America's Top-Rated Cities: A Statistical Handbook

Volume 2

2012

Nineteenth Edition

America's Top-Rated Cities: A Statistical Handbook

Volume 2: Western Region

A UNIVERSAL REFERENCE BOOK

Grey House Publishing

PUBLISHER: Leslie Mackenzie
EDITORIAL DIRECTOR: Laura Mars
EDITOR: David Garoogian

CONTRIBUTING WRITER: Alison Amorello; Allison Blake
RESEARCH ASSISTANTS: Katrina Doyle; Dawn Jenkins
MARKETING DIRECTOR: Jessica Moody

A Universal Reference Book
Grey House Publishing, Inc.
4919 Route 22
Amenia, NY 12501
518.789.8700
Fax 845.373.6390
www.greyhouse.com
e-mail: books @greyhouse.com

Nineteenth Edition
Printed in Canada

Publisher's Cataloging-in-Publication Data
(Prepared by The Donohue Group, Inc.)

America's top-rated cities. Vol. I, Southern region : a statistical handbook.. -- 1992-

v. : ill. ; cm.
Annual, 1995-
Irregular, 1992-1993
ISSN: 1082-7102

1. Cities and towns--Ratings--Southern States--Statistics--Periodicals. 2. Cities and towns--Southern States--Statistics--Periodicals. 3. Social indicators--Southern States--Periodicals. 4. Quality of life--Southern States--Statistics--Periodicals. 5. Southern States--Social conditions--Statistics--Periodicals. I. Title: America's top rated cities. II. Title: Southern region

HT123.5.S6 A44
307.76/0973/05

95644648

4-Volume Set ISBN: 978-1-59237-857-9
Volume 1 ISBN: 978-1-59237-858-6
Volume 2 ISBN: 978-1-59237-859-3
Volume 3 ISBN: 978-1-59237-860-9
Volume 4 ISBN: 978-1-59237-861-6

Albuquerque, New Mexico

Background 1
Rankings 2
Business Environment 9
City Finances 9
Demographics 10
Economy 12
Income 12
Employment 13
Residential Real Estate 16
Taxes 16
Commercial Real Estate 17
Commercial Utilities 17
Transportation 18
Businesses 19
Hotels 20
Event Sites 20
Living Environment 21
Cost of Living 21
Housing 22
Health 23
Education 24
Presidential Election 25
Employers 26
Public Safety 26
Recreation 27
Climate 27
Hazardous Waste 27
Air & Water Quality 28

Anchorage, Alaska

Background 31
Rankings 33
Business Environment 37
City Finances 37
Demographics 38
Economy 40
Income 40
Employment 41
Residential Real Estate 43
Taxes 44
Commercial Utilities 45
Transportation 45
Businesses 46
Hotels 46
Event Sites 46
Living Environment 48
Cost of Living 48
Housing 49
Health 50
Education 51
Presidential Election 52
Employers 53
Public Safety 53
Recreation 54
Climate 54
Hazardous Waste 54
Air & Water Quality 55

Bellevue, Washington

Background 57
Rankings 58
Business Environment 65
City Finances 65
Demographics 66
Economy 68
Income 68
Employment 69
Residential Real Estate 71
Taxes 72
Commercial Real Estate 73
Commercial Utilities 73
Transportation 73
Businesses 75
Hotels 76
Event Sites 76
Living Environment 77
Cost of Living 77
Housing 78
Health 79
Education 80
Presidential Election 82
Employers 83
Public Safety 83
Recreation 84
Climate 84
Hazardous Waste 84
Air & Water Quality 85

Billings, Montana

Background 87
Rankings 88
Business Environment 91
City Finances 91
Demographics 92
Economy 94
Income 94
Employment 95
Residential Real Estate 97
Taxes 98
Commercial Utilities 99
Transportation 99
Businesses 100
Hotels 101
Event Sites 101
Living Environment 102
Cost of Living 102
Housing 103
Health 104
Education 105
Presidential Election 106
Employers 107
Public Safety 107
Recreation 108
Climate 108
Hazardous Waste 108
Air & Water Quality 109

Boise City, Idaho

Background 111
Rankings 112
Business Environment 117
City Finances 117
Demographics 118
Economy 120
Income 120
Employment 121
Residential Real Estate 123
Taxes 124
Commercial Utilities 125
Transportation 125
Businesses 127
Hotels 127
Event Sites 128
Living Environment 129
Cost of Living 129
Housing 130
Health 131
Education 132
Presidential Election 133
Employers 134
Public Safety 134
Recreation 135
Climate 135
Hazardous Waste 135
Air & Water Quality 136

Boulder, Colorado

Background 139
Rankings 140
Business Environment 144
City Finances 144
Demographics 145
Economy 147
Income 147
Employment 148
Residential Real Estate 150
Taxes 151
Commercial Utilities 152
Transportation 152
Businesses 153
Hotels 154
Event Sites 154
Living Environment 155
Cost of Living 155
Housing 156
Health 157
Education 158
Presidential Election 160
Employers 160
Public Safety 160
Recreation 161
Climate 161
Hazardous Waste 162
Air & Water Quality 162

Carlsbad, California

Background 165
Rankings 166
Business Environment 171
City Finances 171
Demographics 172
Economy 174
Income 174
Employment 175
Residential Real Estate 178
Taxes 178
Commercial Real Estate 179
Commercial Utilities 179
Transportation 180
Businesses 181
Hotels 181
Event Sites 182
Living Environment 183
Cost of Living 183
Housing 184
Health 185
Education 186
Presidential Election 188
Employers 188
Public Safety 188
Recreation 189
Climate 189
Hazardous Waste 189
Air & Water Quality 190

Colorado Springs, Colorado

Background 193
Rankings 194
Business Environment 201
City Finances 201
Demographics 202
Economy 204
Income 204
Employment 205
Residential Real Estate 207
Taxes 208
Commercial Real Estate 209
Commercial Utilities 209
Transportation 209
Businesses 210
Hotels 211
Event Sites 211
Living Environment 212
Cost of Living 212
Housing 213
Health 214
Education 215
Presidential Election 217
Employers 217
Public Safety 218
Recreation 218
Climate 219
Hazardous Waste 219
Air & Water Quality 219

Denver, Colorado

Background **221**
Rankings **222**
Business Environment **233**
City Finances 233
Demographics 234
Economy 236
Income 236
Employment 237
Residential Real Estate 239
Taxes 240
Commercial Real Estate 241
Commercial Utilities 241
Transportation 241
Businesses 243
Hotels 244
Event Sites 244
Living Environment **245**
Cost of Living 245
Housing 246
Health 247
Education 248
Presidential Election 250
Employers 250
Public Safety 251
Recreation 251
Climate 252
Hazardous Waste 252
Air & Water Quality 252

Fort Collins, Colorado

Background **255**
Rankings **256**
Business Environment **259**
City Finances 259
Demographics 260
Economy 262
Income 262
Employment 263
Residential Real Estate 265
Taxes 266
Commercial Utilities 267
Transportation 267
Businesses 268
Hotels 269
Event Sites 269
Living Environment **270**
Cost of Living 270
Housing 271
Health 272
Education 273
Presidential Election 274
Employers 275
Public Safety 275
Recreation 276
Climate 276
Hazardous Waste 276
Air & Water Quality 277

Gilbert, Arizona

Background **279**
Rankings **280**
Business Environment **287**
City Finances 287
Demographics 288
Economy 290
Income 290
Employment 291
Residential Real Estate 293
Taxes 294
Commercial Real Estate 295
Commercial Utilities 295
Transportation 295
Businesses 296
Hotels 297
Event Sites 297
Living Environment **298**
Cost of Living 298
Housing 299
Health 300
Education 301
Presidential Election 303
Employers 303
Public Safety 303
Recreation 304
Climate 304
Hazardous Waste 305
Air & Water Quality 305

Henderson, Nevada

Background **307**
Rankings **308**
Business Environment **314**
City Finances 314
Demographics 315
Economy 317
Income 317
Employment 318
Residential Real Estate 320
Taxes 321
Commercial Real Estate 322
Commercial Utilities 322
Transportation 322
Businesses 323
Hotels 324
Event Sites 324
Living Environment **325**
Cost of Living 325
Housing 326
Health 327
Education 328
Presidential Election 329
Employers 330
Public Safety 330
Recreation 331
Climate 331
Hazardous Waste 332
Air & Water Quality 332

Honolulu, Hawaii

Background **335**
Rankings **337**
Business Environment **345**
City Finances 345
Demographics 346
Economy 348
Income 348
Employment 349
Residential Real Estate 351
Taxes 352
Commercial Utilities 353
Transportation 353
Businesses 354
Hotels 355
Event Sites 355
Living Environment **356**
Cost of Living 356
Housing 357
Health 358
Education 359
Presidential Election 360
Employers 361
Public Safety 361
Recreation 362
Climate 362
Hazardous Waste 362
Air & Water Quality 363

Irvine, California

Background **365**
Rankings **366**
Business Environment **373**
City Finances 373
Demographics 374
Economy 376
Income 376
Employment 377
Residential Real Estate 380
Taxes 380
Commercial Real Estate 381
Commercial Utilities 381
Transportation 382
Businesses 383
Hotels 384
Event Sites 384
Living Environment **385**
Cost of Living 385
Housing 386
Health 387
Education 388
Presidential Election 390
Employers 390
Public Safety 391
Recreation 391
Climate 392
Hazardous Waste 392
Air & Water Quality 392

Las Vegas, Nevada

Background **395**
Rankings **396**
Business Environment **404**
City Finances 404
Demographics 405
Economy 407
Income 407
Employment 408
Residential Real Estate 410
Taxes 411
Commercial Real Estate 412
Commercial Utilities 412
Transportation 412
Businesses 413
Hotels 414
Event Sites 414
Living Environment **416**
Cost of Living 416
Housing 417
Health 418
Education 419
Presidential Election 420
Employers 421
Public Safety 421
Recreation 422
Climate 422
Hazardous Waste 423
Air & Water Quality 423

Los Angeles, California

Background **425**
Rankings **426**
Business Environment **436**
City Finances 436
Demographics 437
Economy 439
Income 439
Employment 440
Residential Real Estate 443
Taxes 443
Commercial Real Estate 444
Commercial Utilities 444
Transportation 445
Businesses 446
Hotels 447
Event Sites 448
Living Environment **449**
Cost of Living 449
Housing 450
Health 451
Education 452
Presidential Election 454
Employers 455
Public Safety 455
Recreation 456
Climate 456
Hazardous Waste 457
Air & Water Quality 457

Phoenix, Arizona

Background 459
Rankings 460
Business Environment 469
City Finances 469
Demographics 470
Economy 472
Income 472
Employment 473
Residential Real Estate 475
Taxes 476
Commercial Real Estate 477
Commercial Utilities 477
Transportation 477
Businesses 479
Hotels 480
Event Sites 480
Living Environment 481
Cost of Living 481
Housing 482
Health 483
Education 485
Presidential Election 486
Employers 487
Public Safety 487
Recreation 488
Climate 488
Hazardous Waste 488
Air & Water Quality 489

Portland, Oregon

Background 491
Rankings 492
Business Environment 502
City Finances 502
Demographics 503
Economy 505
Income 505
Employment 506
Residential Real Estate 508
Taxes 509
Commercial Real Estate 510
Commercial Utilities 510
Transportation 511
Businesses 512
Hotels 512
Event Sites 513
Living Environment 514
Cost of Living 514
Housing 515
Health 516
Education 517
Presidential Election 519
Employers 519
Public Safety 519
Recreation 520
Climate 520
Hazardous Waste 521
Air & Water Quality 521

Provo, Utah

Background 523
Rankings 524
Business Environment 527
City Finances 527
Demographics 528
Economy 530
Income 530
Employment 531
Residential Real Estate 533
Taxes 534
Commercial Utilities 535
Transportation 535
Businesses 536
Hotels 537
Event Sites 537
Living Environment 538
Cost of Living 538
Housing 539
Health 540
Education 541
Presidential Election 543
Employers 543
Public Safety 543
Recreation 544
Climate 544
Hazardous Waste 544
Air & Water Quality 545

Roseville, California

Background 547
Rankings 548
Business Environment 554
City Finances 554
Demographics 555
Economy 557
Income 557
Employment 558
Residential Real Estate 561
Taxes 561
Commercial Real Estate 562
Commercial Utilities 562
Transportation 563
Businesses 564
Hotels 564
Living Environment 565
Cost of Living 565
Housing 566
Health 567
Education 568
Presidential Election 570
Employers 570
Public Safety 570
Recreation 571
Climate 571
Hazardous Waste 572
Air & Water Quality 572

San Diego, California

Background **575**
Rankings **576**
Business Environment **585**
City Finances 585
Demographics 586
Economy 588
Income 588
Employment 589
Residential Real Estate 592
Taxes 592
Commercial Real Estate 593
Commercial Utilities 593
Transportation 594
Businesses 595
Hotels 596
Event Sites 596
Living Environment **598**
Cost of Living 598
Housing 599
Health 600
Education 601
Presidential Election 603
Employers 603
Public Safety 604
Recreation 605
Climate 605
Hazardous Waste 605
Air & Water Quality 606

San Francisco, California

Background **609**
Rankings **610**
Business Environment **622**
City Finances 622
Demographics 623
Economy 625
Income 625
Employment 626
Residential Real Estate 629
Taxes 629
Commercial Real Estate 630
Commercial Utilities 630
Transportation 631
Businesses 632
Hotels 633
Event Sites 634
Living Environment **635**
Cost of Living 635
Housing 636
Health 637
Education 638
Presidential Election 640
Employers 640
Public Safety 641
Recreation 642
Climate 642
Hazardous Waste 642
Air & Water Quality 643

San Jose, California

Background **645**
Rankings **646**
Business Environment **655**
City Finances 655
Demographics 656
Economy 658
Income 658
Employment 659
Residential Real Estate 662
Taxes 662
Commercial Real Estate 663
Commercial Utilities 663
Transportation 664
Businesses 665
Hotels 665
Event Sites 666
Living Environment **667**
Cost of Living 667
Housing 668
Health 669
Education 671
Presidential Election 672
Employers 673
Public Safety 674
Recreation 674
Climate 675
Hazardous Waste 675
Air & Water Quality 675

Scottsdale, Arizona

Background **679**
Rankings **680**
Business Environment **687**
City Finances 687
Demographics 688
Economy 690
Income 690
Employment 691
Residential Real Estate 693
Taxes 694
Commercial Real Estate 695
Commercial Utilities 695
Transportation 695
Businesses 697
Hotels 697
Event Sites 698
Living Environment **699**
Cost of Living 699
Housing 700
Health 701
Education 702
Presidential Election 704
Employers 705
Public Safety 705
Recreation 706
Climate 706
Hazardous Waste 707
Air & Water Quality 707

Seattle, Washington

Background **709**
Rankings **710**
Business Environment **722**
City Finances 722
Demographics 723
Economy 725
Income 725
Employment 726
Residential Real Estate 728
Taxes 729
Commercial Real Estate 730
Commercial Utilities 730
Transportation 730
Businesses 732
Hotels 733
Event Sites 733
Living Environment **734**
Cost of Living 734
Housing 735
Health 736
Education 737
Presidential Election 739
Employers 739
Public Safety 740
Recreation 740
Climate 741
Hazardous Waste 741
Air & Water Quality 741

Sunnyvale, California

Background **745**
Rankings **746**
Business Environment **752**
City Finances 752
Demographics 753
Economy 755
Income 755
Employment 756
Residential Real Estate 759
Taxes 759
Commercial Real Estate 760
Commercial Utilities 760
Transportation 761
Businesses 762
Hotels 762
Event Sites 763
Living Environment **764**
Cost of Living 764
Housing 765
Health 766
Education 767
Presidential Election 769
Employers 769
Public Safety 770
Recreation 770
Climate 771
Hazardous Waste 771
Air & Water Quality 771

Temecula, California

Background **775**
Rankings **776**
Business Environment **780**
City Finances 780
Demographics 781
Economy 783
Income 783
Employment 784
Residential Real Estate 787
Taxes 787
Commercial Real Estate 788
Commercial Utilities 788
Transportation 789
Businesses 790
Hotels 790
Living Environment **791**
Cost of Living 791
Housing 792
Health 793
Education 794
Presidential Election 795
Employers 796
Public Safety 796
Recreation 797
Climate 797
Hazardous Waste 797
Air & Water Quality 798

Thousand Oaks, California

Background **801**
Rankings **802**
Business Environment **805**
City Finances 805
Demographics 806
Economy 808
Income 808
Employment 809
Residential Real Estate 812
Taxes 812
Commercial Utilities 813
Transportation 813
Businesses 814
Hotels 815
Event Sites 815
Living Environment **816**
Cost of Living 816
Housing 817
Health 818
Education 819
Presidential Election 820
Employers 821
Public Safety 821
Recreation 822
Climate 822
Hazardous Waste 822
Air & Water Quality 823

Appendix A: Counties A-1
Appendix B: Metropolitan Statistical Areas A-3
Appendix C: Chambers of Commerce. A-7
Appendix D: State Departments of Labor A-15
Appendix E: Comparative Statistics A-19

Introduction

This nineteenth edition of *America's Top-Rated Cities* is a concise, statistical, 4-volume work identifying America's top-rated cities with populations of at least 95,000. It profiles 100 cities that have received high marks for business and living from prominent publications, such as *Forbes* and *U.S. New & World Report,* from surveys appearing in over 300 sources, such as *BusinessWeek, Inc. Magazine, Fortune, Men's Health, The Wall Street Journal, Women's Health, and CNBC,* and from first-hand visits, interviews and reports.

Each volume covers a different region of the country—Southern, Western, Central and Eastern—and includes a detailed Table of Contents, City Chapters, Appendices, and Maps. Each City Chapter incorporates information from hundreds of resources to create the following major sections:

- **Background**—lively narrative of significant, up-to-date news for both businesses and residents. Each background combines historical facts with up-to-the-minute development, "known-for" annual events, and an annual weather report.
- **Rankings**—fun-to-read, bulleted survey results from 320 books and magazines, such as general (Best Quality of Life Cities), specific (Most Literate Cities), and everything in between (Happiest Cities).
- **Statistical Tables**—118 tables and detailed topics, with several new and expanded topics, offer an unparalleled view of each city's Business and Living Environments. They are carefully organized with data that is easy to read and understand.
- **Appendices**—five in all, follow each volume of City Chapters. These range from listings of Metropolitan Statistical Areas to Comparative Statistics for all 100 cities.

This new edition of *America's Top Rated Cities* includes cites that ranked highest and received the most points, using our unique weighting system. Twenty-four cities have never before appeared as a top-rated city, and 7 cities have shown up again, after a year or more of not making the cut. New cities, by volume, are:

- SOUTHERN: Cape Coral and Pembroke Pines, FL; Clarkesville and Murfreesboro, TN; Round Rock, TX
- WESTERN: Gilbert, AZ; Carlsbad, Roseville, Sunnyvale, and Temecula, CA; Billings, MT; Henderson, NV
- CENTRAL: Olathe, KS; Sterling Heights, MI; Columbia, MO; Broken Arrow and Norman, OK; Kenosha, WI
- EASTERN: Columbia, MD; High Point, NC; Jersey City, NJ; Huntington and Oyster Bay, NY; Chesapeake, VA

Praise for previous editions:

> *"...Smartly compiled with an assortment of useful information, libraries that have purchased earlier editions will want to continue that tradition..."*
>
> —Against the Grain

> *"...Users who are thinking of relocating...or who would like to see if their businesses have the possibility of thriving in a new location will find...valuable information....[S]uitable for large public libraries, academic libraries [with] business schools, business libraries, and corporate libraires."*
>
> —ARBA

> *"...[ATRC] has...proven its worth to a wide audience...from businesspeople and corporations planning to launch, relocate, or expand their operations to market researchers, real estate professionals, urban planners, job-seekers, students...interested in...reliable, attractively presented statistical infomation about larger U.S. cities."*
>
> —ARBA

BACKGROUND

Each city begins with an informative **Background** that combines history with current events. These narratives reflect changes that have occurred during the past year, and touch on the city's environment, politics, employment, cultural offerings, climate, and often include interesting trivia. For example, Henderson supplied most of the magnesium needed for WWII planes and weapons, both Presidents Franklin and Theodore Roosevelt went to Harvard, Gatorade was invented to hydrate University of Florida's football team (the Gators), and Temecula harvests more than 50 varieties of wine grapes.

RANKINGS
This section has rankings from a possible 320 (up from 289) books, articles, and reports. For easy reference, these Rankings are categorized into 18 topics including Business/Finance, Dating/Romance, and Health/Fitness.

The Rankings are presented in an easy-to-read, bulleted format and include results from both annual surveys and one-shot studies. **Fastest-Growing Wages . . . Best for Having a Baby . . . Most Well-Read . . . Most Playful . . . Most Wired . . . Healthiest for Women . . . Best for Minority Entrepreneurs . . . Most Romantic . . . Safest . . . Best to Grow Old . . . Most Polite . . . Best for Moviemakers . . . Noisiest . . . Most Vegetarian-Friendly . . . Least Stressful . . . Best Sleeping . . . Best to Ride out a Recession . . . Most Sex Happy . . . Most Political . . . Most Charitable . . . Most Miserable . . . Most Tax Friendly . . . Best for Telecommuters . . . Most Road Rage . . . Greediest . . . Gayest . . . Best for Cats . . . Most Tattooed . . . Best for Wheelchair Users . . . and more.**

Sources for these Rankings include both well-known magazines and other media, including *Forbes, Fortune, Inc. Magazine, Working Mother, Popular Science, Prevention, Field & Stream, BusinessWeek, Kiplinger's Personal Finance, Men's Journal,* and *Travel + Leisure,* as well as resources not as well known, such as the *Asthma & Allergy Foundation of America, Christopher & Dana Reeve Foundation, The Advocate, Black Enterprise, National Civic League, The National Coalition for the Homeless, MovieMaker Magazine, Center for Digital Government, U.S. Conference of Mayors, Milken Institue,* and the *Centre for International Competitiveness.*

STATISTICAL TABLES
Each city chapter includes a possible 118 tables and detailed topics—66 in BUSINESS and 52 in LIVING. Nearly 95% of statistical data has been updated. New topics include *Housing Affordability* and *Consumer Fraud.* Expanded topics include the breakdown of Mexican, Cuban and Puerto Rican for *Hispanic Orgin;* the addition of American Indian/Alaska Native and Native Hawaiian to *Race;* and the addition of: PSA Testing and Seniors Receiving Flu Shots to *Health Risks.*

Business Environment includes hard facts and figures on 12 topics, including City Finances, Demographics, Income, Economy, Employment, and Real Estate. *Living Environment* includes 11 topics, such as Cost of Living, Housing, Health, Education, Safety, Recreation, and Sports Teams.

To compile the Statistical Tables, our editors have again turned to a wide range of sources, some well known, such as the *U.S. Census Bureau, U.S. Environmental Protection Agency, Bureau of Labor Statistics, Centers for Disease Control and Prevention,* and the *Federal Bureau of Investigation*, and some more obscure, like *The Council for Community and Economic Research, Texas Transportation Institute,* and *Federation of Tax Administrators.*

APPENDICES
- **Appendix A**—*Counties*
- **Appendix B**—*Metropolitan Area Definitions*
- **Appendix C**—*Chambers of Commerce and Economic Development Organizations*: Addresses, phone, fax, web sites of these resources help readers find more detailed information on each city.
- **Appendix D**—*State Departments of Labor and Employment*: Additional economic and employment data, with address, phone and web site for easy access.
- **Appendix E**—*Comparative Statistics*: City-by-city comparison comprised of 73 tables. All volumes include all 100 cities.

Material provided by public and private agencies and organizations was supplemented by original research, numerous library sources and Internet sites. *America's Top-Rated Cities, 2012*, is designed for a wide range of readers: private individuals considering relocating a residence or business; professionals considering expanding their businesses or changing careers; corporations considering relocation, opening up additional offices or creating new divisions; government agencies; general and market researchers; real estate consultants; human resource personnel; urban planners; investors; and urban government students.

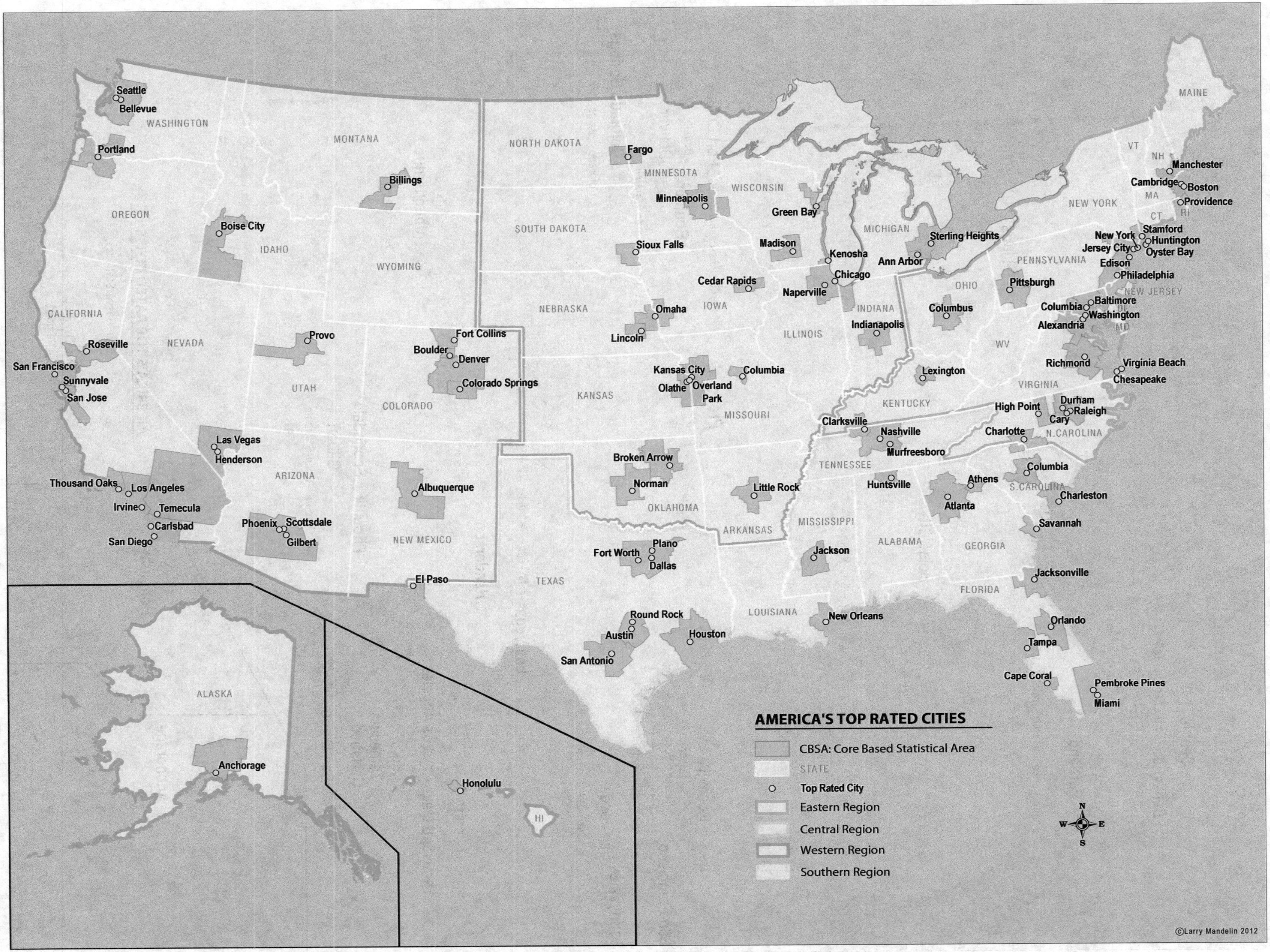

AMERICA'S TOP RATED CITIES
CBSA: Core Based Statistical Area
STATE
Top Rated City
Eastern Region
Central Region
Western Region
Southern Region
N
S
E
W
Seattle
Bellevue
Portland
Billings
Boise City
Fargo
Minneapolis
Sioux Falls
Green Bay
Madison
Kenosha
Chicago
Naperville
Ann Arbor
Sterling Heights
Cedar Rapids
Omaha
Lincoln
Provo
Roseville
San Francisco
Sunnyvale
San Jose
Fort Collins
Boulder
Denver
Colorado Springs
Kansas City
Olathe
Overland Park
Columbia
Indianapolis
Columbus
Pittsburgh
Lexington
Las Vegas
Henderson
Thousand Oaks
Los Angeles
Irvine
Temecula
Carlsbad
San Diego
Phoenix
Scottsdale
Gilbert
Albuquerque
El Paso
Broken Arrow
Norman
Little Rock
Clarksville
Nashville
Murfreesboro
Huntsville
Athens
Atlanta
Fort Worth
Plano
Dallas
Jackson
Round Rock
Austin
San Antonio
Houston
New Orleans
Manchester
Cambridge
Boston
Providence
New York
Stamford
Huntington
Oyster Bay
Jersey City
Edison
Philadelphia
Baltimore
Columbia
Washington
Alexandria
Richmond
Virginia Beach
Chesapeake
High Point
Durham
Raleigh
Cary
Charlotte
Columbia
Charleston
Savannah
Jacksonville
Orlando
Tampa
Cape Coral
Pembroke Pines
Miami
Anchorage
Honolulu
WASHINGTON
OREGON
CALIFORNIA
NEVADA
IDAHO
MONTANA
WYOMING
UTAH
ARIZONA
COLORADO
NEW MEXICO
NORTH DAKOTA
SOUTH DAKOTA
NEBRASKA
KANSAS
OKLAHOMA
TEXAS
MINNESOTA
IOWA
MISSOURI
ARKANSAS
LOUISIANA
WISCONSIN
ILLINOIS
MICHIGAN
INDIANA
OHIO
KENTUCKY
TENNESSEE
MISSISSIPPI
ALABAMA
GEORGIA
FLORIDA
S.CAROLINA
N.CAROLINA
VIRGINIA
WV
PENNSYLVANIA
NEW YORK
NEW JERSEY
MD
DE
VT
NH
MA
CT
RI
MAINE
ALASKA
HI
©Larry Mandelin 2012

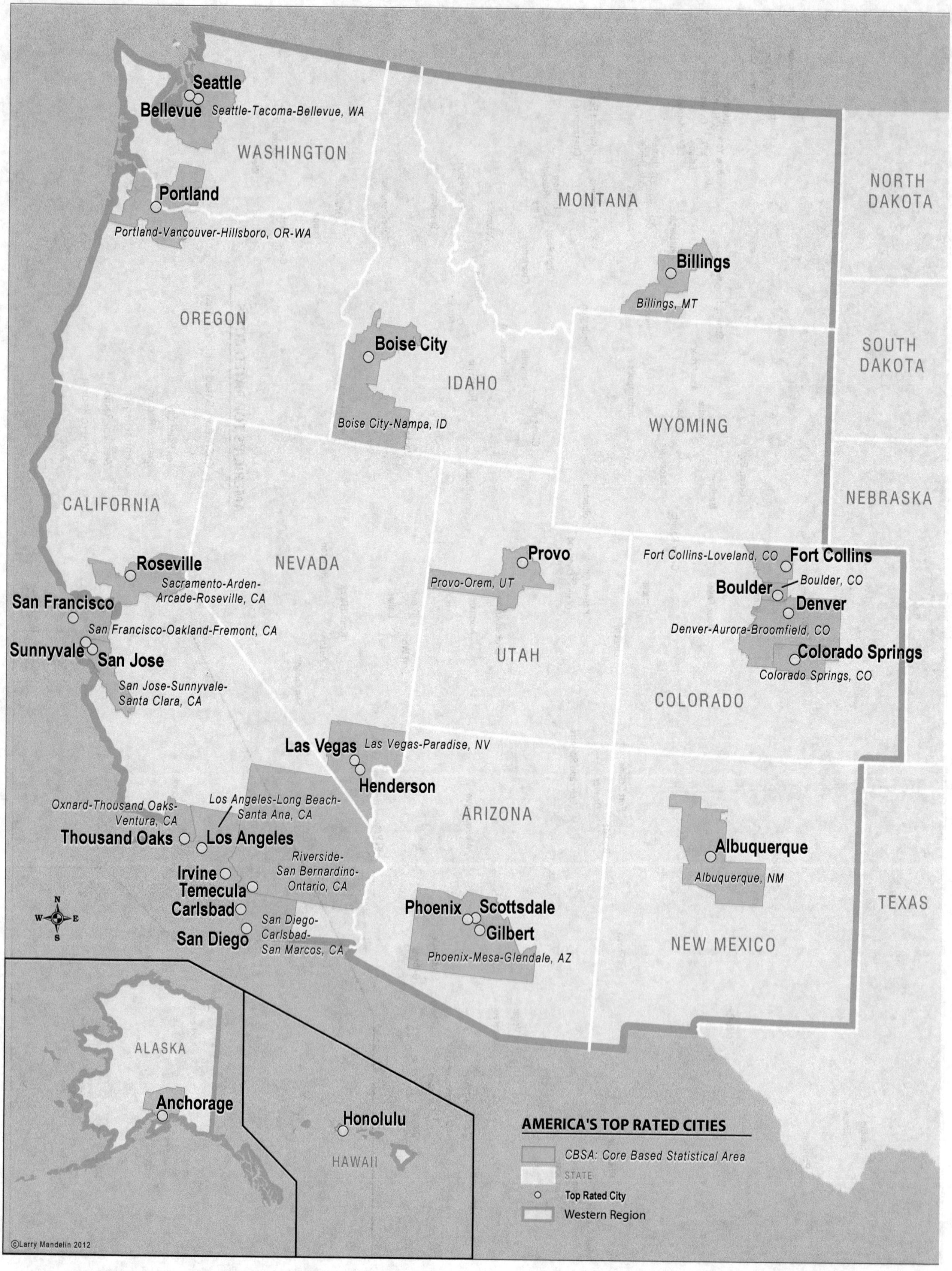

Seattle
Bellevue
Seattle-Tacoma-Bellevue, WA
WASHINGTON
Portland
Portland-Vancouver-Hillsboro, OR-WA
MONTANA
NORTH DAKOTA
Billings
Billings, MT
OREGON
Boise City
IDAHO
Boise City-Nampa, ID
SOUTH DAKOTA
WYOMING
CALIFORNIA
NEBRASKA
Provo
Provo-Orem, UT
NEVADA
Roseville
Sacramento-Arden-Arcade-Roseville, CA
San Francisco
San Francisco-Oakland-Fremont, CA
Sunnyvale
San Jose
San Jose-Sunnyvale-Santa Clara, CA
Fort Collins-Loveland, CO
Fort Collins
Boulder
Boulder, CO
Denver
Denver-Aurora-Broomfield, CO
Colorado Springs
Colorado Springs, CO
UTAH
COLORADO
Las Vegas
Las Vegas-Paradise, NV
Henderson
Oxnard-Thousand Oaks-Ventura, CA
Los Angeles-Long Beach-Santa Ana, CA
ARIZONA
Thousand Oaks
Los Angeles
Riverside-San Bernardino-Ontario, CA
Irvine
Temecula
Carlsbad
San Diego
San Diego-Carlsbad-San Marcos, CA
Albuquerque
Albuquerque, NM
Phoenix
Scottsdale
Gilbert
Phoenix-Mesa-Glendale, AZ
TEXAS
NEW MEXICO
ALASKA
Anchorage
Honolulu
HAWAII
AMERICA'S TOP RATED CITIES
CBSA: Core Based Statistical Area
STATE
Top Rated City
Western Region
©Larry Mandelin 2012

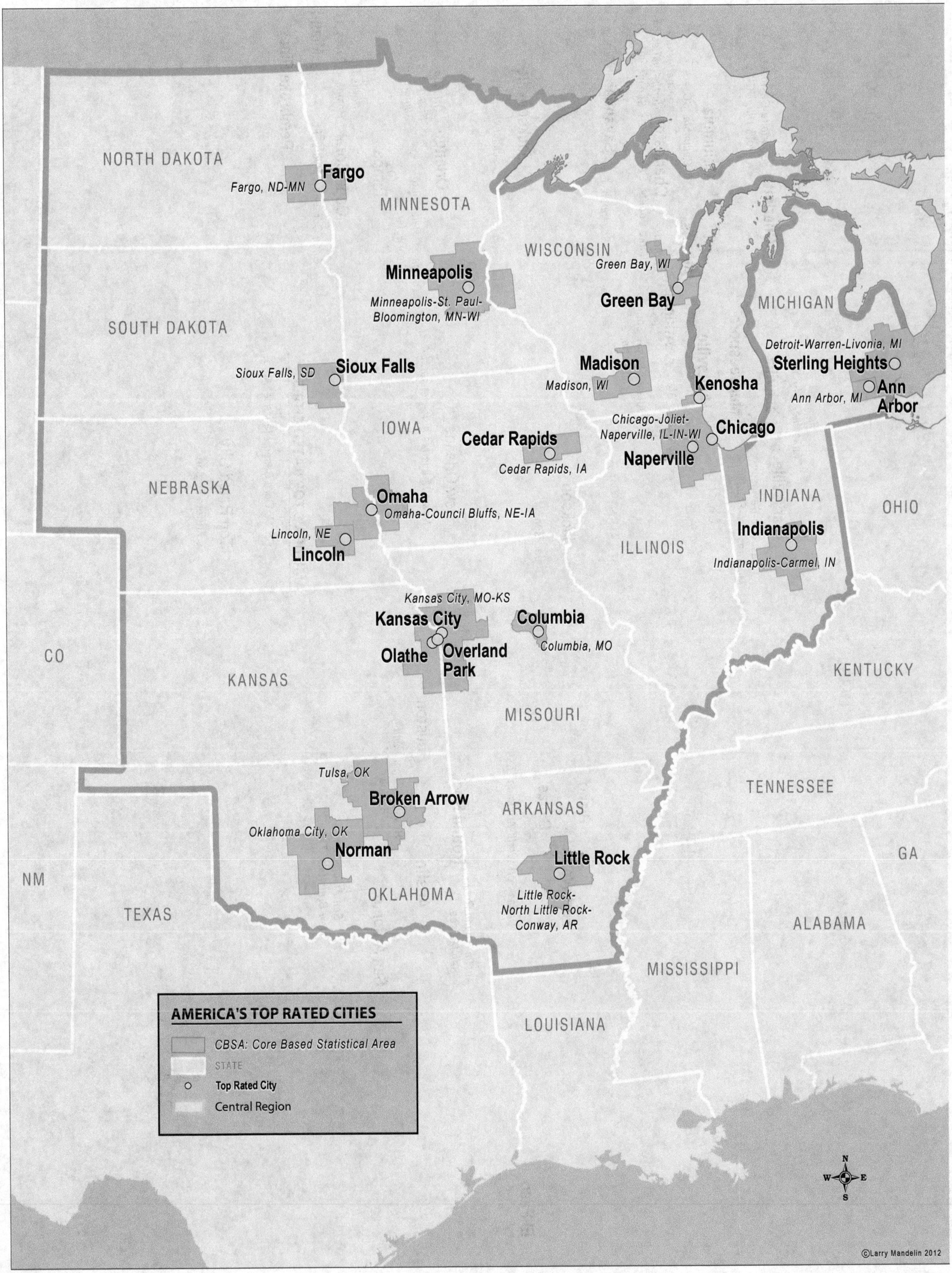
NORTH DAKOTA
Fargo
Fargo, ND-MN
MINNESOTA
WISCONSIN
Green Bay, WI
Minneapolis
Minneapolis-St. Paul-Bloomington, MN-WI
Green Bay
MICHIGAN
SOUTH DAKOTA
Detroit-Warren-Livonia, MI
Sterling Heights
Madison
Sioux Falls
Sioux Falls, SD
Madison, WI
Kenosha
Ann Arbor
Ann Arbor, MI
IOWA
Chicago-Joliet-Naperville, IL-IN-WI
Chicago
Cedar Rapids
Naperville
Cedar Rapids, IA
NEBRASKA
INDIANA
OHIO
Omaha
Omaha-Council Bluffs, NE-IA
Indianapolis
Lincoln, NE
ILLINOIS
Lincoln
Indianapolis-Carmel, IN
Kansas City, MO-KS
Kansas City
Columbia
Columbia, MO
CO
Olathe
Overland Park
KENTUCKY
KANSAS
MISSOURI
Tulsa, OK
TENNESSEE
Broken Arrow
ARKANSAS
Oklahoma City, OK
Norman
Little Rock
GA
NM
OKLAHOMA
Little Rock-North Little Rock-Conway, AR
TEXAS
ALABAMA
MISSISSIPPI
AMERICA'S TOP RATED CITIES
CBSA: Core Based Statistical Area
STATE
Top Rated City
Central Region
LOUISIANA
N
W
E
S
©Larry Mandelin 2012

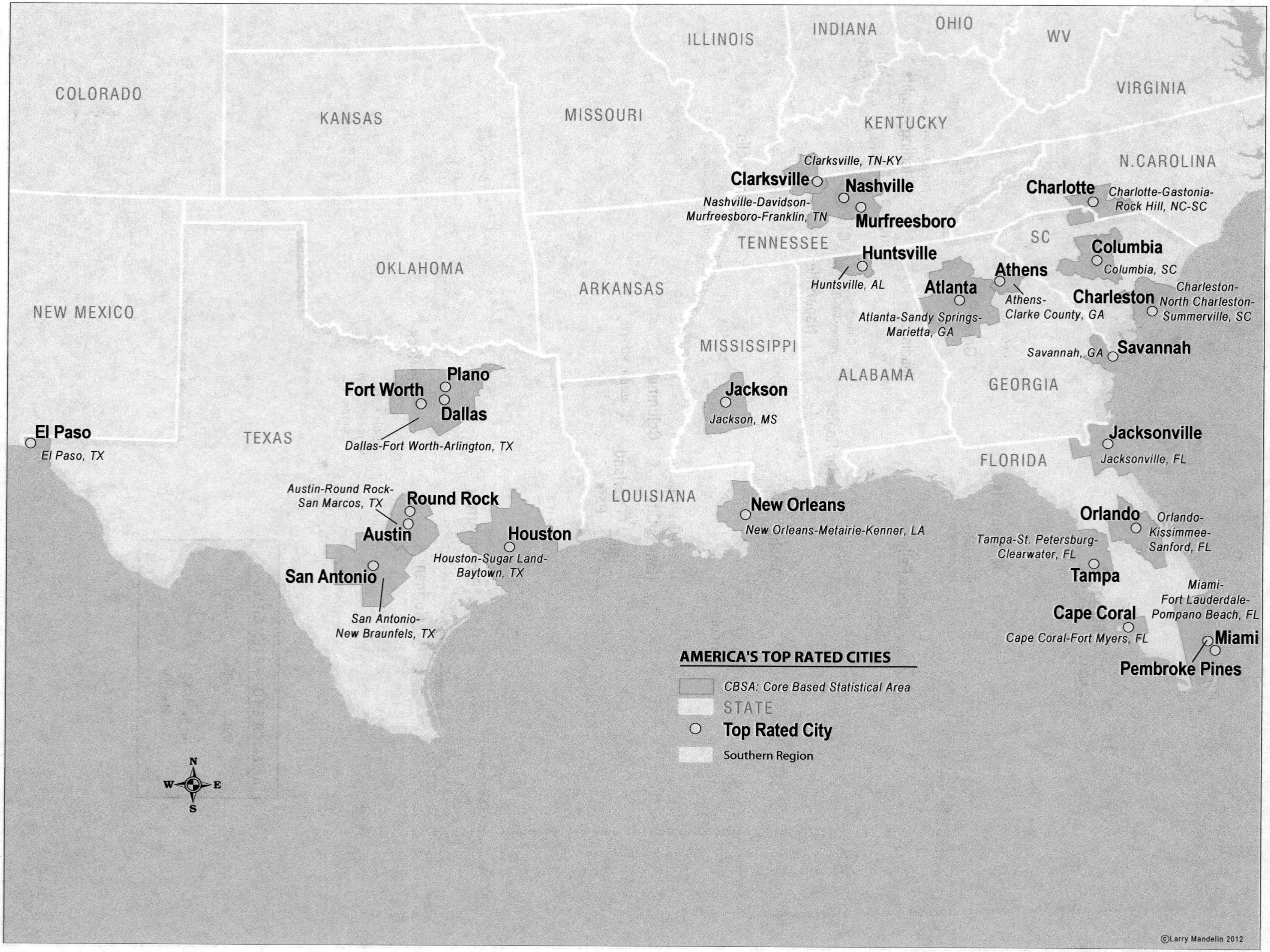
AMERICA'S TOP RATED CITIES
CBSA: Core Based Statistical Area
STATE
Top Rated City
Southern Region
COLORADO
KANSAS
MISSOURI
ILLINOIS
INDIANA
OHIO
WV
VIRGINIA
KENTUCKY
N.CAROLINA
NEW MEXICO
OKLAHOMA
ARKANSAS
TENNESSEE
SC
MISSISSIPPI
ALABAMA
GEORGIA
TEXAS
LOUISIANA
FLORIDA
El Paso
El Paso, TX
Fort Worth
Plano
Dallas
Dallas-Fort Worth-Arlington, TX
Austin-Round Rock-San Marcos, TX
Round Rock
Austin
San Antonio
San Antonio-New Braunfels, TX
Houston
Houston-Sugar Land-Baytown, TX
Jackson
Jackson, MS
New Orleans
New Orleans-Metairie-Kenner, LA
Clarksville
Clarksville, TN-KY
Nashville
Murfreesboro
Nashville-Davidson-Murfreesboro-Franklin, TN
Huntsville
Huntsville, AL
Atlanta
Atlanta-Sandy Springs-Marietta, GA
Athens
Athens-Clarke County, GA
Charlotte
Charlotte-Gastonia-Rock Hill, NC-SC
Columbia
Columbia, SC
Charleston
Charleston-North Charleston-Summerville, SC
Savannah
Savannah, GA
Jacksonville
Jacksonville, FL
Orlando
Orlando-Kissimmee-Sanford, FL
Tampa
Tampa-St. Petersburg-Clearwater, FL
Cape Coral
Cape Coral-Fort Myers, FL
Miami
Pembroke Pines
Miami-Fort Lauderdale-Pompano Beach, FL
N
W
E
S
©Larry Mandelin 2012

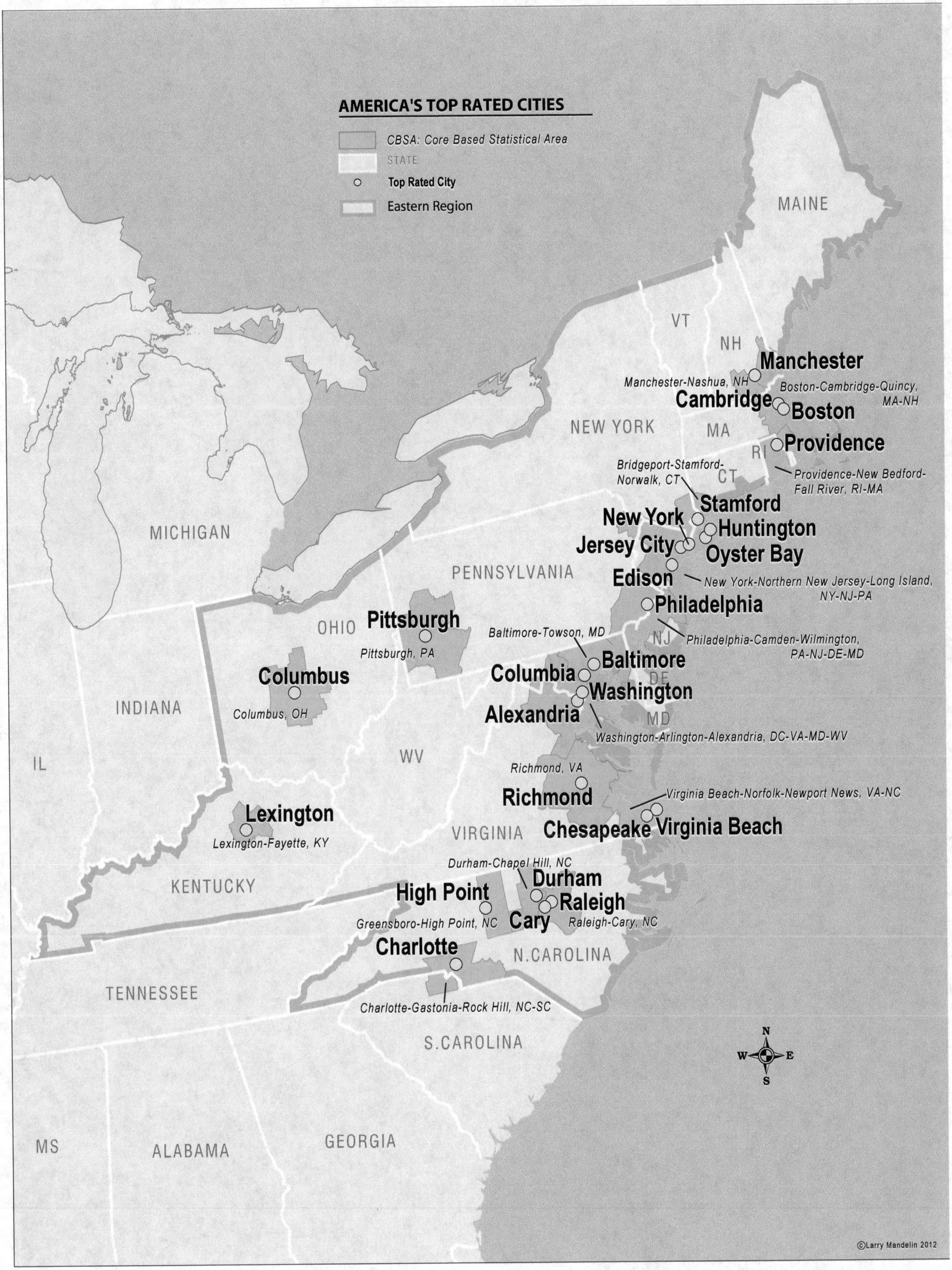
AMERICA'S TOP RATED CITIES
CBSA: Core Based Statistical Area
STATE
Top Rated City
Eastern Region
MAINE
VT
NH
MA
RI
CT
NEW YORK
MICHIGAN
PENNSYLVANIA
OHIO
NJ
DE
MD
INDIANA
IL
WV
VIRGINIA
KENTUCKY
TENNESSEE
N.CAROLINA
S.CAROLINA
MS
ALABAMA
GEORGIA
Manchester
Manchester-Nashua, NH
Boston-Cambridge-Quincy, MA-NH
Cambridge
Boston
Providence
Providence-New Bedford-Fall River, RI-MA
Bridgeport-Stamford-Norwalk, CT
Stamford
New York
Huntington
Jersey City
Oyster Bay
Edison
New York-Northern New Jersey-Long Island, NY-NJ-PA
Philadelphia
Philadelphia-Camden-Wilmington, PA-NJ-DE-MD
Pittsburgh
Pittsburgh, PA
Baltimore-Towson, MD
Baltimore
Columbia
Washington
Alexandria
Washington-Arlington-Alexandria, DC-VA-MD-WV
Columbus
Columbus, OH
Richmond, VA
Richmond
Virginia Beach-Norfolk-Newport News, VA-NC
Chesapeake
Virginia Beach
Lexington
Lexington-Fayette, KY
Durham-Chapel Hill, NC
Durham
Raleigh
Cary
Raleigh-Cary, NC
High Point
Greensboro-High Point, NC
Charlotte
Charlotte-Gastonia-Rock Hill, NC-SC
N
S
E
W
©Larry Mandelin 2012

Albuquerque, New Mexico

Background

Pueblo Indians originally inhabited what is now the Albuquerque metropolitan area. In the sixteenth century, Spaniards began pushing up from Mexico in search of riches, but it was not until 1706 that they founded the settlement, naming it after the viceroy of New Spain, San Francisco Xavier de Alburquerque, a duke whose permission was needed to set up the town. Eventually, the city's name would lose a consonant and become Albuquerque. The city earned the sobriquet "Duke City" because of its namesake.

In the early nineteenth century, Mexico secured her independence from Spanish rule and allowed Americans to enter the province of New Mexico to trade. During the Mexican War of the 1840s, Americans under the command of General Stephen Kearny captured the town, and New Mexico was transferred to the United States in the Treaty of Guadalupe Hidalgo, ending the war.

During the Civil War, Confederates held the town for a few weeks, eventually surrendering it to a besieging Union army. After the war, the railroad arrived in 1880, bringing with it people and business. In 1891 the town received a city charter. Albuquerque became an important site for tuberculosis sanatoriums during the next few decades because of the healing nature of the dry desert air.

World War II had a great impact on Albuquerque, as Kirtland Air Force Base became an important site for the making of the atomic bomb. Sandia National Laboratories was founded in the city after the war and played an important role in defense-related research during the Cold War.

The defense industry is of prime significance to Albuquerque. Institutions once dedicated to defense research are now involved in applying such technology to the private sector, making the city a perfect place for high-tech concerns. In addition to Sandia, the city hosts a branch of the Air Force Research Laboratories and the Los Alamos National Laboratory. Biotechnical and semiconductor industries also have had a positive impact on the city's economy.

Albuquerque and New Mexico have many programs to assist business. The state has property taxes that are among the lowest in the nation.

More traditional forms of making a living are still present, as the city is located in an area where ranchers raise sheep and other livestock.

Albuquerque is also a critical transportation center for the American Southwest, with two major interstates that intersect there. Its airport, Albuquerque International Sunport, is served by seven major commercial carriers and at least five commuter airlines. A recent expansion included an "aerotropolis" of state-of-the-art manufacturing and shipping facilities and Mesa del Sol, a mixed-used development site on 20 square miles of land, connected to the airport by light-rail and a commuter rail line that also serves the region. The New Mexico Rail Runner Express system began operation in July 2006; in 2010, the train's new Wi-Fi network became operational. An 11-mile bus service, Rapid Ride, was so popular that a new Green Line of service was added. Interestingly, the city was voted one of the most walkable American cities in 2011.

There are various venues for higher education located in Albuquerque, the most significant of which is the University of New Mexico.

There are festive events scheduled throughout the year. The annual International Albuquerque International Balloon Fiesta has become a "must" for residents and visitors alike. The city is also home to the annual Gathering of Nations Powwow, an international event featuring over 3,000 indigenous Native American dancers and singers representing more than 500 tribes from Canada and the United States.

Albuquerque enjoys a dry, arid climate, with plenty of sunshine, low humidity, and scant rainfall. More than three-fourths of the daylight hours have sunshine, summer and winter. As in all desert climates, temperatures can fluctuate widely between day and night, all year round. Precipitation is meager during the winter, more abundant in summer with afternoon and evening thunderstorms.

Rankings

General Rankings

- The Albuquerque metro area was selected one of America's "Best Cities" by *Kiplinger's Personal Finance.* Criteria: stable employment; income growth; cost of living; percentage of workforce in the creative class (scientists, engineers, educators, writers, artists, entertainers, etc.). *Kiplinger's Personal Finance, "Best Cities 2009: It's All About Jobs," July 2009*
- *Men's Health Living* ranked 100 U.S. cities in terms of quality of life. Albuquerque was ranked #29 and received a grade of B-. Criteria: number of fitness facilities; air quality; number of physicians; male/female ratio; education levels; household income; cost of living. *Men's Health Living, Spring 2008*
- Albuquerque was selected as one of America's best cities by *Bloomberg Businessweek.* The city ranked #15 out of 50. Criteria: number of restaurants, bars and museums per capita; number of colleges, libraries, and professional sports teams; income, poverty, unemployment, crime, and foreclosure rates; percent of population with bachelor's degrees; public school performance; park acres per capita; air quality. *BusinessWeek, "America's 50 Best Cities," September 20, 2011*
- Albuquerque appeared on RelocateAmerica's list of best places to live in America. The annual "Top 100 Places to Live" list recognizes the top communities as nominated by their residents & local businesses. RelocateAmerica's Research Group determines the list based on review of various data gathered for economic, employment, housing, education, industry, opportunity, environment and recreation along with feedback from area leaders and residents. *RelocateAmerica.com, "Top 100 Places to Live for 2011"*

Business/Finance Rankings

- Albuquerque was identified as one of the 20 strongest-performing metro areas during the recession and recovery from trough quarter through the third quarter of 2011. Criteria: percent change in employment; percentage point change in unemployment rate; percent change in gross metropolitan product; percent change in House Price Index. *Brookings Institution, MetroMonitor: Tracking Economic Recession and Recovery in America's 100 Largest Metropolitan Areas, December 2011*
- The Albuquerque metro area was identified as one of the 10 best cities for job growth in 2010 by *USAToday* based on data from *Moody's Economy.com.* The metro area was ranked #8. Criteria: one-year forecast change in jobs from the 4th quarter 2009 to the 4th quarter 2010. *USAToday, "Jobs May Rebound in 2010," April 7, 2010*
- Albuquerque was selected as one of the best places to ride out a recession in the U.S. by *BusinessWeek.* Twenty cities were identified as places where large portions of the population worked in anticyclical industries such as government, health care, education, agriculture, and legal services. *BusinessWeek, "Some Cities Will Be Safer in a Recession," October 14, 2008*
- Albuquerque was identified as one of the "Unhappiest Cities to Work in 2012" by *CareerBliss.com,* an online community for career advancement. The city ranked #5 out of 30. Criteria: independent company reviews from employees all over the country on: relationship with their boss and co-workers; work environment; job resources; growth opportunities; compensation; company culture; company reputation; daily tasks; job control over work performed on a daily basis. *CareerBliss.com, "Happiest and Unhappiest Cities to Work in 2012"*
- *American City Business Journals* ranked America's 261 largest cities in terms of their resident's wealth. Albuquerque ranked #163. Criteria: per capita income; median household income; percentage of households with annual incomes of $200,000 or more; median home value. *American City Business Journals, "Where the Money Is: America's Wealth Centers," August 18, 2008*
- The Albuquerque metro area appeared on the Milken Institute "2011 Best Performing Metros" list. Rank: #94 out of 200 large metro areas. Criteria: job growth; wage and salary growth; high-tech output growth. *Milken Institute, "2011 Best Performing Metros"*

- *Forbes* ranked the 200 most populous metro areas in the U.S. in terms of the "Best Places for Business and Careers." The Albuquerque metro area was ranked #38. Criteria: costs (business and living); job growth (past and projected); income growth; educational attainment; projected economic growth; crime; cultural and recreational opportunities; net migration patterns; number of highly ranked colleges. *Forbes, "Best Places for Business and Careers," June 2011*

Children/Family Rankings

- The Albuquerque metro area was selected as one of the "Best Cities for Relocating Families" by Worldwide ERC and Primacy Relocation. The 2008 study looked at nearly 50 factors important to relocating families including: recent job growth; nearby top-ranked colleges; in-state tuition for four-year public colleges; population growth since 2000; pediatricians per 100,000 population; and a Green Living index. *Worldwide ERC and Primacy Relocation, "2008 Best Cities for Relocating Families"*

- *Fit Pregnancy* magazine ranked the 50 best U.S. cities in which to have a baby. Albuquerque was ranked #10. Criteria: access to hospitals and doctors; affordability; birthing options; breastfeeding; child care; fertility laws/resources; maternal and infant health risk; parks/stroller friendliness; safety. *Fit Pregnancy, "The Best Cities in America to Have a Baby 2008"*

Culture/Performing Arts Rankings

- Albuquerque was selected as one of 10 best U.S. cities to be a moviemaker. The city was ranked #3. Criteria: cost of living; average salary; unemployment rate; job growth; median home price; crime rate; number of film schools, festivals, movie-related vendors and local movie theaters; current production scene (i.e. production days, size of talent pool); financial incentives for shooting in a particular area. *MovieMaker Magazine, "Top 10 Cities to be a Moviemaker: 2012," January 16, 2012*

- Albuquerque was selected as one of "America's Top 25 Arts Destinations." The city ranked #7 in the big city (population 500,000 and over) category. Criteria: readers' top choices for arts travel destinations based on the richness and variety of visual arts sites, activities and events. *American Style, "America's Top 25 Arts Destinations," May 2010*

Dating/Romance Rankings

- Albuquerque appeared on *Men's Health's* list of the most sex-happy cities in America. The city ranked #57 of 100. Criteria: condom sales; birth rates; sex toy sales; rates of chlamydia, gonorrhea, and syphilis. *Men's Health, "America's Most Sex-Happy Cities," October 2010*
- *Men's Health* ranked 100 U.S. cities in terms of best (and worst) marriages. Albuquerque was ranked #8 (#1 = worst). Criteria: rate of failed marriages; stringency of divorce laws; percentage of population who've split; number of licensed marriage and family therapists. *Men's Health, "Splitsville, USA," May 2010*

- The Albuquerque metro area was selected as one of the "Best Cities for Relocating Singles" by Worldwide ERC and Primacy Relocation. The area ranked #78 out of the 100 largest metro areas in the U.S. Criteria: recent job growth; recent singles population growth; overall population growth; affordable rental housing; cost-of-living index; expanded arts and recreation opportunities; ratio of single men and single women; affordability of quality higher education (including state residency requirements); diversity index; climate; population density. *Worldwide ERC and Primacy Relocation, "2008 Best Cities for Relocating Singles"*

Education Rankings

- *Men's Health* ranked 100 U.S. cities in terms of their education levels. Albuquerque was ranked #40 (#1 = most educated city). Criteria: high school graduation rates; school enrollment; educational attainment; number of households who have outstanding student loans; number of households whose members have taken adult-education courses. *Men's Health, "Where School Is In: The Most and Least Educated Cities," September 12, 2011*

- Albuquerque was selected as one of "America's Most Literate Cities." The city ranked #38 out of the 75 largest U.S. cities. Criteria: number of booksellers; library resources; Internet resources; educational attainment; periodical publishing resources; newspaper circulation. *Central Connecticut State University, "America's Most Literate Cities 2011"*

- Albuquerque was identified as one of the 100 "smartest" metro areas in the U.S. The area ranked #45. Criteria: the editors rated the collective brainpower of the 100 largest metro areas in the U.S. based on their residents' educational attainment. *American City Business Journals, April 14, 2008*

- Albuquerque was identified as one of "America's Brainiest Bastions" by *Portfolio.com.* The metro area ranked #69 out of 200. *Portfolio.com* analyzed levels of educational attainment in the nation's 200 largest metropolitan areas. The editors established scores for five levels of educational attainment, based on relative earning power of adult workers age 25 or older. Scores were determined by comparing the median income for all workers with the median income for those workers at a specified educational level. *Portfolio.com, "America's Brainiest Bastions," December 1, 2010*

Environmental Rankings

- Albuquerque was selected as one of 22 "Smarter Cities" for energy by the Natural Resources Defense Council. Criteria: investment in green power; energy efficiency measures; conservation. *Natural Resources Defense Council, "2010 Smarter Cities," July 19, 2010*

- *American City Business Journal* ranked 43 metropolitan areas in terms of their "greenness." The Albuquerque metro area ranked #9. Criteria: Forty-one metros in which *ACBJ* has business weeklies, plus Indianapolis and Cleveland, were ranked based on 20 different indicators such as adoption of green technologies, utilization of environmentally sound practices, and air and water quality. *American City Business Journals, "Green City Index," March 11, 2010*

- Albuquerque was selected as one of "America's 50 Greenest Cities" by *Popular Science.* The city ranked #16. Criteria: electricity; transportation; green living; recycling and green perspective. *Popular Science, February 2008*

- 100 of the largest metro areas in the U.S. were analyzed in terms of their current drought severity. The Albuquerque metro area ranked #92 (#1 = driest). The rankings were based on statistics such as long-term precipitation trends and patterns and the Palmer drought indices. *Sperling's BestPlaces, www.BestPlaces.net, "America's Drought-Riskiest Cities," November 2007*

- The Albuquerque metro area appeared in *Country Home's* "Best Green Places" report. The area ranked #102 out of 379. Criteria: official energy policies; green power; green buildings; availability of fresh, locally grown food. *Country Home, "Best Green Places," 2008*

- Albuquerque was highlighted as one of the top 25 cleanest metro areas for year-round particle pollution (Annual PM 2.5) in the U.S. The area ranked #7. *American Lung Association, State of the Air 2011*

Food/Drink Rankings

- Albuquerque was selected as one of North America's most vegetarian- and vegan-friendly large cities (population 300,000 or more). The city was ranked #3. Criteria: number of vegetarian restaurants and vegetarian-friendly restaurants per capita; input from PETA supporters and staff members on the quality of the options. *People for the Ethical Treatment of Animals, "North America's Best Vegetarian- and Vegan-Friendly Cities," July 23, 2010*

Health/Fitness Rankings

- Albuquerque was selected as one of the 25 fittest cities in America by *Men's Fitness Online*. It ranked #3 out of America's 50 largest cities. Criteria: fitness centers and sport stores; nutrition; sports participation; TV viewing; overweight/sedentary; junk food; air quality; geography; commute; parks and open space; city recreational facilities; access to healthcare; motivation; mayor and city initiatives; state obesity initiatives. *Men's Fitness, "The Fittest and Fattest Cities in America," March 5, 2012*

- Albuquerque was identified as a "2011 Asthma Capital." The area ranked #89 out of the nation's 100 largest metropolitan areas. Twelve factors were used to identify the most challenging places to live for people with asthma: estimated prevalence; self-reported prevalence; crude death rate for asthma; annual pollen score; annual air quality; public smoking laws; number of board-certified asthma specialists; school inhaler access laws; rescue medication use; controller medication use; uninsured rate; poverty rate. *Asthma and Allergy Foundation of America, "2011 Asthma Capitals"*
- Albuquerque was identified as a "2011 Fall Allergy Capital." The area ranked #73 out of 100. Three groups of factors were used to identify the most severe cities for people with allergies during the fall season: annual pollen levels; medicine utilization; access to board-certified allergists. *Asthma and Allergy Foundation of America, "2011 Fall Allergy Capitals"*
- Albuquerque was identified as a "2012 Spring Allergy Capital." The area ranked #52 out of 100. Three groups of factors were used to identify the most severe cities for people with allergies during the spring season: annual pollen levels; medicine utilization; access to board-certified allergists. *Asthma and Allergy Foundation of America, "2012 Spring Allergy Capitals"*
- *Men's Health* examined 100 major U.S. cities and selected the best and worst cities for men. Albuquerque ranked #50. Criteria: 35 statistical parameters of long life in the categories of health, quality of life, and fitness. *Men's Health, "The 10 Best and Worst Cities for Men 2012," January/February 2012*
- Albuquerque was selected as one of the most accident-prone cities in America by *Men's Health.* The city ranked #9 of 10. Criteria: workplace accident rates; traffic fatalities; emergency room visits; accidental poisonings; incidents of drowning; fires; injury-producing falls. *Men's Health, "Ranking America's Cities: Accident City, USA," October 2009*
- The Albuquerque metro area appeared in the 2011 Gallup-Healthways Well-Being Index. The index, based on interviews with more than 350,000 Americans, measured jobs, finances, physical health, emotional state of mind and communities. The metro area ranked #79 out of 190. Criteria: life evaluation; emotional health; work environment; physical health; healthy behaviors; basic access (basic needs optimal for a healthy life, such as access to food and medicine, having health insurance and feeling safe while walking at night). *Gallup-Healthways, "State of Well-Being 2011"*
- *Men's Health* ranked 100 U.S. cities in terms of their activity levels. Albuquerque was ranked #46 (#1 = most active city). Criteria: where and how often residents exercise; percentage of households that watch more than 15 hours of cable television a week and buy more than 11 video games a year; death rate from deep-vein thrombosis, a condition linked to sitting for extended periods of time. *Men's Health, "Where Sit Happens: The Most and Least Active Cities in America," June 20, 2011*
- Albuquerque was selected as one of the "20 Most Livable U.S. Cities for Wheelchair Users" by the Christopher & Dana Reeve Foundation. The city ranked #2. Criteria: Medicaid eligibility and spending; access to physicians and rehabilitation facilities; access to fitness facilities and recreation; access to paratransit; percentage of people living with disabilities who are employed; clean air; climate. *Christopher & Dana Reeve Foundation, "20 Most Livable U.S. Cities for Wheelchair Users," July 26, 2010*

Pet Rankings

- Albuquerque was selected as one of the best places to live with pets by *Livability.com.* The city was ranked #8. Criteria: pet-friendly parks and trails; quality veterinary care; active animal welfare groups; abundance of pet boutiques and retail shops; excellent quality of life for pet owners. *Livability.com, "Top 10 Pet Friendly Cities," October 20, 2010*

Real Estate Rankings

- *Fortune* ranked the 100 largest metro areas in the U.S. in terms of projected median home price change in 2010. The Albuquerque metro area ranked #69. *Fortune, "The 2010 Housing Outlook," December 9, 2009*

- Albuquerque appeared on *ApartmentRatings.com* "Top Cities for Renters" list in 2009." The area ranked #58. Overall satisfaction ratings were ranked using thousands of user submitted scores for hundreds of apartment complexes located in the 100 most populated U.S. municipalities. *ApartmentRatings.com, "2009 Renter Satisfaction Rankings"*
- Albuquerque appeared on *ApartmentRatings.com* "Top College Towns & Cities" for renters list in 2011." The area ranked #37 out of 87. Overall satisfaction ratings were ranked using thousands of user submitted scores for hundreds of apartment complexes located in cities and towns that are home to the 100 largest four-year institutions in the U.S. *ApartmentRatings.com, "2011 College Town Renter Satisfaction Rankings"*
- Albuquerque appeared on *CNNMoney.com's* list of "Foreclosure Hotspots." The list includes the 10 cities with the fastest-growing foreclosure rates out of the 100 worst-hit places. *CNNMoney.com, "Foreclosure Hotspots," February 14, 2011*
- The Center for Housing Policy ranked 210 U.S. metropolitan areas by the fair market rent for a two-bedroom unit. The Albuquerque metro area was ranked #127. (#1 = most expensive) with a rent of $782. Criteria: Fair Market Rent (FMR) in effect during the fourth quarter of 2009 based on HUD's fiscal year 2010 FMRs. *The Center for Housing Policy, "Paycheck to Paycheck: Most to Least Expensive Rental Markets in 2009"*
- The Albuquerque metro area was identified as one of the best U.S. markets to invest in rental property" by HomeVestors and Local Market Monitor. The area ranked #61 out of 100. Criteria: risk-return premium relative to national average. *HomeVestors and Local Market Monitor, "Best 100 U.S. Markets to Invest in Rental Property," March 9, 2012*

Safety Rankings

- Symantec, the makers of Norton, in partnership with Sperling's BestPlaces, ranked the 50 largest cities in the U.S. in terms of their vulnerability to cybercrime. The city ranked #41. Criteria: number of cyberattacks and potential infections; level of Internet access; expenditures on smartphones and computer hardware/software; wireless hotspots; broadband connectivity; Internet usage; online purchases. *Symantec, "Riskiest Online Cities of 2012" February 15, 2012*
- Allstate ranked the 193 largest cities in America in terms of driver safety. Albuquerque ranked #83. In addition, drivers were 5.0% more likely to have had an accident compared to the national average. Allstate researchers analyzed internal property damage reported claims over a two-year period (from January 2008 to December 2009) to protect findings from external influences such as weather or road construction. A weighted average of the two-year numbers determined the annual percentages. The report defines an auto crash as any collision resulting in a property damage claim. *Allstate, "2011 Allstate America's Best Drivers Report™"*
- Albuquerque was identified as one of the least disaster-proof places in the U.S. in terms of its vulnerability to natural and non-natural disasters. The city ranked #1 out of 5. Rankings are based on the U.S. Center for Disease Control's Cities Readiness Initiative (CRI). As part of the CRI, the CDC and state public health personnel assess local emergency-management plans, protocols and capabilities for 72 Metropolitan Statistical Areas and four non-MSA large cities. *Forbes, "America's Most and Least Disaster-Proof Cities," December 12, 2011*
- The National Insurance Crime Bureau ranked 366 metro areas in the U.S. in terms of per capita rates of vehicle theft. The Albuquerque metro area ranked #20 (#1 = highest rate). Criteria: number of vehicle theft offenses per 100,000 inhabitants in 2010. *National Insurance Crime Bureau, "Hot Spots," June 21, 2011*

Seniors/Retirement Rankings

- Albuquerque was identified as one of the "100 Most Popular Retirement Towns" by *Topretirements.com* The list reflects the 100 cities (out of 815+ total cities reviewed) that visitors to the website are most interested in for retirement. *Topretirements.com, "100 Most Popular Retirement Towns," February 21, 2012*
- Albuquerque was selected as one of the best places to retire by *CNNMoney.com*. Criteria: low cost of living; low violent-crime rate; good medical care; large population over age 50; abundant amenities for retirees. *CNNMoney.com, "Best Places to Retire 2011"*

- Albuquerque was selected as one of "The Best Retirement Places" by *Forbes.* The magazine considered a wide range of factors such as climate, availability of doctors, driving environment, and crime rates, but focused especially on tax burden and cost of living. *Forbes, "The Best Retirement Places," March 27, 2011*

Sports/Recreation Rankings

- Albuquerque was selected as one of "10 Great Golf Cities" by *Livability.com.* The city was ranked #3. *Livability.com* searched 200 of the most livable cities in America to find the top 10 best lesser-known cities for golfers. *Livability.com, "Golf's Best Kept Secrets: 10 Great Golf Cities," March 2, 2010*
- Albuquerque appeared on the *Sporting News* list of the "Best Sports Cities" for 2011. The area ranked #110 out of 271 cities in the U.S. *Sporting News* takes a 12-month snapshot of each city's sports, putting a heavy premium on regular-season won-lost records (from the most recently completed season). Other criteria include: playoff berths, bowl appearances and tournament bids; championships; applicable power ratings; quality of competition; overall fan fervor (measured in part by attendance); abundance of teams (rewarding quality over quantity); stadium and arena quality; ticket availability and prices; franchise ownership; and marquee appeal of athletes. *Sporting News, "Best Sports Cities 2011," October 4, 2011*
- Albuquerque was chosen as a bicycle friendly community by the League of American Bicyclists. A Bicycle Friendly Community welcomes cyclists by providing safe accommodation for cycling and encouraging people to bike for transportation and recreation. There are four award levels: Platinum; Gold; Silver; and Bronze. The community achieved an award level of Bronze. *League of American Bicyclists, "Bicycle Friendly Community Master List 2011"*
- Albuquerque was chosen as one of America's best cities for bicycling. The city ranked #17 out of 50. Criteria: number of segregated bike lanes, municipal bike racks, and bike boulevards; vibrant and diverse bike culture; smart, savvy bike shops; interviews with national and local advocates, bike shops and other experts. The editors only considered cities with populations of 100,000 or more. *Bicycling, "America's Best Bike Cities," April 2010*

Transportation Rankings

- The Albuquerque metro area appeared on *Forbes* list of the best and worst cities for commuters. The metro area ranked #13 out of 60 (#1 is best). Criteria: travel time; road congestion; travel delays. *Forbes.com, "Best and Worst Cities for Commuters," February 16, 2010*

Women/Minorities Rankings

- *Women's Health* examined U.S. cities and identified the 100 best cities for women. Albuquerque was ranked #36. Criteria: 30 categories were examined from obesity and breast cancer rates to commuting times and hours spent working out. *Women's Health, "Best Cities for Women 2012"*
- Albuquerque was ranked #54 out of 100 metro areas in *SELF Magazine's* ranking of America's healthiest places for women." A panel of experts came up with more than 50 criteria including death and disease rates, environmental indicators, community resources, and lifestyle habits. *SELF Magazine, "Secrets of America's Healthiest Women," December 2008*
- Albuquerque was selected as one of the "Top 10 Cities for Hispanics." Criteria: the prospect of a good job; a safe place to raise a family; a manageable cost of living; the ability to buy and keep a home; a culture of inclusion where Hispanics are highly represented; resources to help start a business; the presence of Hispanic or Spanish-language media; representation of Hispanic needs on local government; a thriving arts and culture community; air quality; energy costs; city's state of health and rates of obesity. *Hispanic Magazine, August 2008*

Miscellaneous Rankings

- *Men's Health* ranked 100 U.S. cities by their level of sadness. Albuquerque was ranked #70 (#1 = saddest city). Criteria: suicide rates; unemployment rates; percentage of households that use antidepressants; percent of population who report feeling blue all or most of the time. *Men's Health, "Frown Towns," November 28, 2011*

- Albuquerque was selected as one of the "Worst Hair Cities" by *NaturallyCurly.com.* The city was ranked #12. Criteria: humidity levels; pollution; rainfall; average wind speeds; water hardness; beauty salons per capita. *NaturallyCurly.com, "Best/Worst Hair Cities," April 29, 2009*

- The Albuquerque metro area appeared in *AutoMD.com's* ranking of the "Best and Worst Cities for Auto Repair." The metro area ranked #48 (#1 is best). The 50 most-populated metro areas in the U.S. were ranked on three critical factors: repair affordability; price disparity range; shop integrity factor. *AutoMD.com, "Advocacy for Repair Shop Fairness Report," February 24, 2010*

Business Environment

CITY FINANCES

City Government Finances

Component	2009 ($000)	2009 ($ per capita)
Total Revenues	964,355	1,861
Total Expenditures	933,775	1,802
Debt Outstanding	1,216,074	2,346
Cash and Securities[1]	695,502	1,342

Note: (1) Cash and security holdings of a government at the close of its fiscal year, including those of its dependent agencies, utilities, and liquor stores.
Source: U.S Census Bureau, State & Local Government Finances 2009

City Government Revenue by Source

Source	2009 ($000)	2009 ($ per capita)
General Revenue		
From Federal Government	27,688	53
From State Government	216,428	418
From Local Governments	980	2
Taxes		
Property	125,812	243
Sales and Gross Receipts	186,774	360
Personal Income	0	0
Corporate Income	0	0
Motor Vehicle License	0	0
Other Taxes	7,860	15
Current Charges	238,953	461
Liquor Store	0	0
Utility	99,855	193
Employee Retirement	0	0

Source: U.S Census Bureau, State & Local Government Finances 2009

City Government Expenditures by Function

Function	2009 ($000)	2009 ($ per capita)	2009 (%)
General Direct Expenditures			
Air Transportation	31,122	60	3.3
Corrections	0	0	0.0
Education	0	0	0.0
Employment Security Administration	0	0	0.0
Financial Administration	15,897	31	1.7
Fire Protection	74,972	145	8.0
General Public Buildings	13,437	26	1.4
Governmental Administration, Other	13,460	26	1.4
Health	9,311	18	1.0
Highways	61,055	118	6.5
Hospitals	0	0	0.0
Housing and Community Development	39,761	77	4.3
Interest on General Debt	14,150	27	1.5
Judicial and Legal	9,201	18	1.0
Libraries	11,578	22	1.2
Parking	4,978	10	0.5
Parks and Recreation	84,666	163	9.1
Police Protection	154,131	297	16.5
Public Welfare	15,045	29	1.6
Sewerage	59,738	115	6.4
Solid Waste Management	45,044	87	4.8
Veterans' Services	0	0	0.0
Liquor Store	0	0	0.0
Utility	177,667	343	19.0
Employee Retirement	0	0	0.0

Source: U.S Census Bureau, State & Local Government Finances 2009

Municipal Bond Ratings

Area	Moody's	S&P	Fitch
City	Aa2	AAA	AA+

Rating Systems (shown in declining order of credit quality): Moody's– Aaa, Aa, A, Baa, Ba, B, Caa, Ca, C (numerical modifiers 1, 2, and 3 are added to letter-rating); S&P– AAA, AA, A, BBB, BB, B, CCC, CC, C; Fitch– AAA, AA, A, BBB, BB, B, CCC, CC, C. Ratings may be modified by the addition of a plus or minus sign to show relative standing within the major rating categories.
Notes: n/a Not Available; w/d Withdrawn (1) Not Reviewed; (2) Issuer Rating/No General Obligation; (3) Standard and Poor's Issue Credit Rating (ICR) is a current opinion of an obliger with respect to a specific financial obligation, a specific class of financial obligations, or a specific financial program.
Source: U.S. Census Bureau, 2012 Statistical Abstract, Bond Ratings for City Governments by Largest Cities: 2010

DEMOGRAPHICS

Population Growth

Area	1990 Census	2000 Census	2010 Census	Population Growth (%)	
				1990-2000	2000-2010
City	388,375	448,607	545,852	15.5	21.7
MSA[1]	599,416	729,649	887,077	21.7	21.6
U.S.	248,709,873	281,421,906	308,745,538	13.2	9.7

Note: (1) Figures cover the Albuquerque, NM Metropolitan Statistical Area—see Appendix B for areas included
Source: U.S. Census Bureau, 2010 Census

Household Size

Area	Persons in Household (%)							Average Household Size
	One	Two	Three	Four	Five	Six	Seven or More	
City	31.9	32.1	15.1	11.9	5.6	2.1	1.3	2.40
MSA[1]	28.5	32.8	15.5	12.6	6.3	2.5	1.7	2.51
U.S.	26.7	32.8	16.1	13.4	6.5	2.6	1.9	2.58

Note: (1) Figures cover the Albuquerque, NM Metropolitan Statistical Area—see Appendix B for areas included
Source: U.S. Census Bureau, 2010 Census

Race

Area	White Alone[2] (%)	Black Alone[2] (%)	Asian Alone[2] (%)	AIAN[3] Alone[2] (%)	NHOPI[4] Alone[2] (%)	Other Race Alone[2] (%)	Two or More Races (%)
City	69.7	3.3	2.6	4.6	0.1	15.0	4.6
MSA[1]	69.6	2.7	2.0	5.9	0.1	15.4	4.3
U.S.	72.4	12.6	4.8	0.9	0.2	6.2	2.9

Note: (1) Figures cover the Albuquerque, NM Metropolitan Statistical Area—see Appendix B for areas included; (2) Alone is defined as not being in combination with one or more other races; (3) American Indian and Alaska Native; (4) Native Hawaiian and Other Pacific Islander
Source: U.S. Census Bureau, 2010 Census

Hispanic or Latino Origin

Area	Hispanic or Latino (%)	Mexican (%)	Puerto Rican (%)	Cuban (%)	Other Hispanic or Latino (%)
City	46.7	26.8	0.5	0.5	18.9
MSA[1]	46.7	26.0	0.5	0.4	19.8
U.S.	16.3	10.3	1.5	0.6	4.0

Note: Persons of Hispanic or Latino origin can be of any race; (1) Figures cover the Albuquerque, NM Metropolitan Statistical Area—see Appendix B for areas included
Source: U.S. Census Bureau, 2010 Census

Segregation

Type	Segregation Indices[1]				Percent Change		
	1990	2000	2010	2010 Rank[2]	1990-2000	1990-2010	2000-2010
Black/White	38.0	32.0	30.9	99	-6.0	-7.1	-1.1
Asian/White	25.7	28.1	28.5	93	2.4	2.9	0.4
Hispanic/White	40.5	39.8	36.4	79	-0.8	-4.1	-3.4

Note: Figures are based on an analysis of 1990, 2000, and 2010 Census Decennial Census tract data by William H. Frey, Brookings Institution and the University of Michigan Social Science Data Analysis Network. In this analysis all racial groups (whites, blacks, and asians) are non-Hispanic members of those races. Hispanics are shown as a separate category; All figures cover the Metropolitan Statistical Area (see Appendix B for areas included); (1) Segregation Indices are Dissimilarity Indices that measure the degree to which the minority group is distributed differently than whites across census tracts. They range from 0 (complete integration) to 100 (complete segregation) where the value indicates the percentage of the minority group that needs to move to be distributed exactly like whites; (2) Ranges from 1 (most segregated) to 102 (least segregated); n/a not available.
Source: www.CensusScope.org

Ancestry

Area	German	Irish	English	American	Italian	Polish	French[2]	Scottish	Dutch
City	11.5	8.8	7.1	2.4	3.4	1.5	2.3	1.9	1.1
MSA[1]	11.8	8.5	7.3	2.7	3.3	1.5	2.4	1.9	1.0
U.S.	16.1	11.6	8.8	6.1	5.7	3.2	3.0	1.9	1.6

Note: Figures are the percentage of the total population reporting a particular ancestry. The nine most commonly reported ancestries in the U.S. are shown. Figures include multiple ancestries (e.g. if a person reported being Irish and Italian, they were included in both columns); (1) Figures cover the Albuquerque, NM Metropolitan Statistical Area—see Appendix B for areas included; (2) Excludes Basque
Source: U.S. Census Bureau, 2008-2010 American Community Survey 3-Year Estimates

Foreign-Born Population

Area	Percent of Population Born in								
	Any Foreign Country	Mexico	Asia	Europe	Carribean	South America	Central America[2]	Africa	Canada
City	11.2	6.7	2.1	0.8	0.4	0.4	0.2	0.2	0.2
MSA[1]	10.0	6.5	1.5	0.8	0.3	0.3	0.2	0.1	0.2
U.S.	12.8	3.8	3.6	1.6	1.2	0.9	1.0	0.5	0.3

Note: (1) Figures cover the Albuquerque, NM Metropolitan Statistical Area—see Appendix B for areas included; (2) Excludes Mexico.
Source: U.S. Census Bureau, 2008-2010 American Community Survey 3-Year Estimates

Marital Status

Area	Never Married	Now Married[2]	Separated	Widowed	Divorced
City	35.2	44.1	1.8	5.1	13.8
MSA[1]	32.9	47.2	1.8	5.3	12.9
U.S.	31.6	49.6	2.2	6.1	10.7

Note: Figures are percentages and cover the population 15 years of age and older; (1) Figures cover the Albuquerque, NM Metropolitan Statistical Area—see Appendix B for areas included; (2) Excludes separated
Source: U.S. Census Bureau, 2008-2010 American Community Survey 3-Year Estimates

Age

Area	Percent of Population							Median Age
	Under Age 5	Age 5 to 17	Age 18 to 34	Age 35 to 49	Age 50 to 64	Age 65 to 79	80 Years and Over	
City	7.0	17.0	25.9	19.8	18.3	8.6	3.5	35.1
MSA[1]	6.8	17.8	23.6	20.0	19.5	9.1	3.2	36.4
U.S.	6.5	17.5	23.2	20.7	19.0	9.4	3.6	37.2

Note: (1) Figures cover the Albuquerque, NM Metropolitan Statistical Area—see Appendix B for areas included
Source: U.S. Census Bureau, 2010 Census

Male/Female Ratio

Area	Males	Females	Males per 100 Females
City	265,106	280,746	94.4
MSA[1]	435,807	451,270	96.6
U.S.	151,781,326	156,964,212	96.7

Note: (1) Figures cover the Albuquerque, NM Metropolitan Statistical Area—see Appendix B for areas included
Source: U.S. Census Bureau, 2010 Census

Religious Groups

Area	Catholic	Baptist	Non-Den.	Methodist[2]	Lutheran	LDS[3]	Pente-costal	Presby-terian[4]	Muslim[5]	Judaism
MSA[1]	27.2	3.8	4.2	1.5	1.0	2.4	1.5	1.1	0.3	0.2
U.S.	19.1	9.3	4.0	4.0	2.3	2.0	1.9	1.6	0.8	0.7

Note: Figures are the number of adherents as a percentage of the total population; (1) Figures cover the Albuquerque, NM Metropolitan Statistical Area—see Appendix B for areas included; (2) Methodist/Pietist; (3) Latter Day Saints; (4) Reformed; (5) Figures are estimates
Source: Association of Statisticians of American Religious Bodies, 2010 U.S. Religion Census: Religious Congregations & Membership Study

ECONOMY

Gross Metropolitan Product

Area	2007	2008	2009	2010	2010 Rank[2]
MSA[1]	34.6	35.0	36.7	38.1	60

Note: Figures are in billions of dollars; (1) Figures cover the Albuquerque, NM Metropolitan Statistical Area—see Appendix B for areas included; (2) Rank ranges from 1 to 363
Source: The United States Conference of Mayors, "U.S. Metro Economies: GMP and Employment Forecasts," June 2011

Economic Growth

Area	2007-2009 (%)	2010 (%)	2011 (%)	Rank[2]
MSA[1]	2.4	4.0	1.9	29
U.S.	-1.3	2.9	2.5	–

Note: Figures are real Gross Metropolitan Product growth rates and represent annual average percent change; (1) Figures cover the Albuquerque, NM Metropolitan Statistical Area—see Appendix B for areas included; (2) Rank ranges from 1 to 363
Source: The United States Conference of Mayors, "U.S. Metro Economies: GMP and Employment Forecasts," June 2011

Metropolitan Area Exports

Area	2005	2006	2007	2008	2009	2010	2010 Rank[2]
MSA[1]	1,976.8	2,228.5	978.9	474.9	357.6	519.9	198

Note: Figures are in millions of dollars; (1) Figures cover the Albuquerque, NM Metropolitan Statistical Area—see Appendix B for areas included; (2) Rank ranges from 1 to 369
Source: U.S. Department of Commerce, International Trade Administration, Office of Trade & Industry Information, Manufacturing & Services, data extracted April 2, 2012

INCOME

Income

Area	Per Capita ($)	Median Household ($)	Average Household ($)
City	25,612	46,532	61,500
MSA[1]	25,216	48,047	63,525
U.S.	26,942	51,222	70,116

Note: (1) Figures cover the Albuquerque, NM Metropolitan Statistical Area—see Appendix B for areas included
Source: U.S. Census Bureau, 2008-2010 American Community Survey 3-Year Estimates

Household Income Distribution

Area	Percent of Households Earning							
	Under $15,000	$15,000 -24,999	$25,000 -34,999	$35,000 -49,999	$50,000 -74,999	$75,000 -99,000	$100,000 -149,999	$150,000 and up
City	14.2	11.8	11.7	15.1	19.0	11.0	10.9	6.2
MSA[1]	13.7	11.6	11.1	15.2	18.9	11.6	11.4	6.6
U.S.	13.0	11.0	10.6	14.2	18.5	12.1	12.2	8.4

Note: (1) Figures cover the Albuquerque, NM Metropolitan Statistical Area—see Appendix B for areas included
Source: U.S. Census Bureau, 2008-2010 American Community Survey 3-Year Estimates

Poverty Rate

Area	All Ages	Under 18 Years Old	18 to 64 Years Old	65 Years and Over
City	16.3	23.5	14.6	11.0
MSA[1]	16.0	23.2	14.2	10.8
U.S.	14.4	20.1	13.1	9.4

Note: Figures are percentage of people whose income during the past 12 months was below the poverty level; (1) Figures cover the Albuquerque, NM Metropolitan Statistical Area—see Appendix B for areas included
Source: U.S. Census Bureau, 2008-2010 American Community Survey 3-Year Estimates

Personal Bankruptcy Filing Rate

Area	2006	2007	2008	2009	2010	2011
Bernalillo County	1.35	1.95	2.67	3.44	3.65	3.15
U.S.	2.00	2.73	3.53	4.61	4.97	4.37

Note: Numbers are per 1,000 population and include Chapter 7 and Chapter 13 filings
Source: Federal Deposit Insurance Corporation, Regional Economic Conditions, March 9, 2012

EMPLOYMENT

Labor Force and Employment

Area	Civilian Labor Force			Workers Employed		
	Dec. 2010	Dec. 2011	% Chg.	Dec. 2010	Dec. 2011	% Chg.
City	263,601	259,931	-1.4	242,952	243,858	0.4
MSA[1]	409,834	403,769	-1.5	374,929	376,326	0.4
U.S.	153,156,000	153,373,000	0.1	139,159,000	140,681,000	1.1

Note: Data is not seasonally adjusted and covers workers 16 years of age and older; (1) Metropolitan Statistical Area—see Appendix B for areas included
Source: Bureau of Labor Statistics, http://stats.bls.gov

Unemployment Rate

Area	2011											
	Jan.	Feb.	Mar.	Apr.	May	Jun.	Jul.	Aug.	Sep.	Oct.	Nov.	Dec.
City	8.4	8.4	7.1	6.6	6.2	7.4	6.9	6.5	6.3	6.4	6.1	6.2
MSA[1]	9.0	9.1	7.7	7.2	6.8	8.2	7.7	7.2	6.9	7.0	6.7	6.8
U.S.	9.8	9.5	9.2	8.7	8.7	9.3	9.3	9.1	8.8	8.5	8.2	8.3

Note: Data is not seasonally adjusted and covers workers 16 years of age and older; All figures are percentages; (1) Metropolitan Statistical Area—see Appendix B for areas included
Source: Bureau of Labor Statistics, http://stats.bls.gov

Projected Unemployment Rate

Area	2010 (%)	2011 (%)	2012 (%)	2013 (%)
MSA[1]	9.2	7.9	7.6	7.1

Note: (1) Metropolitan Statistical Area—see Appendix B for areas included
Source: The United States Conference of Mayors, "U.S. Metro Economies: GMP and Employment Forecasts," June 2011

Employment by Occupation

Occupation Classification	City (%)	MSA[1] (%)	U.S. (%)
Management, Business, Science, and Arts	39.0	38.1	35.6
Natural Resources, Construction, and Maintenance	8.7	9.7	9.5
Production, Transportation, and Material Moving	8.2	8.7	12.1
Sales and Office	25.6	25.5	25.2
Service	18.4	18.0	17.6

Note: Figures cover employed civilians 16 years of age and older; (1) Figures cover the Albuquerque, NM Metropolitan Statistical Area—see Appendix B for areas included
Source: U.S. Census Bureau, 2008-2010 American Community Survey 3-Year Estimates

Employment by Industry

Sector	MSA[1]		U.S.
	Number of Employees	Percent of Total	Percent of Total
Construction	n/a	n/a	4.1
Education and Health Services	59,300	15.9	15.2
Financial Activities	17,200	4.6	5.8
Government	83,600	22.4	16.8
Information	8,800	2.4	2.0
Leisure and Hospitality	36,100	9.7	9.9
Manufacturing	18,100	4.8	8.9
Mining and Logging	n/a	n/a	0.6
Other Services	11,500	3.1	4.0
Professional and Business Services	55,700	14.9	13.3
Retail Trade	41,900	11.2	11.5
Transportation and Utilities	9,700	2.6	3.8
Wholesale Trade	11,600	3.1	4.2

Note: Figures cover non-farm employment as of December 2011 and are not seasonally adjusted; (1) Metropolitan Statistical Area—see Appendix B for areas included; n/a not available
Source: Bureau of Labor Statistics, http://stats.bls.gov

Occupations with Greatest Projected Employment Growth: 2008 – 2018

Occupation[1]	2008 Employment	2018 Projected Employment	Numeric Employment Change	Percent Employment Change
Personal and Home Care Aides	13,740	20,370	6,630	48.3
Home Health Aides	8,760	13,180	4,420	50.5
Registered Nurses	13,160	16,300	3,140	23.9
Retail Salespersons	31,130	33,880	2,750	8.8
Customer Service Representatives	13,510	15,670	2,160	16.0
Cashiers	21,150	23,110	1,960	9.3
Postsecondary Teachers	11,390	13,190	1,800	15.8
Nursing Aides, Orderlies, and Attendants	8,060	9,800	1,740	21.6
Construction Laborers	16,170	17,810	1,640	10.1
Elementary School Teachers, Except Special Education	9,350	10,890	1,540	16.5

Note: Projections cover New Mexico; (1) Sorted by numeric employment change
Source: www.projectionscentral.com, State Occupational Projections, 2008–2018 Long-Term Projections

Fastest Growing Occupations: 2008 – 2018

Occupation[1]	2008 Employment	2018 Projected Employment	Numeric Employment Change	Percent Employment Change
Home Health Aides	8,760	13,180	4,420	50.5
Network Systems and Data Communications Analysts	820	1,220	400	48.8
Water and Liquid Waste Treatment Plant and System Operators	860	1,280	420	48.8
Personal and Home Care Aides	13,740	20,370	6,630	48.3
Gaming Dealers	670	970	300	44.8
Self-Enrichment Education Teachers	490	690	200	40.8
Petroleum Engineers	330	460	130	39.4
Compliance Officers, Except Agriculture, Construction, Health and Safety, and Transportation	1,150	1,550	400	34.8
Electrical and Electronics Repairers, Powerhouse, Substation, and Relay	500	670	170	34.0
Fire Fighters	1,560	2,070	510	32.7

Note: Projections cover New Mexico; (1) Sorted by percent employment change and excludes occupations with numeric employment change less than 100
Source: www.projectionscentral.com, State Occupational Projections, 2008–2018 Long-Term Projections

Average Wages

Occupation	$/Hr.	Occupation	$/Hr.
Accountants and Auditors	31.32	Maids and Housekeeping Cleaners	9.21
Automotive Mechanics	17.27	Maintenance and Repair Workers	16.36
Bookkeepers	16.78	Marketing Managers	45.60
Carpenters	20.00	Nuclear Medicine Technologists	33.03
Cashiers	9.94	Nurses, Licensed Practical	23.01
Clerks, General Office	12.22	Nurses, Registered	33.73
Clerks, Receptionists/Information	11.83	Nursing Aides/Orderlies/Attendants	13.35
Clerks, Shipping/Receiving	14.07	Packers and Packagers, Hand	11.64
Computer Programmers	37.22	Physical Therapists	35.16
Computer Support Specialists	23.38	Postal Service Mail Carriers	24.93
Computer Systems Analysts	40.34	Real Estate Brokers	38.36
Cooks, Restaurant	10.13	Retail Salespersons	12.27
Dentists	77.32	Sales Reps., Exc. Tech./Scientific	27.05
Electrical Engineers	43.52	Sales Reps., Tech./Scientific	38.12
Electricians	22.07	Secretaries, Exc. Legal/Med./Exec.	13.94
Financial Managers	46.38	Security Guards	11.78
First-Line Supervisors/Managers, Sales	18.74	Surgeons	n/a
Food Preparation Workers	10.15	Teacher Assistants	10.00
General and Operations Managers	46.43	Teachers, Elementary School	22.90
Hairdressers/Cosmetologists	11.30	Teachers, Secondary School	23.50
Internists	n/a	Telemarketers	n/a
Janitors and Cleaners	10.41	Truck Drivers, Heavy/Tractor-Trailer	18.77
Landscaping/Groundskeeping Workers	10.90	Truck Drivers, Light/Delivery Svcs.	15.51
Lawyers	44.61	Waiters and Waitresses	10.07

Note: Wage data covers the Albuquerque, NM Metropolitan Statistical Area—see Appendix B for areas included. Hourly wages for elementary/secondary school teachers and teacher assistants were calculated by the editors from annual wage data assuming a 40 hour work week; n/a not available.
Source: Bureau of Labor Statistics, Metro Area Occupational Employment and Wage Estimates, May 2011

RESIDENTIAL REAL ESTATE

Building Permits

Area	Single-Family			Multi-Family			Total		
	2010	2011	Pct. Chg.	2010	2011	Pct. Chg.	2010	2011	Pct. Chg.
City	814	754	-7.4	202	270	33.7	1,016	1,024	0.8
MSA[1]	1,553	1,354	-12.8	211	280	32.7	1,764	1,634	-7.4
U.S.	447,311	418,498	-6.4	157,299	205,563	30.7	604,610	624,061	3.2

Note: (1) Metropolitan Statistical Area—see Appendix B for areas included; figures represent new, privately-owned housing units authorized (unadjusted data); All permit data are based on estimates with imputation.
Source: U.S. Census Bureau, Manufacturing, Mining, and Construction Statistics, Building Permits, 2010, 2011

Homeownership Rate

Area	2005 (%)	2006 (%)	2007 (%)	2008 (%)	2009 (%)	2010 (%)	2011 (%)
MSA[1]	69.2	70.0	70.5	68.2	65.7	65.5	67.1
U.S.	68.9	68.8	68.1	67.8	67.4	66.9	66.1

Note: (1) Metropolitan Statistical Area—see Appendix B for areas included
Source: U.S. Census Bureau, Housing Vacancies and Homeownership Annual Statistics: 2011

Housing Vacancy Rates

Area	Gross Vacancy Rate[2] (%)			Year-Round Vacancy Rate[3] (%)			Rental Vacancy Rate[4] (%)			Homeowner Vacancy Rate[5] (%)		
	2009	2010	2011	2009	2010	2011	2009	2010	2011	2009	2010	2011
MSA[1]	8.5	7.4	7.1	7.8	6.6	6.3	8.0	5.0	6.9	1.9	1.7	1.4
U.S.	14.5	14.3	14.2	11.3	11.3	11.1	10.6	10.2	9.5	2.6	2.6	2.5

Note: (1) Metropolitan Statistical Area—see Appendix B for areas included; (2) The percentage of the total housing inventory that is vacant; (3) The percentage of the housing inventory (excluding seasonal units) that is year-round vacant; (4) The percentage of rental inventory that is vacant for rent; (5) The percentage of homeowner inventory that is vacant for sale
Source: U.S. Census Bureau, Housing Vacancies and Homeownership Annual Statistics: 2011

TAXES

State Corporate Income Tax Rates

State	Tax Rate (%)	Income Brackets ($)	Num. of Brackets	Financial Institution Tax Rate (%)[a]	Federal Income Tax Ded.
New Mexico	4.8 - 7.6	500,000 - 1 mil.	3	4.8 - 7.6	No

Note: Tax rates as of January 1, 2012; (a) Rates listed are the corporate income tax rate applied to financial institutions or excise taxes based on income. Some states have other taxes based upon the value of deposits or shares.
Source: Federation of Tax Administrators, "State Corporate Income Tax Rates, 2012"

State Individual Income Tax Rates

State	Tax Rate (%)	Income Brackets ($)	Num. of Brackets	Personal Exempt. ($)[1]		Fed. Inc. Tax Ded.
				Single	Dependents	
New Mexico	1.7 - 4.9	5,500 (o) - 16,001 (o)	4	3,700 (d)	3,700 (d)	No

Note: Tax rates as of January 1, 2012; Local- and county-level taxes are not included; n/a not applicable; (1) Married joint filers generally receive double the single exemption; (d) These states use the personal exemption amounts provided in the federal Internal Revenue Code; (o) The income brackets reported for New Mexico are for single individuals. For married couples filing jointly, the same tax rates apply to income brackets ranging from $8,000, to $24,000.
Source: Federation of Tax Administrators, "State Individual Income Tax Rates, 2012"

Various State and Local Tax Rates

State	State and Local Sales and Use (%)	State Sales and Use (%)	Gasoline[1] (¢/gal.)	Cigarette[2] ($/pack)	Spirits[3] ($/gal.)	Wine[4] ($/gal.)	Beer[5] ($/gal.)
New Mexico	6.9995	5.13 (c)	18.9	1.66	6.06	1.70	0.41

Note: All tax rates as of January 1, 2012 except beer, wine and spirits (September 1, 2011); (1) The American Petroleum Institute has developed a methodology for determining the average tax rate on a gallon of fuel. Rates may include any of the following: excise taxes, environmental fees, storage tank fees, other fees or taxes, general sales tax, and local taxes. In states where gasoline is subject to the general sales tax, or where the fuel tax is based on the average sale price, the average rate determined by API is sensitive to changes in the price of gasoline. States that fully or partially apply general sales taxes to gasoline: CA, CO, GA, IL, IN, MI, NY; (2) The federal excise tax of $1.0066 per pack and local taxes are not included; (3) Rates are those applicable to off-premise sales of 40% alcohol by volume (a.b.v.) distilled spirits in 750ml containers. Local excise taxes are excluded; (4) Rates are those applicable to off-premise sales of 11% a.b.v. non-carbonated wine in 750ml containers; (5) Rates are those applicable to off-premise sales of 4.7% a.b.v. beer in 12 ounce containers; (c) The sales taxes in Hawaii, New Mexico and South Dakota have broad bases that include many services, so their rates are not strictly comparable to other states.
Source: Tax Foundation, 2012 Facts & Figures: How Does Your State Compare?

State-Local Tax Burdens

Area	Rate (%)	Rank[1]	Per Capita Taxes Paid to Home State ($)	Total State and Local Per Capita Taxes Paid ($)	Per Capita Income ($)
New Mexico	8.4	41	2,079	2,997	35,780
U.S. Average	9.8	-	3,057	4,160	42,539

Note: Figures cover 2009; (1) Rank ranges from 1 to 50 where 1 is highest tax burden
Source: Tax Foundation, State-Local Tax Burdens, All States, 2009

State Business Tax Climate Index Rankings

State	Overall Rank	Corporate Tax Index Rank	Individual Income Tax Index Rank	Sales Tax Index Rank	Unemployment Insurance Tax Index Rank	Property Tax Index Rank
New Mexico	38	38	33	45	14	1

Note: The index is a measure of how each state's tax laws affect economic performance. The lower the rank, the more favorable a state's tax system is for business. States without a given tax are given a ranking of 1.
Source: Tax Foundation, Major Components of the State Business Tax Climate Index, FY 2012

COMMERCIAL REAL ESTATE

Office Market

Market Area	Inventory (sq. ft.)	Vacant (sq. ft.)	Vac. Rate (%)	Under Constr. (sq. ft.)	Asking Rent ($/sf/yr) Class A	Asking Rent ($/sf/yr) Class B
Albuquerque	13,734,779	2,544,730	18.5	0	20.13	16.94

Source: Grubb & Ellis, Office Markets Trends, 4th Quarter 2011

Industrial Market

Market Area	Inventory (sq. ft.)	Vacant (sq. ft.)	Vac. Rate (%)	Under Constr. (sq. ft.)	Asking Rent ($/sf/yr) WH/Dist	Asking Rent ($/sf/yr) R&D/Flex
Albuquerque	36,860,255	3,804,414	10.3	79,310	5.43	9.99

Source: Grubb & Ellis, Industrial Markets Trends, 4th Quarter 2011

COMMERCIAL UTILITIES

Typical Monthly Electric Bills

Area	Commercial Service ($/month)		Industrial Service ($/month)	
	1,500 kWh	40 kW demand 14,000 kWh	1,000 kW demand 200,000 kWh	50,000 kW demand 15,000,000 kWh
City	n/a	n/a	n/a	n/a
Average[1]	189	1,616	25,197	1,470,813

Note: Based on total rates in effect July 1, 2011; (1) average based on 184 utilities surveyed; n/a not available
Source: Edison Electric Institute, Typical Bills and Average Rates Report, Summer 2011

TRANSPORTATION

Means of Transportation to Work

Area	Car/Truck/Van: Drove Alone	Car/Truck/Van: Car-pooled	Public Transportation: Bus	Public Transportation: Subway	Public Transportation: Railroad	Bicycle	Walked	Other Means	Worked at Home
City	79.0	10.3	2.1	0.0	0.1	1.5	1.8	1.2	4.0
MSA[1]	78.6	11.0	1.5	0.0	0.3	1.0	1.7	1.3	4.5
U.S.	76.0	10.2	2.7	1.7	0.5	0.5	2.8	1.3	4.2

Note: Figures are percentages and cover workers 16 years of age and older; (1) Figures cover the Albuquerque, NM Metropolitan Statistical Area—see Appendix B for areas included
Source: U.S. Census Bureau, 2008-2010 American Community Survey 3-Year Estimates

Travel Time to Work

Area	Less Than 10 Minutes	10 to 19 Minutes	20 to 29 Minutes	30 to 44 Minutes	45 to 59 Minutes	60 to 89 Minutes	90 Minutes or More
City	11.3	38.1	27.1	16.3	3.2	2.2	1.7
MSA[1]	11.2	33.1	24.4	20.3	6.0	3.2	1.8
U.S.	13.9	30.1	20.8	19.8	7.5	5.5	2.5

Note: Figures are percentages and include workers 16 years old and over; (1) Figures cover the Albuquerque, NM Metropolitan Statistical Area—see Appendix B for areas included
Source: U.S. Census Bureau, 2008-2010 American Community Survey 3-Year Estimates

Travel Time Index

Area	1985	1990	1995	2000	2005	2010
Urban Area[1]	1.06	1.10	1.15	1.17	1.16	1.10
Average[2]	1.11	1.16	1.18	1.21	1.25	1.20

Note: Travel Time Index—the ratio of travel time in the peak period to the travel time at free-flow conditions. A value of 1.30 indicates a 20-minute free-flow trip takes 26 minutes in the peak. Free-flow speeds (60 mph on freeways and 35 mph on principal arterials) are used as the comparison threshold; (1) Covers the Albuquerque NM urban area; (2) average of 439 urban areas
Source: Texas Transportation Institute, Urban Mobility Report 2011, September 2011

Public Transportation

Agency Name / Mode of Transportation	Vehicles Operated in Maximum Service	Annual Unlinked Passenger Trips ('000)	Annual Passenger Miles ('000)
ABQ Ride			
Bus (directly operated)	123	11,177.1	37,443.3
Demand Response (directly operated)	50	203.7	2,018.1

Source: Federal Transit Administration, National Transit Database, 2010

Air Transportation

Airport Name and Code / Type of Service	Passenger Airlines[1]	Passenger Enplanements	Freight Carriers[2]	Freight (lbs.)
Albuquerque International (ABQ)				
Domestic service (U.S. carriers - 2011)	29	2,757,018	11	90,835,512
International service (U.S. carriers - 2010)	4	610	0	0

Note: (1) Includes all U.S.-based major, minor and commuter airlines that carried at least one passenger during the year; (2) Includes all U.S.-based airlines and freight carriers that transported at least one pound of freight during the year
Source: Bureau of Transportation Statistics, The Intermodal Transportation Database, Air Carriers: T-100 Domestic Market (U.S. Carriers), 2011; Bureau of Transportation Statistics, The Intermodal Transportation Database, Air Carriers: T-100 International Market (U.S. Carriers), 2010

Other Transportation Statistics

Major Highways:	I-25; I-40
Amtrak Service:	Yes
Major Waterways/Ports:	None

Source: Amtrak.com; Google Maps

BUSINESSES

Major Business Headquarters

Company Name	Rankings	
	Fortune[1]	Forbes[2]
No companies listed	-	-

Note: (1) Fortune 500—companies that produce a 10-K are ranked 1 to 500 based on 2010 revenue; (2) all private companies with at least $2 billion in annual revenue are ranked 1 to 212; companies listed are headquartered in the city; dashes indicate no ranking
Source: Fortune, "Fortune 500," May 23, 2011; Forbes, "America's Largest Private Companies," November 16, 2011

Fast-Growing Businesses

According to *Initiative for a Competitive Inner City (ICIC)*, Albuquerque is home to one of America's 100 fastest-growing "inner city" companies: **Sacred Power Corporation** (#23). Companies were ranked by their five-year compound annual growth rate. Criteria for inclusion: company must be headquartered in or have 51 percent or more of its physical operations in an economically distressed urban area; must be an independent, for-profit corporation, partnership or proprietorship; must have 10 or more employees and have a five-year sales history that includes sales of at least $200,000 in the base year and at least $1 million in the current year with no decrease in sales over the two most recent years. *Initiative for a Competitive Inner City (ICIC), "Inner City 100 Companies, 2011"*

According to Deloitte, Albuquerque is home to one of North America's 500 fastest-growing high-technology companies: **New Mexico Software** (#301). Companies are ranked by percentage growth in revenue over a five-year period. Criteria for inclusion: company must be headquartered within North America; must own proprietary intellectual property or proprietary technology that contributes to a significant portion of the company's operating revenue, or devote a significant proportion of revenues to research and development of technology; must have been in business for a minumum of five years with 2006 operating revenues of at least $50,000 USD/CD and 2010 operating revenues of at least $5 million USD/CD. *Deloitte Touche Tohmatsu, 2011 Deloitte Technology Fast 500™*

Minority Business Opportunity

Albuquerque is home to 23 companies which are on the *Hispanic Business* 500 list (500 largest U.S. Hispanic-owned companies based on 2010 revenue): **Manuel Lujan Insurance** (#64); **Roses Southwest Papers** (#71); **Holman's** (#107); **David Montoya Construction** (#113); **Abba Technologies** (#126); **A-Tech Corp.** (#127); **L&M Technologies** (#141); **Star Paving Co.** (#157); **Integrated Control Systems** (#203); **Service Electric Co.** (#271); **ADC Ltd. NM** (#280); **Captiva Group** (#287); **San Bar Construction Corp.** (#315); **Apache Construction Company** (#334); **Molzen Corbin** (#342); **Ray's Flooring Specialists** (#346); **Sparkle Maintenance** (#361); **Fiore Industries** (#409); **GenQuest** (#412); **Networx** (#433); **ORION International Technologies** (#442); **Queston Construction** (#482); **Source Technologies** (#484). Companies included must show at least 51 percent ownership by Hispanic U.S. citizens, and must maintain headquarters in one of the 50 states or Washington, D.C. *Hispanic Business, "Hispanic Business 500," June 2011*

Albuquerque is home to five companies which are on the *Hispanic Business* Fastest-Growing 100 list (greatest sales growth from 2006 to 2010): **GenQuest** (#10); **A-Tech Corp.** (#19); **L&M Technologies** (#43); **Holman's** (#73); **Integrated Control Systems** (#79). Companies included must show at least 51 percent ownership by Hispanic U.S. citizens, and must maintain headquarters in one of the 50 states or Washington, D.C. In addition, companies must have minimum revenues of $200,000 for calendar year 2005. *Hispanic Business, July/August 2011*

Minority- and Women-Owned Businesses

Group	All Firms		Firms with Paid Employees			
	Firms	Sales ($000)	Firms	Sales ($000)	Employees	Payroll ($000)
Asian	1,738	574,140	460	530,694	4,242	112,480
Black	912	297,162	45	276,321	928	27,301
Hispanic	10,291	2,799,414	1,690	2,538,011	19,254	553,758
Women	14,187	2,349,306	1,822	2,010,087	16,711	456,681
All Firms	175	4,922,311	171	4,922,288	15,112	769,254

Note: Figures cover firms located in the city; minority- and women-owned business are defined as firms in which the corresponding group own 51% or more of the stock or equity of the company
Source: U.S. Census Bureau, 2007 Economic Census, Survey of Business Owners

HOTELS

Hotels/Motels

Area	5 Star		4 Star		3 Star		2 Star		1 Star		Not Rated	
	Num.	Pct.[3]	Num.	Pct.[3]	Num.	Pct.[3]	Num.	Pct.[3]	Num.	Pct.[3]	Num.	Pct.[3]
City[1]	0	0.0	3	2.4	39	31.0	70	55.6	3	2.4	11	8.7
Total[2]	133	0.9	940	6.5	4,569	31.8	7,033	48.9	351	2.4	1,343	9.3

Note: (1) Figures cover Albuquerque and vicinity; (2) Figures cover all 100 cities in this book; (3) Percentage of hotels which have a given star rating; Star ratings are determined by expedia.com and offer an indication of the general quality of a particular hotel.
Source: expedia.com, April 25, 2012

EVENT SITES

Major Stadiums, Arenas, and Auditoriums

Name	Max. Capacity
Albuquerque Convention Center Auditorium	2,350
Isotopes Park	13,279
Tingley Coliseum	12,000
University Stadium	38,634
University of New Mexico Arena	18,018

Source: Original research

Convention Centers

Name	Overall Space (sq. ft.)	Exhibit Space (sq. ft.)	Meeting Space (sq. ft.)	Meeting Rooms
Albuquerque Convention Center	n/a	n/a	272,746	37

Note: n/a not available
Source: Original research

Living Environment

COST OF LIVING

Cost of Living Index

Composite Index	Groceries	Housing	Utilities	Trans-portation	Health Care	Misc. Goods/ Services
94.7	94.5	87.0	98.6	94.4	100.9	99.6

Note: U.S. = 100; Figures cover the Rio Rancho NM urban area.
Source: The Council for Community and Economic Research, ACCRA Cost of Living Index, 2011

Grocery Prices

Area[1]	T-Bone Steak ($/pound)	Frying Chicken ($/pound)	Whole Milk ($/half gal.)	Eggs ($/dozen)	Orange Juice ($/64 oz.)	Coffee ($/11.5 oz.)
City[2]	8.48	0.97	2.17	1.63	3.25	4.83
Avg.	9.25	1.18	2.22	1.66	3.19	4.40
Min.	6.70	0.88	1.31	0.95	2.46	2.94
Max.	14.30	2.16	3.50	3.18	4.75	6.83

Note: (1) Values for the local area are compared with the average, minimum and maximum values for all 335 areas in the Cost of Living Index; (2) Figures cover the Rio Rancho NM urban area; **T-Bone Steak** *(price per pound);* **Frying Chicken** *(price per pound, whole fryer);* **Whole Milk** *(half gallon carton);* **Eggs** *(price per dozen, Grade A, large);* **Orange Juice** *(64 oz. Tropicana or Florida Natural);* **Coffee** *(11.5 oz. can, vacuum-packed, Maxwell House, Hills Bros, or Folgers).*
Source: The Council for Community and Economic Research, ACCRA Cost of Living Index, 2011

Housing and Utility Costs

Area[1]	New Home Price ($)	Apartment Rent ($/month)	All Electric ($/month)	Part Electric ($/month)	Other Energy ($/month)	Telephone ($/month)
City[2]	253,971	727	-	103.95	76.48	22.15
Avg.	285,990	839	163.23	89.00	77.52	26.92
Min.	188,005	460	125.58	45.39	33.89	17.98
Max.	1,197,028	3,244	339.16	181.97	348.69	40.01

Note: (1) Values for the local area are compared with the average, minimum and maximum values for all 335 areas in the Cost of Living Index; (2) Figures cover the Rio Rancho NM urban area; **New Home Price** *(2,400 sf living area, 8,000 sf lot, in urban area with full utilities);* **Apartment Rent** *(950 sf 2 bedroom/1.5 or 2 bath, unfurnished, excluding all utilities except water);* **All Electric** *(average monthly cost for an all-electric home);* **Part Electric** *(average monthly cost for a part-electric home);* **Other Energy** *(average monthly cost for natural gas, fuel oil, coal, wood, and any other forms of energy except electricity);* **Telephone** *(price includes basic monthly rate for a private residential line plus additional local usage charges incurred by a family of four).*
Source: The Council for Community and Economic Research, ACCRA Cost of Living Index, 2011

Health Care, Transportation, and Other Costs

Area[1]	Doctor ($/visit)	Dentist ($/visit)	Optometrist ($/visit)	Gasoline ($/gallon)	Beauty Salon ($/visit)	Men's Shirt ($)
City[2]	92.97	89.44	90.90	3.33	35.92	24.55
Avg.	93.88	81.72	90.54	3.48	32.65	25.06
Min.	60.00	55.33	53.66	3.18	19.78	13.44
Max.	154.98	145.97	183.72	4.31	63.21	46.00

Note: (1) Values for the local area are compared with the average, minimum and maximum values for all 335 areas in the Cost of Living Index; (2) Figures cover the Rio Rancho NM urban area; **Doctor** *(general practitioners routine exam of an established patient);* **Dentist** *(adult teeth cleaning and periodic oral examination);* **Optometrist** *(full vision eye exam for established adult patient);* **Gasoline** *(one gallon regular unleaded, national brand, including all taxes, cash price at self-service pump if available);* **Beauty Salon** *(woman's shampoo, trim, and blow-dry);* **Men's Shirt** *(cotton/polyester dress shirt, pinpoint weave, long sleeves).*
Source: The Council for Community and Economic Research, ACCRA Cost of Living Index, 2011

HOUSING

House Price Index (HPI)

Area	National Ranking[2]	Quarterly Change (%)	One-Year Change (%)	Five-Year Change (%)
MSA[1]	201	-0.02	-3.93	-11.37
U.S.[3]	-	-0.10	-2.43	-19.16

Note: The HPI is a weighted repeat sales index. It measures average price changes in repeat sales or refinancings on the same properties. This information is obtained by reviewing repeat mortgage transactions on single-family properties whose mortgages have been purchased or securitized by Fannie Mae or Freddie Mac in January 1975; (1) Metropolitan/Micropolitan Statistical Area—see Appendix B for areas included; (2) Rankings are based on annual percentage change for all metro areas containing at least 15,000 transactions over the last 10 years and ranges from 1 to 306; (3) figures based on a weighted average of Census Division estimates using a purchase only index; all figures are for the period ending December 31, 2011
Source: Federal Housing Finance Agency, House Price Index, February 23, 2012

House Price Valuations

Area	Q4 2005		Q4 2006		Q4 2007		Q4 2008		Q4 2009	
	Price ($000)	Over-valuation	Price ($000)	Over-valuation	Price ($000)	Over-valuation	Price ($000)	Over-valuation	Price ($000)	Over-valuation
MSA[1]	170.5	5.9	191.8	12.7	193.4	8.2	189.8	4.8	179.5	-0.8

Note: Figures show the percentage of over- or under-valuation of single family homes relative to statistically normal house values (e.g. a value of 23.6 indicates that house values are 23.6% overvalued). Statistically normal house values are based on house prices, interest rates, household incomes, population densities, and any historical premiums or discounts metropolitan areas have exhibited over time; (1) Figures cover the Albuquerque, NM - see Appendix B for areas included
Source: Global Insight/PNC Financial Services Group, House Prices in America: 4th Quarter 2009 Update

Median Single-Family Home Prices

Area	2009	2010	2011p	Percent Change 2010 to 2011
MSA[1]	180.6	178.7	167.9	-6.0
U.S. Average	172.1	173.1	166.2	-4.0

Note: Figures are median sales prices of existing single-family homes in thousands of dollars; (p) preliminary; n/a not available; (1) Metropolitan Statistical Area—see Appendix B for areas included
Source: National Association of Realtors, Median Sales Price of Existing Single-Family Homes for Metropolitan Areas, 4th Quarter 2011

Affordability Index of Existing Single-Family Homes

Area	2009	2010	2011p	Percent Change 2010 to 2011
MSA[1]	91.5	97.0	108.3	11.6

Note: The housing affordability index measures whether or not a typical family could qualify for a mortgage loan on a typical home. The higher the index, the greater the household purchasing power. An index of 100 is defined as the point where a median-income household has exactly enough income to qualify for the purchase of a median-priced existing single-family home, assuming a 20 percent downpayment and 25 percent of gross income devoted to mortgage principal and interest payments; (p) preliminary; n/a not available; (1) Metropolitan Statistical Area—see Appendix B for areas included
Source: National Association of Realtors, Affordability Index of Existing Single-Family Homes, 2011

Median Apartment Condo-Coop Home Prices

Area	2009	2010	2011p	Percent Change 2010 to 2011
MSA[1]	143.7	142.9	n/a	n/a
U.S. Average	175.6	171.7	165.1	-3.8

Note: Figures are median sales prices of existing apartment condo-coop homes in thousands of dollars; (p) preliminary; n/a not available; (1) Metropolitan Statistical Area—see Appendix B for areas included
Source: National Association of Realtors, Median Sales Price of Existing Apartment Condo-Coop Homes for Metropolitan Areas, 4th Quarter 2011

Year Housing Structure Built

Area	2005 or Later	2000 -2004	1990 -1999	1980 -1989	1970 -1979	1960 -1969	1950 -1959	Before 1950	Median Year
City	5.6	11.7	15.1	14.6	20.4	10.5	13.9	8.2	1979
MSA[1]	6.8	11.9	18.2	16.1	19.3	9.3	10.8	7.6	1982
U.S.	5.0	8.6	14.0	14.1	16.3	11.3	11.2	19.6	1975

Note: Figures are percentages except for Median Year; (1) Figures cover the Albuquerque, NM Metropolitan Statistical Area—see Appendix B for areas included
Source: U.S. Census Bureau, 2008-2010 American Community Survey 3-Year Estimates

HEALTH

Health Risk Data

Category	MSA[1] (%)	U.S. (%)
Adults who have been told they have high blood pressure[2]	24.6	28.7
Adults who have been told they have high blood cholesterol[2]	31.8	37.5
Adults who have been told they have diabetes[3]	7.1	8.7
Adults who have been told they have arthritis[2]	25.3	26.0
Adults who have been told they currently have asthma	9.5	9.1
Adults who are current smokers	19.4	17.3
Adults who are heavy drinkers[4]	4.1	5.0
Adults who are binge drinkers[5]	10.0	15.1
Adults who are overweight (BMI 25.0 - 29.9)	34.9	36.2
Adults who are obese (BMI 30.0 - 99.8)	21.7	27.5
Adults who participated in any physical activities in the past month	82.0	76.1
Adults 50+ who have ever had a sigmoidoscopy or colonoscopy	65.7	65.2
Women aged 40+ who have had a mammogram within the past two years	75.2	75.2
Men aged 40+ who have had a PSA test within the past two years	54.6	53.2
Adults aged 65+ who have had flu shot within the past year	74.0	67.5
Adults aged 18–64 who have any kind of health care coverage	82.6	82.2

Note: Data as of 2010 unless otherwise noted; (1) Figures cover the Albuquerque, NM Metropolitan Statistical Area—see Appendix B for areas included; (2) Data as of 2009; (3) Figures do not include pregnancy-related, borderline, or pre-diabetes; (4) Heavy drinkers are classified as males having more than two drinks per day or females having more than one drink per day; (5) Binge drinkers are classified as males having five or more drinks on one occasion or females having four or more drinks on one occasion
Source: Centers for Disease Control and Prevention, Behaviorial Risk Factor Surveillance System, SMART: Selected Metropolitan/Micropolitan Area Risk Trends, 2009, 2010

Mortality Rates for the Top 10 Causes of Death in the U.S.

ICD-10[a] Sub-Chapter	ICD-10[a] Code	Age-Adjusted Mortality Rate[1] per 100,000 population	
		County[2]	U.S.
Malignant neoplasms	C00-C97	155.9	175.6
Ischaemic heart diseases	I20-I25	100.9	121.6
Other forms of heart disease	I30-I51	38.4	48.6
Chronic lower respiratory diseases	J40-J47	44.0	42.3
Cerebrovascular diseases	I60-I69	40.2	40.6
Organic, including symptomatic, mental disorders	F01-F09	28.8	26.7
Other degenerative diseases of the nervous system	G30-G31	18.9	24.7
Other external causes of accidental injury	W00-X59	49.7	24.4
Diabetes mellitus	E10-E14	25.3	21.7
Hypertensive diseases	I10-I15	13.7	18.2

Note: (a) ICD-10 = International Classification of Diseases 10th Revision; (1) Mortality rates are a three year average covering 2007-2009; (2) Figures cover Bernalillo County
Source: Centers for Disease Control and Prevention, National Center for Health Statistics. Underlying Cause of Death 1999-2009 on CDC WONDER Online Database, released 2012. Data for year 2009 are compiled from the Multiple Cause of Death File 2009, Series 20 No. 2O, 2012, Data for year 2008 are compiled from the Multiple Cause of Death File 2008, Series 20 No. 2N, 2011, Data for year 2007 are compiled from Multiple Cause of Death File 2007, Series 20 No. 2M, 2010.

Mortality Rates for Selected Causes of Death

ICD-10[a] Sub-Chapter	ICD-10[a] Code	Age-Adjusted Mortality Rate[1] per 100,000 population	
		County[2]	U.S.
Assault	X85-Y09	8.1	5.7
Human immunodeficiency virus (HIV) disease	B20-B24	2.7	3.3
Influenza and pneumonia	J09-J18	14.4	16.4
Intentional self-harm	X60-X84	19.7	11.5
Malnutrition	E40-E46	*0.0	0.8
Obesity and other hyperalimentation	E65-E68	2.4	1.6
Transport accidents	V01-V99	13.8	13.7
Viral hepatitis	B15-B19	4.3	2.2

Note: (a) ICD-10 = International Classification of Diseases 10th Revision; (1) Mortality rates are a three year average covering 2007-2009; (2) Figures cover Bernalillo County; (*) Unreliable data as per CDC
Source: Centers for Disease Control and Prevention, National Center for Health Statistics. Underlying Cause of Death 1999-2009 on CDC WONDER Online Database, released 2012. Data for year 2009 are compiled from the Multiple Cause of Death File 2009, Series 20 No. 2O, 2012, Data for year 2008 are compiled from the Multiple Cause of Death File 2008, Series 20 No. 2N, 2011, Data for year 2007 are compiled from Multiple Cause of Death File 2007, Series 20 No. 2M, 2010.

Distribution of Physicians and Dentists

Area[1]	Dentists[2]	D.O.[3]	M.D.[4] Total	M.D.[4] Family/General Practice	M.D.[4] Pediatrics	M.D.[4] Medical Specialties	M.D.[4] Surgical Specialties
Local (number)	263	97	1,603	209	119	572	325
Local (rate[5])	4.2	1.5	25.2	3.3	1.9	9.0	5.1
U.S. (rate[5])	4.5	1.9	18.3	2.5	1.4	6.8	4.1

Note: Data as of 2008 unless noted; (1) Local data covers Bernalillo County; (2) Data as of 2007; (3) Doctor of Osteopathic Medicine; (4) Includes active, non-federal, patient-care, office-based Doctors of Medicine; (5) rate per 10,000 population
Source: Area Resource File (ARF). 2009-2010 Release. U.S. Department of Health and Human Services, Health Resources and Services Administration, Bureau of Health Professions, Rockville, MD, August 2010

EDUCATION

Public School District Statistics

District Name	Schls	Pupils	Pupil/Teacher Ratio	Minority Pupils[1] (%)	Free Lunch Eligible[2] (%)	IEP[3] (%)
Albuquerque Public Schools	172	96,572	14.8	76.1	52.6	13.9

Note: Table includes school districts with 2,000 or more students; (1) Percentage of students that are not non-Hispanic white; (2) Percentage of students that are eligible for the free lunch program; (3) Percentage of students that have an Individualized Education Program.
Source: U.S. Department of Education, National Center for Education Statistics, Common Core of Data, Local Education Agency (School District) Universe Survey: School Year 2009-2010; U.S. Department of Education, National Center for Education Statistics, Common Core of Data, Public Elementary/Secondary School Universe Survey: School Year 2009-2010

Highest Level of Education

Area	Less than H.S.	H.S. Diploma	Some College, No Deg.	Associate Degree	Bachelors Degree	Masters Degree	Profess. School Degree	Doctorate Degree
City	12.7	23.5	24.6	7.2	18.0	9.5	2.4	2.2
MSA[1]	13.4	25.1	24.9	7.3	16.6	8.6	2.1	2.0
U.S.	14.7	28.4	21.3	7.6	17.6	7.2	1.9	1.2

Note: Figures cover persons age 25 and over; (1) Figures cover the Albuquerque, NM Metropolitan Statistical Area—see Appendix B for areas included
Source: U.S. Census Bureau, 2008-2010 American Community Survey 3-Year Estimates

Educational Attainment by Race

Area	High School Graduate or Higher (%)					Bachelor's Degree or Higher (%)				
	Total	White	Black	Asian	Hisp.[2]	Total	White	Black	Asian	Hisp.[2]
City	87.3	89.2	94.2	82.4	75.9	32.0	35.5	28.8	44.7	16.7
MSA[1]	86.6	88.9	93.6	84.1	75.4	29.3	33.1	27.9	44.3	15.1
U.S.	85.3	87.5	81.4	85.5	61.6	28.0	29.3	17.8	50.2	13.0

Note: Figures shown cover persons 25 years old and over; (1) Figures cover the Albuquerque, NM Metropolitan Statistical Area—see Appendix B for areas included; (2) People of Hispanic origin can be of any race
Source: U.S. Census Bureau, 2008-2010 American Community Survey 3-Year Estimates

School Enrollment by Grade and Control

Area	Preschool (%)		Kindergarten (%)		Grades 1 - 4 (%)		Grades 5 - 8 (%)		Grades 9 - 12 (%)	
	Public	Private	Public	Private	Public	Private	Public	Private	Public	Private
City	53.5	46.5	85.4	14.6	87.4	12.6	85.8	14.2	88.7	11.3
MSA[1]	60.0	40.0	86.4	13.6	88.5	11.5	88.0	12.0	89.6	10.4
U.S.	55.4	44.6	87.1	12.9	89.4	10.6	89.5	10.5	90.4	9.6

Note: Figures shown cover persons 3 years old and over; (1) Figures cover the Albuquerque, NM Metropolitan Statistical Area—see Appendix B for areas included
Source: U.S. Census Bureau, 2008-2010 American Community Survey 3-Year Estimates

Average Salaries of Public School Classroom Teachers

Area	2010-11		2011-12		Percent Change 2010-11 to 2011-12	Percent Change 2001-02 to 2011-12
	Dollars	Rank[1]	Dollars	Rank[1]		
New Mexico	46,888	40	48,011	39	2.39	31.80
U.S. Average	55,623	-	56,643	-	1.83	26.8

Note: (1) State rank ranges from 1 to 51 where 1 indicates highest salary.
Source: National Education Association, Rankings & Estimates: Rankings of the States 2011 and Estimates of School Statistics 2012, December 2011

Higher Education

Four-Year Colleges			Two-Year Colleges			Medical Schools[1]	Law Schools[2]	Voc/ Tech[3]
Public	Private Non-profit	Private For-profit	Public	Private Non-profit	Private For-profit			
1	0	6	2	0	2	1	1	6

Note: Figures cover institutions located within the city limits and include main campuses only; (1) includes schools accredited by the Liaison Committee on Medical Education and the American Osteopathic Association's Commission on Osteopathic College Accreditation; (2) includes American Bar Association-accredited law schools; (3) includes all schools with programs that are less than 2 years.
Source: National Center for Education Statistics, Integrated Postsecondary Education System (IPEDS) Peer Analysis System, 2011-12; Association of American Medical Colleges, Member List, April 23, 2012; American Osteopathic Association, Member List, April 23, 2012; Law School Admission Council, Official Guide to ABA-Approved Law Schools Online, April 23, 2012

According to *U.S. News & World Report*, the Albuquerque, NM is home to one of the best national universities in the U.S.: **University of New Mexico** (#181). The indicators used to capture academic quality fall into a number of categories: assessment by administrators at peer institutions; retention of students; faculty resources; student selectivity; financial resources; alumni giving; high school counselor ratings of colleges; and graduation rate. *U.S. News & World Report, "America's Best Colleges 2012"*

PRESIDENTIAL ELECTION

2008 Presidential Election Results

Area	Obama	McCain	Nader	Other
Bernalillo County	60.0	38.7	0.6	0.7
U.S.	52.9	45.6	0.6	0.9

Note: Results are percentages and may not add to 100% due to rounding
Source: Dave Leip's Atlas of U.S. Presidential Elections, www.uselectionatlas.org

EMPLOYERS

Major Employers

Company Name	Industry
Central New Mexico Community College	Vocational schools
City of Albuquerque	Municipal police
City of Albuquerque	City and town managers' office
Fish and Wildlife Services, United States	Fish and wildlife conservation agency, government
Jack Henry & Associates	Computers
Laguna Development Corporation	Grocery stores, independent
Mediplex of Massachusetts	Nursing home, exc skilled & intermediate care facility
Sandia Corporation	Noncommercial research organizations
The Boeing Company	Aircraft
United States Department of Energy	Energy development and conservation agency, government
United States Department of the Air Force	Air force
United States Department of the Air Force	Testing laboratories
University of New Mexico	General medical and surgical hospitals
University of New Mexico	Offices and clinics of medical doctors
University of New Mexico	Pediatrician
University of New Mexico	University
Veterans Health Administration	General medical and surgical hospitals
Veterans Health Administration	Administration of veterans' affiars

Note: Companies shown are located within the Albuquerque, NM metropolitan area.
Source: Hoovers.com, data extracted April 25 2012

PUBLIC SAFETY

Crime Rate

Area	All Crimes	Violent Crimes				Property Crimes		
		Murder	Forcible Rape	Robbery	Aggrav. Assault	Burglary	Larceny -Theft	Motor Vehicle Theft
City	5,622.2	7.7	62.0	172.4	544.7	1,002.0	3,325.0	508.4
Suburbs[1]	2,867.3	2.7	17.1	46.9	416.4	789.5	1,396.9	197.7
Metro[2]	4,566.6	5.8	44.8	124.3	495.6	920.6	2,586.2	389.4
U.S.	3,345.5	4.8	27.5	119.1	252.3	699.6	2,003.5	238.8

Note: Figures are crimes per 100,000 population; (1) All areas within the metro area that are located outside the city limits; (2) Metropolitan Statistical Area—see Appendix B for areas included
Source: FBI Uniform Crime Reports, 2010

Hate Crimes

Area	Number of Quarters Reported	Bias Motivation				
		Race	Religion	Sexual Orientation	Ethnicity	Disability
City	4	9	1	5	6	0

Source: Federal Bureau of Investigation, Hate Crime Statistics 2010

Identity Theft Consumer Complaints

Area	Complaints	Complaints per 100,000 Population	Rank[2]
MSA[1]	820	98.2	103
U.S.	279,156	90.4	-

Note: (1) Metropolitan Statistical Area—see Appendix B for areas included; (2) Rank ranges from 1 to 384 where 1 indicates greatest number of identity theft complaints per 100,000 population
Source: Federal Trade Commission, Consumer Sentinel Network Data Book for January–December 2011

Fraud and Other Consumer Complaints

Area	Complaints	Complaints per 100,000 Population	Rank[2]
MSA[1]	3,627	434.3	244
U.S.	1,533,924	496.8	-

Note: (1) Metropolitan Statistical Area—see Appendix B for areas included; (2) Rank ranges from 1 to 384 where 1 indicates greatest number of fraud and other complaints per 100,000 population
Source: Federal Trade Commission, Consumer Sentinel Network Data Book for January–December 2011

RECREATION

Culture

Dance[1]	Theatre[1]	Instrumental Music[1]	Vocal Music[1]	Series/ Festivals	Museums	Zoos and Aquariums[2]
2	4	2	2	2	18	1

Note: (1) Number of professional perfoming groups; (2) AZA-accredited
Source: The Grey House Performing Arts Directory, 2011-2012; Official Museum Directory, 2011; American Association of Museums, AAM Member Museums, April 2012; Association of Zoos & Aquariums, AZA Member Zoos & Aquariums, April 2012

Professional Sports Teams

Team Name	League
No teams are located in the metro area	

Source: Original research

CLIMATE

Average and Extreme Temperatures

Temperature	Jan	Feb	Mar	Apr	May	Jun	Jul	Aug	Sep	Oct	Nov	Dec	Yr.
Extreme High (°F)	69	76	85	89	98	105	105	101	100	91	77	72	105
Average High (°F)	47	53	61	71	80	90	92	89	83	72	57	48	70
Average Temp. (°F)	35	40	47	56	65	75	79	76	70	58	45	36	57
Average Low (°F)	23	27	33	41	50	59	65	63	56	44	31	24	43
Extreme Low (°F)	-17	-5	8	19	28	40	52	50	37	21	-7	-7	-17

Note: Figures cover the years 1948-1992
Source: National Climatic Data Center, International Station Meteorological Climate Summary, 9/96

Average Precipitation/Snowfall/Humidity

Precip./Humidity	Jan	Feb	Mar	Apr	May	Jun	Jul	Aug	Sep	Oct	Nov	Dec	Yr.
Avg. Precip. (in.)	0.4	0.4	0.5	0.4	0.5	0.5	1.4	1.5	0.9	0.9	0.4	0.5	8.5
Avg. Snowfall (in.)	3	2	2	1	Tr	0	0	0	Tr	Tr	1	3	11
Avg. Rel. Hum. 5am (%)	68	64	55	48	48	45	60	65	61	60	63	68	59
Avg. Rel. Hum. 5pm (%)	41	33	25	20	19	18	27	30	29	29	35	43	29

Note: Figures cover the years 1948-1992; Tr = Trace amounts (<0.05 in. of rain; <0.5 in. of snow)
Source: National Climatic Data Center, International Station Meteorological Climate Summary, 9/96

Weather Conditions

Temperature			Daytime Sky			Precipitation		
10°F & below	32°F & below	90°F & above	Clear	Partly cloudy	Cloudy	0.01 inch or more precip.	0.1 inch or more snow/ice	Thunder-storms
4	114	65	140	161	64	60	9	38

Note: Figures are average number of days per year and cover the years 1948-1992
Source: National Climatic Data Center, International Station Meteorological Climate Summary, 9/96

HAZARDOUS WASTE

Superfund Sites

Albuquerque has three hazardous waste sites on the EPA's Superfund Final National Priorities List: **Fruit Avenue Plume; AT&SF (Albuquerque); South Valley**. *U.S. Environmental Protection Agency, Final National Priorities List, April 17, 2012*

AIR & WATER QUALITY

Air Quality Index

Area	Percent of Days when Air Quality was...[2]					AQI Statistics[2]	
	Good	Moderate	Unhealthy for Sensitive Groups	Unhealthy	Very Unhealthy	Maximum	Median
Area[1]	45.8	50.4	3.3	0.3	0.3	293	52

Note: Air Quality Index (AQI) is an index for reporting daily air quality. EPA calculates the AQI for five major air pollutants regulated by the Clean Air Act: ground-level ozone, particle pollution (aka particulate matter), carbon monoxide, sulfur dioxide, and nitrogen dioxide. The AQI runs from 0 to 500. The higher the AQI value, the greater the level of air pollution and the greater the health concern. There are six AQI categories: "Good" AQI is between 0 and 50. Air quality is considered satisfactory; "Moderate" AQI is between 51 and 100. Air quality is acceptable; "Unhealthy for Sensitive Groups" When AQI values are between 101 and 150, members of sensitive groups may experience health effects; "Unhealthy" When AQI values are between 151 and 200 everyone may begin to experience health effects; "Very Unhealthy" AQI values between 201 and 300 trigger a health alert; "Hazardous" AQI values over 300 trigger warnings of emergency conditions (not shown); (1) Data covers Bernalillo County; (2) Based on 365 days with AQI data in 2011.
Source: U.S. Environmental Protection Agency, AirData Report, 2011

Air Quality Index Pollutants

Area	Percent of Days when AQI Pollutant was...[2]					
	Carbon Monoxide	Nitrogen Dioxide	Ozone	Sulfur Dioxide	Particulate Matter 2.5	Particulate Matter 10
Area[1]	0.0	5.5	51.2	1.1	32.6	9.6

Note: The Air Quality Index (AQI) is an index for reporting daily air quality. EPA calculates the AQI for five major air pollutants regulated by the Clean Air Act: ground-level ozone, particle pollution (also known as particulate matter), carbon monoxide, sulfur dioxide, and nitrogen dioxide. The AQI runs from 0 to 500. The higher the AQI value, the greater the level of air pollution and the greater the health concern; (1) Data covers Bernalillo County; (2) Based on 365 days with AQI data in 2011.
Source: U.S. Environmental Protection Agency, AirData Report, 2011

Air Quality Index Trends

Area	Trend Sites (days)								All Sites (days)
	2003	2004	2005	2006	2007	2008	2009	2010	2010
MSA[1]	16	6	11	8	2	1	0	2	2

Note: Figures are the number of days the AQI value exceeded 100 in a given year. An AQI value greater than 100 indicates that air quality would have been in the unhealthful range on that day. Data from exceptional events are included. These counts are presented in two ways. First, the counts are based on sites having an adequate record of monitoring data during the trend period (trend sites). These counts represent the relative change in the number of days with AQI values greater than 100. In the last column, the counts are based on all sites with data in the most recent year (because it is possible for a site to have data in the most recent year but not enough data to be a trend site); (1) Data covers the Albuquerque, NM—see Appendix B for areas included
Source: U.S. Environmental Protection Agency, Air Quality Index Information, "Number of Days with Air Quality Index Values Greater than 100 at Trend Sites, 2000-2010, and at All Sites in 2010"

Maximum Air Pollutant Concentrations: Particulate Matter, Ozone, CO and Lead

	Particulate Matter 10 (ug/m^3)	Particulate Matter 2.5 Wtd AM (ug/m^3)	Particulate Matter 2.5 24-Hr (ug/m^3)	Ozone (ppm)	Carbon Monoxide (ppm)	Lead (ug/m^3)
MSA[1] Level	122	5.3	18	0.069	3	n/a
NAAQS[2]	150	15	35	0.075	9	0.15
Met NAAQS[2]	Yes	Yes	Yes	Yes	Yes	n/a

Note: Data from exceptional events are not included; (1) Data covers the Albuquerque, NM—see Appendix B for areas included; (2) National Ambient Air Quality Standards; ppm = parts per million; ug/m^3 = micrograms per cubic meter; n/a not available
Concentrations: Particulate Matter 10 (coarse particulate)—highest second maximum 24-hour concentration; Particulate Matter 2.5 Wtd AM (fine particulate)—highest weighted annual mean concentration; Particulate Matter 2.5 24-Hour (fine particulate)—highest 98th percentile 24-hour concentration; Ozone—highest fourth daily maximum 8-hour concentration; Carbon Monoxide—highest second maximum non-overlapping 8-hour concentration; Lead—maximum running 3-month average
Source: U.S. Environmental Protection Agency, CBSA Factbook 2010, Air Quality Statistics by City, 2010

Maximum Air Pollutant Concentrations: Nitrogen Dioxide and Sulfur Dioxide

	Nitrogen Dioxide AM (ppb)	Nitrogen Dioxide 1-Hr (ppb)	Sulfur Dioxide AM (ppb)	Sulfur Dioxide 1-Hr (ppb)	Sulfur Dioxide 24-Hr (ppb)
MSA[1] Level	12.068	53	n/a	n/a	n/a
NAAQS[2]	53	100	30	75	140
Met NAAQS[2]	Yes	Yes	n/a	n/a	n/a

Note: Data from exceptional events are not included; (1) Data covers the Albuquerque, NM—see Appendix B for areas included; (2) National Ambient Air Quality Standards; ppb = parts per billion; n/a not available
Concentrations: Nitrogen Dioxide AM—highest arithmetic mean concentration; Nitrogen Dioxide 1-Hr—highest 98th percentile 1-hour daily maximum concentration; Sulfur Dioxide AM—highest annual mean concentration; Sulfur Dioxide 1-Hr—highest 99th percentile 1-hour daily maximum concentration; Sulfur Dioxide 24-Hr—highest second maximum 24-hour concentration
Source: U.S. Environmental Protection Agency, CBSA Factbook 2010, Air Quality Statistics by City, 2010

Drinking Water

Water System Name	Pop. Served	Primary Water Source Type	Violations[1]	
			Health Based	Monitoring/ Reporting
Albuquerque Water System	601,983	Surface	0	0

Note: (1) Based on violation data from January 1, 2011 to December 31, 2011 (includes unresolved violations from earlier years)
Source: U.S. Environmental Protection Agency, Office of Ground Water and Drinking Water, Safe Drinking Water Information System (based on data extracted April 18, 2012)

Anchorage, Alaska

Background

Anchorage, in south central Alaska, is the state's largest city and a center for the state's communication, transportation, health care, and finance industries. Originally powered by the railroads and the fishing industry, Anchorage's economy has in more recent times been closely tied to petroleum production, which accounts for more than 22 percent of the nation's oil reserves.

This modern city lies in a spectacular natural setting, with the Chugach Mountain Range across its eastern skyline and the waters of the Cook Inlet to the west. The city boasts all the advantages of a dynamic urban center, while its residents enjoy a natural environment that teems with bear, moose, caribou, fox, eagles, wolves, dall sheep, orcas, and beluga whales.

The city is young, having been incorporated in 1920, and grew slowly for the next several decades. During World War II, when airfields and roads were constructed to aid in the war effort, the population expanded dramatically; by 1946, Anchorage was home to more than 40,000 people.

In 1964, the region was hit by the strongest earthquake ever to strike North America. There was extensive damage and some loss of life, but the city was quickly rebuilt; in fact, reconstruction was so prompt, efficient, and successful that many look back on the period with considerable civic pride. Earthquakes are not uncommon to the region, with a moderate 5.7 event occurring in Anchorage in January 2009.

In 1951, Anchorage International Airport, which is now Ted Stevens International Airport (ANC), was completed, and the city became vital to the emerging air transport industry as new routes were created. Ted Stevens International Airport flies more than 560 transcontinental cargo flights each week and is the busiest cargo airport in the country. Elmendorf Air Force Base at the northeast end of town, and Anchorage's pioneering development of "bush" aviation, which serves the entire interior of Alaska, further testify to the importance of air travel to the city's development. Also located at the airport are Fort Richardson Army Post and Kulis Air National Guard Base that together employ 8,500.

Oil in Alaska was first discovered in 1957, and 17 oil companies subsequently set up headquarters in Anchorage, giving the city a tremendous economic boost. In 1968, the large North Slope field was discovered, Anchorage was again a major beneficiary. With the completion of the Trans-Alaskan Pipeline System in 1977, Anchorage entered into its contemporary period of sustained population growth and dynamic economic development.

Alaska's tourism industry accounts for more than 30,000 statewide jobs and an estimated economic impact of nearly $80 million in Anchorage alone.

In 1999, two new fiber-optic cables were installed between Alaska and the continental U.S., increasing capabilities of computer networks statewide.

The city's cultural amenities include the Anchorage Museum at Rasmuson Center and the Alaska Aviation Heritage Museum, which chronicles the story of Alaska's early and pioneering air transport system. Near the city is the Potter Section House Railway Museum, which pays homage to the state's vital rail industry. The city also boasts the Alaska Center for the Performing Arts and the Alaska Botanical Garden. Delaney Park, also known as the Park Strip, is a venerable and valued recreational resource in the city's business district, and its ongoing improvement looks toward a year-round "Central Park" for Anchorage. The Alaska State Fair has been recognized as one of the Top 100 Events in North America.

Because of its long summer days and relatively mild temperatures, Anchorage is called "The City of Lights and Flowers," and is adorned in summer throughout the municipality with open, grassy expanses and flowers. The season brings out a friendly competition among the city's residents, who plant along streets, in parks, private gardens, window boxes, and lobbies.

The natural environment of Anchorage is spectacular, and at nearby Portage Glacier, one can watch the glacier "calving," as huge blocks of ice crash into the lake below. Anchorage is also located at one end of the famous annual Iditarod Trail Sled Dog Race.

The city is an educational center with two universities and many technical, vocational, and private schools. A campus of the University of Alaska has been in Anchorage since 1954, and the city is also home to Alaska Pacific University.

The weather in Anchorage, contrary to what many believe, is not savagely cold. It is tempered by the city's location on the coast and by the Alaska Mountain Range, which acts as a barrier to very cold air from the north. Snow season lasts from October to May. Summers can bring fog and rain.

Rankings

General Rankings

- *Men's Health Living* ranked 100 U.S. cities in terms of quality of life. Anchorage was ranked #25 and received a grade of B-. Criteria: number of fitness facilities; air quality; number of physicians; male/female ratio; education levels; household income; cost of living. *Men's Health Living, Spring 2008*

- Anchorage was selected as one of America's best cities by *Bloomberg Businessweek.* The city ranked #10 out of 50. Criteria: number of restaurants, bars and museums per capita; number of colleges, libraries, and professional sports teams; income, poverty, unemployment, crime, and foreclosure rates; percent of population with bachelor's degrees; public school performance; park acres per capita; air quality. *BusinessWeek, "America's 50 Best Cities," September 20, 2011*

- Anchorage appeared on RelocateAmerica's list of best places to live in America. The annual "Top 100 Places to Live" list recognizes the top communities as nominated by their residents & local businesses. RelocateAmerica's Research Group determines the list based on review of various data gathered for economic, employment, housing, education, industry, opportunity, environment and recreation along with feedback from area leaders and residents. *RelocateAmerica.com, "Top 100 Places to Live for 2011"*

Business/Finance Rankings

- The Anchorage metro area was identified as one of the most debt-ridden places in America by credit reporting agency Equifax. The metro area was ranked #9. Criteria: proportion of average yearly income owed to credit card companies. *Equifax, "The Most Debt-Ridden Cities in America," February 23, 2012*
- Anchorage was selected as one of the best places to ride out a recession in the U.S. by *BusinessWeek.* Twenty cities were identified as places where large portions of the population worked in anticyclical industries such as government, health care, education, agriculture, and legal services. *BusinessWeek, "Some Cities Will Be Safer in a Recession," October 14, 2008*
- Anchorage was selected as one of the best cities in the world for telecommuting. The city ranked #10. The editors at *Cartridge Save* (printer technology news, guides and reviews) identified the 20 best cities in which to be an at-home, tech-using employee. *Cartridge Save, "20 of the Best Cities in the World for Telecommuting," May 14, 2008*

- *American City Business Journals* ranked America's 261 largest cities in terms of their resident's wealth. Anchorage ranked #63. Criteria: per capita income; median household income; percentage of households with annual incomes of $200,000 or more; median home value. *American City Business Journals, "Where the Money Is: America's Wealth Centers," August 18, 2008*

- The Anchorage metro area appeared on the Milken Institute "2011 Best Performing Metros" list. Rank: #7 out of 200 large metro areas. Criteria: job growth; wage and salary growth; high-tech output growth. *Milken Institute, "2011 Best Performing Metros"*

- *Forbes* ranked the 200 most populous metro areas in the U.S. in terms of the "Best Places for Business and Careers." The Anchorage metro area was ranked #39. Criteria: costs (business and living); job growth (past and projected); income growth; educational attainment; projected economic growth; crime; cultural and recreational opportunities; net migration patterns; number of highly ranked colleges. *Forbes, "Best Places for Business and Careers," June 2011*

- Anchorage appeared on *Kiplinger's Personal Finance* list of the "Top Ten Tax-Friendly Cities." The city was ranked #1. Criteria: income tax; sales tax; real estate and car/personal property tax. *Kiplinger's Personal Finance, March 1, 2009*

Children/Family Rankings

- Anchorage was chosen as one of America's "100 Best Communities for Young People." The winners were selected based upon detailed information provided about each community's efforts to fulfill five essential promises critical to the well-being of young people: caring adults who are actively involved in their lives; safe places in which to learn and grow; a healthy start toward adulthood; an effective education that builds marketable skills; and opportunities to help others. *America's Promise Alliance, "100 Best Communities for Young People, 2010"*

Dating/Romance Rankings

- Anchorage appeared on *Men's Health's* list of the most sex-happy cities in America. The city ranked #17 of 100. Criteria: condom sales; birth rates; sex toy sales; rates of chlamydia, gonorrhea, and syphilis. *Men's Health, "America's Most Sex-Happy Cities," October 2010*
- *Men's Health* ranked 100 U.S. cities in terms of best (and worst) marriages. Anchorage was ranked #29 (#1 = worst). Criteria: rate of failed marriages; stringency of divorce laws; percentage of population who've split; number of licensed marriage and family therapists. *Men's Health, "Splitsville, USA," May 2010*

Education Rankings

- *Men's Health* ranked 100 U.S. cities in terms of their education levels. Anchorage was ranked #30 (#1 = most educated city). Criteria: high school graduation rates; school enrollment; educational attainment; number of households who have outstanding student loans; number of households whose members have taken adult-education courses. *Men's Health, "Where School Is In: The Most and Least Educated Cities," September 12, 2011*
- Anchorage was selected as one of "America's Most Literate Cities." The city ranked #61 out of the 75 largest U.S. cities. Criteria: number of booksellers; library resources; Internet resources; educational attainment; periodical publishing resources; newspaper circulation. *Central Connecticut State University, "America's Most Literate Cities 2011"*
- Anchorage was identified as one of "America's Brainiest Bastions" by *Portfolio.com.* The metro area ranked #51 out of 200. *Portfolio.com* analyzed levels of educational attainment in the nation's 200 largest metropolitan areas. The editors established scores for five levels of educational attainment, based on relative earning power of adult workers age 25 or older. Scores were determined by comparing the median income for all workers with the median income for those workers at a specified educational level. *Portfolio.com, "America's Brainiest Bastions," December 1, 2010*

Environmental Rankings

- Anchorage was selected as one of 22 "Smarter Cities" for energy by the Natural Resources Defense Council. Criteria: investment in green power; energy efficiency measures; conservation. *Natural Resources Defense Council, "2010 Smarter Cities," July 19, 2010*
- Anchorage was selected as one of "America's 50 Greenest Cities" by *Popular Science.* The city ranked #32. Criteria: electricity; transportation; green living; recycling and green perspective. *Popular Science, February 2008*
- The Anchorage metro area appeared in *Country Home's* "Best Green Places" report. The area ranked #299 out of 379. Criteria: official energy policies; green power; green buildings; availability of fresh, locally grown food. *Country Home, "Best Green Places," 2008*
- Anchorage was highlighted as one of the top 25 cleanest metro areas for year-round particle pollution (Annual PM 2.5) in the U.S. The area ranked #6. *American Lung Association, State of the Air 2011*

Health/Fitness Rankings

- *Men's Health* examined 100 major U.S. cities and selected the best and worst cities for men. Anchorage ranked #23. Criteria: 35 statistical parameters of long life in the categories of health, quality of life, and fitness. *Men's Health, "The 10 Best and Worst Cities for Men 2012," January/February 2012*

- The Anchorage metro area appeared in the 2011 Gallup-Healthways Well-Being Index. The index, based on interviews with more than 350,000 Americans, measured jobs, finances, physical health, emotional state of mind and communities. The metro area ranked #23 out of 190. Criteria: life evaluation; emotional health; work environment; physical health; healthy behaviors; basic access (basic needs optimal for a healthy life, such as access to food and medicine, having health insurance and feeling safe while walking at night). *Gallup-Healthways, "State of Well-Being 2011"*

- *Men's Health* ranked 100 U.S. cities in terms of their activity levels. Anchorage was ranked #25 (#1 = most active city). Criteria: where and how often residents exercise; percentage of households that watch more than 15 hours of cable television a week and buy more than 11 video games a year; death rate from deep-vein thrombosis, a condition linked to sitting for extended periods of time. *Men's Health, "Where Sit Happens: The Most and Least Active Cities in America," June 20, 2011*

- *Men's Health* examined the nation's largest 100 cities and identified the 10 cities at highest risk of erectile dysfunction. Anchorage ranked #7. Criteria: percentage of current male smokers; percentage of adults with a BMI of at least 30; percentage of adults with diabetes; percentage of men working out three or more times per week; percentage of urologists per 100,000 men; number of ED drug prescriptions filled in 2007. *Men's Health, "Ranking America's Cities: Cities that Need Viagara," April 2009*

Real Estate Rankings

- The Center for Housing Policy ranked 210 U.S. metropolitan areas by the fair market rent for a two-bedroom unit. The Anchorage metro area was ranked #51. (#1 = most expensive) with a rent of $1,031. Criteria: Fair Market Rent (FMR) in effect during the fourth quarter of 2009 based on HUD's fiscal year 2010 FMRs. *The Center for Housing Policy, "Paycheck to Paycheck: Most to Least Expensive Rental Markets in 2009"*

- The Anchorage metro area was identified as one of the top 20 cities in terms of decreasing home equity. The metro area was ranked #10. Criteria: percentage of home equity relative to the home's current value. *Forbes.com, "Where Americans are Losing Home Equity Most," May 1, 2010*

Safety Rankings

- Farmers Insurance Group of Companies, in partnership with Sperling's BestPlaces, ranked 379 metro areas and identified the "Most Secure U.S. Places to Live." The Anchorage metro area ranked #15 out of the top 20 in the mid-size city category (150,000 to 500,000 residents). Criteria: crime statistics; extreme weather; risk of natural disasters; housing depreciation; foreclosures; environmental hazards; terrorist threats; air quality; life expectancy; mortality rates from cancer and motor vehicle accidents; job loss numbers. *Farmers Insurance Group, "Most Secure U.S. Places to Live 2011," December 15, 2011*

- Allstate ranked the 193 largest cities in America in terms of driver safety. Anchorage ranked #126. In addition, drivers were 14.8% more likely to have had an accident compared to the national average. Allstate researchers analyzed internal property damage reported claims over a two-year period (from January 2008 to December 2009) to protect findings from external influences such as weather or road construction. A weighted average of the two-year numbers determined the annual percentages. The report defines an auto crash as any collision resulting in a property damage claim. *Allstate, "2011 Allstate America's Best Drivers Report™"*

- The Anchorage metro area was identified as one of "America's Most Dangerous Cities" by *Forbes*. The area ranked #5 out of 10. Criteria: violent crime (murder and non-negligent manslaughter, forcible rape, robbery, and aggravated assault) rates per capita. The editors only considered metropolitan areas with populations above 200,000. *Forbes, "America's Most Dangerous Cities," October 3, 2011*

- The National Insurance Crime Bureau ranked 366 metro areas in the U.S. in terms of per capita rates of vehicle theft. The Anchorage metro area ranked #105 (#1 = highest rate). Criteria: number of vehicle theft offenses per 100,000 inhabitants in 2010. *National Insurance Crime Bureau, "Hot Spots," June 21, 2011*

Sports/Recreation Rankings

- Anchorage was chosen as a bicycle friendly community by the League of American Bicyclists. A Bicycle Friendly Community welcomes cyclists by providing safe accommodation for cycling and encouraging people to bike for transportation and recreation. There are four award levels: Platinum; Gold; Silver; and Bronze. The community achieved an award level of Bronze. *League of American Bicyclists, "Bicycle Friendly Community Master List 2011"*
- Anchorage was chosen as one of America's best cities for bicycling. The city ranked #47 out of 50. Criteria: number of segregated bike lanes, municipal bike racks, and bike boulevards; vibrant and diverse bike culture; smart, savvy bike shops; interviews with national and local advocates, bike shops and other experts. The editors only considered cities with populations of 100,000 or more. *Bicycling, "America's Best Bike Cities," April 2010*

Women/Minorities Rankings

- *Women's Health* examined U.S. cities and identified the 100 best cities for women. Anchorage was ranked #26. Criteria: 30 categories were examined from obesity and breast cancer rates to commuting times and hours spent working out. *Women's Health, "Best Cities for Women 2012"*

Miscellaneous Rankings

- *Men's Health* ranked 100 U.S. cities by their level of sadness. Anchorage was ranked #26 (#1 = saddest city). Criteria: suicide rates; unemployment rates; percentage of households that use antidepressants; percent of population who report feeling blue all or most of the time. *Men's Health, "Frown Towns," November 28, 2011*
- Anchorage was selected as one of the "Best Hair Cities" by *NaturallyCurly.com.* The city was ranked #4. Criteria: humidity levels; pollution; rainfall; average wind speeds; water hardness; beauty salons per capita. *NaturallyCurly.com, "Best/Worst Hair Cities," April 29, 2009*
- Anchorage was selected as one of the best "Escapes of a Lifetime" by *U.S. News & World Report.* The city was ranked #2 out of 5 in the "Overall" category. *U.S. News & World Report* surveyed over 1,200 TripAdvisor (a popular travel website) travelers and asked them to rank, in various categories, the destinations they most like to visit. *U.S. News & World Report, "Escapes of a Lifetime," October 2010*

Business Environment

CITY FINANCES

City Government Finances

Component	2009 ($000)	2009 ($ per capita)
Total Revenues	1,247,102	4,459
Total Expenditures	1,643,758	5,877
Debt Outstanding	1,805,257	6,455
Cash and Securities[1]	1,000,957	3,579

Note: (1) Cash and security holdings of a government at the close of its fiscal year, including those of its dependent agencies, utilities, and liquor stores.
Source: U.S Census Bureau, State & Local Government Finances 2009

City Government Revenue by Source

Source	2009 ($000)	2009 ($ per capita)
General Revenue		
From Federal Government	32,726	117
From State Government	506,746	1,812
From Local Governments	0	0
Taxes		
Property	437,290	1,564
Sales and Gross Receipts	38,832	139
Personal Income	0	0
Corporate Income	0	0
Motor Vehicle License	10,536	38
Other Taxes	10,951	39
Current Charges	123,992	443
Liquor Store	0	0
Utility	154,280	552
Employee Retirement	-106,927	-382

Source: U.S Census Bureau, State & Local Government Finances 2009

City Government Expenditures by Function

Function	2009 ($000)	2009 ($ per capita)	2009 (%)
General Direct Expenditures			
Air Transportation	4,243	15	0.3
Corrections	0	0	0.0
Education	702,945	2,513	42.8
Employment Security Administration	0	0	0.0
Financial Administration	12,109	43	0.7
Fire Protection	75,189	269	4.6
General Public Buildings	1,433	5	0.1
Governmental Administration, Other	23,891	85	1.5
Health	25,953	93	1.6
Highways	141,469	506	8.6
Hospitals	0	0	0.0
Housing and Community Development	0	0	0.0
Interest on General Debt	33,942	121	2.1
Judicial and Legal	1,371	5	0.1
Libraries	9,578	34	0.6
Parking	7,913	28	0.5
Parks and Recreation	68,334	244	4.2
Police Protection	105,355	377	6.4
Public Welfare	0	0	0.0
Sewerage	41,496	148	2.5
Solid Waste Management	20,820	74	1.3
Veterans' Services	0	0	0.0
Liquor Store	0	0	0.0
Utility	199,051	712	12.1
Employee Retirement	27,388	98	1.7

Source: U.S Census Bureau, State & Local Government Finances 2009

Municipal Bond Ratings

Area	Moody's	S&P	Fitch
City	Aa3	AA	AA+

Rating Systems (shown in declining order of credit quality): Moody's– Aaa, Aa, A, Baa, Ba, B, Caa, Ca, C (numerical modifiers 1, 2, and 3 are added to letter-rating); S&P– AAA, AA, A, BBB, BB, B, CCC, CC, C; Fitch– AAA, AA, A, BBB, BB, B, CCC, CC, C. Ratings may be modified by the addition of a plus or minus sign to show relative standing within the major rating categories.
Notes: n/a Not Available; w/d Withdrawn (1) Not Reviewed; (2) Issuer Rating/No General Obligation; (3) Standard and Poor's Issue Credit Rating (ICR) is a current opinion of an obliger with respect to a specific financial obligation, a specific class of financial obligations, or a specific financial program.
Source: U.S. Census Bureau, 2012 Statistical Abstract, Bond Ratings for City Governments by Largest Cities: 2010

DEMOGRAPHICS

Population Growth

Area	1990 Census	2000 Census	2010 Census	Population Growth (%) 1990-2000	Population Growth (%) 2000-2010
City	226,338	260,283	291,826	15.0	12.1
MSA[1]	266,021	319,605	380,821	20.1	19.2
U.S.	248,709,873	281,421,906	308,745,538	13.2	9.7

Note: (1) Figures cover the Anchorage, AK Metropolitan Statistical Area—see Appendix B for areas included
Source: U.S. Census Bureau, 2010 Census

Household Size

Area	Persons in Household (%)							Average Household Size
	One	Two	Three	Four	Five	Six	Seven or More	
City	24.9	32.6	17.1	13.8	6.5	2.8	2.3	2.64
MSA[1]	24.3	32.8	16.9	13.8	6.7	3.0	2.4	2.67
U.S.	26.7	32.8	16.1	13.4	6.5	2.6	1.9	2.58

Note: (1) Figures cover the Anchorage, AK Metropolitan Statistical Area—see Appendix B for areas included
Source: U.S. Census Bureau, 2010 Census

Race

Area	White Alone[2] (%)	Black Alone[2] (%)	Asian Alone[2] (%)	AIAN[3] Alone[2] (%)	NHOPI[4] Alone[2] (%)	Other Race Alone[2] (%)	Two or More Races (%)
City	66.0	5.6	8.1	7.9	2.0	2.3	8.1
MSA[1]	70.4	4.5	6.5	7.4	1.6	2.0	7.7
U.S.	72.4	12.6	4.8	0.9	0.2	6.2	2.9

Note: (1) Figures cover the Anchorage, AK Metropolitan Statistical Area—see Appendix B for areas included; (2) Alone is defined as not being in combination with one or more other races; (3) American Indian and Alaska Native; (4) Native Hawaiian and Other Pacific Islander
Source: U.S. Census Bureau, 2010 Census

Hispanic or Latino Origin

Area	Hispanic or Latino (%)	Mexican (%)	Puerto Rican (%)	Cuban (%)	Other Hispanic or Latino (%)
City	7.6	3.9	0.9	0.2	2.5
MSA[1]	6.7	3.5	0.8	0.2	2.2
U.S.	16.3	10.3	1.5	0.6	4.0

Note: Persons of Hispanic or Latino origin can be of any race; (1) Figures cover the Anchorage, AK Metropolitan Statistical Area—see Appendix B for areas included
Source: U.S. Census Bureau, 2010 Census

Segregation

Type	Segregation Indices[1]				Percent Change		
	1990	2000	2010	2010 Rank[2]	1990-2000	1990-2010	2000-2010
Black/White	n/a	n/a	n/a	n/a	n/a	n/a	n/a
Asian/White	n/a	n/a	n/a	n/a	n/a	n/a	n/a
Hispanic/White	n/a	n/a	n/a	n/a	n/a	n/a	n/a

Note: Figures are based on an analysis of 1990, 2000, and 2010 Census Decennial Census tract data by William H. Frey, Brookings Institution and the University of Michigan Social Science Data Analysis Network. In this analysis all racial groups (whites, blacks, and asians) are non-Hispanic members of those races. Hispanics are shown as a separate category; All figures cover the Metropolitan Statistical Area (see Appendix B for areas included); (1) Segregation Indices are Dissimilarity Indices that measure the degree to which the minority group is distributed differently than whites across census tracts. They range from 0 (complete integration) to 100 (complete segregation) where the value indicates the percentage of the minority group that needs to move to be distributed exactly like whites; (2) Ranges from 1 (most segregated) to 102 (least segregated); n/a not available.
Source: www.CensusScope.org

Ancestry

Area	German	Irish	English	American	Italian	Polish	French[2]	Scottish	Dutch
City	19.5	12.2	9.4	3.5	3.6	2.8	3.7	3.3	2.1
MSA[1]	20.9	12.9	10.3	3.7	3.8	2.9	4.0	3.5	2.6
U.S.	16.1	11.6	8.8	6.1	5.7	3.2	3.0	1.9	1.6

Note: Figures are the percentage of the total population reporting a particular ancestry. The nine most commonly reported ancestries in the U.S. are shown. Figures include multiple ancestries (e.g. if a person reported being Irish and Italian, they were included in both columns); (1) Figures cover the Anchorage, AK Metropolitan Statistical Area—see Appendix B for areas included; (2) Excludes Basque
Source: U.S. Census Bureau, 2008-2010 American Community Survey 3-Year Estimates

Foreign-Born Population

Area	Percent of Population Born in								
	Any Foreign Country	Mexico	Asia	Europe	Carribean	South America	Central America[2]	Africa	Canada
City	9.2	0.5	5.3	1.1	0.5	0.4	0.3	0.3	0.5
MSA[1]	7.7	0.4	4.3	1.1	0.4	0.4	0.2	0.2	0.5
U.S.	12.8	3.8	3.6	1.6	1.2	0.9	1.0	0.5	0.3

Note: (1) Figures cover the Anchorage, AK Metropolitan Statistical Area—see Appendix B for areas included; (2) Excludes Mexico.
Source: U.S. Census Bureau, 2008-2010 American Community Survey 3-Year Estimates

Marital Status

Area	Never Married	Now Married[2]	Separated	Widowed	Divorced
City	32.0	49.4	2.2	3.5	13.0
MSA[1]	31.0	50.6	2.2	3.6	12.7
U.S.	31.6	49.6	2.2	6.1	10.7

Note: Figures are percentages and cover the population 15 years of age and older; (1) Figures cover the Anchorage, AK Metropolitan Statistical Area—see Appendix B for areas included; (2) Excludes separated
Source: U.S. Census Bureau, 2008-2010 American Community Survey 3-Year Estimates

Age

Area	Percent of Population							Median Age
	Under Age 5	Age 5 to 17	Age 18 to 34	Age 35 to 49	Age 50 to 64	Age 65 to 79	80 Years and Over	
City	7.5	18.4	26.8	21.1	18.9	5.8	1.5	32.9
MSA[1]	7.6	19.1	25.5	21.2	19.2	5.9	1.5	33.3
U.S.	6.5	17.5	23.2	20.7	19.0	9.4	3.6	37.2

Note: (1) Figures cover the Anchorage, AK Metropolitan Statistical Area—see Appendix B for areas included
Source: U.S. Census Bureau, 2010 Census

Male/Female Ratio

Area	Males	Females	Males per 100 Females
City	148,209	143,617	103.2
MSA[1]	194,249	186,572	104.1
U.S.	151,781,326	156,964,212	96.7

Note: (1) Figures cover the Anchorage, AK Metropolitan Statistical Area—see Appendix B for areas included
Source: U.S. Census Bureau, 2010 Census

Religious Groups

Area	Catholic	Baptist	Non-Den.	Methodist[2]	Lutheran	LDS[3]	Pente-costal	Presby-terian[4]	Muslim[5]	Judaism
MSA[1]	6.9	5.0	6.4	1.4	1.9	5.1	1.9	0.7	0.1	0.2
U.S.	19.1	9.3	4.0	4.0	2.3	2.0	1.9	1.6	0.8	0.7

Note: Figures are the number of adherents as a percentage of the total population; (1) Figures cover the Anchorage, AK Metropolitan Statistical Area—see Appendix B for areas included; (2) Methodist/Pietist; (3) Latter Day Saints; (4) Reformed; (5) Figures are estimates
Source: Association of Statisticians of American Religious Bodies, 2010 U.S. Religion Census: Religious Congregations & Membership Study

ECONOMY

Gross Metropolitan Product

Area	2007	2008	2009	2010	2010 Rank[2]
MSA[1]	24.4	26.8	24.9	26.2	84

Note: Figures are in billions of dollars; (1) Figures cover the Anchorage, AK Metropolitan Statistical Area—see Appendix B for areas included; (2) Rank ranges from 1 to 363
Source: The United States Conference of Mayors, "U.S. Metro Economies: GMP and Employment Forecasts," June 2011

Economic Growth

Area	2007-2009 (%)	2010 (%)	2011 (%)	Rank[2]
MSA[1]	3.4	10.9	2.1	18
U.S.	-1.3	2.9	2.5	–

Note: Figures are real Gross Metropolitan Product growth rates and represent annual average percent change; (1) Figures cover the Anchorage, AK Metropolitan Statistical Area—see Appendix B for areas included; (2) Rank ranges from 1 to 363
Source: The United States Conference of Mayors, "U.S. Metro Economies: GMP and Employment Forecasts," June 2011

Metropolitan Area Exports

Area	2005	2006	2007	2008	2009	2010	2010 Rank[2]
MSA[1]	152.4	370.4	416.9	245.8	213.9	n/a	n/a

Note: Figures are in millions of dollars; (1) Figures cover the Anchorage, AK Metropolitan Statistical Area—see Appendix B for areas included; (2) Rank ranges from 1 to 369
Source: U.S. Department of Commerce, International Trade Administration, Office of Trade & Industry Information, Manufacturing & Services, data extracted April 2, 2012

INCOME

Income

Area	Per Capita ($)	Median Household ($)	Average Household ($)
City	34,999	74,272	92,007
MSA[1]	33,461	73,412	89,351
U.S.	26,942	51,222	70,116

Note: (1) Figures cover the Anchorage, AK Metropolitan Statistical Area—see Appendix B for areas included
Source: U.S. Census Bureau, 2008-2010 American Community Survey 3-Year Estimates

Household Income Distribution

Area	Percent of Households Earning							
	Under $15,000	$15,000 -24,999	$25,000 -34,999	$35,000 -49,999	$50,000 -74,999	$75,000 -99,000	$100,000 -149,999	$150,000 and up
City	6.0	5.6	8.5	11.7	18.9	15.9	19.0	14.5
MSA[1]	6.4	6.0	8.4	11.7	18.8	16.1	19.2	13.4
U.S.	13.0	11.0	10.6	14.2	18.5	12.1	12.2	8.4

Note: (1) Figures cover the Anchorage, AK Metropolitan Statistical Area—see Appendix B for areas included
Source: U.S. Census Bureau, 2008-2010 American Community Survey 3-Year Estimates

Poverty Rate

Area	All Ages	Under 18 Years Old	18 to 64 Years Old	65 Years and Over
City	7.7	10.1	7.1	4.5
MSA[1]	8.2	10.8	7.5	4.2
U.S.	14.4	20.1	13.1	9.4

Note: Figures are percentage of people whose income during the past 12 months was below the poverty level; (1) Figures cover the Anchorage, AK Metropolitan Statistical Area—see Appendix B for areas included
Source: U.S. Census Bureau, 2008-2010 American Community Survey 3-Year Estimates

Personal Bankruptcy Filing Rate

Area	2006	2007	2008	2009	2010	2011
Anchorage Borough	1.14	1.24	1.69	1.80	1.94	1.72
U.S.	2.00	2.73	3.53	4.61	4.97	4.37

Note: Numbers are per 1,000 population and include Chapter 7 and Chapter 13 filings
Source: Federal Deposit Insurance Corporation, Regional Economic Conditions, March 9, 2012

EMPLOYMENT

Labor Force and Employment

Area	Civilian Labor Force			Workers Employed		
	Dec. 2010	Dec. 2011	% Chg.	Dec. 2010	Dec. 2011	% Chg.
City	158,312	158,419	0.1	148,244	149,527	0.9
MSA[1]	202,320	202,675	0.2	188,153	189,781	0.9
U.S.	153,156,000	153,373,000	0.1	139,159,000	140,681,000	1.1

Note: Data is not seasonally adjusted and covers workers 16 years of age and older; (1) Metropolitan Statistical Area—see Appendix B for areas included
Source: Bureau of Labor Statistics, http://stats.bls.gov

Unemployment Rate

Area	2011											
	Jan.	Feb.	Mar.	Apr.	May	Jun.	Jul.	Aug.	Sep.	Oct.	Nov.	Dec.
City	6.6	6.5	6.5	6.2	6.1	6.7	6.0	5.8	5.8	5.5	5.4	5.6
MSA[1]	7.4	7.3	7.3	6.8	6.6	7.2	6.4	6.2	6.2	6.0	6.1	6.4
U.S.	9.8	9.5	9.2	8.7	8.7	9.3	9.3	9.1	8.8	8.5	8.2	8.3

Note: Data is not seasonally adjusted and covers workers 16 years of age and older; All figures are percentages; (1) Metropolitan Statistical Area—see Appendix B for areas included
Source: Bureau of Labor Statistics, http://stats.bls.gov

Projected Unemployment Rate

Area	2010 (%)	2011 (%)	2012 (%)	2013 (%)
MSA[1]	7.3	6.8	6.8	6.7

Note: (1) Metropolitan Statistical Area—see Appendix B for areas included
Source: The United States Conference of Mayors, "U.S. Metro Economies: GMP and Employment Forecasts," June 2011

Employment by Occupation

Occupation Classification	City (%)	MSA[1] (%)	U.S. (%)
Management, Business, Science, and Arts	38.7	37.1	35.6
Natural Resources, Construction, and Maintenance	9.1	11.1	9.5
Production, Transportation, and Material Moving	9.4	9.4	12.1
Sales and Office	25.9	25.2	25.2
Service	16.9	17.2	17.6

Note: Figures cover employed civilians 16 years of age and older; (1) Figures cover the Anchorage, AK Metropolitan Statistical Area—see Appendix B for areas included
Source: U.S. Census Bureau, 2008-2010 American Community Survey 3-Year Estimates

Employment by Industry

Sector	MSA[1] Number of Employees	MSA[1] Percent of Total	U.S. Percent of Total
Construction	7,200	4.2	4.1
Education and Health Services	27,400	16.0	15.2
Financial Activities	9,900	5.8	5.8
Government	37,000	21.7	16.8
Information	4,900	2.9	2.0
Leisure and Hospitality	17,200	10.1	9.9
Manufacturing	1,900	1.1	8.9
Mining and Logging	3,000	1.8	0.6
Other Services	6,100	3.6	4.0
Professional and Business Services	20,100	11.8	13.3
Retail Trade	20,000	11.7	11.5
Transportation and Utilities	11,600	6.8	3.8
Wholesale Trade	4,600	2.7	4.2

Note: Figures cover non-farm employment as of December 2011 and are not seasonally adjusted; (1) Metropolitan Statistical Area—see Appendix B for areas included
Source: Bureau of Labor Statistics, http://stats.bls.gov

Occupations with Greatest Projected Employment Growth: 2008 – 2018

Occupation[1]	2008 Employment	2018 Projected Employment	Numeric Employment Change	Percent Employment Change
Registered Nurses	5,030	6,400	1,370	27.2
Retail Salespersons	11,310	12,280	970	8.6
Home Health Aides	1,890	2,780	890	47.1
Personal and Home Care Aides	2,470	3,350	880	35.6
Office Clerks, General	7,000	7,690	690	9.9
Construction Laborers	5,250	5,920	670	12.8
Cashiers	7,200	7,730	530	7.4
Janitors and Cleaners, Except Maids and Housekeeping Cleaners	5,300	5,780	480	9.1
Operating Engineers and Other Construction Equipment Operators	3,420	3,880	460	13.5
Nursing Aides, Orderlies, and Attendants	2,000	2,450	450	22.5

Note: Projections cover Alaska; (1) Sorted by numeric employment change
Source: www.projectionscentral.com, State Occupational Projections, 2008–2018 Long-Term Projections

Fastest Growing Occupations: 2008 – 2018

Occupation[1]	2008 Employment	2018 Projected Employment	Numeric Employment Change	Percent Employment Change
Home Health Aides	1,890	2,780	890	47.1
Pharmacists	360	500	140	38.9
Pharmacy Technicians	530	720	190	35.8
Personal and Home Care Aides	2,470	3,350	880	35.6
Licensed Practical and Licensed Vocational Nurses	640	830	190	29.7
Medical Assistants	830	1,070	240	28.9
Registered Nurses	5,030	6,400	1,370	27.2
Physician Assistants	380	480	100	26.3
Medical Records and Health Information Technicians	400	500	100	25.0
Physicians and surgeons	890	1,110	220	24.7

Note: Projections cover Alaska; (1) Sorted by percent employment change and excludes occupations with numeric employment change less than 100
Source: www.projectionscentral.com, State Occupational Projections, 2008–2018 Long-Term Projections

Average Wages

Occupation	$/Hr.	Occupation	$/Hr.
Accountants and Auditors	33.68	Maids and Housekeeping Cleaners	10.92
Automotive Mechanics	25.41	Maintenance and Repair Workers	21.57
Bookkeepers	19.46	Marketing Managers	39.44
Carpenters	29.15	Nuclear Medicine Technologists	n/a
Cashiers	11.32	Nurses, Licensed Practical	24.82
Clerks, General Office	17.00	Nurses, Registered	39.99
Clerks, Receptionists/Information	14.42	Nursing Aides/Orderlies/Attendants	16.61
Clerks, Shipping/Receiving	19.41	Packers and Packagers, Hand	12.48
Computer Programmers	35.11	Physical Therapists	44.45
Computer Support Specialists	25.21	Postal Service Mail Carriers	25.98
Computer Systems Analysts	37.05	Real Estate Brokers	n/a
Cooks, Restaurant	14.36	Retail Salespersons	13.13
Dentists	82.57	Sales Reps., Exc. Tech./Scientific	26.16
Electrical Engineers	48.13	Sales Reps., Tech./Scientific	37.99
Electricians	33.92	Secretaries, Exc. Legal/Med./Exec.	18.95
Financial Managers	50.67	Security Guards	15.02
First-Line Supervisors/Managers, Sales	20.36	Surgeons	n/a
Food Preparation Workers	11.54	Teacher Assistants	n/a
General and Operations Managers	47.58	Teachers, Elementary School	n/a
Hairdressers/Cosmetologists	13.05	Teachers, Secondary School	n/a
Internists	n/a	Telemarketers	n/a
Janitors and Cleaners	14.28	Truck Drivers, Heavy/Tractor-Trailer	23.41
Landscaping/Groundskeeping Workers	14.55	Truck Drivers, Light/Delivery Svcs.	20.42
Lawyers	56.84	Waiters and Waitresses	10.88

Note: Wage data covers the Anchorage, AK Metropolitan Statistical Area—see Appendix B for areas included. Hourly wages for elementary/secondary school teachers and teacher assistants were calculated by the editors from annual wage data assuming a 40 hour work week; n/a not available.
Source: Bureau of Labor Statistics, Metro Area Occupational Employment and Wage Estimates, May 2011

RESIDENTIAL REAL ESTATE

Building Permits

Area	Single-Family 2010	Single-Family 2011	Single-Family Pct. Chg.	Multi-Family 2010	Multi-Family 2011	Multi-Family Pct. Chg.	Total 2010	Total 2011	Total Pct. Chg.
City	381	344	-9.7	99	103	4.0	480	447	-6.9
MSA[1]	424	401	-5.4	109	123	12.8	533	524	-1.7
U.S.	447,311	418,498	-6.4	157,299	205,563	30.7	604,610	624,061	3.2

Note: (1) Metropolitan Statistical Area—see Appendix B for areas included; figures represent new, privately-owned housing units authorized (unadjusted data); All permit data are based on estimates with imputation.
Source: U.S. Census Bureau, Manufacturing, Mining, and Construction Statistics, Building Permits, 2010, 2011

Homeownership Rate

Area	2005 (%)	2006 (%)	2007 (%)	2008 (%)	2009 (%)	2010 (%)	2011 (%)
MSA[1]	n/a	n/a	n/a	n/a	n/a	n/a	n/a
U.S.	68.9	68.8	68.1	67.8	67.4	66.9	66.1

Note: (1) Metropolitan Statistical Area—see Appendix B for areas included; n/a not available
Source: U.S. Census Bureau, Housing Vacancies and Homeownership Annual Statistics: 2011

Housing Vacancy Rates

Area	Gross Vacancy Rate[2] (%)			Year-Round Vacancy Rate[3] (%)			Rental Vacancy Rate[4] (%)			Homeowner Vacancy Rate[5] (%)		
	2009	2010	2011	2009	2010	2011	2009	2010	2011	2009	2010	2011
MSA[1]	n/a	n/a	n/a	n/a	n/a	n/a	n/a	n/a	n/a	n/a	n/a	n/a
U.S.	14.5	14.3	14.2	11.3	11.3	11.1	10.6	10.2	9.5	2.6	2.6	2.5

Note: (1) Metropolitan Statistical Area—see Appendix B for areas included; (2) The percentage of the total housing inventory that is vacant; (3) The percentage of the housing inventory (excluding seasonal units) that is year-round vacant; (4) The percentage of rental inventory that is vacant for rent; (5) The percentage of homeowner inventory that is vacant for sale; n/a not available
Source: U.S. Census Bureau, Housing Vacancies and Homeownership Annual Statistics: 2011

TAXES

State Corporate Income Tax Rates

State	Tax Rate (%)	Income Brackets ($)	Num. of Brackets	Financial Institution Tax Rate (%)[a]	Federal Income Tax Ded.
Alaska	1.0 - 9.4	9,999 - 90,000	10	1.0 - 9.4	No

Note: Tax rates as of January 1, 2012; (a) Rates listed are the corporate income tax rate applied to financial institutions or excise taxes based on income. Some states have other taxes based upon the value of deposits or shares.
Source: Federation of Tax Administrators, "State Corporate Income Tax Rates, 2012"

State Individual Income Tax Rates

State	Tax Rate (%)	Income Brackets ($)	Num. of Brackets	Personal Exempt. ($)[1] Single	Personal Exempt. ($)[1] Dependents	Fed. Inc. Tax Ded.
Alaska – No State Income Tax						

Note: Tax rates as of January 1, 2012; Local- and county-level taxes are not included; n/a not applicable; (1) Married joint filers generally receive double the single exemption
Source: Federation of Tax Administrators, "State Individual Income Tax Rates, 2012"

Various State and Local Tax Rates

State	State and Local Sales and Use (%)	State Sales and Use (%)	Gasoline[1] (¢/gal.)	Cigarette[2] ($/pack)	Spirits[3] ($/gal.)	Wine[4] ($/gal.)	Beer[5] ($/gal.)
Alaska	None	None	8.0	2.00	12.80	2.50	1.07

Note: All tax rates as of January 1, 2012 except beer, wine and spirits (September 1, 2011); (1) The American Petroleum Institute has developed a methodology for determining the average tax rate on a gallon of fuel. Rates may include any of the following: excise taxes, environmental fees, storage tank fees, other fees or taxes, general sales tax, and local taxes. In states where gasoline is subject to the general sales tax, or where the fuel tax is based on the average sale price, the average rate determined by API is sensitive to changes in the price of gasoline. States that fully or partially apply general sales taxes to gasoline: CA, CO, GA, IL, IN, MI, NY; (2) The federal excise tax of $1.0066 per pack and local taxes are not included; (3) Rates are those applicable to off-premise sales of 40% alcohol by volume (a.b.v.) distilled spirits in 750ml containers. Local excise taxes are excluded; (4) Rates are those applicable to off-premise sales of 11% a.b.v. non-carbonated wine in 750ml containers; (5) Rates are those applicable to off-premise sales of 4.7% a.b.v. beer in 12 ounce containers.
Source: Tax Foundation, 2012 Facts & Figures: How Does Your State Compare?

State-Local Tax Burdens

Area	Rate (%)	Rank[1]	Per Capita Taxes Paid to Home State ($)	Total State and Local Per Capita Taxes Paid ($)	Per Capita Income ($)
Alaska	6.3	50	1,893	2,973	46,841
U.S. Average	9.8	-	3,057	4,160	42,539

Note: Figures cover 2009; (1) Rank ranges from 1 to 50 where 1 is highest tax burden
Source: Tax Foundation, State-Local Tax Burdens, All States, 2009

State Business Tax Climate Index Rankings

State	Overall Rank	Corporate Tax Index Rank	Individual Income Tax Index Rank	Sales Tax Index Rank	Unemployment Insurance Tax Index Rank	Property Tax Index Rank
Alaska	4	27	1	5	28	13

Note: The index is a measure of how each state's tax laws affect economic performance. The lower the rank, the more favorable a state's tax system is for business. States without a given tax are given a ranking of 1.
Source: Tax Foundation, Major Components of the State Business Tax Climate Index, FY 2012

COMMERCIAL UTILITIES

Typical Monthly Electric Bills

Area	Commercial Service ($/month)		Industrial Service ($/month)	
	1,500 kWh	40 kW demand 14,000 kWh	1,000 kW demand 200,000 kWh	50,000 kW demand 15,000,000 kWh
City	n/a	n/a	n/a	n/a
Average[1]	189	1,616	25,197	1,470,813

Note: Based on total rates in effect July 1, 2011; (1) average based on 184 utilities surveyed; n/a not available
Source: Edison Electric Institute, Typical Bills and Average Rates Report, Summer 2011

TRANSPORTATION

Means of Transportation to Work

Area	Car/Truck/Van		Public Transportation			Bicycle	Walked	Other Means	Worked at Home
	Drove Alone	Car-pooled	Bus	Subway	Railroad				
City	75.7	13.7	1.5	0.0	0.0	1.1	2.6	2.2	3.3
MSA[1]	74.7	13.8	1.3	0.0	0.0	0.9	2.5	2.6	4.1
U.S.	76.0	10.2	2.7	1.7	0.5	0.5	2.8	1.3	4.2

Note: Figures are percentages and cover workers 16 years of age and older; (1) Figures cover the Anchorage, AK Metropolitan Statistical Area—see Appendix B for areas included
Source: U.S. Census Bureau, 2008-2010 American Community Survey 3-Year Estimates

Travel Time to Work

Area	Less Than 10 Minutes	10 to 19 Minutes	20 to 29 Minutes	30 to 44 Minutes	45 to 59 Minutes	60 to 89 Minutes	90 Minutes or More
City	16.4	44.1	22.3	12.0	2.8	1.2	1.2
MSA[1]	16.3	40.7	20.4	11.9	4.8	4.0	1.8
U.S.	13.9	30.1	20.8	19.8	7.5	5.5	2.5

Note: Figures are percentages and include workers 16 years old and over; (1) Figures cover the Anchorage, AK Metropolitan Statistical Area—see Appendix B for areas included
Source: U.S. Census Bureau, 2008-2010 American Community Survey 3-Year Estimates

Travel Time Index

Area	1985	1990	1995	2000	2005	2010
Urban Area[1]	1.05	1.05	1.05	1.05	1.06	1.05
Average[2]	1.11	1.16	1.18	1.21	1.25	1.20

Note: Travel Time Index—the ratio of travel time in the peak period to the travel time at free-flow conditions. A value of 1.30 indicates a 20-minute free-flow trip takes 26 minutes in the peak. Free-flow speeds (60 mph on freeways and 35 mph on principal arterials) are used as the comparison threshold; (1) Covers the Anchorage AK urban area; (2) average of 439 urban areas
Source: Texas Transportation Institute, Urban Mobility Report 2011, September 2011

Public Transportation

Agency Name / Mode of Transportation	Vehicles Operated in Maximum Service	Annual Unlinked Passenger Trips ('000)	Annual Passenger Miles ('000)
Anchorage Public Transportation Dept. (People Mover)			
Bus (directly operated)	45	4,145.6	18,509.8
Demand Response (purchased transportation)	42	197.8	1,287.4

Source: Federal Transit Administration, National Transit Database, 2010

Air Transportation

Airport Name and Code / Type of Service	Passenger Airlines[1]	Passenger Enplanements	Freight Carriers[2]	Freight (lbs.)
Anchorage International (ANC)				
Domestic service (U.S. carriers - 2011)	25	2,208,490	30	1,169,620,718
International service (U.S. carriers - 2010)	9	444	11	371,044,730

Note: (1) Includes all U.S.-based major, minor and commuter airlines that carried at least one passenger during the year; (2) Includes all U.S.-based airlines and freight carriers that transported at least one pound of freight during the year
Source: Bureau of Transportation Statistics, The Intermodal Transportation Database, Air Carriers: T-100 Domestic Market (U.S. Carriers), 2011; Bureau of Transportation Statistics, The Intermodal Transportation Database, Air Carriers: T-100 International Market (U.S. Carriers), 2010

Other Transportation Statistics

Major Highways:	None
Amtrak Service:	No
Major Waterways/Ports:	Gulf of Alaska

Source: Amtrak.com; Google Maps

BUSINESSES

Major Business Headquarters

Company Name	Rankings: Fortune[1]	Rankings: Forbes[2]
No companies listed	-	-

Note: (1) Fortune 500—companies that produce a 10-K are ranked 1 to 500 based on 2010 revenue; (2) all private companies with at least $2 billion in annual revenue are ranked 1 to 212; companies listed are headquartered in the city; dashes indicate no ranking
Source: Fortune, "Fortune 500," May 23, 2011; Forbes, "America's Largest Private Companies," November 16, 2011

Minority- and Women-Owned Businesses

Group	All Firms: Firms	All Firms: Sales ($000)	Firms with Paid Employees: Firms	Sales ($000)	Employees	Payroll ($000)
Asian	1,415	331,168	397	290,202	2,836	66,437
Black	680	72,101	87	54,292	1,030	22,278
Hispanic	825	121,023	141	91,944	930	28,512
Women	8,063	1,665,467	1,288	1,492,529	9,775	335,936
All Firms	26,726	42,963,995	6,947	42,051,422	112,855	5,330,369

Note: Figures cover firms located in the city; minority- and women-owned business are defined as firms in which the corresponding group own 51% or more of the stock or equity of the company
Source: U.S. Census Bureau, 2007 Economic Census, Survey of Business Owners

HOTELS

Hotels/Motels

Area	5 Star Num.	5 Star Pct.[3]	4 Star Num.	4 Star Pct.[3]	3 Star Num.	3 Star Pct.[3]	2 Star Num.	2 Star Pct.[3]	1 Star Num.	1 Star Pct.[3]	Not Rated Num.	Not Rated Pct.[3]
City[1]	0	0.0	2	2.9	17	24.6	30	43.5	2	2.9	18	26.1
Total[2]	133	0.9	940	6.5	4,569	31.8	7,033	48.9	351	2.4	1,343	9.3

Note: (1) Figures cover Anchorage and vicinity; (2) Figures cover all 100 cities in this book; (3) Percentage of hotels which have a given star rating; Star ratings are determined by expedia.com and offer an indication of the general quality of a particular hotel.
Source: expedia.com, April 25, 2012

EVENT SITES

Major Stadiums, Arenas, and Auditoriums

Name	Max. Capacity
George M. Sullivan Arena	6,290
William A. Egan Civic and Convention Center	2,540

Source: Original research

Convention Centers

Name	Overall Space (sq. ft.)	Exhibit Space (sq. ft.)	Meeting Space (sq. ft.)	Meeting Rooms
Dena'ina Civic and Convention Center	n/a	n/a	50,000	n/a
William A. Egan Civic Center	45,000	19,306	19,306	n/a

Note: n/a not available
Source: Original research

Living Environment

COST OF LIVING

Cost of Living Index

Composite Index	Groceries	Housing	Utilities	Trans-portation	Health Care	Misc. Goods/ Services
130.8	137.6	150.2	98.2	112.0	139.1	126.3

Note: U.S. = 100; Figures cover the Anchorage AK urban area.
Source: The Council for Community and Economic Research, ACCRA Cost of Living Index, 2011

Grocery Prices

Area[1]	T-Bone Steak ($/pound)	Frying Chicken ($/pound)	Whole Milk ($/half gal.)	Eggs ($/dozen)	Orange Juice ($/64 oz.)	Coffee ($/11.5 oz.)
City[2]	10.51	1.44	2.12	2.57	4.41	6.00
Avg.	9.25	1.18	2.22	1.66	3.19	4.40
Min.	6.70	0.88	1.31	0.95	2.46	2.94
Max.	14.30	2.16	3.50	3.18	4.75	6.83

Note: (1) Values for the local area are compared with the average, minimum and maximum values for all 335 areas in the Cost of Living Index; (2) Figures cover the Anchorage AK urban area; **T-Bone Steak** *(price per pound);* **Frying Chicken** *(price per pound, whole fryer);* **Whole Milk** *(half gallon carton);* **Eggs** *(price per dozen, Grade A, large);* **Orange Juice** *(64 oz. Tropicana or Florida Natural);* **Coffee** *(11.5 oz. can, vacuum-packed, Maxwell House, Hills Bros, or Folgers).*
Source: The Council for Community and Economic Research, ACCRA Cost of Living Index, 2011

Housing and Utility Costs

Area[1]	New Home Price ($)	Apartment Rent ($/month)	All Electric ($/month)	Part Electric ($/month)	Other Energy ($/month)	Telephone ($/month)
City[2]	422,933	1,302	-	73.24	104.51	22.55
Avg.	285,990	839	163.23	89.00	77.52	26.92
Min.	188,005	460	125.58	45.39	33.89	17.98
Max.	1,197,028	3,244	339.16	181.97	348.69	40.01

Note: (1) Values for the local area are compared with the average, minimum and maximum values for all 335 areas in the Cost of Living Index; (2) Figures cover the Anchorage AK urban area; **New Home Price** *(2,400 sf living area, 8,000 sf lot, in urban area with full utilities);* **Apartment Rent** *(950 sf 2 bedroom/1.5 or 2 bath, unfurnished, excluding all utilities except water);* **All Electric** *(average monthly cost for an all-electric home);* **Part Electric** *(average monthly cost for a part-electric home);* **Other Energy** *(average monthly cost for natural gas, fuel oil, coal, wood, and any other forms of energy except electricity);* **Telephone** *(price includes basic monthly rate for a private residential line plus additional local usage charges incurred by a family of four).*
Source: The Council for Community and Economic Research, ACCRA Cost of Living Index, 2011

Health Care, Transportation, and Other Costs

Area[1]	Doctor ($/visit)	Dentist ($/visit)	Optometrist ($/visit)	Gasoline ($/gallon)	Beauty Salon ($/visit)	Men's Shirt ($)
City[2]	154.98	127.82	156.44	3.82	40.38	27.67
Avg.	93.88	81.72	90.54	3.48	32.65	25.06
Min.	60.00	55.33	53.66	3.18	19.78	13.44
Max.	154.98	145.97	183.72	4.31	63.21	46.00

Note: (1) Values for the local area are compared with the average, minimum and maximum values for all 335 areas in the Cost of Living Index; (2) Figures cover the Anchorage AK urban area; **Doctor** *(general practitioners routine exam of an established patient);* **Dentist** *(adult teeth cleaning and periodic oral examination);* **Optometrist** *(full vision eye exam for established adult patient);* **Gasoline** *(one gallon regular unleaded, national brand, including all taxes, cash price at self-service pump if available);* **Beauty Salon** *(woman's shampoo, trim, and blow-dry);* **Men's Shirt** *(cotton/polyester dress shirt, pinpoint weave, long sleeves).*
Source: The Council for Community and Economic Research, ACCRA Cost of Living Index, 2011

HOUSING

House Price Index (HPI)

Area	National Ranking[2]	Quarterly Change (%)	One-Year Change (%)	Five-Year Change (%)
MSA[1]	22	0.30	0.31	1.75
U.S.[3]	-	-0.10	-2.43	-19.16

Note: The HPI is a weighted repeat sales index. It measures average price changes in repeat sales or refinancings on the same properties. This information is obtained by reviewing repeat mortgage transactions on single-family properties whose mortgages have been purchased or securitized by Fannie Mae or Freddie Mac in January 1975; (1) Metropolitan/Micropolitan Statistical Area—see Appendix B for areas included; (2) Rankings are based on annual percentage change for all metro areas containing at least 15,000 transactions over the last 10 years and ranges from 1 to 306; (3) figures based on a weighted average of Census Division estimates using a purchase only index; all figures are for the period ending December 31, 2011
Source: Federal Housing Finance Agency, House Price Index, February 23, 2012

House Price Valuations

Area	Q4 2005		Q4 2006		Q4 2007		Q4 2008		Q4 2009	
	Price ($000)	Over-valuation	Price ($000)	Over-valuation	Price ($000)	Over-valuation	Price ($000)	Over-valuation	Price ($000)	Over-valuation
MSA[1]	230.0	14.5	237.1	12.6	235.6	7.6	238.6	0.4	231.1	-0.3

Note: Figures show the percentage of over- or under-valuation of single family homes relative to statistically normal house values (e.g. a value of 23.6 indicates that house values are 23.6% overvalued). Statistically normal house values are based on house prices, interest rates, household incomes, population densities, and any historical premiums or discounts metropolitan areas have exhibited over time; (1) Figures cover the Anchorage, AK - see Appendix B for areas included
Source: Global Insight/PNC Financial Services Group, House Prices in America: 4th Quarter 2009 Update

Median Single-Family Home Prices

Area	2009	2010	2011[p]	Percent Change 2010 to 2011
MSA[1]	n/a	n/a	n/a	n/a
U.S. Average	172.1	173.1	166.2	-4.0

Note: Figures are median sales prices of existing single-family homes in thousands of dollars; (p) preliminary; n/a not available; (1) Metropolitan Statistical Area—see Appendix B for areas included
Source: National Association of Realtors, Median Sales Price of Existing Single-Family Homes for Metropolitan Areas, 4th Quarter 2011

Affordability Index of Existing Single-Family Homes

Area	2009	2010	2011[p]	Percent Change 2010 to 2011
MSA[1]	n/a	n/a	n/a	n/a

Note: The housing affordability index measures whether or not a typical family could qualify for a mortgage loan on a typical home. The higher the index, the greater the household purchasing power. An index of 100 is defined as the point where a median-income household has exactly enough income to qualify for the purchase of a median-priced existing single-family home, assuming a 20 percent downpayment and 25 percent of gross income devoted to mortgage principal and interest payments; (p) preliminary; n/a not available; (1) Metropolitan Statistical Area—see Appendix B for areas included
Source: National Association of Realtors, Affordability Index of Existing Single-Family Homes, 2011

Median Apartment Condo-Coop Home Prices

Area	2009	2010	2011[p]	Percent Change 2010 to 2011
MSA[1]	n/a	n/a	n/a	n/a
U.S. Average	175.6	171.7	165.1	-3.8

Note: Figures are median sales prices of existing apartment condo-coop homes in thousands of dollars; (p) preliminary; n/a not available; (1) Metropolitan Statistical Area—see Appendix B for areas included
Source: National Association of Realtors, Median Sales Price of Existing Apartment Condo-Coop Homes for Metropolitan Areas, 4th Quarter 2011

Year Housing Structure Built

Area	2005 or Later	2000 -2004	1990 -1999	1980 -1989	1970 -1979	1960 -1969	1950 -1959	Before 1950	Median Year
City	4.8	7.9	10.9	27.2	28.8	11.2	7.3	1.8	1980
MSA[1]	5.6	10.0	13.0	27.8	25.8	9.8	6.3	1.8	1982
U.S.	5.0	8.6	14.0	14.1	16.3	11.3	11.2	19.6	1975

Note: Figures are percentages except for Median Year; (1) Figures cover the Anchorage, AK Metropolitan Statistical Area—see Appendix B for areas included
Source: U.S. Census Bureau, 2008-2010 American Community Survey 3-Year Estimates

HEALTH

Health Risk Data

Category	MSA[1] (%)	U.S. (%)
Adults who have been told they have high blood pressure[2]	n/a	28.7
Adults who have been told they have high blood cholesterol[2]	n/a	37.5
Adults who have been told they have diabetes[3]	n/a	8.7
Adults who have been told they have arthritis[2]	n/a	26.0
Adults who have been told they currently have asthma	n/a	9.1
Adults who are current smokers	n/a	17.3
Adults who are heavy drinkers[4]	n/a	5.0
Adults who are binge drinkers[5]	n/a	15.1
Adults who are overweight (BMI 25.0 - 29.9)	n/a	36.2
Adults who are obese (BMI 30.0 - 99.8)	n/a	27.5
Adults who participated in any physical activities in the past month	n/a	76.1
Adults 50+ who have ever had a sigmoidoscopy or colonoscopy	n/a	65.2
Women aged 40+ who have had a mammogram within the past two years	n/a	75.2
Men aged 40+ who have had a PSA test within the past two years	n/a	53.2
Adults aged 65+ who have had flu shot within the past year	n/a	67.5
Adults aged 18–64 who have any kind of health care coverage	n/a	82.2

Note: Data as of 2010 unless otherwise noted; n/a not available; (1) Figures cover the Anchorage, AK—see Appendix B for areas included; (2) Data as of 2009; (3) Figures do not include pregnancy-related, borderline, or pre-diabetes; (4) Heavy drinkers are classified as males having more than two drinks per day or females having more than one drink per day; (5) Binge drinkers are classified as males having five or more drinks on one occasion or females having four or more drinks on one occasion
Source: Centers for Disease Control and Prevention, Behaviorial Risk Factor Surveillance System, SMART: Selected Metropolitan/Micropolitan Area Risk Trends, 2009, 2010

Mortality Rates for the Top 10 Causes of Death in the U.S.

ICD-10[a] Sub-Chapter	ICD-10[a] Code	Age-Adjusted Mortality Rate[1] per 100,000 population	
		County[2]	U.S.
Malignant neoplasms	C00-C97	180.9	175.6
Ischaemic heart diseases	I20-I25	81.3	121.6
Other forms of heart disease	I30-I51	45.5	48.6
Chronic lower respiratory diseases	J40-J47	43.5	42.3
Cerebrovascular diseases	I60-I69	42.4	40.6
Organic, including symptomatic, mental disorders	F01-F09	38.0	26.7
Other degenerative diseases of the nervous system	G30-G31	27.8	24.7
Other external causes of accidental injury	W00-X59	34.0	24.4
Diabetes mellitus	E10-E14	20.8	21.7
Hypertensive diseases	I10-I15	12.4	18.2

Note: (a) ICD-10 = International Classification of Diseases 10th Revision; (1) Mortality rates are a three year average covering 2007-2009; (2) Figures cover Anchorage Borough
Source: Centers for Disease Control and Prevention, National Center for Health Statistics. Underlying Cause of Death 1999-2009 on CDC WONDER Online Database, released 2012. Data for year 2009 are compiled from the Multiple Cause of Death File 2009, Series 20 No. 2O, 2012, Data for year 2008 are compiled from the Multiple Cause of Death File 2008, Series 20 No. 2N, 2011, Data for year 2007 are compiled from Multiple Cause of Death File 2007, Series 20 No. 2M, 2010.

Mortality Rates for Selected Causes of Death

ICD-10[a] Sub-Chapter	ICD-10[a] Code	Age-Adjusted Mortality Rate[1] per 100,000 population	
		County[2]	U.S.
Assault	X85-Y09	5.2	5.7
Human immunodeficiency virus (HIV) disease	B20-B24	*Unreliable	3.3
Influenza and pneumonia	J09-J18	11.2	16.4
Intentional self-harm	X60-X84	16.5	11.5
Malnutrition	E40-E46	*0.0	0.8
Obesity and other hyperalimentation	E65-E68	*Unreliable	1.6
Transport accidents	V01-V99	11.0	13.7
Viral hepatitis	B15-B19	3.9	2.2

Note: (a) ICD-10 = International Classification of Diseases 10th Revision; (1) Mortality rates are a three year average covering 2007-2009; (2) Figures cover Anchorage Borough; (*) Unreliable data as per CDC
Source: Centers for Disease Control and Prevention, National Center for Health Statistics. Underlying Cause of Death 1999-2009 on CDC WONDER Online Database, released 2012. Data for year 2009 are compiled from the Multiple Cause of Death File 2009, Series 20 No. 2O, 2012, Data for year 2008 are compiled from the Multiple Cause of Death File 2008, Series 20 No. 2N, 2011, Data for year 2007 are compiled from Multiple Cause of Death File 2007, Series 20 No. 2M, 2010.

Distribution of Physicians and Dentists

Area[1]	Dentists[2]	D.O.[3]	M.D.[4] Total	Family/General Practice	Pediatrics	Medical Specialties	Surgical Specialties
Local (number)	161	63	671	124	50	181	175
Local (rate[5])	5.8	2.2	23.9	4.4	1.8	6.5	6.2
U.S. (rate[5])	4.5	1.9	18.3	2.5	1.4	6.8	4.1

Note: Data as of 2008 unless noted; (1) Local data covers Anchorage Borough; (2) Data as of 2007; (3) Doctor of Osteopathic Medicine; (4) Includes active, non-federal, patient-care, office-based Doctors of Medicine; (5) rate per 10,000 population
Source: Area Resource File (ARF). 2009-2010 Release. U.S. Department of Health and Human Services, Health Resources and Services Administration, Bureau of Health Professions, Rockville, MD, August 2010

EDUCATION

Public School District Statistics

District Name	Schls	Pupils	Pupil/ Teacher Ratio	Minority Pupils[1] (%)	Free Lunch Eligible[2] (%)	IEP[3] (%)
Anchorage School District	98	49,592	17.0	51.9	28.0	14.0

Note: Table includes school districts with 2,000 or more students; (1) Percentage of students that are not non-Hispanic white; (2) Percentage of students that are eligible for the free lunch program; (3) Percentage of students that have an Individualized Education Program.
Source: U.S. Department of Education, National Center for Education Statistics, Common Core of Data, Local Education Agency (School District) Universe Survey: School Year 2009-2010; U.S. Department of Education, National Center for Education Statistics, Common Core of Data, Public Elementary/Secondary School Universe Survey: School Year 2009-2010

Highest Level of Education

Area	Less than H.S.	H.S. Diploma	Some College, No Deg.	Associate Degree	Bachelors Degree	Masters Degree	Profess. School Degree	Doctorate Degree
City	7.5	22.4	28.8	8.4	21.7	7.7	2.1	1.4
MSA[1]	7.6	24.3	29.4	8.5	20.1	7.0	1.8	1.2
U.S.	14.7	28.4	21.3	7.6	17.6	7.2	1.9	1.2

Note: Figures cover persons age 25 and over; (1) Figures cover the Anchorage, AK Metropolitan Statistical Area—see Appendix B for areas included
Source: U.S. Census Bureau, 2008-2010 American Community Survey 3-Year Estimates

Educational Attainment by Race

Area	High School Graduate or Higher (%)					Bachelor's Degree or Higher (%)				
	Total	White	Black	Asian	Hisp.[2]	Total	White	Black	Asian	Hisp.[2]
City	92.5	95.2	90.8	81.1	80.1	32.9	37.4	21.2	25.3	22.7
MSA[1]	92.4	94.6	90.8	80.1	80.7	30.2	33.4	20.3	25.0	22.0
U.S.	85.3	87.5	81.4	85.5	61.6	28.0	29.3	17.8	50.2	13.0

Note: Figures shown cover persons 25 years old and over; (1) Figures cover the Anchorage, AK Metropolitan Statistical Area—see Appendix B for areas included; (2) People of Hispanic origin can be of any race
Source: U.S. Census Bureau, 2008-2010 American Community Survey 3-Year Estimates

School Enrollment by Grade and Control

Area	Preschool (%)		Kindergarten (%)		Grades 1 - 4 (%)		Grades 5 - 8 (%)		Grades 9 - 12 (%)	
	Public	Private	Public	Private	Public	Private	Public	Private	Public	Private
City	48.7	51.3	91.6	8.4	93.1	6.9	91.5	8.5	93.3	6.7
MSA[1]	49.9	50.1	91.5	8.5	91.0	9.0	89.7	10.3	91.1	8.9
U.S.	55.4	44.6	87.1	12.9	89.4	10.6	89.5	10.5	90.4	9.6

Note: Figures shown cover persons 3 years old and over; (1) Figures cover the Anchorage, AK Metropolitan Statistical Area—see Appendix B for areas included
Source: U.S. Census Bureau, 2008-2010 American Community Survey 3-Year Estimates

Average Salaries of Public School Classroom Teachers

Area	2010-11		2011-12		Percent Change 2010-11 to 2011-12	Percent Change 2001-02 to 2011-12
	Dollars	Rank[1]	Dollars	Rank[1]		
Alaska	62,918	10	62,425	10	-0.78	26.30
U.S. Average	55,623	-	56,643	-	1.83	26.8

Note: (1) State rank ranges from 1 to 51 where 1 indicates highest salary.
Source: National Education Association, Rankings & Estimates: Rankings of the States 2011 and Estimates of School Statistics 2012, December 2011

Higher Education

Four-Year Colleges			Two-Year Colleges			Medical Schools[1]	Law Schools[2]	Voc/ Tech[3]
Public	Private Non-profit	Private For-profit	Public	Private Non-profit	Private For-profit			
1	1	1	0	0	1	0	0	0

Note: Figures cover institutions located within the city limits and include main campuses only; (1) includes schools accredited by the Liaison Committee on Medical Education and the American Osteopathic Association's Commission on Osteopathic College Accreditation; (2) includes American Bar Association-accredited law schools; (3) includes all schools with programs that are less than 2 years.
Source: National Center for Education Statistics, Integrated Postsecondary Education System (IPEDS) Peer Analysis System, 2011-12; Association of American Medical Colleges, Member List, April 23, 2012; American Osteopathic Association, Member List, April 23, 2012; Law School Admission Council, Official Guide to ABA-Approved Law Schools Online, April 23, 2012

PRESIDENTIAL ELECTION

2008 Presidential Election Results

Area	Obama	McCain	Nader	Other
Anchorage: Districts 18 - 32	43.0	55.9	1.0	0.0
U.S.	52.9	45.6	0.6	0.9

Note: Results are percentages and may not add to 100% due to rounding
Source: Dave Leip's Atlas of U.S. Presidential Elections, www.uselectionatlas.org

EMPLOYERS

Major Employers

Company Name	Industry
Ahtna Technical Services	Building maintenance services
Akima Logistics Services	General warehousing and storage
Alaska Native Tribal Health Consortium	General medical and surgical hospitals
Alaskan Professional Employers	Employee leasing service
ASRC Energy Services	Oil and gas field services
AT&T Alas.com	Telephone communication, except radio
BP Transportation (Alaska)	Crude petroleum production
Bureau of Land Management	Information bureau
Federal Aviation Administration	Aircraft regulating agencies
Federal Express Corporation	Air cargo carrier, scheduled
Fish and Wildlife Services, United States	Fish and wildlife conservation agency, government
Galen Hospital Alaska	General medical and surgical hospitals
Indian Health Service	General medical and surgical hospitals
Municipality of Anchorage	Mayors' office
Nabors Alaska Drilling	Drilling oil and gas wells
United States Department of the Air Force	Air force
Usphs AK Native Medical Center	General medical and surgical hospitals

Note: Companies shown are located within the Anchorage, AK metropolitan area.
Source: Hoovers.com, data extracted April 25 2012

PUBLIC SAFETY

Crime Rate

Area	All Crimes	Violent Crimes				Property Crimes		
		Murder	Forcible Rape	Robbery	Aggrav. Assault	Burglary	Larceny -Theft	Motor Vehicle Theft
City	4,355.7	4.5	90.9	156.4	585.9	421.2	2,816.8	280.0
Suburbs[1]	3,856.1	0.0	21.9	48.1	428.9	350.2	2,770.6	236.4
Metro[2]	4,319.2	4.2	85.9	148.5	574.4	416.1	2,813.4	276.8
U.S.	3,345.5	4.8	27.5	119.1	252.3	699.6	2,003.5	238.8

Note: Figures are crimes per 100,000 population; (1) All areas within the metro area that are located outside the city limits; (2) Metropolitan Statistical Area—see Appendix B for areas included
Source: FBI Uniform Crime Reports, 2010

Hate Crimes

Area	Number of Quarters Reported	Bias Motivation				
		Race	Religion	Sexual Orientation	Ethnicity	Disability
City	4	3	1	1	1	1

Source: Federal Bureau of Investigation, Hate Crime Statistics 2010

Identity Theft Consumer Complaints

Area	Complaints	Complaints per 100,000 Population	Rank[2]
MSA[1]	206	56.9	295
U.S.	279,156	90.4	-

Note: (1) Metropolitan Statistical Area—see Appendix B for areas included; (2) Rank ranges from 1 to 384 where 1 indicates greatest number of identity theft complaints per 100,000 population
Source: Federal Trade Commission, Consumer Sentinel Network Data Book for January–December 2011

Fraud and Other Consumer Complaints

Area	Complaints	Complaints per 100,000 Population	Rank[2]
MSA[1]	2,037	562.2	76
U.S.	1,533,924	496.8	-

Note: (1) Metropolitan Statistical Area—see Appendix B for areas included; (2) Rank ranges from 1 to 384 where 1 indicates greatest number of fraud and other complaints per 100,000 population
Source: Federal Trade Commission, Consumer Sentinel Network Data Book for January–December 2011

RECREATION

Culture

Dance[1]	Theatre[1]	Instrumental Music[1]	Vocal Music[1]	Series/ Festivals	Museums	Zoos and Aquariums[2]
1	4	2	3	2	10	0

Note: (1) Number of professional perfoming groups; (2) AZA-accredited
Source: The Grey House Performing Arts Directory, 2011-2012; Official Museum Directory, 2011; American Association of Museums, AAM Member Museums, April 2012; Association of Zoos & Aquariums, AZA Member Zoos & Aquariums, April 2012

Professional Sports Teams

Team Name	League
No teams are located in the metro area	

Source: Original research

CLIMATE

Average and Extreme Temperatures

Temperature	Jan	Feb	Mar	Apr	May	Jun	Jul	Aug	Sep	Oct	Nov	Dec	Yr.
Extreme High (°F)	50	48	51	65	77	85	82	82	73	61	53	48	85
Average High (°F)	22	25	33	43	55	62	65	63	55	41	28	22	43
Average Temp. (°F)	15	18	25	36	47	55	59	57	48	35	22	16	36
Average Low (°F)	8	11	17	28	39	47	51	49	41	28	15	10	29
Extreme Low (°F)	-34	-26	-24	-4	17	33	36	31	19	-5	-21	-30	-34

Note: Figures cover the years 1953-1995
Source: National Climatic Data Center, International Station Meteorological Climate Summary, 9/96

Average Precipitation/Snowfall/Humidity

Precip./Humidity	Jan	Feb	Mar	Apr	May	Jun	Jul	Aug	Sep	Oct	Nov	Dec	Yr.
Avg. Precip. (in.)	0.8	0.8	0.7	0.6	0.7	1.0	1.9	2.4	2.7	1.9	1.1	1.1	15.7
Avg. Snowfall (in.)	10	12	10	5	Tr	0	0	0	Tr	8	12	15	71
Avg. Rel. Hum. 6am (%)	74	74	72	75	73	74	80	84	84	78	78	78	77
Avg. Rel. Hum. 3pm (%)	73	67	57	54	50	55	62	64	64	67	74	76	64

Note: Figures cover the years 1953-1995; Tr = Trace amounts (<0.05 in. of rain; <0.5 in. of snow)
Source: National Climatic Data Center, International Station Meteorological Climate Summary, 9/96

Weather Conditions

Temperature			Daytime Sky			Precipitation		
0°F & below	32°F & below	65°F & above	Clear	Partly cloudy	Cloudy	0.01 inch or more precip.	0.1 inch or more snow/ice	Thunder-storms
32	194	41	50	115	200	113	49	2

Note: Figures are average number of days per year and cover the years 1953-1995
Source: National Climatic Data Center, International Station Meteorological Climate Summary, 9/96

HAZARDOUS WASTE

Superfund Sites

Anchorage has two hazardous waste sites on the EPA's Superfund Final National Priorities List: **Fort Richardson (USARMY)**; **Elmendorf Air Force Base**. *U.S. Environmental Protection Agency, Final National Priorities List, April 17, 2012*

AIR & WATER QUALITY

Air Quality Index

Area	Percent of Days when Air Quality was...[2]					AQI Statistics[2]	
	Good	Moderate	Unhealthy for Sensitive Groups	Unhealthy	Very Unhealthy	Maximum	Median
Area[1]	89.6	10.4	0.0	0.0	0.0	88	25

Note: Air Quality Index (AQI) is an index for reporting daily air quality. EPA calculates the AQI for five major air pollutants regulated by the Clean Air Act: ground-level ozone, particle pollution (aka particulate matter), carbon monoxide, sulfur dioxide, and nitrogen dioxide. The AQI runs from 0 to 500. The higher the AQI value, the greater the level of air pollution and the greater the health concern. There are six AQI categories: "Good" AQI is between 0 and 50. Air quality is considered satisfactory; "Moderate" AQI is between 51 and 100. Air quality is acceptable; "Unhealthy for Sensitive Groups" When AQI values are between 101 and 150, members of sensitive groups may experience health effects; "Unhealthy" When AQI values are between 151 and 200 everyone may begin to experience health effects; "Very Unhealthy" AQI values between 201 and 300 trigger a health alert; "Hazardous" AQI values over 300 trigger warnings of emergency conditions (not shown); (1) Data covers Anchorage Municipality; (2) Based on 365 days with AQI data in 2011.
Source: U.S. Environmental Protection Agency, AirData Report, 2011

Air Quality Index Pollutants

Area	Percent of Days when AQI Pollutant was...[2]					
	Carbon Monoxide	Nitrogen Dioxide	Ozone	Sulfur Dioxide	Particulate Matter 2.5	Particulate Matter 10
Area[1]	7.1	0.0	38.6	0.0	28.8	25.5

Note: The Air Quality Index (AQI) is an index for reporting daily air quality. EPA calculates the AQI for five major air pollutants regulated by the Clean Air Act: ground-level ozone, particle pollution (also known as particulate matter), carbon monoxide, sulfur dioxide, and nitrogen dioxide. The AQI runs from 0 to 500. The higher the AQI value, the greater the level of air pollution and the greater the health concern; (1) Data covers Anchorage Municipality; (2) Based on 365 days with AQI data in 2011.
Source: U.S. Environmental Protection Agency, AirData Report, 2011

Air Quality Index Trends

Area	Trend Sites (days)								All Sites (days)
	2003	2004	2005	2006	2007	2008	2009	2010	2010
MSA[1]	n/a	n/a	n/a	n/a	n/a	n/a	n/a	n/a	n/a

Note: Figures are the number of days the AQI value exceeded 100 in a given year. An AQI value greater than 100 indicates that air quality would have been in the unhealthful range on that day. Data from exceptional events are included. These counts are presented in two ways. First, the counts are based on sites having an adequate record of monitoring data during the trend period (trend sites). These counts represent the relative change in the number of days with AQI values greater than 100. In the last column, the counts are based on all sites with data in the most recent year (because it is possible for a site to have data in the most recent year but not enough data to be a trend site); (1) Data covers the Anchorage, AK—see Appendix B for areas included; n/a not available.
Source: U.S. Environmental Protection Agency, Air Quality Index Information, "Number of Days with Air Quality Index Values Greater than 100 at Trend Sites, 2000-2010, and at All Sites in 2010"

Maximum Air Pollutant Concentrations: Particulate Matter, Ozone, CO and Lead

	Particulate Matter 10 (ug/m^3)	Particulate Matter 2.5 Wtd AM (ug/m^3)	Particulate Matter 2.5 24-Hr (ug/m^3)	Ozone (ppm)	Carbon Monoxide (ppm)	Lead (ug/m^3)
MSA[1] Level	98	5.5	38	0.045	6	n/a
NAAQS[2]	150	15	35	0.075	9	0.15
Met NAAQS[2]	Yes	Yes	No	Yes	Yes	n/a

Note: Data from exceptional events are not included; (1) Data covers the Anchorage, AK—see Appendix B for areas included; (2) National Ambient Air Quality Standards; ppm = parts per million; ug/m^3 = micrograms per cubic meter; n/a not available
Concentrations: Particulate Matter 10 (coarse particulate)—highest second maximum 24-hour concentration; Particulate Matter 2.5 Wtd AM (fine particulate)—highest weighted annual mean concentration; Particulate Matter 2.5 24-Hour (fine particulate)—highest 98th percentile 24-hour concentration; Ozone—highest fourth daily maximum 8-hour concentration; Carbon Monoxide—highest second maximum non-overlapping 8-hour concentration; Lead—maximum running 3-month average
Source: U.S. Environmental Protection Agency, CBSA Factbook 2010, Air Quality Statistics by City, 2010

Maximum Air Pollutant Concentrations: Nitrogen Dioxide and Sulfur Dioxide

	Nitrogen Dioxide AM (ppb)	Nitrogen Dioxide 1-Hr (ppb)	Sulfur Dioxide AM (ppb)	Sulfur Dioxide 1-Hr (ppb)	Sulfur Dioxide 24-Hr (ppb)
MSA[1] Level	n/a	n/a	n/a	n/a	n/a
NAAQS[2]	53	100	30	75	140
Met NAAQS[2]	n/a	n/a	n/a	n/a	n/a

Note: Data from exceptional events are not included; (1) Data covers the Anchorage, AK—see Appendix B for areas included; (2) National Ambient Air Quality Standards; ppb = parts per billion; n/a not available

Concentrations: Nitrogen Dioxide AM—highest arithmetic mean concentration; Nitrogen Dioxide 1-Hr—highest 98th percentile 1-hour daily maximum concentration; Sulfur Dioxide AM—highest annual mean concentration; Sulfur Dioxide 1-Hr—highest 99th percentile 1-hour daily maximum concentration; Sulfur Dioxide 24-Hr—highest second maximum 24-hour concentration

Source: U.S. Environmental Protection Agency, CBSA Factbook 2010, Air Quality Statistics by City, 2010

Drinking Water

Water System Name	Pop. Served	Primary Water Source Type	Violations[1]	
			Health Based	Monitoring/ Reporting
MOA Municipality of Anchorage	221,351	Surface	0	0

Note: (1) Based on violation data from January 1, 2011 to December 31, 2011 (includes unresolved violations from earlier years)

Source: U.S. Environmental Protection Agency, Office of Ground Water and Drinking Water, Safe Drinking Water Information System (based on data extracted April 18, 2012)

Bellevue, Washington

Background

Bellevue, Washington, is situated in a postcard-perfect site between Lake Washington and Lake Sammamish, west of the Cascade Mountains and east of the Olympics. To its south is Mt. Rainier, and to the north, Mt. Baker, marking the Canadian border. Linked by bridges to the charms and resources of Seattle, two miles away, Bellevue is both an elegant suburban community and a thriving high-tech business site, well known for the production of cutting-edge systems and products.

Bellevue enjoys the benefits of a highly trained, increasingly diverse workforce. In 2009, the state's highest proportion of foreign-born residents lived in Bellevue. The city is also the second-largest city in King County, and is included in the Seattle-Tacoma-Bellevue Metropolitan Statistical Area (MSA).

Bellevue was founded in 1869 by William Meydenbauer, but not incorporated as a city until 1953. Growth was slow until 1941, when the Floating Bridge first directly linked Bellevue to Seattle. In 1963, a second bridge to Seattle, the Evergreen Point Floating Bridge, was constructed, and Bellevue took its modern shape.

A thriving community, the city experienced considerable economic growth well above the U.S. average in recent decades. Among its high-tech corporate citizens is Microsoft, which is headquartered next-door in Redmond but has offices in Bellevue. Retailer Eddie Bauer is headquartered here.

The city has worked with regional transit authorities to improve transportation in the eastern Puget Sound corridor. After upgrading downtown access with new highway ramps and facilitating commuters with a Rider Services Building—replete with bike racks—Bellevue is among the regional partners now tackling light rail. Sound Transit plans to extend light rail service into Bellevue and Redmond via the East Link. Construction is slated to start in 2015.

Although the park-filled city is located next door to Seattle, it offers much within its own borders. Bellevue's Meydenbauer Center is the hub of an active and varied arts community. In addition to its function as a convention center, the Meydenbauer annually hosts a wide array of regional, national, and local performing arts groups, including the Bellevue Philharmonic Orchestra, Bellevue Opera, the Bellevue Chamber Chorus, and the Bellevue Civic Theater. The Bellevue Arts Museum, designed by architect Steven Holl, was extensively renovated in 2005 and features works by regional artists. Also in Bellevue are the Rosalie Whyel Museum of Doll Art, the Bellevue Botanical Garden, many private art galleries, publicly sited artworks, and an annual Jazz Festival.

Retail includes Neiman Marcus among the city's numerous upscale shopping options.

Institutions of higher education in the city and environs include Bellevue College (formerly Bellevue Community College), City University of Seattle, Lake Washington Technical College, the University of Washington at Bothell, and Cascadia Community College. The Bellevue Public Schools are widely recognized for achievement.

Bellevue's climate is best described as marine—mild and moist. The Pacific Ocean governs weather year-round, and in addition the city is protected from the extremes of continental weather by the Cascade Mountains to the east. Most rain falls between October and April, but not in the huge amounts for which the Northwest is famous elsewhere. In summer, weather is drier and sunnier, but not hot.

Rankings

General Rankings

- The Seattle metro area was identified as one of the 10 most popular big cities by Pew Research Center. The results are based on a telephone survey of 2,260 adults conducted during October 2008. The report explored a range of attitudes related to where Americans live, where they would like to live, and why. *Pew Research Center, "For Nearly Half of America, Grass is Greener Somewhere Else," January 29, 2009*
- Bellevue appeared on RelocateAmerica's list of best places to live in America. The annual "Top 100 Places to Live" list recognizes the top communities as nominated by their residents & local businesses. RelocateAmerica's Research Group determines the list based on review of various data gathered for economic, employment, housing, education, industry, opportunity, environment and recreation along with feedback from area leaders and residents. *RelocateAmerica.com, "Top 100 Places to Live for 2011"*
- Bellevue was selected as one of the "Best Places to Live in America" by *Money* magazine. The city ranked #4 out of 100. This year's list focused on cities with populations of 50,000 to 300,000. Criteria: job opportunities; economic strength; top-notch schools; low crime; good health care; recreation; and many other factors that help make a town great for raising a family. *CNNMoney.com, "Best Places to Live in America 2010," August 2010*

Business/Finance Rankings

- The Seattle metro area was identified as one of 10 places with the fastest-growing wages in America. The area ranked #5. Criteria: private-sector wage growth between the 4th quarter of 2010 and the 4th quarter of 2011. *PayScale, "The 10 Cities with the Fastest-Growing Wages in America," January 12, 2012*
- Experian ranked the top 20 major U.S. metropolitan areas by average debt per consumer. The Seattle metro area was ranked #1. Criteria: average debt per consumer. Debt for this study includes credit cards, auto loans and personal loans. It does not include mortgages. *Experian, May 13, 2010*
- Bellevue was selected as one of the "100 Best Places to Live and Launch" in the U.S. The city ranked #1. The editors at *Fortune Small Business* ranked 296 Census-designated metro areas by business friendliness (Launching Score, % New Businesses) and lifestyle offerings (Living Score). Then they picked the town within each of the top 100 metro areas that best blends business and pleasure. *Fortune Small Business, "100 Best Places to Live and Launch 2008," April 2008*
- *American City Business Journals* ranked America's 261 largest cities in terms of their resident's wealth. Bellevue ranked #13. Criteria: per capita income; median household income; percentage of households with annual incomes of $200,000 or more; median home value. *American City Business Journals, "Where the Money Is: America's Wealth Centers," August 18, 2008*
- The Seattle metro area appeared on the Milken Institute "2011 Best Performing Metros" list. Rank: #27 out of 200 large metro areas. Criteria: job growth; wage and salary growth; high-tech output growth. *Milken Institute, "2011 Best Performing Metros"*
- The Seattle metro area is projected to be one the best performing housing markets in 2012. The metro area ranked #6 out of 10. Criteria: forecast home price gains by September 2012. *CNNMoney.com, "Housing Markets: Best Recovery Bets," 2011*
- The Seattle metro area was selected as one of the best cities for entrepreneurs in America by *Inc. Magazine.* Criteria: job-growth data for 335 metro areas was analyzed for: recent growth trend; mid-term growth; long-term trend; current year growth. The Seattle metro area ranked #10 among large metro areas and #54 overall. *Inc. Magazine, "The Best Cities for Doing Business," July 2008*
- Seattle was ranked #7 out of 145 regions worldwide in terms of its "Knowledge Competitiveness Index." The index attempts to measure the knowledge-based development taking place throughout the world and is based on 19 measures of economic performance that indicate a region's ability to translate its knowledge capacity into economic value. *Centre for International Competitiveness, World Knowledge Competitiveness Index 2008*

- *Forbes* ranked the 200 most populous metro areas in the U.S. in terms of the "Best Places for Business and Careers." The Seattle metro area was ranked #13. Criteria: costs (business and living); job growth (past and projected); income growth; educational attainment; projected economic growth; crime; cultural and recreational opportunities; net migration patterns; number of highly ranked colleges. *Forbes, "Best Places for Business and Careers," June 2011*

Children/Family Rankings

- The Seattle metro area was selected as one of the "Best Cities for Relocating Families" by Worldwide ERC and Primacy Relocation. The 2008 study looked at nearly 50 factors important to relocating families including: recent job growth; nearby top-ranked colleges; in-state tuition for four-year public colleges; population growth since 2000; pediatricians per 100,000 population; and a Green Living index. *Worldwide ERC and Primacy Relocation, "2008 Best Cities for Relocating Families"*

- Bellevue was chosen as one of America's "100 Best Communities for Young People." The winners were selected based upon detailed information provided about each community's efforts to fulfill five essential promises critical to the well-being of young people: caring adults who are actively involved in their lives; safe places in which to learn and grow; a healthy start toward adulthood; an effective education that builds marketable skills; and opportunities to help others. *America's Promise Alliance, "100 Best Communities for Young People, 2010"*

Dating/Romance Rankings

- Eli Lily and Company, in partnership with Sperling's BestPlaces, ranked the nation's 50 largest metro areas in terms of the "Most Romantic Cities for Baby Boomers." The Seattle metro area ranked #30. Criteria: marriage and divorce rates among baby boomers age 45 to 60; great restaurants; dance studios; chocolate, jewelry and flower sales. *Eli Lily and Company, "Most Romantic Cities for Baby Boomers," April 20, 2007*

- The Seattle metro area was selected as one of the "Best Cities for Relocating Singles" by Worldwide ERC and Primacy Relocation. The area ranked #36 out of the 100 largest metro areas in the U.S. Criteria: recent job growth; recent singles population growth; overall population growth; affordable rental housing; cost-of-living index; expanded arts and recreation opportunities; ratio of single men and single women; affordability of quality higher education (including state residency requirements); diversity index; climate; population density. *Worldwide ERC and Primacy Relocation, "2008 Best Cities for Relocating Singles"*

- *Forbes* ranked the 40 most populous urbanized areas in the U.S. in terms of the "Best Cities for Singles." The Seattle metro area ranked #4. Criteria: number of singles; cost of living alone; nightlife; culture; job growth; coolness; and online dating participation. *Forbes.com, "Best Cities for Singles," July 27, 2009*

Education Rankings

- Bellevue was identified as one of America's smartest cities by *The Business Journals On Numbers*. The city ranked #9 in the large city category (population 100,000 or more). Each city's score was based on its percentage of adults (25 or older) at each of the following rungs: dropped out before high school graduation; stopped at high school diploma; stopped at associate degree or attended college but stopped without any degree; stopped at bachelor's degree; earned graduate degree and/or professional degree. The point value of a specific rung was determined by the relative earning power of people at that level. *The Business Journals On Numbers, "Brainpower Ratings," November 17, 2011*

- Bellevue was selected as one of the most well-read cities in America by *Amazon.com*. The city ranked #15 of 20. Cities with populations greater than 100,000 were evaluated based on per capita sales of books, magazines and newspapers. *Amazon.com, "Top 20 Most Well-Read Cities in America," June 4, 2011*

- Bellevue was selected as one of "America's Geekiest Cities" by *Forbes.com*. The city ranked #10 of 20. Criteria: percentage of workers with jobs in science, technology, engineering and mathematics. *Forbes.com, "America's Geekiest Cities," August 5, 2011*

- Seattle was identified as one of the 100 "smartest" metro areas in the U.S. The area ranked #9. Criteria: the editors rated the collective brainpower of the 100 largest metro areas in the U.S. based on their residents' educational attainment. *American City Business Journals, April 14, 2008*
- Seattle was identified as one of "America's Smartest Cities" by *The Daily Beast.* The metro area ranked #6 out of 55. The editors ranked metropolitan areas with one million or more residents on the following criteria: percentage of residents over age 25 with bachelor's or graduate degrees; non-fiction book sales; ratio of institutions of higher education; libraries per capita. *The Daily Beast, "America's Smartest Cities," October 24, 2010*
- Seattle was identified as one of "America's Brainiest Bastions" by *Portfolio.com.* The metro area ranked #16 out of 200. *Portfolio.com* analyzed levels of educational attainment in the nation's 200 largest metropolitan areas. The editors established scores for five levels of educational attainment, based on relative earning power of adult workers age 25 or older. Scores were determined by comparing the median income for all workers with the median income for those workers at a specified educational level. *Portfolio.com, "America's Brainiest Bastions," December 1, 2010*
- Seattle was identified as one of "America's Smartest Cities" by *CNNMoney.com.* The area ranked #9. Criteria: percentage of residents with bachelors or graduate degrees. *CNNMoney.com, "America's Smartest Cities," October 1, 2010*

Environmental Rankings

- The Seattle was identified as one of North America's greenest metropolitan areas. The area ranked #4. The Green City Index is comprised of 31 indicators, and scores cities across nine categories: carbon dioxide; energy; land use; buildings; transport; water; waste; air quality; environmental governance. The 27 largest metropolitan areas in the U.S. and Canada were considered. *Economist Intelligence Unit, sponsored by Siemens, "U.S. and Canada Green City Index, 2011"*
- The Seattle was identified as one of America's cities with the most ENERGY STAR certified buildings. The area ranked #16 out of 25. Criteria: number of ENERGY STAR labeled buildings in 2010. *U.S. Environmental Protection Agency, "Top Cities With the Most ENERGY STAR Certified Buildings," March 15, 2011*
- Bellevue was selected as one of 22 "Smarter Cities" for energy by the Natural Resources Defense Council. Criteria: investment in green power; energy efficiency measures; conservation. *Natural Resources Defense Council, "2010 Smarter Cities," July 19, 2010*
- *American City Business Journal* ranked 43 metropolitan areas in terms of their "greenness." The Seattle metro area ranked #6. Criteria: Forty-one metros in which *ACBJ* has business weeklies, plus Indianapolis and Cleveland, were ranked based on 20 different indicators such as adoption of green technologies, utilization of environmentally sound practices, and air and water quality. *American City Business Journals, "Green City Index," March 11, 2010*
- 100 of the largest metro areas in the U.S. were analyzed in terms of their current drought severity. The Seattle metro area ranked #66 (#1 = driest). The rankings were based on statistics such as long-term precipitation trends and patterns and the Palmer drought indices. *Sperling's BestPlaces, www.BestPlaces.net, "America's Drought-Riskiest Cities," November 2007*
- The Seattle metro area appeared in *Country Home's* "Best Green Places" report. The area ranked #13 out of 379. Criteria: official energy policies; green power; green buildings; availability of fresh, locally grown food. *Country Home, "Best Green Places," 2008*
- Seattle was highlighted as one of the 25 metro areas most polluted by short-term particle pollution (24-hour PM 2.5) in the U.S. The area ranked #18. *American Lung Association, State of the Air 2011*

Food/Drink Rankings

- The Seattle metro area was selected as one of the best cities for "foodies" in America by Sperling's BestPlaces. The metro area ranked #8 out of 10. A "foodie" is defined as a person whose hobby is food—not just eating it, but also learning about its origins and preparation. Criteria: ratio of local restaurants to chain restaurants; number of local and accessible CSA (Community Supported Agriculture) and farmers markets; number of Whole Foods stores; number of cookware stores; number of craft breweries, brew pubs, wine shops, and wine bars. *Sperling's BestPlaces, www.BestPlaces.net, "America's Best Cities for Foodies," January 2011*

Health/Fitness Rankings

- The Seattle metro area was selected as one of the worst cities for bed bugs in America by Rollins corporation, the owner of seven pest control companies, including Orkin. The area ranked #27 based on the number of bed bug treatments from January to December 2011. *Rollins, "The Top 50 U.S. Cities for Bed Bugs," March 19, 2012*
- Seattle was identified as a "2011 Asthma Capital." The area ranked #90 out of the nation's 100 largest metropolitan areas. Twelve factors were used to identify the most challenging places to live for people with asthma: estimated prevalence; self-reported prevalence; crude death rate for asthma; annual pollen score; annual air quality; public smoking laws; number of board-certified asthma specialists; school inhaler access laws; rescue medication use; controller medication use; uninsured rate; poverty rate. *Asthma and Allergy Foundation of America, "2011 Asthma Capitals"*
- Seattle was identified as a "2011 Fall Allergy Capital." The area ranked #99 out of 100. Three groups of factors were used to identify the most severe cities for people with allergies during the fall season: annual pollen levels; medicine utilization; access to board-certified allergists. *Asthma and Allergy Foundation of America, "2011 Fall Allergy Capitals"*
- Seattle was identified as a "2012 Spring Allergy Capital." The area ranked #95 out of 100. Three groups of factors were used to identify the most severe cities for people with allergies during the spring season: annual pollen levels; medicine utilization; access to board-certified allergists. *Asthma and Allergy Foundation of America, "2012 Spring Allergy Capitals"*
- The Seattle metropolitan area was selected as one of the best metros for hospital care in America by *HealthGrades.com.* The rankings are based on a comprehensive study of patient death and complication rates in the nation's nearly 5,000 hospitals. Hospitals performing in the top 5% nationwide across 26 different medical procedures and diagnoses were identified. *HealthGrades.com* then ranked cities by the highest percentage of these Distinguished Hospitals for Clinical Excellence™. The Seattle metro area ranked #35. *HealthGrades.com, "America's Top 50 Cities for Hospital Care," January 21, 2012*
- The American Academy of Dermatology ranked 26 U.S. metropolitan regions in terms of their residents knowledge, attitude and behaviors towards tanning, sun protection and skin cancer detection. The Seattle metro area ranked #23. The results of the study are based on an online survey of over 7,000 adults nationwide. *American Academy of Dermatology, "Suntelligence: How Sun Smart is Your City," May 3, 2010*
- The Seattle metro area appeared in the 2011 Gallup-Healthways Well-Being Index. The index, based on interviews with more than 350,000 Americans, measured jobs, finances, physical health, emotional state of mind and communities. The metro area ranked #44 out of 190. Criteria: life evaluation; emotional health; work environment; physical health; healthy behaviors; basic access (basic needs optimal for a healthy life, such as access to food and medicine, having health insurance and feeling safe while walking at night). *Gallup-Healthways, "State of Well-Being 2011"*
- The Seattle metro area was identified as one of "America's Most Stressful Cities" by *Sperling's BestPlaces.* The metro area ranked #9 out of 50. Criteria: unemployment rate; suicide rate; commute time; mental health; poor rest; alcohol use; violent crime rate; property crime rate; cloudy days annually. *Sperling's BestPlaces, www.BestPlaces.net, "Stressful Cities 2012*
- The Seattle metro area was identified as one of "America's Most Stressful Cities" by *Forbes.* The metro area ranked #10 out of 40. Criteria: housing affordability; unemployment rate; cost of living; air quality; traffic congestion; sunny days; population density. *Forbes.com, "America's Most Stressful Cities," September 23, 2011*

- 50 of the largest metro areas in the U.S. were analyzed in terms of their health and fitness by the American College of Sports Medicine in their "American Fitness Index." The Seattle metro area ranked #4 (#1 = healthiest). Criteria: preventative health behaviors; levels of chronic disease; health care access; community resources and policies that support physical activity. *American College of Sports Medicine, "Health and Community Fitness Status of the 50 Largest Metropolitan Areas," August 1, 2011*

- The Seattle metro area was selected as one of "America's Most Relaxed Cities" by *Forbes.* The metro area ranked #7 out of 10. Criteria: unemployment rates; numbers of commuters that spend an hour or more in traffic on the way to work; average weekly hours people spend at work; access to health care; overall health of residents; percentage of population who exercise. *Forbes, "America's Most Relaxed Cities," November 5, 2010*

Pet Rankings

- Seattle was selected as one of the "Top 10 Cat-Friendly Cities" in the U.S. The area ranked #7. Criteria: cat ownership per capita; level of veterinary care; microchipping; cat-friendly local ordinances. *CATalyst Council, "Top 10 Cat-Friendly Cities," March 27, 2009*

Real Estate Rankings

- *Fortune* ranked the 100 largest metro areas in the U.S. in terms of projected median home price change in 2010. The Seattle metro area ranked #27. *Fortune, "The 2010 Housing Outlook," December 9, 2009*

- The Seattle metro area was identified as one of the 20 least affordable housing markets in the U.S. in 2011. The area ranked #20 out of 152 markets with an affordability index of 94.7%. The index measures whether or not a typical family could qualify for a mortgage loan on a typical home. The calculation used assumes a down payment of 20 percent of the home price and a qualifying ratio of 25 percent, meaning that the monthly P&I payment cannot exceed 25 percent of a the median family monthly income. *National Association of Realtors®, Affordability Index of Existing Single-Family Homes for Metropolitan Areas, 2011*

- The nation's largest metro areas were analyzed in terms of the best places to buy bank-owned properties. The Seattle metro area ranked #8 out of 10. Criteria: at least 500 REO sales during the fourth quarter and an REO sales increase of at least five percent from a year ago. The areas selected posted the biggest discounts on the sales of bank-owned properties. *RealtyTrac, "Fourth Quarter and Year-End 2011 U.S. Foreclosure Sales Report: Shifting Towards Short Sales," February 28, 2012*

- The nation's largest metro areas were analyzed in terms of the best places to buy pre-foreclosures (short sales). The Seattle metro area ranked #10 out of 10. Criteria: at least 500 pre-foreclosure sales during the fourth quarter and a short sales increase of at least five percent from a year ago. The areas selected posted the biggest discounts on the sales of pre-foreclosure properties. *RealtyTrac, "Fourth Quarter and Year-End 2011 U.S. Foreclosure Sales Report: Shifting Towards Short Sales," February 28, 2012*

- The Seattle metro area appeared in a *Wall Street Journal* article ranking cities by "housing stress." The metro area was ranked #23 (#1 = most stress). Criteria: fraction of mortgage-holding homeowners with a monthly housing payment in excess of 30 percent of income; percentage of people without health insurance; unemployment rate. *The Wall Street Journal, "Which Cities Face Biggest Housing Risk," October 5, 2010*

- The Center for Housing Policy ranked 210 U.S. metropolitan areas by the fair market rent for a two-bedroom unit. The Seattle metro area was ranked #47. (#1 = most expensive) with a rent of $1,056. Criteria: Fair Market Rent (FMR) in effect during the fourth quarter of 2009 based on HUD's fiscal year 2010 FMRs. *The Center for Housing Policy, "Paycheck to Paycheck: Most to Least Expensive Rental Markets in 2009"*

- The Seattle metro area was identified as one of the best U.S. markets to invest in rental property" by HomeVestors and Local Market Monitor. The area ranked #83 out of 100. Criteria: risk-return premium relative to national average. *HomeVestors and Local Market Monitor, "Best 100 U.S. Markets to Invest in Rental Property," March 9, 2012*

Safety Rankings

- Allstate ranked the 193 largest cities in America in terms of driver safety. Bellevue ranked #145. In addition, drivers were 24.1% more likely to have had an accident compared to the national average. Allstate researchers analyzed internal property damage reported claims over a two-year period (from January 2008 to December 2009) to protect findings from external influences such as weather or road construction. A weighted average of the two-year numbers determined the annual percentages. The report defines an auto crash as any collision resulting in a property damage claim. *Allstate, "2011 Allstate America's Best Drivers Report™"*
- Seattle was identified as one of the least disaster-proof places in the U.S. in terms of its vulnerability to natural and non-natural disasters. The city ranked #2 out of 5. Rankings are based on the U.S. Center for Disease Control's Cities Readiness Initiative (CRI). As part of the CRI, the CDC and state public health personnel assess local emergency-management plans, protocols and capabilities for 72 Metropolitan Statistical Areas and four non-MSA large cities. *Forbes, "America's Most and Least Disaster-Proof Cities," December 12, 2011*
- The National Insurance Crime Bureau ranked 366 metro areas in the U.S. in terms of per capita rates of vehicle theft. The Seattle metro area ranked #13 (#1 = highest rate). Criteria: number of vehicle theft offenses per 100,000 inhabitants in 2010. *National Insurance Crime Bureau, "Hot Spots," June 21, 2011*
- The Seattle metro area was identified as one of the most dangerous metro areas for pedestrians by Transportation for America. The metro area ranked #46 out of 52 metro areas with over 1 million residents. Criteria: area's population divided by the number of pedestrian fatalities in that area. *Transportation for America, "Dangerous by Design 2011"*

Seniors/Retirement Rankings

- Bankers Life and Casualty Company, in partnership with Sperling's BestPlaces, ranked the nation's 50 largest metro areas in terms of the "Best U.S. Cities for Seniors." The Seattle metro area ranked #19. Criteria: healthcare; transportation; housing; environment; economy; health and longevity; social and spiritual life; crime. *Bankers Life and Casualty Company, Center for a Secure Retirement, "Best U.S. Cities for Seniors 2011," September 2011*

Sports/Recreation Rankings

- Scarborough Sports Marketing, a leading market research firm, identified the Seattle DMA (Designated Market Area) as one of the top markets for Summer Olympics fans with more than 65% of adults reporting that they are "very, somewhat, or a little bit interested" in the Summer Olympics. *Scarborough Sports Marketing, July 30, 2008*
- The Seattle was selected as one of the best metro areas for golf in America by *Golf Digest*. The Seattle area was ranked #6 out of 20. Criteria: climate; cost of public golf; quality of public golf; accessibility. *Golf Digest, "The Top 20 Cities for Golf," October 2011*
- *Golf.com* and the research arm of the National Golf Foundation analyzed the 50 largest metropolitan areas in the U.S. in terms of golf. The Seattle metro area ranked #6. Criteria: weather; affordability; quality of courses; accessibility; number of courses designed by esteemed architects; availability; crowdedness. *Golf.com, November 15, 2007*

Technology Rankings

- The Seattle metro area was selected as one of "America's Most Wired Cities" by *Forbes*. The metro area was ranked #3 out of 20. Criteria: percentage of Internet users with high-speed access; number of companies providing high-speed Internet; number of public wireless hot spots. *Forbes, "America's Most Wired Cities," March 2, 2010*
- The Seattle metro area was selected as one of "America's Most Innovative Cities" by *Forbes*. The metro area was ranked #5 out of 20. Criteria: patents per capita; venture capital investment per capita; ratio of high-tech, science and "creative" jobs. *Forbes, "America's Most Innovative Cities," May 24, 2010*

- The Seattle metro area was identified as one of the "Top 14 Nano Metros" in the U.S. by the Project on Emerging Nanotechnologies. The metro area is home to 25 companies, universities, government laboratories and/or organizations working in nanotechnology. *Project on Emerging Nanotechnologies, "Nano Metros 2009"*

Transportation Rankings

- The Seattle metro area was identified as one of the best U.S. cities to live in without a car by *24/7 Wall St.* The area ranked #5 out of 10. Criteria: percentage of neighborhoods covered by public transit; frequency of service for those neighborhoods; share of jobs reachable within 90 minutes or less by public transit; how accessible amenities are for residents on foot; percentage of commuters who bike to work. The 100 largest metropolitan areas in the U.S. were examined. *24/7 Wall St., "The Best Cities to Live in Car-Free," November 28, 2011*
- The Seattle metro area appeared on *Forbes* list of the best and worst cities for commuters. The metro area ranked #28 out of 60 (#1 is best). Criteria: travel time; road congestion; travel delays. *Forbes.com, "Best and Worst Cities for Commuters," February 16, 2010*

Women/Minorities Rankings

- Seattle was ranked #10 out of 100 metro areas in *SELF Magazine's* ranking of America's healthiest places for women." A panel of experts came up with more than 50 criteria including death and disease rates, environmental indicators, community resources, and lifestyle habits. *SELF Magazine, "Secrets of America's Healthiest Women," December 2008*
- The Seattle metro area appeared on *Forbes'* list of the "Best Cities for Minority Entrepreneurs." The area ranked #10 out of 10. Criteria: 52 metropolitan statistical areas were examined. For each ethnicity (African Americans, Asians and Hispanics), the editors measured housing affordability, population growth, income growth, and entrepreneurship (per capita self-employment). *Forbes, "Best Cities for Minority Entrepreneurs," March 23, 2011*

Miscellaneous Rankings

- The Seattle metro area was selected as one of "5 Great Cities for Young Adults" by *Kiplinger.com.* Criteria: high starting salaries for college graduates; cost of living near or below national average; affordable monthly rent; percentage of residents ages 20 to 29 near or above national average. *Kiplinger.com, "5 Great Cities for Young Adults," October 25, 2011*
- Energizer Holdings, the makers of Edge® shave gel, in partnership with Sperling's BestPlaces, ranked 50 major metro areas in terms of everyday irritations. The Seattle metro area ranked #35. Criteria: humidity levels; weather conditions; incidence of traffic delays and congestion; average commute times; frequency of flight delays and cancellations; rates of sleeplessness; underemployment; pollens and allergens; pests; comedy clubs per capita. *Energizer Holdings, "Most Irritation Prone Cities," July 23, 2010*
- Mars Chocolate North America, the makers of COMBOS®, in partnership with Sperling's BestPlaces, ranked 50 major metro areas in terms of their "manliness." The Seattle metro area ranked #41. Criteria: number of professional sports teams; number of nearby NASCAR tracks and racing events; manly lifestyle; concentration of manly retail stores; manly occupations per capita; salty snack sales; "Board of Manliness" rankings. *Mars Chocolate North America, "America's Manliest Cities 2011," September 1, 2011*
- The Seattle metro area was selected as one of "America's Greediest Cities" by *Forbes*. The area was ranked #3 out of 10. Criteria: number of Forbes 400 (*Forbes* annual list of the richest Americans) members per capita. *Forbes, "America's Greediest Cities," December 7, 2007*
- Scarborough Research, a leading market research firm, identified the top local markets for volunteers in the U.S. The Seattle DMA (Designated Market Area) ranked in the top 10 with 31% of adults 18+ reporting that they have participated in volunteer work in the past 12 months. *Scarborough Research, December 13, 2011*

Business Environment

CITY FINANCES

City Government Finances

Component	2009 ($000)	2009 ($ per capita)
Total Revenues	305,924	2,521
Total Expenditures	284,539	2,345
Debt Outstanding	178,379	1,470
Cash and Securities[1]	179,988	1,483

Note: (1) Cash and security holdings of a government at the close of its fiscal year, including those of its dependent agencies, utilities, and liquor stores.
Source: U.S Census Bureau, State & Local Government Finances 2009

City Government Revenue by Source

Source	2009 ($000)	2009 ($ per capita)
General Revenue		
From Federal Government	1,144	9
From State Government	10,952	90
From Local Governments	19,575	161
Taxes		
Property	28,815	237
Sales and Gross Receipts	84,699	698
Personal Income	0	0
Corporate Income	0	0
Motor Vehicle License	0	0
Other Taxes	44,966	371
Current Charges	68,095	561
Liquor Store	0	0
Utility	33,805	279
Employee Retirement	0	0

Source: U.S Census Bureau, State & Local Government Finances 2009

City Government Expenditures by Function

Function	2009 ($000)	2009 ($ per capita)	2009 (%)
General Direct Expenditures			
Air Transportation	0	0	0.0
Corrections	1,727	14	0.6
Education	0	0	0.0
Employment Security Administration	0	0	0.0
Financial Administration	26,734	220	9.4
Fire Protection	15,743	130	5.5
General Public Buildings	4,304	35	1.5
Governmental Administration, Other	8,751	72	3.1
Health	14,593	120	5.1
Highways	30,662	253	10.8
Hospitals	0	0	0.0
Housing and Community Development	13,810	114	4.9
Interest on General Debt	7,927	65	2.8
Judicial and Legal	2,953	24	1.0
Libraries	0	0	0.0
Parking	0	0	0.0
Parks and Recreation	35,496	293	12.5
Police Protection	25,635	211	9.0
Public Welfare	108	1	0.0
Sewerage	33,840	279	11.9
Solid Waste Management	1,301	11	0.5
Veterans' Services	0	0	0.0
Liquor Store	0	0	0.0
Utility	28,281	233	9.9
Employee Retirement	0	0	0.0

Source: U.S Census Bureau, State & Local Government Finances 2009

Municipal Bond Ratings

Area	Moody's	S&P	Fitch
City	Aaa	AAA	n/a

Rating Systems (shown in declining order of credit quality): Moody's– Aaa, Aa, A, Baa, Ba, B, Caa, Ca, C (numerical modifiers 1, 2, and 3 are added to letter-rating); S&P– AAA, AA, A, BBB, BB, B, CCC, CC, C; Fitch– AAA, AA, A, BBB, BB, B, CCC, CC, C. Ratings may be modified by the addition of a plus or minus sign to show relative standing within the major rating categories.
Notes: n/a Not Available; w/d Withdrawn (1) Not Reviewed; (2) Issuer Rating/No General Obligation; (3) Standard and Poor's Issue Credit Rating (ICR) is a current opinion of an obliger with respect to a specific financial obligation, a specific class of financial obligations, or a specific financial program.
Source: City of Bellevue, Washington, Comprehensive Annual Financial Report, Fiscal Year Ended December 31, 2009

DEMOGRAPHICS

Population Growth

Area	1990 Census	2000 Census	2010 Census	Population Growth (%) 1990-2000	Population Growth (%) 2000-2010
City	99,057	109,569	122,363	10.6	11.7
MSA[1]	2,559,164	3,043,878	3,439,809	18.9	13.0
U.S.	248,709,873	281,421,906	308,745,538	13.2	9.7

Note: (1) Figures cover the Seattle-Tacoma-Bellevue, WA Metropolitan Statistical Area—see Appendix B for areas included
Source: U.S. Census Bureau, 2010 Census

Household Size

Area	Persons in Household (%) One	Two	Three	Four	Five	Six	Seven or More	Average Household Size
City	28.1	34.8	16.4	13.7	4.7	1.6	0.8	2.41
MSA[1]	28.4	33.2	15.9	13.3	5.5	2.2	1.5	2.49
U.S.	26.7	32.8	16.1	13.4	6.5	2.6	1.9	2.58

Note: (1) Figures cover the Seattle-Tacoma-Bellevue, WA Metropolitan Statistical Area—see Appendix B for areas included
Source: U.S. Census Bureau, 2010 Census

Race

Area	White Alone[2] (%)	Black Alone[2] (%)	Asian Alone[2] (%)	AIAN[3] Alone[2] (%)	NHOPI[4] Alone[2] (%)	Other Race Alone[2] (%)	Two or More Races (%)
City	62.6	2.3	27.6	0.4	0.2	3.1	3.9
MSA[1]	71.9	5.6	11.4	1.1	0.8	3.8	5.3
U.S.	72.4	12.6	4.8	0.9	0.2	6.2	2.9

Note: (1) Figures cover the Seattle-Tacoma-Bellevue, WA Metropolitan Statistical Area—see Appendix B for areas included; (2) Alone is defined as not being in combination with one or more other races; (3) American Indian and Alaska Native; (4) Native Hawaiian and Other Pacific Islander
Source: U.S. Census Bureau, 2010 Census

Hispanic or Latino Origin

Area	Hispanic or Latino (%)	Mexican (%)	Puerto Rican (%)	Cuban (%)	Other Hispanic or Latino (%)
City	7.0	4.7	0.2	0.1	2.0
MSA[1]	9.0	6.4	0.5	0.1	2.0
U.S.	16.3	10.3	1.5	0.6	4.0

Note: Persons of Hispanic or Latino origin can be of any race; (1) Figures cover the Seattle-Tacoma-Bellevue, WA Metropolitan Statistical Area—see Appendix B for areas included
Source: U.S. Census Bureau, 2010 Census

Segregation

Type	Segregation Indices[1]				Percent Change		
	1990	2000	2010	2010 Rank[2]	1990-2000	1990-2010	2000-2010
Black/White	56.5	52.4	49.1	72	-4.1	-7.4	-3.3
Asian/White	36.8	37.6	37.6	69	0.8	0.8	0.0
Hispanic/White	22.3	30.4	32.8	87	8.1	10.5	2.4

Note: Figures are based on an analysis of 1990, 2000, and 2010 Census Decennial Census tract data by William H. Frey, Brookings Institution and the University of Michigan Social Science Data Analysis Network. In this analysis all racial groups (whites, blacks, and asians) are non-Hispanic members of those races. Hispanics are shown as a separate category; All figures cover the Metropolitan Statistical Area (see Appendix B for areas included); (1) Segregation Indices are Dissimilarity Indices that measure the degree to which the minority group is distributed differently than whites across census tracts. They range from 0 (complete integration) to 100 (complete segregation) where the value indicates the percentage of the minority group that needs to move to be distributed exactly like whites; (2) Ranges from 1 (most segregated) to 102 (least segregated); n/a not available.
Source: www.CensusScope.org

Ancestry

Area	German	Irish	English	American	Italian	Polish	French[2]	Scottish	Dutch
City	14.4	8.4	10.3	2.2	3.3	2.1	3.1	2.9	1.6
MSA[1]	18.1	11.7	11.1	3.3	3.8	2.1	3.5	3.1	2.0
U.S.	16.1	11.6	8.8	6.1	5.7	3.2	3.0	1.9	1.6

Note: Figures are the percentage of the total population reporting a particular ancestry. The nine most commonly reported ancestries in the U.S. are shown. Figures include multiple ancestries (e.g. if a person reported being Irish and Italian, they were included in both columns); (1) Figures cover the Seattle-Tacoma-Bellevue, WA Metropolitan Statistical Area—see Appendix B for areas included; (2) Excludes Basque
Source: U.S. Census Bureau, 2008-2010 American Community Survey 3-Year Estimates

Foreign-Born Population

Area	Percent of Population Born in								
	Any Foreign Country	Mexico	Asia	Europe	Carribean	South America	Central America[2]	Africa	Canada
City	33.0	2.5	21.4	4.9	0.0	1.0	0.4	0.9	1.4
MSA[1]	16.4	2.7	8.0	2.7	0.1	0.4	0.4	1.1	0.8
U.S.	12.8	3.8	3.6	1.6	1.2	0.9	1.0	0.5	0.3

Note: (1) Figures cover the Seattle-Tacoma-Bellevue, WA Metropolitan Statistical Area—see Appendix B for areas included; (2) Excludes Mexico.
Source: U.S. Census Bureau, 2008-2010 American Community Survey 3-Year Estimates

Marital Status

Area	Never Married	Now Married[2]	Separated	Widowed	Divorced
City	27.0	57.0	1.6	4.6	9.8
MSA[1]	31.6	50.5	1.7	4.5	11.8
U.S.	31.6	49.6	2.2	6.1	10.7

Note: Figures are percentages and cover the population 15 years of age and older; (1) Figures cover the Seattle-Tacoma-Bellevue, WA Metropolitan Statistical Area—see Appendix B for areas included; (2) Excludes separated
Source: U.S. Census Bureau, 2008-2010 American Community Survey 3-Year Estimates

Age

Area	Percent of Population							Median Age
	Under Age 5	Age 5 to 17	Age 18 to 34	Age 35 to 49	Age 50 to 64	Age 65 to 79	80 Years and Over	
City	5.6	15.6	24.1	22.0	18.8	9.7	4.3	38.5
MSA[1]	6.5	16.4	24.5	22.5	19.3	7.7	3.1	36.8
U.S.	6.5	17.5	23.2	20.7	19.0	9.4	3.6	37.2

Note: (1) Figures cover the Seattle-Tacoma-Bellevue, WA Metropolitan Statistical Area—see Appendix B for areas included
Source: U.S. Census Bureau, 2010 Census

Male/Female Ratio

Area	Males	Females	Males per 100 Females
City	61,330	61,033	100.5
MSA[1]	1,711,982	1,727,827	99.1
U.S.	151,781,326	156,964,212	96.7

Note: (1) Figures cover the Seattle-Tacoma-Bellevue, WA Metropolitan Statistical Area—see Appendix B for areas included
Source: U.S. Census Bureau, 2010 Census

Religious Groups

Area	Catholic	Baptist	Non-Den.	Methodist[2]	Lutheran	LDS[3]	Pente-costal	Presby-terian[4]	Muslim[5]	Judaism
MSA[1]	12.3	2.2	5.0	1.2	2.1	3.3	2.8	1.4	0.5	0.5
U.S.	19.1	9.3	4.0	4.0	2.3	2.0	1.9	1.6	0.8	0.7

Note: Figures are the number of adherents as a percentage of the total population; (1) Figures cover the Seattle-Tacoma-Bellevue, WA Metropolitan Statistical Area—see Appendix B for areas included; (2) Methodist/Pietist; (3) Latter Day Saints; (4) Reformed; (5) Figures are estimates
Source: Association of Statisticians of American Religious Bodies, 2010 U.S. Religion Census: Religious Congregations & Membership Study

ECONOMY

Gross Metropolitan Product

Area	2007	2008	2009	2010	2010 Rank[2]
MSA[1]	220.9	227.9	225.6	231.4	12

Note: Figures are in billions of dollars; (1) Figures cover the Seattle-Tacoma-Bellevue, WA Metropolitan Statistical Area—see Appendix B for areas included; (2) Rank ranges from 1 to 363
Source: The United States Conference of Mayors, "U.S. Metro Economies: GMP and Employment Forecasts," June 2011

Economic Growth

Area	2007-2009 (%)	2010 (%)	2011 (%)	Rank[2]
MSA[1]	-0.8	1.6	2.8	144
U.S.	-1.3	2.9	2.5	–

Note: Figures are real Gross Metropolitan Product growth rates and represent annual average percent change; (1) Figures cover the Seattle-Tacoma-Bellevue, WA Metropolitan Statistical Area—see Appendix B for areas included; (2) Rank ranges from 1 to 363
Source: The United States Conference of Mayors, "U.S. Metro Economies: GMP and Employment Forecasts," June 2011

Metropolitan Area Exports

Area	2005	2006	2007	2008	2009	2010	2010 Rank[2]
MSA[1]	30,676.0	46,309.2	53,893.1	46,911.2	36,942.3	35,409.6	6

Note: Figures are in millions of dollars; (1) Figures cover the Seattle-Tacoma-Bellevue, WA Metropolitan Statistical Area—see Appendix B for areas included; (2) Rank ranges from 1 to 369
Source: U.S. Department of Commerce, International Trade Administration, Office of Trade & Industry Information, Manufacturing & Services, data extracted April 2, 2012

INCOME

Income

Area	Per Capita ($)	Median Household ($)	Average Household ($)
City	45,470	81,113	107,984
MSA[1]	33,755	64,821	83,560
U.S.	26,942	51,222	70,116

Note: (1) Figures cover the Seattle-Tacoma-Bellevue, WA Metropolitan Statistical Area—see Appendix B for areas included
Source: U.S. Census Bureau, 2008-2010 American Community Survey 3-Year Estimates

Household Income Distribution

Area	Percent of Households Earning							
	Under $15,000	$15,000 -24,999	$25,000 -34,999	$35,000 -49,999	$50,000 -74,999	$75,000 -99,000	$100,000 -149,999	$150,000 and up
City	6.9	5.7	6.0	10.1	17.5	12.9	19.7	21.2
MSA[1]	9.1	7.8	8.4	12.9	18.9	14.1	16.6	12.2
U.S.	13.0	11.0	10.6	14.2	18.5	12.1	12.2	8.4

Note: (1) Figures cover the Seattle-Tacoma-Bellevue, WA Metropolitan Statistical Area—see Appendix B for areas included
Source: U.S. Census Bureau, 2008-2010 American Community Survey 3-Year Estimates

Poverty Rate

Area	All Ages	Under 18 Years Old	18 to 64 Years Old	65 Years and Over
City	5.8	4.1	6.1	6.9
MSA[1]	10.5	13.3	10.0	8.0
U.S.	14.4	20.1	13.1	9.4

Note: Figures are percentage of people whose income during the past 12 months was below the poverty level; (1) Figures cover the Seattle-Tacoma-Bellevue, WA Metropolitan Statistical Area—see Appendix B for areas included
Source: U.S. Census Bureau, 2008-2010 American Community Survey 3-Year Estimates

Personal Bankruptcy Filing Rate

Area	2006	2007	2008	2009	2010	2011
King County	1.44	1.79	2.42	3.76	4.32	4.09
U.S.	2.00	2.73	3.53	4.61	4.97	4.37

Note: Numbers are per 1,000 population and include Chapter 7 and Chapter 13 filings
Source: Federal Deposit Insurance Corporation, Regional Economic Conditions, March 9, 2012

EMPLOYMENT

Labor Force and Employment

Area	Civilian Labor Force			Workers Employed		
	Dec. 2010	Dec. 2011	% Chg.	Dec. 2010	Dec. 2011	% Chg.
City	70,579	70,735	0.2	65,672	66,650	1.5
MD[1]	1,483,979	1,492,083	0.5	1,350,324	1,383,080	2.4
U.S.	153,156,000	153,373,000	0.1	139,159,000	140,681,000	1.1

Note: Data is not seasonally adjusted and covers workers 16 years of age and older; (1) Metropolitan Division—see Appendix B for areas included
Source: Bureau of Labor Statistics, http://stats.bls.gov

Unemployment Rate

Area	2011											
	Jan.	Feb.	Mar.	Apr.	May	Jun.	Jul.	Aug.	Sep.	Oct.	Nov.	Dec.
City	7.0	7.3	7.2	6.5	6.6	7.4	7.3	6.8	6.8	6.6	6.1	5.8
MD[1]	9.3	9.3	8.8	8.1	8.3	9.0	8.7	8.0	8.2	8.1	7.7	7.3
U.S.	9.8	9.5	9.2	8.7	8.7	9.3	9.3	9.1	8.8	8.5	8.2	8.3

Note: Data is not seasonally adjusted and covers workers 16 years of age and older; All figures are percentages; (1) Metropolitan Division—see Appendix B for areas included
Source: Bureau of Labor Statistics, http://stats.bls.gov

Projected Unemployment Rate

Area	2010 (%)	2011 (%)	2012 (%)	2013 (%)
MSA[1]	9.3	8.3	7.8	7.0

Note: (1) Metropolitan Statistical Area—see Appendix B for areas included
Source: The United States Conference of Mayors, "U.S. Metro Economies: GMP and Employment Forecasts," June 2011

Employment by Occupation

Occupation Classification	City (%)	MSA[1] (%)	U.S. (%)
Management, Business, Science, and Arts	60.4	42.2	35.6
Natural Resources, Construction, and Maintenance	3.2	8.3	9.5
Production, Transportation, and Material Moving	5.3	10.0	12.1
Sales and Office	18.3	23.7	25.2
Service	12.7	15.8	17.6

Note: Figures cover employed civilians 16 years of age and older; (1) Figures cover the Seattle-Tacoma-Bellevue, WA Metropolitan Statistical Area—see Appendix B for areas included
Source: U.S. Census Bureau, 2008-2010 American Community Survey 3-Year Estimates

Employment by Industry

Sector	MD[1] Number of Employees	MD[1] Percent of Total	U.S. Percent of Total
Construction	63,800	4.5	4.1
Education and Health Services	173,400	12.2	15.2
Financial Activities	77,200	5.4	5.8
Government	201,000	14.1	16.8
Information	85,600	6.0	2.0
Leisure and Hospitality	134,600	9.5	9.9
Manufacturing	165,000	11.6	8.9
Mining and Logging	600	<0.1	0.6
Other Services	50,500	3.6	4.0
Professional and Business Services	207,900	14.6	13.3
Retail Trade	146,800	10.3	11.5
Transportation and Utilities	47,900	3.4	3.8
Wholesale Trade	67,700	4.8	4.2

Note: Figures cover non-farm employment as of December 2011 and are not seasonally adjusted; (1) Metropolitan Division—see Appendix B for areas included
Source: Bureau of Labor Statistics, http://stats.bls.gov

Occupations with Greatest Projected Employment Growth: 2008 – 2018

Occupation[1]	2008 Employment	2018 Projected Employment	Numeric Employment Change	Percent Employment Change
Registered Nurses	54,560	71,220	16,660	30.5
Personal and Home Care Aides	27,270	36,390	9,120	33.4
Combined Food Preparation and Serving Workers, Including Fast Food	64,840	72,570	7,730	11.9
Janitors and Cleaners, Except Maids and Housekeeping Cleaners	44,620	52,050	7,430	16.7
Retail Salespersons	96,740	104,100	7,360	7.6
Landscaping and Groundskeeping Workers	25,340	32,160	6,820	26.9
Home Health Aides	12,940	19,400	6,460	49.9
Office Clerks, General	59,940	65,840	5,900	9.8
Laborers and Freight, Stock, and Material Movers, Hand	47,530	53,280	5,750	12.1
Computer Software Engineers, Applications	25,000	30,240	5,240	21.0

Note: Projections cover Washington; (1) Sorted by numeric employment change
Source: www.projectionscentral.com, State Occupational Projections, 2008–2018 Long-Term Projections

Fastest Growing Occupations: 2008 – 2018

Occupation[1]	2008 Employment	2018 Projected Employment	Numeric Employment Change	Percent Employment Change
Biomedical Engineers	420	670	250	59.5
Home Health Aides	12,940	19,400	6,460	49.9
Employment, Recruitment, and Placement Specialists	4,320	6,100	1,780	41.2
Physical Therapist Aides	1,110	1,530	420	37.8
Network Systems and Data Communications Analysts	11,880	16,180	4,300	36.2
Veterinarians	1,520	2,060	540	35.5
Veterinary Technologists and Technicians	1,690	2,290	600	35.5
Chiropractors	1,320	1,780	460	34.8
Personal and Home Care Aides	27,270	36,390	9,120	33.4
Physician Assistants	2,020	2,690	670	33.2

Note: Projections cover Washington; (1) Sorted by percent employment change and excludes occupations with numeric employment change less than 100
Source: www.projectionscentral.com, State Occupational Projections, 2008–2018 Long-Term Projections

Average Wages

Occupation	$/Hr.	Occupation	$/Hr.
Accountants and Auditors	33.93	Maids and Housekeeping Cleaners	12.10
Automotive Mechanics	19.26	Maintenance and Repair Workers	20.35
Bookkeepers	19.53	Marketing Managers	63.21
Carpenters	25.62	Nuclear Medicine Technologists	41.27
Cashiers	12.86	Nurses, Licensed Practical	24.18
Clerks, General Office	16.09	Nurses, Registered	37.68
Clerks, Receptionists/Information	14.48	Nursing Aides/Orderlies/Attendants	14.77
Clerks, Shipping/Receiving	17.95	Packers and Packagers, Hand	11.79
Computer Programmers	45.55	Physical Therapists	37.65
Computer Support Specialists	28.14	Postal Service Mail Carriers	25.70
Computer Systems Analysts	43.29	Real Estate Brokers	41.03
Cooks, Restaurant	12.88	Retail Salespersons	14.24
Dentists	106.68	Sales Reps., Exc. Tech./Scientific	33.18
Electrical Engineers	45.46	Sales Reps., Tech./Scientific	43.02
Electricians	31.80	Secretaries, Exc. Legal/Med./Exec.	19.27
Financial Managers	60.69	Security Guards	18.98
First-Line Supervisors/Managers, Sales	22.33	Surgeons	n/a
Food Preparation Workers	11.95	Teacher Assistants	15.40
General and Operations Managers	66.28	Teachers, Elementary School	29.00
Hairdressers/Cosmetologists	18.08	Teachers, Secondary School	29.50
Internists	86.31	Telemarketers	12.43
Janitors and Cleaners	14.35	Truck Drivers, Heavy/Tractor-Trailer	21.25
Landscaping/Groundskeeping Workers	15.62	Truck Drivers, Light/Delivery Svcs.	17.47
Lawyers	59.08	Waiters and Waitresses	14.87

Note: Wage data covers the Seattle-Bellevue-Everett, WA Metropolitan Division—see Appendix B for areas included. Hourly wages for elementary/secondary school teachers and teacher assistants were calculated by the editors from annual wage data assuming a 40 hour work week; n/a not available.
Source: Bureau of Labor Statistics, Metro Area Occupational Employment and Wage Estimates, May 2011

RESIDENTIAL REAL ESTATE

Building Permits

Area	Single-Family			Multi-Family			Total		
	2010	2011	Pct. Chg.	2010	2011	Pct. Chg.	2010	2011	Pct. Chg.
City	75	68	-9.3	129	66	-48.8	204	134	-34.3
MSA[1]	6,139	6,078	-1.0	3,901	5,152	32.1	10,040	11,230	11.9
U.S.	447,311	418,498	-6.4	157,299	205,563	30.7	604,610	624,061	3.2

Note: (1) Metropolitan Statistical Area—see Appendix B for areas included; figures represent new, privately-owned housing units authorized (unadjusted data); All permit data are based on estimates with imputation.
Source: U.S. Census Bureau, Manufacturing, Mining, and Construction Statistics, Building Permits, 2010, 2011

Homeownership Rate

Area	2005 (%)	2006 (%)	2007 (%)	2008 (%)	2009 (%)	2010 (%)	2011 (%)
MSA[1]	64.5	63.7	62.8	61.3	61.2	60.9	60.7
U.S.	68.9	68.8	68.1	67.8	67.4	66.9	66.1

Note: (1) Metropolitan Statistical Area—see Appendix B for areas included
Source: U.S. Census Bureau, Housing Vacancies and Homeownership Annual Statistics: 2011

Housing Vacancy Rates

Area	Gross Vacancy Rate[2] (%)			Year-Round Vacancy Rate[3] (%)			Rental Vacancy Rate[4] (%)			Homeowner Vacancy Rate[5] (%)		
	2009	2010	2011	2009	2010	2011	2009	2010	2011	2009	2010	2011
MSA[1]	9.0	8.8	8.6	8.8	8.6	8.3	8.0	7.4	6.7	2.8	3.2	2.6
U.S.	14.5	14.3	14.2	11.3	11.3	11.1	10.6	10.2	9.5	2.6	2.6	2.5

Note: (1) Metropolitan Statistical Area—see Appendix B for areas included; (2) The percentage of the total housing inventory that is vacant; (3) The percentage of the housing inventory (excluding seasonal units) that is year-round vacant; (4) The percentage of rental inventory that is vacant for rent; (5) The percentage of homeowner inventory that is vacant for sale
Source: U.S. Census Bureau, Housing Vacancies and Homeownership Annual Statistics: 2011

TAXES

State Corporate Income Tax Rates

State	Tax Rate (%)	Income Brackets ($)	Num. of Brackets	Financial Institution Tax Rate (%)[a]	Federal Income Tax Ded.
Washington	No corporate tax	–	-	–	No

Note: Tax rates as of January 1, 2012; (a) Rates listed are the corporate income tax rate applied to financial institutions or excise taxes based on income. Some states have other taxes based upon the value of deposits or shares.
Source: Federation of Tax Administrators, "State Corporate Income Tax Rates, 2012"

State Individual Income Tax Rates

State	Tax Rate (%)	Income Brackets ($)	Num. of Brackets	Personal Exempt. ($)[1] Single	Personal Exempt. ($)[1] Dependents	Fed. Inc. Tax Ded.
Washington – No State Income Tax						

Note: Tax rates as of January 1, 2012; Local- and county-level taxes are not included; n/a not applicable; (1) Married joint filers generally receive double the single exemption
Source: Federation of Tax Administrators, "State Individual Income Tax Rates, 2012"

Various State and Local Tax Rates

State	State and Local Sales and Use (%)	State Sales and Use (%)	Gasoline[1] (¢/gal.)	Cigarette[2] ($/pack)	Spirits[3] ($/gal.)	Wine[4] ($/gal.)	Beer[5] ($/gal.)
Washington	9.5	6.50	37.5	3.03	26.70 (f)	0.88	0.26

Note: All tax rates as of January 1, 2012 except beer, wine and spirits (September 1, 2011); (1) The American Petroleum Institute has developed a methodology for determining the average tax rate on a gallon of fuel. Rates may include any of the following: excise taxes, environmental fees, storage tank fees, other fees or taxes, general sales tax, and local taxes. In states where gasoline is subject to the general sales tax, or where the fuel tax is based on the average sale price, the average rate determined by API is sensitive to changes in the price of gasoline. States that fully or partially apply general sales taxes to gasoline: CA, CO, GA, IL, IN, MI, NY; (2) The federal excise tax of $1.0066 per pack and local taxes are not included; (3) Rates are those applicable to off-premise sales of 40% alcohol by volume (a.b.v.) distilled spirits in 750ml containers. Local excise taxes are excluded; (4) Rates are those applicable to off-premise sales of 11% a.b.v. non-carbonated wine in 750ml containers; (5) Rates are those applicable to off-premise sales of 4.7% a.b.v. beer in 12 ounce containers; (f) States where the government controls sales. In these "control states," products are subject to ad valorem mark-up and excise taxes. The excise tax rate is calculated using a methodology developed by the Distilled Spirits Council of the United States.
Source: Tax Foundation, 2012 Facts & Figures: How Does Your State Compare?

State-Local Tax Burdens

Area	Rate (%)	Rank[1]	Per Capita Taxes Paid to Home State ($)	Total State and Local Per Capita Taxes Paid ($)	Per Capita Income ($)
Washington	9.3	29	3,141	4,408	47,361
U.S. Average	9.8	-	3,057	4,160	42,539

Note: Figures cover 2009; (1) Rank ranges from 1 to 50 where 1 is highest tax burden
Source: Tax Foundation, State-Local Tax Burdens, All States, 2009

State Business Tax Climate Index Rankings

State	Overall Rank	Corporate Tax Index Rank	Individual Income Tax Index Rank	Sales Tax Index Rank	Unemployment Insurance Tax Index Rank	Property Tax Index Rank
Washington	7	30	1	48	18	22

Note: The index is a measure of how each state's tax laws affect economic performance. The lower the rank, the more favorable a state's tax system is for business. States without a given tax are given a ranking of 1.
Source: Tax Foundation, Major Components of the State Business Tax Climate Index, FY 2012

COMMERCIAL REAL ESTATE

Office Market

Market Area	Inventory (sq. ft.)	Vacant (sq. ft.)	Vac. Rate (%)	Under Constr. (sq. ft.)	Asking Rent ($/sf/yr)	
					Class A	Class B
Seattle	90,570,911	14,842,822	16.4	276,842	30.48	23.09

Source: Grubb & Ellis, Office Markets Trends, 4th Quarter 2011

Industrial Market

Market Area	Inventory (sq. ft.)	Vacant (sq. ft.)	Vac. Rate (%)	Under Constr. (sq. ft.)	Asking Rent ($/sf/yr)	
					WH/Dist	R&D/Flex
Seattle	163,327,607	14,463,624	8.9	137,284	5.88	11.52

Source: Grubb & Ellis, Industrial Markets Trends, 4th Quarter 2011

COMMERCIAL UTILITIES

Typical Monthly Electric Bills

Area	Commercial Service ($/month)		Industrial Service ($/month)	
	1,500 kWh	40 kW demand 14,000 kWh	1,000 kW demand 200,000 kWh	50,000 kW demand 15,000,000 kWh
City	146	1,302	19,279	1,091,465
Average[1]	189	1,616	25,197	1,470,813

Note: Based on total rates in effect July 1, 2011; (1) average based on 184 utilities surveyed
Source: Edison Electric Institute, Typical Bills and Average Rates Report, Summer 2011

TRANSPORTATION

Means of Transportation to Work

Area	Car/Truck/Van		Public Transportation			Bicycle	Walked	Other Means	Worked at Home
	Drove Alone	Car-pooled	Bus	Subway	Railroad				
City	66.5	9.8	10.9	0.0	0.0	0.7	5.1	1.2	5.8
MSA[1]	69.5	11.3	7.8	0.1	0.3	1.0	3.6	1.2	5.1
U.S.	76.0	10.2	2.7	1.7	0.5	0.5	2.8	1.3	4.2

Note: Figures are percentages and cover workers 16 years of age and older; (1) Figures cover the Seattle-Tacoma-Bellevue, WA Metropolitan Statistical Area—see Appendix B for areas included
Source: U.S. Census Bureau, 2008-2010 American Community Survey 3-Year Estimates

Travel Time to Work

Area	Less Than 10 Minutes	10 to 19 Minutes	20 to 29 Minutes	30 to 44 Minutes	45 to 59 Minutes	60 to 89 Minutes	90 Minutes or More
City	12.3	34.2	24.9	20.9	4.4	2.8	0.5
MSA[1]	9.8	26.1	22.4	24.2	9.0	6.3	2.2
U.S.	13.9	30.1	20.8	19.8	7.5	5.5	2.5

Note: Figures are percentages and include workers 16 years old and over; (1) Figures cover the Seattle-Tacoma-Bellevue, WA Metropolitan Statistical Area—see Appendix B for areas included
Source: U.S. Census Bureau, 2008-2010 American Community Survey 3-Year Estimates

Travel Time Index

Area	1985	1990	1995	2000	2005	2010
Urban Area[1]	1.13	1.27	1.30	1.31	1.33	1.27
Average[2]	1.11	1.16	1.18	1.21	1.25	1.20

Note: Travel Time Index—the ratio of travel time in the peak period to the travel time at free-flow conditions. A value of 1.30 indicates a 20-minute free-flow trip takes 26 minutes in the peak. Free-flow speeds (60 mph on freeways and 35 mph on principal arterials) are used as the comparison threshold; (1) Covers the Seattle WA urban area; (2) average of 439 urban areas
Source: Texas Transportation Institute, Urban Mobility Report 2011, September 2011

Public Transportation

Agency Name / Mode of Transportation	Vehicles Operated in Maximum Service	Annual Unlinked Passenger Trips ('000)	Annual Passenger Miles ('000)
King County Department of Transportation (KC Metro)			
Bus (directly operated)	932	87,470.8	419,705.3
Bus (purchased transportation)	30	817.0	2,626.7
Demand Response (purchased transportation)	336	1,177.2	12,191.4
Demand Response Taxi (purchased transportation)	44	80.7	640.6
Light Rail (directly operated)	2	520.9	471.6
Trolleybus (directly operated)	116	20,721.1	36,274.4
Vanpool (directly operated)	1,154	2,849.6	58,134.0

Source: Federal Transit Administration, National Transit Database, 2010

Air Transportation

Airport Name and Code / Type of Service	Passenger Airlines[1]	Passenger Enplanements	Freight Carriers[2]	Freight (lbs.)
Seattle-Tacoma International (SEA)				
Domestic service (U.S. carriers - 2011)	24	14,484,254	20	195,835,210
International service (U.S. carriers - 2010)	8	793,481	6	14,430,439

Note: (1) Includes all U.S.-based major, minor and commuter airlines that carried at least one passenger during the year; (2) Includes all U.S.-based airlines and freight carriers that transported at least one pound of freight during the year
Source: Bureau of Transportation Statistics, The Intermodal Transportation Database, Air Carriers: T-100 Domestic Market (U.S. Carriers), 2011; Bureau of Transportation Statistics, The Intermodal Transportation Database, Air Carriers: T-100 International Market (U.S. Carriers), 2010

Other Transportation Statistics

Major Highways:	I-50; I-90
Amtrak Service:	No
Major Waterways/Ports:	Lake Washington; Near Puget Sound (8 miles)

Source: Amtrak.com; Google Maps

BUSINESSES

Major Business Headquarters

Company Name	Rankings	
	Fortune[1]	Forbes[2]
Paccar	238	-

Note: (1) Fortune 500—companies that produce a 10-K are ranked 1 to 500 based on 2010 revenue; (2) all private companies with at least $2 billion in annual revenue are ranked 1 to 212; companies listed are headquartered in the city; dashes indicate no ranking
Source: Fortune, "Fortune 500," May 23, 2011; Forbes, "America's Largest Private Companies," November 16, 2011

Fast-Growing Businesses

According to *Inc.*, Bellevue is home to four of America's 500 fastest-growing private companies: **Vega Consulting** (#201); **110 Consulting** (#314); **Clarisonic** (#435); **Derflan** (#484). Criteria: must be an independent, privately-held, for-profit, U.S. corporation, proprietorship or partnership; revenues must be at least $80,000 in 2007 and $2 million in 2010; must have four-year operating/sales history. Holding companies, regulated banks, and utilities were excluded. *Inc., "America's 500 Fastest-Growing Private Companies," September 2011*

According to *Fortune*, Bellevue is home to one of the 100 fastest-growing companies in the world: **Coinstar** (#22). Companies were ranked by their revenue growth rate; their EPS growth rate; and their three-year annualized total return to investors for the period ending June 30, 2011. Criteria for inclusion: a company, foreign or domestic, must trade on a major U.S. stock exchange; must file quarterly reports with the SEC; must have a minimum market capitalization of $250 million; must have a stock price of at least $5 on June 30, 2011; must have been trading continuously since June 30, 2008; must have revenue and net income for the four quarters ended on or before April 30, 2011, of at least $50 million and $10 million, respectively; and must have posted a compound annual growth in revenue and earnings per share of at least 15% annually over the three years ending on or before April 30, 2011. REITs, limited-liability companies, limited parterships, companies about to be acquired, and companies that lost money in the quarter ending April 30, 2011 were excluded. *Fortune, "100 Fastest-Growing Companies," September 26, 2011*

According to Deloitte, Bellevue is home to two of North America's 500 fastest-growing high-technology companies: **Edifecs** (#254); **eMagin Corp.** (#311). Companies are ranked by percentage growth in revenue over a five-year period. Criteria for inclusion: company must be headquartered within North America; must own proprietary intellectual property or proprietary technology that contributes to a significant portion of the company's operating revenue, or devote a significant proportion of revenues to research and development of technology; must have been in business for a minumum of five years with 2006 operating revenues of at least $50,000 USD/CD and 2010 operating revenues of at least $5 million USD/CD. *Deloitte Touche Tohmatsu, 2011 Deloitte Technology Fast 500™*

Minority- and Women-Owned Businesses

Group	All Firms		Firms with Paid Employees			
	Firms	Sales ($000)	Firms	Sales ($000)	Employees	Payroll ($000)
Asian	n/a	n/a	n/a	n/a	n/a	n/a
Black	n/a	n/a	n/a	n/a	n/a	n/a
Hispanic	n/a	n/a	n/a	n/a	n/a	n/a
Women	n/a	n/a	n/a	n/a	n/a	n/a
All Firms	1,956	207,651	405	151,671	1,346	32,383

Note: Figures cover firms located in the city; minority- and women-owned business are defined as firms in which the corresponding group own 51% or more of the stock or equity of the company; n/a not available
Source: U.S. Census Bureau, 2007 Economic Census, Survey of Business Owners

HOTELS

Hotels/Motels

Area	5 Star		4 Star		3 Star		2 Star		1 Star		Not Rated	
	Num.	Pct.[3]	Num.	Pct.[3]	Num.	Pct.[3]	Num.	Pct.[3]	Num.	Pct.[3]	Num.	Pct.[3]
City[1]	0	0.0	5	12.2	22	53.7	11	26.8	0	0.0	3	7.3
Total[2]	133	0.9	940	6.5	4,569	31.8	7,033	48.9	351	2.4	1,343	9.3

Note: (1) Figures cover Bellevue and vicinity; (2) Figures cover all 100 cities in this book; (3) Percentage of hotels which have a given star rating; Star ratings are determined by expedia.com and offer an indication of the general quality of a particular hotel.
Source: expedia.com, April 25, 2012

The Seattle-Bellevue-Everett, WA metro area is home to four of the best hotels in the U.S. according to *Travel & Leisure*: **Willows Lodge** (#21); **Four Seasons Hotel, Seattle** (#57); **Hotel 1000** (#58); **The Fairmont Olympic Hotel Seattle** (#110). Criteria: service; location; rooms; food; and value. *Travel & Leisure, "T+L 500, The World's Best Hotels 2012"*

The Seattle-Bellevue-Everett, WA metro area is home to five of the best hotels in the U.S. according to *Condé Nast Traveler*: **Hotel 1000** (#14); **Inn at The Market** (#40); **Fairmont Olympic Hotel** (#62); **Salish Lodge & Spa** (#75); **Hyatt at Olive 8** (#91). The selections are based on over 25,000 responses to the magazine's annual Readers' Choice Survey. *Condé Nast Traveler, "2011 Readers' Choice Awards"*

EVENT SITES

Convention Centers

Name	Overall Space (sq. ft.)	Exhibit Space (sq. ft.)	Meeting Space (sq. ft.)	Meeting Rooms
Meydenbaur Center	n/a	12,000	36,000	n/a

Note: n/a not available
Source: Original research

Living Environment

COST OF LIVING

Cost of Living Index

Composite Index	Groceries	Housing	Utilities	Trans-portation	Health Care	Misc. Goods/ Services
117.2	111.7	129.5	90.4	112.4	118.4	118.7

Note: U.S. = 100; Figures cover the Seattle WA urban area.
Source: The Council for Community and Economic Research, ACCRA Cost of Living Index, 2011

Grocery Prices

Area[1]	T-Bone Steak ($/pound)	Frying Chicken ($/pound)	Whole Milk ($/half gal.)	Eggs ($/dozen)	Orange Juice ($/64 oz.)	Coffee ($/11.5 oz.)
City[2]	9.32	1.36	1.90	1.99	3.75	5.45
Avg.	9.25	1.18	2.22	1.66	3.19	4.40
Min.	6.70	0.88	1.31	0.95	2.46	2.94
Max.	14.30	2.16	3.50	3.18	4.75	6.83

Note: (1) Values for the local area are compared with the average, minimum and maximum values for all 335 areas in the Cost of Living Index; (2) Figures cover the Seattle WA urban area; **T-Bone Steak** *(price per pound);* **Frying Chicken** *(price per pound, whole fryer);* **Whole Milk** *(half gallon carton);* **Eggs** *(price per dozen, Grade A, large);* **Orange Juice** *(64 oz. Tropicana or Florida Natural);* **Coffee** *(11.5 oz. can, vacuum-packed, Maxwell House, Hills Bros, or Folgers).*
Source: The Council for Community and Economic Research, ACCRA Cost of Living Index, 2011

Housing and Utility Costs

Area[1]	New Home Price ($)	Apartment Rent ($/month)	All Electric ($/month)	Part Electric ($/month)	Other Energy ($/month)	Telephone ($/month)
City[2]	342,917	1,473	143.76	-	-	25.99
Avg.	285,990	839	163.23	89.00	77.52	26.92
Min.	188,005	460	125.58	45.39	33.89	17.98
Max.	1,197,028	3,244	339.16	181.97	348.69	40.01

Note: (1) Values for the local area are compared with the average, minimum and maximum values for all 335 areas in the Cost of Living Index; (2) Figures cover the Seattle WA urban area; **New Home Price** *(2,400 sf living area, 8,000 sf lot, in urban area with full utilities);* **Apartment Rent** *(950 sf 2 bedroom/1.5 or 2 bath, unfurnished, excluding all utilities except water);* **All Electric** *(average monthly cost for an all-electric home);* **Part Electric** *(average monthly cost for a part-electric home);* **Other Energy** *(average monthly cost for natural gas, fuel oil, coal, wood, and any other forms of energy except electricity);* **Telephone** *(price includes basic monthly rate for a private residential line plus additional local usage charges incurred by a family of four).*
Source: The Council for Community and Economic Research, ACCRA Cost of Living Index, 2011

Health Care, Transportation, and Other Costs

Area[1]	Doctor ($/visit)	Dentist ($/visit)	Optometrist ($/visit)	Gasoline ($/gallon)	Beauty Salon ($/visit)	Men's Shirt ($)
City[2]	119.29	106.93	115.25	3.65	41.48	35.93
Avg.	93.88	81.72	90.54	3.48	32.65	25.06
Min.	60.00	55.33	53.66	3.18	19.78	13.44
Max.	154.98	145.97	183.72	4.31	63.21	46.00

Note: (1) Values for the local area are compared with the average, minimum and maximum values for all 335 areas in the Cost of Living Index; (2) Figures cover the Seattle WA urban area; **Doctor** *(general practitioners routine exam of an established patient);* **Dentist** *(adult teeth cleaning and periodic oral examination);* **Optometrist** *(full vision eye exam for established adult patient);* **Gasoline** *(one gallon regular unleaded, national brand, including all taxes, cash price at self-service pump if available);* **Beauty Salon** *(woman's shampoo, trim, and blow-dry);* **Men's Shirt** *(cotton/polyester dress shirt, pinpoint weave, long sleeves).*
Source: The Council for Community and Economic Research, ACCRA Cost of Living Index, 2011

HOUSING

House Price Index (HPI)

Area	National Ranking[2]	Quarterly Change (%)	One-Year Change (%)	Five-Year Change (%)
MD[1]	227	-0.28	-4.64	-19.92
U.S.[3]	-	-0.10	-2.43	-19.16

Note: The HPI is a weighted repeat sales index. It measures average price changes in repeat sales or refinancings on the same properties. This information is obtained by reviewing repeat mortgage transactions on single-family properties whose mortgages have been purchased or securitized by Fannie Mae or Freddie Mac in January 1975; (1) Metropolitan Division - see Appendix B for areas included; (2) Rankings are based on annual percentage change for all metro areas containing at least 15,000 transactions over the last 10 years and ranges from 1 to 306; (3) figures based on a weighted average of Census Division estimates using a purchase only index; all figures are for the period ending December 31, 2011
Source: Federal Housing Finance Agency, House Price Index, February 23, 2012

House Price Valuations

Area	Q4 2005		Q4 2006		Q4 2007		Q4 2008		Q4 2009	
	Price ($000)	Over-valuation	Price ($000)	Over-valuation	Price ($000)	Over-valuation	Price ($000)	Over-valuation	Price ($000)	Over-valuation
MD[1]	347.9	24.3	395.6	28.8	408.1	23.1	370.8	11.6	350.6	5.5

Note: Figures show the percentage of over- or under-valuation of single family homes relative to statistically normal house values (e.g. a value of 23.6 indicates that house values are 23.6% overvalued). Statistically normal house values are based on house prices, interest rates, household incomes, population densities, and any historical premiums or discounts metropolitan areas have exhibited over time; (1) Figures cover the Seattle-Bellevue-Everett, WA - see Appendix B for areas included
Source: Global Insight/PNC Financial Services Group, House Prices in America: 4th Quarter 2009 Update

Median Single-Family Home Prices

Area	2009	2010	2011p	Percent Change 2010 to 2011
MSA[1]	306.2	295.7	285.0	-3.6
U.S. Average	172.1	173.1	166.2	-4.0

Note: Figures are median sales prices of existing single-family homes in thousands of dollars; (p) preliminary; n/a not available; (1) Metropolitan Statistical Area—see Appendix B for areas included
Source: National Association of Realtors, Median Sales Price of Existing Single-Family Homes for Metropolitan Areas, 4th Quarter 2011

Affordability Index of Existing Single-Family Homes

Area	2009	2010	2011p	Percent Change 2010 to 2011
MSA[1]	78.5	85.9	94.7	10.2

Note: The housing affordability index measures whether or not a typical family could qualify for a mortgage loan on a typical home. The higher the index, the greater the household purchasing power. An index of 100 is defined as the point where a median-income household has exactly enough income to qualify for the purchase of a median-priced existing single-family home, assuming a 20 percent downpayment and 25 percent of gross income devoted to mortgage principal and interest payments; (p) preliminary; n/a not available; (1) Metropolitan Statistical Area—see Appendix B for areas included
Source: National Association of Realtors, Affordability Index of Existing Single-Family Homes, 2011

Median Apartment Condo-Coop Home Prices

Area	2009	2010	2011p	Percent Change 2010 to 2011
MSA[1]	n/a	n/a	n/a	n/a
U.S. Average	175.6	171.7	165.1	-3.8

Note: Figures are median sales prices of existing apartment condo-coop homes in thousands of dollars; (p) preliminary; n/a not available; (1) Metropolitan Statistical Area—see Appendix B for areas included
Source: National Association of Realtors, Median Sales Price of Existing Apartment Condo-Coop Homes for Metropolitan Areas, 4th Quarter 2011

Year Housing Structure Built

Area	2005 or Later	2000 -2004	1990 -1999	1980 -1989	1970 -1979	1960 -1969	1950 -1959	Before 1950	Median Year
City	3.4	8.0	15.1	18.5	21.6	19.2	12.2	2.1	1978
MSA[1]	5.9	9.4	16.5	15.8	16.0	11.8	8.4	16.2	1978
U.S.	5.0	8.6	14.0	14.1	16.3	11.3	11.2	19.6	1975

Note: Figures are percentages except for Median Year; (1) Figures cover the Seattle-Tacoma-Bellevue, WA Metropolitan Statistical Area—see Appendix B for areas included
Source: U.S. Census Bureau, 2008-2010 American Community Survey 3-Year Estimates

HEALTH

Health Risk Data

Category	MSA[1] (%)	U.S. (%)
Adults who have been told they have high blood pressure[2]	25.7	28.7
Adults who have been told they have high blood cholesterol[2]	37.3	37.5
Adults who have been told they have diabetes[3]	6.4	8.7
Adults who have been told they have arthritis[2]	23.7	26.0
Adults who have been told they currently have asthma	8.9	9.1
Adults who are current smokers	12.9	17.3
Adults who are heavy drinkers[4]	6.1	5.0
Adults who are binge drinkers[5]	16.9	15.1
Adults who are overweight (BMI 25.0 - 29.9)	34.9	36.2
Adults who are obese (BMI 30.0 - 99.8)	22.8	27.5
Adults who participated in any physical activities in the past month	83.4	76.1
Adults 50+ who have ever had a sigmoidoscopy or colonoscopy	71.4	65.2
Women aged 40+ who have had a mammogram within the past two years	76.6	75.2
Men aged 40+ who have had a PSA test within the past two years	43.9	53.2
Adults aged 65+ who have had flu shot within the past year	70.8	67.5
Adults aged 18–64 who have any kind of health care coverage	83.7	82.2

Note: Data as of 2010 unless otherwise noted; (1) Figures cover the Seattle-Bellevue-Everett, WA Metropolitan Division—see Appendix B for areas included; (2) Data as of 2009; (3) Figures do not include pregnancy-related, borderline, or pre-diabetes; (4) Heavy drinkers are classified as males having more than two drinks per day or females having more than one drink per day; (5) Binge drinkers are classified as males having five or more drinks on one occasion or females having four or more drinks on one occasion
Source: Centers for Disease Control and Prevention, Behaviorial Risk Factor Surveillance System, SMART: Selected Metropolitan/Micropolitan Area Risk Trends, 2009, 2010

Mortality Rates for the Top 10 Causes of Death in the U.S.

ICD-10[a] Sub-Chapter	ICD-10[a] Code	Age-Adjusted Mortality Rate[1] per 100,000 population	
		County[2]	U.S.
Malignant neoplasms	C00-C97	159.5	175.6
Ischaemic heart diseases	I20-I25	94.2	121.6
Other forms of heart disease	I30-I51	28.1	48.6
Chronic lower respiratory diseases	J40-J47	33.0	42.3
Cerebrovascular diseases	I60-I69	36.5	40.6
Organic, including symptomatic, mental disorders	F01-F09	16.5	26.7
Other degenerative diseases of the nervous system	G30-G31	44.9	24.7
Other external causes of accidental injury	W00-X59	24.2	24.4
Diabetes mellitus	E10-E14	19.5	21.7
Hypertensive diseases	I10-I15	19.9	18.2

Note: (a) ICD-10 = International Classification of Diseases 10th Revision; (1) Mortality rates are a three year average covering 2007-2009; (2) Figures cover King County
Source: Centers for Disease Control and Prevention, National Center for Health Statistics. Underlying Cause of Death 1999-2009 on CDC WONDER Online Database, released 2012. Data for year 2009 are compiled from the Multiple Cause of Death File 2009, Series 20 No. 2O, 2012, Data for year 2008 are compiled from the Multiple Cause of Death File 2008, Series 20 No. 2N, 2011, Data for year 2007 are compiled from Multiple Cause of Death File 2007, Series 20 No. 2M, 2010.

Mortality Rates for Selected Causes of Death

ICD-10[a] Sub-Chapter	ICD-10[a] Code	Age-Adjusted Mortality Rate[1] per 100,000 population	
		County[2]	U.S.
Assault	X85-Y09	3.2	5.7
Human immunodeficiency virus (HIV) disease	B20-B24	2.3	3.3
Influenza and pneumonia	J09-J18	10.1	16.4
Intentional self-harm	X60-X84	10.8	11.5
Malnutrition	E40-E46	0.5	0.8
Obesity and other hyperalimentation	E65-E68	1.5	1.6
Transport accidents	V01-V99	7.1	13.7
Viral hepatitis	B15-B19	2.6	2.2

Note: (a) ICD-10 = International Classification of Diseases 10th Revision; (1) Mortality rates are a three year average covering 2007-2009; (2) Figures cover King County
Source: Centers for Disease Control and Prevention, National Center for Health Statistics. Underlying Cause of Death 1999-2009 on CDC WONDER Online Database, released 2012. Data for year 2009 are compiled from the Multiple Cause of Death File 2009, Series 20 No. 2O, 2012, Data for year 2008 are compiled from the Multiple Cause of Death File 2008, Series 20 No. 2N, 2011, Data for year 2007 are compiled from Multiple Cause of Death File 2007, Series 20 No. 2M, 2010.

Distribution of Physicians and Dentists

Area[1]	Dentists[2]	D.O.[3]	M.D.[4]				
			Total	Family/ General Practice	Pediatrics	Medical Specialties	Surgical Specialties
Local (number)	1,416	199	5,541	874	363	1,921	1,076
Local (rate[5])	7.6	1.1	29.4	4.6	1.9	10.2	5.7
U.S. (rate[5])	4.5	1.9	18.3	2.5	1.4	6.8	4.1

Note: Data as of 2008 unless noted; (1) Local data covers King County; (2) Data as of 2007; (3) Doctor of Osteopathic Medicine; (4) Includes active, non-federal, patient-care, office-based Doctors of Medicine; (5) rate per 10,000 population
Source: Area Resource File (ARF). 2009-2010 Release. U.S. Department of Health and Human Services, Health Resources and Services Administration, Bureau of Health Professions, Rockville, MD, August 2010

Best Hospitals

According to *U.S. News,* the Seattle-Bellevue-Everett, WA is home to three of the best hospitals in the U.S.: **Harborview Medical Center** (2 specialties); **University of Washington Medical Center** (11 specialties); **Virginia Mason Medical Center** (1 specialty). The hospitals listed were highly ranked in at least one adult specialty. *U.S. News Online, "America's Best Hospitals 2011-12"*

According to *U.S. News,* the Seattle-Bellevue-Everett, WA is home to one of the best children's hospitals in the U.S.: **Seattle Children's Hospital** (10 specialties). The hospital listed was highly ranked in at least one pediatric specialty. *U.S. News Online, "America's Best Children's Hospitals 2011-12"*

EDUCATION

Public School District Statistics

District Name	Schls	Pupils	Pupil/ Teacher Ratio	Minority Pupils[1] (%)	Free Lunch Eligible[2] (%)	IEP[3] (%)
Bellevue School District	30	17,578	19.3	48.8	16.0	9.6

Note: Table includes school districts with 2,000 or more students; (1) Percentage of students that are not non-Hispanic white; (2) Percentage of students that are eligible for the free lunch program; (3) Percentage of students that have an Individualized Education Program.
Source: U.S. Department of Education, National Center for Education Statistics, Common Core of Data, Local Education Agency (School District) Universe Survey: School Year 2009-2010; U.S. Department of Education, National Center for Education Statistics, Common Core of Data, Public Elementary/Secondary School Universe Survey: School Year 2009-2010

Top Public High Schools

High School Name	Rank[1]	Score[1]	Grad. Rate[2] (%)	College[3] (%)	AP/IB/ AICE[4] (%)	SAT/ ACT[5] (%)
Bellevue	148	0.590	94	96	4.0	1672
Interlake	48	1.036	86	97	7.6	1740
International School	12	1.658	100	100	8.2	1893
Newport	56	0.973	95	97	5.5	1750
Sammamish	369	0.279	85	94	4.8	1634

Note: (1) Public schools are ranked from 1 to 500 based on the following self-reported statistics (with their corresponding weight in the final score). Schools that had fewer than 10 graduates, as well as those that were newly founded and did not have a graduating senior class in 2010 were excluded; (2) Four-year, on-time graduation rate (25%); (3) Percent of 2010 graduates who enrolled immediately in college (25%); (4) AP/IB/AICE tests per graduate (25%); (5) Average SAT and/or ACT score (10%); Average AP/IB/AICE exam score (10%); AP/IB/AICE courses offered per graduate (5%); (6) School is unranked, but has been identified by Newsweek as one of the nation's most elite public high schools.
Source: Newsweek Online, "Top High Schools 2011"

Highest Level of Education

Area	Less than H.S.	H.S. Diploma	Some College, No Deg.	Associate Degree	Bachelors Degree	Masters Degree	Profess. School Degree	Doctorate Degree
City	4.3	11.3	16.1	7.1	38.0	16.5	3.9	2.8
MSA[1]	8.8	21.4	24.0	8.8	24.0	9.0	2.4	1.5
U.S.	14.7	28.4	21.3	7.6	17.6	7.2	1.9	1.2

Note: Figures cover persons age 25 and over; (1) Figures cover the Seattle-Tacoma-Bellevue, WA Metropolitan Statistical Area—see Appendix B for areas included
Source: U.S. Census Bureau, 2008-2010 American Community Survey 3-Year Estimates

Educational Attainment by Race

Area	High School Graduate or Higher (%)					Bachelor's Degree or Higher (%)				
	Total	White	Black	Asian	Hisp.[2]	Total	White	Black	Asian	Hisp.[2]
City	95.7	96.5	100.0	94.9	72.3	61.2	58.7	43.6	72.2	29.8
MSA[1]	91.2	93.2	87.7	85.9	67.4	37.0	37.7	20.0	48.8	17.1
U.S.	85.3	87.5	81.4	85.5	61.6	28.0	29.3	17.8	50.2	13.0

Note: Figures shown cover persons 25 years old and over; (1) Figures cover the Seattle-Tacoma-Bellevue, WA Metropolitan Statistical Area—see Appendix B for areas included; (2) People of Hispanic origin can be of any race
Source: U.S. Census Bureau, 2008-2010 American Community Survey 3-Year Estimates

School Enrollment by Grade and Control

Area	Preschool (%)		Kindergarten (%)		Grades 1 - 4 (%)		Grades 5 - 8 (%)		Grades 9 - 12 (%)	
	Public	Private	Public	Private	Public	Private	Public	Private	Public	Private
City	25.4	74.6	82.9	17.1	83.2	16.8	87.1	12.9	89.1	10.9
MSA[1]	39.5	60.5	84.9	15.1	89.0	11.0	88.7	11.3	89.9	10.1
U.S.	55.4	44.6	87.1	12.9	89.4	10.6	89.5	10.5	90.4	9.6

Note: Figures shown cover persons 3 years old and over; (1) Figures cover the Seattle-Tacoma-Bellevue, WA Metropolitan Statistical Area—see Appendix B for areas included
Source: U.S. Census Bureau, 2008-2010 American Community Survey 3-Year Estimates

Average Salaries of Public School Classroom Teachers

Area	2010-11		2011-12		Percent Change 2010-11 to 2011-12	Percent Change 2001-02 to 2011-12
	Dollars	Rank[1]	Dollars	Rank[1]		
Washington	52,926	21	54,193	21	2.39	24.70
U.S. Average	55,623	-	56,643	-	1.83	26.8

Note: (1) State rank ranges from 1 to 51 where 1 indicates highest salary.
Source: National Education Association, Rankings & Estimates: Rankings of the States 2011 and Estimates of School Statistics 2012, December 2011

Higher Education

Four-Year Colleges			Two-Year Colleges			Medical Schools[1]	Law Schools[2]	Voc/ Tech[3]
Public	Private Non-profit	Private For-profit	Public	Private Non-profit	Private For-profit			
1	1	0	0	0	1	0	0	0

Note: Figures cover institutions located within the city limits and include main campuses only; (1) includes schools accredited by the Liaison Committee on Medical Education and the American Osteopathic Association's Commission on Osteopathic College Accreditation; (2) includes American Bar Association-accredited law schools; (3) includes all schools with programs that are less than 2 years.
Source: National Center for Education Statistics, Integrated Postsecondary Education System (IPEDS) Peer Analysis System, 2011-12; Association of American Medical Colleges, Member List, April 23, 2012; American Osteopathic Association, Member List, April 23, 2012; Law School Admission Council, Official Guide to ABA-Approved Law Schools Online, April 23, 2012

According to *U.S. News & World Report,* the Seattle-Bellevue-Everett, WA is home to one of the best national universities in the U.S.: **University of Washington** (#42). The indicators used to capture academic quality fall into a number of categories: assessment by administrators at peer institutions; retention of students; faculty resources; student selectivity; financial resources; alumni giving; high school counselor ratings of colleges; and graduation rate.*U.S. News & World Report, "America's Best Colleges 2012"*

According to *U.S. News & World Report,* the Seattle-Bellevue-Everett, WA is home to one of the top 50 law schools in the U.S.: **University of Washington** (#20). The rankings are based on a weighted average of 12 measures of quality: peer assessment score; assessment score by lawyers/judges; median LSAT scores; median undergrad GPA; acceptance rate; employment rates for graduates; placement success; bar passage rate; faculty resources; expenditures per student; student/faculty ratio; and library resources. *U.S. News & World Report, "America's Best Law Schools 2013"*

According to *Forbes,* the Seattle-Bellevue-Everett, WA is home to one of the best business schools in the U.S.: **Washington (Foster)** (#36). The rankings are based on the return on investment that graduates of the Class of 2006 received (median salary five years after graduation). *Forbes, "Best Business Schools," August 3, 2011*

PRESIDENTIAL ELECTION

2008 Presidential Election Results

Area	Obama	McCain	Nader	Other
King County	70.0	28.0	0.8	1.2
U.S.	52.9	45.6	0.6	0.9

Note: Results are percentages and may not add to 100% due to rounding
Source: Dave Leip's Atlas of U.S. Presidential Elections, www.uselectionatlas.org

EMPLOYERS

Major Employers

Company Name	Industry
City of Tacoma	Switching and terminal services
Costco Wholesale Corporation	Miscellaneous general merchandise stores
County of Snohomish	Bureau of public roads
Evergreen Healthcare	General medical and surgical hospitals
Harborview Medical Center	General medical and surgical hospitals
King County Public Hospital District No. 2	Hospital and health services consultant
Microsoft Corporation	Prepackaged software
Prologix Distribution Services (west)	General merchandise, non-durable
R U Corporation	American restaurant
SNC-Lavalin Constructors	Heavy construction, nec
Social & Health Svcs, Washington Dept of	General medical and surgical hospitals
Swedish Health Services	General medical and surgical hospitals
T-Mobile USA	Radio, telephone communication
The Boeing Company	Airplanes, fixed or rotary wing
Tulalip Resort Casino	Casino hotel
United States Department of the Army	Medical centers
University of Washington	Colleges and universities
Virginia Mason Medical Center	General medical and surgical hospitals
Virginia Mason Medical Center	Clinic, operated by physicians
Virginia Mason Seattle Main Clinic	Clinic, operated by physicians

Note: Companies shown are located within the Seattle-Tacoma-Bellevue, WA metropolitan area.
Source: Hoovers.com, data extracted April 25 2012

PUBLIC SAFETY

Crime Rate

Area	All Crimes	Violent Crimes				Property Crimes		
		Murder	Forcible Rape	Robbery	Aggrav. Assault	Burglary	Larceny -Theft	Motor Vehicle Theft
City	3,058.7	0.0	7.8	46.2	54.0	514.3	2,274.2	162.1
Suburbs[1]	4,256.6	2.1	32.3	118.1	174.9	787.0	2,674.8	467.5
Metro[2]	4,198.4	2.0	31.1	114.6	169.0	773.8	2,655.3	452.6
U.S.	3,345.5	4.8	27.5	119.1	252.3	699.6	2,003.5	238.8

Note: Figures are crimes per 100,000 population; (1) All areas within the metro area that are located outside the city limits; (2) Metropolitan Division—see Appendix B for areas included
Source: FBI Uniform Crime Reports, 2010

Hate Crimes

Area	Number of Quarters Reported	Bias Motivation				
		Race	Religion	Sexual Orientation	Ethnicity	Disability
City	4	3	2	1	1	0

Source: Federal Bureau of Investigation, Hate Crime Statistics 2010

Identity Theft Consumer Complaints

Area	Complaints	Complaints per 100,000 Population	Rank[2]
MSA[1]	2,796	84.5	147
U.S.	279,156	90.4	-

Note: (1) Metropolitan Statistical Area—see Appendix B for areas included; (2) Rank ranges from 1 to 384 where 1 indicates greatest number of identity theft complaints per 100,000 population
Source: Federal Trade Commission, Consumer Sentinel Network Data Book for January–December 2011

Fraud and Other Consumer Complaints

Area	Complaints	Complaints per 100,000 Population	Rank[2]
MSA[1]	17,212	520.1	124
U.S.	1,533,924	496.8	-

Note: (1) Metropolitan Statistical Area—see Appendix B for areas included; (2) Rank ranges from 1 to 384 where 1 indicates greatest number of fraud and other complaints per 100,000 population
Source: Federal Trade Commission, Consumer Sentinel Network Data Book for January–December 2011

RECREATION

Culture

Dance[1]	Theatre[1]	Instrumental Music[1]	Vocal Music[1]	Series/ Festivals	Museums	Zoos and Aquariums[2]
0	0	1	0	0	4	0

Note: (1) Number of professional perfoming groups; (2) AZA-accredited
Source: The Grey House Performing Arts Directory, 2011-2012; Official Museum Directory, 2011; American Association of Museums, AAM Member Museums, April 2012; Association of Zoos & Aquariums, AZA Member Zoos & Aquariums, April 2012

Professional Sports Teams

Team Name	League
Seattle Mariners	Major League Baseball (MLB)
Seattle Seahawks	National Football League (NFL)
Seattle Sounders FC	Major League Soccer (MLS)

Note: Includes teams located in the Seattle metro area.
Source: Original research

CLIMATE

Average and Extreme Temperatures

Temperature	Jan	Feb	Mar	Apr	May	Jun	Jul	Aug	Sep	Oct	Nov	Dec	Yr.
Extreme High (°F)	64	70	75	85	93	96	98	99	98	89	74	63	99
Average High (°F)	44	48	52	57	64	69	75	74	69	59	50	45	59
Average Temp. (°F)	39	43	45	49	55	61	65	65	60	52	45	41	52
Average Low (°F)	34	36	38	41	46	51	54	55	51	45	39	36	44
Extreme Low (°F)	0	1	11	29	28	38	43	44	35	28	6	6	0

Note: Figures cover the years 1948-1990
Source: National Climatic Data Center, International Station Meteorological Climate Summary, 9/96

Average Precipitation/Snowfall/Humidity

Precip./Humidity	Jan	Feb	Mar	Apr	May	Jun	Jul	Aug	Sep	Oct	Nov	Dec	Yr.
Avg. Precip. (in.)	5.7	4.2	3.7	2.4	1.7	1.4	0.8	1.1	1.9	3.5	5.9	5.9	38.4
Avg. Snowfall (in.)	5	2	1	Tr	Tr	0	0	0	0	Tr	1	3	13
Avg. Rel. Hum. 7am (%)	83	83	84	83	80	79	79	84	87	88	85	85	83
Avg. Rel. Hum. 4pm (%)	76	69	63	57	54	54	49	51	57	68	76	79	63

Note: Figures cover the years 1948-1990; Tr = Trace amounts (<0.05 in. of rain; <0.5 in. of snow)
Source: National Climatic Data Center, International Station Meteorological Climate Summary, 9/96

Weather Conditions

Temperature			Daytime Sky			Precipitation		
5°F & below	32°F & below	90°F & above	Clear	Partly cloudy	Cloudy	0.01 inch or more precip.	0.1 inch or more snow/ice	Thunder-storms
< 1	38	3	57	121	187	157	8	8

Note: Figures are average number of days per year and cover the years 1948-1990
Source: National Climatic Data Center, International Station Meteorological Climate Summary, 9/96

HAZARDOUS WASTE

Superfund Sites

Bellevue has no sites on the EPA's Superfund Final National Priorities List.
U.S. Environmental Protection Agency, Final National Priorities List, April 17, 2012

AIR & WATER QUALITY

Air Quality Index

Area	Percent of Days when Air Quality was...[2]					AQI Statistics[2]	
	Good	Moderate	Unhealthy for Sensitive Groups	Unhealthy	Very Unhealthy	Maximum	Median
Area[1]	86.8	13.2	0.0	0.0	0.0	89	33

Note: Air Quality Index (AQI) is an index for reporting daily air quality. EPA calculates the AQI for five major air pollutants regulated by the Clean Air Act: ground-level ozone, particle pollution (aka particulate matter), carbon monoxide, sulfur dioxide, and nitrogen dioxide. The AQI runs from 0 to 500. The higher the AQI value, the greater the level of air pollution and the greater the health concern. There are six AQI categories: "Good" AQI is between 0 and 50. Air quality is considered satisfactory; "Moderate" AQI is between 51 and 100. Air quality is acceptable; "Unhealthy for Sensitive Groups" When AQI values are between 101 and 150, members of sensitive groups may experience health effects; "Unhealthy" When AQI values are between 151 and 200 everyone may begin to experience health effects; "Very Unhealthy" AQI values between 201 and 300 trigger a health alert; "Hazardous" AQI values over 300 trigger warnings of emergency conditions (not shown); (1) Data covers King County; (2) Based on 365 days with AQI data in 2011.
Source: U.S. Environmental Protection Agency, AirData Report, 2011

Air Quality Index Pollutants

Area	Percent of Days when AQI Pollutant was...[2]					
	Carbon Monoxide	Nitrogen Dioxide	Ozone	Sulfur Dioxide	Particulate Matter 2.5	Particulate Matter 10
Area[1]	0.0	0.0	47.4	0.8	51.8	0.0

Note: The Air Quality Index (AQI) is an index for reporting daily air quality. EPA calculates the AQI for five major air pollutants regulated by the Clean Air Act: ground-level ozone, particle pollution (also known as particulate matter), carbon monoxide, sulfur dioxide, and nitrogen dioxide. The AQI runs from 0 to 500. The higher the AQI value, the greater the level of air pollution and the greater the health concern; (1) Data covers King County; (2) Based on 365 days with AQI data in 2011.
Source: U.S. Environmental Protection Agency, AirData Report, 2011

Air Quality Index Trends

Area	Trend Sites (days)								All Sites (days)
	2003	2004	2005	2006	2007	2008	2009	2010	2010
MSA[1]	16	7	7	14	10	7	12	1	1

Note: Figures are the number of days the AQI value exceeded 100 in a given year. An AQI value greater than 100 indicates that air quality would have been in the unhealthful range on that day. Data from exceptional events are included. These counts are presented in two ways. First, the counts are based on sites having an adequate record of monitoring data during the trend period (trend sites). These counts represent the relative change in the number of days with AQI values greater than 100. In the last column, the counts are based on all sites with data in the most recent year (because it is possible for a site to have data in the most recent year but not enough data to be a trend site); (1) Data covers the Seattle-Tacoma-Bellevue, WA—see Appendix B for areas included
Source: U.S. Environmental Protection Agency, Air Quality Index Information, "Number of Days with Air Quality Index Values Greater than 100 at Trend Sites, 2000-2010, and at All Sites in 2010"

Maximum Air Pollutant Concentrations: Particulate Matter, Ozone, CO and Lead

	Particulate Matter 10 (ug/m^3)	Particulate Matter 2.5 Wtd AM (ug/m^3)	Particulate Matter 2.5 24-Hr (ug/m^3)	Ozone (ppm)	Carbon Monoxide (ppm)	Lead (ug/m^3)
MSA[1] Level	n/a	7.1	24	0.068	1	n/a
NAAQS[2]	150	15	35	0.075	9	0.15
Met NAAQS[2]	n/a	Yes	Yes	Yes	Yes	n/a

Note: Data from exceptional events are not included; (1) Data covers the Seattle-Tacoma-Bellevue, WA—see Appendix B for areas included; (2) National Ambient Air Quality Standards; ppm = parts per million; ug/m^3 = micrograms per cubic meter; n/a not available
Concentrations: Particulate Matter 10 (coarse particulate)—highest second maximum 24-hour concentration; Particulate Matter 2.5 Wtd AM (fine particulate)—highest weighted annual mean concentration; Particulate Matter 2.5 24-Hour (fine particulate)—highest 98th percentile 24-hour concentration; Ozone—highest fourth daily maximum 8-hour concentration; Carbon Monoxide—highest second maximum non-overlapping 8-hour concentration; Lead—maximum running 3-month average
Source: U.S. Environmental Protection Agency, CBSA Factbook 2010, Air Quality Statistics by City, 2010

Maximum Air Pollutant Concentrations: Nitrogen Dioxide and Sulfur Dioxide

	Nitrogen Dioxide AM (ppb)	Nitrogen Dioxide 1-Hr (ppb)	Sulfur Dioxide AM (ppb)	Sulfur Dioxide 1-Hr (ppb)	Sulfur Dioxide 24-Hr (ppb)
MSA[1] Level	n/a	n/a	1.136	24.5	8
NAAQS[2]	53	100	30	75	140
Met NAAQS[2]	n/a	n/a	Yes	Yes	Yes

Note: Data from exceptional events are not included; (1) Data covers the Seattle-Tacoma-Bellevue, WA—see Appendix B for areas included; (2) National Ambient Air Quality Standards; ppb = parts per billion; n/a not available

Concentrations: Nitrogen Dioxide AM—highest arithmetic mean concentration; Nitrogen Dioxide 1-Hr—highest 98th percentile 1-hour daily maximum concentration; Sulfur Dioxide AM—highest annual mean concentration; Sulfur Dioxide 1-Hr—highest 99th percentile 1-hour daily maximum concentration; Sulfur Dioxide 24-Hr—highest second maximum 24-hour concentration

Source: U.S. Environmental Protection Agency, CBSA Factbook 2010, Air Quality Statistics by City, 2010

Drinking Water

Water System Name	Pop. Served	Primary Water Source Type	Violations[1] Health Based	Violations[1] Monitoring/ Reporting
City of Bellevue	135,100	Purchased Surface	0	1

Note: (1) Based on violation data from January 1, 2011 to December 31, 2011 (includes unresolved violations from earlier years)

Source: U.S. Environmental Protection Agency, Office of Ground Water and Drinking Water, Safe Drinking Water Information System (based on data extracted April 18, 2012)

Billings, Montana

Background

Established in 1882 in Montana Territory, Billings is the largest city in the state. Located in the Yellowstone Valley, it was once home to prehistoric hunters and the Crow Indians. In 1806, William Clark (of the Lewis and Clark expedition) visited the area and inscribed his name on a pillar in 1806. Shortly after the city's establishment, it prospered as a rail hub by the Northern Pacific Railroad, which came to be known as Clark's Fork Bottom. Billings' location on the Yellowstone River made it a natural central point for traveling steamboats.

Shortly following Billings' settlement, entrepreneur Herman Clark arrived and announced ambitious plans to house 20,000 residents, build nearly a dozen sawmills, roads, and most importantly a massive railroad system. Clark's dream became a reality when the city added a transcontinental railroad in 1883 and had a growing population of 1,500 by 1888. In 1909, the Great Northern Railway laid tracks through Billings and congress passed the Enlarged Homestead act, allowing settlers to lay claims to 320 acres of farmlands. This encouraged more growth, and settlers from around the world arrived in Billings.

Throughout the early half of the 20th Century, Billings established itself as an industrial metropolis in Yellowstone Valley. By 1910, the population had peaked above 10,000 and the city included banks, hotels, shopping districts and government buildings. The discovery of oil and natural gas in the area helped Billings to propel itself into the post-war era of the 1940s and 50s. Due to its oil boom, the city secured a dominant role in the energy industry throughout the 1970s and onward. In the 1970s and 80s, while the rest of the country was experiencing a severe economic recession, Billings constructed the first high rise buildings in Montana and welcomed a handful of development companies to construct local shopping districts and residential areas.

Even in the 1990s, Billings continued to grow by expanding its I-90 corridor, welcoming large hotel chains and Fortune 500 corporations. This trend continued into the 21st century, as companies like GE and Wells Fargo aided in the development of Billings' downtown business district, resulting in Skypoint, the city's highest elevated building and observation point. The rapid pace of construction coupled with low tax rates placed Billings at the top of a number of "best cities" lists. Today, Billings maintains high levels of employment, construction, and investments in the local community.

There is no lack of local flavor and attractions in Billings. The Western Romance Company offers wagons, horses, and equipment for visitors who wish to explore like the cowboys did. For kids and families, Billings offers multiple nearby water parks like Big Splash, the Amusement Park Drive In, and local sports teams like the Billings Mustangs baseball team. Cultural attractions are abundant in the Downtown Historic District, with local theaters and museums, notably the Yellowstone Art Museum and the Billings Symphony Orchestra.

Billings also boasts stunning geography, nestled between the Yellowstone Valley and the Yellowstone River. The surrounding Bighorn and Pyror Mountains help create its desirable semi-arid climate with hot summers and tepid winters.

Rankings

General Rankings

- Billings appeared on RelocateAmerica's list of best places to live in America. The annual "Top 100 Places to Live" list recognizes the top communities as nominated by their residents & local businesses. RelocateAmerica's Research Group determines the list based on review of various data gathered for economic, employment, housing, education, industry, opportunity, environment and recreation along with feedback from area leaders and residents. *RelocateAmerica.com, "Top 100 Places to Live for 2011"*

Business/Finance Rankings

- Billings was selected as one of the "100 Best Places to Live and Launch" in the U.S. The city ranked #89. The editors at *Fortune Small Business* ranked 296 Census-designated metro areas by business friendliness (Launching Score, % New Businesses) and lifestyle offerings (Living Score). Then they picked the town within each of the top 100 metro areas that best blends business and pleasure. *Fortune Small Business, "100 Best Places to Live and Launch 2008," April 2008*
- The Billings metro area appeared on the Milken Institute "2011 Best Performing Metros" list. Rank: #37 out of 179 small metro areas. Criteria: job growth; wage and salary growth; high-tech output growth. *Milken Institute, "2011 Best Performing Metros"*
- The Billings metro area was selected as one of the best cities for entrepreneurs in America by *Inc. Magazine.* Criteria: job-growth data for 335 metro areas was analyzed for: recent growth trend; mid-term growth; long-term trend; current year growth. The Billings metro area ranked #23 among small metro areas and #31 overall. *Inc. Magazine, "The Best Cities for Doing Business," July 2008*
- Billings appeared on *Kiplinger's Personal Finance* list of the "Top Ten Tax-Friendly Cities." The city was ranked #9. Criteria: income tax; sales tax; real estate and car/personal property tax. *Kiplinger's Personal Finance, March 1, 2009*

Dating/Romance Rankings

- Billings appeared on *Men's Health's* list of the most sex-happy cities in America. The city ranked #91 of 100. Criteria: condom sales; birth rates; sex toy sales; rates of chlamydia, gonorrhea, and syphilis. *Men's Health, "America's Most Sex-Happy Cities," October 2010*
- *Men's Health* ranked 100 U.S. cities in terms of best (and worst) marriages. Billings was ranked #3 (#1 = worst). Criteria: rate of failed marriages; stringency of divorce laws; percentage of population who've split; number of licensed marriage and family therapists. *Men's Health, "Splitsville, USA," May 2010*

Education Rankings

- *Men's Health* ranked 100 U.S. cities in terms of their education levels. Billings was ranked #43 (#1 = most educated city). Criteria: high school graduation rates; school enrollment; educational attainment; number of households who have outstanding student loans; number of households whose members have taken adult-education courses. *Men's Health, "Where School Is In: The Most and Least Educated Cities," September 12, 2011*

Environmental Rankings

- Billings was selected as one of 22 "Smarter Cities" for energy by the Natural Resources Defense Council. Criteria: investment in green power; energy efficiency measures; conservation. *Natural Resources Defense Council, "2010 Smarter Cities," July 19, 2010*
- The Billings metro area appeared in *Country Home's* "Best Green Places" report. The area ranked #157 out of 379. Criteria: official energy policies; green power; green buildings; availability of fresh, locally grown food. *Country Home, "Best Green Places," 2008*

- Billings was highlighted as one of the top 25 cleanest metro areas for year-round particle pollution (Annual PM 2.5) in the U.S. The area ranked #13. *American Lung Association, State of the Air 2011*
- Billings was highlighted as one of the top 25 cleanest metro areas for short-term particle pollution (24-hour PM 2.5) in the U.S. Monitors in these cities reported no days with unhealthful PM 2.5 levels. *American Lung Association, State of the Air 2011*

Health/Fitness Rankings

- *Men's Health* examined 100 major U.S. cities and selected the best and worst cities for men. Billings ranked #35. Criteria: 35 statistical parameters of long life in the categories of health, quality of life, and fitness. *Men's Health, "The 10 Best and Worst Cities for Men 2012," January/February 2012*
- Billings was selected as one of the most accident-prone cities in America by *Men's Health.* The city ranked #10 of 10. Criteria: workplace accident rates; traffic fatalities; emergency room visits; accidental poisonings; incidents of drowning; fires; injury-producing falls. *Men's Health, "Ranking America's Cities: Accident City, USA," October 2009*
- The Billings metro area appeared in the 2011 Gallup-Healthways Well-Being Index. The index, based on interviews with more than 350,000 Americans, measured jobs, finances, physical health, emotional state of mind and communities. The metro area ranked #25 out of 190. Criteria: life evaluation; emotional health; work environment; physical health; healthy behaviors; basic access (basic needs optimal for a healthy life, such as access to food and medicine, having health insurance and feeling safe while walking at night). *Gallup-Healthways, "State of Well-Being 2011"*
- *Men's Health* ranked 100 U.S. cities in terms of their activity levels. Billings was ranked #74 (#1 = most active city). Criteria: where and how often residents exercise; percentage of households that watch more than 15 hours of cable television a week and buy more than 11 video games a year; death rate from deep-vein thrombosis, a condition linked to sitting for extended periods of time. *Men's Health, "Where Sit Happens: The Most and Least Active Cities in America," June 20, 2011*

Safety Rankings

- The National Insurance Crime Bureau ranked 366 metro areas in the U.S. in terms of per capita rates of vehicle theft. The Billings metro area ranked #119 (#1 = highest rate). Criteria: number of vehicle theft offenses per 100,000 inhabitants in 2010. *National Insurance Crime Bureau, "Hot Spots," June 21, 2011*

Sports/Recreation Rankings

- Billings was chosen as a bicycle friendly community by the League of American Bicyclists. A Bicycle Friendly Community welcomes cyclists by providing safe accommodation for cycling and encouraging people to bike for transportation and recreation. There are four award levels: Platinum; Gold; Silver; and Bronze. The community achieved an award level of Bronze. *League of American Bicyclists, "Bicycle Friendly Community Master List 2011"*
- Billings was chosen as one of America's best cities for bicycling. The city ranked #37 out of 50. Criteria: number of segregated bike lanes, municipal bike racks, and bike boulevards; vibrant and diverse bike culture; smart, savvy bike shops; interviews with national and local advocates, bike shops and other experts. The editors only considered cities with populations of 100,000 or more. *Bicycling, "America's Best Bike Cities," April 2010*

Women/Minorities Rankings

- *Women's Health* examined U.S. cities and identified the 100 best cities for women. Billings was ranked #30. Criteria: 30 categories were examined from obesity and breast cancer rates to commuting times and hours spent working out. *Women's Health, "Best Cities for Women 2012"*

Miscellaneous Rankings

- *Men's Health* ranked 100 U.S. cities by their level of sadness. Billings was ranked #28 (#1 = saddest city). Criteria: suicide rates; unemployment rates; percentage of households that use antidepressants; percent of population who report feeling blue all or most of the time. *Men's Health, "Frown Towns," November 28, 2011*

Business Environment

CITY FINANCES

City Government Finances

Component	2009 ($000)	2009 ($ per capita)
Total Revenues	164,254	1,612
Total Expenditures	170,668	1,675
Debt Outstanding	102,668	1,008
Cash and Securities[1]	132,543	1,301

Note: (1) Cash and security holdings of a government at the close of its fiscal year, including those of its dependent agencies, utilities, and liquor stores.
Source: U.S Census Bureau, State & Local Government Finances 2009

City Government Revenue by Source

Source	2009 ($000)	2009 ($ per capita)
General Revenue		
From Federal Government	9,161	90
From State Government	16,068	158
From Local Governments	1,839	18
Taxes		
Property	27,750	272
Sales and Gross Receipts	0	0
Personal Income	0	0
Corporate Income	0	0
Motor Vehicle License	1,744	17
Other Taxes	4,852	48
Current Charges	41,640	409
Liquor Store	0	0
Utility	20,094	197
Employee Retirement	0	0

Source: U.S Census Bureau, State & Local Government Finances 2009

City Government Expenditures by Function

Function	2009 ($000)	2009 ($ per capita)	2009 (%)
General Direct Expenditures			
Air Transportation	10,350	102	6.1
Corrections	0	0	0.0
Education	0	0	0.0
Employment Security Administration	0	0	0.0
Financial Administration	1,152	11	0.7
Fire Protection	15,299	150	9.0
General Public Buildings	1,161	11	0.7
Governmental Administration, Other	3,187	31	1.9
Health	745	7	0.4
Highways	24,787	243	14.5
Hospitals	0	0	0.0
Housing and Community Development	3,948	39	2.3
Interest on General Debt	3,247	32	1.9
Judicial and Legal	2,578	25	1.5
Libraries	2,808	28	1.6
Parking	1,558	15	0.9
Parks and Recreation	5,092	50	3.0
Police Protection	16,622	163	9.7
Public Welfare	0	0	0.0
Sewerage	20,586	202	12.1
Solid Waste Management	10,452	103	6.1
Veterans' Services	0	0	0.0
Liquor Store	0	0	0.0
Utility	27,809	273	16.3
Employee Retirement	0	0	0.0

Source: U.S Census Bureau, State & Local Government Finances 2009

Municipal Bond Ratings

Area	Moody's	S&P	Fitch
City	n/a	n/a	n/a

Rating Systems (shown in declining order of credit quality): Moody's– Aaa, Aa, A, Baa, Ba, B, Caa, Ca, C (numerical modifiers 1, 2, and 3 are added to letter-rating); S&P– AAA, AA, A, BBB, BB, B, CCC, CC, C; Fitch– AAA, AA, A, BBB, BB, B, CCC, CC, C. Ratings may be modified by the addition of a plus or minus sign to show relative standing within the major rating categories.
Notes: n/a Not Available; w/d Withdrawn (1) Not Reviewed; (2) Issuer Rating/No General Obligation; (3) Standard and Poor's Issue Credit Rating (ICR) is a current opinion of an obliger with respect to a specific financial obligation, a specific class of financial obligations, or a specific financial program.
Source: U.S. Census Bureau, 2012 Statistical Abstract, Bond Ratings for City Governments by Largest Cities: 2010

DEMOGRAPHICS

Population Growth

Area	1990 Census	2000 Census	2010 Census	Population Growth (%) 1990-2000	Population Growth (%) 2000-2010
City	81,812	89,847	104,170	9.8	15.9
MSA[1]	121,499	138,904	158,050	14.3	13.8
U.S.	248,709,873	281,421,906	308,745,538	13.2	9.7

Note: (1) Figures cover the Billings, MT Metropolitan Statistical Area—see Appendix B for areas included
Source: U.S. Census Bureau, 2010 Census

Household Size

Area	Persons in Household (%)							Average Household Size
	One	Two	Three	Four	Five	Six	Seven or More	
City	32.6	34.7	14.6	10.7	4.8	1.6	0.9	2.29
MSA[1]	29.8	36.0	14.7	11.5	5.2	1.8	1.0	2.37
U.S.	26.7	32.8	16.1	13.4	6.5	2.6	1.9	2.58

Note: (1) Figures cover the Billings, MT Metropolitan Statistical Area—see Appendix B for areas included
Source: U.S. Census Bureau, 2010 Census

Race

Area	White Alone[2] (%)	Black Alone[2] (%)	Asian Alone[2] (%)	AIAN[3] Alone[2] (%)	NHOPI[4] Alone[2] (%)	Other Race Alone[2] (%)	Two or More Races (%)
City	89.6	0.8	0.7	4.4	0.1	1.4	2.9
MSA[1]	91.1	0.6	0.6	3.8	0.1	1.1	2.7
U.S.	72.4	12.6	4.8	0.9	0.2	6.2	2.9

Note: (1) Figures cover the Billings, MT Metropolitan Statistical Area—see Appendix B for areas included; (2) Alone is defined as not being in combination with one or more other races; (3) American Indian and Alaska Native; (4) Native Hawaiian and Other Pacific Islander
Source: U.S. Census Bureau, 2010 Census

Hispanic or Latino Origin

Area	Hispanic or Latino (%)	Mexican (%)	Puerto Rican (%)	Cuban (%)	Other Hispanic or Latino (%)
City	5.2	4.0	0.2	0.0	0.9
MSA[1]	4.5	3.5	0.2	0.0	0.8
U.S.	16.3	10.3	1.5	0.6	4.0

Note: Persons of Hispanic or Latino origin can be of any race; (1) Figures cover the Billings, MT Metropolitan Statistical Area—see Appendix B for areas included
Source: U.S. Census Bureau, 2010 Census

Segregation

Type	Segregation Indices[1]				Percent Change		
	1990	2000	2010	2010 Rank[2]	1990-2000	1990-2010	2000-2010
Black/White	n/a	n/a	n/a	n/a	n/a	n/a	n/a
Asian/White	n/a	n/a	n/a	n/a	n/a	n/a	n/a
Hispanic/White	n/a	n/a	n/a	n/a	n/a	n/a	n/a

Note: Figures are based on an analysis of 1990, 2000, and 2010 Census Decennial Census tract data by William H. Frey, Brookings Institution and the University of Michigan Social Science Data Analysis Network. In this analysis all racial groups (whites, blacks, and asians) are non-Hispanic members of those races. Hispanics are shown as a separate category; All figures cover the Metropolitan Statistical Area (see Appendix B for areas included); (1) Segregation Indices are Dissimilarity Indices that measure the degree to which the minority group is distributed differently than whites across census tracts. They range from 0 (complete integration) to 100 (complete segregation) where the value indicates the percentage of the minority group that needs to move to be distributed exactly like whites; (2) Ranges from 1 (most segregated) to 102 (least segregated); n/a not available.
Source: www.CensusScope.org

Ancestry

Area	German	Irish	English	American	Italian	Polish	French[2]	Scottish	Dutch
City	30.2	13.7	10.4	10.0	2.8	1.6	3.6	3.0	1.8
MSA[1]	30.7	13.7	11.4	10.9	2.5	1.8	3.3	3.1	2.2
U.S.	16.1	11.6	8.8	6.1	5.7	3.2	3.0	1.9	1.6

Note: Figures are the percentage of the total population reporting a particular ancestry. The nine most commonly reported ancestries in the U.S. are shown. Figures include multiple ancestries (e.g. if a person reported being Irish and Italian, they were included in both columns); (1) Figures cover the Billings, MT Metropolitan Statistical Area—see Appendix B for areas included; (2) Excludes Basque
Source: U.S. Census Bureau, 2008-2010 American Community Survey 3-Year Estimates

Foreign-Born Population

Area	Percent of Population Born in								
	Any Foreign Country	Mexico	Asia	Europe	Carribean	South America	Central America[2]	Africa	Canada
City	n/a	n/a	n/a	n/a	n/a	n/a	n/a	n/a	n/a
MSA[1]	n/a	n/a	n/a	n/a	n/a	n/a	n/a	n/a	n/a
U.S.	12.8	3.8	3.6	1.6	1.2	0.9	1.0	0.5	0.3

Note: (1) Figures cover the Billings, MT Metropolitan Statistical Area—see Appendix B for areas included; (2) Excludes Mexico.
Source: U.S. Census Bureau, 2008-2010 American Community Survey 3-Year Estimates

Marital Status

Area	Never Married	Now Married[2]	Separated	Widowed	Divorced
City	29.4	48.4	1.6	6.3	14.3
MSA[1]	26.8	52.6	1.3	5.9	13.4
U.S.	31.6	49.6	2.2	6.1	10.7

Note: Figures are percentages and cover the population 15 years of age and older; (1) Figures cover the Billings, MT Metropolitan Statistical Area—see Appendix B for areas included; (2) Excludes separated
Source: U.S. Census Bureau, 2008-2010 American Community Survey 3-Year Estimates

Age

Area	Percent of Population							Median Age
	Under Age 5	Age 5 to 17	Age 18 to 34	Age 35 to 49	Age 50 to 64	Age 65 to 79	80 Years and Over	
City	7.0	15.6	24.5	18.4	19.5	9.9	5.1	37.5
MSA[1]	6.7	16.8	22.0	19.2	21.0	10.0	4.4	39.0
U.S.	6.5	17.5	23.2	20.7	19.0	9.4	3.6	37.2

Note: (1) Figures cover the Billings, MT Metropolitan Statistical Area—see Appendix B for areas included
Source: U.S. Census Bureau, 2010 Census

Male/Female Ratio

Area	Males	Females	Males per 100 Females
City	50,266	53,904	93.3
MSA[1]	77,490	80,560	96.2
U.S.	151,781,326	156,964,212	96.7

Note: (1) Figures cover the Billings, MT Metropolitan Statistical Area—see Appendix B for areas included
Source: U.S. Census Bureau, 2010 Census

Religious Groups

Area	Catholic	Baptist	Non-Den.	Methodist[2]	Lutheran	LDS[3]	Pente-costal	Presby-terian[4]	Muslim[5]	Judaism
MSA[1]	12.1	2.5	3.8	2.1	6.1	4.9	4.1	1.8	0.1	0.0
U.S.	19.1	9.3	4.0	4.0	2.3	2.0	1.9	1.6	0.8	0.7

Note: Figures are the number of adherents as a percentage of the total population; (1) Figures cover the Billings, MT Metropolitan Statistical Area—see Appendix B for areas included; (2) Methodist/Pietist; (3) Latter Day Saints; (4) Reformed; (5) Figures are estimates
Source: Association of Statisticians of American Religious Bodies, 2010 U.S. Religion Census: Religious Congregations & Membership Study

ECONOMY

Gross Metropolitan Product

Area	2007	2008	2009	2010	2010 Rank[2]
MSA[1]	7.4	7.2	7.1	7.2	216

Note: Figures are in billions of dollars; (1) Figures cover the Billings, MT Metropolitan Statistical Area—see Appendix B for areas included; (2) Rank ranges from 1 to 363
Source: The United States Conference of Mayors, "U.S. Metro Economies: GMP and Employment Forecasts," June 2011

Economic Growth

Area	2007-2009 (%)	2010 (%)	2011 (%)	Rank[2]
MSA[1]	-1.3	0.3	2.4	174
U.S.	-1.3	2.9	2.5	–

Note: Figures are real Gross Metropolitan Product growth rates and represent annual average percent change; (1) Figures cover the Billings, MT Metropolitan Statistical Area—see Appendix B for areas included; (2) Rank ranges from 1 to 363
Source: The United States Conference of Mayors, "U.S. Metro Economies: GMP and Employment Forecasts," June 2011

Metropolitan Area Exports

Area	2005	2006	2007	2008	2009	2010	2010 Rank[2]
MSA[1]	66.2	75.4	61.7	88.6	70.7	86.7	334

Note: Figures are in millions of dollars; (1) Figures cover the Billings, MT Metropolitan Statistical Area—see Appendix B for areas included; (2) Rank ranges from 1 to 369
Source: U.S. Department of Commerce, International Trade Administration, Office of Trade & Industry Information, Manufacturing & Services, data extracted April 2, 2012

INCOME

Income

Area	Per Capita ($)	Median Household ($)	Average Household ($)
City	26,556	46,065	61,537
MSA[1]	26,386	47,959	62,687
U.S.	26,942	51,222	70,116

Note: (1) Figures cover the Billings, MT Metropolitan Statistical Area—see Appendix B for areas included
Source: U.S. Census Bureau, 2008-2010 American Community Survey 3-Year Estimates

Household Income Distribution

Area	Percent of Households Earning							
	Under $15,000	$15,000 -24,999	$25,000 -34,999	$35,000 -49,999	$50,000 -74,999	$75,000 -99,000	$100,000 -149,999	$150,000 and up
City	11.4	13.4	12.2	16.9	19.9	11.5	9.9	4.9
MSA[1]	10.6	13.5	11.6	16.0	20.5	12.1	10.5	5.0
U.S.	13.0	11.0	10.6	14.2	18.5	12.1	12.2	8.4

Note: (1) Figures cover the Billings, MT Metropolitan Statistical Area—see Appendix B for areas included
Source: U.S. Census Bureau, 2008-2010 American Community Survey 3-Year Estimates

Poverty Rate

Area	All Ages	Under 18 Years Old	18 to 64 Years Old	65 Years and Over
City	12.5	19.8	11.1	7.0
MSA[1]	12.0	18.4	10.6	7.2
U.S.	14.4	20.1	13.1	9.4

Note: Figures are percentage of people whose income during the past 12 months was below the poverty level; (1) Figures cover the Billings, MT Metropolitan Statistical Area—see Appendix B for areas included
Source: U.S. Census Bureau, 2008-2010 American Community Survey 3-Year Estimates

Personal Bankruptcy Filing Rate

Area	2006	2007	2008	2009	2010	2011
Yellowstone County	1.94	2.33	2.34	2.60	3.33	3.32
U.S.	2.00	2.73	3.53	4.61	4.97	4.37

Note: Numbers are per 1,000 population and include Chapter 7 and Chapter 13 filings
Source: Federal Deposit Insurance Corporation, Regional Economic Conditions, March 9, 2012

EMPLOYMENT

Labor Force and Employment

Area	Civilian Labor Force			Workers Employed		
	Dec. 2010	Dec. 2011	% Chg.	Dec. 2010	Dec. 2011	% Chg.
City	58,498	58,675	0.3	55,316	55,995	1.2
MSA[1]	85,204	85,505	0.4	80,398	81,385	1.2
U.S.	153,156,000	153,373,000	0.1	139,159,000	140,681,000	1.1

Note: Data is not seasonally adjusted and covers workers 16 years of age and older; (1) Metropolitan Statistical Area—see Appendix B for areas included
Source: Bureau of Labor Statistics, http://stats.bls.gov

Unemployment Rate

Area	2011											
	Jan.	Feb.	Mar.	Apr.	May	Jun.	Jul.	Aug.	Sep.	Oct.	Nov.	Dec.
City	6.1	5.6	5.6	4.8	5.0	5.9	5.5	5.5	5.2	5.0	4.6	4.6
MSA[1]	6.4	6.0	5.9	5.1	5.2	6.0	5.6	5.6	5.4	5.2	4.7	4.8
U.S.	9.8	9.5	9.2	8.7	8.7	9.3	9.3	9.1	8.8	8.5	8.2	8.3

Note: Data is not seasonally adjusted and covers workers 16 years of age and older; All figures are percentages; (1) Metropolitan Statistical Area—see Appendix B for areas included
Source: Bureau of Labor Statistics, http://stats.bls.gov

Projected Unemployment Rate

Area	2010 (%)	2011 (%)	2012 (%)	2013 (%)
MSA[1]	5.8	5.1	4.6	4.4

Note: (1) Metropolitan Statistical Area—see Appendix B for areas included
Source: The United States Conference of Mayors, "U.S. Metro Economies: GMP and Employment Forecasts," June 2011

Employment by Occupation

Occupation Classification	City (%)	MSA[1] (%)	U.S. (%)
Management, Business, Science, and Arts	33.5	32.7	35.6
Natural Resources, Construction, and Maintenance	9.7	11.4	9.5
Production, Transportation, and Material Moving	11.2	11.9	12.1
Sales and Office	27.2	26.3	25.2
Service	18.4	17.7	17.6

Note: Figures cover employed civilians 16 years of age and older; (1) Figures cover the Billings, MT Metropolitan Statistical Area—see Appendix B for areas included
Source: U.S. Census Bureau, 2008-2010 American Community Survey 3-Year Estimates

Employment by Industry

Sector	MSA[1]		U.S.
	Number of Employees	Percent of Total	Percent of Total
Construction	n/a	n/a	4.1
Education and Health Services	13,400	17.4	15.2
Financial Activities	n/a	n/a	5.8
Government	9,300	12.0	16.8
Information	n/a	n/a	2.0
Leisure and Hospitality	9,400	12.2	9.9
Manufacturing	n/a	n/a	8.9
Mining and Logging	n/a	n/a	0.6
Other Services	n/a	n/a	4.0
Professional and Business Services	10,200	13.2	13.3
Retail Trade	n/a	n/a	11.5
Transportation and Utilities	n/a	n/a	3.8
Wholesale Trade	n/a	n/a	4.2

Note: Figures cover non-farm employment as of December 2011 and are not seasonally adjusted; (1) Metropolitan Statistical Area—see Appendix B for areas included; n/a not available
Source: Bureau of Labor Statistics, http://stats.bls.gov

Occupations with Greatest Projected Employment Growth: 2008 – 2018

Occupation[1]	2008 Employment	2018 Projected Employment	Numeric Employment Change	Percent Employment Change
Retail Salespersons	18,740	21,160	2,420	12.9
Bookkeeping, Accounting, and Auditing Clerks	12,360	14,070	1,710	13.8
Registered Nurses	8,320	9,970	1,650	19.8
Janitors and Cleaners, Except Maids and Housekeeping Cleaners	8,950	10,370	1,420	15.9
Combined Food Preparation and Serving Workers, Including Fast Food	9,150	10,420	1,270	13.9
Customer Service Representatives	5,150	6,280	1,130	21.9
Waiters and Waitresses	9,380	10,460	1,080	11.5
Maids and Housekeeping Cleaners	5,740	6,600	860	15.0
Landscaping and Groundskeeping Workers	4,210	5,040	830	19.7
Nursing Aides, Orderlies, and Attendants	5,670	6,490	820	14.5

Note: Projections cover Montana; (1) Sorted by numeric employment change
Source: www.projectionscentral.com, State Occupational Projections, 2008–2018 Long-Term Projections

Fastest Growing Occupations: 2008 – 2018

Occupation[1]	2008 Employment	2018 Projected Employment	Numeric Employment Change	Percent Employment Change
Medical Assistants	1,110	1,450	340	30.6
Network Systems and Data Communications Analysts	420	540	120	28.6
Social and Human Service Assistants	1,590	2,010	420	26.4
Gaming and Sports Book Writers and Runners	720	910	190	26.4
Dental Assistants	1,040	1,310	270	26.0
Mental Health Counselors	620	780	160	25.8
Fitness Trainers and Aerobics Instructors	1,050	1,320	270	25.7
Substance Abuse and Behavioral Disorder Counselors	470	590	120	25.5
Physical Therapists	800	1,000	200	25.0
Child, Family, and School Social Workers	980	1,220	240	24.5

Note: Projections cover Montana; (1) Sorted by percent employment change and excludes occupations with numeric employment change less than 100
Source: www.projectionscentral.com, State Occupational Projections, 2008–2018 Long-Term Projections

Average Wages

Occupation	$/Hr.	Occupation	$/Hr.
Accountants and Auditors	31.72	Maids and Housekeeping Cleaners	9.30
Automotive Mechanics	17.39	Maintenance and Repair Workers	15.01
Bookkeepers	15.52	Marketing Managers	38.80
Carpenters	17.21	Nuclear Medicine Technologists	n/a
Cashiers	9.26	Nurses, Licensed Practical	16.95
Clerks, General Office	12.99	Nurses, Registered	30.66
Clerks, Receptionists/Information	11.87	Nursing Aides/Orderlies/Attendants	12.41
Clerks, Shipping/Receiving	12.27	Packers and Packagers, Hand	9.36
Computer Programmers	27.08	Physical Therapists	31.15
Computer Support Specialists	18.49	Postal Service Mail Carriers	24.77
Computer Systems Analysts	33.38	Real Estate Brokers	n/a
Cooks, Restaurant	11.08	Retail Salespersons	12.55
Dentists	55.11	Sales Reps., Exc. Tech./Scientific	27.02
Electrical Engineers	32.19	Sales Reps., Tech./Scientific	28.18
Electricians	22.32	Secretaries, Exc. Legal/Med./Exec.	12.85
Financial Managers	50.49	Security Guards	12.66
First-Line Supervisors/Managers, Sales	19.12	Surgeons	118.29
Food Preparation Workers	9.48	Teacher Assistants	9.30
General and Operations Managers	42.76	Teachers, Elementary School	20.60
Hairdressers/Cosmetologists	12.15	Teachers, Secondary School	20.20
Internists	n/a	Telemarketers	11.73
Janitors and Cleaners	10.47	Truck Drivers, Heavy/Tractor-Trailer	19.27
Landscaping/Groundskeeping Workers	12.16	Truck Drivers, Light/Delivery Svcs.	14.35
Lawyers	34.89	Waiters and Waitresses	9.11

Note: Wage data covers the Billings, MT Metropolitan Statistical Area—see Appendix B for areas included. Hourly wages for elementary/secondary school teachers and teacher assistants were calculated by the editors from annual wage data assuming a 40 hour work week; n/a not available.
Source: Bureau of Labor Statistics, Metro Area Occupational Employment and Wage Estimates, May 2011

RESIDENTIAL REAL ESTATE

Building Permits

Area	Single-Family			Multi-Family			Total		
	2010	2011	Pct. Chg.	2010	2011	Pct. Chg.	2010	2011	Pct. Chg.
City	308	243	-21.1	125	10	-92.0	433	253	-41.6
MSA[1]	321	256	-20.2	136	16	-88.2	457	272	-40.5
U.S.	447,311	418,498	-6.4	157,299	205,563	30.7	604,610	624,061	3.2

Note: (1) Metropolitan Statistical Area—see Appendix B for areas included; figures represent new, privately-owned housing units authorized (unadjusted data); All permit data are based on estimates with imputation.
Source: U.S. Census Bureau, Manufacturing, Mining, and Construction Statistics, Building Permits, 2010, 2011

Homeownership Rate

Area	2005 (%)	2006 (%)	2007 (%)	2008 (%)	2009 (%)	2010 (%)	2011 (%)
MSA[1]	n/a	n/a	n/a	n/a	n/a	n/a	n/a
U.S.	68.9	68.8	68.1	67.8	67.4	66.9	66.1

Note: (1) Metropolitan Statistical Area—see Appendix B for areas included; n/a not available
Source: U.S. Census Bureau, Housing Vacancies and Homeownership Annual Statistics: 2011

Housing Vacancy Rates

Area	Gross Vacancy Rate[2] (%)			Year-Round Vacancy Rate[3] (%)			Rental Vacancy Rate[4] (%)			Homeowner Vacancy Rate[5] (%)		
	2009	2010	2011	2009	2010	2011	2009	2010	2011	2009	2010	2011
MSA[1]	n/a	n/a	n/a	n/a	n/a	n/a	n/a	n/a	n/a	n/a	n/a	n/a
U.S.	14.5	14.3	14.2	11.3	11.3	11.1	10.6	10.2	9.5	2.6	2.6	2.5

Note: (1) Metropolitan Statistical Area—see Appendix B for areas included; (2) The percentage of the total housing inventory that is vacant; (3) The percentage of the housing inventory (excluding seasonal units) that is year-round vacant; (4) The percentage of rental inventory that is vacant for rent; (5) The percentage of homeowner inventory that is vacant for sale; n/a not available
Source: U.S. Census Bureau, Housing Vacancies and Homeownership Annual Statistics: 2011

TAXES

State Corporate Income Tax Rates

State	Tax Rate (%)	Income Brackets ($)	Num. of Brackets	Financial Institution Tax Rate (%)[a]	Federal Income Tax Ded.
Montana	6.75 (p)	Flat rate	1	6.75 (p)	No

Note: Tax rates as of January 1, 2012; (a) Rates listed are the corporate income tax rate applied to financial institutions or excise taxes based on income. Some states have other taxes based upon the value of deposits or shares; (p) Montana levies a 7% tax on taxpayers using water's edge combination. The minimum tax per corporation is $50; the $50 minimum applies to each corporation included on a combined tax return. Taxpayers with gross sales in Montana of $100,000 or less maypay an alternative tax of 0.5% on such sales, instead of the net income tax.
Source: Federation of Tax Administrators, "State Corporate Income Tax Rates, 2012"

State Individual Income Tax Rates

State	Tax Rate (%)	Income Brackets ($)	Num. of Brackets	Personal Exempt. ($)[1] Single	Personal Exempt. ($)[1] Dependents	Fed. Inc. Tax Ded.
Montana (a)	1.0 - 6.9	2,700 - 16,000	7	2,190	2,190	Yes (m)

Note: Tax rates as of January 1, 2012; Local- and county-level taxes are not included; n/a not applicable; (1) Married joint filers generally receive double the single exemption; (a) 17 states have statutory provision for automatically adjusting to the rate of inflation the dollar values of the income tax brackets, standard deductions, and/or personal exemptions. Massachusetts, Michigan, and Nebraska index the personal exemptiononly. Oregon does not index the income brackets for $125,000 and over. Because the inflation-adjustments for 2012 are not yet available in some cases, the table may report the 2011 amounts; (m) The deduction for federal income tax is limited to $5,000 for individuals and $10,000 for joint returns in Missouri and Montana, and to $5,950 for all filers in Oregon.
Source: Federation of Tax Administrators, "State Individual Income Tax Rates, 2012"

Various State and Local Tax Rates

State	State and Local Sales and Use (%)	State Sales and Use (%)	Gasoline[1] (¢/gal.)	Cigarette[2] ($/pack)	Spirits[3] ($/gal.)	Wine[4] ($/gal.)	Beer[5] ($/gal.)
Montana	None	None (d)	27.8	1.70	9.45 (f)	1.06	0.14

Note: All tax rates as of January 1, 2012 except beer, wine and spirits (September 1, 2011); (1) The American Petroleum Institute has developed a methodology for determining the average tax rate on a gallon of fuel. Rates may include any of the following: excise taxes, environmental fees, storage tank fees, other fees or taxes, general sales tax, and local taxes. In states where gasoline is subject to the general sales tax, or where the fuel tax is based on the average sale price, the average rate determined by API is sensitive to changes in the price of gasoline. States that fully or partially apply general sales taxes to gasoline: CA, CO, GA, IL, IN, MI, NY; (2) The federal excise tax of $1.0066 per pack and local taxes are not included; (3) Rates are those applicable to off-premise sales of 40% alcohol by volume (a.b.v.) distilled spirits in 750ml containers. Local excise taxes are excluded; (4) Rates are those applicable to off-premise sales of 11% a.b.v. non-carbonated wine in 750ml containers; (5) Rates are those applicable to off-premise sales of 4.7% a.b.v. beer in 12 ounce containers; (d) Due to data limitations, table does not include sales taxes in local resort areas in Montana; (f) States where the government controls sales. In these "control states," products are subject to ad valorem mark-up and excise taxes. The excise tax rate is calculated using a methodology developed by the Distilled Spirits Council of the United States.
Source: Tax Foundation, 2012 Facts & Figures: How Does Your State Compare?

State-Local Tax Burdens

Area	Rate (%)	Rank[1]	Per Capita Taxes Paid to Home State ($)	Total State and Local Per Capita Taxes Paid ($)	Per Capita Income ($)
Montana	8.7	35	2,111	3,216	36,784
U.S. Average	9.8	-	3,057	4,160	42,539

Note: Figures cover 2009; (1) Rank ranges from 1 to 50 where 1 is highest tax burden
Source: Tax Foundation, State-Local Tax Burdens, All States, 2009

State Business Tax Climate Index Rankings

State	Overall Rank	Corporate Tax Index Rank	Individual Income Tax Index Rank	Sales Tax Index Rank	Unemployment Insurance Tax Index Rank	Property Tax Index Rank
Montana	8	15	20	3	20	8

Note: The index is a measure of how each state's tax laws affect economic performance. The lower the rank, the more favorable a state's tax system is for business. States without a given tax are given a ranking of 1.
Source: Tax Foundation, Major Components of the State Business Tax Climate Index, FY 2012

COMMERCIAL UTILITIES

Typical Monthly Electric Bills

Area	Commercial Service ($/month)		Industrial Service ($/month)	
	1,500 kWh	40 kW demand 14,000 kWh	1,000 kW demand 200,000 kWh	50,000 kW demand 15,000,000 kWh
City	n/a	n/a	n/a	n/a
Average[1]	189	1,616	25,197	1,470,813

Note: Based on total rates in effect July 1, 2011; (1) average based on 184 utilities surveyed; n/a not available
Source: Edison Electric Institute, Typical Bills and Average Rates Report, Summer 2011

TRANSPORTATION

Means of Transportation to Work

Area	Car/Truck/Van		Public Transportation			Bicycle	Walked	Other Means	Worked at Home
	Drove Alone	Car-pooled	Bus	Subway	Railroad				
City	80.8	8.9	1.7	0.0	0.0	0.6	3.8	0.8	3.5
MSA[1]	79.6	9.3	1.3	0.0	0.0	0.6	3.9	1.0	4.3
U.S.	76.0	10.2	2.7	1.7	0.5	0.5	2.8	1.3	4.2

Note: Figures are percentages and cover workers 16 years of age and older; (1) Figures cover the Billings, MT Metropolitan Statistical Area—see Appendix B for areas included
Source: U.S. Census Bureau, 2008-2010 American Community Survey 3-Year Estimates

Travel Time to Work

Area	Less Than 10 Minutes	10 to 19 Minutes	20 to 29 Minutes	30 to 44 Minutes	45 to 59 Minutes	60 to 89 Minutes	90 Minutes or More
City	20.3	50.3	19.7	5.6	1.5	1.1	1.6
MSA[1]	20.2	43.6	22.3	8.6	2.2	1.4	1.8
U.S.	13.9	30.1	20.8	19.8	7.5	5.5	2.5

Note: Figures are percentages and include workers 16 years old and over; (1) Figures cover the Billings, MT Metropolitan Statistical Area—see Appendix B for areas included
Source: U.S. Census Bureau, 2008-2010 American Community Survey 3-Year Estimates

Travel Time Index

Area	1985	1990	1995	2000	2005	2010
Urban Area[1]	n/a	n/a	n/a	n/a	n/a	n/a
Average[2]	1.11	1.16	1.18	1.21	1.25	1.20

Note: Travel Time Index—the ratio of travel time in the peak period to the travel time at free-flow conditions. A value of 1.30 indicates a 20-minute free-flow trip takes 26 minutes in the peak. Free-flow speeds (60 mph on freeways and 35 mph on principal arterials) are used as the comparison threshold; (1) Data for the Billings, MT urban area was not available; (2) average of 439 urban areas
Source: Texas Transportation Institute, Urban Mobility Report 2011, September 2011

Public Transportation

Agency Name / Mode of Transportation	Vehicles Operated in Maximum Service	Annual Unlinked Passenger Trips ('000)	Annual Passenger Miles ('000)
Billings Metropolitan Transit (Billings MET Transit)			
Bus (directly operated)	20	630.1	2,335.1
Demand Response (directly operated)	11	59.5	320.1

Source: Federal Transit Administration, National Transit Database, 2010

Air Transportation

Airport Name and Code / Type of Service	Passenger Airlines[1]	Passenger Enplanements	Freight Carriers[2]	Freight (lbs.)
Logan International (BIL)				
Domestic service (U.S. carriers - 2011)	15	407,084	8	27,952,801
International service (U.S. carriers - 2010)	0	0	1	44,500

Note: (1) Includes all U.S.-based major, minor and commuter airlines that carried at least one passenger during the year; (2) Includes all U.S.-based airlines and freight carriers that transported at least one pound of freight during the year
Source: Bureau of Transportation Statistics, The Intermodal Transportation Database, Air Carriers: T-100 Domestic Market (U.S. Carriers), 2011; Bureau of Transportation Statistics, The Intermodal Transportation Database, Air Carriers: T-100 International Market (U.S. Carriers), 2010

Other Transportation Statistics

Major Highways:	I-90; I-94; SR-87
Amtrak Service:	No
Major Waterways/Ports:	Yellowstone River

Source: Amtrak.com; Google Maps

BUSINESSES

Major Business Headquarters

Company Name	Rankings: Fortune[1]	Rankings: Forbes[2]
No companies listed	-	-

Note: (1) Fortune 500—companies that produce a 10-K are ranked 1 to 500 based on 2010 revenue; (2) all private companies with at least $2 billion in annual revenue are ranked 1 to 212; companies listed are headquartered in the city; dashes indicate no ranking
Source: Fortune, "Fortune 500," May 23, 2011; Forbes, "America's Largest Private Companies," November 16, 2011

Minority- and Women-Owned Businesses

Group	All Firms		Firms with Paid Employees			
	Firms	Sales ($000)	Firms	Sales ($000)	Employees	Payroll ($000)
Asian	122	30,909	24	29,099	152	6,409
Black	58	15,535	16	12,804	21	1,297
Hispanic					,	
Women	3,122	402,079	585	334,328	3,706	72,251
All Firms					,	

Note: Figures cover firms located in the city; minority- and women-owned business are defined as firms in which the corresponding group own 51% or more of the stock or equity of the company
Source: U.S. Census Bureau, 2007 Economic Census, Survey of Business Owners

HOTELS

Hotels/Motels

Area	5 Star		4 Star		3 Star		2 Star		1 Star		Not Rated	
	Num.	Pct.[3]	Num.	Pct.[3]	Num.	Pct.[3]	Num.	Pct.[3]	Num.	Pct.[3]	Num.	Pct.[3]
City[1]	0	0.0	0	0.0	3	8.8	18	52.9	1	2.9	12	35.3
Total[2]	133	0.9	940	6.5	4,569	31.8	7,033	48.9	351	2.4	1,343	9.3

Note: (1) Figures cover Billings and vicinity; (2) Figures cover all 100 cities in this book; (3) Percentage of hotels which have a given star rating; Star ratings are determined by expedia.com and offer an indication of the general quality of a particular hotel.
Source: expedia.com, April 25, 2012

EVENT SITES

Major Stadiums, Arenas, and Auditoriums

Name	Max. Capacity
Expo Center	1,250
Metrapark	12,000
Montana Pavillion	2,500
RimRock Auto Arena	10,093

Source: Original research

Convention Centers

Name	Overall Space (sq. ft.)	Exhibit Space (sq. ft.)	Meeting Space (sq. ft.)	Meeting Rooms
Billings Convention Center	50,000	n/a	n/a	n/a

Note: n/a not available
Source: Original research

Living Environment

COST OF LIVING

Cost of Living Index

Composite Index	Groceries	Housing	Utilities	Transportation	Health Care	Misc. Goods/ Services
n/a	n/a	n/a	n/a	n/a	n/a	n/a

Note: U.S. = 100; n/a not available
Source: The Council for Community and Economic Research, ACCRA Cost of Living Index, 2011

Grocery Prices

Area[1]	T-Bone Steak ($/pound)	Frying Chicken ($/pound)	Whole Milk ($/half gal.)	Eggs ($/dozen)	Orange Juice ($/64 oz.)	Coffee ($/11.5 oz.)
City[2]	n/a	n/a	n/a	n/a	n/a	n/a
Avg.	9.25	1.18	2.22	1.66	3.19	4.40
Min.	6.70	0.88	1.31	0.95	2.46	2.94
Max.	14.30	2.16	3.50	3.18	4.75	6.83

Note: (1) Values for the local area are compared with the average, minimum and maximum values for all 335 areas in the Cost of Living Index; (2) Figures cover the Billings MT urban area; n/a not available; **T-Bone Steak** *(price per pound);* **Frying Chicken** *(price per pound, whole fryer);* **Whole Milk** *(half gallon carton);* **Eggs** *(price per dozen, Grade A, large);* **Orange Juice** *(64 oz. Tropicana or Florida Natural);* **Coffee** *(11.5 oz. can, vacuum-packed, Maxwell House, Hills Bros, or Folgers).*
Source: The Council for Community and Economic Research, ACCRA Cost of Living Index, 2011

Housing and Utility Costs

Area[1]	New Home Price ($)	Apartment Rent ($/month)	All Electric ($/month)	Part Electric ($/month)	Other Energy ($/month)	Telephone ($/month)
City[2]	n/a	n/a	n/a	n/a	n/a	n/a
Avg.	285,990	839	163.23	89.00	77.52	26.92
Min.	188,005	460	125.58	45.39	33.89	17.98
Max.	1,197,028	3,244	339.16	181.97	348.69	40.01

Note: (1) Values for the local area are compared with the average, minimum and maximum values for all 335 areas in the Cost of Living Index; (2) Figures cover the Billings MT urban area; n/a not available; **New Home Price** *(2,400 sf living area, 8,000 sf lot, in urban area with full utilities);* **Apartment Rent** *(950 sf 2 bedroom/1.5 or 2 bath, unfurnished, excluding all utilities except water);* **All Electric** *(average monthly cost for an all-electric home);* **Part Electric** *(average monthly cost for a part-electric home);* **Other Energy** *(average monthly cost for natural gas, fuel oil, coal, wood, and any other forms of energy except electricity);* **Telephone** *(price includes basic monthly rate for a private residential line plus additional local usage charges incurred by a family of four).*
Source: The Council for Community and Economic Research, ACCRA Cost of Living Index, 2011

Health Care, Transportation, and Other Costs

Area[1]	Doctor ($/visit)	Dentist ($/visit)	Optometrist ($/visit)	Gasoline ($/gallon)	Beauty Salon ($/visit)	Men's Shirt ($)
City[2]	n/a	n/a	n/a	n/a	n/a	n/a
Avg.	93.88	81.72	90.54	3.48	32.65	25.06
Min.	60.00	55.33	53.66	3.18	19.78	13.44
Max.	154.98	145.97	183.72	4.31	63.21	46.00

Note: (1) Values for the local area are compared with the average, minimum and maximum values for all 335 areas in the Cost of Living Index; (2) Figures cover the Billings MT urban area; n/a not available; **Doctor** *(general practitioners routine exam of an established patient);* **Dentist** *(adult teeth cleaning and periodic oral examination);* **Optometrist** *(full vision eye exam for established adult patient);* **Gasoline** *(one gallon regular unleaded, national brand, including all taxes, cash price at self-service pump if available);* **Beauty Salon** *(woman's shampoo, trim, and blow-dry);* **Men's Shirt** *(cotton/polyester dress shirt, pinpoint weave, long sleeves).*
Source: The Council for Community and Economic Research, ACCRA Cost of Living Index, 2011

HOUSING

House Price Index (HPI)

Area	National Ranking[2]	Quarterly Change (%)	One-Year Change (%)	Five-Year Change (%)
MSA[1]	115	-0.16	-1.90	5.84
U.S.[3]	-	-0.10	-2.43	-19.16

Note: The HPI is a weighted repeat sales index. It measures average price changes in repeat sales or refinancings on the same properties. This information is obtained by reviewing repeat mortgage transactions on single-family properties whose mortgages have been purchased or securitized by Fannie Mae or Freddie Mac in January 1975; (1) Metropolitan/Micropolitan Statistical Area-see Appendix B for areas included; (2) Rankings are based on annual percentage change for all metro areas containing at least 15,000 transactions over the last 10 years and ranges from 1 to 306; (3) figures based on a weighted average of Census Division estimates using a purchase only index; all figures are for the period ending December 31, 2011
Source: Federal Housing Finance Agency, House Price Index, February 23, 2012

House Price Valuations

Area	Q4 2005		Q4 2006		Q4 2007		Q4 2008		Q4 2009	
	Price ($000)	Over-valuation	Price ($000)	Over-valuation	Price ($000)	Over-valuation	Price ($000)	Over-valuation	Price ($000)	Over-valuation
MSA[1]	144.8	4.2	154.4	3.9	163.5	3.2	161.6	1.5	158.4	-0.8

Note: Figures show the percentage of over- or under-valuation of single family homes relative to statistically normal house values (e.g. a value of 23.6 indicates that house values are 23.6% overvalued). Statistically normal house values are based on house prices, interest rates, household incomes, population densities, and any historical premiums or discounts metropolitan areas have exhibited over time; (1) Figures cover the Billings, MT MSA - see Appendix B for areas included; n/a not available
Source: Global Insight/PNC Financial Services Group, House Prices in America: 4th Quarter 2009 Update

Median Single-Family Home Prices

Area	2009	2010	2011p	Percent Change 2010 to 2011
MSA[1]	n/a	n/a	n/a	n/a
U.S. Average	172.1	173.1	166.2	-4.0

Note: Figures are median sales prices of existing single-family homes in thousands of dollars; (p) preliminary; n/a not available; (1) Metropolitan Statistical Area-see Appendix B for areas included
Source: National Association of Realtors, Median Sales Price of Existing Single-Family Homes for Metropolitan Areas, 4th Quarter 2011

Affordability Index of Existing Single-Family Homes

Area	2009	2010	2011p	Percent Change 2010 to 2011
MSA[1]	n/a	n/a	n/a	n/a

Note: The housing affordability index measures whether or not a typical family could qualify for a mortgage loan on a typical home. The higher the index, the greater the household purchasing power. An index of 100 is defined as the point where a median-income household has exactly enough income to qualify for the purchase of a median-priced existing single-family home, assuming a 20 percent downpayment and 25 percent of gross income devoted to mortgage principal and interest payments; (p) preliminary; n/a not available; (1) Metropolitan Statistical Area-see Appendix B for areas included
Source: National Association of Realtors, Affordability Index of Existing Single-Family Homes, 2011

Median Apartment Condo-Coop Home Prices

Area	2009	2010	2011p	Percent Change 2010 to 2011
MSA[1]	n/a	n/a	n/a	n/a
U.S. Average	175.6	171.7	165.1	-3.8

Note: Figures are median sales prices of existing apartment condo-coop homes in thousands of dollars; (p) preliminary; n/a not available; (1) Metropolitan Statistical Area-see Appendix B for areas included
Source: National Association of Realtors, Median Sales Price of Existing Apartment Condo-Coop Homes for Metropolitan Areas, 4th Quarter 2011

Year Housing Structure Built

Area	2005 or Later	2000 -2004	1990 -1999	1980 -1989	1970 -1979	1960 -1969	1950 -1959	Before 1950	Median Year
City	5.2	6.1	11.1	14.2	20.4	9.8	16.8	16.3	1973
MSA[1]	5.0	7.2	13.6	13.8	21.3	8.9	13.2	16.9	1975
U.S.	5.0	8.6	14.0	14.1	16.3	11.3	11.2	19.6	1975

Note: Figures are percentages except for Median Year; (1) Figures cover the Billings, MT Metropolitan Statistical Area—see Appendix B for areas included
Source: U.S. Census Bureau, 2008-2010 American Community Survey 3-Year Estimates

HEALTH

Health Risk Data

Category	MSA[1] (%)	U.S. (%)
Adults who have been told they have high blood pressure[2]	28.8	28.7
Adults who have been told they have high blood cholesterol[2]	35.9	37.5
Adults who have been told they have diabetes[3]	7.1	8.7
Adults who have been told they have arthritis[2]	25.4	26.0
Adults who have been told they currently have asthma	10.4	9.1
Adults who are current smokers	16.0	17.3
Adults who are heavy drinkers[4]	4.1	5.0
Adults who are binge drinkers[5]	14.8	15.1
Adults who are overweight (BMI 25.0 - 29.9)	37.4	36.2
Adults who are obese (BMI 30.0 - 99.8)	27.2	27.5
Adults who participated in any physical activities in the past month	76.0	76.1
Adults 50+ who have ever had a sigmoidoscopy or colonoscopy	67.3	65.2
Women aged 40+ who have had a mammogram within the past two years	70.9	75.2
Men aged 40+ who have had a PSA test within the past two years	45.9	53.2
Adults aged 65+ who have had flu shot within the past year	70.0	67.5
Adults aged 18–64 who have any kind of health care coverage	82.5	82.2

Note: Data as of 2010 unless otherwise noted; (1) Figures cover the Billings, MT Metropolitan Statistical Area—see Appendix B for areas included; (2) Data as of 2009; (3) Figures do not include pregnancy-related, borderline, or pre-diabetes; (4) Heavy drinkers are classified as males having more than two drinks per day or females having more than one drink per day; (5) Binge drinkers are classified as males having five or more drinks on one occasion or females having four or more drinks on one occasion
Source: Centers for Disease Control and Prevention, Behaviorial Risk Factor Surveillance System, SMART: Selected Metropolitan/Micropolitan Area Risk Trends, 2009, 2010

Mortality Rates for the Top 10 Causes of Death in the U.S.

ICD-10[a] Sub-Chapter	ICD-10[a] Code	Age-Adjusted Mortality Rate[1] per 100,000 population	
		County[2]	U.S.
Malignant neoplasms	C00-C97	170.1	175.6
Ischaemic heart diseases	I20-I25	69.9	121.6
Other forms of heart disease	I30-I51	75.8	48.6
Chronic lower respiratory diseases	J40-J47	62.0	42.3
Cerebrovascular diseases	I60-I69	43.1	40.6
Organic, including symptomatic, mental disorders	F01-F09	45.5	26.7
Other degenerative diseases of the nervous system	G30-G31	24.8	24.7
Other external causes of accidental injury	W00-X59	21.8	24.4
Diabetes mellitus	E10-E14	19.5	21.7
Hypertensive diseases	I10-I15	16.6	18.2

Note: (a) ICD-10 = International Classification of Diseases 10th Revision; (1) Mortality rates are a three year average covering 2007-2009; (2) Figures cover
Source: Centers for Disease Control and Prevention, National Center for Health Statistics. Underlying Cause of Death 1999-2009 on CDC WONDER Online Database, released 2012. Data for year 2009 are compiled from the Multiple Cause of Death File 2009, Series 20 No. 2O, 2012, Data for year 2008 are compiled from the Multiple Cause of Death File 2008, Series 20 No. 2N, 2011, Data for year 2007 are compiled from Multiple Cause of Death File 2007, Series 20 No. 2M, 2010.

Mortality Rates for Selected Causes of Death

ICD-10[a] Sub-Chapter	ICD-10[a] Code	Age-Adjusted Mortality Rate[1] per 100,000 population	
		County[2]	U.S.
Assault	X85-Y09	*0.0	5.7
Human immunodeficiency virus (HIV) disease	B20-B24	*0.0	3.3
Influenza and pneumonia	J09-J18	13.2	16.4
Intentional self-harm	X60-X84	16.8	11.5
Malnutrition	E40-E46	*0.0	0.8
Obesity and other hyperalimentation	E65-E68	*0.0	1.6
Transport accidents	V01-V99	18.3	13.7
Viral hepatitis	B15-B19	*0.0	2.2

Note: (a) ICD-10 = International Classification of Diseases 10th Revision; (1) Mortality rates are a three year average covering 2007-2009; (2) Figures cover; (*) Unreliable data as per CDC
Source: Centers for Disease Control and Prevention, National Center for Health Statistics. Underlying Cause of Death 1999-2009 on CDC WONDER Online Database, released 2012. Data for year 2009 are compiled from the Multiple Cause of Death File 2009, Series 20 No. 2O, 2012, Data for year 2008 are compiled from the Multiple Cause of Death File 2008, Series 20 No. 2N, 2011, Data for year 2007 are compiled from Multiple Cause of Death File 2007, Series 20 No. 2M, 2010.

Distribution of Physicians and Dentists

Area[1]	Dentists[2]	D.O.[3]	M.D.[4] Total	M.D.[4] Family/General Practice	M.D.[4] Pediatrics	M.D.[4] Medical Specialties	M.D.[4] Surgical Specialties
Local (number)	71	20	394	46	20	118	113
Local (rate[5])	5.1	1.4	27.6	3.2	1.4	8.3	7.9
U.S. (rate[5])	4.5	1.9	18.3	2.5	1.4	6.8	4.1

Note: Data as of 2008 unless noted; (1) Local data covers Yellowstone County; (2) Data as of 2007; (3) Doctor of Osteopathic Medicine; (4) Includes active, non-federal, patient-care, office-based Doctors of Medicine; (5) rate per 10,000 population
Source: Area Resource File (ARF). 2009-2010 Release. U.S. Department of Health and Human Services, Health Resources and Services Administration, Bureau of Health Professions, Rockville, MD, August 2010

EDUCATION

Public School District Statistics

District Name	Schls	Pupils	Pupil/ Teacher Ratio	Minority Pupils[1] (%)	Free Lunch Eligible[2] (%)	IEP[3] (%)
Billings Elem	26	10,496	16.1	20.5	30.7	10.5
Billings H S	3	5,179	16.3	14.8	16.5	12.2

Note: Table includes school districts with 2,000 or more students; (1) Percentage of students that are not non-Hispanic white; (2) Percentage of students that are eligible for the free lunch program; (3) Percentage of students that have an Individualized Education Program.
Source: U.S. Department of Education, National Center for Education Statistics, Common Core of Data, Local Education Agency (School District) Universe Survey: School Year 2009-2010; U.S. Department of Education, National Center for Education Statistics, Common Core of Data, Public Elementary/Secondary School Universe Survey: School Year 2009-2010

Highest Level of Education

Area	Less than H.S.	H.S. Diploma	Some College, No Deg.	Associate Degree	Bachelors Degree	Masters Degree	Profess. School Degree	Doctorate Degree
City	7.8	29.6	23.7	7.8	22.2	5.9	2.2	0.8
MSA[1]	8.2	32.0	22.9	7.6	21.3	5.2	2.0	0.7
U.S.	14.7	28.4	21.3	7.6	17.6	7.2	1.9	1.2

Note: Figures cover persons age 25 and over; (1) Figures cover the Billings, MT Metropolitan Statistical Area—see Appendix B for areas included
Source: U.S. Census Bureau, 2008-2010 American Community Survey 3-Year Estimates

Educational Attainment by Race

Area	High School Graduate or Higher (%)					Bachelor's Degree or Higher (%)				
	Total	White	Black	Asian	Hisp.[2]	Total	White	Black	Asian	Hisp.[2]
City	92.2	93.2	n/a	n/a	72.6	31.0	32.2	n/a	n/a	13.9
MSA[1]	91.8	92.4	n/a	80.1	74.8	29.3	29.8	n/a	33.6	14.6
U.S.	85.3	87.5	81.4	85.5	61.6	28.0	29.3	17.8	50.2	13.0

Note: Figures shown cover persons 25 years old and over; (1) Figures cover the Billings, MT Metropolitan Statistical Area—see Appendix B for areas included; (2) People of Hispanic origin can be of any race
Source: U.S. Census Bureau, 2008-2010 American Community Survey 3-Year Estimates

School Enrollment by Grade and Control

Area	Preschool (%)		Kindergarten (%)		Grades 1 - 4 (%)		Grades 5 - 8 (%)		Grades 9 - 12 (%)	
	Public	Private	Public	Private	Public	Private	Public	Private	Public	Private
City	51.0	49.0	93.1	6.9	94.3	5.7	92.8	7.2	93.8	6.2
MSA[1]	51.4	48.6	89.6	10.4	93.7	6.3	92.9	7.1	92.5	7.5
U.S.	55.4	44.6	87.1	12.9	89.4	10.6	89.5	10.5	90.4	9.6

Note: Figures shown cover persons 3 years old and over; (1) Figures cover the Billings, MT Metropolitan Statistical Area—see Appendix B for areas included
Source: U.S. Census Bureau, 2008-2010 American Community Survey 3-Year Estimates

Average Salaries of Public School Classroom Teachers

Area	2010-11		2011-12		Percent Change 2010-11 to 2011-12	Percent Change 2001-02 to 2011-12
	Dollars	Rank[1]	Dollars	Rank[1]		
Montana	47,132	37	48,546	35	3.00	41.20
U.S. Average	55,623	-	56,643	-	1.83	26.8

Note: (1) State rank ranges from 1 to 51 where 1 indicates highest salary.
Source: National Education Association, Rankings & Estimates: Rankings of the States 2011 and Estimates of School Statistics 2012, December 2011

Higher Education

Four-Year Colleges			Two-Year Colleges			Medical Schools[1]	Law Schools[2]	Voc/ Tech[3]
Public	Private Non-profit	Private For-profit	Public	Private Non-profit	Private For-profit			
1	1	0	0	0	1	0	0	0

Note: Figures cover institutions located within the city limits and include main campuses only; (1) includes schools accredited by the Liaison Committee on Medical Education and the American Osteopathic Association's Commission on Osteopathic College Accreditation; (2) includes American Bar Association-accredited law schools; (3) includes all schools with programs that are less than 2 years.
Source: National Center for Education Statistics, Integrated Postsecondary Education System (IPEDS) Peer Analysis System, 2011-12; Association of American Medical Colleges, Member List, April 23, 2012; American Osteopathic Association, Member List, April 23, 2012; Law School Admission Council, Official Guide to ABA-Approved Law Schools Online, April 23, 2012

PRESIDENTIAL ELECTION

2008 Presidential Election Results

Area	Obama	McCain	Nader	Other
Yellowstone County	45.3	51.6	0.7	2.3
U.S.	52.9	45.6	0.6	0.9

Note: Results are percentages and may not add to 100% due to rounding
Source: Dave Leip's Atlas of U.S. Presidential Elections, www.uselectionatlas.org

EMPLOYERS

Major Employers

Company Name	Industry
Beall Trailers of Montana	Tanks, standard or custom fabricated: metal plate
Billings Clinic	Offices and clinics of medical doctors
Billings Clinic	General medical and surgical hospitals
Bureau of Land Management	Land management agency, government
Employee Benefit Management Services	Med. insurance claim processing, contract or fee basis
EXXON Mobil Corporation	Nonaromatic chemical products
First Interstate Bank	State commercial banks
Interstate Brands Corporation	Bread, cake, and related products
Montana Dept of Environmental Quality	Air, water, and solid waste management
Montana State University-Billings	Colleges and universities
Sears, Roebuck and Co	Department stores
St. John's Lutheran Ministries	Skilled nursing care facilities
St. Vincent Healthcare Foundation	Trusts
St. Vincent Healthcare Foundation	General medical and surgical hospitals
St. Vincent Hospital Auxilliary	Charitable organization
SYSCO Montana	Groceries and related products
Wal-Mart Stores	Department stores, discount
Yellowstone Boys and Girls Ranch	Emotionally disturbed home
Yellowstone City-County Health Department	Medical service organization

Note: Companies shown are located within the Billings, MT metropolitan area.
Source: Hoovers.com, data extracted April 25 2012

PUBLIC SAFETY

Crime Rate

Area	All Crimes	Violent Crimes				Property Crimes		
		Murder	Forcible Rape	Robbery	Aggrav. Assault	Burglary	Larceny -Theft	Motor Vehicle Theft
City	4,906.6	1.9	23.1	38.9	195.3	784.9	3,527.4	335.1
Suburbs[1]	2,074.6	2.0	12.2	6.1	107.8	362.0	1,436.0	148.5
Metro[2]	4,020.9	1.9	19.7	28.6	167.9	652.7	2,873.3	276.7
U.S.	3,345.5	4.8	27.5	119.1	252.3	699.6	2,003.5	238.8

Note: Figures are crimes per 100,000 population; (1) All areas within the metro area that are located outside the city limits; (2) Metropolitan Statistical Area—see Appendix B for areas included
Source: FBI Uniform Crime Reports, 2010

Hate Crimes

Area	Number of Quarters Reported	Bias Motivation				
		Race	Religion	Sexual Orientation	Ethnicity	Disability
City	4	1	0	0	0	0

Source: Federal Bureau of Investigation, Hate Crime Statistics 2010

Identity Theft Consumer Complaints

Area	Complaints	Complaints per 100,000 Population	Rank[2]
MSA[1]	63	42.1	362
U.S.	279,156	90.4	-

Note: (1) Metropolitan Statistical Area—see Appendix B for areas included; (2) Rank ranges from 1 to 384 where 1 indicates greatest number of identity theft complaints per 100,000 population
Source: Federal Trade Commission, Consumer Sentinel Network Data Book for January–December 2011

Fraud and Other Consumer Complaints

Area	Complaints	Complaints per 100,000 Population	Rank[2]
MSA[1]	587	392.2	309
U.S.	1,533,924	496.8	-

Note: (1) Metropolitan Statistical Area—see Appendix B for areas included; (2) Rank ranges from 1 to 384 where 1 indicates greatest number of fraud and other complaints per 100,000 population
Source: Federal Trade Commission, Consumer Sentinel Network Data Book for January–December 2011

RECREATION

Culture

Dance[1]	Theatre[1]	Instrumental Music[1]	Vocal Music[1]	Series/ Festivals	Museums	Zoos and Aquariums[2]
0	1	2	1	1	n/a	0

Note: (1) Number of professional perfoming groups; (2) AZA-accredited; n/a not available
Source: The Grey House Performing Arts Directory, 2011-2012; Official Museum Directory, 2011; American Association of Museums, AAM Member Museums, April 2012; Association of Zoos & Aquariums, AZA Member Zoos & Aquariums, April 2012

Professional Sports Teams

Team Name	League
No teams are located in the metro area	

Source: Original research

CLIMATE

Average and Extreme Temperatures

Temperature	Jan	Feb	Mar	Apr	May	Jun	Jul	Aug	Sep	Oct	Nov	Dec	Yr.
Extreme High (°F)	68	72	79	90	95	105	105	105	103	90	77	69	105
Average High (°F)	32	38	45	57	67	77	86	85	72	61	45	36	59
Average Temp. (°F)	23	29	35	46	56	65	72	71	60	49	36	27	47
Average Low (°F)	14	19	25	34	44	52	58	57	47	37	26	18	36
Extreme Low (°F)	-28	-28	-19	9	14	32	41	35	22	-7	-22	-32	-32

Note: Figures cover the years 1948-1995
Source: National Climatic Data Center, International Station Meteorological Climate Summary, 9/96

Average Precipitation/Snowfall/Humidity

Precip./Humidity	Jan	Feb	Mar	Apr	May	Jun	Jul	Aug	Sep	Oct	Nov	Dec	Yr.
Avg. Precip. (in.)	0.8	0.6	1.1	1.8	2.4	2.1	1.1	0.9	1.3	1.1	0.8	0.7	14.6
Avg. Snowfall (in.)	10	7	10	9	2	Tr	0	Tr	1	4	7	9	59
Avg. Rel. Hum. 5am (%)	64	66	69	68	71	72	64	61	64	63	65	64	66
Avg. Rel. Hum. 5pm (%)	56	53	48	42	42	41	32	30	37	42	53	56	44

Note: Figures cover the years 1948-1995; Tr = Trace amounts (<0.05 in. of rain; <0.5 in. of snow)
Source: National Climatic Data Center, International Station Meteorological Climate Summary, 9/96

Weather Conditions

Temperature			Daytime Sky			Precipitation		
5°F & below	32°F & below	90°F & above	Clear	Partly cloudy	Cloudy	0.01 inch or more precip.	0.1 inch or more snow/ice	Thunder-storms
25	149	29	75	163	127	97	41	27

Note: Figures are average number of days per year and cover the years 1948-1995
Source: National Climatic Data Center, International Station Meteorological Climate Summary, 9/96

HAZARDOUS WASTE

Superfund Sites

Billings has one hazardous waste site on the EPA's Superfund Final National Priorities List: **Lockwood Solvent Ground Water Plume**. *U.S. Environmental Protection Agency, Final National Priorities List, April 17, 2012*

AIR & WATER QUALITY

Air Quality Index

Area	Percent of Days when Air Quality was...[2]					AQI Statistics[2]	
	Good	Moderate	Unhealthy for Sensitive Groups	Unhealthy	Very Unhealthy	Maximum	Median
Area[1]	87.7	11.5	0.8	0.0	0.0	131	23

Note: Air Quality Index (AQI) is an index for reporting daily air quality. EPA calculates the AQI for five major air pollutants regulated by the Clean Air Act: ground-level ozone, particle pollution (aka particulate matter), carbon monoxide, sulfur dioxide, and nitrogen dioxide. The AQI runs from 0 to 500. The higher the AQI value, the greater the level of air pollution and the greater the health concern. There are six AQI categories: "Good" AQI is between 0 and 50. Air quality is considered satisfactory; "Moderate" AQI is between 51 and 100. Air quality is acceptable; "Unhealthy for Sensitive Groups" When AQI values are between 101 and 150, members of sensitive groups may experience health effects; "Unhealthy" When AQI values are between 151 and 200 everyone may begin to experience health effects; "Very Unhealthy" AQI values between 201 and 300 trigger a health alert; "Hazardous" AQI values over 300 trigger warnings of emergency conditions (not shown); (1) Data covers Yellowstone County; (2) Based on 365 days with AQI data in 2011.
Source: U.S. Environmental Protection Agency, AirData Report, 2011

Air Quality Index Pollutants

Area	Percent of Days when AQI Pollutant was...[2]					
	Carbon Monoxide	Nitrogen Dioxide	Ozone	Sulfur Dioxide	Particulate Matter 2.5	Particulate Matter 10
Area[1]	1.1	0.0	0.0	54.2	44.7	0.0

Note: The Air Quality Index (AQI) is an index for reporting daily air quality. EPA calculates the AQI for five major air pollutants regulated by the Clean Air Act: ground-level ozone, particle pollution (also known as particulate matter), carbon monoxide, sulfur dioxide, and nitrogen dioxide. The AQI runs from 0 to 500. The higher the AQI value, the greater the level of air pollution and the greater the health concern; (1) Data covers Yellowstone County; (2) Based on 365 days with AQI data in 2011.
Source: U.S. Environmental Protection Agency, AirData Report, 2011

Air Quality Index Trends

Area	Trend Sites (days)								All Sites (days)
	2003	2004	2005	2006	2007	2008	2009	2010	2010
MSA[1]	n/a	n/a	n/a	n/a	n/a	n/a	n/a	n/a	n/a

Note: Figures are the number of days the AQI value exceeded 100 in a given year. An AQI value greater than 100 indicates that air quality would have been in the unhealthful range on that day. Data from exceptional events are included. These counts are presented in two ways. First, the counts are based on sites having an adequate record of monitoring data during the trend period (trend sites). These counts represent the relative change in the number of days with AQI values greater than 100. In the last column, the counts are based on all sites with data in the most recent year (because it is possible for a site to have data in the most recent year but not enough data to be a trend site); (1) Data covers the Billings, MT—see Appendix B for areas included; n/a not available.
Source: U.S. Environmental Protection Agency, Air Quality Index Information, "Number of Days with Air Quality Index Values Greater than 100 at Trend Sites, 2000-2010, and at All Sites in 2010"

Maximum Air Pollutant Concentrations: Particulate Matter, Ozone, CO and Lead

	Particulate Matter 10 (ug/m^3)	Particulate Matter 2.5 Wtd AM (ug/m^3)	Particulate Matter 2.5 24-Hr (ug/m^3)	Ozone (ppm)	Carbon Monoxide (ppm)	Lead (ug/m^3)
MSA[1] Level	n/a	n/a	n/a	n/a	2	n/a
NAAQS[2]	150	15	35	0.075	9	0.15
Met NAAQS[2]	n/a	n/a	n/a	n/a	Yes	n/a

Note: Data from exceptional events are not included; (1) Data covers the Billings, MT—see Appendix B for areas included; (2) National Ambient Air Quality Standards; ppm = parts per million; ug/m^3 = micrograms per cubic meter; n/a not available
Concentrations: Particulate Matter 10 (coarse particulate)—highest second maximum 24-hour concentration; Particulate Matter 2.5 Wtd AM (fine particulate)—highest weighted annual mean concentration; Particulate Matter 2.5 24-Hour (fine particulate)—highest 98th percentile 24-hour concentration; Ozone—highest fourth daily maximum 8-hour concentration; Carbon Monoxide—highest second maximum non-overlapping 8-hour concentration; Lead—maximum running 3-month average
Source: U.S. Environmental Protection Agency, CBSA Factbook 2010, Air Quality Statistics by City, 2010

Maximum Air Pollutant Concentrations: Nitrogen Dioxide and Sulfur Dioxide

	Nitrogen Dioxide AM (ppb)	Nitrogen Dioxide 1-Hr (ppb)	Sulfur Dioxide AM (ppb)	Sulfur Dioxide 1-Hr (ppb)	Sulfur Dioxide 24-Hr (ppb)
MSA[1] Level	n/a	n/a	3.876	91	23.4
NAAQS[2]	53	100	30	75	140
Met NAAQS[2]	n/a	n/a	Yes	No	Yes

Note: Data from exceptional events are not included; (1) Data covers the Billings, MT—see Appendix B for areas included; (2) National Ambient Air Quality Standards; ppb = parts per billion; n/a not available

Concentrations: Nitrogen Dioxide AM—highest arithmetic mean concentration; Nitrogen Dioxide 1-Hr—highest 98th percentile 1-hour daily maximum concentration; Sulfur Dioxide AM—highest annual mean concentration; Sulfur Dioxide 1-Hr—highest 99th percentile 1-hour daily maximum concentration; Sulfur Dioxide 24-Hr—highest second maximum 24-hour concentration

Source: U.S. Environmental Protection Agency, CBSA Factbook 2010, Air Quality Statistics by City, 2010

Drinking Water

Water System Name	Pop. Served	Primary Water Source Type	Violations[1] Health Based	Violations[1] Monitoring/ Reporting
City of Billings	114,000	Surface	0	0

Note: (1) Based on violation data from January 1, 2011 to December 31, 2011 (includes unresolved violations from earlier years)

Source: U.S. Environmental Protection Agency, Office of Ground Water and Drinking Water, Safe Drinking Water Information System (based on data extracted April 18, 2012)

Boise City, Idaho

Background

Boise (boy-see) is the capital and largest city in Idaho, lying along the Boise River adjacent to the foothills of the Rocky Mountains. The city is located south and west of the western slopes of the Rockies, and is the site of a great system of natural warm water springs.

Boise's spectacular natural location is its first and most obvious attraction, and this, coupled with its dynamic economic growth in recent decades, makes Boise an altogether remarkable city. The splendor of its surroundings, together with an average 18-minute drive to work, has allowed the city to combine pleasure and efficiency in an enviable mix.

French-Canadian trappers were familiar with Boise and its environs by 1811, and the name of the city is an Anglicization of the French Les Bois—the trees. The first substantial European settlement dates to 1863 when, in the spring of that year, I.M. Coston built from pegged driftwood a great house that served as a hub for the activities of prospectors, traders, and Native Americans. In the same year, the U.S. Army built Fort Boise, and considerable deposits of gold and silver were discovered in the area. The U.S. Assay Office in Boise, in 1870-71 alone, is said to have valuated more than $75 million in precious metals.

The area is rich in gold rush lore, and six miles above Boise, on the south side of the river, there may even be buried treasure from that era. The eastbound stagecoach from Boise was said to have been waylaid by a robber who, though wounded in the attack by a resourceful passenger, managed to drag off a strongbox filled with $50,000 in gold. The robber died of his wounds and was discovered the next day, but he had apparently buried his loot. No one has ever located it.

The Boise area was subsequently developed for farming, as crops of grains, vegetables, and fruits, replaced the mines as its source of wealth. It became the territorial capital of Idaho in 1864 and the state capital in 1890. Education was served with the opening of a university in 1932, which became Boise State University in 1974 and now enrolls almost 20,000 students.

The city's natural setting offers a great range of outdoor activities that are pursued energetically by its citizens. Its rivers, mountains, deserts, and lakes offer world-class skiing, hiking, camping, kayaking, river rafting, hunting, and fishing. Bike paths run throughout the city and into Boise's large outdoor trail network, the Boise River Greenbelt. Recreational wilderness exists extensively just outside the city's limits. The Word Center for Birds of Prey is located on the city's southern frontier, and is the site of the Peregrine Falcon's rehabilitation and release into the wild.

Many large regional, national, and international companies are headquartered there, including Boise Cascade, Micron Technology, and Simplot, plue major call centers for DIRECTV and T-Mobile.

The city produces high- and low-tech products and everything in between: software, computer components, steel and sheet metal products, mobile homes, lumber products, farm machinery, packed meats, and processed foods. Increasingly an advanced technological center, it continues to serve as a trading center for the greater agricultural region.

By virtue of its history and geographical character, the city can be considered a presence on the Pacific Rim. In a more tangible vein, Boise, with ten airlines operating at its airport, is conveniently tied to the wider world.

Boise's Basque community, numbering about 15,000, is the largest in the United States and the third largest in the world outside Argentina and the Basque Country in Spain and France. A large Basque festival known as Jaialdi is held once every five years, most recently in 2010. Boise (along with Valley and Boise Counties) recently hosted the 2009 Special Olympics World Winter Games. More than 2,500 athletes from over100 countries participated.

The city is protected by the mountains to the north in such a way that it is largely unbothered by the extreme blizzards that affect eastern Idaho and parts of neighboring states. Boise, and this section of western Idaho generally, are affected by climatic influences from the Pacific Ocean and exhibits an unusually mild climate for this latitude. Summers can be hot, but nights are almost always cool, and sunshine generally prevails.

Rankings

General Rankings

- The Boise City metro area was selected one of America's "Best Cities to Live, Work and Play" by *Kiplinger's Personal Finance.* Criteria: population growth; percentage of workforce in the creative class (scientists, engineers, educators, writers, artists, entertainers, etc.); job quality; income growth; cost of living. *Kiplinger's Personal Finance, "Best Cities to Live, Work and Play," July 2008*
- Boise City was selected as one of America's best cities by *Bloomberg Businessweek.* The city ranked #33 out of 50. Criteria: number of restaurants, bars and museums per capita; number of colleges, libraries, and professional sports teams; income, poverty, unemployment, crime, and foreclosure rates; percent of population with bachelor's degrees; public school performance; park acres per capita; air quality. *BusinessWeek, "America's 50 Best Cities," September 20, 2011*
- Boise City appeared on RelocateAmerica's list of best places to live in America. The annual "Top 100 Places to Live" list recognizes the top communities as nominated by their residents & local businesses. RelocateAmerica's Research Group determines the list based on review of various data gathered for economic, employment, housing, education, industry, opportunity, environment and recreation along with feedback from area leaders and residents. *RelocateAmerica.com, "Top 100 Places to Live for 2011"*
- Boise City was selected as one of "America's Top 10 Places to Live" by *RelocateAmerica.com.* The city ranked #8. Criteria: real estate and housing; economic health; recreation; safety; input from local residents, business and community leaders. *RelocateAmerica.com, "Top 10 Places to Live for 2011"*
- Boise City was chosen as one of America's best cities by *Outside Magazine* in the "Best Overall in the West" category. Criteria: educational attainment; cost of living; cultural vibrancy; economic resilience; housing market sanity; sport-specific facts such as the miles of trail within a hour's drive, frequency of group rides, and proximity to worthy ski areas. *Outside Magazine, "Best Towns 2010," August 2010*

Business/Finance Rankings

- Boise City was selected as one of the "100 Best Places to Live and Launch" in the U.S. The city ranked #19. The editors at *Fortune Small Business* ranked 296 Census-designated metro areas by business friendliness (Launching Score, % New Businesses) and lifestyle offerings (Living Score). Then they picked the town within each of the top 100 metro areas that best blends business and pleasure. *Fortune Small Business, "100 Best Places to Live and Launch 2008," April 2008*
- *American City Business Journals* ranked America's 261 largest cities in terms of their resident's wealth. Boise City ranked #128. Criteria: per capita income; median household income; percentage of households with annual incomes of $200,000 or more; median home value. *American City Business Journals, "Where the Money Is: America's Wealth Centers," August 18, 2008*
- The Boise City metro area appeared on the Milken Institute "2011 Best Performing Metros" list. Rank: #130 out of 200 large metro areas. Criteria: job growth; wage and salary growth; high-tech output growth. *Milken Institute, "2011 Best Performing Metros"*
- The Boise City metro area was selected as one of the best cities for entrepreneurs in America by *Inc. Magazine.* Criteria: job-growth data for 335 metro areas was analyzed for: recent growth trend; mid-term growth; long-term trend; current year growth. The Boise City metro area ranked #12 among mid-sized metro areas and #44 overall. *Inc. Magazine, "The Best Cities for Doing Business," July 2008*
- *Forbes* ranked the 200 most populous metro areas in the U.S. in terms of the "Best Places for Business and Careers." The Boise City metro area was ranked #18. Criteria: costs (business and living); job growth (past and projected); income growth; educational attainment; projected economic growth; crime; cultural and recreational opportunities; net migration patterns; number of highly ranked colleges. *Forbes, "Best Places for Business and Careers," June 2011*

Children/Family Rankings

- Boise City was identified as one of the best cities for raising a family by *24/7 Wall St.* The city ranked #9. The nation's 100 largest cities were evaluated on the following criteria: large public outdoor spaces; top hospitals; strong schools; low unemployment; high educational attainment; low violent crime rates. *24/7 Wall St., "The 10 Best U.S. Cities for Raising a Family," January 13, 2012*
- The Boise City metro area was selected as one of the "Best Cities for Relocating Families" by Worldwide ERC and Primacy Relocation. The 2008 study looked at nearly 50 factors important to relocating families including: recent job growth; nearby top-ranked colleges; in-state tuition for four-year public colleges; population growth since 2000; pediatricians per 100,000 population; and a Green Living index. *Worldwide ERC and Primacy Relocation, "2008 Best Cities for Relocating Families"*
- Boise City was chosen as one of America's "100 Best Communities for Young People." The winners were selected based upon detailed information provided about each community's efforts to fulfill five essential promises critical to the well-being of young people: caring adults who are actively involved in their lives; safe places in which to learn and grow; a healthy start toward adulthood; an effective education that builds marketable skills; and opportunities to help others. *America's Promise Alliance, "100 Best Communities for Young People, 2010"*

Dating/Romance Rankings

- Boise City appeared on *Men's Health's* list of the most sex-happy cities in America. The city ranked #60 of 100. Criteria: condom sales; birth rates; sex toy sales; rates of chlamydia, gonorrhea, and syphilis. *Men's Health, "America's Most Sex-Happy Cities," October 2010*
- *Men's Health* ranked 100 U.S. cities in terms of best (and worst) marriages. Boise City was ranked #23 (#1 = worst). Criteria: rate of failed marriages; stringency of divorce laws; percentage of population who've split; number of licensed marriage and family therapists. *Men's Health, "Splitsville, USA," May 2010*
- The Boise City metro area was selected as one of the "Best Cities for Relocating Singles" by Worldwide ERC and Primacy Relocation. The area ranked #57 out of the 100 largest metro areas in the U.S. Criteria: recent job growth; recent singles population growth; overall population growth; affordable rental housing; cost-of-living index; expanded arts and recreation opportunities; ratio of single men and single women; affordability of quality higher education (including state residency requirements); diversity index; climate; population density. *Worldwide ERC and Primacy Relocation, "2008 Best Cities for Relocating Singles"*

Education Rankings

- *Men's Health* ranked 100 U.S. cities in terms of their education levels. Boise City was ranked #11 (#1 = most educated city). Criteria: high school graduation rates; school enrollment; educational attainment; number of households who have outstanding student loans; number of households whose members have taken adult-education courses. *Men's Health, "Where School Is In: The Most and Least Educated Cities," September 12, 2011*
- Boise City was identified as one of the 100 "smartest" metro areas in the U.S. The area ranked #41. Criteria: the editors rated the collective brainpower of the 100 largest metro areas in the U.S. based on their residents' educational attainment. *American City Business Journals, April 14, 2008*
- Boise City was identified as one of America's most inventive cities by *The Daily Beast.* The city ranked #8 out of 25. The 200 largest cities in the U.S. were ranked by the number of patents (applied and approved) per capita. *The Daily Beast, "The 25 Most Inventive Cities," October 2, 2011*
- Boise City was identified as one of "America's Brainiest Bastions" by *Portfolio.com.* The metro area ranked #83 out of 200. *Portfolio.com* analyzed levels of educational attainment in the nation's 200 largest metropolitan areas. The editors established scores for five levels of educational attainment, based on relative earning power of adult workers age 25 or older. Scores were determined by comparing the median income for all workers with the median income for those workers at a specified educational level. *Portfolio.com, "America's Brainiest Bastions," December 1, 2010*

Environmental Rankings

- Boise City was selected as one of 22 "Smarter Cities" for energy by the Natural Resources Defense Council. Criteria: investment in green power; energy efficiency measures; conservation. *Natural Resources Defense Council, "2010 Smarter Cities," July 19, 2010*
- 100 of the largest metro areas in the U.S. were analyzed in terms of their current drought severity. The Boise City metro area ranked #46 (#1 = driest). The rankings were based on statistics such as long-term precipitation trends and patterns and the Palmer drought indices. *Sperling's BestPlaces, www.BestPlaces.net, "America's Drought-Riskiest Cities," November 2007*
- The Boise City metro area appeared in *Country Home's* "Best Green Places" report. The area ranked #98 out of 379. Criteria: official energy policies; green power; green buildings; availability of fresh, locally grown food. *Country Home, "Best Green Places," 2008*
- Boise City was highlighted as one of the top 25 cleanest metro areas for year-round particle pollution (Annual PM 2.5) in the U.S. The area ranked #12. *American Lung Association, State of the Air 2011*

Food/Drink Rankings

- Boise City was selected as one of North America's most vegetarian- and vegan-friendly small cities (population under 300,000). The city was ranked #10. Criteria: number of vegetarian restaurants and vegetarian-friendly restaurants per capita; input from PETA supporters and staff members on the quality of the options. *People for the Ethical Treatment of Animals, "North America's Best Vegetarian- and Vegan-Friendly Cities," July 23, 2010*

Health/Fitness Rankings

- Boise City was identified as a "2011 Asthma Capital." The area ranked #69 out of the nation's 100 largest metropolitan areas. Twelve factors were used to identify the most challenging places to live for people with asthma: estimated prevalence; self-reported prevalence; crude death rate for asthma; annual pollen score; annual air quality; public smoking laws; number of board-certified asthma specialists; school inhaler access laws; rescue medication use; controller medication use; uninsured rate; poverty rate. *Asthma and Allergy Foundation of America, "2011 Asthma Capitals"*
- Boise City was identified as a "2011 Fall Allergy Capital." The area ranked #94 out of 100. Three groups of factors were used to identify the most severe cities for people with allergies during the fall season: annual pollen levels; medicine utilization; access to board-certified allergists. *Asthma and Allergy Foundation of America, "2011 Fall Allergy Capitals"*
- Boise City was identified as a "2012 Spring Allergy Capital." The area ranked #99 out of 100. Three groups of factors were used to identify the most severe cities for people with allergies during the spring season: annual pollen levels; medicine utilization; access to board-certified allergists. *Asthma and Allergy Foundation of America, "2012 Spring Allergy Capitals"*
- *Men's Health* examined 100 major U.S. cities and selected the best and worst cities for men. Boise City ranked #5. Criteria: 35 statistical parameters of long life in the categories of health, quality of life, and fitness. *Men's Health, "The 10 Best and Worst Cities for Men 2012," January/February 2012*
- *Men's Health* examined 100 U.S. cities and selected the best and worst cities for women. Boise City was ranked among the ten best at #7. Criteria: dozens of statistical parameters of long life in the categories of health, quality of life, and fitness. *Men's Health, "The 10 Best and Worst Cities for Women 2011," January/February 2011*
- The Boise City metro area appeared in the 2011 Gallup-Healthways Well-Being Index. The index, based on interviews with more than 350,000 Americans, measured jobs, finances, physical health, emotional state of mind and communities. The metro area ranked #43 out of 190. Criteria: life evaluation; emotional health; work environment; physical health; healthy behaviors; basic access (basic needs optimal for a healthy life, such as access to food and medicine, having health insurance and feeling safe while walking at night). *Gallup-Healthways, "State of Well-Being 2011"*

- *Men's Health* ranked 100 U.S. cities in terms of their activity levels. Boise City was ranked #26 (#1 = most active city). Criteria: where and how often residents exercise; percentage of households that watch more than 15 hours of cable television a week and buy more than 11 video games a year; death rate from deep-vein thrombosis, a condition linked to sitting for extended periods of time. *Men's Health, "Where Sit Happens: The Most and Least Active Cities in America," June 20, 2011*

Real Estate Rankings

- Boise City was identified as one of 13 metro areas where home prices are falling dangerously. Criteria: home price change from October 2010 to September 2011; projected home price change through 2012. *Forbes.com, "Cities Where Home Prices are Falling Dangerously," January 10, 2012*

- Boise City was identified as one of the "Top Turnaround Housing Markets for 2012." The area ranked #6 out of 10. Criteria: year-over-year median home price appreciation; year-over-year median inventory age; year-over-year inventory reduction. *AOL Real Estate, "Top Turnaround Housing Markets for 2012," February 4, 2012*

- Boise City was identified as one of the top 20 metro areas with the lowest rate of house price appreciation in 2011. The area ranked #17 with a one-year price appreciation of -8.3% through the 4th quarter 2011. *Federal Housing Finance Agency, House Price Index, 4th Quarter 2011*

- The Boise City metro area was identified as one of the 25 worst housing markets in the U.S. in 2011. The area ranked #1 out of 149 markets with a home price appreciation of -20.2%. Criteria: year-over-year change of median sales price of existing single-family homes between the 4th quarter of 2010 and the 4th quarter of 2011. *National Association of Realtors®, Median Sales Price of Existing Single-Family Homes for Metropolitan Areas, 4th Quarter 2011*

- The Boise City metro area was identified as one of "America's 25 Weakest Housing Markets" by *Forbes*. The metro area ranked #10. Criteria: metro areas with populations over 500,000 were ranked based on projected home values through 2011. *Forbes.com, "America's 25 Weakest Housing Markets," January 7, 2009*

- The nation's largest metro areas were analyzed in terms of the percentage of households entering some stage of foreclosure in 2011. The Boise City metro area ranked #19 out of 20 (#1 = highest foreclosure rate). *RealtyTrac, 2011 Year-End Foreclosure Market Report, January 12, 2012*

- The Center for Housing Policy ranked 210 U.S. metropolitan areas by the fair market rent for a two-bedroom unit. The Boise City metro area was ranked #152. (#1 = most expensive) with a rent of $721. Criteria: Fair Market Rent (FMR) in effect during the fourth quarter of 2009 based on HUD's fiscal year 2010 FMRs. *The Center for Housing Policy, "Paycheck to Paycheck: Most to Least Expensive Rental Markets in 2009"*

- The Boise City metro area was identified as one of the markets with the worst expected performance in home prices over the next 12 months. *Local Market Monitor, "First Quarter Home Price Forecast for Smallest US Markets," March 2, 2011*

- The Boise City metro area was identified as one of the best U.S. markets to invest in rental property" by HomeVestors and Local Market Monitor. The area ranked #10 out of 100. Criteria: risk-return premium relative to national average. *HomeVestors and Local Market Monitor, "Best 100 U.S. Markets to Invest in Rental Property," March 9, 2012*

Safety Rankings

- Allstate ranked the 193 largest cities in America in terms of driver safety. Boise City ranked #2. In addition, drivers were 25.5% less likely to have had an accident compared to the national average. Allstate researchers analyzed internal property damage reported claims over a two-year period (from January 2008 to December 2009) to protect findings from external influences such as weather or road construction. A weighted average of the two-year numbers determined the annual percentages. The report defines an auto crash as any collision resulting in a property damage claim. *Allstate, "2011 Allstate America's Best Drivers Report™"*

- Boise City was identified as one of the safest places in the U.S. in terms of its vulnerability to natural disasters and weather extremes. The city ranked #2 out of 10. Data was analyzed to show a metro areas' relative tendency to experience natural disasters (hail, tornadoes, high winds, hurricanes, earthquakes, and brush fires) or extreme weather (abundant rain or snowfall or days that are below freezing or above 90 degrees Fahrenheit). *Forbes, "Safest and Least Safe Places in the U.S.," August 30, 2005*

- The National Insurance Crime Bureau ranked 366 metro areas in the U.S. in terms of per capita rates of vehicle theft. The Boise City metro area ranked #316 (#1 = highest rate). Criteria: number of vehicle theft offenses per 100,000 inhabitants in 2010. *National Insurance Crime Bureau, "Hot Spots," June 21, 2011*

Seniors/Retirement Rankings

- Boise City was selected as one of the best places to retire by *CNNMoney.com*. Criteria: low cost of living; low violent-crime rate; good medical care; large population over age 50; abundant amenities for retirees. *CNNMoney.com, "Best Places to Retire 2011"*

Sports/Recreation Rankings

- Boise City appeared on the *Sporting News* list of the "Best Sports Cities" for 2011. The area ranked #62 out of 271 cities in the U.S. *Sporting News* takes a 12-month snapshot of each city's sports, putting a heavy premium on regular-season won-lost records (from the most recently completed season). Other criteria include: playoff berths, bowl appearances and tournament bids; championships; applicable power ratings; quality of competition; overall fan fervor (measured in part by attendance); abundance of teams (rewarding quality over quantity); stadium and arena quality; ticket availability and prices; franchise ownership; and marquee appeal of athletes. *Sporting News, "Best Sports Cities 2011," October 4, 2011*

- Boise City was chosen as one of America's best cities for bicycling. The city ranked #32 out of 50. Criteria: number of segregated bike lanes, municipal bike racks, and bike boulevards; vibrant and diverse bike culture; smart, savvy bike shops; interviews with national and local advocates, bike shops and other experts. The editors only considered cities with populations of 100,000 or more. *Bicycling, "America's Best Bike Cities," April 2010*

Technology Rankings

- The Boise City metro area was selected as one of "America's Most Innovative Cities" by *Forbes*. The metro area was ranked #16 out of 20. Criteria: patents per capita; venture capital investment per capita; ratio of high-tech, science and "creative" jobs. *Forbes, "America's Most Innovative Cities," May 24, 2010*

- The Boise City metro area was identified as one of 10 "Top Up-and-Coming Tech Cities" by *Forbes*. The metro area ranked #7. Criteria: regional innovation trends; important patents. *Forbes.com, "Top Up-and-Coming Tech Cities," March 11, 2008*

Women/Minorities Rankings

- *Women's Health* examined U.S. cities and identified the 100 best cities for women. Boise City was ranked #4. Criteria: 30 categories were examined from obesity and breast cancer rates to commuting times and hours spent working out. *Women's Health, "Best Cities for Women 2012"*

Miscellaneous Rankings

- *Men's Health* ranked 100 U.S. cities by their level of sadness. Boise City was ranked #45 (#1 = saddest city). Criteria: suicide rates; unemployment rates; percentage of households that use antidepressants; percent of population who report feeling blue all or most of the time. *Men's Health, "Frown Towns," November 28, 2011*

Business Environment

CITY FINANCES

City Government Finances

Component	2009 ($000)	2009 ($ per capita)
Total Revenues	271,526	1,339
Total Expenditures	252,677	1,246
Debt Outstanding	126,970	626
Cash and Securities[1]	143,763	709

Note: (1) Cash and security holdings of a government at the close of its fiscal year, including those of its dependent agencies, utilities, and liquor stores.
Source: U.S Census Bureau, State & Local Government Finances 2009

City Government Revenue by Source

Source	2009 ($000)	2009 ($ per capita)
General Revenue		
From Federal Government	19,972	98
From State Government	16,505	81
From Local Governments	0	0
Taxes		
Property	92,501	456
Sales and Gross Receipts	7,343	36
Personal Income	0	0
Corporate Income	0	0
Motor Vehicle License	0	0
Other Taxes	6,687	33
Current Charges	111,046	547
Liquor Store	0	0
Utility	0	0
Employee Retirement	0	0

Source: U.S Census Bureau, State & Local Government Finances 2009

City Government Expenditures by Function

Function	2009 ($000)	2009 ($ per capita)	2009 (%)
General Direct Expenditures			
Air Transportation	27,909	138	11.0
Corrections	0	0	0.0
Education	0	0	0.0
Employment Security Administration	0	0	0.0
Financial Administration	8,244	41	3.3
Fire Protection	32,553	160	12.9
General Public Buildings	1,654	8	0.7
Governmental Administration, Other	8,118	40	3.2
Health	0	0	0.0
Highways	2,915	14	1.2
Hospitals	0	0	0.0
Housing and Community Development	3,074	15	1.2
Interest on General Debt	2,053	10	0.8
Judicial and Legal	7,041	35	2.8
Libraries	7,923	39	3.1
Parking	1,309	6	0.5
Parks and Recreation	19,923	98	7.9
Police Protection	39,466	195	15.6
Public Welfare	0	0	0.0
Sewerage	37,749	186	14.9
Solid Waste Management	23,742	117	9.4
Veterans' Services	0	0	0.0
Liquor Store	0	0	0.0
Utility	0	0	0.0
Employee Retirement	0	0	0.0

Source: U.S Census Bureau, State & Local Government Finances 2009

Municipal Bond Ratings

Area	Moody's	S&P	Fitch
City	n/a	n/a	n/a

Rating Systems (shown in declining order of credit quality): Moody's– Aaa, Aa, A, Baa, Ba, B, Caa, Ca, C (numerical modifiers 1, 2, and 3 are added to letter-rating); S&P– AAA, AA, A, BBB, BB, B, CCC, CC, C; Fitch– AAA, AA, A, BBB, BB, B, CCC, CC, C. Ratings may be modified by the addition of a plus or minus sign to show relative standing within the major rating categories.
Notes: n/a Not Available; w/d Withdrawn (1) Not Reviewed; (2) Issuer Rating/No General Obligation; (3) Standard and Poor's Issue Credit Rating (ICR) is a current opinion of an obliger with respect to a specific financial obligation, a specific class of financial obligations, or a specific financial program.
Source: U.S. Census Bureau, 2012 Statistical Abstract, Bond Ratings for City Governments by Largest Cities: 2010

DEMOGRAPHICS

Population Growth

Area	1990 Census	2000 Census	2010 Census	Population Growth (%) 1990-2000	Population Growth (%) 2000-2010
City	144,317	185,787	205,671	28.7	10.7
MSA[1]	319,596	464,840	616,561	45.4	32.6
U.S.	248,709,873	281,421,906	308,745,538	13.2	9.7

Note: (1) Figures cover the Boise City-Nampa, ID Metropolitan Statistical Area—see Appendix B for areas included
Source: U.S. Census Bureau, 2010 Census

Household Size

Area	Persons in Household (%) One	Two	Three	Four	Five	Six	Seven or More	Average Household Size
City	30.6	34.9	15.4	11.5	4.7	1.9	1.1	2.36
MSA[1]	23.6	33.9	15.7	14.1	7.3	3.3	2.0	2.67
U.S.	26.7	32.8	16.1	13.4	6.5	2.6	1.9	2.58

Note: (1) Figures cover the Boise City-Nampa, ID Metropolitan Statistical Area—see Appendix B for areas included
Source: U.S. Census Bureau, 2010 Census

Race

Area	White Alone[2] (%)	Black Alone[2] (%)	Asian Alone[2] (%)	AIAN[3] Alone[2] (%)	NHOPI[4] Alone[2] (%)	Other Race Alone[2] (%)	Two or More Races (%)
City	89.0	1.5	3.2	0.7	0.2	2.5	3.0
MSA[1]	87.9	0.9	1.8	0.9	0.2	5.4	2.9
U.S.	72.4	12.6	4.8	0.9	0.2	6.2	2.9

Note: (1) Figures cover the Boise City-Nampa, ID Metropolitan Statistical Area—see Appendix B for areas included; (2) Alone is defined as not being in combination with one or more other races; (3) American Indian and Alaska Native; (4) Native Hawaiian and Other Pacific Islander
Source: U.S. Census Bureau, 2010 Census

Hispanic or Latino Origin

Area	Hispanic or Latino (%)	Mexican (%)	Puerto Rican (%)	Cuban (%)	Other Hispanic or Latino (%)
City	7.1	5.4	0.2	0.1	1.4
MSA[1]	12.6	10.5	0.2	0.1	1.8
U.S.	16.3	10.3	1.5	0.6	4.0

Note: Persons of Hispanic or Latino origin can be of any race; (1) Figures cover the Boise City-Nampa, ID Metropolitan Statistical Area—see Appendix B for areas included
Source: U.S. Census Bureau, 2010 Census

Segregation

Type	Segregation Indices[1]				Percent Change		
	1990	2000	2010	2010 Rank[2]	1990-2000	1990-2010	2000-2010
Black/White	31.6	26.8	30.2	101	-4.8	-1.4	3.4
Asian/White	19.2	23.4	27.6	95	4.1	8.4	4.3
Hispanic/White	41.1	39.0	36.2	80	-2.1	-4.9	-2.8

Note: Figures are based on an analysis of 1990, 2000, and 2010 Census Decennial Census tract data by William H. Frey, Brookings Institution and the University of Michigan Social Science Data Analysis Network. In this analysis all racial groups (whites, blacks, and asians) are non-Hispanic members of those races. Hispanics are shown as a separate category; All figures cover the Metropolitan Statistical Area (see Appendix B for areas included); (1) Segregation Indices are Dissimilarity Indices that measure the degree to which the minority group is distributed differently than whites across census tracts. They range from 0 (complete integration) to 100 (complete segregation) where the value indicates the percentage of the minority group that needs to move to be distributed exactly like whites; (2) Ranges from 1 (most segregated) to 102 (least segregated); n/a not available.
Source: www.CensusScope.org

Ancestry

Area	German	Irish	English	American	Italian	Polish	French[2]	Scottish	Dutch
City	17.7	12.3	15.0	8.1	3.5	1.6	2.9	3.1	1.9
MSA[1]	17.7	10.1	14.2	12.7	3.0	1.4	2.7	3.1	2.1
U.S.	16.1	11.6	8.8	6.1	5.7	3.2	3.0	1.9	1.6

Note: Figures are the percentage of the total population reporting a particular ancestry. The nine most commonly reported ancestries in the U.S. are shown. Figures include multiple ancestries (e.g. if a person reported being Irish and Italian, they were included in both columns); (1) Figures cover the Boise City-Nampa, ID Metropolitan Statistical Area—see Appendix B for areas included; (2) Excludes Basque
Source: U.S. Census Bureau, 2008-2010 American Community Survey 3-Year Estimates

Foreign-Born Population

Area	Percent of Population Born in								
	Any Foreign Country	Mexico	Asia	Europe	Carribean	South America	Central America[2]	Africa	Canada
City	n/a	n/a	n/a	n/a	n/a	n/a	n/a	n/a	n/a
MSA[1]	7.2	3.1	1.5	1.3	0.1	0.2	0.3	0.4	0.3
U.S.	12.8	3.8	3.6	1.6	1.2	0.9	1.0	0.5	0.3

Note: (1) Figures cover the Boise City-Nampa, ID Metropolitan Statistical Area—see Appendix B for areas included; (2) Excludes Mexico.
Source: U.S. Census Bureau, 2008-2010 American Community Survey 3-Year Estimates

Marital Status

Area	Never Married	Now Married[2]	Separated	Widowed	Divorced
City	31.7	49.1	1.5	4.5	13.3
MSA[1]	26.2	55.6	1.7	4.4	12.1
U.S.	31.6	49.6	2.2	6.1	10.7

Note: Figures are percentages and cover the population 15 years of age and older; (1) Figures cover the Boise City-Nampa, ID Metropolitan Statistical Area—see Appendix B for areas included; (2) Excludes separated
Source: U.S. Census Bureau, 2008-2010 American Community Survey 3-Year Estimates

Age

Area	Percent of Population							Median Age
	Under Age 5	Age 5 to 17	Age 18 to 34	Age 35 to 49	Age 50 to 64	Age 65 to 79	80 Years and Over	
City	6.4	16.3	26.8	20.3	19.0	7.8	3.4	35.3
MSA[1]	7.8	20.2	23.2	20.5	17.4	8.0	2.9	34.1
U.S.	6.5	17.5	23.2	20.7	19.0	9.4	3.6	37.2

Note: (1) Figures cover the Boise City-Nampa, ID Metropolitan Statistical Area—see Appendix B for areas included
Source: U.S. Census Bureau, 2010 Census

Male/Female Ratio

Area	Males	Females	Males per 100 Females
City	101,690	103,981	97.8
MSA[1]	307,856	308,705	99.7
U.S.	151,781,326	156,964,212	96.7

Note: (1) Figures cover the Boise City-Nampa, ID Metropolitan Statistical Area—see Appendix B for areas included
Source: U.S. Census Bureau, 2010 Census

Religious Groups

Area	Catholic	Baptist	Non-Den.	Methodist[2]	Lutheran	LDS[3]	Pente-costal	Presby-terian[4]	Muslim[5]	Judaism
MSA[1]	8.0	2.9	4.2	2.1	1.2	15.9	2.3	0.6	0.1	0.1
U.S.	19.1	9.3	4.0	4.0	2.3	2.0	1.9	1.6	0.8	0.7

Note: Figures are the number of adherents as a percentage of the total population; (1) Figures cover the Boise City-Nampa, ID Metropolitan Statistical Area—see Appendix B for areas included; (2) Methodist/Pietist; (3) Latter Day Saints; (4) Reformed; (5) Figures are estimates
Source: Association of Statisticians of American Religious Bodies, 2010 U.S. Religion Census: Religious Congregations & Membership Study

ECONOMY

Gross Metropolitan Product

Area	2007	2008	2009	2010	2010 Rank[2]
MSA[1]	25.6	25.6	24.9	25.5	87

Note: Figures are in billions of dollars; (1) Figures cover the Boise City-Nampa, ID Metropolitan Statistical Area—see Appendix B for areas included; (2) Rank ranges from 1 to 363
Source: The United States Conference of Mayors, "U.S. Metro Economies: GMP and Employment Forecasts," June 2011

Economic Growth

Area	2007-2009 (%)	2010 (%)	2011 (%)	Rank[2]
MSA[1]	-2.2	1.9	3.1	238
U.S.	-1.3	2.9	2.5	–

Note: Figures are real Gross Metropolitan Product growth rates and represent annual average percent change; (1) Figures cover the Boise City-Nampa, ID Metropolitan Statistical Area—see Appendix B for areas included; (2) Rank ranges from 1 to 363
Source: The United States Conference of Mayors, "U.S. Metro Economies: GMP and Employment Forecasts," June 2011

Metropolitan Area Exports

Area	2005	2006	2007	2008	2009	2010	2010 Rank[2]
MSA[1]	2,670.3	3,040.0	3,852.9	3,851.2	2,849.7	3,647.7	57

Note: Figures are in millions of dollars; (1) Figures cover the Boise City-Nampa, ID Metropolitan Statistical Area—see Appendix B for areas included; (2) Rank ranges from 1 to 369
Source: U.S. Department of Commerce, International Trade Administration, Office of Trade & Industry Information, Manufacturing & Services, data extracted April 2, 2012

INCOME

Income

Area	Per Capita ($)	Median Household ($)	Average Household ($)
City	27,221	48,506	64,930
MSA[1]	23,502	50,026	63,351
U.S.	26,942	51,222	70,116

Note: (1) Figures cover the Boise City-Nampa, ID Metropolitan Statistical Area—see Appendix B for areas included
Source: U.S. Census Bureau, 2008-2010 American Community Survey 3-Year Estimates

Household Income Distribution

Area	Percent of Households Earning							
	Under $15,000	$15,000 -24,999	$25,000 -34,999	$35,000 -49,999	$50,000 -74,999	$75,000 -99,000	$100,000 -149,999	$150,000 and up
City	12.9	10.7	12.0	15.6	19.3	12.0	10.7	6.8
MSA[1]	11.7	11.1	11.8	15.3	21.6	12.4	10.2	5.9
U.S.	13.0	11.0	10.6	14.2	18.5	12.1	12.2	8.4

Note: (1) Figures cover the Boise City-Nampa, ID Metropolitan Statistical Area—see Appendix B for areas included
Source: U.S. Census Bureau, 2008-2010 American Community Survey 3-Year Estimates

Poverty Rate

Area	All Ages	Under 18 Years Old	18 to 64 Years Old	65 Years and Over
City	14.2	17.7	13.9	8.6
MSA[1]	14.2	18.5	13.4	7.7
U.S.	14.4	20.1	13.1	9.4

Note: Figures are percentage of people whose income during the past 12 months was below the poverty level; (1) Figures cover the Boise City-Nampa, ID Metropolitan Statistical Area—see Appendix B for areas included
Source: U.S. Census Bureau, 2008-2010 American Community Survey 3-Year Estimates

Personal Bankruptcy Filing Rate

Area	2006	2007	2008	2009	2010	2011
Ada County	2.46	2.97	4.26	6.17	6.11	5.62
U.S.	2.00	2.73	3.53	4.61	4.97	4.37

Note: Numbers are per 1,000 population and include Chapter 7 and Chapter 13 filings
Source: Federal Deposit Insurance Corporation, Regional Economic Conditions, March 9, 2012

EMPLOYMENT

Labor Force and Employment

Area	Civilian Labor Force			Workers Employed		
	Dec. 2010	Dec. 2011	% Chg.	Dec. 2010	Dec. 2011	% Chg.
City	106,962	109,041	1.9	97,521	100,874	3.4
MSA[1]	292,392	297,808	1.9	263,652	272,718	3.4
U.S.	153,156,000	153,373,000	0.1	139,159,000	140,681,000	1.1

Note: Data is not seasonally adjusted and covers workers 16 years of age and older; (1) Metropolitan Statistical Area—see Appendix B for areas included
Source: Bureau of Labor Statistics, http://stats.bls.gov

Unemployment Rate

Area	2011											
	Jan.	Feb.	Mar.	Apr.	May	Jun.	Jul.	Aug.	Sep.	Oct.	Nov.	Dec.
City	9.5	9.3	9.0	8.6	8.1	8.5	7.9	7.9	7.8	7.7	7.7	7.5
MSA[1]	10.8	10.5	10.1	9.5	8.8	9.7	9.1	9.0	8.5	8.4	8.5	8.4
U.S.	9.8	9.5	9.2	8.7	8.7	9.3	9.3	9.1	8.8	8.5	8.2	8.3

Note: Data is not seasonally adjusted and covers workers 16 years of age and older; All figures are percentages; (1) Metropolitan Statistical Area—see Appendix B for areas included
Source: Bureau of Labor Statistics, http://stats.bls.gov

Projected Unemployment Rate

Area	2010 (%)	2011 (%)	2012 (%)	2013 (%)
MSA[1]	10.0	8.9	8.1	7.6

Note: (1) Metropolitan Statistical Area—see Appendix B for areas included
Source: The United States Conference of Mayors, "U.S. Metro Economies: GMP and Employment Forecasts," June 2011

Employment by Occupation

Occupation Classification	City (%)	MSA[1] (%)	U.S. (%)
Management, Business, Science, and Arts	41.1	37.0	35.6
Natural Resources, Construction, and Maintenance	7.1	9.8	9.5
Production, Transportation, and Material Moving	8.3	10.5	12.1
Sales and Office	25.1	26.0	25.2
Service	18.3	16.7	17.6

Note: Figures cover employed civilians 16 years of age and older; (1) Figures cover the Boise City-Nampa, ID Metropolitan Statistical Area—see Appendix B for areas included
Source: U.S. Census Bureau, 2008-2010 American Community Survey 3-Year Estimates

Employment by Industry

Sector	MSA[1]		U.S.
	Number of Employees	Percent of Total	Percent of Total
Construction	n/a	n/a	4.1
Education and Health Services	39,400	15.2	15.2
Financial Activities	13,700	5.3	5.8
Government	43,000	16.6	16.8
Information	4,300	1.7	2.0
Leisure and Hospitality	22,100	8.5	9.9
Manufacturing	23,200	9.0	8.9
Mining and Logging	n/a	n/a	0.6
Other Services	9,100	3.5	4.0
Professional and Business Services	39,000	15.1	13.3
Retail Trade	31,100	12.0	11.5
Transportation and Utilities	8,300	3.2	3.8
Wholesale Trade	12,000	4.6	4.2

Note: Figures cover non-farm employment as of December 2011 and are not seasonally adjusted; (1) Metropolitan Statistical Area—see Appendix B for areas included; n/a not available
Source: Bureau of Labor Statistics, http://stats.bls.gov

Occupations with Greatest Projected Employment Growth: 2008 – 2018

Occupation[1]	2008 Employment	2018 Projected Employment	Numeric Employment Change	Percent Employment Change
Retail Salespersons	23,640	28,650	5,010	21.2
Customer Service Representatives	11,800	15,960	4,160	35.3
Office Clerks, General	18,690	22,090	3,400	18.2
Registered Nurses	10,500	13,340	2,840	27.0
Combined Food Preparation and Serving Workers, Including Fast Food	12,260	15,060	2,800	22.8
Truck Drivers, Heavy and Tractor-Trailer	14,130	16,800	2,670	18.9
Cashiers	14,540	17,170	2,630	18.1
Personal and Home Care Aides	3,490	5,750	2,260	64.8
Nursing Aides, Orderlies, and Attendants	7,200	9,300	2,100	29.2
Home Health Aides	3,900	5,930	2,030	52.1

Note: Projections cover Idaho; (1) Sorted by numeric employment change
Source: www.projectionscentral.com, State Occupational Projections, 2008–2018 Long-Term Projections

Fastest Growing Occupations: 2008 – 2018

Occupation[1]	2008 Employment	2018 Projected Employment	Numeric Employment Change	Percent Employment Change
Personal and Home Care Aides	3,490	5,750	2,260	64.8
Network Systems and Data Communications Analysts	900	1,410	510	56.7
Home Health Aides	3,900	5,930	2,030	52.1
Fitness Trainers and Aerobics Instructors	1,480	2,220	740	50.0
Personal Financial Advisors	960	1,390	430	44.8
Computer Software Engineers, Applications	1,010	1,460	450	44.6
Pharmacy Technicians	1,550	2,240	690	44.5
Social and Human Service Assistants	2,010	2,860	850	42.3
Hazardous Materials Removal Workers	310	440	130	41.9
Fiberglass Laminators and Fabricators	290	410	120	41.4

Note: Projections cover Idaho; (1) Sorted by percent employment change and excludes occupations with numeric employment change less than 100
Source: www.projectionscentral.com, State Occupational Projections, 2008–2018 Long-Term Projections

Average Wages

Occupation	$/Hr.	Occupation	$/Hr.
Accountants and Auditors	29.96	Maids and Housekeeping Cleaners	9.47
Automotive Mechanics	17.63	Maintenance and Repair Workers	15.69
Bookkeepers	16.54	Marketing Managers	47.44
Carpenters	19.46	Nuclear Medicine Technologists	n/a
Cashiers	9.52	Nurses, Licensed Practical	19.60
Clerks, General Office	13.48	Nurses, Registered	31.49
Clerks, Receptionists/Information	12.37	Nursing Aides/Orderlies/Attendants	11.32
Clerks, Shipping/Receiving	13.39	Packers and Packagers, Hand	8.98
Computer Programmers	30.53	Physical Therapists	33.98
Computer Support Specialists	19.12	Postal Service Mail Carriers	24.47
Computer Systems Analysts	33.46	Real Estate Brokers	n/a
Cooks, Restaurant	10.21	Retail Salespersons	11.73
Dentists	92.45	Sales Reps., Exc. Tech./Scientific	24.13
Electrical Engineers	43.91	Sales Reps., Tech./Scientific	37.81
Electricians	22.03	Secretaries, Exc. Legal/Med./Exec.	14.47
Financial Managers	40.93	Security Guards	12.44
First-Line Supervisors/Managers, Sales	16.90	Surgeons	n/a
Food Preparation Workers	9.04	Teacher Assistants	10.30
General and Operations Managers	38.37	Teachers, Elementary School	23.30
Hairdressers/Cosmetologists	10.45	Teachers, Secondary School	22.80
Internists	n/a	Telemarketers	11.88
Janitors and Cleaners	10.74	Truck Drivers, Heavy/Tractor-Trailer	17.51
Landscaping/Groundskeeping Workers	12.31	Truck Drivers, Light/Delivery Svcs.	14.09
Lawyers	49.86	Waiters and Waitresses	9.58

Note: Wage data covers the Boise City-Nampa, ID Metropolitan Statistical Area—see Appendix B for areas included. Hourly wages for elementary/secondary school teachers and teacher assistants were calculated by the editors from annual wage data assuming a 40 hour work week; n/a not available.
Source: Bureau of Labor Statistics, Metro Area Occupational Employment and Wage Estimates, May 2011

RESIDENTIAL REAL ESTATE

Building Permits

Area	Single-Family			Multi-Family			Total		
	2010	2011	Pct. Chg.	2010	2011	Pct. Chg.	2010	2011	Pct. Chg.
City	352	359	2.0	0	59	-	352	418	18.8
MSA[1]	1,630	1,578	-3.2	63	262	315.9	1,693	1,840	8.7
U.S.	447,311	418,498	-6.4	157,299	205,563	30.7	604,610	624,061	3.2

Note: (1) Metropolitan Statistical Area—see Appendix B for areas included; figures represent new, privately-owned housing units authorized (unadjusted data); All permit data are based on estimates with imputation.
Source: U.S. Census Bureau, Manufacturing, Mining, and Construction Statistics, Building Permits, 2010, 2011

Homeownership Rate

Area	2005 (%)	2006 (%)	2007 (%)	2008 (%)	2009 (%)	2010 (%)	2011 (%)
MSA[1]	n/a	n/a	n/a	n/a	n/a	n/a	n/a
U.S.	68.9	68.8	68.1	67.8	67.4	66.9	66.1

Note: (1) Metropolitan Statistical Area—see Appendix B for areas included; n/a not available
Source: U.S. Census Bureau, Housing Vacancies and Homeownership Annual Statistics: 2011

Housing Vacancy Rates

Area	Gross Vacancy Rate[2] (%)			Year-Round Vacancy Rate[3] (%)			Rental Vacancy Rate[4] (%)			Homeowner Vacancy Rate[5] (%)		
	2009	2010	2011	2009	2010	2011	2009	2010	2011	2009	2010	2011
MSA[1]	n/a	n/a	n/a	n/a	n/a	n/a	n/a	n/a	n/a	n/a	n/a	n/a
U.S.	14.5	14.3	14.2	11.3	11.3	11.1	10.6	10.2	9.5	2.6	2.6	2.5

Note: (1) Metropolitan Statistical Area—see Appendix B for areas included; (2) The percentage of the total housing inventory that is vacant; (3) The percentage of the housing inventory (excluding seasonal units) that is year-round vacant; (4) The percentage of rental inventory that is vacant for rent; (5) The percentage of homeowner inventory that is vacant for sale; n/a not available
Source: U.S. Census Bureau, Housing Vacancies and Homeownership Annual Statistics: 2011

TAXES

State Corporate Income Tax Rates

State	Tax Rate (%)	Income Brackets ($)	Num. of Brackets	Financial Institution Tax Rate (%)[a]	Federal Income Tax Ded.
Idaho	7.6 (h)	Flat rate	1	7.6 (h)	No

Note: Tax rates as of January 1, 2012; (a) Rates listed are the corporate income tax rate applied to financial institutions or excise taxes based on income. Some states have other taxes based upon the value of deposits or shares; (h) Idaho's minimum tax on a corporation is $20. The $10 Permanent Building Fund Tax must be paid by each corporation in a unitary group filing a combined return. Taxpayers with gross sales in Idaho under $100,000, and with no property or payroll in Idaho, may elect to pay 1% on such sales (instead of the tax on net income).
Source: Federation of Tax Administrators, "State Corporate Income Tax Rates, 2012"

State Individual Income Tax Rates

State	Tax Rate (%)	Income Brackets ($)	Num. of Brackets	Personal Exempt. ($)[1] Single	Personal Exempt. ($)[1] Dependents	Fed. Inc. Tax Ded.
Idaho (a)	1.6 - 7.8	1,338 (b) - 26,760 (b)	8	3,700 (d)	3,700 (d)	No

Note: Tax rates as of January 1, 2012; Local- and county-level taxes are not included; n/a not applicable; (1) Married joint filers generally receive double the single exemption; (a) 17 states have statutory provision for automatically adjusting to the rate of inflation the dollar values of the income tax brackets, standard deductions, and/or personal exemptions. Massachusetts, Michigan, and Nebraska index the personal exemptiononly. Oregon does not index the income brackets for $125,000 and over. Because the inflation-adjustments for 2012 are not yet available in some cases, the table may report the 2011 amounts; (b) For joint returns, taxes are twice the tax on half the couple's income; (d) These states use the personal exemption amounts provided in the federal Internal Revenue Code.
Source: Federation of Tax Administrators, "State Individual Income Tax Rates, 2012"

Various State and Local Tax Rates

State	State and Local Sales and Use (%)	State Sales and Use (%)	Gasoline[1] (¢/gal.)	Cigarette[2] ($/pack)	Spirits[3] ($/gal.)	Wine[4] ($/gal.)	Beer[5] ($/gal.)
Idaho	6.0	6.00	25.0	0.57	11.28 (f)	0.45	0.15

Note: All tax rates as of January 1, 2012 except beer, wine and spirits (September 1, 2011); (1) The American Petroleum Institute has developed a methodology for determining the average tax rate on a gallon of fuel. Rates may include any of the following: excise taxes, environmental fees, storage tank fees, other fees or taxes, general sales tax, and local taxes. In states where gasoline is subject to the general sales tax, or where the fuel tax is based on the average sale price, the average rate determined by API is sensitive to changes in the price of gasoline. States that fully or partially apply general sales taxes to gasoline: CA, CO, GA, IL, IN, MI, NY; (2) The federal excise tax of $1.0066 per pack and local taxes are not included; (3) Rates are those applicable to off-premise sales of 40% alcohol by volume (a.b.v.) distilled spirits in 750ml containers. Local excise taxes are excluded; (4) Rates are those applicable to off-premise sales of 11% a.b.v. non-carbonated wine in 750ml containers; (5) Rates are those applicable to off-premise sales of 4.7% a.b.v. beer in 12 ounce containers; (f) States where the government controls sales. In these "control states," products are subject to ad valorem mark-up and excise taxes. The excise tax rate is calculated using a methodology developed by the Distilled Spirits Council of the United States.
Source: Tax Foundation, 2012 Facts & Figures: How Does Your State Compare?

State-Local Tax Burdens

Area	Rate (%)	Rank[1]	Per Capita Taxes Paid to Home State ($)	Total State and Local Per Capita Taxes Paid ($)	Per Capita Income ($)
Idaho	9.4	28	2,227	3,276	34,973
U.S. Average	9.8	-	3,057	4,160	42,539

Note: Figures cover 2009; (1) Rank ranges from 1 to 50 where 1 is highest tax burden
Source: Tax Foundation, State-Local Tax Burdens, All States, 2009

State Business Tax Climate Index Rankings

State	Overall Rank	Corporate Tax Index Rank	Individual Income Tax Index Rank	Sales Tax Index Rank	Unemployment Insurance Tax Index Rank	Property Tax Index Rank
Idaho	21	19	26	23	48	2

Note: The index is a measure of how each state's tax laws affect economic performance. The lower the rank, the more favorable a state's tax system is for business. States without a given tax are given a ranking of 1.
Source: Tax Foundation, Major Components of the State Business Tax Climate Index, FY 2012

COMMERCIAL UTILITIES

Typical Monthly Electric Bills

Area	Commercial Service ($/month)		Industrial Service ($/month)	
	1,500 kWh	40 kW demand 14,000 kWh	1,000 kW demand 200,000 kWh	50,000 kW demand 15,000,000 kWh
City	106	810	13,566	n/a
Average[1]	189	1,616	25,197	1,470,813

Note: Based on total rates in effect July 1, 2011; (1) average based on 184 utilities surveyed; n/a not available
Source: Edison Electric Institute, Typical Bills and Average Rates Report, Summer 2011

TRANSPORTATION

Means of Transportation to Work

Area	Car/Truck/Van		Public Transportation			Bicycle	Walked	Other Means	Worked at Home
	Drove Alone	Car-pooled	Bus	Subway	Railroad				
City	78.2	7.7	0.8	0.1	0.0	4.3	2.5	1.4	5.0
MSA[1]	78.4	9.5	0.5	0.0	0.0	1.9	2.0	2.0	5.6
U.S.	76.0	10.2	2.7	1.7	0.5	0.5	2.8	1.3	4.2

Note: Figures are percentages and cover workers 16 years of age and older; (1) Figures cover the Boise City-Nampa, ID Metropolitan Statistical Area—see Appendix B for areas included
Source: U.S. Census Bureau, 2008-2010 American Community Survey 3-Year Estimates

Travel Time to Work

Area	Less Than 10 Minutes	10 to 19 Minutes	20 to 29 Minutes	30 to 44 Minutes	45 to 59 Minutes	60 to 89 Minutes	90 Minutes or More
City	16.8	47.3	22.2	10.0	1.7	1.2	0.9
MSA[1]	14.8	35.6	23.5	17.6	4.8	2.6	1.1
U.S.	13.9	30.1	20.8	19.8	7.5	5.5	2.5

Note: Figures are percentages and include workers 16 years old and over; (1) Figures cover the Boise City-Nampa, ID Metropolitan Statistical Area—see Appendix B for areas included
Source: U.S. Census Bureau, 2008-2010 American Community Survey 3-Year Estimates

Travel Time Index

Area	1985	1990	1995	2000	2005	2010
Urban Area[1]	1.03	1.07	1.07	1.12	1.15	1.10
Average[2]	1.11	1.16	1.18	1.21	1.25	1.20

Note: Travel Time Index—the ratio of travel time in the peak period to the travel time at free-flow conditions. A value of 1.30 indicates a 20-minute free-flow trip takes 26 minutes in the peak. Free-flow speeds (60 mph on freeways and 35 mph on principal arterials) are used as the comparison threshold; (1) Covers the Boise City ID urban area; (2) average of 439 urban areas
Source: Texas Transportation Institute, Urban Mobility Report 2011, September 2011

Public Transportation

Agency Name / Mode of Transportation	Vehicles Operated in Maximum Service	Annual Unlinked Passenger Trips ('000)	Annual Passenger Miles ('000)
ValleyRide			
Bus (directly operated)	27	1,203.2	5,073.1
Bus (purchased transportation)	11	172.4	2,599.6
Demand Response (directly operated)	10	40.9	258.3
Demand Response (purchased transportation)	2	1.8	11.9

Source: Federal Transit Administration, National Transit Database, 2010

Air Transportation

Airport Name and Code / Type of Service	Passenger Airlines[1]	Passenger Enplanements	Freight Carriers[2]	Freight (lbs.)
Boise Air Terminal-Gowen Field (BOI)				
Domestic service (U.S. carriers - 2011)	19	1,381,035	11	39,598,992
International service (U.S. carriers - 2010)	3	444	0	0

Note: (1) Includes all U.S.-based major, minor and commuter airlines that carried at least one passenger during the year; (2) Includes all U.S.-based airlines and freight carriers that transported at least one pound of freight during the year
Source: Bureau of Transportation Statistics, The Intermodal Transportation Database, Air Carriers: T-100 Domestic Market (U.S. Carriers), 2011; Bureau of Transportation Statistics, The Intermodal Transportation Database, Air Carriers: T-100 International Market (U.S. Carriers), 2010

Other Transportation Statistics

Major Highways:	I-84
Amtrak Service:	Bus connection
Major Waterways/Ports:	None

Source: Amtrak.com; Google Maps

BUSINESSES

Major Business Headquarters

Company Name	Rankings	
	Fortune[1]	Forbes[2]
Boise Cascade	-	200
JR Simplot	-	64
Micron Technology	287	-
WinCo Foods	-	66

Note: (1) Fortune 500—companies that produce a 10-K are ranked 1 to 500 based on 2010 revenue; (2) all private companies with at least $2 billion in annual revenue are ranked 1 to 212; companies listed are headquartered in the city; dashes indicate no ranking
Source: Fortune, "Fortune 500," May 23, 2011; Forbes, "America's Largest Private Companies," November 16, 2011

Fast-Growing Businesses

According to *Fortune*, Boise City is home to one of the 100 fastest-growing companies in the world: **MWI Veterinary Supply** (#92). Companies were ranked by their revenue growth rate; their EPS growth rate; and their three-year annualized total return to investors for the period ending June 30, 2011. Criteria for inclusion: a company, foreign or domestic, must trade on a major U.S. stock exchange; must file quarterly reports with the SEC; must have a minimum market capitalization of $250 million; must have a stock price of at least $5 on June 30, 2011; must have been trading continuously since June 30, 2008; must have revenue and net income for the four quarters ended on or before April 30, 2011, of at least $50 million and $10 million, respectively; and must have posted a compound annual growth in revenue and earnings per share of at least 15% annually over the three years ending on or before April 30, 2011. REITs, limited-liability companies, limited parterships, companies about to be acquired, and companies that lost money in the quarter ending April 30, 2011 were excluded. *Fortune, "100 Fastest-Growing Companies," September 26, 2011*

Minority Business Opportunity

Boise City is home to one company which is on the *Hispanic Business* 500 list (500 largest U.S. Hispanic-owned companies based on 2010 revenue): **Metalcraft** (#478). Companies included must show at least 51 percent ownership by Hispanic U.S. citizens, and must maintain headquarters in one of the 50 states or Washington, D.C. *Hispanic Business, "Hispanic Business 500," June 2011*

Minority- and Women-Owned Businesses

Group	All Firms		Firms with Paid Employees			
	Firms	Sales ($000)	Firms	Sales ($000)	Employees	Payroll ($000)
Asian	334	87,192	127	78,909	818	12,425
Black	115	10,503	8	6,281	47	702
Hispanic	447	35,995	104	30,376	465	8,701
Women	6,314	730,171	849	606,840	5,526	146,859
All Firms	24,611	47,523,495	6,802	46,786,667	173,758	7,366,058

Note: Figures cover firms located in the city; minority- and women-owned business are defined as firms in which the corresponding group own 51% or more of the stock or equity of the company
Source: U.S. Census Bureau, 2007 Economic Census, Survey of Business Owners

HOTELS

Hotels/Motels

Area	5 Star		4 Star		3 Star		2 Star		1 Star		Not Rated	
	Num.	Pct.[3]	Num.	Pct.[3]	Num.	Pct.[3]	Num.	Pct.[3]	Num.	Pct.[3]	Num.	Pct.[3]
City[1]	0	0.0	1	1.4	22	31.4	37	52.9	0	0.0	10	14.3
Total[2]	133	0.9	940	6.5	4,569	31.8	7,033	48.9	351	2.4	1,343	9.3

Note: (1) Figures cover Boise City and vicinity; (2) Figures cover all 100 cities in this book; (3) Percentage of hotels which have a given star rating; Star ratings are determined by expedia.com and offer an indication of the general quality of a particular hotel.
Source: expedia.com, April 25, 2012

EVENT SITES

Major Stadiums, Arenas, and Auditoriums

Name	Max. Capacity
Boise State University, Bronco Stadium	32,000
Boise State University, Taco Bell Arena	12,380
Qwest Arena	5,000

Source: Original research

Convention Centers

Name	Overall Space (sq. ft.)	Exhibit Space (sq. ft.)	Meeting Space (sq. ft.)	Meeting Rooms
Boise Centre on the Grove	n/a	n/a	45,000	n/a

Note: n/a not available
Source: Original research

Living Environment

COST OF LIVING

Cost of Living Index

Composite Index	Groceries	Housing	Utilities	Trans-portation	Health Care	Misc. Goods/ Services
96.1	101.3	83.7	97.2	101.3	101.4	102.2

Note: U.S. = 100; Figures cover the Boise ID urban area.
Source: The Council for Community and Economic Research, ACCRA Cost of Living Index, 2011

Grocery Prices

Area[1]	T-Bone Steak ($/pound)	Frying Chicken ($/pound)	Whole Milk ($/half gal.)	Eggs ($/dozen)	Orange Juice ($/64 oz.)	Coffee ($/11.5 oz.)
City[2]	8.23	1.58	1.83	1.63	3.32	4.52
Avg.	9.25	1.18	2.22	1.66	3.19	4.40
Min.	6.70	0.88	1.31	0.95	2.46	2.94
Max.	14.30	2.16	3.50	3.18	4.75	6.83

Note: (1) Values for the local area are compared with the average, minimum and maximum values for all 335 areas in the Cost of Living Index; (2) Figures cover the Boise ID urban area; **T-Bone Steak** *(price per pound);* **Frying Chicken** *(price per pound, whole fryer);* **Whole Milk** *(half gallon carton);* **Eggs** *(price per dozen, Grade A, large);* **Orange Juice** *(64 oz. Tropicana or Florida Natural);* **Coffee** *(11.5 oz. can, vacuum-packed, Maxwell House, Hills Bros, or Folgers).*
Source: The Council for Community and Economic Research, ACCRA Cost of Living Index, 2011

Housing and Utility Costs

Area[1]	New Home Price ($)	Apartment Rent ($/month)	All Electric ($/month)	Part Electric ($/month)	Other Energy ($/month)	Telephone ($/month)
City[2]	238,006	703	-	84.47	67.46	28.64
Avg.	285,990	839	163.23	89.00	77.52	26.92
Min.	188,005	460	125.58	45.39	33.89	17.98
Max.	1,197,028	3,244	339.16	181.97	348.69	40.01

Note: (1) Values for the local area are compared with the average, minimum and maximum values for all 335 areas in the Cost of Living Index; (2) Figures cover the Boise ID urban area; **New Home Price** *(2,400 sf living area, 8,000 sf lot, in urban area with full utilities);* **Apartment Rent** *(950 sf 2 bedroom/1.5 or 2 bath, unfurnished, excluding all utilities except water);* **All Electric** *(average monthly cost for an all-electric home);* **Part Electric** *(average monthly cost for a part-electric home);* **Other Energy** *(average monthly cost for natural gas, fuel oil, coal, wood, and any other forms of energy except electricity);* **Telephone** *(price includes basic monthly rate for a private residential line plus additional local usage charges incurred by a family of four).*
Source: The Council for Community and Economic Research, ACCRA Cost of Living Index, 2011

Health Care, Transportation, and Other Costs

Area[1]	Doctor ($/visit)	Dentist ($/visit)	Optometrist ($/visit)	Gasoline ($/gallon)	Beauty Salon ($/visit)	Men's Shirt ($)
City[2]	102.63	83.07	87.80	3.42	24.94	33.45
Avg.	93.88	81.72	90.54	3.48	32.65	25.06
Min.	60.00	55.33	53.66	3.18	19.78	13.44
Max.	154.98	145.97	183.72	4.31	63.21	46.00

Note: (1) Values for the local area are compared with the average, minimum and maximum values for all 335 areas in the Cost of Living Index; (2) Figures cover the Boise ID urban area; **Doctor** *(general practitioners routine exam of an established patient);* **Dentist** *(adult teeth cleaning and periodic oral examination);* **Optometrist** *(full vision eye exam for established adult patient);* **Gasoline** *(one gallon regular unleaded, national brand, including all taxes, cash price at self-service pump if available);* **Beauty Salon** *(woman's shampoo, trim, and blow-dry);* **Men's Shirt** *(cotton/polyester dress shirt, pinpoint weave, long sleeves).*
Source: The Council for Community and Economic Research, ACCRA Cost of Living Index, 2011

HOUSING

House Price Index (HPI)

Area	National Ranking[2]	Quarterly Change (%)	One-Year Change (%)	Five-Year Change (%)
MSA[1]	289	2.70	-8.36	-35.65
U.S.[3]	-	-0.10	-2.43	-19.16

Note: The HPI is a weighted repeat sales index. It measures average price changes in repeat sales or refinancings on the same properties. This information is obtained by reviewing repeat mortgage transactions on single-family properties whose mortgages have been purchased or securitized by Fannie Mae or Freddie Mac in January 1975; (1) Metropolitan/Micropolitan Statistical Area—see Appendix B for areas included; (2) Rankings are based on annual percentage change for all metro areas containing at least 15,000 transactions over the last 10 years and ranges from 1 to 306; (3) figures based on a weighted average of Census Division estimates using a purchase only index; all figures are for the period ending December 31, 2011
Source: Federal Housing Finance Agency, House Price Index, February 23, 2012

House Price Valuations

Area	Q4 2005		Q4 2006		Q4 2007		Q4 2008		Q4 2009	
	Price ($000)	Over-valuation	Price ($000)	Over-valuation	Price ($000)	Over-valuation	Price ($000)	Over-valuation	Price ($000)	Over-valuation
MSA[1]	172.5	14.6	200.6	24.0	201.3	21.7	176.9	9.7	154.2	-0.7

Note: Figures show the percentage of over- or under-valuation of single family homes relative to statistically normal house values (e.g. a value of 23.6 indicates that house values are 23.6% overvalued). Statistically normal house values are based on house prices, interest rates, household incomes, population densities, and any historical premiums or discounts metropolitan areas have exhibited over time; (1) Figures cover the Boise City-Nampa, ID - see Appendix B for areas included
Source: Global Insight/PNC Financial Services Group, House Prices in America: 4th Quarter 2009 Update

Median Single-Family Home Prices

Area	2009	2010	2011p	Percent Change 2010 to 2011
MSA[1]	153.8	136.2	115.4	-15.3
U.S. Average	172.1	173.1	166.2	-4.0

Note: Figures are median sales prices of existing single-family homes in thousands of dollars; (p) preliminary; n/a not available; (1) Metropolitan Statistical Area—see Appendix B for areas included
Source: National Association of Realtors, Median Sales Price of Existing Single-Family Homes for Metropolitan Areas, 4th Quarter 2011

Affordability Index of Existing Single-Family Homes

Area	2009	2010	2011p	Percent Change 2010 to 2011
MSA[1]	104.7	124.8	152.5	22.2

Note: The housing affordability index measures whether or not a typical family could qualify for a mortgage loan on a typical home. The higher the index, the greater the household purchasing power. An index of 100 is defined as the point where a median-income household has exactly enough income to qualify for the purchase of a median-priced existing single-family home, assuming a 20 percent downpayment and 25 percent of gross income devoted to mortgage principal and interest payments; (p) preliminary; n/a not available; (1) Metropolitan Statistical Area—see Appendix B for areas included
Source: National Association of Realtors, Affordability Index of Existing Single-Family Homes, 2011

Median Apartment Condo-Coop Home Prices

Area	2009	2010	2011p	Percent Change 2010 to 2011
MSA[1]	n/a	n/a	n/a	n/a
U.S. Average	175.6	171.7	165.1	-3.8

Note: Figures are median sales prices of existing apartment condo-coop homes in thousands of dollars; (p) preliminary; n/a not available; (1) Metropolitan Statistical Area—see Appendix B for areas included
Source: National Association of Realtors, Median Sales Price of Existing Apartment Condo-Coop Homes for Metropolitan Areas, 4th Quarter 2011

Year Housing Structure Built

Area	2005 or Later	2000 -2004	1990 -1999	1980 -1989	1970 -1979	1960 -1969	1950 -1959	Before 1950	Median Year
City	3.8	9.5	21.3	15.0	22.2	7.8	8.5	11.9	1980
MSA[1]	10.9	16.8	22.8	10.1	18.9	5.4	5.5	9.5	1990
U.S.	5.0	8.6	14.0	14.1	16.3	11.3	11.2	19.6	1975

Note: Figures are percentages except for Median Year; (1) Figures cover the Boise City-Nampa, ID Metropolitan Statistical Area—see Appendix B for areas included
Source: U.S. Census Bureau, 2008-2010 American Community Survey 3-Year Estimates

HEALTH

Health Risk Data

Category	MSA[1] (%)	U.S. (%)
Adults who have been told they have high blood pressure[2]	25.2	28.7
Adults who have been told they have high blood cholesterol[2]	37.2	37.5
Adults who have been told they have diabetes[3]	7.4	8.7
Adults who have been told they have arthritis[2]	21.6	26.0
Adults who have been told they currently have asthma	10.8	9.1
Adults who are current smokers	15.2	17.3
Adults who are heavy drinkers[4]	3.5	5.0
Adults who are binge drinkers[5]	12.4	15.1
Adults who are overweight (BMI 25.0 - 29.9)	36.6	36.2
Adults who are obese (BMI 30.0 - 99.8)	25.3	27.5
Adults who participated in any physical activities in the past month	83.4	76.1
Adults 50+ who have ever had a sigmoidoscopy or colonoscopy	62.2	65.2
Women aged 40+ who have had a mammogram within the past two years	67.8	75.2
Men aged 40+ who have had a PSA test within the past two years	50.5	53.2
Adults aged 65+ who have had flu shot within the past year	61.6	67.5
Adults aged 18–64 who have any kind of health care coverage	77.3	82.2

Note: Data as of 2010 unless otherwise noted; (1) Figures cover the Boise City-Nampa, ID Metropolitan Statistical Area—see Appendix B for areas included; (2) Data as of 2009; (3) Figures do not include pregnancy-related, borderline, or pre-diabetes; (4) Heavy drinkers are classified as males having more than two drinks per day or females having more than one drink per day; (5) Binge drinkers are classified as males having five or more drinks on one occasion or females having four or more drinks on one occasion
Source: Centers for Disease Control and Prevention, Behaviorial Risk Factor Surveillance System, SMART: Selected Metropolitan/Micropolitan Area Risk Trends, 2009, 2010

Mortality Rates for the Top 10 Causes of Death in the U.S.

ICD-10[a] Sub-Chapter	ICD-10[a] Code	Age-Adjusted Mortality Rate[1] per 100,000 population	
		County[2]	U.S.
Malignant neoplasms	C00-C97	156.0	175.6
Ischaemic heart diseases	I20-I25	94.7	121.6
Other forms of heart disease	I30-I51	37.8	48.6
Chronic lower respiratory diseases	J40-J47	47.1	42.3
Cerebrovascular diseases	I60-I69	36.7	40.6
Organic, including symptomatic, mental disorders	F01-F09	43.5	26.7
Other degenerative diseases of the nervous system	G30-G31	35.1	24.7
Other external causes of accidental injury	W00-X59	19.8	24.4
Diabetes mellitus	E10-E14	17.8	21.7
Hypertensive diseases	I10-I15	13.6	18.2

Note: (a) ICD-10 = International Classification of Diseases 10th Revision; (1) Mortality rates are a three year average covering 2007-2009; (2) Figures cover Ada County
Source: Centers for Disease Control and Prevention, National Center for Health Statistics. Underlying Cause of Death 1999-2009 on CDC WONDER Online Database, released 2012. Data for year 2009 are compiled from the Multiple Cause of Death File 2009, Series 20 No. 2O, 2012, Data for year 2008 are compiled from the Multiple Cause of Death File 2008, Series 20 No. 2N, 2011, Data for year 2007 are compiled from Multiple Cause of Death File 2007, Series 20 No. 2M, 2010.

Mortality Rates for Selected Causes of Death

ICD-10[a] Sub-Chapter	ICD-10[a] Code	Age-Adjusted Mortality Rate[1] per 100,000 population County[2]	U.S.
Assault	X85-Y09	2.1	5.7
Human immunodeficiency virus (HIV) disease	B20-B24	*0.0	3.3
Influenza and pneumonia	J09-J18	11.3	16.4
Intentional self-harm	X60-X84	15.1	11.5
Malnutrition	E40-E46	*0.0	0.8
Obesity and other hyperalimentation	E65-E68	*Unreliable	1.6
Transport accidents	V01-V99	9.7	13.7
Viral hepatitis	B15-B19	2.5	2.2

Note: (a) ICD-10 = International Classification of Diseases 10th Revision; (1) Mortality rates are a three year average covering 2007-2009; (2) Figures cover Ada County; (*) Unreliable data as per CDC
Source: Centers for Disease Control and Prevention, National Center for Health Statistics. Underlying Cause of Death 1999-2009 on CDC WONDER Online Database, released 2012. Data for year 2009 are compiled from the Multiple Cause of Death File 2009, Series 20 No. 2O, 2012, Data for year 2008 are compiled from the Multiple Cause of Death File 2008, Series 20 No. 2N, 2011, Data for year 2007 are compiled from Multiple Cause of Death File 2007, Series 20 No. 2M, 2010.

Distribution of Physicians and Dentists

Area[1]	Dentists[2]	D.O.[3]	M.D.[4] Total	Family/ General Practice	Pediatrics	Medical Specialties	Surgical Specialties
Local (number)	241	61	854	135	38	242	246
Local (rate[5])	6.5	1.6	22.5	3.6	1.0	6.4	6.5
U.S. (rate[5])	4.5	1.9	18.3	2.5	1.4	6.8	4.1

Note: Data as of 2008 unless noted; (1) Local data covers Ada County; (2) Data as of 2007; (3) Doctor of Osteopathic Medicine; (4) Includes active, non-federal, patient-care, office-based Doctors of Medicine; (5) rate per 10,000 population
Source: Area Resource File (ARF). 2009-2010 Release. U.S. Department of Health and Human Services, Health Resources and Services Administration, Bureau of Health Professions, Rockville, MD, August 2010

EDUCATION

Public School District Statistics

District Name	Schls	Pupils	Pupil/ Teacher Ratio	Minority Pupils[1] (%)	Free Lunch Eligible[2] (%)	IEP[3] (%)
Boise Independent District	53	25,453	17.3	17.9	30.1	10.9

Note: Table includes school districts with 2,000 or more students; (1) Percentage of students that are not non-Hispanic white; (2) Percentage of students that are eligible for the free lunch program; (3) Percentage of students that have an Individualized Education Program.
Source: U.S. Department of Education, National Center for Education Statistics, Common Core of Data, Local Education Agency (School District) Universe Survey: School Year 2009-2010; U.S. Department of Education, National Center for Education Statistics, Common Core of Data, Public Elementary/Secondary School Universe Survey: School Year 2009-2010

Highest Level of Education

Area	Less than H.S.	H.S. Diploma	Some College, No Deg.	Associate Degree	Bachelors Degree	Masters Degree	Profess. School Degree	Doctorate Degree
City	6.8	22.0	26.9	7.5	24.2	8.5	2.6	1.4
MSA[1]	11.0	25.9	27.5	7.7	19.1	6.1	1.7	1.0
U.S.	14.7	28.4	21.3	7.6	17.6	7.2	1.9	1.2

Note: Figures cover persons age 25 and over; (1) Figures cover the Boise City-Nampa, ID Metropolitan Statistical Area—see Appendix B for areas included
Source: U.S. Census Bureau, 2008-2010 American Community Survey 3-Year Estimates

Educational Attainment by Race

Area	High School Graduate or Higher (%)					Bachelor's Degree or Higher (%)				
	Total	White	Black	Asian	Hisp.[2]	Total	White	Black	Asian	Hisp.[2]
City	93.2	93.9	73.3	88.8	72.5	36.8	36.7	16.0	53.6	20.4
MSA[1]	89.0	89.7	80.9	86.7	56.3	28.0	28.2	15.1	49.2	9.6
U.S.	85.3	87.5	81.4	85.5	61.6	28.0	29.3	17.8	50.2	13.0

Note: Figures shown cover persons 25 years old and over; (1) Figures cover the Boise City-Nampa, ID Metropolitan Statistical Area—see Appendix B for areas included; (2) People of Hispanic origin can be of any race
Source: U.S. Census Bureau, 2008-2010 American Community Survey 3-Year Estimates

School Enrollment by Grade and Control

Area	Preschool (%)		Kindergarten (%)		Grades 1 - 4 (%)		Grades 5 - 8 (%)		Grades 9 - 12 (%)	
	Public	Private	Public	Private	Public	Private	Public	Private	Public	Private
City	51.8	48.2	84.6	15.4	90.7	9.3	90.9	9.1	92.3	7.7
MSA[1]	45.9	54.1	90.0	10.0	92.6	7.4	92.3	7.7	92.6	7.4
U.S.	55.4	44.6	87.1	12.9	89.4	10.6	89.5	10.5	90.4	9.6

Note: Figures shown cover persons 3 years old and over; (1) Figures cover the Boise City-Nampa, ID Metropolitan Statistical Area—see Appendix B for areas included
Source: U.S. Census Bureau, 2008-2010 American Community Survey 3-Year Estimates

Average Salaries of Public School Classroom Teachers

Area	2010-11		2011-12		Percent Change 2010-11 to 2011-12	Percent Change 2001-02 to 2011-12
	Dollars	Rank[1]	Dollars	Rank[1]		
Idaho	47,416	34	48,551	34	2.39	23.90
U.S. Average	55,623	-	56,643	-	1.83	26.8

Note: (1) State rank ranges from 1 to 51 where 1 indicates highest salary.
Source: National Education Association, Rankings & Estimates: Rankings of the States 2011 and Estimates of School Statistics 2012, December 2011

Higher Education

Four-Year Colleges			Two-Year Colleges			Medical Schools[1]	Law Schools[2]	Voc/ Tech[3]
Public	Private Non-profit	Private For-profit	Public	Private Non-profit	Private For-profit			
1	1	3	0	0	5	0	0	1

Note: Figures cover institutions located within the city limits and include main campuses only; (1) includes schools accredited by the Liaison Committee on Medical Education and the American Osteopathic Association's Commission on Osteopathic College Accreditation; (2) includes American Bar Association-accredited law schools; (3) includes all schools with programs that are less than 2 years.
Source: National Center for Education Statistics, Integrated Postsecondary Education System (IPEDS) Peer Analysis System, 2011-12; Association of American Medical Colleges, Member List, April 23, 2012; American Osteopathic Association, Member List, April 23, 2012; Law School Admission Council, Official Guide to ABA-Approved Law Schools Online, April 23, 2012

According to *U.S. News & World Report,* the Boise City-Nampa, ID is home to one of the best liberal arts colleges in the U.S.: **College of Idaho** (#171). The indicators used to capture academic quality fall into a number of categories: assessment by administrators at peer institutions; retention of students; faculty resources; student selectivity; financial resources; alumni giving; high school counselor ratings of colleges; and graduation rate.*U.S. News & World Report, "America's Best Colleges 2012"*

PRESIDENTIAL ELECTION

2008 Presidential Election Results

Area	Obama	McCain	Nader	Other
Ada County	45.5	51.6	1.1	1.8
U.S.	52.9	45.6	0.6	0.9

Note: Results are percentages and may not add to 100% due to rounding
Source: Dave Leip's Atlas of U.S. Presidential Elections, www.uselectionatlas.org

EMPLOYERS

Major Employers

Company Name	Industry
Albertson's	Grocery stores
American Drug Stores	Drug stores
Blue Cross of Idaho Health Service	Hospital and medical service plans
Boise State University	Colleges and universities
Bureau of Land Management	Land management agency, government
Hewlett-Packard Company	Computers
Idaho Division of Military	National security
Kit Manufacturing Company	Travel trailers and campers
Lactalis American Group	Cheese; natural and processed
Micron Technology	Semiconductors and related devices
Mk Capital Corporation	Bridge, tunnel, and elevated highway construction
Morrison-Knudsen Engineers	Bridge construction
Motivepower	Railroad car rebuilding
Saint Alphonsus Regional Medical Center	General medical and surgical hospitals
St. Luke's Health System	General medical and surgical hospitals
St. Luke's Regional Medical Center	Hospital, affiliated with ama residency
URS Energy & Construction	Personal service agents, brokers, and bureaus
URS Energy & Construction	Bridge, tunnel, and elevated highway construction
URS Energy & Construction	Highway and street
Veterans Health Administration	Administration of veterans' affairs
Washington Closure Co	Environmental cleanup services
Washington Group International	Equipment rental and leasing
Wells Fargo Bank National Association	National commercial banks
Young Men's Christian Assn of Boise	Youth organizations

Note: Companies shown are located within the Boise City-Nampa, ID metropolitan area.
Source: Hoovers.com, data extracted April 25 2012

PUBLIC SAFETY

Crime Rate

Area	All Crimes	Violent Crimes: Murder	Violent Crimes: Forcible Rape	Violent Crimes: Robbery	Violent Crimes: Aggrav. Assault	Property Crimes: Burglary	Property Crimes: Larceny -Theft	Property Crimes: Motor Vehicle Theft
City	3,033.5	1.5	43.2	28.2	188.9	431.3	2,263.2	77.2
Suburbs[1]	1,910.1	1.7	29.0	13.3	149.8	385.1	1,251.0	80.2
Metro[2]	2,283.3	1.6	33.7	18.2	162.8	400.4	1,587.3	79.2
U.S.	3,345.5	4.8	27.5	119.1	252.3	699.6	2,003.5	238.8

Note: Figures are crimes per 100,000 population; (1) All areas within the metro area that are located outside the city limits; (2) Metropolitan Statistical Area—see Appendix B for areas included
Source: FBI Uniform Crime Reports, 2010

Hate Crimes

Area	Number of Quarters Reported	Bias Motivation: Race	Bias Motivation: Religion	Bias Motivation: Sexual Orientation	Bias Motivation: Ethnicity	Bias Motivation: Disability
Area[2]	4	4	1	0	1	0

Note: (2) Figures cover Boise.
Source: Federal Bureau of Investigation, Hate Crime Statistics 2010

Identity Theft Consumer Complaints

Area	Complaints	Complaints per 100,000 Population	Rank[2]
MSA[1]	298	50.7	326
U.S.	279,156	90.4	-

Note: (1) Metropolitan Statistical Area—see Appendix B for areas included; (2) Rank ranges from 1 to 384 where 1 indicates greatest number of identity theft complaints per 100,000 population
Source: Federal Trade Commission, Consumer Sentinel Network Data Book for January–December 2011

Fraud and Other Consumer Complaints

Area	Complaints	Complaints per 100,000 Population	Rank[2]
MSA[1]	3,047	518.5	127
U.S.	1,533,924	496.8	-

Note: (1) Metropolitan Statistical Area—see Appendix B for areas included; (2) Rank ranges from 1 to 384 where 1 indicates greatest number of fraud and other complaints per 100,000 population
Source: Federal Trade Commission, Consumer Sentinel Network Data Book for January–December 2011

RECREATION

Culture

Dance[1]	Theatre[1]	Instrumental Music[1]	Vocal Music[1]	Series/ Festivals	Museums	Zoos and Aquariums[2]
2	1	3	3	3	7	1

Note: (1) Number of professional perfoming groups; (2) AZA-accredited
Source: The Grey House Performing Arts Directory, 2011-2012; Official Museum Directory, 2011; American Association of Museums, AAM Member Museums, April 2012; Association of Zoos & Aquariums, AZA Member Zoos & Aquariums, April 2012

Professional Sports Teams

Team Name	League
No teams are located in the metro area	

Source: Original research

CLIMATE

Average and Extreme Temperatures

Temperature	Jan	Feb	Mar	Apr	May	Jun	Jul	Aug	Sep	Oct	Nov	Dec	Yr.
Extreme High (°F)	63	70	81	92	98	105	111	110	101	94	74	65	111
Average High (°F)	36	44	53	62	71	80	90	88	78	65	48	38	63
Average Temp. (°F)	29	36	42	49	58	66	74	73	63	52	40	31	51
Average Low (°F)	22	27	31	37	44	52	58	57	48	39	30	23	39
Extreme Low (°F)	-17	-15	6	19	22	31	35	34	23	11	-3	-25	-25

Note: Figures cover the years 1948-1995
Source: National Climatic Data Center, International Station Meteorological Climate Summary, 9/96

Average Precipitation/Snowfall/Humidity

Precip./Humidity	Jan	Feb	Mar	Apr	May	Jun	Jul	Aug	Sep	Oct	Nov	Dec	Yr.
Avg. Precip. (in.)	1.4	1.1	1.2	1.2	1.2	0.9	0.3	0.3	0.6	0.7	1.4	1.4	11.8
Avg. Snowfall (in.)	7	4	2	1	Tr	Tr	0	0	0	Tr	2	6	22
Avg. Rel. Hum. 7am (%)	81	80	75	69	65	59	48	50	58	67	77	81	68
Avg. Rel. Hum. 4pm (%)	68	58	45	35	34	29	22	23	28	36	55	67	42

Note: Figures cover the years 1948-1995; Tr = Trace amounts (<0.05 in. of rain; <0.5 in. of snow)
Source: National Climatic Data Center, International Station Meteorological Climate Summary, 9/96

Weather Conditions

Temperature			Daytime Sky			Precipitation		
5°F & below	32°F & below	90°F & above	Clear	Partly cloudy	Cloudy	0.01 inch or more precip.	0.1 inch or more snow/ice	Thunder-storms
6	124	45	106	133	126	91	22	14

Note: Figures are average number of days per year and cover the years 1948-1995
Source: National Climatic Data Center, International Station Meteorological Climate Summary, 9/96

HAZARDOUS WASTE

Superfund Sites

Boise City has no sites on the EPA's Superfund Final National Priorities List.
U.S. Environmental Protection Agency, Final National Priorities List, April 17, 2012

AIR & WATER QUALITY

Air Quality Index

Area	Percent of Days when Air Quality was...[2]					AQI Statistics[2]	
	Good	Moderate	Unhealthy for Sensitive Groups	Unhealthy	Very Unhealthy	Maximum	Median
Area[1]	88.2	11.2	0.5	0.0	0.0	115	38

Note: Air Quality Index (AQI) is an index for reporting daily air quality. EPA calculates the AQI for five major air pollutants regulated by the Clean Air Act: ground-level ozone, particle pollution (aka particulate matter), carbon monoxide, sulfur dioxide, and nitrogen dioxide. The AQI runs from 0 to 500. The higher the AQI value, the greater the level of air pollution and the greater the health concern. There are six AQI categories: "Good" AQI is between 0 and 50. Air quality is considered satisfactory; "Moderate" AQI is between 51 and 100. Air quality is acceptable; "Unhealthy for Sensitive Groups" When AQI values are between 101 and 150, members of sensitive groups may experience health effects; "Unhealthy" When AQI values are between 151 and 200 everyone may begin to experience health effects; "Very Unhealthy" AQI values between 201 and 300 trigger a health alert; "Hazardous" AQI values over 300 trigger warnings of emergency conditions (not shown); (1) Data covers Ada County; (2) Based on 365 days with AQI data in 2011.
Source: U.S. Environmental Protection Agency, AirData Report, 2011

Air Quality Index Pollutants

Area	Percent of Days when AQI Pollutant was...[2]					
	Carbon Monoxide	Nitrogen Dioxide	Ozone	Sulfur Dioxide	Particulate Matter 2.5	Particulate Matter 10
Area[1]	0.8	2.5	81.6	0.0	7.4	7.7

Note: The Air Quality Index (AQI) is an index for reporting daily air quality. EPA calculates the AQI for five major air pollutants regulated by the Clean Air Act: ground-level ozone, particle pollution (also known as particulate matter), carbon monoxide, sulfur dioxide, and nitrogen dioxide. The AQI runs from 0 to 500. The higher the AQI value, the greater the level of air pollution and the greater the health concern; (1) Data covers Ada County; (2) Based on 365 days with AQI data in 2011.
Source: U.S. Environmental Protection Agency, AirData Report, 2011

Air Quality Index Trends

Area	Trend Sites (days)								All Sites (days)
	2003	2004	2005	2006	2007	2008	2009	2010	2010
MSA[1]	n/a	n/a	n/a	n/a	n/a	n/a	n/a	n/a	n/a

Note: Figures are the number of days the AQI value exceeded 100 in a given year. An AQI value greater than 100 indicates that air quality would have been in the unhealthful range on that day. Data from exceptional events are included. These counts are presented in two ways. First, the counts are based on sites having an adequate record of monitoring data during the trend period (trend sites). These counts represent the relative change in the number of days with AQI values greater than 100. In the last column, the counts are based on all sites with data in the most recent year (because it is possible for a site to have data in the most recent year but not enough data to be a trend site); (1) Data covers the Boise City-Nampa, ID—see Appendix B for areas included; n/a not available.
Source: U.S. Environmental Protection Agency, Air Quality Index Information, "Number of Days with Air Quality Index Values Greater than 100 at Trend Sites, 2000-2010, and at All Sites in 2010"

Maximum Air Pollutant Concentrations: Particulate Matter, Ozone, CO and Lead

	Particulate Matter 10 (ug/m³)	Particulate Matter 2.5 Wtd AM (ug/m³)	Particulate Matter 2.5 24-Hr (ug/m³)	Ozone (ppm)	Carbon Monoxide (ppm)	Lead (ug/m³)
MSA[1] Level	66	5.9	15	0.069	2	n/a
NAAQS[2]	150	15	35	0.075	9	0.15
Met NAAQS[2]	Yes	Yes	Yes	Yes	Yes	n/a

Note: Data from exceptional events are not included; (1) Data covers the Boise City-Nampa, ID—see Appendix B for areas included; (2) National Ambient Air Quality Standards; ppm = parts per million; ug/m³ = micrograms per cubic meter; n/a not available
Concentrations: Particulate Matter 10 (coarse particulate)—highest second maximum 24-hour concentration; Particulate Matter 2.5 Wtd AM (fine particulate)—highest weighted annual mean concentration; Particulate Matter 2.5 24-Hour (fine particulate)—highest 98th percentile 24-hour concentration; Ozone—highest fourth daily maximum 8-hour concentration; Carbon Monoxide—highest second maximum non-overlapping 8-hour concentration; Lead—maximum running 3-month average
Source: U.S. Environmental Protection Agency, CBSA Factbook 2010, Air Quality Statistics by City, 2010

Maximum Air Pollutant Concentrations: Nitrogen Dioxide and Sulfur Dioxide

	Nitrogen Dioxide AM (ppb)	Nitrogen Dioxide 1-Hr (ppb)	Sulfur Dioxide AM (ppb)	Sulfur Dioxide 1-Hr (ppb)	Sulfur Dioxide 24-Hr (ppb)
MSA[1] Level	9.51	45	0.366	n/a	1.1
NAAQS[2]	53	100	30	75	140
Met NAAQS[2]	Yes	Yes	Yes	n/a	Yes

Note: Data from exceptional events are not included; (1) Data covers the Boise City-Nampa, ID—see Appendix B for areas included; (2) National Ambient Air Quality Standards; ppb = parts per billion; n/a not available
Concentrations: Nitrogen Dioxide AM—highest arithmetic mean concentration; Nitrogen Dioxide 1-Hr—highest 98th percentile 1-hour daily maximum concentration; Sulfur Dioxide AM—highest annual mean concentration; Sulfur Dioxide 1-Hr—highest 99th percentile 1-hour daily maximum concentration; Sulfur Dioxide 24-Hr—highest second maximum 24-hour concentration
Source: U.S. Environmental Protection Agency, CBSA Factbook 2010, Air Quality Statistics by City, 2010

Drinking Water

Water System Name	Pop. Served	Primary Water Source Type	Violations[1]	
			Health Based	Monitoring/ Reporting
United Water Idaho	218,978	Surface	0	0

Note: (1) Based on violation data from January 1, 2011 to December 31, 2011 (includes unresolved violations from earlier years)
Source: U.S. Environmental Protection Agency, Office of Ground Water and Drinking Water, Safe Drinking Water Information System (based on data extracted April 18, 2012)

Boulder, Colorado

Background

Boulder, Colorado, lies at the foot of the Rocky Mountains in Boulder County. It is the eighth largest city in Colorado, with 27.8 square miles. Tourism is a major industry in Boulder, which offers spectacular views from its elevation of 5,430 feet and many outdoor recreation opportunities in over 31,000 acres of open space.

Boulder Valley originally was home to the Southern Arapahoe tribe. The first white settlement was established by gold miners in 1858 near the entrance to Boulder Canyon at Red Rocks. In 1859, the Boulder City Town Company was formed. The town's first schoolhouse was built in 1860, and in 1874, the University of Colorado opened.

Boulder was incorporated as a town in 1871 and as a city in 1882. By 1890, the railroad provided service from Boulder to Golden, Denver, and the western mining camps. In 1905, amidst a weakening economy, Boulder began promoting tourism to boost its finances. The city raised money to construct a first-class hotel, which was completed in 1908 and named Hotel Boulderado.

Although tourism remained strong until the late 1930s, it had begun to decline by World War II. However, the U.S. Navy's Japanese language school, housed at the city's University of Colorado, proved to be an impressive introduction to the area, and many people later returned to Boulder as students, professionals, and veterans attending the university on the GI Bill. Consequently, Boulder's population grew from 12,958 in 1940 to 20,000 in 1950. To accommodate this huge increase, new public buildings, highways, residential areas, and shopping centers developed, spurring further economic expansion.

Major employers in the Boulder area include Sun Microsystems, IBM, Ball AerospaceCorp, Covidien, and Level 3 Communications, one of the largest communications and Internet backbones in the world. NOAA, the National Oceanic and Atmospheric Administration, also operates here.

Boulder is home to the University of Colorado, which houses a research park that includes corporate tenants such as Qwest. Cultural venues in the city include the Boulder Dushanbe Teahouse, a gift to the city from its sister city of Dushanbe in Tajikistan, and the Pearl Street Mall, an open-air walkway that was the city's original downtown and is today rich with restaurants, cafes, bookstores, and street entertainers. Boulder offers many scenic opportunities for outdoor activities, with parks, recreation areas, and hiking trails. The city boasts hundreds of miles of bike trails, lanes and paths as a part of their renowned network of citywide bikeways. In 2008, Boulder was recognized by the League of American Bicyclists for being a leading bicyclist-friendly city.

Keeping with Boulder's tradition of outdoor recreation, each Memorial Day, over 50,000 runners, joggers, walkers and wheelers participate in the "Bolder Boulder," a popular race that lures more than 100,000 spectators.

Annual attractions include the Creek Festival in May, Art Fair in July, Fall Festival, and Lights of December Parade. The Boulder International Film Festival (BIFF) held their sixth annual event in February 2010 featuring 47 films and 31 filmmakers. Since its creation in 2005, BIFF has created a name for itself in the international film community. Ticket sales rose 14 percent in 2010.

Like the rest of Colorado, Boulder enjoys a cool, dry highland continental climate. In winter, the mountains to the west shield the city from the coldest temperatures. Humidity is generally low. Winter storms moving east from the Pacific drop most of their moisture on the mountains to the west, while summer precipitation comes from scattered thunderstorms.

Rankings

General Rankings

- Boulder was selected as one of the "10 Best Cities for the Next Decade" by *Kiplinger's Personal Finance.* The city ranked #4. Criteria: innovation factor (smart people, great ideas, and collaboration between governments, universities, and businesses); economic growth and growth potential; creativity in music, arts and culture; neighborhoods and recreational facilities that rank high for "coolness." *Kiplinger's Personal Finance, "10 Best Cities for the Next Decade," July 2010*
- Boulder appeared on RelocateAmerica's list of best places to live in America. The annual "Top 100 Places to Live" list recognizes the top communities as nominated by their residents & local businesses. RelocateAmerica's Research Group determines the list based on review of various data gathered for economic, employment, housing, education, industry, opportunity, environment and recreation along with feedback from area leaders and residents. *RelocateAmerica.com, "Top 100 Places to Live for 2011"*
- Boulder was selected as one of "America's Top 10 Places to Live" by *RelocateAmerica.com.* The city ranked #3. Criteria: real estate and housing; economic health; recreation; safety; input from local residents, business and community leaders. *RelocateAmerica.com, "Top 10 Places to Live for 2011"*
- Boulder was chosen as one of America's best cities by *Outside Magazine* in the "Best for Road Biking (Runner-up)" category. Criteria: educational attainment; cost of living; cultural vibrancy; economic resilience; housing market sanity; sport-specific facts such as the miles of trail within a hour's drive, frequency of group rides, and proximity to worthy ski areas. *Outside Magazine, "Best Towns 2010," August 2010*
- Boulder was selected as one the "finest places you'd ever want to call home" by *Outside Magazine.* Criteria: affordable homes; solid job prospects; vibrant nightlife. *Outside Magazine, "Life is Better Here," October 2011*

Business/Finance Rankings

- Boulder was identified as one of "America's Hardest-Working Towns." The city ranked #16 out of 25. Criteria: average hours worked per capita; willingness to work during personal time; number of dual income households; local employment rate. *Parade, "What is America's Hardest-Working Town?," April 15, 2012*
- Boulder was identified as one of the "Unhappiest Cities to Work in 2012" by *CareerBliss.com,* an online community for career advancement. The city ranked #11 out of 30. Criteria: independent company reviews from employees all over the country on: relationship with their boss and co-workers; work environment; job resources; growth opportunities; compensation; company culture; company reputation; daily tasks; job control over work performed on a daily basis. *CareerBliss.com, "Happiest and Unhappiest Cities to Work in 2012"*
- The Boulder metro area appeared on the Milken Institute "2011 Best Performing Metros" list. Rank: #59 out of 200 large metro areas. Criteria: job growth; wage and salary growth; high-tech output growth. *Milken Institute, "2011 Best Performing Metros"*
- *Forbes* ranked the 200 most populous metro areas in the U.S. in terms of the "Best Places for Business and Careers." The Boulder metro area was ranked #44. Criteria: costs (business and living); job growth (past and projected); income growth; educational attainment; projected economic growth; crime; cultural and recreational opportunities; net migration patterns; number of highly ranked colleges. *Forbes, "Best Places for Business and Careers," June 2011*

Culture/Performing Arts Rankings

- Boulder was selected as one of "America's Top 25 Arts Destinations." The city ranked #9 in the small city (population under 100,000) category. Criteria: readers' top choices for arts travel destinations based on the richness and variety of visual arts sites, activities and events. *American Style, "America's Top 25 Arts Destinations," May 2010*

Dating/Romance Rankings

- Boulder was selected as one of the best cities to date a nerd by *Match.com.* The city ranked #7 out of 10. Criteria: top 10 cities with the highest educated *Match.com* members in either technical or educational occupations. *Match.com, "Top 10 Cities to Date a Nerd," March 16, 2011*

Education Rankings

- Boulder was identified as one of America's smartest cities by *The Business Journals On Numbers.* The city ranked #8 in the mid-sized city category (population 50,000 to 99,999). Each city's score was based on its percentage of adults (25 or older) at each of the following rungs: dropped out before high school graduation; stopped at high school diploma; stopped at associate degree or attended college but stopped without any degree; stopped at bachelor's degree; earned graduate degree and/or professional degree. The point value of a specific rung was determined by the relative earning power of people at that level. *The Business Journals On Numbers, "Brainpower Ratings," November 17, 2011*
- Boulder was selected as one of the most well-read cities in America by *Amazon.com.* The city ranked #5 of 20. Cities with populations greater than 100,000 were evaluated based on per capita sales of books, magazines and newspapers. *Amazon.com, "Top 20 Most Well-Read Cities in America," June 4, 2011*
- Boulder was selected as one of "America's Geekiest Cities" by *Forbes.com.* The city ranked #2 of 20. Criteria: percentage of workers with jobs in science, technology, engineering and mathematics. *Forbes.com, "America's Geekiest Cities," August 5, 2011*
- Boulder was identified as one of "America's Brainiest Bastions" by *Portfolio.com.* The metro area ranked #1 out of 200. *Portfolio.com* analyzed levels of educational attainment in the nation's 200 largest metropolitan areas. The editors established scores for five levels of educational attainment, based on relative earning power of adult workers age 25 or older. Scores were determined by comparing the median income for all workers with the median income for those workers at a specified educational level. *Portfolio.com, "America's Brainiest Bastions," December 1, 2010*
- Boulder was identified as one of America's smartest cities" by *Forbes.* The area ranked #1 out of 25. Criteria: percentage of the population age 25 and over with at least a bachelor's degree. *Forbes.com, "The Smartest Cities in America," February 8, 2008*

Environmental Rankings

- Boulder was selected as one of 22 "Smarter Cities" for energy by the Natural Resources Defense Council. Criteria: investment in green power; energy efficiency measures; conservation. *Natural Resources Defense Council, "2010 Smarter Cities," July 19, 2010*
- The Boulder metro area appeared in *Country Home's* "Best Green Places" report. The area ranked #5 out of 379. Criteria: official energy policies; green power; green buildings; availability of fresh, locally grown food. *Country Home, "Best Green Places," 2008*

Health/Fitness Rankings

- The Boulder metro area was identified as one of America's "Healthiest Hometowns" by AARP. The metro area ranked #6 out of 10. More than 20 measures of vitality were analyzed including air and water quality and the health and habits of the populace. *AARP, "Healthiest Hometowns," September/October 2008*
- The Boulder metro area appeared in the 2011 Gallup-Healthways Well-Being Index. The index, based on interviews with more than 350,000 Americans, measured jobs, finances, physical health, emotional state of mind and communities. The metro area ranked #5 out of 190. Criteria: life evaluation; emotional health; work environment; physical health; healthy behaviors; basic access (basic needs optimal for a healthy life, such as access to food and medicine, having health insurance and feeling safe while walking at night). *Gallup-Healthways, "State of Well-Being 2011"*

Pet Rankings

- Boulder was selected as one of the best places to live with pets by *Livability.com.* The city was ranked #4. Criteria: pet-friendly parks and trails; quality veterinary care; active animal welfare groups; abundance of pet boutiques and retail shops; excellent quality of life for pet owners. *Livability.com, "Top 10 Pet Friendly Cities," October 20, 2010*

Real Estate Rankings

- The Boulder metro area was identified as one of the 20 least affordable housing markets in the U.S. in 2011. The area ranked #8 out of 152 markets with an affordability index of 74.4%. The index measures whether or not a typical family could qualify for a mortgage loan on a typical home. The calculation used assumes a down payment of 20 percent of the home price and a qualifying ratio of 25 percent, meaning that the monthly P&I payment cannot exceed 25 percent of a the median family monthly income. *National Association of Realtors®, Affordability Index of Existing Single-Family Homes for Metropolitan Areas, 2011*
- Boulder appeared on *ApartmentRatings.com* "Top College Towns & Cities" for renters list in 2011." The area ranked #13 out of 87. Overall satisfaction ratings were ranked using thousands of user submitted scores for hundreds of apartment complexes located in cities and towns that are home to the 100 largest four-year institutions in the U.S. *ApartmentRatings.com, "2011 College Town Renter Satisfaction Rankings"*
- The Center for Housing Policy ranked 210 U.S. metropolitan areas by the fair market rent for a two-bedroom unit. The Boulder metro area was ranked #46. (#1 = most expensive) with a rent of $1,059. Criteria: Fair Market Rent (FMR) in effect during the fourth quarter of 2009 based on HUD's fiscal year 2010 FMRs. *The Center for Housing Policy, "Paycheck to Paycheck: Most to Least Expensive Rental Markets in 2009"*

Safety Rankings

- Farmers Insurance Group of Companies, in partnership with Sperling's BestPlaces, ranked 379 metro areas and identified the "Most Secure U.S. Places to Live." The Boulder metro area ranked #2 out of the top 20 in the mid-size city category (150,000 to 500,000 residents). Criteria: crime statistics; extreme weather; risk of natural disasters; housing depreciation; foreclosures; environmental hazards; terrorist threats; air quality; life expectancy; mortality rates from cancer and motor vehicle accidents; job loss numbers. *Farmers Insurance Group, "Most Secure U.S. Places to Live 2011," December 15, 2011*
- The National Insurance Crime Bureau ranked 366 metro areas in the U.S. in terms of per capita rates of vehicle theft. The Boulder metro area ranked #286 (#1 = highest rate). Criteria: number of vehicle theft offenses per 100,000 inhabitants in 2010. *National Insurance Crime Bureau, "Hot Spots," June 21, 2011*

Seniors/Retirement Rankings

- Boulder was identified as one of the "100 Most Popular Retirement Towns" by *Topretirements.com* The list reflects the 100 cities (out of 815+ total cities reviewed) that visitors to the website are most interested in for retirement. *Topretirements.com, "100 Most Popular Retirement Towns," February 21, 2012*
- Boulder was selected as one of America's "10 Brainiest Places to Retire" by *U.S. News & World Report.* Criteria: 10 retirement destinations were selected that attract highly educated folks. *U.S. News & World Report, "10 Brainiest Places to Retire," August 8, 2008*
- Boulder was selected as one of "America's Best Healthy Places to Retire" by *U.S. News & World Report.* Criteria: editors traveled the country and selected 10 cities that provide numerous places to exercise, promote strong social support, and encourage healthful lifestyle habits. *U.S. News & World Report, "America's Best Healthy Places to Retire," September 29/October 6, 2008*

Sports/Recreation Rankings

- Boulder appeared on the *Sporting News* list of the "Best Sports Cities" for 2011. The area ranked #20 out of 271 cities in the U.S. *Sporting News* takes a 12-month snapshot of each city's sports, putting a heavy premium on regular-season won-lost records (from the most recently completed season). Other criteria include: playoff berths, bowl appearances and tournament bids; championships; applicable power ratings; quality of competition; overall fan fervor (measured in part by attendance); abundance of teams (rewarding quality over quantity); stadium and arena quality; ticket availability and prices; franchise ownership; and marquee appeal of athletes. *Sporting News, "Best Sports Cities 2011," October 4, 2011*
- Boulder was chosen as a bicycle friendly community by the League of American Bicyclists. A Bicycle Friendly Community welcomes cyclists by providing safe accommodation for cycling and encouraging people to bike for transportation and recreation. There are four award levels: Platinum; Gold; Silver; and Bronze. The community achieved an award level of Platinum. *League of American Bicyclists, "Bicycle Friendly Community Master List 2011"*
- Boulder was chosen as one of America's best cities for bicycling. The city ranked #3 out of 50. Criteria: number of segregated bike lanes, municipal bike racks, and bike boulevards; vibrant and diverse bike culture; smart, savvy bike shops; interviews with national and local advocates, bike shops and other experts. The editors only considered cities with populations of 100,000 or more. *Bicycling, "America's Best Bike Cities," April 2010*

Transportation Rankings

- The Boulder metro area was selected as one of 15 "Smarter Cities" for transportation by the Natural Resources Defense Council. The area appeared in the mid-sized metro area (population 250,000 to one million) category. Criteria: public transit availability and use; household automobile ownership and use; innovative, sustainable and affordable transportation programs. *Natural Resources Defense Council, "2011 Smarter Cities," February 23, 2011*

Business Environment

CITY FINANCES

City Government Finances

Component	2009 ($000)	2009 ($ per capita)
Total Revenues	216,428	2,313
Total Expenditures	221,700	2,370
Debt Outstanding	182,492	1,951
Cash and Securities[1]	175,875	1,880

Note: (1) Cash and security holdings of a government at the close of its fiscal year, including those of its dependent agencies, utilities, and liquor stores.
Source: U.S Census Bureau, State & Local Government Finances 2009

City Government Revenue by Source

Source	2009 ($000)	2009 ($ per capita)
General Revenue		
From Federal Government	2,809	30
From State Government	11,610	124
From Local Governments	939	10
Taxes		
Property	31,066	332
Sales and Gross Receipts	96,574	1,032
Personal Income	0	0
Corporate Income	0	0
Motor Vehicle License	0	0
Other Taxes	9,912	106
Current Charges	37,676	403
Liquor Store	0	0
Utility	21,093	225
Employee Retirement	-8,594	-92

Source: U.S Census Bureau, State & Local Government Finances 2009

City Government Expenditures by Function

Function	2009 ($000)	2009 ($ per capita)	2009 (%)
General Direct Expenditures			
Air Transportation	1,425	15	0.6
Corrections	0	0	0.0
Education	0	0	0.0
Employment Security Administration	0	0	0.0
Financial Administration	5,889	63	2.7
Fire Protection	21,721	232	9.8
General Public Buildings	8,376	90	3.8
Governmental Administration, Other	8,414	90	3.8
Health	0	0	0.0
Highways	32,504	347	14.7
Hospitals	0	0	0.0
Housing and Community Development	11,437	122	5.2
Interest on General Debt	5,934	63	2.7
Judicial and Legal	6,731	72	3.0
Libraries	6,916	74	3.1
Parking	4,104	44	1.9
Parks and Recreation	37,832	404	17.1
Police Protection	21,301	228	9.6
Public Welfare	0	0	0.0
Sewerage	26,631	285	12.0
Solid Waste Management	0	0	0.0
Veterans' Services	0	0	0.0
Liquor Store	0	0	0.0
Utility	19,996	214	9.0
Employee Retirement	2,413	26	1.1

Source: U.S Census Bureau, State & Local Government Finances 2009

Municipal Bond Ratings

Area	Moody's	S&P	Fitch
City	Aa1	AAA	n/a

Rating Systems (shown in declining order of credit quality): Moody's– Aaa, Aa, A, Baa, Ba, B, Caa, Ca, C (numerical modifiers 1, 2, and 3 are added to letter-rating); S&P– AAA, AA, A, BBB, BB, B, CCC, CC, C; Fitch– AAA, AA, A, BBB, BB, B, CCC, CC, C. Ratings may be modified by the addition of a plus or minus sign to show relative standing within the major rating categories.
Notes: n/a Not Available; w/d Withdrawn (1) Not Reviewed; (2) Issuer Rating/No General Obligation; (3) Standard and Poor's Issue Credit Rating (ICR) is a current opinion of an obliger with respect to a specific financial obligation, a specific class of financial obligations, or a specific financial program.
Source: City of Boulder, Colorado, Comprehensive Annual Financial Report, Fiscal Year Ended December 31, 2009

DEMOGRAPHICS

Population Growth

Area	1990 Census	2000 Census	2010 Census	Population Growth (%) 1990-2000	Population Growth (%) 2000-2010
City	87,737	94,673	97,385	7.9	2.9
MSA[1]	208,898	269,758	294,567	29.1	9.2
U.S.	248,709,873	281,421,906	308,745,538	13.2	9.7

Note: (1) Figures cover the Boulder, CO Metropolitan Statistical Area—see Appendix B for areas included
Source: U.S. Census Bureau, 2010 Census

Household Size

Area	Persons in Household (%) One	Two	Three	Four	Five	Six	Seven or More	Average Household Size
City	35.8	34.7	14.3	10.7	3.2	0.9	0.4	2.16
MSA[1]	29.0	34.8	15.7	13.2	4.8	1.6	0.9	2.39
U.S.	26.7	32.8	16.1	13.4	6.5	2.6	1.9	2.58

Note: (1) Figures cover the Boulder, CO Metropolitan Statistical Area—see Appendix B for areas included
Source: U.S. Census Bureau, 2010 Census

Race

Area	White Alone[2] (%)	Black Alone[2] (%)	Asian Alone[2] (%)	AIAN[3] Alone[2] (%)	NHOPI[4] Alone[2] (%)	Other Race Alone[2] (%)	Two or More Races (%)
City	88.0	0.9	4.7	0.4	0.1	3.2	2.6
MSA[1]	87.2	0.9	4.1	0.6	0.1	4.5	2.7
U.S.	72.4	12.6	4.8	0.9	0.2	6.2	2.9

Note: (1) Figures cover the Boulder, CO Metropolitan Statistical Area—see Appendix B for areas included; (2) Alone is defined as not being in combination with one or more other races; (3) American Indian and Alaska Native; (4) Native Hawaiian and Other Pacific Islander
Source: U.S. Census Bureau, 2010 Census

Hispanic or Latino Origin

Area	Hispanic or Latino (%)	Mexican (%)	Puerto Rican (%)	Cuban (%)	Other Hispanic or Latino (%)
City	8.7	6.1	0.3	0.2	2.2
MSA[1]	13.3	10.3	0.3	0.1	2.6
U.S.	16.3	10.3	1.5	0.6	4.0

Note: Persons of Hispanic or Latino origin can be of any race; (1) Figures cover the Boulder, CO Metropolitan Statistical Area—see Appendix B for areas included
Source: U.S. Census Bureau, 2010 Census

Segregation

Type	Segregation Indices[1]				Percent Change		
	1990	2000	2010	2010 Rank[2]	1990-2000	1990-2010	2000-2010
Black/White	n/a	n/a	n/a	n/a	n/a	n/a	n/a
Asian/White	n/a	n/a	n/a	n/a	n/a	n/a	n/a
Hispanic/White	n/a	n/a	n/a	n/a	n/a	n/a	n/a

Note: Figures are based on an analysis of 1990, 2000, and 2010 Census Decennial Census tract data by William H. Frey, Brookings Institution and the University of Michigan Social Science Data Analysis Network. In this analysis all racial groups (whites, blacks, and asians) are non-Hispanic members of those races. Hispanics are shown as a separate category; All figures cover the Metropolitan Statistical Area (see Appendix B for areas included); (1) Segregation Indices are Dissimilarity Indices that measure the degree to which the minority group is distributed differently than whites across census tracts. They range from 0 (complete integration) to 100 (complete segregation) where the value indicates the percentage of the minority group that needs to move to be distributed exactly like whites; (2) Ranges from 1 (most segregated) to 102 (least segregated); n/a not available.
Source: www.CensusScope.org

Ancestry

Area	German	Irish	English	American	Italian	Polish	French[2]	Scottish	Dutch
City	23.4	13.9	16.2	2.0	7.1	4.4	4.1	4.7	2.6
MSA[1]	23.7	14.3	14.4	3.0	6.2	3.9	4.0	4.3	2.4
U.S.	16.1	11.6	8.8	6.1	5.7	3.2	3.0	1.9	1.6

Note: Figures are the percentage of the total population reporting a particular ancestry. The nine most commonly reported ancestries in the U.S. are shown. Figures include multiple ancestries (e.g. if a person reported being Irish and Italian, they were included in both columns); (1) Figures cover the Boulder, CO Metropolitan Statistical Area—see Appendix B for areas included; (2) Excludes Basque
Source: U.S. Census Bureau, 2008-2010 American Community Survey 3-Year Estimates

Foreign-Born Population

Area	Percent of Population Born in								
	Any Foreign Country	Mexico	Asia	Europe	Carribean	South America	Central America[2]	Africa	Canada
City	11.3	2.8	3.5	3.3	0.2	0.5	0.2	0.2	0.5
MSA[1]	11.0	3.8	3.1	2.3	0.1	0.4	0.6	0.1	0.5
U.S.	12.8	3.8	3.6	1.6	1.2	0.9	1.0	0.5	0.3

Note: (1) Figures cover the Boulder, CO Metropolitan Statistical Area—see Appendix B for areas included; (2) Excludes Mexico.
Source: U.S. Census Bureau, 2008-2010 American Community Survey 3-Year Estimates

Marital Status

Area	Never Married	Now Married[2]	Separated	Widowed	Divorced
City	53.5	34.2	0.6	3.0	8.8
MSA[1]	35.9	49.2	1.1	3.5	10.4
U.S.	31.6	49.6	2.2	6.1	10.7

Note: Figures are percentages and cover the population 15 years of age and older; (1) Figures cover the Boulder, CO Metropolitan Statistical Area—see Appendix B for areas included; (2) Excludes separated
Source: U.S. Census Bureau, 2008-2010 American Community Survey 3-Year Estimates

Age

Area	Percent of Population							Median Age
	Under Age 5	Age 5 to 17	Age 18 to 34	Age 35 to 49	Age 50 to 64	Age 65 to 79	80 Years and Over	
City	4.1	9.8	45.1	17.1	15.0	6.0	2.9	28.7
MSA[1]	5.6	15.7	27.6	21.4	19.7	7.4	2.7	35.8
U.S.	6.5	17.5	23.2	20.7	19.0	9.4	3.6	37.2

Note: (1) Figures cover the Boulder, CO Metropolitan Statistical Area—see Appendix B for areas included
Source: U.S. Census Bureau, 2010 Census

Male/Female Ratio

Area	Males	Females	Males per 100 Females
City	50,004	47,381	105.5
MSA[1]	147,916	146,651	100.9
U.S.	151,781,326	156,964,212	96.7

Note: (1) Figures cover the Boulder, CO Metropolitan Statistical Area—see Appendix B for areas included
Source: U.S. Census Bureau, 2010 Census

Religious Groups

Area	Catholic	Baptist	Non-Den.	Methodist[2]	Lutheran	LDS[3]	Pente-costal	Presby-terian[4]	Muslim[5]	Judaism
MSA[1]	20.1	2.3	4.8	1.8	3.1	3.0	0.5	2.0	0.8	0.1
U.S.	19.1	9.3	4.0	4.0	2.3	2.0	1.9	1.6	0.8	0.7

Note: Figures are the number of adherents as a percentage of the total population; (1) Figures cover the Boulder, CO Metropolitan Statistical Area—see Appendix B for areas included; (2) Methodist/Pietist; (3) Latter Day Saints; (4) Reformed; (5) Figures are estimates
Source: Association of Statisticians of American Religious Bodies, 2010 U.S. Religion Census: Religious Congregations & Membership Study

ECONOMY

Gross Metropolitan Product

Area	2007	2008	2009	2010	2010 Rank[2]
MSA[1]	17.6	18.0	17.6	18.1	113

Note: Figures are in billions of dollars; (1) Figures cover the Boulder, CO Metropolitan Statistical Area—see Appendix B for areas included; (2) Rank ranges from 1 to 363
Source: The United States Conference of Mayors, "U.S. Metro Economies: GMP and Employment Forecasts," June 2011

Economic Growth

Area	2007-2009 (%)	2010 (%)	2011 (%)	Rank[2]
MSA[1]	-1.4	2.0	2.6	184
U.S.	-1.3	2.9	2.5	–

Note: Figures are real Gross Metropolitan Product growth rates and represent annual average percent change; (1) Figures cover the Boulder, CO Metropolitan Statistical Area—see Appendix B for areas included; (2) Rank ranges from 1 to 363
Source: The United States Conference of Mayors, "U.S. Metro Economies: GMP and Employment Forecasts," June 2011

Metropolitan Area Exports

Area	2005	2006	2007	2008	2009	2010	2010 Rank[2]
MSA[1]	702.6	937.4	898.9	891.7	727.2	1,058.7	127

Note: Figures are in millions of dollars; (1) Figures cover the Boulder, CO Metropolitan Statistical Area—see Appendix B for areas included; (2) Rank ranges from 1 to 369
Source: U.S. Department of Commerce, International Trade Administration, Office of Trade & Industry Information, Manufacturing & Services, data extracted April 2, 2012

INCOME

Income

Area	Per Capita ($)	Median Household ($)	Average Household ($)
City	36,036	52,276	84,329
MSA[1]	37,099	64,314	89,944
U.S.	26,942	51,222	70,116

Note: (1) Figures cover the Boulder, CO Metropolitan Statistical Area—see Appendix B for areas included
Source: U.S. Census Bureau, 2008-2010 American Community Survey 3-Year Estimates

Household Income Distribution

Area	Percent of Households Earning							
	Under $15,000	$15,000 -24,999	$25,000 -34,999	$35,000 -49,999	$50,000 -74,999	$75,000 -99,000	$100,000 -149,999	$150,000 and up
City	15.5	11.3	10.5	11.5	15.1	9.4	12.5	14.3
MSA[1]	10.0	8.7	9.2	12.3	16.5	12.1	15.9	15.2
U.S.	13.0	11.0	10.6	14.2	18.5	12.1	12.2	8.4

Note: (1) Figures cover the Boulder, CO Metropolitan Statistical Area—see Appendix B for areas included
Source: U.S. Census Bureau, 2008-2010 American Community Survey 3-Year Estimates

Poverty Rate

Area	All Ages	Under 18 Years Old	18 to 64 Years Old	65 Years and Over
City	20.1	12.5	23.4	6.3
MSA[1]	12.7	12.9	13.6	5.6
U.S.	14.4	20.1	13.1	9.4

Note: Figures are percentage of people whose income during the past 12 months was below the poverty level; (1) Figures cover the Boulder, CO Metropolitan Statistical Area—see Appendix B for areas included
Source: U.S. Census Bureau, 2008-2010 American Community Survey 3-Year Estimates

Personal Bankruptcy Filing Rate

Area	2006	2007	2008	2009	2010	2011
Boulder County	1.37	2.19	2.90	3.82	4.22	3.86
U.S.	2.00	2.73	3.53	4.61	4.97	4.37

Note: Numbers are per 1,000 population and include Chapter 7 and Chapter 13 filings
Source: Federal Deposit Insurance Corporation, Regional Economic Conditions, March 9, 2012

EMPLOYMENT

Labor Force and Employment

Area	Civilian Labor Force			Workers Employed		
	Dec. 2010	Dec. 2011	% Chg.	Dec. 2010	Dec. 2011	% Chg.
City	61,762	63,548	2.9	56,942	59,248	4.0
MSA[1]	171,897	177,145	3.1	160,365	166,859	4.0
U.S.	153,156,000	153,373,000	0.1	139,159,000	140,681,000	1.1

Note: Data is not seasonally adjusted and covers workers 16 years of age and older; (1) Metropolitan Statistical Area—see Appendix B for areas included
Source: Bureau of Labor Statistics, http://stats.bls.gov

Unemployment Rate

Area	2011											
	Jan.	Feb.	Mar.	Apr.	May	Jun.	Jul.	Aug.	Sep.	Oct.	Nov.	Dec.
City	9.0	8.7	8.0	7.2	7.3	8.1	8.0	7.6	6.9	6.9	6.9	6.8
MSA[1]	7.7	7.5	6.9	6.2	6.3	7.0	6.9	6.6	5.9	5.9	5.9	5.8
U.S.	9.8	9.5	9.2	8.7	8.7	9.3	9.3	9.1	8.8	8.5	8.2	8.3

Note: Data is not seasonally adjusted and covers workers 16 years of age and older; All figures are percentages; (1) Metropolitan Statistical Area—see Appendix B for areas included
Source: Bureau of Labor Statistics, http://stats.bls.gov

Projected Unemployment Rate

Area	2010 (%)	2011 (%)	2012 (%)	2013 (%)
MSA[1]	7.4	6.4	5.9	5.4

Note: (1) Metropolitan Statistical Area—see Appendix B for areas included
Source: The United States Conference of Mayors, "U.S. Metro Economies: GMP and Employment Forecasts," June 2011

Employment by Occupation

Occupation Classification	City (%)	MSA[1] (%)	U.S. (%)
Management, Business, Science, and Arts	56.6	52.5	35.6
Natural Resources, Construction, and Maintenance	3.3	5.5	9.5
Production, Transportation, and Material Moving	3.9	6.5	12.1
Sales and Office	20.0	20.6	25.2
Service	16.2	14.8	17.6

Note: Figures cover employed civilians 16 years of age and older; (1) Figures cover the Boulder, CO Metropolitan Statistical Area—see Appendix B for areas included
Source: U.S. Census Bureau, 2008-2010 American Community Survey 3-Year Estimates

Employment by Industry

Sector	MSA[1] Number of Employees	MSA[1] Percent of Total	U.S. Percent of Total
Construction	n/a	n/a	4.1
Education and Health Services	20,600	12.4	15.2
Financial Activities	7,300	4.4	5.8
Government	33,400	20.1	16.8
Information	8,900	5.4	2.0
Leisure and Hospitality	18,200	11.0	9.9
Manufacturing	15,900	9.6	8.9
Mining and Logging	n/a	n/a	0.6
Other Services	5,300	3.2	4.0
Professional and Business Services	30,500	18.4	13.3
Retail Trade	15,200	9.2	11.5
Transportation and Utilities	1,500	0.9	3.8
Wholesale Trade	5,100	3.1	4.2

Note: Figures cover non-farm employment as of December 2011 and are not seasonally adjusted; (1) Metropolitan Statistical Area—see Appendix B for areas included; n/a not available
Source: Bureau of Labor Statistics, http://stats.bls.gov

Occupations with Greatest Projected Employment Growth: 2008 – 2018

Occupation[1]	2008 Employment	2018 Projected Employment	Numeric Employment Change	Percent Employment Change
Registered Nurses	40,880	53,130	12,250	30.0
Combined Food Preparation and Serving Workers, Including Fast Food	51,320	62,180	10,860	21.2
Customer Service Representatives	38,300	44,710	6,410	16.7
Postsecondary Teachers	24,980	31,030	6,050	24.2
Waiters and Waitresses	45,430	50,990	5,560	12.2
Computer Software Engineers, Applications	16,410	21,540	5,130	31.3
Personal and Home Care Aides	11,520	16,460	4,940	42.9
Retail Salespersons	79,820	84,660	4,840	6.1
Janitors and Cleaners, Except Maids and Housekeeping Cleaners	36,660	41,040	4,380	11.9
Nursing Aides, Orderlies, and Attendants	18,580	22,160	3,580	19.3

Note: Projections cover Colorado; (1) Sorted by numeric employment change
Source: www.projectionscentral.com, State Occupational Projections, 2008–2018 Long-Term Projections

Fastest Growing Occupations: 2008 – 2018

Occupation[1]	2008 Employment	2018 Projected Employment	Numeric Employment Change	Percent Employment Change
Personal and Home Care Aides	11,520	16,460	4,940	42.9
Network Systems and Data Communications Analysts	6,070	8,650	2,580	42.5
Air Traffic Controllers	640	900	260	40.6
Forensic Science Technicians	310	430	120	38.7
Pharmacy Technicians	4,250	5,860	1,610	37.9
Cardiovascular Technologists and Technicians	650	870	220	33.8
Physical Therapist Assistants	700	930	230	32.9
Medical Assistants	7,080	9,400	2,320	32.8
Skin Care Specialists	1,130	1,500	370	32.7
Computer Software Engineers, Applications	16,410	21,540	5,130	31.3

Note: Projections cover Colorado; (1) Sorted by percent employment change and excludes occupations with numeric employment change less than 100
Source: www.projectionscentral.com, State Occupational Projections, 2008–2018 Long-Term Projections

Average Wages

Occupation	$/Hr.	Occupation	$/Hr.
Accountants and Auditors	35.82	Maids and Housekeeping Cleaners	10.53
Automotive Mechanics	17.99	Maintenance and Repair Workers	19.40
Bookkeepers	18.53	Marketing Managers	67.50
Carpenters	19.50	Nuclear Medicine Technologists	n/a
Cashiers	10.87	Nurses, Licensed Practical	22.00
Clerks, General Office	14.83	Nurses, Registered	32.84
Clerks, Receptionists/Information	13.63	Nursing Aides/Orderlies/Attendants	13.37
Clerks, Shipping/Receiving	15.53	Packers and Packagers, Hand	12.09
Computer Programmers	n/a	Physical Therapists	33.15
Computer Support Specialists	29.14	Postal Service Mail Carriers	25.22
Computer Systems Analysts	40.69	Real Estate Brokers	31.47
Cooks, Restaurant	11.39	Retail Salespersons	13.59
Dentists	n/a	Sales Reps., Exc. Tech./Scientific	36.76
Electrical Engineers	51.95	Sales Reps., Tech./Scientific	42.23
Electricians	21.27	Secretaries, Exc. Legal/Med./Exec.	17.08
Financial Managers	65.49	Security Guards	13.46
First-Line Supervisors/Managers, Sales	20.74	Surgeons	88.85
Food Preparation Workers	10.13	Teacher Assistants	13.60
General and Operations Managers	62.22	Teachers, Elementary School	25.30
Hairdressers/Cosmetologists	18.08	Teachers, Secondary School	n/a
Internists	n/a	Telemarketers	13.29
Janitors and Cleaners	13.28	Truck Drivers, Heavy/Tractor-Trailer	19.27
Landscaping/Groundskeeping Workers	13.25	Truck Drivers, Light/Delivery Svcs.	15.31
Lawyers	56.35	Waiters and Waitresses	11.72

Note: Wage data covers the Boulder, CO Metropolitan Statistical Area—see Appendix B for areas included. Hourly wages for elementary/secondary school teachers and teacher assistants were calculated by the editors from annual wage data assuming a 40 hour work week; n/a not available.
Source: Bureau of Labor Statistics, Metro Area Occupational Employment and Wage Estimates, May 2011

RESIDENTIAL REAL ESTATE

Building Permits

Area	Single-Family			Multi-Family			Total		
	2010	2011	Pct. Chg.	2010	2011	Pct. Chg.	2010	2011	Pct. Chg.
City	115	59	-48.7	338	56	-83.4	453	115	-74.6
MSA[1]	276	390	41.3	381	271	-28.9	657	661	0.6
U.S.	447,311	418,498	-6.4	157,299	205,563	30.7	604,610	624,061	3.2

Note: (1) Metropolitan Statistical Area—see Appendix B for areas included; figures represent new, privately-owned housing units authorized (unadjusted data); All permit data are based on estimates with imputation.
Source: U.S. Census Bureau, Manufacturing, Mining, and Construction Statistics, Building Permits, 2010, 2011

Homeownership Rate

Area	2005 (%)	2006 (%)	2007 (%)	2008 (%)	2009 (%)	2010 (%)	2011 (%)
MSA[1]	n/a	n/a	n/a	n/a	n/a	n/a	n/a
U.S.	68.9	68.8	68.1	67.8	67.4	66.9	66.1

Note: (1) Metropolitan Statistical Area—see Appendix B for areas included; n/a not available
Source: U.S. Census Bureau, Housing Vacancies and Homeownership Annual Statistics: 2011

Housing Vacancy Rates

Area	Gross Vacancy Rate[2] (%)			Year-Round Vacancy Rate[3] (%)			Rental Vacancy Rate[4] (%)			Homeowner Vacancy Rate[5] (%)		
	2009	2010	2011	2009	2010	2011	2009	2010	2011	2009	2010	2011
MSA[1]	n/a	n/a	n/a	n/a	n/a	n/a	n/a	n/a	n/a	n/a	n/a	n/a
U.S.	14.5	14.3	14.2	11.3	11.3	11.1	10.6	10.2	9.5	2.6	2.6	2.5

Note: (1) Metropolitan Statistical Area—see Appendix B for areas included; (2) The percentage of the total housing inventory that is vacant; (3) The percentage of the housing inventory (excluding seasonal units) that is year-round vacant; (4) The percentage of rental inventory that is vacant for rent; (5) The percentage of homeowner inventory that is vacant for sale; n/a not available
Source: U.S. Census Bureau, Housing Vacancies and Homeownership Annual Statistics: 2011

TAXES

State Corporate Income Tax Rates

State	Tax Rate (%)	Income Brackets ($)	Num. of Brackets	Financial Institution Tax Rate (%)[a]	Federal Income Tax Ded.
Colorado	4.63	Flat rate	1	4.63	No

Note: Tax rates as of January 1, 2012; (a) Rates listed are the corporate income tax rate applied to financial institutions or excise taxes based on income. Some states have other taxes based upon the value of deposits or shares.
Source: Federation of Tax Administrators, "State Corporate Income Tax Rates, 2012"

State Individual Income Tax Rates

State	Tax Rate (%)	Income Brackets ($)	Num. of Brackets	Personal Exempt. ($)[1]		Fed. Inc. Tax Ded.
				Single	Dependents	
Colorado	4.63	Flat rate	1	3,700 (d)	3,700 (d)	No

Note: Tax rates as of January 1, 2012; Local- and county-level taxes are not included; n/a not applicable; (1) Married joint filers generally receive double the single exemption; (d) These states use the personal exemption amounts provided in the federal Internal Revenue Code.
Source: Federation of Tax Administrators, "State Individual Income Tax Rates, 2012"

Various State and Local Tax Rates

State	State and Local Sales and Use (%)	State Sales and Use (%)	Gasoline[1] (¢/gal.)	Cigarette[2] ($/pack)	Spirits[3] ($/gal.)	Wine[4] ($/gal.)	Beer[5] ($/gal.)
Colorado	8.21	2.90	22.0	0.84	2.28	0.32	0.08

Note: All tax rates as of January 1, 2012 except beer, wine and spirits (September 1, 2011); (1) The American Petroleum Institute has developed a methodology for determining the average tax rate on a gallon of fuel. Rates may include any of the following: excise taxes, environmental fees, storage tank fees, other fees or taxes, general sales tax, and local taxes. In states where gasoline is subject to the general sales tax, or where the fuel tax is based on the average sale price, the average rate determined by API is sensitive to changes in the price of gasoline. States that fully or partially apply general sales taxes to gasoline: CA, CO, GA, IL, IN, MI, NY; (2) The federal excise tax of $1.0066 per pack and local taxes are not included; (3) Rates are those applicable to off-premise sales of 40% alcohol by volume (a.b.v.) distilled spirits in 750ml containers. Local excise taxes are excluded; (4) Rates are those applicable to off-premise sales of 11% a.b.v. non-carbonated wine in 750ml containers; (5) Rates are those applicable to off-premise sales of 4.7% a.b.v. beer in 12 ounce containers.
Source: Tax Foundation, 2012 Facts & Figures: How Does Your State Compare?

State-Local Tax Burdens

Area	Rate (%)	Rank[1]	Per Capita Taxes Paid to Home State ($)	Total State and Local Per Capita Taxes Paid ($)	Per Capita Income ($)
Colorado	8.6	39	2,776	4,011	46,716
U.S. Average	9.8		3,057	4,160	42,539

Note: Figures cover 2009; (1) Rank ranges from 1 to 50 where 1 is highest tax burden
Source: Tax Foundation, State-Local Tax Burdens, All States, 2009

State Business Tax Climate Index Rankings

State	Overall Rank	Corporate Tax Index Rank	Individual Income Tax Index Rank	Sales Tax Index Rank	Unemployment Insurance Tax Index Rank	Property Tax Index Rank
Colorado	16	20	16	44	23	9

Note: The index is a measure of how each state's tax laws affect economic performance. The lower the rank, the more favorable a state's tax system is for business. States without a given tax are given a ranking of 1.
Source: Tax Foundation, Major Components of the State Business Tax Climate Index, FY 2012

COMMERCIAL UTILITIES

Typical Monthly Electric Bills

Area	Commercial Service ($/month)		Industrial Service ($/month)	
	1,500 kWh	40 kW demand 14,000 kWh	1,000 kW demand 200,000 kWh	50,000 kW demand 15,000,000 kWh
City	185	1,446	27,105	1,542,956
Average[1]	189	1,616	25,197	1,470,813

Note: Based on total rates in effect July 1, 2011; (1) average based on 184 utilities surveyed
Source: Edison Electric Institute, Typical Bills and Average Rates Report, Summer 2011

TRANSPORTATION

Means of Transportation to Work

Area	Car/Truck/Van		Public Transportation			Bicycle	Walked	Other Means	Worked at Home
	Drove Alone	Car-pooled	Bus	Subway	Railroad				
City	52.0	6.4	9.4	0.0	0.0	10.5	9.1	1.5	11.2
MSA[1]	65.9	8.1	5.1	0.0	0.0	4.2	4.3	1.2	11.1
U.S.	76.0	10.2	2.7	1.7	0.5	0.5	2.8	1.3	4.2

Note: Figures are percentages and cover workers 16 years of age and older; (1) Figures cover the Boulder, CO Metropolitan Statistical Area—see Appendix B for areas included
Source: U.S. Census Bureau, 2008-2010 American Community Survey 3-Year Estimates

Travel Time to Work

Area	Less Than 10 Minutes	10 to 19 Minutes	20 to 29 Minutes	30 to 44 Minutes	45 to 59 Minutes	60 to 89 Minutes	90 Minutes or More
City	19.5	44.9	17.3	9.6	4.9	2.7	1.1
MSA[1]	16.8	35.2	21.1	15.6	6.3	3.7	1.3
U.S.	13.9	30.1	20.8	19.8	7.5	5.5	2.5

Note: Figures are percentages and include workers 16 years old and over; (1) Figures cover the Boulder, CO Metropolitan Statistical Area—see Appendix B for areas included
Source: U.S. Census Bureau, 2008-2010 American Community Survey 3-Year Estimates

Travel Time Index

Area	1985	1990	1995	2000	2005	2010
Urban Area[1]	1.06	1.08	1.14	1.15	1.14	1.14
Average[2]	1.11	1.16	1.18	1.21	1.25	1.20

Note: Travel Time Index—the ratio of travel time in the peak period to the travel time at free-flow conditions. A value of 1.30 indicates a 20-minute free-flow trip takes 26 minutes in the peak. Free-flow speeds (60 mph on freeways and 35 mph on principal arterials) are used as the comparison threshold; (1) Covers the Boulder CO urban area; (2) average of 439 urban areas
Source: Texas Transportation Institute, Urban Mobility Report 2011, September 2011

Public Transportation

Agency Name / Mode of Transportation	Vehicles Operated in Maximum Service	Annual Unlinked Passenger Trips ('000)	Annual Passenger Miles ('000)
Community Transit Network			
Bus (directly operated)	458	49,898.0	258,792.8
Bus (purchased transportation)	358	26,270.1	126,617.3
Demand Response (directly operated)	8	64.2	668.4
Demand Response (purchased transportation)	351	1,108.2	9,926.3
Light Rail (directly operated)	104	20,087.7	139,416.7

Note: n/a not available
Source: City of Boulder, www.bouldercolorado.gov

Air Transportation

Airport Name and Code / Type of Service	Passenger Airlines[1]	Passenger Enplanements	Freight Carriers[2]	Freight (lbs.)
Denver International (40 miles) (DEN)				
Domestic service (U.S. carriers - 2011)	39	24,658,918	22	222,944,070
International service (U.S. carriers - 2010)	10	681,601	5	2,937,908

Note: (1) Includes all U.S.-based major, minor and commuter airlines that carried at least one passenger during the year; (2) Includes all U.S.-based airlines and freight carriers that transported at least one pound of freight during the year
Source: Bureau of Transportation Statistics, The Intermodal Transportation Database, Air Carriers: T-100 Domestic Market (U.S. Carriers), 2011; Bureau of Transportation Statistics, The Intermodal Transportation Database, Air Carriers: T-100 International Market (U.S. Carriers), 2010

Other Transportation Statistics

Major Highways:	SR-36 connecting to I-25, I-70 and I-76
Amtrak Service:	No
Major Waterways/Ports:	None

Source: Amtrak.com; Google Maps

BUSINESSES

Major Business Headquarters

Company Name	Rankings	
	Fortune[1]	Forbes[2]
No companies listed	-	-

Note: (1) Fortune 500—companies that produce a 10-K are ranked 1 to 500 based on 2010 revenue; (2) all private companies with at least $2 billion in annual revenue are ranked 1 to 212; companies listed are headquartered in the city; dashes indicate no ranking
Source: Fortune, "Fortune 500," May 23, 2011; Forbes, "America's Largest Private Companies," November 16, 2011

Fast-Growing Businesses

According to *Inc.*, Boulder is home to two of America's 500 fastest-growing private companies: **SurveyGizmo** (#144); **Albeo Technologies** (#447). Criteria: must be an independent, privately-held, for-profit, U.S. corporation, proprietorship or partnership; revenues must be at least $80,000 in 2007 and $2 million in 2010; must have four-year operating/sales history. Holding companies, regulated banks, and utilities were excluded. *Inc., "America's 500 Fastest-Growing Private Companies," September 2011*

Minority- and Women-Owned Businesses

Group	All Firms		Firms with Paid Employees			
	Firms	Sales ($000)	Firms	Sales ($000)	Employees	Payroll ($000)
Asian	304	135,831	98	126,651	933	20,421
Black	86	21,745	16	18,546	285	6,350
Hispanic	324	64,376	92	59,990	544	14,621
Women	4,923	532,099	919	408,550	4,467	119,646
All Firms	16,762	16,610,865	4,853	16,023,312	71,677	3,680,870

Note: Figures cover firms located in the city; minority- and women-owned business are defined as firms in which the corresponding group own 51% or more of the stock or equity of the company
Source: U.S. Census Bureau, 2007 Economic Census, Survey of Business Owners

HOTELS

Hotels/Motels

Area	5 Star		4 Star		3 Star		2 Star		1 Star		Not Rated	
	Num.	Pct.[3]	Num.	Pct.[3]	Num.	Pct.[3]	Num.	Pct.[3]	Num.	Pct.[3]	Num.	Pct.[3]
City[1]	0	0.0	2	3.8	20	38.5	19	36.5	1	1.9	10	19.2
Total[2]	133	0.9	940	6.5	4,569	31.8	7,033	48.9	351	2.4	1,343	9.3

Note: (1) Figures cover Boulder and vicinity; (2) Figures cover all 100 cities in this book; (3) Percentage of hotels which have a given star rating; Star ratings are determined by expedia.com and offer an indication of the general quality of a particular hotel.
Source: expedia.com, April 25, 2012

EVENT SITES

Major Stadiums, Arenas, and Auditoriums

Name	Max. Capacity
Folsom Field	53,750

Source: Original research

Living Environment

COST OF LIVING

Cost of Living Index

Composite Index	Groceries	Housing	Utilities	Transportation	Health Care	Misc. Goods/ Services
n/a	n/a	n/a	n/a	n/a	n/a	n/a

Note: U.S. = 100; n/a not available
Source: The Council for Community and Economic Research, ACCRA Cost of Living Index, 2011

Grocery Prices

Area[1]	T-Bone Steak ($/pound)	Frying Chicken ($/pound)	Whole Milk ($/half gal.)	Eggs ($/dozen)	Orange Juice ($/64 oz.)	Coffee ($/11.5 oz.)
City[2]	n/a	n/a	n/a	n/a	n/a	n/a
Avg.	9.25	1.18	2.22	1.66	3.19	4.40
Min.	6.70	0.88	1.31	0.95	2.46	2.94
Max.	14.30	2.16	3.50	3.18	4.75	6.83

Note: (1) Values for the local area are compared with the average, minimum and maximum values for all 335 areas in the Cost of Living Index; (2) Figures cover the Boulder CO urban area; n/a not available; **T-Bone Steak** *(price per pound);* **Frying Chicken** *(price per pound, whole fryer);* **Whole Milk** *(half gallon carton);* **Eggs** *(price per dozen, Grade A, large);* **Orange Juice** *(64 oz. Tropicana or Florida Natural);* **Coffee** *(11.5 oz. can, vacuum-packed, Maxwell House, Hills Bros, or Folgers).*
Source: The Council for Community and Economic Research, ACCRA Cost of Living Index, 2011

Housing and Utility Costs

Area[1]	New Home Price ($)	Apartment Rent ($/month)	All Electric ($/month)	Part Electric ($/month)	Other Energy ($/month)	Telephone ($/month)
City[2]	n/a	n/a	n/a	n/a	n/a	n/a
Avg.	285,990	839	163.23	89.00	77.52	26.92
Min.	188,005	460	125.58	45.39	33.89	17.98
Max.	1,197,028	3,244	339.16	181.97	348.69	40.01

Note: (1) Values for the local area are compared with the average, minimum and maximum values for all 335 areas in the Cost of Living Index; (2) Figures cover the Boulder CO urban area; n/a not available; **New Home Price** *(2,400 sf living area, 8,000 sf lot, in urban area with full utilities);* **Apartment Rent** *(950 sf 2 bedroom/1.5 or 2 bath, unfurnished, excluding all utilities except water);* **All Electric** *(average monthly cost for an all-electric home);* **Part Electric** *(average monthly cost for a part-electric home);* **Other Energy** *(average monthly cost for natural gas, fuel oil, coal, wood, and any other forms of energy except electricity);* **Telephone** *(price includes basic monthly rate for a private residential line plus additional local usage charges incurred by a family of four).*
Source: The Council for Community and Economic Research, ACCRA Cost of Living Index, 2011

Health Care, Transportation, and Other Costs

Area[1]	Doctor ($/visit)	Dentist ($/visit)	Optometrist ($/visit)	Gasoline ($/gallon)	Beauty Salon ($/visit)	Men's Shirt ($)
City[2]	n/a	n/a	n/a	n/a	n/a	n/a
Avg.	93.88	81.72	90.54	3.48	32.65	25.06
Min.	60.00	55.33	53.66	3.18	19.78	13.44
Max.	154.98	145.97	183.72	4.31	63.21	46.00

Note: (1) Values for the local area are compared with the average, minimum and maximum values for all 335 areas in the Cost of Living Index; (2) Figures cover the Boulder CO urban area; n/a not available; **Doctor** *(general practitioners routine exam of an established patient);* **Dentist** *(adult teeth cleaning and periodic oral examination);* **Optometrist** *(full vision eye exam for established adult patient);* **Gasoline** *(one gallon regular unleaded, national brand, including all taxes, cash price at self-service pump if available);* **Beauty Salon** *(woman's shampoo, trim, and blow-dry);* **Men's Shirt** *(cotton/polyester dress shirt, pinpoint weave, long sleeves).*
Source: The Council for Community and Economic Research, ACCRA Cost of Living Index, 2011

HOUSING

House Price Index (HPI)

Area	National Ranking[2]	Quarterly Change (%)	One-Year Change (%)	Five-Year Change (%)
MSA[1]	57	0.63	-0.75	1.56
U.S.[3]	-	-0.10	-2.43	-19.16

Note: The HPI is a weighted repeat sales index. It measures average price changes in repeat sales or refinancings on the same properties. This information is obtained by reviewing repeat mortgage transactions on single-family properties whose mortgages have been purchased or securitized by Fannie Mae or Freddie Mac in January 1975; (1) Metropolitan/Micropolitan Statistical Area—see Appendix B for areas included; (2) Rankings are based on annual percentage change for all metro areas containing at least 15,000 transactions over the last 10 years and ranges from 1 to 306; (3) figures based on a weighted average of Census Division estimates using a purchase only index; all figures are for the period ending December 31, 2011
Source: Federal Housing Finance Agency, House Price Index, February 23, 2012

House Price Valuations

Area	Q4 2005		Q4 2006		Q4 2007		Q4 2008		Q4 2009	
	Price ($000)	Over-valuation	Price ($000)	Over-valuation	Price ($000)	Over-valuation	Price ($000)	Over-valuation	Price ($000)	Over-valuation
MSA[1]	297.7	8.8	303.5	4.6	304.5	-1.3	300.1	-2.2	311.0	3.3

Note: Figures show the percentage of over- or under-valuation of single family homes relative to statistically normal house values (e.g. a value of 23.6 indicates that house values are 23.6% overvalued). Statistically normal house values are based on house prices, interest rates, household incomes, population densities, and any historical premiums or discounts metropolitan areas have exhibited over time; (1) Figures cover the Boulder, CO - see Appendix B for areas included
Source: Global Insight/PNC Financial Services Group, House Prices in America: 4th Quarter 2009 Update

Median Single-Family Home Prices

Area	2009	2010	2011p	Percent Change 2010 to 2011
MSA[1]	345.5	358.1	353.1	-1.4
U.S. Average	172.1	173.1	166.2	-4.0

Note: Figures are median sales prices of existing single-family homes in thousands of dollars; (p) preliminary; n/a not available; (1) Metropolitan Statistical Area—see Appendix B for areas included
Source: National Association of Realtors, Median Sales Price of Existing Single-Family Homes for Metropolitan Areas, 4th Quarter 2011

Affordability Index of Existing Single-Family Homes

Area	2009	2010	2011p	Percent Change 2010 to 2011
MSA[1]	68.8	70.5	74.4	5.5

Note: The housing affordability index measures whether or not a typical family could qualify for a mortgage loan on a typical home. The higher the index, the greater the household purchasing power. An index of 100 is defined as the point where a median-income household has exactly enough income to qualify for the purchase of a median-priced existing single-family home, assuming a 20 percent downpayment and 25 percent of gross income devoted to mortgage principal and interest payments; (p) preliminary; n/a not available; (1) Metropolitan Statistical Area—see Appendix B for areas included
Source: National Association of Realtors, Affordability Index of Existing Single-Family Homes, 2011

Median Apartment Condo-Coop Home Prices

Area	2009	2010	2011p	Percent Change 2010 to 2011
MSA[1]	203.0	206.2	210.1	1.9
U.S. Average	175.6	171.7	165.1	-3.8

Note: Figures are median sales prices of existing apartment condo-coop homes in thousands of dollars; (p) preliminary; n/a not available; (1) Metropolitan Statistical Area—see Appendix B for areas included
Source: National Association of Realtors, Median Sales Price of Existing Apartment Condo-Coop Homes for Metropolitan Areas, 4th Quarter 2011

Year Housing Structure Built

Area	2005 or Later	2000 -2004	1990 -1999	1980 -1989	1970 -1979	1960 -1969	1950 -1959	Before 1950	Median Year
City	2.7	4.9	11.3	15.7	24.1	20.0	10.4	11.0	1974
MSA[1]	3.3	9.6	21.0	16.1	22.5	13.0	6.0	8.6	1980
U.S.	5.0	8.6	14.0	14.1	16.3	11.3	11.2	19.6	1975

Note: Figures are percentages except for Median Year; (1) Figures cover the Boulder, CO Metropolitan Statistical Area—see Appendix B for areas included
Source: U.S. Census Bureau, 2008-2010 American Community Survey 3-Year Estimates

HEALTH

Health Risk Data

Category	MSA[1] (%)	U.S. (%)
Adults who have been told they have high blood pressure[2]	n/a	28.7
Adults who have been told they have high blood cholesterol[2]	n/a	37.5
Adults who have been told they have diabetes[3]	n/a	8.7
Adults who have been told they have arthritis[2]	n/a	26.0
Adults who have been told they currently have asthma	n/a	9.1
Adults who are current smokers	n/a	17.3
Adults who are heavy drinkers[4]	n/a	5.0
Adults who are binge drinkers[5]	n/a	15.1
Adults who are overweight (BMI 25.0 - 29.9)	n/a	36.2
Adults who are obese (BMI 30.0 - 99.8)	n/a	27.5
Adults who participated in any physical activities in the past month	n/a	76.1
Adults 50+ who have ever had a sigmoidoscopy or colonoscopy	n/a	65.2
Women aged 40+ who have had a mammogram within the past two years	n/a	75.2
Men aged 40+ who have had a PSA test within the past two years	n/a	53.2
Adults aged 65+ who have had flu shot within the past year	n/a	67.5
Adults aged 18–64 who have any kind of health care coverage	n/a	82.2

Note: Data as of 2010 unless otherwise noted; n/a not available; (1) Figures cover the Boulder, CO—see Appendix B for areas included; (2) Data as of 2009; (3) Figures do not include pregnancy-related, borderline, or pre-diabetes; (4) Heavy drinkers are classified as males having more than two drinks per day or females having more than one drink per day; (5) Binge drinkers are classified as males having five or more drinks on one occasion or females having four or more drinks on one occasion
Source: Centers for Disease Control and Prevention, Behaviorial Risk Factor Surveillance System, SMART: Selected Metropolitan/Micropolitan Area Risk Trends, 2009, 2010

Mortality Rates for the Top 10 Causes of Death in the U.S.

ICD-10[a] Sub-Chapter	ICD-10[a] Code	Age-Adjusted Mortality Rate[1] per 100,000 population	
		County[2]	U.S.
Malignant neoplasms	C00-C97	143.8	175.6
Ischaemic heart diseases	I20-I25	84.7	121.6
Other forms of heart disease	I30-I51	46.6	48.6
Chronic lower respiratory diseases	J40-J47	44.2	42.3
Cerebrovascular diseases	I60-I69	39.9	40.6
Organic, including symptomatic, mental disorders	F01-F09	39.6	26.7
Other degenerative diseases of the nervous system	G30-G31	37.6	24.7
Other external causes of accidental injury	W00-X59	42.1	24.4
Diabetes mellitus	E10-E14	11.5	21.7
Hypertensive diseases	I10-I15	11.1	18.2

Note: (a) ICD-10 = International Classification of Diseases 10th Revision; (1) Mortality rates are a three year average covering 2007-2009; (2) Figures cover Boulder County
Source: Centers for Disease Control and Prevention, National Center for Health Statistics. Underlying Cause of Death 1999-2009 on CDC WONDER Online Database, released 2012. Data for year 2009 are compiled from the Multiple Cause of Death File 2009, Series 20 No. 2O, 2012, Data for year 2008 are compiled from the Multiple Cause of Death File 2008, Series 20 No. 2N, 2011, Data for year 2007 are compiled from Multiple Cause of Death File 2007, Series 20 No. 2M, 2010.

Mortality Rates for Selected Causes of Death

ICD-10[a] Sub-Chapter	ICD-10[a] Code	Age-Adjusted Mortality Rate[1] per 100,000 population: County[2]	Age-Adjusted Mortality Rate[1] per 100,000 population: U.S.
Assault	X85-Y09	*Unreliable	5.7
Human immunodeficiency virus (HIV) disease	B20-B24	*0.0	3.3
Influenza and pneumonia	J09-J18	17.0	16.4
Intentional self-harm	X60-X84	16.5	11.5
Malnutrition	E40-E46	*0.0	0.8
Obesity and other hyperalimentation	E65-E68	*0.0	1.6
Transport accidents	V01-V99	8.5	13.7
Viral hepatitis	B15-B19	*Unreliable	2.2

Note: (a) ICD-10 = International Classification of Diseases 10th Revision; (1) Mortality rates are a three year average covering 2007-2009; (2) Figures cover Boulder County; (*) Unreliable data as per CDC
Source: Centers for Disease Control and Prevention, National Center for Health Statistics. Underlying Cause of Death 1999-2009 on CDC WONDER Online Database, released 2012. Data for year 2009 are compiled from the Multiple Cause of Death File 2009, Series 20 No. 2O, 2012, Data for year 2008 are compiled from the Multiple Cause of Death File 2008, Series 20 No. 2N, 2011, Data for year 2007 are compiled from Multiple Cause of Death File 2007, Series 20 No. 2M, 2010.

Distribution of Physicians and Dentists

Area[1]	Dentists[2]	D.O.[3]	M.D.[4] Total	M.D.[4] Family/General Practice	M.D.[4] Pediatrics	M.D.[4] Medical Specialties	M.D.[4] Surgical Specialties
Local (number)	179	61	852	162	62	250	193
Local (rate[5])	6.1	2.0	28.4	5.4	2.1	8.3	6.4
U.S. (rate[5])	4.5	1.9	18.3	2.5	1.4	6.8	4.1

Note: Data as of 2008 unless noted; (1) Local data covers Boulder County; (2) Data as of 2007; (3) Doctor of Osteopathic Medicine; (4) Includes active, non-federal, patient-care, office-based Doctors of Medicine; (5) rate per 10,000 population
Source: Area Resource File (ARF). 2009-2010 Release. U.S. Department of Health and Human Services, Health Resources and Services Administration, Bureau of Health Professions, Rockville, MD, August 2010

EDUCATION

Public School District Statistics

District Name	Schls	Pupils	Pupil/Teacher Ratio	Minority Pupils[1] (%)	Free Lunch Eligible[2] (%)	IEP[3] (%)
Boulder Valley School District #RE2	54	29,011	16.9	24.9	13.8	n/a

Note: Table includes school districts with 2,000 or more students; (1) Percentage of students that are not non-Hispanic white; (2) Percentage of students that are eligible for the free lunch program; (3) Percentage of students that have an Individualized Education Program.
Source: U.S. Department of Education, National Center for Education Statistics, Common Core of Data, Local Education Agency (School District) Universe Survey: School Year 2009-2010; U.S. Department of Education, National Center for Education Statistics, Common Core of Data, Public Elementary/Secondary School Universe Survey: School Year 2009-2010

Top Public High Schools

High School Name	Rank[1]	Score[1]	Grad. Rate[2] (%)	College[3] (%)	AP/IB/AICE[4] (%)	SAT/ACT[5] (%)
Fairview	212	0.500	94	87	3.3	1817

Note: (1) Public schools are ranked from 1 to 500 based on the following self-reported statistics (with their corresponding weight in the final score). Schools that had fewer than 10 graduates, as well as those that were newly founded and did not have a graduating senior class in 2010 were excluded; (2) Four-year, on-time graduation rate (25%); (3) Percent of 2010 graduates who enrolled immediately in college (25%); (4) AP/IB/AICE tests per graduate (25%); (5) Average SAT and/or ACT score (10%); Average AP/IB/AICE exam score (10%); AP/IB/AICE courses offered per graduate (5%); (6) School is unranked, but has been identified by Newsweek as one of the nation's most elite public high schools.
Source: Newsweek Online, "Top High Schools 2011"

Highest Level of Education

Area	Less than H.S.	H.S. Diploma	Some College, No Deg.	Associate Degree	Bachelors Degree	Masters Degree	Profess. School Degree	Doctorate Degree
City	5.1	7.0	14.0	4.2	34.4	22.3	5.6	7.3
MSA[1]	6.3	12.2	17.8	5.8	32.8	17.1	3.6	4.4
U.S.	14.7	28.4	21.3	7.6	17.6	7.2	1.9	1.2

Note: Figures cover persons age 25 and over; (1) Figures cover the Boulder, CO Metropolitan Statistical Area—see Appendix B for areas included
Source: U.S. Census Bureau, 2008-2010 American Community Survey 3-Year Estimates

Educational Attainment by Race

Area	High School Graduate or Higher (%)					Bachelor's Degree or Higher (%)				
	Total	White	Black	Asian	Hisp.[2]	Total	White	Black	Asian	Hisp.[2]
City	94.9	96.7	n/a	93.9	55.7	69.7	71.3	n/a	79.4	25.5
MSA[1]	93.7	95.6	91.0	94.0	62.0	57.9	59.5	44.1	72.0	22.2
U.S.	85.3	87.5	81.4	85.5	61.6	28.0	29.3	17.8	50.2	13.0

Note: Figures shown cover persons 25 years old and over; (1) Figures cover the Boulder, CO Metropolitan Statistical Area—see Appendix B for areas included; (2) People of Hispanic origin can be of any race
Source: U.S. Census Bureau, 2008-2010 American Community Survey 3-Year Estimates

School Enrollment by Grade and Control

Area	Preschool (%)		Kindergarten (%)		Grades 1 - 4 (%)		Grades 5 - 8 (%)		Grades 9 - 12 (%)	
	Public	Private	Public	Private	Public	Private	Public	Private	Public	Private
City	43.8	56.2	82.9	17.1	93.5	6.5	90.0	10.0	91.9	8.1
MSA[1]	42.6	57.4	87.3	12.7	91.0	9.0	88.9	11.1	92.5	7.5
U.S.	55.4	44.6	87.1	12.9	89.4	10.6	89.5	10.5	90.4	9.6

Note: Figures shown cover persons 3 years old and over; (1) Figures cover the Boulder, CO Metropolitan Statistical Area—see Appendix B for areas included
Source: U.S. Census Bureau, 2008-2010 American Community Survey 3-Year Estimates

Average Salaries of Public School Classroom Teachers

Area	2010-11		2011-12		Percent Change 2010-11 to 2011-12	Percent Change 2001-02 to 2011-12
	Dollars	Rank[1]	Dollars	Rank[1]		
Colorado	49,228	27	50,407	27	2.39	24.00
U.S. Average	55,623	-	56,643	-	1.83	26.8

Note: (1) State rank ranges from 1 to 51 where 1 indicates highest salary.
Source: National Education Association, Rankings & Estimates: Rankings of the States 2011 and Estimates of School Statistics 2012, December 2011

Higher Education

Four-Year Colleges			Two-Year Colleges			Medical Schools[1]	Law Schools[2]	Voc/ Tech[3]
Public	Private Non-profit	Private For-profit	Public	Private Non-profit	Private For-profit			
1	2	1	0	1	0	0	1	2

Note: Figures cover institutions located within the city limits and include main campuses only; (1) includes schools accredited by the Liaison Committee on Medical Education and the American Osteopathic Association's Commission on Osteopathic College Accreditation; (2) includes American Bar Association-accredited law schools; (3) includes all schools with programs that are less than 2 years.
Source: National Center for Education Statistics, Integrated Postsecondary Education System (IPEDS) Peer Analysis System, 2011-12; Association of American Medical Colleges, Member List, April 23, 2012; American Osteopathic Association, Member List, April 23, 2012; Law School Admission Council, Official Guide to ABA-Approved Law Schools Online, April 23, 2012

According to *U.S. News & World Report,* the Boulder, CO is home to one of the best national universities in the U.S.: **University of Colorado–Boulder** (#94). The indicators used to capture academic quality fall into a number of categories: assessment by administrators at peer institutions; retention of students; faculty resources; student selectivity; financial resources; alumni giving; high school counselor ratings of colleges; and graduation rate. *U.S. News & World Report, "America's Best Colleges 2012"*

According to *U.S. News & World Report,* the Boulder, CO is home to one of the best law schools in the U.S.: **University of Colorado–Boulder** (#44). The rankings are based on a weighted average of 12 measures of quality: peer assessment score; assessment score by lawyers/judges; median LSAT scores; median undergrad GPA; acceptance rate; employment rates for graduates; placement success; bar passage rate; faculty resources; expenditures per student; student/faculty ratio; and library resources. *U.S. News & World Report, "America's Best Law Schools 2013"*

PRESIDENTIAL ELECTION

2008 Presidential Election Results

Area	Obama	McCain	Nader	Other
Boulder County	72.3	26.1	0.5	1.1
U.S.	52.9	45.6	0.6	0.9

Note: Results are percentages and may not add to 100% due to rounding
Source: Dave Leip's Atlas of U.S. Presidential Elections, www.uselectionatlas.org

EMPLOYERS

Major Employers

Company Name	Industry
Agilent Technologies	Instruments to measure electricity
America's Note Network	Mortgage bankers and loan correspondents
Ball Aerospace & Technologies Corp.	Search and navigation equipment
Ball Corporation	Space research and technology
Corden Pharma Colorado	Pharmaceutical preparations
County of Boulder	Sheriffs' office
Crispin Porter Bogusky	Business services at non-commercial site
Health Carechain	Medical field-related associations
IBM	Magnetic storage devices, computer
IBM	Computer related consulting services
Lockheed Martin Corporation	Search and navigation equipment
Micro Motion	Liquid meters
National Oceanic and Atmospheric Admin	Environmental protection agency, government
Natl Inst of Standards & Technology	Commercial physical research
Qualcomm Incorporated	Integrated circuits, semiconductor networks
Staffing Solutions Southwest	Temporary help service
The Regents of the University of Colorado	Colleges and universities
The Regents of the University of Colorado	Noncommercial research organizations
The Regents of the University of Colorado	Libraries
Tyco Healthcare Group, LP	Medical instruments & equipment, blood & bone work
University Corp for Atmospheric Research	Noncommercial research organizations
Wall Street On Demand	Financial services
Whole Foods Market	Grocery stores

Note: Companies shown are located within the Boulder, CO metropolitan area.
Source: Hoovers.com, data extracted April 25 2012

PUBLIC SAFETY

Crime Rate

Area	All Crimes	Violent Crimes				Property Crimes		
		Murder	Forcible Rape	Robbery	Aggrav. Assault	Burglary	Larceny -Theft	Motor Vehicle Theft
City	2,954.0	4.0	33.2	29.2	145.1	481.6	2,171.2	89.7
Suburbs[1]	2,249.5	1.5	11.8	20.7	157.1	341.7	1,621.3	95.5
Metro[2]	2,480.8	2.3	18.9	23.5	153.1	387.6	1,801.8	93.6
U.S.	3,345.5	4.8	27.5	119.1	252.3	699.6	2,003.5	238.8

Note: Figures are crimes per 100,000 population; (1) All areas within the metro area that are located outside the city limits; (2) Metropolitan Statistical Area—see Appendix B for areas included
Source: FBI Uniform Crime Reports, 2010

Hate Crimes

Area	Number of Quarters Reported	Bias Motivation				
		Race	Religion	Sexual Orientation	Ethnicity	Disability
City	4	2	0	0	0	1

Source: Federal Bureau of Investigation, Hate Crime Statistics 2010

Identity Theft Consumer Complaints

Area	Complaints	Complaints per 100,000 Population	Rank[2]
MSA[1]	293	100.9	91
U.S.	279,156	90.4	-

Note: (1) Metropolitan Statistical Area—see Appendix B for areas included; (2) Rank ranges from 1 to 384 where 1 indicates greatest number of identity theft complaints per 100,000 population
Source: Federal Trade Commission, Consumer Sentinel Network Data Book for January–December 2011

Fraud and Other Consumer Complaints

Area	Complaints	Complaints per 100,000 Population	Rank[2]
MSA[1]	2,566	884.0	5
U.S.	1,533,924	496.8	-

Note: (1) Metropolitan Statistical Area—see Appendix B for areas included; (2) Rank ranges from 1 to 384 where 1 indicates greatest number of fraud and other complaints per 100,000 population
Source: Federal Trade Commission, Consumer Sentinel Network Data Book for January–December 2011

RECREATION

Culture

Dance[1]	Theatre[1]	Instrumental Music[1]	Vocal Music[1]	Series/ Festivals	Museums	Zoos and Aquariums[2]
2	3	2	0	9	7	0

Note: (1) Number of professional perfoming groups; (2) AZA-accredited
Source: The Grey House Performing Arts Directory, 2011-2012; Official Museum Directory, 2011; American Association of Museums, AAM Member Museums, April 2012; Association of Zoos & Aquariums, AZA Member Zoos & Aquariums, April 2012

Professional Sports Teams

Team Name	League
No teams are located in the metro area	

Source: Original research

CLIMATE

Average and Extreme Temperatures

Temperature	Jan	Feb	Mar	Apr	May	Jun	Jul	Aug	Sep	Oct	Nov	Dec	Yr.
Extreme High (°F)	73	76	84	90	93	102	103	100	97	89	79	75	103
Average High (°F)	43	47	52	62	71	81	88	86	77	67	52	45	64
Average Temp. (°F)	30	34	39	48	58	67	73	72	63	52	39	32	51
Average Low (°F)	16	20	25	34	44	53	59	57	48	37	25	18	37
Extreme Low (°F)	-25	-25	-10	-2	22	30	43	41	17	3	-8	-25	-25

Note: Figures cover the years 1948-1992
Source: National Climatic Data Center, International Station Meteorological Climate Summary, 9/96

Average Precipitation/Snowfall/Humidity

Precip./Humidity	Jan	Feb	Mar	Apr	May	Jun	Jul	Aug	Sep	Oct	Nov	Dec	Yr.
Avg. Precip. (in.)	0.6	0.6	1.3	1.7	2.5	1.7	1.9	1.5	1.1	1.0	0.9	0.6	15.5
Avg. Snowfall (in.)	9	7	14	9	2	Tr	0	0	2	4	9	8	63
Avg. Rel. Hum. 5am (%)	62	65	67	66	70	68	67	68	66	63	66	63	66
Avg. Rel. Hum. 5pm (%)	49	44	40	35	38	34	34	34	32	34	47	50	39

Note: Figures cover the years 1948-1992; Tr = Trace amounts (<0.05 in. of rain; <0.5 in. of snow)
Source: National Climatic Data Center, International Station Meteorological Climate Summary, 9/96

Weather Conditions

Temperature			Daytime Sky			Precipitation		
10°F & below	32°F & below	90°F & above	Clear	Partly cloudy	Cloudy	0.01 inch or more precip.	0.1 inch or more snow/ice	Thunder-storms
24	155	33	99	177	89	90	38	39

Note: Figures are average number of days per year and cover the years 1948-1992
Source: National Climatic Data Center, International Station Meteorological Climate Summary, 9/96

HAZARDOUS WASTE

Superfund Sites

Boulder has one hazardous waste site on the EPA's Superfund Final National Priorities List: **Marshall Landfill (Boulder County).** *U.S. Environmental Protection Agency, Final National Priorities List, April 17, 2012*

AIR & WATER QUALITY

Air Quality Index

Area	Percent of Days when Air Quality was...[2]					AQI Statistics[2]	
	Good	Moderate	Unhealthy for Sensitive Groups	Unhealthy	Very Unhealthy	Maximum	Median
Area[1]	80.0	18.9	1.1	0.0	0.0	116	42

Note: Air Quality Index (AQI) is an index for reporting daily air quality. EPA calculates the AQI for five major air pollutants regulated by the Clean Air Act: ground-level ozone, particle pollution (aka particulate matter), carbon monoxide, sulfur dioxide, and nitrogen dioxide. The AQI runs from 0 to 500. The higher the AQI value, the greater the level of air pollution and the greater the health concern. There are six AQI categories: "Good" AQI is between 0 and 50. Air quality is considered satisfactory; "Moderate" AQI is between 51 and 100. Air quality is acceptable; "Unhealthy for Sensitive Groups" When AQI values are between 101 and 150, members of sensitive groups may experience health effects; "Unhealthy" When AQI values are between 151 and 200 everyone may begin to experience health effects; "Very Unhealthy" AQI values between 201 and 300 trigger a health alert; "Hazardous" AQI values over 300 trigger warnings of emergency conditions (not shown); (1) Data covers Boulder County; (2) Based on 365 days with AQI data in 2011.
Source: U.S. Environmental Protection Agency, AirData Report, 2011

Air Quality Index Pollutants

Area	Percent of Days when AQI Pollutant was...[2]					
	Carbon Monoxide	Nitrogen Dioxide	Ozone	Sulfur Dioxide	Particulate Matter 2.5	Particulate Matter 10
Area[1]	0.0	0.0	95.1	0.0	4.7	0.3

Note: The Air Quality Index (AQI) is an index for reporting daily air quality. EPA calculates the AQI for five major air pollutants regulated by the Clean Air Act: ground-level ozone, particle pollution (also known as particulate matter), carbon monoxide, sulfur dioxide, and nitrogen dioxide. The AQI runs from 0 to 500. The higher the AQI value, the greater the level of air pollution and the greater the health concern; (1) Data covers Boulder County; (2) Based on 365 days with AQI data in 2011.
Source: U.S. Environmental Protection Agency, AirData Report, 2011

Air Quality Index Trends

Area	Trend Sites (days)								All Sites (days)
	2003	2004	2005	2006	2007	2008	2009	2010	2010
MSA[1]	n/a	n/a	n/a	n/a	n/a	n/a	n/a	n/a	n/a

Note: Figures are the number of days the AQI value exceeded 100 in a given year. An AQI value greater than 100 indicates that air quality would have been in the unhealthful range on that day. Data from exceptional events are included. These counts are presented in two ways. First, the counts are based on sites having an adequate record of monitoring data during the trend period (trend sites). These counts represent the relative change in the number of days with AQI values greater than 100. In the last column, the counts are based on all sites with data in the most recent year (because it is possible for a site to have data in the most recent year but not enough data to be a trend site); (1) Data covers the Boulder, CO—see Appendix B for areas included; n/a not available.
Source: U.S. Environmental Protection Agency, Air Quality Index Information, "Number of Days with Air Quality Index Values Greater than 100 at Trend Sites, 2000-2010, and at All Sites in 2010"

Maximum Air Pollutant Concentrations: Particulate Matter, Ozone, CO and Lead

	Particulate Matter 10 (ug/m^3)	Particulate Matter 2.5 Wtd AM (ug/m^3)	Particulate Matter 2.5 24-Hr (ug/m^3)	Ozone (ppm)	Carbon Monoxide (ppm)	Lead (ug/m^3)
MSA[1] Level	36	7.1	23	0.072	2	n/a
NAAQS[2]	150	15	35	0.075	9	0.15
Met NAAQS[2]	Yes	Yes	Yes	Yes	Yes	n/a

Note: Data from exceptional events are not included; (1) Data covers the Boulder, CO—see Appendix B for areas included; (2) National Ambient Air Quality Standards; ppm = parts per million; ug/m^3 = micrograms per cubic meter; n/a not available

Concentrations: Particulate Matter 10 (coarse particulate)—highest second maximum 24-hour concentration; Particulate Matter 2.5 Wtd AM (fine particulate)—highest weighted annual mean concentration; Particulate Matter 2.5 24-Hour (fine particulate)—highest 98th percentile 24-hour concentration; Ozone—highest fourth daily maximum 8-hour concentration; Carbon Monoxide—highest second maximum non-overlapping 8-hour concentration; Lead—maximum running 3-month average

Source: U.S. Environmental Protection Agency, CBSA Factbook 2010, Air Quality Statistics by City, 2010

Maximum Air Pollutant Concentrations: Nitrogen Dioxide and Sulfur Dioxide

	Nitrogen Dioxide AM (ppb)	Nitrogen Dioxide 1-Hr (ppb)	Sulfur Dioxide AM (ppb)	Sulfur Dioxide 1-Hr (ppb)	Sulfur Dioxide 24-Hr (ppb)
MSA[1] Level	n/a	n/a	n/a	n/a	n/a
NAAQS[2]	53	100	30	75	140
Met NAAQS[2]	n/a	n/a	n/a	n/a	n/a

Note: Data from exceptional events are not included; (1) Data covers the Boulder, CO—see Appendix B for areas included; (2) National Ambient Air Quality Standards; ppb = parts per billion; n/a not available

Concentrations: Nitrogen Dioxide AM—highest arithmetic mean concentration; Nitrogen Dioxide 1-Hr—highest 98th percentile 1-hour daily maximum concentration; Sulfur Dioxide AM—highest annual mean concentration; Sulfur Dioxide 1-Hr—highest 99th percentile 1-hour daily maximum concentration; Sulfur Dioxide 24-Hr—highest second maximum 24-hour concentration

Source: U.S. Environmental Protection Agency, CBSA Factbook 2010, Air Quality Statistics by City, 2010

Drinking Water

Water System Name	Pop. Served	Primary Water Source Type	Violations[1]	
			Health Based	Monitoring/ Reporting
City of Boulder	166,080	Surface	0	0

Note: (1) Based on violation data from January 1, 2011 to December 31, 2011 (includes unresolved violations from earlier years)

Source: U.S. Environmental Protection Agency, Office of Ground Water and Drinking Water, Safe Drinking Water Information System (based on data extracted April 18, 2012)

Carlsbad, California

Background

Carlsbad, a coastal town in Northern San Diego County, began its life near what is now Agua Hedionda Lagoon, as the village of Palamai. In the 1880s, John Frazier dug a fresh-water well, and distributed it to the townsfolk, who quickly confirmed that this was no ordinary water. Tests showed that all fresh-water wells in the area produced water that was chemically similar to that from the most famous spas in the world. This discovery made Carlsbad an instant attraction. Gerhard Schutte, a German-born American, came from the Midwest to form the Carlsbad Land and Mineral Water Company, along with Samuel Church Smith, D.D. Wadsworth and Henry Nelson. The town was named for the Austro-Hungarian town of Karlsbad, which contains a popular spa.

The physical beauty of this beachside city added to its popularity, and it was a tourist town right from the get go. Homes and businesses began forming in the 1880s during a period of growth that coincided with a marketing campaign to attract visitors. Farming changed the landscape, and avocados, citrus fruits, and olives helped keep the community going through the late 1880s when land prices fell in San Diego County.

An affluent community with award winning school systems, Carlsbad is now a desirable place to live and work. The economy is diversified and Carlsbad is known for tourism, shopping, resort living and a successful high tech industry.

The Northwest part of town includes "The Barrio" as well as "Olde Carlsbad," the first area to be settled. It's heavily influenced by Latino culture, and includes a wide range of homes from humble cottages to ocean view mansions. Along the Pacific Ocean, Southwest Carlsbad is home to the famous—and very expensive—Aviara resort neighborhood.

Northeast Carlsbad is made up of mostly single family homes and contains the Palomar Airport, while the more heavily populated Southeast includes the luxurious La Costa Resort and spa.

The ocean is a large part of the Carlsbad identity. In addition to seven miles of beautiful beaches, Carlsbad is home to three lagoons, which cover more than 1,000 acres and provide nature preserves, hiking trails and spectacular views.

In 1976, the city became the first in the world to have an outdoor skateboard park—designed and built by local inventors Jack Graham and John O'Malley. Action sports such as skateboarding remain popular in the city.

Carlsbad boasts LegoLand California, the first Lego park outside of Europe. Since opening in 1999, the park has become one of Carlsbad's top employers, as well as a popular place for recreation and family fun. In celebration of the arts, Carlsbad welcomed the Museum of Making Music in 2000. The museum organizes performances and public events whose goals are to teach the public about making music.

Carlsbad has a sub-tropical Mediterranean climate—hot, dry summers and mild, wet winters, similar to many coastal towns in Southern California towns.

Rankings

General Rankings

- The San Diego metro area was identified as one of the 10 most popular big cities by Pew Research Center. The results are based on a telephone survey of 2,260 adults conducted during October 2008. The report explored a range of attitudes related to where Americans live, where they would like to live, and why. *Pew Research Center, "For Nearly Half of America, Grass is Greener Somewhere Else," January 29, 2009*

Business/Finance Rankings

- The San Diego metro area was identified as one of 10 places with the fastest-growing wages in America. The area ranked #10. Criteria: private-sector wage growth between the 4th quarter of 2010 and the 4th quarter of 2011. *PayScale, "The 10 Cities with the Fastest-Growing Wages in America," January 12, 2012*
- Carlsbad was selected as one of the "100 Best Places to Live and Launch" in the U.S. The city ranked #32. The editors at *Fortune Small Business* ranked 296 Census-designated metro areas by business friendliness (Launching Score, % New Businesses) and lifestyle offerings (Living Score). Then they picked the town within each of the top 100 metro areas that best blends business and pleasure. *Fortune Small Business, "100 Best Places to Live and Launch 2008," April 2008*
- The San Diego metro area appeared on the Milken Institute "2011 Best Performing Metros" list. Rank: #69 out of 200 large metro areas. Criteria: job growth; wage and salary growth; high-tech output growth. *Milken Institute, "2011 Best Performing Metros"*
- San Diego was ranked #10 out of 145 regions worldwide in terms of its "Knowledge Competitiveness Index." The index attempts to measure the knowledge-based development taking place throughout the world and is based on 19 measures of economic performance that indicate a region's ability to translate its knowledge capacity into economic value. *Centre for International Competitiveness, World Knowledge Competitiveness Index 2008*
- *Forbes* ranked the 200 most populous metro areas in the U.S. in terms of the "Best Places for Business and Careers." The San Diego metro area was ranked #64. Criteria: costs (business and living); job growth (past and projected); income growth; educational attainment; projected economic growth; crime; cultural and recreational opportunities; net migration patterns; number of highly ranked colleges. *Forbes, "Best Places for Business and Careers," June 2011*

Children/Family Rankings

- The San Diego metro area was selected as one of the "Best Cities for Relocating Families" by Worldwide ERC and Primacy Relocation. The 2008 study looked at nearly 50 factors important to relocating families including: recent job growth; nearby top-ranked colleges; in-state tuition for four-year public colleges; population growth since 2000; pediatricians per 100,000 population; and a Green Living index. *Worldwide ERC and Primacy Relocation, "2008 Best Cities for Relocating Families"*

Dating/Romance Rankings

- Eli Lily and Company, in partnership with Sperling's BestPlaces, ranked the nation's 50 largest metro areas in terms of the "Most Romantic Cities for Baby Boomers." The San Diego metro area ranked #45. Criteria: marriage and divorce rates among baby boomers age 45 to 60; great restaurants; dance studios; chocolate, jewelry and flower sales. *Eli Lily and Company, "Most Romantic Cities for Baby Boomers," April 20, 2007*
- The San Diego metro area was selected as one of the "Best Cities for Relocating Singles" by Worldwide ERC and Primacy Relocation. The area ranked #25 out of the 100 largest metro areas in the U.S. Criteria: recent job growth; recent singles population growth; overall population growth; affordable rental housing; cost-of-living index; expanded arts and recreation opportunities; ratio of single men and single women; affordability of quality higher education (including state residency requirements); diversity index; climate; population density. *Worldwide ERC and Primacy Relocation, "2008 Best Cities for Relocating Singles"*

- *Forbes* ranked the 40 most populous urbanized areas in the U.S. in terms of the "Best Cities for Singles." The San Diego metro area ranked #12. Criteria: number of singles; cost of living alone; nightlife; culture; job growth; coolness; and online dating participation. *Forbes.com, "Best Cities for Singles," July 27, 2009*

Education Rankings

- San Diego was identified as one of the 100 "smartest" metro areas in the U.S. The area ranked #24. Criteria: the editors rated the collective brainpower of the 100 largest metro areas in the U.S. based on their residents' educational attainment. *American City Business Journals, April 14, 2008*
- San Diego was identified as one of "America's Smartest Cities" by *The Daily Beast.* The metro area ranked #18 out of 55. The editors ranked metropolitan areas with one million or more residents on the following criteria: percentage of residents over age 25 with bachelor's or graduate degrees; non-fiction book sales; ratio of institutions of higher education; libraries per capita. *The Daily Beast, "America's Smartest Cities," October 24, 2010*
- San Diego was identified as one of "America's Brainiest Bastions" by *Portfolio.com.* The metro area ranked #33 out of 200. *Portfolio.com* analyzed levels of educational attainment in the nation's 200 largest metropolitan areas. The editors established scores for five levels of educational attainment, based on relative earning power of adult workers age 25 or older. Scores were determined by comparing the median income for all workers with the median income for those workers at a specified educational level. *Portfolio.com, "America's Brainiest Bastions," December 1, 2010*

Environmental Rankings

- The San Diego was identified as one of America's dirtiest metro areas by *Forbes.* The area ranked #9 out of 10. Criteria: year-round particulate pollution; short-term particulate pollution; ozone pollution. *Forbes, "Dirtiest Cities in America," November 4, 2011*
- The San Diego was identified as one of America's cities with the most ENERGY STAR certified buildings. The area ranked #20 out of 25. Criteria: number of ENERGY STAR labeled buildings in 2010. *U.S. Environmental Protection Agency, "Top Cities With the Most ENERGY STAR Certified Buildings," March 15, 2011*
- Carlsbad was selected as one of 22 "Smarter Cities" for energy by the Natural Resources Defense Council. Criteria: investment in green power; energy efficiency measures; conservation. *Natural Resources Defense Council, "2010 Smarter Cities," July 19, 2010*
- 100 of the largest metro areas in the U.S. were analyzed in terms of their current drought severity. The San Diego metro area ranked #2 (#1 = driest). The rankings were based on statistics such as long-term precipitation trends and patterns and the Palmer drought indices. *Sperling's BestPlaces, www.BestPlaces.net, "America's Drought-Riskiest Cities," November 2007*
- The San Diego metro area appeared in *Country Home's* "Best Green Places" report. The area ranked #32 out of 379. Criteria: official energy policies; green power; green buildings; availability of fresh, locally grown food. *Country Home, "Best Green Places," 2008*
- San Diego was highlighted as one of the 25 metro areas most polluted by short-term particle pollution (24-hour PM 2.5) in the U.S. The area ranked #15. *American Lung Association, State of the Air 2011*
- San Diego was highlighted as one of the 25 most ozone-polluted metro areas in the U.S. The area ranked #7. *American Lung Association, State of the Air 2011*

Health/Fitness Rankings

- The San Diego metro area was selected as one of the worst cities for bed bugs in America by Rollins corporation, the owner of seven pest control companies, including Orkin. The area ranked #26 based on the number of bed bug treatments from January to December 2011. *Rollins, "The Top 50 U.S. Cities for Bed Bugs," March 19, 2012*

- San Diego was identified as a "2011 Asthma Capital." The area ranked #82 out of the nation's 100 largest metropolitan areas. Twelve factors were used to identify the most challenging places to live for people with asthma: estimated prevalence; self-reported prevalence; crude death rate for asthma; annual pollen score; annual air quality; public smoking laws; number of board-certified asthma specialists; school inhaler access laws; rescue medication use; controller medication use; uninsured rate; poverty rate. *Asthma and Allergy Foundation of America, "2011 Asthma Capitals"*

- San Diego was identified as a "2011 Fall Allergy Capital." The area ranked #98 out of 100. Three groups of factors were used to identify the most severe cities for people with allergies during the fall season: annual pollen levels; medicine utilization; access to board-certified allergists. *Asthma and Allergy Foundation of America, "2011 Fall Allergy Capitals"*

- San Diego was identified as a "2012 Spring Allergy Capital." The area ranked #94 out of 100. Three groups of factors were used to identify the most severe cities for people with allergies during the spring season: annual pollen levels; medicine utilization; access to board-certified allergists. *Asthma and Allergy Foundation of America, "2012 Spring Allergy Capitals"*

- The San Diego metropolitan area was selected as one of the best metros for hospital care in America by *HealthGrades.com.* The rankings are based on a comprehensive study of patient death and complication rates in the nation's nearly 5,000 hospitals. Hospitals performing in the top 5% nationwide across 26 different medical procedures and diagnoses were identified. *HealthGrades.com* then ranked cities by the highest percentage of these Distinguished Hospitals for Clinical Excellence™. The San Diego metro area ranked #29. *HealthGrades.com, "America's Top 50 Cities for Hospital Care," January 21, 2012*

- The American Academy of Dermatology ranked 26 U.S. metropolitan regions in terms of their residents knowledge, attitude and behaviors towards tanning, sun protection and skin cancer detection. The San Diego metro area ranked #17. The results of the study are based on an online survey of over 7,000 adults nationwide. *American Academy of Dermatology, "Suntelligence: How Sun Smart is Your City," May 3, 2010*

- The San Diego metro area appeared in the 2011 Gallup-Healthways Well-Being Index. The index, based on interviews with more than 350,000 Americans, measured jobs, finances, physical health, emotional state of mind and communities. The metro area ranked #35 out of 190. Criteria: life evaluation; emotional health; work environment; physical health; healthy behaviors; basic access (basic needs optimal for a healthy life, such as access to food and medicine, having health insurance and feeling safe while walking at night). *Gallup-Healthways, "State of Well-Being 2011"*

- The San Diego metro area was identified as one of "America's Most Stressful Cities" by *Sperling's BestPlaces.* The metro area ranked #21 out of 50. Criteria: unemployment rate; suicide rate; commute time; mental health; poor rest; alcohol use; violent crime rate; property crime rate; cloudy days annually. *Sperling's BestPlaces, www.BestPlaces.net, "Stressful Cities 2012*

- The San Diego metro area was identified as one of "America's Most Stressful Cities" by *Forbes.* The metro area ranked #5 out of 40. Criteria: housing affordability; unemployment rate; cost of living; air quality; traffic congestion; sunny days; population density. *Forbes.com, "America's Most Stressful Cities," September 23, 2011*

- 50 of the largest metro areas in the U.S. were analyzed in terms of their health and fitness by the American College of Sports Medicine in their "American Fitness Index." The San Diego metro area ranked #13 (#1 = healthiest). Criteria: preventative health behaviors; levels of chronic disease; health care access; community resources and policies that support physical activity. *American College of Sports Medicine, "Health and Community Fitness Status of the 50 Largest Metropolitan Areas," August 1, 2011*

Pet Rankings

- San Diego was selected as one of the "Top 10 Cat-Friendly Cities" in the U.S. The area ranked #8. Criteria: cat ownership per capita; level of veterinary care; microchipping; cat-friendly local ordinances. *CATalyst Council, "Top 10 Cat-Friendly Cities," March 27, 2009*

Real Estate Rankings

- San Diego was identified as one of the priciest cities to rent in the U.S. The area ranked #7 out of 10. Criteria: rent-to-income ratio. *CNBC, "Priciest Cities to Rent," March 14, 2012*
- *Fortune* ranked the 100 largest metro areas in the U.S. in terms of projected median home price change in 2010. The San Diego metro area ranked #72. *Fortune, "The 2010 Housing Outlook," December 9, 2009*
- The San Diego metro area was identified as one of the 20 least affordable housing markets in the U.S. in 2011. The area ranked #5 out of 152 markets with an affordability index of 65.0%. The index measures whether or not a typical family could qualify for a mortgage loan on a typical home. The calculation used assumes a down payment of 20 percent of the home price and a qualifying ratio of 25 percent, meaning that the monthly P&I payment cannot exceed 25 percent of a the median family monthly income. *National Association of Realtors®, Affordability Index of Existing Single-Family Homes for Metropolitan Areas, 2011*
- The San Diego metro area appeared in a *Wall Street Journal* article ranking cities by "housing stress." The metro area was ranked #4 (#1 = most stress). Criteria: fraction of mortgage-holding homeowners with a monthly housing payment in excess of 30 percent of income; percentage of people without health insurance; unemployment rate. *The Wall Street Journal, "Which Cities Face Biggest Housing Risk," October 5, 2010*
- The Center for Housing Policy ranked 210 U.S. metropolitan areas by the fair market rent for a two-bedroom unit. The San Diego metro area was ranked #18. (#1 = most expensive) with a rent of $1,324. Criteria: Fair Market Rent (FMR) in effect during the fourth quarter of 2009 based on HUD's fiscal year 2010 FMRs. *The Center for Housing Policy, "Paycheck to Paycheck: Most to Least Expensive Rental Markets in 2009"*
- The San Diego metro area was identified as one of the best housing markets of the decade by *Forbes*. Criteria: increase in housing values per square foot since January 2000. *Forbes, "America's 5 Best (and Worst) Housing Markets of the Decade," December 7, 2010*
- The San Diego metro area was identified as one of the best U.S. markets to invest in rental property" by HomeVestors and Local Market Monitor. The area ranked #90 out of 100. Criteria: risk-return premium relative to national average. *HomeVestors and Local Market Monitor, "Best 100 U.S. Markets to Invest in Rental Property," March 9, 2012*

Safety Rankings

- The National Insurance Crime Bureau ranked 366 metro areas in the U.S. in terms of per capita rates of vehicle theft. The San Diego metro area ranked #15 (#1 = highest rate). Criteria: number of vehicle theft offenses per 100,000 inhabitants in 2010. *National Insurance Crime Bureau, "Hot Spots," June 21, 2011*
- The San Diego metro area was identified as one of the most dangerous metro areas for pedestrians by Transportation for America. The metro area ranked #28 out of 52 metro areas with over 1 million residents. Criteria: area's population divided by the number of pedestrian fatalities in that area. *Transportation for America, "Dangerous by Design 2011"*

Seniors/Retirement Rankings

- Bankers Life and Casualty Company, in partnership with Sperling's BestPlaces, ranked the nation's 50 largest metro areas in terms of the "Best U.S. Cities for Seniors." The San Diego metro area ranked #32. Criteria: healthcare; transportation; housing; environment; economy; health and longevity; social and spiritual life; crime. *Bankers Life and Casualty Company, Center for a Secure Retirement, "Best U.S. Cities for Seniors 2011," September 2011*
- Carlsbad was selected as one of America's "10 Best Outdoorsy Places to Retire" by *U.S. News & World Report. U.S. News & World Report, "10 Best Outdoorsy Places to Retire," August 8, 2008*

Sports/Recreation Rankings

- The San Diego was selected as one of the best metro areas for golf in America by *Golf Digest.* The San Diego area was ranked #17 out of 20. Criteria: climate; cost of public golf; quality of public golf; accessibility. *Golf Digest, "The Top 20 Cities for Golf," October 2011*

Technology Rankings

- The San Diego metro area was selected as one of "America's Most Wired Cities" by *Forbes*. The metro area was ranked #14 out of 20. Criteria: percentage of Internet users with high-speed access; number of companies providing high-speed Internet; number of public wireless hot spots. *Forbes, "America's Most Wired Cities," March 2, 2010*
- The San Diego metro area was selected as one of "America's Most Innovative Cities" by *Forbes*. The metro area was ranked #6 out of 20. Criteria: patents per capita; venture capital investment per capita; ratio of high-tech, science and "creative" jobs. *Forbes, "America's Most Innovative Cities," May 24, 2010*
- The San Diego metro area was identified as one of the "Top 14 Nano Metros" in the U.S. by the Project on Emerging Nanotechnologies. The metro area is home to 27 companies, universities, government laboratories and/or organizations working in nanotechnology. *Project on Emerging Nanotechnologies, "Nano Metros 2009"*

Transportation Rankings

- The San Diego metro area appeared on *Forbes* list of the best and worst cities for commuters. The metro area ranked #43 out of 60 (#1 is best). Criteria: travel time; road congestion; travel delays. *Forbes.com, "Best and Worst Cities for Commuters," February 16, 2010*

Women/Minorities Rankings

- San Diego was ranked #31 out of 100 metro areas in *SELF Magazine's* ranking of America's healthiest places for women." A panel of experts came up with more than 50 criteria including death and disease rates, environmental indicators, community resources, and lifestyle habits. *SELF Magazine, "Secrets of America's Healthiest Women," December 2008*
- The San Diego metro area appeared on *Forbes'* list of the "Best Cities for Minority Entrepreneurs." The area ranked #31 out of 10. Criteria: 52 metropolitan statistical areas were examined. For each ethnicity (African Americans, Asians and Hispanics), the editors measured housing affordability, population growth, income growth, and entrepreneurship (per capita self-employment). *Forbes, "Best Cities for Minority Entrepreneurs," March 23, 2011*

Miscellaneous Rankings

- Energizer Holdings, the makers of Edge® shave gel, in partnership with Sperling's BestPlaces, ranked 50 major metro areas in terms of everyday irritations. The San Diego metro area ranked #18. Criteria: humidity levels; weather conditions; incidence of traffic delays and congestion; average commute times; frequency of flight delays and cancellations; rates of sleeplessness; underemployment; pollens and allergens; pests; comedy clubs per capita. *Energizer Holdings, "Most Irritation Prone Cities," July 23, 2010*
- Mars Chocolate North America, the makers of COMBOS®, in partnership with Sperling's BestPlaces, ranked 50 major metro areas in terms of their "manliness." The San Diego metro area ranked #49. Criteria: number of professional sports teams; number of nearby NASCAR tracks and racing events; manly lifestyle; concentration of manly retail stores; manly occupations per capita; salty snack sales; "Board of Manliness" rankings. *Mars Chocolate North America, "America's Manliest Cities 2011," September 1, 2011*

Business Environment

CITY FINANCES

City Government Finances

Component	2009 ($000)	2009 ($ per capita)
Total Revenues	220,487	2,310
Total Expenditures	220,602	2,311
Debt Outstanding	71,226	746
Cash and Securities[1]	553,266	5,797

Note: (1) Cash and security holdings of a government at the close of its fiscal year, including those of its dependent agencies, utilities, and liquor stores.
Source: U.S Census Bureau, State & Local Government Finances 2009

City Government Revenue by Source

Source	2009 ($000)	2009 ($ per capita)
General Revenue		
From Federal Government	7,302	77
From State Government	4,470	47
From Local Governments	0	0
Taxes		
Property	60,979	639
Sales and Gross Receipts	36,016	377
Personal Income	0	0
Corporate Income	0	0
Motor Vehicle License	0	0
Other Taxes	8,813	92
Current Charges	30,806	323
Liquor Store	0	0
Utility	27,114	284
Employee Retirement	0	0

Source: U.S Census Bureau, State & Local Government Finances 2009

City Government Expenditures by Function

Function	2009 ($000)	2009 ($ per capita)	2009 (%)
General Direct Expenditures			
Air Transportation	0	0	0.0
Corrections	0	0	0.0
Education	0	0	0.0
Employment Security Administration	0	0	0.0
Financial Administration	0	0	0.0
Fire Protection	4,822	51	2.2
General Public Buildings	0	0	0.0
Governmental Administration, Other	21,758	228	9.9
Health	15,484	162	7.0
Highways	15,647	164	7.1
Hospitals	209	2	0.1
Housing and Community Development	7,503	79	3.4
Interest on General Debt	6,116	64	2.8
Judicial and Legal	0	0	0.0
Libraries	11,560	121	5.2
Parking	0	0	0.0
Parks and Recreation	26,695	280	12.1
Police Protection	28,126	295	12.7
Public Welfare	0	0	0.0
Sewerage	19,204	201	8.7
Solid Waste Management	2,580	27	1.2
Veterans' Services	0	0	0.0
Liquor Store	0	0	0.0
Utility	48,729	511	22.1
Employee Retirement	0	0	0.0

Source: U.S Census Bureau, State & Local Government Finances 2009

Municipal Bond Ratings

Area	Moody's	S&P	Fitch
City	n/a	n/a	n/a

Rating Systems (shown in declining order of credit quality): Moody's– Aaa, Aa, A, Baa, Ba, B, Caa, Ca, C (numerical modifiers 1, 2, and 3 are added to letter-rating); S&P– AAA, AA, A, BBB, BB, B, CCC, CC, C; Fitch– AAA, AA, A, BBB, BB, B, CCC, CC, C. Ratings may be modified by the addition of a plus or minus sign to show relative standing within the major rating categories.
Notes: n/a Not Available; w/d Withdrawn (1) Not Reviewed; (2) Issuer Rating/No General Obligation; (3) Standard and Poor's Issue Credit Rating (ICR) is a current opinion of an obliger with respect to a specific financial obligation, a specific class of financial obligations, or a specific financial program.
Source: U.S. Census Bureau, 2012 Statistical Abstract, Bond Ratings for City Governments by Largest Cities: 2010

DEMOGRAPHICS

Population Growth

Area	1990 Census	2000 Census	2010 Census	Population Growth (%) 1990-2000	Population Growth (%) 2000-2010
City	62,753	78,247	105,328	24.7	34.6
MSA[1]	2,498,016	2,813,833	3,095,313	12.6	10.0
U.S.	248,709,873	281,421,906	308,745,538	13.2	9.7

Note: (1) Figures cover the San Diego-Carlsbad-San Marcos, CA Metropolitan Statistical Area—see Appendix B for areas included
Source: U.S. Census Bureau, 2010 Census

Household Size

Area	Persons in Household (%)							Average Household Size
	One	Two	Three	Four	Five	Six	Seven or More	
City	23.9	35.6	16.7	15.6	5.6	1.8	0.8	2.53
MSA[1]	24.0	31.2	16.5	14.5	7.4	3.3	3.0	2.75
U.S.	26.7	32.8	16.1	13.4	6.5	2.6	1.9	2.58

Note: (1) Figures cover the San Diego-Carlsbad-San Marcos, CA Metropolitan Statistical Area—see Appendix B for areas included
Source: U.S. Census Bureau, 2010 Census

Race

Area	White Alone[2] (%)	Black Alone[2] (%)	Asian Alone[2] (%)	AIAN[3] Alone[2] (%)	NHOPI[4] Alone[2] (%)	Other Race Alone[2] (%)	Two or More Races (%)
City	82.8	1.3	7.1	0.5	0.2	4.0	4.2
MSA[1]	64.0	5.1	10.9	0.9	0.5	13.6	5.1
U.S.	72.4	12.6	4.8	0.9	0.2	6.2	2.9

Note: (1) Figures cover the San Diego-Carlsbad-San Marcos, CA Metropolitan Statistical Area—see Appendix B for areas included; (2) Alone is defined as not being in combination with one or more other races; (3) American Indian and Alaska Native; (4) Native Hawaiian and Other Pacific Islander
Source: U.S. Census Bureau, 2010 Census

Hispanic or Latino Origin

Area	Hispanic or Latino (%)	Mexican (%)	Puerto Rican (%)	Cuban (%)	Other Hispanic or Latino (%)
City	13.3	10.2	0.4	0.2	2.5
MSA[1]	32.0	28.1	0.7	0.2	3.1
U.S.	16.3	10.3	1.5	0.6	4.0

Note: Persons of Hispanic or Latino origin can be of any race; (1) Figures cover the San Diego-Carlsbad-San Marcos, CA Metropolitan Statistical Area—see Appendix B for areas included
Source: U.S. Census Bureau, 2010 Census

Segregation

Type	Segregation Indices[1]				Percent Change		
	1990	2000	2010	2010 Rank[2]	1990-2000	1990-2010	2000-2010
Black/White	58.1	55.5	51.2	68	-2.6	-6.9	-4.3
Asian/White	47.9	49.9	48.2	13	2.0	0.3	-1.7
Hispanic/White	45.2	50.6	49.6	25	5.4	4.4	-1.0

Note: Figures are based on an analysis of 1990, 2000, and 2010 Census Decennial Census tract data by William H. Frey, Brookings Institution and the University of Michigan Social Science Data Analysis Network. In this analysis all racial groups (whites, blacks, and asians) are non-Hispanic members of those races. Hispanics are shown as a separate category; All figures cover the Metropolitan Statistical Area (see Appendix B for areas included); (1) Segregation Indices are Dissimilarity Indices that measure the degree to which the minority group is distributed differently than whites across census tracts. They range from 0 (complete integration) to 100 (complete segregation) where the value indicates the percentage of the minority group that needs to move to be distributed exactly like whites; (2) Ranges from 1 (most segregated) to 102 (least segregated); n/a not available.
Source: www.CensusScope.org

Ancestry

Area	German	Irish	English	American	Italian	Polish	French[2]	Scottish	Dutch
City	16.8	11.4	17.5	3.1	7.2	3.9	3.6	2.4	1.9
MSA[1]	12.3	9.0	8.7	2.3	4.6	2.1	2.6	1.9	1.3
U.S.	16.1	11.6	8.8	6.1	5.7	3.2	3.0	1.9	1.6

Note: Figures are the percentage of the total population reporting a particular ancestry. The nine most commonly reported ancestries in the U.S. are shown. Figures include multiple ancestries (e.g. if a person reported being Irish and Italian, they were included in both columns); (1) Figures cover the San Diego-Carlsbad-San Marcos, CA Metropolitan Statistical Area—see Appendix B for areas included; (2) Excludes Basque
Source: U.S. Census Bureau, 2008-2010 American Community Survey 3-Year Estimates

Foreign-Born Population

Area	Percent of Population Born in								
	Any Foreign Country	Mexico	Asia	Europe	Carribean	South America	Central America[2]	Africa	Canada
City	14.8	3.5	5.4	3.6	0.2	0.8	0.1	0.4	0.8
MSA[1]	23.2	10.9	8.2	1.9	0.2	0.5	0.5	0.5	0.4
U.S.	12.8	3.8	3.6	1.6	1.2	0.9	1.0	0.5	0.3

Note: (1) Figures cover the San Diego-Carlsbad-San Marcos, CA Metropolitan Statistical Area—see Appendix B for areas included; (2) Excludes Mexico.
Source: U.S. Census Bureau, 2008-2010 American Community Survey 3-Year Estimates

Marital Status

Area	Never Married	Now Married[2]	Separated	Widowed	Divorced
City	26.3	55.3	1.3	5.1	12.0
MSA[1]	35.2	47.6	2.0	4.9	10.3
U.S.	31.6	49.6	2.2	6.1	10.7

Note: Figures are percentages and cover the population 15 years of age and older; (1) Figures cover the San Diego-Carlsbad-San Marcos, CA Metropolitan Statistical Area—see Appendix B for areas included; (2) Excludes separated
Source: U.S. Census Bureau, 2008-2010 American Community Survey 3-Year Estimates

Age

Area	Percent of Population							Median Age
	Under Age 5	Age 5 to 17	Age 18 to 34	Age 35 to 49	Age 50 to 64	Age 65 to 79	80 Years and Over	
City	6.0	18.1	18.0	23.5	20.4	9.2	4.8	40.4
MSA[1]	6.6	16.8	27.1	20.7	17.5	7.9	3.4	34.6
U.S.	6.5	17.5	23.2	20.7	19.0	9.4	3.6	37.2

Note: (1) Figures cover the San Diego-Carlsbad-San Marcos, CA Metropolitan Statistical Area—see Appendix B for areas included
Source: U.S. Census Bureau, 2010 Census

Male/Female Ratio

Area	Males	Females	Males per 100 Females
City	51,485	53,843	95.6
MSA[1]	1,553,679	1,541,634	100.8
U.S.	151,781,326	156,964,212	96.7

Note: (1) Figures cover the San Diego-Carlsbad-San Marcos, CA Metropolitan Statistical Area—see Appendix B for areas included
Source: U.S. Census Bureau, 2010 Census

Religious Groups

Area	Catholic	Baptist	Non-Den.	Methodist[2]	Lutheran	LDS[3]	Pente-costal	Presby-terian[4]	Muslim[5]	Judaism
MSA[1]	25.9	2.0	4.8	1.1	1.0	2.3	1.0	0.9	0.5	0.7
U.S.	19.1	9.3	4.0	4.0	2.3	2.0	1.9	1.6	0.8	0.7

Note: Figures are the number of adherents as a percentage of the total population; (1) Figures cover the San Diego-Carlsbad-San Marcos, CA Metropolitan Statistical Area—see Appendix B for areas included; (2) Methodist/Pietist; (3) Latter Day Saints; (4) Reformed; (5) Figures are estimates
Source: Association of Statisticians of American Religious Bodies, 2010 U.S. Religion Census: Religious Congregations & Membership Study

ECONOMY

Gross Metropolitan Product

Area	2007	2008	2009	2010	2010 Rank[2]
MSA[1]	166.4	171.2	168.1	172.7	16

Note: Figures are in billions of dollars; (1) Figures cover the San Diego-Carlsbad-San Marcos, CA Metropolitan Statistical Area—see Appendix B for areas included; (2) Rank ranges from 1 to 363
Source: The United States Conference of Mayors, "U.S. Metro Economies: GMP and Employment Forecasts," June 2011

Economic Growth

Area	2007-2009 (%)	2010 (%)	2011 (%)	Rank[2]
MSA[1]	-1.2	1.9	2.2	168
U.S.	-1.3	2.9	2.5	–

Note: Figures are real Gross Metropolitan Product growth rates and represent annual average percent change; (1) Figures cover the San Diego-Carlsbad-San Marcos, CA Metropolitan Statistical Area—see Appendix B for areas included; (2) Rank ranges from 1 to 363
Source: The United States Conference of Mayors, "U.S. Metro Economies: GMP and Employment Forecasts," June 2011

Metropolitan Area Exports

Area	2005	2006	2007	2008	2009	2010	2010 Rank[2]
MSA[1]	13,192.7	13,617.8	14,341.7	15,855.9	13,418.6	16,464.3	17

Note: Figures are in millions of dollars; (1) Figures cover the San Diego-Carlsbad-San Marcos, CA Metropolitan Statistical Area—see Appendix B for areas included; (2) Rank ranges from 1 to 369
Source: U.S. Department of Commerce, International Trade Administration, Office of Trade & Industry Information, Manufacturing & Services, data extracted April 2, 2012

INCOME

Income

Area	Per Capita ($)	Median Household ($)	Average Household ($)
City	42,012	83,238	105,409
MSA[1]	29,792	61,469	82,033
U.S.	26,942	51,222	70,116

Note: (1) Figures cover the San Diego-Carlsbad-San Marcos, CA Metropolitan Statistical Area—see Appendix B for areas included
Source: U.S. Census Bureau, 2008-2010 American Community Survey 3-Year Estimates

Household Income Distribution

Area	Percent of Households Earning							
	Under $15,000	$15,000 -24,999	$25,000 -34,999	$35,000 -49,999	$50,000 -74,999	$75,000 -99,000	$100,000 -149,999	$150,000 and up
City	6.8	6.2	6.5	11.7	15.3	11.5	20.5	21.4
MSA[1]	9.9	8.8	9.0	13.4	17.7	13.5	15.3	12.5
U.S.	13.0	11.0	10.6	14.2	18.5	12.1	12.2	8.4

Note: (1) Figures cover the San Diego-Carlsbad-San Marcos, CA Metropolitan Statistical Area—see Appendix B for areas included
Source: U.S. Census Bureau, 2008-2010 American Community Survey 3-Year Estimates

Poverty Rate

Area	All Ages	Under 18 Years Old	18 to 64 Years Old	65 Years and Over
City	8.0	10.3	8.1	3.3
MSA[1]	13.2	17.4	12.6	8.0
U.S.	14.4	20.1	13.1	9.4

Note: Figures are percentage of people whose income during the past 12 months was below the poverty level; (1) Figures cover the San Diego-Carlsbad-San Marcos, CA Metropolitan Statistical Area—see Appendix B for areas included
Source: U.S. Census Bureau, 2008-2010 American Community Survey 3-Year Estimates

Personal Bankruptcy Filing Rate

Area	2006	2007	2008	2009	2010	2011
San Diego County	1.40	2.55	4.46	6.50	7.23	6.48
U.S.	2.00	2.73	3.53	4.61	4.97	4.37

Note: Numbers are per 1,000 population and include Chapter 7 and Chapter 13 filings
Source: Federal Deposit Insurance Corporation, Regional Economic Conditions, March 9, 2012

EMPLOYMENT

Labor Force and Employment

Area	Civilian Labor Force			Workers Employed		
	Dec. 2010	Dec. 2011	% Chg.	Dec. 2010	Dec. 2011	% Chg.
City	47,115	48,251	2.4	43,939	45,410	3.3
MSA[1]	1,555,853	1,586,031	1.9	1,398,252	1,445,067	3.3
U.S.	153,156,000	153,373,000	0.1	139,159,000	140,681,000	1.1

Note: Data is not seasonally adjusted and covers workers 16 years of age and older; (1) Metropolitan Statistical Area—see Appendix B for areas included
Source: Bureau of Labor Statistics, http://stats.bls.gov

Unemployment Rate

Area	2011											
	Jan.	Feb.	Mar.	Apr.	May	Jun.	Jul.	Aug.	Sep.	Oct.	Nov.	Dec.
City	6.9	6.7	6.8	6.5	6.4	6.9	7.1	6.8	6.5	6.4	6.1	5.9
MSA[1]	10.4	10.1	10.2	9.8	9.6	10.4	10.6	10.2	9.8	9.7	9.2	8.9
U.S.	9.8	9.5	9.2	8.7	8.7	9.3	9.3	9.1	8.8	8.5	8.2	8.3

Note: Data is not seasonally adjusted and covers workers 16 years of age and older; All figures are percentages; (1) Metropolitan Statistical Area—see Appendix B for areas included
Source: Bureau of Labor Statistics, http://stats.bls.gov

Projected Unemployment Rate

Area	2010 (%)	2011 (%)	2012 (%)	2013 (%)
MSA[1]	10.7	9.7	9.2	8.4

Note: (1) Metropolitan Statistical Area—see Appendix B for areas included
Source: The United States Conference of Mayors, "U.S. Metro Economies: GMP and Employment Forecasts," June 2011

Employment by Occupation

Occupation Classification	City (%)	MSA[1] (%)	U.S. (%)
Management, Business, Science, and Arts	51.1	39.5	35.6
Natural Resources, Construction, and Maintenance	4.7	8.2	9.5
Production, Transportation, and Material Moving	4.9	8.1	12.1
Sales and Office	26.8	25.5	25.2
Service	12.4	18.7	17.6

Note: Figures cover employed civilians 16 years of age and older; (1) Figures cover the San Diego-Carlsbad-San Marcos, CA Metropolitan Statistical Area—see Appendix B for areas included
Source: U.S. Census Bureau, 2008-2010 American Community Survey 3-Year Estimates

Employment by Industry

Sector	MSA[1] Number of Employees	MSA[1] Percent of Total	U.S. Percent of Total
Construction	55,900	4.5	4.1
Education and Health Services	153,500	12.3	15.2
Financial Activities	66,500	5.3	5.8
Government	230,700	18.4	16.8
Information	24,000	1.9	2.0
Leisure and Hospitality	157,100	12.6	9.9
Manufacturing	92,100	7.4	8.9
Mining and Logging	400	<0.1	0.6
Other Services	46,900	3.7	4.0
Professional and Business Services	216,800	17.3	13.3
Retail Trade	139,700	11.2	11.5
Transportation and Utilities	26,800	2.1	3.8
Wholesale Trade	40,600	3.2	4.2

Note: Figures cover non-farm employment as of December 2011 and are not seasonally adjusted; (1) Metropolitan Statistical Area—see Appendix B for areas included
Source: Bureau of Labor Statistics, http://stats.bls.gov

Occupations with Greatest Projected Employment Growth: 2008 – 2018

Occupation[1]	2008 Employment	2018 Projected Employment	Numeric Employment Change	Percent Employment Change
Personal and Home Care Aides	346,500	504,700	158,200	45.7
Registered Nurses	236,400	297,200	60,800	25.7
Retail Salespersons	499,400	559,100	59,700	12.0
Combined Food Preparation and Serving Workers, Including Fast Food	260,600	308,800	48,200	18.5
Elementary School Teachers, Except Special Education	197,500	233,400	35,900	18.2
Office Clerks, General	372,500	407,400	34,900	9.4
Customer Service Representatives	202,200	236,600	34,400	17.0
Waiters and Waitresses	245,600	279,900	34,300	14.0
Stock Clerks and Order Fillers	207,700	237,100	29,400	14.2
Postsecondary Teachers	168,000	196,100	28,100	16.7

Note: Projections cover California; (1) Sorted by numeric employment change
Source: www.projectionscentral.com, State Occupational Projections, 2008–2018 Long-Term Projections

Fastest Growing Occupations: 2008 – 2018

Occupation[1]	2008 Employment	2018 Projected Employment	Numeric Employment Change	Percent Employment Change
Biomedical Engineers	3,100	5,600	2,500	80.6
Network Systems and Data Communications Analysts	35,000	52,600	17,600	50.3
Biochemists and Biophysicists	4,800	7,100	2,300	47.9
Medical Scientists, Except Epidemiologists	26,200	38,500	12,300	46.9
Personal and Home Care Aides	346,500	504,700	158,200	45.7
Home Health Aides	54,300	78,000	23,700	43.6
Physician Assistants	8,100	11,500	3,400	42.0
Separating, Filtering, Clarifying, Precipitating, and Still Machine Setters, Operators, and Te	7,300	10,200	2,900	39.7
Physical Therapist Aides	5,900	8,100	2,200	37.3
Electrical and Electronics Repairers, Powerhouse, Substation, and Relay	1,100	1,500	400	36.4

Note: Projections cover California; (1) Sorted by percent employment change and excludes occupations with numeric employment change less than 100
Source: www.projectionscentral.com, State Occupational Projections, 2008–2018 Long-Term Projections

Average Wages

Occupation	$/Hr.	Occupation	$/Hr.
Accountants and Auditors	35.75	Maids and Housekeeping Cleaners	10.12
Automotive Mechanics	20.90	Maintenance and Repair Workers	17.57
Bookkeepers	19.21	Marketing Managers	62.90
Carpenters	25.56	Nuclear Medicine Technologists	39.31
Cashiers	10.68	Nurses, Licensed Practical	23.19
Clerks, General Office	14.81	Nurses, Registered	40.82
Clerks, Receptionists/Information	13.88	Nursing Aides/Orderlies/Attendants	12.68
Clerks, Shipping/Receiving	14.82	Packers and Packagers, Hand	9.96
Computer Programmers	36.63	Physical Therapists	42.57
Computer Support Specialists	24.22	Postal Service Mail Carriers	25.79
Computer Systems Analysts	41.73	Real Estate Brokers	33.89
Cooks, Restaurant	12.22	Retail Salespersons	12.76
Dentists	77.88	Sales Reps., Exc. Tech./Scientific	29.99
Electrical Engineers	47.72	Sales Reps., Tech./Scientific	41.40
Electricians	26.26	Secretaries, Exc. Legal/Med./Exec.	18.21
Financial Managers	61.05	Security Guards	13.27
First-Line Supervisors/Managers, Sales	21.20	Surgeons	92.00
Food Preparation Workers	9.84	Teacher Assistants	13.70
General and Operations Managers	61.96	Teachers, Elementary School	31.10
Hairdressers/Cosmetologists	12.04	Teachers, Secondary School	32.30
Internists	90.55	Telemarketers	12.10
Janitors and Cleaners	12.83	Truck Drivers, Heavy/Tractor-Trailer	19.72
Landscaping/Groundskeeping Workers	12.71	Truck Drivers, Light/Delivery Svcs.	17.14
Lawyers	69.30	Waiters and Waitresses	9.43

Note: Wage data covers the San Diego-Carlsbad-San Marcos, CA Metropolitan Statistical Area—see Appendix B for areas included. Hourly wages for elementary/secondary school teachers and teacher assistants were calculated by the editors from annual wage data assuming a 40 hour work week; n/a not available.
Source: Bureau of Labor Statistics, Metro Area Occupational Employment and Wage Estimates, May 2011

RESIDENTIAL REAL ESTATE

Building Permits

Area	Single-Family 2010	Single-Family 2011	Single-Family Pct. Chg.	Multi-Family 2010	Multi-Family 2011	Multi-Family Pct. Chg.	Total 2010	Total 2011	Total Pct. Chg.
City	376	267	-29.0	2	50	2,400.0	378	317	-16.1
MSA[1]	2,270	2,245	-1.1	1,224	3,125	155.3	3,494	5,370	53.7
U.S.	447,311	418,498	-6.4	157,299	205,563	30.7	604,610	624,061	3.2

Note: (1) Metropolitan Statistical Area—see Appendix B for areas included; figures represent new, privately-owned housing units authorized (unadjusted data); All permit data are based on estimates with imputation.
Source: U.S. Census Bureau, Manufacturing, Mining, and Construction Statistics, Building Permits, 2010, 2011

Homeownership Rate

Area	2005 (%)	2006 (%)	2007 (%)	2008 (%)	2009 (%)	2010 (%)	2011 (%)
MSA[1]	60.5	61.2	59.6	57.1	56.4	54.4	55.2
U.S.	68.9	68.8	68.1	67.8	67.4	66.9	66.1

Note: (1) Metropolitan Statistical Area—see Appendix B for areas included
Source: U.S. Census Bureau, Housing Vacancies and Homeownership Annual Statistics: 2011

Housing Vacancy Rates

Area	Gross Vacancy Rate[2] (%)			Year-Round Vacancy Rate[3] (%)			Rental Vacancy Rate[4] (%)			Homeowner Vacancy Rate[5] (%)		
	2009	2010	2011	2009	2010	2011	2009	2010	2011	2009	2010	2011
MSA[1]	10.4	10.5	9.9	9.8	10.0	9.5	8.8	7.8	6.9	2.1	2.9	1.9
U.S.	14.5	14.3	14.2	11.3	11.3	11.1	10.6	10.2	9.5	2.6	2.6	2.5

Note: (1) Metropolitan Statistical Area—see Appendix B for areas included; (2) The percentage of the total housing inventory that is vacant; (3) The percentage of the housing inventory (excluding seasonal units) that is year-round vacant; (4) The percentage of rental inventory that is vacant for rent; (5) The percentage of homeowner inventory that is vacant for sale
Source: U.S. Census Bureau, Housing Vacancies and Homeownership Annual Statistics: 2011

TAXES

State Corporate Income Tax Rates

State	Tax Rate (%)	Income Brackets ($)	Num. of Brackets	Financial Institution Tax Rate (%)[a]	Federal Income Tax Ded.
California	8.84 (c)	Flat rate	1	10.84 (c)	No

Note: Tax rates as of January 1, 2012; (a) Rates listed are the corporate income tax rate applied to financial institutions or excise taxes based on income. Some states have other taxes based upon the value of deposits or shares; (c) The minimum corporation franchise tax in California is $800. The additional alternative minimum tax is levied at a 6.65% rate.
Source: Federation of Tax Administrators, "State Corporate Income Tax Rates, 2012"

State Individual Income Tax Rates

State	Tax Rate (%)	Income Brackets ($)	Num. of Brackets	Personal Exempt. ($)[1] Single	Personal Exempt. ($)[1] Dependents	Fed. Inc. Tax Ded.
California (a)	1.0 - 9.3 (f)	7,316 (b) - 48,029 (b)	6	102 (c)	315 (c)	No

Note: Tax rates as of January 1, 2012; Local- and county-level taxes are not included; n/a not applicable; (1) Married joint filers generally receive double the single exemption; (a) 17 states have statutory provision for automatically adjusting to the rate of inflation the dollar values of the income tax brackets, standard deductions, and/or personal exemptions. Massachusetts, Michigan, and Nebraska index the personal exemptiononly. Oregon does not index the income brackets for $125,000 and over. Because the inflation-adjustments for 2012 are not yet available in some cases, the table may report the 2011 amounts; (b) For joint returns, taxes are twice the tax on half the couple's income; (c) The personal exemption takes the form of a tax credit instead of a deduction; (f) California imposes an additional 1% tax on taxable income over $1 million, making the maximum rate 10.3% over $1 million.
Source: Federation of Tax Administrators, "State Individual Income Tax Rates, 2012"

Various State and Local Tax Rates

State	State and Local Sales and Use (%)	State Sales and Use (%)	Gasoline[1] (¢/gal.)	Cigarette[2] ($/pack)	Spirits[3] ($/gal.)	Wine[4] ($/gal.)	Beer[5] ($/gal.)
California	7.75	7.25 (b)	48.6	0.87	3.30	0.20	0.20

Note: All tax rates as of January 1, 2012 except beer, wine and spirits (September 1, 2011); (1) The American Petroleum Institute has developed a methodology for determining the average tax rate on a gallon of fuel. Rates may include any of the following: excise taxes, environmental fees, storage tank fees, other fees or taxes, general sales tax, and local taxes. In states where gasoline is subject to the general sales tax, or where the fuel tax is based on the average sale price, the average rate determined by API is sensitive to changes in the price of gasoline. States that fully or partially apply general sales taxes to gasoline: CA, CO, GA, IL, IN, MI, NY; (2) The federal excise tax of $1.0066 per pack and local taxes are not included; (3) Rates are those applicable to off-premise sales of 40% alcohol by volume (a.b.v.) distilled spirits in 750ml containers. Local excise taxes are excluded; (4) Rates are those applicable to off-premise sales of 11% a.b.v. non-carbonated wine in 750ml containers; (5) Rates are those applicable to off-premise sales of 4.7% a.b.v. beer in 12 ounce containers; (b) Three states collect a separate, uniform "local" add-on sales tax: California (1%), Utah (1.25%), Virginia (1%). These amounts are included in the state sales tax column.
Source: Tax Foundation, 2012 Facts & Figures: How Does Your State Compare?

State-Local Tax Burdens

Area	Rate (%)	Rank[1]	Per Capita Taxes Paid to Home State ($)	Total State and Local Per Capita Taxes Paid ($)	Per Capita Income ($)
California	10.6	6	3,874	4,910	46,366
U.S. Average	9.8	-	3,057	4,160	42,539

Note: Figures cover 2009; (1) Rank ranges from 1 to 50 where 1 is highest tax burden
Source: Tax Foundation, State-Local Tax Burdens, All States, 2009

State Business Tax Climate Index Rankings

State	Overall Rank	Corporate Tax Index Rank	Individual Income Tax Index Rank	Sales Tax Index Rank	Unemployment Insurance Tax Index Rank	Property Tax Index Rank
California	48	43	50	40	13	17

Note: The index is a measure of how each state's tax laws affect economic performance. The lower the rank, the more favorable a state's tax system is for business. States without a given tax are given a ranking of 1.
Source: Tax Foundation, Major Components of the State Business Tax Climate Index, FY 2012

COMMERCIAL REAL ESTATE

Office Market

Market Area	Inventory (sq. ft.)	Vacant (sq. ft.)	Vac. Rate (%)	Under Constr. (sq. ft.)	Asking Rent ($/sf/yr)	
					Class A	Class B
San Diego	69,062,692	12,327,059	17.8	123,429	26.16	23.40

Source: Grubb & Ellis, Office Markets Trends, 4th Quarter 2011

Industrial Market

Market Area	Inventory (sq. ft.)	Vacant (sq. ft.)	Vac. Rate (%)	Under Constr. (sq. ft.)	Asking Rent ($/sf/yr)	
					WH/Dist	R&D/Flex
San Diego	176,583,584	18,601,673	10.5	31,246	7.56	12.96

Source: Grubb & Ellis, Industrial Markets Trends, 4th Quarter 2011

COMMERCIAL UTILITIES

Typical Monthly Electric Bills

Area	Commercial Service ($/month)		Industrial Service ($/month)	
	1,500 kWh	40 kW demand 14,000 kWh	1,000 kW demand 200,000 kWh	50,000 kW demand 15,000,000 kWh
City	299	2,280	43,146	1,739,327
Average[1]	189	1,616	25,197	1,470,813

Note: Based on total rates in effect July 1, 2011; (1) average based on 184 utilities surveyed
Source: Edison Electric Institute, Typical Bills and Average Rates Report, Summer 2011

TRANSPORTATION

Means of Transportation to Work

Area	Car/Truck/Van Drove Alone	Car/Truck/Van Car-pooled	Public Transportation Bus	Public Transportation Subway	Public Transportation Railroad	Bicycle	Walked	Other Means	Worked at Home
City	77.7	6.6	0.6	0.1	1.2	0.8	1.4	1.5	10.1
MSA[1]	75.4	10.4	2.7	0.0	0.3	0.7	3.0	1.4	6.1
U.S.	76.0	10.2	2.7	1.7	0.5	0.5	2.8	1.3	4.2

Note: Figures are percentages and cover workers 16 years of age and older; (1) Figures cover the San Diego-Carlsbad-San Marcos, CA Metropolitan Statistical Area—see Appendix B for areas included
Source: U.S. Census Bureau, 2008-2010 American Community Survey 3-Year Estimates

Travel Time to Work

Area	Less Than 10 Minutes	10 to 19 Minutes	20 to 29 Minutes	30 to 44 Minutes	45 to 59 Minutes	60 to 89 Minutes	90 Minutes or More
City	9.4	30.2	20.3	20.5	10.7	4.9	4.0
MSA[1]	10.8	31.9	25.2	20.9	5.8	3.5	1.9
U.S.	13.9	30.1	20.8	19.8	7.5	5.5	2.5

Note: Figures are percentages and include workers 16 years old and over; (1) Figures cover the San Diego-Carlsbad-San Marcos, CA Metropolitan Statistical Area—see Appendix B for areas included
Source: U.S. Census Bureau, 2008-2010 American Community Survey 3-Year Estimates

Travel Time Index

Area	1985	1990	1995	2000	2005	2010
Urban Area[1]	1.06	1.14	1.13	1.20	1.25	1.19
Average[2]	1.11	1.16	1.18	1.21	1.25	1.20

Note: Travel Time Index—the ratio of travel time in the peak period to the travel time at free-flow conditions. A value of 1.30 indicates a 20-minute free-flow trip takes 26 minutes in the peak. Free-flow speeds (60 mph on freeways and 35 mph on principal arterials) are used as the comparison threshold; (1) Covers the San Diego CA urban area; (2) average of 439 urban areas
Source: Texas Transportation Institute, Urban Mobility Report 2011, September 2011

Public Transportation

Agency Name / Mode of Transportation	Vehicles Operated in Maximum Service	Annual Unlinked Passenger Trips ('000)	Annual Passenger Miles ('000)
North County Transit District (NCTD)			
Bus (directly operated)	123	7,018.4	34,873.2
Bus (purchased transportation)	22	806.8	4,008.9
Commuter Rail (purchased transportation)	26	1,271.6	35,916.3
Demand Response (purchased transportation)	26	119.2	1,559.5
Light Rail (purchased transportation)	6	2,117.9	18,400.5

Source: Federal Transit Administration, National Transit Database, 2010

Air Transportation

Airport Name and Code / Type of Service	Passenger Airlines[1]	Passenger Enplanements	Freight Carriers[2]	Freight (lbs.)
San Diego International-Lindbergh Field (SAN)				
Domestic service (U.S. carriers - 2011)	25	8,235,357	20	135,275,135
International service (U.S. carriers - 2010)	6	45,368	4	29,807

Note: (1) Includes all U.S.-based major, minor and commuter airlines that carried at least one passenger during the year; (2) Includes all U.S.-based airlines and freight carriers that transported at least one pound of freight during the year
Source: Bureau of Transportation Statistics, The Intermodal Transportation Database, Air Carriers: T-100 Domestic Market (U.S. Carriers), 2011; Bureau of Transportation Statistics, The Intermodal Transportation Database, Air Carriers: T-100 International Market (U.S. Carriers), 2010

Other Transportation Statistics

Major Highways:	I-5; CR-78 connecting to I-15
Amtrak Service:	Yes (station is located in Oceanside)
Major Waterways/Ports:	Pacific Ocean

Source: Amtrak.com; Google Maps

BUSINESSES

Major Business Headquarters

Company Name	Rankings	
	Fortune[1]	Forbes[2]
No companies listed	-	-

Note: (1) Fortune 500—companies that produce a 10-K are ranked 1 to 500 based on 2010 revenue; (2) all private companies with at least $2 billion in annual revenue are ranked 1 to 212; companies listed are headquartered in the city; dashes indicate no ranking
Source: Fortune, "Fortune 500," May 23, 2011; Forbes, "America's Largest Private Companies," November 16, 2011

Fast-Growing Businesses

According to *Fortune*, Carlsbad is home to one of the 100 fastest-growing companies in the world: **Life Technologies** (#72). Companies were ranked by their revenue growth rate; their EPS growth rate; and their three-year annualized total return to investors for the period ending June 30, 2011. Criteria for inclusion: a company, foreign or domestic, must trade on a major U.S. stock exchange; must file quarterly reports with the SEC; must have a minimum market capitalization of $250 million; must have a stock price of at least $5 on June 30, 2011; must have been trading continuously since June 30, 2008; must have revenue and net income for the four quarters ended on or before April 30, 2011, of at least $50 million and $10 million, respectively; and must have posted a compound annual growth in revenue and earnings per share of at least 15% annually over the three years ending on or before April 30, 2011. REITs, limited-liability companies, limited parterships, companies about to be acquired, and companies that lost money in the quarter ending April 30, 2011 were excluded. *Fortune, "100 Fastest-Growing Companies," September 26, 2011*

According to Deloitte, Carlsbad is home to five of North America's 500 fastest-growing high-technology companies: **MaxLinear** (#17); **Isis Pharmaceuticals** (#158); **AutoClaims Direct** (#202); **Life Technologies Corp.** (#373); **Alphatec Spine** (#449). Companies are ranked by percentage growth in revenue over a five-year period. Criteria for inclusion: company must be headquartered within North America; must own proprietary intellectual property or proprietary technology that contributes to a significant portion of the company's operating revenue, or devote a significant proportion of revenues to research and development of technology; must have been in business for a minumum of five years with 2006 operating revenues of at least $50,000 USD/CD and 2010 operating revenues of at least $5 million USD/CD. *Deloitte Touche Tohmatsu, 2011 Deloitte Technology Fast 500™*

Minority- and Women-Owned Businesses

Group	All Firms		Firms with Paid Employees			
	Firms	Sales ($000)	Firms	Sales ($000)	Employees	Payroll ($000)
Asian	(s)	(s)	(s)	(s)	(s)	(s)
Black	(s)	(s)	(s)	(s)	(s)	(s)
Hispanic	1,078	397,355	240	364,903	1,128	43,204
Women	4,010	1,098,618	458	990,929	4,082	147,049
All Firms	14,442	15,158,881	3,526	14,460,029	61,311	2,985,937

Note: Figures cover firms located in the city; minority- and women-owned business are defined as firms in which the corresponding group own 51% or more of the stock or equity of the company; (s) estimates are suppressed when publication standards are not met
Source: U.S. Census Bureau, 2007 Economic Census, Survey of Business Owners

HOTELS

Hotels/Motels

Area	5 Star		4 Star		3 Star		2 Star		1 Star		Not Rated	
	Num.	Pct.[3]	Num.	Pct.[3]	Num.	Pct.[3]	Num.	Pct.[3]	Num.	Pct.[3]	Num.	Pct.[3]
City[1]	1	2.6	2	5.3	14	36.8	17	44.7	0	0.0	4	10.5
Total[2]	133	0.9	940	6.5	4,569	31.8	7,033	48.9	351	2.4	1,343	9.3

Note: (1) Figures cover Carlsbad and vicinity; (2) Figures cover all 100 cities in this book; (3) Percentage of hotels which have a given star rating; Star ratings are determined by expedia.com and offer an indication of the general quality of a particular hotel.
Source: expedia.com, April 25, 2012

EVENT SITES

Convention Centers

Name	Overall Space (sq. ft.)	Exhibit Space (sq. ft.)	Meeting Space (sq. ft.)	Meeting Rooms
La Costa Coastal Events Center	n/a	4,000	8,140	7

Note: n/a not available
Source: Original research

Living Environment

COST OF LIVING

Cost of Living Index

Composite Index	Groceries	Housing	Utilities	Trans-portation	Health Care	Misc. Goods/ Services
130.8	107.4	189.1	113.0	111.2	112.4	103.6

Note: U.S. = 100; Figures cover the San Diego CA urban area.
Source: The Council for Community and Economic Research, ACCRA Cost of Living Index, 2011

Grocery Prices

Area[1]	T-Bone Steak ($/pound)	Frying Chicken ($/pound)	Whole Milk ($/half gal.)	Eggs ($/dozen)	Orange Juice ($/64 oz.)	Coffee ($/11.5 oz.)
City[2]	9.85	1.06	2.14	2.28	3.33	5.58
Avg.	9.25	1.18	2.22	1.66	3.19	4.40
Min.	6.70	0.88	1.31	0.95	2.46	2.94
Max.	14.30	2.16	3.50	3.18	4.75	6.83

Note: (1) Values for the local area are compared with the average, minimum and maximum values for all 335 areas in the Cost of Living Index; (2) Figures cover the San Diego CA urban area; **T-Bone Steak** *(price per pound);* **Frying Chicken** *(price per pound, whole fryer);* **Whole Milk** *(half gallon carton);* **Eggs** *(price per dozen, Grade A, large);* **Orange Juice** *(64 oz. Tropicana or Florida Natural);* **Coffee** *(11.5 oz. can, vacuum-packed, Maxwell House, Hills Bros, or Folgers).*
Source: The Council for Community and Economic Research, ACCRA Cost of Living Index, 2011

Housing and Utility Costs

Area[1]	New Home Price ($)	Apartment Rent ($/month)	All Electric ($/month)	Part Electric ($/month)	Other Energy ($/month)	Telephone ($/month)
City[2]	525,576	1,712	-	121.58	67.99	29.85
Avg.	285,990	839	163.23	89.00	77.52	26.92
Min.	188,005	460	125.58	45.39	33.89	17.98
Max.	1,197,028	3,244	339.16	181.97	348.69	40.01

Note: (1) Values for the local area are compared with the average, minimum and maximum values for all 335 areas in the Cost of Living Index; (2) Figures cover the San Diego CA urban area; **New Home Price** *(2,400 sf living area, 8,000 sf lot, in urban area with full utilities);* **Apartment Rent** *(950 sf 2 bedroom/1.5 or 2 bath, unfurnished, excluding all utilities except water);* **All Electric** *(average monthly cost for an all-electric home);* **Part Electric** *(average monthly cost for a part-electric home);* **Other Energy** *(average monthly cost for natural gas, fuel oil, coal, wood, and any other forms of energy except electricity);* **Telephone** *(price includes basic monthly rate for a private residential line plus additional local usage charges incurred by a family of four).*
Source: The Council for Community and Economic Research, ACCRA Cost of Living Index, 2011

Health Care, Transportation, and Other Costs

Area[1]	Doctor ($/visit)	Dentist ($/visit)	Optometrist ($/visit)	Gasoline ($/gallon)	Beauty Salon ($/visit)	Men's Shirt ($)
City[2]	98.80	98.60	98.80	3.83	46.67	22.25
Avg.	93.88	81.72	90.54	3.48	32.65	25.06
Min.	60.00	55.33	53.66	3.18	19.78	13.44
Max.	154.98	145.97	183.72	4.31	63.21	46.00

Note: (1) Values for the local area are compared with the average, minimum and maximum values for all 335 areas in the Cost of Living Index; (2) Figures cover the San Diego CA urban area; **Doctor** *(general practitioners routine exam of an established patient);* **Dentist** *(adult teeth cleaning and periodic oral examination);* **Optometrist** *(full vision eye exam for established adult patient);* **Gasoline** *(one gallon regular unleaded, national brand, including all taxes, cash price at self-service pump if available);* **Beauty Salon** *(woman's shampoo, trim, and blow-dry);* **Men's Shirt** *(cotton/polyester dress shirt, pinpoint weave, long sleeves).*
Source: The Council for Community and Economic Research, ACCRA Cost of Living Index, 2011

HOUSING

House Price Index (HPI)

Area	National Ranking[2]	Quarterly Change (%)	One-Year Change (%)	Five-Year Change (%)
MSA[1]	215	-0.39	-4.25	-31.71
U.S.[3]	-	-0.10	-2.43	-19.16

Note: The HPI is a weighted repeat sales index. It measures average price changes in repeat sales or refinancings on the same properties. This information is obtained by reviewing repeat mortgage transactions on single-family properties whose mortgages have been purchased or securitized by Fannie Mae or Freddie Mac in January 1975; (1) Metropolitan/Micropolitan Statistical Area—see Appendix B for areas included; (2) Rankings are based on annual percentage change for all metro areas containing at least 15,000 transactions over the last 10 years and ranges from 1 to 306; (3) figures based on a weighted average of Census Division estimates using a purchase only index; all figures are for the period ending December 31, 2011

Source: Federal Housing Finance Agency, House Price Index, February 23, 2012

House Price Valuations

Area	Q4 2005		Q4 2006		Q4 2007		Q4 2008		Q4 2009	
	Price ($000)	Over-valuation	Price ($000)	Over-valuation	Price ($000)	Over-valuation	Price ($000)	Over-valuation	Price ($000)	Over-valuation
MSA[1]	498.3	36.8	478.3	24.3	419.1	3.6	334.6	-17.3	341.3	-15.8

Note: Figures show the percentage of over- or under-valuation of single family homes relative to statistically normal house values (e.g. a value of 23.6 indicates that house values are 23.6% overvalued). Statistically normal house values are based on house prices, interest rates, household incomes, population densities, and any historical premiums or discounts metropolitan areas have exhibited over time; (1) Figures cover the San Diego-Carlsbad-San Marcos, CA - see Appendix B for areas included

Source: Global Insight/PNC Financial Services Group, House Prices in America: 4th Quarter 2009 Update

Median Single-Family Home Prices

Area	2009	2010	2011p	Percent Change 2010 to 2011
MSA[1]	359.5	385.7	370.3	-4.0
U.S. Average	172.1	173.1	166.2	-4.0

Note: Figures are median sales prices of existing single-family homes in thousands of dollars; (p) preliminary; n/a not available; (1) Metropolitan Statistical Area—see Appendix B for areas included

Source: National Association of Realtors, Median Sales Price of Existing Single-Family Homes for Metropolitan Areas, 4th Quarter 2011

Affordability Index of Existing Single-Family Homes

Area	2009	2010	2011p	Percent Change 2010 to 2011
MSA[1]	60.6	59.5	65.0	9.2

Note: The housing affordability index measures whether or not a typical family could qualify for a mortgage loan on a typical home. The higher the index, the greater the household purchasing power. An index of 100 is defined as the point where a median-income household has exactly enough income to qualify for the purchase of a median-priced existing single-family home, assuming a 20 percent downpayment and 25 percent of gross income devoted to mortgage principal and interest payments; (p) preliminary; n/a not available; (1) Metropolitan Statistical Area—see Appendix B for areas included

Source: National Association of Realtors, Affordability Index of Existing Single-Family Homes, 2011

Median Apartment Condo-Coop Home Prices

Area	2009	2010	2011p	Percent Change 2010 to 2011
MSA[1]	212.5	219.8	207.7	-5.5
U.S. Average	175.6	171.7	165.1	-3.8

Note: Figures are median sales prices of existing apartment condo-coop homes in thousands of dollars; (p) preliminary; n/a not available; (1) Metropolitan Statistical Area—see Appendix B for areas included

Source: National Association of Realtors, Median Sales Price of Existing Apartment Condo-Coop Homes for Metropolitan Areas, 4th Quarter 2011

Year Housing Structure Built

Area	2005 or Later	2000 -2004	1990 -1999	1980 -1989	1970 -1979	1960 -1969	1950 -1959	Before 1950	Median Year
City	7.0	13.8	19.2	25.1	25.6	5.4	2.9	1.0	1986
MSA[1]	3.8	7.9	11.7	19.0	24.9	12.8	11.4	8.3	1977
U.S.	5.0	8.6	14.0	14.1	16.3	11.3	11.2	19.6	1975

Note: Figures are percentages except for Median Year; (1) Figures cover the San Diego-Carlsbad-San Marcos, CA Metropolitan Statistical Area—see Appendix B for areas included
Source: U.S. Census Bureau, 2008-2010 American Community Survey 3-Year Estimates

HEALTH

Health Risk Data

Category	MSA[1] (%)	U.S. (%)
Adults who have been told they have high blood pressure[2]	23.5	28.7
Adults who have been told they have high blood cholesterol[2]	34.4	37.5
Adults who have been told they have diabetes[3]	8.9	8.7
Adults who have been told they have arthritis[2]	18.7	26.0
Adults who have been told they currently have asthma	7.7	9.1
Adults who are current smokers	13.0	17.3
Adults who are heavy drinkers[4]	7.3	5.0
Adults who are binge drinkers[5]	17.7	15.1
Adults who are overweight (BMI 25.0 - 29.9)	32.8	36.2
Adults who are obese (BMI 30.0 - 99.8)	26.1	27.5
Adults who participated in any physical activities in the past month	81.0	76.1
Adults 50+ who have ever had a sigmoidoscopy or colonoscopy	64.5	65.2
Women aged 40+ who have had a mammogram within the past two years	77.5	75.2
Men aged 40+ who have had a PSA test within the past two years	51.7	53.2
Adults aged 65+ who have had flu shot within the past year	62.2	67.5
Adults aged 18–64 who have any kind of health care coverage	79.3	82.2

Note: Data as of 2010 unless otherwise noted; (1) Figures cover the San Diego-Carlsbad-San Marcos, CA Metropolitan Statistical Area—see Appendix B for areas included; (2) Data as of 2009; (3) Figures do not include pregnancy-related, borderline, or pre-diabetes; (4) Heavy drinkers are classified as males having more than two drinks per day or females having more than one drink per day; (5) Binge drinkers are classified as males having five or more drinks on one occasion or females having four or more drinks on one occasion
Source: Centers for Disease Control and Prevention, Behaviorial Risk Factor Surveillance System, SMART: Selected Metropolitan/Micropolitan Area Risk Trends, 2009, 2010

Mortality Rates for the Top 10 Causes of Death in the U.S.

ICD-10[a] Sub-Chapter	ICD-10[a] Code	Age-Adjusted Mortality Rate[1] per 100,000 population	
		County[2]	U.S.
Malignant neoplasms	C00-C97	165.1	175.6
Ischaemic heart diseases	I20-I25	107.1	121.6
Other forms of heart disease	I30-I51	36.0	48.6
Chronic lower respiratory diseases	J40-J47	34.7	42.3
Cerebrovascular diseases	I60-I69	38.0	40.6
Organic, including symptomatic, mental disorders	F01-F09	15.4	26.7
Other degenerative diseases of the nervous system	G30-G31	36.6	24.7
Other external causes of accidental injury	W00-X59	20.7	24.4
Diabetes mellitus	E10-E14	18.9	21.7
Hypertensive diseases	I10-I15	18.8	18.2

Note: (a) ICD-10 = International Classification of Diseases 10th Revision; (1) Mortality rates are a three year average covering 2007-2009; (2) Figures cover San Diego County
Source: Centers for Disease Control and Prevention, National Center for Health Statistics. Underlying Cause of Death 1999-2009 on CDC WONDER Online Database, released 2012. Data for year 2009 are compiled from the Multiple Cause of Death File 2009, Series 20 No. 2O, 2012, Data for year 2008 are compiled from the Multiple Cause of Death File 2008, Series 20 No. 2N, 2011, Data for year 2007 are compiled from Multiple Cause of Death File 2007, Series 20 No. 2M, 2010.

Mortality Rates for Selected Causes of Death

ICD-10[a] Sub-Chapter	ICD-10[a] Code	Age-Adjusted Mortality Rate[1] per 100,000 population	
		County[2]	U.S.
Assault	X85-Y09	3.2	5.7
Human immunodeficiency virus (HIV) disease	B20-B24	2.5	3.3
Influenza and pneumonia	J09-J18	10.4	16.4
Intentional self-harm	X60-X84	12.1	11.5
Malnutrition	E40-E46	0.5	0.8
Obesity and other hyperalimentation	E65-E68	1.8	1.6
Transport accidents	V01-V99	10.1	13.7
Viral hepatitis	B15-B19	3.9	2.2

Note: (a) ICD-10 = International Classification of Diseases 10th Revision; (1) Mortality rates are a three year average covering 2007-2009; (2) Figures cover San Diego County

Source: Centers for Disease Control and Prevention, National Center for Health Statistics. Underlying Cause of Death 1999-2009 on CDC WONDER Online Database, released 2012. Data for year 2009 are compiled from the Multiple Cause of Death File 2009, Series 20 No. 2O, 2012, Data for year 2008 are compiled from the Multiple Cause of Death File 2008, Series 20 No. 2N, 2011, Data for year 2007 are compiled from Multiple Cause of Death File 2007, Series 20 No. 2M, 2010.

Distribution of Physicians and Dentists

Area[1]	Dentists[2]	D.O.[3]	M.D.[4] Total	M.D.[4] Family/ General Practice	M.D.[4] Pediatrics	M.D.[4] Medical Specialties	M.D.[4] Surgical Specialties
Local (number)	1,796	393	6,342	804	483	2,254	1,372
Local (rate[5])	6.0	1.3	21.0	2.7	1.6	7.5	4.5
U.S. (rate[5])	4.5	1.9	18.3	2.5	1.4	6.8	4.1

Note: Data as of 2008 unless noted; (1) Local data covers San Diego County; (2) Data as of 2007; (3) Doctor of Osteopathic Medicine; (4) Includes active, non-federal, patient-care, office-based Doctors of Medicine; (5) rate per 10,000 population

Source: Area Resource File (ARF). 2009-2010 Release. U.S. Department of Health and Human Services, Health Resources and Services Administration, Bureau of Health Professions, Rockville, MD, August 2010

Best Hospitals

According to *U.S. News,* the San Diego-Carlsbad-San Marcos, CA is home to two of the best hospitals in the U.S.: **Scripps La Jolla Hospitals and Clinics** (1 specialty); **UC San Diego Medical Center** (6 specialties). The hospitals listed were highly ranked in at least one adult specialty. *U.S. News Online, "America's Best Hospitals 2011-12"*

According to *U.S. News,* the San Diego-Carlsbad-San Marcos, CA is home to one of the best children's hospitals in the U.S.: **Rady Children's Hospital** (10 specialties). The hospital listed was highly ranked in at least one pediatric specialty. *U.S. News Online, "America's Best Children's Hospitals 2011-12"*

EDUCATION

Public School District Statistics

District Name	Schls	Pupils	Pupil/ Teacher Ratio	Minority Pupils[1] (%)	Free Lunch Eligible[2] (%)	IEP[3] (%)
Carlsbad Unified	15	10,906	22.0	41.9	16.7	9.9

Note: Table includes school districts with 2,000 or more students; (1) Percentage of students that are not non-Hispanic white; (2) Percentage of students that are eligible for the free lunch program; (3) Percentage of students that have an Individualized Education Program.

Source: U.S. Department of Education, National Center for Education Statistics, Common Core of Data, Local Education Agency (School District) Universe Survey: School Year 2009-2010; U.S. Department of Education, National Center for Education Statistics, Common Core of Data, Public Elementary/Secondary School Universe Survey: School Year 2009-2010

Highest Level of Education

Area	Less than H.S.	H.S. Diploma	Some College, No Deg.	Associate Degree	Bachelors Degree	Masters Degree	Profess. School Degree	Doctorate Degree
City	4.6	13.6	20.9	10.3	31.7	12.9	3.4	2.7
MSA[1]	14.9	19.1	23.5	8.4	21.3	8.2	2.6	2.0
U.S.	14.7	28.4	21.3	7.6	17.6	7.2	1.9	1.2

Note: Figures cover persons age 25 and over; (1) Figures cover the San Diego-Carlsbad-San Marcos, CA Metropolitan Statistical Area—see Appendix B for areas included
Source: U.S. Census Bureau, 2008-2010 American Community Survey 3-Year Estimates

Educational Attainment by Race

Area	High School Graduate or Higher (%)					Bachelor's Degree or Higher (%)				
	Total	White	Black	Asian	Hisp.[2]	Total	White	Black	Asian	Hisp.[2]
City	95.4	96.0	n/a	97.1	74.6	50.7	50.1	n/a	67.4	27.3
MSA[1]	85.1	86.1	90.1	88.0	61.9	34.1	34.9	22.8	45.8	14.5
U.S.	85.3	87.5	81.4	85.5	61.6	28.0	29.3	17.8	50.2	13.0

Note: Figures shown cover persons 25 years old and over; (1) Figures cover the San Diego-Carlsbad-San Marcos, CA Metropolitan Statistical Area—see Appendix B for areas included; (2) People of Hispanic origin can be of any race
Source: U.S. Census Bureau, 2008-2010 American Community Survey 3-Year Estimates

School Enrollment by Grade and Control

Area	Preschool (%)		Kindergarten (%)		Grades 1 - 4 (%)		Grades 5 - 8 (%)		Grades 9 - 12 (%)	
	Public	Private	Public	Private	Public	Private	Public	Private	Public	Private
City	21.3	78.7	88.7	11.3	90.7	9.3	87.7	12.3	94.9	5.1
MSA[1]	52.5	47.5	90.2	9.8	91.5	8.5	91.6	8.4	93.0	7.0
U.S.	55.4	44.6	87.1	12.9	89.4	10.6	89.5	10.5	90.4	9.6

Note: Figures shown cover persons 3 years old and over; (1) Figures cover the San Diego-Carlsbad-San Marcos, CA Metropolitan Statistical Area—see Appendix B for areas included
Source: U.S. Census Bureau, 2008-2010 American Community Survey 3-Year Estimates

Average Salaries of Public School Classroom Teachers

Area	2010-11		2011-12		Percent Change 2010-11 to 2011-12	Percent Change 2001-02 to 2011-12
	Dollars	Rank[1]	Dollars	Rank[1]		
California	67,871	4	69,496	4	2.39	27.90
U.S. Average	55,623	-	56,643	-	1.83	26.8

Note: (1) State rank ranges from 1 to 51 where 1 indicates highest salary.
Source: National Education Association, Rankings & Estimates: Rankings of the States 2011 and Estimates of School Statistics 2012, December 2011

Higher Education

Four-Year Colleges			Two-Year Colleges			Medical Schools[1]	Law Schools[2]	Voc/ Tech[3]
Public	Private Non-profit	Private For-profit	Public	Private Non-profit	Private For-profit			
0	0	0	0	0	1	0	0	1

Note: Figures cover institutions located within the city limits and include main campuses only; (1) includes schools accredited by the Liaison Committee on Medical Education and the American Osteopathic Association's Commission on Osteopathic College Accreditation; (2) includes American Bar Association-accredited law schools; (3) includes all schools with programs that are less than 2 years.
Source: National Center for Education Statistics, Integrated Postsecondary Education System (IPEDS) Peer Analysis System, 2011-12; Association of American Medical Colleges, Member List, April 23, 2012; American Osteopathic Association, Member List, April 23, 2012; Law School Admission Council, Official Guide to ABA-Approved Law Schools Online, April 23, 2012

According to *U.S. News & World Report,* the San Diego-Carlsbad-San Marcos, CA is home to three of the best national universities in the U.S.: **University of California–San Diego** (#37); **University of San Diego** (#97); **San Diego State University** (#164). The indicators used to capture academic quality fall into a number of categories: assessment by administrators at peer institutions; retention of students; faculty resources; student selectivity; financial resources; alumni giving; high school counselor ratings of colleges; and graduation rate. *U.S. News & World Report, "America's Best Colleges 2012"*

PRESIDENTIAL ELECTION

2008 Presidential Election Results

Area	Obama	McCain	Nader	Other
San Diego County	54.1	43.9	0.7	1.2
U.S.	52.9	45.6	0.6	0.9

Note: Results are percentages and may not add to 100% due to rounding
Source: Dave Leip's Atlas of U.S. Presidential Elections, www.uselectionatlas.org

EMPLOYERS

Major Employers

Company Name	Industry
Barona Resort & Casino	Resort hotel
CA Dept of Housing & Comm Dev	Housing agency, government
City of San Diego	Municipal police
Elite Show Services	Help supply services
Forestry and Fire Protection, CA Dept of	Fire department, not including volunteer
Go-Staff	Temporary help service
Kaiser Foundation Hospitals	Trusts, nec
Marine Corps, United States	Marine corps
Palomar Community College District	Junior colleges
Qualcomm International	Patent buying, licensing, leasing
Risk Management Strategies	Employee programs administration
San Diego State University	Colleges and universities
Sharp Memorial Hospital	General medical and surgical hospitals
Solar Turbines Incorporated	Turbines and turbine generator sets
The Navy United States Department of	Navy
The Navy United States Department of	Medical centers
University of California, San Diego	General medical and surgical hospitals
Veterans Health Administration	Administration of veterans' affairs

Note: Companies shown are located within the San Diego-Carlsbad-San Marcos, CA metropolitan area.
Source: Hoovers.com, data extracted April 25 2012

PUBLIC SAFETY

Crime Rate

Area	All Crimes	Violent Crimes				Property Crimes		
		Murder	Forcible Rape	Robbery	Aggrav. Assault	Burglary	Larceny -Theft	Motor Vehicle Theft
City	2,005.8	0.0	19.9	40.8	133.4	397.2	1,307.0	107.5
Suburbs[1]	2,604.5	2.3	22.0	111.2	249.2	459.6	1,341.6	418.5
Metro[2]	2,584.9	2.2	22.0	108.9	245.4	457.6	1,340.5	408.3
U.S.	3,345.5	4.8	27.5	119.1	252.3	699.6	2,003.5	238.8

Note: Figures are crimes per 100,000 population; (1) All areas within the metro area that are located outside the city limits; (2) Metropolitan Statistical Area—see Appendix B for areas included
Source: FBI Uniform Crime Reports, 2010

Hate Crimes

Area	Number of Quarters Reported	Bias Motivation				
		Race	Religion	Sexual Orientation	Ethnicity	Disability
City	4	0	0	1	0	0

Source: Federal Bureau of Investigation, Hate Crime Statistics 2010

Identity Theft Consumer Complaints

Area	Complaints	Complaints per 100,000 Population	Rank[2]
MSA[1]	2,722	91.5	122
U.S.	279,156	90.4	-

Note: (1) Metropolitan Statistical Area—see Appendix B for areas included; (2) Rank ranges from 1 to 384 where 1 indicates greatest number of identity theft complaints per 100,000 population
Source: Federal Trade Commission, Consumer Sentinel Network Data Book for January–December 2011

Fraud and Other Consumer Complaints

Area	Complaints	Complaints per 100,000 Population	Rank[2]
MSA[1]	15,072	506.6	140
U.S.	1,533,924	496.8	-

Note: (1) Metropolitan Statistical Area—see Appendix B for areas included; (2) Rank ranges from 1 to 384 where 1 indicates greatest number of fraud and other complaints per 100,000 population
Source: Federal Trade Commission, Consumer Sentinel Network Data Book for January–December 2011

RECREATION

Culture

Dance[1]	Theatre[1]	Instrumental Music[1]	Vocal Music[1]	Series/ Festivals	Museums	Zoos and Aquariums[2]
0	0	0	0	0	n/a	0

Note: (1) Number of professional perfoming groups; (2) AZA-accredited; n/a not available
Source: The Grey House Performing Arts Directory, 2011-2012; Official Museum Directory, 2011; American Association of Museums, AAM Member Museums, April 2012; Association of Zoos & Aquariums, AZA Member Zoos & Aquariums, April 2012

Professional Sports Teams

Team Name	League
San Diego Chargers	National Football League (NFL)
San Diego Padres	Major League Baseball (MLB)

Note: Includes teams located in the San Diego metro area.
Source: Original research

CLIMATE

Average and Extreme Temperatures

Temperature	Jan	Feb	Mar	Apr	May	Jun	Jul	Aug	Sep	Oct	Nov	Dec	Yr.
Extreme High (°F)	88	88	93	98	96	101	95	98	111	107	97	88	111
Average High (°F)	65	66	66	68	69	72	76	77	77	74	71	66	71
Average Temp. (°F)	57	58	59	62	64	67	71	72	71	67	62	58	64
Average Low (°F)	48	50	52	55	58	61	65	66	65	60	53	49	57
Extreme Low (°F)	29	36	39	44	48	51	55	58	51	43	38	34	29

Note: Figures cover the years 1948-1990
Source: National Climatic Data Center, International Station Meteorological Climate Summary, 9/96

Average Precipitation/Snowfall/Humidity

Precip./Humidity	Jan	Feb	Mar	Apr	May	Jun	Jul	Aug	Sep	Oct	Nov	Dec	Yr.
Avg. Precip. (in.)	1.9	1.4	1.7	0.8	0.2	0.1	Tr	0.1	0.2	0.4	1.2	1.4	9.5
Avg. Snowfall (in.)	Tr	0	0	0	0	0	0	0	0	0	0	Tr	Tr
Avg. Rel. Hum. 7am (%)	70	72	73	72	73	77	79	79	78	74	69	68	74
Avg. Rel. Hum. 4pm (%)	57	58	59	59	63	66	65	66	65	63	60	58	62

Note: Figures cover the years 1948-1990; Tr = Trace amounts (<0.05 in. of rain; <0.5 in. of snow)
Source: National Climatic Data Center, International Station Meteorological Climate Summary, 9/96

Weather Conditions

Temperature			Daytime Sky			Precipitation		
10°F & below	32°F & below	90°F & above	Clear	Partly cloudy	Cloudy	0.01 inch or more precip.	0.1 inch or more snow/ice	Thunder-storms
0	< 1	4	115	126	124	40	0	5

Note: Figures are average number of days per year and cover the years 1948-1990
Source: National Climatic Data Center, International Station Meteorological Climate Summary, 9/96

HAZARDOUS WASTE

Superfund Sites

Carlsbad has no sites on the EPA's Superfund Final National Priorities List.
U.S. Environmental Protection Agency, Final National Priorities List, April 17, 2012

AIR & WATER QUALITY

Air Quality Index

Area	Percent of Days when Air Quality was...[2]					AQI Statistics[2]	
	Good	Moderate	Unhealthy for Sensitive Groups	Unhealthy	Very Unhealthy	Maximum	Median
Area[1]	33.7	62.7	3.3	0.3	0.0	155	54

Note: Air Quality Index (AQI) is an index for reporting daily air quality. EPA calculates the AQI for five major air pollutants regulated by the Clean Air Act: ground-level ozone, particle pollution (aka particulate matter), carbon monoxide, sulfur dioxide, and nitrogen dioxide. The AQI runs from 0 to 500. The higher the AQI value, the greater the level of air pollution and the greater the health concern. There are six AQI categories: "Good" AQI is between 0 and 50. Air quality is considered satisfactory; "Moderate" AQI is between 51 and 100. Air quality is acceptable; "Unhealthy for Sensitive Groups" When AQI values are between 101 and 150, members of sensitive groups may experience health effects; "Unhealthy" When AQI values are between 151 and 200 everyone may begin to experience health effects; "Very Unhealthy" AQI values between 201 and 300 trigger a health alert; "Hazardous" AQI values over 300 trigger warnings of emergency conditions (not shown); (1) Data covers San Diego County; (2) Based on 365 days with AQI data in 2011.
Source: U.S. Environmental Protection Agency, AirData Report, 2011

Air Quality Index Pollutants

Area	Percent of Days when AQI Pollutant was...[2]					
	Carbon Monoxide	Nitrogen Dioxide	Ozone	Sulfur Dioxide	Particulate Matter 2.5	Particulate Matter 10
Area[1]	0.0	15.1	38.1	0.0	44.4	2.5

Note: The Air Quality Index (AQI) is an index for reporting daily air quality. EPA calculates the AQI for five major air pollutants regulated by the Clean Air Act: ground-level ozone, particle pollution (also known as particulate matter), carbon monoxide, sulfur dioxide, and nitrogen dioxide. The AQI runs from 0 to 500. The higher the AQI value, the greater the level of air pollution and the greater the health concern; (1) Data covers San Diego County; (2) Based on 365 days with AQI data in 2011.
Source: U.S. Environmental Protection Agency, AirData Report, 2011

Air Quality Index Trends

Area	Trend Sites (days)								All Sites (days)
	2003	2004	2005	2006	2007	2008	2009	2010	2010
MSA[1]	50	31	30	39	34	43	25	14	15

Note: Figures are the number of days the AQI value exceeded 100 in a given year. An AQI value greater than 100 indicates that air quality would have been in the unhealthful range on that day. Data from exceptional events are included. These counts are presented in two ways. First, the counts are based on sites having an adequate record of monitoring data during the trend period (trend sites). These counts represent the relative change in the number of days with AQI values greater than 100. In the last column, the counts are based on all sites with data in the most recent year (because it is possible for a site to have data in the most recent year but not enough data to be a trend site); (1) Data covers the San Diego-Carlsbad-San Marcos, CA—see Appendix B for areas included
Source: U.S. Environmental Protection Agency, Air Quality Index Information, "Number of Days with Air Quality Index Values Greater than 100 at Trend Sites, 2000-2010, and at All Sites in 2010"

Maximum Air Pollutant Concentrations: Particulate Matter, Ozone, CO and Lead

	Particulate Matter 10 (ug/m³)	Particulate Matter 2.5 Wtd AM (ug/m³)	Particulate Matter 2.5 24-Hr (ug/m³)	Ozone (ppm)	Carbon Monoxide (ppm)	Lead (ug/m³)
MSA[1] Level	101	13.3	114	0.081	2	n/a
NAAQS[2]	150	15	35	0.075	9	0.15
Met NAAQS[2]	Yes	Yes	No	No	Yes	n/a

Note: Data from exceptional events are not included; (1) Data covers the San Diego-Carlsbad-San Marcos, CA—see Appendix B for areas included; (2) National Ambient Air Quality Standards; ppm = parts per million; ug/m³ = micrograms per cubic meter; n/a not available
Concentrations: Particulate Matter 10 (coarse particulate)—highest second maximum 24-hour concentration; Particulate Matter 2.5 Wtd AM (fine particulate)—highest weighted annual mean concentration; Particulate Matter 2.5 24-Hour (fine particulate)—highest 98th percentile 24-hour concentration; Ozone—highest fourth daily maximum 8-hour concentration; Carbon Monoxide—highest second maximum non-overlapping 8-hour concentration; Lead—maximum running 3-month average
Source: U.S. Environmental Protection Agency, CBSA Factbook 2010, Air Quality Statistics by City, 2010

Maximum Air Pollutant Concentrations: Nitrogen Dioxide and Sulfur Dioxide

	Nitrogen Dioxide AM (ppb)	Nitrogen Dioxide 1-Hr (ppb)	Sulfur Dioxide AM (ppb)	Sulfur Dioxide 1-Hr (ppb)	Sulfur Dioxide 24-Hr (ppb)
MSA[1] Level	20.975	74	1.765	18	7.1
NAAQS[2]	53	100	30	75	140
Met NAAQS[2]	Yes	Yes	Yes	Yes	Yes

Note: Data from exceptional events are not included; (1) Data covers the San Diego-Carlsbad-San Marcos, CA—see Appendix B for areas included; (2) National Ambient Air Quality Standards; ppb = parts per billion; n/a not available

Concentrations: Nitrogen Dioxide AM—highest arithmetic mean concentration; Nitrogen Dioxide 1-Hr—highest 98th percentile 1-hour daily maximum concentration; Sulfur Dioxide AM—highest annual mean concentration; Sulfur Dioxide 1-Hr—highest 99th percentile 1-hour daily maximum concentration; Sulfur Dioxide 24-Hr—highest second maximum 24-hour concentration

Source: U.S. Environmental Protection Agency, CBSA Factbook 2010, Air Quality Statistics by City, 2010

Drinking Water

Water System Name	Pop. Served	Primary Water Source Type	Violations[1]	
			Health Based	Monitoring/ Reporting
Carlsbad MWD	80,800	Purchased Surface	0	0

Note: (1) Based on violation data from January 1, 2011 to December 31, 2011 (includes unresolved violations from earlier years)

Source: U.S. Environmental Protection Agency, Office of Ground Water and Drinking Water, Safe Drinking Water Information System (based on data extracted April 18, 2012)

Colorado Springs, Colorado

Background

Colorado Springs is the seat of El Paso County in central Colorado and sits at the foot of Pike's Peak. A dynamic and growing city, its economy is based on health care, high-tech manufacturing, tourism, and sports, with strong employment links to nearby military installations. With such an economic base and gorgeous surroundings, it is no wonder that Colorado Springs ranks as one of the fastest-growing cities in the country.

In 1806, Lieutenant Zebulon Pike visited the site and the mountain that now bears his name, but true settlement did not begin in earnest until gold was discovered in 1859 and miners flooded into the area.

In 1871, General William Jackson Palmer, a railroad tycoon, purchased the site for $10,000 and began promoting the area as a health and recreation resort. Pike's Peak was already well known as a scenic landmark, and very soon the Garden of the Gods, Seven Falls, Cheyenne Mountain, and Manitou Springs were also widely known as spectacular natural sites. The extraordinary nature of the natural environment has long been celebrated, but perhaps the highest testimonial came from Katherine Lee Bates, who, after a trip to Pike's Peak in 1893, wrote "America the Beautiful."

The planned community of Colorado Springs was incorporated in 1876. As a resort, it was wildly successful, hosting the likes of Oscar Wilde and John D. Rockefeller. It became a special favorite of English visitors, one of whom made the claim that there were two "civilized" places between the Atlantic and the Pacific—Chicago and Colorado Springs.

The English were so enamored of the place, in fact, that it came to be called "Little London," as English visitors settled in the area, introducing golf, cricket, polo, and fox hunting; but since there were no local foxes, an artificial scent was spread out for the hounds, or sometimes a coyote was substituted. Several sumptuous hotels were built during this period, as was an elegantly appointed opera house.

In 1891, gold was again discovered, and the city's population tripled to 35,000 in the following decade. Sufficient gold deposits allowed a lucky few to amass considerable fortunes and build huge houses north of the city. However, not all of the newly minted millionaires were inclined toward conspicuous display; Winfield Scott Stratton, "Midas of the Rockies," bruised emerging aesthetic sensibilities by constructing a crude wooden frame house near the business district.

After the 1890s rush ended, Colorado Springs resumed a more measured pace of growth. During and after World War II, though, the town again saw considerable development as Fort Carson and the Peterson Air Force Base were established, followed by the North American Aerospace Defense Command (NORAD) and the U.S. Air Force Academy in the 1950s. Today NORAD is primarily concerned with the tracking of ICBMs, and celebrated its 51st anniversary in 2009. The city's military connection has contributed in large part to the economic base of the area, and to the presence of a highly educated and technically skilled workforce. In late 2008, Fort Carson became the home station of the 4th Infantry Division, nearly doubling the population of the base.

The area's major employers include Verizon, Hewlett Packard, Memorial Health Services, Penrose-St. Francis Health Services, and Lockheed Martin. Military establishments also provide employment. Colorado Springs is the site of the headquarters of the United States Olympics Committee, which maintains an important Olympic training center there. It is also home to the World Figure Skating Museum and Hall of Fame and the Pro Rodeo Hall of Fame and Museum of the American Cowboy.

The city hosts several institutions of higher learning, including Colorado College (1874), the U.S. Air Force Academy (1954), a campus of the University of Colorado (1965), and Nazarene Bible College (1967). Cultural amenities include the Fine Arts Center and Theatreworks at the University of Colorado.

The region enjoys four seasons, with plenty of sunshine—300 days each year. Rainfall is relatively minimal, but snow can pile up.

Rankings

General Rankings

- Colorado Springs was selected as one of 12 "Distinctive Destinations" for 2011, an annual list of unique and lovingly preserved communities in the U.S. Each year the National Trust for Historic Preservation selects 12 communities where residents have taken forceful action to protect their town's character and sense of place. *National Trust for Historic Preservation, "2011 Dozen Distinctive Destinations"*
- The Colorado Springs metro area was selected one of America's "Best Cities to Live, Work and Play" by *Kiplinger's Personal Finance.* Criteria: population growth; percentage of workforce in the creative class (scientists, engineers, educators, writers, artists, entertainers, etc.); job quality; income growth; cost of living. *Kiplinger's Personal Finance, "Best Cities to Live, Work and Play," July 2008*
- Colorado Springs was selected as one of America's best cities by *Bloomberg Businessweek.* The city ranked #18 out of 50. Criteria: number of restaurants, bars and museums per capita; number of colleges, libraries, and professional sports teams; income, poverty, unemployment, crime, and foreclosure rates; percent of population with bachelor's degrees; public school performance; park acres per capita; air quality. *BusinessWeek, "America's 50 Best Cities," September 20, 2011*
- The Colorado Springs metro area was selected as one of 10 "Best Value Cities" for 2011 by *Kiplinger.com* The area ranked #4. Criteria: vibrant economy; low cost of living; abundant lifestyle amenities. *Kiplinger.com, "Best Value Cities 2011"*

Business/Finance Rankings

- *Forbes* ranked the largest metro areas in the U.S. in terms of the "Best Cities for Young Professionals." The Colorado Springs metro area ranked #8out of 15. Criteria: job growth; unemployment rate; median salary of college graduates age 24 to 34; cost of living; number of small businesses per capita; number of large companies; percentage of population 25 years of age and older with college degrees. *Forbes.com, "America's Best Cities for Young Professionals," July 12, 2011*
- Colorado Springs was identified as one of the 20 weakest-performing metro areas during the recession and recovery from trough quarter through the third quarter of 2011. Criteria: percent change in employment; percentage point change in unemployment rate; percent change in gross metropolitan product; percent change in House Price Index. *Brookings Institution, MetroMonitor: Tracking Economic Recession and Recovery in America's 100 Largest Metropolitan Areas, December 2011*
- The Colorado Springs metro area was identified as one of the most debt-ridden places in America by credit reporting agency Equifax. The metro area was ranked #5. Criteria: proportion of average yearly income owed to credit card companies. *Equifax, "The Most Debt-Ridden Cities in America," February 23, 2012*
- Colorado Springs was identified as one of the top 25 U.S. cities with the most credit card debt by credit reporting bureau Experian. The city was ranked #15. *Experian, March 4, 2011*
- Colorado Springs was identified as one of the "Happiest Cities to Work in 2012" by *CareerBliss.com,* an online community for career advancement. The city ranked #43 out of 50. Criteria: independent company reviews from employees all over the country on: relationship with their boss and co-workers; work environment; job resources; growth opportunities; compensation; company culture; company reputation; daily tasks; job control over work performed on a daily basis. *CareerBliss.com, "Happiest and Unhappiest Cities to Work in 2012"*
- Colorado Springs was selected as one of the "100 Best Places to Live and Launch" in the U.S. The city ranked #28. The editors at *Fortune Small Business* ranked 296 Census-designated metro areas by business friendliness (Launching Score, % New Businesses) and lifestyle offerings (Living Score). Then they picked the town within each of the top 100 metro areas that best blends business and pleasure. *Fortune Small Business, "100 Best Places to Live and Launch 2008," April 2008*

- Colorado Springs was selected as one of the best cities in the world for telecommuting. The city ranked #19. The editors at *Cartridge Save* (printer technology news, guides and reviews) identified the 20 best cities in which to be an at-home, tech-using employee. *Cartridge Save, "20 of the Best Cities in the World for Telecommuting," May 14, 2008*

- *American City Business Journals* ranked America's 261 largest cities in terms of their resident's wealth. Colorado Springs ranked #125. Criteria: per capita income; median household income; percentage of households with annual incomes of $200,000 or more; median home value. *American City Business Journals, "Where the Money Is: America's Wealth Centers," August 18, 2008*

- The Colorado Springs metro area appeared on the Milken Institute "2011 Best Performing Metros" list. Rank: #81 out of 200 large metro areas. Criteria: job growth; wage and salary growth; high-tech output growth. *Milken Institute, "2011 Best Performing Metros"*

- The Colorado Springs metro area is projected to be one the best performing housing markets in 2012. The metro area ranked #8 out of 10. Criteria: forecast home price gains by September 2012. *CNNMoney.com, "Housing Markets: Best Recovery Bets," 2011*

- Colorado Springs was identified as one of the top 10 cities with the greatest number of *Inc. 500* companies per million residents. The city ranked #5. *Inc. Magazine, September 2008*

- Colorado Springs was ranked #26 out of 145 regions worldwide in terms of its "Knowledge Competitiveness Index." The index attempts to measure the knowledge-based development taking place throughout the world and is based on 19 measures of economic performance that indicate a region's ability to translate its knowledge capacity into economic value. *Centre for International Competitiveness, World Knowledge Competitiveness Index 2008*

- *Forbes* ranked the 200 most populous metro areas in the U.S. in terms of the "Best Places for Business and Careers." The Colorado Springs metro area was ranked #30. Criteria: costs (business and living); job growth (past and projected); income growth; educational attainment; projected economic growth; crime; cultural and recreational opportunities; net migration patterns; number of highly ranked colleges. *Forbes, "Best Places for Business and Careers," June 2011*

Children/Family Rankings

- Colorado Springs was selected as one of the safest cities for children in America by *Men's Health*. The city ranked #8 of 10. Criteria: accidental death rates for kids ages 5 to 14; number of car seat inspection locations per child; sex offenders per capita; percentage of abused children protected from further abuse; strength of child-restraint and bike-helmet laws. *Men's Health, "The Safest (and Least Safe) Cities for Children," September 2010*

- The Colorado Springs metro area was selected as one of the "Best Cities for Relocating Families" by Worldwide ERC and Primacy Relocation. The 2008 study looked at nearly 50 factors important to relocating families including: recent job growth; nearby top-ranked colleges; in-state tuition for four-year public colleges; population growth since 2000; pediatricians per 100,000 population; and a Green Living index. *Worldwide ERC and Primacy Relocation, "2008 Best Cities for Relocating Families"*

- *Fit Pregnancy* magazine ranked the 50 best U.S. cities in which to have a baby. Colorado Springs was ranked #14. Criteria: access to hospitals and doctors; affordability; birthing options; breastfeeding; child care; fertility laws/resources; maternal and infant health risk; parks/stroller friendliness; safety. *Fit Pregnancy, "The Best Cities in America to Have a Baby 2008"*

Culture/Performing Arts Rankings

- Colorado Springs was selected as one of "America's Top 25 Arts Destinations." The city ranked #17 in the mid-sized city (population 100,000 to 499,999) category. Criteria: readers' top choices for arts travel destinations based on the richness and variety of visual arts sites, activities and events. *American Style, "America's Top 25 Arts Destinations," May 2010*

Dating/Romance Rankings

- Colorado Springs appeared on *Men's Health's* list of the most sex-happy cities in America. The city ranked #52 of 100. Criteria: condom sales; birth rates; sex toy sales; rates of chlamydia, gonorrhea, and syphilis. *Men's Health, "America's Most Sex-Happy Cities," October 2010*
- *Men's Health* ranked 100 U.S. cities in terms of best (and worst) marriages. Colorado Springs was ranked #30 (#1 = worst). Criteria: rate of failed marriages; stringency of divorce laws; percentage of population who've split; number of licensed marriage and family therapists. *Men's Health, "Splitsville, USA," May 2010*
- The Colorado Springs metro area was selected as one of the "Best Cities for Relocating Singles" by Worldwide ERC and Primacy Relocation. The area ranked #38 out of the 100 largest metro areas in the U.S. Criteria: recent job growth; recent singles population growth; overall population growth; affordable rental housing; cost-of-living index; expanded arts and recreation opportunities; ratio of single men and single women; affordability of quality higher education (including state residency requirements); diversity index; climate; population density. *Worldwide ERC and Primacy Relocation, "2008 Best Cities for Relocating Singles"*

Education Rankings

- *Men's Health* ranked 100 U.S. cities in terms of their education levels. Colorado Springs was ranked #13 (#1 = most educated city). Criteria: high school graduation rates; school enrollment; educational attainment; number of households who have outstanding student loans; number of households whose members have taken adult-education courses. *Men's Health, "Where School Is In: The Most and Least Educated Cities," September 12, 2011*
- Colorado Springs was selected as one of "America's Most Literate Cities." The city ranked #26 out of the 75 largest U.S. cities. Criteria: number of booksellers; library resources; Internet resources; educational attainment; periodical publishing resources; newspaper circulation. *Central Connecticut State University, "America's Most Literate Cities 2011"*
- Colorado Springs was identified as one of the 100 "smartest" metro areas in the U.S. The area ranked #10. Criteria: the editors rated the collective brainpower of the 100 largest metro areas in the U.S. based on their residents' educational attainment. *American City Business Journals, April 14, 2008*
- Colorado Springs was identified as one of "America's Brainiest Bastions" by *Portfolio.com.* The metro area ranked #15 out of 200. *Portfolio.com* analyzed levels of educational attainment in the nation's 200 largest metropolitan areas. The editors established scores for five levels of educational attainment, based on relative earning power of adult workers age 25 or older. Scores were determined by comparing the median income for all workers with the median income for those workers at a specified educational level. *Portfolio.com, "America's Brainiest Bastions," December 1, 2010*

Environmental Rankings

- Colorado Springs was selected as one of 22 "Smarter Cities" for energy by the Natural Resources Defense Council. Criteria: investment in green power; energy efficiency measures; conservation. *Natural Resources Defense Council, "2010 Smarter Cities," July 19, 2010*
- 100 of the largest metro areas in the U.S. were analyzed in terms of their current drought severity. The Colorado Springs metro area ranked #81 (#1 = driest). The rankings were based on statistics such as long-term precipitation trends and patterns and the Palmer drought indices. *Sperling's BestPlaces, www.BestPlaces.net, "America's Drought-Riskiest Cities," November 2007*
- The U.S. Conference of Mayors and Wal-Mart Stores sponsor the Mayors' Climate Protection Awards Program. The awards recognize and honor mayors for outstanding and innovative practices that mayors are taking to increase energy efficiency in their cities, and to help curb global warming. Colorado Springs was a Large City Best Practice Model. *U.S. Conference of Mayors, "2009 Mayors' Climate Protection Awards Program"*
- The Colorado Springs metro area appeared in *Country Home's* "Best Green Places" report. The area ranked #41 out of 379. Criteria: official energy policies; green power; green buildings; availability of fresh, locally grown food. *Country Home, "Best Green Places," 2008*

- Colorado Springs was highlighted as one of the top 25 cleanest metro areas for short-term particle pollution (24-hour PM 2.5) in the U.S. Monitors in these cities reported no days with unhealthful PM 2.5 levels. *American Lung Association, State of the Air 2011*

Health/Fitness Rankings

- The Colorado Springs metro area was selected as one of the worst cities for bed bugs in America by Rollins corporation, the owner of seven pest control companies, including Orkin. The area ranked #25 based on the number of bed bug treatments from January to December 2011. *Rollins, "The Top 50 U.S. Cities for Bed Bugs," March 19, 2012*
- Colorado Springs was selected as one of the 25 fittest cities in America by *Men's Fitness Online*. It ranked #13 out of America's 50 largest cities. Criteria: fitness centers and sport stores; nutrition; sports participation; TV viewing; overweight/sedentary; junk food; air quality; geography; commute; parks and open space; city recreational facilities; access to healthcare; motivation; mayor and city initiatives; state obesity initiatives. *Men's Fitness, "The Fittest and Fattest Cities in America," March 5, 2012*
- Colorado Springs was identified as a "2011 Asthma Capital." The area ranked #98 out of the nation's 100 largest metropolitan areas. Twelve factors were used to identify the most challenging places to live for people with asthma: estimated prevalence; self-reported prevalence; crude death rate for asthma; annual pollen score; annual air quality; public smoking laws; number of board-certified asthma specialists; school inhaler access laws; rescue medication use; controller medication use; uninsured rate; poverty rate. *Asthma and Allergy Foundation of America, "2011 Asthma Capitals"*
- Colorado Springs was identified as a "2011 Fall Allergy Capital." The area ranked #87 out of 100. Three groups of factors were used to identify the most severe cities for people with allergies during the fall season: annual pollen levels; medicine utilization; access to board-certified allergists. *Asthma and Allergy Foundation of America, "2011 Fall Allergy Capitals"*
- Colorado Springs was identified as a "2012 Spring Allergy Capital." The area ranked #93 out of 100. Three groups of factors were used to identify the most severe cities for people with allergies during the spring season: annual pollen levels; medicine utilization; access to board-certified allergists. *Asthma and Allergy Foundation of America, "2012 Spring Allergy Capitals"*
- *Men's Health* examined 100 major U.S. cities and selected the best and worst cities for men. Colorado Springs ranked #18. Criteria: 35 statistical parameters of long life in the categories of health, quality of life, and fitness. *Men's Health, "The 10 Best and Worst Cities for Men 2012," January/February 2012*
- The Colorado Springs metropolitan area was selected as one of the best metros for hospital care in America by *HealthGrades.com.* The rankings are based on a comprehensive study of patient death and complication rates in the nation's nearly 5,000 hospitals. Hospitals performing in the top 5% nationwide across 26 different medical procedures and diagnoses were identified. *HealthGrades.com* then ranked cities by the highest percentage of these Distinguished Hospitals for Clinical Excellence™. The Colorado Springs metro area ranked #28. *HealthGrades.com, "America's Top 50 Cities for Hospital Care," January 21, 2012*
- The Colorado Springs metro area appeared in the 2011 Gallup-Healthways Well-Being Index. The index, based on interviews with more than 350,000 Americans, measured jobs, finances, physical health, emotional state of mind and communities. The metro area ranked #38 out of 190. Criteria: life evaluation; emotional health; work environment; physical health; healthy behaviors; basic access (basic needs optimal for a healthy life, such as access to food and medicine, having health insurance and feeling safe while walking at night). *Gallup-Healthways, "State of Well-Being 2011"*
- *Men's Health* ranked 100 U.S. cities in terms of their activity levels. Colorado Springs was ranked #29 (#1 = most active city). Criteria: where and how often residents exercise; percentage of households that watch more than 15 hours of cable television a week and buy more than 11 video games a year; death rate from deep-vein thrombosis, a condition linked to sitting for extended periods of time. *Men's Health, "Where Sit Happens: The Most and Least Active Cities in America," June 20, 2011*

Pet Rankings

- Colorado Springs was selected as one of the best places to live with pets by *Livability.com.* The city was ranked #2. Criteria: pet-friendly parks and trails; quality veterinary care; active animal welfare groups; abundance of pet boutiques and retail shops; excellent quality of life for pet owners. *Livability.com, "Top 10 Pet Friendly Cities," October 20, 2010*

Real Estate Rankings

- Colorado Springs was selected as one of five U.S. cities that may offer exceptional values for home buyers in this economy by *Kiplinger's Personal Finance.* The city ranked #4. Criteria: reasonable living costs; high quality of life; vibrant economies; great amenities. *Kiplinger's Personal Finance, "Best Cities for Housing Values, 2011" August 9, 2011*
- Colorado Springs appeared on *ApartmentRatings.com* "Top Cities for Renters" list in 2009." The area ranked #18. Overall satisfaction ratings were ranked using thousands of user submitted scores for hundreds of apartment complexes located in the 100 most populated U.S. municipalities. *ApartmentRatings.com, "2009 Renter Satisfaction Rankings"*
- The Center for Housing Policy ranked 210 U.S. metropolitan areas by the fair market rent for a two-bedroom unit. The Colorado Springs metro area was ranked #121. (#1 = most expensive) with a rent of $795. Criteria: Fair Market Rent (FMR) in effect during the fourth quarter of 2009 based on HUD's fiscal year 2010 FMRs. *The Center for Housing Policy, "Paycheck to Paycheck: Most to Least Expensive Rental Markets in 2009"*
- The Colorado Springs metro area was identified as one of the best U.S. markets to invest in rental property" by HomeVestors and Local Market Monitor. The area ranked #41 out of 100. Criteria: risk-return premium relative to national average. *HomeVestors and Local Market Monitor, "Best 100 U.S. Markets to Invest in Rental Property," March 9, 2012*

Safety Rankings

- Symantec, the makers of Norton, in partnership with Sperling's BestPlaces, ranked the 50 largest cities in the U.S. in terms of their vulnerability to cybercrime. The city ranked #20. Criteria: number of cyberattacks and potential infections; level of Internet access; expenditures on smartphones and computer hardware/software; wireless hotspots; broadband connectivity; Internet usage; online purchases. *Symantec, "Riskiest Online Cities of 2012" February 15, 2012*
- Farmers Insurance Group of Companies, in partnership with Sperling's BestPlaces, ranked 379 metro areas and identified the "Most Secure U.S. Places to Live." The Colorado Springs metro area ranked #17 out of the top 20 in the large metro area category (500,000 or more residents). Criteria: crime statistics; extreme weather; risk of natural disasters; housing depreciation; foreclosures; environmental hazards; terrorist threats; air quality; life expectancy; mortality rates from cancer and motor vehicle accidents; job loss numbers. *Farmers Insurance Group, "Most Secure U.S. Places to Live 2011," December 15, 2011*
- Allstate ranked the 193 largest cities in America in terms of driver safety. Colorado Springs ranked #11. In addition, drivers were 16.1% less likely to have had an accident compared to the national average. Allstate researchers analyzed internal property damage reported claims over a two-year period (from January 2008 to December 2009) to protect findings from external influences such as weather or road construction. A weighted average of the two-year numbers determined the annual percentages. The report defines an auto crash as any collision resulting in a property damage claim. *Allstate, "2011 Allstate America's Best Drivers Report™"*
- Colorado Springs was selected as one of "America's Safest Cities" by *Forbes.* The city ranked #8 out of 10. Criteria: violent crime rates; traffic fatalities per 100,000 residents. The editors only considered cities with populations above 250,000. *Forbes, "America's Safest Cities," December 15, 2011*
- The National Insurance Crime Bureau ranked 366 metro areas in the U.S. in terms of per capita rates of vehicle theft. The Colorado Springs metro area ranked #97 (#1 = highest rate). Criteria: number of vehicle theft offenses per 100,000 inhabitants in 2010. *National Insurance Crime Bureau, "Hot Spots," June 21, 2011*

Seniors/Retirement Rankings

- The Colorado Springs metro area was identified as one of the "Best Places for Bargain Retirement Homes" by *Forbes*. The metro area ranked #10 out of 10. Criteria: low cost of living; stable home prices; low taxes; reasonable average home prices. *Forbes.com, "Best Places for Bargain Retirement Homes," January 12, 2011*
- Colorado Springs was selected as one of the best affordable mountain towns for retirement by *U.S. News & World Report.* Criteria: access to skiing, trails, and wildlife; affordable housing; reasonable cost of living; access to healthcare; low crime rate. *U.S. News & World Report, "10 Best Affordable Mountain Towns for Retirement," July 12, 2010*
- Colorado Springs was identified as one of the "100 Most Popular Retirement Towns" by *Topretirements.com* The list reflects the 100 cities (out of 815+ total cities reviewed) that visitors to the website are most interested in for retirement. *Topretirements.com, "100 Most Popular Retirement Towns," February 21, 2012*
- Colorado Springs was selected as one of "The Best Retirement Places" by *Forbes.* The magazine considered a wide range of factors such as climate, availability of doctors, driving environment, and crime rates, but focused especially on tax burden and cost of living. *Forbes, "The Best Retirement Places," March 27, 2011*

Sports/Recreation Rankings

- Colorado Springs appeared on the *Sporting News* list of the "Best Sports Cities" for 2011. The area ranked #87 out of 271 cities in the U.S. *Sporting News* takes a 12-month snapshot of each city's sports, putting a heavy premium on regular-season won-lost records (from the most recently completed season). Other criteria include: playoff berths, bowl appearances and tournament bids; championships; applicable power ratings; quality of competition; overall fan fervor (measured in part by attendance); abundance of teams (rewarding quality over quantity); stadium and arena quality; ticket availability and prices; franchise ownership; and marquee appeal of athletes. *Sporting News, "Best Sports Cities 2011," October 4, 2011*
- Colorado Springs was chosen as a bicycle friendly community by the League of American Bicyclists. A Bicycle Friendly Community welcomes cyclists by providing safe accommodation for cycling and encouraging people to bike for transportation and recreation. There are four award levels: Platinum; Gold; Silver; and Bronze. The community achieved an award level of Silver. *League of American Bicyclists, "Bicycle Friendly Community Master List 2011"*
- Colorado Springs was chosen as one of America's best cities for bicycling. The city ranked #18 out of 50. Criteria: number of segregated bike lanes, municipal bike racks, and bike boulevards; vibrant and diverse bike culture; smart, savvy bike shops; interviews with national and local advocates, bike shops and other experts. The editors only considered cities with populations of 100,000 or more. *Bicycling, "America's Best Bike Cities," April 2010*

Technology Rankings

- The Colorado Springs metro area was selected as one of "America's Most Wired Cities" by *Forbes*. The metro area was ranked #6 out of 20. Criteria: percentage of Internet users with high-speed access; number of companies providing high-speed Internet; number of public wireless hot spots. *Forbes, "America's Most Wired Cities," March 2, 2010*
- Scarborough Research, a leading market research firm, identified the Colorado Springs DMA (Designated Market Area) as one of the top markets for text messaging with more than 50% of cell phone subscribers age 18+ utilizing the text messaging feature on their phone. *Scarborough Research, November 24, 2008*

Transportation Rankings

- Colorado Springs appeared on *Trapster.com's* list of the 10 most-active U.S. cities for speed traps. The city ranked #9 of 10. *Trapster.com* is a community platform accessed online and via smartphone app that alerts drivers to traps, hazards and other traffic issues nearby. *Trapster.com, "Speeders Beware: Cities With the Most Speed Traps," February 10, 2012*

- Colorado Springs was identified as one of America's worst cities for speed traps by the National Motorists Association. The city ranked #8 out of 25. Criteria: speed trap locations per 100,000 residents. *National Motorists Association, September 2011*

Women/Minorities Rankings

- *Women's Health* examined U.S. cities and identified the 100 best cities for women. Colorado Springs was ranked #29. Criteria: 30 categories were examined from obesity and breast cancer rates to commuting times and hours spent working out. *Women's Health, "Best Cities for Women 2012"*

- Colorado Springs was ranked #43 out of 100 metro areas in *SELF Magazine's* ranking of America's healthiest places for women." A panel of experts came up with more than 50 criteria including death and disease rates, environmental indicators, community resources, and lifestyle habits. *SELF Magazine, "Secrets of America's Healthiest Women," December 2008*

Miscellaneous Rankings

- *Men's Health* ranked 100 U.S. cities by their level of sadness. Colorado Springs was ranked #63 (#1 = saddest city). Criteria: suicide rates; unemployment rates; percentage of households that use antidepressants; percent of population who report feeling blue all or most of the time. *Men's Health, "Frown Towns," November 28, 2011*

- The Colorado Springs metro area was selected as one of "5 Great Cities for Young Adults" by *Kiplinger.com.* Criteria: high starting salaries for college graduates; cost of living near or below national average; affordable monthly rent; percentage of residents ages 20 to 29 near or above national average. *Kiplinger.com, "5 Great Cities for Young Adults," October 25, 2011*

- The Colorado Springs metro area appeared in *AutoMD.com's* ranking of the "Best and Worst Cities for Auto Repair." The metro area ranked #18 (#1 is best). The 50 most-populated metro areas in the U.S. were ranked on three critical factors: repair affordability; price disparity range; shop integrity factor. *AutoMD.com, "Advocacy for Repair Shop Fairness Report," February 24, 2010*

Business Environment

CITY FINANCES

City Government Finances

Component	2009 ($000)	2009 ($ per capita)
Total Revenues	1,775,707	4,717
Total Expenditures	1,793,217	4,764
Debt Outstanding	2,838,531	7,541
Cash and Securities[1]	181,445	482

Note: (1) Cash and security holdings of a government at the close of its fiscal year, including those of its dependent agencies, utilities, and liquor stores.
Source: U.S Census Bureau, State & Local Government Finances 2009

City Government Revenue by Source

Source	2009 ($000)	2009 ($ per capita)
General Revenue		
From Federal Government	30,184	80
From State Government	17,482	46
From Local Governments	8,607	23
Taxes		
Property	24,685	66
Sales and Gross Receipts	180,857	480
Personal Income	0	0
Corporate Income	0	0
Motor Vehicle License	0	0
Other Taxes	651	2
Current Charges	670,816	1,782
Liquor Store	0	0
Utility	728,154	1,934
Employee Retirement	0	0

Source: U.S Census Bureau, State & Local Government Finances 2009

City Government Expenditures by Function

Function	2009 ($000)	2009 ($ per capita)	2009 (%)
General Direct Expenditures			
Air Transportation	36,908	98	2.1
Corrections	0	0	0.0
Education	0	0	0.0
Employment Security Administration	0	0	0.0
Financial Administration	69,041	183	3.9
Fire Protection	39,575	105	2.2
General Public Buildings	0	0	0.0
Governmental Administration, Other	5,682	15	0.3
Health	1,174	3	0.1
Highways	77,453	206	4.3
Hospitals	499,446	1,327	27.9
Housing and Community Development	5,957	16	0.3
Interest on General Debt	7,429	20	0.4
Judicial and Legal	7,832	21	0.4
Libraries	8	< 1	< 0.1
Parking	2,464	7	0.1
Parks and Recreation	24,993	66	1.4
Police Protection	81,530	217	4.5
Public Welfare	0	0	0.0
Sewerage	66,287	176	3.7
Solid Waste Management	0	0	0.0
Veterans' Services	0	0	0.0
Liquor Store	0	0	0.0
Utility	775,487	2,060	43.2
Employee Retirement	0	0	0.0

Source: U.S Census Bureau, State & Local Government Finances 2009

Municipal Bond Ratings

Area	Moody's	S&P	Fitch
City	n/a	n/a	n/a

Rating Systems (shown in declining order of credit quality): Moody's– Aaa, Aa, A, Baa, Ba, B, Caa, Ca, C (numerical modifiers 1, 2, and 3 are added to letter-rating); S&P– AAA, AA, A, BBB, BB, B, CCC, CC, C; Fitch– AAA, AA, A, BBB, BB, B, CCC, CC, C. Ratings may be modified by the addition of a plus or minus sign to show relative standing within the major rating categories.
Notes: n/a Not Available; w/d Withdrawn (1) Not Reviewed; (2) Issuer Rating/No General Obligation; (3) Standard and Poor's Issue Credit Rating (ICR) is a current opinion of an obliger with respect to a specific financial obligation, a specific class of financial obligations, or a specific financial program.
Source: U.S. Census Bureau, 2012 Statistical Abstract, Bond Ratings for City Governments by Largest Cities: 2010

DEMOGRAPHICS

Population Growth

Area	1990 Census	2000 Census	2010 Census	Population Growth (%)	
				1990-2000	2000-2010
City	283,798	360,890	416,427	27.2	15.4
MSA[1]	409,482	537,484	645,613	31.3	20.1
U.S.	248,709,873	281,421,906	308,745,538	13.2	9.7

Note: (1) Figures cover the Colorado Springs, CO Metropolitan Statistical Area—see Appendix B for areas included
Source: U.S. Census Bureau, 2010 Census

Household Size

Area	Persons in Household (%)							Average Household Size
	One	Two	Three	Four	Five	Six	Seven or More	
City	29.6	33.2	15.6	12.5	5.7	2.2	1.2	2.44
MSA[1]	25.9	33.8	16.3	13.8	6.4	2.5	1.3	2.55
U.S.	26.7	32.8	16.1	13.4	6.5	2.6	1.9	2.58

Note: (1) Figures cover the Colorado Springs, CO Metropolitan Statistical Area—see Appendix B for areas included
Source: U.S. Census Bureau, 2010 Census

Race

Area	White Alone[2] (%)	Black Alone[2] (%)	Asian Alone[2] (%)	AIAN[3] Alone[2] (%)	NHOPI[4] Alone[2] (%)	Other Race Alone[2] (%)	Two or More Races (%)
City	78.8	6.3	3.0	1.0	0.3	5.5	5.1
MSA[1]	80.3	6.0	2.7	1.0	0.3	4.8	5.0
U.S.	72.4	12.6	4.8	0.9	0.2	6.2	2.9

Note: (1) Figures cover the Colorado Springs, CO Metropolitan Statistical Area—see Appendix B for areas included; (2) Alone is defined as not being in combination with one or more other races; (3) American Indian and Alaska Native; (4) Native Hawaiian and Other Pacific Islander
Source: U.S. Census Bureau, 2010 Census

Hispanic or Latino Origin

Area	Hispanic or Latino (%)	Mexican (%)	Puerto Rican (%)	Cuban (%)	Other Hispanic or Latino (%)
City	16.1	10.6	1.1	0.2	4.1
MSA[1]	14.7	9.5	1.2	0.2	3.8
U.S.	16.3	10.3	1.5	0.6	4.0

Note: Persons of Hispanic or Latino origin can be of any race; (1) Figures cover the Colorado Springs, CO Metropolitan Statistical Area—see Appendix B for areas included
Source: U.S. Census Bureau, 2010 Census

Segregation

Type	Segregation Indices[1]				Percent Change		
	1990	2000	2010	2010 Rank[2]	1990-2000	1990-2010	2000-2010
Black/White	44.6	43.3	39.3	92	-1.3	-5.3	-4.0
Asian/White	28.5	25.2	24.1	98	-3.2	-4.3	-1.1
Hispanic/White	27.8	31.5	30.3	95	3.7	2.5	-1.3

Note: Figures are based on an analysis of 1990, 2000, and 2010 Census Decennial Census tract data by William H. Frey, Brookings Institution and the University of Michigan Social Science Data Analysis Network. In this analysis all racial groups (whites, blacks, and asians) are non-Hispanic members of those races. Hispanics are shown as a separate category; All figures cover the Metropolitan Statistical Area (see Appendix B for areas included); (1) Segregation Indices are Dissimilarity Indices that measure the degree to which the minority group is distributed differently than whites across census tracts. They range from 0 (complete integration) to 100 (complete segregation) where the value indicates the percentage of the minority group that needs to move to be distributed exactly like whites; (2) Ranges from 1 (most segregated) to 102 (least segregated); n/a not available.
Source: www.CensusScope.org

Ancestry

Area	German	Irish	English	American	Italian	Polish	French[2]	Scottish	Dutch
City	22.0	13.2	12.1	4.5	5.5	2.5	3.8	2.8	1.8
MSA[1]	22.4	13.5	12.1	5.1	5.1	2.7	3.7	2.8	1.9
U.S.	16.1	11.6	8.8	6.1	5.7	3.2	3.0	1.9	1.6

Note: Figures are the percentage of the total population reporting a particular ancestry. The nine most commonly reported ancestries in the U.S. are shown. Figures include multiple ancestries (e.g. if a person reported being Irish and Italian, they were included in both columns); (1) Figures cover the Colorado Springs, CO Metropolitan Statistical Area—see Appendix B for areas included; (2) Excludes Basque
Source: U.S. Census Bureau, 2008-2010 American Community Survey 3-Year Estimates

Foreign-Born Population

Area	Percent of Population Born in								
	Any Foreign Country	Mexico	Asia	Europe	Carribean	South America	Central America[2]	Africa	Canada
City	7.9	2.2	2.3	1.7	0.2	0.2	0.4	0.3	0.5
MSA[1]	6.9	1.8	2.0	1.7	0.2	0.2	0.4	0.2	0.4
U.S.	12.8	3.8	3.6	1.6	1.2	0.9	1.0	0.5	0.3

Note: (1) Figures cover the Colorado Springs, CO Metropolitan Statistical Area—see Appendix B for areas included; (2) Excludes Mexico.
Source: U.S. Census Bureau, 2008-2010 American Community Survey 3-Year Estimates

Marital Status

Area	Never Married	Now Married[2]	Separated	Widowed	Divorced
City	28.6	51.1	2.3	4.8	13.2
MSA[1]	27.7	53.7	2.0	4.4	12.2
U.S.	31.6	49.6	2.2	6.1	10.7

Note: Figures are percentages and cover the population 15 years of age and older; (1) Figures cover the Colorado Springs, CO Metropolitan Statistical Area—see Appendix B for areas included; (2) Excludes separated
Source: U.S. Census Bureau, 2008-2010 American Community Survey 3-Year Estimates

Age

Area	Percent of Population							Median Age
	Under Age 5	Age 5 to 17	Age 18 to 34	Age 35 to 49	Age 50 to 64	Age 65 to 79	80 Years and Over	
City	7.1	17.9	25.1	20.6	18.4	8.0	2.9	34.9
MSA[1]	7.2	18.8	24.6	20.8	18.6	7.7	2.4	34.6
U.S.	6.5	17.5	23.2	20.7	19.0	9.4	3.6	37.2

Note: (1) Figures cover the Colorado Springs, CO Metropolitan Statistical Area—see Appendix B for areas included
Source: U.S. Census Bureau, 2010 Census

Male/Female Ratio

Area	Males	Females	Males per 100 Females
City	203,944	212,483	96.0
MSA[1]	322,047	323,566	99.5
U.S.	151,781,326	156,964,212	96.7

Note: (1) Figures cover the Colorado Springs, CO Metropolitan Statistical Area—see Appendix B for areas included
Source: U.S. Census Bureau, 2010 Census

Religious Groups

Area	Catholic	Baptist	Non-Den.	Methodist[2]	Lutheran	LDS[3]	Pentecostal	Presbyterian[4]	Muslim[5]	Judaism
MSA[1]	8.4	4.3	7.4	2.4	2.0	3.0	1.1	2.1	0.1	0.1
U.S.	19.1	9.3	4.0	4.0	2.3	2.0	1.9	1.6	0.8	0.7

Note: Figures are the number of adherents as a percentage of the total population; (1) Figures cover the Colorado Springs, CO Metropolitan Statistical Area—see Appendix B for areas included; (2) Methodist/Pietist; (3) Latter Day Saints; (4) Reformed; (5) Figures are estimates
Source: Association of Statisticians of American Religious Bodies, 2010 U.S. Religion Census: Religious Congregations & Membership Study

ECONOMY

Gross Metropolitan Product

Area	2007	2008	2009	2010	2010 Rank[2]
MSA[1]	23.9	24.5	25.2	26.4	81

Note: Figures are in billions of dollars; (1) Figures cover the Colorado Springs, CO Metropolitan Statistical Area—see Appendix B for areas included; (2) Rank ranges from 1 to 363
Source: The United States Conference of Mayors, "U.S. Metro Economies: GMP and Employment Forecasts," June 2011

Economic Growth

Area	2007-2009 (%)	2010 (%)	2011 (%)	Rank[2]
MSA[1]	1.8	4.1	2.7	37
U.S.	-1.3	2.9	2.5	–

Note: Figures are real Gross Metropolitan Product growth rates and represent annual average percent change; (1) Figures cover the Colorado Springs, CO Metropolitan Statistical Area—see Appendix B for areas included; (2) Rank ranges from 1 to 363
Source: The United States Conference of Mayors, "U.S. Metro Economies: GMP and Employment Forecasts," June 2011

Metropolitan Area Exports

Area	2005	2006	2007	2008	2009	2010	2010 Rank[2]
MSA[1]	1,968.2	2,227.4	1,825.8	1,932.4	1,281.1	1,193.1	119

Note: Figures are in millions of dollars; (1) Figures cover the Colorado Springs, CO Metropolitan Statistical Area—see Appendix B for areas included; (2) Rank ranges from 1 to 369
Source: U.S. Department of Commerce, International Trade Administration, Office of Trade & Industry Information, Manufacturing & Services, data extracted April 2, 2012

INCOME

Income

Area	Per Capita ($)	Median Household ($)	Average Household ($)
City	27,753	52,179	68,046
MSA[1]	27,391	55,166	70,491
U.S.	26,942	51,222	70,116

Note: (1) Figures cover the Colorado Springs, CO Metropolitan Statistical Area—see Appendix B for areas included
Source: U.S. Census Bureau, 2008-2010 American Community Survey 3-Year Estimates

Household Income Distribution

Area	Under $15,000	$15,000 -24,999	$25,000 -34,999	$35,000 -49,999	$50,000 -74,999	$75,000 -99,000	$100,000 -149,999	$150,000 and up
	Percent of Households Earning							
City	11.9	11.0	10.4	14.2	20.6	11.7	13.0	7.3
MSA[1]	10.8	9.9	9.7	14.3	20.9	12.7	14.1	7.8
U.S.	13.0	11.0	10.6	14.2	18.5	12.1	12.2	8.4

Note: (1) Figures cover the Colorado Springs, CO Metropolitan Statistical Area—see Appendix B for areas included
Source: U.S. Census Bureau, 2008-2010 American Community Survey 3-Year Estimates

Poverty Rate

Area	All Ages	Under 18 Years Old	18 to 64 Years Old	65 Years and Over
City	13.0	18.1	12.1	6.1
MSA[1]	12.1	17.0	11.0	5.7
U.S.	14.4	20.1	13.1	9.4

Note: Figures are percentage of people whose income during the past 12 months was below the poverty level; (1) Figures cover the Colorado Springs, CO Metropolitan Statistical Area—see Appendix B for areas included
Source: U.S. Census Bureau, 2008-2010 American Community Survey 3-Year Estimates

Personal Bankruptcy Filing Rate

Area	2006	2007	2008	2009	2010	2011
El Paso County	1.94	3.27	4.59	5.55	6.08	5.07
U.S.	2.00	2.73	3.53	4.61	4.97	4.37

Note: Numbers are per 1,000 population and include Chapter 7 and Chapter 13 filings
Source: Federal Deposit Insurance Corporation, Regional Economic Conditions, March 9, 2012

EMPLOYMENT

Labor Force and Employment

Area	Civilian Labor Force			Workers Employed		
	Dec. 2010	Dec. 2011	% Chg.	Dec. 2010	Dec. 2011	% Chg.
City	209,764	210,018	0.1	190,593	191,463	0.5
MSA[1]	304,273	304,234	0.0	275,536	276,793	0.5
U.S.	153,156,000	153,373,000	0.1	139,159,000	140,681,000	1.1

Note: Data is not seasonally adjusted and covers workers 16 years of age and older; (1) Metropolitan Statistical Area—see Appendix B for areas included
Source: Bureau of Labor Statistics, http://stats.bls.gov

Unemployment Rate

Area	2011											
	Jan.	Feb.	Mar.	Apr.	May	Jun.	Jul.	Aug.	Sep.	Oct.	Nov.	Dec.
City	10.4	10.2	9.8	8.9	9.1	9.6	9.4	9.1	8.4	8.5	8.5	8.8
MSA[1]	10.7	10.5	10.1	9.1	9.3	9.8	9.6	9.3	8.6	8.6	8.7	9.0
U.S.	9.8	9.5	9.2	8.7	8.7	9.3	9.3	9.1	8.8	8.5	8.2	8.3

Note: Data is not seasonally adjusted and covers workers 16 years of age and older; All figures are percentages; (1) Metropolitan Statistical Area—see Appendix B for areas included
Source: Bureau of Labor Statistics, http://stats.bls.gov

Projected Unemployment Rate

Area	2010 (%)	2011 (%)	2012 (%)	2013 (%)
MSA[1]	9.9	9.4	8.6	7.8

Note: (1) Metropolitan Statistical Area—see Appendix B for areas included
Source: The United States Conference of Mayors, "U.S. Metro Economies: GMP and Employment Forecasts," June 2011

Employment by Occupation

Occupation Classification	City (%)	MSA[1] (%)	U.S. (%)
Management, Business, Science, and Arts	39.8	40.1	35.6
Natural Resources, Construction, and Maintenance	8.5	8.6	9.5
Production, Transportation, and Material Moving	8.5	8.6	12.1
Sales and Office	24.7	24.4	25.2
Service	18.5	18.2	17.6

Note: Figures cover employed civilians 16 years of age and older; (1) Figures cover the Colorado Springs, CO Metropolitan Statistical Area—see Appendix B for areas included
Source: U.S. Census Bureau, 2008-2010 American Community Survey 3-Year Estimates

Employment by Industry

Sector	MSA[1]		U.S.
	Number of Employees	Percent of Total	Percent of Total
Construction	n/a	n/a	4.1
Education and Health Services	30,900	12.5	15.2
Financial Activities	16,200	6.5	5.8
Government	49,500	20.0	16.8
Information	7,200	2.9	2.0
Leisure and Hospitality	29,000	11.7	9.9
Manufacturing	12,600	5.1	8.9
Mining and Logging	n/a	n/a	0.6
Other Services	14,200	5.7	4.0
Professional and Business Services	38,300	15.5	13.3
Retail Trade	29,200	11.8	11.5
Transportation and Utilities	4,500	1.8	3.8
Wholesale Trade	4,900	2.0	4.2

Note: Figures cover non-farm employment as of December 2011 and are not seasonally adjusted; (1) Metropolitan Statistical Area—see Appendix B for areas included; n/a not available
Source: Bureau of Labor Statistics, http://stats.bls.gov

Occupations with Greatest Projected Employment Growth: 2008 – 2018

Occupation[1]	2008 Employment	2018 Projected Employment	Numeric Employment Change	Percent Employment Change
Registered Nurses	40,880	53,130	12,250	30.0
Combined Food Preparation and Serving Workers, Including Fast Food	51,320	62,180	10,860	21.2
Customer Service Representatives	38,300	44,710	6,410	16.7
Postsecondary Teachers	24,980	31,030	6,050	24.2
Waiters and Waitresses	45,430	50,990	5,560	12.2
Computer Software Engineers, Applications	16,410	21,540	5,130	31.3
Personal and Home Care Aides	11,520	16,460	4,940	42.9
Retail Salespersons	79,820	84,660	4,840	6.1
Janitors and Cleaners, Except Maids and Housekeeping Cleaners	36,660	41,040	4,380	11.9
Nursing Aides, Orderlies, and Attendants	18,580	22,160	3,580	19.3

Note: Projections cover Colorado; (1) Sorted by numeric employment change
Source: www.projectionscentral.com, State Occupational Projections, 2008–2018 Long-Term Projections

Fastest Growing Occupations: 2008 – 2018

Occupation[1]	2008 Employment	2018 Projected Employment	Numeric Employment Change	Percent Employment Change
Personal and Home Care Aides	11,520	16,460	4,940	42.9
Network Systems and Data Communications Analysts	6,070	8,650	2,580	42.5
Air Traffic Controllers	640	900	260	40.6
Forensic Science Technicians	310	430	120	38.7
Pharmacy Technicians	4,250	5,860	1,610	37.9
Cardiovascular Technologists and Technicians	650	870	220	33.8
Physical Therapist Assistants	700	930	230	32.9
Medical Assistants	7,080	9,400	2,320	32.8
Skin Care Specialists	1,130	1,500	370	32.7
Computer Software Engineers, Applications	16,410	21,540	5,130	31.3

Note: Projections cover Colorado; (1) Sorted by percent employment change and excludes occupations with numeric employment change less than 100
Source: www.projectionscentral.com, State Occupational Projections, 2008–2018 Long-Term Projections

Average Wages

Occupation	$/Hr.	Occupation	$/Hr.
Accountants and Auditors	29.17	Maids and Housekeeping Cleaners	9.70
Automotive Mechanics	22.11	Maintenance and Repair Workers	17.32
Bookkeepers	16.11	Marketing Managers	53.96
Carpenters	18.63	Nuclear Medicine Technologists	33.32
Cashiers	9.47	Nurses, Licensed Practical	20.27
Clerks, General Office	13.57	Nurses, Registered	31.91
Clerks, Receptionists/Information	12.62	Nursing Aides/Orderlies/Attendants	12.33
Clerks, Shipping/Receiving	14.51	Packers and Packagers, Hand	10.10
Computer Programmers	39.49	Physical Therapists	34.27
Computer Support Specialists	25.76	Postal Service Mail Carriers	25.20
Computer Systems Analysts	41.38	Real Estate Brokers	24.31
Cooks, Restaurant	11.48	Retail Salespersons	12.71
Dentists	65.74	Sales Reps., Exc. Tech./Scientific	28.07
Electrical Engineers	40.22	Sales Reps., Tech./Scientific	35.20
Electricians	23.70	Secretaries, Exc. Legal/Med./Exec.	15.48
Financial Managers	55.99	Security Guards	14.02
First-Line Supervisors/Managers, Sales	18.08	Surgeons	n/a
Food Preparation Workers	9.69	Teacher Assistants	11.80
General and Operations Managers	49.73	Teachers, Elementary School	22.00
Hairdressers/Cosmetologists	12.33	Teachers, Secondary School	22.30
Internists	n/a	Telemarketers	11.15
Janitors and Cleaners	12.91	Truck Drivers, Heavy/Tractor-Trailer	16.82
Landscaping/Groundskeeping Workers	12.76	Truck Drivers, Light/Delivery Svcs.	15.00
Lawyers	49.49	Waiters and Waitresses	9.27

Note: Wage data covers the Colorado Springs, CO Metropolitan Statistical Area—see Appendix B for areas included. Hourly wages for elementary/secondary school teachers and teacher assistants were calculated by the editors from annual wage data assuming a 40 hour work week; n/a not available.
Source: Bureau of Labor Statistics, Metro Area Occupational Employment and Wage Estimates, May 2011

RESIDENTIAL REAL ESTATE

Building Permits

Area	Single-Family			Multi-Family			Total		
	2010	2011	Pct. Chg.	2010	2011	Pct. Chg.	2010	2011	Pct. Chg.
City	n/a	n/a	n/a	n/a	n/a	n/a	n/a	n/a	n/a
MSA[1]	1,676	1,616	-3.6	84	659	684.5	1,760	2,275	29.3
U.S.	447,311	418,498	-6.4	157,299	205,563	30.7	604,610	624,061	3.2

Note: (1) Metropolitan Statistical Area—see Appendix B for areas included; figures represent new, privately-owned housing units authorized (unadjusted data); All permit data are based on estimates with imputation.
Source: U.S. Census Bureau, Manufacturing, Mining, and Construction Statistics, Building Permits, 2010, 2011

Homeownership Rate

Area	2005 (%)	2006 (%)	2007 (%)	2008 (%)	2009 (%)	2010 (%)	2011 (%)
MSA[1]	n/a	n/a	n/a	n/a	n/a	n/a	n/a
U.S.	68.9	68.8	68.1	67.8	67.4	66.9	66.1

Note: (1) Metropolitan Statistical Area—see Appendix B for areas included; n/a not available
Source: U.S. Census Bureau, Housing Vacancies and Homeownership Annual Statistics: 2011

Housing Vacancy Rates

Area	Gross Vacancy Rate[2] (%)			Year-Round Vacancy Rate[3] (%)			Rental Vacancy Rate[4] (%)			Homeowner Vacancy Rate[5] (%)		
	2009	2010	2011	2009	2010	2011	2009	2010	2011	2009	2010	2011
MSA[1]	n/a	n/a	n/a	n/a	n/a	n/a	n/a	n/a	n/a	n/a	n/a	n/a
U.S.	14.5	14.3	14.2	11.3	11.3	11.1	10.6	10.2	9.5	2.6	2.6	2.5

Note: (1) Metropolitan Statistical Area—see Appendix B for areas included; (2) The percentage of the total housing inventory that is vacant; (3) The percentage of the housing inventory (excluding seasonal units) that is year-round vacant; (4) The percentage of rental inventory that is vacant for rent; (5) The percentage of homeowner inventory that is vacant for sale; n/a not available
Source: U.S. Census Bureau, Housing Vacancies and Homeownership Annual Statistics: 2011

TAXES

State Corporate Income Tax Rates

State	Tax Rate (%)	Income Brackets ($)	Num. of Brackets	Financial Institution Tax Rate (%)[a]	Federal Income Tax Ded.
Colorado	4.63	Flat rate	1	4.63	No

Note: Tax rates as of January 1, 2012; (a) Rates listed are the corporate income tax rate applied to financial institutions or excise taxes based on income. Some states have other taxes based upon the value of deposits or shares.
Source: Federation of Tax Administrators, "State Corporate Income Tax Rates, 2012"

State Individual Income Tax Rates

State	Tax Rate (%)	Income Brackets ($)	Num. of Brackets	Personal Exempt. ($)[1] Single	Personal Exempt. ($)[1] Dependents	Fed. Inc. Tax Ded.
Colorado	4.63	Flat rate	1	3,700 (d)	3,700 (d)	No

Note: Tax rates as of January 1, 2012; Local- and county-level taxes are not included; n/a not applicable; (1) Married joint filers generally receive double the single exemption; (d) These states use the personal exemption amounts provided in the federal Internal Revenue Code.
Source: Federation of Tax Administrators, "State Individual Income Tax Rates, 2012"

Various State and Local Tax Rates

State	State and Local Sales and Use (%)	State Sales and Use (%)	Gasoline[1] (¢/gal.)	Cigarette[2] ($/pack)	Spirits[3] ($/gal.)	Wine[4] ($/gal.)	Beer[5] ($/gal.)
Colorado	7.4	2.90	22.0	0.84	2.28	0.32	0.08

Note: All tax rates as of January 1, 2012 except beer, wine and spirits (September 1, 2011); (1) The American Petroleum Institute has developed a methodology for determining the average tax rate on a gallon of fuel. Rates may include any of the following: excise taxes, environmental fees, storage tank fees, other fees or taxes, general sales tax, and local taxes. In states where gasoline is subject to the general sales tax, or where the fuel tax is based on the average sale price, the average rate determined by API is sensitive to changes in the price of gasoline. States that fully or partially apply general sales taxes to gasoline: CA, CO, GA, IL, IN, MI, NY; (2) The federal excise tax of $1.0066 per pack and local taxes are not included; (3) Rates are those applicable to off-premise sales of 40% alcohol by volume (a.b.v.) distilled spirits in 750ml containers. Local excise taxes are excluded; (4) Rates are those applicable to off-premise sales of 11% a.b.v. non-carbonated wine in 750ml containers; (5) Rates are those applicable to off-premise sales of 4.7% a.b.v. beer in 12 ounce containers.
Source: Tax Foundation, 2012 Facts & Figures: How Does Your State Compare?

State-Local Tax Burdens

Area	Rate (%)	Rank[1]	Per Capita Taxes Paid to Home State ($)	Total State and Local Per Capita Taxes Paid ($)	Per Capita Income ($)
Colorado	8.6	39	2,776	4,011	46,716
U.S. Average	9.8	-	3,057	4,160	42,539

Note: Figures cover 2009; (1) Rank ranges from 1 to 50 where 1 is highest tax burden
Source: Tax Foundation, State-Local Tax Burdens, All States, 2009

State Business Tax Climate Index Rankings

State	Overall Rank	Corporate Tax Index Rank	Individual Income Tax Index Rank	Sales Tax Index Rank	Unemployment Insurance Tax Index Rank	Property Tax Index Rank
Colorado	16	20	16	44	23	9

Note: The index is a measure of how each state's tax laws affect economic performance. The lower the rank, the more favorable a state's tax system is for business. States without a given tax are given a ranking of 1.
Source: Tax Foundation, Major Components of the State Business Tax Climate Index, FY 2012

COMMERCIAL REAL ESTATE

Office Market

Market Area	Inventory (sq. ft.)	Vacant (sq. ft.)	Vac. Rate (%)	Under Constr. (sq. ft.)	Asking Rent ($/sf/yr)	
					Class A	Class B
Colorado Springs	24,485,255	3,812,357	15.6	120,000	21.78	15.58

Source: Grubb & Ellis, Office Markets Trends, 4th Quarter 2011

Industrial Market

Market Area	Inventory (sq. ft.)	Vacant (sq. ft.)	Vac. Rate (%)	Under Constr. (sq. ft.)	Asking Rent ($/sf/yr)	
					WH/Dist	R&D/Flex
Colorado Springs	33,319,994	2,641,122	7.4	0	5.81	n/a

Source: Grubb & Ellis, Industrial Markets Trends, 4th Quarter 2011

COMMERCIAL UTILITIES

Typical Monthly Electric Bills

Area	Commercial Service ($/month)		Industrial Service ($/month)	
	1,500 kWh	40 kW demand 14,000 kWh	1,000 kW demand 200,000 kWh	50,000 kW demand 15,000,000 kWh
City	n/a	n/a	n/a	n/a
Average[1]	189	1,616	25,197	1,470,813

Note: Based on total rates in effect July 1, 2011; (1) average based on 184 utilities surveyed; n/a not available
Source: Edison Electric Institute, Typical Bills and Average Rates Report, Summer 2011

TRANSPORTATION

Means of Transportation to Work

Area	Car/Truck/Van		Public Transportation			Bicycle	Walked	Other Means	Worked at Home
	Drove Alone	Car-pooled	Bus	Subway	Railroad				
City	79.1	9.9	1.5	0.0	0.0	0.6	2.8	1.1	5.1
MSA[1]	77.1	9.5	1.2	0.0	0.0	0.4	4.6	1.2	6.0
U.S.	76.0	10.2	2.7	1.7	0.5	0.5	2.8	1.3	4.2

Note: Figures are percentages and cover workers 16 years of age and older; (1) Figures cover the Colorado Springs, CO Metropolitan Statistical Area—see Appendix B for areas included
Source: U.S. Census Bureau, 2008-2010 American Community Survey 3-Year Estimates

Travel Time to Work

Area	Less Than 10 Minutes	10 to 19 Minutes	20 to 29 Minutes	30 to 44 Minutes	45 to 59 Minutes	60 to 89 Minutes	90 Minutes or More
City	13.9	38.4	26.7	13.7	3.2	2.6	1.6
MSA[1]	15.0	33.3	25.8	16.6	4.5	3.0	1.8
U.S.	13.9	30.1	20.8	19.8	7.5	5.5	2.5

Note: Figures are percentages and include workers 16 years old and over; (1) Figures cover the Colorado Springs, CO Metropolitan Statistical Area—see Appendix B for areas included
Source: U.S. Census Bureau, 2008-2010 American Community Survey 3-Year Estimates

Travel Time Index

Area	1985	1990	1995	2000	2005	2010
Urban Area[1]	1.03	1.04	1.09	1.18	1.18	1.13
Average[2]	1.11	1.16	1.18	1.21	1.25	1.20

Note: Travel Time Index—the ratio of travel time in the peak period to the travel time at free-flow conditions. A value of 1.30 indicates a 20-minute free-flow trip takes 26 minutes in the peak. Free-flow speeds (60 mph on freeways and 35 mph on principal arterials) are used as the comparison threshold; (1) Covers the Colorado Springs CO urban area; (2) average of 439 urban areas
Source: Texas Transportation Institute, Urban Mobility Report 2011, September 2011

Public Transportation

Agency Name / Mode of Transportation	Vehicles Operated in Maximum Service	Annual Unlinked Passenger Trips ('000)	Annual Passenger Miles ('000)
Colorado Springs Transit System			
Bus (purchased transportation)	41	2,537.9	15,412.8
Demand Response (purchased transportation)	85	258.8	1,617.5
Vanpool (directly operated)	25	49.5	2,909.8

Source: Federal Transit Administration, National Transit Database, 2010

Air Transportation

Airport Name and Code / Type of Service	Passenger Airlines[1]	Passenger Enplanements	Freight Carriers[2]	Freight (lbs.)
City of Colorado Springs Municipal (COS)				
Domestic service (U.S. carriers - 2011)	18	796,637	4	13,452,680
International service (U.S. carriers - 2010)	3	270	0	0

Note: (1) Includes all U.S.-based major, minor and commuter airlines that carried at least one passenger during the year; (2) Includes all U.S.-based airlines and freight carriers that transported at least one pound of freight during the year
Source: Bureau of Transportation Statistics, The Intermodal Transportation Database, Air Carriers: T-100 Domestic Market (U.S. Carriers), 2011; Bureau of Transportation Statistics, The Intermodal Transportation Database, Air Carriers: T-100 International Market (U.S. Carriers), 2010

Other Transportation Statistics

Major Highways:	I-25
Amtrak Service:	Bus connection
Major Waterways/Ports:	None

Source: Amtrak.com; Google Maps

BUSINESSES

Major Business Headquarters

Company Name	Rankings Fortune[1]	Forbes[2]
No companies listed	-	-

Note: (1) Fortune 500—companies that produce a 10-K are ranked 1 to 500 based on 2010 revenue; (2) all private companies with at least $2 billion in annual revenue are ranked 1 to 212; companies listed are headquartered in the city; dashes indicate no ranking
Source: Fortune, "Fortune 500," May 23, 2011; Forbes, "America's Largest Private Companies," November 16, 2011

Fast-Growing Businesses

According to Deloitte, Colorado Springs is home to two of North America's 500 fastest-growing high-technology companies: **RadiantBlue Technologies** (#197); **Intelligent Software Solutions (ISS)** (#352). Companies are ranked by percentage growth in revenue over a five-year period. Criteria for inclusion: company must be headquartered within North America; must own proprietary intellectual property or proprietary technology that contributes to a significant portion of the company's operating revenue, or devote a significant proportion of revenues to research and development of technology; must have been in business for a minumum of five years with 2006 operating revenues of at least $50,000 USD/CD and 2010 operating revenues of at least $5 million USD/CD. *Deloitte Touche Tohmatsu, 2011 Deloitte Technology Fast 500™*

Minority- and Women-Owned Businesses

Group	All Firms		Firms with Paid Employees			
	Firms	Sales ($000)	Firms	Sales ($000)	Employees	Payroll ($000)
Asian	1,422	296,184	370	259,767	2,180	49,218
Black	1,108	41,563	48	19,675	322	7,302
Hispanic	2,040	325,147	325	288,389	2,072	62,148
Women	12,933	1,527,256	1,833	1,280,462	12,859	327,221
All Firms	41,019	38,769,299	10,051	37,456,398	181,328	7,036,810

Note: Figures cover firms located in the city; minority- and women-owned business are defined as firms in which the corresponding group own 51% or more of the stock or equity of the company
Source: U.S. Census Bureau, 2007 Economic Census, Survey of Business Owners

HOTELS

Hotels/Motels

Area	5 Star		4 Star		3 Star		2 Star		1 Star		Not Rated	
	Num.	Pct.[3]	Num.	Pct.[3]	Num.	Pct.[3]	Num.	Pct.[3]	Num.	Pct.[3]	Num.	Pct.[3]
City[1]	0	0.0	1	1.0	26	26.0	54	54.0	1	1.0	18	18.0
Total[2]	133	0.9	940	6.5	4,569	31.8	7,033	48.9	351	2.4	1,343	9.3

Note: (1) Figures cover Colorado Springs and vicinity; (2) Figures cover all 100 cities in this book; (3) Percentage of hotels which have a given star rating; Star ratings are determined by expedia.com and offer an indication of the general quality of a particular hotel.
Source: expedia.com, April 25, 2012

The Colorado Springs, CO metro area is home to one of the best hotels in the U.S. according to *Travel & Leisure*: **The Broadmoor** (#36). Criteria: service; location; rooms; food; and value. *Travel & Leisure, "T+L 500, The World's Best Hotels 2012"*

EVENT SITES

Major Stadiums, Arenas, and Auditoriums

Name	Max. Capacity
Falcon Stadium	52,480

Source: Original research

Living Environment

COST OF LIVING

Cost of Living Index

Composite Index	Groceries	Housing	Utilities	Trans-portation	Health Care	Misc. Goods/ Services
92.6	94.1	89.3	89.8	96.8	102.2	93.1

Note: U.S. = 100; Figures cover the Colorado Springs CO urban area.
Source: The Council for Community and Economic Research, ACCRA Cost of Living Index, 2011

Grocery Prices

Area[1]	T-Bone Steak ($/pound)	Frying Chicken ($/pound)	Whole Milk ($/half gal.)	Eggs ($/dozen)	Orange Juice ($/64 oz.)	Coffee ($/11.5 oz.)
City[2]	9.83	1.05	2.01	1.68	3.21	4.91
Avg.	9.25	1.18	2.22	1.66	3.19	4.40
Min.	6.70	0.88	1.31	0.95	2.46	2.94
Max.	14.30	2.16	3.50	3.18	4.75	6.83

Note: (1) Values for the local area are compared with the average, minimum and maximum values for all 335 areas in the Cost of Living Index; (2) Figures cover the Colorado Springs CO urban area; **T-Bone Steak** *(price per pound);* **Frying Chicken** *(price per pound, whole fryer);* **Whole Milk** *(half gallon carton);* **Eggs** *(price per dozen, Grade A, large);* **Orange Juice** *(64 oz. Tropicana or Florida Natural);* **Coffee** *(11.5 oz. can, vacuum-packed, Maxwell House, Hills Bros, or Folgers).*
Source: The Council for Community and Economic Research, ACCRA Cost of Living Index, 2011

Housing and Utility Costs

Area[1]	New Home Price ($)	Apartment Rent ($/month)	All Electric ($/month)	Part Electric ($/month)	Other Energy ($/month)	Telephone ($/month)
City[2]	247,964	808	-	67.47	58.34	30.25
Avg.	285,990	839	163.23	89.00	77.52	26.92
Min.	188,005	460	125.58	45.39	33.89	17.98
Max.	1,197,028	3,244	339.16	181.97	348.69	40.01

Note: (1) Values for the local area are compared with the average, minimum and maximum values for all 335 areas in the Cost of Living Index; (2) Figures cover the Colorado Springs CO urban area; **New Home Price** *(2,400 sf living area, 8,000 sf lot, in urban area with full utilities);* **Apartment Rent** *(950 sf 2 bedroom/1.5 or 2 bath, unfurnished, excluding all utilities except water);* **All Electric** *(average monthly cost for an all-electric home);* **Part Electric** *(average monthly cost for a part-electric home);* **Other Energy** *(average monthly cost for natural gas, fuel oil, coal, wood, and any other forms of energy except electricity);* **Telephone** *(price includes basic monthly rate for a private residential line plus additional local usage charges incurred by a family of four).*
Source: The Council for Community and Economic Research, ACCRA Cost of Living Index, 2011

Health Care, Transportation, and Other Costs

Area[1]	Doctor ($/visit)	Dentist ($/visit)	Optometrist ($/visit)	Gasoline ($/gallon)	Beauty Salon ($/visit)	Men's Shirt ($)
City[2]	96.13	87.47	93.29	3.22	35.20	28.13
Avg.	93.88	81.72	90.54	3.48	32.65	25.06
Min.	60.00	55.33	53.66	3.18	19.78	13.44
Max.	154.98	145.97	183.72	4.31	63.21	46.00

Note: (1) Values for the local area are compared with the average, minimum and maximum values for all 335 areas in the Cost of Living Index; (2) Figures cover the Colorado Springs CO urban area; **Doctor** *(general practitioners routine exam of an established patient);* **Dentist** *(adult teeth cleaning and periodic oral examination);* **Optometrist** *(full vision eye exam for established adult patient);* **Gasoline** *(one gallon regular unleaded, national brand, including all taxes, cash price at self-service pump if available);* **Beauty Salon** *(woman's shampoo, trim, and blow-dry);* **Men's Shirt** *(cotton/polyester dress shirt, pinpoint weave, long sleeves).*
Source: The Council for Community and Economic Research, ACCRA Cost of Living Index, 2011

HOUSING

House Price Index (HPI)

Area	National Ranking[2]	Quarterly Change (%)	One-Year Change (%)	Five-Year Change (%)
MSA[1]	154	0.91	-2.72	-8.78
U.S.[3]	-	-0.10	-2.43	-19.16

Note: The HPI is a weighted repeat sales index. It measures average price changes in repeat sales or refinancings on the same properties. This information is obtained by reviewing repeat mortgage transactions on single-family properties whose mortgages have been purchased or securitized by Fannie Mae or Freddie Mac in January 1975; (1) Metropolitan/Micropolitan Statistical Area—see Appendix B for areas included; (2) Rankings are based on annual percentage change for all metro areas containing at least 15,000 transactions over the last 10 years and ranges from 1 to 306; (3) figures based on a weighted average of Census Division estimates using a purchase only index; all figures are for the period ending December 31, 2011

Source: Federal Housing Finance Agency, House Price Index, February 23, 2012

House Price Valuations

Area	Q4 2005		Q4 2006		Q4 2007		Q4 2008		Q4 2009	
	Price ($000)	Over-valuation	Price ($000)	Over-valuation	Price ($000)	Over-valuation	Price ($000)	Over-valuation	Price ($000)	Over-valuation
MSA[1]	196.6	9.6	204.9	8.8	199.4	1.6	190.5	0.2	194.0	6.3

Note: Figures show the percentage of over- or under-valuation of single family homes relative to statistically normal house values (e.g. a value of 23.6 indicates that house values are 23.6% overvalued). Statistically normal house values are based on house prices, interest rates, household incomes, population densities, and any historical premiums or discounts metropolitan areas have exhibited over time; (1) Figures cover the Colorado Springs, CO - see Appendix B for areas included

Source: Global Insight/PNC Financial Services Group, House Prices in America: 4th Quarter 2009 Update

Median Single-Family Home Prices

Area	2009	2010	2011p	Percent Change 2010 to 2011
MSA[1]	189.8	195.5	187.2	-4.2
U.S. Average	172.1	173.1	166.2	-4.0

Note: Figures are median sales prices of existing single-family homes in thousands of dollars; (p) preliminary; n/a not available; (1) Metropolitan Statistical Area—see Appendix B for areas included

Source: National Association of Realtors, Median Sales Price of Existing Single-Family Homes for Metropolitan Areas, 4th Quarter 2011

Affordability Index of Existing Single-Family Homes

Area	2009	2010	2011p	Percent Change 2010 to 2011
MSA[1]	96.0	98.4	108.2	10.0

Note: The housing affordability index measures whether or not a typical family could qualify for a mortgage loan on a typical home. The higher the index, the greater the household purchasing power. An index of 100 is defined as the point where a median-income household has exactly enough income to qualify for the purchase of a median-priced existing single-family home, assuming a 20 percent downpayment and 25 percent of gross income devoted to mortgage principal and interest payments; (p) preliminary; n/a not available; (1) Metropolitan Statistical Area—see Appendix B for areas included

Source: National Association of Realtors, Affordability Index of Existing Single-Family Homes, 2011

Median Apartment Condo-Coop Home Prices

Area	2009	2010	2011p	Percent Change 2010 to 2011
MSA[1]	134.6	132.4	125.5	-5.2
U.S. Average	175.6	171.7	165.1	-3.8

Note: Figures are median sales prices of existing apartment condo-coop homes in thousands of dollars; (p) preliminary; n/a not available; (1) Metropolitan Statistical Area—see Appendix B for areas included

Source: National Association of Realtors, Median Sales Price of Existing Apartment Condo-Coop Homes for Metropolitan Areas, 4th Quarter 2011

Year Housing Structure Built

Area	2005 or Later	2000 -2004	1990 -1999	1980 -1989	1970 -1979	1960 -1969	1950 -1959	Before 1950	Median Year
City	5.4	12.0	15.5	18.5	20.6	11.4	8.3	8.3	1981
MSA[1]	6.6	13.1	17.2	18.1	19.6	10.5	7.4	7.5	1983
U.S.	5.0	8.6	14.0	14.1	16.3	11.3	11.2	19.6	1975

Note: Figures are percentages except for Median Year; (1) Figures cover the Colorado Springs, CO Metropolitan Statistical Area—see Appendix B for areas included
Source: U.S. Census Bureau, 2008-2010 American Community Survey 3-Year Estimates

HEALTH

Health Risk Data

Category	MSA[1] (%)	U.S. (%)
Adults who have been told they have high blood pressure[2]	20.1	28.7
Adults who have been told they have high blood cholesterol[2]	35.2	37.5
Adults who have been told they have diabetes[3]	5.9	8.7
Adults who have been told they have arthritis[2]	27.3	26.0
Adults who have been told they currently have asthma	9.1	9.1
Adults who are current smokers	17.9	17.3
Adults who are heavy drinkers[4]	3.6	5.0
Adults who are binge drinkers[5]	14.0	15.1
Adults who are overweight (BMI 25.0 - 29.9)	37.8	36.2
Adults who are obese (BMI 30.0 - 99.8)	23.6	27.5
Adults who participated in any physical activities in the past month	80.9	76.1
Adults 50+ who have ever had a sigmoidoscopy or colonoscopy	65.3	65.2
Women aged 40+ who have had a mammogram within the past two years	74.0	75.2
Men aged 40+ who have had a PSA test within the past two years	46.8	53.2
Adults aged 65+ who have had flu shot within the past year	69.5	67.5
Adults aged 18–64 who have any kind of health care coverage	83.2	82.2

Note: Data as of 2010 unless otherwise noted; (1) Figures cover the Colorado Springs, CO Metropolitan Statistical Area—see Appendix B for areas included; (2) Data as of 2009; (3) Figures do not include pregnancy-related, borderline, or pre-diabetes; (4) Heavy drinkers are classified as males having more than two drinks per day or females having more than one drink per day; (5) Binge drinkers are classified as males having five or more drinks on one occasion or females having four or more drinks on one occasion
Source: Centers for Disease Control and Prevention, Behaviorial Risk Factor Surveillance System, SMART: Selected Metropolitan/Micropolitan Area Risk Trends, 2009, 2010

Mortality Rates for the Top 10 Causes of Death in the U.S.

ICD-10[a] Sub-Chapter	ICD-10[a] Code	Age-Adjusted Mortality Rate[1] per 100,000 population	
		County[2]	U.S.
Malignant neoplasms	C00-C97	155.5	175.6
Ischaemic heart diseases	I20-I25	91.3	121.6
Other forms of heart disease	I30-I51	36.0	48.6
Chronic lower respiratory diseases	J40-J47	49.6	42.3
Cerebrovascular diseases	I60-I69	44.3	40.6
Organic, including symptomatic, mental disorders	F01-F09	37.1	26.7
Other degenerative diseases of the nervous system	G30-G31	23.1	24.7
Other external causes of accidental injury	W00-X59	31.6	24.4
Diabetes mellitus	E10-E14	16.0	21.7
Hypertensive diseases	I10-I15	17.4	18.2

Note: (a) ICD-10 = International Classification of Diseases 10th Revision; (1) Mortality rates are a three year average covering 2007-2009; (2) Figures cover El Paso County
Source: Centers for Disease Control and Prevention, National Center for Health Statistics. Underlying Cause of Death 1999-2009 on CDC WONDER Online Database, released 2012. Data for year 2009 are compiled from the Multiple Cause of Death File 2009, Series 20 No. 2O, 2012, Data for year 2008 are compiled from the Multiple Cause of Death File 2008, Series 20 No. 2N, 2011, Data for year 2007 are compiled from Multiple Cause of Death File 2007, Series 20 No. 2M, 2010.

Mortality Rates for Selected Causes of Death

ICD-10[a] Sub-Chapter	ICD-10[a] Code	Age-Adjusted Mortality Rate[1] per 100,000 population	
		County[2]	U.S.
Assault	X85-Y09	4.5	5.7
Human immunodeficiency virus (HIV) disease	B20-B24	*Unreliable	3.3
Influenza and pneumonia	J09-J18	11.9	16.4
Intentional self-harm	X60-X84	18.7	11.5
Malnutrition	E40-E46	*0.0	0.8
Obesity and other hyperalimentation	E65-E68	1.3	1.6
Transport accidents	V01-V99	11.0	13.7
Viral hepatitis	B15-B19	1.9	2.2

Note: (a) ICD-10 = International Classification of Diseases 10th Revision; (1) Mortality rates are a three year average covering 2007-2009; (2) Figures cover El Paso County; (*) Unreliable data as per CDC
Source: Centers for Disease Control and Prevention, National Center for Health Statistics. Underlying Cause of Death 1999-2009 on CDC WONDER Online Database, released 2012. Data for year 2009 are compiled from the Multiple Cause of Death File 2009, Series 20 No. 2O, 2012, Data for year 2008 are compiled from the Multiple Cause of Death File 2008, Series 20 No. 2N, 2011, Data for year 2007 are compiled from Multiple Cause of Death File 2007, Series 20 No. 2M, 2010.

Distribution of Physicians and Dentists

Area[1]	Dentists[2]	D.O.[3]	M.D.[4]				
			Total	Family/ General Practice	Pediatrics	Medical Specialties	Surgical Specialties
Local (number)	328	152	951	117	68	289	236
Local (rate[5])	5.6	2.6	16.0	2.0	1.1	4.9	4.0
U.S. (rate[5])	4.5	1.9	18.3	2.5	1.4	6.8	4.1

Note: Data as of 2008 unless noted; (1) Local data covers El Paso County; (2) Data as of 2007; (3) Doctor of Osteopathic Medicine; (4) Includes active, non-federal, patient-care, office-based Doctors of Medicine; (5) rate per 10,000 population
Source: Area Resource File (ARF). 2009-2010 Release. U.S. Department of Health and Human Services, Health Resources and Services Administration, Bureau of Health Professions, Rockville, MD, August 2010

EDUCATION

Public School District Statistics

District Name	Schls	Pupils	Pupil/ Teacher Ratio	Minority Pupils[1] (%)	Free Lunch Eligible[2] (%)	IEP[3] (%)
Academy School District No. 20	32	22,620	16.4	19.1	7.1	n/a
Cheyenne Mountain School Dist No. 12	9	4,578	16.2	21.8	10.1	n/a
Colorado Springs School Dist No. 11	59	29,673	17.1	39.0	41.0	n/a
Harrison School District No. 2	26	11,309	13.9	69.3	57.8	n/a
SD No. 3 in the County of El Paso	17	8,851	17.6	41.2	28.3	n/a

Note: Table includes school districts with 2,000 or more students; (1) Percentage of students that are not non-Hispanic white; (2) Percentage of students that are eligible for the free lunch program; (3) Percentage of students that have an Individualized Education Program.
Source: U.S. Department of Education, National Center for Education Statistics, Common Core of Data, Local Education Agency (School District) Universe Survey: School Year 2009-2010; U.S. Department of Education, National Center for Education Statistics, Common Core of Data, Public Elementary/Secondary School Universe Survey: School Year 2009-2010

Top Public High Schools

High School Name	Rank[1]	Score[1]	Grad. Rate[2] (%)	College[3] (%)	AP/IB/AICE[4] (%)	SAT/ACT[5] (%)
Rampart	285	0.388	92	95	2.8	1724
The Vanguard School at Cheyenne Mountain Charter Academy	130	0.634	100	89	1.5	1782

Note: (1) Public schools are ranked from 1 to 500 based on the following self-reported statistics (with their corresponding weight in the final score). Schools that had fewer than 10 graduates, as well as those that were newly founded and did not have a graduating senior class in 2010 were excluded; (2) Four-year, on-time graduation rate (25%); (3) Percent of 2010 graduates who enrolled immediately in college (25%); (4) AP/IB/AICE tests per graduate (25%); (5) Average SAT and/or ACT score (10%); Average AP/IB/AICE exam score (10%); AP/IB/AICE courses offered per graduate (5%); (6) School is unranked, but has been identified by Newsweek as one of the nation's most elite public high schools.
Source: Newsweek Online, "Top High Schools 2011"

Highest Level of Education

Area	Less than H.S.	H.S. Diploma	Some College, No Deg.	Associate Degree	Bachelors Degree	Masters Degree	Profess. School Degree	Doctorate Degree
City	7.6	21.1	25.7	9.4	22.1	10.7	1.9	1.4
MSA[1]	7.0	22.1	26.1	9.6	21.6	10.6	1.7	1.3
U.S.	14.7	28.4	21.3	7.6	17.6	7.2	1.9	1.2

Note: Figures cover persons age 25 and over; (1) Figures cover the Colorado Springs, CO Metropolitan Statistical Area—see Appendix B for areas included
Source: U.S. Census Bureau, 2008-2010 American Community Survey 3-Year Estimates

Educational Attainment by Race

Area	High School Graduate or Higher (%)					Bachelor's Degree or Higher (%)				
	Total	White	Black	Asian	Hisp.[2]	Total	White	Black	Asian	Hisp.[2]
City	92.4	93.6	90.9	86.2	75.8	36.1	38.8	19.2	36.5	13.4
MSA[1]	93.0	94.1	92.5	84.4	78.6	35.1	37.3	21.6	35.6	15.3
U.S.	85.3	87.5	81.4	85.5	61.6	28.0	29.3	17.8	50.2	13.0

Note: Figures shown cover persons 25 years old and over; (1) Figures cover the Colorado Springs, CO Metropolitan Statistical Area—see Appendix B for areas included; (2) People of Hispanic origin can be of any race
Source: U.S. Census Bureau, 2008-2010 American Community Survey 3-Year Estimates

School Enrollment by Grade and Control

Area	Preschool (%)		Kindergarten (%)		Grades 1 - 4 (%)		Grades 5 - 8 (%)		Grades 9 - 12 (%)	
	Public	Private	Public	Private	Public	Private	Public	Private	Public	Private
City	53.3	46.7	91.9	8.1	93.9	6.1	90.6	9.4	92.3	7.7
MSA[1]	59.5	40.5	89.0	11.0	90.2	9.8	89.4	10.6	91.7	8.3
U.S.	55.4	44.6	87.1	12.9	89.4	10.6	89.5	10.5	90.4	9.6

Note: Figures shown cover persons 3 years old and over; (1) Figures cover the Colorado Springs, CO Metropolitan Statistical Area—see Appendix B for areas included
Source: U.S. Census Bureau, 2008-2010 American Community Survey 3-Year Estimates

Average Salaries of Public School Classroom Teachers

Area	2010-11		2011-12		Percent Change 2010-11 to 2011-12	Percent Change 2001-02 to 2011-12
	Dollars	Rank[1]	Dollars	Rank[1]		
Colorado	49,228	27	50,407	27	2.39	24.00
U.S. Average	55,623	-	56,643	-	1.83	26.8

Note: (1) State rank ranges from 1 to 51 where 1 indicates highest salary.
Source: National Education Association, Rankings & Estimates: Rankings of the States 2011 and Estimates of School Statistics 2012, December 2011

Higher Education

Four-Year Colleges: Public	Four-Year Colleges: Private Non-profit	Four-Year Colleges: Private For-profit	Two-Year Colleges: Public	Two-Year Colleges: Private Non-profit	Two-Year Colleges: Private For-profit	Medical Schools[1]	Law Schools[2]	Voc/ Tech[3]
1	3	7	1	0	8	0	0	2

Note: Figures cover institutions located within the city limits and include main campuses only; (1) includes schools accredited by the Liaison Committee on Medical Education and the American Osteopathic Association's Commission on Osteopathic College Accreditation; (2) includes American Bar Association-accredited law schools; (3) includes all schools with programs that are less than 2 years.
Source: National Center for Education Statistics, Integrated Postsecondary Education System (IPEDS) Peer Analysis System, 2011-12; Association of American Medical Colleges, Member List, April 23, 2012; American Osteopathic Association, Member List, April 23, 2012; Law School Admission Council, Official Guide to ABA-Approved Law Schools Online, April 23, 2012

According to *U.S. News & World Report,* the Colorado Springs, CO is home to two of the best liberal arts colleges in the U.S.: **Colorado College** (#27); **United States Air Force Academy** (#33). The indicators used to capture academic quality fall into a number of categories: assessment by administrators at peer institutions; retention of students; faculty resources; student selectivity; financial resources; alumni giving; high school counselor ratings of colleges; and graduation rate.*U.S. News & World Report, "America's Best Colleges 2012"*

PRESIDENTIAL ELECTION

2008 Presidential Election Results

Area	Obama	McCain	Nader	Other
El Paso County	39.9	58.7	0.4	1.0
U.S.	52.9	45.6	0.6	0.9

Note: Results are percentages and may not add to 100% due to rounding
Source: Dave Leip's Atlas of U.S. Presidential Elections, www.uselectionatlas.org

EMPLOYERS

Major Employers

Company Name	Industry
Agilent Technologies	Instruments to measure electricity
Air Force, United States Dept of the	Air force
Broadmoor Hotel	Hotels and motels
Catholic Health Initiatives Colorado	Charitable organization
Centura Health Corporation	General medical and surgical hospitals
CISCO Systems	Data conversion equipment, media-to-media: computer
Direct Checks Unlimited	Checkbooks
Hewlett-Packard Company	Computer rental and leasing
ITT Federal Services Intl Corp	Electrical or electronic engineering
Lockheed Martin Corporation	Search and navigation equipment
Lockheed Martin Corporation	Acceleration indicators & systems components, aerospace
Lockheed Martin Corporation	Defense systems and equipment
Lockheed Martin Corporation	Systems integration services
Lockheed Martin Corporation	Engineering services
Memorial Health System	General medical and surgical hospitals
United States Department of Defense	National security, federal government
World Radio Missionary Fellowship	Nonchurch religious organizations
YMCA of The Pikes Peak Region	Recreation association

Note: Companies shown are located within the Colorado Springs, CO metropolitan area.
Source: Hoovers.com, data extracted April 25 2012

PUBLIC SAFETY

Crime Rate

Area	All Crimes	Violent Crimes				Property Crimes		
		Murder	Forcible Rape	Robbery	Aggrav. Assault	Burglary	Larceny -Theft	Motor Vehicle Theft
City	4,712.7	5.0	80.2	132.2	274.5	867.6	3,029.5	323.7
Suburbs[1]	1,928.9	1.3	38.1	19.3	352.5	377.5	1,001.4	138.8
Metro[2]	3,697.5	3.7	64.8	91.0	302.9	688.9	2,289.9	256.3
U.S.	3,345.5	4.8	27.5	119.1	252.3	699.6	2,003.5	238.8

Note: Figures are crimes per 100,000 population; (1) All areas within the metro area that are located outside the city limits; (2) Metropolitan Statistical Area—see Appendix B for areas included
Source: FBI Uniform Crime Reports, 2010

Hate Crimes

Area	Number of Quarters Reported	Bias Motivation				
		Race	Religion	Sexual Orientation	Ethnicity	Disability
City	4	10	1	4	0	0

Source: Federal Bureau of Investigation, Hate Crime Statistics 2010

Identity Theft Consumer Complaints

Area	Complaints	Complaints per 100,000 Population	Rank[2]
MSA[1]	496	81.4	169
U.S.	279,156	90.4	-

Note: (1) Metropolitan Statistical Area—see Appendix B for areas included; (2) Rank ranges from 1 to 384 where 1 indicates greatest number of identity theft complaints per 100,000 population
Source: Federal Trade Commission, Consumer Sentinel Network Data Book for January–December 2011

Fraud and Other Consumer Complaints

Area	Complaints	Complaints per 100,000 Population	Rank[2]
MSA[1]	5,495	902.2	3
U.S.	1,533,924	496.8	-

Note: (1) Metropolitan Statistical Area—see Appendix B for areas included; (2) Rank ranges from 1 to 384 where 1 indicates greatest number of fraud and other complaints per 100,000 population
Source: Federal Trade Commission, Consumer Sentinel Network Data Book for January–December 2011

RECREATION

Culture

Dance[1]	Theatre[1]	Instrumental Music[1]	Vocal Music[1]	Series/ Festivals	Museums	Zoos and Aquariums[2]
0	0	1	2	2	12	1

Note: (1) Number of professional perfoming groups; (2) AZA-accredited
Source: The Grey House Performing Arts Directory, 2011-2012; Official Museum Directory, 2011; American Association of Museums, AAM Member Museums, April 2012; Association of Zoos & Aquariums, AZA Member Zoos & Aquariums, April 2012

Professional Sports Teams

Team Name	League
No teams are located in the metro area	

Source: Original research

CLIMATE

Average and Extreme Temperatures

Temperature	Jan	Feb	Mar	Apr	May	Jun	Jul	Aug	Sep	Oct	Nov	Dec	Yr.
Extreme High (°F)	71	72	78	87	93	99	98	97	94	86	78	75	99
Average High (°F)	41	44	51	61	68	79	85	81	75	63	49	41	62
Average Temp. (°F)	29	32	39	48	55	66	71	69	61	50	37	30	49
Average Low (°F)	17	20	26	34	42	52	57	55	48	36	24	17	36
Extreme Low (°F)	-20	-19	-3	8	22	36	48	39	22	7	-5	-24	-24

Note: Figures cover the years 1948-1993
Source: National Climatic Data Center, International Station Meteorological Climate Summary, 9/96

Average Precipitation/Snowfall/Humidity

Precip./Humidity	Jan	Feb	Mar	Apr	May	Jun	Jul	Aug	Sep	Oct	Nov	Dec	Yr.
Avg. Precip. (in.)	0.3	0.4	1.3	1.3	2.6	2.1	2.6	3.4	1.0	0.9	0.6	0.5	17.0
Avg. Snowfall (in.)	6	6	10	5	2	0	0	0	Tr	3	7	8	48
Avg. Rel. Hum. 5am (%)	57	60	62	62	69	67	66	71	66	59	60	59	63
Avg. Rel. Hum. 5pm (%)	48	43	39	34	39	36	36	43	36	36	45	52	41

Note: Figures cover the years 1948-1993; Tr = Trace amounts (<0.05 in. of rain; <0.5 in. of snow)
Source: National Climatic Data Center, International Station Meteorological Climate Summary, 9/96

Weather Conditions

Temperature			Daytime Sky			Precipitation		
10°F & below	32°F & below	90°F & above	Clear	Partly cloudy	Cloudy	0.01 inch or more precip.	0.1 inch or more snow/ice	Thunder-storms
21	161	18	108	157	100	98	33	49

Note: Figures are average number of days per year and cover the years 1948-1993
Source: National Climatic Data Center, International Station Meteorological Climate Summary, 9/96

HAZARDOUS WASTE

Superfund Sites

Colorado Springs has no sites on the EPA's Superfund Final National Priorities List.
U.S. Environmental Protection Agency, Final National Priorities List, April 17, 2012

AIR & WATER QUALITY

Air Quality Index

Area	Percent of Days when Air Quality was...[2]					AQI Statistics[2]	
	Good	Moderate	Unhealthy for Sensitive Groups	Unhealthy	Very Unhealthy	Maximum	Median
Area[1]	74.8	24.4	0.8	0.0	0.0	119	43

Note: Air Quality Index (AQI) is an index for reporting daily air quality. EPA calculates the AQI for five major air pollutants regulated by the Clean Air Act: ground-level ozone, particle pollution (aka particulate matter), carbon monoxide, sulfur dioxide, and nitrogen dioxide. The AQI runs from 0 to 500. The higher the AQI value, the greater the level of air pollution and the greater the health concern. There are six AQI categories: "Good" AQI is between 0 and 50. Air quality is considered satisfactory; "Moderate" AQI is between 51 and 100. Air quality is acceptable; "Unhealthy for Sensitive Groups" When AQI values are between 101 and 150, members of sensitive groups may experience health effects; "Unhealthy" When AQI values are between 151 and 200 everyone may begin to experience health effects; "Very Unhealthy" AQI values between 201 and 300 trigger a health alert; "Hazardous" AQI values over 300 trigger warnings of emergency conditions (not shown); (1) Data covers El Paso County; (2) Based on 365 days with AQI data in 2011.
Source: U.S. Environmental Protection Agency, AirData Report, 2011

Air Quality Index Pollutants

Area	Percent of Days when AQI Pollutant was...[2]					
	Carbon Monoxide	Nitrogen Dioxide	Ozone	Sulfur Dioxide	Particulate Matter 2.5	Particulate Matter 10
Area[1]	0.0	0.0	98.4	0.0	1.4	0.3

Note: The Air Quality Index (AQI) is an index for reporting daily air quality. EPA calculates the AQI for five major air pollutants regulated by the Clean Air Act: ground-level ozone, particle pollution (also known as particulate matter), carbon monoxide, sulfur dioxide, and nitrogen dioxide. The AQI runs from 0 to 500. The higher the AQI value, the greater the level of air pollution and the greater the health concern; (1) Data covers El Paso County; (2) Based on 365 days with AQI data in 2011.
Source: U.S. Environmental Protection Agency, AirData Report, 2011

Air Quality Index Trends

Area	Trend Sites (days)								All Sites (days)
	2003	2004	2005	2006	2007	2008	2009	2010	2010
MSA[1]	4	0	6	0	1	2	0	1	2

Note: Figures are the number of days the AQI value exceeded 100 in a given year. An AQI value greater than 100 indicates that air quality would have been in the unhealthful range on that day. Data from exceptional events are included. These counts are presented in two ways. First, the counts are based on sites having an adequate record of monitoring data during the trend period (trend sites). These counts represent the relative change in the number of days with AQI values greater than 100. In the last column, the counts are based on all sites with data in the most recent year (because it is possible for a site to have data in the most recent year but not enough data to be a trend site); (1) Data covers the Colorado Springs, CO—see Appendix B for areas included

Source: U.S. Environmental Protection Agency, Air Quality Index Information, "Number of Days with Air Quality Index Values Greater than 100 at Trend Sites, 2000-2010, and at All Sites in 2010"

Maximum Air Pollutant Concentrations: Particulate Matter, Ozone, CO and Lead

	Particulate Matter 10 (ug/m^3)	Particulate Matter 2.5 Wtd AM (ug/m^3)	Particulate Matter 2.5 24-Hr (ug/m^3)	Ozone (ppm)	Carbon Monoxide (ppm)	Lead (ug/m^3)
MSA[1] Level	38	6.2	12	0.072	2	n/a
NAAQS[2]	150	15	35	0.075	9	0.15
Met NAAQS[2]	Yes	Yes	Yes	Yes	Yes	n/a

Note: Data from exceptional events are not included; (1) Data covers the Colorado Springs, CO—see Appendix B for areas included; (2) National Ambient Air Quality Standards; ppm = parts per million; ug/m^3 = micrograms per cubic meter; n/a not available

Concentrations: Particulate Matter 10 (coarse particulate)—highest second maximum 24-hour concentration; Particulate Matter 2.5 Wtd AM (fine particulate)—highest weighted annual mean concentration; Particulate Matter 2.5 24-Hour (fine particulate)—highest 98th percentile 24-hour concentration; Ozone—highest fourth daily maximum 8-hour concentration; Carbon Monoxide—highest second maximum non-overlapping 8-hour concentration; Lead—maximum running 3-month average

Source: U.S. Environmental Protection Agency, CBSA Factbook 2010, Air Quality Statistics by City, 2010

Maximum Air Pollutant Concentrations: Nitrogen Dioxide and Sulfur Dioxide

	Nitrogen Dioxide AM (ppb)	Nitrogen Dioxide 1-Hr (ppb)	Sulfur Dioxide AM (ppb)	Sulfur Dioxide 1-Hr (ppb)	Sulfur Dioxide 24-Hr (ppb)
MSA[1] Level	n/a	n/a	n/a	n/a	n/a
NAAQS[2]	53	100	30	75	140
Met NAAQS[2]	n/a	n/a	n/a	n/a	n/a

Note: Data from exceptional events are not included; (1) Data covers the Colorado Springs, CO—see Appendix B for areas included; (2) National Ambient Air Quality Standards; ppb = parts per billion; n/a not available

Concentrations: Nitrogen Dioxide AM—highest arithmetic mean concentration; Nitrogen Dioxide 1-Hr—highest 98th percentile 1-hour daily maximum concentration; Sulfur Dioxide AM—highest annual mean concentration; Sulfur Dioxide 1-Hr—highest 99th percentile 1-hour daily maximum concentration; Sulfur Dioxide 24-Hr—highest second maximum 24-hour concentration

Source: U.S. Environmental Protection Agency, CBSA Factbook 2010, Air Quality Statistics by City, 2010

Drinking Water

Water System Name	Pop. Served	Primary Water Source Type	Violations[1]	
			Health Based	Monitoring/ Reporting
Colorado Springs Utilities	418,096	Surface	0	0

Note: (1) Based on violation data from January 1, 2011 to December 31, 2011 (includes unresolved violations from earlier years)

Source: U.S. Environmental Protection Agency, Office of Ground Water and Drinking Water, Safe Drinking Water Information System (based on data extracted April 18, 2012)

Denver, Colorado

Background

From almost anywhere in Denver, you can command a breathtaking view of the 14,000-foot Rocky Mountains. However, the early settlers of Denver were not attracted to the city because of its vistas; they were there in search of gold.

In 1858, there were rumors that gold had been discovered in Cherry Creek, one of the waterways on which Denver stands. Although prospectors came and went without much luck, later it was discovered that there really was gold, and silver as well. By 1867, Denver had been established.

Today, Denver, with its sparkling, dramatic skyline of glass and steel towers, bears little resemblance to the dusty frontier village of the nineteenth century. With an excellent location, the "Mile High City" has become a manufacturing, distribution, and transportation center that serves not only the western regions of the United States, but the entire nation. Denver is also home to many companies that are engaged in alternative fuel research and development.

Denver has been the host city of the Democratic National Convention twice: first in 1908 and again in 2008. The city also hosted the international G7 (now G8) summit in 1997. These events bolstered Denver's international reputation both on a political and socioeconomic level.

The massively renovated Colorado Convention Center—now 584,000 square feet—is a magnet for regional and national conferences and shows, and is enhanced by the 5,000 seat Wells Fargo Theatre and new Light Rail Train Station. Major construction is underway at the historic Denver Union Station, which will operate as a mixed-use retail and multi-modal transportation hub. Another architecturally interesting building is the Jeppesen Terminal at Denver's airport, the largest international hub in the United States. The unique roof is made of heat- and light-reflecting tension fabric. The airport is huge, with 53 square miles and 6 million square feet of public space and 93 gates.

The city is also home to a lively cultural, recreational, and educational scene. There are concerts at the Boettcher Concert Hall of the Denver Center for the Performing Arts, seasonal drives through the Denver Mountain Park Circle Drive, and skiing and hiking the Rockies just 90 minutes away. Other area attractions include the Denver Museum of Nature and Science, the Colorado History Museum, and the Denver Art Museum, which increased its exhibition space in 2006 with the dramatic new Frederick C. Hamilton building designed by Daniel Libeskind. Opposite the museum, a new condominium complex, Museum Residences, also by Libeskind, recently opened it sales office.

The city has developed a 12-year, $4.7 billion public transportation expansion plan, FasTracks, for the Denver-Aurora and Boulder Metropolitan Areas, developed by the Regional Transportation District. The plan calls for six light rail and diesel commuter rail lines with a combined length of 119 miles to be opened between 2013 and 2016.

The city also has its share of offbeat, distinctive places to have fun including the hip Capitol Hill district, which offers small music venues and dank bars that appeal to University of Denver students. Sports fans have the Colorado Avalanche hockey team, the Denver Nuggets basketball team, the Colorado Rockies baseball team, and the Denver Broncos football team. The city also has the Six Flags Elitch Gardens amusement park.

The Denver Zoo is open year-round and houses nearly 4,000 animals representing 700 species, including the okapi, red-bellied lemur, Amur leopard, black rhino, and Siberian tiger. In recent years, the zoo has been implementing features of a master modernization plan of habitats. Most recently was the completion of Predator Ridge, home to 14 African species of mammals, birds and reptiles, and an indoor tropical rain forest.

The University of Denver, Community College of Denver, Metropolitan State College, and the University of Colorado at Denver are only a few of the many excellent educational opportunities available in the city.

Denver's invigorating climate matches much of the central Rocky Mountain region, without the frigidly cold mornings of the higher elevations during winter, or the hot afternoons of summer at lower altitudes. Extreme cold and heat are generally short-lived. Low relative humidity, light precipitation, and abundant sunshine characterize Denver's weather. Spring is the cloudiest, wettest, and windiest season, while autumn is the most pleasant. Air pollution, known locally as the "brown cloud," which the city has spent decades combating, continues to be a problem.

Rankings

General Rankings

- The Denver metro area was selected as one of the best cities to relocate to in America by Sperling's BestPlaces. The metro area ranked #9 out of 10. Criteria: unemployment; cost of living; crime rates; population health; cultural events; economic stability. *Sperling's BestPlaces, www.BestPlaces.net, "The Best Cities to Relocate to in America," October 2010*
- The Denver metro area was identified as one of the 10 most popular big cities by Pew Research Center. The results are based on a telephone survey of 2,260 adults conducted during October 2008. The report explored a range of attitudes related to where Americans live, where they would like to live, and why. *Pew Research Center, "For Nearly Half of America, Grass is Greener Somewhere Else," January 29, 2009*
- *Men's Health Living* ranked 100 U.S. cities in terms of quality of life. Denver was ranked #50 and received a grade of C. Criteria: number of fitness facilities; air quality; number of physicians; male/female ratio; education levels; household income; cost of living. *Men's Health Living, Spring 2008*
- Denver was selected as one of America's ten "Best Cities to Work and Live." The city ranked #7. The results are based on a survey of 2,500 employees and entrepreneurs who were asked about 40 large cities. *BusinessWeek, "America's Most and Least Favorite Cities," January 5, 2009*
- Denver was selected as one of America's best cities by *Bloomberg Businessweek.* The city ranked #27 out of 50. Criteria: number of restaurants, bars and museums per capita; number of colleges, libraries, and professional sports teams; income, poverty, unemployment, crime, and foreclosure rates; percent of population with bachelor's degrees; public school performance; park acres per capita; air quality. *BusinessWeek, "America's 50 Best Cities," September 20, 2011*
- Denver appeared on RelocateAmerica's list of best places to live in America. The annual "Top 100 Places to Live" list recognizes the top communities as nominated by their residents & local businesses. RelocateAmerica's Research Group determines the list based on review of various data gathered for economic, employment, housing, education, industry, opportunity, environment and recreation along with feedback from area leaders and residents. *RelocateAmerica.com, "Top 100 Places to Live for 2011"*
- Denver was chosen as one of America's best cities by *Outside Magazine* in the "Best for Road Running" category. Criteria: educational attainment; cost of living; cultural vibrancy; economic resilience; housing market sanity; sport-specific facts such as the miles of trail within a hour's drive, frequency of group rides, and proximity to worthy ski areas. *Outside Magazine, "Best Towns 2010," August 2010*
- Denver was identified as one of the top places to live in the U.S. by Harris Interactive. The city ranked #10 out of 15. Criteria: 2,463 adults (age 18 and over) were polled and asked "if you could live in or near any city in the country except the one you live in or nearest to now, which city would you choose?" The poll was conducted online within the U.S. between September 14 and 20, 2010. *Harris Interactive, November 9, 2011*
- Denver was selected as one of "America's Favorite Cities." The city ranked #6 in the "Quality of Life and Visitor Experience" category. Respondents to an online survey were asked to rate 35 top urban destinations in the U.S. from a visitor's perspective. Criteria: noteworthy neighborhoods; skyline/views; public parks and outdoor access; cleanliness; public transportation and pedestrian friendliness; safety; weather; peace and quiet; people-watching; environmental friendliness. *Travelandleisure.com, "America's Favorite Cities 2010," November 2010*
- Denver was selected as one of "America's Favorite Cities." The city ranked #7 in the "People" category. Respondents to an online survey were asked to rate 35 top urban destinations in the U.S. from a visitor's perspective. Criteria: attractive; friendly; stylish; intelligent; athletic/active; diverse. *Travelandleisure.com, "America's Favorite Cities 2010," November 2010*

- Denver was selected as one of "America's Favorite Cities." The city ranked #10 in the "Nightlife" category. Respondents to an online survey were asked to rate 35 top urban destinations in the U.S. from a visitor's perspective. Criteria: cocktail hour; live music/concerts and bands; singles/bar scene. *Travelandleisure.com, "America's Favorite Cities 2010," November 2010*

Business/Finance Rankings

- *Forbes* ranked the largest metro areas in the U.S. in terms of the "Best Cities for Young Professionals." The Denver metro area ranked #7out of 15. Criteria: job growth; unemployment rate; median salary of college graduates age 24 to 34; cost of living; number of small businesses per capita; number of large companies; percentage of population 25 years of age and older with college degrees. *Forbes.com, "America's Best Cities for Young Professionals," July 12, 2011*
- The Denver metro area was identified as one of 10 "Cities Where the Recession is Easing." The metro area was ranked #6. Criteria: job growth; goods produced; home sale prices; unemployment rates. *Forbes.com, "Cities Where the Recession is Easing," March 3, 2010*
- Experian ranked the top 20 major U.S. metropolitan areas by average debt per consumer. The Denver metro area was ranked #3. Criteria: average debt per consumer. Debt for this study includes credit cards, auto loans and personal loans. It does not include mortgages. *Experian, May 13, 2010*
- Denver was identified as one of America's most coupon-loving cities by *Coupons.com.* The city ranked #19 out of 25. Criteria: online coupon usage. *Coupons.com, "Top 25 Most Frugal Cities of 2011," February 23, 2012*
- Denver was identified as one of the top 25 U.S. cities with the most credit card debt by credit reporting bureau Experian. The city was ranked #13. *Experian, March 4, 2011*
- Denver was identified as one of the "Best Cities for Recent College Graduates." The city ranked #4. Criteria: concentration of young adults (age 20 to 24); inventory of jobs requiring less than one year of experience; average cost of rent for a one bedroom apartment. *CareerBuilder.com, "Top 10 Best Cities for Recent College Graduates," August 30, 2011*
- Denver was identified as one of the "Unhappiest Cities to Work in 2012" by *CareerBliss.com,* an online community for career advancement. The city ranked #21 out of 30. Criteria: independent company reviews from employees all over the country on: relationship with their boss and co-workers; work environment; job resources; growth opportunities; compensation; company culture; company reputation; daily tasks; job control over work performed on a daily basis. *CareerBliss.com, "Happiest and Unhappiest Cities to Work in 2012"*
- Denver was identified as one of the best cities for new college graduates. The city ranked #8. Criteria: cost of living; average annual salary; unemployment rate; number of employers looking to hire people at entry-level. *Business Week, "The Best Cities for New Grads," July 20, 2010*
- Denver was selected as one of the "100 Best Places to Live and Launch" in the U.S. The city ranked #7. The editors at *Fortune Small Business* ranked 296 Census-designated metro areas by business friendliness (Launching Score, % New Businesses) and lifestyle offerings (Living Score). Then they picked the town within each of the top 100 metro areas that best blends business and pleasure. *Fortune Small Business, "100 Best Places to Live and Launch 2008," April 2008*
- *American City Business Journals* ranked America's 261 largest cities in terms of their resident's wealth. Denver ranked #106. Criteria: per capita income; median household income; percentage of households with annual incomes of $200,000 or more; median home value. *American City Business Journals, "Where the Money Is: America's Wealth Centers," August 18, 2008*
- The Denver metro area appeared on the Milken Institute "2011 Best Performing Metros" list. Rank: #44 out of 200 large metro areas. Criteria: job growth; wage and salary growth; high-tech output growth. *Milken Institute, "2011 Best Performing Metros"*

- The Denver metro area was selected as one of the best cities for entrepreneurs in America by *Inc. Magazine.* Criteria: job-growth data for 335 metro areas was analyzed for: recent growth trend; mid-term growth; long-term trend; current year growth. The Denver metro area ranked #20 among large metro areas and #108 overall. *Inc. Magazine, "The Best Cities for Doing Business," July 2008*

- Denver was ranked #45 out of 145 regions worldwide in terms of its "Knowledge Competitiveness Index." The index attempts to measure the knowledge-based development taking place throughout the world and is based on 19 measures of economic performance that indicate a region's ability to translate its knowledge capacity into economic value. *Centre for International Competitiveness, World Knowledge Competitiveness Index 2008*

- *Forbes* ranked the 200 most populous metro areas in the U.S. in terms of the "Best Places for Business and Careers." The Denver metro area was ranked #9. Criteria: costs (business and living); job growth (past and projected); income growth; educational attainment; projected economic growth; crime; cultural and recreational opportunities; net migration patterns; number of highly ranked colleges. *Forbes, "Best Places for Business and Careers," June 2011*

Children/Family Rankings

- The Denver metro area was selected as one of the "Best Cities for Relocating Families" by Worldwide ERC and Primacy Relocation. The 2008 study looked at nearly 50 factors important to relocating families including: recent job growth; nearby top-ranked colleges; in-state tuition for four-year public colleges; population growth since 2000; pediatricians per 100,000 population; and a Green Living index. *Worldwide ERC and Primacy Relocation, "2008 Best Cities for Relocating Families"*

- *Fit Pregnancy* magazine ranked the 50 best U.S. cities in which to have a baby. Denver was ranked #5. Criteria: access to hospitals and doctors; affordability; birthing options; breastfeeding; child care; fertility laws/resources; maternal and infant health risk; parks/stroller friendliness; safety. *Fit Pregnancy, "The Best Cities in America to Have a Baby 2008"*

Culture/Performing Arts Rankings

- Denver was selected as one of the top 10 cities for design in America by architectural firm RMJM Hillier. The city was ranked #8. American cities with more than 500,000 residents were ranked according to criteria such as the quality of public transit, the number of LEED-registered buildings (indicating sustainable design) and how many of the city's employees work within creative industries such as performing arts or publishing. Resident interviews were used to rate a city's design factor, which takes in elements of a city's architecture as well as its creative appeal. *RMJM Hillier, "America's Best Cities for Design," June 25, 2008*

- Denver was selected as one of "America's Top 25 Arts Destinations." The city ranked #15 in the big city (population 500,000 and over) category. Criteria: readers' top choices for arts travel destinations based on the richness and variety of visual arts sites, activities and events. *American Style, "America's Top 25 Arts Destinations," May 2010*

Dating/Romance Rankings

- Denver was selected as one of the best cities for single women by *Rent.com.* The city ranked #4 of 10. Criteria: high single male-to-female ratio; lively nightlife; low divorce rate; low cost of living. *Rent.com, "Top 10 Cities for Single Women," August 19, 2011*

- Denver appeared on *Men's Health's* list of the most sex-happy cities in America. The city ranked #5 of 100. Criteria: condom sales; birth rates; sex toy sales; rates of chlamydia, gonorrhea, and syphilis. *Men's Health, "America's Most Sex-Happy Cities," October 2010*

- *Men's Health* ranked 100 U.S. cities in terms of best (and worst) marriages. Denver was ranked #34 (#1 = worst). Criteria: rate of failed marriages; stringency of divorce laws; percentage of population who've split; number of licensed marriage and family therapists. *Men's Health, "Splitsville, USA," May 2010*

- Eli Lily and Company, in partnership with Sperling's BestPlaces, ranked the nation's 50 largest metro areas in terms of the "Most Romantic Cities for Baby Boomers." The Denver metro area ranked #42. Criteria: marriage and divorce rates among baby boomers age 45 to 60; great restaurants; dance studios; chocolate, jewelry and flower sales. *Eli Lily and Company, "Most Romantic Cities for Baby Boomers," April 20, 2007*
- The Denver metro area was selected as one of the "Best Cities for Relocating Singles" by Worldwide ERC and Primacy Relocation. The area ranked #56 out of the 100 largest metro areas in the U.S. Criteria: recent job growth; recent singles population growth; overall population growth; affordable rental housing; cost-of-living index; expanded arts and recreation opportunities; ratio of single men and single women; affordability of quality higher education (including state residency requirements); diversity index; climate; population density. *Worldwide ERC and Primacy Relocation, "2008 Best Cities for Relocating Singles"*
- *Forbes* ranked the 40 most populous urbanized areas in the U.S. in terms of the "Best Cities for Singles." The Denver metro area ranked #13. Criteria: number of singles; cost of living alone; nightlife; culture; job growth; coolness; and online dating participation. *Forbes.com, "Best Cities for Singles," July 27, 2009*

Education Rankings

- *Men's Health* ranked 100 U.S. cities in terms of their education levels. Denver was ranked #50 (#1 = most educated city). Criteria: high school graduation rates; school enrollment; educational attainment; number of households who have outstanding student loans; number of households whose members have taken adult-education courses. *Men's Health, "Where School Is In: The Most and Least Educated Cities," September 12, 2011*
- Denver was selected as one of "America's Most Literate Cities." The city ranked #10 out of the 75 largest U.S. cities. Criteria: number of booksellers; library resources; Internet resources; educational attainment; periodical publishing resources; newspaper circulation. *Central Connecticut State University, "America's Most Literate Cities 2011"*
- Denver was identified as one of the 100 "smartest" metro areas in the U.S. The area ranked #15. Criteria: the editors rated the collective brainpower of the 100 largest metro areas in the U.S. based on their residents' educational attainment. *American City Business Journals, April 14, 2008*
- Denver was identified as one of "America's Smartest Cities" by *The Daily Beast.* The metro area ranked #5 out of 55. The editors ranked metropolitan areas with one million or more residents on the following criteria: percentage of residents over age 25 with bachelor's or graduate degrees; non-fiction book sales; ratio of institutions of higher education; libraries per capita. *The Daily Beast, "America's Smartest Cities," October 24, 2010*
- Denver was identified as one of "America's Brainiest Bastions" by *Portfolio.com.* The metro area ranked #21 out of 200. *Portfolio.com* analyzed levels of educational attainment in the nation's 200 largest metropolitan areas. The editors established scores for five levels of educational attainment, based on relative earning power of adult workers age 25 or older. Scores were determined by comparing the median income for all workers with the median income for those workers at a specified educational level. *Portfolio.com, "America's Brainiest Bastions," December 1, 2010*
- Denver was identified as one of "America's Smartest Cities" by *CNNMoney.com.* The area ranked #8. Criteria: percentage of residents with bachelors or graduate degrees. *CNNMoney.com, "America's Smartest Cities," October 1, 2010*

Environmental Rankings

- The Denver was identified as one of North America's greenest metropolitan areas. The area ranked #5. The Green City Index is comprised of 31 indicators, and scores cities across nine categories: carbon dioxide; energy; land use; buildings; transport; water; waste; air quality; environmental governance. The 27 largest metropolitan areas in the U.S. and Canada were considered. *Economist Intelligence Unit, sponsored by Siemens, "U.S. and Canada Green City Index, 2011"*

- The Denver was identified as one of America's cities with the most ENERGY STAR certified buildings. The area ranked #11 out of 25. Criteria: number of ENERGY STAR labeled buildings in 2010. *U.S. Environmental Protection Agency, "Top Cities With the Most ENERGY STAR Certified Buildings," March 15, 2011*

- The Denver metro area was identified as one of the snowiest major metropolitan areas in the U.S. by *Forbes.* The metro area ranked #1 out of 10. Criteria: average annual snowfall. *Forbes, "America's Snowiest Cities," January 12, 2011*

- Denver was selected as one of 22 "Smarter Cities" for energy by the Natural Resources Defense Council. Criteria: investment in green power; energy efficiency measures; conservation. *Natural Resources Defense Council, "2010 Smarter Cities," July 19, 2010*

- *American City Business Journal* ranked 43 metropolitan areas in terms of their "greenness." The Denver metro area ranked #7. Criteria: Forty-one metros in which *ACBJ* has business weeklies, plus Indianapolis and Cleveland, were ranked based on 20 different indicators such as adoption of green technologies, utilization of environmentally sound practices, and air and water quality. *American City Business Journals, "Green City Index," March 11, 2010*

- Denver was selected as one of "America's 50 Greenest Cities" by *Popular Science.* The city ranked #19. Criteria: electricity; transportation; green living; recycling and green perspective. *Popular Science, February 2008*

- 100 of the largest metro areas in the U.S. were analyzed in terms of their current drought severity. The Denver metro area ranked #85 (#1 = driest). The rankings were based on statistics such as long-term precipitation trends and patterns and the Palmer drought indices. *Sperling's BestPlaces, www.BestPlaces.net, "America's Drought-Riskiest Cities," November 2007*

- The U.S. Conference of Mayors and Wal-Mart Stores sponsor the Mayors' Climate Protection Awards Program. The awards recognize and honor mayors for outstanding and innovative practices that mayors are taking to increase energy efficiency in their cities, and to help curb global warming. Denver received First Place Honors in the large cities category. *U.S. Conference of Mayors, "2009 Mayors' Climate Protection Awards Program"*

- The Denver metro area appeared in *Country Home's* "Best Green Places" report. The area ranked #29 out of 379. Criteria: official energy policies; green power; green buildings; availability of fresh, locally grown food. *Country Home, "Best Green Places," 2008*

Food/Drink Rankings

- Denver was identified as one of "America's Drunkest Cities of 2011" by *The Daily Beast.* The city ranked #13 out of 25. Criteria: binge drinking; drinks consumed per month. *The Daily Beast, "Tipsy Towns: Where are America's Drunkest Cities?," December 31, 2011*

- Denver was selected as one of America's best cities for hamburgers by the readers of *Travel + Leisure* in their annual America's Favorite Cities survey. The city was ranked #4 out of 10. Criteria:. *Travel + Leisure, "America's Best Burger Cities," May 2011*

- Coors Field (Colorado Rockies) was selected as one of PETA's "2011 Top 10 Vegetarian-Friendly Major League Ballparks." The park ranked #5. *People for the Ethical Treatment of Animals, "2011 Top 10 Vegetarian-Friendly Major League Ballparks"*

Health/Fitness Rankings

- The American Podiatric Medical Association and *Prevention* magazine ranked 100 American cities based on walkability. Nineteen walking criteria were evaluated including the percentage of adults who walk to work, number of parks per square mile, number of trails for walking and hiking, air pollution, use of mass transit, crime rate, pedestrian fatalities, and percentage of adults who walk for fitness. Denver ranked #20. *Prevention, "The Best Walking Cities of 2009," May 2009; American Podiatric Medical Association, "2009 Best Fitness-Walking Cities," April 7, 2009*

- Denver was identified as one of the "Worst Bed Bug-Infested Cities" in the U.S. by *Forbes.* Orkin and Terminix, the nation's largest pest control companies, both compiled lists based on the number of calls they've received and bed bug jobs performed relative to population. *Forbes* selected the 13 cities that appeared on both lists. *Forbes, "America's Worst Bed Bug-Infested Cities," December 23, 2010*

- The Denver metro area was selected as one of the worst cities for bed bugs in America by Rollins corporation, the owner of seven pest control companies, including Orkin. The area ranked #4 based on the number of bed bug treatments from January to December 2011. *Rollins, "The Top 50 U.S. Cities for Bed Bugs," March 19, 2012*

- Denver was identified as one of the most bed bug-infested cities in the U.S. by Terminix. Denver ranked #6.Criteria: complaint calls from customers; confirmed cases by professionals. *Terminix, "2011 Most Bedbug-Infested Cities," May 24, 2011*

- Denver was named a finalist in the "2009 Accessible America Contest" by the National Organization on Disability. The award recognizes communities that have made extraordinary efforts to create an accessible environment for people with disabilities. *National Organization on Disability, 2009 Accessible America Contest*

- Denver was selected as one of the 25 fittest cities in America by *Men's Fitness Online*. It ranked #7 out of America's 50 largest cities. Criteria: fitness centers and sport stores; nutrition; sports participation; TV viewing; overweight/sedentary; junk food; air quality; geography; commute; parks and open space; city recreational facilities; access to healthcare; motivation; mayor and city initiatives; state obesity initiatives. *Men's Fitness, "The Fittest and Fattest Cities in America," March 5, 2012*

- Denver was identified as a "2011 Asthma Capital." The area ranked #78 out of the nation's 100 largest metropolitan areas. Twelve factors were used to identify the most challenging places to live for people with asthma: estimated prevalence; self-reported prevalence; crude death rate for asthma; annual pollen score; annual air quality; public smoking laws; number of board-certified asthma specialists; school inhaler access laws; rescue medication use; controller medication use; uninsured rate; poverty rate. *Asthma and Allergy Foundation of America, "2011 Asthma Capitals"*

- Denver was identified as a "2011 Fall Allergy Capital." The area ranked #82 out of 100. Three groups of factors were used to identify the most severe cities for people with allergies during the fall season: annual pollen levels; medicine utilization; access to board-certified allergists. *Asthma and Allergy Foundation of America, "2011 Fall Allergy Capitals"*

- Denver was identified as a "2012 Spring Allergy Capital." The area ranked #97 out of 100. Three groups of factors were used to identify the most severe cities for people with allergies during the spring season: annual pollen levels; medicine utilization; access to board-certified allergists. *Asthma and Allergy Foundation of America, "2012 Spring Allergy Capitals"*

- *Men's Health* examined 100 major U.S. cities and selected the best and worst cities for men. Denver ranked #33. Criteria: 35 statistical parameters of long life in the categories of health, quality of life, and fitness. *Men's Health, "The 10 Best and Worst Cities for Men 2012," January/February 2012*

- The Denver metropolitan area was selected as one of the best metros for hospital care in America by *HealthGrades.com.* The rankings are based on a comprehensive study of patient death and complication rates in the nation's nearly 5,000 hospitals. Hospitals performing in the top 5% nationwide across 26 different medical procedures and diagnoses were identified. *HealthGrades.com* then ranked cities by the highest percentage of these Distinguished Hospitals for Clinical Excellence™. The Denver metro area ranked #39. *HealthGrades.com, "America's Top 50 Cities for Hospital Care," January 21, 2012*

- The American Academy of Dermatology ranked 26 U.S. metropolitan regions in terms of their residents knowledge, attitude and behaviors towards tanning, sun protection and skin cancer detection. The Denver metro area ranked #3. The results of the study are based on an online survey of over 7,000 adults nationwide. *American Academy of Dermatology, "Suntelligence: How Sun Smart is Your City," May 3, 2010*

- The Denver metro area appeared in the 2011 Gallup-Healthways Well-Being Index. The index, based on interviews with more than 350,000 Americans, measured jobs, finances, physical health, emotional state of mind and communities. The metro area ranked #42 out of 190. Criteria: life evaluation; emotional health; work environment; physical health; healthy behaviors; basic access (basic needs optimal for a healthy life, such as access to food and medicine, having health insurance and feeling safe while walking at night). *Gallup-Healthways, "State of Well-Being 2011"*

- The Denver metro area was identified as one of "America's Most Stressful Cities" by *Sperling's BestPlaces*. The metro area ranked #19 out of 50. Criteria: unemployment rate; suicide rate; commute time; mental health; poor rest; alcohol use; violent crime rate; property crime rate; cloudy days annually. *Sperling's BestPlaces, www.BestPlaces.net, "Stressful Cities 2012*
- *Men's Health* ranked 100 U.S. cities in terms of their activity levels. Denver was ranked #9 (#1 = most active city). Criteria: where and how often residents exercise; percentage of households that watch more than 15 hours of cable television a week and buy more than 11 video games a year; death rate from deep-vein thrombosis, a condition linked to sitting for extended periods of time. *Men's Health, "Where Sit Happens: The Most and Least Active Cities in America," June 20, 2011*
- 50 of the largest metro areas in the U.S. were analyzed in terms of their health and fitness by the American College of Sports Medicine in their "American Fitness Index." The Denver metro area ranked #6 (#1 = healthiest). Criteria: preventative health behaviors; levels of chronic disease; health care access; community resources and policies that support physical activity. *American College of Sports Medicine, "Health and Community Fitness Status of the 50 Largest Metropolitan Areas," August 1, 2011*
- Denver was selected as one of the "20 Most Livable U.S. Cities for Wheelchair Users" by the Christopher & Dana Reeve Foundation. The city ranked #4. Criteria: Medicaid eligibility and spending; access to physicians and rehabilitation facilities; access to fitness facilities and recreation; access to paratransit; percentage of people living with disabilities who are employed; clean air; climate. *Christopher & Dana Reeve Foundation, "20 Most Livable U.S. Cities for Wheelchair Users," July 26, 2010*
- The Denver metro area was selected as one of "America's Most Relaxed Cities" by *Forbes*. The metro area ranked #6 out of 10. Criteria: unemployment rates; numbers of commuters that spend an hour or more in traffic on the way to work; average weekly hours people spend at work; access to health care; overall health of residents; percentage of population who exercise. *Forbes, "America's Most Relaxed Cities," November 5, 2010*

Pet Rankings

- Denver was selected as one of the "Top 10 Cat-Friendly Cities" in the U.S. The area ranked #5. Criteria: cat ownership per capita; level of veterinary care; microchipping; cat-friendly local ordinances. *CATalyst Council, "Top 10 Cat-Friendly Cities," March 27, 2009*

Real Estate Rankings

- *Fortune* ranked the 100 largest metro areas in the U.S. in terms of projected median home price change in 2010. The Denver metro area ranked #17. *Fortune, "The 2010 Housing Outlook," December 9, 2009*
- Denver appeared on *ApartmentRatings.com* "Top Cities for Renters" list in 2009." The area ranked #54. Overall satisfaction ratings were ranked using thousands of user submitted scores for hundreds of apartment complexes located in the 100 most populated U.S. municipalities. *ApartmentRatings.com, "2009 Renter Satisfaction Rankings"*
- The Denver metro area was identified as one of the "Top 25 Real Estate Investment Markets" by *FinestExperts.com*. The metro area ranked #21. Over 10,000 real estate markets were analyzed to identify the most suitable places for real estate investors to seek stability and growth. Criteria: employment; rental markets; growth levels as offset by foreclosures. *FinestExperts.com, "Top 25 Real Estate Investment Markets," January 7, 2010*
- The Denver metro area appeared in a *Wall Street Journal* article ranking cities by "housing stress." The metro area was ranked #30 (#1 = most stress). Criteria: fraction of mortgage-holding homeowners with a monthly housing payment in excess of 30 percent of income; percentage of people without health insurance; unemployment rate. *The Wall Street Journal, "Which Cities Face Biggest Housing Risk," October 5, 2010*
- The Center for Housing Policy ranked 210 U.S. metropolitan areas by the fair market rent for a two-bedroom unit. The Denver metro area was ranked #75. (#1 = most expensive) with a rent of $921. Criteria: Fair Market Rent (FMR) in effect during the fourth quarter of 2009 based on HUD's fiscal year 2010 FMRs. *The Center for Housing Policy, "Paycheck to Paycheck: Most to Least Expensive Rental Markets in 2009"*

- The Denver metro area was identified as one of the best U.S. markets to invest in rental property" by HomeVestors and Local Market Monitor. The area ranked #52 out of 100. Criteria: risk-return premium relative to national average. *HomeVestors and Local Market Monitor, "Best 100 U.S. Markets to Invest in Rental Property," March 9, 2012*

Safety Rankings

- Symantec, the makers of Norton, in partnership with Sperling's BestPlaces, ranked the 50 largest cities in the U.S. in terms of their vulnerability to cybercrime. The city ranked #6. Criteria: number of cyberattacks and potential infections; level of Internet access; expenditures on smartphones and computer hardware/software; wireless hotspots; broadband connectivity; Internet usage; online purchases. *Symantec, "Riskiest Online Cities of 2012" February 15, 2012*
- Farmers Insurance Group of Companies, in partnership with Sperling's BestPlaces, ranked 379 metro areas and identified the "Most Secure U.S. Places to Live." The Denver metro area ranked #9 out of the top 20 in the large metro area category (500,000 or more residents). Criteria: crime statistics; extreme weather; risk of natural disasters; housing depreciation; foreclosures; environmental hazards; terrorist threats; air quality; life expectancy; mortality rates from cancer and motor vehicle accidents; job loss numbers. *Farmers Insurance Group, "Most Secure U.S. Places to Live 2011," December 15, 2011*
- Allstate ranked the 193 largest cities in America in terms of driver safety. Denver ranked #51. In addition, drivers were 1.8% less likely to have had an accident compared to the national average. Allstate researchers analyzed internal property damage reported claims over a two-year period (from January 2008 to December 2009) to protect findings from external influences such as weather or road construction. A weighted average of the two-year numbers determined the annual percentages. The report defines an auto crash as any collision resulting in a property damage claim. *Allstate, "2011 Allstate America's Best Drivers Report™"*
- Denver was identified as one of the safest large cities in America by CQ Press. All 34 cities with populations of 500,000 or more that reported crime rates in 2010 for murder, rape, robbery, aggravated assault, burglary, and motor vehicle thefts were ranked. The city ranked #10 out of the top 10. *CQ Press, City Crime Rankings 2011-2012*
- The National Insurance Crime Bureau ranked 366 metro areas in the U.S. in terms of per capita rates of vehicle theft. The Denver metro area ranked #68 (#1 = highest rate). Criteria: number of vehicle theft offenses per 100,000 inhabitants in 2010. *National Insurance Crime Bureau, "Hot Spots," June 21, 2011*
- The Denver metro area was identified as one of the most dangerous metro areas for pedestrians by Transportation for America. The metro area ranked #29 out of 52 metro areas with over 1 million residents. Criteria: area's population divided by the number of pedestrian fatalities in that area. *Transportation for America, "Dangerous by Design 2011"*

Seniors/Retirement Rankings

- Bankers Life and Casualty Company, in partnership with Sperling's BestPlaces, ranked the nation's 50 largest metro areas in terms of the "Best U.S. Cities for Seniors." The Denver metro area ranked #5. Criteria: healthcare; transportation; housing; environment; economy; health and longevity; social and spiritual life; crime. *Bankers Life and Casualty Company, Center for a Secure Retirement, "Best U.S. Cities for Seniors 2011," September 2011*
- The Denver metro area was identified as one of "America's Most Affordable Places to Retire" by *Forbes*. The metro area ranked #7. Criteria: housing affordability; inflation; number of persons over 65 who are employed; net migration for persons over 65; percent of persons over 65 living below poverty level; doctors per capita; number of citizens tapping their Medicare benefits per thousand people. *Forbes.com, "America's Most Affordable Places to Retire," September 5, 2008*
- The Denver metro area was selected as one of "America's Best Places to Grow Old" by *Forbes*. The area was ranked #7 out of 10. Criteria: housing affordability; inflationary pressures; number of persons over 65 who are currently employed; net migration for persons over 65; percent of seniors living below poverty level; doctors per capita; number of citizens tapping their Medicare benefits per 1,000 people. *Forbes, "America's Best Places to Grow Old," December 12, 2008*

- Denver was identified as one of the "100 Most Popular Retirement Towns" by *Topretirements.com* The list reflects the 100 cities (out of 815+ total cities reviewed) that visitors to the website are most interested in for retirement. *Topretirements.com, "100 Most Popular Retirement Towns," February 21, 2012*

Sports/Recreation Rankings

- Denver was selected as one of "America's Most Miserable Sports Cities" by *Forbes.* The city was ranked #7. Criteria: postseason losses; years since last title; ratio of cumulative seasons to championships won. Contenders were limited to cities with at least 75 total seasons of NFL, NBA, NHL and MLB play. *Forbes, "America's Most Miserable Sports Cities," February 28, 2012*

- Denver appeared on the *Sporting News* list of the "Best Sports Cities" for 2011. The area ranked #20 out of 271 cities in the U.S. *Sporting News* takes a 12-month snapshot of each city's sports, putting a heavy premium on regular-season won-lost records (from the most recently completed season). Other criteria include: playoff berths, bowl appearances and tournament bids; championships; applicable power ratings; quality of competition; overall fan fervor (measured in part by attendance); abundance of teams (rewarding quality over quantity); stadium and arena quality; ticket availability and prices; franchise ownership; and marquee appeal of athletes. *Sporting News, "Best Sports Cities 2011," October 4, 2011*

- Scarborough Sports Marketing, a leading market research firm, identified the Denver DMA (Designated Market Area) as one of the top markets for Summer Olympics fans with more than 65% of adults reporting that they are "very, somewhat, or a little bit interested" in the Summer Olympics. *Scarborough Sports Marketing, July 30, 2008*

- Scarborough Sports Marketing, a leading market research firm, identified the Denver DMA (Designated Market Area) as one of the top markets for sports with more than 60% of adults reporting that they are "very" interested in any of the sports measured by Scarborough. *Scarborough Sports Marketing, October 1, 2008*

- Denver was chosen as a bicycle friendly community by the League of American Bicyclists. A Bicycle Friendly Community welcomes cyclists by providing safe accommodation for cycling and encouraging people to bike for transportation and recreation. There are four award levels: Platinum; Gold; Silver; and Bronze. The community achieved an award level of Silver. *League of American Bicyclists, "Bicycle Friendly Community Master List 2011"*

- Denver was chosen as one of America's best cities for bicycling. The city ranked #12 out of 50. Criteria: number of segregated bike lanes, municipal bike racks, and bike boulevards; vibrant and diverse bike culture; smart, savvy bike shops; interviews with national and local advocates, bike shops and other experts. The editors only considered cities with populations of 100,000 or more. *Bicycling, "America's Best Bike Cities," April 2010*

Technology Rankings

- Denver was selected as one of the best cities for broadband by Ookla, the company behind the broadband speed testing site Speedtest.net. The city ranked #9 out of 10. Criteria: U.S. cities were ranked based on their 30-day average speeds. Only cities with more than 75,000 people connecting for more than three months were measured. *Ookla, "The Top 10 Cities With the Best Broadband," May 25, 2010*

- The Denver metro area was selected as one of "America's Most Wired Cities" by *Forbes*. The metro area was ranked #7 out of 20. Criteria: percentage of Internet users with high-speed access; number of companies providing high-speed Internet; number of public wireless hot spots. *Forbes, "America's Most Wired Cities," March 2, 2010*

- The Denver metro area was selected as one of "America's Most Innovative Cities" by *Forbes*. The metro area was ranked #18 out of 20. Criteria: patents per capita; venture capital investment per capita; ratio of high-tech, science and "creative" jobs. *Forbes, "America's Most Innovative Cities," May 24, 2010*

Transportation Rankings

- Denver was identified as one of America's "10 Best Cities for Public Transportation" by *U.S. News & World Report.* The city ranked #9. The ten cities selected had the best combination of public transportation investment, ridership, and safety. *U.S. News & World Report, "10 Best Cities for Public Transportation," February 8, 2011*

- Denver was identified as one of America's worst cities for speed traps by the National Motorists Association. The city ranked #5 out of 25. Criteria: speed trap locations per 100,000 residents. *National Motorists Association, September 2011*

- The Denver metro area was identified as one of the best U.S. cities to live in without a car by *24/7 Wall St.* The area ranked #7 out of 10. Criteria: percentage of neighborhoods covered by public transit; frequency of service for those neighborhoods; share of jobs reachable within 90 minutes or less by public transit; how accessible amenities are for residents on foot; percentage of commuters who bike to work. The 100 largest metropolitan areas in the U.S. were examined. *24/7 Wall St., "The Best Cities to Live in Car-Free," November 28, 2011*

- The Denver metro area appeared on *Forbes* list of the best and worst cities for commuters. The metro area ranked #32 out of 60 (#1 is best). Criteria: travel time; road congestion; travel delays. *Forbes.com, "Best and Worst Cities for Commuters," February 16, 2010*

Women/Minorities Rankings

- *Women's Health* examined U.S. cities and identified the 100 best cities for women. Denver was ranked #25. Criteria: 30 categories were examined from obesity and breast cancer rates to commuting times and hours spent working out. *Women's Health, "Best Cities for Women 2012"*

- Denver was ranked #52 out of 100 metro areas in *SELF Magazine's* ranking of America's healthiest places for women." A panel of experts came up with more than 50 criteria including death and disease rates, environmental indicators, community resources, and lifestyle habits. *SELF Magazine, "Secrets of America's Healthiest Women," December 2008*

- Denver was selected as one of the "Gayest Cities in America" by *The Advocate.* The city ranked #15 out of 15. *The Advocate* used several different measures to establish "per capita queerness"—including a city's number of teams entered in the Gay Softball World Series, gay bookstores, openly gay elected officials and semifinalists in the International Mr. Leather Contest. *The Advocate, "Gayest Cities in America, 2012" January 2012*

- Denver was selected as one of the 25 healthiest cities for Latinas by *Latina Magazine.* The city ranked #3. Criteria: U.S. cities with populations over 500,000 residents were evaluated on the following criteria: percentage of 18-34 year-olds per city; Latino college graduation rates; number of colleges and universities; affordability; housing costs; income growth over time; average salary; percentage of singles; climate; safety; how the city's diversity compares to the national average; opportunities for minority entrepreneurs. *Latina Magazine, "Top 15 U.S. Cities for Young Latinos to Live In," August 19, 2011*

- The Denver metro area appeared on *Forbes'* list of the "Best Cities for Minority Entrepreneurs." The area ranked #3 out of 10. Criteria: 52 metropolitan statistical areas were examined. For each ethnicity (African Americans, Asians and Hispanics), the editors measured housing affordability, population growth, income growth, and entrepreneurship (per capita self-employment). *Forbes, "Best Cities for Minority Entrepreneurs," March 23, 2011*

- Denver was selected as one of the "Top 10 Cities for Hispanics." Criteria: the prospect of a good job; a safe place to raise a family; a manageable cost of living; the ability to buy and keep a home; a culture of inclusion where Hispanics are highly represented; resources to help start a business; the presence of Hispanic or Spanish-language media; representation of Hispanic needs on local government; a thriving arts and culture community; air quality; energy costs; city's state of health and rates of obesity. *Hispanic Magazine, August 2008*

Miscellaneous Rankings

- *Men's Health* ranked 100 U.S. cities by their level of sadness. Denver was ranked #64 (#1 = saddest city). Criteria: suicide rates; unemployment rates; percentage of households that use antidepressants; percent of population who report feeling blue all or most of the time. *Men's Health, "Frown Towns," November 28, 2011*

- Energizer Holdings, the makers of Edge® shave gel, in partnership with Sperling's BestPlaces, ranked 50 major metro areas in terms of everyday irritations. The Denver metro area ranked #41. Criteria: humidity levels; weather conditions; incidence of traffic delays and congestion; average commute times; frequency of flight delays and cancellations; rates of sleeplessness; underemployment; pollens and allergens; pests; comedy clubs per capita. *Energizer Holdings, "Most Irritation Prone Cities," July 23, 2010*

- Mars Chocolate North America, the makers of COMBOS®, in partnership with Sperling's BestPlaces, ranked 50 major metro areas in terms of their "manliness." The Denver metro area ranked #31. Criteria: number of professional sports teams; number of nearby NASCAR tracks and racing events; manly lifestyle; concentration of manly retail stores; manly occupations per capita; salty snack sales; "Board of Manliness" rankings. *Mars Chocolate North America, "America's Manliest Cities 2011," September 1, 2011*

- Denver was selected as one of the "Best Hair Cities" by *NaturallyCurly.com.* The city was ranked #9. Criteria: humidity levels; pollution; rainfall; average wind speeds; water hardness; beauty salons per capita. *NaturallyCurly.com, "Best/Worst Hair Cities," April 29, 2009*

- Denver was selected as one of "America's Best Cities for Hipsters" by *Travel + Leisure*. The city was ranked #10 out of 10. Criteria: live music; coffee bars; independent boutiques; best microbrews; offbeat and tech-savvy locals. *Travel + Leisure, "America's Best Cities for Hipsters," April 11, 2012*

- The Denver metro area was selected as one of "America's Greediest Cities" by *Forbes*. The area was ranked #4 out of 10. Criteria: number of Forbes 400 (*Forbes* annual list of the richest Americans) members per capita. *Forbes, "America's Greediest Cities," December 7, 2007*

- The Denver metro area appeared in *AutoMD.com's* ranking of the "Best and Worst Cities for Auto Repair." The metro area ranked #16 (#1 is best). The 50 most-populated metro areas in the U.S. were ranked on three critical factors: repair affordability; price disparity range; shop integrity factor. *AutoMD.com, "Advocacy for Repair Shop Fairness Report," February 24, 2010*

Business Environment

CITY FINANCES

City Government Finances

Component	2009 ($000)	2009 ($ per capita)
Total Revenues	1,831,623	3,113
Total Expenditures	2,566,495	4,362
Debt Outstanding	5,879,530	9,993
Cash and Securities[1]	4,761,008	8,092

Note: (1) Cash and security holdings of a government at the close of its fiscal year, including those of its dependent agencies, utilities, and liquor stores.
Source: U.S Census Bureau, State & Local Government Finances 2009

City Government Revenue by Source

Source	2009 ($000)	2009 ($ per capita)
General Revenue		
From Federal Government	204,856	348
From State Government	93,680	159
From Local Governments	0	0
Taxes		
Property	274,809	467
Sales and Gross Receipts	540,739	919
Personal Income	0	0
Corporate Income	0	0
Motor Vehicle License	19,514	33
Other Taxes	100,544	171
Current Charges	765,033	1,300
Liquor Store	0	0
Utility	216,262	368
Employee Retirement	-603,375	-1,026

Source: U.S Census Bureau, State & Local Government Finances 2009

City Government Expenditures by Function

Function	2009 ($000)	2009 ($ per capita)	2009 (%)
General Direct Expenditures			
Air Transportation	429,313	730	16.7
Corrections	94,460	161	3.7
Education	14,459	25	0.6
Employment Security Administration	0	0	0.0
Financial Administration	154,328	262	6.0
Fire Protection	102,844	175	4.0
General Public Buildings	49,780	85	1.9
Governmental Administration, Other	50,900	87	2.0
Health	52,191	89	2.0
Highways	107,668	183	4.2
Hospitals	0	0	0.0
Housing and Community Development	31,486	54	1.2
Interest on General Debt	76,073	129	3.0
Judicial and Legal	78,823	134	3.1
Libraries	40,826	69	1.6
Parking	9,627	16	0.4
Parks and Recreation	100,928	172	3.9
Police Protection	174,117	296	6.8
Public Welfare	190,035	323	7.4
Sewerage	96,041	163	3.7
Solid Waste Management	24,000	41	0.9
Veterans' Services	0	0	0.0
Liquor Store	0	0	0.0
Utility	277,348	471	10.8
Employee Retirement	141,042	240	5.5

Source: U.S Census Bureau, State & Local Government Finances 2009

Municipal Bond Ratings

Area	Moody's	S&P	Fitch
City	Aa1	AAA	AAA

Rating Systems (shown in declining order of credit quality): Moody's– Aaa, Aa, A, Baa, Ba, B, Caa, Ca, C (numerical modifiers 1, 2, and 3 are added to letter-rating); S&P– AAA, AA, A, BBB, BB, B, CCC, CC, C; Fitch– AAA, AA, A, BBB, BB, B, CCC, CC, C. Ratings may be modified by the addition of a plus or minus sign to show relative standing within the major rating categories.
Notes: n/a Not Available; w/d Withdrawn (1) Not Reviewed; (2) Issuer Rating/No General Obligation; (3) Standard and Poor's Issue Credit Rating (ICR) is a current opinion of an obliger with respect to a specific financial obligation, a specific class of financial obligations, or a specific financial program.
Source: U.S. Census Bureau, 2012 Statistical Abstract, Bond Ratings for City Governments by Largest Cities: 2010

DEMOGRAPHICS

Population Growth

Area	1990 Census	2000 Census	2010 Census	Population Growth (%) 1990-2000	Population Growth (%) 2000-2010
City	467,153	554,636	600,158	18.7	8.2
MSA[1]	1,666,935	2,179,296	2,543,482	30.7	16.7
U.S.	248,709,873	281,421,906	308,745,538	13.2	9.7

Note: (1) Figures cover the Denver-Aurora-Broomfield, CO Metropolitan Statistical Area—see Appendix B for areas included
Source: U.S. Census Bureau, 2010 Census

Household Size

Area	Persons in Household (%) One	Two	Three	Four	Five	Six	Seven or More	Average Household Size
City	40.6	30.4	11.7	8.9	4.4	2.0	2.0	2.22
MSA[1]	29.1	32.6	15.1	13.2	6.0	2.4	1.7	2.50
U.S.	26.7	32.8	16.1	13.4	6.5	2.6	1.9	2.58

Note: (1) Figures cover the Denver-Aurora-Broomfield, CO Metropolitan Statistical Area—see Appendix B for areas included
Source: U.S. Census Bureau, 2010 Census

Race

Area	White Alone[2] (%)	Black Alone[2] (%)	Asian Alone[2] (%)	AIAN[3] Alone[2] (%)	NHOPI[4] Alone[2] (%)	Other Race Alone[2] (%)	Two or More Races (%)
City	68.9	10.2	3.4	1.4	0.1	11.9	4.1
MSA[1]	78.0	5.6	3.7	1.0	0.1	8.0	3.6
U.S.	72.4	12.6	4.8	0.9	0.2	6.2	2.9

Note: (1) Figures cover the Denver-Aurora-Broomfield, CO Metropolitan Statistical Area—see Appendix B for areas included; (2) Alone is defined as not being in combination with one or more other races; (3) American Indian and Alaska Native; (4) Native Hawaiian and Other Pacific Islander
Source: U.S. Census Bureau, 2010 Census

Hispanic or Latino Origin

Area	Hispanic or Latino (%)	Mexican (%)	Puerto Rican (%)	Cuban (%)	Other Hispanic or Latino (%)
City	31.8	24.9	0.4	0.2	6.4
MSA[1]	22.5	16.7	0.4	0.1	5.2
U.S.	16.3	10.3	1.5	0.6	4.0

Note: Persons of Hispanic or Latino origin can be of any race; (1) Figures cover the Denver-Aurora-Broomfield, CO Metropolitan Statistical Area—see Appendix B for areas included
Source: U.S. Census Bureau, 2010 Census

Segregation

Type	Segregation Indices[1]				Percent Change		
	1990	2000	2010	2010 Rank[2]	1990-2000	1990-2010	2000-2010
Black/White	64.8	64.2	62.6	31	-0.5	-2.2	-1.6
Asian/White	29.5	32.3	33.4	83	2.9	3.9	1.1
Hispanic/White	46.7	50.3	48.8	31	3.6	2.1	-1.5

Note: Figures are based on an analysis of 1990, 2000, and 2010 Census Decennial Census tract data by William H. Frey, Brookings Institution and the University of Michigan Social Science Data Analysis Network. In this analysis all racial groups (whites, blacks, and asians) are non-Hispanic members of those races. Hispanics are shown as a separate category; All figures cover the Metropolitan Statistical Area (see Appendix B for areas included); (1) Segregation Indices are Dissimilarity Indices that measure the degree to which the minority group is distributed differently than whites across census tracts. They range from 0 (complete integration) to 100 (complete segregation) where the value indicates the percentage of the minority group that needs to move to be distributed exactly like whites; (2) Ranges from 1 (most segregated) to 102 (least segregated); n/a not available.
Source: www.CensusScope.org

Ancestry

Area	German	Irish	English	American	Italian	Polish	French[2]	Scottish	Dutch
City	14.7	10.0	8.4	3.3	4.4	2.2	2.6	1.9	1.4
MSA[1]	20.6	12.0	10.8	4.7	5.3	2.7	3.1	2.5	1.8
U.S.	16.1	11.6	8.8	6.1	5.7	3.2	3.0	1.9	1.6

Note: Figures are the percentage of the total population reporting a particular ancestry. The nine most commonly reported ancestries in the U.S. are shown. Figures include multiple ancestries (e.g. if a person reported being Irish and Italian, they were included in both columns); (1) Figures cover the Denver-Aurora-Broomfield, CO Metropolitan Statistical Area—see Appendix B for areas included; (2) Excludes Basque
Source: U.S. Census Bureau, 2008-2010 American Community Survey 3-Year Estimates

Foreign-Born Population

Area	Percent of Population Born in								
	Any Foreign Country	Mexico	Asia	Europe	Carribean	South America	Central America[2]	Africa	Canada
City	16.4	9.4	3.0	1.8	0.1	0.3	0.4	1.0	0.2
MSA[1]	12.2	5.7	2.8	1.6	0.1	0.3	0.5	0.7	0.3
U.S.	12.8	3.8	3.6	1.6	1.2	0.9	1.0	0.5	0.3

Note: (1) Figures cover the Denver-Aurora-Broomfield, CO Metropolitan Statistical Area—see Appendix B for areas included; (2) Excludes Mexico.
Source: U.S. Census Bureau, 2008-2010 American Community Survey 3-Year Estimates

Marital Status

Area	Never Married	Now Married[2]	Separated	Widowed	Divorced
City	41.4	39.0	2.4	5.0	12.2
MSA[1]	30.9	51.4	1.8	4.4	11.5
U.S.	31.6	49.6	2.2	6.1	10.7

Note: Figures are percentages and cover the population 15 years of age and older; (1) Figures cover the Denver-Aurora-Broomfield, CO Metropolitan Statistical Area—see Appendix B for areas included; (2) Excludes separated
Source: U.S. Census Bureau, 2008-2010 American Community Survey 3-Year Estimates

Age

Area	Percent of Population							Median Age
	Under Age 5	Age 5 to 17	Age 18 to 34	Age 35 to 49	Age 50 to 64	Age 65 to 79	80 Years and Over	
City	7.3	14.2	30.9	21.1	16.3	7.2	3.2	33.7
MSA[1]	7.1	17.8	24.0	22.3	18.7	7.4	2.6	35.7
U.S.	6.5	17.5	23.2	20.7	19.0	9.4	3.6	37.2

Note: (1) Figures cover the Denver-Aurora-Broomfield, CO Metropolitan Statistical Area—see Appendix B for areas included
Source: U.S. Census Bureau, 2010 Census

Male/Female Ratio

Area	Males	Females	Males per 100 Females
City	300,089	300,069	100.0
MSA[1]	1,264,550	1,278,932	98.9
U.S.	151,781,326	156,964,212	96.7

Note: (1) Figures cover the Denver-Aurora-Broomfield, CO Metropolitan Statistical Area—see Appendix B for areas included
Source: U.S. Census Bureau, 2010 Census

Religious Groups

Area	Catholic	Baptist	Non-Den.	Methodist[2]	Lutheran	LDS[3]	Pente-costal	Presby-terian[4]	Muslim[5]	Judaism
MSA[1]	16.1	3.0	4.6	1.7	2.1	2.4	1.2	1.6	0.6	0.6
U.S.	19.1	9.3	4.0	4.0	2.3	2.0	1.9	1.6	0.8	0.7

Note: Figures are the number of adherents as a percentage of the total population; (1) Figures cover the Denver-Aurora-Broomfield, CO Metropolitan Statistical Area—see Appendix B for areas included; (2) Methodist/Pietist; (3) Latter Day Saints; (4) Reformed; (5) Figures are estimates
Source: Association of Statisticians of American Religious Bodies, 2010 U.S. Religion Census: Religious Congregations & Membership Study

ECONOMY

Gross Metropolitan Product

Area	2007	2008	2009	2010	2010 Rank[2]
MSA[1]	147.1	154.3	152.7	157.1	17

Note: Figures are in billions of dollars; (1) Figures cover the Denver-Aurora-Broomfield, CO Metropolitan Statistical Area—see Appendix B for areas included; (2) Rank ranges from 1 to 363
Source: The United States Conference of Mayors, "U.S. Metro Economies: GMP and Employment Forecasts," June 2011

Economic Growth

Area	2007-2009 (%)	2010 (%)	2011 (%)	Rank[2]
MSA[1]	1.4	2.9	2.6	47
U.S.	-1.3	2.9	2.5	–

Note: Figures are real Gross Metropolitan Product growth rates and represent annual average percent change; (1) Figures cover the Denver-Aurora-Broomfield, CO Metropolitan Statistical Area—see Appendix B for areas included; (2) Rank ranges from 1 to 363
Source: The United States Conference of Mayors, "U.S. Metro Economies: GMP and Employment Forecasts," June 2011

Metropolitan Area Exports

Area	2005	2006	2007	2008	2009	2010	2010 Rank[2]
MSA[1]	2,918.0	3,844.0	4,195.8	4,633.5	4,309.8	4,990.9	47

Note: Figures are in millions of dollars; (1) Figures cover the Denver-Aurora-Broomfield, CO Metropolitan Statistical Area—see Appendix B for areas included; (2) Rank ranges from 1 to 369
Source: U.S. Department of Commerce, International Trade Administration, Office of Trade & Industry Information, Manufacturing & Services, data extracted April 2, 2012

INCOME

Income

Area	Per Capita ($)	Median Household ($)	Average Household ($)
City	30,806	45,526	68,791
MSA[1]	31,829	59,919	79,382
U.S.	26,942	51,222	70,116

Note: (1) Figures cover the Denver-Aurora-Broomfield, CO Metropolitan Statistical Area—see Appendix B for areas included
Source: U.S. Census Bureau, 2008-2010 American Community Survey 3-Year Estimates

Household Income Distribution

Area	Under $15,000	$15,000 -24,999	$25,000 -34,999	$35,000 -49,999	$50,000 -74,999	$75,000 -99,000	$100,000 -149,999	$150,000 and up
	Percent of Households Earning							
City	16.6	11.9	11.0	14.2	16.3	10.5	10.3	9.2
MSA[1]	10.6	9.0	9.3	13.3	18.3	13.3	15.2	11.0
U.S.	13.0	11.0	10.6	14.2	18.5	12.1	12.2	8.4

Note: (1) Figures cover the Denver-Aurora-Broomfield, CO Metropolitan Statistical Area—see Appendix B for areas included
Source: U.S. Census Bureau, 2008-2010 American Community Survey 3-Year Estimates

Poverty Rate

Area	All Ages	Under 18 Years Old	18 to 64 Years Old	65 Years and Over
City	19.8	30.1	17.2	15.0
MSA[1]	12.0	16.4	10.7	9.4
U.S.	14.4	20.1	13.1	9.4

Note: Figures are percentage of people whose income during the past 12 months was below the poverty level; (1) Figures cover the Denver-Aurora-Broomfield, CO Metropolitan Statistical Area—see Appendix B for areas included
Source: U.S. Census Bureau, 2008-2010 American Community Survey 3-Year Estimates

Personal Bankruptcy Filing Rate

Area	2006	2007	2008	2009	2010	2011
Denver County	2.24	3.24	4.38	5.54	6.30	6.20
U.S.	2.00	2.73	3.53	4.61	4.97	4.37

Note: Numbers are per 1,000 population and include Chapter 7 and Chapter 13 filings
Source: Federal Deposit Insurance Corporation, Regional Economic Conditions, March 9, 2012

EMPLOYMENT

Labor Force and Employment

Area	Civilian Labor Force Dec. 2010	Civilian Labor Force Dec. 2011	Civilian Labor Force % Chg.	Workers Employed Dec. 2010	Workers Employed Dec. 2011	Workers Employed % Chg.
City	319,329	325,874	2.0	288,061	295,836	2.7
MSA[1]	1,366,243	1,391,518	1.8	1,245,326	1,278,938	2.7
U.S.	153,156,000	153,373,000	0.1	139,159,000	140,681,000	1.1

Note: Data is not seasonally adjusted and covers workers 16 years of age and older; (1) Metropolitan Statistical Area—see Appendix B for areas included
Source: Bureau of Labor Statistics, http://stats.bls.gov

Unemployment Rate

Area	Jan.	Feb.	Mar.	Apr.	May	Jun.	Jul.	Aug.	Sep.	Oct.	Nov.	Dec.
	2011											
City	10.9	10.7	10.2	9.1	9.2	9.4	9.3	9.3	8.7	8.7	8.8	9.2
MSA[1]	9.9	9.8	9.3	8.3	8.5	8.8	8.6	8.5	7.9	7.8	7.9	8.1
U.S.	9.8	9.5	9.2	8.7	8.7	9.3	9.3	9.1	8.8	8.5	8.2	8.3

Note: Data is not seasonally adjusted and covers workers 16 years of age and older; All figures are percentages; (1) Metropolitan Statistical Area—see Appendix B for areas included
Source: Bureau of Labor Statistics, http://stats.bls.gov

Projected Unemployment Rate

Area	2010 (%)	2011 (%)	2012 (%)	2013 (%)
MSA[1]	9.3	8.4	7.6	6.8

Note: (1) Metropolitan Statistical Area—see Appendix B for areas included
Source: The United States Conference of Mayors, "U.S. Metro Economies: GMP and Employment Forecasts," June 2011

Employment by Occupation

Occupation Classification	City (%)	MSA[1] (%)	U.S. (%)
Management, Business, Science, and Arts	40.9	40.4	35.6
Natural Resources, Construction, and Maintenance	8.2	9.0	9.5
Production, Transportation, and Material Moving	8.7	9.0	12.1
Sales and Office	23.9	25.9	25.2
Service	18.4	15.7	17.6

Note: Figures cover employed civilians 16 years of age and older; (1) Figures cover the Denver-Aurora-Broomfield, CO Metropolitan Statistical Area—see Appendix B for areas included
Source: U.S. Census Bureau, 2008-2010 American Community Survey 3-Year Estimates

Employment by Industry

Sector	MSA[1]		U.S.
	Number of Employees	Percent of Total	Percent of Total
Construction	n/a	n/a	4.1
Education and Health Services	149,500	12.2	15.2
Financial Activities	90,900	7.4	5.8
Government	177,400	14.5	16.8
Information	43,900	3.6	2.0
Leisure and Hospitality	127,100	10.4	9.9
Manufacturing	61,300	5.0	8.9
Mining and Logging	n/a	n/a	0.6
Other Services	50,000	4.1	4.0
Professional and Business Services	214,000	17.5	13.3
Retail Trade	129,700	10.6	11.5
Transportation and Utilities	46,200	3.8	3.8
Wholesale Trade	62,900	5.1	4.2

Note: Figures cover non-farm employment as of December 2011 and are not seasonally adjusted; (1) Metropolitan Statistical Area—see Appendix B for areas included; n/a not available
Source: Bureau of Labor Statistics, http://stats.bls.gov

Occupations with Greatest Projected Employment Growth: 2008 – 2018

Occupation[1]	2008 Employment	2018 Projected Employment	Numeric Employment Change	Percent Employment Change
Registered Nurses	40,880	53,130	12,250	30.0
Combined Food Preparation and Serving Workers, Including Fast Food	51,320	62,180	10,860	21.2
Customer Service Representatives	38,300	44,710	6,410	16.7
Postsecondary Teachers	24,980	31,030	6,050	24.2
Waiters and Waitresses	45,430	50,990	5,560	12.2
Computer Software Engineers, Applications	16,410	21,540	5,130	31.3
Personal and Home Care Aides	11,520	16,460	4,940	42.9
Retail Salespersons	79,820	84,660	4,840	6.1
Janitors and Cleaners, Except Maids and Housekeeping Cleaners	36,660	41,040	4,380	11.9
Nursing Aides, Orderlies, and Attendants	18,580	22,160	3,580	19.3

Note: Projections cover Colorado; (1) Sorted by numeric employment change
Source: www.projectionscentral.com, State Occupational Projections, 2008–2018 Long-Term Projections

Fastest Growing Occupations: 2008 – 2018

Occupation[1]	2008 Employment	2018 Projected Employment	Numeric Employment Change	Percent Employment Change
Personal and Home Care Aides	11,520	16,460	4,940	42.9
Network Systems and Data Communications Analysts	6,070	8,650	2,580	42.5
Air Traffic Controllers	640	900	260	40.6
Forensic Science Technicians	310	430	120	38.7
Pharmacy Technicians	4,250	5,860	1,610	37.9
Cardiovascular Technologists and Technicians	650	870	220	33.8
Physical Therapist Assistants	700	930	230	32.9
Medical Assistants	7,080	9,400	2,320	32.8
Skin Care Specialists	1,130	1,500	370	32.7
Computer Software Engineers, Applications	16,410	21,540	5,130	31.3

Note: Projections cover Colorado; (1) Sorted by percent employment change and excludes occupations with numeric employment change less than 100
Source: www.projectionscentral.com, State Occupational Projections, 2008–2018 Long-Term Projections

Average Wages

Occupation	$/Hr.	Occupation	$/Hr.
Accountants and Auditors	36.14	Maids and Housekeeping Cleaners	9.70
Automotive Mechanics	19.46	Maintenance and Repair Workers	18.32
Bookkeepers	17.90	Marketing Managers	61.53
Carpenters	19.07	Nuclear Medicine Technologists	38.16
Cashiers	10.28	Nurses, Licensed Practical	22.47
Clerks, General Office	16.09	Nurses, Registered	34.46
Clerks, Receptionists/Information	14.04	Nursing Aides/Orderlies/Attendants	14.11
Clerks, Shipping/Receiving	15.41	Packers and Packagers, Hand	11.04
Computer Programmers	38.39	Physical Therapists	34.46
Computer Support Specialists	28.18	Postal Service Mail Carriers	25.63
Computer Systems Analysts	42.31	Real Estate Brokers	43.80
Cooks, Restaurant	10.87	Retail Salespersons	13.31
Dentists	66.03	Sales Reps., Exc. Tech./Scientific	33.23
Electrical Engineers	40.82	Sales Reps., Tech./Scientific	43.23
Electricians	23.49	Secretaries, Exc. Legal/Med./Exec.	17.43
Financial Managers	63.95	Security Guards	13.73
First-Line Supervisors/Managers, Sales	20.73	Surgeons	103.52
Food Preparation Workers	10.44	Teacher Assistants	13.80
General and Operations Managers	62.34	Teachers, Elementary School	25.40
Hairdressers/Cosmetologists	13.41	Teachers, Secondary School	27.00
Internists	67.02	Telemarketers	13.58
Janitors and Cleaners	11.15	Truck Drivers, Heavy/Tractor-Trailer	20.43
Landscaping/Groundskeeping Workers	12.90	Truck Drivers, Light/Delivery Svcs.	16.74
Lawyers	67.62	Waiters and Waitresses	10.21

Note: Wage data covers the Denver-Aurora-Broomfield, CO Metropolitan Statistical Area—see Appendix B for areas included. Hourly wages for elementary/secondary school teachers and teacher assistants were calculated by the editors from annual wage data assuming a 40 hour work week; n/a not available.
Source: Bureau of Labor Statistics, Metro Area Occupational Employment and Wage Estimates, May 2011

RESIDENTIAL REAL ESTATE

Building Permits

Area	Single-Family			Multi-Family			Total		
	2010	2011	Pct. Chg.	2010	2011	Pct. Chg.	2010	2011	Pct. Chg.
City	632	703	11.2	600	1,982	230.3	1,232	2,685	117.9
MSA[1]	3,660	3,630	-0.8	1,382	3,043	120.2	5,042	6,673	32.3
U.S.	447,311	418,498	-6.4	157,299	205,563	30.7	604,610	624,061	3.2

Note: (1) Metropolitan Statistical Area—see Appendix B for areas included; figures represent new, privately-owned housing units authorized (unadjusted data); All permit data are based on estimates with imputation.
Source: U.S. Census Bureau, Manufacturing, Mining, and Construction Statistics, Building Permits, 2010, 2011

Homeownership Rate

Area	2005 (%)	2006 (%)	2007 (%)	2008 (%)	2009 (%)	2010 (%)	2011 (%)
MSA[1]	70.7	70.0	69.5	66.9	65.3	65.7	63.0
U.S.	68.9	68.8	68.1	67.8	67.4	66.9	66.1

Note: (1) Metropolitan Statistical Area—see Appendix B for areas included
Source: U.S. Census Bureau, Housing Vacancies and Homeownership Annual Statistics: 2011

Housing Vacancy Rates

Area	Gross Vacancy Rate[2] (%)			Year-Round Vacancy Rate[3] (%)			Rental Vacancy Rate[4] (%)			Homeowner Vacancy Rate[5] (%)		
	2009	2010	2011	2009	2010	2011	2009	2010	2011	2009	2010	2011
MSA[1]	9.2	7.2	7.0	8.7	6.8	6.5	10.2	8.2	6.8	2.7	1.7	1.8
U.S.	14.5	14.3	14.2	11.3	11.3	11.1	10.6	10.2	9.5	2.6	2.6	2.5

Note: (1) Metropolitan Statistical Area—see Appendix B for areas included; (2) The percentage of the total housing inventory that is vacant; (3) The percentage of the housing inventory (excluding seasonal units) that is year-round vacant; (4) The percentage of rental inventory that is vacant for rent; (5) The percentage of homeowner inventory that is vacant for sale
Source: U.S. Census Bureau, Housing Vacancies and Homeownership Annual Statistics: 2011

TAXES

State Corporate Income Tax Rates

State	Tax Rate (%)	Income Brackets ($)	Num. of Brackets	Financial Institution Tax Rate (%)[a]	Federal Income Tax Ded.
Colorado	4.63	Flat rate	1	4.63	No

Note: Tax rates as of January 1, 2012; (a) Rates listed are the corporate income tax rate applied to financial institutions or excise taxes based on income. Some states have other taxes based upon the value of deposits or shares.
Source: Federation of Tax Administrators, "State Corporate Income Tax Rates, 2012"

State Individual Income Tax Rates

State	Tax Rate (%)	Income Brackets ($)	Num. of Brackets	Personal Exempt. ($)[1] Single	Personal Exempt. ($)[1] Dependents	Fed. Inc. Tax Ded.
Colorado	4.63	Flat rate	1	3,700 (d)	3,700 (d)	No

Note: Tax rates as of January 1, 2012; Local- and county-level taxes are not included; n/a not applicable; (1) Married joint filers generally receive double the single exemption; (d) These states use the personal exemption amounts provided in the federal Internal Revenue Code.
Source: Federation of Tax Administrators, "State Individual Income Tax Rates, 2012"

Various State and Local Tax Rates

State	State and Local Sales and Use (%)	State Sales and Use (%)	Gasoline[1] (¢/gal.)	Cigarette[2] ($/pack)	Spirits[3] ($/gal.)	Wine[4] ($/gal.)	Beer[5] ($/gal.)
Colorado	7.62	2.90	22.0	0.84	2.28	0.32	0.08

Note: All tax rates as of January 1, 2012 except beer, wine and spirits (September 1, 2011); (1) The American Petroleum Institute has developed a methodology for determining the average tax rate on a gallon of fuel. Rates may include any of the following: excise taxes, environmental fees, storage tank fees, other fees or taxes, general sales tax, and local taxes. In states where gasoline is subject to the general sales tax, or where the fuel tax is based on the average sale price, the average rate determined by API is sensitive to changes in the price of gasoline. States that fully or partially apply general sales taxes to gasoline: CA, CO, GA, IL, IN, MI, NY; (2) The federal excise tax of $1.0066 per pack and local taxes are not included; (3) Rates are those applicable to off-premise sales of 40% alcohol by volume (a.b.v.) distilled spirits in 750ml containers. Local excise taxes are excluded; (4) Rates are those applicable to off-premise sales of 11% a.b.v. non-carbonated wine in 750ml containers; (5) Rates are those applicable to off-premise sales of 4.7% a.b.v. beer in 12 ounce containers.
Source: Tax Foundation, 2012 Facts & Figures: How Does Your State Compare?

COMMERCIAL REAL ESTATE

COMMERCIAL UTILITIES

TRANSPORTATION

State-Local Tax Burdens

Area	Rate (%)	Rank[1]	Per Capita Taxes Paid to Home State ($)	Total State and Local Per Capita Taxes Paid ($)	Per Capita Income ($)
Colorado	8.6	39	2,776	4,011	46,716
U.S. Average	9.8	-	3,057	4,160	42,539

Note: Figures cover 2009; (1) Rank ranges from 1 to 50 where 1 is highest tax burden
Source: Tax Foundation, State-Local Tax Burdens, All States, 2009

State Business Tax Climate Index Rankings

State	Overall Rank	Corporate Tax Index Rank	Individual Income Tax Index Rank	Sales Tax Index Rank	Unemployment Insurance Tax Index Rank	Property Tax Index Rank
Colorado	16	20	16	44	23	9

Note: The index is a measure of how each state's tax laws affect economic performance. The lower the rank, the more favorable a state's tax system is for business. States without a given tax are given a ranking of 1.
Source: Tax Foundation, Major Components of the State Business Tax Climate Index, FY 2012

Office Market

Market Area	Inventory (sq. ft.)	Vacant (sq. ft.)	Vac. Rate (%)	Under Constr. (sq. ft.)	Asking Rent ($/sf/yr)	
					Class A	Class B
Denver	108,368,721	18,559,716	17.1	0	23.40	19.33

Source: Grubb & Ellis, Office Markets Trends, 4th Quarter 2011

Industrial Market

Market Area	Inventory (sq. ft.)	Vacant (sq. ft.)	Vac. Rate (%)	Under Constr. (sq. ft.)	Asking Rent ($/sf/yr)	
					WH/Dist	R&D/Flex
Denver	220,120,912	18,522,425	8.4	58,800	4.09	9.01

Source: Grubb & Ellis, Industrial Markets Trends, 4th Quarter 2011

Typical Monthly Electric Bills

Area	Commercial Service ($/month)		Industrial Service ($/month)	
	1,500 kWh	40 kW demand 14,000 kWh	1,000 kW demand 200,000 kWh	50,000 kW demand 15,000,000 kWh
City	185	1,446	27,105	1,542,956
Average[1]	189	1,616	25,197	1,470,813

Note: Based on total rates in effect July 1, 2011; (1) average based on 184 utilities surveyed
Source: Edison Electric Institute, Typical Bills and Average Rates Report, Summer 2011

Means of Transportation to Work

Area	Car/Truck/Van		Public Transportation			Bicycle	Walked	Other Means	Worked at Home
	Drove Alone	Car-pooled	Bus	Subway	Railroad				
City	69.1	10.3	6.5	0.8	0.3	2.0	4.0	1.3	5.7
MSA[1]	75.5	9.8	3.8	0.5	0.2	0.8	2.1	1.3	6.1
U.S.	76.0	10.2	2.7	1.7	0.5	0.5	2.8	1.3	4.2

Note: Figures are percentages and cover workers 16 years of age and older; (1) Figures cover the Denver-Aurora-Broomfield, CO Metropolitan Statistical Area—see Appendix B for areas included
Source: U.S. Census Bureau, 2008-2010 American Community Survey 3-Year Estimates

Travel Time to Work

Area	Less Than 10 Minutes	10 to 19 Minutes	20 to 29 Minutes	30 to 44 Minutes	45 to 59 Minutes	60 to 89 Minutes	90 Minutes or More
City	9.1	29.7	26.3	21.7	7.7	3.5	2.0
MSA[1]	9.3	25.6	24.5	24.9	9.5	4.3	1.9
U.S.	13.9	30.1	20.8	19.8	7.5	5.5	2.5

Note: Figures are percentages and include workers 16 years old and over; (1) Figures cover the Denver-Aurora-Broomfield, CO Metropolitan Statistical Area—see Appendix B for areas included
Source: U.S. Census Bureau, 2008-2010 American Community Survey 3-Year Estimates

Travel Time Index

Area	1985	1990	1995	2000	2005	2010
Urban Area[1]	1.09	1.11	1.19	1.26	1.28	1.24
Average[2]	1.11	1.16	1.18	1.21	1.25	1.20

Note: Travel Time Index—the ratio of travel time in the peak period to the travel time at free-flow conditions. A value of 1.30 indicates a 20-minute free-flow trip takes 26 minutes in the peak. Free-flow speeds (60 mph on freeways and 35 mph on principal arterials) are used as the comparison threshold; (1) Covers the Denver-Aurora CO urban area; (2) average of 439 urban areas
Source: Texas Transportation Institute, Urban Mobility Report 2011, September 2011

Public Transportation

Agency Name / Mode of Transportation	Vehicles Operated in Maximum Service	Annual Unlinked Passenger Trips ('000)	Annual Passenger Miles ('000)
Denver Regional Transportation District (RTD)			
Bus (directly operated)	458	49,898.0	258,792.8
Bus (purchased transportation)	358	26,270.1	126,617.3
Demand Response (directly operated)	8	64.2	668.4
Demand Response (purchased transportation)	351	1,108.2	9,926.3
Light Rail (directly operated)	104	20,087.7	139,416.7

Source: Federal Transit Administration, National Transit Database, 2010

Air Transportation

Airport Name and Code / Type of Service	Passenger Airlines[1]	Passenger Enplanements	Freight Carriers[2]	Freight (lbs.)
Denver International (DEN)				
Domestic service (U.S. carriers - 2011)	39	24,658,918	22	222,944,070
International service (U.S. carriers - 2010)	10	681,601	5	2,937,908

Note: (1) Includes all U.S.-based major, minor and commuter airlines that carried at least one passenger during the year; (2) Includes all U.S.-based airlines and freight carriers that transported at least one pound of freight during the year
Source: Bureau of Transportation Statistics, The Intermodal Transportation Database, Air Carriers: T-100 Domestic Market (U.S. Carriers), 2011; Bureau of Transportation Statistics, The Intermodal Transportation Database, Air Carriers: T-100 International Market (U.S. Carriers), 2010

Other Transportation Statistics

Major Highways:	I-25; I-70; I-76
Amtrak Service:	Yes
Major Waterways/Ports:	None

Source: Amtrak.com; Google Maps

BUSINESSES

Major Business Headquarters

Company Name	Rankings	
	Fortune[1]	Forbes[2]
DaVita	359	-
Leprino Foods	-	164
ProBuild Holdings	-	113
Qwest Communications	209	-
TransMontaigne		21

Note: (1) Fortune 500—companies that produce a 10-K are ranked 1 to 500 based on 2010 revenue; (2) all private companies with at least $2 billion in annual revenue are ranked 1 to 212; companies listed are headquartered in the city; dashes indicate no ranking

Source: Fortune, "Fortune 500," May 23, 2011; Forbes, "America's Largest Private Companies," November 16, 2011

Fast-Growing Businesses

According to *Inc.*, Denver is home to four of America's 500 fastest-growing private companies: **Rivet Software** (#60); **Smashburger** (#99); **BuyMyTronics.com** (#146); **Methodical** (#357). Criteria: must be an independent, privately-held, for-profit, U.S. corporation, proprietorship or partnership; revenues must be at least $80,000 in 2007 and $2 million in 2010; must have four-year operating/sales history. Holding companies, regulated banks, and utilities were excluded. *Inc., "America's 500 Fastest-Growing Private Companies," September 2011*

According to *Fortune*, Denver is home to one of the 100 fastest-growing companies in the world: **Chipotle Mexican Grill** (#54). Companies were ranked by their revenue growth rate; their EPS growth rate; and their three-year annualized total return to investors for the period ending June 30, 2011. Criteria for inclusion: a company, foreign or domestic, must trade on a major U.S. stock exchange; must file quarterly reports with the SEC; must have a minimum market capitalization of $250 million; must have a stock price of at least $5 on June 30, 2011; must have been trading continuously since June 30, 2008; must have revenue and net income for the four quarters ended on or before April 30, 2011, of at least $50 million and $10 million, respectively; and must have posted a compound annual growth in revenue and earnings per share of at least 15% annually over the three years ending on or before April 30, 2011. REITs, limited-liability companies, limited parterships, companies about to be acquired, and companies that lost money in the quarter ending April 30, 2011 were excluded. *Fortune, "100 Fastest-Growing Companies," September 26, 2011*

According to *Initiative for a Competitive Inner City (ICIC)*, Denver is home to four of America's 100 fastest-growing "inner city" companies: **RTL Networks** (#18); **Catalyst Repository Systems** (#35); **Postmodern Company** (#57); **CAM Services** (#67). Companies were ranked by their five-year compound annual growth rate. Criteria for inclusion: company must be headquartered in or have 51 percent or more of its physical operations in an economically distressed urban area; must be an independent, for-profit corporation, partnership or proprietorship; must have 10 or more employees and have a five-year sales history that includes sales of at least $200,000 in the base year and at least $1 million in the current year with no decrease in sales over the two most recent years. *Initiative for a Competitive Inner City (ICIC), "Inner City 100 Companies, 2011"*

According to Deloitte, Denver is home to four of North America's 500 fastest-growing high-technology companies: **NewsGator Technologies** (#192); **ReadyTalk** (#251); **Catalyst Repository Systems** (#264); **Transzap** (#496). Companies are ranked by percentage growth in revenue over a five-year period. Criteria for inclusion: company must be headquartered within North America; must own proprietary intellectual property or proprietary technology that contributes to a significant portion of the company's operating revenue, or devote a significant proportion of revenues to research and development of technology; must have been in business for a minumum of five years with 2006 operating revenues of at least $50,000 USD/CD and 2010 operating revenues of at least $5 million USD/CD. *Deloitte Touche Tohmatsu, 2011 Deloitte Technology Fast 500™*

Minority Business Opportunity

Denver is home to three companies which are on the *Hispanic Business* 500 list (500 largest U.S. Hispanic-owned companies based on 2010 revenue): **Venoco** (#20); **Mike Shaw Automotive** (#29); **Alpine Buick GMC** (#130). Companies included must show at least 51 percent ownership by Hispanic U.S. citizens, and must maintain headquarters in one of the 50 states or Washington, D.C. *Hispanic Business, "Hispanic Business 500," June 2011*

Minority- and Women-Owned Businesses

Group	All Firms		Firms with Paid Employees			
	Firms	Sales ($000)	Firms	Sales ($000)	Employees	Payroll ($000)
Asian	2,498	800,497	834	744,502	6,198	148,319
Black	2,922	289,901	265	227,986	2,260	59,624
Hispanic	5,893	1,099,027	824	894,252	7,765	231,497
Women	20,354	4,462,192	3,023	3,949,844	22,574	750,709
All Firms	67,500	107,004,756	17,531	104,443,789	393,770	20,209,927

Note: Figures cover firms located in the city; minority- and women-owned business are defined as firms in which the corresponding group own 51% or more of the stock or equity of the company
Source: U.S. Census Bureau, 2007 Economic Census, Survey of Business Owners

HOTELS

Hotels/Motels

Area	5 Star		4 Star		3 Star		2 Star		1 Star		Not Rated	
	Num.	Pct.[3]	Num.	Pct.[3]	Num.	Pct.[3]	Num.	Pct.[3]	Num.	Pct.[3]	Num.	Pct.[3]
City[1]	2	0.8	15	6.0	94	37.3	119	47.2	8	3.2	14	5.6
Total[2]	133	0.9	940	6.5	4,569	31.8	7,033	48.9	351	2.4	1,343	9.3

Note: (1) Figures cover Denver and vicinity; (2) Figures cover all 100 cities in this book; (3) Percentage of hotels which have a given star rating; Star ratings are determined by expedia.com and offer an indication of the general quality of a particular hotel.
Source: expedia.com, April 25, 2012

The Denver-Aurora-Broomfield, CO metro area is home to three of the best hotels in the U.S. according to *Travel & Leisure*: **Hotel Teatro** (#95); **Ritz-Carlton, Denver** (#138); **Hotel Monaco, Denver** (#200). Criteria: service; location; rooms; food; and value. *Travel & Leisure, "T+L 500, The World's Best Hotels 2012"*

The Denver-Aurora-Broomfield, CO metro area is home to one of the best hotels in the U.S. according to *Condé Nast Traveler*: **Oxford Hotel** (#47). The selections are based on over 25,000 responses to the magazine's annual Readers' Choice Survey. *Condé Nast Traveler, "2011 Readers' Choice Awards"*

EVENT SITES

Major Stadiums, Arenas, and Auditoriums

Name	Max. Capacity
Coors Field	50,455
Denver Coliseum	10,200
Denver Performing Arts Complex	10,000
INVESCO Field at Mile High	76,125
Pepsi Center	21,000
University of Denver's Magness Arena	7,200

Source: Original research

Convention Centers

Name	Overall Space (sq. ft.)	Exhibit Space (sq. ft.)	Meeting Space (sq. ft.)	Meeting Rooms
Colorado Convention Center	2,200,000	100,000	584,000	63

Source: Original research

Living Environment

COST OF LIVING

Cost of Living Index

Composite Index	Groceries	Housing	Utilities	Transportation	Health Care	Misc. Goods/ Services
105.1	102.7	113.2	90.0	95.1	106.5	106.9

Note: U.S. = 100; Figures cover the Denver CO urban area.
Source: The Council for Community and Economic Research, ACCRA Cost of Living Index, 2011

Grocery Prices

Area[1]	T-Bone Steak ($/pound)	Frying Chicken ($/pound)	Whole Milk ($/half gal.)	Eggs ($/dozen)	Orange Juice ($/64 oz.)	Coffee ($/11.5 oz.)
City[2]	9.80	1.16	1.87	1.71	3.08	5.18
Avg.	9.25	1.18	2.22	1.66	3.19	4.40
Min.	6.70	0.88	1.31	0.95	2.46	2.94
Max.	14.30	2.16	3.50	3.18	4.75	6.83

Note: (1) Values for the local area are compared with the average, minimum and maximum values for all 335 areas in the Cost of Living Index; (2) Figures cover the Denver CO urban area; **T-Bone Steak** *(price per pound);* **Frying Chicken** *(price per pound, whole fryer);* **Whole Milk** *(half gallon carton);* **Eggs** *(price per dozen, Grade A, large);* **Orange Juice** *(64 oz. Tropicana or Florida Natural);* **Coffee** *(11.5 oz. can, vacuum-packed, Maxwell House, Hills Bros, or Folgers).*
Source: The Council for Community and Economic Research, ACCRA Cost of Living Index, 2011

Housing and Utility Costs

Area[1]	New Home Price ($)	Apartment Rent ($/month)	All Electric ($/month)	Part Electric ($/month)	Other Energy ($/month)	Telephone ($/month)
City[2]	339,420	853	-	78.86	58.85	27.26
Avg.	285,990	839	163.23	89.00	77.52	26.92
Min.	188,005	460	125.58	45.39	33.89	17.98
Max.	1,197,028	3,244	339.16	181.97	348.69	40.01

Note: (1) Values for the local area are compared with the average, minimum and maximum values for all 335 areas in the Cost of Living Index; (2) Figures cover the Denver CO urban area; **New Home Price** *(2,400 sf living area, 8,000 sf lot, in urban area with full utilities);* **Apartment Rent** *(950 sf 2 bedroom/1.5 or 2 bath, unfurnished, excluding all utilities except water);* **All Electric** *(average monthly cost for an all-electric home);* **Part Electric** *(average monthly cost for a part-electric home);* **Other Energy** *(average monthly cost for natural gas, fuel oil, coal, wood, and any other forms of energy except electricity);* **Telephone** *(price includes basic monthly rate for a private residential line plus additional local usage charges incurred by a family of four).*
Source: The Council for Community and Economic Research, ACCRA Cost of Living Index, 2011

Health Care, Transportation, and Other Costs

Area[1]	Doctor ($/visit)	Dentist ($/visit)	Optometrist ($/visit)	Gasoline ($/gallon)	Beauty Salon ($/visit)	Men's Shirt ($)
City[2]	108.17	88.32	100.29	3.28	33.76	18.88
Avg.	93.88	81.72	90.54	3.48	32.65	25.06
Min.	60.00	55.33	53.66	3.18	19.78	13.44
Max.	154.98	145.97	183.72	4.31	63.21	46.00

Note: (1) Values for the local area are compared with the average, minimum and maximum values for all 335 areas in the Cost of Living Index; (2) Figures cover the Denver CO urban area; **Doctor** *(general practitioners routine exam of an established patient);* **Dentist** *(adult teeth cleaning and periodic oral examination);* **Optometrist** *(full vision eye exam for established adult patient);* **Gasoline** *(one gallon regular unleaded, national brand, including all taxes, cash price at self-service pump if available);* **Beauty Salon** *(woman's shampoo, trim, and blow-dry);* **Men's Shirt** *(cotton/polyester dress shirt, pinpoint weave, long sleeves).*
Source: The Council for Community and Economic Research, ACCRA Cost of Living Index, 2011

HOUSING

House Price Index (HPI)

Area	National Ranking[2]	Quarterly Change (%)	One-Year Change (%)	Five-Year Change (%)
MSA[1]	123	0.36	-1.99	-5.56
U.S.[3]	-	-0.10	-2.43	-19.16

Note: The HPI is a weighted repeat sales index. It measures average price changes in repeat sales or refinancings on the same properties. This information is obtained by reviewing repeat mortgage transactions on single-family properties whose mortgages have been purchased or securitized by Fannie Mae or Freddie Mac in January 1975; (1) Metropolitan/Micropolitan Statistical Area—see Appendix B for areas included; (2) Rankings are based on annual percentage change for all metro areas containing at least 15,000 transactions over the last 10 years and ranges from 1 to 306; (3) figures based on a weighted average of Census Division estimates using a purchase only index; all figures are for the period ending December 31, 2011
Source: Federal Housing Finance Agency, House Price Index, February 23, 2012

House Price Valuations

Area	Q4 2005		Q4 2006		Q4 2007		Q4 2008		Q4 2009	
	Price ($000)	Over-valuation	Price ($000)	Over-valuation	Price ($000)	Over-valuation	Price ($000)	Over-valuation	Price ($000)	Over-valuation
MSA[1]	226.2	7.9	226.9	1.1	222.7	-6.1	213.8	-8.3	225.2	-2.0

Note: Figures show the percentage of over- or under-valuation of single family homes relative to statistically normal house values (e.g. a value of 23.6 indicates that house values are 23.6% overvalued). Statistically normal house values are based on house prices, interest rates, household incomes, population densities, and any historical premiums or discounts metropolitan areas have exhibited over time; (1) Figures cover the Denver-Aurora-Broomfield, CO - see Appendix B for areas included
Source: Global Insight/PNC Financial Services Group, House Prices in America: 4th Quarter 2009 Update

Median Single-Family Home Prices

Area	2009	2010	2011p	Percent Change 2010 to 2011
MSA[1]	219.9	232.4	231.4	-0.4
U.S. Average	172.1	173.1	166.2	-4.0

Note: Figures are median sales prices of existing single-family homes in thousands of dollars; (p) preliminary; n/a not available; (1) Metropolitan Statistical Area—see Appendix B for areas included
Source: National Association of Realtors, Median Sales Price of Existing Single-Family Homes for Metropolitan Areas, 4th Quarter 2011

Affordability Index of Existing Single-Family Homes

Area	2009	2010	2011p	Percent Change 2010 to 2011
MSA[1]	103.1	102.2	107.3	5.0

Note: The housing affordability index measures whether or not a typical family could qualify for a mortgage loan on a typical home. The higher the index, the greater the household purchasing power. An index of 100 is defined as the point where a median-income household has exactly enough income to qualify for the purchase of a median-priced existing single-family home, assuming a 20 percent downpayment and 25 percent of gross income devoted to mortgage principal and interest payments; (p) preliminary; n/a not available; (1) Metropolitan Statistical Area—see Appendix B for areas included
Source: National Association of Realtors, Affordability Index of Existing Single-Family Homes, 2011

Median Apartment Condo-Coop Home Prices

Area	2009	2010	2011p	Percent Change 2010 to 2011
MSA[1]	n/a	n/a	n/a	n/a
U.S. Average	175.6	171.7	165.1	-3.8

Note: Figures are median sales prices of existing apartment condo-coop homes in thousands of dollars; (p) preliminary; n/a not available; (1) Metropolitan Statistical Area—see Appendix B for areas included
Source: National Association of Realtors, Median Sales Price of Existing Apartment Condo-Coop Homes for Metropolitan Areas, 4th Quarter 2011

Year Housing Structure Built

Area	2005 or Later	2000 -2004	1990 -1999	1980 -1989	1970 -1979	1960 -1969	1950 -1959	Before 1950	Median Year
City	4.7	7.8	6.7	8.0	15.9	12.0	15.7	29.2	1964
MSA[1]	5.6	11.4	15.8	15.1	20.7	10.6	10.1	10.7	1979
U.S.	5.0	8.6	14.0	14.1	16.3	11.3	11.2	19.6	1975

Note: Figures are percentages except for Median Year; (1) Figures cover the Denver-Aurora-Broomfield, CO Metropolitan Statistical Area—see Appendix B for areas included
Source: U.S. Census Bureau, 2008-2010 American Community Survey 3-Year Estimates

HEALTH

Health Risk Data

Category	MSA[1] (%)	U.S. (%)
Adults who have been told they have high blood pressure[2]	23.5	28.7
Adults who have been told they have high blood cholesterol[2]	36.1	37.5
Adults who have been told they have diabetes[3]	5.4	8.7
Adults who have been told they have arthritis[2]	23.0	26.0
Adults who have been told they currently have asthma	9.9	9.1
Adults who are current smokers	14.6	17.3
Adults who are heavy drinkers[4]	5.1	5.0
Adults who are binge drinkers[5]	16.8	15.1
Adults who are overweight (BMI 25.0 - 29.9)	37.4	36.2
Adults who are obese (BMI 30.0 - 99.8)	19.6	27.5
Adults who participated in any physical activities in the past month	83.8	76.1
Adults 50+ who have ever had a sigmoidoscopy or colonoscopy	67.9	65.2
Women aged 40+ who have had a mammogram within the past two years	71.1	75.2
Men aged 40+ who have had a PSA test within the past two years	50.5	53.2
Adults aged 65+ who have had flu shot within the past year	76.4	67.5
Adults aged 18–64 who have any kind of health care coverage	85.0	82.2

Note: Data as of 2010 unless otherwise noted; (1) Figures cover the Denver-Aurora, CO Metropolitan Statistical Area—see Appendix B for areas included; (2) Data as of 2009; (3) Figures do not include pregnancy-related, borderline, or pre-diabetes; (4) Heavy drinkers are classified as males having more than two drinks per day or females having more than one drink per day; (5) Binge drinkers are classified as males having five or more drinks on one occasion or females having four or more drinks on one occasion
Source: Centers for Disease Control and Prevention, Behaviorial Risk Factor Surveillance System, SMART: Selected Metropolitan/Micropolitan Area Risk Trends, 2009, 2010

Mortality Rates for the Top 10 Causes of Death in the U.S.

ICD-10[a] Sub-Chapter	ICD-10[a] Code	Age-Adjusted Mortality Rate[1] per 100,000 population	
		County[2]	U.S.
Malignant neoplasms	C00-C97	158.7	175.6
Ischaemic heart diseases	I20-I25	97.3	121.6
Other forms of heart disease	I30-I51	37.0	48.6
Chronic lower respiratory diseases	J40-J47	48.3	42.3
Cerebrovascular diseases	I60-I69	35.6	40.6
Organic, including symptomatic, mental disorders	F01-F09	24.4	26.7
Other degenerative diseases of the nervous system	G30-G31	28.8	24.7
Other external causes of accidental injury	W00-X59	46.3	24.4
Diabetes mellitus	E10-E14	19.1	21.7
Hypertensive diseases	I10-I15	12.3	18.2

Note: (a) ICD-10 = International Classification of Diseases 10th Revision; (1) Mortality rates are a three year average covering 2007-2009; (2) Figures cover Denver County
Source: Centers for Disease Control and Prevention, National Center for Health Statistics. Underlying Cause of Death 1999-2009 on CDC WONDER Online Database, released 2012. Data for year 2009 are compiled from the Multiple Cause of Death File 2009, Series 20 No. 2O, 2012, Data for year 2008 are compiled from the Multiple Cause of Death File 2008, Series 20 No. 2N, 2011, Data for year 2007 are compiled from Multiple Cause of Death File 2007, Series 20 No. 2M, 2010.

Mortality Rates for Selected Causes of Death

ICD-10[a] Sub-Chapter	ICD-10[a] Code	Age-Adjusted Mortality Rate[1] per 100,000 population	
		County[2]	U.S.
Assault	X85-Y09	7.5	5.7
Human immunodeficiency virus (HIV) disease	B20-B24	5.1	3.3
Influenza and pneumonia	J09-J18	17.1	16.4
Intentional self-harm	X60-X84	16.6	11.5
Malnutrition	E40-E46	*Unreliable	0.8
Obesity and other hyperalimentation	E65-E68	1.3	1.6
Transport accidents	V01-V99	10.7	13.7
Viral hepatitis	B15-B19	5.3	2.2

Note: (a) ICD-10 = International Classification of Diseases 10th Revision; (1) Mortality rates are a three year average covering 2007-2009; (2) Figures cover Denver County; (*) Unreliable data as per CDC
Source: Centers for Disease Control and Prevention, National Center for Health Statistics. Underlying Cause of Death 1999-2009 on CDC WONDER Online Database, released 2012. Data for year 2009 are compiled from the Multiple Cause of Death File 2009, Series 20 No. 2O, 2012, Data for year 2008 are compiled from the Multiple Cause of Death File 2008, Series 20 No. 2N, 2011, Data for year 2007 are compiled from Multiple Cause of Death File 2007, Series 20 No. 2M, 2010.

Distribution of Physicians and Dentists

Area[1]	Dentists[2]	D.O.[3]	M.D.[4] Total	Family/ General Practice	Pediatrics	Medical Specialties	Surgical Specialties
Local (number)	310	152	2,092	173	136	781	459
Local (rate[5])	5.4	2.6	35.3	2.9	2.3	13.2	7.7
U.S. (rate[5])	4.5	1.9	18.3	2.5	1.4	6.8	4.1

Note: Data as of 2008 unless noted; (1) Local data covers Denver County; (2) Data as of 2007; (3) Doctor of Osteopathic Medicine; (4) Includes active, non-federal, patient-care, office-based Doctors of Medicine; (5) rate per 10,000 population
Source: Area Resource File (ARF). 2009-2010 Release. U.S. Department of Health and Human Services, Health Resources and Services Administration, Bureau of Health Professions, Rockville, MD, August 2010

Best Hospitals

According to *U.S. News,* the Denver-Aurora-Broomfield, CO is home to three of the best hospitals in the U.S.: **Craig Hospital** (1 specialty); **National Jewish Health Denver-University of Colorado Hospital** (1 specialty); **University of Colorado Hospital** (4 specialties). The hospitals listed were highly ranked in at least one adult specialty. *U.S. News Online, "America's Best Hospitals 2011-12"*

According to *U.S. News,* the Denver-Aurora-Broomfield, CO is home to one of the best children's hospitals in the U.S.: **Children's Hospital Colorado** (10 specialties). The hospital listed was highly ranked in at least one pediatric specialty. *U.S. News Online, "America's Best Children's Hospitals 2011-12"*

EDUCATION

Public School District Statistics

District Name	Schls	Pupils	Pupil/ Teacher Ratio	Minority Pupils[1] (%)	Free Lunch Eligible[2] (%)	IEP[3] (%)
Charter School Institute	21	6,581	17.7	46.7	28.6	n/a
Mapleton School District No. 1	17	5,775	17.9	68.1	56.1	n/a
SD No. 1 in the County of Denver	148	77,267	16.9	75.1	61.6	n/a
Westminster School District No. 50	20	9,862	18.0	78.2	64.1	n/a

Note: Table includes school districts with 2,000 or more students; (1) Percentage of students that are not non-Hispanic white; (2) Percentage of students that are eligible for the free lunch program; (3) Percentage of students that have an Individualized Education Program.
Source: U.S. Department of Education, National Center for Education Statistics, Common Core of Data, Local Education Agency (School District) Universe Survey: School Year 2009-2010; U.S. Department of Education, National Center for Education Statistics, Common Core of Data, Public Elementary/Secondary School Universe Survey: School Year 2009-2010

Highest Level of Education

Area	Less than H.S.	H.S. Diploma	Some College, No Deg.	Associate Degree	Bachelors Degree	Masters Degree	Profess. School Degree	Doctorate Degree
City	15.8	20.0	18.5	5.0	24.9	10.2	4.0	1.5
MSA[1]	11.0	21.8	21.8	7.3	24.9	9.6	2.4	1.2
U.S.	14.7	28.4	21.3	7.6	17.6	7.2	1.9	1.2

Note: Figures cover persons age 25 and over; (1) Figures cover the Denver-Aurora-Broomfield, CO Metropolitan Statistical Area—see Appendix B for areas included
Source: U.S. Census Bureau, 2008-2010 American Community Survey 3-Year Estimates

Educational Attainment by Race

Area	High School Graduate or Higher (%)					Bachelor's Degree or Higher (%)				
	Total	White	Black	Asian	Hisp.[2]	Total	White	Black	Asian	Hisp.[2]
City	84.2	86.6	85.6	83.1	55.5	40.6	46.0	19.7	50.0	10.8
MSA[1]	89.0	91.1	87.5	84.8	62.5	38.1	40.8	22.0	46.1	12.6
U.S.	85.3	87.5	81.4	85.5	61.6	28.0	29.3	17.8	50.2	13.0

Note: Figures shown cover persons 25 years old and over; (1) Figures cover the Denver-Aurora-Broomfield, CO Metropolitan Statistical Area—see Appendix B for areas included; (2) People of Hispanic origin can be of any race
Source: U.S. Census Bureau, 2008-2010 American Community Survey 3-Year Estimates

School Enrollment by Grade and Control

Area	Preschool (%)		Kindergarten (%)		Grades 1 - 4 (%)		Grades 5 - 8 (%)		Grades 9 - 12 (%)	
	Public	Private	Public	Private	Public	Private	Public	Private	Public	Private
City	53.8	46.2	89.1	10.9	88.7	11.3	89.3	10.7	90.4	9.6
MSA[1]	52.7	47.3	87.7	12.3	91.4	8.6	91.9	8.1	91.7	8.3
U.S.	55.4	44.6	87.1	12.9	89.4	10.6	89.5	10.5	90.4	9.6

Note: Figures shown cover persons 3 years old and over; (1) Figures cover the Denver-Aurora-Broomfield, CO Metropolitan Statistical Area—see Appendix B for areas included
Source: U.S. Census Bureau, 2008-2010 American Community Survey 3-Year Estimates

Average Salaries of Public School Classroom Teachers

Area	2010-11		2011-12		Percent Change 2010-11 to 2011-12	Percent Change 2001-02 to 2011-12
	Dollars	Rank[1]	Dollars	Rank[1]		
Colorado	49,228	27	50,407	27	2.39	24.00
U.S. Average	55,623	-	56,643	-	1.83	26.8

Note: (1) State rank ranges from 1 to 51 where 1 indicates highest salary.
Source: National Education Association, Rankings & Estimates: Rankings of the States 2011 and Estimates of School Statistics 2012, December 2011

Higher Education

Four-Year Colleges			Two-Year Colleges			Medical Schools[1]	Law Schools[2]	Voc/ Tech[3]
Public	Private Non-profit	Private For-profit	Public	Private Non-profit	Private For-profit			
2	7	10	1	0	8	0	1	3

Note: Figures cover institutions located within the city limits and include main campuses only; (1) includes schools accredited by the Liaison Committee on Medical Education and the American Osteopathic Association's Commission on Osteopathic College Accreditation; (2) includes American Bar Association-accredited law schools; (3) includes all schools with programs that are less than 2 years.
Source: National Center for Education Statistics, Integrated Postsecondary Education System (IPEDS) Peer Analysis System, 2011-12; Association of American Medical Colleges, Member List, April 23, 2012; American Osteopathic Association, Member List, April 23, 2012; Law School Admission Council, Official Guide to ABA-Approved Law Schools Online, April 23, 2012

According to *U.S. News & World Report,* the Denver-Aurora-Broomfield, CO is home to three of the best national universities in the U.S.: **Colorado School of Mines** (#75); **University of Denver** (#82); **University of Colorado–Denver** (#181). The indicators used to capture academic quality fall into a number of categories: assessment by administrators at peer institutions; retention of students; faculty resources; student selectivity; financial resources; alumni giving; high school counselor ratings of colleges; and graduation rate. *U.S. News & World Report, "America's Best Colleges 2012"*

PRESIDENTIAL ELECTION

2008 Presidential Election Results

Area	Obama	McCain	Nader	Other
Denver County	75.5	23.0	0.6	0.9
U.S.	52.9	45.6	0.6	0.9

Note: Results are percentages and may not add to 100% due to rounding
Source: Dave Leip's Atlas of U.S. Presidential Elections, www.uselectionatlas.org

EMPLOYERS

Major Employers

Company Name	Industry
Arvada House Preservation	Apartment building operators
Centura Health Corporation	General medical and surgical hospitals
Colorado Department of Transportation	Regulation, administration of transportation
County of Jefferson	County commissioner
DISH Network Corporation	Cable and other pay television services
Gart Bros Sporting Goods Company	Sporting goods and bicycle shops
HCA-Healthone	General medical and surgical hospitals
IBM	Printers, computer
Level 3 Communications	Telephone communication, except radio
Lockheed Martin Corporation	Space vehicles, complete
Lockheed Martin Corporation	Aircraft
Lockheed Martin Corporation	Search and navigation equipment
Mormon Church	Mormon Church
MWH/Fni Joint Venture	Engineering services
Newmont Gold Company	Gold ores mining
Noodles and Company	Eating places
Strasburg Telephone Company	Telephone communication, except radio
Synergy Services	Payroll accounting service
TW Telecom Holdings	Telephone communication, except radio
Western Union Financial Services	Electronic funds transfer network, including switching

Note: Companies shown are located within the Denver-Aurora-Broomfield, CO metropolitan area.
Source: Hoovers.com, data extracted April 25 2012

Best Companies to Work For

PCL Construction, headquartered in Denver, is among "The 100 Best Companies to Work For." To pick the 100 Best Companies to Work For, *Fortune* partnered with the Great Place to Work Institute. Two hundred eighty firms participated in this year's survey. Two-thirds of a company's score is based on the results of the Institute's Trust Index survey, which is sent to a random sample of employees from each company. The questions related to attitudes about management's credibility, job satisfaction, and camaraderie. The other third of the scoring is based on the company's responses to the Institute's Culture Audit, which includes detailed questions about pay and benefit programs, and a series of open-ended questions about hiring practices, internal communication, training, recognition programs, and diversity efforts. Any company that is at least five years old with more than 1,000 U.S. employees is eligible. *Fortune, "The 100 Best Companies to Work For," February 6, 2012*

Pinnacol Assurance, headquartered in Denver, is among the "50 Best Employers for Workers Over 50." Criteria: recruiting practices; opportunities for training, education, and career development; workplace accommodations; alternative work options, such as flexible scheduling, job sharing, and phased retirement; employee health and pension benefits; and retiree benefits. Employers with at least 50 employees based in the U.S. are eligible, including for-profit companies, not-for-profit organizations, and government employers. *AARP, "2011 AARP Best Employers for Workers Over 50"*

PUBLIC SAFETY

Crime Rate

Area	All Crimes	Violent Crimes				Property Crimes		
		Murder	Forcible Rape	Robbery	Aggrav. Assault	Burglary	Larceny -Theft	Motor Vehicle Theft
City	3,947.3	3.6	60.5	152.5	325.5	741.5	2,132.3	531.4
Suburbs[1]	2,847.3	2.2	45.3	57.2	168.5	462.2	1,895.2	216.6
Metro[2]	3,108.6	2.5	48.9	79.9	205.8	528.6	1,951.5	291.4
U.S.	3,345.5	4.8	27.5	119.1	252.3	699.6	2,003.5	238.8

Note: Figures are crimes per 100,000 population; (1) All areas within the metro area that are located outside the city limits; (2) Metropolitan Statistical Area—see Appendix B for areas included
Source: FBI Uniform Crime Reports, 2010

Hate Crimes

Area	Number of Quarters Reported	Bias Motivation				
		Race	Religion	Sexual Orientation	Ethnicity	Disability
City	4	14	10	16	3	0

Source: Federal Bureau of Investigation, Hate Crime Statistics 2010

Identity Theft Consumer Complaints

Area	Complaints	Complaints per 100,000 Population	Rank[2]
MSA[1]	2,394	97.1	107
U.S.	279,156	90.4	-

Note: (1) Metropolitan Statistical Area—see Appendix B for areas included; (2) Rank ranges from 1 to 384 where 1 indicates greatest number of identity theft complaints per 100,000 population
Source: Federal Trade Commission, Consumer Sentinel Network Data Book for January–December 2011

Fraud and Other Consumer Complaints

Area	Complaints	Complaints per 100,000 Population	Rank[2]
MSA[1]	15,234	618.0	36
U.S.	1,533,924	496.8	-

Note: (1) Metropolitan Statistical Area—see Appendix B for areas included; (2) Rank ranges from 1 to 384 where 1 indicates greatest number of fraud and other complaints per 100,000 population
Source: Federal Trade Commission, Consumer Sentinel Network Data Book for January–December 2011

RECREATION

Culture

Dance[1]	Theatre[1]	Instrumental Music[1]	Vocal Music[1]	Series/ Festivals	Museums	Zoos and Aquariums[2]
5	13	3	3	2	17	2

Note: (1) Number of professional perfoming groups; (2) AZA-accredited
Source: The Grey House Performing Arts Directory, 2011-2012; Official Museum Directory, 2011; American Association of Museums, AAM Member Museums, April 2012; Association of Zoos & Aquariums, AZA Member Zoos & Aquariums, April 2012

Professional Sports Teams

Team Name	League
Colorado Avalanche	National Hockey League (NHL)
Colorado Rapids	Major League Soccer (MLS)
Colorado Rockies	Major League Baseball (MLB)
Denver Broncos	National Football League (NFL)
Denver Nuggets	National Basketball Association (NBA)

Note: Includes teams located in the Denver metro area.
Source: Original research

CLIMATE

Average and Extreme Temperatures

Temperature	Jan	Feb	Mar	Apr	May	Jun	Jul	Aug	Sep	Oct	Nov	Dec	Yr.
Extreme High (°F)	73	76	84	90	93	102	103	100	97	89	79	75	103
Average High (°F)	43	47	52	62	71	81	88	86	77	67	52	45	64
Average Temp. (°F)	30	34	39	48	58	67	73	72	63	52	39	32	51
Average Low (°F)	16	20	25	34	44	53	59	57	48	37	25	18	37
Extreme Low (°F)	-25	-25	-10	-2	22	30	43	41	17	3	-8	-25	-25

Note: Figures cover the years 1948-1992
Source: National Climatic Data Center, International Station Meteorological Climate Summary, 9/96

Average Precipitation/Snowfall/Humidity

Precip./Humidity	Jan	Feb	Mar	Apr	May	Jun	Jul	Aug	Sep	Oct	Nov	Dec	Yr.
Avg. Precip. (in.)	0.6	0.6	1.3	1.7	2.5	1.7	1.9	1.5	1.1	1.0	0.9	0.6	15.5
Avg. Snowfall (in.)	9	7	14	9	2	Tr	0	0	2	4	9	8	63
Avg. Rel. Hum. 5am (%)	62	65	67	66	70	68	67	68	66	63	66	63	66
Avg. Rel. Hum. 5pm (%)	49	44	40	35	38	34	34	34	32	34	47	50	39

Note: Figures cover the years 1948-1992; Tr = Trace amounts (<0.05 in. of rain; <0.5 in. of snow)
Source: National Climatic Data Center, International Station Meteorological Climate Summary, 9/96

Weather Conditions

Temperature			Daytime Sky			Precipitation		
10°F & below	32°F & below	90°F & above	Clear	Partly cloudy	Cloudy	0.01 inch or more precip.	0.1 inch or more snow/ice	Thunderstorms
24	155	33	99	177	89	90	38	39

Note: Figures are average number of days per year and cover the years 1948-1992
Source: National Climatic Data Center, International Station Meteorological Climate Summary, 9/96

HAZARDOUS WASTE

Superfund Sites

Denver has four hazardous waste sites on the EPA's Superfund Final National Priorities List: **Vasquez Boulevard and I-70; Chemical Sales Co.; Broderick Wood Products; Denver Radium Site**. *U.S. Environmental Protection Agency, Final National Priorities List, April 17, 2012*

AIR & WATER QUALITY

Air Quality Index

Area	Percent of Days when Air Quality was...[2]					AQI Statistics[2]	
	Good	Moderate	Unhealthy for Sensitive Groups	Unhealthy	Very Unhealthy	Maximum	Median
Area[1]	57.8	41.1	1.1	0.0	0.0	137	48

Note: Air Quality Index (AQI) is an index for reporting daily air quality. EPA calculates the AQI for five major air pollutants regulated by the Clean Air Act: ground-level ozone, particle pollution (aka particulate matter), carbon monoxide, sulfur dioxide, and nitrogen dioxide. The AQI runs from 0 to 500. The higher the AQI value, the greater the level of air pollution and the greater the health concern. There are six AQI categories: "Good" AQI is between 0 and 50. Air quality is considered satisfactory; "Moderate" AQI is between 51 and 100. Air quality is acceptable; "Unhealthy for Sensitive Groups" When AQI values are between 101 and 150, members of sensitive groups may experience health effects; "Unhealthy" When AQI values are between 151 and 200 everyone may begin to experience health effects; "Very Unhealthy" AQI values between 201 and 300 trigger a health alert; "Hazardous" AQI values over 300 trigger warnings of emergency conditions (not shown); (1) Data covers Denver County; (2) Based on 365 days with AQI data in 2011.
Source: U.S. Environmental Protection Agency, AirData Report, 2011

Air Quality Index Pollutants

Area	Percent of Days when AQI Pollutant was...[2]					
	Carbon Monoxide	Nitrogen Dioxide	Ozone	Sulfur Dioxide	Particulate Matter 2.5	Particulate Matter 10
Area[1]	0.0	40.8	38.6	1.9	7.7	11.0

Note: The Air Quality Index (AQI) is an index for reporting daily air quality. EPA calculates the AQI for five major air pollutants regulated by the Clean Air Act: ground-level ozone, particle pollution (also known as particulate matter), carbon monoxide, sulfur dioxide, and nitrogen dioxide. The AQI runs from 0 to 500. The higher the AQI value, the greater the level of air pollution and the greater the health concern; (1) Data covers Denver County; (2) Based on 365 days with AQI data in 2011.
Source: U.S. Environmental Protection Agency, AirData Report, 2011

Air Quality Index Trends

Area	Trend Sites (days)								All Sites (days)
	2003	2004	2005	2006	2007	2008	2009	2010	2010
MSA[1]	35	6	13	27	23	10	7	8	11

Note: Figures are the number of days the AQI value exceeded 100 in a given year. An AQI value greater than 100 indicates that air quality would have been in the unhealthful range on that day. Data from exceptional events are included. These counts are presented in two ways. First, the counts are based on sites having an adequate record of monitoring data during the trend period (trend sites). These counts represent the relative change in the number of days with AQI values greater than 100. In the last column, the counts are based on all sites with data in the most recent year (because it is possible for a site to have data in the most recent year but not enough data to be a trend site); (1) Data covers the Denver-Aurora-Broomfield, CO—see Appendix B for areas included
Source: U.S. Environmental Protection Agency, Air Quality Index Information, "Number of Days with Air Quality Index Values Greater than 100 at Trend Sites, 2000-2010, and at All Sites in 2010"

Maximum Air Pollutant Concentrations: Particulate Matter, Ozone, CO and Lead

	Particulate Matter 10 (ug/m^3)	Particulate Matter 2.5 Wtd AM (ug/m^3)	Particulate Matter 2.5 24-Hr (ug/m^3)	Ozone (ppm)	Carbon Monoxide (ppm)	Lead (ug/m^3)
MSA[1] Level	68	8.6	22	0.079	2	0.01
NAAQS[2]	150	15	35	0.075	9	0.15
Met NAAQS[2]	Yes	Yes	Yes	No	Yes	Yes

Note: Data from exceptional events are not included; (1) Data covers the Denver-Aurora-Broomfield, CO—see Appendix B for areas included; (2) National Ambient Air Quality Standards; ppm = parts per million; ug/m^3 = micrograms per cubic meter; n/a not available
Concentrations: Particulate Matter 10 (coarse particulate)—highest second maximum 24-hour concentration; Particulate Matter 2.5 Wtd AM (fine particulate)—highest weighted annual mean concentration; Particulate Matter 2.5 24-Hour (fine particulate)—highest 98th percentile 24-hour concentration; Ozone—highest fourth daily maximum 8-hour concentration; Carbon Monoxide—highest second maximum non-overlapping 8-hour concentration; Lead—maximum running 3-month average
Source: U.S. Environmental Protection Agency, CBSA Factbook 2010, Air Quality Statistics by City, 2010

Maximum Air Pollutant Concentrations: Nitrogen Dioxide and Sulfur Dioxide

	Nitrogen Dioxide AM (ppb)	Nitrogen Dioxide 1-Hr (ppb)	Sulfur Dioxide AM (ppb)	Sulfur Dioxide 1-Hr (ppb)	Sulfur Dioxide 24-Hr (ppb)
MSA[1] Level	27.704	71	1.644	37	8.8
NAAQS[2]	53	100	30	75	140
Met NAAQS[2]	Yes	Yes	Yes	Yes	Yes

Note: Data from exceptional events are not included; (1) Data covers the Denver-Aurora-Broomfield, CO—see Appendix B for areas included; (2) National Ambient Air Quality Standards; ppb = parts per billion; n/a not available
Concentrations: Nitrogen Dioxide AM—highest arithmetic mean concentration; Nitrogen Dioxide 1-Hr—highest 98th percentile 1-hour daily maximum concentration; Sulfur Dioxide AM—highest annual mean concentration; Sulfur Dioxide 1-Hr—highest 99th percentile 1-hour daily maximum concentration; Sulfur Dioxide 24-Hr—highest second maximum 24-hour concentration
Source: U.S. Environmental Protection Agency, CBSA Factbook 2010, Air Quality Statistics by City, 2010

Drinking Water

Water System Name	Pop. Served	Primary Water Source Type	Violations[1]	
			Health Based	Monitoring/ Reporting
Denver Water Board	1,000,000	Surface	0	0

Note: (1) Based on violation data from January 1, 2011 to December 31, 2011 (includes unresolved violations from earlier years)
Source: U.S. Environmental Protection Agency, Office of Ground Water and Drinking Water, Safe Drinking Water Information System (based on data extracted April 18, 2012)

Fort Collins, Colorado

Background

At 4,985 feet, Fort Collins lies high in the eastern base of the Rocky Mountains' front range along the Cache la Poudre River about one hour from Denver. Although not quite as large as Denver, Fort Collins, home to Colorado State University and its own symphony orchestra, offers virtually everything its citizens need, all within a spectacular landscape.

Fort Collins owes its name to Colonel William Collins of the Civil War era, who was sent with a regiment of Union soldiers to guard farmers and ranchers scattered throughout the valley, and to provide security for the Overland Stage trail. Originally called Camp Collins, the place remained a military reservation until 1866 and was incorporated in 1879.

The early economy of the town depended first on lumber, and then on the raising of livestock and produce, with alfalfa, grain, and sugar beets as the chief crops. Sugar refiners, dairies, and meatpacking plants bolstered the wealth of the town, as did the products of mining and quarrying. Fort Collins is still the commercial center for a rich agricultural region that produces hay, barley, and sugar beets.

Colorado State University, the land grant University of Colorado, was established in Fort Collins in 1879, and offers innumerable cultural, economic, and educational benefits to residents. More than 24,000 students are enrolled at CSU, which is the largest employer in the city. CSU offers a world-class range of undergraduate and graduate programs, and is an internationally recognized center for forestry, agricultural science, veterinary medicine, and civil engineering.

Fort Collins' businesses produce motion-picture film, combustion engines, prefabricated metal buildings, arc welders and rods, cement products, dental hygiene appliances, and miscellaneous plastics. Large employers in the area include Colorado State University, Hewlett-Packard, Eastman-Kodak, Agilent Technologies, Water Pik, LSI Logic, Anheuser-Busch and Intel. With fabulous scenery, a symphony orchestra, and all the attractions of Denver an hour away, Fort Collins offers an attractive site for relocation. For outdoor sporting enthusiasts, the area is irresistible. The town is only a few hours from Colorado's world-famous ski areas, and cross-country skiing is nearby.

The Fort Collins public school system, within the Poudre School District, is one of the area's largest employers. New construction in the Poudre School District has recently been completed with the opening of the city's 32nd elementary school. The city's public library system, Poudre River Public Libraries, recently finished new construction in the Front Range Village Shopping Center on the city's third public library.

Gateway Natural Area, 15 miles from Fort Collins, offers several recreation opportunities, including a quarter-mile nature trail and a designated boat launching area. Lakes are easily accessible for all water sports, and the Cache La Poudre River itself offers some of the best trout fishing in Colorado. For hunters, the area is a paradise, with ample supplies of antelope, black bear, deer, elk, mountain lion, and small game.

Fort Collins also offers a great range of cultural amenities. The city's Lincoln Center presents year-round performances by a variety of artists. Old Town, a historic downtown shopping district, hosts a number of large festivals each year. Fort Collins Symphony, the Larimer Chorale, Open Stage Theatre, and the Canyon Concert Ballet call Fort Collins their home. The city also cultivates the visual arts, with "Art in Public Places" sponsored by the city, and provides exhibits at the Lincoln Center, Fort Collins Museum, and private galleries.

Transportation in and around the city is convenient. The municipality operates its own bus service on 10 daily routes, and interstate bus service is available. Residents are served by three nearby airports, Fort Collins/Loveland Airport, Cheyenne Municipal Airport, and Denver International Airport, which is one of the nation's busiest airports.

Fort Collins features four distinct seasons and, though high in the foothills, is buffered from both summer and winter extremes of temperature. The most typical day in Fort Collins is warm and dry, and mild nights are the rule. The town enjoys 296 days per year of sun, and an annual snowfall of 51 inches. Rainfall is far less. Summers are comfortable, while winters are cold.

Rankings

General Rankings

- Fort Collins appeared on RelocateAmerica's list of best places to live in America. The annual "Top 100 Places to Live" list recognizes the top communities as nominated by their residents & local businesses. RelocateAmerica's Research Group determines the list based on review of various data gathered for economic, employment, housing, education, industry, opportunity, environment and recreation along with feedback from area leaders and residents. *RelocateAmerica.com, "Top 100 Places to Live for 2011"*

- Fort Collins was selected as one of the "Best Places to Live in America" by *Money* magazine. The city ranked #6 out of 100. This year's list focused on cities with populations of 50,000 to 300,000. Criteria: job opportunities; economic strength; top-notch schools; low crime; good health care; recreation; and many other factors that help make a town great for raising a family. *CNNMoney.com, "Best Places to Live in America 2010," August 2010*

Business/Finance Rankings

- Fort Collins was identified as one of the "Unhappiest Cities to Work in 2012" by *CareerBliss.com,* an online community for career advancement. The city ranked #6 out of 30. Criteria: independent company reviews from employees all over the country on: relationship with their boss and co-workers; work environment; job resources; growth opportunities; compensation; company culture; company reputation; daily tasks; job control over work performed on a daily basis. *CareerBliss.com, "Happiest and Unhappiest Cities to Work in 2012"*

- Fort Collins was selected as one of the "100 Best Places to Live and Launch" in the U.S. The city ranked #39. The editors at *Fortune Small Business* ranked 296 Census-designated metro areas by business friendliness (Launching Score, % New Businesses) and lifestyle offerings (Living Score). Then they picked the town within each of the top 100 metro areas that best blends business and pleasure. *Fortune Small Business, "100 Best Places to Live and Launch 2008," April 2008*

- *American City Business Journals* ranked America's 261 largest cities in terms of their resident's wealth. Fort Collins ranked #116. Criteria: per capita income; median household income; percentage of households with annual incomes of $200,000 or more; median home value. *American City Business Journals, "Where the Money Is: America's Wealth Centers," August 18, 2008*

- The Fort Collins metro area appeared on the Milken Institute "2011 Best Performing Metros" list. Rank: #3 out of 200 large metro areas. Criteria: job growth; wage and salary growth; high-tech output growth. *Milken Institute, "2011 Best Performing Metros"*

- *Forbes* ranked the 200 most populous metro areas in the U.S. in terms of the "Best Places for Business and Careers." The Fort Collins metro area was ranked #5. Criteria: costs (business and living); job growth (past and projected); income growth; educational attainment; projected economic growth; crime; cultural and recreational opportunities; net migration patterns; number of highly ranked colleges. *Forbes, "Best Places for Business and Careers," June 2011*

Education Rankings

- Fort Collins was identified as one of America's most inventive cities by *The Daily Beast.* The city ranked #20 out of 25. The 200 largest cities in the U.S. were ranked by the number of patents (applied and approved) per capita. *The Daily Beast, "The 25 Most Inventive Cities," October 2, 2011*

- Fort Collins was identified as one of "America's Brainiest Bastions" by *Portfolio.com.* The metro area ranked #5 out of 200. *Portfolio.com* analyzed levels of educational attainment in the nation's 200 largest metropolitan areas. The editors established scores for five levels of educational attainment, based on relative earning power of adult workers age 25 or older. Scores were determined by comparing the median income for all workers with the median income for those workers at a specified educational level. *Portfolio.com, "America's Brainiest Bastions," December 1, 2010*

- Fort Collins was identified as one of America's smartest cities" by *Forbes*. The area ranked #12 out of 25. Criteria: percentage of the population age 25 and over with at least a bachelor's degree. *Forbes.com, "The Smartest Cities in America," February 8, 2008*

Environmental Rankings

- Fort Collins was selected as one of 22 "Smarter Cities" for energy by the Natural Resources Defense Council. The city appeared as one of 6 cities in the mid-sized city (population 100,000 to 249,999) category. Criteria: investment in green power; energy efficiency measures; conservation. *Natural Resources Defense Council, "2010 Smarter Cities," July 19, 2010*

- The Fort Collins metro area appeared in *Country Home's* "Best Green Places" report. The area ranked #14 out of 379. Criteria: official energy policies; green power; green buildings; availability of fresh, locally grown food. *Country Home, "Best Green Places," 2008*

- Fort Collins was highlighted as one of the top 25 cleanest metro areas for year-round particle pollution (Annual PM 2.5) in the U.S. The area ranked #14. *American Lung Association, State of the Air 2011*

Health/Fitness Rankings

- The Fort Collins metro area appeared in the 2011 Gallup-Healthways Well-Being Index. The index, based on interviews with more than 350,000 Americans, measured jobs, finances, physical health, emotional state of mind and communities. The metro area ranked #9 out of 190. Criteria: life evaluation; emotional health; work environment; physical health; healthy behaviors; basic access (basic needs optimal for a healthy life, such as access to food and medicine, having health insurance and feeling safe while walking at night). *Gallup-Healthways, "State of Well-Being 2011"*

Real Estate Rankings

- Fort Collins was identified as one of the top 20 metro areas with the highest rate of house price appreciation in 2011. The area ranked #6 with a one-year price appreciation of 1.4% through the 4th quarter 2011. *Federal Housing Finance Agency, House Price Index, 4th Quarter 2011*
- Fort Collins appeared on *ApartmentRatings.com* "Top College Towns & Cities" for renters list in 2011." The area ranked #32 out of 87. Overall satisfaction ratings were ranked using thousands of user submitted scores for hundreds of apartment complexes located in cities and towns that are home to the 100 largest four-year institutions in the U.S. *ApartmentRatings.com, "2011 College Town Renter Satisfaction Rankings"*
- The Fort Collins metro area was identified as one of "10 Housing Markets for the Next Decade" by *U.S. News and World Report*. The metro area was ranked #9. Criteria: 10-year home price projections from 2009 to 2019. *U.S. News and World Report, "10 Housing Markets for the Next Decade," March 2010*

- The Center for Housing Policy ranked 210 U.S. metropolitan areas by the fair market rent for a two-bedroom unit. The Fort Collins metro area was ranked #104. (#1 = most expensive) with a rent of $832. Criteria: Fair Market Rent (FMR) in effect during the fourth quarter of 2009 based on HUD's fiscal year 2010 FMRs. *The Center for Housing Policy, "Paycheck to Paycheck: Most to Least Expensive Rental Markets in 2009"*

Safety Rankings

- Farmers Insurance Group of Companies, in partnership with Sperling's BestPlaces, ranked 379 metro areas and identified the "Most Secure U.S. Places to Live." The Fort Collins metro area ranked #9 out of the top 20 in the mid-size city category (150,000 to 500,000 residents). Criteria: crime statistics; extreme weather; risk of natural disasters; housing depreciation; foreclosures; environmental hazards; terrorist threats; air quality; life expectancy; mortality rates from cancer and motor vehicle accidents; job loss numbers. *Farmers Insurance Group, "Most Secure U.S. Places to Live 2011," December 15, 2011*

- Allstate ranked the 193 largest cities in America in terms of driver safety. Fort Collins ranked #1. In addition, drivers were 28.6% less likely to have had an accident compared to the national average. Allstate researchers analyzed internal property damage reported claims over a two-year period (from January 2008 to December 2009) to protect findings from external influences such as weather or road construction. A weighted average of the two-year numbers determined the annual percentages. The report defines an auto crash as any collision resulting in a property damage claim. *Allstate, "2011 Allstate America's Best Drivers Report™"*

- The National Insurance Crime Bureau ranked 366 metro areas in the U.S. in terms of per capita rates of vehicle theft. The Fort Collins metro area ranked #275 (#1 = highest rate). Criteria: number of vehicle theft offenses per 100,000 inhabitants in 2010. *National Insurance Crime Bureau, "Hot Spots," June 21, 2011*

Seniors/Retirement Rankings

- Fort Collins was selected as one of "10 Best Places to Reinvent Your Life in Retirement" by *U.S. News & World Report.* Criteria: recreational and cultural activities; affordable housing; reasonable cost of living; employers or industries that are generally open to hiring older workers; nearby colleges, universities, hospitals, and in-home and residential long-term care facilities. *U.S. News & World Report, "10 Best Places to Reinvent Your Life in Retirement," August 4, 2010*

- Fort Collins was identified as one of the "100 Most Popular Retirement Towns" by *Topretirements.com* The list reflects the 100 cities (out of 815+ total cities reviewed) that visitors to the website are most interested in for retirement. *Topretirements.com, "100 Most Popular Retirement Towns," February 21, 2012*

Sports/Recreation Rankings

- Fort Collins appeared on the *Sporting News* list of the "Best Sports Cities" for 2011. The area ranked #108 out of 271 cities in the U.S. *Sporting News* takes a 12-month snapshot of each city's sports, putting a heavy premium on regular-season won-lost records (from the most recently completed season). Other criteria include: playoff berths, bowl appearances and tournament bids; championships; applicable power ratings; quality of competition; overall fan fervor (measured in part by attendance); abundance of teams (rewarding quality over quantity); stadium and arena quality; ticket availability and prices; franchise ownership; and marquee appeal of athletes. *Sporting News, "Best Sports Cities 2011," October 4, 2011*

- Fort Collins was chosen as a bicycle friendly community by the League of American Bicyclists. A Bicycle Friendly Community welcomes cyclists by providing safe accommodation for cycling and encouraging people to bike for transportation and recreation. There are four award levels: Platinum; Gold; Silver; and Bronze. The community achieved an award level of Gold. *League of American Bicyclists, "Bicycle Friendly Community Master List 2011"*

Business Environment

CITY FINANCES

City Government Finances

Component	2009 ($000)	2009 ($ per capita)
Total Revenues	359,366	2,684
Total Expenditures	348,617	2,604
Debt Outstanding	209,619	1,566
Cash and Securities[1]	388,795	2,904

Note: (1) Cash and security holdings of a government at the close of its fiscal year, including those of its dependent agencies, utilities, and liquor stores.
Source: U.S Census Bureau, State & Local Government Finances 2009

City Government Revenue by Source

Source	2009 ($000)	2009 ($ per capita)
General Revenue		
From Federal Government	11,765	88
From State Government	3,907	29
From Local Governments	3,585	27
Taxes		
Property	16,683	125
Sales and Gross Receipts	82,095	613
Personal Income	0	0
Corporate Income	0	0
Motor Vehicle License	1,819	14
Other Taxes	2,143	16
Current Charges	72,235	539
Liquor Store	0	0
Utility	116,138	867
Employee Retirement	0	0

Source: U.S Census Bureau, State & Local Government Finances 2009

City Government Expenditures by Function

Function	2009 ($000)	2009 ($ per capita)	2009 (%)
General Direct Expenditures			
Air Transportation	0	0	0.0
Corrections	0	0	0.0
Education	0	0	0.0
Employment Security Administration	0	0	0.0
Financial Administration	34,938	261	10.0
Fire Protection	0	0	0.0
General Public Buildings	0	0	0.0
Governmental Administration, Other	0	0	0.0
Health	0	0	0.0
Highways	53,621	400	15.4
Hospitals	0	0	0.0
Housing and Community Development	0	0	0.0
Interest on General Debt	6,054	45	1.7
Judicial and Legal	0	0	0.0
Libraries	0	0	0.0
Parking	0	0	0.0
Parks and Recreation	46,276	346	13.3
Police Protection	29,859	223	8.6
Public Welfare	0	0	0.0
Sewerage	17,627	132	5.1
Solid Waste Management	0	0	0.0
Veterans' Services	0	0	0.0
Liquor Store	0	0	0.0
Utility	121,312	906	34.8
Employee Retirement	0	0	0.0

Source: U.S Census Bureau, State & Local Government Finances 2009

Municipal Bond Ratings

Area	Moody's	S&P	Fitch
City	n/a	n/a	n/a

Rating Systems (shown in declining order of credit quality): Moody's–Aaa, Aa, A, Baa, Ba, B, Caa, Ca, C (numerical modifiers 1, 2, and 3 are added to letter-rating); S&P–AAA, AA, A, BBB, BB, B, CCC, CC, C; Fitch–AAA, AA, A, BBB, BB, B, CCC, CC, C. Ratings may be modified by the addition of a plus or minus sign to show relative standing within the major rating categories.
Notes: n/a Not Available; w/d Withdrawn (1) Not Reviewed; (2) Issuer Rating/No General Obligation; (3) Standard and Poor's Issue Credit Rating (ICR) is a current opinion of an obliger with respect to a specific financial obligation, a specific class of financial obligations, or a specific financial program.
Source: U.S. Census Bureau, 2012 Statistical Abstract, Bond Ratings for City Governments by Largest Cities: 2010

DEMOGRAPHICS

Population Growth

Area	1990 Census	2000 Census	2010 Census	Population Growth (%) 1990-2000	Population Growth (%) 2000-2010
City	89,555	118,652	143,986	32.5	21.4
MSA[1]	186,136	251,494	299,630	35.1	19.1
U.S.	248,709,873	281,421,906	308,745,538	13.2	9.7

Note: (1) Figures cover the Fort Collins-Loveland, CO Metropolitan Statistical Area—see Appendix B for areas included
Source: U.S. Census Bureau, 2010 Census

Household Size

Area	Persons in Household (%) One	Two	Three	Four	Five	Six	Seven or More	Average Household Size
City	28.4	35.6	16.8	12.6	4.3	1.5	0.7	2.37
MSA[1]	25.9	38.0	15.9	12.7	4.9	1.8	0.9	2.42
U.S.	26.7	32.8	16.1	13.4	6.5	2.6	1.9	2.58

Note: (1) Figures cover the Fort Collins-Loveland, CO Metropolitan Statistical Area—see Appendix B for areas included
Source: U.S. Census Bureau, 2010 Census

Race

Area	White Alone[2] (%)	Black Alone[2] (%)	Asian Alone[2] (%)	AIAN[3] Alone[2] (%)	NHOPI[4] Alone[2] (%)	Other Race Alone[2] (%)	Two or More Races (%)
City	89.0	1.2	2.9	0.6	0.1	3.0	3.1
MSA[1]	90.5	0.8	1.9	0.7	0.1	3.2	2.6
U.S.	72.4	12.6	4.8	0.9	0.2	6.2	2.9

Note: (1) Figures cover the Fort Collins-Loveland, CO Metropolitan Statistical Area—see Appendix B for areas included; (2) Alone is defined as not being in combination with one or more other races; (3) American Indian and Alaska Native; (4) Native Hawaiian and Other Pacific Islander
Source: U.S. Census Bureau, 2010 Census

Hispanic or Latino Origin

Area	Hispanic or Latino (%)	Mexican (%)	Puerto Rican (%)	Cuban (%)	Other Hispanic or Latino (%)
City	10.1	6.9	0.3	0.1	2.8
MSA[1]	10.6	7.7	0.3	0.1	2.5
U.S.	16.3	10.3	1.5	0.6	4.0

Note: Persons of Hispanic or Latino origin can be of any race; (1) Figures cover the Fort Collins-Loveland, CO Metropolitan Statistical Area—see Appendix B for areas included
Source: U.S. Census Bureau, 2010 Census

Segregation

Type	Segregation Indices[1]				Percent Change		
	1990	2000	2010	2010 Rank[2]	1990-2000	1990-2010	2000-2010
Black/White	n/a	n/a	n/a	n/a	n/a	n/a	n/a
Asian/White	n/a	n/a	n/a	n/a	n/a	n/a	n/a
Hispanic/White	n/a	n/a	n/a	n/a	n/a	n/a	n/a

Note: Figures are based on an analysis of 1990, 2000, and 2010 Census Decennial Census tract data by William H. Frey, Brookings Institution and the University of Michigan Social Science Data Analysis Network. In this analysis all racial groups (whites, blacks, and asians) are non-Hispanic members of those races. Hispanics are shown as a separate category; All figures cover the Metropolitan Statistical Area (see Appendix B for areas included); (1) Segregation Indices are Dissimilarity Indices that measure the degree to which the minority group is distributed differently than whites across census tracts. They range from 0 (complete integration) to 100 (complete segregation) where the value indicates the percentage of the minority group that needs to move to be distributed exactly like whites; (2) Ranges from 1 (most segregated) to 102 (least segregated); n/a not available.
Source: www.CensusScope.org

Ancestry

Area	German	Irish	English	American	Italian	Polish	French[2]	Scottish	Dutch
City	29.7	14.9	12.8	3.3	5.7	2.7	2.9	3.1	2.9
MSA[1]	31.1	14.8	13.6	3.7	5.0	2.7	3.3	3.2	2.6
U.S.	16.1	11.6	8.8	6.1	5.7	3.2	3.0	1.9	1.6

Note: Figures are the percentage of the total population reporting a particular ancestry. The nine most commonly reported ancestries in the U.S. are shown. Figures include multiple ancestries (e.g. if a person reported being Irish and Italian, they were included in both columns); (1) Figures cover the Fort Collins-Loveland, CO Metropolitan Statistical Area—see Appendix B for areas included; (2) Excludes Basque
Source: U.S. Census Bureau, 2008-2010 American Community Survey 3-Year Estimates

Foreign-Born Population

Area	Percent of Population Born in								
	Any Foreign Country	Mexico	Asia	Europe	Carribean	South America	Central America[2]	Africa	Canada
City	n/a	n/a	n/a	n/a	n/a	n/a	n/a	n/a	n/a
MSA[1]	5.5	1.9	1.4	1.2	0.1	0.2	0.2	0.1	0.3
U.S.	12.8	3.8	3.6	1.6	1.2	0.9	1.0	0.5	0.3

Note: (1) Figures cover the Fort Collins-Loveland, CO Metropolitan Statistical Area—see Appendix B for areas included; (2) Excludes Mexico.
Source: U.S. Census Bureau, 2008-2010 American Community Survey 3-Year Estimates

Marital Status

Area	Never Married	Now Married[2]	Separated	Widowed	Divorced
City	43.2	43.1	1.2	3.1	9.5
MSA[1]	31.9	52.7	1.1	3.9	10.4
U.S.	31.6	49.6	2.2	6.1	10.7

Note: Figures are percentages and cover the population 15 years of age and older; (1) Figures cover the Fort Collins-Loveland, CO Metropolitan Statistical Area—see Appendix B for areas included; (2) Excludes separated
Source: U.S. Census Bureau, 2008-2010 American Community Survey 3-Year Estimates

Age

Area	Percent of Population							Median Age
	Under Age 5	Age 5 to 17	Age 18 to 34	Age 35 to 49	Age 50 to 64	Age 65 to 79	80 Years and Over	
City	5.7	14.2	38.3	17.8	15.2	6.0	2.8	29.6
MSA[1]	5.9	15.5	28.0	19.0	19.7	8.7	3.2	35.5
U.S.	6.5	17.5	23.2	20.7	19.0	9.4	3.6	37.2

Note: (1) Figures cover the Fort Collins-Loveland, CO Metropolitan Statistical Area—see Appendix B for areas included
Source: U.S. Census Bureau, 2010 Census

Male/Female Ratio

Area	Males	Females	Males per 100 Females
City	71,909	72,077	99.8
MSA[1]	148,637	150,993	98.4
U.S.	151,781,326	156,964,212	96.7

Note: (1) Figures cover the Fort Collins-Loveland, CO Metropolitan Statistical Area—see Appendix B for areas included
Source: U.S. Census Bureau, 2010 Census

Religious Groups

Area	Catholic	Baptist	Non-Den.	Methodist[2]	Lutheran	LDS[3]	Pente-costal	Presby-terian[4]	Muslim[5]	Judaism
MSA[1]	11.8	2.2	6.4	4.4	3.5	3.0	4.7	1.9	0.0	0.1
U.S.	19.1	9.3	4.0	4.0	2.3	2.0	1.9	1.6	0.8	0.7

Note: Figures are the number of adherents as a percentage of the total population; (1) Figures cover the Fort Collins-Loveland, CO Metropolitan Statistical Area—see Appendix B for areas included; (2) Methodist/Pietist; (3) Latter Day Saints; (4) Reformed; (5) Figures are estimates
Source: Association of Statisticians of American Religious Bodies, 2010 U.S. Religion Census: Religious Congregations & Membership Study

ECONOMY

Gross Metropolitan Product

Area	2007	2008	2009	2010	2010 Rank[2]
MSA[1]	10.9	11.2	11.2	11.7	157

Note: Figures are in billions of dollars; (1) Figures cover the Fort Collins-Loveland, CO Metropolitan Statistical Area—see Appendix B for areas included; (2) Rank ranges from 1 to 363
Source: The United States Conference of Mayors, "U.S. Metro Economies: GMP and Employment Forecasts," June 2011

Economic Growth

Area	2007-2009 (%)	2010 (%)	2011 (%)	Rank[2]
MSA[1]	-0.6	3.1	2.7	132
U.S.	-1.3	2.9	2.5	–

Note: Figures are real Gross Metropolitan Product growth rates and represent annual average percent change; (1) Figures cover the Fort Collins-Loveland, CO Metropolitan Statistical Area—see Appendix B for areas included; (2) Rank ranges from 1 to 363
Source: The United States Conference of Mayors, "U.S. Metro Economies: GMP and Employment Forecasts," June 2011

Metropolitan Area Exports

Area	2005	2006	2007	2008	2009	2010	2010 Rank[2]
MSA[1]	588.8	698.0	557.0	631.5	584.0	694.1	170

Note: Figures are in millions of dollars; (1) Figures cover the Fort Collins-Loveland, CO Metropolitan Statistical Area—see Appendix B for areas included; (2) Rank ranges from 1 to 369
Source: U.S. Department of Commerce, International Trade Administration, Office of Trade & Industry Information, Manufacturing & Services, data extracted April 2, 2012

INCOME

Income

Area	Per Capita ($)	Median Household ($)	Average Household ($)
City	27,491	49,512	67,958
MSA[1]	29,733	55,896	73,201
U.S.	26,942	51,222	70,116

Note: (1) Figures cover the Fort Collins-Loveland, CO Metropolitan Statistical Area—see Appendix B for areas included
Source: U.S. Census Bureau, 2008-2010 American Community Survey 3-Year Estimates

Household Income Distribution

Area	Percent of Households Earning							
	Under $15,000	$15,000 -24,999	$25,000 -34,999	$35,000 -49,999	$50,000 -74,999	$75,000 -99,000	$100,000 -149,999	$150,000 and up
City	14.6	11.4	9.8	14.5	17.1	11.8	13.1	7.6
MSA[1]	12.2	9.7	9.3	13.8	19.0	13.0	14.1	8.8
U.S.	13.0	11.0	10.6	14.2	18.5	12.1	12.2	8.4

Note: (1) Figures cover the Fort Collins-Loveland, CO Metropolitan Statistical Area—see Appendix B for areas included
Source: U.S. Census Bureau, 2008-2010 American Community Survey 3-Year Estimates

Poverty Rate

Area	All Ages	Under 18 Years Old	18 to 64 Years Old	65 Years and Over
City	18.4	13.2	21.4	6.6
MSA[1]	14.0	13.1	15.7	6.2
U.S.	14.4	20.1	13.1	9.4

Note: Figures are percentage of people whose income during the past 12 months was below the poverty level; (1) Figures cover the Fort Collins-Loveland, CO Metropolitan Statistical Area—see Appendix B for areas included
Source: U.S. Census Bureau, 2008-2010 American Community Survey 3-Year Estimates

Personal Bankruptcy Filing Rate

Area	2006	2007	2008	2009	2010	2011
Larimer County	2.37	3.49	4.30	5.39	6.26	5.31
U.S.	2.00	2.73	3.53	4.61	4.97	4.37

Note: Numbers are per 1,000 population and include Chapter 7 and Chapter 13 filings
Source: Federal Deposit Insurance Corporation, Regional Economic Conditions, March 9, 2012

EMPLOYMENT

Labor Force and Employment

Area	Civilian Labor Force			Workers Employed		
	Dec. 2010	Dec. 2011	% Chg.	Dec. 2010	Dec. 2011	% Chg.
City	82,975	85,576	3.1	76,097	79,425	4.4
MSA[1]	173,200	178,902	3.3	160,659	167,686	4.4
U.S.	153,156,000	153,373,000	0.1	139,159,000	140,681,000	1.1

Note: Data is not seasonally adjusted and covers workers 16 years of age and older; (1) Metropolitan Statistical Area—see Appendix B for areas included
Source: Bureau of Labor Statistics, http://stats.bls.gov

Unemployment Rate

Area	2011											
	Jan.	Feb.	Mar.	Apr.	May	Jun.	Jul.	Aug.	Sep.	Oct.	Nov.	Dec.
City	9.7	9.5	8.8	7.7	7.6	8.0	7.9	7.6	6.9	7.0	7.1	7.2
MSA[1]	8.5	8.3	7.7	6.7	6.6	7.0	6.9	6.6	6.0	6.1	6.2	6.3
U.S.	9.8	9.5	9.2	8.7	8.7	9.3	9.3	9.1	8.8	8.5	8.2	8.3

Note: Data is not seasonally adjusted and covers workers 16 years of age and older; All figures are percentages; (1) Metropolitan Statistical Area—see Appendix B for areas included
Source: Bureau of Labor Statistics, http://stats.bls.gov

Projected Unemployment Rate

Area	2010 (%)	2011 (%)	2012 (%)	2013 (%)
MSA[1]	7.7	7.0	7.3	7.3

Note: (1) Metropolitan Statistical Area—see Appendix B for areas included
Source: The United States Conference of Mayors, "U.S. Metro Economies: GMP and Employment Forecasts," June 2011

Employment by Occupation

Occupation Classification	City (%)	MSA[1] (%)	U.S. (%)
Management, Business, Science, and Arts	45.0	42.3	35.6
Natural Resources, Construction, and Maintenance	6.3	8.7	9.5
Production, Transportation, and Material Moving	7.6	8.8	12.1
Sales and Office	22.3	22.6	25.2
Service	18.7	17.6	17.6

Note: Figures cover employed civilians 16 years of age and older; (1) Figures cover the Fort Collins-Loveland, CO Metropolitan Statistical Area—see Appendix B for areas included
Source: U.S. Census Bureau, 2008-2010 American Community Survey 3-Year Estimates

Employment by Industry

Sector	MSA[1]		U.S.
	Number of Employees	Percent of Total	Percent of Total
Construction	n/a	n/a	4.1
Education and Health Services	18,700	13.7	15.2
Financial Activities	5,600	4.1	5.8
Government	30,200	22.1	16.8
Information	2,400	1.8	2.0
Leisure and Hospitality	16,100	11.8	9.9
Manufacturing	11,100	8.1	8.9
Mining and Logging	n/a	n/a	0.6
Other Services	5,000	3.7	4.0
Professional and Business Services	17,600	12.9	13.3
Retail Trade	17,500	12.8	11.5
Transportation and Utilities	2,600	1.9	3.8
Wholesale Trade	3,000	2.2	4.2

Note: Figures cover non-farm employment as of December 2011 and are not seasonally adjusted; (1) Metropolitan Statistical Area—see Appendix B for areas included; n/a not available
Source: Bureau of Labor Statistics, http://stats.bls.gov

Occupations with Greatest Projected Employment Growth: 2008 – 2018

Occupation[1]	2008 Employment	2018 Projected Employment	Numeric Employment Change	Percent Employment Change
Registered Nurses	40,880	53,130	12,250	30.0
Combined Food Preparation and Serving Workers, Including Fast Food	51,320	62,180	10,860	21.2
Customer Service Representatives	38,300	44,710	6,410	16.7
Postsecondary Teachers	24,980	31,030	6,050	24.2
Waiters and Waitresses	45,430	50,990	5,560	12.2
Computer Software Engineers, Applications	16,410	21,540	5,130	31.3
Personal and Home Care Aides	11,520	16,460	4,940	42.9
Retail Salespersons	79,820	84,660	4,840	6.1
Janitors and Cleaners, Except Maids and Housekeeping Cleaners	36,660	41,040	4,380	11.9
Nursing Aides, Orderlies, and Attendants	18,580	22,160	3,580	19.3

Note: Projections cover Colorado; (1) Sorted by numeric employment change
Source: www.projectionscentral.com, State Occupational Projections, 2008–2018 Long-Term Projections

Fastest Growing Occupations: 2008 – 2018

Occupation[1]	2008 Employment	2018 Projected Employment	Numeric Employment Change	Percent Employment Change
Personal and Home Care Aides	11,520	16,460	4,940	42.9
Network Systems and Data Communications Analysts	6,070	8,650	2,580	42.5
Air Traffic Controllers	640	900	260	40.6
Forensic Science Technicians	310	430	120	38.7
Pharmacy Technicians	4,250	5,860	1,610	37.9
Cardiovascular Technologists and Technicians	650	870	220	33.8
Physical Therapist Assistants	700	930	230	32.9
Medical Assistants	7,080	9,400	2,320	32.8
Skin Care Specialists	1,130	1,500	370	32.7
Computer Software Engineers, Applications	16,410	21,540	5,130	31.3

Note: Projections cover Colorado; (1) Sorted by percent employment change and excludes occupations with numeric employment change less than 100
Source: www.projectionscentral.com, State Occupational Projections, 2008–2018 Long-Term Projections

Average Wages

Occupation	$/Hr.	Occupation	$/Hr.
Accountants and Auditors	31.89	Maids and Housekeeping Cleaners	10.33
Automotive Mechanics	20.64	Maintenance and Repair Workers	16.87
Bookkeepers	15.91	Marketing Managers	56.43
Carpenters	19.26	Nuclear Medicine Technologists	n/a
Cashiers	9.79	Nurses, Licensed Practical	22.17
Clerks, General Office	13.91	Nurses, Registered	31.03
Clerks, Receptionists/Information	13.25	Nursing Aides/Orderlies/Attendants	12.29
Clerks, Shipping/Receiving	14.16	Packers and Packagers, Hand	10.49
Computer Programmers	36.07	Physical Therapists	35.30
Computer Support Specialists	24.55	Postal Service Mail Carriers	25.21
Computer Systems Analysts	37.49	Real Estate Brokers	25.47
Cooks, Restaurant	11.09	Retail Salespersons	11.78
Dentists	99.42	Sales Reps., Exc. Tech./Scientific	30.94
Electrical Engineers	40.34	Sales Reps., Tech./Scientific	37.64
Electricians	25.31	Secretaries, Exc. Legal/Med./Exec.	15.46
Financial Managers	59.83	Security Guards	10.29
First-Line Supervisors/Managers, Sales	19.08	Surgeons	108.04
Food Preparation Workers	9.78	Teacher Assistants	12.10
General and Operations Managers	50.08	Teachers, Elementary School	n/a
Hairdressers/Cosmetologists	11.61	Teachers, Secondary School	n/a
Internists	n/a	Telemarketers	n/a
Janitors and Cleaners	11.59	Truck Drivers, Heavy/Tractor-Trailer	19.01
Landscaping/Groundskeeping Workers	12.87	Truck Drivers, Light/Delivery Svcs.	14.59
Lawyers	46.74	Waiters and Waitresses	9.59

Note: Wage data covers the Fort Collins-Loveland, CO Metropolitan Statistical Area—see Appendix B for areas included. Hourly wages for elementary/secondary school teachers and teacher assistants were calculated by the editors from annual wage data assuming a 40 hour work week; n/a not available.
Source: Bureau of Labor Statistics, Metro Area Occupational Employment and Wage Estimates, May 2011

RESIDENTIAL REAL ESTATE

Building Permits

Area	Single-Family			Multi-Family			Total		
	2010	2011	Pct. Chg.	2010	2011	Pct. Chg.	2010	2011	Pct. Chg.
City	180	258	43.3	66	456	590.9	246	714	190.2
MSA[1]	477	702	47.2	676	490	-27.5	1,153	1,192	3.4
U.S.	447,311	418,498	-6.4	157,299	205,563	30.7	604,610	624,061	3.2

Note: (1) Metropolitan Statistical Area—see Appendix B for areas included; figures represent new, privately-owned housing units authorized (unadjusted data); All permit data are based on estimates with imputation.
Source: U.S. Census Bureau, Manufacturing, Mining, and Construction Statistics, Building Permits, 2010, 2011

Homeownership Rate

Area	2005 (%)	2006 (%)	2007 (%)	2008 (%)	2009 (%)	2010 (%)	2011 (%)
MSA[1]	n/a	n/a	n/a	n/a	n/a	n/a	n/a
U.S.	68.9	68.8	68.1	67.8	67.4	66.9	66.1

Note: (1) Metropolitan Statistical Area—see Appendix B for areas included; n/a not available
Source: U.S. Census Bureau, Housing Vacancies and Homeownership Annual Statistics: 2011

Housing Vacancy Rates

Area	Gross Vacancy Rate[2] (%)			Year-Round Vacancy Rate[3] (%)			Rental Vacancy Rate[4] (%)			Homeowner Vacancy Rate[5] (%)		
	2009	2010	2011	2009	2010	2011	2009	2010	2011	2009	2010	2011
MSA[1]	n/a	n/a	n/a	n/a	n/a	n/a	n/a	n/a	n/a	n/a	n/a	n/a
U.S.	14.5	14.3	14.2	11.3	11.3	11.1	10.6	10.2	9.5	2.6	2.6	2.5

Note: (1) Metropolitan Statistical Area—see Appendix B for areas included; (2) The percentage of the total housing inventory that is vacant; (3) The percentage of the housing inventory (excluding seasonal units) that is year-round vacant; (4) The percentage of rental inventory that is vacant for rent; (5) The percentage of homeowner inventory that is vacant for sale; n/a not available
Source: U.S. Census Bureau, Housing Vacancies and Homeownership Annual Statistics: 2011

TAXES

State Corporate Income Tax Rates

State	Tax Rate (%)	Income Brackets ($)	Num. of Brackets	Financial Institution Tax Rate (%)[a]	Federal Income Tax Ded.
Colorado	4.63	Flat rate	1	4.63	No

Note: Tax rates as of January 1, 2012; (a) Rates listed are the corporate income tax rate applied to financial institutions or excise taxes based on income. Some states have other taxes based upon the value of deposits or shares.
Source: Federation of Tax Administrators, "State Corporate Income Tax Rates, 2012"

State Individual Income Tax Rates

State	Tax Rate (%)	Income Brackets ($)	Num. of Brackets	Personal Exempt. ($)[1]		Fed. Inc. Tax Ded.
				Single	Dependents	
Colorado	4.63	Flat rate	1	3,700 (d)	3,700 (d)	No

Note: Tax rates as of January 1, 2012; Local- and county-level taxes are not included; n/a not applicable; (1) Married joint filers generally receive double the single exemption; (d) These states use the personal exemption amounts provided in the federal Internal Revenue Code.
Source: Federation of Tax Administrators, "State Individual Income Tax Rates, 2012"

Various State and Local Tax Rates

State	State and Local Sales and Use (%)	State Sales and Use (%)	Gasoline[1] (¢/gal.)	Cigarette[2] ($/pack)	Spirits[3] ($/gal.)	Wine[4] ($/gal.)	Beer[5] ($/gal.)
Colorado	7.55	2.90	22.0	0.84	2.28	0.32	0.08

Note: All tax rates as of January 1, 2012 except beer, wine and spirits (September 1, 2011); (1) The American Petroleum Institute has developed a methodology for determining the average tax rate on a gallon of fuel. Rates may include any of the following: excise taxes, environmental fees, storage tank fees, other fees or taxes, general sales tax, and local taxes. In states where gasoline is subject to the general sales tax, or where the fuel tax is based on the average sale price, the average rate determined by API is sensitive to changes in the price of gasoline. States that fully or partially apply general sales taxes to gasoline: CA, CO, GA, IL, IN, MI, NY; (2) The federal excise tax of $1.0066 per pack and local taxes are not included; (3) Rates are those applicable to off-premise sales of 40% alcohol by volume (a.b.v.) distilled spirits in 750ml containers. Local excise taxes are excluded; (4) Rates are those applicable to off-premise sales of 11% a.b.v. non-carbonated wine in 750ml containers; (5) Rates are those applicable to off-premise sales of 4.7% a.b.v. beer in 12 ounce containers.
Source: Tax Foundation, 2012 Facts & Figures: How Does Your State Compare?

State-Local Tax Burdens

Area	Rate (%)	Rank[1]	Per Capita Taxes Paid to Home State ($)	Total State and Local Per Capita Taxes Paid ($)	Per Capita Income ($)
Colorado	8.6	39	2,776	4,011	46,716
U.S. Average	9.8	-	3,057	4,160	42,539

Note: Figures cover 2009; (1) Rank ranges from 1 to 50 where 1 is highest tax burden
Source: Tax Foundation, State-Local Tax Burdens, All States, 2009

State Business Tax Climate Index Rankings

State	Overall Rank	Corporate Tax Index Rank	Individual Income Tax Index Rank	Sales Tax Index Rank	Unemployment Insurance Tax Index Rank	Property Tax Index Rank
Colorado	16	20	16	44	23	9

Note: The index is a measure of how each state's tax laws affect economic performance. The lower the rank, the more favorable a state's tax system is for business. States without a given tax are given a ranking of 1.
Source: Tax Foundation, Major Components of the State Business Tax Climate Index, FY 2012

COMMERCIAL UTILITIES

Typical Monthly Electric Bills

Area	Commercial Service ($/month)		Industrial Service ($/month)	
	1,500 kWh	40 kW demand 14,000 kWh	1,000 kW demand 200,000 kWh	50,000 kW demand 15,000,000 kWh
City	n/a	n/a	n/a	n/a
Average[1]	189	1,616	25,197	1,470,813

Note: Based on total rates in effect July 1, 2011; (1) average based on 184 utilities surveyed; n/a not available
Source: Edison Electric Institute, Typical Bills and Average Rates Report, Summer 2011

TRANSPORTATION

Means of Transportation to Work

Area	Car/Truck/Van		Public Transportation			Bicycle	Walked	Other Means	Worked at Home
	Drove Alone	Car-pooled	Bus	Subway	Railroad				
City	72.7	8.9	1.1	0.0	0.0	7.2	3.1	1.1	5.9
MSA[1]	75.6	9.4	0.8	0.0	0.0	4.1	2.3	1.1	6.6
U.S.	76.0	10.2	2.7	1.7	0.5	0.5	2.8	1.3	4.2

Note: Figures are percentages and cover workers 16 years of age and older; (1) Figures cover the Fort Collins-Loveland, CO Metropolitan Statistical Area—see Appendix B for areas included
Source: U.S. Census Bureau, 2008-2010 American Community Survey 3-Year Estimates

Travel Time to Work

Area	Less Than 10 Minutes	10 to 19 Minutes	20 to 29 Minutes	30 to 44 Minutes	45 to 59 Minutes	60 to 89 Minutes	90 Minutes or More
City	19.1	47.0	16.9	8.7	3.5	3.1	1.8
MSA[1]	16.9	38.4	20.2	13.4	5.1	4.2	1.9
U.S.	13.9	30.1	20.8	19.8	7.5	5.5	2.5

Note: Figures are percentages and include workers 16 years old and over; (1) Figures cover the Fort Collins-Loveland, CO Metropolitan Statistical Area—see Appendix B for areas included
Source: U.S. Census Bureau, 2008-2010 American Community Survey 3-Year Estimates

Travel Time Index

Area	1985	1990	1995	2000	2005	2010
Urban Area[1]	n/a	n/a	n/a	n/a	n/a	n/a
Average[2]	1.11	1.16	1.18	1.21	1.25	1.20

Note: Travel Time Index—the ratio of travel time in the peak period to the travel time at free-flow conditions. A value of 1.30 indicates a 20-minute free-flow trip takes 26 minutes in the peak. Free-flow speeds (60 mph on freeways and 35 mph on principal arterials) are used as the comparison threshold; (1) Data for the Fort Collins-Loveland, CO urban area was not available; (2) average of 439 urban areas
Source: Texas Transportation Institute, Urban Mobility Report 2011, September 2011

Public Transportation

Agency Name / Mode of Transportation	Vehicles Operated in Maximum Service	Annual Unlinked Passenger Trips ('000)	Annual Passenger Miles ('000)
Transfort			
Bus (directly operated)	26	2,034.2	7,079.0
Demand Response (directly operated)	7	8.5	55.5
Demand Response (purchased transportation)	16	31.9	189.3

Source: Federal Transit Administration, National Transit Database, 2010

Air Transportation

Airport Name and Code / Type of Service	Passenger Airlines[1]	Passenger Enplanements	Freight Carriers[2]	Freight (lbs.)
Denver International (60 miles) (DEN)				
Domestic service (U.S. carriers - 2011)	39	24,658,918	22	222,944,070
International service (U.S. carriers - 2010)	10	681,601	5	2,937,908

Note: (1) Includes all U.S.-based major, minor and commuter airlines that carried at least one passenger during the year; (2) Includes all U.S.-based airlines and freight carriers that transported at least one pound of freight during the year

Source: Bureau of Transportation Statistics, The Intermodal Transportation Database, Air Carriers: T-100 Domestic Market (U.S. Carriers), 2011; Bureau of Transportation Statistics, The Intermodal Transportation Database, Air Carriers: T-100 International Market (U.S. Carriers), 2010

Other Transportation Statistics

Major Highways:	I-25
Amtrak Service:	Bus connection
Major Waterways/Ports:	None

Source: Amtrak.com; Google Maps

BUSINESSES

Major Business Headquarters

Company Name	Rankings	
	Fortune[1]	Forbes[2]
No companies listed	-	-

Note: (1) Fortune 500—companies that produce a 10-K are ranked 1 to 500 based on 2010 revenue; (2) all private companies with at least $2 billion in annual revenue are ranked 1 to 212; companies listed are headquartered in the city; dashes indicate no ranking

Source: Fortune, "Fortune 500," May 23, 2011; Forbes, "America's Largest Private Companies," November 16, 2011

Fast-Growing Businesses

According to *Inc.*, Fort Collins is home to one of America's 500 fastest-growing private companies: **OtterBox** (#70). Criteria: must be an independent, privately-held, for-profit, U.S. corporation, proprietorship or partnership; revenues must be at least $80,000 in 2007 and $2 million in 2010; must have four-year operating/sales history. Holding companies, regulated banks, and utilities were excluded. *Inc., "America's 500 Fastest-Growing Private Companies," September 2011*

Minority Business Opportunity

Fort Collins is home to one company which is on the *Hispanic Business* 500 list (500 largest U.S. Hispanic-owned companies based on 2010 revenue): **Gallegos Sanitation** (#275). Companies included must show at least 51 percent ownership by Hispanic U.S. citizens, and must maintain headquarters in one of the 50 states or Washington, D.C. *Hispanic Business, "Hispanic Business 500," June 2011*

Fort Collins is home to one company which is on the *Hispanic Business* Fastest-Growing 100 list (greatest sales growth from 2006 to 2010): **Gallegos Sanitation** (#84). Companies included must show at least 51 percent ownership by Hispanic U.S. citizens, and must maintain headquarters in one of the 50 states or Washington, D.C. In addition, companies must have minimum revenues of $200,000 for calendar year 2005. *Hispanic Business, July/August 2011*

Minority- and Women-Owned Businesses

Group	All Firms		Firms with Paid Employees			
	Firms	Sales ($000)	Firms	Sales ($000)	Employees	Payroll ($000)
Asian	290	104,508	80	98,664	1,086	27,846
Black	93	5,047	6	3,468	62	2,148
Hispanic	564	46,054	(s)	(s)	(s)	(s)
Women	4,372	474,930	608	391,512	3,868	115,341
All Firms	14,921	11,436,748	3,866	10,959,813	57,564	2,139,714

Note: Figures cover firms located in the city; minority- and women-owned business are defined as firms in which the corresponding group own 51% or more of the stock or equity of the company; (s) estimates are suppressed when publication standards are not met
Source: U.S. Census Bureau, 2007 Economic Census, Survey of Business Owners

HOTELS

Hotels/Motels

Area	5 Star		4 Star		3 Star		2 Star		1 Star		Not Rated	
	Num.	Pct.[3]	Num.	Pct.[3]	Num.	Pct.[3]	Num.	Pct.[3]	Num.	Pct.[3]	Num.	Pct.[3]
City[1]	0	0.0	0	0.0	11	21.6	31	60.8	1	2.0	8	15.7
Total[2]	133	0.9	940	6.5	4,569	31.8	7,033	48.9	351	2.4	1,343	9.3

Note: (1) Figures cover Fort Collins and vicinity; (2) Figures cover all 100 cities in this book; (3) Percentage of hotels which have a given star rating; Star ratings are determined by expedia.com and offer an indication of the general quality of a particular hotel.
Source: expedia.com, April 25, 2012

EVENT SITES

Major Stadiums, Arenas, and Auditoriums

Name	Max. Capacity
Moby Arena	8,745
Sonny Lubick Field at Hughes Stadium	34,400

Source: Original research

Living Environment

COST OF LIVING

Cost of Living Index

Composite Index	Groceries	Housing	Utilities	Trans-portation	Health Care	Misc. Goods/ Services
n/a	n/a	n/a	n/a	n/a	n/a	n/a

Note: U.S. = 100; n/a not available
Source: The Council for Community and Economic Research, ACCRA Cost of Living Index, 2011

Grocery Prices

Area[1]	T-Bone Steak ($/pound)	Frying Chicken ($/pound)	Whole Milk ($/half gal.)	Eggs ($/dozen)	Orange Juice ($/64 oz.)	Coffee ($/11.5 oz.)
City[2]	n/a	n/a	n/a	n/a	n/a	n/a
Avg.	9.25	1.18	2.22	1.66	3.19	4.40
Min.	6.70	0.88	1.31	0.95	2.46	2.94
Max.	14.30	2.16	3.50	3.18	4.75	6.83

Note: (1) Values for the local area are compared with the average, minimum and maximum values for all 335 areas in the Cost of Living Index; (2) Figures cover the Fort Collins CO urban area; n/a not available; **T-Bone Steak** *(price per pound);* **Frying Chicken** *(price per pound, whole fryer);* **Whole Milk** *(half gallon carton);* **Eggs** *(price per dozen, Grade A, large);* **Orange Juice** *(64 oz. Tropicana or Florida Natural);* **Coffee** *(11.5 oz. can, vacuum-packed, Maxwell House, Hills Bros, or Folgers).*
Source: The Council for Community and Economic Research, ACCRA Cost of Living Index, 2011

Housing and Utility Costs

Area[1]	New Home Price ($)	Apartment Rent ($/month)	All Electric ($/month)	Part Electric ($/month)	Other Energy ($/month)	Telephone ($/month)
City[2]	n/a	n/a	n/a	n/a	n/a	n/a
Avg.	285,990	839	163.23	89.00	77.52	26.92
Min.	188,005	460	125.58	45.39	33.89	17.98
Max.	1,197,028	3,244	339.16	181.97	348.69	40.01

Note: (1) Values for the local area are compared with the average, minimum and maximum values for all 335 areas in the Cost of Living Index; (2) Figures cover the Fort Collins CO urban area; n/a not available; **New Home Price** *(2,400 sf living area, 8,000 sf lot, in urban area with full utilities);* **Apartment Rent** *(950 sf 2 bedroom/1.5 or 2 bath, unfurnished, excluding all utilities except water);* **All Electric** *(average monthly cost for an all-electric home);* **Part Electric** *(average monthly cost for a part-electric home);* **Other Energy** *(average monthly cost for natural gas, fuel oil, coal, wood, and any other forms of energy except electricity);* **Telephone** *(price includes basic monthly rate for a private residential line plus additional local usage charges incurred by a family of four).*
Source: The Council for Community and Economic Research, ACCRA Cost of Living Index, 2011

Health Care, Transportation, and Other Costs

Area[1]	Doctor ($/visit)	Dentist ($/visit)	Optometrist ($/visit)	Gasoline ($/gallon)	Beauty Salon ($/visit)	Men's Shirt ($)
City[2]	n/a	n/a	n/a	n/a	n/a	n/a
Avg.	93.88	81.72	90.54	3.48	32.65	25.06
Min.	60.00	55.33	53.66	3.18	19.78	13.44
Max.	154.98	145.97	183.72	4.31	63.21	46.00

Note: (1) Values for the local area are compared with the average, minimum and maximum values for all 335 areas in the Cost of Living Index; (2) Figures cover the Fort Collins CO urban area; n/a not available; **Doctor** *(general practitioners routine exam of an established patient);* **Dentist** *(adult teeth cleaning and periodic oral examination);* **Optometrist** *(full vision eye exam for established adult patient);* **Gasoline** *(one gallon regular unleaded, national brand, including all taxes, cash price at self-service pump if available);* **Beauty Salon** *(woman's shampoo, trim, and blow-dry);* **Men's Shirt** *(cotton/polyester dress shirt, pinpoint weave, long sleeves).*
Source: The Council for Community and Economic Research, ACCRA Cost of Living Index, 2011

HOUSING

House Price Index (HPI)

Area	National Ranking[2]	Quarterly Change (%)	One-Year Change (%)	Five-Year Change (%)
MSA[1]	6	1.10	1.49	-1.82
U.S.[3]	-	-0.10	-2.43	-19.16

Note: The HPI is a weighted repeat sales index. It measures average price changes in repeat sales or refinancings on the same properties. This information is obtained by reviewing repeat mortgage transactions on single-family properties whose mortgages have been purchased or securitized by Fannie Mae or Freddie Mac in January 1975; (1) Metropolitan/Micropolitan Statistical Area—see Appendix B for areas included; (2) Rankings are based on annual percentage change for all metro areas containing at least 15,000 transactions over the last 10 years and ranges from 1 to 306; (3) figures based on a weighted average of Census Division estimates using a purchase only index; all figures are for the period ending December 31, 2011
Source: Federal Housing Finance Agency, House Price Index, February 23, 2012

House Price Valuations

Area	Q4 2005		Q4 2006		Q4 2007		Q4 2008		Q4 2009	
	Price ($000)	Over-valuation	Price ($000)	Over-valuation	Price ($000)	Over-valuation	Price ($000)	Over-valuation	Price ($000)	Over-valuation
MSA[1]	217.9	8.8	221.7	3.6	218.0	-3.5	207.7	-6.5	215.3	-1.4

Note: Figures show the percentage of over- or under-valuation of single family homes relative to statistically normal house values (e.g. a value of 23.6 indicates that house values are 23.6% overvalued). Statistically normal house values are based on house prices, interest rates, household incomes, population densities, and any historical premiums or discounts metropolitan areas have exhibited over time; (1) Figures cover the Fort Collins-Loveland, CO - see Appendix B for areas included
Source: Global Insight/PNC Financial Services Group, House Prices in America: 4th Quarter 2009 Update

Median Single-Family Home Prices

Area	2009	2010	2011p	Percent Change 2010 to 2011
MSA[1]	n/a	n/a	n/a	n/a
U.S. Average	172.1	173.1	166.2	-4.0

Note: Figures are median sales prices of existing single-family homes in thousands of dollars; (p) preliminary; n/a not available; (1) Metropolitan Statistical Area—see Appendix B for areas included
Source: National Association of Realtors, Median Sales Price of Existing Single-Family Homes for Metropolitan Areas, 4th Quarter 2011

Affordability Index of Existing Single-Family Homes

Area	2009	2010	2011p	Percent Change 2010 to 2011
MSA[1]	n/a	n/a	n/a	n/a

Note: The housing affordability index measures whether or not a typical family could qualify for a mortgage loan on a typical home. The higher the index, the greater the household purchasing power. An index of 100 is defined as the point where a median-income household has exactly enough income to qualify for the purchase of a median-priced existing single-family home, assuming a 20 percent downpayment and 25 percent of gross income devoted to mortgage principal and interest payments; (p) preliminary; n/a not available; (1) Metropolitan Statistical Area—see Appendix B for areas included
Source: National Association of Realtors, Affordability Index of Existing Single-Family Homes, 2011

Median Apartment Condo-Coop Home Prices

Area	2009	2010	2011p	Percent Change 2010 to 2011
MSA[1]	n/a	n/a	n/a	n/a
U.S. Average	175.6	171.7	165.1	-3.8

Note: Figures are median sales prices of existing apartment condo-coop homes in thousands of dollars; (p) preliminary; n/a not available; (1) Metropolitan Statistical Area—see Appendix B for areas included
Source: National Association of Realtors, Median Sales Price of Existing Apartment Condo-Coop Homes for Metropolitan Areas, 4th Quarter 2011

Year Housing Structure Built

Area	2005 or Later	2000 -2004	1990 -1999	1980 -1989	1970 -1979	1960 -1969	1950 -1959	Before 1950	Median Year
City	5.9	13.7	20.7	17.5	22.7	7.8	4.2	7.5	1984
MSA[1]	7.2	14.0	20.8	14.9	22.0	8.1	4.5	8.4	1985
U.S.	5.0	8.6	14.0	14.1	16.3	11.3	11.2	19.6	1975

Note: Figures are percentages except for Median Year; (1) Figures cover the Fort Collins-Loveland, CO Metropolitan Statistical Area—see Appendix B for areas included
Source: U.S. Census Bureau, 2008-2010 American Community Survey 3-Year Estimates

HEALTH

Health Risk Data

Category	MSA[1] (%)	U.S. (%)
Adults who have been told they have high blood pressure[2]	20.4	28.7
Adults who have been told they have high blood cholesterol[2]	35.4	37.5
Adults who have been told they have diabetes[3]	4.7	8.7
Adults who have been told they have arthritis[2]	21.1	26.0
Adults who have been told they currently have asthma	8.4	9.1
Adults who are current smokers	17.2	17.3
Adults who are heavy drinkers[4]	5.7	5.0
Adults who are binge drinkers[5]	14.0	15.1
Adults who are overweight (BMI 25.0 - 29.9)	28.5	36.2
Adults who are obese (BMI 30.0 - 99.8)	21.3	27.5
Adults who participated in any physical activities in the past month	86.9	76.1
Adults 50+ who have ever had a sigmoidoscopy or colonoscopy	70.3	65.2
Women aged 40+ who have had a mammogram within the past two years	71.4	75.2
Men aged 40+ who have had a PSA test within the past two years	56.5	53.2
Adults aged 65+ who have had flu shot within the past year	73.6	67.5
Adults aged 18–64 who have any kind of health care coverage	85.6	82.2

Note: Data as of 2010 unless otherwise noted; (1) Figures cover the Fort Collins-Loveland, CO Metropolitan Statistical Area—see Appendix B for areas included; (2) Data as of 2009; (3) Figures do not include pregnancy-related, borderline, or pre-diabetes; (4) Heavy drinkers are classified as males having more than two drinks per day or females having more than one drink per day; (5) Binge drinkers are classified as males having five or more drinks on one occasion or females having four or more drinks on one occasion
Source: Centers for Disease Control and Prevention, Behaviorial Risk Factor Surveillance System, SMART: Selected Metropolitan/Micropolitan Area Risk Trends, 2009, 2010

Mortality Rates for the Top 10 Causes of Death in the U.S.

ICD-10[a] Sub-Chapter	ICD-10[a] Code	Age-Adjusted Mortality Rate[1] per 100,000 population	
		County[2]	U.S.
Malignant neoplasms	C00-C97	142.0	175.6
Ischaemic heart diseases	I20-I25	75.4	121.6
Other forms of heart disease	I30-I51	41.6	48.6
Chronic lower respiratory diseases	J40-J47	34.3	42.3
Cerebrovascular diseases	I60-I69	44.5	40.6
Organic, including symptomatic, mental disorders	F01-F09	20.9	26.7
Other degenerative diseases of the nervous system	G30-G31	26.3	24.7
Other external causes of accidental injury	W00-X59	24.3	24.4
Diabetes mellitus	E10-E14	14.9	21.7
Hypertensive diseases	I10-I15	16.1	18.2

Note: (a) ICD-10 = International Classification of Diseases 10th Revision; (1) Mortality rates are a three year average covering 2007-2009; (2) Figures cover Larimer County
Source: Centers for Disease Control and Prevention, National Center for Health Statistics. Underlying Cause of Death 1999-2009 on CDC WONDER Online Database, released 2012. Data for year 2009 are compiled from the Multiple Cause of Death File 2009, Series 20 No. 2O, 2012, Data for year 2008 are compiled from the Multiple Cause of Death File 2008, Series 20 No. 2N, 2011, Data for year 2007 are compiled from Multiple Cause of Death File 2007, Series 20 No. 2M, 2010.

Mortality Rates for Selected Causes of Death

ICD-10[a] Sub-Chapter	ICD-10[a] Code	Age-Adjusted Mortality Rate[1] per 100,000 population County[2]	U.S.
Assault	X85-Y09	*Unreliable	5.7
Human immunodeficiency virus (HIV) disease	B20-B24	*0.0	3.3
Influenza and pneumonia	J09-J18	12.6	16.4
Intentional self-harm	X60-X84	14.2	11.5
Malnutrition	E40-E46	*Unreliable	0.8
Obesity and other hyperalimentation	E65-E68	*0.0	1.6
Transport accidents	V01-V99	9.9	13.7
Viral hepatitis	B15-B19	*Unreliable	2.2

Note: (a) ICD-10 = International Classification of Diseases 10th Revision; (1) Mortality rates are a three year average covering 2007-2009; (2) Figures cover Larimer County; (*) Unreliable data as per CDC
Source: Centers for Disease Control and Prevention, National Center for Health Statistics. Underlying Cause of Death 1999-2009 on CDC WONDER Online Database, released 2012. Data for year 2009 are compiled from the Multiple Cause of Death File 2009, Series 20 No. 2O, 2012, Data for year 2008 are compiled from the Multiple Cause of Death File 2008, Series 20 No. 2N, 2011, Data for year 2007 are compiled from Multiple Cause of Death File 2007, Series 20 No. 2M, 2010.

Distribution of Physicians and Dentists

Area[1]	Dentists[2]	D.O.[3]	M.D.[4] Total	Family/ General Practice	Pediatrics	Medical Specialties	Surgical Specialties
Local (number)	147	62	560	134	33	148	127
Local (rate[5])	5.1	2.1	19.1	4.6	1.1	5.1	4.3
U.S. (rate[5])	4.5	1.9	18.3	2.5	1.4	6.8	4.1

Note: Data as of 2008 unless noted; (1) Local data covers Larimer County; (2) Data as of 2007; (3) Doctor of Osteopathic Medicine; (4) Includes active, non-federal, patient-care, office-based Doctors of Medicine; (5) rate per 10,000 population
Source: Area Resource File (ARF). 2009-2010 Release. U.S. Department of Health and Human Services, Health Resources and Services Administration, Bureau of Health Professions, Rockville, MD, August 2010

EDUCATION

Public School District Statistics

District Name	Schls	Pupils	Pupil/ Teacher Ratio	Minority Pupils[1] (%)	Free Lunch Eligible[2] (%)	IEP[3] (%)
Poudre School District R-1	52	26,520	17.0	23.5	21.6	n/a

Note: Table includes school districts with 2,000 or more students; (1) Percentage of students that are not non-Hispanic white; (2) Percentage of students that are eligible for the free lunch program; (3) Percentage of students that have an Individualized Education Program.
Source: U.S. Department of Education, National Center for Education Statistics, Common Core of Data, Local Education Agency (School District) Universe Survey: School Year 2009-2010; U.S. Department of Education, National Center for Education Statistics, Common Core of Data, Public Elementary/Secondary School Universe Survey: School Year 2009-2010

Highest Level of Education

Area	Less than H.S.	H.S. Diploma	Some College, No Deg.	Associate Degree	Bachelors Degree	Masters Degree	Profess. School Degree	Doctorate Degree
City	4.9	15.0	21.9	7.4	30.4	14.1	2.8	3.5
MSA[1]	6.4	19.9	22.5	8.3	25.9	11.7	2.4	2.9
U.S.	14.7	28.4	21.3	7.6	17.6	7.2	1.9	1.2

Note: Figures cover persons age 25 and over; (1) Figures cover the Fort Collins-Loveland, CO Metropolitan Statistical Area—see Appendix B for areas included
Source: U.S. Census Bureau, 2008-2010 American Community Survey 3-Year Estimates

Educational Attainment by Race

Area	High School Graduate or Higher (%)					Bachelor's Degree or Higher (%)				
	Total	White	Black	Asian	Hisp.[2]	Total	White	Black	Asian	Hisp.[2]
City	95.1	95.7	n/a	97.5	76.5	50.8	52.1	n/a	61.7	22.6
MSA[1]	93.6	94.3	90.1	98.0	67.8	43.0	43.8	27.4	61.6	16.3
U.S.	85.3	87.5	81.4	85.5	61.6	28.0	29.3	17.8	50.2	13.0

Note: Figures shown cover persons 25 years old and over; (1) Figures cover the Fort Collins-Loveland, CO Metropolitan Statistical Area—see Appendix B for areas included; (2) People of Hispanic origin can be of any race
Source: U.S. Census Bureau, 2008-2010 American Community Survey 3-Year Estimates

School Enrollment by Grade and Control

Area	Preschool (%)		Kindergarten (%)		Grades 1 - 4 (%)		Grades 5 - 8 (%)		Grades 9 - 12 (%)	
	Public	Private	Public	Private	Public	Private	Public	Private	Public	Private
City	27.2	72.8	98.7	1.3	92.2	7.8	88.2	11.8	96.3	3.7
MSA[1]	29.7	70.3	92.8	7.2	91.2	8.8	91.3	8.7	94.9	5.1
U.S.	55.4	44.6	87.1	12.9	89.4	10.6	89.5	10.5	90.4	9.6

Note: Figures shown cover persons 3 years old and over; (1) Figures cover the Fort Collins-Loveland, CO Metropolitan Statistical Area—see Appendix B for areas included
Source: U.S. Census Bureau, 2008-2010 American Community Survey 3-Year Estimates

Average Salaries of Public School Classroom Teachers

Area	2010-11		2011-12		Percent Change 2010-11 to 2011-12	Percent Change 2001-02 to 2011-12
	Dollars	Rank[1]	Dollars	Rank[1]		
Colorado	49,228	27	50,407	27	2.39	24.00
U.S. Average	55,623	-	56,643	-	1.83	26.8

Note: (1) State rank ranges from 1 to 51 where 1 indicates highest salary.
Source: National Education Association, Rankings & Estimates: Rankings of the States 2011 and Estimates of School Statistics 2012, December 2011

Higher Education

Four-Year Colleges			Two-Year Colleges			Medical Schools[1]	Law Schools[2]	Voc/ Tech[3]
Public	Private Non-profit	Private For-profit	Public	Private Non-profit	Private For-profit			
1	0	1	0	0	2	0	0	3

Note: Figures cover institutions located within the city limits and include main campuses only; (1) includes schools accredited by the Liaison Committee on Medical Education and the American Osteopathic Association's Commission on Osteopathic College Accreditation; (2) includes American Bar Association-accredited law schools; (3) includes all schools with programs that are less than 2 years.
Source: National Center for Education Statistics, Integrated Postsecondary Education System (IPEDS) Peer Analysis System, 2011-12; Association of American Medical Colleges, Member List, April 23, 2012; American Osteopathic Association, Member List, April 23, 2012; Law School Admission Council, Official Guide to ABA-Approved Law Schools Online, April 23, 2012

According to *U.S. News & World Report,* the Fort Collins-Loveland, CO is home to one of the best national universities in the U.S.: **Colorado State University** (#128). The indicators used to capture academic quality fall into a number of categories: assessment by administrators at peer institutions; retention of students; faculty resources; student selectivity; financial resources; alumni giving; high school counselor ratings of colleges; and graduation rate. *U.S. News & World Report, "America's Best Colleges 2012"*

PRESIDENTIAL ELECTION

2008 Presidential Election Results

Area	Obama	McCain	Nader	Other
Larimer County	54.0	44.3	0.5	1.2
U.S.	52.9	45.6	0.6	0.9

Note: Results are percentages and may not add to 100% due to rounding
Source: Dave Leip's Atlas of U.S. Presidential Elections, www.uselectionatlas.org

EMPLOYERS

Major Employers

Company Name	Industry
Advanced Energy Industrials	Special industry machinery
Anheuser Busch Incorporated	Malt beverages
Animal and Plant Health Inspection	Management services
Aramark Corporation	Food/bars
Center Partners Inc	Business services
City of Loveland	City and town managers office
Colorado State University	Colleges/universities
Colorado State University	College/university library
Contibeef	Beef cattle feedlots
Deere and Company	Farm machinery/equipment
Hach Company	Analytical instruments
Hewlett Packard Co	Electronic computers
Hewlett Packard Co	Tape storage units/computers
Medical Center of the Rockies	General medical/surgical hospitals
Poudre School District	Building cleaning service
Poudre Valley Health Systems	General medical/surgical hospitals
Woodward Inc	Relays/industrial controls
Woodward Inc	Governors/aircraft propeller feathering
Woodward Inc	Aircraft engines/parts

Note: Companies shown are located within the Fort Collins-Loveland, CO metropolitan area.
Source: Hoovers.com, data extracted April 25 2012

PUBLIC SAFETY

Crime Rate

Area	All Crimes	Violent Crimes				Property Crimes		
		Murder	Forcible Rape	Robbery	Aggrav. Assault	Burglary	Larceny -Theft	Motor Vehicle Theft
City	3,597.3	0.0	46.1	36.1	233.6	463.6	2,672.2	145.6
Suburbs[1]	2,143.0	0.0	30.6	20.6	120.5	307.8	1,578.1	85.5
Metro[2]	2,817.8	0.0	37.8	27.8	173.0	380.1	2,085.8	113.4
U.S.	3,345.5	4.8	27.5	119.1	252.3	699.6	2,003.5	238.8

Note: Figures are crimes per 100,000 population; (1) All areas within the metro area that are located outside the city limits; (2) Metropolitan Statistical Area—see Appendix B for areas included
Source: FBI Uniform Crime Reports, 2010

Hate Crimes

Area	Number of Quarters Reported	Bias Motivation				
		Race	Religion	Sexual Orientation	Ethnicity	Disability
City	4	2	0	4	1	0

Source: Federal Bureau of Investigation, Hate Crime Statistics 2010

Identity Theft Consumer Complaints

Area	Complaints	Complaints per 100,000 Population	Rank[2]
MSA[1]	281	97.7	105
U.S.	279,156	90.4	-

Note: (1) Metropolitan Statistical Area—see Appendix B for areas included; (2) Rank ranges from 1 to 384 where 1 indicates greatest number of identity theft complaints per 100,000 population
Source: Federal Trade Commission, Consumer Sentinel Network Data Book for January–December 2011

Fraud and Other Consumer Complaints

Area	Complaints	Complaints per 100,000 Population	Rank[2]
MSA[1]	2,192	762.2	13
U.S.	1,533,924	496.8	-

Note: (1) Metropolitan Statistical Area—see Appendix B for areas included; (2) Rank ranges from 1 to 384 where 1 indicates greatest number of fraud and other complaints per 100,000 population
Source: Federal Trade Commission, Consumer Sentinel Network Data Book for January–December 2011

RECREATION

Culture

Dance[1]	Theatre[1]	Instrumental Music[1]	Vocal Music[1]	Series/ Festivals	Museums	Zoos and Aquariums[2]
1	1	2	2	0	6	0

Note: (1) Number of professional perfoming groups; (2) AZA-accredited
Source: The Grey House Performing Arts Directory, 2011-2012; Official Museum Directory, 2011; American Association of Museums, AAM Member Museums, April 2012; Association of Zoos & Aquariums, AZA Member Zoos & Aquariums, April 2012

Professional Sports Teams

Team Name	League

No teams are located in the metro area
Source: Original research

CLIMATE

Average and Extreme Temperatures

Temperature	Jan	Feb	Mar	Apr	May	Jun	Jul	Aug	Sep	Oct	Nov	Dec	Yr.
Extreme High (°F)	73	76	84	90	93	102	103	100	97	89	79	75	103
Average High (°F)	43	47	52	62	71	81	88	86	77	67	52	45	64
Average Temp. (°F)	30	34	39	48	58	67	73	72	63	52	39	32	51
Average Low (°F)	16	20	25	34	44	53	59	57	48	37	25	18	37
Extreme Low (°F)	-25	-25	-10	-2	22	30	43	41	17	3	-8	-25	-25

Note: Figures cover the years 1948-1992
Source: National Climatic Data Center, International Station Meteorological Climate Summary, 9/96

Average Precipitation/Snowfall/Humidity

Precip./Humidity	Jan	Feb	Mar	Apr	May	Jun	Jul	Aug	Sep	Oct	Nov	Dec	Yr.
Avg. Precip. (in.)	0.6	0.6	1.3	1.7	2.5	1.7	1.9	1.5	1.1	1.0	0.9	0.6	15.5
Avg. Snowfall (in.)	9	7	14	9	2	Tr	0	0	2	4	9	8	63
Avg. Rel. Hum. 5am (%)	62	65	67	66	70	68	67	68	66	63	66	63	66
Avg. Rel. Hum. 5pm (%)	49	44	40	35	38	34	34	34	32	34	47	50	39

Note: Figures cover the years 1948-1992; Tr = Trace amounts (<0.05 in. of rain; <0.5 in. of snow)
Source: National Climatic Data Center, International Station Meteorological Climate Summary, 9/96

Weather Conditions

Temperature			Daytime Sky			Precipitation		
10°F & below	32°F & below	90°F & above	Clear	Partly cloudy	Cloudy	0.01 inch or more precip.	0.1 inch or more snow/ice	Thunder-storms
24	155	33	99	177	89	90	38	39

Note: Figures are average number of days per year and cover the years 1948-1992
Source: National Climatic Data Center, International Station Meteorological Climate Summary, 9/96

HAZARDOUS WASTE

Superfund Sites

Fort Collins has no sites on the EPA's Superfund Final National Priorities List.
U.S. Environmental Protection Agency, Final National Priorities List, April 17, 2012

AIR & WATER QUALITY

Air Quality Index

Area	Percent of Days when Air Quality was...[2]					AQI Statistics[2]	
	Good	Moderate	Unhealthy for Sensitive Groups	Unhealthy	Very Unhealthy	Maximum	Median
Area[1]	60.3	36.2	3.6	0.0	0.0	127	48

Note: Air Quality Index (AQI) is an index for reporting daily air quality. EPA calculates the AQI for five major air pollutants regulated by the Clean Air Act: ground-level ozone, particle pollution (aka particulate matter), carbon monoxide, sulfur dioxide, and nitrogen dioxide. The AQI runs from 0 to 500. The higher the AQI value, the greater the level of air pollution and the greater the health concern. There are six AQI categories: "Good" AQI is between 0 and 50. Air quality is considered satisfactory; "Moderate" AQI is between 51 and 100. Air quality is acceptable; "Unhealthy for Sensitive Groups" When AQI values are between 101 and 150, members of sensitive groups may experience health effects; "Unhealthy" When AQI values are between 151 and 200 everyone may begin to experience health effects; "Very Unhealthy" AQI values between 201 and 300 trigger a health alert; "Hazardous" AQI values over 300 trigger warnings of emergency conditions (not shown); (1) Data covers Larimer County; (2) Based on 365 days with AQI data in 2011.
Source: U.S. Environmental Protection Agency, AirData Report, 2011

Air Quality Index Pollutants

Area	Percent of Days when AQI Pollutant was...[2]					
	Carbon Monoxide	Nitrogen Dioxide	Ozone	Sulfur Dioxide	Particulate Matter 2.5	Particulate Matter 10
Area[1]	0.0	0.0	98.9	0.0	1.1	0.0

Note: The Air Quality Index (AQI) is an index for reporting daily air quality. EPA calculates the AQI for five major air pollutants regulated by the Clean Air Act: ground-level ozone, particle pollution (also known as particulate matter), carbon monoxide, sulfur dioxide, and nitrogen dioxide. The AQI runs from 0 to 500. The higher the AQI value, the greater the level of air pollution and the greater the health concern; (1) Data covers Larimer County; (2) Based on 365 days with AQI data in 2011.
Source: U.S. Environmental Protection Agency, AirData Report, 2011

Air Quality Index Trends

Area	Trend Sites (days)								All Sites (days)
	2003	2004	2005	2006	2007	2008	2009	2010	2010
MSA[1]	n/a	n/a	n/a	n/a	n/a	n/a	n/a	n/a	n/a

Note: Figures are the number of days the AQI value exceeded 100 in a given year. An AQI value greater than 100 indicates that air quality would have been in the unhealthful range on that day. Data from exceptional events are included. These counts are presented in two ways. First, the counts are based on sites having an adequate record of monitoring data during the trend period (trend sites). These counts represent the relative change in the number of days with AQI values greater than 100. In the last column, the counts are based on all sites with data in the most recent year (because it is possible for a site to have data in the most recent year but not enough data to be a trend site); (1) Data covers the Fort Collins-Loveland, CO—see Appendix B for areas included; n/a not available.
Source: U.S. Environmental Protection Agency, Air Quality Index Information, "Number of Days with Air Quality Index Values Greater than 100 at Trend Sites, 2000-2010, and at All Sites in 2010"

Maximum Air Pollutant Concentrations: Particulate Matter, Ozone, CO and Lead

	Particulate Matter 10 (ug/m^3)	Particulate Matter 2.5 Wtd AM (ug/m^3)	Particulate Matter 2.5 24-Hr (ug/m^3)	Ozone (ppm)	Carbon Monoxide (ppm)	Lead (ug/m^3)
MSA[1] Level	43	6.5	22	0.077	2	n/a
NAAQS[2]	150	15	35	0.075	9	0.15
Met NAAQS[2]	Yes	Yes	Yes	No	Yes	n/a

Note: Data from exceptional events are not included; (1) Data covers the Fort Collins-Loveland, CO—see Appendix B for areas included; (2) National Ambient Air Quality Standards; ppm = parts per million; ug/m^3 = micrograms per cubic meter; n/a not available
Concentrations: Particulate Matter 10 (coarse particulate)—highest second maximum 24-hour concentration; Particulate Matter 2.5 Wtd AM (fine particulate)—highest weighted annual mean concentration; Particulate Matter 2.5 24-Hour (fine particulate)—highest 98th percentile 24-hour concentration; Ozone—highest fourth daily maximum 8-hour concentration; Carbon Monoxide—highest second maximum non-overlapping 8-hour concentration; Lead—maximum running 3-month average
Source: U.S. Environmental Protection Agency, CBSA Factbook 2010, Air Quality Statistics by City, 2010

Maximum Air Pollutant Concentrations: Nitrogen Dioxide and Sulfur Dioxide

	Nitrogen Dioxide AM (ppb)	Nitrogen Dioxide 1-Hr (ppb)	Sulfur Dioxide AM (ppb)	Sulfur Dioxide 1-Hr (ppb)	Sulfur Dioxide 24-Hr (ppb)
MSA[1] Level	n/a	n/a	n/a	n/a	n/a
NAAQS[2]	53	100	30	75	140
Met NAAQS[2]	n/a	n/a	n/a	n/a	n/a

Note: Data from exceptional events are not included; (1) Data covers the Fort Collins-Loveland, CO—see Appendix B for areas included; (2) National Ambient Air Quality Standards; ppb = parts per billion; n/a not available

Concentrations: Nitrogen Dioxide AM—highest arithmetic mean concentration; Nitrogen Dioxide 1-Hr—highest 98th percentile 1-hour daily maximum concentration; Sulfur Dioxide AM—highest annual mean concentration; Sulfur Dioxide 1-Hr—highest 99th percentile 1-hour daily maximum concentration; Sulfur Dioxide 24-Hr—highest second maximum 24-hour concentration

Source: U.S. Environmental Protection Agency, CBSA Factbook 2010, Air Quality Statistics by City, 2010

Drinking Water

Water System Name	Pop. Served	Primary Water Source Type	Violations[1]	
			Health Based	Monitoring/ Reporting
City of Fort Collins	125,500	Surface	0	0

Note: (1) Based on violation data from January 1, 2011 to December 31, 2011 (includes unresolved violations from earlier years)

Source: U.S. Environmental Protection Agency, Office of Ground Water and Drinking Water, Safe Drinking Water Information System (based on data extracted April 18, 2012)

Gilbert, Arizona

Background

Located just southeast of Phoenix, Gilbert began after land owner, William Gilbert, allowed the Arizona Eastern Railway to develop railroad tracks through his property. With the rail line stretching from Phoenix to Florence, a farming community sprung up around it, and the construction of the Roosevelt Dam and the Eastern and Consolidated Canals resulted in a town of agricultural excellence. Gilbert was incorporated on July 6, 1920 and is now part of Maricopa County.

The town carried on this way for many years and was labeled the "Hay Capitol of the World" until the late 1920s. Since then Gilbert has made tremendous developmental strides. The economic focus has evolved from agriculture into a more diverse suburban community. Many Gilbert residents hold positions in management or related professional occupations, while many others are in sales or office jobs. The community is affluent, rapidly expanding, and considered one of the safest communities in the United States.

In wise anticipation of Gilbert's growth, the town council approved a strip annexation of 53 miles of land the 1970s. Humble in population until recent decades, Gilbert became the fastest growing municipality in the United States between 1980 to 2010.

One factor responsible for the population increase is Gilbert's highly reputable school system, consisting of twenty-four elementary schools, six junior high schools, and four high schools. The first district in Arizona to acquire a national pre-engineering program, Desert Ridge High School proudly offers "Project Lead the Way"- a four year high school college prep program with an emphasis on math and science. In support of the arts, the Mayor recently established the Town of Gilbert Schools of Distinction Award for Outstanding Achievement in Arts Education, which seeks to reward artistic excellence in all Gilbert schools.

Gilbert also hosts several cultural events, including GilbertFest, an annual music & arts festival, and in February and March, monthly showcases called the Gilbert Art Walk, which are held outdoors and free to the public.

Gilbert has some of the nations most highly regarded parks and recreational areas. Beautiful trails, parks and wildlife have led to a community appreciation for the outdoors. The city is a bicycle friendly community, and has implemented a pedestrian and bicycle plan that provides a system of on-road bike lanes and off-road trails. The Santan Vista trail intersects with the Riparian Preserve—home to many rare species of birds and a National Audubon Society recognized "Important Bird Area." Other notable trails include The Heritage Trail, which intersects with the popular Freestone Park, and The Santan Freeway Trail, known for its breathtaking scenery and proximity to various parks and shopping areas along the Santan Freeway.

Gilbert has a subtropic desert climate, with extremely hot summers and warm winters. The average summer lasts from late May to early September. There is typically little precipitation throughout the summer but humidity levels are high, leading to occasional flooding and heavy localized precipitation.

Rankings

General Rankings

- The Phoenix metro area was identified as one of the 10 most popular big cities by Pew Research Center. The results are based on a telephone survey of 2,260 adults conducted during October 2008. The report explored a range of attitudes related to where Americans live, where they would like to live, and why. *Pew Research Center, "For Nearly Half of America, Grass is Greener Somewhere Else," January 29, 2009*
- Gilbert was selected as one of America's best cities by *Bloomberg Businessweek.* The city ranked #41 out of 50. Criteria: number of restaurants, bars and museums per capita; number of colleges, libraries, and professional sports teams; income, poverty, unemployment, crime, and foreclosure rates; percent of population with bachelor's degrees; public school performance; park acres per capita; air quality. *BusinessWeek, "America's 50 Best Cities," September 20, 2011*
- Gilbert was selected as one of the "Best Places to Live in America" by *Money* magazine. The city ranked #36 out of 100. This year's list focused on cities with populations of 50,000 to 300,000. Criteria: job opportunities; economic strength; top-notch schools; low crime; good health care; recreation; and many other factors that help make a town great for raising a family. *CNNMoney.com, "Best Places to Live in America 2010," August 2010*

Business/Finance Rankings

- Phoenix was identified as one of the 20 strongest-performing metro areas during the recession and recovery from trough quarter through the third quarter of 2011. Criteria: percent change in employment; percentage point change in unemployment rate; percent change in gross metropolitan product; percent change in House Price Index. *Brookings Institution, MetroMonitor: Tracking Economic Recession and Recovery in America's 100 Largest Metropolitan Areas, December 2011*
- Experian ranked the top 20 major U.S. metropolitan areas by average debt per consumer. The Phoenix metro area was ranked #5. Criteria: average debt per consumer. Debt for this study includes credit cards, auto loans and personal loans. It does not include mortgages. *Experian, May 13, 2010*
- *American City Business Journals* ranked America's 261 largest cities in terms of their resident's wealth. Gilbert ranked #51. Criteria: per capita income; median household income; percentage of households with annual incomes of $200,000 or more; median home value. *American City Business Journals, "Where the Money Is: America's Wealth Centers," August 18, 2008*
- The Phoenix metro area appeared on the Milken Institute "2011 Best Performing Metros" list. Rank: #136 out of 200 large metro areas. Criteria: job growth; wage and salary growth; high-tech output growth. *Milken Institute, "2011 Best Performing Metros"*
- The Phoenix metro area was selected as one of the best cities for entrepreneurs in America by *Inc. Magazine.* Criteria: job-growth data for 335 metro areas was analyzed for: recent growth trend; mid-term growth; long-term trend; current year growth. The Phoenix metro area ranked #14 among large metro areas and #61 overall. *Inc. Magazine, "The Best Cities for Doing Business," July 2008*
- Phoenix was ranked #58 out of 145 regions worldwide in terms of its "Knowledge Competitiveness Index." The index attempts to measure the knowledge-based development taking place throughout the world and is based on 19 measures of economic performance that indicate a region's ability to translate its knowledge capacity into economic value. *Centre for International Competitiveness, World Knowledge Competitiveness Index 2008*
- *Forbes* ranked the 200 most populous metro areas in the U.S. in terms of the "Best Places for Business and Careers." The Phoenix metro area was ranked #88. Criteria: costs (business and living); job growth (past and projected); income growth; educational attainment; projected economic growth; crime; cultural and recreational opportunities; net migration patterns; number of highly ranked colleges. *Forbes, "Best Places for Business and Careers," June 2011*

Children/Family Rankings

- The Phoenix metro area was selected as one of the "Best Cities for Relocating Families" by Worldwide ERC and Primacy Relocation. The 2008 study looked at nearly 50 factors important to relocating families including: recent job growth; nearby top-ranked colleges; in-state tuition for four-year public colleges; population growth since 2000; pediatricians per 100,000 population; and a Green Living index. *Worldwide ERC and Primacy Relocation, "2008 Best Cities for Relocating Families"*

Dating/Romance Rankings

- Eli Lily and Company, in partnership with Sperling's BestPlaces, ranked the nation's 50 largest metro areas in terms of the "Most Romantic Cities for Baby Boomers." The Phoenix metro area ranked #38. Criteria: marriage and divorce rates among baby boomers age 45 to 60; great restaurants; dance studios; chocolate, jewelry and flower sales. *Eli Lily and Company, "Most Romantic Cities for Baby Boomers," April 20, 2007*

- The Phoenix metro area was selected as one of the "Best Cities for Relocating Singles" by Worldwide ERC and Primacy Relocation. The area ranked #71 out of the 100 largest metro areas in the U.S. Criteria: recent job growth; recent singles population growth; overall population growth; affordable rental housing; cost-of-living index; expanded arts and recreation opportunities; ratio of single men and single women; affordability of quality higher education (including state residency requirements); diversity index; climate; population density. *Worldwide ERC and Primacy Relocation, "2008 Best Cities for Relocating Singles"*

- *Forbes* ranked the 40 most populous urbanized areas in the U.S. in terms of the "Best Cities for Singles." The Phoenix metro area ranked #30. Criteria: number of singles; cost of living alone; nightlife; culture; job growth; coolness; and online dating participation. *Forbes.com, "Best Cities for Singles," July 27, 2009*

Education Rankings

- Phoenix was identified as one of the 100 "smartest" metro areas in the U.S. The area ranked #70. Criteria: the editors rated the collective brainpower of the 100 largest metro areas in the U.S. based on their residents' educational attainment. *American City Business Journals, April 14, 2008*

- Phoenix was identified as one of "America's Brainiest Bastions" by *Portfolio.com.* The metro area ranked #100 out of 200. *Portfolio.com* analyzed levels of educational attainment in the nation's 200 largest metropolitan areas. The editors established scores for five levels of educational attainment, based on relative earning power of adult workers age 25 or older. Scores were determined by comparing the median income for all workers with the median income for those workers at a specified educational level. *Portfolio.com, "America's Brainiest Bastions," December 1, 2010*

Environmental Rankings

- The Phoenix was identified as one of America's dirtiest metro areas by *Forbes.* The area ranked #8 out of 10. Criteria: year-round particulate pollution; short-term particulate pollution; ozone pollution. *Forbes, "Dirtiest Cities in America," November 4, 2011*

- The Phoenix was identified as one of North America's greenest metropolitan areas. The area ranked #24. The Green City Index is comprised of 31 indicators, and scores cities across nine categories: carbon dioxide; energy; land use; buildings; transport; water; waste; air quality; environmental governance. The 27 largest metropolitan areas in the U.S. and Canada were considered. *Economist Intelligence Unit, sponsored by Siemens, "U.S. and Canada Green City Index, 2011"*

- The Phoenix was identified as one of America's cities with the most ENERGY STAR certified buildings. The area ranked #17 out of 25. Criteria: number of ENERGY STAR labeled buildings in 2010. *U.S. Environmental Protection Agency, "Top Cities With the Most ENERGY STAR Certified Buildings," March 15, 2011*

- The Phoenix metro area was identified as one of "The Ten Biggest American Cities that are Running Out of Water" by *24/7 Wall St.* The metro area ranked #3 out of 10. *24/7 Wall St.* did an analysis of the water supply and consumption in the 30 largest metropolitan areas in the U.S. Criteria include: projected water demand as a share of available precipitation; groundwater use as a share or projected available precipitation; susceptibility to drought; projected increase in freshwater withdrawals; projected increase in summer water deficit. *24/7 Wall St., "The Ten Biggest American Cities that are Running Out of Water," November 1, 2010*

- Gilbert was selected as one of 22 "Smarter Cities" for energy by the Natural Resources Defense Council. Criteria: investment in green power; energy efficiency measures; conservation. *Natural Resources Defense Council, "2010 Smarter Cities," July 19, 2010*

- *American City Business Journal* ranked 43 metropolitan areas in terms of their "greenness." The Phoenix metro area ranked #21. Criteria: Forty-one metros in which *ACBJ* has business weeklies, plus Indianapolis and Cleveland, were ranked based on 20 different indicators such as adoption of green technologies, utilization of environmentally sound practices, and air and water quality. *American City Business Journals, "Green City Index," March 11, 2010*

- 100 of the largest metro areas in the U.S. were analyzed in terms of their current drought severity. The Phoenix metro area ranked #23 (#1 = driest). The rankings were based on statistics such as long-term precipitation trends and patterns and the Palmer drought indices. *Sperling's BestPlaces, www.BestPlaces.net, "America's Drought-Riskiest Cities," November 2007*

- The Phoenix metro area appeared in *Country Home's* "Best Green Places" report. The area ranked #130 out of 379. Criteria: official energy policies; green power; green buildings; availability of fresh, locally grown food. *Country Home, "Best Green Places," 2008*

- Phoenix was highlighted as one of the 25 metro areas most polluted by short-term particle pollution (24-hour PM 2.5) in the U.S. The area ranked #24. *American Lung Association, State of the Air 2011*

- Phoenix was highlighted as one of the 25 metro areas most polluted by year-round particle pollution (Annual PM 2.5) in the U.S. The area ranked #2. *American Lung Association, State of the Air 2011*

- Phoenix was highlighted as one of the 25 most ozone-polluted metro areas in the U.S. The area ranked #19. *American Lung Association, State of the Air 2011*

Health/Fitness Rankings

- The Phoenix metro area was selected as one of the worst cities for bed bugs in America by Rollins corporation, the owner of seven pest control companies, including Orkin. The area ranked #34 based on the number of bed bug treatments from January to December 2011. *Rollins, "The Top 50 U.S. Cities for Bed Bugs," March 19, 2012*

- Phoenix was identified as a "2011 Asthma Capital." The area ranked #81 out of the nation's 100 largest metropolitan areas. Twelve factors were used to identify the most challenging places to live for people with asthma: estimated prevalence; self-reported prevalence; crude death rate for asthma; annual pollen score; annual air quality; public smoking laws; number of board-certified asthma specialists; school inhaler access laws; rescue medication use; controller medication use; uninsured rate; poverty rate. *Asthma and Allergy Foundation of America, "2011 Asthma Capitals"*

- Phoenix was identified as a "2011 Fall Allergy Capital." The area ranked #91 out of 100. Three groups of factors were used to identify the most severe cities for people with allergies during the fall season: annual pollen levels; medicine utilization; access to board-certified allergists. *Asthma and Allergy Foundation of America, "2011 Fall Allergy Capitals"*

- Phoenix was identified as a "2012 Spring Allergy Capital." The area ranked #72 out of 100. Three groups of factors were used to identify the most severe cities for people with allergies during the spring season: annual pollen levels; medicine utilization; access to board-certified allergists. *Asthma and Allergy Foundation of America, "2012 Spring Allergy Capitals"*

- The Phoenix metropolitan area was selected as one of the best metros for hospital care in America by *HealthGrades.com.* The rankings are based on a comprehensive study of patient death and complication rates in the nation's nearly 5,000 hospitals. Hospitals performing in the top 5% nationwide across 26 different medical procedures and diagnoses were identified. *HealthGrades.com* then ranked cities by the highest percentage of these Distinguished Hospitals for Clinical Excellence™. The Phoenix metro area ranked #2. *HealthGrades.com, "America's Top 50 Cities for Hospital Care," January 21, 2012*
- The American Academy of Dermatology ranked 26 U.S. metropolitan regions in terms of their residents knowledge, attitude and behaviors towards tanning, sun protection and skin cancer detection. The Phoenix metro area ranked #6. The results of the study are based on an online survey of over 7,000 adults nationwide. *American Academy of Dermatology, "Suntelligence: How Sun Smart is Your City," May 3, 2010*
- The Phoenix metro area appeared in the 2011 Gallup-Healthways Well-Being Index. The index, based on interviews with more than 350,000 Americans, measured jobs, finances, physical health, emotional state of mind and communities. The metro area ranked #69 out of 190. Criteria: life evaluation; emotional health; work environment; physical health; healthy behaviors; basic access (basic needs optimal for a healthy life, such as access to food and medicine, having health insurance and feeling safe while walking at night). *Gallup-Healthways, "State of Well-Being 2011"*
- The Phoenix metro area was identified as one of "America's Most Stressful Cities" by *Sperling's BestPlaces.* The metro area ranked #18 out of 50. Criteria: unemployment rate; suicide rate; commute time; mental health; poor rest; alcohol use; violent crime rate; property crime rate; cloudy days annually. *Sperling's BestPlaces, www.BestPlaces.net, "Stressful Cities 2012*
- 50 of the largest metro areas in the U.S. were analyzed in terms of their health and fitness by the American College of Sports Medicine in their "American Fitness Index." The Phoenix metro area ranked #32 (#1 = healthiest). Criteria: preventative health behaviors; levels of chronic disease; health care access; community resources and policies that support physical activity. *American College of Sports Medicine, "Health and Community Fitness Status of the 50 Largest Metropolitan Areas," August 1, 2011*

Pet Rankings

- Phoenix was selected as one of the "Top 10 Cat-Friendly Cities" in the U.S. The area ranked #2. Criteria: cat ownership per capita; level of veterinary care; microchipping; cat-friendly local ordinances. *CATalyst Council, "Top 10 Cat-Friendly Cities," March 27, 2009*

Real Estate Rankings

- Phoenix was identified as one of 13 metro areas where home prices are falling dangerously. Criteria: home price change from October 2010 to September 2011; projected home price change through 2012. *Forbes.com, "Cities Where Home Prices are Falling Dangerously," January 10, 2012*
- Phoenix was identified as one of the "Top Turnaround Housing Markets for 2012." The area ranked #2 out of 10. Criteria: year-over-year median home price appreciation; year-over-year median inventory age; year-over-year inventory reduction. *AOL Real Estate, "Top Turnaround Housing Markets for 2012," February 4, 2012*
- *Fortune* ranked the 100 largest metro areas in the U.S. in terms of projected median home price change in 2010. The Phoenix metro area ranked #92. *Fortune, "The 2010 Housing Outlook," December 9, 2009*
- The Phoenix metro area was identified as one of the "Top 25 Real Estate Investment Markets" by *FinestExperts.com.* The metro area ranked #17. Over 10,000 real estate markets were analyzed to identify the most suitable places for real estate investors to seek stability and growth. Criteria: employment; rental markets; growth levels as offset by foreclosures. *FinestExperts.com, "Top 25 Real Estate Investment Markets," January 7, 2010*
- The Phoenix metro area was identified as one of "America's 25 Weakest Housing Markets" by *Forbes.* The metro area ranked #12. Criteria: metro areas with populations over 500,000 were ranked based on projected home values through 2011. *Forbes.com, "America's 25 Weakest Housing Markets," January 7, 2009*

- The nation's largest metro areas were analyzed in terms of the percentage of households entering some stage of foreclosure in 2011. The Phoenix metro area ranked #6 out of 20 (#1 = highest foreclosure rate). *RealtyTrac, 2011 Year-End Foreclosure Market Report, January 12, 2012*
- The nation's largest metro areas were analyzed in terms of the best places to buy pre-foreclosures (short sales). The Phoenix metro area ranked #9 out of 10. Criteria: at least 500 pre-foreclosure sales during the fourth quarter and a short sales increase of at least five percent from a year ago. The areas selected posted the biggest discounts on the sales of pre-foreclosure properties. *RealtyTrac, "Fourth Quarter and Year-End 2011 U.S. Foreclosure Sales Report: Shifting Towards Short Sales," February 28, 2012*
- The Phoenix metro area was identified as one of the 10 best cities for "Real Estate Steals" in the U.S. by *U.S. News and World Report.* The metro area was ranked #8. Criteria: average and quarterly price-to-income ratios. *U.S. News and World Report, "10 Cities for Real Estate Steals," February 18, 2010*
- The Phoenix metro area appeared in a *Wall Street Journal* article ranking cities by "housing stress." The metro area was ranked #11 (#1 = most stress). Criteria: fraction of mortgage-holding homeowners with a monthly housing payment in excess of 30 percent of income; percentage of people without health insurance; unemployment rate. *The Wall Street Journal, "Which Cities Face Biggest Housing Risk," October 5, 2010*
- The Center for Housing Policy ranked 210 U.S. metropolitan areas by the fair market rent for a two-bedroom unit. The Phoenix metro area was ranked #76. (#1 = most expensive) with a rent of $919. Criteria: Fair Market Rent (FMR) in effect during the fourth quarter of 2009 based on HUD's fiscal year 2010 FMRs. *The Center for Housing Policy, "Paycheck to Paycheck: Most to Least Expensive Rental Markets in 2009"*
- The Phoenix metro area was identified as one of the worst housing markets of the decade by *Forbes.* Criteria: decrease in housing values per square foot since January 2000. *Forbes, "America's 5 Best (and Worst) Housing Markets of the Decade," December 7, 2010*
- The Phoenix metro area was identified as one of the top 20 cities in terms of decreasing home equity. The metro area was ranked #3. Criteria: percentage of home equity relative to the home's current value. *Forbes.com, "Where Americans are Losing Home Equity Most," May 1, 2010*
- The Phoenix metro area was identified as one of the markets with the worst expected performance in home prices over the next 12 months. *Local Market Monitor, "First Quarter Home Price Forecast for Largest US Markets," March 2, 2011*
- The Phoenix metro area was identified as one of the best U.S. markets to invest in rental property" by HomeVestors and Local Market Monitor. The area ranked #8 out of 100. Criteria: risk-return premium relative to national average. *HomeVestors and Local Market Monitor, "Best 100 U.S. Markets to Invest in Rental Property," March 9, 2012*

Safety Rankings

- Allstate ranked the 193 largest cities in America in terms of driver safety. Gilbert ranked #18. In addition, drivers were 12.9% less likely to have had an accident compared to the national average. Allstate researchers analyzed internal property damage reported claims over a two-year period (from January 2008 to December 2009) to protect findings from external influences such as weather or road construction. A weighted average of the two-year numbers determined the annual percentages. The report defines an auto crash as any collision resulting in a property damage claim. *Allstate, "2011 Allstate America's Best Drivers Report™"*
- Gilbert was identified as one of the safest mid-size cities in America by CQ Press. All 234 cities with populations of 100,000 to 499,999 that reported crime rates in 2010 for murder, rape, robbery, aggravated assault, burglary, and motor vehicle thefts were ranked. The city ranked #8 out of the top 10. *CQ Press, City Crime Rankings 2011-2012*
- The National Insurance Crime Bureau ranked 366 metro areas in the U.S. in terms of per capita rates of vehicle theft. The Phoenix metro area ranked #56 (#1 = highest rate). Criteria: number of vehicle theft offenses per 100,000 inhabitants in 2010. *National Insurance Crime Bureau, "Hot Spots," June 21, 2011*

- The Phoenix metro area was identified as one of the most dangerous metro areas for pedestrians by Transportation for America. The metro area ranked #8 out of 52 metro areas with over 1 million residents. Criteria: area's population divided by the number of pedestrian fatalities in that area. *Transportation for America, "Dangerous by Design 2011"*

Seniors/Retirement Rankings

- Bankers Life and Casualty Company, in partnership with Sperling's BestPlaces, ranked the nation's 50 largest metro areas in terms of the "Best U.S. Cities for Seniors." The Phoenix metro area ranked #40. Criteria: healthcare; transportation; housing; environment; economy; health and longevity; social and spiritual life; crime. *Bankers Life and Casualty Company, Center for a Secure Retirement, "Best U.S. Cities for Seniors 2011," September 2011*
- The Phoenix metro area was identified as one of the "Best Places for Bargain Retirement Homes" by *Forbes*. The metro area ranked #9 out of 10. Criteria: low cost of living; stable home prices; low taxes; reasonable average home prices. *Forbes.com, "Best Places for Bargain Retirement Homes," January 12, 2011*
- The Phoenix metro area was selected as one of "The 10 Most Affordable Cities for Long-Term Care" by *U.S. News & World Report*. Criteria: costs at nursing homes, assisted living facilities, and adult day health care facilities; cost for licensed home health aides. *U.S. News & World Report, "The 10 Most Affordable Cities for Long-Term Care," May 17, 2010*

Sports/Recreation Rankings

- Gilbert was chosen as a bicycle friendly community by the League of American Bicyclists. A Bicycle Friendly Community welcomes cyclists by providing safe accommodation for cycling and encouraging people to bike for transportation and recreation. There are four award levels: Platinum; Gold; Silver; and Bronze. The community achieved an award level of Bronze. *League of American Bicyclists, "Bicycle Friendly Community Master List 2011"*
- Gilbert was selected as one of the most playful cities in the U.S. by KaBOOM! The organization's Playful City USA initiative is a national recognition program that honors cities and towns across the nation for a vision, plan and commitment to creating an agenda for play. Cities were recognized based on a pledge to five specific commitments to play: creating a local play commission or task force; designing an annual action plan for play; conducting a play space audit; outlining a financial investment in play for the current fiscal year; and proclaiming and celebrating an annual "play day." *KaBOOM! National Campaign for Play, "2011 Playful City USA Communities"*
- The Phoenix was selected as one of the best metro areas for golf in America by *Golf Digest*. The Phoenix area was ranked #15 out of 20. Criteria: climate; cost of public golf; quality of public golf; accessibility. *Golf Digest, "The Top 20 Cities for Golf," October 2011*

Transportation Rankings

- The Phoenix metro area appeared on *Forbes* list of the best and worst cities for commuters. The metro area ranked #36 out of 60 (#1 is best). Criteria: travel time; road congestion; travel delays. *Forbes.com, "Best and Worst Cities for Commuters," February 16, 2010*

Women/Minorities Rankings

- Phoenix was ranked #48 out of 100 metro areas in *SELF Magazine's* ranking of America's healthiest places for women." A panel of experts came up with more than 50 criteria including death and disease rates, environmental indicators, community resources, and lifestyle habits. *SELF Magazine, "Secrets of America's Healthiest Women," December 2008*
- The Phoenix metro area appeared on *Forbes'* list of the "Best Cities for Minority Entrepreneurs." The area ranked #48 out of 10. Criteria: 52 metropolitan statistical areas were examined. For each ethnicity (African Americans, Asians and Hispanics), the editors measured housing affordability, population growth, income growth, and entrepreneurship (per capita self-employment). *Forbes, "Best Cities for Minority Entrepreneurs," March 23, 2011*

Miscellaneous Rankings

- The Phoenix metro area was selected as one of "The Best U.S. Cities for Bargain Shopping" by *Forbes.* The area ranked #3 out of 10. Criteria: number of outlet stores; gross leasable retail space in major malls; low consumer price index; low sales tax rate. Indicators were examined in the nation's 50 largest metropolitan areas. *Forbes, "The Best U.S. Cities for Bargain Shopping," January 20, 2012*

- Energizer Holdings, the makers of Edge® shave gel, in partnership with Sperling's BestPlaces, ranked 50 major metro areas in terms of everyday irritations. The Phoenix metro area ranked #10. Criteria: humidity levels; weather conditions; incidence of traffic delays and congestion; average commute times; frequency of flight delays and cancellations; rates of sleeplessness; underemployment; pollens and allergens; pests; comedy clubs per capita. *Energizer Holdings, "Most Irritation Prone Cities," July 23, 2010*

- Mars Chocolate North America, the makers of COMBOS®, in partnership with Sperling's BestPlaces, ranked 50 major metro areas in terms of their "manliness." The Phoenix metro area ranked #32. Criteria: number of professional sports teams; number of nearby NASCAR tracks and racing events; manly lifestyle; concentration of manly retail stores; manly occupations per capita; salty snack sales; "Board of Manliness" rankings. *Mars Chocolate North America, "America's Manliest Cities 2011," September 1, 2011*

Business Environment

CITY FINANCES

City Government Finances

Component	2009 ($000)	2009 ($ per capita)
Total Revenues	280,360	1,351
Total Expenditures	360,240	1,736
Debt Outstanding	638,185	3,075
Cash and Securities[1]	430,739	2,075

Note: (1) Cash and security holdings of a government at the close of its fiscal year, including those of its dependent agencies, utilities, and liquor stores.
Source: U.S Census Bureau, State & Local Government Finances 2009

City Government Revenue by Source

Source	2009 ($000)	2009 ($ per capita)
General Revenue		
From Federal Government	2,207	11
From State Government	60,647	292
From Local Governments	5,337	26
Taxes		
Property	33,130	160
Sales and Gross Receipts	51,280	247
Personal Income	0	0
Corporate Income	0	0
Motor Vehicle License	0	0
Other Taxes	26,058	126
Current Charges	43,486	210
Liquor Store	0	0
Utility	33,575	162
Employee Retirement	0	0

Source: U.S Census Bureau, State & Local Government Finances 2009

City Government Expenditures by Function

Function	2009 ($000)	2009 ($ per capita)	2009 (%)
General Direct Expenditures			
Air Transportation	0	0	0.0
Corrections	0	0	0.0
Education	0	0	0.0
Employment Security Administration	0	0	0.0
Financial Administration	9,187	44	2.6
Fire Protection	21,382	103	5.9
General Public Buildings	6,264	30	1.7
Governmental Administration, Other	4,947	24	1.4
Health	0	0	0.0
Highways	67,055	323	18.6
Hospitals	0	0	0.0
Housing and Community Development	2,867	14	0.8
Interest on General Debt	16,501	80	4.6
Judicial and Legal	5,203	25	1.4
Libraries	0	0	0.0
Parking	0	0	0.0
Parks and Recreation	78,507	378	21.8
Police Protection	35,834	173	9.9
Public Welfare	0	0	0.0
Sewerage	13,480	65	3.7
Solid Waste Management	13,816	67	3.8
Veterans' Services	0	0	0.0
Liquor Store	0	0	0.0
Utility	64,459	311	17.9
Employee Retirement	0	0	0.0

Source: U.S Census Bureau, State & Local Government Finances 2009

Municipal Bond Ratings

Area	Moody's	S&P	Fitch
City	n/a	n/a	n/a

Rating Systems (shown in declining order of credit quality): Moody's– Aaa, Aa, A, Baa, Ba, B, Caa, Ca, C (numerical modifiers 1, 2, and 3 are added to letter-rating); S&P– AAA, AA, A, BBB, BB, B, CCC, CC, C; Fitch– AAA, AA, A, BBB, BB, B, CCC, CC, C. Ratings may be modified by the addition of a plus or minus sign to show relative standing within the major rating categories.
Notes: n/a Not Available; w/d Withdrawn (1) Not Reviewed; (2) Issuer Rating/No General Obligation; (3) Standard and Poor's Issue Credit Rating (ICR) is a current opinion of an obliger with respect to a specific financial obligation, a specific class of financial obligations, or a specific financial program.
Source: U.S. Census Bureau, 2012 Statistical Abstract, Bond Ratings for City Governments by Largest Cities: 2010

DEMOGRAPHICS

Population Growth

Area	1990 Census	2000 Census	2010 Census	Population Growth (%)	
				1990-2000	2000-2010
City	33,229	109,697	208,453	230.1	90.0
MSA[1]	2,238,480	3,251,876	4,192,887	45.3	28.9
U.S.	248,709,873	281,421,906	308,745,538	13.2	9.7

Note: (1) Figures cover the Phoenix-Mesa-Glendale, AZ Metropolitan Statistical Area—see Appendix B for areas included
Source: U.S. Census Bureau, 2010 Census

Household Size

Area	Persons in Household (%)							Average Household Size
	One	Two	Three	Four	Five	Six	Seven or More	
City	16.1	30.0	18.1	19.6	9.6	4.2	2.3	3.00
MSA[1]	25.4	33.2	14.8	13.2	7.3	3.4	2.8	2.68
U.S.	26.7	32.8	16.1	13.4	6.5	2.6	1.9	2.58

Note: (1) Figures cover the Phoenix-Mesa-Glendale, AZ Metropolitan Statistical Area—see Appendix B for areas included
Source: U.S. Census Bureau, 2010 Census

Race

Area	White Alone[2] (%)	Black Alone[2] (%)	Asian Alone[2] (%)	AIAN[3] Alone[2] (%)	NHOPI[4] Alone[2] (%)	Other Race Alone[2] (%)	Two or More Races (%)
City	81.8	3.4	5.8	0.8	0.2	4.5	3.5
MSA[1]	73.0	5.0	3.3	2.4	0.2	12.7	3.5
U.S.	72.4	12.6	4.8	0.9	0.2	6.2	2.9

Note: (1) Figures cover the Phoenix-Mesa-Glendale, AZ Metropolitan Statistical Area—see Appendix B for areas included; (2) Alone is defined as not being in combination with one or more other races; (3) American Indian and Alaska Native; (4) Native Hawaiian and Other Pacific Islander
Source: U.S. Census Bureau, 2010 Census

Hispanic or Latino Origin

Area	Hispanic or Latino (%)	Mexican (%)	Puerto Rican (%)	Cuban (%)	Other Hispanic or Latino (%)
City	14.9	11.4	0.7	0.2	2.6
MSA[1]	29.5	25.5	0.6	0.2	3.2
U.S.	16.3	10.3	1.5	0.6	4.0

Note: Persons of Hispanic or Latino origin can be of any race; (1) Figures cover the Phoenix-Mesa-Glendale, AZ Metropolitan Statistical Area—see Appendix B for areas included
Source: U.S. Census Bureau, 2010 Census

Segregation

Type	Segregation Indices[1]				Percent Change		
	1990	2000	2010	2010 Rank[2]	1990-2000	1990-2010	2000-2010
Black/White	50.1	45.1	43.6	86	-5.0	-6.4	-1.5
Asian/White	28.1	30.1	32.7	85	2.0	4.6	2.6
Hispanic/White	48.6	52.2	49.3	28	3.5	0.7	-2.8

Note: Figures are based on an analysis of 1990, 2000, and 2010 Census Decennial Census tract data by William H. Frey, Brookings Institution and the University of Michigan Social Science Data Analysis Network. In this analysis all racial groups (whites, blacks, and asians) are non-Hispanic members of those races. Hispanics are shown as a separate category; All figures cover the Metropolitan Statistical Area (see Appendix B for areas included); (1) Segregation Indices are Dissimilarity Indices that measure the degree to which the minority group is distributed differently than whites across census tracts. They range from 0 (complete integration) to 100 (complete segregation) where the value indicates the percentage of the minority group that needs to move to be distributed exactly like whites; (2) Ranges from 1 (most segregated) to 102 (least segregated); n/a not available.
Source: www.CensusScope.org

Ancestry

Area	German	Irish	English	American	Italian	Polish	French[2]	Scottish	Dutch
City	22.8	13.0	13.8	3.4	5.9	3.6	3.3	2.0	1.6
MSA[1]	16.0	10.5	9.3	5.1	4.9	2.8	2.7	1.9	1.5
U.S.	16.1	11.6	8.8	6.1	5.7	3.2	3.0	1.9	1.6

Note: Figures are the percentage of the total population reporting a particular ancestry. The nine most commonly reported ancestries in the U.S. are shown. Figures include multiple ancestries (e.g. if a person reported being Irish and Italian, they were included in both columns); (1) Figures cover the Phoenix-Mesa-Glendale, AZ Metropolitan Statistical Area—see Appendix B for areas included; (2) Excludes Basque
Source: U.S. Census Bureau, 2008-2010 American Community Survey 3-Year Estimates

Foreign-Born Population

Area	Percent of Population Born in								
	Any Foreign Country	Mexico	Asia	Europe	Carribean	South America	Central America[2]	Africa	Canada
City	8.6	1.5	3.8	0.9	0.3	0.6	0.1	0.7	0.5
MSA[1]	14.9	8.8	2.7	1.4	0.2	0.3	0.5	0.4	0.6
U.S.	12.8	3.8	3.6	1.6	1.2	0.9	1.0	0.5	0.3

Note: (1) Figures cover the Phoenix-Mesa-Glendale, AZ Metropolitan Statistical Area—see Appendix B for areas included; (2) Excludes Mexico.
Source: U.S. Census Bureau, 2008-2010 American Community Survey 3-Year Estimates

Marital Status

Area	Never Married	Now Married[2]	Separated	Widowed	Divorced
City	27.5	56.9	1.5	2.5	11.5
MSA[1]	31.8	49.9	1.6	5.0	11.7
U.S.	31.6	49.6	2.2	6.1	10.7

Note: Figures are percentages and cover the population 15 years of age and older; (1) Figures cover the Phoenix-Mesa-Glendale, AZ Metropolitan Statistical Area—see Appendix B for areas included; (2) Excludes separated
Source: U.S. Census Bureau, 2008-2010 American Community Survey 3-Year Estimates

Age

Area	Percent of Population							Median Age
	Under Age 5	Age 5 to 17	Age 18 to 34	Age 35 to 49	Age 50 to 64	Age 65 to 79	80 Years and Over	
City	8.5	23.6	22.7	24.6	14.5	5.0	1.0	31.9
MSA[1]	7.5	19.0	24.0	20.5	16.8	9.1	3.2	34.7
U.S.	6.5	17.5	23.2	20.7	19.0	9.4	3.6	37.2

Note: (1) Figures cover the Phoenix-Mesa-Glendale, AZ Metropolitan Statistical Area—see Appendix B for areas included
Source: U.S. Census Bureau, 2010 Census

Male/Female Ratio

Area	Males	Females	Males per 100 Females
City	102,634	105,819	97.0
MSA[1]	2,085,630	2,107,257	99.0
U.S.	151,781,326	156,964,212	96.7

Note: (1) Figures cover the Phoenix-Mesa-Glendale, AZ Metropolitan Statistical Area—see Appendix B for areas included
Source: U.S. Census Bureau, 2010 Census

Religious Groups

Area	Catholic	Baptist	Non-Den.	Methodist[2]	Lutheran	LDS[3]	Pente-costal	Presby-terian[4]	Muslim[5]	Judaism
MSA[1]	13.4	3.5	5.2	1.0	1.6	6.1	2.9	0.6	0.3	0.2
U.S.	19.1	9.3	4.0	4.0	2.3	2.0	1.9	1.6	0.8	0.7

Note: Figures are the number of adherents as a percentage of the total population; (1) Figures cover the Phoenix-Mesa-Glendale, AZ Metropolitan Statistical Area—see Appendix B for areas included; (2) Methodist/Pietist; (3) Latter Day Saints; (4) Reformed; (5) Figures are estimates
Source: Association of Statisticians of American Religious Bodies, 2010 U.S. Religion Census: Religious Congregations & Membership Study

ECONOMY

Gross Metropolitan Product

Area	2007	2008	2009	2010	2010 Rank[2]
MSA[1]	196.4	196.0	187.4	190.6	15

Note: Figures are in billions of dollars; (1) Figures cover the Phoenix-Mesa-Glendale, AZ Metropolitan Statistical Area—see Appendix B for areas included; (2) Rank ranges from 1 to 363
Source: The United States Conference of Mayors, "U.S. Metro Economies: GMP and Employment Forecasts," June 2011

Economic Growth

Area	2007-2009 (%)	2010 (%)	2011 (%)	Rank[2]
MSA[1]	-3.9	0.9	2.1	303
U.S.	-1.3	2.9	2.5	–

Note: Figures are real Gross Metropolitan Product growth rates and represent annual average percent change; (1) Figures cover the Phoenix-Mesa-Glendale, AZ Metropolitan Statistical Area—see Appendix B for areas included; (2) Rank ranges from 1 to 363
Source: The United States Conference of Mayors, "U.S. Metro Economies: GMP and Employment Forecasts," June 2011

Metropolitan Area Exports

Area	2005	2006	2007	2008	2009	2010	2010 Rank[2]
MSA[1]	8,473.0	10,954.8	12,818.2	12,623.6	7,947.5	9,342.7	29

Note: Figures are in millions of dollars; (1) Figures cover the Phoenix-Mesa-Glendale, AZ Metropolitan Statistical Area—see Appendix B for areas included; (2) Rank ranges from 1 to 369
Source: U.S. Department of Commerce, International Trade Administration, Office of Trade & Industry Information, Manufacturing & Services, data extracted April 2, 2012

INCOME

Income

Area	Per Capita ($)	Median Household ($)	Average Household ($)
City	30,005	75,895	88,751
MSA[1]	26,243	52,904	70,586
U.S.	26,942	51,222	70,116

Note: (1) Figures cover the Phoenix-Mesa-Glendale, AZ Metropolitan Statistical Area—see Appendix B for areas included
Source: U.S. Census Bureau, 2008-2010 American Community Survey 3-Year Estimates

Household Income Distribution

Area	Percent of Households Earning							
	Under $15,000	$15,000 -24,999	$25,000 -34,999	$35,000 -49,999	$50,000 -74,999	$75,000 -99,000	$100,000 -149,999	$150,000 and up
City	4.7	4.9	6.6	12.5	20.6	16.6	22.6	11.5
MSA[1]	11.1	10.1	10.7	15.1	19.5	12.7	12.9	7.9
U.S.	13.0	11.0	10.6	14.2	18.5	12.1	12.2	8.4

Note: (1) Figures cover the Phoenix-Mesa-Glendale, AZ Metropolitan Statistical Area—see Appendix B for areas included
Source: U.S. Census Bureau, 2008-2010 American Community Survey 3-Year Estimates

Poverty Rate

Area	All Ages	Under 18 Years Old	18 to 64 Years Old	65 Years and Over
City	6.3	8.1	5.8	2.9
MSA[1]	14.9	21.2	13.6	7.1
U.S.	14.4	20.1	13.1	9.4

Note: Figures are percentage of people whose income during the past 12 months was below the poverty level; (1) Figures cover the Phoenix-Mesa-Glendale, AZ Metropolitan Statistical Area—see Appendix B for areas included
Source: U.S. Census Bureau, 2008-2010 American Community Survey 3-Year Estimates

Personal Bankruptcy Filing Rate

Area	2006	2007	2008	2009	2010	2011
Maricopa County	1.40	1.87	3.47	6.22	7.81	6.60
U.S.	2.00	2.73	3.53	4.61	4.97	4.37

Note: Numbers are per 1,000 population and include Chapter 7 and Chapter 13 filings
Source: Federal Deposit Insurance Corporation, Regional Economic Conditions, March 9, 2012

EMPLOYMENT

Labor Force and Employment

Area	Civilian Labor Force			Workers Employed		
	Dec. 2010	Dec. 2011	% Chg.	Dec. 2010	Dec. 2011	% Chg.
City	118,345	118,842	0.4	112,626	113,586	0.9
MSA[1]	2,125,593	2,127,867	0.1	1,944,188	1,960,752	0.9
U.S.	153,156,000	153,373,000	0.1	139,159,000	140,681,000	1.1

Note: Data is not seasonally adjusted and covers workers 16 years of age and older; (1) Metropolitan Statistical Area—see Appendix B for areas included
Source: Bureau of Labor Statistics, http://stats.bls.gov

Unemployment Rate

Area	2011											
	Jan.	Feb.	Mar.	Apr.	May	Jun.	Jul.	Aug.	Sep.	Oct.	Nov.	Dec.
City	5.3	5.0	4.9	4.6	4.5	5.1	4.9	4.8	4.5	4.5	4.3	4.4
MSA[1]	9.3	8.8	8.7	8.1	8.0	9.0	8.7	8.4	8.0	8.1	7.7	7.9
U.S.	9.8	9.5	9.2	8.7	8.7	9.3	9.3	9.1	8.8	8.5	8.2	8.3

Note: Data is not seasonally adjusted and covers workers 16 years of age and older; All figures are percentages; (1) Metropolitan Statistical Area—see Appendix B for areas included
Source: Bureau of Labor Statistics, http://stats.bls.gov

Projected Unemployment Rate

Area	2010 (%)	2011 (%)	2012 (%)	2013 (%)
MSA[1]	8.9	8.4	7.9	7.3

Note: (1) Metropolitan Statistical Area—see Appendix B for areas included
Source: The United States Conference of Mayors, "U.S. Metro Economies: GMP and Employment Forecasts," June 2011

Employment by Occupation

Occupation Classification	City (%)	MSA[1] (%)	U.S. (%)
Management, Business, Science, and Arts	43.9	35.7	35.6
Natural Resources, Construction, and Maintenance	6.7	9.5	9.5
Production, Transportation, and Material Moving	6.9	9.4	12.1
Sales and Office	28.4	27.7	25.2
Service	14.1	17.6	17.6

Note: Figures cover employed civilians 16 years of age and older; (1) Figures cover the Phoenix-Mesa-Glendale, AZ Metropolitan Statistical Area—see Appendix B for areas included
Source: U.S. Census Bureau, 2008-2010 American Community Survey 3-Year Estimates

Employment by Industry

Sector	MSA[1]		U.S.
	Number of Employees	Percent of Total	Percent of Total
Construction	82,200	4.7	4.1
Education and Health Services	255,000	14.6	15.2
Financial Activities	143,100	8.2	5.8
Government	236,600	13.5	16.8
Information	28,600	1.6	2.0
Leisure and Hospitality	180,200	10.3	9.9
Manufacturing	112,000	6.4	8.9
Mining and Logging	3,300	0.2	0.6
Other Services	63,500	3.6	4.0
Professional and Business Services	282,900	16.2	13.3
Retail Trade	218,700	12.5	11.5
Transportation and Utilities	62,200	3.6	3.8
Wholesale Trade	81,800	4.7	4.2

Note: Figures cover non-farm employment as of December 2011 and are not seasonally adjusted; (1) Metropolitan Statistical Area—see Appendix B for areas included
Source: Bureau of Labor Statistics, http://stats.bls.gov

Occupations with Greatest Projected Employment Growth: 2008 – 2018

Occupation[1]	2008 Employment	2018 Projected Employment	Numeric Employment Change	Percent Employment Change
Customer Service Representatives	64,870	74,760	9,890	15.2
Registered Nurses	40,510	50,010	9,500	23.5
Combined Food Preparation and Serving Workers, Including Fast Food	43,970	52,950	8,980	20.4
Retail Salespersons	86,670	94,880	8,210	9.5
Cashiers	62,340	67,580	5,240	8.4
Waiters and Waitresses	50,230	55,440	5,210	10.4
Stock Clerks and Order Fillers	41,050	46,200	5,150	12.5
Office Clerks, General	60,330	64,570	4,240	7.0
Postsecondary Teachers	32,770	36,940	4,170	12.7
Accountants and Auditors	28,320	32,250	3,930	13.9

Note: Projections cover Arizona; (1) Sorted by numeric employment change
Source: www.projectionscentral.com, State Occupational Projections, 2008–2018 Long-Term Projections

Fastest Growing Occupations: 2008 – 2018

Occupation[1]	2008 Employment	2018 Projected Employment	Numeric Employment Change	Percent Employment Change
Biomedical Engineers	240	370	130	54.2
Credit Authorizers, Checkers, and Clerks	7,080	10,760	3,680	52.0
Network Systems and Data Communications Analysts	4,590	6,450	1,860	40.5
Medical Scientists, Except Epidemiologists	880	1,220	340	38.6
Radiation Therapists	610	820	210	34.4
Physician Assistants	1,290	1,730	440	34.1
Dental Hygienists	2,690	3,570	880	32.7
Pharmacy Technicians	7,700	10,170	2,470	32.1
Surgical Technologists	1,560	2,050	490	31.4
Dental Assistants	6,320	8,280	1,960	31.0

Note: Projections cover Arizona; (1) Sorted by percent employment change and excludes occupations with numeric employment change less than 100
Source: www.projectionscentral.com, State Occupational Projections, 2008–2018 Long-Term Projections

Average Wages

Occupation	$/Hr.	Occupation	$/Hr.
Accountants and Auditors	29.62	Maids and Housekeeping Cleaners	9.60
Automotive Mechanics	19.98	Maintenance and Repair Workers	17.63
Bookkeepers	17.77	Marketing Managers	52.33
Carpenters	19.96	Nuclear Medicine Technologists	35.95
Cashiers	10.97	Nurses, Licensed Practical	25.14
Clerks, General Office	14.89	Nurses, Registered	35.74
Clerks, Receptionists/Information	13.73	Nursing Aides/Orderlies/Attendants	13.23
Clerks, Shipping/Receiving	14.26	Packers and Packagers, Hand	10.78
Computer Programmers	37.73	Physical Therapists	37.94
Computer Support Specialists	23.79	Postal Service Mail Carriers	25.15
Computer Systems Analysts	36.35	Real Estate Brokers	n/a
Cooks, Restaurant	14.05	Retail Salespersons	12.05
Dentists	89.20	Sales Reps., Exc. Tech./Scientific	30.16
Electrical Engineers	47.97	Sales Reps., Tech./Scientific	39.60
Electricians	21.37	Secretaries, Exc. Legal/Med./Exec.	15.99
Financial Managers	51.98	Security Guards	13.08
First-Line Supervisors/Managers, Sales	19.48	Surgeons	n/a
Food Preparation Workers	10.57	Teacher Assistants	11.00
General and Operations Managers	51.63	Teachers, Elementary School	20.60
Hairdressers/Cosmetologists	11.42	Teachers, Secondary School	21.00
Internists	93.77	Telemarketers	14.81
Janitors and Cleaners	11.50	Truck Drivers, Heavy/Tractor-Trailer	20.92
Landscaping/Groundskeeping Workers	11.12	Truck Drivers, Light/Delivery Svcs.	17.50
Lawyers	62.72	Waiters and Waitresses	10.36

Note: Wage data covers the Phoenix-Mesa-Glendale, AZ Metropolitan Statistical Area—see Appendix B for areas included. Hourly wages for elementary/secondary school teachers and teacher assistants were calculated by the editors from annual wage data assuming a 40 hour work week; n/a not available.
Source: Bureau of Labor Statistics, Metro Area Occupational Employment and Wage Estimates, May 2011

RESIDENTIAL REAL ESTATE

Building Permits

Area	Single-Family			Multi-Family			Total		
	2010	2011	Pct. Chg.	2010	2011	Pct. Chg.	2010	2011	Pct. Chg.
City	1,060	1,541	45.4	0	0	-	1,060	1,541	45.4
MSA[1]	7,212	7,297	1.2	1,088	1,784	64.0	8,300	9,081	9.4
U.S.	447,311	418,498	-6.4	157,299	205,563	30.7	604,610	624,061	3.2

Note: (1) Metropolitan Statistical Area—see Appendix B for areas included; figures represent new, privately-owned housing units authorized (unadjusted data); All permit data are based on estimates with imputation.
Source: U.S. Census Bureau, Manufacturing, Mining, and Construction Statistics, Building Permits, 2010, 2011

Homeownership Rate

Area	2005 (%)	2006 (%)	2007 (%)	2008 (%)	2009 (%)	2010 (%)	2011 (%)
MSA[1]	71.2	72.5	70.8	70.2	69.8	66.5	63.3
U.S.	68.9	68.8	68.1	67.8	67.4	66.9	66.1

Note: (1) Metropolitan Statistical Area—see Appendix B for areas included
Source: U.S. Census Bureau, Housing Vacancies and Homeownership Annual Statistics: 2011

Housing Vacancy Rates

Area	Gross Vacancy Rate[2] (%)			Year-Round Vacancy Rate[3] (%)			Rental Vacancy Rate[4] (%)			Homeowner Vacancy Rate[5] (%)		
	2009	2010	2011	2009	2010	2011	2009	2010	2011	2009	2010	2011
MSA[1]	18.6	18.4	16.7	13.2	12.9	10.8	18.3	16.3	10.9	3.1	2.9	3.1
U.S.	14.5	14.3	14.2	11.3	11.3	11.1	10.6	10.2	9.5	2.6	2.6	2.5

Note: (1) Metropolitan Statistical Area—see Appendix B for areas included; (2) The percentage of the total housing inventory that is vacant; (3) The percentage of the housing inventory (excluding seasonal units) that is year-round vacant; (4) The percentage of rental inventory that is vacant for rent; (5) The percentage of homeowner inventory that is vacant for sale
Source: U.S. Census Bureau, Housing Vacancies and Homeownership Annual Statistics: 2011

TAXES

State Corporate Income Tax Rates

State	Tax Rate (%)	Income Brackets ($)	Num. of Brackets	Financial Institution Tax Rate (%)[a]	Federal Income Tax Ded.
Arizona	6.968 (b)	Flat rate	1	6.968 (b)	No

Note: Tax rates as of January 1, 2012; (a) Rates listed are the corporate income tax rate applied to financial institutions or excise taxes based on income. Some states have other taxes based upon the value of deposits or shares; (b) Minimum tax is $50 in Arizona, $100 in District of Columbia, $50 in North Dakota (banks), $500 in Rhode Island, $200 per location in South Dakota (banks), $100 in Utah, $250 in Vermont.
Source: Federation of Tax Administrators, "State Corporate Income Tax Rates, 2012"

State Individual Income Tax Rates

State	Tax Rate (%)	Income Brackets ($)	Num. of Brackets	Personal Exempt. ($)[1] Single	Personal Exempt. ($)[1] Dependents	Fed. Inc. Tax Ded.
Arizona	2.59 - 4.54	10,000 (b)-150,001 (b)	5	2,100	2,100	No

Note: Tax rates as of January 1, 2012; Local- and county-level taxes are not included; n/a not applicable; (1) Married joint filers generally receive double the single exemption; (b) For joint returns, taxes are twice the tax on half the couple's income.
Source: Federation of Tax Administrators, "State Individual Income Tax Rates, 2012"

Various State and Local Tax Rates

State	State and Local Sales and Use (%)	State Sales and Use (%)	Gasoline[1] (¢/gal.)	Cigarette[2] ($/pack)	Spirits[3] ($/gal.)	Wine[4] ($/gal.)	Beer[5] ($/gal.)
Arizona	8.8	6.60	19.0	2.00	3.00	0.84	0.16

Note: All tax rates as of January 1, 2012 except beer, wine and spirits (September 1, 2011); (1) The American Petroleum Institute has developed a methodology for determining the average tax rate on a gallon of fuel. Rates may include any of the following: excise taxes, environmental fees, storage tank fees, other fees or taxes, general sales tax, and local taxes. In states where gasoline is subject to the general sales tax, or where the fuel tax is based on the average sale price, the average rate determined by API is sensitive to changes in the price of gasoline. States that fully or partially apply general sales taxes to gasoline: CA, CO, GA, IL, IN, MI, NY; (2) The federal excise tax of $1.0066 per pack and local taxes are not included; (3) Rates are those applicable to off-premise sales of 40% alcohol by volume (a.b.v.) distilled spirits in 750ml containers. Local excise taxes are excluded; (4) Rates are those applicable to off-premise sales of 11% a.b.v. non-carbonated wine in 750ml containers; (5) Rates are those applicable to off-premise sales of 4.7% a.b.v. beer in 12 ounce containers.
Source: Tax Foundation, 2012 Facts & Figures: How Does Your State Compare?

State-Local Tax Burdens

Area	Rate (%)	Rank[1]	Per Capita Taxes Paid to Home State ($)	Total State and Local Per Capita Taxes Paid ($)	Per Capita Income ($)
Arizona	8.7	38	2,177	3,140	36,228
U.S. Average	9.8	-	3,057	4,160	42,539

Note: Figures cover 2009; (1) Rank ranges from 1 to 50 where 1 is highest tax burden
Source: Tax Foundation, State-Local Tax Burdens, All States, 2009

State Business Tax Climate Index Rankings

State	Overall Rank	Corporate Tax Index Rank	Individual Income Tax Index Rank	Sales Tax Index Rank	Unemployment Insurance Tax Index Rank	Property Tax Index Rank
Arizona	27	28	17	50	1	5

Note: The index is a measure of how each state's tax laws affect economic performance. The lower the rank, the more favorable a state's tax system is for business. States without a given tax are given a ranking of 1.
Source: Tax Foundation, Major Components of the State Business Tax Climate Index, FY 2012

COMMERCIAL REAL ESTATE

Office Market

Market Area	Inventory (sq. ft.)	Vacant (sq. ft.)	Vac. Rate (%)	Under Constr. (sq. ft.)	Asking Rent ($/sf/yr) Class A	Class B
Phoenix	68,508,745	18,987,702	27.7	210,202	23.46	18.55

Source: Grubb & Ellis, Office Markets Trends, 4th Quarter 2011

Industrial Market

Market Area	Inventory (sq. ft.)	Vacant (sq. ft.)	Vac. Rate (%)	Under Constr. (sq. ft.)	Asking Rent ($/sf/yr) WH/Dist	R&D/Flex
Phoenix	272,186,144	35,152,622	12.9	1,713,983	4.44	11.64

Source: Grubb & Ellis, Industrial Markets Trends, 4th Quarter 2011

COMMERCIAL UTILITIES

Typical Monthly Electric Bills

Area	Commercial Service ($/month) 1,500 kWh	Commercial Service ($/month) 40 kW demand 14,000 kWh	Industrial Service ($/month) 1,000 kW demand 200,000 kWh	Industrial Service ($/month) 50,000 kW demand 15,000,000 kWh
City	253	1,761	27,301	1,499,060
Average[1]	189	1,616	25,197	1,470,813

Note: Based on total rates in effect July 1, 2011; (1) average based on 184 utilities surveyed
Source: Edison Electric Institute, Typical Bills and Average Rates Report, Summer 2011

TRANSPORTATION

Means of Transportation to Work

Area	Car/Truck/Van Drove Alone	Car/Truck/Van Car-pooled	Public Transportation Bus	Public Transportation Subway	Public Transportation Railroad	Bicycle	Walked	Other Means	Worked at Home
City	78.7	13.0	0.7	0.0	0.0	0.3	0.5	1.2	5.5
MSA[1]	76.2	12.2	2.1	0.0	0.0	0.7	1.6	1.6	5.5
U.S.	76.0	10.2	2.7	1.7	0.5	0.5	2.8	1.3	4.2

Note: Figures are percentages and cover workers 16 years of age and older; (1) Figures cover the Phoenix-Mesa-Glendale, AZ Metropolitan Statistical Area—see Appendix B for areas included
Source: U.S. Census Bureau, 2008-2010 American Community Survey 3-Year Estimates

Travel Time to Work

Area	Less Than 10 Minutes	10 to 19 Minutes	20 to 29 Minutes	30 to 44 Minutes	45 to 59 Minutes	60 to 89 Minutes	90 Minutes or More
City	10.6	23.7	25.0	24.6	9.3	5.7	1.1
MSA[1]	10.6	27.5	21.9	24.9	8.7	4.9	1.5
U.S.	13.9	30.1	20.8	19.8	7.5	5.5	2.5

Note: Figures are percentages and include workers 16 years old and over; (1) Figures cover the Phoenix-Mesa-Glendale, AZ Metropolitan Statistical Area—see Appendix B for areas included
Source: U.S. Census Bureau, 2008-2010 American Community Survey 3-Year Estimates

Travel Time Index

Area	1985	1990	1995	2000	2005	2010
Urban Area[1]	1.10	1.11	1.11	1.18	1.21	1.21
Average[2]	1.11	1.16	1.18	1.21	1.25	1.20

Note: Travel Time Index—the ratio of travel time in the peak period to the travel time at free-flow conditions. A value of 1.30 indicates a 20-minute free-flow trip takes 26 minutes in the peak. Free-flow speeds (60 mph on freeways and 35 mph on principal arterials) are used as the comparison threshold; (1) Covers the Phoenix AZ urban area; (2) average of 439 urban areas
Source: Texas Transportation Institute, Urban Mobility Report 2011, September 2011

Public Transportation

Agency Name / Mode of Transportation	Vehicles Operated in Maximum Service	Annual Unlinked Passenger Trips ('000)	Annual Passenger Miles ('000)
Valley Metro			
Bus (purchased transportation)	450	37,181.5	138,158.1
Demand Response (directly operated)	45	160.8	1,113.9
Demand Response (purchased transportation)	105	358.4	3,103.6

Source: Federal Transit Administration, National Transit Database, 2010

Air Transportation

Airport Name and Code / Type of Service	Passenger Airlines[1]	Passenger Enplanements	Freight Carriers[2]	Freight (lbs.)
Sky Harbor International (PHX)				
Domestic service (U.S. carriers - 2011)	31	18,643,720	29	236,320,096
International service (U.S. carriers - 2010)	8	811,320	5	448,583

Note: (1) Includes all U.S.-based major, minor and commuter airlines that carried at least one passenger during the year; (2) Includes all U.S.-based airlines and freight carriers that transported at least one pound of freight during the year
Source: Bureau of Transportation Statistics, The Intermodal Transportation Database, Air Carriers: T-100 Domestic Market (U.S. Carriers), 2011; Bureau of Transportation Statistics, The Intermodal Transportation Database, Air Carriers: T-100 International Market (U.S. Carriers), 2010

Other Transportation Statistics

Major Highways:	Loop-202 connecting to I-10 and I-17
Amtrak Service:	Yes (station is located in Phoenix)
Major Waterways/Ports:	None

Source: Amtrak.com; Google Maps

BUSINESSES

Major Business Headquarters

Company Name	Rankings	
	Fortune[1]	Forbes[2]
No companies listed	-	-

Note: (1) Fortune 500—companies that produce a 10-K are ranked 1 to 500 based on 2010 revenue; (2) all private companies with at least $2 billion in annual revenue are ranked 1 to 212; companies listed are headquartered in the city; dashes indicate no ranking
Source: Fortune, "Fortune 500," May 23, 2011; Forbes, "America's Largest Private Companies," November 16, 2011

Fast-Growing Businesses

According to *Inc.*, Gilbert is home to one of America's 500 fastest-growing private companies: **American Group** (#51). Criteria: must be an independent, privately-held, for-profit, U.S. corporation, proprietorship or partnership; revenues must be at least $80,000 in 2007 and $2 million in 2010; must have four-year operating/sales history. Holding companies, regulated banks, and utilities were excluded. *Inc., "America's 500 Fastest-Growing Private Companies," September 2011*

Minority- and Women-Owned Businesses

Group	All Firms		Firms with Paid Employees			
	Firms	Sales ($000)	Firms	Sales ($000)	Employees	Payroll ($000)
Asian	893	88,364	132	51,033	532	11,737
Black	467	12,280	23	3,642	18	790
Hispanic	1,117	147,943	71	113,515	1,273	42,937
Women	5,050	691,382	507	579,552	5,101	147,177
All Firms	17,097	9,037,980	3,298	8,378,768	46,208	1,587,034

Note: Figures cover firms located in the city; minority- and women-owned business are defined as firms in which the corresponding group own 51% or more of the stock or equity of the company
Source: U.S. Census Bureau, 2007 Economic Census, Survey of Business Owners

HOTELS

Hotels/Motels

Area	5 Star		4 Star		3 Star		2 Star		1 Star		Not Rated	
	Num.	Pct.[3]	Num.	Pct.[3]	Num.	Pct.[3]	Num.	Pct.[3]	Num.	Pct.[3]	Num.	Pct.[3]
City[1]	0	0.0	0	0.0	14	34.1	19	46.3	1	2.4	7	17.1
Total[2]	133	0.9	940	6.5	4,569	31.8	7,033	48.9	351	2.4	1,343	9.3

Note: (1) Figures cover Gilbert and vicinity; (2) Figures cover all 100 cities in this book; (3) Percentage of hotels which have a given star rating; Star ratings are determined by expedia.com and offer an indication of the general quality of a particular hotel.
Source: expedia.com, April 25, 2012

The Phoenix-Mesa-Glendale, AZ metro area is home to six of the best hotels in the U.S. according to *Travel & Leisure*: **Sanctuary on Camelback Mountain Resort & Spa** (#70); **Four Seasons Resort Scottsdale at Troon North** (#75); **Royal Palms Resort and Spa** (#99); **Hermosa Inn** (#141); **The Phoenician, A Luxury Collection Resort** (#146); **Montelucia Resort & Spa** (#163). Criteria: service; location; rooms; food; and value. *Travel & Leisure, "T+L 500, The World's Best Hotels 2012"*

EVENT SITES

Major Stadiums, Arenas, and Auditoriums

Name	Max. Capacity
Hohokam Stadium	12,500

Source: Original research

Convention Centers

Name	Overall Space (sq. ft.)	Exhibit Space (sq. ft.)	Meeting Space (sq. ft.)	Meeting Rooms
Elegante Convention and Event Center	n/a	10,000	n/a	7

Note: n/a not available
Source: Original research

Living Environment

COST OF LIVING

Cost of Living Index

Composite Index	Groceries	Housing	Utilities	Transportation	Health Care	Misc. Goods/ Services
96.6	103.9	87.4	100.3	102.9	102.6	97.6

Note: U.S. = 100; Figures cover the Phoenix AZ urban area.
Source: The Council for Community and Economic Research, ACCRA Cost of Living Index, 2011

Grocery Prices

Area[1]	T-Bone Steak ($/pound)	Frying Chicken ($/pound)	Whole Milk ($/half gal.)	Eggs ($/dozen)	Orange Juice ($/64 oz.)	Coffee ($/11.5 oz.)
City[2]	9.12	1.20	2.26	1.77	3.18	4.97
Avg.	9.25	1.18	2.22	1.66	3.19	4.40
Min.	6.70	0.88	1.31	0.95	2.46	2.94
Max.	14.30	2.16	3.50	3.18	4.75	6.83

Note: (1) Values for the local area are compared with the average, minimum and maximum values for all 335 areas in the Cost of Living Index; (2) Figures cover the Phoenix AZ urban area; **T-Bone Steak** *(price per pound);* **Frying Chicken** *(price per pound, whole fryer);* **Whole Milk** *(half gallon carton);* **Eggs** *(price per dozen, Grade A, large);* **Orange Juice** *(64 oz. Tropicana or Florida Natural);* **Coffee** *(11.5 oz. can, vacuum-packed, Maxwell House, Hills Bros, or Folgers).*
Source: The Council for Community and Economic Research, ACCRA Cost of Living Index, 2011

Housing and Utility Costs

Area[1]	New Home Price ($)	Apartment Rent ($/month)	All Electric ($/month)	Part Electric ($/month)	Other Energy ($/month)	Telephone ($/month)
City[2]	241,396	889	184.74	-	-	22.17
Avg.	285,990	839	163.23	89.00	77.52	26.92
Min.	188,005	460	125.58	45.39	33.89	17.98
Max.	1,197,028	3,244	339.16	181.97	348.69	40.01

Note: (1) Values for the local area are compared with the average, minimum and maximum values for all 335 areas in the Cost of Living Index; (2) Figures cover the Phoenix AZ urban area; **New Home Price** *(2,400 sf living area, 8,000 sf lot, in urban area with full utilities);* **Apartment Rent** *(950 sf 2 bedroom/1.5 or 2 bath, unfurnished, excluding all utilities except water);* **All Electric** *(average monthly cost for an all-electric home);* **Part Electric** *(average monthly cost for a part-electric home);* **Other Energy** *(average monthly cost for natural gas, fuel oil, coal, wood, and any other forms of energy except electricity);* **Telephone** *(price includes basic monthly rate for a private residential line plus additional local usage charges incurred by a family of four).*
Source: The Council for Community and Economic Research, ACCRA Cost of Living Index, 2011

Health Care, Transportation, and Other Costs

Area[1]	Doctor ($/visit)	Dentist ($/visit)	Optometrist ($/visit)	Gasoline ($/gallon)	Beauty Salon ($/visit)	Men's Shirt ($)
City[2]	91.10	89.66	97.16	3.32	41.43	21.20
Avg.	93.88	81.72	90.54	3.48	32.65	25.06
Min.	60.00	55.33	53.66	3.18	19.78	13.44
Max.	154.98	145.97	183.72	4.31	63.21	46.00

Note: (1) Values for the local area are compared with the average, minimum and maximum values for all 335 areas in the Cost of Living Index; (2) Figures cover the Phoenix AZ urban area; **Doctor** *(general practitioners routine exam of an established patient);* **Dentist** *(adult teeth cleaning and periodic oral examination);* **Optometrist** *(full vision eye exam for established adult patient);* **Gasoline** *(one gallon regular unleaded, national brand, including all taxes, cash price at self-service pump if available);* **Beauty Salon** *(woman's shampoo, trim, and blow-dry);* **Men's Shirt** *(cotton/polyester dress shirt, pinpoint weave, long sleeves).*
Source: The Council for Community and Economic Research, ACCRA Cost of Living Index, 2011

HOUSING

House Price Index (HPI)

Area	National Ranking[2]	Quarterly Change (%)	One-Year Change (%)	Five-Year Change (%)
MSA[1]	275	2.67	-7.12	-47.78
U.S.[3]	-	-0.10	-2.43	-19.16

Note: The HPI is a weighted repeat sales index. It measures average price changes in repeat sales or refinancings on the same properties. This information is obtained by reviewing repeat mortgage transactions on single-family properties whose mortgages have been purchased or securitized by Fannie Mae or Freddie Mac in January 1975; (1) Metropolitan/Micropolitan Statistical Area—see Appendix B for areas included; (2) Rankings are based on annual percentage change for all metro areas containing at least 15,000 transactions over the last 10 years and ranges from 1 to 306; (3) figures based on a weighted average of Census Division estimates using a purchase only index; all figures are for the period ending December 31, 2011
Source: Federal Housing Finance Agency, House Price Index, February 23, 2012

House Price Valuations

Area	Q4 2005		Q4 2006		Q4 2007		Q4 2008		Q4 2009	
	Price ($000)	Over-valuation	Price ($000)	Over-valuation	Price ($000)	Over-valuation	Price ($000)	Over-valuation	Price ($000)	Over-valuation
MSA[1]	242.1	38.9	255.3	35.8	227.8	17.7	166.6	-12.9	146.5	-22.3

Note: Figures show the percentage of over- or under-valuation of single family homes relative to statistically normal house values (e.g. a value of 23.6 indicates that house values are 23.6% overvalued). Statistically normal house values are based on house prices, interest rates, household incomes, population densities, and any historical premiums or discounts metropolitan areas have exhibited over time; (1) Figures cover the Phoenix-Mesa-Glendale, AZ - see Appendix B for areas included
Source: Global Insight/PNC Financial Services Group, House Prices in America: 4th Quarter 2009 Update

Median Single-Family Home Prices

Area	2009	2010	2011[p]	Percent Change 2010 to 2011
MSA[1]	137.0	139.2	115.5	-17.0
U.S. Average	172.1	173.1	166.2	-4.0

Note: Figures are median sales prices of existing single-family homes in thousands of dollars; (p) preliminary; n/a not available; (1) Metropolitan Statistical Area—see Appendix B for areas included
Source: National Association of Realtors, Median Sales Price of Existing Single-Family Homes for Metropolitan Areas, 4th Quarter 2011

Affordability Index of Existing Single-Family Homes

Area	2009	2010	2011[p]	Percent Change 2010 to 2011
MSA[1]	126.3	129.7	162.0	24.9

Note: The housing affordability index measures whether or not a typical family could qualify for a mortgage loan on a typical home. The higher the index, the greater the household purchasing power. An index of 100 is defined as the point where a median-income household has exactly enough income to qualify for the purchase of a median-priced existing single-family home, assuming a 20 percent downpayment and 25 percent of gross income devoted to mortgage principal and interest payments; (p) preliminary; n/a not available; (1) Metropolitan Statistical Area—see Appendix B for areas included
Source: National Association of Realtors, Affordability Index of Existing Single-Family Homes, 2011

Median Apartment Condo-Coop Home Prices

Area	2009	2010	2011[p]	Percent Change 2010 to 2011
MSA[1]	101.1	79.4	65.9	-17.0
U.S. Average	175.6	171.7	165.1	-3.8

Note: Figures are median sales prices of existing apartment condo-coop homes in thousands of dollars; (p) preliminary; n/a not available; (1) Metropolitan Statistical Area—see Appendix B for areas included
Source: National Association of Realtors, Median Sales Price of Existing Apartment Condo-Coop Homes for Metropolitan Areas, 4th Quarter 2011

Year Housing Structure Built

Area	2005 or Later	2000 -2004	1990 -1999	1980 -1989	1970 -1979	1960 -1969	1950 -1959	Before 1950	Median Year
City	15.1	25.1	41.4	13.0	3.4	1.3	0.6	0.2	1998
MSA[1]	9.6	16.4	21.6	19.1	17.4	7.4	5.8	2.5	1989
U.S.	5.0	8.6	14.0	14.1	16.3	11.3	11.2	19.6	1975

Note: Figures are percentages except for Median Year; (1) Figures cover the Phoenix-Mesa-Glendale, AZ Metropolitan Statistical Area—see Appendix B for areas included
Source: U.S. Census Bureau, 2008-2010 American Community Survey 3-Year Estimates

HEALTH

Health Risk Data

Category	MSA[1] (%)	U.S. (%)
Adults who have been told they have high blood pressure[2]	25.2	28.7
Adults who have been told they have high blood cholesterol[2]	41.1	37.5
Adults who have been told they have diabetes[3]	7.1	8.7
Adults who have been told they have arthritis[2]	22.9	26.0
Adults who have been told they currently have asthma	9.6	9.1
Adults who are current smokers	14.8	17.3
Adults who are heavy drinkers[4]	4.5	5.0
Adults who are binge drinkers[5]	15.9	15.1
Adults who are overweight (BMI 25.0 - 29.9)	41.1	36.2
Adults who are obese (BMI 30.0 - 99.8)	22.8	27.5
Adults who participated in any physical activities in the past month	81.5	76.1
Adults 50+ who have ever had a sigmoidoscopy or colonoscopy	64.4	65.2
Women aged 40+ who have had a mammogram within the past two years	73.8	75.2
Men aged 40+ who have had a PSA test within the past two years	51.8	53.2
Adults aged 65+ who have had flu shot within the past year	68.8	67.5
Adults aged 18–64 who have any kind of health care coverage	84.8	82.2

Note: Data as of 2010 unless otherwise noted; (1) Figures cover the Phoenix-Mesa-Scottsdale, AZ Metropolitan Statistical Area—see Appendix B for areas included; (2) Data as of 2009; (3) Figures do not include pregnancy-related, borderline, or pre-diabetes; (4) Heavy drinkers are classified as males having more than two drinks per day or females having more than one drink per day; (5) Binge drinkers are classified as males having five or more drinks on one occasion or females having four or more drinks on one occasion
Source: Centers for Disease Control and Prevention, Behaviorial Risk Factor Surveillance System, SMART: Selected Metropolitan/Micropolitan Area Risk Trends, 2009, 2010

Mortality Rates for the Top 10 Causes of Death in the U.S.

ICD-10[a] Sub-Chapter	ICD-10[a] Code	Age-Adjusted Mortality Rate[1] per 100,000 population	
		County[2]	U.S.
Malignant neoplasms	C00-C97	145.7	175.6
Ischaemic heart diseases	I20-I25	111.8	121.6
Other forms of heart disease	I30-I51	20.0	48.6
Chronic lower respiratory diseases	J40-J47	39.8	42.3
Cerebrovascular diseases	I60-I69	30.2	40.6
Organic, including symptomatic, mental disorders	F01-F09	18.0	26.7
Other degenerative diseases of the nervous system	G30-G31	39.2	24.7
Other external causes of accidental injury	W00-X59	30.0	24.4
Diabetes mellitus	E10-E14	15.8	21.7
Hypertensive diseases	I10-I15	18.7	18.2

Note: (a) ICD-10 = International Classification of Diseases 10th Revision; (1) Mortality rates are a three year average covering 2007-2009; (2) Figures cover Maricopa County
Source: Centers for Disease Control and Prevention, National Center for Health Statistics. Underlying Cause of Death 1999-2009 on CDC WONDER Online Database, released 2012. Data for year 2009 are compiled from the Multiple Cause of Death File 2009, Series 20 No. 2O, 2012, Data for year 2008 are compiled from the Multiple Cause of Death File 2008, Series 20 No. 2N, 2011, Data for year 2007 are compiled from Multiple Cause of Death File 2007, Series 20 No. 2M, 2010.

Mortality Rates for Selected Causes of Death

ICD-10[a] Sub-Chapter	ICD-10[a] Code	Age-Adjusted Mortality Rate[1] per 100,000 population	
		County[2]	U.S.
Assault	X85-Y09	7.2	5.7
Human immunodeficiency virus (HIV) disease	B20-B24	1.9	3.3
Influenza and pneumonia	J09-J18	13.5	16.4
Intentional self-harm	X60-X84	14.1	11.5
Malnutrition	E40-E46	0.4	0.8
Obesity and other hyperalimentation	E65-E68	1.2	1.6
Transport accidents	V01-V99	12.5	13.7
Viral hepatitis	B15-B19	2.8	2.2

Note: (a) ICD-10 = International Classification of Diseases 10th Revision; (1) Mortality rates are a three year average covering 2007-2009; (2) Figures cover Maricopa County
Source: Centers for Disease Control and Prevention, National Center for Health Statistics. Underlying Cause of Death 1999-2009 on CDC WONDER Online Database, released 2012. Data for year 2009 are compiled from the Multiple Cause of Death File 2009, Series 20 No. 2O, 2012, Data for year 2008 are compiled from the Multiple Cause of Death File 2008, Series 20 No. 2N, 2011, Data for year 2007 are compiled from Multiple Cause of Death File 2007, Series 20 No. 2M, 2010.

Distribution of Physicians and Dentists

Area[1]	Dentists[2]	D.O.[3]	M.D.[4] Total	Family/ General Practice	Pediatrics	Medical Specialties	Surgical Specialties
Local (number)	1,754	1,213	6,438	712	454	2,415	1,424
Local (rate[5])	4.5	3.1	16.3	1.8	1.1	6.1	3.6
U.S. (rate[5])	4.5	1.9	18.3	2.5	1.4	6.8	4.1

Note: Data as of 2008 unless noted; (1) Local data covers Maricopa County; (2) Data as of 2007; (3) Doctor of Osteopathic Medicine; (4) Includes active, non-federal, patient-care, office-based Doctors of Medicine; (5) rate per 10,000 population
Source: Area Resource File (ARF). 2009-2010 Release. U.S. Department of Health and Human Services, Health Resources and Services Administration, Bureau of Health Professions, Rockville, MD, August 2010

Best Hospitals

According to *U.S. News,* the Phoenix-Mesa-Glendale, AZ is home to three of the best hospitals in the U.S.: **Banner Good Samaritan Medical Center** (4 specialties); **Mayo Clinic** (3 specialties); **St. Joseph's Hospital and Medical Center** (1 specialty). The hospitals listed were highly ranked in at least one adult specialty. *U.S. News Online, "America's Best Hospitals 2011-12"*

According to *U.S. News,* the Phoenix-Mesa-Glendale, AZ is home to one of the best children's hospitals in the U.S.: **Phoenix Children's Hospital** (5 specialties). The hospital listed was highly ranked in at least one pediatric specialty. *U.S. News Online, "America's Best Children's Hospitals 2011-12"*

EDUCATION

Public School District Statistics

District Name	Schls	Pupils	Pupil/ Teacher Ratio	Minority Pupils[1] (%)	Free Lunch Eligible[2] (%)	IEP[3] (%)
Benjamin Franklin Charter School	4	2,170	n/a	15.7	0.1	5.6
Gilbert Public Schools	42	38,800	18.5	28.2	15.6	12.4
Higley Unified School District	10	9,751	20.8	30.7	17.9	11.6

Note: Table includes school districts with 2,000 or more students; (1) Percentage of students that are not non-Hispanic white; (2) Percentage of students that are eligible for the free lunch program; (3) Percentage of students that have an Individualized Education Program.
Source: U.S. Department of Education, National Center for Education Statistics, Common Core of Data, Local Education Agency (School District) Universe Survey: School Year 2009-2010; U.S. Department of Education, National Center for Education Statistics, Common Core of Data, Public Elementary/Secondary School Universe Survey: School Year 2009-2010

Highest Level of Education

Area	Less than H.S.	H.S. Diploma	Some College, No Deg.	Associate Degree	Bachelors Degree	Masters Degree	Profess. School Degree	Doctorate Degree
City	4.1	18.6	28.3	11.4	25.8	8.7	1.7	1.5
MSA[1]	14.4	24.0	25.7	8.1	18.1	7.0	1.8	1.0
U.S.	14.7	28.4	21.3	7.6	17.6	7.2	1.9	1.2

Note: Figures cover persons age 25 and over; (1) Figures cover the Phoenix-Mesa-Glendale, AZ Metropolitan Statistical Area—see Appendix B for areas included
Source: U.S. Census Bureau, 2008-2010 American Community Survey 3-Year Estimates

Educational Attainment by Race

Area	High School Graduate or Higher (%)					Bachelor's Degree or Higher (%)				
	Total	White	Black	Asian	Hisp.[2]	Total	White	Black	Asian	Hisp.[2]
City	95.9	96.5	96.1	92.0	87.7	37.6	37.6	29.3	51.0	24.7
MSA[1]	85.6	86.7	89.3	89.3	60.3	27.8	28.5	23.0	53.4	10.1
U.S.	85.3	87.5	81.4	85.5	61.6	28.0	29.3	17.8	50.2	13.0

Note: Figures shown cover persons 25 years old and over; (1) Figures cover the Phoenix-Mesa-Glendale, AZ Metropolitan Statistical Area—see Appendix B for areas included; (2) People of Hispanic origin can be of any race
Source: U.S. Census Bureau, 2008-2010 American Community Survey 3-Year Estimates

School Enrollment by Grade and Control

Area	Preschool (%)		Kindergarten (%)		Grades 1 - 4 (%)		Grades 5 - 8 (%)		Grades 9 - 12 (%)	
	Public	Private	Public	Private	Public	Private	Public	Private	Public	Private
City	48.6	51.4	89.2	10.8	90.8	9.2	93.6	6.4	96.1	3.9
MSA[1]	55.9	44.1	91.0	9.0	92.9	7.1	94.0	6.0	94.4	5.6
U.S.	55.4	44.6	87.1	12.9	89.4	10.6	89.5	10.5	90.4	9.6

Note: Figures shown cover persons 3 years old and over; (1) Figures cover the Phoenix-Mesa-Glendale, AZ Metropolitan Statistical Area—see Appendix B for areas included
Source: U.S. Census Bureau, 2008-2010 American Community Survey 3-Year Estimates

Average Salaries of Public School Classroom Teachers

Area	2010-11		2011-12		Percent Change 2010-11 to 2011-12	Percent Change 2001-02 to 2011-12
	Dollars	Rank[1]	Dollars	Rank[1]		
Arizona	47,553	33	48,691	33	2.39	21.80
U.S. Average	55,623	-	56,643	-	1.83	26.8

Note: (1) State rank ranges from 1 to 51 where 1 indicates highest salary.
Source: National Education Association, Rankings & Estimates: Rankings of the States 2011 and Estimates of School Statistics 2012, December 2011

Higher Education

Four-Year Colleges			Two-Year Colleges			Medical Schools[1]	Law Schools[2]	Voc/ Tech[3]
Public	Private Non-profit	Private For-profit	Public	Private Non-profit	Private For-profit			
0	0	0	0	0	0	0	0	0

Note: Figures cover institutions located within the city limits and include main campuses only; (1) includes schools accredited by the Liaison Committee on Medical Education and the American Osteopathic Association's Commission on Osteopathic College Accreditation; (2) includes American Bar Association-accredited law schools; (3) includes all schools with programs that are less than 2 years.
Source: National Center for Education Statistics, Integrated Postsecondary Education System (IPEDS) Peer Analysis System, 2011-12; Association of American Medical Colleges, Member List, April 23, 2012; American Osteopathic Association, Member List, April 23, 2012; Law School Admission Council, Official Guide to ABA-Approved Law Schools Online, April 23, 2012

According to *U.S. News & World Report,* the Phoenix-Mesa-Glendale, AZ is home to one of the best national universities in the U.S.: **Arizona State University** (#132). The indicators used to capture academic quality fall into a number of categories: assessment by administrators at peer institutions; retention of students; faculty resources; student selectivity; financial resources; alumni giving; high school counselor ratings of colleges; and graduation rate.*U.S. News & World Report, "America's Best Colleges 2012"*

According to *U.S. News & World Report,* the Phoenix-Mesa-Glendale, AZ is home to one of the best law schools in the U.S.: **Arizona State University (O'Connor)** (#26). The rankings are based on a weighted average of 12 measures of quality: peer assessment score; assessment score by lawyers/judges; median LSAT scores; median undergrad GPA; acceptance rate; employment rates for graduates; placement success; bar passage rate; faculty resources; expenditures per student; student/faculty ratio; and library resources. *U.S. News & World Report, "America's Best Law Schools 2013"*

According to *Forbes,* the Phoenix-Mesa-Glendale, AZ is home to one of the best business schools in the U.S.: **Arizona State (Carey)** (#66). The rankings are based on the return on investment that graduates of the Class of 2006 received (median salary five years after graduation). *Forbes, "Best Business Schools," August 3, 2011*

PRESIDENTIAL ELECTION

2008 Presidential Election Results

Area	Obama	McCain	Nader	Other
Maricopa County	43.9	54.4	0.4	1.2
U.S.	52.9	45.6	0.6	0.9

Note: Results are percentages and may not add to 100% due to rounding
Source: Dave Leip's Atlas of U.S. Presidential Elections, www.uselectionatlas.org

EMPLOYERS

Major Employers

Company Name	Industry
Arizona Dept of Transportation	Regulation, administration of transportation
Arizona State University	University
Arizona State University	Libraries
Avnet	Electronic parts and equipment, nec
Carter & Burgess	Engineering services
Chase Bankcard Services	State commercial banks
City of Mesa	Executive offices
City of Phoenix	Administration of social and human resources
City of Phoenix	Executive offices
General Dynamics C4 Systems	Communications equipment, nec
Grand Canyon Education	Colleges and universities
Honeywell International	Aircraft engines and engine parts
Lockheed Martin Corporation	Search and navigation equipment
Paramount Building Solutions	Janitorial service, contract basis
Salt River Pima-Maricopa Indian Community	Gambling establishment
Scottsdale Healthcare Corp.	Hospital management
Scottsdale Healthcare Osborn Med Ctr	General medical and surgical hospitals
Swift Transportation Company	Trucking, except local
The Boeing Company	Helicopters
Veterans Health Administration	General medical and surgical hospitals

Note: Companies shown are located within the Phoenix-Mesa-Glendale, AZ metropolitan area.
Source: Hoovers.com, data extracted April 25 2012

PUBLIC SAFETY

Crime Rate

Area	All Crimes	Violent Crimes: Murder	Violent Crimes: Forcible Rape	Violent Crimes: Robbery	Violent Crimes: Aggrav. Assault	Property Crimes: Burglary	Property Crimes: Larceny -Theft	Property Crimes: Motor Vehicle Theft
City	1,991.0	2.3	12.1	28.3	52.5	367.5	1,456.7	71.6
Suburbs[1]	4,008.0	5.6	26.7	129.2	224.0	818.5	2,453.0	351.0
Metro[2]	3,905.4	5.5	25.9	124.1	215.3	795.6	2,402.3	336.8
U.S.	3,345.5	4.8	27.5	119.1	252.3	699.6	2,003.5	238.8

Note: Figures are crimes per 100,000 population; (1) All areas within the metro area that are located outside the city limits; (2) Metropolitan Statistical Area—see Appendix B for areas included
Source: FBI Uniform Crime Reports, 2010

Hate Crimes

Area	Number of Quarters Reported	Bias Motivation				
		Race	Religion	Sexual Orientation	Ethnicity	Disability
City	4	0	0	0	0	0

Source: Federal Bureau of Investigation, Hate Crime Statistics 2010

Identity Theft Consumer Complaints

Area	Complaints	Complaints per 100,000 Population	Rank[2]
MSA[1]	4,078	97.6	106
U.S.	279,156	90.4	-

Note: (1) Metropolitan Statistical Area—see Appendix B for areas included; (2) Rank ranges from 1 to 384 where 1 indicates greatest number of identity theft complaints per 100,000 population
Source: Federal Trade Commission, Consumer Sentinel Network Data Book for January–December 2011

Fraud and Other Consumer Complaints

Area	Complaints	Complaints per 100,000 Population	Rank[2]
MSA[1]	19,577	468.4	196
U.S.	1,533,924	496.8	-

Note: (1) Metropolitan Statistical Area—see Appendix B for areas included; (2) Rank ranges from 1 to 384 where 1 indicates greatest number of fraud and other complaints per 100,000 population
Source: Federal Trade Commission, Consumer Sentinel Network Data Book for January–December 2011

RECREATION

Culture

Dance[1]	Theatre[1]	Instrumental Music[1]	Vocal Music[1]	Series/ Festivals	Museums	Zoos and Aquariums[2]
0	0	0	0	0	n/a	0

Note: (1) Number of professional perfoming groups; (2) AZA-accredited; n/a not available
Source: The Grey House Performing Arts Directory, 2011-2012; Official Museum Directory, 2011; American Association of Museums, AAM Member Museums, April 2012; Association of Zoos & Aquariums, AZA Member Zoos & Aquariums, April 2012

Professional Sports Teams

Team Name	League
Arizona Cardinals	National Football League (NFL)
Arizona Diamondbacks	Major League Baseball (MLB)
Phoenix Coyotes	National Hockey League (NHL)
Phoenix Suns	National Basketball Association (NBA)

Note: Includes teams located in the Phoenix metro area.
Source: Original research

CLIMATE

Average and Extreme Temperatures

Temperature	Jan	Feb	Mar	Apr	May	Jun	Jul	Aug	Sep	Oct	Nov	Dec	Yr.
Extreme High (°F)	88	92	100	105	113	122	118	116	118	107	93	88	122
Average High (°F)	66	70	75	84	93	103	105	103	99	88	75	67	86
Average Temp. (°F)	53	57	62	70	78	88	93	91	85	74	62	54	72
Average Low (°F)	40	44	48	55	63	72	80	78	72	60	48	41	59
Extreme Low (°F)	17	22	25	37	40	51	66	61	47	34	27	22	17

Note: Figures cover the years 1948-1990
Source: National Climatic Data Center, International Station Meteorological Climate Summary, 9/96

Average Precipitation/Snowfall/Humidity

Precip./Humidity	Jan	Feb	Mar	Apr	May	Jun	Jul	Aug	Sep	Oct	Nov	Dec	Yr.
Avg. Precip. (in.)	0.7	0.6	0.8	0.3	0.1	0.1	0.8	1.0	0.7	0.6	0.6	0.9	7.3
Avg. Snowfall (in.)	Tr	Tr	0	0	0	0	0	0	0	0	0	Tr	Tr
Avg. Rel. Hum. 5am (%)	68	63	56	45	37	33	47	53	50	53	59	66	53
Avg. Rel. Hum. 5pm (%)	34	28	24	17	14	12	21	24	23	24	28	34	24

Note: Figures cover the years 1948-1990; Tr = Trace amounts (<0.05 in. of rain; <0.5 in. of snow)
Source: National Climatic Data Center, International Station Meteorological Climate Summary, 9/96

Weather Conditions

Temperature			Daytime Sky			Precipitation		
10°F & below	32°F & below	90°F & above	Clear	Partly cloudy	Cloudy	0.01 inch or more precip.	0.1 inch or more snow/ice	Thunder-storms
0	10	167	186	125	54	37	< 1	23

Note: Figures are average number of days per year and cover the years 1948-1990
Source: National Climatic Data Center, International Station Meteorological Climate Summary, 9/96

HAZARDOUS WASTE

Superfund Sites

Gilbert has no sites on the EPA's Superfund Final National Priorities List.
U.S. Environmental Protection Agency, Final National Priorities List, April 17, 2012

AIR & WATER QUALITY

Air Quality Index

Area	Percent of Days when Air Quality was...[2]					AQI Statistics[2]	
	Good	Moderate	Unhealthy for Sensitive Groups	Unhealthy	Very Unhealthy	Maximum	Median
Area[1]	23.6	65.2	7.1	2.2	1.9	565	61

Note: Air Quality Index (AQI) is an index for reporting daily air quality. EPA calculates the AQI for five major air pollutants regulated by the Clean Air Act: ground-level ozone, particle pollution (aka particulate matter), carbon monoxide, sulfur dioxide, and nitrogen dioxide. The AQI runs from 0 to 500. The higher the AQI value, the greater the level of air pollution and the greater the health concern. There are six AQI categories: "Good" AQI is between 0 and 50. Air quality is considered satisfactory; "Moderate" AQI is between 51 and 100. Air quality is acceptable; "Unhealthy for Sensitive Groups" When AQI values are between 101 and 150, members of sensitive groups may experience health effects; "Unhealthy" When AQI values are between 151 and 200 everyone may begin to experience health effects; "Very Unhealthy" AQI values between 201 and 300 trigger a health alert; "Hazardous" AQI values over 300 trigger warnings of emergency conditions (not shown); (1) Data covers Maricopa County; (2) Based on 365 days with AQI data in 2011.
Source: U.S. Environmental Protection Agency, AirData Report, 2011

Air Quality Index Pollutants

Area	Percent of Days when AQI Pollutant was...[2]					
	Carbon Monoxide	Nitrogen Dioxide	Ozone	Sulfur Dioxide	Particulate Matter 2.5	Particulate Matter 10
Area[1]	0.0	19.2	38.9	0.0	15.6	26.3

Note: The Air Quality Index (AQI) is an index for reporting daily air quality. EPA calculates the AQI for five major air pollutants regulated by the Clean Air Act: ground-level ozone, particle pollution (also known as particulate matter), carbon monoxide, sulfur dioxide, and nitrogen dioxide. The AQI runs from 0 to 500. The higher the AQI value, the greater the level of air pollution and the greater the health concern; (1) Data covers Maricopa County; (2) Based on 365 days with AQI data in 2011.
Source: U.S. Environmental Protection Agency, AirData Report, 2011

Air Quality Index Trends

Area	Trend Sites (days)								All Sites (days)
	2003	2004	2005	2006	2007	2008	2009	2010	2010
MSA[1]	51	23	49	50	21	27	10	11	43

Note: Figures are the number of days the AQI value exceeded 100 in a given year. An AQI value greater than 100 indicates that air quality would have been in the unhealthful range on that day. Data from exceptional events are included. These counts are presented in two ways. First, the counts are based on sites having an adequate record of monitoring data during the trend period (trend sites). These counts represent the relative change in the number of days with AQI values greater than 100. In the last column, the counts are based on all sites with data in the most recent year (because it is possible for a site to have data in the most recent year but not enough data to be a trend site); (1) Data covers the Phoenix-Mesa-Glendale, AZ—see Appendix B for areas included

Source: U.S. Environmental Protection Agency, Air Quality Index Information, "Number of Days with Air Quality Index Values Greater than 100 at Trend Sites, 2000-2010, and at All Sites in 2010"

Maximum Air Pollutant Concentrations: Particulate Matter, Ozone, CO and Lead

	Particulate Matter 10 (ug/m^3)	Particulate Matter 2.5 Wtd AM (ug/m^3)	Particulate Matter 2.5 24-Hr (ug/m^3)	Ozone (ppm)	Carbon Monoxide (ppm)	Lead (ug/m^3)
MSA[1] Level	226	12.4	27	0.079	3	n/a
NAAQS[2]	150	15	35	0.075	9	0.15
Met NAAQS[2]	No	Yes	Yes	No	Yes	n/a

Note: Data from exceptional events are not included; (1) Data covers the Phoenix-Mesa-Glendale, AZ—see Appendix B for areas included; (2) National Ambient Air Quality Standards; ppm = parts per million; ug/m^3 = micrograms per cubic meter; n/a not available

Concentrations: Particulate Matter 10 (coarse particulate)—highest second maximum 24-hour concentration; Particulate Matter 2.5 Wtd AM (fine particulate)—highest weighted annual mean concentration; Particulate Matter 2.5 24-Hour (fine particulate)—highest 98th percentile 24-hour concentration; Ozone—highest fourth daily maximum 8-hour concentration; Carbon Monoxide—highest second maximum non-overlapping 8-hour concentration; Lead—maximum running 3-month average

Source: U.S. Environmental Protection Agency, CBSA Factbook 2010, Air Quality Statistics by City, 2010

Maximum Air Pollutant Concentrations: Nitrogen Dioxide and Sulfur Dioxide

	Nitrogen Dioxide AM (ppb)	Nitrogen Dioxide 1-Hr (ppb)	Sulfur Dioxide AM (ppb)	Sulfur Dioxide 1-Hr (ppb)	Sulfur Dioxide 24-Hr (ppb)
MSA[1] Level	24.524	68	1.742	10	5.3
NAAQS[2]	53	100	30	75	140
Met NAAQS[2]	Yes	Yes	Yes	Yes	Yes

Note: Data from exceptional events are not included; (1) Data covers the Phoenix-Mesa-Glendale, AZ—see Appendix B for areas included; (2) National Ambient Air Quality Standards; ppb = parts per billion; n/a not available

Concentrations: Nitrogen Dioxide AM—highest arithmetic mean concentration; Nitrogen Dioxide 1-Hr—highest 98th percentile 1-hour daily maximum concentration; Sulfur Dioxide AM—highest annual mean concentration; Sulfur Dioxide 1-Hr—highest 99th percentile 1-hour daily maximum concentration; Sulfur Dioxide 24-Hr—highest second maximum 24-hour concentration

Source: U.S. Environmental Protection Agency, CBSA Factbook 2010, Air Quality Statistics by City, 2010

Drinking Water

Water System Name	Pop. Served	Primary Water Source Type	Violations[1]	
			Health Based	Monitoring/ Reporting
Town of Gilbert	210,000	Surface	0	0

Note: (1) Based on violation data from January 1, 2011 to December 31, 2011 (includes unresolved violations from earlier years)

Source: U.S. Environmental Protection Agency, Office of Ground Water and Drinking Water, Safe Drinking Water Information System (based on data extracted April 18, 2012)

Henderson, Nevada

Background

Lying in the Las Vegas Metropolitan area of the Mojave Desert, Henderson is the second largest city in Nevada, despite its fairly recent incorporation in 1953. Named for Senator Charles B. Henderson, the town was created when a magnesium plant was needed during World War II and was built there. Henderson became vital to American success, providing a quarter of U.S. war-time magnesium used for airplane engines, frames, and military weapons.

After the war, the majority of the magnesium plant workers left, and Henderson's population decreased by two thirds. Nevada legislature stepped in to rebuild the community, which soon regained economic stability and began to flourish. To this day, it is one of the nations fastest growing communities.

Surrounded by gently sloped mountains, Henderson's immediate landscape is desert, with trails and open spaces that bring a great deal of natural beauty to the city. The unique appeal of the desert environment is celebrated, and The Acacia Demonstration Gardens educates residents about authentic desert plants and landscape ideas, also promoting water conservation.

An amazing place for outdoor activities, Henderson has breathtaking bike trails. The River Mountains Loop Trail creates opportunity for hiking, climbing and horseback riding through 35 miles of the River Mountains. The Bird Watching Preserve is another gorgeous attraction, where visitors can see and learn about over 200 birds, native to the area.

In addition to the natural attractions, Henderson is also close to some significant man made wonders such as the Las Vegas strip and the Hoover Dam. As a highly developed area with shopping malls, restaurants, theaters and casino resorts, Henderson attracts residents and tourists alike.

Art is an important part of Henderson's culture. Historic Water Street is brimming with art and culture. The Country Fresh Farmers Market offers produce, handmade crafts and more. The Pinnacle Children's Art Museum is also a Water Street attraction, featuring art made by Henderson's own youth.

City Lights Art Museum is a modern, interactive museum that aims to encourage understanding and expression of art from both artists and observers. Springtime brings an annual Art Festival in Henderson, and fall means Shakespeare in the Park, a program that was initiated in the 1980s.

Higher education in Henderson includes Nevada State College, located in the southern foothills of the city, that has graduated many first generation college students since opening in 2002. Roseman University of Health Sciences is also located in Henderson, and offers a Doctor of Pharmacy program. The city is also home to the College of Southern Nevada, a community college, as well as secondary campuses from California's National University.

Henderson's climate is subtropical that produces sunshine year round, as is typical in the Mojave Desert. Rainfall is scarce, resulting in dry terrain and unique plant life. Temperatures drop in the winter but weather remains mild, and the season only lasts about two months.

Rankings

General Rankings

- Henderson was selected as one of America's best cities by *Bloomberg Businessweek.* The city ranked #38 out of 50. Criteria: number of restaurants, bars and museums per capita; number of colleges, libraries, and professional sports teams; income, poverty, unemployment, crime, and foreclosure rates; percent of population with bachelor's degrees; public school performance; park acres per capita; air quality. *BusinessWeek, "America's 50 Best Cities," September 20, 2011*

Business/Finance Rankings

- Henderson was selected as one of the "100 Best Places to Live and Launch" in the U.S. The city ranked #98. The editors at *Fortune Small Business* ranked 296 Census-designated metro areas by business friendliness (Launching Score, % New Businesses) and lifestyle offerings (Living Score). Then they picked the town within each of the top 100 metro areas that best blends business and pleasure. *Fortune Small Business, "100 Best Places to Live and Launch 2008," April 2008*
- *American City Business Journals* ranked America's 261 largest cities in terms of their resident's wealth. Henderson ranked #53. Criteria: per capita income; median household income; percentage of households with annual incomes of $200,000 or more; median home value. *American City Business Journals, "Where the Money Is: America's Wealth Centers," August 18, 2008*
- The Las Vegas metro area appeared on the Milken Institute "2011 Best Performing Metros" list. Rank: #197 out of 200 large metro areas. Criteria: job growth; wage and salary growth; high-tech output growth. *Milken Institute, "2011 Best Performing Metros"*
- The Las Vegas metro area was selected as one of the best cities for entrepreneurs in America by *Inc. Magazine.* Criteria: job-growth data for 335 metro areas was analyzed for: recent growth trend; mid-term growth; long-term trend; current year growth. The Las Vegas metro area ranked #8 among large metro areas and #49 overall. *Inc. Magazine, "The Best Cities for Doing Business," July 2008*
- Las Vegas was ranked #109 out of 145 regions worldwide in terms of its "Knowledge Competitiveness Index." The index attempts to measure the knowledge-based development taking place throughout the world and is based on 19 measures of economic performance that indicate a region's ability to translate its knowledge capacity into economic value. *Centre for International Competitiveness, World Knowledge Competitiveness Index 2008*
- *Forbes* ranked the 200 most populous metro areas in the U.S. in terms of the "Best Places for Business and Careers." The Las Vegas metro area was ranked #135. Criteria: costs (business and living); job growth (past and projected); income growth; educational attainment; projected economic growth; crime; cultural and recreational opportunities; net migration patterns; number of highly ranked colleges. *Forbes, "Best Places for Business and Careers," June 2011*

Children/Family Rankings

- The Las Vegas metro area was selected as one of the "Best Cities for Relocating Families" by Worldwide ERC and Primacy Relocation. The 2008 study looked at nearly 50 factors important to relocating families including: recent job growth; nearby top-ranked colleges; in-state tuition for four-year public colleges; population growth since 2000; pediatricians per 100,000 population; and a Green Living index. *Worldwide ERC and Primacy Relocation, "2008 Best Cities for Relocating Families"*

Dating/Romance Rankings

- Eli Lily and Company, in partnership with Sperling's BestPlaces, ranked the nation's 50 largest metro areas in terms of the "Most Romantic Cities for Baby Boomers." The Las Vegas metro area ranked #47. Criteria: marriage and divorce rates among baby boomers age 45 to 60; great restaurants; dance studios; chocolate, jewelry and flower sales. *Eli Lily and Company, "Most Romantic Cities for Baby Boomers," April 20, 2007*

- The Las Vegas metro area was selected as one of the "Best Cities for Relocating Singles" by Worldwide ERC and Primacy Relocation. The area ranked #84 out of the 100 largest metro areas in the U.S. Criteria: recent job growth; recent singles population growth; overall population growth; affordable rental housing; cost-of-living index; expanded arts and recreation opportunities; ratio of single men and single women; affordability of quality higher education (including state residency requirements); diversity index; climate; population density. *Worldwide ERC and Primacy Relocation, "2008 Best Cities for Relocating Singles"*
- *Forbes* ranked the 40 most populous urbanized areas in the U.S. in terms of the "Best Cities for Singles." The Las Vegas metro area ranked #22. Criteria: number of singles; cost of living alone; nightlife; culture; job growth; coolness; and online dating participation. *Forbes.com, "Best Cities for Singles," July 27, 2009*

Education Rankings

- Henderson was selected as one of "America's Most Literate Cities." The city ranked #53 out of the 75 largest U.S. cities. Criteria: number of booksellers; library resources; Internet resources; educational attainment; periodical publishing resources; newspaper circulation. *Central Connecticut State University, "America's Most Literate Cities 2011"*
- Las Vegas was identified as one of the 100 "smartest" metro areas in the U.S. The area ranked #91. Criteria: the editors rated the collective brainpower of the 100 largest metro areas in the U.S. based on their residents' educational attainment. *American City Business Journals, April 14, 2008*
- Las Vegas was identified as one of "America's Brainiest Bastions" by *Portfolio.com.* The metro area ranked #159 out of 200. *Portfolio.com* analyzed levels of educational attainment in the nation's 200 largest metropolitan areas. The editors established scores for five levels of educational attainment, based on relative earning power of adult workers age 25 or older. Scores were determined by comparing the median income for all workers with the median income for those workers at a specified educational level. *Portfolio.com, "America's Brainiest Bastions," December 1, 2010*

Environmental Rankings

- The Las Vegas metro area was identified as one of "The Ten Biggest American Cities that are Running Out of Water" by *24/7 Wall St.* The metro area ranked #7 out of 10. *24/7 Wall St.* did an analysis of the water supply and consumption in the 30 largest metropolitan areas in the U.S. Criteria include: projected water demand as a share of available precipitation; groundwater use as a share or projected available precipitation; susceptibility to drought; projected increase in freshwater withdrawals; projected increase in summer water deficit. *24/7 Wall St., "The Ten Biggest American Cities that are Running Out of Water," November 1, 2010*
- Henderson was selected as one of 22 "Smarter Cities" for energy by the Natural Resources Defense Council. Criteria: investment in green power; energy efficiency measures; conservation. *Natural Resources Defense Council, "2010 Smarter Cities," July 19, 2010*
- The Las Vegas metro area was selected as one of "America's Cleanest Cities" by *Forbes*. The metro area ranked #5 out of 10. Criteria: toxic releases; air and water quality; per capita spending on Superfund site cleanup. *Forbes.com, "America's Cleanest Cities 2011," March 11, 2011*
- 100 of the largest metro areas in the U.S. were analyzed in terms of their current drought severity. The Las Vegas metro area ranked #29 (#1 = driest). The rankings were based on statistics such as long-term precipitation trends and patterns and the Palmer drought indices. *Sperling's BestPlaces, www.BestPlaces.net, "America's Drought-Riskiest Cities," November 2007*
- The Las Vegas metro area appeared in *Country Home's* "Best Green Places" report. The area ranked #132 out of 379. Criteria: official energy policies; green power; green buildings; availability of fresh, locally grown food. *Country Home, "Best Green Places," 2008*
- Las Vegas was highlighted as one of the 25 most ozone-polluted metro areas in the U.S. The area ranked #25. *American Lung Association, State of the Air 2011*

Health/Fitness Rankings

- The Las Vegas metro area was selected as one of the worst cities for bed bugs in America by Rollins corporation, the owner of seven pest control companies, including Orkin. The area ranked #16 based on the number of bed bug treatments from January to December 2011. *Rollins, "The Top 50 U.S. Cities for Bed Bugs," March 19, 2012*
- Las Vegas was identified as a "2011 Asthma Capital." The area ranked #73 out of the nation's 100 largest metropolitan areas. Twelve factors were used to identify the most challenging places to live for people with asthma: estimated prevalence; self-reported prevalence; crude death rate for asthma; annual pollen score; annual air quality; public smoking laws; number of board-certified asthma specialists; school inhaler access laws; rescue medication use; controller medication use; uninsured rate; poverty rate. *Asthma and Allergy Foundation of America, "2011 Asthma Capitals"*
- Las Vegas was identified as a "2011 Fall Allergy Capital." The area ranked #80 out of 100. Three groups of factors were used to identify the most severe cities for people with allergies during the fall season: annual pollen levels; medicine utilization; access to board-certified allergists. *Asthma and Allergy Foundation of America, "2011 Fall Allergy Capitals"*
- Las Vegas was identified as a "2012 Spring Allergy Capital." The area ranked #42 out of 100. Three groups of factors were used to identify the most severe cities for people with allergies during the spring season: annual pollen levels; medicine utilization; access to board-certified allergists. *Asthma and Allergy Foundation of America, "2012 Spring Allergy Capitals"*
- The Las Vegas metro area appeared in the 2011 Gallup-Healthways Well-Being Index. The index, based on interviews with more than 350,000 Americans, measured jobs, finances, physical health, emotional state of mind and communities. The metro area ranked #156 out of 190. Criteria: life evaluation; emotional health; work environment; physical health; healthy behaviors; basic access (basic needs optimal for a healthy life, such as access to food and medicine, having health insurance and feeling safe while walking at night). *Gallup-Healthways, "State of Well-Being 2011"*
- The Las Vegas metro area was identified as one of "America's Most Stressful Cities" by *Sperling's BestPlaces.* The metro area ranked #2 out of 50. Criteria: unemployment rate; suicide rate; commute time; mental health; poor rest; alcohol use; violent crime rate; property crime rate; cloudy days annually. *Sperling's BestPlaces, www.BestPlaces.net, "Stressful Cities 2012*
- 50 of the largest metro areas in the U.S. were analyzed in terms of their health and fitness by the American College of Sports Medicine in their "American Fitness Index." The Las Vegas metro area ranked #45 (#1 = healthiest). Criteria: preventative health behaviors; levels of chronic disease; health care access; community resources and policies that support physical activity. *American College of Sports Medicine, "Health and Community Fitness Status of the 50 Largest Metropolitan Areas," August 1, 2011*
- *The Daily Beast* identified the 30 U.S. metro areas with the worst smoking habits. The Las Vegas metro area ranked #10. Sixty urban centers with populations of more than one million were ranked based on the following criteria: number of smokers; number of cigarettes smoked per day; fewest attempts to quit. *The Daily Beast, "30 Cities With Smoking Problems," January 3, 2011*

Real Estate Rankings

- Las Vegas was identified as one of 13 metro areas where home prices are falling dangerously. Criteria: home price change from October 2010 to September 2011; projected home price change through 2012. *Forbes.com, "Cities Where Home Prices are Falling Dangerously," January 10, 2012*
- Las Vegas was identified as one of the best cities for home buyers in the U.S. The area ranked #6 out of 10. The affordability of home ownership was calculated by comparing the cost of renting vs. owning. Criteria: cost to rent as a percent of after-tax mortgage payment. *Fortune, "The 10 Best Cities for Buyers," April 11, 2011*
- *Fortune* ranked the 100 largest metro areas in the U.S. in terms of projected median home price change in 2010. The Las Vegas metro area ranked #95. *Fortune, "The 2010 Housing Outlook," December 9, 2009*

- Las Vegas was identified as one of the top 20 metro areas with the lowest rate of house price appreciation in 2011. The area ranked #1 with a one-year price appreciation of -12.6% through the 4th quarter 2011. *Federal Housing Finance Agency, House Price Index, 4th Quarter 2011*

- The Las Vegas metro area was identified as one of "America's 25 Weakest Housing Markets" by *Forbes*. The metro area ranked #1. Criteria: metro areas with populations over 500,000 were ranked based on projected home values through 2011. *Forbes.com, "America's 25 Weakest Housing Markets," January 7, 2009*

- The nation's largest metro areas were analyzed in terms of the percentage of households entering some stage of foreclosure in 2011. The Las Vegas metro area ranked #1 out of 20 (#1 = highest foreclosure rate). *RealtyTrac, 2011 Year-End Foreclosure Market Report, January 12, 2012*

- The Las Vegas metro area was identified as one of America's most undervalued cities in 2011 by *CNNMoney.com* based on data from Local Market Monitor. Criteria: median home prices; local interest rates; economic and population growth; construction costs; vacancies; household income. *CNNMoney.com, "America's Most Overvalued (and Undervalued) Cities," January 16, 2011*

- The Las Vegas metro area appeared in a *Wall Street Journal* article ranking cities by "housing stress." The metro area was ranked #5 (#1 = most stress). Criteria: fraction of mortgage-holding homeowners with a monthly housing payment in excess of 30 percent of income; percentage of people without health insurance; unemployment rate. *The Wall Street Journal, "Which Cities Face Biggest Housing Risk," October 5, 2010*

- The Center for Housing Policy ranked 210 U.S. metropolitan areas by the fair market rent for a two-bedroom unit. The Las Vegas metro area was ranked #45. (#1 = most expensive) with a rent of $1,063. Criteria: Fair Market Rent (FMR) in effect during the fourth quarter of 2009 based on HUD's fiscal year 2010 FMRs. *The Center for Housing Policy, "Paycheck to Paycheck: Most to Least Expensive Rental Markets in 2009"*

- The Las Vegas metro area was identified as one of the worst housing markets of the decade by *Forbes*. Criteria: decrease in housing values per square foot since January 2000. *Forbes, "America's 5 Best (and Worst) Housing Markets of the Decade," December 7, 2010*

- The Las Vegas metro area was identified as one of the top 20 cities in terms of decreasing home equity. The metro area was ranked #4. Criteria: percentage of home equity relative to the home's current value. *Forbes.com, "Where Americans are Losing Home Equity Most," May 1, 2010*

- The Las Vegas metro area was identified as one of the markets with the worst expected performance in home prices over the next 12 months. *Local Market Monitor, "First Quarter Home Price Forecast for Largest US Markets," March 2, 2011*

- The Las Vegas metro area was identified as one of the best U.S. markets to invest in rental property" by HomeVestors and Local Market Monitor. The area ranked #1 out of 100. Criteria: risk-return premium relative to national average. *HomeVestors and Local Market Monitor, "Best 100 U.S. Markets to Invest in Rental Property," March 9, 2012*

Safety Rankings

- Allstate ranked the 193 largest cities in America in terms of driver safety. Henderson ranked #97. In addition, drivers were 7.7% more likely to have had an accident compared to the national average. Allstate researchers analyzed internal property damage reported claims over a two-year period (from January 2008 to December 2009) to protect findings from external influences such as weather or road construction. A weighted average of the two-year numbers determined the annual percentages. The report defines an auto crash as any collision resulting in a property damage claim. *Allstate, "2011 Allstate America's Best Drivers Report™"*

- Henderson was selected as one of "America's Safest Cities" by *Forbes*. The city ranked #2 out of 10. Criteria: violent crime rates; traffic fatalities per 100,000 residents. The editors only considered cities with populations above 250,000. *Forbes, "America's Safest Cities," December 15, 2011*

- The Las Vegas metro area was identified as one of "America's Most Dangerous Cities" by *Forbes*. The area ranked #9 out of 10. Criteria: violent crime (murder and non-negligent manslaughter, forcible rape, robbery, and aggravated assault) rates per capita. The editors only considered metropolitan areas with populations above 200,000. *Forbes, "America's Most Dangerous Cities," October 3, 2011*
- The National Insurance Crime Bureau ranked 366 metro areas in the U.S. in terms of per capita rates of vehicle theft. The Las Vegas metro area ranked #17 (#1 = highest rate). Criteria: number of vehicle theft offenses per 100,000 inhabitants in 2010. *National Insurance Crime Bureau, "Hot Spots," June 21, 2011*
- The Las Vegas metro area was identified as one of the most dangerous metro areas for pedestrians by Transportation for America. The metro area ranked #6 out of 52 metro areas with over 1 million residents. Criteria: area's population divided by the number of pedestrian fatalities in that area. *Transportation for America, "Dangerous by Design 2011"*

Seniors/Retirement Rankings

- Bankers Life and Casualty Company, in partnership with Sperling's BestPlaces, ranked the nation's 50 largest metro areas in terms of the "Best U.S. Cities for Seniors." The Las Vegas metro area ranked #49. Criteria: healthcare; transportation; housing; environment; economy; health and longevity; social and spiritual life; crime. *Bankers Life and Casualty Company, Center for a Secure Retirement, "Best U.S. Cities for Seniors 2011," September 2011*
- Henderson was identified as one of the "100 Most Popular Retirement Towns" by *Topretirements.com* The list reflects the 100 cities (out of 815+ total cities reviewed) that visitors to the website are most interested in for retirement. *Topretirements.com, "100 Most Popular Retirement Towns," February 21, 2012*
- The Las Vegas metro area was selected as one of "The 10 Most Affordable Cities for Long-Term Care" by *U.S. News & World Report.* Criteria: costs at nursing homes, assisted living facilities, and adult day health care facilities; cost for licensed home health aides. *U.S. News & World Report, "The 10 Most Affordable Cities for Long-Term Care," May 17, 2010*

Sports/Recreation Rankings

- Henderson was selected as one of the most playful cities in the U.S. by KaBOOM! The organization's Playful City USA initiative is a national recognition program that honors cities and towns across the nation for a vision, plan and commitment to creating an agenda for play. Cities were recognized based on a pledge to five specific commitments to play: creating a local play commission or task force; designing an annual action plan for play; conducting a play space audit; outlining a financial investment in play for the current fiscal year; and proclaiming and celebrating an annual "play day." *KaBOOM! National Campaign for Play, "2011 Playful City USA Communities"*
- *Golf.com* and the research arm of the National Golf Foundation analyzed the 50 largest metropolitan areas in the U.S. in terms of golf. The Las Vegas metro area ranked #3. Criteria: weather; affordability; quality of courses; accessibility; number of courses designed by esteemed architects; availability; crowdedness. *Golf.com, November 15, 2007*

Technology Rankings

- Scarborough Research, a leading market research firm, identified the Las Vegas DMA (Designated Market Area) as one of the top markets for text messaging with more than 50% of cell phone subscribers age 18+ utilizing the text messaging feature on their phone. *Scarborough Research, November 24, 2008*

Transportation Rankings

- The Las Vegas metro area appeared on *Forbes* list of the best and worst cities for commuters. The metro area ranked #16 out of 60 (#1 is best). Criteria: travel time; road congestion; travel delays. *Forbes.com, "Best and Worst Cities for Commuters," February 16, 2010*

Women/Minorities Rankings

- Las Vegas was ranked #82 out of 100 metro areas in *SELF Magazine's* ranking of America's healthiest places for women." A panel of experts came up with more than 50 criteria including death and disease rates, environmental indicators, community resources, and lifestyle habits. *SELF Magazine, "Secrets of America's Healthiest Women," December 2008*
- The Las Vegas metro area appeared on *Forbes'* list of the "Best Cities for Minority Entrepreneurs." The area ranked #82 out of 10. Criteria: 52 metropolitan statistical areas were examined. For each ethnicity (African Americans, Asians and Hispanics), the editors measured housing affordability, population growth, income growth, and entrepreneurship (per capita self-employment). *Forbes, "Best Cities for Minority Entrepreneurs," March 23, 2011*

Miscellaneous Rankings

- The Las Vegas metro area was selected as one of "The Best U.S. Cities for Bargain Shopping" by *Forbes.* The area ranked #4 out of 10. Criteria: number of outlet stores; gross leasable retail space in major malls; low consumer price index; low sales tax rate. Indicators were examined in the nation's 50 largest metropolitan areas. *Forbes, "The Best U.S. Cities for Bargain Shopping," January 20, 2012*
- Proctor & Gamble, the makers of Pepto-Bismol, in partnership with Sperling's BestPlaces, ranked the nation's 100 most populated metro areas in terms of the "Best Places for Thanksgiving Celebrations." The Las Vegas metro area ranked #5. Criteria: turkey consumption per capita; increase in inbound air traffic during Thanksgiving; Pepto-Bismol sales; results from a consumer poll of 4,800 Americans recording the number of people attending Thanksgiving, the number of dishes served, and ways people intended to celebrate. *Proctor & Gamble, "Top 10 Best Places for Thanksgiving Celebrations," November 18, 2010*
- Energizer Holdings, the makers of Edge® shave gel, in partnership with Sperling's BestPlaces, ranked 50 major metro areas in terms of everyday irritations. The Las Vegas metro area ranked #25. Criteria: humidity levels; weather conditions; incidence of traffic delays and congestion; average commute times; frequency of flight delays and cancellations; rates of sleeplessness; underemployment; pollens and allergens; pests; comedy clubs per capita. *Energizer Holdings, "Most Irritation Prone Cities," July 23, 2010*
- Mars Chocolate North America, the makers of COMBOS®, in partnership with Sperling's BestPlaces, ranked 50 major metro areas in terms of their "manliness." The Las Vegas metro area ranked #38. Criteria: number of professional sports teams; number of nearby NASCAR tracks and racing events; manly lifestyle; concentration of manly retail stores; manly occupations per capita; salty snack sales; "Board of Manliness" rankings. *Mars Chocolate North America, "America's Manliest Cities 2011," September 1, 2011*

Business Environment

CITY FINANCES

City Government Finances

Component	2009 ($000)	2009 ($ per capita)
Total Revenues	426,503	1,710
Total Expenditures	444,086	1,781
Debt Outstanding	413,188	1,657
Cash and Securities[1]	734,594	2,946

Note: (1) Cash and security holdings of a government at the close of its fiscal year, including those of its dependent agencies, utilities, and liquor stores.
Source: U.S Census Bureau, State & Local Government Finances 2009

City Government Revenue by Source

Source	2009 ($000)	2009 ($ per capita)
General Revenue		
From Federal Government	3,174	13
From State Government	86,592	347
From Local Governments	30,765	123
Taxes		
Property	95,311	382
Sales and Gross Receipts	40,616	163
Personal Income	0	0
Corporate Income	0	0
Motor Vehicle License	0	0
Other Taxes	12,805	51
Current Charges	58,075	233
Liquor Store	0	0
Utility	56,850	228
Employee Retirement	0	0

Source: U.S Census Bureau, State & Local Government Finances 2009

City Government Expenditures by Function

Function	2009 ($000)	2009 ($ per capita)	2009 (%)
General Direct Expenditures			
Air Transportation	0	0	0.0
Corrections	0	0	0.0
Education	0	0	0.0
Employment Security Administration	0	0	0.0
Financial Administration	13,717	55	3.1
Fire Protection	39,120	157	8.8
General Public Buildings	54,916	220	12.4
Governmental Administration, Other	8,924	36	2.0
Health	0	0	0.0
Highways	9,597	38	2.2
Hospitals	0	0	0.0
Housing and Community Development	17,082	68	3.8
Interest on General Debt	13,266	53	3.0
Judicial and Legal	16,722	67	3.8
Libraries	0	0	0.0
Parking	0	0	0.0
Parks and Recreation	76,532	307	17.2
Police Protection	74,592	299	16.8
Public Welfare	0	0	0.0
Sewerage	27,533	110	6.2
Solid Waste Management	0	0	0.0
Veterans' Services	0	0	0.0
Liquor Store	0	0	0.0
Utility	56,432	226	12.7
Employee Retirement	0	0	0.0

Source: U.S Census Bureau, State & Local Government Finances 2009

Municipal Bond Ratings

Area	Moody's	S&P	Fitch
City	n/a	n/a	n/a

Rating Systems (shown in declining order of credit quality): Moody's– Aaa, Aa, A, Baa, Ba, B, Caa, Ca, C (numerical modifiers 1, 2, and 3 are added to letter-rating); S&P– AAA, AA, A, BBB, BB, B, CCC, CC, C; Fitch– AAA, AA, A, BBB, BB, B, CCC, CC, C. Ratings may be modified by the addition of a plus or minus sign to show relative standing within the major rating categories.

Notes: n/a Not Available; w/d Withdrawn (1) Not Reviewed; (2) Issuer Rating/No General Obligation; (3) Standard and Poor's Issue Credit Rating (ICR) is a current opinion of an obliger with respect to a specific financial obligation, a specific class of financial obligations, or a specific financial program.

Source: U.S. Census Bureau, 2012 Statistical Abstract, Bond Ratings for City Governments by Largest Cities: 2010

DEMOGRAPHICS

Population Growth

Area	1990 Census	2000 Census	2010 Census	Population Growth (%)	
				1990-2000	2000-2010
City	66,093	175,381	257,729	165.4	47.0
MSA[1]	741,459	1,375,765	1,951,269	85.5	41.8
U.S.	248,709,873	281,421,906	308,745,538	13.2	9.7

Note: (1) Figures cover the Las Vegas-Paradise, NV Metropolitan Statistical Area—see Appendix B for areas included

Source: U.S. Census Bureau, 2010 Census

Household Size

Area	Persons in Household (%)							Average Household Size
	One	Two	Three	Four	Five	Six	Seven or More	
City	24.2	37.2	15.9	12.8	5.9	2.5	1.4	2.53
MSA[1]	25.3	32.0	15.9	13.0	7.4	3.5	2.8	2.70
U.S.	26.7	32.8	16.1	13.4	6.5	2.6	1.9	2.58

Note: (1) Figures cover the Las Vegas-Paradise, NV Metropolitan Statistical Area—see Appendix B for areas included

Source: U.S. Census Bureau, 2010 Census

Race

Area	White Alone[2] (%)	Black Alone[2] (%)	Asian Alone[2] (%)	AIAN[3] Alone[2] (%)	NHOPI[4] Alone[2] (%)	Other Race Alone[2] (%)	Two or More Races (%)
City	76.9	5.1	7.2	0.7	0.6	4.8	4.8
MSA[1]	60.9	10.5	8.7	0.7	0.7	13.5	5.1
U.S.	72.4	12.6	4.8	0.9	0.2	6.2	2.9

Note: (1) Figures cover the Las Vegas-Paradise, NV Metropolitan Statistical Area—see Appendix B for areas included; (2) Alone is defined as not being in combination with one or more other races; (3) American Indian and Alaska Native; (4) Native Hawaiian and Other Pacific Islander

Source: U.S. Census Bureau, 2010 Census

Hispanic or Latino Origin

Area	Hispanic or Latino (%)	Mexican (%)	Puerto Rican (%)	Cuban (%)	Other Hispanic or Latino (%)
City	14.9	9.9	0.9	0.6	3.5
MSA[1]	29.1	21.7	0.9	1.1	5.5
U.S.	16.3	10.3	1.5	0.6	4.0

Note: Persons of Hispanic or Latino origin can be of any race; (1) Figures cover the Las Vegas-Paradise, NV Metropolitan Statistical Area—see Appendix B for areas included

Source: U.S. Census Bureau, 2010 Census

Segregation

Type	Segregation Indices[1]				Percent Change		
	1990	2000	2010	2010 Rank[2]	1990-2000	1990-2010	2000-2010
Black/White	49.0	40.4	37.6	94	-8.7	-11.5	-2.8
Asian/White	23.3	25.4	28.8	92	2.1	5.5	3.5
Hispanic/White	28.8	42.4	42.0	58	13.6	13.3	-0.4

Note: Figures are based on an analysis of 1990, 2000, and 2010 Census Decennial Census tract data by William H. Frey, Brookings Institution and the University of Michigan Social Science Data Analysis Network. In this analysis all racial groups (whites, blacks, and asians) are non-Hispanic members of those races. Hispanics are shown as a separate category; All figures cover the Metropolitan Statistical Area (see Appendix B for areas included); (1) Segregation Indices are Dissimilarity Indices that measure the degree to which the minority group is distributed differently than whites across census tracts. They range from 0 (complete integration) to 100 (complete segregation) where the value indicates the percentage of the minority group that needs to move to be distributed exactly like whites; (2) Ranges from 1 (most segregated) to 102 (least segregated); n/a not available.
Source: www.CensusScope.org

Ancestry

Area	German	Irish	English	American	Italian	Polish	French[2]	Scottish	Dutch
City	17.0	12.8	11.5	4.8	8.9	3.8	2.9	2.3	1.8
MSA[1]	11.1	8.7	7.2	2.7	6.2	2.5	2.2	1.5	1.1
U.S.	16.1	11.6	8.8	6.1	5.7	3.2	3.0	1.9	1.6

Note: Figures are the percentage of the total population reporting a particular ancestry. The nine most commonly reported ancestries in the U.S. are shown. Figures include multiple ancestries (e.g. if a person reported being Irish and Italian, they were included in both columns); (1) Figures cover the Las Vegas-Paradise, NV Metropolitan Statistical Area—see Appendix B for areas included; (2) Excludes Basque
Source: U.S. Census Bureau, 2008-2010 American Community Survey 3-Year Estimates

Foreign-Born Population

Area	Percent of Population Born in								
	Any Foreign Country	Mexico	Asia	Europe	Carribean	South America	Central America[2]	Africa	Canada
City	11.4	1.8	5.4	1.8	0.4	0.6	0.4	0.3	0.6
MSA[1]	22.0	9.4	6.5	1.9	0.8	0.6	1.7	0.7	0.4
U.S.	12.8	3.8	3.6	1.6	1.2	0.9	1.0	0.5	0.3

Note: (1) Figures cover the Las Vegas-Paradise, NV Metropolitan Statistical Area—see Appendix B for areas included; (2) Excludes Mexico.
Source: U.S. Census Bureau, 2008-2010 American Community Survey 3-Year Estimates

Marital Status

Area	Never Married	Now Married[2]	Separated	Widowed	Divorced
City	25.6	53.4	1.8	5.5	13.6
MSA[1]	31.9	47.2	2.4	4.9	13.6
U.S.	31.6	49.6	2.2	6.1	10.7

Note: Figures are percentages and cover the population 15 years of age and older; (1) Figures cover the Las Vegas-Paradise, NV Metropolitan Statistical Area—see Appendix B for areas included; (2) Excludes separated
Source: U.S. Census Bureau, 2008-2010 American Community Survey 3-Year Estimates

Age

Area	Percent of Population							Median Age
	Under Age 5	Age 5 to 17	Age 18 to 34	Age 35 to 49	Age 50 to 64	Age 65 to 79	80 Years and Over	
City	5.9	16.8	20.8	21.9	20.4	11.6	2.7	39.6
MSA[1]	7.1	17.9	24.3	21.9	17.5	8.9	2.4	35.5
U.S.	6.5	17.5	23.2	20.7	19.0	9.4	3.6	37.2

Note: (1) Figures cover the Las Vegas-Paradise, NV Metropolitan Statistical Area—see Appendix B for areas included
Source: U.S. Census Bureau, 2010 Census

Male/Female Ratio

Area	Males	Females	Males per 100 Females
City	126,779	130,950	96.8
MSA[1]	982,193	969,076	101.4
U.S.	151,781,326	156,964,212	96.7

Note: (1) Figures cover the Las Vegas-Paradise, NV Metropolitan Statistical Area—see Appendix B for areas included
Source: U.S. Census Bureau, 2010 Census

Religious Groups

Area	Catholic	Baptist	Non-Den.	Methodist[2]	Lutheran	LDS[3]	Pente-costal	Presby-terian[4]	Muslim[5]	Judaism
MSA[1]	18.1	3.0	3.1	0.4	0.7	6.4	1.5	0.2	0.3	0.1
U.S.	19.1	9.3	4.0	4.0	2.3	2.0	1.9	1.6	0.8	0.7

Note: Figures are the number of adherents as a percentage of the total population; (1) Figures cover the Las Vegas-Paradise, NV Metropolitan Statistical Area—see Appendix B for areas included; (2) Methodist/Pietist; (3) Latter Day Saints; (4) Reformed; (5) Figures are estimates
Source: Association of Statisticians of American Religious Bodies, 2010 U.S. Religion Census: Religious Congregations & Membership Study

ECONOMY

Gross Metropolitan Product

Area	2007	2008	2009	2010	2010 Rank[2]
MSA[1]	99.5	97.8	91.7	91.4	33

Note: Figures are in billions of dollars; (1) Figures cover the Las Vegas-Paradise, NV Metropolitan Statistical Area—see Appendix B for areas included; (2) Rank ranges from 1 to 363
Source: The United States Conference of Mayors, "U.S. Metro Economies: GMP and Employment Forecasts," June 2011

Economic Growth

Area	2007-2009 (%)	2010 (%)	2011 (%)	Rank[2]
MSA[1]	-5.7	-1.1	1.6	342
U.S.	-1.3	2.9	2.5	–

Note: Figures are real Gross Metropolitan Product growth rates and represent annual average percent change; (1) Figures cover the Las Vegas-Paradise, NV Metropolitan Statistical Area—see Appendix B for areas included; (2) Rank ranges from 1 to 363
Source: The United States Conference of Mayors, "U.S. Metro Economies: GMP and Employment Forecasts," June 2011

Metropolitan Area Exports

Area	2005	2006	2007	2008	2009	2010	2010 Rank[2]
MSA[1]	716.8	1,051.8	1,182.1	1,167.7	1,022.7	1,187.8	120

Note: Figures are in millions of dollars; (1) Figures cover the Las Vegas-Paradise, NV Metropolitan Statistical Area—see Appendix B for areas included; (2) Rank ranges from 1 to 369
Source: U.S. Department of Commerce, International Trade Administration, Office of Trade & Industry Information, Manufacturing & Services, data extracted April 2, 2012

INCOME

Income

Area	Per Capita ($)	Median Household ($)	Average Household ($)
City	34,075	65,047	84,449
MSA[1]	26,211	54,458	69,877
U.S.	26,942	51,222	70,116

Note: (1) Figures cover the Las Vegas-Paradise, NV Metropolitan Statistical Area—see Appendix B for areas included
Source: U.S. Census Bureau, 2008-2010 American Community Survey 3-Year Estimates

Household Income Distribution

Area	Percent of Households Earning							
	Under $15,000	$15,000 -24,999	$25,000 -34,999	$35,000 -49,999	$50,000 -74,999	$75,000 -99,000	$100,000 -149,999	$150,000 and up
City	8.2	6.6	8.4	13.8	20.5	13.7	17.2	11.6
MSA[1]	10.0	9.6	11.0	14.9	21.0	13.4	12.8	7.4
U.S.	13.0	11.0	10.6	14.2	18.5	12.1	12.2	8.4

Note: (1) Figures cover the Las Vegas-Paradise, NV Metropolitan Statistical Area—see Appendix B for areas included
Source: U.S. Census Bureau, 2008-2010 American Community Survey 3-Year Estimates

Poverty Rate

Area	All Ages	Under 18 Years Old	18 to 64 Years Old	65 Years and Over
City	8.0	10.3	7.2	7.5
MSA[1]	12.9	18.6	11.4	8.1
U.S.	14.4	20.1	13.1	9.4

Note: Figures are percentage of people whose income during the past 12 months was below the poverty level; (1) Figures cover the Las Vegas-Paradise, NV Metropolitan Statistical Area—see Appendix B for areas included
Source: U.S. Census Bureau, 2008-2010 American Community Survey 3-Year Estimates

Personal Bankruptcy Filing Rate

Area	2006	2007	2008	2009	2010	2011
Clark County	2.44	4.80	8.25	12.68	12.53	10.24
U.S.	2.00	2.73	3.53	4.61	4.97	4.37

Note: Numbers are per 1,000 population and include Chapter 7 and Chapter 13 filings
Source: Federal Deposit Insurance Corporation, Regional Economic Conditions, March 9, 2012

EMPLOYMENT

Labor Force and Employment

Area	Civilian Labor Force			Workers Employed		
	Dec. 2010	Dec. 2011	% Chg.	Dec. 2010	Dec. 2011	% Chg.
City	139,492	138,309	-0.8	119,913	122,019	1.8
MSA[1]	952,734	942,225	-1.1	808,526	822,726	1.8
U.S.	153,156,000	153,373,000	0.1	139,159,000	140,681,000	1.1

Note: Data is not seasonally adjusted and covers workers 16 years of age and older; (1) Metropolitan Statistical Area—see Appendix B for areas included
Source: Bureau of Labor Statistics, http://stats.bls.gov

Unemployment Rate

Area	2011											
	Jan.	Feb.	Mar.	Apr.	May	Jun.	Jul.	Aug.	Sep.	Oct.	Nov.	Dec.
City	12.1	12.8	12.4	11.1	11.3	12.7	12.8	13.0	12.5	12.0	11.6	11.8
MSA[1]	13.7	13.7	13.3	12.0	12.4	13.8	14.0	14.3	13.6	13.1	12.4	12.7
U.S.	9.8	9.5	9.2	8.7	8.7	9.3	9.3	9.1	8.8	8.5	8.2	8.3

Note: Data is not seasonally adjusted and covers workers 16 years of age and older; All figures are percentages; (1) Metropolitan Statistical Area—see Appendix B for areas included
Source: Bureau of Labor Statistics, http://stats.bls.gov

Projected Unemployment Rate

Area	2010 (%)	2011 (%)	2012 (%)	2013 (%)
MSA[1]	15.4	13.4	12.8	11.9

Note: (1) Metropolitan Statistical Area—see Appendix B for areas included
Source: The United States Conference of Mayors, "U.S. Metro Economies: GMP and Employment Forecasts," June 2011

Employment by Occupation

Occupation Classification	City (%)	MSA[1] (%)	U.S. (%)
Management, Business, Science, and Arts	35.9	26.6	35.6
Natural Resources, Construction, and Maintenance	7.9	9.6	9.5
Production, Transportation, and Material Moving	6.9	9.0	12.1
Sales and Office	28.8	26.2	25.2
Service	20.5	28.6	17.6

Note: Figures cover employed civilians 16 years of age and older; (1) Figures cover the Las Vegas-Paradise, NV Metropolitan Statistical Area—see Appendix B for areas included
Source: U.S. Census Bureau, 2008-2010 American Community Survey 3-Year Estimates

Employment by Industry

Sector	MSA[1] Number of Employees	MSA[1] Percent of Total	U.S. Percent of Total
Construction	38,400	4.7	4.1
Education and Health Services	72,200	8.9	15.2
Financial Activities	39,000	4.8	5.8
Government	93,400	11.5	16.8
Information	9,300	1.1	2.0
Leisure and Hospitality	262,900	32.3	9.9
Manufacturing	19,800	2.4	8.9
Mining and Logging	200	<0.1	0.6
Other Services	24,000	2.9	4.0
Professional and Business Services	100,900	12.4	13.3
Retail Trade	97,700	12.0	11.5
Transportation and Utilities	36,200	4.4	3.8
Wholesale Trade	20,900	2.6	4.2

Note: Figures cover non-farm employment as of December 2011 and are not seasonally adjusted; (1) Metropolitan Statistical Area—see Appendix B for areas included
Source: Bureau of Labor Statistics, http://stats.bls.gov

Occupations with Greatest Projected Employment Growth: 2008 – 2018

Occupation[1]	2008 Employment	2018 Projected Employment	Numeric Employment Change	Percent Employment Change
Retail Salespersons	43,200	50,270	7,070	16.4
Combined Food Preparation and Serving Workers, Including Fast Food	27,380	31,340	3,960	14.5
Registered Nurses	16,900	20,240	3,340	19.8
Customer Service Representatives	15,480	18,250	2,770	17.9
Sales Representatives, Wholesale and Manufacturing, Except Technical and Scientific Products	9,940	12,110	2,170	21.8
General and Operations Managers	17,820	19,840	2,020	11.3
Cashiers	33,010	34,870	1,860	5.6
Gaming Dealers	23,790	25,600	1,810	7.6
Janitors and Cleaners, Except Maids and Housekeeping Cleaners	31,820	33,440	1,620	5.1
Postsecondary Teachers	8,990	10,600	1,610	17.9

Note: Projections cover Nevada; (1) Sorted by numeric employment change
Source: www.projectionscentral.com, State Occupational Projections, 2008–2018 Long-Term Projections

Fastest Growing Occupations: 2008 – 2018

Occupation[1]	2008 Employment	2018 Projected Employment	Numeric Employment Change	Percent Employment Change
Computer Software Engineers, Systems Software	1,620	2,370	750	46.3
Computer Software Engineers, Applications	1,430	2,050	620	43.4
Network Systems and Data Communications Analysts	990	1,400	410	41.4
Physician Assistants	470	650	180	38.3
Physical Therapist Assistants	340	470	130	38.2
Industrial Engineering Technicians	270	370	100	37.0
Dental Hygienists	1,420	1,940	520	36.6
Physical Therapist Aides	360	490	130	36.1
Network and Computer Systems Administrators	1,250	1,700	450	36.0
Dental Assistants	2,550	3,450	900	35.3

Note: Projections cover Nevada; (1) Sorted by percent employment change and excludes occupations with numeric employment change less than 100
Source: www.projectionscentral.com, State Occupational Projections, 2008–2018 Long-Term Projections

Average Wages

Occupation	$/Hr.	Occupation	$/Hr.
Accountants and Auditors	30.67	Maids and Housekeeping Cleaners	13.73
Automotive Mechanics	19.70	Maintenance and Repair Workers	21.61
Bookkeepers	17.63	Marketing Managers	59.31
Carpenters	28.18	Nuclear Medicine Technologists	38.14
Cashiers	10.52	Nurses, Licensed Practical	25.75
Clerks, General Office	14.60	Nurses, Registered	37.40
Clerks, Receptionists/Information	13.25	Nursing Aides/Orderlies/Attendants	16.22
Clerks, Shipping/Receiving	14.00	Packers and Packagers, Hand	12.06
Computer Programmers	33.34	Physical Therapists	47.65
Computer Support Specialists	22.25	Postal Service Mail Carriers	25.51
Computer Systems Analysts	39.57	Real Estate Brokers	39.47
Cooks, Restaurant	14.48	Retail Salespersons	12.51
Dentists	69.94	Sales Reps., Exc. Tech./Scientific	27.10
Electrical Engineers	41.18	Sales Reps., Tech./Scientific	52.63
Electricians	32.37	Secretaries, Exc. Legal/Med./Exec.	17.96
Financial Managers	50.71	Security Guards	13.25
First-Line Supervisors/Managers, Sales	19.67	Surgeons	93.59
Food Preparation Workers	13.93	Teacher Assistants	15.30
General and Operations Managers	53.29	Teachers, Elementary School	25.10
Hairdressers/Cosmetologists	10.30	Teachers, Secondary School	25.20
Internists	95.39	Telemarketers	15.49
Janitors and Cleaners	13.43	Truck Drivers, Heavy/Tractor-Trailer	22.68
Landscaping/Groundskeeping Workers	12.32	Truck Drivers, Light/Delivery Svcs.	16.25
Lawyers	56.92	Waiters and Waitresses	11.09

Note: Wage data covers the Las Vegas-Paradise, NV Metropolitan Statistical Area—see Appendix B for areas included. Hourly wages for elementary/secondary school teachers and teacher assistants were calculated by the editors from annual wage data assuming a 40 hour work week; n/a not available.
Source: Bureau of Labor Statistics, Metro Area Occupational Employment and Wage Estimates, May 2011

RESIDENTIAL REAL ESTATE

Building Permits

Area	Single-Family			Multi-Family			Total		
	2010	2011	Pct. Chg.	2010	2011	Pct. Chg.	2010	2011	Pct. Chg.
City	700	752	7.4	68	368	441.2	768	1,120	45.8
MSA[1]	4,623	3,817	-17.4	851	1,330	56.3	5,474	5,147	-6.0
U.S.	447,311	418,498	-6.4	157,299	205,563	30.7	604,610	624,061	3.2

Note: (1) Metropolitan Statistical Area—see Appendix B for areas included; figures represent new, privately-owned housing units authorized (unadjusted data); All permit data are based on estimates with imputation.
Source: U.S. Census Bureau, Manufacturing, Mining, and Construction Statistics, Building Permits, 2010, 2011

Homeownership Rate

Area	2005 (%)	2006 (%)	2007 (%)	2008 (%)	2009 (%)	2010 (%)	2011 (%)
MSA[1]	61.4	63.3	60.5	60.3	59.0	55.7	52.9
U.S.	68.9	68.8	68.1	67.8	67.4	66.9	66.1

Note: (1) Metropolitan Statistical Area—see Appendix B for areas included
Source: U.S. Census Bureau, Housing Vacancies and Homeownership Annual Statistics: 2011

Housing Vacancy Rates

Area	Gross Vacancy Rate[2] (%)			Year-Round Vacancy Rate[3] (%)			Rental Vacancy Rate[4] (%)			Homeowner Vacancy Rate[5] (%)		
	2009	2010	2011	2009	2010	2011	2009	2010	2011	2009	2010	2011
MSA[1]	16.7	17.2	16.4	16.5	16.8	16.0	14.3	13.8	12.1	5.0	5.1	4.1
U.S.	14.5	14.3	14.2	11.3	11.3	11.1	10.6	10.2	9.5	2.6	2.6	2.5

Note: (1) Metropolitan Statistical Area—see Appendix B for areas included; (2) The percentage of the total housing inventory that is vacant; (3) The percentage of the housing inventory (excluding seasonal units) that is year-round vacant; (4) The percentage of rental inventory that is vacant for rent; (5) The percentage of homeowner inventory that is vacant for sale
Source: U.S. Census Bureau, Housing Vacancies and Homeownership Annual Statistics: 2011

TAXES

State Corporate Income Tax Rates

State	Tax Rate (%)	Income Brackets ($)	Num. of Brackets	Financial Institution Tax Rate (%)[a]	Federal Income Tax Ded.
Nevada	No corporate tax		–	–	No

Note: Tax rates as of January 1, 2012; (a) Rates listed are the corporate income tax rate applied to financial institutions or excise taxes based on income. Some states have other taxes based upon the value of deposits or shares.
Source: Federation of Tax Administrators, "State Corporate Income Tax Rates, 2012"

State Individual Income Tax Rates

State	Tax Rate (%)	Income Brackets ($)	Num. of Brackets	Personal Exempt. ($)[1] Single	Personal Exempt. ($)[1] Dependents	Fed. Inc. Tax Ded.
Nevada – No State Income Tax						

Note: Tax rates as of January 1, 2012; Local- and county-level taxes are not included; n/a not applicable; (1) Married joint filers generally receive double the single exemption
Source: Federation of Tax Administrators, "State Individual Income Tax Rates, 2012"

Various State and Local Tax Rates

State	State and Local Sales and Use (%)	State Sales and Use (%)	Gasoline[1] (¢/gal.)	Cigarette[2] ($/pack)	Spirits[3] ($/gal.)	Wine[4] ($/gal.)	Beer[5] ($/gal.)
Nevada	8.1	6.85	33.1	0.80	3.60	0.70	0.16

Note: All tax rates as of January 1, 2012 except beer, wine and spirits (September 1, 2011); (1) The American Petroleum Institute has developed a methodology for determining the average tax rate on a gallon of fuel. Rates may include any of the following: excise taxes, environmental fees, storage tank fees, other fees or taxes, general sales tax, and local taxes. In states where gasoline is subject to the general sales tax, or where the fuel tax is based on the average sale price, the average rate determined by API is sensitive to changes in the price of gasoline. States that fully or partially apply general sales taxes to gasoline: CA, CO, GA, IL, IN, MI, NY; (2) The federal excise tax of \$1.0066 per pack and local taxes are not included; (3) Rates are those applicable to off-premise sales of 40% alcohol by volume (a.b.v.) distilled spirits in 750ml containers. Local excise taxes are excluded; (4) Rates are those applicable to off-premise sales of 11% a.b.v. non-carbonated wine in 750ml containers; (5) Rates are those applicable to off-premise sales of 4.7% a.b.v. beer in 12 ounce containers.
Source: Tax Foundation, 2012 Facts & Figures: How Does Your State Compare?

State-Local Tax Burdens

Area	Rate (%)	Rank[1]	Per Capita Taxes Paid to Home State ($)	Total State and Local Per Capita Taxes Paid ($)	Per Capita Income ($)
Nevada	7.5	49	1,988	3,311	44,241
U.S. Average	9.8	-	3,057	4,160	42,539

Note: Figures cover 2009; (1) Rank ranges from 1 to 50 where 1 is highest tax burden
Source: Tax Foundation, State-Local Tax Burdens, All States, 2009

State Business Tax Climate Index Rankings

State	Overall Rank	Corporate Tax Index Rank	Individual Income Tax Index Rank	Sales Tax Index Rank	Unemployment Insurance Tax Index Rank	Property Tax Index Rank
Nevada	3	1	1	42	42	16

Note: The index is a measure of how each state's tax laws affect economic performance. The lower the rank, the more favorable a state's tax system is for business. States without a given tax are given a ranking of 1.
Source: Tax Foundation, Major Components of the State Business Tax Climate Index, FY 2012

COMMERCIAL REAL ESTATE

Office Market

Market Area	Inventory (sq. ft.)	Vacant (sq. ft.)	Vac. Rate (%)	Under Constr. (sq. ft.)	Asking Rent ($/sf/yr) Class A	Asking Rent ($/sf/yr) Class B
Las Vegas	35,867,489	8,502,874	23.7	150,069	29.19	20.42

Source: Grubb & Ellis, Office Markets Trends, 4th Quarter 2011

Industrial Market

Market Area	Inventory (sq. ft.)	Vacant (sq. ft.)	Vac. Rate (%)	Under Constr. (sq. ft.)	Asking Rent ($/sf/yr) WH/Dist	Asking Rent ($/sf/yr) R&D/Flex
Las Vegas	99,377,925	15,450,909	15.5	0	4.80	8.76

Source: Grubb & Ellis, Industrial Markets Trends, 4th Quarter 2011

COMMERCIAL UTILITIES

Typical Monthly Electric Bills

Area	Commercial Service ($/month) 1,500 kWh	Commercial Service ($/month) 40 kW demand 14,000 kWh	Industrial Service ($/month) 1,000 kW demand 200,000 kWh	Industrial Service ($/month) 50,000 kW demand 15,000,000 kWh
City	n/a	n/a	n/a	n/a
Average[1]	189	1,616	25,197	1,470,813

Note: Based on total rates in effect July 1, 2011; (1) average based on 184 utilities surveyed; n/a not available
Source: Edison Electric Institute, Typical Bills and Average Rates Report, Summer 2011

TRANSPORTATION

Means of Transportation to Work

Area	Car/Truck/Van: Drove Alone	Car/Truck/Van: Car-pooled	Public Transportation: Bus	Public Transportation: Subway	Public Transportation: Railroad	Bicycle	Walked	Other Means	Worked at Home
City	82.1	8.5	1.2	0.0	0.0	0.1	1.4	1.6	5.1
MSA[1]	78.5	11.0	3.6	0.0	0.0	0.5	1.8	1.5	3.1
U.S.	76.0	10.2	2.7	1.7	0.5	0.5	2.8	1.3	4.2

Note: Figures are percentages and cover workers 16 years of age and older; (1) Figures cover the Las Vegas-Paradise, NV Metropolitan Statistical Area—see Appendix B for areas included
Source: U.S. Census Bureau, 2008-2010 American Community Survey 3-Year Estimates

Travel Time to Work

Area	Less Than 10 Minutes	10 to 19 Minutes	20 to 29 Minutes	30 to 44 Minutes	45 to 59 Minutes	60 to 89 Minutes	90 Minutes or More
City	9.3	29.8	33.6	21.5	3.1	1.4	1.3
MSA[1]	8.8	28.7	29.6	23.9	4.8	2.6	1.6
U.S.	13.9	30.1	20.8	19.8	7.5	5.5	2.5

Note: Figures are percentages and include workers 16 years old and over; (1) Figures cover the Las Vegas-Paradise, NV Metropolitan Statistical Area—see Appendix B for areas included
Source: U.S. Census Bureau, 2008-2010 American Community Survey 3-Year Estimates

Travel Time Index

Area	1985	1990	1995	2000	2005	2010
Urban Area[1]	1.07	1.16	1.23	1.25	1.29	1.24
Average[2]	1.11	1.16	1.18	1.21	1.25	1.20

Note: Travel Time Index—the ratio of travel time in the peak period to the travel time at free-flow conditions. A value of 1.30 indicates a 20-minute free-flow trip takes 26 minutes in the peak. Free-flow speeds (60 mph on freeways and 35 mph on principal arterials) are used as the comparison threshold; (1) Covers the Las Vegas NV urban area; (2) average of 439 urban areas

Source: Texas Transportation Institute, Urban Mobility Report 2011, September 2011

Public Transportation

Agency Name / Mode of Transportation	Vehicles Operated in Maximum Service	Annual Unlinked Passenger Trips ('000)	Annual Passenger Miles ('000)
Regional Transportation Commission of Southern Nevada (RTC)			
Bus (purchased transportation)	298	56,382.3	187,753.0
Demand Response (purchased transportation)	230	1,031.8	11,835.2

Source: Federal Transit Administration, National Transit Database, 2010

Air Transportation

Airport Name and Code / Type of Service	Passenger Airlines[1]	Passenger Enplanements	Freight Carriers[2]	Freight (lbs.)
McCarran International (LAS)				
Domestic service (U.S. carriers - 2011)	33	18,475,168	13	81,886,640
International service (U.S. carriers - 2010)	8	17,389	2	4,357

Note: (1) Includes all U.S.-based major, minor and commuter airlines that carried at least one passenger during the year; (2) Includes all U.S.-based airlines and freight carriers that transported at least one pound of freight during the year

Source: Bureau of Transportation Statistics, The Intermodal Transportation Database, Air Carriers: T-100 Domestic Market (U.S. Carriers), 2011; Bureau of Transportation Statistics, The Intermodal Transportation Database, Air Carriers: T-100 International Market (U.S. Carriers), 2010

Other Transportation Statistics

Major Highways:	CR-564 connecting to I-515 and I-215
Amtrak Service:	Bus service only (station is in Las Vegas)
Major Waterways/Ports:	Near Lake Mead

Source: Amtrak.com; Google Maps

BUSINESSES

Major Business Headquarters

Company Name	Rankings: Fortune[1]	Rankings: Forbes[2]
No companies listed	-	-

Note: (1) Fortune 500—companies that produce a 10-K are ranked 1 to 500 based on 2010 revenue; (2) all private companies with at least $2 billion in annual revenue are ranked 1 to 212; companies listed are headquartered in the city; dashes indicate no ranking

Source: Fortune, "Fortune 500," May 23, 2011; Forbes, "America's Largest Private Companies," November 16, 2011

Fast-Growing Businesses

According to *Inc.*, Henderson is home to one of America's 500 fastest-growing private companies: **K2 Energy Solutions** (#79). Criteria: must be an independent, privately-held, for-profit, U.S. corporation, proprietorship or partnership; revenues must be at least $80,000 in 2007 and $2 million in 2010; must have four-year operating/sales history. Holding companies, regulated banks, and utilities were excluded. *Inc., "America's 500 Fastest-Growing Private Companies," September 2011*

According to Deloitte, Henderson is home to one of North America's 500 fastest-growing high-technology companies: **Spectrum Pharmaceuticals** (#86). Companies are ranked by percentage growth in revenue over a five-year period. Criteria for inclusion: company must be headquartered within North America; must own proprietary intellectual property or proprietary technology that contributes to a significant portion of the company's operating revenue, or devote a significant proportion of revenues to research and development of technology; must have been in business for a minumum of five years with 2006 operating revenues of at least $50,000 USD/CD and 2010 operating revenues of at least $5 million USD/CD. *Deloitte Touche Tohmatsu, 2011 Deloitte Technology Fast 500™*

Minority- and Women-Owned Businesses

Group	All Firms		Firms with Paid Employees			
	Firms	Sales ($000)	Firms	Sales ($000)	Employees	Payroll ($000)
Asian	1,998	382,444	324	274,641	2,000	64,635
Black	688	56,553				
Hispanic	1,936	259,321	231	190,855	1,791	57,150
Women	7,331	1,897,712	871	1,677,350	6,666	298,119
All Firms	345	3,057,828	271	3,037,401	18,052	668,840

Note: Figures cover firms located in the city; minority- and women-owned business are defined as firms in which the corresponding group own 51% or more of the stock or equity of the company
Source: U.S. Census Bureau, 2007 Economic Census, Survey of Business Owners

HOTELS

Hotels/Motels

Area	5 Star		4 Star		3 Star		2 Star		1 Star		Not Rated	
	Num.	Pct.[3]	Num.	Pct.[3]	Num.	Pct.[3]	Num.	Pct.[3]	Num.	Pct.[3]	Num.	Pct.[3]
City[1]	0	0.0	3	7.5	16	40.0	17	42.5	1	2.5	3	7.5
Total[2]	133	0.9	940	6.5	4,569	31.8	7,033	48.9	351	2.4	1,343	9.3

Note: (1) Figures cover Henderson and vicinity; (2) Figures cover all 100 cities in this book; (3) Percentage of hotels which have a given star rating; Star ratings are determined by expedia.com and offer an indication of the general quality of a particular hotel.
Source: expedia.com, April 25, 2012

The Las Vegas-Paradise, NV metro area is home to eight of the best hotels in the U.S. according to *Travel & Leisure*: **Wynn Las Vegas** (#73); **The Palazzo** (#76); **Encore Las Vegas** (#78); **Mandarin Oriental, Las Vegas** (#112); **Bellagio, Las Vegas** (#122); **Trump International Hotel Las Vegas** (#155); **Four Seasons Hotel, Las Vegas** (#171); **The Venetian** (#198). Criteria: service; location; rooms; food; and value. *Travel & Leisure, "T+L 500, The World's Best Hotels 2012"*

The Las Vegas-Paradise, NV metro area is home to six of the best hotels in the U.S. according to *Condé Nast Traveler*: **The Cosmopolitan of Las Vegas** (#27); **Four Seasons** (#34); **Encore Wynn Las Vegas** (#45); **Bellagio** (#56); **The Venetian Resort Hotel Casino** (#66); **Mandarin Oriental** (#77). The selections are based on over 25,000 responses to the magazine's annual Readers' Choice Survey. *Condé Nast Traveler, "2011 Readers' Choice Awards"*

EVENT SITES

Major Stadiums, Arenas, and Auditoriums

Name	Max. Capacity
Henderson Convention Center	10,000
Henderson Events Plaza	900
Henderson Pavillion	2,444

Source: Original research

Convention Centers

Name	Overall Space (sq. ft.)	Exhibit Space (sq. ft.)	Meeting Space (sq. ft.)	Meeting Rooms
Henderson Convention Center	n/a	3,765	10,000	6
Henderson Events Plaza	60,000	n/a	n/a	n/a

Note: n/a not available
Source: Original research

Living Environment

COST OF LIVING

Cost of Living Index

Composite Index	Groceries	Housing	Utilities	Transportation	Health Care	Misc. Goods/ Services
100.2	105.1	92.5	91.4	103.8	106.4	105.8

Note: U.S. = 100; Figures cover the Las Vegas NV urban area.
Source: The Council for Community and Economic Research, ACCRA Cost of Living Index, 2011

Grocery Prices

Area[1]	T-Bone Steak ($/pound)	Frying Chicken ($/pound)	Whole Milk ($/half gal.)	Eggs ($/dozen)	Orange Juice ($/64 oz.)	Coffee ($/11.5 oz.)
City[2]	9.29	1.08	2.34	1.90	3.25	4.89
Avg.	9.25	1.18	2.22	1.66	3.19	4.40
Min.	6.70	0.88	1.31	0.95	2.46	2.94
Max.	14.30	2.16	3.50	3.18	4.75	6.83

Note: (1) Values for the local area are compared with the average, minimum and maximum values for all 335 areas in the Cost of Living Index; (2) Figures cover the Las Vegas NV urban area; **T-Bone Steak** *(price per pound);* **Frying Chicken** *(price per pound, whole fryer);* **Whole Milk** *(half gallon carton);* **Eggs** *(price per dozen, Grade A, large);* **Orange Juice** *(64 oz. Tropicana or Florida Natural);* **Coffee** *(11.5 oz. can, vacuum-packed, Maxwell House, Hills Bros, or Folgers).*
Source: The Council for Community and Economic Research, ACCRA Cost of Living Index, 2011

Housing and Utility Costs

Area[1]	New Home Price ($)	Apartment Rent ($/month)	All Electric ($/month)	Part Electric ($/month)	Other Energy ($/month)	Telephone ($/month)
City[2]	261,021	766	-	124.12	44.17	20.26
Avg.	285,990	839	163.23	89.00	77.52	26.92
Min.	188,005	460	125.58	45.39	33.89	17.98
Max.	1,197,028	3,244	339.16	181.97	348.69	40.01

Note: (1) Values for the local area are compared with the average, minimum and maximum values for all 335 areas in the Cost of Living Index; (2) Figures cover the Las Vegas NV urban area; **New Home Price** *(2,400 sf living area, 8,000 sf lot, in urban area with full utilities);* **Apartment Rent** *(950 sf 2 bedroom/1.5 or 2 bath, unfurnished, excluding all utilities except water);* **All Electric** *(average monthly cost for an all-electric home);* **Part Electric** *(average monthly cost for a part-electric home);* **Other Energy** *(average monthly cost for natural gas, fuel oil, coal, wood, and any other forms of energy except electricity);* **Telephone** *(price includes basic monthly rate for a private residential line plus additional local usage charges incurred by a family of four).*
Source: The Council for Community and Economic Research, ACCRA Cost of Living Index, 2011

Health Care, Transportation, and Other Costs

Area[1]	Doctor ($/visit)	Dentist ($/visit)	Optometrist ($/visit)	Gasoline ($/gallon)	Beauty Salon ($/visit)	Men's Shirt ($)
City[2]	98.33	89.33	110.48	3.46	46.37	35.71
Avg.	93.88	81.72	90.54	3.48	32.65	25.06
Min.	60.00	55.33	53.66	3.18	19.78	13.44
Max.	154.98	145.97	183.72	4.31	63.21	46.00

Note: (1) Values for the local area are compared with the average, minimum and maximum values for all 335 areas in the Cost of Living Index; (2) Figures cover the Las Vegas NV urban area; **Doctor** *(general practitioners routine exam of an established patient);* **Dentist** *(adult teeth cleaning and periodic oral examination);* **Optometrist** *(full vision eye exam for established adult patient);* **Gasoline** *(one gallon regular unleaded, national brand, including all taxes, cash price at self-service pump if available);* **Beauty Salon** *(woman's shampoo, trim, and blow-dry);* **Men's Shirt** *(cotton/polyester dress shirt, pinpoint weave, long sleeves).*
Source: The Council for Community and Economic Research, ACCRA Cost of Living Index, 2011

HOUSING

House Price Index (HPI)

Area	National Ranking[2]	Quarterly Change (%)	One-Year Change (%)	Five-Year Change (%)
MSA[1]	306	-0.37	-12.60	-59.81
U.S.[3]	-	-0.10	-2.43	-19.16

Note: The HPI is a weighted repeat sales index. It measures average price changes in repeat sales or refinancings on the same properties. This information is obtained by reviewing repeat mortgage transactions on single-family properties whose mortgages have been purchased or securitized by Fannie Mae or Freddie Mac in January 1975; (1) Metropolitan/Micropolitan Statistical Area—see Appendix B for areas included; (2) Rankings are based on annual percentage change for all metro areas containing at least 15,000 transactions over the last 10 years and ranges from 1 to 306; (3) figures based on a weighted average of Census Division estimates using a purchase only index; all figures are for the period ending December 31, 2011
Source: Federal Housing Finance Agency, House Price Index, February 23, 2012

House Price Valuations

Area	Q4 2005		Q4 2006		Q4 2007		Q4 2008		Q4 2009	
	Price ($000)	Over-valuation	Price ($000)	Over-valuation	Price ($000)	Over-valuation	Price ($000)	Over-valuation	Price ($000)	Over-valuation
MSA[1]	287.0	35.3	288.8	30.5	254.1	5.9	152.7	-34.4	123.0	-45.3

Note: Figures show the percentage of over- or under-valuation of single family homes relative to statistically normal house values (e.g. a value of 23.6 indicates that house values are 23.6% overvalued). Statistically normal house values are based on house prices, interest rates, household incomes, population densities, and any historical premiums or discounts metropolitan areas have exhibited over time; (1) Figures cover the Las Vegas-Paradise, NV - see Appendix B for areas included
Source: Global Insight/PNC Financial Services Group, House Prices in America: 4th Quarter 2009 Update

Median Single-Family Home Prices

Area	2009	2010	2011p	Percent Change 2010 to 2011
MSA[1]	142.9	138.0	124.7	-9.6
U.S. Average	172.1	173.1	166.2	-4.0

Note: Figures are median sales prices of existing single-family homes in thousands of dollars; (p) preliminary; n/a not available; (1) Metropolitan Statistical Area—see Appendix B for areas included
Source: National Association of Realtors, Median Sales Price of Existing Single-Family Homes for Metropolitan Areas, 4th Quarter 2011

Affordability Index of Existing Single-Family Homes

Area	2009	2010	2011p	Percent Change 2010 to 2011
MSA[1]	120.5	127.9	144.2	12.7

Note: The housing affordability index measures whether or not a typical family could qualify for a mortgage loan on a typical home. The higher the index, the greater the household purchasing power. An index of 100 is defined as the point where a median-income household has exactly enough income to qualify for the purchase of a median-priced existing single-family home, assuming a 20 percent downpayment and 25 percent of gross income devoted to mortgage principal and interest payments; (p) preliminary; n/a not available; (1) Metropolitan Statistical Area—see Appendix B for areas included
Source: National Association of Realtors, Affordability Index of Existing Single-Family Homes, 2011

Median Apartment Condo-Coop Home Prices

Area	2009	2010	2011p	Percent Change 2010 to 2011
MSA[1]	68.6	64.4	55.7	-13.5
U.S. Average	175.6	171.7	165.1	-3.8

Note: Figures are median sales prices of existing apartment condo-coop homes in thousands of dollars; (p) preliminary; n/a not available; (1) Metropolitan Statistical Area—see Appendix B for areas included
Source: National Association of Realtors, Median Sales Price of Existing Apartment Condo-Coop Homes for Metropolitan Areas, 4th Quarter 2011

Year Housing Structure Built

Area	2005 or Later	2000 -2004	1990 -1999	1980 -1989	1970 -1979	1960 -1969	1950 -1959	Before 1950	Median Year
City	12.1	25.3	38.5	16.5	4.4	1.1	1.4	0.7	1997
MSA[1]	11.5	22.2	28.6	15.9	12.8	5.6	2.4	1.0	1994
U.S.	5.0	8.6	14.0	14.1	16.3	11.3	11.2	19.6	1975

Note: Figures are percentages except for Median Year; (1) Figures cover the Las Vegas-Paradise, NV Metropolitan Statistical Area—see Appendix B for areas included
Source: U.S. Census Bureau, 2008-2010 American Community Survey 3-Year Estimates

HEALTH

Health Risk Data

Category	MSA[1] (%)	U.S. (%)
Adults who have been told they have high blood pressure[2]	27.4	28.7
Adults who have been told they have high blood cholesterol[2]	39.1	37.5
Adults who have been told they have diabetes[3]	9.0	8.7
Adults who have been told they have arthritis[2]	23.9	26.0
Adults who have been told they currently have asthma	9.3	9.1
Adults who are current smokers	22.1	17.3
Adults who are heavy drinkers[4]	5.1	5.0
Adults who are binge drinkers[5]	17.5	15.1
Adults who are overweight (BMI 25.0 - 29.9)	37.3	36.2
Adults who are obese (BMI 30.0 - 99.8)	23.1	27.5
Adults who participated in any physical activities in the past month	76.3	76.1
Adults 50+ who have ever had a sigmoidoscopy or colonoscopy	60.5	65.2
Women aged 40+ who have had a mammogram within the past two years	66.8	75.2
Men aged 40+ who have had a PSA test within the past two years	51.6	53.2
Adults aged 65+ who have had flu shot within the past year	59.4	67.5
Adults aged 18–64 who have any kind of health care coverage	77.2	82.2

Note: Data as of 2010 unless otherwise noted; (1) Figures cover the Las Vegas-Paradise, NV Metropolitan Statistical Area—see Appendix B for areas included; (2) Data as of 2009; (3) Figures do not include pregnancy-related, borderline, or pre-diabetes; (4) Heavy drinkers are classified as males having more than two drinks per day or females having more than one drink per day; (5) Binge drinkers are classified as males having five or more drinks on one occasion or females having four or more drinks on one occasion
Source: Centers for Disease Control and Prevention, Behaviorial Risk Factor Surveillance System, SMART: Selected Metropolitan/Micropolitan Area Risk Trends, 2009, 2010

Mortality Rates for the Top 10 Causes of Death in the U.S.

ICD-10[a] Sub-Chapter	ICD-10[a] Code	Age-Adjusted Mortality Rate[1] per 100,000 population	
		County[2]	U.S.
Malignant neoplasms	C00-C97	177.5	175.6
Ischaemic heart diseases	I20-I25	94.8	121.6
Other forms of heart disease	I30-I51	86.4	48.6
Chronic lower respiratory diseases	J40-J47	48.0	42.3
Cerebrovascular diseases	I60-I69	38.8	40.6
Organic, including symptomatic, mental disorders	F01-F09	36.7	26.7
Other degenerative diseases of the nervous system	G30-G31	11.9	24.7
Other external causes of accidental injury	W00-X59	28.1	24.4
Diabetes mellitus	E10-E14	11.3	21.7
Hypertensive diseases	I10-I15	20.4	18.2

Note: (a) ICD-10 = International Classification of Diseases 10th Revision; (1) Mortality rates are a three year average covering 2007-2009; (2) Figures cover Clark County
Source: Centers for Disease Control and Prevention, National Center for Health Statistics. Underlying Cause of Death 1999-2009 on CDC WONDER Online Database, released 2012. Data for year 2009 are compiled from the Multiple Cause of Death File 2009, Series 20 No. 2O, 2012, Data for year 2008 are compiled from the Multiple Cause of Death File 2008, Series 20 No. 2N, 2011, Data for year 2007 are compiled from Multiple Cause of Death File 2007, Series 20 No. 2M, 2010.

Mortality Rates for Selected Causes of Death

ICD-10[a] Sub-Chapter	ICD-10[a] Code	Age-Adjusted Mortality Rate[1] per 100,000 population County[2]	U.S.
Assault	X85-Y09	7.2	5.7
Human immunodeficiency virus (HIV) disease	B20-B24	3.4	3.3
Influenza and pneumonia	J09-J18	21.8	16.4
Intentional self-harm	X60-X84	18.3	11.5
Malnutrition	E40-E46	*Unreliable	0.8
Obesity and other hyperalimentation	E65-E68	0.8	1.6
Transport accidents	V01-V99	12.6	13.7
Viral hepatitis	B15-B19	2.0	2.2

Note: (a) ICD-10 = International Classification of Diseases 10th Revision; (1) Mortality rates are a three year average covering 2007-2009; (2) Figures cover Clark County; (*) Unreliable data as per CDC
Source: Centers for Disease Control and Prevention, National Center for Health Statistics. Underlying Cause of Death 1999-2009 on CDC WONDER Online Database, released 2012. Data for year 2009 are compiled from the Multiple Cause of Death File 2009, Series 20 No. 2O, 2012, Data for year 2008 are compiled from the Multiple Cause of Death File 2008, Series 20 No. 2N, 2011, Data for year 2007 are compiled from Multiple Cause of Death File 2007, Series 20 No. 2M, 2010.

Distribution of Physicians and Dentists

Area[1]	Dentists[2]	D.O.[3]	M.D.[4] Total	Family/General Practice	Pediatrics	Medical Specialties	Surgical Specialties
Local (number)	741	390	2,671	303	170	1,046	568
Local (rate[5])	4.0	2.1	14.2	1.6	0.9	5.6	3.0
U.S. (rate[5])	4.5	1.9	18.3	2.5	1.4	6.8	4.1

Note: Data as of 2008 unless noted; (1) Local data covers Clark County; (2) Data as of 2007; (3) Doctor of Osteopathic Medicine; (4) Includes active, non-federal, patient-care, office-based Doctors of Medicine; (5) rate per 10,000 population
Source: Area Resource File (ARF). 2009-2010 Release. U.S. Department of Health and Human Services, Health Resources and Services Administration, Bureau of Health Professions, Rockville, MD, August 2010

EDUCATION

Public School District Statistics

District Name	Schls	Pupils	Pupil/Teacher Ratio	Minority Pupils[1] (%)	Free Lunch Eligible[2] (%)	IEP[3] (%)
Clark County School District	358	307,059	19.8	65.9	38.0	10.5

Note: Table includes school districts with 2,000 or more students; (1) Percentage of students that are not non-Hispanic white; (2) Percentage of students that are eligible for the free lunch program; (3) Percentage of students that have an Individualized Education Program.
Source: U.S. Department of Education, National Center for Education Statistics, Common Core of Data, Local Education Agency (School District) Universe Survey: School Year 2009-2010; U.S. Department of Education, National Center for Education Statistics, Common Core of Data, Public Elementary/Secondary School Universe Survey: School Year 2009-2010

Highest Level of Education

Area	Less than H.S.	H.S. Diploma	Some College, No Deg.	Associate Degree	Bachelors Degree	Masters Degree	Profess. School Degree	Doctorate Degree
City	7.3	26.7	27.2	7.9	20.0	7.3	2.2	1.4
MSA[1]	16.6	29.3	25.3	7.0	14.7	4.9	1.5	0.7
U.S.	14.7	28.4	21.3	7.6	17.6	7.2	1.9	1.2

Note: Figures cover persons age 25 and over; (1) Figures cover the Las Vegas-Paradise, NV Metropolitan Statistical Area—see Appendix B for areas included
Source: U.S. Census Bureau, 2008-2010 American Community Survey 3-Year Estimates

Educational Attainment by Race

Area	High School Graduate or Higher (%)					Bachelor's Degree or Higher (%)				
	Total	White	Black	Asian	Hisp.[2]	Total	White	Black	Asian	Hisp.[2]
City	92.7	92.8	93.6	95.6	80.3	30.8	30.4	23.0	53.0	18.1
MSA[1]	83.4	83.4	87.0	89.7	57.9	21.8	21.5	16.2	38.6	8.2
U.S.	85.3	87.5	81.4	85.5	61.6	28.0	29.3	17.8	50.2	13.0

Note: Figures shown cover persons 25 years old and over; (1) Figures cover the Las Vegas-Paradise, NV Metropolitan Statistical Area—see Appendix B for areas included; (2) People of Hispanic origin can be of any race
Source: U.S. Census Bureau, 2008-2010 American Community Survey 3-Year Estimates

School Enrollment by Grade and Control

Area	Preschool (%)		Kindergarten (%)		Grades 1 - 4 (%)		Grades 5 - 8 (%)		Grades 9 - 12 (%)	
	Public	Private	Public	Private	Public	Private	Public	Private	Public	Private
City	51.2	48.8	85.3	14.7	91.8	8.2	96.2	3.8	94.6	5.4
MSA[1]	56.2	43.8	92.4	7.6	93.6	6.4	95.6	4.4	95.2	4.8
U.S.	55.4	44.6	87.1	12.9	89.4	10.6	89.5	10.5	90.4	9.6

Note: Figures shown cover persons 3 years old and over; (1) Figures cover the Las Vegas-Paradise, NV Metropolitan Statistical Area—see Appendix B for areas included
Source: U.S. Census Bureau, 2008-2010 American Community Survey 3-Year Estimates

Average Salaries of Public School Classroom Teachers

Area	2010-11		2011-12		Percent Change 2010-11 to 2011-12	Percent Change 2001-02 to 2011-12
	Dollars	Rank[1]	Dollars	Rank[1]		
Nevada	53,023	20	54,559	19	2.90	33.80
U.S. Average	55,623	-	56,643	-	1.83	26.8

Note: (1) State rank ranges from 1 to 51 where 1 indicates highest salary.
Source: National Education Association, Rankings & Estimates: Rankings of the States 2011 and Estimates of School Statistics 2012, December 2011

Higher Education

Four-Year Colleges			Two-Year Colleges			Medical Schools[1]	Law Schools[2]	Voc/ Tech[3]
Public	Private Non-profit	Private For-profit	Public	Private Non-profit	Private For-profit			
1	2	5	0	0	2	1	0	0

Note: Figures cover institutions located within the city limits and include main campuses only; (1) includes schools accredited by the Liaison Committee on Medical Education and the American Osteopathic Association's Commission on Osteopathic College Accreditation; (2) includes American Bar Association-accredited law schools; (3) includes all schools with programs that are less than 2 years.
Source: National Center for Education Statistics, Integrated Postsecondary Education System (IPEDS) Peer Analysis System, 2011-12; Association of American Medical Colleges, Member List, April 23, 2012; American Osteopathic Association, Member List, April 23, 2012; Law School Admission Council, Official Guide to ABA-Approved Law Schools Online, April 23, 2012

PRESIDENTIAL ELECTION

2008 Presidential Election Results

Area	Obama	McCain	Nader	Other
Clark County	58.5	39.5	0.6	1.4
U.S.	52.9	45.6	0.6	0.9

Note: Results are percentages and may not add to 100% due to rounding
Source: Dave Leip's Atlas of U.S. Presidential Elections, www.uselectionatlas.org

EMPLOYERS

Major Employers

Company Name	Industry
Barrick Gaming Operations	Casino hotel
City of Las vegas	Executive offices
Coast Casinos Inc	Hotels/motels
Consolidated Electric	Electrical apparatus equipment
Donald J Laughlin	Gambling machines, coin operated
E-T-T	Slot machines
Gaughan South	Casino hotel
Las Vegas Sands	Casino hotel
M Arthur Gensler Jr & Associates Inc	Architectual services
Nevada System of Higher Education	Colleges/universities
Nevada System of Higher Education	General medical/surgical hospitals
New Castle Corp	Casino hotel
New York - New York Hotel and Casino	Casino hotel
Paris Hotel Casino Resort	Casino hotel
Primm Casinos	Hotels/motels
Sam-Will Inc	Casino hotel
Station Casinos Inc	Hotels/motels
Station Casinos Inc	Casino hotel
Stratosphere Gaming	Hotels/motels
Sunrise Hospitality and Medical Center	General medical/surgical hospitals
University Medical Center of Southern NV	General medical/surgical hospitals
Venetian Casino/Resort	Resort hotel

Note: Companies shown are located within the Las Vegas-Paradise, NV metropolitan area.
Source: Hoovers.com, data extracted April 25 2012

Best Companies to Work For

Zappos.com, headquartered in Henderson, is among "The 100 Best Companies to Work For." To pick the 100 Best Companies to Work For, *Fortune* partnered with the Great Place to Work Institute. Two hundred eighty firms participated in this year's survey. Two-thirds of a company's score is based on the results of the Institute's Trust Index survey, which is sent to a random sample of employees from each company. The questions related to attitudes about management's credibility, job satisfaction, and camaraderie. The other third of the scoring is based on the company's responses to the Institute's Culture Audit, which includes detailed questions about pay and benefit programs, and a series of open-ended questions about hiring practices, internal communication, training, recognition programs, and diversity efforts. Any company that is at least five years old with more than 1,000 U.S. employees is eligible. *Fortune, "The 100 Best Companies to Work For," February 6, 2012*

PUBLIC SAFETY

Crime Rate

Area	All Crimes	Violent Crimes: Murder	Violent Crimes: Forcible Rape	Violent Crimes: Robbery	Violent Crimes: Aggrav. Assault	Property Crimes: Burglary	Property Crimes: Larceny -Theft	Property Crimes: Motor Vehicle Theft
City	2,171.6	3.0	13.2	71.5	117.7	484.3	1,288.8	193.0
Suburbs[1]	3,922.4	7.3	43.9	267.1	532.5	965.5	1,625.6	480.5
Metro[2]	3,685.3	6.7	39.8	240.6	476.3	900.3	1,580.0	441.6
U.S.	3,345.5	4.8	27.5	119.1	252.3	699.6	2,003.5	238.8

Note: Figures are crimes per 100,000 population; (1) All areas within the metro area that are located outside the city limits; (2) Metropolitan Statistical Area—see Appendix B for areas included
Source: FBI Uniform Crime Reports, 2010

Hate Crimes

Area	Number of Quarters Reported	Bias Motivation: Race	Religion	Sexual Orientation	Ethnicity	Disability
City	4	1	3	1	1	0

Source: Federal Bureau of Investigation, Hate Crime Statistics 2010

Identity Theft Consumer Complaints

Area	Complaints	Complaints per 100,000 Population	Rank[2]
MSA[1]	1,839	100.1	94
U.S.	279,156	90.4	-

Note: (1) Metropolitan Statistical Area—see Appendix B for areas included; (2) Rank ranges from 1 to 384 where 1 indicates greatest number of identity theft complaints per 100,000 population
Source: Federal Trade Commission, Consumer Sentinel Network Data Book for January–December 2011

Fraud and Other Consumer Complaints

Area	Complaints	Complaints per 100,000 Population	Rank[2]
MSA[1]	9,548	519.9	126
U.S.	1,533,924	496.8	-

Note: (1) Metropolitan Statistical Area—see Appendix B for areas included; (2) Rank ranges from 1 to 384 where 1 indicates greatest number of fraud and other complaints per 100,000 population
Source: Federal Trade Commission, Consumer Sentinel Network Data Book for January–December 2011

RECREATION

Culture

Dance[1]	Theatre[1]	Instrumental Music[1]	Vocal Music[1]	Series/ Festivals	Museums	Zoos and Aquariums[2]
0	0	0	0	0	n/a	0

Note: (1) Number of professional perfoming groups; (2) AZA-accredited; n/a not available
Source: The Grey House Performing Arts Directory, 2011-2012; Official Museum Directory, 2011; American Association of Museums, AAM Member Museums, April 2012; Association of Zoos & Aquariums, AZA Member Zoos & Aquariums, April 2012

Professional Sports Teams

Team Name	League
No teams are located in the metro area	

Source: Original research

CLIMATE

Average and Extreme Temperatures

Temperature	Jan	Feb	Mar	Apr	May	Jun	Jul	Aug	Sep	Oct	Nov	Dec	Yr.
Extreme High (°F)	77	87	91	99	109	115	116	116	113	103	87	77	116
Average High (°F)	56	62	69	78	88	99	104	102	94	81	66	57	80
Average Temp. (°F)	45	50	56	65	74	84	90	88	80	68	54	46	67
Average Low (°F)	33	38	43	51	60	69	76	74	66	54	41	34	53
Extreme Low (°F)	8	16	23	31	40	49	60	56	43	26	21	11	8

Note: Figures cover the years 1948-1990
Source: National Climatic Data Center, International Station Meteorological Climate Summary, 9/96

Average Precipitation/Snowfall/Humidity

Precip./Humidity	Jan	Feb	Mar	Apr	May	Jun	Jul	Aug	Sep	Oct	Nov	Dec	Yr.
Avg. Precip. (in.)	0.5	0.4	0.4	0.2	0.2	0.1	0.4	0.5	0.3	0.2	0.4	0.3	4.0
Avg. Snowfall (in.)	1	Tr	Tr	Tr	0	0	0	0	0	0	Tr	Tr	1
Avg. Rel. Hum. 7am (%)	59	52	41	31	26	20	26	31	30	36	47	56	38
Avg. Rel. Hum. 4pm (%)	32	25	20	15	13	10	14	16	16	18	26	31	20

Note: Figures cover the years 1948-1990; Tr = Trace amounts (<0.05 in. of rain; <0.5 in. of snow)
Source: National Climatic Data Center, International Station Meteorological Climate Summary, 9/96

Weather Conditions

Temperature			Daytime Sky			Precipitation		
10°F & below	32°F & below	90°F & above	Clear	Partly cloudy	Cloudy	0.01 inch or more precip.	0.1 inch or more snow/ice	Thunder-storms
< 1	37	134	185	132	48	27	2	13

Note: Figures are average number of days per year and cover the years 1948-1990
Source: National Climatic Data Center, International Station Meteorological Climate Summary, 9/96

HAZARDOUS WASTE

Superfund Sites

Henderson has no sites on the EPA's Superfund Final National Priorities List.

U.S. Environmental Protection Agency, Final National Priorities List, April 17, 2012

AIR & WATER QUALITY

Air Quality Index

Area	Percent of Days when Air Quality was...[2]					AQI Statistics[2]	
	Good	Moderate	Unhealthy for Sensitive Groups	Unhealthy	Very Unhealthy	Maximum	Median
Area[1]	57.5	35.9	6.6	0.0	0.0	144	47

Note: Air Quality Index (AQI) is an index for reporting daily air quality. EPA calculates the AQI for five major air pollutants regulated by the Clean Air Act: ground-level ozone, particle pollution (aka particulate matter), carbon monoxide, sulfur dioxide, and nitrogen dioxide. The AQI runs from 0 to 500. The higher the AQI value, the greater the level of air pollution and the greater the health concern. There are six AQI categories: "Good" AQI is between 0 and 50. Air quality is considered satisfactory; "Moderate" AQI is between 51 and 100. Air quality is acceptable; "Unhealthy for Sensitive Groups" When AQI values are between 101 and 150, members of sensitive groups may experience health effects; "Unhealthy" When AQI values are between 151 and 200 everyone may begin to experience health effects; "Very Unhealthy" AQI values between 201 and 300 trigger a health alert; "Hazardous" AQI values over 300 trigger warnings of emergency conditions (not shown); (1) Data covers Clark County; (2) Based on 365 days with AQI data in 2011.

Source: U.S. Environmental Protection Agency, AirData Report, 2011

Air Quality Index Pollutants

Area	Percent of Days when AQI Pollutant was...[2]					
	Carbon Monoxide	Nitrogen Dioxide	Ozone	Sulfur Dioxide	Particulate Matter 2.5	Particulate Matter 10
Area[1]	0.0	2.2	78.6	0.0	15.9	3.3

Note: The Air Quality Index (AQI) is an index for reporting daily air quality. EPA calculates the AQI for five major air pollutants regulated by the Clean Air Act: ground-level ozone, particle pollution (also known as particulate matter), carbon monoxide, sulfur dioxide, and nitrogen dioxide. The AQI runs from 0 to 500. The higher the AQI value, the greater the level of air pollution and the greater the health concern; (1) Data covers Clark County; (2) Based on 365 days with AQI data in 2011.

Source: U.S. Environmental Protection Agency, AirData Report, 2011

Air Quality Index Trends

Area	Trend Sites (days)								All Sites (days)
	2003	2004	2005	2006	2007	2008	2009	2010	2010
MSA[1]	42	22	34	35	24	12	5	2	10

Note: Figures are the number of days the AQI value exceeded 100 in a given year. An AQI value greater than 100 indicates that air quality would have been in the unhealthful range on that day. Data from exceptional events are included. These counts are presented in two ways. First, the counts are based on sites having an adequate record of monitoring data during the trend period (trend sites). These counts represent the relative change in the number of days with AQI values greater than 100. In the last column, the counts are based on all sites with data in the most recent year (because it is possible for a site to have data in the most recent year but not enough data to be a trend site); (1) Data covers the Las Vegas-Paradise, NV—see Appendix B for areas included

Source: U.S. Environmental Protection Agency, Air Quality Index Information, "Number of Days with Air Quality Index Values Greater than 100 at Trend Sites, 2000-2010, and at All Sites in 2010"

Maximum Air Pollutant Concentrations: Particulate Matter, Ozone, CO and Lead

	Particulate Matter 10 (ug/m³)	Particulate Matter 2.5 Wtd AM (ug/m³)	Particulate Matter 2.5 24-Hr (ug/m³)	Ozone (ppm)	Carbon Monoxide (ppm)	Lead (ug/m³)
MSA[1] Level	61	7.4	22	0.079	3	n/a
NAAQS[2]	150	15	35	0.075	9	0.15
Met NAAQS[2]	Yes	Yes	Yes	No	Yes	n/a

Note: Data from exceptional events are not included; (1) Data covers the Las Vegas-Paradise, NV—see Appendix B for areas included; (2) National Ambient Air Quality Standards; ppm = parts per million; ug/m³ = micrograms per cubic meter; n/a not available

Concentrations: Particulate Matter 10 (coarse particulate)—highest second maximum 24-hour concentration; Particulate Matter 2.5 Wtd AM (fine particulate)—highest weighted annual mean concentration; Particulate Matter 2.5 24-Hour (fine particulate)—highest 98th percentile 24-hour concentration; Ozone—highest fourth daily maximum 8-hour concentration; Carbon Monoxide—highest second maximum non-overlapping 8-hour concentration; Lead—maximum running 3-month average

Source: U.S. Environmental Protection Agency, CBSA Factbook 2010, Air Quality Statistics by City, 2010

Maximum Air Pollutant Concentrations: Nitrogen Dioxide and Sulfur Dioxide

	Nitrogen Dioxide AM (ppb)	Nitrogen Dioxide 1-Hr (ppb)	Sulfur Dioxide AM (ppb)	Sulfur Dioxide 1-Hr (ppb)	Sulfur Dioxide 24-Hr (ppb)
MSA[1] Level	13.308	55.9	n/a	n/a	n/a
NAAQS[2]	53	100	30	75	140
Met NAAQS[2]	Yes	Yes	n/a	n/a	n/a

Note: Data from exceptional events are not included; (1) Data covers the Las Vegas-Paradise, NV—see Appendix B for areas included; (2) National Ambient Air Quality Standards; ppb = parts per billion; n/a not available

Concentrations: Nitrogen Dioxide AM—highest arithmetic mean concentration; Nitrogen Dioxide 1-Hr—highest 98th percentile 1-hour daily maximum concentration; Sulfur Dioxide AM—highest annual mean concentration; Sulfur Dioxide 1-Hr—highest 99th percentile 1-hour daily maximum concentration; Sulfur Dioxide 24-Hr—highest second maximum 24-hour concentration

Source: U.S. Environmental Protection Agency, CBSA Factbook 2010, Air Quality Statistics by City, 2010

Drinking Water

Water System Name	Pop. Served	Primary Water Source Type	Violations[1]	
			Health Based	Monitoring/ Reporting
City of Henderson	246,000	Surface	0	0

Note: (1) Based on violation data from January 1, 2011 to December 31, 2011 (includes unresolved violations from earlier years)

Source: U.S. Environmental Protection Agency, Office of Ground Water and Drinking Water, Safe Drinking Water Information System (based on data extracted April 18, 2012)

Honolulu, Hawaii

Background

Honolulu, whose name in Hawaiian means "sheltered harbor," is the capital of Hawaii and the seat of Honolulu County. The city sits in one of the most famously attractive areas of the world, on the island of Oahu, with the extinct volcano Diamond Head and Waikiki Beach to the east, and two mountain ranges, the Koolau and the Waianae, in the background. Honolulu is the economic hub of Hawaii, a major seaport and, most importantly, home to a $10 billion tourist industry.

Traditionally home to fishing and horticultural tribal groups, the Hawaiian islands were politically united under the reign of King Kamehameha I, who first moved his triumphant court to Waikiki and subsequently to a site in what is now downtown Honolulu (1804). It was during his time that the port became a center for the sandalwood trade, thus establishing the region as an international presence even before the political interventions of non-Hawaiians.

European activity dates from 1794, when the English sea captain William Brown entered Honolulu, dubbing it Fair Harbor, though many of the Europeans who followed called it Brown's Harbor. Two decades later, the first missionaries arrived. American Congregationalists were followed by French Catholics and, later, Mormons and Anglicans. By the end of the nineteenth century, non-Hawaiians owned most of the land. This economic situation was soon echoed in the area's political developments, which culminated in the 1898 annexation of Hawaii by the U.S.

As is true for many strategically located cities, the events of World War II had a profound effect on Honolulu. The Japanese attack on December 7, 1941, forever etched the name of Pearl Harbor into the national memory. During the war, existing military bases were expanded and new bases built, providing considerable economic stimuli. The Vietnam War also had a dramatic effect on Honolulu; by the end of the twentieth century, military families accounted for 10 percent of the population.

Today, the U.S. military is still a major employer in the city employing more than 45,000 personnel throughout the state. Nearby are the Nimitz-MacArthur Pacific Command Center, Hickam Air Force Base and the Tripler Army Medical Center. Fruit, primarily pineapple, processing and light manufacturing are also important to the economy. Aquaculture, which includes cultivated species of shellfish, finfish and algae, has grown in recent years. There is a small but fast-growing biotechnology sector.

Increasingly, however, tourism has been the private-sector mainstay of Honolulu's economy, with most of the millions of tourists who visit Hawaii annually coming through its port or airport. Honolulu is a required stop for any holiday ship cruising these waters, and it is also the center for the inter-island air services that ferry tourists to various resort locations.

The center of Honolulu's downtown district is dominated by the Iolani Palace, once home to Hawaii's original royal family. Nearby are the State Capitol Building and the State Supreme Court Building, known as Aliiolani Hall. The Aloha Tower Development Corporation, a state agency tasked with redeveloping underused state property, continues its work with plans to modernize the mixed-use space in and around the Aloha Tower Complex along the city's piers.

In 2008 Honolulu residents voted to go forward with the proposed Honolulu High-Capacity Transit Corridor Project. The project details include building a rail line connecting Kapolei in West Oahu to the University of Hawaii at Manoa, and construction began in February 2011. Completion is planned in three phases—2015, 2017, and 2019.

Honolulu, as it has grown along the southern coast of Oahu, has established a mix of residential zones, with single-family dwellings and relatively small multi-unit buildings. The result is that large parts of what is a major metropolitan area feel like cozy neighborhoods. In fact, Honolulu is governed in part through the device of a Neighborhood Board System, which insures maximal local input with regard to planning decisions and city services.

Cultural amenities include the Bishop Museum, the Honolulu Academy of Arts, and the Contemporary Museum, which together offer world-class collections in Polynesian art and artifacts, Japanese, Chinese, and Korean art, and modern art from the world over. Honolulu also hosts a symphony orchestra, the oldest U.S. symphony orchestra west of the Rocky Mountains, which performs at the Neal S. Blaisdell Center.

Barack Obama, the United States' 44th president, is the first president from Hawaii. Obama was born in Honolulu, causing the city a fair amount of attention during the 2008 presidential election.

Honolulu's weather is subtropical, with temperatures moderated by the surrounding ocean and the trade winds. There are only slight variations in temperature from summer to winter. Rain is moderate, though heavier in summer, when it sometimes comes in the form of quick showers while the sun is shining—an effect known locally as "liquid sunshine."

Rankings

General Rankings

- *Men's Health Living* ranked 100 U.S. cities in terms of quality of life. Honolulu was ranked #7 and received a grade of A-. Criteria: number of fitness facilities; air quality; number of physicians; male/female ratio; education levels; household income; cost of living. *Men's Health Living, Spring 2008*
- Honolulu was selected as one of America's best cities by *Bloomberg Businessweek.* The city ranked #3 out of 50. Criteria: number of restaurants, bars and museums per capita; number of colleges, libraries, and professional sports teams; income, poverty, unemployment, crime, and foreclosure rates; percent of population with bachelor's degrees; public school performance; park acres per capita; air quality. *BusinessWeek, "America's 50 Best Cities," September 20, 2011*
- Honolulu was identified as one of the top places to live in the U.S. by Harris Interactive. The city ranked #9 out of 15. Criteria: 2,463 adults (age 18 and over) were polled and asked "if you could live in or near any city in the country except the one you live in or nearest to now, which city would you choose?" The poll was conducted online within the U.S. between September 14 and 20, 2010. *Harris Interactive, November 9, 2011*
- Honolulu was selected as one of "America's Favorite Cities." The city ranked #5 in the "Quality of Life and Visitor Experience" category. Respondents to an online survey were asked to rate 35 top urban destinations in the U.S. from a visitor's perspective. Criteria: noteworthy neighborhoods; skyline/views; public parks and outdoor access; cleanliness; public transportation and pedestrian friendliness; safety; weather; peace and quiet; people-watching; environmental friendliness. *Travelandleisure.com, "America's Favorite Cities 2010," November 2010*
- Honolulu was selected as one of "America's Favorite Cities." The city ranked #5 in the "People" category. Respondents to an online survey were asked to rate 35 top urban destinations in the U.S. from a visitor's perspective. Criteria: attractive; friendly; stylish; intelligent; athletic/active; diverse. *Travelandleisure.com, "America's Favorite Cities 2010," November 2010*
- *Condé Nast Traveler* polled thousands of readers for travel satisfaction. American cities were ranked based on the following criteria: friendliness; atmosphere/ambiance; culture/sites; restaurants; lodging; and shopping. Honolulu appeared in the top 10, ranking #5. *Condé Nast Traveler, 2011 Readers' Choice Awards*

Business/Finance Rankings

- Honolulu was identified as one of the 20 weakest-performing metro areas during the recession and recovery from trough quarter through the third quarter of 2011. Criteria: percent change in employment; percentage point change in unemployment rate; percent change in gross metropolitan product; percent change in House Price Index. *Brookings Institution, MetroMonitor: Tracking Economic Recession and Recovery in America's 100 Largest Metropolitan Areas, December 2011*
- The Honolulu metro area was identified as one of the most debt-ridden places in America by credit reporting agency Equifax. The metro area was ranked #8. Criteria: proportion of average yearly income owed to credit card companies. *Equifax, "The Most Debt-Ridden Cities in America," February 23, 2012*
- Honolulu was identified as one of the top 25 U.S. cities with the most credit card debt by credit reporting bureau Experian. The city was ranked #4. *Experian, March 4, 2011*
- Honolulu was selected as one of the "100 Best Places to Live and Launch" in the U.S. The city ranked #67. The editors at *Fortune Small Business* ranked 296 Census-designated metro areas by business friendliness (Launching Score, % New Businesses) and lifestyle offerings (Living Score). Then they picked the town within each of the top 100 metro areas that best blends business and pleasure. *Fortune Small Business, "100 Best Places to Live and Launch 2008," April 2008*

- *American City Business Journals* ranked America's 261 largest cities in terms of their resident's wealth. Honolulu ranked #23. Criteria: per capita income; median household income; percentage of households with annual incomes of $200,000 or more; median home value. *American City Business Journals, "Where the Money Is: America's Wealth Centers," August 18, 2008*

- The Honolulu metro area appeared on the Milken Institute "2011 Best Performing Metros" list. Rank: #43 out of 200 large metro areas. Criteria: job growth; wage and salary growth; high-tech output growth. *Milken Institute, "2011 Best Performing Metros"*

- The Honolulu metro area was selected as one of the best cities for entrepreneurs in America by *Inc. Magazine.* Criteria: job-growth data for 335 metro areas was analyzed for: recent growth trend; mid-term growth; long-term trend; current year growth. The Honolulu metro area ranked #15 among large metro areas and #80 overall. *Inc. Magazine, "The Best Cities for Doing Business," July 2008*

- *Forbes* ranked the 200 most populous metro areas in the U.S. in terms of the "Best Places for Business and Careers." The Honolulu metro area was ranked #185. Criteria: costs (business and living); job growth (past and projected); income growth; educational attainment; projected economic growth; crime; cultural and recreational opportunities; net migration patterns; number of highly ranked colleges. *Forbes, "Best Places for Business and Careers," June 2011*

Children/Family Rankings

- Honolulu was selected as one of the safest cities for children in America by *Men's Health*. The city ranked #2 of 10. Criteria: accidental death rates for kids ages 5 to 14; number of car seat inspection locations per child; sex offenders per capita; percentage of abused children protected from further abuse; strength of child-restraint and bike-helmet laws. *Men's Health, "The Safest (and Least Safe) Cities for Children," September 2010*

- The Honolulu metro area was selected as one of the "Best Cities for Relocating Families" by Worldwide ERC and Primacy Relocation. The 2008 study looked at nearly 50 factors important to relocating families including: recent job growth; nearby top-ranked colleges; in-state tuition for four-year public colleges; population growth since 2000; pediatricians per 100,000 population; and a Green Living index. *Worldwide ERC and Primacy Relocation, "2008 Best Cities for Relocating Families"*

- *Fit Pregnancy* magazine ranked the 50 best U.S. cities in which to have a baby. Honolulu was ranked #13. Criteria: access to hospitals and doctors; affordability; birthing options; breastfeeding; child care; fertility laws/resources; maternal and infant health risk; parks/stroller friendliness; safety. *Fit Pregnancy, "The Best Cities in America to Have a Baby 2008"*

- Honolulu was chosen as one of America's "100 Best Communities for Young People." The winners were selected based upon detailed information provided about each community's efforts to fulfill five essential promises critical to the well-being of young people: caring adults who are actively involved in their lives; safe places in which to learn and grow; a healthy start toward adulthood; an effective education that builds marketable skills; and opportunities to help others. *America's Promise Alliance, "100 Best Communities for Young People, 2010"*

Culture/Performing Arts Rankings

- Honolulu was selected as one of "America's Top 25 Arts Destinations." The city ranked #24 in the mid-sized city (population 100,000 to 499,999) category. Criteria: readers' top choices for arts travel destinations based on the richness and variety of visual arts sites, activities and events. *American Style, "America's Top 25 Arts Destinations," May 2010*

Dating/Romance Rankings

- Honolulu appeared on *Men's Health's* list of the most sex-happy cities in America. The city ranked #82 of 100. Criteria: condom sales; birth rates; sex toy sales; rates of chlamydia, gonorrhea, and syphilis. *Men's Health, "America's Most Sex-Happy Cities," October 2010*
- *Men's Health* ranked 100 U.S. cities in terms of best (and worst) marriages. Honolulu was ranked #44 (#1 = worst). Criteria: rate of failed marriages; stringency of divorce laws; percentage of population who've split; number of licensed marriage and family therapists. *Men's Health, "Splitsville, USA," May 2010*

- Eli Lily and Company, in partnership with Sperling's BestPlaces, ranked the nation's 50 largest metro areas in terms of the "Most Romantic Cities for Baby Boomers." The Honolulu metro area ranked #13. Criteria: marriage and divorce rates among baby boomers age 45 to 60; great restaurants; dance studios; chocolate, jewelry and flower sales. *Eli Lily and Company, "Most Romantic Cities for Baby Boomers," April 20, 2007*

- The Honolulu metro area was selected as one of the "Best Cities for Relocating Singles" by Worldwide ERC and Primacy Relocation. The area ranked #51 out of the 100 largest metro areas in the U.S. Criteria: recent job growth; recent singles population growth; overall population growth; affordable rental housing; cost-of-living index; expanded arts and recreation opportunities; ratio of single men and single women; affordability of quality higher education (including state residency requirements); diversity index; climate; population density. *Worldwide ERC and Primacy Relocation, "2008 Best Cities for Relocating Singles"*

Education Rankings

- *Men's Health* ranked 100 U.S. cities in terms of their education levels. Honolulu was ranked #7 (#1 = most educated city). Criteria: high school graduation rates; school enrollment; educational attainment; number of households who have outstanding student loans; number of households whose members have taken adult-education courses. *Men's Health, "Where School Is In: The Most and Least Educated Cities," September 12, 2011*

- Honolulu was selected as one of "America's Most Literate Cities." The city ranked #19 out of the 75 largest U.S. cities. Criteria: number of booksellers; library resources; Internet resources; educational attainment; periodical publishing resources; newspaper circulation. *Central Connecticut State University, "America's Most Literate Cities 2011"*

- Honolulu was identified as one of the 100 "smartest" metro areas in the U.S. The area ranked #13. Criteria: the editors rated the collective brainpower of the 100 largest metro areas in the U.S. based on their residents' educational attainment. *American City Business Journals, April 14, 2008*

- Honolulu was identified as one of "America's Brainiest Bastions" by *Portfolio.com.* The metro area ranked #50 out of 200. *Portfolio.com* analyzed levels of educational attainment in the nation's 200 largest metropolitan areas. The editors established scores for five levels of educational attainment, based on relative earning power of adult workers age 25 or older. Scores were determined by comparing the median income for all workers with the median income for those workers at a specified educational level. *Portfolio.com, "America's Brainiest Bastions," December 1, 2010*

Environmental Rankings

- Scarborough Research, a leading market research firm, identified the top local markets for green appliance households. The Honolulu DMA (Designated Market Area) ranked in the top 16 with 40% of consumers reporting that they own an energy-efficient appliance. *Scarborough Research, March 23, 2010*

- Honolulu was selected as one of 22 "Smarter Cities" for energy by the Natural Resources Defense Council. Criteria: investment in green power; energy efficiency measures; conservation. *Natural Resources Defense Council, "2010 Smarter Cities," July 19, 2010*

- Mercer Human Resources Consulting ranked 221 cities worldwide in terms of their eco-ranking. Honolulu ranked #2. Criteria: water availability; water potability; waste removal; sewage; air pollution; traffic congestion. *Mercer Human Resources Consulting, "Mercer 2010 Quality of Living Survey, Eco-City Ranking," May 26, 2010*

- *American City Business Journal* ranked 43 metropolitan areas in terms of their "greenness." The Honolulu metro area ranked #3. Criteria: Forty-one metros in which *ACBJ* has business weeklies, plus Indianapolis and Cleveland, were ranked based on 20 different indicators such as adoption of green technologies, utilization of environmentally sound practices, and air and water quality. *American City Business Journals, "Green City Index," March 11, 2010*

- Honolulu was selected as one of "America's 50 Greenest Cities" by *Popular Science.* The city ranked #14. Criteria: electricity; transportation; green living; recycling and green perspective. *Popular Science, February 2008*

- 100 of the largest metro areas in the U.S. were analyzed in terms of their current drought severity. The Honolulu metro area ranked #52 (#1 = driest). The rankings were based on statistics such as long-term precipitation trends and patterns and the Palmer drought indices. *Sperling's BestPlaces, www.BestPlaces.net, "America's Drought-Riskiest Cities," November 2007*

- The U.S. Conference of Mayors and Wal-Mart Stores sponsor the Mayors' Climate Protection Awards Program. The awards recognize and honor mayors for outstanding and innovative practices that mayors are taking to increase energy efficiency in their cities, and to help curb global warming. Honolulu was a Large City Best Practice Model. *U.S. Conference of Mayors, "2009 Mayors' Climate Protection Awards Program"*

- The Honolulu metro area appeared in *Country Home's* "Best Green Places" report. The area ranked #78 out of 379. Criteria: official energy policies; green power; green buildings; availability of fresh, locally grown food. *Country Home, "Best Green Places," 2008*

- Honolulu was highlighted as one of the top 25 cleanest metro areas for year-round particle pollution (Annual PM 2.5) in the U.S. The area ranked #4. *American Lung Association, State of the Air 2011*

- Honolulu was highlighted as one of the top 25 cleanest metro areas for short-term particle pollution (24-hour PM 2.5) in the U.S. Monitors in these cities reported no days with unhealthful PM 2.5 levels. *American Lung Association, State of the Air 2011*

- Honolulu was highlighted as one of the cleanest metro areas for ozone air pollution in the U.S. The list represents cities with no monitored ozone air pollution in unhealthful ranges. *American Lung Association, State of the Air 2011*

Health/Fitness Rankings

- The American Podiatric Medical Association and *Prevention* magazine ranked 100 American cities based on walkability. Nineteen walking criteria were evaluated including the percentage of adults who walk to work, number of parks per square mile, number of trails for walking and hiking, air pollution, use of mass transit, crime rate, pedestrian fatalities, and percentage of adults who walk for fitness. Honolulu ranked #8. *Prevention, "The Best Walking Cities of 2009," May 2009; American Podiatric Medical Association, "2009 Best Fitness-Walking Cities," April 7, 2009*

- Honolulu was identified as one of the most walkable cities in the U.S. by *WalkScore.com,* a Seattle-based service that rates the convenience and transit access of 10,000 neighborhoods in 2,500 cities. The editors at Grey House Publishing used *WalkScore.com's* online service to look at the scores of 280 cities with populations greater than or equal to 100,000. The top 50 cities were selected. *WalkScore.com, April 2, 2012*

- The Honolulu metro area was selected as one of the worst cities for bed bugs in America by Rollins corporation, the owner of seven pest control companies, including Orkin. The area ranked #17 based on the number of bed bug treatments from January to December 2011. *Rollins, "The Top 50 U.S. Cities for Bed Bugs," March 19, 2012*

- Honolulu was selected as one of the 25 fittest cities in America by *Men's Fitness Online*. It ranked #10 out of America's 50 largest cities. Criteria: fitness centers and sport stores; nutrition; sports participation; TV viewing; overweight/sedentary; junk food; air quality; geography; commute; parks and open space; city recreational facilities; access to healthcare; motivation; mayor and city initiatives; state obesity initiatives. *Men's Fitness, "The Fittest and Fattest Cities in America," March 5, 2012*

- *Men's Health* examined 100 major U.S. cities and selected the best and worst cities for men. Honolulu ranked #19. Criteria: 35 statistical parameters of long life in the categories of health, quality of life, and fitness. *Men's Health, "The 10 Best and Worst Cities for Men 2012," January/February 2012*

- The Honolulu metropolitan area was selected as one of the best metros for hospital care in America by *HealthGrades.com.* The rankings are based on a comprehensive study of patient death and complication rates in the nation's nearly 5,000 hospitals. Hospitals performing in the top 5% nationwide across 26 different medical procedures and diagnoses were identified. *HealthGrades.com* then ranked cities by the highest percentage of these Distinguished Hospitals for Clinical Excellence™. The Honolulu metro area ranked #33. *HealthGrades.com, "America's Top 50 Cities for Hospital Care," January 21, 2012*

- The Honolulu metro area was identified as one of America's "Healthiest Hometowns" by AARP. The metro area ranked #2 out of 10. More than 20 measures of vitality were analyzed including air and water quality and the health and habits of the populace. *AARP, "Healthiest Hometowns," September/October 2008*
- The Honolulu metro area appeared in the 2011 Gallup-Healthways Well-Being Index. The index, based on interviews with more than 350,000 Americans, measured jobs, finances, physical health, emotional state of mind and communities. The metro area ranked #6 out of 190. Criteria: life evaluation; emotional health; work environment; physical health; healthy behaviors; basic access (basic needs optimal for a healthy life, such as access to food and medicine, having health insurance and feeling safe while walking at night). *Gallup-Healthways, "State of Well-Being 2011"*
- *Men's Health* ranked 100 U.S. cities in terms of their activity levels. Honolulu was ranked #24 (#1 = most active city). Criteria: where and how often residents exercise; percentage of households that watch more than 15 hours of cable television a week and buy more than 11 video games a year; death rate from deep-vein thrombosis, a condition linked to sitting for extended periods of time. *Men's Health, "Where Sit Happens: The Most and Least Active Cities in America," June 20, 2011*
- *The Daily Beast* identified the 30 U.S. metro areas with the worst smoking habits. The Honolulu metro area ranked #13. Sixty urban centers with populations of more than one million were ranked based on the following criteria: number of smokers; number of cigarettes smoked per day; fewest attempts to quit. *The Daily Beast, "30 Cities With Smoking Problems," January 3, 2011*

Real Estate Rankings

- *Fortune* ranked the 100 largest metro areas in the U.S. in terms of projected median home price change in 2010. The Honolulu metro area ranked #74. *Fortune, "The 2010 Housing Outlook," December 9, 2009*
- The Honolulu metro area was identified as one of the 20 least affordable housing markets in the U.S. in 2011. The area ranked #1 out of 152 markets with an affordability index of 39.2%. The index measures whether or not a typical family could qualify for a mortgage loan on a typical home. The calculation used assumes a down payment of 20 percent of the home price and a qualifying ratio of 25 percent, meaning that the monthly P&I payment cannot exceed 25 percent of a the median family monthly income. *National Association of Realtors®, Affordability Index of Existing Single-Family Homes for Metropolitan Areas, 2011*
- The Honolulu metro area was identified as one of "America's 25 Weakest Housing Markets" by *Forbes*. The metro area ranked #13. Criteria: metro areas with populations over 500,000 were ranked based on projected home values through 2011. *Forbes.com, "America's 25 Weakest Housing Markets," January 7, 2009*
- The Honolulu metro area was identified as one of America's least affordable cities to buy a house in 2010 by *CNNMoney.com.* The metro area was ranked #3 out of 5. Criteria: median home prices; median family income *CNNMoney.com, "America's Most and Least Affordable Cities to Buy a House," May 21, 2010*
- The Center for Housing Policy ranked 210 U.S. metropolitan areas by the fair market rent for a two-bedroom unit. The Honolulu metro area was ranked #2. (#1 = most expensive) with a rent of $1,704. Criteria: Fair Market Rent (FMR) in effect during the fourth quarter of 2009 based on HUD's fiscal year 2010 FMRs. *The Center for Housing Policy, "Paycheck to Paycheck: Most to Least Expensive Rental Markets in 2009"*
- The Honolulu metro area was identified as one of the markets with the best expected performance in home prices over the next 12 months. *Local Market Monitor, "First Quarter Home Price Forecast for Largest US Markets," March 2, 2011*
- The Honolulu metro area was identified as one of the best U.S. markets to invest in rental property" by HomeVestors and Local Market Monitor. The area ranked #93 out of 100. Criteria: risk-return premium relative to national average. *HomeVestors and Local Market Monitor, "Best 100 U.S. Markets to Invest in Rental Property," March 9, 2012*

Safety Rankings

- Symantec, the makers of Norton, in partnership with Sperling's BestPlaces, ranked the 50 largest cities in the U.S. in terms of their vulnerability to cybercrime. The city ranked #14. Criteria: number of cyberattacks and potential infections; level of Internet access; expenditures on smartphones and computer hardware/software; wireless hotspots; broadband connectivity; Internet usage; online purchases. *Symantec, "Riskiest Online Cities of 2012" February 15, 2012*
- Farmers Insurance Group of Companies, in partnership with Sperling's BestPlaces, ranked 379 metro areas and identified the "Most Secure U.S. Places to Live." The Honolulu metro area ranked #15 out of the top 20 in the large metro area category (500,000 or more residents). Criteria: crime statistics; extreme weather; risk of natural disasters; housing depreciation; foreclosures; environmental hazards; terrorist threats; air quality; life expectancy; mortality rates from cancer and motor vehicle accidents; job loss numbers. *Farmers Insurance Group, "Most Secure U.S. Places to Live 2011," December 15, 2011*
- Allstate ranked the 193 largest cities in America in terms of driver safety. Honolulu ranked #89. In addition, drivers were 6.3% more likely to have had an accident compared to the national average. Allstate researchers analyzed internal property damage reported claims over a two-year period (from January 2008 to December 2009) to protect findings from external influences such as weather or road construction. A weighted average of the two-year numbers determined the annual percentages. The report defines an auto crash as any collision resulting in a property damage claim. *Allstate, "2011 Allstate America's Best Drivers Report™"*
- Honolulu was identified as one of the safest places in the U.S. in terms of its vulnerability to natural disasters and weather extremes. The city ranked #1 out of 10. Data was analyzed to show a metro areas' relative tendency to experience natural disasters (hail, tornadoes, high winds, hurricanes, earthquakes, and brush fires) or extreme weather (abundant rain or snowfall or days that are below freezing or above 90 degrees Fahrenheit). *Forbes, "Safest and Least Safe Places in the U.S.," August 30, 2005*
- Honolulu was selected as one of "America's Safest Cities" by *Forbes*. The city ranked #3 out of 10. Criteria: violent crime rates; traffic fatalities per 100,000 residents. The editors only considered cities with populations above 250,000. *Forbes, "America's Safest Cities," December 15, 2011*
- Honolulu was identified as one of the safest large cities in America by CQ Press. All 34 cities with populations of 500,000 or more that reported crime rates in 2010 for murder, rape, robbery, aggravated assault, burglary, and motor vehicle thefts were ranked. The city ranked #2 out of the top 10. *CQ Press, City Crime Rankings 2011-2012*
- The National Insurance Crime Bureau ranked 366 metro areas in the U.S. in terms of per capita rates of vehicle theft. The Honolulu metro area ranked #50 (#1 = highest rate). Criteria: number of vehicle theft offenses per 100,000 inhabitants in 2010. *National Insurance Crime Bureau, "Hot Spots," June 21, 2011*

Sports/Recreation Rankings

- Honolulu appeared on the *Sporting News* list of the "Best Sports Cities" for 2011. The area ranked #94 out of 271 cities in the U.S. *Sporting News* takes a 12-month snapshot of each city's sports, putting a heavy premium on regular-season won-lost records (from the most recently completed season). Other criteria include: playoff berths, bowl appearances and tournament bids; championships; applicable power ratings; quality of competition; overall fan fervor (measured in part by attendance); abundance of teams (rewarding quality over quantity); stadium and arena quality; ticket availability and prices; franchise ownership; and marquee appeal of athletes. *Sporting News, "Best Sports Cities 2011," October 4, 2011*
- Scarborough Sports Marketing, a leading market research firm, identified the Honolulu DMA (Designated Market Area) as one of the top markets for Summer Olympics fans with more than 65% of adults reporting that they are "very, somewhat, or a little bit interested" in the Summer Olympics. *Scarborough Sports Marketing, July 30, 2008*

Technology Rankings

- Honolulu was selected as a 2011 Digital Cities Survey winner. The city ranked #1 in the large city (250,000 or more population) category. The survey examined and assessed how city governments are utilizing information technology to operate and deliver quality service to their customers and citizens. Survey questions focused on implementation and adoption of online service delivery; planning and governance; and the infrastructure and architecture that make the transformation to digital government possible. *Center for Digital Government, "2011 Digital Cities Survey"*

Transportation Rankings

- Honolulu was identified as one of America's "10 Best Cities for Public Transportation" by *U.S. News & World Report.* The city ranked #8. The ten cities selected had the best combination of public transportation investment, ridership, and safety. *U.S. News & World Report, "10 Best Cities for Public Transportation," February 8, 2011*

- The Honolulu metro area was identified as one of the best U.S. cities to live in without a car by *24/7 Wall St.* The area ranked #4 out of 10. Criteria: percentage of neighborhoods covered by public transit; frequency of service for those neighborhoods; share of jobs reachable within 90 minutes or less by public transit; how accessible amenities are for residents on foot; percentage of commuters who bike to work. The 100 largest metropolitan areas in the U.S. were examined. *24/7 Wall St., "The Best Cities to Live in Car-Free," November 28, 2011*

- The Honolulu metro area was selected as one of 15 "Smarter Cities" for transportation by the Natural Resources Defense Council. The area appeared in the mid-sized metro area (population 250,000 to one million) category. Criteria: public transit availability and use; household automobile ownership and use; innovative, sustainable and affordable transportation programs. *Natural Resources Defense Council, "2011 Smarter Cities," February 23, 2011*

- The Honolulu metro area appeared on *Forbes* list of the best and worst cities for commuters. The metro area ranked #18 out of 60 (#1 is best). Criteria: travel time; road congestion; travel delays. *Forbes.com, "Best and Worst Cities for Commuters," February 16, 2010*

Women/Minorities Rankings

- *Women's Health* examined U.S. cities and identified the 100 best cities for women. Honolulu was ranked #20. Criteria: 30 categories were examined from obesity and breast cancer rates to commuting times and hours spent working out. *Women's Health, "Best Cities for Women 2012"*

- Honolulu was ranked #3 out of 100 metro areas in *SELF Magazine's* ranking of America's healthiest places for women." A panel of experts came up with more than 50 criteria including death and disease rates, environmental indicators, community resources, and lifestyle habits. *SELF Magazine, "Secrets of America's Healthiest Women," December 2008*

Miscellaneous Rankings

- *Men's Health* ranked 100 U.S. cities by their level of sadness. Honolulu was ranked #1 (#1 = saddest city). Criteria: suicide rates; unemployment rates; percentage of households that use antidepressants; percent of population who report feeling blue all or most of the time. *Men's Health, "Frown Towns," November 28, 2011*

- Honolulu was selected as one of the "Best Hair Cities" by *NaturallyCurly.com.* The city was ranked #2. Criteria: humidity levels; pollution; rainfall; average wind speeds; water hardness; beauty salons per capita. *NaturallyCurly.com, "Best/Worst Hair Cities," April 29, 2009*

- Honolulu was selected as one of the most tattooed cities in America by *TotalBeauty.com.* The city was ranked #8. Criteria: number of tattoo and permanent makeup shops per capita; number of tattoo conventions hosted. *TotalBeauty.com, "Top 10 Most Tattooed Cities in America," August 2010*

- The Honolulu metro area appeared in *AutoMD.com's* ranking of the "Best and Worst Cities for Auto Repair." The metro area ranked #49 (#1 is best). The 50 most-populated metro areas in the U.S. were ranked on three critical factors: repair affordability; price disparity range; shop integrity factor. *AutoMD.com, "Advocacy for Repair Shop Fairness Report," February 24, 2010*
- Honolulu was selected as one of America's "10 Meanest Cities" by the National Coalition for the Homeless and The National Law Center on Homelessness & Poverty. The city was ranked #8. Criteria: the number of anti-homeless laws; the enforcement of those laws and severity of penalties; the general political climate towards homeless people; local advocate support for the meanest designation; the city's history of criminalization measures; and the existence of pending or recently enacted criminalization legislation in the city. *National Coalition for the Homeless and The National Law Center on Homelessness & Poverty, "Homes Not Handcuffs: The Criminalization of Homelessness in U.S. Cities," July 2009*

Business Environment

CITY FINANCES

City Government Finances

Component	2009 ($000)	2009 ($ per capita)
Total Revenues	1,919,722	2,120
Total Expenditures	2,027,776	2,239
Debt Outstanding	3,894,964	4,301
Cash and Securities[1]	1,079,682	1,192

Note: (1) Cash and security holdings of a government at the close of its fiscal year, including those of its dependent agencies, utilities, and liquor stores.
Source: U.S Census Bureau, State & Local Government Finances 2009

City Government Revenue by Source

Source	2009 ($000)	2009 ($ per capita)
General Revenue		
From Federal Government	145,765	161
From State Government	84,961	94
From Local Governments	470	1
Taxes		
Property	801,669	885
Sales and Gross Receipts	150,862	167
Personal Income	0	0
Corporate Income	0	0
Motor Vehicle License	92,868	103
Other Taxes	19,559	22
Current Charges	392,519	433
Liquor Store	0	0
Utility	184,687	204
Employee Retirement	0	0

Source: U.S Census Bureau, State & Local Government Finances 2009

City Government Expenditures by Function

Function	2009 ($000)	2009 ($ per capita)	2009 (%)
General Direct Expenditures			
Air Transportation	0	0	0.0
Corrections	0	0	0.0
Education	0	0	0.0
Employment Security Administration	0	0	0.0
Financial Administration	36,567	40	1.8
Fire Protection	95,101	105	4.7
General Public Buildings	44,319	49	2.2
Governmental Administration, Other	36,257	40	1.8
Health	31,954	35	1.6
Highways	130,575	144	6.4
Hospitals	0	0	0.0
Housing and Community Development	61,881	68	3.1
Interest on General Debt	161,374	178	8.0
Judicial and Legal	24,372	27	1.2
Libraries	0	0	0.0
Parking	14	< 1	< 0.1
Parks and Recreation	116,567	129	5.7
Police Protection	230,174	254	11.4
Public Welfare	0	0	0.0
Sewerage	284,287	314	14.0
Solid Waste Management	213,228	235	10.5
Veterans' Services	0	0	0.0
Liquor Store	0	0	0.0
Utility	382,765	423	18.9
Employee Retirement	0	0	0.0

Source: U.S Census Bureau, State & Local Government Finances 2009

Municipal Bond Ratings

Area	Moody's	S&P	Fitch
City	Aa2	AA	AA+

Rating Systems (shown in declining order of credit quality): Moody's– Aaa, Aa, A, Baa, Ba, B, Caa, Ca, C (numerical modifiers 1, 2, and 3 are added to letter-rating); S&P– AAA, AA, A, BBB, BB, B, CCC, CC, C; Fitch– AAA, AA, A, BBB, BB, B, CCC, CC, C. Ratings may be modified by the addition of a plus or minus sign to show relative standing within the major rating categories.
Notes: n/a Not Available; w/d Withdrawn (1) Not Reviewed; (2) Issuer Rating/No General Obligation; (3) Standard and Poor's Issue Credit Rating (ICR) is a current opinion of an obliger with respect to a specific financial obligation, a specific class of financial obligations, or a specific financial program.
Source: U.S. Census Bureau, 2012 Statistical Abstract, Bond Ratings for City Governments by Largest Cities: 2010

DEMOGRAPHICS

Population Growth

Area	1990 Census	2000 Census	2010 Census	Population Growth (%) 1990-2000	Population Growth (%) 2000-2010
City	376,465	371,657	337,256	-1.3	-9.3
MSA[1]	836,231	876,156	953,207	4.8	8.8
U.S.	248,709,873	281,421,906	308,745,538	13.2	9.7

Note: (1) Figures cover the Honolulu, HI Metropolitan Statistical Area—see Appendix B for areas included
Source: U.S. Census Bureau, 2010 Census

Household Size

Area	Persons in Household (%)							Average Household Size
	One	Two	Three	Four	Five	Six	Seven or More	
City	32.9	31.1	14.9	10.2	5.0	2.6	3.4	2.51
MSA[1]	22.8	29.4	17.2	13.9	7.5	4.0	5.2	2.95
U.S.	26.7	32.8	16.1	13.4	6.5	2.6	1.9	2.58

Note: (1) Figures cover the Honolulu, HI Metropolitan Statistical Area—see Appendix B for areas included
Source: U.S. Census Bureau, 2010 Census

Race

Area	White Alone[2] (%)	Black Alone[2] (%)	Asian Alone[2] (%)	AIAN[3] Alone[2] (%)	NHOPI[4] Alone[2] (%)	Other Race Alone[2] (%)	Two or More Races (%)
City	17.9	1.5	54.8	0.2	8.4	0.8	16.3
MSA[1]	20.8	2.0	43.9	0.3	9.5	1.1	22.3
U.S.	72.4	12.6	4.8	0.9	0.2	6.2	2.9

Note: (1) Figures cover the Honolulu, HI Metropolitan Statistical Area—see Appendix B for areas included; (2) Alone is defined as not being in combination with one or more other races; (3) American Indian and Alaska Native; (4) Native Hawaiian and Other Pacific Islander
Source: U.S. Census Bureau, 2010 Census

Hispanic or Latino Origin

Area	Hispanic or Latino (%)	Mexican (%)	Puerto Rican (%)	Cuban (%)	Other Hispanic or Latino (%)
City	5.4	1.7	1.6	0.1	2.1
MSA[1]	8.1	2.3	2.9	0.1	2.9
U.S.	16.3	10.3	1.5	0.6	4.0

Note: Persons of Hispanic or Latino origin can be of any race; (1) Figures cover the Honolulu, HI Metropolitan Statistical Area—see Appendix B for areas included
Source: U.S. Census Bureau, 2010 Census

Segregation

Type	Segregation Indices[1]				Percent Change		
	1990	2000	2010	2010 Rank[2]	1990-2000	1990-2010	2000-2010
Black/White	43.4	41.4	36.9	95	-2.0	-6.4	-4.5
Asian/White	38.5	41.4	42.1	44	2.9	3.5	0.7
Hispanic/White	32.4	32.8	31.9	91	0.3	-0.5	-0.8

Note: Figures are based on an analysis of 1990, 2000, and 2010 Census Decennial Census tract data by William H. Frey, Brookings Institution and the University of Michigan Social Science Data Analysis Network. In this analysis all racial groups (whites, blacks, and asians) are non-Hispanic members of those races. Hispanics are shown as a separate category; All figures cover the Metropolitan Statistical Area (see Appendix B for areas included); (1) Segregation Indices are Dissimilarity Indices that measure the degree to which the minority group is distributed differently than whites across census tracts. They range from 0 (complete integration) to 100 (complete segregation) where the value indicates the percentage of the minority group that needs to move to be distributed exactly like whites; (2) Ranges from 1 (most segregated) to 102 (least segregated); n/a not available.
Source: www.CensusScope.org

Ancestry

Area	German	Irish	English	American	Italian	Polish	French[2]	Scottish	Dutch
City	4.1	3.5	3.3	0.6	1.5	0.8	1.1	0.8	0.6
MSA[1]	5.7	4.4	3.7	0.7	1.8	0.8	1.3	0.9	0.7
U.S.	16.1	11.6	8.8	6.1	5.7	3.2	3.0	1.9	1.6

Note: Figures are the percentage of the total population reporting a particular ancestry. The nine most commonly reported ancestries in the U.S. are shown. Figures include multiple ancestries (e.g. if a person reported being Irish and Italian, they were included in both columns); (1) Figures cover the Honolulu, HI Metropolitan Statistical Area—see Appendix B for areas included; (2) Excludes Basque
Source: U.S. Census Bureau, 2008-2010 American Community Survey 3-Year Estimates

Foreign-Born Population

Area	Percent of Population Born in								
	Any Foreign Country	Mexico	Asia	Europe	Carribean	South America	Central America[2]	Africa	Canada
City	28.3	0.2	23.5	1.2	0.1	0.3	0.1	0.1	0.4
MSA[1]	19.9	0.2	16.0	0.8	0.2	0.3	0.1	0.1	0.3
U.S.	12.8	3.8	3.6	1.6	1.2	0.9	1.0	0.5	0.3

Note: (1) Figures cover the Honolulu, HI Metropolitan Statistical Area—see Appendix B for areas included; (2) Excludes Mexico.
Source: U.S. Census Bureau, 2008-2010 American Community Survey 3-Year Estimates

Marital Status

Area	Never Married	Now Married[2]	Separated	Widowed	Divorced
City	35.8	45.1	1.4	7.4	10.3
MSA[1]	33.2	50.5	1.3	6.1	8.8
U.S.	31.6	49.6	2.2	6.1	10.7

Note: Figures are percentages and cover the population 15 years of age and older; (1) Figures cover the Honolulu, HI Metropolitan Statistical Area—see Appendix B for areas included; (2) Excludes separated
Source: U.S. Census Bureau, 2008-2010 American Community Survey 3-Year Estimates

Age

Area	Percent of Population							Median Age
	Under Age 5	Age 5 to 17	Age 18 to 34	Age 35 to 49	Age 50 to 64	Age 65 to 79	80 Years and Over	
City	4.9	12.5	24.1	20.3	20.4	11.3	6.5	41.3
MSA[1]	6.4	15.7	24.4	20.1	18.9	9.9	4.7	37.8
U.S.	6.5	17.5	23.2	20.7	19.0	9.4	3.6	37.2

Note: (1) Figures cover the Honolulu, HI Metropolitan Statistical Area—see Appendix B for areas included
Source: U.S. Census Bureau, 2010 Census

Male/Female Ratio

Area	Males	Females	Males per 100 Females
City	166,500	170,756	97.5
MSA[1]	477,092	476,115	100.2
U.S.	151,781,326	156,964,212	96.7

Note: (1) Figures cover the Honolulu, HI Metropolitan Statistical Area—see Appendix B for areas included
Source: U.S. Census Bureau, 2010 Census

Religious Groups

Area	Catholic	Baptist	Non-Den.	Methodist[2]	Lutheran	LDS[3]	Pente-costal	Presby-terian[4]	Muslim[5]	Judaism
MSA[1]	18.2	1.9	2.2	0.8	0.3	5.1	4.2	1.5	0.1	0.0
U.S.	19.1	9.3	4.0	4.0	2.3	2.0	1.9	1.6	0.8	0.7

Note: Figures are the number of adherents as a percentage of the total population; (1) Figures cover the Honolulu, HI Metropolitan Statistical Area—see Appendix B for areas included; (2) Methodist/Pietist; (3) Latter Day Saints; (4) Reformed; (5) Figures are estimates
Source: Association of Statisticians of American Religious Bodies, 2010 U.S. Religion Census: Religious Congregations & Membership Study

ECONOMY

Gross Metropolitan Product

Area	2007	2008	2009	2010	2010 Rank[2]
MSA[1]	47.9	49.8	49.9	51.0	51

Note: Figures are in billions of dollars; (1) Figures cover the Honolulu, HI Metropolitan Statistical Area—see Appendix B for areas included; (2) Rank ranges from 1 to 363
Source: The United States Conference of Mayors, "U.S. Metro Economies: GMP and Employment Forecasts," June 2011

Economic Growth

Area	2007-2009 (%)	2010 (%)	2011 (%)	Rank[2]
MSA[1]	0.3	1.2	1.8	90
U.S.	-1.3	2.9	2.5	–

Note: Figures are real Gross Metropolitan Product growth rates and represent annual average percent change; (1) Figures cover the Honolulu, HI Metropolitan Statistical Area—see Appendix B for areas included; (2) Rank ranges from 1 to 363
Source: The United States Conference of Mayors, "U.S. Metro Economies: GMP and Employment Forecasts," June 2011

Metropolitan Area Exports

Area	2005	2006	2007	2008	2009	2010	2010 Rank[2]
MSA[1]	209.6	265.9	359.6	546.0	357.9	439.5	206

Note: Figures are in millions of dollars; (1) Figures cover the Honolulu, HI Metropolitan Statistical Area—see Appendix B for areas included; (2) Rank ranges from 1 to 369
Source: U.S. Department of Commerce, International Trade Administration, Office of Trade & Industry Information, Manufacturing & Services, data extracted April 2, 2012

INCOME

Income

Area	Per Capita ($)	Median Household ($)	Average Household ($)
City	29,609	55,809	74,676
MSA[1]	29,303	70,356	86,269
U.S.	26,942	51,222	70,116

Note: (1) Figures cover the Honolulu, HI Metropolitan Statistical Area—see Appendix B for areas included
Source: U.S. Census Bureau, 2008-2010 American Community Survey 3-Year Estimates

Household Income Distribution

Area	Under $15,000	$15,000 -24,999	$25,000 -34,999	$35,000 -49,999	$50,000 -74,999	$75,000 -99,000	$100,000 -149,999	$150,000 and up
	Percent of Households Earning							
City	11.7	9.4	10.3	13.2	18.3	13.7	13.8	9.6
MSA[1]	8.4	7.0	7.8	11.8	18.3	15.4	18.4	12.9
U.S.	13.0	11.0	10.6	14.2	18.5	12.1	12.2	8.4

Note: (1) Figures cover the Honolulu, HI Metropolitan Statistical Area—see Appendix B for areas included
Source: U.S. Census Bureau, 2008-2010 American Community Survey 3-Year Estimates

Poverty Rate

Area	All Ages	Under 18 Years Old	18 to 64 Years Old	65 Years and Over
City	11.7	14.1	12.0	8.3
MSA[1]	9.2	11.7	8.9	6.8
U.S.	14.4	20.1	13.1	9.4

Note: Figures are percentage of people whose income during the past 12 months was below the poverty level; (1) Figures cover the Honolulu, HI Metropolitan Statistical Area—see Appendix B for areas included
Source: U.S. Census Bureau, 2008-2010 American Community Survey 3-Year Estimates

Personal Bankruptcy Filing Rate

Area	2006	2007	2008	2009	2010	2011
Honolulu County	0.82	1.08	1.44	1.98	2.41	2.06
U.S.	2.00	2.73	3.53	4.61	4.97	4.37

Note: Numbers are per 1,000 population and include Chapter 7 and Chapter 13 filings
Source: Federal Deposit Insurance Corporation, Regional Economic Conditions, March 9, 2012

EMPLOYMENT

Labor Force and Employment

Area	Civilian Labor Force			Workers Employed		
	Dec. 2010	Dec. 2011	% Chg.	Dec. 2010	Dec. 2011	% Chg.
City	441,056	444,744	0.8	419,892	421,022	0.3
MSA[1]	441,056	444,744	0.8	419,892	421,022	0.3
U.S.	153,156,000	153,373,000	0.1	139,159,000	140,681,000	1.1

Note: Data is not seasonally adjusted and covers workers 16 years of age and older; (1) Metropolitan Statistical Area—see Appendix B for areas included
Source: Bureau of Labor Statistics, http://stats.bls.gov

Unemployment Rate

Area	2011											
	Jan.	Feb.	Mar.	Apr.	May	Jun.	Jul.	Aug.	Sep.	Oct.	Nov.	Dec.
City	5.4	5.3	5.0	4.6	4.9	5.7	5.4	5.5	5.7	5.6	5.7	5.3
MSA[1]	5.4	5.3	5.0	4.6	4.9	5.7	5.4	5.5	5.7	5.6	5.7	5.3
U.S.	9.8	9.5	9.2	8.7	8.7	9.3	9.3	9.1	8.8	8.5	8.2	8.3

Note: Data is not seasonally adjusted and covers workers 16 years of age and older; All figures are percentages; (1) Metropolitan Statistical Area—see Appendix B for areas included
Source: Bureau of Labor Statistics, http://stats.bls.gov

Projected Unemployment Rate

Area	2010 (%)	2011 (%)	2012 (%)	2013 (%)
MSA[1]	5.6	5.1	4.9	4.5

Note: (1) Metropolitan Statistical Area—see Appendix B for areas included
Source: The United States Conference of Mayors, "U.S. Metro Economies: GMP and Employment Forecasts," June 2011

Employment by Occupation

Occupation Classification	City (%)	MSA[1] (%)	U.S. (%)
Management, Business, Science, and Arts	34.8	35.0	35.6
Natural Resources, Construction, and Maintenance	6.0	9.4	9.5
Production, Transportation, and Material Moving	7.8	8.3	12.1
Sales and Office	27.8	26.2	25.2
Service	23.6	21.1	17.6

Note: Figures cover employed civilians 16 years of age and older; (1) Figures cover the Honolulu, HI Metropolitan Statistical Area—see Appendix B for areas included
Source: U.S. Census Bureau, 2008-2010 American Community Survey 3-Year Estimates

Employment by Industry

Sector	MSA[1]		U.S.
	Number of Employees	Percent of Total	Percent of Total
Construction	n/a	n/a	4.1
Education and Health Services	59,100	13.2	15.2
Financial Activities	21,100	4.7	5.8
Government	101,300	22.7	16.8
Information	6,600	1.5	2.0
Leisure and Hospitality	64,400	14.4	9.9
Manufacturing	10,700	2.4	8.9
Mining and Logging	n/a	n/a	0.6
Other Services	20,200	4.5	4.0
Professional and Business Services	60,900	13.6	13.3
Retail Trade	47,100	10.5	11.5
Transportation and Utilities	20,000	4.5	3.8
Wholesale Trade	13,700	3.1	4.2

Note: Figures cover non-farm employment as of December 2011 and are not seasonally adjusted; (1) Metropolitan Statistical Area—see Appendix B for areas included; n/a not available
Source: Bureau of Labor Statistics, http://stats.bls.gov

Occupations with Greatest Projected Employment Growth: 2008 – 2018

Occupation[1]	2008 Employment	2018 Projected Employment	Numeric Employment Change	Percent Employment Change
Personal and Home Care Aides	5,110	7,840	2,730	53.4
Retail Salespersons	26,140	28,270	2,130	8.1
Registered Nurses	9,120	10,850	1,730	19.0
Combined Food Preparation and Serving Workers, Including Fast Food	12,720	14,120	1,400	11.0
Elementary School Teachers, Except Special Education	9,450	10,840	1,390	14.7
Postsecondary Teachers	8,720	9,950	1,230	14.1
Nursing Aides, Orderlies, and Attendants	4,970	6,160	1,190	23.9
Landscaping and Groundskeeping Workers	10,140	11,310	1,170	11.5
Security Guards	11,090	12,170	1,080	9.7
Customer Service Representatives	7,020	8,000	980	14.0

Note: Projections cover Hawaii; (1) Sorted by numeric employment change
Source: www.projectionscentral.com, State Occupational Projections, 2008–2018 Long-Term Projections

Fastest Growing Occupations: 2008 – 2018

Occupation[1]	2008 Employment	2018 Projected Employment	Numeric Employment Change	Percent Employment Change
Personal and Home Care Aides	5,110	7,840	2,730	53.4
Home Health Aides	720	1,070	350	48.6
Network Systems and Data Communications Analysts	1,540	2,120	580	37.7
Medical Scientists, Except Epidemiologists	410	540	130	31.7
Self-Enrichment Education Teachers	2,080	2,690	610	29.3
Skin Care Specialists	380	490	110	28.9
Pharmacy Technicians	910	1,170	260	28.6
Captains, Mates, and Pilots of Water Vessels	530	660	130	24.5
Respiratory Therapists	410	510	100	24.4
Hairdressers, Hairstylists, and Cosmetologists	2,130	2,650	520	24.4

Note: Projections cover Hawaii; (1) Sorted by percent employment change and excludes occupations with numeric employment change less than 100
Source: www.projectionscentral.com, State Occupational Projections, 2008–2018 Long-Term Projections

Average Wages

Occupation	$/Hr.	Occupation	$/Hr.
Accountants and Auditors	30.56	Maids and Housekeeping Cleaners	14.88
Automotive Mechanics	22.37	Maintenance and Repair Workers	20.28
Bookkeepers	17.73	Marketing Managers	45.74
Carpenters	33.41	Nuclear Medicine Technologists	37.59
Cashiers	10.79	Nurses, Licensed Practical	21.49
Clerks, General Office	14.69	Nurses, Registered	41.60
Clerks, Receptionists/Information	14.52	Nursing Aides/Orderlies/Attendants	13.85
Clerks, Shipping/Receiving	15.62	Packers and Packagers, Hand	10.01
Computer Programmers	32.91	Physical Therapists	36.72
Computer Support Specialists	24.28	Postal Service Mail Carriers	26.30
Computer Systems Analysts	33.00	Real Estate Brokers	n/a
Cooks, Restaurant	13.99	Retail Salespersons	13.11
Dentists	71.85	Sales Reps., Exc. Tech./Scientific	20.99
Electrical Engineers	39.48	Sales Reps., Tech./Scientific	31.88
Electricians	34.74	Secretaries, Exc. Legal/Med./Exec.	18.51
Financial Managers	44.59	Security Guards	12.01
First-Line Supervisors/Managers, Sales	22.47	Surgeons	93.71
Food Preparation Workers	11.31	Teacher Assistants	13.20
General and Operations Managers	49.88	Teachers, Elementary School	26.40
Hairdressers/Cosmetologists	18.04	Teachers, Secondary School	26.00
Internists	112.29	Telemarketers	13.11
Janitors and Cleaners	12.05	Truck Drivers, Heavy/Tractor-Trailer	21.19
Landscaping/Groundskeeping Workers	13.24	Truck Drivers, Light/Delivery Svcs.	15.58
Lawyers	55.89	Waiters and Waitresses	11.68

Note: Wage data covers the Honolulu, HI Metropolitan Statistical Area—see Appendix B for areas included. Hourly wages for elementary/secondary school teachers and teacher assistants were calculated by the editors from annual wage data assuming a 40 hour work week; n/a not available.
Source: Bureau of Labor Statistics, Metro Area Occupational Employment and Wage Estimates, May 2011

RESIDENTIAL REAL ESTATE

Building Permits

Area	Single-Family			Multi-Family			Total		
	2010	2011	Pct. Chg.	2010	2011	Pct. Chg.	2010	2011	Pct. Chg.
City	n/a	n/a	n/a	n/a	n/a	n/a	n/a	n/a	n/a
MSA[1]	879	734	-16.5	1,012	990	-2.2	1,891	1,724	-8.8
U.S.	447,311	418,498	-6.4	157,299	205,563	30.7	604,610	624,061	3.2

Note: (1) Metropolitan Statistical Area—see Appendix B for areas included; figures represent new, privately-owned housing units authorized (unadjusted data); All permit data are based on estimates with imputation.
Source: U.S. Census Bureau, Manufacturing, Mining, and Construction Statistics, Building Permits, 2010, 2011

Homeownership Rate

Area	2005 (%)	2006 (%)	2007 (%)	2008 (%)	2009 (%)	2010 (%)	2011 (%)
MSA[1]	58.0	58.4	58.8	57.2	57.6	54.9	54.1
U.S.	68.9	68.8	68.1	67.8	67.4	66.9	66.1

Note: (1) Metropolitan Statistical Area—see Appendix B for areas included
Source: U.S. Census Bureau, Housing Vacancies and Homeownership Annual Statistics: 2011

Housing Vacancy Rates

Area	Gross Vacancy Rate[2] (%)			Year-Round Vacancy Rate[3] (%)			Rental Vacancy Rate[4] (%)			Homeowner Vacancy Rate[5] (%)		
	2009	2010	2011	2009	2010	2011	2009	2010	2011	2009	2010	2011
MSA[1]	10.9	11.5	12.1	9.4	10.0	10.9	6.9	7.2	6.9	0.8	1.0	0.7
U.S.	14.5	14.3	14.2	11.3	11.3	11.1	10.6	10.2	9.5	2.6	2.6	2.5

Note: (1) Metropolitan Statistical Area—see Appendix B for areas included; (2) The percentage of the total housing inventory that is vacant; (3) The percentage of the housing inventory (excluding seasonal units) that is year-round vacant; (4) The percentage of rental inventory that is vacant for rent; (5) The percentage of homeowner inventory that is vacant for sale
Source: U.S. Census Bureau, Housing Vacancies and Homeownership Annual Statistics: 2011

TAXES

State Corporate Income Tax Rates

State	Tax Rate (%)	Income Brackets ($)	Num. of Brackets	Financial Institution Tax Rate (%)[a]	Federal Income Tax Ded.
Hawaii	4.4 - 6.4 (g)	25,000 - 100,001	3	7.92 (g)	No

Note: Tax rates as of January 1, 2012; (a) Rates listed are the corporate income tax rate applied to financial institutions or excise taxes based on income. Some states have other taxes based upon the value of deposits or shares; (g) Hawaii taxes capital gains at 4%. Financial institutions pay a franchise tax of 7.92% of taxable income (in lieu of the corporate income tax and general excise taxes).
Source: Federation of Tax Administrators, "State Corporate Income Tax Rates, 2012"

State Individual Income Tax Rates

State	Tax Rate (%)	Income Brackets ($)	Num. of Brackets	Personal Exempt. ($)[1] Single	Personal Exempt. ($)[1] Dependents	Fed. Inc. Tax Ded.
Hawaii	1.4 - 11.00	2,400 (b)-200,001 (b)	12	1,040	1,040	No

Note: Tax rates as of January 1, 2012; Local- and county-level taxes are not included; n/a not applicable; (1) Married joint filers generally receive double the single exemption; (b) For joint returns, taxes are twice the tax on half the couple's income.
Source: Federation of Tax Administrators, "State Individual Income Tax Rates, 2012"

Various State and Local Tax Rates

State	State and Local Sales and Use (%)	State Sales and Use (%)	Gasoline[1] (¢/gal.)	Cigarette[2] ($/pack)	Spirits[3] ($/gal.)	Wine[4] ($/gal.)	Beer[5] ($/gal.)
Hawaii	4.5	4.00 (c)	47.1	3.20	5.98	1.38	0.93

Note: All tax rates as of January 1, 2012 except beer, wine and spirits (September 1, 2011); (1) The American Petroleum Institute has developed a methodology for determining the average tax rate on a gallon of fuel. Rates may include any of the following: excise taxes, environmental fees, storage tank fees, other fees or taxes, general sales tax, and local taxes. In states where gasoline is subject to the general sales tax, or where the fuel tax is based on the average sale price, the average rate determined by API is sensitive to changes in the price of gasoline. States that fully or partially apply general sales taxes to gasoline: CA, CO, GA, IL, IN, MI, NY; (2) The federal excise tax of $1.0066 per pack and local taxes are not included; (3) Rates are those applicable to off-premise sales of 40% alcohol by volume (a.b.v.) distilled spirits in 750ml containers. Local excise taxes are excluded; (4) Rates are those applicable to off-premise sales of 11% a.b.v. non-carbonated wine in 750ml containers; (5) Rates are those applicable to off-premise sales of 4.7% a.b.v. beer in 12 ounce containers; (c) The sales taxes in Hawaii, New Mexico and South Dakota have broad bases that include many services, so their rates are not strictly comparable to other states.
Source: Tax Foundation, 2012 Facts & Figures: How Does Your State Compare?

State-Local Tax Burdens

Area	Rate (%)	Rank[1]	Per Capita Taxes Paid to Home State ($)	Total State and Local Per Capita Taxes Paid ($)	Per Capita Income ($)
Hawaii	9.6	22	3,356	4,399	45,725
U.S. Average	9.8	-	3,057	4,160	42,539

Note: Figures cover 2009; (1) Rank ranges from 1 to 50 where 1 is highest tax burden
Source: Tax Foundation, State-Local Tax Burdens, All States, 2009

State Business Tax Climate Index Rankings

State	Overall Rank	Corporate Tax Index Rank	Individual Income Tax Index Rank	Sales Tax Index Rank	Unemployment Insurance Tax Index Rank	Property Tax Index Rank
Hawaii	35	4	41	31	30	15

Note: The index is a measure of how each state's tax laws affect economic performance. The lower the rank, the more favorable a state's tax system is for business. States without a given tax are given a ranking of 1.
Source: Tax Foundation, Major Components of the State Business Tax Climate Index, FY 2012

COMMERCIAL UTILITIES

Typical Monthly Electric Bills

Area	Commercial Service ($/month)		Industrial Service ($/month)	
	1,500 kWh	40 kW demand 14,000 kWh	1,000 kW demand 200,000 kWh	50,000 kW demand 15,000,000 kWh
City	518	4,209	69,167	4,677,360
Average[1]	189	1,616	25,197	1,470,813

Note: Based on total rates in effect July 1, 2011; (1) average based on 184 utilities surveyed
Source: Edison Electric Institute, Typical Bills and Average Rates Report, Summer 2011

TRANSPORTATION

Means of Transportation to Work

Area	Car/Truck/Van		Public Transportation			Bicycle	Walked	Other Means	Worked at Home
	Drove Alone	Car-pooled	Bus	Subway	Railroad				
City	57.0	12.7	12.6	0.0	0.0	1.8	9.7	3.2	3.0
MSA[1]	64.4	14.9	8.1	0.0	0.0	1.1	5.5	2.6	3.4
U.S.	76.0	10.2	2.7	1.7	0.5	0.5	2.8	1.3	4.2

Note: Figures are percentages and cover workers 16 years of age and older; (1) Figures cover the Honolulu, HI Metropolitan Statistical Area—see Appendix B for areas included
Source: U.S. Census Bureau, 2008-2010 American Community Survey 3-Year Estimates

Travel Time to Work

Area	Less Than 10 Minutes	10 to 19 Minutes	20 to 29 Minutes	30 to 44 Minutes	45 to 59 Minutes	60 to 89 Minutes	90 Minutes or More
City	10.0	34.2	22.0	25.4	4.9	2.7	0.8
MSA[1]	9.8	25.0	20.0	27.6	9.3	6.6	1.7
U.S.	13.9	30.1	20.8	19.8	7.5	5.5	2.5

Note: Figures are percentages and include workers 16 years old and over; (1) Figures cover the Honolulu, HI Metropolitan Statistical Area—see Appendix B for areas included
Source: U.S. Census Bureau, 2008-2010 American Community Survey 3-Year Estimates

Travel Time Index

Area	1985	1990	1995	2000	2005	2010
Urban Area[1]	1.10	1.16	1.17	1.15	1.18	1.18
Average[2]	1.11	1.16	1.18	1.21	1.25	1.20

Note: Travel Time Index—the ratio of travel time in the peak period to the travel time at free-flow conditions. A value of 1.30 indicates a 20-minute free-flow trip takes 26 minutes in the peak. Free-flow speeds (60 mph on freeways and 35 mph on principal arterials) are used as the comparison threshold; (1) Covers the Honolulu HI urban area; (2) average of 439 urban areas
Source: Texas Transportation Institute, Urban Mobility Report 2011, September 2011

Public Transportation

Agency Name / Mode of Transportation	Vehicles Operated in Maximum Service	Annual Unlinked Passenger Trips ('000)	Annual Passenger Miles ('000)
City and County of Honolulu Dept. of Transportation Services (DTS)			
Bus (purchased transportation)	428	73,158.6	386,225.0
Demand Response (purchased transportation)	134	790.4	9,485.4
Demand Response Taxi (purchased transportation)	114	92.2	391.7

Source: Federal Transit Administration, National Transit Database, 2010

Air Transportation

Airport Name and Code / Type of Service	Passenger Airlines[1]	Passenger Enplanements	Freight Carriers[2]	Freight (lbs.)
Honolulu International (HNL)				
Domestic service (U.S. carriers - 2011)	15	6,744,217	15	283,177,378
International service (U.S. carriers - 2010)	8	562,697	10	123,692,883

Note: (1) Includes all U.S.-based major, minor and commuter airlines that carried at least one passenger during the year; (2) Includes all U.S.-based airlines and freight carriers that transported at least one pound of freight during the year

Source: Bureau of Transportation Statistics, The Intermodal Transportation Database, Air Carriers: T-100 Domestic Market (U.S. Carriers), 2011; Bureau of Transportation Statistics, The Intermodal Transportation Database, Air Carriers: T-100 International Market (U.S. Carriers), 2010

Other Transportation Statistics

Major Highways:	None
Amtrak Service:	No
Major Waterways/Ports:	Port of Honolulu

Source: Amtrak.com; Google Maps

BUSINESSES

Major Business Headquarters

Company Name	Rankings	
	Fortune[1]	Forbes[2]
No companies listed	-	-

Note: (1) Fortune 500—companies that produce a 10-K are ranked 1 to 500 based on 2010 revenue; (2) all private companies with at least $2 billion in annual revenue are ranked 1 to 212; companies listed are headquartered in the city; dashes indicate no ranking

Source: Fortune, "Fortune 500," May 23, 2011; Forbes, "America's Largest Private Companies," November 16, 2011

Minority- and Women-Owned Businesses

Group	All Firms		Firms with Paid Employees			
	Firms	Sales ($000)	Firms	Sales ($000)	Employees	Payroll ($000)
Asian	24,262	10,337,119	6,013	9,505,117	58,665	2,020,268
Black	373	155,621	51	148,102	1,143	58,161
Hispanic	1,133	138,484	111	114,435	1,275	32,060
Women	12,530	2,456,477	2,063	2,068,992	18,903	518,607
All Firms	42,030	46,813,051	11,887	45,343,943	250,071	9,395,949

Note: Figures cover firms located in the city; minority- and women-owned business are defined as firms in which the corresponding group own 51% or more of the stock or equity of the company

Source: U.S. Census Bureau, 2007 Economic Census, Survey of Business Owners

HOTELS

Hotels/Motels

Area	5 Star		4 Star		3 Star		2 Star		1 Star		Not Rated	
	Num.	Pct.[3]	Num.	Pct.[3]	Num.	Pct.[3]	Num.	Pct.[3]	Num.	Pct.[3]	Num.	Pct.[3]
City[1]	4	4.5	13	14.6	39	43.8	28	31.5	0	0.0	5	5.6
Total[2]	133	0.9	940	6.5	4,569	31.8	7,033	48.9	351	2.4	1,343	9.3

Note: (1) Figures cover Honolulu and vicinity; (2) Figures cover all 100 cities in this book; (3) Percentage of hotels which have a given star rating; Star ratings are determined by expedia.com and offer an indication of the general quality of a particular hotel.
Source: expedia.com, April 25, 2012

The Honolulu, HI metro area is home to two of the best hotels in the U.S. according to *Travel & Leisure*: **Halekulani (#15); Royal Hawaiian, A Luxury Collection Resort** (#193). Criteria: service; location; rooms; food; and value. *Travel & Leisure, "T+L 500, The World's Best Hotels 2012"*

The Honolulu, HI metro area is home to one of the best hotels in the U.S. according to *Condé Nast Traveler*: **Halekulani** (#36). The selections are based on over 25,000 responses to the magazine's annual Readers' Choice Survey. *Condé Nast Traveler, "2011 Readers' Choice Awards"*

EVENT SITES

Major Stadiums, Arenas, and Auditoriums

Name	Max. Capacity
Aloha Stadium	50,000
Neal S. Blaisdell Center	8,800

Source: Original research

Convention Centers

Name	Overall Space (sq. ft.)	Exhibit Space (sq. ft.)	Meeting Space (sq. ft.)	Meeting Rooms
Hawaii Convention Center	n/a	149,768	200,000	47

Note: n/a not available
Source: Original research

Living Environment

COST OF LIVING

Cost of Living Index

Composite Index	Groceries	Housing	Utilities	Trans-portation	Health Care	Misc. Goods/ Services
168.0	155.8	252.5	161.8	125.9	123.4	120.4

Note: U.S. = 100; Figures cover the Honolulu HI urban area.
Source: The Council for Community and Economic Research, ACCRA Cost of Living Index, 2011

Grocery Prices

Area[1]	T-Bone Steak ($/pound)	Frying Chicken ($/pound)	Whole Milk ($/half gal.)	Eggs ($/dozen)	Orange Juice ($/64 oz.)	Coffee ($/11.5 oz.)
City[2]	8.32	1.85	3.50	3.18	4.68	6.83
Avg.	9.25	1.18	2.22	1.66	3.19	4.40
Min.	6.70	0.88	1.31	0.95	2.46	2.94
Max.	14.30	2.16	3.50	3.18	4.75	6.83

Note: (1) Values for the local area are compared with the average, minimum and maximum values for all 335 areas in the Cost of Living Index; (2) Figures cover the Honolulu HI urban area; **T-Bone Steak** *(price per pound);* **Frying Chicken** *(price per pound, whole fryer);* **Whole Milk** *(half gallon carton);* **Eggs** *(price per dozen, Grade A, large);* **Orange Juice** *(64 oz. Tropicana or Florida Natural);* **Coffee** *(11.5 oz. can, vacuum-packed, Maxwell House, Hills Bros, or Folgers).*
Source: The Council for Community and Economic Research, ACCRA Cost of Living Index, 2011

Housing and Utility Costs

Area[1]	New Home Price ($)	Apartment Rent ($/month)	All Electric ($/month)	Part Electric ($/month)	Other Energy ($/month)	Telephone ($/month)
City[2]	666,923	2,702	339.16	-	-	24.97
Avg.	285,990	839	163.23	89.00	77.52	26.92
Min.	188,005	460	125.58	45.39	33.89	17.98
Max.	1,197,028	3,244	339.16	181.97	348.69	40.01

Note: (1) Values for the local area are compared with the average, minimum and maximum values for all 335 areas in the Cost of Living Index; (2) Figures cover the Honolulu HI urban area; **New Home Price** *(2,400 sf living area, 8,000 sf lot, in urban area with full utilities);* **Apartment Rent** *(950 sf 2 bedroom/1.5 or 2 bath, unfurnished, excluding all utilities except water);* **All Electric** *(average monthly cost for an all-electric home);* **Part Electric** *(average monthly cost for a part-electric home);* **Other Energy** *(average monthly cost for natural gas, fuel oil, coal, wood, and any other forms of energy except electricity);* **Telephone** *(price includes basic monthly rate for a private residential line plus additional local usage charges incurred by a family of four).*
Source: The Council for Community and Economic Research, ACCRA Cost of Living Index, 2011

Health Care, Transportation, and Other Costs

Area[1]	Doctor ($/visit)	Dentist ($/visit)	Optometrist ($/visit)	Gasoline ($/gallon)	Beauty Salon ($/visit)	Men's Shirt ($)
City[2]	128.23	94.93	126.91	3.99	48.51	45.37
Avg.	93.88	81.72	90.54	3.48	32.65	25.06
Min.	60.00	55.33	53.66	3.18	19.78	13.44
Max.	154.98	145.97	183.72	4.31	63.21	46.00

Note: (1) Values for the local area are compared with the average, minimum and maximum values for all 335 areas in the Cost of Living Index; (2) Figures cover the Honolulu HI urban area; **Doctor** *(general practitioners routine exam of an established patient);* **Dentist** *(adult teeth cleaning and periodic oral examination);* **Optometrist** *(full vision eye exam for established adult patient);* **Gasoline** *(one gallon regular unleaded, national brand, including all taxes, cash price at self-service pump if available);* **Beauty Salon** *(woman's shampoo, trim, and blow-dry);* **Men's Shirt** *(cotton/polyester dress shirt, pinpoint weave, long sleeves).*
Source: The Council for Community and Economic Research, ACCRA Cost of Living Index, 2011

HOUSING

House Price Index (HPI)

Area	National Ranking[2]	Quarterly Change (%)	One-Year Change (%)	Five-Year Change (%)
MSA[1]	24	-0.02	0.25	-5.00
U.S.[3]	-	-0.10	-2.43	-19.16

Note: The HPI is a weighted repeat sales index. It measures average price changes in repeat sales or refinancings on the same properties. This information is obtained by reviewing repeat mortgage transactions on single-family properties whose mortgages have been purchased or securitized by Fannie Mae or Freddie Mac in January 1975; (1) Metropolitan/Micropolitan Statistical Area—see Appendix B for areas included; (2) Rankings are based on annual percentage change for all metro areas containing at least 15,000 transactions over the last 10 years and ranges from 1 to 306; (3) figures based on a weighted average of Census Division estimates using a purchase only index; all figures are for the period ending December 31, 2011
Source: Federal Housing Finance Agency, House Price Index, February 23, 2012

House Price Valuations

Area	Q4 2005		Q4 2006		Q4 2007		Q4 2008		Q4 2009	
	Price ($000)	Over-valuation	Price ($000)	Over-valuation	Price ($000)	Over-valuation	Price ($000)	Over-valuation	Price ($000)	Over-valuation
MSA[1]	607.6	39.9	616.3	31.9	642.3	29.7	658.1	29.5	587.8	13.6

Note: Figures show the percentage of over- or under-valuation of single family homes relative to statistically normal house values (e.g. a value of 23.6 indicates that house values are 23.6% overvalued). Statistically normal house values are based on house prices, interest rates, household incomes, population densities, and any historical premiums or discounts metropolitan areas have exhibited over time; (1) Figures cover the Honolulu, HI - see Appendix B for areas included
Source: Global Insight/PNC Financial Services Group, House Prices in America: 4th Quarter 2009 Update

Median Single-Family Home Prices

Area	2009	2010	2011p	Percent Change 2010 to 2011
MSA[1]	596.2	607.6	597.0	-1.7
U.S. Average	172.1	173.1	166.2	-4.0

Note: Figures are median sales prices of existing single-family homes in thousands of dollars; (p) preliminary; n/a not available; (1) Metropolitan Statistical Area—see Appendix B for areas included
Source: National Association of Realtors, Median Sales Price of Existing Single-Family Homes for Metropolitan Areas, 4th Quarter 2011

Affordability Index of Existing Single-Family Homes

Area	2009	2010	2011p	Percent Change 2010 to 2011
MSA[1]	35.1	36.2	39.2	8.3

Note: The housing affordability index measures whether or not a typical family could qualify for a mortgage loan on a typical home. The higher the index, the greater the household purchasing power. An index of 100 is defined as the point where a median-income household has exactly enough income to qualify for the purchase of a median-priced existing single-family home, assuming a 20 percent downpayment and 25 percent of gross income devoted to mortgage principal and interest payments; (p) preliminary; n/a not available; (1) Metropolitan Statistical Area—see Appendix B for areas included
Source: National Association of Realtors, Affordability Index of Existing Single-Family Homes, 2011

Median Apartment Condo-Coop Home Prices

Area	2009	2010	2011p	Percent Change 2010 to 2011
MSA[1]	310.0	312.1	300.7	-3.7
U.S. Average	175.6	171.7	165.1	-3.8

Note: Figures are median sales prices of existing apartment condo-coop homes in thousands of dollars; (p) preliminary; n/a not available; (1) Metropolitan Statistical Area—see Appendix B for areas included
Source: National Association of Realtors, Median Sales Price of Existing Apartment Condo-Coop Homes for Metropolitan Areas, 4th Quarter 2011

Year Housing Structure Built

Area	2005 or Later	2000 -2004	1990 -1999	1980 -1989	1970 -1979	1960 -1969	1950 -1959	Before 1950	Median Year
City	3.2	2.4	8.2	9.4	27.6	23.1	13.6	12.5	1970
MSA[1]	4.0	5.5	12.3	12.6	26.2	19.7	11.6	8.2	1974
U.S.	5.0	8.6	14.0	14.1	16.3	11.3	11.2	19.6	1975

Note: Figures are percentages except for Median Year; (1) Figures cover the Honolulu, HI Metropolitan Statistical Area—see Appendix B for areas included
Source: U.S. Census Bureau, 2008-2010 American Community Survey 3-Year Estimates

HEALTH

Health Risk Data

Category	MSA[1] (%)	U.S. (%)
Adults who have been told they have high blood pressure[2]	31.1	28.7
Adults who have been told they have high blood cholesterol[2]	39.0	37.5
Adults who have been told they have diabetes[3]	8.5	8.7
Adults who have been told they have arthritis[2]	20.3	26.0
Adults who have been told they currently have asthma	9.0	9.1
Adults who are current smokers	13.1	17.3
Adults who are heavy drinkers[4]	6.3	5.0
Adults who are binge drinkers[5]	17.4	15.1
Adults who are overweight (BMI 25.0 - 29.9)	34.2	36.2
Adults who are obese (BMI 30.0 - 99.8)	21.9	27.5
Adults who participated in any physical activities in the past month	80.3	76.1
Adults 50+ who have ever had a sigmoidoscopy or colonoscopy	61.8	65.2
Women aged 40+ who have had a mammogram within the past two years	78.4	75.2
Men aged 40+ who have had a PSA test within the past two years	41.2	53.2
Adults aged 65+ who have had flu shot within the past year	75.4	67.5
Adults aged 18–64 who have any kind of health care coverage	92.6	82.2

Note: Data as of 2010 unless otherwise noted; (1) Figures cover the Honolulu, HI Metropolitan Statistical Area—see Appendix B for areas included; (2) Data as of 2009; (3) Figures do not include pregnancy-related, borderline, or pre-diabetes; (4) Heavy drinkers are classified as males having more than two drinks per day or females having more than one drink per day; (5) Binge drinkers are classified as males having five or more drinks on one occasion or females having four or more drinks on one occasion
Source: Centers for Disease Control and Prevention, Behaviorial Risk Factor Surveillance System, SMART: Selected Metropolitan/Micropolitan Area Risk Trends, 2009, 2010

Mortality Rates for the Top 10 Causes of Death in the U.S.

ICD-10[a] Sub-Chapter	ICD-10[a] Code	Age-Adjusted Mortality Rate[1] per 100,000 population	
		County[2]	U.S.
Malignant neoplasms	C00-C97	137.8	175.6
Ischaemic heart diseases	I20-I25	70.4	121.6
Other forms of heart disease	I30-I51	56.5	48.6
Chronic lower respiratory diseases	J40-J47	17.3	42.3
Cerebrovascular diseases	I60-I69	38.2	40.6
Organic, including symptomatic, mental disorders	F01-F09	30.7	26.7
Other degenerative diseases of the nervous system	G30-G31	12.3	24.7
Other external causes of accidental injury	W00-X59	21.7	24.4
Diabetes mellitus	E10-E14	17.1	21.7
Hypertensive diseases	I10-I15	9.4	18.2

Note: (a) ICD-10 = International Classification of Diseases 10th Revision; (1) Mortality rates are a three year average covering 2007-2009; (2) Figures cover Honolulu County
Source: Centers for Disease Control and Prevention, National Center for Health Statistics. Underlying Cause of Death 1999-2009 on CDC WONDER Online Database, released 2012. Data for year 2009 are compiled from the Multiple Cause of Death File 2009, Series 20 No. 2O, 2012, Data for year 2008 are compiled from the Multiple Cause of Death File 2008, Series 20 No. 2N, 2011, Data for year 2007 are compiled from Multiple Cause of Death File 2007, Series 20 No. 2M, 2010.

Mortality Rates for Selected Causes of Death

ICD-10[a] Sub-Chapter	ICD-10[a] Code	Age-Adjusted Mortality Rate[1] per 100,000 population	
		County[2]	U.S.
Assault	X85-Y09	1.9	5.7
Human immunodeficiency virus (HIV) disease	B20-B24	1.5	3.3
Influenza and pneumonia	J09-J18	14.9	16.4
Intentional self-harm	X60-X84	9.0	11.5
Malnutrition	E40-E46	0.8	0.8
Obesity and other hyperalimentation	E65-E68	1.8	1.6
Transport accidents	V01-V99	6.9	13.7
Viral hepatitis	B15-B19	2.7	2.2

Note: (a) ICD-10 = International Classification of Diseases 10th Revision; (1) Mortality rates are a three year average covering 2007-2009; (2) Figures cover Honolulu County
Source: Centers for Disease Control and Prevention, National Center for Health Statistics. Underlying Cause of Death 1999-2009 on CDC WONDER Online Database, released 2012. Data for year 2009 are compiled from the Multiple Cause of Death File 2009, Series 20 No. 2O, 2012, Data for year 2008 are compiled from the Multiple Cause of Death File 2008, Series 20 No. 2N, 2011, Data for year 2007 are compiled from Multiple Cause of Death File 2007, Series 20 No. 2M, 2010.

Distribution of Physicians and Dentists

Area[1]	Dentists[2]	D.O.[3]	M.D.[4] Total	M.D.[4] Family/General Practice	M.D.[4] Pediatrics	M.D.[4] Medical Specialties	M.D.[4] Surgical Specialties
Local (number)	568	138	2,178	195	189	866	481
Local (rate[5])	6.3	1.5	24.1	2.2	2.1	9.6	5.3
U.S. (rate[5])	4.5	1.9	18.3	2.5	1.4	6.8	4.1

Note: Data as of 2008 unless noted; (1) Local data covers Honolulu County; (2) Data as of 2007; (3) Doctor of Osteopathic Medicine; (4) Includes active, non-federal, patient-care, office-based Doctors of Medicine; (5) rate per 10,000 population
Source: Area Resource File (ARF). 2009-2010 Release. U.S. Department of Health and Human Services, Health Resources and Services Administration, Bureau of Health Professions, Rockville, MD, August 2010

EDUCATION

Public School District Statistics

District Name	Schls	Pupils	Pupil/ Teacher Ratio	Minority Pupils[1] (%)	Free Lunch Eligible[2] (%)	IEP[3] (%)
Hawaii Department of Education	289	180,196	15.8	80.3	32.7	11.1

Note: Table includes school districts with 2,000 or more students; (1) Percentage of students that are not non-Hispanic white; (2) Percentage of students that are eligible for the free lunch program; (3) Percentage of students that have an Individualized Education Program.
Source: U.S. Department of Education, National Center for Education Statistics, Common Core of Data, Local Education Agency (School District) Universe Survey: School Year 2009-2010; U.S. Department of Education, National Center for Education Statistics, Common Core of Data, Public Elementary/Secondary School Universe Survey: School Year 2009-2010

Highest Level of Education

Area	Less than H.S.	H.S. Diploma	Some College, No Deg.	Associate Degree	Bachelors Degree	Masters Degree	Profess. School Degree	Doctorate Degree
City	11.8	26.6	19.9	8.5	21.7	7.3	2.7	1.6
MSA[1]	9.7	27.9	21.7	9.5	20.6	6.7	2.5	1.3
U.S.	14.7	28.4	21.3	7.6	17.6	7.2	1.9	1.2

Note: Figures cover persons age 25 and over; (1) Figures cover the Honolulu, HI Metropolitan Statistical Area—see Appendix B for areas included
Source: U.S. Census Bureau, 2008-2010 American Community Survey 3-Year Estimates

Educational Attainment by Race

Area	High School Graduate or Higher (%)					Bachelor's Degree or Higher (%)				
	Total	White	Black	Asian	Hisp.[2]	Total	White	Black	Asian	Hisp.[2]
City	88.2	95.7	95.6	84.9	87.2	33.3	47.7	26.9	32.0	24.4
MSA[1]	90.3	96.2	97.1	87.3	89.6	31.2	44.7	26.4	31.7	21.4
U.S.	85.3	87.5	81.4	85.5	61.6	28.0	29.3	17.8	50.2	13.0

Note: Figures shown cover persons 25 years old and over; (1) Figures cover the Honolulu, HI Metropolitan Statistical Area—see Appendix B for areas included; (2) People of Hispanic origin can be of any race
Source: U.S. Census Bureau, 2008-2010 American Community Survey 3-Year Estimates

School Enrollment by Grade and Control

Area	Preschool (%)		Kindergarten (%)		Grades 1 - 4 (%)		Grades 5 - 8 (%)		Grades 9 - 12 (%)	
	Public	Private	Public	Private	Public	Private	Public	Private	Public	Private
City	36.8	63.2	71.3	28.7	79.8	20.2	75.9	24.1	76.1	23.9
MSA[1]	30.5	69.5	79.3	20.7	83.5	16.5	78.1	21.9	76.8	23.2
U.S.	55.4	44.6	87.1	12.9	89.4	10.6	89.5	10.5	90.4	9.6

Note: Figures shown cover persons 3 years old and over; (1) Figures cover the Honolulu, HI Metropolitan Statistical Area—see Appendix B for areas included
Source: U.S. Census Bureau, 2008-2010 American Community Survey 3-Year Estimates

Average Salaries of Public School Classroom Teachers

Area	2010-11		2011-12		Percent Change 2010-11 to 2011-12	Percent Change 2001-02 to 2011-12
	Dollars	Rank[1]	Dollars	Rank[1]		
Hawaii	55,063	17	54,268	20	-1.44	27.30
U.S. Average	55,623	-	56,643	-	1.83	26.8

Note: (1) State rank ranges from 1 to 51 where 1 indicates highest salary.
Source: National Education Association, Rankings & Estimates: Rankings of the States 2011 and Estimates of School Statistics 2012, December 2011

Higher Education

Four-Year Colleges			Two-Year Colleges			Medical Schools[1]	Law Schools[2]	Voc/ Tech[3]
Public	Private Non-profit	Private For-profit	Public	Private Non-profit	Private For-profit			
1	5	3	2	0	2	1	1	5

Note: Figures cover institutions located within the city limits and include main campuses only; (1) includes schools accredited by the Liaison Committee on Medical Education and the American Osteopathic Association's Commission on Osteopathic College Accreditation; (2) includes American Bar Association-accredited law schools; (3) includes all schools with programs that are less than 2 years.
Source: National Center for Education Statistics, Integrated Postsecondary Education System (IPEDS) Peer Analysis System, 2011-12; Association of American Medical Colleges, Member List, April 23, 2012; American Osteopathic Association, Member List, April 23, 2012; Law School Admission Council, Official Guide to ABA-Approved Law Schools Online, April 23, 2012

According to *U.S. News & World Report,* the Honolulu, HI is home to one of the best national universities in the U.S.: **University of Hawaii–Manoa** (#164). The indicators used to capture academic quality fall into a number of categories: assessment by administrators at peer institutions; retention of students; faculty resources; student selectivity; financial resources; alumni giving; high school counselor ratings of colleges; and graduation rate. *U.S. News & World Report, "America's Best Colleges 2012"*

PRESIDENTIAL ELECTION

2008 Presidential Election Results

Area	Obama	McCain	Nader	Other
Honolulu County	69.8	28.7	0.8	0.6
U.S.	52.9	45.6	0.6	0.9

Note: Results are percentages and may not add to 100% due to rounding
Source: Dave Leip's Atlas of U.S. Presidential Elections, www.uselectionatlas.org

EMPLOYERS

Major Employers

Company Name	Industry
City and County of Honolulu	General government/local government
City and County of Honolulu	Civil service/commission government
First Hawaiin Bank	State commercial banks
Hawaii Dept of Health	Admin of public health programs
Hawaii Dept of Health	Administration of public health programs
Hawaii Dept of Transportation	Admin of transportation
Hawaii Mediacal Services Assoc	Hospital and medical service plans
Hawaii Pacific Health	General medical/surgical hospitals
Hawaiin Telecom Inc	Local and long distance telephone
KYO YA Hotels and Resorts	Hotels/motels
Mormon Church	Misc denominational church
OAHU transit Services	Bus line operations
St Francis Healthcare Sys of Hawaii	Skilled nursing facility
State of Hawaii	Public order and safety/state gov't
The Boeing Company	Airplanes fixed or rotary wing
The Queens Medical Center	Medical centers
The Queens Medical Center	General medical/surgical hospitals
Trustess of the Estate of Bernice Bishop	Private elementary/secondary schools
University of Hawaii System	Colleges/universities
University of Hawaii System	University

Note: Companies shown are located within the Honolulu, HI metropolitan area.
Source: Hoovers.com, data extracted April 25 2012

PUBLIC SAFETY

Crime Rate

Area	All Crimes	Violent Crimes				Property Crimes		
		Murder	Forcible Rape	Robbery	Aggrav. Assault	Burglary	Larceny -Theft	Motor Vehicle Theft
County[3]	3,600.7	2.0	22.9	93.8	149.4	606.1	2,315.9	410.5
Suburbs[1]	n/a	n/a	n/a	n/a	n/a	n/a	n/a	n/a
Metro[2]	3,600.7	2.0	22.9	93.8	149.4	606.1	2,315.9	410.5
U.S.	3,345.5	4.8	27.5	119.1	252.3	699.6	2,003.5	238.8

Note: Figures are crimes per 100,000 population; (1) All areas within the metro area that are located outside the city limits; (2) Metropolitan Statistical Area—see Appendix B for areas included; (3) Figures are for Honolulu County; n/a not available
Source: FBI Uniform Crime Reports, 2010

Hate Crimes

Area	Number of Quarters Reported	Bias Motivation				
		Race	Religion	Sexual Orientation	Ethnicity	Disability
City	n/a	n/a	n/a	n/a	n/a	n/a

Note: n/a not available.
Source: Federal Bureau of Investigation, Hate Crime Statistics 2010

Identity Theft Consumer Complaints

Area	Complaints	Complaints per 100,000 Population	Rank[2]
MSA[1]	411	45.4	349
U.S.	279,156	90.4	-

Note: (1) Metropolitan Statistical Area—see Appendix B for areas included; (2) Rank ranges from 1 to 384 where 1 indicates greatest number of identity theft complaints per 100,000 population
Source: Federal Trade Commission, Consumer Sentinel Network Data Book for January–December 2011

Fraud and Other Consumer Complaints

Area	Complaints	Complaints per 100,000 Population	Rank[2]
MSA[1]	3,693	407.8	279
U.S.	1,533,924	496.8	-

Note: (1) Metropolitan Statistical Area—see Appendix B for areas included; (2) Rank ranges from 1 to 384 where 1 indicates greatest number of fraud and other complaints per 100,000 population
Source: Federal Trade Commission, Consumer Sentinel Network Data Book for January–December 2011

RECREATION

Culture

Dance[1]	Theatre[1]	Instrumental Music[1]	Vocal Music[1]	Series/ Festivals	Museums	Zoos and Aquariums[2]
0	4	6	4	2	21	1

Note: (1) Number of professional perfoming groups; (2) AZA-accredited
Source: The Grey House Performing Arts Directory, 2011-2012; Official Museum Directory, 2011; American Association of Museums, AAM Member Museums, April 2012; Association of Zoos & Aquariums, AZA Member Zoos & Aquariums, April 2012

Professional Sports Teams

Team Name	League
No teams are located in the metro area	

Source: Original research

CLIMATE

Average and Extreme Temperatures

Temperature	Jan	Feb	Mar	Apr	May	Jun	Jul	Aug	Sep	Oct	Nov	Dec	Yr.
Extreme High (°F)	87	88	89	89	93	92	92	93	94	94	93	89	94
Average High (°F)	80	80	81	82	84	86	87	88	88	86	84	81	84
Average Temp. (°F)	73	73	74	76	77	79	80	81	81	79	77	74	77
Average Low (°F)	66	66	67	69	70	72	73	74	73	72	70	67	70
Extreme Low (°F)	52	53	55	56	60	65	66	67	66	64	57	54	52

Note: Figures cover the years 1949-1990
Source: National Climatic Data Center, International Station Meteorological Climate Summary, 9/96

Average Precipitation/Snowfall/Humidity

Precip./Humidity	Jan	Feb	Mar	Apr	May	Jun	Jul	Aug	Sep	Oct	Nov	Dec	Yr.
Avg. Precip. (in.)	3.7	2.5	2.8	1.4	1.0	0.4	0.5	0.6	0.7	2.0	2.8	3.7	22.4
Avg. Snowfall (in.)	0	0	0	0	0	0	0	0	0	0	0	0	0
Avg. Rel. Hum. 5am (%)	82	80	78	77	76	75	75	75	76	78	79	80	78
Avg. Rel. Hum. 5pm (%)	66	64	62	61	60	58	58	58	60	63	66	66	62

Note: Figures cover the years 1949-1990; Tr = Trace amounts (<0.05 in. of rain; <0.5 in. of snow)
Source: National Climatic Data Center, International Station Meteorological Climate Summary, 9/96

Weather Conditions

Temperature			Daytime Sky			Precipitation		
32°F & below	45°F & below	90°F & above	Clear	Partly cloudy	Cloudy	0.01 inch or more precip.	0.1 inch or more snow/ice	Thunder-storms
0	0	23	25	286	54	98	0	7

Note: Figures are average number of days per year and cover the years 1949-1990
Source: National Climatic Data Center, International Station Meteorological Climate Summary, 9/96

HAZARDOUS WASTE

Superfund Sites

Honolulu has one hazardous waste site on the EPA's Superfund Final National Priorities List: **Del Monte Corp. (Oahu Plantation)**. *U.S. Environmental Protection Agency, Final National Priorities List, April 17, 2012*

AIR & WATER QUALITY

Air Quality Index

Area	Percent of Days when Air Quality was...[2]					AQI Statistics[2]	
	Good	Moderate	Unhealthy for Sensitive Groups	Unhealthy	Very Unhealthy	Maximum	Median
Area[1]	92.6	7.4	0.0	0.0	0.0	91	32

Note: Air Quality Index (AQI) is an index for reporting daily air quality. EPA calculates the AQI for five major air pollutants regulated by the Clean Air Act: ground-level ozone, particle pollution (aka particulate matter), carbon monoxide, sulfur dioxide, and nitrogen dioxide. The AQI runs from 0 to 500. The higher the AQI value, the greater the level of air pollution and the greater the health concern. There are six AQI categories: "Good" AQI is between 0 and 50. Air quality is considered satisfactory; "Moderate" AQI is between 51 and 100. Air quality is acceptable; "Unhealthy for Sensitive Groups" When AQI values are between 101 and 150, members of sensitive groups may experience health effects; "Unhealthy" When AQI values are between 151 and 200 everyone may begin to experience health effects; "Very Unhealthy" AQI values between 201 and 300 trigger a health alert; "Hazardous" AQI values over 300 trigger warnings of emergency conditions (not shown); (1) Data covers Honolulu County; (2) Based on 365 days with AQI data in 2011.
Source: U.S. Environmental Protection Agency, AirData Report, 2011

Air Quality Index Pollutants

Area	Percent of Days when AQI Pollutant was...[2]					
	Carbon Monoxide	Nitrogen Dioxide	Ozone	Sulfur Dioxide	Particulate Matter 2.5	Particulate Matter 10
Area[1]	0.0	0.0	44.7	0.3	50.1	4.9

Note: The Air Quality Index (AQI) is an index for reporting daily air quality. EPA calculates the AQI for five major air pollutants regulated by the Clean Air Act: ground-level ozone, particle pollution (also known as particulate matter), carbon monoxide, sulfur dioxide, and nitrogen dioxide. The AQI runs from 0 to 500. The higher the AQI value, the greater the level of air pollution and the greater the health concern; (1) Data covers Honolulu County; (2) Based on 365 days with AQI data in 2011.
Source: U.S. Environmental Protection Agency, AirData Report, 2011

Air Quality Index Trends

Area	Trend Sites (days)								All Sites (days)
	2003	2004	2005	2006	2007	2008	2009	2010	2010
MSA[1]	2	2	2	1	0	0	0	0	0

Note: Figures are the number of days the AQI value exceeded 100 in a given year. An AQI value greater than 100 indicates that air quality would have been in the unhealthful range on that day. Data from exceptional events are included. These counts are presented in two ways. First, the counts are based on sites having an adequate record of monitoring data during the trend period (trend sites). These counts represent the relative change in the number of days with AQI values greater than 100. In the last column, the counts are based on all sites with data in the most recent year (because it is possible for a site to have data in the most recent year but not enough data to be a trend site); (1) Data covers the Honolulu, HI—see Appendix B for areas included
Source: U.S. Environmental Protection Agency, Air Quality Index Information, "Number of Days with Air Quality Index Values Greater than 100 at Trend Sites, 2000-2010, and at All Sites in 2010"

Maximum Air Pollutant Concentrations: Particulate Matter, Ozone, CO and Lead

	Particulate Matter 10 (ug/m3)	Particulate Matter 2.5 Wtd AM (ug/m3)	Particulate Matter 2.5 24-Hr (ug/m3)	Ozone (ppm)	Carbon Monoxide (ppm)	Lead (ug/m3)
MSA[1] Level	70	4.7	12	0.047	1	0
NAAQS[2]	150	15	35	0.075	9	0.15
Met NAAQS[2]	Yes	Yes	Yes	Yes	Yes	Yes

Note: Data from exceptional events are not included; (1) Data covers the Honolulu, HI—see Appendix B for areas included; (2) National Ambient Air Quality Standards; ppm = parts per million; ug/m3 = micrograms per cubic meter; n/a not available
Concentrations: Particulate Matter 10 (coarse particulate)—highest second maximum 24-hour concentration; Particulate Matter 2.5 Wtd AM (fine particulate)—highest weighted annual mean concentration; Particulate Matter 2.5 24-Hour (fine particulate)—highest 98th percentile 24-hour concentration; Ozone—highest fourth daily maximum 8-hour concentration; Carbon Monoxide—highest second maximum non-overlapping 8-hour concentration; Lead—maximum running 3-month average
Source: U.S. Environmental Protection Agency, CBSA Factbook 2010, Air Quality Statistics by City, 2010

Maximum Air Pollutant Concentrations: Nitrogen Dioxide and Sulfur Dioxide

	Nitrogen Dioxide AM (ppb)	Nitrogen Dioxide 1-Hr (ppb)	Sulfur Dioxide AM (ppb)	Sulfur Dioxide 1-Hr (ppb)	Sulfur Dioxide 24-Hr (ppb)
MSA[1] Level	3.411	24	1.272	18	4
NAAQS[2]	53	100	30	75	140
Met NAAQS[2]	Yes	Yes	Yes	Yes	Yes

Note: Data from exceptional events are not included; (1) Data covers the Honolulu, HI—see Appendix B for areas included; (2) National Ambient Air Quality Standards; ppb = parts per billion; n/a not available

Concentrations: Nitrogen Dioxide AM—highest arithmetic mean concentration; Nitrogen Dioxide 1-Hr—highest 98th percentile 1-hour daily maximum concentration; Sulfur Dioxide AM—highest annual mean concentration; Sulfur Dioxide 1-Hr—highest 99th percentile 1-hour daily maximum concentration; Sulfur Dioxide 24-Hr—highest second maximum 24-hour concentration

Source: U.S. Environmental Protection Agency, CBSA Factbook 2010, Air Quality Statistics by City, 2010

Drinking Water

Water System Name	Pop. Served	Primary Water Source Type	Violations[1] Health Based	Violations[1] Monitoring/ Reporting
Honolulu-Windward-Pearl Harbor	665,735	Ground	0	0

Note: (1) Based on violation data from January 1, 2011 to December 31, 2011 (includes unresolved violations from earlier years)

Source: U.S. Environmental Protection Agency, Office of Ground Water and Drinking Water, Safe Drinking Water Information System (based on data extracted April 18, 2012)

Irvine, California

Background

Irvine, in Orange County, California, is located on the southern portion of the vast Los Angeles-Riverside-Orange County metropolitan area. The planned city offers a mix of careful residential and business cluster development coupled with a shrewd eye to the Pacific Rim's ever-expanding economic opportunities.

The area is rich in pre-colonial, Spanish, Mexican, and American history. Gabrielino Indians, a tribe of the Shoshonean language group, occupied the Irvine area for some 2,000 years before Europeans arrived, and subsisted well on a rich supply of shellfish, water fowl, and game animals.

Gaspar de Portola, leading a Spanish expedition into the area in 1769, ended the Gabrielino way of life, establishing forts, missions, and cattle-herding, and the king of Spain began to allocate land to missions and private individuals. Three large grants made up the land that later became the Irvine Ranch. In the years after California's acquisition by the United States, this vast plot was extensively litigated in a maze of conflicting land claims, but by 1878, James Irvine controlled the property, 110,000 acres stretching 23 miles from the Pacific Ocean to the Santa Ana River.

At the end of the nineteenth century, the ranch had shifted its focus from grazing to a mixed agricultural operation producing field crops and olive and citrus orchards, and by 1918 almost 60,000 acres were devoted exclusively to the cultivation of lima beans. From this time on, the pace of development quickened dramatically. Marine air facilities were built during World War II on land sold to the government by the Irvine Company, and by 1947 the company started to parcel out small sections of the ranch for residential and commercial use.

In 1959, the University of California received a large plot from the Irvine Company for the establishment of a new campus, thus making Irvine one of the few American communities to have been largely planned around the expansion of a university system. In 1970, the Irvine Business Complex was developed, along with the residential sites of Turtle Rock, University Park, Culverdale, The Ranch, and Walnut. In 1971, voting residents of these communities elected to incorporate, forming a city considerably larger than had been envisioned by the original university planners.

The University has gone on to further strengthen its ties to businesses in the community by launching a 180-acre University Research Park and the Irvine Biomedical Research Center. More recently, the university's School of Law opened in the fall of 2009.

Irvine is a self-sufficient city with an economy that depends on a mix of industries and services including biotechnology products, electronics, software/digital media, and even action/apparel makers. Major employers include Allergan, Blizzard Entertainment, Broadcom Corp, eMachines, and Vizio. Kia Motors, Mazda Motor Corp., Samsung Electronics and Toshiba are some of the businesses who are headquartered in Irvine.

Irvine continues to carefully plan its efforts to preserve aspects of its natural environment, but nonetheless offers unique access to the great Los Angeles-Riverside-Orange County megalopolis. A major convenience for traveling Irvinites and businesspeople is the fully modern John Wayne Airport located just at the western edge of the city.

The city is home to the Ayn Rand Institute, the Verizon Wireless Amphitheater, and the Irvine Fine Arts Center devoted to visual arts programming.

Irvine specifically, and Orange County generally, feature southern California's famously salubrious climate. The sun shines almost all the time, temperatures are moderate, and rainfall is rare.

Rankings

General Rankings

- Irvine was selected as one of America's best cities by *Bloomberg Businessweek.* The city ranked #5 out of 50. Criteria: number of restaurants, bars and museums per capita; number of colleges, libraries, and professional sports teams; income, poverty, unemployment, crime, and foreclosure rates; percent of population with bachelor's degrees; public school performance; park acres per capita; air quality. *BusinessWeek, "America's 50 Best Cities," September 20, 2011*
- Irvine appeared on RelocateAmerica's list of best places to live in America. The annual "Top 100 Places to Live" list recognizes the top communities as nominated by their residents & local businesses. RelocateAmerica's Research Group determines the list based on review of various data gathered for economic, employment, housing, education, industry, opportunity, environment and recreation along with feedback from area leaders and residents. *RelocateAmerica.com, "Top 100 Places to Live for 2011"*
- Irvine was selected as one of the "Best Places to Live in America" by *Money* magazine. The city ranked #22 out of 100. This year's list focused on cities with populations of 50,000 to 300,000. Criteria: job opportunities; economic strength; top-notch schools; low crime; good health care; recreation; and many other factors that help make a town great for raising a family. *CNNMoney.com, "Best Places to Live in America 2010," August 2010*

Business/Finance Rankings

- The Santa Ana metro area was identified as one of 10 "Cities Where the Recession is Easing." The metro area was ranked #9. Criteria: job growth; goods produced; home sale prices; unemployment rates. *Forbes.com, "Cities Where the Recession is Easing," March 3, 2010*
- Experian ranked the top 20 major U.S. metropolitan areas by average debt per consumer. The Los Angeles metro area was ranked #20. Criteria: average debt per consumer. Debt for this study includes credit cards, auto loans and personal loans. It does not include mortgages. *Experian, May 13, 2010*
- Irvine was selected as one of the best places to ride out a recession in the U.S. by *BusinessWeek.* Twenty cities were identified as places where large portions of the population worked in anticyclical industries such as government, health care, education, agriculture, and legal services. *BusinessWeek, "Some Cities Will Be Safer in a Recession," October 14, 2008*
- *American City Business Journals* ranked America's 261 largest cities in terms of their resident's wealth. Irvine ranked #6. Criteria: per capita income; median household income; percentage of households with annual incomes of $200,000 or more; median home value. *American City Business Journals, "Where the Money Is: America's Wealth Centers," August 18, 2008*
- The Santa Ana metro area appeared on the Milken Institute "2011 Best Performing Metros" list. Rank: #165 out of 200 large metro areas. Criteria: job growth; wage and salary growth; high-tech output growth. *Milken Institute, "2011 Best Performing Metros"*
- Santa Ana was ranked #11 out of 145 regions worldwide in terms of its "Knowledge Competitiveness Index." The index attempts to measure the knowledge-based development taking place throughout the world and is based on 19 measures of economic performance that indicate a region's ability to translate its knowledge capacity into economic value. *Centre for International Competitiveness, World Knowledge Competitiveness Index 2008*
- *Forbes* ranked the 200 most populous metro areas in the U.S. in terms of the "Best Places for Business and Careers." The Santa Ana metro area was ranked #109. Criteria: costs (business and living); job growth (past and projected); income growth; educational attainment; projected economic growth; crime; cultural and recreational opportunities; net migration patterns; number of highly ranked colleges. *Forbes, "Best Places for Business and Careers," June 2011*

Children/Family Rankings

- Irvine was identified as one of the best cities for raising a family by *24/7 Wall St.* The city ranked #4. The nation's 100 largest cities were evaluated on the following criteria: large public outdoor spaces; top hospitals; strong schools; low unemployment; high educational attainment; low violent crime rates. *24/7 Wall St., "The 10 Best U.S. Cities for Raising a Family," January 13, 2012*

- The Santa Ana metro area was selected as one of the "Best Cities for Relocating Families" by Worldwide ERC and Primacy Relocation. The 2008 study looked at nearly 50 factors important to relocating families including: recent job growth; nearby top-ranked colleges; in-state tuition for four-year public colleges; population growth since 2000; pediatricians per 100,000 population; and a Green Living index. *Worldwide ERC and Primacy Relocation, "2008 Best Cities for Relocating Families"*

- Irvine was chosen as one of America's "100 Best Communities for Young People." The winners were selected based upon detailed information provided about each community's efforts to fulfill five essential promises critical to the well-being of young people: caring adults who are actively involved in their lives; safe places in which to learn and grow; a healthy start toward adulthood; an effective education that builds marketable skills; and opportunities to help others. *America's Promise Alliance, "100 Best Communities for Young People, 2010"*

Dating/Romance Rankings

- Eli Lily and Company, in partnership with Sperling's BestPlaces, ranked the nation's 50 largest metro areas in terms of the "Most Romantic Cities for Baby Boomers." The Los Angeles metro area ranked #41. Criteria: marriage and divorce rates among baby boomers age 45 to 60; great restaurants; dance studios; chocolate, jewelry and flower sales. *Eli Lily and Company, "Most Romantic Cities for Baby Boomers," April 20, 2007*
- The Santa Ana metro area was selected as one of the "Best Cities for Relocating Singles" by Worldwide ERC and Primacy Relocation. The area ranked #9 out of the 100 largest metro areas in the U.S. Criteria: recent job growth; recent singles population growth; overall population growth; affordable rental housing; cost-of-living index; expanded arts and recreation opportunities; ratio of single men and single women; affordability of quality higher education (including state residency requirements); diversity index; climate; population density. *Worldwide ERC and Primacy Relocation, "2008 Best Cities for Relocating Singles"*

- *Forbes* ranked the 40 most populous urbanized areas in the U.S. in terms of the "Best Cities for Singles." The Los Angeles metro area ranked #8. Criteria: number of singles; cost of living alone; nightlife; culture; job growth; coolness; and online dating participation. *Forbes.com, "Best Cities for Singles," July 27, 2009*

Education Rankings

- Irvine was identified as one of America's smartest cities by *The Business Journals On Numbers*. The city ranked #5 in the large city category (population 100,000 or more). Each city's score was based on its percentage of adults (25 or older) at each of the following rungs: dropped out before high school graduation; stopped at high school diploma; stopped at associate degree or attended college but stopped without any degree; stopped at bachelor's degree; earned graduate degree and/or professional degree. The point value of a specific rung was determined by the relative earning power of people at that level. *The Business Journals On Numbers, "Brainpower Ratings," November 17, 2011*

- Los Angeles was identified as one of the 100 "smartest" metro areas in the U.S. The area ranked #76. Criteria: the editors rated the collective brainpower of the 100 largest metro areas in the U.S. based on their residents' educational attainment. *American City Business Journals, April 14, 2008*

- Irvine was identified as one of America's most inventive cities by *The Daily Beast.* The city ranked #4 out of 25. The 200 largest cities in the U.S. were ranked by the number of patents (applied and approved) per capita. *The Daily Beast, "The 25 Most Inventive Cities," October 2, 2011*

- Los Angeles was identified as one of "America's Brainiest Bastions" by *Portfolio.com.* The metro area ranked #111 out of 200. *Portfolio.com* analyzed levels of educational attainment in the nation's 200 largest metropolitan areas. The editors established scores for five levels of educational attainment, based on relative earning power of adult workers age 25 or older. Scores were determined by comparing the median income for all workers with the median income for those workers at a specified educational level. *Portfolio.com, "America's Brainiest Bastions," December 1, 2010*

Environmental Rankings

- The Los Angeles was identified as one of America's dirtiest metro areas by *Forbes.* The area ranked #2 out of 10. Criteria: year-round particulate pollution; short-term particulate pollution; ozone pollution. *Forbes, "Dirtiest Cities in America," November 4, 2011*

- The Los Angeles was identified as one of North America's greenest metropolitan areas. The area ranked #7. The Green City Index is comprised of 31 indicators, and scores cities across nine categories: carbon dioxide; energy; land use; buildings; transport; water; waste; air quality; environmental governance. The 27 largest metropolitan areas in the U.S. and Canada were considered. *Economist Intelligence Unit, sponsored by Siemens, "U.S. and Canada Green City Index, 2011"*

- The Los Angeles was identified as one of America's cities with the most ENERGY STAR certified buildings. The area ranked #1 out of 25. Criteria: number of ENERGY STAR labeled buildings in 2010. *U.S. Environmental Protection Agency, "Top Cities With the Most ENERGY STAR Certified Buildings," March 15, 2011*

- The Los Angeles metro area was identified as one of "The Ten Biggest American Cities that are Running Out of Water" by *24/7 Wall St.* The metro area ranked #1 out of 10. *24/7 Wall St.* did an analysis of the water supply and consumption in the 30 largest metropolitan areas in the U.S. Criteria include: projected water demand as a share of available precipitation; groundwater use as a share or projected available precipitation; susceptibility to drought; projected increase in freshwater withdrawals; projected increase in summer water deficit. *24/7 Wall St., "The Ten Biggest American Cities that are Running Out of Water," November 1, 2010*

- Irvine was selected as one of 22 "Smarter Cities" for energy by the Natural Resources Defense Council. Criteria: investment in green power; energy efficiency measures; conservation. *Natural Resources Defense Council, "2010 Smarter Cities," July 19, 2010*

- The Los Angeles metro area was selected as one of "America's Most Toxic Cities" by *Forbes.* The metro area ranked #6 out of 10. The 80 largest metropolitan areas were ranked on the following criteria: air quality; water quality; Superfund sites; toxic releases. *Forbes, "America's Most Toxic Cities, 2011," February 28, 2011*

- *American City Business Journal* ranked 43 metropolitan areas in terms of their "greenness." The Santa Ana metro area ranked #29. Criteria: Forty-one metros in which *ACBJ* has business weeklies, plus Indianapolis and Cleveland, were ranked based on 20 different indicators such as adoption of green technologies, utilization of environmentally sound practices, and air and water quality. *American City Business Journals, "Green City Index," March 11, 2010*

- Irvine was selected as one of "America's 50 Greenest Cities" by *Popular Science.* The city ranked #21. Criteria: electricity; transportation; green living; recycling and green perspective. *Popular Science, February 2008*

- 100 of the largest metro areas in the U.S. were analyzed in terms of their current drought severity. The Santa Ana metro area ranked #1 (#1 = driest). The rankings were based on statistics such as long-term precipitation trends and patterns and the Palmer drought indices. *Sperling's BestPlaces, www.BestPlaces.net, "America's Drought-Riskiest Cities," November 2007*

- The Santa Ana metro area appeared in *Country Home's* "Best Green Places" report. The area ranked #47 out of 379. Criteria: official energy policies; green power; green buildings; availability of fresh, locally grown food. *Country Home, "Best Green Places," 2008*

- Los Angeles was highlighted as one of the 25 metro areas most polluted by short-term particle pollution (24-hour PM 2.5) in the U.S. The area ranked #4. *American Lung Association, State of the Air 2011*

- Los Angeles was highlighted as one of the 25 metro areas most polluted by year-round particle pollution (Annual PM 2.5) in the U.S. The area ranked #2. *American Lung Association, State of the Air 2011*
- Los Angeles was highlighted as one of the 25 most ozone-polluted metro areas in the U.S. The area ranked #1. *American Lung Association, State of the Air 2011*

Health/Fitness Rankings

- The Los Angeles metro area was selected as one of the worst cities for bed bugs in America by Rollins corporation, the owner of seven pest control companies, including Orkin. The area ranked #5 based on the number of bed bug treatments from January to December 2011. *Rollins, "The Top 50 U.S. Cities for Bed Bugs," March 19, 2012*
- Los Angeles was identified as a "2011 Asthma Capital." The area ranked #57 out of the nation's 100 largest metropolitan areas. Twelve factors were used to identify the most challenging places to live for people with asthma: estimated prevalence; self-reported prevalence; crude death rate for asthma; annual pollen score; annual air quality; public smoking laws; number of board-certified asthma specialists; school inhaler access laws; rescue medication use; controller medication use; uninsured rate; poverty rate. *Asthma and Allergy Foundation of America, "2011 Asthma Capitals"*
- Los Angeles was identified as a "2011 Fall Allergy Capital." The area ranked #77 out of 100. Three groups of factors were used to identify the most severe cities for people with allergies during the fall season: annual pollen levels; medicine utilization; access to board-certified allergists. *Asthma and Allergy Foundation of America, "2011 Fall Allergy Capitals"*
- Los Angeles was identified as a "2012 Spring Allergy Capital." The area ranked #63 out of 100. Three groups of factors were used to identify the most severe cities for people with allergies during the spring season: annual pollen levels; medicine utilization; access to board-certified allergists. *Asthma and Allergy Foundation of America, "2012 Spring Allergy Capitals"*
- The Los Angeles metropolitan area was selected as one of the best metros for hospital care in America by *HealthGrades.com.* The rankings are based on a comprehensive study of patient death and complication rates in the nation's nearly 5,000 hospitals. Hospitals performing in the top 5% nationwide across 26 different medical procedures and diagnoses were identified. *HealthGrades.com* then ranked cities by the highest percentage of these Distinguished Hospitals for Clinical Excellence™. The Los Angeles metro area ranked #22. *HealthGrades.com, "America's Top 50 Cities for Hospital Care," January 21, 2012*
- The American Academy of Dermatology ranked 26 U.S. metropolitan regions in terms of their residents knowledge, attitude and behaviors towards tanning, sun protection and skin cancer detection. The Los Angeles metro area ranked #22. The results of the study are based on an online survey of over 7,000 adults nationwide. *American Academy of Dermatology, "Suntelligence: How Sun Smart is Your City," May 3, 2010*
- The Los Angeles metro area appeared in the 2011 Gallup-Healthways Well-Being Index. The index, based on interviews with more than 350,000 Americans, measured jobs, finances, physical health, emotional state of mind and communities. The metro area ranked #63 out of 190. Criteria: life evaluation; emotional health; work environment; physical health; healthy behaviors; basic access (basic needs optimal for a healthy life, such as access to food and medicine, having health insurance and feeling safe while walking at night). *Gallup-Healthways, "State of Well-Being 2011"*
- The Santa Ana metro area was identified as one of "America's Most Stressful Cities" by *Sperling's BestPlaces.* The metro area ranked #42 out of 50. Criteria: unemployment rate; suicide rate; commute time; mental health; poor rest; alcohol use; violent crime rate; property crime rate; cloudy days annually. *Sperling's BestPlaces, www.BestPlaces.net, "Stressful Cities 2012*
- The Los Angeles metro area was identified as one of "America's Most Stressful Cities" by *Forbes*. The metro area ranked #1 out of 40. Criteria: housing affordability; unemployment rate; cost of living; air quality; traffic congestion; sunny days; population density. *Forbes.com, "America's Most Stressful Cities," September 23, 2011*

- 50 of the largest metro areas in the U.S. were analyzed in terms of their health and fitness by the American College of Sports Medicine in their "American Fitness Index." The Los Angeles metro area ranked #38 (#1 = healthiest). Criteria: preventative health behaviors; levels of chronic disease; health care access; community resources and policies that support physical activity. *American College of Sports Medicine, "Health and Community Fitness Status of the 50 Largest Metropolitan Areas," August 1, 2011*

Real Estate Rankings

- Santa Ana was identified as one of the priciest cities to rent in the U.S. The area ranked #8 out of 10. Criteria: rent-to-income ratio. *CNBC, "Priciest Cities to Rent," March 14, 2012*
- *Fortune* ranked the 100 largest metro areas in the U.S. in terms of projected median home price change in 2010. The Santa Ana metro area ranked #77. *Fortune, "The 2010 Housing Outlook," December 9, 2009*
- The Santa Ana metro area was identified as one of the 20 least affordable housing markets in the U.S. in 2011. The area ranked #2 out of 152 markets with an affordability index of 51.1%. The index measures whether or not a typical family could qualify for a mortgage loan on a typical home. The calculation used assumes a down payment of 20 percent of the home price and a qualifying ratio of 25 percent, meaning that the monthly P&I payment cannot exceed 25 percent of a the median family monthly income. *National Association of Realtors®, Affordability Index of Existing Single-Family Homes for Metropolitan Areas, 2011*
- Irvine appeared on *ApartmentRatings.com* "Top College Towns & Cities" for renters list in 2011." The area ranked #16 out of 87. Overall satisfaction ratings were ranked using thousands of user submitted scores for hundreds of apartment complexes located in cities and towns that are home to the 100 largest four-year institutions in the U.S. *ApartmentRatings.com, "2011 College Town Renter Satisfaction Rankings"*
- The Santa Ana metro area was identified as one of the most expensive places to rent in the U.S. The area ranked #16 out of 10 markets with an average effective rent of $1,490 per month. The rental figures cover apartment properties in complexes with 40 or more units (20 or more units in California and Arizona). The figures are blended average rents, which include all unit sizes. Effective rents include free rent incentives and other landlord concessions. *Wall Street Journal Online, January 17, 2008*
- The Santa Ana metro area was identified as one of "America's 25 Weakest Housing Markets" by *Forbes*. The metro area ranked #16. Criteria: metro areas with populations over 500,000 were ranked based on projected home values through 2011. *Forbes.com, "America's 25 Weakest Housing Markets," January 7, 2009*
- The nation's largest metro areas were analyzed in terms of the best places to buy pre-foreclosures (short sales). The Santa Ana metro area ranked #7 out of 10. Criteria: at least 500 pre-foreclosure sales during the fourth quarter and a short sales increase of at least five percent from a year ago. The areas selected posted the biggest discounts on the sales of pre-foreclosure properties. *RealtyTrac, "Fourth Quarter and Year-End 2011 U.S. Foreclosure Sales Report: Shifting Towards Short Sales," February 28, 2012*
- The Santa Ana metro area was identified as one of America's most overvalued cities in 2011 by *CNNMoney.com* based on data from Local Market Monitor. Criteria: median home prices; local interest rates; economic and population growth; construction costs; vacancies; household income. *CNNMoney.com, "America's Most Overvalued (and Undervalued) Cities," January 16, 2011*
- The Santa Ana metro area was identified as one of America's least affordable cities to buy a house in 2010 by *CNNMoney.com.* The metro area was ranked #4 out of 5. Criteria: median home prices; median family income *CNNMoney.com, "America's Most and Least Affordable Cities to Buy a House," May 21, 2010*
- The Santa Ana metro area appeared in a *Wall Street Journal* article ranking cities by "housing stress." The metro area was ranked #3 (#1 = most stress). Criteria: fraction of mortgage-holding homeowners with a monthly housing payment in excess of 30 percent of income; percentage of people without health insurance; unemployment rate. *The Wall Street Journal, "Which Cities Face Biggest Housing Risk," October 5, 2010*

- The Center for Housing Policy ranked 210 U.S. metropolitan areas by the fair market rent for a two-bedroom unit. The Santa Ana metro area was ranked #4. (#1 = most expensive) with a rent of $1,594. Criteria: Fair Market Rent (FMR) in effect during the fourth quarter of 2009 based on HUD's fiscal year 2010 FMRs. *The Center for Housing Policy, "Paycheck to Paycheck: Most to Least Expensive Rental Markets in 2009"*
- The Los Angeles metro area was identified as one of the best housing markets of the decade by *Forbes.* Criteria: increase in housing values per square foot since January 2000. *Forbes, "America's 5 Best (and Worst) Housing Markets of the Decade," December 7, 2010*
- The Santa Ana metro area was identified as one of the markets with the best expected performance in home prices over the next 12 months. *Local Market Monitor, "First Quarter Home Price Forecast for Largest US Markets," March 2, 2011*
- The Santa Ana metro area was identified as one of the best U.S. markets to invest in rental property" by HomeVestors and Local Market Monitor. The area ranked #94 out of 100. Criteria: risk-return premium relative to national average. *HomeVestors and Local Market Monitor, "Best 100 U.S. Markets to Invest in Rental Property," March 9, 2012*

Safety Rankings

- Allstate ranked the 193 largest cities in America in terms of driver safety. Irvine ranked #160. In addition, drivers were 30.5% more likely to have had an accident compared to the national average. Allstate researchers analyzed internal property damage reported claims over a two-year period (from January 2008 to December 2009) to protect findings from external influences such as weather or road construction. A weighted average of the two-year numbers determined the annual percentages. The report defines an auto crash as any collision resulting in a property damage claim. *Allstate, "2011 Allstate America's Best Drivers Report™"*
- Irvine was identified as one of the safest mid-size cities in America by CQ Press. All 234 cities with populations of 100,000 to 499,999 that reported crime rates in 2010 for murder, rape, robbery, aggravated assault, burglary, and motor vehicle thefts were ranked. The city ranked #1 out of the top 10. *CQ Press, City Crime Rankings 2011-2012*
- The National Insurance Crime Bureau ranked 366 metro areas in the U.S. in terms of per capita rates of vehicle theft. The Los Angeles metro area ranked #23 (#1 = highest rate). Criteria: number of vehicle theft offenses per 100,000 inhabitants in 2010. *National Insurance Crime Bureau, "Hot Spots," June 21, 2011*
- The Los Angeles metro area was identified as one of the most dangerous metro areas for pedestrians by Transportation for America. The metro area ranked #27 out of 52 metro areas with over 1 million residents. Criteria: area's population divided by the number of pedestrian fatalities in that area. *Transportation for America, "Dangerous by Design 2011"*

Seniors/Retirement Rankings

- Bankers Life and Casualty Company, in partnership with Sperling's BestPlaces, ranked the nation's 50 largest metro areas in terms of the "Best U.S. Cities for Seniors." The Santa Ana metro area ranked #42. Criteria: healthcare; transportation; housing; environment; economy; health and longevity; social and spiritual life; crime. *Bankers Life and Casualty Company, Center for a Secure Retirement, "Best U.S. Cities for Seniors 2011," September 2011*

Sports/Recreation Rankings

- Irvine was chosen as a bicycle friendly community by the League of American Bicyclists. A Bicycle Friendly Community welcomes cyclists by providing safe accommodation for cycling and encouraging people to bike for transportation and recreation. There are four award levels: Platinum; Gold; Silver; and Bronze. The community achieved an award level of Bronze. *League of American Bicyclists, "Bicycle Friendly Community Master List 2011"*
- The Los Angeles was selected as one of the best metro areas for golf in America by *Golf Digest.* The Los Angeles area was ranked #4 out of 20. Criteria: climate; cost of public golf; quality of public golf; accessibility. *Golf Digest, "The Top 20 Cities for Golf," October 2011*

Technology Rankings

- Scarborough Research, a leading market research firm, identified the Los Angeles DMA (Designated Market Area) as one of the top markets for text messaging with more than 50% of cell phone subscribers age 18+ utilizing the text messaging feature on their phone. *Scarborough Research, November 24, 2008*

- The Santa Ana metro area was identified as one of the "Top 14 Nano Metros" in the U.S. by the Project on Emerging Nanotechnologies. The metro area is home to 23 companies, universities, government laboratories and/or organizations working in nanotechnology. *Project on Emerging Nanotechnologies, "Nano Metros 2009"*

Transportation Rankings

- The Santa Ana metro area was identified as one of the best U.S. cities to live in without a car by *24/7 Wall St.* The area ranked #9 out of 10. Criteria: percentage of neighborhoods covered by public transit; frequency of service for those neighborhoods; share of jobs reachable within 90 minutes or less by public transit; how accessible amenities are for residents on foot; percentage of commuters who bike to work. The 100 largest metropolitan areas in the U.S. were examined. *24/7 Wall St., "The Best Cities to Live in Car-Free," November 28, 2011*

- The Santa Ana metro area appeared on *Forbes* list of the best and worst cities for commuters. The metro area ranked #51 out of 60 (#1 is best). Criteria: travel time; road congestion; travel delays. *Forbes.com, "Best and Worst Cities for Commuters," February 16, 2010*

Women/Minorities Rankings

- Santa Ana was ranked #8 out of 100 metro areas in *SELF Magazine's* ranking of America's healthiest places for women." A panel of experts came up with more than 50 criteria including death and disease rates, environmental indicators, community resources, and lifestyle habits. *SELF Magazine, "Secrets of America's Healthiest Women," December 2008*

- The Los Angeles metro area appeared on *Forbes'* list of the "Best Cities for Minority Entrepreneurs." The area ranked #8 out of 10. Criteria: 52 metropolitan statistical areas were examined. For each ethnicity (African Americans, Asians and Hispanics), the editors measured housing affordability, population growth, income growth, and entrepreneurship (per capita self-employment). *Forbes, "Best Cities for Minority Entrepreneurs," March 23, 2011*

Miscellaneous Rankings

- Energizer Holdings, the makers of Edge® shave gel, in partnership with Sperling's BestPlaces, ranked 50 major metro areas in terms of everyday irritations. The Los Angeles metro area ranked #5. Criteria: humidity levels; weather conditions; incidence of traffic delays and congestion; average commute times; frequency of flight delays and cancellations; rates of sleeplessness; underemployment; pollens and allergens; pests; comedy clubs per capita. *Energizer Holdings, "Most Irritation Prone Cities," July 23, 2010*

- Mars Chocolate North America, the makers of COMBOS®, in partnership with Sperling's BestPlaces, ranked 50 major metro areas in terms of their "manliness." The Los Angeles metro area ranked #50. Criteria: number of professional sports teams; number of nearby NASCAR tracks and racing events; manly lifestyle; concentration of manly retail stores; manly occupations per capita; salty snack sales; "Board of Manliness" rankings. *Mars Chocolate North America, "America's Manliest Cities 2011," September 1, 2011*

- The Los Angeles metro area was selected as one of "America's Greediest Cities" by *Forbes*. The area was ranked #8 out of 10. Criteria: number of Forbes 400 (*Forbes* annual list of the richest Americans) members per capita. *Forbes, "America's Greediest Cities," December 7, 2007*

Business Environment

CITY FINANCES

City Government Finances

Component	2009 ($000)	2009 ($ per capita)
Total Revenues	248,069	1,233
Total Expenditures	321,427	1,598
Debt Outstanding	1,259,257	6,260
Cash and Securities[1]	470,876	2,341

Note: (1) Cash and security holdings of a government at the close of its fiscal year, including those of its dependent agencies, utilities, and liquor stores.
Source: U.S Census Bureau, State & Local Government Finances 2009

City Government Revenue by Source

Source	2009 ($000)	2009 ($ per capita)
General Revenue		
From Federal Government	8,997	45
From State Government	24,557	122
From Local Governments	3,403	17
Taxes		
Property	67,404	335
Sales and Gross Receipts	71,236	354
Personal Income	0	0
Corporate Income	0	0
Motor Vehicle License	0	0
Other Taxes	3,271	16
Current Charges	40,274	200
Liquor Store	0	0
Utility	0	0
Employee Retirement	0	0

Source: U.S Census Bureau, State & Local Government Finances 2009

City Government Expenditures by Function

Function	2009 ($000)	2009 ($ per capita)	2009 (%)
General Direct Expenditures			
Air Transportation	0	0	0.0
Corrections	0	0	0.0
Education	0	0	0.0
Employment Security Administration	0	0	0.0
Financial Administration	5,073	25	1.6
Fire Protection	0	0	0.0
General Public Buildings	0	0	0.0
Governmental Administration, Other	54,645	272	17.0
Health	2,525	13	0.8
Highways	80,138	398	24.9
Hospitals	0	0	0.0
Housing and Community Development	9,179	46	2.9
Interest on General Debt	43,078	214	13.4
Judicial and Legal	405	2	0.1
Libraries	0	0	0.0
Parking	0	0	0.0
Parks and Recreation	37,280	185	11.6
Police Protection	61,168	304	19.0
Public Welfare	0	0	0.0
Sewerage	0	0	0.0
Solid Waste Management	0	0	0.0
Veterans' Services	0	0	0.0
Liquor Store	0	0	0.0
Utility	0	0	0.0
Employee Retirement	0	0	0.0

Source: U.S Census Bureau, State & Local Government Finances 2009

Municipal Bond Ratings

Area	Moody's	S&P	Fitch
City	n/a	n/a	n/a

Rating Systems (shown in declining order of credit quality): Moody's– Aaa, Aa, A, Baa, Ba, B, Caa, Ca, C (numerical modifiers 1, 2, and 3 are added to letter-rating); S&P– AAA, AA, A, BBB, BB, B, CCC, CC, C; Fitch– AAA, AA, A, BBB, BB, B, CCC, CC, C. Ratings may be modified by the addition of a plus or minus sign to show relative standing within the major rating categories.
Notes: n/a Not Available; w/d Withdrawn (1) Not Reviewed; (2) Issuer Rating/No General Obligation; (3) Standard and Poor's Issue Credit Rating (ICR) is a current opinion of an obliger with respect to a specific financial obligation, a specific class of financial obligations, or a specific financial program.
Source: U.S. Census Bureau, 2012 Statistical Abstract, Bond Ratings for City Governments by Largest Cities: 2010

DEMOGRAPHICS

Population Growth

Area	1990 Census	2000 Census	2010 Census	Population Growth (%) 1990-2000	Population Growth (%) 2000-2010
City	111,754	143,072	212,375	28.0	48.4
MSA[1]	11,273,720	12,365,627	12,828,837	9.7	3.7
U.S.	248,709,873	281,421,906	308,745,538	13.2	9.7

Note: (1) Figures cover the Los Angeles-Long Beach-Santa Ana, CA Metropolitan Statistical Area—see Appendix B for areas included
Source: U.S. Census Bureau, 2010 Census

Household Size

Area	Persons in Household (%) One	Two	Three	Four	Five	Six	Seven or More	Average Household Size
City	23.4	31.4	18.7	18.0	5.8	1.9	0.8	2.61
MSA[1]	23.4	27.0	16.3	15.3	8.7	4.4	4.9	2.98
U.S.	26.7	32.8	16.1	13.4	6.5	2.6	1.9	2.58

Note: (1) Figures cover the Los Angeles-Long Beach-Santa Ana, CA Metropolitan Statistical Area—see Appendix B for areas included
Source: U.S. Census Bureau, 2010 Census

Race

Area	White Alone[2] (%)	Black Alone[2] (%)	Asian Alone[2] (%)	AIAN[3] Alone[2] (%)	NHOPI[4] Alone[2] (%)	Other Race Alone[2] (%)	Two or More Races (%)
City	50.5	1.8	39.2	0.2	0.2	2.8	5.5
MSA[1]	52.8	7.1	14.7	0.7	0.3	20.1	4.4
U.S.	72.4	12.6	4.8	0.9	0.2	6.2	2.9

Note: (1) Figures cover the Los Angeles-Long Beach-Santa Ana, CA Metropolitan Statistical Area—see Appendix B for areas included; (2) Alone is defined as not being in combination with one or more other races; (3) American Indian and Alaska Native; (4) Native Hawaiian and Other Pacific Islander
Source: U.S. Census Bureau, 2010 Census

Hispanic or Latino Origin

Area	Hispanic or Latino (%)	Mexican (%)	Puerto Rican (%)	Cuban (%)	Other Hispanic or Latino (%)
City	9.2	6.0	0.3	0.2	2.7
MSA[1]	44.4	34.1	0.4	0.4	9.6
U.S.	16.3	10.3	1.5	0.6	4.0

Note: Persons of Hispanic or Latino origin can be of any race; (1) Figures cover the Los Angeles-Long Beach-Santa Ana, CA Metropolitan Statistical Area—see Appendix B for areas included
Source: U.S. Census Bureau, 2010 Census

Segregation

Type	Segregation Indices[1]				Percent Change		
	1990	2000	2010	2010 Rank[2]	1990-2000	1990-2010	2000-2010
Black/White	72.7	70.0	67.8	10	-2.8	-4.9	-2.1
Asian/White	43.5	47.9	48.4	12	4.4	4.9	0.5
Hispanic/White	60.3	62.5	62.2	2	2.2	1.9	-0.3

Note: Figures are based on an analysis of 1990, 2000, and 2010 Census Decennial Census tract data by William H. Frey, Brookings Institution and the University of Michigan Social Science Data Analysis Network. In this analysis all racial groups (whites, blacks, and asians) are non-Hispanic members of those races. Hispanics are shown as a separate category; All figures cover the Metropolitan Statistical Area (see Appendix B for areas included); (1) Segregation Indices are Dissimilarity Indices that measure the degree to which the minority group is distributed differently than whites across census tracts. They range from 0 (complete integration) to 100 (complete segregation) where the value indicates the percentage of the minority group that needs to move to be distributed exactly like whites; (2) Ranges from 1 (most segregated) to 102 (least segregated); n/a not available.
Source: www.CensusScope.org

Ancestry

Area	German	Irish	English	American	Italian	Polish	French[2]	Scottish	Dutch
City	9.1	6.3	6.6	2.1	3.5	1.8	2.2	1.5	0.8
MSA[1]	6.7	5.2	4.8	2.0	3.2	1.4	1.5	1.1	0.8
U.S.	16.1	11.6	8.8	6.1	5.7	3.2	3.0	1.9	1.6

Note: Figures are the percentage of the total population reporting a particular ancestry. The nine most commonly reported ancestries in the U.S. are shown. Figures include multiple ancestries (e.g. if a person reported being Irish and Italian, they were included in both columns); (1) Figures cover the Los Angeles-Long Beach-Santa Ana, CA Metropolitan Statistical Area—see Appendix B for areas included; (2) Excludes Basque
Source: U.S. Census Bureau, 2008-2010 American Community Survey 3-Year Estimates

Foreign-Born Population

Area	Percent of Population Born in								
	Any Foreign Country	Mexico	Asia	Europe	Carribean	South America	Central America[2]	Africa	Canada
City	35.0	1.5	27.7	2.7	0.1	0.8	0.3	0.9	0.8
MSA[1]	34.5	13.9	12.2	1.8	0.3	0.9	4.3	0.5	0.3
U.S.	12.8	3.8	3.6	1.6	1.2	0.9	1.0	0.5	0.3

Note: (1) Figures cover the Los Angeles-Long Beach-Santa Ana, CA Metropolitan Statistical Area—see Appendix B for areas included; (2) Excludes Mexico.
Source: U.S. Census Bureau, 2008-2010 American Community Survey 3-Year Estimates

Marital Status

Area	Never Married	Now Married[2]	Separated	Widowed	Divorced
City	38.1	50.1	1.0	3.2	7.6
MSA[1]	38.5	45.3	2.5	5.0	8.6
U.S.	31.6	49.6	2.2	6.1	10.7

Note: Figures are percentages and cover the population 15 years of age and older; (1) Figures cover the Los Angeles-Long Beach-Santa Ana, CA Metropolitan Statistical Area—see Appendix B for areas included; (2) Excludes separated
Source: U.S. Census Bureau, 2008-2010 American Community Survey 3-Year Estimates

Age

Area	Percent of Population							Median Age
	Under Age 5	Age 5 to 17	Age 18 to 34	Age 35 to 49	Age 50 to 64	Age 65 to 79	80 Years and Over	
City	5.7	15.9	30.1	23.0	16.7	6.5	2.1	33.9
MSA[1]	6.5	17.9	25.4	21.9	17.2	7.9	3.1	35.1
U.S.	6.5	17.5	23.2	20.7	19.0	9.4	3.6	37.2

Note: (1) Figures cover the Los Angeles-Long Beach-Santa Ana, CA Metropolitan Statistical Area—see Appendix B for areas included
Source: U.S. Census Bureau, 2010 Census

Male/Female Ratio

Area	Males	Females	Males per 100 Females
City	103,434	108,941	94.9
MSA[1]	6,328,434	6,500,403	97.4
U.S.	151,781,326	156,964,212	96.7

Note: (1) Figures cover the Los Angeles-Long Beach-Santa Ana, CA Metropolitan Statistical Area—see Appendix B for areas included
Source: U.S. Census Bureau, 2010 Census

Religious Groups

Area	Catholic	Baptist	Non-Den.	Methodist[2]	Lutheran	LDS[3]	Pente-costal	Presby-terian[4]	Muslim[5]	Judaism
MSA[1]	33.8	2.8	3.6	1.1	0.7	1.7	1.8	0.9	1.0	0.7
U.S.	19.1	9.3	4.0	4.0	2.3	2.0	1.9	1.6	0.8	0.7

Note: Figures are the number of adherents as a percentage of the total population; (1) Figures cover the Los Angeles-Long Beach-Santa Ana, CA Metropolitan Statistical Area—see Appendix B for areas included; (2) Methodist/Pietist; (3) Latter Day Saints; (4) Reformed; (5) Figures are estimates
Source: Association of Statisticians of American Religious Bodies, 2010 U.S. Religion Census: Religious Congregations & Membership Study

ECONOMY

Gross Metropolitan Product

Area	2007	2008	2009	2010	2010 Rank[2]
MSA[1]	731.6	747.0	716.4	737.9	2

Note: Figures are in billions of dollars; (1) Figures cover the Los Angeles-Long Beach-Santa Ana, CA Metropolitan Statistical Area—see Appendix B for areas included; (2) Rank ranges from 1 to 363
Source: The United States Conference of Mayors, "U.S. Metro Economies: GMP and Employment Forecasts," June 2011

Economic Growth

Area	2007-2009 (%)	2010 (%)	2011 (%)	Rank[2]
MSA[1]	-2.3	2.5	2.2	240
U.S.	-1.3	2.9	2.5	–

Note: Figures are real Gross Metropolitan Product growth rates and represent annual average percent change; (1) Figures cover the Los Angeles-Long Beach-Santa Ana, CA Metropolitan Statistical Area—see Appendix B for areas included; (2) Rank ranges from 1 to 363
Source: The United States Conference of Mayors, "U.S. Metro Economies: GMP and Employment Forecasts," June 2011

Metropolitan Area Exports

Area	2005	2006	2007	2008	2009	2010	2010 Rank[2]
MSA[1]	43,814.2	48,718.1	54,433.0	59,985.6	51,528.4	62,167.6	3

Note: Figures are in millions of dollars; (1) Figures cover the Los Angeles-Long Beach-Santa Ana, CA Metropolitan Statistical Area—see Appendix B for areas included; (2) Rank ranges from 1 to 369
Source: U.S. Department of Commerce, International Trade Administration, Office of Trade & Industry Information, Manufacturing & Services, data extracted April 2, 2012

INCOME

Income

Area	Per Capita ($)	Median Household ($)	Average Household ($)
City	41,175	88,571	111,618
MSA[1]	28,405	59,129	83,389
U.S.	26,942	51,222	70,116

Note: (1) Figures cover the Los Angeles-Long Beach-Santa Ana, CA Metropolitan Statistical Area—see Appendix B for areas included
Source: U.S. Census Bureau, 2008-2010 American Community Survey 3-Year Estimates

Household Income Distribution

Area	Percent of Households Earning							
	Under $15,000	$15,000 -24,999	$25,000 -34,999	$35,000 -49,999	$50,000 -74,999	$75,000 -99,000	$100,000 -149,999	$150,000 and up
City	9.6	5.2	4.7	6.7	15.3	14.0	21.3	23.1
MSA[1]	11.1	9.9	9.2	12.7	17.5	12.3	14.4	12.7
U.S.	13.0	11.0	10.6	14.2	18.5	12.1	12.2	8.4

Note: (1) Figures cover the Los Angeles-Long Beach-Santa Ana, CA Metropolitan Statistical Area—see Appendix B for areas included
Source: U.S. Census Bureau, 2008-2010 American Community Survey 3-Year Estimates

Poverty Rate

Area	All Ages	Under 18 Years Old	18 to 64 Years Old	65 Years and Over
City	10.9	7.1	12.4	8.2
MSA[1]	15.1	21.2	13.4	10.8
U.S.	14.4	20.1	13.1	9.4

Note: Figures are percentage of people whose income during the past 12 months was below the poverty level; (1) Figures cover the Los Angeles-Long Beach-Santa Ana, CA Metropolitan Statistical Area—see Appendix B for areas included
Source: U.S. Census Bureau, 2008-2010 American Community Survey 3-Year Estimates

Personal Bankruptcy Filing Rate

Area	2006	2007	2008	2009	2010	2011
Orange County	0.88	1.61	3.03	4.93	6.26	6.03
U.S.	2.00	2.73	3.53	4.61	4.97	4.37

Note: Numbers are per 1,000 population and include Chapter 7 and Chapter 13 filings
Source: Federal Deposit Insurance Corporation, Regional Economic Conditions, March 9, 2012

EMPLOYMENT

Labor Force and Employment

Area	Civilian Labor Force			Workers Employed		
	Dec. 2010	Dec. 2011	% Chg.	Dec. 2010	Dec. 2011	% Chg.
City	81,681	83,158	1.8	76,160	78,312	2.8
MD[1]	1,573,923	1,597,153	1.5	1,432,760	1,473,258	2.8
U.S.	153,156,000	153,373,000	0.1	139,159,000	140,681,000	1.1

Note: Data is not seasonally adjusted and covers workers 16 years of age and older; (1) Metropolitan Division—see Appendix B for areas included
Source: Bureau of Labor Statistics, http://stats.bls.gov

Unemployment Rate

Area	2011											
	Jan.	Feb.	Mar.	Apr.	May	Jun.	Jul.	Aug.	Sep.	Oct.	Nov.	Dec.
City	6.9	6.7	6.8	6.5	6.4	6.9	7.0	6.8	6.5	6.4	6.1	5.8
MD[1]	9.2	8.9	9.1	8.6	8.5	9.2	9.3	9.0	8.6	8.5	8.1	7.8
U.S.	9.8	9.5	9.2	8.7	8.7	9.3	9.3	9.1	8.8	8.5	8.2	8.3

Note: Data is not seasonally adjusted and covers workers 16 years of age and older; All figures are percentages; (1) Metropolitan Division—see Appendix B for areas included
Source: Bureau of Labor Statistics, http://stats.bls.gov

Projected Unemployment Rate

Area	2010 (%)	2011 (%)	2012 (%)	2013 (%)
MSA[1]	12.1	10.8	10.1	9.3

Note: (1) Metropolitan Statistical Area—see Appendix B for areas included
Source: The United States Conference of Mayors, "U.S. Metro Economies: GMP and Employment Forecasts," June 2011

Employment by Occupation

Occupation Classification	City (%)	MSA[1] (%)	U.S. (%)
Management, Business, Science, and Arts	61.8	36.0	35.6
Natural Resources, Construction, and Maintenance	2.4	7.9	9.5
Production, Transportation, and Material Moving	3.8	12.3	12.1
Sales and Office	24.4	26.0	25.2
Service	7.6	17.8	17.6

Note: Figures cover employed civilians 16 years of age and older; (1) Figures cover the Los Angeles-Long Beach-Santa Ana, CA Metropolitan Statistical Area—see Appendix B for areas included
Source: U.S. Census Bureau, 2008-2010 American Community Survey 3-Year Estimates

Employment by Industry

Sector	MD[1]		U.S.
	Number of Employees	Percent of Total	Percent of Total
Construction	66,900	4.8	4.1
Education and Health Services	160,500	11.5	15.2
Financial Activities	104,200	7.5	5.8
Government	151,800	10.9	16.8
Information	24,100	1.7	2.0
Leisure and Hospitality	174,800	12.6	9.9
Manufacturing	155,300	11.2	8.9
Mining and Logging	500	<0.1	0.6
Other Services	42,600	3.1	4.0
Professional and Business Services	254,500	18.3	13.3
Retail Trade	150,600	10.8	11.5
Transportation and Utilities	27,900	2.0	3.8
Wholesale Trade	78,500	5.6	4.2

Note: Figures cover non-farm employment as of December 2011 and are not seasonally adjusted; (1) Metropolitan Division—see Appendix B for areas included
Source: Bureau of Labor Statistics, http://stats.bls.gov

Occupations with Greatest Projected Employment Growth: 2008 – 2018

Occupation[1]	2008 Employment	2018 Projected Employment	Numeric Employment Change	Percent Employment Change
Personal and Home Care Aides	346,500	504,700	158,200	45.7
Registered Nurses	236,400	297,200	60,800	25.7
Retail Salespersons	499,400	559,100	59,700	12.0
Combined Food Preparation and Serving Workers, Including Fast Food	260,600	308,800	48,200	18.5
Elementary School Teachers, Except Special Education	197,500	233,400	35,900	18.2
Office Clerks, General	372,500	407,400	34,900	9.4
Customer Service Representatives	202,200	236,600	34,400	17.0
Waiters and Waitresses	245,600	279,900	34,300	14.0
Stock Clerks and Order Fillers	207,700	237,100	29,400	14.2
Postsecondary Teachers	168,000	196,100	28,100	16.7

Note: Projections cover California; (1) Sorted by numeric employment change
Source: www.projectionscentral.com, State Occupational Projections, 2008–2018 Long-Term Projections

Fastest Growing Occupations: 2008 – 2018

Occupation[1]	2008 Employment	2018 Projected Employment	Numeric Employment Change	Percent Employment Change
Biomedical Engineers	3,100	5,600	2,500	80.6
Network Systems and Data Communications Analysts	35,000	52,600	17,600	50.3
Biochemists and Biophysicists	4,800	7,100	2,300	47.9
Medical Scientists, Except Epidemiologists	26,200	38,500	12,300	46.9
Personal and Home Care Aides	346,500	504,700	158,200	45.7
Home Health Aides	54,300	78,000	23,700	43.6
Physician Assistants	8,100	11,500	3,400	42.0
Separating, Filtering, Clarifying, Precipitating, and Still Machine Setters, Operators, and Te	7,300	10,200	2,900	39.7
Physical Therapist Aides	5,900	8,100	2,200	37.3
Electrical and Electronics Repairers, Powerhouse, Substation, and Relay	1,100	1,500	400	36.4

Note: Projections cover California; (1) Sorted by percent employment change and excludes occupations with numeric employment change less than 100
Source: www.projectionscentral.com, State Occupational Projections, 2008–2018 Long-Term Projections

Average Wages

Occupation	$/Hr.	Occupation	$/Hr.
Accountants and Auditors	35.34	Maids and Housekeeping Cleaners	10.33
Automotive Mechanics	21.61	Maintenance and Repair Workers	18.09
Bookkeepers	20.04	Marketing Managers	66.97
Carpenters	27.99	Nuclear Medicine Technologists	45.74
Cashiers	11.00	Nurses, Licensed Practical	23.45
Clerks, General Office	15.22	Nurses, Registered	39.33
Clerks, Receptionists/Information	13.65	Nursing Aides/Orderlies/Attendants	13.86
Clerks, Shipping/Receiving	15.39	Packers and Packagers, Hand	10.50
Computer Programmers	35.93	Physical Therapists	40.02
Computer Support Specialists	28.47	Postal Service Mail Carriers	26.15
Computer Systems Analysts	41.41	Real Estate Brokers	47.09
Cooks, Restaurant	11.68	Retail Salespersons	13.42
Dentists	56.38	Sales Reps., Exc. Tech./Scientific	32.23
Electrical Engineers	47.12	Sales Reps., Tech./Scientific	43.66
Electricians	27.78	Secretaries, Exc. Legal/Med./Exec.	18.40
Financial Managers	67.44	Security Guards	14.09
First-Line Supervisors/Managers, Sales	21.14	Surgeons	86.61
Food Preparation Workers	11.06	Teacher Assistants	15.50
General and Operations Managers	65.01	Teachers, Elementary School	33.00
Hairdressers/Cosmetologists	12.29	Teachers, Secondary School	35.10
Internists	84.72	Telemarketers	16.54
Janitors and Cleaners	11.86	Truck Drivers, Heavy/Tractor-Trailer	22.37
Landscaping/Groundskeeping Workers	12.41	Truck Drivers, Light/Delivery Svcs.	16.70
Lawyers	72.46	Waiters and Waitresses	10.52

Note: Wage data covers the Santa Ana-Anaheim-Irvine, CA Metropolitan Division—see Appendix B for areas included. Hourly wages for elementary/secondary school teachers and teacher assistants were calculated by the editors from annual wage data assuming a 40 hour work week; n/a not available.
Source: Bureau of Labor Statistics, Metro Area Occupational Employment and Wage Estimates, May 2011

RESIDENTIAL REAL ESTATE

Building Permits

Area	Single-Family			Multi-Family			Total		
	2010	2011	Pct. Chg.	2010	2011	Pct. Chg.	2010	2011	Pct. Chg.
City	641	857	33.7	1,113	1,776	59.6	1,754	2,633	50.1
MSA[1]	4,008	4,097	2.2	6,386	10,150	58.9	10,394	14,247	37.1
U.S.	447,311	418,498	-6.4	157,299	205,563	30.7	604,610	624,061	3.2

Note: (1) Metropolitan Statistical Area—see Appendix B for areas included; figures represent new, privately-owned housing units authorized (unadjusted data); All permit data are based on estimates with imputation.
Source: U.S. Census Bureau, Manufacturing, Mining, and Construction Statistics, Building Permits, 2010, 2011

Homeownership Rate

Area	2005 (%)	2006 (%)	2007 (%)	2008 (%)	2009 (%)	2010 (%)	2011 (%)
MSA[1]	54.6	54.4	52.3	52.1	50.4	49.7	50.1
U.S.	68.9	68.8	68.1	67.8	67.4	66.9	66.1

Note: (1) Metropolitan Statistical Area—see Appendix B for areas included
Source: U.S. Census Bureau, Housing Vacancies and Homeownership Annual Statistics: 2011

Housing Vacancy Rates

Area	Gross Vacancy Rate[2] (%)			Year-Round Vacancy Rate[3] (%)			Rental Vacancy Rate[4] (%)			Homeowner Vacancy Rate[5] (%)		
	2009	2010	2011	2009	2010	2011	2009	2010	2011	2009	2010	2011
MSA[1]	6.6	7.2	6.7	6.3	6.9	6.4	6.4	6.7	5.3	1.3	1.8	1.8
U.S.	14.5	14.3	14.2	11.3	11.3	11.1	10.6	10.2	9.5	2.6	2.6	2.5

Note: (1) Metropolitan Statistical Area—see Appendix B for areas included; (2) The percentage of the total housing inventory that is vacant; (3) The percentage of the housing inventory (excluding seasonal units) that is year-round vacant; (4) The percentage of rental inventory that is vacant for rent; (5) The percentage of homeowner inventory that is vacant for sale
Source: U.S. Census Bureau, Housing Vacancies and Homeownership Annual Statistics: 2011

TAXES

State Corporate Income Tax Rates

State	Tax Rate (%)	Income Brackets ($)	Num. of Brackets	Financial Institution Tax Rate (%)[a]	Federal Income Tax Ded.
California	8.84 (c)	Flat rate	1	10.84 (c)	No

Note: Tax rates as of January 1, 2012; (a) Rates listed are the corporate income tax rate applied to financial institutions or excise taxes based on income. Some states have other taxes based upon the value of deposits or shares; (c) The minimum corporation franchise tax in California is $800. The additional alternative minimum tax is levied at a 6.65% rate.
Source: Federation of Tax Administrators, "State Corporate Income Tax Rates, 2012"

State Individual Income Tax Rates

State	Tax Rate (%)	Income Brackets ($)	Num. of Brackets	Personal Exempt. ($)[1]		Fed. Inc. Tax Ded.
				Single	Dependents	
California (a)	1.0 - 9.3 (f)	7,316 (b) - 48,029 (b)	6	102 (c)	315 (c)	No

Note: Tax rates as of January 1, 2012; Local- and county-level taxes are not included; n/a not applicable; (1) Married joint filers generally receive double the single exemption; (a) 17 states have statutory provision for automatically adjusting to the rate of inflation the dollar values of the income tax brackets, standard deductions, and/or personal exemptions. Massachusetts, Michigan, and Nebraska index the personal exemptiononly. Oregon does not index the income brackets for $125,000 and over. Because the inflation-adjustments for 2012 are not yet available in some cases, the table may report the 2011 amounts; (b) For joint returns, taxes are twice the tax on half the couple's income; (c) The personal exemption takes the form of a tax credit instead of a deduction; (f) California imposes an additional 1% tax on taxable income over $1 million, making the maximum rate 10.3% over $1 million.
Source: Federation of Tax Administrators, "State Individual Income Tax Rates, 2012"

Various State and Local Tax Rates

State	State and Local Sales and Use (%)	State Sales and Use (%)	Gasoline[1] (¢/gal.)	Cigarette[2] ($/pack)	Spirits[3] ($/gal.)	Wine[4] ($/gal.)	Beer[5] ($/gal.)
California	7.75	7.25 (b)	48.6	0.87	3.30	0.20	0.20

Note: All tax rates as of January 1, 2012 except beer, wine and spirits (September 1, 2011); (1) The American Petroleum Institute has developed a methodology for determining the average tax rate on a gallon of fuel. Rates may include any of the following: excise taxes, environmental fees, storage tank fees, other fees or taxes, general sales tax, and local taxes. In states where gasoline is subject to the general sales tax, or where the fuel tax is based on the average sale price, the average rate determined by API is sensitive to changes in the price of gasoline. States that fully or partially apply general sales taxes to gasoline: CA, CO, GA, IL, IN, MI, NY; (2) The federal excise tax of $1.0066 per pack and local taxes are not included; (3) Rates are those applicable to off-premise sales of 40% alcohol by volume (a.b.v.) distilled spirits in 750ml containers. Local excise taxes are excluded; (4) Rates are those applicable to off-premise sales of 11% a.b.v. non-carbonated wine in 750ml containers; (5) Rates are those applicable to off-premise sales of 4.7% a.b.v. beer in 12 ounce containers; (b) Three states collect a separate, uniform "local" add-on sales tax: California (1%), Utah (1.25%), Virginia (1%). These amounts are included in the state sales tax column.
Source: Tax Foundation, 2012 Facts & Figures: How Does Your State Compare?

State-Local Tax Burdens

Area	Rate (%)	Rank[1]	Per Capita Taxes Paid to Home State ($)	Total State and Local Per Capita Taxes Paid ($)	Per Capita Income ($)
California	10.6	6	3,874	4,910	46,366
U.S. Average	9.8	-	3,057	4,160	42,539

Note: Figures cover 2009; (1) Rank ranges from 1 to 50 where 1 is highest tax burden
Source: Tax Foundation, State-Local Tax Burdens, All States, 2009

State Business Tax Climate Index Rankings

State	Overall Rank	Corporate Tax Index Rank	Individual Income Tax Index Rank	Sales Tax Index Rank	Unemployment Insurance Tax Index Rank	Property Tax Index Rank
California	48	43	50	40	13	17

Note: The index is a measure of how each state's tax laws affect economic performance. The lower the rank, the more favorable a state's tax system is for business. States without a given tax are given a ranking of 1.
Source: Tax Foundation, Major Components of the State Business Tax Climate Index, FY 2012

COMMERCIAL REAL ESTATE

Office Market

Market Area	Inventory (sq. ft.)	Vacant (sq. ft.)	Vac. Rate (%)	Under Constr. (sq. ft.)	Asking Rent ($/sf/yr) Class A	Asking Rent ($/sf/yr) Class B
Orange County	86,167,565	15,366,985	17.8	0	26.11	21.72

Source: Grubb & Ellis, Office Markets Trends, 4th Quarter 2011

Industrial Market

Market Area	Inventory (sq. ft.)	Vacant (sq. ft.)	Vac. Rate (%)	Under Constr. (sq. ft.)	Asking Rent ($/sf/yr) WH/Dist	Asking Rent ($/sf/yr) R&D/Flex
Orange County	265,104,992	13,805,137	5.2	0	6.00	11.64

Source: Grubb & Ellis, Industrial Markets Trends, 4th Quarter 2011

COMMERCIAL UTILITIES

Typical Monthly Electric Bills

Area	Commercial Service ($/month) 1,500 kWh	Commercial Service ($/month) 40 kW demand 14,000 kWh	Industrial Service ($/month) 1,000 kW demand 200,000 kWh	Industrial Service ($/month) 50,000 kW demand 15,000,000 kWh
City	283	2,469	52,039	2,061,098
Average[1]	189	1,616	25,197	1,470,813

Note: Based on total rates in effect July 1, 2011; (1) average based on 184 utilities surveyed
Source: Edison Electric Institute, Typical Bills and Average Rates Report, Summer 2011

TRANSPORTATION

Means of Transportation to Work

Area	Car/Truck/Van: Drove Alone	Car/Truck/Van: Car-pooled	Public Transportation: Bus	Public Transportation: Subway	Public Transportation: Railroad	Bicycle	Walked	Other Means	Worked at Home
City	76.2	7.7	0.9	0.1	0.5	2.2	5.0	1.0	6.4
MSA[1]	73.3	11.0	5.6	0.3	0.2	0.8	2.6	1.3	4.8
U.S.	76.0	10.2	2.7	1.7	0.5	0.5	2.8	1.3	4.2

Note: Figures are percentages and cover workers 16 years of age and older; (1) Figures cover the Los Angeles-Long Beach-Santa Ana, CA Metropolitan Statistical Area—see Appendix B for areas included
Source: U.S. Census Bureau, 2008-2010 American Community Survey 3-Year Estimates

Travel Time to Work

Area	Less Than 10 Minutes	10 to 19 Minutes	20 to 29 Minutes	30 to 44 Minutes	45 to 59 Minutes	60 to 89 Minutes	90 Minutes or More
City	8.8	41.1	23.6	16.1	3.9	4.9	1.5
MSA[1]	8.8	26.8	20.5	24.6	8.9	7.7	2.8
U.S.	13.9	30.1	20.8	19.8	7.5	5.5	2.5

Note: Figures are percentages and include workers 16 years old and over; (1) Figures cover the Los Angeles-Long Beach-Santa Ana, CA Metropolitan Statistical Area—see Appendix B for areas included
Source: U.S. Census Bureau, 2008-2010 American Community Survey 3-Year Estimates

Travel Time Index

Area	1985	1990	1995	2000	2005	2010
Urban Area[1]	1.23	1.41	1.36	1.39	1.42	1.38
Average[2]	1.11	1.16	1.18	1.21	1.25	1.20

Note: Travel Time Index—the ratio of travel time in the peak period to the travel time at free-flow conditions. A value of 1.30 indicates a 20-minute free-flow trip takes 26 minutes in the peak. Free-flow speeds (60 mph on freeways and 35 mph on principal arterials) are used as the comparison threshold; (1) Covers the Los Angeles-Long Beach-Santa Ana CA urban area; (2) average of 439 urban areas
Source: Texas Transportation Institute, Urban Mobility Report 2011, September 2011

Public Transportation

Agency Name / Mode of Transportation	Vehicles Operated in Maximum Service	Annual Unlinked Passenger Trips ('000)	Annual Passenger Miles ('000)
Orange County Transportation Authority (OCTA)			
Bus (directly operated)	442	52,472.6	228,594.5
Bus (purchased transportation)	80	904.0	6,452.5
Demand Response (purchased transportation)	350	1,431.1	15,093.0
Demand Response Taxi (purchased transportation)	55	51.8	202.4
Vanpool (purchased transportation)	286	848.7	30,208.6

Source: Federal Transit Administration, National Transit Database, 2010

Air Transportation

Airport Name and Code / Type of Service	Passenger Airlines[1]	Passenger Enplanements	Freight Carriers[2]	Freight (lbs.)
John Wayne International (Santa Ana) (SNA)				
Domestic service (U.S. carriers - 2011)	13	4,198,351	9	27,623,220
International service (U.S. carriers - 2010)	4	1,106	0	0

Note: (1) Includes all U.S.-based major, minor and commuter airlines that carried at least one passenger during the year; (2) Includes all U.S.-based airlines and freight carriers that transported at least one pound of freight during the year
Source: Bureau of Transportation Statistics, The Intermodal Transportation Database, Air Carriers: T-100 Domestic Market (U.S. Carriers), 2011; Bureau of Transportation Statistics, The Intermodal Transportation Database, Air Carriers: T-100 International Market (U.S. Carriers), 2010

Other Transportation Statistics

Major Highways:	I-5
Amtrak Service:	Yes
Major Waterways/Ports:	Near the Pacific Ocean (5 miles)

Source: Amtrak.com; Google Maps

BUSINESSES

Major Business Headquarters

Company Name	Rankings	
	Fortune[1]	Forbes[2]
Allergan	457	-
Broadcom	343	-
Golden State Foods	-	71
Spectrum Group International	381	-
Vizio	-	146

Note: (1) Fortune 500—companies that produce a 10-K are ranked 1 to 500 based on 2010 revenue; (2) all private companies with at least $2 billion in annual revenue are ranked 1 to 212; companies listed are headquartered in the city; dashes indicate no ranking
Source: Fortune, "Fortune 500," May 23, 2011; Forbes, "America's Largest Private Companies," November 16, 2011

Fast-Growing Businesses

According to *Inc.*, Irvine is home to five of America's 500 fastest-growing private companies: **eGumBall** (#89); **Vinculums** (#341); **Cosemi Technologies** (#426); **Source Consulting** (#469); **US Lighting Tech** (#499). Criteria: must be an independent, privately-held, for-profit, U.S. corporation, proprietorship or partnership; revenues must be at least $80,000 in 2007 and $2 million in 2010; must have four-year operating/sales history. Holding companies, regulated banks, and utilities were excluded. *Inc., "America's 500 Fastest-Growing Private Companies," September 2011*

According to *Fortune*, Irvine is home to one of the 100 fastest-growing companies in the world: **Broadcom** (#84). Companies were ranked by their revenue growth rate; their EPS growth rate; and their three-year annualized total return to investors for the period ending June 30, 2011. Criteria for inclusion: a company, foreign or domestic, must trade on a major U.S. stock exchange; must file quarterly reports with the SEC; must have a minimum market capitalization of $250 million; must have a stock price of at least $5 on June 30, 2011; must have been trading continuously since June 30, 2008; must have revenue and net income for the four quarters ended on or before April 30, 2011, of at least $50 million and $10 million, respectively; and must have posted a compound annual growth in revenue and earnings per share of at least 15% annually over the three years ending on or before April 30, 2011. REITs, limited-liability companies, limited parterships, companies about to be acquired, and companies that lost money in the quarter ending April 30, 2011 were excluded. *Fortune, "100 Fastest-Growing Companies," September 26, 2011*

According to Deloitte, Irvine is home to four of North America's 500 fastest-growing high-technology companies: **Cortex Pharmaceuticals** (#136); **Local.com Corp.** (#191); **ISTA Pharmaceuticals** (#239); **Endologix** (#248). Companies are ranked by percentage growth in revenue over a five-year period. Criteria for inclusion: company must be headquartered within North America; must own proprietary intellectual property or proprietary technology that contributes to a significant portion of the company's operating revenue, or devote a significant proportion of revenues to research and development of technology; must have been in business for a minumum of five years with 2006 operating revenues of at least $50,000 USD/CD and 2010 operating revenues of at least $5 million USD/CD. *Deloitte Touche Tohmatsu, 2011 Deloitte Technology Fast 500™*

Minority- and Women-Owned Businesses

Group	All Firms		Firms with Paid Employees			
	Firms	Sales ($000)	Firms	Sales ($000)	Employees	Payroll ($000)
Asian	6,509	2,395,785	1,245	2,074,142	12,493	487,654
Black	331	151,512	(s)	(s)	(s)	(s)
Hispanic	(s)	(s)	(s)	(s)	(s)	(s)
Women	7,408	1,818,566	1,107	1,551,101	12,178	528,628
All Firms	28,549	108,138,725	8,721	106,752,284	254,282	15,288,563

Note: Figures cover firms located in the city; minority- and women-owned business are defined as firms in which the corresponding group own 51% or more of the stock or equity of the company; (s) estimates are suppressed when publication standards are not met
Source: U.S. Census Bureau, 2007 Economic Census, Survey of Business Owners

HOTELS

Hotels/Motels

Area	5 Star		4 Star		3 Star		2 Star		1 Star		Not Rated	
	Num.	Pct.[3]	Num.	Pct.[3]	Num.	Pct.[3]	Num.	Pct.[3]	Num.	Pct.[3]	Num.	Pct.[3]
City[1]	0	0.0	3	6.5	24	52.2	17	37.0	1	2.2	1	2.2
Total[2]	133	0.9	940	6.5	4,569	31.8	7,033	48.9	351	2.4	1,343	9.3

Note: (1) Figures cover Irvine and vicinity; (2) Figures cover all 100 cities in this book; (3) Percentage of hotels which have a given star rating; Star ratings are determined by expedia.com and offer an indication of the general quality of a particular hotel.
Source: expedia.com, April 25, 2012

The Santa Ana-Anaheim-Irvine, CA metro area is home to six of the best hotels in the U.S. according to *Travel & Leisure*: **Pelican Hill** (#11); **Montage Laguna Beach** (#72); **Surf & Sand** (#85); **Ritz-Carlton, Laguna Niguel** (#116); **St. Regis Monarch Beach** (#167); **Hyatt Regency Huntington Beach Resort & Spa** (#184). Criteria: service; location; rooms; food; and value. *Travel & Leisure, "T+L 500, The World's Best Hotels 2012"*

EVENT SITES

Major Stadiums, Arenas, and Auditoriums

Name	Max. Capacity
Bren Events Center, UC Irvine	5,710
Verizon Wireless Amphitheater Irvine	16,085

Source: Original research

Living Environment

COST OF LIVING

Cost of Living Index

Composite Index	Groceries	Housing	Utilities	Trans-portation	Health Care	Misc. Goods/ Services
142.9	108.2	230.3	112.8	112.0	109.0	104.4

Note: U.S. = 100; Figures cover the Orange County CA urban area.
Source: The Council for Community and Economic Research, ACCRA Cost of Living Index, 2011

Grocery Prices

Area[1]	T-Bone Steak ($/pound)	Frying Chicken ($/pound)	Whole Milk ($/half gal.)	Eggs ($/dozen)	Orange Juice ($/64 oz.)	Coffee ($/11.5 oz.)
City[2]	9.34	1.08	2.23	2.26	3.30	5.48
Avg.	9.25	1.18	2.22	1.66	3.19	4.40
Min.	6.70	0.88	1.31	0.95	2.46	2.94
Max.	14.30	2.16	3.50	3.18	4.75	6.83

Note: (1) Values for the local area are compared with the average, minimum and maximum values for all 335 areas in the Cost of Living Index; (2) Figures cover the Orange County CA urban area; **T-Bone Steak** *(price per pound);* **Frying Chicken** *(price per pound, whole fryer);* **Whole Milk** *(half gallon carton);* **Eggs** *(price per dozen, Grade A, large);* **Orange Juice** *(64 oz. Tropicana or Florida Natural);* **Coffee** *(11.5 oz. can, vacuum-packed, Maxwell House, Hills Bros, or Folgers).*
Source: The Council for Community and Economic Research, ACCRA Cost of Living Index, 2011

Housing and Utility Costs

Area[1]	New Home Price ($)	Apartment Rent ($/month)	All Electric ($/month)	Part Electric ($/month)	Other Energy ($/month)	Telephone ($/month)
City[2]	681,690	1,678	-	134.27	54.93	29.85
Avg.	285,990	839	163.23	89.00	77.52	26.92
Min.	188,005	460	125.58	45.39	33.89	17.98
Max.	1,197,028	3,244	339.16	181.97	348.69	40.01

Note: (1) Values for the local area are compared with the average, minimum and maximum values for all 335 areas in the Cost of Living Index; (2) Figures cover the Orange County CA urban area; **New Home Price** *(2,400 sf living area, 8,000 sf lot, in urban area with full utilities);* **Apartment Rent** *(950 sf 2 bedroom/1.5 or 2 bath, unfurnished, excluding all utilities except water);* **All Electric** *(average monthly cost for an all-electric home);* **Part Electric** *(average monthly cost for a part-electric home);* **Other Energy** *(average monthly cost for natural gas, fuel oil, coal, wood, and any other forms of energy except electricity);* **Telephone** *(price includes basic monthly rate for a private residential line plus additional local usage charges incurred by a family of four).*
Source: The Council for Community and Economic Research, ACCRA Cost of Living Index, 2011

Health Care, Transportation, and Other Costs

Area[1]	Doctor ($/visit)	Dentist ($/visit)	Optometrist ($/visit)	Gasoline ($/gallon)	Beauty Salon ($/visit)	Men's Shirt ($)
City[2]	91.85	95.00	102.90	3.81	58.46	24.56
Avg.	93.88	81.72	90.54	3.48	32.65	25.06
Min.	60.00	55.33	53.66	3.18	19.78	13.44
Max.	154.98	145.97	183.72	4.31	63.21	46.00

Note: (1) Values for the local area are compared with the average, minimum and maximum values for all 335 areas in the Cost of Living Index; (2) Figures cover the Orange County CA urban area; **Doctor** *(general practitioners routine exam of an established patient);* **Dentist** *(adult teeth cleaning and periodic oral examination);* **Optometrist** *(full vision eye exam for established adult patient);* **Gasoline** *(one gallon regular unleaded, national brand, including all taxes, cash price at self-service pump if available);* **Beauty Salon** *(woman's shampoo, trim, and blow-dry);* **Men's Shirt** *(cotton/polyester dress shirt, pinpoint weave, long sleeves).*
Source: The Council for Community and Economic Research, ACCRA Cost of Living Index, 2011

HOUSING

House Price Index (HPI)

Area	National Ranking[2]	Quarterly Change (%)	One-Year Change (%)	Five-Year Change (%)
MD[1]	199	-0.44	-3.89	-30.93
U.S.[3]	-	-0.10	-2.43	-19.16

Note: The HPI is a weighted repeat sales index. It measures average price changes in repeat sales or refinancings on the same properties. This information is obtained by reviewing repeat mortgage transactions on single-family properties whose mortgages have been purchased or securitized by Fannie Mae or Freddie Mac in January 1975; (1) Metropolitan Division - see Appendix B for areas included; (2) Rankings are based on annual percentage change for all metro areas containing at least 15,000 transactions over the last 10 years and ranges from 1 to 306; (3) figures based on a weighted average of Census Division estimates using a purchase only index; all figures are for the period ending December 31, 2011
Source: Federal Housing Finance Agency, House Price Index, February 23, 2012

House Price Valuations

Area	Q4 2005		Q4 2006		Q4 2007		Q4 2008		Q4 2009	
	Price ($000)	Over-valuation	Price ($000)	Over-valuation	Price ($000)	Over-valuation	Price ($000)	Over-valuation	Price ($000)	Over-valuation
MD[1]	612.8	31.1	616.5	24.1	545.6	6.4	446.1	-11.4	474.6	-5.6

Note: Figures show the percentage of over- or under-valuation of single family homes relative to statistically normal house values (e.g. a value of 23.6 indicates that house values are 23.6% overvalued). Statistically normal house values are based on house prices, interest rates, household incomes, population densities, and any historical premiums or discounts metropolitan areas have exhibited over time; (1) Figures cover the Santa Ana-Anaheim-Irvine, CA - see Appendix B for areas included
Source: Global Insight/PNC Financial Services Group, House Prices in America: 4th Quarter 2009 Update

Median Single-Family Home Prices

Area	2009	2010	2011p	Percent Change 2010 to 2011
MD[1]	477.2	546.4	512.5	-6.2
U.S. Average	172.1	173.1	166.2	-4.0

Note: Figures are median sales prices of existing single-family homes in thousands of dollars; (p) preliminary; n/a not available; (1) Metropolitan Division—see Appendix B for areas included
Source: National Association of Realtors, Median Sales Price of Existing Single-Family Homes for Metropolitan Areas, 4th Quarter 2011

Affordability Index of Existing Single-Family Homes

Area	2009	2010	2011p	Percent Change 2010 to 2011
MSA[1]	49.1	45.6	51.1	12.1

Note: The housing affordability index measures whether or not a typical family could qualify for a mortgage loan on a typical home. The higher the index, the greater the household purchasing power. An index of 100 is defined as the point where a median-income household has exactly enough income to qualify for the purchase of a median-priced existing single-family home, assuming a 20 percent downpayment and 25 percent of gross income devoted to mortgage principal and interest payments; (p) preliminary; n/a not available; (1) Metropolitan Statistical Area—see Appendix B for areas included
Source: National Association of Realtors, Affordability Index of Existing Single-Family Homes, 2011

Median Apartment Condo-Coop Home Prices

Area	2009	2010	2011p	Percent Change 2010 to 2011
MSA[1]	n/a	n/a	n/a	n/a
U.S. Average	175.6	171.7	165.1	-3.8

Note: Figures are median sales prices of existing apartment condo-coop homes in thousands of dollars; (p) preliminary; n/a not available; (1) Metropolitan Statistical Area—see Appendix B for areas included
Source: National Association of Realtors, Median Sales Price of Existing Apartment Condo-Coop Homes for Metropolitan Areas, 4th Quarter 2011

Year Housing Structure Built

Area	2005 or Later	2000 -2004	1990 -1999	1980 -1989	1970 -1979	1960 -1969	1950 -1959	Before 1950	Median Year
City	10.7	20.9	16.5	20.1	26.0	4.5	0.7	0.6	1989
MSA[1]	2.1	3.9	7.2	12.6	17.0	16.5	19.1	21.6	1966
U.S.	5.0	8.6	14.0	14.1	16.3	11.3	11.2	19.6	1975

Note: Figures are percentages except for Median Year; (1) Figures cover the Los Angeles-Long Beach-Santa Ana, CA Metropolitan Statistical Area—see Appendix B for areas included
Source: U.S. Census Bureau, 2008-2010 American Community Survey 3-Year Estimates

HEALTH

Health Risk Data

Category	MSA[1] (%)	U.S. (%)
Adults who have been told they have high blood pressure[2]	22.8	28.7
Adults who have been told they have high blood cholesterol[2]	35.9	37.5
Adults who have been told they have diabetes[3]	8.1	8.7
Adults who have been told they have arthritis[2]	18.5	26.0
Adults who have been told they currently have asthma	6.5	9.1
Adults who are current smokers	9.0	17.3
Adults who are heavy drinkers[4]	4.3	5.0
Adults who are binge drinkers[5]	14.9	15.1
Adults who are overweight (BMI 25.0 - 29.9)	36.3	36.2
Adults who are obese (BMI 30.0 - 99.8)	20.7	27.5
Adults who participated in any physical activities in the past month	78.9	76.1
Adults 50+ who have ever had a sigmoidoscopy or colonoscopy	64.8	65.2
Women aged 40+ who have had a mammogram within the past two years	81.0	75.2
Men aged 40+ who have had a PSA test within the past two years	54.1	53.2
Adults aged 65+ who have had flu shot within the past year	68.2	67.5
Adults aged 18–64 who have any kind of health care coverage	81.5	82.2

Note: Data as of 2010 unless otherwise noted; (1) Figures cover the Santa Ana-Anaheim-Irvine, CA Metropolitan Division—see Appendix B for areas included; (2) Data as of 2009; (3) Figures do not include pregnancy-related, borderline, or pre-diabetes; (4) Heavy drinkers are classified as males having more than two drinks per day or females having more than one drink per day; (5) Binge drinkers are classified as males having five or more drinks on one occasion or females having four or more drinks on one occasion
Source: Centers for Disease Control and Prevention, Behaviorial Risk Factor Surveillance System, SMART: Selected Metropolitan/Micropolitan Area Risk Trends, 2009, 2010

Mortality Rates for the Top 10 Causes of Death in the U.S.

ICD-10[a] Sub-Chapter	ICD-10[a] Code	Age-Adjusted Mortality Rate[1] per 100,000 population	
		County[2]	U.S.
Malignant neoplasms	C00-C97	148.1	175.6
Ischaemic heart diseases	I20-I25	110.7	121.6
Other forms of heart disease	I30-I51	34.2	48.6
Chronic lower respiratory diseases	J40-J47	32.4	42.3
Cerebrovascular diseases	I60-I69	37.2	40.6
Organic, including symptomatic, mental disorders	F01-F09	15.1	26.7
Other degenerative diseases of the nervous system	G30-G31	30.7	24.7
Other external causes of accidental injury	W00-X59	16.2	24.4
Diabetes mellitus	E10-E14	14.1	21.7
Hypertensive diseases	I10-I15	16.1	18.2

Note: (a) ICD-10 = International Classification of Diseases 10th Revision; (1) Mortality rates are a three year average covering 2007-2009; (2) Figures cover Orange County
Source: Centers for Disease Control and Prevention, National Center for Health Statistics. Underlying Cause of Death 1999-2009 on CDC WONDER Online Database, released 2012. Data for year 2009 are compiled from the Multiple Cause of Death File 2009, Series 20 No. 2O, 2012, Data for year 2008 are compiled from the Multiple Cause of Death File 2008, Series 20 No. 2N, 2011, Data for year 2007 are compiled from Multiple Cause of Death File 2007, Series 20 No. 2M, 2010.

Mortality Rates for Selected Causes of Death

ICD-10[a] Sub-Chapter	ICD-10[a] Code	Age-Adjusted Mortality Rate[1] per 100,000 population	
		County[2]	U.S.
Assault	X85-Y09	2.5	5.7
Human immunodeficiency virus (HIV) disease	B20-B24	1.3	3.3
Influenza and pneumonia	J09-J18	18.5	16.4
Intentional self-harm	X60-X84	9.0	11.5
Malnutrition	E40-E46	*Unreliable	0.8
Obesity and other hyperalimentation	E65-E68	0.6	1.6
Transport accidents	V01-V99	7.4	13.7
Viral hepatitis	B15-B19	2.4	2.2

Note: (a) ICD-10 = International Classification of Diseases 10th Revision; (1) Mortality rates are a three year average covering 2007-2009; (2) Figures cover Orange County; (*) Unreliable data as per CDC
Source: Centers for Disease Control and Prevention, National Center for Health Statistics. Underlying Cause of Death 1999-2009 on CDC WONDER Online Database, released 2012. Data for year 2009 are compiled from the Multiple Cause of Death File 2009, Series 20 No. 2O, 2012, Data for year 2008 are compiled from the Multiple Cause of Death File 2008, Series 20 No. 2N, 2011, Data for year 2007 are compiled from Multiple Cause of Death File 2007, Series 20 No. 2M, 2010.

Distribution of Physicians and Dentists

Area[1]	Dentists[2]	D.O.[3]	M.D.[4] Total	M.D.[4] Family/General Practice	M.D.[4] Pediatrics	M.D.[4] Medical Specialties	M.D.[4] Surgical Specialties
Local (number)	2,436	445	6,953	948	579	2,575	1,555
Local (rate[5])	8.2	1.5	23.3	3.2	1.9	8.6	5.2
U.S. (rate[5])	4.5	1.9	18.3	2.5	1.4	6.8	4.1

Note: Data as of 2008 unless noted; (1) Local data covers Orange County; (2) Data as of 2007; (3) Doctor of Osteopathic Medicine; (4) Includes active, non-federal, patient-care, office-based Doctors of Medicine; (5) rate per 10,000 population
Source: Area Resource File (ARF). 2009-2010 Release. U.S. Department of Health and Human Services, Health Resources and Services Administration, Bureau of Health Professions, Rockville, MD, August 2010

Best Hospitals

According to *U.S. News,* the Santa Ana-Anaheim-Irvine, CA is home to one of the best hospitals in the U.S.: **University of California-Irvine Medical Center** (4 specialties). The hospital listed was highly ranked in at least one adult specialty. *U.S. News Online, "America's Best Hospitals 2011-12"*

According to *U.S. News,* the Santa Ana-Anaheim-Irvine, CA is home to one of the best children's hospitals in the U.S.: **Children's Hospital of Orange County** (8 specialties). The hospital listed was highly ranked in at least one pediatric specialty. *U.S. News Online, "America's Best Children's Hospitals 2011-12"*

EDUCATION

Public School District Statistics

District Name	Schls	Pupils	Pupil/Teacher Ratio	Minority Pupils[1] (%)	Free Lunch Eligible[2] (%)	IEP[3] (%)
Irvine Unified	35	26,822	26.1	63.4	7.2	9.6

Note: Table includes school districts with 2,000 or more students; (1) Percentage of students that are not non-Hispanic white; (2) Percentage of students that are eligible for the free lunch program; (3) Percentage of students that have an Individualized Education Program.
Source: U.S. Department of Education, National Center for Education Statistics, Common Core of Data, Local Education Agency (School District) Universe Survey: School Year 2009-2010; U.S. Department of Education, National Center for Education Statistics, Common Core of Data, Public Elementary/Secondary School Universe Survey: School Year 2009-2010

Top Public High Schools

High School Name	Rank[1]	Score[1]	Grad. Rate[2] (%)	College[3] (%)	AP/IB/ AICE[4] (%)	SAT/ ACT[5] (%)
Northwood	96	0.781	99	96	2.2	1808
University	8	1.824	98	96	3.2	1920
Woodbridge	477	0.119	87	94	1.4	1766

Note: (1) Public schools are ranked from 1 to 500 based on the following self-reported statistics (with their corresponding weight in the final score). Schools that had fewer than 10 graduates, as well as those that were newly founded and did not have a graduating senior class in 2010 were excluded; (2) Four-year, on-time graduation rate (25%); (3) Percent of 2010 graduates who enrolled immediately in college (25%); (4) AP/IB/AICE tests per graduate (25%); (5) Average SAT and/or ACT score (10%); Average AP/IB/AICE exam score (10%); AP/IB/AICE courses offered per graduate (5%); (6) School is unranked, but has been identified by Newsweek as one of the nation's most elite public high schools.
Source: Newsweek Online, "Top High Schools 2011"

Highest Level of Education

Area	Less than H.S.	H.S. Diploma	Some College, No Deg.	Associate Degree	Bachelors Degree	Masters Degree	Profess. School Degree	Doctorate Degree
City	4.1	8.8	14.7	6.7	37.4	18.6	5.2	4.6
MSA[1]	22.4	19.9	20.0	7.0	20.1	6.9	2.4	1.3
U.S.	14.7	28.4	21.3	7.6	17.6	7.2	1.9	1.2

Note: Figures cover persons age 25 and over; (1) Figures cover the Los Angeles-Long Beach-Santa Ana, CA Metropolitan Statistical Area—see Appendix B for areas included
Source: U.S. Census Bureau, 2008-2010 American Community Survey 3-Year Estimates

Educational Attainment by Race

Area	High School Graduate or Higher (%)					Bachelor's Degree or Higher (%)				
	Total	White	Black	Asian	Hisp.[2]	Total	White	Black	Asian	Hisp.[2]
City	95.9	96.3	90.4	96.3	85.7	65.7	60.6	32.7	77.8	41.2
MSA[1]	77.6	81.4	87.7	86.6	54.8	30.7	33.4	23.2	49.0	10.2
U.S.	85.3	87.5	81.4	85.5	61.6	28.0	29.3	17.8	50.2	13.0

Note: Figures shown cover persons 25 years old and over; (1) Figures cover the Los Angeles-Long Beach-Santa Ana, CA Metropolitan Statistical Area—see Appendix B for areas included; (2) People of Hispanic origin can be of any race
Source: U.S. Census Bureau, 2008-2010 American Community Survey 3-Year Estimates

School Enrollment by Grade and Control

Area	Preschool (%)		Kindergarten (%)		Grades 1 - 4 (%)		Grades 5 - 8 (%)		Grades 9 - 12 (%)	
	Public	Private	Public	Private	Public	Private	Public	Private	Public	Private
City	24.1	75.9	89.2	10.8	91.0	9.0	91.9	8.1	93.9	6.1
MSA[1]	57.7	42.3	87.4	12.6	90.2	9.8	90.3	9.7	91.8	8.2
U.S.	55.4	44.6	87.1	12.9	89.4	10.6	89.5	10.5	90.4	9.6

Note: Figures shown cover persons 3 years old and over; (1) Figures cover the Los Angeles-Long Beach-Santa Ana, CA Metropolitan Statistical Area—see Appendix B for areas included
Source: U.S. Census Bureau, 2008-2010 American Community Survey 3-Year Estimates

Average Salaries of Public School Classroom Teachers

Area	2010-11		2011-12		Percent Change 2010-11 to 2011-12	Percent Change 2001-02 to 2011-12
	Dollars	Rank[1]	Dollars	Rank[1]		
California	67,871	4	69,496	4	2.39	27.90
U.S. Average	55,623	-	56,643	-	1.83	26.8

Note: (1) State rank ranges from 1 to 51 where 1 indicates highest salary.
Source: National Education Association, Rankings & Estimates: Rankings of the States 2011 and Estimates of School Statistics 2012, December 2011

Higher Education

Four-Year Colleges			Two-Year Colleges			Medical Schools[1]	Law Schools[2]	Voc/ Tech[3]
Public	Private Non-profit	Private For-profit	Public	Private Non-profit	Private For-profit			
1	3	1	1	0	1	1	1	0

Note: Figures cover institutions located within the city limits and include main campuses only; (1) includes schools accredited by the Liaison Committee on Medical Education and the American Osteopathic Association's Commission on Osteopathic College Accreditation; (2) includes American Bar Association-accredited law schools; (3) includes all schools with programs that are less than 2 years.
Source: National Center for Education Statistics, Integrated Postsecondary Education System (IPEDS) Peer Analysis System, 2011-12; Association of American Medical Colleges, Member List, April 23, 2012; American Osteopathic Association, Member List, April 23, 2012; Law School Admission Council, Official Guide to ABA-Approved Law Schools Online, April 23, 2012

According to *U.S. News & World Report,* the Santa Ana-Anaheim-Irvine, CA is home to one of the best national universities in the U.S.: **University of California–Irvine** (#45). The indicators used to capture academic quality fall into a number of categories: assessment by administrators at peer institutions; retention of students; faculty resources; student selectivity; financial resources; alumni giving; high school counselor ratings of colleges; and graduation rate.*U.S. News & World Report, "America's Best Colleges 2012"*

According to *U.S. News & World Report,* the Santa Ana-Anaheim-Irvine, CA is home to one of the best liberal arts colleges in the U.S.: **Soka University of America** (#64). The indicators used to capture academic quality fall into a number of categories: assessment by administrators at peer institutions; retention of students; faculty resources; student selectivity; financial resources; alumni giving; high school counselor ratings of colleges; and graduation rate.*U.S. News & World Report, "America's Best Colleges 2012"*

According to *Forbes,* the Santa Ana-Anaheim-Irvine, CA is home to one of the best business schools in the U.S.: **UC Irvine (Merage)** (#69). The rankings are based on the return on investment that graduates of the Class of 2006 received (median salary five years after graduation). *Forbes, "Best Business Schools," August 3, 2011*

PRESIDENTIAL ELECTION

2008 Presidential Election Results

Area	Obama	McCain	Nader	Other
Orange County	47.6	50.2	0.7	1.5
U.S.	52.9	45.6	0.6	0.9

Note: Results are percentages and may not add to 100% due to rounding
Source: Dave Leip's Atlas of U.S. Presidential Elections, www.uselectionatlas.org

EMPLOYERS

Major Employers

Company Name	Industry
City of Los Angeles	General government
County of Los Angeles	General government
County of Los Angeles	Pubblic welfare administration: nonoperating, government
Decton	Employment agencies
Disney Enterprises	Motion picture production and distribution
Disney Worldwide Services	Telecommunication equipment repair (except telephones)
Electronic Arts	Home entertainment computer software
King Holding Corporation	Bolts, nuts, rivets, and washers
Securitas Security Services USA	Security guard service
Team-One Employment Specialists	Employment agencies
The Boeing Company	Aircraft
The Boeing Company	Aircraft engines and engine parts
The Walt Disney Company	Television broadcasting stations
U C L A Medical Group	Medical centers
Ucla Health System	Home health care services
University of California, Irvine	University
University of Southern California	Colleges and universities
Veterans Health Administration	Administration of veterans' affairs
Warner Bros. Entertainment	Motion picture and video production

Note: Companies shown are located within the Los Angeles-Long Beach-Santa Ana, CA metropolitan area.
Source: Hoovers.com, data extracted April 25 2012

PUBLIC SAFETY

Crime Rate

Area	All Crimes	Violent Crimes: Murder	Violent Crimes: Forcible Rape	Violent Crimes: Robbery	Violent Crimes: Aggrav. Assault	Property Crimes: Burglary	Property Crimes: Larceny -Theft	Property Crimes: Motor Vehicle Theft
City	1,343.5	0.0	11.1	18.4	25.8	221.0	1,011.5	55.7
Suburbs[1]	2,295.4	2.4	15.0	89.7	133.1	369.6	1,475.0	210.5
Metro[2]	2,227.4	2.2	14.8	84.6	125.5	359.0	1,441.9	199.4
U.S.	3,345.5	4.8	27.5	119.1	252.3	699.6	2,003.5	238.8

Note: Figures are crimes per 100,000 population; (1) All areas within the metro area that are located outside the city limits; (2) Metropolitan Division—see Appendix B for areas included
Source: FBI Uniform Crime Reports, 2010

Hate Crimes

Area	Number of Quarters Reported	Bias Motivation: Race	Bias Motivation: Religion	Bias Motivation: Sexual Orientation	Bias Motivation: Ethnicity	Bias Motivation: Disability
City	4	0	0	0	0	0

Source: Federal Bureau of Investigation, Hate Crime Statistics 2010

Identity Theft Consumer Complaints

Area	Complaints	Complaints per 100,000 Population	Rank[2]
MSA[1]	15,380	119.5	40
U.S.	279,156	90.4	-

Note: (1) Metropolitan Statistical Area—see Appendix B for areas included; (2) Rank ranges from 1 to 384 where 1 indicates greatest number of identity theft complaints per 100,000 population
Source: Federal Trade Commission, Consumer Sentinel Network Data Book for January–December 2011

Fraud and Other Consumer Complaints

Area	Complaints	Complaints per 100,000 Population	Rank[2]
MSA[1]	49,239	382.4	324
U.S.	1,533,924	496.8	-

Note: (1) Metropolitan Statistical Area—see Appendix B for areas included; (2) Rank ranges from 1 to 384 where 1 indicates greatest number of fraud and other complaints per 100,000 population
Source: Federal Trade Commission, Consumer Sentinel Network Data Book for January–December 2011

RECREATION

Culture

Dance[1]	Theatre[1]	Instrumental Music[1]	Vocal Music[1]	Series/ Festivals	Museums	Zoos and Aquariums[2]
0	0	2	0	2	3	0

Note: (1) Number of professional perfoming groups; (2) AZA-accredited
Source: The Grey House Performing Arts Directory, 2011-2012; Official Museum Directory, 2011; American Association of Museums, AAM Member Museums, April 2012; Association of Zoos & Aquariums, AZA Member Zoos & Aquariums, April 2012

Professional Sports Teams

Team Name	League
Anaheim Ducks	National Hockey League (NHL)
C.D. Chivas USA	Major League Soccer (MLS)
Los Angeles Angels of Anaheim	Major League Baseball (MLB)
Los Angeles Clippers	National Basketball Association (NBA)
Los Angeles Dodgers	Major League Baseball (MLB)
Los Angeles Galaxy	Major League Soccer (MLS)
Los Angeles Kings	National Hockey League (NHL)
Los Angeles Lakers	National Basketball Association (NBA)

Note: Includes teams located in the Los Angeles-Santa Ana metro area.
Source: Original research

CLIMATE

Average and Extreme Temperatures

Temperature	Jan	Feb	Mar	Apr	May	Jun	Jul	Aug	Sep	Oct	Nov	Dec	Yr.
Extreme High (°F)	89	91	97	108	102	107	112	104	112	105	95	93	112
Average High (°F)	68	69	69	72	73	77	82	83	83	79	73	68	75
Average Temp. (°F)	56	58	58	61	64	68	72	74	72	67	61	56	64
Average Low (°F)	44	46	48	50	55	59	62	64	61	56	48	43	53
Extreme Low (°F)	28	29	31	34	38	42	45	48	44	30	32	25	25

Note: Figures cover the years 1945-1995
Source: National Climatic Data Center, International Station Meteorological Climate Summary, 9/96

Average Precipitation/Snowfall/Humidity

Precip./Humidity	Jan	Feb	Mar	Apr	May	Jun	Jul	Aug	Sep	Oct	Nov	Dec	Yr.
Avg. Precip. (in.)	2.7	2.4	2.2	0.8	0.2	0.1	Tr	0.1	0.4	0.3	1.3	1.5	11.9
Avg. Snowfall (in.)	0	0	0	0	0	0	0	0	0	0	0	Tr	Tr
Avg. Rel. Hum. 7am (%)	78	81	82	79	77	79	80	81	81	80	79	79	80
Avg. Rel. Hum. 4pm (%)	56	57	57	55	58	59	57	57	56	57	56	57	57

Note: Figures cover the years 1945-1995; Tr = Trace amounts (<0.05 in. of rain; <0.5 in. of snow)
Source: National Climatic Data Center, International Station Meteorological Climate Summary, 9/96

Weather Conditions

Temperature			Daytime Sky			Precipitation		
10°F & below	32°F & below	90°F & above	Clear	Partly cloudy	Cloudy	0.01 inch or more precip.	0.1 inch or more snow/ice	Thunderstorms
0	2	18	95	192	78	41	0	4

Note: Figures are average number of days per year and cover the years 1945-1995
Source: National Climatic Data Center, International Station Meteorological Climate Summary, 9/96

HAZARDOUS WASTE

Superfund Sites

Irvine has no sites on the EPA's Superfund Final National Priorities List.
U.S. Environmental Protection Agency, Final National Priorities List, April 17, 2012

AIR & WATER QUALITY

Air Quality Index

Area	Percent of Days when Air Quality was...[2]					AQI Statistics[2]	
	Good	Moderate	Unhealthy for Sensitive Groups	Unhealthy	Very Unhealthy	Maximum	Median
Area[1]	50.1	47.9	1.9	0.0	0.0	119	50

Note: Air Quality Index (AQI) is an index for reporting daily air quality. EPA calculates the AQI for five major air pollutants regulated by the Clean Air Act: ground-level ozone, particle pollution (aka particulate matter), carbon monoxide, sulfur dioxide, and nitrogen dioxide. The AQI runs from 0 to 500. The higher the AQI value, the greater the level of air pollution and the greater the health concern. There are six AQI categories: "Good" AQI is between 0 and 50. Air quality is considered satisfactory; "Moderate" AQI is between 51 and 100. Air quality is acceptable; "Unhealthy for Sensitive Groups" When AQI values are between 101 and 150, members of sensitive groups may experience health effects; "Unhealthy" When AQI values are between 151 and 200 everyone may begin to experience health effects; "Very Unhealthy" AQI values between 201 and 300 trigger a health alert; "Hazardous" AQI values over 300 trigger warnings of emergency conditions (not shown); (1) Data covers Orange County; (2) Based on 365 days with AQI data in 2011.
Source: U.S. Environmental Protection Agency, AirData Report, 2011

Air Quality Index Pollutants

Area	Percent of Days when AQI Pollutant was...[2]					
	Carbon Monoxide	Nitrogen Dioxide	Ozone	Sulfur Dioxide	Particulate Matter 2.5	Particulate Matter 10
Area[1]	0.0	9.0	27.9	0.0	61.6	1.4

Note: The Air Quality Index (AQI) is an index for reporting daily air quality. EPA calculates the AQI for five major air pollutants regulated by the Clean Air Act: ground-level ozone, particle pollution (also known as particulate matter), carbon monoxide, sulfur dioxide, and nitrogen dioxide. The AQI runs from 0 to 500. The higher the AQI value, the greater the level of air pollution and the greater the health concern; (1) Data covers Orange County; (2) Based on 365 days with AQI data in 2011.
Source: U.S. Environmental Protection Agency, AirData Report, 2011

Air Quality Index Trends

Area	Trend Sites (days)								All Sites (days)
	2003	2004	2005	2006	2007	2008	2009	2010	2010
MSA[1]	147	134	113	98	102	94	99	74	79

Note: Figures are the number of days the AQI value exceeded 100 in a given year. An AQI value greater than 100 indicates that air quality would have been in the unhealthful range on that day. Data from exceptional events are included. These counts are presented in two ways. First, the counts are based on sites having an adequate record of monitoring data during the trend period (trend sites). These counts represent the relative change in the number of days with AQI values greater than 100. In the last column, the counts are based on all sites with data in the most recent year (because it is possible for a site to have data in the most recent year but not enough data to be a trend site); (1) Data covers the Los Angeles-Long Beach-Santa Ana, CA—see Appendix B for areas included

Source: U.S. Environmental Protection Agency, Air Quality Index Information, "Number of Days with Air Quality Index Values Greater than 100 at Trend Sites, 2000-2010, and at All Sites in 2010"

Maximum Air Pollutant Concentrations: Particulate Matter, Ozone, CO and Lead

	Particulate Matter 10 (ug/m^3)	Particulate Matter 2.5 Wtd AM (ug/m^3)	Particulate Matter 2.5 24-Hr (ug/m^3)	Ozone (ppm)	Carbon Monoxide (ppm)	Lead (ug/m^3)
MSA[1] Level	71	12.6	32	0.09	4	0.39
NAAQS[2]	150	15	35	0.075	9	0.15
Met NAAQS[2]	Yes	Yes	Yes	No	Yes	No

Note: Data from exceptional events are not included; (1) Data covers the Los Angeles-Long Beach-Santa Ana, CA—see Appendix B for areas included; (2) National Ambient Air Quality Standards; ppm = parts per million; ug/m^3 = micrograms per cubic meter; n/a not available

Concentrations: Particulate Matter 10 (coarse particulate)—highest second maximum 24-hour concentration; Particulate Matter 2.5 Wtd AM (fine particulate)—highest weighted annual mean concentration; Particulate Matter 2.5 24-Hour (fine particulate)—highest 98th percentile 24-hour concentration; Ozone—highest fourth daily maximum 8-hour concentration; Carbon Monoxide—highest second maximum non-overlapping 8-hour concentration; Lead—maximum running 3-month average

Source: U.S. Environmental Protection Agency, CBSA Factbook 2010, Air Quality Statistics by City, 2010

Maximum Air Pollutant Concentrations: Nitrogen Dioxide and Sulfur Dioxide

	Nitrogen Dioxide AM (ppb)	Nitrogen Dioxide 1-Hr (ppb)	Sulfur Dioxide AM (ppb)	Sulfur Dioxide 1-Hr (ppb)	Sulfur Dioxide 24-Hr (ppb)
MSA[1] Level	26.179	72.5	1.394	16.2	4.8
NAAQS[2]	53	100	30	75	140
Met NAAQS[2]	Yes	Yes	Yes	Yes	Yes

Note: Data from exceptional events are not included; (1) Data covers the Los Angeles-Long Beach-Santa Ana, CA—see Appendix B for areas included; (2) National Ambient Air Quality Standards; ppb = parts per billion; n/a not available

Concentrations: Nitrogen Dioxide AM—highest arithmetic mean concentration; Nitrogen Dioxide 1-Hr—highest 98th percentile 1-hour daily maximum concentration; Sulfur Dioxide AM—highest annual mean concentration; Sulfur Dioxide 1-Hr—highest 99th percentile 1-hour daily maximum concentration; Sulfur Dioxide 24-Hr—highest second maximum 24-hour concentration

Source: U.S. Environmental Protection Agency, CBSA Factbook 2010, Air Quality Statistics by City, 2010

Drinking Water

Water System Name	Pop. Served	Primary Water Source Type	Violations[1]	
			Health Based	Monitoring/ Reporting
Irvine Ranch Water District	330,000	Surface	1	0

Note: (1) Based on violation data from January 1, 2011 to December 31, 2011 (includes unresolved violations from earlier years)

Source: U.S. Environmental Protection Agency, Office of Ground Water and Drinking Water, Safe Drinking Water Information System (based on data extracted April 18, 2012)

Las Vegas, Nevada

Background

Upright citizens can accuse Las Vegas of many vices, but not of hypocrisy. Back in 1931, the city officials of this desert town, located 225 miles northeast of Los Angeles, saw gambling to be a growing popular pastime. To capitalize upon that trend, the city simply legalized it. Gambling, combined with spectacular, neon-lit entertainment, lures more than 36.4 million visitors a year to its more than 1,700 casinos and 140,000 hotel rooms.

Before Wayne Newton ever saw his name in lights or Siegfried and Roy made white tigers disappear, Las Vegas was a temporary stopping place for a diverse group of people. In the early 1880s, Las Vegas was a watering hole for those on the trail to California. Areas of the Las Vegas Valley contained artesian wells that supported extensive green meadows, or *vega* in Spanish, hence the name Las Vegas. In 1855 the area was settled by Mormon missionaries, but they left two years later. Finally, in the late 1800s, the land was used for ranching.

In the beginning of the twentieth century, the seeds of the present Las Vegas began to sprout. In 1905 the arrival of the Union Pacific Railroad sprinkled businesses, saloons, and gambling houses along it tracks; the city was formally founded on May 15, 1905. Then, during the Great Depression, men working on the nearby Hoover Dam spent their extra money in the establishments. Finally, gambling was legalized, hydroelectric power from the Hoover Dam lit the city in neon, and hotels began to compete for the brightest stars and the plushest surroundings. Las Vegas was an overnight success, luring many people with get-rich-quick dreams. The dream has thus far endured, and in 2005 the city celebrated its centennial with a suitably festive media blitz, many special events, and the world's largest birthday cake at 130,000 pounds.

Las Vegas is home to the World Series of Poker, which began in Texas in 1969. Winners can pocket close to $10 million.

For the past 25 years, senior citizens have constituted the fastest-growing segment of the Las Vegas population, as people over 60 years arrive to take advantage of the dry climate, reasonably priced housing, low property taxes, no sales tax, and plenty of entertainment. Today, the state leads the nation in growth of its senior citizen population, and this is expected to continue. Many programs exist to ensure their comfort and welfare, including quality economic, legal, and medical plans.

In 2005 the World Market Center opened. Intended to be the nation's preeminent furniture wholesale showroom and marketplace, it was built to compete with the current furniture market capital of High Point, North Carolina. In recent years, several megahotels and many smaller projects have been completed. At least $6 billion has been spent in hotel and casino construction. At the highest point of this activity, some 3,000 people moved to the city each month, most of them in construction and casino-related work. The new $3.7 million Durango Drive Improvement project has helped to ease traffic congestion with new ramps, a trails system underpass, new auxiliary lanes, and a new traffic signal system.

One of the more serious problems facing the fast-growing city is its diminishing water supply. Las Vegas uses approximately 350 gallons daily per person, more than any city in the world. The city has raised water rates and encourages conservation by homeowners and businesses through desert landscaping, which can reduce water use by as much as 80 percent.

Las Vegas is located near the center of a broad desert valley, which is almost surrounded by mountains ranging from 2,000 to 10,000 feet. The four seasons are well defined. Summers display desert conditions with extreme high temperatures, but nights are relatively cool due to the closeness of the mountains. For about two weeks almost every summer, warm, moist air predominates, causing higher-than-average humidity and scattered, sever thunderstorms. Winters are generally mild and pleasant with clear skies prevailing. Strong winds, associated with major storms, usually reach the valley from the southwest or through the pass from the northwest. Winds over 50 miles per hour are infrequent but, when they do occur, are the most troublesome of the elements because of the dust and sand they stir up.

Rankings

General Rankings

- *Men's Health Living* ranked 100 U.S. cities in terms of quality of life. Las Vegas was ranked #96 and received a grade of F. Criteria: number of fitness facilities; air quality; number of physicians; male/female ratio; education levels; household income; cost of living. *Men's Health Living, Spring 2008*
- Las Vegas was selected as one of America's ten "Best Cities to Work and Live." The city ranked #4. The results are based on a survey of 2,500 employees and entrepreneurs who were asked about 40 large cities. *BusinessWeek, "America's Most and Least Favorite Cities," January 5, 2009*
- Las Vegas was identified as one of the top places to live in the U.S. by Harris Interactive. The city ranked #5 out of 15. Criteria: 2,463 adults (age 18 and over) were polled and asked "if you could live in or near any city in the country except the one you live in or nearest to now, which city would you choose?" The poll was conducted online within the U.S. between September 14 and 20, 2010. *Harris Interactive, November 9, 2011*
- Las Vegas was selected as one of "America's Favorite Cities." The city ranked #3 in the "Nightlife" category. Respondents to an online survey were asked to rate 35 top urban destinations in the U.S. from a visitor's perspective. Criteria: cocktail hour; live music/concerts and bands; singles/bar scene. *Travelandleisure.com, "America's Favorite Cities 2010," November 2010*

Business/Finance Rankings

- Las Vegas was identified as one of the top 25 U.S. cities with the most credit card debt by credit reporting bureau Experian. The city was ranked #16. *Experian, March 4, 2011*
- Las Vegas was identified as one of the "Happiest Cities to Work in 2012" by *CareerBliss.com,* an online community for career advancement. The city ranked #40 out of 50. Criteria: independent company reviews from employees all over the country on: relationship with their boss and co-workers; work environment; job resources; growth opportunities; compensation; company culture; company reputation; daily tasks; job control over work performed on a daily basis. *CareerBliss.com, "Happiest and Unhappiest Cities to Work in 2012"*
- *American City Business Journals* ranked America's 261 largest cities in terms of their resident's wealth. Las Vegas ranked #80. Criteria: per capita income; median household income; percentage of households with annual incomes of $200,000 or more; median home value. *American City Business Journals, "Where the Money Is: America's Wealth Centers," August 18, 2008*
- The Las Vegas metro area appeared on the Milken Institute "2011 Best Performing Metros" list. Rank: #197 out of 200 large metro areas. Criteria: job growth; wage and salary growth; high-tech output growth. *Milken Institute, "2011 Best Performing Metros"*
- The Las Vegas metro area was selected as one of the best cities for entrepreneurs in America by *Inc. Magazine.* Criteria: job-growth data for 335 metro areas was analyzed for: recent growth trend; mid-term growth; long-term trend; current year growth. The Las Vegas metro area ranked #8 among large metro areas and #49 overall. *Inc. Magazine, "The Best Cities for Doing Business," July 2008*
- Las Vegas was ranked #109 out of 145 regions worldwide in terms of its "Knowledge Competitiveness Index." The index attempts to measure the knowledge-based development taking place throughout the world and is based on 19 measures of economic performance that indicate a region's ability to translate its knowledge capacity into economic value. *Centre for International Competitiveness, World Knowledge Competitiveness Index 2008*
- *Forbes* ranked the 200 most populous metro areas in the U.S. in terms of the "Best Places for Business and Careers." The Las Vegas metro area was ranked #135. Criteria: costs (business and living); job growth (past and projected); income growth; educational attainment; projected economic growth; crime; cultural and recreational opportunities; net migration patterns; number of highly ranked colleges. *Forbes, "Best Places for Business and Careers," June 2011*

- Las Vegas appeared on *Kiplinger's Personal Finance* list of the "Top Ten Tax-Friendly Cities." The city was ranked #5. Criteria: income tax; sales tax; real estate and car/personal property tax. *Kiplinger's Personal Finance, March 1, 2009*

Children/Family Rankings

- Las Vegas was selected as one of the 10 worst cities to raise children in the U.S. by *KidFriendlyCities.org*. Criteria: education; environment; health; employment; crime; diversity; cost of living. *KidFriendlyCities.org, "Top Rated Kid/Family Friendly Cities 2009"*
- The Las Vegas metro area was selected as one of the "Best Cities for Relocating Families" by Worldwide ERC and Primacy Relocation. The 2008 study looked at nearly 50 factors important to relocating families including: recent job growth; nearby top-ranked colleges; in-state tuition for four-year public colleges; population growth since 2000; pediatricians per 100,000 population; and a Green Living index. *Worldwide ERC and Primacy Relocation, "2008 Best Cities for Relocating Families"*
- *Fit Pregnancy* magazine ranked the 50 best U.S. cities in which to have a baby. Las Vegas was ranked #49. Criteria: access to hospitals and doctors; affordability; birthing options; breastfeeding; child care; fertility laws/resources; maternal and infant health risk; parks/stroller friendliness; safety. *Fit Pregnancy, "The Best Cities in America to Have a Baby 2008"*

Culture/Performing Arts Rankings

- Las Vegas was selected as one of "America's Top 25 Arts Destinations." The city ranked #23 in the big city (population 500,000 and over) category. Criteria: readers' top choices for arts travel destinations based on the richness and variety of visual arts sites, activities and events. *American Style, "America's Top 25 Arts Destinations," May 2010*

Dating/Romance Rankings

- Las Vegas was selected as one of the least romantic cities in the U.S. by video-rental kiosk company Redbox. The city ranked #7 out of 10. Criteria: number of romantic comedies rented in 2011. *Redbox, "10 Most/Least Romantic Cities," February 1, 2012*
- Las Vegas was selected as one of the most romantic cities in America by *Amazon.com*. The city ranked #18 of 20. Criteria: per capita sales of romance novels and relationship books, romantic comedy movies, Barry White albums, and sexual wellness products. *Amazon.com, "America's Most Romantic Cities Revealed," February 14, 2012*
- Las Vegas was selected as one of the best cities for single women by *Rent.com*. The city ranked #8 of 10. Criteria: high single male-to-female ratio; lively nightlife; low divorce rate; low cost of living. *Rent.com, "Top 10 Cities for Single Women," August 19, 2011*
- Las Vegas appeared on *Men's Health's* list of the most sex-happy cities in America. The city ranked #70 of 100. Criteria: condom sales; birth rates; sex toy sales; rates of chlamydia, gonorrhea, and syphilis. *Men's Health, "America's Most Sex-Happy Cities," October 2010*
- *Men's Health* ranked 100 U.S. cities in terms of best (and worst) marriages. Las Vegas was ranked #2 (#1 = worst). Criteria: rate of failed marriages; stringency of divorce laws; percentage of population who've split; number of licensed marriage and family therapists. *Men's Health, "Splitsville, USA," May 2010*
- Eli Lily and Company, in partnership with Sperling's BestPlaces, ranked the nation's 50 largest metro areas in terms of the "Most Romantic Cities for Baby Boomers." The Las Vegas metro area ranked #47. Criteria: marriage and divorce rates among baby boomers age 45 to 60; great restaurants; dance studios; chocolate, jewelry and flower sales. *Eli Lily and Company, "Most Romantic Cities for Baby Boomers," April 20, 2007*
- The Las Vegas metro area was selected as one of the "Best Cities for Relocating Singles" by Worldwide ERC and Primacy Relocation. The area ranked #84 out of the 100 largest metro areas in the U.S. Criteria: recent job growth; recent singles population growth; overall population growth; affordable rental housing; cost-of-living index; expanded arts and recreation opportunities; ratio of single men and single women; affordability of quality higher education (including state residency requirements); diversity index; climate; population density. *Worldwide ERC and Primacy Relocation, "2008 Best Cities for Relocating Singles"*

- *Forbes* ranked the 40 most populous urbanized areas in the U.S. in terms of the "Best Cities for Singles." The Las Vegas metro area ranked #22. Criteria: number of singles; cost of living alone; nightlife; culture; job growth; coolness; and online dating participation. *Forbes.com, "Best Cities for Singles," July 27, 2009*

Education Rankings

- *Men's Health* ranked 100 U.S. cities in terms of their education levels. Las Vegas was ranked #98 (#1 = most educated city). Criteria: high school graduation rates; school enrollment; educational attainment; number of households who have outstanding student loans; number of households whose members have taken adult-education courses. *Men's Health, "Where School Is In: The Most and Least Educated Cities," September 12, 2011*
- Las Vegas was selected as one of "America's Most Literate Cities." The city ranked #47 out of the 75 largest U.S. cities. Criteria: number of booksellers; library resources; Internet resources; educational attainment; periodical publishing resources; newspaper circulation. *Central Connecticut State University, "America's Most Literate Cities 2011"*
- Las Vegas was identified as one of the 100 "smartest" metro areas in the U.S. The area ranked #91. Criteria: the editors rated the collective brainpower of the 100 largest metro areas in the U.S. based on their residents' educational attainment. *American City Business Journals, April 14, 2008*
- Las Vegas was identified as one of "America's Brainiest Bastions" by *Portfolio.com.* The metro area ranked #159 out of 200. *Portfolio.com* analyzed levels of educational attainment in the nation's 200 largest metropolitan areas. The editors established scores for five levels of educational attainment, based on relative earning power of adult workers age 25 or older. Scores were determined by comparing the median income for all workers with the median income for those workers at a specified educational level. *Portfolio.com, "America's Brainiest Bastions," December 1, 2010*

Environmental Rankings

- The Las Vegas metro area was identified as one of "The Ten Biggest American Cities that are Running Out of Water" by *24/7 Wall St.* The metro area ranked #7 out of 10. *24/7 Wall St.* did an analysis of the water supply and consumption in the 30 largest metropolitan areas in the U.S. Criteria include: projected water demand as a share of available precipitation; groundwater use as a share or projected available precipitation; susceptibility to drought; projected increase in freshwater withdrawals; projected increase in summer water deficit. *24/7 Wall St., "The Ten Biggest American Cities that are Running Out of Water," November 1, 2010*
- Las Vegas was selected as one of 22 "Smarter Cities" for energy by the Natural Resources Defense Council. Criteria: investment in green power; energy efficiency measures; conservation. *Natural Resources Defense Council, "2010 Smarter Cities," July 19, 2010*
- The Las Vegas metro area was selected as one of "America's Cleanest Cities" by *Forbes*. The metro area ranked #5 out of 10. Criteria: toxic releases; air and water quality; per capita spending on Superfund site cleanup. *Forbes.com, "America's Cleanest Cities 2011," March 11, 2011*
- 100 of the largest metro areas in the U.S. were analyzed in terms of their current drought severity. The Las Vegas metro area ranked #29 (#1 = driest). The rankings were based on statistics such as long-term precipitation trends and patterns and the Palmer drought indices. *Sperling's BestPlaces, www.BestPlaces.net, "America's Drought-Riskiest Cities," November 2007*
- The Las Vegas metro area appeared in *Country Home's* "Best Green Places" report. The area ranked #132 out of 379. Criteria: official energy policies; green power; green buildings; availability of fresh, locally grown food. *Country Home, "Best Green Places," 2008*
- Las Vegas was highlighted as one of the 25 most ozone-polluted metro areas in the U.S. The area ranked #25. *American Lung Association, State of the Air 2011*

Food/Drink Rankings

- Las Vegas was identified as one of "America's Drunkest Cities of 2011" by *The Daily Beast.* The city ranked #14 out of 25. Criteria: binge drinking; drinks consumed per month. *The Daily Beast, "Tipsy Towns: Where are America's Drunkest Cities?," December 31, 2011*

Health/Fitness Rankings

- The Las Vegas metro area was selected as one of the worst cities for bed bugs in America by Rollins corporation, the owner of seven pest control companies, including Orkin. The area ranked #16 based on the number of bed bug treatments from January to December 2011. *Rollins, "The Top 50 U.S. Cities for Bed Bugs," March 19, 2012*

- Las Vegas was selected as one of the 25 fattest cities in America by *Men's Fitness Online*. It ranked #6 out of America's 50 largest cities. Criteria: fitness centers and sport stores; nutrition; sports participation; TV viewing; overweight/sedentary; junk food; air quality; geography; commute; parks and open space; city recreational facilities; access to healthcare; motivation; mayor and city initiatives; state obesity initiatives. *Men's Fitness, "The Fittest and Fattest Cities in America," March 5, 2012*

- Las Vegas was identified as a "2011 Asthma Capital." The area ranked #73 out of the nation's 100 largest metropolitan areas. Twelve factors were used to identify the most challenging places to live for people with asthma: estimated prevalence; self-reported prevalence; crude death rate for asthma; annual pollen score; annual air quality; public smoking laws; number of board-certified asthma specialists; school inhaler access laws; rescue medication use; controller medication use; uninsured rate; poverty rate. *Asthma and Allergy Foundation of America, "2011 Asthma Capitals"*

- Las Vegas was identified as a "2011 Fall Allergy Capital." The area ranked #80 out of 100. Three groups of factors were used to identify the most severe cities for people with allergies during the fall season: annual pollen levels; medicine utilization; access to board-certified allergists. *Asthma and Allergy Foundation of America, "2011 Fall Allergy Capitals"*

- Las Vegas was identified as a "2012 Spring Allergy Capital." The area ranked #42 out of 100. Three groups of factors were used to identify the most severe cities for people with allergies during the spring season: annual pollen levels; medicine utilization; access to board-certified allergists. *Asthma and Allergy Foundation of America, "2012 Spring Allergy Capitals"*

- *Men's Health* examined 100 major U.S. cities and selected the best and worst cities for men. Las Vegas ranked #85. Criteria: 35 statistical parameters of long life in the categories of health, quality of life, and fitness. *Men's Health, "The 10 Best and Worst Cities for Men 2012," January/February 2012*

- The Las Vegas metro area appeared in the 2011 Gallup-Healthways Well-Being Index. The index, based on interviews with more than 350,000 Americans, measured jobs, finances, physical health, emotional state of mind and communities. The metro area ranked #156 out of 190. Criteria: life evaluation; emotional health; work environment; physical health; healthy behaviors; basic access (basic needs optimal for a healthy life, such as access to food and medicine, having health insurance and feeling safe while walking at night). *Gallup-Healthways, "State of Well-Being 2011"*

- The Las Vegas metro area was identified as one of "America's Most Stressful Cities" by *Sperling's BestPlaces.* The metro area ranked #2 out of 50. Criteria: unemployment rate; suicide rate; commute time; mental health; poor rest; alcohol use; violent crime rate; property crime rate; cloudy days annually. *Sperling's BestPlaces, www.BestPlaces.net, "Stressful Cities 2012*

- *Men's Health* ranked 100 U.S. cities in terms of their activity levels. Las Vegas was ranked #77 (#1 = most active city). Criteria: where and how often residents exercise; percentage of households that watch more than 15 hours of cable television a week and buy more than 11 video games a year; death rate from deep-vein thrombosis, a condition linked to sitting for extended periods of time. *Men's Health, "Where Sit Happens: The Most and Least Active Cities in America," June 20, 2011*

- 50 of the largest metro areas in the U.S. were analyzed in terms of their health and fitness by the American College of Sports Medicine in their "American Fitness Index." The Las Vegas metro area ranked #45 (#1 = healthiest). Criteria: preventative health behaviors; levels of chronic disease; health care access; community resources and policies that support physical activity. *American College of Sports Medicine, "Health and Community Fitness Status of the 50 Largest Metropolitan Areas," August 1, 2011*

- *The Daily Beast* identified the 30 U.S. metro areas with the worst smoking habits. The Las Vegas metro area ranked #10. Sixty urban centers with populations of more than one million were ranked based on the following criteria: number of smokers; number of cigarettes smoked per day; fewest attempts to quit. *The Daily Beast, "30 Cities With Smoking Problems," January 3, 2011*

Real Estate Rankings

- Las Vegas was identified as one of 13 metro areas where home prices are falling dangerously. Criteria: home price change from October 2010 to September 2011; projected home price change through 2012. *Forbes.com, "Cities Where Home Prices are Falling Dangerously," January 10, 2012*

- Las Vegas was identified as one of the best cities for home buyers in the U.S. The area ranked #6 out of 10. The affordability of home ownership was calculated by comparing the cost of renting vs. owning. Criteria: cost to rent as a percent of after-tax mortgage payment. *Fortune, "The 10 Best Cities for Buyers," April 11, 2011*

- *Fortune* ranked the 100 largest metro areas in the U.S. in terms of projected median home price change in 2010. The Las Vegas metro area ranked #95. *Fortune, "The 2010 Housing Outlook," December 9, 2009*

- Las Vegas was identified as one of the top 20 metro areas with the lowest rate of house price appreciation in 2011. The area ranked #1 with a one-year price appreciation of -12.6% through the 4th quarter 2011. *Federal Housing Finance Agency, House Price Index, 4th Quarter 2011*

- Las Vegas appeared on *ApartmentRatings.com* "Top Cities for Renters" list in 2009." The area ranked #86. Overall satisfaction ratings were ranked using thousands of user submitted scores for hundreds of apartment complexes located in the 100 most populated U.S. municipalities. *ApartmentRatings.com, "2009 Renter Satisfaction Rankings"*

- Las Vegas appeared on *ApartmentRatings.com* "Top College Towns & Cities" for renters list in 2011." The area ranked #77 out of 87. Overall satisfaction ratings were ranked using thousands of user submitted scores for hundreds of apartment complexes located in cities and towns that are home to the 100 largest four-year institutions in the U.S. *ApartmentRatings.com, "2011 College Town Renter Satisfaction Rankings"*

- The Las Vegas metro area was identified as one of "America's 25 Weakest Housing Markets" by *Forbes*. The metro area ranked #1. Criteria: metro areas with populations over 500,000 were ranked based on projected home values through 2011. *Forbes.com, "America's 25 Weakest Housing Markets," January 7, 2009*

- The nation's largest metro areas were analyzed in terms of the percentage of households entering some stage of foreclosure in 2011. The Las Vegas metro area ranked #1 out of 20 (#1 = highest foreclosure rate). *RealtyTrac, 2011 Year-End Foreclosure Market Report, January 12, 2012*

- The Las Vegas metro area was identified as one of America's most undervalued cities in 2011 by *CNNMoney.com* based on data from Local Market Monitor. Criteria: median home prices; local interest rates; economic and population growth; construction costs; vacancies; household income. *CNNMoney.com, "America's Most Overvalued (and Undervalued) Cities," January 16, 2011*

- The Las Vegas metro area appeared in a *Wall Street Journal* article ranking cities by "housing stress." The metro area was ranked #5 (#1 = most stress). Criteria: fraction of mortgage-holding homeowners with a monthly housing payment in excess of 30 percent of income; percentage of people without health insurance; unemployment rate. *The Wall Street Journal, "Which Cities Face Biggest Housing Risk," October 5, 2010*

- The Center for Housing Policy ranked 210 U.S. metropolitan areas by the fair market rent for a two-bedroom unit. The Las Vegas metro area was ranked #45. (#1 = most expensive) with a rent of $1,063. Criteria: Fair Market Rent (FMR) in effect during the fourth quarter of 2009 based on HUD's fiscal year 2010 FMRs. *The Center for Housing Policy, "Paycheck to Paycheck: Most to Least Expensive Rental Markets in 2009"*
- The Las Vegas metro area was identified as one of the worst housing markets of the decade by *Forbes*. Criteria: decrease in housing values per square foot since January 2000. *Forbes, "America's 5 Best (and Worst) Housing Markets of the Decade," December 7, 2010*
- The Las Vegas metro area was identified as one of the top 20 cities in terms of decreasing home equity. The metro area was ranked #4. Criteria: percentage of home equity relative to the home's current value. *Forbes.com, "Where Americans are Losing Home Equity Most," May 1, 2010*
- The Las Vegas metro area was identified as one of the markets with the worst expected performance in home prices over the next 12 months. *Local Market Monitor, "First Quarter Home Price Forecast for Largest US Markets," March 2, 2011*
- The Las Vegas metro area was identified as one of the best U.S. markets to invest in rental property" by HomeVestors and Local Market Monitor. The area ranked #1 out of 100. Criteria: risk-return premium relative to national average. *HomeVestors and Local Market Monitor, "Best 100 U.S. Markets to Invest in Rental Property," March 9, 2012*

Safety Rankings

- Symantec, the makers of Norton, in partnership with Sperling's BestPlaces, ranked the 50 largest cities in the U.S. in terms of their vulnerability to cybercrime. The city ranked #11. Criteria: number of cyberattacks and potential infections; level of Internet access; expenditures on smartphones and computer hardware/software; wireless hotspots; broadband connectivity; Internet usage; online purchases. *Symantec, "Riskiest Online Cities of 2012" February 15, 2012*
- Allstate ranked the 193 largest cities in America in terms of driver safety. Las Vegas ranked #138. In addition, drivers were 22.2% more likely to have had an accident compared to the national average. Allstate researchers analyzed internal property damage reported claims over a two-year period (from January 2008 to December 2009) to protect findings from external influences such as weather or road construction. A weighted average of the two-year numbers determined the annual percentages. The report defines an auto crash as any collision resulting in a property damage claim. *Allstate, "2011 Allstate America's Best Drivers Report™"*
- The Las Vegas metro area was identified as one of "America's Most Dangerous Cities" by *Forbes*. The area ranked #9 out of 10. Criteria: violent crime (murder and non-negligent manslaughter, forcible rape, robbery, and aggravated assault) rates per capita. The editors only considered metropolitan areas with populations above 200,000. *Forbes, "America's Most Dangerous Cities," October 3, 2011*
- The National Insurance Crime Bureau ranked 366 metro areas in the U.S. in terms of per capita rates of vehicle theft. The Las Vegas metro area ranked #17 (#1 = highest rate). Criteria: number of vehicle theft offenses per 100,000 inhabitants in 2010. *National Insurance Crime Bureau, "Hot Spots," June 21, 2011*
- The Las Vegas metro area was identified as one of the most dangerous metro areas for pedestrians by Transportation for America. The metro area ranked #6 out of 52 metro areas with over 1 million residents. Criteria: area's population divided by the number of pedestrian fatalities in that area. *Transportation for America, "Dangerous by Design 2011"*

Seniors/Retirement Rankings

- Bankers Life and Casualty Company, in partnership with Sperling's BestPlaces, ranked the nation's 50 largest metro areas in terms of the "Best U.S. Cities for Seniors." The Las Vegas metro area ranked #49. Criteria: healthcare; transportation; housing; environment; economy; health and longevity; social and spiritual life; crime. *Bankers Life and Casualty Company, Center for a Secure Retirement, "Best U.S. Cities for Seniors 2011," September 2011*

- The Las Vegas metro area was selected as one of "The 10 Most Affordable Cities for Long-Term Care" by *U.S. News & World Report.* Criteria: costs at nursing homes, assisted living facilities, and adult day health care facilities; cost for licensed home health aides. *U.S. News & World Report, "The 10 Most Affordable Cities for Long-Term Care," May 17, 2010*

Sports/Recreation Rankings

- Las Vegas appeared on the *Sporting News* list of the "Best Sports Cities" for 2011. The area ranked #97 out of 271 cities in the U.S. *Sporting News* takes a 12-month snapshot of each city's sports, putting a heavy premium on regular-season won-lost records (from the most recently completed season). Other criteria include: playoff berths, bowl appearances and tournament bids; championships; applicable power ratings; quality of competition; overall fan fervor (measured in part by attendance); abundance of teams (rewarding quality over quantity); stadium and arena quality; ticket availability and prices; franchise ownership; and marquee appeal of athletes. *Sporting News, "Best Sports Cities 2011," October 4, 2011*
- *Golf.com* and the research arm of the National Golf Foundation analyzed the 50 largest metropolitan areas in the U.S. in terms of golf. The Las Vegas metro area ranked #3. Criteria: weather; affordability; quality of courses; accessibility; number of courses designed by esteemed architects; availability; crowdedness. *Golf.com, November 15, 2007*

Technology Rankings

- Scarborough Research, a leading market research firm, identified the Las Vegas DMA (Designated Market Area) as one of the top markets for text messaging with more than 50% of cell phone subscribers age 18+ utilizing the text messaging feature on their phone. *Scarborough Research, November 24, 2008*

Transportation Rankings

- Las Vegas appeared on *Trapster.com's* list of the 10 most-active U.S. cities for speed traps. The city ranked #4 of 10. *Trapster.com* is a community platform accessed online and via smartphone app that alerts drivers to traps, hazards and other traffic issues nearby. *Trapster.com, "Speeders Beware: Cities With the Most Speed Traps," February 10, 2012*
- Las Vegas was identified as one of America's worst cities for speed traps by the National Motorists Association. The city ranked #4 out of 25. Criteria: speed trap locations per 100,000 residents. *National Motorists Association, September 2011*
- The Las Vegas metro area appeared on *Forbes* list of the best and worst cities for commuters. The metro area ranked #16 out of 60 (#1 is best). Criteria: travel time; road congestion; travel delays. *Forbes.com, "Best and Worst Cities for Commuters," February 16, 2010*

Women/Minorities Rankings

- *Women's Health* examined U.S. cities and identified the 100 best cities for women. Las Vegas was ranked #87. Criteria: 30 categories were examined from obesity and breast cancer rates to commuting times and hours spent working out. *Women's Health, "Best Cities for Women 2012"*
- Las Vegas was ranked #82 out of 100 metro areas in *SELF Magazine's* ranking of America's healthiest places for women." A panel of experts came up with more than 50 criteria including death and disease rates, environmental indicators, community resources, and lifestyle habits. *SELF Magazine, "Secrets of America's Healthiest Women," December 2008*
- Las Vegas was selected as one of the 25 healthiest cities for Latinas by *Latina Magazine.* The city ranked #15. Criteria: U.S. cities with populations over 500,000 residents were evaluated on the following criteria: percentage of 18-34 year-olds per city; Latino college graduation rates; number of colleges and universities; affordability; housing costs; income growth over time; average salary; percentage of singles; climate; safety; how the city's diversity compares to the national average; opportunities for minority entrepreneurs. *Latina Magazine, "Top 15 U.S. Cities for Young Latinos to Live In," August 19, 2011*

- The Las Vegas metro area appeared on *Forbes'* list of the "Best Cities for Minority Entrepreneurs." The area ranked #15 out of 10. Criteria: 52 metropolitan statistical areas were examined. For each ethnicity (African Americans, Asians and Hispanics), the editors measured housing affordability, population growth, income growth, and entrepreneurship (per capita self-employment). *Forbes, "Best Cities for Minority Entrepreneurs," March 23, 2011*

Miscellaneous Rankings

- *Men's Health* ranked 100 U.S. cities by their level of sadness. Las Vegas was ranked #91 (#1 = saddest city). Criteria: suicide rates; unemployment rates; percentage of households that use antidepressants; percent of population who report feeling blue all or most of the time. *Men's Health, "Frown Towns," November 28, 2011*
- The Las Vegas metro area was selected as one of "The Best U.S. Cities for Bargain Shopping" by *Forbes.* The area ranked #4 out of 10. Criteria: number of outlet stores; gross leasable retail space in major malls; low consumer price index; low sales tax rate. Indicators were examined in the nation's 50 largest metropolitan areas. *Forbes, "The Best U.S. Cities for Bargain Shopping," January 20, 2012*
- Proctor & Gamble, the makers of Pepto-Bismol, in partnership with Sperling's BestPlaces, ranked the nation's 100 most populated metro areas in terms of the "Best Places for Thanksgiving Celebrations." The Las Vegas metro area ranked #5. Criteria: turkey consumption per capita; increase in inbound air traffic during Thanksgiving; Pepto-Bismol sales; results from a consumer poll of 4,800 Americans recording the number of people attending Thanksgiving, the number of dishes served, and ways people intended to celebrate. *Proctor & Gamble, "Top 10 Best Places for Thanksgiving Celebrations," November 18, 2010*
- Energizer Holdings, the makers of Edge® shave gel, in partnership with Sperling's BestPlaces, ranked 50 major metro areas in terms of everyday irritations. The Las Vegas metro area ranked #25. Criteria: humidity levels; weather conditions; incidence of traffic delays and congestion; average commute times; frequency of flight delays and cancellations; rates of sleeplessness; underemployment; pollens and allergens; pests; comedy clubs per capita. *Energizer Holdings, "Most Irritation Prone Cities," July 23, 2010*
- Mars Chocolate North America, the makers of COMBOS®, in partnership with Sperling's BestPlaces, ranked 50 major metro areas in terms of their "manliness." The Las Vegas metro area ranked #38. Criteria: number of professional sports teams; number of nearby NASCAR tracks and racing events; manly lifestyle; concentration of manly retail stores; manly occupations per capita; salty snack sales; "Board of Manliness" rankings. *Mars Chocolate North America, "America's Manliest Cities 2011," September 1, 2011*
- Las Vegas was selected as one of the "Worst Hair Cities" by *NaturallyCurly.com.* The city was ranked #4. Criteria: humidity levels; pollution; rainfall; average wind speeds; water hardness; beauty salons per capita. *NaturallyCurly.com, "Best/Worst Hair Cities," April 29, 2009*
- Las Vegas was selected as one of the most tattooed cities in America by *TotalBeauty.com.* The city was ranked #2. Criteria: number of tattoo and permanent makeup shops per capita; number of tattoo conventions hosted. *TotalBeauty.com, "Top 10 Most Tattooed Cities in America," August 2010*
- The Las Vegas metro area appeared in *AutoMD.com's* ranking of the "Best and Worst Cities for Auto Repair." The metro area ranked #10 (#1 is best). The 50 most-populated metro areas in the U.S. were ranked on three critical factors: repair affordability; price disparity range; shop integrity factor. *AutoMD.com, "Advocacy for Repair Shop Fairness Report," February 24, 2010*
- Las Vegas appeared on Procter & Gamble's list of the "Top-20 All-Time Sweatiest Cities." The city was ranked #3. The rankings are based on computer simulations of the amount of sweat a person of average height and weight would produce walking around for an hour in the average temperatures during the summer months, based on historical weather data during June, July and August from 2001-2008 for each city. *Procter & Gamble, Old Spice Press Release, "Top-20 All-Time Sweatiest Cities," July 1, 2009*

Business Environment

CITY FINANCES

City Government Finances

Component	2009 ($000)	2009 ($ per capita)
Total Revenues	1,137,666	2,036
Total Expenditures	920,615	1,647
Debt Outstanding	491,792	880
Cash and Securities[1]	741,069	1,326

Note: (1) Cash and security holdings of a government at the close of its fiscal year, including those of its dependent agencies, utilities, and liquor stores.
Source: U.S Census Bureau, State & Local Government Finances 2009

City Government Revenue by Source

Source	2009 ($000)	2009 ($ per capita)
General Revenue		
From Federal Government	67,342	120
From State Government	231,138	414
From Local Governments	124,153	222
Taxes		
Property	165,870	297
Sales and Gross Receipts	66,076	118
Personal Income	0	0
Corporate Income	0	0
Motor Vehicle License	0	0
Other Taxes	34,620	62
Current Charges	365,256	654
Liquor Store	0	0
Utility	116	0
Employee Retirement	0	0

Source: U.S Census Bureau, State & Local Government Finances 2009

City Government Expenditures by Function

Function	2009 ($000)	2009 ($ per capita)	2009 (%)
General Direct Expenditures			
Air Transportation	0	0	0.0
Corrections	47,702	85	5.2
Education	0	0	0.0
Employment Security Administration	0	0	0.0
Financial Administration	52,230	93	5.7
Fire Protection	124,151	222	13.5
General Public Buildings	33,438	60	3.6
Governmental Administration, Other	19,787	35	2.1
Health	3,476	6	0.4
Highways	108,673	194	11.8
Hospitals	0	0	0.0
Housing and Community Development	29,222	52	3.2
Interest on General Debt	12,798	23	1.4
Judicial and Legal	30,260	54	3.3
Libraries	0	0	0.0
Parking	4,086	7	0.4
Parks and Recreation	134,004	240	14.6
Police Protection	11,623	21	1.3
Public Welfare	1,129	2	0.1
Sewerage	48,935	88	5.3
Solid Waste Management	5,483	10	0.6
Veterans' Services	0	0	0.0
Liquor Store	0	0	0.0
Utility	1,257	2	0.1
Employee Retirement	0	0	0.0

Source: U.S Census Bureau, State & Local Government Finances 2009

Municipal Bond Ratings

Area	Moody's	S&P	Fitch
City	Aa2	AA	AA

Rating Systems (shown in declining order of credit quality): Moody's– Aaa, Aa, A, Baa, Ba, B, Caa, Ca, C (numerical modifiers 1, 2, and 3 are added to letter-rating); S&P– AAA, AA, A, BBB, BB, B, CCC, CC, C; Fitch– AAA, AA, A, BBB, BB, B, CCC, CC, C. Ratings may be modified by the addition of a plus or minus sign to show relative standing within the major rating categories.
Notes: n/a Not Available; w/d Withdrawn (1) Not Reviewed; (2) Issuer Rating/No General Obligation; (3) Standard and Poor's Issue Credit Rating (ICR) is a current opinion of an obliger with respect to a specific financial obligation, a specific class of financial obligations, or a specific financial program.
Source: U.S. Census Bureau, 2012 Statistical Abstract, Bond Ratings for City Governments by Largest Cities: 2010

DEMOGRAPHICS

Population Growth

Area	1990 Census	2000 Census	2010 Census	Population Growth (%)	
				1990-2000	2000-2010
City	261,374	478,434	583,756	83.0	22.0
MSA[1]	741,459	1,375,765	1,951,269	85.5	41.8
U.S.	248,709,873	281,421,906	308,745,538	13.2	9.7

Note: (1) Figures cover the Las Vegas-Paradise, NV Metropolitan Statistical Area—see Appendix B for areas included
Source: U.S. Census Bureau, 2010 Census

Household Size

Area	Persons in Household (%)							Average Household Size
	One	Two	Three	Four	Five	Six	Seven or More	
City	26.0	31.1	15.7	12.9	7.5	3.7	3.1	2.71
MSA[1]	25.3	32.0	15.9	13.0	7.4	3.5	2.8	2.70
U.S.	26.7	32.8	16.1	13.4	6.5	2.6	1.9	2.58

Note: (1) Figures cover the Las Vegas-Paradise, NV Metropolitan Statistical Area—see Appendix B for areas included
Source: U.S. Census Bureau, 2010 Census

Race

Area	White Alone[2] (%)	Black Alone[2] (%)	Asian Alone[2] (%)	AIAN[3] Alone[2] (%)	NHOPI[4] Alone[2] (%)	Other Race Alone[2] (%)	Two or More Races (%)
City	62.1	11.1	6.1	0.7	0.6	14.5	4.9
MSA[1]	60.9	10.5	8.7	0.7	0.7	13.5	5.1
U.S.	72.4	12.6	4.8	0.9	0.2	6.2	2.9

Note: (1) Figures cover the Las Vegas-Paradise, NV Metropolitan Statistical Area—see Appendix B for areas included; (2) Alone is defined as not being in combination with one or more other races; (3) American Indian and Alaska Native; (4) Native Hawaiian and Other Pacific Islander
Source: U.S. Census Bureau, 2010 Census

Hispanic or Latino Origin

Area	Hispanic or Latino (%)	Mexican (%)	Puerto Rican (%)	Cuban (%)	Other Hispanic or Latino (%)
City	31.5	24.0	0.9	0.9	5.7
MSA[1]	29.1	21.7	0.9	1.1	5.5
U.S.	16.3	10.3	1.5	0.6	4.0

Note: Persons of Hispanic or Latino origin can be of any race; (1) Figures cover the Las Vegas-Paradise, NV Metropolitan Statistical Area—see Appendix B for areas included
Source: U.S. Census Bureau, 2010 Census

Segregation

Type	Segregation Indices[1]				Percent Change		
	1990	2000	2010	2010 Rank[2]	1990-2000	1990-2010	2000-2010
Black/White	49.0	40.4	37.6	94	-8.7	-11.5	-2.8
Asian/White	23.3	25.4	28.8	92	2.1	5.5	3.5
Hispanic/White	28.8	42.4	42.0	58	13.6	13.3	-0.4

Note: Figures are based on an analysis of 1990, 2000, and 2010 Census Decennial Census tract data by William H. Frey, Brookings Institution and the University of Michigan Social Science Data Analysis Network. In this analysis all racial groups (whites, blacks, and asians) are non-Hispanic members of those races. Hispanics are shown as a separate category; All figures cover the Metropolitan Statistical Area (see Appendix B for areas included); (1) Segregation Indices are Dissimilarity Indices that measure the degree to which the minority group is distributed differently than whites across census tracts. They range from 0 (complete integration) to 100 (complete segregation) where the value indicates the percentage of the minority group that needs to move to be distributed exactly like whites; (2) Ranges from 1 (most segregated) to 102 (least segregated); n/a not available.
Source: www.CensusScope.org

Ancestry

Area	German	Irish	English	American	Italian	Polish	French[2]	Scottish	Dutch
City	11.2	8.6	6.9	2.4	6.2	2.8	2.1	1.5	1.0
MSA[1]	11.1	8.7	7.2	2.7	6.2	2.5	2.2	1.5	1.1
U.S.	16.1	11.6	8.8	6.1	5.7	3.2	3.0	1.9	1.6

Note: Figures are the percentage of the total population reporting a particular ancestry. The nine most commonly reported ancestries in the U.S. are shown. Figures include multiple ancestries (e.g. if a person reported being Irish and Italian, they were included in both columns); (1) Figures cover the Las Vegas-Paradise, NV Metropolitan Statistical Area—see Appendix B for areas included; (2) Excludes Basque
Source: U.S. Census Bureau, 2008-2010 American Community Survey 3-Year Estimates

Foreign-Born Population

Area	Percent of Population Born in								
	Any Foreign Country	Mexico	Asia	Europe	Carribean	South America	Central America[2]	Africa	Canada
City	22.2	10.9	5.0	1.8	0.8	0.6	2.1	0.4	0.4
MSA[1]	22.0	9.4	6.5	1.9	0.8	0.6	1.7	0.7	0.4
U.S.	12.8	3.8	3.6	1.6	1.2	0.9	1.0	0.5	0.3

Note: (1) Figures cover the Las Vegas-Paradise, NV Metropolitan Statistical Area—see Appendix B for areas included; (2) Excludes Mexico.
Source: U.S. Census Bureau, 2008-2010 American Community Survey 3-Year Estimates

Marital Status

Area	Never Married	Now Married[2]	Separated	Widowed	Divorced
City	31.8	46.0	2.7	5.3	14.2
MSA[1]	31.9	47.2	2.4	4.9	13.6
U.S.	31.6	49.6	2.2	6.1	10.7

Note: Figures are percentages and cover the population 15 years of age and older; (1) Figures cover the Las Vegas-Paradise, NV Metropolitan Statistical Area—see Appendix B for areas included; (2) Excludes separated
Source: U.S. Census Bureau, 2008-2010 American Community Survey 3-Year Estimates

Age

Area	Percent of Population							Median Age
	Under Age 5	Age 5 to 17	Age 18 to 34	Age 35 to 49	Age 50 to 64	Age 65 to 79	80 Years and Over	
City	7.2	18.4	23.1	21.9	17.3	9.3	2.7	35.9
MSA[1]	7.1	17.9	24.3	21.9	17.5	8.9	2.4	35.5
U.S.	6.5	17.5	23.2	20.7	19.0	9.4	3.6	37.2

Note: (1) Figures cover the Las Vegas-Paradise, NV Metropolitan Statistical Area—see Appendix B for areas included
Source: U.S. Census Bureau, 2010 Census

Male/Female Ratio

Area	Males	Females	Males per 100 Females
City	294,100	289,656	101.5
MSA[1]	982,193	969,076	101.4
U.S.	151,781,326	156,964,212	96.7

Note: (1) Figures cover the Las Vegas-Paradise, NV Metropolitan Statistical Area—see Appendix B for areas included
Source: U.S. Census Bureau, 2010 Census

Religious Groups

Area	Catholic	Baptist	Non-Den.	Methodist[2]	Lutheran	LDS[3]	Pentecostal	Presbyterian[4]	Muslim[5]	Judaism
MSA[1]	18.1	3.0	3.1	0.4	0.7	6.4	1.5	0.2	0.3	0.1
U.S.	19.1	9.3	4.0	4.0	2.3	2.0	1.9	1.6	0.8	0.7

Note: Figures are the number of adherents as a percentage of the total population; (1) Figures cover the Las Vegas-Paradise, NV Metropolitan Statistical Area—see Appendix B for areas included; (2) Methodist/Pietist; (3) Latter Day Saints; (4) Reformed; (5) Figures are estimates
Source: Association of Statisticians of American Religious Bodies, 2010 U.S. Religion Census: Religious Congregations & Membership Study

ECONOMY

Gross Metropolitan Product

Area	2007	2008	2009	2010	2010 Rank[2]
MSA[1]	99.5	97.8	91.7	91.4	33

Note: Figures are in billions of dollars; (1) Figures cover the Las Vegas-Paradise, NV Metropolitan Statistical Area—see Appendix B for areas included; (2) Rank ranges from 1 to 363
Source: The United States Conference of Mayors, "U.S. Metro Economies: GMP and Employment Forecasts," June 2011

Economic Growth

Area	2007-2009 (%)	2010 (%)	2011 (%)	Rank[2]
MSA[1]	-5.7	-1.1	1.6	342
U.S.	-1.3	2.9	2.5	–

Note: Figures are real Gross Metropolitan Product growth rates and represent annual average percent change; (1) Figures cover the Las Vegas-Paradise, NV Metropolitan Statistical Area—see Appendix B for areas included; (2) Rank ranges from 1 to 363
Source: The United States Conference of Mayors, "U.S. Metro Economies: GMP and Employment Forecasts," June 2011

Metropolitan Area Exports

Area	2005	2006	2007	2008	2009	2010	2010 Rank[2]
MSA[1]	716.8	1,051.8	1,182.1	1,167.7	1,022.7	1,187.8	120

Note: Figures are in millions of dollars; (1) Figures cover the Las Vegas-Paradise, NV Metropolitan Statistical Area—see Appendix B for areas included; (2) Rank ranges from 1 to 369
Source: U.S. Department of Commerce, International Trade Administration, Office of Trade & Industry Information, Manufacturing & Services, data extracted April 2, 2012

INCOME

Income

Area	Per Capita ($)	Median Household ($)	Average Household ($)
City	25,549	52,382	68,296
MSA[1]	26,211	54,458	69,877
U.S.	26,942	51,222	70,116

Note: (1) Figures cover the Las Vegas-Paradise, NV Metropolitan Statistical Area—see Appendix B for areas included
Source: U.S. Census Bureau, 2008-2010 American Community Survey 3-Year Estimates

EMPLOYMENT

Household Income Distribution

Area	Under $15,000	$15,000 -24,999	$25,000 -34,999	$35,000 -49,999	$50,000 -74,999	$75,000 -99,000	$100,000 -149,999	$150,000 and up
	Percent of Households Earning							
City	11.9	10.2	11.1	14.3	20.5	12.5	12.1	7.3
MSA[1]	10.0	9.6	11.0	14.9	21.0	13.4	12.8	7.4
U.S.	13.0	11.0	10.6	14.2	18.5	12.1	12.2	8.4

Note: (1) Figures cover the Las Vegas-Paradise, NV Metropolitan Statistical Area—see Appendix B for areas included
Source: U.S. Census Bureau, 2008-2010 American Community Survey 3-Year Estimates

Poverty Rate

Area	All Ages	Under 18 Years Old	18 to 64 Years Old	65 Years and Over
City	14.6	20.3	13.3	9.1
MSA[1]	12.9	18.6	11.4	8.1
U.S.	14.4	20.1	13.1	9.4

Note: Figures are percentage of people whose income during the past 12 months was below the poverty level; (1) Figures cover the Las Vegas-Paradise, NV Metropolitan Statistical Area—see Appendix B for areas included
Source: U.S. Census Bureau, 2008-2010 American Community Survey 3-Year Estimates

Personal Bankruptcy Filing Rate

Area	2006	2007	2008	2009	2010	2011
Clark County	2.44	4.80	8.25	12.68	12.53	10.24
U.S.	2.00	2.73	3.53	4.61	4.97	4.37

Note: Numbers are per 1,000 population and include Chapter 7 and Chapter 13 filings
Source: Federal Deposit Insurance Corporation, Regional Economic Conditions, March 9, 2012

Labor Force and Employment

Area	Civilian Labor Force			Workers Employed		
	Dec. 2010	Dec. 2011	% Chg.	Dec. 2010	Dec. 2011	% Chg.
City	277,063	273,342	-1.3	233,762	237,867	1.8
MSA[1]	952,734	942,225	-1.1	808,526	822,726	1.8
U.S.	153,156,000	153,373,000	0.1	139,159,000	140,681,000	1.1

Note: Data is not seasonally adjusted and covers workers 16 years of age and older; (1) Metropolitan Statistical Area—see Appendix B for areas included
Source: Bureau of Labor Statistics, http://stats.bls.gov

Unemployment Rate

Area	2011											
	Jan.	Feb.	Mar.	Apr.	May	Jun.	Jul.	Aug.	Sep.	Oct.	Nov.	Dec.
City	13.5	14.3	13.8	12.3	12.7	14.1	14.3	14.6	13.9	13.3	12.6	13.0
MSA[1]	13.7	13.7	13.3	12.0	12.4	13.8	14.0	14.3	13.6	13.1	12.4	12.7
U.S.	9.8	9.5	9.2	8.7	8.7	9.3	9.3	9.1	8.8	8.5	8.2	8.3

Note: Data is not seasonally adjusted and covers workers 16 years of age and older; All figures are percentages; (1) Metropolitan Statistical Area—see Appendix B for areas included
Source: Bureau of Labor Statistics, http://stats.bls.gov

Projected Unemployment Rate

Area	2010 (%)	2011 (%)	2012 (%)	2013 (%)
MSA[1]	15.4	13.4	12.8	11.9

Note: (1) Metropolitan Statistical Area—see Appendix B for areas included
Source: The United States Conference of Mayors, "U.S. Metro Economies: GMP and Employment Forecasts," June 2011

Employment by Occupation

Occupation Classification	City (%)	MSA[1] (%)	U.S. (%)
Management, Business, Science, and Arts	27.3	26.6	35.6
Natural Resources, Construction, and Maintenance	10.4	9.6	9.5
Production, Transportation, and Material Moving	9.0	9.0	12.1
Sales and Office	25.1	26.2	25.2
Service	28.2	28.6	17.6

Note: Figures cover employed civilians 16 years of age and older; (1) Figures cover the Las Vegas-Paradise, NV Metropolitan Statistical Area—see Appendix B for areas included
Source: U.S. Census Bureau, 2008-2010 American Community Survey 3-Year Estimates

Employment by Industry

Sector	MSA[1] Number of Employees	MSA[1] Percent of Total	U.S. Percent of Total
Construction	38,400	4.7	4.1
Education and Health Services	72,200	8.9	15.2
Financial Activities	39,000	4.8	5.8
Government	93,400	11.5	16.8
Information	9,300	1.1	2.0
Leisure and Hospitality	262,900	32.3	9.9
Manufacturing	19,800	2.4	8.9
Mining and Logging	200	<0.1	0.6
Other Services	24,000	2.9	4.0
Professional and Business Services	100,900	12.4	13.3
Retail Trade	97,700	12.0	11.5
Transportation and Utilities	36,200	4.4	3.8
Wholesale Trade	20,900	2.6	4.2

Note: Figures cover non-farm employment as of December 2011 and are not seasonally adjusted; (1) Metropolitan Statistical Area—see Appendix B for areas included
Source: Bureau of Labor Statistics, http://stats.bls.gov

Occupations with Greatest Projected Employment Growth: 2008 – 2018

Occupation[1]	2008 Employment	2018 Projected Employment	Numeric Employment Change	Percent Employment Change
Retail Salespersons	43,200	50,270	7,070	16.4
Combined Food Preparation and Serving Workers, Including Fast Food	27,380	31,340	3,960	14.5
Registered Nurses	16,900	20,240	3,340	19.8
Customer Service Representatives	15,480	18,250	2,770	17.9
Sales Representatives, Wholesale and Manufacturing, Except Technical and Scientific Products	9,940	12,110	2,170	21.8
General and Operations Managers	17,820	19,840	2,020	11.3
Cashiers	33,010	34,870	1,860	5.6
Gaming Dealers	23,790	25,600	1,810	7.6
Janitors and Cleaners, Except Maids and Housekeeping Cleaners	31,820	33,440	1,620	5.1
Postsecondary Teachers	8,990	10,600	1,610	17.9

Note: Projections cover Nevada; (1) Sorted by numeric employment change
Source: www.projectionscentral.com, State Occupational Projections, 2008–2018 Long-Term Projections

Fastest Growing Occupations: 2008 – 2018

Occupation[1]	2008 Employment	2018 Projected Employment	Numeric Employment Change	Percent Employment Change
Computer Software Engineers, Systems Software	1,620	2,370	750	46.3
Computer Software Engineers, Applications	1,430	2,050	620	43.4
Network Systems and Data Communications Analysts	990	1,400	410	41.4
Physician Assistants	470	650	180	38.3
Physical Therapist Assistants	340	470	130	38.2
Industrial Engineering Technicians	270	370	100	37.0
Dental Hygienists	1,420	1,940	520	36.6
Physical Therapist Aides	360	490	130	36.1
Network and Computer Systems Administrators	1,250	1,700	450	36.0
Dental Assistants	2,550	3,450	900	35.3

Note: Projections cover Nevada; (1) Sorted by percent employment change and excludes occupations with numeric employment change less than 100
Source: www.projectionscentral.com, State Occupational Projections, 2008–2018 Long-Term Projections

Average Wages

Occupation	$/Hr.	Occupation	$/Hr.
Accountants and Auditors	30.67	Maids and Housekeeping Cleaners	13.73
Automotive Mechanics	19.70	Maintenance and Repair Workers	21.61
Bookkeepers	17.63	Marketing Managers	59.31
Carpenters	28.18	Nuclear Medicine Technologists	38.14
Cashiers	10.52	Nurses, Licensed Practical	25.75
Clerks, General Office	14.60	Nurses, Registered	37.40
Clerks, Receptionists/Information	13.25	Nursing Aides/Orderlies/Attendants	16.22
Clerks, Shipping/Receiving	14.00	Packers and Packagers, Hand	12.06
Computer Programmers	33.34	Physical Therapists	47.65
Computer Support Specialists	22.25	Postal Service Mail Carriers	25.51
Computer Systems Analysts	39.57	Real Estate Brokers	39.47
Cooks, Restaurant	14.48	Retail Salespersons	12.51
Dentists	69.94	Sales Reps., Exc. Tech./Scientific	27.10
Electrical Engineers	41.18	Sales Reps., Tech./Scientific	52.63
Electricians	32.37	Secretaries, Exc. Legal/Med./Exec.	17.96
Financial Managers	50.71	Security Guards	13.25
First-Line Supervisors/Managers, Sales	19.67	Surgeons	93.59
Food Preparation Workers	13.93	Teacher Assistants	15.30
General and Operations Managers	53.29	Teachers, Elementary School	25.10
Hairdressers/Cosmetologists	10.30	Teachers, Secondary School	25.20
Internists	95.39	Telemarketers	15.49
Janitors and Cleaners	13.43	Truck Drivers, Heavy/Tractor-Trailer	22.68
Landscaping/Groundskeeping Workers	12.32	Truck Drivers, Light/Delivery Svcs.	16.25
Lawyers	56.92	Waiters and Waitresses	11.09

Note: Wage data covers the Las Vegas-Paradise, NV Metropolitan Statistical Area—see Appendix B for areas included. Hourly wages for elementary/secondary school teachers and teacher assistants were calculated by the editors from annual wage data assuming a 40 hour work week; n/a not available.
Source: Bureau of Labor Statistics, Metro Area Occupational Employment and Wage Estimates, May 2011

RESIDENTIAL REAL ESTATE

Building Permits

Area	Single-Family			Multi-Family			Total		
	2010	2011	Pct. Chg.	2010	2011	Pct. Chg.	2010	2011	Pct. Chg.
City	926	814	-12.1	362	114	-68.5	1,288	928	-28.0
MSA[1]	4,623	3,817	-17.4	851	1,330	56.3	5,474	5,147	-6.0
U.S.	447,311	418,498	-6.4	157,299	205,563	30.7	604,610	624,061	3.2

Note: (1) Metropolitan Statistical Area—see Appendix B for areas included; figures represent new, privately-owned housing units authorized (unadjusted data); All permit data are based on estimates with imputation.
Source: U.S. Census Bureau, Manufacturing, Mining, and Construction Statistics, Building Permits, 2010, 2011

Homeownership Rate

Area	2005 (%)	2006 (%)	2007 (%)	2008 (%)	2009 (%)	2010 (%)	2011 (%)
MSA[1]	61.4	63.3	60.5	60.3	59.0	55.7	52.9
U.S.	68.9	68.8	68.1	67.8	67.4	66.9	66.1

Note: (1) Metropolitan Statistical Area—see Appendix B for areas included
Source: U.S. Census Bureau, Housing Vacancies and Homeownership Annual Statistics: 2011

Housing Vacancy Rates

Area	Gross Vacancy Rate[2] (%)			Year-Round Vacancy Rate[3] (%)			Rental Vacancy Rate[4] (%)			Homeowner Vacancy Rate[5] (%)		
	2009	2010	2011	2009	2010	2011	2009	2010	2011	2009	2010	2011
MSA[1]	16.7	17.2	16.4	16.5	16.8	16.0	14.3	13.8	12.1	5.0	5.1	4.1
U.S.	14.5	14.3	14.2	11.3	11.3	11.1	10.6	10.2	9.5	2.6	2.6	2.5

Note: (1) Metropolitan Statistical Area—see Appendix B for areas included; (2) The percentage of the total housing inventory that is vacant; (3) The percentage of the housing inventory (excluding seasonal units) that is year-round vacant; (4) The percentage of rental inventory that is vacant for rent; (5) The percentage of homeowner inventory that is vacant for sale
Source: U.S. Census Bureau, Housing Vacancies and Homeownership Annual Statistics: 2011

TAXES

State Corporate Income Tax Rates

State	Tax Rate (%)	Income Brackets ($)	Num. of Brackets	Financial Institution Tax Rate (%)[a]	Federal Income Tax Ded.
Nevada	No corporate tax	–	-	–	No

Note: Tax rates as of January 1, 2012; (a) Rates listed are the corporate income tax rate applied to financial institutions or excise taxes based on income. Some states have other taxes based upon the value of deposits or shares.
Source: Federation of Tax Administrators, "State Corporate Income Tax Rates, 2012"

State Individual Income Tax Rates

State	Tax Rate (%)	Income Brackets ($)	Num. of Brackets	Personal Exempt. ($)[1] Single	Personal Exempt. ($)[1] Dependents	Fed. Inc. Tax Ded.

Nevada – No State Income Tax

Note: Tax rates as of January 1, 2012; Local- and county-level taxes are not included; n/a not applicable; (1) Married joint filers generally receive double the single exemption
Source: Federation of Tax Administrators, "State Individual Income Tax Rates, 2012"

Various State and Local Tax Rates

State	State and Local Sales and Use (%)	State Sales and Use (%)	Gasoline[1] (¢/gal.)	Cigarette[2] ($/pack)	Spirits[3] ($/gal.)	Wine[4] ($/gal.)	Beer[5] ($/gal.)
Nevada	8.1	6.85	33.1	0.80	3.60	0.70	0.16

Note: All tax rates as of January 1, 2012 except beer, wine and spirits (September 1, 2011); (1) The American Petroleum Institute has developed a methodology for determining the average tax rate on a gallon of fuel. Rates may include any of the following: excise taxes, environmental fees, storage tank fees, other fees or taxes, general sales tax, and local taxes. In states where gasoline is subject to the general sales tax, or where the fuel tax is based on the average sale price, the average rate determined by API is sensitive to changes in the price of gasoline. States that fully or partially apply general sales taxes to gasoline: CA, CO, GA, IL, IN, MI, NY; (2) The federal excise tax of $1.0066 per pack and local taxes are not included; (3) Rates are those applicable to off-premise sales of 40% alcohol by volume (a.b.v.) distilled spirits in 750ml containers. Local excise taxes are excluded; (4) Rates are those applicable to off-premise sales of 11% a.b.v. non-carbonated wine in 750ml containers; (5) Rates are those applicable to off-premise sales of 4.7% a.b.v. beer in 12 ounce containers.
Source: Tax Foundation, 2012 Facts & Figures: How Does Your State Compare?

State-Local Tax Burdens

Area	Rate (%)	Rank[1]	Per Capita Taxes Paid to Home State ($)	Total State and Local Per Capita Taxes Paid ($)	Per Capita Income ($)
Nevada	7.5	49	1,988	3,311	44,241
U.S. Average	9.8	-	3,057	4,160	42,539

Note: Figures cover 2009; (1) Rank ranges from 1 to 50 where 1 is highest tax burden
Source: Tax Foundation, State-Local Tax Burdens, All States, 2009

State Business Tax Climate Index Rankings

State	Overall Rank	Corporate Tax Index Rank	Individual Income Tax Index Rank	Sales Tax Index Rank	Unemployment Insurance Tax Index Rank	Property Tax Index Rank
Nevada	3	1	1	42	42	16

Note: The index is a measure of how each state's tax laws affect economic performance. The lower the rank, the more favorable a state's tax system is for business. States without a given tax are given a ranking of 1.
Source: Tax Foundation, Major Components of the State Business Tax Climate Index, FY 2012

COMMERCIAL REAL ESTATE

Office Market

Market Area	Inventory (sq. ft.)	Vacant (sq. ft.)	Vac. Rate (%)	Under Constr. (sq. ft.)	Asking Rent ($/sf/yr)	
					Class A	Class B
Las Vegas	35,867,489	8,502,874	23.7	150,069	29.19	20.42

Source: Grubb & Ellis, Office Markets Trends, 4th Quarter 2011

Industrial Market

Market Area	Inventory (sq. ft.)	Vacant (sq. ft.)	Vac. Rate (%)	Under Constr. (sq. ft.)	Asking Rent ($/sf/yr)	
					WH/Dist	R&D/Flex
Las Vegas	99,377,925	15,450,909	15.5	0	4.80	8.76

Source: Grubb & Ellis, Industrial Markets Trends, 4th Quarter 2011

COMMERCIAL UTILITIES

Typical Monthly Electric Bills

Area	Commercial Service ($/month)		Industrial Service ($/month)	
	1,500 kWh	40 kW demand 14,000 kWh	1,000 kW demand 200,000 kWh	50,000 kW demand 15,000,000 kWh
City	129	1,155	14,987	1,011,615
Average[1]	189	1,616	25,197	1,470,813

Note: Based on total rates in effect July 1, 2011; (1) average based on 184 utilities surveyed
Source: Edison Electric Institute, Typical Bills and Average Rates Report, Summer 2011

TRANSPORTATION

Means of Transportation to Work

Area	Car/Truck/Van: Drove Alone	Car/Truck/Van: Car-pooled	Public Transportation: Bus	Public Transportation: Subway	Public Transportation: Railroad	Bicycle	Walked	Other Means	Worked at Home
City	77.6	11.2	4.2	0.0	0.0	0.3	2.0	1.7	3.0
MSA[1]	78.5	11.0	3.6	0.0	0.0	0.5	1.8	1.5	3.1
U.S.	76.0	10.2	2.7	1.7	0.5	0.5	2.8	1.3	4.2

Note: Figures are percentages and cover workers 16 years of age and older; (1) Figures cover the Las Vegas-Paradise, NV Metropolitan Statistical Area—see Appendix B for areas included
Source: U.S. Census Bureau, 2008-2010 American Community Survey 3-Year Estimates

Travel Time to Work

Area	Less Than 10 Minutes	10 to 19 Minutes	20 to 29 Minutes	30 to 44 Minutes	45 to 59 Minutes	60 to 89 Minutes	90 Minutes or More
City	8.2	25.9	29.5	26.5	5.3	2.9	1.8
MSA[1]	8.8	28.7	29.6	23.9	4.8	2.6	1.6
U.S.	13.9	30.1	20.8	19.8	7.5	5.5	2.5

Note: Figures are percentages and include workers 16 years old and over; (1) Figures cover the Las Vegas-Paradise, NV Metropolitan Statistical Area—see Appendix B for areas included
Source: U.S. Census Bureau, 2008-2010 American Community Survey 3-Year Estimates

Travel Time Index

Area	1985	1990	1995	2000	2005	2010
Urban Area[1]	1.07	1.16	1.23	1.25	1.29	1.24
Average[2]	1.11	1.16	1.18	1.21	1.25	1.20

Note: Travel Time Index—the ratio of travel time in the peak period to the travel time at free-flow conditions. A value of 1.30 indicates a 20-minute free-flow trip takes 26 minutes in the peak. Free-flow speeds (60 mph on freeways and 35 mph on principal arterials) are used as the comparison threshold; (1) Covers the Las Vegas NV urban area; (2) average of 439 urban areas

Source: Texas Transportation Institute, Urban Mobility Report 2011, September 2011

Public Transportation

Agency Name / Mode of Transportation	Vehicles Operated in Maximum Service	Annual Unlinked Passenger Trips ('000)	Annual Passenger Miles ('000)
Regional Transportation Commission of Southern Nevada (RTC)			
Bus (purchased transportation)	298	56,382.3	187,753.0
Demand Response (purchased transportation)	230	1,031.8	11,835.2

Source: Federal Transit Administration, National Transit Database, 2010

Air Transportation

Airport Name and Code / Type of Service	Passenger Airlines[1]	Passenger Enplanements	Freight Carriers[2]	Freight (lbs.)
McCarran International (LAS)				
Domestic service (U.S. carriers - 2011)	33	18,475,168	13	81,886,640
International service (U.S. carriers - 2010)	8	17,389	2	4,357

Note: (1) Includes all U.S.-based major, minor and commuter airlines that carried at least one passenger during the year; (2) Includes all U.S.-based airlines and freight carriers that transported at least one pound of freight during the year

Source: Bureau of Transportation Statistics, The Intermodal Transportation Database, Air Carriers: T-100 Domestic Market (U.S. Carriers), 2011; Bureau of Transportation Statistics, The Intermodal Transportation Database, Air Carriers: T-100 International Market (U.S. Carriers), 2010

Other Transportation Statistics

Major Highways:	I-15
Amtrak Service:	Bus connection
Major Waterways/Ports:	None

Source: Amtrak.com; Google Maps

BUSINESSES

Major Business Headquarters

Company Name	Rankings	
	Fortune[1]	Forbes[2]
Caesars Entertainment	277	-
Caesars Entertainment	-	31
Las Vegas Sands	342	-
MGM Resorts International	380	-

Note: (1) Fortune 500—companies that produce a 10-K are ranked 1 to 500 based on 2010 revenue; (2) all private companies with at least $2 billion in annual revenue are ranked 1 to 212; companies listed are headquartered in the city; dashes indicate no ranking

Source: Fortune, "Fortune 500," May 23, 2011; Forbes, "America's Largest Private Companies," November 16, 2011

Fast-Growing Businesses

According to *Inc.*, Las Vegas is home to four of America's 500 fastest-growing private companies: **CPAlead** (#40); **Rimini Street** (#204); **Deluxe Marketing** (#227); **Local Leads HQ** (#375). Criteria: must be an independent, privately-held, for-profit, U.S. corporation, proprietorship or partnership; revenues must be at least $80,000 in 2007 and $2 million in 2010; must have four-year operating/sales history. Holding companies, regulated banks, and utilities were excluded. *Inc., "America's 500 Fastest-Growing Private Companies," September 2011*

According to *Fortune*, Las Vegas is home to one of the 100 fastest-growing companies in the world: **Allegiant Travel** (#64). Companies were ranked by their revenue growth rate; their EPS growth rate; and their three-year annualized total return to investors for the period ending June 30, 2011. Criteria for inclusion: a company, foreign or domestic, must trade on a major U.S. stock exchange; must file quarterly reports with the SEC; must have a minimum market capitalization of $250 million; must have a stock price of at least $5 on June 30, 2011; must have been trading continuously since June 30, 2008; must have revenue and net income for the four quarters ended on or before April 30, 2011, of at least $50 million and $10 million, respectively; and must have posted a compound annual growth in revenue and earnings per share of at least 15% annually over the three years ending on or before April 30, 2011. REITs, limited-liability companies, limited parterships, companies about to be acquired, and companies that lost money in the quarter ending April 30, 2011 were excluded. *Fortune, "100 Fastest-Growing Companies," September 26, 2011*

Minority- and Women-Owned Businesses

Group	All Firms		Firms with Paid Employees			
	Firms	Sales ($000)	Firms	Sales ($000)	Employees	Payroll ($000)
Asian	5,710	1,037,064	804	856,837	5,412	184,775
Black	2,929	376,877	203	306,884	3,779	96,193
Hispanic	5,387	1,061,966	589	901,531	4,758	158,683
Women	16,073	3,984,163	1,673	3,402,002	14,667	503,397
All Firms	1,189	7,506,514	766	7,439,323	38,701	1,335,354

Note: Figures cover firms located in the city; minority- and women-owned business are defined as firms in which the corresponding group own 51% or more of the stock or equity of the company
Source: U.S. Census Bureau, 2007 Economic Census, Survey of Business Owners

HOTELS

Hotels/Motels

Area	5 Star		4 Star		3 Star		2 Star		1 Star		Not Rated	
	Num.	Pct.[3]	Num.	Pct.[3]	Num.	Pct.[3]	Num.	Pct.[3]	Num.	Pct.[3]	Num.	Pct.[3]
City[1]	13	6.2	27	12.8	79	37.4	76	36.0	6	2.8	10	4.7
Total[2]	133	0.9	940	6.5	4,569	31.8	7,033	48.9	351	2.4	1,343	9.3

Note: (1) Figures cover Las Vegas and vicinity; (2) Figures cover all 100 cities in this book; (3) Percentage of hotels which have a given star rating; Star ratings are determined by expedia.com and offer an indication of the general quality of a particular hotel.
Source: expedia.com, April 25, 2012

The Las Vegas-Paradise, NV metro area is home to eight of the best hotels in the U.S. according to *Travel & Leisure*: **Wynn Las Vegas** (#73); **The Palazzo** (#76); **Encore Las Vegas** (#78); **Mandarin Oriental, Las Vegas** (#112); **Bellagio, Las Vegas** (#122); **Trump International Hotel Las Vegas** (#155); **Four Seasons Hotel, Las Vegas** (#171); **The Venetian** (#198). Criteria: service; location; rooms; food; and value. *Travel & Leisure, "T+L 500, The World's Best Hotels 2012"*

The Las Vegas-Paradise, NV metro area is home to six of the best hotels in the U.S. according to *Condé Nast Traveler*: **The Cosmopolitan of Las Vegas** (#27); **Four Seasons** (#34); **Encore Wynn Las Vegas** (#45); **Bellagio** (#56); **The Venetian Resort Hotel Casino** (#66); **Mandarin Oriental** (#77). The selections are based on over 25,000 responses to the magazine's annual Readers' Choice Survey. *Condé Nast Traveler, "2011 Readers' Choice Awards"*

EVENT SITES

Major Stadiums, Arenas, and Auditoriums

Name	Max. Capacity
Cashman Field	9,334
Orleans Arena	9,500
Sam Boyd Stadium	36,800
Terrible's Star of the Desert Arena	6,500
Thomas & Mack Center	18,776

Source: Original research

Convention Centers

Name	Overall Space (sq. ft.)	Exhibit Space (sq. ft.)	Meeting Space (sq. ft.)	Meeting Rooms
Cashman Center	483,000	n/a	98,100	12
Las Vegas Convention Center	3,200,000	241,000	2,000,000	144
Mandalay Bay Convention Center	1,700,000	n/a	934,731	n/a
Sands Expo and Convention Center	1,800,000	n/a	n/a	n/a

Note: n/a not available
Source: Original research

Living Environment

COST OF LIVING

Cost of Living Index

Composite Index	Groceries	Housing	Utilities	Transportation	Health Care	Misc. Goods/ Services
100.2	105.1	92.5	91.4	103.8	106.4	105.8

Note: U.S. = 100; Figures cover the Las Vegas NV urban area.
Source: The Council for Community and Economic Research, ACCRA Cost of Living Index, 2011

Grocery Prices

Area[1]	T-Bone Steak ($/pound)	Frying Chicken ($/pound)	Whole Milk ($/half gal.)	Eggs ($/dozen)	Orange Juice ($/64 oz.)	Coffee ($/11.5 oz.)
City[2]	9.29	1.08	2.34	1.90	3.25	4.89
Avg.	9.25	1.18	2.22	1.66	3.19	4.40
Min.	6.70	0.88	1.31	0.95	2.46	2.94
Max.	14.30	2.16	3.50	3.18	4.75	6.83

Note: (1) Values for the local area are compared with the average, minimum and maximum values for all 335 areas in the Cost of Living Index; (2) Figures cover the Las Vegas NV urban area; **T-Bone Steak** *(price per pound);* **Frying Chicken** *(price per pound, whole fryer);* **Whole Milk** *(half gallon carton);* **Eggs** *(price per dozen, Grade A, large);* **Orange Juice** *(64 oz. Tropicana or Florida Natural);* **Coffee** *(11.5 oz. can, vacuum-packed, Maxwell House, Hills Bros, or Folgers).*
Source: The Council for Community and Economic Research, ACCRA Cost of Living Index, 2011

Housing and Utility Costs

Area[1]	New Home Price ($)	Apartment Rent ($/month)	All Electric ($/month)	Part Electric ($/month)	Other Energy ($/month)	Telephone ($/month)
City[2]	261,021	766	-	124.12	44.17	20.26
Avg.	285,990	839	163.23	89.00	77.52	26.92
Min.	188,005	460	125.58	45.39	33.89	17.98
Max.	1,197,028	3,244	339.16	181.97	348.69	40.01

Note: (1) Values for the local area are compared with the average, minimum and maximum values for all 335 areas in the Cost of Living Index; (2) Figures cover the Las Vegas NV urban area; **New Home Price** *(2,400 sf living area, 8,000 sf lot, in urban area with full utilities);* **Apartment Rent** *(950 sf 2 bedroom/1.5 or 2 bath, unfurnished, excluding all utilities except water);* **All Electric** *(average monthly cost for an all-electric home);* **Part Electric** *(average monthly cost for a part-electric home);* **Other Energy** *(average monthly cost for natural gas, fuel oil, coal, wood, and any other forms of energy except electricity);* **Telephone** *(price includes basic monthly rate for a private residential line plus additional local usage charges incurred by a family of four).*
Source: The Council for Community and Economic Research, ACCRA Cost of Living Index, 2011

Health Care, Transportation, and Other Costs

Area[1]	Doctor ($/visit)	Dentist ($/visit)	Optometrist ($/visit)	Gasoline ($/gallon)	Beauty Salon ($/visit)	Men's Shirt ($)
City[2]	98.33	89.33	110.48	3.46	46.37	35.71
Avg.	93.88	81.72	90.54	3.48	32.65	25.06
Min.	60.00	55.33	53.66	3.18	19.78	13.44
Max.	154.98	145.97	183.72	4.31	63.21	46.00

Note: (1) Values for the local area are compared with the average, minimum and maximum values for all 335 areas in the Cost of Living Index; (2) Figures cover the Las Vegas NV urban area; **Doctor** *(general practitioners routine exam of an established patient);* **Dentist** *(adult teeth cleaning and periodic oral examination);* **Optometrist** *(full vision eye exam for established adult patient);* **Gasoline** *(one gallon regular unleaded, national brand, including all taxes, cash price at self-service pump if available);* **Beauty Salon** *(woman's shampoo, trim, and blow-dry);* **Men's Shirt** *(cotton/polyester dress shirt, pinpoint weave, long sleeves).*
Source: The Council for Community and Economic Research, ACCRA Cost of Living Index, 2011

HOUSING

House Price Index (HPI)

Area	National Ranking[2]	Quarterly Change (%)	One-Year Change (%)	Five-Year Change (%)
MSA[1]	306	-0.37	-12.60	-59.81
U.S.[3]	-	-0.10	-2.43	-19.16

Note: The HPI is a weighted repeat sales index. It measures average price changes in repeat sales or refinancings on the same properties. This information is obtained by reviewing repeat mortgage transactions on single-family properties whose mortgages have been purchased or securitized by Fannie Mae or Freddie Mac in January 1975; (1) Metropolitan/Micropolitan Statistical Area—see Appendix B for areas included; (2) Rankings are based on annual percentage change for all metro areas containing at least 15,000 transactions over the last 10 years and ranges from 1 to 306; (3) figures based on a weighted average of Census Division estimates using a purchase only index; all figures are for the period ending December 31, 2011
Source: Federal Housing Finance Agency, House Price Index, February 23, 2012

House Price Valuations

Area	Q4 2005		Q4 2006		Q4 2007		Q4 2008		Q4 2009	
	Price ($000)	Over-valuation	Price ($000)	Over-valuation	Price ($000)	Over-valuation	Price ($000)	Over-valuation	Price ($000)	Over-valuation
MSA[1]	287.0	35.3	288.8	30.5	254.1	5.9	152.7	-34.4	123.0	-45.3

Note: Figures show the percentage of over- or under-valuation of single family homes relative to statistically normal house values (e.g. a value of 23.6 indicates that house values are 23.6% overvalued). Statistically normal house values are based on house prices, interest rates, household incomes, population densities, and any historical premiums or discounts metropolitan areas have exhibited over time; (1) Figures cover the Las Vegas-Paradise, NV - see Appendix B for areas included
Source: Global Insight/PNC Financial Services Group, House Prices in America: 4th Quarter 2009 Update

Median Single-Family Home Prices

Area	2009	2010	2011[p]	Percent Change 2010 to 2011
MSA[1]	142.9	138.0	124.7	-9.6
U.S. Average	172.1	173.1	166.2	-4.0

Note: Figures are median sales prices of existing single-family homes in thousands of dollars; (p) preliminary; n/a not available; (1) Metropolitan Statistical Area—see Appendix B for areas included
Source: National Association of Realtors, Median Sales Price of Existing Single-Family Homes for Metropolitan Areas, 4th Quarter 2011

Affordability Index of Existing Single-Family Homes

Area	2009	2010	2011[p]	Percent Change 2010 to 2011
MSA[1]	120.5	127.9	144.2	12.7

Note: The housing affordability index measures whether or not a typical family could qualify for a mortgage loan on a typical home. The higher the index, the greater the household purchasing power. An index of 100 is defined as the point where a median-income household has exactly enough income to qualify for the purchase of a median-priced existing single-family home, assuming a 20 percent downpayment and 25 percent of gross income devoted to mortgage principal and interest payments; (p) preliminary; n/a not available; (1) Metropolitan Statistical Area—see Appendix B for areas included
Source: National Association of Realtors, Affordability Index of Existing Single-Family Homes, 2011

Median Apartment Condo-Coop Home Prices

Area	2009	2010	2011[p]	Percent Change 2010 to 2011
MSA[1]	68.6	64.4	55.7	-13.5
U.S. Average	175.6	171.7	165.1	-3.8

Note: Figures are median sales prices of existing apartment condo-coop homes in thousands of dollars; (p) preliminary; n/a not available; (1) Metropolitan Statistical Area—see Appendix B for areas included
Source: National Association of Realtors, Median Sales Price of Existing Apartment Condo-Coop Homes for Metropolitan Areas, 4th Quarter 2011

Year Housing Structure Built

Area	2005 or Later	2000 -2004	1990 -1999	1980 -1989	1970 -1979	1960 -1969	1950 -1959	Before 1950	Median Year
City	7.2	15.6	33.6	18.4	11.3	8.0	4.4	1.5	1992
MSA[1]	11.5	22.2	28.6	15.9	12.8	5.6	2.4	1.0	1994
U.S.	5.0	8.6	14.0	14.1	16.3	11.3	11.2	19.6	1975

Note: Figures are percentages except for Median Year; (1) Figures cover the Las Vegas-Paradise, NV Metropolitan Statistical Area—see Appendix B for areas included
Source: U.S. Census Bureau, 2008-2010 American Community Survey 3-Year Estimates

HEALTH

Health Risk Data

Category	MSA[1] (%)	U.S. (%)
Adults who have been told they have high blood pressure[2]	27.4	28.7
Adults who have been told they have high blood cholesterol[2]	39.1	37.5
Adults who have been told they have diabetes[3]	9.0	8.7
Adults who have been told they have arthritis[2]	23.9	26.0
Adults who have been told they currently have asthma	9.3	9.1
Adults who are current smokers	22.1	17.3
Adults who are heavy drinkers[4]	5.1	5.0
Adults who are binge drinkers[5]	17.5	15.1
Adults who are overweight (BMI 25.0 - 29.9)	37.3	36.2
Adults who are obese (BMI 30.0 - 99.8)	23.1	27.5
Adults who participated in any physical activities in the past month	76.3	76.1
Adults 50+ who have ever had a sigmoidoscopy or colonoscopy	60.5	65.2
Women aged 40+ who have had a mammogram within the past two years	66.8	75.2
Men aged 40+ who have had a PSA test within the past two years	51.6	53.2
Adults aged 65+ who have had flu shot within the past year	59.4	67.5
Adults aged 18–64 who have any kind of health care coverage	77.2	82.2

Note: Data as of 2010 unless otherwise noted; (1) Figures cover the Las Vegas-Paradise, NV Metropolitan Statistical Area—see Appendix B for areas included; (2) Data as of 2009; (3) Figures do not include pregnancy-related, borderline, or pre-diabetes; (4) Heavy drinkers are classified as males having more than two drinks per day or females having more than one drink per day; (5) Binge drinkers are classified as males having five or more drinks on one occasion or females having four or more drinks on one occasion
Source: Centers for Disease Control and Prevention, Behaviorial Risk Factor Surveillance System, SMART: Selected Metropolitan/Micropolitan Area Risk Trends, 2009, 2010

Mortality Rates for the Top 10 Causes of Death in the U.S.

ICD-10[a] Sub-Chapter	ICD-10[a] Code	Age-Adjusted Mortality Rate[1] per 100,000 population	
		County[2]	U.S.
Malignant neoplasms	C00-C97	177.5	175.6
Ischaemic heart diseases	I20-I25	94.8	121.6
Other forms of heart disease	I30-I51	86.4	48.6
Chronic lower respiratory diseases	J40-J47	48.0	42.3
Cerebrovascular diseases	I60-I69	38.8	40.6
Organic, including symptomatic, mental disorders	F01-F09	36.7	26.7
Other degenerative diseases of the nervous system	G30-G31	11.9	24.7
Other external causes of accidental injury	W00-X59	28.1	24.4
Diabetes mellitus	E10-E14	11.3	21.7
Hypertensive diseases	I10-I15	20.4	18.2

Note: (a) ICD-10 = International Classification of Diseases 10th Revision; (1) Mortality rates are a three year average covering 2007-2009; (2) Figures cover Clark County
Source: Centers for Disease Control and Prevention, National Center for Health Statistics. Underlying Cause of Death 1999-2009 on CDC WONDER Online Database, released 2012. Data for year 2009 are compiled from the Multiple Cause of Death File 2009, Series 20 No. 2O, 2012, Data for year 2008 are compiled from the Multiple Cause of Death File 2008, Series 20 No. 2N, 2011, Data for year 2007 are compiled from Multiple Cause of Death File 2007, Series 20 No. 2M, 2010.

Mortality Rates for Selected Causes of Death

ICD-10[a] Sub-Chapter	ICD-10[a] Code	Age-Adjusted Mortality Rate[1] per 100,000 population County[2]	U.S.
Assault	X85-Y09	7.2	5.7
Human immunodeficiency virus (HIV) disease	B20-B24	3.4	3.3
Influenza and pneumonia	J09-J18	21.8	16.4
Intentional self-harm	X60-X84	18.3	11.5
Malnutrition	E40-E46	*Unreliable	0.8
Obesity and other hyperalimentation	E65-E68	0.8	1.6
Transport accidents	V01-V99	12.6	13.7
Viral hepatitis	B15-B19	2.0	2.2

Note: (a) ICD-10 = International Classification of Diseases 10th Revision; (1) Mortality rates are a three year average covering 2007-2009; (2) Figures cover Clark County; (*) Unreliable data as per CDC
Source: Centers for Disease Control and Prevention, National Center for Health Statistics. Underlying Cause of Death 1999-2009 on CDC WONDER Online Database, released 2012. Data for year 2009 are compiled from the Multiple Cause of Death File 2009, Series 20 No. 2O, 2012, Data for year 2008 are compiled from the Multiple Cause of Death File 2008, Series 20 No. 2N, 2011, Data for year 2007 are compiled from Multiple Cause of Death File 2007, Series 20 No. 2M, 2010.

Distribution of Physicians and Dentists

Area[1]	Dentists[2]	D.O.[3]	M.D.[4] Total	Family/General Practice	Pediatrics	Medical Specialties	Surgical Specialties
Local (number)	741	390	2,671	303	170	1,046	568
Local (rate[5])	4.0	2.1	14.2	1.6	0.9	5.6	3.0
U.S. (rate[5])	4.5	1.9	18.3	2.5	1.4	6.8	4.1

Note: Data as of 2008 unless noted; (1) Local data covers Clark County; (2) Data as of 2007; (3) Doctor of Osteopathic Medicine; (4) Includes active, non-federal, patient-care, office-based Doctors of Medicine; (5) rate per 10,000 population
Source: Area Resource File (ARF). 2009-2010 Release. U.S. Department of Health and Human Services, Health Resources and Services Administration, Bureau of Health Professions, Rockville, MD, August 2010

EDUCATION

Public School District Statistics

District Name	Schls	Pupils	Pupil/Teacher Ratio	Minority Pupils[1] (%)	Free Lunch Eligible[2] (%)	IEP[3] (%)
Clark County School District	358	307,059	19.8	65.9	38.0	10.5

Note: Table includes school districts with 2,000 or more students; (1) Percentage of students that are not non-Hispanic white; (2) Percentage of students that are eligible for the free lunch program; (3) Percentage of students that have an Individualized Education Program.
Source: U.S. Department of Education, National Center for Education Statistics, Common Core of Data, Local Education Agency (School District) Universe Survey: School Year 2009-2010; U.S. Department of Education, National Center for Education Statistics, Common Core of Data, Public Elementary/Secondary School Universe Survey: School Year 2009-2010

Highest Level of Education

Area	Less than H.S.	H.S. Diploma	Some College, No Deg.	Associate Degree	Bachelors Degree	Masters Degree	Profess. School Degree	Doctorate Degree
City	18.7	28.7	25.0	7.0	13.4	4.9	1.7	0.7
MSA[1]	16.6	29.3	25.3	7.0	14.7	4.9	1.5	0.7
U.S.	14.7	28.4	21.3	7.6	17.6	7.2	1.9	1.2

Note: Figures cover persons age 25 and over; (1) Figures cover the Las Vegas-Paradise, NV Metropolitan Statistical Area—see Appendix B for areas included
Source: U.S. Census Bureau, 2008-2010 American Community Survey 3-Year Estimates

Educational Attainment by Race

Area	High School Graduate or Higher (%)					Bachelor's Degree or Higher (%)				
	Total	White	Black	Asian	Hisp.[2]	Total	White	Black	Asian	Hisp.[2]
City	81.3	81.0	84.8	90.9	52.9	20.6	20.8	14.6	38.5	7.4
MSA[1]	83.4	83.4	87.0	89.7	57.9	21.8	21.5	16.2	38.6	8.2
U.S.	85.3	87.5	81.4	85.5	61.6	28.0	29.3	17.8	50.2	13.0

Note: Figures shown cover persons 25 years old and over; (1) Figures cover the Las Vegas-Paradise, NV Metropolitan Statistical Area—see Appendix B for areas included; (2) People of Hispanic origin can be of any race
Source: U.S. Census Bureau, 2008-2010 American Community Survey 3-Year Estimates

School Enrollment by Grade and Control

Area	Preschool (%)		Kindergarten (%)		Grades 1 - 4 (%)		Grades 5 - 8 (%)		Grades 9 - 12 (%)	
	Public	Private	Public	Private	Public	Private	Public	Private	Public	Private
City	49.9	50.1	93.6	6.4	93.3	6.7	93.5	6.5	94.4	5.6
MSA[1]	56.2	43.8	92.4	7.6	93.6	6.4	95.6	4.4	95.2	4.8
U.S.	55.4	44.6	87.1	12.9	89.4	10.6	89.5	10.5	90.4	9.6

Note: Figures shown cover persons 3 years old and over; (1) Figures cover the Las Vegas-Paradise, NV Metropolitan Statistical Area—see Appendix B for areas included
Source: U.S. Census Bureau, 2008-2010 American Community Survey 3-Year Estimates

Average Salaries of Public School Classroom Teachers

Area	2010-11		2011-12		Percent Change 2010-11 to 2011-12	Percent Change 2001-02 to 2011-12
	Dollars	Rank[1]	Dollars	Rank[1]		
Nevada	53,023	20	54,559	19	2.90	33.80
U.S. Average	55,623	-	56,643	-	1.83	26.8

Note: (1) State rank ranges from 1 to 51 where 1 indicates highest salary.
Source: National Education Association, Rankings & Estimates: Rankings of the States 2011 and Estimates of School Statistics 2012, December 2011

Higher Education

Four-Year Colleges			Two-Year Colleges			Medical Schools[1]	Law Schools[2]	Voc/ Tech[3]
Public	Private Non-profit	Private For-profit	Public	Private Non-profit	Private For-profit			
2	0	1	0	1	10	0	1	8

Note: Figures cover institutions located within the city limits and include main campuses only; (1) includes schools accredited by the Liaison Committee on Medical Education and the American Osteopathic Association's Commission on Osteopathic College Accreditation; (2) includes American Bar Association-accredited law schools; (3) includes all schools with programs that are less than 2 years.
Source: National Center for Education Statistics, Integrated Postsecondary Education System (IPEDS) Peer Analysis System, 2011-12; Association of American Medical Colleges, Member List, April 23, 2012; American Osteopathic Association, Member List, April 23, 2012; Law School Admission Council, Official Guide to ABA-Approved Law Schools Online, April 23, 2012

PRESIDENTIAL ELECTION

2008 Presidential Election Results

Area	Obama	McCain	Nader	Other
Clark County	58.5	39.5	0.6	1.4
U.S.	52.9	45.6	0.6	0.9

Note: Results are percentages and may not add to 100% due to rounding
Source: Dave Leip's Atlas of U.S. Presidential Elections, www.uselectionatlas.org

EMPLOYERS

Major Employers

Company Name	Industry
Barrick Gaming Operations	Casino hotel
City of Las vegas	Executive offices
Coast Casinos Inc	Hotels/motels
Consolidated Electric	Electrical apparatus equipment
Donald J Laughlin	Gambling machines, coin operated
E-T-T	Slot machines
Gaughan South	Casino hotel
Las Vegas Sands	Casino hotel
M Arthur Gensler Jr & Associates Inc	Architectual services
Nevada System of Higher Education	Colleges/universities
Nevada System of Higher Education	General medical/surgical hospitals
New Castle Corp	Casino hotel
New York - New York Hotel and Casino	Casino hotel
Paris Hotel Casino Resort	Casino hotel
Primm Casinos	Hotels/motels
Sam-Will Inc	Casino hotel
Station Casinos Inc	Hotels/motels
Station Casinos Inc	Casino hotel
Stratosphere Gaming	Hotels/motels
Sunrise Hospitality and Medical Center	General medical/surgical hospitals
University Medical Center of Southern NV	General medical/surgical hospitals
Venetian Casino/Resort	Resort hotel

Note: Companies shown are located within the Las Vegas-Paradise, NV metropolitan area.
Source: Hoovers.com, data extracted April 25 2012

Best Companies to Work For

Nevada Federal Credit Union, headquartered in Las Vegas, is among the "50 Best Employers for Workers Over 50." Criteria: recruiting practices; opportunities for training, education, and career development; workplace accommodations; alternative work options, such as flexible scheduling, job sharing, and phased retirement; employee health and pension benefits; and retiree benefits. Employers with at least 50 employees based in the U.S. are eligible, including for-profit companies, not-for-profit organizations, and government employers. *AARP, "2011 AARP Best Employers for Workers Over 50"*

Caesars Entertainment Corp, headquartered in Las Vegas, is among the "100 Best Places to Work in IT." To qualify, companies, both public and private, had to have a minimum of 50 IT employees and were selected based on average salary and bonus increases, the percentage of IT staffers promoted, IT staff turnover rates, training and development programs, and the percentage of women and minorities in IT staff and management positions. In addition, *Computerworld* looked at retention efforts, programs for recognizing and rewarding outstanding performances, and benefits such as flextime, elder care and child care, and reimbursement for college tuition and the cost of pursuing technology certifications. *Computerworld, "100 Best Places to Work in IT 2011"*

PUBLIC SAFETY

Crime Rate

Area	All Crimes	Violent Crimes				Property Crimes		
		Murder	Forcible Rape	Robbery	Aggrav. Assault	Burglary	Larceny -Theft	Motor Vehicle Theft
City	3,944.3	7.6	46.0	282.6	556.8	976.0	1,569.5	505.8
Suburbs[1]	3,000.0	4.5	23.2	129.5	263.4	700.1	1,607.6	271.7
Metro[2]	3,685.3	6.7	39.8	240.6	476.3	900.3	1,580.0	441.6
U.S.	3,345.5	4.8	27.5	119.1	252.3	699.6	2,003.5	238.8

Note: Figures are crimes per 100,000 population; (1) All areas within the metro area that are located outside the city limits; (2) Metropolitan Statistical Area—see Appendix B for areas included
Source: FBI Uniform Crime Reports, 2010

Hate Crimes

Area	Number of Quarters Reported	Bias Motivation				
		Race	Religion	Sexual Orientation	Ethnicity	Disability
Area[2]	4	19	13	13	7	0

Note: (2) Figures cover Las Vegas Metropolitan Police.
Source: Federal Bureau of Investigation, Hate Crime Statistics 2010

Identity Theft Consumer Complaints

Area	Complaints	Complaints per 100,000 Population	Rank[2]
MSA[1]	1,839	100.1	94
U.S.	279,156	90.4	-

Note: (1) Metropolitan Statistical Area—see Appendix B for areas included; (2) Rank ranges from 1 to 384 where 1 indicates greatest number of identity theft complaints per 100,000 population
Source: Federal Trade Commission, Consumer Sentinel Network Data Book for January–December 2011

Fraud and Other Consumer Complaints

Area	Complaints	Complaints per 100,000 Population	Rank[2]
MSA[1]	9,548	519.9	126
U.S.	1,533,924	496.8	-

Note: (1) Metropolitan Statistical Area—see Appendix B for areas included; (2) Rank ranges from 1 to 384 where 1 indicates greatest number of fraud and other complaints per 100,000 population
Source: Federal Trade Commission, Consumer Sentinel Network Data Book for January–December 2011

RECREATION

Culture

Dance[1]	Theatre[1]	Instrumental Music[1]	Vocal Music[1]	Series/ Festivals	Museums	Zoos and Aquariums[2]
1	2	3	0	2	16	1

Note: (1) Number of professional perfoming groups; (2) AZA-accredited
Source: The Grey House Performing Arts Directory, 2011-2012; Official Museum Directory, 2011; American Association of Museums, AAM Member Museums, April 2012; Association of Zoos & Aquariums, AZA Member Zoos & Aquariums, April 2012

Professional Sports Teams

Team Name	League
No teams are located in the metro area	

Source: Original research

CLIMATE

Average and Extreme Temperatures

Temperature	Jan	Feb	Mar	Apr	May	Jun	Jul	Aug	Sep	Oct	Nov	Dec	Yr.
Extreme High (°F)	77	87	91	99	109	115	116	116	113	103	87	77	116
Average High (°F)	56	62	69	78	88	99	104	102	94	81	66	57	80
Average Temp. (°F)	45	50	56	65	74	84	90	88	80	68	54	46	67
Average Low (°F)	33	38	43	51	60	69	76	74	66	54	41	34	53
Extreme Low (°F)	8	16	23	31	40	49	60	56	43	26	21	11	8

Note: Figures cover the years 1948-1990
Source: National Climatic Data Center, International Station Meteorological Climate Summary, 9/96

Average Precipitation/Snowfall/Humidity

Precip./Humidity	Jan	Feb	Mar	Apr	May	Jun	Jul	Aug	Sep	Oct	Nov	Dec	Yr.
Avg. Precip. (in.)	0.5	0.4	0.4	0.2	0.2	0.1	0.4	0.5	0.3	0.2	0.4	0.3	4.0
Avg. Snowfall (in.)	1	Tr	Tr	Tr	0	0	0	0	0	0	Tr	Tr	1
Avg. Rel. Hum. 7am (%)	59	52	41	31	26	20	26	31	30	36	47	56	38
Avg. Rel. Hum. 4pm (%)	32	25	20	15	13	10	14	16	16	18	26	31	20

Note: Figures cover the years 1948-1990; Tr = Trace amounts (<0.05 in. of rain; <0.5 in. of snow)
Source: National Climatic Data Center, International Station Meteorological Climate Summary, 9/96

Weather Conditions

Temperature			Daytime Sky			Precipitation		
10°F & below	32°F & below	90°F & above	Clear	Partly cloudy	Cloudy	0.01 inch or more precip.	0.1 inch or more snow/ice	Thunder-storms
< 1	37	134	185	132	48	27	2	13

Note: Figures are average number of days per year and cover the years 1948-1990
Source: National Climatic Data Center, International Station Meteorological Climate Summary, 9/96

HAZARDOUS WASTE

Superfund Sites

Las Vegas has no sites on the EPA's Superfund Final National Priorities List.
U.S. Environmental Protection Agency, Final National Priorities List, April 17, 2012

AIR & WATER QUALITY

Air Quality Index

Area	Percent of Days when Air Quality was...[2]					AQI Statistics[2]	
	Good	Moderate	Unhealthy for Sensitive Groups	Unhealthy	Very Unhealthy	Maximum	Median
Area[1]	57.5	35.9	6.6	0.0	0.0	144	47

Note: Air Quality Index (AQI) is an index for reporting daily air quality. EPA calculates the AQI for five major air pollutants regulated by the Clean Air Act: ground-level ozone, particle pollution (aka particulate matter), carbon monoxide, sulfur dioxide, and nitrogen dioxide. The AQI runs from 0 to 500. The higher the AQI value, the greater the level of air pollution and the greater the health concern. There are six AQI categories: "Good" AQI is between 0 and 50. Air quality is considered satisfactory; "Moderate" AQI is between 51 and 100. Air quality is acceptable; "Unhealthy for Sensitive Groups" When AQI values are between 101 and 150, members of sensitive groups may experience health effects; "Unhealthy" When AQI values are between 151 and 200 everyone may begin to experience health effects; "Very Unhealthy" AQI values between 201 and 300 trigger a health alert; "Hazardous" AQI values over 300 trigger warnings of emergency conditions (not shown); (1) Data covers Clark County; (2) Based on 365 days with AQI data in 2011.
Source: U.S. Environmental Protection Agency, AirData Report, 2011

Air Quality Index Pollutants

Area	Percent of Days when AQI Pollutant was...[2]					
	Carbon Monoxide	Nitrogen Dioxide	Ozone	Sulfur Dioxide	Particulate Matter 2.5	Particulate Matter 10
Area[1]	0.0	2.2	78.6	0.0	15.9	3.3

Note: The Air Quality Index (AQI) is an index for reporting daily air quality. EPA calculates the AQI for five major air pollutants regulated by the Clean Air Act: ground-level ozone, particle pollution (also known as particulate matter), carbon monoxide, sulfur dioxide, and nitrogen dioxide. The AQI runs from 0 to 500. The higher the AQI value, the greater the level of air pollution and the greater the health concern; (1) Data covers Clark County; (2) Based on 365 days with AQI data in 2011.
Source: U.S. Environmental Protection Agency, AirData Report, 2011

Air Quality Index Trends

Area	Trend Sites (days)								All Sites (days)
	2003	2004	2005	2006	2007	2008	2009	2010	2010
MSA[1]	42	22	34	35	24	12	5	2	10

Note: Figures are the number of days the AQI value exceeded 100 in a given year. An AQI value greater than 100 indicates that air quality would have been in the unhealthful range on that day. Data from exceptional events are included. These counts are presented in two ways. First, the counts are based on sites having an adequate record of monitoring data during the trend period (trend sites). These counts represent the relative change in the number of days with AQI values greater than 100. In the last column, the counts are based on all sites with data in the most recent year (because it is possible for a site to have data in the most recent year but not enough data to be a trend site); (1) Data covers the Las Vegas-Paradise, NV—see Appendix B for areas included
Source: U.S. Environmental Protection Agency, Air Quality Index Information, "Number of Days with Air Quality Index Values Greater than 100 at Trend Sites, 2000-2010, and at All Sites in 2010"

Maximum Air Pollutant Concentrations: Particulate Matter, Ozone, CO and Lead

	Particulate Matter 10 (ug/m3)	Particulate Matter 2.5 Wtd AM (ug/m3)	Particulate Matter 2.5 24-Hr (ug/m3)	Ozone (ppm)	Carbon Monoxide (ppm)	Lead (ug/m3)
MSA[1] Level	61	7.4	22	0.079	3	n/a
NAAQS[2]	150	15	35	0.075	9	0.15
Met NAAQS[2]	Yes	Yes	Yes	No	Yes	n/a

Note: Data from exceptional events are not included; (1) Data covers the Las Vegas-Paradise, NV—see Appendix B for areas included; (2) National Ambient Air Quality Standards; ppm = parts per million; ug/m³ = micrograms per cubic meter; n/a not available

Concentrations: Particulate Matter 10 (coarse particulate)—highest second maximum 24-hour concentration; Particulate Matter 2.5 Wtd AM (fine particulate)—highest weighted annual mean concentration; Particulate Matter 2.5 24-Hour (fine particulate)—highest 98th percentile 24-hour concentration; Ozone—highest fourth daily maximum 8-hour concentration; Carbon Monoxide—highest second maximum non-overlapping 8-hour concentration; Lead—maximum running 3-month average

Source: U.S. Environmental Protection Agency, CBSA Factbook 2010, Air Quality Statistics by City, 2010

Maximum Air Pollutant Concentrations: Nitrogen Dioxide and Sulfur Dioxide

	Nitrogen Dioxide AM (ppb)	Nitrogen Dioxide 1-Hr (ppb)	Sulfur Dioxide AM (ppb)	Sulfur Dioxide 1-Hr (ppb)	Sulfur Dioxide 24-Hr (ppb)
MSA[1] Level	13.308	55.9	n/a	n/a	n/a
NAAQS[2]	53	100	30	75	140
Met NAAQS[2]	Yes	Yes	n/a	n/a	n/a

Note: Data from exceptional events are not included; (1) Data covers the Las Vegas-Paradise, NV—see Appendix B for areas included; (2) National Ambient Air Quality Standards; ppb = parts per billion; n/a not available

Concentrations: Nitrogen Dioxide AM—highest arithmetic mean concentration; Nitrogen Dioxide 1-Hr—highest 98th percentile 1-hour daily maximum concentration; Sulfur Dioxide AM—highest annual mean concentration; Sulfur Dioxide 1-Hr—highest 99th percentile 1-hour daily maximum concentration; Sulfur Dioxide 24-Hr—highest second maximum 24-hour concentration

Source: U.S. Environmental Protection Agency, CBSA Factbook 2010, Air Quality Statistics by City, 2010

Drinking Water

Water System Name	Pop. Served	Primary Water Source Type	Violations[1] Health Based	Violations[1] Monitoring/ Reporting
Las Vegas Valley Water District	1,276,091	Purchased Surface	0	0

Note: (1) Based on violation data from January 1, 2011 to December 31, 2011 (includes unresolved violations from earlier years)

Source: U.S. Environmental Protection Agency, Office of Ground Water and Drinking Water, Safe Drinking Water Information System (based on data extracted April 18, 2012)

Los Angeles, California

Background

There is as much to say about Los Angeles as there are unincorporated and incorporated municipalities under its jurisdiction. The city is immense, and in the words of one of its residents, "If you want a life in LA, you need a car."

Los Angeles acquired its many neighborhoods and communities such as Hollywood, Glendale, Burbank, and Alhambra when those cities wanted to share in the water piped into Los Angeles from the Owens River. To obtain it, the cities were required to join the Los Angeles municipal system. Due to those annexations, Los Angeles is now one of the largest U.S. cities in both acreage and population. It is also one of the most racially diverse.

The city tries to connect the communities in its far-flung empire through a rather Byzantine system of freeways which gives Los Angeles its reputation as a congested, car-oriented culture, where people have to schedule their days around the three-hour rush hour.

Despite these challenges, Los Angeles is a city with a diversified economy and 325 days of sunshine a year. What was founded in 1781 as a sleepy pueblo of 44 people, with chickens roaming the footpaths, is now a city leading the nation in commerce, transportation, finance, and, especially, entertainment—with three-quarters of all motion pictures made in the United States still produced in the Los Angeles area, and headquarters of such major studios as MGM and Universal located in "municipalities" unto themselves.

Playa Vista, the first new community to be established on the Westside of Los Angeles in more than 50 years, is home to Electronic Arts, the world's leading video game publisher. Lincoln Properties is currently building office buildings totaling more than 820,000 square feet in the eastern portion of Playa Vista community known as "The Campus at Playa Vista." The National Basketball Association Clippers has a new training facility at the Campus, which will also be home to a basketball-themed public park, a fitting way to celebrate the 2011 NBA champion Lakers.

The arts are center-stage in Los Angeles. The new home of the Getty Center and Museum, an architectural masterpiece designed by Richard Meier and built on a commanding hill, is a dramatic venue for visual arts and other events. The Los Angeles Opera, under the direction of Placido Domingo, offers a lively season of operas as well as recitals by such luminaries as Cecilia Bartoli and Renee Fleming. The Los Angeles Philharmonic now performs in the Walt Disney Concert Hall, dedicated in October of 2003. This hall was designed by Frank Gehry, famous as the architect of the Guggenheim Museum at Bilbao.

The downtown's first modern industrial park, The Los Angeles World Trade Center, is a 20-acre project that is downtown's only foreign trade zone.

Inland and up foothill slopes, both high and low temperatures become more extreme and the average relative humidity drops. Relative humidity is frequently high near the coast, but may be quite low along the foothills. Most rain falls November through March, while the summers are very dry. Destructive flash floods occasionally develop in and below some mountain canyons. Snow is often visible on the nearby mountains in the winter, but is extremely rare in the coastal basin. Thunderstorms are infrequent.

The climate of Los Angeles is normally pleasant and mild throughout the year, with unusual differences in temperature, humidity, cloudiness, fog, rain, and sunshine over fairly short distances in the metro area. Low clouds are common at night and in the morning along the coast during spring and summer. Near the foothills, clouds form later in the day and clear earlier. Annual percentages of fog and cloudiness are greatest near the ocean. Sunshine totals are highest on the inland side of the city.

At times, high concentrations of air pollution affect the Los Angeles coastal basin and adjacent areas, when lack of air movement combines with an atmospheric inversion. In the fall and winter, the Santa Ana winds pick up considerable amounts of dust and can blow strongly in the northern and eastern sections of the city and in outlying areas in the north and east; these rarely reach coastal sections of the city.

Rankings

General Rankings

- *Men's Health Living* ranked 100 U.S. cities in terms of quality of life. Los Angeles was ranked #78 and received a grade of D+. Criteria: number of fitness facilities; air quality; number of physicians; male/female ratio; education levels; household income; cost of living. *Men's Health Living, Spring 2008*
- Los Angeles was selected as one of America's ten "Best Cities to Work and Live." The city ranked #5. The results are based on a survey of 2,500 employees and entrepreneurs who were asked about 40 large cities. *BusinessWeek, "America's Most and Least Favorite Cities," January 5, 2009*
- Los Angeles was identified as one of the top places to live in the U.S. by Harris Interactive. The city ranked #13 out of 15. Criteria: 2,463 adults (age 18 and over) were polled and asked "if you could live in or near any city in the country except the one you live in or nearest to now, which city would you choose?" The poll was conducted online within the U.S. between September 14 and 20, 2010. *Harris Interactive, November 9, 2011*

Business/Finance Rankings

- The Los Angeles metro area was identified as one of 10 "Cities Where the Recession is Easing." The metro area was ranked #9. Criteria: job growth; goods produced; home sale prices; unemployment rates. *Forbes.com, "Cities Where the Recession is Easing," March 3, 2010*
- Experian ranked the top 20 major U.S. metropolitan areas by average debt per consumer. The Los Angeles metro area was ranked #20. Criteria: average debt per consumer. Debt for this study includes credit cards, auto loans and personal loans. It does not include mortgages. *Experian, May 13, 2010*
- Los Angeles was identified as one of "America's Hardest-Working Towns." The city ranked #13 out of 25. Criteria: average hours worked per capita; willingness to work during personal time; number of dual income households; local employment rate. *Parade, "What is America's Hardest-Working Town?," April 15, 2012*
- Los Angeles was identified as one of the "Happiest Cities to Work in 2012" by *CareerBliss.com,* an online community for career advancement. The city ranked #21 out of 50. Criteria: independent company reviews from employees all over the country on: relationship with their boss and co-workers; work environment; job resources; growth opportunities; compensation; company culture; company reputation; daily tasks; job control over work performed on a daily basis. *CareerBliss.com, "Happiest and Unhappiest Cities to Work in 2012"*
- *American City Business Journals* ranked America's 261 largest cities in terms of their resident's wealth. Los Angeles ranked #28. Criteria: per capita income; median household income; percentage of households with annual incomes of $200,000 or more; median home value. *American City Business Journals, "Where the Money Is: America's Wealth Centers," August 18, 2008*
- The Los Angeles metro area appeared on the Milken Institute "2011 Best Performing Metros" list. Rank: #135 out of 200 large metro areas. Criteria: job growth; wage and salary growth; high-tech output growth. *Milken Institute, "2011 Best Performing Metros"*
- Los Angeles was ranked #11 out of 145 regions worldwide in terms of its "Knowledge Competitiveness Index." The index attempts to measure the knowledge-based development taking place throughout the world and is based on 19 measures of economic performance that indicate a region's ability to translate its knowledge capacity into economic value. *Centre for International Competitiveness, World Knowledge Competitiveness Index 2008*
- *Forbes* ranked the 200 most populous metro areas in the U.S. in terms of the "Best Places for Business and Careers." The Los Angeles metro area was ranked #114. Criteria: costs (business and living); job growth (past and projected); income growth; educational attainment; projected economic growth; crime; cultural and recreational opportunities; net migration patterns; number of highly ranked colleges. *Forbes, "Best Places for Business and Careers," June 2011*

Children/Family Rankings

- Los Angeles was selected as one of the 10 worst cities to raise children in the U.S. by *KidFriendlyCities.org*. Criteria: education; environment; health; employment; crime; diversity; cost of living. *KidFriendlyCities.org, "Top Rated Kid/Family Friendly Cities 2009"*

- The Los Angeles metro area was selected as one of the "Best Cities for Relocating Families" by Worldwide ERC and Primacy Relocation. The 2008 study looked at nearly 50 factors important to relocating families including: recent job growth; nearby top-ranked colleges; in-state tuition for four-year public colleges; population growth since 2000; pediatricians per 100,000 population; and a Green Living index. *Worldwide ERC and Primacy Relocation, "2008 Best Cities for Relocating Families"*

- *Fit Pregnancy* magazine ranked the 50 best U.S. cities in which to have a baby. Los Angeles was ranked #36. Criteria: access to hospitals and doctors; affordability; birthing options; breastfeeding; child care; fertility laws/resources; maternal and infant health risk; parks/stroller friendliness; safety. *Fit Pregnancy, "The Best Cities in America to Have a Baby 2008"*

Culture/Performing Arts Rankings

- Los Angeles was selected as one of the top 10 cities for design in America by architectural firm RMJM Hillier. The city was ranked #4. American cities with more than 500,000 residents were ranked according to criteria such as the quality of public transit, the number of LEED-registered buildings (indicating sustainable design) and how many of the city's employees work within creative industries such as performing arts or publishing. Resident interviews were used to rate a city's design factor, which takes in elements of a city's architecture as well as its creative appeal. *RMJM Hillier, "America's Best Cities for Design," June 25, 2008*
- Los Angeles was selected as one of "America's Top 25 Arts Destinations." The city ranked #12 in the big city (population 500,000 and over) category. Criteria: readers' top choices for arts travel destinations based on the richness and variety of visual arts sites, activities and events. *American Style, "America's Top 25 Arts Destinations," May 2010*

Dating/Romance Rankings

- Los Angeles was selected as one of the best cities for single men by *Rent.com*. The city ranked #6 of 10. Criteria: high single female-to-male ratio; lively nightlife; low divorce rate; low cost of living. *Rent.com, "Top 10 Cities for Single Men," May 2, 2011*
- Los Angeles was selected as one of the best cities for single women by *Rent.com*. The city ranked #7 of 10. Criteria: high single male-to-female ratio; lively nightlife; low divorce rate; low cost of living. *Rent.com, "Top 10 Cities for Single Women," August 19, 2011*

- Los Angeles appeared on *Men's Health's* list of the most sex-happy cities in America. The city ranked #54 of 100. Criteria: condom sales; birth rates; sex toy sales; rates of chlamydia, gonorrhea, and syphilis. *Men's Health, "America's Most Sex-Happy Cities," October 2010*

- *Men's Health* ranked 100 U.S. cities in terms of best (and worst) marriages. Los Angeles was ranked #93 (#1 = worst). Criteria: rate of failed marriages; stringency of divorce laws; percentage of population who've split; number of licensed marriage and family therapists. *Men's Health, "Splitsville, USA," May 2010*

- Eli Lily and Company, in partnership with Sperling's BestPlaces, ranked the nation's 50 largest metro areas in terms of the "Most Romantic Cities for Baby Boomers." The Los Angeles metro area ranked #41. Criteria: marriage and divorce rates among baby boomers age 45 to 60; great restaurants; dance studios; chocolate, jewelry and flower sales. *Eli Lily and Company, "Most Romantic Cities for Baby Boomers," April 20, 2007*

- The Los Angeles metro area was selected as one of the "Best Cities for Relocating Singles" by Worldwide ERC and Primacy Relocation. The area ranked #12 out of the 100 largest metro areas in the U.S. Criteria: recent job growth; recent singles population growth; overall population growth; affordable rental housing; cost-of-living index; expanded arts and recreation opportunities; ratio of single men and single women; affordability of quality higher education (including state residency requirements); diversity index; climate; population density. *Worldwide ERC and Primacy Relocation, "2008 Best Cities for Relocating Singles"*

- *Forbes* ranked the 40 most populous urbanized areas in the U.S. in terms of the "Best Cities for Singles." The Los Angeles metro area ranked #8. Criteria: number of singles; cost of living alone; nightlife; culture; job growth; coolness; and online dating participation. *Forbes.com, "Best Cities for Singles," July 27, 2009*

Education Rankings

- *Men's Health* ranked 100 U.S. cities in terms of their education levels. Los Angeles was ranked #67 (#1 = most educated city). Criteria: high school graduation rates; school enrollment; educational attainment; number of households who have outstanding student loans; number of households whose members have taken adult-education courses. *Men's Health, "Where School Is In: The Most and Least Educated Cities," September 12, 2011*
- Los Angeles was selected as one of "America's Most Literate Cities." The city ranked #59 out of the 75 largest U.S. cities. Criteria: number of booksellers; library resources; Internet resources; educational attainment; periodical publishing resources; newspaper circulation. *Central Connecticut State University, "America's Most Literate Cities 2011"*
- Los Angeles was identified as one of the 100 "smartest" metro areas in the U.S. The area ranked #76. Criteria: the editors rated the collective brainpower of the 100 largest metro areas in the U.S. based on their residents' educational attainment. *American City Business Journals, April 14, 2008*
- Los Angeles was identified as one of "America's Brainiest Bastions" by *Portfolio.com.* The metro area ranked #111 out of 200. *Portfolio.com* analyzed levels of educational attainment in the nation's 200 largest metropolitan areas. The editors established scores for five levels of educational attainment, based on relative earning power of adult workers age 25 or older. Scores were determined by comparing the median income for all workers with the median income for those workers at a specified educational level. *Portfolio.com, "America's Brainiest Bastions," December 1, 2010*

Environmental Rankings

- The Los Angeles was identified as one of America's dirtiest metro areas by *Forbes.* The area ranked #2 out of 10. Criteria: year-round particulate pollution; short-term particulate pollution; ozone pollution. *Forbes, "Dirtiest Cities in America," November 4, 2011*
- The Los Angeles was identified as one of North America's greenest metropolitan areas. The area ranked #7. The Green City Index is comprised of 31 indicators, and scores cities across nine categories: carbon dioxide; energy; land use; buildings; transport; water; waste; air quality; environmental governance. The 27 largest metropolitan areas in the U.S. and Canada were considered. *Economist Intelligence Unit, sponsored by Siemens, "U.S. and Canada Green City Index, 2011"*
- The Los Angeles was identified as one of America's cities with the most ENERGY STAR certified buildings. The area ranked #1 out of 25. Criteria: number of ENERGY STAR labeled buildings in 2010. *U.S. Environmental Protection Agency, "Top Cities With the Most ENERGY STAR Certified Buildings," March 15, 2011*
- The Los Angeles metro area was identified as one of "The Ten Biggest American Cities that are Running Out of Water" by *24/7 Wall St.* The metro area ranked #1 out of 10. *24/7 Wall St.* did an analysis of the water supply and consumption in the 30 largest metropolitan areas in the U.S. Criteria include: projected water demand as a share of available precipitation; groundwater use as a share or projected available precipitation; susceptibility to drought; projected increase in freshwater withdrawals; projected increase in summer water deficit. *24/7 Wall St., "The Ten Biggest American Cities that are Running Out of Water," November 1, 2010*
- Los Angeles was selected as one of 22 "Smarter Cities" for energy by the Natural Resources Defense Council. Criteria: investment in green power; energy efficiency measures; conservation. *Natural Resources Defense Council, "2010 Smarter Cities," July 19, 2010*
- The Los Angeles metro area was selected as one of "America's Most Toxic Cities" by *Forbes.* The metro area ranked #6 out of 10. The 80 largest metropolitan areas were ranked on the following criteria: air quality; water quality; Superfund sites; toxic releases. *Forbes, "America's Most Toxic Cities, 2011," February 28, 2011*

- *American City Business Journal* ranked 43 metropolitan areas in terms of their "greenness." The Los Angeles metro area ranked #29. Criteria: Forty-one metros in which *ACBJ* has business weeklies, plus Indianapolis and Cleveland, were ranked based on 20 different indicators such as adoption of green technologies, utilization of environmentally sound practices, and air and water quality. *American City Business Journals, "Green City Index," March 11, 2010*

- 100 of the largest metro areas in the U.S. were analyzed in terms of their current drought severity. The Los Angeles metro area ranked #1 (#1 = driest). The rankings were based on statistics such as long-term precipitation trends and patterns and the Palmer drought indices. *Sperling's BestPlaces, www.BestPlaces.net, "America's Drought-Riskiest Cities," November 2007*

- The Los Angeles metro area appeared in *Country Home's* "Best Green Places" report. The area ranked #40 out of 379. Criteria: official energy policies; green power; green buildings; availability of fresh, locally grown food. *Country Home, "Best Green Places," 2008*

- Los Angeles was highlighted as one of the 25 metro areas most polluted by short-term particle pollution (24-hour PM 2.5) in the U.S. The area ranked #4. *American Lung Association, State of the Air 2011*

- Los Angeles was highlighted as one of the 25 metro areas most polluted by year-round particle pollution (Annual PM 2.5) in the U.S. The area ranked #2. *American Lung Association, State of the Air 2011*

- Los Angeles was highlighted as one of the 25 most ozone-polluted metro areas in the U.S. The area ranked #1. *American Lung Association, State of the Air 2011*

Food/Drink Rankings

- Los Angeles was identified as one of "America's Most Caffeinated Cities" by *Bundle.com.* The city was ranked #5 out of 10. The rankings were determined by examining consumer spending at 16 widely known coffee chains during the second quarter of 2011. *Bundle.com, "America's Most Caffeinated Cities," September 19, 2011*

- Angel Stadium (Los Angeles Angels of Anaheim) was selected as one of PETA's "2011 Top 10 Vegetarian-Friendly Major League Ballparks." The park ranked #8. *People for the Ethical Treatment of Animals, "2011 Top 10 Vegetarian-Friendly Major League Ballparks"*

- Los Angeles was selected as one of North America's most vegetarian- and vegan-friendly large cities (population 300,000 or more). The city was ranked #8. Criteria: number of vegetarian restaurants and vegetarian-friendly restaurants per capita; input from PETA supporters and staff members on the quality of the options. *People for the Ethical Treatment of Animals, "North America's Best Vegetarian- and Vegan-Friendly Cities," July 23, 2010*

- Los Angeles was selected as one of the "Top 10 Places to Eat Classic American Chow." *USA Weekend, "Summer Travel Report," May 18-20, 2007*

Health/Fitness Rankings

- The American Podiatric Medical Association and *Prevention* magazine ranked 100 American cities based on walkability. Nineteen walking criteria were evaluated including the percentage of adults who walk to work, number of parks per square mile, number of trails for walking and hiking, air pollution, use of mass transit, crime rate, pedestrian fatalities, and percentage of adults who walk for fitness. Los Angeles ranked #14. *Prevention, "The Best Walking Cities of 2009," May 2009; American Podiatric Medical Association, "2009 Best Fitness-Walking Cities," April 7, 2009*

- Los Angeles was identified as one of the most walkable cities in the U.S. by *WalkScore.com,* a Seattle-based service that rates the convenience and transit access of 10,000 neighborhoods in 2,500 cities. The editors at Grey House Publishing used *WalkScore.com's* online service to look at the scores of 280 cities with populations greater than or equal to 100,000. The top 50 cities were selected. *WalkScore.com, April 2, 2012*

- Los Angeles was identified as one of the "Worst Bed Bug-Infested Cities" in the U.S. by *Forbes.* Orkin and Terminix, the nation's largest pest control companies, both compiled lists based on the number of calls they've received and bed bug jobs performed relative to population. *Forbes* selected the 13 cities that appeared on both lists. *Forbes, "America's Worst Bed Bug-Infested Cities," December 23, 2010*

- The Los Angeles metro area was selected as one of the worst cities for bed bugs in America by Rollins corporation, the owner of seven pest control companies, including Orkin. The area ranked #5 based on the number of bed bug treatments from January to December 2011. *Rollins, "The Top 50 U.S. Cities for Bed Bugs," March 19, 2012*

- Los Angeles was identified as one of the most bed bug-infested cities in the U.S. by Terminix. Los Angeles ranked #8.Criteria: complaint calls from customers; confirmed cases by professionals. *Terminix, "2011 Most Bedbug-Infested Cities," May 24, 2011*

- Los Angeles was selected as one of the 25 fattest cities in America by *Men's Fitness Online*. It ranked #9 out of America's 50 largest cities. Criteria: fitness centers and sport stores; nutrition; sports participation; TV viewing; overweight/sedentary; junk food; air quality; geography; commute; parks and open space; city recreational facilities; access to healthcare; motivation; mayor and city initiatives; state obesity initiatives. *Men's Fitness, "The Fittest and Fattest Cities in America," March 5, 2012*

- Los Angeles was identified as a "2011 Asthma Capital." The area ranked #57 out of the nation's 100 largest metropolitan areas. Twelve factors were used to identify the most challenging places to live for people with asthma: estimated prevalence; self-reported prevalence; crude death rate for asthma; annual pollen score; annual air quality; public smoking laws; number of board-certified asthma specialists; school inhaler access laws; rescue medication use; controller medication use; uninsured rate; poverty rate. *Asthma and Allergy Foundation of America, "2011 Asthma Capitals"*

- Los Angeles was identified as a "2011 Fall Allergy Capital." The area ranked #77 out of 100. Three groups of factors were used to identify the most severe cities for people with allergies during the fall season: annual pollen levels; medicine utilization; access to board-certified allergists. *Asthma and Allergy Foundation of America, "2011 Fall Allergy Capitals"*

- Los Angeles was identified as a "2012 Spring Allergy Capital." The area ranked #63 out of 100. Three groups of factors were used to identify the most severe cities for people with allergies during the spring season: annual pollen levels; medicine utilization; access to board-certified allergists. *Asthma and Allergy Foundation of America, "2012 Spring Allergy Capitals"*

- *Men's Health* examined 100 major U.S. cities and selected the best and worst cities for men. Los Angeles ranked #39. Criteria: 35 statistical parameters of long life in the categories of health, quality of life, and fitness. *Men's Health, "The 10 Best and Worst Cities for Men 2012," January/February 2012*

- Los Angeles was selected as one of the least accident-prone cities in America by *Men's Health*. The city ranked #3 of 10. Criteria: workplace accident rates; traffic fatalities; emergency room visits; accidental poisonings; incidents of drowning; fires; injury-producing falls. *Men's Health, "Ranking America's Cities: Accident City, USA," October 2009*

- The Los Angeles metropolitan area was selected as one of the best metros for hospital care in America by *HealthGrades.com.* The rankings are based on a comprehensive study of patient death and complication rates in the nation's nearly 5,000 hospitals. Hospitals performing in the top 5% nationwide across 26 different medical procedures and diagnoses were identified. *HealthGrades.com* then ranked cities by the highest percentage of these Distinguished Hospitals for Clinical Excellence™. The Los Angeles metro area ranked #22. *HealthGrades.com, "America's Top 50 Cities for Hospital Care," January 21, 2012*

- The American Academy of Dermatology ranked 26 U.S. metropolitan regions in terms of their residents knowledge, attitude and behaviors towards tanning, sun protection and skin cancer detection. The Los Angeles metro area ranked #22. The results of the study are based on an online survey of over 7,000 adults nationwide. *American Academy of Dermatology, "Suntelligence: How Sun Smart is Your City," May 3, 2010*

- The Los Angeles metro area appeared in the 2011 Gallup-Healthways Well-Being Index. The index, based on interviews with more than 350,000 Americans, measured jobs, finances, physical health, emotional state of mind and communities. The metro area ranked #63 out of 190. Criteria: life evaluation; emotional health; work environment; physical health; healthy behaviors; basic access (basic needs optimal for a healthy life, such as access to food and medicine, having health insurance and feeling safe while walking at night). *Gallup-Healthways, "State of Well-Being 2011"*
- The Los Angeles metro area was identified as one of "America's Most Stressful Cities" by *Sperling's BestPlaces*. The metro area ranked #14 out of 50. Criteria: unemployment rate; suicide rate; commute time; mental health; poor rest; alcohol use; violent crime rate; property crime rate; cloudy days annually. *Sperling's BestPlaces, www.BestPlaces.net, "Stressful Cities 2012*
- The Los Angeles metro area was identified as one of "America's Most Stressful Cities" by *Forbes*. The metro area ranked #1 out of 40. Criteria: housing affordability; unemployment rate; cost of living; air quality; traffic congestion; sunny days; population density. *Forbes.com, "America's Most Stressful Cities," September 23, 2011*
- *Men's Health* ranked 100 U.S. cities in terms of their activity levels. Los Angeles was ranked #27 (#1 = most active city). Criteria: where and how often residents exercise; percentage of households that watch more than 15 hours of cable television a week and buy more than 11 video games a year; death rate from deep-vein thrombosis, a condition linked to sitting for extended periods of time. *Men's Health, "Where Sit Happens: The Most and Least Active Cities in America," June 20, 2011*
- 50 of the largest metro areas in the U.S. were analyzed in terms of their health and fitness by the American College of Sports Medicine in their "American Fitness Index." The Los Angeles metro area ranked #38 (#1 = healthiest). Criteria: preventative health behaviors; levels of chronic disease; health care access; community resources and policies that support physical activity. *American College of Sports Medicine, "Health and Community Fitness Status of the 50 Largest Metropolitan Areas," August 1, 2011*

Real Estate Rankings

- Los Angeles was identified as one of the priciest cities to rent in the U.S. The area ranked #2 out of 10. Criteria: rent-to-income ratio. *CNBC, "Priciest Cities to Rent," March 14, 2012*
- *Fortune* ranked the 100 largest metro areas in the U.S. in terms of projected median home price change in 2010. The Los Angeles metro area ranked #91. *Fortune, "The 2010 Housing Outlook," December 9, 2009*
- Los Angeles was selected as one of the 10 best U.S. cities for real estate investment. The city ranked #5. *Association of Foreign Investors in Real Estate, "AFIRE News," January/February, 2011*
- The Los Angeles metro area was identified as one of the 20 least affordable housing markets in the U.S. in 2011. The area ranked #7 out of 152 markets with an affordability index of 72.7%. The index measures whether or not a typical family could qualify for a mortgage loan on a typical home. The calculation used assumes a down payment of 20 percent of the home price and a qualifying ratio of 25 percent, meaning that the monthly P&I payment cannot exceed 25 percent of a the median family monthly income. *National Association of Realtors®, Affordability Index of Existing Single-Family Homes for Metropolitan Areas, 2011*
- Los Angeles appeared on *ApartmentRatings.com* "Top Cities for Renters" list in 2009." The area ranked #81. Overall satisfaction ratings were ranked using thousands of user submitted scores for hundreds of apartment complexes located in the 100 most populated U.S. municipalities. *ApartmentRatings.com, "2009 Renter Satisfaction Rankings"*
- Los Angeles appeared on *ApartmentRatings.com* "Top College Towns & Cities" for renters list in 2011." The area ranked #67 out of 87. Overall satisfaction ratings were ranked using thousands of user submitted scores for hundreds of apartment complexes located in cities and towns that are home to the 100 largest four-year institutions in the U.S. *ApartmentRatings.com, "2011 College Town Renter Satisfaction Rankings"*

- The Los Angeles metro area was identified as one of the most expensive places to rent in the U.S. The area ranked #67 out of 10 markets with an average effective rent of $1,380 per month. The rental figures cover apartment properties in complexes with 40 or more units (20 or more units in California and Arizona). The figures are blended average rents, which include all unit sizes. Effective rents include free rent incentives and other landlord concessions. *Wall Street Journal Online, January 17, 2008*

- The Los Angeles metro area was identified as one of "America's 25 Weakest Housing Markets" by *Forbes*. The metro area ranked #19. Criteria: metro areas with populations over 500,000 were ranked based on projected home values through 2011. *Forbes.com, "America's 25 Weakest Housing Markets," January 7, 2009*

- The nation's largest metro areas were analyzed in terms of the best places to buy pre-foreclosures (short sales). The Los Angeles metro area ranked #7 out of 10. Criteria: at least 500 pre-foreclosure sales during the fourth quarter and a short sales increase of at least five percent from a year ago. The areas selected posted the biggest discounts on the sales of pre-foreclosure properties. *RealtyTrac, "Fourth Quarter and Year-End 2011 U.S. Foreclosure Sales Report: Shifting Towards Short Sales," February 28, 2012*

- The Los Angeles metro area was identified as one of America's most overvalued cities in 2011 by *CNNMoney.com* based on data from Local Market Monitor. Criteria: median home prices; local interest rates; economic and population growth; construction costs; vacancies; household income. *CNNMoney.com, "America's Most Overvalued (and Undervalued) Cities," January 16, 2011*

- The Los Angeles metro area was identified as one of America's least affordable cities to buy a house in 2010 by *CNNMoney.com.* The metro area was ranked #5 out of 5. Criteria: median home prices; median family income *CNNMoney.com, "America's Most and Least Affordable Cities to Buy a House," May 21, 2010*

- The Los Angeles metro area appeared in a *Wall Street Journal* article ranking cities by "housing stress." The metro area was ranked #3 (#1 = most stress). Criteria: fraction of mortgage-holding homeowners with a monthly housing payment in excess of 30 percent of income; percentage of people without health insurance; unemployment rate. *The Wall Street Journal, "Which Cities Face Biggest Housing Risk," October 5, 2010*

- The Center for Housing Policy ranked 210 U.S. metropolitan areas by the fair market rent for a two-bedroom unit. The Los Angeles metro area was ranked #10. (#1 = most expensive) with a rent of $1,420. Criteria: Fair Market Rent (FMR) in effect during the fourth quarter of 2009 based on HUD's fiscal year 2010 FMRs. *The Center for Housing Policy, "Paycheck to Paycheck: Most to Least Expensive Rental Markets in 2009"*

- The Los Angeles metro area was identified as one of the best housing markets of the decade by *Forbes.* Criteria: increase in housing values per square foot since January 2000. *Forbes, "America's 5 Best (and Worst) Housing Markets of the Decade," December 7, 2010*

- The Los Angeles metro area was identified as one of the markets with the best expected performance in home prices over the next 12 months. *Local Market Monitor, "First Quarter Home Price Forecast for Largest US Markets," March 2, 2011*

- The Los Angeles metro area was identified as one of the best U.S. markets to invest in rental property" by HomeVestors and Local Market Monitor. The area ranked #97 out of 100. Criteria: risk-return premium relative to national average. *HomeVestors and Local Market Monitor, "Best 100 U.S. Markets to Invest in Rental Property," March 9, 2012*

Safety Rankings

- Symantec, the makers of Norton, in partnership with Sperling's BestPlaces, ranked the 50 largest cities in the U.S. in terms of their vulnerability to cybercrime. The city ranked #35. Criteria: number of cyberattacks and potential infections; level of Internet access; expenditures on smartphones and computer hardware/software; wireless hotspots; broadband connectivity; Internet usage; online purchases. *Symantec, "Riskiest Online Cities of 2012" February 15, 2012*

- Allstate ranked the 193 largest cities in America in terms of driver safety. Los Angeles ranked #182. In addition, drivers were 50.8% more likely to have had an accident compared to the national average. Allstate researchers analyzed internal property damage reported claims over a two-year period (from January 2008 to December 2009) to protect findings from external influences such as weather or road construction. A weighted average of the two-year numbers determined the annual percentages. The report defines an auto crash as any collision resulting in a property damage claim. *Allstate, "2011 Allstate America's Best Drivers Report™"*

- Los Angeles was identified as one of the safest large cities in America by CQ Press. All 34 cities with populations of 500,000 or more that reported crime rates in 2010 for murder, rape, robbery, aggravated assault, burglary, and motor vehicle thefts were ranked. The city ranked #8 out of the top 10. *CQ Press, City Crime Rankings 2011-2012*

- The National Insurance Crime Bureau ranked 366 metro areas in the U.S. in terms of per capita rates of vehicle theft. The Los Angeles metro area ranked #23 (#1 = highest rate). Criteria: number of vehicle theft offenses per 100,000 inhabitants in 2010. *National Insurance Crime Bureau, "Hot Spots," June 21, 2011*

- The Los Angeles metro area was identified as one of the most dangerous metro areas for pedestrians by Transportation for America. The metro area ranked #27 out of 52 metro areas with over 1 million residents. Criteria: area's population divided by the number of pedestrian fatalities in that area. *Transportation for America, "Dangerous by Design 2011"*

Seniors/Retirement Rankings

- Bankers Life and Casualty Company, in partnership with Sperling's BestPlaces, ranked the nation's 50 largest metro areas in terms of the "Best U.S. Cities for Seniors." The Los Angeles metro area ranked #37. Criteria: healthcare; transportation; housing; environment; economy; health and longevity; social and spiritual life; crime. *Bankers Life and Casualty Company, Center for a Secure Retirement, "Best U.S. Cities for Seniors 2011," September 2011*

Sports/Recreation Rankings

- Los Angeles appeared on the *Sporting News* list of the "Best Sports Cities" for 2011. The area ranked #8 out of 271 cities in the U.S. *Sporting News* takes a 12-month snapshot of each city's sports, putting a heavy premium on regular-season won-lost records (from the most recently completed season). Other criteria include: playoff berths, bowl appearances and tournament bids; championships; applicable power ratings; quality of competition; overall fan fervor (measured in part by attendance); abundance of teams (rewarding quality over quantity); stadium and arena quality; ticket availability and prices; franchise ownership; and marquee appeal of athletes. *Sporting News, "Best Sports Cities 2011," October 4, 2011*

- The Los Angeles was selected as one of the best metro areas for golf in America by *Golf Digest.* The Los Angeles area was ranked #4 out of 20. Criteria: climate; cost of public golf; quality of public golf; accessibility. *Golf Digest, "The Top 20 Cities for Golf," October 2011*

Technology Rankings

- Scarborough Research, a leading market research firm, identified the Los Angeles DMA (Designated Market Area) as one of the top markets for text messaging with more than 50% of cell phone subscribers age 18+ utilizing the text messaging feature on their phone. *Scarborough Research, November 24, 2008*

- The Los Angeles metro area was identified as one of the "Top 14 Nano Metros" in the U.S. by the Project on Emerging Nanotechnologies. The metro area is home to 20 companies, universities, government laboratories and/or organizations working in nanotechnology. *Project on Emerging Nanotechnologies, "Nano Metros 2009"*

Transportation Rankings

- Los Angeles appeared on *Trapster.com's* list of the 10 most-active U.S. cities for speed traps. The city ranked #2 of 10. *Trapster.com* is a community platform accessed online and via smartphone app that alerts drivers to traps, hazards and other traffic issues nearby. *Trapster.com, "Speeders Beware: Cities With the Most Speed Traps," February 10, 2012*

- Los Angeles was identified as one of America's "10 Best Cities for Public Transportation" by *U.S. News & World Report.* The city ranked #7. The ten cities selected had the best combination of public transportation investment, ridership, and safety. *U.S. News & World Report, "10 Best Cities for Public Transportation," February 8, 2011*

- Los Angeles was identified as one of America's worst cities for speed traps by the National Motorists Association. The city ranked #24 out of 25. Criteria: speed trap locations per 100,000 residents. *National Motorists Association, September 2011*

- The Los Angeles metro area was identified as one of the best U.S. cities to live in without a car by *24/7 Wall St.* The area ranked #9 out of 10. Criteria: percentage of neighborhoods covered by public transit; frequency of service for those neighborhoods; share of jobs reachable within 90 minutes or less by public transit; how accessible amenities are for residents on foot; percentage of commuters who bike to work. The 100 largest metropolitan areas in the U.S. were examined. *24/7 Wall St., "The Best Cities to Live in Car-Free," November 28, 2011*

- The Los Angeles metro area appeared on *Forbes* list of the best and worst cities for commuters. The metro area ranked #51 out of 60 (#1 is best). Criteria: travel time; road congestion; travel delays. *Forbes.com, "Best and Worst Cities for Commuters," February 16, 2010*

Women/Minorities Rankings

- *Women's Health* examined U.S. cities and identified the 100 best cities for women. Los Angeles was ranked #45. Criteria: 30 categories were examined from obesity and breast cancer rates to commuting times and hours spent working out. *Women's Health, "Best Cities for Women 2012"*

- Los Angeles was ranked #30 out of 100 metro areas in *SELF Magazine's* ranking of America's healthiest places for women." A panel of experts came up with more than 50 criteria including death and disease rates, environmental indicators, community resources, and lifestyle habits. *SELF Magazine, "Secrets of America's Healthiest Women," December 2008*

- Los Angeles was selected as one of the 25 healthiest cities for Latinas by *Latina Magazine.* The city ranked #6. Criteria: U.S. cities with populations over 500,000 residents were evaluated on the following criteria: percentage of 18-34 year-olds per city; Latino college graduation rates; number of colleges and universities; affordability; housing costs; income growth over time; average salary; percentage of singles; climate; safety; how the city's diversity compares to the national average; opportunities for minority entrepreneurs. *Latina Magazine, "Top 15 U.S. Cities for Young Latinos to Live In," August 19, 2011*

- The Los Angeles metro area appeared on *Forbes'* list of the "Best Cities for Minority Entrepreneurs." The area ranked #6 out of 10. Criteria: 52 metropolitan statistical areas were examined. For each ethnicity (African Americans, Asians and Hispanics), the editors measured housing affordability, population growth, income growth, and entrepreneurship (per capita self-employment). *Forbes, "Best Cities for Minority Entrepreneurs," March 23, 2011*

Miscellaneous Rankings

- *Men's Health* ranked 100 U.S. cities by their level of sadness. Los Angeles was ranked #65 (#1 = saddest city). Criteria: suicide rates; unemployment rates; percentage of households that use antidepressants; percent of population who report feeling blue all or most of the time. *Men's Health, "Frown Towns," November 28, 2011*

- Energizer Holdings, the makers of Edge® shave gel, in partnership with Sperling's BestPlaces, ranked 50 major metro areas in terms of everyday irritations. The Los Angeles metro area ranked #5. Criteria: humidity levels; weather conditions; incidence of traffic delays and congestion; average commute times; frequency of flight delays and cancellations; rates of sleeplessness; underemployment; pollens and allergens; pests; comedy clubs per capita. *Energizer Holdings, "Most Irritation Prone Cities," July 23, 2010*

- Mars Chocolate North America, the makers of COMBOS®, in partnership with Sperling's BestPlaces, ranked 50 major metro areas in terms of their "manliness." The Los Angeles metro area ranked #50. Criteria: number of professional sports teams; number of nearby NASCAR tracks and racing events; manly lifestyle; concentration of manly retail stores; manly occupations per capita; salty snack sales; "Board of Manliness" rankings. *Mars Chocolate North America, "America's Manliest Cities 2011," September 1, 2011*
- Los Angeles was selected as one of the "Best Hair Cities" by *NaturallyCurly.com.* The city was ranked #8. Criteria: humidity levels; pollution; rainfall; average wind speeds; water hardness; beauty salons per capita. *NaturallyCurly.com, "Best/Worst Hair Cities," April 29, 2009*
- Los Angeles was selected as one of the most tattooed cities in America by *TotalBeauty.com.* The city was ranked #10. Criteria: number of tattoo and permanent makeup shops per capita; number of tattoo conventions hosted. *TotalBeauty.com, "Top 10 Most Tattooed Cities in America," August 2010*
- The Los Angeles metro area was selected as one of "America's Greediest Cities" by *Forbes*. The area was ranked #8 out of 10. Criteria: number of Forbes 400 (*Forbes* annual list of the richest Americans) members per capita. *Forbes, "America's Greediest Cities," December 7, 2007*
- The Los Angeles metro area appeared in *AutoMD.com's* ranking of the "Best and Worst Cities for Auto Repair." The metro area ranked #19 (#1 is best). The 50 most-populated metro areas in the U.S. were ranked on three critical factors: repair affordability; price disparity range; shop integrity factor. *AutoMD.com, "Advocacy for Repair Shop Fairness Report," February 24, 2010*
- Los Angeles was identified as one of "America's Vainest Cities" by *Forbes.com.* The city ranked #8. Criteria: highest number of cosmetic surgeons per 100,000 people in America's 50 largest cities. *Forbes.com, "America's Vainest Cities," November 29, 2007*
- Los Angeles was selected as one of America's "10 Meanest Cities" by the National Coalition for the Homeless and The National Law Center on Homelessness & Poverty. The city was ranked #1. Criteria: the number of anti-homeless laws; the enforcement of those laws and severity of penalties; the general political climate towards homeless people; local advocate support for the meanest designation; the city's history of criminalization measures; and the existence of pending or recently enacted criminalization legislation in the city. *National Coalition for the Homeless and The National Law Center on Homelessness & Poverty, "Homes Not Handcuffs: The Criminalization of Homelessness in U.S. Cities," July 2009*

Business Environment

CITY FINANCES

City Government Finances

Component	2009 ($000)	2009 ($ per capita)
Total Revenues	7,412,976	1,933
Total Expenditures	15,207,300	3,966
Debt Outstanding	18,720,393	4,882
Cash and Securities[1]	33,944,588	8,853

Note: (1) Cash and security holdings of a government at the close of its fiscal year, including those of its dependent agencies, utilities, and liquor stores.
Source: U.S Census Bureau, State & Local Government Finances 2009

City Government Revenue by Source

Source	2009 ($000)	2009 ($ per capita)
General Revenue		
From Federal Government	368,190	96
From State Government	340,227	89
From Local Governments	0	0
Taxes		
Property	1,938,624	506
Sales and Gross Receipts	1,374,329	358
Personal Income	0	0
Corporate Income	0	0
Motor Vehicle License	0	0
Other Taxes	666,097	174
Current Charges	2,806,662	732
Liquor Store	0	0
Utility	3,664,614	956
Employee Retirement	-5,453,593	-1,422

Source: U.S Census Bureau, State & Local Government Finances 2009

City Government Expenditures by Function

Function	2009 ($000)	2009 ($ per capita)	2009 (%)
General Direct Expenditures			
Air Transportation	1,138,710	297	7.5
Corrections	0	0	0.0
Education	0	0	0.0
Employment Security Administration	0	0	0.0
Financial Administration	221,327	58	1.5
Fire Protection	685,199	179	4.5
General Public Buildings	0	0	0.0
Governmental Administration, Other	126,393	33	0.8
Health	198,802	52	1.3
Highways	706,818	184	4.6
Hospitals	0	0	0.0
Housing and Community Development	488,173	127	3.2
Interest on General Debt	419,871	110	2.8
Judicial and Legal	118,041	31	0.8
Libraries	118,227	31	0.8
Parking	32,339	8	0.2
Parks and Recreation	425,366	111	2.8
Police Protection	2,050,733	535	13.5
Public Welfare	0	0	0.0
Sewerage	384,757	100	2.5
Solid Waste Management	246,049	64	1.6
Veterans' Services	0	0	0.0
Liquor Store	0	0	0.0
Utility	4,303,856	1,122	28.3
Employee Retirement	1,760,844	459	11.6

Source: U.S Census Bureau, State & Local Government Finances 2009

Municipal Bond Ratings

Area	Moody's	S&P	Fitch
City	Aa2	AA-	AA-

Rating Systems (shown in declining order of credit quality): Moody's– Aaa, Aa, A, Baa, Ba, B, Caa, Ca, C (numerical modifiers 1, 2, and 3 are added to letter-rating); S&P– AAA, AA, A, BBB, BB, B, CCC, CC, C; Fitch– AAA, AA, A, BBB, BB, B, CCC, CC, C. Ratings may be modified by the addition of a plus or minus sign to show relative standing within the major rating categories.
Notes: n/a Not Available; w/d Withdrawn (1) Not Reviewed; (2) Issuer Rating/No General Obligation; (3) Standard and Poor's Issue Credit Rating (ICR) is a current opinion of an obliger with respect to a specific financial obligation, a specific class of financial obligations, or a specific financial program.
Source: U.S. Census Bureau, 2012 Statistical Abstract, Bond Ratings for City Governments by Largest Cities: 2010

DEMOGRAPHICS

Population Growth

Area	1990 Census	2000 Census	2010 Census	Population Growth (%) 1990-2000	Population Growth (%) 2000-2010
City	3,487,671	3,694,820	3,792,621	5.9	2.6
MSA[1]	11,273,720	12,365,627	12,828,837	9.7	3.7
U.S.	248,709,873	281,421,906	308,745,538	13.2	9.7

Note: (1) Figures cover the Los Angeles-Long Beach-Santa Ana, CA Metropolitan Statistical Area—see Appendix B for areas included
Source: U.S. Census Bureau, 2010 Census

Household Size

Area	Persons in Household (%) One	Two	Three	Four	Five	Six	Seven or More	Average Household Size
City	28.3	27.0	15.2	13.2	7.7	4.0	4.6	2.81
MSA[1]	23.4	27.0	16.3	15.3	8.7	4.4	4.9	2.98
U.S.	26.7	32.8	16.1	13.4	6.5	2.6	1.9	2.58

Note: (1) Figures cover the Los Angeles-Long Beach-Santa Ana, CA Metropolitan Statistical Area—see Appendix B for areas included
Source: U.S. Census Bureau, 2010 Census

Race

Area	White Alone[2] (%)	Black Alone[2] (%)	Asian Alone[2] (%)	AIAN[3] Alone[2] (%)	NHOPI[4] Alone[2] (%)	Other Race Alone[2] (%)	Two or More Races (%)
City	49.8	9.6	11.3	0.7	0.1	23.8	4.6
MSA[1]	52.8	7.1	14.7	0.7	0.3	20.1	4.4
U.S.	72.4	12.6	4.8	0.9	0.2	6.2	2.9

Note: (1) Figures cover the Los Angeles-Long Beach-Santa Ana, CA Metropolitan Statistical Area—see Appendix B for areas included; (2) Alone is defined as not being in combination with one or more other races; (3) American Indian and Alaska Native; (4) Native Hawaiian and Other Pacific Islander
Source: U.S. Census Bureau, 2010 Census

Hispanic or Latino Origin

Area	Hispanic or Latino (%)	Mexican (%)	Puerto Rican (%)	Cuban (%)	Other Hispanic or Latino (%)
City	48.5	31.9	0.4	0.4	15.8
MSA[1]	44.4	34.1	0.4	0.4	9.6
U.S.	16.3	10.3	1.5	0.6	4.0

Note: Persons of Hispanic or Latino origin can be of any race; (1) Figures cover the Los Angeles-Long Beach-Santa Ana, CA Metropolitan Statistical Area—see Appendix B for areas included
Source: U.S. Census Bureau, 2010 Census

Segregation

Type	Segregation Indices[1]				Percent Change		
	1990	2000	2010	2010 Rank[2]	1990-2000	1990-2010	2000-2010
Black/White	72.7	70.0	67.8	10	-2.8	-4.9	-2.1
Asian/White	43.5	47.9	48.4	12	4.4	4.9	0.5
Hispanic/White	60.3	62.5	62.2	2	2.2	1.9	-0.3

Note: Figures are based on an analysis of 1990, 2000, and 2010 Census Decennial Census tract data by William H. Frey, Brookings Institution and the University of Michigan Social Science Data Analysis Network. In this analysis all racial groups (whites, blacks, and asians) are non-Hispanic members of those races. Hispanics are shown as a separate category; All figures cover the Metropolitan Statistical Area (see Appendix B for areas included); (1) Segregation Indices are Dissimilarity Indices that measure the degree to which the minority group is distributed differently than whites across census tracts. They range from 0 (complete integration) to 100 (complete segregation) where the value indicates the percentage of the minority group that needs to move to be distributed exactly like whites; (2) Ranges from 1 (most segregated) to 102 (least segregated); n/a not available.
Source: www.CensusScope.org

Ancestry

Area	German	Irish	English	American	Italian	Polish	French[2]	Scottish	Dutch
City	4.8	3.8	3.4	1.5	2.7	1.6	1.2	0.7	0.5
MSA[1]	6.7	5.2	4.8	2.0	3.2	1.4	1.5	1.1	0.8
U.S.	16.1	11.6	8.8	6.1	5.7	3.2	3.0	1.9	1.6

Note: Figures are the percentage of the total population reporting a particular ancestry. The nine most commonly reported ancestries in the U.S. are shown. Figures include multiple ancestries (e.g. if a person reported being Irish and Italian, they were included in both columns); (1) Figures cover the Los Angeles-Long Beach-Santa Ana, CA Metropolitan Statistical Area—see Appendix B for areas included; (2) Excludes Basque
Source: U.S. Census Bureau, 2008-2010 American Community Survey 3-Year Estimates

Foreign-Born Population

Area	Percent of Population Born in								
	Any Foreign Country	Mexico	Asia	Europe	Carribean	South America	Central America[2]	Africa	Canada
City	39.6	14.9	11.2	2.4	0.3	1.1	8.5	0.6	0.4
MSA[1]	34.5	13.9	12.2	1.8	0.3	0.9	4.3	0.5	0.3
U.S.	12.8	3.8	3.6	1.6	1.2	0.9	1.0	0.5	0.3

Note: (1) Figures cover the Los Angeles-Long Beach-Santa Ana, CA Metropolitan Statistical Area—see Appendix B for areas included; (2) Excludes Mexico.
Source: U.S. Census Bureau, 2008-2010 American Community Survey 3-Year Estimates

Marital Status

Area	Never Married	Now Married[2]	Separated	Widowed	Divorced
City	44.2	39.7	2.9	4.9	8.4
MSA[1]	38.5	45.3	2.5	5.0	8.6
U.S.	31.6	49.6	2.2	6.1	10.7

Note: Figures are percentages and cover the population 15 years of age and older; (1) Figures cover the Los Angeles-Long Beach-Santa Ana, CA Metropolitan Statistical Area—see Appendix B for areas included; (2) Excludes separated
Source: U.S. Census Bureau, 2008-2010 American Community Survey 3-Year Estimates

Age

Area	Percent of Population							Median Age
	Under Age 5	Age 5 to 17	Age 18 to 34	Age 35 to 49	Age 50 to 64	Age 65 to 79	80 Years and Over	
City	6.6	16.4	28.3	21.9	16.3	7.4	3.1	34.1
MSA[1]	6.5	17.9	25.4	21.9	17.2	7.9	3.1	35.1
U.S.	6.5	17.5	23.2	20.7	19.0	9.4	3.6	37.2

Note: (1) Figures cover the Los Angeles-Long Beach-Santa Ana, CA Metropolitan Statistical Area—see Appendix B for areas included
Source: U.S. Census Bureau, 2010 Census

Male/Female Ratio

Area	Males	Females	Males per 100 Females
City	1,889,064	1,903,557	99.2
MSA[1]	6,328,434	6,500,403	97.4
U.S.	151,781,326	156,964,212	96.7

Note: (1) Figures cover the Los Angeles-Long Beach-Santa Ana, CA Metropolitan Statistical Area—see Appendix B for areas included
Source: U.S. Census Bureau, 2010 Census

Religious Groups

Area	Catholic	Baptist	Non-Den.	Methodist[2]	Lutheran	LDS[3]	Pente-costal	Presby-terian[4]	Muslim[5]	Judaism
MSA[1]	33.8	2.8	3.6	1.1	0.7	1.7	1.8	0.9	1.0	0.7
U.S.	19.1	9.3	4.0	4.0	2.3	2.0	1.9	1.6	0.8	0.7

Note: Figures are the number of adherents as a percentage of the total population; (1) Figures cover the Los Angeles-Long Beach-Santa Ana, CA Metropolitan Statistical Area—see Appendix B for areas included; (2) Methodist/Pietist; (3) Latter Day Saints; (4) Reformed; (5) Figures are estimates
Source: Association of Statisticians of American Religious Bodies, 2010 U.S. Religion Census: Religious Congregations & Membership Study

ECONOMY

Gross Metropolitan Product

Area	2007	2008	2009	2010	2010 Rank[2]
MSA[1]	731.6	747.0	716.4	737.9	2

Note: Figures are in billions of dollars; (1) Figures cover the Los Angeles-Long Beach-Santa Ana, CA Metropolitan Statistical Area—see Appendix B for areas included; (2) Rank ranges from 1 to 363
Source: The United States Conference of Mayors, "U.S. Metro Economies: GMP and Employment Forecasts," June 2011

Economic Growth

Area	2007-2009 (%)	2010 (%)	2011 (%)	Rank[2]
MSA[1]	-2.3	2.5	2.2	240
U.S.	-1.3	2.9	2.5	–

Note: Figures are real Gross Metropolitan Product growth rates and represent annual average percent change; (1) Figures cover the Los Angeles-Long Beach-Santa Ana, CA Metropolitan Statistical Area—see Appendix B for areas included; (2) Rank ranges from 1 to 363
Source: The United States Conference of Mayors, "U.S. Metro Economies: GMP and Employment Forecasts," June 2011

Metropolitan Area Exports

Area	2005	2006	2007	2008	2009	2010	2010 Rank[2]
MSA[1]	43,814.2	48,718.1	54,433.0	59,985.6	51,528.4	62,167.6	3

Note: Figures are in millions of dollars; (1) Figures cover the Los Angeles-Long Beach-Santa Ana, CA Metropolitan Statistical Area—see Appendix B for areas included; (2) Rank ranges from 1 to 369
Source: U.S. Department of Commerce, International Trade Administration, Office of Trade & Industry Information, Manufacturing & Services, data extracted April 2, 2012

INCOME

Income

Area	Per Capita ($)	Median Household ($)	Average Household ($)
City	27,346	48,746	75,691
MSA[1]	28,405	59,129	83,389
U.S.	26,942	51,222	70,116

Note: (1) Figures cover the Los Angeles-Long Beach-Santa Ana, CA Metropolitan Statistical Area—see Appendix B for areas included
Source: U.S. Census Bureau, 2008-2010 American Community Survey 3-Year Estimates

Household Income Distribution

Area	Percent of Households Earning							
	Under $15,000	$15,000 -24,999	$25,000 -34,999	$35,000 -49,999	$50,000 -74,999	$75,000 -99,000	$100,000 -149,999	$150,000 and up
City	15.0	12.0	10.4	13.5	16.6	10.5	11.4	10.6
MSA[1]	11.1	9.9	9.2	12.7	17.5	12.3	14.4	12.7
U.S.	13.0	11.0	10.6	14.2	18.5	12.1	12.2	8.4

Note: (1) Figures cover the Los Angeles-Long Beach-Santa Ana, CA Metropolitan Statistical Area—see Appendix B for areas included
Source: U.S. Census Bureau, 2008-2010 American Community Survey 3-Year Estimates

Poverty Rate

Area	All Ages	Under 18 Years Old	18 to 64 Years Old	65 Years and Over
City	20.2	29.2	17.9	14.2
MSA[1]	15.1	21.2	13.4	10.8
U.S.	14.4	20.1	13.1	9.4

Note: Figures are percentage of people whose income during the past 12 months was below the poverty level; (1) Figures cover the Los Angeles-Long Beach-Santa Ana, CA Metropolitan Statistical Area—see Appendix B for areas included
Source: U.S. Census Bureau, 2008-2010 American Community Survey 3-Year Estimates

Personal Bankruptcy Filing Rate

Area	2006	2007	2008	2009	2010	2011
Los Angeles County	1.01	1.82	3.43	5.57	7.34	6.86
U.S.	2.00	2.73	3.53	4.61	4.97	4.37

Note: Numbers are per 1,000 population and include Chapter 7 and Chapter 13 filings
Source: Federal Deposit Insurance Corporation, Regional Economic Conditions, March 9, 2012

EMPLOYMENT

Labor Force and Employment

Area	Civilian Labor Force			Workers Employed		
	Dec. 2010	Dec. 2011	% Chg.	Dec. 2010	Dec. 2011	% Chg.
City	1,920,895	1,906,816	-0.7	1,653,729	1,663,084	0.6
MD[1]	4,943,016	4,931,592	-0.2	4,329,943	4,358,225	0.7
U.S.	153,156,000	153,373,000	0.1	139,159,000	140,681,000	1.1

Note: Data is not seasonally adjusted and covers workers 16 years of age and older; (1) Metropolitan Division—see Appendix B for areas included
Source: Bureau of Labor Statistics, http://stats.bls.gov

Unemployment Rate

Area	2011											
	Jan.	Feb.	Mar.	Apr.	May	Jun.	Jul.	Aug.	Sep.	Oct.	Nov.	Dec.
City	14.4	13.5	13.4	12.9	13.0	13.6	14.6	13.9	13.4	13.1	12.7	12.8
MD[1]	12.9	12.3	12.1	11.7	12.0	12.5	13.2	12.9	12.5	12.1	11.6	11.6
U.S.	9.8	9.5	9.2	8.7	8.7	9.3	9.3	9.1	8.8	8.5	8.2	8.3

Note: Data is not seasonally adjusted and covers workers 16 years of age and older; All figures are percentages; (1) Metropolitan Division—see Appendix B for areas included
Source: Bureau of Labor Statistics, http://stats.bls.gov

Projected Unemployment Rate

Area	2010 (%)	2011 (%)	2012 (%)	2013 (%)
MSA[1]	12.1	10.8	10.1	9.3

Note: (1) Metropolitan Statistical Area—see Appendix B for areas included
Source: The United States Conference of Mayors, "U.S. Metro Economies: GMP and Employment Forecasts," June 2011

Employment by Occupation

Occupation Classification	City (%)	MSA[1] (%)	U.S. (%)
Management, Business, Science, and Arts	34.6	36.0	35.6
Natural Resources, Construction, and Maintenance	8.5	7.9	9.5
Production, Transportation, and Material Moving	12.4	12.3	12.1
Sales and Office	23.9	26.0	25.2
Service	20.5	17.8	17.6

Note: Figures cover employed civilians 16 years of age and older; (1) Figures cover the Los Angeles-Long Beach-Santa Ana, CA Metropolitan Statistical Area—see Appendix B for areas included
Source: U.S. Census Bureau, 2008-2010 American Community Survey 3-Year Estimates

Employment by Industry

Sector	MD[1] Number of Employees	MD[1] Percent of Total	U.S. Percent of Total
Construction	105,300	2.7	4.1
Education and Health Services	544,600	14.1	15.2
Financial Activities	211,700	5.5	5.8
Government	569,100	14.8	16.8
Information	205,600	5.3	2.0
Leisure and Hospitality	393,600	10.2	9.9
Manufacturing	361,200	9.4	8.9
Mining and Logging	4,000	0.1	0.6
Other Services	135,200	3.5	4.0
Professional and Business Services	550,800	14.3	13.3
Retail Trade	410,800	10.7	11.5
Transportation and Utilities	151,400	3.9	3.8
Wholesale Trade	210,100	5.5	4.2

Note: Figures cover non-farm employment as of December 2011 and are not seasonally adjusted; (1) Metropolitan Division—see Appendix B for areas included
Source: Bureau of Labor Statistics, http://stats.bls.gov

Occupations with Greatest Projected Employment Growth: 2008 – 2018

Occupation[1]	2008 Employment	2018 Projected Employment	Numeric Employment Change	Percent Employment Change
Personal and Home Care Aides	346,500	504,700	158,200	45.7
Registered Nurses	236,400	297,200	60,800	25.7
Retail Salespersons	499,400	559,100	59,700	12.0
Combined Food Preparation and Serving Workers, Including Fast Food	260,600	308,800	48,200	18.5
Elementary School Teachers, Except Special Education	197,500	233,400	35,900	18.2
Office Clerks, General	372,500	407,400	34,900	9.4
Customer Service Representatives	202,200	236,600	34,400	17.0
Waiters and Waitresses	245,600	279,900	34,300	14.0
Stock Clerks and Order Fillers	207,700	237,100	29,400	14.2
Postsecondary Teachers	168,000	196,100	28,100	16.7

Note: Projections cover California; (1) Sorted by numeric employment change
Source: www.projectionscentral.com, State Occupational Projections, 2008–2018 Long-Term Projections

Fastest Growing Occupations: 2008 – 2018

Occupation[1]	2008 Employment	2018 Projected Employment	Numeric Employment Change	Percent Employment Change
Biomedical Engineers	3,100	5,600	2,500	80.6
Network Systems and Data Communications Analysts	35,000	52,600	17,600	50.3
Biochemists and Biophysicists	4,800	7,100	2,300	47.9
Medical Scientists, Except Epidemiologists	26,200	38,500	12,300	46.9
Personal and Home Care Aides	346,500	504,700	158,200	45.7
Home Health Aides	54,300	78,000	23,700	43.6
Physician Assistants	8,100	11,500	3,400	42.0
Separating, Filtering, Clarifying, Precipitating, and Still Machine Setters, Operators, and Te	7,300	10,200	2,900	39.7
Physical Therapist Aides	5,900	8,100	2,200	37.3
Electrical and Electronics Repairers, Powerhouse, Substation, and Relay	1,100	1,500	400	36.4

Note: Projections cover California; (1) Sorted by percent employment change and excludes occupations with numeric employment change less than 100
Source: www.projectionscentral.com, State Occupational Projections, 2008–2018 Long-Term Projections

Average Wages

Occupation	$/Hr.	Occupation	$/Hr.
Accountants and Auditors	35.72	Maids and Housekeeping Cleaners	10.89
Automotive Mechanics	19.00	Maintenance and Repair Workers	19.24
Bookkeepers	19.14	Marketing Managers	63.88
Carpenters	25.79	Nuclear Medicine Technologists	42.62
Cashiers	10.84	Nurses, Licensed Practical	23.91
Clerks, General Office	15.06	Nurses, Registered	41.03
Clerks, Receptionists/Information	13.54	Nursing Aides/Orderlies/Attendants	12.75
Clerks, Shipping/Receiving	14.38	Packers and Packagers, Hand	10.22
Computer Programmers	40.73	Physical Therapists	41.74
Computer Support Specialists	26.04	Postal Service Mail Carriers	26.15
Computer Systems Analysts	42.62	Real Estate Brokers	58.15
Cooks, Restaurant	11.20	Retail Salespersons	12.42
Dentists	63.44	Sales Reps., Exc. Tech./Scientific	30.78
Electrical Engineers	48.09	Sales Reps., Tech./Scientific	38.68
Electricians	29.72	Secretaries, Exc. Legal/Med./Exec.	17.76
Financial Managers	66.04	Security Guards	13.10
First-Line Supervisors/Managers, Sales	21.64	Surgeons	114.00
Food Preparation Workers	9.72	Teacher Assistants	14.30
General and Operations Managers	63.08	Teachers, Elementary School	32.30
Hairdressers/Cosmetologists	13.20	Teachers, Secondary School	30.80
Internists	93.12	Telemarketers	13.04
Janitors and Cleaners	12.43	Truck Drivers, Heavy/Tractor-Trailer	20.25
Landscaping/Groundskeeping Workers	13.60	Truck Drivers, Light/Delivery Svcs.	15.97
Lawyers	80.43	Waiters and Waitresses	10.20

Note: Wage data covers the Los Angeles-Long Beach-Glendale, CA Metropolitan Division—see Appendix B for areas included. Hourly wages for elementary/secondary school teachers and teacher assistants were calculated by the editors from annual wage data assuming a 40 hour work week; n/a not available.
Source: Bureau of Labor Statistics, Metro Area Occupational Employment and Wage Estimates, May 2011

RESIDENTIAL REAL ESTATE

Building Permits

Area	Single-Family			Multi-Family			Total		
	2010	2011	Pct. Chg.	2010	2011	Pct. Chg.	2010	2011	Pct. Chg.
City	636	525	-17.5	3,473	5,422	56.1	4,109	5,947	44.7
MSA[1]	4,008	4,097	2.2	6,386	10,150	58.9	10,394	14,247	37.1
U.S.	447,311	418,498	-6.4	157,299	205,563	30.7	604,610	624,061	3.2

Note: (1) Metropolitan Statistical Area—see Appendix B for areas included; figures represent new, privately-owned housing units authorized (unadjusted data); All permit data are based on estimates with imputation.
Source: U.S. Census Bureau, Manufacturing, Mining, and Construction Statistics, Building Permits, 2010, 2011

Homeownership Rate

Area	2005 (%)	2006 (%)	2007 (%)	2008 (%)	2009 (%)	2010 (%)	2011 (%)
MSA[1]	54.6	54.4	52.3	52.1	50.4	49.7	50.1
U.S.	68.9	68.8	68.1	67.8	67.4	66.9	66.1

Note: (1) Metropolitan Statistical Area—see Appendix B for areas included
Source: U.S. Census Bureau, Housing Vacancies and Homeownership Annual Statistics: 2011

Housing Vacancy Rates

Area	Gross Vacancy Rate[2] (%)			Year-Round Vacancy Rate[3] (%)			Rental Vacancy Rate[4] (%)			Homeowner Vacancy Rate[5] (%)		
	2009	2010	2011	2009	2010	2011	2009	2010	2011	2009	2010	2011
MSA[1]	6.6	7.2	6.7	6.3	6.9	6.4	6.4	6.7	5.3	1.3	1.8	1.8
U.S.	14.5	14.3	14.2	11.3	11.3	11.1	10.6	10.2	9.5	2.6	2.6	2.5

Note: (1) Metropolitan Statistical Area—see Appendix B for areas included; (2) The percentage of the total housing inventory that is vacant; (3) The percentage of the housing inventory (excluding seasonal units) that is year-round vacant; (4) The percentage of rental inventory that is vacant for rent; (5) The percentage of homeowner inventory that is vacant for sale
Source: U.S. Census Bureau, Housing Vacancies and Homeownership Annual Statistics: 2011

TAXES

State Corporate Income Tax Rates

State	Tax Rate (%)	Income Brackets ($)	Num. of Brackets	Financial Institution Tax Rate (%)[a]	Federal Income Tax Ded.
California	8.84 (c)	Flat rate	1	10.84 (c)	No

Note: Tax rates as of January 1, 2012; (a) Rates listed are the corporate income tax rate applied to financial institutions or excise taxes based on income. Some states have other taxes based upon the value of deposits or shares; (c) The minimum corporation franchise tax in California is $800. The additional alternative minimum tax is levied at a 6.65% rate.
Source: Federation of Tax Administrators, "State Corporate Income Tax Rates, 2012"

State Individual Income Tax Rates

State	Tax Rate (%)	Income Brackets ($)	Num. of Brackets	Personal Exempt. ($)[1]		Fed. Inc. Tax Ded.
				Single	Dependents	
California (a)	1.0 - 9.3 (f)	7,316 (b) - 48,029 (b)	6	102 (c)	315 (c)	No

Note: Tax rates as of January 1, 2012; Local- and county-level taxes are not included; n/a not applicable; (1) Married joint filers generally receive double the single exemption; (a) 17 states have statutory provision for automatically adjusting to the rate of inflation the dollar values of the income tax brackets, standard deductions, and/or personal exemptions. Massachusetts, Michigan, and Nebraska index the personal exemptiononly. Oregon does not index the income brackets for $125,000 and over. Because the inflation-adjustments for 2012 are not yet available in some cases, the table may report the 2011 amounts; (b) For joint returns, taxes are twice the tax on half the couple's income; (c) The personal exemption takes the form of a tax credit instead of a deduction; (f) California imposes an additional 1% tax on taxable income over $1 million, making the maximum rate 10.3% over $1 million.
Source: Federation of Tax Administrators, "State Individual Income Tax Rates, 2012"

Various State and Local Tax Rates

State	State and Local Sales and Use (%)	State Sales and Use (%)	Gasoline[1] (¢/gal.)	Cigarette[2] ($/pack)	Spirits[3] ($/gal.)	Wine[4] ($/gal.)	Beer[5] ($/gal.)
California	8.75	7.25 (b)	48.6	0.87	3.30	0.20	0.20

Note: All tax rates as of January 1, 2012 except beer, wine and spirits (September 1, 2011); (1) The American Petroleum Institute has developed a methodology for determining the average tax rate on a gallon of fuel. Rates may include any of the following: excise taxes, environmental fees, storage tank fees, other fees or taxes, general sales tax, and local taxes. In states where gasoline is subject to the general sales tax, or where the fuel tax is based on the average sale price, the average rate determined by API is sensitive to changes in the price of gasoline. States that fully or partially apply general sales taxes to gasoline: CA, CO, GA, IL, IN, MI, NY; (2) The federal excise tax of $1.0066 per pack and local taxes are not included; (3) Rates are those applicable to off-premise sales of 40% alcohol by volume (a.b.v.) distilled spirits in 750ml containers. Local excise taxes are excluded; (4) Rates are those applicable to off-premise sales of 11% a.b.v. non-carbonated wine in 750ml containers; (5) Rates are those applicable to off-premise sales of 4.7% a.b.v. beer in 12 ounce containers; (b) Three states collect a separate, uniform "local" add-on sales tax: California (1%), Utah (1.25%), Virginia (1%). These amounts are included in the state sales tax column.
Source: Tax Foundation, 2012 Facts & Figures: How Does Your State Compare?

State-Local Tax Burdens

Area	Rate (%)	Rank[1]	Per Capita Taxes Paid to Home State ($)	Total State and Local Per Capita Taxes Paid ($)	Per Capita Income ($)
California	10.6	6	3,874	4,910	46,366
U.S. Average	9.8	-	3,057	4,160	42,539

Note: Figures cover 2009; (1) Rank ranges from 1 to 50 where 1 is highest tax burden
Source: Tax Foundation, State-Local Tax Burdens, All States, 2009

State Business Tax Climate Index Rankings

State	Overall Rank	Corporate Tax Index Rank	Individual Income Tax Index Rank	Sales Tax Index Rank	Unemployment Insurance Tax Index Rank	Property Tax Index Rank
California	48	43	50	40	13	17

Note: The index is a measure of how each state's tax laws affect economic performance. The lower the rank, the more favorable a state's tax system is for business. States without a given tax are given a ranking of 1.
Source: Tax Foundation, Major Components of the State Business Tax Climate Index, FY 2012

COMMERCIAL REAL ESTATE

Office Market

Market Area	Inventory (sq. ft.)	Vacant (sq. ft.)	Vac. Rate (%)	Under Constr. (sq. ft.)	Asking Rent ($/sf/yr) Class A	Asking Rent ($/sf/yr) Class B
Los Angeles	190,451,454	32,331,296	17.0	526,000	34.76	26.04

Source: Grubb & Ellis, Office Markets Trends, 4th Quarter 2011

Industrial Market

Market Area	Inventory (sq. ft.)	Vacant (sq. ft.)	Vac. Rate (%)	Under Constr. (sq. ft.)	Asking Rent ($/sf/yr) WH/Dist	Asking Rent ($/sf/yr) R&D/Flex
Los Angeles	997,579,619	29,240,816	2.9	531,390	5.76	8.40

Source: Grubb & Ellis, Industrial Markets Trends, 4th Quarter 2011

COMMERCIAL UTILITIES

Typical Monthly Electric Bills

Area	Commercial Service ($/month)		Industrial Service ($/month)	
	40 kW demand 5,000 kWh	500 kW demand 100,000 kWh	5,000 kW demand 1,500,000 kWh	70,000 kW demand 50,000,000 kWh
City	936	20,398	281,370	8,465,975

Note: Based on rates in effect January 1, 2011
Source: Memphis Light, Gas and Water, 2011 Utility Bill Comparisons for Selected U.S. Cities

TRANSPORTATION

Means of Transportation to Work

Area	Car/Truck/Van: Drove Alone	Car/Truck/Van: Car-pooled	Public Transportation: Bus	Public Transportation: Subway	Public Transportation: Railroad	Bicycle	Walked	Other Means	Worked at Home
City	66.9	10.6	10.4	0.5	0.1	1.0	3.5	1.5	5.4
MSA[1]	73.3	11.0	5.6	0.3	0.2	0.8	2.6	1.3	4.8
U.S.	76.0	10.2	2.7	1.7	0.5	0.5	2.8	1.3	4.2

Note: Figures are percentages and cover workers 16 years of age and older; (1) Figures cover the Los Angeles-Long Beach-Santa Ana, CA Metropolitan Statistical Area—see Appendix B for areas included
Source: U.S. Census Bureau, 2008-2010 American Community Survey 3-Year Estimates

Travel Time to Work

Area	Less Than 10 Minutes	10 to 19 Minutes	20 to 29 Minutes	30 to 44 Minutes	45 to 59 Minutes	60 to 89 Minutes	90 Minutes or More
City	7.7	24.9	20.1	27.3	9.2	7.9	2.9
MSA[1]	8.8	26.8	20.5	24.6	8.9	7.7	2.8
U.S.	13.9	30.1	20.8	19.8	7.5	5.5	2.5

Note: Figures are percentages and include workers 16 years old and over; (1) Figures cover the Los Angeles-Long Beach-Santa Ana, CA Metropolitan Statistical Area—see Appendix B for areas included
Source: U.S. Census Bureau, 2008-2010 American Community Survey 3-Year Estimates

Travel Time Index

Area	1985	1990	1995	2000	2005	2010
Urban Area[1]	1.23	1.41	1.36	1.39	1.42	1.38
Average[2]	1.11	1.16	1.18	1.21	1.25	1.20

Note: Travel Time Index—the ratio of travel time in the peak period to the travel time at free-flow conditions. A value of 1.30 indicates a 20-minute free-flow trip takes 26 minutes in the peak. Free-flow speeds (60 mph on freeways and 35 mph on principal arterials) are used as the comparison threshold; (1) Covers the Los Angeles-Long Beach-Santa Ana CA urban area; (2) average of 439 urban areas
Source: Texas Transportation Institute, Urban Mobility Report 2011, September 2011

Public Transportation

Agency Name / Mode of Transportation	Vehicles Operated in Maximum Service	Annual Unlinked Passenger Trips ('000)	Annual Passenger Miles ('000)
Los Angeles Co. Metro Transportation Authority (LACMTA)			
Bus (directly operated)	2,089	353,046.5	1,442,067.1
Bus (purchased transportation)	145	12,929.0	44,734.4
Heavy Rail (directly operated)	70	47,905.9	231,935.8
Light Rail (directly operated)	118	46,409.1	333,334.4
Vanpool (purchased transportation)	907	2,725.1	124,260.7
City of Los Angeles Department of Transportation (LADOT)			
Bus (purchased transportation)	256	30,341.0	69,281.4
Demand Response (purchased transportation)	122	334.5	1,675.0
Demand Response Taxi (purchased transportation)	38	675.4	1,629.0
LACMTA - Small Operators			
Bus (purchased transportation)	190	11,283.7	28,718.4
Demand Response (purchased transportation)	193	1,021.4	3,543.8
Demand Response Taxi (purchased transportation)	60	439.9	1,407.4

Source: Federal Transit Administration, National Transit Database, 2010

Air Transportation

Airport Name and Code / Type of Service	Passenger Airlines[1]	Passenger Enplanements	Freight Carriers[2]	Freight (lbs.)
Los Angeles International (LAX)				
Domestic service (U.S. carriers - 2011)	29	22,395,162	27	706,902,661
International service (U.S. carriers - 2010)	12	1,675,488	14	146,137,036

Note: (1) Includes all U.S.-based major, minor and commuter airlines that carried at least one passenger during the year; (2) Includes all U.S.-based airlines and freight carriers that transported at least one pound of freight during the year

Source: Bureau of Transportation Statistics, The Intermodal Transportation Database, Air Carriers: T-100 Domestic Market (U.S. Carriers), 2011; Bureau of Transportation Statistics, The Intermodal Transportation Database, Air Carriers: T-100 International Market (U.S. Carriers), 2010

Other Transportation Statistics

Major Highways:	I-10; I-5
Amtrak Service:	Yes
Major Waterways/Ports:	Port of Los Angeles

Source: Amtrak.com; Google Maps

BUSINESSES

Major Business Headquarters

Company Name	Rankings	
	Fortune[1]	Forbes[2]
AECOM Technology	353	-
CB Richard Ellis Group	440	-
Capital Group Cos	-	41
Forever 21	-	162
Northrop Grumman	72	-
Occidental Petroleum	129	-
Reliance Steel & Aluminum	367	-
Roll Global	-	183

Note: (1) Fortune 500—companies that produce a 10-K are ranked 1 to 500 based on 2010 revenue; (2) all private companies with at least $2 billion in annual revenue are ranked 1 to 212; companies listed are headquartered in the city; dashes indicate no ranking

Source: Fortune, "Fortune 500," May 23, 2011; Forbes, "America's Largest Private Companies," November 16, 2011

Fast-Growing Businesses

According to *Inc.*, Los Angeles is home to 10 of America's 500 fastest-growing private companies: **I.T. Source** (#26); **Aurum Advisors** (#111); **Savings.com** (#135); **Calvin Group** (#170); **VeeV Acai Spirit** (#242); **Phenomenon** (#251); **BeautyChoice.com** (#387); **CloseOutStore.net** (#392); **ElJet Aviation Services** (#420); **Round Sky** (#463). Criteria: must be an independent, privately-held, for-profit, U.S. corporation, proprietorship or partnership; revenues must be at least $80,000 in 2007 and $2 million in 2010; must have four-year operating/sales history. Holding companies, regulated banks, and utilities were excluded. *Inc., "America's 500 Fastest-Growing Private Companies," September 2011*

According to *Initiative for a Competitive Inner City (ICIC)*, Los Angeles is home to one of America's 100 fastest-growing "inner city" companies: **El Clasificado** (#83). Companies were ranked by their five-year compound annual growth rate. Criteria for inclusion: company must be headquartered in or have 51 percent or more of its physical operations in an economically distressed urban area; must be an independent, for-profit corporation, partnership or proprietorship; must have 10 or more employees and have a five-year sales history that includes sales of at least $200,000 in the base year and at least $1 million in the current year with no decrease in sales over the two most recent years. *Initiative for a Competitive Inner City (ICIC), "Inner City 100 Companies, 2011"*

According to Deloitte, Los Angeles is home to six of North America's 500 fastest-growing high-technology companies: **CyberDefender Corp.** (#98); **BlackLine Systems** (#111); **Awareness Technologies** (#188); **Boingo Wireless** (#278); **Response Genetics** (#329); **Evolve Media Corp.** (#451). Companies are ranked by percentage growth in revenue over a five-year period. Criteria for inclusion: company must be headquartered within North America; must own proprietary intellectual property or proprietary technology that contributes to a significant portion of the company's operating revenue, or devote a significant proportion of revenues to research and development of technology; must have been in business for a minumum of five years with 2006 operating revenues of at least $50,000 USD/CD and 2010 operating revenues of at least $5 million USD/CD. *Deloitte Touche Tohmatsu, 2011 Deloitte Technology Fast 500™*

Minority Business Opportunity

Los Angeles is home to one company which is on the *Black Enterprise* Industrial/Service 100 list (100 largest companies based on gross sales): **The Client Base Funding Group** (#73). Criteria: operational in previous calendar year; at least 51% black-owned and manufactures/owns the product it sells or provides industrial or consumer services. Brokerages, real estate firms and firms that provide professional services are not eligible. *Black Enterprise, B.E. 100s, 2011*

Los Angeles is home to one company which is on the *Black Enterprise* Bank 20 list (20 largest banks based on total assets, capital, deposits and loans, including mortgage-backed securities for the calendar year): **Broadway Federal Bank F.S.B.** (#4). Only commercial banks or savings and loans that are classified by the Federal Reserve as black institutions and have been fully operational for the previous calendar year were considered. *Black Enterprise, B.E. 100s, 2011*

Los Angeles is home to 12 companies which are on the *Hispanic Business* 500 list (500 largest U.S. Hispanic-owned companies based on 2010 revenue): **TELACU Industries** (#50); **Jules & Associates** (#68); **E.J. De La Rosa & Co.** (#114); **Field Fresh Foods** (#138); **PromoShop** (#155); **El Clasificado** (#257); **RBB Architects** (#262); **Vista Investments** (#306); **Avcogas Propane Sales & Services** (#312); **Quijote Corp.** (#394); **Art Lewin & Co. Custom Clothiers** (#437); **General Transistor Corp.** (#465). Companies included must show at least 51 percent ownership by Hispanic U.S. citizens, and must maintain headquarters in one of the 50 states or Washington, D.C. *Hispanic Business, "Hispanic Business 500," June 2011*

Los Angeles is home to three companies which are on the *Hispanic Business* Fastest-Growing 100 list (greatest sales growth from 2006 to 2010): **Quijote Corp.** (#11); **E.J. De La Rosa & Co.** (#17); **El Clasificado** (#55). Companies included must show at least 51 percent ownership by Hispanic U.S. citizens, and must maintain headquarters in one of the 50 states or Washington, D.C. In addition, companies must have minimum revenues of $200,000 for calendar year 2005. *Hispanic Business, July/August 2011*

Minority- and Women-Owned Businesses

Group	All Firms		Firms with Paid Employees			
	Firms	Sales ($000)	Firms	Sales ($000)	Employees	Payroll ($000)
Asian	61,606	25,468,797	17,779	23,159,723	116,912	3,326,715
Black	26,002	2,936,749	2,073	2,214,730	15,385	570,684
Hispanic	94,643	11,214,207	7,162	8,442,631	54,236	1,603,109
Women	136,579	21,535,185	15,674	17,247,176	99,164	3,688,050
All Firms	450,050	379,390,317	91,908	360,903,264	1,448,871	68,250,202

Note: Figures cover firms located in the city; minority- and women-owned business are defined as firms in which the corresponding group own 51% or more of the stock or equity of the company
Source: U.S. Census Bureau, 2007 Economic Census, Survey of Business Owners

HOTELS

Hotels/Motels

Area	5 Star		4 Star		3 Star		2 Star		1 Star		Not Rated	
	Num.	Pct.[3]	Num.	Pct.[3]	Num.	Pct.[3]	Num.	Pct.[3]	Num.	Pct.[3]	Num.	Pct.[3]
City[1]	13	2.1	47	7.6	173	27.8	302	48.6	22	3.5	65	10.5
Total[2]	133	0.9	940	6.5	4,569	31.8	7,033	48.9	351	2.4	1,343	9.3

Note: (1) Figures cover Los Angeles and vicinity; (2) Figures cover all 100 cities in this book; (3) Percentage of hotels which have a given star rating; Star ratings are determined by expedia.com and offer an indication of the general quality of a particular hotel.
Source: expedia.com, April 25, 2012

The Los Angeles-Long Beach-Glendale, CA metro area is home to 10 of the best hotels in the U.S. according to *Travel & Leisure*: **Hotel Bel-Air, Dorchester Collection** (#39); **Shutters on the Beach** (#46); **Montage Beverly Hills** (#77); **Peninsula Beverly Hills** (#79); **L'Ermitage Beverly Hills** (#86); **Beverly Wilshire, A Four Seasons Hotel** (#147); **Four**

Seasons Hotel Los Angeles at Beverly Hills (#169); **Langham Huntington, Pasadena** (#192); **Ritz-Carlton, Marina del Rey** (#202); **Beverly Hills Hotel & Bungalows** (#204). Criteria: service; location; rooms; food; and value. *Travel & Leisure, "T+L 500, The World's Best Hotels 2012"*

The Los Angeles-Long Beach-Glendale, CA metro area is home to six of the best hotels in the U.S. according to *Condé Nast Traveler*: **The Peninsula** (#7); **Beverly Hills Hotel And Bungalows** (#34); **Beverly Wilshire** (#54); **Langham Huntington, Pasadena** (#77); **Four Seasons** (#91); **Sunset Marquis Hotel & Villas** (#100). The selections are based on over 25,000 responses to the magazine's annual Readers' Choice Survey. *Condé Nast Traveler, "2011 Readers' Choice Awards"*

EVENT SITES

Major Stadiums, Arenas, and Auditoriums

Name	Max. Capacity
Dodger Stadium	56,000
Los Angeles Memorial Coliseum	93,607
Los Angeles Sports Arena	16,740
Music Center Performing Arts Ctr of L.A. County	6,015
Shrine Auditorium	6,300
Staples Center	20,000
The Greek Theatre	5,801

Source: Original research

Convention Centers

Name	Overall Space (sq. ft.)	Exhibit Space (sq. ft.)	Meeting Space (sq. ft.)	Meeting Rooms
Los Angeles Convention Center	n/a	n/a	720,000	64

Note: n/a not available
Source: Original research

Living Environment

COST OF LIVING

Cost of Living Index

Composite Index	Groceries	Housing	Utilities	Trans-portation	Health Care	Misc. Goods/ Services
133.0	107.6	197.3	112.3	109.0	110.0	104.5

Note: U.S. = 100; Figures cover the Los Angeles-Long Beach CA urban area.
Source: The Council for Community and Economic Research, ACCRA Cost of Living Index, 2011

Grocery Prices

Area[1]	T-Bone Steak ($/pound)	Frying Chicken ($/pound)	Whole Milk ($/half gal.)	Eggs ($/dozen)	Orange Juice ($/64 oz.)	Coffee ($/11.5 oz.)
City[2]	9.99	1.16	2.18	2.28	3.26	5.55
Avg.	9.25	1.18	2.22	1.66	3.19	4.40
Min.	6.70	0.88	1.31	0.95	2.46	2.94
Max.	14.30	2.16	3.50	3.18	4.75	6.83

Note: (1) Values for the local area are compared with the average, minimum and maximum values for all 335 areas in the Cost of Living Index; (2) Figures cover the Los Angeles-Long Beach CA urban area; **T-Bone Steak** *(price per pound);* **Frying Chicken** *(price per pound, whole fryer);* **Whole Milk** *(half gallon carton);* **Eggs** *(price per dozen, Grade A, large);* **Orange Juice** *(64 oz. Tropicana or Florida Natural);* **Coffee** *(11.5 oz. can, vacuum-packed, Maxwell House, Hills Bros, or Folgers).*
Source: The Council for Community and Economic Research, ACCRA Cost of Living Index, 2011

Housing and Utility Costs

Area[1]	New Home Price ($)	Apartment Rent ($/month)	All Electric ($/month)	Part Electric ($/month)	Other Energy ($/month)	Telephone ($/month)
City[2]	540,850	1,863	-	125.12	62.59	29.85
Avg.	285,990	839	163.23	89.00	77.52	26.92
Min.	188,005	460	125.58	45.39	33.89	17.98
Max.	1,197,028	3,244	339.16	181.97	348.69	40.01

Note: (1) Values for the local area are compared with the average, minimum and maximum values for all 335 areas in the Cost of Living Index; (2) Figures cover the Los Angeles-Long Beach CA urban area; **New Home Price** *(2,400 sf living area, 8,000 sf lot, in urban area with full utilities);* **Apartment Rent** *(950 sf 2 bedroom/1.5 or 2 bath, unfurnished, excluding all utilities except water);* **All Electric** *(average monthly cost for an all-electric home);* **Part Electric** *(average monthly cost for a part-electric home);* **Other Energy** *(average monthly cost for natural gas, fuel oil, coal, wood, and any other forms of energy except electricity);* **Telephone** *(price includes basic monthly rate for a private residential line plus additional local usage charges incurred by a family of four).*
Source: The Council for Community and Economic Research, ACCRA Cost of Living Index, 2011

Health Care, Transportation, and Other Costs

Area[1]	Doctor ($/visit)	Dentist ($/visit)	Optometrist ($/visit)	Gasoline ($/gallon)	Beauty Salon ($/visit)	Men's Shirt ($)
City[2]	91.20	95.47	113.07	3.83	59.53	24.52
Avg.	93.88	81.72	90.54	3.48	32.65	25.06
Min.	60.00	55.33	53.66	3.18	19.78	13.44
Max.	154.98	145.97	183.72	4.31	63.21	46.00

Note: (1) Values for the local area are compared with the average, minimum and maximum values for all 335 areas in the Cost of Living Index; (2) Figures cover the Los Angeles-Long Beach CA urban area; **Doctor** *(general practitioners routine exam of an established patient);* **Dentist** *(adult teeth cleaning and periodic oral examination);* **Optometrist** *(full vision eye exam for established adult patient);* **Gasoline** *(one gallon regular unleaded, national brand, including all taxes, cash price at self-service pump if available);* **Beauty Salon** *(woman's shampoo, trim, and blow-dry);* **Men's Shirt** *(cotton/polyester dress shirt, pinpoint weave, long sleeves).*
Source: The Council for Community and Economic Research, ACCRA Cost of Living Index, 2011

HOUSING

House Price Index (HPI)

Area	National Ranking[2]	Quarterly Change (%)	One-Year Change (%)	Five-Year Change (%)
MD[1]	200	-0.46	-3.92	-32.83
U.S.[3]	-	-0.10	-2.43	-19.16

Note: The HPI is a weighted repeat sales index. It measures average price changes in repeat sales or refinancings on the same properties. This information is obtained by reviewing repeat mortgage transactions on single-family properties whose mortgages have been purchased or securitized by Fannie Mae or Freddie Mac in January 1975; (1) Metropolitan Division - see Appendix B for areas included; (2) Rankings are based on annual percentage change for all metro areas containing at least 15,000 transactions over the last 10 years and ranges from 1 to 306; (3) figures based on a weighted average of Census Division estimates using a purchase only index; all figures are for the period ending December 31, 2011
Source: Federal Housing Finance Agency, House Price Index, February 23, 2012

House Price Valuations

Area	Q4 2005		Q4 2006		Q4 2007		Q4 2008		Q4 2009	
	Price ($000)	Over-valuation	Price ($000)	Over-valuation	Price ($000)	Over-valuation	Price ($000)	Over-valuation	Price ($000)	Over-valuation
MD[1]	525.1	55.9	540.5	50.0	481.2	27.4	368.8	-2.0	368.6	-2.0

Note: Figures show the percentage of over- or under-valuation of single family homes relative to statistically normal house values (e.g. a value of 23.6 indicates that house values are 23.6% overvalued). Statistically normal house values are based on house prices, interest rates, household incomes, population densities, and any historical premiums or discounts metropolitan areas have exhibited over time; (1) Figures cover the Los Angeles-Long Beach-Glendale, CA - see Appendix B for areas included
Source: Global Insight/PNC Financial Services Group, House Prices in America: 4th Quarter 2009 Update

Median Single-Family Home Prices

Area	2009	2010	2011p	Percent Change 2010 to 2011
MSA[1]	333.9	323.3	307.7	-4.8
U.S. Average	172.1	173.1	166.2	-4.0

Note: Figures are median sales prices of existing single-family homes in thousands of dollars; (p) preliminary; n/a not available; (1) Metropolitan Statistical Area—see Appendix B for areas included
Source: National Association of Realtors, Median Sales Price of Existing Single-Family Homes for Metropolitan Areas, 4th Quarter 2011

Affordability Index of Existing Single-Family Homes

Area	2009	2010	2011p	Percent Change 2010 to 2011
MSA[1]	58.5	65.1	72.7	11.7

Note: The housing affordability index measures whether or not a typical family could qualify for a mortgage loan on a typical home. The higher the index, the greater the household purchasing power. An index of 100 is defined as the point where a median-income household has exactly enough income to qualify for the purchase of a median-priced existing single-family home, assuming a 20 percent downpayment and 25 percent of gross income devoted to mortgage principal and interest payments; (p) preliminary; n/a not available; (1) Metropolitan Statistical Area—see Appendix B for areas included
Source: National Association of Realtors, Affordability Index of Existing Single-Family Homes, 2011

Median Apartment Condo-Coop Home Prices

Area	2009	2010	2011p	Percent Change 2010 to 2011
MSA[1]	221.8	231.8	226.1	-2.5
U.S. Average	175.6	171.7	165.1	-3.8

Note: Figures are median sales prices of existing apartment condo-coop homes in thousands of dollars; (p) preliminary; n/a not available; (1) Metropolitan Statistical Area—see Appendix B for areas included
Source: National Association of Realtors, Median Sales Price of Existing Apartment Condo-Coop Homes for Metropolitan Areas, 4th Quarter 2011

Year Housing Structure Built

Area	2005 or Later	2000 -2004	1990 -1999	1980 -1989	1970 -1979	1960 -1969	1950 -1959	Before 1950	Median Year
City	2.2	3.0	5.5	10.2	14.1	14.7	18.4	31.9	1960
MSA[1]	2.1	3.9	7.2	12.6	17.0	16.5	19.1	21.6	1966
U.S.	5.0	8.6	14.0	14.1	16.3	11.3	11.2	19.6	1975

Note: Figures are percentages except for Median Year; (1) Figures cover the Los Angeles-Long Beach-Santa Ana, CA Metropolitan Statistical Area—see Appendix B for areas included
Source: U.S. Census Bureau, 2008-2010 American Community Survey 3-Year Estimates

HEALTH

Health Risk Data

Category	MSA[1] (%)	U.S. (%)
Adults who have been told they have high blood pressure[2]	25.7	28.7
Adults who have been told they have high blood cholesterol[2]	37.8	37.5
Adults who have been told they have diabetes[3]	8.7	8.7
Adults who have been told they have arthritis[2]	18.1	26.0
Adults who have been told they currently have asthma	6.4	9.1
Adults who are current smokers	11.7	17.3
Adults who are heavy drinkers[4]	5.2	5.0
Adults who are binge drinkers[5]	15.4	15.1
Adults who are overweight (BMI 25.0 - 29.9)	38.2	36.2
Adults who are obese (BMI 30.0 - 99.8)	24.3	27.5
Adults who participated in any physical activities in the past month	79.2	76.1
Adults 50+ who have ever had a sigmoidoscopy or colonoscopy	56.3	65.2
Women aged 40+ who have had a mammogram within the past two years	81.3	75.2
Men aged 40+ who have had a PSA test within the past two years	48.1	53.2
Adults aged 65+ who have had flu shot within the past year	57.9	67.5
Adults aged 18–64 who have any kind of health care coverage	74.0	82.2

Note: Data as of 2010 unless otherwise noted; (1) Figures cover the Los Angeles-Long Beach-Glendale, CA Metropolitan Division—see Appendix B for areas included; (2) Data as of 2009; (3) Figures do not include pregnancy-related, borderline, or pre-diabetes; (4) Heavy drinkers are classified as males having more than two drinks per day or females having more than one drink per day; (5) Binge drinkers are classified as males having five or more drinks on one occasion or females having four or more drinks on one occasion
Source: Centers for Disease Control and Prevention, Behaviorial Risk Factor Surveillance System, SMART: Selected Metropolitan/Micropolitan Area Risk Trends, 2009, 2010

Mortality Rates for the Top 10 Causes of Death in the U.S.

ICD-10[a] Sub-Chapter	ICD-10[a] Code	Age-Adjusted Mortality Rate[1] per 100,000 population	
		County[2]	U.S.
Malignant neoplasms	C00-C97	153.2	175.6
Ischaemic heart diseases	I20-I25	139.4	121.6
Other forms of heart disease	I30-I51	31.6	48.6
Chronic lower respiratory diseases	J40-J47	33.8	42.3
Cerebrovascular diseases	I60-I69	37.7	40.6
Organic, including symptomatic, mental disorders	F01-F09	14.0	26.7
Other degenerative diseases of the nervous system	G30-G31	22.6	24.7
Other external causes of accidental injury	W00-X59	13.5	24.4
Diabetes mellitus	E10-E14	23.6	21.7
Hypertensive diseases	I10-I15	20.3	18.2

Note: (a) ICD-10 = International Classification of Diseases 10th Revision; (1) Mortality rates are a three year average covering 2007-2009; (2) Figures cover Los Angeles County
Source: Centers for Disease Control and Prevention, National Center for Health Statistics. Underlying Cause of Death 1999-2009 on CDC WONDER Online Database, released 2012. Data for year 2009 are compiled from the Multiple Cause of Death File 2009, Series 20 No. 2O, 2012, Data for year 2008 are compiled from the Multiple Cause of Death File 2008, Series 20 No. 2N, 2011, Data for year 2007 are compiled from Multiple Cause of Death File 2007, Series 20 No. 2M, 2010.

Mortality Rates for Selected Causes of Death

ICD-10[a] Sub-Chapter	ICD-10[a] Code	Age-Adjusted Mortality Rate[1] per 100,000 population	
		County[2]	U.S.
Assault	X85-Y09	7.8	5.7
Human immunodeficiency virus (HIV) disease	B20-B24	3.7	3.3
Influenza and pneumonia	J09-J18	24.1	16.4
Intentional self-harm	X60-X84	7.7	11.5
Malnutrition	E40-E46	0.4	0.8
Obesity and other hyperalimentation	E65-E68	1.2	1.6
Transport accidents	V01-V99	8.8	13.7
Viral hepatitis	B15-B19	3.2	2.2

Note: (a) ICD-10 = International Classification of Diseases 10th Revision; (1) Mortality rates are a three year average covering 2007-2009; (2) Figures cover Los Angeles County
Source: Centers for Disease Control and Prevention, National Center for Health Statistics. Underlying Cause of Death 1999-2009 on CDC WONDER Online Database, released 2012. Data for year 2009 are compiled from the Multiple Cause of Death File 2009, Series 20 No. 2O, 2012, Data for year 2008 are compiled from the Multiple Cause of Death File 2008, Series 20 No. 2N, 2011, Data for year 2007 are compiled from Multiple Cause of Death File 2007, Series 20 No. 2M, 2010.

Distribution of Physicians and Dentists

Area[1]	Dentists[2]	D.O.[3]	M.D.[4] Total	Family/General Practice	Pediatrics	Medical Specialties	Surgical Specialties
Local (number)	5,952	949	19,255	2,160	1,494	7,496	4,242
Local (rate[5])	6.1	1.0	19.7	2.2	1.5	7.7	4.3
U.S. (rate[5])	4.5	1.9	18.3	2.5	1.4	6.8	4.1

Note: Data as of 2008 unless noted; (1) Local data covers Los Angeles County; (2) Data as of 2007; (3) Doctor of Osteopathic Medicine; (4) Includes active, non-federal, patient-care, office-based Doctors of Medicine; (5) rate per 10,000 population
Source: Area Resource File (ARF). 2009-2010 Release. U.S. Department of Health and Human Services, Health Resources and Services Administration, Bureau of Health Professions, Rockville, MD, August 2010

Best Hospitals

According to *U.S. News,* the Los Angeles-Long Beach-Glendale, CA is home to 10 of the best hospitals in the U.S.: **Cedars-Sinai Medical Center** (12 specialties); **City of Hope** (1 specialty); **Doheny Eye Institute-USC University Hospital** (1 specialty); **Jules Stein Eye Institute-UCLA Medical Center** (1 specialty); **Rancho Los Amigos National Rehabilitation Center** (1 specialty); **Resnick Neuropsychiatric Hospital at UCLA** (1 specialty); **Ronald Reagan UCLA Medical Center** (13 specialties); **St. Vincent Medical Center** (1 specialty); **USC Norris Cancer Hospital** (1 specialty); **USC University Hospital** (7 specialties). The hospitals listed were highly ranked in at least one adult specialty. *U.S. News Online, "America's Best Hospitals 2011-12"*

According to *U.S. News,* the Los Angeles-Long Beach-Glendale, CA is home to two of the best children's hospitals in the U.S.: **Children's Hospital Los Angeles** (10 specialties); **Mattel Children's Hospital UCLA** (9 specialties). The hospitals listed were highly ranked in at least one pediatric specialty. *U.S. News Online, "America's Best Children's Hospitals 2011-12"*

EDUCATION

Public School District Statistics

District Name	Schls	Pupils	Pupil/Teacher Ratio	Minority Pupils[1] (%)	Free Lunch Eligible[2] (%)	IEP[3] (%)
Los Angeles Unified	870	670,746	21.4	91.2	70.1	12.2

Note: Table includes school districts with 2,000 or more students; (1) Percentage of students that are not non-Hispanic white; (2) Percentage of students that are eligible for the free lunch program; (3) Percentage of students that have an Individualized Education Program.
Source: U.S. Department of Education, National Center for Education Statistics, Common Core of Data, Local Education Agency (School District) Universe Survey: School Year 2009-2010; U.S. Department of Education, National Center for Education Statistics, Common Core of Data, Public Elementary/Secondary School Universe Survey: School Year 2009-2010

Top Public High Schools

High School Name	Rank[1]	Score[1]	Grad. Rate[2] (%)	College[3] (%)	AP/IB/ AICE[4] (%)	SAT/ ACT[5] (%)
Los Angeles Center for Enriched Studies	311	0.360	82	99	5.0	1601

Note: (1) Public schools are ranked from 1 to 500 based on the following self-reported statistics (with their corresponding weight in the final score). Schools that had fewer than 10 graduates, as well as those that were newly founded and did not have a graduating senior class in 2010 were excluded; (2) Four-year, on-time graduation rate (25%); (3) Percent of 2010 graduates who enrolled immediately in college (25%); (4) AP/IB/AICE tests per graduate (25%); (5) Average SAT and/or ACT score (10%); Average AP/IB/AICE exam score (10%); AP/IB/AICE courses offered per graduate (5%); (6) School is unranked, but has been identified by Newsweek as one of the nation's most elite public high schools.
Source: Newsweek Online, "Top High Schools 2011"

Highest Level of Education

Area	Less than H.S.	H.S. Diploma	Some College, No Deg.	Associate Degree	Bachelors Degree	Masters Degree	Profess. School Degree	Doctorate Degree
City	26.3	19.2	18.1	6.1	20.2	6.3	2.7	1.2
MSA[1]	22.4	19.9	20.0	7.0	20.1	6.9	2.4	1.3
U.S.	14.7	28.4	21.3	7.6	17.6	7.2	1.9	1.2

Note: Figures cover persons age 25 and over; (1) Figures cover the Los Angeles-Long Beach-Santa Ana, CA Metropolitan Statistical Area—see Appendix B for areas included
Source: U.S. Census Bureau, 2008-2010 American Community Survey 3-Year Estimates

Educational Attainment by Race

Area	High School Graduate or Higher (%)					Bachelor's Degree or Higher (%)				
	Total	White	Black	Asian	Hisp.[2]	Total	White	Black	Asian	Hisp.[2]
City	73.7	78.3	85.6	88.6	48.8	30.4	36.0	21.7	50.3	9.2
MSA[1]	77.6	81.4	87.7	86.6	54.8	30.7	33.4	23.2	49.0	10.2
U.S.	85.3	87.5	81.4	85.5	61.6	28.0	29.3	17.8	50.2	13.0

Note: Figures shown cover persons 25 years old and over; (1) Figures cover the Los Angeles-Long Beach-Santa Ana, CA Metropolitan Statistical Area—see Appendix B for areas included; (2) People of Hispanic origin can be of any race
Source: U.S. Census Bureau, 2008-2010 American Community Survey 3-Year Estimates

School Enrollment by Grade and Control

Area	Preschool (%)		Kindergarten (%)		Grades 1 - 4 (%)		Grades 5 - 8 (%)		Grades 9 - 12 (%)	
	Public	Private	Public	Private	Public	Private	Public	Private	Public	Private
City	61.7	38.3	87.5	12.5	89.0	11.0	88.9	11.1	89.6	10.4
MSA[1]	57.7	42.3	87.4	12.6	90.2	9.8	90.3	9.7	91.8	8.2
U.S.	55.4	44.6	87.1	12.9	89.4	10.6	89.5	10.5	90.4	9.6

Note: Figures shown cover persons 3 years old and over; (1) Figures cover the Los Angeles-Long Beach-Santa Ana, CA Metropolitan Statistical Area—see Appendix B for areas included
Source: U.S. Census Bureau, 2008-2010 American Community Survey 3-Year Estimates

Average Salaries of Public School Classroom Teachers

Area	2010-11		2011-12		Percent Change 2010-11 to 2011-12	Percent Change 2001-02 to 2011-12
	Dollars	Rank[1]	Dollars	Rank[1]		
California	67,871	4	69,496	4	2.39	27.90
U.S. Average	55,623	-	56,643	-	1.83	26.8

Note: (1) State rank ranges from 1 to 51 where 1 indicates highest salary.
Source: National Education Association, Rankings & Estimates: Rankings of the States 2011 and Estimates of School Statistics 2012, December 2011

Higher Education

Four-Year Colleges			Two-Year Colleges			Medical Schools[1]	Law Schools[2]	Voc/ Tech[3]
Public	Private Non-profit	Private For-profit	Public	Private Non-profit	Private For-profit			
2	20	5	4	3	6	2	4	23

Note: Figures cover institutions located within the city limits and include main campuses only; (1) includes schools accredited by the Liaison Committee on Medical Education and the American Osteopathic Association's Commission on Osteopathic College Accreditation; (2) includes American Bar Association-accredited law schools; (3) includes all schools with programs that are less than 2 years.
Source: National Center for Education Statistics, Integrated Postsecondary Education System (IPEDS) Peer Analysis System, 2011-12; Association of American Medical Colleges, Member List, April 23, 2012; American Osteopathic Association, Member List, April 23, 2012; Law School Admission Council, Official Guide to ABA-Approved Law Schools Online, April 23, 2012

According to *U.S. News & World Report,* the Los Angeles-Long Beach-Glendale, CA is home to seven of the best national universities in the U.S.: **California Institute of Technology** (#5); **University of Southern California** (#23); **University of California–Los Angeles** (#25); **Pepperdine University** (#55); **University of La Verne** (#152); **Azusa Pacific University** (#170); **Biola University** (#170). The indicators used to capture academic quality fall into a number of categories: assessment by administrators at peer institutions; retention of students; faculty resources; student selectivity; financial resources; alumni giving; high school counselor ratings of colleges; and graduation rate. *U.S. News & World Report, "America's Best Colleges 2012"*

According to *U.S. News & World Report,* the Los Angeles-Long Beach-Glendale, CA is home to seven of the best liberal arts colleges in the U.S.: **Pomona College** (#4); **Claremont McKenna College** (#9); **Harvey Mudd College** (#18); **Scripps College** (#29); **Occidental College** (#37); **Pitzer College** (#42); **Whittier College** (#133). The indicators used to capture academic quality fall into a number of categories: assessment by administrators at peer institutions; retention of students; faculty resources; student selectivity; financial resources; alumni giving; high school counselor ratings of colleges; and graduation rate. *U.S. News & World Report, "America's Best Colleges 2012"*

According to *U.S. News & World Report,* the Los Angeles-Long Beach-Glendale, CA is home to three of the top 50 law schools in the U.S.: **University of California–Los Angeles** (#15); **University of Southern California (Gould)** (#18); **Pepperdine University** (#49). The rankings are based on a weighted average of 12 measures of quality: peer assessment score; assessment score by lawyers/judges; median LSAT scores; median undergrad GPA; acceptance rate; employment rates for graduates; placement success; bar passage rate; faculty resources; expenditures per student; student/faculty ratio; and library resources. *U.S. News & World Report, "America's Best Law Schools 2013"*

According to *Forbes,* the Los Angeles-Long Beach-Glendale, CA is home to three of the best business schools in the U.S.: **UCLA (Anderson)** (#20); **USC (Marshall)** (#39); **Pepperdine (Graziadio)** (#74). The rankings are based on the return on investment that graduates of the Class of 2006 received (median salary five years after graduation). *Forbes, "Best Business Schools," August 3, 2011*

PRESIDENTIAL ELECTION

2008 Presidential Election Results

Area	Obama	McCain	Nader	Other
Los Angeles County	69.2	28.8	0.8	1.2
U.S.	52.9	45.6	0.6	0.9

Note: Results are percentages and may not add to 100% due to rounding
Source: Dave Leip's Atlas of U.S. Presidential Elections, www.uselectionatlas.org

EMPLOYERS

Major Employers

Company Name	Industry
City of Los Angeles	General government
County of Los Angeles	General government
County of Los Angeles	Pubblic welfare administration: nonoperating, government
Decton	Employment agencies
Disney Enterprises	Motion picture production and distribution
Disney Worldwide Services	Telecommunication equipment repair (except telephones)
Electronic Arts	Home entertainment computer software
King Holding Corporation	Bolts, nuts, rivets, and washers
Securitas Security Services USA	Security guard service
Team-One Employment Specialists	Employment agencies
The Boeing Company	Aircraft
The Boeing Company	Aircraft engines and engine parts
The Walt Disney Company	Television broadcasting stations
U C L A Medical Group	Medical centers
Ucla Health System	Home health care services
University of California, Irvine	University
University of Southern California	Colleges and universities
Veterans Health Administration	Administration of veterans' affairs
Warner Bros. Entertainment	Motion picture and video production

Note: Companies shown are located within the Los Angeles-Long Beach-Santa Ana, CA metropolitan area.
Source: Hoovers.com, data extracted April 25 2012

Best Companies to Work For

University of Southern California, headquartered in Los Angeles, is among the "50 Best Employers for Workers Over 50." Criteria: recruiting practices; opportunities for training, education, and career development; workplace accommodations; alternative work options, such as flexible scheduling, job sharing, and phased retirement; employee health and pension benefits; and retiree benefits. Employers with at least 50 employees based in the U.S. are eligible, including for-profit companies, not-for-profit organizations, and government employers. *AARP, "2011 AARP Best Employers for Workers Over 50"*

PUBLIC SAFETY

Crime Rate

Area	All Crimes	Violent Crimes: Murder	Violent Crimes: Forcible Rape	Violent Crimes: Robbery	Violent Crimes: Aggrav. Assault	Property Crimes: Burglary	Property Crimes: Larceny -Theft	Property Crimes: Motor Vehicle Theft
City	2,894.2	7.6	24.0	284.4	243.2	453.2	1,438.1	443.7
Suburbs[1]	2,856.6	5.4	19.0	182.0	270.5	527.1	1,415.2	437.4
Metro[2]	2,871.3	6.3	21.0	221.8	259.9	498.3	1,424.1	439.9
U.S.	3,345.5	4.8	27.5	119.1	252.3	699.6	2,003.5	238.8

Note: Figures are crimes per 100,000 population; (1) All areas within the metro area that are located outside the city limits; (2) Metropolitan Division—see Appendix B for areas included
Source: FBI Uniform Crime Reports, 2010

Hate Crimes

Area	Number of Quarters Reported	Bias Motivation: Race	Religion	Sexual Orientation	Ethnicity	Disability
City	4	39	28	37	33	1

Source: Federal Bureau of Investigation, Hate Crime Statistics 2010

Identity Theft Consumer Complaints

Area	Complaints	Complaints per 100,000 Population	Rank[2]
MSA[1]	15,380	119.5	40
U.S.	279,156	90.4	-

Note: (1) Metropolitan Statistical Area—see Appendix B for areas included; (2) Rank ranges from 1 to 384 where 1 indicates greatest number of identity theft complaints per 100,000 population
Source: Federal Trade Commission, Consumer Sentinel Network Data Book for January–December 2011

Fraud and Other Consumer Complaints

Area	Complaints	Complaints per 100,000 Population	Rank[2]
MSA[1]	49,239	382.4	324
U.S.	1,533,924	496.8	-

Note: (1) Metropolitan Statistical Area—see Appendix B for areas included; (2) Rank ranges from 1 to 384 where 1 indicates greatest number of fraud and other complaints per 100,000 population
Source: Federal Trade Commission, Consumer Sentinel Network Data Book for January–December 2011

RECREATION

Culture

Dance[1]	Theatre[1]	Instrumental Music[1]	Vocal Music[1]	Series/ Festivals	Museums	Zoos and Aquariums[2]
8	32	8	5	13	42	2

Note: (1) Number of professional perfoming groups; (2) AZA-accredited
Source: The Grey House Performing Arts Directory, 2011-2012; Official Museum Directory, 2011; American Association of Museums, AAM Member Museums, April 2012; Association of Zoos & Aquariums, AZA Member Zoos & Aquariums, April 2012

Professional Sports Teams

Team Name	League
Anaheim Ducks	National Hockey League (NHL)
C.D. Chivas USA	Major League Soccer (MLS)
Los Angeles Angels of Anaheim	Major League Baseball (MLB)
Los Angeles Clippers	National Basketball Association (NBA)
Los Angeles Dodgers	Major League Baseball (MLB)
Los Angeles Galaxy	Major League Soccer (MLS)
Los Angeles Kings	National Hockey League (NHL)
Los Angeles Lakers	National Basketball Association (NBA)

Note: Includes teams located in the Los Angeles-Santa Ana metro area.
Source: Original research

CLIMATE

Average and Extreme Temperatures

Temperature	Jan	Feb	Mar	Apr	May	Jun	Jul	Aug	Sep	Oct	Nov	Dec	Yr.
Extreme High (°F)	88	92	95	102	97	104	97	98	110	106	101	94	110
Average High (°F)	65	66	65	67	69	72	75	76	76	74	71	66	70
Average Temp. (°F)	56	57	58	60	63	66	69	70	70	67	62	57	63
Average Low (°F)	47	49	50	53	56	59	63	64	63	59	52	48	55
Extreme Low (°F)	27	34	37	43	45	48	52	51	47	43	38	32	27

Note: Figures cover the years 1947-1990
Source: National Climatic Data Center, International Station Meteorological Climate Summary, 9/96

Average Precipitation/Snowfall/Humidity

Precip./Humidity	Jan	Feb	Mar	Apr	May	Jun	Jul	Aug	Sep	Oct	Nov	Dec	Yr.
Avg. Precip. (in.)	2.6	2.3	1.8	0.8	0.1	Tr	Tr	0.1	0.2	0.3	1.5	1.5	11.3
Avg. Snowfall (in.)	Tr	0	0	0	0	0	0	0	0	0	0	0	Tr
Avg. Rel. Hum. 7am (%)	69	72	76	76	77	80	80	81	80	76	69	67	75
Avg. Rel. Hum. 4pm (%)	60	62	64	64	66	67	67	68	67	66	61	60	64

Note: Figures cover the years 1947-1990; Tr = Trace amounts (<0.05 in. of rain; <0.5 in. of snow)
Source: National Climatic Data Center, International Station Meteorological Climate Summary, 9/96

Weather Conditions

Temperature			Daytime Sky			Precipitation		
10°F & below	32°F & below	90°F & above	Clear	Partly cloudy	Cloudy	0.01 inch or more precip.	0.1 inch or more snow/ice	Thunder-storms
0	< 1	5	131	125	109	34	0	1

Note: Figures are average number of days per year and cover the years 1947-1990
Source: National Climatic Data Center, International Station Meteorological Climate Summary, 9/96

HAZARDOUS WASTE

Superfund Sites

Los Angeles has four hazardous waste sites on the EPA's Superfund Final National Priorities List: **Del Amo; San Fernando Valley (Area 1); San Fernando Valley (Area 2); San Fernando Valley (Area 4)**. *U.S. Environmental Protection Agency, Final National Priorities List, April 17, 2012*

AIR & WATER QUALITY

Air Quality Index

Area	Percent of Days when Air Quality was...[2]					AQI Statistics[2]	
	Good	Moderate	Unhealthy for Sensitive Groups	Unhealthy	Very Unhealthy	Maximum	Median
Area[1]	14.5	59.5	23.0	2.7	0.3	203	69

Note: Air Quality Index (AQI) is an index for reporting daily air quality. EPA calculates the AQI for five major air pollutants regulated by the Clean Air Act: ground-level ozone, particle pollution (aka particulate matter), carbon monoxide, sulfur dioxide, and nitrogen dioxide. The AQI runs from 0 to 500. The higher the AQI value, the greater the level of air pollution and the greater the health concern. There are six AQI categories: "Good" AQI is between 0 and 50. Air quality is considered satisfactory; "Moderate" AQI is between 51 and 100. Air quality is acceptable; "Unhealthy for Sensitive Groups" When AQI values are between 101 and 150, members of sensitive groups may experience health effects; "Unhealthy" When AQI values are between 151 and 200 everyone may begin to experience health effects; "Very Unhealthy" AQI values between 201 and 300 trigger a health alert; "Hazardous" AQI values over 300 trigger warnings of emergency conditions (not shown); (1) Data covers Los Angeles County; (2) Based on 365 days with AQI data in 2011.
Source: U.S. Environmental Protection Agency, AirData Report, 2011

Air Quality Index Pollutants

Area	Percent of Days when AQI Pollutant was...[2]					
	Carbon Monoxide	Nitrogen Dioxide	Ozone	Sulfur Dioxide	Particulate Matter 2.5	Particulate Matter 10
Area[1]	0.0	10.1	42.7	0.3	46.3	0.5

Note: The Air Quality Index (AQI) is an index for reporting daily air quality. EPA calculates the AQI for five major air pollutants regulated by the Clean Air Act: ground-level ozone, particle pollution (also known as particulate matter), carbon monoxide, sulfur dioxide, and nitrogen dioxide. The AQI runs from 0 to 500. The higher the AQI value, the greater the level of air pollution and the greater the health concern; (1) Data covers Los Angeles County; (2) Based on 365 days with AQI data in 2011.
Source: U.S. Environmental Protection Agency, AirData Report, 2011

Air Quality Index Trends

Area	Trend Sites (days)								All Sites (days)
	2003	2004	2005	2006	2007	2008	2009	2010	2010
MSA[1]	147	134	113	98	102	94	99	74	79

Note: Figures are the number of days the AQI value exceeded 100 in a given year. An AQI value greater than 100 indicates that air quality would have been in the unhealthful range on that day. Data from exceptional events are included. These counts are presented in two ways. First, the counts are based on sites having an adequate record of monitoring data during the trend period (trend sites). These counts represent the relative change in the number of days with AQI values greater than 100. In the last column, the counts are based on all sites with data in the most recent year (because it is possible for a site to have data in the most recent year but not enough data to be a trend site); (1) Data covers the Los Angeles-Long Beach-Santa Ana, CA—see Appendix B for areas included
Source: U.S. Environmental Protection Agency, Air Quality Index Information, "Number of Days with Air Quality Index Values Greater than 100 at Trend Sites, 2000-2010, and at All Sites in 2010"

Maximum Air Pollutant Concentrations: Particulate Matter, Ozone, CO and Lead

	Particulate Matter 10 (ug/m^3)	Particulate Matter 2.5 Wtd AM (ug/m^3)	Particulate Matter 2.5 24-Hr (ug/m^3)	Ozone (ppm)	Carbon Monoxide (ppm)	Lead (ug/m^3)
MSA[1] Level	71	12.6	32	0.09	4	0.39
NAAQS[2]	150	15	35	0.075	9	0.15
Met NAAQS[2]	Yes	Yes	Yes	No	Yes	No

Note: Data from exceptional events are not included; (1) Data covers the Los Angeles-Long Beach-Santa Ana, CA—see Appendix B for areas included; (2) National Ambient Air Quality Standards; ppm = parts per million; ug/m^3 = micrograms per cubic meter; n/a not available

Concentrations: Particulate Matter 10 (coarse particulate)—highest second maximum 24-hour concentration; Particulate Matter 2.5 Wtd AM (fine particulate)—highest weighted annual mean concentration; Particulate Matter 2.5 24-Hour (fine particulate)—highest 98th percentile 24-hour concentration; Ozone—highest fourth daily maximum 8-hour concentration; Carbon Monoxide—highest second maximum non-overlapping 8-hour concentration; Lead—maximum running 3-month average

Source: U.S. Environmental Protection Agency, CBSA Factbook 2010, Air Quality Statistics by City, 2010

Maximum Air Pollutant Concentrations: Nitrogen Dioxide and Sulfur Dioxide

	Nitrogen Dioxide AM (ppb)	Nitrogen Dioxide 1-Hr (ppb)	Sulfur Dioxide AM (ppb)	Sulfur Dioxide 1-Hr (ppb)	Sulfur Dioxide 24-Hr (ppb)
MSA[1] Level	26.179	72.5	1.394	16.2	4.8
NAAQS[2]	53	100	30	75	140
Met NAAQS[2]	Yes	Yes	Yes	Yes	Yes

Note: Data from exceptional events are not included; (1) Data covers the Los Angeles-Long Beach-Santa Ana, CA—see Appendix B for areas included; (2) National Ambient Air Quality Standards; ppb = parts per billion; n/a not available

Concentrations: Nitrogen Dioxide AM—highest arithmetic mean concentration; Nitrogen Dioxide 1-Hr—highest 98th percentile 1-hour daily maximum concentration; Sulfur Dioxide AM—highest annual mean concentration; Sulfur Dioxide 1-Hr—highest 99th percentile 1-hour daily maximum concentration; Sulfur Dioxide 24-Hr—highest second maximum 24-hour concentration

Source: U.S. Environmental Protection Agency, CBSA Factbook 2010, Air Quality Statistics by City, 2010

Drinking Water

Water System Name	Pop. Served	Primary Water Source Type	Violations[1]	
			Health Based	Monitoring/ Reporting
LA Dept of Water & Power	4,094,764	Surface	0	0

Note: (1) Based on violation data from January 1, 2011 to December 31, 2011 (includes unresolved violations from earlier years)

Source: U.S. Environmental Protection Agency, Office of Ground Water and Drinking Water, Safe Drinking Water Information System (based on data extracted April 18, 2012)

Phoenix, Arizona

Background

Phoenix, the arid "Valley of the Sun," and the capital of Arizona, was named by the English soldier and prospector, "Lord Darell" Duppa for the mythical bird of ancient Greek/Phoenician lore. According to the legend, the Phoenix was a beautiful bird that destroyed itself with its own flames. When nothing remained but embers, it would rise again from the ashes, more awesome and beautiful than before. Like the romantic tale, Duppa hoped that his city of Phoenix would rise again from the mysteriously abandoned Hohokam village.

Many might agree that Phoenix fulfilled Duppa's wish. Within 15 years after its second founding in 1867, Phoenix had grown to be an important supply point for the mining districts of north-central Arizona, as well as an important trading site for farmers, cattlemen, and prospectors.

Around this time, Phoenix entered its Wild West phase, complete with stagecoaches, saloons, gambling houses, soldiers, cowboys, miners, and the pungent air of outlawry. Two public hangings near the end of the 1800s set a dramatic example, and helped turn the tide.

Today, Phoenix is just as exciting as ever, but more law-abiding, and many continue to be attracted to Phoenix's natural beauty. Despite occasional sprawling suburbs and shopping malls, the sophisticated blend of Spanish, Native American, and cowboy culture is obvious in the city's architecture, arts, and crafts.

Downtown Phoenix underwent a major renaissance in the 1990s with the completion of a history museum, expanded art museum, new central library, and a renovated concert hall. In 2010 the Musical Instrument Museum opened in the city, featuring the largest musical instrument collection in the world. The $48 million Arizona Science Center opened in 1998, as did Chase Field, where, in 2001, the Arizona Diamondbacks won their first World Series.

Phoenix is the country's sixth-largest city, with more than one million people, while the Phoenix metro area population has grown to nearly four million. This increase in population continues to make Phoenix an attractive location for companies that are expanding into the fields of electronics and communications. The city hosts headquarters for U-HAUL and Best Western, as well as the entire website for American Express—all financial transactions and customer service. Other top employers in the city include Intel and Honeywell.

The completion of the city's Valley Metro Rail light rail project has sparked interest in a commuter rail system operating on existing railroad lines connecting several neighboring cities.

Contrary to some thinking, the Phoenix Chamber of Commerce reports that ample water sources are available to support the growth of Greater Phoenix well into the twenty-second century. Sources include seven reservoirs, local groundwater aquifers, and Colorado River water supplied through the Central Arizona Project Canal.

Temperatures in Phoenix are mild in winter and very hot in summer. However, with the low humidity, the summer heat is somewhat more bearable than one might expect. Rainfall is slight and comes in two seasons. In winter rain comes on winds from the Pacific, ending by April. In summer, especially during July and August, there are severe thunderstorms from the southeast.

Rankings

General Rankings

- The Phoenix metro area was identified as one of the 10 most popular big cities by Pew Research Center. The results are based on a telephone survey of 2,260 adults conducted during October 2008. The report explored a range of attitudes related to where Americans live, where they would like to live, and why. *Pew Research Center, "For Nearly Half of America, Grass is Greener Somewhere Else," January 29, 2009*
- *Men's Health Living* ranked 100 U.S. cities in terms of quality of life. Phoenix was ranked #91 and received a grade of D-. Criteria: number of fitness facilities; air quality; number of physicians; male/female ratio; education levels; household income; cost of living. *Men's Health Living, Spring 2008*
- Phoenix was selected as one of America's ten "Best Cities to Work and Live." The city ranked #8. The results are based on a survey of 2,500 employees and entrepreneurs who were asked about 40 large cities. *BusinessWeek, "America's Most and Least Favorite Cities," January 5, 2009*
- Phoenix was selected as one of America's best cities by *Bloomberg Businessweek.* The city ranked #49 out of 50. Criteria: number of restaurants, bars and museums per capita; number of colleges, libraries, and professional sports teams; income, poverty, unemployment, crime, and foreclosure rates; percent of population with bachelor's degrees; public school performance; park acres per capita; air quality. *BusinessWeek, "America's 50 Best Cities," September 20, 2011*
- Phoenix appeared on RelocateAmerica's list of best places to live in America. The annual "Top 100 Places to Live" list recognizes the top communities as nominated by their residents & local businesses. RelocateAmerica's Research Group determines the list based on review of various data gathered for economic, employment, housing, education, industry, opportunity, environment and recreation along with feedback from area leaders and residents. *RelocateAmerica.com, "Top 100 Places to Live for 2011"*
- Phoenix was identified as one of the top places to live in the U.S. by Harris Interactive. The city ranked #15 out of 15. Criteria: 2,463 adults (age 18 and over) were polled and asked "if you could live in or near any city in the country except the one you live in or nearest to now, which city would you choose?" The poll was conducted online within the U.S. between September 14 and 20, 2010. *Harris Interactive, November 9, 2011*

Business/Finance Rankings

- Phoenix was identified as one of the 20 strongest-performing metro areas during the recession and recovery from trough quarter through the third quarter of 2011. Criteria: percent change in employment; percentage point change in unemployment rate; percent change in gross metropolitan product; percent change in House Price Index. *Brookings Institution, MetroMonitor: Tracking Economic Recession and Recovery in America's 100 Largest Metropolitan Areas, December 2011*
- Experian ranked the top 20 major U.S. metropolitan areas by average debt per consumer. The Phoenix metro area was ranked #5. Criteria: average debt per consumer. Debt for this study includes credit cards, auto loans and personal loans. It does not include mortgages. *Experian, May 13, 2010*
- Phoenix was identified as one of America's most coupon-loving cities by *Coupons.com.* The city ranked #23 out of 25. Criteria: online coupon usage. *Coupons.com, "Top 25 Most Frugal Cities of 2011," February 23, 2012*
- Phoenix was identified as one of the top 25 U.S. cities with the most credit card debt by credit reporting bureau Experian. The city was ranked #22. *Experian, March 4, 2011*
- Phoenix was identified as one of the "Happiest Cities to Work in 2012" by *CareerBliss.com,* an online community for career advancement. The city ranked #39 out of 50. Criteria: independent company reviews from employees all over the country on: relationship with their boss and co-workers; work environment; job resources; growth opportunities; compensation; company culture; company reputation; daily tasks; job control over work performed on a daily basis. *CareerBliss.com, "Happiest and Unhappiest Cities to Work in 2012"*

- Phoenix was selected as one of the best cities in the world for telecommuting. The city ranked #7. The editors at *Cartridge Save* (printer technology news, guides and reviews) identified the 20 best cities in which to be an at-home, tech-using employee. *Cartridge Save, "20 of the Best Cities in the World for Telecommuting," May 14, 2008*
- *American City Business Journals* ranked America's 261 largest cities in terms of their resident's wealth. Phoenix ranked #113. Criteria: per capita income; median household income; percentage of households with annual incomes of $200,000 or more; median home value. *American City Business Journals, "Where the Money Is: America's Wealth Centers," August 18, 2008*
- The Phoenix metro area appeared on the Milken Institute "2011 Best Performing Metros" list. Rank: #136 out of 200 large metro areas. Criteria: job growth; wage and salary growth; high-tech output growth. *Milken Institute, "2011 Best Performing Metros"*
- The Phoenix metro area was selected as one of the best cities for entrepreneurs in America by *Inc. Magazine.* Criteria: job-growth data for 335 metro areas was analyzed for: recent growth trend; mid-term growth; long-term trend; current year growth. The Phoenix metro area ranked #14 among large metro areas and #61 overall. *Inc. Magazine, "The Best Cities for Doing Business," July 2008*
- Phoenix was ranked #58 out of 145 regions worldwide in terms of its "Knowledge Competitiveness Index." The index attempts to measure the knowledge-based development taking place throughout the world and is based on 19 measures of economic performance that indicate a region's ability to translate its knowledge capacity into economic value. *Centre for International Competitiveness, World Knowledge Competitiveness Index 2008*
- *Forbes* ranked the 200 most populous metro areas in the U.S. in terms of the "Best Places for Business and Careers." The Phoenix metro area was ranked #88. Criteria: costs (business and living); job growth (past and projected); income growth; educational attainment; projected economic growth; crime; cultural and recreational opportunities; net migration patterns; number of highly ranked colleges. *Forbes, "Best Places for Business and Careers," June 2011*
- Phoenix appeared on *Kiplinger's Personal Finance* list of the "Top Ten Tax-Friendly Cities." The city was ranked #8. Criteria: income tax; sales tax; real estate and car/personal property tax. *Kiplinger's Personal Finance, March 1, 2009*

Children/Family Rankings

- The Phoenix metro area was selected as one of the "Best Cities for Relocating Families" by Worldwide ERC and Primacy Relocation. The 2008 study looked at nearly 50 factors important to relocating families including: recent job growth; nearby top-ranked colleges; in-state tuition for four-year public colleges; population growth since 2000; pediatricians per 100,000 population; and a Green Living index. *Worldwide ERC and Primacy Relocation, "2008 Best Cities for Relocating Families"*
- *Fit Pregnancy* magazine ranked the 50 best U.S. cities in which to have a baby. Phoenix was ranked #40. Criteria: access to hospitals and doctors; affordability; birthing options; breastfeeding; child care; fertility laws/resources; maternal and infant health risk; parks/stroller friendliness; safety. *Fit Pregnancy, "The Best Cities in America to Have a Baby 2008"*

Culture/Performing Arts Rankings

- Phoenix was selected as one of "America's Top 25 Arts Destinations." The city ranked #19 in the big city (population 500,000 and over) category. Criteria: readers' top choices for arts travel destinations based on the richness and variety of visual arts sites, activities and events. *American Style, "America's Top 25 Arts Destinations," May 2010*

Dating/Romance Rankings

- Phoenix was selected as one of the best cities for single women by *Rent.com.* The city ranked #1 of 10. Criteria: high single male-to-female ratio; lively nightlife; low divorce rate; low cost of living. *Rent.com, "Top 10 Cities for Single Women," August 19, 2011*

- Phoenix was selected as one of "America's Best Cities for Dating" by *Yahoo! Travel.* Criteria: high proportion of singles; excellent dating venues and/or stunning natural settings. *Yahoo! Travel, "America's Best Cities for Dating," February 7, 2012*

- Phoenix appeared on *Men's Health's* list of the most sex-happy cities in America. The city ranked #45 of 100. Criteria: condom sales; birth rates; sex toy sales; rates of chlamydia, gonorrhea, and syphilis. *Men's Health, "America's Most Sex-Happy Cities," October 2010*

- Phoenix was selected as one of the best cities for single women in America by *SingleMindedWomen.com.* The city ranked #4. Criteria: ratio of women to men; singles population; healthy lifestyle; employment opportunities; cost of living; access to travel; entertainment options; social opportunities. *SingleMindedWomen.com, "Top 10 Cities for Single Women," 2011*

- *Men's Health* ranked 100 U.S. cities in terms of best (and worst) marriages. Phoenix was ranked #31 (#1 = worst). Criteria: rate of failed marriages; stringency of divorce laws; percentage of population who've split; number of licensed marriage and family therapists. *Men's Health, "Splitsville, USA," May 2010*

- Eli Lily and Company, in partnership with Sperling's BestPlaces, ranked the nation's 50 largest metro areas in terms of the "Most Romantic Cities for Baby Boomers." The Phoenix metro area ranked #38. Criteria: marriage and divorce rates among baby boomers age 45 to 60; great restaurants; dance studios; chocolate, jewelry and flower sales. *Eli Lily and Company, "Most Romantic Cities for Baby Boomers," April 20, 2007*

- The Phoenix metro area was selected as one of the "Best Cities for Relocating Singles" by Worldwide ERC and Primacy Relocation. The area ranked #71 out of the 100 largest metro areas in the U.S. Criteria: recent job growth; recent singles population growth; overall population growth; affordable rental housing; cost-of-living index; expanded arts and recreation opportunities; ratio of single men and single women; affordability of quality higher education (including state residency requirements); diversity index; climate; population density. *Worldwide ERC and Primacy Relocation, "2008 Best Cities for Relocating Singles"*

- *Forbes* ranked the 40 most populous urbanized areas in the U.S. in terms of the "Best Cities for Singles." The Phoenix metro area ranked #30. Criteria: number of singles; cost of living alone; nightlife; culture; job growth; coolness; and online dating participation. *Forbes.com, "Best Cities for Singles," July 27, 2009*

Education Rankings

- *Men's Health* ranked 100 U.S. cities in terms of their education levels. Phoenix was ranked #80 (#1 = most educated city). Criteria: high school graduation rates; school enrollment; educational attainment; number of households who have outstanding student loans; number of households whose members have taken adult-education courses. *Men's Health, "Where School Is In: The Most and Least Educated Cities," September 12, 2011*

- Phoenix was selected as one of "America's Most Literate Cities." The city ranked #56 out of the 75 largest U.S. cities. Criteria: number of booksellers; library resources; Internet resources; educational attainment; periodical publishing resources; newspaper circulation. *Central Connecticut State University, "America's Most Literate Cities 2011"*

- Phoenix was identified as one of the 100 "smartest" metro areas in the U.S. The area ranked #70. Criteria: the editors rated the collective brainpower of the 100 largest metro areas in the U.S. based on their residents' educational attainment. *American City Business Journals, April 14, 2008*

- Phoenix was identified as one of "America's Brainiest Bastions" by *Portfolio.com.* The metro area ranked #100 out of 200. *Portfolio.com* analyzed levels of educational attainment in the nation's 200 largest metropolitan areas. The editors established scores for five levels of educational attainment, based on relative earning power of adult workers age 25 or older. Scores were determined by comparing the median income for all workers with the median income for those workers at a specified educational level. *Portfolio.com, "America's Brainiest Bastions," December 1, 2010*

Environmental Rankings

- The Phoenix was identified as one of America's dirtiest metro areas by *Forbes.* The area ranked #8 out of 10. Criteria: year-round particulate pollution; short-term particulate pollution; ozone pollution. *Forbes, "Dirtiest Cities in America," November 4, 2011*

- The Phoenix was identified as one of North America's greenest metropolitan areas. The area ranked #24. The Green City Index is comprised of 31 indicators, and scores cities across nine categories: carbon dioxide; energy; land use; buildings; transport; water; waste; air quality; environmental governance. The 27 largest metropolitan areas in the U.S. and Canada were considered. *Economist Intelligence Unit, sponsored by Siemens, "U.S. and Canada Green City Index, 2011"*

- The Phoenix was identified as one of America's cities with the most ENERGY STAR certified buildings. The area ranked #17 out of 25. Criteria: number of ENERGY STAR labeled buildings in 2010. *U.S. Environmental Protection Agency, "Top Cities With the Most ENERGY STAR Certified Buildings," March 15, 2011*

- The Phoenix metro area was identified as one of "The Ten Biggest American Cities that are Running Out of Water" by *24/7 Wall St.* The metro area ranked #3 out of 10. *24/7 Wall St.* did an analysis of the water supply and consumption in the 30 largest metropolitan areas in the U.S. Criteria include: projected water demand as a share of available precipitation; groundwater use as a share or projected available precipitation; susceptibility to drought; projected increase in freshwater withdrawals; projected increase in summer water deficit. *24/7 Wall St., "The Ten Biggest American Cities that are Running Out of Water," November 1, 2010*

- Phoenix was selected as one of 22 "Smarter Cities" for energy by the Natural Resources Defense Council. Criteria: investment in green power; energy efficiency measures; conservation. *Natural Resources Defense Council, "2010 Smarter Cities," July 19, 2010*

- *American City Business Journal* ranked 43 metropolitan areas in terms of their "greenness." The Phoenix metro area ranked #21. Criteria: Forty-one metros in which *ACBJ* has business weeklies, plus Indianapolis and Cleveland, were ranked based on 20 different indicators such as adoption of green technologies, utilization of environmentally sound practices, and air and water quality. *American City Business Journals, "Green City Index," March 11, 2010*

- 100 of the largest metro areas in the U.S. were analyzed in terms of their current drought severity. The Phoenix metro area ranked #23 (#1 = driest). The rankings were based on statistics such as long-term precipitation trends and patterns and the Palmer drought indices. *Sperling's BestPlaces, www.BestPlaces.net, "America's Drought-Riskiest Cities," November 2007*

- The Phoenix metro area appeared in *Country Home's* "Best Green Places" report. The area ranked #130 out of 379. Criteria: official energy policies; green power; green buildings; availability of fresh, locally grown food. *Country Home, "Best Green Places," 2008*

- Phoenix was highlighted as one of the 25 metro areas most polluted by short-term particle pollution (24-hour PM 2.5) in the U.S. The area ranked #24. *American Lung Association, State of the Air 2011*

- Phoenix was highlighted as one of the 25 metro areas most polluted by year-round particle pollution (Annual PM 2.5) in the U.S. The area ranked #2. *American Lung Association, State of the Air 2011*

- Phoenix was highlighted as one of the 25 most ozone-polluted metro areas in the U.S. The area ranked #19. *American Lung Association, State of the Air 2011*

Health/Fitness Rankings

- The Phoenix metro area was selected as one of the worst cities for bed bugs in America by Rollins corporation, the owner of seven pest control companies, including Orkin. The area ranked #34 based on the number of bed bug treatments from January to December 2011. *Rollins, "The Top 50 U.S. Cities for Bed Bugs," March 19, 2012*

- Phoenix was selected as one of the 25 fattest cities in America by *Men's Fitness Online*. It ranked #18 out of America's 50 largest cities. Criteria: fitness centers and sport stores; nutrition; sports participation; TV viewing; overweight/sedentary; junk food; air quality; geography; commute; parks and open space; city recreational facilities; access to healthcare; motivation; mayor and city initiatives; state obesity initiatives. *Men's Fitness, "The Fittest and Fattest Cities in America," March 5, 2012*

- Phoenix was identified as a "2011 Asthma Capital." The area ranked #81 out of the nation's 100 largest metropolitan areas. Twelve factors were used to identify the most challenging places to live for people with asthma: estimated prevalence; self-reported prevalence; crude death rate for asthma; annual pollen score; annual air quality; public smoking laws; number of board-certified asthma specialists; school inhaler access laws; rescue medication use; controller medication use; uninsured rate; poverty rate. *Asthma and Allergy Foundation of America, "2011 Asthma Capitals"*

- Phoenix was identified as a "2011 Fall Allergy Capital." The area ranked #91 out of 100. Three groups of factors were used to identify the most severe cities for people with allergies during the fall season: annual pollen levels; medicine utilization; access to board-certified allergists. *Asthma and Allergy Foundation of America, "2011 Fall Allergy Capitals"*

- Phoenix was identified as a "2012 Spring Allergy Capital." The area ranked #72 out of 100. Three groups of factors were used to identify the most severe cities for people with allergies during the spring season: annual pollen levels; medicine utilization; access to board-certified allergists. *Asthma and Allergy Foundation of America, "2012 Spring Allergy Capitals"*

- *Men's Health* examined 100 major U.S. cities and selected the best and worst cities for men. Phoenix ranked #40. Criteria: 35 statistical parameters of long life in the categories of health, quality of life, and fitness. *Men's Health, "The 10 Best and Worst Cities for Men 2012," January/February 2012*

- The Phoenix metropolitan area was selected as one of the best metros for hospital care in America by *HealthGrades.com*. The rankings are based on a comprehensive study of patient death and complication rates in the nation's nearly 5,000 hospitals. Hospitals performing in the top 5% nationwide across 26 different medical procedures and diagnoses were identified. *HealthGrades.com* then ranked cities by the highest percentage of these Distinguished Hospitals for Clinical Excellence™. The Phoenix metro area ranked #2. *HealthGrades.com, "America's Top 50 Cities for Hospital Care," January 21, 2012*

- The American Academy of Dermatology ranked 26 U.S. metropolitan regions in terms of their residents knowledge, attitude and behaviors towards tanning, sun protection and skin cancer detection. The Phoenix metro area ranked #6. The results of the study are based on an online survey of over 7,000 adults nationwide. *American Academy of Dermatology, "Suntelligence: How Sun Smart is Your City," May 3, 2010*

- The Phoenix metro area appeared in the 2011 Gallup-Healthways Well-Being Index. The index, based on interviews with more than 350,000 Americans, measured jobs, finances, physical health, emotional state of mind and communities. The metro area ranked #69 out of 190. Criteria: life evaluation; emotional health; work environment; physical health; healthy behaviors; basic access (basic needs optimal for a healthy life, such as access to food and medicine, having health insurance and feeling safe while walking at night). *Gallup-Healthways, "State of Well-Being 2011"*

- The Phoenix metro area was identified as one of "America's Most Stressful Cities" by *Sperling's BestPlaces*. The metro area ranked #18 out of 50. Criteria: unemployment rate; suicide rate; commute time; mental health; poor rest; alcohol use; violent crime rate; property crime rate; cloudy days annually. *Sperling's BestPlaces, www.BestPlaces.net, "Stressful Cities 2012*

- *Men's Health* ranked 100 U.S. cities in terms of their activity levels. Phoenix was ranked #35 (#1 = most active city). Criteria: where and how often residents exercise; percentage of households that watch more than 15 hours of cable television a week and buy more than 11 video games a year; death rate from deep-vein thrombosis, a condition linked to sitting for extended periods of time. *Men's Health, "Where Sit Happens: The Most and Least Active Cities in America," June 20, 2011*

- 50 of the largest metro areas in the U.S. were analyzed in terms of their health and fitness by the American College of Sports Medicine in their "American Fitness Index." The Phoenix metro area ranked #32 (#1 = healthiest). Criteria: preventative health behaviors; levels of chronic disease; health care access; community resources and policies that support physical activity. *American College of Sports Medicine, "Health and Community Fitness Status of the 50 Largest Metropolitan Areas," August 1, 2011*

Pet Rankings

- Phoenix was selected as one of the "Top 10 Cat-Friendly Cities" in the U.S. The area ranked #2. Criteria: cat ownership per capita; level of veterinary care; microchipping; cat-friendly local ordinances. *CATalyst Council, "Top 10 Cat-Friendly Cities," March 27, 2009*

Real Estate Rankings

- Phoenix was selected as one of the best cities for renters by *Forbes.* The city ranked #3 out of 5. The 44 largest cities in the U.S. were rated on four criteria: average rent in the first quarter of 2011 and how much it changed year-over-year; vacancy rates; cost of renting versus buying. *Forbes, "Best and Worst Cities for Renters," June 20, 2011*
- Phoenix was identified as one of 13 metro areas where home prices are falling dangerously. Criteria: home price change from October 2010 to September 2011; projected home price change through 2012. *Forbes.com, "Cities Where Home Prices are Falling Dangerously," January 10, 2012*
- Phoenix was identified as one of the "Top Turnaround Housing Markets for 2012." The area ranked #2 out of 10. Criteria: year-over-year median home price appreciation; year-over-year median inventory age; year-over-year inventory reduction. *AOL Real Estate, "Top Turnaround Housing Markets for 2012," February 4, 2012*
- *Fortune* ranked the 100 largest metro areas in the U.S. in terms of projected median home price change in 2010. The Phoenix metro area ranked #92. *Fortune, "The 2010 Housing Outlook," December 9, 2009*
- Phoenix appeared on *ApartmentRatings.com* "Top Cities for Renters" list in 2009." The area ranked #55. Overall satisfaction ratings were ranked using thousands of user submitted scores for hundreds of apartment complexes located in the 100 most populated U.S. municipalities. *ApartmentRatings.com, "2009 Renter Satisfaction Rankings"*
- The Phoenix metro area was identified as one of the "Top 25 Real Estate Investment Markets" by *FinestExperts.com.* The metro area ranked #17. Over 10,000 real estate markets were analyzed to identify the most suitable places for real estate investors to seek stability and growth. Criteria: employment; rental markets; growth levels as offset by foreclosures. *FinestExperts.com, "Top 25 Real Estate Investment Markets," January 7, 2010*
- The Phoenix metro area was identified as one of "America's 25 Weakest Housing Markets" by *Forbes*. The metro area ranked #12. Criteria: metro areas with populations over 500,000 were ranked based on projected home values through 2011. *Forbes.com, "America's 25 Weakest Housing Markets," January 7, 2009*
- The nation's largest metro areas were analyzed in terms of the percentage of households entering some stage of foreclosure in 2011. The Phoenix metro area ranked #6 out of 20 (#1 = highest foreclosure rate). *RealtyTrac, 2011 Year-End Foreclosure Market Report, January 12, 2012*
- The nation's largest metro areas were analyzed in terms of the best places to buy pre-foreclosures (short sales). The Phoenix metro area ranked #9 out of 10. Criteria: at least 500 pre-foreclosure sales during the fourth quarter and a short sales increase of at least five percent from a year ago. The areas selected posted the biggest discounts on the sales of pre-foreclosure properties. *RealtyTrac, "Fourth Quarter and Year-End 2011 U.S. Foreclosure Sales Report: Shifting Towards Short Sales," February 28, 2012*
- The Phoenix metro area was identified as one of the 10 best cities for "Real Estate Steals" in the U.S. by *U.S. News and World Report.* The metro area was ranked #8. Criteria: average and quarterly price-to-income ratios. *U.S. News and World Report, "10 Cities for Real Estate Steals," February 18, 2010*

- The Phoenix metro area appeared in a *Wall Street Journal* article ranking cities by "housing stress." The metro area was ranked #11 (#1 = most stress). Criteria: fraction of mortgage-holding homeowners with a monthly housing payment in excess of 30 percent of income; percentage of people without health insurance; unemployment rate. *The Wall Street Journal, "Which Cities Face Biggest Housing Risk," October 5, 2010*

- The Center for Housing Policy ranked 210 U.S. metropolitan areas by the fair market rent for a two-bedroom unit. The Phoenix metro area was ranked #76. (#1 = most expensive) with a rent of $919. Criteria: Fair Market Rent (FMR) in effect during the fourth quarter of 2009 based on HUD's fiscal year 2010 FMRs. *The Center for Housing Policy, "Paycheck to Paycheck: Most to Least Expensive Rental Markets in 2009"*

- The Phoenix metro area was identified as one of the worst housing markets of the decade by *Forbes.* Criteria: decrease in housing values per square foot since January 2000. *Forbes, "America's 5 Best (and Worst) Housing Markets of the Decade," December 7, 2010*

- The Phoenix metro area was identified as one of the top 20 cities in terms of decreasing home equity. The metro area was ranked #3. Criteria: percentage of home equity relative to the home's current value. *Forbes.com, "Where Americans are Losing Home Equity Most," May 1, 2010*

- The Phoenix metro area was identified as one of the markets with the worst expected performance in home prices over the next 12 months. *Local Market Monitor, "First Quarter Home Price Forecast for Largest US Markets," March 2, 2011*

- The Phoenix metro area was identified as one of the best U.S. markets to invest in rental property" by HomeVestors and Local Market Monitor. The area ranked #8 out of 100. Criteria: risk-return premium relative to national average. *HomeVestors and Local Market Monitor, "Best 100 U.S. Markets to Invest in Rental Property," March 9, 2012*

Safety Rankings

- Symantec, the makers of Norton, in partnership with Sperling's BestPlaces, ranked the 50 largest cities in the U.S. in terms of their vulnerability to cybercrime. The city ranked #31. Criteria: number of cyberattacks and potential infections; level of Internet access; expenditures on smartphones and computer hardware/software; wireless hotspots; broadband connectivity; Internet usage; online purchases. *Symantec, "Riskiest Online Cities of 2012" February 15, 2012*

- Allstate ranked the 193 largest cities in America in terms of driver safety. Phoenix ranked #55. In addition, drivers were 1.1% less likely to have had an accident compared to the national average. Allstate researchers analyzed internal property damage reported claims over a two-year period (from January 2008 to December 2009) to protect findings from external influences such as weather or road construction. A weighted average of the two-year numbers determined the annual percentages. The report defines an auto crash as any collision resulting in a property damage claim. *Allstate, "2011 Allstate America's Best Drivers Report™"*

- The National Insurance Crime Bureau ranked 366 metro areas in the U.S. in terms of per capita rates of vehicle theft. The Phoenix metro area ranked #56 (#1 = highest rate). Criteria: number of vehicle theft offenses per 100,000 inhabitants in 2010. *National Insurance Crime Bureau, "Hot Spots," June 21, 2011*

- The Phoenix metro area was identified as one of the most dangerous metro areas for pedestrians by Transportation for America. The metro area ranked #8 out of 52 metro areas with over 1 million residents. Criteria: area's population divided by the number of pedestrian fatalities in that area. *Transportation for America, "Dangerous by Design 2011"*

Seniors/Retirement Rankings

- Bankers Life and Casualty Company, in partnership with Sperling's BestPlaces, ranked the nation's 50 largest metro areas in terms of the "Best U.S. Cities for Seniors." The Phoenix metro area ranked #40. Criteria: healthcare; transportation; housing; environment; economy; health and longevity; social and spiritual life; crime. *Bankers Life and Casualty Company, Center for a Secure Retirement, "Best U.S. Cities for Seniors 2011," September 2011*

- The Phoenix metro area was identified as one of the "Best Places for Bargain Retirement Homes" by *Forbes*. The metro area ranked #9 out of 10. Criteria: low cost of living; stable home prices; low taxes; reasonable average home prices. *Forbes.com, "Best Places for Bargain Retirement Homes," January 12, 2011*
- Phoenix was identified as one of the "100 Most Popular Retirement Towns" by *Topretirements.com* The list reflects the 100 cities (out of 815+ total cities reviewed) that visitors to the website are most interested in for retirement. *Topretirements.com, "100 Most Popular Retirement Towns," February 21, 2012*
- The Phoenix metro area was selected as one of "The 10 Most Affordable Cities for Long-Term Care" by *U.S. News & World Report.* Criteria: costs at nursing homes, assisted living facilities, and adult day health care facilities; cost for licensed home health aides. *U.S. News & World Report, "The 10 Most Affordable Cities for Long-Term Care," May 17, 2010*

Sports/Recreation Rankings

- Phoenix was selected as one of "America's Most Miserable Sports Cities" by *Forbes.* The city was ranked #3. Criteria: postseason losses; years since last title; ratio of cumulative seasons to championships won. Contenders were limited to cities with at least 75 total seasons of NFL, NBA, NHL and MLB play. *Forbes, "America's Most Miserable Sports Cities," February 28, 2012*
- Phoenix appeared on the *Sporting News* list of the "Best Sports Cities" for 2011. The area ranked #18 out of 271 cities in the U.S. *Sporting News* takes a 12-month snapshot of each city's sports, putting a heavy premium on regular-season won-lost records (from the most recently completed season). Other criteria include: playoff berths, bowl appearances and tournament bids; championships; applicable power ratings; quality of competition; overall fan fervor (measured in part by attendance); abundance of teams (rewarding quality over quantity); stadium and arena quality; ticket availability and prices; franchise ownership; and marquee appeal of athletes. *Sporting News, "Best Sports Cities 2011," October 4, 2011*
- Phoenix was selected as one of the most playful cities in the U.S. by KaBOOM! The organization's Playful City USA initiative is a national recognition program that honors cities and towns across the nation for a vision, plan and commitment to creating an agenda for play. Cities were recognized based on a pledge to five specific commitments to play: creating a local play commission or task force; designing an annual action plan for play; conducting a play space audit; outlining a financial investment in play for the current fiscal year; and proclaiming and celebrating an annual "play day." *KaBOOM! National Campaign for Play, "2011 Playful City USA Communities"*
- Phoenix was chosen as one of America's best cities for bicycling. The city ranked #15 out of 50. Criteria: number of segregated bike lanes, municipal bike racks, and bike boulevards; vibrant and diverse bike culture; smart, savvy bike shops; interviews with national and local advocates, bike shops and other experts. The editors only considered cities with populations of 100,000 or more. *Bicycling, "America's Best Bike Cities," April 2010*
- The Phoenix was selected as one of the best metro areas for golf in America by *Golf Digest.* The Phoenix area was ranked #15 out of 20. Criteria: climate; cost of public golf; quality of public golf; accessibility. *Golf Digest, "The Top 20 Cities for Golf," October 2011*

Transportation Rankings

- The Phoenix metro area appeared on *Forbes* list of the best and worst cities for commuters. The metro area ranked #36 out of 60 (#1 is best). Criteria: travel time; road congestion; travel delays. *Forbes.com, "Best and Worst Cities for Commuters," February 16, 2010*

Women/Minorities Rankings

- *Women's Health* examined U.S. cities and identified the 100 best cities for women. Phoenix was ranked #33. Criteria: 30 categories were examined from obesity and breast cancer rates to commuting times and hours spent working out. *Women's Health, "Best Cities for Women 2012"*

- Phoenix was ranked #48 out of 100 metro areas in *SELF Magazine's* ranking of America's healthiest places for women." A panel of experts came up with more than 50 criteria including death and disease rates, environmental indicators, community resources, and lifestyle habits. *SELF Magazine, "Secrets of America's Healthiest Women," December 2008*
- Phoenix was selected as one of the 25 healthiest cities for Latinas by *Latina Magazine.* The city ranked #5. Criteria: U.S. cities with populations over 500,000 residents were evaluated on the following criteria: percentage of 18-34 year-olds per city; Latino college graduation rates; number of colleges and universities; affordability; housing costs; income growth over time; average salary; percentage of singles; climate; safety; how the city's diversity compares to the national average; opportunities for minority entrepreneurs. *Latina Magazine, "Top 15 U.S. Cities for Young Latinos to Live In," August 19, 2011*
- The Phoenix metro area appeared on *Forbes'* list of the "Best Cities for Minority Entrepreneurs." The area ranked #5 out of 10. Criteria: 52 metropolitan statistical areas were examined. For each ethnicity (African Americans, Asians and Hispanics), the editors measured housing affordability, population growth, income growth, and entrepreneurship (per capita self-employment). *Forbes, "Best Cities for Minority Entrepreneurs," March 23, 2011*

Miscellaneous Rankings

- *Men's Health* ranked 100 U.S. cities by their level of sadness. Phoenix was ranked #83 (#1 = saddest city). Criteria: suicide rates; unemployment rates; percentage of households that use antidepressants; percent of population who report feeling blue all or most of the time. *Men's Health, "Frown Towns," November 28, 2011*
- The Phoenix metro area was selected as one of "The Best U.S. Cities for Bargain Shopping" by *Forbes.* The area ranked #3 out of 10. Criteria: number of outlet stores; gross leasable retail space in major malls; low consumer price index; low sales tax rate. Indicators were examined in the nation's 50 largest metropolitan areas. *Forbes, "The Best U.S. Cities for Bargain Shopping," January 20, 2012*
- Energizer Holdings, the makers of Edge® shave gel, in partnership with Sperling's BestPlaces, ranked 50 major metro areas in terms of everyday irritations. The Phoenix metro area ranked #10. Criteria: humidity levels; weather conditions; incidence of traffic delays and congestion; average commute times; frequency of flight delays and cancellations; rates of sleeplessness; underemployment; pollens and allergens; pests; comedy clubs per capita. *Energizer Holdings, "Most Irritation Prone Cities," July 23, 2010*
- Mars Chocolate North America, the makers of COMBOS®, in partnership with Sperling's BestPlaces, ranked 50 major metro areas in terms of their "manliness." The Phoenix metro area ranked #32. Criteria: number of professional sports teams; number of nearby NASCAR tracks and racing events; manly lifestyle; concentration of manly retail stores; manly occupations per capita; salty snack sales; "Board of Manliness" rankings. *Mars Chocolate North America, "America's Manliest Cities 2011," September 1, 2011*
- Phoenix was selected as one of the "Worst Hair Cities" by *NaturallyCurly.com.* The city was ranked #5. Criteria: humidity levels; pollution; rainfall; average wind speeds; water hardness; beauty salons per capita. *NaturallyCurly.com, "Best/Worst Hair Cities," April 29, 2009*
- Phoenix was selected as one of the best cities for shopping in the U.S. by *Forbes.* The city was ranked #2.Criteria: number of major shopping centers; retail locations; Consumer Price Index (CPI); combined state and local sales tax. *Forbes, "America's 25 Best Cities for Shopping," December 13, 2010*
- The Phoenix metro area appeared in *AutoMD.com's* ranking of the "Best and Worst Cities for Auto Repair." The metro area ranked #43 (#1 is best). The 50 most-populated metro areas in the U.S. were ranked on three critical factors: repair affordability; price disparity range; shop integrity factor. *AutoMD.com, "Advocacy for Repair Shop Fairness Report," February 24, 2010*
- Phoenix appeared on Procter & Gamble's list of the "Top-20 All-Time Sweatiest Cities." The city was ranked #1. The rankings are based on computer simulations of the amount of sweat a person of average height and weight would produce walking around for an hour in the average temperatures during the summer months, based on historical weather data during June, July and August from 2001-2008 for each city. *Procter & Gamble, Old Spice Press Release, "Top-20 All-Time Sweatiest Cities," July 1, 2009*

Business Environment

CITY FINANCES

City Government Finances

Component	2009 ($000)	2009 ($ per capita)
Total Revenues	3,147,551	2,028
Total Expenditures	3,887,206	2,504
Debt Outstanding	7,814,925	5,035
Cash and Securities[1]	5,301,566	3,415

Note: (1) Cash and security holdings of a government at the close of its fiscal year, including those of its dependent agencies, utilities, and liquor stores.
Source: U.S Census Bureau, State & Local Government Finances 2009

City Government Revenue by Source

Source	2009 ($000)	2009 ($ per capita)
General Revenue		
From Federal Government	254,226	164
From State Government	709,970	457
From Local Governments	98,010	63
Taxes		
Property	315,549	203
Sales and Gross Receipts	676,845	436
Personal Income	0	0
Corporate Income	0	0
Motor Vehicle License	0	0
Other Taxes	65,623	42
Current Charges	809,417	521
Liquor Store	0	0
Utility	345,682	223
Employee Retirement	-335,727	-216

Source: U.S Census Bureau, State & Local Government Finances 2009

City Government Expenditures by Function

Function	2009 ($000)	2009 ($ per capita)	2009 (%)
General Direct Expenditures			
Air Transportation	437,286	282	11.2
Corrections	0	0	0.0
Education	19,837	13	0.5
Employment Security Administration	0	0	0.0
Financial Administration	29,721	19	0.8
Fire Protection	281,413	181	7.2
General Public Buildings	16,822	11	0.4
Governmental Administration, Other	25,106	16	0.6
Health	0	0	0.0
Highways	219,366	141	5.6
Hospitals	0	0	0.0
Housing and Community Development	171,522	110	4.4
Interest on General Debt	236,374	152	6.1
Judicial and Legal	51,662	33	1.3
Libraries	46,096	30	1.2
Parking	1,561	1	0.0
Parks and Recreation	425,391	274	10.9
Police Protection	473,862	305	12.2
Public Welfare	12,801	8	0.3
Sewerage	466,153	300	12.0
Solid Waste Management	122,233	79	3.1
Veterans' Services	0	0	0.0
Liquor Store	0	0	0.0
Utility	617,538	398	15.9
Employee Retirement	124,035	80	3.2

Source: U.S Census Bureau, State & Local Government Finances 2009

Municipal Bond Ratings

Area	Moody's	S&P	Fitch
City	Aa1	AAA	n/a

Rating Systems (shown in declining order of credit quality): Moody's– Aaa, Aa, A, Baa, Ba, B, Caa, Ca, C (numerical modifiers 1, 2, and 3 are added to letter-rating); S&P– AAA, AA, A, BBB, BB, B, CCC, CC, C; Fitch– AAA, AA, A, BBB, BB, B, CCC, CC, C. Ratings may be modified by the addition of a plus or minus sign to show relative standing within the major rating categories.
Notes: n/a Not Available; w/d Withdrawn (1) Not Reviewed; (2) Issuer Rating/No General Obligation; (3) Standard and Poor's Issue Credit Rating (ICR) is a current opinion of an obliger with respect to a specific financial obligation, a specific class of financial obligations, or a specific financial program.
Source: U.S. Census Bureau, 2012 Statistical Abstract, Bond Ratings for City Governments by Largest Cities: 2010

DEMOGRAPHICS

Population Growth

Area	1990 Census	2000 Census	2010 Census	Population Growth (%) 1990-2000	Population Growth (%) 2000-2010
City	989,873	1,321,045	1,445,632	33.5	9.4
MSA[1]	2,238,480	3,251,876	4,192,887	45.3	28.9
U.S.	248,709,873	281,421,906	308,745,538	13.2	9.7

Note: (1) Figures cover the Phoenix-Mesa-Glendale, AZ Metropolitan Statistical Area—see Appendix B for areas included
Source: U.S. Census Bureau, 2010 Census

Household Size

Area	Persons in Household (%) One	Two	Three	Four	Five	Six	Seven or More	Average Household Size
City	27.1	28.8	15.3	13.3	7.9	4.0	3.7	2.77
MSA[1]	25.4	33.2	14.8	13.2	7.3	3.4	2.8	2.68
U.S.	26.7	32.8	16.1	13.4	6.5	2.6	1.9	2.58

Note: (1) Figures cover the Phoenix-Mesa-Glendale, AZ Metropolitan Statistical Area—see Appendix B for areas included
Source: U.S. Census Bureau, 2010 Census

Race

Area	White Alone[2] (%)	Black Alone[2] (%)	Asian Alone[2] (%)	AIAN[3] Alone[2] (%)	NHOPI[4] Alone[2] (%)	Other Race Alone[2] (%)	Two or More Races (%)
City	65.9	6.5	3.2	2.2	0.2	18.5	3.6
MSA[1]	73.0	5.0	3.3	2.4	0.2	12.7	3.5
U.S.	72.4	12.6	4.8	0.9	0.2	6.2	2.9

Note: (1) Figures cover the Phoenix-Mesa-Glendale, AZ Metropolitan Statistical Area—see Appendix B for areas included; (2) Alone is defined as not being in combination with one or more other races; (3) American Indian and Alaska Native; (4) Native Hawaiian and Other Pacific Islander
Source: U.S. Census Bureau, 2010 Census

Hispanic or Latino Origin

Area	Hispanic or Latino (%)	Mexican (%)	Puerto Rican (%)	Cuban (%)	Other Hispanic or Latino (%)
City	40.8	35.9	0.6	0.3	4.0
MSA[1]	29.5	25.5	0.6	0.2	3.2
U.S.	16.3	10.3	1.5	0.6	4.0

Note: Persons of Hispanic or Latino origin can be of any race; (1) Figures cover the Phoenix-Mesa-Glendale, AZ Metropolitan Statistical Area—see Appendix B for areas included
Source: U.S. Census Bureau, 2010 Census

Segregation

Type	Segregation Indices[1]				Percent Change		
	1990	2000	2010	2010 Rank[2]	1990-2000	1990-2010	2000-2010
Black/White	50.1	45.1	43.6	86	-5.0	-6.4	-1.5
Asian/White	28.1	30.1	32.7	85	2.0	4.6	2.6
Hispanic/White	48.6	52.2	49.3	28	3.5	0.7	-2.8

Note: Figures are based on an analysis of 1990, 2000, and 2010 Census Decennial Census tract data by William H. Frey, Brookings Institution and the University of Michigan Social Science Data Analysis Network. In this analysis all racial groups (whites, blacks, and asians) are non-Hispanic members of those races. Hispanics are shown as a separate category; All figures cover the Metropolitan Statistical Area (see Appendix B for areas included); (1) Segregation Indices are Dissimilarity Indices that measure the degree to which the minority group is distributed differently than whites across census tracts. They range from 0 (complete integration) to 100 (complete segregation) where the value indicates the percentage of the minority group that needs to move to be distributed exactly like whites; (2) Ranges from 1 (most segregated) to 102 (least segregated); n/a not available.
Source: www.CensusScope.org

Ancestry

Area	German	Irish	English	American	Italian	Polish	French[2]	Scottish	Dutch
City	12.8	9.0	7.0	3.7	4.1	2.4	2.1	1.5	1.2
MSA[1]	16.0	10.5	9.3	5.1	4.9	2.8	2.7	1.9	1.5
U.S.	16.1	11.6	8.8	6.1	5.7	3.2	3.0	1.9	1.6

Note: Figures are the percentage of the total population reporting a particular ancestry. The nine most commonly reported ancestries in the U.S. are shown. Figures include multiple ancestries (e.g. if a person reported being Irish and Italian, they were included in both columns); (1) Figures cover the Phoenix-Mesa-Glendale, AZ Metropolitan Statistical Area—see Appendix B for areas included; (2) Excludes Basque
Source: U.S. Census Bureau, 2008-2010 American Community Survey 3-Year Estimates

Foreign-Born Population

Area	Percent of Population Born in								
	Any Foreign Country	Mexico	Asia	Europe	Carribean	South America	Central America[2]	Africa	Canada
City	21.0	14.7	2.7	1.4	0.3	0.3	0.7	0.7	0.3
MSA[1]	14.9	8.8	2.7	1.4	0.2	0.3	0.5	0.4	0.6
U.S.	12.8	3.8	3.6	1.6	1.2	0.9	1.0	0.5	0.3

Note: (1) Figures cover the Phoenix-Mesa-Glendale, AZ Metropolitan Statistical Area—see Appendix B for areas included; (2) Excludes Mexico.
Source: U.S. Census Bureau, 2008-2010 American Community Survey 3-Year Estimates

Marital Status

Area	Never Married	Now Married[2]	Separated	Widowed	Divorced
City	37.4	44.3	1.9	4.2	12.1
MSA[1]	31.8	49.9	1.6	5.0	11.7
U.S.	31.6	49.6	2.2	6.1	10.7

Note: Figures are percentages and cover the population 15 years of age and older; (1) Figures cover the Phoenix-Mesa-Glendale, AZ Metropolitan Statistical Area—see Appendix B for areas included; (2) Excludes separated
Source: U.S. Census Bureau, 2008-2010 American Community Survey 3-Year Estimates

Age

Area	Percent of Population							Median Age
	Under Age 5	Age 5 to 17	Age 18 to 34	Age 35 to 49	Age 50 to 64	Age 65 to 79	80 Years and Over	
City	8.3	20.0	25.9	21.3	16.1	6.3	2.1	32.2
MSA[1]	7.5	19.0	24.0	20.5	16.8	9.1	3.2	34.7
U.S.	6.5	17.5	23.2	20.7	19.0	9.4	3.6	37.2

Note: (1) Figures cover the Phoenix-Mesa-Glendale, AZ Metropolitan Statistical Area—see Appendix B for areas included
Source: U.S. Census Bureau, 2010 Census

Male/Female Ratio

Area	Males	Females	Males per 100 Females
City	725,020	720,612	100.6
MSA[1]	2,085,630	2,107,257	99.0
U.S.	151,781,326	156,964,212	96.7

Note: (1) Figures cover the Phoenix-Mesa-Glendale, AZ Metropolitan Statistical Area—see Appendix B for areas included
Source: U.S. Census Bureau, 2010 Census

Religious Groups

Area	Catholic	Baptist	Non-Den.	Methodist[2]	Lutheran	LDS[3]	Pente-costal	Presby-terian[4]	Muslim[5]	Judaism
MSA[1]	13.4	3.5	5.2	1.0	1.6	6.1	2.9	0.6	0.3	0.2
U.S.	19.1	9.3	4.0	4.0	2.3	2.0	1.9	1.6	0.8	0.7

Note: Figures are the number of adherents as a percentage of the total population; (1) Figures cover the Phoenix-Mesa-Glendale, AZ Metropolitan Statistical Area—see Appendix B for areas included; (2) Methodist/Pietist; (3) Latter Day Saints; (4) Reformed; (5) Figures are estimates
Source: Association of Statisticians of American Religious Bodies, 2010 U.S. Religion Census: Religious Congregations & Membership Study

ECONOMY

Gross Metropolitan Product

Area	2007	2008	2009	2010	2010 Rank[2]
MSA[1]	196.4	196.0	187.4	190.6	15

Note: Figures are in billions of dollars; (1) Figures cover the Phoenix-Mesa-Glendale, AZ Metropolitan Statistical Area—see Appendix B for areas included; (2) Rank ranges from 1 to 363
Source: The United States Conference of Mayors, "U.S. Metro Economies: GMP and Employment Forecasts," June 2011

Economic Growth

Area	2007-2009 (%)	2010 (%)	2011 (%)	Rank[2]
MSA[1]	-3.9	0.9	2.1	303
U.S.	-1.3	2.9	2.5	–

Note: Figures are real Gross Metropolitan Product growth rates and represent annual average percent change; (1) Figures cover the Phoenix-Mesa-Glendale, AZ Metropolitan Statistical Area—see Appendix B for areas included; (2) Rank ranges from 1 to 363
Source: The United States Conference of Mayors, "U.S. Metro Economies: GMP and Employment Forecasts," June 2011

Metropolitan Area Exports

Area	2005	2006	2007	2008	2009	2010	2010 Rank[2]
MSA[1]	8,473.0	10,954.8	12,818.2	12,623.6	7,947.5	9,342.7	29

Note: Figures are in millions of dollars; (1) Figures cover the Phoenix-Mesa-Glendale, AZ Metropolitan Statistical Area—see Appendix B for areas included; (2) Rank ranges from 1 to 369
Source: U.S. Department of Commerce, International Trade Administration, Office of Trade & Industry Information, Manufacturing & Services, data extracted April 2, 2012

INCOME

Income

Area	Per Capita ($)	Median Household ($)	Average Household ($)
City	23,626	47,187	65,034
MSA[1]	26,243	52,904	70,586
U.S.	26,942	51,222	70,116

Note: (1) Figures cover the Phoenix-Mesa-Glendale, AZ Metropolitan Statistical Area—see Appendix B for areas included
Source: U.S. Census Bureau, 2008-2010 American Community Survey 3-Year Estimates

Household Income Distribution

Area	Percent of Households Earning							
	Under $15,000	$15,000 -24,999	$25,000 -34,999	$35,000 -49,999	$50,000 -74,999	$75,000 -99,000	$100,000 -149,999	$150,000 and up
City	14.3	11.3	11.7	15.3	17.8	11.3	11.3	7.1
MSA[1]	11.1	10.1	10.7	15.1	19.5	12.7	12.9	7.9
U.S.	13.0	11.0	10.6	14.2	18.5	12.1	12.2	8.4

Note: (1) Figures cover the Phoenix-Mesa-Glendale, AZ Metropolitan Statistical Area—see Appendix B for areas included
Source: U.S. Census Bureau, 2008-2010 American Community Survey 3-Year Estimates

Poverty Rate

Area	All Ages	Under 18 Years Old	18 to 64 Years Old	65 Years and Over
City	20.7	29.8	18.1	9.7
MSA[1]	14.9	21.2	13.6	7.1
U.S.	14.4	20.1	13.1	9.4

Note: Figures are percentage of people whose income during the past 12 months was below the poverty level; (1) Figures cover the Phoenix-Mesa-Glendale, AZ Metropolitan Statistical Area—see Appendix B for areas included
Source: U.S. Census Bureau, 2008-2010 American Community Survey 3-Year Estimates

Personal Bankruptcy Filing Rate

Area	2006	2007	2008	2009	2010	2011
Maricopa County	1.40	1.87	3.47	6.22	7.81	6.60
U.S.	2.00	2.73	3.53	4.61	4.97	4.37

Note: Numbers are per 1,000 population and include Chapter 7 and Chapter 13 filings
Source: Federal Deposit Insurance Corporation, Regional Economic Conditions, March 9, 2012

EMPLOYMENT

Labor Force and Employment

Area	Civilian Labor Force			Workers Employed		
	Dec. 2010	Dec. 2011	% Chg.	Dec. 2010	Dec. 2011	% Chg.
City	800,878	800,658	0.0	722,214	728,367	0.9
MSA[1]	2,125,593	2,127,867	0.1	1,944,188	1,960,752	0.9
U.S.	153,156,000	153,373,000	0.1	139,159,000	140,681,000	1.1

Note: Data is not seasonally adjusted and covers workers 16 years of age and older; (1) Metropolitan Statistical Area—see Appendix B for areas included
Source: Bureau of Labor Statistics, http://stats.bls.gov

Unemployment Rate

Area	2011											
	Jan.	Feb.	Mar.	Apr.	May	Jun.	Jul.	Aug.	Sep.	Oct.	Nov.	Dec.
City	10.7	10.2	10.0	9.4	9.2	10.3	10.0	9.7	9.3	9.3	8.8	9.0
MSA[1]	9.3	8.8	8.7	8.1	8.0	9.0	8.7	8.4	8.0	8.1	7.7	7.9
U.S.	9.8	9.5	9.2	8.7	8.7	9.3	9.3	9.1	8.8	8.5	8.2	8.3

Note: Data is not seasonally adjusted and covers workers 16 years of age and older; All figures are percentages; (1) Metropolitan Statistical Area—see Appendix B for areas included
Source: Bureau of Labor Statistics, http://stats.bls.gov

Projected Unemployment Rate

Area	2010 (%)	2011 (%)	2012 (%)	2013 (%)
MSA[1]	8.9	8.4	7.9	7.3

Note: (1) Metropolitan Statistical Area—see Appendix B for areas included
Source: The United States Conference of Mayors, "U.S. Metro Economies: GMP and Employment Forecasts," June 2011

Employment by Occupation

Occupation Classification	City (%)	MSA[1] (%)	U.S. (%)
Management, Business, Science, and Arts	33.4	35.7	35.6
Natural Resources, Construction, and Maintenance	10.7	9.5	9.5
Production, Transportation, and Material Moving	10.3	9.4	12.1
Sales and Office	26.9	27.7	25.2
Service	18.6	17.6	17.6

Note: Figures cover employed civilians 16 years of age and older; (1) Figures cover the Phoenix-Mesa-Glendale, AZ Metropolitan Statistical Area—see Appendix B for areas included
Source: U.S. Census Bureau, 2008-2010 American Community Survey 3-Year Estimates

Employment by Industry

Sector	MSA[1]		U.S.
	Number of Employees	Percent of Total	Percent of Total
Construction	82,200	4.7	4.1
Education and Health Services	255,000	14.6	15.2
Financial Activities	143,100	8.2	5.8
Government	236,600	13.5	16.8
Information	28,600	1.6	2.0
Leisure and Hospitality	180,200	10.3	9.9
Manufacturing	112,000	6.4	8.9
Mining and Logging	3,300	0.2	0.6
Other Services	63,500	3.6	4.0
Professional and Business Services	282,900	16.2	13.3
Retail Trade	218,700	12.5	11.5
Transportation and Utilities	62,200	3.6	3.8
Wholesale Trade	81,800	4.7	4.2

Note: Figures cover non-farm employment as of December 2011 and are not seasonally adjusted; (1) Metropolitan Statistical Area—see Appendix B for areas included
Source: Bureau of Labor Statistics, http://stats.bls.gov

Occupations with Greatest Projected Employment Growth: 2008 – 2018

Occupation[1]	2008 Employment	2018 Projected Employment	Numeric Employment Change	Percent Employment Change
Customer Service Representatives	64,870	74,760	9,890	15.2
Registered Nurses	40,510	50,010	9,500	23.5
Combined Food Preparation and Serving Workers, Including Fast Food	43,970	52,950	8,980	20.4
Retail Salespersons	86,670	94,880	8,210	9.5
Cashiers	62,340	67,580	5,240	8.4
Waiters and Waitresses	50,230	55,440	5,210	10.4
Stock Clerks and Order Fillers	41,050	46,200	5,150	12.5
Office Clerks, General	60,330	64,570	4,240	7.0
Postsecondary Teachers	32,770	36,940	4,170	12.7
Accountants and Auditors	28,320	32,250	3,930	13.9

Note: Projections cover Arizona; (1) Sorted by numeric employment change
Source: www.projectionscentral.com, State Occupational Projections, 2008–2018 Long-Term Projections

Fastest Growing Occupations: 2008 – 2018

Occupation[1]	2008 Employment	2018 Projected Employment	Numeric Employment Change	Percent Employment Change
Biomedical Engineers	240	370	130	54.2
Credit Authorizers, Checkers, and Clerks	7,080	10,760	3,680	52.0
Network Systems and Data Communications Analysts	4,590	6,450	1,860	40.5
Medical Scientists, Except Epidemiologists	880	1,220	340	38.6
Radiation Therapists	610	820	210	34.4
Physician Assistants	1,290	1,730	440	34.1
Dental Hygienists	2,690	3,570	880	32.7
Pharmacy Technicians	7,700	10,170	2,470	32.1
Surgical Technologists	1,560	2,050	490	31.4
Dental Assistants	6,320	8,280	1,960	31.0

Note: Projections cover Arizona; (1) Sorted by percent employment change and excludes occupations with numeric employment change less than 100
Source: www.projectionscentral.com, State Occupational Projections, 2008–2018 Long-Term Projections

Average Wages

Occupation	$/Hr.	Occupation	$/Hr.
Accountants and Auditors	29.62	Maids and Housekeeping Cleaners	9.60
Automotive Mechanics	19.98	Maintenance and Repair Workers	17.63
Bookkeepers	17.77	Marketing Managers	52.33
Carpenters	19.96	Nuclear Medicine Technologists	35.95
Cashiers	10.97	Nurses, Licensed Practical	25.14
Clerks, General Office	14.89	Nurses, Registered	35.74
Clerks, Receptionists/Information	13.73	Nursing Aides/Orderlies/Attendants	13.23
Clerks, Shipping/Receiving	14.26	Packers and Packagers, Hand	10.78
Computer Programmers	37.73	Physical Therapists	37.94
Computer Support Specialists	23.79	Postal Service Mail Carriers	25.15
Computer Systems Analysts	36.35	Real Estate Brokers	n/a
Cooks, Restaurant	14.05	Retail Salespersons	12.05
Dentists	89.20	Sales Reps., Exc. Tech./Scientific	30.16
Electrical Engineers	47.97	Sales Reps., Tech./Scientific	39.60
Electricians	21.37	Secretaries, Exc. Legal/Med./Exec.	15.99
Financial Managers	51.98	Security Guards	13.08
First-Line Supervisors/Managers, Sales	19.48	Surgeons	n/a
Food Preparation Workers	10.57	Teacher Assistants	11.00
General and Operations Managers	51.63	Teachers, Elementary School	20.60
Hairdressers/Cosmetologists	11.42	Teachers, Secondary School	21.00
Internists	93.77	Telemarketers	14.81
Janitors and Cleaners	11.50	Truck Drivers, Heavy/Tractor-Trailer	20.92
Landscaping/Groundskeeping Workers	11.12	Truck Drivers, Light/Delivery Svcs.	17.50
Lawyers	62.72	Waiters and Waitresses	10.36

Note: Wage data covers the Phoenix-Mesa-Glendale, AZ Metropolitan Statistical Area—see Appendix B for areas included. Hourly wages for elementary/secondary school teachers and teacher assistants were calculated by the editors from annual wage data assuming a 40 hour work week; n/a not available.
Source: Bureau of Labor Statistics, Metro Area Occupational Employment and Wage Estimates, May 2011

RESIDENTIAL REAL ESTATE

Building Permits

Area	Single-Family			Multi-Family			Total		
	2010	2011	Pct. Chg.	2010	2011	Pct. Chg.	2010	2011	Pct. Chg.
City	1,111	952	-14.3	584	676	15.8	1,695	1,628	-4.0
MSA[1]	7,212	7,297	1.2	1,088	1,784	64.0	8,300	9,081	9.4
U.S.	447,311	418,498	-6.4	157,299	205,563	30.7	604,610	624,061	3.2

Note: (1) Metropolitan Statistical Area—see Appendix B for areas included; figures represent new, privately-owned housing units authorized (unadjusted data); All permit data are based on estimates with imputation.
Source: U.S. Census Bureau, Manufacturing, Mining, and Construction Statistics, Building Permits, 2010, 2011

Homeownership Rate

Area	2005 (%)	2006 (%)	2007 (%)	2008 (%)	2009 (%)	2010 (%)	2011 (%)
MSA[1]	71.2	72.5	70.8	70.2	69.8	66.5	63.3
U.S.	68.9	68.8	68.1	67.8	67.4	66.9	66.1

Note: (1) Metropolitan Statistical Area—see Appendix B for areas included
Source: U.S. Census Bureau, Housing Vacancies and Homeownership Annual Statistics: 2011

Housing Vacancy Rates

Area	Gross Vacancy Rate[2] (%)			Year-Round Vacancy Rate[3] (%)			Rental Vacancy Rate[4] (%)			Homeowner Vacancy Rate[5] (%)		
	2009	2010	2011	2009	2010	2011	2009	2010	2011	2009	2010	2011
MSA[1]	18.6	18.4	16.7	13.2	12.9	10.8	18.3	16.3	10.9	3.1	2.9	3.1
U.S.	14.5	14.3	14.2	11.3	11.3	11.1	10.6	10.2	9.5	2.6	2.6	2.5

Note: (1) Metropolitan Statistical Area—see Appendix B for areas included; (2) The percentage of the total housing inventory that is vacant; (3) The percentage of the housing inventory (excluding seasonal units) that is year-round vacant; (4) The percentage of rental inventory that is vacant for rent; (5) The percentage of homeowner inventory that is vacant for sale
Source: U.S. Census Bureau, Housing Vacancies and Homeownership Annual Statistics: 2011

TAXES

State Corporate Income Tax Rates

State	Tax Rate (%)	Income Brackets ($)	Num. of Brackets	Financial Institution Tax Rate (%)[a]	Federal Income Tax Ded.
Arizona	6.968 (b)	Flat rate	1	6.968 (b)	No

Note: Tax rates as of January 1, 2012; (a) Rates listed are the corporate income tax rate applied to financial institutions or excise taxes based on income. Some states have other taxes based upon the value of deposits or shares; (b) Minimum tax is $50 in Arizona, $100 in District of Columbia, $50 in North Dakota (banks), $500 in Rhode Island, $200 per location in South Dakota (banks), $100 in Utah, $250 in Vermont.
Source: Federation of Tax Administrators, "State Corporate Income Tax Rates, 2012"

State Individual Income Tax Rates

State	Tax Rate (%)	Income Brackets ($)	Num. of Brackets	Personal Exempt. ($)[1] Single	Personal Exempt. ($)[1] Dependents	Fed. Inc. Tax Ded.
Arizona	2.59 - 4.54	10,000 (b)-150,001 (b)	5	2,100	2,100	No

Note: Tax rates as of January 1, 2012; Local- and county-level taxes are not included; n/a not applicable; (1) Married joint filers generally receive double the single exemption; (b) For joint returns, taxes are twice the tax on half the couple's income.
Source: Federation of Tax Administrators, "State Individual Income Tax Rates, 2012"

Various State and Local Tax Rates

State	State and Local Sales and Use (%)	State Sales and Use (%)	Gasoline[1] (¢/gal.)	Cigarette[2] ($/pack)	Spirits[3] ($/gal.)	Wine[4] ($/gal.)	Beer[5] ($/gal.)
Arizona	9.3	6.60	19.0	2.00	3.00	0.84	0.16

Note: All tax rates as of January 1, 2012 except beer, wine and spirits (September 1, 2011); (1) The American Petroleum Institute has developed a methodology for determining the average tax rate on a gallon of fuel. Rates may include any of the following: excise taxes, environmental fees, storage tank fees, other fees or taxes, general sales tax, and local taxes. In states where gasoline is subject to the general sales tax, or where the fuel tax is based on the average sale price, the average rate determined by API is sensitive to changes in the price of gasoline. States that fully or partially apply general sales taxes to gasoline: CA, CO, GA, IL, IN, MI, NY; (2) The federal excise tax of $1.0066 per pack and local taxes are not included; (3) Rates are those applicable to off-premise sales of 40% alcohol by volume (a.b.v.) distilled spirits in 750ml containers. Local excise taxes are excluded; (4) Rates are those applicable to off-premise sales of 11% a.b.v. non-carbonated wine in 750ml containers; (5) Rates are those applicable to off-premise sales of 4.7% a.b.v. beer in 12 ounce containers.
Source: Tax Foundation, 2012 Facts & Figures: How Does Your State Compare?

State-Local Tax Burdens

Area	Rate (%)	Rank[1]	Per Capita Taxes Paid to Home State ($)	Total State and Local Per Capita Taxes Paid ($)	Per Capita Income ($)
Arizona	8.7	38	2,177	3,140	36,228
U.S. Average	9.8	-	3,057	4,160	42,539

Note: Figures cover 2009; (1) Rank ranges from 1 to 50 where 1 is highest tax burden
Source: Tax Foundation, State-Local Tax Burdens, All States, 2009

State Business Tax Climate Index Rankings

State	Overall Rank	Corporate Tax Index Rank	Individual Income Tax Index Rank	Sales Tax Index Rank	Unemployment Insurance Tax Index Rank	Property Tax Index Rank
Arizona	27	28	17	50	1	5

Note: The index is a measure of how each state's tax laws affect economic performance. The lower the rank, the more favorable a state's tax system is for business. States without a given tax are given a ranking of 1.
Source: Tax Foundation, Major Components of the State Business Tax Climate Index, FY 2012

COMMERCIAL REAL ESTATE

Office Market

Market Area	Inventory (sq. ft.)	Vacant (sq. ft.)	Vac. Rate (%)	Under Constr. (sq. ft.)	Asking Rent ($/sf/yr) Class A	Asking Rent ($/sf/yr) Class B
Phoenix	68,508,745	18,987,702	27.7	210,202	23.46	18.55

Source: Grubb & Ellis, Office Markets Trends, 4th Quarter 2011

Industrial Market

Market Area	Inventory (sq. ft.)	Vacant (sq. ft.)	Vac. Rate (%)	Under Constr. (sq. ft.)	Asking Rent ($/sf/yr) WH/Dist	Asking Rent ($/sf/yr) R&D/Flex
Phoenix	272,186,144	35,152,622	12.9	1,713,983	4.44	11.64

Source: Grubb & Ellis, Industrial Markets Trends, 4th Quarter 2011

COMMERCIAL UTILITIES

Typical Monthly Electric Bills

Area	Commercial Service ($/month) 1,500 kWh	Commercial Service ($/month) 40 kW demand 14,000 kWh	Industrial Service ($/month) 1,000 kW demand 200,000 kWh	Industrial Service ($/month) 50,000 kW demand 15,000,000 kWh
City	253	1,761	27,301	1,499,060
Average[1]	189	1,616	25,197	1,470,813

Note: Based on total rates in effect July 1, 2011; (1) average based on 184 utilities surveyed
Source: Edison Electric Institute, Typical Bills and Average Rates Report, Summer 2011

TRANSPORTATION

Means of Transportation to Work

Area	Car/Truck/Van Drove Alone	Car/Truck/Van Car-pooled	Public Transportation Bus	Public Transportation Subway	Public Transportation Railroad	Bicycle	Walked	Other Means	Worked at Home
City	74.4	13.2	3.3	0.0	0.0	0.7	1.8	1.5	5.1
MSA[1]	76.2	12.2	2.1	0.0	0.0	0.7	1.6	1.6	5.5
U.S.	76.0	10.2	2.7	1.7	0.5	0.5	2.8	1.3	4.2

Note: Figures are percentages and cover workers 16 years of age and older; (1) Figures cover the Phoenix-Mesa-Glendale, AZ Metropolitan Statistical Area—see Appendix B for areas included
Source: U.S. Census Bureau, 2008-2010 American Community Survey 3-Year Estimates

Travel Time to Work

Area	Less Than 10 Minutes	10 to 19 Minutes	20 to 29 Minutes	30 to 44 Minutes	45 to 59 Minutes	60 to 89 Minutes	90 Minutes or More
City	9.9	29.5	23.9	25.2	6.6	3.6	1.3
MSA[1]	10.6	27.5	21.9	24.9	8.7	4.9	1.5
U.S.	13.9	30.1	20.8	19.8	7.5	5.5	2.5

Note: Figures are percentages and include workers 16 years old and over; (1) Figures cover the Phoenix-Mesa-Glendale, AZ Metropolitan Statistical Area—see Appendix B for areas included
Source: U.S. Census Bureau, 2008-2010 American Community Survey 3-Year Estimates

Travel Time Index

Area	1985	1990	1995	2000	2005	2010
Urban Area[1]	1.10	1.11	1.11	1.18	1.21	1.21
Average[2]	1.11	1.16	1.18	1.21	1.25	1.20

Note: Travel Time Index—the ratio of travel time in the peak period to the travel time at free-flow conditions. A value of 1.30 indicates a 20-minute free-flow trip takes 26 minutes in the peak. Free-flow speeds (60 mph on freeways and 35 mph on principal arterials) are used as the comparison threshold; (1) Covers the Phoenix AZ urban area; (2) average of 439 urban areas
Source: Texas Transportation Institute, Urban Mobility Report 2011, September 2011

Public Transportation

Agency Name / Mode of Transportation	Vehicles Operated in Maximum Service	Annual Unlinked Passenger Trips ('000)	Annual Passenger Miles ('000)
City of Phoenix Public Transit Dept. (Valley Metro)			
Bus (purchased transportation)	450	37,181.5	138,158.1
Demand Response (directly operated)	45	160.8	1,113.9
Demand Response (purchased transportation)	105	358.4	3,103.6
Phoenix - VPSI Inc.			
Vanpool (directly operated)	342	1,049.6	26,836.8

Source: Federal Transit Administration, National Transit Database, 2010

Air Transportation

Airport Name and Code / Type of Service	Passenger Airlines[1]	Passenger Enplanements	Freight Carriers[2]	Freight (lbs.)
Phoenix Sky Harbor International (PHX)				
Domestic service (U.S. carriers - 2011)	31	18,643,720	29	236,320,096
International service (U.S. carriers - 2010)	8	811,320	5	448,583

Note: (1) Includes all U.S.-based major, minor and commuter airlines that carried at least one passenger during the year; (2) Includes all U.S.-based airlines and freight carriers that transported at least one pound of freight during the year
Source: Bureau of Transportation Statistics, The Intermodal Transportation Database, Air Carriers: T-100 Domestic Market (U.S. Carriers), 2011; Bureau of Transportation Statistics, The Intermodal Transportation Database, Air Carriers: T-100 International Market (U.S. Carriers), 2010

Other Transportation Statistics

Major Highways:	I-10; I-17
Amtrak Service:	Bus connection
Major Waterways/Ports:	None

Source: Amtrak.com; Google Maps

BUSINESSES

Major Business Headquarters

Company Name	Rankings	
	Fortune[1]	Forbes[2]
Apollo Group	452	-
Avnet	132	-
Freeport-McMoRan Copper & Gold	136	-
PetSmart	400	-
Republic Services	296	-

Note: (1) Fortune 500—companies that produce a 10-K are ranked 1 to 500 based on 2010 revenue; (2) all private companies with at least $2 billion in annual revenue are ranked 1 to 212; companies listed are headquartered in the city; dashes indicate no ranking
Source: Fortune, "Fortune 500," May 23, 2011; Forbes, "America's Largest Private Companies," November 16, 2011

Fast-Growing Businesses

According to *Inc.*, Phoenix is home to one of America's 500 fastest-growing private companies: **Celestech** (#443). Criteria: must be an independent, privately-held, for-profit, U.S. corporation, proprietorship or partnership; revenues must be at least $80,000 in 2007 and $2 million in 2010; must have four-year operating/sales history. Holding companies, regulated banks, and utilities were excluded. *Inc., "America's 500 Fastest-Growing Private Companies," September 2011*

According to *Initiative for a Competitive Inner City (ICIC)*, Phoenix is home to two of America's 100 fastest-growing "inner city" companies: **Auction Systems Auctioneers & Appraisers** (#27); **Keller Electrical Industries** (#98). Companies were ranked by their five-year compound annual growth rate. Criteria for inclusion: company must be headquartered in or have 51 percent or more of its physical operations in an economically distressed urban area; must be an independent, for-profit corporation, partnership or proprietorship; must have 10 or more employees and have a five-year sales history that includes sales of at least $200,000 in the base year and at least $1 million in the current year with no decrease in sales over the two most recent years. *Initiative for a Competitive Inner City (ICIC), "Inner City 100 Companies, 2011"*

Minority Business Opportunity

Phoenix is home to nine companies which are on the *Hispanic Business* 500 list (500 largest U.S. Hispanic-owned companies based on 2010 revenue): **Leadpoint Business Services** (#235); **Gaucho Ltd.** (#316); **Apodaca Wall System** (#392); **Garcia Express** (#395); **LawLogix Group** (#418); **Hernandez Companies** (#456); **ATL** (#468); **Gutierrez-Palmenberg** (#479); **State Technology & Manufacturing** (#483). Companies included must show at least 51 percent ownership by Hispanic U.S. citizens, and must maintain headquarters in one of the 50 states or Washington, D.C. *Hispanic Business, "Hispanic Business 500," June 2011*

Phoenix is home to one company which is on the *Hispanic Business* Fastest-Growing 100 list (greatest sales growth from 2006 to 2010): **LawLogix Group** (#30). Companies included must show at least 51 percent ownership by Hispanic U.S. citizens, and must maintain headquarters in one of the 50 states or Washington, D.C. In addition, companies must have minimum revenues of $200,000 for calendar year 2005. *Hispanic Business, July/August 2011*

Minority- and Women-Owned Businesses

Group	All Firms		Firms with Paid Employees			
	Firms	Sales ($000)	Firms	Sales ($000)	Employees	Payroll ($000)
Asian	4,173	1,441,105	1,240	1,301,808	8,257	229,530
Black	3,409	250,109	239	169,296	2,483	58,288
Hispanic	12,658	2,245,759	1,618	1,847,147	15,846	494,736
Women	30,006	6,885,198	4,152	6,036,357	44,707	1,451,500
All Firms	112,192	175,477,167	28,685	170,955,625	773,842	32,674,607

Note: Figures cover firms located in the city; minority- and women-owned business are defined as firms in which the corresponding group own 51% or more of the stock or equity of the company
Source: U.S. Census Bureau, 2007 Economic Census, Survey of Business Owners

HOTELS

Hotels/Motels

Area	5 Star Num.	5 Star Pct.[3]	4 Star Num.	4 Star Pct.[3]	3 Star Num.	3 Star Pct.[3]	2 Star Num.	2 Star Pct.[3]	1 Star Num.	1 Star Pct.[3]	Not Rated Num.	Not Rated Pct.[3]
City[1]	8	2.1	28	7.3	144	37.7	165	43.2	8	2.1	29	7.6
Total[2]	133	0.9	940	6.5	4,569	31.8	7,033	48.9	351	2.4	1,343	9.3

Note: (1) Figures cover Phoenix and vicinity; (2) Figures cover all 100 cities in this book; (3) Percentage of hotels which have a given star rating; Star ratings are determined by expedia.com and offer an indication of the general quality of a particular hotel.
Source: expedia.com, April 25, 2012

The Phoenix-Mesa-Glendale, AZ metro area is home to six of the best hotels in the U.S. according to *Travel & Leisure*: **Sanctuary on Camelback Mountain Resort & Spa** (#70); **Four Seasons Resort Scottsdale at Troon North** (#75); **Royal Palms Resort and Spa** (#99); **Hermosa Inn** (#141); **The Phoenician, A Luxury Collection Resort** (#146); **Montelucia Resort & Spa** (#163). Criteria: service; location; rooms; food; and value. *Travel & Leisure, "T+L 500, The World's Best Hotels 2012"*

EVENT SITES

Major Stadiums, Arenas, and Auditoriums

Name	Max. Capacity
Chase Field	49,033
Phoenix Convention Center	36,320
US Airways Center	18,422

Source: Original research

Convention Centers

Name	Overall Space (sq. ft.)	Exhibit Space (sq. ft.)	Meeting Space (sq. ft.)	Meeting Rooms
Phoenix Convention Center	2,000,000	n/a	900,000	n/a

Note: n/a not available
Source: Original research

Living Environment

COST OF LIVING

Cost of Living Index

Composite Index	Groceries	Housing	Utilities	Trans-portation	Health Care	Misc. Goods/Services
96.6	103.9	87.4	100.3	102.9	102.6	97.6

Note: U.S. = 100; Figures cover the Phoenix AZ urban area.
Source: The Council for Community and Economic Research, ACCRA Cost of Living Index, 2011

Grocery Prices

Area[1]	T-Bone Steak ($/pound)	Frying Chicken ($/pound)	Whole Milk ($/half gal.)	Eggs ($/dozen)	Orange Juice ($/64 oz.)	Coffee ($/11.5 oz.)
City[2]	9.12	1.20	2.26	1.77	3.18	4.97
Avg.	9.25	1.18	2.22	1.66	3.19	4.40
Min.	6.70	0.88	1.31	0.95	2.46	2.94
Max.	14.30	2.16	3.50	3.18	4.75	6.83

Note: (1) Values for the local area are compared with the average, minimum and maximum values for all 335 areas in the Cost of Living Index; (2) Figures cover the Phoenix AZ urban area; **T-Bone Steak** *(price per pound);* **Frying Chicken** *(price per pound, whole fryer);* **Whole Milk** *(half gallon carton);* **Eggs** *(price per dozen, Grade A, large);* **Orange Juice** *(64 oz. Tropicana or Florida Natural);* **Coffee** *(11.5 oz. can, vacuum-packed, Maxwell House, Hills Bros, or Folgers).*
Source: The Council for Community and Economic Research, ACCRA Cost of Living Index, 2011

Housing and Utility Costs

Area[1]	New Home Price ($)	Apartment Rent ($/month)	All Electric ($/month)	Part Electric ($/month)	Other Energy ($/month)	Telephone ($/month)
City[2]	241,396	889	184.74	-	-	22.17
Avg.	285,990	839	163.23	89.00	77.52	26.92
Min.	188,005	460	125.58	45.39	33.89	17.98
Max.	1,197,028	3,244	339.16	181.97	348.69	40.01

Note: (1) Values for the local area are compared with the average, minimum and maximum values for all 335 areas in the Cost of Living Index; (2) Figures cover the Phoenix AZ urban area; **New Home Price** *(2,400 sf living area, 8,000 sf lot, in urban area with full utilities);* **Apartment Rent** *(950 sf 2 bedroom/1.5 or 2 bath, unfurnished, excluding all utilities except water);* **All Electric** *(average monthly cost for an all-electric home);* **Part Electric** *(average monthly cost for a part-electric home);* **Other Energy** *(average monthly cost for natural gas, fuel oil, coal, wood, and any other forms of energy except electricity);* **Telephone** *(price includes basic monthly rate for a private residential line plus additional local usage charges incurred by a family of four).*
Source: The Council for Community and Economic Research, ACCRA Cost of Living Index, 2011

Health Care, Transportation, and Other Costs

Area[1]	Doctor ($/visit)	Dentist ($/visit)	Optometrist ($/visit)	Gasoline ($/gallon)	Beauty Salon ($/visit)	Men's Shirt ($)
City[2]	91.10	89.66	97.16	3.32	41.43	21.20
Avg.	93.88	81.72	90.54	3.48	32.65	25.06
Min.	60.00	55.33	53.66	3.18	19.78	13.44
Max.	154.98	145.97	183.72	4.31	63.21	46.00

Note: (1) Values for the local area are compared with the average, minimum and maximum values for all 335 areas in the Cost of Living Index; (2) Figures cover the Phoenix AZ urban area; **Doctor** *(general practitioners routine exam of an established patient);* **Dentist** *(adult teeth cleaning and periodic oral examination);* **Optometrist** *(full vision eye exam for established adult patient);* **Gasoline** *(one gallon regular unleaded, national brand, including all taxes, cash price at self-service pump if available);* **Beauty Salon** *(woman's shampoo, trim, and blow-dry);* **Men's Shirt** *(cotton/polyester dress shirt, pinpoint weave, long sleeves).*
Source: The Council for Community and Economic Research, ACCRA Cost of Living Index, 2011

HOUSING

House Price Index (HPI)

Area	National Ranking[2]	Quarterly Change (%)	One-Year Change (%)	Five-Year Change (%)
MSA[1]	275	2.67	-7.12	-47.78
U.S.[3]	-	-0.10	-2.43	-19.16

Note: The HPI is a weighted repeat sales index. It measures average price changes in repeat sales or refinancings on the same properties. This information is obtained by reviewing repeat mortgage transactions on single-family properties whose mortgages have been purchased or securitized by Fannie Mae or Freddie Mac in January 1975; (1) Metropolitan/Micropolitan Statistical Area—see Appendix B for areas included; (2) Rankings are based on annual percentage change for all metro areas containing at least 15,000 transactions over the last 10 years and ranges from 1 to 306; (3) figures based on a weighted average of Census Division estimates using a purchase only index; all figures are for the period ending December 31, 2011
Source: Federal Housing Finance Agency, House Price Index, February 23, 2012

House Price Valuations

Area	Q4 2005		Q4 2006		Q4 2007		Q4 2008		Q4 2009	
	Price ($000)	Over-valuation	Price ($000)	Over-valuation	Price ($000)	Over-valuation	Price ($000)	Over-valuation	Price ($000)	Over-valuation
MSA[1]	242.1	38.9	255.3	35.8	227.8	17.7	166.6	-12.9	146.5	-22.3

Note: Figures show the percentage of over- or under-valuation of single family homes relative to statistically normal house values (e.g. a value of 23.6 indicates that house values are 23.6% overvalued). Statistically normal house values are based on house prices, interest rates, household incomes, population densities, and any historical premiums or discounts metropolitan areas have exhibited over time; (1) Figures cover the Phoenix-Mesa-Glendale, AZ - see Appendix B for areas included
Source: Global Insight/PNC Financial Services Group, House Prices in America: 4th Quarter 2009 Update

Median Single-Family Home Prices

Area	2009	2010	2011p	Percent Change 2010 to 2011
MSA[1]	137.0	139.2	115.5	-17.0
U.S. Average	172.1	173.1	166.2	-4.0

Note: Figures are median sales prices of existing single-family homes in thousands of dollars; (p) preliminary; n/a not available; (1) Metropolitan Statistical Area—see Appendix B for areas included
Source: National Association of Realtors, Median Sales Price of Existing Single-Family Homes for Metropolitan Areas, 4th Quarter 2011

Affordability Index of Existing Single-Family Homes

Area	2009	2010	2011p	Percent Change 2010 to 2011
MSA[1]	126.3	129.7	162.0	24.9

Note: The housing affordability index measures whether or not a typical family could qualify for a mortgage loan on a typical home. The higher the index, the greater the household purchasing power. An index of 100 is defined as the point where a median-income household has exactly enough income to qualify for the purchase of a median-priced existing single-family home, assuming a 20 percent downpayment and 25 percent of gross income devoted to mortgage principal and interest payments; (p) preliminary; n/a not available; (1) Metropolitan Statistical Area—see Appendix B for areas included
Source: National Association of Realtors, Affordability Index of Existing Single-Family Homes, 2011

Median Apartment Condo-Coop Home Prices

Area	2009	2010	2011p	Percent Change 2010 to 2011
MSA[1]	101.1	79.4	65.9	-17.0
U.S. Average	175.6	171.7	165.1	-3.8

Note: Figures are median sales prices of existing apartment condo-coop homes in thousands of dollars; (p) preliminary; n/a not available; (1) Metropolitan Statistical Area—see Appendix B for areas included
Source: National Association of Realtors, Median Sales Price of Existing Apartment Condo-Coop Homes for Metropolitan Areas, 4th Quarter 2011

Year Housing Structure Built

Area	2005 or Later	2000 -2004	1990 -1999	1980 -1989	1970 -1979	1960 -1969	1950 -1959	Before 1950	Median Year
City	7.3	10.2	16.2	18.7	21.1	10.8	10.9	4.9	1981
MSA[1]	9.6	16.4	21.6	19.1	17.4	7.4	5.8	2.5	1989
U.S.	5.0	8.6	14.0	14.1	16.3	11.3	11.2	19.6	1975

Note: Figures are percentages except for Median Year; (1) Figures cover the Phoenix-Mesa-Glendale, AZ Metropolitan Statistical Area—see Appendix B for areas included
Source: U.S. Census Bureau, 2008-2010 American Community Survey 3-Year Estimates

HEALTH

Health Risk Data

Category	MSA[1] (%)	U.S. (%)
Adults who have been told they have high blood pressure[2]	25.2	28.7
Adults who have been told they have high blood cholesterol[2]	41.1	37.5
Adults who have been told they have diabetes[3]	7.1	8.7
Adults who have been told they have arthritis[2]	22.9	26.0
Adults who have been told they currently have asthma	9.6	9.1
Adults who are current smokers	14.8	17.3
Adults who are heavy drinkers[4]	4.5	5.0
Adults who are binge drinkers[5]	15.9	15.1
Adults who are overweight (BMI 25.0 - 29.9)	41.1	36.2
Adults who are obese (BMI 30.0 - 99.8)	22.8	27.5
Adults who participated in any physical activities in the past month	81.5	76.1
Adults 50+ who have ever had a sigmoidoscopy or colonoscopy	64.4	65.2
Women aged 40+ who have had a mammogram within the past two years	73.8	75.2
Men aged 40+ who have had a PSA test within the past two years	51.8	53.2
Adults aged 65+ who have had flu shot within the past year	68.8	67.5
Adults aged 18–64 who have any kind of health care coverage	84.8	82.2

Note: Data as of 2010 unless otherwise noted; (1) Figures cover the Phoenix-Mesa-Scottsdale, AZ Metropolitan Statistical Area—see Appendix B for areas included; (2) Data as of 2009; (3) Figures do not include pregnancy-related, borderline, or pre-diabetes; (4) Heavy drinkers are classified as males having more than two drinks per day or females having more than one drink per day; (5) Binge drinkers are classified as males having five or more drinks on one occasion or females having four or more drinks on one occasion
Source: Centers for Disease Control and Prevention, Behaviorial Risk Factor Surveillance System, SMART: Selected Metropolitan/Micropolitan Area Risk Trends, 2009, 2010

Mortality Rates for the Top 10 Causes of Death in the U.S.

ICD-10[a] Sub-Chapter	ICD-10[a] Code	Age-Adjusted Mortality Rate[1] per 100,000 population	
		County[2]	U.S.
Malignant neoplasms	C00-C97	145.7	175.6
Ischaemic heart diseases	I20-I25	111.8	121.6
Other forms of heart disease	I30-I51	20.0	48.6
Chronic lower respiratory diseases	J40-J47	39.8	42.3
Cerebrovascular diseases	I60-I69	30.2	40.6
Organic, including symptomatic, mental disorders	F01-F09	18.0	26.7
Other degenerative diseases of the nervous system	G30-G31	39.2	24.7
Other external causes of accidental injury	W00-X59	30.0	24.4
Diabetes mellitus	E10-E14	15.8	21.7
Hypertensive diseases	I10-I15	18.7	18.2

Note: (a) ICD-10 = International Classification of Diseases 10th Revision; (1) Mortality rates are a three year average covering 2007-2009; (2) Figures cover Maricopa County
Source: Centers for Disease Control and Prevention, National Center for Health Statistics. Underlying Cause of Death 1999-2009 on CDC WONDER Online Database, released 2012. Data for year 2009 are compiled from the Multiple Cause of Death File 2009, Series 20 No. 2O, 2012, Data for year 2008 are compiled from the Multiple Cause of Death File 2008, Series 20 No. 2N, 2011, Data for year 2007 are compiled from Multiple Cause of Death File 2007, Series 20 No. 2M, 2010.

Mortality Rates for Selected Causes of Death

ICD-10[a] Sub-Chapter	ICD-10[a] Code	Age-Adjusted Mortality Rate[1] per 100,000 population	
		County[2]	U.S.
Assault	X85-Y09	7.2	5.7
Human immunodeficiency virus (HIV) disease	B20-B24	1.9	3.3
Influenza and pneumonia	J09-J18	13.5	16.4
Intentional self-harm	X60-X84	14.1	11.5
Malnutrition	E40-E46	0.4	0.8
Obesity and other hyperalimentation	E65-E68	1.2	1.6
Transport accidents	V01-V99	12.5	13.7
Viral hepatitis	B15-B19	2.8	2.2

Note: (a) ICD-10 = International Classification of Diseases 10th Revision; (1) Mortality rates are a three year average covering 2007-2009; (2) Figures cover Maricopa County
Source: Centers for Disease Control and Prevention, National Center for Health Statistics. Underlying Cause of Death 1999-2009 on CDC WONDER Online Database, released 2012. Data for year 2009 are compiled from the Multiple Cause of Death File 2009, Series 20 No. 2O, 2012, Data for year 2008 are compiled from the Multiple Cause of Death File 2008, Series 20 No. 2N, 2011, Data for year 2007 are compiled from Multiple Cause of Death File 2007, Series 20 No. 2M, 2010.

Distribution of Physicians and Dentists

Area[1]	Dentists[2]	D.O.[3]	M.D.[4] Total	Family/ General Practice	Pediatrics	Medical Specialties	Surgical Specialties
Local (number)	1,754	1,213	6,438	712	454	2,415	1,424
Local (rate[5])	4.5	3.1	16.3	1.8	1.1	6.1	3.6
U.S. (rate[5])	4.5	1.9	18.3	2.5	1.4	6.8	4.1

Note: Data as of 2008 unless noted; (1) Local data covers Maricopa County; (2) Data as of 2007; (3) Doctor of Osteopathic Medicine; (4) Includes active, non-federal, patient-care, office-based Doctors of Medicine; (5) rate per 10,000 population
Source: Area Resource File (ARF). 2009-2010 Release. U.S. Department of Health and Human Services, Health Resources and Services Administration, Bureau of Health Professions, Rockville, MD, August 2010

Best Hospitals

According to *U.S. News,* the Phoenix-Mesa-Glendale, AZ is home to three of the best hospitals in the U.S.: **Banner Good Samaritan Medical Center** (4 specialties); **Mayo Clinic** (3 specialties); **St. Joseph's Hospital and Medical Center** (1 specialty). The hospitals listed were highly ranked in at least one adult specialty. *U.S. News Online, "America's Best Hospitals 2011-12"*

According to *U.S. News,* the Phoenix-Mesa-Glendale, AZ is home to one of the best children's hospitals in the U.S.: **Phoenix Children's Hospital** (5 specialties). The hospital listed was highly ranked in at least one pediatric specialty. *U.S. News Online, "America's Best Children's Hospitals 2011-12"*

EDUCATION

Public School District Statistics

District Name	Schls	Pupils	Pupil/ Teacher Ratio	Minority Pupils[1] (%)	Free Lunch Eligible[2] (%)	IEP[3] (%)
Alhambra Elementary District	15	14,498	21.8	92.4	72.0	9.6
Arizona Virtual Academy	1	4,276	n/a	23.5	34.1	12.9
Balsz Elementary District	5	2,848	17.5	92.7	3.9	10.5
Cartwright Elementary District	21	18,351	19.9	95.6	70.7	10.4
Creighton Elementary District	10	7,209	16.5	94.5	85.3	12.4
Deer Valley Unified District	38	36,241	19.3	22.8	14.9	9.1
Fowler Elementary District	7	4,551	17.5	91.4	71.6	10.7
Isaac Elementary District	14	7,936	19.5	98.8	1.4	10.8
Madison Elementary District	8	5,494	18.7	47.5	1.5	3.7
Murphy Elementary District	4	2,215	19.6	97.8	87.8	11.7
Osborn Elementary District	6	3,297	17.2	86.7	79.6	15.8
Paradise Valley Unified District	47	33,146	18.6	32.8	24.8	12.6
Pendergast Elementary District	15	10,290	20.2	80.1	53.7	10.8
Phoenix Elementary District	15	7,073	16.2	94.9	2.8	11.7
Phoenix Union High School District	16	25,187	16.9	93.9	70.6	12.3
Roosevelt Elementary District	21	11,129	18.0	97.1	80.1	11.0
Scottsdale Unified District	31	26,588	17.8	27.4	13.9	11.7

Note: Table includes school districts with 2,000 or more students; (1) Percentage of students that are not non-Hispanic white; (2) Percentage of students that are eligible for the free lunch program; (3) Percentage of students that have an Individualized Education Program.
Source: U.S. Department of Education, National Center for Education Statistics, Common Core of Data, Local Education Agency (School District) Universe Survey: School Year 2009-2010; U.S. Department of Education, National Center for Education Statistics, Common Core of Data, Public Elementary/Secondary School Universe Survey: School Year 2009-2010

Highest Level of Education

Area	Less than H.S.	H.S. Diploma	Some College, No Deg.	Associate Degree	Bachelors Degree	Masters Degree	Profess. School Degree	Doctorate Degree
City	20.2	24.3	23.2	7.1	16.2	6.3	1.9	0.8
MSA[1]	14.4	24.0	25.7	8.1	18.1	7.0	1.8	1.0
U.S.	14.7	28.4	21.3	7.6	17.6	7.2	1.9	1.2

Note: Figures cover persons age 25 and over; (1) Figures cover the Phoenix-Mesa-Glendale, AZ Metropolitan Statistical Area—see Appendix B for areas included
Source: U.S. Census Bureau, 2008-2010 American Community Survey 3-Year Estimates

Educational Attainment by Race

Area	High School Graduate or Higher (%)					Bachelor's Degree or Higher (%)				
	Total	White	Black	Asian	Hisp.[2]	Total	White	Black	Asian	Hisp.[2]
City	79.8	80.6	86.5	85.6	54.2	25.3	26.1	19.8	52.1	7.5
MSA[1]	85.6	86.7	89.3	89.3	60.3	27.8	28.5	23.0	53.4	10.1
U.S.	85.3	87.5	81.4	85.5	61.6	28.0	29.3	17.8	50.2	13.0

Note: Figures shown cover persons 25 years old and over; (1) Figures cover the Phoenix-Mesa-Glendale, AZ Metropolitan Statistical Area—see Appendix B for areas included; (2) People of Hispanic origin can be of any race
Source: U.S. Census Bureau, 2008-2010 American Community Survey 3-Year Estimates

School Enrollment by Grade and Control

Area	Preschool (%)		Kindergarten (%)		Grades 1 - 4 (%)		Grades 5 - 8 (%)		Grades 9 - 12 (%)	
	Public	Private	Public	Private	Public	Private	Public	Private	Public	Private
City	63.1	36.9	92.5	7.5	93.6	6.4	93.9	6.1	93.7	6.3
MSA[1]	55.9	44.1	91.0	9.0	92.9	7.1	94.0	6.0	94.4	5.6
U.S.	55.4	44.6	87.1	12.9	89.4	10.6	89.5	10.5	90.4	9.6

Note: Figures shown cover persons 3 years old and over; (1) Figures cover the Phoenix-Mesa-Glendale, AZ Metropolitan Statistical Area—see Appendix B for areas included
Source: U.S. Census Bureau, 2008-2010 American Community Survey 3-Year Estimates

Average Salaries of Public School Classroom Teachers

Area	2010-11 Dollars	2010-11 Rank[1]	2011-12 Dollars	2011-12 Rank[1]	Percent Change 2010-11 to 2011-12	Percent Change 2001-02 to 2011-12
Arizona	47,553	33	48,691	33	2.39	21.80
U.S. Average	55,623	-	56,643	-	1.83	26.8

Note: (1) State rank ranges from 1 to 51 where 1 indicates highest salary.
Source: National Education Association, Rankings & Estimates: Rankings of the States 2011 and Estimates of School Statistics 2012, December 2011

Higher Education

Four-Year Colleges			Two-Year Colleges			Medical Schools[1]	Law Schools[2]	Voc/ Tech[3]
Public	Private Non-profit	Private For-profit	Public	Private Non-profit	Private For-profit			
0	4	22	4	0	7	0	1	11

Note: Figures cover institutions located within the city limits and include main campuses only; (1) includes schools accredited by the Liaison Committee on Medical Education and the American Osteopathic Association's Commission on Osteopathic College Accreditation; (2) includes American Bar Association-accredited law schools; (3) includes all schools with programs that are less than 2 years.
Source: National Center for Education Statistics, Integrated Postsecondary Education System (IPEDS) Peer Analysis System, 2011-12; Association of American Medical Colleges, Member List, April 23, 2012; American Osteopathic Association, Member List, April 23, 2012; Law School Admission Council, Official Guide to ABA-Approved Law Schools Online, April 23, 2012

According to *U.S. News & World Report,* the Phoenix-Mesa-Glendale, AZ is home to one of the best national universities in the U.S.: **Arizona State University** (#132). The indicators used to capture academic quality fall into a number of categories: assessment by administrators at peer institutions; retention of students; faculty resources; student selectivity; financial resources; alumni giving; high school counselor ratings of colleges; and graduation rate.*U.S. News & World Report, "America's Best Colleges 2012"*

According to *U.S. News & World Report,* the Phoenix-Mesa-Glendale, AZ is home to one of the best law schools in the U.S.: **Arizona State University (O'Connor)** (#26). The rankings are based on a weighted average of 12 measures of quality: peer assessment score; assessment score by lawyers/judges; median LSAT scores; median undergrad GPA; acceptance rate; employment rates for graduates; placement success; bar passage rate; faculty resources; expenditures per student; student/faculty ratio; and library resources. *U.S. News & World Report, "America's Best Law Schools 2013"*

According to *Forbes,* the Phoenix-Mesa-Glendale, AZ is home to one of the best business schools in the U.S.: **Arizona State (Carey)** (#66). The rankings are based on the return on investment that graduates of the Class of 2006 received (median salary five years after graduation). *Forbes, "Best Business Schools," August 3, 2011*

PRESIDENTIAL ELECTION

2008 Presidential Election Results

Area	Obama	McCain	Nader	Other
Maricopa County	43.9	54.4	0.4	1.2
U.S.	52.9	45.6	0.6	0.9

Note: Results are percentages and may not add to 100% due to rounding
Source: Dave Leip's Atlas of U.S. Presidential Elections, www.uselectionatlas.org

EMPLOYERS

Major Employers

Company Name	Industry
Arizona Dept of Transportation	Regulation, administration of transportation
Arizona State University	University
Arizona State University	Libraries
Avnet	Electronic parts and equipment, nec
Carter & Burgess	Engineering services
Chase Bankcard Services	State commercial banks
City of Mesa	Executive offices
City of Phoenix	Administration of social and human resources
City of Phoenix	Executive offices
General Dynamics C4 Systems	Communications equipment, nec
Grand Canyon Education	Colleges and universities
Honeywell International	Aircraft engines and engine parts
Lockheed Martin Corporation	Search and navigation equipment
Paramount Building Solutions	Janitorial service, contract basis
Salt River Pima-Maricopa Indian Community	Gambling establishment
Scottsdale Healthcare Corp.	Hospital management
Scottsdale Healthcare Osborn Med Ctr	General medical and surgical hospitals
Swift Transportation Company	Trucking, except local
The Boeing Company	Helicopters
Veterans Health Administration	General medical and surgical hospitals

Note: Companies shown are located within the Phoenix-Mesa-Glendale, AZ metropolitan area.
Source: Hoovers.com, data extracted April 25 2012

PUBLIC SAFETY

Crime Rate

Area	All Crimes	Violent Crimes				Property Crimes		
		Murder	Forcible Rape	Robbery	Aggrav. Assault	Burglary	Larceny -Theft	Motor Vehicle Theft
City	4,491.2	7.6	33.8	210.4	266.3	1,011.8	2,461.2	500.1
Suburbs[1]	3,568.4	4.2	21.4	74.4	186.0	671.2	2,368.4	242.8
Metro[2]	3,905.4	5.5	25.9	124.1	215.3	795.6	2,402.3	336.8
U.S.	3,345.5	4.8	27.5	119.1	252.3	699.6	2,003.5	238.8

Note: Figures are crimes per 100,000 population; (1) All areas within the metro area that are located outside the city limits; (2) Metropolitan Statistical Area—see Appendix B for areas included
Source: FBI Uniform Crime Reports, 2010

Hate Crimes

Area	Number of Quarters Reported	Bias Motivation				
		Race	Religion	Sexual Orientation	Ethnicity	Disability
City	4	50	19	37	27	2

Source: Federal Bureau of Investigation, Hate Crime Statistics 2010

Identity Theft Consumer Complaints

Area	Complaints	Complaints per 100,000 Population	Rank[2]
MSA[1]	4,078	97.6	106
U.S.	279,156	90.4	-

Note: (1) Metropolitan Statistical Area—see Appendix B for areas included; (2) Rank ranges from 1 to 384 where 1 indicates greatest number of identity theft complaints per 100,000 population
Source: Federal Trade Commission, Consumer Sentinel Network Data Book for January–December 2011

Fraud and Other Consumer Complaints

Area	Complaints	Complaints per 100,000 Population	Rank[2]
MSA[1]	19,577	468.4	196
U.S.	1,533,924	496.8	-

Note: (1) Metropolitan Statistical Area—see Appendix B for areas included; (2) Rank ranges from 1 to 384 where 1 indicates greatest number of fraud and other complaints per 100,000 population
Source: Federal Trade Commission, Consumer Sentinel Network Data Book for January–December 2011

RECREATION

Culture

Dance[1]	Theatre[1]	Instrumental Music[1]	Vocal Music[1]	Series/ Festivals	Museums	Zoos and Aquariums[2]
1	1	2	4	3	22	1

Note: (1) Number of professional perfoming groups; (2) AZA-accredited
Source: The Grey House Performing Arts Directory, 2011-2012; Official Museum Directory, 2011; American Association of Museums, AAM Member Museums, April 2012; Association of Zoos & Aquariums, AZA Member Zoos & Aquariums, April 2012

Professional Sports Teams

Team Name	League
Arizona Cardinals	National Football League (NFL)
Arizona Diamondbacks	Major League Baseball (MLB)
Phoenix Coyotes	National Hockey League (NHL)
Phoenix Suns	National Basketball Association (NBA)

Note: Includes teams located in the Phoenix metro area.
Source: Original research

CLIMATE

Average and Extreme Temperatures

Temperature	Jan	Feb	Mar	Apr	May	Jun	Jul	Aug	Sep	Oct	Nov	Dec	Yr.
Extreme High (°F)	88	92	100	105	113	122	118	116	118	107	93	88	122
Average High (°F)	66	70	75	84	93	103	105	103	99	88	75	67	86
Average Temp. (°F)	53	57	62	70	78	88	93	91	85	74	62	54	72
Average Low (°F)	40	44	48	55	63	72	80	78	72	60	48	41	59
Extreme Low (°F)	17	22	25	37	40	51	66	61	47	34	27	22	17

Note: Figures cover the years 1948-1990
Source: National Climatic Data Center, International Station Meteorological Climate Summary, 9/96

Average Precipitation/Snowfall/Humidity

Precip./Humidity	Jan	Feb	Mar	Apr	May	Jun	Jul	Aug	Sep	Oct	Nov	Dec	Yr.
Avg. Precip. (in.)	0.7	0.6	0.8	0.3	0.1	0.1	0.8	1.0	0.7	0.6	0.6	0.9	7.3
Avg. Snowfall (in.)	Tr	Tr	0	0	0	0	0	0	0	0	0	Tr	Tr
Avg. Rel. Hum. 5am (%)	68	63	56	45	37	33	47	53	50	53	59	66	53
Avg. Rel. Hum. 5pm (%)	34	28	24	17	14	12	21	24	23	24	28	34	24

Note: Figures cover the years 1948-1990; Tr = Trace amounts (<0.05 in. of rain; <0.5 in. of snow)
Source: National Climatic Data Center, International Station Meteorological Climate Summary, 9/96

Weather Conditions

Temperature			Daytime Sky			Precipitation		
10°F & below	32°F & below	90°F & above	Clear	Partly cloudy	Cloudy	0.01 inch or more precip.	0.1 inch or more snow/ice	Thunder-storms
0	10	167	186	125	54	37	< 1	23

Note: Figures are average number of days per year and cover the years 1948-1990
Source: National Climatic Data Center, International Station Meteorological Climate Summary, 9/96

HAZARDOUS WASTE

Superfund Sites

Phoenix has one hazardous waste site on the EPA's Superfund Final National Priorities List: **Motorola, Inc. (52nd Street Plant)**. *U.S. Environmental Protection Agency, Final National Priorities List, April 17, 2012*

AIR & WATER QUALITY

Air Quality Index

Area	Percent of Days when Air Quality was...[2]					AQI Statistics[2]	
	Good	Moderate	Unhealthy for Sensitive Groups	Unhealthy	Very Unhealthy	Maximum	Median
Area[1]	23.6	65.2	7.1	2.2	1.9	565	61

Note: Air Quality Index (AQI) is an index for reporting daily air quality. EPA calculates the AQI for five major air pollutants regulated by the Clean Air Act: ground-level ozone, particle pollution (aka particulate matter), carbon monoxide, sulfur dioxide, and nitrogen dioxide. The AQI runs from 0 to 500. The higher the AQI value, the greater the level of air pollution and the greater the health concern. There are six AQI categories: "Good" AQI is between 0 and 50. Air quality is considered satisfactory; "Moderate" AQI is between 51 and 100. Air quality is acceptable; "Unhealthy for Sensitive Groups" When AQI values are between 101 and 150, members of sensitive groups may experience health effects; "Unhealthy" When AQI values are between 151 and 200 everyone may begin to experience health effects; "Very Unhealthy" AQI values between 201 and 300 trigger a health alert; "Hazardous" AQI values over 300 trigger warnings of emergency conditions (not shown); (1) Data covers Maricopa County; (2) Based on 365 days with AQI data in 2011.
Source: U.S. Environmental Protection Agency, AirData Report, 2011

Air Quality Index Pollutants

Area	Percent of Days when AQI Pollutant was...[2]					
	Carbon Monoxide	Nitrogen Dioxide	Ozone	Sulfur Dioxide	Particulate Matter 2.5	Particulate Matter 10
Area[1]	0.0	19.2	38.9	0.0	15.6	26.3

Note: The Air Quality Index (AQI) is an index for reporting daily air quality. EPA calculates the AQI for five major air pollutants regulated by the Clean Air Act: ground-level ozone, particle pollution (also known as particulate matter), carbon monoxide, sulfur dioxide, and nitrogen dioxide. The AQI runs from 0 to 500. The higher the AQI value, the greater the level of air pollution and the greater the health concern; (1) Data covers Maricopa County; (2) Based on 365 days with AQI data in 2011.
Source: U.S. Environmental Protection Agency, AirData Report, 2011

Air Quality Index Trends

Area	Trend Sites (days)								All Sites (days)
	2003	2004	2005	2006	2007	2008	2009	2010	2010
MSA[1]	51	23	49	50	21	27	10	11	43

Note: Figures are the number of days the AQI value exceeded 100 in a given year. An AQI value greater than 100 indicates that air quality would have been in the unhealthful range on that day. Data from exceptional events are included. These counts are presented in two ways. First, the counts are based on sites having an adequate record of monitoring data during the trend period (trend sites). These counts represent the relative change in the number of days with AQI values greater than 100. In the last column, the counts are based on all sites with data in the most recent year (because it is possible for a site to have data in the most recent year but not enough data to be a trend site); (1) Data covers the Phoenix-Mesa-Glendale, AZ—see Appendix B for areas included
Source: U.S. Environmental Protection Agency, Air Quality Index Information, "Number of Days with Air Quality Index Values Greater than 100 at Trend Sites, 2000-2010, and at All Sites in 2010"

Maximum Air Pollutant Concentrations: Particulate Matter, Ozone, CO and Lead

	Particulate Matter 10 (ug/m^3)	Particulate Matter 2.5 Wtd AM (ug/m^3)	Particulate Matter 2.5 24-Hr (ug/m^3)	Ozone (ppm)	Carbon Monoxide (ppm)	Lead (ug/m^3)
MSA[1] Level	226	12.4	27	0.079	3	n/a
NAAQS[2]	150	15	35	0.075	9	0.15
Met NAAQS[2]	No	Yes	Yes	No	Yes	n/a

Note: Data from exceptional events are not included; (1) Data covers the Phoenix-Mesa-Glendale, AZ—see Appendix B for areas included; (2) National Ambient Air Quality Standards; ppm = parts per million; ug/m^3 = micrograms per cubic meter; n/a not available
Concentrations: Particulate Matter 10 (coarse particulate)—highest second maximum 24-hour concentration; Particulate Matter 2.5 Wtd AM (fine particulate)—highest weighted annual mean concentration; Particulate Matter 2.5 24-Hour (fine particulate)—highest 98th percentile 24-hour concentration; Ozone—highest fourth daily maximum 8-hour concentration; Carbon Monoxide—highest second maximum non-overlapping 8-hour concentration; Lead—maximum running 3-month average
Source: U.S. Environmental Protection Agency, CBSA Factbook 2010, Air Quality Statistics by City, 2010

Maximum Air Pollutant Concentrations: Nitrogen Dioxide and Sulfur Dioxide

	Nitrogen Dioxide AM (ppb)	Nitrogen Dioxide 1-Hr (ppb)	Sulfur Dioxide AM (ppb)	Sulfur Dioxide 1-Hr (ppb)	Sulfur Dioxide 24-Hr (ppb)
MSA[1] Level	24.524	68	1.742	10	5.3
NAAQS[2]	53	100	30	75	140
Met NAAQS[2]	Yes	Yes	Yes	Yes	Yes

Note: Data from exceptional events are not included; (1) Data covers the Phoenix-Mesa-Glendale, AZ—see Appendix B for areas included; (2) National Ambient Air Quality Standards; ppb = parts per billion; n/a not available

Concentrations: Nitrogen Dioxide AM—highest arithmetic mean concentration; Nitrogen Dioxide 1-Hr—highest 98th percentile 1-hour daily maximum concentration; Sulfur Dioxide AM—highest annual mean concentration; Sulfur Dioxide 1-Hr—highest 99th percentile 1-hour daily maximum concentration; Sulfur Dioxide 24-Hr—highest second maximum 24-hour concentration

Source: U.S. Environmental Protection Agency, CBSA Factbook 2010, Air Quality Statistics by City, 2010

Drinking Water

Water System Name	Pop. Served	Primary Water Source Type	Violations[1] Health Based	Violations[1] Monitoring/ Reporting
City of Phoenix	1,533,582	Surface	0	0

Note: (1) Based on violation data from January 1, 2011 to December 31, 2011 (includes unresolved violations from earlier years)

Source: U.S. Environmental Protection Agency, Office of Ground Water and Drinking Water, Safe Drinking Water Information System (based on data extracted April 18, 2012)

Portland, Oregon

Background

Portland is the kind of city that inspires civic pride and the desire to preserve. For who among us could be indifferent to the magnificent views of the Cascade Mountains, the mild climate, and the historical brick structures that blend so well with its more contemporary structures?

Nature is undisputedly "Queen" in Portland. The symbol of the city, she is embodied in Portlandia, a statue of an earth mother kneeling among her sculpture animal children. The number of activities, such as fishing, skiing, and hunting, as well as the number of outdoor zoological gardens, attest to the mindset of the typical Portlander. And to think that in 1845 Portland held the unromantic name of "Stumptown!"

For the concerned citizen looking for a place that espouses the ideals of the early 1990s television series *Northern Exposure,* Portland may be its real-world, big city counterpart. Portland is a major industrial and commercial center that can still boast clean air and water within its city limits as many of the factories use the electricity generated by mountain rivers; thus, little soot or smoke is belched out. The largest employers in the city are in the health services and Oregon State University.

Portland is a major cultural center, with art museums such as the Portland Art Museum and the Oregon Museum of Science and Industry, and fine educational institutions such as Reed College and the University of Portland. The site where Portland's PGE Park sports stadium now stands was first used for athletic competition in 1893, when the Multnomah Amateur Athletic Club rented a piece of Tanner Creek Gulch pasture there. More recently, in 2001, the PGE was given a $38.5 facelift, and now meets more contemporary tastes and standards, with accommodations that include a field level bar and grill and pavilion suites, all state-of-the-art and seismic code compliant.

The Portland area's regional government is referred to as Metro and includes 24 cities and parts of three counties. Established in the late 1970s, it is the nation's first and only elected regional government. It attempts to control growth by using its authority over land use, transportation, and the environment. This experiment in urban planning is designed to protect farms, forests, and open space. Portland today has a downtown area that caters to pedestrians and includes a heavily used city park where once there was a freeway. Visible from the air is a clear line against sprawl—with cities on one side and open spaces on the other.

Portland is Oregon's biggest city, and has long been considered a shining example of effective sprawl control. Urban planners and visiting city officials see Portland as a "role model for twenty-first century urban development." The city, with its seven-member Metro Council, faces the question of whether further growth will be more sprawling or more dense for Portland and other communities inside the UGB (urban growth boundary), with homebuilders and other advocates on one side of the debate and local officials on the other side.

Finally, Portland's well-organized mass-transit system makes living there all the more enjoyable; this is a city that takes history, progress, and environmental protection seriously. The Portland Streetcar is adding 3.3 miles of track in 2012 and more in 2013.

In 2000, the Portland Art Museum completed its "Program for the Millennium," a multi-stage expansion program that brought total exhibition space to 240,000 square feet. In 2005, restoration of the North Building, a former Masonic Temple, was completed. While preserving the historical integrity, the restoration provides space for the Portland Art Museum's Center for Modern and Contemporary Art.

Portland has a very definite winter rainfall climate, with the most rain falling October through May. The winter season is marked by relatively mild temperatures, cloudy skies, and rain with southeasterly surface winds predominating. Summer produces pleasant, mild temperatures with very little precipitation. Fall and spring are transitional. Fall and early winter bring the most frequent fog. Destructive storms are infrequent, with thunderstorms occurring once a month through the spring and summer.

Rankings

General Rankings

- The Portland metro area was identified as one of the 10 most popular big cities by Pew Research Center. The results are based on a telephone survey of 2,260 adults conducted during October 2008. The report explored a range of attitudes related to where Americans live, where they would like to live, and why. *Pew Research Center, "For Nearly Half of America, Grass is Greener Somewhere Else," January 29, 2009*

- *Men's Health Living* ranked 100 U.S. cities in terms of quality of life. Portland was ranked #26 and received a grade of B-. Criteria: number of fitness facilities; air quality; number of physicians; male/female ratio; education levels; household income; cost of living. *Men's Health Living, Spring 2008*

- Portland was selected as one of America's best cities by *Bloomberg Businessweek.* The city ranked #19 out of 50. Criteria: number of restaurants, bars and museums per capita; number of colleges, libraries, and professional sports teams; income, poverty, unemployment, crime, and foreclosure rates; percent of population with bachelor's degrees; public school performance; park acres per capita; air quality. *BusinessWeek, "America's 50 Best Cities," September 20, 2011*

- Portland appeared on RelocateAmerica's list of best places to live in America. The annual "Top 100 Places to Live" list recognizes the top communities as nominated by their residents & local businesses. RelocateAmerica's Research Group determines the list based on review of various data gathered for economic, employment, housing, education, industry, opportunity, environment and recreation along with feedback from area leaders and residents. *RelocateAmerica.com, "Top 100 Places to Live for 2011"*

- Portland was selected as one the "finest places you'd ever want to call home" by *Outside Magazine.* Criteria: affordable homes; solid job prospects; vibrant nightlife. *Outside Magazine, "Life is Better Here," October 2011*

- Portland was identified as one of the top places to live in the U.S. by Harris Interactive. The city ranked #13 out of 15. Criteria: 2,463 adults (age 18 and over) were polled and asked "if you could live in or near any city in the country except the one you live in or nearest to now, which city would you choose?" The poll was conducted online within the U.S. between September 14 and 20, 2010. *Harris Interactive, November 9, 2011*

- Portland was selected as one of "America's Favorite Cities." The city ranked #3 in the "Quality of Life and Visitor Experience" category. Respondents to an online survey were asked to rate 35 top urban destinations in the U.S. from a visitor's perspective. Criteria: noteworthy neighborhoods; skyline/views; public parks and outdoor access; cleanliness; public transportation and pedestrian friendliness; safety; weather; peace and quiet; people-watching; environmental friendliness. *Travelandleisure.com, "America's Favorite Cities 2010," November 2010*

- Portland was selected as one of "America's Favorite Cities." The city ranked #8 in the "People" category. Respondents to an online survey were asked to rate 35 top urban destinations in the U.S. from a visitor's perspective. Criteria: attractive; friendly; stylish; intelligent; athletic/active; diverse. *Travelandleisure.com, "America's Favorite Cities 2010," November 2010*

Business/Finance Rankings

- Portland was identified as one of the "Happiest Cities to Work in 2012" by *CareerBliss.com,* an online community for career advancement. The city ranked #31 out of 50. Criteria: independent company reviews from employees all over the country on: relationship with their boss and co-workers; work environment; job resources; growth opportunities; compensation; company culture; company reputation; daily tasks; job control over work performed on a daily basis. *CareerBliss.com, "Happiest and Unhappiest Cities to Work in 2012"*

- Portland was selected as one of the "100 Best Places to Live and Launch" in the U.S. The city ranked #6. The editors at *Fortune Small Business* ranked 296 Census-designated metro areas by business friendliness (Launching Score, % New Businesses) and lifestyle offerings (Living Score). Then they picked the town within each of the top 100 metro areas that best blends business and pleasure. *Fortune Small Business, "100 Best Places to Live and Launch 2008," April 2008*

- *American City Business Journals* ranked America's 261 largest cities in terms of their resident's wealth. Portland ranked #94. Criteria: per capita income; median household income; percentage of households with annual incomes of $200,000 or more; median home value. *American City Business Journals, "Where the Money Is: America's Wealth Centers," August 18, 2008*

- The Portland metro area appeared on the Milken Institute "2011 Best Performing Metros" list. Rank: #65 out of 200 large metro areas. Criteria: job growth; wage and salary growth; high-tech output growth. *Milken Institute, "2011 Best Performing Metros"*

- The Portland metro area was selected as one of the best cities for entrepreneurs in America by *Inc. Magazine.* Criteria: job-growth data for 335 metro areas was analyzed for: recent growth trend; mid-term growth; long-term trend; current year growth. The Portland metro area ranked #11 among large metro areas and #56 overall. *Inc. Magazine, "The Best Cities for Doing Business," July 2008*

- Portland was ranked #22 out of 145 regions worldwide in terms of its "Knowledge Competitiveness Index." The index attempts to measure the knowledge-based development taking place throughout the world and is based on 19 measures of economic performance that indicate a region's ability to translate its knowledge capacity into economic value. *Centre for International Competitiveness, World Knowledge Competitiveness Index 2008*

- *Forbes* ranked the 200 most populous metro areas in the U.S. in terms of the "Best Places for Business and Careers." The Portland metro area was ranked #15. Criteria: costs (business and living); job growth (past and projected); income growth; educational attainment; projected economic growth; crime; cultural and recreational opportunities; net migration patterns; number of highly ranked colleges. *Forbes, "Best Places for Business and Careers," June 2011*

Children/Family Rankings

- Underwriters Laboratories (UL), in partnership with Sperling's BestPlaces, ranked the 50 largest cities in the U.S. in terms of the safest for families with young children. Each city was measured on 25 criteria encompassing child-focused, safety-oriented behaviors and regulatory best practices. The study filtered out cities with the highest crime rates and considered air quality, incidence of child pedestrian accidents, injuries and drowning. The study also focused on accessibility to hospitals; response time for fire and police personnel; and laws, codes and regulations that address smoking, home inspections, smoke and carbon monoxide alarms, pool safety and bike helmets. The top 10 cities had the highest frequency or values in these categories. *Underwriters Laboratories, "Safest Cities for Families with Young Children," September 29, 2010*

- The Portland metro area was selected as one of the "Best Cities for Relocating Families" by Worldwide ERC and Primacy Relocation. The 2008 study looked at nearly 50 factors important to relocating families including: recent job growth; nearby top-ranked colleges; in-state tuition for four-year public colleges; population growth since 2000; pediatricians per 100,000 population; and a Green Living index. *Worldwide ERC and Primacy Relocation, "2008 Best Cities for Relocating Families"*

- *Fit Pregnancy* magazine ranked the 50 best U.S. cities in which to have a baby. Portland was ranked #1. Criteria: access to hospitals and doctors; affordability; birthing options; breastfeeding; child care; fertility laws/resources; maternal and infant health risk; parks/stroller friendliness; safety. *Fit Pregnancy, "The Best Cities in America to Have a Baby 2008"*

Culture/Performing Arts Rankings

- Portland was selected as one of the top 10 cities for design in America by architectural firm RMJM Hillier. The city was ranked #5. American cities with more than 500,000 residents were ranked according to criteria such as the quality of public transit, the number of LEED-registered buildings (indicating sustainable design) and how many of the city's employees work within creative industries such as performing arts or publishing. Resident interviews were used to rate a city's design factor, which takes in elements of a city's architecture as well as its creative appeal. *RMJM Hillier, "America's Best Cities for Design," June 25, 2008*
- Portland was selected as one of "America's Top 25 Arts Destinations." The city ranked #11 in the big city (population 500,000 and over) category. Criteria: readers' top choices for arts travel destinations based on the richness and variety of visual arts sites, activities and events. *American Style, "America's Top 25 Arts Destinations," May 2010*

Dating/Romance Rankings

- Portland appeared on *Men's Health's* list of the most sex-happy cities in America. The city ranked #59 of 100. Criteria: condom sales; birth rates; sex toy sales; rates of chlamydia, gonorrhea, and syphilis. *Men's Health, "America's Most Sex-Happy Cities," October 2010*
- *Men's Health* ranked 100 U.S. cities in terms of best (and worst) marriages. Portland was ranked #52 (#1 = worst). Criteria: rate of failed marriages; stringency of divorce laws; percentage of population who've split; number of licensed marriage and family therapists. *Men's Health, "Splitsville, USA," May 2010*
- Eli Lily and Company, in partnership with Sperling's BestPlaces, ranked the nation's 50 largest metro areas in terms of the "Most Romantic Cities for Baby Boomers." The Portland metro area ranked #27. Criteria: marriage and divorce rates among baby boomers age 45 to 60; great restaurants; dance studios; chocolate, jewelry and flower sales. *Eli Lily and Company, "Most Romantic Cities for Baby Boomers," April 20, 2007*
- The Portland metro area was selected as one of the "Best Cities for Relocating Singles" by Worldwide ERC and Primacy Relocation. The area ranked #43 out of the 100 largest metro areas in the U.S. Criteria: recent job growth; recent singles population growth; overall population growth; affordable rental housing; cost-of-living index; expanded arts and recreation opportunities; ratio of single men and single women; affordability of quality higher education (including state residency requirements); diversity index; climate; population density. *Worldwide ERC and Primacy Relocation, "2008 Best Cities for Relocating Singles"*
- *Forbes* ranked the 40 most populous urbanized areas in the U.S. in terms of the "Best Cities for Singles." The Portland metro area ranked #16. Criteria: number of singles; cost of living alone; nightlife; culture; job growth; coolness; and online dating participation. *Forbes.com, "Best Cities for Singles," July 27, 2009*

Education Rankings

- *Men's Health* ranked 100 U.S. cities in terms of their education levels. Portland was ranked #27 (#1 = most educated city). Criteria: high school graduation rates; school enrollment; educational attainment; number of households who have outstanding student loans; number of households whose members have taken adult-education courses. *Men's Health, "Where School Is In: The Most and Least Educated Cities," September 12, 2011*
- Portland was selected as one of the most well-read cities in America by *Amazon.com*. The city ranked #19 of 20. Cities with populations greater than 100,000 were evaluated based on per capita sales of books, magazines and newspapers. *Amazon.com, "Top 20 Most Well-Read Cities in America," June 4, 2011*
- Portland was selected as one of "America's Most Literate Cities." The city ranked #11 out of the 75 largest U.S. cities. Criteria: number of booksellers; library resources; Internet resources; educational attainment; periodical publishing resources; newspaper circulation. *Central Connecticut State University, "America's Most Literate Cities 2011"*

- Portland was identified as one of the 100 "smartest" metro areas in the U.S. The area ranked #21. Criteria: the editors rated the collective brainpower of the 100 largest metro areas in the U.S. based on their residents' educational attainment. *American City Business Journals, April 14, 2008*

- Portland was identified as one of "America's Smartest Cities" by *The Daily Beast.* The metro area ranked #11 out of 55. The editors ranked metropolitan areas with one million or more residents on the following criteria: percentage of residents over age 25 with bachelor's or graduate degrees; non-fiction book sales; ratio of institutions of higher education; libraries per capita. *The Daily Beast, "America's Smartest Cities," October 24, 2010*

- Portland was identified as one of America's most inventive cities by *The Daily Beast.* The city ranked #21 out of 25. The 200 largest cities in the U.S. were ranked by the number of patents (applied and approved) per capita. *The Daily Beast, "The 25 Most Inventive Cities," October 2, 2011*

- Portland was identified as one of "America's Brainiest Bastions" by *Portfolio.com.* The metro area ranked #27 out of 200. *Portfolio.com* analyzed levels of educational attainment in the nation's 200 largest metropolitan areas. The editors established scores for five levels of educational attainment, based on relative earning power of adult workers age 25 or older. Scores were determined by comparing the median income for all workers with the median income for those workers at a specified educational level. *Portfolio.com, "America's Brainiest Bastions," December 1, 2010*

Environmental Rankings

- The Portland was identified as one of America's cities with the most ENERGY STAR certified buildings. The area ranked #15 out of 25. Criteria: number of ENERGY STAR labeled buildings in 2010. *U.S. Environmental Protection Agency, "Top Cities With the Most ENERGY STAR Certified Buildings," March 15, 2011*

- Scarborough Research, a leading market research firm, identified the top local markets for green appliance households. The Portland DMA (Designated Market Area) ranked in the top 16 with 39% of consumers reporting that they own an energy-efficient appliance. *Scarborough Research, March 23, 2010*

- Portland was selected as one of 22 "Smarter Cities" for energy by the Natural Resources Defense Council. The city appeared as one of 12 cities in the large city (population 250,000 and over) category. Criteria: investment in green power; energy efficiency measures; conservation. *Natural Resources Defense Council, "2010 Smarter Cities," July 19, 2010*

- *American City Business Journal* ranked 43 metropolitan areas in terms of their "greenness." The Portland metro area ranked #1. Criteria: Forty-one metros in which *ACBJ* has business weeklies, plus Indianapolis and Cleveland, were ranked based on 20 different indicators such as adoption of green technologies, utilization of environmentally sound practices, and air and water quality. *American City Business Journals, "Green City Index," March 11, 2010*

- Portland was selected as one of "America's 50 Greenest Cities" by *Popular Science.* The city ranked #1. Criteria: electricity; transportation; green living; recycling and green perspective. *Popular Science, February 2008*

- 100 of the largest metro areas in the U.S. were analyzed in terms of their current drought severity. The Portland metro area ranked #51 (#1 = driest). The rankings were based on statistics such as long-term precipitation trends and patterns and the Palmer drought indices. *Sperling's BestPlaces, www.BestPlaces.net, "America's Drought-Riskiest Cities," November 2007*

- The Portland metro area appeared in *Country Home's* "Best Green Places" report. The area ranked #2 out of 379. Criteria: official energy policies; green power; green buildings; availability of fresh, locally grown food. *Country Home, "Best Green Places," 2008*

- Portland was highlighted as one of the 25 metro areas most polluted by short-term particle pollution (24-hour PM 2.5) in the U.S. The area ranked #24. *American Lung Association, State of the Air 2011*

Food/Drink Rankings

- Portland was identified as one of "America's Most Caffeinated Cities" by *Bundle.com.* The city was ranked #8 out of 10. The rankings were determined by examining consumer spending at 16 widely known coffee chains during the second quarter of 2011. *Bundle.com, "America's Most Caffeinated Cities," September 19, 2011*
- Portland was selected as one of the best beer towns in the U.S. by *Men's Journal.* The city was ranked #3.Criteria: beer culture; drinking establishments; breweries. *Men's Journal, "The Top Five Beer Towns in the U.S.," October 2009*
- Portland was selected as one of "America's Favorite Cities." The city ranked #6 in the "Food/Dining" category. Respondents to an online survey were asked to rate 35 top urban destinations in the U.S. from a visitor's perspective. Criteria: big-name restaurants; ethnic food; farmers' markets; neighborhood joints and cafes. *Travelandleisure.com, "America's Favorite Cities 2010," November 2010*
- Portland was selected as one of North America's most vegetarian- and vegan-friendly large cities (population 300,000 or more). The city was ranked #2. Criteria: number of vegetarian restaurants and vegetarian-friendly restaurants per capita; input from PETA supporters and staff members on the quality of the options. *People for the Ethical Treatment of Animals, "North America's Best Vegetarian- and Vegan-Friendly Cities," July 23, 2010*
- The Portland metro area was selected as one of the best cities for "foodies" in America by Sperling's BestPlaces. The metro area ranked #2 out of 10. A "foodie" is defined as a person whose hobby is food—not just eating it, but also learning about its origins and preparation. Criteria: ratio of local restaurants to chain restaurants; number of local and accessible CSA (Community Supported Agriculture) and farmers markets; number of Whole Foods stores; number of cookware stores; number of craft breweries, brew pubs, wine shops, and wine bars. *Sperling's BestPlaces, www.BestPlaces.net, "America's Best Cities for Foodies," January 2011*

Health/Fitness Rankings

- The American Podiatric Medical Association and *Prevention* magazine ranked 100 American cities based on walkability. Nineteen walking criteria were evaluated including the percentage of adults who walk to work, number of parks per square mile, number of trails for walking and hiking, air pollution, use of mass transit, crime rate, pedestrian fatalities, and percentage of adults who walk for fitness. Portland ranked #9. *Prevention, "The Best Walking Cities of 2009," May 2009; American Podiatric Medical Association, "2009 Best Fitness-Walking Cities," April 7, 2009*
- Portland was identified as one of the most walkable cities in the U.S. by *WalkScore.com,* a Seattle-based service that rates the convenience and transit access of 10,000 neighborhoods in 2,500 cities. The editors at Grey House Publishing used *WalkScore.com's* online service to look at the scores of 280 cities with populations greater than or equal to 100,000. The top 50 cities were selected. *WalkScore.com, April 2, 2012*
- Portland was selected as one of the 25 fittest cities in America by *Men's Fitness Online.* It ranked #1 out of America's 50 largest cities. Criteria: fitness centers and sport stores; nutrition; sports participation; TV viewing; overweight/sedentary; junk food; air quality; geography; commute; parks and open space; city recreational facilities; access to healthcare; motivation; mayor and city initiatives; state obesity initiatives. *Men's Fitness, "The Fittest and Fattest Cities in America," March 5, 2012*
- Portland was identified as a "2011 Asthma Capital." The area ranked #100 out of the nation's 100 largest metropolitan areas. Twelve factors were used to identify the most challenging places to live for people with asthma: estimated prevalence; self-reported prevalence; crude death rate for asthma; annual pollen score; annual air quality; public smoking laws; number of board-certified asthma specialists; school inhaler access laws; rescue medication use; controller medication use; uninsured rate; poverty rate. *Asthma and Allergy Foundation of America, "2011 Asthma Capitals"*
- Portland was identified as a "2011 Fall Allergy Capital." The area ranked #100 out of 100. Three groups of factors were used to identify the most severe cities for people with allergies during the fall season: annual pollen levels; medicine utilization; access to board-certified allergists. *Asthma and Allergy Foundation of America, "2011 Fall Allergy Capitals"*

- Portland was identified as a "2012 Spring Allergy Capital." The area ranked #100 out of 100. Three groups of factors were used to identify the most severe cities for people with allergies during the spring season: annual pollen levels; medicine utilization; access to board-certified allergists. *Asthma and Allergy Foundation of America, "2012 Spring Allergy Capitals"*

- *Men's Health* examined 100 major U.S. cities and selected the best and worst cities for men. Portland ranked #28. Criteria: 35 statistical parameters of long life in the categories of health, quality of life, and fitness. *Men's Health, "The 10 Best and Worst Cities for Men 2012," January/February 2012*

- *Men's Health* examined the nation's largest 100 cities and identified the cities with the best and worst teeth. Portland was ranked among the ten worst at #7. Criteria: annual dentist visits; canceled appointments; regular flossers; fluoride usage; dental extractions. *Men's Health, April 2008*

- The American Academy of Dermatology ranked 26 U.S. metropolitan regions in terms of their residents knowledge, attitude and behaviors towards tanning, sun protection and skin cancer detection. The Portland metro area ranked #9. The results of the study are based on an online survey of over 7,000 adults nationwide. *American Academy of Dermatology, "Suntelligence: How Sun Smart is Your City," May 3, 2010*

- The Portland metro area appeared in the 2011 Gallup-Healthways Well-Being Index. The index, based on interviews with more than 350,000 Americans, measured jobs, finances, physical health, emotional state of mind and communities. The metro area ranked #72 out of 190. Criteria: life evaluation; emotional health; work environment; physical health; healthy behaviors; basic access (basic needs optimal for a healthy life, such as access to food and medicine, having health insurance and feeling safe while walking at night). *Gallup-Healthways, "State of Well-Being 2011"*

- The Portland metro area was identified as one of "America's Most Stressful Cities" by *Sperling's BestPlaces.* The metro area ranked #20 out of 50. Criteria: unemployment rate; suicide rate; commute time; mental health; poor rest; alcohol use; violent crime rate; property crime rate; cloudy days annually. *Sperling's BestPlaces, www.BestPlaces.net, "Stressful Cities 2012*

- *Men's Health* ranked 100 U.S. cities in terms of their activity levels. Portland was ranked #15 (#1 = most active city). Criteria: where and how often residents exercise; percentage of households that watch more than 15 hours of cable television a week and buy more than 11 video games a year; death rate from deep-vein thrombosis, a condition linked to sitting for extended periods of time. *Men's Health, "Where Sit Happens: The Most and Least Active Cities in America," June 20, 2011*

- 50 of the largest metro areas in the U.S. were analyzed in terms of their health and fitness by the American College of Sports Medicine in their "American Fitness Index." The Portland metro area ranked #5 (#1 = healthiest). Criteria: preventative health behaviors; levels of chronic disease; health care access; community resources and policies that support physical activity. *American College of Sports Medicine, "Health and Community Fitness Status of the 50 Largest Metropolitan Areas," August 1, 2011*

- Portland was selected as one of the "20 Most Livable U.S. Cities for Wheelchair Users" by the Christopher & Dana Reeve Foundation. The city ranked #5. Criteria: Medicaid eligibility and spending; access to physicians and rehabilitation facilities; access to fitness facilities and recreation; access to paratransit; percentage of people living with disabilities who are employed; clean air; climate. *Christopher & Dana Reeve Foundation, "20 Most Livable U.S. Cities for Wheelchair Users," July 26, 2010*

- The Portland metro area was selected as one of "America's Most Relaxed Cities" by *Forbes.* The metro area ranked #4 out of 10. Criteria: unemployment rates; numbers of commuters that spend an hour or more in traffic on the way to work; average weekly hours people spend at work; access to health care; overall health of residents; percentage of population who exercise. *Forbes, "America's Most Relaxed Cities," November 5, 2010*

Pet Rankings

- Portland was selected as one of the "Top 10 Cat-Friendly Cities" in the U.S. The area ranked #4. Criteria: cat ownership per capita; level of veterinary care; microchipping; cat-friendly local ordinances. *CATalyst Council, "Top 10 Cat-Friendly Cities," March 27, 2009*

- Portland was selected as one of the best places to live with pets by *Livability.com.* The city was ranked #1. Criteria: pet-friendly parks and trails; quality veterinary care; active animal welfare groups; abundance of pet boutiques and retail shops; excellent quality of life for pet owners. *Livability.com, "Top 10 Pet Friendly Cities," October 20, 2010*

Real Estate Rankings

- *Fortune* ranked the 100 largest metro areas in the U.S. in terms of projected median home price change in 2010. The Portland metro area ranked #60. *Fortune, "The 2010 Housing Outlook," December 9, 2009*
- Portland appeared on *ApartmentRatings.com* "Top Cities for Renters" list in 2009." The area ranked #32. Overall satisfaction ratings were ranked using thousands of user submitted scores for hundreds of apartment complexes located in the 100 most populated U.S. municipalities. *ApartmentRatings.com, "2009 Renter Satisfaction Rankings"*
- Portland appeared on *ApartmentRatings.com* "Top College Towns & Cities" for renters list in 2011." The area ranked #43 out of 87. Overall satisfaction ratings were ranked using thousands of user submitted scores for hundreds of apartment complexes located in cities and towns that are home to the 100 largest four-year institutions in the U.S. *ApartmentRatings.com, "2011 College Town Renter Satisfaction Rankings"*
- The nation's largest metro areas were analyzed in terms of the best places to buy pre-foreclosures (short sales). The Portland metro area ranked #8 out of 10. Criteria: at least 500 pre-foreclosure sales during the fourth quarter and a short sales increase of at least five percent from a year ago. The areas selected posted the biggest discounts on the sales of pre-foreclosure properties. *RealtyTrac, "Fourth Quarter and Year-End 2011 U.S. Foreclosure Sales Report: Shifting Towards Short Sales," February 28, 2012*
- The Portland metro area was identified as one of America's most overvalued cities in 2011 by *CNNMoney.com* based on data from Local Market Monitor. Criteria: median home prices; local interest rates; economic and population growth; construction costs; vacancies; household income. *CNNMoney.com, "America's Most Overvalued (and Undervalued) Cities," January 16, 2011*
- The Portland metro area appeared in a *Wall Street Journal* article ranking cities by "housing stress." The metro area was ranked #21 (#1 = most stress). Criteria: fraction of mortgage-holding homeowners with a monthly housing payment in excess of 30 percent of income; percentage of people without health insurance; unemployment rate. *The Wall Street Journal, "Which Cities Face Biggest Housing Risk," October 5, 2010*
- The Center for Housing Policy ranked 210 U.S. metropolitan areas by the fair market rent for a two-bedroom unit. The Portland metro area was ranked #99. (#1 = most expensive) with a rent of $839. Criteria: Fair Market Rent (FMR) in effect during the fourth quarter of 2009 based on HUD's fiscal year 2010 FMRs. *The Center for Housing Policy, "Paycheck to Paycheck: Most to Least Expensive Rental Markets in 2009"*
- The Portland metro area was identified as one of the best U.S. markets to invest in rental property" by HomeVestors and Local Market Monitor. The area ranked #70 out of 100. Criteria: risk-return premium relative to national average. *HomeVestors and Local Market Monitor, "Best 100 U.S. Markets to Invest in Rental Property," March 9, 2012*

Safety Rankings

- Symantec, the makers of Norton, in partnership with Sperling's BestPlaces, ranked the 50 largest cities in the U.S. in terms of their vulnerability to cybercrime. The city ranked #16. Criteria: number of cyberattacks and potential infections; level of Internet access; expenditures on smartphones and computer hardware/software; wireless hotspots; broadband connectivity; Internet usage; online purchases. *Symantec, "Riskiest Online Cities of 2012" February 15, 2012*

- Allstate ranked the 193 largest cities in America in terms of driver safety. Portland ranked #128. In addition, drivers were 17.8% more likely to have had an accident compared to the national average. Allstate researchers analyzed internal property damage reported claims over a two-year period (from January 2008 to December 2009) to protect findings from external influences such as weather or road construction. A weighted average of the two-year numbers determined the annual percentages. The report defines an auto crash as any collision resulting in a property damage claim. *Allstate, "2011 Allstate America's Best Drivers Report™"*
- Portland was identified as one of the safest large cities in America by CQ Press. All 34 cities with populations of 500,000 or more that reported crime rates in 2010 for murder, rape, robbery, aggravated assault, burglary, and motor vehicle thefts were ranked. The city ranked #9 out of the top 10. *CQ Press, City Crime Rankings 2011-2012*
- The National Insurance Crime Bureau ranked 366 metro areas in the U.S. in terms of per capita rates of vehicle theft. The Portland metro area ranked #65 (#1 = highest rate). Criteria: number of vehicle theft offenses per 100,000 inhabitants in 2010. *National Insurance Crime Bureau, "Hot Spots," June 21, 2011*
- The Portland metro area was identified as one of the most dangerous metro areas for pedestrians by Transportation for America. The metro area ranked #45 out of 52 metro areas with over 1 million residents. Criteria: area's population divided by the number of pedestrian fatalities in that area. *Transportation for America, "Dangerous by Design 2011"*

Seniors/Retirement Rankings

- Bankers Life and Casualty Company, in partnership with Sperling's BestPlaces, ranked the nation's 50 largest metro areas in terms of the "Best U.S. Cities for Seniors." The Portland metro area ranked #8. Criteria: healthcare; transportation; housing; environment; economy; health and longevity; social and spiritual life; crime. *Bankers Life and Casualty Company, Center for a Secure Retirement, "Best U.S. Cities for Seniors 2011," September 2011*
- Portland was selected as one of "10 Bargain Retirement Spots" by *U.S. News & World Report.* Criteria: cities where home prices are falling fast. *U.S. News & World Report, "10 Bargain Retirement Spots," February 22, 2011*
- Portland was identified as one of the "100 Most Popular Retirement Towns" by *Topretirements.com* The list reflects the 100 cities (out of 815+ total cities reviewed) that visitors to the website are most interested in for retirement. *Topretirements.com, "100 Most Popular Retirement Towns," February 21, 2012*
- Portland was selected as one of "Seven Places to Retire During an Economic Downturn." The city ranked #5. The editors at *Smart Money* selected seven recession-proof places soon-to-be retirees should consider. *SmartMoney.com, "Seven Places to Retire During an Economic Downturn," February 29, 2008*

Sports/Recreation Rankings

- Portland appeared on the *Sporting News* list of the "Best Sports Cities" for 2011. The area ranked #40 out of 271 cities in the U.S. *Sporting News* takes a 12-month snapshot of each city's sports, putting a heavy premium on regular-season won-lost records (from the most recently completed season). Other criteria include: playoff berths, bowl appearances and tournament bids; championships; applicable power ratings; quality of competition; overall fan fervor (measured in part by attendance); abundance of teams (rewarding quality over quantity); stadium and arena quality; ticket availability and prices; franchise ownership; and marquee appeal of athletes. *Sporting News, "Best Sports Cities 2011," October 4, 2011*
- Scarborough Sports Marketing, a leading market research firm, identified the Portland DMA (Designated Market Area) as one of the top markets for Summer Olympics fans with more than 65% of adults reporting that they are "very, somewhat, or a little bit interested" in the Summer Olympics. *Scarborough Sports Marketing, July 30, 2008*
- Portland was chosen as a bicycle friendly community by the League of American Bicyclists. A Bicycle Friendly Community welcomes cyclists by providing safe accommodation for cycling and encouraging people to bike for transportation and recreation. There are four award levels: Platinum; Gold; Silver; and Bronze. The community achieved an award level of Platinum. *League of American Bicyclists, "Bicycle Friendly Community Master List 2011"*

- Portland was chosen as one of America's best cities for bicycling. The city ranked #2 out of 50. Criteria: number of segregated bike lanes, municipal bike racks, and bike boulevards; vibrant and diverse bike culture; smart, savvy bike shops; interviews with national and local advocates, bike shops and other experts. The editors only considered cities with populations of 100,000 or more. *Bicycling, "America's Best Bike Cities," April 2010*
- The Portland was selected as one of the best metro areas for golf in America by *Golf Digest.* The Portland area was ranked #10 out of 20. Criteria: climate; cost of public golf; quality of public golf; accessibility. *Golf Digest, "The Top 20 Cities for Golf," October 2011*
- *Golf.com* and the research arm of the National Golf Foundation analyzed the 50 largest metropolitan areas in the U.S. in terms of golf. The Portland metro area ranked #9. Criteria: weather; affordability; quality of courses; accessibility; number of courses designed by esteemed architects; availability; crowdedness. *Golf.com, November 15, 2007*

Technology Rankings

- The Portland metro area was selected as one of "America's Most Wired Cities" by *Forbes*. The metro area was ranked #10 out of 20. Criteria: percentage of Internet users with high-speed access; number of companies providing high-speed Internet; number of public wireless hot spots. *Forbes, "America's Most Wired Cities," March 2, 2010*
- The Portland metro area was selected as one of "America's Most Innovative Cities" by *Forbes*. The metro area was ranked #10 out of 20. Criteria: patents per capita; venture capital investment per capita; ratio of high-tech, science and "creative" jobs. *Forbes, "America's Most Innovative Cities," May 24, 2010*

Transportation Rankings

- Portland was identified as one of America's "10 Best Cities for Public Transportation" by *U.S. News & World Report.* The city ranked #1. The ten cities selected had the best combination of public transportation investment, ridership, and safety. *U.S. News & World Report, "10 Best Cities for Public Transportation," February 8, 2011*
- Portland was identified as one of America's worst cities for speed traps by the National Motorists Association. The city ranked #11 out of 25. Criteria: speed trap locations per 100,000 residents. *National Motorists Association, September 2011*
- The Portland metro area was identified as one of the best U.S. cities to live in without a car by *24/7 Wall St.* The area ranked #2 out of 10. Criteria: percentage of neighborhoods covered by public transit; frequency of service for those neighborhoods; share of jobs reachable within 90 minutes or less by public transit; how accessible amenities are for residents on foot; percentage of commuters who bike to work. The 100 largest metropolitan areas in the U.S. were examined. *24/7 Wall St., "The Best Cities to Live in Car-Free," November 28, 2011*
- The Portland metro area was selected as one of 15 "Smarter Cities" for transportation by the Natural Resources Defense Council. The area appeared in the large metro area (population greater than one million) category. Criteria: public transit availability and use; household automobile ownership and use; innovative, sustainable and affordable transportation programs. *Natural Resources Defense Council, "2011 Smarter Cities," February 23, 2011*
- Portland was selected as one of the "Most Courteous Cities (Least Road Rage)" in the U.S. by AutoVantage. The city ranked #1. Criteria: 2,518 consumers were interviewed in 25 major metropolitan areas about their views on road rage. *AutoVantage, "2009 AutoVantage Road Rage Survey"*
- The Portland metro area appeared on *Forbes* list of the best and worst cities for commuters. The metro area ranked #11 out of 60 (#1 is best). Criteria: travel time; road congestion; travel delays. *Forbes.com, "Best and Worst Cities for Commuters," February 16, 2010*

Women/Minorities Rankings

- *Women's Health* examined U.S. cities and identified the 100 best cities for women. Portland was ranked #32. Criteria: 30 categories were examined from obesity and breast cancer rates to commuting times and hours spent working out. *Women's Health, "Best Cities for Women 2012"*

- Portland was ranked #27 out of 100 metro areas in *SELF Magazine's* ranking of America's healthiest places for women." A panel of experts came up with more than 50 criteria including death and disease rates, environmental indicators, community resources, and lifestyle habits. *SELF Magazine, "Secrets of America's Healthiest Women," December 2008*

- Portland was selected as one of the "Gayest Cities in America" by *The Advocate.* The city ranked #12 out of 15. *The Advocate* used several different measures to establish "per capita queerness"—including a city's number of teams entered in the Gay Softball World Series, gay bookstores, openly gay elected officials and semifinalists in the International Mr. Leather Contest. *The Advocate, "Gayest Cities in America, 2012" January 2012*

- The Portland metro area appeared on *Forbes'* list of the "Best Cities for Minority Entrepreneurs." The area ranked #12 out of 10. Criteria: 52 metropolitan statistical areas were examined. For each ethnicity (African Americans, Asians and Hispanics), the editors measured housing affordability, population growth, income growth, and entrepreneurship (per capita self-employment). *Forbes, "Best Cities for Minority Entrepreneurs," March 23, 2011*

Miscellaneous Rankings

- *Men's Health* ranked 100 U.S. cities by their level of sadness. Portland was ranked #69 (#1 = saddest city). Criteria: suicide rates; unemployment rates; percentage of households that use antidepressants; percent of population who report feeling blue all or most of the time. *Men's Health, "Frown Towns," November 28, 2011*

- Energizer Holdings, the makers of Edge® shave gel, in partnership with Sperling's BestPlaces, ranked 50 major metro areas in terms of everyday irritations. The Portland metro area ranked #43. Criteria: humidity levels; weather conditions; incidence of traffic delays and congestion; average commute times; frequency of flight delays and cancellations; rates of sleeplessness; underemployment; pollens and allergens; pests; comedy clubs per capita. *Energizer Holdings, "Most Irritation Prone Cities," July 23, 2010*

- Mars Chocolate North America, the makers of COMBOS®, in partnership with Sperling's BestPlaces, ranked 50 major metro areas in terms of their "manliness." The Portland metro area ranked #37. Criteria: number of professional sports teams; number of nearby NASCAR tracks and racing events; manly lifestyle; concentration of manly retail stores; manly occupations per capita; salty snack sales; "Board of Manliness" rankings. *Mars Chocolate North America, "America's Manliest Cities 2011," September 1, 2011*

- Portland was selected as one of the most tattooed cities in America by *TotalBeauty.com.* The city was ranked #5. Criteria: number of tattoo and permanent makeup shops per capita; number of tattoo conventions hosted. *TotalBeauty.com, "Top 10 Most Tattooed Cities in America," August 2010*

- Portland was selected as one of "America's Best Cities for Hipsters" by *Travel + Leisure.* The city was ranked #2 out of 10. Criteria: live music; coffee bars; independent boutiques; best microbrews; offbeat and tech-savvy locals. *Travel + Leisure, "America's Best Cities for Hipsters," April 11, 2012*

- The Portland metro area appeared in *AutoMD.com's* ranking of the "Best and Worst Cities for Auto Repair." The metro area ranked #24 (#1 is best). The 50 most-populated metro areas in the U.S. were ranked on three critical factors: repair affordability; price disparity range; shop integrity factor. *AutoMD.com, "Advocacy for Repair Shop Fairness Report," February 24, 2010*

- *Men's Health* examined the nation's largest 100 cities and identified "America's Most Political Cities." Portland was ranked among the ten most political at #9. Criteria: percentage of active registered voters; percentage of ballots counted of active registration; percentage of income donated to 2008 presidential election; campaign spending; percentage of registrants who voted in the 2008 primaries; percentage of voters in the 2004/2006 Senate election; percentage of voters in the 2004-2007 gubernatorial election. *Men's Health, "Ranking America's Cities: America's Most Political Cities," October 2008*

- Scarborough Research, a leading market research firm, identified the top local markets for volunteers in the U.S. The Portland DMA (Designated Market Area) ranked in the top 10 with 33% of adults 18+ reporting that they have participated in volunteer work in the past 12 months. *Scarborough Research, December 13, 2011*

Business Environment

CITY FINANCES

City Government Finances

Component	2009 ($000)	2009 ($ per capita)
Total Revenues	1,093,852	1,987
Total Expenditures	1,470,300	2,671
Debt Outstanding	2,844,692	5,168
Cash and Securities[1]	797,815	1,450

Note: (1) Cash and security holdings of a government at the close of its fiscal year, including those of its dependent agencies, utilities, and liquor stores.
Source: U.S Census Bureau, State & Local Government Finances 2009

City Government Revenue by Source

Source	2009 ($000)	2009 ($ per capita)
General Revenue		
From Federal Government	20,429	37
From State Government	62,630	114
From Local Governments	45,742	83
Taxes		
Property	277,991	505
Sales and Gross Receipts	77,978	142
Personal Income	0	0
Corporate Income	0	0
Motor Vehicle License	0	0
Other Taxes	106,865	194
Current Charges	325,378	591
Liquor Store	0	0
Utility	105,093	191
Employee Retirement	1,437	3

Source: U.S Census Bureau, State & Local Government Finances 2009

City Government Expenditures by Function

Function	2009 ($000)	2009 ($ per capita)	2009 (%)
General Direct Expenditures			
Air Transportation	0	0	0.0
Corrections	0	0	0.0
Education	0	0	0.0
Employment Security Administration	0	0	0.0
Financial Administration	49,366	90	3.4
Fire Protection	94,510	172	6.4
General Public Buildings	4,450	8	0.3
Governmental Administration, Other	33,848	61	2.3
Health	0	0	0.0
Highways	117,743	214	8.0
Hospitals	0	0	0.0
Housing and Community Development	50,697	92	3.4
Interest on General Debt	101,720	185	6.9
Judicial and Legal	8,016	15	0.5
Libraries	0	0	0.0
Parking	6,125	11	0.4
Parks and Recreation	120,778	219	8.2
Police Protection	153,063	278	10.4
Public Welfare	0	0	0.0
Sewerage	282,422	513	19.2
Solid Waste Management	3,529	6	0.2
Veterans' Services	0	0	0.0
Liquor Store	0	0	0.0
Utility	150,641	274	10.2
Employee Retirement	94,361	171	6.4

Source: U.S Census Bureau, State & Local Government Finances 2009

Municipal Bond Ratings

Area	Moody's	S&P	Fitch
City	Aaa	(1)	n/a

Rating Systems (shown in declining order of credit quality): Moody's– Aaa, Aa, A, Baa, Ba, B, Caa, Ca, C (numerical modifiers 1, 2, and 3 are added to letter-rating); S&P– AAA, AA, A, BBB, BB, B, CCC, CC, C; Fitch– AAA, AA, A, BBB, BB, B, CCC, CC, C. Ratings may be modified by the addition of a plus or minus sign to show relative standing within the major rating categories.

Notes: n/a Not Available; w/d Withdrawn (1) Not Reviewed; (2) Issuer Rating/No General Obligation; (3) Standard and Poor's Issue Credit Rating (ICR) is a current opinion of an obliger with respect to a specific financial obligation, a specific class of financial obligations, or a specific financial program.

Source: U.S. Census Bureau, 2012 Statistical Abstract, Bond Ratings for City Governments by Largest Cities: 2010

DEMOGRAPHICS

Population Growth

Area	1990 Census	2000 Census	2010 Census	Population Growth (%) 1990-2000	Population Growth (%) 2000-2010
City	485,833	529,121	583,776	8.9	10.3
MSA[1]	1,523,741	1,927,881	2,226,009	26.5	15.5
U.S.	248,709,873	281,421,906	308,745,538	13.2	9.7

Note: (1) Figures cover the Portland-Vancouver-Hillsboro, OR-WA Metropolitan Statistical Area—see Appendix B for areas included

Source: U.S. Census Bureau, 2010 Census

Household Size

Area	Persons in Household (%) One	Two	Three	Four	Five	Six	Seven or More	Average Household Size
City	34.5	33.7	14.3	10.3	4.1	1.7	1.4	2.28
MSA[1]	27.0	34.1	15.8	13.2	5.8	2.4	1.7	2.52
U.S.	26.7	32.8	16.1	13.4	6.5	2.6	1.9	2.58

Note: (1) Figures cover the Portland-Vancouver-Hillsboro, OR-WA Metropolitan Statistical Area—see Appendix B for areas included

Source: U.S. Census Bureau, 2010 Census

Race

Area	White Alone[2] (%)	Black Alone[2] (%)	Asian Alone[2] (%)	AIAN[3] Alone[2] (%)	NHOPI[4] Alone[2] (%)	Other Race Alone[2] (%)	Two or More Races (%)
City	76.1	6.3	7.1	1.0	0.5	4.2	4.7
MSA[1]	81.0	2.9	5.7	0.9	0.5	4.9	4.1
U.S.	72.4	12.6	4.8	0.9	0.2	6.2	2.9

Note: (1) Figures cover the Portland-Vancouver-Hillsboro, OR-WA Metropolitan Statistical Area—see Appendix B for areas included; (2) Alone is defined as not being in combination with one or more other races; (3) American Indian and Alaska Native; (4) Native Hawaiian and Other Pacific Islander

Source: U.S. Census Bureau, 2010 Census

Hispanic or Latino Origin

Area	Hispanic or Latino (%)	Mexican (%)	Puerto Rican (%)	Cuban (%)	Other Hispanic or Latino (%)
City	9.4	6.7	0.3	0.4	2.0
MSA[1]	10.9	8.5	0.3	0.2	1.9
U.S.	16.3	10.3	1.5	0.6	4.0

Note: Persons of Hispanic or Latino origin can be of any race; (1) Figures cover the Portland-Vancouver-Hillsboro, OR-WA Metropolitan Statistical Area—see Appendix B for areas included

Source: U.S. Census Bureau, 2010 Census

Segregation

Type	Segregation Indices[1]				Percent Change		
	1990	2000	2010	2010 Rank[2]	1990-2000	1990-2010	2000-2010
Black/White	63.2	51.8	46.0	81	-11.4	-17.2	-5.9
Asian/White	31.2	35.1	35.8	75	3.9	4.7	0.8
Hispanic/White	25.6	34.2	34.3	83	8.6	8.6	0.0

Note: Figures are based on an analysis of 1990, 2000, and 2010 Census Decennial Census tract data by William H. Frey, Brookings Institution and the University of Michigan Social Science Data Analysis Network. In this analysis all racial groups (whites, blacks, and asians) are non-Hispanic members of thoses races. Hispanics are shown as a separate category; All figures cover the Metropolitan Statistical Area (see Appendix B for areas included); (1) Segregation Indices are Dissimilarity Indices that measure the degree to which the minority group is distributed differently than whites across census tracts. They range from 0 (complete integration) to 100 (complete segregation) where the value indicates the percentage of the minority group that needs to move to be distributed exactly like whites; (2) Ranges from 1 (most segregated) to 102 (least segregated); n/a not available.
Source: www.CensusScope.org

Ancestry

Area	German	Irish	English	American	Italian	Polish	French[2]	Scottish	Dutch
City	19.2	12.4	11.8	4.2	4.2	2.2	3.6	3.5	1.9
MSA[1]	21.6	12.6	12.5	4.1	3.9	1.9	3.7	3.4	2.3
U.S.	16.1	11.6	8.8	6.1	5.7	3.2	3.0	1.9	1.6

Note: Figures are the percentage of the total population reporting a particular ancestry. The nine most commonly reported ancestries in the U.S. are shown. Figures include multiple ancestries (e.g. if a person reported being Irish and Italian, they were included in both columns); (1) Figures cover the Portland-Vancouver-Hillsboro, OR-WA Metropolitan Statistical Area—see Appendix B for areas included; (2) Excludes Basque
Source: U.S. Census Bureau, 2008-2010 American Community Survey 3-Year Estimates

Foreign-Born Population

Area	Percent of Population Born in								
	Any Foreign Country	Mexico	Asia	Europe	Carribean	South America	Central America[2]	Africa	Canada
City	13.5	2.5	5.4	2.8	0.3	0.2	0.6	0.6	0.6
MSA[1]	12.6	3.5	4.3	2.6	0.2	0.3	0.5	0.4	0.5
U.S.	12.8	3.8	3.6	1.6	1.2	0.9	1.0	0.5	0.3

Note: (1) Figures cover the Portland-Vancouver-Hillsboro, OR-WA Metropolitan Statistical Area—see Appendix B for areas included; (2) Excludes Mexico.
Source: U.S. Census Bureau, 2008-2010 American Community Survey 3-Year Estimates

Marital Status

Area	Never Married	Now Married[2]	Separated	Widowed	Divorced
City	40.1	40.7	1.7	4.9	12.6
MSA[1]	30.5	50.7	1.8	4.8	12.2
U.S.	31.6	49.6	2.2	6.1	10.7

Note: Figures are percentages and cover the population 15 years of age and older; (1) Figures cover the Portland-Vancouver-Hillsboro, OR-WA Metropolitan Statistical Area—see Appendix B for areas included; (2) Excludes separated
Source: U.S. Census Bureau, 2008-2010 American Community Survey 3-Year Estimates

Age

Area	Percent of Population							Median Age
	Under Age 5	Age 5 to 17	Age 18 to 34	Age 35 to 49	Age 50 to 64	Age 65 to 79	80 Years and Over	
City	6.0	13.1	29.3	22.6	18.5	7.1	3.3	35.8
MSA[1]	6.5	17.2	23.8	21.7	19.4	8.1	3.3	36.7
U.S.	6.5	17.5	23.2	20.7	19.0	9.4	3.6	37.2

Note: (1) Figures cover the Portland-Vancouver-Hillsboro, OR-WA Metropolitan Statistical Area—see Appendix B for areas included
Source: U.S. Census Bureau, 2010 Census

Male/Female Ratio

Area	Males	Females	Males per 100 Females
City	289,211	294,565	98.2
MSA[1]	1,099,122	1,126,887	97.5
U.S.	151,781,326	156,964,212	96.7

Note: (1) Figures cover the Portland-Vancouver-Hillsboro, OR-WA Metropolitan Statistical Area—see Appendix B for areas included
Source: U.S. Census Bureau, 2010 Census

Religious Groups

Area	Catholic	Baptist	Non-Den.	Methodist[2]	Lutheran	LDS[3]	Pente-costal	Presby-terian[4]	Muslim[5]	Judaism
MSA[1]	10.6	2.3	4.5	1.0	1.6	3.8	2.0	1.0	0.3	0.1
U.S.	19.1	9.3	4.0	4.0	2.3	2.0	1.9	1.6	0.8	0.7

Note: Figures are the number of adherents as a percentage of the total population; (1) Figures cover the Portland-Vancouver-Hillsboro, OR-WA Metropolitan Statistical Area—see Appendix B for areas included; (2) Methodist/Pietist; (3) Latter Day Saints; (4) Reformed; (5) Figures are estimates
Source: Association of Statisticians of American Religious Bodies, 2010 U.S. Religion Census: Religious Congregations & Membership Study

ECONOMY

Gross Metropolitan Product

Area	2007	2008	2009	2010	2010 Rank[2]
MSA[1]	116.8	122.4	118.2	122.8	21

Note: Figures are in billions of dollars; (1) Figures cover the Portland-Vancouver-Hillsboro, OR-WA Metropolitan Statistical Area—see Appendix B for areas included; (2) Rank ranges from 1 to 363
Source: The United States Conference of Mayors, "U.S. Metro Economies: GMP and Employment Forecasts," June 2011

Economic Growth

Area	2007-2009 (%)	2010 (%)	2011 (%)	Rank[2]
MSA[1]	0.5	3.6	3.4	79
U.S.	-1.3	2.9	2.5	–

Note: Figures are real Gross Metropolitan Product growth rates and represent annual average percent change; (1) Figures cover the Portland-Vancouver-Hillsboro, OR-WA Metropolitan Statistical Area—see Appendix B for areas included; (2) Rank ranges from 1 to 363
Source: The United States Conference of Mayors, "U.S. Metro Economies: GMP and Employment Forecasts," June 2011

Metropolitan Area Exports

Area	2005	2006	2007	2008	2009	2010	2010 Rank[2]
MSA[1]	11,202.1	14,580.6	15,783.9	19,477.1	15,482.4	18,544.9	15

Note: Figures are in millions of dollars; (1) Figures cover the Portland-Vancouver-Hillsboro, OR-WA Metropolitan Statistical Area—see Appendix B for areas included; (2) Rank ranges from 1 to 369
Source: U.S. Department of Commerce, International Trade Administration, Office of Trade & Industry Information, Manufacturing & Services, data extracted April 2, 2012

INCOME

Income

Area	Per Capita ($)	Median Household ($)	Average Household ($)
City	29,634	49,326	67,714
MSA[1]	28,651	55,618	72,200
U.S.	26,942	51,222	70,116

Note: (1) Figures cover the Portland-Vancouver-Hillsboro, OR-WA Metropolitan Statistical Area—see Appendix B for areas included
Source: U.S. Census Bureau, 2008-2010 American Community Survey 3-Year Estimates

Household Income Distribution

Area	Percent of Households Earning							
	Under $15,000	$15,000 -24,999	$25,000 -34,999	$35,000 -49,999	$50,000 -74,999	$75,000 -99,000	$100,000 -149,999	$150,000 and up
City	14.8	11.0	10.3	14.4	18.6	11.3	11.4	8.1
MSA[1]	10.7	9.6	10.0	14.5	19.9	13.4	13.6	8.4
U.S.	13.0	11.0	10.6	14.2	18.5	12.1	12.2	8.4

Note: (1) Figures cover the Portland-Vancouver-Hillsboro, OR-WA Metropolitan Statistical Area—see Appendix B for areas included
Source: U.S. Census Bureau, 2008-2010 American Community Survey 3-Year Estimates

Poverty Rate

Area	All Ages	Under 18 Years Old	18 to 64 Years Old	65 Years and Over
City	16.7	21.4	16.0	12.6
MSA[1]	12.4	16.3	11.7	8.4
U.S.	14.4	20.1	13.1	9.4

Note: Figures are percentage of people whose income during the past 12 months was below the poverty level; (1) Figures cover the Portland-Vancouver-Hillsboro, OR-WA Metropolitan Statistical Area—see Appendix B for areas included
Source: U.S. Census Bureau, 2008-2010 American Community Survey 3-Year Estimates

Personal Bankruptcy Filing Rate

Area	2006	2007	2008	2009	2010	2011
Multnomah County	2.18	2.63	3.18	4.30	4.82	4.43
U.S.	2.00	2.73	3.53	4.61	4.97	4.37

Note: Numbers are per 1,000 population and include Chapter 7 and Chapter 13 filings
Source: Federal Deposit Insurance Corporation, Regional Economic Conditions, March 9, 2012

EMPLOYMENT

Labor Force and Employment

Area	Civilian Labor Force			Workers Employed		
	Dec. 2010	Dec. 2011	% Chg.	Dec. 2010	Dec. 2011	% Chg.
City	310,800	315,295	1.4	282,198	290,279	2.9
MSA[1]	1,193,027	1,197,593	0.4	1,076,210	1,100,953	2.3
U.S.	153,156,000	153,373,000	0.1	139,159,000	140,681,000	1.1

Note: Data is not seasonally adjusted and covers workers 16 years of age and older; (1) Metropolitan Statistical Area—see Appendix B for areas included
Source: Bureau of Labor Statistics, http://stats.bls.gov

Unemployment Rate

Area	2011											
	Jan.	Feb.	Mar.	Apr.	May	Jun.	Jul.	Aug.	Sep.	Oct.	Nov.	Dec.
City	9.8	9.7	9.3	8.3	8.2	9.0	8.6	8.7	8.4	8.3	7.6	7.9
MSA[1]	10.3	10.2	9.9	9.1	8.9	9.5	9.1	9.2	8.7	8.6	8.0	8.1
U.S.	9.8	9.5	9.2	8.7	8.7	9.3	9.3	9.1	8.8	8.5	8.2	8.3

Note: Data is not seasonally adjusted and covers workers 16 years of age and older; All figures are percentages; (1) Metropolitan Statistical Area—see Appendix B for areas included
Source: Bureau of Labor Statistics, http://stats.bls.gov

Projected Unemployment Rate

Area	2010 (%)	2011 (%)	2012 (%)	2013 (%)
MSA[1]	10.5	8.9	8.3	7.5

Note: (1) Metropolitan Statistical Area—see Appendix B for areas included
Source: The United States Conference of Mayors, "U.S. Metro Economies: GMP and Employment Forecasts," June 2011

Employment by Occupation

Occupation Classification	City (%)	MSA[1] (%)	U.S. (%)
Management, Business, Science, and Arts	44.5	39.2	35.6
Natural Resources, Construction, and Maintenance	5.2	8.1	9.5
Production, Transportation, and Material Moving	10.9	11.5	12.1
Sales and Office	22.4	24.9	25.2
Service	17.0	16.3	17.6

Note: Figures cover employed civilians 16 years of age and older; (1) Figures cover the Portland-Vancouver-Hillsboro, OR-WA Metropolitan Statistical Area—see Appendix B for areas included
Source: U.S. Census Bureau, 2008-2010 American Community Survey 3-Year Estimates

Employment by Industry

Sector	MSA[1] Number of Employees	MSA[1] Percent of Total	U.S. Percent of Total
Construction	50,300	5.0	4.1
Education and Health Services	145,400	14.6	15.2
Financial Activities	62,100	6.2	5.8
Government	146,100	14.6	16.8
Information	22,000	2.2	2.0
Leisure and Hospitality	97,900	9.8	9.9
Manufacturing	109,800	11.0	8.9
Mining and Logging	1,000	0.1	0.6
Other Services	34,300	3.4	4.0
Professional and Business Services	131,300	13.2	13.3
Retail Trade	107,300	10.8	11.5
Transportation and Utilities	34,500	3.5	3.8
Wholesale Trade	56,100	5.6	4.2

Note: Figures cover non-farm employment as of December 2011 and are not seasonally adjusted; (1) Metropolitan Statistical Area—see Appendix B for areas included
Source: Bureau of Labor Statistics, http://stats.bls.gov

Occupations with Greatest Projected Employment Growth: 2008 – 2018

Occupation[1]	2008 Employment	2018 Projected Employment	Numeric Employment Change	Percent Employment Change
Registered Nurses	30,660	37,430	6,770	22.1
Retail Salespersons	60,240	66,000	5,760	9.6
Combined Food Preparation and Serving Workers, Including Fast Food	35,430	40,270	4,840	13.7
Cashiers	34,400	38,190	3,790	11.0
Waiters and Waitresses	29,160	32,450	3,290	11.3
Office Clerks, General	37,450	40,730	3,280	8.8
Nursing Aides, Orderlies, and Attendants	12,840	15,950	3,110	24.2
Janitors and Cleaners, Except Maids and Housekeeping Cleaners	23,800	26,350	2,550	10.7
Bookkeeping, Accounting, and Auditing Clerks	27,510	30,050	2,540	9.2
Home Health Aides	8,600	10,780	2,180	25.3

Note: Projections cover Oregon; (1) Sorted by numeric employment change
Source: www.projectionscentral.com, State Occupational Projections, 2008–2018 Long-Term Projections

Fastest Growing Occupations: 2008 – 2018

Occupation[1]	2008 Employment	2018 Projected Employment	Numeric Employment Change	Percent Employment Change
Psychiatric Technicians	440	870	430	97.7
Psychiatric Aides	670	1,000	330	49.3
Chiropractors	380	490	110	28.9
Optometrists	350	450	100	28.6
Dental Hygienists	3,140	4,000	860	27.4
Dental Assistants	4,360	5,530	1,170	26.8
Physical Therapist Aides	600	760	160	26.7
Physician Assistants	640	810	170	26.6
Medical Assistants	7,110	8,950	1,840	25.9
Medical and Clinical Laboratory Technicians	1,060	1,330	270	25.5

Note: Projections cover Oregon; (1) Sorted by percent employment change and excludes occupations with numeric employment change less than 100
Source: www.projectionscentral.com, State Occupational Projections, 2008–2018 Long-Term Projections

Average Wages

Occupation	$/Hr.	Occupation	$/Hr.
Accountants and Auditors	30.49	Maids and Housekeeping Cleaners	10.92
Automotive Mechanics	20.09	Maintenance and Repair Workers	18.72
Bookkeepers	18.47	Marketing Managers	51.57
Carpenters	22.48	Nuclear Medicine Technologists	39.20
Cashiers	11.55	Nurses, Licensed Practical	23.20
Clerks, General Office	15.01	Nurses, Registered	38.36
Clerks, Receptionists/Information	13.57	Nursing Aides/Orderlies/Attendants	13.17
Clerks, Shipping/Receiving	15.23	Packers and Packagers, Hand	10.83
Computer Programmers	34.01	Physical Therapists	37.27
Computer Support Specialists	25.80	Postal Service Mail Carriers	25.16
Computer Systems Analysts	40.89	Real Estate Brokers	37.46
Cooks, Restaurant	12.08	Retail Salespersons	12.97
Dentists	99.99	Sales Reps., Exc. Tech./Scientific	30.60
Electrical Engineers	42.45	Sales Reps., Tech./Scientific	49.83
Electricians	33.43	Secretaries, Exc. Legal/Med./Exec.	16.97
Financial Managers	52.55	Security Guards	13.56
First-Line Supervisors/Managers, Sales	19.37	Surgeons	n/a
Food Preparation Workers	10.68	Teacher Assistants	14.10
General and Operations Managers	53.15	Teachers, Elementary School	27.00
Hairdressers/Cosmetologists	13.53	Teachers, Secondary School	27.50
Internists	96.43	Telemarketers	13.09
Janitors and Cleaners	12.36	Truck Drivers, Heavy/Tractor-Trailer	19.51
Landscaping/Groundskeeping Workers	13.43	Truck Drivers, Light/Delivery Svcs.	18.22
Lawyers	49.96	Waiters and Waitresses	12.86

Note: Wage data covers the Portland-Vancouver-Hillsboro, OR-WA Metropolitan Statistical Area—see Appendix B for areas included. Hourly wages for elementary/secondary school teachers and teacher assistants were calculated by the editors from annual wage data assuming a 40 hour work week; n/a not available.
Source: Bureau of Labor Statistics, Metro Area Occupational Employment and Wage Estimates, May 2011

RESIDENTIAL REAL ESTATE

Building Permits

Area	Single-Family			Multi-Family			Total		
	2010	2011	Pct. Chg.	2010	2011	Pct. Chg.	2010	2011	Pct. Chg.
City	435	451	3.7	665	913	37.3	1,100	1,364	24.0
MSA[1]	3,359	3,132	-6.8	1,117	2,081	86.3	4,476	5,213	16.5
U.S.	447,311	418,498	-6.4	157,299	205,563	30.7	604,610	624,061	3.2

Note: (1) Metropolitan Statistical Area—see Appendix B for areas included; figures represent new, privately-owned housing units authorized (unadjusted data); All permit data are based on estimates with imputation.
Source: U.S. Census Bureau, Manufacturing, Mining, and Construction Statistics, Building Permits, 2010, 2011

Homeownership Rate

Area	2005 (%)	2006 (%)	2007 (%)	2008 (%)	2009 (%)	2010 (%)	2011 (%)
MSA[1]	68.3	66.0	61.2	62.6	64.0	63.7	63.7
U.S.	68.9	68.8	68.1	67.8	67.4	66.9	66.1

Note: (1) Metropolitan Statistical Area—see Appendix B for areas included
Source: U.S. Census Bureau, Housing Vacancies and Homeownership Annual Statistics: 2011

Housing Vacancy Rates

Area	Gross Vacancy Rate[2] (%)			Year-Round Vacancy Rate[3] (%)			Rental Vacancy Rate[4] (%)			Homeowner Vacancy Rate[5] (%)		
	2009	2010	2011	2009	2010	2011	2009	2010	2011	2009	2010	2011
MSA[1]	8.2	7.2	6.5	7.9	7.0	6.3	4.3	4.2	3.4	4.8	3.2	2.0
U.S.	14.5	14.3	14.2	11.3	11.3	11.1	10.6	10.2	9.5	2.6	2.6	2.5

Note: (1) Metropolitan Statistical Area—see Appendix B for areas included; (2) The percentage of the total housing inventory that is vacant; (3) The percentage of the housing inventory (excluding seasonal units) that is year-round vacant; (4) The percentage of rental inventory that is vacant for rent; (5) The percentage of homeowner inventory that is vacant for sale
Source: U.S. Census Bureau, Housing Vacancies and Homeownership Annual Statistics: 2011

TAXES

State Corporate Income Tax Rates

State	Tax Rate (%)	Income Brackets ($)	Num. of Brackets	Financial Institution Tax Rate (%)[a]	Federal Income Tax Ded.
Oregon	6.6 - 7.6 (v)	250,001	2	6.6 - 7.6 (v)	No

Note: Tax rates as of January 1, 2012; (a) Rates listed are the corporate income tax rate applied to financial institutions or excise taxes based on income. Some states have other taxes based upon the value of deposits or shares; (v) Oregon's minimum tax for C corporations depends on the Oregon sales of the filing group. The minimum tax ranges from $150 for corporations with sales under $500,000, up to $100,000 for companies with sales of $100 million or above.
Source: Federation of Tax Administrators, "State Corporate Income Tax Rates, 2012"

State Individual Income Tax Rates

State	Tax Rate (%)	Income Brackets ($)	Num. of Brackets	Personal Exempt. ($)[1] Single	Personal Exempt. ($)[1] Dependents	Fed. Inc. Tax Ded.
Oregon (a)	5.0 - 9.9	2,000 (b)-125,000 (b)	4	183 (c)	183 (c)	Yes (m)

Note: Tax rates as of January 1, 2012; Local- and county-level taxes are not included; n/a not applicable; (1) Married joint filers generally receive double the single exemption; (a) 17 states have statutory provision for automatically adjusting to the rate of inflation the dollar values of the income tax brackets, standard deductions, and/or personal exemptions. Massachusetts, Michigan, and Nebraska index the personal exemptiononly. Oregon does not index the income brackets for $125,000 and over. Because the inflation-adjustments for 2012 are not yet available in some cases, the table may report the 2011 amounts; (b) For joint returns, taxes are twice the tax on half the couple's income; (c) The personal exemption takes the form of a tax credit instead of a deduction; (m) The deduction for federal income tax is limited to $5,000 for individuals and $10,000 for joint returns in Missouri and Montana, and to $5,950 for all filers in Oregon.
Source: Federation of Tax Administrators, "State Individual Income Tax Rates, 2012"

Various State and Local Tax Rates

State	State and Local Sales and Use (%)	State Sales and Use (%)	Gasoline[1] (¢/gal.)	Cigarette[2] ($/pack)	Spirits[3] ($/gal.)	Wine[4] ($/gal.)	Beer[5] ($/gal.)
Oregon	None	None	31.0	1.18	23.03 (f)	0.67	0.08

Note: All tax rates as of January 1, 2012 except beer, wine and spirits (September 1, 2011); (1) The American Petroleum Institute has developed a methodology for determining the average tax rate on a gallon of fuel. Rates may include any of the following: excise taxes, environmental fees, storage tank fees, other fees or taxes, general sales tax, and local taxes. In states where gasoline is subject to the general sales tax, or where the fuel tax is based on the average sale price, the average rate determined by API is sensitive to changes in the price of gasoline. States that fully or partially apply general sales taxes to gasoline: CA, CO, GA, IL, IN, MI, NY; (2) The federal excise tax of $1.0066 per pack and local taxes are not included; (3) Rates are those applicable to off-premise sales of 40% alcohol by volume (a.b.v.) distilled spirits in 750ml containers. Local excise taxes are excluded; (4) Rates are those applicable to off-premise sales of 11% a.b.v. non-carbonated wine in 750ml containers; (5) Rates are those applicable to off-premise sales of 4.7% a.b.v. beer in 12 ounce containers; (f) States where the government controls sales. In these "control states," products are subject to ad valorem mark-up and excise taxes. The excise tax rate is calculated using a methodology developed by the Distilled Spirits Council of the United States.
Source: Tax Foundation, 2012 Facts & Figures: How Does Your State Compare?

State-Local Tax Burdens

Area	Rate (%)	Rank[1]	Per Capita Taxes Paid to Home State ($)	Total State and Local Per Capita Taxes Paid ($)	Per Capita Income ($)
Oregon	9.8	17	2,732	3,761	38,527
U.S. Average	9.8	-	3,057	4,160	42,539

Note: Figures cover 2009; (1) Rank ranges from 1 to 50 where 1 is highest tax burden
Source: Tax Foundation, State-Local Tax Burdens, All States, 2009

State Business Tax Climate Index Rankings

State	Overall Rank	Corporate Tax Index Rank	Individual Income Tax Index Rank	Sales Tax Index Rank	Unemployment Insurance Tax Index Rank	Property Tax Index Rank
Oregon	13	31	34	4	33	10

Note: The index is a measure of how each state's tax laws affect economic performance. The lower the rank, the more favorable a state's tax system is for business. States without a given tax are given a ranking of 1.
Source: Tax Foundation, Major Components of the State Business Tax Climate Index, FY 2012

COMMERCIAL REAL ESTATE

Office Market

Market Area	Inventory (sq. ft.)	Vacant (sq. ft.)	Vac. Rate (%)	Under Constr. (sq. ft.)	Asking Rent ($/sf/yr) Class A	Asking Rent ($/sf/yr) Class B
Portland	52,546,054	7,250,133	13.8	393,851	23.22	18.63

Source: Grubb & Ellis, Office Markets Trends, 4th Quarter 2011

Industrial Market

Market Area	Inventory (sq. ft.)	Vacant (sq. ft.)	Vac. Rate (%)	Under Constr. (sq. ft.)	Asking Rent ($/sf/yr) WH/Dist	Asking Rent ($/sf/yr) R&D/Flex
Portland	164,549,220	13,345,053	8.1	2,516,823	4.92	7.92

Source: Grubb & Ellis, Industrial Markets Trends, 4th Quarter 2011

COMMERCIAL UTILITIES

Typical Monthly Electric Bills

Area	Commercial Service ($/month) 1,500 kWh	Commercial Service ($/month) 40 kW demand 14,000 kWh	Industrial Service ($/month) 1,000 kW demand 200,000 kWh	Industrial Service ($/month) 50,000 kW demand 15,000,000 kWh
City	171	1,283	17,561	999,064
Average[1]	189	1,616	25,197	1,470,813

Note: Based on total rates in effect July 1, 2011; (1) average based on 184 utilities surveyed
Source: Edison Electric Institute, Typical Bills and Average Rates Report, Summer 2011

TRANSPORTATION

Means of Transportation to Work

Area	Car/Truck/Van: Drove Alone	Car/Truck/Van: Car-pooled	Public Transportation: Bus	Public Transportation: Subway	Public Transportation: Railroad	Bicycle	Walked	Other Means	Worked at Home
City	59.9	8.8	10.1	0.6	0.2	6.1	5.6	2.1	6.6
MSA[1]	71.3	9.7	5.0	0.4	0.2	2.2	3.4	1.6	6.2
U.S.	76.0	10.2	2.7	1.7	0.5	0.5	2.8	1.3	4.2

Note: Figures are percentages and cover workers 16 years of age and older; (1) Figures cover the Portland-Vancouver-Hillsboro, OR-WA Metropolitan Statistical Area—see Appendix B for areas included
Source: U.S. Census Bureau, 2008-2010 American Community Survey 3-Year Estimates

Travel Time to Work

Area	Less Than 10 Minutes	10 to 19 Minutes	20 to 29 Minutes	30 to 44 Minutes	45 to 59 Minutes	60 to 89 Minutes	90 Minutes or More
City	9.2	31.3	27.4	21.7	5.3	3.5	1.7
MSA[1]	11.7	29.1	23.8	21.9	7.2	4.4	1.8
U.S.	13.9	30.1	20.8	19.8	7.5	5.5	2.5

Note: Figures are percentages and include workers 16 years old and over; (1) Figures cover the Portland-Vancouver-Hillsboro, OR-WA Metropolitan Statistical Area—see Appendix B for areas included
Source: U.S. Census Bureau, 2008-2010 American Community Survey 3-Year Estimates

Travel Time Index

Area	1985	1990	1995	2000	2005	2010
Urban Area[1]	1.07	1.12	1.19	1.26	1.27	1.25
Average[2]	1.11	1.16	1.18	1.21	1.25	1.20

Note: Travel Time Index—the ratio of travel time in the peak period to the travel time at free-flow conditions. A value of 1.30 indicates a 20-minute free-flow trip takes 26 minutes in the peak. Free-flow speeds (60 mph on freeways and 35 mph on principal arterials) are used as the comparison threshold; (1) Covers the Portland OR-WA urban area; (2) average of 439 urban areas
Source: Texas Transportation Institute, Urban Mobility Report 2011, September 2011

Public Transportation

Agency Name / Mode of Transportation	Vehicles Operated in Maximum Service	Annual Unlinked Passenger Trips ('000)	Annual Passenger Miles ('000)
Tri-County Metropolitan Transportation District of Oregon (Tri-Met)			
Bus (directly operated)	540	60,508.2	231,580.9
Commuter Rail (purchased transportation)	4	306.2	2,558.1
Demand Response (purchased transportation)	217	966.9	9,251.0
Demand Response Taxi (purchased transportation)	44	105.8	1,117.2
Light Rail (directly operated)	110	42,452.6	208,779.2

Source: Federal Transit Administration, National Transit Database, 2010

Air Transportation

Airport Name and Code / Type of Service	Passenger Airlines[1]	Passenger Enplanements	Freight Carriers[2]	Freight (lbs.)
Portland International (PDX)				
Domestic service (U.S. carriers - 2011)	25	6,536,020	16	193,830,980
International service (U.S. carriers - 2010)	9	172,208	4	4,476,566

Note: (1) Includes all U.S.-based major, minor and commuter airlines that carried at least one passenger during the year; (2) Includes all U.S.-based airlines and freight carriers that transported at least one pound of freight during the year
Source: Bureau of Transportation Statistics, The Intermodal Transportation Database, Air Carriers: T-100 Domestic Market (U.S. Carriers), 2011; Bureau of Transportation Statistics, The Intermodal Transportation Database, Air Carriers: T-100 International Market (U.S. Carriers), 2010

Other Transportation Statistics

Major Highways:	I-5; I-80
Amtrak Service:	Yes
Major Waterways/Ports:	Port of Portland

Source: Amtrak.com; Google Maps

BUSINESSES

Major Business Headquarters

Company Name	Rankings	
	Fortune[1]	Forbes[2]
Precision Castparts	409	-

Note: (1) Fortune 500—companies that produce a 10-K are ranked 1 to 500 based on 2010 revenue; (2) all private companies with at least $2 billion in annual revenue are ranked 1 to 212; companies listed are headquartered in the city; dashes indicate no ranking
Source: Fortune, "Fortune 500," May 23, 2011; Forbes, "America's Largest Private Companies," November 16, 2011

Fast-Growing Businesses

According to *Inc.*, Portland is home to one of America's 500 fastest-growing private companies: **Jama Software** (#202). Criteria: must be an independent, privately-held, for-profit, U.S. corporation, proprietorship or partnership; revenues must be at least $80,000 in 2007 and $2 million in 2010; must have four-year operating/sales history. Holding companies, regulated banks, and utilities were excluded. *Inc., "America's 500 Fastest-Growing Private Companies," September 2011*

According to Deloitte, Portland is home to one of North America's 500 fastest-growing high-technology companies: **Smarsh** (#151). Companies are ranked by percentage growth in revenue over a five-year period. Criteria for inclusion: company must be headquartered within North America; must own proprietary intellectual property or proprietary technology that contributes to a significant portion of the company's operating revenue, or devote a significant proportion of revenues to research and development of technology; must have been in business for a minumum of five years with 2006 operating revenues of at least $50,000 USD/CD and 2010 operating revenues of at least $5 million USD/CD. *Deloitte Touche Tohmatsu, 2011 Deloitte Technology Fast 500™*

Minority- and Women-Owned Businesses

Group	All Firms		Firms with Paid Employees			
	Firms	Sales ($000)	Firms	Sales ($000)	Employees	Payroll ($000)
Asian	n/a	n/a	n/a	n/a	n/a	n/a
Black	n/a	n/a	n/a	n/a	n/a	n/a
Hispanic	n/a	n/a	n/a	n/a	n/a	n/a
Women	n/a	n/a	n/a	n/a	n/a	n/a
All Firms	1,880	1,244,730	518	1,180,998	5,725	215,847

Note: Figures cover firms located in the city; minority- and women-owned business are defined as firms in which the corresponding group own 51% or more of the stock or equity of the company; n/a not available
Source: U.S. Census Bureau, 2007 Economic Census, Survey of Business Owners

HOTELS

Hotels/Motels

Area	5 Star		4 Star		3 Star		2 Star		1 Star		Not Rated	
	Num.	Pct.[3]	Num.	Pct.[3]	Num.	Pct.[3]	Num.	Pct.[3]	Num.	Pct.[3]	Num.	Pct.[3]
City[1]	1	0.5	12	5.7	61	28.8	103	48.6	6	2.8	29	13.7
Total[2]	133	0.9	940	6.5	4,569	31.8	7,033	48.9	351	2.4	1,343	9.3

Note: (1) Figures cover Portland and vicinity; (2) Figures cover all 100 cities in this book; (3) Percentage of hotels which have a given star rating; Star ratings are determined by expedia.com and offer an indication of the general quality of a particular hotel.
Source: expedia.com, April 25, 2012

The Portland-Vancouver-Hillsboro, OR-WA metro area is home to three of the best hotels in the U.S. according to *Condé Nast Traveler*: **The Nines** (#45); **Allison Inn & Spa, Newburg** (#56); **Hotel Modera** (#72). The selections are based on over 25,000 responses to the magazine's annual Readers' Choice Survey. *Condé Nast Traveler, "2011 Readers' Choice Awards"*

EVENT SITES

Major Stadiums, Arenas, and Auditoriums

Name	Max. Capacity
Memorial Coliseum	12,000
PGE Park	23,136
Portland Center for the Performing Arts	6,940
Rose Garden	20,630

Source: Original research

Convention Centers

Name	Overall Space (sq. ft.)	Exhibit Space (sq. ft.)	Meeting Space (sq. ft.)	Meeting Rooms
Oregon Convention Center	n/a	22,800	255,000	50

Note: n/a not available
Source: Original research

Living Environment

COST OF LIVING

Cost of Living Index

Composite Index	Groceries	Housing	Utilities	Trans-portation	Health Care	Misc. Goods/ Services
113.7	111.3	131.0	88.3	113.7	113.7	107.6

Note: U.S. = 100; Figures cover the Portland OR urban area.
Source: The Council for Community and Economic Research, ACCRA Cost of Living Index, 2011

Grocery Prices

Area[1]	T-Bone Steak ($/pound)	Frying Chicken ($/pound)	Whole Milk ($/half gal.)	Eggs ($/dozen)	Orange Juice ($/64 oz.)	Coffee ($/11.5 oz.)
City[2]	9.90	1.47	1.86	1.83	3.52	5.36
Avg.	9.25	1.18	2.22	1.66	3.19	4.40
Min.	6.70	0.88	1.31	0.95	2.46	2.94
Max.	14.30	2.16	3.50	3.18	4.75	6.83

Note: (1) Values for the local area are compared with the average, minimum and maximum values for all 335 areas in the Cost of Living Index; (2) Figures cover the Portland OR urban area; **T-Bone Steak** *(price per pound);* **Frying Chicken** *(price per pound, whole fryer);* **Whole Milk** *(half gallon carton);* **Eggs** *(price per dozen, Grade A, large);* **Orange Juice** *(64 oz. Tropicana or Florida Natural);* **Coffee** *(11.5 oz. can, vacuum-packed, Maxwell House, Hills Bros, or Folgers).*
Source: The Council for Community and Economic Research, ACCRA Cost of Living Index, 2011

Housing and Utility Costs

Area[1]	New Home Price ($)	Apartment Rent ($/month)	All Electric ($/month)	Part Electric ($/month)	Other Energy ($/month)	Telephone ($/month)
City[2]	356,341	1,289	-	71.51	80.84	22.26
Avg.	285,990	839	163.23	89.00	77.52	26.92
Min.	188,005	460	125.58	45.39	33.89	17.98
Max.	1,197,028	3,244	339.16	181.97	348.69	40.01

Note: (1) Values for the local area are compared with the average, minimum and maximum values for all 335 areas in the Cost of Living Index; (2) Figures cover the Portland OR urban area; **New Home Price** *(2,400 sf living area, 8,000 sf lot, in urban area with full utilities);* **Apartment Rent** *(950 sf 2 bedroom/1.5 or 2 bath, unfurnished, excluding all utilities except water);* **All Electric** *(average monthly cost for an all-electric home);* **Part Electric** *(average monthly cost for a part-electric home);* **Other Energy** *(average monthly cost for natural gas, fuel oil, coal, wood, and any other forms of energy except electricity);* **Telephone** *(price includes basic monthly rate for a private residential line plus additional local usage charges incurred by a family of four).*
Source: The Council for Community and Economic Research, ACCRA Cost of Living Index, 2011

Health Care, Transportation, and Other Costs

Area[1]	Doctor ($/visit)	Dentist ($/visit)	Optometrist ($/visit)	Gasoline ($/gallon)	Beauty Salon ($/visit)	Men's Shirt ($)
City[2]	122.00	93.64	112.39	3.66	38.75	23.24
Avg.	93.88	81.72	90.54	3.48	32.65	25.06
Min.	60.00	55.33	53.66	3.18	19.78	13.44
Max.	154.98	145.97	183.72	4.31	63.21	46.00

Note: (1) Values for the local area are compared with the average, minimum and maximum values for all 335 areas in the Cost of Living Index; (2) Figures cover the Portland OR urban area; **Doctor** *(general practitioners routine exam of an established patient);* **Dentist** *(adult teeth cleaning and periodic oral examination);* **Optometrist** *(full vision eye exam for established adult patient);* **Gasoline** *(one gallon regular unleaded, national brand, including all taxes, cash price at self-service pump if available);* **Beauty Salon** *(woman's shampoo, trim, and blow-dry);* **Men's Shirt** *(cotton/polyester dress shirt, pinpoint weave, long sleeves).*
Source: The Council for Community and Economic Research, ACCRA Cost of Living Index, 2011

HOUSING

House Price Index (HPI)

Area	National Ranking[2]	Quarterly Change (%)	One-Year Change (%)	Five-Year Change (%)
MSA[1]	220	0.77	-4.43	-19.54
U.S.[3]	-	-0.10	-2.43	-19.16

Note: The HPI is a weighted repeat sales index. It measures average price changes in repeat sales or refinancings on the same properties. This information is obtained by reviewing repeat mortgage transactions on single-family properties whose mortgages have been purchased or securitized by Fannie Mae or Freddie Mac in January 1975; (1) Metropolitan/Micropolitan Statistical Area—see Appendix B for areas included; (2) Rankings are based on annual percentage change for all metro areas containing at least 15,000 transactions over the last 10 years and ranges from 1 to 306; (3) figures based on a weighted average of Census Division estimates using a purchase only index; all figures are for the period ending December 31, 2011
Source: Federal Housing Finance Agency, House Price Index, February 23, 2012

House Price Valuations

Area	Q4 2005		Q4 2006		Q4 2007		Q4 2008		Q4 2009	
	Price ($000)	Over-valuation	Price ($000)	Over-valuation	Price ($000)	Over-valuation	Price ($000)	Over-valuation	Price ($000)	Over-valuation
MSA[1]	271.9	33.6	298.3	37.6	305.6	35.3	281.4	23.8	262.2	15.2

Note: Figures show the percentage of over- or under-valuation of single family homes relative to statistically normal house values (e.g. a value of 23.6 indicates that house values are 23.6% overvalued). Statistically normal house values are based on house prices, interest rates, household incomes, population densities, and any historical premiums or discounts metropolitan areas have exhibited over time; (1) Figures cover the Portland-Vancouver-Hillsboro, OR-WA - see Appendix B for areas included
Source: Global Insight/PNC Financial Services Group, House Prices in America: 4th Quarter 2009 Update

Median Single-Family Home Prices

Area	2009	2010	2011[p]	Percent Change 2010 to 2011
MSA[1]	244.1	237.3	219.5	-7.5
U.S. Average	172.1	173.1	166.2	-4.0

Note: Figures are median sales prices of existing single-family homes in thousands of dollars; (p) preliminary; n/a not available; (1) Metropolitan Statistical Area—see Appendix B for areas included
Source: National Association of Realtors, Median Sales Price of Existing Single-Family Homes for Metropolitan Areas, 4th Quarter 2011

Affordability Index of Existing Single-Family Homes

Area	2009	2010	2011[p]	Percent Change 2010 to 2011
MSA[1]	78.0	85.1	96.8	13.7

Note: The housing affordability index measures whether or not a typical family could qualify for a mortgage loan on a typical home. The higher the index, the greater the household purchasing power. An index of 100 is defined as the point where a median-income household has exactly enough income to qualify for the purchase of a median-priced existing single-family home, assuming a 20 percent downpayment and 25 percent of gross income devoted to mortgage principal and interest payments; (p) preliminary; n/a not available; (1) Metropolitan Statistical Area—see Appendix B for areas included
Source: National Association of Realtors, Affordability Index of Existing Single-Family Homes, 2011

Median Apartment Condo-Coop Home Prices

Area	2009	2010	2011[p]	Percent Change 2010 to 2011
MSA[1]	183.0	173.7	152.6	-12.1
U.S. Average	175.6	171.7	165.1	-3.8

Note: Figures are median sales prices of existing apartment condo-coop homes in thousands of dollars; (p) preliminary; n/a not available; (1) Metropolitan Statistical Area—see Appendix B for areas included
Source: National Association of Realtors, Median Sales Price of Existing Apartment Condo-Coop Homes for Metropolitan Areas, 4th Quarter 2011

Year Housing Structure Built

Area	2005 or Later	2000 -2004	1990 -1999	1980 -1989	1970 -1979	1960 -1969	1950 -1959	Before 1950	Median Year
City	4.2	6.7	8.7	5.6	11.5	10.0	13.2	40.1	1957
MSA[1]	5.5	9.8	19.5	11.7	18.3	9.4	7.7	18.1	1978
U.S.	5.0	8.6	14.0	14.1	16.3	11.3	11.2	19.6	1975

Note: Figures are percentages except for Median Year; (1) Figures cover the Portland-Vancouver-Hillsboro, OR-WA Metropolitan Statistical Area—see Appendix B for areas included
Source: U.S. Census Bureau, 2008-2010 American Community Survey 3-Year Estimates

HEALTH

Health Risk Data

Category	MSA[1] (%)	U.S. (%)
Adults who have been told they have high blood pressure[2]	25.4	28.7
Adults who have been told they have high blood cholesterol[2]	33.8	37.5
Adults who have been told they have diabetes[3]	6.5	8.7
Adults who have been told they have arthritis[2]	25.3	26.0
Adults who have been told they currently have asthma	8.5	9.1
Adults who are current smokers	13.9	17.3
Adults who are heavy drinkers[4]	5.9	5.0
Adults who are binge drinkers[5]	14.7	15.1
Adults who are overweight (BMI 25.0 - 29.9)	33.7	36.2
Adults who are obese (BMI 30.0 - 99.8)	26.0	27.5
Adults who participated in any physical activities in the past month	84.2	76.1
Adults 50+ who have ever had a sigmoidoscopy or colonoscopy	69.7	65.2
Women aged 40+ who have had a mammogram within the past two years	72.6	75.2
Men aged 40+ who have had a PSA test within the past two years	47.8	53.2
Adults aged 65+ who have had flu shot within the past year	66.8	67.5
Adults aged 18–64 who have any kind of health care coverage	83.7	82.2

Note: Data as of 2010 unless otherwise noted; (1) Figures cover the Portland-Vancouver-Beaverton, OR-WA Metropolitan Statistical Area—see Appendix B for areas included; (2) Data as of 2009; (3) Figures do not include pregnancy-related, borderline, or pre-diabetes; (4) Heavy drinkers are classified as males having more than two drinks per day or females having more than one drink per day; (5) Binge drinkers are classified as males having five or more drinks on one occasion or females having four or more drinks on one occasion
Source: Centers for Disease Control and Prevention, Behaviorial Risk Factor Surveillance System, SMART: Selected Metropolitan/Micropolitan Area Risk Trends, 2009, 2010

Mortality Rates for the Top 10 Causes of Death in the U.S.

ICD-10[a] Sub-Chapter	ICD-10[a] Code	Age-Adjusted Mortality Rate[1] per 100,000 population	
		County[2]	U.S.
Malignant neoplasms	C00-C97	191.0	175.6
Ischaemic heart diseases	I20-I25	91.3	121.6
Other forms of heart disease	I30-I51	51.4	48.6
Chronic lower respiratory diseases	J40-J47	46.7	42.3
Cerebrovascular diseases	I60-I69	45.1	40.6
Organic, including symptomatic, mental disorders	F01-F09	44.7	26.7
Other degenerative diseases of the nervous system	G30-G31	32.6	24.7
Other external causes of accidental injury	W00-X59	33.7	24.4
Diabetes mellitus	E10-E14	28.9	21.7
Hypertensive diseases	I10-I15	17.0	18.2

Note: (a) ICD-10 = International Classification of Diseases 10th Revision; (1) Mortality rates are a three year average covering 2007-2009; (2) Figures cover Multnomah County
Source: Centers for Disease Control and Prevention, National Center for Health Statistics. Underlying Cause of Death 1999-2009 on CDC WONDER Online Database, released 2012. Data for year 2009 are compiled from the Multiple Cause of Death File 2009, Series 20 No. 2O, 2012, Data for year 2008 are compiled from the Multiple Cause of Death File 2008, Series 20 No. 2N, 2011, Data for year 2007 are compiled from Multiple Cause of Death File 2007, Series 20 No. 2M, 2010.

Mortality Rates for Selected Causes of Death

ICD-10[a] Sub-Chapter	ICD-10[a] Code	Age-Adjusted Mortality Rate[1] per 100,000 population	
		County[2]	U.S.
Assault	X85-Y09	3.5	5.7
Human immunodeficiency virus (HIV) disease	B20-B24	2.7	3.3
Influenza and pneumonia	J09-J18	12.7	16.4
Intentional self-harm	X60-X84	14.3	11.5
Malnutrition	E40-E46	*Unreliable	0.8
Obesity and other hyperalimentation	E65-E68	2.1	1.6
Transport accidents	V01-V99	7.8	13.7
Viral hepatitis	B15-B19	5.0	2.2

Note: (a) ICD-10 = International Classification of Diseases 10th Revision; (1) Mortality rates are a three year average covering 2007-2009; (2) Figures cover Multnomah County; (*) Unreliable data as per CDC
Source: Centers for Disease Control and Prevention, National Center for Health Statistics. Underlying Cause of Death 1999-2009 on CDC WONDER Online Database, released 2012. Data for year 2009 are compiled from the Multiple Cause of Death File 2009, Series 20 No. 2O, 2012, Data for year 2008 are compiled from the Multiple Cause of Death File 2008, Series 20 No. 2N, 2011, Data for year 2007 are compiled from Multiple Cause of Death File 2007, Series 20 No. 2M, 2010.

Distribution of Physicians and Dentists

Area[1]	Dentists[2]	D.O.[3]	M.D.[4] Total	M.D.[4] Family/General Practice	M.D.[4] Pediatrics	M.D.[4] Medical Specialties	M.D.[4] Surgical Specialties
Local (number)	380	173	2,372	222	143	901	511
Local (rate[5])	5.5	2.4	33.3	3.1	2.0	12.6	7.2
U.S. (rate[5])	4.5	1.9	18.3	2.5	1.4	6.8	4.1

Note: Data as of 2008 unless noted; (1) Local data covers Multnomah County; (2) Data as of 2007; (3) Doctor of Osteopathic Medicine; (4) Includes active, non-federal, patient-care, office-based Doctors of Medicine; (5) rate per 10,000 population
Source: Area Resource File (ARF). 2009-2010 Release. U.S. Department of Health and Human Services, Health Resources and Services Administration, Bureau of Health Professions, Rockville, MD, August 2010

Best Hospitals

According to *U.S. News*, the Portland-Vancouver-Hillsboro, OR-WA is home to one of the best hospitals in the U.S.: **Oregon Health and Science University** (1 specialty). The hospital listed was highly ranked in at least one adult specialty. *U.S. News Online, "America's Best Hospitals 2011-12"*

According to *U.S. News*, the Portland-Vancouver-Hillsboro, OR-WA is home to one of the best children's hospitals in the U.S.: **Doernbecher Children's Hospital at Oregon Health and Science University** (8 specialties). The hospital listed was highly ranked in at least one pediatric specialty. *U.S. News Online, "America's Best Children's Hospitals 2011-12"*

EDUCATION

Public School District Statistics

District Name	Schls	Pupils	Pupil/Teacher Ratio	Minority Pupils[1] (%)	Free Lunch Eligible[2] (%)	IEP[3] (%)
Centennial SD 28J	10	6,687	21.3	45.1	50.7	14.8
David Douglas SD 40	16	10,855	19.1	52.6	61.6	13.5
Parkrose SD 3	6	3,456	20.4	61.5	60.8	14.1
Portland SD 1J	91	45,748	18.5	47.7	35.8	15.1

Note: Table includes school districts with 2,000 or more students; (1) Percentage of students that are not non-Hispanic white; (2) Percentage of students that are eligible for the free lunch program; (3) Percentage of students that have an Individualized Education Program.
Source: U.S. Department of Education, National Center for Education Statistics, Common Core of Data, Local Education Agency (School District) Universe Survey: School Year 2009-2010; U.S. Department of Education, National Center for Education Statistics, Common Core of Data, Public Elementary/Secondary School Universe Survey: School Year 2009-2010

Highest Level of Education

Area	Less than H.S.	H.S. Diploma	Some College, No Deg.	Associate Degree	Bachelors Degree	Masters Degree	Profess. School Degree	Doctorate Degree
City	10.4	18.3	22.8	6.2	26.0	10.7	3.8	1.9
MSA[1]	9.9	22.3	26.2	8.0	21.6	8.2	2.3	1.5
U.S.	14.7	28.4	21.3	7.6	17.6	7.2	1.9	1.2

Note: Figures cover persons age 25 and over; (1) Figures cover the Portland-Vancouver-Hillsboro, OR-WA Metropolitan Statistical Area—see Appendix B for areas included
Source: U.S. Census Bureau, 2008-2010 American Community Survey 3-Year Estimates

Educational Attainment by Race

Area	High School Graduate or Higher (%)					Bachelor's Degree or Higher (%)				
	Total	White	Black	Asian	Hisp.[2]	Total	White	Black	Asian	Hisp.[2]
City	89.6	92.7	83.1	75.7	59.3	42.4	45.9	21.3	36.4	20.5
MSA[1]	90.1	92.2	85.0	84.7	58.8	33.6	34.4	24.0	45.5	13.5
U.S.	85.3	87.5	81.4	85.5	61.6	28.0	29.3	17.8	50.2	13.0

Note: Figures shown cover persons 25 years old and over; (1) Figures cover the Portland-Vancouver-Hillsboro, OR-WA Metropolitan Statistical Area—see Appendix B for areas included; (2) People of Hispanic origin can be of any race
Source: U.S. Census Bureau, 2008-2010 American Community Survey 3-Year Estimates

School Enrollment by Grade and Control

Area	Preschool (%)		Kindergarten (%)		Grades 1 - 4 (%)		Grades 5 - 8 (%)		Grades 9 - 12 (%)	
	Public	Private	Public	Private	Public	Private	Public	Private	Public	Private
City	42.4	57.6	84.9	15.1	87.5	12.5	89.2	10.8	88.8	11.2
MSA[1]	38.0	62.0	84.0	16.0	89.4	10.6	90.9	9.1	91.4	8.6
U.S.	55.4	44.6	87.1	12.9	89.4	10.6	89.5	10.5	90.4	9.6

Note: Figures shown cover persons 3 years old and over; (1) Figures cover the Portland-Vancouver-Hillsboro, OR-WA Metropolitan Statistical Area—see Appendix B for areas included
Source: U.S. Census Bureau, 2008-2010 American Community Survey 3-Year Estimates

Average Salaries of Public School Classroom Teachers

Area	2010-11		2011-12		Percent Change 2010-11 to 2011-12	Percent Change 2001-02 to 2011-12
	Dollars	Rank[1]	Dollars	Rank[1]		
Oregon	56,503	15	57,348	15	1.50	24.30
U.S. Average	55,623	-	56,643	-	1.83	26.8

Note: (1) State rank ranges from 1 to 51 where 1 indicates highest salary.
Source: National Education Association, Rankings & Estimates: Rankings of the States 2011 and Estimates of School Statistics 2012, December 2011

Higher Education

Four-Year Colleges			Two-Year Colleges			Medical Schools[1]	Law Schools[2]	Voc/ Tech[3]
Public	Private Non-profit	Private For-profit	Public	Private Non-profit	Private For-profit			
2	14	4	1	1	10	1	1	1

Note: Figures cover institutions located within the city limits and include main campuses only; (1) includes schools accredited by the Liaison Committee on Medical Education and the American Osteopathic Association's Commission on Osteopathic College Accreditation; (2) includes American Bar Association-accredited law schools; (3) includes all schools with programs that are less than 2 years.
Source: National Center for Education Statistics, Integrated Postsecondary Education System (IPEDS) Peer Analysis System, 2011-12; Association of American Medical Colleges, Member List, April 23, 2012; American Osteopathic Association, Member List, April 23, 2012; Law School Admission Council, Official Guide to ABA-Approved Law Schools Online, April 23, 2012

According to *U.S. News & World Report,* the Portland-Vancouver-Hillsboro, OR-WA is home to three of the best liberal arts colleges in the U.S.: **Reed College** (#57); **Lewis & Clark College** (#71); **Linfield College** (#121). The indicators used to capture academic quality fall into a number of categories: assessment by administrators at peer institutions; retention of students; faculty resources; student selectivity; financial resources; alumni giving; high school counselor ratings of colleges; and graduation rate. *U.S. News & World Report, "America's Best Colleges 2012"*

PRESIDENTIAL ELECTION

2008 Presidential Election Results

Area	Obama	McCain	Nader	Other
Multnomah County	76.7	20.6	1.1	1.6
U.S.	52.9	45.6	0.6	0.9

Note: Results are percentages and may not add to 100% due to rounding
Source: Dave Leip's Atlas of U.S. Presidential Elections, www.uselectionatlas.org

EMPLOYERS

Major Employers

Company Name	Industry
Children's Creative Learning Center	Child day care services
Clackamas Community College	Community college
Coho Distributing	Liquor
Con-Way Enterprise Services	Accounting, auditing, and bookkeeping
Legacy Emanuel Hospital and Health Center	General medical and surgical hospitals
Nike	Rubber and plastics footwear
Oregon Health & Science University	Colleges and universities
PCC Structurals	Aircraft parts and equipment, nec
Portland Adventist Medical Center	General medical and surgical hospitals
Portland Community College	Community college
Portland State University	Colleges and universities
Providence Health & Services - Oregon	Skilled nursing care facilities
School Dist 1 Multnomah County	Public elementary and secondary schools
Shilo Management Corp.	Motels
Southwest Washington Medical Center	General medical and surgical hospitals
Stancorp Mortgage Investors	Life insurance
SW Washington Hospital	General medical and surgical hospitals
Tektronix	Instruments to measure elasticity
The Evergreen Aviation and Space Museum	Museums and art galleries
Veterans Health Administration	Administration of veterans' affairs

Note: Companies shown are located within the Portland-Vancouver-Hillsboro, OR-WA metropolitan area.
Source: Hoovers.com, data extracted April 25 2012

Best Companies to Work For

Umpqua Bank, headquartered in Portland, is among "The 100 Best Companies to Work For." To pick the 100 Best Companies to Work For, *Fortune* partnered with the Great Place to Work Institute. Two hundred eighty firms participated in this year's survey. Two-thirds of a company's score is based on the results of the Institute's Trust Index survey, which is sent to a random sample of employees from each company. The questions related to attitudes about management's credibility, job satisfaction, and camaraderie. The other third of the scoring is based on the company's responses to the Institute's Culture Audit, which includes detailed questions about pay and benefit programs, and a series of open-ended questions about hiring practices, internal communication, training, recognition programs, and diversity efforts. Any company that is at least five years old with more than 1,000 U.S. employees is eligible. *Fortune, "The 100 Best Companies to Work For," February 6, 2012*

PUBLIC SAFETY

Crime Rate

Area	All Crimes	Violent Crimes				Property Crimes		
		Murder	Forcible Rape	Robbery	Aggrav. Assault	Burglary	Larceny -Theft	Motor Vehicle Theft
City	5,571.0	3.9	40.8	178.1	317.9	730.0	3,725.4	575.0
Suburbs[1]	n/a	n/a	n/a	n/a	n/a	n/a	n/a	n/a
Metro[2]	n/a	n/a	n/a	n/a	n/a	n/a	n/a	n/a
U.S.	3,345.5	4.8	27.5	119.1	252.3	699.6	2,003.5	238.8

Note: Figures are crimes per 100,000 population; (1) All areas within the metro area that are located outside the city limits; (2) Metropolitan Statistical Area—see Appendix B for areas included; n/a not available
Source: FBI Uniform Crime Reports, 2010

Hate Crimes

Area	Number of Quarters Reported	Bias Motivation				
		Race	Religion	Sexual Orientation	Ethnicity	Disability
City	4	11	2	13	3	0

Source: Federal Bureau of Investigation, Hate Crime Statistics 2010

Identity Theft Consumer Complaints

Area	Complaints	Complaints per 100,000 Population	Rank[2]
MSA[1]	1,460	67.1	234
U.S.	279,156	90.4	-

Note: (1) Metropolitan Statistical Area—see Appendix B for areas included; (2) Rank ranges from 1 to 384 where 1 indicates greatest number of identity theft complaints per 100,000 population
Source: Federal Trade Commission, Consumer Sentinel Network Data Book for January–December 2011

Fraud and Other Consumer Complaints

Area	Complaints	Complaints per 100,000 Population	Rank[2]
MSA[1]	10,945	503.2	147
U.S.	1,533,924	496.8	-

Note: (1) Metropolitan Statistical Area—see Appendix B for areas included; (2) Rank ranges from 1 to 384 where 1 indicates greatest number of fraud and other complaints per 100,000 population
Source: Federal Trade Commission, Consumer Sentinel Network Data Book for January–December 2011

RECREATION

Culture

Dance[1]	Theatre[1]	Instrumental Music[1]	Vocal Music[1]	Series/ Festivals	Museums	Zoos and Aquariums[2]
4	7	12	1	7	14	1

Note: (1) Number of professional perfoming groups; (2) AZA-accredited
Source: The Grey House Performing Arts Directory, 2011-2012; Official Museum Directory, 2011; American Association of Museums, AAM Member Museums, April 2012; Association of Zoos & Aquariums, AZA Member Zoos & Aquariums, April 2012

Professional Sports Teams

Team Name	League
Portland Timbers	Major League Soccer (MLS)
Portland Trail Blazers	National Basketball Association (NBA)

Note: Includes teams located in the Portland metro area.
Source: Original research

CLIMATE

Average and Extreme Temperatures

Temperature	Jan	Feb	Mar	Apr	May	Jun	Jul	Aug	Sep	Oct	Nov	Dec	Yr.
Extreme High (°F)	65	71	83	93	100	102	107	107	105	92	73	64	107
Average High (°F)	45	50	56	61	68	73	80	79	74	64	53	46	62
Average Temp. (°F)	39	43	48	52	58	63	68	68	63	55	46	41	54
Average Low (°F)	34	36	39	42	48	53	57	57	52	46	40	36	45
Extreme Low (°F)	-2	-3	19	29	29	39	43	44	34	26	13	6	-3

Note: Figures cover the years 1926-1992
Source: National Climatic Data Center, International Station Meteorological Climate Summary, 9/96

Average Precipitation/Snowfall/Humidity

Precip./Humidity	Jan	Feb	Mar	Apr	May	Jun	Jul	Aug	Sep	Oct	Nov	Dec	Yr.
Avg. Precip. (in.)	5.5	4.2	3.8	2.4	2.0	1.5	0.5	0.9	1.7	3.0	5.5	6.6	37.5
Avg. Snowfall (in.)	3	1	1	Tr	Tr	0	0	0	0	0	1	2	7
Avg. Rel. Hum. 7am (%)	85	86	86	84	80	78	77	81	87	90	88	87	84
Avg. Rel. Hum. 4pm (%)	75	67	60	55	53	50	45	45	49	61	74	79	59

Note: Figures cover the years 1926-1992; Tr = Trace amounts (<0.05 in. of rain; <0.5 in. of snow)
Source: National Climatic Data Center, International Station Meteorological Climate Summary, 9/96

Weather Conditions

Temperature			Daytime Sky			Precipitation		
5°F & below	32°F & below	90°F & above	Clear	Partly cloudy	Cloudy	0.01 inch or more precip.	0.1 inch or more snow/ice	Thunder-storms
< 1	37	11	67	116	182	152	4	7

Note: Figures are average number of days per year and cover the years 1926-1992
Source: National Climatic Data Center, International Station Meteorological Climate Summary, 9/96

HAZARDOUS WASTE

Superfund Sites

Portland has three hazardous waste sites on the EPA's Superfund Final National Priorities List: **Harbor Oil; Portland Harbor; McCormick & Baxter Creosoting Co. (Portland Plant).** *U.S. Environmental Protection Agency, Final National Priorities List, April 17, 2012*

AIR & WATER QUALITY

Air Quality Index

Area	Percent of Days when Air Quality was...[2]					AQI Statistics[2]	
	Good	Moderate	Unhealthy for Sensitive Groups	Unhealthy	Very Unhealthy	Maximum	Median
Area[1]	85.5	13.7	0.8	0.0	0.0	112	31

Note: Air Quality Index (AQI) is an index for reporting daily air quality. EPA calculates the AQI for five major air pollutants regulated by the Clean Air Act: ground-level ozone, particle pollution (aka particulate matter), carbon monoxide, sulfur dioxide, and nitrogen dioxide. The AQI runs from 0 to 500. The higher the AQI value, the greater the level of air pollution and the greater the health concern. There are six AQI categories: "Good" AQI is between 0 and 50. Air quality is considered satisfactory; "Moderate" AQI is between 51 and 100. Air quality is acceptable; "Unhealthy for Sensitive Groups" When AQI values are between 101 and 150, members of sensitive groups may experience health effects; "Unhealthy" When AQI values are between 151 and 200 everyone may begin to experience health effects; "Very Unhealthy" AQI values between 201 and 300 trigger a health alert; "Hazardous" AQI values over 300 trigger warnings of emergency conditions (not shown); (1) Data covers Multnomah County; (2) Based on 365 days with AQI data in 2011.
Source: U.S. Environmental Protection Agency, AirData Report, 2011

Air Quality Index Pollutants

Area	Percent of Days when AQI Pollutant was...[2]					
	Carbon Monoxide	Nitrogen Dioxide	Ozone	Sulfur Dioxide	Particulate Matter 2.5	Particulate Matter 10
Area[1]	0.0	3.6	59.5	0.0	37.0	0.0

Note: The Air Quality Index (AQI) is an index for reporting daily air quality. EPA calculates the AQI for five major air pollutants regulated by the Clean Air Act: ground-level ozone, particle pollution (also known as particulate matter), carbon monoxide, sulfur dioxide, and nitrogen dioxide. The AQI runs from 0 to 500. The higher the AQI value, the greater the level of air pollution and the greater the health concern; (1) Data covers Multnomah County; (2) Based on 365 days with AQI data in 2011.
Source: U.S. Environmental Protection Agency, AirData Report, 2011

Air Quality Index Trends

Area	Trend Sites (days)								All Sites (days)
	2003	2004	2005	2006	2007	2008	2009	2010	2010
MSA[1]	2	4	4	2	5	3	5	1	1

Note: Figures are the number of days the AQI value exceeded 100 in a given year. An AQI value greater than 100 indicates that air quality would have been in the unhealthful range on that day. Data from exceptional events are included. These counts are presented in two ways. First, the counts are based on sites having an adequate record of monitoring data during the trend period (trend sites). These counts represent the relative change in the number of days with AQI values greater than 100. In the last column, the counts are based on all sites with data in the most recent year (because it is possible for a site to have data in the most recent year but not enough data to be a trend site); (1) Data covers the Portland-Vancouver-Hillsboro, OR-WA—see Appendix B for areas included
Source: U.S. Environmental Protection Agency, Air Quality Index Information, "Number of Days with Air Quality Index Values Greater than 100 at Trend Sites, 2000-2010, and at All Sites in 2010"

Maximum Air Pollutant Concentrations: Particulate Matter, Ozone, CO and Lead

	Particulate Matter 10 (ug/m^3)	Particulate Matter 2.5 Wtd AM (ug/m^3)	Particulate Matter 2.5 24-Hr (ug/m^3)	Ozone (ppm)	Carbon Monoxide (ppm)	Lead (ug/m^3)
MSA[1] Level	29	6.6	18	0.066	2	0.03
NAAQS[2]	150	15	35	0.075	9	0.15
Met NAAQS[2]	Yes	Yes	Yes	Yes	Yes	Yes

Note: Data from exceptional events are not included; (1) Data covers the Portland-Vancouver-Hillsboro, OR-WA—see Appendix B for areas included; (2) National Ambient Air Quality Standards; ppm = parts per million; ug/m^3 = micrograms per cubic meter; n/a not available

Concentrations: Particulate Matter 10 (coarse particulate)—highest second maximum 24-hour concentration; Particulate Matter 2.5 Wtd AM (fine particulate)—highest weighted annual mean concentration; Particulate Matter 2.5 24-Hour (fine particulate)—highest 98th percentile 24-hour concentration; Ozone—highest fourth daily maximum 8-hour concentration; Carbon Monoxide—highest second maximum non-overlapping 8-hour concentration; Lead—maximum running 3-month average

Source: U.S. Environmental Protection Agency, CBSA Factbook 2010, Air Quality Statistics by City, 2010

Maximum Air Pollutant Concentrations: Nitrogen Dioxide and Sulfur Dioxide

	Nitrogen Dioxide AM (ppb)	Nitrogen Dioxide 1-Hr (ppb)	Sulfur Dioxide AM (ppb)	Sulfur Dioxide 1-Hr (ppb)	Sulfur Dioxide 24-Hr (ppb)
MSA[1] Level	8.635	33	1.35	8	3.2
NAAQS[2]	53	100	30	75	140
Met NAAQS[2]	Yes	Yes	Yes	Yes	Yes

Note: Data from exceptional events are not included; (1) Data covers the Portland-Vancouver-Hillsboro, OR-WA—see Appendix B for areas included; (2) National Ambient Air Quality Standards; ppb = parts per billion; n/a not available

Concentrations: Nitrogen Dioxide AM—highest arithmetic mean concentration; Nitrogen Dioxide 1-Hr—highest 98th percentile 1-hour daily maximum concentration; Sulfur Dioxide AM—highest annual mean concentration; Sulfur Dioxide 1-Hr—highest 99th percentile 1-hour daily maximum concentration; Sulfur Dioxide 24-Hr—highest second maximum 24-hour concentration

Source: U.S. Environmental Protection Agency, CBSA Factbook 2010, Air Quality Statistics by City, 2010

Drinking Water

Water System Name	Pop. Served	Primary Water Source Type	Violations[1] Health Based	Violations[1] Monitoring/ Reporting
Portland Water Bureau	539,200	Surface	0	0

Note: (1) Based on violation data from January 1, 2011 to December 31, 2011 (includes unresolved violations from earlier years)

Source: U.S. Environmental Protection Agency, Office of Ground Water and Drinking Water, Safe Drinking Water Information System (based on data extracted April 18, 2012)

Provo, Utah

Background

Provo is situated on the Provo River at a site that was once under the waters of Lake Bonneville in a prehistoric period. Year after year, Provo enjoys one of the country's highest employment rates, a growing high-tech economy, a minuscule crime rate, and a magnificent natural environment. The seat of Utah County, it lies at the base of the steep Wasatch Mountains, with Provo Peak rising to a height of 11,054 feet just east of the city, making Provo convenient to many of Utah's famed ski areas and to the Uinta National Forest.

The Spanish missionaries Francisco Silvestre Velez de Escalante and Francisco Atanasio Dominguez, exploring for a more direct route from present-day New Mexico to California, were probably the first Europeans to view the area, but they did not stay long or establish a permanent mission. They did, however, note that the area could easily be irrigated and developed into an important agricultural settlement. Etienne Prevot, a Canadian trapper and explorer, likewise visited but did not settle, though he too remarked on the beauty and potential of the site. They also noted the presence of the site's original inhabitants, the Ute Indians, who held an important fish festival on the river every spring.

Permanent European settlement of Provo is strongly linked to Mormon history. In 1849, John S. Higbee, with 30 families in a wagon train, left the larger Salt Lake City community to move north. As they arrived at the site, they confronted a group of Ute, with whom white settlers had already been in some conflict. A short-lived peace agreement gave way to further conflict and a series of battles, after which the Indians agreed to resettlement. Peace ensued, and Provo was not subject to long periods of Indian hostilities as were many other young Western towns.

Irrigation has been central to Provo's success, and in the very year of Higbee's arrival, two large canals were dug, taking water from the Provo River. Thereafter, grain mills were constructed to serve the needs of nearby farmers. Important rail links were completed in the 1870s connecting Provo to Salt Lake City and to the Union Pacific System, and giving impetus to the region's agricultural and mining industries.

Provo's growth then took off, with an electric generating plant built in 1890, and in 1914, an interurban commuter rail service established between Provo and Salt Lake City. The town had become a major regional industrial center, with ironworks, flourmills, and brickyards. Today, industries include computer hardware and software (Novell), food processing, clothing, and electronic equipment.

Provo's industrial dynamism and creativity is reflected in the careers of two of its favorite sons. Dr. Harvey Fletcher, who was associated with Bell Laboratories, was the inventor of many aids to the deaf and hearing-impaired, and was an important early leader of the National Acoustic Association. Philo T. Farnsworth, born in Beaver, Utah, but raised in Provo, was a college student in 1924 when he developed the fundamental concepts of television at the age of 18.

Provo is home to Farnsworth's alma mater, Brigham Young University, a private university operated by The Church of Jesus Christ of Latter-day Saints. The school was founded in 1875 and has earned national respect for everything from its football team and undergraduate liberal arts program to its graduate programs in business and law. The Provo Tabernacle that was destroyed by fire in 2010 is being rebuilt.

In 2001, Provo resident Larry H. Miller donated the Larry H. Miller Field to Brigham Young University. Initially, the stadium hosted the Provo Angels minor league professional baseball team, but the stadium in recent years has been used as a training and competitive facility by other teams, including the Brigham Young Cougars. In 2009, the city of Provo implemented CITYWATCH, a city-wide emergency notification system. The Utah Valley Convention Center was completed in early 2012.

The climate of Provo is semi-arid continental. Summers are generally hot and dry. Winters are cold but not severe. Precipitation is generally light, with most of the rain falling in the spring.

Rankings

General Rankings

- The Provo metro area was selected one of America's "Best Cities to Live, Work and Play" by *Kiplinger's Personal Finance.* Criteria: population growth; percentage of workforce in the creative class (scientists, engineers, educators, writers, artists, entertainers, etc.); job quality; income growth; cost of living. *Kiplinger's Personal Finance, "Best Cities to Live, Work and Play," July 2008*

Business/Finance Rankings

- Provo was identified as one of the 20 strongest-performing metro areas during the recession and recovery from trough quarter through the third quarter of 2011. Criteria: percent change in employment; percentage point change in unemployment rate; percent change in gross metropolitan product; percent change in House Price Index. *Brookings Institution, MetroMonitor: Tracking Economic Recession and Recovery in America's 100 Largest Metropolitan Areas, December 2011*
- The Provo metro area was identified as one of the best places for finding a job by *U.S. News & World Report.* The metro area ranked #10 out of 10. Methodology was based on percent change in unemployment rate from November 2010 to November 2011 which was then subtracted from a given city's November 2011 unemployment rate. The 10 cities with the lowest results were selected. The editors only considered metropolitan areas with 200,000 people or more. *U.S. News & World Report, "The 10 Best Cities for Finding a Job," January 13, 2012*
- Provo was identified as one of the "Happiest Cities to Work in 2012" by *CareerBliss.com,* an online community for career advancement. The city ranked #10 out of 50. Criteria: independent company reviews from employees all over the country on: relationship with their boss and co-workers; work environment; job resources; growth opportunities; compensation; company culture; company reputation; daily tasks; job control over work performed on a daily basis. *CareerBliss.com, "Happiest and Unhappiest Cities to Work in 2012"*
- *American City Business Journals* ranked America's 261 largest cities in terms of their resident's wealth. Provo ranked #203. Criteria: per capita income; median household income; percentage of households with annual incomes of $200,000 or more; median home value. *American City Business Journals, "Where the Money Is: America's Wealth Centers," August 18, 2008*
- The Provo metro area appeared on the Milken Institute "2011 Best Performing Metros" list. Rank: #9 out of 200 large metro areas. Criteria: job growth; wage and salary growth; high-tech output growth. *Milken Institute, "2011 Best Performing Metros"*
- The Provo metro area was selected as one of the best cities for entrepreneurs in America by *Inc. Magazine.* Criteria: job-growth data for 335 metro areas was analyzed for: recent growth trend; mid-term growth; long-term trend; current year growth. The Provo metro area ranked #1 among mid-sized metro areas and #7 overall. *Inc. Magazine, "The Best Cities for Doing Business," July 2008*
- Provo was identified as one of the top 10 cities with the greatest number of *Inc. 500* companies per million residents. The city ranked #1. *Inc. Magazine, September 2008*
- *Forbes* ranked the 200 most populous metro areas in the U.S. in terms of the "Best Places for Business and Careers." The Provo metro area was ranked #3. Criteria: costs (business and living); job growth (past and projected); income growth; educational attainment; projected economic growth; crime; cultural and recreational opportunities; net migration patterns; number of highly ranked colleges. *Forbes, "Best Places for Business and Careers," June 2011*

Children/Family Rankings

- The Provo metro area was selected as one of the "Best Cities for Relocating Families" by Worldwide ERC and Primacy Relocation. The 2008 study looked at nearly 50 factors important to relocating families including: recent job growth; nearby top-ranked colleges; in-state tuition for four-year public colleges; population growth since 2000; pediatricians per 100,000 population; and a Green Living index. *Worldwide ERC and Primacy Relocation, "2008 Best Cities for Relocating Families"*

Education Rankings

- Provo was identified as one of "America's Brainiest Bastions" by *Portfolio.com.* The metro area ranked #23 out of 200. *Portfolio.com* analyzed levels of educational attainment in the nation's 200 largest metropolitan areas. The editors established scores for five levels of educational attainment, based on relative earning power of adult workers age 25 or older. Scores were determined by comparing the median income for all workers with the median income for those workers at a specified educational level. *Portfolio.com, "America's Brainiest Bastions," December 1, 2010*

Environmental Rankings

- Provo was selected as one of 22 "Smarter Cities" for energy by the Natural Resources Defense Council. Criteria: investment in green power; energy efficiency measures; conservation. *Natural Resources Defense Council, "2010 Smarter Cities," July 19, 2010*
- The Provo metro area appeared in *Country Home's* "Best Green Places" report. The area ranked #155 out of 379. Criteria: official energy policies; green power; green buildings; availability of fresh, locally grown food. *Country Home, "Best Green Places," 2008*
- Provo was highlighted as one of the 25 metro areas most polluted by short-term particle pollution (24-hour PM 2.5) in the U.S. The area ranked #6. *American Lung Association, State of the Air 2011*

Health/Fitness Rankings

- The Provo metro area appeared in the 2011 Gallup-Healthways Well-Being Index. The index, based on interviews with more than 350,000 Americans, measured jobs, finances, physical health, emotional state of mind and communities. The metro area ranked #4 out of 190. Criteria: life evaluation; emotional health; work environment; physical health; healthy behaviors; basic access (basic needs optimal for a healthy life, such as access to food and medicine, having health insurance and feeling safe while walking at night). *Gallup-Healthways, "State of Well-Being 2011"*

Real Estate Rankings

- Provo appeared on *ApartmentRatings.com* "Top College Towns & Cities" for renters list in 2011." The area ranked #55 out of 87. Overall satisfaction ratings were ranked using thousands of user submitted scores for hundreds of apartment complexes located in cities and towns that are home to the 100 largest four-year institutions in the U.S. *ApartmentRatings.com, "2011 College Town Renter Satisfaction Rankings"*
- The Provo metro area was identified as one of "America's 25 Weakest Housing Markets" by *Forbes*. The metro area ranked #5. Criteria: metro areas with populations over 500,000 were ranked based on projected home values through 2011. *Forbes.com, "America's 25 Weakest Housing Markets," January 7, 2009*
- The Center for Housing Policy ranked 210 U.S. metropolitan areas by the fair market rent for a two-bedroom unit. The Provo metro area was ranked #163. (#1 = most expensive) with a rent of $699. Criteria: Fair Market Rent (FMR) in effect during the fourth quarter of 2009 based on HUD's fiscal year 2010 FMRs. *The Center for Housing Policy, "Paycheck to Paycheck: Most to Least Expensive Rental Markets in 2009"*

- The Provo metro area was identified as one of the best U.S. markets to invest in rental property" by HomeVestors and Local Market Monitor. The area ranked #51 out of 100. Criteria: risk-return premium relative to national average. *HomeVestors and Local Market Monitor, "Best 100 U.S. Markets to Invest in Rental Property," March 9, 2012*

Safety Rankings

- The National Insurance Crime Bureau ranked 366 metro areas in the U.S. in terms of per capita rates of vehicle theft. The Provo metro area ranked #330 (#1 = highest rate). Criteria: number of vehicle theft offenses per 100,000 inhabitants in 2010. *National Insurance Crime Bureau, "Hot Spots," June 21, 2011*

Sports/Recreation Rankings

- Provo appeared on the *Sporting News* list of the "Best Sports Cities" for 2011. The area ranked #28 out of 271 cities in the U.S. *Sporting News* takes a 12-month snapshot of each city's sports, putting a heavy premium on regular-season won-lost records (from the most recently completed season). Other criteria include: playoff berths, bowl appearances and tournament bids; championships; applicable power ratings; quality of competition; overall fan fervor (measured in part by attendance); abundance of teams (rewarding quality over quantity); stadium and arena quality; ticket availability and prices; franchise ownership; and marquee appeal of athletes. *Sporting News, "Best Sports Cities 2011," October 4, 2011*

Technology Rankings

- The Provo metro area was selected as one of "America's Most Innovative Cities" by *Forbes*. The metro area was ranked #9 out of 20. Criteria: patents per capita; venture capital investment per capita; ratio of high-tech, science and "creative" jobs. *Forbes, "America's Most Innovative Cities," May 24, 2010*

Business Environment

CITY FINANCES

City Government Finances

Component	2009 ($000)	2009 ($ per capita)
Total Revenues	131,812	1,121
Total Expenditures	128,465	1,092
Debt Outstanding	82,189	699
Cash and Securities[1]	8,368	71

Note: (1) Cash and security holdings of a government at the close of its fiscal year, including those of its dependent agencies, utilities, and liquor stores.
Source: U.S Census Bureau, State & Local Government Finances 2009

City Government Revenue by Source

Source	2009 ($000)	2009 ($ per capita)
General Revenue		
From Federal Government	4,969	42
From State Government	4,516	38
From Local Governments	828	7
Taxes		
Property	12,326	105
Sales and Gross Receipts	22,625	192
Personal Income	0	0
Corporate Income	0	0
Motor Vehicle License	0	0
Other Taxes	1,117	9
Current Charges	23,260	198
Liquor Store	0	0
Utility	54,479	463
Employee Retirement	0	0

Source: U.S Census Bureau, State & Local Government Finances 2009

City Government Expenditures by Function

Function	2009 ($000)	2009 ($ per capita)	2009 (%)
General Direct Expenditures			
Air Transportation	2,448	21	1.9
Corrections	0	0	0.0
Education	0	0	0.0
Employment Security Administration	0	0	0.0
Financial Administration	3,455	29	2.7
Fire Protection	8,592	73	6.7
General Public Buildings	2,835	24	2.2
Governmental Administration, Other	2,181	19	1.7
Health	0	0	0.0
Highways	5,959	51	4.6
Hospitals	0	0	0.0
Housing and Community Development	6,926	59	5.4
Interest on General Debt	3,509	30	2.7
Judicial and Legal	1,153	10	0.9
Libraries	3,733	32	2.9
Parking	0	0	0.0
Parks and Recreation	11,026	94	8.6
Police Protection	13,972	119	10.9
Public Welfare	0	0	0.0
Sewerage	6,127	52	4.8
Solid Waste Management	2,854	24	2.2
Veterans' Services	0	0	0.0
Liquor Store	0	0	0.0
Utility	49,644	422	38.6
Employee Retirement	0	0	0.0

Source: U.S Census Bureau, State & Local Government Finances 2009

Municipal Bond Ratings

Area	Moody's	S&P	Fitch
City	n/a	n/a	n/a

Rating Systems (shown in declining order of credit quality): Moody's– Aaa, Aa, A, Baa, Ba, B, Caa, Ca, C (numerical modifiers 1, 2, and 3 are added to letter-rating); S&P– AAA, AA, A, BBB, BB, B, CCC, CC, C; Fitch– AAA, AA, A, BBB, BB, B, CCC, CC, C. Ratings may be modified by the addition of a plus or minus sign to show relative standing within the major rating categories.
Notes: n/a Not Available; w/d Withdrawn (1) Not Reviewed; (2) Issuer Rating/No General Obligation; (3) Standard and Poor's Issue Credit Rating (ICR) is a current opinion of an obliger with respect to a specific financial obligation, a specific class of financial obligations, or a specific financial program.
Source: U.S. Census Bureau, 2012 Statistical Abstract, Bond Ratings for City Governments by Largest Cities: 2010

DEMOGRAPHICS

Population Growth

Area	1990 Census	2000 Census	2010 Census	Population Growth (%) 1990-2000	Population Growth (%) 2000-2010
City	87,148	105,166	112,488	20.7	7.0
MSA[1]	269,407	376,774	526,810	39.9	39.8
U.S.	248,709,873	281,421,906	308,745,538	13.2	9.7

Note: (1) Figures cover the Provo-Orem, UT Metropolitan Statistical Area—see Appendix B for areas included
Source: U.S. Census Bureau, 2010 Census

Household Size

Area	Persons in Household (%)							Average Household Size
	One	Two	Three	Four	Five	Six	Seven or More	
City	12.8	29.5	18.8	18.3	8.7	7.6	4.2	3.24
MSA[1]	11.7	25.2	16.4	17.0	13.1	9.5	7.0	3.57
U.S.	26.7	32.8	16.1	13.4	6.5	2.6	1.9	2.58

Note: (1) Figures cover the Provo-Orem, UT Metropolitan Statistical Area—see Appendix B for areas included
Source: U.S. Census Bureau, 2010 Census

Race

Area	White Alone[2] (%)	Black Alone[2] (%)	Asian Alone[2] (%)	AIAN[3] Alone[2] (%)	NHOPI[4] Alone[2] (%)	Other Race Alone[2] (%)	Two or More Races (%)
City	84.8	0.7	2.5	0.8	1.1	6.6	3.4
MSA[1]	89.5	0.5	1.3	0.6	0.7	4.6	2.7
U.S.	72.4	12.6	4.8	0.9	0.2	6.2	2.9

Note: (1) Figures cover the Provo-Orem, UT Metropolitan Statistical Area—see Appendix B for areas included; (2) Alone is defined as not being in combination with one or more other races; (3) American Indian and Alaska Native; (4) Native Hawaiian and Other Pacific Islander
Source: U.S. Census Bureau, 2010 Census

Hispanic or Latino Origin

Area	Hispanic or Latino (%)	Mexican (%)	Puerto Rican (%)	Cuban (%)	Other Hispanic or Latino (%)
City	15.2	10.2	0.3	0.1	4.6
MSA[1]	10.7	7.2	0.2	0.1	3.2
U.S.	16.3	10.3	1.5	0.6	4.0

Note: Persons of Hispanic or Latino origin can be of any race; (1) Figures cover the Provo-Orem, UT Metropolitan Statistical Area—see Appendix B for areas included
Source: U.S. Census Bureau, 2010 Census

Segregation

Type	Segregation Indices[1]				Percent Change		
	1990	2000	2010	2010 Rank[2]	1990-2000	1990-2010	2000-2010
Black/White	38.6	29.4	21.9	102	-9.2	-16.7	-7.5
Asian/White	32.3	31.5	28.2	94	-0.8	-4.1	-3.3
Hispanic/White	20.9	33.3	30.9	93	12.4	10.0	-2.4

Note: Figures are based on an analysis of 1990, 2000, and 2010 Census Decennial Census tract data by William H. Frey, Brookings Institution and the University of Michigan Social Science Data Analysis Network. In this analysis all racial groups (whites, blacks, and asians) are non-Hispanic members of those races. Hispanics are shown as a separate category; All figures cover the Metropolitan Statistical Area (see Appendix B for areas included); (1) Segregation Indices are Dissimilarity Indices that measure the degree to which the minority group is distributed differently than whites across census tracts. They range from 0 (complete integration) to 100 (complete segregation) where the value indicates the percentage of the minority group that needs to move to be distributed exactly like whites; (2) Ranges from 1 (most segregated) to 102 (least segregated); n/a not available.
Source: www.CensusScope.org

Ancestry

Area	German	Irish	English	American	Italian	Polish	French[2]	Scottish	Dutch
City	11.0	5.3	28.3	2.7	2.5	0.7	2.2	5.8	1.2
MSA[1]	11.9	5.0	30.6	4.6	2.2	0.6	2.1	6.0	2.1
U.S.	16.1	11.6	8.8	6.1	5.7	3.2	3.0	1.9	1.6

Note: Figures are the percentage of the total population reporting a particular ancestry. The nine most commonly reported ancestries in the U.S. are shown. Figures include multiple ancestries (e.g. if a person reported being Irish and Italian, they were included in both columns); (1) Figures cover the Provo-Orem, UT Metropolitan Statistical Area—see Appendix B for areas included; (2) Excludes Basque
Source: U.S. Census Bureau, 2008-2010 American Community Survey 3-Year Estimates

Foreign-Born Population

Area	Percent of Population Born in								
	Any Foreign Country	Mexico	Asia	Europe	Carribean	South America	Central America[2]	Africa	Canada
City	n/a	n/a	n/a	n/a	n/a	n/a	n/a	n/a	n/a
MSA[1]	7.0	2.9	0.9	0.6	0.0	1.2	0.5	0.1	0.5
U.S.	12.8	3.8	3.6	1.6	1.2	0.9	1.0	0.5	0.3

Note: (1) Figures cover the Provo-Orem, UT Metropolitan Statistical Area—see Appendix B for areas included; (2) Excludes Mexico.
Source: U.S. Census Bureau, 2008-2010 American Community Survey 3-Year Estimates

Marital Status

Area	Never Married	Now Married[2]	Separated	Widowed	Divorced
City	53.8	38.6	1.0	2.2	4.4
MSA[1]	31.7	58.5	1.1	2.8	5.8
U.S.	31.6	49.6	2.2	6.1	10.7

Note: Figures are percentages and cover the population 15 years of age and older; (1) Figures cover the Provo-Orem, UT Metropolitan Statistical Area—see Appendix B for areas included; (2) Excludes separated
Source: U.S. Census Bureau, 2008-2010 American Community Survey 3-Year Estimates

Age

Area	Percent of Population							Median Age
	Under Age 5	Age 5 to 17	Age 18 to 34	Age 35 to 49	Age 50 to 64	Age 65 to 79	80 Years and Over	
City	8.5	13.9	54.5	9.8	7.5	4.0	1.8	23.3
MSA[1]	11.3	24.0	32.6	15.3	10.3	4.9	1.7	24.6
U.S.	6.5	17.5	23.2	20.7	19.0	9.4	3.6	37.2

Note: (1) Figures cover the Provo-Orem, UT Metropolitan Statistical Area—see Appendix B for areas included
Source: U.S. Census Bureau, 2010 Census

Male/Female Ratio

Area	Males	Females	Males per 100 Females
City	55,737	56,751	98.2
MSA[1]	263,989	262,821	100.4
U.S.	151,781,326	156,964,212	96.7

Note: (1) Figures cover the Provo-Orem, UT Metropolitan Statistical Area—see Appendix B for areas included
Source: U.S. Census Bureau, 2010 Census

Religious Groups

Area	Catholic	Baptist	Non-Den.	Methodist[2]	Lutheran	LDS[3]	Pentecostal	Presbyterian[4]	Muslim[5]	Judaism
MSA[1]	1.3	0.1	0.1	0.2	0.0	88.6	0.1	0.1	n/a	n/a
U.S.	19.1	9.3	4.0	4.0	2.3	2.0	1.9	1.6	0.8	0.7

Note: Figures are the number of adherents as a percentage of the total population; (1) Figures cover the Provo-Orem, UT Metropolitan Statistical Area—see Appendix B for areas included; (2) Methodist/Pietist; (3) Latter Day Saints; (4) Reformed; (5) Figures are estimates
Source: Association of Statisticians of American Religious Bodies, 2010 U.S. Religion Census: Religious Congregations & Membership Study

ECONOMY

Gross Metropolitan Product

Area	2007	2008	2009	2010	2010 Rank[2]
MSA[1]	14.3	14.6	14.2	14.6	136

Note: Figures are in billions of dollars; (1) Figures cover the Provo-Orem, UT Metropolitan Statistical Area—see Appendix B for areas included; (2) Rank ranges from 1 to 363
Source: The United States Conference of Mayors, "U.S. Metro Economies: GMP and Employment Forecasts," June 2011

Economic Growth

Area	2007-2009 (%)	2010 (%)	2011 (%)	Rank[2]
MSA[1]	-1.6	1.6	2.3	203
U.S.	-1.3	2.9	2.5	–

Note: Figures are real Gross Metropolitan Product growth rates and represent annual average percent change; (1) Figures cover the Provo-Orem, UT Metropolitan Statistical Area—see Appendix B for areas included; (2) Rank ranges from 1 to 363
Source: The United States Conference of Mayors, "U.S. Metro Economies: GMP and Employment Forecasts," June 2011

Metropolitan Area Exports

Area	2005	2006	2007	2008	2009	2010	2010 Rank[2]
MSA[1]	1,014.5	787.4	1,205.1	2,218.0	1,772.8	2,024.6	86

Note: Figures are in millions of dollars; (1) Figures cover the Provo-Orem, UT Metropolitan Statistical Area—see Appendix B for areas included; (2) Rank ranges from 1 to 369
Source: U.S. Department of Commerce, International Trade Administration, Office of Trade & Industry Information, Manufacturing & Services, data extracted April 2, 2012

INCOME

Income

Area	Per Capita ($)	Median Household ($)	Average Household ($)
City	16,130	38,807	55,571
MSA[1]	20,098	56,594	70,927
U.S.	26,942	51,222	70,116

Note: (1) Figures cover the Provo-Orem, UT Metropolitan Statistical Area—see Appendix B for areas included
Source: U.S. Census Bureau, 2008-2010 American Community Survey 3-Year Estimates

Household Income Distribution

Area	Percent of Households Earning							
	Under $15,000	$15,000 -24,999	$25,000 -34,999	$35,000 -49,999	$50,000 -74,999	$75,000 -99,000	$100,000 -149,999	$150,000 and up
City	16.6	14.4	14.4	16.1	17.9	8.8	7.1	4.6
MSA[1]	8.8	9.2	9.6	15.4	22.3	14.2	13.5	7.0
U.S.	13.0	11.0	10.6	14.2	18.5	12.1	12.2	8.4

Note: (1) Figures cover the Provo-Orem, UT Metropolitan Statistical Area—see Appendix B for areas included
Source: U.S. Census Bureau, 2008-2010 American Community Survey 3-Year Estimates

Poverty Rate

Area	All Ages	Under 18 Years Old	18 to 64 Years Old	65 Years and Over
City	31.2	17.9	37.4	7.4
MSA[1]	13.4	11.2	15.7	5.0
U.S.	14.4	20.1	13.1	9.4

Note: Figures are percentage of people whose income during the past 12 months was below the poverty level; (1) Figures cover the Provo-Orem, UT Metropolitan Statistical Area—see Appendix B for areas included
Source: U.S. Census Bureau, 2008-2010 American Community Survey 3-Year Estimates

Personal Bankruptcy Filing Rate

Area	2006	2007	2008	2009	2010	2011
Utah County	1.59	1.74	2.64	4.59	5.94	5.81
U.S.	2.00	2.73	3.53	4.61	4.97	4.37

Note: Numbers are per 1,000 population and include Chapter 7 and Chapter 13 filings
Source: Federal Deposit Insurance Corporation, Regional Economic Conditions, March 9, 2012

EMPLOYMENT

Labor Force and Employment

Area	Civilian Labor Force			Workers Employed		
	Dec. 2010	Dec. 2011	% Chg.	Dec. 2010	Dec. 2011	% Chg.
City	68,637	68,566	-0.1	63,343	64,523	1.9
MSA[1]	225,671	225,769	0.0	209,836	213,746	1.9
U.S.	153,156,000	153,373,000	0.1	139,159,000	140,681,000	1.1

Note: Data is not seasonally adjusted and covers workers 16 years of age and older; (1) Metropolitan Statistical Area—see Appendix B for areas included
Source: Bureau of Labor Statistics, http://stats.bls.gov

Unemployment Rate

Area	2011											
	Jan.	Feb.	Mar.	Apr.	May	Jun.	Jul.	Aug.	Sep.	Oct.	Nov.	Dec.
City	9.1	9.1	8.4	7.7	8.3	8.7	8.8	8.7	7.5	7.0	6.0	5.9
MSA[1]	8.3	8.3	7.6	7.0	7.5	7.9	8.0	7.9	6.8	6.3	5.4	5.3
U.S.	9.8	9.5	9.2	8.7	8.7	9.3	9.3	9.1	8.8	8.5	8.2	8.3

Note: Data is not seasonally adjusted and covers workers 16 years of age and older; All figures are percentages; (1) Metropolitan Statistical Area—see Appendix B for areas included
Source: Bureau of Labor Statistics, http://stats.bls.gov

Projected Unemployment Rate

Area	2010 (%)	2011 (%)	2012 (%)	2013 (%)
MSA[1]	8.0	6.9	6.6	6.3

Note: (1) Metropolitan Statistical Area—see Appendix B for areas included
Source: The United States Conference of Mayors, "U.S. Metro Economies: GMP and Employment Forecasts," June 2011

Employment by Occupation

Occupation Classification	City (%)	MSA[1] (%)	U.S. (%)
Management, Business, Science, and Arts	37.6	38.2	35.6
Natural Resources, Construction, and Maintenance	5.4	8.8	9.5
Production, Transportation, and Material Moving	8.8	9.6	12.1
Sales and Office	28.2	27.9	25.2
Service	20.1	15.5	17.6

Note: Figures cover employed civilians 16 years of age and older; (1) Figures cover the Provo-Orem, UT Metropolitan Statistical Area—see Appendix B for areas included
Source: U.S. Census Bureau, 2008-2010 American Community Survey 3-Year Estimates

Employment by Industry

Sector	MSA[1]		U.S.
	Number of Employees	Percent of Total	Percent of Total
Construction	n/a	n/a	4.1
Education and Health Services	43,300	23.1	15.2
Financial Activities	6,200	3.3	5.8
Government	27,800	14.8	16.8
Information	8,200	4.4	2.0
Leisure and Hospitality	13,000	6.9	9.9
Manufacturing	17,400	9.3	8.9
Mining and Logging	n/a	n/a	0.6
Other Services	4,200	2.2	4.0
Professional and Business Services	25,300	13.5	13.3
Retail Trade	23,200	12.4	11.5
Transportation and Utilities	2,800	1.5	3.8
Wholesale Trade	5,100	2.7	4.2

Note: Figures cover non-farm employment as of December 2011 and are not seasonally adjusted; (1) Metropolitan Statistical Area—see Appendix B for areas included; n/a not available
Source: Bureau of Labor Statistics, http://stats.bls.gov

Occupations with Greatest Projected Employment Growth: 2008 – 2018

Occupation[1]	2008 Employment	2018 Projected Employment	Numeric Employment Change	Percent Employment Change
Customer Service Representatives	30,900	41,650	10,750	34.8
Retail Salespersons	45,240	55,210	9,970	22.0
Registered Nurses	19,790	27,890	8,100	40.9
Combined Food Preparation and Serving Workers, Including Fast Food	26,500	34,290	7,790	29.4
Office Clerks, General	27,110	33,110	6,000	22.1
Cashiers	32,570	38,460	5,890	18.1
Construction Laborers	19,720	24,530	4,810	24.4
Truck Drivers, Heavy and Tractor-Trailer	22,090	26,870	4,780	21.6
Home Health Aides	6,080	10,670	4,590	75.5
Accountants and Auditors	12,370	16,700	4,330	35.0

Note: Projections cover Utah; (1) Sorted by numeric employment change
Source: www.projectionscentral.com, State Occupational Projections, 2008–2018 Long-Term Projections

Fastest Growing Occupations: 2008 – 2018

Occupation[1]	2008 Employment	2018 Projected Employment	Numeric Employment Change	Percent Employment Change
Home Health Aides	6,080	10,670	4,590	75.5
Biochemists and Biophysicists	230	400	170	73.9
Personal and Home Care Aides	2,900	4,940	2,040	70.3
Biomedical Engineers	430	730	300	69.8
Network Systems and Data Communications Analysts	1,780	3,020	1,240	69.7
Petroleum Engineers	160	270	110	68.8
Physical Therapist Aides	810	1,340	530	65.4
Physical Therapist Assistants	400	640	240	60.0
Physician Assistants	830	1,320	490	59.0
Psychiatric Aides	290	460	170	58.6

Note: Projections cover Utah; (1) Sorted by percent employment change and excludes occupations with numeric employment change less than 100
Source: www.projectionscentral.com, State Occupational Projections, 2008–2018 Long-Term Projections

Average Wages

Occupation	$/Hr.	Occupation	$/Hr.
Accountants and Auditors	29.78	Maids and Housekeeping Cleaners	9.21
Automotive Mechanics	19.84	Maintenance and Repair Workers	16.72
Bookkeepers	15.32	Marketing Managers	47.29
Carpenters	18.97	Nuclear Medicine Technologists	n/a
Cashiers	9.14	Nurses, Licensed Practical	17.99
Clerks, General Office	11.72	Nurses, Registered	29.01
Clerks, Receptionists/Information	10.73	Nursing Aides/Orderlies/Attendants	10.50
Clerks, Shipping/Receiving	13.42	Packers and Packagers, Hand	9.38
Computer Programmers	31.70	Physical Therapists	39.24
Computer Support Specialists	20.24	Postal Service Mail Carriers	24.77
Computer Systems Analysts	33.44	Real Estate Brokers	n/a
Cooks, Restaurant	10.25	Retail Salespersons	11.81
Dentists	85.00	Sales Reps., Exc. Tech./Scientific	24.32
Electrical Engineers	37.25	Sales Reps., Tech./Scientific	28.32
Electricians	25.18	Secretaries, Exc. Legal/Med./Exec.	14.47
Financial Managers	50.90	Security Guards	13.63
First-Line Supervisors/Managers, Sales	16.69	Surgeons	n/a
Food Preparation Workers	9.27	Teacher Assistants	11.30
General and Operations Managers	42.84	Teachers, Elementary School	20.50
Hairdressers/Cosmetologists	15.49	Teachers, Secondary School	24.60
Internists	n/a	Telemarketers	11.22
Janitors and Cleaners	10.50	Truck Drivers, Heavy/Tractor-Trailer	18.38
Landscaping/Groundskeeping Workers	12.48	Truck Drivers, Light/Delivery Svcs.	14.00
Lawyers	52.77	Waiters and Waitresses	10.76

Note: Wage data covers the Provo-Orem, UT Metropolitan Statistical Area—see Appendix B for areas included. Hourly wages for elementary/secondary school teachers and teacher assistants were calculated by the editors from annual wage data assuming a 40 hour work week; n/a not available.
Source: Bureau of Labor Statistics, Metro Area Occupational Employment and Wage Estimates, May 2011

RESIDENTIAL REAL ESTATE

Building Permits

Area	Single-Family			Multi-Family			Total		
	2010	2011	Pct. Chg.	2010	2011	Pct. Chg.	2010	2011	Pct. Chg.
City	76	75	-1.3	238	28	-88.2	314	103	-67.2
MSA[1]	1,553	1,452	-6.5	432	480	11.1	1,985	1,932	-2.7
U.S.	447,311	418,498	-6.4	157,299	205,563	30.7	604,610	624,061	3.2

Note: (1) Metropolitan Statistical Area—see Appendix B for areas included; figures represent new, privately-owned housing units authorized (unadjusted data); All permit data are based on estimates with imputation.
Source: U.S. Census Bureau, Manufacturing, Mining, and Construction Statistics, Building Permits, 2010, 2011

Homeownership Rate

Area	2005 (%)	2006 (%)	2007 (%)	2008 (%)	2009 (%)	2010 (%)	2011 (%)
MSA[1]	n/a	n/a	n/a	n/a	n/a	n/a	n/a
U.S.	68.9	68.8	68.1	67.8	67.4	66.9	66.1

Note: (1) Metropolitan Statistical Area—see Appendix B for areas included; n/a not available
Source: U.S. Census Bureau, Housing Vacancies and Homeownership Annual Statistics: 2011

Housing Vacancy Rates

Area	Gross Vacancy Rate[2] (%)			Year-Round Vacancy Rate[3] (%)			Rental Vacancy Rate[4] (%)			Homeowner Vacancy Rate[5] (%)		
	2009	2010	2011	2009	2010	2011	2009	2010	2011	2009	2010	2011
MSA[1]	n/a	n/a	n/a	n/a	n/a	n/a	n/a	n/a	n/a	n/a	n/a	n/a
U.S.	14.5	14.3	14.2	11.3	11.3	11.1	10.6	10.2	9.5	2.6	2.6	2.5

Note: (1) Metropolitan Statistical Area—see Appendix B for areas included; (2) The percentage of the total housing inventory that is vacant; (3) The percentage of the housing inventory (excluding seasonal units) that is year-round vacant; (4) The percentage of rental inventory that is vacant for rent; (5) The percentage of homeowner inventory that is vacant for sale; n/a not available
Source: U.S. Census Bureau, Housing Vacancies and Homeownership Annual Statistics: 2011

TAXES

State Corporate Income Tax Rates

State	Tax Rate (%)	Income Brackets ($)	Num. of Brackets	Financial Institution Tax Rate (%)[a]	Federal Income Tax Ded.
Utah	5.0 (b)	Flat rate	-	5.0 (b)	No

Note: Tax rates as of January 1, 2012; (a) Rates listed are the corporate income tax rate applied to financial institutions or excise taxes based on income. Some states have other taxes based upon the value of deposits or shares; (b) Minimum tax is $50 in Arizona, $100 in District of Columbia, $50 in North Dakota (banks), $500 in Rhode Island, $200 per location in South Dakota (banks), $100 in Utah, $250 in Vermont.
Source: Federation of Tax Administrators, "State Corporate Income Tax Rates, 2012"

State Individual Income Tax Rates

State	Tax Rate (%)	Income Brackets ($)	Num. of Brackets	Personal Exempt. ($)[1]		Fed. Inc. Tax Ded.
				Single	Dependents	
Utah	5.0	Flat rate	1	(t)	(t)	No

Note: Tax rates as of January 1, 2012; Local- and county-level taxes are not included; n/a not applicable; (1) Married joint filers generally receive double the single exemption; (t) Utah provides a tax credit equal to 6% of the federal personal exemption amounts (an applicable standard deduction).
Source: Federation of Tax Administrators, "State Individual Income Tax Rates, 2012"

Various State and Local Tax Rates

State	State and Local Sales and Use (%)	State Sales and Use (%)	Gasoline[1] (¢/gal.)	Cigarette[2] ($/pack)	Spirits[3] ($/gal.)	Wine[4] ($/gal.)	Beer[5] ($/gal.)
Utah	6.75	5.95 (b)	24.5	1.70	11.63 (f)	- (j)	0.41

Note: All tax rates as of January 1, 2012 except beer, wine and spirits (September 1, 2011); (1) The American Petroleum Institute has developed a methodology for determining the average tax rate on a gallon of fuel. Rates may include any of the following: excise taxes, environmental fees, storage tank fees, other fees or taxes, general sales tax, and local taxes. In states where gasoline is subject to the general sales tax, or where the fuel tax is based on the average sale price, the average rate determined by API is sensitive to changes in the price of gasoline. States that fully or partially apply general sales taxes to gasoline: CA, CO, GA, IL, IN, MI, NY; (2) The federal excise tax of $1.0066 per pack and local taxes are not included; (3) Rates are those applicable to off-premise sales of 40% alcohol by volume (a.b.v.) distilled spirits in 750ml containers. Local excise taxes are excluded; (4) Rates are those applicable to off-premise sales of 11% a.b.v. non-carbonated wine in 750ml containers; (5) Rates are those applicable to off-premise sales of 4.7% a.b.v. beer in 12 ounce containers; (b) Three states collect a separate, uniform "local" add-on sales tax: California (1%), Utah (1.25%), Virginia (1%). These amounts are included in the state sales tax column; (f) States where the government controls sales. In these "control states," products are subject to ad valorem mark-up and excise taxes. The excise tax rate is calculated using a methodology developed by the Distilled Spirits Council of the United States; (j) Control states, where the government controls all sales. Products can be subject to ad valorem mark-up and excise taxes.
Source: Tax Foundation, 2012 Facts & Figures: How Does Your State Compare?

State-Local Tax Burdens

Area	Rate (%)	Rank[1]	Per Capita Taxes Paid to Home State ($)	Total State and Local Per Capita Taxes Paid ($)	Per Capita Income ($)
Utah	9.7	20	2,355	3,349	34,596
U.S. Average	9.8	-	3,057	4,160	42,539

Note: Figures cover 2009; (1) Rank ranges from 1 to 50 where 1 is highest tax burden
Source: Tax Foundation, State-Local Tax Burdens, All States, 2009

State Business Tax Climate Index Rankings

State	Overall Rank	Corporate Tax Index Rank	Individual Income Tax Index Rank	Sales Tax Index Rank	Unemployment Insurance Tax Index Rank	Property Tax Index Rank
Utah	10	5	14	22	24	3

Note: The index is a measure of how each state's tax laws affect economic performance. The lower the rank, the more favorable a state's tax system is for business. States without a given tax are given a ranking of 1.
Source: Tax Foundation, Major Components of the State Business Tax Climate Index, FY 2012

COMMERCIAL UTILITIES

Typical Monthly Electric Bills

Area	Commercial Service ($/month)		Industrial Service ($/month)	
	1,500 kWh	40 kW demand 14,000 kWh	1,000 kW demand 200,000 kWh	50,000 kW demand 15,000,000 kWh
City	n/a	n/a	n/a	n/a
Average[1]	189	1,616	25,197	1,470,813

Note: Based on total rates in effect July 1, 2011; (1) average based on 184 utilities surveyed; n/a not available
Source: Edison Electric Institute, Typical Bills and Average Rates Report, Summer 2011

TRANSPORTATION

Means of Transportation to Work

Area	Car/Truck/Van		Public Transportation			Bicycle	Walked	Other Means	Worked at Home
	Drove Alone	Car-pooled	Bus	Subway	Railroad				
City	61.2	12.5	2.9	0.0	0.0	2.4	15.8	0.5	4.7
MSA[1]	73.4	11.8	2.1	0.0	0.0	1.0	4.9	0.9	5.8
U.S.	76.0	10.2	2.7	1.7	0.5	0.5	2.8	1.3	4.2

Note: Figures are percentages and cover workers 16 years of age and older; (1) Figures cover the Provo-Orem, UT Metropolitan Statistical Area—see Appendix B for areas included
Source: U.S. Census Bureau, 2008-2010 American Community Survey 3-Year Estimates

Travel Time to Work

Area	Less Than 10 Minutes	10 to 19 Minutes	20 to 29 Minutes	30 to 44 Minutes	45 to 59 Minutes	60 to 89 Minutes	90 Minutes or More
City	27.0	46.2	14.0	7.1	2.8	1.9	1.0
MSA[1]	20.5	35.8	18.5	14.8	5.5	3.2	1.6
U.S.	13.9	30.1	20.8	19.8	7.5	5.5	2.5

Note: Figures are percentages and include workers 16 years old and over; (1) Figures cover the Provo-Orem, UT Metropolitan Statistical Area—see Appendix B for areas included
Source: U.S. Census Bureau, 2008-2010 American Community Survey 3-Year Estimates

Travel Time Index

Area	1985	1990	1995	2000	2005	2010
Urban Area[1]	1.02	1.02	1.03	1.04	1.05	1.08
Average[2]	1.11	1.16	1.18	1.21	1.25	1.20

Note: Travel Time Index—the ratio of travel time in the peak period to the travel time at free-flow conditions. A value of 1.30 indicates a 20-minute free-flow trip takes 26 minutes in the peak. Free-flow speeds (60 mph on freeways and 35 mph on principal arterials) are used as the comparison threshold; (1) Covers the Provo UT urban area; (2) average of 439 urban areas
Source: Texas Transportation Institute, Urban Mobility Report 2011, September 2011

Public Transportation

Agency Name / Mode of Transportation	Vehicles Operated in Maximum Service	Annual Unlinked Passenger Trips ('000)	Annual Passenger Miles ('000)
Utah Transit Authority (UT)			
Bus (directly operated)	415	21,716.9	128,375.8
Commuter Rail (directly operated)	34	1,389.9	36,276.3
Demand Response (directly operated)	75	322.5	3,089.1
Demand Response (purchased transportation)	54	183.4	2,181.4
Demand Response Taxi (purchased transportation)	13	3.8	24.1
Light Rail (directly operated)	43	13,400.5	57,228.6
Vanpool (directly operated)	420	1,346.9	54,429.4

Source: Federal Transit Administration, National Transit Database, 2010

Air Transportation

Airport Name and Code / Type of Service	Passenger Airlines[1]	Passenger Enplanements	Freight Carriers[2]	Freight (lbs.)
Salt Lake City International (50 miles) (SLC)				
Domestic service (U.S. carriers - 2011)	28	9,481,923	19	171,750,131
International service (U.S. carriers - 2010)	7	233,893	3	1,580,434

Note: (1) Includes all U.S.-based major, minor and commuter airlines that carried at least one passenger during the year; (2) Includes all U.S.-based airlines and freight carriers that transported at least one pound of freight during the year

Source: Bureau of Transportation Statistics, The Intermodal Transportation Database, Air Carriers: T-100 Domestic Market (U.S. Carriers), 2011; Bureau of Transportation Statistics, The Intermodal Transportation Database, Air Carriers: T-100 International Market (U.S. Carriers), 2010

Other Transportation Statistics

Major Highways:	I-15
Amtrak Service:	Yes
Major Waterways/Ports:	None

Source: Amtrak.com; Google Maps

BUSINESSES

Major Business Headquarters

Company Name	Rankings	
	Fortune[1]	Forbes[2]
No companies listed	-	-

Note: (1) Fortune 500—companies that produce a 10-K are ranked 1 to 500 based on 2010 revenue; (2) all private companies with at least $2 billion in annual revenue are ranked 1 to 212; companies listed are headquartered in the city; dashes indicate no ranking

Source: Fortune, "Fortune 500," May 23, 2011; Forbes, "America's Largest Private Companies," November 16, 2011

Minority- and Women-Owned Businesses

Group	All Firms		Firms with Paid Employees			
	Firms	Sales ($000)	Firms	Sales ($000)	Employees	Payroll ($000)
Asian	n/a	n/a	n/a	n/a	n/a	n/a
Black	n/a	n/a	n/a	n/a	n/a	n/a
Hispanic	n/a	n/a	n/a	n/a	n/a	n/a
Women	n/a	n/a	n/a	n/a	n/a	n/a
All Firms	3,824	619,998	546	517,793	3,475	100,573

Note: Figures cover firms located in the city; minority- and women-owned business are defined as firms in which the corresponding group own 51% or more of the stock or equity of the company; n/a not available

Source: U.S. Census Bureau, 2007 Economic Census, Survey of Business Owners

HOTELS

Hotels/Motels

Area	5 Star		4 Star		3 Star		2 Star		1 Star		Not Rated	
	Num.	Pct.[3]	Num.	Pct.[3]	Num.	Pct.[3]	Num.	Pct.[3]	Num.	Pct.[3]	Num.	Pct.[3]
City[1]	0	0.0	1	3.1	5	15.6	22	68.8	1	3.1	3	9.4
Total[2]	133	0.9	940	6.5	4,569	31.8	7,033	48.9	351	2.4	1,343	9.3

Note: (1) Figures cover Provo and vicinity; (2) Figures cover all 100 cities in this book; (3) Percentage of hotels which have a given star rating; Star ratings are determined by expedia.com and offer an indication of the general quality of a particular hotel.
Source: expedia.com, April 25, 2012

The Provo-Orem, UT metro area is home to one of the best hotels in the U.S. according to *Travel & Leisure*: **Sundance Resort** (#30). Criteria: service; location; rooms; food; and value. *Travel & Leisure, "T+L 500, The World's Best Hotels 2012"*

EVENT SITES

Major Stadiums, Arenas, and Auditoriums

Name	Max. Capacity
LaVell Edwards Stadium	64,045

Source: Original research

Convention Centers

Name	Overall Space (sq. ft.)	Exhibit Space (sq. ft.)	Meeting Space (sq. ft.)	Meeting Rooms
Provo Convention Center (planned)	80,000	n/a	n/a	n/a

Note: n/a not available
Source: Original research

Living Environment

COST OF LIVING

Cost of Living Index

Composite Index	Groceries	Housing	Utilities	Trans-portation	Health Care	Misc. Goods/ Services
90.1	89.6	82.3	82.8	93.9	89.2	98.4

Note: U.S. = 100; Figures cover the Provo-Orem UT urban area.
Source: The Council for Community and Economic Research, ACCRA Cost of Living Index, 2011

Grocery Prices

Area[1]	T-Bone Steak ($/pound)	Frying Chicken ($/pound)	Whole Milk ($/half gal.)	Eggs ($/dozen)	Orange Juice ($/64 oz.)	Coffee ($/11.5 oz.)
City[2]	8.13	1.14	2.02	1.09	2.91	4.97
Avg.	9.25	1.18	2.22	1.66	3.19	4.40
Min.	6.70	0.88	1.31	0.95	2.46	2.94
Max.	14.30	2.16	3.50	3.18	4.75	6.83

Note: (1) Values for the local area are compared with the average, minimum and maximum values for all 335 areas in the Cost of Living Index; (2) Figures cover the Provo-Orem UT urban area; **T-Bone Steak** *(price per pound);* **Frying Chicken** *(price per pound, whole fryer);* **Whole Milk** *(half gallon carton);* **Eggs** *(price per dozen, Grade A, large);* **Orange Juice** *(64 oz. Tropicana or Florida Natural);* **Coffee** *(11.5 oz. can, vacuum-packed, Maxwell House, Hills Bros, or Folgers).*
Source: The Council for Community and Economic Research, ACCRA Cost of Living Index, 2011

Housing and Utility Costs

Area[1]	New Home Price ($)	Apartment Rent ($/month)	All Electric ($/month)	Part Electric ($/month)	Other Energy ($/month)	Telephone ($/month)
City[2]	230,965	838	-	55.36	63.86	27.08
Avg.	285,990	839	163.23	89.00	77.52	26.92
Min.	188,005	460	125.58	45.39	33.89	17.98
Max.	1,197,028	3,244	339.16	181.97	348.69	40.01

Note: (1) Values for the local area are compared with the average, minimum and maximum values for all 335 areas in the Cost of Living Index; (2) Figures cover the Provo-Orem UT urban area; **New Home Price** *(2,400 sf living area, 8,000 sf lot, in urban area with full utilities);* **Apartment Rent** *(950 sf 2 bedroom/1.5 or 2 bath, unfurnished, excluding all utilities except water);* **All Electric** *(average monthly cost for an all-electric home);* **Part Electric** *(average monthly cost for a part-electric home);* **Other Energy** *(average monthly cost for natural gas, fuel oil, coal, wood, and any other forms of energy except electricity);* **Telephone** *(price includes basic monthly rate for a private residential line plus additional local usage charges incurred by a family of four).*
Source: The Council for Community and Economic Research, ACCRA Cost of Living Index, 2011

Health Care, Transportation, and Other Costs

Area[1]	Doctor ($/visit)	Dentist ($/visit)	Optometrist ($/visit)	Gasoline ($/gallon)	Beauty Salon ($/visit)	Men's Shirt ($)
City[2]	81.73	65.71	83.88	3.22	28.53	26.75
Avg.	93.88	81.72	90.54	3.48	32.65	25.06
Min.	60.00	55.33	53.66	3.18	19.78	13.44
Max.	154.98	145.97	183.72	4.31	63.21	46.00

Note: (1) Values for the local area are compared with the average, minimum and maximum values for all 335 areas in the Cost of Living Index; (2) Figures cover the Provo-Orem UT urban area; **Doctor** *(general practitioners routine exam of an established patient);* **Dentist** *(adult teeth cleaning and periodic oral examination);* **Optometrist** *(full vision eye exam for established adult patient);* **Gasoline** *(one gallon regular unleaded, national brand, including all taxes, cash price at self-service pump if available);* **Beauty Salon** *(woman's shampoo, trim, and blow-dry);* **Men's Shirt** *(cotton/polyester dress shirt, pinpoint weave, long sleeves).*
Source: The Council for Community and Economic Research, ACCRA Cost of Living Index, 2011

HOUSING

House Price Index (HPI)

Area	National Ranking[2]	Quarterly Change (%)	One-Year Change (%)	Five-Year Change (%)
MSA[1]	221	0.30	-4.46	-16.82
U.S.[3]	-	-0.10	-2.43	-19.16

Note: The HPI is a weighted repeat sales index. It measures average price changes in repeat sales or refinancings on the same properties. This information is obtained by reviewing repeat mortgage transactions on single-family properties whose mortgages have been purchased or securitized by Fannie Mae or Freddie Mac in January 1975; (1) Metropolitan/Micropolitan Statistical Area—see Appendix B for areas included; (2) Rankings are based on annual percentage change for all metro areas containing at least 15,000 transactions over the last 10 years and ranges from 1 to 306; (3) figures based on a weighted average of Census Division estimates using a purchase only index; all figures are for the period ending December 31, 2011
Source: Federal Housing Finance Agency, House Price Index, February 23, 2012

House Price Valuations

Area	Q4 2005		Q4 2006		Q4 2007		Q4 2008		Q4 2009	
	Price ($000)	Over-valuation	Price ($000)	Over-valuation	Price ($000)	Over-valuation	Price ($000)	Over-valuation	Price ($000)	Over-valuation
MSA[1]	194.4	10.7	232.4	24.0	248.0	24.6	223.7	14.7	200.0	4.1

Note: Figures show the percentage of over- or under-valuation of single family homes relative to statistically normal house values (e.g. a value of 23.6 indicates that house values are 23.6% overvalued). Statistically normal house values are based on house prices, interest rates, household incomes, population densities, and any historical premiums or discounts metropolitan areas have exhibited over time; (1) Figures cover the Provo-Orem, UT - see Appendix B for areas included
Source: Global Insight/PNC Financial Services Group, House Prices in America: 4th Quarter 2009 Update

Median Single-Family Home Prices

Area	2009	2010	2011p	Percent Change 2010 to 2011
MSA[1]	n/a	n/a	n/a	n/a
U.S. Average	172.1	173.1	166.2	-4.0

Note: Figures are median sales prices of existing single-family homes in thousands of dollars; (p) preliminary; n/a not available; (1) Metropolitan Statistical Area—see Appendix B for areas included
Source: National Association of Realtors, Median Sales Price of Existing Single-Family Homes for Metropolitan Areas, 4th Quarter 2011

Affordability Index of Existing Single-Family Homes

Area	2009	2010	2011p	Percent Change 2010 to 2011
MSA[1]	n/a	n/a	n/a	n/a

Note: The housing affordability index measures whether or not a typical family could qualify for a mortgage loan on a typical home. The higher the index, the greater the household purchasing power. An index of 100 is defined as the point where a median-income household has exactly enough income to qualify for the purchase of a median-priced existing single-family home, assuming a 20 percent downpayment and 25 percent of gross income devoted to mortgage principal and interest payments; (p) preliminary; n/a not available; (1) Metropolitan Statistical Area—see Appendix B for areas included
Source: National Association of Realtors, Affordability Index of Existing Single-Family Homes, 2011

Median Apartment Condo-Coop Home Prices

Area	2009	2010	2011p	Percent Change 2010 to 2011
MSA[1]	n/a	n/a	n/a	n/a
U.S. Average	175.6	171.7	165.1	-3.8

Note: Figures are median sales prices of existing apartment condo-coop homes in thousands of dollars; (p) preliminary; n/a not available; (1) Metropolitan Statistical Area—see Appendix B for areas included
Source: National Association of Realtors, Median Sales Price of Existing Apartment Condo-Coop Homes for Metropolitan Areas, 4th Quarter 2011

Year Housing Structure Built

Area	2005 or Later	2000 -2004	1990 -1999	1980 -1989	1970 -1979	1960 -1969	1950 -1959	Before 1950	Median Year
City	4.9	9.9	18.5	10.3	21.3	12.2	8.1	14.8	1977
MSA[1]	12.2	16.9	22.4	9.8	15.8	6.1	5.9	10.9	1991
U.S.	5.0	8.6	14.0	14.1	16.3	11.3	11.2	19.6	1975

Note: Figures are percentages except for Median Year; (1) Figures cover the Provo-Orem, UT Metropolitan Statistical Area—see Appendix B for areas included
Source: U.S. Census Bureau, 2008-2010 American Community Survey 3-Year Estimates

HEALTH

Health Risk Data

Category	MSA[1] (%)	U.S. (%)
Adults who have been told they have high blood pressure[2]	19.1	28.7
Adults who have been told they have high blood cholesterol[2]	27.3	37.5
Adults who have been told they have diabetes[3]	4.8	8.7
Adults who have been told they have arthritis[2]	16.2	26.0
Adults who have been told they currently have asthma	10.7	9.1
Adults who are current smokers	5.8	17.3
Adults who are heavy drinkers[4]	1.5	5.0
Adults who are binge drinkers[5]	3.8	15.1
Adults who are overweight (BMI 25.0 - 29.9)	33.9	36.2
Adults who are obese (BMI 30.0 - 99.8)	21.8	27.5
Adults who participated in any physical activities in the past month	83.8	76.1
Adults 50+ who have ever had a sigmoidoscopy or colonoscopy	68.9	65.2
Women aged 40+ who have had a mammogram within the past two years	66.5	75.2
Men aged 40+ who have had a PSA test within the past two years	48.4	53.2
Adults aged 65+ who have had flu shot within the past year	64.4	67.5
Adults aged 18–64 who have any kind of health care coverage	83.9	82.2

Note: Data as of 2010 unless otherwise noted; (1) Figures cover the Provo-Orem, UT Metropolitan Statistical Area—see Appendix B for areas included; (2) Data as of 2009; (3) Figures do not include pregnancy-related, borderline, or pre-diabetes; (4) Heavy drinkers are classified as males having more than two drinks per day or females having more than one drink per day; (5) Binge drinkers are classified as males having five or more drinks on one occasion or females having four or more drinks on one occasion
Source: Centers for Disease Control and Prevention, Behaviorial Risk Factor Surveillance System, SMART: Selected Metropolitan/Micropolitan Area Risk Trends, 2009, 2010

Mortality Rates for the Top 10 Causes of Death in the U.S.

ICD-10[a] Sub-Chapter	ICD-10[a] Code	Age-Adjusted Mortality Rate[1] per 100,000 population	
		County[2]	U.S.
Malignant neoplasms	C00-C97	117.7	175.6
Ischaemic heart diseases	I20-I25	68.6	121.6
Other forms of heart disease	I30-I51	64.0	48.6
Chronic lower respiratory diseases	J40-J47	18.7	42.3
Cerebrovascular diseases	I60-I69	43.7	40.6
Organic, including symptomatic, mental disorders	F01-F09	31.1	26.7
Other degenerative diseases of the nervous system	G30-G31	22.3	24.7
Other external causes of accidental injury	W00-X59	21.4	24.4
Diabetes mellitus	E10-E14	24.7	21.7
Hypertensive diseases	I10-I15	15.8	18.2

Note: (a) ICD-10 = International Classification of Diseases 10th Revision; (1) Mortality rates are a three year average covering 2007-2009; (2) Figures cover Utah County
Source: Centers for Disease Control and Prevention, National Center for Health Statistics. Underlying Cause of Death 1999-2009 on CDC WONDER Online Database, released 2012. Data for year 2009 are compiled from the Multiple Cause of Death File 2009, Series 20 No. 2O, 2012, Data for year 2008 are compiled from the Multiple Cause of Death File 2008, Series 20 No. 2N, 2011, Data for year 2007 are compiled from Multiple Cause of Death File 2007, Series 20 No. 2M, 2010.

Mortality Rates for Selected Causes of Death

ICD-10[a] Sub-Chapter	ICD-10[a] Code	Age-Adjusted Mortality Rate[1] per 100,000 population	
		County[2]	U.S.
Assault	X85-Y09	*Unreliable	5.7
Human immunodeficiency virus (HIV) disease	B20-B24	*0.0	3.3
Influenza and pneumonia	J09-J18	13.2	16.4
Intentional self-harm	X60-X84	11.0	11.5
Malnutrition	E40-E46	*0.0	0.8
Obesity and other hyperalimentation	E65-E68	2.2	1.6
Transport accidents	V01-V99	9.6	13.7
Viral hepatitis	B15-B19	*Unreliable	2.2

Note: (a) ICD-10 = International Classification of Diseases 10th Revision; (1) Mortality rates are a three year average covering 2007-2009; (2) Figures cover Utah County; (*) Unreliable data as per CDC
Source: Centers for Disease Control and Prevention, National Center for Health Statistics. Underlying Cause of Death 1999-2009 on CDC WONDER Online Database, released 2012. Data for year 2009 are compiled from the Multiple Cause of Death File 2009, Series 20 No. 2O, 2012, Data for year 2008 are compiled from the Multiple Cause of Death File 2008, Series 20 No. 2N, 2011, Data for year 2007 are compiled from Multiple Cause of Death File 2007, Series 20 No. 2M, 2010.

Distribution of Physicians and Dentists

Area[1]	Dentists[2]	D.O.[3]	M.D.[4] Total	Family/General Practice	Pediatrics	Medical Specialties	Surgical Specialties
Local (number)	256	60	496	104	49	138	125
Local (rate[5])	5.0	1.1	9.4	2.0	0.9	2.6	2.4
U.S. (rate[5])	4.5	1.9	18.3	2.5	1.4	6.8	4.1

Note: Data as of 2008 unless noted; (1) Local data covers Utah County; (2) Data as of 2007; (3) Doctor of Osteopathic Medicine; (4) Includes active, non-federal, patient-care, office-based Doctors of Medicine; (5) rate per 10,000 population
Source: Area Resource File (ARF). 2009-2010 Release. U.S. Department of Health and Human Services, Health Resources and Services Administration, Bureau of Health Professions, Rockville, MD, August 2010

EDUCATION

Public School District Statistics

District Name	Schls	Pupils	Pupil/Teacher Ratio	Minority Pupils[1] (%)	Free Lunch Eligible[2] (%)	IEP[3] (%)
Provo District	24	13,769	22.0	42.2	39.7	13.8

Note: Table includes school districts with 2,000 or more students; (1) Percentage of students that are not non-Hispanic white; (2) Percentage of students that are eligible for the free lunch program; (3) Percentage of students that have an Individualized Education Program.
Source: U.S. Department of Education, National Center for Education Statistics, Common Core of Data, Local Education Agency (School District) Universe Survey: School Year 2009-2010; U.S. Department of Education, National Center for Education Statistics, Common Core of Data, Public Elementary/Secondary School Universe Survey: School Year 2009-2010

Highest Level of Education

Area	Less than H.S.	H.S. Diploma	Some College, No Deg.	Associate Degree	Bachelors Degree	Masters Degree	Profess. School Degree	Doctorate Degree
City	8.1	15.3	27.7	8.9	27.8	7.1	1.7	3.2
MSA[1]	6.4	18.0	29.9	11.0	24.1	7.4	1.6	1.6
U.S.	14.7	28.4	21.3	7.6	17.6	7.2	1.9	1.2

Note: Figures cover persons age 25 and over; (1) Figures cover the Provo-Orem, UT Metropolitan Statistical Area—see Appendix B for areas included
Source: U.S. Census Bureau, 2008-2010 American Community Survey 3-Year Estimates

Educational Attainment by Race

Area	High School Graduate or Higher (%)					Bachelor's Degree or Higher (%)				
	Total	White	Black	Asian	Hisp.[2]	Total	White	Black	Asian	Hisp.[2]
City	91.9	93.6	n/a	96.5	67.6	39.9	41.3	n/a	52.6	16.1
MSA[1]	93.6	94.6	88.1	92.0	73.1	34.7	35.1	35.0	46.0	18.5
U.S.	85.3	87.5	81.4	85.5	61.6	28.0	29.3	17.8	50.2	13.0

Note: Figures shown cover persons 25 years old and over; (1) Figures cover the Provo-Orem, UT Metropolitan Statistical Area—see Appendix B for areas included; (2) People of Hispanic origin can be of any race
Source: U.S. Census Bureau, 2008-2010 American Community Survey 3-Year Estimates

School Enrollment by Grade and Control

Area	Preschool (%)		Kindergarten (%)		Grades 1 - 4 (%)		Grades 5 - 8 (%)		Grades 9 - 12 (%)	
	Public	Private	Public	Private	Public	Private	Public	Private	Public	Private
City	43.1	56.9	93.9	6.1	94.3	5.7	94.6	5.4	77.9	22.1
MSA[1]	41.2	58.8	92.4	7.6	94.9	5.1	94.6	5.4	93.5	6.5
U.S.	55.4	44.6	87.1	12.9	89.4	10.6	89.5	10.5	90.4	9.6

Note: Figures shown cover persons 3 years old and over; (1) Figures cover the Provo-Orem, UT Metropolitan Statistical Area—see Appendix B for areas included
Source: U.S. Census Bureau, 2008-2010 American Community Survey 3-Year Estimates

Average Salaries of Public School Classroom Teachers

Area	2010-11		2011-12		Percent Change 2010-11 to 2011-12	Percent Change 2001-02 to 2011-12
	Dollars	Rank[1]	Dollars	Rank[1]		
Utah	47,033	39	48,159	38	2.39	26.30
U.S. Average	55,623	-	56,643	-	1.83	26.8

Note: (1) State rank ranges from 1 to 51 where 1 indicates highest salary.
Source: National Education Association, Rankings & Estimates: Rankings of the States 2011 and Estimates of School Statistics 2012, December 2011

Higher Education

Four-Year Colleges			Two-Year Colleges			Medical Schools[1]	Law Schools[2]	Voc/ Tech[3]
Public	Private Non-profit	Private For-profit	Public	Private Non-profit	Private For-profit			
0	1	0	0	0	5	0	1	2

Note: Figures cover institutions located within the city limits and include main campuses only; (1) includes schools accredited by the Liaison Committee on Medical Education and the American Osteopathic Association's Commission on Osteopathic College Accreditation; (2) includes American Bar Association-accredited law schools; (3) includes all schools with programs that are less than 2 years.
Source: National Center for Education Statistics, Integrated Postsecondary Education System (IPEDS) Peer Analysis System, 2011-12; Association of American Medical Colleges, Member List, April 23, 2012; American Osteopathic Association, Member List, April 23, 2012; Law School Admission Council, Official Guide to ABA-Approved Law Schools Online, April 23, 2012

According to *U.S. News & World Report,* the Provo-Orem, UT is home to one of the best national universities in the U.S.: **Brigham Young University–Provo** (#71). The indicators used to capture academic quality fall into a number of categories: assessment by administrators at peer institutions; retention of students; faculty resources; student selectivity; financial resources; alumni giving; high school counselor ratings of colleges; and graduation rate.*U.S. News & World Report, "America's Best Colleges 2012"*

According to *U.S. News & World Report,* the Provo-Orem, UT is home to one of the best law schools in the U.S.: **Brigham Young University (Clark)** (#39). The rankings are based on a weighted average of 12 measures of quality: peer assessment score; assessment score by lawyers/judges; median LSAT scores; median undergrad GPA; acceptance rate; employment rates for graduates; placement success; bar passage rate; faculty resources; expenditures per student; student/faculty ratio; and library resources. *U.S. News & World Report, "America's Best Law Schools 2013"*

According to *Forbes,* the Provo-Orem, UT is home to one of the best business schools in the U.S.: **Brigham Young (Marriott)** (#15). The rankings are based on the return on investment that graduates of the Class of 2006 received (median salary five years after graduation). *Forbes, "Best Business Schools," August 3, 2011*

PRESIDENTIAL ELECTION

2008 Presidential Election Results

Area	Obama	McCain	Nader	Other
Utah County	18.8	77.7	0.7	2.8
U.S.	52.9	45.6	0.6	0.9

Note: Results are percentages and may not add to 100% due to rounding
Source: Dave Leip's Atlas of U.S. Presidential Elections, www.uselectionatlas.org

EMPLOYERS

Major Employers

Company Name	Industry
About Time Technologies	Movements, clock or watch
Ancestry.com	Communication services, nec
Brigham Young University	Colleges and universities
Brigham Young University	Libraries
City of Provo	Mayors' office
Intermountain Health Care	General medical and surgical hospitals
Morinda Holdings	Bottled and canned soft drinks
Novell	Prepackaged software
Nu Skin Enterprises United States	Drugs, proprietaries, and sundries
Nu Skin International	Toilet preparations
Phone Directories Company	Directories, phone: publish only, not printed on site
Rbm Services	Building cleaning service
TPUSA	Telemarketing services
Utah Dept of Human Services	Mental hospital, except for the mentally retarded
Utah Dept of Human Services	Intermediate care facilities
Utah Valley University	College, except junior
Wal-Mart Stores	Department stores, discount
Wasatch Summit	Management consulting services
Xango	Drugs, proprietaries, and sundries

Note: Companies shown are located within the Provo-Orem, UT metropolitan area.
Source: Hoovers.com, data extracted April 25 2012

PUBLIC SAFETY

Crime Rate

Area	All Crimes	Violent Crimes				Property Crimes		
		Murder	Forcible Rape	Robbery	Aggrav. Assault	Burglary	Larceny -Theft	Motor Vehicle Theft
City	2,491.2	1.7	39.1	22.9	101.1	314.3	1,924.7	87.5
Suburbs[1]	2,099.1	0.9	17.6	11.8	28.9	312.5	1,658.6	68.7
Metro[2]	2,181.5	1.1	22.1	14.1	44.1	312.9	1,714.5	72.6
U.S.	3,345.5	4.8	27.5	119.1	252.3	699.6	2,003.5	238.8

Note: Figures are crimes per 100,000 population; (1) All areas within the metro area that are located outside the city limits; (2) Metropolitan Statistical Area—see Appendix B for areas included
Source: FBI Uniform Crime Reports, 2010

Hate Crimes

Area	Number of Quarters Reported	Bias Motivation				
		Race	Religion	Sexual Orientation	Ethnicity	Disability
City	4	0	1	1	0	0

Source: Federal Bureau of Investigation, Hate Crime Statistics 2010

Identity Theft Consumer Complaints

Area	Complaints	Complaints per 100,000 Population	Rank[2]
MSA[1]	249	50.5	328
U.S.	279,156	90.4	-

Note: (1) Metropolitan Statistical Area—see Appendix B for areas included; (2) Rank ranges from 1 to 384 where 1 indicates greatest number of identity theft complaints per 100,000 population
Source: Federal Trade Commission, Consumer Sentinel Network Data Book for January–December 2011

Fraud and Other Consumer Complaints

Area	Complaints	Complaints per 100,000 Population	Rank[2]
MSA[1]	1,846	374.2	336
U.S.	1,533,924	496.8	-

Note: (1) Metropolitan Statistical Area—see Appendix B for areas included; (2) Rank ranges from 1 to 384 where 1 indicates greatest number of fraud and other complaints per 100,000 population
Source: Federal Trade Commission, Consumer Sentinel Network Data Book for January–December 2011

RECREATION

Culture

Dance[1]	Theatre[1]	Instrumental Music[1]	Vocal Music[1]	Series/ Festivals	Museums	Zoos and Aquariums[2]
0	0	1	0	1	5	0

Note: (1) Number of professional perfoming groups; (2) AZA-accredited
Source: The Grey House Performing Arts Directory, 2011-2012; Official Museum Directory, 2011; American Association of Museums, AAM Member Museums, April 2012; Association of Zoos & Aquariums, AZA Member Zoos & Aquariums, April 2012

Professional Sports Teams

Team Name	League
No teams are located in the metro area	

Source: Original research

CLIMATE

Average and Extreme Temperatures

Temperature	Jan	Feb	Mar	Apr	May	Jun	Jul	Aug	Sep	Oct	Nov	Dec	Yr.
Extreme High (°F)	62	69	78	85	93	104	107	104	100	89	75	67	107
Average High (°F)	37	43	52	62	72	83	93	90	80	66	50	38	64
Average Temp. (°F)	28	34	41	50	59	69	78	76	65	53	40	30	52
Average Low (°F)	19	24	31	38	46	54	62	61	51	40	30	22	40
Extreme Low (°F)	-22	-14	2	15	25	35	40	37	27	16	-14	-15	-22

Note: Figures cover the years 1948-1990
Source: National Climatic Data Center, International Station Meteorological Climate Summary, 9/96

Average Precipitation/Snowfall/Humidity

Precip./Humidity	Jan	Feb	Mar	Apr	May	Jun	Jul	Aug	Sep	Oct	Nov	Dec	Yr.
Avg. Precip. (in.)	1.3	1.2	1.8	2.0	1.7	0.9	0.8	0.9	1.1	1.3	1.3	1.4	15.6
Avg. Snowfall (in.)	13	10	11	6	1	Tr	0	0	Tr	2	6	13	63
Avg. Rel. Hum. 5am (%)	79	77	71	67	66	60	53	54	60	68	75	79	67
Avg. Rel. Hum. 5pm (%)	69	59	47	38	33	26	22	23	28	40	59	71	43

Note: Figures cover the years 1948-1990; Tr = Trace amounts (<0.05 in. of rain; <0.5 in. of snow)
Source: National Climatic Data Center, International Station Meteorological Climate Summary, 9/96

Weather Conditions

Temperature			Daytime Sky			Precipitation		
5°F & below	32°F & below	90°F & above	Clear	Partly cloudy	Cloudy	0.01 inch or more precip.	0.1 inch or more snow/ice	Thunder-storms
7	128	56	94	152	119	92	38	38

Note: Figures are average number of days per year and cover the years 1948-1990
Source: National Climatic Data Center, International Station Meteorological Climate Summary, 9/96

HAZARDOUS WASTE

Superfund Sites

Provo has no sites on the EPA's Superfund Final National Priorities List.
U.S. Environmental Protection Agency, Final National Priorities List, April 17, 2012

AIR & WATER QUALITY

Air Quality Index

Area	Percent of Days when Air Quality was...[2]					AQI Statistics[2]	
	Good	Moderate	Unhealthy for Sensitive Groups	Unhealthy	Very Unhealthy	Maximum	Median
Area[1]	73.2	25.5	1.4	0.0	0.0	120	43

Note: Air Quality Index (AQI) is an index for reporting daily air quality. EPA calculates the AQI for five major air pollutants regulated by the Clean Air Act: ground-level ozone, particle pollution (aka particulate matter), carbon monoxide, sulfur dioxide, and nitrogen dioxide. The AQI runs from 0 to 500. The higher the AQI value, the greater the level of air pollution and the greater the health concern. There are six AQI categories: "Good" AQI is between 0 and 50. Air quality is considered satisfactory; "Moderate" AQI is between 51 and 100. Air quality is acceptable; "Unhealthy for Sensitive Groups" When AQI values are between 101 and 150, members of sensitive groups may experience health effects; "Unhealthy" When AQI values are between 151 and 200 everyone may begin to experience health effects; "Very Unhealthy" AQI values between 201 and 300 trigger a health alert; "Hazardous" AQI values over 300 trigger warnings of emergency conditions (not shown); (1) Data covers Utah County; (2) Based on 365 days with AQI data in 2011.
Source: U.S. Environmental Protection Agency, AirData Report, 2011

Air Quality Index Pollutants

Area	Percent of Days when AQI Pollutant was...[2]					
	Carbon Monoxide	Nitrogen Dioxide	Ozone	Sulfur Dioxide	Particulate Matter 2.5	Particulate Matter 10
Area[1]	0.0	21.1	58.6	0.0	19.5	0.8

Note: The Air Quality Index (AQI) is an index for reporting daily air quality. EPA calculates the AQI for five major air pollutants regulated by the Clean Air Act: ground-level ozone, particle pollution (also known as particulate matter), carbon monoxide, sulfur dioxide, and nitrogen dioxide. The AQI runs from 0 to 500. The higher the AQI value, the greater the level of air pollution and the greater the health concern; (1) Data covers Utah County; (2) Based on 365 days with AQI data in 2011.
Source: U.S. Environmental Protection Agency, AirData Report, 2011

Air Quality Index Trends

Area	Trend Sites (days)								All Sites (days)
	2003	2004	2005	2006	2007	2008	2009	2010	2010
MSA[1]	n/a	n/a	n/a	n/a	n/a	n/a	n/a	n/a	n/a

Note: Figures are the number of days the AQI value exceeded 100 in a given year. An AQI value greater than 100 indicates that air quality would have been in the unhealthful range on that day. Data from exceptional events are included. These counts are presented in two ways. First, the counts are based on sites having an adequate record of monitoring data during the trend period (trend sites). These counts represent the relative change in the number of days with AQI values greater than 100. In the last column, the counts are based on all sites with data in the most recent year (because it is possible for a site to have data in the most recent year but not enough data to be a trend site); (1) Data covers the Provo-Orem, UT—see Appendix B for areas included; n/a not available.
Source: U.S. Environmental Protection Agency, Air Quality Index Information, "Number of Days with Air Quality Index Values Greater than 100 at Trend Sites, 2000-2010, and at All Sites in 2010"

Maximum Air Pollutant Concentrations: Particulate Matter, Ozone, CO and Lead

	Particulate Matter 10 (ug/m³)	Particulate Matter 2.5 Wtd AM (ug/m³)	Particulate Matter 2.5 24-Hr (ug/m³)	Ozone (ppm)	Carbon Monoxide (ppm)	Lead (ug/m³)
MSA[1] Level	108	8.9	48	0.071	2	n/a
NAAQS[2]	150	15	35	0.075	9	0.15
Met NAAQS[2]	Yes	Yes	No	Yes	Yes	n/a

Note: Data from exceptional events are not included; (1) Data covers the Provo-Orem, UT—see Appendix B for areas included; (2) National Ambient Air Quality Standards; ppm = parts per million; ug/m^3 = micrograms per cubic meter; n/a not available
Concentrations: Particulate Matter 10 (coarse particulate)—highest second maximum 24-hour concentration; Particulate Matter 2.5 Wtd AM (fine particulate)—highest weighted annual mean concentration; Particulate Matter 2.5 24-Hour (fine particulate)—highest 98th percentile 24-hour concentration; Ozone—highest fourth daily maximum 8-hour concentration; Carbon Monoxide—highest second maximum non-overlapping 8-hour concentration; Lead—maximum running 3-month average
Source: U.S. Environmental Protection Agency, CBSA Factbook 2010, Air Quality Statistics by City, 2010

Maximum Air Pollutant Concentrations: Nitrogen Dioxide and Sulfur Dioxide

	Nitrogen Dioxide AM (ppb)	Nitrogen Dioxide 1-Hr (ppb)	Sulfur Dioxide AM (ppb)	Sulfur Dioxide 1-Hr (ppb)	Sulfur Dioxide 24-Hr (ppb)
MSA[1] Level	14.56	50	n/a	n/a	n/a
NAAQS[2]	53	100	30	75	140
Met NAAQS[2]	Yes	Yes	n/a	n/a	n/a

Note: Data from exceptional events are not included; (1) Data covers the Provo-Orem, UT—see Appendix B for areas included; (2) National Ambient Air Quality Standards; ppb = parts per billion; n/a not available
Concentrations: Nitrogen Dioxide AM—highest arithmetic mean concentration; Nitrogen Dioxide 1-Hr—highest 98th percentile 1-hour daily maximum concentration; Sulfur Dioxide AM—highest annual mean concentration; Sulfur Dioxide 1-Hr—highest 99th percentile 1-hour daily maximum concentration; Sulfur Dioxide 24-Hr—highest second maximum 24-hour concentration
Source: U.S. Environmental Protection Agency, CBSA Factbook 2010, Air Quality Statistics by City, 2010

Drinking Water

Water System Name	Pop. Served	Primary Water Source Type	Violations[1]	
			Health Based	Monitoring/ Reporting
Provo City	115,000	Purchased Surface	0	1

Note: (1) Based on violation data from January 1, 2011 to December 31, 2011 (includes unresolved violations from earlier years)
Source: U.S. Environmental Protection Agency, Office of Ground Water and Drinking Water, Safe Drinking Water Information System (based on data extracted April 18, 2012)

Roseville, California

Background

Long before Roseville became official, it was a breathtaking place of miles of natural grasslands, covered in gorgeous wild flowers growing in the shade of thick oak tree groves. Fresh water streams ran throughout the area and Native tribes, including the Maidu people, lived here for thousands of years before the first Europeans set foot in the area.

After the California Gold Rush in the late 1840s, many who came to this area in search of riches with no intention to settle, claimed land and began farming when panning for gold was unsuccessful. These people made up a core community considered Roseville's first families, and some of their descendants remain in town today. At that time, the economic focus was exclusively agriculture. Eventually the addition of the railroad led this simple farming town to expand into a city, and Roseville was officially incorporated in 1909.

As part of Placer County in the metropolitan area of Sacramento, Roseville maintains and celebrates its roots. The flourishing community now has a diverse economy that includes healthcare, technology, and agriculture. The town thrives on large retailers, as well as the auto industry. Roseville is considered a regional shopping destination with several high-end shopping centers that employ a large number of its residents.

There is an emphasis on culture and entertainment in Roseville with venues all around the city, including the Magic Circle Theater, a non-profit running since 1987, providing live performances. A popular Roseville tradition is Music in the Park, with musical events held in the local parks.

The breathtaking Maidu Museum and Historic Site has been preserved for its historic significance as home to the native Maidu people for over 3,000 years, and a place to take in the lands natural beauty. The museum provides information and artifacts from the Maidu people, and visitors can walk down the trails—observing changing views with the changing seasons.

Summertime brings about live bands and vendors along the historic Old Town Vernon Street, as well as Denio's Farmer Market & Swap Meet. Golf courses, neighborhood parks and acres of open space abound in Roseville.

Higher education in Roseville includes several colleges and universities. Heald College offers two-year programs, and Chapman University offers night classes, both designed to make education available to working professionals in the community. Plans are in the works for Sacramento State University to establish a satellite campus in Roseville.

Summers in Roseville are generally hot and dry while winters are fairly mild, much like many other California cities. Snow fall is uncommon, though October through April is considered the "wet season" as is usually met with an increase in precipitation.

Rankings

General Rankings

- The Sacramento metro area was selected one of America's "Best Cities to Live, Work and Play" by *Kiplinger's Personal Finance.* Criteria: population growth; percentage of workforce in the creative class (scientists, engineers, educators, writers, artists, entertainers, etc.); job quality; income growth; cost of living. *Kiplinger's Personal Finance, "Best Cities to Live, Work and Play," July 2008*
- The Sacramento metro area was identified as one of the 10 most popular big cities by Pew Research Center. The results are based on a telephone survey of 2,260 adults conducted during October 2008. The report explored a range of attitudes related to where Americans live, where they would like to live, and why. *Pew Research Center, "For Nearly Half of America, Grass is Greener Somewhere Else," January 29, 2009*

Business/Finance Rankings

- Experian ranked the top 20 major U.S. metropolitan areas by average debt per consumer. The Sacramento metro area was ranked #13. Criteria: average debt per consumer. Debt for this study includes credit cards, auto loans and personal loans. It does not include mortgages. *Experian, May 13, 2010*
- *American City Business Journals* ranked America's 261 largest cities in terms of their resident's wealth. Roseville ranked #37. Criteria: per capita income; median household income; percentage of households with annual incomes of $200,000 or more; median home value. *American City Business Journals, "Where the Money Is: America's Wealth Centers," August 18, 2008*
- The Sacramento metro area appeared on the Milken Institute "2011 Best Performing Metros" list. Rank: #144 out of 200 large metro areas. Criteria: job growth; wage and salary growth; high-tech output growth. *Milken Institute, "2011 Best Performing Metros"*
- Sacramento was ranked #18 out of 145 regions worldwide in terms of its "Knowledge Competitiveness Index." The index attempts to measure the knowledge-based development taking place throughout the world and is based on 19 measures of economic performance that indicate a region's ability to translate its knowledge capacity into economic value. *Centre for International Competitiveness, World Knowledge Competitiveness Index 2008*
- *Forbes* ranked the 200 most populous metro areas in the U.S. in terms of the "Best Places for Business and Careers." The Sacramento metro area was ranked #180. Criteria: costs (business and living); job growth (past and projected); income growth; educational attainment; projected economic growth; crime; cultural and recreational opportunities; net migration patterns; number of highly ranked colleges. *Forbes, "Best Places for Business and Careers," June 2011*

Children/Family Rankings

- The Sacramento metro area was selected as one of the "Best Cities for Relocating Families" by Worldwide ERC and Primacy Relocation. The 2008 study looked at nearly 50 factors important to relocating families including: recent job growth; nearby top-ranked colleges; in-state tuition for four-year public colleges; population growth since 2000; pediatricians per 100,000 population; and a Green Living index. *Worldwide ERC and Primacy Relocation, "2008 Best Cities for Relocating Families"*

Dating/Romance Rankings

- Eli Lily and Company, in partnership with Sperling's BestPlaces, ranked the nation's 50 largest metro areas in terms of the "Most Romantic Cities for Baby Boomers." The Sacramento metro area ranked #48. Criteria: marriage and divorce rates among baby boomers age 45 to 60; great restaurants; dance studios; chocolate, jewelry and flower sales. *Eli Lily and Company, "Most Romantic Cities for Baby Boomers," April 20, 2007*

- The Sacramento metro area was selected as one of the "Best Cities for Relocating Singles" by Worldwide ERC and Primacy Relocation. The area ranked #48 out of the 100 largest metro areas in the U.S. Criteria: recent job growth; recent singles population growth; overall population growth; affordable rental housing; cost-of-living index; expanded arts and recreation opportunities; ratio of single men and single women; affordability of quality higher education (including state residency requirements); diversity index; climate; population density. *Worldwide ERC and Primacy Relocation, "2008 Best Cities for Relocating Singles"*
- *Forbes* ranked the 40 most populous urbanized areas in the U.S. in terms of the "Best Cities for Singles." The Sacramento metro area ranked #35. Criteria: number of singles; cost of living alone; nightlife; culture; job growth; coolness; and online dating participation. *Forbes.com, "Best Cities for Singles," July 27, 2009*

Education Rankings

- Sacramento was identified as one of the 100 "smartest" metro areas in the U.S. The area ranked #35. Criteria: the editors rated the collective brainpower of the 100 largest metro areas in the U.S. based on their residents' educational attainment. *American City Business Journals, April 14, 2008*
- Sacramento was identified as one of "America's Brainiest Bastions" by *Portfolio.com.* The metro area ranked #68 out of 200. *Portfolio.com* analyzed levels of educational attainment in the nation's 200 largest metropolitan areas. The editors established scores for five levels of educational attainment, based on relative earning power of adult workers age 25 or older. Scores were determined by comparing the median income for all workers with the median income for those workers at a specified educational level. *Portfolio.com, "America's Brainiest Bastions," December 1, 2010*

Environmental Rankings

- The Sacramento was identified as one of America's dirtiest metro areas by *Forbes.* The area ranked #10 out of 10. Criteria: year-round particulate pollution; short-term particulate pollution; ozone pollution. *Forbes, "Dirtiest Cities in America," November 4, 2011*
- The Sacramento was identified as one of North America's greenest metropolitan areas. The area ranked #15. The Green City Index is comprised of 31 indicators, and scores cities across nine categories: carbon dioxide; energy; land use; buildings; transport; water; waste; air quality; environmental governance. The 27 largest metropolitan areas in the U.S. and Canada were considered. *Economist Intelligence Unit, sponsored by Siemens, "U.S. and Canada Green City Index, 2011"*
- The Sacramento was identified as one of America's cities with the most ENERGY STAR certified buildings. The area ranked #8 out of 25. Criteria: number of ENERGY STAR labeled buildings in 2010. *U.S. Environmental Protection Agency, "Top Cities With the Most ENERGY STAR Certified Buildings," March 15, 2011*
- Scarborough Research, a leading market research firm, identified the top local markets for green appliance households. The Sacramento DMA (Designated Market Area) ranked in the top 16 with 36% of consumers reporting that they own an energy-efficient appliance. *Scarborough Research, March 23, 2010*
- Roseville was selected as one of 22 "Smarter Cities" for energy by the Natural Resources Defense Council. Criteria: investment in green power; energy efficiency measures; conservation. *Natural Resources Defense Council, "2010 Smarter Cities," July 19, 2010*
- *American City Business Journal* ranked 43 metropolitan areas in terms of their "greenness." The Sacramento metro area ranked #13. Criteria: Forty-one metros in which *ACBJ* has business weeklies, plus Indianapolis and Cleveland, were ranked based on 20 different indicators such as adoption of green technologies, utilization of environmentally sound practices, and air and water quality. *American City Business Journals, "Green City Index," March 11, 2010*
- 100 of the largest metro areas in the U.S. were analyzed in terms of their current drought severity. The Sacramento metro area ranked #31 (#1 = driest). The rankings were based on statistics such as long-term precipitation trends and patterns and the Palmer drought indices. *Sperling's BestPlaces, www.BestPlaces.net, "America's Drought-Riskiest Cities," November 2007*

- The Sacramento metro area appeared in *Country Home's* "Best Green Places" report. The area ranked #31 out of 379. Criteria: official energy policies; green power; green buildings; availability of fresh, locally grown food. *Country Home, "Best Green Places," 2008*
- Sacramento was highlighted as one of the 25 metro areas most polluted by short-term particle pollution (24-hour PM 2.5) in the U.S. The area ranked #9. *American Lung Association, State of the Air 2011*
- Sacramento was highlighted as one of the 25 most ozone-polluted metro areas in the U.S. The area ranked #5. *American Lung Association, State of the Air 2011*

Health/Fitness Rankings

- The Sacramento metro area was selected as one of the worst cities for bed bugs in America by Rollins corporation, the owner of seven pest control companies, including Orkin. The area ranked #41 based on the number of bed bug treatments from January to December 2011. *Rollins, "The Top 50 U.S. Cities for Bed Bugs," March 19, 2012*
- Sacramento was identified as a "2011 Asthma Capital." The area ranked #72 out of the nation's 100 largest metropolitan areas. Twelve factors were used to identify the most challenging places to live for people with asthma: estimated prevalence; self-reported prevalence; crude death rate for asthma; annual pollen score; annual air quality; public smoking laws; number of board-certified asthma specialists; school inhaler access laws; rescue medication use; controller medication use; uninsured rate; poverty rate. *Asthma and Allergy Foundation of America, "2011 Asthma Capitals"*
- Sacramento was identified as a "2011 Fall Allergy Capital." The area ranked #97 out of 100. Three groups of factors were used to identify the most severe cities for people with allergies during the fall season: annual pollen levels; medicine utilization; access to board-certified allergists. *Asthma and Allergy Foundation of America, "2011 Fall Allergy Capitals"*
- Sacramento was identified as a "2012 Spring Allergy Capital." The area ranked #89 out of 100. Three groups of factors were used to identify the most severe cities for people with allergies during the spring season: annual pollen levels; medicine utilization; access to board-certified allergists. *Asthma and Allergy Foundation of America, "2012 Spring Allergy Capitals"*
- The Sacramento metropolitan area was selected as one of the best metros for hospital care in America by *HealthGrades.com.* The rankings are based on a comprehensive study of patient death and complication rates in the nation's nearly 5,000 hospitals. Hospitals performing in the top 5% nationwide across 26 different medical procedures and diagnoses were identified. *HealthGrades.com* then ranked cities by the highest percentage of these Distinguished Hospitals for Clinical Excellence™. The Sacramento metro area ranked #41. *HealthGrades.com, "America's Top 50 Cities for Hospital Care," January 21, 2012*
- The Sacramento metro area appeared in the 2011 Gallup-Healthways Well-Being Index. The index, based on interviews with more than 350,000 Americans, measured jobs, finances, physical health, emotional state of mind and communities. The metro area ranked #88 out of 190. Criteria: life evaluation; emotional health; work environment; physical health; healthy behaviors; basic access (basic needs optimal for a healthy life, such as access to food and medicine, having health insurance and feeling safe while walking at night). *Gallup-Healthways, "State of Well-Being 2011"*
- The Sacramento metro area was identified as one of "America's Most Stressful Cities" by *Sperling's BestPlaces.* The metro area ranked #8 out of 50. Criteria: unemployment rate; suicide rate; commute time; mental health; poor rest; alcohol use; violent crime rate; property crime rate; cloudy days annually. *Sperling's BestPlaces, www.BestPlaces.net, "Stressful Cities 2012*
- The Sacramento metro area was identified as one of "America's Most Stressful Cities" by *Forbes*. The metro area ranked #15 out of 40. Criteria: housing affordability; unemployment rate; cost of living; air quality; traffic congestion; sunny days; population density. *Forbes.com, "America's Most Stressful Cities," September 23, 2011*

- 50 of the largest metro areas in the U.S. were analyzed in terms of their health and fitness by the American College of Sports Medicine in their "American Fitness Index." The Sacramento metro area ranked #7 (#1 = healthiest). Criteria: preventative health behaviors; levels of chronic disease; health care access; community resources and policies that support physical activity. *American College of Sports Medicine, "Health and Community Fitness Status of the 50 Largest Metropolitan Areas," August 1, 2011*

Real Estate Rankings

- Sacramento was identified as one of 13 metro areas where home prices are falling dangerously. Criteria: home price change from October 2010 to September 2011; projected home price change through 2012. *Forbes.com, "Cities Where Home Prices are Falling Dangerously," January 10, 2012*
- *Fortune* ranked the 100 largest metro areas in the U.S. in terms of projected median home price change in 2010. The Sacramento metro area ranked #75. *Fortune, "The 2010 Housing Outlook," December 9, 2009*
- The nation's largest metro areas were analyzed in terms of the percentage of households entering some stage of foreclosure in 2011. The Sacramento metro area ranked #10 out of 20 (#1 = highest foreclosure rate). *RealtyTrac, 2011 Year-End Foreclosure Market Report, January 12, 2012*
- The Sacramento metro area appeared in a *Wall Street Journal* article ranking cities by "housing stress." The metro area was ranked #8 (#1 = most stress). Criteria: fraction of mortgage-holding homeowners with a monthly housing payment in excess of 30 percent of income; percentage of people without health insurance; unemployment rate. *The Wall Street Journal, "Which Cities Face Biggest Housing Risk," October 5, 2010*
- The Center for Housing Policy ranked 210 U.S. metropolitan areas by the fair market rent for a two-bedroom unit. The Sacramento metro area was ranked #50. (#1 = most expensive) with a rent of $1,039. Criteria: Fair Market Rent (FMR) in effect during the fourth quarter of 2009 based on HUD's fiscal year 2010 FMRs. *The Center for Housing Policy, "Paycheck to Paycheck: Most to Least Expensive Rental Markets in 2009"*
- The Sacramento metro area was identified as one of the top 20 cities in terms of decreasing home equity. The metro area was ranked #12. Criteria: percentage of home equity relative to the home's current value. *Forbes.com, "Where Americans are Losing Home Equity Most," May 1, 2010*
- The Sacramento metro area was identified as one of the markets with the worst expected performance in home prices over the next 12 months. *Local Market Monitor, "First Quarter Home Price Forecast for Largest US Markets," March 2, 2011*
- The Sacramento metro area was identified as one of the best U.S. markets to invest in rental property" by HomeVestors and Local Market Monitor. The area ranked #38 out of 100. Criteria: risk-return premium relative to national average. *HomeVestors and Local Market Monitor, "Best 100 U.S. Markets to Invest in Rental Property," March 9, 2012*

Safety Rankings

- The National Insurance Crime Bureau ranked 366 metro areas in the U.S. in terms of per capita rates of vehicle theft. The Sacramento metro area ranked #6 (#1 = highest rate). Criteria: number of vehicle theft offenses per 100,000 inhabitants in 2010. *National Insurance Crime Bureau, "Hot Spots," June 21, 2011*
- The Sacramento metro area was identified as one of the most dangerous metro areas for pedestrians by Transportation for America. The metro area ranked #21 out of 52 metro areas with over 1 million residents. Criteria: area's population divided by the number of pedestrian fatalities in that area. *Transportation for America, "Dangerous by Design 2011"*

Seniors/Retirement Rankings

- Bankers Life and Casualty Company, in partnership with Sperling's BestPlaces, ranked the nation's 50 largest metro areas in terms of the "Best U.S. Cities for Seniors." The Sacramento metro area ranked #47. Criteria: healthcare; transportation; housing; environment; economy; health and longevity; social and spiritual life; crime. *Bankers Life and Casualty Company, Center for a Secure Retirement, "Best U.S. Cities for Seniors 2011," September 2011*

Sports/Recreation Rankings

- Roseville was chosen as a bicycle friendly community by the League of American Bicyclists. A Bicycle Friendly Community welcomes cyclists by providing safe accommodation for cycling and encouraging people to bike for transportation and recreation. There are four award levels: Platinum; Gold; Silver; and Bronze. The community achieved an award level of Bronze. *League of American Bicyclists, "Bicycle Friendly Community Master List 2011"*

Technology Rankings

- Roseville was selected as a 2011 Digital Cities Survey winner. The city ranked #1 in the small city (75,000 to 124,999 population) category. The survey examined and assessed how city governments are utilizing information technology to operate and deliver quality service to their customers and citizens. Survey questions focused on implementation and adoption of online service delivery; planning and governance; and the infrastructure and architecture that make the transformation to digital government possible. *Center for Digital Government, "2011 Digital Cities Survey"*
- Scarborough Research, a leading market research firm, identified the Sacramento DMA (Designated Market Area) as one of the top markets for text messaging with more than 50% of cell phone subscribers age 18+ utilizing the text messaging feature on their phone. *Scarborough Research, November 24, 2008*

Transportation Rankings

- The Sacramento metro area appeared on *Forbes* list of the best and worst cities for commuters. The metro area ranked #36 out of 60 (#1 is best). Criteria: travel time; road congestion; travel delays. *Forbes.com, "Best and Worst Cities for Commuters," February 16, 2010*

Women/Minorities Rankings

- Sacramento was ranked #35 out of 100 metro areas in *SELF Magazine's* ranking of America's healthiest places for women." A panel of experts came up with more than 50 criteria including death and disease rates, environmental indicators, community resources, and lifestyle habits. *SELF Magazine, "Secrets of America's Healthiest Women," December 2008*
- The Sacramento metro area appeared on *Forbes'* list of the "Best Cities for Minority Entrepreneurs." The area ranked #35 out of 10. Criteria: 52 metropolitan statistical areas were examined. For each ethnicity (African Americans, Asians and Hispanics), the editors measured housing affordability, population growth, income growth, and entrepreneurship (per capita self-employment). *Forbes, "Best Cities for Minority Entrepreneurs," March 23, 2011*

Miscellaneous Rankings

- Energizer Holdings, the makers of Edge® shave gel, in partnership with Sperling's BestPlaces, ranked 50 major metro areas in terms of everyday irritations. The Sacramento metro area ranked #12. Criteria: humidity levels; weather conditions; incidence of traffic delays and congestion; average commute times; frequency of flight delays and cancellations; rates of sleeplessness; underemployment; pollens and allergens; pests; comedy clubs per capita. *Energizer Holdings, "Most Irritation Prone Cities," July 23, 2010*

- Mars Chocolate North America, the makers of COMBOS®, in partnership with Sperling's BestPlaces, ranked 50 major metro areas in terms of their "manliness." The Sacramento metro area ranked #43. Criteria: number of professional sports teams; number of nearby NASCAR tracks and racing events; manly lifestyle; concentration of manly retail stores; manly occupations per capita; salty snack sales; "Board of Manliness" rankings. *Mars Chocolate North America, "America's Manliest Cities 2011," September 1, 2011*
- The Sacramento metro area was selected as one of "America's Most Miserable Cities" by *Forbes.com.* The metro area ranked #5 out of 10. Criteria: violent crime; unemployment; foreclosures; income and property taxes; home prices; political corruption; commute times; climate; pro sports team records. *Forbes.com, "America's Most Miserable Cities, 2012" February 2, 2012*

Business Environment

CITY FINANCES

City Government Finances

Component	2009 ($000)	2009 ($ per capita)
Total Revenues	500,552	4,602
Total Expenditures	561,258	5,161
Debt Outstanding	1,170,435	10,762
Cash and Securities[1]	367,808	3,382

Note: (1) Cash and security holdings of a government at the close of its fiscal year, including those of its dependent agencies, utilities, and liquor stores.
Source: U.S Census Bureau, State & Local Government Finances 2009

City Government Revenue by Source

Source	2009 ($000)	2009 ($ per capita)
General Revenue		
From Federal Government	9,955	92
From State Government	17,858	164
From Local Governments	0	0
Taxes		
Property	49,441	455
Sales and Gross Receipts	29,417	270
Personal Income	0	0
Corporate Income	0	0
Motor Vehicle License	0	0
Other Taxes	6,514	60
Current Charges	99,604	916
Liquor Store	0	0
Utility	196,806	1,810
Employee Retirement	0	0

Source: U.S Census Bureau, State & Local Government Finances 2009

City Government Expenditures by Function

Function	2009 ($000)	2009 ($ per capita)	2009 (%)
General Direct Expenditures			
Air Transportation	0	0	0.0
Corrections	0	0	0.0
Education	0	0	0.0
Employment Security Administration	0	0	0.0
Financial Administration	11,564	106	2.1
Fire Protection	24,781	228	4.4
General Public Buildings	0	0	0.0
Governmental Administration, Other	45,285	416	8.1
Health	0	0	0.0
Highways	48,317	444	8.6
Hospitals	0	0	0.0
Housing and Community Development	15,780	145	2.8
Interest on General Debt	35,736	329	6.4
Judicial and Legal	1,658	15	0.3
Libraries	3,487	32	0.6
Parking	0	0	0.0
Parks and Recreation	27,150	250	4.8
Police Protection	30,636	282	5.5
Public Welfare	0	0	0.0
Sewerage	37,016	340	6.6
Solid Waste Management	15,040	138	2.7
Veterans' Services	0	0	0.0
Liquor Store	0	0	0.0
Utility	262,273	2,412	46.7
Employee Retirement	0	0	0.0

Source: U.S Census Bureau, State & Local Government Finances 2009

Municipal Bond Ratings

Area	Moody's	S&P	Fitch
City	n/a	n/a	n/a

Rating Systems (shown in declining order of credit quality): Moody's– Aaa, Aa, A, Baa, Ba, B, Caa, Ca, C (numerical modifiers 1, 2, and 3 are added to letter-rating); S&P– AAA, AA, A, BBB, BB, B, CCC, CC, C; Fitch– AAA, AA, A, BBB, BB, B, CCC, CC, C. Ratings may be modified by the addition of a plus or minus sign to show relative standing within the major rating categories.

Notes: n/a Not Available; w/d Withdrawn (1) Not Reviewed; (2) Issuer Rating/No General Obligation; (3) Standard and Poor's Issue Credit Rating (ICR) is a current opinion of an obliger with respect to a specific financial obligation, a specific class of financial obligations, or a specific financial program.

Source: U.S. Census Bureau, 2012 Statistical Abstract, Bond Ratings for City Governments by Largest Cities: 2010

DEMOGRAPHICS

Population Growth

Area	1990 Census	2000 Census	2010 Census	Population Growth (%) 1990-2000	2000-2010
City	44,692	79,921	118,788	78.8	48.6
MSA[1]	1,481,126	1,796,857	2,149,127	21.3	19.6
U.S.	248,709,873	281,421,906	308,745,538	13.2	9.7

Note: (1) Figures cover the Sacramento—Arden-Arcade—Roseville, CA Metropolitan Statistical Area—see Appendix B for areas included

Source: U.S. Census Bureau, 2010 Census

Household Size

Area	Persons in Household (%)							Average Household Size
	One	Two	Three	Four	Five	Six	Seven or More	
City	24.5	32.4	16.4	16.0	7.0	2.4	1.3	2.62
MSA[1]	24.8	32.1	16.2	14.2	7.0	3.1	2.5	2.68
U.S.	26.7	32.8	16.1	13.4	6.5	2.6	1.9	2.58

Note: (1) Figures cover the Sacramento—Arden-Arcade—Roseville, CA Metropolitan Statistical Area—see Appendix B for areas included

Source: U.S. Census Bureau, 2010 Census

Race

Area	White Alone[2] (%)	Black Alone[2] (%)	Asian Alone[2] (%)	AIAN[3] Alone[2] (%)	NHOPI[4] Alone[2] (%)	Other Race Alone[2] (%)	Two or More Races (%)
City	79.3	2.0	8.4	0.7	0.3	4.3	5.0
MSA[1]	64.7	7.4	11.9	1.0	0.7	8.4	5.9
U.S.	72.4	12.6	4.8	0.9	0.2	6.2	2.9

Note: (1) Figures cover the Sacramento—Arden-Arcade—Roseville, CA Metropolitan Statistical Area—see Appendix B for areas included; (2) Alone is defined as not being in combination with one or more other races; (3) American Indian and Alaska Native; (4) Native Hawaiian and Other Pacific Islander

Source: U.S. Census Bureau, 2010 Census

Hispanic or Latino Origin

Area	Hispanic or Latino (%)	Mexican (%)	Puerto Rican (%)	Cuban (%)	Other Hispanic or Latino (%)
City	14.6	11.0	0.5	0.1	3.0
MSA[1]	20.2	16.4	0.6	0.1	3.1
U.S.	16.3	10.3	1.5	0.6	4.0

Note: Persons of Hispanic or Latino origin can be of any race; (1) Figures cover the Sacramento—Arden-Arcade—Roseville, CA Metropolitan Statistical Area—see Appendix B for areas included

Source: U.S. Census Bureau, 2010 Census

Segregation

Type	Segregation Indices[1]				Percent Change		
	1990	2000	2010	2010 Rank[2]	1990-2000	1990-2010	2000-2010
Black/White	55.7	57.9	56.9	46	2.2	1.2	-1.0
Asian/White	48.1	50.0	49.9	8	1.9	1.8	-0.1
Hispanic/White	37.0	40.3	38.9	71	3.3	1.9	-1.4

Note: Figures are based on an analysis of 1990, 2000, and 2010 Census Decennial Census tract data by William H. Frey, Brookings Institution and the University of Michigan Social Science Data Analysis Network. In this analysis all racial groups (whites, blacks, and asians) are non-Hispanic members of those races. Hispanics are shown as a separate category; All figures cover the Metropolitan Statistical Area (see Appendix B for areas included); (1) Segregation Indices are Dissimilarity Indices that measure the degree to which the minority group is distributed differently than whites across census tracts. They range from 0 (complete integration) to 100 (complete segregation) where the value indicates the percentage of the minority group that needs to move to be distributed exactly like whites; (2) Ranges from 1 (most segregated) to 102 (least segregated); n/a not available.
Source: www.CensusScope.org

Ancestry

Area	German	Irish	English	American	Italian	Polish	French[2]	Scottish	Dutch
City	18.5	15.2	12.4	3.1	7.6	2.2	3.2	2.2	1.3
MSA[1]	14.1	10.9	9.8	2.6	5.8	1.5	2.8	2.3	1.5
U.S.	16.1	11.6	8.8	6.1	5.7	3.2	3.0	1.9	1.6

Note: Figures are the percentage of the total population reporting a particular ancestry. The nine most commonly reported ancestries in the U.S. are shown. Figures include multiple ancestries (e.g. if a person reported being Irish and Italian, they were included in both columns); (1) Figures cover the Sacramento—Arden-Arcade—Roseville, CA Metropolitan Statistical Area—see Appendix B for areas included; (2) Excludes Basque
Source: U.S. Census Bureau, 2008-2010 American Community Survey 3-Year Estimates

Foreign-Born Population

Area	Percent of Population Born in								
	Any Foreign Country	Mexico	Asia	Europe	Carribean	South America	Central America[2]	Africa	Canada
City	n/a	n/a	n/a	n/a	n/a	n/a	n/a	n/a	n/a
MSA[1]	17.3	4.9	7.4	2.7	0.1	0.3	0.6	0.4	0.3
U.S.	12.8	3.8	3.6	1.6	1.2	0.9	1.0	0.5	0.3

Note: (1) Figures cover the Sacramento—Arden-Arcade—Roseville, CA Metropolitan Statistical Area—see Appendix B for areas included; (2) Excludes Mexico.
Source: U.S. Census Bureau, 2008-2010 American Community Survey 3-Year Estimates

Marital Status

Area	Never Married	Now Married[2]	Separated	Widowed	Divorced
City	25.8	55.4	2.1	5.7	10.9
MSA[1]	32.6	48.5	2.2	5.4	11.2
U.S.	31.6	49.6	2.2	6.1	10.7

Note: Figures are percentages and cover the population 15 years of age and older; (1) Figures cover the Sacramento—Arden-Arcade—Roseville, CA Metropolitan Statistical Area—see Appendix B for areas included; (2) Excludes separated
Source: U.S. Census Bureau, 2008-2010 American Community Survey 3-Year Estimates

Age

Area	Percent of Population							Median Age
	Under Age 5	Age 5 to 17	Age 18 to 34	Age 35 to 49	Age 50 to 64	Age 65 to 79	80 Years and Over	
City	6.8	19.5	21.2	22.4	16.7	9.1	4.3	36.8
MSA[1]	6.7	18.2	23.9	20.5	18.7	8.6	3.4	36.0
U.S.	6.5	17.5	23.2	20.7	19.0	9.4	3.6	37.2

Note: (1) Figures cover the Sacramento—Arden-Arcade—Roseville, CA Metropolitan Statistical Area—see Appendix B for areas included
Source: U.S. Census Bureau, 2010 Census

Male/Female Ratio

Area	Males	Females	Males per 100 Females
City	56,894	61,894	91.9
MSA[1]	1,053,450	1,095,677	96.1
U.S.	151,781,326	156,964,212	96.7

Note: (1) Figures cover the Sacramento—Arden-Arcade—Roseville, CA Metropolitan Statistical Area—see Appendix B for areas included
Source: U.S. Census Bureau, 2010 Census

Religious Groups

Area	Catholic	Baptist	Non-Den.	Methodist[2]	Lutheran	LDS[3]	Pente-costal	Presby-terian[4]	Muslim[5]	Judaism
MSA[1]	16.2	3.2	4.0	1.8	0.8	3.4	2.0	0.8	0.3	0.8
U.S.	19.1	9.3	4.0	4.0	2.3	2.0	1.9	1.6	0.8	0.7

Note: Figures are the number of adherents as a percentage of the total population; (1) Figures cover the Sacramento—Arden-Arcade—Roseville, CA Metropolitan Statistical Area—see Appendix B for areas included; (2) Methodist/Pietist; (3) Latter Day Saints; (4) Reformed; (5) Figures are estimates
Source: Association of Statisticians of American Religious Bodies, 2010 U.S. Religion Census: Religious Congregations & Membership Study

ECONOMY

Gross Metropolitan Product

Area	2007	2008	2009	2010	2010 Rank[2]
MSA[1]	95.3	94.7	92.5	93.5	32

Note: Figures are in billions of dollars; (1) Figures cover the Sacramento—Arden-Arcade—Roseville, CA Metropolitan Statistical Area—see Appendix B for areas included; (2) Rank ranges from 1 to 363
Source: The United States Conference of Mayors, "U.S. Metro Economies: GMP and Employment Forecasts," June 2011

Economic Growth

Area	2007-2009 (%)	2010 (%)	2011 (%)	Rank[2]
MSA[1]	-3.4	0.1	0.0	287
U.S.	-1.3	2.9	2.5	–

Note: Figures are real Gross Metropolitan Product growth rates and represent annual average percent change; (1) Figures cover the Sacramento—Arden-Arcade—Roseville, CA Metropolitan Statistical Area—see Appendix B for areas included; (2) Rank ranges from 1 to 363
Source: The United States Conference of Mayors, "U.S. Metro Economies: GMP and Employment Forecasts," June 2011

Metropolitan Area Exports

Area	2005	2006	2007	2008	2009	2010	2010 Rank[2]
MSA[1]	2,924.4	3,398.5	3,318.8	3,608.0	3,502.0	4,070.5	51

Note: Figures are in millions of dollars; (1) Figures cover the Sacramento—Arden-Arcade—Roseville, CA Metropolitan Statistical Area—see Appendix B for areas included; (2) Rank ranges from 1 to 369
Source: U.S. Department of Commerce, International Trade Administration, Office of Trade & Industry Information, Manufacturing & Services, data extracted April 2, 2012

INCOME

Income

Area	Per Capita ($)	Median Household ($)	Average Household ($)
City	32,249	72,857	84,691
MSA[1]	27,995	58,733	75,256
U.S.	26,942	51,222	70,116

Note: (1) Figures cover the Sacramento—Arden-Arcade—Roseville, CA Metropolitan Statistical Area—see Appendix B for areas included
Source: U.S. Census Bureau, 2008-2010 American Community Survey 3-Year Estimates

Household Income Distribution

Area	Percent of Households Earning							
	Under $15,000	$15,000 -24,999	$25,000 -34,999	$35,000 -49,999	$50,000 -74,999	$75,000 -99,000	$100,000 -149,999	$150,000 and up
City	7.1	6.5	8.5	12.0	17.0	15.1	20.2	13.7
MSA[1]	10.0	9.4	9.8	13.3	19.1	13.3	15.1	10.0
U.S.	13.0	11.0	10.6	14.2	18.5	12.1	12.2	8.4

Note: (1) Figures cover the Sacramento—Arden-Arcade—Roseville, CA Metropolitan Statistical Area—see Appendix B for areas included
Source: U.S. Census Bureau, 2008-2010 American Community Survey 3-Year Estimates

Poverty Rate

Area	All Ages	Under 18 Years Old	18 to 64 Years Old	65 Years and Over
City	8.3	10.2	7.3	8.7
MSA[1]	13.6	18.4	12.8	7.4
U.S.	14.4	20.1	13.1	9.4

Note: Figures are percentage of people whose income during the past 12 months was below the poverty level; (1) Figures cover the Sacramento—Arden-Arcade—Roseville, CA Metropolitan Statistical Area—see Appendix B for areas included
Source: U.S. Census Bureau, 2008-2010 American Community Survey 3-Year Estimates

Personal Bankruptcy Filing Rate

Area	2006	2007	2008	2009	2010	2011
Placer County	1.34	2.84	5.61	8.55	9.63	8.28
U.S.	2.00	2.73	3.53	4.61	4.97	4.37

Note: Numbers are per 1,000 population and include Chapter 7 and Chapter 13 filings
Source: Federal Deposit Insurance Corporation, Regional Economic Conditions, March 9, 2012

EMPLOYMENT

Labor Force and Employment

Area	Civilian Labor Force			Workers Employed		
	Dec. 2010	Dec. 2011	% Chg.	Dec. 2010	Dec. 2011	% Chg.
City	54,742	54,780	0.1	48,587	49,540	2.0
MSA[1]	1,026,651	1,026,925	0.0	897,351	914,943	2.0
U.S.	153,156,000	153,373,000	0.1	139,159,000	140,681,000	1.1

Note: Data is not seasonally adjusted and covers workers 16 years of age and older; (1) Metropolitan Statistical Area—see Appendix B for areas included
Source: Bureau of Labor Statistics, http://stats.bls.gov

Unemployment Rate

Area	2011											
	Jan.	Feb.	Mar.	Apr.	May	Jun.	Jul.	Aug.	Sep.	Oct.	Nov.	Dec.
City	11.6	11.5	11.6	11.0	10.9	11.4	11.3	10.9	10.4	10.4	9.9	9.6
MSA[1]	12.9	12.6	12.7	12.0	11.7	12.4	12.5	11.9	11.4	11.4	10.9	10.9
U.S.	9.8	9.5	9.2	8.7	8.7	9.3	9.3	9.1	8.8	8.5	8.2	8.3

Note: Data is not seasonally adjusted and covers workers 16 years of age and older; All figures are percentages; (1) Metropolitan Statistical Area—see Appendix B for areas included
Source: Bureau of Labor Statistics, http://stats.bls.gov

Projected Unemployment Rate

Area	2010 (%)	2011 (%)	2012 (%)	2013 (%)
MSA[1]	12.9	11.6	10.9	10.0

Note: (1) Metropolitan Statistical Area—see Appendix B for areas included
Source: The United States Conference of Mayors, "U.S. Metro Economies: GMP and Employment Forecasts," June 2011

Employment by Occupation

Occupation Classification	City (%)	MSA[1] (%)	U.S. (%)
Management, Business, Science, and Arts	41.4	38.6	35.6
Natural Resources, Construction, and Maintenance	6.6	8.2	9.5
Production, Transportation, and Material Moving	7.0	8.4	12.1
Sales and Office	29.3	26.8	25.2
Service	15.7	18.0	17.6

Note: Figures cover employed civilians 16 years of age and older; (1) Figures cover the Sacramento—Arden-Arcade—Roseville, CA Metropolitan Statistical Area—see Appendix B for areas included
Source: U.S. Census Bureau, 2008-2010 American Community Survey 3-Year Estimates

Employment by Industry

Sector	MSA[1]		U.S.
	Number of Employees	Percent of Total	Percent of Total
Construction	34,800	4.3	4.1
Education and Health Services	105,200	13.1	15.2
Financial Activities	47,100	5.9	5.8
Government	222,100	27.6	16.8
Information	16,800	2.1	2.0
Leisure and Hospitality	77,300	9.6	9.9
Manufacturing	32,700	4.1	8.9
Mining and Logging	400	<0.1	0.6
Other Services	27,700	3.4	4.0
Professional and Business Services	101,800	12.7	13.3
Retail Trade	93,900	11.7	11.5
Transportation and Utilities	21,400	2.7	3.8
Wholesale Trade	23,000	2.9	4.2

Note: Figures cover non-farm employment as of December 2011 and are not seasonally adjusted; (1) Metropolitan Statistical Area—see Appendix B for areas included
Source: Bureau of Labor Statistics, http://stats.bls.gov

Occupations with Greatest Projected Employment Growth: 2008 – 2018

Occupation[1]	2008 Employment	2018 Projected Employment	Numeric Employment Change	Percent Employment Change
Personal and Home Care Aides	346,500	504,700	158,200	45.7
Registered Nurses	236,400	297,200	60,800	25.7
Retail Salespersons	499,400	559,100	59,700	12.0
Combined Food Preparation and Serving Workers, Including Fast Food	260,600	308,800	48,200	18.5
Elementary School Teachers, Except Special Education	197,500	233,400	35,900	18.2
Office Clerks, General	372,500	407,400	34,900	9.4
Customer Service Representatives	202,200	236,600	34,400	17.0
Waiters and Waitresses	245,600	279,900	34,300	14.0
Stock Clerks and Order Fillers	207,700	237,100	29,400	14.2
Postsecondary Teachers	168,000	196,100	28,100	16.7

Note: Projections cover California; (1) Sorted by numeric employment change
Source: www.projectionscentral.com, State Occupational Projections, 2008–2018 Long-Term Projections

Fastest Growing Occupations: 2008 – 2018

Occupation[1]	2008 Employment	2018 Projected Employment	Numeric Employment Change	Percent Employment Change
Biomedical Engineers	3,100	5,600	2,500	80.6
Network Systems and Data Communications Analysts	35,000	52,600	17,600	50.3
Biochemists and Biophysicists	4,800	7,100	2,300	47.9
Medical Scientists, Except Epidemiologists	26,200	38,500	12,300	46.9
Personal and Home Care Aides	346,500	504,700	158,200	45.7
Home Health Aides	54,300	78,000	23,700	43.6
Physician Assistants	8,100	11,500	3,400	42.0
Separating, Filtering, Clarifying, Precipitating, and Still Machine Setters, Operators, and Te	7,300	10,200	2,900	39.7
Physical Therapist Aides	5,900	8,100	2,200	37.3
Electrical and Electronics Repairers, Powerhouse, Substation, and Relay	1,100	1,500	400	36.4

Note: Projections cover California; (1) Sorted by percent employment change and excludes occupations with numeric employment change less than 100
Source: www.projectionscentral.com, State Occupational Projections, 2008–2018 Long-Term Projections

Average Wages

Occupation	$/Hr.	Occupation	$/Hr.
Accountants and Auditors	31.77	Maids and Housekeeping Cleaners	11.64
Automotive Mechanics	21.78	Maintenance and Repair Workers	20.40
Bookkeepers	19.82	Marketing Managers	52.30
Carpenters	25.23	Nuclear Medicine Technologists	51.53
Cashiers	11.35	Nurses, Licensed Practical	26.08
Clerks, General Office	16.16	Nurses, Registered	47.71
Clerks, Receptionists/Information	13.76	Nursing Aides/Orderlies/Attendants	15.40
Clerks, Shipping/Receiving	15.59	Packers and Packagers, Hand	12.45
Computer Programmers	38.33	Physical Therapists	42.79
Computer Support Specialists	28.76	Postal Service Mail Carriers	24.88
Computer Systems Analysts	37.48	Real Estate Brokers	30.05
Cooks, Restaurant	11.39	Retail Salespersons	12.32
Dentists	67.02	Sales Reps., Exc. Tech./Scientific	32.15
Electrical Engineers	51.08	Sales Reps., Tech./Scientific	42.87
Electricians	28.49	Secretaries, Exc. Legal/Med./Exec.	17.88
Financial Managers	52.89	Security Guards	12.52
First-Line Supervisors/Managers, Sales	19.67	Surgeons	n/a
Food Preparation Workers	10.48	Teacher Assistants	14.70
General and Operations Managers	57.72	Teachers, Elementary School	31.80
Hairdressers/Cosmetologists	12.55	Teachers, Secondary School	31.10
Internists	109.55	Telemarketers	13.16
Janitors and Cleaners	13.16	Truck Drivers, Heavy/Tractor-Trailer	19.58
Landscaping/Groundskeeping Workers	13.33	Truck Drivers, Light/Delivery Svcs.	17.34
Lawyers	58.86	Waiters and Waitresses	10.06

Note: Wage data covers the Sacramento—Arden-Arcade—Roseville, CA Metropolitan Statistical Area—see Appendix B for areas included. Hourly wages for elementary/secondary school teachers and teacher assistants were calculated by the editors from annual wage data assuming a 40 hour work week; n/a not available.
Source: Bureau of Labor Statistics, Metro Area Occupational Employment and Wage Estimates, May 2011

RESIDENTIAL REAL ESTATE

Building Permits

Area	Single-Family			Multi-Family			Total		
	2010	2011	Pct. Chg.	2010	2011	Pct. Chg.	2010	2011	Pct. Chg.
City	635	411	-35.3	0	0		635	411	-35.3
MSA[1]	2,166	1,873	-13.5	536	618	15.3	2,702	2,491	-7.8
U.S.	447,311	418,498	-6.4	157,299	205,563	30.7	604,610	624,061	3.2

Note: (1) Metropolitan Statistical Area—see Appendix B for areas included; figures represent new, privately-owned housing units authorized (unadjusted data); All permit data are based on estimates with imputation.
Source: U.S. Census Bureau, Manufacturing, Mining, and Construction Statistics, Building Permits, 2010, 2011

Homeownership Rate

Area	2005 (%)	2006 (%)	2007 (%)	2008 (%)	2009 (%)	2010 (%)	2011 (%)
MSA[1]	64.1	64.2	60.8	61.1	64.3	61.1	57.2
U.S.	68.9	68.8	68.1	67.8	67.4	66.9	66.1

Note: (1) Metropolitan Statistical Area—see Appendix B for areas included
Source: U.S. Census Bureau, Housing Vacancies and Homeownership Annual Statistics: 2011

Housing Vacancy Rates

Area	Gross Vacancy Rate[2] (%)			Year-Round Vacancy Rate[3] (%)			Rental Vacancy Rate[4] (%)			Homeowner Vacancy Rate[5] (%)		
	2009	2010	2011	2009	2010	2011	2009	2010	2011	2009	2010	2011
MSA[1]	15.2	14.0	10.5	12.7	11.3	9.2	10.6	8.4	7.1	4.0	2.9	2.4
U.S.	14.5	14.3	14.2	11.3	11.3	11.1	10.6	10.2	9.5	2.6	2.6	2.5

Note: (1) Metropolitan Statistical Area—see Appendix B for areas included; (2) The percentage of the total housing inventory that is vacant; (3) The percentage of the housing inventory (excluding seasonal units) that is year-round vacant; (4) The percentage of rental inventory that is vacant for rent; (5) The percentage of homeowner inventory that is vacant for sale
Source: U.S. Census Bureau, Housing Vacancies and Homeownership Annual Statistics: 2011

TAXES

State Corporate Income Tax Rates

State	Tax Rate (%)	Income Brackets ($)	Num. of Brackets	Financial Institution Tax Rate (%)[a]	Federal Income Tax Ded.
California	8.84 (c)	Flat rate	1	10.84 (c)	No

Note: Tax rates as of January 1, 2012; (a) Rates listed are the corporate income tax rate applied to financial institutions or excise taxes based on income. Some states have other taxes based upon the value of deposits or shares; (c) The minimum corporation franchise tax in California is $800. The additional alternative minimum tax is levied at a 6.65% rate.
Source: Federation of Tax Administrators, "State Corporate Income Tax Rates, 2012"

State Individual Income Tax Rates

State	Tax Rate (%)	Income Brackets ($)	Num. of Brackets	Personal Exempt. ($)[1]		Fed. Inc. Tax Ded.
				Single	Dependents	
California (a)	1.0 - 9.3 (f)	7,316 (b) - 48,029 (b)	6	102 (c)	315 (c)	No

Note: Tax rates as of January 1, 2012; Local- and county-level taxes are not included; n/a not applicable; (1) Married joint filers generally receive double the single exemption; (a) 17 states have statutory provision for automatically adjusting to the rate of inflation the dollar values of the income tax brackets, standard deductions, and/or personal exemptions. Massachusetts, Michigan, and Nebraska index the personal exemptiononly. Oregon does not index the income brackets for $125,000 and over. Because the inflation-adjustments for 2012 are not yet available in some cases, the table may report the 2011 amounts; (b) For joint returns, taxes are twice the tax on half the couple's income; (c) The personal exemption takes the form of a tax credit instead of a deduction; (f) California imposes an additional 1% tax on taxable income over $1 million, making the maximum rate 10.3% over $1 million.
Source: Federation of Tax Administrators, "State Individual Income Tax Rates, 2012"

Various State and Local Tax Rates

State	State and Local Sales and Use (%)	State Sales and Use (%)	Gasoline[1] (¢/gal.)	Cigarette[2] ($/pack)	Spirits[3] ($/gal.)	Wine[4] ($/gal.)	Beer[5] ($/gal.)
California	7.25	7.25 (b)	48.6	0.87	3.30	0.20	0.20

Note: All tax rates as of January 1, 2012 except beer, wine and spirits (September 1, 2011); (1) The American Petroleum Institute has developed a methodology for determining the average tax rate on a gallon of fuel. Rates may include any of the following: excise taxes, environmental fees, storage tank fees, other fees or taxes, general sales tax, and local taxes. In states where gasoline is subject to the general sales tax, or where the fuel tax is based on the average sale price, the average rate determined by API is sensitive to changes in the price of gasoline. States that fully or partially apply general sales taxes to gasoline: CA, CO, GA, IL, IN, MI, NY; (2) The federal excise tax of $1.0066 per pack and local taxes are not included; (3) Rates are those applicable to off-premise sales of 40% alcohol by volume (a.b.v.) distilled spirits in 750ml containers. Local excise taxes are excluded; (4) Rates are those applicable to off-premise sales of 11% a.b.v. non-carbonated wine in 750ml containers; (5) Rates are those applicable to off-premise sales of 4.7% a.b.v. beer in 12 ounce containers; (b) Three states collect a separate, uniform "local" add-on sales tax: California (1%), Utah (1.25%), Virginia (1%). These amounts are included in the state sales tax column.
Source: Tax Foundation, 2012 Facts & Figures: How Does Your State Compare?

State-Local Tax Burdens

Area	Rate (%)	Rank[1]	Per Capita Taxes Paid to Home State ($)	Total State and Local Per Capita Taxes Paid ($)	Per Capita Income ($)
California	10.6	6	3,874	4,910	46,366
U.S. Average	9.8	-	3,057	4,160	42,539

Note: Figures cover 2009; (1) Rank ranges from 1 to 50 where 1 is highest tax burden
Source: Tax Foundation, State-Local Tax Burdens, All States, 2009

State Business Tax Climate Index Rankings

State	Overall Rank	Corporate Tax Index Rank	Individual Income Tax Index Rank	Sales Tax Index Rank	Unemployment Insurance Tax Index Rank	Property Tax Index Rank
California	48	43	50	40	13	17

Note: The index is a measure of how each state's tax laws affect economic performance. The lower the rank, the more favorable a state's tax system is for business. States without a given tax are given a ranking of 1.
Source: Tax Foundation, Major Components of the State Business Tax Climate Index, FY 2012

COMMERCIAL REAL ESTATE

Office Market

Market Area	Inventory (sq. ft.)	Vacant (sq. ft.)	Vac. Rate (%)	Under Constr. (sq. ft.)	Asking Rent ($/sf/yr) Class A	Asking Rent ($/sf/yr) Class B
Oakland-East Bay	26,955,875	4,795,061	17.8	94,000	24.07	21.00

Source: Grubb & Ellis, Office Markets Trends, 4th Quarter 2011

Industrial Market

Market Area	Inventory (sq. ft.)	Vacant (sq. ft.)	Vac. Rate (%)	Under Constr. (sq. ft.)	Asking Rent ($/sf/yr) WH/Dist	Asking Rent ($/sf/yr) R&D/Flex
Oakland-East Bay	126,350,472	10,347,270	8.2	0	4.68	8.16

Source: Grubb & Ellis, Industrial Markets Trends, 4th Quarter 2011

COMMERCIAL UTILITIES

Typical Monthly Electric Bills

Area	Commercial Service ($/month) 1,500 kWh	Commercial Service ($/month) 40 kW demand 14,000 kWh	Industrial Service ($/month) 1,000 kW demand 200,000 kWh	Industrial Service ($/month) 50,000 kW demand 15,000,000 kWh
City	n/a	n/a	n/a	n/a
Average[1]	189	1,616	25,197	1,470,813

Note: Based on total rates in effect July 1, 2011; (1) average based on 184 utilities surveyed; n/a not available
Source: Edison Electric Institute, Typical Bills and Average Rates Report, Summer 2011

TRANSPORTATION

Means of Transportation to Work

Area	Car/Truck/Van		Public Transportation			Bicycle	Walked	Other Means	Worked at Home
	Drove Alone	Car-pooled	Bus	Subway	Railroad				
City	79.8	9.4	0.7	0.0	0.4	0.5	1.5	1.3	6.5
MSA[1]	75.2	11.7	2.0	0.2	0.3	1.7	2.0	1.6	5.3
U.S.	76.0	10.2	2.7	1.7	0.5	0.5	2.8	1.3	4.2

Note: Figures are percentages and cover workers 16 years of age and older; (1) Figures cover the Sacramento—Arden-Arcade—Roseville, CA Metropolitan Statistical Area—see Appendix B for areas included
Source: U.S. Census Bureau, 2008-2010 American Community Survey 3-Year Estimates

Travel Time to Work

Area	Less Than 10 Minutes	10 to 19 Minutes	20 to 29 Minutes	30 to 44 Minutes	45 to 59 Minutes	60 to 89 Minutes	90 Minutes or More
City	15.7	30.1	16.9	24.1	7.0	3.1	3.1
MSA[1]	12.2	30.0	22.0	21.5	6.9	4.4	2.9
U.S.	13.9	30.1	20.8	19.8	7.5	5.5	2.5

Note: Figures are percentages and include workers 16 years old and over; (1) Figures cover the Sacramento—Arden-Arcade—Roseville, CA Metropolitan Statistical Area—see Appendix B for areas included
Source: U.S. Census Bureau, 2008-2010 American Community Survey 3-Year Estimates

Travel Time Index

Area	1985	1990	1995	2000	2005	2010
Urban Area[1]	1.07	1.15	1.16	1.20	1.26	1.19
Average[2]	1.11	1.16	1.18	1.21	1.25	1.20

Note: Travel Time Index—the ratio of travel time in the peak period to the travel time at free-flow conditions. A value of 1.30 indicates a 20-minute free-flow trip takes 26 minutes in the peak. Free-flow speeds (60 mph on freeways and 35 mph on principal arterials) are used as the comparison threshold; (1) Covers the Sacramento CA urban area; (2) average of 439 urban areas
Source: Texas Transportation Institute, Urban Mobility Report 2011, September 2011

Public Transportation

Agency Name / Mode of Transportation	Vehicles Operated in Maximum Service	Annual Unlinked Passenger Trips ('000)	Annual Passenger Miles ('000)
Roseville Transit			
Bus (purchased transportation)	17	363.3	2,652.3
Demand Response (purchased transportation)	5	32.8	136.5

Source: Federal Transit Administration, National Transit Database, 2010

Air Transportation

Airport Name and Code / Type of Service	Passenger Airlines[1]	Passenger Enplanements	Freight Carriers[2]	Freight (lbs.)
Sacramento Metropolitan (SMF)				
Domestic service (U.S. carriers - 2011)	23	4,327,864	14	65,258,738
International service (U.S. carriers - 2010)	5	1,855	1	410

Note: (1) Includes all U.S.-based major, minor and commuter airlines that carried at least one passenger during the year; (2) Includes all U.S.-based airlines and freight carriers that transported at least one pound of freight during the year
Source: Bureau of Transportation Statistics, The Intermodal Transportation Database, Air Carriers: T-100 Domestic Market (U.S. Carriers), 2011; Bureau of Transportation Statistics, The Intermodal Transportation Database, Air Carriers: T-100 International Market (U.S. Carriers), 2010

Other Transportation Statistics

Major Highways:	I-80
Amtrak Service:	Yes
Major Waterways/Ports:	Near Folsom Lake

Source: Amtrak.com; Google Maps

BUSINESSES

Major Business Headquarters

Company Name	Rankings	
	Fortune[1]	Forbes[2]
No companies listed	-	-

Note: (1) Fortune 500—companies that produce a 10-K are ranked 1 to 500 based on 2010 revenue; (2) all private companies with at least $2 billion in annual revenue are ranked 1 to 212; companies listed are headquartered in the city; dashes indicate no ranking
Source: Fortune, "Fortune 500," May 23, 2011; Forbes, "America's Largest Private Companies," November 16, 2011

Fast-Growing Businesses

According to Deloitte, Roseville is home to one of North America's 500 fastest-growing high-technology companies: **Solar Power Incorporated** (#150). Companies are ranked by percentage growth in revenue over a five-year period. Criteria for inclusion: company must be headquartered within North America; must own proprietary intellectual property or proprietary technology that contributes to a significant portion of the company's operating revenue, or devote a significant proportion of revenues to research and development of technology; must have been in business for a minumum of five years with 2006 operating revenues of at least $50,000 USD/CD and 2010 operating revenues of at least $5 million USD/CD. *Deloitte Touche Tohmatsu, 2011 Deloitte Technology Fast 500*™

Minority- and Women-Owned Businesses

Group	All Firms		Firms with Paid Employees			
	Firms	Sales ($000)	Firms	Sales ($000)	Employees	Payroll ($000)
Asian	(s)	(s)	(s)	(s)	(s)	(s)
Black	(s)	(s)	(s)	(s)	(s)	(s)
Hispanic	(s)	(s)	(s)	(s)	(s)	(s)
Women	3,256	521,731	263	422,812	3,027	85,458
All Firms	11,321	18,763,677	3,036	18,330,113	66,700	2,931,196

Note: Figures cover firms located in the city; minority- and women-owned business are defined as firms in which the corresponding group own 51% or more of the stock or equity of the company; (s) estimates are suppressed when publication standards are not met
Source: U.S. Census Bureau, 2007 Economic Census, Survey of Business Owners

HOTELS

Hotels/Motels

Area	5 Star		4 Star		3 Star		2 Star		1 Star		Not Rated	
	Num.	Pct.[3]	Num.	Pct.[3]	Num.	Pct.[3]	Num.	Pct.[3]	Num.	Pct.[3]	Num.	Pct.[3]
City[1]	0	0.0	1	2.4	18	42.9	20	47.6	0	0.0	3	7.1
Total[2]	133	0.9	940	6.5	4,569	31.8	7,033	48.9	351	2.4	1,343	9.3

Note: (1) Figures cover Roseville and vicinity; (2) Figures cover all 100 cities in this book; (3) Percentage of hotels which have a given star rating; Star ratings are determined by expedia.com and offer an indication of the general quality of a particular hotel.
Source: expedia.com, April 25, 2012

Living Environment

COST OF LIVING

Cost of Living Index

Composite Index	Groceries	Housing	Utilities	Trans-portation	Health Care	Misc. Goods/ Services
116.3	109.7	138.6	117.4	114.0	114.2	100.1

Note: U.S. = 100; Figures cover the Sacramento CA urban area.
Source: The Council for Community and Economic Research, ACCRA Cost of Living Index, 2011

Grocery Prices

Area[1]	T-Bone Steak ($/pound)	Frying Chicken ($/pound)	Whole Milk ($/half gal.)	Eggs ($/dozen)	Orange Juice ($/64 oz.)	Coffee ($/11.5 oz.)
City[2]	10.64	1.10	2.19	2.27	2.94	4.98
Avg.	9.25	1.18	2.22	1.66	3.19	4.40
Min.	6.70	0.88	1.31	0.95	2.46	2.94
Max.	14.30	2.16	3.50	3.18	4.75	6.83

Note: (1) Values for the local area are compared with the average, minimum and maximum values for all 335 areas in the Cost of Living Index; (2) Figures cover the Sacramento CA urban area; **T-Bone Steak** *(price per pound);* **Frying Chicken** *(price per pound, whole fryer);* **Whole Milk** *(half gallon carton);* **Eggs** *(price per dozen, Grade A, large);* **Orange Juice** *(64 oz. Tropicana or Florida Natural);* **Coffee** *(11.5 oz. can, vacuum-packed, Maxwell House, Hills Bros, or Folgers).*
Source: The Council for Community and Economic Research, ACCRA Cost of Living Index, 2011

Housing and Utility Costs

Area[1]	New Home Price ($)	Apartment Rent ($/month)	All Electric ($/month)	Part Electric ($/month)	Other Energy ($/month)	Telephone ($/month)
City[2]	401,500	1,095	-	163.54	38.11	29.84
Avg.	285,990	839	163.23	89.00	77.52	26.92
Min.	188,005	460	125.58	45.39	33.89	17.98
Max.	1,197,028	3,244	339.16	181.97	348.69	40.01

Note: (1) Values for the local area are compared with the average, minimum and maximum values for all 335 areas in the Cost of Living Index; (2) Figures cover the Sacramento CA urban area; **New Home Price** *(2,400 sf living area, 8,000 sf lot, in urban area with full utilities);* **Apartment Rent** *(950 sf 2 bedroom/1.5 or 2 bath, unfurnished, excluding all utilities except water);* **All Electric** *(average monthly cost for an all-electric home);* **Part Electric** *(average monthly cost for a part-electric home);* **Other Energy** *(average monthly cost for natural gas, fuel oil, coal, wood, and any other forms of energy except electricity);* **Telephone** *(price includes basic monthly rate for a private residential line plus additional local usage charges incurred by a family of four).*
Source: The Council for Community and Economic Research, ACCRA Cost of Living Index, 2011

Health Care, Transportation, and Other Costs

Area[1]	Doctor ($/visit)	Dentist ($/visit)	Optometrist ($/visit)	Gasoline ($/gallon)	Beauty Salon ($/visit)	Men's Shirt ($)
City[2]	112.86	93.49	112.13	3.82	46.05	25.41
Avg.	93.88	81.72	90.54	3.48	32.65	25.06
Min.	60.00	55.33	53.66	3.18	19.78	13.44
Max.	154.98	145.97	183.72	4.31	63.21	46.00

Note: (1) Values for the local area are compared with the average, minimum and maximum values for all 335 areas in the Cost of Living Index; (2) Figures cover the Sacramento CA urban area; **Doctor** *(general practitioners routine exam of an established patient);* **Dentist** *(adult teeth cleaning and periodic oral examination);* **Optometrist** *(full vision eye exam for established adult patient);* **Gasoline** *(one gallon regular unleaded, national brand, including all taxes, cash price at self-service pump if available);* **Beauty Salon** *(woman's shampoo, trim, and blow-dry);* **Men's Shirt** *(cotton/polyester dress shirt, pinpoint weave, long sleeves).*
Source: The Council for Community and Economic Research, ACCRA Cost of Living Index, 2011

HOUSING

House Price Index (HPI)

Area	National Ranking[2]	Quarterly Change (%)	One-Year Change (%)	Five-Year Change (%)
MSA[1]	277	0.14	-7.16	-43.52
U.S.[3]	-	-0.10	-2.43	-19.16

Note: The HPI is a weighted repeat sales index. It measures average price changes in repeat sales or refinancings on the same properties. This information is obtained by reviewing repeat mortgage transactions on single-family properties whose mortgages have been purchased or securitized by Fannie Mae or Freddie Mac in January 1975; (1) Metropolitan/Micropolitan Statistical Area—see Appendix B for areas included; (2) Rankings are based on annual percentage change for all metro areas containing at least 15,000 transactions over the last 10 years and ranges from 1 to 306; (3) figures based on a weighted average of Census Division estimates using a purchase only index; all figures are for the period ending December 31, 2011
Source: Federal Housing Finance Agency, House Price Index, February 23, 2012

House Price Valuations

Area	Q4 2005		Q4 2006		Q4 2007		Q4 2008		Q4 2009	
	Price ($000)	Over-valuation	Price ($000)	Over-valuation	Price ($000)	Over-valuation	Price ($000)	Over-valuation	Price ($000)	Over-valuation
MSA[1]	391.2	54.5	358.1	34.9	295.7	7.4	220.1	-18.9	215.5	-19.2

Note: Figures show the percentage of over- or under-valuation of single family homes relative to statistically normal house values (e.g. a value of 23.6 indicates that house values are 23.6% overvalued). Statistically normal house values are based on house prices, interest rates, household incomes, population densities, and any historical premiums or discounts metropolitan areas have exhibited over time; (1) Figures cover the Sacramento—Arden-Arcade—Roseville, CA - see Appendix B for areas included
Source: Global Insight/PNC Financial Services Group, House Prices in America: 4th Quarter 2009 Update

Median Single-Family Home Prices

Area	2009	2010	2011p	Percent Change 2010 to 2011
MSA[1]	180.5	184.2	167.1	-9.3
U.S. Average	172.1	173.1	166.2	-4.0

Note: Figures are median sales prices of existing single-family homes in thousands of dollars; (p) preliminary; n/a not available; (1) Metropolitan Statistical Area—see Appendix B for areas included
Source: National Association of Realtors, Median Sales Price of Existing Single-Family Homes for Metropolitan Areas, 4th Quarter 2011

Affordability Index of Existing Single-Family Homes

Area	2009	2010	2011p	Percent Change 2010 to 2011
MSA[1]	106.5	109.1	125.8	15.3

Note: The housing affordability index measures whether or not a typical family could qualify for a mortgage loan on a typical home. The higher the index, the greater the household purchasing power. An index of 100 is defined as the point where a median-income household has exactly enough income to qualify for the purchase of a median-priced existing single-family home, assuming a 20 percent downpayment and 25 percent of gross income devoted to mortgage principal and interest payments; (p) preliminary; n/a not available; (1) Metropolitan Statistical Area—see Appendix B for areas included
Source: National Association of Realtors, Affordability Index of Existing Single-Family Homes, 2011

Median Apartment Condo-Coop Home Prices

Area	2009	2010	2011p	Percent Change 2010 to 2011
MSA[1]	98.5	88.5	79.5	-10.2
U.S. Average	175.6	171.7	165.1	-3.8

Note: Figures are median sales prices of existing apartment condo-coop homes in thousands of dollars; (p) preliminary; n/a not available; (1) Metropolitan Statistical Area—see Appendix B for areas included
Source: National Association of Realtors, Median Sales Price of Existing Apartment Condo-Coop Homes for Metropolitan Areas, 4th Quarter 2011

Year Housing Structure Built

Area	2005 or Later	2000 -2004	1990 -1999	1980 -1989	1970 -1979	1960 -1969	1950 -1959	Before 1950	Median Year
City	9.2	22.9	28.5	18.6	8.2	4.4	3.6	4.7	1994
MSA[1]	5.7	12.0	14.3	16.8	19.4	11.6	11.2	8.9	1979
U.S.	5.0	8.6	14.0	14.1	16.3	11.3	11.2	19.6	1975

Note: Figures are percentages except for Median Year; (1) Figures cover the Sacramento—Arden-Arcade—Roseville, CA Metropolitan Statistical Area—see Appendix B for areas included
Source: U.S. Census Bureau, 2008-2010 American Community Survey 3-Year Estimates

HEALTH

Health Risk Data

Category	MSA[1] (%)	U.S. (%)
Adults who have been told they have high blood pressure[2]	25.0	28.7
Adults who have been told they have high blood cholesterol[2]	31.3	37.5
Adults who have been told they have diabetes[3]	8.3	8.7
Adults who have been told they have arthritis[2]	22.1	26.0
Adults who have been told they currently have asthma	8.6	9.1
Adults who are current smokers	10.9	17.3
Adults who are heavy drinkers[4]	5.1	5.0
Adults who are binge drinkers[5]	14.3	15.1
Adults who are overweight (BMI 25.0 - 29.9)	35.1	36.2
Adults who are obese (BMI 30.0 - 99.8)	24.0	27.5
Adults who participated in any physical activities in the past month	84.7	76.1
Adults 50+ who have ever had a sigmoidoscopy or colonoscopy	70.9	65.2
Women aged 40+ who have had a mammogram within the past two years	81.1	75.2
Men aged 40+ who have had a PSA test within the past two years	46.0	53.2
Adults aged 65+ who have had flu shot within the past year	73.1	67.5
Adults aged 18–64 who have any kind of health care coverage	84.8	82.2

Note: Data as of 2010 unless otherwise noted; (1) Figures cover the Sacramento-Arden-Arcade-Roseville, CA Metropolitan Statistical Area—see Appendix B for areas included; (2) Data as of 2009; (3) Figures do not include pregnancy-related, borderline, or pre-diabetes; (4) Heavy drinkers are classified as males having more than two drinks per day or females having more than one drink per day; (5) Binge drinkers are classified as males having five or more drinks on one occasion or females having four or more drinks on one occasion
Source: Centers for Disease Control and Prevention, Behaviorial Risk Factor Surveillance System, SMART: Selected Metropolitan/Micropolitan Area Risk Trends, 2009, 2010

Mortality Rates for the Top 10 Causes of Death in the U.S.

ICD-10[a] Sub-Chapter	ICD-10[a] Code	Age-Adjusted Mortality Rate[1] per 100,000 population	
		County[2]	U.S.
Malignant neoplasms	C00-C97	161.1	175.6
Ischaemic heart diseases	I20-I25	100.8	121.6
Other forms of heart disease	I30-I51	36.2	48.6
Chronic lower respiratory diseases	J40-J47	36.5	42.3
Cerebrovascular diseases	I60-I69	40.4	40.6
Organic, including symptomatic, mental disorders	F01-F09	14.0	26.7
Other degenerative diseases of the nervous system	G30-G31	31.7	24.7
Other external causes of accidental injury	W00-X59	18.7	24.4
Diabetes mellitus	E10-E14	14.7	21.7
Hypertensive diseases	I10-I15	12.7	18.2

Note: (a) ICD-10 = International Classification of Diseases 10th Revision; (1) Mortality rates are a three year average covering 2007-2009; (2) Figures cover Placer County
Source: Centers for Disease Control and Prevention, National Center for Health Statistics. Underlying Cause of Death 1999-2009 on CDC WONDER Online Database, released 2012. Data for year 2009 are compiled from the Multiple Cause of Death File 2009, Series 20 No. 2O, 2012, Data for year 2008 are compiled from the Multiple Cause of Death File 2008, Series 20 No. 2N, 2011, Data for year 2007 are compiled from Multiple Cause of Death File 2007, Series 20 No. 2M, 2010.

Mortality Rates for Selected Causes of Death

ICD-10[a] Sub-Chapter	ICD-10[a] Code	Age-Adjusted Mortality Rate[1] per 100,000 population County[2]	U.S.
Assault	X85-Y09	*Unreliable	5.7
Human immunodeficiency virus (HIV) disease	B20-B24	*0.0	3.3
Influenza and pneumonia	J09-J18	11.5	16.4
Intentional self-harm	X60-X84	12.6	11.5
Malnutrition	E40-E46	*0.0	0.8
Obesity and other hyperalimentation	E65-E68	*0.0	1.6
Transport accidents	V01-V99	7.6	13.7
Viral hepatitis	B15-B19	2.8	2.2

Note: (a) ICD-10 = International Classification of Diseases 10th Revision; (1) Mortality rates are a three year average covering 2007-2009; (2) Figures cover Placer County; (*) Unreliable data as per CDC
Source: Centers for Disease Control and Prevention, National Center for Health Statistics. Underlying Cause of Death 1999-2009 on CDC WONDER Online Database, released 2012. Data for year 2009 are compiled from the Multiple Cause of Death File 2009, Series 20 No. 2O, 2012, Data for year 2008 are compiled from the Multiple Cause of Death File 2008, Series 20 No. 2N, 2011, Data for year 2007 are compiled from Multiple Cause of Death File 2007, Series 20 No. 2M, 2010.

Distribution of Physicians and Dentists

Area[1]	Dentists[2]	D.O.[3]	M.D.[4] Total	Family/ General Practice	Pediatrics	Medical Specialties	Surgical Specialties
Local (number)	261	44	775	135	67	275	164
Local (rate[5])	7.9	1.3	22.7	4.0	2.0	8.1	4.8
U.S. (rate[5])	4.5	1.9	18.3	2.5	1.4	6.8	4.1

Note: Data as of 2008 unless noted; (1) Local data covers Placer County; (2) Data as of 2007; (3) Doctor of Osteopathic Medicine; (4) Includes active, non-federal, patient-care, office-based Doctors of Medicine; (5) rate per 10,000 population
Source: Area Resource File (ARF). 2009-2010 Release. U.S. Department of Health and Human Services, Health Resources and Services Administration, Bureau of Health Professions, Rockville, MD, August 2010

Best Hospitals

According to *U.S. News*, the Sacramento—Arden-Arcade—Roseville, CA is home to one of the best hospitals in the U.S.: **University of California-Davis Medical Center** (2 specialties). The hospital listed was highly ranked in at least one adult specialty. *U.S. News Online, "America's Best Hospitals 2011-12"*

According to *U.S. News*, the Sacramento—Arden-Arcade—Roseville, CA is home to one of the best children's hospitals in the U.S.: **University of California Davis Children's Hospital** (1 specialty). The hospital listed was highly ranked in at least one pediatric specialty. *U.S. News Online, "America's Best Children's Hospitals 2011-12"*

EDUCATION

Public School District Statistics

District Name	Schls	Pupils	Pupil/ Teacher Ratio	Minority Pupils[1] (%)	Free Lunch Eligible[2] (%)	IEP[3] (%)
Dry Creek Joint Elementary	10	7,237	21.4	37.1	21.4	10.9
Roseville City Elementary	17	9,573	22.1	35.4	20.2	10.6
Roseville Joint Union High	7	9,868	23.5	33.9	16.3	6.7

Note: Table includes school districts with 2,000 or more students; (1) Percentage of students that are not non-Hispanic white; (2) Percentage of students that are eligible for the free lunch program; (3) Percentage of students that have an Individualized Education Program.
Source: U.S. Department of Education, National Center for Education Statistics, Common Core of Data, Local Education Agency (School District) Universe Survey: School Year 2009-2010; U.S. Department of Education, National Center for Education Statistics, Common Core of Data, Public Elementary/Secondary School Universe Survey: School Year 2009-2010

Highest Level of Education

Area	Less than H.S.	H.S. Diploma	Some College, No Deg.	Associate Degree	Bachelors Degree	Masters Degree	Profess. School Degree	Doctorate Degree
City	6.3	19.9	28.2	11.7	23.2	7.2	2.3	1.2
MSA[1]	13.0	21.1	26.7	9.4	19.8	6.4	2.2	1.3
U.S.	14.7	28.4	21.3	7.6	17.6	7.2	1.9	1.2

Note: Figures cover persons age 25 and over; (1) Figures cover the Sacramento—Arden-Arcade—Roseville, CA Metropolitan Statistical Area—see Appendix B for areas included
Source: U.S. Census Bureau, 2008-2010 American Community Survey 3-Year Estimates

Educational Attainment by Race

Area	High School Graduate or Higher (%)					Bachelor's Degree or Higher (%)				
	Total	White	Black	Asian	Hisp.[2]	Total	White	Black	Asian	Hisp.[2]
City	93.7	94.4	89.8	92.9	79.4	33.9	32.8	29.3	48.8	17.5
MSA[1]	87.0	90.3	86.9	80.8	65.8	29.7	31.3	18.4	38.4	14.1
U.S.	85.3	87.5	81.4	85.5	61.6	28.0	29.3	17.8	50.2	13.0

Note: Figures shown cover persons 25 years old and over; (1) Figures cover the Sacramento—Arden-Arcade—Roseville, CA Metropolitan Statistical Area—see Appendix B for areas included; (2) People of Hispanic origin can be of any race
Source: U.S. Census Bureau, 2008-2010 American Community Survey 3-Year Estimates

School Enrollment by Grade and Control

Area	Preschool (%)		Kindergarten (%)		Grades 1 - 4 (%)		Grades 5 - 8 (%)		Grades 9 - 12 (%)	
	Public	Private	Public	Private	Public	Private	Public	Private	Public	Private
City	49.7	50.3	89.4	10.6	88.7	11.3	89.6	10.4	92.7	7.3
MSA[1]	52.9	47.1	86.9	13.1	90.6	9.4	91.8	8.2	91.5	8.5
U.S.	55.4	44.6	87.1	12.9	89.4	10.6	89.5	10.5	90.4	9.6

Note: Figures shown cover persons 3 years old and over; (1) Figures cover the Sacramento—Arden-Arcade—Roseville, CA Metropolitan Statistical Area—see Appendix B for areas included
Source: U.S. Census Bureau, 2008-2010 American Community Survey 3-Year Estimates

Average Salaries of Public School Classroom Teachers

Area	2010-11		2011-12		Percent Change 2010-11 to 2011-12	Percent Change 2001-02 to 2011-12
	Dollars	Rank[1]	Dollars	Rank[1]		
California	67,871	4	69,496	4	2.39	27.90
U.S. Average	55,623	-	56,643	-	1.83	26.8

Note: (1) State rank ranges from 1 to 51 where 1 indicates highest salary.
Source: National Education Association, Rankings & Estimates: Rankings of the States 2011 and Estimates of School Statistics 2012, December 2011

Higher Education

Four-Year Colleges			Two-Year Colleges			Medical Schools[1]	Law Schools[2]	Voc/ Tech[3]
Public	Private Non-profit	Private For-profit	Public	Private Non-profit	Private For-profit			
0	0	0	0	0	1	0	0	1

Note: Figures cover institutions located within the city limits and include main campuses only; (1) includes schools accredited by the Liaison Committee on Medical Education and the American Osteopathic Association's Commission on Osteopathic College Accreditation; (2) includes American Bar Association-accredited law schools; (3) includes all schools with programs that are less than 2 years.
Source: National Center for Education Statistics, Integrated Postsecondary Education System (IPEDS) Peer Analysis System, 2011-12; Association of American Medical Colleges, Member List, April 23, 2012; American Osteopathic Association, Member List, April 23, 2012; Law School Admission Council, Official Guide to ABA-Approved Law Schools Online, April 23, 2012

According to *U.S. News & World Report*, the Sacramento—Arden-Arcade—Roseville, CA is home to one of the best national universities in the U.S.: **University of California–Davis** (#38). The indicators used to capture academic quality fall into a number of categories: assessment by administrators at peer institutions; retention of students; faculty resources; student selectivity; financial resources; alumni giving; high school counselor ratings of colleges; and graduation rate. *U.S. News & World Report, "America's Best Colleges 2012"*

According to *U.S. News & World Report,* the Sacramento—Arden-Arcade—Roseville, CA is home to one of the best law schools in the U.S.: **University of California–Davis** (#29). The rankings are based on a weighted average of 12 measures of quality: peer assessment score; assessment score by lawyers/judges; median LSAT scores; median undergrad GPA; acceptance rate; employment rates for graduates; placement success; bar passage rate; faculty resources; expenditures per student; student/faculty ratio; and library resources. *U.S. News & World Report, "America's Best Law Schools 2013"*

According to *Forbes,* the Sacramento—Arden-Arcade—Roseville, CA is home to one of the best business schools in the U.S.: **UC Davis** (#72). The rankings are based on the return on investment that graduates of the Class of 2006 received (median salary five years after graduation). *Forbes, "Best Business Schools," August 3, 2011*

PRESIDENTIAL ELECTION

2008 Presidential Election Results

Area	Obama	McCain	Nader	Other
Placer County	43.2	54.5	0.7	1.6
U.S.	52.9	45.6	0.6	0.9

Note: Results are percentages and may not add to 100% due to rounding
Source: Dave Leip's Atlas of U.S. Presidential Elections, www.uselectionatlas.org

EMPLOYERS

Major Employers

Company Name	Industry
C H W Mercy Healthcare	X-ray laboratory, including dental
CA Dept of Corrections and Rehab	Correctional institutions
Cache Creek Casino Resorts	Casino hotel
Calif Employment Dev Dept	Administration of social and manpower programs
Calif. Dept of Health Care Services	Administration of public health programs
California Department of General Services	Building maintenance services, nec
California Department of Justice	Legal counsel and prosecution
California Department of Transportation	Regulation, administration of transportation
Food & Agriculture, Calif. Dept of	Marketing and consumer service, government
Kaiser Foundation Hospitals	Trusts, nec
Los Rios Community College District	Colleges and universities
McClatchy Newspapers	Newspapers, publishing and printing
Red Hawk Casino	Gambling establishment
Sacramento Municipal Utility District	Electrical services
Shaw Environmental & Infrastructure	Engineering services
Sutter Health Sacramento Sierra Region	Health screening service
Sutter Roseville Medical Center	General medical and surgical hospitals
University Enterprises	Educational services
University of California, Davis	General medical and surgical hospitals
Water Resources, California Dept of	Air, water, and solid waste management

Note: Companies shown are located within the Sacramento—Arden-Arcade—Roseville, CA metropolitan area.
Source: Hoovers.com, data extracted April 25 2012

PUBLIC SAFETY

Crime Rate

Area	All Crimes	Violent Crimes: Murder	Violent Crimes: Forcible Rape	Violent Crimes: Robbery	Violent Crimes: Aggrav. Assault	Property Crimes: Burglary	Property Crimes: Larceny-Theft	Property Crimes: Motor Vehicle Theft
City	3,453.7	0.8	14.2	72.6	191.2	452.6	2,529.3	192.9
Suburbs[1]	3,592.5	4.4	26.8	165.5	293.1	787.9	1,850.5	464.2
Metro[2]	3,584.8	4.2	26.1	160.4	287.5	769.3	1,888.1	449.2
U.S.	3,345.5	4.8	27.5	119.1	252.3	699.6	2,003.5	238.8

Note: Figures are crimes per 100,000 population; (1) All areas within the metro area that are located outside the city limits; (2) Metropolitan Statistical Area—see Appendix B for areas included
Source: FBI Uniform Crime Reports, 2010

Hate Crimes

Area	Number of Quarters Reported	Bias Motivation				
		Race	Religion	Sexual Orientation	Ethnicity	Disability
City	4	1	1	0	1	0

Source: Federal Bureau of Investigation, Hate Crime Statistics 2010

Identity Theft Consumer Complaints

Area	Complaints	Complaints per 100,000 Population	Rank[2]
MSA[1]	1,979	94.6	112
U.S.	279,156	90.4	-

Note: (1) Metropolitan Statistical Area—see Appendix B for areas included; (2) Rank ranges from 1 to 384 where 1 indicates greatest number of identity theft complaints per 100,000 population
Source: Federal Trade Commission, Consumer Sentinel Network Data Book for January–December 2011

Fraud and Other Consumer Complaints

Area	Complaints	Complaints per 100,000 Population	Rank[2]
MSA[1]	9,931	474.9	187
U.S.	1,533,924	496.8	-

Note: (1) Metropolitan Statistical Area—see Appendix B for areas included; (2) Rank ranges from 1 to 384 where 1 indicates greatest number of fraud and other complaints per 100,000 population
Source: Federal Trade Commission, Consumer Sentinel Network Data Book for January–December 2011

RECREATION

Culture

Dance[1]	Theatre[1]	Instrumental Music[1]	Vocal Music[1]	Series/ Festivals	Museums	Zoos and Aquariums[2]
1	2	0	0	0	n/a	0

Note: (1) Number of professional perfoming groups; (2) AZA-accredited; n/a not available
Source: The Grey House Performing Arts Directory, 2011-2012; Official Museum Directory, 2011; American Association of Museums, AAM Member Museums, April 2012; Association of Zoos & Aquariums, AZA Member Zoos & Aquariums, April 2012

Professional Sports Teams

Team Name	League
Sacramento Kings	National Basketball Association (NBA)

Note: Includes teams located in the Sacramento metro area.
Source: Original research

CLIMATE

Average and Extreme Temperatures

Temperature	Jan	Feb	Mar	Apr	May	Jun	Jul	Aug	Sep	Oct	Nov	Dec	Yr.
Extreme High (°F)	70	76	88	93	105	115	114	109	108	101	87	72	115
Average High (°F)	53	60	64	71	80	87	93	91	87	78	63	53	73
Average Temp. (°F)	45	51	54	59	65	72	76	75	72	64	53	46	61
Average Low (°F)	38	41	43	46	50	55	58	58	56	50	43	38	48
Extreme Low (°F)	20	23	26	32	34	41	48	48	43	35	26	18	18

Note: Figures cover the years 1947-1990
Source: National Climatic Data Center, International Station Meteorological Climate Summary, 9/96

Average Precipitation/Snowfall/Humidity

Precip./Humidity	Jan	Feb	Mar	Apr	May	Jun	Jul	Aug	Sep	Oct	Nov	Dec	Yr.
Avg. Precip. (in.)	3.6	2.8	2.4	1.3	0.4	0.1	Tr	0.1	0.3	1.0	2.4	2.8	17.3
Avg. Snowfall (in.)	Tr	Tr	Tr	Tr	0	0	0	0	0	0	0	Tr	Tr
Avg. Rel. Hum. 7am (%)	90	88	84	78	71	67	68	73	75	80	87	90	79
Avg. Rel. Hum. 4pm (%)	70	59	51	43	36	31	28	29	31	39	57	70	45

Note: Figures cover the years 1947-1990; Tr = Trace amounts (<0.05 in. of rain; <0.5 in. of snow)
Source: National Climatic Data Center, International Station Meteorological Climate Summary, 9/96

Weather Conditions

Temperature			Daytime Sky			Precipitation		
10°F & below	32°F & below	90°F & above	Clear	Partly cloudy	Cloudy	0.01 inch or more precip.	0.1 inch or more snow/ice	Thunder-storms
0	21	73	175	111	79	58	< 1	2

Note: Figures are average number of days per year and cover the years 1947-1990
Source: National Climatic Data Center, International Station Meteorological Climate Summary, 9/96

HAZARDOUS WASTE

Superfund Sites

Roseville has no sites on the EPA's Superfund Final National Priorities List.
U.S. Environmental Protection Agency, Final National Priorities List, April 17, 2012

AIR & WATER QUALITY

Air Quality Index

Area	Percent of Days when Air Quality was...[2]					AQI Statistics[2]	
	Good	Moderate	Unhealthy for Sensitive Groups	Unhealthy	Very Unhealthy	Maximum	Median
Area[1]	75.6	18.4	6.0	0.0	0.0	147	41

Note: Air Quality Index (AQI) is an index for reporting daily air quality. EPA calculates the AQI for five major air pollutants regulated by the Clean Air Act: ground-level ozone, particle pollution (aka particulate matter), carbon monoxide, sulfur dioxide, and nitrogen dioxide. The AQI runs from 0 to 500. The higher the AQI value, the greater the level of air pollution and the greater the health concern. There are six AQI categories: "Good" AQI is between 0 and 50. Air quality is considered satisfactory; "Moderate" AQI is between 51 and 100. Air quality is acceptable; "Unhealthy for Sensitive Groups" When AQI values are between 101 and 150, members of sensitive groups may experience health effects; "Unhealthy" When AQI values are between 151 and 200 everyone may begin to experience health effects; "Very Unhealthy" AQI values between 201 and 300 trigger a health alert; "Hazardous" AQI values over 300 trigger warnings of emergency conditions (not shown); (1) Data covers Placer County; (2) Based on 365 days with AQI data in 2011.
Source: U.S. Environmental Protection Agency, AirData Report, 2011

Air Quality Index Pollutants

Area	Percent of Days when AQI Pollutant was...[2]					
	Carbon Monoxide	Nitrogen Dioxide	Ozone	Sulfur Dioxide	Particulate Matter 2.5	Particulate Matter 10
Area[1]	0.0	21.9	74.0	0.0	4.1	0.0

Note: The Air Quality Index (AQI) is an index for reporting daily air quality. EPA calculates the AQI for five major air pollutants regulated by the Clean Air Act: ground-level ozone, particle pollution (also known as particulate matter), carbon monoxide, sulfur dioxide, and nitrogen dioxide. The AQI runs from 0 to 500. The higher the AQI value, the greater the level of air pollution and the greater the health concern; (1) Data covers Placer County; (2) Based on 365 days with AQI data in 2011.
Source: U.S. Environmental Protection Agency, AirData Report, 2011

Air Quality Index Trends

Area	Trend Sites (days)								All Sites (days)
	2003	2004	2005	2006	2007	2008	2009	2010	2010
MSA[1]	79	66	62	79	53	61	43	23	24

Note: Figures are the number of days the AQI value exceeded 100 in a given year. An AQI value greater than 100 indicates that air quality would have been in the unhealthful range on that day. Data from exceptional events are included. These counts are presented in two ways. First, the counts are based on sites having an adequate record of monitoring data during the trend period (trend sites). These counts represent the relative change in the number of days with AQI values greater than 100. In the last column, the counts are based on all sites with data in the most recent year (because it is possible for a site to have data in the most recent year but not enough data to be a trend site); (1) Data covers the Sacramento—Arden-Arcade—Roseville, CA—see Appendix B for areas included
Source: U.S. Environmental Protection Agency, Air Quality Index Information, "Number of Days with Air Quality Index Values Greater than 100 at Trend Sites, 2000-2010, and at All Sites in 2010"

Maximum Air Pollutant Concentrations: Particulate Matter, Ozone, CO and Lead

	Particulate Matter 10 (ug/m^3)	Particulate Matter 2.5 Wtd AM (ug/m^3)	Particulate Matter 2.5 24-Hr (ug/m^3)	Ozone (ppm)	Carbon Monoxide (ppm)	Lead (ug/m^3)
MSA[1] Level	54	8.7	27	0.096	2	n/a
NAAQS[2]	150	15	35	0.075	9	0.15
Met NAAQS[2]	Yes	Yes	Yes	No	Yes	n/a

Note: Data from exceptional events are not included; (1) Data covers the Sacramento—Arden-Arcade—Roseville, CA—see Appendix B for areas included; (2) National Ambient Air Quality Standards; ppm = parts per million; ug/m^3 = micrograms per cubic meter; n/a not available
Concentrations: Particulate Matter 10 (coarse particulate)—highest second maximum 24-hour concentration; Particulate Matter 2.5 Wtd AM (fine particulate)—highest weighted annual mean concentration; Particulate Matter 2.5 24-Hour (fine particulate)—highest 98th percentile 24-hour concentration; Ozone—highest fourth daily maximum 8-hour concentration; Carbon Monoxide—highest second maximum non-overlapping 8-hour concentration; Lead—maximum running 3-month average
Source: U.S. Environmental Protection Agency, CBSA Factbook 2010, Air Quality Statistics by City, 2010

Maximum Air Pollutant Concentrations: Nitrogen Dioxide and Sulfur Dioxide

	Nitrogen Dioxide AM (ppb)	Nitrogen Dioxide 1-Hr (ppb)	Sulfur Dioxide AM (ppb)	Sulfur Dioxide 1-Hr (ppb)	Sulfur Dioxide 24-Hr (ppb)
MSA[1] Level	12.494	54	0.462	1	1.9
NAAQS[2]	53	100	30	75	140
Met NAAQS[2]	Yes	Yes	Yes	Yes	Yes

Note: Data from exceptional events are not included; (1) Data covers the Sacramento—Arden-Arcade—Roseville, CA—see Appendix B for areas included; (2) National Ambient Air Quality Standards; ppb = parts per billion; n/a not available
Concentrations: Nitrogen Dioxide AM—highest arithmetic mean concentration; Nitrogen Dioxide 1-Hr—highest 98th percentile 1-hour daily maximum concentration; Sulfur Dioxide AM—highest annual mean concentration; Sulfur Dioxide 1-Hr—highest 99th percentile 1-hour daily maximum concentration; Sulfur Dioxide 24-Hr—highest second maximum 24-hour concentration
Source: U.S. Environmental Protection Agency, CBSA Factbook 2010, Air Quality Statistics by City, 2010

Drinking Water

Water System Name	Pop. Served	Primary Water Source Type	Violations[1]	
			Health Based	Monitoring/ Reporting
City of Roseville	119,000	Surface	0	0

Note: (1) Based on violation data from January 1, 2011 to December 31, 2011 (includes unresolved violations from earlier years)
Source: U.S. Environmental Protection Agency, Office of Ground Water and Drinking Water, Safe Drinking Water Information System (based on data extracted April 18, 2012)

San Diego, California

Background

San Diego is the archetypal southern California City. Located 100 miles south of Los Angeles, near the Mexican border, San Diego is characterized by sunny days, an excellent harbor, a populous citizenry that alludes to its Spanish heritage, and recreational activities based on ideal weather conditions.

San Diego was first claimed in 1542 for Spain by Juan Rodriquez Cabrillo, a Portuguese navigator in the service of the Spanish crown. The site remained uneventful until 1769, when Spanish colonizer, Gaspar de Portola, established the first European settlement in California. Accompanying de Portola was a Franciscan monk named Junipero Serra, who established the Mission Basilica San Diega de Alcala, the first of a chain of missions along the California Coast.

After San Diego fell under the U.S. flag during the Mexican War of 1846, the city existed in relative isolation, deferring status and importance to its sister cities in the north, Los Angeles and San Francisco. Even when San Francisco businessman Alonzo Horton bought 1,000 acres of land near the harbor to establish a logical and practical downtown there, San Diego remained secondary to both these cities, and saw a decrease in population from 40,000 in 1880 to 17,000 at the turn of the century.

World War II repopulated the city, when the Navy moved one of its bases from Pearl Harbor to San Diego. The naval base brought personnel and a number of related industries, such as nuclear and oceanographic research, and aviation development. In celebration of this past, the famed IMidway, a 1,000-foot World War II aircraft carrier, has undergone a $6.5 million reconstruction and has been moved to Navy Pier, where it opened in 2004 as a floating museum.

Today, San Diego is the second most populous city in California, with plenty of outdoor activities, jobs, fine educational institutions, theaters, and museums with which to attract new residents, young and old alike. San Diego's downtown redevelopment agency has transformed what was largely an abandoned downtown into a glittering showcase of waterfront skyscrapers, live-work loft developments, five-star hotels, and many cafes, restaurants, and shops. The once-industrial East Village adjacent to PETCO ballpark is now the new frontier in San Diego's downtown urban renewal.

According to recent studies, the western part of the U.S., from Seattle to the Silicon Valley, and from San Diego to Denver, is becoming the center for all the hot growth industries, namely telecommunications, biomedical products, software, and financial services. San Diego leads the country in biotechnology companies that are attracting venture capital.

The San Diego Convention Center underwent expansion in 2001 that increased exhibit space from 250,000 to 615,000 square feet. The water supply system, always a significant issue in this part of California, has been upgraded and improved in recent years. The San Diego International Airport, at present trends, will shift from serving 16 million passengers in 2004 to serving more than 27 million by 2030, and appropriate airport renovations are being discussed.

San Diego summers are cool and winters are warm in comparison with other locations along the same general latitude, due to the Pacific Ocean. A marked feature of the climate is the wide variation in temperature. In nearby valleys, for example, daytime temperatures are much warmer in summer and noticeably cooler on winter nights than in the city proper. As is usual on the Pacific Coast, nighttime and early morning cloudiness is the norm. Considerable fog occurs along the coast, especially during the winter months.

Rankings

General Rankings

- The San Diego metro area was identified as one of the 10 most popular big cities by Pew Research Center. The results are based on a telephone survey of 2,260 adults conducted during October 2008. The report explored a range of attitudes related to where Americans live, where they would like to live, and why. *Pew Research Center, "For Nearly Half of America, Grass is Greener Somewhere Else," January 29, 2009*
- *Men's Health Living* ranked 100 U.S. cities in terms of quality of life. San Diego was ranked #17 and received a grade of B. Criteria: number of fitness facilities; air quality; number of physicians; male/female ratio; education levels; household income; cost of living. *Men's Health Living, Spring 2008*
- San Diego was selected as one of America's ten "Best Cities to Work and Live." The city ranked #2. The results are based on a survey of 2,500 employees and entrepreneurs who were asked about 40 large cities. *BusinessWeek, "America's Most and Least Favorite Cities," January 5, 2009*
- San Diego was selected as one of America's best cities by *Bloomberg Businessweek.* The city ranked #7 out of 50. Criteria: number of restaurants, bars and museums per capita; number of colleges, libraries, and professional sports teams; income, poverty, unemployment, crime, and foreclosure rates; percent of population with bachelor's degrees; public school performance; park acres per capita; air quality. *BusinessWeek, "America's 50 Best Cities," September 20, 2011*
- San Diego appeared on RelocateAmerica's list of best places to live in America. The annual "Top 100 Places to Live" list recognizes the top communities as nominated by their residents & local businesses. RelocateAmerica's Research Group determines the list based on review of various data gathered for economic, employment, housing, education, industry, opportunity, environment and recreation along with feedback from area leaders and residents. *RelocateAmerica.com, "Top 100 Places to Live for 2011"*
- San Diego was identified as one of the top places to live in the U.S. by Harris Interactive. The city ranked #2 out of 15. Criteria: 2,463 adults (age 18 and over) were polled and asked "if you could live in or near any city in the country except the one you live in or nearest to now, which city would you choose?" The poll was conducted online within the U.S. between September 14 and 20, 2010. *Harris Interactive, November 9, 2011*
- San Diego was selected as one of "America's Favorite Cities." The city ranked #7 in the "Quality of Life and Visitor Experience" category. Respondents to an online survey were asked to rate 35 top urban destinations in the U.S. from a visitor's perspective. Criteria: noteworthy neighborhoods; skyline/views; public parks and outdoor access; cleanliness; public transportation and pedestrian friendliness; safety; weather; peace and quiet; people-watching; environmental friendliness. *Travelandleisure.com, "America's Favorite Cities 2010," November 2010*
- San Diego was selected as one of "America's Favorite Cities." The city ranked #6 in the "People" category. Respondents to an online survey were asked to rate 35 top urban destinations in the U.S. from a visitor's perspective. Criteria: attractive; friendly; stylish; intelligent; athletic/active; diverse. *Travelandleisure.com, "America's Favorite Cities 2010," November 2010*

Business/Finance Rankings

- The San Diego metro area was identified as one of 10 places with the fastest-growing wages in America. The area ranked #10. Criteria: private-sector wage growth between the 4th quarter of 2010 and the 4th quarter of 2011. *PayScale, "The 10 Cities with the Fastest-Growing Wages in America," January 12, 2012*
- San Diego was identified as one of the top 25 U.S. cities with the most credit card debt by credit reporting bureau Experian. The city was ranked #10. *Experian, March 4, 2011*

- San Diego was identified as one of the "Happiest Cities to Work in 2012" by *CareerBliss.com,* an online community for career advancement. The city ranked #22 out of 50. Criteria: independent company reviews from employees all over the country on: relationship with their boss and co-workers; work environment; job resources; growth opportunities; compensation; company culture; company reputation; daily tasks; job control over work performed on a daily basis. *CareerBliss.com, "Happiest and Unhappiest Cities to Work in 2012"*

- *American City Business Journals* ranked America's 261 largest cities in terms of their resident's wealth. San Diego ranked #31. Criteria: per capita income; median household income; percentage of households with annual incomes of $200,000 or more; median home value. *American City Business Journals, "Where the Money Is: America's Wealth Centers," August 18, 2008*

- The San Diego metro area appeared on the Milken Institute "2011 Best Performing Metros" list. Rank: #69 out of 200 large metro areas. Criteria: job growth; wage and salary growth; high-tech output growth. *Milken Institute, "2011 Best Performing Metros"*

- San Diego was ranked #10 out of 145 regions worldwide in terms of its "Knowledge Competitiveness Index." The index attempts to measure the knowledge-based development taking place throughout the world and is based on 19 measures of economic performance that indicate a region's ability to translate its knowledge capacity into economic value. *Centre for International Competitiveness, World Knowledge Competitiveness Index 2008*

- *Forbes* ranked the 200 most populous metro areas in the U.S. in terms of the "Best Places for Business and Careers." The San Diego metro area was ranked #64. Criteria: costs (business and living); job growth (past and projected); income growth; educational attainment; projected economic growth; crime; cultural and recreational opportunities; net migration patterns; number of highly ranked colleges. *Forbes, "Best Places for Business and Careers," June 2011*

Children/Family Rankings

- San Diego was selected as one of the 10 worst cities to raise children in the U.S. by *KidFriendlyCities.org.* Criteria: education; environment; health; employment; crime; diversity; cost of living. *KidFriendlyCities.org, "Top Rated Kid/Family Friendly Cities 2009"*

- The San Diego metro area was selected as one of the "Best Cities for Relocating Families" by Worldwide ERC and Primacy Relocation. The 2008 study looked at nearly 50 factors important to relocating families including: recent job growth; nearby top-ranked colleges; in-state tuition for four-year public colleges; population growth since 2000; pediatricians per 100,000 population; and a Green Living index. *Worldwide ERC and Primacy Relocation, "2008 Best Cities for Relocating Families"*

- *Fit Pregnancy* magazine ranked the 50 best U.S. cities in which to have a baby. San Diego was ranked #12. Criteria: access to hospitals and doctors; affordability; birthing options; breastfeeding; child care; fertility laws/resources; maternal and infant health risk; parks/stroller friendliness; safety. *Fit Pregnancy, "The Best Cities in America to Have a Baby 2008"*

Culture/Performing Arts Rankings

- San Diego was selected as one of "America's Top 25 Arts Destinations." The city ranked #16 in the big city (population 500,000 and over) category. Criteria: readers' top choices for arts travel destinations based on the richness and variety of visual arts sites, activities and events. *American Style, "America's Top 25 Arts Destinations," May 2010*

Dating/Romance Rankings

- San Diego was selected as one of "America's Best Cities for Dating" by *Yahoo! Travel.* Criteria: high proportion of singles; excellent dating venues and/or stunning natural settings. *Yahoo! Travel, "America's Best Cities for Dating," February 7, 2012*

- San Diego appeared on *Men's Health's* list of the most sex-happy cities in America. The city ranked #43 of 100. Criteria: condom sales; birth rates; sex toy sales; rates of chlamydia, gonorrhea, and syphilis. *Men's Health, "America's Most Sex-Happy Cities," October 2010*

- *Men's Health* ranked 100 U.S. cities in terms of best (and worst) marriages. San Diego was ranked #60 (#1 = worst). Criteria: rate of failed marriages; stringency of divorce laws; percentage of population who've split; number of licensed marriage and family therapists. *Men's Health, "Splitsville, USA," May 2010*

- Eli Lily and Company, in partnership with Sperling's BestPlaces, ranked the nation's 50 largest metro areas in terms of the "Most Romantic Cities for Baby Boomers." The San Diego metro area ranked #45. Criteria: marriage and divorce rates among baby boomers age 45 to 60; great restaurants; dance studios; chocolate, jewelry and flower sales. *Eli Lily and Company, "Most Romantic Cities for Baby Boomers," April 20, 2007*

- The San Diego metro area was selected as one of the "Best Cities for Relocating Singles" by Worldwide ERC and Primacy Relocation. The area ranked #25 out of the 100 largest metro areas in the U.S. Criteria: recent job growth; recent singles population growth; overall population growth; affordable rental housing; cost-of-living index; expanded arts and recreation opportunities; ratio of single men and single women; affordability of quality higher education (including state residency requirements); diversity index; climate; population density. *Worldwide ERC and Primacy Relocation, "2008 Best Cities for Relocating Singles"*

- *Forbes* ranked the 40 most populous urbanized areas in the U.S. in terms of the "Best Cities for Singles." The San Diego metro area ranked #12. Criteria: number of singles; cost of living alone; nightlife; culture; job growth; coolness; and online dating participation. *Forbes.com, "Best Cities for Singles," July 27, 2009*

Education Rankings

- *Men's Health* ranked 100 U.S. cities in terms of their education levels. San Diego was ranked #6 (#1 = most educated city). Criteria: high school graduation rates; school enrollment; educational attainment; number of households who have outstanding student loans; number of households whose members have taken adult-education courses. *Men's Health, "Where School Is In: The Most and Least Educated Cities," September 12, 2011*

- San Diego was selected as one of "America's Most Literate Cities." The city ranked #33 out of the 75 largest U.S. cities. Criteria: number of booksellers; library resources; Internet resources; educational attainment; periodical publishing resources; newspaper circulation. *Central Connecticut State University, "America's Most Literate Cities 2011"*

- San Diego was identified as one of the 100 "smartest" metro areas in the U.S. The area ranked #24. Criteria: the editors rated the collective brainpower of the 100 largest metro areas in the U.S. based on their residents' educational attainment. *American City Business Journals, April 14, 2008*

- San Diego was identified as one of "America's Smartest Cities" by *The Daily Beast.* The metro area ranked #18 out of 55. The editors ranked metropolitan areas with one million or more residents on the following criteria: percentage of residents over age 25 with bachelor's or graduate degrees; non-fiction book sales; ratio of institutions of higher education; libraries per capita. *The Daily Beast, "America's Smartest Cities," October 24, 2010*

- San Diego was identified as one of America's most inventive cities by *The Daily Beast.* The city ranked #15 out of 25. The 200 largest cities in the U.S. were ranked by the number of patents (applied and approved) per capita. *The Daily Beast, "The 25 Most Inventive Cities," October 2, 2011*

- San Diego was identified as one of "America's Brainiest Bastions" by *Portfolio.com.* The metro area ranked #33 out of 200. *Portfolio.com* analyzed levels of educational attainment in the nation's 200 largest metropolitan areas. The editors established scores for five levels of educational attainment, based on relative earning power of adult workers age 25 or older. Scores were determined by comparing the median income for all workers with the median income for those workers at a specified educational level. *Portfolio.com, "America's Brainiest Bastions," December 1, 2010*

Environmental Rankings

- The San Diego was identified as one of America's dirtiest metro areas by *Forbes.* The area ranked #9 out of 10. Criteria: year-round particulate pollution; short-term particulate pollution; ozone pollution. *Forbes, "Dirtiest Cities in America," November 4, 2011*

- The San Diego was identified as one of America's cities with the most ENERGY STAR certified buildings. The area ranked #20 out of 25. Criteria: number of ENERGY STAR labeled buildings in 2010. *U.S. Environmental Protection Agency, "Top Cities With the Most ENERGY STAR Certified Buildings," March 15, 2011*

- San Diego was selected as one of 22 "Smarter Cities" for energy by the Natural Resources Defense Council. Criteria: investment in green power; energy efficiency measures; conservation. *Natural Resources Defense Council, "2010 Smarter Cities," July 19, 2010*

- 100 of the largest metro areas in the U.S. were analyzed in terms of their current drought severity. The San Diego metro area ranked #2 (#1 = driest). The rankings were based on statistics such as long-term precipitation trends and patterns and the Palmer drought indices. *Sperling's BestPlaces, www.BestPlaces.net, "America's Drought-Riskiest Cities," November 2007*

- The San Diego metro area appeared in *Country Home's* "Best Green Places" report. The area ranked #32 out of 379. Criteria: official energy policies; green power; green buildings; availability of fresh, locally grown food. *Country Home, "Best Green Places," 2008*

- San Diego was highlighted as one of the 25 metro areas most polluted by short-term particle pollution (24-hour PM 2.5) in the U.S. The area ranked #15. *American Lung Association, State of the Air 2011*

- San Diego was highlighted as one of the 25 most ozone-polluted metro areas in the U.S. The area ranked #7. *American Lung Association, State of the Air 2011*

Food/Drink Rankings

- San Diego was identified as one of "America's Drunkest Cities of 2011" by *The Daily Beast.* The city ranked #9 out of 25. Criteria: binge drinking; drinks consumed per month. *The Daily Beast, "Tipsy Towns: Where are America's Drunkest Cities?," December 31, 2011*
- San Diego was selected as one of the best beer towns in the U.S. by *Men's Journal.* The city was ranked #1.Criteria: beer culture; drinking establishments; breweries. *Men's Journal, "The Top Five Beer Towns in the U.S.," October 2009*

- PETCO Park (San Diego Padres) was selected as one of PETA's "2011 Top 10 Vegetarian-Friendly Major League Ballparks." The park ranked #7. *People for the Ethical Treatment of Animals, "2011 Top 10 Vegetarian-Friendly Major League Ballparks"*

Health/Fitness Rankings

- The American Podiatric Medical Association and *Prevention* magazine ranked 100 American cities based on walkability. Nineteen walking criteria were evaluated including the percentage of adults who walk to work, number of parks per square mile, number of trails for walking and hiking, air pollution, use of mass transit, crime rate, pedestrian fatalities, and percentage of adults who walk for fitness. San Diego ranked #13. *Prevention, "The Best Walking Cities of 2009," May 2009; American Podiatric Medical Association, "2009 Best Fitness-Walking Cities," April 7, 2009*

- The San Diego metro area was selected as one of the worst cities for bed bugs in America by Rollins corporation, the owner of seven pest control companies, including Orkin. The area ranked #26 based on the number of bed bug treatments from January to December 2011. *Rollins, "The Top 50 U.S. Cities for Bed Bugs," March 19, 2012*

- San Diego was selected as one of the 25 fittest cities in America by *Men's Fitness Online*. It ranked #8 out of America's 50 largest cities. Criteria: fitness centers and sport stores; nutrition; sports participation; TV viewing; overweight/sedentary; junk food; air quality; geography; commute; parks and open space; city recreational facilities; access to healthcare; motivation; mayor and city initiatives; state obesity initiatives. *Men's Fitness, "The Fittest and Fattest Cities in America," March 5, 2012*

- San Diego was identified as a "2011 Asthma Capital." The area ranked #82 out of the nation's 100 largest metropolitan areas. Twelve factors were used to identify the most challenging places to live for people with asthma: estimated prevalence; self-reported prevalence; crude death rate for asthma; annual pollen score; annual air quality; public smoking laws; number of board-certified asthma specialists; school inhaler access laws; rescue medication use; controller medication use; uninsured rate; poverty rate. *Asthma and Allergy Foundation of America, "2011 Asthma Capitals"*
- San Diego was identified as a "2011 Fall Allergy Capital." The area ranked #98 out of 100. Three groups of factors were used to identify the most severe cities for people with allergies during the fall season: annual pollen levels; medicine utilization; access to board-certified allergists. *Asthma and Allergy Foundation of America, "2011 Fall Allergy Capitals"*
- San Diego was identified as a "2012 Spring Allergy Capital." The area ranked #94 out of 100. Three groups of factors were used to identify the most severe cities for people with allergies during the spring season: annual pollen levels; medicine utilization; access to board-certified allergists. *Asthma and Allergy Foundation of America, "2012 Spring Allergy Capitals"*
- *Men's Health* examined 100 major U.S. cities and selected the best and worst cities for men. San Diego ranked #15. Criteria: 35 statistical parameters of long life in the categories of health, quality of life, and fitness. *Men's Health, "The 10 Best and Worst Cities for Men 2012," January/February 2012*
- The San Diego metropolitan area was selected as one of the best metros for hospital care in America by *HealthGrades.com.* The rankings are based on a comprehensive study of patient death and complication rates in the nation's nearly 5,000 hospitals. Hospitals performing in the top 5% nationwide across 26 different medical procedures and diagnoses were identified. *HealthGrades.com* then ranked cities by the highest percentage of these Distinguished Hospitals for Clinical Excellence™. The San Diego metro area ranked #29. *HealthGrades.com, "America's Top 50 Cities for Hospital Care," January 21, 2012*
- The American Academy of Dermatology ranked 26 U.S. metropolitan regions in terms of their residents knowledge, attitude and behaviors towards tanning, sun protection and skin cancer detection. The San Diego metro area ranked #17. The results of the study are based on an online survey of over 7,000 adults nationwide. *American Academy of Dermatology, "Suntelligence: How Sun Smart is Your City," May 3, 2010*
- The San Diego metro area appeared in the 2011 Gallup-Healthways Well-Being Index. The index, based on interviews with more than 350,000 Americans, measured jobs, finances, physical health, emotional state of mind and communities. The metro area ranked #35 out of 190. Criteria: life evaluation; emotional health; work environment; physical health; healthy behaviors; basic access (basic needs optimal for a healthy life, such as access to food and medicine, having health insurance and feeling safe while walking at night). *Gallup-Healthways, "State of Well-Being 2011"*
- The San Diego metro area was identified as one of "America's Most Stressful Cities" by *Sperling's BestPlaces.* The metro area ranked #21 out of 50. Criteria: unemployment rate; suicide rate; commute time; mental health; poor rest; alcohol use; violent crime rate; property crime rate; cloudy days annually. *Sperling's BestPlaces, www.BestPlaces.net, "Stressful Cities 2012*
- The San Diego metro area was identified as one of "America's Most Stressful Cities" by *Forbes*. The metro area ranked #5 out of 40. Criteria: housing affordability; unemployment rate; cost of living; air quality; traffic congestion; sunny days; population density. *Forbes.com, "America's Most Stressful Cities," September 23, 2011*
- *Men's Health* ranked 100 U.S. cities in terms of their activity levels. San Diego was ranked #21 (#1 = most active city). Criteria: where and how often residents exercise; percentage of households that watch more than 15 hours of cable television a week and buy more than 11 video games a year; death rate from deep-vein thrombosis, a condition linked to sitting for extended periods of time. *Men's Health, "Where Sit Happens: The Most and Least Active Cities in America," June 20, 2011*

- 50 of the largest metro areas in the U.S. were analyzed in terms of their health and fitness by the American College of Sports Medicine in their "American Fitness Index." The San Diego metro area ranked #13 (#1 = healthiest). Criteria: preventative health behaviors; levels of chronic disease; health care access; community resources and policies that support physical activity. *American College of Sports Medicine, "Health and Community Fitness Status of the 50 Largest Metropolitan Areas," August 1, 2011*

Pet Rankings

- San Diego was selected as one of the "Top 10 Cat-Friendly Cities" in the U.S. The area ranked #8. Criteria: cat ownership per capita; level of veterinary care; microchipping; cat-friendly local ordinances. *CATalyst Council, "Top 10 Cat-Friendly Cities," March 27, 2009*

Real Estate Rankings

- San Diego was identified as one of the priciest cities to rent in the U.S. The area ranked #7 out of 10. Criteria: rent-to-income ratio. *CNBC, "Priciest Cities to Rent," March 14, 2012*
- *Fortune* ranked the 100 largest metro areas in the U.S. in terms of projected median home price change in 2010. The San Diego metro area ranked #72. *Fortune, "The 2010 Housing Outlook," December 9, 2009*
- The San Diego metro area was identified as one of the 20 least affordable housing markets in the U.S. in 2011. The area ranked #5 out of 152 markets with an affordability index of 65.0%. The index measures whether or not a typical family could qualify for a mortgage loan on a typical home. The calculation used assumes a down payment of 20 percent of the home price and a qualifying ratio of 25 percent, meaning that the monthly P&I payment cannot exceed 25 percent of a the median family monthly income. *National Association of Realtors®, Affordability Index of Existing Single-Family Homes for Metropolitan Areas, 2011*
- San Diego appeared on *ApartmentRatings.com* "Top Cities for Renters" list in 2009." The area ranked #48. Overall satisfaction ratings were ranked using thousands of user submitted scores for hundreds of apartment complexes located in the 100 most populated U.S. municipalities. *ApartmentRatings.com, "2009 Renter Satisfaction Rankings"*
- San Diego appeared on *ApartmentRatings.com* "Top College Towns & Cities" for renters list in 2011." The area ranked #46 out of 87. Overall satisfaction ratings were ranked using thousands of user submitted scores for hundreds of apartment complexes located in cities and towns that are home to the 100 largest four-year institutions in the U.S. *ApartmentRatings.com, "2011 College Town Renter Satisfaction Rankings"*
- The San Diego metro area appeared in a *Wall Street Journal* article ranking cities by "housing stress." The metro area was ranked #4 (#1 = most stress). Criteria: fraction of mortgage-holding homeowners with a monthly housing payment in excess of 30 percent of income; percentage of people without health insurance; unemployment rate. *The Wall Street Journal, "Which Cities Face Biggest Housing Risk," October 5, 2010*
- The Center for Housing Policy ranked 210 U.S. metropolitan areas by the fair market rent for a two-bedroom unit. The San Diego metro area was ranked #18. (#1 = most expensive) with a rent of $1,324. Criteria: Fair Market Rent (FMR) in effect during the fourth quarter of 2009 based on HUD's fiscal year 2010 FMRs. *The Center for Housing Policy, "Paycheck to Paycheck: Most to Least Expensive Rental Markets in 2009"*
- The San Diego metro area was identified as one of the best housing markets of the decade by *Forbes*. Criteria: increase in housing values per square foot since January 2000. *Forbes, "America's 5 Best (and Worst) Housing Markets of the Decade," December 7, 2010*
- The San Diego metro area was identified as one of the best U.S. markets to invest in rental property" by HomeVestors and Local Market Monitor. The area ranked #90 out of 100. Criteria: risk-return premium relative to national average. *HomeVestors and Local Market Monitor, "Best 100 U.S. Markets to Invest in Rental Property," March 9, 2012*

Safety Rankings

- Symantec, the makers of Norton, in partnership with Sperling's BestPlaces, ranked the 50 largest cities in the U.S. in terms of their vulnerability to cybercrime. The city ranked #12. Criteria: number of cyberattacks and potential infections; level of Internet access; expenditures on smartphones and computer hardware/software; wireless hotspots; broadband connectivity; Internet usage; online purchases. *Symantec, "Riskiest Online Cities of 2012" February 15, 2012*

- Allstate ranked the 193 largest cities in America in terms of driver safety. San Diego ranked #117. In addition, drivers were 12.7% more likely to have had an accident compared to the national average. Allstate researchers analyzed internal property damage reported claims over a two-year period (from January 2008 to December 2009) to protect findings from external influences such as weather or road construction. A weighted average of the two-year numbers determined the annual percentages. The report defines an auto crash as any collision resulting in a property damage claim. *Allstate, "2011 Allstate America's Best Drivers Report™"*

- San Diego was identified as one of the safest large cities in America by CQ Press. All 34 cities with populations of 500,000 or more that reported crime rates in 2010 for murder, rape, robbery, aggravated assault, burglary, and motor vehicle thefts were ranked. The city ranked #5 out of the top 10. *CQ Press, City Crime Rankings 2011-2012*

- The National Insurance Crime Bureau ranked 366 metro areas in the U.S. in terms of per capita rates of vehicle theft. The San Diego metro area ranked #15 (#1 = highest rate). Criteria: number of vehicle theft offenses per 100,000 inhabitants in 2010. *National Insurance Crime Bureau, "Hot Spots," June 21, 2011*

- The San Diego metro area was identified as one of the most dangerous metro areas for pedestrians by Transportation for America. The metro area ranked #28 out of 52 metro areas with over 1 million residents. Criteria: area's population divided by the number of pedestrian fatalities in that area. *Transportation for America, "Dangerous by Design 2011"*

Seniors/Retirement Rankings

- Bankers Life and Casualty Company, in partnership with Sperling's BestPlaces, ranked the nation's 50 largest metro areas in terms of the "Best U.S. Cities for Seniors." The San Diego metro area ranked #32. Criteria: healthcare; transportation; housing; environment; economy; health and longevity; social and spiritual life; crime. *Bankers Life and Casualty Company, Center for a Secure Retirement, "Best U.S. Cities for Seniors 2011," September 2011*

- San Diego was identified as one of the "100 Most Popular Retirement Towns" by *Topretirements.com* The list reflects the 100 cities (out of 815+ total cities reviewed) that visitors to the website are most interested in for retirement. *Topretirements.com, "100 Most Popular Retirement Towns," February 21, 2012*

Sports/Recreation Rankings

- San Diego was selected as one of "America's Most Miserable Sports Cities" by *Forbes.* The city was ranked #5. Criteria: postseason losses; years since last title; ratio of cumulative seasons to championships won. Contenders were limited to cities with at least 75 total seasons of NFL, NBA, NHL and MLB play. *Forbes, "America's Most Miserable Sports Cities," February 28, 2012*

- San Diego appeared on the *Sporting News* list of the "Best Sports Cities" for 2011. The area ranked #17 out of 271 cities in the U.S. *Sporting News* takes a 12-month snapshot of each city's sports, putting a heavy premium on regular-season won-lost records (from the most recently completed season). Other criteria include: playoff berths, bowl appearances and tournament bids; championships; applicable power ratings; quality of competition; overall fan fervor (measured in part by attendance); abundance of teams (rewarding quality over quantity); stadium and arena quality; ticket availability and prices; franchise ownership; and marquee appeal of athletes. *Sporting News, "Best Sports Cities 2011," October 4, 2011*

- San Diego was selected as one of the five best boat cities in the U.S. The city ranked #1. Criteria: climate; scenery; fishing; boat communities with water access. *Best Boat News, "The 5 Best Boat Cities to Live In (in the U.S.)," April 16, 2010*

- San Diego was chosen as one of America's 10 best places to live and boat. Criteria: boating opportunities; boat-friendly regulations; water access; availability of waterfront homes; health of the local economy; and overall lifestyle for boaters. *Boating Magazine, "10 Best Places to Live and Boat," June 2010*

- The San Diego was selected as one of the best metro areas for golf in America by *Golf Digest*. The San Diego area was ranked #17 out of 20. Criteria: climate; cost of public golf; quality of public golf; accessibility. *Golf Digest, "The Top 20 Cities for Golf," October 2011*

Technology Rankings

- The San Diego metro area was selected as one of "America's Most Wired Cities" by *Forbes*. The metro area was ranked #14 out of 20. Criteria: percentage of Internet users with high-speed access; number of companies providing high-speed Internet; number of public wireless hot spots. *Forbes, "America's Most Wired Cities," March 2, 2010*

- The San Diego metro area was selected as one of "America's Most Innovative Cities" by *Forbes*. The metro area was ranked #6 out of 20. Criteria: patents per capita; venture capital investment per capita; ratio of high-tech, science and "creative" jobs. *Forbes, "America's Most Innovative Cities," May 24, 2010*

- The San Diego metro area was identified as one of the "Top 14 Nano Metros" in the U.S. by the Project on Emerging Nanotechnologies. The metro area is home to 27 companies, universities, government laboratories and/or organizations working in nanotechnology. *Project on Emerging Nanotechnologies, "Nano Metros 2009"*

Transportation Rankings

- San Diego was identified as one of America's worst cities for speed traps by the National Motorists Association. The city ranked #20 out of 25. Criteria: speed trap locations per 100,000 residents. *National Motorists Association, September 2011*

- The San Diego metro area appeared on *Forbes* list of the best and worst cities for commuters. The metro area ranked #43 out of 60 (#1 is best). Criteria: travel time; road congestion; travel delays. *Forbes.com, "Best and Worst Cities for Commuters," February 16, 2010*

Women/Minorities Rankings

- *Women's Health* examined U.S. cities and identified the 100 best cities for women. San Diego was ranked #18. Criteria: 30 categories were examined from obesity and breast cancer rates to commuting times and hours spent working out. *Women's Health, "Best Cities for Women 2012"*

- San Diego was ranked #31 out of 100 metro areas in *SELF Magazine's* ranking of America's healthiest places for women." A panel of experts came up with more than 50 criteria including death and disease rates, environmental indicators, community resources, and lifestyle habits. *SELF Magazine, "Secrets of America's Healthiest Women," December 2008*

- San Diego was selected as one of the 25 healthiest cities for Latinas by *Latina Magazine*. The city ranked #9. Criteria: U.S. cities with populations over 500,000 residents were evaluated on the following criteria: percentage of 18-34 year-olds per city; Latino college graduation rates; number of colleges and universities; affordability; housing costs; income growth over time; average salary; percentage of singles; climate; safety; how the city's diversity compares to the national average; opportunities for minority entrepreneurs. *Latina Magazine, "Top 15 U.S. Cities for Young Latinos to Live In," August 19, 2011*

- The San Diego metro area appeared on *Forbes'* list of the "Best Cities for Minority Entrepreneurs." The area ranked #9 out of 10. Criteria: 52 metropolitan statistical areas were examined. For each ethnicity (African Americans, Asians and Hispanics), the editors measured housing affordability, population growth, income growth, and entrepreneurship (per capita self-employment). *Forbes, "Best Cities for Minority Entrepreneurs," March 23, 2011*

- San Diego was selected as one of the "Top 10 Cities for Hispanics." Criteria: the prospect of a good job; a safe place to raise a family; a manageable cost of living; the ability to buy and keep a home; a culture of inclusion where Hispanics are highly represented; resources to help start a business; the presence of Hispanic or Spanish-language media; representation of Hispanic needs on local government; a thriving arts and culture community; air quality; energy costs; city's state of health and rates of obesity. *Hispanic Magazine, August 2008*

Miscellaneous Rankings

- *Men's Health* ranked 100 U.S. cities by their level of sadness. San Diego was ranked #34 (#1 = saddest city). Criteria: suicide rates; unemployment rates; percentage of households that use antidepressants; percent of population who report feeling blue all or most of the time. *Men's Health, "Frown Towns," November 28, 2011*
- Energizer Holdings, the makers of Edge® shave gel, in partnership with Sperling's BestPlaces, ranked 50 major metro areas in terms of everyday irritations. The San Diego metro area ranked #18. Criteria: humidity levels; weather conditions; incidence of traffic delays and congestion; average commute times; frequency of flight delays and cancellations; rates of sleeplessness; underemployment; pollens and allergens; pests; comedy clubs per capita. *Energizer Holdings, "Most Irritation Prone Cities," July 23, 2010*
- Mars Chocolate North America, the makers of COMBOS®, in partnership with Sperling's BestPlaces, ranked 50 major metro areas in terms of their "manliness." The San Diego metro area ranked #49. Criteria: number of professional sports teams; number of nearby NASCAR tracks and racing events; manly lifestyle; concentration of manly retail stores; manly occupations per capita; salty snack sales; "Board of Manliness" rankings. *Mars Chocolate North America, "America's Manliest Cities 2011," September 1, 2011*
- San Diego was selected as one of the "Best Hair Cities" by *NaturallyCurly.com.* The city was ranked #3. Criteria: humidity levels; pollution; rainfall; average wind speeds; water hardness; beauty salons per capita. *NaturallyCurly.com, "Best/Worst Hair Cities," April 29, 2009*
- San Diego was selected as one of the best cities for shopping in the U.S. by *Forbes.* The city was ranked #10.Criteria: number of major shopping centers; retail locations; Consumer Price Index (CPI); combined state and local sales tax. *Forbes, "America's 25 Best Cities for Shopping," December 13, 2010*
- The San Diego metro area appeared in *AutoMD.com's* ranking of the "Best and Worst Cities for Auto Repair." The metro area ranked #45 (#1 is best). The 50 most-populated metro areas in the U.S. were ranked on three critical factors: repair affordability; price disparity range; shop integrity factor. *AutoMD.com, "Advocacy for Repair Shop Fairness Report," February 24, 2010*
- San Diego was identified as one of "America's Vainest Cities" by *Forbes.com.* The city ranked #3. Criteria: highest number of cosmetic surgeons per 100,000 people in America's 50 largest cities. *Forbes.com, "America's Vainest Cities," November 29, 2007*

Business Environment

CITY FINANCES

City Government Finances

Component	2009 ($000)	2009 ($ per capita)
Total Revenues	265,133	209
Total Expenditures	3,212,039	2,536
Debt Outstanding	3,633,124	2,868
Cash and Securities[1]	6,105,999	4,820

Note: (1) Cash and security holdings of a government at the close of its fiscal year, including those of its dependent agencies, utilities, and liquor stores.
Source: U.S Census Bureau, State & Local Government Finances 2009

City Government Revenue by Source

Source	2009 ($000)	2009 ($ per capita)
General Revenue		
From Federal Government	211,018	167
From State Government	114,874	91
From Local Governments	4,266	3
Taxes		
Property	765,242	604
Sales and Gross Receipts	439,978	347
Personal Income	0	0
Corporate Income	0	0
Motor Vehicle License	0	0
Other Taxes	36,529	29
Current Charges	752,318	594
Liquor Store	0	0
Utility	342,949	271
Employee Retirement	-2,747,973	-2,169

Source: U.S Census Bureau, State & Local Government Finances 2009

City Government Expenditures by Function

Function	2009 ($000)	2009 ($ per capita)	2009 (%)
General Direct Expenditures			
Air Transportation	6,297	5	0.2
Corrections	0	0	0.0
Education	0	0	0.0
Employment Security Administration	0	0	0.0
Financial Administration	40,276	32	1.3
Fire Protection	217,201	171	6.8
General Public Buildings	59,019	47	1.8
Governmental Administration, Other	111,387	88	3.5
Health	50,026	39	1.6
Highways	162,465	128	5.1
Hospitals	0	0	0.0
Housing and Community Development	405,599	320	12.6
Interest on General Debt	127,001	100	4.0
Judicial and Legal	36,773	29	1.1
Libraries	36,012	28	1.1
Parking	4,787	4	0.1
Parks and Recreation	212,714	168	6.6
Police Protection	407,684	322	12.7
Public Welfare	0	0	0.0
Sewerage	318,554	251	9.9
Solid Waste Management	48,705	38	1.5
Veterans' Services	0	0	0.0
Liquor Store	0	0	0.0
Utility	414,901	328	12.9
Employee Retirement	272,338	215	8.5

Source: U.S Census Bureau, State & Local Government Finances 2009

Municipal Bond Ratings

Area	Moody's	S&P	Fitch
City	A2	A	AA-

Rating Systems (shown in declining order of credit quality): Moody's– Aaa, Aa, A, Baa, Ba, B, Caa, Ca, C (numerical modifiers 1, 2, and 3 are added to letter-rating); S&P– AAA, AA, A, BBB, BB, B, CCC, CC, C; Fitch– AAA, AA, A, BBB, BB, B, CCC, CC, C. Ratings may be modified by the addition of a plus or minus sign to show relative standing within the major rating categories.
Notes: n/a Not Available; w/d Withdrawn (1) Not Reviewed; (2) Issuer Rating/No General Obligation; (3) Standard and Poor's Issue Credit Rating (ICR) is a current opinion of an obliger with respect to a specific financial obligation, a specific class of financial obligations, or a specific financial program.
Source: U.S. Census Bureau, 2012 Statistical Abstract, Bond Ratings for City Governments by Largest Cities: 2010

DEMOGRAPHICS

Population Growth

Area	1990 Census	2000 Census	2010 Census	Population Growth (%) 1990-2000	Population Growth (%) 2000-2010
City	1,111,048	1,223,400	1,307,402	10.1	6.9
MSA[1]	2,498,016	2,813,833	3,095,313	12.6	10.0
U.S.	248,709,873	281,421,906	308,745,538	13.2	9.7

Note: (1) Figures cover the San Diego-Carlsbad-San Marcos, CA Metropolitan Statistical Area—see Appendix B for areas included
Source: U.S. Census Bureau, 2010 Census

Household Size

Area	Persons in Household (%)							Average Household Size
	One	Two	Three	Four	Five	Six	Seven or More	
City	28.0	31.6	15.6	13.0	6.4	2.9	2.6	2.60
MSA[1]	24.0	31.2	16.5	14.5	7.4	3.3	3.0	2.75
U.S.	26.7	32.8	16.1	13.4	6.5	2.6	1.9	2.58

Note: (1) Figures cover the San Diego-Carlsbad-San Marcos, CA Metropolitan Statistical Area—see Appendix B for areas included
Source: U.S. Census Bureau, 2010 Census

Race

Area	White Alone[2] (%)	Black Alone[2] (%)	Asian Alone[2] (%)	AIAN[3] Alone[2] (%)	NHOPI[4] Alone[2] (%)	Other Race Alone[2] (%)	Two or More Races (%)
City	58.9	6.7	15.9	0.6	0.5	12.3	5.1
MSA[1]	64.0	5.1	10.9	0.9	0.5	13.6	5.1
U.S.	72.4	12.6	4.8	0.9	0.2	6.2	2.9

Note: (1) Figures cover the San Diego-Carlsbad-San Marcos, CA Metropolitan Statistical Area—see Appendix B for areas included; (2) Alone is defined as not being in combination with one or more other races; (3) American Indian and Alaska Native; (4) Native Hawaiian and Other Pacific Islander
Source: U.S. Census Bureau, 2010 Census

Hispanic or Latino Origin

Area	Hispanic or Latino (%)	Mexican (%)	Puerto Rican (%)	Cuban (%)	Other Hispanic or Latino (%)
City	28.8	24.9	0.6	0.2	3.0
MSA[1]	32.0	28.1	0.7	0.2	3.1
U.S.	16.3	10.3	1.5	0.6	4.0

Note: Persons of Hispanic or Latino origin can be of any race; (1) Figures cover the San Diego-Carlsbad-San Marcos, CA Metropolitan Statistical Area—see Appendix B for areas included
Source: U.S. Census Bureau, 2010 Census

Segregation

Type	Segregation Indices[1]				Percent Change		
	1990	2000	2010	2010 Rank[2]	1990-2000	1990-2010	2000-2010
Black/White	58.1	55.5	51.2	68	-2.6	-6.9	-4.3
Asian/White	47.9	49.9	48.2	13	2.0	0.3	-1.7
Hispanic/White	45.2	50.6	49.6	25	5.4	4.4	-1.0

Note: Figures are based on an analysis of 1990, 2000, and 2010 Census Decennial Census tract data by William H. Frey, Brookings Institution and the University of Michigan Social Science Data Analysis Network. In this analysis all racial groups (whites, blacks, and asians) are non-Hispanic members of those races. Hispanics are shown as a separate category; All figures cover the Metropolitan Statistical Area (see Appendix B for areas included); (1) Segregation Indices are Dissimilarity Indices that measure the degree to which the minority group is distributed differently than whites across census tracts. They range from 0 (complete integration) to 100 (complete segregation) where the value indicates the percentage of the minority group that needs to move to be distributed exactly like whites; (2) Ranges from 1 (most segregated) to 102 (least segregated); n/a not available.
Source: www.CensusScope.org

Ancestry

Area	German	Irish	English	American	Italian	Polish	French[2]	Scottish	Dutch
City	10.9	8.3	7.0	2.3	4.7	2.1	2.3	1.9	1.1
MSA[1]	12.3	9.0	8.7	2.3	4.6	2.1	2.6	1.9	1.3
U.S.	16.1	11.6	8.8	6.1	5.7	3.2	3.0	1.9	1.6

Note: Figures are the percentage of the total population reporting a particular ancestry. The nine most commonly reported ancestries in the U.S. are shown. Figures include multiple ancestries (e.g. if a person reported being Irish and Italian, they were included in both columns); (1) Figures cover the San Diego-Carlsbad-San Marcos, CA Metropolitan Statistical Area—see Appendix B for areas included; (2) Excludes Basque
Source: U.S. Census Bureau, 2008-2010 American Community Survey 3-Year Estimates

Foreign-Born Population

Area	Percent of Population Born in								
	Any Foreign Country	Mexico	Asia	Europe	Carribean	South America	Central America[2]	Africa	Canada
City	25.8	9.5	11.3	2.3	0.2	0.6	0.5	0.7	0.5
MSA[1]	23.2	10.9	8.2	1.9	0.2	0.5	0.5	0.5	0.4
U.S.	12.8	3.8	3.6	1.6	1.2	0.9	1.0	0.5	0.3

Note: (1) Figures cover the San Diego-Carlsbad-San Marcos, CA Metropolitan Statistical Area—see Appendix B for areas included; (2) Excludes Mexico.
Source: U.S. Census Bureau, 2008-2010 American Community Survey 3-Year Estimates

Marital Status

Area	Never Married	Now Married[2]	Separated	Widowed	Divorced
City	40.5	42.9	2.1	4.5	10.0
MSA[1]	35.2	47.6	2.0	4.9	10.3
U.S.	31.6	49.6	2.2	6.1	10.7

Note: Figures are percentages and cover the population 15 years of age and older; (1) Figures cover the San Diego-Carlsbad-San Marcos, CA Metropolitan Statistical Area—see Appendix B for areas included; (2) Excludes separated
Source: U.S. Census Bureau, 2008-2010 American Community Survey 3-Year Estimates

Age

Area	Percent of Population							Median Age
	Under Age 5	Age 5 to 17	Age 18 to 34	Age 35 to 49	Age 50 to 64	Age 65 to 79	80 Years and Over	
City	6.2	15.2	30.7	20.9	16.4	7.5	3.2	33.6
MSA[1]	6.6	16.8	27.1	20.7	17.5	7.9	3.4	34.6
U.S.	6.5	17.5	23.2	20.7	19.0	9.4	3.6	37.2

Note: (1) Figures cover the San Diego-Carlsbad-San Marcos, CA Metropolitan Statistical Area—see Appendix B for areas included
Source: U.S. Census Bureau, 2010 Census

Male/Female Ratio

Area	Males	Females	Males per 100 Females
City	660,626	646,776	102.1
MSA[1]	1,553,679	1,541,634	100.8
U.S.	151,781,326	156,964,212	96.7

Note: (1) Figures cover the San Diego-Carlsbad-San Marcos, CA Metropolitan Statistical Area—see Appendix B for areas included
Source: U.S. Census Bureau, 2010 Census

Religious Groups

Area	Catholic	Baptist	Non-Den.	Methodist[2]	Lutheran	LDS[3]	Pentecostal	Presbyterian[4]	Muslim[5]	Judaism
MSA[1]	25.9	2.0	4.8	1.1	1.0	2.3	1.0	0.9	0.5	0.7
U.S.	19.1	9.3	4.0	4.0	2.3	2.0	1.9	1.6	0.8	0.7

Note: Figures are the number of adherents as a percentage of the total population; (1) Figures cover the San Diego-Carlsbad-San Marcos, CA Metropolitan Statistical Area—see Appendix B for areas included; (2) Methodist/Pietist; (3) Latter Day Saints; (4) Reformed; (5) Figures are estimates
Source: Association of Statisticians of American Religious Bodies, 2010 U.S. Religion Census: Religious Congregations & Membership Study

ECONOMY

Gross Metropolitan Product

Area	2007	2008	2009	2010	2010 Rank[2]
MSA[1]	166.4	171.2	168.1	172.7	16

Note: Figures are in billions of dollars; (1) Figures cover the San Diego-Carlsbad-San Marcos, CA Metropolitan Statistical Area—see Appendix B for areas included; (2) Rank ranges from 1 to 363
Source: The United States Conference of Mayors, "U.S. Metro Economies: GMP and Employment Forecasts," June 2011

Economic Growth

Area	2007-2009 (%)	2010 (%)	2011 (%)	Rank[2]
MSA[1]	-1.2	1.9	2.2	168
U.S.	-1.3	2.9	2.5	–

Note: Figures are real Gross Metropolitan Product growth rates and represent annual average percent change; (1) Figures cover the San Diego-Carlsbad-San Marcos, CA Metropolitan Statistical Area—see Appendix B for areas included; (2) Rank ranges from 1 to 363
Source: The United States Conference of Mayors, "U.S. Metro Economies: GMP and Employment Forecasts," June 2011

Metropolitan Area Exports

Area	2005	2006	2007	2008	2009	2010	2010 Rank[2]
MSA[1]	13,192.7	13,617.8	14,341.7	15,855.9	13,418.6	16,464.3	17

Note: Figures are in millions of dollars; (1) Figures cover the San Diego-Carlsbad-San Marcos, CA Metropolitan Statistical Area—see Appendix B for areas included; (2) Rank ranges from 1 to 369
Source: U.S. Department of Commerce, International Trade Administration, Office of Trade & Industry Information, Manufacturing & Services, data extracted April 2, 2012

INCOME

Income

Area	Per Capita ($)	Median Household ($)	Average Household ($)
City	31,981	61,282	83,172
MSA[1]	29,792	61,469	82,033
U.S.	26,942	51,222	70,116

Note: (1) Figures cover the San Diego-Carlsbad-San Marcos, CA Metropolitan Statistical Area—see Appendix B for areas included
Source: U.S. Census Bureau, 2008-2010 American Community Survey 3-Year Estimates

Household Income Distribution

Area	Under $15,000	$15,000 -24,999	$25,000 -34,999	$35,000 -49,999	$50,000 -74,999	$75,000 -99,000	$100,000 -149,999	$150,000 and up
	Percent of Households Earning							
City	11.2	8.9	8.3	12.8	17.6	13.4	14.7	13.2
MSA[1]	9.9	8.8	9.0	13.4	17.7	13.5	15.3	12.5
U.S.	13.0	11.0	10.6	14.2	18.5	12.1	12.2	8.4

Note: (1) Figures cover the San Diego-Carlsbad-San Marcos, CA Metropolitan Statistical Area—see Appendix B for areas included
Source: U.S. Census Bureau, 2008-2010 American Community Survey 3-Year Estimates

Poverty Rate

Area	All Ages	Under 18 Years Old	18 to 64 Years Old	65 Years and Over
City	15.2	19.6	14.9	8.4
MSA[1]	13.2	17.4	12.6	8.0
U.S.	14.4	20.1	13.1	9.4

Note: Figures are percentage of people whose income during the past 12 months was below the poverty level; (1) Figures cover the San Diego-Carlsbad-San Marcos, CA Metropolitan Statistical Area—see Appendix B for areas included
Source: U.S. Census Bureau, 2008-2010 American Community Survey 3-Year Estimates

Personal Bankruptcy Filing Rate

Area	2006	2007	2008	2009	2010	2011
San Diego County	1.40	2.55	4.46	6.50	7.23	6.48
U.S.	2.00	2.73	3.53	4.61	4.97	4.37

Note: Numbers are per 1,000 population and include Chapter 7 and Chapter 13 filings
Source: Federal Deposit Insurance Corporation, Regional Economic Conditions, March 9, 2012

EMPLOYMENT

Labor Force and Employment

Area	Civilian Labor Force			Workers Employed		
	Dec. 2010	Dec. 2011	% Chg.	Dec. 2010	Dec. 2011	% Chg.
City	694,528	708,004	1.9	624,205	645,104	3.3
MSA[1]	1,555,853	1,586,031	1.9	1,398,252	1,445,067	3.3
U.S.	153,156,000	153,373,000	0.1	139,159,000	140,681,000	1.1

Note: Data is not seasonally adjusted and covers workers 16 years of age and older; (1) Metropolitan Statistical Area—see Appendix B for areas included
Source: Bureau of Labor Statistics, http://stats.bls.gov

Unemployment Rate

Area	2011											
	Jan.	Feb.	Mar.	Apr.	May	Jun.	Jul.	Aug.	Sep.	Oct.	Nov.	Dec.
City	10.3	10.1	10.2	9.8	9.6	10.4	10.6	10.2	9.8	9.7	9.2	8.9
MSA[1]	10.4	10.1	10.2	9.8	9.6	10.4	10.6	10.2	9.8	9.7	9.2	8.9
U.S.	9.8	9.5	9.2	8.7	8.7	9.3	9.3	9.1	8.8	8.5	8.2	8.3

Note: Data is not seasonally adjusted and covers workers 16 years of age and older; All figures are percentages; (1) Metropolitan Statistical Area—see Appendix B for areas included
Source: Bureau of Labor Statistics, http://stats.bls.gov

Projected Unemployment Rate

Area	2010 (%)	2011 (%)	2012 (%)	2013 (%)
MSA[1]	10.7	9.7	9.2	8.4

Note: (1) Metropolitan Statistical Area—see Appendix B for areas included
Source: The United States Conference of Mayors, "U.S. Metro Economies: GMP and Employment Forecasts," June 2011

Employment by Occupation

Occupation Classification	City (%)	MSA[1] (%)	U.S. (%)
Management, Business, Science, and Arts	44.7	39.5	35.6
Natural Resources, Construction, and Maintenance	6.1	8.2	9.5
Production, Transportation, and Material Moving	7.2	8.1	12.1
Sales and Office	24.2	25.5	25.2
Service	17.8	18.7	17.6

Note: Figures cover employed civilians 16 years of age and older; (1) Figures cover the San Diego-Carlsbad-San Marcos, CA Metropolitan Statistical Area—see Appendix B for areas included
Source: U.S. Census Bureau, 2008-2010 American Community Survey 3-Year Estimates

Employment by Industry

Sector	MSA[1]		U.S.
	Number of Employees	Percent of Total	Percent of Total
Construction	55,900	4.5	4.1
Education and Health Services	153,500	12.3	15.2
Financial Activities	66,500	5.3	5.8
Government	230,700	18.4	16.8
Information	24,000	1.9	2.0
Leisure and Hospitality	157,100	12.6	9.9
Manufacturing	92,100	7.4	8.9
Mining and Logging	400	<0.1	0.6
Other Services	46,900	3.7	4.0
Professional and Business Services	216,800	17.3	13.3
Retail Trade	139,700	11.2	11.5
Transportation and Utilities	26,800	2.1	3.8
Wholesale Trade	40,600	3.2	4.2

Note: Figures cover non-farm employment as of December 2011 and are not seasonally adjusted; (1) Metropolitan Statistical Area—see Appendix B for areas included
Source: Bureau of Labor Statistics, http://stats.bls.gov

Occupations with Greatest Projected Employment Growth: 2008 – 2018

Occupation[1]	2008 Employment	2018 Projected Employment	Numeric Employment Change	Percent Employment Change
Personal and Home Care Aides	346,500	504,700	158,200	45.7
Registered Nurses	236,400	297,200	60,800	25.7
Retail Salespersons	499,400	559,100	59,700	12.0
Combined Food Preparation and Serving Workers, Including Fast Food	260,600	308,800	48,200	18.5
Elementary School Teachers, Except Special Education	197,500	233,400	35,900	18.2
Office Clerks, General	372,500	407,400	34,900	9.4
Customer Service Representatives	202,200	236,600	34,400	17.0
Waiters and Waitresses	245,600	279,900	34,300	14.0
Stock Clerks and Order Fillers	207,700	237,100	29,400	14.2
Postsecondary Teachers	168,000	196,100	28,100	16.7

Note: Projections cover California; (1) Sorted by numeric employment change
Source: www.projectionscentral.com, State Occupational Projections, 2008–2018 Long-Term Projections

Fastest Growing Occupations: 2008 – 2018

Occupation[1]	2008 Employment	2018 Projected Employment	Numeric Employment Change	Percent Employment Change
Biomedical Engineers	3,100	5,600	2,500	80.6
Network Systems and Data Communications Analysts	35,000	52,600	17,600	50.3
Biochemists and Biophysicists	4,800	7,100	2,300	47.9
Medical Scientists, Except Epidemiologists	26,200	38,500	12,300	46.9
Personal and Home Care Aides	346,500	504,700	158,200	45.7
Home Health Aides	54,300	78,000	23,700	43.6
Physician Assistants	8,100	11,500	3,400	42.0
Separating, Filtering, Clarifying, Precipitating, and Still Machine Setters, Operators, and Te	7,300	10,200	2,900	39.7
Physical Therapist Aides	5,900	8,100	2,200	37.3
Electrical and Electronics Repairers, Powerhouse, Substation, and Relay	1,100	1,500	400	36.4

Note: Projections cover California; (1) Sorted by percent employment change and excludes occupations with numeric employment change less than 100
Source: www.projectionscentral.com, State Occupational Projections, 2008–2018 Long-Term Projections

Average Wages

Occupation	$/Hr.	Occupation	$/Hr.
Accountants and Auditors	35.75	Maids and Housekeeping Cleaners	10.12
Automotive Mechanics	20.90	Maintenance and Repair Workers	17.57
Bookkeepers	19.21	Marketing Managers	62.90
Carpenters	25.56	Nuclear Medicine Technologists	39.31
Cashiers	10.68	Nurses, Licensed Practical	23.19
Clerks, General Office	14.81	Nurses, Registered	40.82
Clerks, Receptionists/Information	13.88	Nursing Aides/Orderlies/Attendants	12.68
Clerks, Shipping/Receiving	14.82	Packers and Packagers, Hand	9.96
Computer Programmers	36.63	Physical Therapists	42.57
Computer Support Specialists	24.22	Postal Service Mail Carriers	25.79
Computer Systems Analysts	41.73	Real Estate Brokers	33.89
Cooks, Restaurant	12.22	Retail Salespersons	12.76
Dentists	77.88	Sales Reps., Exc. Tech./Scientific	29.99
Electrical Engineers	47.72	Sales Reps., Tech./Scientific	41.40
Electricians	26.26	Secretaries, Exc. Legal/Med./Exec.	18.21
Financial Managers	61.05	Security Guards	13.27
First-Line Supervisors/Managers, Sales	21.20	Surgeons	92.00
Food Preparation Workers	9.84	Teacher Assistants	13.70
General and Operations Managers	61.96	Teachers, Elementary School	31.10
Hairdressers/Cosmetologists	12.04	Teachers, Secondary School	32.30
Internists	90.55	Telemarketers	12.10
Janitors and Cleaners	12.83	Truck Drivers, Heavy/Tractor-Trailer	19.72
Landscaping/Groundskeeping Workers	12.71	Truck Drivers, Light/Delivery Svcs.	17.14
Lawyers	69.30	Waiters and Waitresses	9.43

Note: Wage data covers the San Diego-Carlsbad-San Marcos, CA Metropolitan Statistical Area—see Appendix B for areas included. Hourly wages for elementary/secondary school teachers and teacher assistants were calculated by the editors from annual wage data assuming a 40 hour work week; n/a not available.
Source: Bureau of Labor Statistics, Metro Area Occupational Employment and Wage Estimates, May 2011

RESIDENTIAL REAL ESTATE

Building Permits

Area	Single-Family			Multi-Family			Total		
	2010	2011	Pct. Chg.	2010	2011	Pct. Chg.	2010	2011	Pct. Chg.
City	557	451	-19.0	519	2,241	331.8	1,076	2,692	150.2
MSA[1]	2,270	2,245	-1.1	1,224	3,125	155.3	3,494	5,370	53.7
U.S.	447,311	418,498	-6.4	157,299	205,563	30.7	604,610	624,061	3.2

Note: (1) Metropolitan Statistical Area—see Appendix B for areas included; figures represent new, privately-owned housing units authorized (unadjusted data); All permit data are based on estimates with imputation.
Source: U.S. Census Bureau, Manufacturing, Mining, and Construction Statistics, Building Permits, 2010, 2011

Homeownership Rate

Area	2005 (%)	2006 (%)	2007 (%)	2008 (%)	2009 (%)	2010 (%)	2011 (%)
MSA[1]	60.5	61.2	59.6	57.1	56.4	54.4	55.2
U.S.	68.9	68.8	68.1	67.8	67.4	66.9	66.1

Note: (1) Metropolitan Statistical Area—see Appendix B for areas included
Source: U.S. Census Bureau, Housing Vacancies and Homeownership Annual Statistics: 2011

Housing Vacancy Rates

Area	Gross Vacancy Rate[2] (%)			Year-Round Vacancy Rate[3] (%)			Rental Vacancy Rate[4] (%)			Homeowner Vacancy Rate[5] (%)		
	2009	2010	2011	2009	2010	2011	2009	2010	2011	2009	2010	2011
MSA[1]	10.4	10.5	9.9	9.8	10.0	9.5	8.8	7.8	6.9	2.1	2.9	1.9
U.S.	14.5	14.3	14.2	11.3	11.3	11.1	10.6	10.2	9.5	2.6	2.6	2.5

Note: (1) Metropolitan Statistical Area—see Appendix B for areas included; (2) The percentage of the total housing inventory that is vacant; (3) The percentage of the housing inventory (excluding seasonal units) that is year-round vacant; (4) The percentage of rental inventory that is vacant for rent; (5) The percentage of homeowner inventory that is vacant for sale
Source: U.S. Census Bureau, Housing Vacancies and Homeownership Annual Statistics: 2011

TAXES

State Corporate Income Tax Rates

State	Tax Rate (%)	Income Brackets ($)	Num. of Brackets	Financial Institution Tax Rate (%)[a]	Federal Income Tax Ded.
California	8.84 (c)	Flat rate	1	10.84 (c)	No

Note: Tax rates as of January 1, 2012; (a) Rates listed are the corporate income tax rate applied to financial institutions or excise taxes based on income. Some states have other taxes based upon the value of deposits or shares; (c) The minimum corporation franchise tax in California is $800. The additional alternative minimum tax is levied at a 6.65% rate.
Source: Federation of Tax Administrators, "State Corporate Income Tax Rates, 2012"

State Individual Income Tax Rates

State	Tax Rate (%)	Income Brackets ($)	Num. of Brackets	Personal Exempt. ($)[1]		Fed. Inc. Tax Ded.
				Single	Dependents	
California (a)	1.0 - 9.3 (f)	7,316 (b) - 48,029 (b)	6	102 (c)	315 (c)	No

Note: Tax rates as of January 1, 2012; Local- and county-level taxes are not included; n/a not applicable; (1) Married joint filers generally receive double the single exemption; (a) 17 states have statutory provision for automatically adjusting to the rate of inflation the dollar values of the income tax brackets, standard deductions, and/or personal exemptions. Massachusetts, Michigan, and Nebraska index the personal exemptiononly. Oregon does not index the income brackets for $125,000 and over. Because the inflation-adjustments for 2012 are not yet available in some cases, the table may report the 2011 amounts; (b) For joint returns, taxes are twice the tax on half the couple's income; (c) The personal exemption takes the form of a tax credit instead of a deduction; (f) California imposes an additional 1% tax on taxable income over $1 million, making the maximum rate 10.3% over $1 million.
Source: Federation of Tax Administrators, "State Individual Income Tax Rates, 2012"

Various State and Local Tax Rates

State	State and Local Sales and Use (%)	State Sales and Use (%)	Gasoline[1] (¢/gal.)	Cigarette[2] ($/pack)	Spirits[3] ($/gal.)	Wine[4] ($/gal.)	Beer[5] ($/gal.)
California	7.75	7.25 (b)	48.6	0.87	3.30	0.20	0.20

Note: All tax rates as of January 1, 2012 except beer, wine and spirits (September 1, 2011); (1) The American Petroleum Institute has developed a methodology for determining the average tax rate on a gallon of fuel. Rates may include any of the following: excise taxes, environmental fees, storage tank fees, other fees or taxes, general sales tax, and local taxes. In states where gasoline is subject to the general sales tax, or where the fuel tax is based on the average sale price, the average rate determined by API is sensitive to changes in the price of gasoline. States that fully or partially apply general sales taxes to gasoline: CA, CO, GA, IL, IN, MI, NY; (2) The federal excise tax of $1.0066 per pack and local taxes are not included; (3) Rates are those applicable to off-premise sales of 40% alcohol by volume (a.b.v.) distilled spirits in 750ml containers. Local excise taxes are excluded; (4) Rates are those applicable to off-premise sales of 11% a.b.v. non-carbonated wine in 750ml containers; (5) Rates are those applicable to off-premise sales of 4.7% a.b.v. beer in 12 ounce containers; (b) Three states collect a separate, uniform "local" add-on sales tax: California (1%), Utah (1.25%), Virginia (1%). These amounts are included in the state sales tax column.
Source: Tax Foundation, 2012 Facts & Figures: How Does Your State Compare?

State-Local Tax Burdens

Area	Rate (%)	Rank[1]	Per Capita Taxes Paid to Home State ($)	Total State and Local Per Capita Taxes Paid ($)	Per Capita Income ($)
California	10.6	6	3,874	4,910	46,366
U.S. Average	9.8	-	3,057	4,160	42,539

Note: Figures cover 2009; (1) Rank ranges from 1 to 50 where 1 is highest tax burden
Source: Tax Foundation, State-Local Tax Burdens, All States, 2009

State Business Tax Climate Index Rankings

State	Overall Rank	Corporate Tax Index Rank	Individual Income Tax Index Rank	Sales Tax Index Rank	Unemployment Insurance Tax Index Rank	Property Tax Index Rank
California	48	43	50	40	13	17

Note: The index is a measure of how each state's tax laws affect economic performance. The lower the rank, the more favorable a state's tax system is for business. States without a given tax are given a ranking of 1.
Source: Tax Foundation, Major Components of the State Business Tax Climate Index, FY 2012

COMMERCIAL REAL ESTATE

Office Market

Market Area	Inventory (sq. ft.)	Vacant (sq. ft.)	Vac. Rate (%)	Under Constr. (sq. ft.)	Asking Rent ($/sf/yr)	
					Class A	Class B
San Diego	69,062,692	12,327,059	17.8	123,429	26.16	23.40

Source: Grubb & Ellis, Office Markets Trends, 4th Quarter 2011

Industrial Market

Market Area	Inventory (sq. ft.)	Vacant (sq. ft.)	Vac. Rate (%)	Under Constr. (sq. ft.)	Asking Rent ($/sf/yr)	
					WH/Dist	R&D/Flex
San Diego	176,583,584	18,601,673	10.5	31,246	7.56	12.96

Source: Grubb & Ellis, Industrial Markets Trends, 4th Quarter 2011

COMMERCIAL UTILITIES

Typical Monthly Electric Bills

Area	Commercial Service ($/month)		Industrial Service ($/month)	
	1,500 kWh	40 kW demand 14,000 kWh	1,000 kW demand 200,000 kWh	50,000 kW demand 15,000,000 kWh
City	299	2,280	43,146	1,739,327
Average[1]	189	1,616	25,197	1,470,813

Note: Based on total rates in effect July 1, 2011; (1) average based on 184 utilities surveyed
Source: Edison Electric Institute, Typical Bills and Average Rates Report, Summer 2011

TRANSPORTATION

Means of Transportation to Work

Area	Car/Truck/Van: Drove Alone	Car/Truck/Van: Car-pooled	Public Transportation: Bus	Public Transportation: Subway	Public Transportation: Railroad	Bicycle	Walked	Other Means	Worked at Home
City	75.5	9.1	3.6	0.0	0.1	0.9	3.0	1.2	6.5
MSA[1]	75.4	10.4	2.7	0.0	0.3	0.7	3.0	1.4	6.1
U.S.	76.0	10.2	2.7	1.7	0.5	0.5	2.8	1.3	4.2

Note: Figures are percentages and cover workers 16 years of age and older; (1) Figures cover the San Diego-Carlsbad-San Marcos, CA Metropolitan Statistical Area—see Appendix B for areas included
Source: U.S. Census Bureau, 2008-2010 American Community Survey 3-Year Estimates

Travel Time to Work

Area	Less Than 10 Minutes	10 to 19 Minutes	20 to 29 Minutes	30 to 44 Minutes	45 to 59 Minutes	60 to 89 Minutes	90 Minutes or More
City	10.2	36.2	27.3	19.2	3.5	2.2	1.4
MSA[1]	10.8	31.9	25.2	20.9	5.8	3.5	1.9
U.S.	13.9	30.1	20.8	19.8	7.5	5.5	2.5

Note: Figures are percentages and include workers 16 years old and over; (1) Figures cover the San Diego-Carlsbad-San Marcos, CA Metropolitan Statistical Area—see Appendix B for areas included
Source: U.S. Census Bureau, 2008-2010 American Community Survey 3-Year Estimates

Travel Time Index

Area	1985	1990	1995	2000	2005	2010
Urban Area[1]	1.06	1.14	1.13	1.20	1.25	1.19
Average[2]	1.11	1.16	1.18	1.21	1.25	1.20

Note: Travel Time Index—the ratio of travel time in the peak period to the travel time at free-flow conditions. A value of 1.30 indicates a 20-minute free-flow trip takes 26 minutes in the peak. Free-flow speeds (60 mph on freeways and 35 mph on principal arterials) are used as the comparison threshold; (1) Covers the San Diego CA urban area; (2) average of 439 urban areas
Source: Texas Transportation Institute, Urban Mobility Report 2011, September 2011

Public Transportation

Agency Name / Mode of Transportation	Vehicles Operated in Maximum Service	Annual Unlinked Passenger Trips ('000)	Annual Passenger Miles ('000)
San Diego Metropolitan Transit System (MTS)			
Bus (directly operated)	198	26,920.5	98,162.8
Bus (purchased transportation)	213	21,558.9	75,929.0
Demand Response (purchased transportation)	121	429.4	3,307.6
Light Rail (directly operated)	93	30,469.0	186,509.3
North San Diego County Transit District (NCTD)			
Bus (directly operated)	123	7,018.4	34,873.2
Bus (purchased transportation)	22	806.8	4,008.9
Commuter Rail (purchased transportation)	26	1,271.6	35,916.3
Demand Response (purchased transportation)	26	119.2	1,559.5
Light Rail (purchased transportation)	6	2,117.9	18,400.5
San Diego Association of Governments (SANDAG)			
Vanpool (purchased transportation)	667	2,042.6	97,611.2

Source: Federal Transit Administration, National Transit Database, 2010

Air Transportation

Airport Name and Code / Type of Service	Passenger Airlines[1]	Passenger Enplanements	Freight Carriers[2]	Freight (lbs.)
San Diego International-Lindbergh Field (SAN)				
Domestic service (U.S. carriers - 2011)	25	8,235,357	20	135,275,135
International service (U.S. carriers - 2010)	6	45,368	4	29,807

Note: (1) Includes all U.S.-based major, minor and commuter airlines that carried at least one passenger during the year; (2) Includes all U.S.-based airlines and freight carriers that transported at least one pound of freight during the year

Source: Bureau of Transportation Statistics, The Intermodal Transportation Database, Air Carriers: T-100 Domestic Market (U.S. Carriers), 2011; Bureau of Transportation Statistics, The Intermodal Transportation Database, Air Carriers: T-100 International Market (U.S. Carriers), 2010

Other Transportation Statistics

Major Highways:	I-5; I-8; I-15
Amtrak Service:	Yes
Major Waterways/Ports:	San Diego Harbor

Source: Amtrak.com; Google Maps

BUSINESSES

Major Business Headquarters

Company Name	Rankings	
	Fortune[1]	Forbes[2]
Petco Animal Supplies	-	151
Qualcomm	222	-
Sempra Energy	274	-

Note: (1) Fortune 500—companies that produce a 10-K are ranked 1 to 500 based on 2010 revenue; (2) all private companies with at least $2 billion in annual revenue are ranked 1 to 212; companies listed are headquartered in the city; dashes indicate no ranking

Source: Fortune, "Fortune 500," May 23, 2011; Forbes, "America's Largest Private Companies," November 16, 2011

Fast-Growing Businesses

According to *Inc.*, San Diego is home to eight of America's 500 fastest-growing private companies: **Cask** (#57); **Black Mountain Systems** (#63); **FortuneBuilders** (#104); **Integrity First Financial Group** (#215); **Aztec Awards** (#229); **Ludus Sports** (#256); **ServiceNow** (#260); **PayLease** (#344). Criteria: must be an independent, privately-held, for-profit, U.S. corporation, proprietorship or partnership; revenues must be at least $80,000 in 2007 and $2 million in 2010; must have four-year operating/sales history. Holding companies, regulated banks, and utilities were excluded. *Inc., "America's 500 Fastest-Growing Private Companies," September 2011*

According to *Fortune*, San Diego is home to two of the 100 fastest-growing companies in the world: **Illumina** (#23); **Encore Capital Group** (#40). Companies were ranked by their revenue growth rate; their EPS growth rate; and their three-year annualized total return to investors for the period ending June 30, 2011. Criteria for inclusion: a company, foreign or domestic, must trade on a major U.S. stock exchange; must file quarterly reports with the SEC; must have a minimum market capitalization of $250 million; must have a stock price of at least $5 on June 30, 2011; must have been trading continuously since June 30, 2008; must have revenue and net income for the four quarters ended on or before April 30, 2011, of at least $50 million and $10 million, respectively; and must have posted a compound annual growth in revenue and earnings per share of at least 15% annually over the three years ending on or before April 30, 2011. REITs, limited-liability companies, limited parterships, companies about to be acquired, and companies that lost money in the quarter ending April 30, 2011 were excluded. *Fortune, "100 Fastest-Growing Companies," September 26, 2011*

According to *Initiative for a Competitive Inner City (ICIC)*, San Diego is home to three of America's 100 fastest-growing "inner city" companies: **Red Door Interactive** (#39); **Montbleau and Associates** (#50); **Silva General Construction** (#100). Companies were ranked by their five-year compound annual growth rate. Criteria for inclusion: company must be headquartered in or have 51 percent or more of its physical operations in an economically distressed urban area; must be an independent, for-profit corporation, partnership or proprietorship; must have 10 or more employees and have a five-year sales history that includes sales of at least $200,000 in the base year and at least $1 million in the current year with no decrease in sales over the two most recent years. *Initiative for a Competitive Inner City (ICIC), "Inner City 100 Companies, 2011"*

According to Deloitte, San Diego is home to 15 of North America's 500 fastest-growing high-technology companies: **ServiceNow** (#5); **Franklin Wireless Corp.** (#18); **Dexcom** (#57); **Halozyme Therapeutics** (#82); **Nik Software** (#217); **ACADIA Pharmaceuticals** (#219); **Entropic Communications** (#224); **Trius Therapeutics** (#226); **Illumina** (#232); **NuVasive** (#234); **The Active Network** (#256); **XIFIN** (#298); **Kratos** (#398); **Volcano Corp.** (#410); **Santarus** (#465). Companies are ranked by percentage growth in revenue over a five-year period. Criteria for inclusion: company must be headquartered within North America; must own proprietary intellectual property or proprietary technology that contributes to a significant portion of the company's operating revenue, or devote a significant proportion of revenues to research and development of technology; must have been in business for a minumum of five years with 2006 operating revenues of at least $50,000 USD/CD and 2010 operating revenues of at least $5 million USD/CD. *Deloitte Touche Tohmatsu, 2011 Deloitte Technology Fast 500™*

Minority Business Opportunity

San Diego is home to one company which is on the *Hispanic Business* 500 list (500 largest U.S. Hispanic-owned companies based on 2010 revenue): **WSA Distributing** (#104). Companies included must show at least 51 percent ownership by Hispanic U.S. citizens, and must maintain headquarters in one of the 50 states or Washington, D.C. *Hispanic Business, "Hispanic Business 500," June 2011*

Minority- and Women-Owned Businesses

Group	All Firms		Firms with Paid Employees			
	Firms	Sales ($000)	Firms	Sales ($000)	Employees	Payroll ($000)
Asian	17,449	6,050,362	3,628	5,596,220	30,837	931,286
Black	4,471	415,928	365	315,648	4,011	113,382
Hispanic	16,669	2,900,814	2,376	2,375,728	17,377	429,264
Women	40,020	6,853,430	5,173	5,718,438	53,352	1,610,742
All Firms	130,519	151,762,267	32,437	146,973,850	677,509	32,704,056

Note: Figures cover firms located in the city; minority- and women-owned business are defined as firms in which the corresponding group own 51% or more of the stock or equity of the company
Source: U.S. Census Bureau, 2007 Economic Census, Survey of Business Owners

HOTELS

Hotels/Motels

Area	5 Star		4 Star		3 Star		2 Star		1 Star		Not Rated	
	Num.	Pct.[3]	Num.	Pct.[3]	Num.	Pct.[3]	Num.	Pct.[3]	Num.	Pct.[3]	Num.	Pct.[3]
City[1]	6	1.5	34	8.4	120	29.8	176	43.7	7	1.7	60	14.9
Total[2]	133	0.9	940	6.5	4,569	31.8	7,033	48.9	351	2.4	1,343	9.3

Note: (1) Figures cover San Diego and vicinity; (2) Figures cover all 100 cities in this book; (3) Percentage of hotels which have a given star rating; Star ratings are determined by expedia.com and offer an indication of the general quality of a particular hotel.
Source: expedia.com, April 25, 2012

EVENT SITES

Major Stadiums, Arenas, and Auditoriums

Name	Max. Capacity
PETCO Park	42,445
Qualcomm Stadium	70,561
San Diego Sports Arena	14,000
Starlight Musical Theatre	3,575
Tony Gwynn Stadium, San Diego State	3,000
Viejas Arena, San Diego State	12,414

Source: Original research

Convention Centers

Name	Overall Space (sq. ft.)	Exhibit Space (sq. ft.)	Meeting Space (sq. ft.)	Meeting Rooms
San Diego Convention Center	2,600,000	204,114	615,701	72

Source: Original research

Living Environment

COST OF LIVING

Cost of Living Index

Composite Index	Groceries	Housing	Utilities	Trans-portation	Health Care	Misc. Goods/ Services
130.8	107.4	189.1	113.0	111.2	112.4	103.6

Note: U.S. = 100; Figures cover the San Diego CA urban area.
Source: The Council for Community and Economic Research, ACCRA Cost of Living Index, 2011

Grocery Prices

Area[1]	T-Bone Steak ($/pound)	Frying Chicken ($/pound)	Whole Milk ($/half gal.)	Eggs ($/dozen)	Orange Juice ($/64 oz.)	Coffee ($/11.5 oz.)
City[2]	9.85	1.06	2.14	2.28	3.33	5.58
Avg.	9.25	1.18	2.22	1.66	3.19	4.40
Min.	6.70	0.88	1.31	0.95	2.46	2.94
Max.	14.30	2.16	3.50	3.18	4.75	6.83

Note: (1) Values for the local area are compared with the average, minimum and maximum values for all 335 areas in the Cost of Living Index; (2) Figures cover the San Diego CA urban area; **T-Bone Steak** *(price per pound);* **Frying Chicken** *(price per pound, whole fryer);* **Whole Milk** *(half gallon carton);* **Eggs** *(price per dozen, Grade A, large);* **Orange Juice** *(64 oz. Tropicana or Florida Natural);* **Coffee** *(11.5 oz. can, vacuum-packed, Maxwell House, Hills Bros, or Folgers).*
Source: The Council for Community and Economic Research, ACCRA Cost of Living Index, 2011

Housing and Utility Costs

Area[1]	New Home Price ($)	Apartment Rent ($/month)	All Electric ($/month)	Part Electric ($/month)	Other Energy ($/month)	Telephone ($/month)
City[2]	525,576	1,712	-	121.58	67.99	29.85
Avg.	285,990	839	163.23	89.00	77.52	26.92
Min.	188,005	460	125.58	45.39	33.89	17.98
Max.	1,197,028	3,244	339.16	181.97	348.69	40.01

Note: (1) Values for the local area are compared with the average, minimum and maximum values for all 335 areas in the Cost of Living Index; (2) Figures cover the San Diego CA urban area; **New Home Price** *(2,400 sf living area, 8,000 sf lot, in urban area with full utilities);* **Apartment Rent** *(950 sf 2 bedroom/1.5 or 2 bath, unfurnished, excluding all utilities except water);* **All Electric** *(average monthly cost for an all-electric home);* **Part Electric** *(average monthly cost for a part-electric home);* **Other Energy** *(average monthly cost for natural gas, fuel oil, coal, wood, and any other forms of energy except electricity);* **Telephone** *(price includes basic monthly rate for a private residential line plus additional local usage charges incurred by a family of four).*
Source: The Council for Community and Economic Research, ACCRA Cost of Living Index, 2011

Health Care, Transportation, and Other Costs

Area[1]	Doctor ($/visit)	Dentist ($/visit)	Optometrist ($/visit)	Gasoline ($/gallon)	Beauty Salon ($/visit)	Men's Shirt ($)
City[2]	98.80	98.60	98.80	3.83	46.67	22.25
Avg.	93.88	81.72	90.54	3.48	32.65	25.06
Min.	60.00	55.33	53.66	3.18	19.78	13.44
Max.	154.98	145.97	183.72	4.31	63.21	46.00

Note: (1) Values for the local area are compared with the average, minimum and maximum values for all 335 areas in the Cost of Living Index; (2) Figures cover the San Diego CA urban area; **Doctor** *(general practitioners routine exam of an established patient);* **Dentist** *(adult teeth cleaning and periodic oral examination);* **Optometrist** *(full vision eye exam for established adult patient);* **Gasoline** *(one gallon regular unleaded, national brand, including all taxes, cash price at self-service pump if available);* **Beauty Salon** *(woman's shampoo, trim, and blow-dry);* **Men's Shirt** *(cotton/polyester dress shirt, pinpoint weave, long sleeves).*
Source: The Council for Community and Economic Research, ACCRA Cost of Living Index, 2011

HOUSING

House Price Index (HPI)

Area	National Ranking[2]	Quarterly Change (%)	One-Year Change (%)	Five-Year Change (%)
MSA[1]	215	-0.39	-4.25	-31.71
U.S.[3]	-	-0.10	-2.43	-19.16

Note: The HPI is a weighted repeat sales index. It measures average price changes in repeat sales or refinancings on the same properties. This information is obtained by reviewing repeat mortgage transactions on single-family properties whose mortgages have been purchased or securitized by Fannie Mae or Freddie Mac in January 1975; (1) Metropolitan/Micropolitan Statistical Area—see Appendix B for areas included; (2) Rankings are based on annual percentage change for all metro areas containing at least 15,000 transactions over the last 10 years and ranges from 1 to 306; (3) figures based on a weighted average of Census Division estimates using a purchase only index; all figures are for the period ending December 31, 2011
Source: Federal Housing Finance Agency, House Price Index, February 23, 2012

House Price Valuations

Area	Q4 2005		Q4 2006		Q4 2007		Q4 2008		Q4 2009	
	Price ($000)	Over-valuation	Price ($000)	Over-valuation	Price ($000)	Over-valuation	Price ($000)	Over-valuation	Price ($000)	Over-valuation
MSA[1]	498.3	36.8	478.3	24.3	419.1	3.6	334.6	-17.3	341.3	-15.8

Note: Figures show the percentage of over- or under-valuation of single family homes relative to statistically normal house values (e.g. a value of 23.6 indicates that house values are 23.6% overvalued). Statistically normal house values are based on house prices, interest rates, household incomes, population densities, and any historical premiums or discounts metropolitan areas have exhibited over time; (1) Figures cover the San Diego-Carlsbad-San Marcos, CA - see Appendix B for areas included
Source: Global Insight/PNC Financial Services Group, House Prices in America: 4th Quarter 2009 Update

Median Single-Family Home Prices

Area	2009	2010	2011p	Percent Change 2010 to 2011
MSA[1]	359.5	385.7	370.3	-4.0
U.S. Average	172.1	173.1	166.2	-4.0

Note: Figures are median sales prices of existing single-family homes in thousands of dollars; (p) preliminary; n/a not available; (1) Metropolitan Statistical Area—see Appendix B for areas included
Source: National Association of Realtors, Median Sales Price of Existing Single-Family Homes for Metropolitan Areas, 4th Quarter 2011

Affordability Index of Existing Single-Family Homes

Area	2009	2010	2011p	Percent Change 2010 to 2011
MSA[1]	60.6	59.5	65.0	9.2

Note: The housing affordability index measures whether or not a typical family could qualify for a mortgage loan on a typical home. The higher the index, the greater the household purchasing power. An index of 100 is defined as the point where a median-income household has exactly enough income to qualify for the purchase of a median-priced existing single-family home, assuming a 20 percent downpayment and 25 percent of gross income devoted to mortgage principal and interest payments; (p) preliminary; n/a not available; (1) Metropolitan Statistical Area—see Appendix B for areas included
Source: National Association of Realtors, Affordability Index of Existing Single-Family Homes, 2011

Median Apartment Condo-Coop Home Prices

Area	2009	2010	2011p	Percent Change 2010 to 2011
MSA[1]	212.5	219.8	207.7	-5.5
U.S. Average	175.6	171.7	165.1	-3.8

Note: Figures are median sales prices of existing apartment condo-coop homes in thousands of dollars; (p) preliminary; n/a not available; (1) Metropolitan Statistical Area—see Appendix B for areas included
Source: National Association of Realtors, Median Sales Price of Existing Apartment Condo-Coop Homes for Metropolitan Areas, 4th Quarter 2011

Year Housing Structure Built

Area	2005 or Later	2000 -2004	1990 -1999	1980 -1989	1970 -1979	1960 -1969	1950 -1959	Before 1950	Median Year
City	3.1	7.1	10.4	17.7	23.3	13.2	13.2	12.0	1975
MSA[1]	3.8	7.9	11.7	19.0	24.9	12.8	11.4	8.3	1977
U.S.	5.0	8.6	14.0	14.1	16.3	11.3	11.2	19.6	1975

Note: Figures are percentages except for Median Year; (1) Figures cover the San Diego-Carlsbad-San Marcos, CA Metropolitan Statistical Area—see Appendix B for areas included
Source: U.S. Census Bureau, 2008-2010 American Community Survey 3-Year Estimates

HEALTH

Health Risk Data

Category	MSA[1] (%)	U.S. (%)
Adults who have been told they have high blood pressure[2]	23.5	28.7
Adults who have been told they have high blood cholesterol[2]	34.4	37.5
Adults who have been told they have diabetes[3]	8.9	8.7
Adults who have been told they have arthritis[2]	18.7	26.0
Adults who have been told they currently have asthma	7.7	9.1
Adults who are current smokers	13.0	17.3
Adults who are heavy drinkers[4]	7.3	5.0
Adults who are binge drinkers[5]	17.7	15.1
Adults who are overweight (BMI 25.0 - 29.9)	32.8	36.2
Adults who are obese (BMI 30.0 - 99.8)	26.1	27.5
Adults who participated in any physical activities in the past month	81.0	76.1
Adults 50+ who have ever had a sigmoidoscopy or colonoscopy	64.5	65.2
Women aged 40+ who have had a mammogram within the past two years	77.5	75.2
Men aged 40+ who have had a PSA test within the past two years	51.7	53.2
Adults aged 65+ who have had flu shot within the past year	62.2	67.5
Adults aged 18–64 who have any kind of health care coverage	79.3	82.2

Note: Data as of 2010 unless otherwise noted; (1) Figures cover the San Diego-Carlsbad-San Marcos, CA Metropolitan Statistical Area—see Appendix B for areas included; (2) Data as of 2009; (3) Figures do not include pregnancy-related, borderline, or pre-diabetes; (4) Heavy drinkers are classified as males having more than two drinks per day or females having more than one drink per day; (5) Binge drinkers are classified as males having five or more drinks on one occasion or females having four or more drinks on one occasion
Source: Centers for Disease Control and Prevention, Behaviorial Risk Factor Surveillance System, SMART: Selected Metropolitan/Micropolitan Area Risk Trends, 2009, 2010

Mortality Rates for the Top 10 Causes of Death in the U.S.

ICD-10[a] Sub-Chapter	ICD-10[a] Code	Age-Adjusted Mortality Rate[1] per 100,000 population	
		County[2]	U.S.
Malignant neoplasms	C00-C97	165.1	175.6
Ischaemic heart diseases	I20-I25	107.1	121.6
Other forms of heart disease	I30-I51	36.0	48.6
Chronic lower respiratory diseases	J40-J47	34.7	42.3
Cerebrovascular diseases	I60-I69	38.0	40.6
Organic, including symptomatic, mental disorders	F01-F09	15.4	26.7
Other degenerative diseases of the nervous system	G30-G31	36.6	24.7
Other external causes of accidental injury	W00-X59	20.7	24.4
Diabetes mellitus	E10-E14	18.9	21.7
Hypertensive diseases	I10-I15	18.8	18.2

Note: (a) ICD-10 = International Classification of Diseases 10th Revision; (1) Mortality rates are a three year average covering 2007-2009; (2) Figures cover San Diego County
Source: Centers for Disease Control and Prevention, National Center for Health Statistics. Underlying Cause of Death 1999-2009 on CDC WONDER Online Database, released 2012. Data for year 2009 are compiled from the Multiple Cause of Death File 2009, Series 20 No. 2O, 2012, Data for year 2008 are compiled from the Multiple Cause of Death File 2008, Series 20 No. 2N, 2011, Data for year 2007 are compiled from Multiple Cause of Death File 2007, Series 20 No. 2M, 2010.

Mortality Rates for Selected Causes of Death

ICD-10[a] Sub-Chapter	ICD-10[a] Code	Age-Adjusted Mortality Rate[1] per 100,000 population	
		County[2]	U.S.
Assault	X85-Y09	3.2	5.7
Human immunodeficiency virus (HIV) disease	B20-B24	2.5	3.3
Influenza and pneumonia	J09-J18	10.4	16.4
Intentional self-harm	X60-X84	12.1	11.5
Malnutrition	E40-E46	0.5	0.8
Obesity and other hyperalimentation	E65-E68	1.8	1.6
Transport accidents	V01-V99	10.1	13.7
Viral hepatitis	B15-B19	3.9	2.2

Note: (a) ICD-10 = International Classification of Diseases 10th Revision; (1) Mortality rates are a three year average covering 2007-2009; (2) Figures cover San Diego County
Source: Centers for Disease Control and Prevention, National Center for Health Statistics. Underlying Cause of Death 1999-2009 on CDC WONDER Online Database, released 2012. Data for year 2009 are compiled from the Multiple Cause of Death File 2009, Series 20 No. 2O, 2012, Data for year 2008 are compiled from the Multiple Cause of Death File 2008, Series 20 No. 2N, 2011, Data for year 2007 are compiled from Multiple Cause of Death File 2007, Series 20 No. 2M, 2010.

Distribution of Physicians and Dentists

Area[1]	Dentists[2]	D.O.[3]	M.D.[4] Total	M.D.[4] Family/General Practice	M.D.[4] Pediatrics	M.D.[4] Medical Specialties	M.D.[4] Surgical Specialties
Local (number)	1,796	393	6,342	804	483	2,254	1,372
Local (rate[5])	6.0	1.3	21.0	2.7	1.6	7.5	4.5
U.S. (rate[5])	4.5	1.9	18.3	2.5	1.4	6.8	4.1

Note: Data as of 2008 unless noted; (1) Local data covers San Diego County; (2) Data as of 2007; (3) Doctor of Osteopathic Medicine; (4) Includes active, non-federal, patient-care, office-based Doctors of Medicine; (5) rate per 10,000 population
Source: Area Resource File (ARF). 2009-2010 Release. U.S. Department of Health and Human Services, Health Resources and Services Administration, Bureau of Health Professions, Rockville, MD, August 2010

Best Hospitals

According to *U.S. News,* the San Diego-Carlsbad-San Marcos, CA is home to two of the best hospitals in the U.S.: **Scripps La Jolla Hospitals and Clinics** (1 specialty); **UC San Diego Medical Center** (6 specialties). The hospitals listed were highly ranked in at least one adult specialty. *U.S. News Online, "America's Best Hospitals 2011-12"*

According to *U.S. News,* the San Diego-Carlsbad-San Marcos, CA is home to one of the best children's hospitals in the U.S.: **Rady Children's Hospital** (10 specialties). The hospital listed was highly ranked in at least one pediatric specialty. *U.S. News Online, "America's Best Children's Hospitals 2011-12"*

EDUCATION

Public School District Statistics

District Name	Schls	Pupils	Pupil/ Teacher Ratio	Minority Pupils[1] (%)	Free Lunch Eligible[2] (%)	IEP[3] (%)
San Diego County Office of Education	16	3,776	16.1	74.3	65.2	15.5
San Diego Unified	218	131,417	20.2	76.6	56.7	12.0

Note: Table includes school districts with 2,000 or more students; (1) Percentage of students that are not non-Hispanic white; (2) Percentage of students that are eligible for the free lunch program; (3) Percentage of students that have an Individualized Education Program.
Source: U.S. Department of Education, National Center for Education Statistics, Common Core of Data, Local Education Agency (School District) Universe Survey: School Year 2009-2010; U.S. Department of Education, National Center for Education Statistics, Common Core of Data, Public Elementary/Secondary School Universe Survey: School Year 2009-2010

Top Public High Schools

High School Name	Rank[1]	Score[1]	Grad. Rate[2] (%)	College[3] (%)	AP/IB/ AICE[4] (%)	SAT/ ACT[5] (%)
Canyon Crest Academy	306	0.364	100	70	3.2	1800
Torrey Pines	90	0.799	95	92	4.1	1834

Note: (1) Public schools are ranked from 1 to 500 based on the following self-reported statistics (with their corresponding weight in the final score). Schools that had fewer than 10 graduates, as well as those that were newly founded and did not have a graduating senior class in 2010 were excluded; (2) Four-year, on-time graduation rate (25%); (3) Percent of 2010 graduates who enrolled immediately in college (25%); (4) AP/IB/AICE tests per graduate (25%); (5) Average SAT and/or ACT score (10%); Average AP/IB/AICE exam score (10%); AP/IB/AICE courses offered per graduate (5%); (6) School is unranked, but has been identified by Newsweek as one of the nation's most elite public high schools.
Source: Newsweek Online, "Top High Schools 2011"

Highest Level of Education

Area	Less than H.S.	H.S. Diploma	Some College, No Deg.	Associate Degree	Bachelors Degree	Masters Degree	Profess. School Degree	Doctorate Degree
City	13.6	16.4	21.7	7.5	24.6	10.0	3.3	2.9
MSA[1]	14.9	19.1	23.5	8.4	21.3	8.2	2.6	2.0
U.S.	14.7	28.4	21.3	7.6	17.6	7.2	1.9	1.2

Note: Figures cover persons age 25 and over; (1) Figures cover the San Diego-Carlsbad-San Marcos, CA Metropolitan Statistical Area—see Appendix B for areas included
Source: U.S. Census Bureau, 2008-2010 American Community Survey 3-Year Estimates

Educational Attainment by Race

Area	High School Graduate or Higher (%)					Bachelor's Degree or Higher (%)				
	Total	White	Black	Asian	Hisp.[2]	Total	White	Black	Asian	Hisp.[2]
City	86.4	87.5	89.4	87.5	62.4	40.8	43.0	22.8	48.2	16.5
MSA[1]	85.1	86.1	90.1	88.0	61.9	34.1	34.9	22.8	45.8	14.5
U.S.	85.3	87.5	81.4	85.5	61.6	28.0	29.3	17.8	50.2	13.0

Note: Figures shown cover persons 25 years old and over; (1) Figures cover the San Diego-Carlsbad-San Marcos, CA Metropolitan Statistical Area—see Appendix B for areas included; (2) People of Hispanic origin can be of any race
Source: U.S. Census Bureau, 2008-2010 American Community Survey 3-Year Estimates

School Enrollment by Grade and Control

Area	Preschool (%)		Kindergarten (%)		Grades 1 - 4 (%)		Grades 5 - 8 (%)		Grades 9 - 12 (%)	
	Public	Private	Public	Private	Public	Private	Public	Private	Public	Private
City	54.0	46.0	90.6	9.4	91.4	8.6	91.6	8.4	92.7	7.3
MSA[1]	52.5	47.5	90.2	9.8	91.5	8.5	91.6	8.4	93.0	7.0
U.S.	55.4	44.6	87.1	12.9	89.4	10.6	89.5	10.5	90.4	9.6

Note: Figures shown cover persons 3 years old and over; (1) Figures cover the San Diego-Carlsbad-San Marcos, CA Metropolitan Statistical Area—see Appendix B for areas included
Source: U.S. Census Bureau, 2008-2010 American Community Survey 3-Year Estimates

Average Salaries of Public School Classroom Teachers

Area	2010-11		2011-12		Percent Change 2010-11 to 2011-12	Percent Change 2001-02 to 2011-12
	Dollars	Rank[1]	Dollars	Rank[1]		
California	67,871	4	69,496	4	2.39	27.90
U.S. Average	55,623	-	56,643	-	1.83	26.8

Note: (1) State rank ranges from 1 to 51 where 1 indicates highest salary.
Source: National Education Association, Rankings & Estimates: Rankings of the States 2011 and Estimates of School Statistics 2012, December 2011

Higher Education

Four-Year Colleges			Two-Year Colleges			Medical Schools[1]	Law Schools[2]	Voc/ Tech[3]
Public	Private Non-profit	Private For-profit	Public	Private Non-profit	Private For-profit			
1	9	9	3	0	5	0	3	9

Note: Figures cover institutions located within the city limits and include main campuses only; (1) includes schools accredited by the Liaison Committee on Medical Education and the American Osteopathic Association's Commission on Osteopathic College Accreditation; (2) includes American Bar Association-accredited law schools; (3) includes all schools with programs that are less than 2 years.
Source: National Center for Education Statistics, Integrated Postsecondary Education System (IPEDS) Peer Analysis System, 2011-12; Association of American Medical Colleges, Member List, April 23, 2012; American Osteopathic Association, Member List, April 23, 2012; Law School Admission Council, Official Guide to ABA-Approved Law Schools Online, April 23, 2012

According to *U.S. News & World Report,* the San Diego-Carlsbad-San Marcos, CA is home to three of the best national universities in the U.S.: **University of California–San Diego** (#37); **University of San Diego** (#97); **San Diego State University** (#164). The indicators used to capture academic quality fall into a number of categories: assessment by administrators at peer institutions; retention of students; faculty resources; student selectivity; financial resources; alumni giving; high school counselor ratings of colleges; and graduation rate. *U.S. News & World Report, "America's Best Colleges 2012"*

PRESIDENTIAL ELECTION

2008 Presidential Election Results

Area	Obama	McCain	Nader	Other
San Diego County	54.1	43.9	0.7	1.2
U.S.	52.9	45.6	0.6	0.9

Note: Results are percentages and may not add to 100% due to rounding
Source: Dave Leip's Atlas of U.S. Presidential Elections, www.uselectionatlas.org

EMPLOYERS

Major Employers

Company Name	Industry
Barona Resort & Casino	Resort hotel
CA Dept of Housing & Comm Dev	Housing agency, government
City of San Diego	Municipal police
Elite Show Services	Help supply services
Forestry and Fire Protection, CA Dept of	Fire department, not including volunteer
Go-Staff	Temporary help service
Kaiser Foundation Hospitals	Trusts, nec
Marine Corps, United States	Marine corps
Palomar Community College District	Junior colleges
Qualcomm International	Patent buying, licensing, leasing
Risk Management Strategies	Employee programs administration
San Diego State University	Colleges and universities
Sharp Memorial Hospital	General medical and surgical hospitals
Solar Turbines Incorporated	Turbines and turbine generator sets
The Navy United States Department of	Navy
The Navy United States Department of	Medical centers
University of California, San Diego	General medical and surgical hospitals
Veterans Health Administration	Administration of veterans' affairs

Note: Companies shown are located within the San Diego-Carlsbad-San Marcos, CA metropolitan area.
Source: Hoovers.com, data extracted April 25 2012

Best Companies to Work For

Qualcomm; Scripps Health, headquartered in San Diego, are among "The 100 Best Companies to Work For." To pick the 100 Best Companies to Work For, *Fortune* partnered with the Great Place to Work Institute. Two hundred eighty firms participated in this year's survey. Two-thirds of a company's score is based on the results of the Institute's Trust Index survey, which is sent to a random sample of employees from each company. The questions related to attitudes about management's credibility, job satisfaction, and camaraderie. The other third of the scoring is based on the company's responses to the Institute's Culture Audit, which includes detailed questions about pay and benefit programs, and a series of open-ended questions about hiring practices, internal communication, training, recognition programs, and diversity efforts. Any company that is at least five years old with more than 1,000 U.S. employees is eligible. *Fortune, "The 100 Best Companies to Work For," February 6, 2012*

Scripps Health, headquartered in San Diego, is among the "100 Best Companies for Working Mothers." Criteria: workforce profile; benefits; child care; women's issues and advancement; flexible work; paid time off and leave; company culture; and work-life programs. This year *Working Mother* gave particular weight to workforce profile, paid time off and company culture. *Working Mother, "100 Best Companies 2011"*

Scripps Health, headquartered in San Diego, is among the "50 Best Employers for Workers Over 50." Criteria: recruiting practices; opportunities for training, education, and career development; workplace accommodations; alternative work options, such as flexible scheduling, job sharing, and phased retirement; employee health and pension benefits; and retiree benefits. Employers with at least 50 employees based in the U.S. are eligible, including for-profit companies, not-for-profit organizations, and government employers. *AARP, "2011 AARP Best Employers for Workers Over 50"*

Qualcomm; Sempra Energy, headquartered in San Diego, are among the "100 Best Places to Work in IT." To qualify, companies, both public and private, had to have a minimum of 50 IT employees and were selected based on average salary and bonus increases, the percentage of IT staffers promoted, IT staff turnover rates, training and development programs, and the percentage of women and minorities in IT staff and management positions. In addition, *Computerworld* looked at retention efforts, programs for recognizing and rewarding outstanding performances, and benefits such as flextime, elder care and child care, and reimbursement for college tuition and the cost of pursuing technology certifications. *Computerworld, "100 Best Places to Work in IT 2011"*

PUBLIC SAFETY

Crime Rate

Area	All Crimes	Violent Crimes				Property Crimes		
		Murder	Forcible Rape	Robbery	Aggrav. Assault	Burglary	Larceny -Theft	Motor Vehicle Theft
City	2,769.0	2.2	22.8	124.6	278.0	486.3	1,368.7	486.4
Suburbs[1]	2,447.6	2.2	21.3	97.3	221.2	436.2	1,319.5	350.1
Metro[2]	2,584.9	2.2	22.0	108.9	245.4	457.6	1,340.5	408.3
U.S.	3,345.5	4.8	27.5	119.1	252.3	699.6	2,003.5	238.8

Note: Figures are crimes per 100,000 population; (1) All areas within the metro area that are located outside the city limits; (2) Metropolitan Statistical Area—see Appendix B for areas included
Source: FBI Uniform Crime Reports, 2010

Hate Crimes

Area	Number of Quarters Reported	Bias Motivation				
		Race	Religion	Sexual Orientation	Ethnicity	Disability
City	4	12	8	20	9	0

Source: Federal Bureau of Investigation, Hate Crime Statistics 2010

Identity Theft Consumer Complaints

Area	Complaints	Complaints per 100,000 Population	Rank[2]
MSA[1]	2,722	91.5	122
U.S.	279,156	90.4	-

Note: (1) Metropolitan Statistical Area—see Appendix B for areas included; (2) Rank ranges from 1 to 384 where 1 indicates greatest number of identity theft complaints per 100,000 population
Source: Federal Trade Commission, Consumer Sentinel Network Data Book for January–December 2011

Fraud and Other Consumer Complaints

Area	Complaints	Complaints per 100,000 Population	Rank[2]
MSA[1]	15,072	506.6	140
U.S.	1,533,924	496.8	-

Note: (1) Metropolitan Statistical Area—see Appendix B for areas included; (2) Rank ranges from 1 to 384 where 1 indicates greatest number of fraud and other complaints per 100,000 population
Source: Federal Trade Commission, Consumer Sentinel Network Data Book for January–December 2011

RECREATION

Culture

Dance[1]	Theatre[1]	Instrumental Music[1]	Vocal Music[1]	Series/ Festivals	Museums	Zoos and Aquariums[2]
6	9	6	5	6	31	2

Note: (1) Number of professional perfoming groups; (2) AZA-accredited
Source: The Grey House Performing Arts Directory, 2011-2012; Official Museum Directory, 2011; American Association of Museums, AAM Member Museums, April 2012; Association of Zoos & Aquariums, AZA Member Zoos & Aquariums, April 2012

Professional Sports Teams

Team Name	League
San Diego Chargers	National Football League (NFL)
San Diego Padres	Major League Baseball (MLB)

Note: Includes teams located in the San Diego metro area.
Source: Original research

CLIMATE

Average and Extreme Temperatures

Temperature	Jan	Feb	Mar	Apr	May	Jun	Jul	Aug	Sep	Oct	Nov	Dec	Yr.
Extreme High (°F)	88	88	93	98	96	101	95	98	111	107	97	88	111
Average High (°F)	65	66	66	68	69	72	76	77	77	74	71	66	71
Average Temp. (°F)	57	58	59	62	64	67	71	72	71	67	62	58	64
Average Low (°F)	48	50	52	55	58	61	65	66	65	60	53	49	57
Extreme Low (°F)	29	36	39	44	48	51	55	58	51	43	38	34	29

Note: Figures cover the years 1948-1990
Source: National Climatic Data Center, International Station Meteorological Climate Summary, 9/96

Average Precipitation/Snowfall/Humidity

Precip./Humidity	Jan	Feb	Mar	Apr	May	Jun	Jul	Aug	Sep	Oct	Nov	Dec	Yr.
Avg. Precip. (in.)	1.9	1.4	1.7	0.8	0.2	0.1	Tr	0.1	0.2	0.4	1.2	1.4	9.5
Avg. Snowfall (in.)	Tr	0	0	0	0	0	0	0	0	0	0	Tr	Tr
Avg. Rel. Hum. 7am (%)	70	72	73	72	73	77	79	79	78	74	69	68	74
Avg. Rel. Hum. 4pm (%)	57	58	59	59	63	66	65	66	65	63	60	58	62

Note: Figures cover the years 1948-1990; Tr = Trace amounts (<0.05 in. of rain; <0.5 in. of snow)
Source: National Climatic Data Center, International Station Meteorological Climate Summary, 9/96

Weather Conditions

Temperature			Daytime Sky			Precipitation		
10°F & below	32°F & below	90°F & above	Clear	Partly cloudy	Cloudy	0.01 inch or more precip.	0.1 inch or more snow/ice	Thunder-storms
0	< 1	4	115	126	124	40	0	5

Note: Figures are average number of days per year and cover the years 1948-1990
Source: National Climatic Data Center, International Station Meteorological Climate Summary, 9/96

HAZARDOUS WASTE

Superfund Sites

San Diego has one hazardous waste site on the EPA's Superfund Final National Priorities List: **Camp Pendleton Marine Corps Base**. *U.S. Environmental Protection Agency, Final National Priorities List, April 17, 2012*

AIR & WATER QUALITY

Air Quality Index

Area	Percent of Days when Air Quality was...[2]					AQI Statistics[2]	
	Good	Moderate	Unhealthy for Sensitive Groups	Unhealthy	Very Unhealthy	Maximum	Median
Area[1]	33.7	62.7	3.3	0.3	0.0	155	54

Note: Air Quality Index (AQI) is an index for reporting daily air quality. EPA calculates the AQI for five major air pollutants regulated by the Clean Air Act: ground-level ozone, particle pollution (aka particulate matter), carbon monoxide, sulfur dioxide, and nitrogen dioxide. The AQI runs from 0 to 500. The higher the AQI value, the greater the level of air pollution and the greater the health concern. There are six AQI categories: "Good" AQI is between 0 and 50. Air quality is considered satisfactory; "Moderate" AQI is between 51 and 100. Air quality is acceptable; "Unhealthy for Sensitive Groups" When AQI values are between 101 and 150, members of sensitive groups may experience health effects; "Unhealthy" When AQI values are between 151 and 200 everyone may begin to experience health effects; "Very Unhealthy" AQI values between 201 and 300 trigger a health alert; "Hazardous" AQI values over 300 trigger warnings of emergency conditions (not shown); (1) Data covers San Diego County; (2) Based on 365 days with AQI data in 2011.
Source: U.S. Environmental Protection Agency, AirData Report, 2011

Air Quality Index Pollutants

Area	Percent of Days when AQI Pollutant was...[2]					
	Carbon Monoxide	Nitrogen Dioxide	Ozone	Sulfur Dioxide	Particulate Matter 2.5	Particulate Matter 10
Area[1]	0.0	15.1	38.1	0.0	44.4	2.5

Note: The Air Quality Index (AQI) is an index for reporting daily air quality. EPA calculates the AQI for five major air pollutants regulated by the Clean Air Act: ground-level ozone, particle pollution (also known as particulate matter), carbon monoxide, sulfur dioxide, and nitrogen dioxide. The AQI runs from 0 to 500. The higher the AQI value, the greater the level of air pollution and the greater the health concern; (1) Data covers San Diego County; (2) Based on 365 days with AQI data in 2011.
Source: U.S. Environmental Protection Agency, AirData Report, 2011

Air Quality Index Trends

Area	Trend Sites (days)								All Sites (days)
	2003	2004	2005	2006	2007	2008	2009	2010	2010
MSA[1]	50	31	30	39	34	43	25	14	15

Note: Figures are the number of days the AQI value exceeded 100 in a given year. An AQI value greater than 100 indicates that air quality would have been in the unhealthful range on that day. Data from exceptional events are included. These counts are presented in two ways. First, the counts are based on sites having an adequate record of monitoring data during the trend period (trend sites). These counts represent the relative change in the number of days with AQI values greater than 100. In the last column, the counts are based on all sites with data in the most recent year (because it is possible for a site to have data in the most recent year but not enough data to be a trend site); (1) Data covers the San Diego-Carlsbad-San Marcos, CA—see Appendix B for areas included
Source: U.S. Environmental Protection Agency, Air Quality Index Information, "Number of Days with Air Quality Index Values Greater than 100 at Trend Sites, 2000-2010, and at All Sites in 2010"

Maximum Air Pollutant Concentrations: Particulate Matter, Ozone, CO and Lead

	Particulate Matter 10 (ug/m³)	Particulate Matter 2.5 Wtd AM (ug/m³)	Particulate Matter 2.5 24-Hr (ug/m³)	Ozone (ppm)	Carbon Monoxide (ppm)	Lead (ug/m³)
MSA[1] Level	101	13.3	114	0.081	2	n/a
NAAQS[2]	150	15	35	0.075	9	0.15
Met NAAQS[2]	Yes	Yes	No	No	Yes	n/a

Note: Data from exceptional events are not included; (1) Data covers the San Diego-Carlsbad-San Marcos, CA—see Appendix B for areas included; (2) National Ambient Air Quality Standards; ppm = parts per million; ug/m³ = micrograms per cubic meter; n/a not available
Concentrations: Particulate Matter 10 (coarse particulate)—highest second maximum 24-hour concentration; Particulate Matter 2.5 Wtd AM (fine particulate)—highest weighted annual mean concentration; Particulate Matter 2.5 24-Hour (fine particulate)—highest 98th percentile 24-hour concentration; Ozone—highest fourth daily maximum 8-hour concentration; Carbon Monoxide—highest second maximum non-overlapping 8-hour concentration; Lead—maximum running 3-month average
Source: U.S. Environmental Protection Agency, CBSA Factbook 2010, Air Quality Statistics by City, 2010

Maximum Air Pollutant Concentrations: Nitrogen Dioxide and Sulfur Dioxide

	Nitrogen Dioxide AM (ppb)	Nitrogen Dioxide 1-Hr (ppb)	Sulfur Dioxide AM (ppb)	Sulfur Dioxide 1-Hr (ppb)	Sulfur Dioxide 24-Hr (ppb)
MSA[1] Level	20.975	74	1.765	18	7.1
NAAQS[2]	53	100	30	75	140
Met NAAQS[2]	Yes	Yes	Yes	Yes	Yes

Note: Data from exceptional events are not included; (1) Data covers the San Diego-Carlsbad-San Marcos, CA—see Appendix B for areas included; (2) National Ambient Air Quality Standards; ppb = parts per billion; n/a not available

Concentrations: Nitrogen Dioxide AM—highest arithmetic mean concentration; Nitrogen Dioxide 1-Hr—highest 98th percentile 1-hour daily maximum concentration; Sulfur Dioxide AM—highest annual mean concentration; Sulfur Dioxide 1-Hr—highest 99th percentile 1-hour daily maximum concentration; Sulfur Dioxide 24-Hr—highest second maximum 24-hour concentration

Source: U.S. Environmental Protection Agency, CBSA Factbook 2010, Air Quality Statistics by City, 2010

Drinking Water

Water System Name	Pop. Served	Primary Water Source Type	Violations[1]	
			Health Based	Monitoring/ Reporting
City of San Diego	1,266,731	Surface	0	0

Note: (1) Based on violation data from January 1, 2011 to December 31, 2011 (includes unresolved violations from earlier years)

Source: U.S. Environmental Protection Agency, Office of Ground Water and Drinking Water, Safe Drinking Water Information System (based on data extracted April 18, 2012)

San Francisco, California

Background

San Francisco is one of the most beautiful cities in the world. It is blessed with a mild climate, one of the best landlocked harbors in the world, and a strong sense of civic pride shaped by its unique history. It has been said that San Francisco is "Paris, but populated with Americans, most of them smiling."

The hilly peninsula known today as San Francisco and its bay was largely ignored by explorers during the sixteenth and seventeenth centuries. Until the 1760s, no European had seen the "Golden Gate," or the narrow strip of water leading into what was to become one of the greatest harbors in the world. However, even with the eventual discovery of that prime piece of real estate, San Francisco remained a quiet and pastoral settlement for nearly 90 years.

The discovery of gold in the Sierra Nevada foothills in 1848 changed San Francisco forever. Every hopeful adventurer from around the world docked in San Francisco, aspiring to make his fortune. San Francisco had entered its phase as a rowdy, frontier, gold-prospecting town, with plenty of bachelors, amusing themselves at the gambling houses and saloons.

When the supply of gold dwindled, many of the men went back to their native countries, but some stayed and continued to live in the ethnic neighborhoods they had created—neighborhoods that still exist today, such as Chinatown, the Italian District, and the Japan Center.

The charm of San Francisco lies in its cosmopolitan, yet cohesive, flavor. Ever mindful of its citizenry, newspapers in San Francisco range from English, Irish, Spanish, and Swiss to Chinese, Japanese, and Korean, with many community newspapers in between. In addition, the city has long been home to a significant gay community.

The San Francisco Bay Area is one of the major economic regions of the United States, with one of the highest percentages of college-educated adults in the nation, which translates into a high per-capita real income. The Bay Area is also home to 20 percent of California's environmental companies, and leads the state with the largest concentration of biotech companies. A former warehouse district in San Francisco has become the center for nearly 400 multimedia and Internet-related companies. Before the Internet crash in 2000, this industry cluster, combined with the concentration of multimedia activity in the Bay Area, had produced jobs for nearly 60,000 people. In terms of world trade, high-tech exports from the Silicon Valley area accounted for almost one-third of the nation's high-technology exports.

AT&T Park, home of the San Francisco Giants major league baseball team, was completed in 2000, and the Giants won the World Series in 2010. The city offers excellent convention facilities with its Moscone Center, where a third building, Moscone West, was completed in 2003, bringing exhibit space to 770,000 square feet. The center was named for Mayor George Moscone, who championed controversial causes and who was murdered in office in 1978, along with gay activist Harvey Milk. The film, *The Times of Harvey Milk* won the 2008 Academy Award for best picture.

The Fine Arts Museums of San Francisco include the de Young, which is the city's oldest museum, and the Legion of Honor, a beautiful Beaux-arts museum that is home to Rodin's *Thinker*. In 2005, the de Young Museum reopened in a new building in Golden Gate Park, replacing an earlier structure damaged by the 1989 earthquake.

Also damaged in that quake was the main facility of the California Academy of Sciences, which oversees the Steinhart Aquarium, the Morrison Planetarium and the Natural History Museum. The California Academy of Sciences, also located in Golden Gate Park was reopened in the fall of 2008. Architect Renzo Piano designed the building to be seismically safe, green and sustainable. Dedicated to the study of art and science, the building allows outside views from nearly anywhere inside.

San Francisco is known as the "Air-Conditioned City" with cool pleasant summers and mild winters. It has greater climatic variability than any other urban area of the same size in the country. Sea fogs and associated low stratus clouds are most common in the summertime, when it is not unusual to see perched on the Golden Gate Bridge a low cloud illuminated by the sun.

Rankings

General Rankings

- The San Francisco metro area was identified as one of the 10 most popular big cities by Pew Research Center. The results are based on a telephone survey of 2,260 adults conducted during October 2008. The report explored a range of attitudes related to where Americans live, where they would like to live, and why. *Pew Research Center, "For Nearly Half of America, Grass is Greener Somewhere Else," January 29, 2009*
- *Men's Health Living* ranked 100 U.S. cities in terms of quality of life. San Francisco was ranked #9 and received a grade of A-. Criteria: number of fitness facilities; air quality; number of physicians; male/female ratio; education levels; household income; cost of living. *Men's Health Living, Spring 2008*
- San Francisco was selected as one of America's ten "Best Cities to Work and Live." The city ranked #3. The results are based on a survey of 2,500 employees and entrepreneurs who were asked about 40 large cities. *BusinessWeek, "America's Most and Least Favorite Cities," January 5, 2009*
- San Francisco was selected as one of America's best cities by *Bloomberg Businessweek.* The city ranked #9 out of 50. Criteria: number of restaurants, bars and museums per capita; number of colleges, libraries, and professional sports teams; income, poverty, unemployment, crime, and foreclosure rates; percent of population with bachelor's degrees; public school performance; park acres per capita; air quality. *BusinessWeek, "America's 50 Best Cities," September 20, 2011*
- San Francisco was identified as one of the top places to live in the U.S. by Harris Interactive. The city ranked #6 out of 15. Criteria: 2,463 adults (age 18 and over) were polled and asked "if you could live in or near any city in the country except the one you live in or nearest to now, which city would you choose?" The poll was conducted online within the U.S. between September 14 and 20, 2010. *Harris Interactive, November 9, 2011*
- San Francisco was selected as one of "America's Favorite Cities." The city ranked #9 in the "Quality of Life and Visitor Experience" category. Respondents to an online survey were asked to rate 35 top urban destinations in the U.S. from a visitor's perspective. Criteria: noteworthy neighborhoods; skyline/views; public parks and outdoor access; cleanliness; public transportation and pedestrian friendliness; safety; weather; peace and quiet; people-watching; environmental friendliness. *Travelandleisure.com, "America's Favorite Cities 2010," November 2010*
- San Francisco was selected as one of "America's Favorite Cities." The city ranked #3 in the "People" category. Respondents to an online survey were asked to rate 35 top urban destinations in the U.S. from a visitor's perspective. Criteria: attractive; friendly; stylish; intelligent; athletic/active; diverse. *Travelandleisure.com, "America's Favorite Cities 2010," November 2010*
- Mercer Human Resources Consulting ranked 221 cities worldwide in terms of overall quality of life. San Francisco ranked #30. Criteria: political, social, economic, and socio-cultural factors; medical and health considerations; schools and education; public services and transportation; recreation; consumer goods; housing; and natural environment. *Mercer Human Resources Consulting, "Mercer 2011 Quality of Living Survey,"November 29, 2011*
- San Francisco appeared on *Travel + Leisure's* list of the ten best cities in the continental U.S. and Canada. The city was ranked #4. Criteria: activities/attractions; culture/arts; restaurants/food; people; and value. *Travel + Leisure, "The World's Best Awards 2011"*
- *Condé Nast Traveler* polled thousands of readers for travel satisfaction. American cities were ranked based on the following criteria: friendliness; atmosphere/ambiance; culture/sites; restaurants; lodging; and shopping. San Francisco appeared in the top 10, ranking #2. *Condé Nast Traveler, 2011 Readers' Choice Awards*

Business/Finance Rankings

- The San Francisco metro area was identified as one of 10 places with the fastest-growing wages in America. The area ranked #6. Criteria: private-sector wage growth between the 4th quarter of 2010 and the 4th quarter of 2011. *PayScale, "The 10 Cities with the Fastest-Growing Wages in America," January 12, 2012*

- Experian ranked the top 20 major U.S. metropolitan areas by average debt per consumer. The San Francisco metro area was ranked #18. Criteria: average debt per consumer. Debt for this study includes credit cards, auto loans and personal loans. It does not include mortgages. *Experian, May 13, 2010*

- The San Francisco metro area was identified as one of the "Best U.S. Cities for Earning a Living" by *Forbes*. The metro area ranked #7. Criteria: median income; cost of living; job growth; number of companies on *Forbes* 400 best big company and 200 best small company lists. *Forbes.com, "Best U.S. Cities for Earning a Living," August 21, 2008*

- San Francisco was identified as one of the "Best Cities for Recent College Graduates." The city ranked #6. Criteria: concentration of young adults (age 20 to 24); inventory of jobs requiring less than one year of experience; average cost of rent for a one bedroom apartment. *CareerBuilder.com, "Top 10 Best Cities for Recent College Graduates," August 30, 2011*

- San Francisco was identified as one of the "Happiest Cities to Work in 2012" by *CareerBliss.com,* an online community for career advancement. The city ranked #27 out of 50. Criteria: independent company reviews from employees all over the country on: relationship with their boss and co-workers; work environment; job resources; growth opportunities; compensation; company culture; company reputation; daily tasks; job control over work performed on a daily basis. *CareerBliss.com, "Happiest and Unhappiest Cities to Work in 2012"*

- San Francisco was selected as one of the best cities in the world for telecommuting. The city ranked #1. The editors at *Cartridge Save* (printer technology news, guides and reviews) identified the 20 best cities in which to be an at-home, tech-using employee. *Cartridge Save, "20 of the Best Cities in the World for Telecommuting," May 14, 2008*

- *American City Business Journals* ranked America's 261 largest cities in terms of their resident's wealth. San Francisco ranked #7. Criteria: per capita income; median household income; percentage of households with annual incomes of $200,000 or more; median home value. *American City Business Journals, "Where the Money Is: America's Wealth Centers," August 18, 2008*

- The San Francisco metro area appeared on the Milken Institute "2011 Best Performing Metros" list. Rank: #52 out of 200 large metro areas. Criteria: job growth; wage and salary growth; high-tech output growth. *Milken Institute, "2011 Best Performing Metros"*

- The San Francisco metro area was selected as one of the best cities for entrepreneurs in America by *Inc. Magazine.* Criteria: job-growth data for 335 metro areas was analyzed for: recent growth trend; mid-term growth; long-term trend; current year growth. The San Francisco metro area ranked #29 among large metro areas and #149 overall. *Inc. Magazine, "The Best Cities for Doing Business," July 2008*

- San Francisco was identified as one of the top 10 cities with the greatest number of *Inc. 500* companies per million residents. The city ranked #9. *Inc. Magazine, September 2008*

- San Francisco was ranked #5 out of 145 regions worldwide in terms of its "Knowledge Competitiveness Index." The index attempts to measure the knowledge-based development taking place throughout the world and is based on 19 measures of economic performance that indicate a region's ability to translate its knowledge capacity into economic value. *Centre for International Competitiveness, World Knowledge Competitiveness Index 2008*

- *Forbes* ranked the 200 most populous metro areas in the U.S. in terms of the "Best Places for Business and Careers." The San Francisco metro area was ranked #37. Criteria: costs (business and living); job growth (past and projected); income growth; educational attainment; projected economic growth; crime; cultural and recreational opportunities; net migration patterns; number of highly ranked colleges. *Forbes, "Best Places for Business and Careers," June 2011*

Children/Family Rankings

- Underwriters Laboratories (UL), in partnership with Sperling's BestPlaces, ranked the 50 largest cities in the U.S. in terms of the safest for families with young children. Each city was measured on 25 criteria encompassing child-focused, safety-oriented behaviors and regulatory best practices. The study filtered out cities with the highest crime rates and considered air quality, incidence of child pedestrian accidents, injuries and drowning. The study also focused on accessibility to hospitals; response time for fire and police personnel; and laws, codes and regulations that address smoking, home inspections, smoke and carbon monoxide alarms, pool safety and bike helmets. The top 10 cities had the highest frequency or values in these categories. *Underwriters Laboratories, "Safest Cities for Families with Young Children," September 29, 2010*

- San Francisco was selected as one of the safest cities for children in America by *Men's Health*. The city ranked #3 of 10. Criteria: accidental death rates for kids ages 5 to 14; number of car seat inspection locations per child; sex offenders per capita; percentage of abused children protected from further abuse; strength of child-restraint and bike-helmet laws. *Men's Health, "The Safest (and Least Safe) Cities for Children," September 2010*

- San Francisco was selected as one of the 10 best cities to raise children in the U.S. by *KidFriendlyCities.org*. Criteria: education; environment; health; employment; crime; diversity; cost of living. *KidFriendlyCities.org, "Top Rated Kid/Family Friendly Cities 2009"*

- The San Francisco metro area was selected as one of the "Best Cities for Relocating Families" by Worldwide ERC and Primacy Relocation. The 2008 study looked at nearly 50 factors important to relocating families including: recent job growth; nearby top-ranked colleges; in-state tuition for four-year public colleges; population growth since 2000; pediatricians per 100,000 population; and a Green Living index. *Worldwide ERC and Primacy Relocation, "2008 Best Cities for Relocating Families"*

- *Fit Pregnancy* magazine ranked the 50 best U.S. cities in which to have a baby. San Francisco was ranked #3. Criteria: access to hospitals and doctors; affordability; birthing options; breastfeeding; child care; fertility laws/resources; maternal and infant health risk; parks/stroller friendliness; safety. *Fit Pregnancy, "The Best Cities in America to Have a Baby 2008"*

Culture/Performing Arts Rankings

- San Francisco was selected as one of the top 10 cities for design in America by architectural firm RMJM Hillier. The city was ranked #6. American cities with more than 500,000 residents were ranked according to criteria such as the quality of public transit, the number of LEED-registered buildings (indicating sustainable design) and how many of the city's employees work within creative industries such as performing arts or publishing. Resident interviews were used to rate a city's design factor, which takes in elements of a city's architecture as well as its creative appeal. *RMJM Hillier, "America's Best Cities for Design," June 25, 2008*

- San Francisco was selected as one of "America's Favorite Cities." The city ranked #7 in the "Culture" category. Respondents to an online survey were asked to rate 35 top urban destinations in the U.S. from a visitor's perspective. Criteria: classical music; live music/bands; theater; museums/galleries; historical sites/monuments. *Travelandleisure.com, "America's Favorite Cities 2010," November 2010*

- San Francisco was selected as one of "America's Top 25 Arts Destinations." The city ranked #4 in the big city (population 500,000 and over) category. Criteria: readers' top choices for arts travel destinations based on the richness and variety of visual arts sites, activities and events. *American Style, "America's Top 25 Arts Destinations," May 2010*

Dating/Romance Rankings

- San Francisco was selected as one of "America's Best Cities for Dating" by *Yahoo! Travel*. Criteria: high proportion of singles; excellent dating venues and/or stunning natural settings. *Yahoo! Travel, "America's Best Cities for Dating," February 7, 2012*

- San Francisco appeared on *Men's Health's* list of the most sex-happy cities in America. The city ranked #74 of 100. Criteria: condom sales; birth rates; sex toy sales; rates of chlamydia, gonorrhea, and syphilis. *Men's Health, "America's Most Sex-Happy Cities," October 2010*

- *Men's Health* ranked 100 U.S. cities in terms of best (and worst) marriages. San Francisco was ranked #87 (#1 = worst). Criteria: rate of failed marriages; stringency of divorce laws; percentage of population who've split; number of licensed marriage and family therapists. *Men's Health, "Splitsville, USA," May 2010*

- Eli Lily and Company, in partnership with Sperling's BestPlaces, ranked the nation's 50 largest metro areas in terms of the "Most Romantic Cities for Baby Boomers." The San Francisco metro area ranked #37. Criteria: marriage and divorce rates among baby boomers age 45 to 60; great restaurants; dance studios; chocolate, jewelry and flower sales. *Eli Lily and Company, "Most Romantic Cities for Baby Boomers," April 20, 2007*

- The San Francisco metro area was selected as one of the "Best Cities for Relocating Singles" by Worldwide ERC and Primacy Relocation. The area ranked #8 out of the 100 largest metro areas in the U.S. Criteria: recent job growth; recent singles population growth; overall population growth; affordable rental housing; cost-of-living index; expanded arts and recreation opportunities; ratio of single men and single women; affordability of quality higher education (including state residency requirements); diversity index; climate; population density. *Worldwide ERC and Primacy Relocation, "2008 Best Cities for Relocating Singles"*

- *Forbes* ranked the 40 most populous urbanized areas in the U.S. in terms of the "Best Cities for Singles." The San Francisco metro area ranked #7. Criteria: number of singles; cost of living alone; nightlife; culture; job growth; coolness; and online dating participation. *Forbes.com, "Best Cities for Singles," July 27, 2009*

Education Rankings

- *Men's Health* ranked 100 U.S. cities in terms of their education levels. San Francisco was ranked #20 (#1 = most educated city). Criteria: high school graduation rates; school enrollment; educational attainment; number of households who have outstanding student loans; number of households whose members have taken adult-education courses. *Men's Health, "Where School Is In: The Most and Least Educated Cities," September 12, 2011*

- San Francisco was selected as one of "America's Geekiest Cities" by *Forbes.com*. The city ranked #19 of 20. Criteria: percentage of workers with jobs in science, technology, engineering and mathematics. *Forbes.com, "America's Geekiest Cities," August 5, 2011*

- San Francisco was selected as one of "America's Most Literate Cities." The city ranked #9 out of the 75 largest U.S. cities. Criteria: number of booksellers; library resources; Internet resources; educational attainment; periodical publishing resources; newspaper circulation. *Central Connecticut State University, "America's Most Literate Cities 2011"*

- San Francisco was identified as one of the 100 "smartest" metro areas in the U.S. The area ranked #6. Criteria: the editors rated the collective brainpower of the 100 largest metro areas in the U.S. based on their residents' educational attainment. *American City Business Journals, April 14, 2008*

- San Francisco was identified as one of "America's Smartest Cities" by *The Daily Beast.* The metro area ranked #3 out of 55. The editors ranked metropolitan areas with one million or more residents on the following criteria: percentage of residents over age 25 with bachelor's or graduate degrees; non-fiction book sales; ratio of institutions of higher education; libraries per capita. *The Daily Beast, "America's Smartest Cities," October 24, 2010*

- San Francisco was identified as one of America's most inventive cities by *The Daily Beast.* The city ranked #6 out of 25. The 200 largest cities in the U.S. were ranked by the number of patents (applied and approved) per capita. *The Daily Beast, "The 25 Most Inventive Cities," October 2, 2011*

- San Francisco was identified as one of "America's Brainiest Bastions" by *Portfolio.com.* The metro area ranked #10 out of 200. *Portfolio.com* analyzed levels of educational attainment in the nation's 200 largest metropolitan areas. The editors established scores for five levels of educational attainment, based on relative earning power of adult workers age 25 or older. Scores were determined by comparing the median income for all workers with the median income for those workers at a specified educational level. *Portfolio.com, "America's Brainiest Bastions," December 1, 2010*

- San Francisco was identified as one of "America's Smartest Cities" by *CNNMoney.com.* The area ranked #2. Criteria: percentage of residents with bachelors or graduate degrees. *CNNMoney.com, "America's Smartest Cities," October 1, 2010*

- San Francisco was identified as one of America's smartest cities" by *Forbes*. The area ranked #9 out of 25. Criteria: percentage of the population age 25 and over with at least a bachelor's degree. *Forbes.com, "The Smartest Cities in America," February 8, 2008*

Environmental Rankings

- The San Francisco was identified as one of North America's greenest metropolitan areas. The area ranked #1. The Green City Index is comprised of 31 indicators, and scores cities across nine categories: carbon dioxide; energy; land use; buildings; transport; water; waste; air quality; environmental governance. The 27 largest metropolitan areas in the U.S. and Canada were considered. *Economist Intelligence Unit, sponsored by Siemens, "U.S. and Canada Green City Index, 2011"*
- The San Francisco was identified as one of America's cities with the most ENERGY STAR certified buildings. The area ranked #3 out of 25. Criteria: number of ENERGY STAR labeled buildings in 2010. *U.S. Environmental Protection Agency, "Top Cities With the Most ENERGY STAR Certified Buildings," March 15, 2011*
- The San Francisco metro area was identified as one of "The Ten Biggest American Cities that are Running Out of Water" by *24/7 Wall St.* The metro area ranked #5 out of 10. *24/7 Wall St.* did an analysis of the water supply and consumption in the 30 largest metropolitan areas in the U.S. Criteria include: projected water demand as a share of available precipitation; groundwater use as a share or projected available precipitation; susceptibility to drought; projected increase in freshwater withdrawals; projected increase in summer water deficit. *24/7 Wall St., "The Ten Biggest American Cities that are Running Out of Water," November 1, 2010*
- Scarborough Research, a leading market research firm, identified the top local markets for green appliance households. The San Francisco DMA (Designated Market Area) ranked in the top 16 with 38% of consumers reporting that they own an energy-efficient appliance. *Scarborough Research, March 23, 2010*
- San Francisco was selected as one of 22 "Smarter Cities" for energy by the Natural Resources Defense Council. The city appeared as one of 12 cities in the large city (population 250,000 and over) category. Criteria: investment in green power; energy efficiency measures; conservation. *Natural Resources Defense Council, "2010 Smarter Cities," July 19, 2010*
- *American City Business Journal* ranked 43 metropolitan areas in terms of their "greenness." The San Francisco metro area ranked #2. Criteria: Forty-one metros in which *ACBJ* has business weeklies, plus Indianapolis and Cleveland, were ranked based on 20 different indicators such as adoption of green technologies, utilization of environmentally sound practices, and air and water quality. *American City Business Journals, "Green City Index," March 11, 2010*
- San Francisco was selected as one of "America's 50 Greenest Cities" by *Popular Science.* The city ranked #2. Criteria: electricity; transportation; green living; recycling and green perspective. *Popular Science, February 2008*
- 100 of the largest metro areas in the U.S. were analyzed in terms of their current drought severity. The San Francisco metro area ranked #34 (#1 = driest). The rankings were based on statistics such as long-term precipitation trends and patterns and the Palmer drought indices. *Sperling's BestPlaces, www.BestPlaces.net, "America's Drought-Riskiest Cities," November 2007*
- The U.S. Conference of Mayors and Wal-Mart Stores sponsor the Mayors' Climate Protection Awards Program. The awards recognize and honor mayors for outstanding and innovative practices that mayors are taking to increase energy efficiency in their cities, and to help curb global warming. San Francisco was a Large City Best Practice Model. *U.S. Conference of Mayors, "2009 Mayors' Climate Protection Awards Program"*
- The San Francisco metro area appeared in *Country Home's* "Best Green Places" report. The area ranked #11 out of 379. Criteria: official energy policies; green power; green buildings; availability of fresh, locally grown food. *Country Home, "Best Green Places," 2008*
- San Francisco was highlighted as one of the 25 metro areas most polluted by short-term particle pollution (24-hour PM 2.5) in the U.S. The area ranked #24. *American Lung Association, State of the Air 2011*

Food/Drink Rankings

- San Francisco was identified as one of "America's Drunkest Cities of 2011" by *The Daily Beast.* The city ranked #22 out of 25. Criteria: binge drinking; drinks consumed per month. *The Daily Beast, "Tipsy Towns: Where are America's Drunkest Cities?," December 31, 2011*
- San Francisco was identified as one of "America's Most Caffeinated Cities" by *Bundle.com.* The city was ranked #4 out of 10. The rankings were determined by examining consumer spending at 16 widely known coffee chains during the second quarter of 2011. *Bundle.com, "America's Most Caffeinated Cities," September 19, 2011*
- San Francisco was selected as one of "America's Favorite Cities." The city ranked #2 in the "Food/Dining" category. Respondents to an online survey were asked to rate 35 top urban destinations in the U.S. from a visitor's perspective. Criteria: big-name restaurants; ethnic food; farmers' markets; neighborhood joints and cafes. *Travelandleisure.com, "America's Favorite Cities 2010," November 2010*
- AT&T Park (San Francisco Giants) was selected as one of PETA's "2011 Top 10 Vegetarian-Friendly Major League Ballparks." The park ranked #1. *People for the Ethical Treatment of Animals, "2011 Top 10 Vegetarian-Friendly Major League Ballparks"*
- San Francisco was selected as one of North America's most vegetarian- and vegan-friendly large cities (population 300,000 or more). The city was ranked #7. Criteria: number of vegetarian restaurants and vegetarian-friendly restaurants per capita; input from PETA supporters and staff members on the quality of the options. *People for the Ethical Treatment of Animals, "North America's Best Vegetarian- and Vegan-Friendly Cities," July 23, 2010*
- The San Francisco metro area was selected as one of the best cities for "foodies" in America by Sperling's BestPlaces. The metro area ranked #5 out of 10. A "foodie" is defined as a person whose hobby is food—not just eating it, but also learning about its origins and preparation. Criteria: ratio of local restaurants to chain restaurants; number of local and accessible CSA (Community Supported Agriculture) and farmers markets; number of Whole Foods stores; number of cookware stores; number of craft breweries, brew pubs, wine shops, and wine bars. *Sperling's BestPlaces, www.BestPlaces.net, "America's Best Cities for Foodies," January 2011*
- San Francisco was selected as one of the "Top 10 Places to Eat Classic American Chow." *USA Weekend, "Summer Travel Report," May 18-20, 2007*

Health/Fitness Rankings

- The American Podiatric Medical Association and *Prevention* magazine ranked 100 American cities based on walkability. Nineteen walking criteria were evaluated including the percentage of adults who walk to work, number of parks per square mile, number of trails for walking and hiking, air pollution, use of mass transit, crime rate, pedestrian fatalities, and percentage of adults who walk for fitness. San Francisco ranked #1. *Prevention, "The Best Walking Cities of 2009," May 2009; American Podiatric Medical Association, "2009 Best Fitness-Walking Cities," April 7, 2009*
- San Francisco was identified as one of the most walkable cities in the U.S. by *WalkScore.com,* a Seattle-based service that rates the convenience and transit access of 10,000 neighborhoods in 2,500 cities. The editors at Grey House Publishing used *WalkScore.com's* online service to look at the scores of 280 cities with populations greater than or equal to 100,000. The top 50 cities were selected. *WalkScore.com, April 2, 2012*
- The San Francisco metro area was selected as one of the worst cities for bed bugs in America by Rollins corporation, the owner of seven pest control companies, including Orkin. The area ranked #12 based on the number of bed bug treatments from January to December 2011. *Rollins, "The Top 50 U.S. Cities for Bed Bugs," March 19, 2012*
- San Francisco was identified as one of the most bed bug-infested cities in the U.S. by Terminix. San Francisco ranked #10.Criteria: complaint calls from customers; confirmed cases by professionals. *Terminix, "2011 Most Bedbug-Infested Cities," May 24, 2011*

- San Francisco was selected as one of the 25 fittest cities in America by *Men's Fitness Online*. It ranked #2 out of America's 50 largest cities. Criteria: fitness centers and sport stores; nutrition; sports participation; TV viewing; overweight/sedentary; junk food; air quality; geography; commute; parks and open space; city recreational facilities; access to healthcare; motivation; mayor and city initiatives; state obesity initiatives. *Men's Fitness, "The Fittest and Fattest Cities in America," March 5, 2012*
- San Francisco was identified as a "2011 Asthma Capital." The area ranked #99 out of the nation's 100 largest metropolitan areas. Twelve factors were used to identify the most challenging places to live for people with asthma: estimated prevalence; self-reported prevalence; crude death rate for asthma; annual pollen score; annual air quality; public smoking laws; number of board-certified asthma specialists; school inhaler access laws; rescue medication use; controller medication use; uninsured rate; poverty rate. *Asthma and Allergy Foundation of America, "2011 Asthma Capitals"*
- San Francisco was identified as a "2011 Fall Allergy Capital." The area ranked #86 out of 100. Three groups of factors were used to identify the most severe cities for people with allergies during the fall season: annual pollen levels; medicine utilization; access to board-certified allergists. *Asthma and Allergy Foundation of America, "2011 Fall Allergy Capitals"*
- San Francisco was identified as a "2012 Spring Allergy Capital." The area ranked #83 out of 100. Three groups of factors were used to identify the most severe cities for people with allergies during the spring season: annual pollen levels; medicine utilization; access to board-certified allergists. *Asthma and Allergy Foundation of America, "2012 Spring Allergy Capitals"*
- *Men's Health* examined 100 major U.S. cities and selected the best and worst cities for men. San Francisco ranked #22. Criteria: 35 statistical parameters of long life in the categories of health, quality of life, and fitness. *Men's Health, "The 10 Best and Worst Cities for Men 2012," January/February 2012*
- *Men's Health* examined 100 U.S. cities and selected the best and worst cities for women. San Francisco was ranked among the ten best at #10. Criteria: dozens of statistical parameters of long life in the categories of health, quality of life, and fitness. *Men's Health, "The 10 Best and Worst Cities for Women 2011," January/February 2011*
- San Francisco was selected as one of America's noisiest cities by *Men's Health*. The city ranked #8 of 10. Criteria: laws limiting excessive noise; traffic congestion levels; airports' overnight flight curfews; percentage of people who report sleeping seven hours or less. *Men's Health, "Ranking America's Cities: America's Noisiest Cities," May 2009*
- The San Francisco metropolitan area was selected as one of the best metros for hospital care in America by *HealthGrades.com*. The rankings are based on a comprehensive study of patient death and complication rates in the nation's nearly 5,000 hospitals. Hospitals performing in the top 5% nationwide across 26 different medical procedures and diagnoses were identified. *HealthGrades.com* then ranked cities by the highest percentage of these Distinguished Hospitals for Clinical Excellence™. The San Francisco metro area ranked #49. *HealthGrades.com, "America's Top 50 Cities for Hospital Care," January 21, 2012*
- The American Academy of Dermatology ranked 26 U.S. metropolitan regions in terms of their residents knowledge, attitude and behaviors towards tanning, sun protection and skin cancer detection. The San Francisco metro area ranked #14. The results of the study are based on an online survey of over 7,000 adults nationwide. *American Academy of Dermatology, "Suntelligence: How Sun Smart is Your City," May 3, 2010*
- The San Francisco metro area was identified as one of America's "Healthiest Hometowns" by AARP. The metro area ranked #9 out of 10. More than 20 measures of vitality were analyzed including air and water quality and the health and habits of the populace. *AARP, "Healthiest Hometowns," September/October 2008*
- The San Francisco metro area appeared in the 2011 Gallup-Healthways Well-Being Index. The index, based on interviews with more than 350,000 Americans, measured jobs, finances, physical health, emotional state of mind and communities. The metro area ranked #16 out of 190. Criteria: life evaluation; emotional health; work environment; physical health; healthy behaviors; basic access (basic needs optimal for a healthy life, such as access to food and medicine, having health insurance and feeling safe while walking at night). *Gallup-Healthways, "State of Well-Being 2011"*

- The San Francisco metro area was identified as one of "America's Most Stressful Cities" by *Sperling's BestPlaces.* The metro area ranked #28 out of 50. Criteria: unemployment rate; suicide rate; commute time; mental health; poor rest; alcohol use; violent crime rate; property crime rate; cloudy days annually. *Sperling's BestPlaces, www.BestPlaces.net, "Stressful Cities 2012*

- The San Francisco metro area was identified as one of "America's Most Stressful Cities" by *Forbes*. The metro area ranked #7 out of 40. Criteria: housing affordability; unemployment rate; cost of living; air quality; traffic congestion; sunny days; population density. *Forbes.com, "America's Most Stressful Cities," September 23, 2011*

- *Men's Health* ranked 100 U.S. cities in terms of their activity levels. San Francisco was ranked #2 (#1 = most active city). Criteria: where and how often residents exercise; percentage of households that watch more than 15 hours of cable television a week and buy more than 11 video games a year; death rate from deep-vein thrombosis, a condition linked to sitting for extended periods of time. *Men's Health, "Where Sit Happens: The Most and Least Active Cities in America," June 20, 2011*

- *Men's Health* examined the nation's largest 100 cities and identified the 10 cities at lowest risk of erectile dysfunction. San Francisco ranked #9. Criteria: percentage of current male smokers; percentage of adults with a BMI of at least 30; percentage of adults with diabetes; percentage of men working out three or more times per week; percentage of urologists per 100,000 men; number of ED drug prescriptions filled in 2007. *Men's Health, "Ranking America's Cities: Cities that Need Viagara," April 2009*

- 50 of the largest metro areas in the U.S. were analyzed in terms of their health and fitness by the American College of Sports Medicine in their "American Fitness Index." The San Francisco metro area ranked #8 (#1 = healthiest). Criteria: preventative health behaviors; levels of chronic disease; health care access; community resources and policies that support physical activity. *American College of Sports Medicine, "Health and Community Fitness Status of the 50 Largest Metropolitan Areas," August 1, 2011*

Pet Rankings

- San Francisco was selected as one of the "Top 10 Cat-Friendly Cities" in the U.S. The area ranked #3. Criteria: cat ownership per capita; level of veterinary care; microchipping; cat-friendly local ordinances. *CATalyst Council, "Top 10 Cat-Friendly Cities," March 27, 2009*

Real Estate Rankings

- San Francisco was selected as one of the worst cities for renters by *Forbes.* The city ranked #5 out of 5. The 44 largest cities in the U.S. were rated on four criteria: average rent in the first quarter of 2011 and how much it changed year-over-year; vacancy rates; cost of renting versus buying. *Forbes, "Best and Worst Cities for Renters," June 20, 2011*

- San Francisco was identified as one of the priciest cities to rent in the U.S. The area ranked #3 out of 10. Criteria: rent-to-income ratio. *CNBC, "Priciest Cities to Rent," March 14, 2012*

- *Fortune* ranked the 100 largest metro areas in the U.S. in terms of projected median home price change in 2010. The San Francisco metro area ranked #56. *Fortune, "The 2010 Housing Outlook," December 9, 2009*

- San Francisco was selected as one of the 10 best U.S. cities for real estate investment. The city ranked #4. *Association of Foreign Investors in Real Estate, "AFIRE News," January/February, 2011*

- The San Francisco metro area was identified as one of the 20 least affordable housing markets in the U.S. in 2011. The area ranked #6 out of 152 markets with an affordability index of 66.2%. The index measures whether or not a typical family could qualify for a mortgage loan on a typical home. The calculation used assumes a down payment of 20 percent of the home price and a qualifying ratio of 25 percent, meaning that the monthly P&I payment cannot exceed 25 percent of a the median family monthly income. *National Association of Realtors®, Affordability Index of Existing Single-Family Homes for Metropolitan Areas, 2011*

- San Francisco appeared on *ApartmentRatings.com* "Top Cities for Renters" list in 2009." The area ranked #83. Overall satisfaction ratings were ranked using thousands of user submitted scores for hundreds of apartment complexes located in the 100 most populated U.S. municipalities. *ApartmentRatings.com, "2009 Renter Satisfaction Rankings"*

- San Francisco appeared on *ApartmentRatings.com* "Top College Towns & Cities" for renters list in 2011." The area ranked #47 out of 87. Overall satisfaction ratings were ranked using thousands of user submitted scores for hundreds of apartment complexes located in cities and towns that are home to the 100 largest four-year institutions in the U.S. *ApartmentRatings.com, "2011 College Town Renter Satisfaction Rankings"*

- The San Francisco metro area was identified as one of the most expensive places to rent in the U.S. The area ranked #47 out of 10 markets with an average effective rent of $1,760 per month. The rental figures cover apartment properties in complexes with 40 or more units (20 or more units in California and Arizona). The figures are blended average rents, which include all unit sizes. Effective rents include free rent incentives and other landlord concessions. *Wall Street Journal Online, January 17, 2008*

- The nation's largest metro areas were analyzed in terms of the best places to buy pre-foreclosures (short sales). The San Francisco metro area ranked #1 out of 10. Criteria: at least 500 pre-foreclosure sales during the fourth quarter and a short sales increase of at least five percent from a year ago. The areas selected posted the biggest discounts on the sales of pre-foreclosure properties. *RealtyTrac, "Fourth Quarter and Year-End 2011 U.S. Foreclosure Sales Report: Shifting Towards Short Sales," February 28, 2012*

- The San Francisco metro area was identified as one of America's least affordable cities to buy a house in 2010 by *CNNMoney.com.* The metro area was ranked #2 out of 5. Criteria: median home prices; median family income *CNNMoney.com, "America's Most and Least Affordable Cities to Buy a House," May 21, 2010*

- The San Francisco metro area appeared in a *Wall Street Journal* article ranking cities by "housing stress." The metro area was ranked #11 (#1 = most stress). Criteria: fraction of mortgage-holding homeowners with a monthly housing payment in excess of 30 percent of income; percentage of people without health insurance; unemployment rate. *The Wall Street Journal, "Which Cities Face Biggest Housing Risk," October 5, 2010*

- The Center for Housing Policy ranked 210 U.S. metropolitan areas by the fair market rent for a two-bedroom unit. The San Francisco metro area was ranked #1. (#1 = most expensive) with a rent of $1,760. Criteria: Fair Market Rent (FMR) in effect during the fourth quarter of 2009 based on HUD's fiscal year 2010 FMRs. *The Center for Housing Policy, "Paycheck to Paycheck: Most to Least Expensive Rental Markets in 2009"*

- The San Francisco metro area was identified as one of the best U.S. markets to invest in rental property" by HomeVestors and Local Market Monitor. The area ranked #100 out of 100. Criteria: risk-return premium relative to national average. *HomeVestors and Local Market Monitor, "Best 100 U.S. Markets to Invest in Rental Property," March 9, 2012*

Safety Rankings

- Symantec, the makers of Norton, in partnership with Sperling's BestPlaces, ranked the 50 largest cities in the U.S. in terms of their vulnerability to cybercrime. The city ranked #3. Criteria: number of cyberattacks and potential infections; level of Internet access; expenditures on smartphones and computer hardware/software; wireless hotspots; broadband connectivity; Internet usage; online purchases. *Symantec, "Riskiest Online Cities of 2012" February 15, 2012*

- Allstate ranked the 193 largest cities in America in terms of driver safety. San Francisco ranked #185. In addition, drivers were 57.3% more likely to have had an accident compared to the national average. Allstate researchers analyzed internal property damage reported claims over a two-year period (from January 2008 to December 2009) to protect findings from external influences such as weather or road construction. A weighted average of the two-year numbers determined the annual percentages. The report defines an auto crash as any collision resulting in a property damage claim. *Allstate, "2011 Allstate America's Best Drivers Report™"*

- The National Insurance Crime Bureau ranked 366 metro areas in the U.S. in terms of per capita rates of vehicle theft. The San Francisco metro area ranked #9 (#1 = highest rate). Criteria: number of vehicle theft offenses per 100,000 inhabitants in 2010. *National Insurance Crime Bureau, "Hot Spots," June 21, 2011*

- The San Francisco metro area was identified as one of the most dangerous metro areas for pedestrians by Transportation for America. The metro area ranked #41 out of 52 metro areas with over 1 million residents. Criteria: area's population divided by the number of pedestrian fatalities in that area. *Transportation for America, "Dangerous by Design 2011"*

Seniors/Retirement Rankings

- Bankers Life and Casualty Company, in partnership with Sperling's BestPlaces, ranked the nation's 50 largest metro areas in terms of the "Best U.S. Cities for Seniors." The San Francisco metro area ranked #7. Criteria: healthcare; transportation; housing; environment; economy; health and longevity; social and spiritual life; crime. *Bankers Life and Casualty Company, Center for a Secure Retirement, "Best U.S. Cities for Seniors 2011," September 2011*

- San Francisco was selected as one of "10 Historic Places to Retire" by *U.S. News & World Report.* The editors looked for places filled with museums, libraries, and national historic monuments that also offer a good quality of life and plenty of amenities for seniors. *U.S. News & World Report, "10 Historic Places to Retire," September 6, 2010*

Sports/Recreation Rankings

- San Francisco appeared on the *Sporting News* list of the "Best Sports Cities" for 2011. The area ranked #15 out of 271 cities in the U.S. *Sporting News* takes a 12-month snapshot of each city's sports, putting a heavy premium on regular-season won-lost records (from the most recently completed season). Other criteria include: playoff berths, bowl appearances and tournament bids; championships; applicable power ratings; quality of competition; overall fan fervor (measured in part by attendance); abundance of teams (rewarding quality over quantity); stadium and arena quality; ticket availability and prices; franchise ownership; and marquee appeal of athletes. *Sporting News, "Best Sports Cities 2011," October 4, 2011*

- San Francisco was chosen as a bicycle friendly community by the League of American Bicyclists. A Bicycle Friendly Community welcomes cyclists by providing safe accommodation for cycling and encouraging people to bike for transportation and recreation. There are four award levels: Platinum; Gold; Silver; and Bronze. The community achieved an award level of Gold. *League of American Bicyclists, "Bicycle Friendly Community Master List 2011"*

- San Francisco was selected as one of the most playful cities in the U.S. by KaBOOM! The organization's Playful City USA initiative is a national recognition program that honors cities and towns across the nation for a vision, plan and commitment to creating an agenda for play. Cities were recognized based on a pledge to five specific commitments to play: creating a local play commission or task force; designing an annual action plan for play; conducting a play space audit; outlining a financial investment in play for the current fiscal year; and proclaiming and celebrating an annual "play day." *KaBOOM! National Campaign for Play, "2011 Playful City USA Communities"*

- San Francisco was chosen as one of America's best cities for bicycling. The city ranked #6 out of 50. Criteria: number of segregated bike lanes, municipal bike racks, and bike boulevards; vibrant and diverse bike culture; smart, savvy bike shops; interviews with national and local advocates, bike shops and other experts. The editors only considered cities with populations of 100,000 or more. *Bicycling, "America's Best Bike Cities," April 2010*

Technology Rankings

- The San Francisco metro area was selected as one of "America's Most Wired Cities" by *Forbes*. The metro area was ranked #4 out of 20. Criteria: percentage of Internet users with high-speed access; number of companies providing high-speed Internet; number of public wireless hot spots. *Forbes, "America's Most Wired Cities," March 2, 2010*

- The San Francisco metro area was selected as one of "America's Most Innovative Cities" by *Forbes*. The metro area was ranked #4 out of 20. Criteria: patents per capita; venture capital investment per capita; ratio of high-tech, science and "creative" jobs. *Forbes, "America's Most Innovative Cities," May 24, 2010*
- The San Francisco metro area was identified as one of the "Top 14 Nano Metros" in the U.S. by the Project on Emerging Nanotechnologies. The metro area is home to 48 companies, universities, government laboratories and/or organizations working in nanotechnology. *Project on Emerging Nanotechnologies, "Nano Metros 2009"*

Transportation Rankings

- San Francisco was identified as one of America's "10 Best Cities for Public Transportation" by *U.S. News & World Report.* The city ranked #6. The ten cities selected had the best combination of public transportation investment, ridership, and safety. *U.S. News & World Report, "10 Best Cities for Public Transportation," February 8, 2011*
- The San Francisco metro area was identified as one of the best U.S. cities to live in without a car by *24/7 Wall St.* The area ranked #1 out of 10. Criteria: percentage of neighborhoods covered by public transit; frequency of service for those neighborhoods; share of jobs reachable within 90 minutes or less by public transit; how accessible amenities are for residents on foot; percentage of commuters who bike to work. The 100 largest metropolitan areas in the U.S. were examined. *24/7 Wall St., "The Best Cities to Live in Car-Free," November 28, 2011*
- The San Francisco metro area was selected as one of 15 "Smarter Cities" for transportation by the Natural Resources Defense Council. The area appeared in the large metro area (population greater than one million) category. Criteria: public transit availability and use; household automobile ownership and use; innovative, sustainable and affordable transportation programs. *Natural Resources Defense Council, "2011 Smarter Cities," February 23, 2011*
- The San Francisco metro area appeared on *Forbes* list of the best and worst cities for commuters. The metro area ranked #41 out of 60 (#1 is best). Criteria: travel time; road congestion; travel delays. *Forbes.com, "Best and Worst Cities for Commuters," February 16, 2010*

Women/Minorities Rankings

- *Women's Health* examined U.S. cities and identified the 100 best cities for women. San Francisco was ranked #11. Criteria: 30 categories were examined from obesity and breast cancer rates to commuting times and hours spent working out. *Women's Health, "Best Cities for Women 2012"*
- San Francisco was ranked #2 out of 100 metro areas in *SELF Magazine's* ranking of America's healthiest places for women." A panel of experts came up with more than 50 criteria including death and disease rates, environmental indicators, community resources, and lifestyle habits. *SELF Magazine, "Secrets of America's Healthiest Women," December 2008*
- The San Francisco metro area appeared on *Forbes'* list of the "Best Cities for Minority Entrepreneurs." The area ranked #2 out of 10. Criteria: 52 metropolitan statistical areas were examined. For each ethnicity (African Americans, Asians and Hispanics), the editors measured housing affordability, population growth, income growth, and entrepreneurship (per capita self-employment). *Forbes, "Best Cities for Minority Entrepreneurs," March 23, 2011*

Miscellaneous Rankings

- *Men's Health* ranked 100 U.S. cities by their level of sadness. San Francisco was ranked #20 (#1 = saddest city). Criteria: suicide rates; unemployment rates; percentage of households that use antidepressants; percent of population who report feeling blue all or most of the time. *Men's Health, "Frown Towns," November 28, 2011*

- Energizer Holdings, the makers of Edge® shave gel, in partnership with Sperling's BestPlaces, ranked 50 major metro areas in terms of everyday irritations. The San Francisco metro area ranked #24. Criteria: humidity levels; weather conditions; incidence of traffic delays and congestion; average commute times; frequency of flight delays and cancellations; rates of sleeplessness; underemployment; pollens and allergens; pests; comedy clubs per capita. *Energizer Holdings, "Most Irritation Prone Cities," July 23, 2010*
- Mars Chocolate North America, the makers of COMBOS®, in partnership with Sperling's BestPlaces, ranked 50 major metro areas in terms of their "manliness." The San Francisco metro area ranked #48. Criteria: number of professional sports teams; number of nearby NASCAR tracks and racing events; manly lifestyle; concentration of manly retail stores; manly occupations per capita; salty snack sales; "Board of Manliness" rankings. *Mars Chocolate North America, "America's Manliest Cities 2011," September 1, 2011*
- San Francisco was selected as one of the "Best Hair Cities" by *NaturallyCurly.com.* The city was ranked #5. Criteria: humidity levels; pollution; rainfall; average wind speeds; water hardness; beauty salons per capita. *NaturallyCurly.com, "Best/Worst Hair Cities," April 29, 2009*
- San Francisco was selected as one of the most tattooed cities in America by *TotalBeauty.com.* The city was ranked #7. Criteria: number of tattoo and permanent makeup shops per capita; number of tattoo conventions hosted. *TotalBeauty.com, "Top 10 Most Tattooed Cities in America," August 2010*
- San Francisco was selected as one of "America's Best Cities for Hipsters" by *Travel + Leisure.* The city was ranked #3 out of 10. Criteria: live music; coffee bars; independent boutiques; best microbrews; offbeat and tech-savvy locals. *Travel + Leisure, "America's Best Cities for Hipsters," April 11, 2012*
- The San Francisco metro area was selected as one of "America's Greediest Cities" by *Forbes.* The area was ranked #2 out of 10. Criteria: number of Forbes 400 (*Forbes* annual list of the richest Americans) members per capita. *Forbes, "America's Greediest Cities," December 7, 2007*
- The San Francisco metro area appeared in *AutoMD.com's* ranking of the "Best and Worst Cities for Auto Repair." The metro area ranked #41 (#1 is best). The 50 most-populated metro areas in the U.S. were ranked on three critical factors: repair affordability; price disparity range; shop integrity factor. *AutoMD.com, "Advocacy for Repair Shop Fairness Report," February 24, 2010*
- San Francisco was identified as one of "America's Vainest Cities" by *Forbes.com.* The city ranked #2. Criteria: highest number of cosmetic surgeons per 100,000 people in America's 50 largest cities. *Forbes.com, "America's Vainest Cities," November 29, 2007*
- San Francisco was selected as one of America's "10 Meanest Cities" by the National Coalition for the Homeless and The National Law Center on Homelessness & Poverty. The city was ranked #7. Criteria: the number of anti-homeless laws; the enforcement of those laws and severity of penalties; the general political climate towards homeless people; local advocate support for the meanest designation; the city's history of criminalization measures; and the existence of pending or recently enacted criminalization legislation in the city. *National Coalition for the Homeless and The National Law Center on Homelessness & Poverty, "Homes Not Handcuffs: The Criminalization of Homelessness in U.S. Cities," July 2009*

Business Environment

CITY FINANCES

City Government Finances

Component	2009 ($000)	2009 ($ per capita)
Total Revenues	3,394,717	4,438
Total Expenditures	7,779,693	10,170
Debt Outstanding	8,800,366	11,504
Cash and Securities[1]	15,644,278	20,451

Note: (1) Cash and security holdings of a government at the close of its fiscal year, including those of its dependent agencies, utilities, and liquor stores.
Source: U.S Census Bureau, State & Local Government Finances 2009

City Government Revenue by Source

Source	2009 ($000)	2009 ($ per capita)
General Revenue		
From Federal Government	143,892	188
From State Government	1,419,664	1,856
From Local Governments	334,937	438
Taxes		
Property	1,373,806	1,796
Sales and Gross Receipts	627,725	821
Personal Income	0	0
Corporate Income	0	0
Motor Vehicle License	0	0
Other Taxes	536,494	701
Current Charges	1,389,065	1,816
Liquor Store	0	0
Utility	479,614	627
Employee Retirement	-3,276,425	-4,283

Source: U.S Census Bureau, State & Local Government Finances 2009

City Government Expenditures by Function

Function	2009 ($000)	2009 ($ per capita)	2009 (%)
General Direct Expenditures			
Air Transportation	688,241	900	8.8
Corrections	186,365	244	2.4
Education	0	0	0.0
Employment Security Administration	0	0	0.0
Financial Administration	48,068	63	0.6
Fire Protection	251,142	328	3.2
General Public Buildings	10,656	14	0.1
Governmental Administration, Other	108,640	142	1.4
Health	800,604	1,047	10.3
Highways	166,429	218	2.1
Hospitals	782,439	1,023	10.1
Housing and Community Development	293,122	383	3.8
Interest on General Debt	387,477	507	5.0
Judicial and Legal	89,277	117	1.1
Libraries	76,962	101	1.0
Parking	96,816	127	1.2
Parks and Recreation	241,764	316	3.1
Police Protection	396,069	518	5.1
Public Welfare	518,468	678	6.7
Sewerage	197,775	259	2.5
Solid Waste Management	0	0	0.0
Veterans' Services	0	0	0.0
Liquor Store	0	0	0.0
Utility	1,272,697	1,664	16.4
Employee Retirement	739,056	966	9.5

Source: U.S Census Bureau, State & Local Government Finances 2009

Municipal Bond Ratings

Area	Moody's	S&P	Fitch
City	Aa2	AA	AA

Rating Systems (shown in declining order of credit quality): Moody's– Aaa, Aa, A, Baa, Ba, B, Caa, Ca, C (numerical modifiers 1, 2, and 3 are added to letter-rating); S&P– AAA, AA, A, BBB, BB, B, CCC, CC, C; Fitch– AAA, AA, A, BBB, BB, B, CCC, CC, C. Ratings may be modified by the addition of a plus or minus sign to show relative standing within the major rating categories.

Notes: n/a Not Available; w/d Withdrawn (1) Not Reviewed; (2) Issuer Rating/No General Obligation; (3) Standard and Poor's Issue Credit Rating (ICR) is a current opinion of an obliger with respect to a specific financial obligation, a specific class of financial obligations, or a specific financial program.

Source: U.S. Census Bureau, 2012 Statistical Abstract, Bond Ratings for City Governments by Largest Cities: 2010

DEMOGRAPHICS

Population Growth

Area	1990 Census	2000 Census	2010 Census	Population Growth (%) 1990-2000	Population Growth (%) 2000-2010
City	723,959	776,733	805,235	7.3	3.7
MSA[1]	3,686,592	4,123,740	4,335,391	11.9	5.1
U.S.	248,709,873	281,421,906	308,745,538	13.2	9.7

Note: (1) Figures cover the San Francisco-Oakland-Fremont, CA Metropolitan Statistical Area—see Appendix B for areas included

Source: U.S. Census Bureau, 2010 Census

Household Size

Area	Persons in Household (%)							Average Household Size
	One	Two	Three	Four	Five	Six	Seven or More	
City	38.6	31.4	13.3	8.9	3.7	1.8	2.3	2.26
MSA[1]	28.0	30.8	16.1	13.7	6.2	2.7	2.6	2.61
U.S.	26.7	32.8	16.1	13.4	6.5	2.6	1.9	2.58

Note: (1) Figures cover the San Francisco-Oakland-Fremont, CA Metropolitan Statistical Area—see Appendix B for areas included

Source: U.S. Census Bureau, 2010 Census

Race

Area	White Alone[2] (%)	Black Alone[2] (%)	Asian Alone[2] (%)	AIAN[3] Alone[2] (%)	NHOPI[4] Alone[2] (%)	Other Race Alone[2] (%)	Two or More Races (%)
City	48.5	6.1	33.3	0.5	0.4	6.6	4.7
MSA[1]	51.7	8.4	23.2	0.6	0.7	9.9	5.5
U.S.	72.4	12.6	4.8	0.9	0.2	6.2	2.9

Note: (1) Figures cover the San Francisco-Oakland-Fremont, CA Metropolitan Statistical Area—see Appendix B for areas included; (2) Alone is defined as not being in combination with one or more other races; (3) American Indian and Alaska Native; (4) Native Hawaiian and Other Pacific Islander

Source: U.S. Census Bureau, 2010 Census

Hispanic or Latino Origin

Area	Hispanic or Latino (%)	Mexican (%)	Puerto Rican (%)	Cuban (%)	Other Hispanic or Latino (%)
City	15.1	7.4	0.5	0.2	6.9
MSA[1]	21.7	14.2	0.7	0.2	6.6
U.S.	16.3	10.3	1.5	0.6	4.0

Note: Persons of Hispanic or Latino origin can be of any race; (1) Figures cover the San Francisco-Oakland-Fremont, CA Metropolitan Statistical Area—see Appendix B for areas included

Source: U.S. Census Bureau, 2010 Census

Segregation

Type	Segregation Indices[1]				Percent Change		
	1990	2000	2010	2010 Rank[2]	1990-2000	1990-2010	2000-2010
Black/White	67.0	65.7	62.0	34	-1.3	-5.0	-3.7
Asian/White	45.8	46.7	46.6	18	0.9	0.8	-0.1
Hispanic/White	43.7	49.7	49.6	26	6.0	5.9	-0.1

Note: Figures are based on an analysis of 1990, 2000, and 2010 Census Decennial Census tract data by William H. Frey, Brookings Institution and the University of Michigan Social Science Data Analysis Network. In this analysis all racial groups (whites, blacks, and asians) are non-Hispanic members of those races. Hispanics are shown as a separate category; All figures cover the Metropolitan Statistical Area (see Appendix B for areas included); (1) Segregation Indices are Dissimilarity Indices that measure the degree to which the minority group is distributed differently than whites across census tracts. They range from 0 (complete integration) to 100 (complete segregation) where the value indicates the percentage of the minority group that needs to move to be distributed exactly like whites; (2) Ranges from 1 (most segregated) to 102 (least segregated); n/a not available.
Source: www.CensusScope.org

Ancestry

Area	German	Irish	English	American	Italian	Polish	French[2]	Scottish	Dutch
City	8.2	7.9	5.5	1.0	4.8	2.1	2.3	1.6	0.9
MSA[1]	9.1	8.4	6.8	1.6	5.3	1.6	2.2	1.7	1.0
U.S.	16.1	11.6	8.8	6.1	5.7	3.2	3.0	1.9	1.6

Note: Figures are the percentage of the total population reporting a particular ancestry. The nine most commonly reported ancestries in the U.S. are shown. Figures include multiple ancestries (e.g. if a person reported being Irish and Italian, they were included in both columns); (1) Figures cover the San Francisco-Oakland-Fremont, CA Metropolitan Statistical Area—see Appendix B for areas included; (2) Excludes Basque
Source: U.S. Census Bureau, 2008-2010 American Community Survey 3-Year Estimates

Foreign-Born Population

Area	Percent of Population Born in								
	Any Foreign Country	Mexico	Asia	Europe	Carribean	South America	Central America[2]	Africa	Canada
City	35.5	3.0	22.7	4.6	0.2	1.0	2.8	0.4	0.6
MSA[1]	30.0	6.1	16.0	2.9	0.2	0.8	2.4	0.5	0.4
U.S.	12.8	3.8	3.6	1.6	1.2	0.9	1.0	0.5	0.3

Note: (1) Figures cover the San Francisco-Oakland-Fremont, CA Metropolitan Statistical Area—see Appendix B for areas included; (2) Excludes Mexico.
Source: U.S. Census Bureau, 2008-2010 American Community Survey 3-Year Estimates

Marital Status

Area	Never Married	Now Married[2]	Separated	Widowed	Divorced
City	47.9	37.5	1.5	5.2	7.8
MSA[1]	36.1	47.4	1.9	5.3	9.3
U.S.	31.6	49.6	2.2	6.1	10.7

Note: Figures are percentages and cover the population 15 years of age and older; (1) Figures cover the San Francisco-Oakland-Fremont, CA Metropolitan Statistical Area—see Appendix B for areas included; (2) Excludes separated
Source: U.S. Census Bureau, 2008-2010 American Community Survey 3-Year Estimates

Age

Area	Percent of Population							Median Age
	Under Age 5	Age 5 to 17	Age 18 to 34	Age 35 to 49	Age 50 to 64	Age 65 to 79	80 Years and Over	
City	4.4	9.0	30.5	23.8	18.7	9.3	4.3	38.5
MSA[1]	6.0	15.2	23.9	22.8	19.5	8.9	3.7	38.3
U.S.	6.5	17.5	23.2	20.7	19.0	9.4	3.6	37.2

Note: (1) Figures cover the San Francisco-Oakland-Fremont, CA Metropolitan Statistical Area—see Appendix B for areas included
Source: U.S. Census Bureau, 2010 Census

Male/Female Ratio

Area	Males	Females	Males per 100 Females
City	408,462	396,773	102.9
MSA[1]	2,137,801	2,197,590	97.3
U.S.	151,781,326	156,964,212	96.7

Note: (1) Figures cover the San Francisco-Oakland-Fremont, CA Metropolitan Statistical Area—see Appendix B for areas included
Source: U.S. Census Bureau, 2010 Census

Religious Groups

Area	Catholic	Baptist	Non-Den.	Methodist[2]	Lutheran	LDS[3]	Pente-costal	Presby-terian[4]	Muslim[5]	Judaism
MSA[1]	20.8	2.5	2.5	2.0	0.6	1.6	1.2	1.1	0.9	1.2
U.S.	19.1	9.3	4.0	4.0	2.3	2.0	1.9	1.6	0.8	0.7

Note: Figures are the number of adherents as a percentage of the total population; (1) Figures cover the San Francisco-Oakland-Fremont, CA Metropolitan Statistical Area—see Appendix B for areas included; (2) Methodist/Pietist; (3) Latter Day Saints; (4) Reformed; (5) Figures are estimates
Source: Association of Statisticians of American Religious Bodies, 2010 U.S. Religion Census: Religious Congregations & Membership Study

ECONOMY

Gross Metropolitan Product

Area	2007	2008	2009	2010	2010 Rank[2]
MSA[1]	321.2	336.5	328.9	337.4	8

Note: Figures are in billions of dollars; (1) Figures cover the San Francisco-Oakland-Fremont, CA Metropolitan Statistical Area—see Appendix B for areas included; (2) Rank ranges from 1 to 363
Source: The United States Conference of Mayors, "U.S. Metro Economies: GMP and Employment Forecasts," June 2011

Economic Growth

Area	2007-2009 (%)	2010 (%)	2011 (%)	Rank[2]
MSA[1]	1.2	1.7	1.3	53
U.S.	-1.3	2.9	2.5	–

Note: Figures are real Gross Metropolitan Product growth rates and represent annual average percent change; (1) Figures cover the San Francisco-Oakland-Fremont, CA Metropolitan Statistical Area—see Appendix B for areas included; (2) Rank ranges from 1 to 363
Source: The United States Conference of Mayors, "U.S. Metro Economies: GMP and Employment Forecasts," June 2011

Metropolitan Area Exports

Area	2005	2006	2007	2008	2009	2010	2010 Rank[2]
MSA[1]	14,706.9	18,358.2	20,081.2	20,470.4	16,040.3	21,355.4	13

Note: Figures are in millions of dollars; (1) Figures cover the San Francisco-Oakland-Fremont, CA Metropolitan Statistical Area—see Appendix B for areas included; (2) Rank ranges from 1 to 369
Source: U.S. Department of Commerce, International Trade Administration, Office of Trade & Industry Information, Manufacturing & Services, data extracted April 2, 2012

INCOME

Income

Area	Per Capita ($)	Median Household ($)	Average Household ($)
City	45,078	71,779	102,227
MSA[1]	39,207	74,809	102,229
U.S.	26,942	51,222	70,116

Note: (1) Figures cover the San Francisco-Oakland-Fremont, CA Metropolitan Statistical Area—see Appendix B for areas included
Source: U.S. Census Bureau, 2008-2010 American Community Survey 3-Year Estimates

Household Income Distribution

Area	Percent of Households Earning							
	Under $15,000	$15,000 -24,999	$25,000 -34,999	$35,000 -49,999	$50,000 -74,999	$75,000 -99,000	$100,000 -149,999	$150,000 and up
City	13.1	8.2	6.9	9.4	14.1	11.7	16.0	20.6
MSA[1]	9.5	7.5	7.0	10.3	15.8	12.3	17.5	20.1
U.S.	13.0	11.0	10.6	14.2	18.5	12.1	12.2	8.4

Note: (1) Figures cover the San Francisco-Oakland-Fremont, CA Metropolitan Statistical Area—see Appendix B for areas included
Source: U.S. Census Bureau, 2008-2010 American Community Survey 3-Year Estimates

Poverty Rate

Area	All Ages	Under 18 Years Old	18 to 64 Years Old	65 Years and Over
City	12.0	12.1	11.8	13.0
MSA[1]	10.2	12.5	9.7	8.3
U.S.	14.4	20.1	13.1	9.4

Note: Figures are percentage of people whose income during the past 12 months was below the poverty level; (1) Figures cover the San Francisco-Oakland-Fremont, CA Metropolitan Statistical Area—see Appendix B for areas included
Source: U.S. Census Bureau, 2008-2010 American Community Survey 3-Year Estimates

Personal Bankruptcy Filing Rate

Area	2006	2007	2008	2009	2010	2011
San Francisco County	0.90	1.20	1.52	2.29	2.74	2.30
U.S.	2.00	2.73	3.53	4.61	4.97	4.37

Note: Numbers are per 1,000 population and include Chapter 7 and Chapter 13 filings
Source: Federal Deposit Insurance Corporation, Regional Economic Conditions, March 9, 2012

EMPLOYMENT

Labor Force and Employment

Area	Civilian Labor Force			Workers Employed		
	Dec. 2010	Dec. 2011	% Chg.	Dec. 2010	Dec. 2011	% Chg.
City	456,081	463,288	1.6	414,765	428,039	3.2
MD[1]	956,585	974,257	1.8	875,013	903,017	3.2
U.S.	153,156,000	153,373,000	0.1	139,159,000	140,681,000	1.1

Note: Data is not seasonally adjusted and covers workers 16 years of age and older; (1) Metropolitan Division—see Appendix B for areas included
Source: Bureau of Labor Statistics, http://stats.bls.gov

Unemployment Rate

Area	2011											
	Jan.	Feb.	Mar.	Apr.	May	Jun.	Jul.	Aug.	Sep.	Oct.	Nov.	Dec.
City	9.5	9.1	9.2	8.5	8.4	9.0	9.1	8.8	8.3	8.1	7.8	7.6
MD[1]	8.9	8.6	8.7	8.3	8.1	8.8	8.8	8.5	8.1	7.9	7.6	7.3
U.S.	9.8	9.5	9.2	8.7	8.7	9.3	9.3	9.1	8.8	8.5	8.2	8.3

Note: Data is not seasonally adjusted and covers workers 16 years of age and older; All figures are percentages; (1) Metropolitan Division—see Appendix B for areas included
Source: Bureau of Labor Statistics, http://stats.bls.gov

Projected Unemployment Rate

Area	2010 (%)	2011 (%)	2012 (%)	2013 (%)
MSA[1]	10.5	9.3	8.8	8.1

Note: (1) Metropolitan Statistical Area—see Appendix B for areas included
Source: The United States Conference of Mayors, "U.S. Metro Economies: GMP and Employment Forecasts," June 2011

Employment by Occupation

Occupation Classification	City (%)	MSA[1] (%)	U.S. (%)
Management, Business, Science, and Arts	50.1	45.3	35.6
Natural Resources, Construction, and Maintenance	4.5	6.8	9.5
Production, Transportation, and Material Moving	5.7	7.8	12.1
Sales and Office	22.2	23.5	25.2
Service	17.5	16.6	17.6

Note: Figures cover employed civilians 16 years of age and older; (1) Figures cover the San Francisco-Oakland-Fremont, CA Metropolitan Statistical Area—see Appendix B for areas included
Source: U.S. Census Bureau, 2008-2010 American Community Survey 3-Year Estimates

Employment by Industry

Sector	MD[1]		U.S.
	Number of Employees	Percent of Total	Percent of Total
Construction	31,600	3.3	4.1
Education and Health Services	112,200	11.6	15.2
Financial Activities	76,900	8.0	5.8
Government	135,100	14.0	16.8
Information	42,400	4.4	2.0
Leisure and Hospitality	128,600	13.3	9.9
Manufacturing	37,000	3.8	8.9
Mining and Logging	200	<0.1	0.6
Other Services	41,000	4.2	4.0
Professional and Business Services	209,100	21.6	13.3
Retail Trade	93,100	9.6	11.5
Transportation and Utilities	36,000	3.7	3.8
Wholesale Trade	24,000	2.5	4.2

Note: Figures cover non-farm employment as of December 2011 and are not seasonally adjusted; (1) Metropolitan Division—see Appendix B for areas included
Source: Bureau of Labor Statistics, http://stats.bls.gov

Occupations with Greatest Projected Employment Growth: 2008 – 2018

Occupation[1]	2008 Employment	2018 Projected Employment	Numeric Employment Change	Percent Employment Change
Personal and Home Care Aides	346,500	504,700	158,200	45.7
Registered Nurses	236,400	297,200	60,800	25.7
Retail Salespersons	499,400	559,100	59,700	12.0
Combined Food Preparation and Serving Workers, Including Fast Food	260,600	308,800	48,200	18.5
Elementary School Teachers, Except Special Education	197,500	233,400	35,900	18.2
Office Clerks, General	372,500	407,400	34,900	9.4
Customer Service Representatives	202,200	236,600	34,400	17.0
Waiters and Waitresses	245,600	279,900	34,300	14.0
Stock Clerks and Order Fillers	207,700	237,100	29,400	14.2
Postsecondary Teachers	168,000	196,100	28,100	16.7

Note: Projections cover California; (1) Sorted by numeric employment change
Source: www.projectionscentral.com, State Occupational Projections, 2008–2018 Long-Term Projections

Fastest Growing Occupations: 2008 – 2018

Occupation[1]	2008 Employment	2018 Projected Employment	Numeric Employment Change	Percent Employment Change
Biomedical Engineers	3,100	5,600	2,500	80.6
Network Systems and Data Communications Analysts	35,000	52,600	17,600	50.3
Biochemists and Biophysicists	4,800	7,100	2,300	47.9
Medical Scientists, Except Epidemiologists	26,200	38,500	12,300	46.9
Personal and Home Care Aides	346,500	504,700	158,200	45.7
Home Health Aides	54,300	78,000	23,700	43.6
Physician Assistants	8,100	11,500	3,400	42.0
Separating, Filtering, Clarifying, Precipitating, and Still Machine Setters, Operators, and Te	7,300	10,200	2,900	39.7
Physical Therapist Aides	5,900	8,100	2,200	37.3
Electrical and Electronics Repairers, Powerhouse, Substation, and Relay	1,100	1,500	400	36.4

Note: Projections cover California; (1) Sorted by percent employment change and excludes occupations with numeric employment change less than 100
Source: www.projectionscentral.com, State Occupational Projections, 2008–2018 Long-Term Projections

Average Wages

Occupation	$/Hr.	Occupation	$/Hr.
Accountants and Auditors	41.46	Maids and Housekeeping Cleaners	15.20
Automotive Mechanics	24.38	Maintenance and Repair Workers	23.49
Bookkeepers	23.01	Marketing Managers	81.50
Carpenters	32.26	Nuclear Medicine Technologists	39.71
Cashiers	13.13	Nurses, Licensed Practical	29.44
Clerks, General Office	17.76	Nurses, Registered	50.80
Clerks, Receptionists/Information	17.53	Nursing Aides/Orderlies/Attendants	18.00
Clerks, Shipping/Receiving	16.67	Packers and Packagers, Hand	11.82
Computer Programmers	46.94	Physical Therapists	42.97
Computer Support Specialists	33.49	Postal Service Mail Carriers	26.37
Computer Systems Analysts	46.48	Real Estate Brokers	33.03
Cooks, Restaurant	14.47	Retail Salespersons	13.43
Dentists	76.44	Sales Reps., Exc. Tech./Scientific	35.39
Electrical Engineers	45.59	Sales Reps., Tech./Scientific	52.68
Electricians	37.23	Secretaries, Exc. Legal/Med./Exec.	20.80
Financial Managers	78.22	Security Guards	14.96
First-Line Supervisors/Managers, Sales	22.25	Surgeons	n/a
Food Preparation Workers	10.83	Teacher Assistants	16.00
General and Operations Managers	73.00	Teachers, Elementary School	30.60
Hairdressers/Cosmetologists	19.73	Teachers, Secondary School	32.50
Internists	109.06	Telemarketers	16.04
Janitors and Cleaners	13.39	Truck Drivers, Heavy/Tractor-Trailer	22.23
Landscaping/Groundskeeping Workers	17.47	Truck Drivers, Light/Delivery Svcs.	19.77
Lawyers	84.20	Waiters and Waitresses	12.19

Note: Wage data covers the San Francisco-San Mateo-Redwood City, CA Metropolitan Division—see Appendix B for areas included. Hourly wages for elementary/secondary school teachers and teacher assistants were calculated by the editors from annual wage data assuming a 40 hour work week; n/a not available.
Source: Bureau of Labor Statistics, Metro Area Occupational Employment and Wage Estimates, May 2011

RESIDENTIAL REAL ESTATE

Building Permits

Area	Single-Family			Multi-Family			Total		
	2010	2011	Pct. Chg.	2010	2011	Pct. Chg.	2010	2011	Pct. Chg.
City	22	31	40.9	757	1,787	136.1	779	1,818	133.4
MSA[1]	2,118	1,923	-9.2	2,503	3,860	54.2	4,621	5,783	25.1
U.S.	447,311	418,498	-6.4	157,299	205,563	30.7	604,610	624,061	3.2

Note: (1) Metropolitan Statistical Area—see Appendix B for areas included; figures represent new, privately-owned housing units authorized (unadjusted data); All permit data are based on estimates with imputation.
Source: U.S. Census Bureau, Manufacturing, Mining, and Construction Statistics, Building Permits, 2010, 2011

Homeownership Rate

Area	2005 (%)	2006 (%)	2007 (%)	2008 (%)	2009 (%)	2010 (%)	2011 (%)
MSA[1]	57.8	59.4	58.0	56.4	57.3	58.0	56.1
U.S.	68.9	68.8	68.1	67.8	67.4	66.9	66.1

Note: (1) Metropolitan Statistical Area—see Appendix B for areas included
Source: U.S. Census Bureau, Housing Vacancies and Homeownership Annual Statistics: 2011

Housing Vacancy Rates

Area	Gross Vacancy Rate[2] (%)			Year-Round Vacancy Rate[3] (%)			Rental Vacancy Rate[4] (%)			Homeowner Vacancy Rate[5] (%)		
	2009	2010	2011	2009	2010	2011	2009	2010	2011	2009	2010	2011
MSA[1]	10.3	9.1	8.3	10.1	9.0	8.1	6.7	6.0	6.8	1.8	1.8	1.8
U.S.	14.5	14.3	14.2	11.3	11.3	11.1	10.6	10.2	9.5	2.6	2.6	2.5

Note: (1) Metropolitan Statistical Area—see Appendix B for areas included; (2) The percentage of the total housing inventory that is vacant; (3) The percentage of the housing inventory (excluding seasonal units) that is year-round vacant; (4) The percentage of rental inventory that is vacant for rent; (5) The percentage of homeowner inventory that is vacant for sale
Source: U.S. Census Bureau, Housing Vacancies and Homeownership Annual Statistics: 2011

TAXES

State Corporate Income Tax Rates

State	Tax Rate (%)	Income Brackets ($)	Num. of Brackets	Financial Institution Tax Rate (%)[a]	Federal Income Tax Ded.
California	8.84 (c)	Flat rate	1	10.84 (c)	No

Note: Tax rates as of January 1, 2012; (a) Rates listed are the corporate income tax rate applied to financial institutions or excise taxes based on income. Some states have other taxes based upon the value of deposits or shares; (c) The minimum corporation franchise tax in California is $800. The additional alternative minimum tax is levied at a 6.65% rate.
Source: Federation of Tax Administrators, "State Corporate Income Tax Rates, 2012"

State Individual Income Tax Rates

State	Tax Rate (%)	Income Brackets ($)	Num. of Brackets	Personal Exempt. ($)[1]		Fed. Inc. Tax Ded.
				Single	Dependents	
California (a)	1.0 - 9.3 (f)	7,316 (b) - 48,029 (b)	6	102 (c)	315 (c)	No

Note: Tax rates as of January 1, 2012; Local- and county-level taxes are not included; n/a not applicable; (1) Married joint filers generally receive double the single exemption; (a) 17 states have statutory provision for automatically adjusting to the rate of inflation the dollar values of the income tax brackets, standard deductions, and/or personal exemptions. Massachusetts, Michigan, and Nebraska index the personal exemptiononly. Oregon does not index the income brackets for $125,000 and over. Because the inflation-adjustments for 2012 are not yet available in some cases, the table may report the 2011 amounts; (b) For joint returns, taxes are twice the tax on half the couple's income; (c) The personal exemption takes the form of a tax credit instead of a deduction; (f) California imposes an additional 1% tax on taxable income over $1 million, making the maximum rate 10.3% over $1 million.
Source: Federation of Tax Administrators, "State Individual Income Tax Rates, 2012"

Various State and Local Tax Rates

State	State and Local Sales and Use (%)	State Sales and Use (%)	Gasoline[1] (¢/gal.)	Cigarette[2] ($/pack)	Spirits[3] ($/gal.)	Wine[4] ($/gal.)	Beer[5] ($/gal.)
California	8.5	7.25 (b)	48.6	0.87	3.30	0.20	0.20

Note: All tax rates as of January 1, 2012 except beer, wine and spirits (September 1, 2011); (1) The American Petroleum Institute has developed a methodology for determining the average tax rate on a gallon of fuel. Rates may include any of the following: excise taxes, environmental fees, storage tank fees, other fees or taxes, general sales tax, and local taxes. In states where gasoline is subject to the general sales tax, or where the fuel tax is based on the average sale price, the average rate determined by API is sensitive to changes in the price of gasoline. States that fully or partially apply general sales taxes to gasoline: CA, CO, GA, IL, IN, MI, NY; (2) The federal excise tax of $1.0066 per pack and local taxes are not included; (3) Rates are those applicable to off-premise sales of 40% alcohol by volume (a.b.v.) distilled spirits in 750ml containers. Local excise taxes are excluded; (4) Rates are those applicable to off-premise sales of 11% a.b.v. non-carbonated wine in 750ml containers; (5) Rates are those applicable to off-premise sales of 4.7% a.b.v. beer in 12 ounce containers; (b) Three states collect a separate, uniform "local" add-on sales tax: California (1%), Utah (1.25%), Virginia (1%). These amounts are included in the state sales tax column.
Source: Tax Foundation, 2012 Facts & Figures: How Does Your State Compare?

State-Local Tax Burdens

Area	Rate (%)	Rank[1]	Per Capita Taxes Paid to Home State ($)	Total State and Local Per Capita Taxes Paid ($)	Per Capita Income ($)
California	10.6	6	3,874	4,910	46,366
U.S. Average	9.8	-	3,057	4,160	42,539

Note: Figures cover 2009; (1) Rank ranges from 1 to 50 where 1 is highest tax burden
Source: Tax Foundation, State-Local Tax Burdens, All States, 2009

State Business Tax Climate Index Rankings

State	Overall Rank	Corporate Tax Index Rank	Individual Income Tax Index Rank	Sales Tax Index Rank	Unemployment Insurance Tax Index Rank	Property Tax Index Rank
California	48	43	50	40	13	17

Note: The index is a measure of how each state's tax laws affect economic performance. The lower the rank, the more favorable a state's tax system is for business. States without a given tax are given a ranking of 1.
Source: Tax Foundation, Major Components of the State Business Tax Climate Index, FY 2012

COMMERCIAL REAL ESTATE

Office Market

Market Area	Inventory (sq. ft.)	Vacant (sq. ft.)	Vac. Rate (%)	Under Constr. (sq. ft.)	Asking Rent ($/sf/yr) Class A	Asking Rent ($/sf/yr) Class B
San Francisco Peninsula	27,129,924	4,038,578	14.9	0	36.13	34.56
San Francisco	64,756,381	8,591,781	13.3	70,484	40.76	34.05

Source: Grubb & Ellis, Office Markets Trends, 4th Quarter 2011

COMMERCIAL UTILITIES

Typical Monthly Electric Bills

Area	Commercial Service ($/month)		Industrial Service ($/month)	
	1,500 kWh	40 kW demand 14,000 kWh	1,000 kW demand 200,000 kWh	50,000 kW demand 15,000,000 kWh
City	305	2,474	44,140	2,342,281
Average[1]	189	1,616	25,197	1,470,813

Note: Based on total rates in effect July 1, 2011; (1) average based on 184 utilities surveyed
Source: Edison Electric Institute, Typical Bills and Average Rates Report, Summer 2011

TRANSPORTATION

Means of Transportation to Work

Area	Car/Truck/Van		Public Transportation			Bicycle	Walked	Other Means	Worked at Home
	Drove Alone	Car-pooled	Bus	Subway	Railroad				
City	37.5	8.0	22.7	6.5	1.1	3.1	9.9	4.5	6.7
MSA[1]	61.7	10.5	7.7	5.2	1.0	1.6	4.3	2.2	5.8
U.S.	76.0	10.2	2.7	1.7	0.5	0.5	2.8	1.3	4.2

Note: Figures are percentages and cover workers 16 years of age and older; (1) Figures cover the San Francisco-Oakland-Fremont, CA Metropolitan Statistical Area—see Appendix B for areas included
Source: U.S. Census Bureau, 2008-2010 American Community Survey 3-Year Estimates

Travel Time to Work

Area	Less Than 10 Minutes	10 to 19 Minutes	20 to 29 Minutes	30 to 44 Minutes	45 to 59 Minutes	60 to 89 Minutes	90 Minutes or More
City	5.2	23.7	21.7	28.5	11.2	7.6	2.0
MSA[1]	8.4	26.5	19.6	23.9	10.6	8.5	2.3
U.S.	13.9	30.1	20.8	19.8	7.5	5.5	2.5

Note: Figures are percentages and include workers 16 years old and over; (1) Figures cover the San Francisco-Oakland-Fremont, CA Metropolitan Statistical Area—see Appendix B for areas included
Source: U.S. Census Bureau, 2008-2010 American Community Survey 3-Year Estimates

Travel Time Index

Area	1985	1990	1995	2000	2005	2010
Urban Area[1]	1.23	1.32	1.30	1.34	1.40	1.28
Average[2]	1.11	1.16	1.18	1.21	1.25	1.20

Note: Travel Time Index—the ratio of travel time in the peak period to the travel time at free-flow conditions. A value of 1.30 indicates a 20-minute free-flow trip takes 26 minutes in the peak. Free-flow speeds (60 mph on freeways and 35 mph on principal arterials) are used as the comparison threshold; (1) Covers the San Francisco-Oakland CA urban area; (2) average of 439 urban areas
Source: Texas Transportation Institute, Urban Mobility Report 2011, September 2011

Public Transportation

Agency Name / Mode of Transportation	Vehicles Operated in Maximum Service	Annual Unlinked Passenger Trips ('000)	Annual Passenger Miles ('000)
San Francisco Municipal Railway (MUNI)			
Bus (directly operated)	385	91,609.2	208,583.7
Cable Car (directly operated)	27	8,008.4	10,053.3
Demand Response (purchased transportation)	88	513.9	4,390.5
Demand Response Taxi (purchased transportation)	1,523	524.9	2,296.3
Light Rail (directly operated)	139	49,396.9	131,367.6
Trolleybus (directly operated)	227	66,967.7	98,408.6
San Francisco Bay Area Rapid Transit District (BART)			
Heavy Rail (directly operated)	534	108,298.0	1,390,909.7

Source: Federal Transit Administration, National Transit Database, 2010

Air Transportation

Airport Name and Code / Type of Service	Passenger Airlines[1]	Passenger Enplanements	Freight Carriers[2]	Freight (lbs.)
San Francisco International (SFO)				
Domestic service (U.S. carriers - 2011)	24	15,635,726	19	123,734,989
International service (U.S. carriers - 2010)	10	1,596,636	6	53,970,429

Note: (1) Includes all U.S.-based major, minor and commuter airlines that carried at least one passenger during the year; (2) Includes all U.S.-based airlines and freight carriers that transported at least one pound of freight during the year
Source: Bureau of Transportation Statistics, The Intermodal Transportation Database, Air Carriers: T-100 Domestic Market (U.S. Carriers), 2011; Bureau of Transportation Statistics, The Intermodal Transportation Database, Air Carriers: T-100 International Market (U.S. Carriers), 2010

Other Transportation Statistics

Major Highways:	I-80
Amtrak Service:	Bus connection
Major Waterways/Ports:	Port of San Francisco

Source: Amtrak.com; Google Maps

BUSINESSES

Major Business Headquarters

Company Name	Rankings	
	Fortune[1]	Forbes[2]
Bechtel	-	5
Charles Schwab	491	-
Del Monte Foods	-	104
Gap	167	-
Levi Strauss	496	78
McKesson	15	-
PG&E Corp.	177	-
URS	267	-
Visa	297	-
Wells Fargo	23	-
Wilbur-Ellis	-	188

Note: (1) Fortune 500—companies that produce a 10-K are ranked 1 to 500 based on 2010 revenue; (2) all private companies with at least $2 billion in annual revenue are ranked 1 to 212; companies listed are headquartered in the city; dashes indicate no ranking
Source: Fortune, "Fortune 500," May 23, 2011; Forbes, "America's Largest Private Companies," November 16, 2011

Fast-Growing Businesses

According to *Inc.*, San Francisco is home to eight of America's 500 fastest-growing private companies: **Astro Gaming** (#13); **Advantis Global Services** (#14); **Build Group** (#131); **5th Finger** (#168); **Cantaloupe Systems** (#331); **Demandforce** (#376); **Curse** (#405); **TRX** (#451). Criteria: must be an independent, privately-held, for-profit, U.S. corporation, proprietorship or partnership; revenues must be at least $80,000 in 2007 and $2 million in 2010; must have four-year operating/sales history. Holding companies, regulated banks, and utilities were excluded. *Inc., "America's 500 Fastest-Growing Private Companies," September 2011*

According to *Fortune*, San Francisco is home to two of the 100 fastest-growing companies in the world: **Riverbed Technology** (#27); **Salesforce.com** (#35). Companies were ranked by their revenue growth rate; their EPS growth rate; and their three-year annualized total return to investors for the period ending June 30, 2011. Criteria for inclusion: a company, foreign or domestic, must trade on a major U.S. stock exchange; must file quarterly reports with the SEC; must have a minimum market capitalization of $250 million; must have a stock price of at least $5 on June 30, 2011; must have been trading continuously since June 30, 2008; must have revenue and net income for the four quarters ended on or before April 30, 2011, of at least $50 million and $10 million, respectively; and must have posted a compound annual growth in revenue and earnings per share of at least 15% annually over the three years ending on or before April 30, 2011. REITs, limited-liability companies, limited parterships, companies about to be acquired, and companies that lost money in the quarter ending April 30, 2011 were excluded. *Fortune, "100 Fastest-Growing Companies," September 26, 2011*

According to *Initiative for a Competitive Inner City (ICIC)*, San Francisco is home to six of America's 100 fastest-growing "inner city" companies: **e-Storm International** (#24); **Yerba Buena Engineering & Construction** (#49); **The Online 401(k)** (#64); **Bankserv** (#69); **Gelfand Partners Architects** (#72); **Merriwether and Williams Insurance** (#94). Companies were ranked by their five-year compound annual growth rate. Criteria for inclusion: company must be headquartered in or have 51 percent or more of its physical operations in an economically distressed urban area; must be an independent, for-profit corporation, partnership or proprietorship; must have 10 or more employees and have a five-year sales history that includes sales of at least $200,000 in the base year and at least $1 million in the current year with no decrease in sales over the two most recent years. *Initiative for a Competitive Inner City (ICIC), "Inner City 100 Companies, 2011"*

According to Deloitte, San Francisco is home to 14 of North America's 500 fastest-growing high-technology companies: **SAY Media** (#11); **Healthline Networks** (#75); **Tagged** (#80); **Tora Holdings** (#166); **Riverbed Technology** (#184); **Recommind** (#193); **FiberTower Corp.** (#209); **Suntech Power Holdings Co., Ltd.** (#237); **OpenTable** (#318); **VerticalResponse** (#343); **salesforce.com** (#348); **Coverity** (#351); **WideOrbit** (#456); **Dolby Laboratories** (#498). Companies are ranked by percentage growth in revenue over a five-year period. Criteria for inclusion: company must be headquartered within North America; must own proprietary intellectual property or proprietary technology that contributes to a significant portion of the company's operating revenue, or devote a significant proportion of revenues to research and development of technology; must have been in business for a minumum of five years with 2006 operating revenues of at least $50,000 USD/CD and 2010 operating revenues of at least $5 million USD/CD. *Deloitte Touche Tohmatsu, 2011 Deloitte Technology Fast 500™*

Minority Business Opportunity

San Francisco is home to one company which is on the *Black Enterprise* Private Equity 15 list (15 largest private equity firms based on capital under management): **Vista Equity Partners** (#2). Criteria: company must be operational in previous calendar year and be at least 51% black-owned. *Black Enterprise, B.E. 100s, 2011*

San Francisco is home to one company which is on the *Black Enterprise* Asset Manager 15 list (15 largest asset management firms based on assets under management): **Progress Investment Management Company** (#4). Criteria: company must have been operational in previous calendar year and be at least 51% black-owned. *Black Enterprise, B.E. 100s, 2011*

San Francisco is home to three companies which are on the *Hispanic Business* 500 list (500 largest U.S. Hispanic-owned companies based on 2010 revenue): **Yerba Buena Engineering & Construction** (#223); **A. Ruiz Constr. Co. & Assoc.** (#249); **LUZ** (#335). Companies included must show at least 51 percent ownership by Hispanic U.S. citizens, and must maintain headquarters in one of the 50 states or Washington, D.C. *Hispanic Business, "Hispanic Business 500," June 2011*

San Francisco is home to one company which is on the *Hispanic Business* Fastest-Growing 100 list (greatest sales growth from 2006 to 2010): **LUZ** (#27). Companies included must show at least 51 percent ownership by Hispanic U.S. citizens, and must maintain headquarters in one of the 50 states or Washington, D.C. In addition, companies must have minimum revenues of $200,000 for calendar year 2005. *Hispanic Business, July/August 2011*

Minority- and Women-Owned Businesses

Group	All Firms		Firms with Paid Employees			
	Firms	Sales ($000)	Firms	Sales ($000)	Employees	Payroll ($000)
Asian	25,236	7,638,482	5,880	6,735,069	40,988	1,405,707
Black	2,788	261,763	301	192,245	2,502	75,355
Hispanic	6,915	986,789	989	757,813	6,421	265,414
Women	31,639	5,268,560	4,628	4,186,663	30,502	1,133,912
All Firms	105,030	161,709,354	25,356	156,979,583	511,507	34,727,580

Note: Figures cover firms located in the city; minority- and women-owned business are defined as firms in which the corresponding group own 51% or more of the stock or equity of the company
Source: U.S. Census Bureau, 2007 Economic Census, Survey of Business Owners

HOTELS

Hotels/Motels

Area	5 Star		4 Star		3 Star		2 Star		1 Star		Not Rated	
	Num.	Pct.[3]	Num.	Pct.[3]	Num.	Pct.[3]	Num.	Pct.[3]	Num.	Pct.[3]	Num.	Pct.[3]
City[1]	6	2.0	37	12.2	95	31.3	132	43.4	8	2.6	26	8.6
Total[2]	133	0.9	940	6.5	4,569	31.8	7,033	48.9	351	2.4	1,343	9.3

Note: (1) Figures cover San Francisco and vicinity; (2) Figures cover all 100 cities in this book; (3) Percentage of hotels which have a given star rating; Star ratings are determined by expedia.com and offer an indication of the general quality of a particular hotel.
Source: expedia.com, April 25, 2012

The San Francisco-San Mateo-Redwood City, CA metro area is home to five of the best hotels in the U.S. according to *Travel & Leisure*: **Ritz-Carlton, Half Moon Bay** (#97); **Taj Campton Place** (#113); **St. Regis, San Francisco** (#125); **Four Seasons Hotel San Francisco** (#165); **Mandarin Oriental, San Francisco** (#180). Criteria: service; location; rooms; food; and value. *Travel & Leisure, "T+L 500, The World's Best Hotels 2012"*

The San Francisco-San Mateo-Redwood City, CA metro area is home to six of the best hotels in the U.S. according to *Condé Nast Traveler*: **Ritz-Carlton** (#62); **St. Regis** (#70); **Hotel Vitale** (#80); **Cavallo Point** (#80); **Four Seasons** (#91); **Mandarin Oriental** (#91). The selections are based on over 25,000 responses to the magazine's annual Readers' Choice Survey. *Condé Nast Traveler, "2011 Readers' Choice Awards"*

EVENT SITES

Major Stadiums, Arenas, and Auditoriums

Name	Max. Capacity
AT&T Park	41,503
Bill Graham Civic Auditorium	7,000
Candlestick Park	70,207
Fort Mason Center	5,000

Source: Original research

Convention Centers

Name	Overall Space (sq. ft.)	Exhibit Space (sq. ft.)	Meeting Space (sq. ft.)	Meeting Rooms
Concourse Exhibition Center at Showplace Square	125,000	n/a	125,000	n/a
Moscone Convention Center	1,346,000	159,980	441,960	69

Note: n/a not available
Source: Original research

Living Environment

COST OF LIVING

Cost of Living Index

Composite Index	Groceries	Housing	Utilities	Transportation	Health Care	Misc. Goods/ Services
162.9	115.9	283.8	91.2	111.5	112.3	122.4

Note: U.S. = 100; Figures cover the San Francisco CA urban area.
Source: The Council for Community and Economic Research, ACCRA Cost of Living Index, 2011

Grocery Prices

Area[1]	T-Bone Steak ($/pound)	Frying Chicken ($/pound)	Whole Milk ($/half gal.)	Eggs ($/dozen)	Orange Juice ($/64 oz.)	Coffee ($/11.5 oz.)
City[2]	10.14	1.27	2.20	2.36	3.80	5.56
Avg.	9.25	1.18	2.22	1.66	3.19	4.40
Min.	6.70	0.88	1.31	0.95	2.46	2.94
Max.	14.30	2.16	3.50	3.18	4.75	6.83

Note: (1) Values for the local area are compared with the average, minimum and maximum values for all 335 areas in the Cost of Living Index; (2) Figures cover the San Francisco CA urban area; **T-Bone Steak** *(price per pound);* **Frying Chicken** *(price per pound, whole fryer);* **Whole Milk** *(half gallon carton);* **Eggs** *(price per dozen, Grade A, large);* **Orange Juice** *(64 oz. Tropicana or Florida Natural);* **Coffee** *(11.5 oz. can, vacuum-packed, Maxwell House, Hills Bros, or Folgers).*
Source: The Council for Community and Economic Research, ACCRA Cost of Living Index, 2011

Housing and Utility Costs

Area[1]	New Home Price ($)	Apartment Rent ($/month)	All Electric ($/month)	Part Electric ($/month)	Other Energy ($/month)	Telephone ($/month)
City[2]	796,762	2,518	-	87.94	66.07	23.88
Avg.	285,990	839	163.23	89.00	77.52	26.92
Min.	188,005	460	125.58	45.39	33.89	17.98
Max.	1,197,028	3,244	339.16	181.97	348.69	40.01

Note: (1) Values for the local area are compared with the average, minimum and maximum values for all 335 areas in the Cost of Living Index; (2) Figures cover the San Francisco CA urban area; **New Home Price** *(2,400 sf living area, 8,000 sf lot, in urban area with full utilities);* **Apartment Rent** *(950 sf 2 bedroom/1.5 or 2 bath, unfurnished, excluding all utilities except water);* **All Electric** *(average monthly cost for an all-electric home);* **Part Electric** *(average monthly cost for a part-electric home);* **Other Energy** *(average monthly cost for natural gas, fuel oil, coal, wood, and any other forms of energy except electricity);* **Telephone** *(price includes basic monthly rate for a private residential line plus additional local usage charges incurred by a family of four).*
Source: The Council for Community and Economic Research, ACCRA Cost of Living Index, 2011

Health Care, Transportation, and Other Costs

Area[1]	Doctor ($/visit)	Dentist ($/visit)	Optometrist ($/visit)	Gasoline ($/gallon)	Beauty Salon ($/visit)	Men's Shirt ($)
City[2]	121.22	94.38	110.57	3.78	63.21	42.14
Avg.	93.88	81.72	90.54	3.48	32.65	25.06
Min.	60.00	55.33	53.66	3.18	19.78	13.44
Max.	154.98	145.97	183.72	4.31	63.21	46.00

Note: (1) Values for the local area are compared with the average, minimum and maximum values for all 335 areas in the Cost of Living Index; (2) Figures cover the San Francisco CA urban area; **Doctor** *(general practitioners routine exam of an established patient);* **Dentist** *(adult teeth cleaning and periodic oral examination);* **Optometrist** *(full vision eye exam for established adult patient);* **Gasoline** *(one gallon regular unleaded, national brand, including all taxes, cash price at self-service pump if available);* **Beauty Salon** *(woman's shampoo, trim, and blow-dry);* **Men's Shirt** *(cotton/polyester dress shirt, pinpoint weave, long sleeves).*
Source: The Council for Community and Economic Research, ACCRA Cost of Living Index, 2011

HOUSING

House Price Index (HPI)

Area	National Ranking[2]	Quarterly Change (%)	One-Year Change (%)	Five-Year Change (%)
MD[1]	172	-0.34	-3.14	-20.83
U.S.[3]	-	-0.10	-2.43	-19.16

Note: The HPI is a weighted repeat sales index. It measures average price changes in repeat sales or refinancings on the same properties. This information is obtained by reviewing repeat mortgage transactions on single-family properties whose mortgages have been purchased or securitized by Fannie Mae or Freddie Mac in January 1975; (1) Metropolitan Division - see Appendix B for areas included; (2) Rankings are based on annual percentage change for all metro areas containing at least 15,000 transactions over the last 10 years and ranges from 1 to 306; (3) figures based on a weighted average of Census Division estimates using a purchase only index; all figures are for the period ending December 31, 2011
Source: Federal Housing Finance Agency, House Price Index, February 23, 2012

House Price Valuations

Area	Q4 2005		Q4 2006		Q4 2007		Q4 2008		Q4 2009	
	Price ($000)	Over-valuation	Price ($000)	Over-valuation	Price ($000)	Over-valuation	Price ($000)	Over-valuation	Price ($000)	Over-valuation
MD[1]	813.4	31.8	782.1	15.4	723.8	-1.4	608.7	-18.6	604.9	-18.4

Note: Figures show the percentage of over- or under-valuation of single family homes relative to statistically normal house values (e.g. a value of 23.6 indicates that house values are 23.6% overvalued). Statistically normal house values are based on house prices, interest rates, household incomes, population densities, and any historical premiums or discounts metropolitan areas have exhibited over time; (1) Figures cover the San Francisco-San Mateo-Redwood City, CA - see Appendix B for areas included
Source: Global Insight/PNC Financial Services Group, House Prices in America: 4th Quarter 2009 Update

Median Single-Family Home Prices

Area	2009	2010	2011p	Percent Change 2010 to 2011
MSA[1]	493.3	525.6	483.4	-8.0
U.S. Average	172.1	173.1	166.2	-4.0

Note: Figures are median sales prices of existing single-family homes in thousands of dollars; (p) preliminary; n/a not available; (1) Metropolitan Statistical Area—see Appendix B for areas included
Source: National Association of Realtors, Median Sales Price of Existing Single-Family Homes for Metropolitan Areas, 4th Quarter 2011

Affordability Index of Existing Single-Family Homes

Area	2009	2010	2011p	Percent Change 2010 to 2011
MSA[1]	58.3	58.0	66.2	14.1

Note: The housing affordability index measures whether or not a typical family could qualify for a mortgage loan on a typical home. The higher the index, the greater the household purchasing power. An index of 100 is defined as the point where a median-income household has exactly enough income to qualify for the purchase of a median-priced existing single-family home, assuming a 20 percent downpayment and 25 percent of gross income devoted to mortgage principal and interest payments; (p) preliminary; n/a not available; (1) Metropolitan Statistical Area—see Appendix B for areas included
Source: National Association of Realtors, Affordability Index of Existing Single-Family Homes, 2011

Median Apartment Condo-Coop Home Prices

Area	2009	2010	2011p	Percent Change 2010 to 2011
MSA[1]	395.3	396.0	355.9	-10.1
U.S. Average	175.6	171.7	165.1	-3.8

Note: Figures are median sales prices of existing apartment condo-coop homes in thousands of dollars; (p) preliminary; n/a not available; (1) Metropolitan Statistical Area—see Appendix B for areas included
Source: National Association of Realtors, Median Sales Price of Existing Apartment Condo-Coop Homes for Metropolitan Areas, 4th Quarter 2011

Year Housing Structure Built

Area	2005 or Later	2000 -2004	1990 -1999	1980 -1989	1970 -1979	1960 -1969	1950 -1959	Before 1950	Median Year
City	2.0	3.5	4.4	5.3	7.3	7.9	9.3	60.3	1940
MSA[1]	2.7	4.6	7.7	10.8	15.4	13.9	14.7	30.2	1964
U.S.	5.0	8.6	14.0	14.1	16.3	11.3	11.2	19.6	1975

Note: Figures are percentages except for Median Year; (1) Figures cover the San Francisco-Oakland-Fremont, CA Metropolitan Statistical Area—see Appendix B for areas included
Source: U.S. Census Bureau, 2008-2010 American Community Survey 3-Year Estimates

HEALTH

Health Risk Data

Category	MSA[1] (%)	U.S. (%)
Adults who have been told they have high blood pressure[2]	n/a	28.7
Adults who have been told they have high blood cholesterol[2]	n/a	37.5
Adults who have been told they have diabetes[3]	7.1	8.7
Adults who have been told they have arthritis[2]	n/a	26.0
Adults who have been told they currently have asthma	8.2	9.1
Adults who are current smokers	9.5	17.3
Adults who are heavy drinkers[4]	6.1	5.0
Adults who are binge drinkers[5]	14.0	15.1
Adults who are overweight (BMI 25.0 - 29.9)	36.9	36.2
Adults who are obese (BMI 30.0 - 99.8)	18.2	27.5
Adults who participated in any physical activities in the past month	82.6	76.1
Adults 50+ who have ever had a sigmoidoscopy or colonoscopy	67.6	65.2
Women aged 40+ who have had a mammogram within the past two years	81.5	75.2
Men aged 40+ who have had a PSA test within the past two years	44.4	53.2
Adults aged 65+ who have had flu shot within the past year	63.1	67.5
Adults aged 18–64 who have any kind of health care coverage	89.1	82.2

Note: Data as of 2010 unless otherwise noted; n/a not available; (1) Figures cover the San Francisco-Oakland-Fremont, CA Metropolitan Statistical Area—see Appendix B for areas included; (2) Data as of 2009; (3) Figures do not include pregnancy-related, borderline, or pre-diabetes; (4) Heavy drinkers are classified as males having more than two drinks per day or females having more than one drink per day; (5) Binge drinkers are classified as males having five or more drinks on one occasion or females having four or more drinks on one occasion
Source: Centers for Disease Control and Prevention, Behaviorial Risk Factor Surveillance System, SMART: Selected Metropolitan/Micropolitan Area Risk Trends, 2009, 2010

Mortality Rates for the Top 10 Causes of Death in the U.S.

ICD-10[a] Sub-Chapter	ICD-10[a] Code	Age-Adjusted Mortality Rate[1] per 100,000 population	
		County[2]	U.S.
Malignant neoplasms	C00-C97	144.8	175.6
Ischaemic heart diseases	I20-I25	76.7	121.6
Other forms of heart disease	I30-I51	26.1	48.6
Chronic lower respiratory diseases	J40-J47	22.0	42.3
Cerebrovascular diseases	I60-I69	33.7	40.6
Organic, including symptomatic, mental disorders	F01-F09	15.9	26.7
Other degenerative diseases of the nervous system	G30-G31	18.8	24.7
Other external causes of accidental injury	W00-X59	28.9	24.4
Diabetes mellitus	E10-E14	10.7	21.7
Hypertensive diseases	I10-I15	33.9	18.2

Note: (a) ICD-10 = International Classification of Diseases 10th Revision; (1) Mortality rates are a three year average covering 2007-2009; (2) Figures cover San Francisco County
Source: Centers for Disease Control and Prevention, National Center for Health Statistics. Underlying Cause of Death 1999-2009 on CDC WONDER Online Database, released 2012. Data for year 2009 are compiled from the Multiple Cause of Death File 2009, Series 20 No. 2O, 2012, Data for year 2008 are compiled from the Multiple Cause of Death File 2008, Series 20 No. 2N, 2011, Data for year 2007 are compiled from Multiple Cause of Death File 2007, Series 20 No. 2M, 2010.

Mortality Rates for Selected Causes of Death

ICD-10[a] Sub-Chapter	ICD-10[a] Code	Age-Adjusted Mortality Rate[1] per 100,000 population County[2]	U.S.
Assault	X85-Y09	8.0	5.7
Human immunodeficiency virus (HIV) disease	B20-B24	10.3	3.3
Influenza and pneumonia	J09-J18	18.9	16.4
Intentional self-harm	X60-X84	10.8	11.5
Malnutrition	E40-E46	*0.0	0.8
Obesity and other hyperalimentation	E65-E68	1.0	1.6
Transport accidents	V01-V99	5.1	13.7
Viral hepatitis	B15-B19	3.3	2.2

Note: (a) ICD-10 = International Classification of Diseases 10th Revision; (1) Mortality rates are a three year average covering 2007-2009; (2) Figures cover San Francisco County; (*) Unreliable data as per CDC
Source: Centers for Disease Control and Prevention, National Center for Health Statistics. Underlying Cause of Death 1999-2009 on CDC WONDER Online Database, released 2012. Data for year 2009 are compiled from the Multiple Cause of Death File 2009, Series 20 No. 2O, 2012, Data for year 2008 are compiled from the Multiple Cause of Death File 2008, Series 20 No. 2N, 2011, Data for year 2007 are compiled from Multiple Cause of Death File 2007, Series 20 No. 2M, 2010.

Distribution of Physicians and Dentists

Area[1]	Dentists[2]	D.O.[3]	M.D.[4] Total	Family/ General Practice	Pediatrics	Medical Specialties	Surgical Specialties
Local (number)	814	67	3,422	225	237	1,386	676
Local (rate[5])	10.2	0.8	42.4	2.8	2.9	17.2	8.4
U.S. (rate[5])	4.5	1.9	18.3	2.5	1.4	6.8	4.1

Note: Data as of 2008 unless noted; (1) Local data covers San Francisco County; (2) Data as of 2007; (3) Doctor of Osteopathic Medicine; (4) Includes active, non-federal, patient-care, office-based Doctors of Medicine; (5) rate per 10,000 population
Source: Area Resource File (ARF). 2009-2010 Release. U.S. Department of Health and Human Services, Health Resources and Services Administration, Bureau of Health Professions, Rockville, MD, August 2010

Best Hospitals

According to *U.S. News*, the San Francisco-San Mateo-Redwood City, CA is home to one of the best hospitals in the U.S.: **UCSF Medical Center** (14 specialties). The hospital listed was highly ranked in at least one adult specialty. *U.S. News Online, "America's Best Hospitals 2011-12"*

According to *U.S. News*, the San Francisco-San Mateo-Redwood City, CA is home to one of the best children's hospitals in the U.S.: **UCSF Benioff Children's Hospital** (9 specialties). The hospital listed was highly ranked in at least one pediatric specialty. *U.S. News Online, "America's Best Children's Hospitals 2011-12"*

EDUCATION

Public School District Statistics

District Name	Schls	Pupils	Pupil/ Teacher Ratio	Minority Pupils[1] (%)	Free Lunch Eligible[2] (%)	IEP[3] (%)
San Francisco Unified	116	55,140	17.6	89.3	42.0	11.4

Note: Table includes school districts with 2,000 or more students; (1) Percentage of students that are not non-Hispanic white; (2) Percentage of students that are eligible for the free lunch program; (3) Percentage of students that have an Individualized Education Program.
Source: U.S. Department of Education, National Center for Education Statistics, Common Core of Data, Local Education Agency (School District) Universe Survey: School Year 2009-2010; U.S. Department of Education, National Center for Education Statistics, Common Core of Data, Public Elementary/Secondary School Universe Survey: School Year 2009-2010

Top Public High Schools

High School Name	Rank[1]	Score[1]	Grad. Rate[2] (%)	College[3] (%)	AP/IB/ AICE[4] (%)	SAT/ ACT[5] (%)
George Washington	497	0.092	95	91	1.9	1441

Note: (1) Public schools are ranked from 1 to 500 based on the following self-reported statistics (with their corresponding weight in the final score). Schools that had fewer than 10 graduates, as well as those that were newly founded and did not have a graduating senior class in 2010 were excluded; (2) Four-year, on-time graduation rate (25%); (3) Percent of 2010 graduates who enrolled immediately in college (25%); (4) AP/IB/AICE tests per graduate (25%); (5) Average SAT and/or ACT score (10%); Average AP/IB/AICE exam score (10%); AP/IB/AICE courses offered per graduate (5%); (6) School is unranked, but has been identified by Newsweek as one of the nation's most elite public high schools.
Source: Newsweek Online, "Top High Schools 2011"

Highest Level of Education

Area	Less than H.S.	H.S. Diploma	Some College, No Deg.	Associate Degree	Bachelors Degree	Masters Degree	Profess. School Degree	Doctorate Degree
City	14.5	14.0	14.8	5.4	31.2	12.5	5.0	2.6
MSA[1]	12.9	17.7	19.0	6.9	26.6	11.0	3.5	2.5
U.S.	14.7	28.4	21.3	7.6	17.6	7.2	1.9	1.2

Note: Figures cover persons age 25 and over; (1) Figures cover the San Francisco-Oakland-Fremont, CA Metropolitan Statistical Area—see Appendix B for areas included
Source: U.S. Census Bureau, 2008-2010 American Community Survey 3-Year Estimates

Educational Attainment by Race

Area	High School Graduate or Higher (%)					Bachelor's Degree or Higher (%)				
	Total	White	Black	Asian	Hisp.[2]	Total	White	Black	Asian	Hisp.[2]
City	85.5	93.3	87.1	73.6	73.7	51.2	63.9	23.9	38.7	28.4
MSA[1]	87.1	90.8	87.4	83.8	66.6	43.5	47.9	23.0	48.8	16.9
U.S.	85.3	87.5	81.4	85.5	61.6	28.0	29.3	17.8	50.2	13.0

Note: Figures shown cover persons 25 years old and over; (1) Figures cover the San Francisco-Oakland-Fremont, CA Metropolitan Statistical Area—see Appendix B for areas included; (2) People of Hispanic origin can be of any race
Source: U.S. Census Bureau, 2008-2010 American Community Survey 3-Year Estimates

School Enrollment by Grade and Control

Area	Preschool (%)		Kindergarten (%)		Grades 1 - 4 (%)		Grades 5 - 8 (%)		Grades 9 - 12 (%)	
	Public	Private	Public	Private	Public	Private	Public	Private	Public	Private
City	31.2	68.8	76.4	23.6	74.1	25.9	74.6	25.4	80.8	19.2
MSA[1]	39.6	60.4	84.3	15.7	85.0	15.0	85.6	14.4	87.4	12.6
U.S.	55.4	44.6	87.1	12.9	89.4	10.6	89.5	10.5	90.4	9.6

Note: Figures shown cover persons 3 years old and over; (1) Figures cover the San Francisco-Oakland-Fremont, CA Metropolitan Statistical Area—see Appendix B for areas included
Source: U.S. Census Bureau, 2008-2010 American Community Survey 3-Year Estimates

Average Salaries of Public School Classroom Teachers

Area	2010-11		2011-12		Percent Change 2010-11 to 2011-12	Percent Change 2001-02 to 2011-12
	Dollars	Rank[1]	Dollars	Rank[1]		
California	67,871	4	69,496	4	2.39	27.90
U.S. Average	55,623	-	56,643	-	1.83	26.8

Note: (1) State rank ranges from 1 to 51 where 1 indicates highest salary.
Source: National Education Association, Rankings & Estimates: Rankings of the States 2011 and Estimates of School Statistics 2012, December 2011

Higher Education

Four-Year Colleges			Two-Year Colleges			Medical Schools[1]	Law Schools[2]	Voc/ Tech[3]
Public	Private Non-profit	Private For-profit	Public	Private Non-profit	Private For-profit			
3	8	3	1	0	3	1	3	4

Note: Figures cover institutions located within the city limits and include main campuses only; (1) includes schools accredited by the Liaison Committee on Medical Education and the American Osteopathic Association's Commission on Osteopathic College Accreditation; (2) includes American Bar Association-accredited law schools; (3) includes all schools with programs that are less than 2 years.
Source: National Center for Education Statistics, Integrated Postsecondary Education System (IPEDS) Peer Analysis System, 2011-12; Association of American Medical Colleges, Member List, April 23, 2012; American Osteopathic Association, Member List, April 23, 2012; Law School Admission Council, Official Guide to ABA-Approved Law Schools Online, April 23, 2012

According to *U.S. News & World Report,* the San Francisco-San Mateo-Redwood City, CA is home to one of the best national universities in the U.S.: **University of San Francisco** (#119). The indicators used to capture academic quality fall into a number of categories: assessment by administrators at peer institutions; retention of students; faculty resources; student selectivity; financial resources; alumni giving; high school counselor ratings of colleges; and graduation rate.*U.S. News & World Report, "America's Best Colleges 2012"*

According to *U.S. News & World Report,* the San Francisco-San Mateo-Redwood City, CA is home to one of the top 50 law schools in the U.S.: **University of California (Hastings)** (#44). The rankings are based on a weighted average of 12 measures of quality: peer assessment score; assessment score by lawyers/judges; median LSAT scores; median undergrad GPA; acceptance rate; employment rates for graduates; placement success; bar passage rate; faculty resources; expenditures per student; student/faculty ratio; and library resources. *U.S. News & World Report, "America's Best Law Schools 2013"*

PRESIDENTIAL ELECTION

2008 Presidential Election Results

Area	Obama	McCain	Nader	Other
San Francisco County	84.2	13.7	1.0	1.2
U.S.	52.9	45.6	0.6	0.9

Note: Results are percentages and may not add to 100% due to rounding
Source: Dave Leip's Atlas of U.S. Presidential Elections, www.uselectionatlas.org

EMPLOYERS

Major Employers

Company Name	Industry
All Hallows Preservation	Apartment building operators
AT&T Corp.	Telephone communication, except radio
AT&T Services	Telephone communication, except radio
California Pacific Medical Center	General medical and surgical hospitals
City & County of San Francisco	General medical and surgical hospitals
City & County of San Francisco	Public welfare administration: nonoperating, govt.
Edy's Grand Ice Cream	Ice cream and ice milk
Franklin Templeton Services	Investment advice
Lawrence Berkeley National Laboratory	Supply agency, government
Lawrence Berkeley National Laboratory	Noncommercial research organizations
Lawrence Livermore National Laboratory	Noncommercial research organizations
Menlo Worldwide Forwarding	Letter delivery, private air
Oracle America	Minicomputers
Oracle Systems Corporation	Prepackaged software
Pacific Gas and Electric Company	Electric and other services combined
PACPIZZA	Pizzeria, chain
San Francisco Community College District	Colleges and universities
University of California, Berkeley	University
Veterans Health Administration	Administration of veterans' affairs
Wells Fargo Bank, National Association	National commercial banks

Note: Companies shown are located within the San Francisco-Oakland-Fremont, CA metropolitan area.
Source: Hoovers.com, data extracted April 25 2012

Best Companies to Work For

Kimpton Hotels & Restaurants; Salesforce.com, headquartered in San Francisco, are among "The 100 Best Companies to Work For." To pick the 100 Best Companies to Work For, *Fortune* partnered with the Great Place to Work Institute. Two hundred eighty firms participated in this year's survey. Two-thirds of a company's score is based on the results of the Institute's Trust Index survey, which is sent to a random sample of employees from each company. The questions related to attitudes about management's credibility, job satisfaction, and camaraderie. The other third of the scoring is based on the company's responses to the Institute's Culture Audit, which includes detailed questions about pay and benefit programs, and a series of open-ended questions about hiring practices, internal communication, training, recognition programs, and diversity efforts. Any company that is at least five years old with more than 1,000 U.S. employees is eligible. *Fortune, "The 100 Best Companies to Work For," February 6, 2012*

Salesforce.com, headquartered in San Francisco, is among the "100 Best Places to Work in IT." To qualify, companies, both public and private, had to have a minimum of 50 IT employees and were selected based on average salary and bonus increases, the percentage of IT staffers promoted, IT staff turnover rates, training and development programs, and the percentage of women and minorities in IT staff and management positions. In addition, *Computerworld* looked at retention efforts, programs for recognizing and rewarding outstanding performances, and benefits such as flextime, elder care and child care, and reimbursement for college tuition and the cost of pursuing technology certifications. *Computerworld, "100 Best Places to Work in IT 2011"*

PUBLIC SAFETY

Crime Rate

Area	All Crimes	Violent Crimes: Murder	Violent Crimes: Forcible Rape	Violent Crimes: Robbery	Violent Crimes: Aggrav. Assault	Property Crimes: Burglary	Property Crimes: Larceny -Theft	Property Crimes: Motor Vehicle Theft
City	4,655.8	5.9	16.2	388.5	291.5	556.7	2,920.3	476.8
Suburbs[1]	2,439.8	2.5	18.6	81.3	143.0	449.0	1,490.7	254.8
Metro[2]	3,453.8	4.0	17.5	221.9	211.0	498.3	2,144.8	356.4
U.S.	3,345.5	4.8	27.5	119.1	252.3	699.6	2,003.5	238.8

Note: Figures are crimes per 100,000 population; (1) All areas within the metro area that are located outside the city limits; (2) Metropolitan Division—see Appendix B for areas included
Source: FBI Uniform Crime Reports, 2010

Hate Crimes

Area	Number of Quarters Reported	Bias Motivation: Race	Bias Motivation: Religion	Bias Motivation: Sexual Orientation	Bias Motivation: Ethnicity	Bias Motivation: Disability
City	4	28	7	24	4	0

Source: Federal Bureau of Investigation, Hate Crime Statistics 2010

Identity Theft Consumer Complaints

Area	Complaints	Complaints per 100,000 Population	Rank[2]
MSA[1]	4,521	107.5	72
U.S.	279,156	90.4	-

Note: (1) Metropolitan Statistical Area—see Appendix B for areas included; (2) Rank ranges from 1 to 384 where 1 indicates greatest number of identity theft complaints per 100,000 population
Source: Federal Trade Commission, Consumer Sentinel Network Data Book for January–December 2011

Fraud and Other Consumer Complaints

Area	Complaints	Complaints per 100,000 Population	Rank[2]
MSA[1]	19,833	471.8	194
U.S.	1,533,924	496.8	-

Note: (1) Metropolitan Statistical Area—see Appendix B for areas included; (2) Rank ranges from 1 to 384 where 1 indicates greatest number of fraud and other complaints per 100,000 population
Source: Federal Trade Commission, Consumer Sentinel Network Data Book for January–December 2011

RECREATION

Culture

Dance[1]	Theatre[1]	Instrumental Music[1]	Vocal Music[1]	Series/ Festivals	Museums	Zoos and Aquariums[2]
21	25	12	12	30	30	3

Note: (1) Number of professional perfoming groups; (2) AZA-accredited
Source: The Grey House Performing Arts Directory, 2011-2012; Official Museum Directory, 2011; American Association of Museums, AAM Member Museums, April 2012; Association of Zoos & Aquariums, AZA Member Zoos & Aquariums, April 2012

Professional Sports Teams

Team Name	League
Golden State Warriors	National Basketball Association (NBA)
Oakland Athletics	Major League Baseball (MLB)
Oakland Raiders	National Football League (NFL)
San Francisco 49ers	National Football League (NFL)
San Francisco Giants	Major League Baseball (MLB)

Note: Includes teams located in the San Francisco-Oakland metro area.
Source: Original research

CLIMATE

Average and Extreme Temperatures

Temperature	Jan	Feb	Mar	Apr	May	Jun	Jul	Aug	Sep	Oct	Nov	Dec	Yr.
Extreme High (°F)	72	77	85	92	97	106	105	98	103	99	85	75	106
Average High (°F)	56	59	61	64	66	70	71	72	73	70	63	56	65
Average Temp. (°F)	49	52	53	56	58	61	63	63	64	61	55	50	57
Average Low (°F)	42	44	45	47	49	52	53	54	54	51	47	42	49
Extreme Low (°F)	26	30	31	36	39	43	44	45	41	37	31	24	24

Note: Figures cover the years 1948-1990
Source: National Climatic Data Center, International Station Meteorological Climate Summary, 9/96

Average Precipitation/Snowfall/Humidity

Precip./Humidity	Jan	Feb	Mar	Apr	May	Jun	Jul	Aug	Sep	Oct	Nov	Dec	Yr.
Avg. Precip. (in.)	4.3	3.1	2.9	1.4	0.3	0.1	Tr	Tr	0.2	1.0	2.5	3.4	19.3
Avg. Snowfall (in.)	Tr	Tr	Tr	0	0	0	0	0	0	0	0	Tr	Tr
Avg. Rel. Hum. 7am (%)	86	85	82	79	78	77	81	83	83	83	85	86	82
Avg. Rel. Hum. 4pm (%)	67	65	63	61	61	60	60	62	60	60	64	68	63

Note: Figures cover the years 1948-1990; Tr = Trace amounts (<0.05 in. of rain; <0.5 in. of snow)
Source: National Climatic Data Center, International Station Meteorological Climate Summary, 9/96

Weather Conditions

Temperature			Daytime Sky			Precipitation		
10°F & below	32°F & below	90°F & above	Clear	Partly cloudy	Cloudy	0.01 inch or more precip.	0.1 inch or more snow/ice	Thunder-storms
0	6	4	136	130	99	63	< 1	5

Note: Figures are average number of days per year and cover the years 1948-1990
Source: National Climatic Data Center, International Station Meteorological Climate Summary, 9/96

HAZARDOUS WASTE

Superfund Sites

San Francisco has one hazardous waste site on the EPA's Superfund Final National Priorities List: **Treasure Island Naval Air Station - Hunters Point Annex**. *U.S. Environmental Protection Agency, Final National Priorities List, April 17, 2012*

AIR & WATER QUALITY

Air Quality Index

Area	Percent of Days when Air Quality was...[2]					AQI Statistics[2]	
	Good	Moderate	Unhealthy for Sensitive Groups	Unhealthy	Very Unhealthy	Maximum	Median
Area[1]	78.4	21.4	0.3	0.0	0.0	115	36

Note: Air Quality Index (AQI) is an index for reporting daily air quality. EPA calculates the AQI for five major air pollutants regulated by the Clean Air Act: ground-level ozone, particle pollution (aka particulate matter), carbon monoxide, sulfur dioxide, and nitrogen dioxide. The AQI runs from 0 to 500. The higher the AQI value, the greater the level of air pollution and the greater the health concern. There are six AQI categories: "Good" AQI is between 0 and 50. Air quality is considered satisfactory; "Moderate" AQI is between 51 and 100. Air quality is acceptable; "Unhealthy for Sensitive Groups" When AQI values are between 101 and 150, members of sensitive groups may experience health effects; "Unhealthy" When AQI values are between 151 and 200 everyone may begin to experience health effects; "Very Unhealthy" AQI values between 201 and 300 trigger a health alert; "Hazardous" AQI values over 300 trigger warnings of emergency conditions (not shown); (1) Data covers San Francisco County; (2) Based on 365 days with AQI data in 2011.
Source: U.S. Environmental Protection Agency, AirData Report, 2011

Air Quality Index Pollutants

Area	Percent of Days when AQI Pollutant was...[2]					
	Carbon Monoxide	Nitrogen Dioxide	Ozone	Sulfur Dioxide	Particulate Matter 2.5	Particulate Matter 10
Area[1]	0.0	29.6	36.7	0.0	33.7	0.0

Note: The Air Quality Index (AQI) is an index for reporting daily air quality. EPA calculates the AQI for five major air pollutants regulated by the Clean Air Act: ground-level ozone, particle pollution (also known as particulate matter), carbon monoxide, sulfur dioxide, and nitrogen dioxide. The AQI runs from 0 to 500. The higher the AQI value, the greater the level of air pollution and the greater the health concern; (1) Data covers San Francisco County; (2) Based on 365 days with AQI data in 2011.
Source: U.S. Environmental Protection Agency, AirData Report, 2011

Air Quality Index Trends

Area	Trend Sites (days)								All Sites (days)
	2003	2004	2005	2006	2007	2008	2009	2010	2010
MSA[1]	15	11	7	21	6	13	7	4	4

Note: Figures are the number of days the AQI value exceeded 100 in a given year. An AQI value greater than 100 indicates that air quality would have been in the unhealthful range on that day. Data from exceptional events are included. These counts are presented in two ways. First, the counts are based on sites having an adequate record of monitoring data during the trend period (trend sites). These counts represent the relative change in the number of days with AQI values greater than 100. In the last column, the counts are based on all sites with data in the most recent year (because it is possible for a site to have data in the most recent year but not enough data to be a trend site); (1) Data covers the San Francisco-Oakland-Fremont, CA—see Appendix B for areas included
Source: U.S. Environmental Protection Agency, Air Quality Index Information, "Number of Days with Air Quality Index Values Greater than 100 at Trend Sites, 2000-2010, and at All Sites in 2010"

Maximum Air Pollutant Concentrations: Particulate Matter, Ozone, CO and Lead

	Particulate Matter 10 (ug/m^3)	Particulate Matter 2.5 Wtd AM (ug/m^3)	Particulate Matter 2.5 24-Hr (ug/m^3)	Ozone (ppm)	Carbon Monoxide (ppm)	Lead (ug/m^3)
MSA[1] Level	45	10.5	33	0.078	2	n/a
NAAQS[2]	150	15	35	0.075	9	0.15
Met NAAQS[2]	Yes	Yes	Yes	No	Yes	n/a

Note: Data from exceptional events are not included; (1) Data covers the San Francisco-Oakland-Fremont, CA—see Appendix B for areas included; (2) National Ambient Air Quality Standards; ppm = parts per million; ug/m^3 = micrograms per cubic meter; n/a not available
Concentrations: Particulate Matter 10 (coarse particulate)—highest second maximum 24-hour concentration; Particulate Matter 2.5 Wtd AM (fine particulate)—highest weighted annual mean concentration; Particulate Matter 2.5 24-Hour (fine particulate)—highest 98th percentile 24-hour concentration; Ozone—highest fourth daily maximum 8-hour concentration; Carbon Monoxide—highest second maximum non-overlapping 8-hour concentration; Lead—maximum running 3-month average
Source: U.S. Environmental Protection Agency, CBSA Factbook 2010, Air Quality Statistics by City, 2010

Maximum Air Pollutant Concentrations: Nitrogen Dioxide and Sulfur Dioxide

	Nitrogen Dioxide AM (ppb)	Nitrogen Dioxide 1-Hr (ppb)	Sulfur Dioxide AM (ppb)	Sulfur Dioxide 1-Hr (ppb)	Sulfur Dioxide 24-Hr (ppb)
MSA[1] Level	15.598	76.6	1.188	15.3	5.7
NAAQS[2]	53	100	30	75	140
Met NAAQS[2]	Yes	Yes	Yes	Yes	Yes

Note: Data from exceptional events are not included; (1) Data covers the San Francisco-Oakland-Fremont, CA—see Appendix B for areas included; (2) National Ambient Air Quality Standards; ppb = parts per billion; n/a not available

Concentrations: Nitrogen Dioxide AM—highest arithmetic mean concentration; Nitrogen Dioxide 1-Hr—highest 98th percentile 1-hour daily maximum concentration; Sulfur Dioxide AM—highest annual mean concentration; Sulfur Dioxide 1-Hr—highest 99th percentile 1-hour daily maximum concentration; Sulfur Dioxide 24-Hr—highest second maximum 24-hour concentration

Source: U.S. Environmental Protection Agency, CBSA Factbook 2010, Air Quality Statistics by City, 2010

Drinking Water

Water System Name	Pop. Served	Primary Water Source Type	Violations[1] Health Based	Violations[1] Monitoring/ Reporting
San Francisco Public Utilities	2,400,000	Purchased Surface	n/a	n/a

Note: (1) Based on violation data from January 1, 2011 to December 31, 2011 (includes unresolved violations from earlier years)

Source: U.S. Environmental Protection Agency, Office of Ground Water and Drinking Water, Safe Drinking Water Information System (based on data extracted April 18, 2012)

San Jose, California

Background

Like many cities in the valleys of northern California, San Jose is an abundant cornucopia of wine grapes and produce. Situated only seven miles from the southernmost tip of San Francisco Bay, San Jose is flanked by the Santa Cruz Mountains to the west, and the Mount Hamilton arm of the Diablo Range to the east. The Coyote and Guadalupe rivers gently cut through this landscape, carrying water only in the spring.

San Jose was founded on November 29, 1777, by Spanish colonizers, and can rightfully claim to be the oldest civic settlement in California. Like its present-day role, San Jose was established by the Spanish to be a produce and cattle supplier to the nearby communities and presidios of San Francisco and Monterey.

After U.S. troops wrested the territory of California from Mexican rule, San Jose became its state capital. At the same time, the city served as a supply base to gold prospectors.

Today, San Jose retains much of its history. As in the past, it is still a major shipping and processing center for agricultural produce. Also, San Jose produces some of the best table wines in the country. To remind its citizens of its Spanish heritage, a replica of the Mission of Santa Clara stands on the grounds of the University of Santa Clara.

Due to annexation of surrounding communities after World War II, the population of San Jose has increased more than tenfold. With the additional industries of NASA research, and electronic components and motors production to attract people to the area, San Jose is rapidly becoming a family-oriented community of housing developments and shopping malls.

During the 1990s, San Jose was home to more than half of Silicon Valley's leading semiconductor, networking, and telecommunications companies, giving it the nickname "Capital of Silicon Valley." The newly renovated downtown became headquarters for Adobe Systems, a major developer of computer software, Cisco Systems, e-Bay and Cadence Design Systems.

In the new century, San Jose suffered from the downturn in electronics and computer industries, but the city has developed numerous strategies, including economic incentives and redevelopment programs to solve unemployment and ensure that the city remains economically healthy and grows into the future.

The HP Pavilion, home of the San Jose Sharks hockey team, is one of the most active venues for events in the world, selling the most tickets to non-sporting events of any venue in the United States.

San Jose enjoys a Mediterranean, or dry summer subtropical, climate. The rain that does fall comes mostly during the months of November through March. Severe winter storms with gale winds and heavy rain occur occasionally. The summer weather is dominated by night and morning stratus clouds along with sea breezes blowing from the cold waters of the bay. During the winter months fog is common, causing difficult flying conditions. Inversions causing pollution are not common during the summer months, but become more frequent during the fall and winter.

Rankings

General Rankings

- *Men's Health Living* ranked 100 U.S. cities in terms of quality of life. San Jose was ranked #19 and received a grade of B. Criteria: number of fitness facilities; air quality; number of physicians; male/female ratio; education levels; household income; cost of living. *Men's Health Living, Spring 2008*
- San Jose was selected as one of America's best cities by *Bloomberg Businessweek.* The city ranked #23 out of 50. Criteria: number of restaurants, bars and museums per capita; number of colleges, libraries, and professional sports teams; income, poverty, unemployment, crime, and foreclosure rates; percent of population with bachelor's degrees; public school performance; park acres per capita; air quality. *BusinessWeek, "America's 50 Best Cities," September 20, 2011*
- San Jose appeared on RelocateAmerica's list of best places to live in America. The annual "Top 100 Places to Live" list recognizes the top communities as nominated by their residents & local businesses. RelocateAmerica's Research Group determines the list based on review of various data gathered for economic, employment, housing, education, industry, opportunity, environment and recreation along with feedback from area leaders and residents. *RelocateAmerica.com, "Top 100 Places to Live for 2011"*

Business/Finance Rankings

- San Jose was identified as one of the 20 strongest-performing metro areas during the recession and recovery from trough quarter through the third quarter of 2011. Criteria: percent change in employment; percentage point change in unemployment rate; percent change in gross metropolitan product; percent change in House Price Index. *Brookings Institution, MetroMonitor: Tracking Economic Recession and Recovery in America's 100 Largest Metropolitan Areas, December 2011*
- San Jose was identified as one of the "Happiest Cities to Work in 2012" by *CareerBliss.com,* an online community for career advancement. The city ranked #4 out of 50. Criteria: independent company reviews from employees all over the country on: relationship with their boss and co-workers; work environment; job resources; growth opportunities; compensation; company culture; company reputation; daily tasks; job control over work performed on a daily basis. *CareerBliss.com, "Happiest and Unhappiest Cities to Work in 2012"*
- San Jose was selected as one of the "100 Best Places to Live and Launch" in the U.S. The city ranked #66. The editors at *Fortune Small Business* ranked 296 Census-designated metro areas by business friendliness (Launching Score, % New Businesses) and lifestyle offerings (Living Score). Then they picked the town within each of the top 100 metro areas that best blends business and pleasure. *Fortune Small Business, "100 Best Places to Live and Launch 2008," April 2008*
- *American City Business Journals* ranked America's 261 largest cities in terms of their resident's wealth. San Jose ranked #15. Criteria: per capita income; median household income; percentage of households with annual incomes of $200,000 or more; median home value. *American City Business Journals, "Where the Money Is: America's Wealth Centers," August 18, 2008*
- The San Jose metro area appeared on the Milken Institute "2011 Best Performing Metros" list. Rank: #51 out of 200 large metro areas. Criteria: job growth; wage and salary growth; high-tech output growth. *Milken Institute, "2011 Best Performing Metros"*
- San Jose was identified as one of the top 10 cities with the greatest number of *Inc. 500* companies per million residents. The city ranked #7. *Inc. Magazine, September 2008*
- San Jose was ranked #1 out of 145 regions worldwide in terms of its "Knowledge Competitiveness Index." The index attempts to measure the knowledge-based development taking place throughout the world and is based on 19 measures of economic performance that indicate a region's ability to translate its knowledge capacity into economic value. *Centre for International Competitiveness, World Knowledge Competitiveness Index 2008*

- *Forbes* ranked the 200 most populous metro areas in the U.S. in terms of the "Best Places for Business and Careers." The San Jose metro area was ranked #35. Criteria: costs (business and living); job growth (past and projected); income growth; educational attainment; projected economic growth; crime; cultural and recreational opportunities; net migration patterns; number of highly ranked colleges. *Forbes, "Best Places for Business and Careers," June 2011*

Children/Family Rankings

- San Jose was selected as one of the 10 best cities to raise children in the U.S. by *KidFriendlyCities.org*. Criteria: education; environment; health; employment; crime; diversity; cost of living. *KidFriendlyCities.org, "Top Rated Kid/Family Friendly Cities 2009"*
- The San Jose metro area was selected as one of the "Best Cities for Relocating Families" by Worldwide ERC and Primacy Relocation. The 2008 study looked at nearly 50 factors important to relocating families including: recent job growth; nearby top-ranked colleges; in-state tuition for four-year public colleges; population growth since 2000; pediatricians per 100,000 population; and a Green Living index. *Worldwide ERC and Primacy Relocation, "2008 Best Cities for Relocating Families"*
- *Fit Pregnancy* magazine ranked the 50 best U.S. cities in which to have a baby. San Jose was ranked #31. Criteria: access to hospitals and doctors; affordability; birthing options; breastfeeding; child care; fertility laws/resources; maternal and infant health risk; parks/stroller friendliness; safety. *Fit Pregnancy, "The Best Cities in America to Have a Baby 2008"*

Dating/Romance Rankings

- San Jose was selected as one of the best cities for single women by *Rent.com*. The city ranked #10 of 10. Criteria: high single male-to-female ratio; lively nightlife; low divorce rate; low cost of living. *Rent.com, "Top 10 Cities for Single Women," August 19, 2011*
- San Jose appeared on *Men's Health's* list of the most sex-happy cities in America. The city ranked #81 of 100. Criteria: condom sales; birth rates; sex toy sales; rates of chlamydia, gonorrhea, and syphilis. *Men's Health, "America's Most Sex-Happy Cities," October 2010*
- *Men's Health* ranked 100 U.S. cities in terms of best (and worst) marriages. San Jose was ranked #100 (#1 = worst). Criteria: rate of failed marriages; stringency of divorce laws; percentage of population who've split; number of licensed marriage and family therapists. *Men's Health, "Splitsville, USA," May 2010*
- The San Jose metro area was selected as one of the "Best Cities for Relocating Singles" by Worldwide ERC and Primacy Relocation. The area ranked #29 out of the 100 largest metro areas in the U.S. Criteria: recent job growth; recent singles population growth; overall population growth; affordable rental housing; cost-of-living index; expanded arts and recreation opportunities; ratio of single men and single women; affordability of quality higher education (including state residency requirements); diversity index; climate; population density. *Worldwide ERC and Primacy Relocation, "2008 Best Cities for Relocating Singles"*

Education Rankings

- *Men's Health* ranked 100 U.S. cities in terms of their education levels. San Jose was ranked #19 (#1 = most educated city). Criteria: high school graduation rates; school enrollment; educational attainment; number of households who have outstanding student loans; number of households whose members have taken adult-education courses. *Men's Health, "Where School Is In: The Most and Least Educated Cities," September 12, 2011*
- San Jose was selected as one of "America's Geekiest Cities" by *Forbes.com*. The city ranked #1 of 20. Criteria: percentage of workers with jobs in science, technology, engineering and mathematics. *Forbes.com, "America's Geekiest Cities," August 5, 2011*
- San Jose was selected as one of "America's Most Literate Cities." The city ranked #32 out of the 75 largest U.S. cities. Criteria: number of booksellers; library resources; Internet resources; educational attainment; periodical publishing resources; newspaper circulation. *Central Connecticut State University, "America's Most Literate Cities 2011"*

- San Jose was identified as one of the 100 "smartest" metro areas in the U.S. The area ranked #3. Criteria: the editors rated the collective brainpower of the 100 largest metro areas in the U.S. based on their residents' educational attainment. *American City Business Journals, April 14, 2008*
- San Jose was identified as one of "America's Smartest Cities" by *The Daily Beast.* The metro area ranked #3 out of 55. The editors ranked metropolitan areas with one million or more residents on the following criteria: percentage of residents over age 25 with bachelor's or graduate degrees; non-fiction book sales; ratio of institutions of higher education; libraries per capita. *The Daily Beast, "America's Smartest Cities," October 24, 2010*
- San Jose was identified as one of America's most inventive cities by *The Daily Beast.* The city ranked #3 out of 25. The 200 largest cities in the U.S. were ranked by the number of patents (applied and approved) per capita. *The Daily Beast, "The 25 Most Inventive Cities," October 2, 2011*
- San Jose was identified as one of "America's Brainiest Bastions" by *Portfolio.com.* The metro area ranked #7 out of 200. *Portfolio.com* analyzed levels of educational attainment in the nation's 200 largest metropolitan areas. The editors established scores for five levels of educational attainment, based on relative earning power of adult workers age 25 or older. Scores were determined by comparing the median income for all workers with the median income for those workers at a specified educational level. *Portfolio.com, "America's Brainiest Bastions," December 1, 2010*
- San Jose was identified as one of "America's Smartest Cities" by *CNNMoney.com.* The area ranked #3. Criteria: percentage of residents with bachelors or graduate degrees. *CNNMoney.com, "America's Smartest Cities," October 1, 2010*
- San Jose was identified as one of America's smartest cities" by *Forbes.* The area ranked #16 out of 25. Criteria: percentage of the population age 25 and over with at least a bachelor's degree. *Forbes.com, "The Smartest Cities in America," February 8, 2008*

Environmental Rankings

- The San Jose was identified as one of America's cities with the most ENERGY STAR certified buildings. The area ranked #22 out of 25. Criteria: number of ENERGY STAR labeled buildings in 2010. *U.S. Environmental Protection Agency, "Top Cities With the Most ENERGY STAR Certified Buildings," March 15, 2011*
- The San Jose metro area was identified as one of "The Ten Biggest American Cities that are Running Out of Water" by *24/7 Wall St.* The metro area ranked #5 out of 10. *24/7 Wall St.* did an analysis of the water supply and consumption in the 30 largest metropolitan areas in the U.S. Criteria include: projected water demand as a share of available precipitation; groundwater use as a share or projected available precipitation; susceptibility to drought; projected increase in freshwater withdrawals; projected increase in summer water deficit. *24/7 Wall St., "The Ten Biggest American Cities that are Running Out of Water," November 1, 2010*
- Scarborough Research, a leading market research firm, identified the top local markets for green appliance households. The San Jose DMA (Designated Market Area) ranked in the top 16 with 38% of consumers reporting that they own an energy-efficient appliance. *Scarborough Research, March 23, 2010*
- San Jose was selected as one of 22 "Smarter Cities" for energy by the Natural Resources Defense Council. Criteria: investment in green power; energy efficiency measures; conservation. *Natural Resources Defense Council, "2010 Smarter Cities," July 19, 2010*
- *American City Business Journal* ranked 43 metropolitan areas in terms of their "greenness." The San Jose metro area ranked #18. Criteria: Forty-one metros in which *ACBJ* has business weeklies, plus Indianapolis and Cleveland, were ranked based on 20 different indicators such as adoption of green technologies, utilization of environmentally sound practices, and air and water quality. *American City Business Journals, "Green City Index," March 11, 2010*
- 100 of the largest metro areas in the U.S. were analyzed in terms of their current drought severity. The San Jose metro area ranked #48 (#1 = driest). The rankings were based on statistics such as long-term precipitation trends and patterns and the Palmer drought indices. *Sperling's BestPlaces, www.BestPlaces.net, "America's Drought-Riskiest Cities," November 2007*

- The San Jose metro area appeared in *Country Home's* "Best Green Places" report. The area ranked #45 out of 379. Criteria: official energy policies; green power; green buildings; availability of fresh, locally grown food. *Country Home, "Best Green Places," 2008*
- San Jose was highlighted as one of the 25 metro areas most polluted by short-term particle pollution (24-hour PM 2.5) in the U.S. The area ranked #24. *American Lung Association, State of the Air 2011*

Food/Drink Rankings

- San Jose was identified as one of "America's Most Caffeinated Cities" by *Bundle.com.* The city was ranked #7 out of 10. The rankings were determined by examining consumer spending at 16 widely known coffee chains during the second quarter of 2011. *Bundle.com, "America's Most Caffeinated Cities," September 19, 2011*

Health/Fitness Rankings

- The American Podiatric Medical Association and *Prevention* magazine ranked 100 American cities based on walkability. Nineteen walking criteria were evaluated including the percentage of adults who walk to work, number of parks per square mile, number of trails for walking and hiking, air pollution, use of mass transit, crime rate, pedestrian fatalities, and percentage of adults who walk for fitness. San Jose ranked #19. *Prevention, "The Best Walking Cities of 2009," May 2009; American Podiatric Medical Association, "2009 Best Fitness-Walking Cities," April 7, 2009*
- The San Jose metro area was selected as one of the worst cities for bed bugs in America by Rollins corporation, the owner of seven pest control companies, including Orkin. The area ranked #12 based on the number of bed bug treatments from January to December 2011. *Rollins, "The Top 50 U.S. Cities for Bed Bugs," March 19, 2012*
- San Jose was selected as one of the 25 fittest cities in America by *Men's Fitness Online*. It ranked #14 out of America's 50 largest cities. Criteria: fitness centers and sport stores; nutrition; sports participation; TV viewing; overweight/sedentary; junk food; air quality; geography; commute; parks and open space; city recreational facilities; access to healthcare; motivation; mayor and city initiatives; state obesity initiatives. *Men's Fitness, "The Fittest and Fattest Cities in America," March 5, 2012*
- San Jose was identified as a "2011 Asthma Capital." The area ranked #79 out of the nation's 100 largest metropolitan areas. Twelve factors were used to identify the most challenging places to live for people with asthma: estimated prevalence; self-reported prevalence; crude death rate for asthma; annual pollen score; annual air quality; public smoking laws; number of board-certified asthma specialists; school inhaler access laws; rescue medication use; controller medication use; uninsured rate; poverty rate. *Asthma and Allergy Foundation of America, "2011 Asthma Capitals"*
- San Jose was identified as a "2011 Fall Allergy Capital." The area ranked #92 out of 100. Three groups of factors were used to identify the most severe cities for people with allergies during the fall season: annual pollen levels; medicine utilization; access to board-certified allergists. *Asthma and Allergy Foundation of America, "2011 Fall Allergy Capitals"*
- San Jose was identified as a "2012 Spring Allergy Capital." The area ranked #78 out of 100. Three groups of factors were used to identify the most severe cities for people with allergies during the spring season: annual pollen levels; medicine utilization; access to board-certified allergists. *Asthma and Allergy Foundation of America, "2012 Spring Allergy Capitals"*
- *Men's Health* examined 100 major U.S. cities and selected the best and worst cities for men. San Jose ranked #4. Criteria: 35 statistical parameters of long life in the categories of health, quality of life, and fitness. *Men's Health, "The 10 Best and Worst Cities for Men 2012," January/February 2012*
- *Men's Health* examined 100 U.S. cities and selected the best and worst cities for women. San Jose was ranked among the ten best at #3. Criteria: dozens of statistical parameters of long life in the categories of health, quality of life, and fitness. *Men's Health, "The 10 Best and Worst Cities for Women 2011," January/February 2011*

- San Jose was selected as one of the least accident-prone cities in America by *Men's Health.* The city ranked #9 of 10. Criteria: workplace accident rates; traffic fatalities; emergency room visits; accidental poisonings; incidents of drowning; fires; injury-producing falls. *Men's Health, "Ranking America's Cities: Accident City, USA," October 2009*

- The San Jose metro area appeared in the 2011 Gallup-Healthways Well-Being Index. The index, based on interviews with more than 350,000 Americans, measured jobs, finances, physical health, emotional state of mind and communities. The metro area ranked #8 out of 190. Criteria: life evaluation; emotional health; work environment; physical health; healthy behaviors; basic access (basic needs optimal for a healthy life, such as access to food and medicine, having health insurance and feeling safe while walking at night). *Gallup-Healthways, "State of Well-Being 2011"*

- The San Jose metro area was identified as one of "America's Most Stressful Cities" by *Sperling's BestPlaces.* The metro area ranked #45 out of 50. Criteria: unemployment rate; suicide rate; commute time; mental health; poor rest; alcohol use; violent crime rate; property crime rate; cloudy days annually. *Sperling's BestPlaces, www.BestPlaces.net, "Stressful Cities 2012*

- *Men's Health* ranked 100 U.S. cities in terms of their activity levels. San Jose was ranked #17 (#1 = most active city). Criteria: where and how often residents exercise; percentage of households that watch more than 15 hours of cable television a week and buy more than 11 video games a year; death rate from deep-vein thrombosis, a condition linked to sitting for extended periods of time. *Men's Health, "Where Sit Happens: The Most and Least Active Cities in America," June 20, 2011*

- 50 of the largest metro areas in the U.S. were analyzed in terms of their health and fitness by the American College of Sports Medicine in their "American Fitness Index." The San Jose metro area ranked #14 (#1 = healthiest). Criteria: preventative health behaviors; levels of chronic disease; health care access; community resources and policies that support physical activity. *American College of Sports Medicine, "Health and Community Fitness Status of the 50 Largest Metropolitan Areas," August 1, 2011*

- The San Jose metro area was selected as one of "America's Most Relaxed Cities" by *Forbes.* The metro area ranked #10 out of 10. Criteria: unemployment rates; numbers of commuters that spend an hour or more in traffic on the way to work; average weekly hours people spend at work; access to health care; overall health of residents; percentage of population who exercise. *Forbes, "America's Most Relaxed Cities," November 5, 2010*

Real Estate Rankings

- The San Jose metro area was identified as one of ten places where real estate is ripe for a rebound by *Forbes.* Criteria: change in home price over the past 12 months and three years; unemployment rates; 12-month job-growth projections; population change from 2006 through 2009; new home construction rates for the third quarter of 2011 as compared to the same quarter in 2010. *Forbes.com, "Cities Where Real Estate is Ripe for a Rebound," January 12, 2012*

- San Jose was selected as one of the worst cities for renters by *Forbes.* The city ranked #3 out of 5. The 44 largest cities in the U.S. were rated on four criteria: average rent in the first quarter of 2011 and how much it changed year-over-year; vacancy rates; cost of renting versus buying. *Forbes, "Best and Worst Cities for Renters," June 20, 2011*

- San Jose was identified as one of the priciest cities to rent in the U.S. The area ranked #9 out of 10. Criteria: rent-to-income ratio. *CNBC, "Priciest Cities to Rent," March 14, 2012*

- *Fortune* ranked the 100 largest metro areas in the U.S. in terms of projected median home price change in 2010. The San Jose metro area ranked #83. *Fortune, "The 2010 Housing Outlook," December 9, 2009*

- The San Jose metro area was identified as one of the 20 least affordable housing markets in the U.S. in 2011. The area ranked #3 out of 152 markets with an affordability index of 54.1%. The index measures whether or not a typical family could qualify for a mortgage loan on a typical home. The calculation used assumes a down payment of 20 percent of the home price and a qualifying ratio of 25 percent, meaning that the monthly P&I payment cannot exceed 25 percent of a the median family monthly income. *National Association of Realtors®, Affordability Index of Existing Single-Family Homes for Metropolitan Areas, 2011*

- San Jose appeared on *ApartmentRatings.com* "Top Cities for Renters" list in 2009." The area ranked #65. Overall satisfaction ratings were ranked using thousands of user submitted scores for hundreds of apartment complexes located in the 100 most populated U.S. municipalities. *ApartmentRatings.com, "2009 Renter Satisfaction Rankings"*

- San Jose appeared on *ApartmentRatings.com* "Top College Towns & Cities" for renters list in 2011." The area ranked #63 out of 87. Overall satisfaction ratings were ranked using thousands of user submitted scores for hundreds of apartment complexes located in cities and towns that are home to the 100 largest four-year institutions in the U.S. *ApartmentRatings.com, "2011 College Town Renter Satisfaction Rankings"*

- The San Jose metro area was identified as one of the most expensive places to rent in the U.S. The area ranked #63 out of 10 markets with an average effective rent of $1,470 per month. The rental figures cover apartment properties in complexes with 40 or more units (20 or more units in California and Arizona). The figures are blended average rents, which include all unit sizes. Effective rents include free rent incentives and other landlord concessions. *Wall Street Journal Online, January 17, 2008*

- The nation's largest metro areas were analyzed in terms of the best places to buy pre-foreclosures (short sales). The San Jose metro area ranked #2 out of 10. Criteria: at least 500 pre-foreclosure sales during the fourth quarter and a short sales increase of at least five percent from a year ago. The areas selected posted the biggest discounts on the sales of pre-foreclosure properties. *RealtyTrac, "Fourth Quarter and Year-End 2011 U.S. Foreclosure Sales Report: Shifting Towards Short Sales," February 28, 2012*

- The San Jose metro area was identified as one of America's most overvalued cities in 2011 by *CNNMoney.com* based on data from Local Market Monitor. Criteria: median home prices; local interest rates; economic and population growth; construction costs; vacancies; household income. *CNNMoney.com, "America's Most Overvalued (and Undervalued) Cities," January 16, 2011*

- The San Jose metro area appeared in a *Wall Street Journal* article ranking cities by "housing stress." The metro area was ranked #9 (#1 = most stress). Criteria: fraction of mortgage-holding homeowners with a monthly housing payment in excess of 30 percent of income; percentage of people without health insurance; unemployment rate. *The Wall Street Journal, "Which Cities Face Biggest Housing Risk," October 5, 2010*

- The Center for Housing Policy ranked 210 U.S. metropolitan areas by the fair market rent for a two-bedroom unit. The San Jose metro area was ranked #9. (#1 = most expensive) with a rent of $1,438. Criteria: Fair Market Rent (FMR) in effect during the fourth quarter of 2009 based on HUD's fiscal year 2010 FMRs. *The Center for Housing Policy, "Paycheck to Paycheck: Most to Least Expensive Rental Markets in 2009"*

- The San Jose metro area was identified as one of the markets with the best expected performance in home prices over the next 12 months. *Local Market Monitor, "First Quarter Home Price Forecast for Largest US Markets," March 2, 2011*

- The San Jose metro area was identified as one of the best U.S. markets to invest in rental property" by HomeVestors and Local Market Monitor. The area ranked #96 out of 100. Criteria: risk-return premium relative to national average. *HomeVestors and Local Market Monitor, "Best 100 U.S. Markets to Invest in Rental Property," March 9, 2012*

Safety Rankings

- Symantec, the makers of Norton, in partnership with Sperling's BestPlaces, ranked the 50 largest cities in the U.S. in terms of their vulnerability to cybercrime. The city ranked #13. Criteria: number of cyberattacks and potential infections; level of Internet access; expenditures on smartphones and computer hardware/software; wireless hotspots; broadband connectivity; Internet usage; online purchases. *Symantec, "Riskiest Online Cities of 2012" February 15, 2012*

- Allstate ranked the 193 largest cities in America in terms of driver safety. San Jose ranked #136. In addition, drivers were 21.9% more likely to have had an accident compared to the national average. Allstate researchers analyzed internal property damage reported claims over a two-year period (from January 2008 to December 2009) to protect findings from external influences such as weather or road construction. A weighted average of the two-year numbers determined the annual percentages. The report defines an auto crash as any collision resulting in a property damage claim. *Allstate, "2011 Allstate America's Best Drivers Report™"*

- San Jose was selected as one of "America's Safest Cities" by *Forbes*. The city ranked #6 out of 10. Criteria: violent crime rates; traffic fatalities per 100,000 residents. The editors only considered cities with populations above 250,000. *Forbes, "America's Safest Cities," December 15, 2011*

- San Jose was identified as one of the safest large cities in America by CQ Press. All 34 cities with populations of 500,000 or more that reported crime rates in 2010 for murder, rape, robbery, aggravated assault, burglary, and motor vehicle thefts were ranked. The city ranked #4 out of the top 10. *CQ Press, City Crime Rankings 2011-2012*

- The National Insurance Crime Bureau ranked 366 metro areas in the U.S. in terms of per capita rates of vehicle theft. The San Jose metro area ranked #18 (#1 = highest rate). Criteria: number of vehicle theft offenses per 100,000 inhabitants in 2010. *National Insurance Crime Bureau, "Hot Spots," June 21, 2011*

- The San Jose metro area was identified as one of the most dangerous metro areas for pedestrians by Transportation for America. The metro area ranked #30 out of 52 metro areas with over 1 million residents. Criteria: area's population divided by the number of pedestrian fatalities in that area. *Transportation for America, "Dangerous by Design 2011"*

Seniors/Retirement Rankings

- Bankers Life and Casualty Company, in partnership with Sperling's BestPlaces, ranked the nation's 50 largest metro areas in terms of the "Best U.S. Cities for Seniors." The San Jose metro area ranked #31. Criteria: healthcare; transportation; housing; environment; economy; health and longevity; social and spiritual life; crime. *Bankers Life and Casualty Company, Center for a Secure Retirement, "Best U.S. Cities for Seniors 2011," September 2011*

Sports/Recreation Rankings

- San Jose appeared on the *Sporting News* list of the "Best Sports Cities" for 2011. The area ranked #13 out of 271 cities in the U.S. *Sporting News* takes a 12-month snapshot of each city's sports, putting a heavy premium on regular-season won-lost records (from the most recently completed season). Other criteria include: playoff berths, bowl appearances and tournament bids; championships; applicable power ratings; quality of competition; overall fan fervor (measured in part by attendance); abundance of teams (rewarding quality over quantity); stadium and arena quality; ticket availability and prices; franchise ownership; and marquee appeal of athletes. *Sporting News, "Best Sports Cities 2011," October 4, 2011*

- San Jose was chosen as a bicycle friendly community by the League of American Bicyclists. A Bicycle Friendly Community welcomes cyclists by providing safe accommodation for cycling and encouraging people to bike for transportation and recreation. There are four award levels: Platinum; Gold; Silver; and Bronze. The community achieved an award level of Bronze. *League of American Bicyclists, "Bicycle Friendly Community Master List 2011"*

- *Golf.com* and the research arm of the National Golf Foundation analyzed the 50 largest metropolitan areas in the U.S. in terms of golf. The San Jose metro area ranked #7. Criteria: weather; affordability; quality of courses; accessibility; number of courses designed by esteemed architects; availability; crowdedness. *Golf.com, November 15, 2007*

Technology Rankings

- San Jose was selected as one of the best cities for broadband by Ookla, the company behind the broadband speed testing site Speedtest.net. The city ranked #1 out of 10. Criteria: U.S. cities were ranked based on their 30-day average speeds. Only cities with more than 75,000 people connecting for more than three months were measured. *Ookla, "The Top 10 Cities With the Best Broadband," May 25, 2010*

- The San Jose metro area was selected as one of "America's Most Wired Cities" by *Forbes*. The metro area was ranked #11 out of 20. Criteria: percentage of Internet users with high-speed access; number of companies providing high-speed Internet; number of public wireless hot spots. *Forbes, "America's Most Wired Cities," March 2, 2010*
- The San Jose metro area was selected as one of "America's Most Innovative Cities" by *Forbes*. The metro area was ranked #1 out of 20. Criteria: patents per capita; venture capital investment per capita; ratio of high-tech, science and "creative" jobs. *Forbes, "America's Most Innovative Cities," May 24, 2010*
- The San Jose metro area was identified as one of the "Top 14 Nano Metros" in the U.S. by the Project on Emerging Nanotechnologies. The metro area is home to 46 companies, universities, government laboratories and/or organizations working in nanotechnology. *Project on Emerging Nanotechnologies, "Nano Metros 2009"*

Transportation Rankings

- San Jose was identified as one of America's worst cities for speed traps by the National Motorists Association. The city ranked #22 out of 25. Criteria: speed trap locations per 100,000 residents. *National Motorists Association, September 2011*
- The San Jose metro area was identified as one of the best U.S. cities to live in without a car by *24/7 Wall St.* The area ranked #6 out of 10. Criteria: percentage of neighborhoods covered by public transit; frequency of service for those neighborhoods; share of jobs reachable within 90 minutes or less by public transit; how accessible amenities are for residents on foot; percentage of commuters who bike to work. The 100 largest metropolitan areas in the U.S. were examined. *24/7 Wall St., "The Best Cities to Live in Car-Free," November 28, 2011*
- The San Jose metro area appeared on *Forbes* list of the best and worst cities for commuters. The metro area ranked #36 out of 60 (#1 is best). Criteria: travel time; road congestion; travel delays. *Forbes.com, "Best and Worst Cities for Commuters," February 16, 2010*

Women/Minorities Rankings

- *Women's Health* examined U.S. cities and identified the 100 best cities for women. San Jose was ranked #2. Criteria: 30 categories were examined from obesity and breast cancer rates to commuting times and hours spent working out. *Women's Health, "Best Cities for Women 2012"*
- San Jose was ranked #9 out of 100 metro areas in *SELF Magazine's* ranking of America's healthiest places for women." A panel of experts came up with more than 50 criteria including death and disease rates, environmental indicators, community resources, and lifestyle habits. *SELF Magazine, "Secrets of America's Healthiest Women," December 2008*
- San Jose was selected as one of the 25 healthiest cities for Latinas by *Latina Magazine.* The city ranked #12. Criteria: U.S. cities with populations over 500,000 residents were evaluated on the following criteria: percentage of 18-34 year-olds per city; Latino college graduation rates; number of colleges and universities; affordability; housing costs; income growth over time; average salary; percentage of singles; climate; safety; how the city's diversity compares to the national average; opportunities for minority entrepreneurs. *Latina Magazine, "Top 15 U.S. Cities for Young Latinos to Live In," August 19, 2011*
- The San Jose metro area appeared on *Forbes'* list of the "Best Cities for Minority Entrepreneurs." The area ranked #12 out of 10. Criteria: 52 metropolitan statistical areas were examined. For each ethnicity (African Americans, Asians and Hispanics), the editors measured housing affordability, population growth, income growth, and entrepreneurship (per capita self-employment). *Forbes, "Best Cities for Minority Entrepreneurs," March 23, 2011*

Miscellaneous Rankings

- *Men's Health* ranked 100 U.S. cities by their level of sadness. San Jose was ranked #15 (#1 = saddest city). Criteria: suicide rates; unemployment rates; percentage of households that use antidepressants; percent of population who report feeling blue all or most of the time. *Men's Health, "Frown Towns," November 28, 2011*

- The San Jose metro area was selected as one of "America's Greediest Cities" by *Forbes*. The area was ranked #1 out of 10. Criteria: number of Forbes 400 (*Forbes* annual list of the richest Americans) members per capita. *Forbes, "America's Greediest Cities," December 7, 2007*
- The San Jose metro area appeared in *AutoMD.com's* ranking of the "Best and Worst Cities for Auto Repair." The metro area ranked #39 (#1 is best). The 50 most-populated metro areas in the U.S. were ranked on three critical factors: repair affordability; price disparity range; shop integrity factor. *AutoMD.com, "Advocacy for Repair Shop Fairness Report," February 24, 2010*
- San Jose was identified as one of "America's Vainest Cities" by *Forbes.com.* The city ranked #3. Criteria: highest number of cosmetic surgeons per 100,000 people in America's 50 largest cities. *Forbes.com, "America's Vainest Cities," November 29, 2007*

Business Environment

CITY FINANCES

City Government Finances

Component	2009 ($000)	2009 ($ per capita)
Total Revenues	1,090,956	1,161
Total Expenditures	2,291,763	2,438
Debt Outstanding	5,404,694	5,750
Cash and Securities[1]	6,127,932	6,520

Note: (1) Cash and security holdings of a government at the close of its fiscal year, including those of its dependent agencies, utilities, and liquor stores.
Source: U.S Census Bureau, State & Local Government Finances 2009

City Government Revenue by Source

Source	2009 ($000)	2009 ($ per capita)
General Revenue		
From Federal Government	64,128	68
From State Government	68,090	72
From Local Governments	38,333	41
Taxes		
Property	501,122	533
Sales and Gross Receipts	240,728	256
Personal Income	0	0
Corporate Income	0	0
Motor Vehicle License	0	0
Other Taxes	94,736	101
Current Charges	592,506	630
Liquor Store	0	0
Utility	25,770	27
Employee Retirement	-706,823	-752

Source: U.S Census Bureau, State & Local Government Finances 2009

City Government Expenditures by Function

Function	2009 ($000)	2009 ($ per capita)	2009 (%)
General Direct Expenditures			
Air Transportation	397,631	423	17.4
Corrections	0	0	0.0
Education	0	0	0.0
Employment Security Administration	0	0	0.0
Financial Administration	86,737	92	3.8
Fire Protection	152,919	163	6.7
General Public Buildings	0	0	0.0
Governmental Administration, Other	40,326	43	1.8
Health	11,477	12	0.5
Highways	135,925	145	5.9
Hospitals	0	0	0.0
Housing and Community Development	91,261	97	4.0
Interest on General Debt	261,748	278	11.4
Judicial and Legal	0	0	0.0
Libraries	63,013	67	2.7
Parking	10,109	11	0.4
Parks and Recreation	175,608	187	7.7
Police Protection	302,220	322	13.2
Public Welfare	0	0	0.0
Sewerage	124,193	132	5.4
Solid Waste Management	107,298	114	4.7
Veterans' Services	0	0	0.0
Liquor Store	0	0	0.0
Utility	27,130	29	1.2
Employee Retirement	167,645	178	7.3

Source: U.S Census Bureau, State & Local Government Finances 2009

Municipal Bond Ratings

Area	Moody's	S&P	Fitch
City	Aa1	AAA	AAA

Rating Systems (shown in declining order of credit quality): Moody's– Aaa, Aa, A, Baa, Ba, B, Caa, Ca, C (numerical modifiers 1, 2, and 3 are added to letter-rating); S&P– AAA, AA, A, BBB, BB, B, CCC, CC, C; Fitch– AAA, AA, A, BBB, BB, B, CCC, CC, C. Ratings may be modified by the addition of a plus or minus sign to show relative standing within the major rating categories.
Notes: n/a Not Available; w/d Withdrawn (1) Not Reviewed; (2) Issuer Rating/No General Obligation; (3) Standard and Poor's Issue Credit Rating (ICR) is a current opinion of an obliger with respect to a specific financial obligation, a specific class of financial obligations, or a specific financial program.
Source: U.S. Census Bureau, 2012 Statistical Abstract, Bond Ratings for City Governments by Largest Cities: 2010

DEMOGRAPHICS

Population Growth

Area	1990 Census	2000 Census	2010 Census	Population Growth (%)	
				1990-2000	2000-2010
City	784,324	894,943	945,942	14.1	5.7
MSA[1]	1,534,280	1,735,819	1,836,911	13.1	5.8
U.S.	248,709,873	281,421,906	308,745,538	13.2	9.7

Note: (1) Figures cover the San Jose-Sunnyvale-Santa Clara, CA Metropolitan Statistical Area—see Appendix B for areas included
Source: U.S. Census Bureau, 2010 Census

Household Size

Area	Persons in Household (%)							Average Household Size
	One	Two	Three	Four	Five	Six	Seven or More	
City	19.7	27.0	17.7	17.3	8.8	4.4	5.2	3.09
MSA[1]	21.6	28.9	17.7	16.9	7.7	3.6	3.7	2.91
U.S.	26.7	32.8	16.1	13.4	6.5	2.6	1.9	2.58

Note: (1) Figures cover the San Jose-Sunnyvale-Santa Clara, CA Metropolitan Statistical Area—see Appendix B for areas included
Source: U.S. Census Bureau, 2010 Census

Race

Area	White Alone[2] (%)	Black Alone[2] (%)	Asian Alone[2] (%)	AIAN[3] Alone[2] (%)	NHOPI[4] Alone[2] (%)	Other Race Alone[2] (%)	Two or More Races (%)
City	42.8	3.2	32.0	0.9	0.4	15.7	5.0
MSA[1]	47.5	2.6	31.1	0.8	0.4	12.8	4.9
U.S.	72.4	12.6	4.8	0.9	0.2	6.2	2.9

Note: (1) Figures cover the San Jose-Sunnyvale-Santa Clara, CA Metropolitan Statistical Area—see Appendix B for areas included; (2) Alone is defined as not being in combination with one or more other races; (3) American Indian and Alaska Native; (4) Native Hawaiian and Other Pacific Islander
Source: U.S. Census Bureau, 2010 Census

Hispanic or Latino Origin

Area	Hispanic or Latino (%)	Mexican (%)	Puerto Rican (%)	Cuban (%)	Other Hispanic or Latino (%)
City	33.2	28.4	0.5	0.1	4.1
MSA[1]	27.8	23.4	0.4	0.1	3.9
U.S.	16.3	10.3	1.5	0.6	4.0

Note: Persons of Hispanic or Latino origin can be of any race; (1) Figures cover the San Jose-Sunnyvale-Santa Clara, CA Metropolitan Statistical Area—see Appendix B for areas included
Source: U.S. Census Bureau, 2010 Census

Segregation

Type	Segregation Indices[1]				Percent Change		
	1990	2000	2010	2010 Rank[2]	1990-2000	1990-2010	2000-2010
Black/White	43.2	41.6	40.9	89	-1.7	-2.4	-0.7
Asian/White	38.8	43.4	45.0	25	4.6	6.1	1.6
Hispanic/White	47.9	50.7	47.6	36	2.9	-0.2	-3.1

Note: Figures are based on an analysis of 1990, 2000, and 2010 Census Decennial Census tract data by William H. Frey, Brookings Institution and the University of Michigan Social Science Data Analysis Network. In this analysis all racial groups (whites, blacks, and asians) are non-Hispanic members of those races. Hispanics are shown as a separate category; All figures cover the Metropolitan Statistical Area (see Appendix B for areas included); (1) Segregation Indices are Dissimilarity Indices that measure the degree to which the minority group is distributed differently than whites across census tracts. They range from 0 (complete integration) to 100 (complete segregation) where the value indicates the percentage of the minority group that needs to move to be distributed exactly like whites; (2) Ranges from 1 (most segregated) to 102 (least segregated); n/a not available.
Source: www.CensusScope.org

Ancestry

Area	German	Irish	English	American	Italian	Polish	French[2]	Scottish	Dutch
City	6.7	4.8	4.5	1.1	4.4	0.9	1.5	0.9	0.8
MSA[1]	8.1	6.1	5.9	1.2	4.7	1.2	1.9	1.4	1.0
U.S.	16.1	11.6	8.8	6.1	5.7	3.2	3.0	1.9	1.6

Note: Figures are the percentage of the total population reporting a particular ancestry. The nine most commonly reported ancestries in the U.S. are shown. Figures include multiple ancestries (e.g. if a person reported being Irish and Italian, they were included in both columns); (1) Figures cover the San Jose-Sunnyvale-Santa Clara, CA Metropolitan Statistical Area—see Appendix B for areas included; (2) Excludes Basque
Source: U.S. Census Bureau, 2008-2010 American Community Survey 3-Year Estimates

Foreign-Born Population

Area	Percent of Population Born in								
	Any Foreign Country	Mexico	Asia	Europe	Carribean	South America	Central America[2]	Africa	Canada
City	38.5	10.7	22.8	2.0	0.1	0.6	1.1	0.5	0.4
MSA[1]	36.5	8.6	22.2	2.8	0.1	0.7	1.0	0.5	0.6
U.S.	12.8	3.8	3.6	1.6	1.2	0.9	1.0	0.5	0.3

Note: (1) Figures cover the San Jose-Sunnyvale-Santa Clara, CA Metropolitan Statistical Area—see Appendix B for areas included; (2) Excludes Mexico.
Source: U.S. Census Bureau, 2008-2010 American Community Survey 3-Year Estimates

Marital Status

Area	Never Married	Now Married[2]	Separated	Widowed	Divorced
City	34.5	50.4	1.7	4.9	8.5
MSA[1]	32.5	52.7	1.6	4.8	8.4
U.S.	31.6	49.6	2.2	6.1	10.7

Note: Figures are percentages and cover the population 15 years of age and older; (1) Figures cover the San Jose-Sunnyvale-Santa Clara, CA Metropolitan Statistical Area—see Appendix B for areas included; (2) Excludes separated
Source: U.S. Census Bureau, 2008-2010 American Community Survey 3-Year Estimates

Age

Area	Percent of Population							Median Age
	Under Age 5	Age 5 to 17	Age 18 to 34	Age 35 to 49	Age 50 to 64	Age 65 to 79	80 Years and Over	
City	7.3	17.6	24.8	23.4	16.9	7.5	2.6	35.2
MSA[1]	7.0	17.3	23.9	23.3	17.5	8.0	3.1	36.1
U.S.	6.5	17.5	23.2	20.7	19.0	9.4	3.6	37.2

Note: (1) Figures cover the San Jose-Sunnyvale-Santa Clara, CA Metropolitan Statistical Area—see Appendix B for areas included
Source: U.S. Census Bureau, 2010 Census

Male/Female Ratio

Area	Males	Females	Males per 100 Females
City	475,668	470,274	101.1
MSA[1]	921,480	915,431	100.7
U.S.	151,781,326	156,964,212	96.7

Note: (1) Figures cover the San Jose-Sunnyvale-Santa Clara, CA Metropolitan Statistical Area—see Appendix B for areas included
Source: U.S. Census Bureau, 2010 Census

Religious Groups

Area	Catholic	Baptist	Non-Den.	Methodist[2]	Lutheran	LDS[3]	Pente-costal	Presby-terian[4]	Muslim[5]	Judaism
MSA[1]	26.0	1.4	4.3	1.1	0.6	1.4	1.2	0.7	0.7	1.0
U.S.	19.1	9.3	4.0	4.0	2.3	2.0	1.9	1.6	0.8	0.7

Note: Figures are the number of adherents as a percentage of the total population; (1) Figures cover the San Jose-Sunnyvale-Santa Clara, CA Metropolitan Statistical Area—see Appendix B for areas included; (2) Methodist/Pietist; (3) Latter Day Saints; (4) Reformed; (5) Figures are estimates
Source: Association of Statisticians of American Religious Bodies, 2010 U.S. Religion Census: Religious Congregations & Membership Study

ECONOMY

Gross Metropolitan Product

Area	2007	2008	2009	2010	2010 Rank[2]
MSA[1]	148.6	150.8	144.4	151.6	18

Note: Figures are in billions of dollars; (1) Figures cover the San Jose-Sunnyvale-Santa Clara, CA Metropolitan Statistical Area—see Appendix B for areas included; (2) Rank ranges from 1 to 363
Source: The United States Conference of Mayors, "U.S. Metro Economies: GMP and Employment Forecasts," June 2011

Economic Growth

Area	2007-2009 (%)	2010 (%)	2011 (%)	Rank[2]
MSA[1]	-1.6	3.7	3.9	207
U.S.	-1.3	2.9	2.5	–

Note: Figures are real Gross Metropolitan Product growth rates and represent annual average percent change; (1) Figures cover the San Jose-Sunnyvale-Santa Clara, CA Metropolitan Statistical Area—see Appendix B for areas included; (2) Rank ranges from 1 to 363
Source: The United States Conference of Mayors, "U.S. Metro Economies: GMP and Employment Forecasts," June 2011

Metropolitan Area Exports

Area	2005	2006	2007	2008	2009	2010	2010 Rank[2]
MSA[1]	25,842.5	28,171.3	28,209.5	27,048.6	21,405.8	26,333.0	8

Note: Figures are in millions of dollars; (1) Figures cover the San Jose-Sunnyvale-Santa Clara, CA Metropolitan Statistical Area—see Appendix B for areas included; (2) Rank ranges from 1 to 369
Source: U.S. Department of Commerce, International Trade Administration, Office of Trade & Industry Information, Manufacturing & Services, data extracted April 2, 2012

INCOME

Income

Area	Per Capita ($)	Median Household ($)	Average Household ($)
City	32,237	78,149	97,994
MSA[1]	38,679	85,799	111,612
U.S.	26,942	51,222	70,116

Note: (1) Figures cover the San Jose-Sunnyvale-Santa Clara, CA Metropolitan Statistical Area—see Appendix B for areas included
Source: U.S. Census Bureau, 2008-2010 American Community Survey 3-Year Estimates

Household Income Distribution

Area	Percent of Households Earning							
	Under $15,000	$15,000 -24,999	$25,000 -34,999	$35,000 -49,999	$50,000 -74,999	$75,000 -99,000	$100,000 -149,999	$150,000 and up
City	8.0	7.0	6.6	10.7	15.6	13.3	18.9	19.8
MSA[1]	7.2	6.4	6.0	9.5	14.6	12.7	19.4	24.2
U.S.	13.0	11.0	10.6	14.2	18.5	12.1	12.2	8.4

Note: (1) Figures cover the San Jose-Sunnyvale-Santa Clara, CA Metropolitan Statistical Area—see Appendix B for areas included
Source: U.S. Census Bureau, 2008-2010 American Community Survey 3-Year Estimates

Poverty Rate

Area	All Ages	Under 18 Years Old	18 to 64 Years Old	65 Years and Over
City	11.5	15.6	10.4	8.4
MSA[1]	9.4	12.0	8.7	7.5
U.S.	14.4	20.1	13.1	9.4

Note: Figures are percentage of people whose income during the past 12 months was below the poverty level; (1) Figures cover the San Jose-Sunnyvale-Santa Clara, CA Metropolitan Statistical Area—see Appendix B for areas included
Source: U.S. Census Bureau, 2008-2010 American Community Survey 3-Year Estimates

Personal Bankruptcy Filing Rate

Area	2006	2007	2008	2009	2010	2011
Santa Clara County	0.96	1.37	2.36	3.99	4.91	4.49
U.S.	2.00	2.73	3.53	4.61	4.97	4.37

Note: Numbers are per 1,000 population and include Chapter 7 and Chapter 13 filings
Source: Federal Deposit Insurance Corporation, Regional Economic Conditions, March 9, 2012

EMPLOYMENT

Labor Force and Employment

Area	Civilian Labor Force			Workers Employed		
	Dec. 2010	Dec. 2011	% Chg.	Dec. 2010	Dec. 2011	% Chg.
City	458,015	466,747	1.9	405,371	421,559	4.0
MSA[1]	897,548	915,977	2.1	802,344	834,386	4.0
U.S.	153,156,000	153,373,000	0.1	139,159,000	140,681,000	1.1

Note: Data is not seasonally adjusted and covers workers 16 years of age and older; (1) Metropolitan Statistical Area—see Appendix B for areas included
Source: Bureau of Labor Statistics, http://stats.bls.gov

Unemployment Rate

Area	2011											
	Jan.	Feb.	Mar.	Apr.	May	Jun.	Jul.	Aug.	Sep.	Oct.	Nov.	Dec.
City	11.7	11.4	11.4	11.0	10.8	11.4	11.4	11.0	10.7	10.5	10.1	9.7
MSA[1]	10.8	10.5	10.6	10.1	9.9	10.4	10.4	10.0	9.6	9.5	9.2	8.9
U.S.	9.8	9.5	9.2	8.7	8.7	9.3	9.3	9.1	8.8	8.5	8.2	8.3

Note: Data is not seasonally adjusted and covers workers 16 years of age and older; All figures are percentages; (1) Metropolitan Statistical Area—see Appendix B for areas included
Source: Bureau of Labor Statistics, http://stats.bls.gov

Projected Unemployment Rate

Area	2010 (%)	2011 (%)	2012 (%)	2013 (%)
MSA[1]	11.3	9.7	9.1	8.2

Note: (1) Metropolitan Statistical Area—see Appendix B for areas included
Source: The United States Conference of Mayors, "U.S. Metro Economies: GMP and Employment Forecasts," June 2011

Employment by Occupation

Occupation Classification	City (%)	MSA[1] (%)	U.S. (%)
Management, Business, Science, and Arts	42.5	48.8	35.6
Natural Resources, Construction, and Maintenance	7.8	7.0	9.5
Production, Transportation, and Material Moving	10.2	8.4	12.1
Sales and Office	22.9	21.5	25.2
Service	16.6	14.3	17.6

Note: Figures cover employed civilians 16 years of age and older; (1) Figures cover the San Jose-Sunnyvale-Santa Clara, CA Metropolitan Statistical Area—see Appendix B for areas included
Source: U.S. Census Bureau, 2008-2010 American Community Survey 3-Year Estimates

Employment by Industry

Sector	MSA[1] Number of Employees	MSA[1] Percent of Total	U.S. Percent of Total
Construction	32,100	3.6	4.1
Education and Health Services	121,900	13.6	15.2
Financial Activities	32,500	3.6	5.8
Government	94,200	10.5	16.8
Information	51,200	5.7	2.0
Leisure and Hospitality	76,500	8.5	9.9
Manufacturing	157,900	17.6	8.9
Mining and Logging	200	<0.1	0.6
Other Services	24,300	2.7	4.0
Professional and Business Services	173,800	19.4	13.3
Retail Trade	85,100	9.5	11.5
Transportation and Utilities	12,400	1.4	3.8
Wholesale Trade	35,600	4.0	4.2

Note: Figures cover non-farm employment as of December 2011 and are not seasonally adjusted; (1) Metropolitan Statistical Area—see Appendix B for areas included
Source: Bureau of Labor Statistics, http://stats.bls.gov

Occupations with Greatest Projected Employment Growth: 2008 – 2018

Occupation[1]	2008 Employment	2018 Projected Employment	Numeric Employment Change	Percent Employment Change
Personal and Home Care Aides	346,500	504,700	158,200	45.7
Registered Nurses	236,400	297,200	60,800	25.7
Retail Salespersons	499,400	559,100	59,700	12.0
Combined Food Preparation and Serving Workers, Including Fast Food	260,600	308,800	48,200	18.5
Elementary School Teachers, Except Special Education	197,500	233,400	35,900	18.2
Office Clerks, General	372,500	407,400	34,900	9.4
Customer Service Representatives	202,200	236,600	34,400	17.0
Waiters and Waitresses	245,600	279,900	34,300	14.0
Stock Clerks and Order Fillers	207,700	237,100	29,400	14.2
Postsecondary Teachers	168,000	196,100	28,100	16.7

Note: Projections cover California; (1) Sorted by numeric employment change
Source: www.projectionscentral.com, State Occupational Projections, 2008–2018 Long-Term Projections

Fastest Growing Occupations: 2008 – 2018

Occupation[1]	2008 Employment	2018 Projected Employment	Numeric Employment Change	Percent Employment Change
Biomedical Engineers	3,100	5,600	2,500	80.6
Network Systems and Data Communications Analysts	35,000	52,600	17,600	50.3
Biochemists and Biophysicists	4,800	7,100	2,300	47.9
Medical Scientists, Except Epidemiologists	26,200	38,500	12,300	46.9
Personal and Home Care Aides	346,500	504,700	158,200	45.7
Home Health Aides	54,300	78,000	23,700	43.6
Physician Assistants	8,100	11,500	3,400	42.0
Separating, Filtering, Clarifying, Precipitating, and Still Machine Setters, Operators, and Te	7,300	10,200	2,900	39.7
Physical Therapist Aides	5,900	8,100	2,200	37.3
Electrical and Electronics Repairers, Powerhouse, Substation, and Relay	1,100	1,500	400	36.4

Note: Projections cover California; (1) Sorted by percent employment change and excludes occupations with numeric employment change less than 100
Source: www.projectionscentral.com, State Occupational Projections, 2008–2018 Long-Term Projections

Average Wages

Occupation	$/Hr.	Occupation	$/Hr.
Accountants and Auditors	41.15	Maids and Housekeeping Cleaners	11.63
Automotive Mechanics	24.15	Maintenance and Repair Workers	23.10
Bookkeepers	22.09	Marketing Managers	77.50
Carpenters	29.61	Nuclear Medicine Technologists	53.97
Cashiers	12.05	Nurses, Licensed Practical	27.41
Clerks, General Office	17.82	Nurses, Registered	56.53
Clerks, Receptionists/Information	15.92	Nursing Aides/Orderlies/Attendants	16.97
Clerks, Shipping/Receiving	16.65	Packers and Packagers, Hand	10.41
Computer Programmers	47.87	Physical Therapists	42.78
Computer Support Specialists	35.27	Postal Service Mail Carriers	26.07
Computer Systems Analysts	47.91	Real Estate Brokers	58.81
Cooks, Restaurant	11.70	Retail Salespersons	12.12
Dentists	67.81	Sales Reps., Exc. Tech./Scientific	36.81
Electrical Engineers	53.77	Sales Reps., Tech./Scientific	53.90
Electricians	35.14	Secretaries, Exc. Legal/Med./Exec.	19.87
Financial Managers	72.63	Security Guards	15.84
First-Line Supervisors/Managers, Sales	20.10	Surgeons	116.76
Food Preparation Workers	10.10	Teacher Assistants	14.90
General and Operations Managers	72.59	Teachers, Elementary School	29.80
Hairdressers/Cosmetologists	11.50	Teachers, Secondary School	35.00
Internists	69.01	Telemarketers	20.43
Janitors and Cleaners	13.30	Truck Drivers, Heavy/Tractor-Trailer	19.47
Landscaping/Groundskeeping Workers	15.04	Truck Drivers, Light/Delivery Svcs.	17.06
Lawyers	89.96	Waiters and Waitresses	10.45

Note: Wage data covers the San Jose-Sunnyvale-Santa Clara, CA Metropolitan Statistical Area—see Appendix B for areas included. Hourly wages for elementary/secondary school teachers and teacher assistants were calculated by the editors from annual wage data assuming a 40 hour work week; n/a not available.
Source: Bureau of Labor Statistics, Metro Area Occupational Employment and Wage Estimates, May 2011

RESIDENTIAL REAL ESTATE

Building Permits

Area	Single-Family			Multi-Family			Total		
	2010	2011	Pct. Chg.	2010	2011	Pct. Chg.	2010	2011	Pct. Chg.
City	74	83	12.2	2,348	962	-59.0	2,422	1,045	-56.9
MSA[1]	861	1,002	16.4	3,318	2,095	-36.9	4,179	3,097	-25.9
U.S.	447,311	418,498	-6.4	157,299	205,563	30.7	604,610	624,061	3.2

Note: (1) Metropolitan Statistical Area—see Appendix B for areas included; figures represent new, privately-owned housing units authorized (unadjusted data); All permit data are based on estimates with imputation.
Source: U.S. Census Bureau, Manufacturing, Mining, and Construction Statistics, Building Permits, 2010, 2011

Homeownership Rate

Area	2005 (%)	2006 (%)	2007 (%)	2008 (%)	2009 (%)	2010 (%)	2011 (%)
MSA[1]	59.2	59.4	57.6	54.6	57.2	58.9	60.4
U.S.	68.9	68.8	68.1	67.8	67.4	66.9	66.1

Note: (1) Metropolitan Statistical Area—see Appendix B for areas included
Source: U.S. Census Bureau, Housing Vacancies and Homeownership Annual Statistics: 2011

Housing Vacancy Rates

Area	Gross Vacancy Rate[2] (%)			Year-Round Vacancy Rate[3] (%)			Rental Vacancy Rate[4] (%)			Homeowner Vacancy Rate[5] (%)		
	2009	2010	2011	2009	2010	2011	2009	2010	2011	2009	2010	2011
MSA[1]	6.3	6.4	5.3	6.3	6.4	5.3	7.7	8.2	4.8	1.4	0.9	0.9
U.S.	14.5	14.3	14.2	11.3	11.3	11.1	10.6	10.2	9.5	2.6	2.6	2.5

Note: (1) Metropolitan Statistical Area—see Appendix B for areas included; (2) The percentage of the total housing inventory that is vacant; (3) The percentage of the housing inventory (excluding seasonal units) that is year-round vacant; (4) The percentage of rental inventory that is vacant for rent; (5) The percentage of homeowner inventory that is vacant for sale
Source: U.S. Census Bureau, Housing Vacancies and Homeownership Annual Statistics: 2011

TAXES

State Corporate Income Tax Rates

State	Tax Rate (%)	Income Brackets ($)	Num. of Brackets	Financial Institution Tax Rate (%)[a]	Federal Income Tax Ded.
California	8.84 (c)	Flat rate	1	10.84 (c)	No

Note: Tax rates as of January 1, 2012; (a) Rates listed are the corporate income tax rate applied to financial institutions or excise taxes based on income. Some states have other taxes based upon the value of deposits or shares; (c) The minimum corporation franchise tax in California is $800. The additional alternative minimum tax is levied at a 6.65% rate.
Source: Federation of Tax Administrators, "State Corporate Income Tax Rates, 2012"

State Individual Income Tax Rates

State	Tax Rate (%)	Income Brackets ($)	Num. of Brackets	Personal Exempt. ($)[1]		Fed. Inc. Tax Ded.
				Single	Dependents	
California (a)	1.0 - 9.3 (f)	7,316 (b) - 48,029 (b)	6	102 (c)	315 (c)	No

Note: Tax rates as of January 1, 2012; Local- and county-level taxes are not included; n/a not applicable; (1) Married joint filers generally receive double the single exemption; (a) 17 states have statutory provision for automatically adjusting to the rate of inflation the dollar values of the income tax brackets, standard deductions, and/or personal exemptions. Massachusetts, Michigan, and Nebraska index the personal exemptiononly. Oregon does not index the income brackets for $125,000 and over. Because the inflation-adjustments for 2012 are not yet available in some cases, the table may report the 2011 amounts; (b) For joint returns, taxes are twice the tax on half the couple's income; (c) The personal exemption takes the form of a tax credit instead of a deduction; (f) California imposes an additional 1% tax on taxable income over $1 million, making the maximum rate 10.3% over $1 million.
Source: Federation of Tax Administrators, "State Individual Income Tax Rates, 2012"

Various State and Local Tax Rates

State	State and Local Sales and Use (%)	State Sales and Use (%)	Gasoline[1] (¢/gal.)	Cigarette[2] ($/pack)	Spirits[3] ($/gal.)	Wine[4] ($/gal.)	Beer[5] ($/gal.)
California	8.25	7.25 (b)	48.6	0.87	3.30	0.20	0.20

Note: All tax rates as of January 1, 2012 except beer, wine and spirits (September 1, 2011); (1) The American Petroleum Institute has developed a methodology for determining the average tax rate on a gallon of fuel. Rates may include any of the following: excise taxes, environmental fees, storage tank fees, other fees or taxes, general sales tax, and local taxes. In states where gasoline is subject to the general sales tax, or where the fuel tax is based on the average sale price, the average rate determined by API is sensitive to changes in the price of gasoline. States that fully or partially apply general sales taxes to gasoline: CA, CO, GA, IL, IN, MI, NY; (2) The federal excise tax of $1.0066 per pack and local taxes are not included; (3) Rates are those applicable to off-premise sales of 40% alcohol by volume (a.b.v.) distilled spirits in 750ml containers. Local excise taxes are excluded; (4) Rates are those applicable to off-premise sales of 11% a.b.v. non-carbonated wine in 750ml containers; (5) Rates are those applicable to off-premise sales of 4.7% a.b.v. beer in 12 ounce containers; (b) Three states collect a separate, uniform "local" add-on sales tax: California (1%), Utah (1.25%), Virginia (1%). These amounts are included in the state sales tax column.
Source: Tax Foundation, 2012 Facts & Figures: How Does Your State Compare?

State-Local Tax Burdens

Area	Rate (%)	Rank[1]	Per Capita Taxes Paid to Home State ($)	Total State and Local Per Capita Taxes Paid ($)	Per Capita Income ($)
California	10.6	6	3,874	4,910	46,366
U.S. Average	9.8	-	3,057	4,160	42,539

Note: Figures cover 2009; (1) Rank ranges from 1 to 50 where 1 is highest tax burden
Source: Tax Foundation, State-Local Tax Burdens, All States, 2009

State Business Tax Climate Index Rankings

State	Overall Rank	Corporate Tax Index Rank	Individual Income Tax Index Rank	Sales Tax Index Rank	Unemployment Insurance Tax Index Rank	Property Tax Index Rank
California	48	43	50	40	13	17

Note: The index is a measure of how each state's tax laws affect economic performance. The lower the rank, the more favorable a state's tax system is for business. States without a given tax are given a ranking of 1.
Source: Tax Foundation, Major Components of the State Business Tax Climate Index, FY 2012

COMMERCIAL REAL ESTATE

Office Market

Market Area	Inventory (sq. ft.)	Vacant (sq. ft.)	Vac. Rate (%)	Under Constr. (sq. ft.)	Asking Rent ($/sf/yr)	
					Class A	Class B
San Jose-Silicon Valley	64,106,088	10,501,383	16.4	13,350	36.00	25.68

Source: Grubb & Ellis, Office Markets Trends, 4th Quarter 2011

Industrial Market

Market Area	Inventory (sq. ft.)	Vacant (sq. ft.)	Vac. Rate (%)	Under Constr. (sq. ft.)	Asking Rent ($/sf/yr)	
					WH/Dist	R&D/Flex
San Jose-Silicon Valley	289,147,642	37,579,056	13.0	0	5.64	14.04

Source: Grubb & Ellis, Industrial Markets Trends, 4th Quarter 2011

COMMERCIAL UTILITIES

Typical Monthly Electric Bills

Area	Commercial Service ($/month)		Industrial Service ($/month)	
	1,500 kWh	40 kW demand 14,000 kWh	1,000 kW demand 200,000 kWh	50,000 kW demand 15,000,000 kWh
City	305	2,474	44,140	2,342,281
Average[1]	189	1,616	25,197	1,470,813

Note: Based on total rates in effect July 1, 2011; (1) average based on 184 utilities surveyed
Source: Edison Electric Institute, Typical Bills and Average Rates Report, Summer 2011

TRANSPORTATION

Means of Transportation to Work

Area	Car/Truck/Van		Public Transportation			Bicycle	Walked	Other Means	Worked at Home
	Drove Alone	Car-pooled	Bus	Subway	Railroad				
City	77.8	10.6	2.4	0.2	0.6	0.9	1.8	1.7	3.9
MSA[1]	76.5	10.3	2.1	0.1	0.8	1.6	2.1	1.7	4.7
U.S.	76.0	10.2	2.7	1.7	0.5	0.5	2.8	1.3	4.2

Note: Figures are percentages and cover workers 16 years of age and older; (1) Figures cover the San Jose-Sunnyvale-Santa Clara, CA Metropolitan Statistical Area—see Appendix B for areas included
Source: U.S. Census Bureau, 2008-2010 American Community Survey 3-Year Estimates

Travel Time to Work

Area	Less Than 10 Minutes	10 to 19 Minutes	20 to 29 Minutes	30 to 44 Minutes	45 to 59 Minutes	60 to 89 Minutes	90 Minutes or More
City	7.5	29.2	26.6	24.3	6.3	4.7	1.4
MSA[1]	9.0	32.1	25.4	21.5	6.1	4.4	1.5
U.S.	13.9	30.1	20.8	19.8	7.5	5.5	2.5

Note: Figures are percentages and include workers 16 years old and over; (1) Figures cover the San Jose-Sunnyvale-Santa Clara, CA Metropolitan Statistical Area—see Appendix B for areas included
Source: U.S. Census Bureau, 2008-2010 American Community Survey 3-Year Estimates

Travel Time Index

Area	1985	1990	1995	2000	2005	2010
Urban Area[1]	1.18	1.24	1.22	1.30	1.31	1.25
Average[2]	1.11	1.16	1.18	1.21	1.25	1.20

Note: Travel Time Index—the ratio of travel time in the peak period to the travel time at free-flow conditions. A value of 1.30 indicates a 20-minute free-flow trip takes 26 minutes in the peak. Free-flow speeds (60 mph on freeways and 35 mph on principal arterials) are used as the comparison threshold; (1) Covers the San Jose CA urban area; (2) average of 439 urban areas
Source: Texas Transportation Institute, Urban Mobility Report 2011, September 2011

Public Transportation

Agency Name / Mode of Transportation	Vehicles Operated in Maximum Service	Annual Unlinked Passenger Trips ('000)	Annual Passenger Miles ('000)
Santa Clara Valley Transportation Authority (VTA)			
Bus (directly operated)	350	31,983.5	142,754.3
Bus (purchased transportation)	11	227.3	942.6
Demand Response (purchased transportation)	230	930.2	9,005.4
Light Rail (directly operated)	47	9,749.9	50,000.3

Source: Federal Transit Administration, National Transit Database, 2010

Air Transportation

Airport Name and Code / Type of Service	Passenger Airlines[1]	Passenger Enplanements	Freight Carriers[2]	Freight (lbs.)
San Jose International (SJC)				
Domestic service (U.S. carriers - 2011)	25	4,018,738	15	51,296,955
International service (U.S. carriers - 2010)	5	2,745	1	1,496

Note: (1) Includes all U.S.-based major, minor and commuter airlines that carried at least one passenger during the year; (2) Includes all U.S.-based airlines and freight carriers that transported at least one pound of freight during the year
Source: Bureau of Transportation Statistics, The Intermodal Transportation Database, Air Carriers: T-100 Domestic Market (U.S. Carriers), 2011; Bureau of Transportation Statistics, The Intermodal Transportation Database, Air Carriers: T-100 International Market (U.S. Carriers), 2010

Other Transportation Statistics

Major Highways:	I-80
Amtrak Service:	Yes
Major Waterways/Ports:	None

Source: Amtrak.com; Google Maps

BUSINESSES

Major Business Headquarters

Company Name	Rankings	
	Fortune[1]	Forbes[2]
Cisco Systems	62	-
Fry's Electronics	-	210
Sanmina-SCI	366	-
eBay	269	-

Note: (1) Fortune 500—companies that produce a 10-K are ranked 1 to 500 based on 2010 revenue; (2) all private companies with at least $2 billion in annual revenue are ranked 1 to 212; companies listed are headquartered in the city; dashes indicate no ranking
Source: Fortune, "Fortune 500," May 23, 2011; Forbes, "America's Largest Private Companies," November 16, 2011

Fast-Growing Businesses

According to *Inc.*, San Jose is home to two of America's 500 fastest-growing private companies: **Agiliance** (#39); **A10 Networks** (#54). Criteria: must be an independent, privately-held, for-profit, U.S. corporation, proprietorship or partnership; revenues must be at least $80,000 in 2007 and $2 million in 2010; must have four-year operating/sales history. Holding companies, regulated banks, and utilities were excluded. *Inc., "America's 500 Fastest-Growing Private Companies," September 2011*

According to Deloitte, San Jose is home to three of North America's 500 fastest-growing high-technology companies: **SunPower Corp.** (#129); **Cavium** (#189); **Super Micro Computer** (#493). Companies are ranked by percentage growth in revenue over a five-year period. Criteria for inclusion: company must be headquartered within North America; must own proprietary intellectual property or proprietary technology that contributes to a significant portion of the company's operating revenue, or devote a significant proportion of revenues to research and development of technology; must have been in business for a minumum of five years with 2006 operating revenues of at least $50,000 USD/CD and 2010 operating revenues of at least $5 million USD/CD. *Deloitte Touche Tohmatsu, 2011 Deloitte Technology Fast 500™*

Minority Business Opportunity

San Jose is home to one company which is on the *Hispanic Business* 500 list (500 largest U.S. Hispanic-owned companies based on 2010 revenue): **R.W. Garcia Co.** (#174). Companies included must show at least 51 percent ownership by Hispanic U.S. citizens, and must maintain headquarters in one of the 50 states or Washington, D.C. *Hispanic Business, "Hispanic Business 500," June 2011*

Minority- and Women-Owned Businesses

Group	All Firms		Firms with Paid Employees			
	Firms	Sales ($000)	Firms	Sales ($000)	Employees	Payroll ($000)
Asian	22,088	6,238,740	4,226	5,444,558	29,969	875,716
Black	(s)	(s)	(s)	(s)	(s)	(s)
Hispanic	10,140	1,326,830	1,665	1,040,989	11,274	278,501
Women	22,000	2,791,388	2,535	2,134,168	18,394	543,361
All Firms	71,553	100,139,638	16,163	97,406,346	351,572	22,132,495

Note: Figures cover firms located in the city; minority- and women-owned business are defined as firms in which the corresponding group own 51% or more of the stock or equity of the company; (s) estimates are suppressed when publication standards are not met
Source: U.S. Census Bureau, 2007 Economic Census, Survey of Business Owners

HOTELS

Hotels/Motels

Area	5 Star		4 Star		3 Star		2 Star		1 Star		Not Rated	
	Num.	Pct.[3]	Num.	Pct.[3]	Num.	Pct.[3]	Num.	Pct.[3]	Num.	Pct.[3]	Num.	Pct.[3]
City[1]	2	0.9	14	6.0	76	32.6	115	49.4	4	1.7	22	9.4
Total[2]	133	0.9	940	6.5	4,569	31.8	7,033	48.9	351	2.4	1,343	9.3

Note: (1) Figures cover San Jose and vicinity; (2) Figures cover all 100 cities in this book; (3) Percentage of hotels which have a given star rating; Star ratings are determined by expedia.com and offer an indication of the general quality of a particular hotel.
Source: expedia.com, April 25, 2012

The San Jose-Sunnyvale-Santa Clara, CA metro area is home to one of the best hotels in the U.S. according to *Condé Nast Traveler*: **Rosewood Sand Hill** (#62). The selections are based on over 25,000 responses to the magazine's annual Readers' Choice Survey. *Condé Nast Traveler, "2011 Readers' Choice Awards"*

EVENT SITES

Major Stadiums, Arenas, and Auditoriums

Name	Max. Capacity
Center for Performing Arts	2,665
HP Pavilion at San Jose	20,000
Municipal Stadium	4,200
Parkside Hall	1,800
San Jose Civic	3,001
San Jose McEnery Convention Center	5,000
Spartan Stadium, San Jose State University	30,456

Source: Original research

Convention Centers

Name	Overall Space (sq. ft.)	Exhibit Space (sq. ft.)	Meeting Space (sq. ft.)	Meeting Rooms
San Jose McEnery Convention Center	425,000	n/a	143,000	31

Note: n/a not available
Source: Original research

Living Environment

COST OF LIVING

Cost of Living Index

Composite Index	Groceries	Housing	Utilities	Transportation	Health Care	Misc. Goods/ Services
150.5	114.7	245.3	131.9	114.6	116.2	103.9

Note: U.S. = 100; Figures cover the San Jose CA urban area.
Source: The Council for Community and Economic Research, ACCRA Cost of Living Index, 2011

Grocery Prices

Area[1]	T-Bone Steak ($/pound)	Frying Chicken ($/pound)	Whole Milk ($/half gal.)	Eggs ($/dozen)	Orange Juice ($/64 oz.)	Coffee ($/11.5 oz.)
City[2]	9.78	1.03	2.16	2.32	2.98	5.20
Avg.	9.25	1.18	2.22	1.66	3.19	4.40
Min.	6.70	0.88	1.31	0.95	2.46	2.94
Max.	14.30	2.16	3.50	3.18	4.75	6.83

Note: (1) Values for the local area are compared with the average, minimum and maximum values for all 335 areas in the Cost of Living Index; (2) Figures cover the San Jose CA urban area; **T-Bone Steak** *(price per pound);* **Frying Chicken** *(price per pound, whole fryer);* **Whole Milk** *(half gallon carton);* **Eggs** *(price per dozen, Grade A, large);* **Orange Juice** *(64 oz. Tropicana or Florida Natural);* **Coffee** *(11.5 oz. can, vacuum-packed, Maxwell House, Hills Bros, or Folgers).*
Source: The Council for Community and Economic Research, ACCRA Cost of Living Index, 2011

Housing and Utility Costs

Area[1]	New Home Price ($)	Apartment Rent ($/month)	All Electric ($/month)	Part Electric ($/month)	Other Energy ($/month)	Telephone ($/month)
City[2]	713,145	1,729	-	181.97	64.31	28.30
Avg.	285,990	839	163.23	89.00	77.52	26.92
Min.	188,005	460	125.58	45.39	33.89	17.98
Max.	1,197,028	3,244	339.16	181.97	348.69	40.01

Note: (1) Values for the local area are compared with the average, minimum and maximum values for all 335 areas in the Cost of Living Index; (2) Figures cover the San Jose CA urban area; **New Home Price** *(2,400 sf living area, 8,000 sf lot, in urban area with full utilities);* **Apartment Rent** *(950 sf 2 bedroom/1.5 or 2 bath, unfurnished, excluding all utilities except water);* **All Electric** *(average monthly cost for an all-electric home);* **Part Electric** *(average monthly cost for a part-electric home);* **Other Energy** *(average monthly cost for natural gas, fuel oil, coal, wood, and any other forms of energy except electricity);* **Telephone** *(price includes basic monthly rate for a private residential line plus additional local usage charges incurred by a family of four).*
Source: The Council for Community and Economic Research, ACCRA Cost of Living Index, 2011

Health Care, Transportation, and Other Costs

Area[1]	Doctor ($/visit)	Dentist ($/visit)	Optometrist ($/visit)	Gasoline ($/gallon)	Beauty Salon ($/visit)	Men's Shirt ($)
City[2]	103.14	105.52	139.53	3.81	57.79	23.36
Avg.	93.88	81.72	90.54	3.48	32.65	25.06
Min.	60.00	55.33	53.66	3.18	19.78	13.44
Max.	154.98	145.97	183.72	4.31	63.21	46.00

Note: (1) Values for the local area are compared with the average, minimum and maximum values for all 335 areas in the Cost of Living Index; (2) Figures cover the San Jose CA urban area; **Doctor** *(general practitioners routine exam of an established patient);* **Dentist** *(adult teeth cleaning and periodic oral examination);* **Optometrist** *(full vision eye exam for established adult patient);* **Gasoline** *(one gallon regular unleaded, national brand, including all taxes, cash price at self-service pump if available);* **Beauty Salon** *(woman's shampoo, trim, and blow-dry);* **Men's Shirt** *(cotton/polyester dress shirt, pinpoint weave, long sleeves).*
Source: The Council for Community and Economic Research, ACCRA Cost of Living Index, 2011

HOUSING

House Price Index (HPI)

Area	National Ranking[2]	Quarterly Change (%)	One-Year Change (%)	Five-Year Change (%)
MSA[1]	112	-0.44	-1.84	-23.53
U.S.[3]	-	-0.10	-2.43	-19.16

Note: The HPI is a weighted repeat sales index. It measures average price changes in repeat sales or refinancings on the same properties. This information is obtained by reviewing repeat mortgage transactions on single-family properties whose mortgages have been purchased or securitized by Fannie Mae or Freddie Mac in January 1975; (1) Metropolitan/Micropolitan Statistical Area—see Appendix B for areas included; (2) Rankings are based on annual percentage change for all metro areas containing at least 15,000 transactions over the last 10 years and ranges from 1 to 306; (3) figures based on a weighted average of Census Division estimates using a purchase only index; all figures are for the period ending December 31, 2011
Source: Federal Housing Finance Agency, House Price Index, February 23, 2012

House Price Valuations

Area	Q4 2005		Q4 2006		Q4 2007		Q4 2008		Q4 2009	
	Price ($000)	Over-valuation	Price ($000)	Over-valuation	Price ($000)	Over-valuation	Price ($000)	Over-valuation	Price ($000)	Over-valuation
MSA[1]	723.3	41.6	707.4	26.7	642.6	6.7	524.2	-14.3	513.7	-13.5

Note: Figures show the percentage of over- or under-valuation of single family homes relative to statistically normal house values (e.g. a value of 23.6 indicates that house values are 23.6% overvalued). Statistically normal house values are based on house prices, interest rates, household incomes, population densities, and any historical premiums or discounts metropolitan areas have exhibited over time; (1) Figures cover the San Jose-Sunnyvale-Santa Clara, CA - see Appendix B for areas included
Source: Global Insight/PNC Financial Services Group, House Prices in America: 4th Quarter 2009 Update

Median Single-Family Home Prices

Area	2009	2010	2011p	Percent Change 2010 to 2011
MSA[1]	530.0	595.0	570.0	-4.2
U.S. Average	172.1	173.1	166.2	-4.0

Note: Figures are median sales prices of existing single-family homes in thousands of dollars; (p) preliminary; n/a not available; (1) Metropolitan Statistical Area—see Appendix B for areas included
Source: National Association of Realtors, Median Sales Price of Existing Single-Family Homes for Metropolitan Areas, 4th Quarter 2011

Affordability Index of Existing Single-Family Homes

Area	2009	2010	2011p	Percent Change 2010 to 2011
MSA[1]	50.3	49.1	54.1	10.2

Note: The housing affordability index measures whether or not a typical family could qualify for a mortgage loan on a typical home. The higher the index, the greater the household purchasing power. An index of 100 is defined as the point where a median-income household has exactly enough income to qualify for the purchase of a median-priced existing single-family home, assuming a 20 percent downpayment and 25 percent of gross income devoted to mortgage principal and interest payments; (p) preliminary; n/a not available; (1) Metropolitan Statistical Area—see Appendix B for areas included
Source: National Association of Realtors, Affordability Index of Existing Single-Family Homes, 2011

Median Apartment Condo-Coop Home Prices

Area	2009	2010	2011p	Percent Change 2010 to 2011
MSA[1]	n/a	n/a	n/a	n/a
U.S. Average	175.6	171.7	165.1	-3.8

Note: Figures are median sales prices of existing apartment condo-coop homes in thousands of dollars; (p) preliminary; n/a not available; (1) Metropolitan Statistical Area—see Appendix B for areas included
Source: National Association of Realtors, Median Sales Price of Existing Apartment Condo-Coop Homes for Metropolitan Areas, 4th Quarter 2011

Year Housing Structure Built

Area	2005 or Later	2000 -2004	1990 -1999	1980 -1989	1970 -1979	1960 -1969	1950 -1959	Before 1950	Median Year
City	3.6	6.7	10.4	13.9	24.3	19.6	12.0	9.5	1974
MSA[1]	3.5	6.1	10.4	12.9	22.7	18.9	15.6	9.8	1972
U.S.	5.0	8.6	14.0	14.1	16.3	11.3	11.2	19.6	1975

Note: Figures are percentages except for Median Year; (1) Figures cover the San Jose-Sunnyvale-Santa Clara, CA Metropolitan Statistical Area—see Appendix B for areas included
Source: U.S. Census Bureau, 2008-2010 American Community Survey 3-Year Estimates

HEALTH

Health Risk Data

Category	MSA[1] (%)	U.S. (%)
Adults who have been told they have high blood pressure[2]	21.7	28.7
Adults who have been told they have high blood cholesterol[2]	38.7	37.5
Adults who have been told they have diabetes[3]	8.6	8.7
Adults who have been told they have arthritis[2]	16.5	26.0
Adults who have been told they currently have asthma	7.0	9.1
Adults who are current smokers	8.0	17.3
Adults who are heavy drinkers[4]	4.0	5.0
Adults who are binge drinkers[5]	11.0	15.1
Adults who are overweight (BMI 25.0 - 29.9)	39.1	36.2
Adults who are obese (BMI 30.0 - 99.8)	21.2	27.5
Adults who participated in any physical activities in the past month	83.0	76.1
Adults 50+ who have ever had a sigmoidoscopy or colonoscopy	63.5	65.2
Women aged 40+ who have had a mammogram within the past two years	82.0	75.2
Men aged 40+ who have had a PSA test within the past two years	40.3	53.2
Adults aged 65+ who have had flu shot within the past year	69.0	67.5
Adults aged 18–64 who have any kind of health care coverage	87.6	82.2

Note: Data as of 2010 unless otherwise noted; (1) Figures cover the San Jose-Sunnyvale-Santa Clara, CA Metropolitan Statistical Area—see Appendix B for areas included; (2) Data as of 2009; (3) Figures do not include pregnancy-related, borderline, or pre-diabetes; (4) Heavy drinkers are classified as males having more than two drinks per day or females having more than one drink per day; (5) Binge drinkers are classified as males having five or more drinks on one occasion or females having four or more drinks on one occasion
Source: Centers for Disease Control and Prevention, Behaviorial Risk Factor Surveillance System, SMART: Selected Metropolitan/Micropolitan Area Risk Trends, 2009, 2010

Mortality Rates for the Top 10 Causes of Death in the U.S.

ICD-10[a] Sub-Chapter	ICD-10[a] Code	Age-Adjusted Mortality Rate[1] per 100,000 population	
		County[2]	U.S.
Malignant neoplasms	C00-C97	139.7	175.6
Ischaemic heart diseases	I20-I25	85.5	121.6
Other forms of heart disease	I30-I51	20.3	48.6
Chronic lower respiratory diseases	J40-J47	26.5	42.3
Cerebrovascular diseases	I60-I69	30.9	40.6
Organic, including symptomatic, mental disorders	F01-F09	9.7	26.7
Other degenerative diseases of the nervous system	G30-G31	36.8	24.7
Other external causes of accidental injury	W00-X59	15.8	24.4
Diabetes mellitus	E10-E14	22.6	21.7
Hypertensive diseases	I10-I15	27.0	18.2

Note: (a) ICD-10 = International Classification of Diseases 10th Revision; (1) Mortality rates are a three year average covering 2007-2009; (2) Figures cover Santa Clara County
Source: Centers for Disease Control and Prevention, National Center for Health Statistics. Underlying Cause of Death 1999-2009 on CDC WONDER Online Database, released 2012. Data for year 2009 are compiled from the Multiple Cause of Death File 2009, Series 20 No. 2O, 2012, Data for year 2008 are compiled from the Multiple Cause of Death File 2008, Series 20 No. 2N, 2011, Data for year 2007 are compiled from Multiple Cause of Death File 2007, Series 20 No. 2M, 2010.

Mortality Rates for Selected Causes of Death

ICD-10[a] Sub-Chapter	ICD-10[a] Code	Age-Adjusted Mortality Rate[1] per 100,000 population	
		County[2]	U.S.
Assault	X85-Y09	2.7	5.7
Human immunodeficiency virus (HIV) disease	B20-B24	1.0	3.3
Influenza and pneumonia	J09-J18	17.3	16.4
Intentional self-harm	X60-X84	8.4	11.5
Malnutrition	E40-E46	*0.0	0.8
Obesity and other hyperalimentation	E65-E68	1.3	1.6
Transport accidents	V01-V99	7.2	13.7
Viral hepatitis	B15-B19	2.8	2.2

Note: (a) ICD-10 = International Classification of Diseases 10th Revision; (1) Mortality rates are a three year average covering 2007-2009; (2) Figures cover Santa Clara County; (*) Unreliable data as per CDC
Source: Centers for Disease Control and Prevention, National Center for Health Statistics. Underlying Cause of Death 1999-2009 on CDC WONDER Online Database, released 2012. Data for year 2009 are compiled from the Multiple Cause of Death File 2009, Series 20 No. 2O, 2012, Data for year 2008 are compiled from the Multiple Cause of Death File 2008, Series 20 No. 2N, 2011, Data for year 2007 are compiled from Multiple Cause of Death File 2007, Series 20 No. 2M, 2010.

Distribution of Physicians and Dentists

Area[1]	Dentists[2]	D.O.[3]	M.D.[4] Total	M.D.[4] Family/General Practice	M.D.[4] Pediatrics	M.D.[4] Medical Specialties	M.D.[4] Surgical Specialties
Local (number)	1,503	111	4,402	366	453	1,916	944
Local (rate[5])	8.7	0.6	25.1	2.1	2.6	10.9	5.4
U.S. (rate[5])	4.5	1.9	18.3	2.5	1.4	6.8	4.1

Note: Data as of 2008 unless noted; (1) Local data covers Santa Clara County; (2) Data as of 2007; (3) Doctor of Osteopathic Medicine; (4) Includes active, non-federal, patient-care, office-based Doctors of Medicine; (5) rate per 10,000 population
Source: Area Resource File (ARF). 2009-2010 Release. U.S. Department of Health and Human Services, Health Resources and Services Administration, Bureau of Health Professions, Rockville, MD, August 2010

Best Hospitals

According to *U.S. News,* the San Jose-Sunnyvale-Santa Clara, CA is home to one of the best hospitals in the U.S.: **Stanford Hospital and Clinics** (14 specialties). The hospital listed was highly ranked in at least one adult specialty. *U.S. News Online, "America's Best Hospitals 2011-12"*

According to *U.S. News,* the San Jose-Sunnyvale-Santa Clara, CA is home to one of the best children's hospitals in the U.S.: **Lucile Packard Children's Hospital at Stanford** (10 specialties). The hospital listed was highly ranked in at least one pediatric specialty. *U.S. News Online, "America's Best Children's Hospitals 2011-12"*

EDUCATION

Public School District Statistics

District Name	Schls	Pupils	Pupil/ Teacher Ratio	Minority Pupils[1] (%)	Free Lunch Eligible[2] (%)	IEP[3] (%)
Alum Rock Union Elementary	28	13,372	20.2	97.4	68.1	10.1
Berryessa Union Elementary	14	8,327	22.3	93.8	26.8	9.6
Cambrian	6	3,218	20.8	49.4	15.8	9.4
Campbell Union High	7	7,791	22.1	54.2	18.1	9.9
East Side Union High	20	26,915	24.1	90.6	30.7	9.1
Evergreen Elementary	18	13,323	22.1	91.3	24.4	7.8
Franklin-Mckinley Elementary	17	10,202	23.1	97.8	67.5	8.9
Moreland Elementary	6	4,135	20.8	68.4	27.6	9.0
Mt. Pleasant Elementary	5	2,753	22.0	96.7	62.5	12.9
Oak Grove Elementary	20	11,633	20.8	79.3	40.5	9.2
San Jose Unified	52	32,423	21.5	73.4	37.3	10.4
Santa Clara County Office of Educ	12	4,513	13.8	81.0	45.2	44.0
Union Elementary	8	4,737	22.3	40.9	10.7	9.5

Note: Table includes school districts with 2,000 or more students; (1) Percentage of students that are not non-Hispanic white; (2) Percentage of students that are eligible for the free lunch program; (3) Percentage of students that have an Individualized Education Program.
Source: U.S. Department of Education, National Center for Education Statistics, Common Core of Data, Local Education Agency (School District) Universe Survey: School Year 2009-2010; U.S. Department of Education, National Center for Education Statistics, Common Core of Data, Public Elementary/Secondary School Universe Survey: School Year 2009-2010

Highest Level of Education

Area	Less than H.S.	H.S. Diploma	Some College, No Deg.	Associate Degree	Bachelors Degree	Masters Degree	Profess. School Degree	Doctorate Degree
City	18.1	18.8	19.2	7.6	22.7	10.3	1.8	1.6
MSA[1]	14.1	16.2	17.9	7.3	25.1	13.8	2.6	2.9
U.S.	14.7	28.4	21.3	7.6	17.6	7.2	1.9	1.2

Note: Figures cover persons age 25 and over; (1) Figures cover the San Jose-Sunnyvale-Santa Clara, CA Metropolitan Statistical Area—see Appendix B for areas included
Source: U.S. Census Bureau, 2008-2010 American Community Survey 3-Year Estimates

Educational Attainment by Race

Area	High School Graduate or Higher (%)					Bachelor's Degree or Higher (%)				
	Total	White	Black	Asian	Hisp.[2]	Total	White	Black	Asian	Hisp.[2]
City	81.9	85.0	89.4	85.1	62.0	36.4	34.7	28.4	49.3	11.9
MSA[1]	85.9	88.4	91.2	89.2	62.8	44.5	42.4	29.6	59.4	13.3
U.S.	85.3	87.5	81.4	85.5	61.6	28.0	29.3	17.8	50.2	13.0

Note: Figures shown cover persons 25 years old and over; (1) Figures cover the San Jose-Sunnyvale-Santa Clara, CA Metropolitan Statistical Area—see Appendix B for areas included; (2) People of Hispanic origin can be of any race
Source: U.S. Census Bureau, 2008-2010 American Community Survey 3-Year Estimates

School Enrollment by Grade and Control

Area	Preschool (%)		Kindergarten (%)		Grades 1 - 4 (%)		Grades 5 - 8 (%)		Grades 9 - 12 (%)	
	Public	Private	Public	Private	Public	Private	Public	Private	Public	Private
City	43.3	56.7	84.9	15.1	87.5	12.5	89.5	10.5	90.4	9.6
MSA[1]	35.0	65.0	83.1	16.9	86.2	13.8	88.3	11.7	89.3	10.7
U.S.	55.4	44.6	87.1	12.9	89.4	10.6	89.5	10.5	90.4	9.6

Note: Figures shown cover persons 3 years old and over; (1) Figures cover the San Jose-Sunnyvale-Santa Clara, CA Metropolitan Statistical Area—see Appendix B for areas included
Source: U.S. Census Bureau, 2008-2010 American Community Survey 3-Year Estimates

Average Salaries of Public School Classroom Teachers

Area	2010-11 Dollars	2010-11 Rank[1]	2011-12 Dollars	2011-12 Rank[1]	Percent Change 2010-11 to 2011-12	Percent Change 2001-02 to 2011-12
California	67,871	4	69,496	4	2.39	27.90
U.S. Average	55,623	-	56,643	-	1.83	26.8

Note: (1) State rank ranges from 1 to 51 where 1 indicates highest salary.
Source: National Education Association, Rankings & Estimates: Rankings of the States 2011 and Estimates of School Statistics 2012, December 2011

Higher Education

Four-Year Colleges			Two-Year Colleges			Medical Schools[1]	Law Schools[2]	Voc/ Tech[3]
Public	Private Non-profit	Private For-profit	Public	Private Non-profit	Private For-profit			
1	1	2	2	0	2	0	0	3

Note: Figures cover institutions located within the city limits and include main campuses only; (1) includes schools accredited by the Liaison Committee on Medical Education and the American Osteopathic Association's Commission on Osteopathic College Accreditation; (2) includes American Bar Association-accredited law schools; (3) includes all schools with programs that are less than 2 years.
Source: National Center for Education Statistics, Integrated Postsecondary Education System (IPEDS) Peer Analysis System, 2011-12; Association of American Medical Colleges, Member List, April 23, 2012; American Osteopathic Association, Member List, April 23, 2012; Law School Admission Council, Official Guide to ABA-Approved Law Schools Online, April 23, 2012

According to *U.S. News & World Report,* the San Jose-Sunnyvale-Santa Clara, CA is home to one of the best national universities in the U.S.: **Stanford University** (#5). The indicators used to capture academic quality fall into a number of categories: assessment by administrators at peer institutions; retention of students; faculty resources; student selectivity; financial resources; alumni giving; high school counselor ratings of colleges; and graduation rate.*U.S. News & World Report, "America's Best Colleges 2012"*

According to *U.S. News & World Report,* the San Jose-Sunnyvale-Santa Clara, CA is home to one of the best law schools in the U.S.: **Stanford University** (#2). The rankings are based on a weighted average of 12 measures of quality: peer assessment score; assessment score by lawyers/judges; median LSAT scores; median undergrad GPA; acceptance rate; employment rates for graduates; placement success; bar passage rate; faculty resources; expenditures per student; student/faculty ratio; and library resources. *U.S. News & World Report, "America's Best Law Schools 2013"*

According to *Forbes,* the San Jose-Sunnyvale-Santa Clara, CA is home to one of the best business schools in the U.S.: **Stanford** (#2). The rankings are based on the return on investment that graduates of the Class of 2006 received (median salary five years after graduation). *Forbes, "Best Business Schools," August 3, 2011*

PRESIDENTIAL ELECTION

2008 Presidential Election Results

Area	Obama	McCain	Nader	Other
Santa Clara County	69.4	28.6	0.7	1.3
U.S.	52.9	45.6	0.6	0.9

Note: Results are percentages and may not add to 100% due to rounding
Source: Dave Leip's Atlas of U.S. Presidential Elections, www.uselectionatlas.org

EMPLOYERS

Major Employers

Company Name	Industry
Apple	Radio and tv communications equipment
Cisco Systems	Data conversion equipment, media-to-media: computer
City of San Jose	Executive offices
Cypress Semiconductor International	Semiconductor devices
e4e	Business services, nec
Hadco Santa Clara	Printed circuit boards
Hewlett-Packard Company	Computer (hardware) development
Hewlett-Packard Company	Electronic computers
Hitachi Global Storage Technologies	Computer storage devices
Intel Corporation	Semiconductors and related devices
Juniper Networks	Computer peripheral equipment, nec
LSI Corporation	Semiconductors and related devices
Mormon Church	Churches, temples, and shrines
Rosendin Electric	Electrical work
San Jose State University	Colleges and universities
Seagate Technology	Computer storage devices
Stanford Hospital and Clinics	General medical and surgical hospitals
The Leland Stanford Junior University	General medical and surgical hospitals
Veterans Health Administration	General medical and surgical hospitals

Note: Companies shown are located within the San Jose-Sunnyvale-Santa Clara, CA metropolitan area.
Source: Hoovers.com, data extracted April 25 2012

Best Companies to Work For

Adobe; Cisco, headquartered in San Jose, are among "The 100 Best Companies to Work For." To pick the 100 Best Companies to Work For, *Fortune* partnered with the Great Place to Work Institute. Two hundred eighty firms participated in this year's survey. Two-thirds of a company's score is based on the results of the Institute's Trust Index survey, which is sent to a random sample of employees from each company. The questions related to attitudes about management's credibility, job satisfaction, and camaraderie. The other third of the scoring is based on the company's responses to the Institute's Culture Audit, which includes detailed questions about pay and benefit programs, and a series of open-ended questions about hiring practices, internal communication, training, recognition programs, and diversity efforts. Any company that is at least five years old with more than 1,000 U.S. employees is eligible. *Fortune, "The 100 Best Companies to Work For," February 6, 2012*

Cisco, headquartered in San Jose, is among the "100 Best Companies for Working Mothers." Criteria: workforce profile; benefits; child care; women's issues and advancement; flexible work; paid time off and leave; company culture; and work-life programs. This year *Working Mother* gave particular weight to workforce profile, paid time off and company culture. *Working Mother, "100 Best Companies 2011"*

Cisco, headquartered in San Jose, is among the "Best Companies for Multicultural Women." *Working Mother* selected 23 companies based on a detailed application completed by public and private firms based in the United States, excluding government agencies, companies in the human resources field and non-autonomous divisions. Companies supplied data about the hiring, pay, and promotion of multicultural employees. Applications focused on representation of multicultural women, recruitment, retention and advancement programs, and company culture. *Working Mother, "2011 Best Companies for Multicultural Women"*

Cisco, located in San Jose, is among the "Top Companies for Executive Women." To be named to the list, companies with a minimum of two women on the board complete a comprehensive application that focuses on the number of women in senior ranks. In addition to assessing corporate programs and policies dedicated to advancing women, NAFE examined the number of women in each company overall, in senior management, and on its board of directors, paying particular attention to the number of women with profit-and-loss responsibility. *National Association for Female Executives, "2012 NAFE Top 50 Companies for Executive Women"*

PUBLIC SAFETY

Crime Rate

Area	All Crimes	Violent Crimes				Property Crimes		
		Murder	Forcible Rape	Robbery	Aggrav. Assault	Burglary	Larceny -Theft	Motor Vehicle Theft
City	2,607.2	2.1	26.1	100.6	202.6	406.1	1,312.0	557.7
Suburbs[1]	2,425.6	0.7	16.9	57.5	115.7	437.3	1,587.1	210.5
Metro[2]	2,520.9	1.4	21.7	80.1	161.3	420.9	1,442.7	392.7
U.S.	3,345.5	4.8	27.5	119.1	252.3	699.6	2,003.5	238.8

Note: Figures are crimes per 100,000 population; (1) All areas within the metro area that are located outside the city limits; (2) Metropolitan Statistical Area—see Appendix B for areas included
Source: FBI Uniform Crime Reports, 2010

Hate Crimes

Area	Number of Quarters Reported	Bias Motivation				
		Race	Religion	Sexual Orientation	Ethnicity	Disability
City	4	7	8	6	3	0

Source: Federal Bureau of Investigation, Hate Crime Statistics 2010

Identity Theft Consumer Complaints

Area	Complaints	Complaints per 100,000 Population	Rank[2]
MSA[1]	1,606	89.0	129
U.S.	279,156	90.4	-

Note: (1) Metropolitan Statistical Area—see Appendix B for areas included; (2) Rank ranges from 1 to 384 where 1 indicates greatest number of identity theft complaints per 100,000 population
Source: Federal Trade Commission, Consumer Sentinel Network Data Book for January–December 2011

Fraud and Other Consumer Complaints

Area	Complaints	Complaints per 100,000 Population	Rank[2]
MSA[1]	7,780	431.3	249
U.S.	1,533,924	496.8	-

Note: (1) Metropolitan Statistical Area—see Appendix B for areas included; (2) Rank ranges from 1 to 384 where 1 indicates greatest number of fraud and other complaints per 100,000 population
Source: Federal Trade Commission, Consumer Sentinel Network Data Book for January–December 2011

RECREATION

Culture

Dance[1]	Theatre[1]	Instrumental Music[1]	Vocal Music[1]	Series/ Festivals	Museums	Zoos and Aquariums[2]
2	8	5	2	0	10	1

Note: (1) Number of professional perfoming groups; (2) AZA-accredited
Source: The Grey House Performing Arts Directory, 2011-2012; Official Museum Directory, 2011; American Association of Museums, AAM Member Museums, April 2012; Association of Zoos & Aquariums, AZA Member Zoos & Aquariums, April 2012

Professional Sports Teams

Team Name	League
San Jose Earthquakes	Major League Soccer (MLS)
San Jose Sharks	National Hockey League (NHL)

Note: Includes teams located in the San Jose metro area.
Source: Original research

CLIMATE

Average and Extreme Temperatures

Temperature	Jan	Feb	Mar	Apr	May	Jun	Jul	Aug	Sep	Oct	Nov	Dec	Yr.
Extreme High (°F)	76	82	83	95	103	104	105	101	105	100	87	76	105
Average High (°F)	57	61	63	67	70	74	75	75	76	72	65	58	68
Average Temp. (°F)	50	53	55	58	61	65	66	67	66	63	56	50	59
Average Low (°F)	42	45	46	48	51	55	57	58	57	53	47	42	50
Extreme Low (°F)	21	26	30	32	38	43	45	47	41	33	29	23	21

Note: Figures cover the years 1945-1993
Source: National Climatic Data Center, International Station Meteorological Climate Summary, 9/96

Average Precipitation/Snowfall/Humidity

Precip./Humidity	Jan	Feb	Mar	Apr	May	Jun	Jul	Aug	Sep	Oct	Nov	Dec	Yr.
Avg. Precip. (in.)	2.7	2.3	2.2	0.9	0.3	0.1	Tr	Tr	0.2	0.7	1.7	2.3	13.5
Avg. Snowfall (in.)	Tr	Tr	Tr	0	0	0	0	0	0	0	0	Tr	Tr
Avg. Rel. Hum. 7am (%)	82	82	80	76	74	73	77	79	79	79	81	82	79
Avg. Rel. Hum. 4pm (%)	62	59	56	52	53	54	58	58	55	54	59	63	57

Note: Figures cover the years 1945-1993; Tr = Trace amounts (<0.05 in. of rain; <0.5 in. of snow)
Source: National Climatic Data Center, International Station Meteorological Climate Summary, 9/96

Weather Conditions

Temperature			Daytime Sky			Precipitation		
10°F & below	32°F & below	90°F & above	Clear	Partly cloudy	Cloudy	0.01 inch or more precip.	0.1 inch or more snow/ice	Thunder-storms
0	5	5	106	180	79	57	< 1	6

Note: Figures are average number of days per year and cover the years 1945-1993
Source: National Climatic Data Center, International Station Meteorological Climate Summary, 9/96

HAZARDOUS WASTE

Superfund Sites

San Jose has two hazardous waste sites on the EPA's Superfund Final National Priorities List: **Fairchild Semiconductor Corp. (South San Jose Plant); Lorentz Barrel & Drum Co.** *U.S. Environmental Protection Agency, Final National Priorities List, April 17, 2012*

AIR & WATER QUALITY

Air Quality Index

Area	Percent of Days when Air Quality was...[2]					AQI Statistics[2]	
	Good	Moderate	Unhealthy for Sensitive Groups	Unhealthy	Very Unhealthy	Maximum	Median
Area[1]	71.2	28.5	0.3	0.0	0.0	121	41

Note: Air Quality Index (AQI) is an index for reporting daily air quality. EPA calculates the AQI for five major air pollutants regulated by the Clean Air Act: ground-level ozone, particle pollution (aka particulate matter), carbon monoxide, sulfur dioxide, and nitrogen dioxide. The AQI runs from 0 to 500. The higher the AQI value, the greater the level of air pollution and the greater the health concern. There are six AQI categories: "Good" AQI is between 0 and 50. Air quality is considered satisfactory; "Moderate" AQI is between 51 and 100. Air quality is acceptable; "Unhealthy for Sensitive Groups" When AQI values are between 101 and 150, members of sensitive groups may experience health effects; "Unhealthy" When AQI values are between 151 and 200 everyone may begin to experience health effects; "Very Unhealthy" AQI values between 201 and 300 trigger a health alert; "Hazardous" AQI values over 300 trigger warnings of emergency conditions (not shown); (1) Data covers Santa Clara County; (2) Based on 365 days with AQI data in 2011.
Source: U.S. Environmental Protection Agency, AirData Report, 2011

Air Quality Index Pollutants

Area	Percent of Days when AQI Pollutant was...[2]					
	Carbon Monoxide	Nitrogen Dioxide	Ozone	Sulfur Dioxide	Particulate Matter 2.5	Particulate Matter 10
Area[1]	0.0	5.2	34.8	0.0	60.0	0.0

Note: The Air Quality Index (AQI) is an index for reporting daily air quality. EPA calculates the AQI for five major air pollutants regulated by the Clean Air Act: ground-level ozone, particle pollution (also known as particulate matter), carbon monoxide, sulfur dioxide, and nitrogen dioxide. The AQI runs from 0 to 500. The higher the AQI value, the greater the level of air pollution and the greater the health concern; (1) Data covers Santa Clara County; (2) Based on 365 days with AQI data in 2011.
Source: U.S. Environmental Protection Agency, AirData Report, 2011

Air Quality Index Trends

Area	Trend Sites (days)								All Sites (days)
	2003	2004	2005	2006	2007	2008	2009	2010	2010
MSA[1]	14	8	4	14	3	13	8	6	8

Note: Figures are the number of days the AQI value exceeded 100 in a given year. An AQI value greater than 100 indicates that air quality would have been in the unhealthful range on that day. Data from exceptional events are included. These counts are presented in two ways. First, the counts are based on sites having an adequate record of monitoring data during the trend period (trend sites). These counts represent the relative change in the number of days with AQI values greater than 100. In the last column, the counts are based on all sites with data in the most recent year (because it is possible for a site to have data in the most recent year but not enough data to be a trend site); (1) Data covers the San Jose-Sunnyvale-Santa Clara, CA—see Appendix B for areas included
Source: U.S. Environmental Protection Agency, Air Quality Index Information, "Number of Days with Air Quality Index Values Greater than 100 at Trend Sites, 2000-2010, and at All Sites in 2010"

Maximum Air Pollutant Concentrations: Particulate Matter, Ozone, CO and Lead

	Particulate Matter 10 (ug/m³)	Particulate Matter 2.5 Wtd AM (ug/m³)	Particulate Matter 2.5 24-Hr (ug/m³)	Ozone (ppm)	Carbon Monoxide (ppm)	Lead (ug/m³)
MSA[1] Level	37	8.8	29	0.08	2	n/a
NAAQS[2]	150	15	35	0.075	9	0.15
Met NAAQS[2]	Yes	Yes	Yes	No	Yes	n/a

Note: Data from exceptional events are not included; (1) Data covers the San Jose-Sunnyvale-Santa Clara, CA—see Appendix B for areas included; (2) National Ambient Air Quality Standards; ppm = parts per million; ug/m³ = micrograms per cubic meter; n/a not available
Concentrations: Particulate Matter 10 (coarse particulate)—highest second maximum 24-hour concentration; Particulate Matter 2.5 Wtd AM (fine particulate)—highest weighted annual mean concentration; Particulate Matter 2.5 24-Hour (fine particulate)—highest 98th percentile 24-hour concentration; Ozone—highest fourth daily maximum 8-hour concentration; Carbon Monoxide—highest second maximum non-overlapping 8-hour concentration; Lead—maximum running 3-month average
Source: U.S. Environmental Protection Agency, CBSA Factbook 2010, Air Quality Statistics by City, 2010

Maximum Air Pollutant Concentrations: Nitrogen Dioxide and Sulfur Dioxide

	Nitrogen Dioxide AM (ppb)	Nitrogen Dioxide 1-Hr (ppb)	Sulfur Dioxide AM (ppb)	Sulfur Dioxide 1-Hr (ppb)	Sulfur Dioxide 24-Hr (ppb)
MSA[1] Level	14.394	50.7	0.352	4.1	1.6
NAAQS[2]	53	100	30	75	140
Met NAAQS[2]	Yes	Yes	Yes	Yes	Yes

Note: Data from exceptional events are not included; (1) Data covers the San Jose-Sunnyvale-Santa Clara, CA—see Appendix B for areas included; (2) National Ambient Air Quality Standards; ppb = parts per billion; n/a not available
Concentrations: Nitrogen Dioxide AM—highest arithmetic mean concentration; Nitrogen Dioxide 1-Hr—highest 98th percentile 1-hour daily maximum concentration; Sulfur Dioxide AM—highest annual mean concentration; Sulfur Dioxide 1-Hr—highest 99th percentile 1-hour daily maximum concentration; Sulfur Dioxide 24-Hr—highest second maximum 24-hour concentration
Source: U.S. Environmental Protection Agency, CBSA Factbook 2010, Air Quality Statistics by City, 2010

Drinking Water

Water System Name	Pop. Served	Primary Water Source Type	Violations[1]	
			Health Based	Monitoring/ Reporting
San Jose Water Company	998,000	Surface	0	0

Note: (1) Based on violation data from January 1, 2011 to December 31, 2011 (includes unresolved violations from earlier years)
Source: U.S. Environmental Protection Agency, Office of Ground Water and Drinking Water, Safe Drinking Water Information System (based on data extracted April 18, 2012)

Scottsdale, Arizona

Background

Scottsdale is located in Maricopa County in central Arizona, 10 miles east of Phoenix. The city is known as a center for electronics equipment, the aerial mapping industry, and fine clothing. Most notably, the town is also a major tourism destination and retirement center, with warm winters and strong sunshine most of the year.

From 800 to 1400 AD, the area's residents were the Hohokam Indians, who farmed using a sophisticated irrigation system involving more than 200 miles of canals. After the Hohokam culture declined, Pima and Maricopa Indians were the only inhabitants until the late 1880s, when white settlers established a permanent presence in what is now the town of Scottsdale. Army chaplain Winfield Scott and his wife were the first non-Indian farmers in the region, planting oranges, sweet potatoes, and peanuts.

In 1896, the population had reached a level that justified the establishment of the first school; a year later, J. L. Davis opened a general store, which also served as a post office. Year-round good weather made Scottsdale a natural resort location, and in 1909, the Ingleside Inn was built, the first of many such establishments to follow. Population growth, however, was slow—by 1951, the year of Scottsdale's incorporation as a city, the town had only 2,000 residents. The newly elected mayor, Malcolm White, was a great promoter of his new city, publicizing its old-fashioned virtues and magnificent scenery by dubbing it "The West's Most Western Town."

Scottsdale has distinguished itself in its efforts to preserve the beauty of the desert environment; there are more than 40 miles of walking and biking trails, and many golf courses connect to the Indian Bend Wash Greenbelt, an integrated flood-control and preservation project that avoids as much as possible the use of concrete.

The city is a golfer's paradise, with more than 125 courses in the area open almost year-round. Skiing is available to the north, and the spectacular Sonoran desert is just to the south. Tonto National Forest adjoins Scottsdale, which is also within easy driving distance of some of the nation's most revered natural treasures—Carefree/Cave Creek, McDowell Mountain Regional Park, Camel Back Mountain Park, Montezuma's Castle National Monument, Fort Verde State Historic Park, Casa Grande National Monument, and Picacho Peak State Park.

Taliesin West, the architectural school founded by Frank Lloyd Wright, is in Scottsdale, as is the Cosanti Foundation, which pursues the projects of the visionary architect Paolo Soleri.

The city continues to grow and improve. The McDowell Mountain Ranch major residential community and the Canal Bank improvement project, with pedestrian paths, landscaping, public art, and park-like areas to downtown, were recently completed.

The city is well known for its support of the arts, with more than 100 art galleries and craft shops. The Scottsdale Historical Museum documents the area's rich local history, and the Fleischer Museum exhibits Impressionist painting and sculpture. The city is home to its own symphony orchestra, and hosts a Dixieland Jazz Festival each November. The Scottsdale Museum of Contemporary Art opened in 1999. The town is also host to the world's largest golf tournament, the FBR Open, known as the "Greatest Show on Grass." WestWorld, Scottsdale's premier equestrian center and special event facility, has begun expansion of the Tony Nelseen Equestrian Center, which will be complete in late 2013.

The area features two important sites of interest to horticulturists—the Arboretum at Arizona State University and the Boyce Thompson Southwest Arboretum. Scottsdale is also convenient to Arizona State University and other major educational institutions.

Sunshine in Scottsdale is abundant. The climate is dry, with very hot summers and mild winters. What rainfall occurs generally comes during two seasons, from Thanksgiving to early April, when Pacific storms bring periodic rains, and during July and August, the thunderstorm season.

Rankings

General Rankings

- The Phoenix metro area was identified as one of the 10 most popular big cities by Pew Research Center. The results are based on a telephone survey of 2,260 adults conducted during October 2008. The report explored a range of attitudes related to where Americans live, where they would like to live, and why. *Pew Research Center, "For Nearly Half of America, Grass is Greener Somewhere Else," January 29, 2009*
- Scottsdale was selected as one of America's best cities by *Bloomberg Businessweek.* The city ranked #4 out of 50. Criteria: number of restaurants, bars and museums per capita; number of colleges, libraries, and professional sports teams; income, poverty, unemployment, crime, and foreclosure rates; percent of population with bachelor's degrees; public school performance; park acres per capita; air quality. *BusinessWeek, "America's 50 Best Cities," September 20, 2011*
- Scottsdale appeared on RelocateAmerica's list of best places to live in America. The annual "Top 100 Places to Live" list recognizes the top communities as nominated by their residents & local businesses. RelocateAmerica's Research Group determines the list based on review of various data gathered for economic, employment, housing, education, industry, opportunity, environment and recreation along with feedback from area leaders and residents. *RelocateAmerica.com, "Top 100 Places to Live for 2011"*
- Scottsdale was selected as one of the "Best Places to Live in America" by *Money* magazine. The city ranked #71 out of 100. This year's list focused on cities with populations of 50,000 to 300,000. Criteria: job opportunities; economic strength; top-notch schools; low crime; good health care; recreation; and many other factors that help make a town great for raising a family. *CNNMoney.com, "Best Places to Live in America 2010," August 2010*

Business/Finance Rankings

- Phoenix was identified as one of the 20 strongest-performing metro areas during the recession and recovery from trough quarter through the third quarter of 2011. Criteria: percent change in employment; percentage point change in unemployment rate; percent change in gross metropolitan product; percent change in House Price Index. *Brookings Institution, MetroMonitor: Tracking Economic Recession and Recovery in America's 100 Largest Metropolitan Areas, December 2011*
- Experian ranked the top 20 major U.S. metropolitan areas by average debt per consumer. The Phoenix metro area was ranked #5. Criteria: average debt per consumer. Debt for this study includes credit cards, auto loans and personal loans. It does not include mortgages. *Experian, May 13, 2010*
- Scottsdale was selected as one of the "100 Best Places to Live and Launch" in the U.S. The city ranked #25. The editors at *Fortune Small Business* ranked 296 Census-designated metro areas by business friendliness (Launching Score, % New Businesses) and lifestyle offerings (Living Score). Then they picked the town within each of the top 100 metro areas that best blends business and pleasure. *Fortune Small Business, "100 Best Places to Live and Launch 2008," April 2008*
- *American City Business Journals* ranked America's 261 largest cities in terms of their resident's wealth. Scottsdale ranked #8. Criteria: per capita income; median household income; percentage of households with annual incomes of $200,000 or more; median home value. *American City Business Journals, "Where the Money Is: America's Wealth Centers," August 18, 2008*
- The Phoenix metro area appeared on the Milken Institute "2011 Best Performing Metros" list. Rank: #136 out of 200 large metro areas. Criteria: job growth; wage and salary growth; high-tech output growth. *Milken Institute, "2011 Best Performing Metros"*
- The Phoenix metro area was selected as one of the best cities for entrepreneurs in America by *Inc. Magazine.* Criteria: job-growth data for 335 metro areas was analyzed for: recent growth trend; mid-term growth; long-term trend; current year growth. The Phoenix metro area ranked #14 among large metro areas and #61 overall. *Inc. Magazine, "The Best Cities for Doing Business," July 2008*

- Phoenix was ranked #58 out of 145 regions worldwide in terms of its "Knowledge Competitiveness Index." The index attempts to measure the knowledge-based development taking place throughout the world and is based on 19 measures of economic performance that indicate a region's ability to translate its knowledge capacity into economic value. *Centre for International Competitiveness, World Knowledge Competitiveness Index 2008*

- *Forbes* ranked the 200 most populous metro areas in the U.S. in terms of the "Best Places for Business and Careers." The Phoenix metro area was ranked #88. Criteria: costs (business and living); job growth (past and projected); income growth; educational attainment; projected economic growth; crime; cultural and recreational opportunities; net migration patterns; number of highly ranked colleges. *Forbes, "Best Places for Business and Careers," June 2011*

Children/Family Rankings

- Scottsdale was identified as one of the best cities for raising a family by *24/7 Wall St.* The city ranked #6. The nation's 100 largest cities were evaluated on the following criteria: large public outdoor spaces; top hospitals; strong schools; low unemployment; high educational attainment; low violent crime rates. *24/7 Wall St., "The 10 Best U.S. Cities for Raising a Family," January 13, 2012*

- The Phoenix metro area was selected as one of the "Best Cities for Relocating Families" by Worldwide ERC and Primacy Relocation. The 2008 study looked at nearly 50 factors important to relocating families including: recent job growth; nearby top-ranked colleges; in-state tuition for four-year public colleges; population growth since 2000; pediatricians per 100,000 population; and a Green Living index. *Worldwide ERC and Primacy Relocation, "2008 Best Cities for Relocating Families"*

- Scottsdale was chosen as one of America's "100 Best Communities for Young People." The winners were selected based upon detailed information provided about each community's efforts to fulfill five essential promises critical to the well-being of young people: caring adults who are actively involved in their lives; safe places in which to learn and grow; a healthy start toward adulthood; an effective education that builds marketable skills; and opportunities to help others. *America's Promise Alliance, "100 Best Communities for Young People, 2010"*

Culture/Performing Arts Rankings

- Scottsdale was selected as one of "America's Top 25 Arts Destinations." The city ranked #8 in the mid-sized city (population 100,000 to 499,999) category. Criteria: readers' top choices for arts travel destinations based on the richness and variety of visual arts sites, activities and events. *American Style, "America's Top 25 Arts Destinations," May 2010*

Dating/Romance Rankings

- Scottsdale was selected as one of "America's Best Cities for Dating" by *Yahoo! Travel.* Criteria: high proportion of singles; excellent dating venues and/or stunning natural settings. *Yahoo! Travel, "America's Best Cities for Dating," February 7, 2012*

- Eli Lily and Company, in partnership with Sperling's BestPlaces, ranked the nation's 50 largest metro areas in terms of the "Most Romantic Cities for Baby Boomers." The Phoenix metro area ranked #38. Criteria: marriage and divorce rates among baby boomers age 45 to 60; great restaurants; dance studios; chocolate, jewelry and flower sales. *Eli Lily and Company, "Most Romantic Cities for Baby Boomers," April 20, 2007*

- The Phoenix metro area was selected as one of the "Best Cities for Relocating Singles" by Worldwide ERC and Primacy Relocation. The area ranked #71 out of the 100 largest metro areas in the U.S. Criteria: recent job growth; recent singles population growth; overall population growth; affordable rental housing; cost-of-living index; expanded arts and recreation opportunities; ratio of single men and single women; affordability of quality higher education (including state residency requirements); diversity index; climate; population density. *Worldwide ERC and Primacy Relocation, "2008 Best Cities for Relocating Singles"*

- *Forbes* ranked the 40 most populous urbanized areas in the U.S. in terms of the "Best Cities for Singles." The Phoenix metro area ranked #30. Criteria: number of singles; cost of living alone; nightlife; culture; job growth; coolness; and online dating participation. *Forbes.com, "Best Cities for Singles," July 27, 2009*

Education Rankings

- Phoenix was identified as one of the 100 "smartest" metro areas in the U.S. The area ranked #70. Criteria: the editors rated the collective brainpower of the 100 largest metro areas in the U.S. based on their residents' educational attainment. *American City Business Journals, April 14, 2008*
- Scottsdale was identified as one of America's most inventive cities by *The Daily Beast.* The city ranked #25 out of 25. The 200 largest cities in the U.S. were ranked by the number of patents (applied and approved) per capita. *The Daily Beast, "The 25 Most Inventive Cities," October 2, 2011*
- Phoenix was identified as one of "America's Brainiest Bastions" by *Portfolio.com.* The metro area ranked #100 out of 200. *Portfolio.com* analyzed levels of educational attainment in the nation's 200 largest metropolitan areas. The editors established scores for five levels of educational attainment, based on relative earning power of adult workers age 25 or older. Scores were determined by comparing the median income for all workers with the median income for those workers at a specified educational level. *Portfolio.com, "America's Brainiest Bastions," December 1, 2010*

Environmental Rankings

- The Phoenix was identified as one of America's dirtiest metro areas by *Forbes.* The area ranked #8 out of 10. Criteria: year-round particulate pollution; short-term particulate pollution; ozone pollution. *Forbes, "Dirtiest Cities in America," November 4, 2011*
- The Phoenix was identified as one of North America's greenest metropolitan areas. The area ranked #24. The Green City Index is comprised of 31 indicators, and scores cities across nine categories: carbon dioxide; energy; land use; buildings; transport; water; waste; air quality; environmental governance. The 27 largest metropolitan areas in the U.S. and Canada were considered. *Economist Intelligence Unit, sponsored by Siemens, "U.S. and Canada Green City Index, 2011"*
- The Phoenix was identified as one of America's cities with the most ENERGY STAR certified buildings. The area ranked #17 out of 25. Criteria: number of ENERGY STAR labeled buildings in 2010. *U.S. Environmental Protection Agency, "Top Cities With the Most ENERGY STAR Certified Buildings," March 15, 2011*
- The Phoenix metro area was identified as one of "The Ten Biggest American Cities that are Running Out of Water" by *24/7 Wall St.* The metro area ranked #3 out of 10. *24/7 Wall St.* did an analysis of the water supply and consumption in the 30 largest metropolitan areas in the U.S. Criteria include: projected water demand as a share of available precipitation; groundwater use as a share or projected available precipitation; susceptibility to drought; projected increase in freshwater withdrawals; projected increase in summer water deficit. *24/7 Wall St., "The Ten Biggest American Cities that are Running Out of Water," November 1, 2010*
- Scottsdale was selected as one of 22 "Smarter Cities" for energy by the Natural Resources Defense Council. Criteria: investment in green power; energy efficiency measures; conservation. *Natural Resources Defense Council, "2010 Smarter Cities," July 19, 2010*
- *American City Business Journal* ranked 43 metropolitan areas in terms of their "greenness." The Phoenix metro area ranked #21. Criteria: Forty-one metros in which *ACBJ* has business weeklies, plus Indianapolis and Cleveland, were ranked based on 20 different indicators such as adoption of green technologies, utilization of environmentally sound practices, and air and water quality. *American City Business Journals, "Green City Index," March 11, 2010*
- 100 of the largest metro areas in the U.S. were analyzed in terms of their current drought severity. The Phoenix metro area ranked #23 (#1 = driest). The rankings were based on statistics such as long-term precipitation trends and patterns and the Palmer drought indices. *Sperling's BestPlaces, www.BestPlaces.net, "America's Drought-Riskiest Cities," November 2007*
- The Phoenix metro area appeared in *Country Home's* "Best Green Places" report. The area ranked #130 out of 379. Criteria: official energy policies; green power; green buildings; availability of fresh, locally grown food. *Country Home, "Best Green Places," 2008*

- Phoenix was highlighted as one of the 25 metro areas most polluted by short-term particle pollution (24-hour PM 2.5) in the U.S. The area ranked #24. *American Lung Association, State of the Air 2011*

- Phoenix was highlighted as one of the 25 metro areas most polluted by year-round particle pollution (Annual PM 2.5) in the U.S. The area ranked #2. *American Lung Association, State of the Air 2011*

- Phoenix was highlighted as one of the 25 most ozone-polluted metro areas in the U.S. The area ranked #19. *American Lung Association, State of the Air 2011*

Health/Fitness Rankings

- The Phoenix metro area was selected as one of the worst cities for bed bugs in America by Rollins corporation, the owner of seven pest control companies, including Orkin. The area ranked #34 based on the number of bed bug treatments from January to December 2011. *Rollins, "The Top 50 U.S. Cities for Bed Bugs," March 19, 2012*

- Phoenix was identified as a "2011 Asthma Capital." The area ranked #81 out of the nation's 100 largest metropolitan areas. Twelve factors were used to identify the most challenging places to live for people with asthma: estimated prevalence; self-reported prevalence; crude death rate for asthma; annual pollen score; annual air quality; public smoking laws; number of board-certified asthma specialists; school inhaler access laws; rescue medication use; controller medication use; uninsured rate; poverty rate. *Asthma and Allergy Foundation of America, "2011 Asthma Capitals"*

- Phoenix was identified as a "2011 Fall Allergy Capital." The area ranked #91 out of 100. Three groups of factors were used to identify the most severe cities for people with allergies during the fall season: annual pollen levels; medicine utilization; access to board-certified allergists. *Asthma and Allergy Foundation of America, "2011 Fall Allergy Capitals"*

- Phoenix was identified as a "2012 Spring Allergy Capital." The area ranked #72 out of 100. Three groups of factors were used to identify the most severe cities for people with allergies during the spring season: annual pollen levels; medicine utilization; access to board-certified allergists. *Asthma and Allergy Foundation of America, "2012 Spring Allergy Capitals"*

- The Phoenix metropolitan area was selected as one of the best metros for hospital care in America by *HealthGrades.com.* The rankings are based on a comprehensive study of patient death and complication rates in the nation's nearly 5,000 hospitals. Hospitals performing in the top 5% nationwide across 26 different medical procedures and diagnoses were identified. *HealthGrades.com* then ranked cities by the highest percentage of these Distinguished Hospitals for Clinical Excellence™. The Phoenix metro area ranked #2. *HealthGrades.com, "America's Top 50 Cities for Hospital Care," January 21, 2012*

- The American Academy of Dermatology ranked 26 U.S. metropolitan regions in terms of their residents knowledge, attitude and behaviors towards tanning, sun protection and skin cancer detection. The Phoenix metro area ranked #6. The results of the study are based on an online survey of over 7,000 adults nationwide. *American Academy of Dermatology, "Suntelligence: How Sun Smart is Your City," May 3, 2010*

- The Phoenix metro area appeared in the 2011 Gallup-Healthways Well-Being Index. The index, based on interviews with more than 350,000 Americans, measured jobs, finances, physical health, emotional state of mind and communities. The metro area ranked #69 out of 190. Criteria: life evaluation; emotional health; work environment; physical health; healthy behaviors; basic access (basic needs optimal for a healthy life, such as access to food and medicine, having health insurance and feeling safe while walking at night). *Gallup-Healthways, "State of Well-Being 2011"*

- The Phoenix metro area was identified as one of "America's Most Stressful Cities" by *Sperling's BestPlaces.* The metro area ranked #18 out of 50. Criteria: unemployment rate; suicide rate; commute time; mental health; poor rest; alcohol use; violent crime rate; property crime rate; cloudy days annually. *Sperling's BestPlaces, www.BestPlaces.net, "Stressful Cities 2012*

- 50 of the largest metro areas in the U.S. were analyzed in terms of their health and fitness by the American College of Sports Medicine in their "American Fitness Index." The Phoenix metro area ranked #32 (#1 = healthiest). Criteria: preventative health behaviors; levels of chronic disease; health care access; community resources and policies that support physical activity. *American College of Sports Medicine, "Health and Community Fitness Status of the 50 Largest Metropolitan Areas," August 1, 2011*

Pet Rankings

- Phoenix was selected as one of the "Top 10 Cat-Friendly Cities" in the U.S. The area ranked #2. Criteria: cat ownership per capita; level of veterinary care; microchipping; cat-friendly local ordinances. *CATalyst Council, "Top 10 Cat-Friendly Cities," March 27, 2009*

Real Estate Rankings

- Phoenix was identified as one of 13 metro areas where home prices are falling dangerously. Criteria: home price change from October 2010 to September 2011; projected home price change through 2012. *Forbes.com, "Cities Where Home Prices are Falling Dangerously," January 10, 2012*
- Phoenix was identified as one of the "Top Turnaround Housing Markets for 2012." The area ranked #2 out of 10. Criteria: year-over-year median home price appreciation; year-over-year median inventory age; year-over-year inventory reduction. *AOL Real Estate, "Top Turnaround Housing Markets for 2012," February 4, 2012*
- *Fortune* ranked the 100 largest metro areas in the U.S. in terms of projected median home price change in 2010. The Phoenix metro area ranked #92. *Fortune, "The 2010 Housing Outlook," December 9, 2009*
- Scottsdale appeared on *ApartmentRatings.com* "Top Cities for Renters" list in 2009." The area ranked #24. Overall satisfaction ratings were ranked using thousands of user submitted scores for hundreds of apartment complexes located in the 100 most populated U.S. municipalities. *ApartmentRatings.com, "2009 Renter Satisfaction Rankings"*
- The Phoenix metro area was identified as one of the "Top 25 Real Estate Investment Markets" by *FinestExperts.com.* The metro area ranked #17. Over 10,000 real estate markets were analyzed to identify the most suitable places for real estate investors to seek stability and growth. Criteria: employment; rental markets; growth levels as offset by foreclosures. *FinestExperts.com, "Top 25 Real Estate Investment Markets," January 7, 2010*
- The Phoenix metro area was identified as one of "America's 25 Weakest Housing Markets" by *Forbes*. The metro area ranked #12. Criteria: metro areas with populations over 500,000 were ranked based on projected home values through 2011. *Forbes.com, "America's 25 Weakest Housing Markets," January 7, 2009*
- The nation's largest metro areas were analyzed in terms of the percentage of households entering some stage of foreclosure in 2011. The Phoenix metro area ranked #6 out of 20 (#1 = highest foreclosure rate). *RealtyTrac, 2011 Year-End Foreclosure Market Report, January 12, 2012*
- The nation's largest metro areas were analyzed in terms of the best places to buy pre-foreclosures (short sales). The Phoenix metro area ranked #9 out of 10. Criteria: at least 500 pre-foreclosure sales during the fourth quarter and a short sales increase of at least five percent from a year ago. The areas selected posted the biggest discounts on the sales of pre-foreclosure properties. *RealtyTrac, "Fourth Quarter and Year-End 2011 U.S. Foreclosure Sales Report: Shifting Towards Short Sales," February 28, 2012*
- The Phoenix metro area was identified as one of the 10 best cities for "Real Estate Steals" in the U.S. by *U.S. News and World Report.* The metro area was ranked #8. Criteria: average and quarterly price-to-income ratios. *U.S. News and World Report, "10 Cities for Real Estate Steals," February 18, 2010*
- The Phoenix metro area appeared in a *Wall Street Journal* article ranking cities by "housing stress." The metro area was ranked #11 (#1 = most stress). Criteria: fraction of mortgage-holding homeowners with a monthly housing payment in excess of 30 percent of income; percentage of people without health insurance; unemployment rate. *The Wall Street Journal, "Which Cities Face Biggest Housing Risk," October 5, 2010*

- The Center for Housing Policy ranked 210 U.S. metropolitan areas by the fair market rent for a two-bedroom unit. The Phoenix metro area was ranked #76. (#1 = most expensive) with a rent of $919. Criteria: Fair Market Rent (FMR) in effect during the fourth quarter of 2009 based on HUD's fiscal year 2010 FMRs. *The Center for Housing Policy, "Paycheck to Paycheck: Most to Least Expensive Rental Markets in 2009"*

- The Phoenix metro area was identified as one of the worst housing markets of the decade by *Forbes*. Criteria: decrease in housing values per square foot since January 2000. *Forbes, "America's 5 Best (and Worst) Housing Markets of the Decade," December 7, 2010*

- The Phoenix metro area was identified as one of the top 20 cities in terms of decreasing home equity. The metro area was ranked #3. Criteria: percentage of home equity relative to the home's current value. *Forbes.com, "Where Americans are Losing Home Equity Most," May 1, 2010*

- The Phoenix metro area was identified as one of the markets with the worst expected performance in home prices over the next 12 months. *Local Market Monitor, "First Quarter Home Price Forecast for Largest US Markets," March 2, 2011*

- The Phoenix metro area was identified as one of the best U.S. markets to invest in rental property" by HomeVestors and Local Market Monitor. The area ranked #8 out of 100. Criteria: risk-return premium relative to national average. *HomeVestors and Local Market Monitor, "Best 100 U.S. Markets to Invest in Rental Property," March 9, 2012*

Safety Rankings

- Allstate ranked the 193 largest cities in America in terms of driver safety. Scottsdale ranked #25. In addition, drivers were 10.3% less likely to have had an accident compared to the national average. Allstate researchers analyzed internal property damage reported claims over a two-year period (from January 2008 to December 2009) to protect findings from external influences such as weather or road construction. A weighted average of the two-year numbers determined the annual percentages. The report defines an auto crash as any collision resulting in a property damage claim. *Allstate, "2011 Allstate America's Best Drivers Report™"*

- The National Insurance Crime Bureau ranked 366 metro areas in the U.S. in terms of per capita rates of vehicle theft. The Phoenix metro area ranked #56 (#1 = highest rate). Criteria: number of vehicle theft offenses per 100,000 inhabitants in 2010. *National Insurance Crime Bureau, "Hot Spots," June 21, 2011*

- The Phoenix metro area was identified as one of the most dangerous metro areas for pedestrians by Transportation for America. The metro area ranked #8 out of 52 metro areas with over 1 million residents. Criteria: area's population divided by the number of pedestrian fatalities in that area. *Transportation for America, "Dangerous by Design 2011"*

Seniors/Retirement Rankings

- Bankers Life and Casualty Company, in partnership with Sperling's BestPlaces, ranked the nation's 50 largest metro areas in terms of the "Best U.S. Cities for Seniors." The Phoenix metro area ranked #40. Criteria: healthcare; transportation; housing; environment; economy; health and longevity; social and spiritual life; crime. *Bankers Life and Casualty Company, Center for a Secure Retirement, "Best U.S. Cities for Seniors 2011," September 2011*

- The Phoenix metro area was identified as one of the "Best Places for Bargain Retirement Homes" by *Forbes*. The metro area ranked #9 out of 10. Criteria: low cost of living; stable home prices; low taxes; reasonable average home prices. *Forbes.com, "Best Places for Bargain Retirement Homes," January 12, 2011*

- The Phoenix metro area was selected as one of "The 10 Most Affordable Cities for Long-Term Care" by *U.S. News & World Report*. Criteria: costs at nursing homes, assisted living facilities, and adult day health care facilities; cost for licensed home health aides. *U.S. News & World Report, "The 10 Most Affordable Cities for Long-Term Care," May 17, 2010*

Sports/Recreation Rankings

- Scottsdale was chosen as a bicycle friendly community by the League of American Bicyclists. A Bicycle Friendly Community welcomes cyclists by providing safe accommodation for cycling and encouraging people to bike for transportation and recreation. There are four award levels: Platinum; Gold; Silver; and Bronze. The community achieved an award level of Gold. *League of American Bicyclists, "Bicycle Friendly Community Master List 2011"*
- Scottsdale was chosen as one of America's best cities for bicycling. The city ranked #20 out of 50. Criteria: number of segregated bike lanes, municipal bike racks, and bike boulevards; vibrant and diverse bike culture; smart, savvy bike shops; interviews with national and local advocates, bike shops and other experts. The editors only considered cities with populations of 100,000 or more. *Bicycling, "America's Best Bike Cities," April 2010*
- The Phoenix was selected as one of the best metro areas for golf in America by *Golf Digest.* The Phoenix area was ranked #15 out of 20. Criteria: climate; cost of public golf; quality of public golf; accessibility. *Golf Digest, "The Top 20 Cities for Golf," October 2011*

Transportation Rankings

- The Phoenix metro area appeared on *Forbes* list of the best and worst cities for commuters. The metro area ranked #36 out of 60 (#1 is best). Criteria: travel time; road congestion; travel delays. *Forbes.com, "Best and Worst Cities for Commuters," February 16, 2010*

Women/Minorities Rankings

- Phoenix was ranked #48 out of 100 metro areas in *SELF Magazine's* ranking of America's healthiest places for women." A panel of experts came up with more than 50 criteria including death and disease rates, environmental indicators, community resources, and lifestyle habits. *SELF Magazine, "Secrets of America's Healthiest Women," December 2008*
- The Phoenix metro area appeared on *Forbes'* list of the "Best Cities for Minority Entrepreneurs." The area ranked #48 out of 10. Criteria: 52 metropolitan statistical areas were examined. For each ethnicity (African Americans, Asians and Hispanics), the editors measured housing affordability, population growth, income growth, and entrepreneurship (per capita self-employment). *Forbes, "Best Cities for Minority Entrepreneurs," March 23, 2011*

Miscellaneous Rankings

- The Phoenix metro area was selected as one of "The Best U.S. Cities for Bargain Shopping" by *Forbes.* The area ranked #3 out of 10. Criteria: number of outlet stores; gross leasable retail space in major malls; low consumer price index; low sales tax rate. Indicators were examined in the nation's 50 largest metropolitan areas. *Forbes, "The Best U.S. Cities for Bargain Shopping," January 20, 2012*
- Energizer Holdings, the makers of Edge® shave gel, in partnership with Sperling's BestPlaces, ranked 50 major metro areas in terms of everyday irritations. The Phoenix metro area ranked #10. Criteria: humidity levels; weather conditions; incidence of traffic delays and congestion; average commute times; frequency of flight delays and cancellations; rates of sleeplessness; underemployment; pollens and allergens; pests; comedy clubs per capita. *Energizer Holdings, "Most Irritation Prone Cities," July 23, 2010*
- Mars Chocolate North America, the makers of COMBOS®, in partnership with Sperling's BestPlaces, ranked 50 major metro areas in terms of their "manliness." The Phoenix metro area ranked #32. Criteria: number of professional sports teams; number of nearby NASCAR tracks and racing events; manly lifestyle; concentration of manly retail stores; manly occupations per capita; salty snack sales; "Board of Manliness" rankings. *Mars Chocolate North America, "America's Manliest Cities 2011," September 1, 2011*

Business Environment

CITY FINANCES

City Government Finances

Component	2009 ($000)	2009 ($ per capita)
Total Revenues	619,877	2,630
Total Expenditures	710,701	3,016
Debt Outstanding	1,120,168	4,753
Cash and Securities[1]	498,359	2,115

Note: (1) Cash and security holdings of a government at the close of its fiscal year, including those of its dependent agencies, utilities, and liquor stores.
Source: U.S Census Bureau, State & Local Government Finances 2009

City Government Revenue by Source

Source	2009 ($000)	2009 ($ per capita)
General Revenue		
From Federal Government	7,002	30
From State Government	79,946	339
From Local Governments	22,501	95
Taxes		
Property	60,516	257
Sales and Gross Receipts	158,650	673
Personal Income	0	0
Corporate Income	0	0
Motor Vehicle License	0	0
Other Taxes	8,179	35
Current Charges	73,977	314
Liquor Store	0	0
Utility	85,130	361
Employee Retirement	0	0

Source: U.S Census Bureau, State & Local Government Finances 2009

City Government Expenditures by Function

Function	2009 ($000)	2009 ($ per capita)	2009 (%)
General Direct Expenditures			
Air Transportation	2,751	12	0.4
Corrections	0	0	0.0
Education	0	0	0.0
Employment Security Administration	0	0	0.0
Financial Administration	9,701	41	1.4
Fire Protection	30,733	130	4.3
General Public Buildings	0	0	0.0
Governmental Administration, Other	31,811	135	4.5
Health	0	0	0.0
Highways	75,776	322	10.7
Hospitals	0	0	0.0
Housing and Community Development	7,368	31	1.0
Interest on General Debt	51,023	216	7.2
Judicial and Legal	12,407	53	1.7
Libraries	11,284	48	1.6
Parking	0	0	0.0
Parks and Recreation	51,058	217	7.2
Police Protection	89,264	379	12.6
Public Welfare	0	0	0.0
Sewerage	56,877	241	8.0
Solid Waste Management	17,082	72	2.4
Veterans' Services	0	0	0.0
Liquor Store	0	0	0.0
Utility	132,673	563	18.7
Employee Retirement	0	0	0.0

Source: U.S Census Bureau, State & Local Government Finances 2009

Municipal Bond Ratings

Area	Moody's	S&P	Fitch
City	n/a	n/a	n/a

Rating Systems (shown in declining order of credit quality): Moody's– Aaa, Aa, A, Baa, Ba, B, Caa, Ca, C (numerical modifiers 1, 2, and 3 are added to letter-rating); S&P– AAA, AA, A, BBB, BB, B, CCC, CC, C; Fitch– AAA, AA, A, BBB, BB, B, CCC, CC, C. Ratings may be modified by the addition of a plus or minus sign to show relative standing within the major rating categories.
Notes: n/a Not Available; w/d Withdrawn (1) Not Reviewed; (2) Issuer Rating/No General Obligation; (3) Standard and Poor's Issue Credit Rating (ICR) is a current opinion of an obliger with respect to a specific financial obligation, a specific class of financial obligations, or a specific financial program.
Source: U.S. Census Bureau, 2012 Statistical Abstract, Bond Ratings for City Governments by Largest Cities: 2010

DEMOGRAPHICS

Population Growth

Area	1990 Census	2000 Census	2010 Census	Population Growth (%) 1990-2000	Population Growth (%) 2000-2010
City	130,300	202,705	217,385	55.6	7.2
MSA[1]	2,238,480	3,251,876	4,192,887	45.3	28.9
U.S.	248,709,873	281,421,906	308,745,538	13.2	9.7

Note: (1) Figures cover the Phoenix-Mesa-Glendale, AZ Metropolitan Statistical Area—see Appendix B for areas included
Source: U.S. Census Bureau, 2010 Census

Household Size

Area	Persons in Household (%) One	Two	Three	Four	Five	Six	Seven or More	Average Household Size
City	34.4	39.4	12.0	9.3	3.4	1.1	0.5	2.14
MSA[1]	25.4	33.2	14.8	13.2	7.3	3.4	2.8	2.68
U.S.	26.7	32.8	16.1	13.4	6.5	2.6	1.9	2.58

Note: (1) Figures cover the Phoenix-Mesa-Glendale, AZ Metropolitan Statistical Area—see Appendix B for areas included
Source: U.S. Census Bureau, 2010 Census

Race

Area	White Alone[2] (%)	Black Alone[2] (%)	Asian Alone[2] (%)	AIAN[3] Alone[2] (%)	NHOPI[4] Alone[2] (%)	Other Race Alone[2] (%)	Two or More Races (%)
City	89.3	1.7	3.3	0.8	0.1	2.5	2.3
MSA[1]	73.0	5.0	3.3	2.4	0.2	12.7	3.5
U.S.	72.4	12.6	4.8	0.9	0.2	6.2	2.9

Note: (1) Figures cover the Phoenix-Mesa-Glendale, AZ Metropolitan Statistical Area—see Appendix B for areas included; (2) Alone is defined as not being in combination with one or more other races; (3) American Indian and Alaska Native; (4) Native Hawaiian and Other Pacific Islander
Source: U.S. Census Bureau, 2010 Census

Hispanic or Latino Origin

Area	Hispanic or Latino (%)	Mexican (%)	Puerto Rican (%)	Cuban (%)	Other Hispanic or Latino (%)
City	8.8	6.6	0.4	0.1	1.7
MSA[1]	29.5	25.5	0.6	0.2	3.2
U.S.	16.3	10.3	1.5	0.6	4.0

Note: Persons of Hispanic or Latino origin can be of any race; (1) Figures cover the Phoenix-Mesa-Glendale, AZ Metropolitan Statistical Area—see Appendix B for areas included
Source: U.S. Census Bureau, 2010 Census

Segregation

Type	Segregation Indices[1]				Percent Change		
	1990	2000	2010	2010 Rank[2]	1990-2000	1990-2010	2000-2010
Black/White	50.1	45.1	43.6	86	-5.0	-6.4	-1.5
Asian/White	28.1	30.1	32.7	85	2.0	4.6	2.6
Hispanic/White	48.6	52.2	49.3	28	3.5	0.7	-2.8

Note: Figures are based on an analysis of 1990, 2000, and 2010 Census Decennial Census tract data by William H. Frey, Brookings Institution and the University of Michigan Social Science Data Analysis Network. In this analysis all racial groups (whites, blacks, and asians) are non-Hispanic members of those races. Hispanics are shown as a separate category; All figures cover the Metropolitan Statistical Area (see Appendix B for areas included); (1) Segregation Indices are Dissimilarity Indices that measure the degree to which the minority group is distributed differently than whites across census tracts. They range from 0 (complete integration) to 100 (complete segregation) where the value indicates the percentage of the minority group that needs to move to be distributed exactly like whites; (2) Ranges from 1 (most segregated) to 102 (least segregated); n/a not available.
Source: www.CensusScope.org

Ancestry

Area	German	Irish	English	American	Italian	Polish	French[2]	Scottish	Dutch
City	20.4	14.6	12.6	4.2	8.4	4.8	3.5	3.1	2.0
MSA[1]	16.0	10.5	9.3	5.1	4.9	2.8	2.7	1.9	1.5
U.S.	16.1	11.6	8.8	6.1	5.7	3.2	3.0	1.9	1.6

Note: Figures are the percentage of the total population reporting a particular ancestry. The nine most commonly reported ancestries in the U.S. are shown. Figures include multiple ancestries (e.g. if a person reported being Irish and Italian, they were included in both columns); (1) Figures cover the Phoenix-Mesa-Glendale, AZ Metropolitan Statistical Area—see Appendix B for areas included; (2) Excludes Basque
Source: U.S. Census Bureau, 2008-2010 American Community Survey 3-Year Estimates

Foreign-Born Population

Area	Percent of Population Born in								
	Any Foreign Country	Mexico	Asia	Europe	Carribean	South America	Central America[2]	Africa	Canada
City	11.2	2.1	3.2	2.6	0.2	0.7	0.3	0.5	1.7
MSA[1]	14.9	8.8	2.7	1.4	0.2	0.3	0.5	0.4	0.6
U.S.	12.8	3.8	3.6	1.6	1.2	0.9	1.0	0.5	0.3

Note: (1) Figures cover the Phoenix-Mesa-Glendale, AZ Metropolitan Statistical Area—see Appendix B for areas included; (2) Excludes Mexico.
Source: U.S. Census Bureau, 2008-2010 American Community Survey 3-Year Estimates

Marital Status

Area	Never Married	Now Married[2]	Separated	Widowed	Divorced
City	27.6	52.0	1.0	6.4	13.0
MSA[1]	31.8	49.9	1.6	5.0	11.7
U.S.	31.6	49.6	2.2	6.1	10.7

Note: Figures are percentages and cover the population 15 years of age and older; (1) Figures cover the Phoenix-Mesa-Glendale, AZ Metropolitan Statistical Area—see Appendix B for areas included; (2) Excludes separated
Source: U.S. Census Bureau, 2008-2010 American Community Survey 3-Year Estimates

Age

Area	Percent of Population							Median Age
	Under Age 5	Age 5 to 17	Age 18 to 34	Age 35 to 49	Age 50 to 64	Age 65 to 79	80 Years and Over	
City	4.2	13.6	18.9	20.4	22.9	14.4	5.6	45.4
MSA[1]	7.5	19.0	24.0	20.5	16.8	9.1	3.2	34.7
U.S.	6.5	17.5	23.2	20.7	19.0	9.4	3.6	37.2

Note: (1) Figures cover the Phoenix-Mesa-Glendale, AZ Metropolitan Statistical Area—see Appendix B for areas included
Source: U.S. Census Bureau, 2010 Census

Male/Female Ratio

Area	Males	Females	Males per 100 Females
City	104,930	112,455	93.3
MSA[1]	2,085,630	2,107,257	99.0
U.S.	151,781,326	156,964,212	96.7

Note: (1) Figures cover the Phoenix-Mesa-Glendale, AZ Metropolitan Statistical Area—see Appendix B for areas included
Source: U.S. Census Bureau, 2010 Census

Religious Groups

Area	Catholic	Baptist	Non-Den.	Methodist[2]	Lutheran	LDS[3]	Pente-costal	Presby-terian[4]	Muslim[5]	Judaism
MSA[1]	13.4	3.5	5.2	1.0	1.6	6.1	2.9	0.6	0.3	0.2
U.S.	19.1	9.3	4.0	4.0	2.3	2.0	1.9	1.6	0.8	0.7

Note: Figures are the number of adherents as a percentage of the total population; (1) Figures cover the Phoenix-Mesa-Glendale, AZ Metropolitan Statistical Area—see Appendix B for areas included; (2) Methodist/Pietist; (3) Latter Day Saints; (4) Reformed; (5) Figures are estimates
Source: Association of Statisticians of American Religious Bodies, 2010 U.S. Religion Census: Religious Congregations & Membership Study

ECONOMY

Gross Metropolitan Product

Area	2007	2008	2009	2010	2010 Rank[2]
MSA[1]	196.4	196.0	187.4	190.6	15

Note: Figures are in billions of dollars; (1) Figures cover the Phoenix-Mesa-Glendale, AZ Metropolitan Statistical Area—see Appendix B for areas included; (2) Rank ranges from 1 to 363
Source: The United States Conference of Mayors, "U.S. Metro Economies: GMP and Employment Forecasts," June 2011

Economic Growth

Area	2007-2009 (%)	2010 (%)	2011 (%)	Rank[2]
MSA[1]	-3.9	0.9	2.1	303
U.S.	-1.3	2.9	2.5	–

Note: Figures are real Gross Metropolitan Product growth rates and represent annual average percent change; (1) Figures cover the Phoenix-Mesa-Glendale, AZ Metropolitan Statistical Area—see Appendix B for areas included; (2) Rank ranges from 1 to 363
Source: The United States Conference of Mayors, "U.S. Metro Economies: GMP and Employment Forecasts," June 2011

Metropolitan Area Exports

Area	2005	2006	2007	2008	2009	2010	2010 Rank[2]
MSA[1]	8,473.0	10,954.8	12,818.2	12,623.6	7,947.5	9,342.7	29

Note: Figures are in millions of dollars; (1) Figures cover the Phoenix-Mesa-Glendale, AZ Metropolitan Statistical Area—see Appendix B for areas included; (2) Rank ranges from 1 to 369
Source: U.S. Department of Commerce, International Trade Administration, Office of Trade & Industry Information, Manufacturing & Services, data extracted April 2, 2012

INCOME

Income

Area	Per Capita ($)	Median Household ($)	Average Household ($)
City	49,337	71,021	106,734
MSA[1]	26,243	52,904	70,586
U.S.	26,942	51,222	70,116

Note: (1) Figures cover the Phoenix-Mesa-Glendale, AZ Metropolitan Statistical Area—see Appendix B for areas included
Source: U.S. Census Bureau, 2008-2010 American Community Survey 3-Year Estimates

Household Income Distribution

Area	Percent of Households Earning							
	Under $15,000	$15,000 -24,999	$25,000 -34,999	$35,000 -49,999	$50,000 -74,999	$75,000 -99,000	$100,000 -149,999	$150,000 and up
City	8.2	8.4	8.2	12.0	16.0	12.3	15.1	19.9
MSA[1]	11.1	10.1	10.7	15.1	19.5	12.7	12.9	7.9
U.S.	13.0	11.0	10.6	14.2	18.5	12.1	12.2	8.4

Note: (1) Figures cover the Phoenix-Mesa-Glendale, AZ Metropolitan Statistical Area—see Appendix B for areas included
Source: U.S. Census Bureau, 2008-2010 American Community Survey 3-Year Estimates

Poverty Rate

Area	All Ages	Under 18 Years Old	18 to 64 Years Old	65 Years and Over
City	7.7	9.6	7.9	5.7
MSA[1]	14.9	21.2	13.6	7.1
U.S.	14.4	20.1	13.1	9.4

Note: Figures are percentage of people whose income during the past 12 months was below the poverty level; (1) Figures cover the Phoenix-Mesa-Glendale, AZ Metropolitan Statistical Area—see Appendix B for areas included
Source: U.S. Census Bureau, 2008-2010 American Community Survey 3-Year Estimates

Personal Bankruptcy Filing Rate

Area	2006	2007	2008	2009	2010	2011
Maricopa County	1.40	1.87	3.47	6.22	7.81	6.60
U.S.	2.00	2.73	3.53	4.61	4.97	4.37

Note: Numbers are per 1,000 population and include Chapter 7 and Chapter 13 filings
Source: Federal Deposit Insurance Corporation, Regional Economic Conditions, March 9, 2012

EMPLOYMENT

Labor Force and Employment

Area	Civilian Labor Force			Workers Employed		
	Dec. 2010	Dec. 2011	% Chg.	Dec. 2010	Dec. 2011	% Chg.
City	128,435	128,808	0.3	120,385	121,410	0.9
MSA[1]	2,125,593	2,127,867	0.1	1,944,188	1,960,752	0.9
U.S.	153,156,000	153,373,000	0.1	139,159,000	140,681,000	1.1

Note: Data is not seasonally adjusted and covers workers 16 years of age and older; (1) Metropolitan Statistical Area—see Appendix B for areas included
Source: Bureau of Labor Statistics, http://stats.bls.gov

Unemployment Rate

Area	2011											
	Jan.	Feb.	Mar.	Apr.	May	Jun.	Jul.	Aug.	Sep.	Oct.	Nov.	Dec.
City	6.8	6.5	6.4	6.0	5.9	6.6	6.4	6.2	5.9	5.9	5.6	5.7
MSA[1]	9.3	8.8	8.7	8.1	8.0	9.0	8.7	8.4	8.0	8.1	7.7	7.9
U.S.	9.8	9.5	9.2	8.7	8.7	9.3	9.3	9.1	8.8	8.5	8.2	8.3

Note: Data is not seasonally adjusted and covers workers 16 years of age and older; All figures are percentages; (1) Metropolitan Statistical Area—see Appendix B for areas included
Source: Bureau of Labor Statistics, http://stats.bls.gov

Projected Unemployment Rate

Area	2010 (%)	2011 (%)	2012 (%)	2013 (%)
MSA[1]	8.9	8.4	7.9	7.3

Note: (1) Metropolitan Statistical Area—see Appendix B for areas included
Source: The United States Conference of Mayors, "U.S. Metro Economies: GMP and Employment Forecasts," June 2011

Employment by Occupation

Occupation Classification	City (%)	MSA[1] (%)	U.S. (%)
Management, Business, Science, and Arts	51.0	35.7	35.6
Natural Resources, Construction, and Maintenance	3.6	9.5	9.5
Production, Transportation, and Material Moving	4.5	9.4	12.1
Sales and Office	27.9	27.7	25.2
Service	13.1	17.6	17.6

Note: Figures cover employed civilians 16 years of age and older; (1) Figures cover the Phoenix-Mesa-Glendale, AZ Metropolitan Statistical Area—see Appendix B for areas included
Source: U.S. Census Bureau, 2008-2010 American Community Survey 3-Year Estimates

Employment by Industry

Sector	MSA[1] Number of Employees	MSA[1] Percent of Total	U.S. Percent of Total
Construction	82,200	4.7	4.1
Education and Health Services	255,000	14.6	15.2
Financial Activities	143,100	8.2	5.8
Government	236,600	13.5	16.8
Information	28,600	1.6	2.0
Leisure and Hospitality	180,200	10.3	9.9
Manufacturing	112,000	6.4	8.9
Mining and Logging	3,300	0.2	0.6
Other Services	63,500	3.6	4.0
Professional and Business Services	282,900	16.2	13.3
Retail Trade	218,700	12.5	11.5
Transportation and Utilities	62,200	3.6	3.8
Wholesale Trade	81,800	4.7	4.2

Note: Figures cover non-farm employment as of December 2011 and are not seasonally adjusted; (1) Metropolitan Statistical Area—see Appendix B for areas included
Source: Bureau of Labor Statistics, http://stats.bls.gov

Occupations with Greatest Projected Employment Growth: 2008 – 2018

Occupation[1]	2008 Employment	2018 Projected Employment	Numeric Employment Change	Percent Employment Change
Customer Service Representatives	64,870	74,760	9,890	15.2
Registered Nurses	40,510	50,010	9,500	23.5
Combined Food Preparation and Serving Workers, Including Fast Food	43,970	52,950	8,980	20.4
Retail Salespersons	86,670	94,880	8,210	9.5
Cashiers	62,340	67,580	5,240	8.4
Waiters and Waitresses	50,230	55,440	5,210	10.4
Stock Clerks and Order Fillers	41,050	46,200	5,150	12.5
Office Clerks, General	60,330	64,570	4,240	7.0
Postsecondary Teachers	32,770	36,940	4,170	12.7
Accountants and Auditors	28,320	32,250	3,930	13.9

Note: Projections cover Arizona; (1) Sorted by numeric employment change
Source: www.projectionscentral.com, State Occupational Projections, 2008–2018 Long-Term Projections

Fastest Growing Occupations: 2008 – 2018

Occupation[1]	2008 Employment	2018 Projected Employment	Numeric Employment Change	Percent Employment Change
Biomedical Engineers	240	370	130	54.2
Credit Authorizers, Checkers, and Clerks	7,080	10,760	3,680	52.0
Network Systems and Data Communications Analysts	4,590	6,450	1,860	40.5
Medical Scientists, Except Epidemiologists	880	1,220	340	38.6
Radiation Therapists	610	820	210	34.4
Physician Assistants	1,290	1,730	440	34.1
Dental Hygienists	2,690	3,570	880	32.7
Pharmacy Technicians	7,700	10,170	2,470	32.1
Surgical Technologists	1,560	2,050	490	31.4
Dental Assistants	6,320	8,280	1,960	31.0

Note: Projections cover Arizona; (1) Sorted by percent employment change and excludes occupations with numeric employment change less than 100
Source: www.projectionscentral.com, State Occupational Projections, 2008–2018 Long-Term Projections

Average Wages

Occupation	$/Hr.	Occupation	$/Hr.
Accountants and Auditors	29.62	Maids and Housekeeping Cleaners	9.60
Automotive Mechanics	19.98	Maintenance and Repair Workers	17.63
Bookkeepers	17.77	Marketing Managers	52.33
Carpenters	19.96	Nuclear Medicine Technologists	35.95
Cashiers	10.97	Nurses, Licensed Practical	25.14
Clerks, General Office	14.89	Nurses, Registered	35.74
Clerks, Receptionists/Information	13.73	Nursing Aides/Orderlies/Attendants	13.23
Clerks, Shipping/Receiving	14.26	Packers and Packagers, Hand	10.78
Computer Programmers	37.73	Physical Therapists	37.94
Computer Support Specialists	23.79	Postal Service Mail Carriers	25.15
Computer Systems Analysts	36.35	Real Estate Brokers	n/a
Cooks, Restaurant	14.05	Retail Salespersons	12.05
Dentists	89.20	Sales Reps., Exc. Tech./Scientific	30.16
Electrical Engineers	47.97	Sales Reps., Tech./Scientific	39.60
Electricians	21.37	Secretaries, Exc. Legal/Med./Exec.	15.99
Financial Managers	51.98	Security Guards	13.08
First-Line Supervisors/Managers, Sales	19.48	Surgeons	n/a
Food Preparation Workers	10.57	Teacher Assistants	11.00
General and Operations Managers	51.63	Teachers, Elementary School	20.60
Hairdressers/Cosmetologists	11.42	Teachers, Secondary School	21.00
Internists	93.77	Telemarketers	14.81
Janitors and Cleaners	11.50	Truck Drivers, Heavy/Tractor-Trailer	20.92
Landscaping/Groundskeeping Workers	11.12	Truck Drivers, Light/Delivery Svcs.	17.50
Lawyers	62.72	Waiters and Waitresses	10.36

Note: Wage data covers the Phoenix-Mesa-Glendale, AZ Metropolitan Statistical Area—see Appendix B for areas included. Hourly wages for elementary/secondary school teachers and teacher assistants were calculated by the editors from annual wage data assuming a 40 hour work week; n/a not available.
Source: Bureau of Labor Statistics, Metro Area Occupational Employment and Wage Estimates, May 2011

RESIDENTIAL REAL ESTATE

Building Permits

Area	Single-Family			Multi-Family			Total		
	2010	2011	Pct. Chg.	2010	2011	Pct. Chg.	2010	2011	Pct. Chg.
City	160	148	-7.5	134	257	91.8	294	405	37.8
MSA[1]	7,212	7,297	1.2	1,088	1,784	64.0	8,300	9,081	9.4
U.S.	447,311	418,498	-6.4	157,299	205,563	30.7	604,610	624,061	3.2

Note: (1) Metropolitan Statistical Area—see Appendix B for areas included; figures represent new, privately-owned housing units authorized (unadjusted data); All permit data are based on estimates with imputation.
Source: U.S. Census Bureau, Manufacturing, Mining, and Construction Statistics, Building Permits, 2010, 2011

Homeownership Rate

Area	2005 (%)	2006 (%)	2007 (%)	2008 (%)	2009 (%)	2010 (%)	2011 (%)
MSA[1]	71.2	72.5	70.8	70.2	69.8	66.5	63.3
U.S.	68.9	68.8	68.1	67.8	67.4	66.9	66.1

Note: (1) Metropolitan Statistical Area—see Appendix B for areas included
Source: U.S. Census Bureau, Housing Vacancies and Homeownership Annual Statistics: 2011

Housing Vacancy Rates

Area	Gross Vacancy Rate[2] (%)			Year-Round Vacancy Rate[3] (%)			Rental Vacancy Rate[4] (%)			Homeowner Vacancy Rate[5] (%)		
	2009	2010	2011	2009	2010	2011	2009	2010	2011	2009	2010	2011
MSA[1]	18.6	18.4	16.7	13.2	12.9	10.8	18.3	16.3	10.9	3.1	2.9	3.1
U.S.	14.5	14.3	14.2	11.3	11.3	11.1	10.6	10.2	9.5	2.6	2.6	2.5

Note: (1) Metropolitan Statistical Area—see Appendix B for areas included; (2) The percentage of the total housing inventory that is vacant; (3) The percentage of the housing inventory (excluding seasonal units) that is year-round vacant; (4) The percentage of rental inventory that is vacant for rent; (5) The percentage of homeowner inventory that is vacant for sale
Source: U.S. Census Bureau, Housing Vacancies and Homeownership Annual Statistics: 2011

TAXES

State Corporate Income Tax Rates

State	Tax Rate (%)	Income Brackets ($)	Num. of Brackets	Financial Institution Tax Rate (%)[a]	Federal Income Tax Ded.
Arizona	6.968 (b)	Flat rate	1	6.968 (b)	No

Note: Tax rates as of January 1, 2012; (a) Rates listed are the corporate income tax rate applied to financial institutions or excise taxes based on income. Some states have other taxes based upon the value of deposits or shares; (b) Minimum tax is $50 in Arizona, $100 in District of Columbia, $50 in North Dakota (banks), $500 in Rhode Island, $200 per location in South Dakota (banks), $100 in Utah, $250 in Vermont.
Source: Federation of Tax Administrators, "State Corporate Income Tax Rates, 2012"

State Individual Income Tax Rates

State	Tax Rate (%)	Income Brackets ($)	Num. of Brackets	Personal Exempt. ($)[1] Single	Personal Exempt. ($)[1] Dependents	Fed. Inc. Tax Ded.
Arizona	2.59 - 4.54	10,000 (b)-150,001 (b)	5	2,100	2,100	No

Note: Tax rates as of January 1, 2012; Local- and county-level taxes are not included; n/a not applicable; (1) Married joint filers generally receive double the single exemption; (b) For joint returns, taxes are twice the tax on half the couple's income.
Source: Federation of Tax Administrators, "State Individual Income Tax Rates, 2012"

Various State and Local Tax Rates

State	State and Local Sales and Use (%)	State Sales and Use (%)	Gasoline[1] (¢/gal.)	Cigarette[2] ($/pack)	Spirits[3] ($/gal.)	Wine[4] ($/gal.)	Beer[5] ($/gal.)
Arizona	8.95	6.60	19.0	2.00	3.00	0.84	0.16

Note: All tax rates as of January 1, 2012 except beer, wine and spirits (September 1, 2011); (1) The American Petroleum Institute has developed a methodology for determining the average tax rate on a gallon of fuel. Rates may include any of the following: excise taxes, environmental fees, storage tank fees, other fees or taxes, general sales tax, and local taxes. In states where gasoline is subject to the general sales tax, or where the fuel tax is based on the average sale price, the average rate determined by API is sensitive to changes in the price of gasoline. States that fully or partially apply general sales taxes to gasoline: CA, CO, GA, IL, IN, MI, NY; (2) The federal excise tax of $1.0066 per pack and local taxes are not included; (3) Rates are those applicable to off-premise sales of 40% alcohol by volume (a.b.v.) distilled spirits in 750ml containers. Local excise taxes are excluded; (4) Rates are those applicable to off-premise sales of 11% a.b.v. non-carbonated wine in 750ml containers; (5) Rates are those applicable to off-premise sales of 4.7% a.b.v. beer in 12 ounce containers.
Source: Tax Foundation, 2012 Facts & Figures: How Does Your State Compare?

State-Local Tax Burdens

Area	Rate (%)	Rank[1]	Per Capita Taxes Paid to Home State ($)	Total State and Local Per Capita Taxes Paid ($)	Per Capita Income ($)
Arizona	8.7	38	2,177	3,140	36,228
U.S. Average	9.8	-	3,057	4,160	42,539

Note: Figures cover 2009; (1) Rank ranges from 1 to 50 where 1 is highest tax burden
Source: Tax Foundation, State-Local Tax Burdens, All States, 2009

State Business Tax Climate Index Rankings

State	Overall Rank	Corporate Tax Index Rank	Individual Income Tax Index Rank	Sales Tax Index Rank	Unemployment Insurance Tax Index Rank	Property Tax Index Rank
Arizona	27	28	17	50	1	5

Note: The index is a measure of how each state's tax laws affect economic performance. The lower the rank, the more favorable a state's tax system is for business. States without a given tax are given a ranking of 1.
Source: Tax Foundation, Major Components of the State Business Tax Climate Index, FY 2012

COMMERCIAL REAL ESTATE

Office Market

Market Area	Inventory (sq. ft.)	Vacant (sq. ft.)	Vac. Rate (%)	Under Constr. (sq. ft.)	Asking Rent ($/sf/yr)	
					Class A	Class B
Phoenix	68,508,745	18,987,702	27.7	210,202	23.46	18.55

Source: Grubb & Ellis, Office Markets Trends, 4th Quarter 2011

Industrial Market

Market Area	Inventory (sq. ft.)	Vacant (sq. ft.)	Vac. Rate (%)	Under Constr. (sq. ft.)	Asking Rent ($/sf/yr)	
					WH/Dist	R&D/Flex
Phoenix	272,186,144	35,152,622	12.9	1,713,983	4.44	11.64

Source: Grubb & Ellis, Industrial Markets Trends, 4th Quarter 2011

COMMERCIAL UTILITIES

Typical Monthly Electric Bills

Area	Commercial Service ($/month)		Industrial Service ($/month)	
	1,500 kWh	40 kW demand 14,000 kWh	1,000 kW demand 200,000 kWh	50,000 kW demand 15,000,000 kWh
City	253	1,761	27,301	1,499,060
Average[1]	189	1,616	25,197	1,470,813

Note: Based on total rates in effect July 1, 2011; (1) average based on 184 utilities surveyed
Source: Edison Electric Institute, Typical Bills and Average Rates Report, Summer 2011

TRANSPORTATION

Means of Transportation to Work

Area	Car/Truck/Van		Public Transportation			Bicycle	Walked	Other Means	Worked at Home
	Drove Alone	Car-pooled	Bus	Subway	Railroad				
City	77.5	6.6	1.6	0.1	0.0	0.9	2.1	1.7	9.6
MSA[1]	76.2	12.2	2.1	0.0	0.0	0.7	1.6	1.6	5.5
U.S.	76.0	10.2	2.7	1.7	0.5	0.5	2.8	1.3	4.2

Note: Figures are percentages and cover workers 16 years of age and older; (1) Figures cover the Phoenix-Mesa-Glendale, AZ Metropolitan Statistical Area—see Appendix B for areas included
Source: U.S. Census Bureau, 2008-2010 American Community Survey 3-Year Estimates

Travel Time to Work

Area	Less Than 10 Minutes	10 to 19 Minutes	20 to 29 Minutes	30 to 44 Minutes	45 to 59 Minutes	60 to 89 Minutes	90 Minutes or More
City	14.4	31.1	23.7	23.1	4.6	1.8	1.2
MSA[1]	10.6	27.5	21.9	24.9	8.7	4.9	1.5
U.S.	13.9	30.1	20.8	19.8	7.5	5.5	2.5

Note: Figures are percentages and include workers 16 years old and over; (1) Figures cover the Phoenix-Mesa-Glendale, AZ Metropolitan Statistical Area—see Appendix B for areas included
Source: U.S. Census Bureau, 2008-2010 American Community Survey 3-Year Estimates

Travel Time Index

Area	1985	1990	1995	2000	2005	2010
Urban Area[1]	1.10	1.11	1.11	1.18	1.21	1.21
Average[2]	1.11	1.16	1.18	1.21	1.25	1.20

Note: Travel Time Index—the ratio of travel time in the peak period to the travel time at free-flow conditions. A value of 1.30 indicates a 20-minute free-flow trip takes 26 minutes in the peak. Free-flow speeds (60 mph on freeways and 35 mph on principal arterials) are used as the comparison threshold; (1) Covers the Phoenix AZ urban area; (2) average of 439 urban areas
Source: Texas Transportation Institute, Urban Mobility Report 2011, September 2011

Public Transportation

Agency Name / Mode of Transportation	Vehicles Operated in Maximum Service	Annual Unlinked Passenger Trips ('000)	Annual Passenger Miles ('000)
City of Phoenix Public Transit Dept. (Valley Metro)			
Bus (purchased transportation)	450	37,181.5	138,158.1
Demand Response (directly operated)	45	160.8	1,113.9
Demand Response (purchased transportation)	105	358.4	3,103.6
Phoenix - VPSI Inc.			
Vanpool (directly operated)	342	1,049.6	26,836.8

Source: Federal Transit Administration, National Transit Database, 2010

Air Transportation

Airport Name and Code / Type of Service	Passenger Airlines[1]	Passenger Enplanements	Freight Carriers[2]	Freight (lbs.)
Phoenix Sky Harbor International (PHX)				
Domestic service (U.S. carriers - 2011)	31	18,643,720	29	236,320,096
International service (U.S. carriers - 2010)	8	811,320	5	448,583

Note: (1) Includes all U.S.-based major, minor and commuter airlines that carried at least one passenger during the year; (2) Includes all U.S.-based airlines and freight carriers that transported at least one pound of freight during the year
Source: Bureau of Transportation Statistics, The Intermodal Transportation Database, Air Carriers: T-100 Domestic Market (U.S. Carriers), 2011; Bureau of Transportation Statistics, The Intermodal Transportation Database, Air Carriers: T-100 International Market (U.S. Carriers), 2010

Other Transportation Statistics

Major Highways:	I-10; I-17
Amtrak Service:	No
Major Waterways/Ports:	None

Source: Amtrak.com; Google Maps

BUSINESSES

Major Business Headquarters

Company Name	Rankings	
	Fortune[1]	Forbes[2]
Discount Tire	-	133
Services Group of America	-	166

Note: (1) Fortune 500—companies that produce a 10-K are ranked 1 to 500 based on 2010 revenue; (2) all private companies with at least $2 billion in annual revenue are ranked 1 to 212; companies listed are headquartered in the city; dashes indicate no ranking
Source: Fortune, "Fortune 500," May 23, 2011; Forbes, "America's Largest Private Companies," November 16, 2011

Fast-Growing Businesses

According to *Inc.*, Scottsdale is home to three of America's 500 fastest-growing private companies: **PruGen Pharmaceuticals** (#29); **Blue Global Media** (#179); **GlobalMedia Group** (#300). Criteria: must be an independent, privately-held, for-profit, U.S. corporation, proprietorship or partnership; revenues must be at least $80,000 in 2007 and $2 million in 2010; must have four-year operating/sales history. Holding companies, regulated banks, and utilities were excluded. *Inc., "America's 500 Fastest-Growing Private Companies," September 2011*

According to Deloitte, Scottsdale is home to three of North America's 500 fastest-growing high-technology companies: **GPS Insight** (#74); **GlobalMed** (#122); **GoDaddy.com** (#384). Companies are ranked by percentage growth in revenue over a five-year period. Criteria for inclusion: company must be headquartered within North America; must own proprietary intellectual property or proprietary technology that contributes to a significant portion of the company's operating revenue, or devote a significant proportion of revenues to research and development of technology; must have been in business for a minumum of five years with 2006 operating revenues of at least $50,000 USD/CD and 2010 operating revenues of at least $5 million USD/CD. *Deloitte Touche Tohmatsu, 2011 Deloitte Technology Fast 500™*

Minority- and Women-Owned Businesses

Group	All Firms		Firms with Paid Employees			
	Firms	Sales ($000)	Firms	Sales ($000)	Employees	Payroll ($000)
Asian	775	184,364	219	147,578	989	36,853
Black	207	25,714	46	17,987	181	5,802
Hispanic	1,102	270,632	271	223,819	2,087	56,631
Women	9,074	2,087,282	1,581	1,654,976	12,016	356,173
All Firms	37,104	52,571,657	10,120	50,235,872	196,448	9,093,262

Note: Figures cover firms located in the city; minority- and women-owned business are defined as firms in which the corresponding group own 51% or more of the stock or equity of the company
Source: U.S. Census Bureau, 2007 Economic Census, Survey of Business Owners

HOTELS

Hotels/Motels

Area	5 Star		4 Star		3 Star		2 Star		1 Star		Not Rated	
	Num.	Pct.[3]	Num.	Pct.[3]	Num.	Pct.[3]	Num.	Pct.[3]	Num.	Pct.[3]	Num.	Pct.[3]
City[1]	8	9.1	15	17.0	39	44.3	20	22.7	0	0.0	6	6.8
Total[2]	133	0.9	940	6.5	4,569	31.8	7,033	48.9	351	2.4	1,343	9.3

Note: (1) Figures cover Scottsdale and vicinity; (2) Figures cover all 100 cities in this book; (3) Percentage of hotels which have a given star rating; Star ratings are determined by expedia.com and offer an indication of the general quality of a particular hotel.
Source: expedia.com, April 25, 2012

The Phoenix-Mesa-Glendale, AZ metro area is home to six of the best hotels in the U.S. according to *Travel & Leisure*: **Sanctuary on Camelback Mountain Resort & Spa** (#70); **Four Seasons Resort Scottsdale at Troon North** (#75); **Royal Palms Resort and Spa** (#99); **Hermosa Inn** (#141); **The Phoenician, A Luxury Collection Resort** (#146); **Montelucia Resort & Spa** (#163). Criteria: service; location; rooms; food; and value. *Travel & Leisure, "T+L 500, The World's Best Hotels 2012"*

EVENT SITES

Major Stadiums, Arenas, and Auditoriums

Name	Max. Capacity
Scottsdale Stadium	12,000

Source: Original research

Convention Centers

Name	Overall Space (sq. ft.)	Exhibit Space (sq. ft.)	Meeting Space (sq. ft.)	Meeting Rooms
Scottsdale Resort & Conference Center	10,000	n/a	n/a	n/a

Note: n/a not available
Source: Original research

Living Environment

COST OF LIVING

Cost of Living Index

Composite Index	Groceries	Housing	Utilities	Trans-portation	Health Care	Misc. Goods/ Services
96.6	103.9	87.4	100.3	102.9	102.6	97.6

Note: U.S. = 100; Figures cover the Phoenix AZ urban area.
Source: The Council for Community and Economic Research, ACCRA Cost of Living Index, 2011

Grocery Prices

Area[1]	T-Bone Steak ($/pound)	Frying Chicken ($/pound)	Whole Milk ($/half gal.)	Eggs ($/dozen)	Orange Juice ($/64 oz.)	Coffee ($/11.5 oz.)
City[2]	9.12	1.20	2.26	1.77	3.18	4.97
Avg.	9.25	1.18	2.22	1.66	3.19	4.40
Min.	6.70	0.88	1.31	0.95	2.46	2.94
Max.	14.30	2.16	3.50	3.18	4.75	6.83

Note: (1) Values for the local area are compared with the average, minimum and maximum values for all 335 areas in the Cost of Living Index; (2) Figures cover the Phoenix AZ urban area; **T-Bone Steak** *(price per pound);* **Frying Chicken** *(price per pound, whole fryer);* **Whole Milk** *(half gallon carton);* **Eggs** *(price per dozen, Grade A, large);* **Orange Juice** *(64 oz. Tropicana or Florida Natural);* **Coffee** *(11.5 oz. can, vacuum-packed, Maxwell House, Hills Bros, or Folgers).*
Source: The Council for Community and Economic Research, ACCRA Cost of Living Index, 2011

Housing and Utility Costs

Area[1]	New Home Price ($)	Apartment Rent ($/month)	All Electric ($/month)	Part Electric ($/month)	Other Energy ($/month)	Telephone ($/month)
City[2]	241,396	889	184.74	-	-	22.17
Avg.	285,990	839	163.23	89.00	77.52	26.92
Min.	188,005	460	125.58	45.39	33.89	17.98
Max.	1,197,028	3,244	339.16	181.97	348.69	40.01

Note: (1) Values for the local area are compared with the average, minimum and maximum values for all 335 areas in the Cost of Living Index; (2) Figures cover the Phoenix AZ urban area; **New Home Price** *(2,400 sf living area, 8,000 sf lot, in urban area with full utilities);* **Apartment Rent** *(950 sf 2 bedroom/1.5 or 2 bath, unfurnished, excluding all utilities except water);* **All Electric** *(average monthly cost for an all-electric home);* **Part Electric** *(average monthly cost for a part-electric home);* **Other Energy** *(average monthly cost for natural gas, fuel oil, coal, wood, and any other forms of energy except electricity);* **Telephone** *(price includes basic monthly rate for a private residential line plus additional local usage charges incurred by a family of four).*
Source: The Council for Community and Economic Research, ACCRA Cost of Living Index, 2011

Health Care, Transportation, and Other Costs

Area[1]	Doctor ($/visit)	Dentist ($/visit)	Optometrist ($/visit)	Gasoline ($/gallon)	Beauty Salon ($/visit)	Men's Shirt ($)
City[2]	91.10	89.66	97.16	3.32	41.43	21.20
Avg.	93.88	81.72	90.54	3.48	32.65	25.06
Min.	60.00	55.33	53.66	3.18	19.78	13.44
Max.	154.98	145.97	183.72	4.31	63.21	46.00

Note: (1) Values for the local area are compared with the average, minimum and maximum values for all 335 areas in the Cost of Living Index; (2) Figures cover the Phoenix AZ urban area; **Doctor** *(general practitioners routine exam of an established patient);* **Dentist** *(adult teeth cleaning and periodic oral examination);* **Optometrist** *(full vision eye exam for established adult patient);* **Gasoline** *(one gallon regular unleaded, national brand, including all taxes, cash price at self-service pump if available);* **Beauty Salon** *(woman's shampoo, trim, and blow-dry);* **Men's Shirt** *(cotton/polyester dress shirt, pinpoint weave, long sleeves).*
Source: The Council for Community and Economic Research, ACCRA Cost of Living Index, 2011

HOUSING

House Price Index (HPI)

Area	National Ranking[2]	Quarterly Change (%)	One-Year Change (%)	Five-Year Change (%)
MSA[1]	275	2.67	-7.12	-47.78
U.S.[3]	-	-0.10	-2.43	-19.16

Note: The HPI is a weighted repeat sales index. It measures average price changes in repeat sales or refinancings on the same properties. This information is obtained by reviewing repeat mortgage transactions on single-family properties whose mortgages have been purchased or securitized by Fannie Mae or Freddie Mac in January 1975; (1) Metropolitan/Micropolitan Statistical Area—see Appendix B for areas included; (2) Rankings are based on annual percentage change for all metro areas containing at least 15,000 transactions over the last 10 years and ranges from 1 to 306; (3) figures based on a weighted average of Census Division estimates using a purchase only index; all figures are for the period ending December 31, 2011
Source: Federal Housing Finance Agency, House Price Index, February 23, 2012

House Price Valuations

Area	Q4 2005		Q4 2006		Q4 2007		Q4 2008		Q4 2009	
	Price ($000)	Over-valuation	Price ($000)	Over-valuation	Price ($000)	Over-valuation	Price ($000)	Over-valuation	Price ($000)	Over-valuation
MSA[1]	242.1	38.9	255.3	35.8	227.8	17.7	166.6	-12.9	146.5	-22.3

Note: Figures show the percentage of over- or under-valuation of single family homes relative to statistically normal house values (e.g. a value of 23.6 indicates that house values are 23.6% overvalued). Statistically normal house values are based on house prices, interest rates, household incomes, population densities, and any historical premiums or discounts metropolitan areas have exhibited over time; (1) Figures cover the Phoenix-Mesa-Glendale, AZ - see Appendix B for areas included
Source: Global Insight/PNC Financial Services Group, House Prices in America: 4th Quarter 2009 Update

Median Single-Family Home Prices

Area	2009	2010	2011p	Percent Change 2010 to 2011
MSA[1]	137.0	139.2	115.5	-17.0
U.S. Average	172.1	173.1	166.2	-4.0

Note: Figures are median sales prices of existing single-family homes in thousands of dollars; (p) preliminary; n/a not available; (1) Metropolitan Statistical Area—see Appendix B for areas included
Source: National Association of Realtors, Median Sales Price of Existing Single-Family Homes for Metropolitan Areas, 4th Quarter 2011

Affordability Index of Existing Single-Family Homes

Area	2009	2010	2011p	Percent Change 2010 to 2011
MSA[1]	126.3	129.7	162.0	24.9

Note: The housing affordability index measures whether or not a typical family could qualify for a mortgage loan on a typical home. The higher the index, the greater the household purchasing power. An index of 100 is defined as the point where a median-income household has exactly enough income to qualify for the purchase of a median-priced existing single-family home, assuming a 20 percent downpayment and 25 percent of gross income devoted to mortgage principal and interest payments; (p) preliminary; n/a not available; (1) Metropolitan Statistical Area—see Appendix B for areas included
Source: National Association of Realtors, Affordability Index of Existing Single-Family Homes, 2011

Median Apartment Condo-Coop Home Prices

Area	2009	2010	2011p	Percent Change 2010 to 2011
MSA[1]	101.1	79.4	65.9	-17.0
U.S. Average	175.6	171.7	165.1	-3.8

Note: Figures are median sales prices of existing apartment condo-coop homes in thousands of dollars; (p) preliminary; n/a not available; (1) Metropolitan Statistical Area—see Appendix B for areas included
Source: National Association of Realtors, Median Sales Price of Existing Apartment Condo-Coop Homes for Metropolitan Areas, 4th Quarter 2011

Year Housing Structure Built

Area	2005 or Later	2000 -2004	1990 -1999	1980 -1989	1970 -1979	1960 -1969	1950 -1959	Before 1950	Median Year
City	4.0	11.0	29.1	22.6	16.4	9.9	6.2	0.8	1987
MSA[1]	9.6	16.4	21.6	19.1	17.4	7.4	5.8	2.5	1989
U.S.	5.0	8.6	14.0	14.1	16.3	11.3	11.2	19.6	1975

Note: Figures are percentages except for Median Year; (1) Figures cover the Phoenix-Mesa-Glendale, AZ Metropolitan Statistical Area—see Appendix B for areas included
Source: U.S. Census Bureau, 2008-2010 American Community Survey 3-Year Estimates

HEALTH

Health Risk Data

Category	MSA[1] (%)	U.S. (%)
Adults who have been told they have high blood pressure[2]	25.2	28.7
Adults who have been told they have high blood cholesterol[2]	41.1	37.5
Adults who have been told they have diabetes[3]	7.1	8.7
Adults who have been told they have arthritis[2]	22.9	26.0
Adults who have been told they currently have asthma	9.6	9.1
Adults who are current smokers	14.8	17.3
Adults who are heavy drinkers[4]	4.5	5.0
Adults who are binge drinkers[5]	15.9	15.1
Adults who are overweight (BMI 25.0 - 29.9)	41.1	36.2
Adults who are obese (BMI 30.0 - 99.8)	22.8	27.5
Adults who participated in any physical activities in the past month	81.5	76.1
Adults 50+ who have ever had a sigmoidoscopy or colonoscopy	64.4	65.2
Women aged 40+ who have had a mammogram within the past two years	73.8	75.2
Men aged 40+ who have had a PSA test within the past two years	51.8	53.2
Adults aged 65+ who have had flu shot within the past year	68.8	67.5
Adults aged 18–64 who have any kind of health care coverage	84.8	82.2

Note: Data as of 2010 unless otherwise noted; (1) Figures cover the Phoenix-Mesa-Scottsdale, AZ Metropolitan Statistical Area—see Appendix B for areas included; (2) Data as of 2009; (3) Figures do not include pregnancy-related, borderline, or pre-diabetes; (4) Heavy drinkers are classified as males having more than two drinks per day or females having more than one drink per day; (5) Binge drinkers are classified as males having five or more drinks on one occasion or females having four or more drinks on one occasion
Source: Centers for Disease Control and Prevention, Behaviorial Risk Factor Surveillance System, SMART: Selected Metropolitan/Micropolitan Area Risk Trends, 2009, 2010

Mortality Rates for the Top 10 Causes of Death in the U.S.

ICD-10[a] Sub-Chapter	ICD-10[a] Code	Age-Adjusted Mortality Rate[1] per 100,000 population	
		County[2]	U.S.
Malignant neoplasms	C00-C97	145.7	175.6
Ischaemic heart diseases	I20-I25	111.8	121.6
Other forms of heart disease	I30-I51	20.0	48.6
Chronic lower respiratory diseases	J40-J47	39.8	42.3
Cerebrovascular diseases	I60-I69	30.2	40.6
Organic, including symptomatic, mental disorders	F01-F09	18.0	26.7
Other degenerative diseases of the nervous system	G30-G31	39.2	24.7
Other external causes of accidental injury	W00-X59	30.0	24.4
Diabetes mellitus	E10-E14	15.8	21.7
Hypertensive diseases	I10-I15	18.7	18.2

Note: (a) ICD-10 = International Classification of Diseases 10th Revision; (1) Mortality rates are a three year average covering 2007-2009; (2) Figures cover Maricopa County
Source: Centers for Disease Control and Prevention, National Center for Health Statistics. Underlying Cause of Death 1999-2009 on CDC WONDER Online Database, released 2012. Data for year 2009 are compiled from the Multiple Cause of Death File 2009, Series 20 No. 2O, 2012, Data for year 2008 are compiled from the Multiple Cause of Death File 2008, Series 20 No. 2N, 2011, Data for year 2007 are compiled from Multiple Cause of Death File 2007, Series 20 No. 2M, 2010.

Mortality Rates for Selected Causes of Death

ICD-10[a] Sub-Chapter	ICD-10[a] Code	Age-Adjusted Mortality Rate[1] per 100,000 population	
		County[2]	U.S.
Assault	X85-Y09	7.2	5.7
Human immunodeficiency virus (HIV) disease	B20-B24	1.9	3.3
Influenza and pneumonia	J09-J18	13.5	16.4
Intentional self-harm	X60-X84	14.1	11.5
Malnutrition	E40-E46	0.4	0.8
Obesity and other hyperalimentation	E65-E68	1.2	1.6
Transport accidents	V01-V99	12.5	13.7
Viral hepatitis	B15-B19	2.8	2.2

Note: (a) ICD-10 = International Classification of Diseases 10th Revision; (1) Mortality rates are a three year average covering 2007-2009; (2) Figures cover Maricopa County
Source: Centers for Disease Control and Prevention, National Center for Health Statistics. Underlying Cause of Death 1999-2009 on CDC WONDER Online Database, released 2012. Data for year 2009 are compiled from the Multiple Cause of Death File 2009, Series 20 No. 2O, 2012, Data for year 2008 are compiled from the Multiple Cause of Death File 2008, Series 20 No. 2N, 2011, Data for year 2007 are compiled from Multiple Cause of Death File 2007, Series 20 No. 2M, 2010.

Distribution of Physicians and Dentists

Area[1]	Dentists[2]	D.O.[3]	M.D.[4] Total	M.D.[4] Family/General Practice	M.D.[4] Pediatrics	M.D.[4] Medical Specialties	M.D.[4] Surgical Specialties
Local (number)	1,754	1,213	6,438	712	454	2,415	1,424
Local (rate[5])	4.5	3.1	16.3	1.8	1.1	6.1	3.6
U.S. (rate[5])	4.5	1.9	18.3	2.5	1.4	6.8	4.1

Note: Data as of 2008 unless noted; (1) Local data covers Maricopa County; (2) Data as of 2007; (3) Doctor of Osteopathic Medicine; (4) Includes active, non-federal, patient-care, office-based Doctors of Medicine; (5) rate per 10,000 population
Source: Area Resource File (ARF). 2009-2010 Release. U.S. Department of Health and Human Services, Health Resources and Services Administration, Bureau of Health Professions, Rockville, MD, August 2010

Best Hospitals

According to *U.S. News,* the Phoenix-Mesa-Glendale, AZ is home to three of the best hospitals in the U.S.: **Banner Good Samaritan Medical Center** (4 specialties); **Mayo Clinic** (3 specialties); **St. Joseph's Hospital and Medical Center** (1 specialty). The hospitals listed were highly ranked in at least one adult specialty. *U.S. News Online, "America's Best Hospitals 2011-12"*

According to *U.S. News,* the Phoenix-Mesa-Glendale, AZ is home to one of the best children's hospitals in the U.S.: **Phoenix Children's Hospital** (5 specialties). The hospital listed was highly ranked in at least one pediatric specialty. *U.S. News Online, "America's Best Children's Hospitals 2011-12"*

EDUCATION

Public School District Statistics

District Name	Schls	Pupils	Pupil/Teacher Ratio	Minority Pupils[1] (%)	Free Lunch Eligible[2] (%)	IEP[3] (%)
Cave Creek Unified District	8	5,860	20.5	12.1	8.5	9.6

Note: Table includes school districts with 2,000 or more students; (1) Percentage of students that are not non-Hispanic white; (2) Percentage of students that are eligible for the free lunch program; (3) Percentage of students that have an Individualized Education Program.
Source: U.S. Department of Education, National Center for Education Statistics, Common Core of Data, Local Education Agency (School District) Universe Survey: School Year 2009-2010; U.S. Department of Education, National Center for Education Statistics, Common Core of Data, Public Elementary/Secondary School Universe Survey: School Year 2009-2010

Top Public High Schools

High School Name	Rank[1]	Score[1]	Grad. Rate[2] (%)	College[3] (%)	AP/IB/ AICE[4] (%)	SAT/ ACT[5] (%)
Desert Mountain	253	0.440	99	97	1.6	1662
Horizon	380	0.267	98	88	1.3	1613

Note: (1) Public schools are ranked from 1 to 500 based on the following self-reported statistics (with their corresponding weight in the final score). Schools that had fewer than 10 graduates, as well as those that were newly founded and did not have a graduating senior class in 2010 were excluded; (2) Four-year, on-time graduation rate (25%); (3) Percent of 2010 graduates who enrolled immediately in college (25%); (4) AP/IB/AICE tests per graduate (25%); (5) Average SAT and/or ACT score (10%); Average AP/IB/AICE exam score (10%); AP/IB/AICE courses offered per graduate (5%); (6) School is unranked, but has been identified by Newsweek as one of the nation's most elite public high schools.
Source: Newsweek Online, "Top High Schools 2011"

Highest Level of Education

Area	Less than H.S.	H.S. Diploma	Some College, No Deg.	Associate Degree	Bachelors Degree	Masters Degree	Profess. School Degree	Doctorate Degree
City	4.4	14.8	22.1	6.8	32.5	12.4	4.7	2.3
MSA[1]	14.4	24.0	25.7	8.1	18.1	7.0	1.8	1.0
U.S.	14.7	28.4	21.3	7.6	17.6	7.2	1.9	1.2

Note: Figures cover persons age 25 and over; (1) Figures cover the Phoenix-Mesa-Glendale, AZ Metropolitan Statistical Area—see Appendix B for areas included
Source: U.S. Census Bureau, 2008-2010 American Community Survey 3-Year Estimates

Educational Attainment by Race

Area	High School Graduate or Higher (%)					Bachelor's Degree or Higher (%)				
	Total	White	Black	Asian	Hisp.[2]	Total	White	Black	Asian	Hisp.[2]
City	95.6	96.0	93.9	94.5	75.1	52.0	51.6	49.7	76.4	33.7
MSA[1]	85.6	86.7	89.3	89.3	60.3	27.8	28.5	23.0	53.4	10.1
U.S.	85.3	87.5	81.4	85.5	61.6	28.0	29.3	17.8	50.2	13.0

Note: Figures shown cover persons 25 years old and over; (1) Figures cover the Phoenix-Mesa-Glendale, AZ Metropolitan Statistical Area—see Appendix B for areas included; (2) People of Hispanic origin can be of any race
Source: U.S. Census Bureau, 2008-2010 American Community Survey 3-Year Estimates

School Enrollment by Grade and Control

Area	Preschool (%)		Kindergarten (%)		Grades 1 - 4 (%)		Grades 5 - 8 (%)		Grades 9 - 12 (%)	
	Public	Private	Public	Private	Public	Private	Public	Private	Public	Private
City	31.9	68.1	86.0	14.0	87.0	13.0	88.5	11.5	87.4	12.6
MSA[1]	55.9	44.1	91.0	9.0	92.9	7.1	94.0	6.0	94.4	5.6
U.S.	55.4	44.6	87.1	12.9	89.4	10.6	89.5	10.5	90.4	9.6

Note: Figures shown cover persons 3 years old and over; (1) Figures cover the Phoenix-Mesa-Glendale, AZ Metropolitan Statistical Area—see Appendix B for areas included
Source: U.S. Census Bureau, 2008-2010 American Community Survey 3-Year Estimates

Average Salaries of Public School Classroom Teachers

Area	2010-11		2011-12		Percent Change 2010-11 to 2011-12	Percent Change 2001-02 to 2011-12
	Dollars	Rank[1]	Dollars	Rank[1]		
Arizona	47,553	33	48,691	33	2.39	21.80
U.S. Average	55,623	-	56,643	-	1.83	26.8

Note: (1) State rank ranges from 1 to 51 where 1 indicates highest salary.
Source: National Education Association, Rankings & Estimates: Rankings of the States 2011 and Estimates of School Statistics 2012, December 2011

Higher Education

Four-Year Colleges			Two-Year Colleges			Medical Schools[1]	Law Schools[2]	Voc/ Tech[3]
Public	Private Non-profit	Private For-profit	Public	Private Non-profit	Private For-profit			
0	1	1	1	0	0	0	0	4

Note: Figures cover institutions located within the city limits and include main campuses only; (1) includes schools accredited by the Liaison Committee on Medical Education and the American Osteopathic Association's Commission on Osteopathic College Accreditation; (2) includes American Bar Association-accredited law schools; (3) includes all schools with programs that are less than 2 years.
Source: National Center for Education Statistics, Integrated Postsecondary Education System (IPEDS) Peer Analysis System, 2011-12; Association of American Medical Colleges, Member List, April 23, 2012; American Osteopathic Association, Member List, April 23, 2012; Law School Admission Council, Official Guide to ABA-Approved Law Schools Online, April 23, 2012

According to *U.S. News & World Report,* the Phoenix-Mesa-Glendale, AZ is home to one of the best national universities in the U.S.: **Arizona State University** (#132). The indicators used to capture academic quality fall into a number of categories: assessment by administrators at peer institutions; retention of students; faculty resources; student selectivity; financial resources; alumni giving; high school counselor ratings of colleges; and graduation rate.*U.S. News & World Report, "America's Best Colleges 2012"*

According to *U.S. News & World Report,* the Phoenix-Mesa-Glendale, AZ is home to one of the best law schools in the U.S.: **Arizona State University (O'Connor)** (#26). The rankings are based on a weighted average of 12 measures of quality: peer assessment score; assessment score by lawyers/judges; median LSAT scores; median undergrad GPA; acceptance rate; employment rates for graduates; placement success; bar passage rate; faculty resources; expenditures per student; student/faculty ratio; and library resources. *U.S. News & World Report, "America's Best Law Schools 2013"*

According to *Forbes,* the Phoenix-Mesa-Glendale, AZ is home to one of the best business schools in the U.S.: **Arizona State (Carey)** (#66). The rankings are based on the return on investment that graduates of the Class of 2006 received (median salary five years after graduation). *Forbes, "Best Business Schools," August 3, 2011*

PRESIDENTIAL ELECTION

2008 Presidential Election Results

Area	Obama	McCain	Nader	Other
Maricopa County	43.9	54.4	0.4	1.2
U.S.	52.9	45.6	0.6	0.9

Note: Results are percentages and may not add to 100% due to rounding
Source: Dave Leip's Atlas of U.S. Presidential Elections, www.uselectionatlas.org

EMPLOYERS

Major Employers

Company Name	Industry
Arizona Dept of Transportation	Regulation, administration of transportation
Arizona State University	University
Arizona State University	Libraries
Avnet	Electronic parts and equipment, nec
Carter & Burgess	Engineering services
Chase Bankcard Services	State commercial banks
City of Mesa	Executive offices
City of Phoenix	Administration of social and human resources
City of Phoenix	Executive offices
General Dynamics C4 Systems	Communications equipment, nec
Grand Canyon Education	Colleges and universities
Honeywell International	Aircraft engines and engine parts
Lockheed Martin Corporation	Search and navigation equipment
Paramount Building Solutions	Janitorial service, contract basis
Salt River Pima-Maricopa Indian Community	Gambling establishment
Scottsdale Healthcare Corp.	Hospital management
Scottsdale Healthcare Osborn Med Ctr	General medical and surgical hospitals
Swift Transportation Company	Trucking, except local
The Boeing Company	Helicopters
Veterans Health Administration	General medical and surgical hospitals

Note: Companies shown are located within the Phoenix-Mesa-Glendale, AZ metropolitan area.
Source: Hoovers.com, data extracted April 25 2012

Best Companies to Work For

GoDaddy.com, headquartered in Scottsdale, is among "The 100 Best Companies to Work For." To pick the 100 Best Companies to Work For, *Fortune* partnered with the Great Place to Work Institute. Two hundred eighty firms participated in this year's survey. Two-thirds of a company's score is based on the results of the Institute's Trust Index survey, which is sent to a random sample of employees from each company. The questions related to attitudes about management's credibility, job satisfaction, and camaraderie. The other third of the scoring is based on the company's responses to the Institute's Culture Audit, which includes detailed questions about pay and benefit programs, and a series of open-ended questions about hiring practices, internal communication, training, recognition programs, and diversity efforts. Any company that is at least five years old with more than 1,000 U.S. employees is eligible.
Fortune, "The 100 Best Companies to Work For," February 6, 2012

PUBLIC SAFETY

Crime Rate

Area	All Crimes	Violent Crimes				Property Crimes		
		Murder	Forcible Rape	Robbery	Aggrav. Assault	Burglary	Larceny -Theft	Motor Vehicle Theft
City	3,000.5	1.7	14.3	43.4	93.7	555.8	2,175.3	116.3
Suburbs[1]	3,957.5	5.7	26.6	128.7	222.3	809.4	2,415.4	349.5
Metro[2]	3,905.4	5.5	25.9	124.1	215.3	795.6	2,402.3	336.8
U.S.	3,345.5	4.8	27.5	119.1	252.3	699.6	2,003.5	238.8

Note: Figures are crimes per 100,000 population; (1) All areas within the metro area that are located outside the city limits; (2) Metropolitan Statistical Area—see Appendix B for areas included
Source: FBI Uniform Crime Reports, 2010

Hate Crimes

Area	Number of Quarters Reported	Bias Motivation				
		Race	Religion	Sexual Orientation	Ethnicity	Disability
City	4	7	5	2	2	0

Source: Federal Bureau of Investigation, Hate Crime Statistics 2010

Identity Theft Consumer Complaints

Area	Complaints	Complaints per 100,000 Population	Rank[2]
MSA[1]	4,078	97.6	106
U.S.	279,156	90.4	-

Note: (1) Metropolitan Statistical Area—see Appendix B for areas included; (2) Rank ranges from 1 to 384 where 1 indicates greatest number of identity theft complaints per 100,000 population
Source: Federal Trade Commission, Consumer Sentinel Network Data Book for January–December 2011

Fraud and Other Consumer Complaints

Area	Complaints	Complaints per 100,000 Population	Rank[2]
MSA[1]	19,577	468.4	196
U.S.	1,533,924	496.8	-

Note: (1) Metropolitan Statistical Area—see Appendix B for areas included; (2) Rank ranges from 1 to 384 where 1 indicates greatest number of fraud and other complaints per 100,000 population
Source: Federal Trade Commission, Consumer Sentinel Network Data Book for January–December 2011

RECREATION

Culture

Dance[1]	Theatre[1]	Instrumental Music[1]	Vocal Music[1]	Series/ Festivals	Museums	Zoos and Aquariums[2]
0	0	1	0	2	n/a	0

Note: (1) Number of professional perfoming groups; (2) AZA-accredited; n/a not available
Source: The Grey House Performing Arts Directory, 2011-2012; Official Museum Directory, 2011; American Association of Museums, AAM Member Museums, April 2012; Association of Zoos & Aquariums, AZA Member Zoos & Aquariums, April 2012

Professional Sports Teams

Team Name	League
Arizona Cardinals	National Football League (NFL)
Arizona Diamondbacks	Major League Baseball (MLB)
Phoenix Coyotes	National Hockey League (NHL)
Phoenix Suns	National Basketball Association (NBA)

Note: Includes teams located in the Phoenix metro area.
Source: Original research

CLIMATE

Average and Extreme Temperatures

Temperature	Jan	Feb	Mar	Apr	May	Jun	Jul	Aug	Sep	Oct	Nov	Dec	Yr.
Extreme High (°F)	88	92	100	105	113	122	118	116	118	107	93	88	122
Average High (°F)	66	70	75	84	93	103	105	103	99	88	75	67	86
Average Temp. (°F)	53	57	62	70	78	88	93	91	85	74	62	54	72
Average Low (°F)	40	44	48	55	63	72	80	78	72	60	48	41	59
Extreme Low (°F)	17	22	25	37	40	51	66	61	47	34	27	22	17

Note: Figures cover the years 1948-1990
Source: National Climatic Data Center, International Station Meteorological Climate Summary, 9/96

Average Precipitation/Snowfall/Humidity

Precip./Humidity	Jan	Feb	Mar	Apr	May	Jun	Jul	Aug	Sep	Oct	Nov	Dec	Yr.
Avg. Precip. (in.)	0.7	0.6	0.8	0.3	0.1	0.1	0.8	1.0	0.7	0.6	0.6	0.9	7.3
Avg. Snowfall (in.)	Tr	Tr	0	0	0	0	0	0	0	0	0	Tr	Tr
Avg. Rel. Hum. 5am (%)	68	63	56	45	37	33	47	53	50	53	59	66	53
Avg. Rel. Hum. 5pm (%)	34	28	24	17	14	12	21	24	23	24	28	34	24

Note: Figures cover the years 1948-1990; Tr = Trace amounts (<0.05 in. of rain; <0.5 in. of snow)
Source: National Climatic Data Center, International Station Meteorological Climate Summary, 9/96

Weather Conditions

Temperature			Daytime Sky			Precipitation		
10°F & below	32°F & below	90°F & above	Clear	Partly cloudy	Cloudy	0.01 inch or more precip.	0.1 inch or more snow/ice	Thunder-storms
0	10	167	186	125	54	37	< 1	23

Note: Figures are average number of days per year and cover the years 1948-1990
Source: National Climatic Data Center, International Station Meteorological Climate Summary, 9/96

HAZARDOUS WASTE

Superfund Sites

Scottsdale has one hazardous waste site on the EPA's Superfund Final National Priorities List: **Indian Bend Wash Area.** *U.S. Environmental Protection Agency, Final National Priorities List, April 17, 2012*

AIR & WATER QUALITY

Air Quality Index

Area	Percent of Days when Air Quality was...²					AQI Statistics²	
	Good	Moderate	Unhealthy for Sensitive Groups	Unhealthy	Very Unhealthy	Maximum	Median
Area¹	23.6	65.2	7.1	2.2	1.9	565	61

Note: Air Quality Index (AQI) is an index for reporting daily air quality. EPA calculates the AQI for five major air pollutants regulated by the Clean Air Act: ground-level ozone, particle pollution (aka particulate matter), carbon monoxide, sulfur dioxide, and nitrogen dioxide. The AQI runs from 0 to 500. The higher the AQI value, the greater the level of air pollution and the greater the health concern. There are six AQI categories: "Good" AQI is between 0 and 50. Air quality is considered satisfactory; "Moderate" AQI is between 51 and 100. Air quality is acceptable; "Unhealthy for Sensitive Groups" When AQI values are between 101 and 150, members of sensitive groups may experience health effects; "Unhealthy" When AQI values are between 151 and 200 everyone may begin to experience health effects; "Very Unhealthy" AQI values between 201 and 300 trigger a health alert; "Hazardous" AQI values over 300 trigger warnings of emergency conditions (not shown); (1) Data covers Maricopa County; (2) Based on 365 days with AQI data in 2011.
Source: U.S. Environmental Protection Agency, AirData Report, 2011

Air Quality Index Pollutants

Area	Percent of Days when AQI Pollutant was...²					
	Carbon Monoxide	Nitrogen Dioxide	Ozone	Sulfur Dioxide	Particulate Matter 2.5	Particulate Matter 10
Area¹	0.0	19.2	38.9	0.0	15.6	26.3

Note: The Air Quality Index (AQI) is an index for reporting daily air quality. EPA calculates the AQI for five major air pollutants regulated by the Clean Air Act: ground-level ozone, particle pollution (also known as particulate matter), carbon monoxide, sulfur dioxide, and nitrogen dioxide. The AQI runs from 0 to 500. The higher the AQI value, the greater the level of air pollution and the greater the health concern; (1) Data covers Maricopa County; (2) Based on 365 days with AQI data in 2011.
Source: U.S. Environmental Protection Agency, AirData Report, 2011

Air Quality Index Trends

Area	Trend Sites (days)								All Sites (days)
	2003	2004	2005	2006	2007	2008	2009	2010	2010
MSA¹	51	23	49	50	21	27	10	11	43

Note: Figures are the number of days the AQI value exceeded 100 in a given year. An AQI value greater than 100 indicates that air quality would have been in the unhealthful range on that day. Data from exceptional events are included. These counts are presented in two ways. First, the counts are based on sites having an adequate record of monitoring data during the trend period (trend sites). These counts represent the relative change in the number of days with AQI values greater than 100. In the last column, the counts are based on all sites with data in the most recent year (because it is possible for a site to have data in the most recent year but not enough data to be a trend site); (1) Data covers the Phoenix-Mesa-Glendale, AZ—see Appendix B for areas included
Source: U.S. Environmental Protection Agency, Air Quality Index Information, "Number of Days with Air Quality Index Values Greater than 100 at Trend Sites, 2000-2010, and at All Sites in 2010"

Maximum Air Pollutant Concentrations: Particulate Matter, Ozone, CO and Lead

	Particulate Matter 10 (ug/m3)	Particulate Matter 2.5 Wtd AM (ug/m3)	Particulate Matter 2.5 24-Hr (ug/m3)	Ozone (ppm)	Carbon Monoxide (ppm)	Lead (ug/m3)
MSA[1] Level	226	12.4	27	0.079	3	n/a
NAAQS[2]	150	15	35	0.075	9	0.15
Met NAAQS[2]	No	Yes	Yes	No	Yes	n/a

Note: Data from exceptional events are not included; (1) Data covers the Phoenix-Mesa-Glendale, AZ—see Appendix B for areas included; (2) National Ambient Air Quality Standards; ppm = parts per million; ug/m³ = micrograms per cubic meter; n/a not available

Concentrations: Particulate Matter 10 (coarse particulate)—highest second maximum 24-hour concentration; Particulate Matter 2.5 Wtd AM (fine particulate)—highest weighted annual mean concentration; Particulate Matter 2.5 24-Hour (fine particulate)—highest 98th percentile 24-hour concentration; Ozone—highest fourth daily maximum 8-hour concentration; Carbon Monoxide—highest second maximum non-overlapping 8-hour concentration; Lead—maximum running 3-month average

Source: U.S. Environmental Protection Agency, CBSA Factbook 2010, Air Quality Statistics by City, 2010

Maximum Air Pollutant Concentrations: Nitrogen Dioxide and Sulfur Dioxide

	Nitrogen Dioxide AM (ppb)	Nitrogen Dioxide 1-Hr (ppb)	Sulfur Dioxide AM (ppb)	Sulfur Dioxide 1-Hr (ppb)	Sulfur Dioxide 24-Hr (ppb)
MSA[1] Level	24.524	68	1.742	10	5.3
NAAQS[2]	53	100	30	75	140
Met NAAQS[2]	Yes	Yes	Yes	Yes	Yes

Note: Data from exceptional events are not included; (1) Data covers the Phoenix-Mesa-Glendale, AZ—see Appendix B for areas included; (2) National Ambient Air Quality Standards; ppb = parts per billion; n/a not available

Concentrations: Nitrogen Dioxide AM—highest arithmetic mean concentration; Nitrogen Dioxide 1-Hr—highest 98th percentile 1-hour daily maximum concentration; Sulfur Dioxide AM—highest annual mean concentration; Sulfur Dioxide 1-Hr—highest 99th percentile 1-hour daily maximum concentration; Sulfur Dioxide 24-Hr—highest second maximum 24-hour concentration

Source: U.S. Environmental Protection Agency, CBSA Factbook 2010, Air Quality Statistics by City, 2010

Drinking Water

Water System Name	Pop. Served	Primary Water Source Type	Violations[1] Health Based	Violations[1] Monitoring/ Reporting
City of Scottsdale	230,000	Surface	0	0

Note: (1) Based on violation data from January 1, 2011 to December 31, 2011 (includes unresolved violations from earlier years)

Source: U.S. Environmental Protection Agency, Office of Ground Water and Drinking Water, Safe Drinking Water Information System (based on data extracted April 18, 2012)

Seattle, Washington

Background

Believe it or not, the virgin hinterlands and wide curving arch of Elliot Bay of present-day Seattle were once named New York. The city was renamed Seattle in 1853, for the Native American Indian Chief Seattle, two years after its first five families from Illinois had settled into the narrow strip of land between Puget Sound and Lake Washington.

The lush, green forests of the "Emerald City," created by the infamously frequent rains and its many natural waterways, gave birth to Seattle's first major industry—lumber. However, this industry also bred a society of bearded, rabble-rousing bachelors. To alleviate that problem, Asa Mercer, president of the Territorial University, which later became the University of Washington, trekked back east and recruited marriageable women. Among those "Mercer girls" was Ms. Mercer herself. Seattle was settling down.

Today, the city does not rely on lumber as its major industry, but now boasts commercial aircraft production and missile research, due to the presence of Boeing on the outskirts of the city.

In addition, importing and exporting is a major revenue source. As the closest U.S. mainland port to Asia, Seattle has become a key trade center for goods such as cars, forest products, electronic equipment, bananas, and petroleum products. The city and it surrounding region is also home to the headquarters of Amazon.com, Nordstrom, Starbucks, Costco and Nintendo.

On the technology front, Seattle seems to be moving in the direction of becoming the next Silicon Valley. It is predominantly a software town dominated by Microsoft in nearby Redmond, with its more than 30,000 employees. Early in 2003 Corbis, the online photo-archive company, moved its headquarters to the city's historic Pioneer Square. And an increase in the rise of young firms brings the feeling that the city is ready for more expansion and innovation.

The Seattle Seaport Terminal Project is actually comprised of a number of small-and-large-scale projects designed to improve the port's facilities for businesses, passengers, residents, and tourists. One phase of the project, a major renovation of Terminal 5, cost some $265 million and was completed by 1998. Other construction has included a Cruise Ship Terminal improvement, completed in 2000. More than $2 billion has been invested in port facilities improvements over the past fifteen years, and approximately that much again is expected to be invested in coming years.

Seattle has undergone a cultural and commercial reemergence of its downtown. Tourists and locals are drawn by luxury hotels, restaurants, a 16-screen movie theater, and other entertainment-oriented businesses, and the first in a nationwide chain of Game Works, computerized playgrounds for adults. In Center City Seattle, an estimated $761.6 million in development projects were completed in 2006, and $2.3 billion more are currently under construction.

The arts are a vital part of Seattle life. The world-famous Seattle Opera, now performing in a state-of-the-art hall dedicated in 2003, is perhaps best-known for its summer presentations of Wagner's *Ring* cycle. The Seattle Philharmonic Orchestra celebrated its 50th anniversary in 2004; its annual Bushnell Concerto Competition features promising new area musicians. The Seattle Museum recently constructed Olympic Sculpture Park, which turned disused waterfront property into a permanent green space with plantings native to Puget Sound. The Seattle Museum of Flight's remarkable collection—the largest on the West Coast—includes a Concorde, donated by British Airways, and the Boeing 707 used as Air Force One by presidents from Eisenhower to Nixon.

Seattle has a distinctly marine climate. The city's location on Puget Sound and between two mountain ranges ensures a mild climate year round, with only moderate variations in temperature. Summers are generally sunny and, while winters are rainy, most of the rain falls between October and March. In 2010, Seattle was the sixth busiest port in the United States.

Rankings

General Rankings

- The Seattle metro area was identified as one of the 10 most popular big cities by Pew Research Center. The results are based on a telephone survey of 2,260 adults conducted during October 2008. The report explored a range of attitudes related to where Americans live, where they would like to live, and why. *Pew Research Center, "For Nearly Half of America, Grass is Greener Somewhere Else," January 29, 2009*
- *Men's Health Living* ranked 100 U.S. cities in terms of quality of life. Seattle was ranked #12 and received a grade of B+. Criteria: number of fitness facilities; air quality; number of physicians; male/female ratio; education levels; household income; cost of living. *Men's Health Living, Spring 2008*
- Seattle was selected as one of America's ten "Best Cities to Work and Live." The city ranked #6. The results are based on a survey of 2,500 employees and entrepreneurs who were asked about 40 large cities. *BusinessWeek, "America's Most and Least Favorite Cities," January 5, 2009*
- Seattle was selected as one of America's best cities by *Bloomberg Businessweek.* The city ranked #13 out of 50. Criteria: number of restaurants, bars and museums per capita; number of colleges, libraries, and professional sports teams; income, poverty, unemployment, crime, and foreclosure rates; percent of population with bachelor's degrees; public school performance; park acres per capita; air quality. *BusinessWeek, "America's 50 Best Cities," September 20, 2011*
- Seattle was selected as one of the "10 Best Cities for the Next Decade" by *Kiplinger's Personal Finance.* The city ranked #2. Criteria: innovation factor (smart people, great ideas, and collaboration between governments, universities, and businesses); economic growth and growth potential; creativity in music, arts and culture; neighborhoods and recreational facilities that rank high for "coolness." *Kiplinger's Personal Finance, "10 Best Cities for the Next Decade," July 2010*
- Seattle was identified as one of the top places to live in the U.S. by Harris Interactive. The city ranked #3 out of 15. Criteria: 2,463 adults (age 18 and over) were polled and asked "if you could live in or near any city in the country except the one you live in or nearest to now, which city would you choose?" The poll was conducted online within the U.S. between September 14 and 20, 2010. *Harris Interactive, November 9, 2011*
- Mercer Human Resources Consulting ranked 221 cities worldwide in terms of overall quality of life. Seattle ranked #48. Criteria: political, social, economic, and socio-cultural factors; medical and health considerations; schools and education; public services and transportation; recreation; consumer goods; housing; and natural environment. *Mercer Human Resources Consulting, "Mercer 2011 Quality of Living Survey,"November 29, 2011*
- *Condé Nast Traveler* polled thousands of readers for travel satisfaction. American cities were ranked based on the following criteria: friendliness; atmosphere/ambiance; culture/sites; restaurants; lodging; and shopping. Seattle appeared in the top 10, ranking #9. *Condé Nast Traveler, 2011 Readers' Choice Awards*

Business/Finance Rankings

- The Seattle metro area was identified as one of 10 places with the fastest-growing wages in America. The area ranked #5. Criteria: private-sector wage growth between the 4th quarter of 2010 and the 4th quarter of 2011. *PayScale, "The 10 Cities with the Fastest-Growing Wages in America," January 12, 2012*
- Experian ranked the top 20 major U.S. metropolitan areas by average debt per consumer. The Seattle metro area was ranked #1. Criteria: average debt per consumer. Debt for this study includes credit cards, auto loans and personal loans. It does not include mortgages. *Experian, May 13, 2010*
- Seattle was selected as one of the best places to ride out a recession in the U.S. by *BusinessWeek.* Twenty cities were identified as places where large portions of the population worked in anticyclical industries such as government, health care, education, agriculture, and legal services. *BusinessWeek, "Some Cities Will Be Safer in a Recession," October 14, 2008*

- Seattle was identified as one of America's most coupon-loving cities by *Coupons.com.* The city ranked #14 out of 25. Criteria: online coupon usage. *Coupons.com, "Top 25 Most Frugal Cities of 2011," February 23, 2012*
- Seattle was identified as one of the top 25 U.S. cities with the most credit card debt by credit reporting bureau Experian. The city was ranked #7. *Experian, March 4, 2011*
- Seattle was identified as one of the "Happiest Cities to Work in 2012" by *CareerBliss.com,* an online community for career advancement. The city ranked #50 out of 50. Criteria: independent company reviews from employees all over the country on: relationship with their boss and co-workers; work environment; job resources; growth opportunities; compensation; company culture; company reputation; daily tasks; job control over work performed on a daily basis. *CareerBliss.com, "Happiest and Unhappiest Cities to Work in 2012"*
- Seattle was selected as one of the best cities in the world for telecommuting. The city ranked #5. The editors at *Cartridge Save* (printer technology news, guides and reviews) identified the 20 best cities in which to be an at-home, tech-using employee. *Cartridge Save, "20 of the Best Cities in the World for Telecommuting," May 14, 2008*
- *American City Business Journals* ranked America's 261 largest cities in terms of their resident's wealth. Seattle ranked #27. Criteria: per capita income; median household income; percentage of households with annual incomes of $200,000 or more; median home value. *American City Business Journals, "Where the Money Is: America's Wealth Centers," August 18, 2008*
- The Seattle metro area appeared on the Milken Institute "2011 Best Performing Metros" list. Rank: #27 out of 200 large metro areas. Criteria: job growth; wage and salary growth; high-tech output growth. *Milken Institute, "2011 Best Performing Metros"*
- The Seattle metro area is projected to be one the best performing housing markets in 2012. The metro area ranked #6 out of 10. Criteria: forecast home price gains by September 2012. *CNNMoney.com, "Housing Markets: Best Recovery Bets," 2011*
- The Seattle metro area was selected as one of the best cities for entrepreneurs in America by *Inc. Magazine.* Criteria: job-growth data for 335 metro areas was analyzed for: recent growth trend; mid-term growth; long-term trend; current year growth. The Seattle metro area ranked #10 among large metro areas and #54 overall. *Inc. Magazine, "The Best Cities for Doing Business," July 2008*
- Seattle was ranked #7 out of 145 regions worldwide in terms of its "Knowledge Competitiveness Index." The index attempts to measure the knowledge-based development taking place throughout the world and is based on 19 measures of economic performance that indicate a region's ability to translate its knowledge capacity into economic value. *Centre for International Competitiveness, World Knowledge Competitiveness Index 2008*
- *Forbes* ranked the 200 most populous metro areas in the U.S. in terms of the "Best Places for Business and Careers." The Seattle metro area was ranked #13. Criteria: costs (business and living); job growth (past and projected); income growth; educational attainment; projected economic growth; crime; cultural and recreational opportunities; net migration patterns; number of highly ranked colleges. *Forbes, "Best Places for Business and Careers," June 2011*
- Seattle appeared on *Kiplinger's Personal Finance* list of the "Top Ten Tax-Friendly Cities." The city was ranked #4. Criteria: income tax; sales tax; real estate and car/personal property tax. *Kiplinger's Personal Finance, March 1, 2009*

Children/Family Rankings

- Underwriters Laboratories (UL), in partnership with Sperling's BestPlaces, ranked the 50 largest cities in the U.S. in terms of the safest for families with young children. Each city was measured on 25 criteria encompassing child-focused, safety-oriented behaviors and regulatory best practices. The study filtered out cities with the highest crime rates and considered air quality, incidence of child pedestrian accidents, injuries and drowning. The study also focused on accessibility to hospitals; response time for fire and police personnel; and laws, codes and regulations that address smoking, home inspections, smoke and carbon monoxide alarms, pool safety and bike helmets. The top 10 cities had the highest frequency or values in these categories. *Underwriters Laboratories, "Safest Cities for Families with Young Children," September 29, 2010*

- Seattle was selected as one of the 10 best cities to raise children in the U.S. by *KidFriendlyCities.org.* Criteria: education; environment; health; employment; crime; diversity; cost of living. *KidFriendlyCities.org, "Top Rated Kid/Family Friendly Cities 2009"*

- The Seattle metro area was selected as one of the "Best Cities for Relocating Families" by Worldwide ERC and Primacy Relocation. The 2008 study looked at nearly 50 factors important to relocating families including: recent job growth; nearby top-ranked colleges; in-state tuition for four-year public colleges; population growth since 2000; pediatricians per 100,000 population; and a Green Living index. *Worldwide ERC and Primacy Relocation, "2008 Best Cities for Relocating Families"*

- *Fit Pregnancy* magazine ranked the 50 best U.S. cities in which to have a baby. Seattle was ranked #4. Criteria: access to hospitals and doctors; affordability; birthing options; breastfeeding; child care; fertility laws/resources; maternal and infant health risk; parks/stroller friendliness; safety. *Fit Pregnancy, "The Best Cities in America to Have a Baby 2008"*

Culture/Performing Arts Rankings

- Seattle was selected as one of 10 best U.S. cities to be a moviemaker. The city was ranked #4. Criteria: cost of living; average salary; unemployment rate; job growth; median home price; crime rate; number of film schools, festivals, movie-related vendors and local movie theaters; current production scene (i.e. production days, size of talent pool); financial incentives for shooting in a particular area. *MovieMaker Magazine, "Top 10 Cities to be a Moviemaker: 2012," January 16, 2012*

- Seattle was selected as one of the top 10 cities for design in America by architectural firm RMJM Hillier. The city was ranked #7. American cities with more than 500,000 residents were ranked according to criteria such as the quality of public transit, the number of LEED-registered buildings (indicating sustainable design) and how many of the city's employees work within creative industries such as performing arts or publishing. Resident interviews were used to rate a city's design factor, which takes in elements of a city's architecture as well as its creative appeal. *RMJM Hillier, "America's Best Cities for Design," June 25, 2008*

- Seattle was selected as one of "America's Top 25 Arts Destinations." The city ranked #8 in the big city (population 500,000 and over) category. Criteria: readers' top choices for arts travel destinations based on the richness and variety of visual arts sites, activities and events. *American Style, "America's Top 25 Arts Destinations," May 2010*

Dating/Romance Rankings

- Seattle was selected as one of the best cities for single women by *Rent.com*. The city ranked #2 of 10. Criteria: high single male-to-female ratio; lively nightlife; low divorce rate; low cost of living. *Rent.com, "Top 10 Cities for Single Women," August 19, 2011*

- Seattle was selected as one of "America's Best Cities for Dating" by *Yahoo! Travel*. Criteria: high proportion of singles; excellent dating venues and/or stunning natural settings. *Yahoo! Travel, "America's Best Cities for Dating," February 7, 2012*

- Seattle appeared on *Men's Health's* list of the most sex-happy cities in America. The city ranked #78 of 100. Criteria: condom sales; birth rates; sex toy sales; rates of chlamydia, gonorrhea, and syphilis. *Men's Health, "America's Most Sex-Happy Cities," October 2010*

- *Men's Health* ranked 100 U.S. cities in terms of best (and worst) marriages. Seattle was ranked #68 (#1 = worst). Criteria: rate of failed marriages; stringency of divorce laws; percentage of population who've split; number of licensed marriage and family therapists. *Men's Health, "Splitsville, USA," May 2010*

- Eli Lily and Company, in partnership with Sperling's BestPlaces, ranked the nation's 50 largest metro areas in terms of the "Most Romantic Cities for Baby Boomers." The Seattle metro area ranked #30. Criteria: marriage and divorce rates among baby boomers age 45 to 60; great restaurants; dance studios; chocolate, jewelry and flower sales. *Eli Lily and Company, "Most Romantic Cities for Baby Boomers," April 20, 2007*

- The Seattle metro area was selected as one of the "Best Cities for Relocating Singles" by Worldwide ERC and Primacy Relocation. The area ranked #36 out of the 100 largest metro areas in the U.S. Criteria: recent job growth; recent singles population growth; overall population growth; affordable rental housing; cost-of-living index; expanded arts and recreation opportunities; ratio of single men and single women; affordability of quality higher education (including state residency requirements); diversity index; climate; population density. *Worldwide ERC and Primacy Relocation, "2008 Best Cities for Relocating Singles"*

- *Forbes* ranked the 40 most populous urbanized areas in the U.S. in terms of the "Best Cities for Singles." The Seattle metro area ranked #4. Criteria: number of singles; cost of living alone; nightlife; culture; job growth; coolness; and online dating participation. *Forbes.com, "Best Cities for Singles," July 27, 2009*

Education Rankings

- *Men's Health* ranked 100 U.S. cities in terms of their education levels. Seattle was ranked #5 (#1 = most educated city). Criteria: high school graduation rates; school enrollment; educational attainment; number of households who have outstanding student loans; number of households whose members have taken adult-education courses. *Men's Health, "Where School Is In: The Most and Least Educated Cities," September 12, 2011*
- Seattle was selected as one of the most well-read cities in America by *Amazon.com.* The city ranked #9 of 20. Cities with populations greater than 100,000 were evaluated based on per capita sales of books, magazines and newspapers. *Amazon.com, "Top 20 Most Well-Read Cities in America," June 4, 2011*
- Seattle was selected as one of "America's Geekiest Cities" by *Forbes.com.* The city ranked #10 of 20. Criteria: percentage of workers with jobs in science, technology, engineering and mathematics. *Forbes.com, "America's Geekiest Cities," August 5, 2011*
- Seattle was selected as one of "America's Most Literate Cities." The city ranked #2 out of the 75 largest U.S. cities. Criteria: number of booksellers; library resources; Internet resources; educational attainment; periodical publishing resources; newspaper circulation. *Central Connecticut State University, "America's Most Literate Cities 2011"*
- Seattle was identified as one of the 100 "smartest" metro areas in the U.S. The area ranked #9. Criteria: the editors rated the collective brainpower of the 100 largest metro areas in the U.S. based on their residents' educational attainment. *American City Business Journals, April 14, 2008*
- Seattle was identified as one of "America's Smartest Cities" by *The Daily Beast.* The metro area ranked #6 out of 55. The editors ranked metropolitan areas with one million or more residents on the following criteria: percentage of residents over age 25 with bachelor's or graduate degrees; non-fiction book sales; ratio of institutions of higher education; libraries per capita. *The Daily Beast, "America's Smartest Cities," October 24, 2010*
- Seattle was identified as one of America's most inventive cities by *The Daily Beast.* The city ranked #7 out of 25. The 200 largest cities in the U.S. were ranked by the number of patents (applied and approved) per capita. *The Daily Beast, "The 25 Most Inventive Cities," October 2, 2011*
- Seattle was identified as one of "America's Brainiest Bastions" by *Portfolio.com.* The metro area ranked #16 out of 200. *Portfolio.com* analyzed levels of educational attainment in the nation's 200 largest metropolitan areas. The editors established scores for five levels of educational attainment, based on relative earning power of adult workers age 25 or older. Scores were determined by comparing the median income for all workers with the median income for those workers at a specified educational level. *Portfolio.com, "America's Brainiest Bastions," December 1, 2010*
- Seattle was identified as one of "America's Smartest Cities" by *CNNMoney.com.* The area ranked #9. Criteria: percentage of residents with bachelors or graduate degrees. *CNNMoney.com, "America's Smartest Cities," October 1, 2010*
- Seattle was identified as one of America's smartest cities" by *Forbes*. The area ranked #25 out of 25. Criteria: percentage of the population age 25 and over with at least a bachelor's degree. *Forbes.com, "The Smartest Cities in America," February 8, 2008*

Environmental Rankings

- The Seattle was identified as one of North America's greenest metropolitan areas. The area ranked #4. The Green City Index is comprised of 31 indicators, and scores cities across nine categories: carbon dioxide; energy; land use; buildings; transport; water; waste; air quality; environmental governance. The 27 largest metropolitan areas in the U.S. and Canada were considered. *Economist Intelligence Unit, sponsored by Siemens, "U.S. and Canada Green City Index, 2011"*
- The Seattle was identified as one of America's cities with the most ENERGY STAR certified buildings. The area ranked #16 out of 25. Criteria: number of ENERGY STAR labeled buildings in 2010. *U.S. Environmental Protection Agency, "Top Cities With the Most ENERGY STAR Certified Buildings," March 15, 2011*
- Seattle was selected as one of 22 "Smarter Cities" for energy by the Natural Resources Defense Council. The city appeared as one of 12 cities in the large city (population 250,000 and over) category. Criteria: investment in green power; energy efficiency measures; conservation. *Natural Resources Defense Council, "2010 Smarter Cities," July 19, 2010*
- *American City Business Journal* ranked 43 metropolitan areas in terms of their "greenness." The Seattle metro area ranked #6. Criteria: Forty-one metros in which *ACBJ* has business weeklies, plus Indianapolis and Cleveland, were ranked based on 20 different indicators such as adoption of green technologies, utilization of environmentally sound practices, and air and water quality. *American City Business Journals, "Green City Index," March 11, 2010*
- Seattle was selected as one of "America's 50 Greenest Cities" by *Popular Science.* The city ranked #8. Criteria: electricity; transportation; green living; recycling and green perspective. *Popular Science, February 2008*
- 100 of the largest metro areas in the U.S. were analyzed in terms of their current drought severity. The Seattle metro area ranked #66 (#1 = driest). The rankings were based on statistics such as long-term precipitation trends and patterns and the Palmer drought indices. *Sperling's BestPlaces, www.BestPlaces.net, "America's Drought-Riskiest Cities," November 2007*
- The U.S. Conference of Mayors and Wal-Mart Stores sponsor the Mayors' Climate Protection Awards Program. The awards recognize and honor mayors for outstanding and innovative practices that mayors are taking to increase energy efficiency in their cities, and to help curb global warming. Seattle was a Large City Best Practice Model. *U.S. Conference of Mayors, "2009 Mayors' Climate Protection Awards Program"*
- The Seattle metro area appeared in *Country Home's* "Best Green Places" report. The area ranked #13 out of 379. Criteria: official energy policies; green power; green buildings; availability of fresh, locally grown food. *Country Home, "Best Green Places," 2008*
- Seattle was highlighted as one of the 25 metro areas most polluted by short-term particle pollution (24-hour PM 2.5) in the U.S. The area ranked #18. *American Lung Association, State of the Air 2011*

Food/Drink Rankings

- Seattle was identified as one of "America's Drunkest Cities of 2011" by *The Daily Beast.* The city ranked #19 out of 25. Criteria: binge drinking; drinks consumed per month. *The Daily Beast, "Tipsy Towns: Where are America's Drunkest Cities?," December 31, 2011*
- Seattle was identified as one of "America's Most Caffeinated Cities" by *Bundle.com.* The city was ranked #3 out of 10. The rankings were determined by examining consumer spending at 16 widely known coffee chains during the second quarter of 2011. *Bundle.com, "America's Most Caffeinated Cities," September 19, 2011*
- Seattle was selected as one of "America's Favorite Cities." The city ranked #7 in the "Food/Dining" category. Respondents to an online survey were asked to rate 35 top urban destinations in the U.S. from a visitor's perspective. Criteria: big-name restaurants; ethnic food; farmers' markets; neighborhood joints and cafes. *Travelandleisure.com, "America's Favorite Cities 2010," November 2010*

- Seattle was selected as one of North America's most vegetarian- and vegan-friendly large cities (population 300,000 or more). The city was ranked #5. Criteria: number of vegetarian restaurants and vegetarian-friendly restaurants per capita; input from PETA supporters and staff members on the quality of the options. *People for the Ethical Treatment of Animals, "North America's Best Vegetarian- and Vegan-Friendly Cities," July 23, 2010*

- The Seattle metro area was selected as one of the best cities for "foodies" in America by Sperling's BestPlaces. The metro area ranked #8 out of 10. A "foodie" is defined as a person whose hobby is food—not just eating it, but also learning about its origins and preparation. Criteria: ratio of local restaurants to chain restaurants; number of local and accessible CSA (Community Supported Agriculture) and farmers markets; number of Whole Foods stores; number of cookware stores; number of craft breweries, brew pubs, wine shops, and wine bars. *Sperling's BestPlaces, www.BestPlaces.net, "America's Best Cities for Foodies," January 2011*

Health/Fitness Rankings

- The American Podiatric Medical Association and *Prevention* magazine ranked 100 American cities based on walkability. Nineteen walking criteria were evaluated including the percentage of adults who walk to work, number of parks per square mile, number of trails for walking and hiking, air pollution, use of mass transit, crime rate, pedestrian fatalities, and percentage of adults who walk for fitness. Seattle ranked #7. *Prevention, "The Best Walking Cities of 2009," May 2009; American Podiatric Medical Association, "2009 Best Fitness-Walking Cities," April 7, 2009*

- Seattle was identified as one of the most walkable cities in the U.S. by *WalkScore.com,* a Seattle-based service that rates the convenience and transit access of 10,000 neighborhoods in 2,500 cities. The editors at Grey House Publishing used *WalkScore.com's* online service to look at the scores of 280 cities with populations greater than or equal to 100,000. The top 50 cities were selected. *WalkScore.com, April 2, 2012*

- The Seattle metro area was selected as one of the worst cities for bed bugs in America by Rollins corporation, the owner of seven pest control companies, including Orkin. The area ranked #27 based on the number of bed bug treatments from January to December 2011. *Rollins, "The Top 50 U.S. Cities for Bed Bugs," March 19, 2012*

- Seattle was selected as one of the 25 fittest cities in America by *Men's Fitness Online*. It ranked #6 out of America's 50 largest cities. Criteria: fitness centers and sport stores; nutrition; sports participation; TV viewing; overweight/sedentary; junk food; air quality; geography; commute; parks and open space; city recreational facilities; access to healthcare; motivation; mayor and city initiatives; state obesity initiatives. *Men's Fitness, "The Fittest and Fattest Cities in America," March 5, 2012*

- Seattle was identified as a "2011 Asthma Capital." The area ranked #90 out of the nation's 100 largest metropolitan areas. Twelve factors were used to identify the most challenging places to live for people with asthma: estimated prevalence; self-reported prevalence; crude death rate for asthma; annual pollen score; annual air quality; public smoking laws; number of board-certified asthma specialists; school inhaler access laws; rescue medication use; controller medication use; uninsured rate; poverty rate. *Asthma and Allergy Foundation of America, "2011 Asthma Capitals"*

- Seattle was identified as a "2011 Fall Allergy Capital." The area ranked #99 out of 100. Three groups of factors were used to identify the most severe cities for people with allergies during the fall season: annual pollen levels; medicine utilization; access to board-certified allergists. *Asthma and Allergy Foundation of America, "2011 Fall Allergy Capitals"*

- Seattle was identified as a "2012 Spring Allergy Capital." The area ranked #95 out of 100. Three groups of factors were used to identify the most severe cities for people with allergies during the spring season: annual pollen levels; medicine utilization; access to board-certified allergists. *Asthma and Allergy Foundation of America, "2012 Spring Allergy Capitals"*

- *Men's Health* examined 100 major U.S. cities and selected the best and worst cities for men. Seattle ranked #8. Criteria: 35 statistical parameters of long life in the categories of health, quality of life, and fitness. *Men's Health, "The 10 Best and Worst Cities for Men 2012," January/February 2012*

- The Seattle metropolitan area was selected as one of the best metros for hospital care in America by *HealthGrades.com.* The rankings are based on a comprehensive study of patient death and complication rates in the nation's nearly 5,000 hospitals. Hospitals performing in the top 5% nationwide across 26 different medical procedures and diagnoses were identified. *HealthGrades.com* then ranked cities by the highest percentage of these Distinguished Hospitals for Clinical Excellence™. The Seattle metro area ranked #35. *HealthGrades.com, "America's Top 50 Cities for Hospital Care," January 21, 2012*
- The American Academy of Dermatology ranked 26 U.S. metropolitan regions in terms of their residents knowledge, attitude and behaviors towards tanning, sun protection and skin cancer detection. The Seattle metro area ranked #23. The results of the study are based on an online survey of over 7,000 adults nationwide. *American Academy of Dermatology, "Suntelligence: How Sun Smart is Your City," May 3, 2010*
- The Seattle metro area appeared in the 2011 Gallup-Healthways Well-Being Index. The index, based on interviews with more than 350,000 Americans, measured jobs, finances, physical health, emotional state of mind and communities. The metro area ranked #44 out of 190. Criteria: life evaluation; emotional health; work environment; physical health; healthy behaviors; basic access (basic needs optimal for a healthy life, such as access to food and medicine, having health insurance and feeling safe while walking at night). *Gallup-Healthways, "State of Well-Being 2011"*
- The Seattle metro area was identified as one of "America's Most Stressful Cities" by *Sperling's BestPlaces.* The metro area ranked #9 out of 50. Criteria: unemployment rate; suicide rate; commute time; mental health; poor rest; alcohol use; violent crime rate; property crime rate; cloudy days annually. *Sperling's BestPlaces, www.BestPlaces.net, "Stressful Cities 2012*
- The Seattle metro area was identified as one of "America's Most Stressful Cities" by *Forbes.* The metro area ranked #10 out of 40. Criteria: housing affordability; unemployment rate; cost of living; air quality; traffic congestion; sunny days; population density. *Forbes.com, "America's Most Stressful Cities," September 23, 2011*
- *Men's Health* ranked 100 U.S. cities in terms of their activity levels. Seattle was ranked #1 (#1 = most active city). Criteria: where and how often residents exercise; percentage of households that watch more than 15 hours of cable television a week and buy more than 11 video games a year; death rate from deep-vein thrombosis, a condition linked to sitting for extended periods of time. *Men's Health, "Where Sit Happens: The Most and Least Active Cities in America," June 20, 2011*
- 50 of the largest metro areas in the U.S. were analyzed in terms of their health and fitness by the American College of Sports Medicine in their "American Fitness Index." The Seattle metro area ranked #4 (#1 = healthiest). Criteria: preventative health behaviors; levels of chronic disease; health care access; community resources and policies that support physical activity. *American College of Sports Medicine, "Health and Community Fitness Status of the 50 Largest Metropolitan Areas," August 1, 2011*
- Seattle was selected as one of the "20 Most Livable U.S. Cities for Wheelchair Users" by the Christopher & Dana Reeve Foundation. The city ranked #1. Criteria: Medicaid eligibility and spending; access to physicians and rehabilitation facilities; access to fitness facilities and recreation; access to paratransit; percentage of people living with disabilities who are employed; clean air; climate. *Christopher & Dana Reeve Foundation, "20 Most Livable U.S. Cities for Wheelchair Users," July 26, 2010*
- The Seattle metro area was selected as one of "America's Most Relaxed Cities" by *Forbes.* The metro area ranked #7 out of 10. Criteria: unemployment rates; numbers of commuters that spend an hour or more in traffic on the way to work; average weekly hours people spend at work; access to health care; overall health of residents; percentage of population who exercise. *Forbes, "America's Most Relaxed Cities," November 5, 2010*

Pet Rankings

- Seattle was selected as one of the "Top 10 Cat-Friendly Cities" in the U.S. The area ranked #7. Criteria: cat ownership per capita; level of veterinary care; microchipping; cat-friendly local ordinances. *CATalyst Council, "Top 10 Cat-Friendly Cities," March 27, 2009*

Real Estate Rankings

- *Fortune* ranked the 100 largest metro areas in the U.S. in terms of projected median home price change in 2010. The Seattle metro area ranked #27. *Fortune, "The 2010 Housing Outlook," December 9, 2009*

- Seattle was selected as one of the 10 best U.S. cities for real estate investment. The city ranked #6. *Association of Foreign Investors in Real Estate, "AFIRE News," January/February, 2011*

- The Seattle metro area was identified as one of the 20 least affordable housing markets in the U.S. in 2011. The area ranked #20 out of 152 markets with an affordability index of 94.7%. The index measures whether or not a typical family could qualify for a mortgage loan on a typical home. The calculation used assumes a down payment of 20 percent of the home price and a qualifying ratio of 25 percent, meaning that the monthly P&I payment cannot exceed 25 percent of a the median family monthly income. *National Association of Realtors®, Affordability Index of Existing Single-Family Homes for Metropolitan Areas, 2011*

- Seattle appeared on *ApartmentRatings.com* "Top Cities for Renters" list in 2009." The area ranked #26. Overall satisfaction ratings were ranked using thousands of user submitted scores for hundreds of apartment complexes located in the 100 most populated U.S. municipalities. *ApartmentRatings.com, "2009 Renter Satisfaction Rankings"*

- Seattle appeared on *ApartmentRatings.com* "Top College Towns & Cities" for renters list in 2011." The area ranked #24 out of 87. Overall satisfaction ratings were ranked using thousands of user submitted scores for hundreds of apartment complexes located in cities and towns that are home to the 100 largest four-year institutions in the U.S. *ApartmentRatings.com, "2011 College Town Renter Satisfaction Rankings"*

- The nation's largest metro areas were analyzed in terms of the best places to buy bank-owned properties. The Seattle metro area ranked #8 out of 10. Criteria: at least 500 REO sales during the fourth quarter and an REO sales increase of at least five percent from a year ago. The areas selected posted the biggest discounts on the sales of bank-owned properties. *RealtyTrac, "Fourth Quarter and Year-End 2011 U.S. Foreclosure Sales Report: Shifting Towards Short Sales," February 28, 2012*

- The nation's largest metro areas were analyzed in terms of the best places to buy pre-foreclosures (short sales). The Seattle metro area ranked #10 out of 10. Criteria: at least 500 pre-foreclosure sales during the fourth quarter and a short sales increase of at least five percent from a year ago. The areas selected posted the biggest discounts on the sales of pre-foreclosure properties. *RealtyTrac, "Fourth Quarter and Year-End 2011 U.S. Foreclosure Sales Report: Shifting Towards Short Sales," February 28, 2012*

- The Seattle metro area appeared in a *Wall Street Journal* article ranking cities by "housing stress." The metro area was ranked #23 (#1 = most stress). Criteria: fraction of mortgage-holding homeowners with a monthly housing payment in excess of 30 percent of income; percentage of people without health insurance; unemployment rate. *The Wall Street Journal, "Which Cities Face Biggest Housing Risk," October 5, 2010*

- The Center for Housing Policy ranked 210 U.S. metropolitan areas by the fair market rent for a two-bedroom unit. The Seattle metro area was ranked #47. (#1 = most expensive) with a rent of $1,056. Criteria: Fair Market Rent (FMR) in effect during the fourth quarter of 2009 based on HUD's fiscal year 2010 FMRs. *The Center for Housing Policy, "Paycheck to Paycheck: Most to Least Expensive Rental Markets in 2009"*

- The Seattle metro area was identified as one of the best U.S. markets to invest in rental property" by HomeVestors and Local Market Monitor. The area ranked #83 out of 100. Criteria: risk-return premium relative to national average. *HomeVestors and Local Market Monitor, "Best 100 U.S. Markets to Invest in Rental Property," March 9, 2012*

Safety Rankings

- Symantec, the makers of Norton, in partnership with Sperling's BestPlaces, ranked the 50 largest cities in the U.S. in terms of their vulnerability to cybercrime. The city ranked #2. Criteria: number of cyberattacks and potential infections; level of Internet access; expenditures on smartphones and computer hardware/software; wireless hotspots; broadband connectivity; Internet usage; online purchases. *Symantec, "Riskiest Online Cities of 2012" February 15, 2012*

- Allstate ranked the 193 largest cities in America in terms of driver safety. Seattle ranked #147. In addition, drivers were 25.1% more likely to have had an accident compared to the national average. Allstate researchers analyzed internal property damage reported claims over a two-year period (from January 2008 to December 2009) to protect findings from external influences such as weather or road construction. A weighted average of the two-year numbers determined the annual percentages. The report defines an auto crash as any collision resulting in a property damage claim. *Allstate, "2011 Allstate America's Best Drivers Report™"*

- Seattle was identified as one of the least disaster-proof places in the U.S. in terms of its vulnerability to natural and non-natural disasters. The city ranked #2 out of 5. Rankings are based on the U.S. Center for Disease Control's Cities Readiness Initiative (CRI). As part of the CRI, the CDC and state public health personnel assess local emergency-management plans, protocols and capabilities for 72 Metropolitan Statistical Areas and four non-MSA large cities. *Forbes, "America's Most and Least Disaster-Proof Cities," December 12, 2011*

- Seattle was identified as one of the safest large cities in America by CQ Press. All 34 cities with populations of 500,000 or more that reported crime rates in 2010 for murder, rape, robbery, aggravated assault, burglary, and motor vehicle thefts were ranked. The city ranked #7 out of the top 10. *CQ Press, City Crime Rankings 2011-2012*

- The National Insurance Crime Bureau ranked 366 metro areas in the U.S. in terms of per capita rates of vehicle theft. The Seattle metro area ranked #13 (#1 = highest rate). Criteria: number of vehicle theft offenses per 100,000 inhabitants in 2010. *National Insurance Crime Bureau, "Hot Spots," June 21, 2011*

- The Seattle metro area was identified as one of the most dangerous metro areas for pedestrians by Transportation for America. The metro area ranked #46 out of 52 metro areas with over 1 million residents. Criteria: area's population divided by the number of pedestrian fatalities in that area. *Transportation for America, "Dangerous by Design 2011"*

Seniors/Retirement Rankings

- Bankers Life and Casualty Company, in partnership with Sperling's BestPlaces, ranked the nation's 50 largest metro areas in terms of the "Best U.S. Cities for Seniors." The Seattle metro area ranked #19. Criteria: healthcare; transportation; housing; environment; economy; health and longevity; social and spiritual life; crime. *Bankers Life and Casualty Company, Center for a Secure Retirement, "Best U.S. Cities for Seniors 2011," September 2011*

- Seattle was identified as one of the "100 Most Popular Retirement Towns" by *Topretirements.com* The list reflects the 100 cities (out of 815+ total cities reviewed) that visitors to the website are most interested in for retirement. *Topretirements.com, "100 Most Popular Retirement Towns," February 21, 2012*

Sports/Recreation Rankings

- Seattle was selected as one of "America's Most Miserable Sports Cities" by *Forbes.* The city was ranked #2. Criteria: postseason losses; years since last title; ratio of cumulative seasons to championships won. Contenders were limited to cities with at least 75 total seasons of NFL, NBA, NHL and MLB play. *Forbes, "America's Most Miserable Sports Cities," February 28, 2012*

- Seattle appeared on the *Sporting News* list of the "Best Sports Cities" for 2011. The area ranked #32 out of 271 cities in the U.S. *Sporting News* takes a 12-month snapshot of each city's sports, putting a heavy premium on regular-season won-lost records (from the most recently completed season). Other criteria include: playoff berths, bowl appearances and tournament bids; championships; applicable power ratings; quality of competition; overall fan fervor (measured in part by attendance); abundance of teams (rewarding quality over quantity); stadium and arena quality; ticket availability and prices; franchise ownership; and marquee appeal of athletes. *Sporting News, "Best Sports Cities 2011," October 4, 2011*

- Seattle was selected as one of the five best boat cities in the U.S. The city ranked #2. Criteria: climate; scenery; fishing; boat communities with water access. *Best Boat News, "The 5 Best Boat Cities to Live In (in the U.S.)," April 16, 2010*

- Scarborough Sports Marketing, a leading market research firm, identified the Seattle DMA (Designated Market Area) as one of the top markets for Summer Olympics fans with more than 65% of adults reporting that they are "very, somewhat, or a little bit interested" in the Summer Olympics. *Scarborough Sports Marketing, July 30, 2008*

- Seattle was chosen as a bicycle friendly community by the League of American Bicyclists. A Bicycle Friendly Community welcomes cyclists by providing safe accommodation for cycling and encouraging people to bike for transportation and recreation. There are four award levels: Platinum; Gold; Silver; and Bronze. The community achieved an award level of Gold. *League of American Bicyclists, "Bicycle Friendly Community Master List 2011"*

- Seattle was chosen as one of America's 10 best places to live and boat. Criteria: boating opportunities; boat-friendly regulations; water access; availability of waterfront homes; health of the local economy; and overall lifestyle for boaters. *Boating Magazine, "10 Best Places to Live and Boat," June 2010*

- Seattle was chosen as one of America's best cities for bicycling. The city ranked #4 out of 50. Criteria: number of segregated bike lanes, municipal bike racks, and bike boulevards; vibrant and diverse bike culture; smart, savvy bike shops; interviews with national and local advocates, bike shops and other experts. The editors only considered cities with populations of 100,000 or more. *Bicycling, "America's Best Bike Cities," April 2010*

- The Seattle was selected as one of the best metro areas for golf in America by *Golf Digest*. The Seattle area was ranked #6 out of 20. Criteria: climate; cost of public golf; quality of public golf; accessibility. *Golf Digest, "The Top 20 Cities for Golf," October 2011*

- *Golf.com* and the research arm of the National Golf Foundation analyzed the 50 largest metropolitan areas in the U.S. in terms of golf. The Seattle metro area ranked #6. Criteria: weather; affordability; quality of courses; accessibility; number of courses designed by esteemed architects; availability; crowdedness. *Golf.com, November 15, 2007*

Technology Rankings

- The Seattle metro area was selected as one of "America's Most Wired Cities" by *Forbes*. The metro area was ranked #3 out of 20. Criteria: percentage of Internet users with high-speed access; number of companies providing high-speed Internet; number of public wireless hot spots. *Forbes, "America's Most Wired Cities," March 2, 2010*

- Seattle was selected as a 2011 Digital Cities Survey winner. The city ranked #2 in the large city (250,000 or more population) category. The survey examined and assessed how city governments are utilizing information technology to operate and deliver quality service to their customers and citizens. Survey questions focused on implementation and adoption of online service delivery; planning and governance; and the infrastructure and architecture that make the transformation to digital government possible. *Center for Digital Government, "2011 Digital Cities Survey"*

- The Seattle metro area was selected as one of "America's Most Innovative Cities" by *Forbes*. The metro area was ranked #5 out of 20. Criteria: patents per capita; venture capital investment per capita; ratio of high-tech, science and "creative" jobs. *Forbes, "America's Most Innovative Cities," May 24, 2010*

- The Seattle metro area was identified as one of the "Top 14 Nano Metros" in the U.S. by the Project on Emerging Nanotechnologies. The metro area is home to 25 companies, universities, government laboratories and/or organizations working in nanotechnology. *Project on Emerging Nanotechnologies, "Nano Metros 2009"*

Transportation Rankings

- The Seattle metro area was identified as one of the best U.S. cities to live in without a car by *24/7 Wall St.* The area ranked #5 out of 10. Criteria: percentage of neighborhoods covered by public transit; frequency of service for those neighborhoods; share of jobs reachable within 90 minutes or less by public transit; how accessible amenities are for residents on foot; percentage of commuters who bike to work. The 100 largest metropolitan areas in the U.S. were examined. *24/7 Wall St., "The Best Cities to Live in Car-Free," November 28, 2011*

- The Seattle metro area appeared on *Forbes* list of the best and worst cities for commuters. The metro area ranked #28 out of 60 (#1 is best). Criteria: travel time; road congestion; travel delays. *Forbes.com, "Best and Worst Cities for Commuters," February 16, 2010*

Women/Minorities Rankings

- *Women's Health* examined U.S. cities and identified the 100 best cities for women. Seattle was ranked #13. Criteria: 30 categories were examined from obesity and breast cancer rates to commuting times and hours spent working out. *Women's Health, "Best Cities for Women 2012"*
- Seattle was ranked #10 out of 100 metro areas in *SELF Magazine's* ranking of America's healthiest places for women." A panel of experts came up with more than 50 criteria including death and disease rates, environmental indicators, community resources, and lifestyle habits. *SELF Magazine, "Secrets of America's Healthiest Women," December 2008*
- Seattle was selected as one of the "Gayest Cities in America" by *The Advocate.* The city ranked #5 out of 15. *The Advocate* used several different measures to establish "per capita queerness"—including a city's number of teams entered in the Gay Softball World Series, gay bookstores, openly gay elected officials and semifinalists in the International Mr. Leather Contest. *The Advocate, "Gayest Cities in America, 2012" January 2012*
- The Seattle metro area appeared on *Forbes'* list of the "Best Cities for Minority Entrepreneurs." The area ranked #5 out of 10. Criteria: 52 metropolitan statistical areas were examined. For each ethnicity (African Americans, Asians and Hispanics), the editors measured housing affordability, population growth, income growth, and entrepreneurship (per capita self-employment). *Forbes, "Best Cities for Minority Entrepreneurs," March 23, 2011*

Miscellaneous Rankings

- *Men's Health* ranked 100 U.S. cities by their level of sadness. Seattle was ranked #47 (#1 = saddest city). Criteria: suicide rates; unemployment rates; percentage of households that use antidepressants; percent of population who report feeling blue all or most of the time. *Men's Health, "Frown Towns," November 28, 2011*
- The Seattle metro area was selected as one of "5 Great Cities for Young Adults" by *Kiplinger.com.* Criteria: high starting salaries for college graduates; cost of living near or below national average; affordable monthly rent; percentage of residents ages 20 to 29 near or above national average. *Kiplinger.com, "5 Great Cities for Young Adults," October 25, 2011*
- Energizer Holdings, the makers of Edge® shave gel, in partnership with Sperling's BestPlaces, ranked 50 major metro areas in terms of everyday irritations. The Seattle metro area ranked #35. Criteria: humidity levels; weather conditions; incidence of traffic delays and congestion; average commute times; frequency of flight delays and cancellations; rates of sleeplessness; underemployment; pollens and allergens; pests; comedy clubs per capita. *Energizer Holdings, "Most Irritation Prone Cities," July 23, 2010*
- Mars Chocolate North America, the makers of COMBOS®, in partnership with Sperling's BestPlaces, ranked 50 major metro areas in terms of their "manliness." The Seattle metro area ranked #41. Criteria: number of professional sports teams; number of nearby NASCAR tracks and racing events; manly lifestyle; concentration of manly retail stores; manly occupations per capita; salty snack sales; "Board of Manliness" rankings. *Mars Chocolate North America, "America's Manliest Cities 2011," September 1, 2011*
- Seattle was selected as one of "America's Best Cities for Hipsters" by *Travel + Leisure.* The city was ranked #1 out of 10. Criteria: live music; coffee bars; independent boutiques; best microbrews; offbeat and tech-savvy locals. *Travel + Leisure, "America's Best Cities for Hipsters," April 11, 2012*
- The Seattle metro area was selected as one of "America's Greediest Cities" by *Forbes.* The area was ranked #3 out of 10. Criteria: number of Forbes 400 (*Forbes* annual list of the richest Americans) members per capita. *Forbes, "America's Greediest Cities," December 7, 2007*

- The Seattle metro area appeared in *AutoMD.com's* ranking of the "Best and Worst Cities for Auto Repair." The metro area ranked #38 (#1 is best). The 50 most-populated metro areas in the U.S. were ranked on three critical factors: repair affordability; price disparity range; shop integrity factor. *AutoMD.com, "Advocacy for Repair Shop Fairness Report," February 24, 2010*
- Scarborough Research, a leading market research firm, identified the top local markets for volunteers in the U.S. The Seattle DMA (Designated Market Area) ranked in the top 10 with 31% of adults 18+ reporting that they have participated in volunteer work in the past 12 months. *Scarborough Research, December 13, 2011*

Business Environment

CITY FINANCES

City Government Finances

Component	2009 ($000)	2009 ($ per capita)
Total Revenues	2,811,561	4,732
Total Expenditures	2,827,867	4,759
Debt Outstanding	3,849,317	6,478
Cash and Securities[1]	2,152,433	3,622

Note: (1) Cash and security holdings of a government at the close of its fiscal year, including those of its dependent agencies, utilities, and liquor stores.
Source: U.S Census Bureau, State & Local Government Finances 2009

City Government Revenue by Source

Source	2009 ($000)	2009 ($ per capita)
General Revenue		
From Federal Government	38,826	65
From State Government	118,326	199
From Local Governments	7,331	12
Taxes		
Property	368,360	620
Sales and Gross Receipts	463,626	780
Personal Income	0	0
Corporate Income	0	0
Motor Vehicle License	0	0
Other Taxes	68,396	115
Current Charges	454,927	766
Liquor Store	0	0
Utility	1,023,880	1,723
Employee Retirement	69,538	117

Source: U.S Census Bureau, State & Local Government Finances 2009

City Government Expenditures by Function

Function	2009 ($000)	2009 ($ per capita)	2009 (%)
General Direct Expenditures			
Air Transportation	0	0	0.0
Corrections	442	1	0.0
Education	4,318	7	0.2
Employment Security Administration	0	0	0.0
Financial Administration	10,571	18	0.4
Fire Protection	121,577	205	4.3
General Public Buildings	4,370	7	0.2
Governmental Administration, Other	39,613	67	1.4
Health	6,324	11	0.2
Highways	148,691	250	5.3
Hospitals	0	0	0.0
Housing and Community Development	49,059	83	1.7
Interest on General Debt	59,077	99	2.1
Judicial and Legal	27,728	47	1.0
Libraries	48,894	82	1.7
Parking	7,735	13	0.3
Parks and Recreation	180,213	303	6.4
Police Protection	156,660	264	5.5
Public Welfare	93,806	158	3.3
Sewerage	237,278	399	8.4
Solid Waste Management	133,285	224	4.7
Veterans' Services	0	0	0.0
Liquor Store	0	0	0.0
Utility	1,117,164	1,880	39.5
Employee Retirement	112,926	190	4.0

Source: U.S Census Bureau, State & Local Government Finances 2009

Municipal Bond Ratings

Area	Moody's	S&P	Fitch
City	Aaa	AAA	AA+

Rating Systems (shown in declining order of credit quality): Moody's– Aaa, Aa, A, Baa, Ba, B, Caa, Ca, C (numerical modifiers 1, 2, and 3 are added to letter-rating); S&P– AAA, AA, A, BBB, BB, B, CCC, CC, C; Fitch– AAA, AA, A, BBB, BB, B, CCC, CC, C. Ratings may be modified by the addition of a plus or minus sign to show relative standing within the major rating categories.

Notes: n/a Not Available; w/d Withdrawn (1) Not Reviewed; (2) Issuer Rating/No General Obligation; (3) Standard and Poor's Issue Credit Rating (ICR) is a current opinion of an obliger with respect to a specific financial obligation, a specific class of financial obligations, or a specific financial program.

Source: U.S. Census Bureau, 2012 Statistical Abstract, Bond Ratings for City Governments by Largest Cities: 2010

DEMOGRAPHICS

Population Growth

Area	1990 Census	2000 Census	2010 Census	Population Growth (%) 1990-2000	Population Growth (%) 2000-2010
City	516,262	563,374	608,660	9.1	8.0
MSA[1]	2,559,164	3,043,878	3,439,809	18.9	13.0
U.S.	248,709,873	281,421,906	308,745,538	13.2	9.7

Note: (1) Figures cover the Seattle-Tacoma-Bellevue, WA Metropolitan Statistical Area—see Appendix B for areas included

Source: U.S. Census Bureau, 2010 Census

Household Size

Area	Persons in Household (%) One	Two	Three	Four	Five	Six	Seven or More	Average Household Size
City	41.3	33.3	12.2	8.5	2.8	1.0	0.9	2.06
MSA[1]	28.4	33.2	15.9	13.3	5.5	2.2	1.5	2.49
U.S.	26.7	32.8	16.1	13.4	6.5	2.6	1.9	2.58

Note: (1) Figures cover the Seattle-Tacoma-Bellevue, WA Metropolitan Statistical Area—see Appendix B for areas included

Source: U.S. Census Bureau, 2010 Census

Race

Area	White Alone[2] (%)	Black Alone[2] (%)	Asian Alone[2] (%)	AIAN[3] Alone[2] (%)	NHOPI[4] Alone[2] (%)	Other Race Alone[2] (%)	Two or More Races (%)
City	69.5	7.9	13.8	0.8	0.4	2.4	5.1
MSA[1]	71.9	5.6	11.4	1.1	0.8	3.8	5.3
U.S.	72.4	12.6	4.8	0.9	0.2	6.2	2.9

Note: (1) Figures cover the Seattle-Tacoma-Bellevue, WA Metropolitan Statistical Area—see Appendix B for areas included; (2) Alone is defined as not being in combination with one or more other races; (3) American Indian and Alaska Native; (4) Native Hawaiian and Other Pacific Islander

Source: U.S. Census Bureau, 2010 Census

Hispanic or Latino Origin

Area	Hispanic or Latino (%)	Mexican (%)	Puerto Rican (%)	Cuban (%)	Other Hispanic or Latino (%)
City	6.6	4.1	0.3	0.2	2.0
MSA[1]	9.0	6.4	0.5	0.1	2.0
U.S.	16.3	10.3	1.5	0.6	4.0

Note: Persons of Hispanic or Latino origin can be of any race; (1) Figures cover the Seattle-Tacoma-Bellevue, WA Metropolitan Statistical Area—see Appendix B for areas included

Source: U.S. Census Bureau, 2010 Census

Segregation

Type	Segregation Indices[1]				Percent Change		
	1990	2000	2010	2010 Rank[2]	1990-2000	1990-2010	2000-2010
Black/White	56.5	52.4	49.1	72	-4.1	-7.4	-3.3
Asian/White	36.8	37.6	37.6	69	0.8	0.8	0.0
Hispanic/White	22.3	30.4	32.8	87	8.1	10.5	2.4

Note: Figures are based on an analysis of 1990, 2000, and 2010 Census Decennial Census tract data by William H. Frey, Brookings Institution and the University of Michigan Social Science Data Analysis Network. In this analysis all racial groups (whites, blacks, and asians) are non-Hispanic members of those races. Hispanics are shown as a separate category; All figures cover the Metropolitan Statistical Area (see Appendix B for areas included); (1) Segregation Indices are Dissimilarity Indices that measure the degree to which the minority group is distributed differently than whites across census tracts. They range from 0 (complete integration) to 100 (complete segregation) where the value indicates the percentage of the minority group that needs to move to be distributed exactly like whites; (2) Ranges from 1 (most segregated) to 102 (least segregated); n/a not available.
Source: www.CensusScope.org

Ancestry

Area	German	Irish	English	American	Italian	Polish	French[2]	Scottish	Dutch
City	16.0	11.9	11.3	2.7	4.4	2.5	3.3	3.8	1.9
MSA[1]	18.1	11.7	11.1	3.3	3.8	2.1	3.5	3.1	2.0
U.S.	16.1	11.6	8.8	6.1	5.7	3.2	3.0	1.9	1.6

Note: Figures are the percentage of the total population reporting a particular ancestry. The nine most commonly reported ancestries in the U.S. are shown. Figures include multiple ancestries (e.g. if a person reported being Irish and Italian, they were included in both columns); (1) Figures cover the Seattle-Tacoma-Bellevue, WA Metropolitan Statistical Area—see Appendix B for areas included; (2) Excludes Basque
Source: U.S. Census Bureau, 2008-2010 American Community Survey 3-Year Estimates

Foreign-Born Population

Area	Percent of Population Born in								
	Any Foreign Country	Mexico	Asia	Europe	Carribean	South America	Central America[2]	Africa	Canada
City	16.8	1.3	8.9	2.4	0.1	0.4	0.3	2.0	1.0
MSA[1]	16.4	2.7	8.0	2.7	0.1	0.4	0.4	1.1	0.8
U.S.	12.8	3.8	3.6	1.6	1.2	0.9	1.0	0.5	0.3

Note: (1) Figures cover the Seattle-Tacoma-Bellevue, WA Metropolitan Statistical Area—see Appendix B for areas included; (2) Excludes Mexico.
Source: U.S. Census Bureau, 2008-2010 American Community Survey 3-Year Estimates

Marital Status

Area	Never Married	Now Married[2]	Separated	Widowed	Divorced
City	43.6	39.4	1.4	4.4	11.2
MSA[1]	31.6	50.5	1.7	4.5	11.8
U.S.	31.6	49.6	2.2	6.1	10.7

Note: Figures are percentages and cover the population 15 years of age and older; (1) Figures cover the Seattle-Tacoma-Bellevue, WA Metropolitan Statistical Area—see Appendix B for areas included; (2) Excludes separated
Source: U.S. Census Bureau, 2008-2010 American Community Survey 3-Year Estimates

Age

Area	Percent of Population							Median Age
	Under Age 5	Age 5 to 17	Age 18 to 34	Age 35 to 49	Age 50 to 64	Age 65 to 79	80 Years and Over	
City	5.3	10.1	32.6	23.1	18.1	7.2	3.6	36.1
MSA[1]	6.5	16.4	24.5	22.5	19.3	7.7	3.1	36.8
U.S.	6.5	17.5	23.2	20.7	19.0	9.4	3.6	37.2

Note: (1) Figures cover the Seattle-Tacoma-Bellevue, WA Metropolitan Statistical Area—see Appendix B for areas included
Source: U.S. Census Bureau, 2010 Census

Male/Female Ratio

Area	Males	Females	Males per 100 Females
City	304,030	304,630	99.8
MSA[1]	1,711,982	1,727,827	99.1
U.S.	151,781,326	156,964,212	96.7

Note: (1) Figures cover the Seattle-Tacoma-Bellevue, WA Metropolitan Statistical Area—see Appendix B for areas included
Source: U.S. Census Bureau, 2010 Census

Religious Groups

Area	Catholic	Baptist	Non-Den.	Methodist[2]	Lutheran	LDS[3]	Pente-costal	Presby-terian[4]	Muslim[5]	Judaism
MSA[1]	12.3	2.2	5.0	1.2	2.1	3.3	2.8	1.4	0.5	0.5
U.S.	19.1	9.3	4.0	4.0	2.3	2.0	1.9	1.6	0.8	0.7

Note: Figures are the number of adherents as a percentage of the total population; (1) Figures cover the Seattle-Tacoma-Bellevue, WA Metropolitan Statistical Area—see Appendix B for areas included; (2) Methodist/Pietist; (3) Latter Day Saints; (4) Reformed; (5) Figures are estimates
Source: Association of Statisticians of American Religious Bodies, 2010 U.S. Religion Census: Religious Congregations & Membership Study

ECONOMY

Gross Metropolitan Product

Area	2007	2008	2009	2010	2010 Rank[2]
MSA[1]	220.9	227.9	225.6	231.4	12

Note: Figures are in billions of dollars; (1) Figures cover the Seattle-Tacoma-Bellevue, WA Metropolitan Statistical Area—see Appendix B for areas included; (2) Rank ranges from 1 to 363
Source: The United States Conference of Mayors, "U.S. Metro Economies: GMP and Employment Forecasts," June 2011

Economic Growth

Area	2007-2009 (%)	2010 (%)	2011 (%)	Rank[2]
MSA[1]	-0.8	1.6	2.8	144
U.S.	-1.3	2.9	2.5	–

Note: Figures are real Gross Metropolitan Product growth rates and represent annual average percent change; (1) Figures cover the Seattle-Tacoma-Bellevue, WA Metropolitan Statistical Area—see Appendix B for areas included; (2) Rank ranges from 1 to 363
Source: The United States Conference of Mayors, "U.S. Metro Economies: GMP and Employment Forecasts," June 2011

Metropolitan Area Exports

Area	2005	2006	2007	2008	2009	2010	2010 Rank[2]
MSA[1]	30,676.0	46,309.2	53,893.1	46,911.2	36,942.3	35,409.6	6

Note: Figures are in millions of dollars; (1) Figures cover the Seattle-Tacoma-Bellevue, WA Metropolitan Statistical Area—see Appendix B for areas included; (2) Rank ranges from 1 to 369
Source: U.S. Department of Commerce, International Trade Administration, Office of Trade & Industry Information, Manufacturing & Services, data extracted April 2, 2012

INCOME

Income

Area	Per Capita ($)	Median Household ($)	Average Household ($)
City	40,894	60,619	85,727
MSA[1]	33,755	64,821	83,560
U.S.	26,942	51,222	70,116

Note: (1) Figures cover the Seattle-Tacoma-Bellevue, WA Metropolitan Statistical Area—see Appendix B for areas included
Source: U.S. Census Bureau, 2008-2010 American Community Survey 3-Year Estimates

Household Income Distribution

Area	Percent of Households Earning							
	Under $15,000	$15,000 -24,999	$25,000 -34,999	$35,000 -49,999	$50,000 -74,999	$75,000 -99,000	$100,000 -149,999	$150,000 and up
City	12.0	8.5	8.4	12.9	17.4	12.5	14.5	13.9
MSA[1]	9.1	7.8	8.4	12.9	18.9	14.1	16.6	12.2
U.S.	13.0	11.0	10.6	14.2	18.5	12.1	12.2	8.4

Note: (1) Figures cover the Seattle-Tacoma-Bellevue, WA Metropolitan Statistical Area—see Appendix B for areas included
Source: U.S. Census Bureau, 2008-2010 American Community Survey 3-Year Estimates

Poverty Rate

Area	All Ages	Under 18 Years Old	18 to 64 Years Old	65 Years and Over
City	12.6	11.1	12.9	12.4
MSA[1]	10.5	13.3	10.0	8.0
U.S.	14.4	20.1	13.1	9.4

Note: Figures are percentage of people whose income during the past 12 months was below the poverty level; (1) Figures cover the Seattle-Tacoma-Bellevue, WA Metropolitan Statistical Area—see Appendix B for areas included
Source: U.S. Census Bureau, 2008-2010 American Community Survey 3-Year Estimates

Personal Bankruptcy Filing Rate

Area	2006	2007	2008	2009	2010	2011
King County	1.44	1.79	2.42	3.76	4.32	4.09
U.S.	2.00	2.73	3.53	4.61	4.97	4.37

Note: Numbers are per 1,000 population and include Chapter 7 and Chapter 13 filings
Source: Federal Deposit Insurance Corporation, Regional Economic Conditions, March 9, 2012

EMPLOYMENT

Labor Force and Employment

Area	Civilian Labor Force			Workers Employed		
	Dec. 2010	Dec. 2011	% Chg.	Dec. 2010	Dec. 2011	% Chg.
City	377,030	378,637	0.4	348,306	353,489	1.5
MD[1]	1,483,979	1,492,083	0.5	1,350,324	1,383,080	2.4
U.S.	153,156,000	153,373,000	0.1	139,159,000	140,681,000	1.1

Note: Data is not seasonally adjusted and covers workers 16 years of age and older; (1) Metropolitan Division—see Appendix B for areas included
Source: Bureau of Labor Statistics, http://stats.bls.gov

Unemployment Rate

Area	2011											
	Jan.	Feb.	Mar.	Apr.	May	Jun.	Jul.	Aug.	Sep.	Oct.	Nov.	Dec.
City	7.9	8.0	7.8	7.4	7.3	8.2	8.1	7.6	7.6	7.4	7.0	6.6
MD[1]	9.3	9.3	8.8	8.1	8.3	9.0	8.7	8.0	8.2	8.1	7.7	7.3
U.S.	9.8	9.5	9.2	8.7	8.7	9.3	9.3	9.1	8.8	8.5	8.2	8.3

Note: Data is not seasonally adjusted and covers workers 16 years of age and older; All figures are percentages; (1) Metropolitan Division—see Appendix B for areas included
Source: Bureau of Labor Statistics, http://stats.bls.gov

Projected Unemployment Rate

Area	2010 (%)	2011 (%)	2012 (%)	2013 (%)
MSA[1]	9.3	8.3	7.8	7.0

Note: (1) Metropolitan Statistical Area—see Appendix B for areas included
Source: The United States Conference of Mayors, "U.S. Metro Economies: GMP and Employment Forecasts," June 2011

Employment by Occupation

Occupation Classification	City (%)	MSA[1] (%)	U.S. (%)
Management, Business, Science, and Arts	54.0	42.2	35.6
Natural Resources, Construction, and Maintenance	4.4	8.3	9.5
Production, Transportation, and Material Moving	6.4	10.0	12.1
Sales and Office	20.5	23.7	25.2
Service	14.7	15.8	17.6

Note: Figures cover employed civilians 16 years of age and older; (1) Figures cover the Seattle-Tacoma-Bellevue, WA Metropolitan Statistical Area—see Appendix B for areas included
Source: U.S. Census Bureau, 2008-2010 American Community Survey 3-Year Estimates

Employment by Industry

Sector	MD[1] Number of Employees	MD[1] Percent of Total	U.S. Percent of Total
Construction	63,800	4.5	4.1
Education and Health Services	173,400	12.2	15.2
Financial Activities	77,200	5.4	5.8
Government	201,000	14.1	16.8
Information	85,600	6.0	2.0
Leisure and Hospitality	134,600	9.5	9.9
Manufacturing	165,000	11.6	8.9
Mining and Logging	600	<0.1	0.6
Other Services	50,500	3.6	4.0
Professional and Business Services	207,900	14.6	13.3
Retail Trade	146,800	10.3	11.5
Transportation and Utilities	47,900	3.4	3.8
Wholesale Trade	67,700	4.8	4.2

Note: Figures cover non-farm employment as of December 2011 and are not seasonally adjusted; (1) Metropolitan Division—see Appendix B for areas included
Source: Bureau of Labor Statistics, http://stats.bls.gov

Occupations with Greatest Projected Employment Growth: 2008 – 2018

Occupation[1]	2008 Employment	2018 Projected Employment	Numeric Employment Change	Percent Employment Change
Registered Nurses	54,560	71,220	16,660	30.5
Personal and Home Care Aides	27,270	36,390	9,120	33.4
Combined Food Preparation and Serving Workers, Including Fast Food	64,840	72,570	7,730	11.9
Janitors and Cleaners, Except Maids and Housekeeping Cleaners	44,620	52,050	7,430	16.7
Retail Salespersons	96,740	104,100	7,360	7.6
Landscaping and Groundskeeping Workers	25,340	32,160	6,820	26.9
Home Health Aides	12,940	19,400	6,460	49.9
Office Clerks, General	59,940	65,840	5,900	9.8
Laborers and Freight, Stock, and Material Movers, Hand	47,530	53,280	5,750	12.1
Computer Software Engineers, Applications	25,000	30,240	5,240	21.0

Note: Projections cover Washington; (1) Sorted by numeric employment change
Source: www.projectionscentral.com, State Occupational Projections, 2008–2018 Long-Term Projections

Fastest Growing Occupations: 2008 – 2018

Occupation[1]	2008 Employment	2018 Projected Employment	Numeric Employment Change	Percent Employment Change
Biomedical Engineers	420	670	250	59.5
Home Health Aides	12,940	19,400	6,460	49.9
Employment, Recruitment, and Placement Specialists	4,320	6,100	1,780	41.2
Physical Therapist Aides	1,110	1,530	420	37.8
Network Systems and Data Communications Analysts	11,880	16,180	4,300	36.2
Veterinarians	1,520	2,060	540	35.5
Veterinary Technologists and Technicians	1,690	2,290	600	35.5
Chiropractors	1,320	1,780	460	34.8
Personal and Home Care Aides	27,270	36,390	9,120	33.4
Physician Assistants	2,020	2,690	670	33.2

Note: Projections cover Washington; (1) Sorted by percent employment change and excludes occupations with numeric employment change less than 100
Source: www.projectionscentral.com, State Occupational Projections, 2008–2018 Long-Term Projections

Average Wages

Occupation	$/Hr.	Occupation	$/Hr.
Accountants and Auditors	33.93	Maids and Housekeeping Cleaners	12.10
Automotive Mechanics	19.26	Maintenance and Repair Workers	20.35
Bookkeepers	19.53	Marketing Managers	63.21
Carpenters	25.62	Nuclear Medicine Technologists	41.27
Cashiers	12.86	Nurses, Licensed Practical	24.18
Clerks, General Office	16.09	Nurses, Registered	37.68
Clerks, Receptionists/Information	14.48	Nursing Aides/Orderlies/Attendants	14.77
Clerks, Shipping/Receiving	17.95	Packers and Packagers, Hand	11.79
Computer Programmers	45.55	Physical Therapists	37.65
Computer Support Specialists	28.14	Postal Service Mail Carriers	25.70
Computer Systems Analysts	43.29	Real Estate Brokers	41.03
Cooks, Restaurant	12.88	Retail Salespersons	14.24
Dentists	106.68	Sales Reps., Exc. Tech./Scientific	33.18
Electrical Engineers	45.46	Sales Reps., Tech./Scientific	43.02
Electricians	31.80	Secretaries, Exc. Legal/Med./Exec.	19.27
Financial Managers	60.69	Security Guards	18.98
First-Line Supervisors/Managers, Sales	22.33	Surgeons	n/a
Food Preparation Workers	11.95	Teacher Assistants	15.40
General and Operations Managers	66.28	Teachers, Elementary School	29.00
Hairdressers/Cosmetologists	18.08	Teachers, Secondary School	29.50
Internists	86.31	Telemarketers	12.43
Janitors and Cleaners	14.35	Truck Drivers, Heavy/Tractor-Trailer	21.25
Landscaping/Groundskeeping Workers	15.62	Truck Drivers, Light/Delivery Svcs.	17.47
Lawyers	59.08	Waiters and Waitresses	14.87

Note: Wage data covers the Seattle-Bellevue-Everett, WA Metropolitan Division—see Appendix B for areas included. Hourly wages for elementary/secondary school teachers and teacher assistants were calculated by the editors from annual wage data assuming a 40 hour work week; n/a not available.
Source: Bureau of Labor Statistics, Metro Area Occupational Employment and Wage Estimates, May 2011

RESIDENTIAL REAL ESTATE

Building Permits

Area	Single-Family			Multi-Family			Total		
	2010	2011	Pct. Chg.	2010	2011	Pct. Chg.	2010	2011	Pct. Chg.
City	241	316	31.1	2,456	2,857	16.3	2,697	3,173	17.6
MSA[1]	6,139	6,078	-1.0	3,901	5,152	32.1	10,040	11,230	11.9
U.S.	447,311	418,498	-6.4	157,299	205,563	30.7	604,610	624,061	3.2

Note: (1) Metropolitan Statistical Area—see Appendix B for areas included; figures represent new, privately-owned housing units authorized (unadjusted data); All permit data are based on estimates with imputation.
Source: U.S. Census Bureau, Manufacturing, Mining, and Construction Statistics, Building Permits, 2010, 2011

Homeownership Rate

Area	2005 (%)	2006 (%)	2007 (%)	2008 (%)	2009 (%)	2010 (%)	2011 (%)
MSA[1]	64.5	63.7	62.8	61.3	61.2	60.9	60.7
U.S.	68.9	68.8	68.1	67.8	67.4	66.9	66.1

Note: (1) Metropolitan Statistical Area—see Appendix B for areas included
Source: U.S. Census Bureau, Housing Vacancies and Homeownership Annual Statistics: 2011

Housing Vacancy Rates

Area	Gross Vacancy Rate[2] (%)			Year-Round Vacancy Rate[3] (%)			Rental Vacancy Rate[4] (%)			Homeowner Vacancy Rate[5] (%)		
	2009	2010	2011	2009	2010	2011	2009	2010	2011	2009	2010	2011
MSA[1]	9.0	8.8	8.6	8.8	8.6	8.3	8.0	7.4	6.7	2.8	3.2	2.6
U.S.	14.5	14.3	14.2	11.3	11.3	11.1	10.6	10.2	9.5	2.6	2.6	2.5

Note: (1) Metropolitan Statistical Area—see Appendix B for areas included; (2) The percentage of the total housing inventory that is vacant; (3) The percentage of the housing inventory (excluding seasonal units) that is year-round vacant; (4) The percentage of rental inventory that is vacant for rent; (5) The percentage of homeowner inventory that is vacant for sale
Source: U.S. Census Bureau, Housing Vacancies and Homeownership Annual Statistics: 2011

TAXES

State Corporate Income Tax Rates

State	Tax Rate (%)	Income Brackets ($)	Num. of Brackets	Financial Institution Tax Rate (%)[a]	Federal Income Tax Ded.
Washington	No corporate tax	–	-	–	No

Note: Tax rates as of January 1, 2012; (a) Rates listed are the corporate income tax rate applied to financial institutions or excise taxes based on income. Some states have other taxes based upon the value of deposits or shares.
Source: Federation of Tax Administrators, "State Corporate Income Tax Rates, 2012"

State Individual Income Tax Rates

State	Tax Rate (%)	Income Brackets ($)	Num. of Brackets	Personal Exempt. ($)[1] Single	Personal Exempt. ($)[1] Dependents	Fed. Inc. Tax Ded.
Washington – No State Income Tax						

Note: Tax rates as of January 1, 2012; Local- and county-level taxes are not included; n/a not applicable; (1) Married joint filers generally receive double the single exemption
Source: Federation of Tax Administrators, "State Individual Income Tax Rates, 2012"

Various State and Local Tax Rates

State	State and Local Sales and Use (%)	State Sales and Use (%)	Gasoline[1] (¢/gal.)	Cigarette[2] ($/pack)	Spirits[3] ($/gal.)	Wine[4] ($/gal.)	Beer[5] ($/gal.)
Washington	9.5	6.50	37.5	3.03	26.70 (f)	0.88	0.26

Note: All tax rates as of January 1, 2012 except beer, wine and spirits (September 1, 2011); (1) The American Petroleum Institute has developed a methodology for determining the average tax rate on a gallon of fuel. Rates may include any of the following: excise taxes, environmental fees, storage tank fees, other fees or taxes, general sales tax, and local taxes. In states where gasoline is subject to the general sales tax, or where the fuel tax is based on the average sale price, the average rate determined by API is sensitive to changes in the price of gasoline. States that fully or partially apply general sales taxes to gasoline: CA, CO, GA, IL, IN, MI, NY; (2) The federal excise tax of $1.0066 per pack and local taxes are not included; (3) Rates are those applicable to off-premise sales of 40% alcohol by volume (a.b.v.) distilled spirits in 750ml containers. Local excise taxes are excluded; (4) Rates are those applicable to off-premise sales of 11% a.b.v. non-carbonated wine in 750ml containers; (5) Rates are those applicable to off-premise sales of 4.7% a.b.v. beer in 12 ounce containers; (f) States where the government controls sales. In these "control states," products are subject to ad valorem mark-up and excise taxes. The excise tax rate is calculated using a methodology developed by the Distilled Spirits Council of the United States.
Source: Tax Foundation, 2012 Facts & Figures: How Does Your State Compare?

State-Local Tax Burdens

Area	Rate (%)	Rank[1]	Per Capita Taxes Paid to Home State ($)	Total State and Local Per Capita Taxes Paid ($)	Per Capita Income ($)
Washington	9.3	29	3,141	4,408	47,361
U.S. Average	9.8		3,057	4,160	42,539

Note: Figures cover 2009; (1) Rank ranges from 1 to 50 where 1 is highest tax burden
Source: Tax Foundation, State-Local Tax Burdens, All States, 2009

State Business Tax Climate Index Rankings

State	Overall Rank	Corporate Tax Index Rank	Individual Income Tax Index Rank	Sales Tax Index Rank	Unemployment Insurance Tax Index Rank	Property Tax Index Rank
Washington	7	30	1	48	18	22

Note: The index is a measure of how each state's tax laws affect economic performance. The lower the rank, the more favorable a state's tax system is for business. States without a given tax are given a ranking of 1.
Source: Tax Foundation, Major Components of the State Business Tax Climate Index, FY 2012

COMMERCIAL REAL ESTATE

Office Market

Market Area	Inventory (sq. ft.)	Vacant (sq. ft.)	Vac. Rate (%)	Under Constr. (sq. ft.)	Asking Rent ($/sf/yr) Class A	Asking Rent ($/sf/yr) Class B
Seattle	90,570,911	14,842,822	16.4	276,842	30.48	23.09

Source: Grubb & Ellis, Office Markets Trends, 4th Quarter 2011

Industrial Market

Market Area	Inventory (sq. ft.)	Vacant (sq. ft.)	Vac. Rate (%)	Under Constr. (sq. ft.)	Asking Rent ($/sf/yr) WH/Dist	Asking Rent ($/sf/yr) R&D/Flex
Seattle	163,327,607	14,463,624	8.9	137,284	5.88	11.52

Source: Grubb & Ellis, Industrial Markets Trends, 4th Quarter 2011

COMMERCIAL UTILITIES

Typical Monthly Electric Bills

Area	Commercial Service ($/month)		Industrial Service ($/month)	
	1,500 kWh	40 kW demand 14,000 kWh	1,000 kW demand 200,000 kWh	50,000 kW demand 15,000,000 kWh
City	n/a	n/a	n/a	n/a
Average[1]	189	1,616	25,197	1,470,813

Note: Based on total rates in effect July 1, 2011; (1) average based on 184 utilities surveyed; n/a not available
Source: Edison Electric Institute, Typical Bills and Average Rates Report, Summer 2011

TRANSPORTATION

Means of Transportation to Work

Area	Car/Truck/Van: Drove Alone	Car/Truck/Van: Car-pooled	Public Transportation: Bus	Public Transportation: Subway	Public Transportation: Railroad	Bicycle	Walked	Other Means	Worked at Home
City	52.6	9.4	18.4	0.2	0.0	3.2	8.7	1.3	6.1
MSA[1]	69.5	11.3	7.8	0.1	0.3	1.0	3.6	1.2	5.1
U.S.	76.0	10.2	2.7	1.7	0.5	0.5	2.8	1.3	4.2

Note: Figures are percentages and cover workers 16 years of age and older; (1) Figures cover the Seattle-Tacoma-Bellevue, WA Metropolitan Statistical Area—see Appendix B for areas included
Source: U.S. Census Bureau, 2008-2010 American Community Survey 3-Year Estimates

Travel Time to Work

Area	Less Than 10 Minutes	10 to 19 Minutes	20 to 29 Minutes	30 to 44 Minutes	45 to 59 Minutes	60 to 89 Minutes	90 Minutes or More
City	8.9	29.4	25.4	24.5	6.5	4.1	1.3
MSA[1]	9.8	26.1	22.4	24.2	9.0	6.3	2.2
U.S.	13.9	30.1	20.8	19.8	7.5	5.5	2.5

Note: Figures are percentages and include workers 16 years old and over; (1) Figures cover the Seattle-Tacoma-Bellevue, WA Metropolitan Statistical Area—see Appendix B for areas included
Source: U.S. Census Bureau, 2008-2010 American Community Survey 3-Year Estimates

Travel Time Index

Area	1985	1990	1995	2000	2005	2010
Urban Area[1]	1.13	1.27	1.30	1.31	1.33	1.27
Average[2]	1.11	1.16	1.18	1.21	1.25	1.20

Note: Travel Time Index—the ratio of travel time in the peak period to the travel time at free-flow conditions. A value of 1.30 indicates a 20-minute free-flow trip takes 26 minutes in the peak. Free-flow speeds (60 mph on freeways and 35 mph on principal arterials) are used as the comparison threshold; (1) Covers the Seattle WA urban area; (2) average of 439 urban areas
Source: Texas Transportation Institute, Urban Mobility Report 2011, September 2011

Public Transportation

Agency Name / Mode of Transportation	Vehicles Operated in Maximum Service	Annual Unlinked Passenger Trips ('000)	Annual Passenger Miles ('000)
King County Department of Transportation (KC Metro)			
Bus (directly operated)	932	87,470.8	419,705.3
Bus (purchased transportation)	30	817.0	2,626.7
Demand Response (purchased transportation)	336	1,177.2	12,191.4
Demand Response Taxi (purchased transportation)	44	80.7	640.6
Light Rail (directly operated)	2	520.9	471.6
Trolleybus (directly operated)	116	20,721.1	36,274.4
Vanpool (directly operated)	1,154	2,849.6	58,134.0

Source: Federal Transit Administration, National Transit Database, 2010

Air Transportation

Airport Name and Code / Type of Service	Passenger Airlines[1]	Passenger Enplanements	Freight Carriers[2]	Freight (lbs.)
Seattle-Tacoma International (SEA)				
Domestic service (U.S. carriers - 2011)	24	14,484,254	20	195,835,210
International service (U.S. carriers - 2010)	8	793,481	6	14,430,439

Note: (1) Includes all U.S.-based major, minor and commuter airlines that carried at least one passenger during the year; (2) Includes all U.S.-based airlines and freight carriers that transported at least one pound of freight during the year
Source: Bureau of Transportation Statistics, The Intermodal Transportation Database, Air Carriers: T-100 Domestic Market (U.S. Carriers), 2011; Bureau of Transportation Statistics, The Intermodal Transportation Database, Air Carriers: T-100 International Market (U.S. Carriers), 2010

Other Transportation Statistics

Major Highways:	I-50; I-90
Amtrak Service:	Yes
Major Waterways/Ports:	Puget Sound; Port of Seattle

Source: Amtrak.com; Google Maps

BUSINESSES

Major Business Headquarters

Company Name	Rankings	
	Fortune[1]	Forbes[2]
Amazon.com	78	-
Expeditors International of Washington	384	-
Nordstrom	254	-
Starbucks	229	-

Note: (1) Fortune 500—companies that produce a 10-K are ranked 1 to 500 based on 2010 revenue; (2) all private companies with at least $2 billion in annual revenue are ranked 1 to 212; companies listed are headquartered in the city; dashes indicate no ranking
Source: Fortune, "Fortune 500," May 23, 2011; Forbes, "America's Largest Private Companies," November 16, 2011

Fast-Growing Businesses

According to *Inc.*, Seattle is home to six of America's 500 fastest-growing private companies: **Contour** (#7); **CleanScapes** (#324); **Spring Creek Group** (#325); **BuddyTV** (#368); **DocuSign** (#381); **Remote Medical International** (#430). Criteria: must be an independent, privately-held, for-profit, U.S. corporation, proprietorship or partnership; revenues must be at least $80,000 in 2007 and $2 million in 2010; must have four-year operating/sales history. Holding companies, regulated banks, and utilities were excluded. *Inc., "America's 500 Fastest-Growing Private Companies," September 2011*

According to *Fortune*, Seattle is home to two of the 100 fastest-growing companies in the world: **Amazon.com** (#45); **F5 Networks** (#48). Companies were ranked by their revenue growth rate; their EPS growth rate; and their three-year annualized total return to investors for the period ending June 30, 2011. Criteria for inclusion: a company, foreign or domestic, must trade on a major U.S. stock exchange; must file quarterly reports with the SEC; must have a minimum market capitalization of $250 million; must have a stock price of at least $5 on June 30, 2011; must have been trading continuously since June 30, 2008; must have revenue and net income for the four quarters ended on or before April 30, 2011, of at least $50 million and $10 million, respectively; and must have posted a compound annual growth in revenue and earnings per share of at least 15% annually over the three years ending on or before April 30, 2011. REITs, limited-liability companies, limited parterships, companies about to be acquired, and companies that lost money in the quarter ending April 30, 2011 were excluded. *Fortune, "100 Fastest-Growing Companies," September 26, 2011*

According to *Initiative for a Competitive Inner City (ICIC)*, Seattle is home to two of America's 100 fastest-growing "inner city" companies: **Tutta Bella** (#43); **Lam's Seafood Market** (#89). Companies were ranked by their five-year compound annual growth rate. Criteria for inclusion: company must be headquartered in or have 51 percent or more of its physical operations in an economically distressed urban area; must be an independent, for-profit corporation, partnership or proprietorship; must have 10 or more employees and have a five-year sales history that includes sales of at least $200,000 in the base year and at least $1 million in the current year with no decrease in sales over the two most recent years. *Initiative for a Competitive Inner City (ICIC), "Inner City 100 Companies, 2011"*

According to Deloitte, Seattle is home to 10 of North America's 500 fastest-growing high-technology companies: **Dendreon Corp.** (#12); **Azaleos** (#28); **DocuSign** (#58); **Tableau Software** (#115); **Powerit Solutions** (#119); **Zillow** (#164); **3TIER** (#276); **A Place for Mom** (#277); **Sesame Communications** (#346); **NetMotion Wireless** (#385). Companies are ranked by percentage growth in revenue over a five-year period. Criteria for inclusion: company must be headquartered within North America; must own proprietary intellectual property or proprietary technology that contributes to a significant portion of the company's operating revenue, or devote a significant proportion of revenues to research and development of technology; must have been in business for a minumum of five years with 2006 operating revenues of at least $50,000 USD/CD and 2010 operating revenues of at least $5 million USD/CD. *Deloitte Touche Tohmatsu, 2011 Deloitte Technology Fast 500™*

Minority- and Women-Owned Businesses

Group	All Firms		Firms with Paid Employees			
	Firms	Sales ($000)	Firms	Sales ($000)	Employees	Payroll ($000)
Asian	n/a	n/a	n/a	n/a	n/a	n/a
Black	n/a	n/a	n/a	n/a	n/a	n/a
Hispanic	n/a	n/a	n/a	n/a	n/a	n/a
Women	n/a	n/a	n/a	n/a	n/a	n/a
All Firms	1,799	785,488	354	715,401	6,115	186,891

Note: Figures cover firms located in the city; minority- and women-owned business are defined as firms in which the corresponding group own 51% or more of the stock or equity of the company; n/a not available
Source: U.S. Census Bureau, 2007 Economic Census, Survey of Business Owners

HOTELS

Hotels/Motels

Area	5 Star		4 Star		3 Star		2 Star		1 Star		Not Rated	
	Num.	Pct.[3]	Num.	Pct.[3]	Num.	Pct.[3]	Num.	Pct.[3]	Num.	Pct.[3]	Num.	Pct.[3]
City[1]	2	0.9	23	10.2	84	37.2	89	39.4	12	5.3	16	7.1
Total[2]	133	0.9	940	6.5	4,569	31.8	7,033	48.9	351	2.4	1,343	9.3

Note: (1) Figures cover Seattle and vicinity; (2) Figures cover all 100 cities in this book; (3) Percentage of hotels which have a given star rating; Star ratings are determined by expedia.com and offer an indication of the general quality of a particular hotel.
Source: expedia.com, April 25, 2012

The Seattle-Bellevue-Everett, WA metro area is home to four of the best hotels in the U.S. according to *Travel & Leisure*: **Willows Lodge** (#21); **Four Seasons Hotel, Seattle** (#57); **Hotel 1000** (#58); **The Fairmont Olympic Hotel Seattle** (#110). Criteria: service; location; rooms; food; and value. *Travel & Leisure, "T+L 500, The World's Best Hotels 2012"*

The Seattle-Bellevue-Everett, WA metro area is home to five of the best hotels in the U.S. according to *Condé Nast Traveler*: **Hotel 1000** (#14); **Inn at The Market** (#40); **Fairmont Olympic Hotel** (#62); **Salish Lodge & Spa** (#75); **Hyatt at Olive 8** (#91). The selections are based on over 25,000 responses to the magazine's annual Readers' Choice Survey. *Condé Nast Traveler, "2011 Readers' Choice Awards"*

EVENT SITES

Major Stadiums, Arenas, and Auditoriums

Name	Max. Capacity
HEC Edmundson Pavilion, University of Washington	10,000
Husky Stadium, University of Washington	72,500
KeyArena at Seattle Center	17,072
Qwest Field	67,000
Safeco Field	47,116
Seattle Center	21,100

Source: Original research

Convention Centers

Name	Overall Space (sq. ft.)	Exhibit Space (sq. ft.)	Meeting Space (sq. ft.)	Meeting Rooms
Seattle Center Exhibition Hall	n/a	n/a	34,000	n/a
Washington State Convention & Trade Center	n/a	57,000	205,700	61

Note: n/a not available
Source: Original research

Living Environment

COST OF LIVING

Cost of Living Index

Composite Index	Groceries	Housing	Utilities	Trans-portation	Health Care	Misc. Goods/ Services
117.2	111.7	129.5	90.4	112.4	118.4	118.7

Note: U.S. = 100; Figures cover the Seattle WA urban area.
Source: The Council for Community and Economic Research, ACCRA Cost of Living Index, 2011

Grocery Prices

Area[1]	T-Bone Steak ($/pound)	Frying Chicken ($/pound)	Whole Milk ($/half gal.)	Eggs ($/dozen)	Orange Juice ($/64 oz.)	Coffee ($/11.5 oz.)
City[2]	9.32	1.36	1.90	1.99	3.75	5.45
Avg.	9.25	1.18	2.22	1.66	3.19	4.40
Min.	6.70	0.88	1.31	0.95	2.46	2.94
Max.	14.30	2.16	3.50	3.18	4.75	6.83

Note: (1) Values for the local area are compared with the average, minimum and maximum values for all 335 areas in the Cost of Living Index; (2) Figures cover the Seattle WA urban area; **T-Bone Steak** *(price per pound);* **Frying Chicken** *(price per pound, whole fryer);* **Whole Milk** *(half gallon carton);* **Eggs** *(price per dozen, Grade A, large);* **Orange Juice** *(64 oz. Tropicana or Florida Natural);* **Coffee** *(11.5 oz. can, vacuum-packed, Maxwell House, Hills Bros, or Folgers).*
Source: The Council for Community and Economic Research, ACCRA Cost of Living Index, 2011

Housing and Utility Costs

Area[1]	New Home Price ($)	Apartment Rent ($/month)	All Electric ($/month)	Part Electric ($/month)	Other Energy ($/month)	Telephone ($/month)
City[2]	342,917	1,473	143.76	-	-	25.99
Avg.	285,990	839	163.23	89.00	77.52	26.92
Min.	188,005	460	125.58	45.39	33.89	17.98
Max.	1,197,028	3,244	339.16	181.97	348.69	40.01

Note: (1) Values for the local area are compared with the average, minimum and maximum values for all 335 areas in the Cost of Living Index; (2) Figures cover the Seattle WA urban area; **New Home Price** *(2,400 sf living area, 8,000 sf lot, in urban area with full utilities);* **Apartment Rent** *(950 sf 2 bedroom/1.5 or 2 bath, unfurnished, excluding all utilities except water);* **All Electric** *(average monthly cost for an all-electric home);* **Part Electric** *(average monthly cost for a part-electric home);* **Other Energy** *(average monthly cost for natural gas, fuel oil, coal, wood, and any other forms of energy except electricity);* **Telephone** *(price includes basic monthly rate for a private residential line plus additional local usage charges incurred by a family of four).*
Source: The Council for Community and Economic Research, ACCRA Cost of Living Index, 2011

Health Care, Transportation, and Other Costs

Area[1]	Doctor ($/visit)	Dentist ($/visit)	Optometrist ($/visit)	Gasoline ($/gallon)	Beauty Salon ($/visit)	Men's Shirt ($)
City[2]	119.29	106.93	115.25	3.65	41.48	35.93
Avg.	93.88	81.72	90.54	3.48	32.65	25.06
Min.	60.00	55.33	53.66	3.18	19.78	13.44
Max.	154.98	145.97	183.72	4.31	63.21	46.00

Note: (1) Values for the local area are compared with the average, minimum and maximum values for all 335 areas in the Cost of Living Index; (2) Figures cover the Seattle WA urban area; **Doctor** *(general practitioners routine exam of an established patient);* **Dentist** *(adult teeth cleaning and periodic oral examination);* **Optometrist** *(full vision eye exam for established adult patient);* **Gasoline** *(one gallon regular unleaded, national brand, including all taxes, cash price at self-service pump if available);* **Beauty Salon** *(woman's shampoo, trim, and blow-dry);* **Men's Shirt** *(cotton/polyester dress shirt, pinpoint weave, long sleeves).*
Source: The Council for Community and Economic Research, ACCRA Cost of Living Index, 2011

HOUSING

House Price Index (HPI)

Area	National Ranking[2]	Quarterly Change (%)	One-Year Change (%)	Five-Year Change (%)
MD[1]	227	-0.28	-4.64	-19.92
U.S.[3]	-	-0.10	-2.43	-19.16

Note: The HPI is a weighted repeat sales index. It measures average price changes in repeat sales or refinancings on the same properties. This information is obtained by reviewing repeat mortgage transactions on single-family properties whose mortgages have been purchased or securitized by Fannie Mae or Freddie Mac in January 1975; (1) Metropolitan Division - see Appendix B for areas included; (2) Rankings are based on annual percentage change for all metro areas containing at least 15,000 transactions over the last 10 years and ranges from 1 to 306; (3) figures based on a weighted average of Census Division estimates using a purchase only index; all figures are for the period ending December 31, 2011
Source: Federal Housing Finance Agency, House Price Index, February 23, 2012

House Price Valuations

Area	Q4 2005		Q4 2006		Q4 2007		Q4 2008		Q4 2009	
	Price ($000)	Over-valuation	Price ($000)	Over-valuation	Price ($000)	Over-valuation	Price ($000)	Over-valuation	Price ($000)	Over-valuation
MD[1]	347.9	24.3	395.6	28.8	408.1	23.1	370.8	11.6	350.6	5.5

Note: Figures show the percentage of over- or under-valuation of single family homes relative to statistically normal house values (e.g. a value of 23.6 indicates that house values are 23.6% overvalued). Statistically normal house values are based on house prices, interest rates, household incomes, population densities, and any historical premiums or discounts metropolitan areas have exhibited over time; (1) Figures cover the Seattle-Bellevue-Everett, WA - see Appendix B for areas included
Source: Global Insight/PNC Financial Services Group, House Prices in America: 4th Quarter 2009 Update

Median Single-Family Home Prices

Area	2009	2010	2011p	Percent Change 2010 to 2011
MSA[1]	306.2	295.7	285.0	-3.6
U.S. Average	172.1	173.1	166.2	-4.0

Note: Figures are median sales prices of existing single-family homes in thousands of dollars; (p) preliminary; n/a not available; (1) Metropolitan Statistical Area—see Appendix B for areas included
Source: National Association of Realtors, Median Sales Price of Existing Single-Family Homes for Metropolitan Areas, 4th Quarter 2011

Affordability Index of Existing Single-Family Homes

Area	2009	2010	2011p	Percent Change 2010 to 2011
MSA[1]	78.5	85.9	94.7	10.2

Note: The housing affordability index measures whether or not a typical family could qualify for a mortgage loan on a typical home. The higher the index, the greater the household purchasing power. An index of 100 is defined as the point where a median-income household has exactly enough income to qualify for the purchase of a median-priced existing single-family home, assuming a 20 percent downpayment and 25 percent of gross income devoted to mortgage principal and interest payments; (p) preliminary; n/a not available; (1) Metropolitan Statistical Area—see Appendix B for areas included
Source: National Association of Realtors, Affordability Index of Existing Single-Family Homes, 2011

Median Apartment Condo-Coop Home Prices

Area	2009	2010	2011p	Percent Change 2010 to 2011
MSA[1]	n/a	n/a	n/a	n/a
U.S. Average	175.6	171.7	165.1	-3.8

Note: Figures are median sales prices of existing apartment condo-coop homes in thousands of dollars; (p) preliminary; n/a not available; (1) Metropolitan Statistical Area—see Appendix B for areas included
Source: National Association of Realtors, Median Sales Price of Existing Apartment Condo-Coop Homes for Metropolitan Areas, 4th Quarter 2011

Year Housing Structure Built

Area	2005 or Later	2000 -2004	1990 -1999	1980 -1989	1970 -1979	1960 -1969	1950 -1959	Before 1950	Median Year
City	5.0	6.8	8.6	8.4	9.5	9.4	11.9	40.3	1958
MSA[1]	5.9	9.4	16.5	15.8	16.0	11.8	8.4	16.2	1978
U.S.	5.0	8.6	14.0	14.1	16.3	11.3	11.2	19.6	1975

Note: Figures are percentages except for Median Year; (1) Figures cover the Seattle-Tacoma-Bellevue, WA Metropolitan Statistical Area—see Appendix B for areas included
Source: U.S. Census Bureau, 2008-2010 American Community Survey 3-Year Estimates

HEALTH

Health Risk Data

Category	MSA[1] (%)	U.S. (%)
Adults who have been told they have high blood pressure[2]	25.7	28.7
Adults who have been told they have high blood cholesterol[2]	37.3	37.5
Adults who have been told they have diabetes[3]	6.4	8.7
Adults who have been told they have arthritis[2]	23.7	26.0
Adults who have been told they currently have asthma	8.9	9.1
Adults who are current smokers	12.9	17.3
Adults who are heavy drinkers[4]	6.1	5.0
Adults who are binge drinkers[5]	16.9	15.1
Adults who are overweight (BMI 25.0 - 29.9)	34.9	36.2
Adults who are obese (BMI 30.0 - 99.8)	22.8	27.5
Adults who participated in any physical activities in the past month	83.4	76.1
Adults 50+ who have ever had a sigmoidoscopy or colonoscopy	71.4	65.2
Women aged 40+ who have had a mammogram within the past two years	76.6	75.2
Men aged 40+ who have had a PSA test within the past two years	43.9	53.2
Adults aged 65+ who have had flu shot within the past year	70.8	67.5
Adults aged 18–64 who have any kind of health care coverage	83.7	82.2

Note: Data as of 2010 unless otherwise noted; (1) Figures cover the Seattle-Bellevue-Everett, WA Metropolitan Division—see Appendix B for areas included; (2) Data as of 2009; (3) Figures do not include pregnancy-related, borderline, or pre-diabetes; (4) Heavy drinkers are classified as males having more than two drinks per day or females having more than one drink per day; (5) Binge drinkers are classified as males having five or more drinks on one occasion or females having four or more drinks on one occasion
Source: Centers for Disease Control and Prevention, Behaviorial Risk Factor Surveillance System, SMART: Selected Metropolitan/Micropolitan Area Risk Trends, 2009, 2010

Mortality Rates for the Top 10 Causes of Death in the U.S.

ICD-10[a] Sub-Chapter	ICD-10[a] Code	Age-Adjusted Mortality Rate[1] per 100,000 population	
		County[2]	U.S.
Malignant neoplasms	C00-C97	159.5	175.6
Ischaemic heart diseases	I20-I25	94.2	121.6
Other forms of heart disease	I30-I51	28.1	48.6
Chronic lower respiratory diseases	J40-J47	33.0	42.3
Cerebrovascular diseases	I60-I69	36.5	40.6
Organic, including symptomatic, mental disorders	F01-F09	16.5	26.7
Other degenerative diseases of the nervous system	G30-G31	44.9	24.7
Other external causes of accidental injury	W00-X59	24.2	24.4
Diabetes mellitus	E10-E14	19.5	21.7
Hypertensive diseases	I10-I15	19.9	18.2

Note: (a) ICD-10 = International Classification of Diseases 10th Revision; (1) Mortality rates are a three year average covering 2007-2009; (2) Figures cover King County
Source: Centers for Disease Control and Prevention, National Center for Health Statistics. Underlying Cause of Death 1999-2009 on CDC WONDER Online Database, released 2012. Data for year 2009 are compiled from the Multiple Cause of Death File 2009, Series 20 No. 2O, 2012, Data for year 2008 are compiled from the Multiple Cause of Death File 2008, Series 20 No. 2N, 2011, Data for year 2007 are compiled from Multiple Cause of Death File 2007, Series 20 No. 2M, 2010.

Mortality Rates for Selected Causes of Death

ICD-10[a] Sub-Chapter	ICD-10[a] Code	Age-Adjusted Mortality Rate[1] per 100,000 population	
		County[2]	U.S.
Assault	X85-Y09	3.2	5.7
Human immunodeficiency virus (HIV) disease	B20-B24	2.3	3.3
Influenza and pneumonia	J09-J18	10.1	16.4
Intentional self-harm	X60-X84	10.8	11.5
Malnutrition	E40-E46	0.5	0.8
Obesity and other hyperalimentation	E65-E68	1.5	1.6
Transport accidents	V01-V99	7.1	13.7
Viral hepatitis	B15-B19	2.6	2.2

Note: (a) ICD-10 = International Classification of Diseases 10th Revision; (1) Mortality rates are a three year average covering 2007-2009; (2) Figures cover King County
Source: Centers for Disease Control and Prevention, National Center for Health Statistics. Underlying Cause of Death 1999-2009 on CDC WONDER Online Database, released 2012. Data for year 2009 are compiled from the Multiple Cause of Death File 2009, Series 20 No. 2O, 2012, Data for year 2008 are compiled from the Multiple Cause of Death File 2008, Series 20 No. 2N, 2011, Data for year 2007 are compiled from Multiple Cause of Death File 2007, Series 20 No. 2M, 2010.

Distribution of Physicians and Dentists

Area[1]	Dentists[2]	D.O.[3]	M.D.[4] Total	M.D.[4] Family/General Practice	M.D.[4] Pediatrics	M.D.[4] Medical Specialties	M.D.[4] Surgical Specialties
Local (number)	1,416	199	5,541	874	363	1,921	1,076
Local (rate[5])	7.6	1.1	29.4	4.6	1.9	10.2	5.7
U.S. (rate[5])	4.5	1.9	18.3	2.5	1.4	6.8	4.1

Note: Data as of 2008 unless noted; (1) Local data covers King County; (2) Data as of 2007; (3) Doctor of Osteopathic Medicine; (4) Includes active, non-federal, patient-care, office-based Doctors of Medicine; (5) rate per 10,000 population
Source: Area Resource File (ARF). 2009-2010 Release. U.S. Department of Health and Human Services, Health Resources and Services Administration, Bureau of Health Professions, Rockville, MD, August 2010

Best Hospitals

According to *U.S. News,* the Seattle-Bellevue-Everett, WA is home to three of the best hospitals in the U.S.: **Harborview Medical Center** (2 specialties); **University of Washington Medical Center** (11 specialties); **Virginia Mason Medical Center** (1 specialty). The hospitals listed were highly ranked in at least one adult specialty. *U.S. News Online, "America's Best Hospitals 2011-12"*

According to *U.S. News,* the Seattle-Bellevue-Everett, WA is home to one of the best children's hospitals in the U.S.: **Seattle Children's Hospital** (10 specialties). The hospital listed was highly ranked in at least one pediatric specialty. *U.S. News Online, "America's Best Children's Hospitals 2011-12"*

EDUCATION

Public School District Statistics

District Name	Schls	Pupils	Pupil/Teacher Ratio	Minority Pupils[1] (%)	Free Lunch Eligible[2] (%)	IEP[3] (%)
Seattle Public Schools	100	46,522	18.4	55.9	32.5	12.7

Note: Table includes school districts with 2,000 or more students; (1) Percentage of students that are not non-Hispanic white; (2) Percentage of students that are eligible for the free lunch program; (3) Percentage of students that have an Individualized Education Program.
Source: U.S. Department of Education, National Center for Education Statistics, Common Core of Data, Local Education Agency (School District) Universe Survey: School Year 2009-2010; U.S. Department of Education, National Center for Education Statistics, Common Core of Data, Public Elementary/Secondary School Universe Survey: School Year 2009-2010

Highest Level of Education

Area	Less than H.S.	H.S. Diploma	Some College, No Deg.	Associate Degree	Bachelors Degree	Masters Degree	Profess. School Degree	Doctorate Degree
City	7.1	12.1	18.2	6.8	33.5	14.2	4.9	3.2
MSA[1]	8.8	21.4	24.0	8.8	24.0	9.0	2.4	1.5
U.S.	14.7	28.4	21.3	7.6	17.6	7.2	1.9	1.2

Note: Figures cover persons age 25 and over; (1) Figures cover the Seattle-Tacoma-Bellevue, WA Metropolitan Statistical Area—see Appendix B for areas included
Source: U.S. Census Bureau, 2008-2010 American Community Survey 3-Year Estimates

Educational Attainment by Race

Area	High School Graduate or Higher (%)					Bachelor's Degree or Higher (%)				
	Total	White	Black	Asian	Hisp.[2]	Total	White	Black	Asian	Hisp.[2]
City	92.9	96.1	80.9	81.9	78.6	55.8	61.5	22.3	48.9	34.7
MSA[1]	91.2	93.2	87.7	85.9	67.4	37.0	37.7	20.0	48.8	17.1
U.S.	85.3	87.5	81.4	85.5	61.6	28.0	29.3	17.8	50.2	13.0

Note: Figures shown cover persons 25 years old and over; (1) Figures cover the Seattle-Tacoma-Bellevue, WA Metropolitan Statistical Area—see Appendix B for areas included; (2) People of Hispanic origin can be of any race
Source: U.S. Census Bureau, 2008-2010 American Community Survey 3-Year Estimates

School Enrollment by Grade and Control

Area	Preschool (%)		Kindergarten (%)		Grades 1 - 4 (%)		Grades 5 - 8 (%)		Grades 9 - 12 (%)	
	Public	Private	Public	Private	Public	Private	Public	Private	Public	Private
City	29.6	70.4	75.4	24.6	78.9	21.1	73.9	26.1	78.9	21.1
MSA[1]	39.5	60.5	84.9	15.1	89.0	11.0	88.7	11.3	89.9	10.1
U.S.	55.4	44.6	87.1	12.9	89.4	10.6	89.5	10.5	90.4	9.6

Note: Figures shown cover persons 3 years old and over; (1) Figures cover the Seattle-Tacoma-Bellevue, WA Metropolitan Statistical Area—see Appendix B for areas included
Source: U.S. Census Bureau, 2008-2010 American Community Survey 3-Year Estimates

Average Salaries of Public School Classroom Teachers

Area	2010-11		2011-12		Percent Change 2010-11 to 2011-12	Percent Change 2001-02 to 2011-12
	Dollars	Rank[1]	Dollars	Rank[1]		
Washington	52,926	21	54,193	21	2.39	24.70
U.S. Average	55,623	-	56,643	-	1.83	26.8

Note: (1) State rank ranges from 1 to 51 where 1 indicates highest salary.
Source: National Education Association, Rankings & Estimates: Rankings of the States 2011 and Estimates of School Statistics 2012, December 2011

Higher Education

Four-Year Colleges			Two-Year Colleges			Medical Schools[1]	Law Schools[2]	Voc/ Tech[3]
Public	Private Non-profit	Private For-profit	Public	Private Non-profit	Private For-profit			
3	6	4	1	0	1	1	2	7

Note: Figures cover institutions located within the city limits and include main campuses only; (1) includes schools accredited by the Liaison Committee on Medical Education and the American Osteopathic Association's Commission on Osteopathic College Accreditation; (2) includes American Bar Association-accredited law schools; (3) includes all schools with programs that are less than 2 years.
Source: National Center for Education Statistics, Integrated Postsecondary Education System (IPEDS) Peer Analysis System, 2011-12; Association of American Medical Colleges, Member List, April 23, 2012; American Osteopathic Association, Member List, April 23, 2012; Law School Admission Council, Official Guide to ABA-Approved Law Schools Online, April 23, 2012

According to *U.S. News & World Report,* the Seattle-Bellevue-Everett, WA is home to one of the best national universities in the U.S.: **University of Washington** (#42). The indicators used to capture academic quality fall into a number of categories: assessment by administrators at peer institutions; retention of students; faculty resources; student selectivity; financial resources; alumni giving; high school counselor ratings of colleges; and graduation rate.*U.S. News & World Report, "America's Best Colleges 2012"*

According to *U.S. News & World Report,* the Seattle-Bellevue-Everett, WA is home to one of the top 50 law schools in the U.S.: **University of Washington** (#20). The rankings are based on a weighted average of 12 measures of quality: peer assessment score; assessment score by lawyers/judges; median LSAT scores; median undergrad GPA; acceptance rate; employment rates for graduates; placement success; bar passage rate; faculty resources; expenditures per student; student/faculty ratio; and library resources. *U.S. News & World Report, "America's Best Law Schools 2013"*

According to *Forbes,* the Seattle-Bellevue-Everett, WA is home to one of the best business schools in the U.S.: **Washington (Foster)** (#36). The rankings are based on the return on investment that graduates of the Class of 2006 received (median salary five years after graduation). *Forbes, "Best Business Schools," August 3, 2011*

PRESIDENTIAL ELECTION

2008 Presidential Election Results

Area	Obama	McCain	Nader	Other
King County	70.0	28.0	0.8	1.2
U.S.	52.9	45.6	0.6	0.9

Note: Results are percentages and may not add to 100% due to rounding
Source: Dave Leip's Atlas of U.S. Presidential Elections, www.uselectionatlas.org

EMPLOYERS

Major Employers

Company Name	Industry
City of Tacoma	Switching and terminal services
Costco Wholesale Corporation	Miscellaneous general merchandise stores
County of Snohomish	Bureau of public roads
Evergreen Healthcare	General medical and surgical hospitals
Harborview Medical Center	General medical and surgical hospitals
King County Public Hospital District No. 2	Hospital and health services consultant
Microsoft Corporation	Prepackaged software
Prologix Distribution Services (west)	General merchandise, non-durable
R U Corporation	American restaurant
SNC-Lavalin Constructors	Heavy construction, nec
Social & Health Svcs, Washington Dept of	General medical and surgical hospitals
Swedish Health Services	General medical and surgical hospitals
T-Mobile USA	Radio, telephone communication
The Boeing Company	Airplanes, fixed or rotary wing
Tulalip Resort Casino	Casino hotel
United States Department of the Army	Medical centers
University of Washington	Colleges and universities
Virginia Mason Medical Center	General medical and surgical hospitals
Virginia Mason Medical Center	Clinic, operated by physicians
Virginia Mason Seattle Main Clinic	Clinic, operated by physicians

Note: Companies shown are located within the Seattle-Tacoma-Bellevue, WA metropolitan area.
Source: Hoovers.com, data extracted April 25 2012

Best Companies to Work For

Nordstrom; Perkins Coie; Starbucks, headquartered in Seattle, are among "The 100 Best Companies to Work For." To pick the 100 Best Companies to Work For, *Fortune* partnered with the Great Place to Work Institute. Two hundred eighty firms participated in this year's survey. Two-thirds of a company's score is based on the results of the Institute's Trust Index survey, which is sent to a random sample of employees from each company. The questions related to attitudes about management's credibility, job satisfaction, and camaraderie. The other third of the scoring is based on the company's responses to the Institute's Culture Audit, which includes detailed questions about pay and benefit programs, and a series of open-ended questions about hiring practices, internal communication, training, recognition programs, and diversity efforts. Any company that is at least five years old with more than 1,000 U.S. employees is eligible. *Fortune, "The 100 Best Companies to Work For," February 6, 2012*

Moss Adams, headquartered in Seattle, is among the "100 Best Companies for Working Mothers." Criteria: workforce profile; benefits; child care; women's issues and advancement; flexible work; paid time off and leave; company culture; and work-life programs. This year *Working Mother* gave particular weight to workforce profile, paid time off and company culture. *Working Mother, "100 Best Companies 2011"*

Avanade, headquartered in Seattle, is among the "100 Best Places to Work in IT." To qualify, companies, both public and private, had to have a minimum of 50 IT employees and were selected based on average salary and bonus increases, the percentage of IT staffers promoted, IT staff turnover rates, training and development programs, and the percentage of women and minorities in IT staff and management positions. In addition, *Computerworld* looked at retention efforts, programs for recognizing and rewarding outstanding performances, and benefits such as flextime, elder care and child care, and reimbursement for college tuition and the cost of pursuing technology certifications. *Computerworld, "100 Best Places to Work in IT 2011"*

PUBLIC SAFETY

Crime Rate

Area	All Crimes	Violent Crimes: Murder	Violent Crimes: Forcible Rape	Violent Crimes: Robbery	Violent Crimes: Aggrav. Assault	Property Crimes: Burglary	Property Crimes: Larceny -Theft	Property Crimes: Motor Vehicle Theft
City	5,917.7	3.1	15.5	230.4	317.8	1,039.8	3,754.3	556.8
Suburbs[1]	3,668.1	1.6	36.0	78.8	123.1	691.7	2,316.3	420.5
Metro[2]	4,198.4	2.0	31.1	114.6	169.0	773.8	2,655.3	452.6
U.S.	3,345.5	4.8	27.5	119.1	252.3	699.6	2,003.5	238.8

Note: Figures are crimes per 100,000 population; (1) All areas within the metro area that are located outside the city limits; (2) Metropolitan Division—see Appendix B for areas included
Source: FBI Uniform Crime Reports, 2010

Hate Crimes

Area	Number of Quarters Reported	Bias Motivation: Race	Bias Motivation: Religion	Bias Motivation: Sexual Orientation	Bias Motivation: Ethnicity	Bias Motivation: Disability
City	4	7	0	5	3	0

Source: Federal Bureau of Investigation, Hate Crime Statistics 2010

Identity Theft Consumer Complaints

Area	Complaints	Complaints per 100,000 Population	Rank[2]
MSA[1]	2,796	84.5	147
U.S.	279,156	90.4	-

Note: (1) Metropolitan Statistical Area—see Appendix B for areas included; (2) Rank ranges from 1 to 384 where 1 indicates greatest number of identity theft complaints per 100,000 population
Source: Federal Trade Commission, Consumer Sentinel Network Data Book for January–December 2011

Fraud and Other Consumer Complaints

Area	Complaints	Complaints per 100,000 Population	Rank[2]
MSA[1]	17,212	520.1	124
U.S.	1,533,924	496.8	-

Note: (1) Metropolitan Statistical Area—see Appendix B for areas included; (2) Rank ranges from 1 to 384 where 1 indicates greatest number of fraud and other complaints per 100,000 population
Source: Federal Trade Commission, Consumer Sentinel Network Data Book for January–December 2011

RECREATION

Culture

Dance[1]	Theatre[1]	Instrumental Music[1]	Vocal Music[1]	Series/ Festivals	Museums	Zoos and Aquariums[2]
6	11	10	3	13	19	2

Note: (1) Number of professional perfoming groups; (2) AZA-accredited
Source: The Grey House Performing Arts Directory, 2011-2012; Official Museum Directory, 2011; American Association of Museums, AAM Member Museums, April 2012; Association of Zoos & Aquariums, AZA Member Zoos & Aquariums, April 2012

Professional Sports Teams

Team Name	League
Seattle Mariners	Major League Baseball (MLB)
Seattle Seahawks	National Football League (NFL)
Seattle Sounders FC	Major League Soccer (MLS)

Note: Includes teams located in the Seattle metro area.
Source: Original research

CLIMATE

Average and Extreme Temperatures

Temperature	Jan	Feb	Mar	Apr	May	Jun	Jul	Aug	Sep	Oct	Nov	Dec	Yr.
Extreme High (°F)	64	70	75	85	93	96	98	99	98	89	74	63	99
Average High (°F)	44	48	52	57	64	69	75	74	69	59	50	45	59
Average Temp. (°F)	39	43	45	49	55	61	65	65	60	52	45	41	52
Average Low (°F)	34	36	38	41	46	51	54	55	51	45	39	36	44
Extreme Low (°F)	0	1	11	29	28	38	43	44	35	28	6	6	0

Note: Figures cover the years 1948-1990
Source: National Climatic Data Center, International Station Meteorological Climate Summary, 9/96

Average Precipitation/Snowfall/Humidity

Precip./Humidity	Jan	Feb	Mar	Apr	May	Jun	Jul	Aug	Sep	Oct	Nov	Dec	Yr.
Avg. Precip. (in.)	5.7	4.2	3.7	2.4	1.7	1.4	0.8	1.1	1.9	3.5	5.9	5.9	38.4
Avg. Snowfall (in.)	5	2	1	Tr	Tr	0	0	0	0	Tr	1	3	13
Avg. Rel. Hum. 7am (%)	83	83	84	83	80	79	79	84	87	88	85	85	83
Avg. Rel. Hum. 4pm (%)	76	69	63	57	54	54	49	51	57	68	76	79	63

Note: Figures cover the years 1948-1990; Tr = Trace amounts (<0.05 in. of rain; <0.5 in. of snow)
Source: National Climatic Data Center, International Station Meteorological Climate Summary, 9/96

Weather Conditions

Temperature			Daytime Sky			Precipitation		
5°F & below	32°F & below	90°F & above	Clear	Partly cloudy	Cloudy	0.01 inch or more precip.	0.1 inch or more snow/ice	Thunder-storms
< 1	38	3	57	121	187	157	8	8

Note: Figures are average number of days per year and cover the years 1948-1990
Source: National Climatic Data Center, International Station Meteorological Climate Summary, 9/96

HAZARDOUS WASTE

Superfund Sites

Seattle has four hazardous waste sites on the EPA's Superfund Final National Priorities List: **Lockheed West Seattle; Lower Duwamish Waterway; Pacific Sound Resources; Harbor Island (Lead)**. *U.S. Environmental Protection Agency, Final National Priorities List, April 17, 2012*

AIR & WATER QUALITY

Air Quality Index

Area	Percent of Days when Air Quality was...[2]					AQI Statistics[2]	
	Good	Moderate	Unhealthy for Sensitive Groups	Unhealthy	Very Unhealthy	Maximum	Median
Area[1]	86.8	13.2	0.0	0.0	0.0	89	33

Note: Air Quality Index (AQI) is an index for reporting daily air quality. EPA calculates the AQI for five major air pollutants regulated by the Clean Air Act: ground-level ozone, particle pollution (aka particulate matter), carbon monoxide, sulfur dioxide, and nitrogen dioxide. The AQI runs from 0 to 500. The higher the AQI value, the greater the level of air pollution and the greater the health concern. There are six AQI categories: "Good" AQI is between 0 and 50. Air quality is considered satisfactory; "Moderate" AQI is between 51 and 100. Air quality is acceptable; "Unhealthy for Sensitive Groups" When AQI values are between 101 and 150, members of sensitive groups may experience health effects; "Unhealthy" When AQI values are between 151 and 200 everyone may begin to experience health effects; "Very Unhealthy" AQI values between 201 and 300 trigger a health alert; "Hazardous" AQI values over 300 trigger warnings of emergency conditions (not shown); (1) Data covers King County; (2) Based on 365 days with AQI data in 2011.
Source: U.S. Environmental Protection Agency, AirData Report, 2011

Air Quality Index Pollutants

Area	Percent of Days when AQI Pollutant was...[2]					
	Carbon Monoxide	Nitrogen Dioxide	Ozone	Sulfur Dioxide	Particulate Matter 2.5	Particulate Matter 10
Area[1]	0.0	0.0	47.4	0.8	51.8	0.0

Note: The Air Quality Index (AQI) is an index for reporting daily air quality. EPA calculates the AQI for five major air pollutants regulated by the Clean Air Act: ground-level ozone, particle pollution (also known as particulate matter), carbon monoxide, sulfur dioxide, and nitrogen dioxide. The AQI runs from 0 to 500. The higher the AQI value, the greater the level of air pollution and the greater the health concern; (1) Data covers King County; (2) Based on 365 days with AQI data in 2011.
Source: U.S. Environmental Protection Agency, AirData Report, 2011

Air Quality Index Trends

Area	Trend Sites (days)								All Sites (days)
	2003	2004	2005	2006	2007	2008	2009	2010	2010
MSA[1]	16	7	7	14	10	7	12	1	1

Note: Figures are the number of days the AQI value exceeded 100 in a given year. An AQI value greater than 100 indicates that air quality would have been in the unhealthful range on that day. Data from exceptional events are included. These counts are presented in two ways. First, the counts are based on sites having an adequate record of monitoring data during the trend period (trend sites). These counts represent the relative change in the number of days with AQI values greater than 100. In the last column, the counts are based on all sites with data in the most recent year (because it is possible for a site to have data in the most recent year but not enough data to be a trend site); (1) Data covers the Seattle-Tacoma-Bellevue, WA—see Appendix B for areas included
Source: U.S. Environmental Protection Agency, Air Quality Index Information, "Number of Days with Air Quality Index Values Greater than 100 at Trend Sites, 2000-2010, and at All Sites in 2010"

Maximum Air Pollutant Concentrations: Particulate Matter, Ozone, CO and Lead

	Particulate Matter 10 (ug/m^3)	Particulate Matter 2.5 Wtd AM (ug/m^3)	Particulate Matter 2.5 24-Hr (ug/m^3)	Ozone (ppm)	Carbon Monoxide (ppm)	Lead (ug/m^3)
MSA[1] Level	n/a	7.1	24	0.068	1	n/a
NAAQS[2]	150	15	35	0.075	9	0.15
Met NAAQS[2]	n/a	Yes	Yes	Yes	Yes	n/a

Note: Data from exceptional events are not included; (1) Data covers the Seattle-Tacoma-Bellevue, WA—see Appendix B for areas included; (2) National Ambient Air Quality Standards; ppm = parts per million; ug/m^3 = micrograms per cubic meter; n/a not available
Concentrations: Particulate Matter 10 (coarse particulate)—highest second maximum 24-hour concentration; Particulate Matter 2.5 Wtd AM (fine particulate)—highest weighted annual mean concentration; Particulate Matter 2.5 24-Hour (fine particulate)—highest 98th percentile 24-hour concentration; Ozone—highest fourth daily maximum 8-hour concentration; Carbon Monoxide—highest second maximum non-overlapping 8-hour concentration; Lead—maximum running 3-month average
Source: U.S. Environmental Protection Agency, CBSA Factbook 2010, Air Quality Statistics by City, 2010

Maximum Air Pollutant Concentrations: Nitrogen Dioxide and Sulfur Dioxide

	Nitrogen Dioxide AM (ppb)	Nitrogen Dioxide 1-Hr (ppb)	Sulfur Dioxide AM (ppb)	Sulfur Dioxide 1-Hr (ppb)	Sulfur Dioxide 24-Hr (ppb)
MSA[1] Level	n/a	n/a	1.136	24.5	8
NAAQS[2]	53	100	30	75	140
Met NAAQS[2]	n/a	n/a	Yes	Yes	Yes

Note: Data from exceptional events are not included; (1) Data covers the Seattle-Tacoma-Bellevue, WA—see Appendix B for areas included; (2) National Ambient Air Quality Standards; ppb = parts per billion; n/a not available
Concentrations: Nitrogen Dioxide AM—highest arithmetic mean concentration; Nitrogen Dioxide 1-Hr—highest 98th percentile 1-hour daily maximum concentration; Sulfur Dioxide AM—highest annual mean concentration; Sulfur Dioxide 1-Hr—highest 99th percentile 1-hour daily maximum concentration; Sulfur Dioxide 24-Hr—highest second maximum 24-hour concentration
Source: U.S. Environmental Protection Agency, CBSA Factbook 2010, Air Quality Statistics by City, 2010

Drinking Water

Water System Name	Pop. Served	Primary Water Source Type	Violations[1]	
			Health Based	Monitoring/ Reporting
Seattle Public Utilities	668,800	Surface	0	0

Note: (1) Based on violation data from January 1, 2011 to December 31, 2011 (includes unresolved violations from earlier years)
Source: U.S. Environmental Protection Agency, Office of Ground Water and Drinking Water, Safe Drinking Water Information System (based on data extracted April 18, 2012)

Sunnyvale, California

Background

Part of Santa Clara Valley in Northern California, Sunnyvale was originally home to the Ohlone native Americans prior to Spanish exploration in the late 1700s. The city began with agricultural success, first with wheat harvesting, and then with fruit orchards. The land, full of wide open space and fertile soil, was ideal for this kind of production and gave the first residents a means to survival. Opportunity expanded and economic focus shifted to industry with the addition of the railroad in 1864. Canneries were built near the orchards and fruit could be processed and distributed outside of the area. In 1904, the production of died fruit led to more economic growth.

Hendy Iron Works, relocated to Sunnyvale from San Francisco in 1906 becoming its first non-agricultural industry. It eventually served to support the war effort and led to the arrival of the defense-related industry. In 1956, Lockheed Missiles & Space Company moved to Sunnyvale, strengthening its economy and population. It quickly became Sunnyvale's largest employer, but in the early 1970s, the defense industry was abandoned for the microprocessor.

Sunnyvale was important to the research and development that led to the formation of Silicon Valley, the region that contains most of the world's most prominent technology corporations. Today, various companies such as Yahoo!, Maxim Integrated Products, Juniper Networks, Fortinet, Palm, Inc., AMD, and NetApp are headquartered in Sunnyvale, and are leading employers.

The city has several distinguished neighborhoods, including Cherry Chase, a residential area built on apricot and cherry orchards and featuring fruit trees in many backyards, and The Heritage District, which contains the town center and shopping areas. The northern half of Sunnyvale is mainly industrial, while the southern half is largely residential.

Sunnyvale features many top-notch quality parks, golf courses and farms enjoyed by residents and visitors alike, and hosts events and programs to celebrate the arts, including the Art & Wine Festival, Summer Music Series, Hands On the Arts, and the Downtown Association Holiday Tree Lighting. Sunnyvale is considered one of the safest cities in America, and is one of the few cities to have a single unified Department of Public Safety. All members are trained as police, firefighters, and EMTs so they are able to act in any role during emergencies.

Sunnyvale, like most of the San Francisco Bay Area, is known for year round comfortable temperatures, with mild winters and dry summers. This desirable climate attracts residents and promotes use of the town's outdoor attractions year round, including beautiful west coach beaches, and the famous trails of the peaceful Redwood Forest.

Rankings

Business/Finance Rankings

- San Jose was identified as one of the 20 strongest-performing metro areas during the recession and recovery from trough quarter through the third quarter of 2011. Criteria: percent change in employment; percentage point change in unemployment rate; percent change in gross metropolitan product; percent change in House Price Index. *Brookings Institution, MetroMonitor: Tracking Economic Recession and Recovery in America's 100 Largest Metropolitan Areas, December 2011*
- *American City Business Journals* ranked America's 261 largest cities in terms of their resident's wealth. Sunnyvale ranked #10. Criteria: per capita income; median household income; percentage of households with annual incomes of $200,000 or more; median home value. *American City Business Journals, "Where the Money Is: America's Wealth Centers," August 18, 2008*
- The San Jose metro area appeared on the Milken Institute "2011 Best Performing Metros" list. Rank: #51 out of 200 large metro areas. Criteria: job growth; wage and salary growth; high-tech output growth. *Milken Institute, "2011 Best Performing Metros"*
- San Jose was ranked #1 out of 145 regions worldwide in terms of its "Knowledge Competitiveness Index." The index attempts to measure the knowledge-based development taking place throughout the world and is based on 19 measures of economic performance that indicate a region's ability to translate its knowledge capacity into economic value. *Centre for International Competitiveness, World Knowledge Competitiveness Index 2008*
- *Forbes* ranked the 200 most populous metro areas in the U.S. in terms of the "Best Places for Business and Careers." The San Jose metro area was ranked #35. Criteria: costs (business and living); job growth (past and projected); income growth; educational attainment; projected economic growth; crime; cultural and recreational opportunities; net migration patterns; number of highly ranked colleges. *Forbes, "Best Places for Business and Careers," June 2011*

Children/Family Rankings

- The San Jose metro area was selected as one of the "Best Cities for Relocating Families" by Worldwide ERC and Primacy Relocation. The 2008 study looked at nearly 50 factors important to relocating families including: recent job growth; nearby top-ranked colleges; in-state tuition for four-year public colleges; population growth since 2000; pediatricians per 100,000 population; and a Green Living index. *Worldwide ERC and Primacy Relocation, "2008 Best Cities for Relocating Families"*

Dating/Romance Rankings

- Sunnyvale was selected as one of the best cities to date a nerd by *Match.com.* The city ranked #1 out of 10. Criteria: top 10 cities with the highest educated *Match.com* members in either technical or educational occupations. *Match.com, "Top 10 Cities to Date a Nerd," March 16, 2011*
- The San Jose metro area was selected as one of the "Best Cities for Relocating Singles" by Worldwide ERC and Primacy Relocation. The area ranked #29 out of the 100 largest metro areas in the U.S. Criteria: recent job growth; recent singles population growth; overall population growth; affordable rental housing; cost-of-living index; expanded arts and recreation opportunities; ratio of single men and single women; affordability of quality higher education (including state residency requirements); diversity index; climate; population density. *Worldwide ERC and Primacy Relocation, "2008 Best Cities for Relocating Singles"*

Education Rankings

- Sunnyvale was identified as one of America's smartest cities by *The Business Journals On Numbers*. The city ranked #10 in the large city category (population 100,000 or more). Each city's score was based on its percentage of adults (25 or older) at each of the following rungs: dropped out before high school graduation; stopped at high school diploma; stopped at associate degree or attended college but stopped without any degree; stopped at bachelor's degree; earned graduate degree and/or professional degree. The point value of a specific rung was determined by the relative earning power of people at that level. *The Business Journals On Numbers, "Brainpower Ratings," November 17, 2011*

- San Jose was identified as one of the 100 "smartest" metro areas in the U.S. The area ranked #3. Criteria: the editors rated the collective brainpower of the 100 largest metro areas in the U.S. based on their residents' educational attainment. *American City Business Journals, April 14, 2008*

- San Jose was identified as one of "America's Smartest Cities" by *The Daily Beast.* The metro area ranked #3 out of 55. The editors ranked metropolitan areas with one million or more residents on the following criteria: percentage of residents over age 25 with bachelor's or graduate degrees; non-fiction book sales; ratio of institutions of higher education; libraries per capita. *The Daily Beast, "America's Smartest Cities," October 24, 2010*

- Sunnyvale was identified as one of America's most inventive cities by *The Daily Beast.* The city ranked #1 out of 25. The 200 largest cities in the U.S. were ranked by the number of patents (applied and approved) per capita. *The Daily Beast, "The 25 Most Inventive Cities," October 2, 2011*

- San Jose was identified as one of "America's Brainiest Bastions" by *Portfolio.com.* The metro area ranked #7 out of 200. *Portfolio.com* analyzed levels of educational attainment in the nation's 200 largest metropolitan areas. The editors established scores for five levels of educational attainment, based on relative earning power of adult workers age 25 or older. Scores were determined by comparing the median income for all workers with the median income for those workers at a specified educational level. *Portfolio.com, "America's Brainiest Bastions," December 1, 2010*

- San Jose was identified as one of "America's Smartest Cities" by *CNNMoney.com.* The area ranked #3. Criteria: percentage of residents with bachelors or graduate degrees. *CNNMoney.com, "America's Smartest Cities," October 1, 2010*

Environmental Rankings

- The San Jose was identified as one of America's cities with the most ENERGY STAR certified buildings. The area ranked #22 out of 25. Criteria: number of ENERGY STAR labeled buildings in 2010. *U.S. Environmental Protection Agency, "Top Cities With the Most ENERGY STAR Certified Buildings," March 15, 2011*

- The San Jose metro area was identified as one of "The Ten Biggest American Cities that are Running Out of Water" by *24/7 Wall St.* The metro area ranked #5 out of 10. *24/7 Wall St.* did an analysis of the water supply and consumption in the 30 largest metropolitan areas in the U.S. Criteria include: projected water demand as a share of available precipitation; groundwater use as a share or projected available precipitation; susceptibility to drought; projected increase in freshwater withdrawals; projected increase in summer water deficit. *24/7 Wall St., "The Ten Biggest American Cities that are Running Out of Water," November 1, 2010*

- Scarborough Research, a leading market research firm, identified the top local markets for green appliance households. The San Jose DMA (Designated Market Area) ranked in the top 16 with 38% of consumers reporting that they own an energy-efficient appliance. *Scarborough Research, March 23, 2010*

- Sunnyvale was selected as one of 22 "Smarter Cities" for energy by the Natural Resources Defense Council. Criteria: investment in green power; energy efficiency measures; conservation. *Natural Resources Defense Council, "2010 Smarter Cities," July 19, 2010*

- *American City Business Journal* ranked 43 metropolitan areas in terms of their "greenness." The San Jose metro area ranked #18. Criteria: Forty-one metros in which *ACBJ* has business weeklies, plus Indianapolis and Cleveland, were ranked based on 20 different indicators such as adoption of green technologies, utilization of environmentally sound practices, and air and water quality. *American City Business Journals, "Green City Index," March 11, 2010*

- Sunnyvale was selected as one of "America's 50 Greenest Cities" by *Popular Science*. The city ranked #13. Criteria: electricity; transportation; green living; recycling and green perspective. *Popular Science, February 2008*
- 100 of the largest metro areas in the U.S. were analyzed in terms of their current drought severity. The San Jose metro area ranked #48 (#1 = driest). The rankings were based on statistics such as long-term precipitation trends and patterns and the Palmer drought indices. *Sperling's BestPlaces, www.BestPlaces.net, "America's Drought-Riskiest Cities," November 2007*
- The San Jose metro area appeared in *Country Home's* "Best Green Places" report. The area ranked #45 out of 379. Criteria: official energy policies; green power; green buildings; availability of fresh, locally grown food. *Country Home, "Best Green Places," 2008*
- San Jose was highlighted as one of the 25 metro areas most polluted by short-term particle pollution (24-hour PM 2.5) in the U.S. The area ranked #24. *American Lung Association, State of the Air 2011*

Health/Fitness Rankings

- Sunnyvale was identified as one of the most walkable cities in the U.S. by *WalkScore.com*, a Seattle-based service that rates the convenience and transit access of 10,000 neighborhoods in 2,500 cities. The editors at Grey House Publishing used *WalkScore.com's* online service to look at the scores of 280 cities with populations greater than or equal to 100,000. The top 50 cities were selected. *WalkScore.com, April 2, 2012*
- The San Jose metro area was selected as one of the worst cities for bed bugs in America by Rollins corporation, the owner of seven pest control companies, including Orkin. The area ranked #12 based on the number of bed bug treatments from January to December 2011. *Rollins, "The Top 50 U.S. Cities for Bed Bugs," March 19, 2012*
- San Jose was identified as a "2011 Asthma Capital." The area ranked #79 out of the nation's 100 largest metropolitan areas. Twelve factors were used to identify the most challenging places to live for people with asthma: estimated prevalence; self-reported prevalence; crude death rate for asthma; annual pollen score; annual air quality; public smoking laws; number of board-certified asthma specialists; school inhaler access laws; rescue medication use; controller medication use; uninsured rate; poverty rate. *Asthma and Allergy Foundation of America, "2011 Asthma Capitals"*
- San Jose was identified as a "2011 Fall Allergy Capital." The area ranked #92 out of 100. Three groups of factors were used to identify the most severe cities for people with allergies during the fall season: annual pollen levels; medicine utilization; access to board-certified allergists. *Asthma and Allergy Foundation of America, "2011 Fall Allergy Capitals"*
- San Jose was identified as a "2012 Spring Allergy Capital." The area ranked #78 out of 100. Three groups of factors were used to identify the most severe cities for people with allergies during the spring season: annual pollen levels; medicine utilization; access to board-certified allergists. *Asthma and Allergy Foundation of America, "2012 Spring Allergy Capitals"*
- The San Jose metro area appeared in the 2011 Gallup-Healthways Well-Being Index. The index, based on interviews with more than 350,000 Americans, measured jobs, finances, physical health, emotional state of mind and communities. The metro area ranked #8 out of 190. Criteria: life evaluation; emotional health; work environment; physical health; healthy behaviors; basic access (basic needs optimal for a healthy life, such as access to food and medicine, having health insurance and feeling safe while walking at night). *Gallup-Healthways, "State of Well-Being 2011"*
- The San Jose metro area was identified as one of "America's Most Stressful Cities" by *Sperling's BestPlaces*. The metro area ranked #45 out of 50. Criteria: unemployment rate; suicide rate; commute time; mental health; poor rest; alcohol use; violent crime rate; property crime rate; cloudy days annually. *Sperling's BestPlaces, www.BestPlaces.net, "Stressful Cities 2012*

- 50 of the largest metro areas in the U.S. were analyzed in terms of their health and fitness by the American College of Sports Medicine in their "American Fitness Index." The San Jose metro area ranked #14 (#1 = healthiest). Criteria: preventative health behaviors; levels of chronic disease; health care access; community resources and policies that support physical activity. *American College of Sports Medicine, "Health and Community Fitness Status of the 50 Largest Metropolitan Areas," August 1, 2011*

- The San Jose metro area was selected as one of "America's Most Relaxed Cities" by *Forbes*. The metro area ranked #10 out of 10. Criteria: unemployment rates; numbers of commuters that spend an hour or more in traffic on the way to work; average weekly hours people spend at work; access to health care; overall health of residents; percentage of population who exercise. *Forbes, "America's Most Relaxed Cities," November 5, 2010*

Real Estate Rankings

- The San Jose metro area was identified as one of ten places where real estate is ripe for a rebound by *Forbes*. Criteria: change in home price over the past 12 months and three years; unemployment rates; 12-month job-growth projections; population change from 2006 through 2009; new home construction rates for the third quarter of 2011 as compared to the same quarter in 2010. *Forbes.com, "Cities Where Real Estate is Ripe for a Rebound," January 12, 2012*

- San Jose was identified as one of the priciest cities to rent in the U.S. The area ranked #9 out of 10. Criteria: rent-to-income ratio. *CNBC, "Priciest Cities to Rent," March 14, 2012*

- *Fortune* ranked the 100 largest metro areas in the U.S. in terms of projected median home price change in 2010. The San Jose metro area ranked #83. *Fortune, "The 2010 Housing Outlook," December 9, 2009*

- The San Jose metro area was identified as one of the 20 least affordable housing markets in the U.S. in 2011. The area ranked #3 out of 152 markets with an affordability index of 54.1%. The index measures whether or not a typical family could qualify for a mortgage loan on a typical home. The calculation used assumes a down payment of 20 percent of the home price and a qualifying ratio of 25 percent, meaning that the monthly P&I payment cannot exceed 25 percent of a the median family monthly income. *National Association of Realtors®, Affordability Index of Existing Single-Family Homes for Metropolitan Areas, 2011*

- The San Jose metro area was identified as one of the most expensive places to rent in the U.S. The area ranked #83 out of 10 markets with an average effective rent of $1,470 per month. The rental figures cover apartment properties in complexes with 40 or more units (20 or more units in California and Arizona). The figures are blended average rents, which include all unit sizes. Effective rents include free rent incentives and other landlord concessions. *Wall Street Journal Online, January 17, 2008*

- The nation's largest metro areas were analyzed in terms of the best places to buy pre-foreclosures (short sales). The San Jose metro area ranked #2 out of 10. Criteria: at least 500 pre-foreclosure sales during the fourth quarter and a short sales increase of at least five percent from a year ago. The areas selected posted the biggest discounts on the sales of pre-foreclosure properties. *RealtyTrac, "Fourth Quarter and Year-End 2011 U.S. Foreclosure Sales Report: Shifting Towards Short Sales," February 28, 2012*

- The San Jose metro area was identified as one of America's most overvalued cities in 2011 by *CNNMoney.com* based on data from Local Market Monitor. Criteria: median home prices; local interest rates; economic and population growth; construction costs; vacancies; household income. *CNNMoney.com, "America's Most Overvalued (and Undervalued) Cities," January 16, 2011*

- The San Jose metro area appeared in a *Wall Street Journal* article ranking cities by "housing stress." The metro area was ranked #9 (#1 = most stress). Criteria: fraction of mortgage-holding homeowners with a monthly housing payment in excess of 30 percent of income; percentage of people without health insurance; unemployment rate. *The Wall Street Journal, "Which Cities Face Biggest Housing Risk," October 5, 2010*

- The Center for Housing Policy ranked 210 U.S. metropolitan areas by the fair market rent for a two-bedroom unit. The San Jose metro area was ranked #9. (#1 = most expensive) with a rent of $1,438. Criteria: Fair Market Rent (FMR) in effect during the fourth quarter of 2009 based on HUD's fiscal year 2010 FMRs. *The Center for Housing Policy, "Paycheck to Paycheck: Most to Least Expensive Rental Markets in 2009"*
- The San Jose metro area was identified as one of the markets with the best expected performance in home prices over the next 12 months. *Local Market Monitor, "First Quarter Home Price Forecast for Largest US Markets," March 2, 2011*
- The San Jose metro area was identified as one of the best U.S. markets to invest in rental property" by HomeVestors and Local Market Monitor. The area ranked #96 out of 100. Criteria: risk-return premium relative to national average. *HomeVestors and Local Market Monitor, "Best 100 U.S. Markets to Invest in Rental Property," March 9, 2012*

Safety Rankings

- Allstate ranked the 193 largest cities in America in terms of driver safety. Sunnyvale ranked #144. In addition, drivers were 24.1% more likely to have had an accident compared to the national average. Allstate researchers analyzed internal property damage reported claims over a two-year period (from January 2008 to December 2009) to protect findings from external influences such as weather or road construction. A weighted average of the two-year numbers determined the annual percentages. The report defines an auto crash as any collision resulting in a property damage claim. *Allstate, "2011 Allstate America's Best Drivers Report™"*
- The National Insurance Crime Bureau ranked 366 metro areas in the U.S. in terms of per capita rates of vehicle theft. The San Jose metro area ranked #18 (#1 = highest rate). Criteria: number of vehicle theft offenses per 100,000 inhabitants in 2010. *National Insurance Crime Bureau, "Hot Spots," June 21, 2011*
- The San Jose metro area was identified as one of the most dangerous metro areas for pedestrians by Transportation for America. The metro area ranked #30 out of 52 metro areas with over 1 million residents. Criteria: area's population divided by the number of pedestrian fatalities in that area. *Transportation for America, "Dangerous by Design 2011"*

Seniors/Retirement Rankings

- Bankers Life and Casualty Company, in partnership with Sperling's BestPlaces, ranked the nation's 50 largest metro areas in terms of the "Best U.S. Cities for Seniors." The San Jose metro area ranked #31. Criteria: healthcare; transportation; housing; environment; economy; health and longevity; social and spiritual life; crime. *Bankers Life and Casualty Company, Center for a Secure Retirement, "Best U.S. Cities for Seniors 2011," September 2011*

Sports/Recreation Rankings

- Sunnyvale was chosen as a bicycle friendly community by the League of American Bicyclists. A Bicycle Friendly Community welcomes cyclists by providing safe accommodation for cycling and encouraging people to bike for transportation and recreation. There are four award levels: Platinum; Gold; Silver; and Bronze. The community achieved an award level of Bronze. *League of American Bicyclists, "Bicycle Friendly Community Master List 2011"*
- *Golf.com* and the research arm of the National Golf Foundation analyzed the 50 largest metropolitan areas in the U.S. in terms of golf. The San Jose metro area ranked #7. Criteria: weather; affordability; quality of courses; accessibility; number of courses designed by esteemed architects; availability; crowdedness. *Golf.com, November 15, 2007*

Technology Rankings

- The San Jose metro area was selected as one of "America's Most Wired Cities" by *Forbes*. The metro area was ranked #11 out of 20. Criteria: percentage of Internet users with high-speed access; number of companies providing high-speed Internet; number of public wireless hot spots. *Forbes, "America's Most Wired Cities," March 2, 2010*

- The San Jose metro area was selected as one of "America's Most Innovative Cities" by *Forbes*. The metro area was ranked #1 out of 20. Criteria: patents per capita; venture capital investment per capita; ratio of high-tech, science and "creative" jobs. *Forbes, "America's Most Innovative Cities," May 24, 2010*
- The San Jose metro area was identified as one of the "Top 14 Nano Metros" in the U.S. by the Project on Emerging Nanotechnologies. The metro area is home to 46 companies, universities, government laboratories and/or organizations working in nanotechnology. *Project on Emerging Nanotechnologies, "Nano Metros 2009"*

Transportation Rankings

- The San Jose metro area was identified as one of the best U.S. cities to live in without a car by *24/7 Wall St.* The area ranked #6 out of 10. Criteria: percentage of neighborhoods covered by public transit; frequency of service for those neighborhoods; share of jobs reachable within 90 minutes or less by public transit; how accessible amenities are for residents on foot; percentage of commuters who bike to work. The 100 largest metropolitan areas in the U.S. were examined. *24/7 Wall St., "The Best Cities to Live in Car-Free," November 28, 2011*
- The San Jose metro area appeared on *Forbes* list of the best and worst cities for commuters. The metro area ranked #36 out of 60 (#1 is best). Criteria: travel time; road congestion; travel delays. *Forbes.com, "Best and Worst Cities for Commuters," February 16, 2010*

Women/Minorities Rankings

- San Jose was ranked #9 out of 100 metro areas in *SELF Magazine's* ranking of America's healthiest places for women." A panel of experts came up with more than 50 criteria including death and disease rates, environmental indicators, community resources, and lifestyle habits. *SELF Magazine, "Secrets of America's Healthiest Women," December 2008*
- The San Jose metro area appeared on *Forbes'* list of the "Best Cities for Minority Entrepreneurs." The area ranked #9 out of 10. Criteria: 52 metropolitan statistical areas were examined. For each ethnicity (African Americans, Asians and Hispanics), the editors measured housing affordability, population growth, income growth, and entrepreneurship (per capita self-employment). *Forbes, "Best Cities for Minority Entrepreneurs," March 23, 2011*

Miscellaneous Rankings

- The San Jose metro area was selected as one of "America's Greediest Cities" by *Forbes*. The area was ranked #1 out of 10. Criteria: number of Forbes 400 (*Forbes* annual list of the richest Americans) members per capita. *Forbes, "America's Greediest Cities," December 7, 2007*

Business Environment

CITY FINANCES

City Government Finances

Component	2009 ($000)	2009 ($ per capita)
Total Revenues	254,881	1,944
Total Expenditures	302,738	2,309
Debt Outstanding	96,074	733
Cash and Securities[1]	193,025	1,472

Note: (1) Cash and security holdings of a government at the close of its fiscal year, including those of its dependent agencies, utilities, and liquor stores.
Source: U.S Census Bureau, State & Local Government Finances 2009

City Government Revenue by Source

Source	2009 ($000)	2009 ($ per capita)
General Revenue		
From Federal Government	15,437	118
From State Government	6,292	48
From Local Governments	114	1
Taxes		
Property	57,325	437
Sales and Gross Receipts	37,392	285
Personal Income	0	0
Corporate Income	0	0
Motor Vehicle License	0	0
Other Taxes	7,267	55
Current Charges	96,940	739
Liquor Store	0	0
Utility	25,022	191
Employee Retirement	0	0

Source: U.S Census Bureau, State & Local Government Finances 2009

City Government Expenditures by Function

Function	2009 ($000)	2009 ($ per capita)	2009 (%)
General Direct Expenditures			
Air Transportation	0	0	0.0
Corrections	0	0	0.0
Education	0	0	0.0
Employment Security Administration	0	0	0.0
Financial Administration	7,528	57	2.5
Fire Protection	26,693	204	8.8
General Public Buildings	3	< 1	< 0.1
Governmental Administration, Other	22,003	168	7.3
Health	651	5	0.2
Highways	19,278	147	6.4
Hospitals	0	0	0.0
Housing and Community Development	4,960	38	1.6
Interest on General Debt	3,853	29	1.3
Judicial and Legal	0	0	0.0
Libraries	7,031	54	2.3
Parking	1,737	13	0.6
Parks and Recreation	20,348	155	6.7
Police Protection	30,358	231	10.0
Public Welfare	0	0	0.0
Sewerage	15,354	117	5.1
Solid Waste Management	65,740	501	21.7
Veterans' Services	0	0	0.0
Liquor Store	0	0	0.0
Utility	21,206	162	7.0
Employee Retirement	0	0	0.0

Source: U.S Census Bureau, State & Local Government Finances 2009

Municipal Bond Ratings

Area	Moody's	S&P	Fitch
City	n/a	n/a	n/a

Rating Systems (shown in declining order of credit quality): Moody's– Aaa, Aa, A, Baa, Ba, B, Caa, Ca, C (numerical modifiers 1, 2, and 3 are added to letter-rating); S&P– AAA, AA, A, BBB, BB, B, CCC, CC, C; Fitch– AAA, AA, A, BBB, BB, B, CCC, CC, C. Ratings may be modified by the addition of a plus or minus sign to show relative standing within the major rating categories.

Notes: n/a Not Available; w/d Withdrawn (1) Not Reviewed; (2) Issuer Rating/No General Obligation; (3) Standard and Poor's Issue Credit Rating (ICR) is a current opinion of an obliger with respect to a specific financial obligation, a specific class of financial obligations, or a specific financial program.

Source: U.S. Census Bureau, 2012 Statistical Abstract, Bond Ratings for City Governments by Largest Cities: 2010

DEMOGRAPHICS

Population Growth

Area	1990 Census	2000 Census	2010 Census	Population Growth (%) 1990-2000	Population Growth (%) 2000-2010
City	117,242	131,760	140,081	12.4	6.3
MSA[1]	1,534,280	1,735,819	1,836,911	13.1	5.8
U.S.	248,709,873	281,421,906	308,745,538	13.2	9.7

Note: (1) Figures cover the San Jose-Sunnyvale-Santa Clara, CA Metropolitan Statistical Area—see Appendix B for areas included

Source: U.S. Census Bureau, 2010 Census

Household Size

Area	Persons in Household (%)							Average Household Size
	One	Two	Three	Four	Five	Six	Seven or More	
City	25.2	31.0	18.8	15.5	5.4	2.3	1.8	2.61
MSA[1]	21.6	28.9	17.7	16.9	7.7	3.6	3.7	2.91
U.S.	26.7	32.8	16.1	13.4	6.5	2.6	1.9	2.58

Note: (1) Figures cover the San Jose-Sunnyvale-Santa Clara, CA Metropolitan Statistical Area—see Appendix B for areas included

Source: U.S. Census Bureau, 2010 Census

Race

Area	White Alone[2] (%)	Black Alone[2] (%)	Asian Alone[2] (%)	AIAN[3] Alone[2] (%)	NHOPI[4] Alone[2] (%)	Other Race Alone[2] (%)	Two or More Races (%)
City	43.0	2.0	40.9	0.5	0.5	8.7	4.5
MSA[1]	47.5	2.6	31.1	0.8	0.4	12.8	4.9
U.S.	72.4	12.6	4.8	0.9	0.2	6.2	2.9

Note: (1) Figures cover the San Jose-Sunnyvale-Santa Clara, CA Metropolitan Statistical Area—see Appendix B for areas included; (2) Alone is defined as not being in combination with one or more other races; (3) American Indian and Alaska Native; (4) Native Hawaiian and Other Pacific Islander

Source: U.S. Census Bureau, 2010 Census

Hispanic or Latino Origin

Area	Hispanic or Latino (%)	Mexican (%)	Puerto Rican (%)	Cuban (%)	Other Hispanic or Latino (%)
City	18.9	14.2	0.4	0.1	4.2
MSA[1]	27.8	23.4	0.4	0.1	3.9
U.S.	16.3	10.3	1.5	0.6	4.0

Note: Persons of Hispanic or Latino origin can be of any race; (1) Figures cover the San Jose-Sunnyvale-Santa Clara, CA Metropolitan Statistical Area—see Appendix B for areas included

Source: U.S. Census Bureau, 2010 Census

Segregation

Type	Segregation Indices[1]				Percent Change		
	1990	2000	2010	2010 Rank[2]	1990-2000	1990-2010	2000-2010
Black/White	43.2	41.6	40.9	89	-1.7	-2.4	-0.7
Asian/White	38.8	43.4	45.0	25	4.6	6.1	1.6
Hispanic/White	47.9	50.7	47.6	36	2.9	-0.2	-3.1

Note: Figures are based on an analysis of 1990, 2000, and 2010 Census Decennial Census tract data by William H. Frey, Brookings Institution and the University of Michigan Social Science Data Analysis Network. In this analysis all racial groups (whites, blacks, and asians) are non-Hispanic members of those races. Hispanics are shown as a separate category; All figures cover the Metropolitan Statistical Area (see Appendix B for areas included); (1) Segregation Indices are Dissimilarity Indices that measure the degree to which the minority group is distributed differently than whites across census tracts. They range from 0 (complete integration) to 100 (complete segregation) where the value indicates the percentage of the minority group that needs to move to be distributed exactly like whites; (2) Ranges from 1 (most segregated) to 102 (least segregated); n/a not available.
Source: www.CensusScope.org

Ancestry

Area	German	Irish	English	American	Italian	Polish	French[2]	Scottish	Dutch
City	7.9	6.1	5.7	1.3	3.4	1.4	2.2	1.4	0.8
MSA[1]	8.1	6.1	5.9	1.2	4.7	1.2	1.9	1.4	1.0
U.S.	16.1	11.6	8.8	6.1	5.7	3.2	3.0	1.9	1.6

Note: Figures are the percentage of the total population reporting a particular ancestry. The nine most commonly reported ancestries in the U.S. are shown. Figures include multiple ancestries (e.g. if a person reported being Irish and Italian, they were included in both columns); (1) Figures cover the San Jose-Sunnyvale-Santa Clara, CA Metropolitan Statistical Area—see Appendix B for areas included; (2) Excludes Basque
Source: U.S. Census Bureau, 2008-2010 American Community Survey 3-Year Estimates

Foreign-Born Population

Area	Percent of Population Born in								
	Any Foreign Country	Mexico	Asia	Europe	Carribean	South America	Central America[2]	Africa	Canada
City	43.2	5.6	30.9	3.1	0.1	1.0	1.4	0.2	0.7
MSA[1]	36.5	8.6	22.2	2.8	0.1	0.7	1.0	0.5	0.6
U.S.	12.8	3.8	3.6	1.6	1.2	0.9	1.0	0.5	0.3

Note: (1) Figures cover the San Jose-Sunnyvale-Santa Clara, CA Metropolitan Statistical Area—see Appendix B for areas included; (2) Excludes Mexico.
Source: U.S. Census Bureau, 2008-2010 American Community Survey 3-Year Estimates

Marital Status

Area	Never Married	Now Married[2]	Separated	Widowed	Divorced
City	29.4	57.6	1.0	4.1	7.9
MSA[1]	32.5	52.7	1.6	4.8	8.4
U.S.	31.6	49.6	2.2	6.1	10.7

Note: Figures are percentages and cover the population 15 years of age and older; (1) Figures cover the San Jose-Sunnyvale-Santa Clara, CA Metropolitan Statistical Area—see Appendix B for areas included; (2) Excludes separated
Source: U.S. Census Bureau, 2008-2010 American Community Survey 3-Year Estimates

Age

Area	Percent of Population							Median Age
	Under Age 5	Age 5 to 17	Age 18 to 34	Age 35 to 49	Age 50 to 64	Age 65 to 79	80 Years and Over	
City	8.0	14.4	26.3	23.9	16.2	7.9	3.3	35.6
MSA[1]	7.0	17.3	23.9	23.3	17.5	8.0	3.1	36.1
U.S.	6.5	17.5	23.2	20.7	19.0	9.4	3.6	37.2

Note: (1) Figures cover the San Jose-Sunnyvale-Santa Clara, CA Metropolitan Statistical Area—see Appendix B for areas included
Source: U.S. Census Bureau, 2010 Census

Male/Female Ratio

Area	Males	Females	Males per 100 Females
City	70,560	69,521	101.5
MSA[1]	921,480	915,431	100.7
U.S.	151,781,326	156,964,212	96.7

Note: (1) Figures cover the San Jose-Sunnyvale-Santa Clara, CA Metropolitan Statistical Area—see Appendix B for areas included
Source: U.S. Census Bureau, 2010 Census

Religious Groups

Area	Catholic	Baptist	Non-Den.	Methodist[2]	Lutheran	LDS[3]	Pentecostal	Presbyterian[4]	Muslim[5]	Judaism
MSA[1]	26.0	1.4	4.3	1.1	0.6	1.4	1.2	0.7	0.7	1.0
U.S.	19.1	9.3	4.0	4.0	2.3	2.0	1.9	1.6	0.8	0.7

Note: Figures are the number of adherents as a percentage of the total population; (1) Figures cover the San Jose-Sunnyvale-Santa Clara, CA Metropolitan Statistical Area—see Appendix B for areas included; (2) Methodist/Pietist; (3) Latter Day Saints; (4) Reformed; (5) Figures are estimates
Source: Association of Statisticians of American Religious Bodies, 2010 U.S. Religion Census: Religious Congregations & Membership Study

ECONOMY

Gross Metropolitan Product

Area	2007	2008	2009	2010	2010 Rank[2]
MSA[1]	148.6	150.8	144.4	151.6	18

Note: Figures are in billions of dollars; (1) Figures cover the San Jose-Sunnyvale-Santa Clara, CA Metropolitan Statistical Area—see Appendix B for areas included; (2) Rank ranges from 1 to 363
Source: The United States Conference of Mayors, "U.S. Metro Economies: GMP and Employment Forecasts," June 2011

Economic Growth

Area	2007-2009 (%)	2010 (%)	2011 (%)	Rank[2]
MSA[1]	-1.6	3.7	3.9	207
U.S.	-1.3	2.9	2.5	–

Note: Figures are real Gross Metropolitan Product growth rates and represent annual average percent change; (1) Figures cover the San Jose-Sunnyvale-Santa Clara, CA Metropolitan Statistical Area—see Appendix B for areas included; (2) Rank ranges from 1 to 363
Source: The United States Conference of Mayors, "U.S. Metro Economies: GMP and Employment Forecasts," June 2011

Metropolitan Area Exports

Area	2005	2006	2007	2008	2009	2010	2010 Rank[2]
MSA[1]	25,842.5	28,171.3	28,209.5	27,048.6	21,405.8	26,333.0	8

Note: Figures are in millions of dollars; (1) Figures cover the San Jose-Sunnyvale-Santa Clara, CA Metropolitan Statistical Area—see Appendix B for areas included; (2) Rank ranges from 1 to 369
Source: U.S. Department of Commerce, International Trade Administration, Office of Trade & Industry Information, Manufacturing & Services, data extracted April 2, 2012

INCOME

Income

Area	Per Capita ($)	Median Household ($)	Average Household ($)
City	43,937	90,701	110,963
MSA[1]	38,679	85,799	111,612
U.S.	26,942	51,222	70,116

Note: (1) Figures cover the San Jose-Sunnyvale-Santa Clara, CA Metropolitan Statistical Area—see Appendix B for areas included
Source: U.S. Census Bureau, 2008-2010 American Community Survey 3-Year Estimates

Household Income Distribution

Area	Under $15,000	$15,000 -24,999	$25,000 -34,999	$35,000 -49,999	$50,000 -74,999	$75,000 -99,000	$100,000 -149,999	$150,000 and up
	Percent of Households Earning							
City	6.0	5.7	5.3	8.3	14.9	14.6	20.4	25.0
MSA[1]	7.2	6.4	6.0	9.5	14.6	12.7	19.4	24.2
U.S.	13.0	11.0	10.6	14.2	18.5	12.1	12.2	8.4

Note: (1) Figures cover the San Jose-Sunnyvale-Santa Clara, CA Metropolitan Statistical Area—see Appendix B for areas included
Source: U.S. Census Bureau, 2008-2010 American Community Survey 3-Year Estimates

Poverty Rate

Area	All Ages	Under 18 Years Old	18 to 64 Years Old	65 Years and Over
City	6.6	7.6	6.4	5.8
MSA[1]	9.4	12.0	8.7	7.5
U.S.	14.4	20.1	13.1	9.4

Note: Figures are percentage of people whose income during the past 12 months was below the poverty level; (1) Figures cover the San Jose-Sunnyvale-Santa Clara, CA Metropolitan Statistical Area—see Appendix B for areas included
Source: U.S. Census Bureau, 2008-2010 American Community Survey 3-Year Estimates

Personal Bankruptcy Filing Rate

Area	2006	2007	2008	2009	2010	2011
Santa Clara County	0.96	1.37	2.36	3.99	4.91	4.49
U.S.	2.00	2.73	3.53	4.61	4.97	4.37

Note: Numbers are per 1,000 population and include Chapter 7 and Chapter 13 filings
Source: Federal Deposit Insurance Corporation, Regional Economic Conditions, March 9, 2012

EMPLOYMENT

Labor Force and Employment

Area	Civilian Labor Force			Workers Employed		
	Dec. 2010	Dec. 2011	% Chg.	Dec. 2010	Dec. 2011	% Chg.
City	74,400	76,170	2.4	67,784	70,491	4.0
MSA[1]	897,548	915,977	2.1	802,344	834,386	4.0
U.S.	153,156,000	153,373,000	0.1	139,159,000	140,681,000	1.1

Note: Data is not seasonally adjusted and covers workers 16 years of age and older; (1) Metropolitan Statistical Area—see Appendix B for areas included
Source: Bureau of Labor Statistics, http://stats.bls.gov

Unemployment Rate

Area	2011											
	Jan.	Feb.	Mar.	Apr.	May	Jun.	Jul.	Aug.	Sep.	Oct.	Nov.	Dec.
City	9.0	8.8	8.9	8.5	8.3	8.8	8.8	8.5	8.2	8.1	7.8	7.5
MSA[1]	10.8	10.5	10.6	10.1	9.9	10.4	10.4	10.0	9.6	9.5	9.2	8.9
U.S.	9.8	9.5	9.2	8.7	8.7	9.3	9.3	9.1	8.8	8.5	8.2	8.3

Note: Data is not seasonally adjusted and covers workers 16 years of age and older; All figures are percentages; (1) Metropolitan Statistical Area—see Appendix B for areas included
Source: Bureau of Labor Statistics, http://stats.bls.gov

Projected Unemployment Rate

Area	2010 (%)	2011 (%)	2012 (%)	2013 (%)
MSA[1]	11.3	9.7	9.1	8.2

Note: (1) Metropolitan Statistical Area—see Appendix B for areas included
Source: The United States Conference of Mayors, "U.S. Metro Economies: GMP and Employment Forecasts," June 2011

Employment by Occupation

Occupation Classification	City (%)	MSA[1] (%)	U.S. (%)
Management, Business, Science, and Arts	59.4	48.8	35.6
Natural Resources, Construction, and Maintenance	5.0	7.0	9.5
Production, Transportation, and Material Moving	6.0	8.4	12.1
Sales and Office	19.6	21.5	25.2
Service	10.0	14.3	17.6

Note: Figures cover employed civilians 16 years of age and older; (1) Figures cover the San Jose-Sunnyvale-Santa Clara, CA Metropolitan Statistical Area—see Appendix B for areas included
Source: U.S. Census Bureau, 2008-2010 American Community Survey 3-Year Estimates

Employment by Industry

Sector	MSA[1]		U.S.
	Number of Employees	Percent of Total	Percent of Total
Construction	32,100	3.6	4.1
Education and Health Services	121,900	13.6	15.2
Financial Activities	32,500	3.6	5.8
Government	94,200	10.5	16.8
Information	51,200	5.7	2.0
Leisure and Hospitality	76,500	8.5	9.9
Manufacturing	157,900	17.6	8.9
Mining and Logging	200	<0.1	0.6
Other Services	24,300	2.7	4.0
Professional and Business Services	173,800	19.4	13.3
Retail Trade	85,100	9.5	11.5
Transportation and Utilities	12,400	1.4	3.8
Wholesale Trade	35,600	4.0	4.2

Note: Figures cover non-farm employment as of December 2011 and are not seasonally adjusted; (1) Metropolitan Statistical Area—see Appendix B for areas included
Source: Bureau of Labor Statistics, http://stats.bls.gov

Occupations with Greatest Projected Employment Growth: 2008 – 2018

Occupation[1]	2008 Employment	2018 Projected Employment	Numeric Employment Change	Percent Employment Change
Personal and Home Care Aides	346,500	504,700	158,200	45.7
Registered Nurses	236,400	297,200	60,800	25.7
Retail Salespersons	499,400	559,100	59,700	12.0
Combined Food Preparation and Serving Workers, Including Fast Food	260,600	308,800	48,200	18.5
Elementary School Teachers, Except Special Education	197,500	233,400	35,900	18.2
Office Clerks, General	372,500	407,400	34,900	9.4
Customer Service Representatives	202,200	236,600	34,400	17.0
Waiters and Waitresses	245,600	279,900	34,300	14.0
Stock Clerks and Order Fillers	207,700	237,100	29,400	14.2
Postsecondary Teachers	168,000	196,100	28,100	16.7

Note: Projections cover California; (1) Sorted by numeric employment change
Source: www.projectionscentral.com, State Occupational Projections, 2008–2018 Long-Term Projections

Fastest Growing Occupations: 2008 – 2018

Occupation[1]	2008 Employment	2018 Projected Employment	Numeric Employment Change	Percent Employment Change
Biomedical Engineers	3,100	5,600	2,500	80.6
Network Systems and Data Communications Analysts	35,000	52,600	17,600	50.3
Biochemists and Biophysicists	4,800	7,100	2,300	47.9
Medical Scientists, Except Epidemiologists	26,200	38,500	12,300	46.9
Personal and Home Care Aides	346,500	504,700	158,200	45.7
Home Health Aides	54,300	78,000	23,700	43.6
Physician Assistants	8,100	11,500	3,400	42.0
Separating, Filtering, Clarifying, Precipitating, and Still Machine Setters, Operators, and Te	7,300	10,200	2,900	39.7
Physical Therapist Aides	5,900	8,100	2,200	37.3
Electrical and Electronics Repairers, Powerhouse, Substation, and Relay	1,100	1,500	400	36.4

Note: Projections cover California; (1) Sorted by percent employment change and excludes occupations with numeric employment change less than 100
Source: www.projectionscentral.com, State Occupational Projections, 2008–2018 Long-Term Projections

Average Wages

Occupation	$/Hr.	Occupation	$/Hr.
Accountants and Auditors	41.15	Maids and Housekeeping Cleaners	11.63
Automotive Mechanics	24.15	Maintenance and Repair Workers	23.10
Bookkeepers	22.09	Marketing Managers	77.50
Carpenters	29.61	Nuclear Medicine Technologists	53.97
Cashiers	12.05	Nurses, Licensed Practical	27.41
Clerks, General Office	17.82	Nurses, Registered	56.53
Clerks, Receptionists/Information	15.92	Nursing Aides/Orderlies/Attendants	16.97
Clerks, Shipping/Receiving	16.65	Packers and Packagers, Hand	10.41
Computer Programmers	47.87	Physical Therapists	42.78
Computer Support Specialists	35.27	Postal Service Mail Carriers	26.07
Computer Systems Analysts	47.91	Real Estate Brokers	58.81
Cooks, Restaurant	11.70	Retail Salespersons	12.12
Dentists	67.81	Sales Reps., Exc. Tech./Scientific	36.81
Electrical Engineers	53.77	Sales Reps., Tech./Scientific	53.90
Electricians	35.14	Secretaries, Exc. Legal/Med./Exec.	19.87
Financial Managers	72.63	Security Guards	15.84
First-Line Supervisors/Managers, Sales	20.10	Surgeons	116.76
Food Preparation Workers	10.10	Teacher Assistants	14.90
General and Operations Managers	72.59	Teachers, Elementary School	29.80
Hairdressers/Cosmetologists	11.50	Teachers, Secondary School	35.00
Internists	69.01	Telemarketers	20.43
Janitors and Cleaners	13.30	Truck Drivers, Heavy/Tractor-Trailer	19.47
Landscaping/Groundskeeping Workers	15.04	Truck Drivers, Light/Delivery Svcs.	17.06
Lawyers	89.96	Waiters and Waitresses	10.45

Note: Wage data covers the San Jose-Sunnyvale-Santa Clara, CA Metropolitan Statistical Area—see Appendix B for areas included. Hourly wages for elementary/secondary school teachers and teacher assistants were calculated by the editors from annual wage data assuming a 40 hour work week; n/a not available.
Source: Bureau of Labor Statistics, Metro Area Occupational Employment and Wage Estimates, May 2011

RESIDENTIAL REAL ESTATE

Building Permits

Area	Single-Family 2010	Single-Family 2011	Single-Family Pct. Chg.	Multi-Family 2010	Multi-Family 2011	Multi-Family Pct. Chg.	Total 2010	Total 2011	Total Pct. Chg.
City	112	211	88.4	744	279	-62.5	856	490	-42.8
MSA[1]	861	1,002	16.4	3,318	2,095	-36.9	4,179	3,097	-25.9
U.S.	447,311	418,498	-6.4	157,299	205,563	30.7	604,610	624,061	3.2

Note: (1) Metropolitan Statistical Area—see Appendix B for areas included; figures represent new, privately-owned housing units authorized (unadjusted data); All permit data are based on estimates with imputation.
Source: U.S. Census Bureau, Manufacturing, Mining, and Construction Statistics, Building Permits, 2010, 2011

Homeownership Rate

Area	2005 (%)	2006 (%)	2007 (%)	2008 (%)	2009 (%)	2010 (%)	2011 (%)
MSA[1]	59.2	59.4	57.6	54.6	57.2	58.9	60.4
U.S.	68.9	68.8	68.1	67.8	67.4	66.9	66.1

Note: (1) Metropolitan Statistical Area—see Appendix B for areas included
Source: U.S. Census Bureau, Housing Vacancies and Homeownership Annual Statistics: 2011

Housing Vacancy Rates

Area	Gross Vacancy Rate[2] (%)			Year-Round Vacancy Rate[3] (%)			Rental Vacancy Rate[4] (%)			Homeowner Vacancy Rate[5] (%)		
	2009	2010	2011	2009	2010	2011	2009	2010	2011	2009	2010	2011
MSA[1]	6.3	6.4	5.3	6.3	6.4	5.3	7.7	8.2	4.8	1.4	0.9	0.9
U.S.	14.5	14.3	14.2	11.3	11.3	11.1	10.6	10.2	9.5	2.6	2.6	2.5

Note: (1) Metropolitan Statistical Area—see Appendix B for areas included; (2) The percentage of the total housing inventory that is vacant; (3) The percentage of the housing inventory (excluding seasonal units) that is year-round vacant; (4) The percentage of rental inventory that is vacant for rent; (5) The percentage of homeowner inventory that is vacant for sale
Source: U.S. Census Bureau, Housing Vacancies and Homeownership Annual Statistics: 2011

TAXES

State Corporate Income Tax Rates

State	Tax Rate (%)	Income Brackets ($)	Num. of Brackets	Financial Institution Tax Rate (%)[a]	Federal Income Tax Ded.
California	8.84 (c)	Flat rate	1	10.84 (c)	No

Note: Tax rates as of January 1, 2012; (a) Rates listed are the corporate income tax rate applied to financial institutions or excise taxes based on income. Some states have other taxes based upon the value of deposits or shares; (c) The minimum corporation franchise tax in California is $800. The additional alternative minimum tax is levied at a 6.65% rate.
Source: Federation of Tax Administrators, "State Corporate Income Tax Rates, 2012"

State Individual Income Tax Rates

State	Tax Rate (%)	Income Brackets ($)	Num. of Brackets	Personal Exempt. ($)[1] Single	Personal Exempt. ($)[1] Dependents	Fed. Inc. Tax Ded.
California (a)	1.0 - 9.3 (f)	7,316 (b) - 48,029 (b)	6	102 (c)	315 (c)	No

Note: Tax rates as of January 1, 2012; Local- and county-level taxes are not included; n/a not applicable; (1) Married joint filers generally receive double the single exemption; (a) 17 states have statutory provision for automatically adjusting to the rate of inflation the dollar values of the income tax brackets, standard deductions, and/or personal exemptions. Massachusetts, Michigan, and Nebraska index the personal exemptiononly. Oregon does not index the income brackets for $125,000 and over. Because the inflation-adjustments for 2012 are not yet available in some cases, the table may report the 2011 amounts; (b) For joint returns, taxes are twice the tax on half the couple's income; (c) The personal exemption takes the form of a tax credit instead of a deduction; (f) California imposes an additional 1% tax on taxable income over $1 million, making the maximum rate 10.3% over $1 million.
Source: Federation of Tax Administrators, "State Individual Income Tax Rates, 2012"

Various State and Local Tax Rates

State	State and Local Sales and Use (%)	State Sales and Use (%)	Gasoline[1] (¢/gal.)	Cigarette[2] ($/pack)	Spirits[3] ($/gal.)	Wine[4] ($/gal.)	Beer[5] ($/gal.)
California	8.25	7.25 (b)	48.6	0.87	3.30	0.20	0.20

Note: All tax rates as of January 1, 2012 except beer, wine and spirits (September 1, 2011); (1) The American Petroleum Institute has developed a methodology for determining the average tax rate on a gallon of fuel. Rates may include any of the following: excise taxes, environmental fees, storage tank fees, other fees or taxes, general sales tax, and local taxes. In states where gasoline is subject to the general sales tax, or where the fuel tax is based on the average sale price, the average rate determined by API is sensitive to changes in the price of gasoline. States that fully or partially apply general sales taxes to gasoline: CA, CO, GA, IL, IN, MI, NY; (2) The federal excise tax of $1.0066 per pack and local taxes are not included; (3) Rates are those applicable to off-premise sales of 40% alcohol by volume (a.b.v.) distilled spirits in 750ml containers. Local excise taxes are excluded; (4) Rates are those applicable to off-premise sales of 11% a.b.v. non-carbonated wine in 750ml containers; (5) Rates are those applicable to off-premise sales of 4.7% a.b.v. beer in 12 ounce containers; (b) Three states collect a separate, uniform "local" add-on sales tax: California (1%), Utah (1.25%), Virginia (1%). These amounts are included in the state sales tax column.
Source: Tax Foundation, 2012 Facts & Figures: How Does Your State Compare?

State-Local Tax Burdens

Area	Rate (%)	Rank[1]	Per Capita Taxes Paid to Home State ($)	Total State and Local Per Capita Taxes Paid ($)	Per Capita Income ($)
California	10.6	6	3,874	4,910	46,366
U.S. Average	9.8	-	3,057	4,160	42,539

Note: Figures cover 2009; (1) Rank ranges from 1 to 50 where 1 is highest tax burden
Source: Tax Foundation, State-Local Tax Burdens, All States, 2009

State Business Tax Climate Index Rankings

State	Overall Rank	Corporate Tax Index Rank	Individual Income Tax Index Rank	Sales Tax Index Rank	Unemployment Insurance Tax Index Rank	Property Tax Index Rank
California	48	43	50	40	13	17

Note: The index is a measure of how each state's tax laws affect economic performance. The lower the rank, the more favorable a state's tax system is for business. States without a given tax are given a ranking of 1.
Source: Tax Foundation, Major Components of the State Business Tax Climate Index, FY 2012

COMMERCIAL REAL ESTATE

Office Market

Market Area	Inventory (sq. ft.)	Vacant (sq. ft.)	Vac. Rate (%)	Under Constr. (sq. ft.)	Asking Rent ($/sf/yr)	
					Class A	Class B
San Jose-Silicon Valley	64,106,088	10,501,383	16.4	13,350	36.00	25.68

Source: Grubb & Ellis, Office Markets Trends, 4th Quarter 2011

COMMERCIAL UTILITIES

Typical Monthly Electric Bills

Area	Commercial Service ($/month)		Industrial Service ($/month)	
	1,500 kWh	40 kW demand 14,000 kWh	1,000 kW demand 200,000 kWh	50,000 kW demand 15,000,000 kWh
City	n/a	n/a	n/a	n/a
Average[1]	189	1,616	25,197	1,470,813

Note: Based on total rates in effect July 1, 2011; (1) average based on 184 utilities surveyed; n/a not available
Source: Edison Electric Institute, Typical Bills and Average Rates Report, Summer 2011

TRANSPORTATION

Means of Transportation to Work

Area	Car/Truck/Van: Drove Alone	Car/Truck/Van: Car-pooled	Public Transportation: Bus	Public Transportation: Subway	Public Transportation: Railroad	Bicycle	Walked	Other Means	Worked at Home
City	77.4	9.9	2.8	0.2	1.6	1.3	1.4	1.2	4.3
MSA[1]	76.5	10.3	2.1	0.1	0.8	1.6	2.1	1.7	4.7
U.S.	76.0	10.2	2.7	1.7	0.5	0.5	2.8	1.3	4.2

Note: Figures are percentages and cover workers 16 years of age and older; (1) Figures cover the San Jose-Sunnyvale-Santa Clara, CA Metropolitan Statistical Area—see Appendix B for areas included
Source: U.S. Census Bureau, 2008-2010 American Community Survey 3-Year Estimates

Travel Time to Work

Area	Less Than 10 Minutes	10 to 19 Minutes	20 to 29 Minutes	30 to 44 Minutes	45 to 59 Minutes	60 to 89 Minutes	90 Minutes or More
City	9.4	40.0	25.4	15.2	4.8	3.2	2.1
MSA[1]	9.0	32.1	25.4	21.5	6.1	4.4	1.5
U.S.	13.9	30.1	20.8	19.8	7.5	5.5	2.5

Note: Figures are percentages and include workers 16 years old and over; (1) Figures cover the San Jose-Sunnyvale-Santa Clara, CA Metropolitan Statistical Area—see Appendix B for areas included
Source: U.S. Census Bureau, 2008-2010 American Community Survey 3-Year Estimates

Travel Time Index

Area	1985	1990	1995	2000	2005	2010
Urban Area[1]	1.18	1.24	1.22	1.30	1.31	1.25
Average[2]	1.11	1.16	1.18	1.21	1.25	1.20

Note: Travel Time Index—the ratio of travel time in the peak period to the travel time at free-flow conditions. A value of 1.30 indicates a 20-minute free-flow trip takes 26 minutes in the peak. Free-flow speeds (60 mph on freeways and 35 mph on principal arterials) are used as the comparison threshold; (1) Covers the San Jose CA urban area; (2) average of 439 urban areas
Source: Texas Transportation Institute, Urban Mobility Report 2011, September 2011

Public Transportation

Agency Name / Mode of Transportation	Vehicles Operated in Maximum Service	Annual Unlinked Passenger Trips ('000)	Annual Passenger Miles ('000)
Santa Clara Valley Transportation Authority (VTA)			
Bus (directly operated)	350	31,983.5	142,754.3
Bus (purchased transportation)	11	227.3	942.6
Demand Response (purchased transportation)	230	930.2	9,005.4
Light Rail (directly operated)	47	9,749.9	50,000.3

Source: Federal Transit Administration, National Transit Database, 2010

Air Transportation

Airport Name and Code / Type of Service	Passenger Airlines[1]	Passenger Enplanements	Freight Carriers[2]	Freight (lbs.)
San Jose International (SJC)				
Domestic service (U.S. carriers - 2011)	25	4,018,738	15	51,296,955
International service (U.S. carriers - 2010)	5	2,745	1	1,496

Note: (1) Includes all U.S.-based major, minor and commuter airlines that carried at least one passenger during the year; (2) Includes all U.S.-based airlines and freight carriers that transported at least one pound of freight during the year
Source: Bureau of Transportation Statistics, The Intermodal Transportation Database, Air Carriers: T-100 Domestic Market (U.S. Carriers), 2011; Bureau of Transportation Statistics, The Intermodal Transportation Database, Air Carriers: T-100 International Market (U.S. Carriers), 2010

Other Transportation Statistics

Major Highways:	CR-85 connecting to I-280 and SR-101
Amtrak Service:	Yes (station is located in Santa Clara)
Major Waterways/Ports:	Near San Francisco Bay

Source: Amtrak.com; Google Maps

BUSINESSES

Major Business Headquarters

Company Name	Rankings	
	Fortune[1]	Forbes[2]
Advanced Micro Devices	357	-
Yahoo	365	-

Note: (1) Fortune 500—companies that produce a 10-K are ranked 1 to 500 based on 2010 revenue; (2) all private companies with at least $2 billion in annual revenue are ranked 1 to 212; companies listed are headquartered in the city; dashes indicate no ranking
Source: Fortune, "Fortune 500," May 23, 2011; Forbes, "America's Largest Private Companies," November 16, 2011

Fast-Growing Businesses

According to *Fortune*, Sunnyvale is home to two of the 100 fastest-growing companies in the world: **Intuitive Surgical** (#87); **Blue Coat Systems** (#95). Companies were ranked by their revenue growth rate; their EPS growth rate; and their three-year annualized total return to investors for the period ending June 30, 2011. Criteria for inclusion: a company, foreign or domestic, must trade on a major U.S. stock exchange; must file quarterly reports with the SEC; must have a minimum market capitalization of $250 million; must have a stock price of at least $5 on June 30, 2011; must have been trading continuously since June 30, 2008; must have revenue and net income for the four quarters ended on or before April 30, 2011, of at least $50 million and $10 million, respectively; and must have posted a compound annual growth in revenue and earnings per share of at least 15% annually over the three years ending on or before April 30, 2011. REITs, limited-liability companies, limited parterships, companies about to be acquired, and companies that lost money in the quarter ending April 30, 2011 were excluded. *Fortune, "100 Fastest-Growing Companies," September 26, 2011*

According to Deloitte, Sunnyvale is home to 15 of North America's 500 fastest-growing high-technology companies: **Pharmacyclics** (#31); **Meru Networks** (#66); **TeleNav** (#120); **Infinera Corp.** (#149); **CoAdna** (#201); **Accuray Incorporated** (#274); **Intuitive Surgical** (#303); **Electric Cloud** (#305); **Aruba Networks** (#316); **Blue Coat Systems** (#335); **Serious Energy** (#344); **Mellanox Technologies** (#364); **Fortinet** (#445); **Cepheid** (#483); **ShoreTel** (#486). Companies are ranked by percentage growth in revenue over a five-year period. Criteria for inclusion: company must be headquartered within North America; must own proprietary intellectual property or proprietary technology that contributes to a significant portion of the company's operating revenue, or devote a significant proportion of revenues to research and development of technology; must have been in business for a minumum of five years with 2006 operating revenues of at least $50,000 USD/CD and 2010 operating revenues of at least $5 million USD/CD. *Deloitte Touche Tohmatsu, 2011 Deloitte Technology Fast 500™*

Minority- and Women-Owned Businesses

Group	All Firms		Firms with Paid Employees			
	Firms	Sales ($000)	Firms	Sales ($000)	Employees	Payroll ($000)
Asian	4,076	929,930	676	784,253	2,975	171,395
Black	(s)	(s)	(s)	(s)	(s)	(s)
Hispanic	897	153,878	118	123,434	1,443	52,613
Women	3,532	2,654,707	477	2,570,683	4,251	213,858
All Firms	11,126	40,885,489	2,640	40,522,995	116,286	10,199,651

Note: Figures cover firms located in the city; minority- and women-owned business are defined as firms in which the corresponding group own 51% or more of the stock or equity of the company; (s) estimates are suppressed when publication standards are not met
Source: U.S. Census Bureau, 2007 Economic Census, Survey of Business Owners

HOTELS

Hotels/Motels

Area	5 Star		4 Star		3 Star		2 Star		1 Star		Not Rated	
	Num.	Pct.[3]	Num.	Pct.[3]	Num.	Pct.[3]	Num.	Pct.[3]	Num.	Pct.[3]	Num.	Pct.[3]
City[1]	0	0.0	2	5.3	16	42.1	17	44.7	1	2.6	2	5.3
Total[2]	133	0.9	940	6.5	4,569	31.8	7,033	48.9	351	2.4	1,343	9.3

Note: (1) Figures cover Sunnyvale and vicinity; (2) Figures cover all 100 cities in this book; (3) Percentage of hotels which have a given star rating; Star ratings are determined by expedia.com and offer an indication of the general quality of a particular hotel.
Source: expedia.com, April 25, 2012

The San Jose-Sunnyvale-Santa Clara, CA metro area is home to one of the best hotels in the U.S. according to *Condé Nast Traveler*: **Rosewood Sand Hill** (#62). The selections are based on over 25,000 responses to the magazine's annual Readers' Choice Survey. *Condé Nast Traveler, "2011 Readers' Choice Awards"*

EVENT SITES

Convention Centers

Name	Overall Space (sq. ft.)	Exhibit Space (sq. ft.)	Meeting Space (sq. ft.)	Meeting Rooms
Quality Inn Santa Clara Convention Center	n/a	n/a	n/a	n/a

Note: n/a not available
Source: Original research

Living Environment

COST OF LIVING

Cost of Living Index

Composite Index	Groceries	Housing	Utilities	Transportation	Health Care	Misc. Goods/ Services
150.5	114.7	245.3	131.9	114.6	116.2	103.9

Note: U.S. = 100; Figures cover the San Jose CA urban area.
Source: The Council for Community and Economic Research, ACCRA Cost of Living Index, 2011

Grocery Prices

Area[1]	T-Bone Steak ($/pound)	Frying Chicken ($/pound)	Whole Milk ($/half gal.)	Eggs ($/dozen)	Orange Juice ($/64 oz.)	Coffee ($/11.5 oz.)
City[2]	9.78	1.03	2.16	2.32	2.98	5.20
Avg.	9.25	1.18	2.22	1.66	3.19	4.40
Min.	6.70	0.88	1.31	0.95	2.46	2.94
Max.	14.30	2.16	3.50	3.18	4.75	6.83

Note: (1) Values for the local area are compared with the average, minimum and maximum values for all 335 areas in the Cost of Living Index; (2) Figures cover the San Jose CA urban area; **T-Bone Steak** *(price per pound);* **Frying Chicken** *(price per pound, whole fryer);* **Whole Milk** *(half gallon carton);* **Eggs** *(price per dozen, Grade A, large);* **Orange Juice** *(64 oz. Tropicana or Florida Natural);* **Coffee** *(11.5 oz. can, vacuum-packed, Maxwell House, Hills Bros, or Folgers).*
Source: The Council for Community and Economic Research, ACCRA Cost of Living Index, 2011

Housing and Utility Costs

Area[1]	New Home Price ($)	Apartment Rent ($/month)	All Electric ($/month)	Part Electric ($/month)	Other Energy ($/month)	Telephone ($/month)
City[2]	713,145	1,729	-	181.97	64.31	28.30
Avg.	285,990	839	163.23	89.00	77.52	26.92
Min.	188,005	460	125.58	45.39	33.89	17.98
Max.	1,197,028	3,244	339.16	181.97	348.69	40.01

Note: (1) Values for the local area are compared with the average, minimum and maximum values for all 335 areas in the Cost of Living Index; (2) Figures cover the San Jose CA urban area; **New Home Price** *(2,400 sf living area, 8,000 sf lot, in urban area with full utilities);* **Apartment Rent** *(950 sf 2 bedroom/1.5 or 2 bath, unfurnished, excluding all utilities except water);* **All Electric** *(average monthly cost for an all-electric home);* **Part Electric** *(average monthly cost for a part-electric home);* **Other Energy** *(average monthly cost for natural gas, fuel oil, coal, wood, and any other forms of energy except electricity);* **Telephone** *(price includes basic monthly rate for a private residential line plus additional local usage charges incurred by a family of four).*
Source: The Council for Community and Economic Research, ACCRA Cost of Living Index, 2011

Health Care, Transportation, and Other Costs

Area[1]	Doctor ($/visit)	Dentist ($/visit)	Optometrist ($/visit)	Gasoline ($/gallon)	Beauty Salon ($/visit)	Men's Shirt ($)
City[2]	103.14	105.52	139.53	3.81	57.79	23.36
Avg.	93.88	81.72	90.54	3.48	32.65	25.06
Min.	60.00	55.33	53.66	3.18	19.78	13.44
Max.	154.98	145.97	183.72	4.31	63.21	46.00

Note: (1) Values for the local area are compared with the average, minimum and maximum values for all 335 areas in the Cost of Living Index; (2) Figures cover the San Jose CA urban area; **Doctor** *(general practitioners routine exam of an established patient);* **Dentist** *(adult teeth cleaning and periodic oral examination);* **Optometrist** *(full vision eye exam for established adult patient);* **Gasoline** *(one gallon regular unleaded, national brand, including all taxes, cash price at self-service pump if available);* **Beauty Salon** *(woman's shampoo, trim, and blow-dry);* **Men's Shirt** *(cotton/polyester dress shirt, pinpoint weave, long sleeves).*
Source: The Council for Community and Economic Research, ACCRA Cost of Living Index, 2011

HOUSING

House Price Index (HPI)

Area	National Ranking[2]	Quarterly Change (%)	One-Year Change (%)	Five-Year Change (%)
MSA[1]	112	-0.44	-1.84	-23.53
U.S.[3]	-	-0.10	-2.43	-19.16

Note: The HPI is a weighted repeat sales index. It measures average price changes in repeat sales or refinancings on the same properties. This information is obtained by reviewing repeat mortgage transactions on single-family properties whose mortgages have been purchased or securitized by Fannie Mae or Freddie Mac in January 1975; (1) Metropolitan/Micropolitan Statistical Area—see Appendix B for areas included; (2) Rankings are based on annual percentage change for all metro areas containing at least 15,000 transactions over the last 10 years and ranges from 1 to 306; (3) figures based on a weighted average of Census Division estimates using a purchase only index; all figures are for the period ending December 31, 2011
Source: Federal Housing Finance Agency, House Price Index, February 23, 2012

House Price Valuations

Area	Q4 2005		Q4 2006		Q4 2007		Q4 2008		Q4 2009	
	Price ($000)	Over-valuation	Price ($000)	Over-valuation	Price ($000)	Over-valuation	Price ($000)	Over-valuation	Price ($000)	Over-valuation
MSA[1]	723.3	41.6	707.4	26.7	642.6	6.7	524.2	-14.3	513.7	-13.5

Note: Figures show the percentage of over- or under-valuation of single family homes relative to statistically normal house values (e.g. a value of 23.6 indicates that house values are 23.6% overvalued). Statistically normal house values are based on house prices, interest rates, household incomes, population densities, and any historical premiums or discounts metropolitan areas have exhibited over time; (1) Figures cover the San Jose-Sunnyvale-Santa Clara, CA - see Appendix B for areas included
Source: Global Insight/PNC Financial Services Group, House Prices in America: 4th Quarter 2009 Update

Median Single-Family Home Prices

Area	2009	2010	2011p	Percent Change 2010 to 2011
MSA[1]	530.0	595.0	570.0	-4.2
U.S. Average	172.1	173.1	166.2	-4.0

Note: Figures are median sales prices of existing single-family homes in thousands of dollars; (p) preliminary; n/a not available; (1) Metropolitan Statistical Area—see Appendix B for areas included
Source: National Association of Realtors, Median Sales Price of Existing Single-Family Homes for Metropolitan Areas, 4th Quarter 2011

Affordability Index of Existing Single-Family Homes

Area	2009	2010	2011p	Percent Change 2010 to 2011
MSA[1]	50.3	49.1	54.1	10.2

Note: The housing affordability index measures whether or not a typical family could qualify for a mortgage loan on a typical home. The higher the index, the greater the household purchasing power. An index of 100 is defined as the point where a median-income household has exactly enough income to qualify for the purchase of a median-priced existing single-family home, assuming a 20 percent downpayment and 25 percent of gross income devoted to mortgage principal and interest payments; (p) preliminary; n/a not available; (1) Metropolitan Statistical Area—see Appendix B for areas included
Source: National Association of Realtors, Affordability Index of Existing Single-Family Homes, 2011

Median Apartment Condo-Coop Home Prices

Area	2009	2010	2011p	Percent Change 2010 to 2011
MSA[1]	n/a	n/a	n/a	n/a
U.S. Average	175.6	171.7	165.1	-3.8

Note: Figures are median sales prices of existing apartment condo-coop homes in thousands of dollars; (p) preliminary; n/a not available; (1) Metropolitan Statistical Area—see Appendix B for areas included
Source: National Association of Realtors, Median Sales Price of Existing Apartment Condo-Coop Homes for Metropolitan Areas, 4th Quarter 2011

Year Housing Structure Built

Area	2005 or Later	2000 -2004	1990 -1999	1980 -1989	1970 -1979	1960 -1969	1950 -1959	Before 1950	Median Year
City	2.9	3.9	10.1	10.9	24.5	22.6	19.3	5.8	1971
MSA[1]	3.5	6.1	10.4	12.9	22.7	18.9	15.6	9.8	1972
U.S.	5.0	8.6	14.0	14.1	16.3	11.3	11.2	19.6	1975

Note: Figures are percentages except for Median Year; (1) Figures cover the San Jose-Sunnyvale-Santa Clara, CA Metropolitan Statistical Area—see Appendix B for areas included
Source: U.S. Census Bureau, 2008-2010 American Community Survey 3-Year Estimates

HEALTH

Health Risk Data

Category	MSA[1] (%)	U.S. (%)
Adults who have been told they have high blood pressure[2]	21.7	28.7
Adults who have been told they have high blood cholesterol[2]	38.7	37.5
Adults who have been told they have diabetes[3]	8.6	8.7
Adults who have been told they have arthritis[2]	16.5	26.0
Adults who have been told they currently have asthma	7.0	9.1
Adults who are current smokers	8.0	17.3
Adults who are heavy drinkers[4]	4.0	5.0
Adults who are binge drinkers[5]	11.0	15.1
Adults who are overweight (BMI 25.0 - 29.9)	39.1	36.2
Adults who are obese (BMI 30.0 - 99.8)	21.2	27.5
Adults who participated in any physical activities in the past month	83.0	76.1
Adults 50+ who have ever had a sigmoidoscopy or colonoscopy	63.5	65.2
Women aged 40+ who have had a mammogram within the past two years	82.0	75.2
Men aged 40+ who have had a PSA test within the past two years	40.3	53.2
Adults aged 65+ who have had flu shot within the past year	69.0	67.5
Adults aged 18–64 who have any kind of health care coverage	87.6	82.2

Note: Data as of 2010 unless otherwise noted; (1) Figures cover the San Jose-Sunnyvale-Santa Clara, CA Metropolitan Statistical Area—see Appendix B for areas included; (2) Data as of 2009; (3) Figures do not include pregnancy-related, borderline, or pre-diabetes; (4) Heavy drinkers are classified as males having more than two drinks per day or females having more than one drink per day; (5) Binge drinkers are classified as males having five or more drinks on one occasion or females having four or more drinks on one occasion
Source: Centers for Disease Control and Prevention, Behaviorial Risk Factor Surveillance System, SMART: Selected Metropolitan/Micropolitan Area Risk Trends, 2009, 2010

Mortality Rates for the Top 10 Causes of Death in the U.S.

ICD-10[a] Sub-Chapter	ICD-10[a] Code	Age-Adjusted Mortality Rate[1] per 100,000 population	
		County[2]	U.S.
Malignant neoplasms	C00-C97	139.7	175.6
Ischaemic heart diseases	I20-I25	85.5	121.6
Other forms of heart disease	I30-I51	20.3	48.6
Chronic lower respiratory diseases	J40-J47	26.5	42.3
Cerebrovascular diseases	I60-I69	30.9	40.6
Organic, including symptomatic, mental disorders	F01-F09	9.7	26.7
Other degenerative diseases of the nervous system	G30-G31	36.8	24.7
Other external causes of accidental injury	W00-X59	15.8	24.4
Diabetes mellitus	E10-E14	22.6	21.7
Hypertensive diseases	I10-I15	27.0	18.2

Note: (a) ICD-10 = International Classification of Diseases 10th Revision; (1) Mortality rates are a three year average covering 2007-2009; (2) Figures cover Santa Clara County
Source: Centers for Disease Control and Prevention, National Center for Health Statistics. Underlying Cause of Death 1999-2009 on CDC WONDER Online Database, released 2012. Data for year 2009 are compiled from the Multiple Cause of Death File 2009, Series 20 No. 2O, 2012, Data for year 2008 are compiled from the Multiple Cause of Death File 2008, Series 20 No. 2N, 2011, Data for year 2007 are compiled from Multiple Cause of Death File 2007, Series 20 No. 2M, 2010.

Mortality Rates for Selected Causes of Death

ICD-10[a] Sub-Chapter	ICD-10[a] Code	Age-Adjusted Mortality Rate[1] per 100,000 population	
		County[2]	U.S.
Assault	X85-Y09	2.7	5.7
Human immunodeficiency virus (HIV) disease	B20-B24	1.0	3.3
Influenza and pneumonia	J09-J18	17.3	16.4
Intentional self-harm	X60-X84	8.4	11.5
Malnutrition	E40-E46	*0.0	0.8
Obesity and other hyperalimentation	E65-E68	1.3	1.6
Transport accidents	V01-V99	7.2	13.7
Viral hepatitis	B15-B19	2.8	2.2

Note: (a) ICD-10 = International Classification of Diseases 10th Revision; (1) Mortality rates are a three year average covering 2007-2009; (2) Figures cover Santa Clara County; (*) Unreliable data as per CDC
Source: Centers for Disease Control and Prevention, National Center for Health Statistics. Underlying Cause of Death 1999-2009 on CDC WONDER Online Database, released 2012. Data for year 2009 are compiled from the Multiple Cause of Death File 2009, Series 20 No. 2O, 2012, Data for year 2008 are compiled from the Multiple Cause of Death File 2008, Series 20 No. 2N, 2011, Data for year 2007 are compiled from Multiple Cause of Death File 2007, Series 20 No. 2M, 2010.

Distribution of Physicians and Dentists

Area[1]	Dentists[2]	D.O.[3]	M.D.[4]				
			Total	Family/ General Practice	Pediatrics	Medical Specialties	Surgical Specialties
Local (number)	1,503	111	4,402	366	453	1,916	944
Local (rate[5])	8.7	0.6	25.1	2.1	2.6	10.9	5.4
U.S. (rate[5])	4.5	1.9	18.3	2.5	1.4	6.8	4.1

Note: Data as of 2008 unless noted; (1) Local data covers Santa Clara County; (2) Data as of 2007; (3) Doctor of Osteopathic Medicine; (4) Includes active, non-federal, patient-care, office-based Doctors of Medicine; (5) rate per 10,000 population
Source: Area Resource File (ARF). 2009-2010 Release. U.S. Department of Health and Human Services, Health Resources and Services Administration, Bureau of Health Professions, Rockville, MD, August 2010

Best Hospitals

According to *U.S. News,* the San Jose-Sunnyvale-Santa Clara, CA is home to one of the best hospitals in the U.S.: **Stanford Hospital and Clinics** (14 specialties). The hospital listed was highly ranked in at least one adult specialty. *U.S. News Online, "America's Best Hospitals 2011-12"*

According to *U.S. News,* the San Jose-Sunnyvale-Santa Clara, CA is home to one of the best children's hospitals in the U.S.: **Lucile Packard Children's Hospital at Stanford** (10 specialties). The hospital listed was highly ranked in at least one pediatric specialty. *U.S. News Online, "America's Best Children's Hospitals 2011-12"*

EDUCATION

Public School District Statistics

District Name	Schls	Pupils	Pupil/ Teacher Ratio	Minority Pupils[1] (%)	Free Lunch Eligible[2] (%)	IEP[3] (%)
Fremont Union High	6	10,285	24.3	72.7	9.0	7.8
Sunnyvale	10	6,305	19.7	80.4	38.5	9.9

Note: Table includes school districts with 2,000 or more students; (1) Percentage of students that are not non-Hispanic white; (2) Percentage of students that are eligible for the free lunch program; (3) Percentage of students that have an Individualized Education Program.
Source: U.S. Department of Education, National Center for Education Statistics, Common Core of Data, Local Education Agency (School District) Universe Survey: School Year 2009-2010; U.S. Department of Education, National Center for Education Statistics, Common Core of Data, Public Elementary/Secondary School Universe Survey: School Year 2009-2010

Highest Level of Education

Area	Less than H.S.	H.S. Diploma	Some College, No Deg.	Associate Degree	Bachelors Degree	Masters Degree	Profess. School Degree	Doctorate Degree
City	8.8	12.1	16.0	6.5	29.9	20.3	2.2	4.2
MSA[1]	14.1	16.2	17.9	7.3	25.1	13.8	2.6	2.9
U.S.	14.7	28.4	21.3	7.6	17.6	7.2	1.9	1.2

Note: Figures cover persons age 25 and over; (1) Figures cover the San Jose-Sunnyvale-Santa Clara, CA Metropolitan Statistical Area—see Appendix B for areas included
Source: U.S. Census Bureau, 2008-2010 American Community Survey 3-Year Estimates

Educational Attainment by Race

Area	High School Graduate or Higher (%)					Bachelor's Degree or Higher (%)				
	Total	White	Black	Asian	Hisp.[2]	Total	White	Black	Asian	Hisp.[2]
City	91.2	93.5	97.5	95.5	60.7	56.6	49.0	21.5	75.9	16.0
MSA[1]	85.9	88.4	91.2	89.2	62.8	44.5	42.4	29.6	59.4	13.3
U.S.	85.3	87.5	81.4	85.5	61.6	28.0	29.3	17.8	50.2	13.0

Note: Figures shown cover persons 25 years old and over; (1) Figures cover the San Jose-Sunnyvale-Santa Clara, CA Metropolitan Statistical Area—see Appendix B for areas included; (2) People of Hispanic origin can be of any race
Source: U.S. Census Bureau, 2008-2010 American Community Survey 3-Year Estimates

School Enrollment by Grade and Control

Area	Preschool (%)		Kindergarten (%)		Grades 1 - 4 (%)		Grades 5 - 8 (%)		Grades 9 - 12 (%)	
	Public	Private	Public	Private	Public	Private	Public	Private	Public	Private
City	14.1	85.9	73.1	26.9	74.0	26.0	86.6	13.4	87.2	12.8
MSA[1]	35.0	65.0	83.1	16.9	86.2	13.8	88.3	11.7	89.3	10.7
U.S.	55.4	44.6	87.1	12.9	89.4	10.6	89.5	10.5	90.4	9.6

Note: Figures shown cover persons 3 years old and over; (1) Figures cover the San Jose-Sunnyvale-Santa Clara, CA Metropolitan Statistical Area—see Appendix B for areas included
Source: U.S. Census Bureau, 2008-2010 American Community Survey 3-Year Estimates

Average Salaries of Public School Classroom Teachers

Area	2010-11		2011-12		Percent Change 2010-11 to 2011-12	Percent Change 2001-02 to 2011-12
	Dollars	Rank[1]	Dollars	Rank[1]		
California	67,871	4	69,496	4	2.39	27.90
U.S. Average	55,623	-	56,643	-	1.83	26.8

Note: (1) State rank ranges from 1 to 51 where 1 indicates highest salary.
Source: National Education Association, Rankings & Estimates: Rankings of the States 2011 and Estimates of School Statistics 2012, December 2011

Higher Education

Four-Year Colleges			Two-Year Colleges			Medical Schools[1]	Law Schools[2]	Voc/ Tech[3]
Public	Private Non-profit	Private For-profit	Public	Private Non-profit	Private For-profit			
0	0	3	0	0	0	0	0	0

Note: Figures cover institutions located within the city limits and include main campuses only; (1) includes schools accredited by the Liaison Committee on Medical Education and the American Osteopathic Association's Commission on Osteopathic College Accreditation; (2) includes American Bar Association-accredited law schools; (3) includes all schools with programs that are less than 2 years.
Source: National Center for Education Statistics, Integrated Postsecondary Education System (IPEDS) Peer Analysis System, 2011-12; Association of American Medical Colleges, Member List, April 23, 2012; American Osteopathic Association, Member List, April 23, 2012; Law School Admission Council, Official Guide to ABA-Approved Law Schools Online, April 23, 2012

According to *U.S. News & World Report,* the San Jose-Sunnyvale-Santa Clara, CA is home to one of the best national universities in the U.S.: **Stanford University** (#5). The indicators used to capture academic quality fall into a number of categories: assessment by administrators at peer institutions; retention of students; faculty resources; student selectivity; financial resources; alumni giving; high school counselor ratings of colleges; and graduation rate.*U.S. News & World Report, "America's Best Colleges 2012"*

According to *U.S. News & World Report,* the San Jose-Sunnyvale-Santa Clara, CA is home to one of the best law schools in the U.S.: **Stanford University** (#2). The rankings are based on a weighted average of 12 measures of quality: peer assessment score; assessment score by lawyers/judges; median LSAT scores; median undergrad GPA; acceptance rate; employment rates for graduates; placement success; bar passage rate; faculty resources; expenditures per student; student/faculty ratio; and library resources. *U.S. News & World Report, "America's Best Law Schools 2013"*

According to *Forbes,* the San Jose-Sunnyvale-Santa Clara, CA is home to one of the best business schools in the U.S.: **Stanford** (#2). The rankings are based on the return on investment that graduates of the Class of 2006 received (median salary five years after graduation). *Forbes, "Best Business Schools," August 3, 2011*

PRESIDENTIAL ELECTION

2008 Presidential Election Results

Area	Obama	McCain	Nader	Other
Santa Clara County	69.4	28.6	0.7	1.3
U.S.	52.9	45.6	0.6	0.9

Note: Results are percentages and may not add to 100% due to rounding
Source: Dave Leip's Atlas of U.S. Presidential Elections, www.uselectionatlas.org

EMPLOYERS

Major Employers

Company Name	Industry
Apple	Radio and tv communications equipment
Cisco Systems	Data conversion equipment, media-to-media: computer
City of San Jose	Executive offices
Cypress Semiconductor International	Semiconductor devices
e4e	Business services, nec
Hadco Santa Clara	Printed circuit boards
Hewlett-Packard Company	Computer (hardware) development
Hewlett-Packard Company	Electronic computers
Hitachi Global Storage Technologies	Computer storage devices
Intel Corporation	Semiconductors and related devices
Juniper Networks	Computer peripheral equipment, nec
LSI Corporation	Semiconductors and related devices
Mormon Church	Churches, temples, and shrines
Rosendin Electric	Electrical work
San Jose State University	Colleges and universities
Seagate Technology	Computer storage devices
Stanford Hospital and Clinics	General medical and surgical hospitals
The Leland Stanford Junior University	General medical and surgical hospitals
Veterans Health Administration	General medical and surgical hospitals

Note: Companies shown are located within the San Jose-Sunnyvale-Santa Clara, CA metropolitan area.
Source: Hoovers.com, data extracted April 25 2012

Best Companies to Work For

NetApp, headquartered in Sunnyvale, is among "The 100 Best Companies to Work For." To pick the 100 Best Companies to Work For, *Fortune* partnered with the Great Place to Work Institute. Two hundred eighty firms participated in this year's survey. Two-thirds of a company's score is based on the results of the Institute's Trust Index survey, which is sent to a random sample of employees from each company. The questions related to attitudes about management's credibility, job satisfaction, and camaraderie. The other third of the scoring is based on the company's responses to the Institute's Culture Audit, which includes detailed questions about pay and benefit programs, and a series of open-ended questions about hiring practices, internal communication, training, recognition programs, and diversity efforts. Any company that is at least five years old with more than 1,000 U.S. employees is eligible. *Fortune, "The 100 Best Companies to Work For," February 6, 2012*

PUBLIC SAFETY

Crime Rate

Area	All Crimes	Violent Crimes				Property Crimes		
		Murder	Forcible Rape	Robbery	Aggrav. Assault	Burglary	Larceny -Theft	Motor Vehicle Theft
City	1,787.1	0.0	19.4	44.0	62.7	303.6	1,174.0	183.5
Suburbs[1]	2,578.3	1.5	21.9	82.9	169.0	430.1	1,463.7	409.1
Metro[2]	2,520.9	1.4	21.7	80.1	161.3	420.9	1,442.7	392.7
U.S.	3,345.5	4.8	27.5	119.1	252.3	699.6	2,003.5	238.8

Note: Figures are crimes per 100,000 population; (1) All areas within the metro area that are located outside the city limits; (2) Metropolitan Statistical Area—see Appendix B for areas included
Source: FBI Uniform Crime Reports, 2010

Hate Crimes

Area	Number of Quarters Reported	Bias Motivation				
		Race	Religion	Sexual Orientation	Ethnicity	Disability
City	4	0	1	1	1	0

Source: Federal Bureau of Investigation, Hate Crime Statistics 2010

Identity Theft Consumer Complaints

Area	Complaints	Complaints per 100,000 Population	Rank[2]
MSA[1]	1,606	89.0	129
U.S.	279,156	90.4	-

Note: (1) Metropolitan Statistical Area—see Appendix B for areas included; (2) Rank ranges from 1 to 384 where 1 indicates greatest number of identity theft complaints per 100,000 population
Source: Federal Trade Commission, Consumer Sentinel Network Data Book for January–December 2011

Fraud and Other Consumer Complaints

Area	Complaints	Complaints per 100,000 Population	Rank[2]
MSA[1]	7,780	431.3	249
U.S.	1,533,924	496.8	-

Note: (1) Metropolitan Statistical Area—see Appendix B for areas included; (2) Rank ranges from 1 to 384 where 1 indicates greatest number of fraud and other complaints per 100,000 population
Source: Federal Trade Commission, Consumer Sentinel Network Data Book for January–December 2011

RECREATION

Culture

Dance[1]	Theatre[1]	Instrumental Music[1]	Vocal Music[1]	Series/ Festivals	Museums	Zoos and Aquariums[2]
0	1	0	0	0	n/a	0

Note: (1) Number of professional perfoming groups; (2) AZA-accredited; n/a not available
Source: The Grey House Performing Arts Directory, 2011-2012; Official Museum Directory, 2011; American Association of Museums, AAM Member Museums, April 2012; Association of Zoos & Aquariums, AZA Member Zoos & Aquariums, April 2012

Professional Sports Teams

Team Name	League
San Jose Earthquakes	Major League Soccer (MLS)
San Jose Sharks	National Hockey League (NHL)

Note: Includes teams located in the San Jose metro area.
Source: Original research

CLIMATE

Average and Extreme Temperatures

Temperature	Jan	Feb	Mar	Apr	May	Jun	Jul	Aug	Sep	Oct	Nov	Dec	Yr.
Extreme High (°F)	76	82	83	95	103	104	105	101	105	100	87	76	105
Average High (°F)	57	61	63	67	70	74	75	75	76	72	65	58	68
Average Temp. (°F)	50	53	55	58	61	65	66	67	66	63	56	50	59
Average Low (°F)	42	45	46	48	51	55	57	58	57	53	47	42	50
Extreme Low (°F)	21	26	30	32	38	43	45	47	41	33	29	23	21

Note: Figures cover the years 1945-1993
Source: National Climatic Data Center, International Station Meteorological Climate Summary, 9/96

Average Precipitation/Snowfall/Humidity

Precip./Humidity	Jan	Feb	Mar	Apr	May	Jun	Jul	Aug	Sep	Oct	Nov	Dec	Yr.
Avg. Precip. (in.)	2.7	2.3	2.2	0.9	0.3	0.1	Tr	Tr	0.2	0.7	1.7	2.3	13.5
Avg. Snowfall (in.)	Tr	Tr	Tr	0	0	0	0	0	0	0	0	Tr	Tr
Avg. Rel. Hum. 7am (%)	82	82	80	76	74	73	77	79	79	79	81	82	79
Avg. Rel. Hum. 4pm (%)	62	59	56	52	53	54	58	58	55	54	59	63	57

Note: Figures cover the years 1945-1993; Tr = Trace amounts (<0.05 in. of rain; <0.5 in. of snow)
Source: National Climatic Data Center, International Station Meteorological Climate Summary, 9/96

Weather Conditions

Temperature			Daytime Sky			Precipitation		
10°F & below	32°F & below	90°F & above	Clear	Partly cloudy	Cloudy	0.01 inch or more precip.	0.1 inch or more snow/ice	Thunder-storms
0	5	5	106	180	79	57	< 1	6

Note: Figures are average number of days per year and cover the years 1945-1993
Source: National Climatic Data Center, International Station Meteorological Climate Summary, 9/96

HAZARDOUS WASTE

Superfund Sites

Sunnyvale has six hazardous waste sites on the EPA's Superfund Final National Priorities List: **Advanced Micro Devices, Inc. (Building 915)**; **TRW Microwave, Inc. (Building 825)**; **Moffett Naval Air Station**; **Monolithic Memories**; **Advanced Micro Devices, Inc.**; **Westinghouse Electric Corp. (Sunnyvale Plant)**. *U.S. Environmental Protection Agency, Final National Priorities List, April 17, 2012*

AIR & WATER QUALITY

Air Quality Index

Area	Percent of Days when Air Quality was...[2]					AQI Statistics[2]	
	Good	Moderate	Unhealthy for Sensitive Groups	Unhealthy	Very Unhealthy	Maximum	Median
Area[1]	71.2	28.5	0.3	0.0	0.0	121	41

Note: Air Quality Index (AQI) is an index for reporting daily air quality. EPA calculates the AQI for five major air pollutants regulated by the Clean Air Act: ground-level ozone, particle pollution (aka particulate matter), carbon monoxide, sulfur dioxide, and nitrogen dioxide. The AQI runs from 0 to 500. The higher the AQI value, the greater the level of air pollution and the greater the health concern. There are six AQI categories: "Good" AQI is between 0 and 50. Air quality is considered satisfactory; "Moderate" AQI is between 51 and 100. Air quality is acceptable; "Unhealthy for Sensitive Groups" When AQI values are between 101 and 150, members of sensitive groups may experience health effects; "Unhealthy" When AQI values are between 151 and 200 everyone may begin to experience health effects; "Very Unhealthy" AQI values between 201 and 300 trigger a health alert; "Hazardous" AQI values over 300 trigger warnings of emergency conditions (not shown); (1) Data covers Santa Clara County; (2) Based on 365 days with AQI data in 2011.
Source: U.S. Environmental Protection Agency, AirData Report, 2011

Air Quality Index Pollutants

Area	Percent of Days when AQI Pollutant was...[2]				
	Carbon Monoxide	Nitrogen Dioxide	Ozone	Sulfur Dioxide	Particulate Matter 2.5	Particulate Matter 10
Area[1]	0.0	5.2	34.8	0.0	60.0	0.0

Note: The Air Quality Index (AQI) is an index for reporting daily air quality. EPA calculates the AQI for five major air pollutants regulated by the Clean Air Act: ground-level ozone, particle pollution (also known as particulate matter), carbon monoxide, sulfur dioxide, and nitrogen dioxide. The AQI runs from 0 to 500. The higher the AQI value, the greater the level of air pollution and the greater the health concern; (1) Data covers Santa Clara County; (2) Based on 365 days with AQI data in 2011.
Source: U.S. Environmental Protection Agency, AirData Report, 2011

Air Quality Index Trends

Area	Trend Sites (days)								All Sites (days)
	2003	2004	2005	2006	2007	2008	2009	2010	2010
MSA[1]	14	8	4	14	3	13	8	6	8

Note: Figures are the number of days the AQI value exceeded 100 in a given year. An AQI value greater than 100 indicates that air quality would have been in the unhealthful range on that day. Data from exceptional events are included. These counts are presented in two ways. First, the counts are based on sites having an adequate record of monitoring data during the trend period (trend sites). These counts represent the relative change in the number of days with AQI values greater than 100. In the last column, the counts are based on all sites with data in the most recent year (because it is possible for a site to have data in the most recent year but not enough data to be a trend site); (1) Data covers the San Jose-Sunnyvale-Santa Clara, CA—see Appendix B for areas included
Source: U.S. Environmental Protection Agency, Air Quality Index Information, "Number of Days with Air Quality Index Values Greater than 100 at Trend Sites, 2000-2010, and at All Sites in 2010"

Maximum Air Pollutant Concentrations: Particulate Matter, Ozone, CO and Lead

	Particulate Matter 10 (ug/m³)	Particulate Matter 2.5 Wtd AM (ug/m³)	Particulate Matter 2.5 24-Hr (ug/m³)	Ozone (ppm)	Carbon Monoxide (ppm)	Lead (ug/m³)
MSA[1] Level	37	8.8	29	0.08	2	n/a
NAAQS[2]	150	15	35	0.075	9	0.15
Met NAAQS[2]	Yes	Yes	Yes	No	Yes	n/a

Note: Data from exceptional events are not included; (1) Data covers the San Jose-Sunnyvale-Santa Clara, CA—see Appendix B for areas included; (2) National Ambient Air Quality Standards; ppm = parts per million; ug/m³ = micrograms per cubic meter; n/a not available
Concentrations: Particulate Matter 10 (coarse particulate)—highest second maximum 24-hour concentration; Particulate Matter 2.5 Wtd AM (fine particulate)—highest weighted annual mean concentration; Particulate Matter 2.5 24-Hour (fine particulate)—highest 98th percentile 24-hour concentration; Ozone—highest fourth daily maximum 8-hour concentration; Carbon Monoxide—highest second maximum non-overlapping 8-hour concentration; Lead—maximum running 3-month average
Source: U.S. Environmental Protection Agency, CBSA Factbook 2010, Air Quality Statistics by City, 2010

Maximum Air Pollutant Concentrations: Nitrogen Dioxide and Sulfur Dioxide

	Nitrogen Dioxide AM (ppb)	Nitrogen Dioxide 1-Hr (ppb)	Sulfur Dioxide AM (ppb)	Sulfur Dioxide 1-Hr (ppb)	Sulfur Dioxide 24-Hr (ppb)
MSA[1] Level	14.394	50.7	0.352	4.1	1.6
NAAQS[2]	53	100	30	75	140
Met NAAQS[2]	Yes	Yes	Yes	Yes	Yes

Note: Data from exceptional events are not included; (1) Data covers the San Jose-Sunnyvale-Santa Clara, CA—see Appendix B for areas included; (2) National Ambient Air Quality Standards; ppb = parts per billion; n/a not available
Concentrations: Nitrogen Dioxide AM—highest arithmetic mean concentration; Nitrogen Dioxide 1-Hr—highest 98th percentile 1-hour daily maximum concentration; Sulfur Dioxide AM—highest annual mean concentration; Sulfur Dioxide 1-Hr—highest 99th percentile 1-hour daily maximum concentration; Sulfur Dioxide 24-Hr—highest second maximum 24-hour concentration
Source: U.S. Environmental Protection Agency, CBSA Factbook 2010, Air Quality Statistics by City, 2010

Drinking Water

Water System Name	Pop. Served	Primary Water Source Type	Violations[1]	
			Health Based	Monitoring/ Reporting
City of Sunnyvale	133,751	Purchased Surface	0	0

Note: (1) Based on violation data from January 1, 2011 to December 31, 2011 (includes unresolved violations from earlier years)

Source: U.S. Environmental Protection Agency, Office of Ground Water and Drinking Water, Safe Drinking Water Information System (based on data extracted April 18, 2012)

Temecula, California

Background

Located in California's southwestern Riverside County, Temecula is a tiny piece of the famous Inland Empire. Prior to its founding by Spanish missionaries, Temecula was inhabited by the native Luiseño people. Although rumored that the indigenous natives occupied the land for more than 10,000 years, the first documented visit was by Padre Juan Noberto de Santiago in 1797.

Following the settlement of Spanish missionaries in 1798, several Mexican land grants were given to mission converts. Several years later, these land grants erupted into tribal wars between the Luiseño people and Mexican soldiers during the Mexican-American war. The most notable of these was dubbed the Temecula Massacre. Tensions continued to mount with native tribes, as more Americans began settling the area in the years following the war.

Temecula quickly expanded during the US Industrial Revolution in the late 1850s. By 1857, two stagecoach lines included Temecula on their routes to urban areas like St. Louis and San Francisco. The second post office in the state of California (the first being in San Francisco) was built in Temecula in 1859, and the city became famous during the late 1800s for large-scale shipments of grain and cattle.

In the first half of the 20th century, a family of immigrants from Nova Scotia were the city's primary developers. When Walter L. Vail came to California in 1904, he began buying vast amounts of land, most notably 38,000 acres of Rancho Temecula. Vail's son acquired and ran the trust, when he was killed by a street car in Los Angeles in 1906. Walter's grandson, Mahlon, continued the family's work, opening the First National Bank of Temecula (1915) and paving the city's first two-lane road (1916).

In the mid-1960s, much of the town's economy still thrived around the 87,500 acre Vail family ranch. Many were employed tending cattle and cultivating agriculture at the ranch. It was sold in 1964 and became known as Rancho California. When Rancho California incorporated in 1989, the city was renamed "Temecula" by popular vote.

During its Rancho California years, 56 different types of wine-making grapes were planted along Temecula valley. Today, Temecula boasts 25 diverse wineries that span over 3,500 acres. This contributed to the city's boom in the 1990s, when many moved from San Diego and Orange County to Temecula's affordable housing and employment opportunities.

Temecula offers 153 holes of golf at 8 different courses (7 are championship courses). The city's Old Town District offers a variety of sightseeing and historical adventures, blended with modern elements like the Old Town Community Theatre and various shops, restaurants and nightlife. The area boasts a breathtaking Ecological Reserve in the Santa Rosa Plateau. Hot air balloons have become so popular that the city hosts a yearly Balloon and Wine Festival in addition to its Spring and Summer festivals.

The city's largest employers include Abbott Labs, the local school district, International Rectifier, and Macy's.

Temecula offers a soothing Mediterranean climate.

Rankings

Business/Finance Rankings

- The Riverside metro area was identified as one of the worst places for finding a job by *U.S. News & World Report.* The metro area ranked #9 out of 10. Methodology was based on percent change in unemployment rate from November 2010 to November 2011 which was then subtracted from a given city's November 2011 unemployment rate. The 10 cities with the lowest results were selected. The editors only considered metropolitan areas with 200,000 people or more. *U.S. News & World Report, "The 10 Worst Cities for Finding a Job," January 20, 2012*
- The Riverside metro area was identified as one of five places with the worst wage growth in America. The area ranked #1. Criteria: private-sector wage growth between the 4th quarter of 2010 and the 4th quarter of 2011. *PayScale, "Five Worst Cities for Wage Growth," January 12, 2012*
- The Riverside metro area appeared on the Milken Institute "2011 Best Performing Metros" list. Rank: #162 out of 200 large metro areas. Criteria: job growth; wage and salary growth; high-tech output growth. *Milken Institute, "2011 Best Performing Metros"*
- The Riverside metro area was selected as one of the best cities for entrepreneurs in America by *Inc. Magazine.* Criteria: job-growth data for 335 metro areas was analyzed for: recent growth trend; mid-term growth; long-term trend; current year growth. The Riverside metro area ranked #24 among large metro areas and #136 overall. *Inc. Magazine, "The Best Cities for Doing Business," July 2008*
- Riverside was ranked #32 out of 145 regions worldwide in terms of its "Knowledge Competitiveness Index." The index attempts to measure the knowledge-based development taking place throughout the world and is based on 19 measures of economic performance that indicate a region's ability to translate its knowledge capacity into economic value. *Centre for International Competitiveness, World Knowledge Competitiveness Index 2008*
- *Forbes* ranked the 200 most populous metro areas in the U.S. in terms of the "Best Places for Business and Careers." The Riverside metro area was ranked #99. Criteria: costs (business and living); job growth (past and projected); income growth; educational attainment; projected economic growth; crime; cultural and recreational opportunities; net migration patterns; number of highly ranked colleges. *Forbes, "Best Places for Business and Careers," June 2011*

Children/Family Rankings

- The Riverside metro area was selected as one of the "Best Cities for Relocating Families" by Worldwide ERC and Primacy Relocation. The 2008 study looked at nearly 50 factors important to relocating families including: recent job growth; nearby top-ranked colleges; in-state tuition for four-year public colleges; population growth since 2000; pediatricians per 100,000 population; and a Green Living index. *Worldwide ERC and Primacy Relocation, "2008 Best Cities for Relocating Families"*

Dating/Romance Rankings

- The Riverside metro area was selected as one of the "Best Cities for Relocating Singles" by Worldwide ERC and Primacy Relocation. The area ranked #39 out of the 100 largest metro areas in the U.S. Criteria: recent job growth; recent singles population growth; overall population growth; affordable rental housing; cost-of-living index; expanded arts and recreation opportunities; ratio of single men and single women; affordability of quality higher education (including state residency requirements); diversity index; climate; population density. *Worldwide ERC and Primacy Relocation, "2008 Best Cities for Relocating Singles"*

Education Rankings

- Riverside was identified as one of the 100 "smartest" metro areas in the U.S. The area ranked #94. Criteria: the editors rated the collective brainpower of the 100 largest metro areas in the U.S. based on their residents' educational attainment. *American City Business Journals, April 14, 2008*

- Riverside was identified as one of "America's Brainiest Bastions" by *Portfolio.com.* The metro area ranked #178 out of 200. *Portfolio.com* analyzed levels of educational attainment in the nation's 200 largest metropolitan areas. The editors established scores for five levels of educational attainment, based on relative earning power of adult workers age 25 or older. Scores were determined by comparing the median income for all workers with the median income for those workers at a specified educational level. *Portfolio.com, "America's Brainiest Bastions," December 1, 2010*

Environmental Rankings

- The Riverside was identified as one of America's dirtiest metro areas by *Forbes.* The area ranked #2 out of 10. Criteria: year-round particulate pollution; short-term particulate pollution; ozone pollution. *Forbes, "Dirtiest Cities in America," November 4, 2011*
- Temecula was selected as one of 22 "Smarter Cities" for energy by the Natural Resources Defense Council. Criteria: investment in green power; energy efficiency measures; conservation. *Natural Resources Defense Council, "2010 Smarter Cities," July 19, 2010*
- The Riverside metro area was selected as one of "America's Most Toxic Cities" by *Forbes.* The metro area ranked #10 out of 10. The 80 largest metropolitan areas were ranked on the following criteria: air quality; water quality; Superfund sites; toxic releases. *Forbes, "America's Most Toxic Cities, 2011," February 28, 2011*
- 100 of the largest metro areas in the U.S. were analyzed in terms of their current drought severity. The Riverside metro area ranked #4 (#1 = driest). The rankings were based on statistics such as long-term precipitation trends and patterns and the Palmer drought indices. *Sperling's BestPlaces, www.BestPlaces.net, "America's Drought-Riskiest Cities," November 2007*
- The Riverside metro area appeared in *Country Home's* "Best Green Places" report. The area ranked #124 out of 379. Criteria: official energy policies; green power; green buildings; availability of fresh, locally grown food. *Country Home, "Best Green Places," 2008*
- Riverside was highlighted as one of the 25 metro areas most polluted by short-term particle pollution (24-hour PM 2.5) in the U.S. The area ranked #4. *American Lung Association, State of the Air 2011*
- Riverside was highlighted as one of the 25 most ozone-polluted metro areas in the U.S. The area ranked #1. *American Lung Association, State of the Air 2011*

Health/Fitness Rankings

- Riverside was identified as a "2011 Asthma Capital." The area ranked #55 out of the nation's 100 largest metropolitan areas. Twelve factors were used to identify the most challenging places to live for people with asthma: estimated prevalence; self-reported prevalence; crude death rate for asthma; annual pollen score; annual air quality; public smoking laws; number of board-certified asthma specialists; school inhaler access laws; rescue medication use; controller medication use; uninsured rate; poverty rate. *Asthma and Allergy Foundation of America, "2011 Asthma Capitals"*
- Riverside was identified as a "2011 Fall Allergy Capital." The area ranked #69 out of 100. Three groups of factors were used to identify the most severe cities for people with allergies during the fall season: annual pollen levels; medicine utilization; access to board-certified allergists. *Asthma and Allergy Foundation of America, "2011 Fall Allergy Capitals"*
- Riverside was identified as a "2012 Spring Allergy Capital." The area ranked #43 out of 100. Three groups of factors were used to identify the most severe cities for people with allergies during the spring season: annual pollen levels; medicine utilization; access to board-certified allergists. *Asthma and Allergy Foundation of America, "2012 Spring Allergy Capitals"*
- The Riverside metro area appeared in the 2011 Gallup-Healthways Well-Being Index. The index, based on interviews with more than 350,000 Americans, measured jobs, finances, physical health, emotional state of mind and communities. The metro area ranked #133 out of 190. Criteria: life evaluation; emotional health; work environment; physical health; healthy behaviors; basic access (basic needs optimal for a healthy life, such as access to food and medicine, having health insurance and feeling safe while walking at night). *Gallup-Healthways, "State of Well-Being 2011"*

- The Riverside metro area was identified as one of "America's Most Stressful Cities" by *Sperling's BestPlaces*. The metro area ranked #7 out of 50. Criteria: unemployment rate; suicide rate; commute time; mental health; poor rest; alcohol use; violent crime rate; property crime rate; cloudy days annually. *Sperling's BestPlaces, www.BestPlaces.net, "Stressful Cities 2012*

- The Riverside metro area was identified as one of "America's Most Stressful Cities" by *Forbes*. The metro area ranked #14 out of 40. Criteria: housing affordability; unemployment rate; cost of living; air quality; traffic congestion; sunny days; population density. *Forbes.com, "America's Most Stressful Cities," September 23, 2011*

- 50 of the largest metro areas in the U.S. were analyzed in terms of their health and fitness by the American College of Sports Medicine in their "American Fitness Index." The Riverside metro area ranked #36 (#1 = healthiest). Criteria: preventative health behaviors; levels of chronic disease; health care access; community resources and policies that support physical activity. *American College of Sports Medicine, "Health and Community Fitness Status of the 50 Largest Metropolitan Areas," August 1, 2011*

Real Estate Rankings

- Riverside was identified as one of the priciest cities to rent in the U.S. The area ranked #10 out of 10. Criteria: rent-to-income ratio. *CNBC, "Priciest Cities to Rent," March 14, 2012*

- *Fortune* ranked the 100 largest metro areas in the U.S. in terms of projected median home price change in 2010. The Riverside metro area ranked #90. *Fortune, "The 2010 Housing Outlook," December 9, 2009*

- The Riverside metro area was identified as one of the 20 least affordable housing markets in the U.S. in 2011. The area ranked #14 out of 152 markets with an affordability index of 88.9%. The index measures whether or not a typical family could qualify for a mortgage loan on a typical home. The calculation used assumes a down payment of 20 percent of the home price and a qualifying ratio of 25 percent, meaning that the monthly P&I payment cannot exceed 25 percent of a the median family monthly income. *National Association of Realtors®, Affordability Index of Existing Single-Family Homes for Metropolitan Areas, 2011*

- The Riverside metro area was identified as one of "America's 25 Weakest Housing Markets" by *Forbes*. The metro area ranked #22. Criteria: metro areas with populations over 500,000 were ranked based on projected home values through 2011. *Forbes.com, "America's 25 Weakest Housing Markets," January 7, 2009*

- The nation's largest metro areas were analyzed in terms of the percentage of households entering some stage of foreclosure in 2011. The Riverside metro area ranked #5 out of 20 (#1 = highest foreclosure rate). *RealtyTrac, 2011 Year-End Foreclosure Market Report, January 12, 2012*

- The Riverside metro area appeared in a *Wall Street Journal* article ranking cities by "housing stress." The metro area was ranked #2 (#1 = most stress). Criteria: fraction of mortgage-holding homeowners with a monthly housing payment in excess of 30 percent of income; percentage of people without health insurance; unemployment rate. *The Wall Street Journal, "Which Cities Face Biggest Housing Risk," October 5, 2010*

- The Center for Housing Policy ranked 210 U.S. metropolitan areas by the fair market rent for a two-bedroom unit. The Riverside metro area was ranked #37. (#1 = most expensive) with a rent of $1,108. Criteria: Fair Market Rent (FMR) in effect during the fourth quarter of 2009 based on HUD's fiscal year 2010 FMRs. *The Center for Housing Policy, "Paycheck to Paycheck: Most to Least Expensive Rental Markets in 2009"*

- The Riverside metro area was identified as one of the top 20 cities in terms of decreasing home equity. The metro area was ranked #9. Criteria: percentage of home equity relative to the home's current value. *Forbes.com, "Where Americans are Losing Home Equity Most," May 1, 2010*

- The Riverside metro area was identified as one of the markets with the best expected performance in home prices over the next 12 months. *Local Market Monitor, "First Quarter Home Price Forecast for Largest US Markets," March 2, 2011*

- The Riverside metro area was identified as one of the best U.S. markets to invest in rental property" by HomeVestors and Local Market Monitor. The area ranked #26 out of 100. Criteria: risk-return premium relative to national average. *HomeVestors and Local Market Monitor, "Best 100 U.S. Markets to Invest in Rental Property," March 9, 2012*

Safety Rankings

- The National Insurance Crime Bureau ranked 366 metro areas in the U.S. in terms of per capita rates of vehicle theft. The Riverside metro area ranked #21 (#1 = highest rate). Criteria: number of vehicle theft offenses per 100,000 inhabitants in 2010. *National Insurance Crime Bureau, "Hot Spots," June 21, 2011*
- The Riverside metro area was identified as one of the most dangerous metro areas for pedestrians by Transportation for America. The metro area ranked #5 out of 52 metro areas with over 1 million residents. Criteria: area's population divided by the number of pedestrian fatalities in that area. *Transportation for America, "Dangerous by Design 2011"*

Seniors/Retirement Rankings

- Bankers Life and Casualty Company, in partnership with Sperling's BestPlaces, ranked the nation's 50 largest metro areas in terms of the "Best U.S. Cities for Seniors." The Riverside metro area ranked #50. Criteria: healthcare; transportation; housing; environment; economy; health and longevity; social and spiritual life; crime. *Bankers Life and Casualty Company, Center for a Secure Retirement, "Best U.S. Cities for Seniors 2011," September 2011*

Sports/Recreation Rankings

- The Riverside was selected as one of the best metro areas for golf in America by *Golf Digest*. The Riverside area was ranked #14 out of 20. Criteria: climate; cost of public golf; quality of public golf; accessibility. *Golf Digest, "The Top 20 Cities for Golf," October 2011*

Transportation Rankings

- The Riverside metro area appeared on *Forbes* list of the best and worst cities for commuters. The metro area ranked #54 out of 60 (#1 is best). Criteria: travel time; road congestion; travel delays. *Forbes.com, "Best and Worst Cities for Commuters," February 16, 2010*

Women/Minorities Rankings

- Riverside was ranked #69 out of 100 metro areas in *SELF Magazine's* ranking of America's healthiest places for women." A panel of experts came up with more than 50 criteria including death and disease rates, environmental indicators, community resources, and lifestyle habits. *SELF Magazine, "Secrets of America's Healthiest Women," December 2008*
- The Riverside metro area appeared on *Forbes'* list of the "Best Cities for Minority Entrepreneurs." The area ranked #69 out of 10. Criteria: 52 metropolitan statistical areas were examined. For each ethnicity (African Americans, Asians and Hispanics), the editors measured housing affordability, population growth, income growth, and entrepreneurship (per capita self-employment). *Forbes, "Best Cities for Minority Entrepreneurs," March 23, 2011*

Business Environment

CITY FINANCES

City Government Finances

Component	2009 ($000)	2009 ($ per capita)
Total Revenues	117,300	1,238
Total Expenditures	154,573	1,631
Debt Outstanding	87,088	919
Cash and Securities[1]	159,476	1,683

Note: (1) Cash and security holdings of a government at the close of its fiscal year, including those of its dependent agencies, utilities, and liquor stores.
Source: U.S Census Bureau, State & Local Government Finances 2009

City Government Revenue by Source

Source	2009 ($000)	2009 ($ per capita)
General Revenue		
From Federal Government	1,143	12
From State Government	7,865	83
From Local Governments	7,382	78
Taxes		
Property	40,188	424
Sales and Gross Receipts	25,413	268
Personal Income	0	0
Corporate Income	0	0
Motor Vehicle License	0	0
Other Taxes	2,763	29
Current Charges	9,641	102
Liquor Store	0	0
Utility	0	0
Employee Retirement	0	0

Source: U.S Census Bureau, State & Local Government Finances 2009

City Government Expenditures by Function

Function	2009 ($000)	2009 ($ per capita)	2009 (%)
General Direct Expenditures			
Air Transportation	0	0	0.0
Corrections	0	0	0.0
Education	0	0	0.0
Employment Security Administration	0	0	0.0
Financial Administration	0	0	0.0
Fire Protection	2,948	31	1.9
General Public Buildings	1,112	12	0.7
Governmental Administration, Other	48,823	515	31.6
Health	189	2	0.1
Highways	11,450	121	7.4
Hospitals	0	0	0.0
Housing and Community Development	38,998	412	25.2
Interest on General Debt	4,078	43	2.6
Judicial and Legal	0	0	0.0
Libraries	662	7	0.4
Parking	0	0	0.0
Parks and Recreation	16,738	177	10.8
Police Protection	19,708	208	12.7
Public Welfare	0	0	0.0
Sewerage	5,684	60	3.7
Solid Waste Management	0	0	0.0
Veterans' Services	0	0	0.0
Liquor Store	0	0	0.0
Utility	0	0	0.0
Employee Retirement	0	0	0.0

Source: U.S Census Bureau, State & Local Government Finances 2009

Municipal Bond Ratings

Area	Moody's	S&P	Fitch
City	n/a	n/a	n/a

Rating Systems (shown in declining order of credit quality): Moody's– Aaa, Aa, A, Baa, Ba, B, Caa, Ca, C (numerical modifiers 1, 2, and 3 are added to letter-rating); S&P– AAA, AA, A, BBB, BB, B, CCC, CC, C; Fitch– AAA, AA, A, BBB, BB, B, CCC, CC, C. Ratings may be modified by the addition of a plus or minus sign to show relative standing within the major rating categories.

Notes: n/a Not Available; w/d Withdrawn (1) Not Reviewed; (2) Issuer Rating/No General Obligation; (3) Standard and Poor's Issue Credit Rating (ICR) is a current opinion of an obliger with respect to a specific financial obligation, a specific class of financial obligations, or a specific financial program.

Source: U.S. Census Bureau, 2012 Statistical Abstract, Bond Ratings for City Governments by Largest Cities: 2010

DEMOGRAPHICS

Population Growth

Area	1990 Census	2000 Census	2010 Census	Population Growth (%) 1990-2000	Population Growth (%) 2000-2010
City	27,078	57,716	100,097	113.1	73.4
MSA[1]	2,588,793	3,254,821	4,224,851	25.7	29.8
U.S.	248,709,873	281,421,906	308,745,538	13.2	9.7

Note: (1) Figures cover the Riverside-San Bernardino-Ontario, CA Metropolitan Statistical Area—see Appendix B for areas included

Source: U.S. Census Bureau, 2010 Census

Household Size

Area	Persons in Household (%)							Average Household Size
	One	Two	Three	Four	Five	Six	Seven or More	
City	13.8	27.1	19.2	21.6	11.1	4.5	2.6	3.15
MSA[1]	18.5	27.1	16.1	16.4	10.8	5.6	5.6	3.20
U.S.	26.7	32.8	16.1	13.4	6.5	2.6	1.9	2.58

Note: (1) Figures cover the Riverside-San Bernardino-Ontario, CA Metropolitan Statistical Area—see Appendix B for areas included

Source: U.S. Census Bureau, 2010 Census

Race

Area	White Alone[2] (%)	Black Alone[2] (%)	Asian Alone[2] (%)	AIAN[3] Alone[2] (%)	NHOPI[4] Alone[2] (%)	Other Race Alone[2] (%)	Two or More Races (%)
City	70.8	4.1	9.8	1.1	0.4	7.9	5.9
MSA[1]	58.9	7.6	6.1	1.1	0.3	21.0	4.9
U.S.	72.4	12.6	4.8	0.9	0.2	6.2	2.9

Note: (1) Figures cover the Riverside-San Bernardino-Ontario, CA Metropolitan Statistical Area—see Appendix B for areas included; (2) Alone is defined as not being in combination with one or more other races; (3) American Indian and Alaska Native; (4) Native Hawaiian and Other Pacific Islander

Source: U.S. Census Bureau, 2010 Census

Hispanic or Latino Origin

Area	Hispanic or Latino (%)	Mexican (%)	Puerto Rican (%)	Cuban (%)	Other Hispanic or Latino (%)
City	24.7	19.9	1.0	0.2	3.6
MSA[1]	47.3	40.6	0.7	0.3	5.7
U.S.	16.3	10.3	1.5	0.6	4.0

Note: Persons of Hispanic or Latino origin can be of any race; (1) Figures cover the Riverside-San Bernardino-Ontario, CA Metropolitan Statistical Area—see Appendix B for areas included

Source: U.S. Census Bureau, 2010 Census

Segregation

Type	Segregation Indices[1]				Percent Change		
	1990	2000	2010	2010 Rank[2]	1990-2000	1990-2010	2000-2010
Black/White	43.8	46.8	45.7	82	3.1	1.9	-1.1
Asian/White	33.3	40.0	40.7	53	6.7	7.4	0.7
Hispanic/White	35.8	42.5	42.4	55	6.6	6.5	-0.1

Note: Figures are based on an analysis of 1990, 2000, and 2010 Census Decennial Census tract data by William H. Frey, Brookings Institution and the University of Michigan Social Science Data Analysis Network. In this analysis all racial groups (whites, blacks, and asians) are non-Hispanic members of those races. Hispanics are shown as a separate category; All figures cover the Metropolitan Statistical Area (see Appendix B for areas included); (1) Segregation Indices are Dissimilarity Indices that measure the degree to which the minority group is distributed differently than whites across census tracts. They range from 0 (complete integration) to 100 (complete segregation) where the value indicates the percentage of the minority group that needs to move to be distributed exactly like whites; (2) Ranges from 1 (most segregated) to 102 (least segregated); n/a not available.
Source: www.CensusScope.org

Ancestry

Area	German	Irish	English	American	Italian	Polish	French[2]	Scottish	Dutch
City	12.3	11.6	9.7	1.6	7.5	3.5	3.0	2.1	1.8
MSA[1]	9.6	7.1	6.5	2.5	3.7	1.3	2.1	1.3	1.3
U.S.	16.1	11.6	8.8	6.1	5.7	3.2	3.0	1.9	1.6

Note: Figures are the percentage of the total population reporting a particular ancestry. The nine most commonly reported ancestries in the U.S. are shown. Figures include multiple ancestries (e.g. if a person reported being Irish and Italian, they were included in both columns); (1) Figures cover the Riverside-San Bernardino-Ontario, CA Metropolitan Statistical Area—see Appendix B for areas included; (2) Excludes Basque
Source: U.S. Census Bureau, 2008-2010 American Community Survey 3-Year Estimates

Foreign-Born Population

Area	Percent of Population Born in								
	Any Foreign Country	Mexico	Asia	Europe	Carribean	South America	Central America[2]	Africa	Canada
City	n/a	n/a	n/a	n/a	n/a	n/a	n/a	n/a	n/a
MSA[1]	21.8	13.3	4.3	1.0	0.2	0.5	1.7	0.3	0.4
U.S.	12.8	3.8	3.6	1.6	1.2	0.9	1.0	0.5	0.3

Note: (1) Figures cover the Riverside-San Bernardino-Ontario, CA Metropolitan Statistical Area—see Appendix B for areas included; (2) Excludes Mexico.
Source: U.S. Census Bureau, 2008-2010 American Community Survey 3-Year Estimates

Marital Status

Area	Never Married	Now Married[2]	Separated	Widowed	Divorced
City	29.8	54.2	1.9	3.3	10.9
MSA[1]	33.4	49.0	2.6	5.0	10.1
U.S.	31.6	49.6	2.2	6.1	10.7

Note: Figures are percentages and cover the population 15 years of age and older; (1) Figures cover the Riverside-San Bernardino-Ontario, CA Metropolitan Statistical Area—see Appendix B for areas included; (2) Excludes separated
Source: U.S. Census Bureau, 2008-2010 American Community Survey 3-Year Estimates

Age

Area	Percent of Population							Median Age
	Under Age 5	Age 5 to 17	Age 18 to 34	Age 35 to 49	Age 50 to 64	Age 65 to 79	80 Years and Over	
City	7.0	23.6	21.3	24.3	15.9	6.0	1.8	33.4
MSA[1]	7.6	21.1	24.2	20.4	16.2	7.7	2.7	32.7
U.S.	6.5	17.5	23.2	20.7	19.0	9.4	3.6	37.2

Note: (1) Figures cover the Riverside-San Bernardino-Ontario, CA Metropolitan Statistical Area—see Appendix B for areas included
Source: U.S. Census Bureau, 2010 Census

Male/Female Ratio

Area	Males	Females	Males per 100 Females
City	49,002	51,095	95.9
MSA[1]	2,101,083	2,123,768	98.9
U.S.	151,781,326	156,964,212	96.7

Note: (1) Figures cover the Riverside-San Bernardino-Ontario, CA Metropolitan Statistical Area—see Appendix B for areas included
Source: U.S. Census Bureau, 2010 Census

Religious Groups

Area	Catholic	Baptist	Non-Den.	Methodist[2]	Lutheran	LDS[3]	Pente-costal	Presby-terian[4]	Muslim[5]	Judaism
MSA[1]	24.8	2.6	5.5	0.6	0.5	2.5	1.6	0.6	0.1	0.6
U.S.	19.1	9.3	4.0	4.0	2.3	2.0	1.9	1.6	0.8	0.7

Note: Figures are the number of adherents as a percentage of the total population; (1) Figures cover the Riverside-San Bernardino-Ontario, CA Metropolitan Statistical Area—see Appendix B for areas included; (2) Methodist/Pietist; (3) Latter Day Saints; (4) Reformed; (5) Figures are estimates
Source: Association of Statisticians of American Religious Bodies, 2010 U.S. Religion Census: Religious Congregations & Membership Study

ECONOMY

Gross Metropolitan Product

Area	2007	2008	2009	2010	2010 Rank[2]
MSA[1]	114.8	112.9	108.4	110.8	25

Note: Figures are in billions of dollars; (1) Figures cover the Riverside-San Bernardino-Ontario, CA Metropolitan Statistical Area—see Appendix B for areas included; (2) Rank ranges from 1 to 363
Source: The United States Conference of Mayors, "U.S. Metro Economies: GMP and Employment Forecasts," June 2011

Economic Growth

Area	2007-2009 (%)	2010 (%)	2011 (%)	Rank[2]
MSA[1]	-4.9	1.2	1.3	325
U.S.	-1.3	2.9	2.5	–

Note: Figures are real Gross Metropolitan Product growth rates and represent annual average percent change; (1) Figures cover the Riverside-San Bernardino-Ontario, CA Metropolitan Statistical Area—see Appendix B for areas included; (2) Rank ranges from 1 to 363
Source: The United States Conference of Mayors, "U.S. Metro Economies: GMP and Employment Forecasts," June 2011

Metropolitan Area Exports

Area	2005	2006	2007	2008	2009	2010	2010 Rank[2]
MSA[1]	3,773.6	4,192.0	4,970.9	6,241.5	5,356.5	6,231.2	38

Note: Figures are in millions of dollars; (1) Figures cover the Riverside-San Bernardino-Ontario, CA Metropolitan Statistical Area—see Appendix B for areas included; (2) Rank ranges from 1 to 369
Source: U.S. Department of Commerce, International Trade Administration, Office of Trade & Industry Information, Manufacturing & Services, data extracted April 2, 2012

INCOME

Income

Area	Per Capita ($)	Median Household ($)	Average Household ($)
City	27,706	72,433	86,415
MSA[1]	22,415	55,116	71,049
U.S.	26,942	51,222	70,116

Note: (1) Figures cover the Riverside-San Bernardino-Ontario, CA Metropolitan Statistical Area—see Appendix B for areas included
Source: U.S. Census Bureau, 2008-2010 American Community Survey 3-Year Estimates

Household Income Distribution

Area	Percent of Households Earning							
	Under $15,000	$15,000 -24,999	$25,000 -34,999	$35,000 -49,999	$50,000 -74,999	$75,000 -99,000	$100,000 -149,999	$150,000 and up
City	7.8	6.7	7.0	10.8	19.2	14.6	21.4	12.6
MSA[1]	10.7	10.4	10.2	13.8	19.2	13.1	14.0	8.4
U.S.	13.0	11.0	10.6	14.2	18.5	12.1	12.2	8.4

Note: (1) Figures cover the Riverside-San Bernardino-Ontario, CA Metropolitan Statistical Area—see Appendix B for areas included
Source: U.S. Census Bureau, 2008-2010 American Community Survey 3-Year Estimates

Poverty Rate

Area	All Ages	Under 18 Years Old	18 to 64 Years Old	65 Years and Over
City	9.6	12.2	8.8	5.2
MSA[1]	15.5	21.6	13.6	8.8
U.S.	14.4	20.1	13.1	9.4

Note: Figures are percentage of people whose income during the past 12 months was below the poverty level; (1) Figures cover the Riverside-San Bernardino-Ontario, CA Metropolitan Statistical Area—see Appendix B for areas included
Source: U.S. Census Bureau, 2008-2010 American Community Survey 3-Year Estimates

Personal Bankruptcy Filing Rate

Area	2006	2007	2008	2009	2010	2011
Riverside County	1.20	2.51	5.32	8.64	10.86	9.85
U.S.	2.00	2.73	3.53	4.61	4.97	4.37

Note: Numbers are per 1,000 population and include Chapter 7 and Chapter 13 filings
Source: Federal Deposit Insurance Corporation, Regional Economic Conditions, March 9, 2012

EMPLOYMENT

Labor Force and Employment

Area	Civilian Labor Force			Workers Employed		
	Dec. 2010	Dec. 2011	% Chg.	Dec. 2010	Dec. 2011	% Chg.
City	36,269	36,869	1.7	32,733	33,729	3.0
MSA[1]	1,761,147	1,778,349	1.0	1,514,937	1,561,051	3.0
U.S.	153,156,000	153,373,000	0.1	139,159,000	140,681,000	1.1

Note: Data is not seasonally adjusted and covers workers 16 years of age and older; (1) Metropolitan Statistical Area—see Appendix B for areas included
Source: Bureau of Labor Statistics, http://stats.bls.gov

Unemployment Rate

Area	2011											
	Jan.	Feb.	Mar.	Apr.	May	Jun.	Jul.	Aug.	Sep.	Oct.	Nov.	Dec.
City	9.8	9.7	9.7	9.2	9.0	9.9	10.4	10.0	9.6	9.4	8.7	8.5
MSA[1]	14.2	13.9	13.9	13.4	13.2	14.3	14.7	14.1	13.5	13.3	12.5	12.2
U.S.	9.8	9.5	9.2	8.7	8.7	9.3	9.3	9.1	8.8	8.5	8.2	8.3

Note: Data is not seasonally adjusted and covers workers 16 years of age and older; All figures are percentages; (1) Metropolitan Statistical Area—see Appendix B for areas included
Source: Bureau of Labor Statistics, http://stats.bls.gov

Projected Unemployment Rate

Area	2010 (%)	2011 (%)	2012 (%)	2013 (%)
MSA[1]	14.7	13.3	12.4	11.2

Note: (1) Metropolitan Statistical Area—see Appendix B for areas included
Source: The United States Conference of Mayors, "U.S. Metro Economies: GMP and Employment Forecasts," June 2011

Employment by Occupation

Occupation Classification	City (%)	MSA[1] (%)	U.S. (%)
Management, Business, Science, and Arts	36.7	28.6	35.6
Natural Resources, Construction, and Maintenance	8.4	11.6	9.5
Production, Transportation, and Material Moving	8.6	14.0	12.1
Sales and Office	27.1	26.7	25.2
Service	19.2	19.2	17.6

Note: Figures cover employed civilians 16 years of age and older; (1) Figures cover the Riverside-San Bernardino-Ontario, CA Metropolitan Statistical Area—see Appendix B for areas included
Source: U.S. Census Bureau, 2008-2010 American Community Survey 3-Year Estimates

Employment by Industry

Sector	MSA[1] Number of Employees	MSA[1] Percent of Total	U.S. Percent of Total
Construction	56,100	4.9	4.1
Education and Health Services	141,100	12.2	15.2
Financial Activities	38,700	3.4	5.8
Government	227,100	19.7	16.8
Information	15,000	1.3	2.0
Leisure and Hospitality	130,800	11.3	9.9
Manufacturing	86,500	7.5	8.9
Mining and Logging	1,000	0.1	0.6
Other Services	39,900	3.5	4.0
Professional and Business Services	130,600	11.3	13.3
Retail Trade	165,100	14.3	11.5
Transportation and Utilities	70,900	6.1	3.8
Wholesale Trade	50,300	4.4	4.2

Note: Figures cover non-farm employment as of December 2011 and are not seasonally adjusted; (1) Metropolitan Statistical Area—see Appendix B for areas included
Source: Bureau of Labor Statistics, http://stats.bls.gov

Occupations with Greatest Projected Employment Growth: 2008 – 2018

Occupation[1]	2008 Employment	2018 Projected Employment	Numeric Employment Change	Percent Employment Change
Personal and Home Care Aides	346,500	504,700	158,200	45.7
Registered Nurses	236,400	297,200	60,800	25.7
Retail Salespersons	499,400	559,100	59,700	12.0
Combined Food Preparation and Serving Workers, Including Fast Food	260,600	308,800	48,200	18.5
Elementary School Teachers, Except Special Education	197,500	233,400	35,900	18.2
Office Clerks, General	372,500	407,400	34,900	9.4
Customer Service Representatives	202,200	236,600	34,400	17.0
Waiters and Waitresses	245,600	279,900	34,300	14.0
Stock Clerks and Order Fillers	207,700	237,100	29,400	14.2
Postsecondary Teachers	168,000	196,100	28,100	16.7

Note: Projections cover California; (1) Sorted by numeric employment change
Source: www.projectionscentral.com, State Occupational Projections, 2008–2018 Long-Term Projections

Fastest Growing Occupations: 2008 – 2018

Occupation[1]	2008 Employment	2018 Projected Employment	Numeric Employment Change	Percent Employment Change
Biomedical Engineers	3,100	5,600	2,500	80.6
Network Systems and Data Communications Analysts	35,000	52,600	17,600	50.3
Biochemists and Biophysicists	4,800	7,100	2,300	47.9
Medical Scientists, Except Epidemiologists	26,200	38,500	12,300	46.9
Personal and Home Care Aides	346,500	504,700	158,200	45.7
Home Health Aides	54,300	78,000	23,700	43.6
Physician Assistants	8,100	11,500	3,400	42.0
Separating, Filtering, Clarifying, Precipitating, and Still Machine Setters, Operators, and Te	7,300	10,200	2,900	39.7
Physical Therapist Aides	5,900	8,100	2,200	37.3
Electrical and Electronics Repairers, Powerhouse, Substation, and Relay	1,100	1,500	400	36.4

Note: Projections cover California; (1) Sorted by percent employment change and excludes occupations with numeric employment change less than 100
Source: www.projectionscentral.com, State Occupational Projections, 2008–2018 Long-Term Projections

Average Wages

Occupation	$/Hr.	Occupation	$/Hr.
Accountants and Auditors	31.12	Maids and Housekeeping Cleaners	10.37
Automotive Mechanics	19.26	Maintenance and Repair Workers	18.41
Bookkeepers	18.27	Marketing Managers	53.71
Carpenters	27.20	Nuclear Medicine Technologists	42.15
Cashiers	10.78	Nurses, Licensed Practical	21.99
Clerks, General Office	14.68	Nurses, Registered	39.09
Clerks, Receptionists/Information	12.79	Nursing Aides/Orderlies/Attendants	12.30
Clerks, Shipping/Receiving	14.48	Packers and Packagers, Hand	11.12
Computer Programmers	32.65	Physical Therapists	39.91
Computer Support Specialists	22.98	Postal Service Mail Carriers	25.31
Computer Systems Analysts	35.24	Real Estate Brokers	n/a
Cooks, Restaurant	11.58	Retail Salespersons	11.79
Dentists	83.02	Sales Reps., Exc. Tech./Scientific	28.82
Electrical Engineers	45.72	Sales Reps., Tech./Scientific	37.82
Electricians	29.14	Secretaries, Exc. Legal/Med./Exec.	16.71
Financial Managers	49.84	Security Guards	11.63
First-Line Supervisors/Managers, Sales	21.05	Surgeons	119.83
Food Preparation Workers	9.95	Teacher Assistants	14.10
General and Operations Managers	53.62	Teachers, Elementary School	32.70
Hairdressers/Cosmetologists	10.14	Teachers, Secondary School	32.20
Internists	83.72	Telemarketers	13.66
Janitors and Cleaners	12.88	Truck Drivers, Heavy/Tractor-Trailer	20.95
Landscaping/Groundskeeping Workers	12.24	Truck Drivers, Light/Delivery Svcs.	16.00
Lawyers	57.78	Waiters and Waitresses	9.36

Note: Wage data covers the Riverside-San Bernardino-Ontario, CA Metropolitan Statistical Area—see Appendix B for areas included. Hourly wages for elementary/secondary school teachers and teacher assistants were calculated by the editors from annual wage data assuming a 40 hour work week; n/a not available.
Source: Bureau of Labor Statistics, Metro Area Occupational Employment and Wage Estimates, May 2011

RESIDENTIAL REAL ESTATE

Building Permits

Area	Single-Family			Multi-Family			Total		
	2010	2011	Pct. Chg.	2010	2011	Pct. Chg.	2010	2011	Pct. Chg.
City	348	288	-17.2	0	0	-	348	288	-17.2
MSA[1]	5,287	3,378	-36.1	1,049	1,358	29.5	6,336	4,736	-25.3
U.S.	447,311	418,498	-6.4	157,299	205,563	30.7	604,610	624,061	3.2

Note: (1) Metropolitan Statistical Area—see Appendix B for areas included; figures represent new, privately-owned housing units authorized (unadjusted data); All permit data are based on estimates with imputation.
Source: U.S. Census Bureau, Manufacturing, Mining, and Construction Statistics, Building Permits, 2010, 2011

Homeownership Rate

Area	2005 (%)	2006 (%)	2007 (%)	2008 (%)	2009 (%)	2010 (%)	2011 (%)
MSA[1]	68.5	68.3	66.6	65.8	65.9	63.9	59.2
U.S.	68.9	68.8	68.1	67.8	67.4	66.9	66.1

Note: (1) Metropolitan Statistical Area—see Appendix B for areas included
Source: U.S. Census Bureau, Housing Vacancies and Homeownership Annual Statistics: 2011

Housing Vacancy Rates

Area	Gross Vacancy Rate[2] (%)			Year-Round Vacancy Rate[3] (%)			Rental Vacancy Rate[4] (%)			Homeowner Vacancy Rate[5] (%)		
	2009	2010	2011	2009	2010	2011	2009	2010	2011	2009	2010	2011
MSA[1]	18.7	19.9	17.7	12.2	13.9	11.4	12.3	12.3	8.4	4.0	4.7	3.5
U.S.	14.5	14.3	14.2	11.3	11.3	11.1	10.6	10.2	9.5	2.6	2.6	2.5

Note: (1) Metropolitan Statistical Area—see Appendix B for areas included; (2) The percentage of the total housing inventory that is vacant; (3) The percentage of the housing inventory (excluding seasonal units) that is year-round vacant; (4) The percentage of rental inventory that is vacant for rent; (5) The percentage of homeowner inventory that is vacant for sale
Source: U.S. Census Bureau, Housing Vacancies and Homeownership Annual Statistics: 2011

TAXES

State Corporate Income Tax Rates

State	Tax Rate (%)	Income Brackets ($)	Num. of Brackets	Financial Institution Tax Rate (%)[a]	Federal Income Tax Ded.
California	8.84 (c)	Flat rate	1	10.84 (c)	No

Note: Tax rates as of January 1, 2012; (a) Rates listed are the corporate income tax rate applied to financial institutions or excise taxes based on income. Some states have other taxes based upon the value of deposits or shares; (c) The minimum corporation franchise tax in California is $800. The additional alternative minimum tax is levied at a 6.65% rate.
Source: Federation of Tax Administrators, "State Corporate Income Tax Rates, 2012"

State Individual Income Tax Rates

State	Tax Rate (%)	Income Brackets ($)	Num. of Brackets	Personal Exempt. ($)[1] Single	Personal Exempt. ($)[1] Dependents	Fed. Inc. Tax Ded.
California (a)	1.0 - 9.3 (f)	7,316 (b) - 48,029 (b)	6	102 (c)	315 (c)	No

Note: Tax rates as of January 1, 2012; Local- and county-level taxes are not included; n/a not applicable; (1) Married joint filers generally receive double the single exemption; (a) 17 states have statutory provision for automatically adjusting to the rate of inflation the dollar values of the income tax brackets, standard deductions, and/or personal exemptions. Massachusetts, Michigan, and Nebraska index the personal exemptiononly. Oregon does not index the income brackets for $125,000 and over. Because the inflation-adjustments for 2012 are not yet available in some cases, the table may report the 2011 amounts; (b) For joint returns, taxes are twice the tax on half the couple's income; (c) The personal exemption takes the form of a tax credit instead of a deduction; (f) California imposes an additional 1% tax on taxable income over $1 million, making the maximum rate 10.3% over $1 million.
Source: Federation of Tax Administrators, "State Individual Income Tax Rates, 2012"

Various State and Local Tax Rates

State	State and Local Sales and Use (%)	State Sales and Use (%)	Gasoline[1] (¢/gal.)	Cigarette[2] ($/pack)	Spirits[3] ($/gal.)	Wine[4] ($/gal.)	Beer[5] ($/gal.)
California	7.75	7.25 (b)	48.6	0.87	3.30	0.20	0.20

Note: All tax rates as of January 1, 2012 except beer, wine and spirits (September 1, 2011); (1) The American Petroleum Institute has developed a methodology for determining the average tax rate on a gallon of fuel. Rates may include any of the following: excise taxes, environmental fees, storage tank fees, other fees or taxes, general sales tax, and local taxes. In states where gasoline is subject to the general sales tax, or where the fuel tax is based on the average sale price, the average rate determined by API is sensitive to changes in the price of gasoline. States that fully or partially apply general sales taxes to gasoline: CA, CO, GA, IL, IN, MI, NY; (2) The federal excise tax of $1.0066 per pack and local taxes are not included; (3) Rates are those applicable to off-premise sales of 40% alcohol by volume (a.b.v.) distilled spirits in 750ml containers. Local excise taxes are excluded; (4) Rates are those applicable to off-premise sales of 11% a.b.v. non-carbonated wine in 750ml containers; (5) Rates are those applicable to off-premise sales of 4.7% a.b.v. beer in 12 ounce containers; (b) Three states collect a separate, uniform "local" add-on sales tax: California (1%), Utah (1.25%), Virginia (1%). These amounts are included in the state sales tax column.
Source: Tax Foundation, 2012 Facts & Figures: How Does Your State Compare?

State-Local Tax Burdens

Area	Rate (%)	Rank[1]	Per Capita Taxes Paid to Home State ($)	Total State and Local Per Capita Taxes Paid ($)	Per Capita Income ($)
California	10.6	6	3,874	4,910	46,366
U.S. Average	9.8	-	3,057	4,160	42,539

Note: Figures cover 2009; (1) Rank ranges from 1 to 50 where 1 is highest tax burden
Source: Tax Foundation, State-Local Tax Burdens, All States, 2009

State Business Tax Climate Index Rankings

State	Overall Rank	Corporate Tax Index Rank	Individual Income Tax Index Rank	Sales Tax Index Rank	Unemployment Insurance Tax Index Rank	Property Tax Index Rank
California	48	43	50	40	13	17

Note: The index is a measure of how each state's tax laws affect economic performance. The lower the rank, the more favorable a state's tax system is for business. States without a given tax are given a ranking of 1.
Source: Tax Foundation, Major Components of the State Business Tax Climate Index, FY 2012

COMMERCIAL REAL ESTATE

Office Market

Market Area	Inventory (sq. ft.)	Vacant (sq. ft.)	Vac. Rate (%)	Under Constr. (sq. ft.)	Asking Rent ($/sf/yr) Class A	Class B
Riverside-San Bernardino	27,899,111	6,528,885	23.4	141,133	23.14	17.52

Source: Grubb & Ellis, Office Markets Trends, 4th Quarter 2011

Industrial Market

Market Area	Inventory (sq. ft.)	Vacant (sq. ft.)	Vac. Rate (%)	Under Constr. (sq. ft.)	Asking Rent ($/sf/yr) WH/Dist	R&D/Flex
Inland Empire	441,678,336	27,758,704	6.3	4,515,330	3.84	6.72

Source: Grubb & Ellis, Industrial Markets Trends, 4th Quarter 2011

COMMERCIAL UTILITIES

Typical Monthly Electric Bills

Area	Commercial Service ($/month) 1,500 kWh	Commercial Service ($/month) 40 kW demand 14,000 kWh	Industrial Service ($/month) 1,000 kW demand 200,000 kWh	Industrial Service ($/month) 50,000 kW demand 15,000,000 kWh
City	283	2,469	52,039	2,061,098
Average[1]	189	1,616	25,197	1,470,813

Note: Based on total rates in effect July 1, 2011; (1) average based on 184 utilities surveyed
Source: Edison Electric Institute, Typical Bills and Average Rates Report, Summer 2011

TRANSPORTATION

Means of Transportation to Work

Area	Car/Truck/Van: Drove Alone	Car/Truck/Van: Car-pooled	Public Transportation: Bus	Public Transportation: Subway	Public Transportation: Railroad	Bicycle	Walked	Other Means	Worked at Home
City	76.9	12.9	0.2	0.0	0.0	0.6	1.6	1.8	6.0
MSA[1]	75.7	14.8	1.2	0.1	0.5	0.4	1.9	1.2	4.3
U.S.	76.0	10.2	2.7	1.7	0.5	0.5	2.8	1.3	4.2

Note: Figures are percentages and cover workers 16 years of age and older; (1) Figures cover the Riverside-San Bernardino-Ontario, CA Metropolitan Statistical Area—see Appendix B for areas included
Source: U.S. Census Bureau, 2008-2010 American Community Survey 3-Year Estimates

Travel Time to Work

Area	Less Than 10 Minutes	10 to 19 Minutes	20 to 29 Minutes	30 to 44 Minutes	45 to 59 Minutes	60 to 89 Minutes	90 Minutes or More
City	14.3	30.3	8.3	12.0	12.7	16.8	5.6
MSA[1]	12.0	27.8	17.9	18.4	8.5	9.8	5.7
U.S.	13.9	30.1	20.8	19.8	7.5	5.5	2.5

Note: Figures are percentages and include workers 16 years old and over; (1) Figures cover the Riverside-San Bernardino-Ontario, CA Metropolitan Statistical Area—see Appendix B for areas included
Source: U.S. Census Bureau, 2008-2010 American Community Survey 3-Year Estimates

Travel Time Index

Area	1985	1990	1995	2000	2005	2010
Urban Area[1]	1.03	1.09	1.09	1.13	1.19	1.18
Average[2]	1.11	1.16	1.18	1.21	1.25	1.20

Note: Travel Time Index—the ratio of travel time in the peak period to the travel time at free-flow conditions. A value of 1.30 indicates a 20-minute free-flow trip takes 26 minutes in the peak. Free-flow speeds (60 mph on freeways and 35 mph on principal arterials) are used as the comparison threshold; (1) Covers the Riverside-San Bernardino CA urban area; (2) average of 439 urban areas
Source: Texas Transportation Institute, Urban Mobility Report 2011, September 2011

Public Transportation

Agency Name / Mode of Transportation	Vehicles Operated in Maximum Service	Annual Unlinked Passenger Trips ('000)	Annual Passenger Miles ('000)
Riverside Transit Agency (RTA)			
Bus (directly operated)	75	6,245.6	38,312.3
Bus (purchased transportation)	61	1,350.1	10,755.2
Demand Response (purchased transportation)	73	331.2	4,084.2
Demand Response Taxi (purchased transportation)	12	7.2	89.0

Source: Federal Transit Administration, National Transit Database, 2010

Air Transportation

Airport Name and Code / Type of Service	Passenger Airlines[1]	Passenger Enplanements	Freight Carriers[2]	Freight (lbs.)
Ontario International (ONT)				
Domestic service (U.S. carriers - 2011)	21	2,228,877	20	455,277,639
International service (U.S. carriers - 2010)	1	293	2	8,463

Note: (1) Includes all U.S.-based major, minor and commuter airlines that carried at least one passenger during the year; (2) Includes all U.S.-based airlines and freight carriers that transported at least one pound of freight during the year
Source: Bureau of Transportation Statistics, The Intermodal Transportation Database, Air Carriers: T-100 Domestic Market (U.S. Carriers), 2011; Bureau of Transportation Statistics, The Intermodal Transportation Database, Air Carriers: T-100 International Market (U.S. Carriers), 2010

Other Transportation Statistics

Major Highways:	I-15; I-215
Amtrak Service:	No
Major Waterways/Ports:	Near the Pacific Ocean (20 miles)

Source: Amtrak.com; Google Maps

BUSINESSES

Major Business Headquarters

Company Name	Rankings	
	Fortune[1]	Forbes[2]
No companies listed	-	-

Note: (1) Fortune 500—companies that produce a 10-K are ranked 1 to 500 based on 2010 revenue; (2) all private companies with at least $2 billion in annual revenue are ranked 1 to 212; companies listed are headquartered in the city; dashes indicate no ranking
Source: Fortune, "Fortune 500," May 23, 2011; Forbes, "America's Largest Private Companies," November 16, 2011

Fast-Growing Businesses

According to Deloitte, Temecula is home to one of North America's 500 fastest-growing high-technology companies: **Walz Group** (#110). Companies are ranked by percentage growth in revenue over a five-year period. Criteria for inclusion: company must be headquartered within North America; must own proprietary intellectual property or proprietary technology that contributes to a significant portion of the company's operating revenue, or devote a significant proportion of revenues to research and development of technology; must have been in business for a minumum of five years with 2006 operating revenues of at least $50,000 USD/CD and 2010 operating revenues of at least $5 million USD/CD. *Deloitte Touche Tohmatsu, 2011 Deloitte Technology Fast 500™*

Minority- and Women-Owned Businesses

Group	All Firms		Firms with Paid Employees			
	Firms	Sales ($000)	Firms	Sales ($000)	Employees	Payroll ($000)
Asian	705	115,216	180	93,933	1,274	39,084
Black	294	7,119	(s)	(s)	(s)	(s)
Hispanic	1,420	80,603	49	32,457	180	5,884
Women	3,136	762,459	330	666,467	2,884	85,711
All Firms	10,547	9,097,820	2,839	8,794,287	42,271	1,436,552

Note: Figures cover firms located in the city; minority- and women-owned business are defined as firms in which the corresponding group own 51% or more of the stock or equity of the company; (s) estimates are suppressed when publication standards are not met
Source: U.S. Census Bureau, 2007 Economic Census, Survey of Business Owners

HOTELS

Hotels/Motels

Area	5 Star		4 Star		3 Star		2 Star		1 Star		Not Rated	
	Num.	Pct.[3]	Num.	Pct.[3]	Num.	Pct.[3]	Num.	Pct.[3]	Num.	Pct.[3]	Num.	Pct.[3]
City[1]	0	0.0	2	5.3	5	13.2	25	65.8	0	0.0	6	15.8
Total[2]	133	0.9	940	6.5	4,569	31.8	7,033	48.9	351	2.4	1,343	9.3

Note: (1) Figures cover Temecula and vicinity; (2) Figures cover all 100 cities in this book; (3) Percentage of hotels which have a given star rating; Star ratings are determined by expedia.com and offer an indication of the general quality of a particular hotel.
Source: expedia.com, April 25, 2012

Living Environment

COST OF LIVING

Cost of Living Index

Composite Index	Groceries	Housing	Utilities	Trans-portation	Health Care	Misc. Goods/ Services
112.5	106.7	135.9	110.2	108.9	102.6	97.5

Note: U.S. = 100; Figures cover the Riverside City CA urban area.
Source: The Council for Community and Economic Research, ACCRA Cost of Living Index, 2011

Grocery Prices

Area[1]	T-Bone Steak ($/pound)	Frying Chicken ($/pound)	Whole Milk ($/half gal.)	Eggs ($/dozen)	Orange Juice ($/64 oz.)	Coffee ($/11.5 oz.)
City[2]	8.80	0.97	2.11	2.18	3.16	5.24
Avg.	9.25	1.18	2.22	1.66	3.19	4.40
Min.	6.70	0.88	1.31	0.95	2.46	2.94
Max.	14.30	2.16	3.50	3.18	4.75	6.83

Note: (1) Values for the local area are compared with the average, minimum and maximum values for all 335 areas in the Cost of Living Index; (2) Figures cover the Riverside City CA urban area; **T-Bone Steak** *(price per pound);* **Frying Chicken** *(price per pound, whole fryer);* **Whole Milk** *(half gallon carton);* **Eggs** *(price per dozen, Grade A, large);* **Orange Juice** *(64 oz. Tropicana or Florida Natural);* **Coffee** *(11.5 oz. can, vacuum-packed, Maxwell House, Hills Bros, or Folgers).*
Source: The Council for Community and Economic Research, ACCRA Cost of Living Index, 2011

Housing and Utility Costs

Area[1]	New Home Price ($)	Apartment Rent ($/month)	All Electric ($/month)	Part Electric ($/month)	Other Energy ($/month)	Telephone ($/month)
City[2]	385,798	1,142	-	120.75	65.28	28.81
Avg.	285,990	839	163.23	89.00	77.52	26.92
Min.	188,005	460	125.58	45.39	33.89	17.98
Max.	1,197,028	3,244	339.16	181.97	348.69	40.01

Note: (1) Values for the local area are compared with the average, minimum and maximum values for all 335 areas in the Cost of Living Index; (2) Figures cover the Riverside City CA urban area; **New Home Price** *(2,400 sf living area, 8,000 sf lot, in urban area with full utilities);* **Apartment Rent** *(950 sf 2 bedroom/1.5 or 2 bath, unfurnished, excluding all utilities except water);* **All Electric** *(average monthly cost for an all-electric home);* **Part Electric** *(average monthly cost for a part-electric home);* **Other Energy** *(average monthly cost for natural gas, fuel oil, coal, wood, and any other forms of energy except electricity);* **Telephone** *(price includes basic monthly rate for a private residential line plus additional local usage charges incurred by a family of four).*
Source: The Council for Community and Economic Research, ACCRA Cost of Living Index, 2011

Health Care, Transportation, and Other Costs

Area[1]	Doctor ($/visit)	Dentist ($/visit)	Optometrist ($/visit)	Gasoline ($/gallon)	Beauty Salon ($/visit)	Men's Shirt ($)
City[2]	82.75	86.70	86.80	3.81	36.66	28.75
Avg.	93.88	81.72	90.54	3.48	32.65	25.06
Min.	60.00	55.33	53.66	3.18	19.78	13.44
Max.	154.98	145.97	183.72	4.31	63.21	46.00

Note: (1) Values for the local area are compared with the average, minimum and maximum values for all 335 areas in the Cost of Living Index; (2) Figures cover the Riverside City CA urban area; **Doctor** *(general practitioners routine exam of an established patient);* **Dentist** *(adult teeth cleaning and periodic oral examination);* **Optometrist** *(full vision eye exam for established adult patient);* **Gasoline** *(one gallon regular unleaded, national brand, including all taxes, cash price at self-service pump if available);* **Beauty Salon** *(woman's shampoo, trim, and blow-dry);* **Men's Shirt** *(cotton/polyester dress shirt, pinpoint weave, long sleeves).*
Source: The Council for Community and Economic Research, ACCRA Cost of Living Index, 2011

HOUSING

House Price Index (HPI)

Area	National Ranking[2]	Quarterly Change (%)	One-Year Change (%)	Five-Year Change (%)
MSA[1]	237	0.24	-4.99	-48.04
U.S.[3]	-	-0.10	-2.43	-19.16

Note: The HPI is a weighted repeat sales index. It measures average price changes in repeat sales or refinancings on the same properties. This information is obtained by reviewing repeat mortgage transactions on single-family properties whose mortgages have been purchased or securitized by Fannie Mae or Freddie Mac in January 1975; (1) Metropolitan/Micropolitan Statistical Area—see Appendix B for areas included; (2) Rankings are based on annual percentage change for all metro areas containing at least 15,000 transactions over the last 10 years and ranges from 1 to 306; (3) figures based on a weighted average of Census Division estimates using a purchase only index; all figures are for the period ending December 31, 2011

Source: Federal Housing Finance Agency, House Price Index, February 23, 2012

House Price Valuations

Area	Q4 2005		Q4 2006		Q4 2007		Q4 2008		Q4 2009	
	Price ($000)	Over-valuation	Price ($000)	Over-valuation	Price ($000)	Over-valuation	Price ($000)	Over-valuation	Price ($000)	Over-valuation
MSA[1]	343.5	60.5	347.1	55.8	292.3	28.4	193.2	-12.4	182.2	-16.2

Note: Figures show the percentage of over- or under-valuation of single family homes relative to statistically normal house values (e.g. a value of 23.6 indicates that house values are 23.6% overvalued). Statistically normal house values are based on house prices, interest rates, household incomes, population densities, and any historical premiums or discounts metropolitan areas have exhibited over time; (1) Figures cover the Riverside-San Bernardino-Ontario, CA - see Appendix B for areas included

Source: Global Insight/PNC Financial Services Group, House Prices in America: 4th Quarter 2009 Update

Median Single-Family Home Prices

Area	2009	2010	2011p	Percent Change 2010 to 2011
MSA[1]	169.7	179.3	172.3	-3.9
U.S. Average	172.1	173.1	166.2	-4.0

Note: Figures are median sales prices of existing single-family homes in thousands of dollars; (p) preliminary; n/a not available; (1) Metropolitan Statistical Area—see Appendix B for areas included

Source: National Association of Realtors, Median Sales Price of Existing Single-Family Homes for Metropolitan Areas, 4th Quarter 2011

Affordability Index of Existing Single-Family Homes

Area	2009	2010	2011p	Percent Change 2010 to 2011
MSA[1]	83.3	82.2	88.9	8.2

Note: The housing affordability index measures whether or not a typical family could qualify for a mortgage loan on a typical home. The higher the index, the greater the household purchasing power. An index of 100 is defined as the point where a median-income household has exactly enough income to qualify for the purchase of a median-priced existing single-family home, assuming a 20 percent downpayment and 25 percent of gross income devoted to mortgage principal and interest payments; (p) preliminary; n/a not available; (1) Metropolitan Statistical Area—see Appendix B for areas included

Source: National Association of Realtors, Affordability Index of Existing Single-Family Homes, 2011

Median Apartment Condo-Coop Home Prices

Area	2009	2010	2011p	Percent Change 2010 to 2011
MSA[1]	n/a	n/a	n/a	n/a
U.S. Average	175.6	171.7	165.1	-3.8

Note: Figures are median sales prices of existing apartment condo-coop homes in thousands of dollars; (p) preliminary; n/a not available; (1) Metropolitan Statistical Area—see Appendix B for areas included

Source: National Association of Realtors, Median Sales Price of Existing Apartment Condo-Coop Homes for Metropolitan Areas, 4th Quarter 2011

Year Housing Structure Built

Area	2005 or Later	2000 -2004	1990 -1999	1980 -1989	1970 -1979	1960 -1969	1950 -1959	Before 1950	Median Year
City	9.8	23.1	34.3	24.2	6.5	0.6	1.1	0.6	1995
MSA[1]	8.1	13.1	14.7	23.2	16.3	9.5	9.0	6.0	1984
U.S.	5.0	8.6	14.0	14.1	16.3	11.3	11.2	19.6	1975

Note: Figures are percentages except for Median Year; (1) Figures cover the Riverside-San Bernardino-Ontario, CA Metropolitan Statistical Area—see Appendix B for areas included
Source: U.S. Census Bureau, 2008-2010 American Community Survey 3-Year Estimates

HEALTH

Health Risk Data

Category	MSA[1] (%)	U.S. (%)
Adults who have been told they have high blood pressure[2]	27.4	28.7
Adults who have been told they have high blood cholesterol[2]	37.2	37.5
Adults who have been told they have diabetes[3]	10.2	8.7
Adults who have been told they have arthritis[2]	22.4	26.0
Adults who have been told they currently have asthma	6.6	9.1
Adults who are current smokers	14.0	17.3
Adults who are heavy drinkers[4]	5.8	5.0
Adults who are binge drinkers[5]	17.2	15.1
Adults who are overweight (BMI 25.0 - 29.9)	36.4	36.2
Adults who are obese (BMI 30.0 - 99.8)	28.5	27.5
Adults who participated in any physical activities in the past month	76.4	76.1
Adults 50+ who have ever had a sigmoidoscopy or colonoscopy	55.4	65.2
Women aged 40+ who have had a mammogram within the past two years	75.8	75.2
Men aged 40+ who have had a PSA test within the past two years	43.2	53.2
Adults aged 65+ who have had flu shot within the past year	59.2	67.5
Adults aged 18–64 who have any kind of health care coverage	72.9	82.2

Note: Data as of 2010 unless otherwise noted; (1) Figures cover the Riverside-San Bernardino-Ontario, CA Metropolitan Statistical Area—see Appendix B for areas included; (2) Data as of 2009; (3) Figures do not include pregnancy-related, borderline, or pre-diabetes; (4) Heavy drinkers are classified as males having more than two drinks per day or females having more than one drink per day; (5) Binge drinkers are classified as males having five or more drinks on one occasion or females having four or more drinks on one occasion
Source: Centers for Disease Control and Prevention, Behaviorial Risk Factor Surveillance System, SMART: Selected Metropolitan/Micropolitan Area Risk Trends, 2009, 2010

Mortality Rates for the Top 10 Causes of Death in the U.S.

ICD-10[a] Sub-Chapter	ICD-10[a] Code	Age-Adjusted Mortality Rate[1] per 100,000 population	
		County[2]	U.S.
Malignant neoplasms	C00-C97	166.9	175.6
Ischaemic heart diseases	I20-I25	132.9	121.6
Other forms of heart disease	I30-I51	39.9	48.6
Chronic lower respiratory diseases	J40-J47	47.0	42.3
Cerebrovascular diseases	I60-I69	40.6	40.6
Organic, including symptomatic, mental disorders	F01-F09	19.3	26.7
Other degenerative diseases of the nervous system	G30-G31	27.2	24.7
Other external causes of accidental injury	W00-X59	19.7	24.4
Diabetes mellitus	E10-E14	21.1	21.7
Hypertensive diseases	I10-I15	22.3	18.2

Note: (a) ICD-10 = International Classification of Diseases 10th Revision; (1) Mortality rates are a three year average covering 2007-2009; (2) Figures cover Riverside County
Source: Centers for Disease Control and Prevention, National Center for Health Statistics. Underlying Cause of Death 1999-2009 on CDC WONDER Online Database, released 2012. Data for year 2009 are compiled from the Multiple Cause of Death File 2009, Series 20 No. 2O, 2012, Data for year 2008 are compiled from the Multiple Cause of Death File 2008, Series 20 No. 2N, 2011, Data for year 2007 are compiled from Multiple Cause of Death File 2007, Series 20 No. 2M, 2010.

Mortality Rates for Selected Causes of Death

ICD-10[a] Sub-Chapter	ICD-10[a] Code	Age-Adjusted Mortality Rate[1] per 100,000 population	
		County[2]	U.S.
Assault	X85-Y09	4.9	5.7
Human immunodeficiency virus (HIV) disease	B20-B24	3.0	3.3
Influenza and pneumonia	J09-J18	13.3	16.4
Intentional self-harm	X60-X84	10.5	11.5
Malnutrition	E40-E46	0.4	0.8
Obesity and other hyperalimentation	E65-E68	1.7	1.6
Transport accidents	V01-V99	13.8	13.7
Viral hepatitis	B15-B19	3.8	2.2

Note: (a) ICD-10 = International Classification of Diseases 10th Revision; (1) Mortality rates are a three year average covering 2007-2009; (2) Figures cover Riverside County
Source: Centers for Disease Control and Prevention, National Center for Health Statistics. Underlying Cause of Death 1999-2009 on CDC WONDER Online Database, released 2012. Data for year 2009 are compiled from the Multiple Cause of Death File 2009, Series 20 No. 2O, 2012, Data for year 2008 are compiled from the Multiple Cause of Death File 2008, Series 20 No. 2N, 2011, Data for year 2007 are compiled from Multiple Cause of Death File 2007, Series 20 No. 2M, 2010.

Distribution of Physicians and Dentists

Area[1]	Dentists[2]	D.O.[3]	M.D.[4] Total	Family/General Practice	Pediatrics	Medical Specialties	Surgical Specialties
Local (number)	638	184	2,038	347	151	698	479
Local (rate[5])	3.1	0.9	9.8	1.7	0.7	3.3	2.3
U.S. (rate[5])	4.5	1.9	18.3	2.5	1.4	6.8	4.1

Note: Data as of 2008 unless noted; (1) Local data covers Riverside County; (2) Data as of 2007; (3) Doctor of Osteopathic Medicine; (4) Includes active, non-federal, patient-care, office-based Doctors of Medicine; (5) rate per 10,000 population
Source: Area Resource File (ARF). 2009-2010 Release. U.S. Department of Health and Human Services, Health Resources and Services Administration, Bureau of Health Professions, Rockville, MD, August 2010

EDUCATION

Public School District Statistics

District Name	Schls	Pupils	Pupil/Teacher Ratio	Minority Pupils[1] (%)	Free Lunch Eligible[2] (%)	IEP[3] (%)
Temecula Valley Unified	31	30,184	22.4	50.5	10.8	11.6

Note: Table includes school districts with 2,000 or more students; (1) Percentage of students that are not non-Hispanic white; (2) Percentage of students that are eligible for the free lunch program; (3) Percentage of students that have an Individualized Education Program.
Source: U.S. Department of Education, National Center for Education Statistics, Common Core of Data, Local Education Agency (School District) Universe Survey: School Year 2009-2010; U.S. Department of Education, National Center for Education Statistics, Common Core of Data, Public Elementary/Secondary School Universe Survey: School Year 2009-2010

Highest Level of Education

Area	Less than H.S.	H.S. Diploma	Some College, No Deg.	Associate Degree	Bachelors Degree	Masters Degree	Profess. School Degree	Doctorate Degree
City	8.7	21.2	29.6	10.5	20.1	7.3	1.5	1.1
MSA[1]	21.7	25.6	25.5	7.8	12.7	4.7	1.3	0.8
U.S.	14.7	28.4	21.3	7.6	17.6	7.2	1.9	1.2

Note: Figures cover persons age 25 and over; (1) Figures cover the Riverside-San Bernardino-Ontario, CA Metropolitan Statistical Area—see Appendix B for areas included
Source: U.S. Census Bureau, 2008-2010 American Community Survey 3-Year Estimates

Educational Attainment by Race

Area	High School Graduate or Higher (%)					Bachelor's Degree or Higher (%)				
	Total	White	Black	Asian	Hisp.[2]	Total	White	Black	Asian	Hisp.[2]
City	91.3	92.9	97.9	86.6	75.9	30.0	31.8	27.4	31.8	19.4
MSA[1]	78.3	80.5	88.0	89.1	59.4	19.4	19.5	20.1	46.7	8.1
U.S.	85.3	87.5	81.4	85.5	61.6	28.0	29.3	17.8	50.2	13.0

Note: Figures shown cover persons 25 years old and over; (1) Figures cover the Riverside-San Bernardino-Ontario, CA Metropolitan Statistical Area—see Appendix B for areas included; (2) People of Hispanic origin can be of any race
Source: U.S. Census Bureau, 2008-2010 American Community Survey 3-Year Estimates

School Enrollment by Grade and Control

Area	Preschool (%)		Kindergarten (%)		Grades 1 - 4 (%)		Grades 5 - 8 (%)		Grades 9 - 12 (%)	
	Public	Private	Public	Private	Public	Private	Public	Private	Public	Private
City	43.5	56.5	88.1	11.9	88.7	11.3	86.8	13.2	94.3	5.7
MSA[1]	63.5	36.5	92.3	7.7	94.1	5.9	93.7	6.3	93.9	6.1
U.S.	55.4	44.6	87.1	12.9	89.4	10.6	89.5	10.5	90.4	9.6

Note: Figures shown cover persons 3 years old and over; (1) Figures cover the Riverside-San Bernardino-Ontario, CA Metropolitan Statistical Area—see Appendix B for areas included
Source: U.S. Census Bureau, 2008-2010 American Community Survey 3-Year Estimates

Average Salaries of Public School Classroom Teachers

Area	2010-11		2011-12		Percent Change 2010-11 to 2011-12	Percent Change 2001-02 to 2011-12
	Dollars	Rank[1]	Dollars	Rank[1]		
California	67,871	4	69,496	4	2.39	27.90
U.S. Average	55,623	-	56,643	-	1.83	26.8

Note: (1) State rank ranges from 1 to 51 where 1 indicates highest salary.
Source: National Education Association, Rankings & Estimates: Rankings of the States 2011 and Estimates of School Statistics 2012, December 2011

Higher Education

Four-Year Colleges			Two-Year Colleges			Medical Schools[1]	Law Schools[2]	Voc/ Tech[3]
Public	Private Non-profit	Private For-profit	Public	Private Non-profit	Private For-profit			
0	0	0	0	0	2	0	0	3

Note: Figures cover institutions located within the city limits and include main campuses only; (1) includes schools accredited by the Liaison Committee on Medical Education and the American Osteopathic Association's Commission on Osteopathic College Accreditation; (2) includes American Bar Association-accredited law schools; (3) includes all schools with programs that are less than 2 years.
Source: National Center for Education Statistics, Integrated Postsecondary Education System (IPEDS) Peer Analysis System, 2011-12; Association of American Medical Colleges, Member List, April 23, 2012; American Osteopathic Association, Member List, April 23, 2012; Law School Admission Council, Official Guide to ABA-Approved Law Schools Online, April 23, 2012

According to *U.S. News & World Report,* the Riverside-San Bernardino-Ontario, CA is home to one of the best national universities in the U.S.: **University of California–Riverside** (#97). The indicators used to capture academic quality fall into a number of categories: assessment by administrators at peer institutions; retention of students; faculty resources; student selectivity; financial resources; alumni giving; high school counselor ratings of colleges; and graduation rate.*U.S. News & World Report, "America's Best Colleges 2012"*

PRESIDENTIAL ELECTION

2008 Presidential Election Results

Area	Obama	McCain	Nader	Other
Riverside County	50.2	47.9	0.7	1.1
U.S.	52.9	45.6	0.6	0.9

Note: Results are percentages and may not add to 100% due to rounding
Source: Dave Leip's Atlas of U.S. Presidential Elections, www.uselectionatlas.org

EMPLOYERS

Major Employers

Company Name	Industry
Arrowhead Regional Medical Center	General medical and surgical hospitals
Chaffey Community College District	Community college
County of Riverside	Executive offices
Eisenhower Medical Center	General medical and surgical hospitals
Environmental Systems Research Institute	Prepackaged software
JW Marriott Resort & Spa	Hotels
Kaiser Foundation Hospitals	General medical and surgical hospitals
KSL Recreation Management Operations	Public golf courses
Loma Linda University	Colleges and universities
Loma Linda University Medical Center	General medical and surgical hospitals
Mental Health California	Mental hospital, except for the mentally retarded
PPG Architectural Finishes	Paints and allied products
RHS Corp.	Hospital management
Riverside County Schools	Elementary and secondary schools
San Antonio Community Hospital	General medical and surgical hospitals
San Manuel Entertainment Authority	Bingo hall
Specialty Brands	Frozen specialties, nec
Steno Employment Services	Employee leasing services
United Parcel Service	Mailing and messenger services
Veterans Health Administration	Administration of veterans' affairs

Note: Companies shown are located within the Riverside-San Bernardino-Ontario, CA metropolitan area.
Source: Hoovers.com, data extracted April 25 2012

PUBLIC SAFETY

Crime Rate

Area	All Crimes	Violent Crimes				Property Crimes		
		Murder	Forcible Rape	Robbery	Aggrav. Assault	Burglary	Larceny -Theft	Motor Vehicle Theft
City	2,366.5	2.0	2.9	41.0	26.3	522.1	1,602.4	169.8
Suburbs[1]	3,080.4	4.6	20.8	117.5	233.0	752.1	1,549.4	403.1
Metro[2]	3,063.1	4.5	20.4	115.7	228.0	746.5	1,550.6	397.5
U.S.	3,345.5	4.8	27.5	119.1	252.3	699.6	2,003.5	238.8

Note: Figures are crimes per 100,000 population; (1) All areas within the metro area that are located outside the city limits; (2) Metropolitan Statistical Area—see Appendix B for areas included
Source: FBI Uniform Crime Reports, 2010

Hate Crimes

Area	Number of Quarters Reported	Bias Motivation				
		Race	Religion	Sexual Orientation	Ethnicity	Disability
City	4	0	2	0	0	0

Source: Federal Bureau of Investigation, Hate Crime Statistics 2010

Identity Theft Consumer Complaints

Area	Complaints	Complaints per 100,000 Population	Rank[2]
MSA[1]	5,091	124.7	32
U.S.	279,156	90.4	-

Note: (1) Metropolitan Statistical Area—see Appendix B for areas included; (2) Rank ranges from 1 to 384 where 1 indicates greatest number of identity theft complaints per 100,000 population
Source: Federal Trade Commission, Consumer Sentinel Network Data Book for January–December 2011

Fraud and Other Consumer Complaints

Area	Complaints	Complaints per 100,000 Population	Rank[2]
MSA[1]	16,951	415.3	270
U.S.	1,533,924	496.8	-

Note: (1) Metropolitan Statistical Area—see Appendix B for areas included; (2) Rank ranges from 1 to 384 where 1 indicates greatest number of fraud and other complaints per 100,000 population
Source: Federal Trade Commission, Consumer Sentinel Network Data Book for January–December 2011

RECREATION

Culture

Dance[1]	Theatre[1]	Instrumental Music[1]	Vocal Music[1]	Series/ Festivals	Museums	Zoos and Aquariums[2]
0	0	0	0	0	n/a	0

Note: (1) Number of professional perfoming groups; (2) AZA-accredited; n/a not available
Source: The Grey House Performing Arts Directory, 2011-2012; Official Museum Directory, 2011; American Association of Museums, AAM Member Museums, April 2012; Association of Zoos & Aquariums, AZA Member Zoos & Aquariums, April 2012

Professional Sports Teams

Team Name	League
No teams are located in the metro area	

Source: Original research

CLIMATE

Average and Extreme Temperatures

Temperature	Jan	Feb	Mar	Apr	May	Jun	Jul	Aug	Sep	Oct	Nov	Dec	Yr.
Extreme High (°F)	90	89	97	110	107	114	114	114	112	110	95	99	114
Average High (°F)	66	68	68	75	79	86	92	92	89	83	73	67	78
Average Temp. (°F)	54	57	58	63	67	73	78	78	76	70	61	55	66
Average Low (°F)	42	45	47	50	55	59	63	64	62	56	47	42	53
Extreme Low (°F)	25	29	30	35	38	43	52	51	47	40	31	24	24

Note: Figures cover the years 1973-1993
Source: National Climatic Data Center, International Station Meteorological Climate Summary, 9/96

Average Precipitation/Snowfall/Humidity

Precip./Humidity	Jan	Feb	Mar	Apr	May	Jun	Jul	Aug	Sep	Oct	Nov	Dec	Yr.
Avg. Precip. (in.)	n/a	n/a	n/a	n/a	n/a	n/a	n/a	n/a	n/a	n/a	n/a	n/a	n/a
Avg. Snowfall (in.)	n/a	n/a	n/a	n/a	n/a	n/a	n/a	n/a	n/a	n/a	n/a	n/a	n/a
Avg. Rel. Hum. 6am (%)	45	44	50	42	44	39	35	36	38	37	36	39	40
Avg. Rel. Hum. 3pm (%)	74	75	79	75	77	76	73	72	71	73	69	70	74

Note: Figures cover the years 1973-1993
Source: National Climatic Data Center, International Station Meteorological Climate Summary, 9/96

Weather Conditions

Temperature			Daytime Sky			Precipitation		
10°F & below	32°F & below	90°F & above	Clear	Partly cloudy	Cloudy	0.01 inch or more precip.	0.1 inch or more snow/ice	Thunder-storms
0	4	82	124	178	63	n/a	n/a	5

Note: Figures are average number of days per year and cover the years 1973-1993
Source: National Climatic Data Center, International Station Meteorological Climate Summary, 9/96

HAZARDOUS WASTE

Superfund Sites

Temecula has no sites on the EPA's Superfund Final National Priorities List.
U.S. Environmental Protection Agency, Final National Priorities List, April 17, 2012

AIR & WATER QUALITY

Air Quality Index

Area	Percent of Days when Air Quality was...[2]					AQI Statistics[2]	
	Good	Moderate	Unhealthy for Sensitive Groups	Unhealthy	Very Unhealthy	Maximum	Median
Area[1]	11.2	55.3	27.4	5.2	0.8	320	82

Note: Air Quality Index (AQI) is an index for reporting daily air quality. EPA calculates the AQI for five major air pollutants regulated by the Clean Air Act: ground-level ozone, particle pollution (aka particulate matter), carbon monoxide, sulfur dioxide, and nitrogen dioxide. The AQI runs from 0 to 500. The higher the AQI value, the greater the level of air pollution and the greater the health concern. There are six AQI categories: "Good" AQI is between 0 and 50. Air quality is considered satisfactory; "Moderate" AQI is between 51 and 100. Air quality is acceptable; "Unhealthy for Sensitive Groups" When AQI values are between 101 and 150, members of sensitive groups may experience health effects; "Unhealthy" When AQI values are between 151 and 200 everyone may begin to experience health effects; "Very Unhealthy" AQI values between 201 and 300 trigger a health alert; "Hazardous" AQI values over 300 trigger warnings of emergency conditions (not shown); (1) Data covers Riverside County; (2) Based on 365 days with AQI data in 2011.
Source: U.S. Environmental Protection Agency, AirData Report, 2011

Air Quality Index Pollutants

Area	Percent of Days when AQI Pollutant was...[2]					
	Carbon Monoxide	Nitrogen Dioxide	Ozone	Sulfur Dioxide	Particulate Matter 2.5	Particulate Matter 10
Area[1]	0.0	0.8	45.2	0.5	35.6	17.8

Note: The Air Quality Index (AQI) is an index for reporting daily air quality. EPA calculates the AQI for five major air pollutants regulated by the Clean Air Act: ground-level ozone, particle pollution (also known as particulate matter), carbon monoxide, sulfur dioxide, and nitrogen dioxide. The AQI runs from 0 to 500. The higher the AQI value, the greater the level of air pollution and the greater the health concern; (1) Data covers Riverside County; (2) Based on 365 days with AQI data in 2011.
Source: U.S. Environmental Protection Agency, AirData Report, 2011

Air Quality Index Trends

Area	Trend Sites (days)								All Sites (days)
	2003	2004	2005	2006	2007	2008	2009	2010	2010
MSA[1]	163	157	142	133	144	131	114	115	116

Note: Figures are the number of days the AQI value exceeded 100 in a given year. An AQI value greater than 100 indicates that air quality would have been in the unhealthful range on that day. Data from exceptional events are included. These counts are presented in two ways. First, the counts are based on sites having an adequate record of monitoring data during the trend period (trend sites). These counts represent the relative change in the number of days with AQI values greater than 100. In the last column, the counts are based on all sites with data in the most recent year (because it is possible for a site to have data in the most recent year but not enough data to be a trend site); (1) Data covers the Riverside-San Bernardino-Ontario, CA—see Appendix B for areas included
Source: U.S. Environmental Protection Agency, Air Quality Index Information, "Number of Days with Air Quality Index Values Greater than 100 at Trend Sites, 2000-2010, and at All Sites in 2010"

Maximum Air Pollutant Concentrations: Particulate Matter, Ozone, CO and Lead

	Particulate Matter 10 (ug/m^3)	Particulate Matter 2.5 Wtd AM (ug/m^3)	Particulate Matter 2.5 24-Hr (ug/m^3)	Ozone (ppm)	Carbon Monoxide (ppm)	Lead (ug/m^3)
MSA[1] Level	312	15.2	36	0.109	4	0.01
NAAQS[2]	150	15	35	0.075	9	0.15
Met NAAQS[2]	No	No	No	No	Yes	Yes

Note: Data from exceptional events are not included; (1) Data covers the Riverside-San Bernardino-Ontario, CA—see Appendix B for areas included; (2) National Ambient Air Quality Standards; ppm = parts per million; ug/m^3 = micrograms per cubic meter; n/a not available
Concentrations: Particulate Matter 10 (coarse particulate)—highest second maximum 24-hour concentration; Particulate Matter 2.5 Wtd AM (fine particulate)—highest weighted annual mean concentration; Particulate Matter 2.5 24-Hour (fine particulate)—highest 98th percentile 24-hour concentration; Ozone—highest fourth daily maximum 8-hour concentration; Carbon Monoxide—highest second maximum non-overlapping 8-hour concentration; Lead—maximum running 3-month average
Source: U.S. Environmental Protection Agency, CBSA Factbook 2010, Air Quality Statistics by City, 2010

Maximum Air Pollutant Concentrations: Nitrogen Dioxide and Sulfur Dioxide

	Nitrogen Dioxide AM (ppb)	Nitrogen Dioxide 1-Hr (ppb)	Sulfur Dioxide AM (ppb)	Sulfur Dioxide 1-Hr (ppb)	Sulfur Dioxide 24-Hr (ppb)
MSA[1] Level	23.087	65	1.28	11	6.7
NAAQS[2]	53	100	30	75	140
Met NAAQS[2]	Yes	Yes	Yes	Yes	Yes

Note: Data from exceptional events are not included; (1) Data covers the Riverside-San Bernardino-Ontario, CA—see Appendix B for areas included; (2) National Ambient Air Quality Standards; ppb = parts per billion; n/a not available

Concentrations: Nitrogen Dioxide AM—highest arithmetic mean concentration; Nitrogen Dioxide 1-Hr—highest 98th percentile 1-hour daily maximum concentration; Sulfur Dioxide AM—highest annual mean concentration; Sulfur Dioxide 1-Hr—highest 99th percentile 1-hour daily maximum concentration; Sulfur Dioxide 24-Hr—highest second maximum 24-hour concentration

Source: U.S. Environmental Protection Agency, CBSA Factbook 2010, Air Quality Statistics by City, 2010

Drinking Water

Water System Name	Pop. Served	Primary Water Source Type	Violations[1]	
			Health Based	Monitoring/ Reporting
Rancho California Water District	116,188	Surface	0	0

Note: (1) Based on violation data from January 1, 2011 to December 31, 2011 (includes unresolved violations from earlier years)

Source: U.S. Environmental Protection Agency, Office of Ground Water and Drinking Water, Safe Drinking Water Information System (based on data extracted April 18, 2012)

Thousand Oaks, California

Background

Thousand Oaks, named for the many oak trees that line area hills, was created in 1964 as part of a master city planned by the Janss Corporation. The new city grew from a total plan that incorporates controlled growth and a balanced mix of residential areas, modern shopping centers, schools, business and industrial centers, parks and open spaces.

The area's first recorded European history dates back to 1542, when explorer Juan Rodriguez Cabrillo discovered Alta, California, and explored several local harbors. He placed his country's flag at Point Mugu and claimed the land for the King of Spain. Thereafter, the region remained undisturbed for two and a half centuries until Spanish explorers and missionaries arrived. In the early 1800's, a Spanish governor granted over 48,000 acres of land to two loyal soldiers. One of the grants included the area that became known as the Conejo Valley, (valley of the rabbits), within which Thousand Oaks was later established. For the next half-century, vaqueros roamed the terrain and tended great herds of cattle. In the late 1800s, the valley began to be parceled into ranchos. In the early 1900s, the Janss family, developers of several Southern California subdivisions, purchased 10,000 acres of Conejo farmland. Field crops, orchards, chicken, hog, and dairy farms dotted the landscape when the first local highway made it possible for motorists to escape Los Angeles to see the scenic countryside.

Today the city supports an active "slow growth" city council initiative that encourages protecting the town's oak trees and open land. More than 14,000 acres have been preserved, containing more than 75 miles of trails.

The Thousand Oaks economy centers on a small range of businesses focusing on biotechnology, electronics, and financing. Amgen and Baxter Healthcare offer many high-tech jobs, while Countrywide and Verizon Wireless manage regional offices. Other employers include General Dynamics, Jafra Cosmetics, and WellPoint Health Networks. Thousand Oaks is also home to many entrepreneurs and welcomes small business to the area. As a suburb, many residents also commute to neighboring Los Angeles and Westlake Village, where the regional headquarters of many large businesses, such as General Motors, are located. Commuters are served by a new regional transportation center that offers bus and shuttle lines to Los Angeles, Oxnard, Ventura, Simi Valley, and Santa Barbara.

Residents of Thousand Oaks enjoy a Mediterranean climate—12 miles inland from the Pacific Ocean—with average temperatures between 65 and 75 degrees during the summer and 53 to 69 degrees in the winter. Rain is nearly nonexistent from May through August, and like most of Southern California, sunshine prevails year round.

Rankings

Business/Finance Rankings

- *American City Business Journals* ranked America's 261 largest cities in terms of their resident's wealth. Thousand Oaks ranked #2. Criteria: per capita income; median household income; percentage of households with annual incomes of $200,000 or more; median home value. *American City Business Journals, "Where the Money Is: America's Wealth Centers," August 18, 2008*
- The Oxnard metro area appeared on the Milken Institute "2011 Best Performing Metros" list. Rank: #124 out of 200 large metro areas. Criteria: job growth; wage and salary growth; high-tech output growth. *Milken Institute, "2011 Best Performing Metros"*
- Oxnard was ranked #17 out of 145 regions worldwide in terms of its "Knowledge Competitiveness Index." The index attempts to measure the knowledge-based development taking place throughout the world and is based on 19 measures of economic performance that indicate a region's ability to translate its knowledge capacity into economic value. *Centre for International Competitiveness, World Knowledge Competitiveness Index 2008*
- *Forbes* ranked the 200 most populous metro areas in the U.S. in terms of the "Best Places for Business and Careers." The Oxnard metro area was ranked #118. Criteria: costs (business and living); job growth (past and projected); income growth; educational attainment; projected economic growth; crime; cultural and recreational opportunities; net migration patterns; number of highly ranked colleges. *Forbes, "Best Places for Business and Careers," June 2011*

Children/Family Rankings

- The Oxnard metro area was selected as one of the "Best Cities for Relocating Families" by Worldwide ERC and Primacy Relocation. The 2008 study looked at nearly 50 factors important to relocating families including: recent job growth; nearby top-ranked colleges; in-state tuition for four-year public colleges; population growth since 2000; pediatricians per 100,000 population; and a Green Living index. *Worldwide ERC and Primacy Relocation, "2008 Best Cities for Relocating Families"*

Dating/Romance Rankings

- The Oxnard metro area was selected as one of the "Best Cities for Relocating Singles" by Worldwide ERC and Primacy Relocation. The area ranked #32 out of the 100 largest metro areas in the U.S. Criteria: recent job growth; recent singles population growth; overall population growth; affordable rental housing; cost-of-living index; expanded arts and recreation opportunities; ratio of single men and single women; affordability of quality higher education (including state residency requirements); diversity index; climate; population density. *Worldwide ERC and Primacy Relocation, "2008 Best Cities for Relocating Singles"*

Education Rankings

- Oxnard was identified as one of the 100 "smartest" metro areas in the U.S. The area ranked #53. Criteria: the editors rated the collective brainpower of the 100 largest metro areas in the U.S. based on their residents' educational attainment. *American City Business Journals, April 14, 2008*
- Thousand Oaks was identified as one of America's most inventive cities by *The Daily Beast*. The city ranked #17 out of 25. The 200 largest cities in the U.S. were ranked by the number of patents (applied and approved) per capita. *The Daily Beast, "The 25 Most Inventive Cities," October 2, 2011*
- Oxnard was identified as one of "America's Brainiest Bastions" by *Portfolio.com*. The metro area ranked #65 out of 200. *Portfolio.com* analyzed levels of educational attainment in the nation's 200 largest metropolitan areas. The editors established scores for five levels of educational attainment, based on relative earning power of adult workers age 25 or older. Scores were determined by comparing the median income for all workers with the median income for those workers at a specified educational level. *Portfolio.com, "America's Brainiest Bastions," December 1, 2010*

Environmental Rankings

- Thousand Oaks was selected as one of 22 "Smarter Cities" for energy by the Natural Resources Defense Council. Criteria: investment in green power; energy efficiency measures; conservation. *Natural Resources Defense Council, "2010 Smarter Cities," July 19, 2010*
- Thousand Oaks was selected as one of "America's 50 Greenest Cities" by *Popular Science*. The city ranked #48. Criteria: electricity; transportation; green living; recycling and green perspective. *Popular Science, February 2008*
- 100 of the largest metro areas in the U.S. were analyzed in terms of their current drought severity. The Oxnard metro area ranked #3 (#1 = driest). The rankings were based on statistics such as long-term precipitation trends and patterns and the Palmer drought indices. *Sperling's BestPlaces, www.BestPlaces.net, "America's Drought-Riskiest Cities," November 2007*
- The Oxnard metro area appeared in *Country Home's* "Best Green Places" report. The area ranked #55 out of 379. Criteria: official energy policies; green power; green buildings; availability of fresh, locally grown food. *Country Home, "Best Green Places," 2008*

Health/Fitness Rankings

- Oxnard was identified as a "2011 Asthma Capital." The area ranked #80 out of the nation's 100 largest metropolitan areas. Twelve factors were used to identify the most challenging places to live for people with asthma: estimated prevalence; self-reported prevalence; crude death rate for asthma; annual pollen score; annual air quality; public smoking laws; number of board-certified asthma specialists; school inhaler access laws; rescue medication use; controller medication use; uninsured rate; poverty rate. *Asthma and Allergy Foundation of America, "2011 Asthma Capitals"*
- Oxnard was identified as a "2011 Fall Allergy Capital." The area ranked #81 out of 100. Three groups of factors were used to identify the most severe cities for people with allergies during the fall season: annual pollen levels; medicine utilization; access to board-certified allergists. *Asthma and Allergy Foundation of America, "2011 Fall Allergy Capitals"*
- Oxnard was identified as a "2012 Spring Allergy Capital." The area ranked #77 out of 100. Three groups of factors were used to identify the most severe cities for people with allergies during the spring season: annual pollen levels; medicine utilization; access to board-certified allergists. *Asthma and Allergy Foundation of America, "2012 Spring Allergy Capitals"*
- The Oxnard metro area appeared in the 2011 Gallup-Healthways Well-Being Index. The index, based on interviews with more than 350,000 Americans, measured jobs, finances, physical health, emotional state of mind and communities. The metro area ranked #61 out of 190. Criteria: life evaluation; emotional health; work environment; physical health; healthy behaviors; basic access (basic needs optimal for a healthy life, such as access to food and medicine, having health insurance and feeling safe while walking at night). *Gallup-Healthways, "State of Well-Being 2011"*

Real Estate Rankings

- *Fortune* ranked the 100 largest metro areas in the U.S. in terms of projected median home price change in 2010. The Oxnard metro area ranked #88. *Fortune, "The 2010 Housing Outlook," December 9, 2009*
- The Oxnard metro area was identified as one of the most expensive places to rent in the U.S. The area ranked #88 out of 10 markets with an average effective rent of $1,400 per month. The rental figures cover apartment properties in complexes with 40 or more units (20 or more units in California and Arizona). The figures are blended average rents, which include all unit sizes. Effective rents include free rent incentives and other landlord concessions. *Wall Street Journal Online, January 17, 2008*
- The nation's largest metro areas were analyzed in terms of the percentage of households entering some stage of foreclosure in 2011. The Oxnard metro area ranked #16 out of 20 (#1 = highest foreclosure rate). *RealtyTrac, 2011 Year-End Foreclosure Market Report, January 12, 2012*

- The Center for Housing Policy ranked 210 U.S. metropolitan areas by the fair market rent for a two-bedroom unit. The Oxnard metro area was ranked #8. (#1 = most expensive) with a rent of $1,479. Criteria: Fair Market Rent (FMR) in effect during the fourth quarter of 2009 based on HUD's fiscal year 2010 FMRs. *The Center for Housing Policy, "Paycheck to Paycheck: Most to Least Expensive Rental Markets in 2009"*
- The Oxnard metro area was identified as one of the top 20 cities in terms of decreasing home equity. The metro area was ranked #5. Criteria: percentage of home equity relative to the home's current value. *Forbes.com, "Where Americans are Losing Home Equity Most," May 1, 2010*
- The Oxnard metro area was identified as one of the best U.S. markets to invest in rental property" by HomeVestors and Local Market Monitor. The area ranked #87 out of 100. Criteria: risk-return premium relative to national average. *HomeVestors and Local Market Monitor, "Best 100 U.S. Markets to Invest in Rental Property," March 9, 2012*

Safety Rankings

- Allstate ranked the 193 largest cities in America in terms of driver safety. Thousand Oaks ranked #99. In addition, drivers were 8.4% more likely to have had an accident compared to the national average. Allstate researchers analyzed internal property damage reported claims over a two-year period (from January 2008 to December 2009) to protect findings from external influences such as weather or road construction. A weighted average of the two-year numbers determined the annual percentages. The report defines an auto crash as any collision resulting in a property damage claim. *Allstate, "2011 Allstate America's Best Drivers Report™"*
- Thousand Oaks was identified as one of the safest mid-size cities in America by CQ Press. All 234 cities with populations of 100,000 to 499,999 that reported crime rates in 2010 for murder, rape, robbery, aggravated assault, burglary, and motor vehicle thefts were ranked. The city ranked #4 out of the top 10. *CQ Press, City Crime Rankings 2011-2012*
- The National Insurance Crime Bureau ranked 366 metro areas in the U.S. in terms of per capita rates of vehicle theft. The Oxnard metro area ranked #174 (#1 = highest rate). Criteria: number of vehicle theft offenses per 100,000 inhabitants in 2010. *National Insurance Crime Bureau, "Hot Spots," June 21, 2011*

Sports/Recreation Rankings

- Thousand Oaks was chosen as a bicycle friendly community by the League of American Bicyclists. A Bicycle Friendly Community welcomes cyclists by providing safe accommodation for cycling and encouraging people to bike for transportation and recreation. There are four award levels: Platinum; Gold; Silver; and Bronze. The community achieved an award level of Bronze. *League of American Bicyclists, "Bicycle Friendly Community Master List 2011"*

Technology Rankings

- The Oxnard metro area was selected as one of "America's Most Innovative Cities" by *Forbes*. The metro area was ranked #17 out of 20. Criteria: patents per capita; venture capital investment per capita; ratio of high-tech, science and "creative" jobs. *Forbes, "America's Most Innovative Cities," May 24, 2010*

Women/Minorities Rankings

- Oxnard was ranked #20 out of 100 metro areas in *SELF Magazine's* ranking of America's healthiest places for women." A panel of experts came up with more than 50 criteria including death and disease rates, environmental indicators, community resources, and lifestyle habits. *SELF Magazine, "Secrets of America's Healthiest Women," December 2008*

Business Environment

CITY FINANCES

City Government Finances

Component	2009 ($000)	2009 ($ per capita)
Total Revenues	170,762	1,384
Total Expenditures	175,064	1,419
Debt Outstanding	158,787	1,287
Cash and Securities[1]	268,112	2,174

Note: (1) Cash and security holdings of a government at the close of its fiscal year, including those of its dependent agencies, utilities, and liquor stores.
Source: U.S Census Bureau, State & Local Government Finances 2009

City Government Revenue by Source

Source	2009 ($000)	2009 ($ per capita)
General Revenue		
From Federal Government	2,451	20
From State Government	8,421	68
From Local Governments	0	0
Taxes		
Property	52,430	425
Sales and Gross Receipts	31,789	258
Personal Income	0	0
Corporate Income	0	0
Motor Vehicle License	0	0
Other Taxes	7,334	59
Current Charges	37,727	306
Liquor Store	0	0
Utility	18,320	149
Employee Retirement	0	0

Source: U.S Census Bureau, State & Local Government Finances 2009

City Government Expenditures by Function

Function	2009 ($000)	2009 ($ per capita)	2009 (%)
General Direct Expenditures			
Air Transportation	0	0	0.0
Corrections	0	0	0.0
Education	0	0	0.0
Employment Security Administration	0	0	0.0
Financial Administration	5,883	48	3.4
Fire Protection	0	0	0.0
General Public Buildings	0	0	0.0
Governmental Administration, Other	23,912	194	13.7
Health	1,157	9	0.7
Highways	25,943	210	14.8
Hospitals	0	0	0.0
Housing and Community Development	12,543	102	7.2
Interest on General Debt	7,741	63	4.4
Judicial and Legal	4,401	36	2.5
Libraries	9,843	80	5.6
Parking	0	0	0.0
Parks and Recreation	10,641	86	6.1
Police Protection	102	1	0.1
Public Welfare	0	0	0.0
Sewerage	17,559	142	10.0
Solid Waste Management	1,344	11	0.8
Veterans' Services	0	0	0.0
Liquor Store	0	0	0.0
Utility	22,447	182	12.8
Employee Retirement	0	0	0.0

Source: U.S Census Bureau, State & Local Government Finances 2009

Municipal Bond Ratings

Area	Moody's	S&P	Fitch
City	n/a	n/a	n/a

Rating Systems (shown in declining order of credit quality): Moody's–Aaa, Aa, A, Baa, Ba, B, Caa, Ca, C (numerical modifiers 1, 2, and 3 are added to letter-rating); S&P–AAA, AA, A, BBB, BB, B, CCC, CC, C; Fitch–AAA, AA, A, BBB, BB, B, CCC, CC, C. Ratings may be modified by the addition of a plus or minus sign to show relative standing within the major rating categories.
Notes: n/a Not Available; w/d Withdrawn (1) Not Reviewed; (2) Issuer Rating/No General Obligation; (3) Standard and Poor's Issue Credit Rating (ICR) is a current opinion of an obliger with respect to a specific financial obligation, a specific class of financial obligations, or a specific financial program.
Source: U.S. Census Bureau, 2012 Statistical Abstract, Bond Ratings for City Governments by Largest Cities: 2010

DEMOGRAPHICS

Population Growth

Area	1990 Census	2000 Census	2010 Census	Population Growth (%) 1990-2000	Population Growth (%) 2000-2010
City	104,661	117,005	126,683	11.8	8.3
MSA[1]	669,016	753,197	823,318	12.6	9.3
U.S.	248,709,873	281,421,906	308,745,538	13.2	9.7

Note: (1) Figures cover the Oxnard-Thousand Oaks-Ventura, CA Metropolitan Statistical Area—see Appendix B for areas included
Source: U.S. Census Bureau, 2010 Census

Household Size

Area	Persons in Household (%) One	Two	Three	Four	Five	Six	Seven or More	Average Household Size
City	21.2	32.8	17.6	17.1	7.0	2.6	1.8	2.73
MSA[1]	19.9	29.3	16.9	16.3	8.6	4.1	4.9	3.04
U.S.	26.7	32.8	16.1	13.4	6.5	2.6	1.9	2.58

Note: (1) Figures cover the Oxnard-Thousand Oaks-Ventura, CA Metropolitan Statistical Area—see Appendix B for areas included
Source: U.S. Census Bureau, 2010 Census

Race

Area	White Alone[2] (%)	Black Alone[2] (%)	Asian Alone[2] (%)	AIAN[3] Alone[2] (%)	NHOPI[4] Alone[2] (%)	Other Race Alone[2] (%)	Two or More Races (%)
City	80.3	1.3	8.7	0.4	0.1	5.4	3.8
MSA[1]	68.7	1.8	6.7	1.0	0.2	17.0	4.5
U.S.	72.4	12.6	4.8	0.9	0.2	6.2	2.9

Note: (1) Figures cover the Oxnard-Thousand Oaks-Ventura, CA Metropolitan Statistical Area—see Appendix B for areas included; (2) Alone is defined as not being in combination with one or more other races; (3) American Indian and Alaska Native; (4) Native Hawaiian and Other Pacific Islander
Source: U.S. Census Bureau, 2010 Census

Hispanic or Latino Origin

Area	Hispanic or Latino (%)	Mexican (%)	Puerto Rican (%)	Cuban (%)	Other Hispanic or Latino (%)
City	16.8	11.6	0.4	0.2	4.7
MSA[1]	40.3	35.6	0.4	0.2	4.1
U.S.	16.3	10.3	1.5	0.6	4.0

Note: Persons of Hispanic or Latino origin can be of any race; (1) Figures cover the Oxnard-Thousand Oaks-Ventura, CA Metropolitan Statistical Area—see Appendix B for areas included
Source: U.S. Census Bureau, 2010 Census

Segregation

Type	Segregation Indices[1]				Percent Change		
	1990	2000	2010	2010 Rank[2]	1990-2000	1990-2010	2000-2010
Black/White	47.8	48.9	39.9	91	1.1	-7.9	-9.0
Asian/White	30.0	31.0	31.2	87	1.0	1.2	0.2
Hispanic/White	52.3	56.1	54.6	13	3.8	2.2	-1.6

Note: Figures are based on an analysis of 1990, 2000, and 2010 Census Decennial Census tract data by William H. Frey, Brookings Institution and the University of Michigan Social Science Data Analysis Network. In this analysis all racial groups (whites, blacks, and asians) are non-Hispanic members of those races. Hispanics are shown as a separate category; All figures cover the Metropolitan Statistical Area (see Appendix B for areas included); (1) Segregation Indices are Dissimilarity Indices that measure the degree to which the minority group is distributed differently than whites across census tracts. They range from 0 (complete integration) to 100 (complete segregation) where the value indicates the percentage of the minority group that needs to move to be distributed exactly like whites; (2) Ranges from 1 (most segregated) to 102 (least segregated); n/a not available.
Source: www.CensusScope.org

Ancestry

Area	German	Irish	English	American	Italian	Polish	French[2]	Scottish	Dutch
City	14.4	12.9	10.7	4.1	9.2	3.8	2.9	2.5	1.8
MSA[1]	11.9	9.4	8.7	3.6	5.2	2.3	2.5	2.0	1.3
U.S.	16.1	11.6	8.8	6.1	5.7	3.2	3.0	1.9	1.6

Note: Figures are the percentage of the total population reporting a particular ancestry. The nine most commonly reported ancestries in the U.S. are shown. Figures include multiple ancestries (e.g. if a person reported being Irish and Italian, they were included in both columns); (1) Figures cover the Oxnard-Thousand Oaks-Ventura, CA Metropolitan Statistical Area—see Appendix B for areas included; (2) Excludes Basque
Source: U.S. Census Bureau, 2008-2010 American Community Survey 3-Year Estimates

Foreign-Born Population

Area	Percent of Population Born in								
	Any Foreign Country	Mexico	Asia	Europe	Carribean	South America	Central America[2]	Africa	Canada
City	19.3	4.3	7.0	4.0	0.3	0.9	1.8	0.2	0.6
MSA[1]	23.2	13.6	5.2	1.8	0.1	0.6	1.2	0.2	0.4
U.S.	12.8	3.8	3.6	1.6	1.2	0.9	1.0	0.5	0.3

Note: (1) Figures cover the Oxnard-Thousand Oaks-Ventura, CA Metropolitan Statistical Area—see Appendix B for areas included; (2) Excludes Mexico.
Source: U.S. Census Bureau, 2008-2010 American Community Survey 3-Year Estimates

Marital Status

Area	Never Married	Now Married[2]	Separated	Widowed	Divorced
City	27.9	56.9	1.2	4.9	9.2
MSA[1]	31.2	51.8	1.7	5.1	10.2
U.S.	31.6	49.6	2.2	6.1	10.7

Note: Figures are percentages and cover the population 15 years of age and older; (1) Figures cover the Oxnard-Thousand Oaks-Ventura, CA Metropolitan Statistical Area—see Appendix B for areas included; (2) Excludes separated
Source: U.S. Census Bureau, 2008-2010 American Community Survey 3-Year Estimates

Age

Area	Percent of Population							Median Age
	Under Age 5	Age 5 to 17	Age 18 to 34	Age 35 to 49	Age 50 to 64	Age 65 to 79	80 Years and Over	
City	5.2	18.5	17.9	22.5	21.2	10.4	4.2	41.5
MSA[1]	6.7	19.0	22.7	21.1	18.8	8.4	3.3	36.2
U.S.	6.5	17.5	23.2	20.7	19.0	9.4	3.6	37.2

Note: (1) Figures cover the Oxnard-Thousand Oaks-Ventura, CA Metropolitan Statistical Area—see Appendix B for areas included
Source: U.S. Census Bureau, 2010 Census

Male/Female Ratio

Area	Males	Females	Males per 100 Females
City	61,989	64,694	95.8
MSA[1]	408,969	414,349	98.7
U.S.	151,781,326	156,964,212	96.7

Note: (1) Figures cover the Oxnard-Thousand Oaks-Ventura, CA Metropolitan Statistical Area—see Appendix B for areas included
Source: U.S. Census Bureau, 2010 Census

Religious Groups

Area	Catholic	Baptist	Non-Den.	Methodist[2]	Lutheran	LDS[3]	Pente-costal	Presby-terian[4]	Muslim[5]	Judaism
MSA[1]	28.2	1.9	4.1	1.1	1.5	2.5	1.3	0.7	0.7	0.4
U.S.	19.1	9.3	4.0	4.0	2.3	2.0	1.9	1.6	0.8	0.7

Note: Figures are the number of adherents as a percentage of the total population; (1) Figures cover the Oxnard-Thousand Oaks-Ventura, CA Metropolitan Statistical Area—see Appendix B for areas included; (2) Methodist/Pietist; (3) Latter Day Saints; (4) Reformed; (5) Figures are estimates
Source: Association of Statisticians of American Religious Bodies, 2010 U.S. Religion Census: Religious Congregations & Membership Study

ECONOMY

Gross Metropolitan Product

Area	2007	2008	2009	2010	2010 Rank[2]
MSA[1]	36.0	34.6	34.3	35.5	63

Note: Figures are in billions of dollars; (1) Figures cover the Oxnard-Thousand Oaks-Ventura, CA Metropolitan Statistical Area—see Appendix B for areas included; (2) Rank ranges from 1 to 363
Source: The United States Conference of Mayors, "U.S. Metro Economies: GMP and Employment Forecasts," June 2011

Economic Growth

Area	2007-2009 (%)	2010 (%)	2011 (%)	Rank[2]
MSA[1]	-3.8	3.3	1.9	300
U.S.	-1.3	2.9	2.5	–

Note: Figures are real Gross Metropolitan Product growth rates and represent annual average percent change; (1) Figures cover the Oxnard-Thousand Oaks-Ventura, CA Metropolitan Statistical Area—see Appendix B for areas included; (2) Rank ranges from 1 to 363
Source: The United States Conference of Mayors, "U.S. Metro Economies: GMP and Employment Forecasts," June 2011

Metropolitan Area Exports

Area	2005	2006	2007	2008	2009	2010	2010 Rank[2]
MSA[1]	2,072.6	2,375.3	2,424.9	2,579.1	2,483.8	2,611.2	70

Note: Figures are in millions of dollars; (1) Figures cover the Oxnard-Thousand Oaks-Ventura, CA Metropolitan Statistical Area—see Appendix B for areas included; (2) Rank ranges from 1 to 369
Source: U.S. Department of Commerce, International Trade Administration, Office of Trade & Industry Information, Manufacturing & Services, data extracted April 2, 2012

INCOME

Income

Area	Per Capita ($)	Median Household ($)	Average Household ($)
City	44,263	99,980	122,170
MSA[1]	31,679	73,907	94,648
U.S.	26,942	51,222	70,116

Note: (1) Figures cover the Oxnard-Thousand Oaks-Ventura, CA Metropolitan Statistical Area—see Appendix B for areas included
Source: U.S. Census Bureau, 2008-2010 American Community Survey 3-Year Estimates

Household Income Distribution

Area	Percent of Households Earning							
	Under $15,000	$15,000 -24,999	$25,000 -34,999	$35,000 -49,999	$50,000 -74,999	$75,000 -99,000	$100,000 -149,999	$150,000 and up
City	5.7	5.3	5.9	8.0	12.9	12.3	22.4	27.6
MSA[1]	7.3	7.5	7.6	10.9	17.3	13.7	19.1	16.7
U.S.	13.0	11.0	10.6	14.2	18.5	12.1	12.2	8.4

Note: (1) Figures cover the Oxnard-Thousand Oaks-Ventura, CA Metropolitan Statistical Area—see Appendix B for areas included
Source: U.S. Census Bureau, 2008-2010 American Community Survey 3-Year Estimates

Poverty Rate

Area	All Ages	Under 18 Years Old	18 to 64 Years Old	65 Years and Over
City	5.6	6.8	5.2	5.4
MSA[1]	9.8	13.2	9.0	7.0
U.S.	14.4	20.1	13.1	9.4

Note: Figures are percentage of people whose income during the past 12 months was below the poverty level; (1) Figures cover the Oxnard-Thousand Oaks-Ventura, CA Metropolitan Statistical Area—see Appendix B for areas included
Source: U.S. Census Bureau, 2008-2010 American Community Survey 3-Year Estimates

Personal Bankruptcy Filing Rate

Area	2006	2007	2008	2009	2010	2011
Ventura County	0.77	1.68	3.17	5.04	6.37	5.94
U.S.	2.00	2.73	3.53	4.61	4.97	4.37

Note: Numbers are per 1,000 population and include Chapter 7 and Chapter 13 filings
Source: Federal Deposit Insurance Corporation, Regional Economic Conditions, March 9, 2012

EMPLOYMENT

Labor Force and Employment

Area	Civilian Labor Force			Workers Employed		
	Dec. 2010	Dec. 2011	% Chg.	Dec. 2010	Dec. 2011	% Chg.
City	70,198	71,202	1.4	64,388	66,037	2.6
MSA[1]	427,638	432,361	1.1	382,087	391,874	2.6
U.S.	153,156,000	153,373,000	0.1	139,159,000	140,681,000	1.1

Note: Data is not seasonally adjusted and covers workers 16 years of age and older; (1) Metropolitan Statistical Area—see Appendix B for areas included
Source: Bureau of Labor Statistics, http://stats.bls.gov

Unemployment Rate

Area	2011											
	Jan.	Feb.	Mar.	Apr.	May	Jun.	Jul.	Aug.	Sep.	Oct.	Nov.	Dec.
City	8.5	8.1	8.1	7.5	7.3	8.0	8.2	8.2	7.8	7.6	7.4	7.3
MSA[1]	10.9	10.5	10.4	9.7	9.5	10.3	10.6	10.5	10.1	9.8	9.5	9.4
U.S.	9.8	9.5	9.2	8.7	8.7	9.3	9.3	9.1	8.8	8.5	8.2	8.3

Note: Data is not seasonally adjusted and covers workers 16 years of age and older; All figures are percentages; (1) Metropolitan Statistical Area—see Appendix B for areas included
Source: Bureau of Labor Statistics, http://stats.bls.gov

Projected Unemployment Rate

Area	2010 (%)	2011 (%)	2012 (%)	2013 (%)
MSA[1]	10.8	10.0	9.5	8.8

Note: (1) Metropolitan Statistical Area—see Appendix B for areas included
Source: The United States Conference of Mayors, "U.S. Metro Economies: GMP and Employment Forecasts," June 2011

Employment by Occupation

Occupation Classification	City (%)	MSA[1] (%)	U.S. (%)
Management, Business, Science, and Arts	50.5	37.6	35.6
Natural Resources, Construction, and Maintenance	5.0	11.1	9.5
Production, Transportation, and Material Moving	5.1	9.5	12.1
Sales and Office	25.8	25.5	25.2
Service	13.5	16.3	17.6

Note: Figures cover employed civilians 16 years of age and older; (1) Figures cover the Oxnard-Thousand Oaks-Ventura, CA Metropolitan Statistical Area—see Appendix B for areas included
Source: U.S. Census Bureau, 2008-2010 American Community Survey 3-Year Estimates

Employment by Industry

Sector	MSA[1] Number of Employees	MSA[1] Percent of Total	U.S. Percent of Total
Construction	10,600	3.8	4.1
Education and Health Services	31,800	11.4	15.2
Financial Activities	22,000	7.9	5.8
Government	45,300	16.3	16.8
Information	5,000	1.8	2.0
Leisure and Hospitality	32,300	11.6	9.9
Manufacturing	30,200	10.9	8.9
Mining and Logging	1,100	0.4	0.6
Other Services	9,000	3.2	4.0
Professional and Business Services	32,900	11.8	13.3
Retail Trade	38,800	13.9	11.5
Transportation and Utilities	6,100	2.2	3.8
Wholesale Trade	13,100	4.7	4.2

Note: Figures cover non-farm employment as of December 2011 and are not seasonally adjusted; (1) Metropolitan Statistical Area—see Appendix B for areas included
Source: Bureau of Labor Statistics, http://stats.bls.gov

Occupations with Greatest Projected Employment Growth: 2008 – 2018

Occupation[1]	2008 Employment	2018 Projected Employment	Numeric Employment Change	Percent Employment Change
Personal and Home Care Aides	346,500	504,700	158,200	45.7
Registered Nurses	236,400	297,200	60,800	25.7
Retail Salespersons	499,400	559,100	59,700	12.0
Combined Food Preparation and Serving Workers, Including Fast Food	260,600	308,800	48,200	18.5
Elementary School Teachers, Except Special Education	197,500	233,400	35,900	18.2
Office Clerks, General	372,500	407,400	34,900	9.4
Customer Service Representatives	202,200	236,600	34,400	17.0
Waiters and Waitresses	245,600	279,900	34,300	14.0
Stock Clerks and Order Fillers	207,700	237,100	29,400	14.2
Postsecondary Teachers	168,000	196,100	28,100	16.7

Note: Projections cover California; (1) Sorted by numeric employment change
Source: www.projectionscentral.com, State Occupational Projections, 2008–2018 Long-Term Projections

Fastest Growing Occupations: 2008 – 2018

Occupation[1]	2008 Employment	2018 Projected Employment	Numeric Employment Change	Percent Employment Change
Biomedical Engineers	3,100	5,600	2,500	80.6
Network Systems and Data Communications Analysts	35,000	52,600	17,600	50.3
Biochemists and Biophysicists	4,800	7,100	2,300	47.9
Medical Scientists, Except Epidemiologists	26,200	38,500	12,300	46.9
Personal and Home Care Aides	346,500	504,700	158,200	45.7
Home Health Aides	54,300	78,000	23,700	43.6
Physician Assistants	8,100	11,500	3,400	42.0
Separating, Filtering, Clarifying, Precipitating, and Still Machine Setters, Operators, and Te	7,300	10,200	2,900	39.7
Physical Therapist Aides	5,900	8,100	2,200	37.3
Electrical and Electronics Repairers, Powerhouse, Substation, and Relay	1,100	1,500	400	36.4

Note: Projections cover California; (1) Sorted by percent employment change and excludes occupations with numeric employment change less than 100
Source: www.projectionscentral.com, State Occupational Projections, 2008–2018 Long-Term Projections

Average Wages

Occupation	$/Hr.	Occupation	$/Hr.
Accountants and Auditors	36.15	Maids and Housekeeping Cleaners	10.37
Automotive Mechanics	19.58	Maintenance and Repair Workers	19.54
Bookkeepers	20.51	Marketing Managers	58.67
Carpenters	22.19	Nuclear Medicine Technologists	49.21
Cashiers	10.91	Nurses, Licensed Practical	26.90
Clerks, General Office	14.76	Nurses, Registered	36.89
Clerks, Receptionists/Information	13.87	Nursing Aides/Orderlies/Attendants	13.50
Clerks, Shipping/Receiving	15.02	Packers and Packagers, Hand	10.39
Computer Programmers	42.78	Physical Therapists	42.71
Computer Support Specialists	27.22	Postal Service Mail Carriers	25.44
Computer Systems Analysts	40.19	Real Estate Brokers	23.53
Cooks, Restaurant	11.33	Retail Salespersons	12.18
Dentists	84.35	Sales Reps., Exc. Tech./Scientific	33.22
Electrical Engineers	46.54	Sales Reps., Tech./Scientific	34.45
Electricians	26.84	Secretaries, Exc. Legal/Med./Exec.	17.73
Financial Managers	56.18	Security Guards	11.97
First-Line Supervisors/Managers, Sales	20.41	Surgeons	n/a
Food Preparation Workers	10.02	Teacher Assistants	14.50
General and Operations Managers	61.47	Teachers, Elementary School	31.30
Hairdressers/Cosmetologists	12.36	Teachers, Secondary School	29.30
Internists	69.01	Telemarketers	15.81
Janitors and Cleaners	13.84	Truck Drivers, Heavy/Tractor-Trailer	21.77
Landscaping/Groundskeeping Workers	13.35	Truck Drivers, Light/Delivery Svcs.	17.24
Lawyers	81.47	Waiters and Waitresses	10.28

Note: Wage data covers the Oxnard-Thousand Oaks-Ventura, CA Metropolitan Statistical Area—see Appendix B for areas included. Hourly wages for elementary/secondary school teachers and teacher assistants were calculated by the editors from annual wage data assuming a 40 hour work week; n/a not available.
Source: Bureau of Labor Statistics, Metro Area Occupational Employment and Wage Estimates, May 2011

RESIDENTIAL REAL ESTATE

Building Permits

Area	Single-Family 2010	Single-Family 2011	Single-Family Pct. Chg.	Multi-Family 2010	Multi-Family 2011	Multi-Family Pct. Chg.	Total 2010	Total 2011	Total Pct. Chg.
City	20	18	-10.0	15	21	40.0	35	39	11.4
MSA[1]	209	281	34.4	381	287	-24.7	590	568	-3.7
U.S.	447,311	418,498	-6.4	157,299	205,563	30.7	604,610	624,061	3.2

Note: (1) Metropolitan Statistical Area—see Appendix B for areas included; figures represent new, privately-owned housing units authorized (unadjusted data); All permit data are based on estimates with imputation.
Source: U.S. Census Bureau, Manufacturing, Mining, and Construction Statistics, Building Permits, 2010, 2011

Homeownership Rate

Area	2005 (%)	2006 (%)	2007 (%)	2008 (%)	2009 (%)	2010 (%)	2011 (%)
MSA[1]	73.4	69.8	71.4	71.7	73.1	67.1	67.0
U.S.	68.9	68.8	68.1	67.8	67.4	66.9	66.1

Note: (1) Metropolitan Statistical Area—see Appendix B for areas included
Source: U.S. Census Bureau, Housing Vacancies and Homeownership Annual Statistics: 2011

Housing Vacancy Rates

Area	Gross Vacancy Rate[2] (%)			Year-Round Vacancy Rate[3] (%)			Rental Vacancy Rate[4] (%)			Homeowner Vacancy Rate[5] (%)		
	2009	2010	2011	2009	2010	2011	2009	2010	2011	2009	2010	2011
MSA[1]	5.9	7.3	7.1	5.5	6.6	4.7	5.0	6.4	3.2	1.5	1.1	0.5
U.S.	14.5	14.3	14.2	11.3	11.3	11.1	10.6	10.2	9.5	2.6	2.6	2.5

Note: (1) Metropolitan Statistical Area—see Appendix B for areas included; (2) The percentage of the total housing inventory that is vacant; (3) The percentage of the housing inventory (excluding seasonal units) that is year-round vacant; (4) The percentage of rental inventory that is vacant for rent; (5) The percentage of homeowner inventory that is vacant for sale
Source: U.S. Census Bureau, Housing Vacancies and Homeownership Annual Statistics: 2011

TAXES

State Corporate Income Tax Rates

State	Tax Rate (%)	Income Brackets ($)	Num. of Brackets	Financial Institution Tax Rate (%)[a]	Federal Income Tax Ded.
California	8.84 (c)	Flat rate	1	10.84 (c)	No

Note: Tax rates as of January 1, 2012; (a) Rates listed are the corporate income tax rate applied to financial institutions or excise taxes based on income. Some states have other taxes based upon the value of deposits or shares; (c) The minimum corporation franchise tax in California is $800. The additional alternative minimum tax is levied at a 6.65% rate.
Source: Federation of Tax Administrators, "State Corporate Income Tax Rates, 2012"

State Individual Income Tax Rates

State	Tax Rate (%)	Income Brackets ($)	Num. of Brackets	Personal Exempt. ($)[1] Single	Personal Exempt. ($)[1] Dependents	Fed. Inc. Tax Ded.
California (a)	1.0 - 9.3 (f)	7,316 (b) - 48,029 (b)	6	102 (c)	315 (c)	No

Note: Tax rates as of January 1, 2012; Local- and county-level taxes are not included; n/a not applicable; (1) Married joint filers generally receive double the single exemption; (a) 17 states have statutory provision for automatically adjusting to the rate of inflation the dollar values of the income tax brackets, standard deductions, and/or personal exemptions. Massachusetts, Michigan, and Nebraska index the personal exemptiononly. Oregon does not index the income brackets for $125,000 and over. Because the inflation-adjustments for 2012 are not yet available in some cases, the table may report the 2011 amounts; (b) For joint returns, taxes are twice the tax on half the couple's income; (c) The personal exemption takes the form of a tax credit instead of a deduction; (f) California imposes an additional 1% tax on taxable income over $1 million, making the maximum rate 10.3% over $1 million.
Source: Federation of Tax Administrators, "State Individual Income Tax Rates, 2012"

Various State and Local Tax Rates

State	State and Local Sales and Use (%)	State Sales and Use (%)	Gasoline[1] (¢/gal.)	Cigarette[2] ($/pack)	Spirits[3] ($/gal.)	Wine[4] ($/gal.)	Beer[5] ($/gal.)
California	7.25	7.25 (b)	48.6	0.87	3.30	0.20	0.20

Note: All tax rates as of January 1, 2012 except beer, wine and spirits (September 1, 2011); (1) The American Petroleum Institute has developed a methodology for determining the average tax rate on a gallon of fuel. Rates may include any of the following: excise taxes, environmental fees, storage tank fees, other fees or taxes, general sales tax, and local taxes. In states where gasoline is subject to the general sales tax, or where the fuel tax is based on the average sale price, the average rate determined by API is sensitive to changes in the price of gasoline. States that fully or partially apply general sales taxes to gasoline: CA, CO, GA, IL, IN, MI, NY; (2) The federal excise tax of $1.0066 per pack and local taxes are not included; (3) Rates are those applicable to off-premise sales of 40% alcohol by volume (a.b.v.) distilled spirits in 750ml containers. Local excise taxes are excluded; (4) Rates are those applicable to off-premise sales of 11% a.b.v. non-carbonated wine in 750ml containers; (5) Rates are those applicable to off-premise sales of 4.7% a.b.v. beer in 12 ounce containers; (b) Three states collect a separate, uniform "local" add-on sales tax: California (1%), Utah (1.25%), Virginia (1%). These amounts are included in the state sales tax column.
Source: Tax Foundation, 2012 Facts & Figures: How Does Your State Compare?

State-Local Tax Burdens

Area	Rate (%)	Rank[1]	Per Capita Taxes Paid to Home State ($)	Total State and Local Per Capita Taxes Paid ($)	Per Capita Income ($)
California	10.6	6	3,874	4,910	46,366
U.S. Average	9.8	-	3,057	4,160	42,539

Note: Figures cover 2009; (1) Rank ranges from 1 to 50 where 1 is highest tax burden
Source: Tax Foundation, State-Local Tax Burdens, All States, 2009

State Business Tax Climate Index Rankings

State	Overall Rank	Corporate Tax Index Rank	Individual Income Tax Index Rank	Sales Tax Index Rank	Unemployment Insurance Tax Index Rank	Property Tax Index Rank
California	48	43	50	40	13	17

Note: The index is a measure of how each state's tax laws affect economic performance. The lower the rank, the more favorable a state's tax system is for business. States without a given tax are given a ranking of 1.
Source: Tax Foundation, Major Components of the State Business Tax Climate Index, FY 2012

COMMERCIAL UTILITIES

Typical Monthly Electric Bills

Area	Commercial Service ($/month) 1,500 kWh	Commercial Service ($/month) 40 kW demand 14,000 kWh	Industrial Service ($/month) 1,000 kW demand 200,000 kWh	Industrial Service ($/month) 50,000 kW demand 15,000,000 kWh
City	283	2,469	52,039	2,061,098
Average[1]	189	1,616	25,197	1,470,813

Note: Based on total rates in effect July 1, 2011; (1) average based on 184 utilities surveyed
Source: Edison Electric Institute, Typical Bills and Average Rates Report, Summer 2011

TRANSPORTATION

Means of Transportation to Work

Area	Car/Truck/Van		Public Transportation			Bicycle	Walked	Other Means	Worked at Home
	Drove Alone	Car-pooled	Bus	Subway	Railroad				
City	77.8	9.9	0.6	0.0	0.2	0.9	2.3	1.4	6.8
MSA[1]	77.0	12.6	1.0	0.0	0.2	0.6	2.1	1.1	5.3
U.S.	76.0	10.2	2.7	1.7	0.5	0.5	2.8	1.3	4.2

Note: Figures are percentages and cover workers 16 years of age and older; (1) Figures cover the Oxnard-Thousand Oaks-Ventura, CA Metropolitan Statistical Area—see Appendix B for areas included
Source: U.S. Census Bureau, 2008-2010 American Community Survey 3-Year Estimates

Travel Time to Work

Area	Less Than 10 Minutes	10 to 19 Minutes	20 to 29 Minutes	30 to 44 Minutes	45 to 59 Minutes	60 to 89 Minutes	90 Minutes or More
City	16.1	37.0	16.6	14.2	5.5	7.4	3.3
MSA[1]	14.1	33.0	19.3	18.3	6.8	5.6	2.9
U.S.	13.9	30.1	20.8	19.8	7.5	5.5	2.5

Note: Figures are percentages and include workers 16 years old and over; (1) Figures cover the Oxnard-Thousand Oaks-Ventura, CA Metropolitan Statistical Area—see Appendix B for areas included
Source: U.S. Census Bureau, 2008-2010 American Community Survey 3-Year Estimates

Travel Time Index

Area	1985	1990	1995	2000	2005	2010
Urban Area[1]	1.02	1.03	1.06	1.08	1.12	1.12
Average[2]	1.11	1.16	1.18	1.21	1.25	1.20

Note: Travel Time Index—the ratio of travel time in the peak period to the travel time at free-flow conditions. A value of 1.30 indicates a 20-minute free-flow trip takes 26 minutes in the peak. Free-flow speeds (60 mph on freeways and 35 mph on principal arterials) are used as the comparison threshold; (1) Covers the Oxnard-Ventura CA urban area; (2) average of 439 urban areas
Source: Texas Transportation Institute, Urban Mobility Report 2011, September 2011

Public Transportation

Agency Name / Mode of Transportation	Vehicles Operated in Maximum Service	Annual Unlinked Passenger Trips ('000)	Annual Passenger Miles ('000)
Thousand Oaks Transit (TOT)			
Bus (purchased transportation)	4	184.9	1,179.3
Demand Response (purchased transportation)	15	81.4	387.7

Source: Federal Transit Administration, National Transit Database, 2010

Air Transportation

Airport Name and Code / Type of Service	Passenger Airlines[1]	Passenger Enplanements	Freight Carriers[2]	Freight (lbs.)
Los Angeles International (45 miles) (LAX)				
Domestic service (U.S. carriers - 2011)	29	22,395,162	27	706,902,661
International service (U.S. carriers - 2010)	12	1,675,488	14	146,137,036

Note: (1) Includes all U.S.-based major, minor and commuter airlines that carried at least one passenger during the year; (2) Includes all U.S.-based airlines and freight carriers that transported at least one pound of freight during the year
Source: Bureau of Transportation Statistics, The Intermodal Transportation Database, Air Carriers: T-100 Domestic Market (U.S. Carriers), 2011; Bureau of Transportation Statistics, The Intermodal Transportation Database, Air Carriers: T-100 International Market (U.S. Carriers), 2010

Other Transportation Statistics

Major Highways:	SR-101
Amtrak Service:	No
Major Waterways/Ports:	Near Pacific Ocean

Source: Amtrak.com; Google Maps

BUSINESSES

Major Business Headquarters

Company Name	Rankings	
	Fortune[1]	Forbes[2]
Amgen	163	-

Note: (1) Fortune 500—companies that produce a 10-K are ranked 1 to 500 based on 2010 revenue; (2) all private companies with at least $2 billion in annual revenue are ranked 1 to 212; companies listed are headquartered in the city; dashes indicate no ranking
Source: Fortune, "Fortune 500," May 23, 2011; Forbes, "America's Largest Private Companies," November 16, 2011

Fast-Growing Businesses

According to *Inc.*, Thousand Oaks is home to one of America's 500 fastest-growing private companies: **PaymentMax** (#11). Criteria: must be an independent, privately-held, for-profit, U.S. corporation, proprietorship or partnership; revenues must be at least $80,000 in 2007 and $2 million in 2010; must have four-year operating/sales history. Holding companies, regulated banks, and utilities were excluded. *Inc., "America's 500 Fastest-Growing Private Companies," September 2011*

Minority- and Women-Owned Businesses

Group	All Firms		Firms with Paid Employees			
	Firms	Sales ($000)	Firms	Sales ($000)	Employees	Payroll ($000)
Asian	(s)	(s)	(s)	(s)	(s)	(s)
Black	156	52,537	35	48,577	1,551	17,829
Hispanic	1,004	170,456	(s)	(s)	(s)	(s)
Women	(s)	(s)	(s)	(s)	(s)	(s)
All Firms	18,106	52,876,110	4,479	51,989,284	63,488	3,830,882

Note: Figures cover firms located in the city; minority- and women-owned business are defined as firms in which the corresponding group own 51% or more of the stock or equity of the company; (s) estimates are suppressed when publication standards are not met
Source: U.S. Census Bureau, 2007 Economic Census, Survey of Business Owners

HOTELS

Hotels/Motels

Area	5 Star		4 Star		3 Star		2 Star		1 Star		Not Rated	
	Num.	Pct.[3]	Num.	Pct.[3]	Num.	Pct.[3]	Num.	Pct.[3]	Num.	Pct.[3]	Num.	Pct.[3]
City[1]	1	2.4	0	0.0	17	40.5	20	47.6	0	0.0	4	9.5
Total[2]	133	0.9	940	6.5	4,569	31.8	7,033	48.9	351	2.4	1,343	9.3

Note: (1) Figures cover Thousand Oaks and vicinity; (2) Figures cover all 100 cities in this book; (3) Percentage of hotels which have a given star rating; Star ratings are determined by expedia.com and offer an indication of the general quality of a particular hotel.
Source: expedia.com, April 25, 2012

The Oxnard-Thousand Oaks-Ventura, CA metro area is home to one of the best hotels in the U.S. according to *Travel & Leisure*: **Ojai Valley Inn & Spa** (#169). Criteria: service; location; rooms; food; and value. *Travel & Leisure, "T+L 500, The World's Best Hotels 2012"*

EVENT SITES

Major Stadiums, Arenas, and Auditoriums

Name	Max. Capacity
Fred Kavli Theatre for the Performing Arts	1,800

Source: Original research

Living Environment

COST OF LIVING

Cost of Living Index

Composite Index	Groceries	Housing	Utilities	Trans-portation	Health Care	Misc. Goods/Services
n/a	n/a	n/a	n/a	n/a	n/a	n/a

Note: U.S. = 100; n/a not available
Source: The Council for Community and Economic Research, ACCRA Cost of Living Index, 2011

Grocery Prices

Area[1]	T-Bone Steak ($/pound)	Frying Chicken ($/pound)	Whole Milk ($/half gal.)	Eggs ($/dozen)	Orange Juice ($/64 oz.)	Coffee ($/11.5 oz.)
City[2]	n/a	n/a	n/a	n/a	n/a	n/a
Avg.	9.25	1.18	2.22	1.66	3.19	4.40
Min.	6.70	0.88	1.31	0.95	2.46	2.94
Max.	14.30	2.16	3.50	3.18	4.75	6.83

Note: (1) Values for the local area are compared with the average, minimum and maximum values for all 335 areas in the Cost of Living Index; (2) Figures cover the Thousand Oaks CA urban area; n/a not available; **T-Bone Steak** *(price per pound);* **Frying Chicken** *(price per pound, whole fryer);* **Whole Milk** *(half gallon carton);* **Eggs** *(price per dozen, Grade A, large);* **Orange Juice** *(64 oz. Tropicana or Florida Natural);* **Coffee** *(11.5 oz. can, vacuum-packed, Maxwell House, Hills Bros, or Folgers).*
Source: The Council for Community and Economic Research, ACCRA Cost of Living Index, 2011

Housing and Utility Costs

Area[1]	New Home Price ($)	Apartment Rent ($/month)	All Electric ($/month)	Part Electric ($/month)	Other Energy ($/month)	Telephone ($/month)
City[2]	n/a	n/a	n/a	n/a	n/a	n/a
Avg.	285,990	839	163.23	89.00	77.52	26.92
Min.	188,005	460	125.58	45.39	33.89	17.98
Max.	1,197,028	3,244	339.16	181.97	348.69	40.01

Note: (1) Values for the local area are compared with the average, minimum and maximum values for all 335 areas in the Cost of Living Index; (2) Figures cover the Thousand Oaks CA urban area; n/a not available; **New Home Price** *(2,400 sf living area, 8,000 sf lot, in urban area with full utilities);* **Apartment Rent** *(950 sf 2 bedroom/1.5 or 2 bath, unfurnished, excluding all utilities except water);* **All Electric** *(average monthly cost for an all-electric home);* **Part Electric** *(average monthly cost for a part-electric home);* **Other Energy** *(average monthly cost for natural gas, fuel oil, coal, wood, and any other forms of energy except electricity);* **Telephone** *(price includes basic monthly rate for a private residential line plus additional local usage charges incurred by a family of four).*
Source: The Council for Community and Economic Research, ACCRA Cost of Living Index, 2011

Health Care, Transportation, and Other Costs

Area[1]	Doctor ($/visit)	Dentist ($/visit)	Optometrist ($/visit)	Gasoline ($/gallon)	Beauty Salon ($/visit)	Men's Shirt ($)
City[2]	n/a	n/a	n/a	n/a	n/a	n/a
Avg.	93.88	81.72	90.54	3.48	32.65	25.06
Min.	60.00	55.33	53.66	3.18	19.78	13.44
Max.	154.98	145.97	183.72	4.31	63.21	46.00

Note: (1) Values for the local area are compared with the average, minimum and maximum values for all 335 areas in the Cost of Living Index; (2) Figures cover the Thousand Oaks CA urban area; n/a not available; **Doctor** *(general practitioners routine exam of an established patient);* **Dentist** *(adult teeth cleaning and periodic oral examination);* **Optometrist** *(full vision eye exam for established adult patient);* **Gasoline** *(one gallon regular unleaded, national brand, including all taxes, cash price at self-service pump if available);* **Beauty Salon** *(woman's shampoo, trim, and blow-dry);* **Men's Shirt** *(cotton/polyester dress shirt, pinpoint weave, long sleeves).*
Source: The Council for Community and Economic Research, ACCRA Cost of Living Index, 2011

HOUSING

House Price Index (HPI)

Area	National Ranking[2]	Quarterly Change (%)	One-Year Change (%)	Five-Year Change (%)
MSA[1]	255	-0.06	-5.65	-34.87
U.S.[3]	-	-0.10	-2.43	-19.16

Note: The HPI is a weighted repeat sales index. It measures average price changes in repeat sales or refinancings on the same properties. This information is obtained by reviewing repeat mortgage transactions on single-family properties whose mortgages have been purchased or securitized by Fannie Mae or Freddie Mac in January 1975; (1) Metropolitan/Micropolitan Statistical Area—see Appendix B for areas included; (2) Rankings are based on annual percentage change for all metro areas containing at least 15,000 transactions over the last 10 years and ranges from 1 to 306; (3) figures based on a weighted average of Census Division estimates using a purchase only index; all figures are for the period ending December 31, 2011
Source: Federal Housing Finance Agency, House Price Index, February 23, 2012

House Price Valuations

Area	Q4 2005		Q4 2006		Q4 2007		Q4 2008		Q4 2009	
	Price ($000)	Over-valuation	Price ($000)	Over-valuation	Price ($000)	Over-valuation	Price ($000)	Over-valuation	Price ($000)	Over-valuation
MSA[1]	570.6	49.5	548.0	33.9	469.0	8.9	347.7	-18.7	358.0	-16.0

Note: Figures show the percentage of over- or under-valuation of single family homes relative to statistically normal house values (e.g. a value of 23.6 indicates that house values are 23.6% overvalued). Statistically normal house values are based on house prices, interest rates, household incomes, population densities, and any historical premiums or discounts metropolitan areas have exhibited over time; (1) Figures cover the Oxnard-Thousand Oaks-Ventura, CA - see Appendix B for areas included
Source: Global Insight/PNC Financial Services Group, House Prices in America: 4th Quarter 2009 Update

Median Single-Family Home Prices

Area	2009	2010	2011p	Percent Change 2010 to 2011
MSA[1]	n/a	n/a	n/a	n/a
U.S. Average	172.1	173.1	166.2	-4.0

Note: Figures are median sales prices of existing single-family homes in thousands of dollars; (p) preliminary; n/a not available; (1) Metropolitan Statistical Area—see Appendix B for areas included
Source: National Association of Realtors, Median Sales Price of Existing Single-Family Homes for Metropolitan Areas, 4th Quarter 2011

Affordability Index of Existing Single-Family Homes

Area	2009	2010	2011p	Percent Change 2010 to 2011
MSA[1]	n/a	n/a	n/a	n/a

Note: The housing affordability index measures whether or not a typical family could qualify for a mortgage loan on a typical home. The higher the index, the greater the household purchasing power. An index of 100 is defined as the point where a median-income household has exactly enough income to qualify for the purchase of a median-priced existing single-family home, assuming a 20 percent downpayment and 25 percent of gross income devoted to mortgage principal and interest payments; (p) preliminary; n/a not available; (1) Metropolitan Statistical Area—see Appendix B for areas included
Source: National Association of Realtors, Affordability Index of Existing Single-Family Homes, 2011

Median Apartment Condo-Coop Home Prices

Area	2009	2010	2011p	Percent Change 2010 to 2011
MSA[1]	n/a	n/a	n/a	n/a
U.S. Average	175.6	171.7	165.1	-3.8

Note: Figures are median sales prices of existing apartment condo-coop homes in thousands of dollars; (p) preliminary; n/a not available; (1) Metropolitan Statistical Area—see Appendix B for areas included
Source: National Association of Realtors, Median Sales Price of Existing Apartment Condo-Coop Homes for Metropolitan Areas, 4th Quarter 2011

Year Housing Structure Built

Area	2005 or Later	2000 -2004	1990 -1999	1980 -1989	1970 -1979	1960 -1969	1950 -1959	Before 1950	Median Year
City	2.0	8.7	12.7	17.0	33.3	21.1	4.1	1.1	1977
MSA[1]	3.4	7.4	10.7	16.7	23.6	21.1	10.1	7.0	1975
U.S.	5.0	8.6	14.0	14.1	16.3	11.3	11.2	19.6	1975

Note: Figures are percentages except for Median Year; (1) Figures cover the Oxnard-Thousand Oaks-Ventura, CA Metropolitan Statistical Area—see Appendix B for areas included
Source: U.S. Census Bureau, 2008-2010 American Community Survey 3-Year Estimates

HEALTH

Health Risk Data

Category	MSA[1] (%)	U.S. (%)
Adults who have been told they have high blood pressure[2]	n/a	28.7
Adults who have been told they have high blood cholesterol[2]	n/a	37.5
Adults who have been told they have diabetes[3]	n/a	8.7
Adults who have been told they have arthritis[2]	n/a	26.0
Adults who have been told they currently have asthma	n/a	9.1
Adults who are current smokers	n/a	17.3
Adults who are heavy drinkers[4]	n/a	5.0
Adults who are binge drinkers[5]	n/a	15.1
Adults who are overweight (BMI 25.0 - 29.9)	n/a	36.2
Adults who are obese (BMI 30.0 - 99.8)	n/a	27.5
Adults who participated in any physical activities in the past month	n/a	76.1
Adults 50+ who have ever had a sigmoidoscopy or colonoscopy	n/a	65.2
Women aged 40+ who have had a mammogram within the past two years	n/a	75.2
Men aged 40+ who have had a PSA test within the past two years	n/a	53.2
Adults aged 65+ who have had flu shot within the past year	n/a	67.5
Adults aged 18–64 who have any kind of health care coverage	n/a	82.2

Note: Data as of 2010 unless otherwise noted; n/a not available; (1) Figures cover the Oxnard-Thousand Oaks-Ventura, CA—see Appendix B for areas included; (2) Data as of 2009; (3) Figures do not include pregnancy-related, borderline, or pre-diabetes; (4) Heavy drinkers are classified as males having more than two drinks per day or females having more than one drink per day; (5) Binge drinkers are classified as males having five or more drinks on one occasion or females having four or more drinks on one occasion
Source: Centers for Disease Control and Prevention, Behaviorial Risk Factor Surveillance System, SMART: Selected Metropolitan/Micropolitan Area Risk Trends, 2009, 2010

Mortality Rates for the Top 10 Causes of Death in the U.S.

ICD-10[a] Sub-Chapter	ICD-10[a] Code	Age-Adjusted Mortality Rate[1] per 100,000 population	
		County[2]	U.S.
Malignant neoplasms	C00-C97	154.2	175.6
Ischaemic heart diseases	I20-I25	118.0	121.6
Other forms of heart disease	I30-I51	34.0	48.6
Chronic lower respiratory diseases	J40-J47	36.6	42.3
Cerebrovascular diseases	I60-I69	38.1	40.6
Organic, including symptomatic, mental disorders	F01-F09	13.6	26.7
Other degenerative diseases of the nervous system	G30-G31	27.1	24.7
Other external causes of accidental injury	W00-X59	19.3	24.4
Diabetes mellitus	E10-E14	18.9	21.7
Hypertensive diseases	I10-I15	20.0	18.2

Note: (a) ICD-10 = International Classification of Diseases 10th Revision; (1) Mortality rates are a three year average covering 2007-2009; (2) Figures cover Ventura County
Source: Centers for Disease Control and Prevention, National Center for Health Statistics. Underlying Cause of Death 1999-2009 on CDC WONDER Online Database, released 2012. Data for year 2009 are compiled from the Multiple Cause of Death File 2009, Series 20 No. 2O, 2012, Data for year 2008 are compiled from the Multiple Cause of Death File 2008, Series 20 No. 2N, 2011, Data for year 2007 are compiled from Multiple Cause of Death File 2007, Series 20 No. 2M, 2010.

Mortality Rates for Selected Causes of Death

ICD-10[a] Sub-Chapter	ICD-10[a] Code	Age-Adjusted Mortality Rate[1] per 100,000 population	
		County[2]	U.S.
Assault	X85-Y09	3.2	5.7
Human immunodeficiency virus (HIV) disease	B20-B24	1.0	3.3
Influenza and pneumonia	J09-J18	12.7	16.4
Intentional self-harm	X60-X84	11.1	11.5
Malnutrition	E40-E46	0.9	0.8
Obesity and other hyperalimentation	E65-E68	1.2	1.6
Transport accidents	V01-V99	11.4	13.7
Viral hepatitis	B15-B19	2.9	2.2

Note: (a) ICD-10 = International Classification of Diseases 10th Revision; (1) Mortality rates are a three year average covering 2007-2009; (2) Figures cover Ventura County
Source: Centers for Disease Control and Prevention, National Center for Health Statistics. Underlying Cause of Death 1999-2009 on CDC WONDER Online Database, released 2012. Data for year 2009 are compiled from the Multiple Cause of Death File 2009, Series 20 No. 2O, 2012, Data for year 2008 are compiled from the Multiple Cause of Death File 2008, Series 20 No. 2N, 2011, Data for year 2007 are compiled from Multiple Cause of Death File 2007, Series 20 No. 2M, 2010.

Distribution of Physicians and Dentists

Area[1]	Dentists[2]	D.O.[3]	M.D.[4] Total	Family/General Practice	Pediatrics	Medical Specialties	Surgical Specialties
Local (number)	431	62	1,411	270	99	491	314
Local (rate[5])	5.5	0.8	17.8	3.4	1.2	6.2	4.0
U.S. (rate[5])	4.5	1.9	18.3	2.5	1.4	6.8	4.1

Note: Data as of 2008 unless noted; (1) Local data covers Ventura County; (2) Data as of 2007; (3) Doctor of Osteopathic Medicine; (4) Includes active, non-federal, patient-care, office-based Doctors of Medicine; (5) rate per 10,000 population
Source: Area Resource File (ARF). 2009-2010 Release. U.S. Department of Health and Human Services, Health Resources and Services Administration, Bureau of Health Professions, Rockville, MD, August 2010

EDUCATION

Public School District Statistics

District Name	Schls	Pupils	Pupil/ Teacher Ratio	Minority Pupils[1] (%)	Free Lunch Eligible[2] (%)	IEP[3] (%)
Conejo Valley Unified	27	21,199	23.0	35.7	13.3	10.9

Note: Table includes school districts with 2,000 or more students; (1) Percentage of students that are not non-Hispanic white; (2) Percentage of students that are eligible for the free lunch program; (3) Percentage of students that have an Individualized Education Program.
Source: U.S. Department of Education, National Center for Education Statistics, Common Core of Data, Local Education Agency (School District) Universe Survey: School Year 2009-2010; U.S. Department of Education, National Center for Education Statistics, Common Core of Data, Public Elementary/Secondary School Universe Survey: School Year 2009-2010

Highest Level of Education

Area	Less than H.S.	H.S. Diploma	Some College, No Deg.	Associate Degree	Bachelors Degree	Masters Degree	Profess. School Degree	Doctorate Degree
City	6.0	15.7	21.6	7.8	30.0	12.6	3.5	2.8
MSA[1]	17.7	19.0	24.5	8.2	19.4	7.6	2.3	1.3
U.S.	14.7	28.4	21.3	7.6	17.6	7.2	1.9	1.2

Note: Figures cover persons age 25 and over; (1) Figures cover the Oxnard-Thousand Oaks-Ventura, CA Metropolitan Statistical Area—see Appendix B for areas included
Source: U.S. Census Bureau, 2008-2010 American Community Survey 3-Year Estimates

Educational Attainment by Race

Area	High School Graduate or Higher (%)					Bachelor's Degree or Higher (%)				
	Total	White	Black	Asian	Hisp.[2]	Total	White	Black	Asian	Hisp.[2]
City	94.0	95.4	94.5	95.5	73.4	48.9	48.0	59.9	72.8	23.7
MSA[1]	82.3	86.6	92.8	92.0	56.5	30.6	32.8	27.5	54.9	10.0
U.S.	85.3	87.5	81.4	85.5	61.6	28.0	29.3	17.8	50.2	13.0

Note: Figures shown cover persons 25 years old and over; (1) Figures cover the Oxnard-Thousand Oaks-Ventura, CA Metropolitan Statistical Area—see Appendix B for areas included; (2) People of Hispanic origin can be of any race
Source: U.S. Census Bureau, 2008-2010 American Community Survey 3-Year Estimates

School Enrollment by Grade and Control

Area	Preschool (%)		Kindergarten (%)		Grades 1 - 4 (%)		Grades 5 - 8 (%)		Grades 9 - 12 (%)	
	Public	Private	Public	Private	Public	Private	Public	Private	Public	Private
City	33.1	66.9	80.0	20.0	87.2	12.8	86.3	13.7	90.4	9.6
MSA[1]	46.9	53.1	89.9	10.1	91.2	8.8	90.2	9.8	92.4	7.6
U.S.	55.4	44.6	87.1	12.9	89.4	10.6	89.5	10.5	90.4	9.6

Note: Figures shown cover persons 3 years old and over; (1) Figures cover the Oxnard-Thousand Oaks-Ventura, CA Metropolitan Statistical Area—see Appendix B for areas included
Source: U.S. Census Bureau, 2008-2010 American Community Survey 3-Year Estimates

Average Salaries of Public School Classroom Teachers

Area	2010-11		2011-12		Percent Change 2010-11 to 2011-12	Percent Change 2001-02 to 2011-12
	Dollars	Rank[1]	Dollars	Rank[1]		
California	67,871	4	69,496	4	2.39	27.90
U.S. Average	55,623	-	56,643	-	1.83	26.8

Note: (1) State rank ranges from 1 to 51 where 1 indicates highest salary.
Source: National Education Association, Rankings & Estimates: Rankings of the States 2011 and Estimates of School Statistics 2012, December 2011

Higher Education

Four-Year Colleges			Two-Year Colleges			Medical Schools[1]	Law Schools[2]	Voc/ Tech[3]
Public	Private Non-profit	Private For-profit	Public	Private Non-profit	Private For-profit			
0	1	0	0	0	0	0	0	0

Note: Figures cover institutions located within the city limits and include main campuses only; (1) includes schools accredited by the Liaison Committee on Medical Education and the American Osteopathic Association's Commission on Osteopathic College Accreditation; (2) includes American Bar Association-accredited law schools; (3) includes all schools with programs that are less than 2 years.
Source: National Center for Education Statistics, Integrated Postsecondary Education System (IPEDS) Peer Analysis System, 2011-12; Association of American Medical Colleges, Member List, April 23, 2012; American Osteopathic Association, Member List, April 23, 2012; Law School Admission Council, Official Guide to ABA-Approved Law Schools Online, April 23, 2012

According to *U.S. News & World Report*, the Oxnard-Thousand Oaks-Ventura, CA is home to one of the best liberal arts colleges in the U.S.: **Thomas Aquinas College** (#71). The indicators used to capture academic quality fall into a number of categories: assessment by administrators at peer institutions; retention of students; faculty resources; student selectivity; financial resources; alumni giving; high school counselor ratings of colleges; and graduation rate.*U.S. News & World Report, "America's Best Colleges 2012"*

PRESIDENTIAL ELECTION

2008 Presidential Election Results

Area	Obama	McCain	Nader	Other
Ventura County	55.0	42.8	0.7	1.6
U.S.	52.9	45.6	0.6	0.9

Note: Results are percentages and may not add to 100% due to rounding
Source: Dave Leip's Atlas of U.S. Presidential Elections, www.uselectionatlas.org

EMPLOYERS

Major Employers

Company Name	Industry
Amgen	Biological produtcs, except diagnostic
Amgen Pharmaceuticals	Biotechnical research, noncommercial
Baxter Healthcare Corporation	Drugs, proprietaries, and sundries
California Department of Mental Health	Mental hospital, except for the mentally retarded
Central Purchasing	Hardware, nec
Community Memorial Health System	General medical and surgical hospitals
County of Ventura	Executive offices
Dignity Health	General medical and surgical hospitals
Farmers Group	Insurance agents, brokers, and service
GTE Corporation	Employment agencies
Haas Automation	Machine tools, metal cutting type
Kavlico Corporation	Relays and industrial controls
L-3 Services	Engineering services
Official Police Garage Assn of Los Angeles	Towing and tugboat service
Oxnard School District	Public and elementary secondary schools
Technicolor Thomson Group	Video, tape or disk reproduction
Truck Underwriters Association	Life insurance
US Navy	Primary care medical clinic
Xavient Information Systems	Business consulting, nec
Xmultiple	Connectors and terminals for electrical devices

Note: Companies shown are located within the Oxnard-Thousand Oaks-Ventura, CA metropolitan area.
Source: Hoovers.com, data extracted April 25 2012

PUBLIC SAFETY

Crime Rate

Area	All Crimes	Violent Crimes				Property Crimes		
		Murder	Forcible Rape	Robbery	Aggrav. Assault	Burglary	Larceny -Theft	Motor Vehicle Theft
City	1,753.4	0.8	12.9	40.3	58.0	288.6	1,294.7	58.0
Suburbs[1]	2,283.4	2.5	13.0	84.6	135.4	393.7	1,499.9	154.3
Metro[2]	2,202.0	2.2	13.0	77.8	123.5	377.5	1,468.4	139.5
U.S.	3,345.5	4.8	27.5	119.1	252.3	699.6	2,003.5	238.8

Note: Figures are crimes per 100,000 population; (1) All areas within the metro area that are located outside the city limits; (2) Metropolitan Statistical Area—see Appendix B for areas included
Source: FBI Uniform Crime Reports, 2010

Hate Crimes

Area	Number of Quarters Reported	Bias Motivation				
		Race	Religion	Sexual Orientation	Ethnicity	Disability
City	4	0	3	0	1	0

Source: Federal Bureau of Investigation, Hate Crime Statistics 2010

Identity Theft Consumer Complaints

Area	Complaints	Complaints per 100,000 Population	Rank[2]
MSA[1]	803	100.6	93
U.S.	279,156	90.4	-

Note: (1) Metropolitan Statistical Area—see Appendix B for areas included; (2) Rank ranges from 1 to 384 where 1 indicates greatest number of identity theft complaints per 100,000 population
Source: Federal Trade Commission, Consumer Sentinel Network Data Book for January–December 2011

Fraud and Other Consumer Complaints

Area	Complaints	Complaints per 100,000 Population	Rank[2]
MSA[1]	3,945	494.1	159
U.S.	1,533,924	496.8	-

Note: (1) Metropolitan Statistical Area—see Appendix B for areas included; (2) Rank ranges from 1 to 384 where 1 indicates greatest number of fraud and other complaints per 100,000 population
Source: Federal Trade Commission, Consumer Sentinel Network Data Book for January–December 2011

RECREATION

Culture

Dance[1]	Theatre[1]	Instrumental Music[1]	Vocal Music[1]	Series/ Festivals	Museums	Zoos and Aquariums[2]
0	0	2	0	3	n/a	0

Note: (1) Number of professional perfoming groups; (2) AZA-accredited; n/a not available
Source: The Grey House Performing Arts Directory, 2011-2012; Official Museum Directory, 2011; American Association of Museums, AAM Member Museums, April 2012; Association of Zoos & Aquariums, AZA Member Zoos & Aquariums, April 2012

Professional Sports Teams

Team Name	League
No teams are located in the metro area	

Source: Original research

CLIMATE

Average and Extreme Temperatures

Temperature	Jan	Feb	Mar	Apr	May	Jun	Jul	Aug	Sep	Oct	Nov	Dec	Yr.
Extreme High (°F)	88	92	95	102	97	104	97	98	110	106	101	94	110
Average High (°F)	65	66	65	67	69	72	75	76	76	74	71	66	70
Average Temp. (°F)	56	57	58	60	63	66	69	70	70	67	62	57	63
Average Low (°F)	47	49	50	53	56	59	63	64	63	59	52	48	55
Extreme Low (°F)	27	34	37	43	45	48	52	51	47	43	38	32	27

Note: Figures cover the years 1947-1990
Source: National Climatic Data Center, International Station Meteorological Climate Summary, 9/96

Average Precipitation/Snowfall/Humidity

Precip./Humidity	Jan	Feb	Mar	Apr	May	Jun	Jul	Aug	Sep	Oct	Nov	Dec	Yr.
Avg. Precip. (in.)	2.6	2.3	1.8	0.8	0.1	Tr	Tr	0.1	0.2	0.3	1.5	1.5	11.3
Avg. Snowfall (in.)	Tr	0	0	0	0	0	0	0	0	0	0	0	Tr
Avg. Rel. Hum. 7am (%)	69	72	76	76	77	80	80	81	80	76	69	67	75
Avg. Rel. Hum. 4pm (%)	60	62	64	64	66	67	67	68	67	66	61	60	64

Note: Figures cover the years 1947-1990; Tr = Trace amounts (<0.05 in. of rain; <0.5 in. of snow)
Source: National Climatic Data Center, International Station Meteorological Climate Summary, 9/96

Weather Conditions

Temperature			Daytime Sky			Precipitation		
10°F & below	32°F & below	90°F & above	Clear	Partly cloudy	Cloudy	0.01 inch or more precip.	0.1 inch or more snow/ice	Thunder-storms
0	< 1	5	131	125	109	34	0	1

Note: Figures are average number of days per year and cover the years 1947-1990
Source: National Climatic Data Center, International Station Meteorological Climate Summary, 9/96

HAZARDOUS WASTE

Superfund Sites

Thousand Oaks has no sites on the EPA's Superfund Final National Priorities List.
U.S. Environmental Protection Agency, Final National Priorities List, April 17, 2012

AIR & WATER QUALITY

Air Quality Index

Area	Percent of Days when Air Quality was...[2]					AQI Statistics[2]	
	Good	Moderate	Unhealthy for Sensitive Groups	Unhealthy	Very Unhealthy	Maximum	Median
Area[1]	75.6	21.9	2.2	0.0	0.3	221	43

Note: Air Quality Index (AQI) is an index for reporting daily air quality. EPA calculates the AQI for five major air pollutants regulated by the Clean Air Act: ground-level ozone, particle pollution (aka particulate matter), carbon monoxide, sulfur dioxide, and nitrogen dioxide. The AQI runs from 0 to 500. The higher the AQI value, the greater the level of air pollution and the greater the health concern. There are six AQI categories: "Good" AQI is between 0 and 50. Air quality is considered satisfactory; "Moderate" AQI is between 51 and 100. Air quality is acceptable; "Unhealthy for Sensitive Groups" When AQI values are between 101 and 150, members of sensitive groups may experience health effects; "Unhealthy" When AQI values are between 151 and 200 everyone may begin to experience health effects; "Very Unhealthy" AQI values between 201 and 300 trigger a health alert; "Hazardous" AQI values over 300 trigger warnings of emergency conditions (not shown); (1) Data covers Ventura County; (2) Based on 365 days with AQI data in 2011.
Source: U.S. Environmental Protection Agency, AirData Report, 2011

Air Quality Index Pollutants

Area	Percent of Days when AQI Pollutant was...[2]					
	Carbon Monoxide	Nitrogen Dioxide	Ozone	Sulfur Dioxide	Particulate Matter 2.5	Particulate Matter 10
Area[1]	0.0	3.0	91.0	0.0	5.5	0.5

Note: The Air Quality Index (AQI) is an index for reporting daily air quality. EPA calculates the AQI for five major air pollutants regulated by the Clean Air Act: ground-level ozone, particle pollution (also known as particulate matter), carbon monoxide, sulfur dioxide, and nitrogen dioxide. The AQI runs from 0 to 500. The higher the AQI value, the greater the level of air pollution and the greater the health concern; (1) Data covers Ventura County; (2) Based on 365 days with AQI data in 2011.
Source: U.S. Environmental Protection Agency, AirData Report, 2011

Air Quality Index Trends

Area	Trend Sites (days)								All Sites (days)
	2003	2004	2005	2006	2007	2008	2009	2010	2010
MSA[1]	70	51	40	39	23	31	25	13	13

Note: Figures are the number of days the AQI value exceeded 100 in a given year. An AQI value greater than 100 indicates that air quality would have been in the unhealthful range on that day. Data from exceptional events are included. These counts are presented in two ways. First, the counts are based on sites having an adequate record of monitoring data during the trend period (trend sites). These counts represent the relative change in the number of days with AQI values greater than 100. In the last column, the counts are based on all sites with data in the most recent year (because it is possible for a site to have data in the most recent year but not enough data to be a trend site); (1) Data covers the Oxnard-Thousand Oaks-Ventura, CA—see Appendix B for areas included
Source: U.S. Environmental Protection Agency, Air Quality Index Information, "Number of Days with Air Quality Index Values Greater than 100 at Trend Sites, 2000-2010, and at All Sites in 2010"

Maximum Air Pollutant Concentrations: Particulate Matter, Ozone, CO and Lead

	Particulate Matter 10 (ug/m^3)	Particulate Matter 2.5 Wtd AM (ug/m^3)	Particulate Matter 2.5 24-Hr (ug/m^3)	Ozone (ppm)	Carbon Monoxide (ppm)	Lead (ug/m^3)
MSA[1] Level	45	8.7	21	0.082	n/a	n/a
NAAQS[2]	150	15	35	0.075	9	0.15
Met NAAQS[2]	Yes	Yes	Yes	No	n/a	n/a

Note: Data from exceptional events are not included; (1) Data covers the Oxnard-Thousand Oaks-Ventura, CA—see Appendix B for areas included; (2) National Ambient Air Quality Standards; ppm = parts per million; ug/m^3 = micrograms per cubic meter; n/a not available
Concentrations: Particulate Matter 10 (coarse particulate)—highest second maximum 24-hour concentration; Particulate Matter 2.5 Wtd AM (fine particulate)—highest weighted annual mean concentration; Particulate Matter 2.5 24-Hour (fine particulate)—highest 98th percentile 24-hour concentration; Ozone—highest fourth daily maximum 8-hour concentration; Carbon Monoxide—highest second maximum non-overlapping 8-hour concentration; Lead—maximum running 3-month average
Source: U.S. Environmental Protection Agency, CBSA Factbook 2010, Air Quality Statistics by City, 2010

Maximum Air Pollutant Concentrations: Nitrogen Dioxide and Sulfur Dioxide

	Nitrogen Dioxide AM (ppb)	Nitrogen Dioxide 1-Hr (ppb)	Sulfur Dioxide AM (ppb)	Sulfur Dioxide 1-Hr (ppb)	Sulfur Dioxide 24-Hr (ppb)
MSA[1] Level	10.096	41	n/a	n/a	n/a
NAAQS[2]	53	100	30	75	140
Met NAAQS[2]	Yes	Yes	n/a	n/a	n/a

Note: Data from exceptional events are not included; (1) Data covers the Oxnard-Thousand Oaks-Ventura, CA—see Appendix B for areas included; (2) National Ambient Air Quality Standards; ppb = parts per billion; n/a not available

Concentrations: Nitrogen Dioxide AM—highest arithmetic mean concentration; Nitrogen Dioxide 1-Hr—highest 98th percentile 1-hour daily maximum concentration; Sulfur Dioxide AM—highest annual mean concentration; Sulfur Dioxide 1-Hr—highest 99th percentile 1-hour daily maximum concentration; Sulfur Dioxide 24-Hr—highest second maximum 24-hour concentration

Source: U.S. Environmental Protection Agency, CBSA Factbook 2010, Air Quality Statistics by City, 2010

Drinking Water

Water System Name	Pop. Served	Primary Water Source Type	Violations[1] Health Based	Violations[1] Monitoring/ Reporting
Thousand Oaks Water Dept.	50,000	Purchased Surface	0	0

Note: (1) Based on violation data from January 1, 2011 to December 31, 2011 (includes unresolved violations from earlier years)

Source: U.S. Environmental Protection Agency, Office of Ground Water and Drinking Water, Safe Drinking Water Information System (based on data extracted April 18, 2012)

Appendix A: Counties

Albuquerque, NM
Bernalillo County

Alexandria, VA
Alexandria Independent City

Anchorage, AK
Anchorage County

Ann Arbor, MI
Washtenaw County

Athens, GA
Clarke County

Atlanta, GA
Fulton County

Austin, TX
Travis County

Baltimore, MD
Baltimore Independent City

Bellevue, WA
King County

Billings, MT
Yellowstone County

Boise City, ID
Ada County

Boston, MA
Suffolk County

Boulder, CO
Boulder County

Broken Arrow, OK
Tulsa County

Cambridge, MA
Middlesex County

Cape Coral, FL
Lee County

Carlsbad, CA
San Diego County

Cary, NC
Wake County

Cedar Rapids, IA
Linn County

Charleston, SC
Charleston County

Charlotte, NC
Mecklenburg County

Chesapeake, VA
Chesapeake Independent City

Chicago, IL
Cook County

Clarksville, TN
Montgomery County

Colorado Springs, CO
El Paso County

Columbia, MD
Howard County

Columbia, MO
Boone County

Columbia, SC
Richland County

Columbus, OH
Franklin County

Dallas, TX
Dallas County

Denver, CO
Denver County

Durham, NC
Durham County

Edison, NJ
Middlesex County

El Paso, TX
El Paso County

Fargo, ND
Cass County

Fort Collins, CO
Larimer County

Fort Worth, TX
Tarrant County

Gilbert, AZ
Maricopa County

Green Bay, WI
Brown County

Henderson, NV
Clark County

High Point, NC
Guilford County

Honolulu, HI
Honolulu County

Houston, TX
Harris County

Huntington, NY
Suffolk County

Huntsville, AL
Madison County

Indianapolis, IN
Marion County

Irvine, CA
Orange County

Jackson, MS
Hinds County

Jacksonville, FL
Duval County

Jersey City, NJ
Hudson County

Kansas City, MO
Jackson County

Kenosha, WI
Kenosha County

Las Vegas, NV
Clark County

Lexington, KY
Fayette County

Lincoln, NE
Lancaster County

Little Rock, AR
Pulaski County

Los Angeles, CA
Los Angeles County

Madison, WI
Dane County

Manchester, NH
Hillsborough County

Miami, FL
Miami-Dade County

Minneapolis, MN
Hennepin County

Murfreesboro, TN
Rutherford County

Naperville, IL
DuPage County

Nashville, TN
Davidson County

New Orleans, LA
Orleans Parish

New York, NY
Bronx, Kings, New York, Queens, and Richmond Counties

Norman, OK
Cleveland County

Olathe, KS
Johnson County

Omaha, NE
Douglas County

Orlando, FL
Orange County

Overland Park, KS
Johnson County

Oyster Bay, NY
Nassau County

Pembroke Pines, FL
Broward County

Philadelphia, PA
Philadelphia County

Phoenix, AZ
Maricopa County

Pittsburgh, PA
Allegheny County

Plano, TX
Collin County

Portland, OR
Multnomah County

Providence, RI
Providence County

Provo, UT
Utah County

Raleigh, NC
Wake County

Richmond, VA
Richmond Independent City

Roseville, CA
Placer County

Round Rock, TX
Williamson County

San Antonio, TX
Bexar County

San Diego, CA
San Diego County

San Francisco, CA
San Francisco County

San Jose, CA
Santa Clara County

Savannah, GA
Chatham County

Scottsdale, AZ
Maricopa County

Seattle, WA
King County

Sioux Falls, SD
Minnehaha County

Stamford, CT
Fairfield County

Sterling Heights, MI
Macomb County

Sunnyvale, CA
Santa Clara County

Tampa, FL
Hillsborough County

Temecula, CA
Riverside County

Thousand Oaks, CA
Ventura County

Virginia Beach, VA
Virginia Beach Independent City

Washington, DC
District of Columbia

Note: *In cases where a city's population is split over multiple counties (except New York), data in this book reflects the county where the majority of the population resides.*

Appendix B: Metropolitan Area Definitions

Metropolitan Statistical Areas (MSA), Metropolitan Divisions (MD), New England City and Town Areas (NECTA), and New England City and Town Area Divisions (NECTAD)

Albuquerque, NM MSA
Bernalillo, Sandoval, Torrance, and Valencia Counties

Alexandria, VA
See Washington, DC

Anchorage, AK MSA
Anchorage Municipality and Matanuska-Susitna Borough

Ann Arbor, MI MSA
Washtenaw County

Athens-Clarke County, GA MSA
Clarke, Madison, Oconee, and Oglethorpe Counties

Atlanta-Sandy Springs-Marietta, GA MSA
Barrow, Bartow, Butts, Carroll, Cherokee, Clayton, Cobb, Coweta, Dawson, DeKalb, Douglas, Fayette, Forsyth, Fulton, Gwinnett, Haralson, Heard, Henry, Jasper, Lamar, Meriwether, Newton, Paulding, Pickens, Pike, Rockdale, Spalding, and Walton Counties

Austin-Round Rock-San Marcos, TX MSA
Bastrop, Caldwell, Hays, Travis, and Williamson Counties

Baltimore-Towson, MD MSA
Baltimore city; Anne Arundel, Baltimore, Carroll, Harford, Howard, and Queen Anne's Counties

Bellevue, WA
See Seattle, WA

Billings, MT MSA
Carbon and Yellowstone Counties

Boise City-Nampa, ID MSA
Ada, Boise, Canyon, Gem, and Owyhee Counties

Boston, MA
Boston-Cambridge-Quincy, MA-NH MSA
Essex, Middlesex, Norfolk, Plymouth, and Suffolk Counties, MA; Rockingham and Strafford Counties, NH
Boston-Quincy, MA MD
Norfolk, Plymouth, and Suffolk Counties
Boston-Cambridge-Quincy, MA-NH NECTA
Includes 155 cities and towns in Massachusetts and 38 cities and towns in New Hampshire
Boston-Cambridge-Quincy, MA NECTA Division
Includes 97 cities and towns in Massachusetts

Boulder, CO MSA
Boulder County

Bridgeport, CT
Bridgeport-Stamford-Norwalk, CT MSA
Fairfield County
Bridgeport-Stamford-Norwalk, CT NECTA
Includes 25 cities and towns in Connecticut

Broken Arrow, OK
See Tulsa, OK MSA

Cambridge, MA
See Boston, MA

Cape Coral-Fort Myers, FL MSA
Lee County

Carlsbad, CA
See San Diego-Carlsbad-San Marcos, CA MSA

Cary, NC
See Raleigh-Cary, NC MSA

Cedar Rapids, IA, MSA
Benton, Jones, and Linn Counties

Charleston-North Charleston-Summerville, SC MSA
Berkeley, Charleston, and Dorchester Counties

Charlotte-Gastonia-Rock Hill, NC-SC MSA
Anson, Cabarrus, Gaston, Mecklenburg, and Union Counties, NC; York County, SC

Chattanooga, TN-GA MSA
Catoosa, Dade, and Walker Counties, GA; Hamilton, Marion, and Sequatchie Counties, TN

Chesapeake, VA
See Virginia Beach-Norfolk-Newport News, VA-NC MSA

Chicago, IL
Chicago-Joliet-Naperville, IL-IN-WI MSA
Cook, DeKalb, DuPage, Grundy, Kane, Kendall, Lake, McHenry, and Will Counties, IL; Jasper, Lake, Newton, and Porter Counties, IN; Kenosha County, WI
Chicago-Joliet-Naperville, IL MD
Cook, DeKalb, DuPage, Grundy, Kane, Kendall, McHenry, and Will Counties
Lake County-Kenosha County, IL-WI MD
Lake County, IL; Kenosha County, WI

Clarksville, TN-KY MSA
Mongomery and Stewart Counties, TN; Christian and Trigg Counties, KY

Colorado Springs, CO MSA
El Paso and Teller Counties

Columbia, MD
See Baltimore-Towson, MD MSA

Columbia, MO MSA
Boone and Howard Counties

Columbia, SC MSA
Calhoun, Fairfield, Kershaw, Lexington, Richland, and Saluda Counties

Columbus, OH MSA
Delaware, Fairfield, Franklin, Licking, Madison, Morrow, Pickaway, and Union Counties

Dallas, TX
Dallas-Fort Worth-Arlington, TX MSA
Collin, Dallas, Delta, Denton, Ellis, Hunt, Johnson, Kaufman, Parker, Rockwall, Tarrant, and Wise Counties
Dallas-Plano-Irving, TX MD
Collin, Dallas, Delta, Denton, Ellis, Hunt, Kaufman, and Rockwall Counties

Denver-Aurora-Broomfield, CO MSA
Adams, Arapahoe, Broomfield, Clear Creek, Denver, Douglas, Elbert, Gilpin, Jefferson, and Park Counties

Detroit, MI
Detroit-Warren-Livonia, MI MSA
Lapeer, Livingston, Macomb, Oakland, and St. Clair, and Wayne Counties
Warren-Troy-Farmington Hills, MI MD
Lapeer, Livingston, Macomb, Oakland, and St. Clair Counties

Durham-Chapel Hill, NC MSA
Chatham, Durham, Orange, and and Person Counties

Edison, NJ
Edison-New Brunswick, NJ MD
Hunterdon, Middlesex and Somerset Counties

See also New York-Northern New Jersey-Long Island, NY-NJ-PA MSA

El Paso, TX MSA
El Paso County

Eugene-Springfield, OR MSA
Lane County

Fargo, ND-MN MSA
Cass County, ND; Clay County, MN

Fort Collins-Loveland, CO MSA
Larimer County

Fort Lauderdale, FL
Fort Lauderdale-Pompano Beach-Deerfield Beach, FL MD
Broward County
See also Miami-Fort Lauderdale-Miami Beach, FL MSA

Fort Worth, TX
Fort Worth-Arlington, TX MD
Johnson, Parker, Tarrant, and Wise Counties
See also Dallas-Fort Worth-Arlington, TX MSA

Gilbert, AZ
See Phoenix, AZ MSA

Green Bay, WI MSA
Brown, Kewaunee, and Oconto Counties

Greensboro-High Point, NC MSA
Guilford, Randolph, and Rockingham Counties

Henderson, NV
See Las Vegas-Paradise, NV MSA

High Point, NC
See Greensboro-High Point, NC MSA

Honolulu, HI MSA
Honolulu County

Houston-Sugar Land-Baytown, TX MSA
Austin, Brazoria, Chambers, Fort Bend, Galveston, Harris, Liberty, Montgomery, San Jacinto, and Waller Counties

Huntington, NY
Nassau-Suffolk, NY MD
Nassau and Suffolk Counties
See also New York, NY

Huntsville, AL MSA
Limestone and Madison Counties

Indianapolis-Carmel, IN MSA
Boone, Brown, Hamilton, Hancock, Hendricks, Johnson, Marion, Morgan, Putnam, and Shelby Counties

Irvine, CA
Santa Ana-Anaheim-Irvine, CA MD

Orange County
See also Los Angeles, CA

Jackson, MS MSA
Copiah, Hinds, Madison, Rankin and Simpson Counties, MS

Jacksonville, FL MSA
Baker, Clay, Duval, Nassau, and St. Johns Counties

Jersey City, NJ
New York-White Plains-Wayne, NY-NJ MD
Bergen, Hudson, and Passaic Counties, NJ; Bronx, Kings, New York, Putnam, Queens, Richmond, Rockland, and Westchester Counties, NY
See also New York, NY

Kansas City, MO-KS MSA
Franklin, Johnson, Leavenworth, Linn, Miami, and Wyandotte Counties, KS; Bates, Caldwell, Cass, Clay, Clinton, Jackson, Lafayette, Platte, and Ray Counties, MO

Kenosha, WA
Lake County-Kenosha County, IL-WI MD
Lake County, IL; Kenosha County, WI
See also Chicago, IL

Las Vegas-Paradise, NV MSA
Clark County

Lexington-Fayette, KY MSA
Bourbon, Clark, Fayette, Jessamine, Scott, and Woodford Counties

Lincoln, NE MSA
Lancaster and Seward Counties

Little Rock-North Little Rock-Conway, AR MSA
Faulkner, Grant, Lonoke, Perry, Pulaski and Saline Counties, AR

Los Angeles, CA
Los Angeles-Long Beach-Santa Ana, CA MSA
Los Angeles and Orange Counties
Los Angeles-Long Beach-Glendale, CA MD
Los Angeles County
Santa Ana-Anaheim-Irvine, CA MD
Orange County

Madison, WI MSA
Columbia, Dane, and Iowa Counties

Manchester-Nashua, NH MSA
Hillsborough County
Manchester, NH NECTA
Includes 9 cities and towns in New Hampshire

Miami, FL
Miami-Fort Lauderdale-Pompano Beach, FL MSA
Broward, Miami-Dade, and Palm Beach Counties
Miami-Miami Beach-Kendall, FL MD
Miami-Dade County

Minneapolis-St. Paul-Bloomington, MN-WI MSA
Anoka, Carver, Chisago, Dakota, Hennepin, Isanti, Ramsey, Scott, Sherburne, Washington, and Wright Counties, MN; Pierce and St. Croix Counties, WI

Murfreesboro, TN
See Nashville-Davidson—Murfreesboro—Franklin, TN MSA

Naperville, IL
See Chicago, IL

Nashville-Davidson—Murfreesboro—Franklin, TN MSA
Cannon, Cheatham, Davidson, Dickson, Hickman, Macon, Robertson, Rutherford, Smith, Sumner, Trousdale, Williamson, and Wilson Counties

New Orleans-Metarie-Kenner, LA MSA
Jefferson, Orleans, Plaquemines, St. Bernard, St. Charles, St. John the Baptist, and St. Tammany Parish

New York, NY
Nassau-Suffolk, NY MD
Nassau and Suffolk Counties
New York-Northern New Jersey-Long Island, NY-NJ-PA MSA
Bergen, Essex, Hudson, Hunterdon, Middlesex, Monmouth, Morris, Ocean, Passaic, Somerset, Sussex, and Union Counties, NJ; Bronx, Kings, Nassau, New York, Putnam, Queens, Richmond, Rockland, Suffolk, and Westchester Counties, NY; Pike County, PA
New York-Wayne-White Plains, NY-NJ MD
Bergen, Hudson, and Passaic Counties, NJ; Bronx, Kings, New York, Putnam, Queens, Richmond, Rockland, and Westchester Counties, NY

Norman, OK
See Oklahoma City, OK MSA

Oakland, CA
Oakland-Fremont-Hayward, CA MD
Alameda and Contra Costa Counties
See also San Francisco-Oakland-Fremont, CA MSA

Oklahoma City, OK MSA
Canadian, Cleveland, Grady, Lincoln, Logan, McClain, and Oklahoma Counties

Olathe, KS
See Kansas City, MO-KS MSA

Omaha-Council Bluffs, NE-IA MSA
Harrison, Mills, and Pottawattamie Counties, IA; Cass, Douglas, Sarpy, Saunders, and Washington Counties, NE

Orlando-Kissimmee-Sanford, FL MSA
Lake, Orange, Osceola, and Seminole Counties

Overland Park, KS
See Kansas City, MO-KS MSA

Oyster Bay, NY
Nassau-Suffolk, NY MD
Nassau and Suffolk Counties
See also New York, NY

Oxnard-Thousand Oaks-Ventura, CA MSA
Ventura County

Pembroke Pines, FL
Fort Lauderdale-Pompano Beach-Deerfield Beach, FL MD
Broward County
See also Miami, FL

Philadelphia, PA
Philadelphia-Camden-Wilmington, PA-NJ-DE-MD MSA
New Castle County, DE; Cecil County, MD; Burlington, Camden, Gloucester, and Salem Counties, NJ; Bucks, Chester, Delaware, Montgomery, and Philadelphia Counties, PA
Philadelphia, PA MD
Bucks, Chester, Delaware, Montgomery, and Philadelphia Counties

Phoenix-Mesa-Glendale, AZ MSA
Maricopa and Pinal Counties

Pittsburgh, PA MSA
Allegheny, Armstrong, Beaver, Butler, Fayette, Washington, and Westmoreland Counties

Plano, TX
Dallas-Plano-Irving, TX MD
Collin, Dallas, Delta, Denton, Ellis, Hunt, Kaufman, and Rockwall Counties
See also Dallas, TX

Portland-Vancouver-Hillsboro, OR-WA MSA
Clackamas, Columbia, Multnomah, Washington, and Yamhill Counties, OR; Clark and Skamania Counties, WA

Providence-New Bedford-Fall River, RI-MA MSA
Bristol County, MA; Bristol, Kent, Newport, Providence, and Washington Counties, RI
Providence-Fall River-Warwick, RI-MA NECTA
Includes 12 cities and towns in Massachusetts and 37 cities and towns in Rhode Island

Provo-Orem, UT MSA
Juab and Utah Counties

Raleigh-Cary, NC MSA
Franklin, Johnston, and Wake Counties

Richmond, VA MSA
Petersburg, Colonial Heights, Hopewell, and Richmond cities; Amelia, Caroline, Charles City, Chesterfield, Cumberland, Dinwiddie, Goochland, Hanover, Henrico, King William, King and Queen, Louisa, New Kent, Powhatan, Prince George, and Sussex Counties

Riverside-San Bernardino-Ontario, CA MSA
Riverside and San Bernardino Counties

Roseville, CA
See Sacramento—Arden-Arcade—Roseville, CA MSA

Round Rock, TX
See Austin-Round Rock-San Marcos, TX MSA

Sacramento—Arden-Arcade—Roseville, CA MSA
El Dorado, Placer, Sacramento, and Yolo Counties

San Antonio-New Braunfels, TX MSA
Atascosa, Bandera, Bexar, Comal, Guadalupe, Kendall, Medina, and Wilson Counties

San Diego-Carlsbad-San Marcos, CA MSA
San Diego County

San Francisco, CA
San Francisco-Oakland-Fremont, CA MSA
Alameda, Contra Costa, Marin, San Francisco, and San Mateo Counties
San Francisco-San Mateo-Redwood City, CA MD
Marin, San Francisco, and San Mateo Counties

San Jose-Sunnyvale-Santa Clara, CA MSA
San Benito and Santa Clara Counties

Savannah, GA MSA
Bryan, Chatham, and Effingham Counties

Scottsdale, AZ
See Phoenix-Mesa-Glendale, AZ MSA

Seattle, WA
Seattle-Tacoma-Bellevue, WA MSA
King, Pierce, and Snohomish Counties
Seattle-Bellevue-Everett, WA MD
King and Snohomish Counties

Sioux Falls, SD MSA
Lincoln, McCook, Minnehaha, and Turner Counties

Stamford, CT
See Bridgeport, CT

Sterling Heights, MI
Warren-Troy-Farmington Hills, MI MD
Lapeer, Livingston, Macomb, Oakland, and St. Clair Counties
See also Detroit, MI

Sunnyvale, CA
See San Jose-Sunnyvale-Santa Clara, CA MSA

Tampa-St. Petersburg-Clearwater, FL MSA
Hernando, Hillsborough, Pasco, and Pinellas Counties

Temecula, CA
See Riverside-San Bernardino-Ontario, CA MSA

Thousand Oaks, CA
See Oxnard-Thousand Oaks-Ventura, CA MSA

Tulsa, OK MSA
Creek, Okmulgee, Osage, Pawnee, Rogers, Tulsa, and Wagoner Counties

Virginia Beach-Norfolk-Newport News, VA-NC MSA
Currituck County, NC; Chesapeake, Hampton, Newport News, Norfolk, Poquoson, Portsmouth, Suffolk, Virginia Beach and Williamsburg cities, VA; Gloucester, Isle of Wight, James City, Mathews, Surry, and York Counties, VA

Washington, DC
Washington-Arlington-Alexandria, DC-VA-MD-WV MSA
District of Columbia; Calvert, Charles, Frederick, Montgomery, and Prince George's Counties, MD; Alexandria, Fairfax, Falls Church, Fredericksburg, Manassas Park, and Manassas cities, VA; Arlington, Clarke, Fairfax, Fauquier, Loudoun, Prince William, Spotsylvania, Stafford, and Warren Counties, VA; Jefferson County, WV
Washington-Arlington-Alexandria, DC-VA-MD-WV MD
District of Columbia; Calvert, Charles, and Prince George's Counties, MD; Alexandria, Fairfax, Falls Church, Fredericksburg, Manassas Park, and Manassas cities, VA; Arlington, Clarke, Fairfax, Fauquier, Loudoun, Prince William, Spotsylvania, Stafford, and Warren Counties, VA; Jefferson County, WV

Appendix C: Chambers of Commerce & Economic Development Offices

Albuquerque, NM

Albuquerque Chamber of Commerce
P.O. Box 25100
Albuquerque, NM 87125
Phone: (505) 764-3700
Fax: (505) 764-3714
www.abqchamber.com

Albuquerque Economic Development Dept
851 University Blvd SE
Suite 203
Albuquerque, NM 87106
Phone: (505) 246-6200
Fax: (505) 246-6219
www.cabq.gov/econdev

Alexandria, VA

Alexandria Chamber of Commerce
801 N Fairfax St
Suite 402
Alexandria, VA 22314
Phone: (703) 739-3810
Fax: (703) 739-3805
www.alexchamber.com

Anchorage, AK

Anchorage Chamber of Commerce
1016 W Sixth Avenue
Suite 303
Anchorage, AK 99501
Phone: (907) 272-2401
Fax: (907) 272-4117
www.anchoragechamber.org

Anchorage Economic Development Department
900 W 5th Avenue
Suite 300
Anchorage, AK 99501
Phone: (907) 258-3700
Fax: (907) 258-6646
www.aedcweb.com/aedcdig

Ann Arbor, MI

Ann Arbor Area Chamber of Commerce
115 West Huron
3rd Floor
Ann Arbor, MI 48104
Phone: (734) 665-4433
Fax: (734) 665-4191
www.annarborchamber.org

Ann Arbor Economic Development Department
201 S Division
Suite 430
Ann Arbor, MI 48104
Phone: (734) 761-9317
www.annarborspark.org

Athens, GA

Athens Area Chamber of Commerce
246 W Hancock Avenue
Athens, GA 30601
Phone: (706) 549-6800
Fax: (706) 549-5636
www.aacoc.org

Athens-Clarke Economic Development
150 E. Hancock Avenue
P.O. Box 1692
Athens, GA 30603
Phone: (706) 613-3810
Fax: (706) 613-3812
www.athensbusiness.org/contact.aspx

Atlanta, GA

Metro Atlanta Chamber of Commerce
235 Andrew Young International Blvd NW
Atlanta, GA 30303
Phone: (404) 880-9000
Fax: (404) 586-8464
www.metroatlantachamber.com

Austin, TX

Greater Austin Chamber of Commerce
210 Barton Springs Road
Suite 400
Austin, TX 78704
Phone: (512) 478-9383
Fax: (512) 478-6389
www.austin-chamber.org

Baltimore, MD

Baltimore City Chamber of Commerce
312 Martin Luther King Jr Blvd
Baltimore, MD 21201
Phone: (410) 837-7101
Fax: (410) 837-7104
www.baltimorecitychamber.com

City of Baltimore Development Corporation
36 South Charles Street
Suite 1600
Baltimore, MD 21201
Phone: (410) 837-9305
Fax: (410) 837-6363
www.baltimoredevelopment.com

Bellevue, WA

Bellevue Chamber of Commerce
302 Bellevue Square
Bellevue, WA 98004
Phone: (425) 454-2464
www.bellevuechamber.org

Billings, MT

Billings Area Chamber of Commerce
815 S 27th St
Billings, MT 59101
Phone: (406) 245-4111
Fax: (406) 2457333
www.billingschamber.com

Boise City, ID

Boise Metro Chamber of Commerce
250 S 5th Street
Suite 800
Boise City, ID 83701
Phone: (208) 472-5200
Fax: (208) 472-5201
www.bisechamber.org

Boston, MA

Greater Boston Chamber of Commerce
265 Franklin Street
12th Floor
Boston, MA 02110
Phone: (617) 227-4500
Fax: (617) 227-7505
www.bostonchamber.com

Boulder, CO

Boulder Chamber of Commerce
2440 Pearl Street
Boulder, CO 80302
Phone: (303) 442-1044
Fax: (303) 938-8837
www.boulderchamber.com

City of Boulder Economic Vitality Program
P.O. Box 791
Boulder, CO 80306
Phone: (303) 441-3090
www.bouldercolorado.gov

Broken Arrow, OK

The Broken Arrow Area Chamber of Commerce
210 N Main Street
Suite C
Broken Arrow, OK 74013
Phone: (918) 251-1518
Fax: (918)251-1777
www.brokenarrow.com

Cambridge, MA

Cambridge Chamber of Commerce
859 Massachusetts Ave
Cambridge, MA 02139
Phone: (617) 876-4100
www.cambridgechamber.org

Cape Coral, FL

Chamber of Commerce of Cape Coral
2051 Cape Coral Parkway East
Cape Coral, FL 33904
Phone: (239) 549-6900
Fax: (239) 549-9609
www.capecoralchamber.com

Carlsbad, CA

The City of Carlsbad Chamber of Commerce
5934 Priestly Dr.
Carlsbad, CA 92008
Phone: (760) 931-8400
Fax: (760) 931-9153
www.carlsbad.org

Cary, NC

Cary Chamber of Commerce
307 North Academy St
Cary, NC 27513
Phone: (919) 467-1016
www.carychamber.com

Cedar Rapids, IA

Cedar Rapids Chamber of Commerce
424 First Avenue NE
Cedar Rapids, IA 52401
Phone: (319) 398-5317
Fax: (319) 398-5228
www.cedarrapids.org

Cedar Rapids Economic Development
50 Second Avenue Bridge
Sixth Floor
Cedar Rapids, IA 52401-1256
Phone: (319) 286-5041
Fax: (319) 286-5141
www.cedar-rapids.org

Cedar Rapids Metro Economic Alliance
424 First Avenue NE
Cedar Rapids, IA 52401-1196
Phone: (319) 398-5317
www.cedarrapids.org

Charleston, SC

Charleston Metro Chamber of Commerce
P.O. Box 975
Charleston, SC 29402
Phone: (843) 577-2510
www.charlestonchamber.net

Charlotte, NC

Charlotte Chamber of Commerce
330 S Tryon Street
P.O. Box 32785
Charlotte, NC 28232
Phone: (704) 378-1300
Fax: (704) 374-1903
www.charlottechamber.com

Charlotte Regional Partnership
1001 Morehead Square Drive
Suite 200
Charlotte, NC 28203
Phone: (704) 347-8942
Fax: (704) 347-8981
www.charlotteusa.com

Chesapeake, VA

Hampton Roads Chamber of Commerce
500 East Main Street
Suite 700
Chesapeake, VA 23510
Phone: (757) 622-2312
Fax: (757) 664-2558
www.hamptonroadschamber.com

Chicago, IL

Chicagoland Chamber of Commerce
200 E Randolph Street
Suite 2200
Chicago, IL 60601-6436
Phone: (312) 494-6700
Fax: (312) 861-0660
www.chicagolandchamber.org

City of Chicago Department of Planning and Development
City Hall, Room 1000
121 North La Salle Street
Chicago, IL 60602
Phone: (312) 744-4190
Fax: (312) 744-2271
egov.cityofchicago.org

Clarksville, TN

Clarksville Area Chamber of Commerce
25 Jefferson Street
Suite 300
Clarksville, TN 37040
Phone: (931) 647-2331
www.clarksvillechamber.com

Colorado Springs, CO

Greater Colorado Springs Chamber of Commerce
6 S. Tejon Street
Suite 700
Colorado Springs, CO 80903
Phone: (719) 635-1551
Fax: (719) 635-1571
gcsco.wliinc3.com

Greater Colorado Springs Economic Development Corp
90 South Cascade Avenue
Suite 1050
Colorado Springs, CO 80903
Phone: (719) 471-8183
Fax: (719) 471-9733
www.coloradosprings.org

Columbia, MD

Howard County Chamber of Commerce
5560 Sterrett Pl.
Suite 105
Columbia, MD 21044
Phone: (410) 730-4111
Fax: (410) 730-4584
www.howardchamber.com

Columbia, MO

Columbia Chamber of Commerce
300 South Providence Rd.
PO Box 1016
Columbia, MO 65205-1016
Phone: (573) 874-1132
Fax: (573)443-3986
www.columbiamochamber.com

Columbia, SC

City of Columbia Office of Economic Development
1201 Main Street
Suite 250
Columbia, SC 29201
Phone: (803) 734-2700
Fax: (803) 734-2702
www.columbiascdevelopment.com

Columbia Chamber of Commerce
930 Richmond Street
Columbia, SC 20201
Phone: (803) 733-1110
Fax: (803) 733-1149
www.columbiachamber.com

Columbus, OH

Greater Columbus Chamber
37 North High Street
Columbus, OH 43215
Phone: (614) 221-1321
Fax: (614) 221-1408
www.columbus.org

Dallas, TX

City of Dallas Economic Development Department
1500 Marilla Street
5C South
Dallas, TX 75201
Phone: (214) 670-1685
Fax: (214) 670-0158
www.dallas-edd.org

Greater Dallas Chamber of Commerce
700 North Pearl Street
Suite1200
Dallas, TX 75201
Phone: (214) 746-6600
Fax: (214) 746-6799
www.dallaschamber.org

Denver, CO

Denver Metro Chamber of Commerce
1445 Market Street
Denver, CO 80202
Phone: (303) 534-8500
Fax: (303) 534-3200
www.denverchamber.org

Downtown Denver Partnership
511 16th Street
Suite 200
Denver, CO 80202
Phone: (303) 534-6161
Fax: (303) 534-2803
www.downtowndenver.com

Durham, NC

Durham Chamber of Commerce
PO Box 3829
Durham, NC 27702
Phone: (919) 682-2133
Fax: (919) 688-8351
www.durhamchamber.org

North Carolina Institute of Minority Economic Development
114 W Parish Street
Durham, NC 27701
Phone: (919) 956-8889
Fax: (919) 688-7668
www.ncimed.com

Edison, NJ

Edison Chamber of Commerce
336 Raritan Center Parkway
Campus Plaza 6
Edison, NJ 08837
Phone: (732) 738-9482
Fax: (732) 738-9485
www.edisonchamber.com

El Paso, TX

City of El Paso Department of Economic Development
2 Civic Center Plaza
El Paso, TX 79901
Phone: (915) 541-4000
Fax: (915) 541-1316
www.elpasotexas.gov

Greater El Paso Chamber of Commerce
10 Civic Center Plaza
El Paso, TX 79901
Phone: (915) 534-0500
Fax: (915) 534-0510
www.elpaso.org

Fargo, ND

Chamber of Commerce of Fargo Moorhead
202 First Avenue North
Fargo, ND 56560
Phone: (218) 233-1100
Fax: (218) 233-1200
www.fmchamber.com

Greater Fargo-Moorhead Economic Development Corporation
51 Broadway, Suite 500
Fargo, ND 58102
Phone: (701) 364-1900
Fax: (701) 293-7819
www.gfmedc.com

Fort Collins, CO

Fort Collins Chamber of Commerce
225 South Meldrum
Fort Collins, CO 80521
Phone: (970) 482-3746
Fax: (970) 482-3774
www.fcchamber.org

Fort Worth, TX

City of Fort Worth Economic Development
City Hall
900 Monroe Street, Suite 301
Fort Worth, TX 76102
Phone: (817) 392-6103
Fax: (817) 392-2431
www.fortworthgov.org

Fort Worth Chamber of Commerce
777 Taylor Street
Suite 900
Fort Worth, TX 76102-4997
Phone: (817) 336-2491
Fax: (817) 877-4034
www.fortworthchamber.com

Gilbert, AZ

Gilbert Chamber of Commerce
119 North Gilbert Road
Suite 101
Gilbert, AZ 85299-0527
Phone: (480) 892-0056
Fax: (480) 892-1980
www.gilbertaz.com

Green Bay, WI

Economic Development
100 N Jefferson St
Room 202
Green Bay, WI 54301
Phone: (920) 448-3397
Fax: (920) 448-3063
www.ci.green-bay.wi.us

Green Bay Area Chamber of Commerce
300 N. Broadway
Suite 3A
Green Bay, WI 54305-1660
Phone: (920) 437-8704
Fax: (920) 593-3468
www.titletown.org

Henderson, NV

Henderson Chamber of Commerce
590 S. Boulder Highway
Henderson, NV 89015
Phone: (702) 565-8951
www.hendersonchamber.com

High Point, NC

High Point Chamber of Commerce
1634 N. Main Street
High Point, NC 27262
Phone: (336) 882-5000
Fax: (336) 889-9499
www.highpointchamber.org

Honolulu, HI

The Chamber of Commerce of Hawaii
1132 Bishop Street
Suite 402
Honolulu, HI 96813
Phone: (808) 545-4300
Fax: (808) 545-4369
www.cochawaii.com

Houston, TX

Greater Houston Partnership
1200 Smith Street
Suite 700
Houston, TX 77002-4400
Phone: (713) 844-3600
Fax: (713) 844-0200
www.houston.org

Huntington, NY

Huntington Chamber of Commerce
164 Main Street
Huntington, NY 11743
Phone: (631) 423-6100
Fax: (631) 351-8276
www.huntingtonchamber.com

Huntsville, AL

Chamber of Commerce of Huntsville/Madison County
225 Church Street
Huntsville, AL 35801
Phone: (256) 535-2000
Fax: (256) 535-2015
www.huntsvillealabamausa.com

Indianapolis, IN

Greater Indianapolis Chamber of Commerce
111 Monument Circle
Suite 1950
Indianapolis, IN 46204
Phone: (317) 464-2222
Fax: (317) 464-2217
www.indychamber.com

The Indy Partnership
111 Monument Circle
Suite 1800
Indianapolis, IN 46204
Phone: (317) 236-6262
Fax: (317) 236-6275
www.indypartnership.com

Irvine, CA

Irvine Chamber of Commerce
2485 McCabe Way
Suite 150
Irvine, CA 92614
Phone: (949) 660-9112
Fax: (949) 660-0829
www.irvinechamber.com

Jackson, MS

MetroJackson Chamber of Commerce
PO Box 22548
Jackson, MS 39225
Phone: (601) 948-7575
Fax: (601) 352-5539
www.metrochamber.com

Jacksonville, FL

Jacksonville Chamber of Commerce
3 Independent Drive
Jacksonville, FL 32202
Phone: (904) 366-6600
Fax: (904) 632-0617
www.myjaxchamber.com

Jersey City, NJ

Hudson County Chamber of Commerce
857 Bergen Avenue
3rd Floor
Jersey City, NJ 7306
Phone: (201) 386-0699
Fax: (201) 386-8480
www.hudsonchamber.org

Kansas City, MO

Greater Kansas City Chamber of Commerce
2600 Commerce Tower
911 Main Street
Kansas City, MO 64105
Phone: (816) 221-2424
Fax: (816) 221-7440
www.kcchamber.com

Kansas City Area Development Council
2600 Commerce Tower
911 Main Street
Kansas City, MO 64105
Phone: (816) 221-2121
Fax: (816) 842-2865
www.thinkkc.com

Kenosha, WI

Kenosha Area Chamber of Commerce
600 52nd Street
Suite 130
Kenosha, WI 53140-3423
Phone: (262) 654-1234
Fax: (262) 654-4655
www.kenoshaareachamber.com

Las Vegas, NV

Las Vegas Chamber of Commerce
6671 Las Vegas Blvd South
Suite 300
Las Vegas, NV 89119
Phone: (702) 735-1616
Fax: (702) 735-0406
www.lvchamber.org

Las Vegas Office of Business Development
400 Stewart Avenue
City Hall
Las Vegas, NV 89101
Phone: (702) 229-6011
Fax: (702) 385-3128
www.lasvegasnevada.gov

Lexington, KY

Greater Lexington Chamber of Commerce
330 East Main Street
Suite 100
Lexington, KY 40507
Phone: (859) 254-4447
Fax: (859) 233-3304
www.commercelexington.com

Lexington Downtown Development Authority
101 East Vine Street
Suite 500
Lexington, KY 40507
Phone: (859) 425-2296
Fax: (859) 425-2292
www.lexingtondda.com

Lincoln, NE

Lincoln Chamber of Commerce
1135 M Street
Suite 200
Lincoln, NE 68508
Phone: (402) 436-2350
Fax: (402) 436-2360
www.lcoc.com

Little Rock, AR

Little Rock Regional Chamber of Commerce
One Chamber Plaza
Little Rock, AR 72201-1618
Phone: (501) 374-2001
www.littlerockchamber.com

Los Angeles, CA

Los Angeles Area Chamber of Commerce
350 South Bixel Street
Los Angeles, CA 90017
Phone: (213) 580-7500
Fax: (213) 580-7511
www.lachamber.org

Los Angeles County Economic Development Corporation
444 South Flower Street
34th Floor
Los Angeles, CA 90071
Phone: (213) 622-4300
Fax: (213) 622-7100
www.laedc.org

Madison, WI

Greater Madison Chamber of Commerce
615 East Washington Avenue
P.O. Box 71
Madison, WI 53701-0071
Phone: (608) 256-8348
Fax: (608) 256-0333
www.greatermadisonchamber.com

Manchester, NH

Greater Manchester Chamber of Commerce
889 Elm Street
Manchester, NH 03101
Phone: (603) 666-6600
Fax: (603) 626-0910
www.manchester-chamber.org

Manchester Economic Development Office
One City Hall Plaza
Manchester, NH 03101
Phone: (603) 624-6505
Fax: (603) 624-6308
www.yourmanchesternh.com

Miami, FL

Greater Miami Chamber of Commerce
1601 Biscayne Boulevard
Ballroom Level
Miami, FL 33132-1260
Phone: (305) 350-7700
Fax: (305) 374-6902
www.greatermiami.com

The Beacon Council
80 Southwest 8th Street
Suite 2400
Miami, FL 33130
Phone: (305) 579-1300
Fax: (305) 375-0271
www.beaconcouncil.com

Minneapolis, MN

Minneapolis Community Development Agency
Crown Roller Mill
105 5th Avenue South, Suite 200
Minneapolis, MN 55401
Phone: (612) 673-5095
Fax: (612) 673-5100
www.ci.minneapolis.mn.us

Murfreesboro, TN

Rutherford County Chamber of Commerce
3050 Medical Center Parkway
Murfreesboro, TN 37129
Phone: (615) 893-6565
Fax: (615) 890-7600
www.rutherfordchamber.org

Naperville, IL

Naperville Chamber of Commerce
55 S Main St #351
Naperville, IL 60540
Phone: (630) 355-4141
www.naperville.net

Nashville, TN

Community Development Department
312 Eighth Avenue North
Eleventh Floor
Nashville, TN 37243
Phone: (615) 741-2626
Fax: (615) 532-8715
www.state.tn.us

Nashville Area Chamber of Commerce
211 Commerce Street
Suite 100
Nashville, TN 37201
Phone: (615) 743-3000
Fax: (615) 256-3074
www.nashvillechamber.cm

Tennessee Valley Authority Economic Development Corp.
P.O. Box 292409
Nashville, TN 37229-2409
Phone: (615) 232-6225
www.tvaed.com

New Orleans, LA

New Orleans Chamber of Commerce
1515 Poydras St
Suite 1010
New Orleans, LA 70112
Phone: (504) 799-4260
Fax: (504) 799-4259
neworleanschamber.org

New York, NY

New York City Economic Development Corporation
110 William Street
New York, NY 10038
Phone: (212) 619-5000
www.nycedc.com

The Partnership for New York City
One Battery Park Plaza
5th Floor
New York, NY 10004
Phone: (212) 493-7400
Fax: (212) 344-3344
www.pfnyc.org

Norman, OK

Norman Chamber of Commerce
115 E. Gray
Norman, OK 73070
Phone: (405) 321-7260
Fax: (405) 360-4679
www.normanchamber.com

Olathe, KS

Olathe Chamber of Commerce
18001 W. 106th St.
Suite 160
Olathe, KS 66061-0098
Phone: (913) 764-1050
Fax: (913) 782-4636
www.olathe.org

Omaha, NE

Omaha Chamber of Commerce
1301 Harney Street
Omaha, NE 68102
Phone: (402) 346-5000
Fax: (402) 346-7050
www.omahachamber.org

Orlando, FL

Metro Orlando Economic Development Commission of Mid-Florida
301 East Pine Street
Suite 900
Orlando, FL 32801
Phone: (407) 422-7159
Fax: (407) 425.6428
www.orlandoedc.com

Orlando Regional Chamber of Commerce
75 South Ivanhoe Boulevard
PO Box 1234
Orlando, FL 32802
Phone: (407) 425-1234
Fax: (407) 839-5020
www.orlando.org

Overland Park, KS

Overland Park Chamber of Commerce
9001 W 110th St
Suite 150
Overland Park, KS 66210
Phone: (913) 491-3600
www.opks.org

Oyster Bay, NY

Historic Oyster Bay Chamber of Commerce
PO Box 21
Oyster Bay, NY 11771
Phone: (516) 922-6464
www.visitoysterbay.com

Pembroke Pines, FL

Miramar Pembroke Pines Regional Chamber of Commerce
10100 Pines Boulevard
4th Floor
Pembroke Pines, FL 33026
Phone: (954) 432-9808
Fax: (954) 432-9193
www.miramarpembrokepines.org

Philadelphia, PA

Greater Philadelphia Chamber of Commerce
200 South Broad Street
Suite 700
Philadelphia, PA 19102
Phone: (215) 545-1234
Fax: (215) 790-3600
www.greaterphilachamber.com

Phoenix, AZ

Greater Phoenix Chamber of Commerce
201 North Central Avenue
27th Floor
Phoenix, AZ 85073
Phone: (602) 495-2195
Fax: (602) 495-8913
www.phoenixchamber.com

Greater Phoenix Economic Council
2 North Central Avenue
Suite 2500
Phoenix, AZ 85004
Phone: (602) 256-7700
Fax: (602) 256-7744
www.gpec.org

Pittsburgh, PA

Allegheny County Industrial Development Authority
425 6th Avenue
Suite 800
Pittsburgh, PA 15219
Phone: (412) 350-1067
Fax: (412) 642-2217
www.alleghenycounty.us

Greater Pittsburgh Chamber of Commerce
425 6th Avenue
12th Floor
Pittsburgh, PA 15219
Phone: (412) 392-4500
Fax: (412) 392-4520
www.alleghenyconference.org

Plano, TX

Plano Chamber of Commerce
1200 E 15th St
Plano, TX 75074
Phone: (972) 424-7547
Fax: (972) 422-5182
www.planochamber.org

Portland, OR

Portland Business Alliance
200 SW Market Street
Suite 1770
Portland, OR 97201
Phone: (503) 224-8684
Fax: (503) 323-9186
www.portlandalliance.com

Providence, RI

Greater Providence Chamber of Commerce
30 Exchange Terrace
Fourth Floor
Providence, RI 02903
Phone: (401) 521-5000
Fax: (401) 351-2090
www.provchamber.com

Rhode Island Economic Development Corporation
Providence City Hall
25 Dorrance Street
Providence, RI 02903
Phone: (401) 421-7740
Fax: (401) 751-0203
www.providenceri.com

Provo, UT

Provo-Orem Chamber of Commerce
51 South University Avenue
Suite 215
Provo, UT 84601
Phone: (801) 851-2555
Fax: (801) 851-2557
www.thechamber.org/

Raleigh, NC

Greater Raleigh Chamber of Commerce
800 South Salisbury Street
Raleigh, NC 27601-2978
Phone: (919) 664-7000
Fax: (919) 664-7099
www.raleighchamber.org

Richmond, VA

Greater Richmond Chamber of Commerce
P.O. Box 12280
Richmond, VA 23241-2280
Phone: (804) 648-1234
Fax: (804) 783-9366
www.grcc.com/

Greater Richmond Partnership
901 East Byrd Street
Suite 801
Richmond, VA 23219-4070
Phone: (804) 643-3227
Fax: (804) 343-7167
www.grpva.com/New_pages/home_ted.shtm

Roseville, CA

Roseville Chamber of Commerce
650 Douglas Blvd.
Roseville, CA 95678
Phone: (916) 783-8136
www.rosevillechamber.com

Round Rock, TX

Round Rock Chamber
212 East Main St.
Round Rock, TX 78664
Phone: (512) 255-5805
Fax: (512) 255-3345
www.roundrockchamber.org

San Antonio, TX

San Antonio Economic Development Department
P.O. Box 839966
San Antonio, TX 78283-3966
Phone: (210) 207-8080
Fax: (210) 207-8151
www.sanantonio.gov/edd

The Greater San Antonio Chamber of Commerce
602 E. Commerce Street
San Antonio, TX 78205
Phone: (210) 229-2100
Fax: (210) 229-1600
www.sachamber.org

San Diego, CA

San Diego Economic Development Corporation
401 B Street
Suite 1100
San Diego, CA 92101
Phone: (619) 234-8484
Fax: (619) 234-1935
www.sandiegobusiness.org

San Diego Regional Chamber of Commerce
402 West Broadway
Suite 1000
San Diego, CA 92101-3585
Phone: (619) 544-1300
Fax: (619) 744-7481
www.sdchamber.org

San Francisco, CA

San Francisco Chamber of Commerce
235 Montgomery Street
12th Floor
San Francisco, CA 94104
Phone: (415) 392-4520
Fax: (415) 392-0485
www.sfchamber.com

San Jose, CA

Office of Economic Development
60 South Market Street
Suite 470
San Jose, CA 95113
Phone: (408) 277-5880
Fax: (408) 277-3615
www.sba.gov

San Jose-Silicone Valley Chamber of Commerce
310 South First Street
San Jose, CA 95113
Phone: (408) 291-5250
Fax: (408) 286-5019
www.sjchamber.com

Savannah, GA

Economic Development Authority
131 Hutchinson Island Road
4th Floor
Savannah, GA 31421
Phone: (912) 447-8450
Fax: (912) 447-8455
www.Seda.org

Savannah Chamber of Commerce
101 E. Bay Street
Savannah, GA 31402
Phone: (912) 644-6400
Fax: (912) 644-6499
www.savannahchamber.com

Scottsdale, AZ

Scottsdale Area Chamber of Commerce
4725 N. Scottsdale Rd.
#210
Scottsdale, AZ 85251-4498
Phone: (480) 355-2700
Fax: (480) 355-2710
www.scottsdalechamber.com

Seattle, WA

Greater Seattle Chamber of Commerce
1301 Fifth Avenue
Suite 2500
Seattle, WA 98101
Phone: (206) 389-7200
Fax: (206) 389-7288
www.seattlechamber.com

Sioux Falls, SD

Sioux Falls Area Chamber of Commerce
200 N. Phillips Avenue
Suite 102
Sioux Falls, SD 57104
Phone: (605) 336-1620
Fax: (605) 336-6499
www.siouxfallschamber.com

Stamford, CT

Stamford Chamber of Commerce
733 Summer Street
Stamford, CT 6901
Phone: (203) 359-4761
Fax: (203) 363-5069
www.stamfordchamber.com

Sterling Heights, MI

Sterling Heights Regional Chamber of Commerce & Industry
12900 Hall Road
Suite 100
Sterling Heights, MI 48313
Phone: (586) 731-5400
Fax: (586) 731-3521
www.suscc.com

Sunnyvale, CA

Sunnyvale Chamber of Commerce
260 S. Sunnyvale Ave.
Suite 402
Sunnyvale, CA 94086
Phone: (408) 736-4971
Fax: (408) 736-1919
www.svcoc.org

Tampa, FL

Greater Tampa Chamber of Commerce
P.O. Box 420
Tampa, FL 33601-0420
Phone: (813) 276-9401
Fax: (813) 229-7855
www.tampachamber.com

Temecula, CA

Temecula Valley Chamber of Commerce
26790 Ynez Court
Suite A
Temecula, CA 92591
Phone: (951) 676-5090
Fax: (951) 694-0201
www.temecula.org

Thousand Oaks, CA

Greater Conejo Valley Chamber of Commerce
600 Hampshire Rd.
Suite 200
Thousand Oaks, CA 91361
Phone: (805) 370-0035
Fax: (805) 370-1083
www.conejochamber.org

Virginia Beach, VA

Hampton Roads Chamber of Commerce
500 East Main St
Suite 700
Virginia Beach, VA 23510
Phone: (757) 664-2531
www.hamptonroadschamber.com

Washington, DC

District of Columbia Chamber of Commerce
1213 K Street NW
Washington, DC 20005
Phone: (202) 347-7201
Fax: (202) 638-6762
www.dcchamber.org

District of Columbia Office of Planning and Economic Development
J.A. Wilson Building
1350 Pennsylvania Ave NW, Suite 317
Washington, DC 20004
Phone: (202) 727-6365
Fax: (202) 727-6703
dcbiz.dc.gov/dmped/site/default.asp

Appendix D: State Departments of Labor

Alabama

Jim Bennett, Commissioner
Alabama Department of Labor
P.O. Box 303500
Montgomery, AL 36130-3500
Phone: (334) 242-3072
www.Alalabor.state.al.us

Alaska

Clark Bishop, Commissioner
Dept of Labor and Workforce Devel.
P.O. Box 11149
Juneau, AK 99822-2249
Phone: (907) 465-2700
www.labor.state.AK.us

Arizona

Brian C. Delfs, Director
Arizona Industrial Commission
800 West Washington Street
Phoenix, AZ 85007
Phone: (602) 542-4515
www.ica.state.AZ.us

Arkansas

James Salkeld, Director
Department of Labor
10421 West Markham
Little Rock, AR 72205
Phone: (501) 682-4500
www.Arkansas.gov/labor

California

Victoria Bradshaw, Director
Labor and Workforce Development
445 Golden Gate Ave., 10th Floor
San Francisco, CA 94102
Phone: (916) 263-1811
www.labor.CA.gov

Colorado

Donald J. Mares, Executive Director
Dept of Labor and Employment
633 17th St., 2nd Floor
Denver, CO 80202-3660
Phone: (888) 390-7936
www.COworkforce.com

Connecticut

Patricia H. Mayfield, Commissioner
Department of Labor
200 Folly Brook Blvd.
Wethersfield, CT 06109-1114
Phone: (860) 263-6000
www.CT.gov/dol

Delaware

Thomas B. Sharp, Secretary of Labor
Department of Labor
4425 N. Market St., 4th Floor
Wilmington, DE 19802
Phone: (302) 451-3423
www.Delawareworks.com

District of Columbia

Ms. Summer Spencer, Director
Employment Services Department
614 New York Ave., NE, Suite 300
Washington, DC 20002
Phone: (202) 671-1900
www.DOES.DC.gov

Florida

Monesia T. Brown, Director
Agency for Workforce Innovation
The Caldwell Building
107 East Madison St. Suite 100
Tallahassee, FL 32399-4120
Phone: (800) 342-3450
www.Floridajobs.org

Georgia

Michael Thurmond, Commissioner
Department of Labor
Sussex Place, Room 600
148 Andrew Young Intl Blvd., NE
Atlanta, GA 30303
Phone: (404) 656-3011
www.dol.state.GA.us

Hawaii

Director
Dept of Labor & Industrial Relations
830 Punchbowl Street
Honolulu, HI 96813
Phone: (808) 586-8842
wwwHawaii.gov/labor

Idaho

Robert B. Madsen, Director
Department of Labor
317 W. Main St.
Boise, ID 83735-0001
Phone: (208) 332-3579
www.labor.Idaho.gov

Illinois

Catherine M. Shannon, Director
Department of Labor
160 N. LaSalle Street, 13th Floor
Suite C-1300
Chicago, IL 60601
Phone: (312) 793-2800
www.state.IL.us/agency/idol

Indiana

Lori Torres, Dept of Labor
Indiana Government Center South
402 W. Washington Street
Room W195
Indianapolis, IN 46204
Phone: (317) 232-2655
www.IN.gov/labor

Iowa

David Neil, Labor Commissioner
Iowa Workforce Development
1000 East Grand Avenue
Des Moines, IA 50319-0209
Phone: (515) 242-5870
www.Iowaworkforce.org/labor

Kansas

Jim Garner, Secretary
Department of Labor
401 S.W. Topeka Blvd.
Topeka, KS 66603-3182
Phone: (785) 296-5000
www.dol.KS.gov

Kentucky

Philip Anderson, Commissioner
Department of Labor
1047 U.S. Hwy 127 South, Suite 4
Frankfort, KY 40601-4381
Phone: (502) 564-3070
www.labor.KY.gov

Louisiana

John Warner Smith, Secretary
Department of Labor
P.O. Box 94094
Baton Rouge, LA 70804-9094
Phone: (225) 342-3111
www.LAworks.net

Maine

Laura Fortman, Commissioner
Department of Labor
45 Commerce Street
Augusta, ME 04330
Phone: (207) 623-7900
www.state.ME.us/labor

Maryland

Tom Perez, Secretary
Department of Labor and Industry
500 N. Calvert Street
Suite 401
Baltimore, MD 21202
Phone: (410) 767-2357
www.dllr.state.MD.us

Massachusetts

Greg Noel, Secretary
Dept of Labor & Work Force Devel.
One Ashburton Place
Room 2112
Boston, MA 02108
Phone: (617) 626-7100
www.Mass.gov/eolwd

Michigan

Keith Cooley, Director
Dept of Labor & Economic Growth
P.O. Box 30004
Lansing, MI 48909
Phone: (517) 335-0400
www.Michigan.gov/cis

Minnesota

Steven A. Sviggum, Commissioner
Dept of Labor and Industry
443 Lafayette Road North
Saint Paul, MN 55155
Phone: (651) 284-5070
www.doli.state.MN.us

Mississippi

Tommye Dale Favre, Executive Director
Dept of Employment Security
P.O. Box 1699
Jackson, MS 39215-1699
Phone: (601) 321-6000
www.mdes.MS.gov

Missouri

Todd Smith, Director
Labor and Industrial Relations
P.O. Box 599
3315 W. Truman Boulevard
Jefferson City, MO 65102-0599
Phone: (573) 751-7500
www.dolir.MO.gov/lirc

Montana

Keith Kelly, Commissioner
Dept of Labor and Industry
P.O. Box 1728
Helena, MT 59624-1728
Phone: (406) 444-9091
www.dli.MT.gov

Nebraska

Fernando Lecuona, Commissioner
Department of Labor
550 South 16th Street
Box 94600
Lincoln, NE 68509-4600
Phone: (402) 471-9000
www.Nebraskaworkforce.com

Nevada

Michael Tanchek, Commissioner
Dept of Business and Industry
555 E. Washington Ave.
Suite 4100
Las Vegas, NV 89101-1050
Phone: (702) 486-2650
www.laborcommissioner.com

New Hampshire

George N. Copadis, Commissioner
Department of Labor
State Office Park South
95 Pleasant Street
Concord, NH 03301
Phone: (603) 271-3176
www.labor.state.NH.us

New Jersey

David Socolow, Commissioner
Department of Labor
John Fitch Plaza, 13th Floor
Suite D
Trenton, NJ 08625-0110
Phone: (609) 777-3200
lwd.dol.state.nj.us/labor

New Mexico

Betty D. Sparrow, Secretary
Department of Labor
401 Broadway, NE
Albuquerque, NM 87103-1928
Phone: (505) 841-8450
www.dol.state.NM.us

New York

M. Patricia Smith, Commissioner
Department of Labor
State Office Bldg. # 12
W.A. Harriman Campus
Albany, NY 12240
Phone: (518) 457-5519
www.labor.state.NY.us

North Carolina

Cherie K. Berry, Commissioner
Department of Labor
4 West Edenton Street
Raleigh, NC 27601-1092
Phone: (919) 733-7166
www.nclabor.com

North Dakota

Lisa Fair McEvers, Commissioner
Department of Labor
State Capitol Building
600 East Boulevard, Dept 406
Bismark, ND 58505-0340
Phone: (701) 328-2660
www.nd.gov/labor

Ohio

Kimberly A. Zurz, Director
Department of Commerce
77 South High Street, 22nd Floor
Columbus, OH 43215
Phone: (614) 644-2239
www.com.state.OH.us

Oklahoma

Lloyd Fields, Commissioner
Department of Labor
4001 N. Lincoln Blvd.
Oklahoma City, OK 73105-5212
Phone: (405) 528-1500
www.state.OK.us/~okdol

Oregon

Dan Gardner, Commissioner
Bureau of Labor and Industries
800 NE Oregon St., #32
Portland, OR 97232
Phone: (971) 673-0761
www.Oregon.gov/boli

Pennsylvania

Stephen M. Schmerin, Secretary
Dept of Labor and Industry
1700 Labor and Industry Bldg
7th and Forster Streets
Harrisburg, PA 17120
Phone: (717) 787-5279
www.dli.state.PA.us

Rhode Island

Adelita S. Orefice, Director
Department of Labor and Training
1511 Pontiac Avenue
Cranston, RI 02920
Phone: (401) 462-8000
www.dlt.state.RI.us

South Carolina

Adrienne R. Youmans, Director
Dept of Labor, Licensing & Regulations
P.O. Box 11329
Columbia, SC 29211-1329
Phone: (803) 896-4300
www.llr.state.SC.us

South Dakota

Pamela S. Roberts, Secretary
Department of Labor
700 Governors Drive
Pierre, SD 57501-2291
Phone: (605) 773-3682
www.state.SD.us

Tennessee

James G. Neeley, Commissioner
Dept of Labor & Workforce Development
Andrew Johnson Tower
710 James Robertson Pkwy
Nashville, TN 37243-0655
Phone: (615) 741-6642
www.state.TN.us/labor-wfd

Texas

Ronald Congleton, Labor Commissioner
Texas Workforce Commission
101 East 15th St.
Austin, TX 78778
Phone: (512) 475-2670
www.twc.state.TX.us

Utah

Sherrie Hayashi, Commissioner
Utah Labor Commission
P.O. Box 146610
Salt Lake City, UT 84114-6610
Phone: (801) 530-6800
Laborcommission.Utah.gov

Vermont

Patricia Moulton Pow, Commissioner
Department of Labor
5 Green Mountain Drive
P.O. Box 488
Montpelier, VT 05601-0488
Phone: (802) 828-4000
www.labor.verMont.gov

Virginia

C. Ray Davenport, Commissioner
Dept of Labor and Industry
Powers-Taylor Building
13 S. 13th Street
Richmond, VA 23219
Phone: (804) 371-2327
www.doli.Virginia.gov

Washington

Judy Schurke, Acting Director
Dept of Labor and Industries
P.O. Box 44001
Olympia, WA 98504-4001
Phone: (360) 902-4200
www.lni.WA.gov

West Virginia

David Mullens, Commissioner
Division of Labor
State Capitol Complex, Building #6
1900 Kanawha Blvd.
Charleston, WV 25305
Phone: (304) 558-7890
www.labor.state.WV.us

Wisconsin

Roberta Gassman, Secretary
Dept of Workforce Development
201 E. Washington Ave., #A400
P.O. Box 7946
Madison, WI 53707-7946
Phone: (608) 266-6861
www.dwd.state.WI.us

Wyoming

Cynthia Pomeroy, Director
Department of Employment
1510 East Pershing Blvd.
Cheyenne, WY 82002
Phone: (307) 777-7261
www.doe.state.WY.us

Source: *U.S. Department of Labor*
http://www.dol.gov/esa/contacts/state_of.htm

Appendix E: Comparative Statistics

Demographics
Population Growth: City . . . A-20
Population Growth: Metro Area . . . A-22
Household Size: City . . . A-24
Household Size: Metro Area . . . A-26
Race: City . . . A-28
Race: Metro Area . . . A-30
Hispanic Origin: City . . . A-32
Hispanic Origin: Metro Area . . . A-34
Age: City . . . A-36
Age: Metro Area . . . A-38
Segregation . . . A-40
Religious Groups . . . A-42
Ancestry: City . . . A-44
Ancestry: Metro Area . . . A-46
Foreign-Born Population: City . . . A-48
Foreign-Born Population: Metro Area . . . A-50
Marital Status: City . . . A-52
Marital Status: Metro Area . . . A-54
Male/Female Ratio: City . . . A-56
Male/Female Ratio: Metro Area . . . A-58

Economy
Gross Metropolitan Product . . . A-60

Income
Income: City . . . A-62
Income: Metro Area . . . A-64
Household Income Distribution: City . . . A-66
Household Income Distribution: Metro Area . . . A-68
Poverty Rate: City . . . A-70
Poverty Rate: Metro Area . . . A-72
Personal Bankruptcy Filing Rate . . . A-74

Residential Real Estate
Building Permits: City . . . A-76
Building Permits: Metro Area . . . A-78
Homeownership Rate . . . A-80
Housing Vacancy Rates . . . A-82

Employment & Earnings
Employment by Industry . . . A-84
Labor Force, Employment and Job Growth: City . . . A-86
Labor Force, Employment and Job Growth: Metro Area . . . A-88
Unemployment Rate: City . . . A-90
Unemployment Rate: Metro Area . . . A-92
Average Hourly Wages: Occupations A - C . . . A-94
Average Hourly Wages: Occupations C - E . . . A-96
Average Hourly Wages: Occupations E - I . . . A-98
Average Hourly Wages: Occupations J - N . . . A-100
Average Hourly Wages: Occupations N - R . . . A-102
Average Hourly Wages: Occupations R - T . . . A-104
Average Hourly Wages: Occupations T - Z . . . A-106
Means of Transportation to Work: City . . . A-108
Means of Transportation to Work: Metro Area . . . A-110
Travel Time to Work: City . . . A-112
Travel Time to Work: Metro Area . . . A-114

Election Results
2008 Presidential Election Results . . . A-116

Housing
House Price Index (HPI) . . . A-118
Year Housing Structure Built: City . . . A-120
Year Housing Structure Built: Metro Area . . . A-122

Education
Highest Level of Education: City . . . A-124
Highest Level of Education: Metro Area . . . A-126
School Enrollment by Grade and Control: City . . . A-128
School Enrollment by Grade and Control: Metro Area . . . A-130
Educational Attainment by Race: City . . . A-132
Educational Attainment by Race: Metro Area . . . A-134

Cost of Living
Cost of Living Index . . . A-136
Grocery Prices . . . A-138
Housing and Utility Costs . . . A-140

Health Care
Health Care, Transportation, and Other Costs . . . A-142
Distribution of Physicians and Dentists . . . A-144

Public Safety
Crime Rate: City . . . A-146
Crime Rate: Suburbs . . . A-148
Crime Rate: Metro Area . . . A-150

Climate
Temperature & Precipitation: Yearly Averages and Extremes . . . A-152
Weather Conditions . . . A-154

Air Quality
Air Quality Index . . . A-156
Air Quality Index Pollutants . . . A-158
Air Quality Index Trends . . . A-160
Maximum Air Pollutant Concentrations: Particulate Matter, Ozone, CO and Lead . . . A-162
Maximum Air Pollutant Concentrations: Nitrogen Dioxide and Sulfur Dioxide . . . A-164

Population Growth: City

City	1990 Census	2000 Census	2010 Census	Population Growth (%) 1990-2000	2000-2010
Albuquerque, NM	388,375	448,607	545,852	15.5	21.7
Alexandria, VA	111,526	128,283	139,966	15.0	9.1
Anchorage, AK	226,338	260,283	291,826	15.0	12.1
Ann Arbor, MI	111,018	114,024	113,934	2.7	-0.1
Athens, GA	86,561	100,266	115,452	15.8	15.1
Atlanta, GA	394,092	416,474	420,003	5.7	0.8
Austin, TX	499,053	656,562	790,390	31.6	20.4
Baltimore, MD	736,014	651,154	620,961	-11.5	-4.6
Bellevue, WA	99,057	109,569	122,363	10.6	11.7
Billings, MT	81,812	89,847	104,170	9.8	15.9
Boise City, ID	144,317	185,787	205,671	28.7	10.7
Boston, MA	574,283	589,141	617,594	2.6	4.8
Boulder, CO	87,737	94,673	97,385	7.9	2.9
Broken Arrow, OK	59,372	74,859	98,850	26.1	32.0
Cambridge, MA	95,959	101,355	105,162	5.6	3.8
Cape Coral, FL	75,507	102,286	154,305	35.5	50.9
Carlsbad, CA	62,753	78,247	105,328	24.7	34.6
Cary, NC	49,835	94,536	135,234	89.7	43.1
Cedar Rapids, IA	110,829	120,758	126,326	9.0	4.6
Charleston, SC	96,102	96,650	120,083	0.6	24.2
Charlotte, NC	428,283	540,828	731,424	26.3	35.2
Chesapeake, VA	151,976	199,184	222,209	31.1	11.6
Chicago, IL	2,783,726	2,896,016	2,695,598	4.0	-6.9
Clarksville, TN	78,569	103,455	132,929	31.7	28.5
Colorado Spgs., CO	283,798	360,890	416,427	27.2	15.4
Columbia, MD	76,649	88,254	99,615	15.1	12.9
Columbia, MO	71,069	84,531	108,500	18.9	28.4
Columbia, SC	115,475	116,278	129,272	0.7	11.2
Columbus, OH	648,656	711,470	787,033	9.7	10.6
Dallas, TX	1,006,971	1,188,580	1,197,816	18.0	0.8
Denver, CO	467,153	554,636	600,158	18.7	8.2
Durham, NC	151,737	187,035	228,330	23.3	22.1
Edison, NJ	88,680	97,687	99,967	10.2	2.3
El Paso, TX	515,541	563,662	649,121	9.3	15.2
Fargo, ND	74,372	90,599	105,549	21.8	16.5
Ft. Collins, CO	89,555	118,652	143,986	32.5	21.4
Ft. Worth, TX	448,311	534,694	741,206	19.3	38.6
Gilbert, AZ	33,229	109,697	208,453	230.1	90.0
Green Bay, WI	96,466	102,313	104,057	6.1	1.7
Henderson, NV	66,093	175,381	257,729	165.4	47.0
High Point, NC	72,061	85,839	104,371	19.1	21.6
Honolulu, HI	376,465	371,657	337,256	-1.3	-9.3
Houston, TX	1,697,610	1,953,631	2,099,451	15.1	7.5
Huntington, NY	191,474	195,289	203,264	2.0	4.1
Huntsville, AL	161,842	158,216	180,105	-2.2	13.8
Indianapolis, IN	730,993	781,870	820,445	7.0	4.9
Irvine, CA	111,754	143,072	212,375	28.0	48.4
Jackson, MS	196,469	184,256	173,514	-6.2	-5.8
Jacksonville, FL	635,221	735,617	821,784	15.8	11.7
Jersey City, NJ	228,543	240,055	247,597	5.0	3.1
Kansas City, MO	434,967	441,545	459,787	1.5	4.1
Kenosha, WI	81,575	90,352	99,218	10.8	9.8
Las Vegas, NV	261,374	478,434	583,756	83.0	22.0
Lexington, KY	225,366	260,512	295,803	15.6	13.5
Lincoln, NE	193,629	225,581	258,379	16.5	14.5

Table continued on next page.

City	1990 Census	2000 Census	2010 Census	Population Growth (%) 1990-2000	2000-2010
Little Rock, AR	177,519	183,133	193,524	3.2	5.7
Los Angeles, CA	3,487,671	3,694,820	3,792,621	5.9	2.6
Madison, WI	193,451	208,054	233,209	7.5	12.1
Manchester, NH	99,567	107,006	109,565	7.5	2.4
Miami, FL	358,843	362,470	399,457	1.0	10.2
Minneapolis, MN	368,383	382,618	382,578	3.9	0.0
Murfreesboro, TN	47,905	68,816	108,755	43.7	58.0
Naperville, IL	90,506	128,358	141,853	41.8	10.5
Nashville, TN	488,364	545,524	601,222	11.7	10.2
New Orleans, LA	496,938	484,674	343,829	-2.5	-29.1
New York, NY	7,322,552	8,008,278	8,175,133	9.4	2.1
Norman, OK	80,071	95,694	110,925	19.5	15.9
Olathe, KS	64,592	92,962	125,872	43.9	35.4
Omaha, NE	371,972	390,007	408,958	4.8	4.9
Orlando, FL	161,172	185,951	238,300	15.4	28.2
Overland Park, KS	111,803	149,080	173,372	33.3	16.3
Oyster Bay, NY	293,200	293,925	293,214	0.2	-0.2
Pembroke Pines, FL	66,095	137,427	154,750	107.9	12.6
Philadelphia, PA	1,585,577	1,517,550	1,526,006	-4.3	0.6
Phoenix, AZ	989,873	1,321,045	1,445,632	33.5	9.4
Pittsburgh, PA	369,785	334,563	305,704	-9.5	-8.6
Plano, TX	128,507	222,030	259,841	72.8	17.0
Portland, OR	485,833	529,121	583,776	8.9	10.3
Providence, RI	160,734	173,618	178,042	8.0	2.5
Provo, UT	87,148	105,166	112,488	20.7	7.0
Raleigh, NC	226,841	276,093	403,892	21.7	46.3
Richmond, VA	202,783	197,790	204,214	-2.5	3.2
Roseville, CA	44,692	79,921	118,788	78.8	48.6
Round Rock, TX	32,854	61,136	99,887	86.1	63.4
San Antonio, TX	997,258	1,144,646	1,327,407	14.8	16.0
San Diego, CA	1,111,048	1,223,400	1,307,402	10.1	6.9
San Francisco, CA	723,959	776,733	805,235	7.3	3.7
San Jose, CA	784,324	894,943	945,942	14.1	5.7
Savannah, GA	138,038	131,510	136,286	-4.7	3.6
Scottsdale, AZ	130,300	202,705	217,385	55.6	7.2
Seattle, WA	516,262	563,374	608,660	9.1	8.0
Sioux Falls, SD	102,262	123,975	153,888	21.2	24.1
Stamford, CT	108,087	117,083	122,643	8.3	4.7
Sterling Hgts, MI	117,810	124,471	129,699	5.7	4.2
Sunnyvale, CA	117,242	131,760	140,081	12.4	6.3
Tampa, FL	279,960	303,447	335,709	8.4	10.6
Temecula, CA	27,078	57,716	100,097	113.1	73.4
Thousand Oaks, CA	104,661	117,005	126,683	11.8	8.3
Virginia Beach, VA	393,069	425,257	437,994	8.2	3.0
Washington, DC	606,900	572,059	601,723	-5.7	5.2
U.S.	248,709,873	281,421,906	308,745,538	13.2	9.7

Source: U.S. Census Bureau, 2010 Census

Population Growth: Metro Area

Metro Area	1990 Census	2000 Census	2010 Census	Population Growth (%) 1990-2000	2000-2010
Albuquerque, NM	599,416	729,649	887,077	21.7	21.6
Alexandria, VA	4,122,914	4,796,183	5,582,170	16.3	16.4
Anchorage, AK	266,021	319,605	380,821	20.1	19.2
Ann Arbor, MI	282,937	322,895	344,791	14.1	6.8
Athens, GA	136,025	166,079	192,541	22.1	15.9
Atlanta, GA	3,069,411	4,247,981	5,268,860	38.4	24.0
Austin, TX	846,217	1,249,763	1,716,289	47.7	37.3
Baltimore, MD	2,382,172	2,552,994	2,710,489	7.2	6.2
Bellevue, WA	2,559,164	3,043,878	3,439,809	18.9	13.0
Billings, MT	121,499	138,904	158,050	14.3	13.8
Boise City, ID	319,596	464,840	616,561	45.4	32.6
Boston, MA	4,133,895	4,391,344	4,552,402	6.2	3.7
Boulder, CO	208,898	269,758	294,567	29.1	9.2
Broken Arrow, OK	761,019	859,532	937,478	12.9	9.1
Cambridge, MA	4,133,895	4,391,344	4,552,402	6.2	3.7
Cape Coral, FL	335,113	440,888	618,754	31.6	40.3
Carlsbad, CA	2,498,016	2,813,833	3,095,313	12.6	10.0
Cary, NC	541,081	797,071	1,130,490	47.3	41.8
Cedar Rapids, IA	210,640	237,230	257,940	12.6	8.7
Charleston, SC	506,875	549,033	664,607	8.3	21.1
Charlotte, NC	1,024,331	1,330,448	1,758,038	29.9	32.1
Chesapeake, VA	1,449,389	1,576,370	1,671,683	8.8	6.0
Chicago, IL	8,182,076	9,098,316	9,461,105	11.2	4.0
Clarksville, TN	189,277	232,000	273,949	22.6	18.1
Colorado Spgs., CO	409,482	537,484	645,613	31.3	20.1
Columbia, MD	2,382,172	2,552,994	2,710,489	7.2	6.2
Columbia, MO	122,010	145,666	172,786	19.4	18.6
Columbia, SC	548,325	647,158	767,598	18.0	18.6
Columbus, OH	1,405,176	1,612,694	1,836,536	14.8	13.9
Dallas, TX	3,989,294	5,161,544	6,371,773	29.4	23.4
Denver, CO	1,666,935	2,179,296	2,543,482	30.7	16.7
Durham, NC	344,646	426,493	504,357	23.7	18.3
Edison, NJ	16,845,992	18,323,002	18,897,109	8.8	3.1
El Paso, TX	591,610	679,622	800,647	14.9	17.8
Fargo, ND	153,296	174,367	208,777	13.7	19.7
Ft. Collins, CO	186,136	251,494	299,630	35.1	19.1
Ft. Worth, TX	3,989,294	5,161,544	6,371,773	29.4	23.4
Gilbert, AZ	2,238,480	3,251,876	4,192,887	45.3	28.9
Green Bay, WI	243,698	282,599	306,241	16.0	8.4
Henderson, NV	741,459	1,375,765	1,951,269	85.5	41.8
High Point, NC	540,257	643,430	723,801	19.1	12.5
Honolulu, HI	836,231	876,156	953,207	4.8	8.8
Houston, TX	3,767,335	4,715,407	5,946,800	25.2	26.1
Huntington, NY	16,845,992	18,323,002	18,897,109	8.8	3.1
Huntsville, AL	293,047	342,376	417,593	16.8	22.0
Indianapolis, IN	1,294,217	1,525,104	1,756,241	17.8	15.2
Irvine, CA	11,273,720	12,365,627	12,828,837	9.7	3.7
Jackson, MS	446,941	497,197	539,057	11.2	8.4
Jacksonville, FL	925,213	1,122,750	1,345,596	21.4	19.8
Jersey City, NJ	16,845,992	18,323,002	18,897,109	8.8	3.1
Kansas City, MO	1,636,528	1,836,038	2,035,334	12.2	10.9
Kenosha, WI	8,182,076	9,098,316	9,461,105	11.2	4.0
Las Vegas, NV	741,459	1,375,765	1,951,269	85.5	41.8
Lexington, KY	348,428	408,326	472,099	17.2	15.6
Lincoln, NE	229,091	266,787	302,157	16.5	13.3

Table continued on next page.

Metro Area	1990 Census	2000 Census	2010 Census	Population Growth (%) 1990-2000	2000-2010
Little Rock, AR	535,034	610,518	699,757	14.1	14.6
Los Angeles, CA	11,273,720	12,365,627	12,828,837	9.7	3.7
Madison, WI	432,323	501,774	568,593	16.1	13.3
Manchester, NH	336,073	380,841	400,721	13.3	5.2
Miami, FL	4,056,100	5,007,564	5,564,635	23.5	11.1
Minneapolis, MN	2,538,834	2,968,806	3,279,833	16.9	10.5
Murfreesboro, TN	1,048,218	1,311,789	1,589,934	25.1	21.2
Naperville, IL	8,182,076	9,098,316	9,461,105	11.2	4.0
Nashville, TN	1,048,218	1,311,789	1,589,934	25.1	21.2
New Orleans, LA	1,264,391	1,316,510	1,167,764	4.1	-11.3
New York, NY	16,845,992	18,323,002	18,897,109	8.8	3.1
Norman, OK	971,042	1,095,421	1,252,987	12.8	14.4
Olathe, KS	1,636,528	1,836,038	2,035,334	12.2	10.9
Omaha, NE	685,797	767,041	865,350	11.8	12.8
Orlando, FL	1,224,852	1,644,561	2,134,411	34.3	29.8
Overland Park, KS	1,636,528	1,836,038	2,035,334	12.2	10.9
Oyster Bay, NY	16,845,992	18,323,002	18,897,109	8.8	3.1
Pembroke Pines, FL	4,056,100	5,007,564	5,564,635	23.5	11.1
Philadelphia, PA	5,435,470	5,687,147	5,965,343	4.6	4.9
Phoenix, AZ	2,238,480	3,251,876	4,192,887	45.3	28.9
Pittsburgh, PA	2,468,289	2,431,087	2,356,285	-1.5	-3.1
Plano, TX	3,989,294	5,161,544	6,371,773	29.4	23.4
Portland, OR	1,523,741	1,927,881	2,226,009	26.5	15.5
Providence, RI	1,509,789	1,582,997	1,600,852	4.8	1.1
Provo, UT	269,407	376,774	526,810	39.9	39.8
Raleigh, NC	541,081	797,071	1,130,490	47.3	41.8
Richmond, VA	949,244	1,096,957	1,258,251	15.6	14.7
Roseville, CA	1,481,126	1,796,857	2,149,127	21.3	19.6
Round Rock, TX	846,217	1,249,763	1,716,289	47.7	37.3
San Antonio, TX	1,407,745	1,711,703	2,142,508	21.6	25.2
San Diego, CA	2,498,016	2,813,833	3,095,313	12.6	10.0
San Francisco, CA	3,686,592	4,123,740	4,335,391	11.9	5.1
San Jose, CA	1,534,280	1,735,819	1,836,911	13.1	5.8
Savannah, GA	258,060	293,000	347,611	13.5	18.6
Scottsdale, AZ	2,238,480	3,251,876	4,192,887	45.3	28.9
Seattle, WA	2,559,164	3,043,878	3,439,809	18.9	13.0
Sioux Falls, SD	153,500	187,093	228,261	21.9	22.0
Stamford, CT	827,645	882,567	916,829	6.6	3.9
Sterling Hgts, MI	4,248,699	4,452,557	4,296,250	4.8	-3.5
Sunnyvale, CA	1,534,280	1,735,819	1,836,911	13.1	5.8
Tampa, FL	2,067,959	2,395,997	2,783,243	15.9	16.2
Temecula, CA	2,588,793	3,254,821	4,224,851	25.7	29.8
Thousand Oaks, CA	669,016	753,197	823,318	12.6	9.3
Virginia Beach, VA	1,449,389	1,576,370	1,671,683	8.8	6.0
Washington, DC	4,122,914	4,796,183	5,582,170	16.3	16.4
U.S.	248,709,873	281,421,906	308,745,538	13.2	9.7

Note: Figures cover the Metropolitan Statistical Area (MSA)—see Appendix B for areas included
Source: U.S. Census Bureau, 2010 Census

Household Size: City

City	Persons in Household (%)							Average Household Size
	One	Two	Three	Four	Five	Six	Seven or More	
Albuquerque, NM	31.9	32.1	15.1	11.9	5.6	2.1	1.3	2.40
Alexandria, VA	43.4	31.9	11.7	7.8	3.1	1.3	0.8	2.03
Anchorage, AK	24.9	32.6	17.1	13.8	6.5	2.8	2.3	2.64
Ann Arbor, MI	37.4	33.9	13.2	9.7	3.4	1.5	0.9	2.17
Athens, GA	30.6	34.1	15.9	11.9	4.5	1.8	1.2	2.37
Atlanta, GA	44.0	29.1	11.9	8.0	3.8	1.6	1.5	2.11
Austin, TX	34.0	31.4	14.4	11.2	5.0	2.2	1.8	2.37
Baltimore, MD	36.1	28.7	15.4	9.8	5.3	2.5	2.3	2.38
Bellevue, WA	28.1	34.8	16.4	13.7	4.7	1.6	0.8	2.41
Billings, MT	32.6	34.7	14.6	10.7	4.8	1.6	0.9	2.29
Boise City, ID	30.6	34.9	15.4	11.5	4.7	1.9	1.1	2.36
Boston, MA	37.1	30.9	14.6	9.6	4.6	1.8	1.4	2.26
Boulder, CO	35.8	34.7	14.3	10.7	3.2	0.9	0.4	2.16
Broken Arrow, OK	19.2	34.7	18.3	16.4	7.4	2.7	1.2	2.72
Cambridge, MA	40.7	34.8	13.7	7.2	2.4	0.7	0.4	2.00
Cape Coral, FL	21.4	39.8	16.7	13.2	5.8	2.1	1.0	2.53
Carlsbad, CA	23.9	35.6	16.7	15.6	5.6	1.8	0.8	2.53
Cary, NC	23.9	32.0	17.1	17.9	6.4	2.0	0.8	2.61
Cedar Rapids, IA	32.5	34.4	14.4	11.3	4.8	1.7	0.9	2.31
Charleston, SC	34.6	35.5	14.9	9.5	3.6	1.1	0.7	2.18
Charlotte, NC	30.3	30.8	16.1	13.0	6.0	2.3	1.5	2.48
Chesapeake, VA	19.8	32.0	20.2	16.7	7.1	2.8	1.4	2.75
Chicago, IL	35.0	27.4	14.2	10.8	6.3	3.1	3.2	2.52
Clarksville, TN	23.7	31.4	19.6	14.6	6.8	2.5	1.3	2.63
Colorado Spgs., CO	29.6	33.2	15.6	12.5	5.7	2.2	1.2	2.44
Columbia, MD	27.7	32.1	16.9	14.3	5.7	2.0	1.3	2.50
Columbia, MO	32.0	32.9	16.3	12.8	4.0	1.4	0.7	2.32
Columbia, SC	38.0	31.9	14.6	9.3	4.0	1.4	0.9	2.18
Columbus, OH	35.1	31.4	14.9	10.4	4.9	2.0	1.3	2.31
Dallas, TX	33.9	27.2	13.8	11.4	7.0	3.5	3.3	2.57
Denver, CO	40.6	30.4	11.7	8.9	4.4	2.0	2.0	2.22
Durham, NC	33.7	32.0	15.5	10.7	4.8	2.1	1.3	2.34
Edison, NJ	20.4	27.7	21.2	19.7	6.6	2.8	1.5	2.80
El Paso, TX	21.5	26.0	18.5	16.8	10.0	4.3	3.0	2.95
Fargo, ND	36.6	34.4	13.9	9.8	3.7	1.1	0.5	2.15
Ft. Collins, CO	28.4	35.6	16.8	12.6	4.3	1.5	0.7	2.37
Ft. Worth, TX	26.5	27.4	16.3	14.6	8.3	3.8	3.0	2.77
Gilbert, AZ	16.1	30.0	18.1	19.6	9.6	4.2	2.3	3.00
Green Bay, WI	32.4	32.8	14.6	11.0	5.3	2.2	1.7	2.39
Henderson, NV	24.2	37.2	15.9	12.8	5.9	2.5	1.4	2.53
High Point, NC	29.8	31.7	16.5	12.8	5.5	2.3	1.4	2.46
Honolulu, HI	32.9	31.1	14.9	10.2	5.0	2.6	3.4	2.51
Houston, TX	31.0	27.6	15.1	12.3	7.3	3.6	3.1	2.64
Huntington, NY	18.5	31.2	17.5	18.6	8.9	3.0	2.3	2.89
Huntsville, AL	34.7	33.5	14.6	10.4	4.4	1.5	0.8	2.25
Indianapolis, IN	32.0	31.3	15.5	11.4	5.7	2.4	1.6	2.42
Irvine, CA	23.4	31.4	18.7	18.0	5.8	1.9	0.8	2.61
Jackson, MS	30.2	28.0	16.9	12.4	6.9	3.1	2.5	2.60
Jacksonville, FL	28.2	32.5	17.4	12.8	5.6	2.2	1.3	2.48
Jersey City, NJ	30.2	29.2	17.5	12.4	6.1	2.6	2.0	2.53
Kansas City, MO	34.7	31.1	14.6	10.7	5.2	2.2	1.5	2.34
Kenosha, WI	28.8	29.4	16.7	14.2	6.6	2.6	1.6	2.56
Las Vegas, NV	26.0	31.1	15.7	12.9	7.5	3.7	3.1	2.71
Lexington, KY	32.7	33.6	15.4	11.5	4.5	1.5	0.8	2.30

Table continued on next page.

City	Persons in Household (%)							Average Household Size
	One	Two	Three	Four	Five	Six	Seven or More	
Lincoln, NE	31.3	33.8	14.9	11.8	5.2	1.9	1.0	2.36
Little Rock, AR	34.8	31.6	15.0	10.7	4.9	1.8	1.1	2.30
Los Angeles, CA	28.3	27.0	15.2	13.2	7.7	4.0	4.6	2.81
Madison, WI	36.2	34.8	13.6	9.8	3.6	1.2	0.7	2.17
Manchester, NH	32.4	32.8	16.0	11.3	4.7	1.7	1.2	2.34
Miami, FL	33.3	28.8	16.2	11.0	5.6	2.7	2.4	2.47
Minneapolis, MN	40.3	30.3	12.5	9.0	4.0	1.8	2.1	2.23
Murfreesboro, TN	27.3	32.3	17.6	14.4	5.6	1.8	1.0	2.49
Naperville, IL	20.5	29.1	18.2	20.3	8.7	2.4	0.9	2.79
Nashville, TN	34.8	32.2	14.7	10.0	4.8	2.0	1.5	2.31
New Orleans, LA	35.9	29.9	15.4	10.0	5.1	2.1	1.6	2.33
New York, NY	32.0	27.6	16.0	12.1	6.4	3.0	2.9	2.57
Norman, OK	30.7	34.5	16.1	11.8	4.5	1.6	0.8	2.33
Olathe, KS	20.0	30.7	18.1	18.6	8.3	2.8	1.4	2.80
Omaha, NE	32.3	31.3	14.5	11.5	6.0	2.5	1.9	2.45
Orlando, FL	34.6	32.2	15.3	10.4	4.6	1.8	1.2	2.29
Overland Park, KS	29.8	33.5	14.9	13.6	5.7	1.8	0.8	2.41
Oyster Bay, NY	17.9	29.9	18.4	20.1	9.1	3.0	1.6	2.89
Pembroke Pines, FL	24.0	29.0	18.4	17.2	7.4	2.5	1.5	2.70
Philadelphia, PA	34.1	28.2	15.8	11.2	5.9	2.6	2.1	2.45
Phoenix, AZ	27.1	28.8	15.3	13.3	7.9	4.0	3.7	2.77
Pittsburgh, PA	41.7	31.7	13.4	7.9	3.2	1.2	0.7	2.07
Plano, TX	24.4	31.8	17.5	16.4	6.3	2.3	1.3	2.61
Portland, OR	34.5	33.7	14.3	10.3	4.1	1.7	1.4	2.28
Providence, RI	31.7	26.5	16.2	12.6	7.1	3.3	2.7	2.60
Provo, UT	12.8	29.5	18.8	18.3	8.7	7.6	4.2	3.24
Raleigh, NC	32.8	31.8	15.5	12.0	4.9	1.8	1.2	2.36
Richmond, VA	37.9	32.0	14.6	8.7	3.9	1.6	1.2	2.20
Roseville, CA	24.5	32.4	16.4	16.0	7.0	2.4	1.3	2.62
Round Rock, TX	20.8	28.7	18.9	18.2	8.4	3.1	2.0	2.84
San Antonio, TX	26.9	28.5	16.6	14.0	7.8	3.5	2.7	2.71
San Diego, CA	28.0	31.6	15.6	13.0	6.4	2.9	2.6	2.60
San Francisco, CA	38.6	31.4	13.3	8.9	3.7	1.8	2.3	2.26
San Jose, CA	19.7	27.0	17.7	17.3	8.8	4.4	5.2	3.09
Savannah, GA	32.7	31.1	16.2	10.5	5.5	2.3	1.7	2.40
Scottsdale, AZ	34.4	39.4	12.0	9.3	3.4	1.1	0.5	2.14
Seattle, WA	41.3	33.3	12.2	8.5	2.8	1.0	0.9	2.06
Sioux Falls, SD	30.6	33.6	15.0	12.4	5.4	2.0	1.1	2.40
Stamford, CT	28.9	30.2	16.4	13.6	6.2	2.6	2.1	2.56
Sterling Hgts, MI	26.5	31.3	16.0	14.6	7.2	2.8	1.6	2.61
Sunnyvale, CA	25.2	31.0	18.8	15.5	5.4	2.3	1.8	2.61
Tampa, FL	33.6	30.5	15.5	11.5	5.2	2.1	1.5	2.38
Temecula, CA	13.8	27.1	19.2	21.6	11.1	4.5	2.6	3.15
Thousand Oaks, CA	21.2	32.8	17.6	17.1	7.0	2.6	1.8	2.73
Virginia Beach, VA	23.3	33.3	18.9	14.8	6.2	2.3	1.2	2.60
Washington, DC	44.0	29.2	12.3	7.6	3.7	1.7	1.5	2.11
U.S.	26.7	32.8	16.1	13.4	6.5	2.6	1.9	2.58

U.S. Census Bureau, 2010 Census

Household Size: Metro Area

Metro Area	Persons in Household (%)							Average Household Size
	One	Two	Three	Four	Five	Six	Seven or More	
Albuquerque, NM	28.5	32.8	15.5	12.6	6.3	2.5	1.7	2.51
Alexandria, VA	27.0	30.1	16.5	14.3	6.9	2.9	2.3	2.64
Anchorage, AK	24.3	32.8	16.9	13.8	6.7	3.0	2.4	2.67
Ann Arbor, MI	30.6	33.9	15.1	12.4	5.1	1.9	1.0	2.38
Athens, GA	26.5	34.2	16.9	13.7	5.4	2.0	1.3	2.50
Atlanta, GA	25.3	30.2	17.3	15.1	7.2	2.9	2.1	2.68
Austin, TX	27.3	32.0	16.0	13.7	6.4	2.6	2.0	2.58
Baltimore, MD	27.4	31.8	17.0	13.7	6.1	2.4	1.6	2.54
Bellevue, WA	28.4	33.2	15.9	13.3	5.5	2.2	1.5	2.49
Billings, MT	29.8	36.0	14.7	11.5	5.2	1.8	1.0	2.37
Boise City, ID	23.6	33.9	15.7	14.1	7.3	3.3	2.0	2.67
Boston, MA	28.5	31.6	16.4	14.1	6.1	2.1	1.2	2.50
Boulder, CO	29.0	34.8	15.7	13.2	4.8	1.6	0.9	2.39
Broken Arrow, OK	27.3	33.9	15.8	12.8	6.3	2.5	1.5	2.51
Cambridge, MA	28.5	31.6	16.4	14.1	6.1	2.1	1.2	2.50
Cape Coral, FL	26.7	42.7	12.9	9.8	4.7	1.9	1.2	2.35
Carlsbad, CA	24.0	31.2	16.5	14.5	7.4	3.3	3.0	2.75
Cary, NC	25.6	32.3	17.1	15.2	6.3	2.2	1.3	2.57
Cedar Rapids, IA	28.6	35.9	14.7	12.7	5.5	1.9	0.8	2.40
Charleston, SC	26.4	34.3	17.2	13.0	5.7	2.1	1.2	2.49
Charlotte, NC	25.9	32.1	17.0	14.6	6.5	2.3	1.4	2.58
Chesapeake, VA	25.0	33.4	18.3	13.9	6.0	2.2	1.2	2.55
Chicago, IL	27.2	29.3	15.9	14.3	7.5	3.2	2.5	2.68
Clarksville, TN	23.6	32.6	18.7	14.5	6.7	2.5	1.4	2.62
Colorado Spgs., CO	25.9	33.8	16.3	13.8	6.4	2.5	1.3	2.55
Columbia, MD	27.4	31.8	17.0	13.7	6.1	2.4	1.6	2.54
Columbia, MO	28.7	34.3	16.6	13.2	4.7	1.7	0.8	2.40
Columbia, SC	27.5	33.3	17.1	13.1	5.7	2.1	1.2	2.48
Columbus, OH	28.4	33.2	16.0	13.2	5.9	2.1	1.2	2.47
Dallas, TX	24.8	29.6	16.7	15.2	7.9	3.3	2.5	2.74
Denver, CO	29.1	32.6	15.1	13.2	6.0	2.4	1.7	2.50
Durham, NC	29.8	34.5	15.8	12.0	4.9	1.9	1.1	2.39
Edison, NJ	27.6	28.5	16.7	14.5	7.2	3.0	2.6	2.67
El Paso, TX	19.8	24.9	18.5	17.5	11.0	4.8	3.5	3.06
Fargo, ND	31.4	34.5	14.8	12.1	5.0	1.4	0.7	2.32
Ft. Collins, CO	25.9	38.0	15.9	12.7	4.9	1.8	0.9	2.42
Ft. Worth, TX	24.8	29.6	16.7	15.2	7.9	3.3	2.5	2.74
Gilbert, AZ	25.4	33.2	14.8	13.2	7.3	3.4	2.8	2.68
Green Bay, WI	27.2	36.0	15.1	13.1	5.6	1.9	1.1	2.45
Henderson, NV	25.3	32.0	15.9	13.0	7.4	3.5	2.8	2.70
High Point, NC	28.6	34.1	16.6	12.4	5.3	1.9	1.1	2.43
Honolulu, HI	22.8	29.4	17.2	13.9	7.5	4.0	5.2	2.95
Houston, TX	23.5	28.6	17.0	15.6	8.6	3.8	2.9	2.83
Huntington, NY	27.6	28.5	16.7	14.5	7.2	3.0	2.6	2.67
Huntsville, AL	27.8	33.8	16.8	13.4	5.5	1.8	0.9	2.45
Indianapolis, IN	27.0	32.7	16.3	13.8	6.5	2.4	1.3	2.53
Irvine, CA	23.4	27.0	16.3	15.3	8.7	4.4	4.9	2.98
Jackson, MS	26.4	31.2	17.5	13.9	6.6	2.5	1.8	2.60
Jacksonville, FL	26.0	34.1	17.3	13.4	5.9	2.2	1.2	2.52
Jersey City, NJ	27.6	28.5	16.7	14.5	7.2	3.0	2.6	2.67
Kansas City, MO	27.8	33.2	15.8	13.3	6.2	2.4	1.4	2.51
Kenosha, WI	27.2	29.3	15.9	14.3	7.5	3.2	2.5	2.68
Las Vegas, NV	25.3	32.0	15.9	13.0	7.4	3.5	2.8	2.70
Lexington, KY	29.3	34.1	16.4	12.5	5.1	1.7	0.9	2.39

Table continued on next page.

Metro Area	Persons in Household (%)							Average Household Size
	One	Two	Three	Four	Five	Six	Seven or More	
Lincoln, NE	29.8	34.7	14.9	12.2	5.4	2.0	1.1	2.40
Little Rock, AR	27.7	34.2	16.8	12.7	5.5	2.0	1.1	2.45
Los Angeles, CA	23.4	27.0	16.3	15.3	8.7	4.4	4.9	2.98
Madison, WI	29.9	35.8	14.8	12.4	4.8	1.5	0.8	2.35
Manchester, NH	25.3	34.0	17.0	14.7	5.9	2.0	1.0	2.53
Miami, FL	27.0	31.0	16.6	13.7	6.7	2.8	2.2	2.62
Minneapolis, MN	27.5	33.1	15.5	14.1	6.1	2.2	1.6	2.53
Murfreesboro, TN	26.8	33.3	16.8	13.6	6.0	2.2	1.4	2.52
Naperville, IL	27.2	29.3	15.9	14.3	7.5	3.2	2.5	2.68
Nashville, TN	26.8	33.3	16.8	13.6	6.0	2.2	1.4	2.52
New Orleans, LA	28.4	31.2	17.2	13.0	6.3	2.4	1.6	2.52
New York, NY	27.6	28.5	16.7	14.5	7.2	3.0	2.6	2.67
Norman, OK	27.8	33.5	16.0	12.8	6.1	2.3	1.4	2.49
Olathe, KS	27.8	33.2	15.8	13.3	6.2	2.4	1.4	2.51
Omaha, NE	27.5	33.0	15.6	13.3	6.6	2.5	1.5	2.54
Orlando, FL	24.1	33.4	17.3	14.2	6.7	2.6	1.6	2.62
Overland Park, KS	27.8	33.2	15.8	13.3	6.2	2.4	1.4	2.51
Oyster Bay, NY	27.6	28.5	16.7	14.5	7.2	3.0	2.6	2.67
Pembroke Pines, FL	27.0	31.0	16.6	13.7	6.7	2.8	2.2	2.62
Philadelphia, PA	27.4	31.0	16.8	14.2	6.6	2.5	1.6	2.56
Phoenix, AZ	25.4	33.2	14.8	13.2	7.3	3.4	2.8	2.68
Pittsburgh, PA	31.9	34.7	15.3	11.5	4.5	1.4	0.6	2.29
Plano, TX	24.8	29.6	16.7	15.2	7.9	3.3	2.5	2.74
Portland, OR	27.0	34.1	15.8	13.2	5.8	2.4	1.7	2.52
Providence, RI	28.9	32.1	16.7	13.6	5.7	2.0	1.1	2.46
Provo, UT	11.7	25.2	16.4	17.0	13.1	9.5	7.0	3.57
Raleigh, NC	25.6	32.3	17.1	15.2	6.3	2.2	1.3	2.57
Richmond, VA	26.6	33.5	17.4	13.6	5.7	2.0	1.2	2.50
Roseville, CA	24.8	32.1	16.2	14.2	7.0	3.1	2.5	2.68
Round Rock, TX	27.3	32.0	16.0	13.7	6.4	2.6	2.0	2.58
San Antonio, TX	24.3	30.3	16.8	14.6	7.9	3.4	2.6	2.74
San Diego, CA	24.0	31.2	16.5	14.5	7.4	3.3	3.0	2.75
San Francisco, CA	28.0	30.8	16.1	13.7	6.2	2.7	2.6	2.61
San Jose, CA	21.6	28.9	17.7	16.9	7.7	3.6	3.7	2.91
Savannah, GA	26.2	33.4	17.4	13.1	6.1	2.3	1.4	2.53
Scottsdale, AZ	25.4	33.2	14.8	13.2	7.3	3.4	2.8	2.68
Seattle, WA	28.4	33.2	15.9	13.3	5.5	2.2	1.5	2.49
Sioux Falls, SD	27.4	34.5	15.3	13.4	6.2	2.1	1.0	2.48
Stamford, CT	24.9	30.0	17.0	16.2	7.6	2.7	1.6	2.68
Sterling Hgts, MI	28.8	31.2	16.1	13.5	6.3	2.4	1.6	2.53
Sunnyvale, CA	21.6	28.9	17.7	16.9	7.7	3.6	3.7	2.91
Tampa, FL	29.9	35.7	15.0	11.4	5.0	1.9	1.2	2.37
Temecula, CA	18.5	27.1	16.1	16.4	10.8	5.6	5.6	3.20
Thousand Oaks, CA	19.9	29.3	16.9	16.3	8.6	4.1	4.9	3.04
Virginia Beach, VA	25.0	33.4	18.3	13.9	6.0	2.2	1.2	2.55
Washington, DC	27.0	30.1	16.5	14.3	6.9	2.9	2.3	2.64
U.S.	26.7	32.8	16.1	13.4	6.5	2.6	1.9	2.58

Note: Figures cover the Metropolitan Statistical Area (MSA)—see Appendix B for areas included
Source: U.S. Census Bureau, 2010 Census

Race: City

City	White Alone[1] (%)	Black Alone[1] (%)	Asian Alone[1] (%)	AIAN[2] Alone[1] (%)	NHOPI[3] Alone[1] (%)	Other Race Alone[1] (%)	Two or More Races (%)
Albuquerque, NM	69.7	3.3	2.6	4.6	0.1	15.0	4.6
Alexandria, VA	60.9	21.8	6.0	0.4	0.1	7.1	3.7
Anchorage, AK	66.0	5.6	8.1	7.9	2.0	2.3	8.1
Ann Arbor, MI	73.0	7.7	14.4	0.3	0.0	1.0	3.6
Athens, GA	61.8	26.6	4.2	0.2	0.1	5.0	2.2
Atlanta, GA	38.4	54.0	3.1	0.2	0.0	2.2	2.0
Austin, TX	68.3	8.1	6.3	0.9	0.1	12.9	3.4
Baltimore, MD	29.6	63.7	2.3	0.4	0.0	1.8	2.1
Bellevue, WA	62.6	2.3	27.6	0.4	0.2	3.1	3.9
Billings, MT	89.6	0.8	0.7	4.4	0.1	1.4	2.9
Boise City, ID	89.0	1.5	3.2	0.7	0.2	2.5	3.0
Boston, MA	53.9	24.4	8.9	0.4	0.0	8.4	3.9
Boulder, CO	88.0	0.9	4.7	0.4	0.1	3.2	2.6
Broken Arrow, OK	79.3	4.3	3.6	5.2	0.0	2.2	5.4
Cambridge, MA	66.6	11.7	15.1	0.2	0.0	2.1	4.3
Cape Coral, FL	88.2	4.3	1.5	0.3	0.1	3.3	2.3
Carlsbad, CA	82.8	1.3	7.1	0.5	0.2	4.0	4.2
Cary, NC	73.1	8.0	13.1	0.4	0.0	2.8	2.6
Cedar Rapids, IA	88.0	5.6	2.2	0.3	0.1	0.9	2.9
Charleston, SC	70.2	25.4	1.6	0.2	0.1	1.0	1.5
Charlotte, NC	50.0	35.0	5.0	0.5	0.1	6.8	2.7
Chesapeake, VA	62.6	29.8	2.9	0.4	0.1	1.2	3.0
Chicago, IL	45.0	32.9	5.5	0.5	0.0	13.4	2.7
Clarksville, TN	65.6	23.2	2.3	0.6	0.5	2.8	5.1
Colorado Spgs., CO	78.8	6.3	3.0	1.0	0.3	5.5	5.1
Columbia, MD	55.5	25.3	11.4	0.4	0.0	2.8	4.4
Columbia, MO	79.0	11.3	5.2	0.3	0.1	1.1	3.1
Columbia, SC	51.7	42.2	2.2	0.3	0.1	1.5	2.0
Columbus, OH	61.5	28.0	4.1	0.3	0.1	2.9	3.3
Dallas, TX	50.7	25.0	2.9	0.7	0.0	18.1	2.6
Denver, CO	68.9	10.2	3.4	1.4	0.1	11.9	4.1
Durham, NC	42.5	41.0	5.1	0.5	0.1	8.3	2.7
Edison, NJ	44.1	7.0	43.2	0.2	0.0	2.7	2.7
El Paso, TX	80.8	3.4	1.2	0.7	0.1	11.0	2.7
Fargo, ND	90.2	2.7	3.0	1.4	0.0	0.6	2.1
Ft. Collins, CO	89.0	1.2	2.9	0.6	0.1	3.0	3.1
Ft. Worth, TX	61.1	18.9	3.7	0.6	0.1	12.4	3.1
Gilbert, AZ	81.8	3.4	5.8	0.8	0.2	4.5	3.5
Green Bay, WI	77.9	3.5	4.0	4.1	0.1	7.2	3.1
Henderson, NV	76.9	5.1	7.2	0.7	0.6	4.8	4.8
High Point, NC	53.6	33.0	6.1	0.6	0.0	4.4	2.3
Honolulu, HI	17.9	1.5	54.8	0.2	8.4	0.8	16.3
Houston, TX	50.5	23.7	6.0	0.7	0.1	15.7	3.3
Huntington, NY	84.2	4.7	5.0	0.2	0.0	3.9	2.1
Huntsville, AL	60.3	31.2	2.4	0.6	0.1	2.9	2.5
Indianapolis, IN	61.8	27.5	2.1	0.3	0.0	5.5	2.8
Irvine, CA	50.5	1.8	39.2	0.2	0.2	2.8	5.5
Jackson, MS	18.4	79.4	0.4	0.1	0.0	0.8	0.9
Jacksonville, FL	59.4	30.7	4.3	0.4	0.1	2.2	2.9
Jersey City, NJ	32.7	25.8	23.7	0.5	0.1	12.8	4.4
Kansas City, MO	59.2	29.9	2.5	0.5	0.2	4.5	3.2
Kenosha, WI	77.1	10.0	1.7	0.6	0.1	6.8	3.8
Las Vegas, NV	62.1	11.1	6.1	0.7	0.6	14.5	4.9
Lexington, KY	75.7	14.5	3.2	0.3	0.0	3.7	2.5

Table continued on next page.

City	White Alone[1] (%)	Black Alone[1] (%)	Asian Alone[1] (%)	AIAN[2] Alone[1] (%)	NHOPI[3] Alone[1] (%)	Other Race Alone[1] (%)	Two or More Races (%)
Lincoln, NE	86.0	3.8	3.8	0.8	0.1	2.5	3.0
Little Rock, AR	48.9	42.3	2.7	0.4	0.1	3.9	1.7
Los Angeles, CA	49.8	9.6	11.3	0.7	0.1	23.8	4.6
Madison, WI	78.9	7.3	7.4	0.4	0.0	2.9	3.1
Manchester, NH	86.1	4.1	3.7	0.3	0.1	3.1	2.7
Miami, FL	72.6	19.2	1.0	0.3	0.0	4.2	2.7
Minneapolis, MN	63.8	18.6	5.6	2.0	0.0	5.6	4.4
Murfreesboro, TN	75.6	15.2	3.4	0.3	0.0	2.8	2.7
Naperville, IL	76.5	4.7	14.9	0.1	0.0	1.5	2.3
Nashville, TN	60.5	28.4	3.1	0.3	0.1	5.1	2.5
New Orleans, LA	33.0	60.2	2.9	0.3	0.0	1.9	1.7
New York, NY	44.0	25.5	12.7	0.7	0.1	13.0	4.0
Norman, OK	79.7	4.3	3.8	4.7	0.1	1.9	5.5
Olathe, KS	83.1	5.3	4.1	0.4	0.1	4.1	3.0
Omaha, NE	73.1	13.7	2.4	0.8	0.1	6.9	3.0
Orlando, FL	57.6	28.1	3.8	0.4	0.1	6.8	3.4
Overland Park, KS	84.4	4.3	6.3	0.3	0.0	2.1	2.5
Oyster Bay, NY	85.0	2.3	9.1	0.2	0.0	1.9	1.6
Pembroke Pines, FL	67.3	19.8	4.9	0.3	0.0	4.4	3.3
Philadelphia, PA	41.0	43.4	6.3	0.5	0.0	5.9	2.8
Phoenix, AZ	65.9	6.5	3.2	2.2	0.2	18.5	3.6
Pittsburgh, PA	66.0	26.1	4.4	0.2	0.0	0.8	2.5
Plano, TX	66.9	7.6	16.9	0.4	0.1	5.1	3.0
Portland, OR	76.1	6.3	7.1	1.0	0.5	4.2	4.7
Providence, RI	49.8	16.0	6.4	1.4	0.1	19.8	6.5
Provo, UT	84.8	0.7	2.5	0.8	1.1	6.6	3.4
Raleigh, NC	57.5	29.3	4.3	0.5	0.0	5.7	2.6
Richmond, VA	40.8	50.6	2.3	0.3	0.1	3.6	2.3
Roseville, CA	79.3	2.0	8.4	0.7	0.3	4.3	5.0
Round Rock, TX	70.8	9.8	5.2	0.7	0.1	9.7	3.8
San Antonio, TX	72.6	6.9	2.4	0.9	0.1	13.7	3.4
San Diego, CA	58.9	6.7	15.9	0.6	0.5	12.3	5.1
San Francisco, CA	48.5	6.1	33.3	0.5	0.4	6.6	4.7
San Jose, CA	42.8	3.2	32.0	0.9	0.4	15.7	5.0
Savannah, GA	38.3	55.4	2.0	0.3	0.1	1.8	2.1
Scottsdale, AZ	89.3	1.7	3.3	0.8	0.1	2.5	2.3
Seattle, WA	69.5	7.9	13.8	0.8	0.4	2.4	5.1
Sioux Falls, SD	86.8	4.2	1.8	2.7	0.1	2.0	2.5
Stamford, CT	65.0	13.9	7.9	0.3	0.1	9.7	3.2
Sterling Hgts, MI	85.1	5.2	6.7	0.2	0.0	0.5	2.2
Sunnyvale, CA	43.0	2.0	40.9	0.5	0.5	8.7	4.5
Tampa, FL	62.9	26.2	3.4	0.4	0.1	3.8	3.2
Temecula, CA	70.8	4.1	9.8	1.1	0.4	7.9	5.9
Thousand Oaks, CA	80.3	1.3	8.7	0.4	0.1	5.4	3.8
Virginia Beach, VA	67.7	19.6	6.1	0.4	0.2	2.0	4.0
Washington, DC	38.5	50.7	3.5	0.3	0.1	4.1	2.9
U.S.	72.4	12.6	4.8	0.9	0.2	6.2	2.9

Note: (1) Alone is defined as not being in combination with one or more other races; (2) American Indian and Alaska Native; (3) Native Hawaiian and Other Pacific Islander
Source: U.S. Census Bureau, 2010 Census

Race: Metro Area

Metro Area	White Alone[1] (%)	Black Alone[1] (%)	Asian Alone[1] (%)	AIAN[2] Alone[1] (%)	NHOPI[3] Alone[1] (%)	Other Race Alone[1] (%)	Two or More Races (%)
Albuquerque, NM	69.6	2.7	2.0	5.9	0.1	15.4	4.3
Alexandria, VA	54.8	25.8	9.3	0.4	0.1	6.0	3.7
Anchorage, AK	70.4	4.5	6.5	7.4	1.6	2.0	7.7
Ann Arbor, MI	74.5	12.7	7.9	0.3	0.0	1.2	3.4
Athens, GA	71.4	19.5	3.2	0.2	0.0	3.7	1.9
Atlanta, GA	55.4	32.4	4.8	0.3	0.1	4.5	2.4
Austin, TX	72.9	7.4	4.8	0.8	0.1	10.9	3.2
Baltimore, MD	62.1	28.7	4.5	0.3	0.1	1.7	2.5
Bellevue, WA	71.9	5.6	11.4	1.1	0.8	3.8	5.3
Billings, MT	91.1	0.6	0.6	3.8	0.1	1.1	2.7
Boise City, ID	87.9	0.9	1.8	0.9	0.2	5.4	2.9
Boston, MA	78.8	7.3	6.5	0.2	0.0	4.6	2.6
Boulder, CO	87.2	0.9	4.1	0.6	0.1	4.5	2.7
Broken Arrow, OK	70.9	8.4	1.8	8.3	0.1	4.2	6.4
Cambridge, MA	78.8	7.3	6.5	0.2	0.0	4.6	2.6
Cape Coral, FL	83.0	8.3	1.4	0.4	0.1	4.9	2.1
Carlsbad, CA	64.0	5.1	10.9	0.9	0.5	13.6	5.1
Cary, NC	67.5	20.2	4.4	0.5	0.0	5.0	2.4
Cedar Rapids, IA	92.0	3.4	1.5	0.3	0.1	0.6	2.1
Charleston, SC	65.6	27.7	1.6	0.5	0.1	2.5	2.1
Charlotte, NC	65.1	24.0	3.1	0.5	0.1	5.0	2.2
Chesapeake, VA	59.6	31.3	3.5	0.4	0.1	1.7	3.4
Chicago, IL	65.4	17.4	5.6	0.4	0.0	8.8	2.4
Clarksville, TN	73.2	18.3	1.6	0.6	0.4	2.1	3.8
Colorado Spgs., CO	80.3	6.0	2.7	1.0	0.3	4.8	5.0
Columbia, MD	62.1	28.7	4.5	0.3	0.1	1.7	2.5
Columbia, MO	83.3	9.1	3.6	0.4	0.1	0.9	2.8
Columbia, SC	60.4	33.2	1.7	0.4	0.1	2.3	2.0
Columbus, OH	77.5	14.9	3.1	0.2	0.1	1.7	2.5
Dallas, TX	65.3	15.1	5.4	0.7	0.1	10.6	2.8
Denver, CO	78.0	5.6	3.7	1.0	0.1	8.0	3.6
Durham, NC	59.3	27.1	4.4	0.5	0.0	6.3	2.4
Edison, NJ	59.2	17.8	9.9	0.5	0.0	9.3	3.2
El Paso, TX	82.1	3.1	1.0	0.8	0.1	10.5	2.5
Fargo, ND	92.0	2.0	2.1	1.3	0.0	0.6	2.0
Ft. Collins, CO	90.5	0.8	1.9	0.7	0.1	3.2	2.6
Ft. Worth, TX	65.3	15.1	5.4	0.7	0.1	10.6	2.8
Gilbert, AZ	73.0	5.0	3.3	2.4	0.2	12.7	3.5
Green Bay, WI	88.4	1.8	2.3	2.4	0.0	3.1	2.0
Henderson, NV	60.9	10.5	8.7	0.7	0.7	13.5	5.1
High Point, NC	65.0	25.5	2.9	0.5	0.0	3.8	2.1
Honolulu, HI	20.8	2.0	43.9	0.3	9.5	1.1	22.3
Houston, TX	60.2	17.2	6.5	0.6	0.1	12.3	3.0
Huntington, NY	59.2	17.8	9.9	0.5	0.0	9.3	3.2
Huntsville, AL	70.6	21.7	2.2	0.7	0.1	2.3	2.3
Indianapolis, IN	77.0	15.0	2.3	0.3	0.0	3.2	2.2
Irvine, CA	52.8	7.1	14.7	0.7	0.3	20.1	4.4
Jackson, MS	49.1	47.7	1.1	0.2	0.0	1.1	0.9
Jacksonville, FL	69.9	21.8	3.4	0.4	0.1	1.8	2.6
Jersey City, NJ	59.2	17.8	9.9	0.5	0.0	9.3	3.2
Kansas City, MO	78.4	12.5	2.3	0.5	0.2	3.3	2.8
Kenosha, WI	65.4	17.4	5.6	0.4	0.0	8.8	2.4
Las Vegas, NV	60.9	10.5	8.7	0.7	0.7	13.5	5.1
Lexington, KY	81.4	10.8	2.3	0.2	0.0	3.0	2.2

Table continued on next page.

Metro Area	White Alone[1] (%)	Black Alone[1] (%)	Asian Alone[1] (%)	AIAN[2] Alone[1] (%)	NHOPI[3] Alone[1] (%)	Other Race Alone[1] (%)	Two or More Races (%)
Lincoln, NE	87.7	3.3	3.3	0.7	0.1	2.3	2.7
Little Rock, AR	71.6	22.2	1.5	0.5	0.1	2.4	1.9
Los Angeles, CA	52.8	7.1	14.7	0.7	0.3	20.1	4.4
Madison, WI	86.4	4.6	4.1	0.4	0.0	2.2	2.3
Manchester, NH	90.4	2.1	3.2	0.2	0.0	2.1	2.0
Miami, FL	70.3	21.0	2.3	0.3	0.0	3.5	2.5
Minneapolis, MN	81.0	7.4	5.7	0.7	0.0	2.3	2.8
Murfreesboro, TN	76.9	15.2	2.3	0.3	0.1	3.2	2.1
Naperville, IL	65.4	17.4	5.6	0.4	0.0	8.8	2.4
Nashville, TN	76.9	15.2	2.3	0.3	0.1	3.2	2.1
New Orleans, LA	58.2	34.0	2.7	0.4	0.0	2.6	1.9
New York, NY	59.2	17.8	9.9	0.5	0.0	9.3	3.2
Norman, OK	71.9	10.4	2.8	4.1	0.1	5.5	5.2
Olathe, KS	78.4	12.5	2.3	0.5	0.2	3.3	2.8
Omaha, NE	82.5	7.9	2.1	0.6	0.1	4.3	2.6
Orlando, FL	70.0	16.2	4.0	0.4	0.1	6.1	3.2
Overland Park, KS	78.4	12.5	2.3	0.5	0.2	3.3	2.8
Oyster Bay, NY	59.2	17.8	9.9	0.5	0.0	9.3	3.2
Pembroke Pines, FL	70.3	21.0	2.3	0.3	0.0	3.5	2.5
Philadelphia, PA	68.2	20.8	5.0	0.3	0.0	3.4	2.3
Phoenix, AZ	73.0	5.0	3.3	2.4	0.2	12.7	3.5
Pittsburgh, PA	87.8	8.4	1.8	0.1	0.0	0.4	1.6
Plano, TX	65.3	15.1	5.4	0.7	0.1	10.6	2.8
Portland, OR	81.0	2.9	5.7	0.9	0.5	4.9	4.1
Providence, RI	83.8	4.9	2.5	0.5	0.0	5.1	3.1
Provo, UT	89.5	0.5	1.3	0.6	0.7	4.6	2.7
Raleigh, NC	67.5	20.2	4.4	0.5	0.0	5.0	2.4
Richmond, VA	62.0	29.8	3.1	0.4	0.1	2.3	2.3
Roseville, CA	64.7	7.4	11.9	1.0	0.7	8.4	5.9
Round Rock, TX	72.9	7.4	4.8	0.8	0.1	10.9	3.2
San Antonio, TX	75.5	6.6	2.1	0.8	0.1	11.6	3.3
San Diego, CA	64.0	5.1	10.9	0.9	0.5	13.6	5.1
San Francisco, CA	51.7	8.4	23.2	0.6	0.7	9.9	5.5
San Jose, CA	47.5	2.6	31.1	0.8	0.4	12.8	4.9
Savannah, GA	59.7	33.9	2.1	0.3	0.1	1.9	2.1
Scottsdale, AZ	73.0	5.0	3.3	2.4	0.2	12.7	3.5
Seattle, WA	71.9	5.6	11.4	1.1	0.8	3.8	5.3
Sioux Falls, SD	90.2	3.0	1.3	2.0	0.1	1.4	2.0
Stamford, CT	74.8	10.8	4.6	0.3	0.0	6.8	2.6
Sterling Hgts, MI	70.1	22.8	3.3	0.3	0.0	1.2	2.2
Sunnyvale, CA	47.5	2.6	31.1	0.8	0.4	12.8	4.9
Tampa, FL	78.8	11.8	2.9	0.4	0.1	3.4	2.6
Temecula, CA	58.9	7.6	6.1	1.1	0.3	21.0	4.9
Thousand Oaks, CA	68.7	1.8	6.7	1.0	0.2	17.0	4.5
Virginia Beach, VA	59.6	31.3	3.5	0.4	0.1	1.7	3.4
Washington, DC	54.8	25.8	9.3	0.4	0.1	6.0	3.7
U.S.	72.4	12.6	4.8	0.9	0.2	6.2	2.9

Note: (1) Figures cover the Metropolitan Statistical Area (MSA)—see Appendix B for areas included; (1) Alone is defined as not being in combination with one or more other races; (2) American Indian and Alaska Native; (3) Native Hawaiian and Other Pacific Islander
Source: U.S. Census Bureau, 2010 Census

Hispanic Origin: City

City	Hispanic or Latino (%)	Mexican (%)	Puerto Rican (%)	Cuban (%)	Other Hispanic or Latino (%)
Albuquerque, NM	46.7	26.8	0.5	0.5	18.9
Alexandria, VA	16.1	1.7	1.1	0.3	13.0
Anchorage, AK	7.6	3.9	0.9	0.2	2.5
Ann Arbor, MI	4.1	1.8	0.4	0.2	1.7
Athens, GA	10.5	6.6	0.6	0.3	3.0
Atlanta, GA	5.2	2.8	0.5	0.3	1.5
Austin, TX	35.1	29.1	0.5	0.4	5.1
Baltimore, MD	4.2	1.3	0.5	0.1	2.3
Bellevue, WA	7.0	4.7	0.2	0.1	2.0
Billings, MT	5.2	4.0	0.2	0.0	0.9
Boise City, ID	7.1	5.4	0.2	0.1	1.4
Boston, MA	17.5	1.0	4.9	0.4	11.2
Boulder, CO	8.7	6.1	0.3	0.2	2.2
Broken Arrow, OK	6.5	4.4	0.4	0.1	1.5
Cambridge, MA	7.6	1.4	1.6	0.4	4.3
Cape Coral, FL	19.5	1.8	4.7	6.4	6.6
Carlsbad, CA	13.3	10.2	0.4	0.2	2.5
Cary, NC	7.7	3.7	0.9	0.4	2.7
Cedar Rapids, IA	3.3	2.3	0.2	0.0	0.7
Charleston, SC	2.9	1.3	0.4	0.1	1.0
Charlotte, NC	13.1	5.6	1.0	0.4	6.1
Chesapeake, VA	4.4	1.6	1.2	0.2	1.3
Chicago, IL	28.9	21.4	3.8	0.3	3.3
Clarksville, TN	9.3	4.1	3.0	0.2	2.0
Colorado Spgs., CO	16.1	10.6	1.1	0.2	4.1
Columbia, MD	7.9	2.0	1.1	0.2	4.5
Columbia, MO	3.4	2.1	0.3	0.2	0.9
Columbia, SC	4.3	1.9	1.0	0.2	1.3
Columbus, OH	5.6	3.3	0.6	0.1	1.6
Dallas, TX	42.4	36.7	0.3	0.2	5.2
Denver, CO	31.8	24.9	0.4	0.2	6.4
Durham, NC	14.2	7.7	0.7	0.2	5.6
Edison, NJ	8.1	1.2	2.6	0.6	3.8
El Paso, TX	80.7	74.9	0.9	0.1	4.8
Fargo, ND	2.2	1.5	0.1	0.0	0.5
Ft. Collins, CO	10.1	6.9	0.3	0.1	2.8
Ft. Worth, TX	34.1	29.6	0.8	0.2	3.5
Gilbert, AZ	14.9	11.4	0.7	0.2	2.6
Green Bay, WI	13.4	10.7	0.9	0.1	1.7
Henderson, NV	14.9	9.9	0.9	0.6	3.5
High Point, NC	8.5	4.9	0.8	0.2	2.5
Honolulu, HI	5.4	1.7	1.6	0.1	2.1
Houston, TX	43.8	32.1	0.4	0.4	10.9
Huntington, NY	11.0	0.7	2.1	0.3	7.9
Huntsville, AL	5.8	4.0	0.6	0.1	1.1
Indianapolis, IN	9.4	6.9	0.4	0.1	2.0
Irvine, CA	9.2	6.0	0.3	0.2	2.7
Jackson, MS	1.6	1.0	0.1	0.0	0.5
Jacksonville, FL	7.7	1.7	2.6	0.9	2.6
Jersey City, NJ	27.6	1.8	10.4	0.7	14.7
Kansas City, MO	10.0	7.8	0.3	0.3	1.6
Kenosha, WI	16.3	12.5	1.7	0.1	2.0
Las Vegas, NV	31.5	24.0	0.9	0.9	5.7
Lexington, KY	6.9	5.1	0.3	0.2	1.3
Lincoln, NE	6.3	4.7	0.2	0.1	1.3

Table continued on next page.

City	Hispanic or Latino (%)	Mexican (%)	Puerto Rican (%)	Cuban (%)	Other Hispanic or Latino (%)
Little Rock, AR	6.8	5.0	0.2	0.1	1.5
Los Angeles, CA	48.5	31.9	0.4	0.4	15.8
Madison, WI	6.8	4.5	0.5	0.1	1.7
Manchester, NH	8.1	1.7	3.0	0.1	3.2
Miami, FL	70.0	1.5	3.2	34.4	30.9
Minneapolis, MN	10.5	7.0	0.4	0.1	3.0
Murfreesboro, TN	5.9	3.7	0.5	0.2	1.6
Naperville, IL	5.3	3.4	0.6	0.2	1.2
Nashville, TN	10.0	6.1	0.5	0.3	3.1
New Orleans, LA	5.2	1.3	0.3	0.4	3.4
New York, NY	28.6	3.9	8.9	0.5	15.3
Norman, OK	6.4	4.2	0.4	0.1	1.7
Olathe, KS	10.2	7.9	0.4	0.1	1.8
Omaha, NE	13.1	10.4	0.2	0.1	2.3
Orlando, FL	25.4	1.8	13.1	1.8	8.7
Overland Park, KS	6.3	4.4	0.2	0.1	1.5
Oyster Bay, NY	7.5	0.5	1.6	0.3	5.0
Pembroke Pines, FL	41.4	1.1	6.8	12.8	20.7
Philadelphia, PA	12.3	1.0	8.0	0.3	3.0
Phoenix, AZ	40.8	35.9	0.6	0.3	4.0
Pittsburgh, PA	2.3	0.7	0.4	0.1	1.0
Plano, TX	14.7	10.6	0.5	0.2	3.5
Portland, OR	9.4	6.7	0.3	0.4	2.0
Providence, RI	38.1	1.8	8.3	0.3	27.7
Provo, UT	15.2	10.2	0.3	0.1	4.6
Raleigh, NC	11.4	5.9	1.1	0.3	4.1
Richmond, VA	6.3	2.0	0.7	0.2	3.3
Roseville, CA	14.6	11.0	0.5	0.1	3.0
Round Rock, TX	29.0	23.4	0.9	0.3	4.4
San Antonio, TX	63.2	53.2	1.0	0.2	8.9
San Diego, CA	28.8	24.9	0.6	0.2	3.0
San Francisco, CA	15.1	7.4	0.5	0.2	6.9
San Jose, CA	33.2	28.4	0.5	0.1	4.1
Savannah, GA	4.7	2.1	1.0	0.2	1.4
Scottsdale, AZ	8.8	6.6	0.4	0.1	1.7
Seattle, WA	6.6	4.1	0.3	0.2	2.0
Sioux Falls, SD	4.4	2.2	0.2	0.1	1.9
Stamford, CT	23.8	2.0	2.8	0.3	18.6
Sterling Hgts, MI	1.9	1.2	0.2	0.1	0.5
Sunnyvale, CA	18.9	14.2	0.4	0.1	4.2
Tampa, FL	23.1	2.9	7.2	6.3	6.7
Temecula, CA	24.7	19.9	1.0	0.2	3.6
Thousand Oaks, CA	16.8	11.6	0.4	0.2	4.7
Virginia Beach, VA	6.6	1.9	2.2	0.2	2.3
Washington, DC	9.1	1.4	0.5	0.3	6.9
U.S.	16.3	10.3	1.5	0.6	4.0

Note: Persons of Hispanic or Latino origin can be of any race
Source: U.S. Census Bureau, 2010 Census

Hispanic Origin: Metro Area

Metro Area	Hispanic or Latino (%)	Mexican (%)	Puerto Rican (%)	Cuban (%)	Other Hispanic or Latino (%)
Albuquerque, NM	46.7	26.0	0.5	0.4	19.8
Alexandria, VA	13.8	2.1	0.9	0.3	10.6
Anchorage, AK	6.7	3.5	0.8	0.2	2.2
Ann Arbor, MI	4.0	2.1	0.4	0.1	1.4
Athens, GA	8.0	5.0	0.4	0.2	2.3
Atlanta, GA	10.4	6.0	0.8	0.3	3.3
Austin, TX	31.4	26.2	0.6	0.3	4.3
Baltimore, MD	4.6	1.2	0.7	0.1	2.5
Bellevue, WA	9.0	6.4	0.5	0.1	2.0
Billings, MT	4.5	3.5	0.2	0.0	0.8
Boise City, ID	12.6	10.5	0.2	0.1	1.8
Boston, MA	9.0	0.6	2.5	0.2	5.7
Boulder, CO	13.3	10.3	0.3	0.1	2.6
Broken Arrow, OK	8.4	6.6	0.3	0.1	1.4
Cambridge, MA	9.0	0.6	2.5	0.2	5.7
Cape Coral, FL	18.3	5.5	4.0	3.3	5.5
Carlsbad, CA	32.0	28.1	0.7	0.2	3.1
Cary, NC	10.1	5.9	0.9	0.3	3.1
Cedar Rapids, IA	2.4	1.6	0.2	0.0	0.5
Charleston, SC	5.4	3.1	0.7	0.1	1.5
Charlotte, NC	9.8	4.8	0.9	0.3	3.8
Chesapeake, VA	5.4	1.7	1.6	0.2	1.8
Chicago, IL	20.7	16.3	2.0	0.2	2.1
Clarksville, TN	6.8	3.2	2.0	0.2	1.4
Colorado Spgs., CO	14.7	9.5	1.2	0.2	3.8
Columbia, MD	4.6	1.2	0.7	0.1	2.5
Columbia, MO	2.9	1.8	0.3	0.1	0.7
Columbia, SC	5.1	2.7	0.9	0.1	1.3
Columbus, OH	3.6	2.0	0.4	0.1	1.1
Dallas, TX	27.5	22.9	0.5	0.2	3.9
Denver, CO	22.5	16.7	0.4	0.1	5.2
Durham, NC	11.3	6.7	0.6	0.2	3.8
Edison, NJ	22.9	3.0	6.2	0.7	13.0
El Paso, TX	82.2	76.6	0.8	0.1	4.7
Fargo, ND	2.4	1.7	0.1	0.0	0.5
Ft. Collins, CO	10.6	7.7	0.3	0.1	2.5
Ft. Worth, TX	27.5	22.9	0.5	0.2	3.9
Gilbert, AZ	29.5	25.5	0.6	0.2	3.2
Green Bay, WI	6.2	4.8	0.5	0.0	0.9
Henderson, NV	29.1	21.7	0.9	1.1	5.5
High Point, NC	7.6	5.2	0.5	0.2	1.7
Honolulu, HI	8.1	2.3	2.9	0.1	2.9
Houston, TX	35.3	26.6	0.5	0.3	7.9
Huntington, NY	22.9	3.0	6.2	0.7	13.0
Huntsville, AL	4.8	3.2	0.5	0.1	1.0
Indianapolis, IN	6.2	4.4	0.3	0.1	1.4
Irvine, CA	44.4	34.1	0.4	0.4	9.6
Jackson, MS	2.1	1.3	0.1	0.0	0.7
Jacksonville, FL	6.9	1.5	2.3	0.7	2.3
Jersey City, NJ	22.9	3.0	6.2	0.7	13.0
Kansas City, MO	8.2	6.4	0.3	0.1	1.4
Kenosha, WI	20.7	16.3	2.0	0.2	2.1
Las Vegas, NV	29.1	21.7	0.9	1.1	5.5
Lexington, KY	5.9	4.4	0.3	0.1	1.0
Lincoln, NE	5.6	4.2	0.2	0.1	1.2

Table continued on next page.

Metro Area	Hispanic or Latino (%)	Mexican (%)	Puerto Rican (%)	Cuban (%)	Other Hispanic or Latino (%)
Little Rock, AR	4.8	3.5	0.2	0.1	1.0
Los Angeles, CA	44.4	34.1	0.4	0.4	9.6
Madison, WI	5.4	3.7	0.4	0.1	1.2
Manchester, NH	5.3	1.1	1.8	0.1	2.3
Miami, FL	41.6	2.4	3.7	17.7	17.8
Minneapolis, MN	5.4	3.7	0.3	0.1	1.4
Murfreesboro, TN	6.6	4.1	0.4	0.2	1.9
Naperville, IL	20.7	16.3	2.0	0.2	2.1
Nashville, TN	6.6	4.1	0.4	0.2	1.9
New Orleans, LA	7.9	1.8	0.4	0.6	5.1
New York, NY	22.9	3.0	6.2	0.7	13.0
Norman, OK	11.3	9.1	0.3	0.1	1.8
Olathe, KS	8.2	6.4	0.3	0.1	1.4
Omaha, NE	9.0	7.0	0.2	0.1	1.7
Orlando, FL	25.2	3.0	12.6	1.7	7.9
Overland Park, KS	8.2	6.4	0.3	0.1	1.4
Oyster Bay, NY	22.9	3.0	6.2	0.7	13.0
Pembroke Pines, FL	41.6	2.4	3.7	17.7	17.8
Philadelphia, PA	7.8	1.7	4.0	0.2	2.0
Phoenix, AZ	29.5	25.5	0.6	0.2	3.2
Pittsburgh, PA	1.3	0.5	0.3	0.1	0.5
Plano, TX	27.5	22.9	0.5	0.2	3.9
Portland, OR	10.9	8.5	0.3	0.2	1.9
Providence, RI	10.2	0.7	3.3	0.1	6.1
Provo, UT	10.7	7.2	0.2	0.1	3.2
Raleigh, NC	10.1	5.9	0.9	0.3	3.1
Richmond, VA	5.0	1.7	0.8	0.2	2.4
Roseville, CA	20.2	16.4	0.6	0.1	3.1
Round Rock, TX	31.4	26.2	0.6	0.3	4.3
San Antonio, TX	54.1	45.3	1.0	0.2	7.6
San Diego, CA	32.0	28.1	0.7	0.2	3.1
San Francisco, CA	21.7	14.2	0.7	0.2	6.6
San Jose, CA	27.8	23.4	0.4	0.1	3.9
Savannah, GA	5.0	2.3	1.1	0.2	1.4
Scottsdale, AZ	29.5	25.5	0.6	0.2	3.2
Seattle, WA	9.0	6.4	0.5	0.1	2.0
Sioux Falls, SD	3.4	1.8	0.2	0.0	1.4
Stamford, CT	16.9	2.1	5.5	0.4	9.0
Sterling Hgts, MI	3.9	2.8	0.4	0.1	0.6
Sunnyvale, CA	27.8	23.4	0.4	0.1	3.9
Tampa, FL	16.2	3.6	5.2	2.9	4.5
Temecula, CA	47.3	40.6	0.7	0.3	5.7
Thousand Oaks, CA	40.3	35.6	0.4	0.2	4.1
Virginia Beach, VA	5.4	1.7	1.6	0.2	1.8
Washington, DC	13.8	2.1	0.9	0.3	10.6
U.S.	16.3	10.3	1.5	0.6	4.0

Note: Persons of Hispanic or Latino origin can be of any race; Figures cover the Metropolitan Statistical Area (MSA)—see Appendix B for areas included

Source: U.S. Census Bureau, 2010 Census

Age: City

City	Percent of Population							Median Age
	Under Age 5	Age 5 to 17	Age 18 to 34	Age 35 to 49	Age 50 to 64	Age 65 to 79	80 Years and Over	
Albuquerque, NM	7.0	17.0	25.9	19.8	18.3	8.6	3.5	35.1
Alexandria, VA	7.1	10.0	31.6	24.6	17.5	6.6	2.5	35.6
Anchorage, AK	7.5	18.4	26.8	21.1	18.9	5.8	1.5	32.9
Ann Arbor, MI	4.3	10.1	47.2	14.9	14.1	6.5	2.9	27.8
Athens, GA	6.0	11.5	47.4	14.4	12.3	6.1	2.3	25.8
Atlanta, GA	6.4	13.0	34.1	21.2	15.5	7.2	2.6	32.9
Austin, TX	7.3	14.9	35.2	21.0	14.5	5.1	1.9	31.0
Baltimore, MD	6.6	14.9	29.3	19.3	18.2	8.4	3.4	34.4
Bellevue, WA	5.6	15.6	24.1	22.0	18.8	9.7	4.3	38.5
Billings, MT	7.0	15.6	24.5	18.4	19.5	9.9	5.1	37.5
Boise City, ID	6.4	16.3	26.8	20.3	19.0	7.8	3.4	35.3
Boston, MA	5.2	11.5	40.2	18.4	14.6	7.1	2.9	30.8
Boulder, CO	4.1	9.8	45.1	17.1	15.0	6.0	2.9	28.7
Broken Arrow, OK	7.2	20.2	21.6	21.6	19.0	7.9	2.5	35.7
Cambridge, MA	4.3	7.1	49.5	16.3	13.3	6.9	2.6	30.2
Cape Coral, FL	5.4	17.1	17.8	21.3	21.5	12.9	4.1	42.4
Carlsbad, CA	6.0	18.1	18.0	23.5	20.4	9.2	4.8	40.4
Cary, NC	7.0	20.8	19.7	26.1	17.8	6.6	2.1	36.6
Cedar Rapids, IA	6.7	16.8	26.1	19.3	18.0	8.8	4.3	35.3
Charleston, SC	6.3	11.7	35.4	17.5	16.9	8.6	3.7	32.5
Charlotte, NC	7.6	17.7	27.7	22.8	15.8	6.2	2.3	33.2
Chesapeake, VA	6.5	19.4	21.7	22.7	19.4	7.9	2.5	37.0
Chicago, IL	6.9	16.2	30.3	20.4	15.9	7.5	2.8	32.9
Clarksville, TN	9.6	18.9	32.5	18.9	12.9	5.6	1.6	28.6
Colorado Spgs., CO	7.1	17.9	25.1	20.6	18.4	8.0	2.9	34.9
Columbia, MD	6.4	17.6	22.6	22.6	20.0	8.4	2.5	37.5
Columbia, MO	6.0	12.9	43.5	15.7	13.5	5.7	2.8	26.8
Columbia, SC	5.4	11.5	43.6	16.4	14.4	6.0	2.7	28.1
Columbus, OH	7.6	15.6	33.0	19.7	15.5	6.2	2.4	31.2
Dallas, TX	8.6	17.9	28.8	20.7	15.1	6.4	2.5	31.8
Denver, CO	7.3	14.2	30.9	21.1	16.3	7.2	3.2	33.7
Durham, NC	7.7	15.0	32.4	20.5	15.5	6.1	2.7	32.1
Edison, NJ	6.4	16.2	22.3	22.8	19.6	8.8	3.8	38.1
El Paso, TX	7.9	21.3	24.0	19.6	16.1	8.1	3.1	32.5
Fargo, ND	6.4	12.9	37.7	16.8	16.0	6.5	3.6	30.2
Ft. Collins, CO	5.7	14.2	38.3	17.8	15.2	6.0	2.8	29.6
Ft. Worth, TX	9.0	20.3	26.6	21.2	14.7	6.0	2.2	31.2
Gilbert, AZ	8.5	23.6	22.7	24.6	14.5	5.0	1.0	31.9
Green Bay, WI	7.7	16.9	27.0	19.5	17.5	7.6	3.7	33.7
Henderson, NV	5.9	16.8	20.8	21.9	20.4	11.6	2.7	39.6
High Point, NC	7.1	18.2	23.6	21.5	17.7	8.3	3.6	35.8
Honolulu, HI	4.9	12.5	24.1	20.3	20.4	11.3	6.5	41.3
Houston, TX	8.1	17.7	28.8	20.4	16.0	6.7	2.4	32.1
Huntington, NY	5.3	19.5	15.6	22.9	21.4	10.8	4.6	42.5
Huntsville, AL	6.2	15.3	26.8	19.3	18.3	10.4	3.8	36.5
Indianapolis, IN	7.6	17.4	26.9	20.2	17.5	7.5	3.0	33.7
Irvine, CA	5.7	15.9	30.1	23.0	16.7	6.5	2.1	33.9
Jackson, MS	7.8	19.6	27.6	18.1	17.0	7.1	2.8	31.2
Jacksonville, FL	7.0	16.9	25.4	21.1	18.7	8.0	2.9	35.5
Jersey City, NJ	7.1	14.1	32.4	21.7	15.6	6.9	2.2	33.2
Kansas City, MO	7.5	16.6	26.4	20.3	18.1	7.9	3.2	34.6
Kenosha, WI	7.6	19.2	25.3	21.2	15.9	7.1	3.7	33.5
Las Vegas, NV	7.2	18.4	23.1	21.9	17.3	9.3	2.7	35.9
Lexington, KY	6.5	14.7	30.8	20.1	17.4	7.6	2.9	33.7

Table continued on next page.

City	Percent of Population							Median Age
	Under Age 5	Age 5 to 17	Age 18 to 34	Age 35 to 49	Age 50 to 64	Age 65 to 79	80 Years and Over	
Lincoln, NE	7.2	15.5	31.7	18.1	16.8	7.4	3.4	31.8
Little Rock, AR	7.0	17.2	25.8	20.0	18.8	7.8	3.6	35.1
Los Angeles, CA	6.6	16.4	28.3	21.9	16.3	7.4	3.1	34.1
Madison, WI	5.8	11.7	39.1	17.6	16.2	6.5	3.1	30.9
Manchester, NH	6.7	14.9	27.0	21.1	18.5	7.8	4.0	36.0
Miami, FL	6.0	12.4	25.9	22.4	17.3	11.2	4.8	38.8
Minneapolis, MN	6.9	13.3	36.2	19.9	15.7	5.6	2.4	31.4
Murfreesboro, TN	7.1	16.4	35.7	19.1	13.6	5.9	2.2	29.0
Naperville, IL	5.8	22.9	17.7	24.8	20.1	6.1	2.5	37.9
Nashville, TN	7.2	14.5	30.3	20.5	17.2	7.3	2.9	33.7
New Orleans, LA	6.4	14.9	29.2	19.2	19.4	8.0	3.0	34.6
New York, NY	6.3	15.3	27.7	21.0	17.5	8.7	3.5	35.5
Norman, OK	5.8	14.0	37.4	16.8	15.9	7.3	2.7	29.6
Olathe, KS	8.9	21.1	23.5	23.6	15.8	5.1	2.0	32.9
Omaha, NE	7.5	17.6	26.8	19.1	17.6	7.9	3.4	33.5
Orlando, FL	7.1	14.9	31.7	21.9	15.0	6.7	2.7	32.8
Overland Park, KS	6.4	18.4	21.7	21.7	19.5	8.4	3.9	37.8
Oyster Bay, NY	4.9	18.2	16.8	21.9	21.9	10.8	5.5	43.1
Pembroke Pines, FL	5.7	18.1	20.2	23.3	18.0	9.7	5.1	39.5
Philadelphia, PA	6.6	15.9	29.5	18.8	17.1	8.5	3.7	33.5
Phoenix, AZ	8.3	20.0	25.9	21.3	16.1	6.3	2.1	32.2
Pittsburgh, PA	4.9	11.3	35.8	16.3	17.8	8.9	4.8	33.2
Plano, TX	6.3	19.6	21.0	24.8	19.5	6.9	1.9	37.2
Portland, OR	6.0	13.1	29.3	22.6	18.5	7.1	3.3	35.8
Providence, RI	6.9	16.4	36.5	17.7	13.7	5.8	2.9	28.5
Provo, UT	8.5	13.9	54.5	9.8	7.5	4.0	1.8	23.3
Raleigh, NC	7.2	15.9	32.3	21.7	14.7	5.8	2.4	31.9
Richmond, VA	6.3	12.3	35.3	17.7	17.3	7.5	3.6	32.0
Roseville, CA	6.8	19.5	21.2	22.4	16.7	9.1	4.3	36.8
Round Rock, TX	8.8	22.3	24.4	25.1	14.1	4.2	1.2	32.0
San Antonio, TX	7.6	19.2	26.3	20.1	16.4	7.6	2.9	32.7
San Diego, CA	6.2	15.2	30.7	20.9	16.4	7.5	3.2	33.6
San Francisco, CA	4.4	9.0	30.5	23.8	18.7	9.3	4.3	38.5
San Jose, CA	7.3	17.6	24.8	23.4	16.9	7.5	2.6	35.2
Savannah, GA	7.1	15.2	32.4	17.2	16.4	8.0	3.6	31.3
Scottsdale, AZ	4.2	13.6	18.9	20.4	22.9	14.4	5.6	45.4
Seattle, WA	5.3	10.1	32.6	23.1	18.1	7.2	3.6	36.1
Sioux Falls, SD	8.0	16.6	27.4	19.9	17.1	7.4	3.5	33.6
Stamford, CT	6.8	14.8	25.2	22.5	17.7	8.7	4.4	37.1
Sterling Hgts, MI	5.5	16.2	21.2	20.9	21.0	10.8	4.4	40.4
Sunnyvale, CA	8.0	14.4	26.3	23.9	16.2	7.9	3.3	35.6
Tampa, FL	6.4	16.2	27.9	21.4	17.2	7.9	3.1	34.6
Temecula, CA	7.0	23.6	21.3	24.3	15.9	6.0	1.8	33.4
Thousand Oaks, CA	5.2	18.5	17.9	22.5	21.2	10.4	4.2	41.5
Virginia Beach, VA	6.7	17.4	26.1	21.3	18.0	7.9	2.7	34.9
Washington, DC	5.4	11.3	35.2	19.8	16.8	8.1	3.3	33.8
U.S.	6.5	17.5	23.2	20.7	19.0	9.4	3.6	37.2

Source: U.S. Census Bureau, 2010 Census

Age: Metro Area

Metro Area	Percent of Population							Median Age
	Under Age 5	Age 5 to 17	Age 18 to 34	Age 35 to 49	Age 50 to 64	Age 65 to 79	80 Years and Over	
Albuquerque, NM	6.8	17.8	23.6	20.0	19.5	9.1	3.2	36.4
Alexandria, VA	6.7	17.1	24.6	23.0	18.5	7.4	2.6	36.1
Anchorage, AK	7.6	19.1	25.5	21.2	19.2	5.9	1.5	33.3
Ann Arbor, MI	5.6	15.3	31.2	19.6	18.2	7.3	2.8	33.3
Athens, GA	6.0	14.9	35.7	17.7	15.7	7.6	2.5	29.9
Atlanta, GA	7.2	19.3	23.6	23.6	17.4	6.9	2.0	34.9
Austin, TX	7.4	17.9	28.6	22.1	15.9	6.1	2.0	32.6
Baltimore, MD	6.2	16.8	23.2	21.3	19.8	9.0	3.6	38.1
Bellevue, WA	6.5	16.4	24.5	22.5	19.3	7.7	3.1	36.8
Billings, MT	6.7	16.8	22.0	19.2	21.0	10.0	4.4	39.0
Boise City, ID	7.8	20.2	23.2	20.5	17.4	8.0	2.9	34.1
Boston, MA	5.6	16.0	24.0	21.8	19.6	9.1	4.0	38.5
Boulder, CO	5.6	15.7	27.6	21.4	19.7	7.4	2.7	35.8
Broken Arrow, OK	7.1	18.5	22.6	20.0	19.1	9.5	3.4	36.5
Cambridge, MA	5.6	16.0	24.0	21.8	19.6	9.1	4.0	38.5
Cape Coral, FL	5.3	14.2	18.3	18.0	20.7	17.5	6.0	45.6
Carlsbad, CA	6.6	16.8	27.1	20.7	17.5	7.9	3.4	34.6
Cary, NC	7.3	18.9	23.9	23.9	17.0	6.8	2.2	34.9
Cedar Rapids, IA	6.6	17.9	22.5	20.5	19.0	9.5	4.1	37.5
Charleston, SC	6.9	16.4	26.2	20.3	18.7	8.8	2.7	35.4
Charlotte, NC	7.2	18.7	23.4	23.3	17.3	7.6	2.5	35.4
Chesapeake, VA	6.5	17.0	26.0	20.5	18.4	8.5	3.0	35.4
Chicago, IL	6.7	18.4	23.8	21.3	18.3	8.1	3.3	35.8
Clarksville, TN	8.8	18.8	28.5	19.2	15.1	7.4	2.2	30.7
Colorado Spgs., CO	7.2	18.8	24.6	20.8	18.6	7.7	2.4	34.6
Columbia, MD	6.2	16.8	23.2	21.3	19.8	9.0	3.6	38.1
Columbia, MO	6.2	14.9	35.4	17.6	16.2	6.9	2.8	30.0
Columbia, SC	6.5	17.0	25.7	20.5	18.9	8.6	2.8	35.7
Columbus, OH	6.9	17.8	25.1	21.5	18.1	7.8	2.8	35.1
Dallas, TX	7.8	20.0	24.3	22.5	16.6	6.7	2.1	33.5
Denver, CO	7.1	17.8	24.0	22.3	18.7	7.4	2.6	35.7
Durham, NC	6.5	15.5	27.9	20.5	18.3	8.1	3.1	35.0
Edison, NJ	6.2	16.6	23.7	21.7	18.8	9.2	3.9	37.6
El Paso, TX	8.1	22.0	24.5	19.6	15.6	7.5	2.7	31.3
Fargo, ND	6.9	15.3	32.5	18.2	16.7	7.0	3.4	31.5
Ft. Collins, CO	5.9	15.5	28.0	19.0	19.7	8.7	3.2	35.5
Ft. Worth, TX	7.8	20.0	24.3	22.5	16.6	6.7	2.1	33.5
Gilbert, AZ	7.5	19.0	24.0	20.5	16.8	9.1	3.2	34.7
Green Bay, WI	6.7	17.9	22.3	21.2	19.5	8.9	3.6	37.7
Henderson, NV	7.1	17.9	24.3	21.9	17.5	8.9	2.4	35.5
High Point, NC	6.2	17.3	22.9	21.3	19.2	9.6	3.6	37.8
Honolulu, HI	6.4	15.7	24.4	20.1	18.9	9.9	4.7	37.8
Houston, TX	7.9	20.0	24.7	21.6	17.2	6.6	2.0	33.2
Huntington, NY	6.2	16.6	23.7	21.7	18.8	9.2	3.9	37.6
Huntsville, AL	6.3	17.5	23.0	21.9	19.0	9.4	2.8	37.6
Indianapolis, IN	7.3	18.9	23.1	21.7	18.2	7.9	2.9	35.5
Irvine, CA	6.5	17.9	25.4	21.9	17.2	7.9	3.1	35.1
Jackson, MS	7.2	18.9	24.0	20.1	18.5	8.3	2.9	34.9
Jacksonville, FL	6.5	17.3	23.1	21.4	19.6	9.0	3.1	37.5
Jersey City, NJ	6.2	16.6	23.7	21.7	18.8	9.2	3.9	37.6
Kansas City, MO	7.2	18.5	22.3	21.1	19.0	8.6	3.4	36.5
Kenosha, WI	6.7	18.4	23.8	21.3	18.3	8.1	3.3	35.8
Las Vegas, NV	7.1	17.9	24.3	21.9	17.5	8.9	2.4	35.5
Lexington, KY	6.6	16.1	27.2	20.8	18.3	8.1	3.0	35.1

Table continued on next page.

Metro Area	Percent of Population: Under Age 5	Age 5 to 17	Age 18 to 34	Age 35 to 49	Age 50 to 64	Age 65 to 79	80 Years and Over	Median Age
Lincoln, NE	7.0	16.1	29.7	18.4	17.6	7.7	3.4	32.8
Little Rock, AR	6.9	17.6	24.3	20.4	18.7	9.1	3.1	35.9
Los Angeles, CA	6.5	17.9	25.4	21.9	17.2	7.9	3.1	35.1
Madison, WI	6.2	15.8	27.6	20.6	18.9	7.6	3.2	35.3
Manchester, NH	5.9	17.5	20.8	23.2	20.6	8.5	3.4	39.3
Miami, FL	5.8	15.8	21.8	22.1	18.6	10.9	5.0	39.8
Minneapolis, MN	6.9	18.1	23.7	21.8	18.9	7.6	3.1	36.0
Murfreesboro, TN	6.9	17.5	24.6	21.9	18.4	8.0	2.7	35.7
Naperville, IL	6.7	18.4	23.8	21.3	18.3	8.1	3.3	35.8
Nashville, TN	6.9	17.5	24.6	21.9	18.4	8.0	2.7	35.7
New Orleans, LA	6.6	16.8	24.1	20.2	20.1	8.9	3.3	37.1
New York, NY	6.2	16.6	23.7	21.7	18.8	9.2	3.9	37.6
Norman, OK	7.3	17.7	25.5	19.5	18.2	8.7	3.1	34.6
Olathe, KS	7.2	18.5	22.3	21.1	19.0	8.6	3.4	36.5
Omaha, NE	7.6	18.6	24.2	20.3	18.1	8.0	3.1	34.6
Orlando, FL	6.2	17.2	24.9	21.5	17.8	9.2	3.2	36.3
Overland Park, KS	7.2	18.5	22.3	21.1	19.0	8.6	3.4	36.5
Oyster Bay, NY	6.2	16.6	23.7	21.7	18.8	9.2	3.9	37.6
Pembroke Pines, FL	5.8	15.8	21.8	22.1	18.6	10.9	5.0	39.8
Philadelphia, PA	6.2	17.1	23.0	20.9	19.5	9.2	4.1	38.1
Phoenix, AZ	7.5	19.0	24.0	20.5	16.8	9.1	3.2	34.7
Pittsburgh, PA	5.1	15.0	20.7	19.8	22.0	11.5	5.8	42.6
Plano, TX	7.8	20.0	24.3	22.5	16.6	6.7	2.1	33.5
Portland, OR	6.5	17.2	23.8	21.7	19.4	8.1	3.3	36.7
Providence, RI	5.5	16.1	22.7	21.2	20.1	9.6	4.8	39.6
Provo, UT	11.3	24.0	32.6	15.3	10.3	4.9	1.7	24.6
Raleigh, NC	7.3	18.9	23.9	23.9	17.0	6.8	2.2	34.9
Richmond, VA	6.2	17.1	22.9	21.6	20.0	8.9	3.3	38.0
Roseville, CA	6.7	18.2	23.9	20.5	18.7	8.6	3.4	36.0
Round Rock, TX	7.4	17.9	28.6	22.1	15.9	6.1	2.0	32.6
San Antonio, TX	7.3	19.5	24.3	20.5	17.3	8.1	2.8	34.1
San Diego, CA	6.6	16.8	27.1	20.7	17.5	7.9	3.4	34.6
San Francisco, CA	6.0	15.2	23.9	22.8	19.5	8.9	3.7	38.3
San Jose, CA	7.0	17.3	23.9	23.3	17.5	8.0	3.1	36.1
Savannah, GA	7.0	17.1	26.7	19.6	18.0	8.6	3.0	34.3
Scottsdale, AZ	7.5	19.0	24.0	20.5	16.8	9.1	3.2	34.7
Seattle, WA	6.5	16.4	24.5	22.5	19.3	7.7	3.1	36.8
Sioux Falls, SD	8.0	18.0	24.7	20.4	17.7	7.7	3.5	34.5
Stamford, CT	6.2	18.6	19.4	22.8	19.5	9.2	4.3	39.5
Sterling Hgts, MI	6.0	18.3	20.4	21.6	20.5	9.2	4.0	39.1
Sunnyvale, CA	7.0	17.3	23.9	23.3	17.5	8.0	3.1	36.1
Tampa, FL	5.6	15.6	20.8	20.7	20.1	12.2	5.1	41.2
Temecula, CA	7.6	21.1	24.2	20.4	16.2	7.7	2.7	32.7
Thousand Oaks, CA	6.7	19.0	22.7	21.1	18.8	8.4	3.3	36.2
Virginia Beach, VA	6.5	17.0	26.0	20.5	18.4	8.5	3.0	35.4
Washington, DC	6.7	17.1	24.6	23.0	18.5	7.4	2.6	36.1
U.S.	6.5	17.5	23.2	20.7	19.0	9.4	3.6	37.2

Note: Figures cover the Metropolitan Statistical Area (MSA)—see Appendix B for areas included
Source: U.S. Census Bureau, 2010 Census

Segregation

Area	Black/White		Asian/White		Hispanic/White	
	Index[1]	Rank[2]	Index[1]	Rank[2]	Index[1]	Rank[2]
Albuquerque, NM	30.9	99	28.5	93	36.4	79
Alexandria, VA	62.3	32	38.9	64	48.3	32
Anchorage, AK	n/a	n/a	n/a	n/a	n/a	n/a
Ann Arbor, MI	n/a	n/a	n/a	n/a	n/a	n/a
Athens, GA	n/a	n/a	n/a	n/a	n/a	n/a
Atlanta, GA	59.0	41	48.5	10	49.5	27
Austin, TX	50.1	70	41.2	49	43.2	51
Baltimore, MD	65.4	19	43.6	33	39.8	67
Bellevue, WA	49.1	72	37.6	69	32.8	87
Billings, MT	n/a	n/a	n/a	n/a	n/a	n/a
Boise City, ID	30.2	101	27.6	95	36.2	80
Boston, MA	64.0	27	45.4	23	59.6	5
Boulder, CO	n/a	n/a	n/a	n/a	n/a	n/a
Broken Arrow, OK	56.6	47	42.6	40	45.3	45
Cambridge, MA	64.0	27	45.4	23	59.6	5
Cape Coral, FL	61.6	35	25.3	96	40.2	63
Carlsbad, CA	51.2	68	48.2	13	49.6	25
Cary, NC	42.1	87	46.7	16	37.1	76
Cedar Rapids, IA	n/a	n/a	n/a	n/a	n/a	n/a
Charleston, SC	41.5	88	33.4	84	39.8	66
Charlotte, NC	53.8	56	43.6	34	47.6	35
Chesapeake, VA	47.8	76	34.3	79	32.2	90
Chicago, IL	76.4	3	44.9	26	56.3	10
Clarksville, TN	n/a	n/a	n/a	n/a	n/a	n/a
Colorado Spgs., CO	39.3	92	24.1	98	30.3	95
Columbia, MD	65.4	19	43.6	33	39.8	67
Columbia, MO	n/a	n/a	n/a	n/a	n/a	n/a
Columbia, SC	48.8	74	41.9	46	34.9	82
Columbus, OH	62.2	33	43.3	35	41.5	59
Dallas, TX	56.6	48	46.6	19	50.3	24
Denver, CO	62.6	31	33.4	83	48.8	31
Durham, NC	48.1	75	44.0	30	48.0	33
Edison, NJ	78.0	2	51.9	3	62.0	3
El Paso, TX	30.7	100	22.2	100	43.3	50
Fargo, ND	n/a	n/a	n/a	n/a	n/a	n/a
Ft. Collins, CO	n/a	n/a	n/a	n/a	n/a	n/a
Ft. Worth, TX	56.6	48	46.6	19	50.3	24
Gilbert, AZ	43.6	86	32.7	85	49.3	28
Green Bay, WI	n/a	n/a	n/a	n/a	n/a	n/a
Henderson, NV	37.6	94	28.8	92	42.0	58
High Point, NC	54.7	53	47.7	14	41.1	61
Honolulu, HI	36.9	95	42.1	44	31.9	91
Houston, TX	61.4	36	50.4	7	52.5	18
Huntington, NY	78.0	2	51.9	3	62.0	3
Huntsville, AL	n/a	n/a	n/a	n/a	n/a	n/a
Indianapolis, IN	66.4	15	41.6	47	47.3	37
Irvine, CA	67.8	10	48.4	12	62.2	2
Jackson, MS	56.0	51	38.9	63	42.9	52
Jacksonville, FL	53.1	59	37.5	71	27.6	98
Jersey City, NJ	78.0	2	51.9	3	62.0	3
Kansas City, MO	61.2	39	38.4	65	44.4	48
Kenosha, WI	76.4	3	44.9	26	56.3	10
Las Vegas, NV	37.6	94	28.8	92	42.0	58
Lexington, KY	n/a	n/a	n/a	n/a	n/a	n/a
Lincoln, NE	n/a	n/a	n/a	n/a	n/a	n/a

Table continued on next page.

Area	Black/White		Asian/White		Hispanic/White	
	Index[1]	Rank[2]	Index[1]	Rank[2]	Index[1]	Rank[2]
Little Rock, AR	58.8	42	39.7	59	39.7	68
Los Angeles, CA	67.8	10	48.4	12	62.2	2
Madison, WI	49.6	71	44.2	29	40.1	65
Manchester, NH	n/a	n/a	n/a	n/a	n/a	n/a
Miami, FL	64.8	23	34.2	80	57.4	8
Minneapolis, MN	52.9	60	42.8	39	42.5	54
Murfreesboro, TN	56.2	49	41.0	51	47.9	34
Naperville, IL	76.4	3	44.9	26	56.3	10
Nashville, TN	56.2	49	41.0	51	47.9	34
New Orleans, LA	63.9	28	48.6	9	38.3	74
New York, NY	78.0	2	51.9	3	62.0	3
Norman, OK	51.4	67	39.2	60	47.0	38
Olathe, KS	61.2	39	38.4	65	44.4	48
Omaha, NE	61.3	38	36.3	74	48.8	30
Orlando, FL	50.7	69	33.9	81	40.2	64
Overland Park, KS	61.2	39	38.4	65	44.4	48
Oyster Bay, NY	78.0	2	51.9	3	62.0	3
Pembroke Pines, FL	64.8	23	34.2	80	57.4	8
Philadelphia, PA	68.4	9	42.3	42	55.1	12
Phoenix, AZ	43.6	86	32.7	85	49.3	28
Pittsburgh, PA	65.8	17	52.4	2	28.6	97
Plano, TX	56.6	48	46.6	19	50.3	24
Portland, OR	46.0	81	35.8	75	34.3	83
Providence, RI	53.5	57	40.1	55	60.1	4
Provo, UT	21.9	102	28.2	94	30.9	93
Raleigh, NC	42.1	87	46.7	16	37.1	76
Richmond, VA	52.4	63	43.9	32	44.9	46
Roseville, CA	56.9	46	49.9	8	38.9	71
Round Rock, TX	50.1	70	41.2	49	43.2	51
San Antonio, TX	49.0	73	38.3	66	46.1	43
San Diego, CA	51.2	68	48.2	13	49.6	25
San Francisco, CA	62.0	34	46.6	18	49.6	26
San Jose, CA	40.9	89	45.0	25	47.6	36
Savannah, GA	n/a	n/a	n/a	n/a	n/a	n/a
Scottsdale, AZ	43.6	86	32.7	85	49.3	28
Seattle, WA	49.1	72	37.6	69	32.8	87
Sioux Falls, SD	n/a	n/a	n/a	n/a	n/a	n/a
Stamford, CT	67.5	12	31.4	86	59.2	6
Sterling Hgts, MI	75.3	4	50.6	6	43.3	49
Sunnyvale, CA	40.9	89	45.0	25	47.6	36
Tampa, FL	56.2	50	35.3	78	40.7	62
Temecula, CA	45.7	82	40.7	53	42.4	55
Thousand Oaks, CA	39.9	91	31.2	87	54.6	13
Virginia Beach, VA	47.8	76	34.3	79	32.2	90
Washington, DC	62.3	32	38.9	64	48.3	32

Note: Figures are based on an analysis of 1990, 2000, and 2010 Census Decennial Census tract data by William H. Frey, Brookings Institution and the University of Michigan Social Science Data Analysis Network. In this analysis all racial groups (whites, blacks, and asians) are non-Hispanic members of those races. Hispanics are shown as a separate category; All figures cover the Metropolitan Statistical Area (see Appendix B for areas included); (1) Segregation Indices are Dissimilarity Indices that measure the degree to which the minority group is distributed differently than whites across census tracts. They range from 0 (complete integration) to 100 (complete [segregation) where the value indicates the percentage of the minority group that needs to move to be distributed exactly like whites; (2) Ranges from 1 (most segregated) to 102 (least segregated); n/a not available.
Source: www.CensusScope.org

Religious Groups

Area[1]	Catholic	Baptist	Non-Den.	Methodist[2]	Lutheran	LDS[3]	Pente-costal	Presby-terian[4]	Muslim[5]	Judaism
Albuquerque, NM	27.2	3.8	4.2	1.5	1.0	2.4	1.5	1.1	0.3	0.2
Alexandria, VA	14.5	7.3	4.9	4.5	1.3	1.2	1.1	1.4	1.2	2.4
Anchorage, AK	6.9	5.0	6.4	1.4	1.9	5.1	1.9	0.7	0.1	0.2
Ann Arbor, MI	12.4	2.2	1.6	3.1	2.9	0.9	1.9	3.0	0.9	1.3
Athens, GA	4.4	16.3	2.3	8.4	0.4	0.8	2.8	2.0	0.2	0.4
Atlanta, GA	7.5	17.5	6.9	7.9	0.5	0.8	2.6	1.8	0.6	0.8
Austin, TX	16.0	10.3	4.5	3.6	2.0	1.2	0.8	1.1	0.3	1.2
Baltimore, MD	16.7	4.2	4.8	6.1	2.1	0.5	1.1	1.3	1.8	0.5
Bellevue, WA	12.3	2.2	5.0	1.2	2.1	3.3	2.8	1.4	0.5	0.5
Billings, MT	12.1	2.5	3.8	2.1	6.1	4.9	4.1	1.8	0.1	0.0
Boise City, ID	8.0	2.9	4.2	2.1	1.2	15.9	2.3	0.6	0.1	0.1
Boston, MA	44.4	1.2	1.0	1.0	0.4	0.4	0.6	1.6	1.4	0.4
Boulder, CO	20.1	2.3	4.8	1.8	3.1	3.0	0.5	2.0	0.8	0.1
Broken Arrow, OK	5.8	22.9	7.6	9.2	0.8	1.2	3.3	1.3	0.3	0.3
Cambridge, MA	44.4	1.2	1.0	1.0	0.4	0.4	0.6	1.6	1.4	0.4
Cape Coral, FL	16.2	5.0	3.0	2.5	1.2	0.5	4.4	1.4	0.2	0.9
Carlsbad, CA	25.9	2.0	4.8	1.1	1.0	2.3	1.0	0.9	0.5	0.7
Cary, NC	9.2	12.1	6.0	6.7	0.9	0.9	2.3	2.3	0.3	0.9
Cedar Rapids, IA	18.8	2.4	3.0	7.3	11.3	0.9	1.8	3.3	0.1	0.5
Charleston, SC	6.2	12.4	7.1	10.0	1.1	1.0	2.0	2.4	0.3	0.2
Charlotte, NC	5.9	17.3	6.8	8.6	1.3	0.8	3.3	4.5	0.3	0.2
Chesapeake, VA	6.4	11.6	6.2	5.3	0.7	0.9	1.9	2.0	0.4	2.1
Chicago, IL	34.2	3.2	4.5	1.9	3.0	0.4	1.2	1.9	0.8	3.3
Clarksville, TN	4.1	30.9	2.3	6.2	0.6	1.5	1.8	1.1	n/a	0.1
Colorado Spgs., CO	8.4	4.3	7.4	2.4	2.0	3.0	1.1	2.1	0.1	0.1
Columbia, MD	16.7	4.2	4.8	6.1	2.1	0.5	1.1	1.3	1.8	0.5
Columbia, MO	6.6	14.7	5.4	4.3	1.7	1.4	1.1	2.3	0.3	0.3
Columbia, SC	3.1	18.1	5.2	9.4	3.4	1.1	2.7	3.3	0.2	0.1
Columbus, OH	11.8	5.3	3.6	4.7	2.4	0.7	2.0	2.0	0.5	0.8
Dallas, TX	13.3	18.7	7.8	5.3	0.8	1.2	2.2	1.0	0.4	2.4
Denver, CO	16.1	3.0	4.6	1.7	2.1	2.4	1.2	1.6	0.6	0.6
Durham, NC	5.1	13.9	5.6	8.1	0.5	0.8	1.4	2.5	0.6	0.5
Edison, NJ	36.9	1.9	1.8	1.3	0.8	0.4	0.9	1.1	4.8	2.3
El Paso, TX	43.2	3.8	5.0	0.9	0.3	1.6	1.4	0.2	0.2	0.1
Fargo, ND	17.4	0.4	0.5	3.3	32.5	0.6	1.5	1.9	0.0	0.1
Ft. Collins, CO	11.8	2.2	6.4	4.4	3.5	3.0	4.7	1.9	0.0	0.1
Ft. Worth, TX	13.3	18.7	7.8	5.3	0.8	1.2	2.2	1.0	0.4	2.4
Gilbert, AZ	13.4	3.5	5.2	1.0	1.6	6.1	2.9	0.6	0.3	0.2
Green Bay, WI	42.0	0.7	3.4	2.2	12.7	0.4	0.6	1.0	0.1	0.1
Henderson, NV	18.1	3.0	3.1	0.4	0.7	6.4	1.5	0.2	0.3	0.1
High Point, NC	2.7	12.8	7.4	9.9	0.7	0.8	2.5	3.2	0.4	0.6
Honolulu, HI	18.2	1.9	2.2	0.8	0.3	5.1	4.2	1.5	0.1	0.0
Houston, TX	17.1	16.0	7.3	4.9	1.1	1.1	1.5	0.9	0.4	2.7
Huntington, NY	36.9	1.9	1.8	1.3	0.8	0.4	0.9	1.1	4.8	2.3
Huntsville, AL	4.0	27.6	3.2	7.5	0.7	1.2	1.2	1.7	0.2	0.2
Indianapolis, IN	10.5	10.3	7.2	5.0	1.7	0.7	1.6	1.7	0.4	0.2
Irvine, CA	33.8	2.8	3.6	1.1	0.7	1.7	1.8	0.9	1.0	0.7
Jackson, MS	3.2	34.5	7.7	10.5	0.2	0.7	2.1	2.0	0.1	0.3
Jacksonville, FL	9.9	18.5	7.8	4.5	0.7	1.1	1.9	1.6	0.4	0.6
Jersey City, NJ	36.9	1.9	1.8	1.3	0.8	0.4	0.9	1.1	4.8	2.3
Kansas City, MO	12.7	13.2	5.2	5.9	2.3	2.5	2.6	1.6	0.4	0.3
Kenosha, WI	34.2	3.2	4.5	1.9	3.0	0.4	1.2	1.9	0.8	3.3
Las Vegas, NV	18.1	3.0	3.1	0.4	0.7	6.4	1.5	0.2	0.3	0.1
Lexington, KY	6.8	24.9	2.4	5.9	0.4	1.1	2.1	1.4	0.3	0.1
Lincoln, NE	14.8	2.4	1.9	7.2	11.3	1.2	1.4	3.9	0.2	0.2

Table continued on next page.

Area[1]	Catholic	Baptist	Non-Den.	Methodist[2]	Lutheran	LDS[3]	Pente-costal	Presby-terian[4]	Muslim[5]	Judaism
Little Rock, AR	4.5	25.9	6.1	7.3	0.5	0.9	2.9	0.9	0.1	0.1
Los Angeles, CA	33.8	2.8	3.6	1.1	0.7	1.7	1.8	0.9	1.0	0.7
Madison, WI	21.8	1.1	1.6	3.7	12.8	0.5	0.4	2.2	0.5	0.5
Manchester, NH	31.2	1.4	2.4	1.2	0.5	0.6	0.5	2.0	0.5	0.3
Miami, FL	18.6	5.4	4.2	1.3	0.5	0.5	1.8	0.7	1.6	0.9
Minneapolis, MN	21.7	2.5	3.0	2.8	14.5	0.6	1.8	1.9	0.7	0.4
Murfreesboro, TN	4.1	25.3	5.8	6.1	0.4	0.8	2.2	2.1	0.2	0.4
Naperville, IL	34.2	3.2	4.5	1.9	3.0	0.4	1.2	1.9	0.8	3.3
Nashville, TN	4.1	25.3	5.8	6.1	0.4	0.8	2.2	2.1	0.2	0.4
New Orleans, LA	31.6	8.4	3.7	2.7	0.8	0.6	2.1	0.5	0.5	0.5
New York, NY	36.9	1.9	1.8	1.3	0.8	0.4	0.9	1.1	4.8	2.3
Norman, OK	6.4	25.4	7.1	10.6	0.7	1.3	3.2	1.0	0.1	0.2
Olathe, KS	12.7	13.2	5.2	5.9	2.3	2.5	2.6	1.6	0.4	0.3
Omaha, NE	21.6	4.6	1.8	3.9	7.9	1.8	1.3	2.3	0.4	0.5
Orlando, FL	13.2	7.0	5.7	3.0	0.9	1.0	3.2	1.4	0.3	1.3
Overland Park, KS	12.7	13.2	5.2	5.9	2.3	2.5	2.6	1.6	0.4	0.3
Oyster Bay, NY	36.9	1.9	1.8	1.3	0.8	0.4	0.9	1.1	4.8	2.3
Pembroke Pines, FL	18.6	5.4	4.2	1.3	0.5	0.5	1.8	0.7	1.6	0.9
Philadelphia, PA	33.5	3.9	2.9	3.0	1.9	0.3	0.9	2.1	1.4	1.3
Phoenix, AZ	13.4	3.5	5.2	1.0	1.6	6.1	2.9	0.6	0.3	0.2
Pittsburgh, PA	32.8	2.3	2.8	5.7	3.4	0.4	1.1	4.7	0.7	0.3
Plano, TX	13.3	18.7	7.8	5.3	0.8	1.2	2.2	1.0	0.4	2.4
Portland, OR	10.6	2.3	4.5	1.0	1.6	3.8	2.0	1.0	0.3	0.1
Providence, RI	47.0	1.4	1.2	0.8	0.5	0.3	0.6	1.0	0.7	0.1
Provo, UT	1.3	0.1	0.1	0.2	0.0	88.6	0.1	0.1	n/a	n/a
Raleigh, NC	9.2	12.1	6.0	6.7	0.9	0.9	2.3	2.3	0.3	0.9
Richmond, VA	6.0	19.9	5.5	6.1	0.6	1.0	1.8	2.1	0.4	2.8
Roseville, CA	16.2	3.2	4.0	1.8	0.8	3.4	2.0	0.8	0.3	0.8
Round Rock, TX	16.0	10.3	4.5	3.6	2.0	1.2	0.8	1.1	0.3	1.2
San Antonio, TX	28.4	8.5	6.0	3.1	1.7	1.4	1.3	0.8	0.2	1.0
San Diego, CA	25.9	2.0	4.8	1.1	1.0	2.3	1.0	0.9	0.5	0.7
San Francisco, CA	20.8	2.5	2.5	2.0	0.6	1.6	1.2	1.1	0.9	1.2
San Jose, CA	26.0	1.4	4.3	1.1	0.6	1.4	1.2	0.7	0.7	1.0
Savannah, GA	7.1	19.7	6.9	8.9	1.6	1.0	2.4	1.0	0.8	0.2
Scottsdale, AZ	13.4	3.5	5.2	1.0	1.6	6.1	2.9	0.6	0.3	0.2
Seattle, WA	12.3	2.2	5.0	1.2	2.1	3.3	2.8	1.4	0.5	0.5
Sioux Falls, SD	14.9	3.0	1.5	3.9	21.4	0.7	1.1	6.2	0.1	0.3
Stamford, CT	44.1	2.0	2.4	2.1	0.8	0.5	1.2	3.0	2.0	0.6
Sterling Hgts, MI	21.4	4.5	5.0	2.1	3.1	0.4	1.3	1.4	0.8	1.9
Sunnyvale, CA	26.0	1.4	4.3	1.1	0.6	1.4	1.2	0.7	0.7	1.0
Tampa, FL	10.9	7.1	3.8	3.5	1.0	0.6	2.1	1.0	0.5	1.3
Temecula, CA	24.8	2.6	5.5	0.6	0.5	2.5	1.6	0.6	0.1	0.6
Thousand Oaks, CA	28.2	1.9	4.1	1.1	1.5	2.5	1.3	0.7	0.7	0.4
Virginia Beach, VA	6.4	11.6	6.2	5.3	0.7	0.9	1.9	2.0	0.4	2.1
Washington, DC	14.5	7.3	4.9	4.5	1.3	1.2	1.1	1.4	1.2	2.4
U.S.	19.1	9.3	4.0	4.0	2.3	2.0	1.9	1.6	0.8	0.7

Note: Figures are the number of adherents as a percentage of the total population; (1) Figures cover the Metropolitan Statistical Area—see Appendix B for areas included; (2) Methodist/Pietist; (3) Latter Day Saints; (4) Reformed; (5) Figures are estimates

Source: Association of Statisticians of American Religious Bodies, 2010 U.S. Religion Census: Religious Congregations & Membership Study

Ancestry: City

City	German	Irish	English	American	Italian	Polish	French[1]	Scottish	Dutch
Albuquerque, NM	11.5	8.8	7.1	2.4	3.4	1.5	2.3	1.9	1.1
Alexandria, VA	12.5	11.4	10.5	2.9	5.0	2.5	2.0	2.7	1.2
Anchorage, AK	19.5	12.2	9.4	3.5	3.6	2.8	3.7	3.3	2.1
Ann Arbor, MI	19.7	10.1	11.4	4.0	4.4	6.8	3.7	3.0	1.8
Athens, GA	9.2	8.6	9.8	8.3	2.2	1.8	1.9	3.6	1.1
Atlanta, GA	6.4	5.4	6.6	6.1	1.9	1.3	1.7	1.9	0.7
Austin, TX	12.5	8.6	9.4	2.8	2.7	1.6	2.9	2.6	1.0
Baltimore, MD	7.6	6.4	3.8	2.1	3.1	2.4	0.9	0.8	0.5
Bellevue, WA	14.4	8.4	10.3	2.2	3.3	2.1	3.1	2.9	1.6
Billings, MT	30.2	13.7	10.4	10.0	2.8	1.6	3.6	3.0	1.8
Boise City, ID	17.7	12.3	15.0	8.1	3.5	1.6	2.9	3.1	1.9
Boston, MA	4.8	16.8	5.5	1.7	8.5	2.8	2.4	1.4	0.5
Boulder, CO	23.4	13.9	16.2	2.0	7.1	4.4	4.1	4.7	2.6
Broken Arrow, OK	16.2	11.6	10.6	7.9	2.3	1.8	2.4	2.2	2.4
Cambridge, MA	9.3	15.1	9.7	1.5	8.8	4.1	3.1	2.6	1.1
Cape Coral, FL	17.0	14.0	8.9	12.3	10.9	4.3	3.4	1.8	1.6
Carlsbad, CA	16.8	11.4	17.5	3.1	7.2	3.9	3.6	2.4	1.9
Cary, NC	15.4	11.5	13.0	7.5	7.2	3.5	2.1	2.8	1.3
Cedar Rapids, IA	39.0	18.4	9.2	4.1	2.4	1.2	3.3	1.6	3.4
Charleston, SC	12.9	11.2	12.4	9.6	4.1	1.9	2.9	3.5	1.2
Charlotte, NC	10.0	7.5	8.0	4.1	4.0	1.5	1.7	2.5	1.0
Chesapeake, VA	10.4	10.5	10.5	15.8	4.1	2.0	2.2	2.2	0.7
Chicago, IL	7.6	7.6	2.4	1.3	3.9	6.4	0.9	0.6	0.6
Clarksville, TN	13.2	10.6	6.9	12.4	2.9	1.3	2.3	1.6	1.0
Colorado Spgs., CO	22.0	13.2	12.1	4.5	5.5	2.5	3.8	2.8	1.8
Columbia, MD	14.4	11.7	8.8	3.7	4.7	4.3	2.3	2.0	1.2
Columbia, MO	28.2	12.9	11.2	3.7	3.5	2.0	3.5	2.7	1.5
Columbia, SC	8.4	8.4	9.3	7.0	2.4	1.2	2.1	2.6	0.8
Columbus, OH	21.0	13.2	7.3	3.8	5.1	2.4	1.9	1.8	1.4
Dallas, TX	6.1	4.8	5.3	2.7	1.4	0.8	1.4	1.2	0.6
Denver, CO	14.7	10.0	8.4	3.3	4.4	2.2	2.6	1.9	1.4
Durham, NC	8.6	6.0	8.0	4.2	2.7	1.7	1.5	2.2	0.8
Edison, NJ	6.0	7.4	2.0	2.7	10.3	5.5	0.8	0.6	0.4
El Paso, TX	3.9	2.5	2.2	3.7	1.2	0.5	0.7	0.5	0.3
Fargo, ND	43.8	9.8	4.3	1.3	1.2	2.9	5.1	1.0	0.9
Ft. Collins, CO	29.7	14.9	12.8	3.3	5.7	2.7	2.9	3.1	2.9
Ft. Worth, TX	9.4	7.3	6.7	6.6	1.8	0.9	1.6	1.6	0.8
Gilbert, AZ	22.8	13.0	13.8	3.4	5.9	3.6	3.3	2.0	1.6
Green Bay, WI	33.7	9.4	3.6	2.4	2.2	9.7	5.5	0.6	3.9
Henderson, NV	17.0	12.8	11.5	4.8	8.9	3.8	2.9	2.3	1.8
High Point, NC	9.1	7.0	8.2	5.5	2.4	0.9	1.1	1.7	0.7
Honolulu, HI	4.1	3.5	3.3	0.6	1.5	0.8	1.1	0.8	0.6
Houston, TX	5.7	4.0	4.3	2.3	1.5	0.9	1.6	1.0	0.5
Huntington, NY	16.1	21.5	5.9	3.0	27.1	6.5	1.4	1.1	1.1
Huntsville, AL	8.6	9.4	10.1	10.2	2.5	1.0	2.3	2.5	1.2
Indianapolis, IN	18.2	11.3	7.9	5.7	2.4	1.5	1.8	1.6	1.5
Irvine, CA	9.1	6.3	6.6	2.1	3.5	1.8	2.2	1.5	0.8
Jackson, MS	2.0	3.1	3.0	3.0	0.5	0.1	0.7	0.8	0.2
Jacksonville, FL	9.7	10.3	8.4	6.2	3.6	1.6	2.2	1.9	1.2
Jersey City, NJ	3.5	5.1	1.7	0.7	5.0	2.4	0.6	0.5	0.3
Kansas City, MO	17.8	11.7	7.8	11.8	3.6	1.3	2.3	1.7	1.5
Kenosha, WI	28.7	12.0	6.3	2.1	11.0	8.4	2.8	1.2	1.5
Las Vegas, NV	11.2	8.6	6.9	2.4	6.2	2.8	2.1	1.5	1.0
Lexington, KY	14.0	13.6	12.6	14.4	3.1	1.4	2.1	2.8	1.3
Lincoln, NE	43.7	14.4	9.6	3.6	1.7	2.9	2.5	1.8	2.6
Little Rock, AR	9.1	8.2	9.8	4.3	1.6	0.6	2.1	1.9	1.0

Table continued on next page.

City	German	Irish	English	American	Italian	Polish	French[1]	Scottish	Dutch
Los Angeles, CA	4.8	3.8	3.4	1.5	2.7	1.6	1.2	0.7	0.5
Madison, WI	35.6	13.5	8.8	2.0	4.3	5.5	2.8	1.8	2.3
Manchester, NH	5.3	21.1	10.4	2.4	8.9	5.1	21.2	2.8	0.3
Miami, FL	1.7	1.5	1.0	2.1	1.7	0.6	0.9	0.2	0.2
Minneapolis, MN	23.7	11.2	6.2	1.3	2.5	3.8	3.3	1.5	1.5
Murfreesboro, TN	12.5	11.4	9.7	12.3	2.8	1.2	2.4	2.4	1.3
Naperville, IL	22.8	17.1	8.0	2.0	10.6	11.4	2.1	1.9	1.7
Nashville, TN	10.0	10.0	8.9	7.9	2.5	1.2	2.1	2.2	1.2
New Orleans, LA	6.9	5.6	4.3	2.8	3.4	0.7	6.2	1.1	0.3
New York, NY	3.3	5.0	1.8	2.4	7.6	2.7	0.8	0.5	0.3
Norman, OK	18.0	15.6	12.2	6.7	2.8	1.5	2.4	3.0	1.5
Olathe, KS	31.1	14.4	12.1	4.9	4.0	2.0	3.0	2.1	2.1
Omaha, NE	29.4	17.2	8.3	3.0	4.8	4.2	2.6	1.2	1.5
Orlando, FL	8.5	8.5	6.2	4.4	5.5	1.7	1.9	1.6	0.8
Overland Park, KS	29.4	16.2	13.9	5.5	3.9	2.5	3.4	3.0	2.1
Oyster Bay, NY	13.8	20.8	4.1	3.2	30.2	6.4	1.3	0.8	0.3
Pembroke Pines, FL	5.2	5.5	3.1	5.1	6.1	2.4	1.4	0.7	0.9
Philadelphia, PA	8.1	12.7	3.0	1.3	8.3	3.9	0.8	0.6	0.4
Phoenix, AZ	12.8	9.0	7.0	3.7	4.1	2.4	2.1	1.5	1.2
Pittsburgh, PA	21.2	16.2	5.3	2.8	13.1	7.4	1.3	1.8	0.6
Plano, TX	12.9	10.0	8.7	7.3	3.7	1.7	2.9	2.5	0.9
Portland, OR	19.2	12.4	11.8	4.2	4.2	2.2	3.6	3.5	1.9
Providence, RI	4.0	9.4	4.6	0.6	11.3	2.6	3.7	0.9	0.4
Provo, UT	11.0	5.3	28.3	2.7	2.5	0.7	2.2	5.8	1.2
Raleigh, NC	9.8	8.0	10.2	9.2	3.8	1.9	1.8	2.9	1.0
Richmond, VA	7.5	6.7	8.2	3.9	3.1	1.6	1.7	2.2	0.6
Roseville, CA	18.5	15.2	12.4	3.1	7.6	2.2	3.2	2.2	1.3
Round Rock, TX	16.7	11.3	9.9	4.1	2.8	1.7	3.0	2.0	1.1
San Antonio, TX	8.5	5.1	4.5	3.7	1.9	1.1	1.7	1.2	0.5
San Diego, CA	10.9	8.3	7.0	2.3	4.7	2.1	2.3	1.9	1.1
San Francisco, CA	8.2	7.9	5.5	1.0	4.8	2.1	2.3	1.6	0.9
San Jose, CA	6.7	4.8	4.5	1.1	4.4	0.9	1.5	0.9	0.8
Savannah, GA	5.1	7.3	5.8	2.7	2.0	0.6	1.0	0.9	0.5
Scottsdale, AZ	20.4	14.6	12.6	4.2	8.4	4.8	3.5	3.1	2.0
Seattle, WA	16.0	11.9	11.3	2.7	4.4	2.5	3.3	3.8	1.9
Sioux Falls, SD	41.5	11.8	5.8	3.4	1.5	1.6	2.0	1.0	6.2
Stamford, CT	5.4	8.7	4.6	1.5	14.1	5.6	1.8	1.3	0.5
Sterling Hgts, MI	16.3	8.5	6.6	4.0	10.0	16.9	3.8	1.5	1.0
Sunnyvale, CA	7.9	6.1	5.7	1.3	3.4	1.4	2.2	1.4	0.8
Tampa, FL	9.8	8.5	6.8	3.5	6.4	2.0	2.0	1.5	1.0
Temecula, CA	12.3	11.6	9.7	1.6	7.5	3.5	3.0	2.1	1.8
Thousand Oaks, CA	14.4	12.9	10.7	4.1	9.2	3.8	2.9	2.5	1.8
Virginia Beach, VA	13.5	12.1	10.3	11.9	7.0	2.6	2.6	2.5	1.5
Washington, DC	6.8	7.1	5.3	1.3	3.0	1.9	1.7	1.3	0.6
U.S.	16.1	11.6	8.8	6.1	5.7	3.2	3.0	1.9	1.6

Note: Figures are the percentage of the total population reporting a particular ancestry. The nine most commonly reported ancestries in the U.S. are shown. Figures include multiple ancestries (e.g. if a person reported being Irish and Italian, they were included in both columns); (1) Excludes Basque
Source: U.S. Census Bureau, 2008-2010 American Community Survey 3-Year Estimates

Ancestry: Metro Area

Metro Area	German	Irish	English	American	Italian	Polish	French[1]	Scottish	Dutch
Albuquerque, NM	11.8	8.5	7.3	2.7	3.3	1.5	2.4	1.9	1.0
Alexandria, VA	11.4	9.8	8.4	3.8	4.5	2.4	2.0	1.9	0.9
Anchorage, AK	20.9	12.9	10.3	3.7	3.8	2.9	4.0	3.5	2.6
Ann Arbor, MI	21.6	11.9	12.1	5.1	4.3	7.2	3.8	3.0	2.1
Athens, GA	9.2	9.6	11.3	13.2	2.0	1.5	1.7	3.4	1.2
Atlanta, GA	8.1	8.2	8.1	8.9	2.7	1.3	1.6	1.9	0.9
Austin, TX	15.6	9.5	9.5	3.6	2.7	1.6	2.9	2.5	1.1
Baltimore, MD	19.2	14.2	9.0	4.2	6.5	4.7	1.9	1.8	1.0
Bellevue, WA	18.1	11.7	11.1	3.3	3.8	2.1	3.5	3.1	2.0
Billings, MT	30.7	13.7	11.4	10.9	2.5	1.8	3.3	3.1	2.2
Boise City, ID	17.7	10.1	14.2	12.7	3.0	1.4	2.7	3.1	2.1
Boston, MA	6.6	24.6	11.4	3.0	14.7	3.9	6.2	2.8	0.7
Boulder, CO	23.7	14.3	14.4	3.0	6.2	3.9	4.0	4.3	2.4
Broken Arrow, OK	15.2	13.1	9.3	7.8	1.8	1.0	2.4	2.1	2.2
Cambridge, MA	6.6	24.6	11.4	3.0	14.7	3.9	6.2	2.8	0.7
Cape Coral, FL	16.0	12.5	10.7	12.0	8.0	3.7	3.1	2.2	1.4
Carlsbad, CA	12.3	9.0	8.7	2.3	4.6	2.1	2.6	1.9	1.3
Cary, NC	11.4	9.9	11.5	10.8	4.9	2.3	2.0	2.8	1.1
Cedar Rapids, IA	42.7	18.6	9.9	4.2	2.1	1.2	3.2	1.9	3.6
Charleston, SC	12.0	10.4	9.6	11.7	3.5	1.8	2.7	2.6	1.0
Charlotte, NC	13.0	9.7	9.0	7.9	4.1	1.7	1.9	2.6	1.3
Chesapeake, VA	11.2	10.0	10.6	11.0	4.6	2.0	2.2	2.2	1.1
Chicago, IL	16.6	12.3	4.7	2.2	7.2	9.9	1.6	1.0	1.3
Clarksville, TN	12.3	11.0	8.8	15.0	2.6	1.2	2.2	1.6	1.2
Colorado Spgs., CO	22.4	13.5	12.1	5.1	5.1	2.7	3.7	2.8	1.9
Columbia, MD	19.2	14.2	9.0	4.2	6.5	4.7	1.9	1.8	1.0
Columbia, MO	28.4	13.4	11.4	5.9	3.1	1.6	3.3	2.7	1.8
Columbia, SC	11.9	9.0	9.1	12.4	2.4	1.1	1.8	2.0	0.9
Columbus, OH	26.6	15.3	10.1	6.6	5.6	2.6	2.2	2.3	1.9
Dallas, TX	11.1	8.6	8.2	6.0	2.3	1.1	2.2	1.8	1.1
Denver, CO	20.6	12.0	10.8	4.7	5.3	2.7	3.1	2.5	1.8
Durham, NC	10.8	8.8	11.9	6.1	3.0	2.0	2.1	2.9	1.1
Edison, NJ	7.7	11.1	3.3	2.9	14.3	4.5	1.1	0.8	0.7
El Paso, TX	3.6	2.4	1.9	3.5	1.1	0.5	0.6	0.4	0.2
Fargo, ND	43.1	9.1	4.9	1.5	1.1	3.2	4.7	1.2	1.1
Ft. Collins, CO	31.1	14.8	13.6	3.7	5.0	2.7	3.3	3.2	2.6
Ft. Worth, TX	11.1	8.6	8.2	6.0	2.3	1.1	2.2	1.8	1.1
Gilbert, AZ	16.0	10.5	9.3	5.1	4.9	2.8	2.7	1.9	1.5
Green Bay, WI	40.7	9.6	4.0	3.1	2.2	10.9	5.8	0.8	5.6
Henderson, NV	11.1	8.7	7.2	2.7	6.2	2.5	2.2	1.5	1.1
High Point, NC	9.7	7.5	9.4	8.7	2.3	1.1	1.4	2.2	1.1
Honolulu, HI	5.7	4.4	3.7	0.7	1.8	0.8	1.3	0.9	0.7
Houston, TX	9.5	6.5	6.1	4.3	2.2	1.2	2.6	1.3	0.8
Huntington, NY	7.7	11.1	3.3	2.9	14.3	4.5	1.1	0.8	0.7
Huntsville, AL	9.8	10.8	10.0	13.5	2.4	1.2	2.3	2.3	1.2
Indianapolis, IN	22.7	12.9	10.7	7.6	2.9	1.9	2.2	2.1	1.8
Irvine, CA	6.7	5.2	4.8	2.0	3.2	1.4	1.5	1.1	0.8
Jackson, MS	5.2	8.3	7.6	7.4	1.3	0.4	1.9	1.8	0.5
Jacksonville, FL	11.8	12.2	10.1	8.0	4.8	2.0	2.6	2.1	1.3
Jersey City, NJ	7.7	11.1	3.3	2.9	14.3	4.5	1.1	0.8	0.7
Kansas City, MO	24.7	14.6	10.8	8.3	3.6	1.8	2.8	2.1	2.0
Kenosha, WI	16.6	12.3	4.7	2.2	7.2	9.9	1.6	1.0	1.3
Las Vegas, NV	11.1	8.7	7.2	2.7	6.2	2.5	2.2	1.5	1.1
Lexington, KY	14.0	13.9	12.2	18.3	2.8	1.4	1.9	2.6	1.2
Lincoln, NE	45.1	14.0	9.8	3.6	1.7	2.7	2.5	1.7	2.7
Little Rock, AR	11.5	11.2	10.1	10.0	1.8	0.9	2.4	1.9	1.4

Table continued on next page.

Metro Area	German	Irish	English	American	Italian	Polish	French[1]	Scottish	Dutch
Los Angeles, CA	6.7	5.2	4.8	2.0	3.2	1.4	1.5	1.1	0.8
Madison, WI	41.9	14.7	9.4	2.7	3.7	5.2	2.9	1.7	2.4
Manchester, NH	8.1	22.5	14.6	3.7	10.5	4.9	17.4	3.7	0.8
Miami, FL	5.8	5.5	3.8	4.2	5.6	2.5	1.6	0.8	0.6
Minneapolis, MN	34.0	12.4	6.6	2.6	2.9	4.9	4.2	1.4	1.8
Murfreesboro, TN	11.7	12.1	11.4	12.6	2.7	1.2	2.4	2.6	1.3
Naperville, IL	16.6	12.3	4.7	2.2	7.2	9.9	1.6	1.0	1.3
Nashville, TN	11.7	12.1	11.4	12.6	2.7	1.2	2.4	2.6	1.3
New Orleans, LA	12.5	8.5	5.4	4.6	9.0	0.6	15.7	1.0	0.4
New York, NY	7.7	11.1	3.3	2.9	14.3	4.5	1.1	0.8	0.7
Norman, OK	15.8	12.7	8.8	7.8	1.9	0.9	2.2	2.0	2.0
Olathe, KS	24.7	14.6	10.8	8.3	3.6	1.8	2.8	2.1	2.0
Omaha, NE	34.7	17.0	9.3	3.6	4.5	4.1	2.9	1.5	2.0
Orlando, FL	11.1	9.4	7.8	7.0	6.0	2.3	2.5	1.6	1.2
Overland Park, KS	24.7	14.6	10.8	8.3	3.6	1.8	2.8	2.1	2.0
Oyster Bay, NY	7.7	11.1	3.3	2.9	14.3	4.5	1.1	0.8	0.7
Pembroke Pines, FL	5.8	5.5	3.8	4.2	5.6	2.5	1.6	0.8	0.6
Philadelphia, PA	17.6	20.9	8.5	2.6	14.2	5.8	1.7	1.4	1.1
Phoenix, AZ	16.0	10.5	9.3	5.1	4.9	2.8	2.7	1.9	1.5
Pittsburgh, PA	30.3	19.5	9.2	3.6	16.4	9.2	2.0	2.1	1.5
Plano, TX	11.1	8.6	8.2	6.0	2.3	1.1	2.2	1.8	1.1
Portland, OR	21.6	12.6	12.5	4.1	3.9	1.9	3.7	3.4	2.3
Providence, RI	5.6	19.6	12.6	2.3	15.7	4.1	12.7	2.0	0.5
Provo, UT	11.9	5.0	30.6	4.6	2.2	0.6	2.1	6.0	2.1
Raleigh, NC	11.4	9.9	11.5	10.8	4.9	2.3	2.0	2.8	1.1
Richmond, VA	11.0	9.6	13.4	8.5	3.5	1.7	2.0	2.4	0.9
Roseville, CA	14.1	10.9	9.8	2.6	5.8	1.5	2.8	2.3	1.5
Round Rock, TX	15.6	9.5	9.5	3.6	2.7	1.6	2.9	2.5	1.1
San Antonio, TX	12.3	6.7	5.8	3.9	2.0	1.7	2.1	1.4	0.8
San Diego, CA	12.3	9.0	8.7	2.3	4.6	2.1	2.6	1.9	1.3
San Francisco, CA	9.1	8.4	6.8	1.6	5.3	1.6	2.2	1.7	1.0
San Jose, CA	8.1	6.1	5.9	1.2	4.7	1.2	1.9	1.4	1.0
Savannah, GA	9.3	10.6	9.5	5.5	2.8	1.1	1.8	2.0	1.1
Scottsdale, AZ	16.0	10.5	9.3	5.1	4.9	2.8	2.7	1.9	1.5
Seattle, WA	18.1	11.7	11.1	3.3	3.8	2.1	3.5	3.1	2.0
Sioux Falls, SD	43.8	11.2	5.6	3.5	1.4	1.5	2.3	1.1	6.6
Stamford, CT	9.5	15.3	8.6	2.5	18.0	5.6	2.5	2.0	0.9
Sterling Hgts, MI	17.6	11.0	7.9	3.7	6.5	11.2	4.3	2.4	1.4
Sunnyvale, CA	8.1	6.1	5.9	1.2	4.7	1.2	1.9	1.4	1.0
Tampa, FL	15.4	13.4	10.3	6.4	8.6	3.4	3.4	2.1	1.4
Temecula, CA	9.6	7.1	6.5	2.5	3.7	1.3	2.1	1.3	1.3
Thousand Oaks, CA	11.9	9.4	8.7	3.6	5.2	2.3	2.5	2.0	1.3
Virginia Beach, VA	11.2	10.0	10.6	11.0	4.6	2.0	2.2	2.2	1.1
Washington, DC	11.4	9.8	8.4	3.8	4.5	2.4	2.0	1.9	0.9
U.S.	16.1	11.6	8.8	6.1	5.7	3.2	3.0	1.9	1.6

Note: Figures are the percentage of the total population reporting a particular ancestry. The nine most commonly reported ancestries in the U.S. are shown. Figures include multiple ancestries (e.g. if a person reported being Irish and Italian, they were included in both columns); Figures cover the Metropolitan Statistical Area—see Appendix B for areas included; (1) Excludes Basque
Source: U.S. Census Bureau, 2008-2010 American Community Survey 3-Year Estimates

Foreign-Born Population: City

City	Percent of Population Born in								
	Any Foreign Country	Mexico	Asia	Europe	Carribean	South America	Central America[1]	Africa	Canada
Albuquerque, NM	11.2	6.7	2.1	0.8	0.4	0.4	0.2	0.2	0.2
Alexandria, VA	24.9	1.1	6.7	2.2	0.7	2.6	4.6	6.6	0.3
Anchorage, AK	9.2	0.5	5.3	1.1	0.5	0.4	0.3	0.3	0.5
Ann Arbor, MI	17.4	0.4	10.9	3.5	0.1	0.6	0.2	0.7	0.9
Athens, GA	n/a	n/a	n/a	n/a	n/a	n/a	n/a	n/a	n/a
Atlanta, GA	7.8	1.9	2.4	1.2	0.6	0.5	0.3	0.5	0.2
Austin, TX	19.7	10.5	4.7	1.1	0.3	0.5	1.8	0.5	0.3
Baltimore, MD	7.2	0.7	1.9	1.1	1.0	0.5	0.8	1.1	0.1
Bellevue, WA	33.0	2.5	21.4	4.9	0.0	1.0	0.4	0.9	1.4
Billings, MT	n/a	n/a	n/a	n/a	n/a	n/a	n/a	n/a	n/a
Boise City, ID	n/a	n/a	n/a	n/a	n/a	n/a	n/a	n/a	n/a
Boston, MA	26.7	0.3	6.8	3.9	7.6	2.4	2.4	2.8	0.4
Boulder, CO	11.3	2.8	3.5	3.3	0.2	0.5	0.2	0.2	0.5
Broken Arrow, OK	n/a	n/a	n/a	n/a	n/a	n/a	n/a	n/a	n/a
Cambridge, MA	27.4	0.8	9.5	7.2	3.1	2.0	1.0	2.5	1.0
Cape Coral, FL	n/a	n/a	n/a	n/a	n/a	n/a	n/a	n/a	n/a
Carlsbad, CA	14.8	3.5	5.4	3.6	0.2	0.8	0.1	0.4	0.8
Cary, NC	18.3	2.7	9.6	2.1	0.6	0.7	1.3	0.8	0.5
Cedar Rapids, IA	n/a	n/a	n/a	n/a	n/a	n/a	n/a	n/a	n/a
Charleston, SC	n/a	n/a	n/a	n/a	n/a	n/a	n/a	n/a	n/a
Charlotte, NC	15.0	3.5	4.0	1.4	0.6	1.4	2.6	1.2	0.3
Chesapeake, VA	4.4	0.5	2.0	0.7	0.3	0.3	0.4	0.2	0.1
Chicago, IL	21.0	9.6	4.3	3.9	0.5	0.9	0.8	0.7	0.2
Clarksville, TN	n/a	n/a	n/a	n/a	n/a	n/a	n/a	n/a	n/a
Colorado Spgs., CO	7.9	2.2	2.3	1.7	0.2	0.2	0.4	0.3	0.5
Columbia, MD	17.9	0.9	8.8	2.2	0.6	0.8	1.9	2.5	0.3
Columbia, MO	n/a	n/a	n/a	n/a	n/a	n/a	n/a	n/a	n/a
Columbia, SC	4.6	0.3	2.0	0.8	0.3	0.3	0.1	0.5	0.2
Columbus, OH	10.6	1.8	3.7	0.8	0.4	0.4	0.5	2.9	0.1
Dallas, TX	24.7	17.1	2.6	0.7	0.2	0.4	2.4	1.1	0.1
Denver, CO	16.4	9.4	3.0	1.8	0.1	0.3	0.4	1.0	0.2
Durham, NC	14.6	4.4	4.1	1.2	0.4	0.8	2.4	0.8	0.4
Edison, NJ	40.3	0.9	31.5	2.8	1.6	1.5	0.2	1.2	0.3
El Paso, TX	25.4	22.9	1.1	0.6	0.2	0.2	0.2	0.1	0.1
Fargo, ND	n/a	n/a	n/a	n/a	n/a	n/a	n/a	n/a	n/a
Ft. Collins, CO	n/a	n/a	n/a	n/a	n/a	n/a	n/a	n/a	n/a
Ft. Worth, TX	17.8	11.9	2.9	0.8	0.2	0.4	0.8	0.6	0.1
Gilbert, AZ	8.6	1.5	3.8	0.9	0.3	0.6	0.1	0.7	0.5
Green Bay, WI	n/a	n/a	n/a	n/a	n/a	n/a	n/a	n/a	n/a
Henderson, NV	11.4	1.8	5.4	1.8	0.4	0.6	0.4	0.3	0.6
High Point, NC	n/a	n/a	n/a	n/a	n/a	n/a	n/a	n/a	n/a
Honolulu, HI	28.3	0.2	23.5	1.2	0.1	0.3	0.1	0.1	0.4
Houston, TX	28.9	13.9	5.3	1.1	0.6	1.0	5.5	1.1	0.2
Huntington, NY	14.5	0.4	4.0	3.7	1.3	1.0	3.5	0.5	0.1
Huntsville, AL	7.0	2.4	1.9	0.9	0.6	0.1	0.3	0.6	0.1
Indianapolis, IN	8.5	4.1	1.9	0.5	0.2	0.2	0.7	0.8	0.1
Irvine, CA	35.0	1.5	27.7	2.7	0.1	0.8	0.3	0.9	0.8
Jackson, MS	n/a	n/a	n/a	n/a	n/a	n/a	n/a	n/a	n/a
Jacksonville, FL	9.4	0.6	3.3	1.7	1.5	1.0	0.5	0.6	0.2
Jersey City, NJ	38.4	0.7	18.3	3.1	5.7	5.0	2.4	3.0	0.1
Kansas City, MO	8.0	2.8	2.0	0.8	0.4	0.2	0.5	1.1	0.1
Kenosha, WI	n/a	n/a	n/a	n/a	n/a	n/a	n/a	n/a	n/a
Las Vegas, NV	22.2	10.9	5.0	1.8	0.8	0.6	2.1	0.4	0.4
Lexington, KY	8.6	3.1	2.9	1.1	0.1	0.4	0.4	0.3	0.2

Table continued on next page.

City	Any Foreign Country	Mexico	Asia	Europe	Carribean	South America	Central America[1]	Africa	Canada
	Percent of Population Born in								
Lincoln, NE	7.5	1.2	3.6	0.8	0.1	0.2	0.5	0.8	0.2
Little Rock, AR	n/a	n/a	n/a	n/a	n/a	n/a	n/a	n/a	n/a
Los Angeles, CA	39.6	14.9	11.2	2.4	0.3	1.1	8.5	0.6	0.4
Madison, WI	10.0	1.6	5.3	1.3	0.1	0.7	0.2	0.6	0.3
Manchester, NH	11.9	1.1	3.1	2.7	0.5	1.1	0.5	1.7	1.1
Miami, FL	58.2	1.0	0.8	1.3	33.7	7.5	13.5	0.2	0.1
Minneapolis, MN	15.0	3.2	4.0	1.1	0.2	1.6	0.4	4.0	0.3
Murfreesboro, TN	n/a	n/a	n/a	n/a	n/a	n/a	n/a	n/a	n/a
Naperville, IL	15.9	1.3	10.1	2.3	0.1	0.8	0.1	0.6	0.5
Nashville, TN	12.3	4.0	3.4	0.8	0.4	0.3	1.3	1.9	0.1
New Orleans, LA	5.7	0.5	1.9	0.8	0.2	0.5	1.4	0.4	0.1
New York, NY	36.8	2.2	10.0	5.8	10.2	5.2	1.5	1.4	0.3
Norman, OK	n/a	n/a	n/a	n/a	n/a	n/a	n/a	n/a	n/a
Olathe, KS	n/a	n/a	n/a	n/a	n/a	n/a	n/a	n/a	n/a
Omaha, NE	9.4	4.5	2.1	0.7	0.1	0.1	0.8	0.9	0.1
Orlando, FL	18.3	1.2	2.6	1.5	6.0	5.1	0.8	0.7	0.3
Overland Park, KS	9.5	1.0	5.5	1.5	0.0	0.5	0.2	0.6	0.2
Oyster Bay, NY	14.3	0.1	6.7	3.7	0.8	1.7	0.8	0.3	0.1
Pembroke Pines, FL	36.7	0.5	4.1	1.8	15.8	11.0	2.2	0.6	0.5
Philadelphia, PA	11.4	0.4	4.6	2.3	1.9	0.7	0.3	1.1	0.1
Phoenix, AZ	21.0	14.7	2.7	1.4	0.3	0.3	0.7	0.7	0.3
Pittsburgh, PA	6.8	0.3	3.6	1.6	0.4	0.2	0.1	0.4	0.2
Plano, TX	24.1	4.9	13.1	1.6	0.3	1.2	1.1	1.3	0.4
Portland, OR	13.5	2.5	5.4	2.8	0.3	0.2	0.6	0.6	0.6
Providence, RI	28.9	0.9	4.1	1.9	10.2	1.6	6.6	3.2	0.2
Provo, UT	n/a	n/a	n/a	n/a	n/a	n/a	n/a	n/a	n/a
Raleigh, NC	14.7	4.2	3.9	1.2	0.6	0.6	1.5	2.1	0.3
Richmond, VA	7.9	1.0	1.9	1.0	0.5	0.4	2.1	0.9	0.2
Roseville, CA	n/a	n/a	n/a	n/a	n/a	n/a	n/a	n/a	n/a
Round Rock, TX	n/a	n/a	n/a	n/a	n/a	n/a	n/a	n/a	n/a
San Antonio, TX	13.8	9.6	1.9	0.7	0.2	0.3	0.6	0.3	0.1
San Diego, CA	25.8	9.5	11.3	2.3	0.2	0.6	0.5	0.7	0.5
San Francisco, CA	35.5	3.0	22.7	4.6	0.2	1.0	2.8	0.4	0.6
San Jose, CA	38.5	10.7	22.8	2.0	0.1	0.6	1.1	0.5	0.4
Savannah, GA	n/a	n/a	n/a	n/a	n/a	n/a	n/a	n/a	n/a
Scottsdale, AZ	11.2	2.1	3.2	2.6	0.2	0.7	0.3	0.5	1.7
Seattle, WA	16.8	1.3	8.9	2.4	0.1	0.4	0.3	2.0	1.0
Sioux Falls, SD	n/a	n/a	n/a	n/a	n/a	n/a	n/a	n/a	n/a
Stamford, CT	39.2	1.8	6.5	8.0	6.6	6.9	8.3	0.5	0.4
Sterling Hgts, MI	n/a	n/a	n/a	n/a	n/a	n/a	n/a	n/a	n/a
Sunnyvale, CA	43.2	5.6	30.9	3.1	0.1	1.0	1.4	0.2	0.7
Tampa, FL	15.0	1.5	2.3	1.4	5.8	1.5	1.2	0.7	0.5
Temecula, CA	n/a	n/a	n/a	n/a	n/a	n/a	n/a	n/a	n/a
Thousand Oaks, CA	19.3	4.3	7.0	4.0	0.3	0.9	1.8	0.2	0.6
Virginia Beach, VA	8.9	0.4	4.6	1.7	0.7	0.5	0.4	0.4	0.2
Washington, DC	13.1	0.6	2.6	2.2	1.3	1.0	3.1	1.9	0.3
U.S.	12.8	3.8	3.6	1.6	1.2	0.9	1.0	0.5	0.3

Note: (1) Excludes Mexico
Source: U.S. Census Bureau, 2008-2010 American Community Survey 3-Year Estimates

Foreign-Born Population: Metro Area

Metro Area	Percent of Population Born in								
	Any Foreign Country	Mexico	Asia	Europe	Carribean	South America	Central America[1]	Africa	Canada
Albuquerque, NM	10.0	6.5	1.5	0.8	0.3	0.3	0.2	0.1	0.2
Alexandria, VA	21.4	0.9	7.7	2.0	1.0	2.3	4.5	2.8	0.2
Anchorage, AK	7.7	0.4	4.3	1.1	0.4	0.4	0.2	0.2	0.5
Ann Arbor, MI	11.3	0.3	6.5	2.2	0.1	0.3	0.3	0.8	0.6
Athens, GA	8.1	3.1	2.1	0.8	0.2	0.6	0.6	0.4	0.2
Atlanta, GA	13.7	3.5	3.8	1.3	1.4	1.0	1.1	1.3	0.2
Austin, TX	14.6	7.6	3.6	1.0	0.2	0.4	1.1	0.4	0.3
Baltimore, MD	9.0	0.6	3.6	1.4	0.7	0.4	1.0	1.1	0.1
Bellevue, WA	16.4	2.7	8.0	2.7	0.1	0.4	0.4	1.1	0.8
Billings, MT	n/a	n/a	n/a	n/a	n/a	n/a	n/a	n/a	n/a
Boise City, ID	7.2	3.1	1.5	1.3	0.1	0.2	0.3	0.4	0.3
Boston, MA	16.5	0.2	5.1	3.3	2.7	1.9	1.3	1.3	0.5
Boulder, CO	11.0	3.8	3.1	2.3	0.1	0.4	0.6	0.1	0.5
Broken Arrow, OK	5.5	2.8	1.4	0.4	0.1	0.2	0.3	0.2	0.1
Cambridge, MA	16.5	0.2	5.1	3.3	2.7	1.9	1.3	1.3	0.5
Cape Coral, FL	15.4	2.4	1.3	2.2	4.5	2.3	1.7	0.1	0.8
Carlsbad, CA	23.2	10.9	8.2	1.9	0.2	0.5	0.5	0.5	0.4
Cary, NC	11.8	3.6	3.5	1.2	0.5	0.5	1.1	1.1	0.3
Cedar Rapids, IA	n/a	n/a	n/a	n/a	n/a	n/a	n/a	n/a	n/a
Charleston, SC	5.5	1.7	1.2	1.1	0.2	0.5	0.5	0.1	0.2
Charlotte, NC	10.1	2.8	2.5	1.1	0.4	1.0	1.4	0.7	0.2
Chesapeake, VA	6.2	0.4	2.7	1.1	0.5	0.3	0.6	0.4	0.2
Chicago, IL	17.6	7.2	4.5	4.0	0.3	0.6	0.5	0.4	0.2
Clarksville, TN	n/a	n/a	n/a	n/a	n/a	n/a	n/a	n/a	n/a
Colorado Spgs., CO	6.9	1.8	2.0	1.7	0.2	0.2	0.4	0.2	0.4
Columbia, MD	9.0	0.6	3.6	1.4	0.7	0.4	1.0	1.1	0.1
Columbia, MO	5.9	0.3	3.2	1.1	0.1	0.1	0.1	0.7	0.2
Columbia, SC	4.8	1.5	1.4	0.7	0.3	0.2	0.5	0.2	0.1
Columbus, OH	6.9	1.0	2.6	0.9	0.3	0.2	0.3	1.5	0.2
Dallas, TX	17.5	9.3	4.2	0.8	0.2	0.5	1.3	0.9	0.2
Denver, CO	12.2	5.7	2.8	1.6	0.1	0.3	0.5	0.7	0.3
Durham, NC	12.6	4.0	3.6	1.4	0.4	0.5	1.6	0.7	0.4
Edison, NJ	28.4	1.7	7.9	4.8	6.4	4.4	1.8	1.1	0.2
El Paso, TX	26.5	24.4	0.9	0.5	0.2	0.2	0.2	0.1	0.1
Fargo, ND	n/a	n/a	n/a	n/a	n/a	n/a	n/a	n/a	n/a
Ft. Collins, CO	5.5	1.9	1.4	1.2	0.1	0.2	0.2	0.1	0.3
Ft. Worth, TX	17.5	9.3	4.2	0.8	0.2	0.5	1.3	0.9	0.2
Gilbert, AZ	14.9	8.8	2.7	1.4	0.2	0.3	0.5	0.4	0.6
Green Bay, WI	n/a	n/a	n/a	n/a	n/a	n/a	n/a	n/a	n/a
Henderson, NV	22.0	9.4	6.5	1.9	0.8	0.6	1.7	0.7	0.4
High Point, NC	8.2	3.1	2.3	0.6	0.4	0.4	0.4	0.9	0.2
Honolulu, HI	19.9	0.2	16.0	0.8	0.2	0.3	0.1	0.1	0.3
Houston, TX	22.2	10.2	5.2	1.0	0.5	1.0	3.3	0.8	0.2
Huntington, NY	28.4	1.7	7.9	4.8	6.4	4.4	1.8	1.1	0.2
Huntsville, AL	5.3	1.7	1.6	0.7	0.3	0.1	0.2	0.3	0.2
Indianapolis, IN	6.2	2.3	1.8	0.6	0.1	0.2	0.4	0.5	0.1
Irvine, CA	34.5	13.9	12.2	1.8	0.3	0.9	4.3	0.5	0.3
Jackson, MS	2.4	0.6	0.9	0.2	0.1	0.1	0.2	0.1	0.0
Jacksonville, FL	7.9	0.5	2.6	1.6	1.2	0.9	0.4	0.4	0.2
Jersey City, NJ	28.4	1.7	7.9	4.8	6.4	4.4	1.8	1.1	0.2
Kansas City, MO	6.3	2.3	1.8	0.7	0.2	0.2	0.4	0.5	0.1
Kenosha, WI	17.6	7.2	4.5	4.0	0.3	0.6	0.5	0.4	0.2
Las Vegas, NV	22.0	9.4	6.5	1.9	0.8	0.6	1.7	0.7	0.4
Lexington, KY	6.7	2.4	2.2	0.9	0.1	0.3	0.4	0.2	0.1

Table continued on next page.

Metro Area	Percent of Population Born in								
	Any Foreign Country	Mexico	Asia	Europe	Carribean	South America	Central America[1]	Africa	Canada
Lincoln, NE	6.7	1.1	3.2	0.8	0.1	0.2	0.4	0.7	0.2
Little Rock, AR	4.3	1.8	1.3	0.5	0.1	0.1	0.3	0.1	0.1
Los Angeles, CA	34.5	13.9	12.2	1.8	0.3	0.9	4.3	0.5	0.3
Madison, WI	6.7	1.4	3.0	1.0	0.1	0.5	0.2	0.3	0.2
Manchester, NH	8.1	0.6	2.6	1.7	0.5	1.0	0.3	0.7	0.8
Miami, FL	38.1	1.2	1.9	2.2	19.6	7.7	4.5	0.3	0.6
Minneapolis, MN	9.5	1.6	3.6	1.1	0.1	0.5	0.3	1.9	0.3
Murfreesboro, TN	7.5	2.2	2.2	0.6	0.2	0.3	0.9	0.8	0.2
Naperville, IL	17.6	7.2	4.5	4.0	0.3	0.6	0.5	0.4	0.2
Nashville, TN	7.5	2.2	2.2	0.6	0.2	0.3	0.9	0.8	0.2
New Orleans, LA	7.1	0.8	2.0	0.6	0.5	0.5	2.4	0.2	0.1
New York, NY	28.4	1.7	7.9	4.8	6.4	4.4	1.8	1.1	0.2
Norman, OK	7.6	3.6	2.2	0.5	0.1	0.2	0.5	0.4	0.1
Olathe, KS	6.3	2.3	1.8	0.7	0.2	0.2	0.4	0.5	0.1
Omaha, NE	6.5	2.8	1.7	0.6	0.1	0.1	0.5	0.6	0.1
Orlando, FL	16.2	1.4	2.8	1.7	4.7	3.7	0.9	0.5	0.4
Overland Park, KS	6.3	2.3	1.8	0.7	0.2	0.2	0.4	0.5	0.1
Oyster Bay, NY	28.4	1.7	7.9	4.8	6.4	4.4	1.8	1.1	0.2
Pembroke Pines, FL	38.1	1.2	1.9	2.2	19.6	7.7	4.5	0.3	0.6
Philadelphia, PA	9.5	0.9	3.8	2.0	1.0	0.6	0.3	0.8	0.2
Phoenix, AZ	14.9	8.8	2.7	1.4	0.2	0.3	0.5	0.4	0.6
Pittsburgh, PA	3.2	0.1	1.4	1.0	0.1	0.1	0.0	0.2	0.1
Plano, TX	17.5	9.3	4.2	0.8	0.2	0.5	1.3	0.9	0.2
Portland, OR	12.6	3.5	4.3	2.6	0.2	0.3	0.5	0.4	0.5
Providence, RI	12.4	0.3	1.9	4.4	1.7	0.9	1.3	1.4	0.3
Provo, UT	7.0	2.9	0.9	0.6	0.0	1.2	0.5	0.1	0.5
Raleigh, NC	11.8	3.6	3.5	1.2	0.5	0.5	1.1	1.1	0.3
Richmond, VA	6.8	0.8	2.4	1.0	0.3	0.4	1.1	0.5	0.2
Roseville, CA	17.3	4.9	7.4	2.7	0.1	0.3	0.6	0.4	0.3
Round Rock, TX	14.6	7.6	3.6	1.0	0.2	0.4	1.1	0.4	0.3
San Antonio, TX	11.6	7.7	1.7	0.7	0.2	0.3	0.6	0.2	0.1
San Diego, CA	23.2	10.9	8.2	1.9	0.2	0.5	0.5	0.5	0.4
San Francisco, CA	30.0	6.1	16.0	2.9	0.2	0.8	2.4	0.5	0.4
San Jose, CA	36.5	8.6	22.2	2.8	0.1	0.7	1.0	0.5	0.6
Savannah, GA	5.2	1.4	1.8	0.6	0.3	0.3	0.4	0.2	0.1
Scottsdale, AZ	14.9	8.8	2.7	1.4	0.2	0.3	0.5	0.4	0.6
Seattle, WA	16.4	2.7	8.0	2.7	0.1	0.4	0.4	1.1	0.8
Sioux Falls, SD	n/a	n/a	n/a	n/a	n/a	n/a	n/a	n/a	n/a
Stamford, CT	20.4	1.1	3.7	5.1	3.1	4.2	2.1	0.6	0.4
Sterling Hgts, MI	8.6	0.8	4.2	2.3	0.1	0.1	0.1	0.3	0.6
Sunnyvale, CA	36.5	8.6	22.2	2.8	0.1	0.7	1.0	0.5	0.6
Tampa, FL	12.2	1.4	2.2	2.4	3.0	1.5	0.6	0.4	0.7
Temecula, CA	21.8	13.3	4.3	1.0	0.2	0.5	1.7	0.3	0.4
Thousand Oaks, CA	23.2	13.6	5.2	1.8	0.1	0.6	1.2	0.2	0.4
Virginia Beach, VA	6.2	0.4	2.7	1.1	0.5	0.3	0.6	0.4	0.2
Washington, DC	21.4	0.9	7.7	2.0	1.0	2.3	4.5	2.8	0.2
U.S.	12.8	3.8	3.6	1.6	1.2	0.9	1.0	0.5	0.3

Note: Figures cover the Metropolitan Statistical Area—see Appendix B for areas included; (1) Excludes Mexico
Source: U.S. Census Bureau, 2008-2010 American Community Survey 3-Year Estimates

Marital Status: City

City	Never Married	Now Married[1]	Separated	Widowed	Divorced
Albuquerque, NM	35.2	44.1	1.8	5.1	13.8
Alexandria, VA	39.9	41.6	2.5	4.5	11.6
Anchorage, AK	32.0	49.4	2.2	3.5	13.0
Ann Arbor, MI	56.4	33.6	0.6	2.8	6.6
Athens, GA	55.9	30.5	2.0	3.7	7.8
Atlanta, GA	53.5	27.6	2.4	5.5	11.0
Austin, TX	43.0	41.1	2.1	3.2	10.6
Baltimore, MD	51.2	26.6	4.1	7.3	10.9
Bellevue, WA	27.0	57.0	1.6	4.6	9.8
Billings, MT	29.4	48.4	1.6	6.3	14.3
Boise City, ID	31.7	49.1	1.5	4.5	13.3
Boston, MA	56.7	28.6	2.9	4.4	7.4
Boulder, CO	53.5	34.2	0.6	3.0	8.8
Broken Arrow, OK	23.2	61.8	0.8	4.7	9.5
Cambridge, MA	54.0	33.5	1.6	3.8	7.1
Cape Coral, FL	25.2	55.0	1.3	6.4	12.1
Carlsbad, CA	26.3	55.3	1.3	5.1	12.0
Cary, NC	25.9	61.9	1.4	3.0	7.8
Cedar Rapids, IA	33.4	47.3	1.5	5.4	12.4
Charleston, SC	44.2	38.2	2.8	5.7	9.2
Charlotte, NC	37.4	44.7	3.1	4.6	10.2
Chesapeake, VA	27.6	55.1	2.5	5.1	9.7
Chicago, IL	47.7	35.0	2.7	5.7	8.9
Clarksville, TN	29.0	50.7	3.2	4.8	12.2
Colorado Spgs., CO	28.6	51.1	2.3	4.8	13.2
Columbia, MD	29.6	55.2	2.5	4.0	8.7
Columbia, MO	49.3	36.5	1.6	3.6	9.0
Columbia, SC	54.5	28.2	3.3	5.2	8.8
Columbus, OH	42.8	37.3	2.4	4.7	12.8
Dallas, TX	39.6	40.5	3.7	5.1	11.2
Denver, CO	41.4	39.0	2.4	5.0	12.2
Durham, NC	41.9	40.3	2.9	5.1	9.8
Edison, NJ	29.9	56.2	1.4	5.8	6.7
El Paso, TX	31.9	47.7	3.6	5.7	11.0
Fargo, ND	42.6	43.2	1.1	4.5	8.6
Ft. Collins, CO	43.2	43.1	1.2	3.1	9.5
Ft. Worth, TX	32.0	48.0	3.1	4.8	12.1
Gilbert, AZ	27.5	56.9	1.5	2.5	11.5
Green Bay, WI	36.6	44.2	1.3	5.2	12.7
Henderson, NV	25.6	53.4	1.8	5.5	13.6
High Point, NC	32.6	45.5	3.9	6.6	11.5
Honolulu, HI	35.8	45.1	1.4	7.4	10.3
Houston, TX	38.1	42.8	3.5	5.1	10.4
Huntington, NY	26.8	58.4	1.8	6.3	6.6
Huntsville, AL	33.8	43.9	3.0	6.1	13.2
Indianapolis, IN	38.5	40.1	2.5	5.9	13.0
Irvine, CA	38.1	50.1	1.0	3.2	7.6
Jackson, MS	46.8	30.9	3.5	6.4	12.5
Jacksonville, FL	33.2	44.7	2.8	5.9	13.5
Jersey City, NJ	45.5	38.8	3.0	5.3	7.6
Kansas City, MO	37.4	41.2	2.6	5.6	13.1
Kenosha, WI	35.1	44.7	1.5	6.2	12.6
Las Vegas, NV	31.8	46.0	2.7	5.3	14.2
Lexington, KY	36.6	44.6	1.8	4.6	12.5
Lincoln, NE	35.5	48.0	1.3	4.2	11.0
Little Rock, AR	35.7	42.4	2.5	5.7	13.8

Table continued on next page.

City	Never Married	Now Married[1]	Separated	Widowed	Divorced
Los Angeles, CA	44.2	39.7	2.9	4.9	8.4
Madison, WI	47.1	39.3	1.2	3.7	8.8
Manchester, NH	35.3	44.3	1.7	5.6	13.1
Miami, FL	38.7	36.1	4.3	7.3	13.6
Minneapolis, MN	51.4	32.4	1.8	4.1	10.3
Murfreesboro, TN	39.5	43.9	1.7	4.7	10.3
Naperville, IL	25.2	63.4	0.7	3.7	7.0
Nashville, TN	39.3	39.8	2.6	5.3	13.0
New Orleans, LA	45.8	33.6	2.8	6.1	11.7
New York, NY	43.3	39.5	3.4	5.9	7.9
Norman, OK	41.6	40.8	1.6	5.3	10.6
Olathe, KS	24.5	61.3	1.3	3.7	9.3
Omaha, NE	37.0	44.1	2.0	5.4	11.5
Orlando, FL	43.1	35.7	3.7	4.4	13.1
Overland Park, KS	25.4	56.8	1.1	5.3	11.4
Oyster Bay, NY	26.7	59.2	1.2	7.4	5.5
Pembroke Pines, FL	29.0	48.4	2.8	7.9	12.0
Philadelphia, PA	50.2	29.9	3.7	7.5	8.7
Phoenix, AZ	37.4	44.3	1.9	4.2	12.1
Pittsburgh, PA	50.3	30.5	2.8	7.4	9.0
Plano, TX	26.6	58.7	1.6	3.5	9.6
Portland, OR	40.1	40.7	1.7	4.9	12.6
Providence, RI	53.8	28.1	4.0	5.2	8.9
Provo, UT	53.8	38.6	1.0	2.2	4.4
Raleigh, NC	41.9	41.0	3.1	4.1	10.0
Richmond, VA	51.7	26.2	3.8	6.2	12.1
Roseville, CA	25.8	55.4	2.1	5.7	10.9
Round Rock, TX	29.2	53.8	2.5	3.0	11.6
San Antonio, TX	34.5	44.5	3.1	5.6	12.3
San Diego, CA	40.5	42.9	2.1	4.5	10.0
San Francisco, CA	47.9	37.5	1.5	5.2	7.8
San Jose, CA	34.5	50.4	1.7	4.9	8.5
Savannah, GA	47.3	31.0	2.4	7.6	11.7
Scottsdale, AZ	27.6	52.0	1.0	6.4	13.0
Seattle, WA	43.6	39.4	1.4	4.4	11.2
Sioux Falls, SD	32.5	49.3	1.4	5.2	11.6
Stamford, CT	33.5	50.6	2.3	5.3	8.3
Sterling Hgts, MI	29.1	54.2	0.7	7.4	8.6
Sunnyvale, CA	29.4	57.6	1.0	4.1	7.9
Tampa, FL	39.7	37.4	3.5	5.1	14.3
Temecula, CA	29.8	54.2	1.9	3.3	10.9
Thousand Oaks, CA	27.9	56.9	1.2	4.9	9.2
Virginia Beach, VA	29.5	51.7	3.0	4.8	11.0
Washington, DC	56.7	25.6	2.9	5.2	9.6
U.S.	31.6	49.6	2.2	6.1	10.7

Note: Figures are percentages and cover the population 15 years of age and older; (1) Excludes separated
Source: U.S. Census Bureau, 2008-2010 American Community Survey 3-Year Estimates

Marital Status: Metro Area

Metro Area	Never Married	Now Married[1]	Separated	Widowed	Divorced
Albuquerque, NM	32.9	47.2	1.8	5.3	12.9
Alexandria, VA	35.4	48.9	2.4	4.6	8.8
Anchorage, AK	31.0	50.6	2.2	3.6	12.7
Ann Arbor, MI	41.0	45.0	0.9	3.9	9.2
Athens, GA	45.2	39.7	2.0	4.3	8.8
Atlanta, GA	32.7	49.6	2.3	4.6	10.9
Austin, TX	34.8	49.2	1.9	3.6	10.4
Baltimore, MD	34.6	46.7	2.7	6.4	9.7
Bellevue, WA	31.6	50.5	1.7	4.5	11.8
Billings, MT	26.8	52.6	1.3	5.9	13.4
Boise City, ID	26.2	55.6	1.7	4.4	12.1
Boston, MA	35.6	48.0	1.8	5.7	8.8
Boulder, CO	35.9	49.2	1.1	3.5	10.4
Broken Arrow, OK	25.8	53.1	2.1	6.2	12.8
Cambridge, MA	35.6	48.0	1.8	5.7	8.8
Cape Coral, FL	24.3	53.8	1.8	7.6	12.4
Carlsbad, CA	35.2	47.6	2.0	4.9	10.3
Cary, NC	30.6	53.5	2.6	4.4	9.0
Cedar Rapids, IA	28.6	53.7	1.2	5.6	10.8
Charleston, SC	33.9	47.1	3.0	5.5	10.5
Charlotte, NC	30.9	51.0	2.9	5.2	10.0
Chesapeake, VA	32.0	48.6	3.2	5.5	10.7
Chicago, IL	35.3	48.1	1.8	5.7	9.0
Clarksville, TN	25.7	54.9	2.7	5.1	11.6
Colorado Spgs., CO	27.7	53.7	2.0	4.4	12.2
Columbia, MD	34.6	46.7	2.7	6.4	9.7
Columbia, MO	40.7	44.1	1.6	4.2	9.4
Columbia, SC	34.7	46.4	3.2	5.8	9.9
Columbus, OH	32.9	48.7	1.9	5.0	11.5
Dallas, TX	30.4	51.6	2.6	4.5	10.9
Denver, CO	30.9	51.4	1.8	4.4	11.5
Durham, NC	36.5	46.6	2.7	4.8	9.4
Edison, NJ	37.0	46.5	2.6	6.2	7.7
El Paso, TX	32.1	48.3	3.7	5.5	10.3
Fargo, ND	37.0	49.1	0.7	4.6	8.7
Ft. Collins, CO	31.9	52.7	1.1	3.9	10.4
Ft. Worth, TX	30.4	51.6	2.6	4.5	10.9
Gilbert, AZ	31.8	49.9	1.6	5.0	11.7
Green Bay, WI	30.2	53.7	1.0	5.3	9.8
Henderson, NV	31.9	47.2	2.4	4.9	13.6
High Point, NC	31.3	48.1	3.2	6.5	10.9
Honolulu, HI	33.2	50.5	1.3	6.1	8.8
Houston, TX	31.5	51.0	2.8	4.7	10.0
Huntington, NY	37.0	46.5	2.6	6.2	7.7
Huntsville, AL	28.1	52.3	2.3	5.5	11.8
Indianapolis, IN	30.6	50.4	1.7	5.4	11.9
Irvine, CA	38.5	45.3	2.5	5.0	8.6
Jackson, MS	34.5	44.8	2.8	6.2	11.6
Jacksonville, FL	29.9	48.8	2.4	5.9	13.0
Jersey City, NJ	37.0	46.5	2.6	6.2	7.7
Kansas City, MO	28.6	52.2	1.8	5.5	11.9
Kenosha, WI	35.3	48.1	1.8	5.7	9.0
Las Vegas, NV	31.9	47.2	2.4	4.9	13.6
Lexington, KY	31.8	48.9	2.0	5.2	12.2
Lincoln, NE	33.8	50.5	1.2	4.3	10.2
Little Rock, AR	28.6	49.9	2.5	6.0	13.0

Table continued on next page.

Metro Area	Never Married	Now Married[1]	Separated	Widowed	Divorced
Los Angeles, CA	38.5	45.3	2.5	5.0	8.6
Madison, WI	34.8	50.2	1.0	4.4	9.6
Manchester, NH	28.6	53.1	1.4	5.3	11.6
Miami, FL	32.5	44.9	2.9	7.1	12.6
Minneapolis, MN	32.7	51.9	1.2	4.5	9.7
Murfreesboro, TN	30.3	50.8	2.0	5.2	11.8
Naperville, IL	35.3	48.1	1.8	5.7	9.0
Nashville, TN	30.3	50.8	2.0	5.2	11.8
New Orleans, LA	34.6	44.5	2.6	6.6	11.7
New York, NY	37.0	46.5	2.6	6.2	7.7
Norman, OK	28.9	50.3	2.1	5.9	12.8
Olathe, KS	28.6	52.2	1.8	5.5	11.9
Omaha, NE	30.6	52.2	1.5	5.2	10.5
Orlando, FL	32.6	48.0	2.6	5.4	11.5
Overland Park, KS	28.6	52.2	1.8	5.5	11.9
Oyster Bay, NY	37.0	46.5	2.6	6.2	7.7
Pembroke Pines, FL	32.5	44.9	2.9	7.1	12.6
Philadelphia, PA	35.8	46.5	2.3	6.7	8.6
Phoenix, AZ	31.8	49.9	1.6	5.0	11.7
Pittsburgh, PA	30.8	49.4	2.1	8.3	9.4
Plano, TX	30.4	51.6	2.6	4.5	10.9
Portland, OR	30.5	50.7	1.8	4.8	12.2
Providence, RI	34.1	46.1	2.1	7.1	10.7
Provo, UT	31.7	58.5	1.1	2.8	5.8
Raleigh, NC	30.6	53.5	2.6	4.4	9.0
Richmond, VA	33.1	48.2	2.8	5.7	10.2
Roseville, CA	32.6	48.5	2.2	5.4	11.2
Round Rock, TX	34.8	49.2	1.9	3.6	10.4
San Antonio, TX	30.8	49.7	2.7	5.4	11.3
San Diego, CA	35.2	47.6	2.0	4.9	10.3
San Francisco, CA	36.1	47.4	1.9	5.3	9.3
San Jose, CA	32.5	52.7	1.6	4.8	8.4
Savannah, GA	34.8	46.4	1.9	5.9	11.1
Scottsdale, AZ	31.8	49.9	1.6	5.0	11.7
Seattle, WA	31.6	50.5	1.7	4.5	11.8
Sioux Falls, SD	28.5	54.5	1.2	5.4	10.4
Stamford, CT	30.2	53.3	1.6	6.0	8.9
Sterling Hgts, MI	33.1	47.3	1.7	6.6	11.3
Sunnyvale, CA	32.5	52.7	1.6	4.8	8.4
Tampa, FL	29.0	47.1	2.4	7.5	14.0
Temecula, CA	33.4	49.0	2.6	5.0	10.1
Thousand Oaks, CA	31.2	51.8	1.7	5.1	10.2
Virginia Beach, VA	32.0	48.6	3.2	5.5	10.7
Washington, DC	35.4	48.9	2.4	4.6	8.8
U.S.	31.6	49.6	2.2	6.1	10.7

Note: Figures are percentages and cover the population 15 years of age and older; Figures cover the Metropolitan Statistical Area—see Appendix B for areas included; (1) Excludes separated

Source: U.S. Census Bureau, 2008-2010 American Community Survey 3-Year Estimates

Male/Female Ratio: City

City	Males	Females	Males per 100 Females
Albuquerque, NM	265,106	280,746	94.4
Alexandria, VA	67,262	72,704	92.5
Anchorage, AK	148,209	143,617	103.2
Ann Arbor, MI	56,155	57,779	97.2
Athens, GA	54,781	60,671	90.3
Atlanta, GA	208,968	211,035	99.0
Austin, TX	399,738	390,652	102.3
Baltimore, MD	292,249	328,712	88.9
Bellevue, WA	61,330	61,033	100.5
Billings, MT	50,266	53,904	93.3
Boise City, ID	101,690	103,981	97.8
Boston, MA	295,951	321,643	92.0
Boulder, CO	50,004	47,381	105.5
Broken Arrow, OK	48,048	50,802	94.6
Cambridge, MA	51,109	54,053	94.6
Cape Coral, FL	75,364	78,941	95.5
Carlsbad, CA	51,485	53,843	95.6
Cary, NC	65,819	69,415	94.8
Cedar Rapids, IA	62,065	64,261	96.6
Charleston, SC	56,741	63,342	89.6
Charlotte, NC	353,511	377,913	93.5
Chesapeake, VA	108,051	114,158	94.7
Chicago, IL	1,308,072	1,387,526	94.3
Clarksville, TN	64,768	68,161	95.0
Colorado Spgs., CO	203,944	212,483	96.0
Columbia, MD	47,891	51,724	92.6
Columbia, MO	52,458	56,042	93.6
Columbia, SC	66,532	62,740	106.0
Columbus, OH	384,265	402,768	95.4
Dallas, TX	598,962	598,854	100.0
Denver, CO	300,089	300,069	100.0
Durham, NC	108,556	119,774	90.6
Edison, NJ	48,899	51,068	95.8
El Paso, TX	311,280	337,841	92.1
Fargo, ND	53,248	52,301	101.8
Ft. Collins, CO	71,909	72,077	99.8
Ft. Worth, TX	363,896	377,310	96.4
Gilbert, AZ	102,634	105,819	97.0
Green Bay, WI	51,359	52,698	97.5
Henderson, NV	126,779	130,950	96.8
High Point, NC	49,002	55,369	88.5
Honolulu, HI	166,500	170,756	97.5
Houston, TX	1,053,517	1,045,934	100.7
Huntington, NY	100,042	103,222	96.9
Huntsville, AL	87,530	92,575	94.6
Indianapolis, IN	396,346	424,099	93.5
Irvine, CA	103,434	108,941	94.9
Jackson, MS	80,615	92,899	86.8
Jacksonville, FL	398,294	423,490	94.1
Jersey City, NJ	122,298	125,299	97.6
Kansas City, MO	223,183	236,604	94.3
Kenosha, WI	48,688	50,530	96.4
Las Vegas, NV	294,100	289,656	101.5
Lexington, KY	145,591	150,212	96.9
Lincoln, NE	129,235	129,144	100.1

Table continued on next page.

City	Males	Females	Males per 100 Females
Little Rock, AR	92,245	101,279	91.1
Los Angeles, CA	1,889,064	1,903,557	99.2
Madison, WI	114,832	118,377	97.0
Manchester, NH	54,356	55,209	98.5
Miami, FL	198,927	200,530	99.2
Minneapolis, MN	192,421	190,157	101.2
Murfreesboro, TN	53,422	55,333	96.5
Naperville, IL	68,981	72,872	94.7
Nashville, TN	291,294	309,928	94.0
New Orleans, LA	166,248	177,581	93.6
New York, NY	3,882,544	4,292,589	90.4
Norman, OK	55,172	55,753	99.0
Olathe, KS	62,358	63,514	98.2
Omaha, NE	201,063	207,895	96.7
Orlando, FL	115,883	122,417	94.7
Overland Park, KS	83,735	89,637	93.4
Oyster Bay, NY	142,056	151,158	94.0
Pembroke Pines, FL	71,515	83,235	85.9
Philadelphia, PA	719,813	806,193	89.3
Phoenix, AZ	725,020	720,612	100.6
Pittsburgh, PA	148,101	157,603	94.0
Plano, TX	127,078	132,763	95.7
Portland, OR	289,211	294,565	98.2
Providence, RI	85,802	92,240	93.0
Provo, UT	55,737	56,751	98.2
Raleigh, NC	195,143	208,749	93.5
Richmond, VA	97,331	106,883	91.1
Roseville, CA	56,894	61,894	91.9
Round Rock, TX	49,139	50,748	96.8
San Antonio, TX	647,690	679,717	95.3
San Diego, CA	660,626	646,776	102.1
San Francisco, CA	408,462	396,773	102.9
San Jose, CA	475,668	470,274	101.1
Savannah, GA	65,301	70,985	92.0
Scottsdale, AZ	104,930	112,455	93.3
Seattle, WA	304,030	304,630	99.8
Sioux Falls, SD	76,268	77,620	98.3
Stamford, CT	60,402	62,241	97.0
Sterling Hgts, MI	62,862	66,837	94.1
Sunnyvale, CA	70,560	69,521	101.5
Tampa, FL	164,061	171,648	95.6
Temecula, CA	49,002	51,095	95.9
Thousand Oaks, CA	61,989	64,694	95.8
Virginia Beach, VA	214,441	223,553	95.9
Washington, DC	284,222	317,501	89.5
U.S.	151,781,326	156,964,212	96.7

Source: U.S. Census Bureau, 2010 Census

Male/Female Ratio: Metro Area

Metro Area	Males	Females	Males per 100 Females
Albuquerque, NM	435,807	451,270	96.6
Alexandria, VA	2,716,483	2,865,687	94.8
Anchorage, AK	194,249	186,572	104.1
Ann Arbor, MI	170,132	174,659	97.4
Athens, GA	92,678	99,863	92.8
Atlanta, GA	2,563,887	2,704,973	94.8
Austin, TX	860,101	856,188	100.5
Baltimore, MD	1,304,960	1,405,529	92.8
Bellevue, WA	1,711,982	1,727,827	99.1
Billings, MT	77,490	80,560	96.2
Boise City, ID	307,856	308,705	99.7
Boston, MA	2,202,868	2,349,534	93.8
Boulder, CO	147,916	146,651	100.9
Broken Arrow, OK	460,092	477,386	96.4
Cambridge, MA	2,202,868	2,349,534	93.8
Cape Coral, FL	303,600	315,154	96.3
Carlsbad, CA	1,553,679	1,541,634	100.8
Cary, NC	552,108	578,382	95.5
Cedar Rapids, IA	127,690	130,250	98.0
Charleston, SC	324,981	339,626	95.7
Charlotte, NC	854,016	904,022	94.5
Chesapeake, VA	819,724	851,959	96.2
Chicago, IL	4,622,870	4,838,235	95.5
Clarksville, TN	135,630	138,319	98.1
Colorado Spgs., CO	322,047	323,566	99.5
Columbia, MD	1,304,960	1,405,529	92.8
Columbia, MO	83,991	88,795	94.6
Columbia, SC	374,340	393,258	95.2
Columbus, OH	901,516	935,020	96.4
Dallas, TX	3,141,634	3,230,139	97.3
Denver, CO	1,264,550	1,278,932	98.9
Durham, NC	241,401	262,956	91.8
Edison, NJ	9,099,234	9,797,875	92.9
El Paso, TX	387,876	412,771	94.0
Fargo, ND	104,688	104,089	100.6
Ft. Collins, CO	148,637	150,993	98.4
Ft. Worth, TX	3,141,634	3,230,139	97.3
Gilbert, AZ	2,085,630	2,107,257	99.0
Green Bay, WI	152,312	153,929	98.9
Henderson, NV	982,193	969,076	101.4
High Point, NC	347,487	376,314	92.3
Honolulu, HI	477,092	476,115	100.2
Houston, TX	2,957,442	2,989,358	98.9
Huntington, NY	9,099,234	9,797,875	92.9
Huntsville, AL	206,230	211,363	97.6
Indianapolis, IN	856,916	899,325	95.3
Irvine, CA	6,328,434	6,500,403	97.4
Jackson, MS	256,917	282,140	91.1
Jacksonville, FL	655,647	689,949	95.0
Jersey City, NJ	9,099,234	9,797,875	92.9
Kansas City, MO	996,319	1,039,015	95.9
Kenosha, WI	4,622,870	4,838,235	95.5
Las Vegas, NV	982,193	969,076	101.4
Lexington, KY	231,618	240,481	96.3
Lincoln, NE	151,575	150,582	100.7

Table continued on next page.

Metro Area	Males	Females	Males per 100 Females
Little Rock, AR	340,141	359,616	94.6
Los Angeles, CA	6,328,434	6,500,403	97.4
Madison, WI	282,224	286,369	98.6
Manchester, NH	198,162	202,559	97.8
Miami, FL	2,693,823	2,870,812	93.8
Minneapolis, MN	1,618,907	1,660,926	97.5
Murfreesboro, TN	777,473	812,461	95.7
Naperville, IL	4,622,870	4,838,235	95.5
Nashville, TN	777,473	812,461	95.7
New Orleans, LA	568,375	599,389	94.8
New York, NY	9,099,234	9,797,875	92.9
Norman, OK	617,347	635,640	97.1
Olathe, KS	996,319	1,039,015	95.9
Omaha, NE	426,917	438,433	97.4
Orlando, FL	1,044,696	1,089,715	95.9
Overland Park, KS	996,319	1,039,015	95.9
Oyster Bay, NY	9,099,234	9,797,875	92.9
Pembroke Pines, FL	2,693,823	2,870,812	93.8
Philadelphia, PA	2,878,862	3,086,481	93.3
Phoenix, AZ	2,085,630	2,107,257	99.0
Pittsburgh, PA	1,138,197	1,218,088	93.4
Plano, TX	3,141,634	3,230,139	97.3
Portland, OR	1,099,122	1,126,887	97.5
Providence, RI	773,916	826,936	93.6
Provo, UT	263,989	262,821	100.4
Raleigh, NC	552,108	578,382	95.5
Richmond, VA	608,491	649,760	93.6
Roseville, CA	1,053,450	1,095,677	96.1
Round Rock, TX	860,101	856,188	100.5
San Antonio, TX	1,052,485	1,090,023	96.6
San Diego, CA	1,553,679	1,541,634	100.8
San Francisco, CA	2,137,801	2,197,590	97.3
San Jose, CA	921,480	915,431	100.7
Savannah, GA	168,573	179,038	94.2
Scottsdale, AZ	2,085,630	2,107,257	99.0
Seattle, WA	1,711,982	1,727,827	99.1
Sioux Falls, SD	113,731	114,530	99.3
Stamford, CT	445,601	471,228	94.6
Sterling Hgts, MI	2,082,043	2,214,207	94.0
Sunnyvale, CA	921,480	915,431	100.7
Tampa, FL	1,347,513	1,435,730	93.9
Temecula, CA	2,101,083	2,123,768	98.9
Thousand Oaks, CA	408,969	414,349	98.7
Virginia Beach, VA	819,724	851,959	96.2
Washington, DC	2,716,483	2,865,687	94.8
U.S.	151,781,326	156,964,212	96.7

Note: Figures cover the Metropolitan Statistical Area (MSA)—see Appendix B for areas included
Source: U.S. Census Bureau, 2010 Census

Gross Metropolitan Product

MSA[1]	2007	2008	2009	2010	2010 Rank[2]
Albuquerque, NM	34.6	35.0	36.7	38.1	60
Alexandria, VA	384.3	400.0	409.6	426.1	4
Anchorage, AK	24.4	26.8	24.9	26.2	84
Ann Arbor, MI	18.2	17.4	18.0	19.0	107
Athens, GA	6.1	6.4	6.2	6.4	230
Atlanta, GA	271.9	274.2	265.2	270.6	10
Austin, TX	76.4	79.8	78.8	84.2	37
Baltimore, MD	134.0	137.6	139.1	144.4	19
Bellevue, WA	220.9	227.9	225.6	231.4	12
Billings, MT	7.4	7.2	7.1	7.2	216
Boise City, ID	25.6	25.6	24.9	25.5	87
Boston, MA	290.8	300.4	296.9	311.3	9
Boulder, CO	17.6	18.0	17.6	18.1	113
Broken Arrow, OK	43.4	46.9	43.4	44.6	55
Cambridge, MA	290.8	300.4	296.9	311.3	9
Cape Coral, FL	22.2	20.9	20.0	20.2	98
Carlsbad, CA	166.4	171.2	168.1	172.7	16
Cary, NC	51.3	53.0	53.6	56.1	49
Cedar Rapids, IA	13.1	12.8	13.3	14.0	139
Charleston, SC	26.2	26.7	26.8	27.9	78
Charlotte, NC	111.2	113.4	112.5	117.3	22
Chesapeake, VA	76.4	78.8	80.3	82.4	39
Chicago, IL	522.1	525.3	517.3	531.4	3
Clarksville, TN	9.1	9.6	10.0	10.9	163
Colorado Spgs., CO	23.9	24.5	25.2	26.4	81
Columbia, MD	134.0	137.6	139.1	144.4	19
Columbia, MO	6.2	6.4	6.6	6.9	219
Columbia, SC	30.4	30.8	31.3	32.2	69
Columbus, OH	89.3	89.7	90.5	93.9	31
Dallas, TX	358.1	370.8	358.3	376.8	6
Denver, CO	147.1	154.3	152.7	157.1	17
Durham, NC	33.5	33.8	35.0	36.3	62
Edison, NJ	1,215.9	1,242.1	1,217.4	1,282.6	1
El Paso, TX	25.3	25.7	26.5	28.7	75
Fargo, ND	9.7	10.5	10.6	11.4	158
Ft. Collins, CO	10.9	11.2	11.2	11.7	157
Ft. Worth, TX	358.1	370.8	358.3	376.8	6
Gilbert, AZ	196.4	196.0	187.4	190.6	15
Green Bay, WI	14.4	14.4	14.7	15.4	130
Henderson, NV	99.5	97.8	91.7	91.4	33
High Point, NC	32.2	32.7	32.5	34.0	65
Honolulu, HI	47.9	49.8	49.9	51.0	51
Houston, TX	373.3	396.5	364.9	378.9	5
Huntington, NY	1,215.9	1,242.1	1,217.4	1,282.6	1
Huntsville, AL	18.3	19.1	19.7	20.5	97
Indianapolis, IN	97.4	99.1	99.7	104.3	28
Irvine, CA	731.6	747.0	716.4	737.9	2
Jackson, MS	23.1	23.8	23.5	24.1	88
Jacksonville, FL	60.2	59.3	58.6	59.7	46
Jersey City, NJ	1,215.9	1,242.1	1,217.4	1,282.6	1
Kansas City, MO	101.2	103.9	103.1	105.6	26
Kenosha, WI	522.1	525.3	517.3	531.4	3
Las Vegas, NV	99.5	97.8	91.7	91.4	33
Lexington, KY	22.2	22.5	22.3	23.2	91
Lincoln, NE	13.4	13.5	14.0	14.5	137
Little Rock, AR	31.3	31.4	32.2	33.2	67

Table continued on next page.

MSA[1]	2007	2008	2009	2010	2010 Rank[2]
Los Angeles, CA	731.6	747.0	716.4	737.9	2
Madison, WI	33.0	33.6	34.9	36.4	61
Manchester, NH	20.1	21.1	20.9	21.1	95
Miami, FL	264.3	260.5	253.8	258.8	11
Minneapolis, MN	189.2	193.4	190.5	198.3	13
Murfreesboro, TN	75.4	77.9	76.4	80.3	40
Naperville, IL	522.1	525.3	517.3	531.4	3
Nashville, TN	75.4	77.9	76.4	80.3	40
New Orleans, LA	67.3	69.6	66.9	70.7	41
New York, NY	1,215.9	1,242.1	1,217.4	1,282.6	1
Norman, OK	54.4	59.4	56.4	58.6	48
Olathe, KS	101.2	103.9	103.1	105.6	26
Omaha, NE	44.7	45.4	46.6	48.0	52
Orlando, FL	104.1	103.6	101.2	103.6	29
Overland Park, KS	101.2	103.9	103.1	105.6	26
Oyster Bay, NY	1,215.9	1,242.1	1,217.4	1,282.6	1
Pembroke Pines, FL	264.3	260.5	253.8	258.8	11
Philadelphia, PA	325.3	332.0	335.7	347.7	7
Phoenix, AZ	196.4	196.0	187.4	190.6	15
Pittsburgh, PA	108.2	111.5	111.3	115.6	23
Plano, TX	358.1	370.8	358.3	376.8	6
Portland, OR	116.8	122.4	118.2	122.8	21
Providence, RI	63.8	64.8	64.3	66.8	42
Provo, UT	14.3	14.6	14.2	14.6	136
Raleigh, NC	51.3	53.0	53.6	56.1	49
Richmond, VA	60.3	61.9	62.0	63.8	45
Roseville, CA	95.3	94.7	92.5	93.5	32
Round Rock, TX	76.4	79.8	78.8	84.2	37
San Antonio, TX	75.9	78.2	78.1	82.7	38
San Diego, CA	166.4	171.2	168.1	172.7	16
San Francisco, CA	321.2	336.5	328.9	337.4	8
San Jose, CA	148.6	150.8	144.4	151.6	18
Savannah, GA	13.0	13.1	12.9	13.3	145
Scottsdale, AZ	196.4	196.0	187.4	190.6	15
Seattle, WA	220.9	227.9	225.6	231.4	12
Sioux Falls, SD	14.4	15.5	15.9	16.6	123
Stamford, CT	81.9	82.5	81.4	84.7	36
Sterling Hgts, MI	204.3	196.8	190.2	196.3	14
Sunnyvale, CA	148.6	150.8	144.4	151.6	18
Tampa, FL	114.1	112.6	111.9	113.9	24
Temecula, CA	114.8	112.9	108.4	110.8	25
Thousand Oaks, CA	36.0	34.6	34.3	35.5	63
Virginia Beach, VA	76.4	78.8	80.3	82.4	39
Washington, DC	384.3	400.0	409.6	426.1	4

Note: Figures are in billions of dollars; (1) Metropolitan Statistical Area—see Appendix B for areas included; (2) Rank ranges from 1 to 363.
Source: The U.S. Conference of Mayors, "U.S. Metro Economies: GMP and Employment Forecasts," June 2011

Income: City

City	Per Capita ($)	Median Household ($)	Average Household ($)
Albuquerque, NM	25,612	46,532	61,500
Alexandria, VA	52,547	80,173	108,615
Anchorage, AK	34,999	74,272	92,007
Ann Arbor, MI	29,404	51,783	72,710
Athens, GA	19,023	33,750	51,082
Atlanta, GA	34,475	44,771	77,979
Austin, TX	29,655	50,147	71,045
Baltimore, MD	22,975	39,113	55,603
Bellevue, WA	45,470	81,113	107,984
Billings, MT	26,556	46,065	61,537
Boise City, ID	27,221	48,506	64,930
Boston, MA	32,261	50,710	75,571
Boulder, CO	36,036	52,276	84,329
Broken Arrow, OK	29,127	64,460	79,824
Cambridge, MA	45,176	67,271	99,495
Cape Coral, FL	23,541	49,111	61,493
Carlsbad, CA	42,012	83,238	105,409
Cary, NC	41,322	88,629	110,715
Cedar Rapids, IA	27,714	50,870	65,172
Charleston, SC	30,487	48,773	69,871
Charlotte, NC	30,453	51,419	75,239
Chesapeake, VA	29,503	68,058	80,745
Chicago, IL	26,967	46,195	68,091
Clarksville, TN	20,151	45,676	53,286
Colorado Spgs., CO	27,753	52,179	68,046
Columbia, MD	44,258	93,888	110,184
Columbia, MO	23,833	40,816	58,141
Columbia, SC	23,958	36,546	58,642
Columbus, OH	22,884	42,368	54,316
Dallas, TX	26,032	41,011	66,620
Denver, CO	30,806	45,526	68,791
Durham, NC	26,282	46,556	63,483
Edison, NJ	36,223	86,282	106,245
El Paso, TX	18,119	37,836	52,689
Fargo, ND	26,851	42,144	59,185
Ft. Collins, CO	27,491	49,512	67,958
Ft. Worth, TX	23,482	48,970	64,403
Gilbert, AZ	30,005	75,895	88,751
Green Bay, WI	22,864	41,443	54,422
Henderson, NV	34,075	65,047	84,449
High Point, NC	21,447	42,587	54,636
Honolulu, HI	29,609	55,809	74,676
Houston, TX	25,700	43,349	67,252
Huntington, NY	45,590	101,495	132,016
Huntsville, AL	29,582	47,238	68,304
Indianapolis, IN	23,449	41,170	56,963
Irvine, CA	41,175	88,571	111,618
Jackson, MS	18,454	33,465	49,136
Jacksonville, FL	24,478	47,356	61,797
Jersey City, NJ	31,066	56,119	78,143
Kansas City, MO	25,666	43,587	59,427
Kenosha, WI	22,383	45,669	57,608
Las Vegas, NV	25,549	52,382	68,296
Lexington, KY	27,881	47,104	65,440
Lincoln, NE	24,981	48,203	61,452
Little Rock, AR	28,505	42,466	66,098

Table continued on next page.

City	Per Capita ($)	Median Household ($)	Average Household ($)
Los Angeles, CA	27,346	48,746	75,691
Madison, WI	29,929	51,822	67,341
Manchester, NH	26,980	51,643	64,363
Miami, FL	19,723	28,506	48,561
Minneapolis, MN	29,233	46,232	65,395
Murfreesboro, TN	24,152	47,662	61,727
Naperville, IL	44,331	99,488	126,695
Nashville, TN	26,153	44,630	61,792
New Orleans, LA	24,721	36,208	57,174
New York, NY	30,394	50,038	77,940
Norman, OK	26,485	44,634	66,513
Olathe, KS	30,311	74,320	85,603
Omaha, NE	25,872	45,115	63,175
Orlando, FL	24,643	40,669	57,840
Overland Park, KS	39,170	70,775	92,434
Oyster Bay, NY	46,295	104,110	135,820
Pembroke Pines, FL	26,976	59,968	74,235
Philadelphia, PA	21,061	35,952	50,877
Phoenix, AZ	23,626	47,187	65,034
Pittsburgh, PA	25,233	36,723	55,937
Plano, TX	39,482	80,210	104,026
Portland, OR	29,634	49,326	67,714
Providence, RI	20,513	36,831	55,831
Provo, UT	16,130	38,807	55,571
Raleigh, NC	29,216	51,173	71,402
Richmond, VA	25,814	37,236	59,299
Roseville, CA	32,249	72,857	84,691
Round Rock, TX	27,502	62,664	76,488
San Antonio, TX	21,613	42,656	58,406
San Diego, CA	31,981	61,282	83,172
San Francisco, CA	45,078	71,779	102,227
San Jose, CA	32,237	78,149	97,994
Savannah, GA	19,464	32,699	47,361
Scottsdale, AZ	49,337	71,021	106,734
Seattle, WA	40,894	60,619	85,727
Sioux Falls, SD	27,561	50,415	67,611
Stamford, CT	41,227	73,965	108,992
Sterling Hgts, MI	25,603	54,569	66,463
Sunnyvale, CA	43,937	90,701	110,963
Tampa, FL	27,186	42,359	65,617
Temecula, CA	27,706	72,433	86,415
Thousand Oaks, CA	44,263	99,980	122,170
Virginia Beach, VA	30,763	64,065	79,801
Washington, DC	42,066	59,822	92,555
U.S.	26,942	51,222	70,116

Source: U.S. Census Bureau, 2008-2010 American Community Survey 3-Year Estimates

Income: Metro Area

Metro Area	Per Capita ($)	Median Household ($)	Average Household ($)
Albuquerque, NM	25,216	48,047	63,525
Alexandria, VA	41,347	85,258	109,531
Anchorage, AK	33,461	73,412	89,351
Ann Arbor, MI	30,596	56,708	76,345
Athens, GA	21,326	40,220	59,125
Atlanta, GA	28,075	56,448	75,563
Austin, TX	29,482	56,732	76,321
Baltimore, MD	33,200	65,817	85,525
Bellevue, WA	33,755	64,821	83,560
Billings, MT	26,386	47,959	62,687
Boise City, ID	23,502	50,026	63,351
Boston, MA	36,714	69,784	93,357
Boulder, CO	37,099	64,314	89,944
Broken Arrow, OK	25,182	46,570	62,846
Cambridge, MA	36,714	69,784	93,357
Cape Coral, FL	27,392	47,232	66,948
Carlsbad, CA	29,792	61,469	82,033
Cary, NC	29,979	59,695	78,205
Cedar Rapids, IA	27,843	54,226	68,232
Charleston, SC	26,132	49,606	66,540
Charlotte, NC	28,220	52,321	72,717
Chesapeake, VA	27,943	57,262	72,109
Chicago, IL	29,963	59,707	80,417
Clarksville, TN	20,524	43,491	53,321
Colorado Spgs., CO	27,391	55,166	70,491
Columbia, MD	33,200	65,817	85,525
Columbia, MO	24,837	44,788	61,482
Columbia, SC	24,841	47,511	62,437
Columbus, OH	27,252	52,324	69,132
Dallas, TX	28,035	55,740	76,630
Denver, CO	31,829	59,919	79,382
Durham, NC	28,337	50,686	70,504
Edison, NJ	34,332	63,263	91,988
El Paso, TX	16,991	36,647	51,077
Fargo, ND	26,809	48,455	63,392
Ft. Collins, CO	29,733	55,896	73,201
Ft. Worth, TX	28,035	55,740	76,630
Gilbert, AZ	26,243	52,904	70,586
Green Bay, WI	26,427	50,989	65,233
Henderson, NV	26,211	54,458	69,877
High Point, NC	23,950	42,611	59,312
Honolulu, HI	29,303	70,356	86,269
Houston, TX	27,447	55,408	77,596
Huntington, NY	34,332	63,263	91,988
Huntsville, AL	29,179	53,974	72,853
Indianapolis, IN	27,020	51,571	69,019
Irvine, CA	28,405	59,129	83,389
Jackson, MS	23,237	45,116	61,506
Jacksonville, FL	26,678	51,663	68,189
Jersey City, NJ	34,332	63,263	91,988
Kansas City, MO	28,429	55,308	71,149
Kenosha, WI	29,963	59,707	80,417
Las Vegas, NV	26,211	54,458	69,877
Lexington, KY	26,994	48,188	65,255
Lincoln, NE	25,858	50,644	64,425
Little Rock, AR	25,016	46,076	61,616

Table continued on next page.

Metro Area	Per Capita ($)	Median Household ($)	Average Household ($)
Los Angeles, CA	28,405	59,129	83,389
Madison, WI	31,284	59,011	74,554
Manchester, NH	33,061	67,792	84,122
Miami, FL	26,283	47,086	68,986
Minneapolis, MN	32,422	63,927	82,191
Murfreesboro, TN	26,953	50,837	68,640
Naperville, IL	29,963	59,707	80,417
Nashville, TN	26,953	50,837	68,640
New Orleans, LA	25,870	46,210	64,705
New York, NY	34,332	63,263	91,988
Norman, OK	25,070	46,894	63,378
Olathe, KS	28,429	55,308	71,149
Omaha, NE	27,467	54,318	69,611
Orlando, FL	24,530	48,450	65,091
Overland Park, KS	28,429	55,308	71,149
Oyster Bay, NY	34,332	63,263	91,988
Pembroke Pines, FL	26,283	47,086	68,986
Philadelphia, PA	31,198	60,037	80,924
Phoenix, AZ	26,243	52,904	70,586
Pittsburgh, PA	27,453	47,549	64,272
Plano, TX	28,035	55,740	76,630
Portland, OR	28,651	55,618	72,200
Providence, RI	28,160	53,914	70,571
Provo, UT	20,098	56,594	70,927
Raleigh, NC	29,979	59,695	78,205
Richmond, VA	29,475	56,608	75,408
Roseville, CA	27,995	58,733	75,256
Round Rock, TX	29,482	56,732	76,321
San Antonio, TX	23,641	49,112	65,016
San Diego, CA	29,792	61,469	82,033
San Francisco, CA	39,207	74,809	102,229
San Jose, CA	38,679	85,799	111,612
Savannah, GA	24,660	47,505	62,789
Scottsdale, AZ	26,243	52,904	70,586
Seattle, WA	33,755	64,821	83,560
Sioux Falls, SD	27,502	54,069	69,244
Stamford, CT	47,283	80,122	127,756
Sterling Hgts, MI	26,370	50,439	67,151
Sunnyvale, CA	38,679	85,799	111,612
Tampa, FL	25,801	45,104	61,685
Temecula, CA	22,415	55,116	71,049
Thousand Oaks, CA	31,679	73,907	94,648
Virginia Beach, VA	27,943	57,262	72,109
Washington, DC	41,347	85,258	109,531
U.S.	26,942	51,222	70,116

Note: Figures cover the Metropolitan Statistical Area (MSA)—see Appendix B for areas included
Source: U.S. Census Bureau, 2008-2010 American Community Survey 3-Year Estimates

Household Income Distribution: City

City	Percent of Households Earning							
	Under $15,000	$15,000 -24,999	$25,000 -34,999	$35,000 -49,999	$50,000 -74,999	$75,000 -99,000	$100,000 -149,999	$150,000 and up
Albuquerque, NM	14.2	11.8	11.7	15.1	19.0	11.0	10.9	6.2
Alexandria, VA	6.4	5.7	6.2	10.0	18.5	13.8	19.5	19.8
Anchorage, AK	6.0	5.6	8.5	11.7	18.9	15.9	19.0	14.5
Ann Arbor, MI	16.3	9.0	9.3	13.2	18.3	10.3	12.4	11.2
Athens, GA	27.2	14.0	10.2	13.6	15.4	7.2	6.8	5.7
Atlanta, GA	21.0	11.0	10.2	11.4	14.7	9.0	10.4	12.3
Austin, TX	13.8	10.2	11.0	15.0	17.7	11.2	11.6	9.5
Baltimore, MD	21.5	12.5	11.7	14.1	17.6	9.2	8.1	5.2
Bellevue, WA	6.9	5.7	6.0	10.1	17.5	12.9	19.7	21.2
Billings, MT	11.4	13.4	12.2	16.9	19.9	11.5	9.9	4.9
Boise City, ID	12.9	10.7	12.0	15.6	19.3	12.0	10.7	6.8
Boston, MA	20.3	9.2	8.3	11.6	15.7	10.7	12.7	11.6
Boulder, CO	15.5	11.3	10.5	11.5	15.1	9.4	12.5	14.3
Broken Arrow, OK	5.2	7.1	8.4	14.7	22.8	16.9	16.4	8.5
Cambridge, MA	14.7	8.5	6.9	9.7	14.5	11.7	16.5	17.5
Cape Coral, FL	9.5	11.3	12.9	17.0	22.0	12.5	10.2	4.5
Carlsbad, CA	6.8	6.2	6.5	11.7	15.3	11.5	20.5	21.4
Cary, NC	4.4	5.4	7.1	9.5	16.3	12.7	21.6	23.0
Cedar Rapids, IA	10.9	11.5	11.2	15.4	21.0	12.8	11.5	5.7
Charleston, SC	16.5	10.2	9.9	14.3	17.0	12.2	11.0	8.8
Charlotte, NC	11.5	10.7	11.0	15.3	19.8	10.8	11.6	9.5
Chesapeake, VA	7.8	7.0	8.3	12.1	20.1	16.3	18.7	9.6
Chicago, IL	17.6	12.0	10.1	13.2	17.2	10.8	10.5	8.7
Clarksville, TN	14.9	10.4	11.8	18.1	22.3	11.8	8.1	2.7
Colorado Spgs., CO	11.9	11.0	10.4	14.2	20.6	11.7	13.0	7.3
Columbia, MD	5.1	4.0	5.4	7.8	16.5	14.9	21.6	24.7
Columbia, MO	19.1	12.5	11.8	13.3	18.7	9.4	9.8	5.3
Columbia, SC	20.6	14.2	13.5	14.1	14.1	8.7	8.3	6.6
Columbus, OH	17.4	12.3	11.6	16.0	19.3	10.7	8.7	4.0
Dallas, TX	16.3	13.6	13.0	15.1	16.4	8.5	8.3	8.7
Denver, CO	16.6	11.9	11.0	14.2	16.3	10.5	10.3	9.2
Durham, NC	14.5	11.8	11.0	15.6	17.3	10.8	12.1	6.9
Edison, NJ	6.5	4.6	5.9	8.9	18.3	13.3	20.8	21.8
El Paso, TX	19.0	15.0	12.6	15.3	16.6	8.9	8.5	4.1
Fargo, ND	15.9	11.4	13.7	16.3	18.0	10.0	9.0	5.6
Ft. Collins, CO	14.6	11.4	9.8	14.5	17.1	11.8	13.1	7.6
Ft. Worth, TX	13.5	12.0	11.1	14.2	19.5	12.1	11.1	6.4
Gilbert, AZ	4.7	4.9	6.6	12.5	20.6	16.6	22.6	11.5
Green Bay, WI	14.5	13.3	12.9	17.9	20.2	10.1	8.0	2.9
Henderson, NV	8.2	6.6	8.4	13.8	20.5	13.7	17.2	11.6
High Point, NC	17.7	12.8	11.3	16.1	19.0	9.2	9.3	4.7
Honolulu, HI	11.7	9.4	10.3	13.2	18.3	13.7	13.8	9.6
Houston, TX	15.4	13.4	12.3	14.3	17.0	9.6	9.4	8.6
Huntington, NY	4.4	5.3	4.7	7.7	14.2	12.4	21.0	30.4
Huntsville, AL	15.3	12.5	11.1	13.1	16.7	10.7	12.2	8.3
Indianapolis, IN	15.8	13.6	13.9	15.2	17.6	10.1	9.0	4.8
Irvine, CA	9.6	5.2	4.7	6.7	15.3	14.0	21.3	23.1
Jackson, MS	22.8	15.8	13.3	15.3	15.0	7.5	6.3	4.1
Jacksonville, FL	13.5	11.4	12.0	15.1	20.1	12.4	10.1	5.3
Jersey City, NJ	15.1	9.9	9.1	11.1	17.5	10.6	13.8	12.8
Kansas City, MO	16.5	11.8	12.8	14.9	17.2	10.5	10.9	5.2
Kenosha, WI	14.3	12.5	12.8	15.0	18.9	11.8	10.3	4.3
Las Vegas, NV	11.9	10.2	11.1	14.3	20.5	12.5	12.1	7.3
Lexington, KY	15.5	12.0	11.7	13.0	17.9	11.6	10.9	7.5

Table continued on next page.

City	Percent of Households Earning							
	Under $15,000	$15,000 -24,999	$25,000 -34,999	$35,000 -49,999	$50,000 -74,999	$75,000 -99,000	$100,000 -149,999	$150,000 and up
Lincoln, NE	13.2	12.1	11.7	14.5	20.8	12.1	10.6	5.1
Little Rock, AR	16.6	12.0	12.5	15.6	16.2	9.9	8.8	8.4
Los Angeles, CA	15.0	12.0	10.4	13.5	16.6	10.5	11.4	10.6
Madison, WI	14.6	10.2	9.6	13.7	18.6	13.7	12.0	7.5
Manchester, NH	10.7	11.5	10.6	15.5	20.3	14.8	11.3	5.4
Miami, FL	28.6	16.7	12.0	13.4	12.6	6.0	5.5	5.2
Minneapolis, MN	18.0	11.2	10.2	13.4	17.8	10.9	10.7	7.8
Murfreesboro, TN	14.7	10.7	10.2	16.4	17.8	12.9	12.3	5.1
Naperville, IL	3.9	4.0	5.3	8.0	15.6	13.4	21.5	28.4
Nashville, TN	15.2	12.0	11.9	16.4	18.7	10.5	8.9	6.4
New Orleans, LA	22.6	14.7	11.5	13.7	15.1	8.0	8.2	6.3
New York, NY	17.1	10.8	9.7	12.4	16.3	10.7	11.8	11.3
Norman, OK	15.0	13.2	11.1	15.6	15.7	11.8	10.2	7.4
Olathe, KS	5.2	6.8	7.6	10.6	20.5	17.4	20.9	11.0
Omaha, NE	13.9	12.5	12.6	15.1	18.8	11.3	9.5	6.2
Orlando, FL	14.5	13.8	13.2	18.4	17.9	8.6	7.7	6.0
Overland Park, KS	6.2	7.0	8.1	12.2	19.4	14.7	16.7	15.6
Oyster Bay, NY	4.0	5.3	5.1	8.2	12.6	12.7	21.9	30.1
Pembroke Pines, FL	9.4	9.8	8.9	13.2	18.9	14.7	15.5	9.6
Philadelphia, PA	24.2	13.5	11.3	13.9	16.2	9.2	7.3	4.4
Phoenix, AZ	14.3	11.3	11.7	15.3	17.8	11.3	11.3	7.1
Pittsburgh, PA	22.2	14.9	11.2	14.4	15.7	8.6	7.1	5.9
Plano, TX	5.7	7.1	6.7	10.5	16.9	13.6	19.7	19.8
Portland, OR	14.8	11.0	10.3	14.4	18.6	11.3	11.4	8.1
Providence, RI	24.0	12.8	10.3	14.8	16.1	8.2	7.5	6.3
Provo, UT	16.6	14.4	14.4	16.1	17.9	8.8	7.1	4.6
Raleigh, NC	10.9	11.3	10.9	15.6	18.4	12.0	11.8	9.1
Richmond, VA	21.5	14.3	11.5	15.1	15.6	8.7	6.9	6.4
Roseville, CA	7.1	6.5	8.5	12.0	17.0	15.1	20.2	13.7
Round Rock, TX	4.5	8.0	10.1	15.0	21.8	15.4	16.6	8.5
San Antonio, TX	16.7	12.8	12.0	15.0	18.0	10.7	9.1	5.5
San Diego, CA	11.2	8.9	8.3	12.8	17.6	13.4	14.7	13.2
San Francisco, CA	13.1	8.2	6.9	9.4	14.1	11.7	16.0	20.6
San Jose, CA	8.0	7.0	6.6	10.7	15.6	13.3	18.9	19.8
Savannah, GA	23.3	15.5	13.9	13.6	16.1	8.0	6.7	2.9
Scottsdale, AZ	8.2	8.4	8.2	12.0	16.0	12.3	15.1	19.9
Seattle, WA	12.0	8.5	8.4	12.9	17.4	12.5	14.5	13.9
Sioux Falls, SD	11.6	9.9	11.9	16.2	21.0	13.5	9.3	6.6
Stamford, CT	9.0	9.1	5.5	10.4	16.7	14.0	14.8	20.6
Sterling Hgts, MI	10.0	9.8	9.5	15.7	20.6	14.8	13.4	6.3
Sunnyvale, CA	6.0	5.7	5.3	8.3	14.9	14.6	20.4	25.0
Tampa, FL	17.3	13.1	11.5	15.1	16.1	9.1	9.0	8.8
Temecula, CA	7.8	6.7	7.0	10.8	19.2	14.6	21.4	12.6
Thousand Oaks, CA	5.7	5.3	5.9	8.0	12.9	12.3	22.4	27.6
Virginia Beach, VA	6.2	6.4	8.7	15.4	22.4	15.5	15.9	9.4
Washington, DC	15.9	7.9	7.7	11.6	15.6	11.2	12.9	17.3
U.S.	13.0	11.0	10.6	14.2	18.5	12.1	12.2	8.4

Source: U.S. Census Bureau, 2008-2010 American Community Survey 3-Year Estimates

Household Income Distribution: Metro Area

Metro Area	Percent of Households Earning							
	Under $15,000	$15,000 -24,999	$25,000 -34,999	$35,000 -49,999	$50,000 -74,999	$75,000 -99,000	$100,000 -149,999	$150,000 and up
Albuquerque, NM	13.7	11.6	11.1	15.2	18.9	11.6	11.4	6.6
Alexandria, VA	6.6	5.0	5.7	10.1	16.4	13.8	20.0	22.4
Anchorage, AK	6.4	6.0	8.4	11.7	18.8	16.1	19.2	13.4
Ann Arbor, MI	12.2	9.3	9.6	12.9	17.8	12.6	14.7	10.9
Athens, GA	21.3	12.6	10.3	14.0	16.1	9.5	9.1	7.0
Atlanta, GA	11.1	9.2	10.1	13.8	19.3	12.9	13.6	10.2
Austin, TX	11.0	9.0	9.7	14.2	18.9	12.9	14.0	10.2
Baltimore, MD	10.1	7.6	8.2	11.9	18.2	13.6	16.7	13.6
Bellevue, WA	9.1	7.8	8.4	12.9	18.9	14.1	16.6	12.2
Billings, MT	10.6	13.5	11.6	16.0	20.5	12.1	10.5	5.0
Boise City, ID	11.7	11.1	11.8	15.3	21.6	12.4	10.2	5.9
Boston, MA	11.1	7.6	7.3	10.8	16.5	13.1	17.5	16.1
Boulder, CO	10.0	8.7	9.2	12.3	16.5	12.1	15.9	15.2
Broken Arrow, OK	13.3	12.0	12.2	15.4	19.1	11.9	10.1	5.9
Cambridge, MA	11.1	7.6	7.3	10.8	16.5	13.1	17.5	16.1
Cape Coral, FL	11.6	12.0	11.9	17.2	18.9	11.6	10.0	6.8
Carlsbad, CA	9.9	8.8	9.0	13.4	17.7	13.5	15.3	12.5
Cary, NC	9.3	9.3	9.7	13.7	18.9	13.5	14.8	10.8
Cedar Rapids, IA	9.3	10.5	10.8	15.3	20.3	14.4	13.2	6.3
Charleston, SC	13.4	11.3	10.5	15.2	18.3	12.9	11.2	7.3
Charlotte, NC	11.4	10.4	10.6	15.1	19.2	12.0	12.3	8.9
Chesapeake, VA	9.5	9.1	9.7	14.7	20.8	14.2	14.2	7.8
Chicago, IL	10.9	9.5	9.1	12.8	18.3	13.4	14.7	11.3
Clarksville, TN	15.0	11.4	13.2	17.1	20.3	12.0	8.4	2.6
Colorado Spgs., CO	10.8	9.9	9.7	14.3	20.9	12.7	14.1	7.8
Columbia, MD	10.1	7.6	8.2	11.9	18.2	13.6	16.7	13.6
Columbia, MO	15.9	12.3	11.3	14.4	19.8	11.1	9.9	5.3
Columbia, SC	13.7	11.8	11.5	15.2	19.2	12.2	11.0	5.5
Columbus, OH	12.5	10.4	10.4	14.5	19.4	12.2	12.6	8.0
Dallas, TX	10.3	10.1	10.2	14.0	18.7	12.5	13.8	10.2
Denver, CO	10.6	9.0	9.3	13.3	18.3	13.3	15.2	11.0
Durham, NC	13.4	10.8	10.9	14.2	16.9	12.2	12.5	9.0
Edison, NJ	12.2	8.9	8.3	11.3	16.2	12.0	15.4	15.8
El Paso, TX	19.2	15.7	13.0	15.5	16.3	8.5	8.0	3.8
Fargo, ND	13.3	10.7	12.0	15.5	19.5	13.0	10.7	5.4
Ft. Collins, CO	12.2	9.7	9.3	13.8	19.0	13.0	14.1	8.8
Ft. Worth, TX	10.3	10.1	10.2	14.0	18.7	12.5	13.8	10.2
Gilbert, AZ	11.1	10.1	10.7	15.1	19.5	12.7	12.9	7.9
Green Bay, WI	10.5	11.2	10.6	16.7	20.7	14.3	10.9	5.1
Henderson, NV	10.0	9.6	11.0	14.9	21.0	13.4	12.8	7.4
High Point, NC	14.9	12.8	13.2	16.2	18.3	10.4	8.8	5.5
Honolulu, HI	8.4	7.0	7.8	11.8	18.3	15.4	18.4	12.9
Houston, TX	11.1	10.5	10.3	13.4	17.8	12.2	13.5	11.1
Huntington, NY	12.2	8.9	8.3	11.3	16.2	12.0	15.4	15.8
Huntsville, AL	11.8	10.8	10.2	13.5	17.5	12.0	14.8	9.3
Indianapolis, IN	11.4	11.1	11.2	14.7	18.7	12.7	12.7	7.4
Irvine, CA	11.1	9.9	9.2	12.7	17.5	12.3	14.4	12.7
Jackson, MS	16.1	12.6	11.1	14.8	17.7	11.6	10.2	5.9
Jacksonville, FL	11.9	10.2	11.1	14.9	20.3	12.8	11.8	7.0
Jersey City, NJ	12.2	8.9	8.3	11.3	16.2	12.0	15.4	15.8
Kansas City, MO	10.9	10.0	10.4	14.0	19.5	13.5	13.8	7.8
Kenosha, WI	10.9	9.5	9.1	12.8	18.3	13.4	14.7	11.3
Las Vegas, NV	10.0	9.6	11.0	14.9	21.0	13.4	12.8	7.4
Lexington, KY	15.0	11.2	11.5	13.8	18.9	11.4	11.2	7.0

Table continued on next page.

Metro Area	Percent of Households Earning							
	Under $15,000	$15,000 -24,999	$25,000 -34,999	$35,000 -49,999	$50,000 -74,999	$75,000 -99,000	$100,000 -149,999	$150,000 and up
Lincoln, NE	12.2	11.3	11.6	14.2	20.7	13.1	11.2	5.7
Little Rock, AR	14.1	11.8	12.0	15.8	19.0	11.5	10.2	5.6
Los Angeles, CA	11.1	9.9	9.2	12.7	17.5	12.3	14.4	12.7
Madison, WI	10.2	9.2	9.4	13.0	20.3	15.3	14.4	8.1
Manchester, NH	7.7	8.0	7.7	12.8	18.6	15.3	17.7	12.1
Miami, FL	14.7	11.9	11.3	14.5	17.7	10.7	10.9	8.4
Minneapolis, MN	9.0	8.0	8.7	12.8	19.4	15.0	15.9	11.2
Murfreesboro, TN	12.4	10.3	10.7	15.7	19.4	12.4	11.4	7.6
Naperville, IL	10.9	9.5	9.1	12.8	18.3	13.4	14.7	11.3
Nashville, TN	12.4	10.3	10.7	15.7	19.4	12.4	11.4	7.6
New Orleans, LA	15.4	12.3	11.2	14.5	17.2	11.0	11.4	7.0
New York, NY	12.2	8.9	8.3	11.3	16.2	12.0	15.4	15.8
Norman, OK	13.5	12.2	11.7	15.2	19.3	11.4	10.5	6.0
Olathe, KS	10.9	10.0	10.4	14.0	19.5	13.5	13.8	7.8
Omaha, NE	10.8	10.2	10.6	14.2	20.0	13.8	13.3	7.0
Orlando, FL	11.5	11.5	12.4	16.0	19.9	11.3	10.7	6.8
Overland Park, KS	10.9	10.0	10.4	14.0	19.5	13.5	13.8	7.8
Oyster Bay, NY	12.2	8.9	8.3	11.3	16.2	12.0	15.4	15.8
Pembroke Pines, FL	14.7	11.9	11.3	14.5	17.7	10.7	10.9	8.4
Philadelphia, PA	12.1	9.1	8.9	12.2	17.4	13.1	15.1	12.1
Phoenix, AZ	11.1	10.1	10.7	15.1	19.5	12.7	12.9	7.9
Pittsburgh, PA	13.8	12.7	11.2	14.4	18.8	11.8	10.7	6.6
Plano, TX	10.3	10.1	10.2	14.0	18.7	12.5	13.8	10.2
Portland, OR	10.7	9.6	10.0	14.5	19.9	13.4	13.6	8.4
Providence, RI	14.2	10.3	9.2	12.7	17.9	13.2	14.0	8.5
Provo, UT	8.8	9.2	9.6	15.4	22.3	14.2	13.5	7.0
Raleigh, NC	9.3	9.3	9.7	13.7	18.9	13.5	14.8	10.8
Richmond, VA	10.4	9.2	9.7	14.7	19.2	13.4	14.0	9.5
Roseville, CA	10.0	9.4	9.8	13.3	19.1	13.3	15.1	10.0
Round Rock, TX	11.0	9.0	9.7	14.2	18.9	12.9	14.0	10.2
San Antonio, TX	14.1	11.2	11.0	14.5	18.9	12.3	11.1	6.9
San Diego, CA	9.9	8.8	9.0	13.4	17.7	13.5	15.3	12.5
San Francisco, CA	9.5	7.5	7.0	10.3	15.8	12.3	17.5	20.1
San Jose, CA	7.2	6.4	6.0	9.5	14.6	12.7	19.4	24.2
Savannah, GA	14.4	11.9	11.2	14.4	19.0	11.6	11.8	5.7
Scottsdale, AZ	11.1	10.1	10.7	15.1	19.5	12.7	12.9	7.9
Seattle, WA	9.1	7.8	8.4	12.9	18.9	14.1	16.6	12.2
Sioux Falls, SD	10.2	9.1	11.2	15.8	22.1	14.8	10.6	6.2
Stamford, CT	9.0	7.0	6.7	9.7	14.9	12.0	16.8	23.9
Sterling Hgts, MI	13.8	11.1	10.6	14.1	18.2	12.3	12.4	7.6
Sunnyvale, CA	7.2	6.4	6.0	9.5	14.6	12.7	19.4	24.2
Tampa, FL	13.2	13.0	12.2	16.2	18.8	10.9	9.5	6.1
Temecula, CA	10.7	10.4	10.2	13.8	19.2	13.1	14.0	8.4
Thousand Oaks, CA	7.3	7.5	7.6	10.9	17.3	13.7	19.1	16.7
Virginia Beach, VA	9.5	9.1	9.7	14.7	20.8	14.2	14.2	7.8
Washington, DC	6.6	5.0	5.7	10.1	16.4	13.8	20.0	22.4
U.S.	13.0	11.0	10.6	14.2	18.5	12.1	12.2	8.4

Note: Figures cover the Metropolitan Statistical Area (MSA)—see Appendix B for areas included
Source: Source: U.S. Census Bureau, 2008-2010 American Community Survey 3-Year Estimates

Poverty Rate: City

City	All Ages	Under 18 Years Old	18 to 64 Years Old	65 Years and Over
Albuquerque, NM	16.3	23.5	14.6	11.0
Alexandria, VA	9.0	15.5	7.6	8.8
Anchorage, AK	7.7	10.1	7.1	4.5
Ann Arbor, MI	20.8	14.6	24.0	7.0
Athens, GA	36.2	36.3	39.1	11.6
Atlanta, GA	23.8	35.3	20.9	20.8
Austin, TX	19.2	26.1	18.0	8.7
Baltimore, MD	22.7	32.0	20.3	18.3
Bellevue, WA	5.8	4.1	6.1	6.9
Billings, MT	12.5	19.8	11.1	7.0
Boise City, ID	14.2	17.7	13.9	8.6
Boston, MA	21.1	26.7	19.8	20.7
Boulder, CO	20.1	12.5	23.4	6.3
Broken Arrow, OK	6.0	9.3	4.7	4.5
Cambridge, MA	14.6	14.5	15.2	10.3
Cape Coral, FL	12.1	18.0	10.8	8.9
Carlsbad, CA	8.0	10.3	8.1	3.3
Cary, NC	5.1	5.5	4.9	4.9
Cedar Rapids, IA	11.9	15.9	11.4	6.9
Charleston, SC	18.4	26.2	17.8	9.9
Charlotte, NC	14.9	20.9	13.6	7.5
Chesapeake, VA	6.9	9.7	5.4	8.8
Chicago, IL	21.5	31.8	18.6	17.3
Clarksville, TN	17.1	23.9	14.7	11.1
Colorado Spgs., CO	13.0	18.1	12.1	6.1
Columbia, MD	6.3	7.4	5.7	7.6
Columbia, MO	23.2	16.4	27.3	5.3
Columbia, SC	23.6	31.2	23.1	13.4
Columbus, OH	22.1	30.9	20.1	13.2
Dallas, TX	23.2	36.1	19.2	13.0
Denver, CO	19.8	30.1	17.2	15.0
Durham, NC	18.5	24.8	17.4	9.8
Edison, NJ	8.2	11.3	7.5	5.1
El Paso, TX	22.6	32.2	18.4	19.5
Fargo, ND	15.5	14.2	16.7	9.2
Ft. Collins, CO	18.4	13.2	21.4	6.6
Ft. Worth, TX	17.9	25.8	15.0	11.4
Gilbert, AZ	6.3	8.1	5.8	2.9
Green Bay, WI	14.8	19.7	14.2	6.9
Henderson, NV	8.0	10.3	7.2	7.5
High Point, NC	20.2	29.7	18.1	9.0
Honolulu, HI	11.7	14.1	12.0	8.3
Houston, TX	21.1	32.6	17.5	13.8
Huntington, NY	4.3	4.3	4.5	3.7
Huntsville, AL	16.4	24.4	15.7	7.1
Indianapolis, IN	19.4	28.7	17.4	8.8
Irvine, CA	10.9	7.1	12.4	8.2
Jackson, MS	26.9	38.8	23.3	15.4
Jacksonville, FL	15.2	22.0	13.5	9.8
Jersey City, NJ	17.4	26.7	14.8	15.4
Kansas City, MO	18.2	26.9	16.3	10.7
Kenosha, WI	15.7	22.2	13.9	9.6
Las Vegas, NV	14.6	20.3	13.3	9.1
Lexington, KY	18.1	23.3	18.0	8.6
Lincoln, NE	15.6	19.5	15.8	6.5

Table continued on next page.

City	All Ages	Under 18 Years Old	18 to 64 Years Old	65 Years and Over
Little Rock, AR	19.0	28.6	16.6	11.7
Los Angeles, CA	20.2	29.2	17.9	14.2
Madison, WI	18.5	16.2	21.0	4.4
Manchester, NH	13.6	24.0	11.1	8.6
Miami, FL	28.6	38.9	24.5	33.3
Minneapolis, MN	22.9	32.3	21.1	15.6
Murfreesboro, TN	18.3	21.5	18.8	5.5
Naperville, IL	3.7	4.4	3.2	4.9
Nashville, TN	18.8	30.3	16.3	10.4
New Orleans, LA	25.8	39.1	23.0	16.5
New York, NY	19.4	28.4	16.6	18.2
Norman, OK	17.3	16.5	19.1	5.9
Olathe, KS	6.9	8.4	6.3	6.3
Omaha, NE	15.8	22.2	14.3	9.5
Orlando, FL	17.7	24.3	16.2	13.9
Overland Park, KS	5.7	8.3	4.8	4.8
Oyster Bay, NY	3.2	3.4	3.2	2.8
Pembroke Pines, FL	7.9	9.8	6.7	10.3
Philadelphia, PA	25.6	34.6	23.7	18.4
Phoenix, AZ	20.7	29.8	18.1	9.7
Pittsburgh, PA	22.8	32.1	22.5	12.3
Plano, TX	7.9	11.1	6.7	6.9
Portland, OR	16.7	21.4	16.0	12.6
Providence, RI	27.1	35.0	24.8	21.7
Provo, UT	31.2	17.9	37.4	7.4
Raleigh, NC	16.2	21.8	15.3	7.5
Richmond, VA	27.4	42.3	25.3	14.6
Roseville, CA	8.3	10.2	7.3	8.7
Round Rock, TX	7.6	10.8	6.3	4.2
San Antonio, TX	19.7	28.4	17.0	13.9
San Diego, CA	15.2	19.6	14.9	8.4
San Francisco, CA	12.0	12.1	11.8	13.0
San Jose, CA	11.5	15.6	10.4	8.4
Savannah, GA	24.6	33.1	22.9	17.1
Scottsdale, AZ	7.7	9.6	7.9	5.7
Seattle, WA	12.6	11.1	12.9	12.4
Sioux Falls, SD	10.4	14.0	9.6	7.0
Stamford, CT	12.8	14.9	12.9	8.2
Sterling Hgts, MI	11.3	14.3	10.5	10.1
Sunnyvale, CA	6.6	7.6	6.4	5.8
Tampa, FL	19.9	30.4	16.9	15.1
Temecula, CA	9.6	12.2	8.8	5.2
Thousand Oaks, CA	5.6	6.8	5.2	5.4
Virginia Beach, VA	6.9	10.0	6.1	4.7
Washington, DC	18.7	30.0	16.5	14.3
U.S.	14.4	20.1	13.1	9.4

Note: Figures are percentage of people whose income during the past 12 months was below the poverty level; Source: U.S. Census Bureau, 2008-2010 American Community Survey 3-Year Estimates

Poverty Rate: Metro Area

Metro Area	All Ages	Under 18 Years Old	18 to 64 Years Old	65 Years and Over
Albuquerque, NM	16.0	23.2	14.2	10.8
Alexandria, VA	7.7	9.7	7.1	6.8
Anchorage, AK	8.2	10.8	7.5	4.2
Ann Arbor, MI	13.7	13.7	14.8	6.4
Athens, GA	26.8	26.3	29.2	12.4
Atlanta, GA	13.2	18.1	11.7	9.8
Austin, TX	14.5	18.5	13.9	7.1
Baltimore, MD	10.4	13.6	9.4	9.1
Bellevue, WA	10.5	13.3	10.0	8.0
Billings, MT	12.0	18.4	10.6	7.2
Boise City, ID	14.2	18.5	13.4	7.7
Boston, MA	9.8	11.1	9.5	9.2
Boulder, CO	12.7	12.9	13.6	5.6
Broken Arrow, OK	14.1	20.9	12.4	8.4
Cambridge, MA	9.8	11.1	9.5	9.2
Cape Coral, FL	13.7	20.7	13.8	7.3
Carlsbad, CA	13.2	17.4	12.6	8.0
Cary, NC	11.6	15.0	10.7	8.1
Cedar Rapids, IA	9.2	11.4	8.9	6.6
Charleston, SC	15.4	22.5	13.7	10.2
Charlotte, NC	13.2	18.2	11.9	8.4
Chesapeake, VA	10.5	16.2	9.0	7.1
Chicago, IL	12.7	17.9	11.1	9.3
Clarksville, TN	16.5	23.3	14.2	11.3
Colorado Spgs., CO	12.1	17.0	11.0	5.7
Columbia, MD	10.4	13.6	9.4	9.1
Columbia, MO	19.2	18.5	21.4	5.7
Columbia, SC	14.2	18.4	13.4	10.0
Columbus, OH	14.8	19.8	13.9	8.4
Dallas, TX	14.0	20.1	12.0	8.7
Denver, CO	12.0	16.4	10.7	9.4
Durham, NC	16.0	20.9	15.8	7.6
Edison, NJ	13.1	18.4	11.6	11.5
El Paso, TX	24.3	34.1	19.9	20.2
Fargo, ND	12.5	12.1	13.2	8.8
Ft. Collins, CO	14.0	13.1	15.7	6.2
Ft. Worth, TX	14.0	20.1	12.0	8.7
Gilbert, AZ	14.9	21.2	13.6	7.1
Green Bay, WI	10.4	13.7	9.7	7.3
Henderson, NV	12.9	18.6	11.4	8.1
High Point, NC	16.4	23.6	15.2	9.2
Honolulu, HI	9.2	11.7	8.9	6.8
Houston, TX	15.3	22.2	12.8	10.9
Huntington, NY	13.1	18.4	11.6	11.5
Huntsville, AL	12.3	16.8	11.5	7.6
Indianapolis, IN	13.4	19.0	12.1	7.0
Irvine, CA	15.1	21.2	13.4	10.8
Jackson, MS	18.2	26.3	16.1	11.0
Jacksonville, FL	13.4	19.0	12.1	9.2
Jersey City, NJ	13.1	18.4	11.6	11.5
Kansas City, MO	11.5	16.3	10.3	7.4
Kenosha, WI	12.7	17.9	11.1	9.3
Las Vegas, NV	12.9	18.6	11.4	8.1
Lexington, KY	16.6	21.8	16.1	8.2
Lincoln, NE	14.0	17.0	14.3	6.1

Table continued on next page.

Metro Area	All Ages	Under 18 Years Old	18 to 64 Years Old	65 Years and Over
Little Rock, AR	15.1	21.9	13.7	8.6
Los Angeles, CA	15.1	21.2	13.4	10.8
Madison, WI	11.7	11.8	12.6	5.3
Manchester, NH	7.6	10.7	6.6	6.8
Miami, FL	15.5	20.7	13.8	15.0
Minneapolis, MN	10.0	13.3	9.1	7.5
Murfreesboro, TN	13.9	19.6	12.4	9.3
Naperville, IL	12.7	17.9	11.1	9.3
Nashville, TN	13.9	19.6	12.4	9.3
New Orleans, LA	16.4	23.9	14.7	11.1
New York, NY	13.1	18.4	11.6	11.5
Norman, OK	15.2	21.9	14.0	7.5
Olathe, KS	11.5	16.3	10.3	7.4
Omaha, NE	11.2	15.3	10.2	7.8
Orlando, FL	13.6	18.5	12.7	8.9
Overland Park, KS	11.5	16.3	10.3	7.4
Oyster Bay, NY	13.1	18.4	11.6	11.5
Pembroke Pines, FL	15.5	20.7	13.8	15.0
Philadelphia, PA	12.2	16.2	11.3	8.9
Phoenix, AZ	14.9	21.2	13.6	7.1
Pittsburgh, PA	12.1	17.0	11.5	8.4
Plano, TX	14.0	20.1	12.0	8.7
Portland, OR	12.4	16.3	11.7	8.4
Providence, RI	12.5	16.9	11.5	10.0
Provo, UT	13.4	11.2	15.7	5.0
Raleigh, NC	11.6	15.0	10.7	8.1
Richmond, VA	11.6	15.6	10.8	7.9
Roseville, CA	13.6	18.4	12.8	7.4
Round Rock, TX	14.5	18.5	13.9	7.1
San Antonio, TX	16.4	23.3	14.2	11.7
San Diego, CA	13.2	17.4	12.6	8.0
San Francisco, CA	10.2	12.5	9.7	8.3
San Jose, CA	9.4	12.0	8.7	7.5
Savannah, GA	15.7	21.2	14.4	10.7
Scottsdale, AZ	14.9	21.2	13.6	7.1
Seattle, WA	10.5	13.3	10.0	8.0
Sioux Falls, SD	8.7	11.3	7.7	7.8
Stamford, CT	8.9	10.4	8.7	6.9
Sterling Hgts, MI	15.4	22.1	14.1	9.1
Sunnyvale, CA	9.4	12.0	8.7	7.5
Tampa, FL	14.1	20.4	13.4	8.8
Temecula, CA	15.5	21.6	13.6	8.8
Thousand Oaks, CA	9.8	13.2	9.0	7.0
Virginia Beach, VA	10.5	16.2	9.0	7.1
Washington, DC	7.7	9.7	7.1	6.8
U.S.	14.4	20.1	13.1	9.4

Note: Figures are percentage of people whose income during the past 12 months was below the poverty level; Figures cover the Metropolitan Statistical Area—see Appendix B for areas included
Source: U.S. Census Bureau, 2008-2010 American Community Survey 3-Year Estimates

Personal Bankruptcy Filing Rate

City	Area Covered	2006	2007	2008	2009	2010	2011
Albuquerque, NM	Bernalillo County	1.35	1.95	2.67	3.44	3.65	3.15
Alexandria, VA	Alexandria City	0.86	1.36	2.48	3.27	3.17	2.81
Anchorage, AK	Anchorage Borough	1.14	1.24	1.69	1.80	1.94	1.72
Ann Arbor, MI	Washtenaw County	2.08	3.07	3.98	4.82	4.96	4.07
Athens, GA	Clarke County	2.18	2.66	2.86	3.46	3.54	3.79
Atlanta, GA	Fulton County	3.78	4.89	5.68	7.45	8.21	7.68
Austin, TX	Travis County	1.26	1.34	1.35	1.81	1.86	1.54
Baltimore, MD	Baltimore City County	2.77	3.18	3.08	4.25	5.03	4.84
Bellevue, WA	King County	1.44	1.79	2.42	3.76	4.32	4.09
Billings, MT	Yellowstone County	1.94	2.33	2.34	2.60	3.33	3.32
Boise City, ID	Ada County	2.46	2.97	4.26	6.17	6.11	5.62
Boston, MA	Suffolk County	1.16	1.86	1.95	2.32	2.71	2.35
Boulder, CO	Boulder County	1.37	2.19	2.90	3.82	4.22	3.86
Broken Arrow, OK	Tulsa County	2.38	2.89	3.30	4.23	4.51	3.81
Cambridge, MA	Middlesex County	0.89	1.51	1.79	2.30	2.58	2.25
Cape Coral, FL	Lee County	0.89	2.27	4.92	7.38	7.32	5.33
Carlsbad, CA	San Diego County	1.40	2.55	4.46	6.50	7.23	6.48
Cary, NC	Wake County	1.86	2.35	2.66	3.45	3.08	2.89
Cedar Rapids, IA	Linn County	0.92	2.02	2.26	3.23	2.82	2.62
Charleston, SC	Charleston County	0.91	1.24	1.45	1.71	1.88	1.52
Charlotte, NC	Mecklenburg County	1.66	1.89	1.98	2.50	2.67	2.26
Chesapeake, VA	Chesapeake City	1.92	2.91	4.06	5.31	5.86	5.50
Chicago, IL	Cook County	3.24	3.34	4.72	6.40	7.44	6.69
Clarksville, TN	Montgomery County	2.84	3.29	4.14	4.65	5.03	4.53
Colorado Spgs., CO	El Paso County	1.94	3.27	4.59	5.55	6.08	5.07
Columbia, MD	Howard County	0.93	1.46	2.29	3.08	3.67	3.00
Columbia, MO	Boone County	3.82	5.14	5.43	6.39	5.70	4.75
Columbia, SC	Richland County	2.08	2.20	2.41	2.37	2.26	2.04
Columbus, OH	Franklin County	3.59	4.58	5.41	6.20	6.22	5.53
Dallas, TX	Dallas County	2.20	2.39	2.39	2.90	2.86	2.63
Denver, CO	Denver County	2.24	3.24	4.38	5.54	6.30	6.20
Durham, NC	Durham County	2.18	2.18	2.35	2.80	2.97	2.73
Edison, NJ	Middlesex County	1.04	1.62	2.30	3.27	3.86	3.56
El Paso, TX	El Paso County	2.04	2.19	2.87	3.71	3.41	3.14
Fargo, ND	Cass County	1.29	2.51	2.81	3.42	3.29	2.61
Ft. Collins, CO	Larimer County	2.37	3.49	4.30	5.39	6.26	5.31
Ft. Worth, TX	Tarrant County	2.44	2.91	3.02	3.74	3.76	3.20
Gilbert, AZ	Maricopa County	1.40	1.87	3.47	6.22	7.81	6.60
Green Bay, WI	Brown County	2.06	2.62	3.98	4.59	5.02	4.06
Henderson, NV	Clark County	2.44	4.80	8.25	12.68	12.53	10.24
High Point, NC	Guilford County	1.78	2.00	2.28	2.68	2.54	2.28
Honolulu, HI	Honolulu County	0.82	1.08	1.44	1.98	2.41	2.06
Houston, TX	Harris County	1.50	1.74	1.52	1.78	2.08	1.95
Huntington, NY	Suffolk County	1.56	2.38	3.25	4.32	4.42	4.01
Huntsville, AL	Madison County	3.19	3.65	4.45	4.94	5.11	4.81
Indianapolis, IN	Marion County	4.64	6.18	7.37	8.44	8.64	7.27
Irvine, CA	Orange County	0.88	1.61	3.03	4.93	6.26	6.03
Jackson, MS	Hinds County	5.28	6.95	5.88	6.57	6.44	6.31
Jacksonville, FL	Duval County	2.39	3.46	4.44	5.80	5.97	5.10
Jersey City, NJ	Hudson County	1.65	2.10	2.89	4.09	4.56	4.27
Kansas City, MO	Jackson County	3.98	4.69	5.21	5.89	6.43	5.44
Kenosha, WI	Kenosha County	2.41	3.03	4.13	6.06	6.97	6.05
Las Vegas, NV	Clark County	2.44	4.80	8.25	12.68	12.53	10.24
Lexington, KY	Fayette County	2.20	2.88	3.59	4.58	4.57	3.97
Lincoln, NE	Lancaster County	2.59	3.21	4.02	4.37	4.43	4.03
Little Rock, AR	Pulaski County	4.76	5.52	6.10	6.81	7.14	6.73

Table continued on next page.

City	Area Covered	2006	2007	2008	2009	2010	2011
Los Angeles, CA	Los Angeles County	1.01	1.82	3.43	5.57	7.34	6.86
Madison, WI	Dane County	1.57	2.15	2.66	3.37	3.71	3.03
Manchester, NH	Hillsborough County	1.52	2.26	3.31	3.99	4.62	3.94
Miami, FL	Miami-Dade County	n/a	n/a	n/a	n/a	n/a	n/a
Minneapolis, MN	Hennepin County	1.48	2.14	2.96	3.89	4.22	3.78
Murfreesboro, TN	Rutherford County	3.92	4.78	6.36	7.27	6.86	6.22
Naperville, IL	DuPage County	1.38	2.10	3.30	4.87	5.84	5.22
Nashville, TN	Davidson County	4.67	5.49	6.61	7.29	6.84	6.51
New Orleans, LA	Orleans Parish	1.18	1.42	1.59	2.12	2.31	2.30
New York, NY	Bronx County	1.19	1.66	2.01	2.36	2.34	2.21
New York, NY	Kings County	1.02	1.25	1.49	1.82	1.85	1.67
New York, NY	New York County	0.94	1.17	1.42	2.15	1.96	1.78
New York, NY	Queens County	1.06	1.59	1.99	2.56	2.74	2.43
New York, NY	Richmond County	0.98	1.41	1.92	2.85	3.03	2.73
Norman, OK	Cleveland County	2.04	2.78	3.38	3.86	4.26	3.80
Olathe, KS	Johnson County	1.97	2.60	3.12	4.12	4.10	3.60
Omaha, NE	Douglas County	2.99	3.57	4.39	4.43	4.65	4.04
Orlando, FL	Orange County	1.17	2.14	3.83	6.51	7.70	6.40
Overland Park, KS	Johnson County	1.97	2.60	3.12	4.12	4.10	3.60
Oyster Bay, NY	Nassau County	0.94	1.52	2.12	2.74	2.58	2.40
Pembroke Pines, FL	Broward County	1.34	2.24	3.75	5.48	6.89	5.98
Philadelphia, PA	Philadelphia County	2.11	2.19	2.02	1.88	2.32	2.05
Phoenix, AZ	Maricopa County	1.40	1.87	3.47	6.22	7.81	6.60
Pittsburgh, PA	Allegheny County	2.96	3.57	3.54	3.83	3.69	3.19
Plano, TX	Collin County	1.95	2.47	2.84	3.49	3.85	3.26
Portland, OR	Multnomah County	2.18	2.63	3.18	4.30	4.82	4.43
Providence, RI	Providence County	1.64	2.86	4.49	5.23	5.60	5.10
Provo, UT	Utah County	1.59	1.74	2.64	4.59	5.94	5.81
Raleigh, NC	Wake County	1.86	2.35	2.66	3.45	3.08	2.89
Richmond, VA	Richmond City	3.15	3.92	4.41	4.77	5.80	5.14
Roseville, CA	Placer County	1.34	2.84	5.61	8.55	9.63	8.28
Round Rock, TX	Williamson County	1.65	2.02	2.02	2.52	2.50	2.26
San Antonio, TX	Bexar County	1.46	1.73	1.91	2.39	2.32	2.05
San Diego, CA	San Diego County	1.40	2.55	4.46	6.50	7.23	6.48
San Francisco, CA	San Francisco County	0.90	1.20	1.52	2.29	2.74	2.30
San Jose, CA	Santa Clara County	0.96	1.37	2.36	3.99	4.91	4.49
Savannah, GA	Chatham County	4.85	5.26	6.33	6.98	6.53	6.28
Scottsdale, AZ	Maricopa County	1.40	1.87	3.47	6.22	7.81	6.60
Seattle, WA	King County	1.44	1.79	2.42	3.76	4.32	4.09
Sioux Falls, SD	Minnehaha County	1.72	2.51	2.84	3.22	3.57	3.23
Stamford, CT	Fairfield County	0.90	1.09	1.70	2.33	2.58	2.18
Sterling Hgts, MI	Macomb County	3.85	5.92	7.52	9.69	9.66	7.79
Sunnyvale, CA	Santa Clara County	0.96	1.37	2.36	3.99	4.91	4.49
Tampa, FL	Hillsborough County	1.80	2.76	4.09	5.55	6.26	4.92
Temecula, CA	Riverside County	1.20	2.51	5.32	8.64	10.86	9.85
Thousand Oaks, CA	Ventura County	0.77	1.68	3.17	5.04	6.37	5.94
Virginia Beach, VA	Virginia Beach City	1.72	2.64	4.06	4.99	5.46	5.01
Washington, DC	District of Columbia	n/a	n/a	n/a	n/a	n/a	n/a
U.S.	U.S.	2.00	2.73	3.53	4.61	4.97	4.37

Note: Numbers are per 1,000 population and include Chapter 7 and Chapter 13 filings; n/a not available
Source: Federal Deposit Insurance Corporation (FDIC), Regional Economic Conditions (RECON), March 9, 2012

Building Permits: City

City	Single-Family			Multi-Family			Total		
	2010	2011	Pct. Chg.	2010	2011	Pct. Chg.	2010	2011	Pct. Chg.
Albuquerque, NM	814	754	-7.4	202	270	33.7	1,016	1,024	0.8
Alexandria, VA	65	105	61.5	403	654	62.3	468	759	62.2
Anchorage, AK	381	344	-9.7	99	103	4.0	480	447	-6.9
Ann Arbor, MI	96	14	-85.4	45	277	515.6	141	291	106.4
Athens, GA	94	84	-10.6	0	87	-	94	171	81.9
Atlanta, GA	83	227	173.5	196	510	160.2	279	737	164.2
Austin, TX	1,664	1,713	2.9	1,110	2,465	122.1	2,774	4,178	50.6
Baltimore, MD	118	75	-36.4	251	914	264.1	369	989	168.0
Bellevue, WA	75	68	-9.3	129	66	-48.8	204	134	-34.3
Billings, MT	308	243	-21.1	125	10	-92.0	433	253	-41.6
Boise City, ID	352	359	2.0	0	59	-	352	418	18.8
Boston, MA	23	33	43.5	328	752	129.3	351	785	123.6
Boulder, CO	115	59	-48.7	338	56	-83.4	453	115	-74.6
Broken Arrow, OK	366	386	5.5	0	378	-	366	764	108.7
Cambridge, MA	8	14	75.0	30	20	-33.3	38	34	-10.5
Cape Coral, FL	216	269	24.5	0	8	-	216	277	28.2
Carlsbad, CA	376	267	-29.0	2	50	2,400.0	378	317	-16.1
Cary, NC	1,083	970	-10.4	276	0	-100.0	1,359	970	-28.6
Cedar Rapids, IA	342	249	-27.2	99	77	-22.2	441	326	-26.1
Charleston, SC	400	392	-2.0	164	223	36.0	564	615	9.0
Charlotte, NC	n/a	n/a	n/a	n/a	n/a	n/a	n/a	n/a	n/a
Chesapeake, VA	736	653	-11.3	349	391	12.0	1,085	1,044	-3.8
Chicago, IL	164	214	30.5	1,713	2,392	39.6	1,877	2,606	38.8
Clarksville, TN	675	996	47.6	760	510	-32.9	1,435	1,506	4.9
Colorado Spgs., CO	n/a	n/a	n/a	n/a	n/a	n/a	n/a	n/a	n/a
Columbia, MD	n/a	n/a	n/a	n/a	n/a	n/a	n/a	n/a	n/a
Columbia, MO	401	316	-21.2	50	550	1,000.0	451	866	92.0
Columbia, SC	203	199	-2.0	96	52	-45.8	299	251	-16.1
Columbus, OH	716	667	-6.8	1,391	1,642	18.0	2,107	2,309	9.6
Dallas, TX	865	809	-6.5	1,744	3,441	97.3	2,609	4,250	62.9
Denver, CO	632	703	11.2	600	1,982	230.3	1,232	2,685	117.9
Durham, NC	891	883	-0.9	296	360	21.6	1,187	1,243	4.7
Edison, NJ	28	27	-3.6	22	0	-100.0	50	27	-46.0
El Paso, TX	2,478	2,966	19.7	1,584	871	-45.0	4,062	3,837	-5.5
Fargo, ND	334	283	-15.3	497	683	37.4	831	966	16.2
Ft. Collins, CO	180	258	43.3	66	456	590.9	246	714	190.2
Ft. Worth, TX	2,759	2,426	-12.1	818	1,144	39.9	3,577	3,570	-0.2
Gilbert, AZ	1,060	1,541	45.4	0	0	-	1,060	1,541	45.4
Green Bay, WI	39	40	2.6	186	16	-91.4	225	56	-75.1
Henderson, NV	700	752	7.4	68	368	441.2	768	1,120	45.8
High Point, NC	163	169	3.7	88	0	-100.0	251	169	-32.7
Honolulu, HI	n/a	n/a	n/a	n/a	n/a	n/a	n/a	n/a	n/a
Houston, TX	2,452	2,575	5.0	2,139	5,160	141.2	4,591	7,735	68.5
Huntington, NY	62	40	-35.5	0	0	-	62	40	-35.5
Huntsville, AL	1,073	1,018	-5.1	0	4	-	1,073	1,022	-4.8
Indianapolis, IN	n/a	n/a	n/a	n/a	n/a	n/a	n/a	n/a	n/a
Irvine, CA	641	857	33.7	1,113	1,776	59.6	1,754	2,633	50.1
Jackson, MS	42	148	252.4	88	153	73.9	130	301	131.5
Jacksonville, FL	1,397	957	-31.5	68	558	720.6	1,465	1,515	3.4
Jersey City, NJ	2	0	-100.0	168	548	226.2	170	548	222.4
Kansas City, MO	68	394	479.4	212	115	-45.8	280	509	81.8
Kenosha, WI	65	36	-44.6	89	107	20.2	154	143	-7.1
Las Vegas, NV	926	814	-12.1	362	114	-68.5	1,288	928	-28.0
Lexington, KY	n/a	n/a	n/a	n/a	n/a	n/a	n/a	n/a	n/a

Table continued on next page.

City	Single-Family 2010	Single-Family 2011	Single-Family Pct. Chg.	Multi-Family 2010	Multi-Family 2011	Multi-Family Pct. Chg.	Total 2010	Total 2011	Total Pct. Chg.
Lincoln, NE	501	544	8.6	332	379	14.2	833	923	10.8
Little Rock, AR	344	325	-5.5	84	1,004	1,095.2	428	1,329	210.5
Los Angeles, CA	636	525	-17.5	3,473	5,422	56.1	4,109	5,947	44.7
Madison, WI	186	177	-4.8	340	444	30.6	526	621	18.1
Manchester, NH	45	91	102.2	155	209	34.8	200	300	50.0
Miami, FL	27	21	-22.2	685	266	-61.2	712	287	-59.7
Minneapolis, MN	41	49	19.5	837	567	-32.3	878	616	-29.8
Murfreesboro, TN	346	400	15.6	184	8	-95.7	530	408	-23.0
Naperville, IL	94	186	97.9	0	0	-	94	186	97.9
Nashville, TN	n/a	n/a	n/a	n/a	n/a	n/a	n/a	n/a	n/a
New Orleans, LA	820	717	-12.6	260	377	45.0	1,080	1,094	1.3
New York, NY	325	264	-18.8	6,077	8,672	42.7	6,402	8,936	39.6
Norman, OK	336	350	4.2	446	39	-91.3	782	389	-50.3
Olathe, KS	364	317	-12.9	0	18	-	364	335	-8.0
Omaha, NE	1,191	1,160	-2.6	388	674	73.7	1,579	1,834	16.1
Orlando, FL	224	308	37.5	336	637	89.6	560	945	68.8
Overland Park, KS	211	274	29.9	11	462	4,100.0	222	736	231.5
Oyster Bay, NY	142	72	-49.3	0	0	-	142	72	-49.3
Pembroke Pines, FL	68	44	-35.3	0	0	-	68	44	-35.3
Philadelphia, PA	447	445	-0.4	537	1,107	106.1	984	1,552	57.7
Phoenix, AZ	1,111	952	-14.3	584	676	15.8	1,695	1,628	-4.0
Pittsburgh, PA	147	284	93.2	0	0	-	147	284	93.2
Plano, TX	311	349	12.2	303	673	122.1	614	1,022	66.4
Portland, OR	435	451	3.7	665	913	37.3	1,100	1,364	24.0
Providence, RI	8	12	50.0	13	8	-38.5	21	20	-4.8
Provo, UT	76	75	-1.3	238	28	-88.2	314	103	-67.2
Raleigh, NC	1,024	988	-3.5	226	1,319	483.6	1,250	2,307	84.6
Richmond, VA	126	92	-27.0	481	251	-47.8	607	343	-43.5
Roseville, CA	635	411	-35.3	0	0	-	635	411	-35.3
Round Rock, TX	253	259	2.4	0	0	-	253	259	2.4
San Antonio, TX	2,337	1,594	-31.8	1,237	2,476	100.2	3,574	4,070	13.9
San Diego, CA	557	451	-19.0	519	2,241	331.8	1,076	2,692	150.2
San Francisco, CA	22	31	40.9	757	1,787	136.1	779	1,818	133.4
San Jose, CA	74	83	12.2	2,348	962	-59.0	2,422	1,045	-56.9
Savannah, GA	241	197	-18.3	279	250	-10.4	520	447	-14.0
Scottsdale, AZ	160	148	-7.5	134	257	91.8	294	405	37.8
Seattle, WA	241	316	31.1	2,456	2,857	16.3	2,697	3,173	17.6
Sioux Falls, SD	546	515	-5.7	212	309	45.8	758	824	8.7
Stamford, CT	16	30	87.5	136	177	30.1	152	207	36.2
Sterling Hgts, MI	103	75	-27.2	0	0	-	103	75	-27.2
Sunnyvale, CA	112	211	88.4	744	279	-62.5	856	490	-42.8
Tampa, FL	455	590	29.7	643	104	-83.8	1,098	694	-36.8
Temecula, CA	348	288	-17.2	0	0	-	348	288	-17.2
Thousand Oaks, CA	20	18	-10.0	15	21	40.0	35	39	11.4
Virginia Beach, VA	529	535	1.1	100	944	844.0	629	1,479	135.1
Washington, DC	177	227	28.2	562	4,385	680.2	739	4,612	524.1
U.S.	447,311	418,498	-6.4	157,299	205,563	30.7	604,610	624,061	3.2

Note: Figures represent new, privately-owned housing units authorized (unadjusted data); All permit data are based on estimates with imputation

Source: U.S. Census Bureau, Manufacturing, Mining, and Construction Statistics, Building Permits, 2010, 2011

Building Permits: Metro Area

Metro Area	Single-Family			Multi-Family			Total		
	2009	2010	Pct. Chg.	2009	2010	Pct. Chg.	2009	2010	Pct. Chg.
Albuquerque, NM	1,553	1,354	-12.8	211	280	32.7	1,764	1,634	-7.4
Alexandria, VA	9,488	9,644	1.6	3,577	10,013	179.9	13,065	19,657	50.5
Anchorage, AK	424	401	-5.4	109	123	12.8	533	524	-1.7
Ann Arbor, MI	317	200	-36.9	51	277	443.1	368	477	29.6
Athens, GA	226	240	6.2	0	87	-	226	327	44.7
Atlanta, GA	6,384	6,214	-2.7	1,191	2,420	103.2	7,575	8,634	14.0
Austin, TX	6,200	6,231	0.5	2,586	4,008	55.0	8,786	10,239	16.5
Baltimore, MD	3,554	3,277	-7.8	2,040	2,876	41.0	5,594	6,153	10.0
Bellevue, WA	6,139	6,078	-1.0	3,901	5,152	32.1	10,040	11,230	11.9
Billings, MT	321	256	-20.2	136	16	-88.2	457	272	-40.5
Boise City, ID	1,630	1,578	-3.2	63	262	315.9	1,693	1,840	8.7
Boston, MA	3,748	3,394	-9.4	2,924	2,745	-6.1	6,672	6,139	-8.0
Boulder, CO	276	390	41.3	381	271	-28.9	657	661	0.6
Broken Arrow, OK	2,269	2,033	-10.4	347	1,532	341.5	2,616	3,565	36.3
Cambridge, MA	3,748	3,394	-9.4	2,924	2,745	-6.1	6,672	6,139	-8.0
Cape Coral, FL	1,175	1,262	7.4	101	325	221.8	1,276	1,587	24.4
Carlsbad, CA	2,270	2,245	-1.1	1,224	3,125	155.3	3,494	5,370	53.7
Cary, NC	4,653	4,753	2.1	560	1,613	188.0	5,213	6,366	22.1
Cedar Rapids, IA	691	577	-16.5	164	154	-6.1	855	731	-14.5
Charleston, SC	2,787	2,597	-6.8	273	1,225	348.7	3,060	3,822	24.9
Charlotte, NC	4,338	4,912	13.2	950	1,534	61.5	5,288	6,446	21.9
Chesapeake, VA	3,149	2,954	-6.2	817	2,605	218.8	3,966	5,559	40.2
Chicago, IL	4,244	4,145	-2.3	3,023	3,448	14.1	7,267	7,593	4.5
Clarksville, TN	1,092	1,427	30.7	829	574	-30.8	1,921	2,001	4.2
Colorado Spgs., CO	1,676	1,616	-3.6	84	659	684.5	1,760	2,275	29.3
Columbia, MD	3,554	3,277	-7.8	2,040	2,876	41.0	5,594	6,153	10.0
Columbia, MO	547	478	-12.6	60	574	856.7	607	1,052	73.3
Columbia, SC	2,527	2,390	-5.4	415	507	22.2	2,942	2,897	-1.5
Columbus, OH	2,887	2,420	-16.2	1,557	2,310	48.4	4,444	4,730	6.4
Dallas, TX	14,420	14,039	-2.6	5,138	10,788	110.0	19,558	24,827	26.9
Denver, CO	3,660	3,630	-0.8	1,382	3,043	120.2	5,042	6,673	32.3
Durham, NC	1,530	1,526	-0.3	383	398	3.9	1,913	1,924	0.6
Edison, NJ	7,010	6,003	-14.4	11,658	15,536	33.3	18,668	21,539	15.4
El Paso, TX	2,961	3,280	10.8	1,588	873	-45.0	4,549	4,153	-8.7
Fargo, ND	760	609	-19.9	558	927	66.1	1,318	1,536	16.5
Ft. Collins, CO	477	702	47.2	676	490	-27.5	1,153	1,192	3.4
Ft. Worth, TX	14,420	14,039	-2.6	5,138	10,788	110.0	19,558	24,827	26.9
Gilbert, AZ	7,212	7,297	1.2	1,088	1,784	64.0	8,300	9,081	9.4
Green Bay, WI	611	484	-20.8	523	396	-24.3	1,134	880	-22.4
Henderson, NV	4,623	3,817	-17.4	851	1,330	56.3	5,474	5,147	-6.0
High Point, NC	1,234	1,054	-14.6	669	993	48.4	1,903	2,047	7.6
Honolulu, HI	879	734	-16.5	1,012	990	-2.2	1,891	1,724	-8.8
Houston, TX	22,330	22,889	2.5	5,122	8,382	63.6	27,452	31,271	13.9
Huntington, NY	7,010	6,003	-14.4	11,658	15,536	33.3	18,668	21,539	15.4
Huntsville, AL	2,275	2,015	-11.4	0	4	-	2,275	2,019	-11.3
Indianapolis, IN	3,793	3,614	-4.7	2,128	1,645	-22.7	5,921	5,259	-11.2
Irvine, CA	4,008	4,097	2.2	6,386	10,150	58.9	10,394	14,247	37.1
Jackson, MS	1,303	1,207	-7.4	88	153	73.9	1,391	1,360	-2.2
Jacksonville, FL	3,387	3,245	-4.2	219	666	204.1	3,606	3,911	8.5
Jersey City, NJ	7,010	6,003	-14.4	11,658	15,536	33.3	18,668	21,539	15.4
Kansas City, MO	2,155	2,363	9.7	559	924	65.3	2,714	3,287	21.1
Kenosha, WI	4,244	4,145	-2.3	3,023	3,448	14.1	7,267	7,593	4.5
Las Vegas, NV	4,623	3,817	-17.4	851	1,330	56.3	5,474	5,147	-6.0
Lexington, KY	1,155	1,009	-12.6	206	492	138.8	1,361	1,501	10.3

Table continued on next page.

Metro Area	Single-Family			Multi-Family			Total		
	2009	2010	Pct. Chg.	2009	2010	Pct. Chg.	2009	2010	Pct. Chg.
Lincoln, NE	648	680	4.9	384	379	-1.3	1,032	1,059	2.6
Little Rock, AR	1,896	1,514	-20.1	1,663	1,716	3.2	3,559	3,230	-9.2
Los Angeles, CA	4,008	4,097	2.2	6,386	10,150	58.9	10,394	14,247	37.1
Madison, WI	794	718	-9.6	404	725	79.5	1,198	1,443	20.5
Manchester, NH	367	334	-9.0	315	368	16.8	682	702	2.9
Miami, FL	3,171	4,303	35.7	2,706	3,229	19.3	5,877	7,532	28.2
Minneapolis, MN	3,805	3,756	-1.3	1,921	1,392	-27.5	5,726	5,148	-10.1
Murfreesboro, TN	3,938	4,100	4.1	1,154	1,294	12.1	5,092	5,394	5.9
Naperville, IL	4,244	4,145	-2.3	3,023	3,448	14.1	7,267	7,593	4.5
Nashville, TN	3,938	4,100	4.1	1,154	1,294	12.1	5,092	5,394	5.9
New Orleans, LA	1,875	1,945	3.7	296	383	29.4	2,171	2,328	7.2
New York, NY	7,010	6,003	-14.4	11,658	15,536	33.3	18,668	21,539	15.4
Norman, OK	3,032	3,079	1.6	603	182	-69.8	3,635	3,261	-10.3
Olathe, KS	2,155	2,363	9.7	559	924	65.3	2,714	3,287	21.1
Omaha, NE	2,305	2,156	-6.5	918	977	6.4	3,223	3,133	-2.8
Orlando, FL	4,221	4,533	7.4	1,033	1,972	90.9	5,254	6,505	23.8
Overland Park, KS	2,155	2,363	9.7	559	924	65.3	2,714	3,287	21.1
Oyster Bay, NY	7,010	6,003	-14.4	11,658	15,536	33.3	18,668	21,539	15.4
Pembroke Pines, FL	3,171	4,303	35.7	2,706	3,229	19.3	5,877	7,532	28.2
Philadelphia, PA	5,186	4,456	-14.1	1,867	2,523	35.1	7,053	6,979	-1.0
Phoenix, AZ	7,212	7,297	1.2	1,088	1,784	64.0	8,300	9,081	9.4
Pittsburgh, PA	3,398	2,654	-21.9	217	260	19.8	3,615	2,914	-19.4
Plano, TX	14,420	14,039	-2.6	5,138	10,788	110.0	19,558	24,827	26.9
Portland, OR	3,359	3,132	-6.8	1,117	2,081	86.3	4,476	5,213	16.5
Providence, RI	1,205	963	-20.1	234	215	-8.1	1,439	1,178	-18.1
Provo, UT	1,553	1,452	-6.5	432	480	11.1	1,985	1,932	-2.7
Raleigh, NC	4,653	4,753	2.1	560	1,613	188.0	5,213	6,366	22.1
Richmond, VA	2,472	2,352	-4.9	984	357	-63.7	3,456	2,709	-21.6
Roseville, CA	2,166	1,873	-13.5	536	618	15.3	2,702	2,491	-7.8
Round Rock, TX	6,200	6,231	0.5	2,586	4,008	55.0	8,786	10,239	16.5
San Antonio, TX	5,144	4,410	-14.3	1,721	2,717	57.9	6,865	7,127	3.8
San Diego, CA	2,270	2,245	-1.1	1,224	3,125	155.3	3,494	5,370	53.7
San Francisco, CA	2,118	1,923	-9.2	2,503	3,860	54.2	4,621	5,783	25.1
San Jose, CA	861	1,002	16.4	3,318	2,095	-36.9	4,179	3,097	-25.9
Savannah, GA	1,020	1,049	2.8	281	576	105.0	1,301	1,625	24.9
Scottsdale, AZ	7,212	7,297	1.2	1,088	1,784	64.0	8,300	9,081	9.4
Seattle, WA	6,139	6,078	-1.0	3,901	5,152	32.1	10,040	11,230	11.9
Sioux Falls, SD	755	716	-5.2	326	413	26.7	1,081	1,129	4.4
Stamford, CT	546	583	6.8	380	354	-6.8	926	937	1.2
Sterling Hgts, MI	2,430	2,862	17.8	780	504	-35.4	3,210	3,366	4.9
Sunnyvale, CA	861	1,002	16.4	3,318	2,095	-36.9	4,179	3,097	-25.9
Tampa, FL	4,396	4,511	2.6	2,105	1,831	-13.0	6,501	6,342	-2.4
Temecula, CA	5,287	3,378	-36.1	1,049	1,358	29.5	6,336	4,736	-25.3
Thousand Oaks, CA	209	281	34.4	381	287	-24.7	590	568	-3.7
Virginia Beach, VA	3,149	2,954	-6.2	817	2,605	218.8	3,966	5,559	40.2
Washington, DC	9,488	9,644	1.6	3,577	10,013	179.9	13,065	19,657	50.5
U.S.	447,311	418,498	-6.4	157,299	205,563	30.7	604,610	624,061	3.2

Note: Figures cover the Metropolitan Statistical Area—see Appendix B for areas included; Figures represent new, privately-owned housing units authorized (unadjusted data); All permit data are based on estimates with imputation

Source: U.S. Census Bureau, Manufacturing, Mining, and Construction Statistics, Building Permits, 2010, 2011

Homeownership Rate

Metro Area	2005	2006	2007	2008	2009	2010	2011
Albuquerque, NM	69.2	70.0	70.5	68.2	65.7	65.5	67.1
Alexandria, VA	68.4	68.9	69.2	68.1	67.2	67.3	67.6
Anchorage, AK	n/a	n/a	n/a	n/a	n/a	n/a	n/a
Ann Arbor, MI	n/a	n/a	n/a	n/a	n/a	n/a	n/a
Athens, GA	n/a	n/a	n/a	n/a	n/a	n/a	n/a
Atlanta, GA	66.4	67.9	66.4	67.5	67.7	67.2	65.8
Austin, TX	63.9	66.7	66.4	65.5	64.0	65.8	58.4
Baltimore, MD	70.6	72.9	71.2	69.3	67.7	65.7	66.8
Bellevue, WA	64.5	63.7	62.8	61.3	61.2	60.9	60.7
Billings, MT	n/a	n/a	n/a	n/a	n/a	n/a	n/a
Boise City, ID	n/a	n/a	n/a	n/a	n/a	n/a	n/a
Boston, MA	63.0	64.7	64.8	66.2	65.5	66.0	65.5
Boulder, CO	n/a	n/a	n/a	n/a	n/a	n/a	n/a
Broken Arrow, OK	71.7	67.9	66.7	66.8	67.8	64.2	64.4
Cambridge, MA	63.0	64.7	64.8	66.2	65.5	66.0	65.5
Cape Coral, FL	n/a	n/a	n/a	n/a	n/a	n/a	n/a
Carlsbad, CA	60.5	61.2	59.6	57.1	56.4	54.4	55.2
Cary, NC	71.4	71.1	72.8	70.7	65.7	65.9	66.7
Cedar Rapids, IA	n/a	n/a	n/a	n/a	n/a	n/a	n/a
Charleston, SC	n/a	n/a	n/a	n/a	n/a	n/a	n/a
Charlotte, NC	65.8	66.1	66.5	65.4	66.1	66.1	63.6
Chesapeake, VA	68.0	68.3	66.0	63.9	63.5	61.4	62.3
Chicago, IL	70.0	69.6	69.0	68.4	69.2	68.2	67.7
Clarksville, TN	n/a	n/a	n/a	n/a	n/a	n/a	n/a
Colorado Spgs., CO	n/a	n/a	n/a	n/a	n/a	n/a	n/a
Columbia, MD	70.6	72.9	71.2	69.3	67.7	65.7	66.8
Columbia, MO	n/a	n/a	n/a	n/a	n/a	n/a	n/a
Columbia, SC	76.3	72.2	71.1	71.4	71.5	74.1	69.0
Columbus, OH	68.9	65.8	66.1	61.2	61.5	62.2	59.7
Dallas, TX	62.3	60.7	60.9	60.9	61.6	63.8	62.6
Denver, CO	70.7	70.0	69.5	66.9	65.3	65.7	63.0
Durham, NC	n/a	n/a	n/a	n/a	n/a	n/a	n/a
Edison, NJ	54.6	53.6	53.8	52.6	51.7	51.6	50.9
El Paso, TX	72.6	65.0	68.2	64.8	63.8	70.1	72.0
Fargo, ND	n/a	n/a	n/a	n/a	n/a	n/a	n/a
Ft. Collins, CO	n/a	n/a	n/a	n/a	n/a	n/a	n/a
Ft. Worth, TX	62.3	60.7	60.9	60.9	61.6	63.8	62.6
Gilbert, AZ	71.2	72.5	70.8	70.2	69.8	66.5	63.3
Green Bay, WI	n/a	n/a	n/a	n/a	n/a	n/a	n/a
Henderson, NV	61.4	63.3	60.5	60.3	59.0	55.7	52.9
High Point, NC	66.3	62.2	62.1	68.0	70.7	68.8	62.7
Honolulu, HI	58.0	58.4	58.8	57.2	57.6	54.9	54.1
Houston, TX	61.7	63.5	64.5	64.8	63.6	61.4	61.3
Huntington, NY	54.6	53.6	53.8	52.6	51.7	51.6	50.9
Huntsville, AL	n/a	n/a	n/a	n/a	n/a	n/a	n/a
Indianapolis, IN	77.1	79.0	75.9	75.0	71.0	68.8	68.3
Irvine, CA	54.6	54.4	52.3	52.1	50.4	49.7	50.1
Jackson, MS	n/a	n/a	n/a	n/a	n/a	n/a	n/a
Jacksonville, FL	67.9	70.0	70.9	72.1	72.6	70.0	68.0
Jersey City, NJ	54.6	53.6	53.8	52.6	51.7	51.6	50.9
Kansas City, MO	71.3	69.5	71.3	70.2	69.5	68.8	68.5
Kenosha, WI	70.0	69.6	69.0	68.4	69.2	68.2	67.7
Las Vegas, NV	61.4	63.3	60.5	60.3	59.0	55.7	52.9
Lexington, KY	n/a	n/a	n/a	n/a	n/a	n/a	n/a
Lincoln, NE	n/a	n/a	n/a	n/a	n/a	n/a	n/a
Little Rock, AR	n/a	n/a	n/a	n/a	n/a	n/a	n/a

Table continued on next page.

Metro Area	2005	2006	2007	2008	2009	2010	2011
Los Angeles, CA	54.6	54.4	52.3	52.1	50.4	49.7	50.1
Madison, WI	n/a	n/a	n/a	n/a	n/a	n/a	n/a
Manchester, NH	n/a	n/a	n/a	n/a	n/a	n/a	n/a
Miami, FL	69.2	67.4	66.6	66.0	67.1	63.8	64.2
Minneapolis, MN	74.9	73.4	70.7	69.9	70.9	71.2	69.1
Murfreesboro, TN	73.0	72.4	70.0	71.3	71.8	70.4	69.6
Naperville, IL	70.0	69.6	69.0	68.4	69.2	68.2	67.7
Nashville, TN	73.0	72.4	70.0	71.3	71.8	70.4	69.6
New Orleans, LA	71.2	70.3	67.8	68.0	68.2	66.9	63.9
New York, NY	54.6	53.6	53.8	52.6	51.7	51.6	50.9
Norman, OK	72.9	71.8	68.2	69.5	69.0	70.0	69.6
Olathe, KS	71.3	69.5	71.3	70.2	69.5	68.8	68.5
Omaha, NE	69.7	68.1	67.9	72.5	73.1	73.2	71.6
Orlando, FL	70.5	71.1	71.8	70.5	72.4	70.8	68.6
Overland Park, KS	71.3	69.5	71.3	70.2	69.5	68.8	68.5
Oyster Bay, NY	54.6	53.6	53.8	52.6	51.7	51.6	50.9
Pembroke Pines, FL	69.2	67.4	66.6	66.0	67.1	63.8	64.2
Philadelphia, PA	73.5	73.1	73.1	71.8	69.7	70.7	69.7
Phoenix, AZ	71.2	72.5	70.8	70.2	69.8	66.5	63.3
Pittsburgh, PA	73.1	72.2	73.6	73.2	71.7	70.4	70.3
Plano, TX	62.3	60.7	60.9	60.9	61.6	63.8	62.6
Portland, OR	68.3	66.0	61.2	62.6	64.0	63.7	63.7
Providence, RI	63.1	65.5	64.1	63.9	61.7	61.0	61.3
Provo, UT	n/a	n/a	n/a	n/a	n/a	n/a	n/a
Raleigh, NC	71.4	71.1	72.8	70.7	65.7	65.9	66.7
Richmond, VA	69.7	68.9	72.7	72.4	72.2	68.1	65.2
Roseville, CA	64.1	64.2	60.8	61.1	64.3	61.1	57.2
Round Rock, TX	63.9	66.7	66.4	65.5	64.0	65.8	58.4
San Antonio, TX	66.0	62.6	62.4	66.1	69.8	70.1	66.5
San Diego, CA	60.5	61.2	59.6	57.1	56.4	54.4	55.2
San Francisco, CA	57.8	59.4	58.0	56.4	57.3	58.0	56.1
San Jose, CA	59.2	59.4	57.6	54.6	57.2	58.9	60.4
Savannah, GA	n/a	n/a	n/a	n/a	n/a	n/a	n/a
Scottsdale, AZ	71.2	72.5	70.8	70.2	69.8	66.5	63.3
Seattle, WA	64.5	63.7	62.8	61.3	61.2	60.9	60.7
Sioux Falls, SD	n/a	n/a	n/a	n/a	n/a	n/a	n/a
Stamford, CT	68.2	70.4	70.3	72.6	70.3	71.3	71.6
Sterling Hgts, MI	75.1	75.8	76.1	75.5	73.9	73.6	73.5
Sunnyvale, CA	59.2	59.4	57.6	54.6	57.2	58.9	60.4
Tampa, FL	71.7	71.6	72.9	70.5	68.3	68.3	68.3
Temecula, CA	68.5	68.3	66.6	65.8	65.9	63.9	59.2
Thousand Oaks, CA	73.4	69.8	71.4	71.7	73.1	67.1	67.0
Virginia Beach, VA	68.0	68.3	66.0	63.9	63.5	61.4	62.3
Washington, DC	68.4	68.9	69.2	68.1	67.2	67.3	67.6
U.S.	68.9	68.8	68.1	67.8	67.4	66.9	66.1

Note: Figures are percentages and cover the Metropolitan Statistical Area—see Appendix B for areas included
Source: U.S. Census Bureau, Housing Vacancies and Homeownership Annual Statistics: 2011

Housing Vacancy Rates

Area	Gross Vacancy Rate[2] (%)			Year-Round Vacancy Rate[3] (%)			Rental Vacancy Rate[4] (%)			Homeowner Vacancy Rate[5] (%)		
	2009	2010	2011	2009	2010	2011	2009	2010	2011	2009	2010	2011
Albuquerque, NM	8.5	7.4	7.1	7.8	6.6	6.3	8.0	5.0	6.9	1.9	1.7	1.4
Alexandria, VA	10.3	10.2	9.6	10.0	10.0	9.4	10.0	8.8	7.9	2.3	2.1	1.8
Anchorage, AK	n/a	n/a	n/a	n/a	n/a	n/a	n/a	n/a	n/a	n/a	n/a	n/a
Ann Arbor, MI	n/a	n/a	n/a	n/a	n/a	n/a	n/a	n/a	n/a	n/a	n/a	n/a
Athens, GA	n/a	n/a	n/a	n/a	n/a	n/a	n/a	n/a	n/a	n/a	n/a	n/a
Atlanta, GA	13.0	11.7	12.8	12.8	11.4	12.4	16.6	13.8	11.6	4.1	3.0	4.3
Austin, TX	12.8	15.8	12.6	12.7	15.7	11.7	12.2	11.8	6.4	1.6	1.9	0.6
Baltimore, MD	12.3	11.0	11.7	12.1	10.9	11.6	13.4	11.8	10.7	1.9	2.2	2.8
Bellevue, WA	9.0	8.8	8.6	8.8	8.6	8.3	8.0	7.4	6.7	2.8	3.2	2.6
Billings, MT	n/a	n/a	n/a	n/a	n/a	n/a	n/a	n/a	n/a	n/a	n/a	n/a
Boise City, ID	n/a	n/a	n/a	n/a	n/a	n/a	n/a	n/a	n/a	n/a	n/a	n/a
Boston, MA	8.2	8.5	8.7	6.8	7.0	6.9	6.0	6.2	5.5	1.5	1.2	1.4
Boulder, CO	n/a	n/a	n/a	n/a	n/a	n/a	n/a	n/a	n/a	n/a	n/a	n/a
Broken Arrow, OK	12.7	13.3	13.2	11.8	12.7	12.7	15.1	15.9	13.0	2.4	1.4	2.5
Cambridge, MA	8.2	8.5	8.7	6.8	7.0	6.9	6.0	6.2	5.5	1.5	1.2	1.4
Cape Coral, FL	n/a	n/a	n/a	n/a	n/a	n/a	n/a	n/a	n/a	n/a	n/a	n/a
Carlsbad, CA	10.4	10.5	9.9	9.8	10.0	9.5	8.8	7.8	6.9	2.1	2.9	1.9
Cary, NC	10.5	11.0	9.2	10.5	11.0	9.1	10.3	11.4	8.9	2.8	5.0	2.9
Cedar Rapids, IA	n/a	n/a	n/a	n/a	n/a	n/a	n/a	n/a	n/a	n/a	n/a	n/a
Charleston, SC	n/a	n/a	n/a	n/a	n/a	n/a	n/a	n/a	n/a	n/a	n/a	n/a
Charlotte, NC	12.9	11.7	9.2	12.7	11.5	9.1	12.1	11.2	10.1	5.1	3.1	1.9
Chesapeake, VA	10.4	11.1	10.8	9.9	10.4	10.3	6.2	8.8	9.4	2.3	2.8	3.2
Chicago, IL	11.4	11.9	11.8	11.2	11.6	11.6	12.0	12.1	9.9	2.9	3.4	3.6
Clarksville, TN	n/a	n/a	n/a	n/a	n/a	n/a	n/a	n/a	n/a	n/a	n/a	n/a
Colorado Spgs., CO	n/a	n/a	n/a	n/a	n/a	n/a	n/a	n/a	n/a	n/a	n/a	n/a
Columbia, MD	12.3	11.0	11.7	12.1	10.9	11.6	13.4	11.8	10.7	1.9	2.2	2.8
Columbia, MO	n/a	n/a	n/a	n/a	n/a	n/a	n/a	n/a	n/a	n/a	n/a	n/a
Columbia, SC	13.3	11.1	12.4	13.0	10.9	12.4	8.4	9.4	8.7	3.1	2.5	5.1
Columbus, OH	10.8	11.7	11.8	10.2	11.7	11.7	7.6	8.0	8.2	2.0	4.2	3.2
Dallas, TX	9.4	10.5	9.8	9.3	10.4	9.6	11.7	13.5	11.8	2.1	2.3	2.0
Denver, CO	9.2	7.2	7.0	8.7	6.8	6.5	10.2	8.2	6.8	2.7	1.7	1.8
Durham, NC	n/a	n/a	n/a	n/a	n/a	n/a	n/a	n/a	n/a	n/a	n/a	n/a
Edison, NJ	9.4	9.6	10.0	8.1	8.3	8.7	5.9	6.6	6.4	2.8	2.1	2.6
El Paso, TX	8.6	7.0	6.5	8.4	6.9	5.9	9.6	5.8	9.2	2.5	1.4	1.3
Fargo, ND	n/a	n/a	n/a	n/a	n/a	n/a	n/a	n/a	n/a	n/a	n/a	n/a
Ft. Collins, CO	n/a	n/a	n/a	n/a	n/a	n/a	n/a	n/a	n/a	n/a	n/a	n/a
Ft. Worth, TX	9.4	10.5	9.8	9.3	10.4	9.6	11.7	13.5	11.8	2.1	2.3	2.0
Gilbert, AZ	18.6	18.4	16.7	13.2	12.9	10.8	18.3	16.3	10.9	3.1	2.9	3.1
Green Bay, WI	n/a	n/a	n/a	n/a	n/a	n/a	n/a	n/a	n/a	n/a	n/a	n/a
Henderson, NV	16.7	17.2	16.4	16.5	16.8	16.0	14.3	13.8	12.1	5.0	5.1	4.1
High Point, NC	13.8	12.8	12.4	13.8	12.6	12.4	15.2	12.8	11.9	6.3	4.1	3.0
Honolulu, HI	10.9	11.5	12.1	9.4	10.0	10.9	6.9	7.2	6.9	0.8	1.0	0.7
Houston, TX	12.5	12.2	11.8	12.3	11.9	11.4	15.6	16.2	16.5	1.9	2.8	2.0
Huntington, NY	9.4	9.6	10.0	8.1	8.3	8.7	5.9	6.6	6.4	2.8	2.1	2.6
Huntsville, AL	n/a	n/a	n/a	n/a	n/a	n/a	n/a	n/a	n/a	n/a	n/a	n/a
Indianapolis, IN	10.0	12.1	12.4	9.7	11.8	11.9	12.6	14.1	13.1	2.6	3.0	3.4
Irvine, CA	6.6	7.2	6.7	6.3	6.9	6.4	6.4	6.7	5.3	1.3	1.8	1.8
Jackson, MS	n/a	n/a	n/a	n/a	n/a	n/a	n/a	n/a	n/a	n/a	n/a	n/a
Jacksonville, FL	14.3	14.9	14.7	13.6	14.6	14.1	15.9	13.9	13.3	3.7	4.6	2.8
Jersey City, NJ	9.4	9.6	10.0	8.1	8.3	8.7	5.9	6.6	6.4	2.8	2.1	2.6
Kansas City, MO	11.0	10.7	11.1	10.7	10.5	10.9	14.4	14.0	12.1	3.4	2.7	2.7
Kenosha, WI	11.4	11.9	11.8	11.2	11.6	11.6	12.0	12.1	9.9	2.9	3.4	3.6
Las Vegas, NV	16.7	17.2	16.4	16.5	16.8	16.0	14.3	13.8	12.1	5.0	5.1	4.1
Lexington, KY	n/a	n/a	n/a	n/a	n/a	n/a	n/a	n/a	n/a	n/a	n/a	n/a

Table continued on next page.

Area	Gross Vacancy Rate[2] (%)			Year-Round Vacancy Rate[3] (%)			Rental Vacancy Rate[4] (%)			Homeowner Vacancy Rate[5] (%)		
	2009	2010	2011	2009	2010	2011	2009	2010	2011	2009	2010	2011
Lincoln, NE	n/a	n/a	n/a	n/a	n/a	n/a	n/a	n/a	n/a	n/a	n/a	n/a
Little Rock, AR	n/a	n/a	n/a	n/a	n/a	n/a	n/a	n/a	n/a	n/a	n/a	n/a
Los Angeles, CA	6.6	7.2	6.7	6.3	6.9	6.4	6.4	6.7	5.3	1.3	1.8	1.8
Madison, WI	n/a	n/a	n/a	n/a	n/a	n/a	n/a	n/a	n/a	n/a	n/a	n/a
Manchester, NH	n/a	n/a	n/a	n/a	n/a	n/a	n/a	n/a	n/a	n/a	n/a	n/a
Miami, FL	23.1	21.8	21.0	13.7	13.0	11.7	13.2	10.1	11.8	3.2	3.5	1.8
Minneapolis, MN	7.6	6.8	6.6	7.1	6.3	6.1	8.5	7.4	6.7	2.2	1.4	1.8
Murfreesboro, TN	8.7	10.9	9.0	8.1	10.5	8.3	8.3	8.2	8.2	1.9	2.4	2.2
Naperville, IL	11.4	11.9	11.8	11.2	11.6	11.6	12.0	12.1	9.9	2.9	3.4	3.6
Nashville, TN	8.7	10.9	9.0	8.1	10.5	8.3	8.3	8.2	8.2	1.9	2.4	2.2
New Orleans, LA	16.1	14.6	10.7	15.9	14.4	10.3	18.0	15.2	13.1	2.5	2.6	2.1
New York, NY	9.4	9.6	10.0	8.1	8.3	8.7	5.9	6.6	6.4	2.8	2.1	2.6
Norman, OK	12.6	13.3	15.1	12.2	13.2	14.8	8.3	9.6	9.9	2.8	2.7	3.9
Olathe, KS	11.0	10.7	11.1	10.7	10.5	10.9	14.4	14.0	12.1	3.4	2.7	2.7
Omaha, NE	8.3	9.6	9.3	8.2	9.1	9.0	11.7	10.1	11.1	2.0	3.3	1.9
Orlando, FL	21.2	19.9	20.1	17.5	16.6	14.0	22.8	19.0	19.0	5.8	5.9	2.5
Overland Park, KS	11.0	10.7	11.1	10.7	10.5	10.9	14.4	14.0	12.1	3.4	2.7	2.7
Oyster Bay, NY	9.4	9.6	10.0	8.1	8.3	8.7	5.9	6.6	6.4	2.8	2.1	2.6
Pembroke Pines, FL	23.1	21.8	21.0	13.7	13.0	11.7	13.2	10.1	11.8	3.2	3.5	1.8
Philadelphia, PA	8.9	9.9	10.5	8.7	9.6	10.1	11.4	11.6	12.7	1.6	1.5	1.6
Phoenix, AZ	18.6	18.4	16.7	13.2	12.9	10.8	18.3	16.3	10.9	3.1	2.9	3.1
Pittsburgh, PA	13.2	12.7	12.3	12.1	11.7	11.6	9.7	7.8	6.3	1.6	2.7	2.2
Plano, TX	9.4	10.5	9.8	9.3	10.4	9.6	11.7	13.5	11.8	2.1	2.3	2.0
Portland, OR	8.2	7.2	6.5	7.9	7.0	6.3	4.3	4.2	3.4	4.8	3.2	2.0
Providence, RI	12.8	12.7	13.7	9.2	9.4	10.8	8.5	7.5	8.8	1.7	1.3	2.2
Provo, UT	n/a	n/a	n/a	n/a	n/a	n/a	n/a	n/a	n/a	n/a	n/a	n/a
Raleigh, NC	10.5	11.0	9.2	10.5	11.0	9.1	10.3	11.4	8.9	2.8	5.0	2.9
Richmond, VA	12.7	11.7	12.4	12.0	11.2	12.0	18.5	13.5	13.7	2.2	3.1	2.4
Roseville, CA	15.2	14.0	10.5	12.7	11.3	9.2	10.6	8.4	7.1	4.0	2.9	2.4
Round Rock, TX	12.8	15.8	12.6	12.7	15.7	11.7	12.2	11.8	6.4	1.6	1.9	0.6
San Antonio, TX	10.6	11.1	11.2	10.3	10.6	10.2	12.1	14.0	9.2	1.2	1.6	1.5
San Diego, CA	10.4	10.5	9.9	9.8	10.0	9.5	8.8	7.8	6.9	2.1	2.9	1.9
San Francisco, CA	10.3	9.1	8.3	10.1	9.0	8.1	6.7	6.0	6.8	1.8	1.8	1.8
San Jose, CA	6.3	6.4	5.3	6.3	6.4	5.3	7.7	8.2	4.8	1.4	0.9	0.9
Savannah, GA	n/a	n/a	n/a	n/a	n/a	n/a	n/a	n/a	n/a	n/a	n/a	n/a
Scottsdale, AZ	18.6	18.4	16.7	13.2	12.9	10.8	18.3	16.3	10.9	3.1	2.9	3.1
Seattle, WA	9.0	8.8	8.6	8.8	8.6	8.3	8.0	7.4	6.7	2.8	3.2	2.6
Sioux Falls, SD	n/a	n/a	n/a	n/a	n/a	n/a	n/a	n/a	n/a	n/a	n/a	n/a
Stamford, CT	10.2	11.0	11.1	9.0	9.7	9.8	8.4	8.7	6.3	2.0	1.3	2.0
Sterling Hgts, MI	12.1	12.7	12.4	12.0	12.6	12.2	15.8	16.4	16.8	3.3	2.6	1.8
Sunnyvale, CA	6.3	6.4	5.3	6.3	6.4	5.3	7.7	8.2	4.8	1.4	0.9	0.9
Tampa, FL	20.5	20.2	20.4	14.7	14.2	14.5	12.4	12.6	11.7	4.1	4.0	3.8
Temecula, CA	18.7	19.9	17.7	12.2	13.9	11.4	12.3	12.3	8.4	4.0	4.7	3.5
Thousand Oaks, CA	5.9	7.3	7.1	5.5	6.6	4.7	5.0	6.4	3.2	1.5	1.1	0.5
Virginia Beach, VA	10.4	11.1	10.8	9.9	10.4	10.3	6.2	8.8	9.4	2.3	2.8	3.2
Washington, DC	10.3	10.2	9.6	10.0	10.0	9.4	10.0	8.8	7.9	2.3	2.1	1.8
U.S.	14.5	14.3	14.2	11.3	11.3	11.1	10.6	10.2	9.5	2.6	2.6	2.5

Note: (1) Metropolitan Statistical Area—see Appendix B for areas included; (2) The percentage of the total housing inventory that is vacant; (3) The percentage of the housing inventory (excluding seasonal units) that is year-round vacant; (4) The percentage of rental inventory that is vacant for rent; (5) The percentage of homeowner inventory that is vacant for sale; n/a not available
Source: U.S. Census Bureau, Housing Vacancies and Homeownership Annual Statistics: 2011

Employment by Industry

Metro Area[1]	(A)	(B)	(C)	(D)	(E)	(F)	(G)	(H)	(I)	(J)	(K)	(L)	(M)
Albuquerque, NM	n/a	15.9	4.6	22.4	2.4	9.7	4.8	n/a	3.1	14.9	11.2	2.6	3.1
Alexandria, VA[2]	n/a	12.0	4.4	24.0	2.7	9.1	1.4	n/a	6.2	23.0	8.4	2.4	1.9
Anchorage, AK	4.2	16.0	5.8	21.7	2.9	10.1	1.1	1.8	3.6	11.8	11.7	6.8	2.7
Ann Arbor, MI	n/a	12.5	3.2	37.8	2.0	6.7	7.1	n/a	3.4	13.0	8.3	1.8	2.6
Athens, GA	n/a	n/a	n/a	34.5	n/a	9.0	n/a	n/a	n/a	8.1	11.3	n/a	n/a
Atlanta, GA	3.9	12.6	5.9	13.6	3.4	9.4	6.3	0.1	3.9	17.6	11.4	5.5	6.3
Austin, TX	n/a	11.6	5.7	20.9	2.5	11.5	6.4	n/a	4.2	14.6	10.8	1.7	5.3
Baltimore, MD	n/a	19.3	5.6	18.6	1.3	8.3	4.7	n/a	4.4	14.9	10.8	3.1	3.8
Bellevue, WA[2]	4.5	12.2	5.4	14.1	6.0	9.5	11.6	<0.1	3.6	14.6	10.3	3.4	4.8
Billings, MT	n/a	17.4	n/a	12.0	n/a	12.2	n/a	n/a	n/a	13.2	n/a	n/a	n/a
Boise City, ID	n/a	15.2	5.3	16.6	1.7	8.5	9.0	n/a	3.5	15.1	12.0	3.2	4.6
Boston, MA[4]	2.9	22.2	8.3	11.9	3.3	8.9	5.6	<0.1	3.9	18.0	9.1	2.4	3.5
Boulder, CO	n/a	12.4	4.4	20.1	5.4	11.0	9.6	n/a	3.2	18.4	9.2	0.9	3.1
Broken Arrow, OK	5.0	14.9	5.3	13.6	1.9	8.9	11.5	1.9	4.0	13.3	10.9	5.0	3.7
Cambridge, MA[4]	2.9	22.2	8.3	11.9	3.3	8.9	5.6	<0.1	3.9	18.0	9.1	2.4	3.5
Cape Coral, FL	n/a	11.8	5.0	18.0	1.4	14.6	2.3	n/a	4.2	13.5	16.6	1.7	2.9
Carlsbad, CA	4.5	12.3	5.3	18.4	1.9	12.6	7.4	<0.1	3.7	17.3	11.2	2.1	3.2
Cary, NC	n/a	12.6	5.1	16.6	3.3	10.5	5.3	n/a	4.4	17.9	12.2	2.2	4.2
Cedar Rapids, IA	n/a	14.0	7.2	12.0	3.5	7.6	15.5	n/a	3.5	9.5	11.8	6.7	3.7
Charleston, SC	n/a	12.0	4.3	19.7	1.6	11.8	8.1	n/a	3.5	14.4	12.8	4.0	2.8
Charlotte, NC	n/a	10.5	8.5	14.2	2.6	9.9	8.2	n/a	3.8	16.9	11.4	4.1	5.5
Chesapeake, VA	n/a	13.3	5.1	22.1	1.5	10.3	7.0	n/a	4.7	13.2	11.9	3.3	2.8
Chicago, IL[2]	3.0	15.4	6.9	12.6	2.0	9.0	8.8	<0.1	4.5	17.4	10.2	4.8	5.4
Clarksville, TN	n/a	13.0	3.2	24.7	1.1	11.5	11.7	n/a	3.2	9.6	12.8	2.6	n/a
Colorado Spgs., CO	n/a	12.5	6.5	20.0	2.9	11.7	5.1	n/a	5.7	15.5	11.8	1.8	2.0
Columbia, MD	n/a	19.3	5.6	18.6	1.3	8.3	4.7	n/a	4.4	14.9	10.8	3.1	3.8
Columbia, MO	n/a	n/a	n/a	34.4	n/a	n/a	n/a	n/a	n/a	n/a	11.8	n/a	n/a
Columbia, SC	n/a	12.1	7.8	22.4	1.6	9.1	8.3	n/a	3.6	12.4	11.4	3.3	3.9
Columbus, OH	n/a	14.5	7.7	16.6	1.8	9.3	7.1	n/a	3.8	16.1	11.1	4.8	4.1
Dallas, TX[2]	n/a	12.2	8.9	13.2	3.1	9.6	8.0	n/a	3.4	16.9	10.4	3.8	5.8
Denver, CO	n/a	12.2	7.4	14.5	3.6	10.4	5.0	n/a	4.1	17.5	10.6	3.8	5.1
Durham, NC	n/a	22.1	4.6	20.4	1.2	7.8	12.2	n/a	3.8	12.8	8.4	1.2	2.8
Edison, NJ[2]	n/a	15.3	5.6	14.4	2.5	8.0	5.9	n/a	4.6	17.3	13.1	4.1	5.7
El Paso, TX	n/a	13.7	4.4	23.3	1.7	10.4	6.2	n/a	3.4	11.0	13.0	4.6	3.5
Fargo, ND	n/a	15.1	7.1	14.8	2.7	10.2	7.5	n/a	3.9	11.0	12.2	3.6	6.2
Ft. Collins, CO	n/a	13.7	4.1	22.1	1.8	11.8	8.1	n/a	3.7	12.9	12.8	1.9	2.2
Ft. Worth, TX[2]	n/a	12.4	6.3	13.6	1.6	11.1	10.2	n/a	3.6	11.2	12.0	7.2	4.6
Gilbert, AZ	4.7	14.6	8.2	13.5	1.6	10.3	6.4	0.2	3.6	16.2	12.5	3.6	4.7
Green Bay, WI	n/a	14.0	7.0	12.3	1.1	9.5	16.8	n/a	5.1	11.9	9.9	4.6	4.4
Henderson, NV	4.7	8.9	4.8	11.5	1.1	32.3	2.4	<0.1	2.9	12.4	12.0	4.4	2.6
High Point, NC	n/a	13.7	5.7	12.8	1.6	8.8	15.3	n/a	3.9	13.8	10.3	4.6	5.3
Honolulu, HI	n/a	13.2	4.7	22.7	1.5	14.4	2.4	n/a	4.5	13.6	10.5	4.5	3.1
Houston, TX	6.4	12.5	5.3	14.2	1.2	9.3	8.7	3.5	3.6	14.7	10.6	4.7	5.2
Huntington, NY[2]	n/a	18.8	5.7	16.7	1.9	7.9	5.8	n/a	4.3	12.8	12.9	3.1	5.4
Huntsville, AL	n/a	8.4	2.9	24.4	1.2	8.5	10.6	n/a	3.7	22.2	11.0	1.3	2.7
Indianapolis, IN	4.6	14.3	6.5	14.0	1.6	9.8	9.1	0.1	3.8	15.0	10.2	6.1	4.9
Irvine, CA[2]	4.8	11.5	7.5	10.9	1.7	12.6	11.2	<0.1	3.1	18.3	10.8	2.0	5.6
Jackson, MS	3.9	15.5	5.9	23.0	1.7	8.5	6.3	0.3	4.0	11.2	11.5	4.0	4.1
Jacksonville, FL	4.3	14.8	9.7	12.9	1.6	10.8	4.5	<0.1	3.8	16.1	12.2	5.1	4.2
Jersey City, NJ[2]	n/a	19.6	10.3	14.3	3.9	8.6	3.1	n/a	4.2	15.6	9.7	3.4	4.3
Kansas City, MO	n/a	13.5	7.1	15.4	2.8	9.6	7.7	n/a	4.5	15.6	10.8	4.5	5.0
Kenosha, WI[2]	3.4	12.7	5.3	14.1	1.1	8.7	14.7	<0.1	3.3	14.3	12.8	2.4	7.0
Las Vegas, NV	4.7	8.9	4.8	11.5	1.1	32.3	2.4	<0.1	2.9	12.4	12.0	4.4	2.6
Lexington, KY	n/a	13.2	4.0	20.0	2.3	10.5	11.3	n/a	4.0	12.5	11.2	3.6	3.6
Lincoln, NE	n/a	15.0	7.7	22.6	1.2	9.0	7.3	n/a	4.0	10.2	10.9	6.1	2.3
Little Rock, AR	n/a	14.7	5.6	21.2	2.2	8.7	5.6	n/a	4.4	12.6	11.5	3.9	4.8

Table continued on next page.

Metro Area[1]	(A)	(B)	(C)	(D)	(E)	(F)	(G)	(H)	(I)	(J)	(K)	(L)	(M)
Los Angeles, CA[2]	2.7	14.1	5.5	14.8	5.3	10.2	9.4	0.1	3.5	14.3	10.7	3.9	5.5
Madison, WI	n/a	11.9	7.5	25.3	3.2	8.2	7.8	n/a	5.4	10.7	11.1	2.4	3.5
Manchester, NH[3]	n/a	19.6	6.7	11.5	3.3	8.3	8.0	n/a	4.2	13.9	13.2	n/a	4.1
Miami, FL[2]	2.9	16.7	6.1	14.4	1.7	11.0	3.5	<0.1	3.9	13.4	13.3	6.0	7.0
Minneapolis, MN	n/a	16.2	7.9	13.4	2.2	8.4	10.3	n/a	4.6	15.8	10.2	3.6	4.6
Murfreesboro, TN	n/a	15.9	6.1	13.7	2.5	10.2	8.3	n/a	4.3	14.5	11.3	4.0	4.8
Naperville, IL[2]	3.0	15.4	6.9	12.6	2.0	9.0	8.8	<0.1	4.5	17.4	10.2	4.8	5.4
Nashville, TN	n/a	15.9	6.1	13.7	2.5	10.2	8.3	n/a	4.3	14.5	11.3	4.0	4.8
New Orleans, LA	5.3	14.9	4.7	15.6	1.4	13.8	6.0	1.3	3.5	13.1	11.1	4.9	4.4
New York, NY[2]	n/a	19.6	10.3	14.3	3.9	8.6	3.1	n/a	4.2	15.6	9.7	3.4	4.3
Norman, OK	4.3	13.9	5.6	20.9	1.7	10.1	5.8	3.1	3.9	12.8	11.2	2.7	4.1
Olathe, KS	n/a	13.5	7.1	15.4	2.8	9.6	7.7	n/a	4.5	15.6	10.8	4.5	5.0
Omaha, NE	n/a	15.9	8.8	14.1	2.4	9.1	6.9	n/a	3.7	14.2	11.2	5.9	3.7
Orlando, FL	4.2	12.1	6.3	11.5	2.3	20.4	3.7	<0.1	4.6	15.8	12.3	3.1	3.7
Overland Park, KS	n/a	13.5	7.1	15.4	2.8	9.6	7.7	n/a	4.5	15.6	10.8	4.5	5.0
Oyster Bay, NY[2]	n/a	18.8	5.7	16.7	1.9	7.9	5.8	n/a	4.3	12.8	12.9	3.1	5.4
Pembroke Pines, FL[2]	3.8	13.6	7.4	13.9	2.3	11.1	3.8	n/a	4.3	16.6	14.0	3.1	6.0
Philadelphia, PA[2]	n/a	23.0	6.9	11.3	2.0	8.2	7.0	n/a	4.5	15.8	10.3	3.2	4.4
Phoenix, AZ	4.7	14.6	8.2	13.5	1.6	10.3	6.4	0.2	3.6	16.2	12.5	3.6	4.7
Pittsburgh, PA	4.2	21.6	6.1	10.9	1.6	9.2	7.5	0.8	4.5	14.3	11.5	3.9	4.1
Plano, TX[2]	n/a	12.2	8.9	13.2	3.1	9.6	8.0	n/a	3.4	16.9	10.4	3.8	5.8
Portland, OR	5.0	14.6	6.2	14.6	2.2	9.8	11.0	0.1	3.4	13.2	10.8	3.5	5.6
Providence, RI[3]	3.4	22.2	6.1	13.2	2.1	10.5	9.6	<0.1	4.4	10.9	11.4	2.5	3.6
Provo, UT	n/a	23.1	3.3	14.8	4.4	6.9	9.3	n/a	2.2	13.5	12.4	1.5	2.7
Raleigh, NC	n/a	12.6	5.1	16.6	3.3	10.5	5.3	n/a	4.4	17.9	12.2	2.2	4.2
Richmond, VA	n/a	13.8	7.4	18.6	1.5	8.8	5.0	n/a	4.8	16.1	10.9	3.4	4.5
Roseville, CA	4.3	13.1	5.9	27.6	2.1	9.6	4.1	<0.1	3.4	12.7	11.7	2.7	2.9
Round Rock, TX	n/a	11.6	5.7	20.9	2.5	11.5	6.4	n/a	4.2	14.6	10.8	1.7	5.3
San Antonio, TX	4.7	15.5	8.1	18.7	2.1	12.2	5.4	0.4	3.7	11.7	11.7	2.5	3.4
San Diego, CA	4.5	12.3	5.3	18.4	1.9	12.6	7.4	<0.1	3.7	17.3	11.2	2.1	3.2
San Francisco, CA[2]	3.3	11.6	8.0	14.0	4.4	13.3	3.8	<0.1	4.2	21.6	9.6	3.7	2.5
San Jose, CA	3.6	13.6	3.6	10.5	5.7	8.5	17.6	<0.1	2.7	19.4	9.5	1.4	4.0
Savannah, GA	n/a	15.9	3.4	15.3	0.9	13.0	9.5	n/a	4.5	11.6	11.8	6.6	3.7
Scottsdale, AZ	4.7	14.6	8.2	13.5	1.6	10.3	6.4	0.2	3.6	16.2	12.5	3.6	4.7
Seattle, WA[2]	4.5	12.2	5.4	14.1	6.0	9.5	11.6	<0.1	3.6	14.6	10.3	3.4	4.8
Sioux Falls, SD	n/a	20.5	10.9	9.4	2.1	9.2	8.9	n/a	3.5	8.7	13.7	3.7	5.1
Stamford, CT[3]	n/a	17.4	10.3	11.6	2.7	8.2	8.8	n/a	4.1	16.0	12.1	2.8	3.5
Sterling Hgts, MI[2]	n/a	15.3	6.1	9.5	1.7	8.7	12.4	n/a	4.4	19.7	12.1	1.8	5.0
Sunnyvale, CA	3.6	13.6	3.6	10.5	5.7	8.5	17.6	<0.1	2.7	19.4	9.5	1.4	4.0
Tampa, FL	4.3	16.0	8.0	13.7	2.3	11.2	5.2	<0.1	3.8	16.6	12.7	2.3	4.0
Temecula, CA	4.9	12.2	3.4	19.7	1.3	11.3	7.5	0.1	3.5	11.3	14.3	6.1	4.4
Thousand Oaks, CA	3.8	11.4	7.9	16.3	1.8	11.6	10.9	0.4	3.2	11.8	13.9	2.2	4.7
Virginia Beach, VA	n/a	13.3	5.1	22.1	1.5	10.3	7.0	n/a	4.7	13.2	11.9	3.3	2.8
Washington, DC[2]	n/a	12.0	4.4	24.0	2.7	9.1	1.4	n/a	6.2	23.0	8.4	2.4	1.9
U.S.	4.1	15.2	5.8	16.8	2.0	9.9	8.9	0.6	4.0	13.3	11.5	3.8	4.2

Note: All figures are percentages covering non-farm employment as of December 2011 and are not seasonally adjusted; (1) Figures cover the Metropolitan Statistical Area (MSA) except where noted. See Appendix B for areas included; (2) Metropolitan Division; (3) New England City and Town Area; (4) New England City and Town Area Division; (A) Construction; (B) Education and Health Services; (C) Financial Activities; (D) Government; (E) Information; (F) Leisure and Hospitality; (G) Manufacturing; (H) Mining and Logging; (I) Other Services; (J) Professional and Business Services; (K) Retail Trade; (L) Transportation and Utilities; (M) Wholesale Trade; n/a not available

Source: Bureau of Labor Statistics, http://stats.bls.gov

Labor Force, Employment and Job Growth: City

City	Civilian Labor Force			Workers Employed		
	Dec. 2010	Dec. 2011	% Chg.	Dec. 2010	Dec. 2011	% Chg.
Albuquerque, NM	263,601	259,931	-1.4	242,952	243,858	0.4
Alexandria, VA	96,695	99,117	2.5	92,424	94,516	2.3
Anchorage, AK	158,312	158,419	0.1	148,244	149,527	0.9
Ann Arbor, MI	63,099	62,103	-1.6	58,664	58,474	-0.3
Athens, GA	64,416	65,002	0.9	59,484	60,085	1.0
Atlanta, GA	232,329	235,446	1.3	206,028	210,598	2.2
Austin, TX	429,920	437,604	1.8	402,844	412,519	2.4
Baltimore, MD	274,017	276,429	0.9	245,658	250,713	2.1
Bellevue, WA	70,579	70,735	0.2	65,672	66,650	1.5
Billings, MT	58,498	58,675	0.3	55,316	55,995	1.2
Boise City, ID	106,962	109,041	1.9	97,521	100,874	3.4
Boston, MA	327,437	328,123	0.2	303,503	308,489	1.6
Boulder, CO	61,762	63,548	2.9	56,942	59,248	4.0
Broken Arrow, OK	47,469	47,735	0.6	44,782	45,322	1.2
Cambridge, MA	61,690	61,845	0.3	58,516	59,478	1.6
Cape Coral, FL	79,492	77,945	-1.9	69,476	70,234	1.1
Carlsbad, CA	47,115	48,251	2.4	43,939	45,410	3.3
Cary, NC	67,380	68,240	1.3	63,838	64,425	0.9
Cedar Rapids, IA	73,950	72,027	-2.6	69,600	67,747	-2.7
Charleston, SC	58,080	58,384	0.5	53,354	54,387	1.9
Charlotte, NC	344,387	344,240	0.0	315,035	314,451	-0.2
Chesapeake, VA	115,110	116,021	0.8	107,570	108,539	0.9
Chicago, IL	1,314,404	1,315,611	0.1	1,189,884	1,179,903	-0.8
Clarksville, TN	53,642	55,136	2.8	48,676	50,390	3.5
Colorado Spgs., CO	209,764	210,018	0.1	190,593	191,463	0.5
Columbia, MD	n/a	n/a	n/a	n/a	n/a	n/a
Columbia, MO	58,328	60,051	3.0	55,017	57,394	4.3
Columbia, SC	54,922	54,995	0.1	49,714	50,533	1.6
Columbus, OH	424,902	414,403	-2.5	392,390	387,740	-1.2
Dallas, TX	602,997	609,820	1.1	551,590	562,113	1.9
Denver, CO	319,329	325,874	2.0	288,061	295,836	2.7
Durham, NC	116,938	117,698	0.6	109,337	109,655	0.3
Edison, NJ	53,777	54,648	1.6	50,546	51,180	1.3
El Paso, TX	274,211	276,634	0.9	249,990	253,316	1.3
Fargo, ND	57,385	57,140	-0.4	55,304	55,356	0.1
Ft. Collins, CO	82,975	85,576	3.1	76,097	79,425	4.4
Ft. Worth, TX	338,904	342,699	1.1	311,270	317,744	2.1
Gilbert, AZ	118,345	118,842	0.4	112,626	113,586	0.9
Green Bay, WI	57,410	56,848	-1.0	51,922	51,633	-0.6
Henderson, NV	139,492	138,309	-0.8	119,913	122,019	1.8
High Point, NC	49,686	50,804	2.3	44,768	45,686	2.1
Honolulu, HI	441,056	444,744	0.8	419,892	421,022	0.3
Houston, TX	1,080,233	1,106,150	2.4	994,389	1,028,242	3.4
Huntington, NY	103,518	102,352	-1.1	97,144	95,951	-1.2
Huntsville, AL	90,774	91,862	1.2	84,297	85,874	1.9
Indianapolis, IN	403,445	410,978	1.9	366,365	373,380	1.9
Irvine, CA	81,681	83,158	1.8	76,160	78,312	2.8
Jackson, MS	82,262	83,529	1.5	74,537	75,583	1.4
Jacksonville, FL	417,935	418,417	0.1	371,136	379,176	2.2
Jersey City, NJ	116,396	118,479	1.8	104,596	106,956	2.3
Kansas City, MO	227,884	232,627	2.1	204,805	213,256	4.1
Kenosha, WI	48,638	48,381	-0.5	43,697	44,134	1.0
Las Vegas, NV	277,063	273,342	-1.3	233,762	237,867	1.8
Lexington, KY	157,131	155,894	-0.8	145,319	145,813	0.3
Lincoln, NE	142,326	147,514	3.6	137,422	142,315	3.6

Table continued on next page.

City	Civilian Labor Force Dec. 2010	Civilian Labor Force Dec. 2011	% Chg.	Workers Employed Dec. 2010	Workers Employed Dec. 2011	% Chg.
Little Rock, AR	98,119	97,912	-0.2	91,248	91,395	0.2
Los Angeles, CA	1,920,895	1,906,816	-0.7	1,653,729	1,663,084	0.6
Madison, WI	144,027	144,473	0.3	137,726	138,351	0.5
Manchester, NH	61,974	61,913	-0.1	58,202	58,542	0.6
Miami, FL	200,338	200,590	0.1	172,181	178,782	3.8
Minneapolis, MN	213,279	214,649	0.6	200,008	203,286	1.6
Murfreesboro, TN	56,085	56,571	0.9	51,593	52,687	2.1
Naperville, IL	75,809	75,675	-0.2	71,459	70,861	-0.8
Nashville, TN	332,223	334,839	0.8	305,276	311,750	2.1
New Orleans, LA	148,131	144,947	-2.1	135,477	133,707	-1.3
New York, NY	3,927,942	3,948,044	0.5	3,583,336	3,599,448	0.4
Norman, OK	54,333	54,846	0.9	51,726	52,401	1.3
Olathe, KS	61,009	61,212	0.3	57,271	57,979	1.2
Omaha, NE	236,084	244,589	3.6	225,948	233,849	3.5
Orlando, FL	136,757	135,243	-1.1	121,383	122,868	1.2
Overland Park, KS	95,913	96,238	0.3	90,071	91,185	1.2
Oyster Bay, NY	152,818	150,530	-1.5	143,348	141,589	-1.2
Pembroke Pines, FL	82,381	81,684	-0.8	74,479	75,293	1.1
Philadelphia, PA	646,182	644,690	-0.2	578,561	579,890	0.2
Phoenix, AZ	800,878	800,658	0.0	722,214	728,367	0.9
Pittsburgh, PA	152,110	154,598	1.6	140,667	144,400	2.7
Plano, TX	147,581	149,299	1.2	137,656	140,283	1.9
Portland, OR	310,800	315,295	1.4	282,198	290,279	2.9
Providence, RI	80,643	79,067	-2.0	70,192	69,132	-1.5
Provo, UT	68,637	68,566	-0.1	63,343	64,523	1.9
Raleigh, NC	206,489	209,124	1.3	192,821	194,595	0.9
Richmond, VA	101,190	102,291	1.1	91,741	93,223	1.6
Roseville, CA	54,742	54,780	0.1	48,587	49,540	2.0
Round Rock, TX	53,943	54,845	1.7	50,395	51,605	2.4
San Antonio, TX	646,232	649,341	0.5	602,179	607,078	0.8
San Diego, CA	694,528	708,004	1.9	624,205	645,104	3.3
San Francisco, CA	456,081	463,288	1.6	414,765	428,039	3.2
San Jose, CA	458,015	466,747	1.9	405,371	421,559	4.0
Savannah, GA	63,625	64,361	1.2	56,977	57,626	1.1
Scottsdale, AZ	128,435	128,808	0.3	120,385	121,410	0.9
Seattle, WA	377,030	378,637	0.4	348,306	353,489	1.5
Sioux Falls, SD	86,840	88,314	1.7	82,385	84,389	2.4
Stamford, CT	67,654	67,672	0.0	62,891	63,288	0.6
Sterling Hgts, MI	63,730	63,483	-0.4	58,274	58,796	0.9
Sunnyvale, CA	74,400	76,170	2.4	67,784	70,491	4.0
Tampa, FL	162,264	163,252	0.6	143,133	147,016	2.7
Temecula, CA	36,269	36,869	1.7	32,733	33,729	3.0
Thousand Oaks, CA	70,198	71,202	1.4	64,388	66,037	2.6
Virginia Beach, VA	219,880	221,985	1.0	206,492	208,352	0.9
Washington, DC	340,478	342,348	0.5	307,792	308,647	0.3
U.S.	153,156,000	153,373,000	0.1	139,159,000	140,681,000	1.1

Note: Data is not seasonally adjusted and covers workers 16 years of age and older
Source: Bureau of Labor Statistics, http://stats.bls.gov

Labor Force, Employment and Job Growth: Metro Area

Metro Area[1]	Civilian Labor Force			Workers Employed		
	Dec. 2010	Dec. 2011	% Chg.	Dec. 2010	Dec. 2011	% Chg.
Albuquerque, NM	409,834	403,769	-1.5	374,929	376,326	0.4
Alexandria, VA[2]	2,417,159	2,457,806	1.7	2,277,413	2,317,235	1.7
Anchorage, AK	202,320	202,675	0.2	188,153	189,781	0.9
Ann Arbor, MI	183,061	180,313	-1.5	170,996	170,441	-0.3
Athens, GA	106,744	107,479	0.7	98,651	99,649	1.0
Atlanta, GA	2,661,869	2,697,848	1.4	2,391,846	2,444,914	2.2
Austin, TX	902,646	918,215	1.7	840,510	860,696	2.4
Baltimore, MD	1,383,128	1,401,399	1.3	1,280,277	1,306,623	2.1
Bellevue, WA[2]	1,483,979	1,492,083	0.5	1,350,324	1,383,080	2.4
Billings, MT	85,204	85,505	0.4	80,398	81,385	1.2
Boise City, ID	292,392	297,808	1.9	263,652	272,718	3.4
Boston, MA[4]	1,542,443	1,545,454	0.2	1,437,727	1,461,346	1.6
Boulder, CO	171,897	177,145	3.1	160,365	166,859	4.0
Broken Arrow, OK	434,239	435,748	0.3	402,253	407,100	1.2
Cambridge, MA[4]	1,542,443	1,545,454	0.2	1,437,727	1,461,346	1.6
Cape Coral, FL	275,835	271,425	-1.6	241,175	243,805	1.1
Carlsbad, CA	1,555,853	1,586,031	1.9	1,398,252	1,445,067	3.3
Cary, NC	557,030	563,930	1.2	514,126	518,857	0.9
Cedar Rapids, IA	148,332	144,171	-2.8	139,176	135,472	-2.7
Charleston, SC	319,849	322,117	0.7	291,009	296,646	1.9
Charlotte, NC	851,629	846,945	-0.6	760,716	760,131	-0.1
Chesapeake, VA	816,488	823,932	0.9	759,028	765,680	0.9
Chicago, IL[2]	4,026,455	4,053,839	0.7	3,657,424	3,676,824	0.5
Clarksville, TN	114,219	115,797	1.4	103,012	105,700	2.6
Colorado Spgs., CO	304,273	304,234	0.0	275,536	276,793	0.5
Columbia, MD	1,383,128	1,401,399	1.3	1,280,277	1,306,623	2.1
Columbia, MO	94,543	97,328	2.9	88,690	92,521	4.3
Columbia, SC	366,913	368,534	0.4	333,605	339,100	1.6
Columbus, OH	970,812	946,232	-2.5	895,916	885,299	-1.2
Dallas, TX[2]	2,158,513	2,180,878	1.0	1,985,464	2,023,344	1.9
Denver, CO	1,366,243	1,391,518	1.8	1,245,326	1,278,938	2.7
Durham, NC	260,016	262,346	0.9	242,064	242,767	0.3
Edison, NJ[2]	1,183,238	1,200,353	1.4	1,088,479	1,102,122	1.3
El Paso, TX	322,362	325,199	0.9	291,214	295,088	1.3
Fargo, ND	118,139	118,780	0.5	113,300	114,431	1.0
Ft. Collins, CO	173,200	178,902	3.3	160,659	167,686	4.4
Ft. Worth, TX[2]	1,072,202	1,083,608	1.1	987,399	1,007,942	2.1
Gilbert, AZ	2,125,593	2,127,867	0.1	1,944,188	1,960,752	0.9
Green Bay, WI	171,052	169,643	-0.8	159,800	158,912	-0.6
Henderson, NV	952,734	942,225	-1.1	808,526	822,726	1.8
High Point, NC	355,892	362,706	1.9	319,890	326,336	2.0
Honolulu, HI	441,056	444,744	0.8	419,892	421,022	0.3
Houston, TX	2,917,366	2,986,579	2.4	2,676,277	2,767,389	3.4
Huntington, NY[2]	1,458,781	1,439,419	-1.3	1,356,608	1,339,955	-1.2
Huntsville, AL	206,531	208,703	1.1	191,689	195,276	1.9
Indianapolis, IN	876,004	891,271	1.7	802,574	817,942	1.9
Irvine, CA[2]	1,573,923	1,597,153	1.5	1,432,760	1,473,258	2.8
Jackson, MS	269,419	273,599	1.6	248,550	252,036	1.4
Jacksonville, FL	688,236	688,514	0.0	611,911	625,167	2.2
Jersey City, NJ[2]	5,658,379	5,697,298	0.7	5,184,743	5,213,699	0.6
Kansas City, MO	1,021,911	1,037,809	1.6	934,486	961,572	2.9
Kenosha, WI[2]	450,241	443,917	-1.4	407,790	402,654	-1.3
Las Vegas, NV	952,734	942,225	-1.1	808,526	822,726	1.8
Lexington, KY	244,730	242,479	-0.9	224,961	225,726	0.3
Lincoln, NE	166,153	172,202	3.6	160,218	165,923	3.6

Table continued on next page.

Metro Area[1]	Civilian Labor Force			Workers Employed		
	Dec. 2010	Dec. 2011	% Chg.	Dec. 2010	Dec. 2011	% Chg.
Little Rock, AR	343,271	342,811	-0.1	320,094	320,610	0.2
Los Angeles, CA[2]	4,943,016	4,931,592	-0.2	4,329,943	4,358,225	0.7
Madison, WI	341,563	342,337	0.2	324,709	326,183	0.5
Manchester, NH[3]	107,716	107,839	0.1	102,028	102,624	0.6
Miami, FL[2]	1,253,036	1,279,120	2.1	1,098,081	1,148,960	4.6
Minneapolis, MN	1,824,877	1,833,108	0.5	1,705,057	1,732,939	1.6
Murfreesboro, TN	823,775	831,576	0.9	758,483	774,567	2.1
Naperville, IL[2]	4,026,455	4,053,839	0.7	3,657,424	3,676,824	0.5
Nashville, TN	823,775	831,576	0.9	758,483	774,567	2.1
New Orleans, LA	541,914	531,205	-2.0	503,787	497,205	-1.3
New York, NY[2]	5,658,379	5,697,298	0.7	5,184,743	5,213,699	0.6
Norman, OK	567,828	572,012	0.7	533,083	540,026	1.3
Olathe, KS	1,021,911	1,037,809	1.6	934,486	961,572	2.9
Omaha, NE	444,254	457,378	3.0	423,346	436,050	3.0
Orlando, FL	1,125,039	1,113,686	-1.0	996,137	1,008,325	1.2
Overland Park, KS	1,021,911	1,037,809	1.6	934,486	961,572	2.9
Oyster Bay, NY[2]	1,458,781	1,439,419	-1.3	1,356,608	1,339,955	-1.2
Pembroke Pines, FL[2]	985,607	978,951	-0.7	885,009	894,687	1.1
Philadelphia, PA[2]	1,940,214	1,933,020	-0.4	1,782,318	1,786,411	0.2
Phoenix, AZ	2,125,593	2,127,867	0.1	1,944,188	1,960,752	0.9
Pittsburgh, PA	1,208,450	1,227,585	1.6	1,117,431	1,147,086	2.7
Plano, TX[2]	2,158,513	2,180,878	1.0	1,985,464	2,023,344	1.9
Portland, OR	1,193,027	1,197,593	0.4	1,076,210	1,100,953	2.3
Providence, RI[3]	713,425	701,670	-1.6	636,018	628,393	-1.2
Provo, UT	225,671	225,769	0.0	209,836	213,746	1.9
Raleigh, NC	557,030	563,930	1.2	514,126	518,857	0.9
Richmond, VA	647,263	654,793	1.2	600,602	610,300	1.6
Roseville, CA	1,026,651	1,026,925	0.0	897,351	914,943	2.0
Round Rock, TX	902,646	918,215	1.7	840,510	860,696	2.4
San Antonio, TX	989,732	992,776	0.3	918,035	925,503	0.8
San Diego, CA	1,555,853	1,586,031	1.9	1,398,252	1,445,067	3.3
San Francisco, CA[2]	956,585	974,257	1.8	875,013	903,017	3.2
San Jose, CA	897,548	915,977	2.1	802,344	834,386	4.0
Savannah, GA	175,491	177,044	0.9	159,717	161,537	1.1
Scottsdale, AZ	2,125,593	2,127,867	0.1	1,944,188	1,960,752	0.9
Seattle, WA[2]	1,483,979	1,492,083	0.5	1,350,324	1,383,080	2.4
Sioux Falls, SD	128,476	130,762	1.8	122,169	125,141	2.4
Stamford, CT[3]	477,386	475,420	-0.4	439,033	441,807	0.6
Sterling Hgts, MI[2]	1,195,732	1,187,612	-0.7	1,071,444	1,081,037	0.9
Sunnyvale, CA	897,548	915,977	2.1	802,344	834,386	4.0
Tampa, FL	1,298,265	1,301,885	0.3	1,140,498	1,171,437	2.7
Temecula, CA	1,761,147	1,778,349	1.0	1,514,937	1,561,051	3.0
Thousand Oaks, CA	427,638	432,361	1.1	382,087	391,874	2.6
Virginia Beach, VA	816,488	823,932	0.9	759,028	765,680	0.9
Washington, DC[2]	2,417,159	2,457,806	1.7	2,277,413	2,317,235	1.7
U.S.	153,156,000	153,373,000	0.1	139,159,000	140,681,000	1.1

Note: Data is not seasonally adjusted and covers workers 16 years of age and older; (1) Figures cover the Metropolitan Statistical Area (MSA) except where noted. See Appendix B for areas included; (2) Metropolitan Division; (3) New England City and Town Area; (4) New England City and Town Area Division

Source: Bureau of Labor Statistics, http://stats.bls.gov

Unemployment Rate: City

City	2011 Jan.	Feb.	Mar.	Apr.	May	Jun.	Jul.	Aug.	Sep.	Oct.	Nov.	Dec.
Albuquerque, NM	8.4	8.4	7.1	6.6	6.2	7.4	6.9	6.5	6.3	6.4	6.1	6.2
Alexandria, VA	4.9	4.7	4.5	4.1	4.5	4.8	4.5	4.8	4.8	4.5	4.3	4.6
Anchorage, AK	6.6	6.5	6.5	6.2	6.1	6.7	6.0	5.8	5.8	5.5	5.4	5.6
Ann Arbor, MI	7.4	7.0	7.5	6.6	7.2	8.2	8.3	7.7	7.0	6.1	5.5	5.8
Athens, GA	7.8	7.6	7.5	7.1	7.4	8.8	8.2	8.1	8.3	7.7	7.1	7.6
Atlanta, GA	11.5	11.2	10.7	10.5	10.6	11.7	11.5	11.7	11.5	11.0	10.3	10.6
Austin, TX	6.7	6.4	6.3	6.1	6.3	7.0	7.0	6.8	6.9	6.5	6.0	5.7
Baltimore, MD	10.8	10.2	9.9	9.5	9.9	10.8	11.1	10.9	10.3	9.9	9.2	9.3
Bellevue, WA	7.0	7.3	7.2	6.5	6.6	7.4	7.3	6.8	6.8	6.6	6.1	5.8
Billings, MT	6.1	5.6	5.6	4.8	5.0	5.9	5.5	5.5	5.2	5.0	4.6	4.6
Boise City, ID	9.5	9.3	9.0	8.6	8.1	8.5	7.9	7.9	7.8	7.7	7.7	7.5
Boston, MA	7.9	7.3	6.8	6.6	6.9	7.7	7.8	6.9	7.1	6.7	6.0	6.0
Boulder, CO	9.0	8.7	8.0	7.2	7.3	8.1	8.0	7.6	6.9	6.9	6.9	6.8
Broken Arrow, OK	5.9	6.0	4.9	4.3	4.6	5.2	5.1	4.5	5.0	5.2	4.9	5.1
Cambridge, MA	5.3	4.8	4.3	4.5	4.9	5.7	5.5	4.6	5.0	4.8	4.1	3.8
Cape Coral, FL	12.6	11.8	11.2	10.6	10.7	11.3	11.1	11.1	10.8	10.4	10.3	9.9
Carlsbad, CA	6.9	6.7	6.8	6.5	6.4	6.9	7.1	6.8	6.5	6.4	6.1	5.9
Cary, NC	5.8	5.7	5.5	5.7	5.9	6.3	6.2	6.5	6.1	5.8	5.6	5.6
Cedar Rapids, IA	6.3	6.3	6.4	6.0	5.7	6.1	5.8	6.4	5.8	5.7	5.4	5.9
Charleston, SC	7.5	7.8	7.0	7.1	7.9	9.1	8.8	8.7	7.9	7.2	6.9	6.8
Charlotte, NC	8.8	8.9	8.7	8.7	9.0	10.0	9.9	9.8	9.2	8.9	8.8	8.7
Chesapeake, VA	6.8	6.5	6.3	6.0	6.2	6.7	6.7	7.0	6.9	6.5	6.2	6.4
Chicago, IL	10.1	9.6	9.3	9.5	10.8	11.4	11.7	11.7	11.2	11.2	11.2	10.3
Clarksville, TN	10.3	10.2	9.7	9.4	9.5	10.3	9.8	9.9	9.9	9.6	9.3	8.6
Colorado Spgs., CO	10.4	10.2	9.8	8.9	9.1	9.6	9.4	9.1	8.4	8.5	8.5	8.8
Columbia, MD	n/a	n/a	n/a	n/a	n/a	n/a	n/a	n/a	n/a	n/a	n/a	n/a
Columbia, MO	6.3	5.7	5.6	5.1	5.7	6.5	6.3	6.4	5.3	5.1	4.5	4.4
Columbia, SC	8.3	8.5	8.5	8.3	10.0	11.5	11.3	10.6	9.8	9.0	8.0	8.1
Columbus, OH	8.3	8.1	7.5	7.3	7.5	8.3	8.3	8.0	7.8	7.7	6.8	6.4
Dallas, TX	9.0	8.6	8.5	8.2	8.4	9.2	9.1	8.8	8.9	8.7	8.1	7.8
Denver, CO	10.9	10.7	10.2	9.1	9.2	9.4	9.3	9.3	8.7	8.7	8.8	9.2
Durham, NC	7.1	7.0	6.8	6.9	7.1	7.8	7.7	8.0	7.7	7.2	6.9	6.8
Edison, NJ	6.6	7.0	6.7	7.0	7.2	7.9	8.0	7.0	7.1	6.8	7.0	6.3
El Paso, TX	9.5	9.2	9.2	8.9	9.1	10.0	10.1	9.8	9.7	9.4	8.7	8.4
Fargo, ND	4.3	4.1	4.0	3.3	3.1	3.8	3.1	3.3	2.9	2.9	2.9	3.1
Ft. Collins, CO	9.7	9.5	8.8	7.7	7.6	8.0	7.9	7.6	6.9	7.0	7.1	7.2
Ft. Worth, TX	8.7	8.3	8.4	8.0	8.3	9.1	9.1	8.7	8.7	8.2	7.6	7.3
Gilbert, AZ	5.3	5.0	4.9	4.6	4.5	5.1	4.9	4.8	4.5	4.5	4.3	4.4
Green Bay, WI	11.0	11.2	10.8	10.0	10.1	11.2	10.8	10.1	9.6	9.2	9.4	9.2
Henderson, NV	12.1	12.8	12.4	11.1	11.3	12.7	12.8	13.0	12.5	12.0	11.6	11.8
High Point, NC	10.1	9.8	9.6	9.3	9.9	10.6	10.7	11.0	10.5	10.5	10.1	10.1
Honolulu, HI	5.4	5.3	5.0	4.6	4.9	5.7	5.4	5.5	5.7	5.6	5.7	5.3
Houston, TX	8.4	8.1	8.0	7.7	7.9	8.8	8.7	8.4	8.5	7.9	7.3	7.0
Huntington, NY	7.2	7.0	6.4	5.8	6.1	6.4	6.2	5.8	6.0	5.9	6.0	6.3
Huntsville, AL	8.2	7.7	7.4	7.5	7.9	9.0	8.6	8.2	8.1	7.4	6.8	6.5
Indianapolis, IN	9.4	9.3	8.9	8.5	8.7	9.1	9.0	9.2	9.0	9.4	9.3	9.1
Irvine, CA	6.9	6.7	6.8	6.5	6.4	6.9	7.0	6.8	6.5	6.4	6.1	5.8
Jackson, MS	10.4	10.1	9.8	9.6	9.4	10.5	10.5	9.3	10.1	9.9	9.4	9.5
Jacksonville, FL	11.6	10.7	10.3	10.0	10.1	10.9	11.0	11.0	10.3	9.8	9.7	9.4
Jersey City, NJ	10.5	10.6	10.5	10.4	11.1	11.6	10.9	10.3	10.8	10.4	10.3	9.7
Kansas City, MO	10.9	10.1	9.6	9.3	10.0	9.7	9.7	10.4	9.6	9.1	8.5	8.3
Kenosha, WI	11.1	11.2	10.8	10.3	10.3	10.7	11.2	10.5	9.9	9.6	9.8	8.8
Las Vegas, NV	13.5	14.3	13.8	12.3	12.7	14.1	14.3	14.6	13.9	13.3	12.6	13.0
Lexington, KY	8.7	8.6	7.9	7.7	7.3	7.6	7.5	7.2	7.8	7.0	6.7	6.5
Lincoln, NE	4.1	4.1	4.0	3.8	3.6	4.1	3.8	3.6	3.5	3.3	3.1	3.5

Table continued on next page.

City	2011											
	Jan.	Feb.	Mar.	Apr.	May	Jun.	Jul.	Aug.	Sep.	Oct.	Nov.	Dec.
Little Rock, AR	7.6	7.3	7.1	6.7	7.2	8.1	7.9	7.7	7.5	6.8	6.6	6.7
Los Angeles, CA	14.4	13.5	13.4	12.9	13.0	13.6	14.6	13.9	13.4	13.1	12.7	12.8
Madison, WI	5.0	5.2	4.9	4.7	5.1	6.0	5.5	5.3	5.2	5.0	4.4	4.2
Manchester, NH	6.6	6.4	5.7	5.1	5.3	5.6	5.8	5.8	5.7	5.4	5.4	5.4
Miami, FL	13.0	12.7	13.2	14.2	14.6	14.8	13.3	13.4	12.2	11.3	10.0	10.9
Minneapolis, MN	6.5	6.2	6.1	6.0	6.3	7.4	7.5	7.2	6.3	5.8	5.4	5.3
Murfreesboro, TN	8.9	8.8	8.4	8.7	8.9	9.7	9.2	9.2	9.0	7.9	7.4	6.9
Naperville, IL	6.3	6.0	5.8	6.1	7.3	8.1	8.1	7.9	7.4	7.2	7.1	6.4
Nashville, TN	8.6	8.7	8.3	8.8	8.5	9.1	8.5	8.8	8.7	7.8	7.3	6.9
New Orleans, LA	10.0	9.0	9.1	8.4	9.3	9.6	9.7	9.1	8.6	8.7	7.8	7.8
New York, NY	9.4	9.1	8.6	8.4	8.6	8.9	9.3	9.2	9.1	9.2	8.9	8.8
Norman, OK	5.0	4.9	4.1	3.7	4.0	5.0	4.7	4.2	4.3	4.8	4.4	4.5
Olathe, KS	6.9	6.4	6.6	5.8	5.8	6.0	6.3	6.1	6.2	6.0	5.5	5.3
Omaha, NE	5.0	4.9	4.7	4.5	4.4	4.8	4.7	4.4	4.2	4.1	3.9	4.4
Orlando, FL	11.5	10.6	10.2	9.7	9.7	10.2	10.3	10.3	10.0	9.7	9.4	9.2
Overland Park, KS	6.8	6.4	6.6	5.7	5.8	6.0	6.3	6.1	6.2	6.0	5.5	5.3
Oyster Bay, NY	6.7	6.5	5.9	5.8	6.1	6.5	6.4	6.1	6.2	5.9	6.0	5.9
Pembroke Pines, FL	10.0	9.1	8.7	8.3	8.3	9.0	9.0	9.0	8.7	8.3	8.2	7.8
Philadelphia, PA	10.7	10.4	10.0	9.3	10.2	10.7	11.2	11.6	11.0	10.6	10.5	10.1
Phoenix, AZ	10.7	10.2	10.0	9.4	9.2	10.3	10.0	9.7	9.3	9.3	8.8	9.0
Pittsburgh, PA	7.6	7.4	7.3	6.7	7.3	7.7	8.1	8.4	7.4	6.9	7.0	6.6
Plano, TX	7.4	7.1	7.2	6.9	7.1	7.6	7.4	7.2	7.3	6.9	6.4	6.0
Portland, OR	9.8	9.7	9.3	8.3	8.2	9.0	8.6	8.7	8.4	8.3	7.6	7.9
Providence, RI	13.5	13.3	13.3	13.4	14.2	14.0	15.0	13.4	12.8	13.0	12.7	12.6
Provo, UT	9.1	9.1	8.4	7.7	8.3	8.7	8.8	8.7	7.5	7.0	6.0	5.9
Raleigh, NC	7.2	7.0	6.8	6.8	7.0	7.8	7.7	8.0	7.6	7.2	6.9	6.9
Richmond, VA	9.8	9.2	8.9	8.4	8.9	9.3	9.4	9.9	9.5	9.0	8.5	8.9
Roseville, CA	11.6	11.5	11.6	11.0	10.9	11.4	11.3	10.9	10.4	10.4	9.9	9.6
Round Rock, TX	7.0	6.6	6.7	6.2	6.5	7.4	7.3	6.9	7.0	6.7	6.1	5.9
San Antonio, TX	7.4	7.0	7.0	6.8	7.1	7.9	8.0	7.6	7.7	7.3	6.7	6.5
San Diego, CA	10.3	10.1	10.2	9.8	9.6	10.4	10.6	10.2	9.8	9.7	9.2	8.9
San Francisco, CA	9.5	9.1	9.2	8.5	8.4	9.0	9.1	8.8	8.3	8.1	7.8	7.6
San Jose, CA	11.7	11.4	11.4	11.0	10.8	11.4	11.4	11.0	10.7	10.5	10.1	9.7
Savannah, GA	10.7	10.3	9.9	9.5	9.8	11.4	11.3	11.4	11.2	10.6	9.9	10.5
Scottsdale, AZ	6.8	6.5	6.4	6.0	5.9	6.6	6.4	6.2	5.9	5.9	5.6	5.7
Seattle, WA	7.9	8.0	7.8	7.4	7.3	8.2	8.1	7.6	7.6	7.4	7.0	6.6
Sioux Falls, SD	5.5	5.8	5.7	5.0	4.9	4.8	4.5	4.7	4.2	4.1	3.9	4.4
Stamford, CT	7.9	8.1	7.7	7.1	7.4	7.3	7.5	7.5	7.1	7.1	6.7	6.5
Sterling Hgts, MI	9.0	9.2	9.0	8.6	8.9	9.8	11.2	9.8	9.1	8.3	7.3	7.4
Sunnyvale, CA	9.0	8.8	8.9	8.5	8.3	8.8	8.8	8.5	8.2	8.1	7.8	7.5
Tampa, FL	12.2	11.3	11.0	10.5	10.7	11.3	11.3	11.0	10.8	10.2	10.2	9.9
Temecula, CA	9.8	9.7	9.7	9.2	9.0	9.9	10.4	10.0	9.6	9.4	8.7	8.5
Thousand Oaks, CA	8.5	8.1	8.1	7.5	7.3	8.0	8.2	8.2	7.8	7.6	7.4	7.3
Virginia Beach, VA	6.5	6.1	6.0	5.6	5.6	6.0	5.9	6.3	6.4	6.1	5.8	6.1
Washington, DC	10.5	9.8	10.1	9.4	10.0	11.3	10.9	10.4	10.5	10.1	9.9	9.8
U.S.	9.8	9.5	9.2	8.7	8.7	9.3	9.3	9.1	8.8	8.5	8.2	8.3

Note: Data is not seasonally adjusted and covers workers 16 years of age and older; All figures are percentages
Source: Bureau of Labor Statistics, http://stats.bls.gov

Unemployment Rate: Metro Area

Metro Area[1]	2011											
	Jan.	Feb.	Mar.	Apr.	May	Jun.	Jul.	Aug.	Sep.	Oct.	Nov.	Dec.
Albuquerque, NM	9.0	9.1	7.7	7.2	6.8	8.2	7.7	7.2	6.9	7.0	6.7	6.8
Alexandria, VA[2]	6.2	6.0	5.9	5.5	5.8	6.3	6.2	6.2	6.2	5.8	5.5	5.7
Anchorage, AK	7.4	7.3	7.3	6.8	6.6	7.2	6.4	6.2	6.2	6.0	6.1	6.4
Ann Arbor, MI	6.9	6.5	7.0	6.2	6.8	7.7	7.8	7.2	6.6	5.7	5.1	5.5
Athens, GA	8.0	7.6	7.3	7.1	7.2	8.3	7.8	7.8	8.0	7.5	6.9	7.3
Atlanta, GA	10.4	10.2	9.8	9.6	9.7	10.5	10.3	10.3	10.2	9.9	9.2	9.4
Austin, TX	7.3	6.9	6.8	6.5	6.8	7.6	7.6	7.4	7.5	7.1	6.6	6.3
Baltimore, MD	7.9	7.7	7.4	7.0	7.3	7.8	7.9	7.8	7.6	7.1	6.6	6.8
Bellevue, WA[2]	9.3	9.3	8.8	8.1	8.3	9.0	8.7	8.0	8.2	8.1	7.7	7.3
Billings, MT	6.4	6.0	5.9	5.1	5.2	6.0	5.6	5.6	5.4	5.2	4.7	4.8
Boise City, ID	10.8	10.5	10.1	9.5	8.8	9.7	9.1	9.0	8.5	8.4	8.5	8.4
Boston, MA[4]	7.4	7.1	6.6	6.2	6.3	6.8	6.8	6.0	6.3	6.0	5.4	5.4
Boulder, CO	7.7	7.5	6.9	6.2	6.3	7.0	6.9	6.6	5.9	5.9	5.9	5.8
Broken Arrow, OK	7.7	7.8	6.6	5.6	6.0	6.7	6.4	6.0	6.4	6.7	6.4	6.6
Cambridge, MA[4]	7.4	7.1	6.6	6.2	6.3	6.8	6.8	6.0	6.3	6.0	5.4	5.4
Cape Coral, FL	12.7	11.7	11.2	10.8	10.9	11.7	11.6	11.5	11.3	10.7	10.5	10.2
Carlsbad, CA	10.4	10.1	10.2	9.8	9.6	10.4	10.6	10.2	9.8	9.7	9.2	8.9
Cary, NC	8.3	8.1	7.8	7.8	8.0	8.6	8.5	8.8	8.4	8.1	7.8	8.0
Cedar Rapids, IA	6.8	6.7	6.7	6.0	5.6	5.9	5.6	6.1	5.6	5.6	5.4	6.0
Charleston, SC	8.3	8.4	7.9	8.0	8.7	9.8	9.5	9.5	9.0	8.5	7.8	7.9
Charlotte, NC	11.2	10.9	10.5	10.3	10.6	11.3	11.3	11.3	10.7	10.3	9.9	10.3
Chesapeake, VA	7.6	7.3	7.0	6.5	6.6	7.0	6.9	7.3	7.3	7.0	6.7	7.1
Chicago, IL[2]	9.9	9.6	9.4	9.5	10.1	10.9	10.8	10.5	10.1	9.8	9.5	9.3
Clarksville, TN	11.0	10.9	10.1	10.3	10.1	10.6	10.3	10.0	10.2	9.4	9.0	8.7
Colorado Spgs., CO	10.7	10.5	10.1	9.1	9.3	9.8	9.6	9.3	8.6	8.6	8.7	9.0
Columbia, MD	7.9	7.7	7.4	7.0	7.3	7.8	7.9	7.8	7.6	7.1	6.6	6.8
Columbia, MO	6.9	6.5	6.2	5.6	6.0	6.8	6.6	6.7	5.6	5.5	4.9	4.9
Columbia, SC	8.3	8.5	8.0	8.1	8.9	10.0	9.9	9.7	9.1	8.5	7.8	8.0
Columbus, OH	8.5	8.2	7.6	7.3	7.4	8.2	8.2	7.8	7.6	7.6	6.6	6.4
Dallas, TX[2]	8.5	8.2	8.1	7.7	7.9	8.7	8.7	8.4	8.4	8.1	7.5	7.2
Denver, CO	9.9	9.8	9.3	8.3	8.5	8.8	8.6	8.5	7.9	7.8	7.9	8.1
Durham, NC	7.6	7.4	7.1	7.1	7.3	8.0	8.0	8.3	7.8	7.6	7.3	7.5
Edison, NJ[2]	9.0	9.2	8.8	8.4	8.6	9.0	9.1	8.3	8.3	8.3	8.4	8.2
El Paso, TX	10.4	10.1	10.0	9.7	10.0	10.9	10.9	10.6	10.5	10.2	9.5	9.3
Fargo, ND	4.7	4.7	4.4	3.7	3.5	4.2	3.7	3.9	3.3	3.1	3.1	3.7
Ft. Collins, CO	8.5	8.3	7.7	6.7	6.6	7.0	6.9	6.6	6.0	6.1	6.2	6.3
Ft. Worth, TX[2]	8.4	8.1	8.0	7.6	7.8	8.6	8.5	8.3	8.2	7.8	7.3	7.0
Gilbert, AZ	9.3	8.8	8.7	8.1	8.0	9.0	8.7	8.4	8.0	8.1	7.7	7.9
Green Bay, WI	7.7	8.0	7.6	7.0	7.2	7.9	7.4	7.0	6.7	6.5	6.4	6.3
Henderson, NV	13.7	13.7	13.3	12.0	12.4	13.8	14.0	14.3	13.6	13.1	12.4	12.7
High Point, NC	10.9	10.6	10.2	10.0	10.2	10.9	10.9	11.0	10.5	10.2	9.8	10.0
Honolulu, HI	5.4	5.3	5.0	4.6	4.9	5.7	5.4	5.5	5.7	5.6	5.7	5.3
Houston, TX	8.8	8.4	8.3	8.0	8.2	9.0	8.9	8.6	8.6	8.1	7.5	7.3
Huntington, NY[2]	7.9	7.7	7.1	6.6	6.7	7.1	7.1	6.8	6.9	6.6	6.7	6.9
Huntsville, AL	8.2	7.9	7.5	7.5	7.9	8.9	8.4	8.1	8.1	7.4	6.8	6.4
Indianapolis, IN	8.7	8.6	8.1	7.6	7.8	8.0	8.0	8.3	8.1	8.3	8.3	8.2
Irvine, CA[2]	9.2	8.9	9.1	8.6	8.5	9.2	9.3	9.0	8.6	8.5	8.1	7.8
Jackson, MS	8.6	8.5	8.2	8.0	7.8	8.8	8.8	7.7	8.6	8.4	7.8	7.9
Jacksonville, FL	11.5	10.6	10.2	9.8	9.7	10.4	10.5	10.4	10.0	9.6	9.5	9.2
Jersey City, NJ[2]	9.2	9.0	8.4	8.2	8.5	8.7	8.7	8.5	8.5	8.6	8.7	8.5
Kansas City, MO	9.7	9.2	8.9	8.1	8.4	8.5	8.4	8.7	8.2	7.8	7.4	7.3
Kenosha, WI[2]	10.4	10.6	10.3	8.9	8.1	8.8	9.0	9.1	8.9	9.0	8.6	9.3
Las Vegas, NV	13.7	13.7	13.3	12.0	12.4	13.8	14.0	14.3	13.6	13.1	12.4	12.7
Lexington, KY	9.4	9.2	8.4	8.1	7.8	8.0	8.1	7.4	8.0	7.4	7.0	6.9
Lincoln, NE	4.3	4.2	4.1	3.9	3.7	4.2	3.9	3.6	3.6	3.4	3.2	3.6

Table continued on next page.

Metro Area[1]	2011											
	Jan.	Feb.	Mar.	Apr.	May	Jun.	Jul.	Aug.	Sep.	Oct.	Nov.	Dec.
Little Rock, AR	7.5	7.1	6.8	6.5	7.0	7.7	7.5	7.3	7.1	6.7	6.3	6.5
Los Angeles, CA[2]	12.9	12.3	12.1	11.7	12.0	12.5	13.2	12.9	12.5	12.1	11.6	11.6
Madison, WI	5.7	6.0	5.7	5.2	5.4	6.1	5.5	5.3	5.2	5.1	4.7	4.7
Manchester, NH[3]	5.9	5.7	5.1	4.6	4.8	5.2	5.3	5.2	5.0	4.9	4.8	4.8
Miami, FL[2]	11.6	11.4	11.7	12.2	12.3	12.4	11.5	11.4	10.8	10.7	9.5	10.2
Minneapolis, MN	7.0	6.9	6.8	6.3	6.3	7.0	7.4	6.7	6.0	5.4	5.2	5.5
Murfreesboro, TN	8.8	8.8	8.3	8.6	8.4	8.9	8.4	8.5	8.5	7.6	7.2	6.9
Naperville, IL[2]	9.9	9.6	9.4	9.5	10.1	10.9	10.8	10.5	10.1	9.8	9.5	9.3
Nashville, TN	8.8	8.8	8.3	8.6	8.4	8.9	8.4	8.5	8.5	7.6	7.2	6.9
New Orleans, LA	8.4	7.8	7.9	7.2	8.0	8.0	7.8	7.3	6.9	7.1	6.5	6.4
New York, NY[2]	9.2	9.0	8.4	8.2	8.5	8.7	8.7	8.5	8.5	8.6	8.7	8.5
Norman, OK	6.3	6.2	5.2	4.6	4.9	5.7	5.5	5.0	5.5	5.8	5.4	5.6
Olathe, KS	9.7	9.2	8.9	8.1	8.4	8.5	8.4	8.7	8.2	7.8	7.4	7.3
Omaha, NE	5.5	5.4	5.2	4.8	4.6	5.0	4.8	4.6	4.5	4.3	4.1	4.7
Orlando, FL	11.8	10.8	10.4	10.0	9.9	10.4	10.5	10.4	10.2	9.8	9.7	9.5
Overland Park, KS	9.7	9.2	8.9	8.1	8.4	8.5	8.4	8.7	8.2	7.8	7.4	7.3
Oyster Bay, NY[2]	7.9	7.7	7.1	6.6	6.7	7.1	7.1	6.8	6.9	6.6	6.7	6.9
Pembroke Pines, FL[2]	10.5	9.7	9.3	8.9	9.0	9.6	9.7	9.5	9.4	8.9	8.9	8.6
Philadelphia, PA[2]	8.6	8.5	8.1	7.4	8.0	8.4	8.7	9.1	8.2	7.8	7.9	7.6
Phoenix, AZ	9.3	8.8	8.7	8.1	8.0	9.0	8.7	8.4	8.0	8.1	7.7	7.9
Pittsburgh, PA	8.1	7.9	7.4	6.6	6.9	7.4	7.5	7.8	6.8	6.4	6.6	6.6
Plano, TX[2]	8.5	8.2	8.1	7.7	7.9	8.7	8.7	8.4	8.4	8.1	7.5	7.2
Portland, OR	10.3	10.2	9.9	9.1	8.9	9.5	9.1	9.2	8.7	8.6	8.0	8.1
Providence, RI[3]	12.0	12.1	11.9	10.9	11.1	10.4	11.2	10.3	10.1	10.1	10.2	10.4
Provo, UT	8.3	8.3	7.6	7.0	7.5	7.9	8.0	7.9	6.8	6.3	5.4	5.3
Raleigh, NC	8.3	8.1	7.8	7.8	8.0	8.6	8.5	8.8	8.4	8.1	7.8	8.0
Richmond, VA	7.7	7.3	7.0	6.5	6.7	7.0	7.0	7.3	7.3	6.8	6.5	6.8
Roseville, CA	12.9	12.6	12.7	12.0	11.7	12.4	12.5	11.9	11.4	11.4	10.9	10.9
Round Rock, TX	7.3	6.9	6.8	6.5	6.8	7.6	7.6	7.4	7.5	7.1	6.6	6.3
San Antonio, TX	7.8	7.4	7.3	7.0	7.3	8.1	8.2	7.9	8.0	7.5	7.0	6.8
San Diego, CA	10.4	10.1	10.2	9.8	9.6	10.4	10.6	10.2	9.8	9.7	9.2	8.9
San Francisco, CA[2]	8.9	8.6	8.7	8.3	8.1	8.8	8.8	8.5	8.1	7.9	7.6	7.3
San Jose, CA	10.8	10.5	10.6	10.1	9.9	10.4	10.4	10.0	9.6	9.5	9.2	8.9
Savannah, GA	9.2	9.1	8.6	8.4	8.5	9.5	9.3	9.5	9.3	9.0	8.4	8.8
Scottsdale, AZ	9.3	8.8	8.7	8.1	8.0	9.0	8.7	8.4	8.0	8.1	7.7	7.9
Seattle, WA[2]	9.3	9.3	8.8	8.1	8.3	9.0	8.7	8.0	8.2	8.1	7.7	7.3
Sioux Falls, SD	5.3	5.5	5.4	4.7	4.6	4.5	4.3	4.5	4.0	3.9	3.8	4.3
Stamford, CT[3]	8.9	9.0	8.7	8.3	8.5	8.5	8.5	8.3	7.9	7.8	7.4	7.1
Sterling Hgts, MI[2]	11.1	11.2	11.1	10.5	10.8	11.6	13.0	11.9	10.8	10.0	8.8	9.0
Sunnyvale, CA	10.8	10.5	10.6	10.1	9.9	10.4	10.4	10.0	9.6	9.5	9.2	8.9
Tampa, FL	12.5	11.5	11.0	10.6	10.6	11.1	11.1	11.0	10.8	10.4	10.3	10.0
Temecula, CA	14.2	13.9	13.9	13.4	13.2	14.3	14.7	14.1	13.5	13.3	12.5	12.2
Thousand Oaks, CA	10.9	10.5	10.4	9.7	9.5	10.3	10.6	10.5	10.1	9.8	9.5	9.4
Virginia Beach, VA	7.6	7.3	7.0	6.5	6.6	7.0	6.9	7.3	7.3	7.0	6.7	7.1
Washington, DC[2]	6.2	6.0	5.9	5.5	5.8	6.3	6.2	6.2	6.2	5.8	5.5	5.7
U.S.	9.8	9.5	9.2	8.7	8.7	9.3	9.3	9.1	8.8	8.5	8.2	8.3

Note: Data is not seasonally adjusted and covers workers 16 years of age and older; All figures are percentages; (1) Figures cover the Metropolitan Statistical Area (MSA) except where noted. See Appendix B for areas included; (2) Metropolitan Division; (3) New England City and Town Area; (4) New England City and Town Area Division

Source: Bureau of Labor Statistics, http://stats.bls.gov

Average Hourly Wages: Occupations A – C

Metro Area	Accountants/ Auditors	Automotive Mechanics	Book-keepers	Carpenters	Cashiers	Clerks, Gen. Office	Clerks, Recep./Info.
Albuquerque, NM	31.32	17.27	16.78	20.00	9.94	12.22	11.83
Alexandria, VA	40.35	22.35	21.08	21.54	10.39	16.13	14.63
Anchorage, AK	33.68	25.41	19.46	29.15	11.32	17.00	14.42
Ann Arbor, MI	31.37	22.10	17.80	23.91	10.16	13.88	12.85
Athens, GA	26.19	19.21	14.55	16.56	9.40	11.01	11.62
Atlanta, GA	34.96	18.96	17.81	19.36	9.39	12.78	12.76
Austin, TX	33.31	22.03	18.23	15.60	9.71	15.47	12.65
Baltimore, MD	35.18	19.62	19.69	20.98	10.52	14.75	13.54
Bellevue, WA	33.93	19.26	19.53	25.62	12.86	16.09	14.48
Billings, MT	31.72	17.39	15.52	17.21	9.26	12.99	11.87
Boise City, ID	29.96	17.63	16.54	19.46	9.52	13.48	12.37
Boston, MA	38.02	22.17	20.63	29.24	10.44	17.04	14.75
Boulder, CO	35.82	17.99	18.53	19.50	10.87	14.83	13.63
Broken Arrow, OK	27.71	16.66	15.32	14.33	9.02	12.08	11.59
Cambridge, MA	38.02	22.17	20.63	29.24	10.44	17.04	14.75
Cape Coral, FL	31.82	18.95	16.69	19.21	9.82	12.63	12.90
Carlsbad, CA	35.75	20.90	19.21	25.56	10.68	14.81	13.88
Cary, NC	31.67	20.79	17.33	16.82	9.15	13.46	12.38
Cedar Rapids, IA	27.78	18.97	15.77	20.20	9.05	14.60	12.67
Charleston, SC	29.13	19.27	16.94	17.24	9.10	12.66	12.68
Charlotte, NC	34.36	21.08	16.96	16.80	9.43	13.44	12.88
Chesapeake, VA	30.67	19.95	16.71	18.69	9.19	12.73	12.15
Chicago, IL	35.94	18.50	18.47	25.37	9.93	14.99	13.44
Clarksville, TN	28.47	16.56	15.66	19.68	8.87	12.72	11.71
Colorado Spgs., CO	29.17	22.11	16.11	18.63	9.47	13.57	12.62
Columbia, MD	35.18	19.62	19.69	20.98	10.52	14.75	13.54
Columbia, MO	24.54	19.22	15.51	20.75	9.46	12.53	11.00
Columbia, SC	26.80	19.36	16.97	16.13	8.61	13.51	13.24
Columbus, OH	31.97	18.58	19.70	19.25	9.78	14.54	12.02
Dallas, TX	35.62	17.75	18.20	15.57	9.39	14.88	12.90
Denver, CO	36.14	19.46	17.90	19.07	10.28	16.09	14.04
Durham, NC	35.05	20.23	18.17	17.28	9.68	13.86	12.72
Edison, NJ	37.42	20.89	19.68	23.91	10.08	15.19	13.45
El Paso, TX	24.24	14.67	14.00	12.20	8.69	11.60	10.11
Fargo, ND	26.49	19.26	16.44	17.33	8.74	12.62	12.16
Ft. Collins, CO	31.89	20.64	15.91	19.26	9.79	13.91	13.25
Ft. Worth, TX	34.28	18.26	17.07	14.74	9.34	14.34	12.95
Gilbert, AZ	29.62	19.98	17.77	19.96	10.97	14.89	13.73
Green Bay, WI	29.28	18.36	16.38	21.58	9.32	14.08	13.20
Henderson, NV	30.67	19.70	17.63	28.18	10.52	14.60	13.25
High Point, NC	31.58	18.40	16.36	14.81	8.94	12.70	12.85
Honolulu, HI	30.56	22.37	17.73	33.41	10.79	14.69	14.52
Houston, TX	35.72	18.16	18.56	17.02	9.44	14.59	12.71
Huntington, NY	41.67	20.79	20.39	28.31	10.20	14.77	14.13
Huntsville, AL	31.84	18.02	15.77	15.15	8.95	10.91	11.24
Indianapolis, IN	33.54	20.10	17.39	22.19	9.25	13.29	12.55
Irvine, CA	35.34	21.61	20.04	27.99	11.00	15.22	13.65
Jackson, MS	27.11	16.41	16.10	14.11	8.86	11.51	11.33
Jacksonville, FL	32.41	19.26	16.24	16.70	9.17	13.06	12.75
Jersey City, NJ	43.13	20.02	20.67	29.57	10.28	14.44	14.33
Kansas City, MO	29.67	19.86	17.17	22.36	9.36	14.75	12.81
Kenosha, WI	34.69	21.24	18.81	27.32	9.76	14.79	13.47
Las Vegas, NV	30.67	19.70	17.63	28.18	10.52	14.60	13.25
Lexington, KY	28.79	16.08	16.29	17.06	9.06	12.88	11.97
Lincoln, NE	29.38	17.92	15.37	17.35	8.97	11.24	11.74

Table continued on next page.

Metro Area	Accountants/ Auditors	Automotive Mechanics	Book-keepers	Carpenters	Cashiers	Clerks, Gen. Office	Clerks, Recep./Info.
Little Rock, AR	28.75	16.90	15.92	17.31	9.21	11.32	11.70
Los Angeles, CA	35.72	19.00	19.14	25.79	10.84	15.06	13.54
Madison, WI	29.82	19.29	17.47	23.34	9.71	15.03	12.78
Manchester, NH	31.87	20.24	18.96	20.51	9.38	16.12	13.29
Miami, FL	35.53	17.87	16.28	17.28	9.41	12.50	11.89
Minneapolis, MN	31.31	19.76	18.66	24.09	9.82	14.74	14.14
Murfreesboro, TN	29.64	17.30	16.00	18.06	9.78	14.45	12.64
Naperville, IL	35.94	18.50	18.47	25.37	9.93	14.99	13.44
Nashville, TN	29.64	17.30	16.00	18.06	9.78	14.45	12.64
New Orleans, LA	31.66	18.89	16.95	18.29	9.24	12.09	11.64
New York, NY	43.13	20.02	20.67	29.57	10.28	14.44	14.33
Norman, OK	29.34	19.14	14.72	16.65	8.87	12.29	11.51
Olathe, KS	29.67	19.86	17.17	22.36	9.36	14.75	12.81
Omaha, NE	32.66	18.61	16.02	17.46	9.38	12.65	12.31
Orlando, FL	30.31	16.88	15.51	16.27	8.98	13.05	11.70
Overland Park, KS	29.67	19.86	17.17	22.36	9.36	14.75	12.81
Oyster Bay, NY	41.67	20.79	20.39	28.31	10.20	14.77	14.13
Pembroke Pines, FL	31.08	18.77	16.79	21.04	9.93	12.92	13.00
Philadelphia, PA	37.84	18.99	19.69	23.32	9.97	15.31	14.40
Phoenix, AZ	29.62	19.98	17.77	19.96	10.97	14.89	13.73
Pittsburgh, PA	33.23	16.76	16.45	20.63	9.10	13.75	11.81
Plano, TX	35.62	17.75	18.20	15.57	9.39	14.88	12.90
Portland, OR	30.49	20.09	18.47	22.48	11.55	15.01	13.57
Providence, RI	33.15	17.75	18.30	21.86	9.84	14.91	13.99
Provo, UT	29.78	19.84	15.32	18.97	9.14	11.72	10.73
Raleigh, NC	31.67	20.79	17.33	16.82	9.15	13.46	12.38
Richmond, VA	32.22	20.97	17.35	18.27	9.56	14.29	12.94
Roseville, CA	31.77	21.78	19.82	25.23	11.35	16.16	13.76
Round Rock, TX	33.31	22.03	18.23	15.60	9.71	15.47	12.65
San Antonio, TX	32.20	17.23	16.88	15.25	9.26	13.07	11.79
San Diego, CA	35.75	20.90	19.21	25.56	10.68	14.81	13.88
San Francisco, CA	41.46	24.38	23.01	32.26	13.13	17.76	17.53
San Jose, CA	41.15	24.15	22.09	29.61	12.05	17.82	15.92
Savannah, GA	32.41	18.85	16.56	19.40	9.20	11.24	11.80
Scottsdale, AZ	29.62	19.98	17.77	19.96	10.97	14.89	13.73
Seattle, WA	33.93	19.26	19.53	25.62	12.86	16.09	14.48
Sioux Falls, SD	28.55	18.28	14.08	16.08	9.16	11.08	11.66
Stamford, CT	37.10	23.27	21.57	28.59	10.73	16.13	16.56
Sterling Hgts, MI	32.66	21.27	17.98	21.56	10.45	14.53	12.77
Sunnyvale, CA	41.15	24.15	22.09	29.61	12.05	17.82	15.92
Tampa, FL	30.06	17.49	15.71	17.16	8.99	12.82	12.52
Temecula, CA	31.12	19.26	18.27	27.20	10.78	14.68	12.79
Thousand Oaks, CA	36.15	19.58	20.51	22.19	10.91	14.76	13.87
Virginia Beach, VA	30.67	19.95	16.71	18.69	9.19	12.73	12.15
Washington, DC	40.35	22.35	21.08	21.54	10.39	16.13	14.63

Notes: Wage data is for May 2011 and covers the Metropolitan Statistical Area—see Appendix B for areas included; n/a not available
Source: Bureau of Labor Statistics, May 2011 Metro Area Occupational Employment and Wage Estimates

Average Hourly Wages: Occupations C – E

Metro Area	Clerks, Ship./Rec.	Computer Program-mers	Computer Support Specialists	Computer Systems Analysts	Cooks, Restaurant	Dentists	Electrical Engineers
Albuquerque, NM	14.07	37.22	23.38	40.34	10.13	77.32	43.52
Alexandria, VA	16.08	38.92	29.37	47.85	12.55	88.19	48.17
Anchorage, AK	19.41	35.11	25.21	37.05	14.36	82.57	48.13
Ann Arbor, MI	15.83	29.93	22.15	38.25	11.79	50.97	38.80
Athens, GA	13.80	26.38	17.43	36.33	11.61	n/a	34.22
Atlanta, GA	14.54	37.52	24.14	38.12	10.65	98.25	39.01
Austin, TX	14.00	38.53	26.47	40.99	10.93	90.89	45.14
Baltimore, MD	15.89	37.15	26.93	39.57	12.51	75.76	42.50
Bellevue, WA	17.95	45.55	28.14	43.29	12.88	106.68	45.46
Billings, MT	12.27	27.08	18.49	33.38	11.08	55.11	32.19
Boise City, ID	13.39	30.53	19.12	33.46	10.21	92.45	43.91
Boston, MA	17.12	42.32	30.29	43.41	13.05	84.70	49.22
Boulder, CO	15.53	n/a	29.14	40.69	11.39	n/a	51.95
Broken Arrow, OK	14.15	33.82	22.75	35.42	10.57	90.53	35.91
Cambridge, MA	17.12	42.32	30.29	43.41	13.05	84.70	49.22
Cape Coral, FL	11.94	32.56	22.02	36.58	11.46	42.76	36.16
Carlsbad, CA	14.82	36.63	24.22	41.73	12.22	77.88	47.72
Cary, NC	14.03	34.63	25.82	39.37	10.33	97.51	43.65
Cedar Rapids, IA	15.07	29.51	21.66	31.72	9.60	111.15	n/a
Charleston, SC	16.03	31.64	22.78	30.90	10.38	69.44	38.72
Charlotte, NC	14.59	35.56	26.91	42.34	11.24	90.62	40.18
Chesapeake, VA	14.67	29.81	24.70	38.60	12.51	103.22	38.08
Chicago, IL	14.77	37.72	27.10	34.27	10.69	59.60	42.65
Clarksville, TN	15.09	32.29	20.71	26.81	10.20	n/a	32.34
Colorado Spgs., CO	14.51	39.49	25.76	41.38	11.48	65.74	40.22
Columbia, MD	15.89	37.15	26.93	39.57	12.51	75.76	42.50
Columbia, MO	13.26	43.46	18.20	34.68	10.62	n/a	n/a
Columbia, SC	13.56	30.43	23.42	32.61	9.44	91.03	39.73
Columbus, OH	14.65	34.64	24.15	39.18	10.61	83.86	33.64
Dallas, TX	14.09	41.54	28.05	41.07	10.09	98.53	46.14
Denver, CO	15.41	38.39	28.18	42.31	10.87	66.03	40.82
Durham, NC	13.93	47.91	31.53	38.49	11.95	60.42	42.09
Edison, NJ	15.71	41.15	26.31	42.57	11.62	68.50	42.08
El Paso, TX	11.02	25.66	20.42	35.74	9.09	95.21	40.18
Fargo, ND	14.18	22.74	19.59	28.92	10.38	105.77	34.97
Ft. Collins, CO	14.16	36.07	24.55	37.49	11.09	99.42	40.34
Ft. Worth, TX	14.29	35.64	25.12	37.32	9.75	69.33	39.08
Gilbert, AZ	14.26	37.73	23.79	36.35	14.05	89.20	47.97
Green Bay, WI	15.32	30.27	22.53	34.56	9.84	85.61	38.54
Henderson, NV	14.00	33.34	22.25	39.57	14.48	69.94	41.18
High Point, NC	14.56	35.19	23.17	37.34	10.75	97.61	42.70
Honolulu, HI	15.62	32.91	24.28	33.00	13.99	71.85	39.48
Houston, TX	14.33	37.32	26.49	43.60	9.25	70.87	43.82
Huntington, NY	15.44	38.68	27.75	41.18	13.71	81.99	46.79
Huntsville, AL	14.51	38.31	21.89	42.27	11.08	84.61	49.02
Indianapolis, IN	14.38	37.17	22.44	35.44	10.67	79.81	38.43
Irvine, CA	15.39	35.93	28.47	41.41	11.68	56.38	47.12
Jackson, MS	14.60	26.73	21.39	26.99	9.43	71.38	36.57
Jacksonville, FL	14.10	34.13	21.65	36.27	11.44	79.36	40.92
Jersey City, NJ	14.89	39.81	28.83	44.33	14.27	66.79	43.62
Kansas City, MO	14.26	33.99	23.84	38.56	10.07	59.44	38.66
Kenosha, WI	15.55	34.62	27.26	37.52	10.27	41.46	36.98
Las Vegas, NV	14.00	33.34	22.25	39.57	14.48	69.94	41.18
Lexington, KY	14.34	29.44	21.11	39.30	10.12	46.44	49.64
Lincoln, NE	14.06	30.31	21.00	29.67	9.98	82.35	36.26

Table continued on next page.

Metro Area	Clerks, Ship./Rec.	Computer Program-mers	Computer Support Specialists	Computer Systems Analysts	Cooks, Restaurant	Dentists	Electrical Engineers
Little Rock, AR	13.20	28.80	21.50	32.57	9.42	85.45	39.03
Los Angeles, CA	14.38	40.73	26.04	42.62	11.20	63.44	48.09
Madison, WI	14.69	35.84	25.86	34.46	10.86	84.06	36.82
Manchester, NH	15.35	34.72	26.57	39.67	11.95	n/a	39.50
Miami, FL	13.49	36.56	22.06	40.96	11.90	55.21	42.83
Minneapolis, MN	16.15	33.80	25.64	37.38	11.18	91.83	42.24
Murfreesboro, TN	13.85	35.55	23.80	34.26	11.15	70.70	39.66
Naperville, IL	14.77	37.72	27.10	34.27	10.69	59.60	42.65
Nashville, TN	13.85	35.55	23.80	34.26	11.15	70.70	39.66
New Orleans, LA	15.28	28.87	23.18	29.30	11.36	74.29	47.05
New York, NY	14.89	39.81	28.83	44.33	14.27	66.79	43.62
Norman, OK	14.52	26.49	21.03	30.74	10.31	65.63	43.62
Olathe, KS	14.26	33.99	23.84	38.56	10.07	59.44	38.66
Omaha, NE	14.20	32.18	25.63	34.93	10.92	87.54	38.13
Orlando, FL	12.62	33.08	20.38	38.82	11.78	62.52	35.26
Overland Park, KS	14.26	33.99	23.84	38.56	10.07	59.44	38.66
Oyster Bay, NY	15.44	38.68	27.75	41.18	13.71	81.99	46.79
Pembroke Pines, FL	13.55	31.99	22.73	37.90	11.70	60.26	37.94
Philadelphia, PA	16.76	35.87	25.68	40.52	14.63	78.97	46.02
Phoenix, AZ	14.26	37.73	23.79	36.35	14.05	89.20	47.97
Pittsburgh, PA	15.07	30.80	22.52	34.99	12.68	64.33	40.20
Plano, TX	14.09	41.54	28.05	41.07	10.09	98.53	46.14
Portland, OR	15.23	34.01	25.80	40.89	12.08	99.99	42.45
Providence, RI	15.00	33.98	23.71	38.52	12.81	68.14	43.91
Provo, UT	13.42	31.70	20.24	33.44	10.25	85.00	37.25
Raleigh, NC	14.03	34.63	25.82	39.37	10.33	97.51	43.65
Richmond, VA	15.25	37.03	23.92	37.80	10.44	70.36	39.87
Roseville, CA	15.59	38.33	28.76	37.48	11.39	67.02	51.08
Round Rock, TX	14.00	38.53	26.47	40.99	10.93	90.89	45.14
San Antonio, TX	13.92	37.36	24.98	41.42	9.69	93.56	39.74
San Diego, CA	14.82	36.63	24.22	41.73	12.22	77.88	47.72
San Francisco, CA	16.67	46.94	33.49	46.48	14.47	76.44	45.59
San Jose, CA	16.65	47.87	35.27	47.91	11.70	67.81	53.77
Savannah, GA	14.96	31.16	23.14	32.95	9.62	79.03	41.86
Scottsdale, AZ	14.26	37.73	23.79	36.35	14.05	89.20	47.97
Seattle, WA	17.95	45.55	28.14	43.29	12.88	106.68	45.46
Sioux Falls, SD	14.07	27.34	19.05	31.81	11.61	65.80	38.02
Stamford, CT	17.91	43.35	31.30	50.49	13.59	71.45	39.80
Sterling Hgts, MI	14.44	34.67	22.78	37.84	11.93	61.28	43.01
Sunnyvale, CA	16.65	47.87	35.27	47.91	11.70	67.81	53.77
Tampa, FL	13.17	34.50	21.13	39.51	10.45	89.88	35.43
Temecula, CA	14.48	32.65	22.98	35.24	11.58	83.02	45.72
Thousand Oaks, CA	15.02	42.78	27.22	40.19	11.33	84.35	46.54
Virginia Beach, VA	14.67	29.81	24.70	38.60	12.51	103.22	38.08
Washington, DC	16.08	38.92	29.37	47.85	12.55	88.19	48.17

Notes: Wage data is for May 2011 and covers the Metropolitan Statistical Area—see Appendix B for areas included; n/a not available
Source: Bureau of Labor Statistics, May 2011 Metro Area Occupational Employment and Wage Estimates

Average Hourly Wages: Occupations E – I

Metro Area	Electricians	Financial Managers	First-Line Supervisors/ Mgrs., Sales	Food Preparation Workers	General/ Operations Managers	Hairdressers/ Cosmetologists	Internists
Albuquerque, NM	22.07	46.38	18.74	10.15	46.43	11.30	n/a
Alexandria, VA	26.66	64.81	21.51	10.83	65.53	15.65	93.95
Anchorage, AK	33.92	50.67	20.36	11.54	47.58	13.05	n/a
Ann Arbor, MI	34.11	48.63	20.53	10.48	50.08	13.82	n/a
Athens, GA	18.05	59.94	16.97	10.19	47.10	13.58	80.48
Atlanta, GA	21.62	60.72	19.34	10.24	55.36	10.88	92.73
Austin, TX	19.31	57.82	19.65	9.75	54.61	10.68	100.65
Baltimore, MD	24.69	51.58	20.74	10.83	56.53	13.66	90.93
Bellevue, WA	31.80	60.69	22.33	11.95	66.28	18.08	86.31
Billings, MT	22.32	50.49	19.12	9.48	42.76	12.15	n/a
Boise City, ID	22.03	40.93	16.90	9.04	38.37	10.45	n/a
Boston, MA	30.36	68.84	20.89	11.51	62.06	14.40	99.93
Boulder, CO	21.27	65.49	20.74	10.13	62.22	18.08	n/a
Broken Arrow, OK	23.49	45.47	16.24	9.03	44.95	10.98	113.75
Cambridge, MA	30.36	68.84	20.89	11.51	62.06	14.40	99.93
Cape Coral, FL	16.37	61.00	21.14	10.01	46.02	12.59	113.39
Carlsbad, CA	26.26	61.05	21.20	9.84	61.96	12.04	90.55
Cary, NC	19.28	56.39	19.38	9.43	62.18	14.61	76.57
Cedar Rapids, IA	26.16	53.18	20.16	8.72	50.41	10.87	n/a
Charleston, SC	19.10	49.45	19.32	9.54	52.74	19.98	n/a
Charlotte, NC	19.39	64.23	19.52	9.67	64.03	12.84	108.95
Chesapeake, VA	20.95	50.44	19.07	9.77	52.84	11.77	77.48
Chicago, IL	36.27	59.35	20.56	9.96	56.91	13.62	96.45
Clarksville, TN	19.44	37.77	16.11	9.27	37.50	12.11	n/a
Colorado Spgs., CO	23.70	55.99	18.08	9.69	49.73	12.33	n/a
Columbia, MD	24.69	51.58	20.74	10.83	56.53	13.66	90.93
Columbia, MO	19.55	45.30	16.33	9.18	35.28	13.02	n/a
Columbia, SC	19.61	49.15	19.28	9.10	49.52	13.54	104.61
Columbus, OH	21.58	56.07	19.76	10.84	56.09	11.82	70.00
Dallas, TX	21.29	59.28	20.33	9.15	59.82	14.08	79.49
Denver, CO	23.49	63.95	20.73	10.44	62.34	13.41	67.02
Durham, NC	20.47	58.70	18.10	10.28	63.12	15.09	77.08
Edison, NJ	29.60	65.85	23.40	10.12	77.01	13.94	97.46
El Paso, TX	18.17	47.49	19.16	8.46	45.95	10.47	106.28
Fargo, ND	19.52	45.32	17.27	10.91	49.52	11.82	n/a
Ft. Collins, CO	25.31	59.83	19.08	9.78	50.08	11.61	n/a
Ft. Worth, TX	20.66	52.01	19.25	9.54	52.48	12.21	89.32
Gilbert, AZ	21.37	51.98	19.48	10.57	51.63	11.42	93.77
Green Bay, WI	23.57	50.31	18.21	10.45	50.85	11.69	n/a
Henderson, NV	32.37	50.71	19.67	13.93	53.29	10.30	95.39
High Point, NC	18.81	52.54	18.30	9.58	57.40	10.42	97.21
Honolulu, HI	34.74	44.59	22.47	11.31	49.88	18.04	112.29
Houston, TX	22.37	63.28	20.04	9.73	58.09	12.77	98.23
Huntington, NY	32.39	70.09	23.90	12.02	65.75	12.12	111.13
Huntsville, AL	19.16	53.23	18.35	9.06	59.83	12.52	116.96
Indianapolis, IN	26.78	52.70	20.11	10.03	57.66	13.93	91.80
Irvine, CA	27.78	67.44	21.14	11.06	65.01	12.29	84.72
Jackson, MS	20.70	38.79	17.71	8.36	49.11	13.13	72.02
Jacksonville, FL	20.80	57.19	20.25	9.52	49.47	12.38	94.93
Jersey City, NJ	38.34	84.27	23.87	11.84	78.11	15.57	74.47
Kansas City, MO	28.23	52.94	18.47	10.02	48.38	11.98	96.76
Kenosha, WI	29.26	53.22	18.72	9.59	52.53	13.66	n/a
Las Vegas, NV	32.37	50.71	19.67	13.93	53.29	10.30	95.39
Lexington, KY	20.43	46.16	17.35	10.26	45.29	10.95	n/a
Lincoln, NE	20.25	57.13	19.01	9.66	50.03	9.47	114.01

Table continued on next page.

Metro Area	Electricians	Financial Managers	First-Line Supervisors/ Mgrs., Sales	Food Preparation Workers	General/ Operations Managers	Hairdressers/ Cosmetologists	Internists
Little Rock, AR	19.89	41.77	17.54	9.09	46.45	14.59	n/a
Los Angeles, CA	29.72	66.04	21.64	9.72	63.08	13.20	93.12
Madison, WI	27.75	49.55	19.43	9.58	51.70	10.92	n/a
Manchester, NH	24.02	47.78	20.64	10.99	55.33	11.49	n/a
Miami, FL	20.72	65.40	20.34	9.60	52.48	11.92	94.51
Minneapolis, MN	30.92	59.15	19.26	10.87	56.08	13.73	105.90
Murfreesboro, TN	20.54	51.34	19.94	10.50	47.06	12.59	82.01
Naperville, IL	36.27	59.35	20.56	9.96	56.91	13.62	96.45
Nashville, TN	20.54	51.34	19.94	10.50	47.06	12.59	82.01
New Orleans, LA	22.16	46.42	18.54	9.00	54.57	11.63	n/a
New York, NY	38.34	84.27	23.87	11.84	78.11	15.57	74.47
Norman, OK	18.96	44.79	17.12	8.65	42.74	11.99	109.00
Olathe, KS	28.23	52.94	18.47	10.02	48.38	11.98	96.76
Omaha, NE	21.89	65.54	20.63	10.40	55.65	13.85	94.83
Orlando, FL	18.63	56.61	20.19	9.67	47.91	11.18	n/a
Overland Park, KS	28.23	52.94	18.47	10.02	48.38	11.98	96.76
Oyster Bay, NY	32.39	70.09	23.90	12.02	65.75	12.12	111.13
Pembroke Pines, FL	18.76	61.20	21.21	10.13	51.16	13.47	118.93
Philadelphia, PA	34.04	63.29	24.39	11.22	63.40	13.84	51.37
Phoenix, AZ	21.37	51.98	19.48	10.57	51.63	11.42	93.77
Pittsburgh, PA	26.49	50.96	21.36	10.18	54.17	10.87	106.76
Plano, TX	21.29	59.28	20.33	9.15	59.82	14.08	79.49
Portland, OR	33.43	52.55	19.37	10.68	53.15	13.53	96.43
Providence, RI	27.19	58.42	21.68	11.61	62.44	13.62	87.42
Provo, UT	25.18	50.90	16.69	9.27	42.84	15.49	n/a
Raleigh, NC	19.28	56.39	19.38	9.43	62.18	14.61	76.57
Richmond, VA	22.12	56.66	19.61	10.51	54.37	13.98	n/a
Roseville, CA	28.49	52.89	19.67	10.48	57.72	12.55	109.55
Round Rock, TX	19.31	57.82	19.65	9.75	54.61	10.68	100.65
San Antonio, TX	20.08	56.50	20.41	9.13	49.92	11.23	111.63
San Diego, CA	26.26	61.05	21.20	9.84	61.96	12.04	90.55
San Francisco, CA	37.23	78.22	22.25	10.83	73.00	19.73	109.06
San Jose, CA	35.14	72.63	20.10	10.10	72.59	11.50	69.01
Savannah, GA	24.40	46.08	17.54	10.05	45.29	12.98	104.42
Scottsdale, AZ	21.37	51.98	19.48	10.57	51.63	11.42	93.77
Seattle, WA	31.80	60.69	22.33	11.95	66.28	18.08	86.31
Sioux Falls, SD	21.61	60.98	20.70	9.67	55.19	12.73	119.01
Stamford, CT	28.12	65.29	23.52	11.83	77.03	15.54	87.63
Sterling Hgts, MI	28.53	55.58	21.12	10.84	57.39	12.24	69.15
Sunnyvale, CA	35.14	72.63	20.10	10.10	72.59	11.50	69.01
Tampa, FL	18.16	55.17	21.18	9.37	52.79	10.53	110.77
Temecula, CA	29.14	49.84	21.05	9.95	53.62	10.14	83.72
Thousand Oaks, CA	26.84	56.18	20.41	10.02	61.47	12.36	69.01
Virginia Beach, VA	20.95	50.44	19.07	9.77	52.84	11.77	77.48
Washington, DC	26.66	64.81	21.51	10.83	65.53	15.65	93.95

Notes: Wage data is for May 2011 and covers the Metropolitan Statistical Area—see Appendix B for areas included; n/a not available
Source: Bureau of Labor Statistics, May 2011 Metro Area Occupational Employment and Wage Estimates

Average Hourly Wages: Occupations J – N

Metro Area	Janitors/ Cleaners	Landscapers	Lawyers	Maids/ House-keepers	Main-tenance Repairers	Marketing Managers	Nuclear Medicine Technologists
Albuquerque, NM	10.41	10.90	44.61	9.21	16.36	45.60	33.03
Alexandria, VA	12.11	12.72	75.86	12.02	20.52	69.78	35.51
Anchorage, AK	14.28	14.55	56.84	10.92	21.57	39.44	n/a
Ann Arbor, MI	13.09	12.69	41.29	12.15	17.35	51.06	27.88
Athens, GA	11.23	9.71	56.77	9.19	15.96	55.01	n/a
Atlanta, GA	11.33	12.62	68.30	9.18	17.74	58.21	32.61
Austin, TX	10.51	11.79	47.69	9.22	16.02	65.36	32.42
Baltimore, MD	11.62	12.20	55.89	10.42	19.26	51.62	38.86
Bellevue, WA	14.35	15.62	59.08	12.10	20.35	63.21	41.27
Billings, MT	10.47	12.16	34.89	9.30	15.01	38.80	n/a
Boise City, ID	10.74	12.31	49.86	9.47	15.69	47.44	n/a
Boston, MA	14.96	16.12	63.99	14.23	22.93	66.29	35.79
Boulder, CO	13.28	13.25	56.35	10.53	19.40	67.50	n/a
Broken Arrow, OK	10.32	10.94	63.12	8.98	16.93	40.62	32.46
Cambridge, MA	14.96	16.12	63.99	14.23	22.93	66.29	35.79
Cape Coral, FL	10.47	10.92	46.78	9.60	15.87	43.92	35.94
Carlsbad, CA	12.83	12.71	69.30	10.12	17.57	62.90	39.31
Cary, NC	10.84	11.34	55.47	9.21	17.86	60.01	31.53
Cedar Rapids, IA	11.73	12.60	50.43	9.42	18.68	49.92	n/a
Charleston, SC	10.02	10.84	53.43	9.27	15.28	49.36	31.80
Charlotte, NC	10.12	10.99	60.66	9.03	18.37	60.63	29.76
Chesapeake, VA	10.34	10.69	55.62	9.10	16.70	54.04	28.10
Chicago, IL	12.63	12.73	70.57	11.21	20.20	54.83	35.11
Clarksville, TN	10.79	10.39	45.21	9.00	16.97	37.70	n/a
Colorado Spgs., CO	12.91	12.76	49.49	9.70	17.32	53.96	33.32
Columbia, MD	11.62	12.20	55.89	10.42	19.26	51.62	38.86
Columbia, MO	11.47	10.44	52.89	9.76	14.94	40.76	n/a
Columbia, SC	10.43	9.98	53.98	9.55	16.95	45.82	29.31
Columbus, OH	11.87	11.24	55.49	9.87	17.15	63.49	31.57
Dallas, TX	10.27	10.86	68.66	9.01	16.80	62.63	31.31
Denver, CO	11.15	12.90	67.62	9.70	18.32	61.53	38.16
Durham, NC	11.04	12.35	51.08	9.24	19.89	64.87	32.80
Edison, NJ	13.58	12.45	63.89	10.48	19.78	72.38	40.48
El Paso, TX	9.87	10.09	51.70	8.92	12.47	52.13	30.81
Fargo, ND	11.26	12.20	55.02	9.59	17.22	44.27	n/a
Ft. Collins, CO	11.59	12.87	46.74	10.33	16.87	56.43	n/a
Ft. Worth, TX	11.14	11.15	56.38	9.18	16.59	54.92	34.77
Gilbert, AZ	11.50	11.12	62.72	9.60	17.63	52.33	35.95
Green Bay, WI	11.96	12.18	58.35	9.37	19.14	47.63	n/a
Henderson, NV	13.43	12.32	56.92	13.73	21.61	59.31	38.14
High Point, NC	9.71	11.67	68.09	8.88	18.08	56.11	n/a
Honolulu, HI	12.05	13.24	55.89	14.88	20.28	45.74	37.59
Houston, TX	10.09	10.78	78.76	8.73	16.98	64.43	30.60
Huntington, NY	15.04	14.38	57.39	13.45	20.73	69.03	37.67
Huntsville, AL	10.56	11.57	66.29	8.82	19.82	55.76	n/a
Indianapolis, IN	10.78	11.99	49.13	9.15	17.62	56.72	30.24
Irvine, CA	11.86	12.41	72.46	10.33	18.09	66.97	45.74
Jackson, MS	9.55	10.82	55.86	8.53	14.27	42.99	26.13
Jacksonville, FL	10.68	10.80	46.99	9.07	16.49	56.19	34.06
Jersey City, NJ	15.23	15.56	79.54	16.06	20.03	80.57	37.69
Kansas City, MO	12.11	12.09	56.96	9.43	17.83	52.56	31.32
Kenosha, WI	12.82	12.47	44.91	9.82	20.33	55.15	35.93
Las Vegas, NV	13.43	12.32	56.92	13.73	21.61	59.31	38.14
Lexington, KY	10.79	11.70	48.83	9.01	16.17	41.78	29.04
Lincoln, NE	11.34	11.65	49.92	9.05	16.99	51.29	n/a

Table continued on next page.

Metro Area	Janitors/ Cleaners	Landscapers	Lawyers	Maids/ House-keepers	Main-tenance Repairers	Marketing Managers	Nuclear Medicine Technologists
Little Rock, AR	9.61	11.43	45.17	8.67	15.28	46.19	30.49
Los Angeles, CA	12.43	13.60	80.43	10.89	19.24	63.88	42.62
Madison, WI	11.44	15.43	49.58	9.78	18.43	46.02	n/a
Manchester, NH	11.73	15.90	66.41	9.91	19.87	49.55	n/a
Miami, FL	10.12	10.62	69.52	9.24	15.63	61.78	31.68
Minneapolis, MN	12.52	14.20	60.55	11.17	20.46	58.99	34.34
Murfreesboro, TN	9.99	11.26	53.12	9.10	16.90	46.60	30.05
Naperville, IL	12.63	12.73	70.57	11.21	20.20	54.83	35.11
Nashville, TN	9.99	11.26	53.12	9.10	16.90	46.60	30.05
New Orleans, LA	10.36	10.94	55.05	9.55	17.54	42.58	32.59
New York, NY	15.23	15.56	79.54	16.06	20.03	80.57	37.69
Norman, OK	9.75	10.50	42.55	9.05	15.27	44.63	32.24
Olathe, KS	12.11	12.09	56.96	9.43	17.83	52.56	31.32
Omaha, NE	11.06	11.47	54.02	9.36	16.65	64.32	29.92
Orlando, FL	10.13	10.77	60.74	9.50	14.88	51.91	33.19
Overland Park, KS	12.11	12.09	56.96	9.43	17.83	52.56	31.32
Oyster Bay, NY	15.04	14.38	57.39	13.45	20.73	69.03	37.67
Pembroke Pines, FL	9.95	10.73	58.17	9.74	16.02	53.59	34.17
Philadelphia, PA	13.75	13.43	73.18	11.95	19.09	67.58	36.21
Phoenix, AZ	11.50	11.12	62.72	9.60	17.63	52.33	35.95
Pittsburgh, PA	12.30	12.46	65.19	9.88	17.52	61.96	25.62
Plano, TX	10.27	10.86	68.66	9.01	16.80	62.63	31.31
Portland, OR	12.36	13.43	49.96	10.92	18.72	51.57	39.20
Providence, RI	13.12	12.98	47.55	11.38	18.55	48.54	41.10
Provo, UT	10.50	12.48	52.77	9.21	16.72	47.29	n/a
Raleigh, NC	10.84	11.34	55.47	9.21	17.86	60.01	31.53
Richmond, VA	10.39	11.96	60.87	9.06	17.50	70.03	32.96
Roseville, CA	13.16	13.33	58.86	11.64	20.40	52.30	51.53
Round Rock, TX	10.51	11.79	47.69	9.22	16.02	65.36	32.42
San Antonio, TX	10.02	11.50	45.71	9.32	14.22	61.38	31.18
San Diego, CA	12.83	12.71	69.30	10.12	17.57	62.90	39.31
San Francisco, CA	13.39	17.47	84.20	15.20	23.49	81.50	39.71
San Jose, CA	13.30	15.04	89.96	11.63	23.10	77.50	53.97
Savannah, GA	10.57	12.43	52.91	8.61	15.51	49.22	n/a
Scottsdale, AZ	11.50	11.12	62.72	9.60	17.63	52.33	35.95
Seattle, WA	14.35	15.62	59.08	12.10	20.35	63.21	41.27
Sioux Falls, SD	10.90	12.35	49.87	9.57	15.63	52.97	27.27
Stamford, CT	13.77	15.87	77.33	12.35	22.39	68.28	41.12
Sterling Hgts, MI	11.95	13.55	52.10	10.96	16.71	51.84	29.23
Sunnyvale, CA	13.30	15.04	89.96	11.63	23.10	77.50	53.97
Tampa, FL	10.04	10.87	52.36	8.98	15.64	51.71	31.56
Temecula, CA	12.88	12.24	57.78	10.37	18.41	53.71	42.15
Thousand Oaks, CA	13.84	13.35	81.47	10.37	19.54	58.67	49.21
Virginia Beach, VA	10.34	10.69	55.62	9.10	16.70	54.04	28.10
Washington, DC	12.11	12.72	75.86	12.02	20.52	69.78	35.51

Notes: Wage data is for May 2011 and covers the Metropolitan Statistical Area—see Appendix B for areas included; n/a not available
Source: Bureau of Labor Statistics, May 2011 Metro Area Occupational Employment and Wage Estimates

Average Hourly Wages: Occupations N – R

Metro Area	Nurses, Licensed Practical	Nurses, Registered	Nursing Aides/ Orderlies/ Attendants	Packers/ Packagers	Physical Therapists	Postal Mail Carriers	R.E. Brokers
Albuquerque, NM	23.01	33.73	13.35	11.64	35.16	24.93	38.36
Alexandria, VA	22.67	35.92	13.65	10.83	40.55	25.00	38.67
Anchorage, AK	24.82	39.99	16.61	12.48	44.45	25.98	n/a
Ann Arbor, MI	20.97	29.78	12.70	9.20	35.03	24.62	n/a
Athens, GA	17.91	29.93	9.02	9.63	34.06	23.58	n/a
Atlanta, GA	18.73	31.13	11.18	10.67	36.50	24.66	36.66
Austin, TX	21.93	33.09	11.00	11.36	38.51	25.00	45.04
Baltimore, MD	24.45	37.14	13.64	12.00	40.03	24.89	45.63
Bellevue, WA	24.18	37.68	14.77	11.79	37.65	25.70	41.03
Billings, MT	16.95	30.66	12.41	9.36	31.15	24.77	n/a
Boise City, ID	19.60	31.49	11.32	8.98	33.98	24.47	n/a
Boston, MA	24.37	45.48	14.84	11.08	36.69	25.81	72.64
Boulder, CO	22.00	32.84	13.37	12.09	33.15	25.22	31.47
Broken Arrow, OK	17.52	26.45	10.44	9.87	35.16	24.64	n/a
Cambridge, MA	24.37	45.48	14.84	11.08	36.69	25.81	72.64
Cape Coral, FL	20.26	31.16	12.32	9.89	39.19	24.14	n/a
Carlsbad, CA	23.19	40.82	12.68	9.96	42.57	25.79	33.89
Cary, NC	20.23	28.69	11.46	10.31	33.65	24.14	30.67
Cedar Rapids, IA	16.95	23.84	12.02	12.39	35.16	24.80	n/a
Charleston, SC	20.09	32.68	11.05	10.19	33.51	23.97	25.25
Charlotte, NC	20.02	30.05	11.04	9.83	37.20	24.22	32.71
Chesapeake, VA	17.61	30.40	11.02	10.18	36.74	25.05	35.93
Chicago, IL	21.29	34.05	12.42	10.90	37.98	25.50	37.47
Clarksville, TN	19.21	28.86	10.69	11.48	34.68	23.83	n/a
Colorado Spgs., CO	20.27	31.91	12.33	10.10	34.27	25.20	24.31
Columbia, MD	24.45	37.14	13.64	12.00	40.03	24.89	45.63
Columbia, MO	18.12	27.35	10.43	8.84	32.64	24.07	n/a
Columbia, SC	19.64	28.95	11.39	11.67	37.01	24.01	26.83
Columbus, OH	20.17	30.29	11.81	10.51	36.06	24.44	37.91
Dallas, TX	21.67	32.86	11.46	10.61	45.67	25.10	49.69
Denver, CO	22.47	34.46	14.11	11.04	34.46	25.63	43.80
Durham, NC	21.12	30.91	12.81	9.85	34.94	24.39	27.11
Edison, NJ	24.95	37.07	13.21	10.76	44.91	25.53	n/a
El Paso, TX	19.64	30.75	10.19	8.82	50.67	25.05	n/a
Fargo, ND	17.52	29.06	12.76	9.83	30.26	24.33	n/a
Ft. Collins, CO	22.17	31.03	12.29	10.49	35.30	25.21	25.47
Ft. Worth, TX	20.86	31.74	11.16	9.53	41.00	25.02	n/a
Gilbert, AZ	25.14	35.74	13.23	10.78	37.94	25.15	n/a
Green Bay, WI	18.19	29.67	12.45	11.53	38.79	24.03	n/a
Henderson, NV	25.75	37.40	16.22	12.06	47.65	25.51	39.47
High Point, NC	19.43	29.35	10.81	9.11	38.46	24.13	25.93
Honolulu, HI	21.49	41.60	13.85	10.01	36.72	26.30	n/a
Houston, TX	21.93	35.63	11.44	11.31	40.26	25.24	48.78
Huntington, NY	24.27	39.67	16.90	11.03	40.95	25.69	49.57
Huntsville, AL	18.07	28.70	11.24	10.42	37.50	24.57	25.73
Indianapolis, IN	19.71	29.53	12.07	12.03	35.17	24.66	n/a
Irvine, CA	23.45	39.33	13.86	10.50	40.02	26.15	47.09
Jackson, MS	17.29	31.47	9.48	9.45	34.15	23.92	n/a
Jacksonville, FL	19.78	31.53	11.48	9.62	46.78	24.92	31.18
Jersey City, NJ	24.25	39.93	16.09	10.72	40.18	25.76	68.66
Kansas City, MO	18.99	31.89	11.80	10.34	33.08	24.74	34.16
Kenosha, WI	22.61	34.98	12.33	10.87	37.64	25.01	n/a
Las Vegas, NV	25.75	37.40	16.22	12.06	47.65	25.51	39.47
Lexington, KY	19.02	28.08	11.53	10.93	39.31	25.14	n/a
Lincoln, NE	17.88	27.45	11.86	10.14	36.58	25.07	21.00

Table continued on next page.

Metro Area	Nurses, Licensed Practical	Nurses, Registered	Nursing Aides/ Orderlies/ Attendants	Packers/ Packagers	Physical Therapists	Postal Mail Carriers	R.E. Brokers
Little Rock, AR	18.06	28.46	10.83	8.99	38.61	24.44	45.04
Los Angeles, CA	23.91	41.03	12.75	10.22	41.74	26.15	58.15
Madison, WI	20.71	35.01	13.08	15.44	35.67	24.55	n/a
Manchester, NH	21.31	32.81	14.41	10.21	36.24	25.67	n/a
Miami, FL	20.47	33.02	10.61	9.42	36.47	25.80	45.70
Minneapolis, MN	20.22	36.52	13.74	11.43	34.51	24.98	32.67
Murfreesboro, TN	18.81	30.99	11.45	9.93	35.11	24.48	28.42
Naperville, IL	21.29	34.05	12.42	10.90	37.98	25.50	37.47
Nashville, TN	18.81	30.99	11.45	9.93	35.11	24.48	28.42
New Orleans, LA	20.38	32.72	11.18	11.49	37.57	25.16	n/a
New York, NY	24.25	39.93	16.09	10.72	40.18	25.76	68.66
Norman, OK	17.73	28.19	10.47	9.07	37.21	24.52	20.67
Olathe, KS	18.99	31.89	11.80	10.34	33.08	24.74	34.16
Omaha, NE	19.20	28.72	12.12	10.10	35.39	24.82	42.69
Orlando, FL	18.83	28.25	11.78	11.28	38.75	24.96	58.00
Overland Park, KS	18.99	31.89	11.80	10.34	33.08	24.74	34.16
Oyster Bay, NY	24.27	39.67	16.90	11.03	40.95	25.69	49.57
Pembroke Pines, FL	20.12	32.78	11.94	9.51	41.16	25.81	22.28
Philadelphia, PA	24.25	35.80	13.57	11.38	36.83	25.54	65.00
Phoenix, AZ	25.14	35.74	13.23	10.78	37.94	25.15	n/a
Pittsburgh, PA	19.56	29.87	12.86	11.37	36.53	24.92	64.72
Plano, TX	21.67	32.86	11.46	10.61	45.67	25.10	49.69
Portland, OR	23.20	38.36	13.17	10.83	37.27	25.16	37.46
Providence, RI	24.57	34.53	13.47	10.47	39.32	25.29	n/a
Provo, UT	17.99	29.01	10.50	9.38	39.24	24.77	n/a
Raleigh, NC	20.23	28.69	11.46	10.31	33.65	24.14	30.67
Richmond, VA	19.43	32.30	11.49	12.18	38.53	23.96	n/a
Roseville, CA	26.08	47.71	15.40	12.45	42.79	24.88	30.05
Round Rock, TX	21.93	33.09	11.00	11.36	38.51	25.00	45.04
San Antonio, TX	20.43	33.17	11.70	10.67	45.48	24.92	29.54
San Diego, CA	23.19	40.82	12.68	9.96	42.57	25.79	33.89
San Francisco, CA	29.44	50.80	18.00	11.82	42.97	26.37	33.03
San Jose, CA	27.41	56.53	16.97	10.41	42.78	26.07	58.81
Savannah, GA	18.32	29.22	10.72	9.73	42.69	24.12	n/a
Scottsdale, AZ	25.14	35.74	13.23	10.78	37.94	25.15	n/a
Seattle, WA	24.18	37.68	14.77	11.79	37.65	25.70	41.03
Sioux Falls, SD	17.28	27.58	12.21	10.35	32.32	24.04	n/a
Stamford, CT	26.33	37.28	15.28	11.70	37.96	25.93	38.31
Sterling Hgts, MI	21.45	34.23	12.53	12.13	36.63	25.24	n/a
Sunnyvale, CA	27.41	56.53	16.97	10.41	42.78	26.07	58.81
Tampa, FL	20.00	31.80	11.52	9.58	38.77	24.78	28.72
Temecula, CA	21.99	39.09	12.30	11.12	39.91	25.31	n/a
Thousand Oaks, CA	26.90	36.89	13.50	10.39	42.71	25.44	23.53
Virginia Beach, VA	17.61	30.40	11.02	10.18	36.74	25.05	35.93
Washington, DC	22.67	35.92	13.65	10.83	40.55	25.00	38.67

Notes: Wage data is for May 2011 and covers the Metropolitan Statistical Area—see Appendix B for areas included; n/a not available
Source: Bureau of Labor Statistics, May 2011 Metro Area Occupational Employment and Wage Estimates

Average Hourly Wages: Occupations R – T

Metro Area	Retail Salespersons	Sales Reps., Except Tech./Scien.	Sales Reps., Tech./Scien.	Secretaries, Exc. Leg./ Med./Exec.	Security Guards	Surgeons	Teacher Assistants
Albuquerque, NM	12.27	27.05	38.12	13.94	11.78	n/a	10.00
Alexandria, VA	12.47	33.41	46.73	20.68	18.21	109.77	14.30
Anchorage, AK	13.13	26.16	37.99	18.95	15.02	n/a	n/a
Ann Arbor, MI	12.05	32.25	44.30	16.43	14.46	n/a	12.30
Athens, GA	10.32	25.87	33.67	14.86	13.95	107.28	9.20
Atlanta, GA	11.33	31.30	38.03	15.54	11.44	111.35	10.10
Austin, TX	12.19	33.93	39.52	15.34	11.96	n/a	12.00
Baltimore, MD	12.12	33.18	39.57	17.80	14.85	113.17	15.30
Bellevue, WA	14.24	33.18	43.02	19.27	18.98	n/a	15.40
Billings, MT	12.55	27.02	28.18	12.85	12.66	118.29	9.30
Boise City, ID	11.73	24.13	37.81	14.47	12.44	n/a	10.30
Boston, MA	12.60	41.69	47.40	20.23	14.17	115.62	14.60
Boulder, CO	13.59	36.76	42.23	17.08	13.46	88.85	13.60
Broken Arrow, OK	12.04	27.43	40.52	13.50	13.62	91.90	11.20
Cambridge, MA	12.60	41.69	47.40	20.23	14.17	115.62	14.60
Cape Coral, FL	12.20	27.71	41.79	14.85	11.15	120.15	9.40
Carlsbad, CA	12.76	29.99	41.40	18.21	13.27	92.00	13.70
Cary, NC	11.54	29.00	32.37	16.27	11.76	100.24	10.60
Cedar Rapids, IA	13.96	27.05	44.97	14.05	10.16	n/a	12.20
Charleston, SC	12.15	25.40	40.29	15.43	12.06	n/a	11.10
Charlotte, NC	11.99	28.65	39.16	16.31	13.14	115.06	11.00
Chesapeake, VA	11.18	28.00	37.11	15.64	11.60	119.02	11.40
Chicago, IL	12.39	32.65	37.38	16.68	12.12	119.74	12.00
Clarksville, TN	10.60	20.67	44.24	13.13	11.99	n/a	11.70
Colorado Spgs., CO	12.71	28.07	35.20	15.48	14.02	n/a	11.80
Columbia, MD	12.12	33.18	39.57	17.80	14.85	113.17	15.30
Columbia, MO	11.73	23.47	25.97	13.73	15.81	n/a	9.90
Columbia, SC	11.77	30.05	32.46	14.65	11.16	102.05	9.90
Columbus, OH	11.96	28.28	36.96	17.66	12.28	119.85	13.60
Dallas, TX	12.80	32.42	50.79	15.88	12.77	n/a	11.30
Denver, CO	13.31	33.23	43.23	17.43	13.73	103.52	13.80
Durham, NC	11.21	28.10	46.51	17.05	13.99	115.99	10.90
Edison, NJ	13.12	35.59	50.80	18.54	12.67	n/a	13.00
El Paso, TX	10.68	22.03	32.45	12.63	11.86	n/a	10.40
Fargo, ND	12.89	24.57	33.79	15.17	11.83	111.67	12.70
Ft. Collins, CO	11.78	30.94	37.64	15.46	10.29	108.04	12.10
Ft. Worth, TX	11.79	28.96	48.18	15.65	12.08	77.40	9.90
Gilbert, AZ	12.05	30.16	39.60	15.99	13.08	n/a	11.00
Green Bay, WI	11.35	30.90	36.26	15.79	14.29	120.35	13.90
Henderson, NV	12.51	27.10	52.63	17.96	13.25	93.59	15.30
High Point, NC	11.77	26.98	32.01	15.35	11.10	117.72	10.90
Honolulu, HI	13.11	20.99	31.88	18.51	12.01	93.71	13.20
Houston, TX	11.33	31.84	41.40	15.79	10.52	66.07	10.50
Huntington, NY	13.87	40.95	51.50	17.43	14.76	104.10	13.60
Huntsville, AL	11.31	27.28	36.21	16.22	13.18	n/a	10.90
Indianapolis, IN	11.12	30.29	38.19	16.36	12.73	118.56	11.50
Irvine, CA	13.42	32.23	43.66	18.40	14.09	86.61	15.50
Jackson, MS	12.64	26.78	n/a	13.88	11.69	88.21	8.80
Jacksonville, FL	11.67	28.67	38.14	14.83	10.26	n/a	11.10
Jersey City, NJ	13.33	38.00	48.38	18.52	14.01	82.60	13.70
Kansas City, MO	12.17	32.88	39.20	15.13	13.40	n/a	11.30
Kenosha, WI	12.04	32.95	38.93	16.79	13.93	n/a	11.60
Las Vegas, NV	12.51	27.10	52.63	17.96	13.25	93.59	15.30
Lexington, KY	11.27	23.79	39.29	14.72	10.40	119.61	13.80
Lincoln, NE	10.73	24.99	38.43	14.95	12.45	n/a	11.70

Table continued on next page.

Metro Area	Retail Salespersons	Sales Reps., Except Tech./Scien.	Sales Reps., Tech./Scien.	Secretaries, Exc. Leg./ Med./Exec.	Security Guards	Surgeons	Teacher Assistants
Little Rock, AR	10.87	26.70	31.77	13.75	11.74	109.00	10.00
Los Angeles, CA	12.42	30.78	38.68	17.76	13.10	114.00	14.30
Madison, WI	11.53	31.39	39.50	16.89	11.19	n/a	12.50
Manchester, NH	12.31	30.01	43.75	16.17	10.89	104.47	12.80
Miami, FL	11.31	27.96	40.36	14.86	11.47	116.44	11.10
Minneapolis, MN	11.40	36.26	42.33	18.91	14.53	n/a	13.70
Murfreesboro, TN	11.58	28.49	34.32	14.84	10.98	n/a	10.90
Naperville, IL	12.39	32.65	37.38	16.68	12.12	119.74	12.00
Nashville, TN	11.58	28.49	34.32	14.84	10.98	n/a	10.90
New Orleans, LA	12.01	28.99	31.55	14.64	12.18	120.03	10.70
New York, NY	13.33	38.00	48.38	18.52	14.01	82.60	13.70
Norman, OK	11.64	27.46	30.18	14.22	12.89	110.26	9.20
Olathe, KS	12.17	32.88	39.20	15.13	13.40	n/a	11.30
Omaha, NE	12.36	29.45	41.40	15.00	14.90	n/a	10.20
Orlando, FL	11.47	26.15	42.08	14.78	11.10	107.08	10.80
Overland Park, KS	12.17	32.88	39.20	15.13	13.40	n/a	11.30
Oyster Bay, NY	13.87	40.95	51.50	17.43	14.76	104.10	13.60
Pembroke Pines, FL	11.49	30.80	41.23	15.08	10.24	111.34	10.30
Philadelphia, PA	13.10	33.51	46.26	16.95	14.35	71.72	13.10
Phoenix, AZ	12.05	30.16	39.60	15.99	13.08	n/a	11.00
Pittsburgh, PA	12.70	31.74	43.12	14.52	11.93	98.95	11.10
Plano, TX	12.80	32.42	50.79	15.88	12.77	n/a	11.30
Portland, OR	12.97	30.60	49.83	16.97	13.56	n/a	14.10
Providence, RI	12.18	34.31	37.75	17.36	12.75	n/a	13.60
Provo, UT	11.81	24.32	28.32	14.47	13.63	n/a	11.30
Raleigh, NC	11.54	29.00	32.37	16.27	11.76	100.24	10.60
Richmond, VA	12.39	32.74	40.67	16.23	13.06	116.38	10.20
Roseville, CA	12.32	32.15	42.87	17.88	12.52	n/a	14.70
Round Rock, TX	12.19	33.93	39.52	15.34	11.96	n/a	12.00
San Antonio, TX	11.50	27.20	42.93	15.20	11.40	98.05	10.50
San Diego, CA	12.76	29.99	41.40	18.21	13.27	92.00	13.70
San Francisco, CA	13.43	35.39	52.68	20.80	14.96	n/a	16.00
San Jose, CA	12.12	36.81	53.90	19.87	15.84	116.76	14.90
Savannah, GA	11.37	27.05	34.62	14.67	13.87	118.18	11.60
Scottsdale, AZ	12.05	30.16	39.60	15.99	13.08	n/a	11.00
Seattle, WA	14.24	33.18	43.02	19.27	18.98	n/a	15.40
Sioux Falls, SD	12.01	27.35	49.82	12.84	12.19	n/a	10.80
Stamford, CT	13.78	42.04	46.58	20.08	15.22	n/a	13.30
Sterling Hgts, MI	12.94	33.37	46.77	16.26	12.54	112.79	12.90
Sunnyvale, CA	12.12	36.81	53.90	19.87	15.84	116.76	14.90
Tampa, FL	12.11	28.26	40.55	14.37	10.90	90.41	10.90
Temecula, CA	11.79	28.82	37.82	16.71	11.63	119.83	14.10
Thousand Oaks, CA	12.18	33.22	34.45	17.73	11.97	n/a	14.50
Virginia Beach, VA	11.18	28.00	37.11	15.64	11.60	119.02	11.40
Washington, DC	12.47	33.41	46.73	20.68	18.21	109.77	14.30

Notes: Wage data is for May 2011 and covers the Metropolitan Statistical Area—see Appendix B for areas included; hourly wages for teacher assistants were calculated by the editors from annual wage data assuming a 40 hour work week; n/a not available
Source: Bureau of Labor Statistics, May 2011 Metro Area Occupational Employment and Wage Estimates

Average Hourly Wages: Occupations T – Z

Metro Area	Teachers, Elementary School	Teachers, Secondary School	Tele-marketers	Truck Driv., Heavy/ Trac. Trail.	Truck Drivers, Light	Waiters/ Waitresses
Albuquerque, NM	22.90	23.50	n/a	18.77	15.51	10.07
Alexandria, VA	32.30	34.10	12.50	20.12	19.21	12.11
Anchorage, AK	n/a	n/a	n/a	23.41	20.42	10.88
Ann Arbor, MI	29.40	28.40	12.79	19.42	18.38	10.23
Athens, GA	27.60	25.20	10.02	18.85	16.62	8.98
Atlanta, GA	26.10	26.30	14.02	19.76	16.52	9.63
Austin, TX	24.40	25.10	15.46	16.34	16.12	8.82
Baltimore, MD	29.50	29.70	14.51	20.06	17.18	9.94
Bellevue, WA	29.00	29.50	12.43	21.25	17.47	14.87
Billings, MT	20.60	20.20	11.73	19.27	14.35	9.11
Boise City, ID	23.30	22.80	11.88	17.51	14.09	9.58
Boston, MA	32.40	32.30	16.83	22.04	18.77	14.08
Boulder, CO	25.30	n/a	13.29	19.27	15.31	11.72
Broken Arrow, OK	22.10	22.20	11.40	17.91	15.60	8.54
Cambridge, MA	32.40	32.30	16.83	22.04	18.77	14.08
Cape Coral, FL	16.60	23.50	18.47	16.80	15.29	10.07
Carlsbad, CA	31.10	32.30	12.10	19.72	17.14	9.43
Cary, NC	21.60	23.20	14.12	19.81	15.76	10.02
Cedar Rapids, IA	22.20	22.50	9.29	16.74	13.42	9.15
Charleston, SC	22.70	n/a	17.92	16.94	14.89	9.24
Charlotte, NC	22.40	22.90	13.14	19.38	15.30	9.81
Chesapeake, VA	26.90	27.40	10.50	16.76	15.61	9.90
Chicago, IL	29.70	33.40	13.54	23.08	18.28	10.68
Clarksville, TN	n/a	21.80	10.69	14.70	12.94	8.93
Colorado Spgs., CO	22.00	22.30	11.15	16.82	15.00	9.27
Columbia, MD	29.50	29.70	14.51	20.06	17.18	9.94
Columbia, MO	19.90	19.50	9.20	18.38	16.72	8.76
Columbia, SC	24.00	25.10	10.60	18.38	14.34	8.45
Columbus, OH	28.30	27.20	10.16	20.39	15.95	9.29
Dallas, TX	26.40	27.90	12.69	19.42	16.73	9.75
Denver, CO	25.40	27.00	13.58	20.43	16.74	10.21
Durham, NC	21.50	22.90	13.07	16.94	17.85	11.39
Edison, NJ	30.80	32.30	12.65	21.26	18.07	10.98
El Paso, TX	25.10	25.90	8.77	16.91	15.38	8.52
Fargo, ND	24.70	23.90	10.78	18.97	14.26	9.56
Ft. Collins, CO	n/a	n/a	n/a	19.01	14.59	9.59
Ft. Worth, TX	26.40	27.40	12.61	19.77	15.76	10.08
Gilbert, AZ	20.60	21.00	14.81	20.92	17.50	10.36
Green Bay, WI	26.50	25.70	23.32	18.88	15.41	11.50
Henderson, NV	25.10	25.20	15.49	22.68	16.25	11.09
High Point, NC	22.30	22.40	13.96	19.40	15.43	8.86
Honolulu, HI	26.40	26.00	13.11	21.19	15.58	11.68
Houston, TX	25.60	27.00	16.77	18.15	15.95	9.04
Huntington, NY	43.50	42.50	13.56	24.12	19.13	11.59
Huntsville, AL	25.30	23.80	n/a	17.13	15.28	9.23
Indianapolis, IN	24.20	24.50	12.87	19.33	15.81	9.74
Irvine, CA	33.00	35.10	16.54	22.37	16.70	10.52
Jackson, MS	20.30	20.30	14.52	17.55	14.71	9.50
Jacksonville, FL	25.90	23.10	12.03	17.52	14.95	9.39
Jersey City, NJ	33.50	36.20	14.34	22.42	17.85	12.32
Kansas City, MO	23.20	23.80	13.62	20.26	16.64	9.17
Kenosha, WI	26.60	31.70	18.51	20.63	15.76	9.63
Las Vegas, NV	25.10	25.20	15.49	22.68	16.25	11.09
Lexington, KY	23.90	25.00	n/a	17.23	16.74	9.32
Lincoln, NE	24.00	24.20	8.75	17.09	15.07	8.94

Table continued on next page.

Metro Area	Teachers, Elementary School	Teachers, Secondary School	Tele-marketers	Truck Driv., Heavy/ Trac. Trail.	Truck Drivers, Light	Waiters/ Waitresses
Little Rock, AR	22.60	24.10	12.12	19.99	14.75	8.68
Los Angeles, CA	32.30	30.80	13.04	20.25	15.97	10.20
Madison, WI	24.70	24.10	10.65	18.57	16.17	9.76
Manchester, NH	24.90	n/a	12.01	19.91	16.63	11.87
Miami, FL	21.80	24.70	11.43	19.33	14.37	9.59
Minneapolis, MN	29.20	27.70	13.35	21.15	18.54	10.18
Murfreesboro, TN	22.30	22.70	14.74	18.79	16.57	9.18
Naperville, IL	29.70	33.40	13.54	23.08	18.28	10.68
Nashville, TN	22.30	22.70	14.74	18.79	16.57	9.18
New Orleans, LA	23.60	23.80	14.84	19.44	16.87	9.55
New York, NY	33.50	36.20	14.34	22.42	17.85	12.32
Norman, OK	20.10	21.40	10.49	20.18	14.76	9.25
Olathe, KS	23.20	23.80	13.62	20.26	16.64	9.17
Omaha, NE	21.90	21.80	10.96	22.38	16.17	8.89
Orlando, FL	24.40	24.70	11.87	16.98	14.67	11.28
Overland Park, KS	23.20	23.80	13.62	20.26	16.64	9.17
Oyster Bay, NY	43.50	42.50	13.56	24.12	19.13	11.59
Pembroke Pines, FL	n/a	n/a	11.62	18.90	15.92	9.70
Philadelphia, PA	26.40	29.90	15.16	21.45	17.23	10.72
Phoenix, AZ	20.60	21.00	14.81	20.92	17.50	10.36
Pittsburgh, PA	26.60	27.50	12.13	20.16	14.78	9.89
Plano, TX	26.40	27.90	12.69	19.42	16.73	9.75
Portland, OR	27.00	27.50	13.09	19.51	18.22	12.86
Providence, RI	33.20	33.00	13.43	20.69	16.57	10.61
Provo, UT	20.50	24.60	11.22	18.38	14.00	10.76
Raleigh, NC	21.60	23.20	14.12	19.81	15.76	10.02
Richmond, VA	25.10	24.50	14.02	18.03	17.00	10.35
Roseville, CA	31.80	31.10	13.16	19.58	17.34	10.06
Round Rock, TX	24.40	25.10	15.46	16.34	16.12	8.82
San Antonio, TX	26.60	27.10	10.94	15.74	14.27	9.36
San Diego, CA	31.10	32.30	12.10	19.72	17.14	9.43
San Francisco, CA	30.60	32.50	16.04	22.23	19.77	12.19
San Jose, CA	29.80	35.00	20.43	19.47	17.06	10.45
Savannah, GA	24.10	23.50	8.97	18.62	15.26	9.05
Scottsdale, AZ	20.60	21.00	14.81	20.92	17.50	10.36
Seattle, WA	29.00	29.50	12.43	21.25	17.47	14.87
Sioux Falls, SD	19.50	19.40	10.93	18.84	15.00	8.94
Stamford, CT	33.30	34.00	17.78	21.40	17.00	10.57
Sterling Hgts, MI	28.10	29.20	11.44	18.65	14.84	9.80
Sunnyvale, CA	29.80	35.00	20.43	19.47	17.06	10.45
Tampa, FL	26.40	28.10	12.22	17.86	16.05	10.07
Temecula, CA	32.70	32.20	13.66	20.95	16.00	9.36
Thousand Oaks, CA	31.30	29.30	15.81	21.77	17.24	10.28
Virginia Beach, VA	26.90	27.40	10.50	16.76	15.61	9.90
Washington, DC	32.30	34.10	12.50	20.12	19.21	12.11

Notes: Wage data is for May 2011 and covers the Metropolitan Statistical Area—see Appendix B for areas included; hourly wages for elementary and secondary school teachers were calculated by the editors from annual wage data assuming a 40 hour work week; n/a not available

Source: Bureau of Labor Statistics, May 2011 Metro Area Occupational Employment and Wage Estimates

Means of Transportation to Work: City

City	Car/Truck/Van		Public Transportation			Bicycle	Walked	Other Means	Worked at Home
	Drove Alone	Car-pooled	Bus	Subway	Railroad				
Albuquerque, NM	79.0	10.3	2.1	0.0	0.1	1.5	1.8	1.2	4.0
Alexandria, VA	58.9	8.9	8.2	13.5	0.2	0.9	3.8	1.4	4.3
Anchorage, AK	75.7	13.7	1.5	0.0	0.0	1.1	2.6	2.2	3.3
Ann Arbor, MI	57.4	7.0	9.9	0.1	0.0	3.2	15.6	0.7	6.2
Athens, GA	73.2	10.1	3.9	0.0	0.0	1.6	5.1	1.6	4.4
Atlanta, GA	66.0	8.1	9.3	2.8	0.4	0.8	4.4	1.7	6.5
Austin, TX	71.0	11.1	4.9	0.0	0.0	1.2	2.4	3.1	6.2
Baltimore, MD	59.1	11.0	15.1	1.4	1.5	0.8	6.6	1.7	2.9
Bellevue, WA	66.5	9.8	10.9	0.0	0.0	0.7	5.1	1.2	5.8
Billings, MT	80.8	8.9	1.7	0.0	0.0	0.6	3.8	0.8	3.5
Boise City, ID	78.2	7.7	0.8	0.1	0.0	4.3	2.5	1.4	5.0
Boston, MA	38.4	7.4	12.7	17.4	1.0	1.7	15.2	2.7	3.6
Boulder, CO	52.0	6.4	9.4	0.0	0.0	10.5	9.1	1.5	11.2
Broken Arrow, OK	84.6	9.0	0.4	0.0	0.0	0.0	0.6	1.7	3.7
Cambridge, MA	30.7	4.8	6.9	18.4	0.7	7.1	23.8	1.6	6.1
Cape Coral, FL	81.6	10.1	0.4	0.0	0.0	0.3	0.7	1.6	5.4
Carlsbad, CA	77.7	6.6	0.6	0.1	1.2	0.8	1.4	1.5	10.1
Cary, NC	79.8	8.4	0.6	0.0	0.0	0.2	1.4	1.4	8.2
Cedar Rapids, IA	82.1	9.0	1.3	0.0	0.0	0.3	3.0	1.3	3.0
Charleston, SC	77.6	7.5	3.1	0.0	0.0	2.0	4.9	1.2	3.7
Charlotte, NC	76.1	11.8	3.3	0.4	0.1	0.2	2.1	0.7	5.3
Chesapeake, VA	85.8	7.0	1.0	0.0	0.0	0.2	1.2	1.2	3.5
Chicago, IL	50.4	9.9	14.5	10.1	1.9	1.2	6.1	1.7	4.3
Clarksville, TN	84.5	10.6	0.6	0.1	0.0	0.1	1.1	0.8	2.2
Colorado Spgs., CO	79.1	9.9	1.5	0.0	0.0	0.6	2.8	1.1	5.1
Columbia, MD	80.1	8.0	3.0	0.7	1.8	0.1	1.5	0.6	4.1
Columbia, MO	75.2	11.6	0.7	0.0	0.0	1.4	6.7	1.0	3.4
Columbia, SC	68.4	7.5	2.2	0.2	0.0	0.6	4.5	2.2	14.4
Columbus, OH	80.5	8.5	2.9	0.0	0.0	0.7	2.9	0.9	3.5
Dallas, TX	77.6	11.1	3.5	0.3	0.3	0.1	1.9	1.4	3.8
Denver, CO	69.1	10.3	6.5	0.8	0.3	2.0	4.0	1.3	5.7
Durham, NC	74.1	13.8	3.4	0.0	0.0	0.5	3.6	0.9	3.8
Edison, NJ	71.5	7.8	0.4	0.8	12.6	0.1	2.2	0.8	3.7
El Paso, TX	80.1	10.4	2.1	0.0	0.0	0.2	2.0	2.7	2.5
Fargo, ND	82.6	7.1	1.2	0.0	0.0	1.4	4.0	1.0	2.7
Ft. Collins, CO	72.7	8.9	1.1	0.0	0.0	7.2	3.1	1.1	5.9
Ft. Worth, TX	80.6	11.6	1.0	0.0	0.2	0.1	1.2	1.9	3.3
Gilbert, AZ	78.7	13.0	0.7	0.0	0.0	0.3	0.5	1.2	5.5
Green Bay, WI	81.1	7.7	1.7	0.0	0.0	0.5	2.7	2.7	3.4
Henderson, NV	82.1	8.5	1.2	0.0	0.0	0.1	1.4	1.6	5.1
High Point, NC	83.1	8.6	2.4	0.0	0.1	0.1	1.4	1.1	3.1
Honolulu, HI	57.0	12.7	12.6	0.0	0.0	1.8	9.7	3.2	3.0
Houston, TX	75.0	13.1	4.3	0.1	0.1	0.4	2.2	1.9	3.1
Huntington, NY	76.7	5.4	1.2	0.5	8.5	0.1	1.4	0.6	5.5
Huntsville, AL	83.5	9.9	0.7	0.0	0.0	0.1	1.1	1.5	3.1
Indianapolis, IN	81.8	10.0	2.0	0.0	0.0	0.4	2.1	0.7	3.0
Irvine, CA	76.2	7.7	0.9	0.1	0.5	2.2	5.0	1.0	6.4
Jackson, MS	82.6	10.4	1.0	0.0	0.0	0.1	1.7	0.8	3.4
Jacksonville, FL	81.0	10.7	1.6	0.0	0.0	0.4	1.8	0.9	3.6
Jersey City, NJ	34.2	7.6	16.1	23.3	4.1	0.5	8.4	3.3	2.5
Kansas City, MO	80.6	8.7	3.7	0.0	0.0	0.3	2.2	1.1	3.5
Kenosha, WI	83.6	9.4	1.0	0.0	0.5	0.3	1.8	1.1	2.2
Las Vegas, NV	77.6	11.2	4.2	0.0	0.0	0.3	2.0	1.7	3.0
Lexington, KY	80.2	10.6	1.4	0.0	0.0	0.6	3.7	0.4	3.1

Table continued on next page.

City	Car/Truck/Van		Public Transportation			Bicycle	Walked	Other Means	Worked at Home
	Drove Alone	Car-pooled	Bus	Subway	Railroad				
Lincoln, NE	80.8	9.9	1.2	0.0	0.0	1.3	3.5	0.5	2.7
Little Rock, AR	80.6	13.1	1.1	0.0	0.0	0.0	1.5	0.7	2.9
Los Angeles, CA	66.9	10.6	10.4	0.5	0.1	1.0	3.5	1.5	5.4
Madison, WI	64.0	9.0	8.4	0.0	0.0	5.0	9.3	1.0	3.2
Manchester, NH	83.9	9.3	0.7	0.0	0.0	0.2	2.4	0.7	2.6
Miami, FL	69.4	10.4	10.4	0.6	0.3	0.6	3.7	1.2	3.6
Minneapolis, MN	61.6	7.7	13.3	0.6	0.6	4.0	6.5	1.0	4.8
Murfreesboro, TN	85.0	9.1	0.6	0.0	0.0	0.3	1.6	1.1	2.2
Naperville, IL	75.0	5.6	0.3	0.4	8.7	0.2	1.3	0.9	7.6
Nashville, TN	79.7	10.3	2.0	0.0	0.1	0.3	2.0	1.1	4.5
New Orleans, LA	68.4	12.2	6.2	0.0	0.0	1.8	5.3	2.6	3.4
New York, NY	22.9	5.2	12.1	41.0	1.7	0.7	10.3	2.2	3.9
Norman, OK	81.5	8.4	0.9	0.1	0.0	1.1	3.9	1.4	2.7
Olathe, KS	81.9	9.8	0.5	0.1	0.0	0.1	1.1	0.9	5.6
Omaha, NE	80.0	11.8	1.4	0.0	0.0	0.1	2.7	0.8	3.3
Orlando, FL	78.3	10.2	4.0	0.0	0.0	0.4	1.7	1.5	3.9
Overland Park, KS	86.1	5.7	0.5	0.0	0.0	0.3	0.9	0.8	5.6
Oyster Bay, NY	73.9	6.8	0.8	0.6	10.8	0.1	1.6	0.6	4.7
Pembroke Pines, FL	84.6	9.0	1.1	0.0	0.1	0.1	0.5	0.8	3.8
Philadelphia, PA	50.3	8.8	18.8	4.4	2.8	1.9	8.6	1.4	2.8
Phoenix, AZ	74.4	13.2	3.3	0.0	0.0	0.7	1.8	1.5	5.1
Pittsburgh, PA	53.4	10.5	18.6	0.3	0.0	1.3	11.4	1.3	3.2
Plano, TX	82.0	6.7	0.6	0.4	0.6	0.1	0.7	1.8	7.1
Portland, OR	59.9	8.8	10.1	0.6	0.2	6.1	5.6	2.1	6.6
Providence, RI	61.1	12.4	7.2	0.2	1.0	1.4	10.6	1.2	5.0
Provo, UT	61.2	12.5	2.9	0.0	0.0	2.4	15.8	0.5	4.7
Raleigh, NC	78.6	10.7	2.0	0.0	0.0	0.5	2.2	0.9	5.1
Richmond, VA	69.7	11.6	7.5	0.0	0.0	2.0	3.9	1.2	4.0
Roseville, CA	79.8	9.4	0.7	0.0	0.4	0.5	1.5	1.3	6.5
Round Rock, TX	78.5	12.6	0.1	0.0	0.0	0.4	1.3	1.0	6.2
San Antonio, TX	78.9	11.5	3.3	0.0	0.0	0.1	2.1	1.5	2.6
San Diego, CA	75.5	9.1	3.6	0.0	0.1	0.9	3.0	1.2	6.5
San Francisco, CA	37.5	8.0	22.7	6.5	1.1	3.1	9.9	4.5	6.7
San Jose, CA	77.8	10.6	2.4	0.2	0.6	0.9	1.8	1.7	3.9
Savannah, GA	75.2	11.5	4.4	0.0	0.0	0.7	3.6	1.2	3.4
Scottsdale, AZ	77.5	6.6	1.6	0.1	0.0	0.9	2.1	1.7	9.6
Seattle, WA	52.6	9.4	18.4	0.2	0.0	3.2	8.7	1.3	6.1
Sioux Falls, SD	84.4	7.9	0.5	0.0	0.0	0.5	2.3	1.1	3.2
Stamford, CT	66.5	11.6	5.0	0.3	5.9	0.2	6.7	0.8	3.3
Sterling Hgts, MI	88.3	8.0	0.5	0.0	0.0	0.2	0.5	0.5	2.2
Sunnyvale, CA	77.4	9.9	2.8	0.2	1.6	1.3	1.4	1.2	4.3
Tampa, FL	76.7	9.6	3.1	0.0	0.0	1.3	2.9	1.1	5.3
Temecula, CA	76.9	12.9	0.2	0.0	0.0	0.6	1.6	1.8	6.0
Thousand Oaks, CA	77.8	9.9	0.6	0.0	0.2	0.9	2.3	1.4	6.8
Virginia Beach, VA	82.3	9.3	0.9	0.0	0.0	0.7	1.8	1.0	3.9
Washington, DC	35.7	6.4	16.2	20.4	0.4	2.6	12.0	1.4	5.0
U.S.	76.0	10.2	2.7	1.7	0.5	0.5	2.8	1.3	4.2

Note: Figures are percentages and cover workers 16 years of age and older
Source: U.S. Census Bureau, 2008-2010 American Community Survey 3-Year Estimates

Means of Transportation to Work: Metro Area

Metro Area	Car/Truck/Van		Public Transportation			Bicycle	Walked	Other Means	Worked at Home
	Drove Alone	Car-pooled	Bus	Subway	Railroad				
Albuquerque, NM	78.6	11.0	1.5	0.0	0.3	1.0	1.7	1.3	4.5
Alexandria, VA	65.7	10.9	5.4	7.7	0.7	0.6	3.3	1.0	4.7
Anchorage, AK	74.7	13.8	1.3	0.0	0.0	0.9	2.5	2.6	4.1
Ann Arbor, MI	73.8	8.3	4.1	0.0	0.0	1.3	6.4	0.6	5.5
Athens, GA	76.0	10.8	2.4	0.0	0.0	1.0	3.6	1.2	5.0
Atlanta, GA	77.2	10.8	2.5	0.7	0.1	0.2	1.3	1.6	5.6
Austin, TX	74.9	11.4	2.6	0.0	0.0	0.7	1.8	2.2	6.5
Baltimore, MD	76.2	9.7	4.3	1.0	0.9	0.3	2.8	1.1	3.7
Bellevue, WA	69.5	11.3	7.8	0.1	0.3	1.0	3.6	1.2	5.1
Billings, MT	79.6	9.3	1.3	0.0	0.0	0.6	3.9	1.0	4.3
Boise City, ID	78.4	9.5	0.5	0.0	0.0	1.9	2.0	2.0	5.6
Boston, MA	68.9	8.0	3.8	5.7	2.0	0.8	5.2	1.3	4.3
Boulder, CO	65.9	8.1	5.1	0.0	0.0	4.2	4.3	1.2	11.1
Broken Arrow, OK	81.9	11.1	0.5	0.0	0.0	0.2	1.3	1.2	3.7
Cambridge, MA	68.9	8.0	3.8	5.7	2.0	0.8	5.2	1.3	4.3
Cape Coral, FL	75.1	14.5	1.0	0.0	0.0	0.8	0.9	1.7	6.0
Carlsbad, CA	75.4	10.4	2.7	0.0	0.3	0.7	3.0	1.4	6.1
Cary, NC	80.5	9.9	1.0	0.0	0.0	0.3	1.4	1.2	5.7
Cedar Rapids, IA	82.2	9.0	0.8	0.0	0.0	0.3	2.8	1.1	3.8
Charleston, SC	80.9	9.7	1.2	0.0	0.0	0.7	2.7	1.1	3.7
Charlotte, NC	79.4	11.0	1.8	0.2	0.1	0.1	1.5	0.8	5.1
Chesapeake, VA	80.7	9.4	1.8	0.0	0.0	0.4	3.0	1.0	3.6
Chicago, IL	70.9	8.8	4.7	3.3	3.2	0.6	3.1	1.2	4.2
Clarksville, TN	82.4	11.1	0.3	0.0	0.0	0.2	1.9	1.2	2.9
Colorado Spgs., CO	77.1	9.5	1.2	0.0	0.0	0.4	4.6	1.2	6.0
Columbia, MD	76.2	9.7	4.3	1.0	0.9	0.3	2.8	1.1	3.7
Columbia, MO	76.9	12.4	0.5	0.0	0.0	0.9	4.9	0.8	3.5
Columbia, SC	80.8	8.9	0.7	0.1	0.0	0.2	1.5	2.5	5.3
Columbus, OH	82.5	8.2	1.6	0.0	0.0	0.5	2.2	0.8	4.2
Dallas, TX	80.8	10.6	1.1	0.1	0.2	0.2	1.3	1.4	4.3
Denver, CO	75.5	9.8	3.8	0.5	0.2	0.8	2.1	1.3	6.1
Durham, NC	74.0	12.4	3.7	0.0	0.0	0.9	3.5	0.8	4.7
Edison, NJ	50.3	7.0	8.4	18.1	3.7	0.5	6.2	2.0	3.8
El Paso, TX	79.3	10.8	1.9	0.0	0.0	0.2	2.1	2.9	2.8
Fargo, ND	82.1	7.6	0.9	0.0	0.0	0.9	4.0	1.0	3.6
Ft. Collins, CO	75.6	9.4	0.8	0.0	0.0	4.1	2.3	1.1	6.6
Ft. Worth, TX	80.8	10.6	1.1	0.1	0.2	0.2	1.3	1.4	4.3
Gilbert, AZ	76.2	12.2	2.1	0.0	0.0	0.7	1.6	1.6	5.5
Green Bay, WI	82.0	8.1	0.9	0.0	0.0	0.4	2.6	1.5	4.5
Henderson, NV	78.5	11.0	3.6	0.0	0.0	0.5	1.8	1.5	3.1
High Point, NC	82.9	10.1	1.3	0.0	0.0	0.1	1.5	0.9	3.3
Honolulu, HI	64.4	14.9	8.1	0.0	0.0	1.1	5.5	2.6	3.4
Houston, TX	78.7	12.1	2.3	0.0	0.0	0.3	1.4	1.7	3.4
Huntington, NY	50.3	7.0	8.4	18.1	3.7	0.5	6.2	2.0	3.8
Huntsville, AL	85.5	9.0	0.4	0.0	0.0	0.1	1.1	1.2	2.7
Indianapolis, IN	83.4	9.0	1.1	0.0	0.0	0.3	1.7	0.9	3.8
Irvine, CA	73.3	11.0	5.6	0.3	0.2	0.8	2.6	1.3	4.8
Jackson, MS	84.4	9.6	0.5	0.0	0.0	0.1	1.3	1.0	3.2
Jacksonville, FL	81.2	10.1	1.1	0.0	0.0	0.6	1.6	1.3	4.0
Jersey City, NJ	50.3	7.0	8.4	18.1	3.7	0.5	6.2	2.0	3.8
Kansas City, MO	82.7	9.2	1.3	0.0	0.0	0.2	1.4	1.2	4.1
Kenosha, WI	70.9	8.8	4.7	3.3	3.2	0.6	3.1	1.2	4.2
Las Vegas, NV	78.5	11.0	3.6	0.0	0.0	0.5	1.8	1.5	3.1
Lexington, KY	80.6	10.8	0.9	0.0	0.0	0.4	3.3	0.5	3.4

Table continued on next page.

Metro Area	Car/Truck/Van: Drove Alone	Car/Truck/Van: Car-pooled	Public Transportation: Bus	Public Transportation: Subway	Public Transportation: Railroad	Bicycle	Walked	Other Means	Worked at Home
Lincoln, NE	80.7	9.9	1.1	0.0	0.0	1.2	3.3	0.6	3.3
Little Rock, AR	82.4	11.6	0.7	0.0	0.0	0.1	1.4	0.9	2.9
Los Angeles, CA	73.3	11.0	5.6	0.3	0.2	0.8	2.6	1.3	4.8
Madison, WI	73.9	9.5	4.1	0.0	0.0	2.5	5.0	1.0	4.0
Manchester, NH	83.0	7.9	0.8	0.0	0.1	0.2	1.7	0.8	5.5
Miami, FL	78.3	10.0	3.1	0.2	0.2	0.5	1.8	1.4	4.4
Minneapolis, MN	78.0	8.6	4.6	0.1	0.1	0.8	2.3	0.8	4.6
Murfreesboro, TN	81.2	10.7	1.0	0.0	0.1	0.2	1.3	1.0	4.5
Naperville, IL	70.9	8.8	4.7	3.3	3.2	0.6	3.1	1.2	4.2
Nashville, TN	81.2	10.7	1.0	0.0	0.1	0.2	1.3	1.0	4.5
New Orleans, LA	78.3	11.5	2.5	0.0	0.0	0.7	2.5	1.8	2.7
New York, NY	50.3	7.0	8.4	18.1	3.7	0.5	6.2	2.0	3.8
Norman, OK	83.1	10.4	0.4	0.0	0.0	0.3	1.6	1.0	3.1
Olathe, KS	82.7	9.2	1.3	0.0	0.0	0.2	1.4	1.2	4.1
Omaha, NE	82.3	10.2	0.8	0.0	0.0	0.2	2.1	0.8	3.6
Orlando, FL	81.4	9.3	1.7	0.0	0.0	0.4	1.1	1.7	4.6
Overland Park, KS	82.7	9.2	1.3	0.0	0.0	0.2	1.4	1.2	4.1
Oyster Bay, NY	50.3	7.0	8.4	18.1	3.7	0.5	6.2	2.0	3.8
Pembroke Pines, FL	78.3	10.0	3.1	0.2	0.2	0.5	1.8	1.4	4.4
Philadelphia, PA	73.4	8.3	5.7	1.5	2.2	0.6	3.7	0.9	3.7
Phoenix, AZ	76.2	12.2	2.1	0.0	0.0	0.7	1.6	1.6	5.5
Pittsburgh, PA	76.7	9.4	5.4	0.2	0.0	0.2	3.7	1.1	3.3
Plano, TX	80.8	10.6	1.1	0.1	0.2	0.2	1.3	1.4	4.3
Portland, OR	71.3	9.7	5.0	0.4	0.2	2.2	3.4	1.6	6.2
Providence, RI	80.9	8.8	1.7	0.1	0.8	0.4	3.0	1.0	3.3
Provo, UT	73.4	11.8	2.1	0.0	0.0	1.0	4.9	0.9	5.8
Raleigh, NC	80.5	9.9	1.0	0.0	0.0	0.3	1.4	1.2	5.7
Richmond, VA	80.8	10.1	1.9	0.0	0.1	0.4	1.3	0.8	4.6
Roseville, CA	75.2	11.7	2.0	0.2	0.3	1.7	2.0	1.6	5.3
Round Rock, TX	74.9	11.4	2.6	0.0	0.0	0.7	1.8	2.2	6.5
San Antonio, TX	79.2	11.7	2.2	0.0	0.0	0.1	2.0	1.4	3.4
San Diego, CA	75.4	10.4	2.7	0.0	0.3	0.7	3.0	1.4	6.1
San Francisco, CA	61.7	10.5	7.7	5.2	1.0	1.6	4.3	2.2	5.8
San Jose, CA	76.5	10.3	2.1	0.1	0.8	1.6	2.1	1.7	4.7
Savannah, GA	80.8	10.4	1.9	0.0	0.0	0.4	1.7	1.2	3.8
Scottsdale, AZ	76.2	12.2	2.1	0.0	0.0	0.7	1.6	1.6	5.5
Seattle, WA	69.5	11.3	7.8	0.1	0.3	1.0	3.6	1.2	5.1
Sioux Falls, SD	83.4	8.6	0.4	0.0	0.0	0.3	2.3	1.0	4.0
Stamford, CT	73.2	8.1	2.9	0.3	5.9	0.2	3.2	0.9	5.2
Sterling Hgts, MI	84.3	8.6	1.6	0.0	0.0	0.2	1.4	0.8	3.0
Sunnyvale, CA	76.5	10.3	2.1	0.1	0.8	1.6	2.1	1.7	4.7
Tampa, FL	80.3	9.4	1.4	0.0	0.0	0.7	1.5	1.4	5.2
Temecula, CA	75.7	14.8	1.2	0.1	0.5	0.4	1.9	1.2	4.3
Thousand Oaks, CA	77.0	12.6	1.0	0.0	0.2	0.6	2.1	1.1	5.3
Virginia Beach, VA	80.7	9.4	1.8	0.0	0.0	0.4	3.0	1.0	3.6
Washington, DC	65.7	10.9	5.4	7.7	0.7	0.6	3.3	1.0	4.7
U.S.	76.0	10.2	2.7	1.7	0.5	0.5	2.8	1.3	4.2

Note: Figures are percentages and cover workers 16 years of age and older; (1) Figures cover the Metropolitan Statistical Area—see Appendix B for areas included
Source: U.S. Census Bureau, 2008-2010 American Community Survey 3-Year Estimates

Travel Time to Work: City

City	Less Than 10 Minutes	10 to 19 Minutes	20 to 29 Minutes	30 to 44 Minutes	45 to 59 Minutes	60 to 89 Minutes	90 Minutes or More
Albuquerque, NM	11.3	38.1	27.1	16.3	3.2	2.2	1.7
Alexandria, VA	6.4	20.4	22.4	27.8	14.8	6.9	1.3
Anchorage, AK	16.4	44.1	22.3	12.0	2.8	1.2	1.2
Ann Arbor, MI	19.8	42.9	16.9	12.1	3.9	3.5	0.8
Athens, GA	18.1	51.0	14.2	9.1	2.8	2.9	2.0
Atlanta, GA	9.4	31.8	24.9	20.7	5.6	4.4	3.2
Austin, TX	11.1	35.5	24.8	19.2	4.6	3.1	1.6
Baltimore, MD	7.3	25.8	22.8	23.8	7.5	8.3	4.5
Bellevue, WA	12.3	34.2	24.9	20.9	4.4	2.8	0.5
Billings, MT	20.3	50.3	19.7	5.6	1.5	1.1	1.6
Boise City, ID	16.8	47.3	22.2	10.0	1.7	1.2	0.9
Boston, MA	7.8	22.5	21.7	28.9	10.6	6.7	1.7
Boulder, CO	19.5	44.9	17.3	9.6	4.9	2.7	1.1
Broken Arrow, OK	11.1	36.7	30.8	17.4	1.9	1.1	0.9
Cambridge, MA	10.2	30.1	21.3	25.8	8.4	3.2	1.0
Cape Coral, FL	7.4	29.0	25.4	26.0	6.5	3.4	2.3
Carlsbad, CA	9.4	30.2	20.3	20.5	10.7	4.9	4.0
Cary, NC	10.6	34.1	31.6	18.0	2.9	1.5	1.3
Cedar Rapids, IA	19.6	48.5	17.7	9.8	2.7	0.8	0.9
Charleston, SC	13.4	36.1	29.0	14.8	3.6	1.8	1.3
Charlotte, NC	9.4	31.2	26.4	22.7	5.5	2.9	1.9
Chesapeake, VA	9.9	28.5	25.8	25.0	7.4	1.9	1.4
Chicago, IL	5.3	18.1	17.9	29.6	14.3	11.1	3.6
Clarksville, TN	10.8	39.0	24.4	14.2	5.1	4.9	1.7
Colorado Spgs., CO	13.9	38.4	26.7	13.7	3.2	2.6	1.6
Columbia, MD	8.9	27.6	18.8	20.2	10.6	9.9	4.1
Columbia, MO	22.1	53.9	11.3	7.8	2.8	1.1	1.0
Columbia, SC	19.9	45.7	19.7	9.4	2.5	1.4	1.5
Columbus, OH	11.1	36.5	30.1	16.8	2.7	1.8	1.1
Dallas, TX	9.3	30.4	23.6	23.9	6.8	4.3	1.6
Denver, CO	9.1	29.7	26.3	21.7	7.7	3.5	2.0
Durham, NC	13.9	40.5	23.5	14.5	3.3	2.5	1.8
Edison, NJ	6.7	25.5	15.1	20.7	9.6	13.5	9.0
El Paso, TX	10.4	31.0	30.3	21.3	4.0	2.0	1.1
Fargo, ND	23.7	55.2	14.7	3.2	1.3	1.0	1.0
Ft. Collins, CO	19.1	47.0	16.9	8.7	3.5	3.1	1.8
Ft. Worth, TX	9.4	29.4	23.5	22.6	8.0	5.4	1.8
Gilbert, AZ	10.6	23.7	25.0	24.6	9.3	5.7	1.1
Green Bay, WI	18.2	48.2	19.4	7.4	3.5	2.2	1.0
Henderson, NV	9.3	29.8	33.6	21.5	3.1	1.4	1.3
High Point, NC	12.8	40.5	25.2	16.4	1.9	1.3	2.0
Honolulu, HI	10.0	34.2	22.0	25.4	4.9	2.7	0.8
Houston, TX	8.6	28.0	24.6	24.8	7.2	4.9	1.9
Huntington, NY	12.6	25.0	16.6	20.1	8.4	9.0	8.3
Huntsville, AL	16.1	43.7	25.6	10.8	1.4	1.2	1.2
Indianapolis, IN	10.7	31.8	29.1	20.4	4.2	2.5	1.2
Irvine, CA	8.8	41.1	23.6	16.1	3.9	4.9	1.5
Jackson, MS	9.7	41.0	29.5	15.7	1.8	1.3	0.9
Jacksonville, FL	9.3	30.4	29.0	22.2	5.3	2.5	1.3
Jersey City, NJ	5.0	19.2	16.6	26.6	15.9	12.6	4.1
Kansas City, MO	11.4	35.7	27.1	19.7	3.6	1.6	1.0
Kenosha, WI	18.6	32.8	16.8	15.9	7.6	6.4	1.9
Las Vegas, NV	8.2	25.9	29.5	26.5	5.3	2.9	1.8
Lexington, KY	13.9	41.2	25.2	13.5	3.1	1.9	1.2
Lincoln, NE	18.3	45.5	23.7	7.5	2.1	2.0	0.8

Table continued on next page.

City	Less Than 10 Minutes	10 to 19 Minutes	20 to 29 Minutes	30 to 44 Minutes	45 to 59 Minutes	60 to 89 Minutes	90 Minutes or More
Little Rock, AR	15.9	45.8	23.5	10.4	2.1	1.4	0.8
Los Angeles, CA	7.7	24.9	20.1	27.3	9.2	7.9	2.9
Madison, WI	14.8	42.7	25.1	12.1	2.5	1.6	1.1
Manchester, NH	13.4	37.6	21.7	15.4	5.6	4.1	2.3
Miami, FL	5.7	24.9	29.0	25.6	7.8	5.4	1.6
Minneapolis, MN	8.7	34.8	30.2	18.6	3.9	2.7	1.0
Murfreesboro, TN	14.4	33.8	16.8	17.4	10.4	5.4	1.9
Naperville, IL	8.4	24.3	16.5	20.0	10.6	14.9	5.3
Nashville, TN	9.2	31.3	29.0	22.5	5.1	1.7	1.2
New Orleans, LA	10.8	35.9	24.4	18.6	4.8	3.6	1.9
New York, NY	4.8	14.4	14.2	26.5	15.2	18.3	6.5
Norman, OK	19.8	37.7	16.5	16.9	6.6	1.5	1.2
Olathe, KS	13.5	36.7	27.0	17.2	4.2	0.8	0.7
Omaha, NE	15.9	43.8	26.1	10.5	1.6	1.2	0.7
Orlando, FL	8.4	32.3	26.3	22.1	6.1	2.9	1.8
Overland Park, KS	14.9	40.4	25.3	14.4	2.9	1.1	1.1
Oyster Bay, NY	9.6	24.9	18.3	18.8	7.6	12.6	8.2
Pembroke Pines, FL	7.1	21.2	21.5	27.7	13.9	6.7	1.9
Philadelphia, PA	6.7	21.4	20.5	27.0	12.0	8.4	4.0
Phoenix, AZ	9.9	29.5	23.9	25.2	6.6	3.6	1.3
Pittsburgh, PA	11.9	33.5	25.5	18.2	6.0	3.2	1.8
Plano, TX	9.6	28.3	22.3	24.5	9.3	5.1	1.0
Portland, OR	9.2	31.3	27.4	21.7	5.3	3.5	1.7
Providence, RI	16.0	39.6	18.8	14.0	5.5	4.4	1.8
Provo, UT	27.0	46.2	14.0	7.1	2.8	1.9	1.0
Raleigh, NC	12.2	35.4	27.4	17.7	3.4	2.2	1.6
Richmond, VA	11.9	38.3	27.5	14.3	2.7	2.8	2.5
Roseville, CA	15.7	30.1	16.9	24.1	7.0	3.1	3.1
Round Rock, TX	11.5	36.0	22.5	18.0	7.8	3.0	1.1
San Antonio, TX	10.2	32.0	26.6	22.4	4.7	2.5	1.6
San Diego, CA	10.2	36.2	27.3	19.2	3.5	2.2	1.4
San Francisco, CA	5.2	23.7	21.7	28.5	11.2	7.6	2.0
San Jose, CA	7.5	29.2	26.6	24.3	6.3	4.7	1.4
Savannah, GA	10.1	45.2	27.9	12.1	2.1	2.0	0.5
Scottsdale, AZ	14.4	31.1	23.7	23.1	4.6	1.8	1.2
Seattle, WA	8.9	29.4	25.4	24.5	6.5	4.1	1.3
Sioux Falls, SD	19.2	53.6	20.0	4.0	1.0	1.0	1.0
Stamford, CT	14.0	36.0	23.3	13.8	2.8	6.1	4.1
Sterling Hgts, MI	8.5	28.4	23.5	26.5	7.9	3.7	1.4
Sunnyvale, CA	9.4	40.0	25.4	15.2	4.8	3.2	2.1
Tampa, FL	13.6	34.8	22.7	19.9	4.6	2.9	1.5
Temecula, CA	14.3	30.3	8.3	12.0	12.7	16.8	5.6
Thousand Oaks, CA	16.1	37.0	16.6	14.2	5.5	7.4	3.3
Virginia Beach, VA	9.8	31.5	27.3	23.6	4.7	2.0	1.1
Washington, DC	5.7	21.6	23.8	29.5	10.1	7.2	2.0
U.S.	13.9	30.1	20.8	19.8	7.5	5.5	2.5

Note: Figures are percentages and include workers 16 years old and over
Source: U.S. Census Bureau, 2008-2010 American Community Survey 3-Year Estimates

Travel Time to Work: Metro Area

Metro Area	Less Than 10 Minutes	10 to 19 Minutes	20 to 29 Minutes	30 to 44 Minutes	45 to 59 Minutes	60 to 89 Minutes	90 Minutes or More
Albuquerque, NM	11.2	33.1	24.4	20.3	6.0	3.2	1.8
Alexandria, VA	6.8	19.6	18.5	25.6	13.3	12.3	3.9
Anchorage, AK	16.3	40.7	20.4	11.9	4.8	4.0	1.8
Ann Arbor, MI	13.5	34.2	22.4	17.6	6.9	4.2	1.2
Athens, GA	14.9	44.5	18.6	12.8	3.9	3.3	2.0
Atlanta, GA	8.2	23.5	20.3	24.6	11.6	8.7	3.1
Austin, TX	10.9	30.1	22.9	22.0	7.9	4.4	1.7
Baltimore, MD	8.4	24.4	21.6	23.9	10.1	8.0	3.5
Bellevue, WA	9.8	26.1	22.4	24.2	9.0	6.3	2.2
Billings, MT	20.2	43.6	22.3	8.6	2.2	1.4	1.8
Boise City, ID	14.8	35.6	23.5	17.6	4.8	2.6	1.1
Boston, MA	10.9	24.2	19.5	24.0	10.7	8.4	2.4
Boulder, CO	16.8	35.2	21.1	15.6	6.3	3.7	1.3
Broken Arrow, OK	15.1	35.0	25.6	16.5	4.2	2.2	1.3
Cambridge, MA	10.9	24.2	19.5	24.0	10.7	8.4	2.4
Cape Coral, FL	9.8	29.5	23.0	24.9	7.3	3.3	2.3
Carlsbad, CA	10.8	31.9	25.2	20.9	5.8	3.5	1.9
Cary, NC	10.3	29.0	26.1	22.7	6.8	3.4	1.6
Cedar Rapids, IA	19.0	39.4	21.2	13.4	4.2	1.6	1.3
Charleston, SC	11.2	29.1	24.9	22.1	7.4	3.7	1.6
Charlotte, NC	10.4	29.0	24.4	23.4	7.6	3.5	1.8
Chesapeake, VA	11.1	33.2	23.8	20.8	6.4	3.3	1.5
Chicago, IL	9.2	22.7	18.0	24.7	11.9	10.1	3.4
Clarksville, TN	13.2	36.3	21.8	16.2	6.1	4.4	1.9
Colorado Spgs., CO	15.0	33.3	25.8	16.6	4.5	3.0	1.8
Columbia, MD	8.4	24.4	21.6	23.9	10.1	8.0	3.5
Columbia, MO	18.3	45.7	18.2	12.2	3.1	1.5	1.0
Columbia, SC	11.9	32.2	24.3	20.9	6.2	2.8	1.6
Columbus, OH	12.2	31.4	27.3	20.1	5.4	2.4	1.3
Dallas, TX	10.2	27.1	21.4	24.5	9.5	5.6	1.7
Denver, CO	9.3	25.6	24.5	24.9	9.5	4.3	1.9
Durham, NC	12.4	35.2	24.1	18.3	5.5	3.1	1.5
Edison, NJ	8.1	20.5	16.5	23.2	11.8	13.9	5.9
El Paso, TX	10.2	29.8	29.2	22.8	4.8	2.3	1.0
Fargo, ND	22.1	49.3	17.2	7.0	2.1	1.0	1.4
Ft. Collins, CO	16.9	38.4	20.2	13.4	5.1	4.2	1.9
Ft. Worth, TX	10.2	27.1	21.4	24.5	9.5	5.6	1.7
Gilbert, AZ	10.6	27.5	21.9	24.9	8.7	4.9	1.5
Green Bay, WI	19.4	39.1	21.7	11.9	4.5	2.2	1.3
Henderson, NV	8.8	28.7	29.6	23.9	4.8	2.6	1.6
High Point, NC	12.3	37.0	24.9	17.3	4.8	2.1	1.7
Honolulu, HI	9.8	25.0	20.0	27.6	9.3	6.6	1.7
Houston, TX	8.9	25.5	20.9	25.2	10.2	7.1	2.2
Huntington, NY	8.1	20.5	16.5	23.2	11.8	13.9	5.9
Huntsville, AL	12.2	34.1	27.7	18.4	4.8	1.6	1.1
Indianapolis, IN	11.8	28.2	25.2	23.3	7.0	3.1	1.4
Irvine, CA	8.8	26.8	20.5	24.6	8.9	7.7	2.8
Jackson, MS	10.7	32.3	27.0	20.8	4.8	3.0	1.4
Jacksonville, FL	10.4	27.5	25.2	23.4	8.3	3.6	1.5
Jersey City, NJ	8.1	20.5	16.5	23.2	11.8	13.9	5.9
Kansas City, MO	13.5	31.3	25.1	20.7	5.9	2.3	1.2
Kenosha, WI	9.2	22.7	18.0	24.7	11.9	10.1	3.4
Las Vegas, NV	8.8	28.7	29.6	23.9	4.8	2.6	1.6
Lexington, KY	15.3	36.7	24.0	16.7	4.0	2.1	1.2
Lincoln, NE	18.1	42.5	24.5	9.6	2.4	1.9	1.0

Table continued on next page.

Metro Area	Less Than 10 Minutes	10 to 19 Minutes	20 to 29 Minutes	30 to 44 Minutes	45 to 59 Minutes	60 to 89 Minutes	90 Minutes or More
Little Rock, AR	14.6	33.4	22.8	19.4	6.0	2.7	1.1
Los Angeles, CA	8.8	26.8	20.5	24.6	8.9	7.7	2.8
Madison, WI	15.6	34.6	25.2	16.7	4.3	2.1	1.5
Manchester, NH	12.2	30.3	19.9	20.3	8.0	6.8	2.6
Miami, FL	8.1	25.6	22.9	26.9	8.8	5.9	1.9
Minneapolis, MN	11.6	28.8	24.9	22.2	7.5	3.7	1.3
Murfreesboro, TN	10.3	27.7	23.2	23.4	9.5	4.3	1.6
Naperville, IL	9.2	22.7	18.0	24.7	11.9	10.1	3.4
Nashville, TN	10.3	27.7	23.2	23.4	9.5	4.3	1.6
New Orleans, LA	11.0	32.2	21.2	20.6	7.5	5.2	2.4
New York, NY	8.1	20.5	16.5	23.2	11.8	13.9	5.9
Norman, OK	14.9	34.5	24.5	18.0	4.7	2.0	1.5
Olathe, KS	13.5	31.3	25.1	20.7	5.9	2.3	1.2
Omaha, NE	15.6	37.6	26.5	14.7	3.1	1.6	1.0
Orlando, FL	8.5	26.9	23.4	26.0	9.1	4.3	1.8
Overland Park, KS	13.5	31.3	25.1	20.7	5.9	2.3	1.2
Oyster Bay, NY	8.1	20.5	16.5	23.2	11.8	13.9	5.9
Pembroke Pines, FL	8.1	25.6	22.9	26.9	8.8	5.9	1.9
Philadelphia, PA	10.5	26.2	20.3	22.9	10.1	7.1	2.8
Phoenix, AZ	10.6	27.5	21.9	24.9	8.7	4.9	1.5
Pittsburgh, PA	13.6	28.0	21.2	21.2	8.8	5.3	1.9
Plano, TX	10.2	27.1	21.4	24.5	9.5	5.6	1.7
Portland, OR	11.7	29.1	23.8	21.9	7.2	4.4	1.8
Providence, RI	14.5	32.9	20.9	17.6	6.8	5.1	2.3
Provo, UT	20.5	35.8	18.5	14.8	5.5	3.2	1.6
Raleigh, NC	10.3	29.0	26.1	22.7	6.8	3.4	1.6
Richmond, VA	10.0	30.4	26.4	21.9	5.9	3.0	2.3
Roseville, CA	12.2	30.0	22.0	21.5	6.9	4.4	2.9
Round Rock, TX	10.9	30.1	22.9	22.0	7.9	4.4	1.7
San Antonio, TX	10.7	29.4	24.0	23.1	7.3	3.8	1.8
San Diego, CA	10.8	31.9	25.2	20.9	5.8	3.5	1.9
San Francisco, CA	8.4	26.5	19.6	23.9	10.6	8.5	2.3
San Jose, CA	9.0	32.1	25.4	21.5	6.1	4.4	1.5
Savannah, GA	9.5	34.6	27.4	19.9	5.4	2.2	1.0
Scottsdale, AZ	10.6	27.5	21.9	24.9	8.7	4.9	1.5
Seattle, WA	9.8	26.1	22.4	24.2	9.0	6.3	2.2
Sioux Falls, SD	18.9	44.6	23.4	8.8	1.9	1.3	1.1
Stamford, CT	12.3	31.9	19.3	16.4	7.2	7.8	5.2
Sterling Hgts, MI	10.5	27.0	23.3	23.9	8.9	4.8	1.7
Sunnyvale, CA	9.0	32.1	25.4	21.5	6.1	4.4	1.5
Tampa, FL	11.0	29.7	22.4	22.1	8.2	4.8	1.9
Temecula, CA	12.0	27.8	17.9	18.4	8.5	9.8	5.7
Thousand Oaks, CA	14.1	33.0	19.3	18.3	6.8	5.6	2.9
Virginia Beach, VA	11.1	33.2	23.8	20.8	6.4	3.3	1.5
Washington, DC	6.8	19.6	18.5	25.6	13.3	12.3	3.9
U.S.	13.9	30.1	20.8	19.8	7.5	5.5	2.5

Note: Figures are percentages and include workers 16 years old and over; Figures cover the Metropolitan Statistical Area—see Appendix B for areas included
Source: U.S. Census Bureau, 2008-2010 American Community Survey 3-Year Estimates

2008 Presidential Election Results

City	Area Covered	Obama	McCain	Nader	Other
Albuquerque, NM	Bernalillo County	60.0	38.7	0.6	0.7
Alexandria, VA	Alexandria Independent City	71.7	27.3	0.3	0.7
Anchorage, AK	Districts 18 – 32	43.0	55.9	1.0	0.0
Ann Arbor, MI	Washtenaw County	69.6	28.8	0.5	1.1
Athens, GA	Clarke County	64.8	33.6	0.1	1.5
Atlanta, GA	Fulton County	67.1	32.1	0.0	0.8
Austin, TX	Travis County	63.5	34.3	0.2	2.0
Baltimore, MD	Baltimore Independent City	87.2	11.7	0.4	0.8
Bellevue, WA	King County	70.0	28.0	0.8	1.2
Billings, MT	Yellowstone County	45.3	51.6	0.7	2.3
Boise City, ID	Ada County	45.5	51.6	1.1	1.8
Boston, MA	Suffolk County	77.5	21.1	0.7	0.7
Boulder, CO	Boulder County	72.3	26.1	0.5	1.1
Broken Arrow, OK	Tulsa County	37.8	62.2	0.0	0.0
Cambridge, MA	Middlesex County	64.0	34.3	0.8	0.9
Cape Coral, FL	Lee County	44.3	54.7	0.4	0.6
Carlsbad, CA	San Diego County	54.1	43.9	0.7	1.2
Cary, NC	Wake County	56.7	42.3	0.0	0.9
Cedar Rapids, IA	Linn County	60.0	38.5	0.4	1.1
Charleston, SC	Charleston County	53.5	45.2	0.3	1.0
Charlotte, NC	Mecklenburg County	61.8	37.4	0.0	0.7
Chesapeake, VA	Chesapeake Independent City	50.2	48.9	0.2	0.7
Chicago, IL	Cook County	76.2	22.8	0.4	0.6
Clarksville, TN	Montgomery County	45.5	53.4	0.4	0.7
Colorado Spgs., CO	El Paso County	39.9	58.7	0.4	1.0
Columbia, MD	Howard County	60.0	38.1	0.6	1.3
Columbia, MO	Boone County	55.2	43.2	0.6	1.0
Columbia, SC	Richland County	64.0	35.1	0.2	0.7
Columbus, OH	Franklin County	59.6	38.9	0.5	1.0
Dallas, TX	Dallas County	57.2	41.9	0.1	0.9
Denver, CO	Denver County	75.5	23.0	0.6	0.9
Durham, NC	Durham County	75.6	23.6	0.1	0.7
Edison, NJ	Middlesex County	60.2	38.4	0.6	0.7
El Paso, TX	El Paso County	65.7	33.3	0.1	0.9
Fargo, ND	Cass County	52.4	45.3	1.1	1.2
Ft. Collins, CO	Larimer County	54.0	44.3	0.5	1.2
Ft. Worth, TX	Tarrant County	43.7	55.4	0.1	0.8
Gilbert, AZ	Maricopa County	43.9	54.4	0.4	1.2
Green Bay, WI	Brown County	53.9	44.8	0.5	0.8
Henderson, NV	Clark County	58.5	39.5	0.6	1.4
High Point, NC	Guilford County	58.8	40.4	0.0	0.8
Honolulu, HI	Honolulu County	69.8	28.7	0.8	0.6
Houston, TX	Harris County	50.4	48.8	0.1	0.7
Huntington, NY	Suffolk County	52.5	46.5	0.5	0.5
Huntsville, AL	Madison County	41.9	56.9	0.3	0.9
Indianapolis, IN	Marion County	63.7	35.3	0.0	1.0
Irvine, CA	Orange County	47.6	50.2	0.7	1.5
Jackson, MS	Hinds County	69.2	30.3	0.1	0.4
Jacksonville, FL	Duval County	48.6	50.5	0.2	0.6
Jersey City, NJ	Hudson County	72.8	26.2	0.4	0.6
Kansas City, MO	Jackson County	62.1	36.8	0.5	0.6
Kenosha, WI	Kenosha County	58.2	40.1	0.6	1.1
Las Vegas, NV	Clark County	58.5	39.5	0.6	1.4
Lexington, KY	Fayette County	51.7	46.9	0.6	0.7
Lincoln, NE	Lancaster County	51.6	46.6	0.7	1.2
Little Rock, AR	Pulaski County	55.1	43.5	0.6	0.8

Table continued on next page.

City	Area Covered	Obama	McCain	Nader	Other
Los Angeles, CA	Los Angeles County	69.2	28.8	0.8	1.2
Madison, WI	Dane County	72.8	25.8	0.5	0.8
Manchester, NH	Hillsborough County	51.2	47.5	0.5	0.9
Miami, FL	Miami-Dade County	57.8	41.7	0.2	0.3
Minneapolis, MN	Hennepin County	63.4	34.8	0.8	1.0
Murfreesboro, TN	Rutherford County	39.8	58.9	0.5	0.9
Naperville, IL	Du Page County	54.7	43.9	0.5	0.8
Nashville, TN	Davidson County	59.9	38.9	0.4	0.8
New Orleans, LA	Orleans Parish	79.4	19.1	0.3	1.2
New York, NY	Bronx County	88.7	10.9	0.1	0.2
New York, NY	Kings County	79.4	20.0	0.2	0.4
New York, NY	New York County	85.7	13.5	0.3	0.5
New York, NY	Queens County	74.9	24.4	0.3	0.4
New York, NY	Richmond County	47.6	51.7	0.4	0.4
Norman, OK	Cleveland County	38.0	62.0	0.0	0.0
Olathe, KS	Johnson County	44.7	53.7	0.5	1.1
Omaha, NE	Douglas County	51.5	46.9	0.6	1.0
Orlando, FL	Orange County	59.0	40.4	0.2	0.4
Overland Park, KS	Johnson County	44.7	53.7	0.5	1.1
Oyster Bay, NY	Nassau County	53.8	45.4	0.4	0.4
Pembroke Pines, FL	Broward County	67.0	32.3	0.2	0.4
Philadelphia, PA	Philadelphia County	83.0	16.3	0.4	0.2
Phoenix, AZ	Maricopa County	43.9	54.4	0.4	1.2
Pittsburgh, PA	Allegheny County	57.1	41.6	0.6	0.7
Plano, TX	Collin County	36.7	62.2	0.1	1.1
Portland, OR	Multnomah County	76.7	20.6	1.1	1.6
Providence, RI	Providence County	66.3	32.1	1.0	0.6
Provo, UT	Utah County	18.8	77.7	0.7	2.8
Raleigh, NC	Wake County	56.7	42.3	0.0	0.9
Richmond, VA	Richmond Independent City	79.1	20.0	0.2	0.6
Roseville, CA	Placer County	43.2	54.5	0.7	1.6
Round Rock, TX	Williamson County	42.5	55.5	0.1	1.9
San Antonio, TX	Bexar County	52.2	46.7	0.0	1.0
San Diego, CA	San Diego County	54.1	43.9	0.7	1.2
San Francisco, CA	San Francisco County	84.2	13.7	1.0	1.2
San Jose, CA	Santa Clara County	69.4	28.6	0.7	1.3
Savannah, GA	Chatham County	56.8	42.4	0.0	0.7
Scottsdale, AZ	Maricopa County	43.9	54.4	0.4	1.2
Seattle, WA	King County	70.0	28.0	0.8	1.2
Sioux Falls, SD	Minnehaha County	49.5	48.7	0.9	0.9
Stamford, CT	Fairfield County	58.7	40.5	0.7	0.0
Sterling Hgts, MI	Macomb County	53.4	44.8	0.8	1.0
Sunnyvale, CA	Santa Clara County	69.4	28.6	0.7	1.3
Tampa, FL	Hillsborough County	53.1	45.9	0.4	0.7
Temecula, CA	Riverside County	50.2	47.9	0.7	1.1
Thousand Oaks, CA	Ventura County	55.0	42.8	0.7	1.6
Virginia Beach, VA	Virginia Beach Independent City	49.1	49.8	0.3	0.7
Washington, DC	District of Columbia	92.5	6.5	0.4	0.6
U.S.	U.S.	52.9	45.6	0.6	0.9

Note: Results are percentages and may not add to 100% due to rounding
Source: Dave Leip's Atlas of U.S. Presidential Elections, www.uselectionatlas.org

House Price Index (HPI)

Metro Area[1]	National Ranking[3]	Quarterly Change (%)	One-Year Change (%)	Five-Year Change (%)
Albuquerque, NM	201	-0.02	-3.93	-11.37
Alexandria, VA[2]	27	0.62	0.14	-21.41
Anchorage, AK	22	0.30	0.31	1.75
Ann Arbor, MI	80	0.04	-1.22	-20.92
Athens, GA	291	-3.15	-8.38	-13.77
Atlanta, GA	274	-0.43	-7.04	-19.74
Austin, TX	18	0.87	0.60	9.27
Baltimore, MD	170	0.41	-3.11	-18.40
Bellevue, WA[2]	227	-0.28	-4.64	-19.92
Billings, MT	115	-0.16	-1.90	5.84
Boise City, ID	289	2.70	-8.36	-35.65
Boston, MA[2]	89	-0.22	-1.34	-12.94
Boulder, CO	57	0.63	-0.75	1.56
Broken Arrow, OK	125	1.25	-2.04	5.19
Cambridge, MA[2]	51	0.25	-0.58	-8.62
Cape Coral, FL	187	4.51	-3.44	-51.23
Carlsbad, CA	215	-0.39	-4.25	-31.71
Cary, NC	142	-1.10	-2.57	-0.71
Cedar Rapids, IA	47	-0.35	-0.49	1.72
Charleston, SC	182	1.68	-3.29	-15.04
Charlotte, NC	180	0.57	-3.23	-5.87
Chesapeake, VA	230	0.61	-4.79	-14.57
Chicago, IL[2]	250	-0.13	-5.50	-22.86
Clarksville, TN	n/a	n/a	n/a	n/a
Colorado Spgs., CO	154	0.91	-2.72	-8.78
Columbia, MD	170	0.41	-3.11	-18.40
Columbia, MO	30	0.83	0.00	-0.17
Columbia, SC	192	-0.60	-3.60	-3.40
Columbus, OH	121	0.32	-1.98	-6.22
Dallas, TX[2]	91	-0.11	-1.44	1.58
Denver, CO	123	0.36	-1.99	-5.56
Durham, NC	79	-0.18	-1.22	-0.37
Edison, NJ[2]	210	-0.23	-4.16	-18.18
El Paso, TX	118	0.64	-1.94	-0.07
Fargo, ND	32	-0.65	-0.08	5.27
Ft. Collins, CO	6	1.10	1.49	-1.82
Ft. Worth, TX[2]	70	0.23	-1.02	0.65
Gilbert, AZ	275	2.67	-7.12	-47.78
Green Bay, WI	124	0.10	-2.01	-7.61
Henderson, NV	306	-0.37	-12.60	-59.81
High Point, NC	165	0.49	-2.96	-3.89
Honolulu, HI	24	-0.02	0.25	-5.00
Houston, TX	53	0.67	-0.67	7.03
Huntington, NY[2]	179	1.04	-3.23	-17.13
Huntsville, AL	94	0.62	-1.49	4.97
Indianapolis, IN	52	0.56	-0.65	-2.40
Irvine, CA[2]	199	-0.44	-3.89	-30.93
Jackson, MS	15	0.71	0.73	-0.07
Jacksonville, FL	276	-1.29	-7.13	-33.76
Jersey City, NJ[2]	145	-0.02	-2.62	-14.98
Kansas City, MO	157	0.46	-2.76	-8.21
Kenosha, WI[2]	253	-0.32	-5.61	-21.94
Las Vegas, NV	306	-0.37	-12.60	-59.81
Lexington, KY	90	0.26	-1.37	0.28
Lincoln, NE	21	0.20	0.47	-0.36

Table continued on next page.

Metro Area[1]	National Ranking[3]	Quarterly Change (%)	One-Year Change (%)	Five-Year Change (%)
Little Rock, AR	25	0.04	0.22	2.17
Los Angeles, CA[2]	200	-0.46	-3.92	-32.83
Madison, WI	78	0.12	-1.20	-4.18
Manchester, NH	158	0.04	-2.76	-17.37
Miami, FL[2]	251	0.74	-5.54	-43.62
Minneapolis, MN	234	0.59	-4.93	-22.61
Murfreesboro, TN	122	0.01	-1.98	-2.79
Naperville, IL[2]	250	-0.13	-5.50	-22.86
Nashville, TN	122	0.01	-1.98	-2.79
New Orleans, LA	41	0.89	-0.36	-7.18
New York, NY[2]	145	-0.02	-2.62	-14.98
Norman, OK	42	1.90	-0.37	4.51
Olathe, KS	157	0.46	-2.76	-8.21
Omaha, NE	34	0.47	-0.12	-1.56
Orlando, FL	281	0.93	-7.54	-45.20
Overland Park, KS	157	0.46	-2.76	-8.21
Oyster Bay, NY[2]	179	1.04	-3.23	-17.13
Pembroke Pines, FL[2]	203	0.71	-3.99	-44.84
Philadelphia, PA[2]	139	0.23	-2.45	-8.01
Phoenix, AZ	275	2.67	-7.12	-47.78
Pittsburgh, PA	13	0.26	0.78	6.68
Plano, TX[2]	91	-0.11	-1.44	1.58
Portland, OR	220	0.77	-4.43	-19.54
Providence, RI	198	0.39	-3.81	-21.36
Provo, UT	221	0.30	-4.46	-16.82
Raleigh, NC	142	-1.10	-2.57	-0.71
Richmond, VA	235	0.86	-4.93	-14.08
Roseville, CA	277	0.14	-7.16	-43.52
Round Rock, TX	18	0.87	0.60	9.27
San Antonio, TX	77	-0.11	-1.20	4.49
San Diego, CA	215	-0.39	-4.25	-31.71
San Francisco, CA[2]	172	-0.34	-3.14	-20.83
San Jose, CA	112	-0.44	-1.84	-23.53
Savannah, GA	205	1.61	-4.00	-15.99
Scottsdale, AZ	275	2.67	-7.12	-47.78
Seattle, WA[2]	227	-0.28	-4.64	-19.92
Sioux Falls, SD	49	0.07	-0.57	4.47
Stamford, CT	162	0.28	-2.87	-16.79
Sterling Hgts, MI[2]	46	1.07	-0.47	-30.70
Sunnyvale, CA	112	-0.44	-1.84	-23.53
Tampa, FL	236	-0.17	-4.97	-40.26
Temecula, CA	237	0.24	-4.99	-48.04
Thousand Oaks, CA	255	-0.06	-5.65	-34.87
Virginia Beach, VA	230	0.61	-4.79	-14.57
Washington, DC[2]	27	0.62	0.14	-21.41
U.S.[4]	-	-0.10	-2.43	-19.16

Note: The HPI is a weighted repeat sales index. It measures average price changes in repeat sales or refinancings on the same properties. This information is obtained by reviewing repeat mortgage transactions on single-family properties whose mortgages have been purchased or securitized by Fannie Mae or Freddie Mac in January 1975; (1) figures cover the Metropolitan Statistical Area (MSA) unless noted otherwise—see Appendix B for areas included; (2) Metropolitan Division—see Appendix B for areas included;
(3) Rankings are based on annual percentage change, for all MSAs containing at least 15,000 transactions over the last 10 years and ranges from 1 to 309; (4) figures based on a weighted division average; all figures are for the period ended December 31, 2011; n/a not available; n/r not ranked
Source: Federal Housing Finance Agency, House Price Index, February 23, 2012

Year Housing Structure Built: City

City	2005 or Later	2000 -2004	1990 -1999	1980 -1989	1970 -1979	1960 -1969	1950 -1959	Before 1950	Median Year
Albuquerque, NM	5.6	11.7	15.1	14.6	20.4	10.5	13.9	8.2	1979
Alexandria, VA	3.4	6.9	11.5	9.4	19.4	16.9	13.0	19.4	1970
Anchorage, AK	4.8	7.9	10.9	27.2	28.8	11.2	7.3	1.8	1980
Ann Arbor, MI	2.3	3.2	10.6	10.1	19.8	20.4	13.5	20.2	1968
Athens, GA	5.2	13.3	19.9	16.7	18.0	12.4	6.4	8.1	1983
Atlanta, GA	8.8	13.2	9.4	8.0	11.5	15.2	13.4	20.6	1971
Austin, TX	8.6	11.4	16.2	21.6	20.6	8.9	6.3	6.5	1984
Baltimore, MD	1.6	1.9	3.3	4.3	6.3	8.9	17.1	56.6	1946
Bellevue, WA	3.4	8.0	15.1	18.5	21.6	19.2	12.2	2.1	1978
Billings, MT	5.2	6.1	11.1	14.2	20.4	9.8	16.8	16.3	1973
Boise City, ID	3.8	9.5	21.3	15.0	22.2	7.8	8.5	11.9	1980
Boston, MA	2.6	3.4	4.0	5.0	7.1	7.8	7.0	63.0	<1940
Boulder, CO	2.7	4.9	11.3	15.7	24.1	20.0	10.4	11.0	1974
Broken Arrow, OK	8.2	14.1	18.9	21.9	25.6	5.6	3.3	2.4	1986
Cambridge, MA	3.4	4.2	4.8	7.0	8.7	6.6	4.5	60.8	<1940
Cape Coral, FL	12.6	28.3	17.1	23.1	12.4	5.3	0.6	0.6	1995
Carlsbad, CA	7.0	13.8	19.2	25.1	25.6	5.4	2.9	1.0	1986
Cary, NC	17.0	12.3	32.7	20.6	11.6	3.4	1.5	0.9	1994
Cedar Rapids, IA	4.5	8.1	13.3	6.7	14.9	16.1	13.5	22.9	1968
Charleston, SC	9.3	15.3	13.6	13.2	11.8	9.5	7.9	19.4	1981
Charlotte, NC	8.3	15.7	20.8	16.3	13.8	10.8	7.7	6.5	1987
Chesapeake, VA	5.0	8.2	22.9	22.7	16.2	11.0	8.6	5.5	1984
Chicago, IL	3.1	4.4	4.0	3.8	6.7	9.7	12.7	55.5	1945
Clarksville, TN	13.3	14.1	22.2	13.5	14.9	9.7	6.7	5.6	1990
Colorado Spgs., CO	5.4	12.0	15.5	18.5	20.6	11.4	8.3	8.3	1981
Columbia, MD	2.4	6.1	20.3	27.1	31.7	9.4	1.8	1.2	1982
Columbia, MO	10.8	13.6	19.7	14.3	12.6	11.9	7.8	9.3	1986
Columbia, SC	5.9	8.7	10.2	11.4	11.6	14.2	17.1	21.0	1968
Columbus, OH	3.4	8.6	15.4	12.7	13.9	12.3	14.1	19.7	1973
Dallas, TX	4.4	7.3	9.5	17.7	18.6	15.4	15.2	12.0	1974
Denver, CO	4.7	7.8	6.7	8.0	15.9	12.0	15.7	29.2	1964
Durham, NC	8.2	14.6	20.0	17.1	12.4	9.9	6.6	11.1	1986
Edison, NJ	2.1	3.9	7.9	26.0	14.1	15.2	20.7	9.9	1973
El Paso, TX	6.3	9.0	13.5	15.1	19.9	13.1	12.5	10.6	1977
Fargo, ND	5.8	9.5	21.6	14.6	17.1	7.3	9.6	14.4	1981
Ft. Collins, CO	5.9	13.7	20.7	17.5	22.7	7.8	4.2	7.5	1984
Ft. Worth, TX	12.6	15.0	11.0	14.1	10.9	9.3	12.1	15.0	1982
Gilbert, AZ	15.1	25.1	41.4	13.0	3.4	1.3	0.6	0.2	1998
Green Bay, WI	1.1	4.9	10.2	10.5	16.0	12.3	16.1	28.9	1964
Henderson, NV	12.1	25.3	38.5	16.5	4.4	1.1	1.4	0.7	1997
High Point, NC	7.9	12.6	18.0	12.3	16.2	10.9	10.6	11.5	1981
Honolulu, HI	3.2	2.4	8.2	9.4	27.6	23.1	13.6	12.5	1970
Houston, TX	5.5	8.0	9.0	14.3	26.7	15.4	11.6	9.4	1975
Huntington, NY	1.8	3.9	4.5	6.1	11.2	24.6	28.2	19.9	1961
Huntsville, AL	7.5	6.1	11.2	16.2	17.5	23.8	10.4	7.4	1975
Indianapolis, IN	3.0	6.8	11.7	11.6	14.1	14.9	13.9	24.0	1968
Irvine, CA	10.7	20.9	16.5	20.1	26.0	4.5	0.7	0.6	1989
Jackson, MS	2.4	2.7	6.9	13.4	24.7	22.3	17.5	10.1	1970
Jacksonville, FL	8.2	12.1	15.9	17.5	12.6	11.0	11.7	11.1	1982
Jersey City, NJ	5.3	6.9	7.2	6.1	6.0	7.3	10.2	51.0	1949
Kansas City, MO	4.3	5.6	8.9	9.6	11.9	13.3	14.6	31.8	1963
Kenosha, WI	4.5	7.2	13.5	6.1	12.7	9.4	14.2	32.3	1964
Las Vegas, NV	7.2	15.6	33.6	18.4	11.3	8.0	4.4	1.5	1992
Lexington, KY	5.8	9.7	17.1	16.7	15.8	13.6	9.9	11.6	1979
Lincoln, NE	5.1	10.3	15.5	11.0	16.4	11.4	11.8	18.4	1975

Table continued on next page.

City	2005 or Later	2000 -2004	1990 -1999	1980 -1989	1970 -1979	1960 -1969	1950 -1959	Before 1950	Median Year
Little Rock, AR	4.8	6.0	10.0	17.2	21.6	15.1	11.8	13.4	1974
Los Angeles, CA	2.2	3.0	5.5	10.2	14.1	14.7	18.4	31.9	1960
Madison, WI	5.6	10.8	12.0	9.8	16.5	13.4	11.1	20.7	1973
Manchester, NH	2.4	4.4	6.0	13.2	11.6	8.1	11.1	43.3	1956
Miami, FL	6.6	10.1	6.0	7.2	14.0	11.2	15.6	29.2	1965
Minneapolis, MN	3.4	4.0	2.8	6.5	9.6	8.0	10.0	55.9	1942
Murfreesboro, TN	13.2	19.8	24.9	13.8	11.4	8.0	4.4	4.5	1993
Naperville, IL	3.3	10.8	28.4	28.4	16.9	5.9	3.0	3.3	1987
Nashville, TN	5.9	7.6	12.2	16.6	18.9	14.7	11.7	12.5	1976
New Orleans, LA	3.3	3.2	3.8	7.5	13.7	12.7	11.6	44.2	1955
New York, NY	2.1	3.0	3.5	4.5	7.0	12.3	14.5	53.1	1947
Norman, OK	6.7	10.5	14.7	18.2	20.9	13.5	7.2	8.3	1980
Olathe, KS	8.3	17.4	25.3	19.5	16.7	5.5	3.7	3.6	1990
Omaha, NE	1.9	3.4	9.0	9.8	18.6	16.7	13.2	27.5	1966
Orlando, FL	7.7	15.0	15.8	19.8	13.8	8.9	10.9	8.1	1984
Overland Park, KS	4.0	11.3	22.7	20.9	13.9	14.0	8.9	4.3	1984
Oyster Bay, NY	1.0	2.9	3.0	5.2	6.3	14.6	49.9	17.1	1957
Pembroke Pines, FL	1.6	11.9	41.1	22.0	15.7	5.5	1.9	0.3	1991
Philadelphia, PA	1.5	1.5	2.4	3.6	6.6	10.2	17.3	56.9	1946
Phoenix, AZ	7.3	10.2	16.2	18.7	21.1	10.8	10.9	4.9	1981
Pittsburgh, PA	1.3	2.0	2.6	4.6	6.7	7.9	13.4	61.4	<1940
Plano, TX	5.1	10.7	35.9	28.0	15.7	3.3	0.8	0.6	1990
Portland, OR	4.2	6.7	8.7	5.6	11.5	10.0	13.2	40.1	1957
Providence, RI	2.0	1.9	3.3	5.4	7.2	4.6	8.1	67.4	<1940
Provo, UT	4.9	9.9	18.5	10.3	21.3	12.2	8.1	14.8	1977
Raleigh, NC	11.2	16.6	19.8	19.7	12.4	8.5	5.9	5.8	1989
Richmond, VA	3.4	3.5	3.2	6.9	12.4	11.4	15.7	43.7	1954
Roseville, CA	9.2	22.9	28.5	18.6	8.2	4.4	3.6	4.7	1994
Round Rock, TX	14.7	23.8	28.1	19.9	10.3	1.3	1.3	0.4	1996
San Antonio, TX	6.8	10.7	13.3	17.3	18.4	10.9	11.1	11.5	1979
San Diego, CA	3.1	7.1	10.4	17.7	23.3	13.2	13.2	12.0	1975
San Francisco, CA	2.0	3.5	4.4	5.3	7.3	7.9	9.3	60.3	1940
San Jose, CA	3.6	6.7	10.4	13.9	24.3	19.6	12.0	9.5	1974
Savannah, GA	6.1	4.9	7.5	10.8	16.3	15.0	15.2	24.2	1967
Scottsdale, AZ	4.0	11.0	29.1	22.6	16.4	9.9	6.2	0.8	1987
Seattle, WA	5.0	6.8	8.6	8.4	9.5	9.4	11.9	40.3	1958
Sioux Falls, SD	7.5	15.0	17.6	11.4	14.5	7.6	9.2	17.1	1981
Stamford, CT	2.0	4.9	7.2	16.7	15.9	14.4	16.2	22.7	1968
Sterling Hgts, MI	2.3	8.3	14.2	14.7	32.1	18.6	7.0	2.8	1977
Sunnyvale, CA	2.9	3.9	10.1	10.9	24.5	22.6	19.3	5.8	1971
Tampa, FL	6.0	10.3	10.3	13.2	15.1	13.1	17.0	14.9	1973
Temecula, CA	9.8	23.1	34.3	24.2	6.5	0.6	1.1	0.6	1995
Thousand Oaks, CA	2.0	8.7	12.7	17.0	33.3	21.1	4.1	1.1	1977
Virginia Beach, VA	4.2	6.5	12.2	29.0	25.3	13.5	6.7	2.7	1981
Washington, DC	3.5	3.6	2.7	3.8	7.2	12.9	15.7	50.6	1950
U.S.	5.0	8.6	14.0	14.1	16.3	11.3	11.2	19.6	1975

Note: Figures are percentages except for Median Year
Source: U.S. Census Bureau, 2008-2010 American Community Survey 3-Year Estimates

Year Housing Structure Built: Metro Area

Metro Area	2005 or Later	2000 -2004	1990 -1999	1980 -1989	1970 -1979	1960 -1969	1950 -1959	Before 1950	Median Year
Albuquerque, NM	6.8	11.9	18.2	16.1	19.3	9.3	10.8	7.6	1982
Alexandria, VA	5.2	9.5	14.4	16.6	15.5	13.4	10.7	14.8	1977
Anchorage, AK	5.6	10.0	13.0	27.8	25.8	9.8	6.3	1.8	1982
Ann Arbor, MI	3.3	9.8	16.4	10.8	17.8	14.1	10.7	16.9	1975
Athens, GA	5.1	12.1	21.9	18.6	17.7	10.4	5.3	8.9	1984
Atlanta, GA	8.8	16.8	22.1	19.0	13.8	8.6	5.4	5.5	1989
Austin, TX	12.1	16.6	20.5	19.9	15.5	5.9	4.5	5.1	1990
Baltimore, MD	3.5	6.5	13.2	14.1	13.9	10.9	14.0	23.9	1971
Bellevue, WA	5.9	9.4	16.5	15.8	16.0	11.8	8.4	16.2	1978
Billings, MT	5.0	7.2	13.6	13.8	21.3	8.9	13.2	16.9	1975
Boise City, ID	10.9	16.8	22.8	10.1	18.9	5.4	5.5	9.5	1990
Boston, MA	2.9	4.4	7.1	10.6	11.3	10.5	11.1	42.1	1957
Boulder, CO	3.3	9.6	21.0	16.1	22.5	13.0	6.0	8.6	1980
Broken Arrow, OK	5.6	8.2	12.8	15.7	21.7	11.7	11.3	12.9	1976
Cambridge, MA	2.9	4.4	7.1	10.6	11.3	10.5	11.1	42.1	1957
Cape Coral, FL	8.9	22.6	18.5	23.1	16.7	6.1	2.6	1.4	1990
Carlsbad, CA	3.8	7.9	11.7	19.0	24.9	12.8	11.4	8.3	1977
Cary, NC	12.2	17.1	25.6	17.7	10.9	6.8	4.6	5.1	1992
Cedar Rapids, IA	5.6	9.0	15.4	6.7	14.8	14.2	11.3	23.0	1971
Charleston, SC	10.2	13.4	17.5	19.0	16.2	9.2	6.5	8.2	1985
Charlotte, NC	10.2	15.4	21.4	15.6	13.0	9.2	7.3	7.8	1988
Chesapeake, VA	4.8	7.5	14.5	19.6	17.9	13.3	11.0	11.5	1978
Chicago, IL	4.1	7.4	10.6	8.8	13.8	12.1	13.7	29.5	1966
Clarksville, TN	10.3	12.1	22.1	12.8	16.1	10.9	7.2	8.4	1986
Colorado Spgs., CO	6.6	13.1	17.2	18.1	19.6	10.5	7.4	7.5	1983
Columbia, MD	3.5	6.5	13.2	14.1	13.9	10.9	14.0	23.9	1971
Columbia, MO	9.0	12.4	19.9	13.6	15.8	11.4	7.0	10.8	1984
Columbia, SC	8.1	11.8	19.5	15.4	17.6	11.1	8.4	8.1	1983
Columbus, OH	4.3	10.6	16.7	11.5	14.4	11.7	12.4	18.2	1975
Dallas, TX	8.6	13.9	16.9	20.1	15.5	10.1	8.4	6.5	1985
Denver, CO	5.6	11.4	15.8	15.1	20.7	10.6	10.1	10.7	1979
Durham, NC	7.8	13.3	19.9	17.3	14.6	10.3	7.1	9.7	1985
Edison, NJ	2.3	4.0	5.7	7.5	9.9	13.9	17.2	39.5	1956
El Paso, TX	7.5	10.1	15.0	15.8	18.9	11.9	11.2	9.7	1979
Fargo, ND	7.8	11.1	17.4	12.1	19.2	8.4	9.4	14.7	1979
Ft. Collins, CO	7.2	14.0	20.8	14.9	22.0	8.1	4.5	8.4	1985
Ft. Worth, TX	8.6	13.9	16.9	20.1	15.5	10.1	8.4	6.5	1985
Gilbert, AZ	9.6	16.4	21.6	19.1	17.4	7.4	5.8	2.5	1989
Green Bay, WI	4.5	9.7	16.0	11.8	16.3	10.2	10.3	21.2	1975
Henderson, NV	11.5	22.2	28.6	15.9	12.8	5.6	2.4	1.0	1994
High Point, NC	5.7	10.0	20.0	15.6	15.7	11.8	10.2	11.0	1981
Honolulu, HI	4.0	5.5	12.3	12.6	26.2	19.7	11.6	8.2	1974
Houston, TX	9.8	13.4	14.6	17.2	21.7	10.0	7.4	5.9	1983
Huntington, NY	2.3	4.0	5.7	7.5	9.9	13.9	17.2	39.5	1956
Huntsville, AL	9.6	10.7	18.8	18.3	14.2	15.3	7.1	6.0	1984
Indianapolis, IN	5.9	11.4	16.8	11.1	13.6	11.8	10.8	18.6	1976
Irvine, CA	2.1	3.9	7.2	12.6	17.0	16.5	19.1	21.6	1966
Jackson, MS	7.0	10.2	18.7	16.0	19.3	12.6	9.1	7.1	1981
Jacksonville, FL	9.2	14.4	18.1	18.9	13.4	8.9	8.8	8.4	1986
Jersey City, NJ	2.3	4.0	5.7	7.5	9.9	13.9	17.2	39.5	1956
Kansas City, MO	5.0	9.3	14.3	12.9	16.0	11.9	12.2	18.4	1975
Kenosha, WI	4.1	7.4	10.6	8.8	13.8	12.1	13.7	29.5	1966
Las Vegas, NV	11.5	22.2	28.6	15.9	12.8	5.6	2.4	1.0	1994
Lexington, KY	7.0	10.6	17.9	15.5	15.2	12.6	8.7	12.5	1981
Lincoln, NE	5.3	10.1	15.8	10.7	17.0	11.1	10.8	19.2	1975

Table continued on next page.

Metro Area	2005 or Later	2000 -2004	1990 -1999	1980 -1989	1970 -1979	1960 -1969	1950 -1959	Before 1950	Median Year
Little Rock, AR	8.1	10.5	17.2	16.7	19.6	11.7	8.2	8.0	1982
Los Angeles, CA	2.1	3.9	7.2	12.6	17.0	16.5	19.1	21.6	1966
Madison, WI	6.1	11.3	15.7	10.9	17.0	11.3	8.3	19.4	1977
Manchester, NH	2.9	6.4	9.6	20.0	16.6	9.9	7.7	27.0	1973
Miami, FL	3.6	9.5	14.8	19.7	23.0	13.0	10.5	5.7	1979
Minneapolis, MN	4.6	10.3	14.5	14.7	15.5	10.3	10.3	19.8	1976
Murfreesboro, TN	8.4	11.8	19.3	16.2	16.2	11.1	7.8	9.1	1984
Naperville, IL	4.1	7.4	10.6	8.8	13.8	12.1	13.7	29.5	1966
Nashville, TN	8.4	11.8	19.3	16.2	16.2	11.1	7.8	9.1	1984
New Orleans, LA	5.1	6.5	9.8	14.5	20.0	14.7	10.0	19.5	1973
New York, NY	2.3	4.0	5.7	7.5	9.9	13.9	17.2	39.5	1956
Norman, OK	6.2	8.5	11.4	16.4	19.2	13.9	11.2	13.2	1976
Olathe, KS	5.0	9.3	14.3	12.9	16.0	11.9	12.2	18.4	1975
Omaha, NE	6.0	8.8	12.9	9.9	16.9	12.9	10.3	22.3	1973
Orlando, FL	8.2	17.6	21.3	22.5	14.1	7.1	5.9	3.3	1989
Overland Park, KS	5.0	9.3	14.3	12.9	16.0	11.9	12.2	18.4	1975
Oyster Bay, NY	2.3	4.0	5.7	7.5	9.9	13.9	17.2	39.5	1956
Pembroke Pines, FL	3.6	9.5	14.8	19.7	23.0	13.0	10.5	5.7	1979
Philadelphia, PA	2.9	4.9	9.1	10.1	12.6	12.2	16.4	31.9	1961
Phoenix, AZ	9.6	16.4	21.6	19.1	17.4	7.4	5.8	2.5	1989
Pittsburgh, PA	2.1	4.1	7.3	7.5	11.9	11.2	17.2	38.7	1957
Plano, TX	8.6	13.9	16.9	20.1	15.5	10.1	8.4	6.5	1985
Portland, OR	5.5	9.8	19.5	11.7	18.3	9.4	7.7	18.1	1978
Providence, RI	2.0	3.9	7.6	10.9	12.0	10.5	11.2	41.9	1957
Provo, UT	12.2	16.9	22.4	9.8	15.8	6.1	5.9	10.9	1991
Raleigh, NC	12.2	17.1	25.6	17.7	10.9	6.8	4.6	5.1	1992
Richmond, VA	6.2	9.1	16.0	16.8	16.4	10.8	9.9	14.8	1979
Roseville, CA	5.7	12.0	14.3	16.8	19.4	11.6	11.2	8.9	1979
Round Rock, TX	12.1	16.6	20.5	19.9	15.5	5.9	4.5	5.1	1990
San Antonio, TX	10.2	12.2	15.4	16.8	17.1	9.5	8.8	10.0	1983
San Diego, CA	3.8	7.9	11.7	19.0	24.9	12.8	11.4	8.3	1977
San Francisco, CA	2.7	4.6	7.7	10.8	15.4	13.9	14.7	30.2	1964
San Jose, CA	3.5	6.1	10.4	12.9	22.7	18.9	15.6	9.8	1972
Savannah, GA	10.7	12.8	17.2	14.9	12.9	9.7	8.5	13.3	1984
Scottsdale, AZ	9.6	16.4	21.6	19.1	17.4	7.4	5.8	2.5	1989
Seattle, WA	5.9	9.4	16.5	15.8	16.0	11.8	8.4	16.2	1978
Sioux Falls, SD	7.8	13.7	17.8	9.7	14.5	7.5	8.4	20.5	1979
Stamford, CT	2.2	4.0	6.2	11.6	14.2	14.8	16.9	30.1	1962
Sterling Hgts, MI	2.2	6.2	11.0	8.9	14.3	12.5	19.9	25.0	1964
Sunnyvale, CA	3.5	6.1	10.4	12.9	22.7	18.9	15.6	9.8	1972
Tampa, FL	5.2	10.5	14.4	22.8	21.9	11.3	9.1	4.8	1981
Temecula, CA	8.1	13.1	14.7	23.2	16.3	9.5	9.0	6.0	1984
Thousand Oaks, CA	3.4	7.4	10.7	16.7	23.6	21.1	10.1	7.0	1975
Virginia Beach, VA	4.8	7.5	14.5	19.6	17.9	13.3	11.0	11.5	1978
Washington, DC	5.2	9.5	14.4	16.6	15.5	13.4	10.7	14.8	1977
U.S.	5.0	8.6	14.0	14.1	16.3	11.3	11.2	19.6	1975

Note: Figures are percentages except for Median Year; Figures cover the Metropolitan Statistical Area—see Appendix B for areas included
Source: U.S. Census Bureau, 2008-2010 American Community Survey 3-Year Estimates

Highest Level of Education: City

City	Less than H.S.	H.S. Diploma	Some College, No Deg.	Associate Degree	Bachelors Degree	Masters Degree	Profess. School Degree	Doctorate Degree
Albuquerque, NM	12.7	23.5	24.6	7.2	18.0	9.5	2.4	2.2
Alexandria, VA	9.7	13.5	14.1	4.2	30.2	18.8	6.5	3.0
Anchorage, AK	7.5	22.4	28.8	8.4	21.7	7.7	2.1	1.4
Ann Arbor, MI	3.2	8.3	13.1	4.7	30.0	24.8	6.2	9.7
Athens, GA	16.9	21.4	16.5	4.6	21.5	10.5	3.6	4.9
Atlanta, GA	13.4	21.0	16.3	3.8	27.5	11.5	4.4	2.1
Austin, TX	14.9	16.8	19.1	5.4	27.5	11.2	2.9	2.3
Baltimore, MD	21.7	30.0	19.0	4.1	13.6	7.4	2.6	1.7
Bellevue, WA	4.3	11.3	16.1	7.1	38.0	16.5	3.9	2.8
Billings, MT	7.8	29.6	23.7	7.8	22.2	5.9	2.2	0.8
Boise City, ID	6.8	22.0	26.9	7.5	24.2	8.5	2.6	1.4
Boston, MA	15.5	22.7	13.9	4.8	23.9	12.6	4.1	2.5
Boulder, CO	5.1	7.0	14.0	4.2	34.4	22.3	5.6	7.3
Broken Arrow, OK	6.7	23.3	30.2	8.6	23.1	5.9	1.6	0.7
Cambridge, MA	5.8	10.3	7.6	3.1	29.5	24.5	7.0	12.1
Cape Coral, FL	11.7	34.8	24.6	8.3	14.6	4.0	1.4	0.6
Carlsbad, CA	4.6	13.6	20.9	10.3	31.7	12.9	3.4	2.7
Cary, NC	4.8	10.3	15.3	7.3	37.4	18.4	3.0	3.4
Cedar Rapids, IA	7.3	26.8	25.2	10.3	21.9	6.5	1.4	0.7
Charleston, SC	9.2	17.7	19.7	6.5	29.4	11.3	3.9	2.2
Charlotte, NC	12.6	20.2	21.1	7.4	26.3	9.1	2.4	0.9
Chesapeake, VA	10.6	25.9	26.1	9.1	17.8	7.9	2.0	0.7
Chicago, IL	20.1	23.0	18.4	5.5	19.6	9.1	2.8	1.4
Clarksville, TN	8.8	31.2	29.8	8.4	14.9	5.2	0.8	0.9
Colorado Spgs., CO	7.6	21.1	25.7	9.4	22.1	10.7	1.9	1.4
Columbia, MD	6.1	12.9	14.9	5.9	30.0	20.4	4.9	4.9
Columbia, MO	6.8	19.2	16.3	5.5	28.5	14.6	3.5	5.6
Columbia, SC	14.6	20.7	20.1	6.1	22.1	10.7	3.7	2.0
Columbus, OH	12.3	26.9	21.8	6.6	21.8	7.2	1.9	1.4
Dallas, TX	26.9	21.6	18.3	4.4	18.5	6.8	2.5	1.0
Denver, CO	15.8	20.0	18.5	5.0	24.9	10.2	4.0	1.5
Durham, NC	14.1	16.5	16.5	6.3	25.7	12.5	3.6	4.7
Edison, NJ	7.9	22.8	12.6	5.6	29.2	17.1	2.4	2.3
El Paso, TX	25.3	23.8	22.7	6.3	14.5	5.3	1.5	0.7
Fargo, ND	5.9	20.9	24.3	10.4	26.8	8.2	2.1	1.5
Ft. Collins, CO	4.9	15.0	21.9	7.4	30.4	14.1	2.8	3.5
Ft. Worth, TX	21.7	24.3	22.4	6.0	17.7	5.6	1.4	0.9
Gilbert, AZ	4.1	18.6	28.3	11.4	25.8	8.7	1.7	1.5
Green Bay, WI	15.0	34.2	21.2	9.0	14.8	4.3	1.0	0.5
Henderson, NV	7.3	26.7	27.2	7.9	20.0	7.3	2.2	1.4
High Point, NC	14.6	28.2	21.6	7.1	20.0	6.4	1.2	0.9
Honolulu, HI	11.8	26.6	19.9	8.5	21.7	7.3	2.7	1.6
Houston, TX	25.9	22.3	19.2	4.3	17.5	6.8	2.4	1.5
Huntington, NY	7.7	21.6	14.9	8.7	25.8	14.5	4.7	2.0
Huntsville, AL	12.6	20.2	23.1	6.4	23.9	9.5	2.4	1.8
Indianapolis, IN	16.2	29.3	20.6	6.5	18.0	6.3	2.1	0.9
Irvine, CA	4.1	8.8	14.7	6.7	37.4	18.6	5.2	4.6
Jackson, MS	18.1	25.5	22.9	6.7	15.9	6.8	2.8	1.2
Jacksonville, FL	13.2	29.7	24.8	8.6	16.3	5.2	1.5	0.7
Jersey City, NJ	15.9	23.4	15.6	4.0	25.7	11.8	2.3	1.4
Kansas City, MO	13.5	26.2	23.6	6.8	18.7	8.3	2.0	0.9
Kenosha, WI	13.2	33.1	22.2	9.6	15.5	5.2	0.8	0.4
Las Vegas, NV	18.7	28.7	25.0	7.0	13.4	4.9	1.7	0.7
Lexington, KY	11.6	21.2	21.4	7.0	22.5	9.9	3.5	2.7
Lincoln, NE	7.3	23.5	23.9	10.5	23.4	7.0	2.1	2.3

Table continued on next page.

City	Less than H.S.	H.S. Diploma	Some College, No Deg.	Associate Degree	Bachelors Degree	Masters Degree	Profess. School Degree	Doctorate Degree
Little Rock, AR	12.0	21.1	23.8	6.5	21.7	9.0	4.3	1.5
Los Angeles, CA	26.3	19.2	18.1	6.1	20.2	6.3	2.7	1.2
Madison, WI	5.9	16.6	17.9	7.7	28.6	14.3	4.1	5.0
Manchester, NH	14.5	31.8	18.9	8.8	17.3	6.5	1.7	0.6
Miami, FL	32.0	28.0	10.3	7.2	14.1	4.6	2.6	1.3
Minneapolis, MN	12.2	18.8	18.9	6.4	27.4	10.2	3.7	2.3
Murfreesboro, TN	10.5	24.5	23.3	7.0	23.6	8.0	1.3	1.7
Naperville, IL	3.1	11.1	13.9	6.5	36.5	21.6	4.0	3.3
Nashville, TN	15.2	24.9	20.7	5.9	20.8	8.0	2.5	2.0
New Orleans, LA	15.3	26.4	21.9	4.2	18.5	8.0	3.7	2.0
New York, NY	21.0	24.9	14.6	6.1	19.8	9.3	3.0	1.3
Norman, OK	7.6	19.6	23.7	6.2	24.4	12.3	3.2	2.8
Olathe, KS	5.8	18.7	22.3	8.0	30.3	11.4	2.4	1.1
Omaha, NE	11.8	24.4	25.2	6.6	21.1	7.1	2.5	1.4
Orlando, FL	12.8	26.7	19.9	9.5	21.3	6.8	2.1	0.9
Overland Park, KS	3.6	13.4	19.2	6.8	36.1	15.7	3.0	2.2
Oyster Bay, NY	6.2	25.6	16.0	8.1	24.6	13.7	4.4	1.2
Pembroke Pines, FL	11.6	24.7	21.5	10.4	20.3	8.7	1.5	1.1
Philadelphia, PA	20.3	35.2	16.9	5.2	12.8	6.0	2.2	1.3
Phoenix, AZ	20.2	24.3	23.2	7.1	16.2	6.3	1.9	0.8
Pittsburgh, PA	10.8	30.1	16.9	7.6	17.9	10.0	3.8	2.8
Plano, TX	6.8	14.1	18.8	6.4	34.8	14.9	2.1	2.0
Portland, OR	10.4	18.3	22.8	6.2	26.0	10.7	3.8	1.9
Providence, RI	27.9	23.3	15.7	4.8	15.7	7.3	2.6	2.7
Provo, UT	8.1	15.3	27.7	8.9	27.8	7.1	1.7	3.2
Raleigh, NC	9.3	16.2	20.0	7.4	31.1	10.9	2.8	2.1
Richmond, VA	20.1	22.9	18.9	4.8	20.1	8.5	3.0	1.7
Roseville, CA	6.3	19.9	28.2	11.7	23.2	7.2	2.3	1.2
Round Rock, TX	10.5	19.9	26.8	8.8	23.8	8.6	0.7	0.9
San Antonio, TX	20.6	25.2	24.0	6.6	15.0	5.9	1.8	0.9
San Diego, CA	13.6	16.4	21.7	7.5	24.6	10.0	3.3	2.9
San Francisco, CA	14.5	14.0	14.8	5.4	31.2	12.5	5.0	2.6
San Jose, CA	18.1	18.8	19.2	7.6	22.7	10.3	1.8	1.6
Savannah, GA	15.8	32.7	21.4	6.7	15.7	5.7	1.0	1.0
Scottsdale, AZ	4.4	14.8	22.1	6.8	32.5	12.4	4.7	2.3
Seattle, WA	7.1	12.1	18.2	6.8	33.5	14.2	4.9	3.2
Sioux Falls, SD	9.4	27.4	22.3	9.2	21.7	6.4	2.5	1.0
Stamford, CT	14.8	23.7	14.9	5.3	23.4	13.4	3.4	1.1
Sterling Hgts, MI	15.3	28.3	21.1	9.1	17.2	7.2	1.0	0.7
Sunnyvale, CA	8.8	12.1	16.0	6.5	29.9	20.3	2.2	4.2
Tampa, FL	15.4	27.0	18.0	7.9	19.6	7.3	3.4	1.3
Temecula, CA	8.7	21.2	29.6	10.5	20.1	7.3	1.5	1.1
Thousand Oaks, CA	6.0	15.7	21.6	7.8	30.0	12.6	3.5	2.8
Virginia Beach, VA	7.2	24.3	27.2	9.9	20.8	7.7	2.0	0.8
Washington, DC	12.9	19.8	14.6	2.9	22.2	15.6	8.0	3.9
U.S.	14.7	28.4	21.3	7.6	17.6	7.2	1.9	1.2

Note: Figures cover persons age 25 and over
Source: U.S. Census Bureau, 2008-2010 American Community Survey 3-Year Estimates

Highest Level of Education: Metro Area

Metro Area	Less than H.S.	H.S. Diploma	Some College, No Deg.	Associate Degree	Bachelors Degree	Masters Degree	Profess. School Degree	Doctorate Degree
Albuquerque, NM	13.4	25.1	24.9	7.3	16.6	8.6	2.1	2.0
Alexandria, VA	10.5	19.5	17.6	5.5	24.7	15.0	4.3	2.9
Anchorage, AK	7.6	24.3	29.4	8.5	20.1	7.0	1.8	1.2
Ann Arbor, MI	6.1	16.0	20.5	6.8	25.0	16.3	4.3	5.0
Athens, GA	18.5	24.5	17.6	4.9	18.1	9.2	3.4	3.8
Atlanta, GA	12.6	25.2	21.0	6.7	22.5	8.6	2.1	1.2
Austin, TX	12.7	19.7	22.0	6.4	25.5	9.7	2.3	1.7
Baltimore, MD	12.2	26.9	20.0	6.1	19.9	10.4	2.8	1.7
Bellevue, WA	8.8	21.4	24.0	8.8	24.0	9.0	2.4	1.5
Billings, MT	8.2	32.0	22.9	7.6	21.3	5.2	2.0	0.7
Boise City, ID	11.0	25.9	27.5	7.7	19.1	6.1	1.7	1.0
Boston, MA	9.7	24.7	15.9	7.3	23.8	12.8	3.2	2.6
Boulder, CO	6.3	12.2	17.8	5.8	32.8	17.1	3.6	4.4
Broken Arrow, OK	12.1	30.1	24.7	7.9	17.3	5.3	1.7	0.8
Cambridge, MA	9.7	24.7	15.9	7.3	23.8	12.8	3.2	2.6
Cape Coral, FL	13.2	32.1	22.8	7.4	15.5	6.1	1.9	0.9
Carlsbad, CA	14.9	19.1	23.5	8.4	21.3	8.2	2.6	2.0
Cary, NC	10.2	19.8	20.0	8.4	27.9	10.0	2.1	1.8
Cedar Rapids, IA	7.1	30.0	24.2	11.0	20.1	6.0	1.2	0.6
Charleston, SC	12.5	27.0	21.8	8.3	19.7	7.5	2.0	1.3
Charlotte, NC	13.6	24.1	21.9	8.2	22.1	7.5	1.8	0.8
Chesapeake, VA	10.8	26.8	26.2	8.5	17.3	7.7	1.7	1.0
Chicago, IL	13.9	25.1	20.5	6.6	20.9	9.3	2.4	1.2
Clarksville, TN	12.2	34.0	27.2	8.1	12.0	5.1	0.9	0.6
Colorado Spgs., CO	7.0	22.1	26.1	9.6	21.6	10.6	1.7	1.3
Columbia, MD	12.2	26.9	20.0	6.1	19.9	10.4	2.8	1.7
Columbia, MO	8.5	23.8	17.6	6.0	25.0	12.0	3.0	4.1
Columbia, SC	12.3	26.8	22.4	8.5	18.8	8.0	1.8	1.3
Columbus, OH	10.3	29.3	20.6	6.9	21.7	7.8	2.1	1.3
Dallas, TX	17.1	23.0	22.7	6.4	20.9	7.4	1.6	1.0
Denver, CO	11.0	21.8	21.8	7.3	24.9	9.6	2.4	1.2
Durham, NC	13.4	20.1	16.6	6.4	23.2	12.0	3.6	4.8
Edison, NJ	15.7	26.4	15.7	6.4	21.2	10.2	3.0	1.4
El Paso, TX	28.1	24.1	22.1	6.0	13.1	4.7	1.3	0.6
Fargo, ND	6.2	24.3	23.2	11.4	24.8	6.9	1.7	1.5
Ft. Collins, CO	6.4	19.9	22.5	8.3	25.9	11.7	2.4	2.9
Ft. Worth, TX	17.1	23.0	22.7	6.4	20.9	7.4	1.6	1.0
Gilbert, AZ	14.4	24.0	25.7	8.1	18.1	7.0	1.8	1.0
Green Bay, WI	10.4	35.7	20.7	10.3	16.6	4.6	1.2	0.4
Henderson, NV	16.6	29.3	25.3	7.0	14.7	4.9	1.5	0.7
High Point, NC	16.2	29.3	21.9	6.9	17.9	5.5	1.3	0.9
Honolulu, HI	9.7	27.9	21.7	9.5	20.6	6.7	2.5	1.3
Houston, TX	19.6	23.9	22.3	5.9	18.7	6.6	1.8	1.2
Huntington, NY	15.7	26.4	15.7	6.4	21.2	10.2	3.0	1.4
Huntsville, AL	13.2	23.8	21.9	7.1	21.7	9.2	1.6	1.3
Indianapolis, IN	11.9	29.7	20.4	7.1	20.5	7.3	2.1	1.0
Irvine, CA	22.4	19.9	20.0	7.0	20.1	6.9	2.4	1.3
Jackson, MS	14.8	25.3	23.5	7.7	18.2	6.9	2.3	1.2
Jacksonville, FL	11.7	28.8	24.5	8.8	17.6	6.1	1.6	0.9
Jersey City, NJ	15.7	26.4	15.7	6.4	21.2	10.2	3.0	1.4
Kansas City, MO	10.0	27.2	23.4	6.9	20.9	8.7	2.0	1.0
Kenosha, WI	13.9	25.1	20.5	6.6	20.9	9.3	2.4	1.2
Las Vegas, NV	16.6	29.3	25.3	7.0	14.7	4.9	1.5	0.7
Lexington, KY	12.9	25.8	21.3	6.8	19.7	8.6	2.9	2.1
Lincoln, NE	6.9	24.0	23.6	10.8	23.2	7.1	2.1	2.3

Table continued on next page.

Metro Area	Less than H.S.	H.S. Diploma	Some College, No Deg.	Associate Degree	Bachelors Degree	Masters Degree	Profess. School Degree	Doctorate Degree
Little Rock, AR	12.2	30.9	24.1	6.8	17.0	6.1	1.9	1.0
Los Angeles, CA	22.4	19.9	20.0	7.0	20.1	6.9	2.4	1.3
Madison, WI	6.0	23.6	19.7	9.2	25.2	10.4	2.9	2.9
Manchester, NH	9.7	27.7	18.6	9.5	22.1	9.6	1.8	0.9
Miami, FL	17.3	27.4	18.5	8.3	18.2	6.5	2.7	1.1
Minneapolis, MN	7.4	23.8	21.9	9.2	25.4	8.6	2.4	1.3
Murfreesboro, TN	13.8	28.6	21.1	6.5	19.9	6.7	2.1	1.3
Naperville, IL	13.9	25.1	20.5	6.6	20.9	9.3	2.4	1.2
Nashville, TN	13.8	28.6	21.1	6.5	19.9	6.7	2.1	1.3
New Orleans, LA	15.4	30.2	22.9	5.3	17.0	5.7	2.3	1.1
New York, NY	15.7	26.4	15.7	6.4	21.2	10.2	3.0	1.4
Norman, OK	12.8	27.9	26.1	6.4	17.8	6.2	1.8	1.0
Olathe, KS	10.0	27.2	23.4	6.9	20.9	8.7	2.0	1.0
Omaha, NE	9.1	25.9	24.8	7.9	21.8	7.4	2.1	1.1
Orlando, FL	12.4	29.0	21.7	9.6	18.5	6.3	1.6	0.8
Overland Park, KS	10.0	27.2	23.4	6.9	20.9	8.7	2.0	1.0
Oyster Bay, NY	15.7	26.4	15.7	6.4	21.2	10.2	3.0	1.4
Pembroke Pines, FL	17.3	27.4	18.5	8.3	18.2	6.5	2.7	1.1
Philadelphia, PA	12.0	31.1	17.8	6.4	19.7	8.8	2.5	1.6
Phoenix, AZ	14.4	24.0	25.7	8.1	18.1	7.0	1.8	1.0
Pittsburgh, PA	8.9	36.8	16.7	8.9	18.0	7.6	2.0	1.2
Plano, TX	17.1	23.0	22.7	6.4	20.9	7.4	1.6	1.0
Portland, OR	9.9	22.3	26.2	8.0	21.6	8.2	2.3	1.5
Providence, RI	17.2	28.5	17.9	8.0	17.8	7.7	1.8	1.1
Provo, UT	6.4	18.0	29.9	11.0	24.1	7.4	1.6	1.6
Raleigh, NC	10.2	19.8	20.0	8.4	27.9	10.0	2.1	1.8
Richmond, VA	14.7	27.1	21.2	6.0	19.9	8.1	1.9	1.1
Roseville, CA	13.0	21.1	26.7	9.4	19.8	6.4	2.2	1.3
Round Rock, TX	12.7	19.7	22.0	6.4	25.5	9.7	2.3	1.7
San Antonio, TX	17.8	25.4	24.4	7.1	16.1	6.5	1.7	0.9
San Diego, CA	14.9	19.1	23.5	8.4	21.3	8.2	2.6	2.0
San Francisco, CA	12.9	17.7	19.0	6.9	26.6	11.0	3.5	2.5
San Jose, CA	14.1	16.2	17.9	7.3	25.1	13.8	2.6	2.9
Savannah, GA	12.4	30.5	22.9	7.0	17.8	6.7	1.7	1.0
Scottsdale, AZ	14.4	24.0	25.7	8.1	18.1	7.0	1.8	1.0
Seattle, WA	8.8	21.4	24.0	8.8	24.0	9.0	2.4	1.5
Sioux Falls, SD	8.3	29.1	22.0	10.4	21.4	5.8	2.1	0.9
Stamford, CT	11.8	23.3	15.1	6.1	24.6	14.1	3.5	1.5
Sterling Hgts, MI	12.4	28.6	24.2	7.8	16.5	7.9	1.9	0.8
Sunnyvale, CA	14.1	16.2	17.9	7.3	25.1	13.8	2.6	2.9
Tampa, FL	13.2	30.8	21.7	8.8	17.1	5.8	1.7	0.9
Temecula, CA	21.7	25.6	25.5	7.8	12.7	4.7	1.3	0.8
Thousand Oaks, CA	17.7	19.0	24.5	8.2	19.4	7.6	2.3	1.3
Virginia Beach, VA	10.8	26.8	26.2	8.5	17.3	7.7	1.7	1.0
Washington, DC	10.5	19.5	17.6	5.5	24.7	15.0	4.3	2.9
U.S.	14.7	28.4	21.3	7.6	17.6	7.2	1.9	1.2

Note: Figures cover persons age 25 and over; Figures cover the Metropolitan Statistical Area—see Appendix B for areas included
Source: U.S. Census Bureau, 2008-2010 American Community Survey 3-Year Estimates

School Enrollment by Grade and Control: City

City	Preschool (%)		Kindergarten (%)		Grades 1 - 4 (%)		Grades 5 - 8 (%)		Grades 9 - 12 (%)	
	Public	Private	Public	Private	Public	Private	Public	Private	Public	Private
Albuquerque, NM	53.5	46.5	85.4	14.6	87.4	12.6	85.8	14.2	88.7	11.3
Alexandria, VA	42.7	57.3	82.2	17.8	89.6	10.4	83.0	17.0	80.3	19.7
Anchorage, AK	48.7	51.3	91.6	8.4	93.1	6.9	91.5	8.5	93.3	6.7
Ann Arbor, MI	35.2	64.8	89.1	10.9	89.7	10.3	87.1	12.9	92.1	7.9
Athens, GA	67.7	32.3	81.3	18.7	90.5	9.5	88.0	12.0	94.4	5.6
Atlanta, GA	52.1	47.9	81.9	18.1	86.5	13.5	84.7	15.3	83.6	16.4
Austin, TX	53.7	46.3	92.7	7.3	91.4	8.6	92.5	7.5	93.2	6.8
Baltimore, MD	68.1	31.9	83.0	17.0	90.0	10.0	85.4	14.6	87.2	12.8
Bellevue, WA	25.4	74.6	82.9	17.1	83.2	16.8	87.1	12.9	89.1	10.9
Billings, MT	51.0	49.0	93.1	6.9	94.3	5.7	92.8	7.2	93.8	6.2
Boise City, ID	51.8	48.2	84.6	15.4	90.7	9.3	90.9	9.1	92.3	7.7
Boston, MA	54.7	45.3	79.5	20.5	85.1	14.9	79.5	20.5	86.6	13.4
Boulder, CO	43.8	56.2	82.9	17.1	93.5	6.5	90.0	10.0	91.9	8.1
Broken Arrow, OK	73.1	26.9	84.0	16.0	83.2	16.8	86.0	14.0	84.7	15.3
Cambridge, MA	27.9	72.1	82.1	17.9	76.5	23.5	81.0	19.0	84.3	15.7
Cape Coral, FL	72.9	27.1	90.8	9.2	92.7	7.3	92.9	7.1	94.3	5.7
Carlsbad, CA	21.3	78.7	88.7	11.3	90.7	9.3	87.7	12.3	94.9	5.1
Cary, NC	27.9	72.1	87.0	13.0	89.5	10.5	88.6	11.4	88.6	11.4
Cedar Rapids, IA	57.7	42.3	92.8	7.2	84.1	15.9	84.9	15.1	86.1	13.9
Charleston, SC	31.8	68.2	68.2	31.8	83.4	16.6	85.7	14.3	81.4	18.6
Charlotte, NC	43.0	57.0	87.1	12.9	88.5	11.5	86.5	13.5	86.9	13.1
Chesapeake, VA	36.4	63.6	83.7	16.3	87.5	12.5	87.3	12.7	93.3	6.7
Chicago, IL	63.1	36.9	82.5	17.5	86.0	14.0	87.1	12.9	85.9	14.1
Clarksville, TN	57.4	42.6	84.9	15.1	90.0	10.0	93.6	6.4	92.5	7.5
Colorado Spgs., CO	53.3	46.7	91.9	8.1	93.9	6.1	90.6	9.4	92.3	7.7
Columbia, MD	27.1	72.9	81.6	18.4	84.9	15.1	93.4	6.6	89.0	11.0
Columbia, MO	44.2	55.8	82.3	17.7	88.6	11.4	88.4	11.6	90.5	9.5
Columbia, SC	54.2	45.8	82.9	17.1	84.7	15.3	85.0	15.0	92.6	7.4
Columbus, OH	54.8	45.2	88.8	11.2	89.6	10.4	89.0	11.0	88.7	11.3
Dallas, TX	67.4	32.6	89.1	10.9	90.4	9.6	90.7	9.3	91.1	8.9
Denver, CO	53.8	46.2	89.1	10.9	88.7	11.3	89.3	10.7	90.4	9.6
Durham, NC	42.4	57.6	86.4	13.6	90.1	9.9	87.0	13.0	92.4	7.6
Edison, NJ	19.6	80.4	79.9	20.1	92.9	7.1	89.9	10.1	94.2	5.8
El Paso, TX	80.0	20.0	91.9	8.1	94.8	5.2	94.8	5.2	95.6	4.4
Fargo, ND	45.0	55.0	82.5	17.5	86.0	14.0	86.7	13.3	89.0	11.0
Ft. Collins, CO	27.2	72.8	98.7	1.3	92.2	7.8	88.2	11.8	96.3	3.7
Ft. Worth, TX	61.3	38.7	89.2	10.8	91.1	8.9	92.4	7.6	91.4	8.6
Gilbert, AZ	48.6	51.4	89.2	10.8	90.8	9.2	93.6	6.4	96.1	3.9
Green Bay, WI	69.3	30.7	89.8	10.2	92.4	7.6	92.2	7.8	92.7	7.3
Henderson, NV	51.2	48.8	85.3	14.7	91.8	8.2	96.2	3.8	94.6	5.4
High Point, NC	63.6	36.4	89.2	10.8	89.4	10.6	89.2	10.8	90.1	9.9
Honolulu, HI	36.8	63.2	71.3	28.7	79.8	20.2	75.9	24.1	76.1	23.9
Houston, TX	68.7	31.3	92.3	7.7	93.7	6.3	93.5	6.5	94.3	5.7
Huntington, NY	39.4	60.6	92.6	7.4	93.6	6.4	93.3	6.7	91.4	8.6
Huntsville, AL	44.8	55.2	83.7	16.3	88.3	11.7	84.1	15.9	89.7	10.3
Indianapolis, IN	44.0	56.0	80.7	19.3	86.2	13.8	86.6	13.4	87.3	12.7
Irvine, CA	24.1	75.9	89.2	10.8	91.0	9.0	91.9	8.1	93.9	6.1
Jackson, MS	76.3	23.7	83.1	16.9	90.3	9.7	85.8	14.2	88.4	11.6
Jacksonville, FL	48.7	51.3	80.3	19.7	85.6	14.4	82.3	17.7	83.1	16.9
Jersey City, NJ	71.6	28.4	92.7	7.3	87.6	12.4	88.7	11.3	89.2	10.8
Kansas City, MO	61.4	38.6	88.1	11.9	86.5	13.5	85.6	14.4	84.1	15.9
Kenosha, WI	63.8	36.2	94.7	5.3	87.1	12.9	91.4	8.6	94.4	5.6
Las Vegas, NV	49.9	50.1	93.6	6.4	93.3	6.7	93.5	6.5	94.4	5.6
Lexington, KY	42.1	57.9	86.2	13.8	87.4	12.6	85.7	14.3	88.7	11.3
Lincoln, NE	45.7	54.3	83.7	16.3	83.4	16.6	80.7	19.3	84.9	15.1

Table continued on next page.

City	Preschool (%)		Kindergarten (%)		Grades 1 - 4 (%)		Grades 5 - 8 (%)		Grades 9 - 12 (%)	
	Public	Private	Public	Private	Public	Private	Public	Private	Public	Private
Little Rock, AR	42.7	57.3	86.7	13.3	86.1	13.9	80.0	20.0	79.4	20.6
Los Angeles, CA	61.7	38.3	87.5	12.5	89.0	11.0	88.9	11.1	89.6	10.4
Madison, WI	27.6	72.4	90.9	9.1	87.7	12.3	87.5	12.5	90.5	9.5
Manchester, NH	52.6	47.4	72.0	28.0	87.1	12.9	88.9	11.1	94.4	5.6
Miami, FL	57.7	42.3	83.7	16.3	89.2	10.8	91.5	8.5	93.1	6.9
Minneapolis, MN	54.9	45.1	83.8	16.2	88.7	11.3	86.2	13.8	90.2	9.8
Murfreesboro, TN	45.9	54.1	90.4	9.6	95.0	5.0	94.0	6.0	97.1	2.9
Naperville, IL	36.2	63.8	86.2	13.8	94.8	5.2	95.1	4.9	92.5	7.5
Nashville, TN	50.3	49.7	78.6	21.4	84.2	15.8	80.1	19.9	81.6	18.4
New Orleans, LA	51.2	48.8	64.6	35.4	76.4	23.6	72.0	28.0	78.0	22.0
New York, NY	53.8	46.2	76.8	23.2	80.9	19.1	81.2	18.8	82.7	17.3
Norman, OK	64.9	35.1	83.3	16.7	93.0	7.0	94.0	6.0	92.9	7.1
Olathe, KS	44.8	55.2	87.3	12.7	91.0	9.0	92.7	7.3	90.6	9.4
Omaha, NE	57.1	42.9	80.2	19.8	84.2	15.8	84.7	15.3	88.3	11.7
Orlando, FL	41.4	58.6	85.3	14.7	88.5	11.5	88.0	12.0	88.3	11.7
Overland Park, KS	28.6	71.4	80.3	19.7	83.4	16.6	82.5	17.5	85.3	14.7
Oyster Bay, NY	23.4	76.6	87.5	12.5	92.9	7.1	87.7	12.3	85.8	14.2
Pembroke Pines, FL	27.6	72.4	83.2	16.8	89.6	10.4	90.9	9.1	87.6	12.4
Philadelphia, PA	59.8	40.2	75.8	24.2	80.8	19.2	78.8	21.2	81.7	18.3
Phoenix, AZ	63.1	36.9	92.5	7.5	93.6	6.4	93.9	6.1	93.7	6.3
Pittsburgh, PA	51.6	48.4	73.5	26.5	80.1	19.9	81.3	18.7	81.8	18.2
Plano, TX	43.6	56.4	86.8	13.2	89.4	10.6	89.0	11.0	91.2	8.8
Portland, OR	42.4	57.6	84.9	15.1	87.5	12.5	89.2	10.8	88.8	11.2
Providence, RI	51.2	48.8	82.7	17.3	82.8	17.2	88.7	11.3	89.0	11.0
Provo, UT	43.1	56.9	93.9	6.1	94.3	5.7	94.6	5.4	77.9	22.1
Raleigh, NC	31.5	68.5	82.9	17.1	88.3	11.7	92.1	7.9	90.7	9.3
Richmond, VA	55.5	44.5	83.9	16.1	87.2	12.8	86.0	14.0	85.8	14.2
Roseville, CA	49.7	50.3	89.4	10.6	88.7	11.3	89.6	10.4	92.7	7.3
Round Rock, TX	46.3	53.7	94.8	5.2	94.9	5.1	92.2	7.8	95.3	4.7
San Antonio, TX	68.0	32.0	89.4	10.6	93.5	6.5	92.8	7.2	93.0	7.0
San Diego, CA	54.0	46.0	90.6	9.4	91.4	8.6	91.6	8.4	92.7	7.3
San Francisco, CA	31.2	68.8	76.4	23.6	74.1	25.9	74.6	25.4	80.8	19.2
San Jose, CA	43.3	56.7	84.9	15.1	87.5	12.5	89.5	10.5	90.4	9.6
Savannah, GA	71.9	28.1	86.4	13.6	90.4	9.6	89.7	10.3	91.1	8.9
Scottsdale, AZ	31.9	68.1	86.0	14.0	87.0	13.0	88.5	11.5	87.4	12.6
Seattle, WA	29.6	70.4	75.4	24.6	78.9	21.1	73.9	26.1	78.9	21.1
Sioux Falls, SD	59.2	40.8	87.7	12.3	87.3	12.7	86.0	14.0	89.1	10.9
Stamford, CT	30.4	69.6	77.6	22.4	83.8	16.2	75.1	24.9	79.0	21.0
Sterling Hgts, MI	76.8	23.2	92.3	7.7	93.9	6.1	89.8	10.2	94.8	5.2
Sunnyvale, CA	14.1	85.9	73.1	26.9	74.0	26.0	86.6	13.4	87.2	12.8
Tampa, FL	56.3	43.7	86.9	13.1	91.4	8.6	87.4	12.6	93.5	6.5
Temecula, CA	43.5	56.5	88.1	11.9	88.7	11.3	86.8	13.2	94.3	5.7
Thousand Oaks, CA	33.1	66.9	80.0	20.0	87.2	12.8	86.3	13.7	90.4	9.6
Virginia Beach, VA	32.7	67.3	79.2	20.8	90.2	9.8	91.4	8.6	91.7	8.3
Washington, DC	67.5	32.5	79.1	20.9	84.4	15.6	79.7	20.3	84.5	15.5
U.S.	55.4	44.6	87.1	12.9	89.4	10.6	89.5	10.5	90.4	9.6

Note: Figures shown cover persons 3 years old and over
Source: U.S. Census Bureau, 2008-2010 American Community Survey 3-Year Estimates

School Enrollment by Grade and Control: Metro Area

Metro Area	Preschool (%)		Kindergarten (%)		Grades 1 - 4 (%)		Grades 5 - 8 (%)		Grades 9 - 12 (%)	
	Public	Private	Public	Private	Public	Private	Public	Private	Public	Private
Albuquerque, NM	60.0	40.0	86.4	13.6	88.5	11.5	88.0	12.0	89.6	10.4
Alexandria, VA	38.6	61.4	82.1	17.9	86.5	13.5	87.0	13.0	88.9	11.1
Anchorage, AK	49.9	50.1	91.5	8.5	91.0	9.0	89.7	10.3	91.1	8.9
Ann Arbor, MI	40.8	59.2	85.0	15.0	86.8	13.2	89.1	10.9	91.1	8.9
Athens, GA	61.0	39.0	85.4	14.6	89.5	10.5	87.7	12.3	92.8	7.2
Atlanta, GA	48.3	51.7	86.0	14.0	89.7	10.3	89.1	10.9	90.2	9.8
Austin, TX	50.0	50.0	90.8	9.2	92.4	7.6	93.0	7.0	93.2	6.8
Baltimore, MD	48.0	52.0	82.3	17.7	85.2	14.8	83.7	16.3	84.4	15.6
Bellevue, WA	39.5	60.5	84.9	15.1	89.0	11.0	88.7	11.3	89.9	10.1
Billings, MT	51.4	48.6	89.6	10.4	93.7	6.3	92.9	7.1	92.5	7.5
Boise City, ID	45.9	54.1	90.0	10.0	92.6	7.4	92.3	7.7	92.6	7.4
Boston, MA	38.1	61.9	84.2	15.8	90.0	10.0	87.6	12.4	86.3	13.7
Boulder, CO	42.6	57.4	87.3	12.7	91.0	9.0	88.9	11.1	92.5	7.5
Broken Arrow, OK	72.1	27.9	89.5	10.5	89.9	10.1	89.9	10.1	88.1	11.9
Cambridge, MA	38.1	61.9	84.2	15.8	90.0	10.0	87.6	12.4	86.3	13.7
Cape Coral, FL	62.7	37.3	90.2	9.8	91.4	8.6	90.4	9.6	91.8	8.2
Carlsbad, CA	52.5	47.5	90.2	9.8	91.5	8.5	91.6	8.4	93.0	7.0
Cary, NC	33.0	67.0	85.8	14.2	89.3	10.7	89.6	10.4	90.6	9.4
Cedar Rapids, IA	60.1	39.9	88.9	11.1	85.4	14.6	86.5	13.5	90.7	9.3
Charleston, SC	47.9	52.1	81.9	18.1	87.7	12.3	87.3	12.7	86.3	13.7
Charlotte, NC	44.4	55.6	89.2	10.8	89.7	10.3	88.4	11.6	89.4	10.6
Chesapeake, VA	49.1	50.9	84.5	15.5	89.4	10.6	89.9	10.1	92.2	7.8
Chicago, IL	55.9	44.1	84.4	15.6	88.0	12.0	88.8	11.2	90.0	10.0
Clarksville, TN	71.7	28.3	86.9	13.1	88.1	11.9	91.0	9.0	89.7	10.3
Colorado Spgs., CO	59.5	40.5	89.0	11.0	90.2	9.8	89.4	10.6	91.7	8.3
Columbia, MD	48.0	52.0	82.3	17.7	85.2	14.8	83.7	16.3	84.4	15.6
Columbia, MO	48.4	51.6	85.6	14.4	89.5	10.5	89.7	10.3	93.1	6.9
Columbia, SC	52.7	47.3	86.9	13.1	90.4	9.6	91.5	8.5	92.7	7.3
Columbus, OH	47.7	52.3	85.6	14.4	87.9	12.1	88.6	11.4	89.6	10.4
Dallas, TX	51.9	48.1	89.1	10.9	91.6	8.4	92.4	7.6	92.6	7.4
Denver, CO	52.7	47.3	87.7	12.3	91.4	8.6	91.9	8.1	91.7	8.3
Durham, NC	40.0	60.0	86.1	13.9	88.4	11.6	87.8	12.2	92.3	7.7
Edison, NJ	47.4	52.6	80.7	19.3	85.3	14.7	85.5	14.5	85.5	14.5
El Paso, TX	82.5	17.5	93.0	7.0	95.7	4.3	95.5	4.5	96.2	3.8
Fargo, ND	50.1	49.9	90.0	10.0	88.9	11.1	91.2	8.8	91.3	8.7
Ft. Collins, CO	29.7	70.3	92.8	7.2	91.2	8.8	91.3	8.7	94.9	5.1
Ft. Worth, TX	51.9	48.1	89.1	10.9	91.6	8.4	92.4	7.6	92.6	7.4
Gilbert, AZ	55.9	44.1	91.0	9.0	92.9	7.1	94.0	6.0	94.4	5.6
Green Bay, WI	65.6	34.4	88.2	11.8	87.7	12.3	89.1	10.9	93.6	6.4
Henderson, NV	56.2	43.8	92.4	7.6	93.6	6.4	95.6	4.4	95.2	4.8
High Point, NC	50.9	49.1	89.0	11.0	91.9	8.1	90.6	9.4	92.5	7.5
Honolulu, HI	30.5	69.5	79.3	20.7	83.5	16.5	78.1	21.9	76.8	23.2
Houston, TX	57.5	42.5	90.6	9.4	93.8	6.2	93.8	6.2	94.1	5.9
Huntington, NY	47.4	52.6	80.7	19.3	85.3	14.7	85.5	14.5	85.5	14.5
Huntsville, AL	45.4	54.6	88.3	11.7	87.9	12.1	84.6	15.4	88.9	11.1
Indianapolis, IN	41.3	58.7	82.1	17.9	88.0	12.0	88.9	11.1	89.2	10.8
Irvine, CA	57.7	42.3	87.4	12.6	90.2	9.8	90.3	9.7	91.8	8.2
Jackson, MS	59.9	40.1	84.3	15.7	86.1	13.9	83.3	16.7	86.2	13.8
Jacksonville, FL	47.7	52.3	85.1	14.9	86.7	13.3	84.5	15.5	87.0	13.0
Jersey City, NJ	47.4	52.6	80.7	19.3	85.3	14.7	85.5	14.5	85.5	14.5
Kansas City, MO	52.2	47.8	86.7	13.3	88.6	11.4	89.0	11.0	88.4	11.6
Kenosha, WI	55.9	44.1	84.4	15.6	88.0	12.0	88.8	11.2	90.0	10.0
Las Vegas, NV	56.2	43.8	92.4	7.6	93.6	6.4	95.6	4.4	95.2	4.8
Lexington, KY	46.8	53.2	86.6	13.4	88.2	11.8	86.9	13.1	89.0	11.0
Lincoln, NE	44.0	56.0	85.1	14.9	82.9	17.1	81.0	19.0	85.2	14.8

Table continued on next page.

Metro Area	Preschool (%)		Kindergarten (%)		Grades 1 - 4 (%)		Grades 5 - 8 (%)		Grades 9 - 12 (%)	
	Public	Private	Public	Private	Public	Private	Public	Private	Public	Private
Little Rock, AR	54.0	46.0	87.3	12.7	89.4	10.6	88.8	11.2	86.6	13.4
Los Angeles, CA	57.7	42.3	87.4	12.6	90.2	9.8	90.3	9.7	91.8	8.2
Madison, WI	45.6	54.4	88.2	11.8	88.9	11.1	91.3	8.7	93.9	6.1
Manchester, NH	34.0	66.0	66.0	34.0	91.0	9.0	89.4	10.6	91.3	8.7
Miami, FL	44.6	55.4	82.0	18.0	87.2	12.8	87.3	12.7	88.1	11.9
Minneapolis, MN	53.0	47.0	86.6	13.4	87.2	12.8	87.7	12.3	90.8	9.2
Murfreesboro, TN	44.0	56.0	84.7	15.3	87.6	12.4	85.2	14.8	84.8	15.2
Naperville, IL	55.9	44.1	84.4	15.6	88.0	12.0	88.8	11.2	90.0	10.0
Nashville, TN	44.0	56.0	84.7	15.3	87.6	12.4	85.2	14.8	84.8	15.2
New Orleans, LA	50.4	49.6	67.6	32.4	75.5	24.5	72.9	27.1	74.0	26.0
New York, NY	47.4	52.6	80.7	19.3	85.3	14.7	85.5	14.5	85.5	14.5
Norman, OK	69.1	30.9	87.6	12.4	91.2	8.8	91.4	8.6	92.1	7.9
Olathe, KS	52.2	47.8	86.7	13.3	88.6	11.4	89.0	11.0	88.4	11.6
Omaha, NE	52.3	47.7	83.9	16.1	84.4	15.6	85.1	14.9	87.6	12.4
Orlando, FL	44.9	55.1	82.3	17.7	87.4	12.6	89.1	10.9	90.2	9.8
Overland Park, KS	52.2	47.8	86.7	13.3	88.6	11.4	89.0	11.0	88.4	11.6
Oyster Bay, NY	47.4	52.6	80.7	19.3	85.3	14.7	85.5	14.5	85.5	14.5
Pembroke Pines, FL	44.6	55.4	82.0	18.0	87.2	12.8	87.3	12.7	88.1	11.9
Philadelphia, PA	42.3	57.7	76.9	23.1	83.1	16.9	82.5	17.5	83.5	16.5
Phoenix, AZ	55.9	44.1	91.0	9.0	92.9	7.1	94.0	6.0	94.4	5.6
Pittsburgh, PA	46.5	53.5	85.1	14.9	87.6	12.4	88.1	11.9	90.5	9.5
Plano, TX	51.9	48.1	89.1	10.9	91.6	8.4	92.4	7.6	92.6	7.4
Portland, OR	38.0	62.0	84.0	16.0	89.4	10.6	90.9	9.1	91.4	8.6
Providence, RI	48.7	51.3	84.2	15.8	89.2	10.8	89.3	10.7	87.7	12.3
Provo, UT	41.2	58.8	92.4	7.6	94.9	5.1	94.6	5.4	93.5	6.5
Raleigh, NC	33.0	67.0	85.8	14.2	89.3	10.7	89.6	10.4	90.6	9.4
Richmond, VA	34.8	65.2	90.7	9.3	91.6	8.4	91.1	8.9	91.6	8.4
Roseville, CA	52.9	47.1	86.9	13.1	90.6	9.4	91.8	8.2	91.5	8.5
Round Rock, TX	50.0	50.0	90.8	9.2	92.4	7.6	93.0	7.0	93.2	6.8
San Antonio, TX	64.1	35.9	89.5	10.5	92.6	7.4	92.3	7.7	93.3	6.7
San Diego, CA	52.5	47.5	90.2	9.8	91.5	8.5	91.6	8.4	93.0	7.0
San Francisco, CA	39.6	60.4	84.3	15.7	85.0	15.0	85.6	14.4	87.4	12.6
San Jose, CA	35.0	65.0	83.1	16.9	86.2	13.8	88.3	11.7	89.3	10.7
Savannah, GA	58.7	41.3	84.1	15.9	86.2	13.8	85.5	14.5	86.0	14.0
Scottsdale, AZ	55.9	44.1	91.0	9.0	92.9	7.1	94.0	6.0	94.4	5.6
Seattle, WA	39.5	60.5	84.9	15.1	89.0	11.0	88.7	11.3	89.9	10.1
Sioux Falls, SD	61.1	38.9	89.4	10.6	89.7	10.3	87.9	12.1	91.7	8.3
Stamford, CT	40.8	59.2	84.2	15.8	86.5	13.5	84.6	15.4	84.8	15.2
Sterling Hgts, MI	64.9	35.1	87.5	12.5	89.4	10.6	90.4	9.6	91.7	8.3
Sunnyvale, CA	35.0	65.0	83.1	16.9	86.2	13.8	88.3	11.7	89.3	10.7
Tampa, FL	54.8	45.2	86.4	13.6	88.7	11.3	88.6	11.4	91.6	8.4
Temecula, CA	63.5	36.5	92.3	7.7	94.1	5.9	93.7	6.3	93.9	6.1
Thousand Oaks, CA	46.9	53.1	89.9	10.1	91.2	8.8	90.2	9.8	92.4	7.6
Virginia Beach, VA	49.1	50.9	84.5	15.5	89.4	10.6	89.9	10.1	92.2	7.8
Washington, DC	38.6	61.4	82.1	17.9	86.5	13.5	87.0	13.0	88.9	11.1
U.S.	55.4	44.6	87.1	12.9	89.4	10.6	89.5	10.5	90.4	9.6

Note: Figures shown cover persons 3 years old and over; Figures cover the Metropolitan Statistical Area—see Appendix B for areas included;
Source: U.S. Census Bureau, 2008-2010 American Community Survey 3-Year Estimates

Educational Attainment by Race: City

City	High School Graduate or Higher (%)					Bachelor's Degree or Higher (%)				
	Total	White	Black	Asian	Hisp.[1]	Total	White	Black	Asian	Hisp.[1]
Albuquerque, NM	87.3	89.2	94.2	82.4	75.9	32.0	35.5	28.8	44.7	16.7
Alexandria, VA	90.3	94.5	84.1	93.3	64.6	58.5	69.8	29.2	67.6	28.1
Anchorage, AK	92.5	95.2	90.8	81.1	80.1	32.9	37.4	21.2	25.3	22.7
Ann Arbor, MI	96.8	97.6	91.5	96.1	97.4	70.8	72.7	35.7	85.4	57.0
Athens, GA	83.1	87.7	73.2	94.8	43.7	40.5	52.6	11.1	82.1	13.1
Atlanta, GA	86.6	96.3	79.0	93.8	68.8	45.5	74.0	20.5	77.0	29.2
Austin, TX	85.1	89.8	85.9	92.6	60.6	43.9	49.8	20.8	70.0	17.6
Baltimore, MD	78.3	83.7	75.2	90.7	62.6	25.2	45.4	12.5	74.4	20.2
Bellevue, WA	95.7	96.5	100.0	94.9	72.3	61.2	58.7	43.6	72.2	29.8
Billings, MT	92.2	93.2	n/a	n/a	72.6	31.0	32.2	n/a	n/a	13.9
Boise City, ID	93.2	93.9	73.3	88.8	72.5	36.8	36.7	16.0	53.6	20.4
Boston, MA	84.5	91.9	80.0	74.0	63.8	43.1	57.3	19.4	45.3	17.1
Boulder, CO	94.9	96.7	n/a	93.9	55.7	69.7	71.3	n/a	79.4	25.5
Broken Arrow, OK	93.3	94.6	91.6	85.4	77.5	31.3	31.4	35.5	43.5	22.1
Cambridge, MA	94.2	96.1	83.3	94.6	83.4	73.1	78.7	34.0	82.8	52.4
Cape Coral, FL	88.3	88.6	82.5	87.7	78.6	20.6	20.5	18.1	36.3	19.6
Carlsbad, CA	95.4	96.0	n/a	97.1	74.6	50.7	50.1	n/a	67.4	27.3
Cary, NC	95.2	96.3	98.8	95.5	63.6	62.3	63.0	45.5	81.3	16.1
Cedar Rapids, IA	92.7	93.6	80.0	88.7	81.8	30.4	30.7	18.1	57.6	16.9
Charleston, SC	90.8	95.1	78.1	91.9	72.8	46.8	55.8	19.0	60.9	20.7
Charlotte, NC	87.4	91.5	85.3	84.3	54.9	38.7	48.4	23.3	54.0	14.4
Chesapeake, VA	89.4	91.9	84.8	86.6	77.2	28.4	30.7	21.7	44.7	25.1
Chicago, IL	79.9	84.7	80.2	86.0	57.2	32.9	45.1	17.5	56.3	11.8
Clarksville, TN	91.2	91.5	91.7	89.5	84.4	21.7	23.4	16.5	30.5	18.8
Colorado Spgs., CO	92.4	93.6	90.9	86.2	75.8	36.1	38.8	19.2	36.5	13.4
Columbia, MD	93.9	95.4	93.1	92.9	66.2	60.2	64.4	44.9	75.2	34.8
Columbia, MO	93.2	94.6	82.6	93.6	84.2	52.2	55.3	19.6	74.1	39.1
Columbia, SC	85.4	94.9	74.1	n/a	90.1	38.5	57.7	14.9	n/a	23.2
Columbus, OH	87.7	89.2	84.9	89.2	65.0	32.3	36.7	16.9	62.5	14.9
Dallas, TX	73.1	76.1	81.3	85.5	42.2	28.8	38.8	13.7	58.5	7.6
Denver, CO	84.2	86.6	85.6	83.1	55.5	40.6	46.0	19.7	50.0	10.8
Durham, NC	85.9	93.7	82.9	95.3	49.7	46.5	61.3	30.1	82.9	17.8
Edison, NJ	92.1	91.7	90.2	93.3	82.3	51.1	31.8	37.1	77.2	22.4
El Paso, TX	74.7	75.2	93.7	88.2	69.1	21.9	22.3	27.0	55.5	17.3
Fargo, ND	94.1	95.3	63.5	84.1	85.4	38.6	39.2	14.5	49.4	21.9
Ft. Collins, CO	95.1	95.7	n/a	97.5	76.5	50.8	52.1	n/a	61.7	22.6
Ft. Worth, TX	78.3	82.1	83.3	84.8	47.9	25.6	30.4	16.0	41.5	8.2
Gilbert, AZ	95.9	96.5	96.1	92.0	87.7	37.6	37.6	29.3	51.0	24.7
Green Bay, WI	85.0	86.6	71.8	66.8	32.8	20.6	21.3	13.7	24.1	6.2
Henderson, NV	92.7	92.8	93.6	95.6	80.3	30.8	30.4	23.0	53.0	18.1
High Point, NC	85.4	89.4	80.6	81.5	70.2	28.5	35.0	14.7	44.7	21.9
Honolulu, HI	88.2	95.7	95.6	84.9	87.2	33.3	47.7	26.9	32.0	24.4
Houston, TX	74.1	74.2	82.6	84.1	48.7	28.2	33.5	17.2	53.4	9.6
Huntington, NY	92.3	94.5	85.9	91.9	66.2	47.0	49.0	30.5	62.0	18.5
Huntsville, AL	87.4	89.8	81.2	89.8	47.3	37.6	42.7	21.6	67.2	12.0
Indianapolis, IN	83.8	86.0	82.8	83.6	45.7	27.4	32.2	15.0	54.6	8.6
Irvine, CA	95.9	96.3	90.4	96.3	85.7	65.7	60.6	32.7	77.8	41.2
Jackson, MS	81.9	91.7	79.1	n/a	45.9	26.7	51.5	18.6	n/a	20.9
Jacksonville, FL	86.8	89.3	82.5	85.3	75.8	23.8	26.1	15.3	44.6	19.4
Jersey City, NJ	84.1	83.8	80.9	92.0	72.0	41.2	42.9	20.3	70.2	17.5
Kansas City, MO	86.5	90.9	81.4	79.4	57.6	29.9	38.4	13.2	40.2	11.1
Kenosha, WI	86.8	88.5	77.0	n/a	64.1	21.9	21.9	19.7	n/a	7.6
Las Vegas, NV	81.3	81.0	84.8	90.9	52.9	20.6	20.8	14.6	38.5	7.4
Lexington, KY	88.4	90.9	80.8	95.3	53.5	38.7	42.0	16.9	75.2	13.5
Lincoln, NE	92.7	94.3	83.1	72.6	68.6	34.8	35.0	22.5	48.4	21.1

Table continued on next page.

City	High School Graduate or Higher (%)					Bachelor's Degree or Higher (%)				
	Total	White	Black	Asian	Hisp.[1]	Total	White	Black	Asian	Hisp.[1]
Little Rock, AR	88.0	91.3	83.9	96.2	51.7	36.6	47.2	18.5	73.0	10.9
Los Angeles, CA	73.7	78.3	85.6	88.6	48.8	30.4	36.0	21.7	50.3	9.2
Madison, WI	94.1	95.8	78.4	88.3	76.7	52.0	53.8	18.3	69.8	25.4
Manchester, NH	85.5	86.8	78.7	78.3	66.8	26.1	26.5	19.9	38.0	20.1
Miami, FL	68.0	69.5	61.2	84.9	64.8	22.6	25.1	9.8	60.4	19.3
Minneapolis, MN	87.8	92.9	71.1	75.3	53.2	43.6	51.5	12.9	42.5	14.7
Murfreesboro, TN	89.5	91.7	89.4	84.3	57.2	34.7	37.1	28.3	34.4	13.8
Naperville, IL	96.9	97.3	96.3	96.4	83.3	65.5	63.4	55.4	82.6	39.1
Nashville, TN	84.8	87.3	82.0	85.2	51.2	33.3	37.8	22.6	46.8	9.6
New Orleans, LA	84.7	94.1	80.0	65.2	72.2	32.2	57.1	15.5	34.2	31.7
New York, NY	79.0	85.0	79.8	74.1	62.5	33.4	43.4	20.5	40.5	15.0
Norman, OK	92.4	92.9	91.3	94.0	80.8	42.8	42.3	42.0	75.9	27.1
Olathe, KS	94.2	94.9	97.1	87.8	69.2	45.2	46.2	27.1	60.3	21.5
Omaha, NE	88.2	90.9	85.3	88.0	45.1	32.0	35.7	12.6	58.9	8.8
Orlando, FL	87.2	91.6	79.2	82.8	78.1	31.1	38.2	15.8	42.5	18.9
Overland Park, KS	96.4	97.1	93.2	90.9	80.6	57.0	57.1	41.3	71.2	34.6
Oyster Bay, NY	93.8	94.1	88.0	93.3	85.2	44.0	42.6	43.1	64.8	24.7
Pembroke Pines, FL	88.4	88.0	89.5	87.4	84.9	31.7	29.8	33.4	52.2	29.4
Philadelphia, PA	79.7	84.2	79.3	67.4	60.0	22.4	32.2	11.8	33.4	10.2
Phoenix, AZ	79.8	80.6	86.5	85.6	54.2	25.3	26.1	19.8	52.1	7.5
Pittsburgh, PA	89.2	90.7	83.9	96.7	86.9	34.5	38.7	15.2	82.0	42.9
Plano, TX	93.2	92.6	96.6	96.1	66.3	53.9	50.7	47.4	76.1	22.6
Portland, OR	89.6	92.7	83.1	75.7	59.3	42.4	45.9	21.3	36.4	20.5
Providence, RI	72.1	79.5	73.2	67.6	53.5	28.3	40.3	19.4	35.6	7.4
Provo, UT	91.9	93.6	n/a	96.5	67.6	39.9	41.3	n/a	52.6	16.1
Raleigh, NC	90.7	93.8	88.6	86.3	57.2	47.0	55.7	29.8	59.9	14.7
Richmond, VA	79.9	87.9	73.0	79.1	31.8	33.3	55.6	12.3	58.3	8.0
Roseville, CA	93.7	94.4	89.8	92.9	79.4	33.9	32.8	29.3	48.8	17.5
Round Rock, TX	89.5	89.7	93.3	89.4	70.0	34.0	34.6	23.5	64.0	15.9
San Antonio, TX	79.4	80.7	85.5	87.6	70.0	23.6	25.1	19.9	53.1	12.8
San Diego, CA	86.4	87.5	89.4	87.5	62.4	40.8	43.0	22.8	48.2	16.5
San Francisco, CA	85.5	93.3	87.1	73.6	73.7	51.2	63.9	23.9	38.7	28.4
San Jose, CA	81.9	85.0	89.4	85.1	62.0	36.4	34.7	28.4	49.3	11.9
Savannah, GA	84.2	90.3	79.4	78.2	63.7	23.5	36.3	12.4	33.0	18.3
Scottsdale, AZ	95.6	96.0	93.9	94.5	75.1	52.0	51.6	49.7	76.4	33.7
Seattle, WA	92.9	96.1	80.9	81.9	78.6	55.8	61.5	22.3	48.9	34.7
Sioux Falls, SD	90.6	92.7	72.0	75.7	60.6	31.7	33.5	10.6	34.2	8.1
Stamford, CT	85.2	91.5	76.8	93.7	64.3	41.3	48.1	16.6	73.9	16.0
Sterling Hgts, MI	84.7	84.7	89.0	86.2	79.4	26.1	23.8	22.9	58.1	39.7
Sunnyvale, CA	91.2	93.5	97.5	95.5	60.7	56.6	49.0	21.5	75.9	16.0
Tampa, FL	84.6	87.6	78.2	84.9	71.8	31.7	37.2	13.3	59.5	16.2
Temecula, CA	91.3	92.9	97.9	86.6	75.9	30.0	31.8	27.4	31.8	19.4
Thousand Oaks, CA	94.0	95.4	94.5	95.5	73.4	48.9	48.0	59.9	72.8	23.7
Virginia Beach, VA	92.8	93.8	89.9	90.3	85.7	31.4	33.5	20.4	39.6	17.7
Washington, DC	87.1	94.1	81.8	93.7	60.3	49.8	81.2	21.9	79.2	35.1
U.S.	85.3	87.5	81.4	85.5	61.6	28.0	29.3	17.8	50.2	13.0

Note: Figures shown cover persons 25 years old and over; (1) People of Hispanic origin can be of any race
Source: U.S. Census Bureau, 2008-2010 American Community Survey 3-Year Estimates

Educational Attainment by Race: Metro Area

Metro Area	High School Graduate or Higher (%)					Bachelor's Degree or Higher (%)				
	Total	White	Black	Asian	Hisp.[1]	Total	White	Black	Asian	Hisp.[1]
Albuquerque, NM	86.6	88.9	93.6	84.1	75.4	29.3	33.1	27.9	44.3	15.1
Alexandria, VA	89.5	92.6	88.8	89.6	62.4	46.9	54.7	29.2	60.6	22.4
Anchorage, AK	92.4	94.6	90.8	80.1	80.7	30.2	33.4	20.3	25.0	22.0
Ann Arbor, MI	93.9	94.9	87.2	94.6	87.4	50.6	51.6	27.1	80.5	38.8
Athens, GA	81.5	84.9	68.6	96.0	43.8	34.5	39.8	10.3	79.8	13.3
Atlanta, GA	87.4	89.0	88.1	87.4	59.0	34.5	38.4	26.3	52.9	15.7
Austin, TX	87.3	90.5	87.9	91.6	64.5	39.2	42.5	21.8	66.4	16.9
Baltimore, MD	87.8	90.2	82.4	89.8	68.0	34.8	38.9	20.5	63.0	25.3
Bellevue, WA	91.2	93.2	87.7	85.9	67.4	37.0	37.7	20.0	48.8	17.1
Billings, MT	91.8	92.4	n/a	80.1	74.8	29.3	29.8	n/a	33.6	14.6
Boise City, ID	89.0	89.7	80.9	86.7	56.3	28.0	28.2	15.1	49.2	9.6
Boston, MA	90.3	92.9	82.3	83.2	66.4	42.4	44.4	22.9	56.9	18.4
Boulder, CO	93.7	95.6	91.0	94.0	62.0	57.9	59.5	44.1	72.0	22.2
Broken Arrow, OK	87.9	89.0	86.0	82.8	60.1	25.1	26.7	17.4	41.8	10.9
Cambridge, MA	90.3	92.9	82.3	83.2	66.4	42.4	44.4	22.9	56.9	18.4
Cape Coral, FL	86.8	89.0	73.3	86.7	65.3	24.4	25.5	13.1	41.6	13.8
Carlsbad, CA	85.1	86.1	90.1	88.0	61.9	34.1	34.9	22.8	45.8	14.5
Cary, NC	89.8	92.2	86.9	91.9	55.1	41.7	45.4	26.7	69.2	13.9
Cedar Rapids, IA	92.9	93.6	79.7	84.4	81.0	27.8	27.9	18.0	49.9	17.2
Charleston, SC	87.5	91.1	79.0	84.9	64.7	30.4	36.4	14.4	41.3	14.6
Charlotte, NC	86.4	88.7	83.6	84.6	56.8	32.2	35.4	21.5	53.1	15.8
Chesapeake, VA	89.2	91.9	83.6	88.3	83.6	27.7	31.9	17.3	39.9	20.4
Chicago, IL	86.1	89.5	83.5	90.7	60.2	33.8	37.3	19.5	62.2	12.1
Clarksville, TN	87.8	88.4	87.0	85.2	83.1	18.5	19.8	12.5	32.0	16.2
Colorado Spgs., CO	93.0	94.1	92.5	84.4	78.6	35.1	37.3	21.6	35.6	15.3
Columbia, MD	87.8	90.2	82.4	89.8	68.0	34.8	38.9	20.5	63.0	25.3
Columbia, MO	91.5	92.7	79.5	93.9	84.1	44.1	45.9	17.0	73.5	35.0
Columbia, SC	87.7	90.7	82.9	85.8	62.2	30.0	34.9	19.3	59.2	16.0
Columbus, OH	89.7	90.7	85.3	91.1	69.3	32.9	34.2	18.9	64.9	18.8
Dallas, TX	82.9	85.4	87.2	87.8	51.7	30.9	33.2	22.2	55.8	10.5
Denver, CO	89.0	91.1	87.5	84.8	62.5	38.1	40.8	22.0	46.1	12.6
Durham, NC	86.6	91.3	82.1	91.4	48.4	43.6	50.7	26.8	76.7	15.9
Edison, NJ	84.3	88.6	81.5	82.2	65.9	35.8	40.1	21.4	52.4	15.9
El Paso, TX	71.9	72.5	92.1	86.8	66.3	19.8	20.2	25.7	54.0	15.3
Fargo, ND	93.8	94.6	68.5	83.9	73.3	34.9	35.3	16.8	46.4	15.1
Ft. Collins, CO	93.6	94.3	90.1	98.0	67.8	43.0	43.8	27.4	61.6	16.3
Ft. Worth, TX	82.9	85.4	87.2	87.8	51.7	30.9	33.2	22.2	55.8	10.5
Gilbert, AZ	85.6	86.7	89.3	89.3	60.3	27.8	28.5	23.0	53.4	10.1
Green Bay, WI	89.6	90.5	75.2	78.3	41.7	22.9	23.1	16.5	30.4	7.6
Henderson, NV	83.4	83.4	87.0	89.7	57.9	21.8	21.5	16.2	38.6	8.2
High Point, NC	83.8	85.6	83.2	73.4	55.0	25.7	27.9	19.1	36.0	13.5
Honolulu, HI	90.3	96.2	97.1	87.3	89.6	31.2	44.7	26.4	31.7	21.4
Houston, TX	80.4	81.6	86.6	85.6	55.2	28.4	30.0	21.7	51.6	10.7
Huntington, NY	84.3	88.6	81.5	82.2	65.9	35.8	40.1	21.4	52.4	15.9
Huntsville, AL	86.8	87.7	83.5	90.6	53.3	33.9	35.4	25.6	60.6	15.2
Indianapolis, IN	88.1	89.7	83.6	88.8	52.7	30.9	33.1	16.8	59.6	12.6
Irvine, CA	77.6	81.4	87.7	86.6	54.8	30.7	33.4	23.2	49.0	10.2
Jackson, MS	85.2	90.6	79.1	80.3	48.9	28.7	35.5	19.4	62.0	16.0
Jacksonville, FL	88.3	90.2	82.6	86.7	77.8	26.2	28.4	15.4	45.5	20.5
Jersey City, NJ	84.3	88.6	81.5	82.2	65.9	35.8	40.1	21.4	52.4	15.9
Kansas City, MO	90.0	91.7	85.0	84.2	62.6	32.5	34.8	17.4	52.4	13.7
Kenosha, WI	86.1	89.5	83.5	90.7	60.2	33.8	37.3	19.5	62.2	12.1
Las Vegas, NV	83.4	83.4	87.0	89.7	57.9	21.8	21.5	16.2	38.6	8.2
Lexington, KY	87.1	88.7	81.0	94.8	57.2	33.3	34.9	16.8	71.3	12.0
Lincoln, NE	93.1	94.4	83.5	72.9	69.0	34.7	34.8	22.8	49.0	22.3

Table continued on next page.

Metro Area	High School Graduate or Higher (%)					Bachelor's Degree or Higher (%)				
	Total	White	Black	Asian	Hisp.[1]	Total	White	Black	Asian	Hisp.[1]
Little Rock, AR	87.8	89.1	83.6	91.1	62.8	26.0	27.9	16.7	57.4	13.4
Los Angeles, CA	77.6	81.4	87.7	86.6	54.8	30.7	33.4	23.2	49.0	10.2
Madison, WI	94.0	94.8	79.9	90.9	72.7	41.5	41.9	16.8	66.4	19.8
Manchester, NH	90.3	90.9	83.7	86.4	67.3	34.4	33.9	25.4	62.2	21.9
Miami, FL	82.7	84.6	76.4	85.9	75.0	28.5	31.1	17.3	46.7	23.6
Minneapolis, MN	92.6	94.7	80.3	80.4	62.2	37.7	39.2	19.8	43.4	16.4
Murfreesboro, TN	86.2	87.5	82.8	86.6	56.7	30.0	31.4	22.6	45.2	11.9
Naperville, IL	86.1	89.5	83.5	90.7	60.2	33.8	37.3	19.5	62.2	12.1
Nashville, TN	86.2	87.5	82.8	86.6	56.7	30.0	31.4	22.6	45.2	11.9
New Orleans, LA	84.6	88.5	79.4	70.7	71.8	26.2	31.7	14.9	31.5	20.2
New York, NY	84.3	88.6	81.5	82.2	65.9	35.8	40.1	21.4	52.4	15.9
Norman, OK	87.2	89.2	86.2	80.4	55.4	26.9	28.4	19.0	43.4	10.1
Olathe, KS	90.0	91.7	85.0	84.2	62.6	32.5	34.8	17.4	52.4	13.7
Omaha, NE	90.9	92.6	86.6	88.9	52.7	32.4	33.9	15.8	56.0	11.9
Orlando, FL	87.6	89.5	81.3	86.3	79.2	27.3	28.8	18.2	44.1	18.4
Overland Park, KS	90.0	91.7	85.0	84.2	62.6	32.5	34.8	17.4	52.4	13.7
Oyster Bay, NY	84.3	88.6	81.5	82.2	65.9	35.8	40.1	21.4	52.4	15.9
Pembroke Pines, FL	82.7	84.6	76.4	85.9	75.0	28.5	31.1	17.3	46.7	23.6
Philadelphia, PA	88.0	90.7	82.6	82.3	64.3	32.7	36.3	16.7	53.5	15.0
Phoenix, AZ	85.6	86.7	89.3	89.3	60.3	27.8	28.5	23.0	53.4	10.1
Pittsburgh, PA	91.1	91.5	86.2	91.4	84.6	28.7	29.0	15.6	71.4	33.7
Plano, TX	82.9	85.4	87.2	87.8	51.7	30.9	33.2	22.2	55.8	10.5
Portland, OR	90.1	92.2	85.0	84.7	58.8	33.6	34.4	24.0	45.5	13.5
Providence, RI	82.8	84.3	75.6	80.9	60.3	28.3	29.4	19.8	43.8	11.7
Provo, UT	93.6	94.6	88.1	92.0	73.1	34.7	35.1	35.0	46.0	18.5
Raleigh, NC	89.8	92.2	86.9	91.9	55.1	41.7	45.4	26.7	69.2	13.9
Richmond, VA	85.3	88.8	78.0	84.0	53.5	31.0	36.1	17.4	54.8	15.4
Roseville, CA	87.0	90.3	86.9	80.8	65.8	29.7	31.3	18.4	38.4	14.1
Round Rock, TX	87.3	90.5	87.9	91.6	64.5	39.2	42.5	21.8	66.4	16.9
San Antonio, TX	82.2	83.5	87.5	86.4	71.0	25.3	26.6	22.7	50.1	13.3
San Diego, CA	85.1	86.1	90.1	88.0	61.9	34.1	34.9	22.8	45.8	14.5
San Francisco, CA	87.1	90.8	87.4	83.8	66.6	43.5	47.9	23.0	48.8	16.9
San Jose, CA	85.9	88.4	91.2	89.2	62.8	44.5	42.4	29.6	59.4	13.3
Savannah, GA	87.6	90.6	82.3	80.9	70.4	27.2	33.0	14.6	31.1	19.8
Scottsdale, AZ	85.6	86.7	89.3	89.3	60.3	27.8	28.5	23.0	53.4	10.1
Seattle, WA	91.2	93.2	87.7	85.9	67.4	37.0	37.7	20.0	48.8	17.1
Sioux Falls, SD	91.7	93.2	72.8	75.0	62.8	30.1	31.3	10.9	32.7	10.0
Stamford, CT	88.2	91.1	79.4	88.9	66.0	43.7	47.9	17.9	64.4	16.0
Sterling Hgts, MI	87.6	89.6	82.2	88.1	66.6	27.0	29.0	15.5	63.0	16.0
Sunnyvale, CA	85.9	88.4	91.2	89.2	62.8	44.5	42.4	29.6	59.4	13.3
Tampa, FL	86.8	87.9	80.6	84.0	74.2	25.5	25.9	17.7	47.3	16.8
Temecula, CA	78.3	80.5	88.0	89.1	59.4	19.4	19.5	20.1	46.7	8.1
Thousand Oaks, CA	82.3	86.6	92.8	92.0	56.5	30.6	32.8	27.5	54.9	10.0
Virginia Beach, VA	89.2	91.9	83.6	88.3	83.6	27.7	31.9	17.3	39.9	20.4
Washington, DC	89.5	92.6	88.8	89.6	62.4	46.9	54.7	29.2	60.6	22.4
U.S.	85.3	87.5	81.4	85.5	61.6	28.0	29.3	17.8	50.2	13.0

Note: Figures shown cover persons 25 years old and over; Figures cover the Metropolitan Statistical Area—see Appendix B for areas included; (1) People of Hispanic origin can be of any race

Source: U.S. Census Bureau, 2008-2010 American Community Survey 3-Year Estimates

Cost of Living Index

Urban Area	Composite	Groceries	Housing	Utilities	Transp.	Health	Misc.
Albuquerque[1], NM	94.7	94.5	87.0	98.6	94.4	100.9	99.6
Alexandria[2], VA	143.5	111.4	241.2	103.9	108.1	101.0	100.7
Anchorage, AK	130.8	137.6	150.2	98.2	112.0	139.1	126.3
Ann Arbor, MI	101.0	98.8	105.4	107.7	100.4	97.3	96.4
Athens, GA	n/a	n/a	n/a	n/a	n/a	n/a	n/a
Atlanta, GA	97.4	101.7	89.4	93.4	102.1	101.0	101.8
Austin, TX	92.8	85.0	82.3	99.1	101.1	102.1	99.3
Baltimore, MD	119.2	109.4	160.3	115.3	103.9	96.5	96.5
Bellevue[3], WA	117.2	111.7	129.5	90.4	112.4	118.4	118.7
Billings, MT	n/a	n/a	n/a	n/a	n/a	n/a	n/a
Boise City, ID	96.1	101.3	83.7	97.2	101.3	101.4	102.2
Boston, MA	137.4	118.9	160.6	147.3	106.8	121.1	133.6
Boulder, CO	n/a	n/a	n/a	n/a	n/a	n/a	n/a
Broken Arrow[4], OK	90.1	92.3	69.1	96.9	101.3	99.2	100.5
Cambridge[5], MA	137.4	118.9	160.6	147.3	106.8	121.1	133.6
Cape Coral, FL	95.6	105.2	90.5	81.1	101.8	99.1	98.2
Carlsbad[6], CA	130.8	107.4	189.1	113.0	111.2	112.4	103.6
Cary[7], NC	93.8	101.4	79.9	104.5	96.6	100.3	97.8
Cedar Rapids, IA	93.7	97.4	78.9	101.3	96.7	94.5	101.6
Charleston, SC	99.8	107.6	90.3	107.5	98.3	108.7	101.7
Charlotte, NC	93.3	100.2	82.1	92.7	98.2	105.0	97.4
Chesapeake[8], VA	105.4	100.3	114.0	110.9	97.7	102.3	101.1
Chicago, IL	114.8	114.5	134.2	97.6	114.6	106.9	104.6
Clarksville, TN	97.6	90.9	89.5	93.5	93.0	99.8	110.0
Colorado Springs, CO	92.6	94.1	89.3	89.8	96.8	102.2	93.1
Columbia[9], MD	119.2	109.4	160.3	115.3	103.9	96.5	96.5
Columbia, MO	91.2	95.6	80.7	90.7	96.2	96.0	96.7
Columbia, SC	95.6	104.7	78.7	106.6	104.0	101.2	99.7
Columbus, OH	90.3	94.4	77.1	99.9	99.0	101.8	92.9
Dallas, TX	96.3	100.7	75.4	108.1	105.0	104.5	105.0
Denver, CO	105.1	102.7	113.2	90.0	95.1	106.5	106.9
Durham, NC	92.7	98.8	78.5	92.7	104.0	100.5	98.0
Edison[10], NJ	126.1	110.3	154.7	131.3	102.4	110.2	115.6
El Paso, TX	91.0	100.8	90.9	81.8	94.0	92.5	88.8
Fargo, ND	93.3	103.9	84.4	89.3	97.0	102.6	95.5
Fort Collins, CO	n/a	n/a	n/a	n/a	n/a	n/a	n/a
Fort Worth, TX	93.2	92.1	79.2	110.8	102.1	96.3	96.9
Gilbert[11], AZ	96.6	103.9	87.4	100.3	102.9	102.6	97.6
Green Bay, WI	94.9	87.4	84.3	107.3	102.3	110.1	98.7
Henderson[12], NV	100.2	105.1	92.5	91.4	103.8	106.4	105.8
High Point, NC	n/a	n/a	n/a	n/a	n/a	n/a	n/a
Honolulu, HI	168.0	155.8	252.5	161.8	125.9	123.4	120.4
Houston, TX	89.9	80.8	83.3	89.3	95.3	98.1	96.8
Huntington[13], NY	138.6	118.9	188.5	138.6	109.8	110.5	116.0
Huntsville, AL	93.7	95.9	78.7	96.2	101.8	95.0	102.4
Indianapolis, IN	n/a	n/a	n/a	n/a	n/a	n/a	n/a
Irvine[14], CA	142.9	108.2	230.3	112.8	112.0	109.0	104.4
Jackson, MS	96.7	91.3	95.1	124.3	94.9	98.4	91.7
Jacksonville, FL	94.0	100.5	82.9	101.5	106.4	88.5	95.2
Jersey City[15], NJ	131.4	106.2	171.0	135.0	103.9	103.8	118.4
Kansas City, MO	99.5	98.9	90.1	110.1	98.7	97.0	105.1
Kenosha[16], WI	99.4	94.5	104.5	109.6	101.2	110.2	91.5
Las Vegas, NV	100.2	105.1	92.5	91.4	103.8	106.4	105.8
Lexington, KY	91.9	91.9	82.8	94.5	97.1	98.8	96.6
Lincoln, NE	93.5	95.2	84.6	103.8	106.8	94.8	92.8
Little Rock, AR	95.8	94.5	89.3	105.4	95.0	90.8	99.8

Table continued on next page.

Urban Area	Composite	Groceries	Housing	Utilities	Transp.	Health	Misc.
Los Angeles, CA	133.0	107.6	197.3	112.3	109.0	110.0	104.5
Madison, WI	108.2	100.8	112.7	103.5	109.8	117.4	107.0
Manchester, NH	119.9	101.7	126.6	127.1	99.7	110.8	127.1
Miami, FL	107.2	107.4	112.0	94.3	109.0	106.3	106.4
Minneapolis, MN	110.7	108.2	119.1	100.7	104.9	102.9	110.6
Murfreesboro, TN	88.2	94.7	78.4	84.0	95.6	89.2	93.0
Naperville[17], IL	100.0	98.1	99.1	103.3	106.4	104.4	97.7
Nashville, TN	90.3	97.5	70.6	87.1	93.4	91.6	104.6
New Orleans[18], LA	95.7	95.9	95.2	89.3	99.1	91.2	97.7
New York, NY	219.2	148.8	414.6	143.6	122.9	127.7	144.1
Norman, OK	91.6	94.1	85.7	81.8	104.2	93.2	94.7
Olathe[19], KS	99.5	98.9	90.1	110.1	98.7	97.0	105.1
Omaha, NE	89.5	94.2	80.5	92.3	100.6	98.2	89.7
Orlando, FL	97.3	100.2	79.7	107.8	99.2	94.2	108.1
Overland Park[20], KS	99.5	98.9	90.1	110.1	98.7	97.0	105.1
Oyster Bay[21], NY	138.6	118.9	188.5	138.6	109.8	110.5	116.0
Pembroke Pines[22], FL	111.1	106.8	128.7	94.3	108.2	103.1	104.9
Philadelphia, PA	125.1	124.6	140.6	129.9	107.7	104.6	118.6
Phoenix, AZ	96.6	103.9	87.4	100.3	102.9	102.6	97.6
Pittsburgh, PA	94.9	104.9	76.9	100.6	111.3	93.7	99.6
Plano, TX	96.7	101.8	85.1	106.3	102.3	103.2	99.2
Portland, OR	113.7	111.3	131.0	88.3	113.7	113.7	107.6
Providence, RI	125.7	111.4	134.6	129.6	104.3	111.8	131.5
Provo, UT	90.1	89.6	82.3	82.8	93.9	89.2	98.4
Raleigh, NC	93.8	101.4	79.9	104.5	96.6	100.3	97.8
Richmond, VA	100.2	104.5	95.4	108.5	101.9	108.5	98.3
Roseville[23], CA	116.3	109.7	138.6	117.4	114.0	114.2	100.1
Round Rock, TX	88.7	82.1	76.1	104.9	88.7	93.9	96.6
San Antonio, TX	93.2	84.6	91.4	85.8	102.2	97.2	97.2
San Diego, CA	130.8	107.4	189.1	113.0	111.2	112.4	103.6
San Francisco, CA	162.9	115.9	283.8	91.2	111.5	112.3	122.4
San Jose, CA	150.5	114.7	245.3	131.9	114.6	116.2	103.9
Savannah, GA	91.6	97.1	77.2	100.6	97.7	93.2	97.1
Scottsdale[24], AZ	96.6	103.9	87.4	100.3	102.9	102.6	97.6
Seattle, WA	117.2	111.7	129.5	90.4	112.4	118.4	118.7
Sioux Falls, SD	97.2	95.0	86.2	102.4	92.5	94.4	108.1
Stamford, CT	147.5	116.5	208.0	139.7	116.5	114.4	124.2
Sterling Heights[25], MI	93.8	95.9	84.8	104.0	100.5	95.5	95.1
Sunnyvale[26], CA	150.5	114.7	245.3	131.9	114.6	116.2	103.9
Tampa, FL	91.9	98.2	79.0	96.7	102.9	93.6	95.2
Temecula[27], CA	112.5	106.7	135.9	110.2	108.9	102.6	97.5
Thousand Oaks, CA	n/a	n/a	n/a	n/a	n/a	n/a	n/a
Virginia Beach[28], VA	105.4	100.3	114.0	110.9	97.7	102.3	101.1
Washington, DC	143.5	111.4	241.2	103.9	108.1	101.0	100.7
U.S.	100.0	100.0	100.0	100.0	100.0	100.0	100.0

Note: In cases where data is not available for the city, data for the metro area or for a neighboring city has been provided and noted below; (1) Rio Rancho NM; (2) Washington-Arlington-Alexandria DC-VA; (3) Seattle WA; (4) Tulsa OK; (5) Boston MA; (6) San Diego CA; (7) Raleigh NC; (8) Hampton Roads-SE Virginia VA; (9) Baltimore MD; (10) Middlesex-Monmouth NJ; (11) Phoenix AZ; (12) Las Vegas NV; (13) Nassau County NY; (14) Orange County CA; (15) Newark-Elizabeth NJ; (16) Milwaukee-Waukesha WI; (17) Joliet-Will County IL; (18) Slidell-St. Tammany Parish LA; (19) Kansas City MO-KS; (20) Kansas City MO-KS; (21) Nassau County NY; (22) Fort Lauderdale FL; (23) Sacramento CA; (24) Phoenix AZ; (25) Detroit MI; (26) San Jose CA; (27) Riverside City CA; (28) Hampton Roads-SE Virginia VA
Source: The Council for Community and Economic Research (formerly ACCRA), Cost of Living Index, 2011

Grocery Prices

Urban Area	T-Bone Steak ($/pound)	Frying Chicken ($/pound)	Whole Milk ($/half gal.)	Eggs ($/dozen)	Orange Juice ($/64 oz.)	Coffee ($/11.5 oz.)
Albuquerque[1], NM	8.48	0.97	2.17	1.63	3.25	4.83
Alexandria[2], VA	9.73	1.53	2.54	2.28	3.40	4.57
Anchorage, AK	10.51	1.44	2.12	2.57	4.41	6.00
Ann Arbor, MI	11.43	0.91	2.03	1.70	3.09	3.99
Athens, GA	n/a	n/a	n/a	n/a	n/a	n/a
Atlanta, GA	9.79	1.16	2.12	1.65	3.35	4.30
Austin, TX	9.08	1.17	2.05	1.45	3.43	3.64
Baltimore, MD	9.69	1.67	2.54	2.26	3.46	4.33
Bellevue[3], WA	9.32	1.36	1.90	1.99	3.75	5.45
Billings, MT	n/a	n/a	n/a	n/a	n/a	n/a
Boise City, ID	8.23	1.58	1.83	1.63	3.32	4.52
Boston, MA	10.69	1.31	2.46	2.28	3.54	5.00
Boulder, CO	n/a	n/a	n/a	n/a	n/a	n/a
Broken Arrow[4], OK	7.75	0.93	2.30	1.45	2.95	3.98
Cambridge[5], MA	10.69	1.31	2.46	2.28	3.54	5.00
Cape Coral, FL	9.05	1.33	2.58	1.65	3.71	4.41
Carlsbad[6], CA	9.85	1.06	2.14	2.28	3.33	5.58
Cary[7], NC	9.39	1.17	2.49	1.61	3.03	3.99
Cedar Rapids, IA	8.61	1.04	1.92	1.58	3.22	4.70
Charleston, SC	9.33	1.32	2.59	1.71	3.26	4.49
Charlotte, NC	8.23	1.24	2.59	1.56	3.19	4.32
Chesapeake[8], VA	8.98	1.09	2.45	1.69	3.02	4.19
Chicago, IL	9.04	1.33	2.67	1.72	3.46	5.57
Clarksville, TN	8.53	0.97	2.36	1.98	3.08	3.91
Colorado Springs, CO	9.83	1.05	2.01	1.68	3.21	4.91
Columbia[9], MD	9.69	1.67	2.54	2.26	3.46	4.33
Columbia, MO	9.02	1.05	2.12	1.49	3.03	4.44
Columbia, SC	9.94	1.40	2.46	1.63	3.33	4.21
Columbus, OH	10.15	0.99	1.90	1.39	3.04	4.75
Dallas, TX	8.98	1.07	2.05	1.63	3.32	4.87
Denver, CO	9.80	1.16	1.87	1.71	3.08	5.18
Durham, NC	7.81	1.09	2.38	1.73	3.11	4.31
Edison[10], NJ	10.14	1.51	2.31	2.23	3.29	4.18
El Paso, TX	8.61	1.10	2.01	1.65	3.31	5.04
Fargo, ND	9.36	1.53	2.98	1.59	3.36	4.55
Fort Collins, CO	n/a	n/a	n/a	n/a	n/a	n/a
Fort Worth, TX	8.97	0.98	2.01	1.66	2.90	4.55
Gilbert[11], AZ	9.12	1.20	2.26	1.77	3.18	4.97
Green Bay, WI	9.71	1.31	1.77	1.30	3.04	4.38
Henderson[12], NV	9.29	1.08	2.34	1.90	3.25	4.89
High Point, NC	n/a	n/a	n/a	n/a	n/a	n/a
Honolulu, HI	8.32	1.85	3.50	3.18	4.68	6.83
Houston, TX	7.45	0.94	2.02	1.43	2.68	4.04
Huntington[13], NY	10.82	1.91	2.15	2.08	3.41	4.21
Huntsville, AL	9.94	1.24	2.30	1.55	3.13	4.45
Indianapolis, IN	n/a	n/a	n/a	n/a	n/a	n/a
Irvine[14], CA	9.34	1.08	2.23	2.26	3.30	5.48
Jackson, MS	8.82	1.04	2.47	1.60	2.98	4.16
Jacksonville, FL	9.83	1.23	2.74	1.74	3.21	4.13
Jersey City[15], NJ	9.56	1.24	2.26	2.28	3.01	4.46
Kansas City, MO	8.93	1.14	2.22	1.44	3.10	4.05
Kenosha[16], WI	9.67	1.44	1.93	1.20	3.09	4.38
Las Vegas, NV	9.29	1.08	2.34	1.90	3.25	4.89
Lexington, KY	9.31	1.06	2.07	1.53	2.93	4.13
Lincoln, NE	8.59	1.51	1.97	1.52	3.22	4.44

Table continued on next page.

Urban Area	T-Bone Steak ($/pound)	Frying Chicken ($/pound)	Whole Milk ($/half gal.)	Eggs ($/dozen)	Orange Juice ($/64 oz.)	Coffee ($/11.5 oz.)
Little Rock, AR	9.49	1.01	1.91	1.49	3.02	4.20
Los Angeles, CA	9.99	1.16	2.18	2.28	3.26	5.55
Madison, WI	8.95	1.54	2.07	1.33	3.17	4.10
Manchester, NH	10.11	1.23	2.04	1.48	2.97	4.04
Miami, FL	10.43	1.40	2.64	1.84	3.57	4.24
Minneapolis, MN	14.30	2.16	2.24	1.93	3.37	4.08
Murfreesboro, TN	8.41	1.06	1.76	1.40	2.80	4.00
Naperville[17], IL	9.23	1.02	2.52	1.66	2.96	4.86
Nashville, TN	8.40	1.33	2.54	1.39	3.14	4.26
New Orleans[18], LA	9.07	1.07	2.76	1.67	3.13	3.99
New York, NY	10.80	1.21	2.32	2.43	3.84	4.88
Norman, OK	9.14	1.01	2.18	1.52	3.08	4.13
Olathe[19], KS	8.93	1.14	2.22	1.44	3.10	4.05
Omaha, NE	8.45	1.21	2.01	1.52	3.17	4.42
Orlando, FL	9.03	1.25	2.65	1.71	3.28	4.27
Overland Park[20], KS	8.93	1.14	2.22	1.44	3.10	4.05
Oyster Bay[21], NY	10.82	1.91	2.15	2.08	3.41	4.21
Pembroke Pines[22], FL	10.38	1.40	2.69	1.87	3.16	4.20
Philadelphia, PA	10.15	1.56	2.09	2.21	4.08	4.78
Phoenix, AZ	9.12	1.20	2.26	1.77	3.18	4.97
Pittsburgh, PA	9.80	1.30	1.98	1.52	3.35	4.51
Plano, TX	8.94	1.05	2.09	1.70	3.50	4.98
Portland, OR	9.90	1.47	1.86	1.83	3.52	5.36
Providence, RI	10.38	1.07	2.44	2.22	3.22	4.57
Provo, UT	8.13	1.14	2.02	1.09	2.91	4.97
Raleigh, NC	9.39	1.17	2.49	1.61	3.03	3.99
Richmond, VA	9.15	1.09	2.50	1.71	2.88	4.42
Roseville[23], CA	10.64	1.10	2.19	2.27	2.94	4.98
Round Rock, TX	8.79	0.99	2.33	1.28	2.70	3.27
San Antonio, TX	9.00	1.03	2.08	1.35	3.01	3.51
San Diego, CA	9.85	1.06	2.14	2.28	3.33	5.58
San Francisco, CA	10.14	1.27	2.20	2.36	3.80	5.56
San Jose, CA	9.78	1.03	2.16	2.32	2.98	5.20
Savannah, GA	9.67	1.18	2.22	1.57	2.93	4.20
Scottsdale[24], AZ	9.12	1.20	2.26	1.77	3.18	4.97
Seattle, WA	9.32	1.36	1.90	1.99	3.75	5.45
Sioux Falls, SD	9.55	0.90	2.11	1.63	3.89	4.67
Stamford, CT	10.32	1.20	2.20	2.28	3.35	4.66
Sterling Heights[25], MI	10.22	0.91	2.03	1.66	3.01	3.98
Sunnyvale[26], CA	9.78	1.03	2.16	2.32	2.98	5.20
Tampa, FL	9.32	1.17	2.57	1.66	3.11	3.84
Temecula[27], CA	8.80	0.97	2.11	2.18	3.16	5.24
Thousand Oaks, CA	n/a	n/a	n/a	n/a	n/a	n/a
Virginia Beach[28], VA	8.98	1.09	2.45	1.69	3.02	4.19
Washington, DC	9.73	1.53	2.54	2.28	3.40	4.57
Average[99]	9.25	1.18	2.22	1.66	3.19	4.40
Minimum[99]	6.70	0.88	1.31	0.95	2.46	2.94
Maximum[99]	14.30	2.16	3.50	3.18	4.75	6.83

*Note: **T-Bone Steak** (price per pound); **Frying Chicken** (price per pound, whole fryer); **Whole Milk** (half gallon carton); **Eggs** (price per dozen, Grade A, large); **Orange Juice** (64 oz. Tropicana or Florida Natural); **Coffee** (11.5 oz. can, vacuum-packed, Maxwell House, Hills Bros, or Folgers); (99) Values for the local area are compared with the average, minimum, and maximum values for all 331 areas in the Cost of Living Index report; n/a not available; In cases where data is not available for the city, data for the metro area or for a neighboring city has been provided and noted below;(1) Rio Rancho NM; (2) Washington-Arlington-Alexandria DC-VA; (3) Seattle WA; (4) Tulsa OK; (5) Boston MA; (6) San Diego CA; (7) Raleigh NC; (8) Hampton Roads-SE Virginia VA; (9) Baltimore MD; (10) Middlesex-Monmouth NJ; (11) Phoenix AZ; (12) Las Vegas NV; (13) Nassau County NY; (14) Orange County CA; (15) Newark-Elizabeth NJ; (16) Milwaukee-Waukesha WI; (17) Joliet-Will County IL; (18) Slidell-St. Tammany Parish LA; (19) Kansas City MO-KS; (20) Kansas City MO-KS; (21) Nassau County NY; (22) Fort Lauderdale FL; (23) Sacramento CA; (24) Phoenix AZ; (25) Detroit MI; (26) San Jose CA; (27) Riverside City CA; (28) Hampton Roads-SE Virginia VA*

Source: The Council for Community and Economic Research (formerly ACCRA), Cost of Living Index, 2011

Housing and Utility Costs

Urban Area	New Home Price ($)	Apartment Rent ($/month)	All Electric ($/month)	Part Electric ($/month)	Other Energy ($/month)	Telephone ($/month)
Albuquerque[1], NM	253,971	727	-	103.95	76.48	22.15
Alexandria[2], VA	711,603	1,879	-	84.46	106.75	23.00
Anchorage, AK	422,933	1,302	-	73.24	104.51	22.55
Ann Arbor, MI	315,268	769	-	103.57	78.12	28.23
Athens, GA	n/a	n/a	n/a	n/a	n/a	n/a
Atlanta, GA	244,734	882	-	96.05	59.20	25.06
Austin, TX	222,483	878	-	92.80	79.38	24.67
Baltimore, MD	449,828	1,504	-	124.39	77.23	28.32
Bellevue[3], WA	342,917	1,473	143.76	-	-	25.99
Billings, MT	n/a	n/a	n/a	n/a	n/a	n/a
Boise City, ID	238,006	703	-	84.47	67.46	28.64
Boston, MA	437,400	1,591	-	104.49	145.16	38.25
Boulder, CO	n/a	n/a	n/a	n/a	n/a	n/a
Broken Arrow[4], OK	194,499	599	-	77.88	61.48	31.70
Cambridge[5], MA	437,400	1,591	-	104.49	145.16	38.25
Cape Coral, FL	250,980	817	149.19	-	-	17.98
Carlsbad[6], CA	525,576	1,712	-	121.58	67.99	29.85
Cary[7], NC	229,862	656	-	94.88	62.65	32.33
Cedar Rapids, IA	221,859	719	-	109.14	67.59	24.99
Charleston, SC	240,230	977	185.13	-	-	27.15
Charlotte, NC	228,128	767	141.85	-	-	28.13
Chesapeake[8], VA	313,649	1,061	-	90.31	69.61	36.17
Chicago, IL	367,442	1,369	-	87.29	65.86	28.60
Clarksville, TN	252,269	770	167.24	-	-	22.03
Colorado Springs, CO	247,964	808	-	67.47	58.34	30.25
Columbia[9], MD	449,828	1,504	-	124.39	77.23	28.32
Columbia, MO	232,638	654	-	87.59	69.65	22.62
Columbia, SC	211,375	793	-	95.48	83.90	28.01
Columbus, OH	208,376	778	-	84.44	77.22	27.99
Dallas, TX	207,192	738	-	131.03	51.86	28.15
Denver, CO	339,420	853	-	78.86	58.85	27.26
Durham, NC	216,053	751	142.15	-	-	28.00
Edison[10], NJ	442,983	1,286	-	117.56	121.47	29.75
El Paso, TX	239,227	942	-	83.02	33.89	26.95
Fargo, ND	247,098	674	-	58.85	73.12	28.32
Fort Collins, CO	n/a	n/a	n/a	n/a	n/a	n/a
Fort Worth, TX	199,901	952	-	131.65	51.86	29.95
Gilbert[11], AZ	241,396	889	184.74	-	-	22.17
Green Bay, WI	250,550	616	-	81.08	90.64	30.57
Henderson[12], NV	261,021	766	-	124.12	44.17	20.26
High Point, NC	n/a	n/a	n/a	n/a	n/a	n/a
Honolulu, HI	666,923	2,702	339.16	-	-	24.97
Houston, TX	224,736	892	-	88.47	42.02	28.69
Huntington[13], NY	551,711	1,488	-	124.59	133.23	29.99
Huntsville, AL	221,338	726	142.62	-	-	30.38
Indianapolis, IN	n/a	n/a	n/a	n/a	n/a	n/a
Irvine[14], CA	681,690	1,678	-	134.27	54.93	29.85
Jackson, MS	278,817	730	-	106.80	115.24	29.34
Jacksonville, FL	206,359	974	181.34	-	-	23.94
Jersey City[15], NJ	479,582	1,536	-	119.78	128.79	29.88
Kansas City, MO	259,295	738	-	85.30	82.44	33.57
Kenosha[16], WI	304,289	817	-	92.17	94.08	28.36
Las Vegas, NV	261,021	766	-	124.12	44.17	20.26
Lexington, KY	227,759	785	-	71.82	73.76	28.40
Lincoln, NE	243,057	678	-	65.63	79.84	34.99

Table continued on next page.

Urban Area	New Home Price ($)	Apartment Rent ($/month)	All Electric ($/month)	Part Electric ($/month)	Other Energy ($/month)	Telephone ($/month)
Little Rock, AR	253,330	719	-	82.50	73.02	33.44
Los Angeles, CA	540,850	1,863	-	125.12	62.59	29.85
Madison, WI	342,283	820	-	95.80	88.84	24.49
Manchester, NH	351,427	1,225	-	105.41	97.64	36.25
Miami, FL	290,911	1,298	152.30	-	-	26.51
Minneapolis, MN	329,223	1,103	-	89.03	86.15	24.99
Murfreesboro, TN	213,745	784	-	81.64	56.33	23.01
Naperville[17], IL	261,391	990	-	86.32	66.85	32.61
Nashville, TN	188,005	795	-	82.30	60.69	23.86
New Orleans[18], LA	252,394	988	146.02	-	-	24.58
New York, NY	972,845	2,401	-	115.77	149.07	30.33
Norman, OK	253,965	631	-	51.26	61.48	28.04
Olathe[19], KS	259,295	738	-	85.30	82.44	33.57
Omaha, NE	227,304	676	-	75.48	70.97	26.64
Orlando, FL	209,687	817	179.04	-	-	28.95
Overland Park[20], KS	259,295	738	-	85.30	82.44	33.57
Oyster Bay[21], NY	551,711	1,488	-	124.59	133.23	29.99
Pembroke Pines[22], FL	350,825	1,339	152.30	-	-	26.51
Philadelphia, PA	391,184	1,248	-	124.88	83.77	36.75
Phoenix, AZ	241,396	889	184.74	-	-	22.17
Pittsburgh, PA	208,174	797	-	96.31	86.45	22.90
Plano, TX	226,303	930	-	134.72	51.47	26.01
Portland, OR	356,341	1,289	-	71.51	80.84	22.26
Providence, RI	365,109	1,383	-	100.19	110.00	36.19
Provo, UT	230,965	838	-	55.36	63.86	27.08
Raleigh, NC	229,862	656	-	94.88	62.65	32.33
Richmond, VA	268,326	894	-	89.02	78.36	32.51
Roseville[23], CA	401,500	1,095	-	163.54	38.11	29.84
Round Rock, TX	210,266	761	-	119.07	49.29	29.72
San Antonio, TX	237,886	993	-	92.63	38.54	26.01
San Diego, CA	525,576	1,712	-	121.58	67.99	29.85
San Francisco, CA	796,762	2,518	-	87.94	66.07	23.88
San Jose, CA	713,145	1,729	-	181.97	64.31	28.30
Savannah, GA	210,203	731	165.86	-	-	27.39
Scottsdale[24], AZ	241,396	889	184.74	-	-	22.17
Seattle, WA	342,917	1,473	143.76	-	-	25.99
Sioux Falls, SD	248,539	710	-	71.54	67.18	35.73
Stamford, CT	573,093	2,004	-	112.54	154.49	28.33
Sterling Heights[25], MI	241,092	697	-	101.42	78.60	26.01
Sunnyvale[26], CA	713,145	1,729	-	181.97	64.31	28.30
Tampa, FL	212,171	790	164.70	-	-	24.95
Temecula[27], CA	385,798	1,142	-	120.75	65.28	28.81
Thousand Oaks, CA	n/a	n/a	n/a	n/a	n/a	n/a
Virginia Beach[28], VA	313,649	1,061	-	90.31	69.61	36.17
Washington, DC	711,603	1,879	-	84.46	106.75	23.00
Average[99]	285,990	839	163.23	89.00	77.52	26.92
Minimum[99]	188,005	460	125.58	45.39	33.89	17.98
Maximum[99]	1,197,028	3,244	339.16	181.97	348.69	40.01

*Note: **New Home Price** (2,400 sf living area, 8,000 sf lot, in urban area with full utilities); **Apartment Rent** (950 sf 2 bedroom/1.5 or 2 bath, unfurnished, excluding all utilities except water); **All Electric** (average monthly cost for an all-electric home); **Part Electric** (average monthly cost for a part-electric home); **Other Energy** (average monthly cost for natural gas, fuel oil, coal, wood, and any other forms of energy except electricity); **Telephone** (price includes basic monthly rate for a private residential line plus additional local usage charges incurred by a family of four); (99) Values for the local area are compared with the average, minimum, and maximum values for all 331 areas in the Cost of Living Index report; n/a not available; In cases where data is not available for the city, data for the metro area or for a neighboring city has been provided and noted below;(1) Rio Rancho NM; (2) Washington-Arlington-Alexandria DC-VA; (3) Seattle WA; (4) Tulsa OK; (5) Boston MA; (6) San Diego CA; (7) Raleigh NC; (8) Hampton Roads-SE Virginia VA; (9) Baltimore MD; (10) Middlesex-Monmouth NJ; (11) Phoenix AZ; (12) Las Vegas NV; (13) Nassau County NY; (14) Orange County CA; (15) Newark-Elizabeth NJ; (16) Milwaukee-Waukesha WI; (17) Joliet-Will County IL; (18) Slidell-St. Tammany Parish LA; (19) Kansas City MO-KS; (20) Kansas City MO-KS; (21) Nassau County NY; (22) Fort Lauderdale FL; (23) Sacramento CA; (24) Phoenix AZ; (25) Detroit MI; (26) San Jose CA; (27) Riverside City CA; (28) Hampton Roads-SE Virginia VA*

Source: The Council for Community and Economic Research (formerly ACCRA), Cost of Living Index, 2011

Health Care, Transportation, and Other Costs

Urban Area	Doctor ($/visit)	Dentist ($/visit)	Optometrist ($/visit)	Gasoline ($/gallon)	Beauty Salon ($/visit)	Men's Shirt ($)
Albuquerque[1], NM	92.97	89.44	90.90	3.33	35.92	24.55
Alexandria[2], VA	87.07	87.60	73.93	3.69	48.73	26.07
Anchorage, AK	154.98	127.82	156.44	3.82	40.38	27.67
Ann Arbor, MI	88.47	81.68	73.91	3.66	32.29	28.22
Athens, GA	n/a	n/a	n/a	n/a	n/a	n/a
Atlanta, GA	89.59	93.46	71.27	3.50	43.14	24.03
Austin, TX	80.31	94.25	91.08	3.38	46.67	17.99
Baltimore, MD	82.37	81.77	67.86	3.49	42.94	26.36
Bellevue[3], WA	119.29	106.93	115.25	3.65	41.48	35.93
Billings, MT	n/a	n/a	n/a	n/a	n/a	n/a
Boise City, ID	102.63	83.07	87.80	3.42	24.94	33.45
Boston, MA	149.00	109.11	99.00	3.58	45.32	40.33
Boulder, CO	n/a	n/a	n/a	n/a	n/a	n/a
Broken Arrow[4], OK	102.78	75.55	80.56	3.31	32.78	22.43
Cambridge[5], MA	149.00	109.11	99.00	3.58	45.32	40.33
Cape Coral, FL	86.37	77.36	77.14	3.58	35.30	21.93
Carlsbad[6], CA	98.80	98.60	98.80	3.83	46.67	22.25
Cary[7], NC	100.70	100.00	86.72	3.38	32.82	20.79
Cedar Rapids, IA	94.54	68.48	76.08	3.42	28.94	25.83
Charleston, SC	100.92	93.55	94.45	3.39	39.50	24.57
Charlotte, NC	88.23	97.48	113.34	3.52	34.60	17.40
Chesapeake[8], VA	100.44	85.35	97.73	3.43	31.90	21.84
Chicago, IL	87.76	99.31	99.13	3.89	39.32	27.24
Clarksville, TN	94.02	84.01	80.05	3.33	33.49	36.61
Colorado Springs, CO	96.13	87.47	93.29	3.22	35.20	28.13
Columbia[9], MD	82.37	81.77	67.86	3.49	42.94	26.36
Columbia, MO	89.45	76.70	83.52	3.40	38.51	24.67
Columbia, SC	104.50	83.33	93.94	3.32	29.53	24.13
Columbus, OH	101.33	82.50	95.03	3.45	34.87	24.92
Dallas, TX	100.25	85.21	89.17	3.46	27.60	29.72
Denver, CO	108.17	88.32	100.29	3.28	33.76	18.88
Durham, NC	93.08	79.78	104.11	3.44	40.53	18.89
Edison[10], NJ	73.68	114.41	93.38	3.44	33.65	42.73
El Paso, TX	84.25	78.17	67.17	3.36	24.15	21.49
Fargo, ND	114.50	79.75	70.33	3.41	26.27	27.00
Fort Collins, CO	n/a	n/a	n/a	n/a	n/a	n/a
Fort Worth, TX	86.80	79.10	64.56	3.46	31.61	24.89
Gilbert[11], AZ	91.10	89.66	97.16	3.32	41.43	21.20
Green Bay, WI	134.43	77.99	72.19	3.60	29.18	25.29
Henderson[12], NV	98.33	89.33	110.48	3.46	46.37	35.71
High Point, NC	n/a	n/a	n/a	n/a	n/a	n/a
Honolulu, HI	128.23	94.93	126.91	3.99	48.51	45.37
Houston, TX	92.50	79.30	88.50	3.30	41.27	20.39
Huntington[13], NY	99.33	102.25	94.67	3.76	47.00	28.40
Huntsville, AL	71.67	79.17	106.00	3.48	35.66	21.18
Indianapolis, IN	n/a	n/a	n/a	n/a	n/a	n/a
Irvine[14], CA	91.85	95.00	102.90	3.81	58.46	24.56
Jackson, MS	86.10	87.33	82.32	3.31	28.92	16.10
Jacksonville, FL	69.07	81.07	67.49	3.39	42.37	20.95
Jersey City[15], NJ	87.36	90.52	90.08	3.48	37.03	42.05
Kansas City, MO	84.43	78.00	77.58	3.38	22.43	42.51
Kenosha[16], WI	137.80	82.25	53.66	3.59	29.55	19.61
Las Vegas, NV	98.33	89.33	110.48	3.46	46.37	35.71
Lexington, KY	88.50	84.37	68.29	3.41	34.17	21.71
Lincoln, NE	110.00	62.67	103.00	3.62	25.78	27.33

Table continued on next page.

Urban Area	Doctor ($/visit)	Dentist ($/visit)	Optometrist ($/visit)	Gasoline ($/gallon)	Beauty Salon ($/visit)	Men's Shirt ($)
Little Rock, AR	94.22	66.00	82.00	3.37	41.60	25.91
Los Angeles, CA	91.20	95.47	113.07	3.83	59.53	24.52
Madison, WI	149.00	91.01	58.32	3.55	36.80	19.91
Manchester, NH	149.00	84.33	92.59	3.47	38.76	37.10
Miami, FL	100.88	89.24	82.47	3.58	46.97	22.26
Minneapolis, MN	109.71	83.18	82.60	3.45	37.85	22.44
Murfreesboro, TN	85.00	64.66	88.33	3.34	39.00	20.16
Naperville[17], IL	100.61	82.76	97.54	3.74	32.28	18.88
Nashville, TN	81.47	78.78	86.47	3.34	29.00	24.20
New Orleans[18], LA	81.57	68.39	73.40	3.39	37.95	27.58
New York, NY	113.30	106.35	63.49	3.84	53.85	33.51
Norman, OK	81.49	76.14	88.90	3.33	30.88	23.98
Olathe[19], KS	84.43	78.00	77.58	3.38	22.43	42.51
Omaha, NE	110.40	64.46	90.17	3.52	24.28	16.87
Orlando, FL	77.70	76.16	71.75	3.48	41.54	35.81
Overland Park[20], KS	84.43	78.00	77.58	3.38	22.43	42.51
Oyster Bay[21], NY	99.33	102.25	94.67	3.76	47.00	28.40
Pembroke Pines[22], FL	82.10	88.82	101.81	3.56	45.61	23.10
Philadelphia, PA	118.58	93.05	97.41	3.59	59.61	38.74
Phoenix, AZ	91.10	89.66	97.16	3.32	41.43	21.20
Pittsburgh, PA	76.19	78.97	74.77	3.60	32.77	24.63
Plano, TX	91.01	92.67	69.67	3.39	33.04	22.25
Portland, OR	122.00	93.64	112.39	3.66	38.75	23.24
Providence, RI	149.00	87.14	107.43	3.60	45.38	40.93
Provo, UT	81.73	65.71	83.88	3.22	28.53	26.75
Raleigh, NC	100.70	100.00	86.72	3.38	32.82	20.79
Richmond, VA	83.58	101.11	110.06	3.45	41.62	18.32
Roseville[23], CA	112.86	93.49	112.13	3.82	46.05	25.41
Round Rock, TX	70.96	91.23	75.69	3.36	29.33	20.61
San Antonio, TX	84.47	79.55	86.08	3.35	42.94	34.31
San Diego, CA	98.80	98.60	98.80	3.83	46.67	22.25
San Francisco, CA	121.22	94.38	110.57	3.78	63.21	42.14
San Jose, CA	103.14	105.52	139.53	3.81	57.79	23.36
Savannah, GA	87.56	71.83	74.62	3.46	37.71	19.58
Scottsdale[24], AZ	91.10	89.66	97.16	3.32	41.43	21.20
Seattle, WA	119.29	106.93	115.25	3.65	41.48	35.93
Sioux Falls, SD	79.95	73.89	95.13	3.47	27.43	22.58
Stamford, CT	113.71	101.64	97.83	3.85	52.93	27.18
Sterling Heights[25], MI	83.80	80.50	70.87	3.62	39.30	18.74
Sunnyvale[26], CA	103.14	105.52	139.53	3.81	57.79	23.36
Tampa, FL	78.56	76.67	80.19	3.46	34.23	20.20
Temecula[27], CA	82.75	86.70	86.80	3.81	36.66	28.75
Thousand Oaks, CA	n/a	n/a	n/a	n/a	n/a	n/a
Virginia Beach[28], VA	100.44	85.35	97.73	3.43	31.90	21.84
Washington, DC	87.07	87.60	73.93	3.69	48.73	26.07
Average[99]	93.88	81.72	90.54	3.48	32.65	25.06
Minimum[99]	60.00	55.33	53.66	3.18	19.78	13.44
Maximum[99]	154.98	145.97	183.72	4.31	63.21	46.00

*Note: **Doctor** (general practitioners routine exam of an established patient); **Dentist** (adult teeth cleaning and periodic oral examination); **Optometrist** (full vision eye exam for established adult patient); **Gasoline** (one gallon regular unleaded, national brand, including all taxes, cash price at self-service pump if available); **Beauty Salon** (woman's shampoo, trim, and blow-dry); **Men's Shirt** (cotton/polyester dress shirt, pinpoint weave, long sleeves); (99) Values for the local area are compared with the average, minimum, and maximum values for all 331 areas in the Cost of Living Index report; n/a not available; In cases where data is not available for the city, data for the metro area or for a neighboring city has been provided and noted below;(1) Rio Rancho NM; (2) Washington-Arlington-Alexandria DC-VA; (3) Seattle WA; (4) Tulsa OK; (5) Boston MA; (6) San Diego CA; (7) Raleigh NC; (8) Hampton Roads-SE Virginia VA; (9) Baltimore MD; (10) Middlesex-Monmouth NJ; (11) Phoenix AZ; (12) Las Vegas NV; (13) Nassau County NY; (14) Orange County CA; (15) Newark-Elizabeth NJ; (16) Milwaukee-Waukesha WI; (17) Joliet-Will County IL; (18) Slidell-St. Tammany Parish LA; (19) Kansas City MO-KS; (20) Kansas City MO-KS; (21) Nassau County NY; (22) Fort Lauderdale FL; (23) Sacramento CA; (24) Phoenix AZ; (25) Detroit MI; (26) San Jose CA; (27) Riverside City CA; (28) Hampton Roads-SE Virginia VA*
Source: The Council for Community and Economic Research (formerly ACCRA), Cost of Living Index, 2011

Distribution of Physicians and Dentists

City	Area Covered	Dentists[1]	D.O.[2]	M.D.[3]				
				Total	Family/ General Practice	Pediatrics	Medical Specialties	Surgical Specialties
Albuquerque, NM	Bernalillo County	4.2	1.5	25.2	3.3	1.9	9.0	5.1
Alexandria, VA	Alexandria City	4.8	1.2	21.4	1.8	1.8	7.8	5.7
Anchorage, AK	Anchorage Borough	5.8	2.2	23.9	4.4	1.8	6.5	6.2
Ann Arbor, MI	Washtenaw County	9.0	3.0	47.5	2.9	3.5	19.1	9.0
Athens, GA	Clarke County	4.8	1.0	23.3	1.9	1.0	7.6	7.4
Atlanta, GA	Fulton County	5.7	0.8	31.2	1.8	2.2	11.5	8.5
Austin, TX	Travis County	4.5	1.2	22.6	2.9	1.7	7.7	5.2
Baltimore, MD	Baltimore City	3.2	1.6	29.3	1.3	1.8	12.5	6.2
Bellevue, WA	King County	7.6	1.1	29.4	4.6	1.9	10.2	5.7
Billings, MT	Yellowstone County	5.1	1.4	27.6	3.2	1.4	8.3	7.9
Boise City, ID	Ada County	6.5	1.6	22.5	3.6	1.0	6.4	6.5
Boston, MA	Suffolk County	7.8	1.1	44.4	1.1	3.0	20.4	8.2
Boulder, CO	Boulder County	6.1	2.0	28.4	5.4	2.1	8.3	6.4
Broken Arrow, OK	Tulsa County	5.1	11.2	20.4	2.4	1.3	7.6	4.9
Cambridge, MA	Middlesex County	7.4	0.6	32.2	1.5	2.9	14.4	5.7
Cape Coral, FL	Lee County	3.2	2.8	15.7	1.3	1.1	5.9	4.3
Carlsbad, CA	San Diego County	6.0	1.3	21.0	2.7	1.6	7.5	4.5
Cary, NC	Wake County	5.4	0.6	20.4	2.4	2.2	8.0	4.7
Cedar Rapids, IA	Linn County	3.4	1.4	15.7	4.2	0.9	3.8	3.4
Charleston, SC	Charleston County	7.1	2.1	40.7	3.3	2.7	13.6	10.1
Charlotte, NC	Mecklenburg County	5.4	0.7	23.2	2.4	2.0	9.1	5.6
Chesapeake, VA	Chesapeake City	3.8	1.4	17.8	3.4	1.7	6.6	4.4
Chicago, IL	Cook County	5.5	2.3	21.5	2.2	1.6	9.1	4.4
Clarksville, TN	Montgomery County	3.4	1.5	10.2	1.4	1.2	3.7	2.9
Colorado Spgs., CO	El Paso County	5.6	2.6	16.0	2.0	1.1	4.9	4.0
Columbia, MD	Howard County	9.6	1.8	41.2	3.5	4.3	18.3	6.2
Columbia, MO	Boone County	5.1	5.4	36.7	3.8	1.9	12.6	8.8
Columbia, SC	Richland County	4.9	0.6	26.1	2.9	2.0	9.9	6.3
Columbus, OH	Franklin County	5.6	5.8	22.2	2.9	1.6	8.2	5.1
Dallas, TX	Dallas County	4.5	1.8	18.7	1.5	1.2	6.8	4.6
Denver, CO	Denver County	5.4	2.6	35.3	2.9	2.3	13.2	7.7
Durham, NC	Durham County	5.4	0.9	42.5	2.8	3.3	16.9	9.3
Edison, NJ	Middlesex County	6.6	1.8	22.2	1.3	2.5	11.2	4.5
El Paso, TX	El Paso County	1.7	1.3	11.5	1.3	1.1	4.4	3.1
Fargo, ND	Cass County	5.2	0.9	29.4	4.7	1.9	10.8	6.3
Ft. Collins, CO	Larimer County	5.1	2.1	19.1	4.6	1.1	5.1	4.3
Ft. Worth, TX	Tarrant County	3.7	3.6	13.7	1.7	0.9	4.7	3.6
Gilbert, AZ	Maricopa County	4.5	3.1	16.3	1.8	1.1	6.1	3.6
Green Bay, WI	Brown County	5.3	1.5	20.0	2.5	1.2	6.4	5.7
Henderson, NV	Clark County	4.0	2.1	14.2	1.6	0.9	5.6	3.0
High Point, NC	Guilford County	4.2	0.5	21.5	2.7	1.5	8.2	5.5
Honolulu, HI	Honolulu County	6.3	1.5	24.1	2.2	2.1	9.6	5.3
Houston, TX	Harris County	4.1	0.8	18.2	1.9	1.4	6.8	4.3
Huntington, NY	Suffolk County	5.9	2.6	18.7	1.5	1.7	7.7	4.2
Huntsville, AL	Madison County	4.4	0.9	20.9	3.7	1.4	6.9	5.0
Indianapolis, IN	Marion County	4.5	1.4	24.5	2.9	1.7	9.0	5.5
Irvine, CA	Orange County	8.2	1.5	23.3	3.2	1.9	8.6	5.2
Jackson, MS	Hinds County	4.9	0.7	27.6	2.5	1.8	10.1	7.4
Jacksonville, FL	Duval County	3.7	2.0	22.1	3.2	1.5	8.0	5.0
Jersey City, NJ	Hudson County	4.8	1.0	11.3	1.0	1.4	5.6	2.5
Kansas City, MO	Jackson County	4.6	4.3	14.9	1.7	1.4	6.1	3.2
Kenosha, WI	Kenosha County	3.0	1.2	9.7	1.5	0.6	3.3	2.1
Las Vegas, NV	Clark County	4.0	2.1	14.2	1.6	0.9	5.6	3.0
Lexington, KY	Fayette County	8.1	2.6	39.4	3.7	2.2	14.0	9.8

Table continued on next page.

City	Area Covered	Dentists[1]	D.O.[2]	M.D.[3] Total	Family/ General Practice	Pediatrics	Medical Specialties	Surgical Specialties
Lincoln, NE	Lancaster County	5.5	0.9	19.9	3.9	1.3	6.5	4.4
Little Rock, AR	Pulaski County	5.1	1.3	37.9	4.3	2.2	12.6	8.8
Los Angeles, CA	Los Angeles County	6.1	1.0	19.7	2.2	1.5	7.7	4.3
Madison, WI	Dane County	5.1	1.6	29.9	4.7	1.8	10.3	5.8
Manchester, NH	Hillsborough County	5.3	1.5	18.3	2.5	1.6	7.0	4.3
Miami, FL	Miami-Dade County	4.4	1.4	22.0	2.7	1.9	9.0	4.7
Minneapolis, MN	Hennepin County	5.9	1.1	31.0	4.5	2.2	10.8	6.7
Murfreesboro, TN	Rutherford County	3.4	0.2	11.1	1.3	1.0	4.3	3.1
Naperville, IL	DuPage County	7.4	3.0	32.9	3.6	2.5	13.0	6.8
Nashville, TN	Davidson County	5.7	0.7	32.8	1.7	2.4	12.9	9.0
New Orleans, LA	Orleans Parish	3.4	0.8	32.1	1.8	2.3	11.9	8.0
New York, NY	Kings County	3.8	1.1	12.4	0.8	1.4	6.5	2.3
Norman, OK	Cleveland County	3.8	3.9	10.6	1.7	0.6	3.3	1.9
Olathe, KS	Johnson County	7.1	3.6	30.4	3.6	1.9	10.4	7.0
Omaha, NE	Douglas County	5.9	2.0	29.6	3.8	2.1	10.2	7.6
Orlando, FL	Orange County	4.0	1.9	19.7	2.5	1.8	7.6	4.3
Overland Park, KS	Johnson County	7.1	3.6	30.4	3.6	1.9	10.4	7.0
Oyster Bay, NY	Nassau County	11.4	5.1	39.4	1.5	3.8	18.3	9.4
Pembroke Pines, FL	Broward County	5.0	3.4	19.5	1.6	1.6	8.3	4.5
Philadelphia, PA	Philadelphia County	4.2	5.3	17.8	1.0	1.3	7.4	3.9
Phoenix, AZ	Maricopa County	4.5	3.1	16.3	1.8	1.1	6.1	3.6
Pittsburgh, PA	Allegheny County	6.5	3.3	31.6	2.8	2.0	12.7	6.9
Plano, TX	Collin County	5.7	1.4	18.7	2.3	1.8	7.4	4.0
Portland, OR	Multnomah County	5.5	2.4	33.3	3.1	2.0	12.6	7.2
Providence, RI	Providence County	3.7	1.5	22.4	1.4	1.8	10.5	5.2
Provo, UT	Utah County	5.0	1.1	9.4	2.0	0.9	2.6	2.4
Raleigh, NC	Wake County	5.4	0.6	20.4	2.4	2.2	8.0	4.7
Richmond, VA	Richmond City	6.1	2.0	33.0	2.9	2.4	12.1	8.7
Roseville, CA	Placer County	7.9	1.3	22.7	4.0	2.0	8.1	4.8
Round Rock, TX	Williamson County	3.9	1.4	10.9	2.5	1.2	3.6	2.5
San Antonio, TX	Bexar County	4.6	1.7	20.7	2.7	1.5	7.3	4.7
San Diego, CA	San Diego County	6.0	1.3	21.0	2.7	1.6	7.5	4.5
San Francisco, CA	San Francisco County	10.2	0.8	42.4	2.8	2.9	17.2	8.4
San Jose, CA	Santa Clara County	8.7	0.6	25.1	2.1	2.6	10.9	5.4
Savannah, GA	Chatham County	4.6	1.3	26.7	2.7	1.9	9.5	7.4
Scottsdale, AZ	Maricopa County	4.5	3.1	16.3	1.8	1.1	6.1	3.6
Seattle, WA	King County	7.6	1.1	29.4	4.6	1.9	10.2	5.7
Sioux Falls, SD	Minnehaha County	3.7	2.1	23.6	4.2	1.2	7.6	5.2
Stamford, CT	Fairfield County	6.9	1.1	26.5	1.1	2.3	12.0	6.6
Sterling Hgts, MI	Macomb County	5.1	5.9	9.5	1.6	0.8	4.1	2.3
Sunnyvale, CA	Santa Clara County	8.7	0.6	25.1	2.1	2.6	10.9	5.4
Tampa, FL	Hillsborough County	4.2	2.3	22.2	1.8	1.9	8.8	5.1
Temecula, CA	Riverside County	3.1	0.9	9.8	1.7	0.7	3.3	2.3
Thousand Oaks, CA	Ventura County	5.5	0.8	17.8	3.4	1.2	6.2	4.0
Virginia Beach, VA	Virginia Beach City	5.7	0.8	19.5	3.3	1.6	6.2	4.4
Washington, DC	The District County	7.4	1.7	36.1	2.1	2.9	15.4	7.7
U.S.	U.S.	4.5	1.9	18.3	2.5	1.4	6.8	4.1

Note: All figures are rates per 100,000 population; Data as of 2008 unless noted; (1) Data as of 2007; (2) Doctor of Osteopathic Medicine; (3) Includes active, non-federal, patient-care, office-based Doctors of Medicine

Source: Area Resource File (ARF). 2009-2010 Release. U.S. Department of Health and Human Services, Health Resources and Services Administration, Bureau of Health Professions, Rockville, MD, August 2010

Crime Rate: City

City	All Crimes	Violent Crimes				Property Crimes		
		Murder	Forcible Rape	Robbery	Aggrav. Assault	Burglary	Larceny -Theft	Motor Vehicle Theft
Albuquerque, NM	5,622.2	7.7	62.0	172.4	544.7	1,002.0	3,325.0	508.4
Alexandria, VA	2,302.3	1.3	13.7	81.8	83.8	207.5	1,727.1	187.2
Anchorage, AK	4,355.7	4.5	90.9	156.4	585.9	421.2	2,816.8	280.0
Ann Arbor, MI	2,882.5	0.0	38.5	68.0	147.7	468.9	2,043.9	115.4
Athens, GA	4,698.2	4.4	25.7	97.5	201.2	1,182.1	2,923.3	264.1
Atlanta, GA	6,812.8	17.3	16.6	403.0	634.7	1,494.2	3,307.0	940.0
Austin, TX	6,230.7	4.8	33.3	154.6	283.3	1,098.7	4,373.5	282.6
Baltimore, MD	5,875.0	34.8	41.4	521.3	858.2	1,183.4	2,546.8	689.0
Bellevue, WA	3,058.7	0.0	7.8	46.2	54.0	514.3	2,274.2	162.1
Billings, MT	4,906.6	1.9	23.1	38.9	195.3	784.9	3,527.4	335.1
Boise City, ID	3,033.5	1.5	43.2	28.2	188.9	431.3	2,263.2	77.2
Boston, MA	4,106.3	11.3	39.7	299.0	553.4	556.9	2,329.6	316.3
Boulder, CO	2,954.0	4.0	33.2	29.2	145.1	481.6	2,171.2	89.7
Broken Arrow, OK	2,234.0	2.0	31.8	28.7	84.0	361.8	1,598.7	127.1
Cambridge, MA	3,422.1	0.0	20.3	157.8	261.2	445.8	2,370.9	166.1
Cape Coral, FL	2,532.5	1.9	14.3	39.9	115.9	675.1	1,617.5	67.9
Carlsbad, CA	2,005.8	0.0	19.9	40.8	133.4	397.2	1,307.0	107.5
Cary, NC	1,625.2	0.7	9.9	24.7	49.5	378.2	1,116.9	45.2
Cedar Rapids, IA	4,124.1	0.8	25.5	94.9	171.3	791.6	2,855.6	184.4
Charleston, SC	3,750.7	8.5	15.3	128.5	212.7	511.3	2,679.7	194.8
Charlotte, NC	4,963.1	7.6	30.0	225.0	350.5	1,168.9	2,846.9	334.1
Chesapeake, VA	3,705.2	4.0	11.5	122.3	246.0	523.0	2,624.7	173.7
Chicago, IL	n/a	15.2	n/a	501.6	485.5	924.7	2,638.4	673.3
Clarksville, TN	3,875.2	7.1	43.5	95.6	487.6	1,085.0	1,995.3	161.2
Colorado Springs, CO	4,712.7	5.0	80.2	132.2	274.5	867.6	3,029.5	323.7
Columbia, MD	n/a	n/a	n/a	n/a	n/a	n/a	n/a	n/a
Columbia, MO	4,202.4	2.9	35.8	126.7	347.1	533.8	3,025.6	130.5
Columbia, SC	7,053.0	12.3	56.7	264.4	667.4	1,301.9	4,236.1	514.2
Columbus, OH	7,195.5	12.2	73.2	434.6	185.3	1,970.8	3,982.5	536.9
Dallas, TX	5,608.2	11.3	38.6	343.4	307.7	1,499.4	2,766.1	641.6
Denver, CO	3,947.3	3.6	60.5	152.5	325.5	741.5	2,132.3	531.4
Durham, NC	5,548.1	9.8	25.7	281.9	373.0	1,562.1	2,988.6	307.1
Edison, NJ	1,842.7	2.0	5.0	51.8	81.7	332.7	1,215.2	154.4
El Paso, TX	3,245.9	0.8	28.7	76.7	352.1	312.8	2,226.3	248.6
Fargo, ND	3,075.4	0.0	44.1	35.1	223.7	393.2	2,211.8	167.5
Fort Collins, CO	3,597.3	0.0	46.1	36.1	233.6	463.6	2,672.2	145.6
Fort Worth, TX	5,276.2	8.4	42.6	178.2	345.9	1,252.9	3,118.0	330.1
Gilbert, AZ	1,991.0	2.3	12.1	28.3	52.5	367.5	1,456.7	71.6
Green Bay, WI	2,926.4	2.0	53.3	66.1	243.8	560.6	1,892.0	108.6
Henderson, NV	2,171.6	3.0	13.2	71.5	117.7	484.3	1,288.8	193.0
High Point, NC	5,211.9	1.9	26.6	209.0	340.1	1,247.2	3,178.3	209.0
Honolulu, HI	n/a	n/a	n/a	n/a	n/a	n/a	n/a	n/a
Houston, TX	6,042.2	11.8	31.2	414.3	528.8	1,224.3	3,269.9	561.9
Huntington, NY	n/a	n/a	n/a	n/a	n/a	n/a	n/a	n/a
Huntsville, AL	5,972.0	6.5	41.4	252.5	344.1	1,460.0	3,397.7	469.6
Indianapolis, IN	n/a	n/a	n/a	n/a	n/a	n/a	n/a	n/a
Irvine, CA	1,343.5	0.0	11.1	18.4	25.8	221.0	1,011.5	55.7
Jackson, MS	8,594.7	23.5	58.0	623.6	281.4	2,766.5	3,948.8	892.9
Jacksonville, FL	5,215.5	9.7	38.4	205.9	411.0	1,165.8	3,144.8	239.9
Jersey City, NJ	3,202.7	10.2	18.0	386.2	334.6	623.7	1,499.6	330.5
Kansas City, MO	6,710.6	21.1	48.4	336.5	733.5	1,474.4	3,440.7	656.1
Kenosha, WI	3,272.0	2.0	41.4	89.9	139.4	608.3	2,262.5	128.3
Las Vegas, NV	3,944.3	7.6	46.0	282.6	556.8	976.0	1,569.5	505.8
Lexington, KY	4,248.4	6.0	29.0	197.6	341.9	892.8	2,567.4	213.6

Table continued on next page.

City	All Crimes	Violent Crimes				Property Crimes		
		Murder	Forcible Rape	Robbery	Aggrav. Assault	Burglary	Larceny -Theft	Motor Vehicle Theft
Lincoln, NE	4,419.4	0.8	55.1	70.1	358.5	563.8	3,237.2	134.0
Little Rock, AR	9,192.3	13.0	77.2	445.3	987.4	2,198.3	4,893.2	578.0
Los Angeles, CA	2,894.2	7.6	24.0	284.4	243.2	453.2	1,438.1	443.7
Madison, WI	3,765.4	0.8	36.5	136.8	217.4	691.4	2,529.1	153.2
Manchester, NH	3,975.9	0.9	57.4	142.5	302.5	839.0	2,485.6	148.0
Miami, FL	5,924.6	15.4	10.4	421.4	660.4	1,045.2	3,215.8	556.0
Minneapolis, MN	5,798.0	9.6	113.6	413.8	516.7	1,241.1	3,009.8	493.4
Murfreesboro, TN	4,773.9	4.6	33.9	138.3	375.5	1,199.6	2,879.1	142.9
Naperville, IL	n/a	n/a	n/a	n/a	n/a	n/a	n/a	n/a
Nashville, TN	6,086.0	8.9	59.5	294.8	771.6	1,254.3	3,387.8	309.1
New Orleans, LA	4,276.5	49.1	40.4	267.5	370.7	1,037.0	1,835.4	676.4
New York, NY	2,256.5	6.4	12.4	235.2	327.6	215.0	1,336.0	123.8
Norman, OK	3,307.5	1.8	42.1	32.3	47.5	727.1	2,356.2	100.4
Olathe, KS	2,001.0	3.2	32.5	22.2	113.4	192.7	1,524.3	112.6
Omaha, NE	4,217.8	7.3	41.8	155.6	282.4	655.6	2,602.3	472.9
Orlando, FL	7,550.9	7.5	47.0	279.7	737.2	1,671.4	4,311.4	496.6
Overland Park, KS	2,504.1	0.0	22.4	20.1	119.2	274.8	1,896.8	170.7
Oyster Bay, NY	n/a	n/a	n/a	n/a	n/a	n/a	n/a	n/a
Pembroke Pines, FL	3,598.4	2.7	8.1	62.4	114.0	747.9	2,456.2	207.0
Philadelphia, PA	4,897.6	19.6	60.6	536.6	572.5	692.8	2,561.9	453.5
Phoenix, AZ	4,491.2	7.6	33.8	210.4	266.3	1,011.8	2,461.2	500.1
Pittsburgh, PA	4,506.7	17.6	21.1	380.5	479.3	943.0	2,455.1	210.1
Plano, TX	2,594.5	1.4	19.0	54.6	105.7	444.6	1,830.4	138.7
Portland, OR	5,571.0	3.9	40.8	178.1	317.9	730.0	3,725.4	575.0
Providence, RI	5,504.0	8.7	43.1	236.1	419.7	1,185.6	2,959.8	651.1
Provo, UT	2,491.2	1.7	39.1	22.9	101.1	314.3	1,924.7	87.5
Raleigh, NC	3,510.8	3.3	23.6	153.2	234.5	719.8	2,169.2	207.3
Richmond, VA	4,892.6	19.9	19.4	357.0	335.1	866.0	2,874.4	420.6
Roseville, CA	3,453.7	0.8	14.2	72.6	191.2	452.6	2,529.3	192.9
Round Rock, TX	2,819.1	0.0	23.4	31.5	49.5	417.6	2,207.0	90.0
San Antonio, TX	6,952.1	5.7	33.5	169.5	397.1	1,242.7	4,697.2	406.3
San Diego, CA	2,769.0	2.2	22.8	124.6	278.0	486.3	1,368.7	486.4
San Francisco, CA	4,655.8	5.9	16.2	388.5	291.5	556.7	2,920.3	476.8
San Jose, CA	2,607.2	2.1	26.1	100.6	202.6	406.1	1,312.0	557.7
Savannah, GA	4,766.4	9.5	14.2	215.4	160.9	1,210.9	2,859.4	296.1
Scottsdale, AZ	3,000.5	1.7	14.3	43.4	93.7	555.8	2,175.3	116.3
Seattle, WA	5,917.7	3.1	15.5	230.4	317.8	1,039.8	3,754.3	556.8
Sioux Falls, SD	3,320.9	1.9	59.7	34.2	204.1	615.5	2,263.5	141.9
Stamford, CT	1,887.2	1.6	15.5	123.6	144.8	283.1	1,162.4	156.2
Sterling Heights, MI	2,069.8	0.8	24.5	27.7	104.5	288.2	1,529.0	95.0
Sunnyvale, CA	1,787.1	0.0	19.4	44.0	62.7	303.6	1,174.0	183.5
Tampa, FL	3,916.6	7.8	13.5	196.6	405.9	900.2	2,151.6	240.9
Temecula, CA	2,366.5	2.0	2.9	41.0	26.3	522.1	1,602.4	169.8
Thousand Oaks, CA	1,753.4	0.8	12.9	40.3	58.0	288.6	1,294.7	58.0
Virginia Beach, VA	3,223.9	3.2	12.6	96.8	75.5	493.5	2,393.1	149.1
Washington, DC	5,751.2	21.9	30.6	650.5	538.1	702.0	2,999.7	808.3
U.S.	3,345.5	4.8	27.5	119.1	252.3	699.6	2,003.5	238.8

Note: Figures are crimes per 100,000 population in 2010 except where noted; n/a not available
Source: FBI Uniform Crime Reports, 2010

Crime Rate: Suburbs

Suburbs[1]	All Crimes	Violent Crimes: Murder	Violent Crimes: Forcible Rape	Violent Crimes: Robbery	Violent Crimes: Aggrav. Assault	Property Crimes: Burglary	Property Crimes: Larceny-Theft	Property Crimes: Motor Vehicle Theft
Albuquerque, NM	2,867.3	2.7	17.1	46.9	416.4	789.5	1,396.9	197.7
Alexandria, VA	3,159.7	6.4	19.4	207.3	204.1	419.6	1,954.2	348.7
Anchorage, AK	3,856.1	0.0	21.9	48.1	428.9	350.2	2,770.6	236.4
Ann Arbor, MI	3,132.8	2.1	45.5	70.6	260.3	750.3	1,801.4	202.5
Athens, GA	3,503.9	4.0	10.6	30.4	398.7	773.6	2,088.6	198.0
Atlanta, GA	3,554.7	4.9	21.3	122.0	193.5	898.1	2,007.3	307.5
Austin, TX	2,362.0	2.3	17.5	25.2	159.6	467.5	1,612.2	77.8
Baltimore, MD	3,130.3	2.7	18.1	120.0	307.5	485.3	2,009.0	187.8
Bellevue, WA	4,256.6	2.1	32.3	118.1	174.9	787.0	2,674.8	467.5
Billings, MT	2,074.6	2.0	12.2	6.1	107.8	362.0	1,436.0	148.5
Boise City, ID	1,910.1	1.7	29.0	13.3	149.8	385.1	1,251.0	80.2
Boston, MA	2,396.8	3.0	20.3	93.7	275.9	465.0	1,405.5	133.3
Boulder, CO	2,249.5	1.5	11.8	20.7	157.1	341.7	1,621.3	95.5
Broken Arrow, OK	4,256.1	7.0	43.5	172.9	426.9	1,134.0	2,112.2	359.8
Cambridge, MA	2,161.8	1.4	16.9	54.0	212.6	411.4	1,354.3	111.1
Cape Coral, FL	3,269.3	5.4	25.5	122.0	310.4	873.4	1,751.5	181.2
Carlsbad, CA	2,604.5	2.3	22.0	111.2	249.2	459.6	1,341.6	418.5
Cary, NC	2,831.7	3.8	17.0	82.3	161.4	662.6	1,701.8	202.8
Cedar Rapids, IA	1,356.7	0.8	19.1	5.3	69.4	358.4	826.7	77.0
Charleston, SC	4,165.2	5.4	28.1	121.8	390.0	803.8	2,522.8	293.1
Charlotte, NC	n/a	n/a	n/a	n/a	n/a	n/a	n/a	n/a
Chesapeake, VA	3,837.1	7.0	21.8	134.7	166.2	618.9	2,687.4	201.0
Chicago, IL	n/a	n/a	n/a	n/a	n/a	n/a	n/a	n/a
Clarksville, TN	2,416.0	4.8	33.0	44.7	127.9	641.7	1,449.7	114.2
Colorado Springs, CO	1,928.9	1.3	38.1	19.3	352.5	377.5	1,001.4	138.8
Columbia, MD	n/a	n/a	n/a	n/a	n/a	n/a	n/a	n/a
Columbia, MO	2,085.7	1.6	15.7	11.0	211.4	327.3	1,446.9	72.0
Columbia, SC	4,124.6	3.8	32.0	91.6	530.2	896.7	2,270.3	299.9
Columbus, OH	2,729.6	1.1	21.1	50.2	48.0	573.6	1,955.5	80.2
Dallas, TX	3,066.5	1.9	21.1	57.2	132.2	658.3	1,979.6	216.3
Denver, CO	2,847.3	2.2	45.3	57.2	168.5	462.2	1,895.2	216.6
Durham, NC	3,092.3	4.7	22.1	42.4	134.8	953.8	1,820.0	114.5
Edison, NJ	2,008.0	1.7	8.1	60.1	86.7	349.3	1,429.0	73.1
El Paso, TX	2,980.0	1.5	32.6	38.6	350.0	566.7	1,801.8	188.7
Fargo, ND	n/a	1.8	n/a	10.1	77.3	325.7	1,329.4	68.1
Fort Collins, CO	2,143.0	0.0	30.6	20.6	120.5	307.8	1,578.1	85.5
Fort Worth, TX	3,798.3	2.9	26.4	72.1	212.7	814.2	2,462.5	207.5
Gilbert, AZ	4,008.0	5.6	26.7	129.2	224.0	818.5	2,453.0	351.0
Green Bay, WI	1,534.7	0.5	19.4	3.9	31.1	280.8	1,158.7	40.3
Henderson, NV	3,922.4	7.3	43.9	267.1	532.5	965.5	1,625.6	480.5
High Point, NC	4,258.8	4.7	15.1	125.1	205.9	1,192.8	2,507.5	207.8
Honolulu, HI	n/a	n/a	n/a	n/a	n/a	n/a	n/a	n/a
Houston, TX	3,653.1	4.5	22.5	127.8	240.5	821.0	2,185.5	251.3
Huntington, NY	n/a	n/a	n/a	n/a	n/a	n/a	n/a	n/a
Huntsville, AL	2,326.0	4.3	17.1	43.7	139.2	586.3	1,407.3	128.1
Indianapolis, IN	n/a	n/a	n/a	n/a	n/a	n/a	n/a	n/a
Irvine, CA	2,295.4	2.4	15.0	89.7	133.1	369.6	1,475.0	210.5
Jackson, MS	2,118.5	4.3	19.9	28.8	92.2	513.6	1,326.1	133.6
Jacksonville, FL	2,948.0	3.2	19.1	57.8	308.4	534.9	1,925.7	98.9
Jersey City, NJ	2,132.2	5.3	10.9	199.6	274.7	233.8	1,288.6	119.3
Kansas City, MO	3,103.2	4.4	26.9	54.5	171.5	571.3	2,025.2	249.5
Kenosha, WI	n/a	n/a	n/a	n/a	n/a	n/a	n/a	n/a
Las Vegas, NV	3,000.0	4.5	23.2	129.5	263.4	700.1	1,607.6	271.7
Lexington, KY	3,452.1	2.3	19.8	56.5	118.0	680.5	2,474.6	100.5

Table continued on next page.

Suburbs[1]	All Crimes	Violent Crimes: Murder	Violent Crimes: Forcible Rape	Violent Crimes: Robbery	Violent Crimes: Aggrav. Assault	Property Crimes: Burglary	Property Crimes: Larceny -Theft	Property Crimes: Motor Vehicle Theft
Lincoln, NE	1,843.4	0.0	13.4	2.2	77.9	285.0	1,415.9	49.0
Little Rock, AR	4,341.6	3.8	35.9	74.8	345.9	1,107.2	2,556.8	217.2
Los Angeles, CA	2,856.6	5.4	19.0	182.0	270.5	527.1	1,415.2	437.4
Madison, WI	2,224.7	0.9	15.3	28.6	86.1	306.9	1,720.2	66.6
Manchester, NH	1,862.6	0.7	24.4	24.7	64.4	326.4	1,356.7	65.4
Miami, FL	5,303.1	7.5	23.6	196.9	426.2	888.3	3,354.8	405.9
Minneapolis, MN	n/a	1.4	n/a	49.8	104.7	403.8	2,080.7	165.1
Murfreesboro, TN	3,978.1	6.3	41.6	138.9	463.0	820.9	2,314.4	192.9
Naperville, IL	n/a	n/a	n/a	n/a	n/a	n/a	n/a	n/a
Nashville, TN	2,756.0	4.5	29.5	42.0	261.6	593.4	1,709.7	115.2
New Orleans, LA	n/a	8.9	19.3	78.9	249.2	634.3	2,145.3	n/a
New York, NY	1,900.3	2.8	7.7	124.5	147.3	308.9	1,185.6	123.4
Norman, OK	n/a	6.1	44.0	114.9	n/a	1,236.2	2,671.5	401.0
Olathe, KS	4,061.6	8.6	31.8	126.0	313.5	817.8	2,405.7	358.3
Omaha, NE	2,616.0	1.2	35.5	29.5	204.7	499.3	1,628.3	217.4
Orlando, FL	3,783.3	4.5	31.2	126.8	393.0	918.9	2,098.4	210.5
Overland Park, KS	4,071.3	9.0	32.8	129.0	318.5	827.3	2,395.1	359.6
Oyster Bay, NY	n/a	n/a	n/a	n/a	n/a	n/a	n/a	n/a
Pembroke Pines, FL	4,388.7	3.6	26.2	186.6	293.6	996.0	2,612.3	270.4
Philadelphia, PA	2,133.3	2.6	14.6	72.5	151.1	300.5	1,507.5	84.5
Phoenix, AZ	3,568.4	4.2	21.4	74.4	186.0	671.2	2,368.4	242.8
Pittsburgh, PA	1,957.2	2.7	16.2	53.2	158.9	352.9	1,304.6	68.7
Plano, TX	3,901.1	4.9	26.8	147.8	189.4	938.4	2,238.1	355.9
Portland, OR	n/a	n/a	n/a	n/a	n/a	n/a	n/a	n/a
Providence, RI	2,589.8	1.9	28.7	74.4	225.9	558.2	1,540.1	160.6
Provo, UT	2,099.1	0.9	17.6	11.8	28.9	312.5	1,658.6	68.7
Raleigh, NC	2,220.3	3.5	11.9	31.4	99.0	576.4	1,327.7	170.4
Richmond, VA	2,405.0	4.7	15.1	63.8	95.3	423.3	1,681.9	121.0
Roseville, CA	3,592.5	4.4	26.8	165.5	293.1	787.9	1,850.5	464.2
Round Rock, TX	4,207.9	3.7	24.7	87.5	227.1	777.1	2,911.6	176.3
San Antonio, TX	3,304.7	2.7	30.7	44.6	168.1	736.4	2,183.8	138.5
San Diego, CA	2,447.6	2.2	21.3	97.3	221.2	436.2	1,319.5	350.1
San Francisco, CA	2,439.8	2.5	18.6	81.3	143.0	449.0	1,490.7	254.8
San Jose, CA	2,425.6	0.7	16.9	57.5	115.7	437.3	1,587.1	210.5
Savannah, GA	2,836.9	1.6	30.8	53.7	160.5	645.0	1,784.8	160.5
Scottsdale, AZ	3,957.5	5.7	26.6	128.7	222.3	809.4	2,415.4	349.5
Seattle, WA	3,668.1	1.6	36.0	78.8	123.1	691.7	2,316.3	420.5
Sioux Falls, SD	1,176.6	0.0	11.0	3.7	83.1	372.6	646.3	59.9
Stamford, CT	2,093.4	4.1	16.0	108.5	153.3	384.9	1,236.3	190.2
Sterling Heights, MI	2,306.4	2.1	29.5	53.2	190.4	460.1	1,394.6	176.5
Sunnyvale, CA	2,578.3	1.5	21.9	82.9	169.0	430.1	1,463.7	409.1
Tampa, FL	3,883.0	3.8	28.4	115.8	334.3	840.3	2,363.5	196.8
Temecula, CA	3,080.4	4.6	20.8	117.5	233.0	752.1	1,549.4	403.1
Thousand Oaks, CA	2,283.4	2.5	13.0	84.6	135.4	393.7	1,499.9	154.3
Virginia Beach, VA	4,026.3	7.8	23.1	145.6	212.0	645.2	2,778.4	214.2
Washington, DC	2,709.2	3.7	17.4	131.1	145.6	365.7	1,777.2	268.5
U.S.	3,345.5	4.8	27.5	119.1	252.3	699.6	2,003.5	238.8

Note: Figures are crimes per 100,000 population in 2010 except where noted; n/a not available; (1) All areas within the metro area that are located outside the city limits
Source: FBI Uniform Crime Reports, 2010

Crime Rate: Metro Area

Metro Area[1]	All Crimes	Violent Crimes				Property Crimes		
		Murder	Forcible Rape	Robbery	Aggrav. Assault	Burglary	Larceny-Theft	Motor Vehicle Theft
Albuquerque, NM	4,566.6	5.8	44.8	124.3	495.6	920.6	2,586.2	389.4
Alexandria, VA[2]	3,129.6	6.2	19.2	202.9	199.8	412.2	1,946.2	343.1
Anchorage, AK	4,319.2	4.2	85.9	148.5	574.4	416.1	2,813.4	276.8
Ann Arbor, MI	3,052.1	1.4	43.2	69.8	224.0	659.7	1,879.5	174.4
Athens, GA	4,218.5	4.2	19.6	70.5	280.5	1,018.0	2,588.1	237.5
Atlanta, GA	3,876.4	6.1	20.9	149.7	237.1	957.0	2,135.7	370.0
Austin, TX	4,119.9	3.4	24.7	84.0	215.8	754.3	2,866.9	170.8
Baltimore, MD	3,776.0	10.3	23.6	214.4	437.0	649.5	2,135.5	305.7
Bellevue, WA[2]	4,198.4	2.0	31.1	114.6	169.0	773.8	2,655.3	452.6
Billings, MT	4,020.9	1.9	19.7	28.6	167.9	652.7	2,873.3	276.7
Boise City, ID	2,283.3	1.6	33.7	18.2	162.8	400.4	1,587.3	79.2
Boston, MA[2]	2,973.7	5.8	26.9	163.0	369.5	496.0	1,717.4	195.1
Boulder, CO	2,480.8	2.3	18.9	23.5	153.1	387.6	1,801.8	93.6
Broken Arrow, OK	4,047.6	6.4	42.3	158.0	391.5	1,054.3	2,059.2	335.8
Cambridge, MA[2]	2,253.3	1.3	17.1	61.6	216.1	413.9	1,428.1	115.1
Cape Coral, FL	3,073.3	4.5	22.6	100.2	258.7	820.6	1,715.8	151.1
Carlsbad, CA	2,584.9	2.2	22.0	108.9	245.4	457.6	1,340.5	408.3
Cary, NC	2,685.2	3.4	16.1	75.3	147.8	628.1	1,630.8	183.7
Cedar Rapids, IA	2,732.3	0.8	22.2	49.9	120.0	573.8	1,835.2	130.4
Charleston, SC	4,092.7	6.0	25.9	122.9	359.0	752.7	2,550.3	275.9
Charlotte, NC	n/a	n/a	n/a	n/a	n/a	n/a	n/a	n/a
Chesapeake, VA	3,819.5	6.6	20.4	133.1	176.8	606.1	2,679.1	197.4
Chicago, IL	n/a	n/a	n/a	n/a	n/a	n/a	n/a	n/a
Clarksville, TN	3,095.0	5.9	37.9	68.4	295.3	847.9	1,703.6	136.1
Colorado Springs, CO	3,697.5	3.7	64.8	91.0	302.9	688.9	2,289.9	256.3
Columbia, MD	3,776.0	10.3	23.6	214.4	437.0	649.5	2,135.5	305.7
Columbia, MO	3,394.3	2.4	28.1	82.5	295.3	454.9	2,422.9	108.2
Columbia, SC	4,630.2	5.3	36.3	121.5	553.9	966.7	2,609.8	336.9
Columbus, OH	4,628.7	5.8	43.2	213.6	106.3	1,167.8	2,817.5	274.4
Dallas, TX[2]	3,818.8	4.7	26.3	141.9	184.1	907.2	2,212.4	342.2
Denver, CO	3,108.6	2.5	48.9	79.9	205.8	528.6	1,951.5	291.4
Durham, NC	4,218.4	7.1	23.7	152.2	244.0	1,232.8	2,355.9	202.8
Edison, NJ[2]	2,001.0	1.7	8.0	59.8	86.5	348.6	1,419.9	76.6
El Paso, TX	3,199.5	0.9	29.4	70.1	351.7	357.1	2,152.2	238.1
Fargo, ND	n/a	1.0	n/a	22.1	147.3	358.0	1,751.5	115.6
Fort Collins, CO	2,817.8	0.0	37.8	27.8	173.0	380.1	2,085.8	113.4
Fort Worth, TX[2]	4,309.2	4.8	32.0	108.8	258.8	965.9	2,689.1	249.9
Gilbert, AZ	3,905.4	5.5	25.9	124.1	215.3	795.6	2,402.3	336.8
Green Bay, WI	1,993.7	1.0	30.6	24.4	101.2	373.1	1,400.6	62.8
Henderson, NV	3,685.3	6.7	39.8	240.6	476.3	900.3	1,580.0	441.6
High Point, NC	4,397.7	4.3	16.7	137.3	225.4	1,200.7	2,605.2	208.0
Honolulu, HI	3,600.7	2.0	22.9	93.8	149.4	606.1	2,315.9	410.5
Houston, TX	4,564.6	7.3	25.8	237.1	350.5	974.8	2,599.3	369.8
Huntington, NY[2]	1,845.7	2.8	5.1	67.7	88.1	262.2	1,323.7	96.1
Huntsville, AL	3,929.7	5.3	27.8	135.5	229.3	970.6	2,282.8	278.3
Indianapolis, IN	n/a	n/a	n/a	n/a	n/a	n/a	n/a	n/a
Irvine, CA[2]	2,227.4	2.2	14.8	84.6	125.5	359.0	1,441.9	199.4
Jackson, MS	4,183.9	10.4	32.0	218.5	152.5	1,232.1	2,162.5	375.8
Jacksonville, FL	4,329.3	7.2	30.9	148.0	370.9	919.2	2,668.3	184.8
Jersey City, NJ[2]	2,154.6	5.4	11.1	203.5	276.0	241.9	1,293.0	123.7
Kansas City, MO	3,937.3	8.2	31.9	119.7	301.4	780.1	2,352.5	343.5
Kenosha, WI	n/a	n/a	n/a	n/a	n/a	n/a	n/a	n/a
Las Vegas, NV	3,685.3	6.7	39.8	240.6	476.3	900.3	1,580.0	441.6
Lexington, KY	3,952.8	4.6	25.6	145.2	258.8	814.0	2,533.0	171.6

Table continued on next page.

Metro Area[1]	All Crimes	Violent Crimes				Property Crimes		
		Murder	Forcible Rape	Robbery	Aggrav. Assault	Burglary	Larceny -Theft	Motor Vehicle Theft
Lincoln, NE	4,039.5	0.7	48.9	60.1	317.1	522.7	2,968.6	121.5
Little Rock, AR	5,690.2	6.3	47.4	177.8	524.3	1,410.5	3,206.4	317.5
Los Angeles, CA[2]	2,871.3	6.3	21.0	221.8	259.9	498.3	1,424.1	439.9
Madison, WI	2,860.4	0.9	24.1	73.3	140.3	465.6	2,054.0	102.4
Manchester, NH	2,429.3	0.7	33.2	56.3	128.2	463.8	1,659.4	87.6
Miami, FL[2]	5,411.6	8.9	21.3	236.1	467.0	915.7	3,330.6	432.1
Minneapolis, MN	n/a	2.4	n/a	92.3	152.8	501.6	2,189.2	203.5
Murfreesboro, TN	4,032.1	6.2	41.0	138.9	457.0	846.7	2,352.8	189.5
Naperville, IL	n/a	n/a	n/a	n/a	n/a	n/a	n/a	n/a
Nashville, TN	4,032.1	6.2	41.0	138.9	457.0	846.7	2,352.8	189.5
New Orleans, LA	n/a	20.8	25.6	134.8	285.3	753.7	2,053.4	n/a
New York, NY[2]	2,154.6	5.4	11.1	203.5	276.0	241.9	1,293.0	123.7
Norman, OK	n/a	5.7	43.8	107.6	n/a	1,190.9	2,643.5	374.2
Olathe, KS	3,937.3	8.2	31.9	119.7	301.4	780.1	2,352.5	343.5
Omaha, NE	3,473.8	4.5	38.8	97.0	246.3	583.0	2,149.9	354.2
Orlando, FL	4,208.2	4.8	33.0	144.1	431.8	1,003.8	2,348.0	242.7
Overland Park, KS	3,937.3	8.2	31.9	119.7	301.4	780.1	2,352.5	343.5
Oyster Bay, NY[2]	1,845.7	2.8	5.1	67.7	88.1	262.2	1,323.7	96.1
Pembroke Pines, FL[2]	4,323.2	3.5	24.7	176.3	278.7	975.5	2,599.4	265.1
Philadelphia, PA[2]	3,197.2	9.1	32.3	251.2	313.3	451.5	1,913.3	226.5
Phoenix, AZ	3,905.4	5.5	25.9	124.1	215.3	795.6	2,402.3	336.8
Pittsburgh, PA	2,295.1	4.7	16.9	96.5	201.4	431.1	1,457.1	87.4
Plano, TX[2]	3,818.8	4.7	26.3	141.9	184.1	907.2	2,212.4	342.2
Portland, OR	n/a	n/a	n/a	n/a	n/a	n/a	n/a	n/a
Providence, RI	2,903.2	2.6	30.2	91.8	246.8	625.7	1,692.8	213.4
Provo, UT	2,181.5	1.1	22.1	14.1	44.1	312.9	1,714.5	72.6
Raleigh, NC	2,685.2	3.4	16.1	75.3	147.8	628.1	1,630.8	183.7
Richmond, VA	2,812.2	7.2	15.8	111.8	134.5	495.8	1,877.1	170.1
Roseville, CA	3,584.8	4.2	26.1	160.4	287.5	769.3	1,888.1	449.2
Round Rock, TX	4,119.9	3.4	24.7	84.0	215.8	754.3	2,866.9	170.8
San Antonio, TX	5,717.1	4.7	32.6	127.2	319.5	1,071.3	3,846.2	315.6
San Diego, CA	2,584.9	2.2	22.0	108.9	245.4	457.6	1,340.5	408.3
San Francisco, CA[2]	3,453.8	4.0	17.5	221.9	211.0	498.3	2,144.8	356.4
San Jose, CA	2,520.9	1.4	21.7	80.1	161.3	420.9	1,442.7	392.7
Savannah, GA	4,042.6	6.5	20.5	154.8	160.7	998.6	2,456.3	245.2
Scottsdale, AZ	3,905.4	5.5	25.9	124.1	215.3	795.6	2,402.3	336.8
Seattle, WA[2]	4,198.4	2.0	31.1	114.6	169.0	773.8	2,655.3	452.6
Sioux Falls, SD	2,597.2	1.2	43.3	23.9	163.3	533.5	1,717.7	114.2
Stamford, CT	2,065.1	3.8	16.0	110.6	152.1	370.9	1,226.2	185.5
Sterling Heights, MI[2]	2,294.3	2.0	29.3	51.9	186.0	451.2	1,401.5	172.3
Sunnyvale, CA	2,520.9	1.4	21.7	80.1	161.3	420.9	1,442.7	392.7
Tampa, FL	3,887.2	4.3	26.6	125.9	343.3	847.8	2,337.1	202.3
Temecula, CA	3,063.1	4.5	20.4	115.7	228.0	746.5	1,550.6	397.5
Thousand Oaks, CA	2,202.0	2.2	13.0	77.8	123.5	377.5	1,468.4	139.5
Virginia Beach, VA	3,819.5	6.6	20.4	133.1	176.8	606.1	2,679.1	197.4
Washington, DC[2]	3,129.6	6.2	19.2	202.9	199.8	412.2	1,946.2	343.1
U.S.	3,345.5	4.8	27.5	119.1	252.3	699.6	2,003.5	238.8

Note: Figures are crimes per 100,000 population in 2010 except where noted; n/a not available; (1) Figures cover the Metropolitan Statistical Area except where noted; (2) Metropolitan Division (MD); See Appendix B for counties included in MSAs and MDs
Source: FBI Uniform Crime Reports, 2010

Temperature & Precipitation: Yearly Averages and Extremes

City	Extreme Low (°F)	Average Low (°F)	Average Temp. (°F)	Average High (°F)	Extreme High (°F)	Average Precip. (in.)	Average Snow (in.)
Albuquerque, NM	-17	43	57	70	105	8.5	11
Alexandria, VA	-5	49	58	67	104	39.5	18
Anchorage, AK	-34	29	36	43	85	15.7	71
Ann Arbor, MI	-21	39	49	58	104	32.4	41
Athens, GA	-8	52	62	72	105	49.8	2
Atlanta, GA	-8	52	62	72	105	49.8	2
Austin, TX	-2	58	69	79	109	31.1	1
Baltimore, MD	-7	45	56	65	105	41.2	21
Bellevue, WA	0	44	52	59	99	38.4	13
Billings, MT	-32	36	47	59	105	14.6	59
Boise City, ID	-25	39	51	63	111	11.8	22
Boston, MA	-12	44	52	59	102	42.9	41
Boulder, CO	-25	37	51	64	103	15.5	63
Broken Arrow, OK	-8	50	61	71	112	38.9	10
Cambridge, MA	-12	44	52	59	102	42.9	41
Cape Coral, FL	26	65	75	84	103	53.9	0
Carlsbad, CA	29	57	64	71	111	9.5	Trace
Cary, NC	-9	48	60	71	105	42.0	8
Cedar Rapids, IA	-34	36	47	57	105	34.4	33
Charleston, SC	6	55	66	76	104	52.1	1
Charlotte, NC	-5	50	61	71	104	42.8	6
Chesapeake, VA	-3	51	60	69	104	44.8	8
Chicago, IL	-27	40	49	59	104	35.4	39
Clarksville, TN	-17	49	60	70	107	47.4	11
Colorado Springs, CO	-24	36	49	62	99	17.0	48
Columbia, MD	-7	45	56	65	105	41.2	21
Columbia, MO	-20	44	54	64	111	40.6	25
Columbia, SC	-1	51	64	75	107	48.3	2
Columbus, OH	-19	42	52	62	104	37.9	28
Dallas, TX	-2	56	67	77	112	33.9	3
Denver, CO	-25	37	51	64	103	15.5	63
Durham, NC	-9	48	60	71	105	42.0	8
Edison, NJ	-2	47	55	62	104	47.0	23
El Paso, TX	-8	50	64	78	114	8.6	6
Fargo, ND	-36	31	41	52	106	19.6	40
Fort Collins, CO	-25	37	51	64	103	15.5	63
Fort Worth, TX	-1	55	66	76	113	32.3	3
Gilbert, AZ	17	59	72	86	122	7.3	Trace
Green Bay, WI	-31	34	44	54	99	28.3	46
Henderson, NV	8	53	67	80	116	4.0	1
High Point, NC	-8	47	58	69	103	42.5	10
Honolulu, HI	52	70	77	84	94	22.4	0
Houston, TX	7	58	69	79	107	46.9	Trace
Huntington, NY	-3	48	55	62	107	42.8	24
Huntsville, AL	-11	50	61	71	104	56.8	4
Indianapolis, IN	-23	42	53	62	104	40.2	25
Irvine, CA	25	53	64	75	112	11.9	Trace
Jackson, MS	2	53	65	76	106	55.4	1
Jacksonville, FL	7	58	69	79	103	52.0	0
Jersey City, NJ	-8	46	55	63	105	43.5	27
Kansas City, MO	-23	44	54	64	109	38.1	21
Kenosha, WI	-27	40	49	59	104	35.4	39
Las Vegas, NV	8	53	67	80	116	4.0	1
Lexington, KY	-21	45	55	65	103	45.1	17
Lincoln, NE	-33	39	51	62	108	29.1	27

Table continued on next page.

City	Extreme Low (°F)	Average Low (°F)	Average Temp. (°F)	Average High (°F)	Extreme High (°F)	Average Precip. (in.)	Average Snow (in.)
Little Rock, AR	-5	51	62	73	112	50.7	5
Los Angeles, CA	27	55	63	70	110	11.3	Trace
Madison, WI	-37	35	46	57	104	31.1	42
Manchester, NH	-33	34	46	57	102	36.9	63
Miami, FL	30	69	76	83	98	57.1	0
Minneapolis, MN	-34	35	45	54	105	27.1	52
Murfreesboro, TN	-17	49	60	70	107	47.4	11
Naperville, IL	-27	40	49	59	104	35.4	39
Nashville, TN	-17	49	60	70	107	47.4	11
New Orleans, LA	11	59	69	78	102	60.6	Trace
New York, NY	-2	47	55	62	104	47.0	23
Norman, OK	-8	49	60	71	110	32.8	10
Olathe, KS	-23	44	54	64	109	38.1	21
Omaha, NE	-23	40	51	62	110	30.1	29
Orlando, FL	19	62	72	82	100	47.7	Trace
Overland Park, KS	-23	44	54	64	109	38.1	21
Oyster Bay, NY	-3	48	55	62	107	42.8	24
Pembroke Pines, FL	30	69	76	83	98	57.1	0
Philadelphia, PA	-7	45	55	64	104	41.4	22
Phoenix, AZ	17	59	72	86	122	7.3	Trace
Pittsburgh, PA	-18	41	51	60	103	37.1	43
Plano, TX	-2	56	67	77	112	33.9	3
Portland, OR	-3	45	54	62	107	37.5	7
Providence, RI	-13	42	51	60	104	45.3	35
Provo, UT	-22	40	52	64	107	15.6	63
Raleigh, NC	-9	48	60	71	105	42.0	8
Richmond, VA	-8	48	58	69	105	43.0	13
Roseville, CA	18	48	61	73	115	17.3	Trace
Round Rock, TX	-2	58	69	79	109	31.1	1
San Antonio, TX	0	58	69	80	108	29.6	1
San Diego, CA	29	57	64	71	111	9.5	Trace
San Francisco, CA	24	49	57	65	106	19.3	Trace
San Jose, CA	21	50	59	68	105	13.5	Trace
Savannah, GA	3	56	67	77	105	50.3	Trace
Scottsdale, AZ	17	59	72	86	122	7.3	Trace
Seattle, WA	0	44	52	59	99	38.4	13
Sioux Falls, SD	-36	35	46	57	110	24.6	38
Stamford, CT	-7	44	52	60	103	41.4	25
Sterling Heights, MI	-21	39	49	58	104	32.4	41
Sunnyvale, CA	21	50	59	68	105	13.5	Trace
Tampa, FL	18	63	73	82	99	46.7	Trace
Temecula, CA	24	53	66	78	114	n/a	n/a
Thousand Oaks, CA	27	55	63	70	110	11.3	Trace
Virginia Beach, VA	-3	51	60	69	104	44.8	8
Washington, DC	-5	49	58	67	104	39.5	18

Source: National Climatic Data Center, International Station Meteorological Climate Summary, 9/96

Weather Conditions

City	Temperature			Daytime Sky			Precipitation		
	10°F & below	32°F & below	90°F & above	Clear	Partly cloudy	Cloudy	0.01 inch or more precip.	1.0 inch or more snow/ice	Thunder-storms
Albuquerque, NM	4	114	65	140	161	64	60	9	38
Alexandria, VA	2	71	34	84	144	137	112	9	30
Anchorage, AK	n/a	194	n/a	50	115	200	113	49	2
Ann Arbor, MI	n/a	136	12	74	134	157	135	38	32
Athens, GA	1	49	38	98	147	120	116	3	48
Atlanta, GA	1	49	38	98	147	120	116	3	48
Austin, TX	< 1	20	111	105	148	112	83	1	41
Baltimore, MD	6	97	31	91	143	131	113	13	27
Bellevue, WA	n/a	38	3	57	121	187	157	8	8
Billings, MT	n/a	149	29	75	163	127	97	41	27
Boise City, ID	n/a	124	45	106	133	126	91	22	14
Boston, MA	n/a	97	12	88	127	150	253	48	18
Boulder, CO	24	155	33	99	177	89	90	38	39
Broken Arrow, OK	6	78	74	117	141	107	88	8	50
Cambridge, MA	n/a	97	12	88	127	150	253	48	18
Cape Coral, FL	n/a	n/a	115	93	220	52	110	0	92
Carlsbad, CA	0	< 1	4	115	126	124	40	0	5
Cary, NC	n/a	n/a	39	98	143	124	110	3	42
Cedar Rapids, IA	n/a	156	16	89	132	144	109	28	42
Charleston, SC	< 1	33	53	89	162	114	114	1	59
Charlotte, NC	1	65	44	98	142	125	113	3	41
Chesapeake, VA	< 1	53	33	89	149	127	115	5	38
Chicago, IL	n/a	132	17	83	136	146	125	31	38
Clarksville, TN	5	76	51	98	135	132	119	8	54
Colorado Springs, CO	21	161	18	108	157	100	98	33	49
Columbia, MD	6	97	31	91	143	131	113	13	27
Columbia, MO	17	108	36	99	127	139	110	17	52
Columbia, SC	< 1	58	77	97	149	119	110	1	53
Columbus, OH	n/a	118	19	72	137	156	136	29	40
Dallas, TX	1	34	102	108	160	97	78	2	49
Denver, CO	24	155	33	99	177	89	90	38	39
Durham, NC	n/a	n/a	39	98	143	124	110	3	42
Edison, NJ	n/a	n/a	18	85	166	114	120	11	20
El Paso, TX	1	59	106	147	164	54	49	3	35
Fargo, ND	n/a	180	15	81	145	139	100	38	31
Fort Collins, CO	24	155	33	99	177	89	90	38	39
Fort Worth, TX	1	40	100	123	136	106	79	3	47
Gilbert, AZ	0	10	167	186	125	54	37	< 1	23
Green Bay, WI	n/a	163	7	86	125	154	120	40	33
Henderson, NV	< 1	37	134	185	132	48	27	2	13
High Point, NC	3	85	32	94	143	128	113	5	43
Honolulu, HI	n/a	n/a	23	25	286	54	98	0	7
Houston, TX	n/a	n/a	96	83	168	114	101	1	62
Huntington, NY	n/a	73	16	77	161	127	119	14	23
Huntsville, AL	2	66	49	70	118	177	116	2	54
Indianapolis, IN	19	119	19	83	128	154	127	24	43
Irvine, CA	0	2	18	95	192	78	41	0	4
Jackson, MS	1	50	84	103	144	118	106	2	68
Jacksonville, FL	< 1	16	83	86	181	98	114	1	65
Jersey City, NJ	n/a	90	24	80	146	139	122	16	46
Kansas City, MO	22	110	39	112	134	119	103	17	51
Kenosha, WI	n/a	132	17	83	136	146	125	31	38
Las Vegas, NV	< 1	37	134	185	132	48	27	2	13
Lexington, KY	11	96	22	86	136	143	129	17	44

Table continued on next page.

City	Temperature			Daytime Sky			Precipitation		
	10°F & below	32°F & below	90°F & above	Clear	Partly cloudy	Cloudy	0.01 inch or more precip.	1.0 inch or more snow/ice	Thunder-storms
Lincoln, NE	n/a	145	40	108	135	122	94	19	46
Little Rock, AR	1	57	73	110	142	113	104	4	57
Los Angeles, CA	0	< 1	5	131	125	109	34	0	1
Madison, WI	n/a	161	14	88	119	158	118	38	40
Manchester, NH	n/a	171	12	87	131	147	125	32	19
Miami, FL	n/a	n/a	55	48	263	54	128	0	74
Minneapolis, MN	n/a	156	16	93	125	147	113	41	37
Murfreesboro, TN	5	76	51	98	135	132	119	8	54
Naperville, IL	n/a	132	17	83	136	146	125	31	38
Nashville, TN	5	76	51	98	135	132	119	8	54
New Orleans, LA	0	13	70	90	169	106	114	1	69
New York, NY	n/a	n/a	18	85	166	114	120	11	20
Norman, OK	5	79	70	124	131	110	80	8	50
Olathe, KS	22	110	39	112	134	119	103	17	51
Omaha, NE	n/a	139	35	100	142	123	97	20	46
Orlando, FL	n/a	n/a	90	76	208	81	115	0	80
Overland Park, KS	22	110	39	112	134	119	103	17	51
Oyster Bay, NY	n/a	73	16	77	161	127	119	14	23
Pembroke Pines, FL	n/a	n/a	55	48	263	54	128	0	74
Philadelphia, PA	5	94	23	81	146	138	117	14	27
Phoenix, AZ	0	10	167	186	125	54	37	< 1	23
Pittsburgh, PA	n/a	121	8	62	137	166	154	42	35
Plano, TX	1	34	102	108	160	97	78	2	49
Portland, OR	n/a	37	11	67	116	182	152	4	7
Providence, RI	n/a	117	9	85	134	146	123	21	21
Provo, UT	n/a	128	56	94	152	119	92	38	38
Raleigh, NC	n/a	n/a	39	98	143	124	110	3	42
Richmond, VA	3	79	41	90	147	128	115	7	43
Roseville, CA	0	21	73	175	111	79	58	< 1	2
Round Rock, TX	< 1	20	111	105	148	112	83	1	41
San Antonio, TX	n/a	n/a	112	97	153	115	81	1	36
San Diego, CA	0	< 1	4	115	126	124	40	0	5
San Francisco, CA	0	6	4	136	130	99	63	< 1	5
San Jose, CA	0	5	5	106	180	79	57	< 1	6
Savannah, GA	< 1	29	70	97	155	113	111	< 1	63
Scottsdale, AZ	0	10	167	186	125	54	37	< 1	23
Seattle, WA	n/a	38	3	57	121	187	157	8	8
Sioux Falls, SD	n/a	n/a	n/a	95	136	134	n/a	n/a	n/a
Stamford, CT	n/a	n/a	7	80	146	139	118	17	22
Sterling Heights, MI	n/a	136	12	74	134	157	135	38	32
Sunnyvale, CA	0	5	5	106	180	79	57	< 1	6
Tampa, FL	n/a	n/a	85	81	204	80	107	< 1	87
Temecula, CA	0	4	82	124	178	63	n/a	n/a	5
Thousand Oaks, CA	0	< 1	5	131	125	109	34	0	1
Virginia Beach, VA	< 1	53	33	89	149	127	115	5	38
Washington, DC	2	71	34	84	144	137	112	9	30

Note: Figures are average number of days per year
Source: National Climatic Data Center, International Station Meteorological Climate Summary, 9/96

Air Quality Index

Area[1] (Days[2])	Percent of Days when Air Quality was...					AQI Statistics	
	Good	Moderate	Unhealthy for Sensitive Groups	Unhealthy	Very Unhealthy	Maximum	Median
Albuquerque, NM (365)	45.8	50.4	3.3	0.3	0.3	293	52
Alexandria, VA (365)	86.0	12.1	1.6	0.3	0.0	161	34
Anchorage, AK (365)	89.6	10.4	0.0	0.0	0.0	88	25
Ann Arbor, MI (296)	83.1	15.5	1.4	0.0	0.0	129	35
Athens, GA (365)	71.2	27.7	1.1	0.0	0.0	106	41
Atlanta, GA (365)	66.0	29.9	4.1	0.0	0.0	145	43
Austin, TX (365)	74.0	25.2	0.8	0.0	0.0	116	40
Baltimore, MD (365)	66.6	31.2	2.2	0.0	0.0	129	43
Bellevue, WA (365)	86.8	13.2	0.0	0.0	0.0	89	33
Billings, MT (365)	87.7	11.5	0.8	0.0	0.0	131	23
Boise City, ID (365)	88.2	11.2	0.5	0.0	0.0	115	38
Boston, MA (365)	75.6	23.8	0.5	0.0	0.0	108	42
Boulder, CO (365)	80.0	18.9	1.1	0.0	0.0	116	42
Broken Arrow, OK (365)	44.7	48.2	6.8	0.3	0.0	158	54
Cambridge, MA (365)	96.7	3.0	0.3	0.0	0.0	127	31
Cape Coral, FL (365)	95.1	4.9	0.0	0.0	0.0	74	34
Carlsbad, CA (365)	33.7	62.7	3.3	0.3	0.0	155	54
Cary, NC (365)	72.9	25.5	1.6	0.0	0.0	137	40
Cedar Rapids, IA (365)	78.6	21.4	0.0	0.0	0.0	84	38
Charleston, SC (365)	80.3	18.6	1.1	0.0	0.0	136	37
Charlotte, NC (365)	67.1	28.2	4.7	0.0	0.0	145	44
Chesapeake, VA (n/a)	n/a	n/a	n/a	n/a	n/a	n/a	n/a
Chicago, IL (365)	37.8	57.0	5.2	0.0	0.0	138	56
Clarksville, TN (365)	76.2	23.6	0.3	0.0	0.0	141	35
Colorado Spgs., CO (365)	74.8	24.4	0.8	0.0	0.0	119	43
Columbia, MD (n/a)	n/a	n/a	n/a	n/a	n/a	n/a	n/a
Columbia, MO (245)	91.4	8.6	0.0	0.0	0.0	97	39
Columbia, SC (365)	66.8	30.7	2.5	0.0	0.0	124	43
Columbus, OH (365)	69.9	27.9	2.2	0.0	0.0	132	42
Dallas, TX (365)	66.0	28.2	4.9	0.8	0.0	156	44
Denver, CO (365)	57.8	41.1	1.1	0.0	0.0	137	48
Durham, NC (365)	81.9	17.8	0.3	0.0	0.0	105	36
Edison, NJ (364)	83.5	13.5	3.0	0.0	0.0	142	37
El Paso, TX (365)	46.3	50.4	2.7	0.5	0.0	186	52
Fargo, ND (350)	91.7	8.3	0.0	0.0	0.0	72	31
Ft. Collins, CO (365)	60.3	36.2	3.6	0.0	0.0	127	48
Ft. Worth, TX (365)	63.3	29.0	6.6	1.1	0.0	169	45
Gilbert, AZ (365)	23.6	65.2	7.1	2.2	1.9	565	61
Green Bay, WI (365)	64.9	33.2	1.9	0.0	0.0	122	42
Henderson, NV (365)	57.5	35.9	6.6	0.0	0.0	144	47
High Point, NC (361)	78.9	19.9	1.1	0.0	0.0	116	39
Honolulu, HI (365)	92.6	7.4	0.0	0.0	0.0	91	32
Houston, TX (365)	52.9	38.6	7.4	1.1	0.0	164	49
Huntington, NY (365)	82.7	14.0	2.5	0.8	0.0	197	38
Huntsville, AL (332)	80.7	18.7	0.6	0.0	0.0	106	38
Indianapolis, IN (365)	44.1	52.6	3.3	0.0	0.0	124	53
Irvine, CA (365)	50.1	47.9	1.9	0.0	0.0	119	50
Jackson, MS (365)	68.5	30.7	0.8	0.0	0.0	124	43
Jacksonville, FL (365)	83.6	14.2	1.4	0.8	0.0	173	38
Jersey City, NJ (365)	69.0	29.6	1.4	0.0	0.0	132	41
Kansas City, MO (365)	60.8	31.0	7.7	0.5	0.0	159	43
Kenosha, WI (304)	82.9	14.8	2.0	0.3	0.0	151	36
Las Vegas, NV (365)	57.5	35.9	6.6	0.0	0.0	144	47
Lexington, KY (365)	78.1	21.1	0.8	0.0	0.0	111	39

Table continued on next page.

Area[1] (Days[2])	Percent of Days when Air Quality was...					AQI Statistics	
	Good	Moderate	Unhealthy for Sensitive Groups	Unhealthy	Very Unhealthy	Maximum	Median
Lincoln, NE (365)	96.7	3.3	0.0	0.0	0.0	78	25
Little Rock, AR (365)	64.4	32.6	3.0	0.0	0.0	122	45
Los Angeles, CA (365)	14.5	59.5	23.0	2.7	0.3	203	69
Madison, WI (359)	79.4	20.6	0.0	0.0	0.0	95	36
Manchester, NH (365)	93.4	6.0	0.5	0.0	0.0	137	35
Miami, FL (365)	89.9	9.6	0.5	0.0	0.0	109	36
Minneapolis, MN (365)	84.7	15.3	0.0	0.0	0.0	86	28
Murfreesboro, TN (243)	88.9	11.1	0.0	0.0	0.0	84	40
Naperville, IL (365)	71.8	27.9	0.3	0.0	0.0	101	40
Nashville, TN (365)	74.2	24.9	0.8	0.0	0.0	124	41
New Orleans, LA (365)	89.6	9.9	0.3	0.3	0.0	155	34
New York, NY (365)	79.7	20.3	0.0	0.0	0.0	98	32
Norman, OK (363)	66.7	30.0	3.3	0.0	0.0	127	44
Olathe, KS (365)	86.6	12.6	0.8	0.0	0.0	137	36
Omaha, NE (365)	57.8	41.6	0.5	0.0	0.0	109	45
Orlando, FL (365)	87.9	10.1	1.9	0.0	0.0	111	36
Overland Park, KS (365)	86.6	12.6	0.8	0.0	0.0	137	36
Oyster Bay, NY (365)	81.6	18.4	0.0	0.0	0.0	96	30
Pembroke Pines, FL (365)	95.9	4.1	0.0	0.0	0.0	100	34
Philadelphia, PA (365)	55.1	41.6	3.3	0.0	0.0	147	48
Phoenix, AZ (365)	23.6	65.2	7.1	2.2	1.9	565	61
Pittsburgh, PA (365)	48.2	42.7	8.2	0.8	0.0	175	52
Plano, TX (362)	78.7	14.9	6.4	0.0	0.0	150	36
Portland, OR (365)	85.5	13.7	0.8	0.0	0.0	112	31
Providence, RI (365)	82.2	16.7	1.1	0.0	0.0	108	38
Provo, UT (365)	73.2	25.5	1.4	0.0	0.0	120	43
Raleigh, NC (365)	72.9	25.5	1.6	0.0	0.0	137	40
Richmond, VA (365)	99.7	0.3	0.0	0.0	0.0	64	20
Roseville, CA (365)	75.6	18.4	6.0	0.0	0.0	147	41
Round Rock, TX (n/a)	n/a	n/a	n/a	n/a	n/a	n/a	n/a
San Antonio, TX (365)	71.8	25.2	3.0	0.0	0.0	140	40
San Diego, CA (365)	33.7	62.7	3.3	0.3	0.0	155	54
San Francisco, CA (365)	78.4	21.4	0.3	0.0	0.0	115	36
San Jose, CA (365)	71.2	28.5	0.3	0.0	0.0	121	41
Savannah, GA (365)	60.5	36.7	2.2	0.5	0.0	155	46
Scottsdale, AZ (365)	23.6	65.2	7.1	2.2	1.9	565	61
Seattle, WA (365)	86.8	13.2	0.0	0.0	0.0	89	33
Sioux Falls, SD (365)	88.5	11.5	0.0	0.0	0.0	90	36
Stamford, CT (365)	82.5	13.7	3.6	0.3	0.0	164	36
Sterling Hgts, MI (242)	78.1	18.6	3.3	0.0	0.0	135	37
Sunnyvale, CA (365)	71.2	28.5	0.3	0.0	0.0	121	41
Tampa, FL (365)	75.1	21.4	3.6	0.0	0.0	119	41
Temecula, CA (365)	11.2	55.3	27.4	5.2	0.8	320	82
Thousand Oaks, CA (365)	75.6	21.9	2.2	0.0	0.3	221	43
Virginia Beach, VA (349)	85.4	14.6	0.0	0.0	0.0	88	27
Washington, DC (365)	61.1	35.9	3.0	0.0	0.0	142	47

Note: The Air Quality Index (AQI) is an index for reporting daily air quality. EPA calculates the AQI for five major air pollutants regulated by the Clean Air Act: ground-level ozone, particle pollution (also known as particulate matter), carbon monoxide, sulfur dioxide, and nitrogen dioxide. The AQI runs from 0 to 500. The higher the AQI value, the greater the level of air pollution and the greater the health concern. There are six AQI categories: "Good" The AQI is between 0 and 50. Air quality is considered satisfactory; "Moderate" The AQI is between 51 and 100. Air quality is acceptable; "Unhealthy for Sensitive Groups" When AQI values are between 101 and 150, members of sensitive groups may experience health effects; "Unhealthy" When AQI values are between 151 and 200 everyone may begin to experience health effects; "Very Unhealthy" AQI values between 201 and 300 trigger a health alert; "Hazardous" AQI values over 300 trigger health warnings of emergency conditions; Data covers the entire county unless noted otherwise; (1) Data cover the entire county; (2) Number of days with AQI data in 2011

Source: U.S. Environmental Protection Agency, AirData Report, 2011

Air Quality Index Pollutants

Area[1] (Days[2])	Percent of Days when AQI Pollutant was... Carbon Monoxide	Nitrogen Dioxide	Ozone	Sulfur Dioxide	Particulate Matter 2.5	Particulate Matter 10
Albuquerque, NM (365)	0.0	5.5	51.2	1.1	32.6	9.6
Alexandria, VA (365)	0.0	38.9	48.2	0.3	12.3	0.3
Anchorage, AK (365)	7.1	0.0	38.6	0.0	28.8	25.5
Ann Arbor, MI (296)	0.0	0.0	81.1	0.0	18.9	0.0
Athens, GA (365)	0.0	0.0	45.5	0.0	54.5	0.0
Atlanta, GA (365)	0.0	0.0	39.5	4.7	55.9	0.0
Austin, TX (365)	0.0	0.5	69.9	0.0	29.6	0.0
Baltimore, MD (365)	0.0	18.4	24.1	0.0	57.5	0.0
Bellevue, WA (365)	0.0	0.0	47.4	0.8	51.8	0.0
Billings, MT (365)	1.1	0.0	0.0	54.2	44.7	0.0
Boise City, ID (365)	0.8	2.5	81.6	0.0	7.4	7.7
Boston, MA (365)	0.0	20.0	24.4	0.8	54.8	0.0
Boulder, CO (365)	0.0	0.0	95.1	0.0	4.7	0.3
Broken Arrow, OK (365)	0.0	0.8	47.1	13.4	37.3	1.4
Cambridge, MA (365)	0.3	0.0	96.2	0.0	3.6	0.0
Cape Coral, FL (365)	0.0	0.0	73.2	0.0	26.6	0.3
Carlsbad, CA (365)	0.0	15.1	38.1	0.0	44.4	2.5
Cary, NC (365)	0.0	0.0	63.3	0.0	36.7	0.0
Cedar Rapids, IA (365)	0.0	0.0	40.0	1.1	57.5	1.4
Charleston, SC (365)	0.0	3.3	39.2	0.0	57.0	0.5
Charlotte, NC (365)	0.0	4.7	58.1	0.0	37.3	0.0
Chesapeake, VA (n/a)	n/a	n/a	n/a	n/a	n/a	n/a
Chicago, IL (365)	0.0	20.5	17.3	11.0	50.4	0.8
Clarksville, TN (365)	0.0	0.0	0.0	22.2	77.8	0.0
Colorado Spgs., CO (365)	0.0	0.0	98.4	0.0	1.4	0.3
Columbia, MD (n/a)	n/a	n/a	n/a	n/a	n/a	n/a
Columbia, MO (245)	0.0	0.0	100.0	0.0	0.0	0.0
Columbia, SC (365)	0.0	3.3	56.4	0.0	40.3	0.0
Columbus, OH (365)	1.1	0.0	35.3	0.0	62.7	0.8
Dallas, TX (365)	0.0	13.2	49.0	0.0	35.3	2.5
Denver, CO (365)	0.0	40.8	38.6	1.9	7.7	11.0
Durham, NC (365)	0.0	0.0	43.3	0.0	56.7	0.0
Edison, NJ (364)	0.0	17.9	59.9	0.0	22.3	0.0
El Paso, TX (365)	0.0	16.4	38.4	0.0	36.2	9.0
Fargo, ND (350)	0.0	2.9	56.3	0.0	29.1	11.7
Ft. Collins, CO (365)	0.0	0.0	98.9	0.0	1.1	0.0
Ft. Worth, TX (365)	0.0	12.6	59.5	0.0	27.7	0.3
Gilbert, AZ (365)	0.0	19.2	38.9	0.0	15.6	26.3
Green Bay, WI (365)	0.0	0.0	26.0	9.3	64.7	0.0
Henderson, NV (365)	0.0	2.2	78.6	0.0	15.9	3.3
High Point, NC (361)	0.0	0.0	47.9	0.0	52.1	0.0
Honolulu, HI (365)	0.0	0.0	44.7	0.3	50.1	4.9
Houston, TX (365)	0.0	10.7	32.9	5.2	44.1	7.1
Huntington, NY (365)	0.0	0.0	72.1	0.0	27.9	0.0
Huntsville, AL (332)	0.0	0.0	62.3	0.0	21.7	16.0
Indianapolis, IN (365)	0.0	0.3	15.9	5.5	78.1	0.3
Irvine, CA (365)	0.0	9.0	27.9	0.0	61.6	1.4
Jackson, MS (365)	0.0	0.0	34.8	0.0	65.2	0.0
Jacksonville, FL (365)	0.5	1.1	67.4	2.7	27.9	0.3
Jersey City, NJ (365)	1.1	33.7	24.1	2.2	36.4	2.5
Kansas City, MO (365)	0.0	21.4	0.0	22.7	54.0	1.9
Kenosha, WI (304)	0.0	0.0	65.8	0.0	34.2	0.0
Las Vegas, NV (365)	0.0	2.2	78.6	0.0	15.9	3.3
Lexington, KY (365)	0.0	9.6	32.3	1.6	56.4	0.0

Table continued on next page.

Area[1] (Days[2])	Percent of Days when AQI Pollutant was...					
	Carbon Monoxide	Nitrogen Dioxide	Ozone	Sulfur Dioxide	Particulate Matter 2.5	Particulate Matter 10
Lincoln, NE (365)	30.1	0.0	50.4	0.0	19.5	0.0
Little Rock, AR (365)	0.0	2.7	38.6	0.0	58.6	0.0
Los Angeles, CA (365)	0.0	10.1	42.7	0.3	46.3	0.5
Madison, WI (359)	0.0	0.0	39.6	0.0	60.4	0.0
Manchester, NH (365)	0.0	0.0	90.7	3.8	5.5	0.0
Miami, FL (365)	0.0	1.6	48.2	0.0	50.1	0.0
Minneapolis, MN (365)	3.3	0.0	0.0	0.0	95.1	1.6
Murfreesboro, TN (243)	0.0	0.0	100.0	0.0	0.0	0.0
Naperville, IL (365)	0.0	0.0	27.4	0.0	72.6	0.0
Nashville, TN (365)	0.0	9.9	30.4	0.0	59.5	0.3
New Orleans, LA (365)	0.0	0.0	70.1	0.0	25.8	4.1
New York, NY (365)	0.0	0.0	0.0	0.0	100.0	0.0
Norman, OK (363)	0.0	0.0	63.6	0.0	36.4	0.0
Olathe, KS (365)	0.0	0.0	90.4	0.0	9.6	0.0
Omaha, NE (365)	0.0	0.0	24.1	9.9	27.1	38.9
Orlando, FL (365)	0.0	0.5	68.8	0.0	30.7	0.0
Overland Park, KS (365)	0.0	0.0	90.4	0.0	9.6	0.0
Oyster Bay, NY (365)	0.0	0.0	0.0	6.8	93.2	0.0
Pembroke Pines, FL (365)	0.0	6.8	56.4	0.0	36.7	0.0
Philadelphia, PA (365)	0.0	16.7	35.6	0.0	47.1	0.5
Phoenix, AZ (365)	0.0	19.2	38.9	0.0	15.6	26.3
Pittsburgh, PA (365)	0.0	4.1	29.9	10.1	55.1	0.8
Plano, TX (362)	0.0	0.0	100.0	0.0	0.0	0.0
Portland, OR (365)	0.0	3.6	59.5	0.0	37.0	0.0
Providence, RI (365)	0.0	6.3	58.4	0.0	35.1	0.3
Provo, UT (365)	0.0	21.1	58.6	0.0	19.5	0.8
Raleigh, NC (365)	0.0	0.0	63.3	0.0	36.7	0.0
Richmond, VA (365)	0.3	95.9	0.0	3.8	0.0	0.0
Roseville, CA (365)	0.0	21.9	74.0	0.0	4.1	0.0
Round Rock, TX (n/a)	n/a	n/a	n/a	n/a	n/a	n/a
San Antonio, TX (365)	0.0	0.8	63.8	0.0	35.1	0.3
San Diego, CA (365)	0.0	15.1	38.1	0.0	44.4	2.5
San Francisco, CA (365)	0.0	29.6	36.7	0.0	33.7	0.0
San Jose, CA (365)	0.0	5.2	34.8	0.0	60.0	0.0
Savannah, GA (365)	0.0	0.0	23.8	27.9	48.2	0.0
Scottsdale, AZ (365)	0.0	19.2	38.9	0.0	15.6	26.3
Seattle, WA (365)	0.0	0.0	47.4	0.8	51.8	0.0
Sioux Falls, SD (365)	0.0	4.9	62.2	0.0	28.5	4.4
Stamford, CT (365)	8.8	25.5	45.2	3.3	17.3	0.0
Sterling Hgts, MI (242)	0.0	0.0	72.7	0.0	27.3	0.0
Sunnyvale, CA (365)	0.0	5.2	34.8	0.0	60.0	0.0
Tampa, FL (365)	0.0	0.0	54.0	11.8	32.6	1.6
Temecula, CA (365)	0.0	0.8	45.2	0.5	35.6	17.8
Thousand Oaks, CA (365)	0.0	3.0	91.0	0.0	5.5	0.5
Virginia Beach, VA (349)	0.0	0.0	0.0	0.0	100.0	0.0
Washington, DC (365)	0.0	11.5	30.7	0.3	57.5	0.0

Note: The Air Quality Index (AQI) is an index for reporting daily air quality. EPA calculates the AQI for five major air pollutants regulated by the Clean Air Act: ground-level ozone, particle pollution (also known as particulate matter), carbon monoxide, sulfur dioxide, and nitrogen dioxide. The AQI runs from 0 to 500. The higher the AQI value, the greater the level of air pollution and the greater the health concern; (1) Data covers the entire county; (2) Number of days with AQI data in 2011

Source: U.S. Environmental Protection Agency, AirData Report, 2011

Air Quality Index Trends

Metro Area (# trend sites)	2003	2004	2005	2006	2007	2008	2009	2010
Albuquerque, NM (22)	16	6	11	8	2	1	0	2
Alexandria, VA (50)	32	32	49	37	43	22	5	28
Anchorage, AK (n/a)	n/a	n/a	n/a	n/a	n/a	n/a	n/a	n/a
Ann Arbor, MI (n/a)	n/a	n/a	n/a	n/a	n/a	n/a	n/a	n/a
Athens, GA (n/a)	n/a	n/a	n/a	n/a	n/a	n/a	n/a	n/a
Atlanta, GA (31)	36	32	52	65	56	31	16	27
Austin, TX (5)	10	10	11	14	4	2	4	2
Baltimore, MD (18)	30	31	36	33	45	23	11	33
Bellevue, WA (16)	16	7	7	14	10	7	12	1
Billings, MT (n/a)	n/a	n/a	n/a	n/a	n/a	n/a	n/a	n/a
Boise City, ID (n/a)	n/a	n/a	n/a	n/a	n/a	n/a	n/a	n/a
Boston, MA (28)	16	9	21	10	21	9	5	3
Boulder, CO (n/a)	n/a	n/a	n/a	n/a	n/a	n/a	n/a	n/a
Broken Arrow, OK (13)	23	20	27	26	7	15	5	3
Cambridge, MA (28)	16	9	21	10	21	9	5	3
Cape Coral, FL (n/a)	n/a	n/a	n/a	n/a	n/a	n/a	n/a	n/a
Carlsbad, CA (29)	50	31	30	39	34	43	25	14
Cary, NC (7)	11	10	26	9	24	11	0	3
Cedar Rapids, IA (n/a)	n/a	n/a	n/a	n/a	n/a	n/a	n/a	n/a
Charleston, SC (8)	3	3	8	9	5	1	0	0
Charlotte, NC (13)	16	20	32	24	36	24	3	14
Chesapeake, VA (9)	10	6	12	13	11	16	0	4
Chicago, IL (81)	44	47	61	35	53	48	26	28
Clarksville, TN (n/a)	n/a	n/a	n/a	n/a	n/a	n/a	n/a	n/a
Colorado Spgs., CO (2)	4	0	6	0	1	2	0	1
Columbia, MD (18)	30	31	36	33	45	23	11	33
Columbia, MO (n/a)	n/a	n/a	n/a	n/a	n/a	n/a	n/a	n/a
Columbia, SC (10)	22	24	29	22	21	14	3	9
Columbus, OH (12)	23	13	32	11	30	10	1	6
Dallas, TX (35)	49	50	80	54	34	30	32	15
Denver, CO (23)	35	6	13	27	23	10	7	8
Durham, NC (n/a)	n/a	n/a	n/a	n/a	n/a	n/a	n/a	n/a
Edison, NJ (69)	41	40	50	40	40	31	15	37
El Paso, TX (26)	18	10	18	12	15	10	3	5
Fargo, ND (n/a)	n/a	n/a	n/a	n/a	n/a	n/a	n/a	n/a
Ft. Collins, CO (n/a)	n/a	n/a	n/a	n/a	n/a	n/a	n/a	n/a
Ft. Worth, TX (35)	49	50	80	54	34	30	32	15
Gilbert, AZ (55)	51	23	49	50	21	27	10	11
Green Bay, WI (n/a)	n/a	n/a	n/a	n/a	n/a	n/a	n/a	n/a
Henderson, NV (28)	42	22	34	35	24	12	5	2
High Point, NC (2)	11	2	4	3	9	10	0	3
Honolulu, HI (14)	2	2	2	1	0	0	0	0
Houston, TX (52)	74	66	93	64	47	24	26	33
Huntington, NY (69)	41	40	50	40	40	31	15	37
Huntsville, AL (n/a)	n/a	n/a	n/a	n/a	n/a	n/a	n/a	n/a
Indianapolis, IN (25)	38	22	49	30	42	8	10	9
Irvine, CA (66)	147	134	113	98	102	94	99	74
Jackson, MS (n/a)	n/a	n/a	n/a	n/a	n/a	n/a	n/a	n/a
Jacksonville, FL (13)	10	15	20	35	16	10	3	15
Jersey City, NJ (69)	41	40	50	40	40	31	15	37
Kansas City, MO (23)	56	35	52	74	44	39	43	22
Kenosha, WI (81)	44	47	61	35	53	48	26	28
Las Vegas, NV (28)	42	22	34	35	24	12	5	2
Lexington, KY (n/a)	n/a	n/a	n/a	n/a	n/a	n/a	n/a	n/a
Lincoln, NE (n/a)	n/a	n/a	n/a	n/a	n/a	n/a	n/a	n/a
Little Rock, AR (11)	3	0	19	11	11	2	2	2

Table continued on next page.

Metro Area (# trend sites)	2003	2004	2005	2006	2007	2008	2009	2010
Los Angeles, CA (66)	147	134	113	98	102	94	99	74
Madison, WI (3)	8	1	9	1	10	1	0	2
Manchester, NH (n/a)	n/a	n/a	n/a	n/a	n/a	n/a	n/a	n/a
Miami, FL (32)	4	11	4	12	10	5	2	4
Minneapolis, MN (29)	18	11	11	1	5	1	3	1
Murfreesboro, TN (19)	23	7	29	17	37	11	1	10
Naperville, IL (81)	44	47	61	35	53	48	26	28
Nashville, TN (19)	23	7	29	17	37	11	1	10
New Orleans, LA (7)	15	12	13	13	17	2	6	8
New York, NY (69)	41	40	50	40	40	31	15	37
Norman, OK (13)	16	6	15	33	5	5	5	3
Olathe, KS (23)	56	35	52	74	44	39	43	22
Omaha, NE (16)	4	4	16	3	7	2	4	3
Orlando, FL (15)	8	6	10	8	11	2	1	2
Overland Park, KS (23)	56	35	52	74	44	39	43	22
Oyster Bay, NY (69)	41	40	50	40	40	31	15	37
Pembroke Pines, FL (32)	4	11	4	12	10	5	2	4
Philadelphia, PA (54)	76	39	62	55	46	30	7	32
Phoenix, AZ (55)	51	23	49	50	21	27	10	11
Pittsburgh, PA (54)	129	118	123	94	97	81	58	58
Plano, TX (35)	49	50	80	54	34	30	32	15
Portland, OR (9)	2	4	4	2	5	3	5	1
Providence, RI (12)	19	10	22	16	21	6	2	14
Provo, UT (n/a)	n/a	n/a	n/a	n/a	n/a	n/a	n/a	n/a
Raleigh, NC (7)	11	10	26	9	24	11	0	3
Richmond, VA (15)	28	18	41	21	37	19	1	11
Roseville, CA (41)	79	66	62	79	53	61	43	23
Round Rock, TX (5)	10	10	11	14	4	2	4	2
San Antonio, TX (8)	21	15	15	21	3	9	3	4
San Diego, CA (29)	50	31	30	39	34	43	25	14
San Francisco, CA (46)	15	11	7	21	6	13	7	4
San Jose, CA (6)	14	8	4	14	3	13	8	6
Savannah, GA (n/a)	n/a	n/a	n/a	n/a	n/a	n/a	n/a	n/a
Scottsdale, AZ (55)	51	23	49	50	21	27	10	11
Seattle, WA (16)	16	7	7	14	10	7	12	1
Sioux Falls, SD (n/a)	n/a	n/a	n/a	n/a	n/a	n/a	n/a	n/a
Stamford, CT (14)	19	14	25	21	28	20	5	17
Sterling Hgts, MI (22)	37	37	62	38	35	24	9	23
Sunnyvale, CA (6)	14	8	4	14	3	13	8	6
Tampa, FL (30)	87	50	47	38	47	24	18	11
Temecula, CA (64)	163	157	142	133	144	131	114	115
Thousand Oaks, CA (17)	70	51	40	39	23	31	25	13
Virginia Beach, VA (9)	10	6	12	13	11	16	0	4
Washington, DC (50)	32	32	49	37	43	22	5	28

Note: Figures are the number of days the AQI value exceeded 100 in a given year. An AQI value greater than 100 indicates that air quality would have been in the unhealthful range on that day; Data from exceptional events are included; Figures cover the Metropolitan Statistical Area—see Appendix B for areas included; n/a not available.
Source: U.S. Environmental Protection Agency, Office of Air and Radiation, Air Quality Index Information, "Number of Days with Air Quality Index Values Greater than 100 at Trend Sites, 2000-2010, and at All Sites in 2010"

Maximum Air Pollutant Concentrations: Particulate Matter, Ozone, CO and Lead

Metro Aea	Particulate Matter 10 (ug/m³)	Particulate Matter 2.5 Wtd AM (ug/m³)	Particulate Matter 2.5 24-Hr (ug/m³)	Ozone (ppm)	Carbon Monoxide (ppm)	Lead (ug/m³)
Albuquerque, NM	122	5.3	18	0.069	3	n/a
Alexandria, VA	85	12.1	29	0.089	3	0
Anchorage, AK	98	5.5	38	0.045	6	n/a
Ann Arbor, MI	n/a	9.2	23	0.066	n/a	n/a
Athens, GA	n/a	11.3	23	0.073	n/a	n/a
Atlanta, GA	51	14.5	25	0.08	2	0.02
Austin, TX	34	10	19	0.074	0	n/a
Baltimore, MD	46	12.7	30	0.096	2	n/a
Bellevue, WA	n/a	7.1	24	0.068	1	n/a
Billings, MT	n/a	n/a	n/a	n/a	2	n/a
Boise City, ID	66	5.9	15	0.069	2	n/a
Boston, MA	41	10	25	0.073	2	0.01
Boulder, CO	36	7.1	23	0.072	2	n/a
Broken Arrow, OK	74	10.7	24	0.073	2	0.01
Cambridge, MA	41	10	25	0.073	2	0.01
Cape Coral, FL	67	7	13	0.065	n/a	n/a
Carlsbad, CA	101	13.3	114	0.081	2	n/a
Cary, NC	43	10.2	21	0.074	2	n/a
Cedar Rapids, IA	68	11.1	36	0.064	1	n/a
Charleston, SC	49	9.9	23	0.068	0	n/a
Charlotte, NC	48	12.1	25	0.082	2	n/a
Chesapeake, VA	37	10.2	24	0.078	2	0.01
Chicago, IL	69	14	35	0.081	2	0.24
Clarksville, TN	34	11.2	22	0.074	n/a	n/a
Colorado Spgs., CO	38	6.2	12	0.072	2	n/a
Columbia, MD	46	12.7	30	0.096	2	n/a
Columbia, MO	n/a	n/a	n/a	0.069	n/a	n/a
Columbia, SC	76	11.6	24	0.072	n/a	0
Columbus, OH	126	13.1	34	0.077	2	0.01
Dallas, TX	62	10.8	25	0.085	2	0.77
Denver, CO	68	8.6	22	0.079	2	0.01
Durham, NC	n/a	10.2	21	0.074	n/a	n/a
Edison, NJ	65	11.5	28	0.087	2	n/a
El Paso, TX	249	8.4	61	0.073	3	0.04
Fargo, ND	96	8.5	27	0.063	1	n/a
Ft. Collins, CO	43	6.5	22	0.077	2	n/a
Ft. Worth, TX	62	10.8	25	0.085	2	0.77
Gilbert, AZ	226	12.4	27	0.079	3	n/a
Green Bay, WI	n/a	10.2	36	0.078	n/a	n/a
Henderson, NV	61	7.4	22	0.079	3	n/a
High Point, NC	29	10.5	21	0.076	n/a	n/a
Honolulu, HI	70	4.7	12	0.047	1	0
Houston, TX	82	12.3	24	0.088	2	0.01
Huntington, NY	65	11.5	28	0.087	2	n/a
Huntsville, AL	37	11.6	20	0.071	n/a	n/a
Indianapolis, IN	83	14	37	0.072	3	0.08
Irvine, CA	71	12.6	32	0.09	4	0.39
Jackson, MS	n/a	11.4	22	0.067	n/a	n/a
Jacksonville, FL	62	9.4	20	0.068	2	n/a
Jersey City, NJ	65	11.5	28	0.087	2	n/a
Kansas City, MO	65	11	31	0.076	2	n/a
Kenosha, WI	69	14	35	0.081	2	0.24
Las Vegas, NV	61	7.4	22	0.079	3	n/a
Lexington, KY	35	12.2	23	0.071	n/a	n/a

Table continued on next page.

Metro Aea	Particulate Matter 10 (ug/m³)	Particulate Matter 2.5 Wtd AM (ug/m³)	Particulate Matter 2.5 24-Hr (ug/m³)	Ozone (ppm)	Carbon Monoxide (ppm)	Lead (ug/m³)
Lincoln, NE	n/a	9	26	0.05	2	n/a
Little Rock, AR	38	12.6	23	0.073	2	n/a
Los Angeles, CA	71	12.6	32	0.09	4	0.39
Madison, WI	39	10.1	30	0.063	n/a	n/a
Manchester, NH	29	8	25	0.077	2	n/a
Miami, FL	44	7.8	14	0.069	2	n/a
Minneapolis, MN	74	10	36	0.067	2	0.27
Murfreesboro, TN	42	11.8	24	0.078	2	n/a
Naperville, IL	69	14	35	0.081	2	0.24
Nashville, TN	42	11.8	24	0.078	2	n/a
New Orleans, LA	73	10.1	19	0.081	n/a	n/a
New York, NY	65	11.5	28	0.087	2	n/a
Norman, OK	41	9.2	18	0.072	1	0
Olathe, KS	65	11	31	0.076	2	n/a
Omaha, NE	249	12.2	32	0.067	2	0.26
Orlando, FL	46	7.6	14	0.071	1	n/a
Overland Park, KS	65	11	31	0.076	2	n/a
Oyster Bay, NY	65	11.5	28	0.087	2	n/a
Pembroke Pines, FL	44	7.8	14	0.069	2	n/a
Philadelphia, PA	91	13.8	35	0.088	2	0.05
Phoenix, AZ	226	12.4	27	0.079	3	n/a
Pittsburgh, PA	93	16.1	49	0.083	3	0.21
Plano, TX	62	10.8	25	0.085	2	0.77
Portland, OR	29	6.6	18	0.066	2	0.03
Providence, RI	37	9.2	26	0.079	2	n/a
Provo, UT	108	8.9	48	0.071	2	n/a
Raleigh, NC	43	10.2	21	0.074	2	n/a
Richmond, VA	33	10.2	22	0.081	2	0.01
Roseville, CA	54	8.7	27	0.096	2	n/a
Round Rock, TX	34	10	19	0.074	0	n/a
San Antonio, TX	55	8.7	16	0.078	1	n/a
San Diego, CA	101	13.3	114	0.081	2	n/a
San Francisco, CA	45	10.5	33	0.078	2	n/a
San Jose, CA	37	8.8	29	0.08	2	n/a
Savannah, GA	33	10.5	24	0.065	n/a	n/a
Scottsdale, AZ	226	12.4	27	0.079	3	n/a
Seattle, WA	n/a	7.1	24	0.068	1	n/a
Sioux Falls, SD	60	9.7	28	0.064	n/a	n/a
Stamford, CT	40	9.1	26	0.084	2	n/a
Sterling Hgts, MI	73	11.3	30	0.078	1	0.01
Sunnyvale, CA	37	8.8	29	0.08	2	n/a
Tampa, FL	62	8.1	16	0.072	1	0.73
Temecula, CA	312	15.2	36	0.109	4	0.01
Thousand Oaks, CA	45	8.7	21	0.082	n/a	n/a
Virginia Beach, VA	37	10.2	24	0.078	2	0.01
Washington, DC	85	12.1	29	0.089	3	0
NAAQS[1]	150	15	35	0.075	9	0.15

Note: Data from exceptional events are excluded; Data covers the Metropolitan Statistical Area—see Appendix B for areas included; (1) National Ambient Air Quality Standards; ppm = parts per million; ug/m³ = micrograms per cubic meter; n/a not available
Concentrations: Particulate Matter 10 (coarse particulate)—highest second maximum 24-hour concentration; Particulate Matter 2.5 Wtd AM (fine particulate)—highest weighted annual mean concentration; Particulate Matter 2.5 24-Hour (fine particulate)—highest 98th percentile 24-hour concentration; Ozone—highest fourth daily maximum 8-hour concentration; Carbon Monoxide—highest second maximum non-overlapping 8-hour concentration; Lead—maximum running 3-month average
Source: U.S. Environmental Protection Agency, CBSA Factbook 2010, Air Quality Statistics by City, 2010

Maximum Air Pollutant Concentrations: Nitrogen Dioxide and Sulfur Dioxide

Metro Area	Nitrogen Dioxide AM (ppb)	Nitrogen Dioxide 1-Hr (ppb)	Sulfur Dioxide AM (ppb)	Sulfur Dioxide 1-Hr (ppb)	Sulfur Dioxide 24-Hr (ppb)
Albuquerque, NM	12.068	53	n/a	n/a	n/a
Alexandria, VA	17.595	59	3.372	21	10.5
Anchorage, AK	n/a	n/a	n/a	n/a	n/a
Ann Arbor, MI	n/a	n/a	n/a	n/a	n/a
Athens, GA	n/a	n/a	n/a	n/a	n/a
Atlanta, GA	13.657	58	1.908	33	10
Austin, TX	3.314	21.1	n/a	n/a	n/a
Baltimore, MD	17.549	61	2.152	20	7.3
Bellevue, WA	n/a	n/a	1.136	24.5	8
Billings, MT	n/a	n/a	3.876	91	23.4
Boise City, ID	9.51	45	0.366	n/a	1.1
Boston, MA	19.098	53	2.933	44.9	10.5
Boulder, CO	n/a	n/a	n/a	n/a	n/a
Broken Arrow, OK	8.311	38	5.3	63	26.2
Cambridge, MA	19.098	53	2.933	44.9	10.5
Cape Coral, FL	n/a	n/a	n/a	n/a	n/a
Carlsbad, CA	20.975	74	1.765	18	7.1
Cary, NC	n/a	n/a	1.017	12.4	5.7
Cedar Rapids, IA	n/a	n/a	0.984	28.9	8.6
Charleston, SC	7.573	n/a	1.07	21	9.5
Charlotte, NC	11.738	50	0.926	19.8	5.7
Chesapeake, VA	n/a	n/a	2.128	41	8.3
Chicago, IL	24.869	71	4.138	90	23.5
Clarksville, TN	n/a	n/a	3.654	51	12
Colorado Spgs., CO	n/a	n/a	n/a	n/a	n/a
Columbia, MD	17.549	61	2.152	20	7.3
Columbia, MO	n/a	n/a	n/a	n/a	n/a
Columbia, SC	5.345	n/a	1.974	85	12
Columbus, OH	n/a	n/a	n/a	n/a	n/a
Dallas, TX	13.186	56.9	0.808	17.3	4.5
Denver, CO	27.704	71	1.644	37	8.8
Durham, NC	n/a	n/a	n/a	n/a	n/a
Edison, NJ	22.192	71	4.829	50.2	23.6
El Paso, TX	17.067	62.7	0.756	10.3	3
Fargo, ND	5.435	44	0.293	6.1	2.5
Ft. Collins, CO	n/a	n/a	n/a	n/a	n/a
Ft. Worth, TX	13.186	56.9	0.808	17.3	4.5
Gilbert, AZ	24.524	68	1.742	10	5.3
Green Bay, WI	n/a	n/a	2.273	69	15.7
Henderson, NV	13.308	55.9	n/a	n/a	n/a
High Point, NC	n/a	n/a	n/a	n/a	n/a
Honolulu, HI	3.411	24	1.272	18	4
Houston, TX	14.941	60	2.336	45.6	13.8
Huntington, NY	22.192	71	4.829	50.2	23.6
Huntsville, AL	n/a	n/a	n/a	n/a	n/a
Indianapolis, IN	12.683	53.5	3.347	105	28.8
Irvine, CA	26.179	72.5	1.394	16.2	4.8
Jackson, MS	n/a	n/a	n/a	n/a	n/a
Jacksonville, FL	9.324	44	3.949	216	58.4
Jersey City, NJ	22.192	71	4.829	50.2	23.6
Kansas City, MO	14.93	54	5.499	49	46.5
Kenosha, WI	24.869	71	4.138	90	23.5
Las Vegas, NV	13.308	55.9	n/a	n/a	n/a
Lexington, KY	9.463	56	2.214	48	11.3
Lincoln, NE	n/a	n/a	n/a	n/a	n/a

Table continued on next page.

Metro Area	Nitrogen Dioxide AM (ppb)	Nitrogen Dioxide 1-Hr (ppb)	Sulfur Dioxide AM (ppb)	Sulfur Dioxide 1-Hr (ppb)	Sulfur Dioxide 24-Hr (ppb)
Little Rock, AR	9.982	51	1.698	9	3.7
Los Angeles, CA	26.179	72.5	1.394	16.2	4.8
Madison, WI	n/a	n/a	n/a	n/a	n/a
Manchester, NH	7.99	42.2	1.453	57.7	12
Miami, FL	9.651	49	0.831	38	5.9
Minneapolis, MN	9.673	51	0.787	29	10.2
Murfreesboro, TN	12.526	46	2.246	14	5.5
Naperville, IL	24.869	71	4.138	90	23.5
Nashville, TN	12.526	46	2.246	14	5.5
New Orleans, LA	7.759	47	7.743	248	75.6
New York, NY	22.192	71	4.829	50.2	23.6
Norman, OK	8.921	47	0.777	6	3.5
Olathe, KS	14.93	54	5.499	49	46.5
Omaha, NE	n/a	n/a	2.124	58	25.9
Orlando, FL	5.627	40	0.157	7	2.2
Overland Park, KS	14.93	54	5.499	49	46.5
Oyster Bay, NY	22.192	71	4.829	50.2	23.6
Pembroke Pines, FL	9.651	49	0.831	38	5.9
Philadelphia, PA	22.609	61.6	3.03	34	17.9
Phoenix, AZ	24.524	68	1.742	10	5.3
Pittsburgh, PA	15.254	51	7.106	161	39.6
Plano, TX	13.186	56.9	0.808	17.3	4.5
Portland, OR	8.635	33	1.35	8	3.2
Providence, RI	9.83	40	3.081	84.3	33.1
Provo, UT	14.56	50	n/a	n/a	n/a
Raleigh, NC	n/a	n/a	1.017	12.4	5.7
Richmond, VA	11.998	57	2.013	44	9.3
Roseville, CA	12.494	54	0.462	1	1.9
Round Rock, TX	3.314	21.1	n/a	n/a	n/a
San Antonio, TX	3.831	31.9	n/a	n/a	n/a
San Diego, CA	20.975	74	1.765	18	7.1
San Francisco, CA	15.598	76.6	1.188	15.3	5.7
San Jose, CA	14.394	50.7	0.352	4.1	1.6
Savannah, GA	n/a	n/a	3.42	83	33.2
Scottsdale, AZ	24.524	68	1.742	10	5.3
Seattle, WA	n/a	n/a	1.136	24.5	8
Sioux Falls, SD	6.583	48	0.247	5	1.7
Stamford, CT	10.132	50	1.529	17.8	10.4
Sterling Hgts, MI	11.96	54	3.385	107	48.8
Sunnyvale, CA	14.394	50.7	0.352	4.1	1.6
Tampa, FL	6.079	38	2.852	104	28.7
Temecula, CA	23.087	65	1.28	11	6.7
Thousand Oaks, CA	10.096	41	n/a	n/a	n/a
Virginia Beach, VA	n/a	n/a	2.128	41	8.3
Washington, DC	17.595	59	3.372	21	10.5
NAAQS[1]	53	100	30	75	140

Note: Data from exceptional events are excluded; Data covers the Metropolitan Statistical Area—see Appendix B for areas included; (1) National Ambient Air Quality Standards; ppb = parts per billion; n/a not available
Concentrations: Nitrogen Dioxide AM—highest arithmetic mean concentration; Nitrogen Dioxide 1-Hr—highest 98th percentile 1-hour daily maximum concentration; Sulfur Dioxide AM—highest annual mean concentration; Sulfur Dioxide 1-Hr—highest 99th percentile 1-hour daily maximum concentration; Sulfur Dioxide 24-Hr—highest second maximum 24-hour concentration
Source: U.S. Environmental Protection Agency, CBSA Factbook 2010, Air Quality Statistics by City, 2010

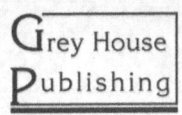

Grey House Publishing

Grey House Publishing
2012 Title List

Visit **www.greyhouse.com** for Product Information, Table of Contents and Sample Pages

General Reference

America's College Museums
American Environmental Leaders: From Colonial Times to the Present
An African Biographical Dictionary
An Encyclopedia of Human Rights in the United States
Encyclopedia of African-American Writing
Encyclopedia of Gun Control & Gun Rights
Encyclopedia of Invasions & Conquests
Encyclopedia of Prisoners of War & Internment
Encyclopedia of Religion & Law in America
Encyclopedia of Rural America
Encyclopedia of the United States Cabinet, 1789-2010
Encyclopedia of War Journalism
Encyclopedia of Warrior Peoples & Fighting Groups
From Suffrage to the Senate: America's Political Women
Nations of the World
Political Corruption in America
Speakers of the House of Representatives, 1789-2009
The Environmental Debate: A Documentary History
The Evolution Wars: A Guide to the Debates
The Religious Right: A Reference Handbook
The Value of a Dollar: 1860-2009
The Value of a Dollar: Colonial Era
US Land & Natural Resource Policy
Weather America
Working Americans 1770-1869 Vol. IX: Revol. War to the Civil War
Working Americans 1880-1999 Vol. I: The Working Class
Working Americans 1880-1999 Vol. II: The Middle Class
Working Americans 1880-1999 Vol. III: The Upper Class
Working Americans 1880-1999 Vol. IV: Their Children
Working Americans 1880-2003 Vol. V: At War
Working Americans 1880-2005 Vol. VI: Women at Work
Working Americans 1880-2006 Vol. VII: Social Movements
Working Americans 1880-2007 Vol. VIII: Immigrants
Working Americans 1880-2009 Vol. X: Sports & Recreation
Working Americans 1880-2010 Vol. XI: Inventors & Entrepreneurs
Working Americans 1880-2011 Vol. XII: Our History through Music
World Cultural Leaders of the 20th & 21st Centuries

Business Information

Directory of Business Information Resources
Directory of Mail Order Catalogs
Directory of Venture Capital & Private Equity Firms
Environmental Resource Handbook
Food & Beverage Market Place
Grey House Homeland Security Directory
Grey House Performing Arts Directory
Hudson's Washington News Media Contacts Directory
New York State Directory
Sports Market Place Directory
The Rauch Guides – Industry Market Research Reports
Sweets Directory by McGraw Hill Construction

Statistics & Demographics

America's Top-Rated Cities
America's Top-Rated Small Towns & Cities
America's Top-Rated Smaller Cities
Comparative Guide to American Hospitals
Comparative Guide to American Suburbs
Profiles of… Series – State Handbooks

Health Information

Comparative Guide to American Hospitals
Complete Directory for Pediatric Disorders
Complete Directory for People with Chronic Illness
Complete Directory for People with Disabilities
Complete Mental Health Directory
Directory of Health Care Group Purchasing Organizations
Directory of Hospital Personnel
HMO/PPO Directory
Medical Device Register
Older Americans Information Directory

Education Information

Charter School Movement
Comparative Guide to American Elementary & Secondary Schools
Complete Learning Disabilities Directory
Educators Resource Directory
Special Education

Financial Ratings Series

TheStreet.com Ratings Guide to Bond & Money Market Mutual Funds
TheStreet.com Ratings Guide to Common Stocks
TheStreet.com Ratings Guide to Exchange-Traded Funds
TheStreet.com Ratings Guide to Stock Mutual Funds
TheStreet.com Ratings Ultimate Guided Tour of Stock Investing
Weiss Ratings Consumer Box Set
Weiss Ratings Guide to Banks & Thrifts
Weiss Ratings Guide to Credit Unions
Weiss Ratings Guide to Health Insurers
Weiss Ratings Guide to Life & Annuity Insurers
Weiss Ratings Guide to Property & Casualty Insurers

Bowker's Books In Print® Titles

Books In Print®
Books In Print® Supplement
American Book Publishing Record® Annual
American Book Publishing Record® Monthly
Books Out Loud™
Bowker's Complete Video Directory™
Children's Books In Print®
Complete Directory of Large Print Books & Serials™
El-Hi Textbooks & Serials In Print®
Forthcoming Books®
Law Books & Serials In Print™
Medical & Health Care Books In Print™
Publishers, Distributors & Wholesalers of the US™
Subject Guide to Books In Print®
Subject Guide to Children's Books In Print®

Canadian General Reference

Associations Canada
Canadian Almanac & Directory
Canadian Environmental Resource Guide
Canadian Parliamentary Guide
Financial Services Canada
Governments Canada
Libraries Canada
The History of Canada

Grey House Publishing
4919 Route 22, PO Box 56, Amenia NY 12501-0056 | (800) 562-2139 | www.greyhouse.com | books@greyhouse.com